adult learning pedagogy = conversational, relates new matls to Mannschreck
prior knowledge

Emphasizes legal relationships among the and between the parties in basic bus. org., the
fundamental structural law of bus. org. as well as when to spot potential bus concepts necessary to
violated bus
claim

Derived from agency law

LLC found 20 years ago

CORPORATIONS AND OTHER BUSINESS ORGANIZATIONS

Statutes, Rules, Materials, and Forms

2006 Edition

③ essay questions allow students to show appreciation for the interrelationship
between learned fact and exhibit diagnostic skills

④ exam allows students to test his confidence in answers and allows for many self-
assessment and reflection that educational philosophers now emphasize for
effective pro. educ. and provides discipline to review the case material

Selected and edited by

MELVIN ARON EISENBERG

Koret Professor of Law,
University of California at Berkeley

Pedagogical purposes

① terminology and nomenclature are very important for understanding, communicating and using matls in
one competes to research in this substantive area. Fill in blanks and "define and explain"
are unique in their focus for students to know terms; knowing cases and their facts
patterns provide a template for analogical reasoning

② sample cases so T and F and multiple choice allow for sampling of knowledge at various
depths across breadth of subject area and encourage studying whole course; help
prepare for law exam; provide practice in careful reading and analysis

FOUNDATION PRESS
2006

THOMSON
W
D0565528

Income statement = profits and loss statement → computes profit of business for the period (usually 1 year)
   Revenues − expenses = Net Income − interest paid on debt = income tax = Profits or Earnings

Cash flow statement = measure of how much more cash a business has at the year end
   Profits from Income Stmt + depreciation − net changes in balance sheet assets (not cash) + changes in lia. +

Balance sheet = picture on given day
   Assets = liabilities + owner equity

Financial Accounting = representation of financial statements to 3rd parties   CPA do this
Managerial or Internal Acct. = for internal use   CMA do this
Regulatory Acct = banking and security law
Tax Acct

□ Acct Concepts:
① Accounting Period Concept = period over which a statement of income is prepared → fiscal year or calendar
② Cash concept = checkbook accounting; income/expenses are measured when cash actually received or paid
③ Accrual = income
   measured at time
   of major effort
   or accomplishment
   occur

④ Realization/recognition = when is a contingent
   liability certain enough to book
⑤ Matching concept = expenses associated w/ revenue are identified and measured
⑥ Money Measurement = all measured in a common monetary unit
⑦ Business entity = delineates boundaries of the org.

Consistency = an acct. method for an event
   or asset must continue to use

Depreciation = tangible assets
Amortization = intangible (copyrights, trademarks)
Goodwill → not in GAAP

CPA = 150 hours of class and 2 years practical experience

FASB = group that writes standards

Leverage = use of debt to create income

□ Tort → frolic or detour

How to make money
① make money and retain earnings
② contributions
③ if loss - must retain
   before contributions

PREFACE

This Supplement is designed to provide students with the essential statutory provisions, rules, materials and forms needed in courses in Corporations and Business Associations, and to give students a hand's-on grasp of the tools with which the profession works in these areas.

This Supplement includes state and federal statutes and rules; extensive excerpts from Restatement (Second) of Agency; the virtually complete text of the ALI's Principles of Corporate Governance together with selected Comments; selected forms; and other materials.

In general, the federal materials have been edited much more heavily than the other materials, because much of the federal material is more relevant to courses in Securities Regulation than to courses in Corporations and Business Associations. The aim of the editing of the federal materials has been to preserve the substance and the flow of the material, but to winnow out details that are unnecessary for the study of corporation law.

The following conventions have been used in the preparation of this Supplement:

(1) Omissions within a statutory section, rule, form, official comment, instruction, note, or other material are indicated by ellipses (. . . .). The omission of an entire statutory section, rule, form, official comment, instruction, or note is not so indicated. However, in the case of the Delaware statute, the Revised Model Business Corporation Act, the Uniform Partnership Act, the Revised Uniform Partnership Act, the Uniform Limited Partnership Act, the Securities Act, and the Securities Exchange Act, the Delaware Limited Liablity Company Act, and the Uniform Limited Liability Company Act, the omission of an entire section is indicated in the Table of Contents by an asterisk following the title of the omitted section.

(2) Editorial insertions in the text are indicated by brackets. In some cases, an official text itself includes bracketed material, but the context usually makes clear whether bracketed material consists of editorial insertions or original text.

(3) Sections of the securities acts have been numbered serially, beginning with Section 1, rather than with the number-and-letter combinations used in the United States Code. Rules and forms under those acts have been numbered without the prefatory Part numbers that appear in the Code of Federal Regulations.

I thank the authors, publishers and copyrightholders who permitted me to reprint all or portions of the following works, including:

PREFACE

American Bar Association, Section of Business Law, Committee on Corporate Laws, Revised Model Business Corporation Act.

American Bar Foundation, Commentaries on Model Debenture and Indenture Provisions (1971).

American Law Institute, Restatement (Second) of Agency, Restatement (Third) of Agency, and Principles of Corporate Governance: Analysis and Recommendations.

Aspen Law & Business, Model Business Corporation Act Annotated.

R. F. Balotti and J. Finkelstein, The Delaware Law of Corporations and Business Organizations (3d ed. 1998).

Robert R. Keatinge and Holland & Hart, Form of Operating Agreement of Limited Liability Company.

National Conference of Commissioners on Uniform State Laws, Uniform Limited Liability Company Act (1995), Uniform Partnership Act, Revised Uniform Limited Partnership Act (1995), and Revised Uniform Limited Partnership Act.

Wachtell, Lipton, Rosen & Katz, Form of Preferred Shareholder Rights Agreement.

MELVIN A. EISENBERG

April, 2006

<!-- handwritten marginalia right margin -->
2 of byol
① Getting &
② On going
③ Getting On

Business Plan
① tax status
② exposure to legal liabil
③ flexibility
– central mang
– transferab of interest
– corp is an agent who
– partnership is binding
④ life of busin

<!-- handwritten notes bottom -->
Legal structures of business

① Sole proprietorship – individual and business the same for tax and legal liability

② Partnership – General = aggregate of sole proprietors, treated like proprietorship for tax + liability, jointly and severally liable

Limited = partnership for tax, like corp for liability, limited and general partners

Limited Liability Part.

Limited Liability Limited Part.

③ Corporation – Regular "C" = corp owners generally protected from personal liability, corp tax entity   double tax for dividends

– "S" = usually closely held → ① only one class of stock ② must be domestic corp (owned 80 by U.S. citizens) ③ 75 or fewer shareholders ④ no more than 25% of revenue from passive sources ⑤ only individuals, estate, certain trusts

④ LLC – protection from liability and 2x tax – taxes paid by owner when earning distributed

⑤ others = joint venture, real estate Investment Trust, Business Trust, Cooperative, Not for profit

Sole Proprietorship = ① personality of owner ② overview of debt and equity ③ cash flow ④ borrows money

iv

ntwo capital firms can not be shareholders in "S" corp

Agency — restatements helpful but statute is still law

TABLE OF CONTENTS

TABLE OF CONTENTS

masters / servant

employer / employee

Principal - disclosed = §320

undisclosed = §322

Partial disclosed = §321

TABLE OF CONTENTS

*

Actual Authority = §26

- actual express authority
- express implied authority = A has authority to do reasonably necessary to get job done

Apparent Authority = §27

- created by manifestation by P to a 3P · must be attributable to P, must get to 3P, must lead 3P reasonably to conclude that A is an agent for P
- does not require detrimental reliance by 3P or P manifestation

Liability of sole proprietor for K of employee = §8

RSA §82 - 3P has to reasonably believe A is the agent of principal

RSA §32, §376, §385

General v. Special Agents = G have broader authority than S. S. prone specific area

engaged in by today because of co.

Express Authority / Implied Authority

Apparent Authority

P

A

3P

misattributed authority

Inherent Authority

(doesn't really go anywhere, but lat here)

Ratification
Estoppel

Principal = one for whom action is to be taken

Agent = one who is to act

Winding UP = UPA v. RUPA

§40 UPA
Stg 1 = each recieves capital account
Stg 2 = default rule is to share profits evenly

RUPA §807 (a) and (b)

Stg 1 = divide amount left and allocate to the capital accounts of each partner
Stg 2 = total new capital account balances
Stg 3 = figure out "loss" "short fall" and allocate equally to each account
Stg 4 = allocate loss
Stg 5 = make sure it balances (capital accounts = cash for distribution)

Sara Cap. Account only $20,000 left

UPA

Stg 1 = $20K left

Stg 2 = determine liabilities owing to partner of cap. acct. (total amount to partners)
↳ $100K + 8K + 2K = 110K

Stg 3 = A110K (cap. acct.) − $20K (amount left) = $90 (shortfall)

Stg 4 = allocate evenly = $30K

Stg 5 = C = $100K − $30 = $70

P = $8 − $30 = ($22)

A → $2 − $30 = ($28)

RUPA

Stg 1 → $20,000 left
Stg 2 → share equally $6,666
Stg 3 → add to cap. acct.   C → $106,666   P → $8 + 6666 = 14,666   A = 8666
Stg 4 → add cap. acct. = $130,000
Stg 5 = shortfall of $110K $130 − $20 = $110   and allocate $36,666
Stg 6 = adjust   C → $106,666 − 36,666 = $70K   P = ($22K)   A = ($28K)

Capital Accounts

C = $100K
P = $8K
A = $2K

Partnership has $200K left

Step 1 give Capital Accounts = $110K so $90K left

Step 2 divide $90 by 3 = $30K add to each

answer   C = $130K   P = $38K   A = $32K

RUPA

Step 1 = divide $200K by 3 = $66,666 add to Capital Account so   C = $166,666
P = $74,666   A = $68,666

Step 2 →

Step 3 = allocate loss ⅓ of
$109,998 = $36,666

Step 4 = $166,666 - 36,666 = $130
etc.

Total = $309,998

CORPORATIONS AND OTHER BUSINESS ORGANIZATIONS

Statutes, Rules, Materials, and Forms

Under RUPA § 807 (b) → partners shall contribute to the partnership an amount equal
to any excess of the charges over credits

so P pay $22K to partnership
A pay $28K to partnership
C receives $50K leaving $20K unpaid   no one liable for $20→last
+ $30 less for rebate

UPA strictly part of — does not require negative Account repayment

partnership owes $70K so split as $23,333

C pays $23,333 so new balance $46,667

P and A give partnership $23,333 each   so   C gets $46,666

P loses $31,333 A loses $25,333   C loses 53,333 (insert + $70,000 should less)
↳ $70 split + loss share

UPA requires negative Account repayment

Part A pay C $50,000

shortfall of $20,000 so split 3X = $6,666

Part A pay $6,666 each
↳ goes to C

RESTATEMENT (SECOND) OF AGENCY

(Selected Sections)

Chapter 1

INTRODUCTORY MATTERS

TOPIC 1. DEFINITIONS

TOPIC 3. ESSENTIAL CHARACTERISTICS OF RELATION

TOPIC 4. AGENCY DISTINGUISHED FROM OTHER RELATIONS

Chapter 2

CREATION OF RELATION

TOPIC 1. MUTUAL CONSENT AND CONSIDERATION

TOPIC 3. CAPACITY OF PARTIES TO RELATION

Chapter 3

CREATION AND INTERPRETATION OF AUTHORITY AND APPARENT AUTHORITY

TOPIC 1. METHODS OF MANIFESTING CONSENT

1

RESTATEMENT (SECOND) OF AGENCY

5

Chapter 14

DUTIES AND LIABILITIES OF PRINCIPAL TO AGENT

TOPIC 1. CONTRACTUAL AND RESTITUTIONAL DUTIES AND LIABILITIES

TITLE A. INTERPRETATION OF CONTRACTS AND LIABILITIES THEREUNDER

Chapter 1

INTRODUCTORY MATTERS

TOPIC 1. DEFINITIONS

§ 1. Agency; Principal; Agent

(1) Agency is the fiduciary relation which results from the manifestation of consent by one person to another that the other shall act on his behalf and subject to his control, and consent by the other so to act.

(2) The one for whom action is to be taken is the principal.

(3) The one who is to act is the agent.

§ 2. Master; Servant; Independent Contractor

(1) A master is a principal who employs an agent to perform service in his affairs and who controls or has the right to control the physical conduct of the other in the performance of the service.

(2) A servant is an agent employed by a master to perform service in his affairs whose physical conduct in the performance of the service is controlled or is subject to the right to control by the master.

(3) An independent contractor is a person who contracts with another to do something for him but who is not controlled by the other nor subject to the other's right to control with respect to his physical conduct in the performance of the undertaking. He may or may not be an agent.

6

Comment:

a. Servants and non-servant agents. A master is a species of principal, and a servant is a species of agent. . . .

b. Servant contrasted with independent contractor. The word "servant" is used in contrast with "independent contractor". The latter term includes all persons who contract to do something for another but who are not servants in doing the work undertaken. An agent who is not a servant is, therefore, an independent contractor when he contracts to act on account of the principal. Thus, a broker who contracts to sell goods for his principal is an independent contractor as distinguished from a servant. Although, under some circumstances, the principal is bound by the broker's unauthorized contracts and representations, the principal is not liable to third persons for tangible harm resulting from his unauthorized physical conduct within the scope of the employment, as the principal would be for similar conduct by a servant; nor does the principal have the duties or immunities of a master towards the broker. Although an agent who contracts to act and who is not a servant is therefore an independent contractor, not all independent contractors are agents. Thus, one who contracts for a stipulated price to build a house for another and who reserves no direction over the conduct of the work is an independent contractor; but he is not an agent, since he is not a fiduciary, has no power to make the one employing him a party to a transaction, and is subject to no control over his conduct.

. . .

c. Servants not necessarily menials. As stated more fully in Section 220, the term servant does not denote menial or manual service. Many servants perform exacting work requiring intelligence rather than muscle. Thus the officers of a corporation or a ship, the interne in a hospital, all of whom give their time to their employers, are servants equally with the janitor and others performing manual labor. . . .

§ 3. General Agent; Special Agent

(1) A general agent is an agent authorized to conduct a series of transactions involving a continuity of service.

(2) A special agent is an agent authorized to conduct a single transaction or a series of transactions not involving continuity of service.

§ 4. Disclosed Principal; Partially Disclosed Principal; Undisclosed Principal

(1) If, at the time of a transaction conducted by an agent, the other party thereto has notice that the agent is acting for a principal and of the principal's identity, the principal is a disclosed principal.

(2) If the other party has notice that the agent is or may be acting for a principal but has no notice of the principal's identity, the principal for whom the agent is acting is a partially disclosed principal.

(3) If the other party has no notice that the agent is acting for a principal, the one for whom he acts is an undisclosed principal.

§ 7. Authority

Authority is the power of the agent to affect the legal relations of the principal by acts done in accordance with the principal's manifestations of consent to him.

§ 8. Apparent Authority

Apparent authority is the power to affect the legal relations of another person by transactions with third persons, professedly as agent for the other, arising from and in accordance with the other's manifestations to such third persons.

§ 8A. Inherent Agency Power

Inherent agency power is a term used in the restatement of this subject to indicate the power of an agent which is derived not from authority, apparent authority or estoppel, but solely from the agency relation and exists for the protection of persons harmed by or dealing with a servant or other agent.

§ 8B. Estoppel; Change of Position

(1) A person who is not otherwise liable as a party to a transaction purported to be done on his account, is nevertheless subject to liability to persons who have changed their positions because of their belief that the transaction was entered into by or for him, if

(a) he intentionally or carelessly caused such belief, or

(b) knowing of such belief and that others might change their positions because of it, he did not take reasonable steps to notify them of the facts.

(2) An owner of property who represents to third persons that another is the owner of the property or who permits the other so to represent, or who realizes that third persons believe that another is the owner of the property, and that he could easily inform the third persons of the facts, is subject to the loss of the property if the other disposes of it to third persons who, in ignorance of the facts, purchase the property or otherwise change their position with reference to it.

(3) Change of position, as the phrase is used in the restatement of this subject, indicates payment of money, expenditure of labor, suffering a loss or subjection to legal liability.

TOPIC 3. ESSENTIAL CHARACTERISTICS OF RELATION

§ 13. Agent as a Fiduciary

An agent is a <u>fiduciary</u> with respect to matters within the scope of his agency.

§ 14. Control by Principal

A principal has the right to control the conduct of the agent with respect to matters entrusted to him.

TOPIC 4. AGENCY DISTINGUISHED FROM OTHER RELATIONS

§ 14H. Agents or Holders of a Power Given for Their Benefit

One who holds a power created in the form of an agency authority, but given for the benefit of the power holder or of a third person, is not an agent of the one creating the power.

§ 14O. Security Holder Becoming a Principal

A creditor who assumes control of his debtor's business for the mutual benefit of himself and his debtor, may become a principal, with liability for the acts and transactions of the debtor in connection with the business.

Chapter 2

CREATION OF RELATION

TOPIC 1. MUTUAL CONSENT AND CONSIDERATION

§ 15. Manifestations of Consent

An agency relation exists only if there has been a manifestation by the principal to the agent that the agent may act on his account, and consent by the agent so to act.

TOPIC 3. CAPACITY OF PARTIES TO RELATION

§ 23. Agent Having Interests Adverse to Principal

One whose interests are adverse to those of another can be authorized to act on behalf of the other; it is a breach of duty for him so to act without revealing the existence and extent of such adverse interests.

Chapter 3

CREATION AND INTERPRETATION OF AUTHORITY AND APPARENT AUTHORITY

TOPIC 1.   METHODS OF MANIFESTING CONSENT

§ 26.   Creation of Authority: General Rule

Except for the execution of instruments under seal or for the performance of transactions required by statute to be authorized in a particular way, authority to do an act can be created by written or spoken words or other conduct of the principal which, reasonably interpreted, causes the agent to believe that the principal desires him so to act on the principal's account.

§ 27.   Creation of Apparent Authority: General Rule

Except for the execution of instruments under seal or for the conduct of transactions required by statute to be authorized in a particular way, apparent authority to do an act is created as to a third person by written or spoken words or any other conduct of the principal which, reasonably interpreted, causes the third person to believe that the principal consents to have the act done on his behalf by the person purporting to act for him.

TOPIC 2.   INTERPRETATION OF AUTHORITY AND APPARENT AUTHORITY

TITLE A.   AUTHORITY

§ 32.   Applicability of Rules for Interpretation of Agreements

Except to the extent that the fiduciary relation between principal and agent requires special rules, the rules for the interpretation of contracts apply to the interpretation of authority.

§ 33.   General Principle of Interpretation

An agent is authorized to do, and to do only, what it is reasonable for him to infer that the principal desires him to do in the light of the principal's manifestations and the facts as he knows or should know them at the time he acts.

Comment:

   a. Authority an ambulatory power.   The agency relation is normally the result of a contract and is always the result of an agreement between the parties. For the purpose of interpreting the words used, the effect of customs and all similar matters, the normal rules for the interpretation of contracts are applicable, as stated in Section 32. Nevertheless, an agreement creating an agency relation has elements different from those of other contracts. The implicit, basic understanding of the parties to the agency relation is that the agent is to act only in accordance with the principal's desires as manifested to him. . . . Whatever the original agreement or authority may have been, he is authorized at any given moment to do, and to do only, what he reasonably believes the principal desires him to do, in the light of what he knows or should know of the principal's purpose and the existing circumstances. . . .

Illustrations:

1. P, a mill owner, directs A, his purchasing agent, to purchase a large quantity of raw material, to be used in executing an order for goods. The following day the order for goods is rescinded, as A learns. Without inquiry as to whether or not P still wishes the material, A has no authority to purchase the raw material.

2. P, the owner of a factory running on half time for lack of orders, before leaving for his vacation, directs his purchasing agent to "put in our usual monthly coal supply of 1000 tons." The following day a large order comes in which will immediately put the factory on full running time. It may be found that A is authorized to purchase sufficient coal to keep the factory running, this depending upon whether or not P can easily be reached, the amount of discretion usually given to A, the condition of P's bank balance, and other factors.

3. Same facts as in Illustration 2, except that P is present when the large order is received. A has no authority to order more than 1000 tons.

b. Authority distinct from contract of agency. An agent is a fiduciary under a duty to obey the will of the principal as he knows it or should know it. This will may change, either with or without a change in events. Whatever it is at any given time, if the agent has reason to know it, his duty is not to act contrary to it. The fact that in changing his mind the principal is violating his contract with the agent does not diminish the agent's duty of obedience to it. Hence the rule applicable to the interpretation of authority must be as flexible as the will of the principal may be. Thus, whether or not the agent is authorized to do a particular act at a particular time depends, not only on what the principal told the agent, but upon a great variety of other factors, including changes in the situation after the instructions were given. The interpretation of authority, therefore, differs in this respect from the interpretation of a contract, even the contract of agency.

The agent's authority may therefore be increased, diminished, become dormant or be destroyed, not only by further manifestations by the principal but also by the happening of events, dependent, in many situations, upon what the agent knows or should know as to the principal's purposes. This does not mean that the agent can do anything merely because he believes it to be of advantage to the principal. Nor does it mean that the agent is authorized to act if he believes the principal would authorize him to act if he knew the facts. The agent's scope of authority is limited to the authorized subject matter and the kind of transaction contemplated. An agent of a dealer in property, whose function is limited to selling, is not authorized to buy property even if he reasonably believes the principal would authorize its purchase if he knew of the opportunity. The ordinary store manager, in the absence of an emergency, is not authorized to borrow, even though he knows the principal would welcome the opportunity.

It is in accordance with this continuous comparison between the communication to the agent and the circumstances under which he acts, that his authority may broaden ... or may be diminished, suspended or terminated ..., however irrevocable the terms in which the authority is expressed. Whether or not the principal is liable for a breach of contract for revoking the authority, nevertheless he can do so.... Further, because the agent is under a duty to protect the principal's interests within the authorized field, if the circumstances are or become ambiguous, either intrinsically or because of extrinsic facts, and he cannot communicate with the principal, the agent is authorized to act reasonably in accordance with the facts as he knows or should know them....

§ 35.   When Incidental Authority Is Inferred

Unless otherwise agreed, authority to conduct a transaction includes authority to do acts which are incidental to it, usually accompany it, or are reasonably necessary to accomplish it.

§ 39.   Inference That Agent Is to Act Only for Principal's Benefit

Unless otherwise agreed, authority to act as agent includes only authority to act for the benefit of the principal.

§ 43.   Acquiescence by Principal in Agent's Conduct

(1) Acquiescence by the principal in conduct of an agent whose previously conferred authorization reasonably might include it, indicates

that the conduct was authorized; if clearly not included in the authorization, acquiescence in it indicates affirmance.

(2) Acquiescence by the principal in a series of acts by the agent indicates authorization to perform similar acts in the future.

TITLE B. APPARENT AUTHORITY

§ 49. Interpretation of Apparent Authority Compared with Interpretation of Authority

The rules applicable to the interpretation of authority are applicable to the interpretation of apparent authority except that:

(a) manifestations of the principal to the other party to the transaction are interpreted in light of what the other party knows or should know instead of what the agent knows or should know....

Chapter 4

RATIFICATION

TOPIC 1. DEFINITIONS

§ 82. Ratification

Ratification is the affirmance by a person of a prior act which did not bind him but which was done or professedly done on his account, whereby the act, as to some or all persons, is given effect as if originally authorized by him.

Comment ...

c. *A unique concept.* The concept of ratification ... is unique. It does not conform to the rules of contracts, since it can be accomplished without consideration to or manifestation by the purported principal and without fresh consent by the other party. Further, it operates as if the transaction were complete at the time and place of the first event, rather than the last, as in the normal case of offer and acceptance. It does not conform to the rules of torts, since the ratifier may become responsible for a harm which was not caused by him, his property or his agent. It can not be justified on a theory of restitution, since the ratifier may not have received a benefit, nor the third person a deprivation. Nor is ratification dependent upon a doctrine of estoppel, since there may be ratification although neither the agent nor the other party suffer a loss resulting from a statement of affirmance or a failure to disavow. However, in some cases in which ratification is claimed, the principal's liability can be based upon unjust enrichment or estoppel, either in addition to or as alternative to his liability based on ratification....

d. *Justification*. That the doctrine of ratification may at times operate unfairly must be admitted, since it gives to the purported principal an election to blow hot or cold upon a transaction to which, in contract cases, the other party normally believes himself to be bound. But this hardship is minimized by denying a power to ratify when it would obviously be unfair. See §§ 88–90. Further, if the transaction is not ratified normally the pseudo-agent is responsible; if not, it is because the third party knew, or agreed to take the risk, of lack of authority by the agent. In many cases, the third person is a distinct gainer as where the purported principal ratifies a tort or a loan for which he was not liable and for which he receives nothing. This result is not, however, unjust, since although the creation of liability against the ratifier may run counter to established tort or contract principles, the liability is self-imposed. Even one who ratifies to protect his business reputation or who retains unwanted goods rather than defend a law suit, chooses ratification as preferable to the alternative. Further, the sometimes-derided doctrine of relation back not only is one used in other parts of the law, but it tends to give the parties what they wanted or said they wanted. If it sometimes happens that a mistaken or over-zealous agent is relieved from liability to the third person, the net result causes no harm to anyone. However, perhaps the best defense of ratification is pragmatic; that it is needed in the prosecution of business. It operates normally to cure minor defects in an agent's authority, minimizing technical defenses and preventing unnecessary law suits. In this aspect, it is a beneficial doctrine, which has been adopted in most systems of law.

§ 83. Affirmance

Affirmance is either

(a) a manifestation of an election by one on whose account an unauthorized act has been done to treat the act as authorized, or

(b) conduct by him justifiable only if there were such an election.

TOPIC 2. WHEN AFFIRMANCE RESULTS IN RATIFICATION

§ 84. What Acts Can Be Ratified

(1) An act which, when done, could have been authorized by a purported principal, or if an act of service by an intended principal, can be ratified if, at the time of affirmance, he could authorize such an act.

(2) An act which, when done, the purported or intended principal could not have authorized, he cannot ratify, except an act affirmed by a legal representative whose appointment relates back to or before the time of such act.

§ 85.   Purporting to Act as Agent as a Requisite for Ratification

(1) Ratification does not result from the affirmance of a transaction with a third person unless the one acting purported to be acting for the ratifier.

(2) An act of service not involving a transaction with a third person is subject to ratification if, but only if, the one doing the act intends or purports to perform it as the servant of another.

§ 87.   Who Can Affirm

To become effective as ratification, the affirmance must be by the person identified as the principal at the time of the original act or, if no person was then identified, by the one for whom the agent intended to act.

§ 88.   Affirmance After Withdrawal of Other Party or Other Termination of Original Transaction

To constitute ratification, the affirmance of a transaction must occur before the other party has manifested his withdrawal from it either to the purported principal or to the agent, and before the offer or agreement has otherwise terminated or been discharged.

§ 89.   Affirmance After Change of Circumstances

If the affirmance of a transaction occurs at a time when the situation has so materially changed that it would be inequitable to subject the other party to liability thereon, the other party has an election to avoid liability.

§ 90.   Affirmance After Rights Have Crystallized

If an act to be effective in creating a right against another or to deprive him of a right must be performed before a specific time, an affirmance is not effective against the other unless made before such time.

TOPIC 3.   WHAT CONSTITUTES AFFIRMANCE

§ 93.   Methods and Formalities of Affirmance

(1) Except as stated in Subsection (2), affirmance can be established by any conduct of the purported principal manifesting that he consents to be a party to the transaction, or by conduct justifiable only if there is ratification.

(2) Where formalities are requisite for the authorization of an act, its affirmance must be by the same formalities in order to constitute a ratification.

(3) The affirmance can be made by an agent authorized so to do.

§ 94. Failure to Act as Affirmance

An affirmance of an unauthorized transaction can be inferred from a failure to repudiate it.

§ 97. Bringing Suit or Basing Defense as Affirmance

There is affirmance if the purported principal, with knowledge of the facts, in an action in which the third person or the purported agent is an adverse party:

(a) brings suit to enforce promises which were part of the unauthorized transaction or to secure interests which were the fruit of such transaction and to which he would be entitled only if the act had been authorized; or

(b) bases a defense upon the unauthorized transaction as though it were authorized; or

(c) continues to maintain such suit or base such defense.

§ 98. Receipt of Benefits as Affirmance

The receipt by a purported principal, with knowledge of the facts, of something to which he would not be entitled unless an act purported to be done for him were affirmed, and to which he makes no claim except through such act, constitutes an affirmance unless at the time of such receipt he repudiates the act. If he repudiates the act, his receipt of benefits constitutes an affirmance at the election of the other party to the transaction.

§ 99. Retention of Benefits as Affirmance

The retention by a purported principal, with knowledge of the facts and before he has changed his position, of something which he is not entitled to retain unless an act purported to be done on his account is affirmed, and to which he makes no claim except through such act, constitutes an affirmance unless at the time of such retention he repudiates the act. Even if he repudiates the act, his retention constitutes an affirmance at the election of the other party to the transaction.

TOPIC 4. LIABILITIES

§ 100. Effect of Ratification; In General

[T]he liabilities resulting from ratification are the same as those resulting from authorization if, between the time when the original act was performed and when it was affirmed, there has been no change in the capacity of the principal or third person or in the legality of authorizing or performing the original act.

§ 100A. Relation Back in Time and Place

The liabilities of the parties to a ratified act or contract are determined in accordance with the law governing the act or contract at the time and place it was done or made. Whether the conduct of the purported principal is an affirmance depends upon the law at the time and place when and where the principal consents or acts.

Chapter 5

TERMINATION OF AGENCY POWERS

TOPIC 1. TERMINATION OF AUTHORITY

TITLE B. TERMINATION BY MUTUAL CONSENT, REVOCATION, OR RENUNCIATION

§ 118. Revocation or Renunciation

Authority terminates if the principal or the agent manifests to the other dissent to its continuance.

Comment:

a. Such termination by act of the principal is revocation; by act of the agent, it is renunciation.

b. Power to revoke or renounce. The principal has power to revoke and the agent has power to renounce, although doing so is in violation of a contract between the parties and although the authority is expressed to be irrevocable. A statement in a contract that the authority cannot be terminated by either party is effective only to create liability for its wrongful termination.

Illustrations:

1. In consideration of A's agreement to advertise and give his best energies to the sale of Blackacre, its owner, P, grants to A "a power of attorney, irrevocable for one year" to sell it. A advertises and spends time trying to sell Blackacre. At the end of three months P informs A that he revokes. A's authority is terminated.

2. In consideration of $1000 and A's promise to endeavor to sell, P grants to A for a period of one year a power of attorney to sell property, with compensation at 25 per cent. of the selling price, the power of attorney ending with this phrase: "Hereby intending and agreeing that this power shall be irrevocable during one year, and that during this period A shall have a power coupled with an interest which shall not be affected by my death or other circumstances." At the end of three months P informs A that he revokes. A's authority is terminated.

Comment:

    c. Liabilities. If there is a contract between principal and agent that the authority shall not be revoked or renounced, a party who revokes or renounces, unless privileged by the conduct of the other or by supervening circumstances, is subject to liability to the other. ...

    d. Non-agency powers. A power in the form of an agency authority given for the protection of a person described as an agent, but who is not one, is not an agency authority and cannot be revoked by the power giver; if such a power is held for the benefit of a third person, it can be terminated neither by revocation nor renunciation. See § 139. ...

TOPIC 5. TERMINATION OF POWERS GIVEN AS SECURITY

§ 138. Definition

    A power given as security is a power to affect the legal relations of another, created in the form of an agency authority, but held for the benefit of the power holder or a third person and given to secure the performance of a duty or to protect a title, either legal or equitable, such power being given when the duty or title is created or given for consideration.

Comment:

    a. A power given as security arises when a person manifests consent that the one to whom it is given can properly act to create liability against him, or to dispose of some of his interests, or to perfect or otherwise protect a title already in the power holder or in the person for whom he is to act. If the power is given as security for the performance of a duty, it must be supported by consideration, but consideration is not necessary if the power is in aid of and accompanies a transfer of a title to the power holder.

    b. Distinguished from authority. A power given as security is one held for the benefit of a person other than the power giver....

§ 139. Termination of Powers Given as Security

    (1) Unless otherwise agreed, a power given as security is not terminated by:

    (a) revocation by the creator of the power;

    (b) surrender by the holder of the power, if he holds for the benefit of another;

    (c) the loss of capacity during the lifetime of either the creator of the power or the holder of the power; or

(d) the death of the holder of the power, or, if the power is given as security for a duty which does not terminate at the death of the creator of the power, by his death.

(2) A power given as security is terminated by its surrender by the beneficiary, if of full capacity; or by the happening of events which, by its terms, discharges the obligations secured by it, or which makes its execution illegal or impossible.

Chapter 6

LIABILITY OF PRINCIPAL TO THIRD PERSONS; CONTRACTS AND CONVEYANCES

TOPIC 1. GENERAL PRINCIPLES

§ 140. Liability Based Upon Agency Principles

The liability of the principal to a third person upon a transaction conducted by an agent, or the transfer of his interests by an agent, may be based upon the fact that:

(a) the agent was authorized;

(b) the agent was apparently authorized; or

(c) the agent had a power arising from the agency relation and not dependent upon authority or apparent authority.

§ 143. Effect of Ratification

Upon ratification with knowledge of the material facts, the principal becomes responsible for contracts and conveyances made for him by one purporting to act on his account as if the transaction had been authorized, if there has been no supervening loss of capacity by the principal or change in the law which would render illegal the authorization or performance of such a transaction.

TOPIC 2. DISCLOSED OR PARTIALLY DISCLOSED PRINCIPAL

TITLE A. CREATION OF LIABILITY BY AUTHORIZED ACTS

§ 144. General Rule

A disclosed or partially disclosed principal is subject to liability upon contracts made by an agent acting within his authority if made in proper form and with the understanding that the principal is a party.

TITLE C.   CREATION OF LIABILITY BY UNAUTHORIZED ACTS

§ 159.   Apparent Authority

A disclosed or partially disclosed principal is subject to liability upon contracts made by an agent acting within his apparent authority if made in proper form and with the understanding that the apparent principal is a party.   The rules as to the liability of a principal for authorized acts, are applicable to unauthorized acts which are apparently authorized.

§ 160.   Violation of Secret Instructions

A disclosed or partially disclosed principal authorizing an agent to make a contract, but imposing upon him limitations as to incidental terms intended not to be revealed, is subject to liability upon a contract made in violation of such limitations with a third person who has no notice of them.

§ 161.   Unauthorized Acts of General Agent

A general agent for a disclosed or partially disclosed principal subjects his principal to liability for acts done on his account which usually accompany or are incidental to transactions which the agent is authorized to conduct if, although they are forbidden by the principal, the other party reasonably believes that the agent is authorized to do them and has no notice that he is not so authorized.

§ 161A.   Unauthorized Acts of Special Agents

A special agent for a disclosed or partly disclosed principal has no power to bind his principal by contracts or conveyances which he is not authorized or apparently authorized to make, unless the principal is estopped, or unless:

> (a) the agent's only departure from his authority or apparent authority is
>
> > i.   in naming or disclosing the principal, or
> >
> > ii.   in having an improper motive, or
> >
> > iii.   in being negligent in determining the facts upon which his authority is based, or
> >
> > iv.   in making misrepresentations; or
>
> (b) the agent is given possession of goods or commercial documents with authority to deal with them.

TITLE D. DEFENSES AND LIABILITY AFFECTED BY SUBSEQUENT EVENTS

§ 179. Rights Between Third Person and Agent

Unless otherwise agreed, the liability of a disclosed or partially disclosed principal is not affected by any rights or liabilities existing between the other party and the agent at the time the contract is made.

§ 180. Defenses of Principal—In General

A disclosed or partially disclosed principal is entitled to all defenses arising out of a transaction between his agent and a third person. He is not entitled to defenses which are personal to the agent.

TOPIC 3. UNDISCLOSED PRINCIPAL

TITLE A. CREATION OF LIABILITY BY AUTHORIZED ACTS

§ 186. General Rule

An undisclosed principal is bound by contracts and conveyances made on his account by an agent acting within his authority, except that the principal is not bound by a contract which is under seal or which is negotiable, or upon a contract which excludes him.

TITLE B. CREATION OF LIABILITY BY UNAUTHORIZED ACTS

§ 194. Acts of General Agents

A general agent for an undisclosed principal authorized to conduct transactions subjects his principal to liability for acts done on his account, if usual or necessary in such transactions, although forbidden by the principal to do them.

§ 195. Acts of Manager Appearing to Be Owner

An undisclosed principal who entrusts an agent with the management of his business is subject to liability to third persons with whom the agent enters into transactions usual in such businesses and on the principal's account, although contrary to the directions of the principal.

§ 195A. Unauthorized Acts of Special Agents

A special agent for an undisclosed principal has no power to bind his principal by contracts or conveyances which he is not authorized to make unless:

    (a) the agent's only departure from his authority is

        (i) in not disclosing his principal, or

        (ii) in having an improper motive, or

(iii) in being negligent in determining the facts upon which his authority is based, or

(iv) in making misrepresentations; or

(b) the agent is given possession of goods or commercial documents with authority to deal with them.

TITLE C.   DEFENSES AND LIABILITY AFFECTED BY SUBSEQUENT EVENTS

§ 203. Defenses of Undisclosed Principal—In General

An undisclosed principal is entitled to all defenses arising out of a transaction with an agent, but not defenses which are personal to the agent.

§ 205. Power of Agent to Modify Contract Before Disclosure of Principal

Until the existence of the principal is disclosed, an agent who has made a contract for an undisclosed principal has power to cancel the contract and to modify it with binding effect upon the principal if the contract or conveyance, as modified, is authorized or is within the inherent power of the agent to make.

Chapter 7

LIABILITY OF PRINCIPAL TO THIRD PERSON; TORTS

TOPIC 2.   LIABILITY FOR AUTHORIZED CONDUCT OR CONDUCT INCIDENTAL THERETO

TITLE B.   TORTS OF SERVANTS

§ 219. When Master is Liable for Torts of His Servants

(1) A master is subject to liability for the torts of his servants committed while acting in the scope of their employment.

(2) A master is not subject to liability for the torts of his servants acting outside the scope of their employment, unless:

(a) the master intended the conduct or the consequences, or

(b) the master was negligent or reckless, or

(c) the conduct violated a non-delegable duty of the master, or

(d) the servant purported to act or to speak on behalf of the principal and there was reliance upon apparent authority, or he was aided in accomplishing the tort by the existence of the agency relation.

WHO IS A SERVANT

§ 220. Definition of Servant

(1) A servant is a person employed to perform services in the affairs of another and who with respect to the physical conduct in the performance of the services is subject to the other's control or right to control.

(2) In determining whether one acting for another is a servant or an independent contractor, the following matters of fact, among others, are considered:

(a) the extent of control which, by the agreement, the master may exercise over the details of the work;

(b) whether or not the one employed is engaged in a distinct occupation or business;

(c) the kind of occupation, with reference to whether, in the locality, the work is usually done under the direction of the employer or by a specialist without supervision;

(d) the skill required in the particular occupation;

(e) whether the employer or the workman supplies the instrumentalities, tools, and the place of work for the person doing the work;

(f) the length of time for which the person is employed;

(g) the method of payment, whether by the time or by the job;

(h) whether or not the work is a part of the regular business of the employer;

(i) whether or not the parties believe they are creating the relation of master and servant; and

(j) whether the principal is or is not in business.

SCOPE OF EMPLOYMENT

§ 228. General Statement

(1) Conduct of a servant is within the scope of employment if, but only if:

(a) it is of the kind he is employed to perform;

(b) it occurs substantially within the authorized time and space limits;

(c) it is actuated, at least in part, by a purpose to serve the master, and

(d) if force is intentionally used by the servant against another, the use of force is not unexpectable by the master.

(2) Conduct of a servant is not within the scope of employment if it is different in kind from that authorized, far beyond the authorized time or space limits, or too little actuated by a purpose to serve the master.

§ 229. Kind of Conduct Within Scope of Employment

(1) To be within the scope of the employment, conduct must be of the same general nature as that authorized, or incidental to the conduct authorized.

(2) In determining whether or not the conduct, although not authorized, is nevertheless so similar to or incidental to the conduct authorized as to be within the scope of employment, the following matters of fact are to be considered:

(a) whether or not the act is one commonly done by such servants;

(b) the time, place and purpose of the act;

(c) the previous relations between the master and the servant;

(d) the extent to which the business of the master is apportioned between different servants;

(e) whether or not the act is outside the enterprise of the master or, if within the enterprise, has not been entrusted to any servant;

(f) whether or not the master has reason to expect that such an act will be done;

(g) the similarity in quality of the act done to the act authorized;

(h) whether or not the instrumentality by which the harm is done has been furnished by the master to the servant;

(i) the extent of departure from the normal method of accomplishing an authorized result; and

(j) whether or not the act is seriously criminal.

§ 230. Forbidden Acts

An act, although forbidden, or done in a forbidden manner, may be within the scope of employment.

§ 231. Criminal or Tortious Acts

An act may be within the scope of employment although consciously criminal or tortious.

TITLE C.   AGENTS' TORTS—LIABILITY NOT DEPENDENT
UPON RELATION OF MASTER AND SERVANT

IN GENERAL

§ 250.   Non-liability for Physical Harm by Non-servant Agents

A principal is not liable for physical harm caused by the negligent physical conduct of a non-servant agent during the performance of the principal's business, if he neither intended nor authorized the result nor the manner of performance, unless he was under a duty to have the act performed with due care.

Chapter 10

LIABILITY OF THIRD PERSON TO PRINCIPAL

TOPIC 1.   CONTRACTS; DISCLOSED AGENCY

§ 292.   General Rule

The other party to a contract made by an agent for a disclosed or partially disclosed principal, acting within his authority, apparent authority or other agency power, is liable to the principal as if he had contracted directly with the principal, unless the principal is excluded as a party by the form or terms of the contract.

§ 298.   Defenses of Other Party

The other party to a contract made by an agent on behalf of a disclosed or partially disclosed principal has all the defenses which he would have had against the principal if the principal had made the contract under the same circumstances.

§ 299.   Rights Between Other Party and Agent

Unless otherwise agreed, the liability of the other party to a disclosed or partially disclosed principal upon a contract made by an agent is not affected by any rights or liabilities then existing between the other party and the agent.

TOPIC 2.   CONTRACTS; UNDISCLOSED AGENCY

§ 302.   General Rule

A person who makes a contract with an agent of an undisclosed principal, intended by the agent to be on account of his principal and within the power of such agent to bind his principal, is liable to the principal as if the principal himself had made the contract with him, unless he is excluded by the form or terms of the contract, unless his existence is fraudulently concealed or unless there is set-off or a similar defense against the agent.

§ 303. Principal Excluded From Transaction

A person with whom an agent makes a contract on account of an undisclosed principal is not liable in an action at law brought upon the contract by such principal:

> (a) if the contract is in the form of a sealed or negotiable instrument; or

> (b) if the terms of the contract exclude liability to any undisclosed principal or to the particular principal.

§ 306. Rights Between Other Party and Agent

(1) If the agent has been authorized to conceal the existence of the principal, the liability to an undisclosed principal of a person dealing with the agent within his power to bind the principal is diminished by any claim which such person may have against the agent at the time of making the contract and until the existence of the principal becomes known to him, if he could set off such claim in an action against the agent.

(2) If the agent is authorized only to contract in the principal's name, the other party does not have set-off for a claim due him from the agent unless the agent has been entrusted with the possession of chattels which he disposes of as directed or unless the principal has otherwise misled the third person into extending credit to the agent.

§ 308. Defenses of Other Party

In an action by an undisclosed principal against the other party to a contract, the other party has all the defenses, except those of a purely procedural nature:

> (a) which he would have had against the principal if the principal had made the contract under the same circumstances,

> (b) which he had against the agent until the discovery of the principal, unless the agent was authorized to contract only in the principal's name.

TOPIC 5.   EFFECT OF RATIFICATION

§ 319. General Rule

Where a purported servant or other agent has entered into a transaction with a third person, its ratification by the purported master or other principal has the same effect upon the liabilities of the third person to the principal as an original authorization.

Chapter 11

LIABILITY OF AGENT TO THIRD PERSONS

TOPIC 1. CONTRACTS AND CONVEYANCES

TITLE A. AGENT A PARTY TO A TRANSACTION CONDUCTED BY HIMSELF

§ 320. Principal Disclosed

Unless otherwise agreed, a person making or purporting to make a contract with another as agent for a disclosed principal does not become a party to the contract.

§ 321. Principal Partially Disclosed

Unless otherwise agreed, a person purporting to make a contract with another for a partially disclosed principal is a party to the contract.

§ 322. Principal Undisclosed

An agent purporting to act upon his own account, but in fact making a contract on account of an undisclosed principal, is a party to the contract.

§ 326. Principal Known to Be Nonexistent or Incompetent

Unless otherwise agreed, a person who, in dealing with another, purports to act as agent for a principal whom both know to be nonexistent or wholly incompetent, becomes a party to such a contract.

Comment ...

b. Promoters. The classic illustration of the rule stated in this Section is the promoter. When a promoter makes an agreement with another on behalf of a corporation to be formed, the following alternatives may represent the intent of the parties:

> (1) They may understand that the other party is making a revocable offer to the nonexistent corporation which will result in a contract if the corporation is formed and accepts the offer prior to withdrawal. This is the normal understanding.

> (2) They may understand that the other party is making an irrevocable offer for a limited time. Consideration to support the promise to keep the offer open can be found in an express or limited promise by the promoter to organize the corporation and use his best efforts to cause it to accept the offer.

> (3) They may agree to a present contract by which the promoter is bound, but with an agreement that his liability

terminates if the corporation is formed and manifests its willingness to become a party. There can be no ratification by the newly formed corporation, since it was not in existence when the agreement was made . . . .

(4) They may agree to a present contract on which, even though the corporation becomes a party, the promoter remains liable either primarily or as surety for the performance of the corporation's obligation.

Which one of these possible alternatives, or variants thereof, is intended is a matter of interpretation on the facts of the individual case.

TITLE B. AGENT NOT PARTY TO TRANSACTION CONDUCTED BY HIMSELF

§ 328. Liability of Authorized Agent for Performance of Contract

An agent, by making a contract only on behalf of a competent disclosed or partially disclosed principal whom he has power so to bind, does not thereby become liable for its nonperformance.

§ 329. Agent Who Warrants Authority

A person who purports to make a contract, conveyance or representation on behalf of another who has full capacity but whom he has no power to bind, thereby becomes subject to liability to the other party thereto upon an implied warranty of authority, unless he has manifested that he does not make such warranty or the other party knows that the agent is not so authorized.

§ 330. Liability for Misrepresentation of Authority

A person who tortiously misrepresents to another that he has authority to make a contract, conveyance, or representation on behalf of a principal whom he has no power to bind, is subject to liability to the other in an action of tort for loss caused by reliance upon such misrepresentation.

TITLE C. DEFENSES AND EFFECTS OF SUBSEQUENT EVENTS

§ 333. Rights Between Other Party and Principal

Unless otherwise agreed, the liability of an agent upon a contract between a third person and the principal to which the agent is a party is not affected by any rights or liabilities existing between the third person and the principal not arising from the transaction, except that, with the consent of the principal, the agent can set off a claim which the principal would have in an action brought against him.

§ 334. Defenses of Agent—In General

In an action against an agent upon a contract between a third person and the principal to which the agent is a party, the agent has all the defenses which arise out of the transaction itself and also those which he has personally against the third person; defenses which are personal to the principal are not available to the agent.

§ 335. Agent Surety for Principal

In an action brought against an agent upon a contract to which the agent is a party but under which the primary duty of performance rests upon the principal, the agent has the defenses available to a surety.

§ 336. Election by Other Party to Hold Principal; Agency Disclosed

Unless otherwise agreed, the agent of a disclosed or partially disclosed principal who is a party to a contract made by another with such principal is not relieved from liability upon the contract by the determination of the other party to look to the principal alone, nor, unless the agent and the principal are joint contractors, by the fact that the other gets a judgment against the principal. He is relieved from liability to the extent that he is prejudiced thereby if he changes his position in justifiable reliance upon a manifestation of the other that he will look solely to the principal for performance.

§ 337. Election by Other Party to Hold Principal; Agency Undisclosed

An agent who has made a contract on behalf of an undisclosed principal is not relieved from liability by the determination of the other party thereto to look to the principal alone for the performance of the contract. He is discharged from liability if the other obtains a judgment against the principal, or, to the extent that he is prejudiced thereby, if he changes his position in justifiable reliance upon the other's manifestation that he will look solely to the principal for payment.

Chapter 13

DUTIES AND LIABILITIES OF AGENT TO PRINCIPAL

TOPIC 1. DUTIES

TITLE B. DUTIES OF SERVICE AND OBEDIENCE

§ 377. Contractual Duties

A person who makes a contract with another to perform services as an agent for him is subject to a duty to act in accordance with his promise.

29

§ 379. Duty of Care and Skill

(1) Unless otherwise agreed, a paid agent is subject to a duty to the principal to act with standard care and with the skill which is standard in the locality for the kind of work which he is employed to perform and, in addition, to exercise any special skill that he has.

(2) Unless otherwise agreed, a gratuitous agent is under a duty to the principal to act with the care and skill which is required of persons not agents performing similar gratuitous undertakings for others.

TITLE C. DUTIES OF LOYALTY

§ 387. General Principle

Unless otherwise agreed, an agent is subject to a duty to his principal to act solely for the benefit of the principal in all matters connected with his agency.

§ 388. Duty to Account for Profits Arising Out of Employment

Unless otherwise agreed, an agent who makes a profit in connection with transactions conducted by him on behalf of the principal is under a duty to give such profit to the principal.

Comment:

a. Ordinarily, the agent's primary function is to make profits for the principal, and his duty to account includes accounting for any unexpected and incidental accretions whether or not received in violation of duty. Thus, an agent who, without the knowledge of the principal, receives something in connection with, or because of, a transaction conducted for the principal, has a duty to pay this to the principal even though otherwise he has acted with perfect fairness to the principal and violates no duty of loyalty in receiving the amount. . . .

Illustrations:

1. A, a real estate broker acting for P, the seller, in order to assure himself of his commission, makes a contract with T, a purchaser, by which, if T cancels the contract with P, as he is given the right to do, T is to pay A the amount of A's commission. T repudiates the contract with P but pays A. A holds his commission as a constructive trustee for P.

2. P authorizes A to sell land held in A's name for a fixed sum. A makes a contract to sell the land to T, who makes a deposit which is to be forfeited if the transaction is not carried out. T forfeits the amount. A sells the land to another person at the price fixed by P. A is under a duty to account to P for the amount received from T. . . .

Comment:

b. Gratuities to agent. An agent can properly retain gratuities received on account of the principal's business if, because of custom or otherwise, an agreement to this effect is found. Except in such a case, the receipt and retention of a gratuity by an agent from a party with interests adverse to those of the principal is evidence that the agent is committing a breach of duty to the principal by not acting in his interests.

Illustrations:

4. A, the purchasing agent for the P railroad, purchases honestly and for a fair price fifty trucks from T, who is going out of business. In gratitude for A's favorable action and without ulterior motive or agreement, T makes A a gift of a car. A holds the automobile as a constructive trustee for P, although A is not otherwise liable to P. . . .

Comment:

c. Use of confidential information. An agent who acquires confidential information in the course of his employment or in violation of his duties has a duty not to use it to the disadvantage of the principal. . . . He also has a duty to account for any profits made by the use of such information, although this does not harm the principal. Thus, where a corporation has decided to operate an enterprise at a place where land values will be increased because of such operation, a corporate officer who takes advantage of his special knowledge to buy land in the vicinity is accountable for the profits he makes, even though such purchases have no adverse effect upon the enterprise. So, if he has "inside" information that the corporation is about to purchase or sell securities, or to declare or to pass a dividend, profits made by him in stock transactions undertaken because of his knowledge are held in constructive trust for the principal. He is also liable for profits made by selling confidential information to third persons, even though the principal is not adversely affected.

§ 389. Acting as Adverse Party Without Principal's Consent

Unless otherwise agreed, an agent is subject to a duty not to deal with his principal as an adverse party in a transaction connected with his agency without the principal's knowledge.

Comment:

a. The rule stated in this Section applies to transactions which the agent conducts for his principal, dealing therein with himself, and also to transactions in which the agent deals with his principal, who acts in person or through another agent; it is applicable to

31

transactions in which the agent is acting entirely for himself and to those in which he has such a substantial interest that it reasonably might affect his judgment. Thus, an agent who is appointed to sell or to give advice concerning sales violates his duty if, without the principal's knowledge, he sells to himself or purchases from the principal through the medium of a "straw," or induces his principal to sell to a corporation in which he has a large concealed interest . . . .

   c. *Where no harm to principal.* The rule stated in this Section is not based upon the existence of harm to the principal in the particular case. It exists to prevent a conflict of opposing interests in the minds of agents whose duty it is to act solely for the benefit of their principals. The rule applies, therefore, even though the transaction between the principal and the agent is beneficial to the principal. Thus, in the absence of a known custom or an agreement, an agent employed to sell at the market price cannot, without disclosure to the principal, properly buy the goods on his own account, even though he pays a higher price for them than the principal could obtain elsewhere. The rule applies also although the transaction is a public sale and the price received is above that stated by the principal to be adequate. Likewise, ordinarily, an agent appointed to buy or to sell at a fixed price violates his duty to the principal if, without the principal's acquiescence, he buys from or sells the specified article to himself at the specified price, even though it is impossible to obtain more or as much. However, if a broker is employed to sell property with an agreement that he is to retain all above a specified price, it may be inferred that the transaction gives him an option to purchase at that price without notice to the principal that he is acting for himself . . . .

§ 390. Acting as Adverse Party With Principal's Consent

An agent who, to the knowledge of the principal, acts on his own account in a transaction in which he is employed has a duty to deal fairly with the principal and to disclose to him all facts which the agent knows or should know would reasonably affect the principal's judgment, unless the principal has manifested that he knows such facts or that he does not care to know them.

Comment:

   a. *Facts to be disclosed.* One employed as agent violates no duty to the principal by acting for his own benefit if he makes a full disclosure of the facts to an acquiescent principal and takes no unfair advantage of him. Before dealing with the principal on his own account, however, an agent has a duty, not only to make no misstatements of fact, but also to disclose to the principal all relevant facts fully and completely. A fact is relevant if it is one which the agent should realize would be likely to affect the judgment of the principal in giving his consent to the agent to enter into the particular transaction on the specified terms. Hence, the disclosure must include not only the fact that the agent is acting on his own account (see § 389), but also all other facts which he should realize have or are likely to have a bearing upon the desirability of the transaction from the viewpoint of the principal. This includes, in the case of sales to him by the principal, not only the price which can be obtained, but also all facts affecting the desirability of sale, such as the likelihood of a higher price being obtained later, the possibilities of dealing with the property in another way, and all other matters which a disinterested and skillful agent advising the principal would think reasonably relevant.

If the principal has limited business experience, an agent cannot properly fail to give such information merely because the principal says he does not care for it; the agent's duty of fair dealing is satisfied only if he reasonably believes that the principal understands the implications of the transaction.

Illustrations:

1. P employs A to sell Blackacre for $1,000. A, having sought a customer, is unable to find one and reports such fact to P. He then states that he is willing to pay $1,000, telling P truthfully that he believes that a better sale might be made later in view of the chance that the locality will develop. A pays P $1,000. A month later, A sells the land for $1,500. In the absence of other facts, A has violated no duty to P.

2. P employs A to purchase a suitable manufacturing site for him. A owns one which is suitable and sells it to P at the fair price of $25,000, telling P all relevant facts except that, a short time previously, he purchased the land for $15,000. The transaction can be rescinded by P....

Comment:

c. *Fairness.* The agent must not take advantage of his position to persuade the principal into making a hard or improvident bargain. If the agent is one upon whom the principal naturally would rely for advice, the fact that the agent discloses that he is acting as an adverse party does not relieve him from the duty of giving the principal impartial advice based upon a carefully formed judgment as to the principal's interests. If he cannot or does not wish to do so, he has a duty to see that the principal secures the advice of a competent and disinterested third person. An agent who is in a close confidential relation to the principal, such as a family attorney, has the burden of proving that a substantial gift to him was not the result of undue influence. Even though an agent employed to sell is not in such a position, payment of less than the reasonable market value for property he buys from the principal is evidence that the bargain was unfair. If the principal is not in a dependent position, however, and the agent fully performs his duties of disclosure, a transaction of purchase and sale between them is not voidable merely because the principal receives an inadequate price or pays too great a price.

Illustrations:

> 4. P, a young physician with some inherited wealth and no business experience, places his property in charge of A to manage. Desiring a particular piece of land which represents a large share of P's assets, A waits until there is a slump in the price of land and, believing correctly that the slump is only temporary, suggests to P that it be sold, offering as an incentive that P's income from his profession will increase and that, although the price to be obtained is low, P can well afford to get more enjoyment from the proceeds now than from a larger amount later. P thereupon agrees to sell to A at a price which is as much as could be obtained at that time for the property. It may be found that A violated his duty of dealing fairly with P.

> 5. Same facts as in Illustration 4, except that A provides P with an independent experienced adviser, who gives disinterested advice, setting out the possibilities of accretion in values. It may be found that A has satisfied his duty of loyalty....

e. Agreements for compensation. A person is not ordinarily subject to a fiduciary duty in making terms as to compensation with a prospective principal....

§ 391. Acting for Adverse Party Without Principal's Consent

Unless otherwise agreed, an agent is subject to a duty to his principal not to act on behalf of an adverse party in a transaction connected with his agency without the principal's knowledge.

§ 392. Acting for Adverse Party With Principal's Consent

An agent who, to the knowledge of two principals, acts for both of them in a transaction between them, has a duty to act with fairness to each and to disclose to each all facts which he knows or should know would reasonably affect the judgment of each in permitting such dual agency, except as to a principal who has manifested that he knows such facts or does not care to know them.

§ 393. Competition as to Subject Matter of Agency

Unless otherwise agreed, an agent is subject to a duty not to compete with the principal concerning the subject matter of his agency.

§ 394. Acting for One With Conflicting Interests

Unless otherwise agreed, an agent is subject to a duty not to act or to agree to act during the period of his agency for persons whose interests conflict with those of the principal in matters in which the agent is employed.

§ 395. Using or Disclosing Confidential Information

Unless otherwise agreed, an agent is subject to a duty to the principal not to use or to communicate information confidentially given him by the principal or acquired by him during the course of or on account of his agency or in violation of his duties as agent, in competition with or to the injury of the principal, on his own account or on behalf of another, although such information does not relate to the transaction in which he is then employed, unless the information is a matter of general knowledge.

§ 396. Using Confidential Information After Termination of Agency

Unless otherwise agreed, after the termination of the agency, the agent:

(a) has no duty not to compete with the principal;

(b) has a duty to the principal not to use or to disclose to third persons, on his own account or on account of others, in competition with the principal or to his injury, trade secrets, written lists of names, or other similar confidential matters given to him only for the principal's use or acquired by the agent in violation of duty. The agent is entitled to use general information concerning the method of business of the principal and the names of the customers retained in his memory, if not acquired in violation of his duty as agent;

(c) has a duty to account for profits made by the sale or use of trade secrets and other confidential information, whether or not in competition with the principal;

(d) has a duty to the principal not to take advantage of a still subsisting confidential relation created during the prior agency relation.

TOPIC 2. LIABILITIES

§ 401. Liability for Loss Caused

An agent is subject to liability for loss caused to the principal by any breach of duty.

§ 403. Liability for Things Received in Violation of Duty of Loyalty

If an agent receives anything as a result of his violation of a duty of loyalty to the principal, he is subject to a liability to deliver it, its value, or its proceeds, to the principal.

§ 404. Liability for Use of Principal's Assets

An agent who, in violation of duty to his principal, uses for his own purposes or those of a third person assets of the principal's business is subject to liability to the principal for the value of the use. If the use predominates in producing a profit he is subject to liability, at the principal's election, for such profit; he is not, however, liable for profits made by him merely by the use of time which he has contracted to devote to the principal unless he violates his duty not to act adversely or in competition with the principal.

Comment:

a. The rule stated in this Section applies whether or not the agent uses the principal's facilities or other assets in competition with him. It applies irrespective of any harm done to the things used and irrespective of the use which the principal would have made of them.

Illustration:

1. P employs A to take care of the horses which P uses for driving purposes. P does not use them for a month and, during this period, without P's consent, A rents the horses to various persons who benefit the horses by the exercise thereby given them. A is subject to liability to P for the amount which he has received as rental.

Comment:

b. What are assets of the principal. The agent is subject to liability not only for the use of tangible things but also for the use of trade secrets, good-will, credit, and other intangible assets of the principal. Thus, an agent is subject to liability if, in selling his own goods, he uses the principal's trade-mark in territory in which the trade-mark is known but in which the principal does not sell and does not intend to sell similar goods.

Although the right to the services of an agent is a business asset of the principal, the agent's liability for profits made by his use of the principal's assets does not include a liability for profits made by him during hours which he should have devoted to the principal's service, unless he has thereby violated a fiduciary duty owed by him to the principal.

Illustration:

> 2. P employs A to give his full time to P as a bookkeeper. A uses portions of the time which he should have devoted to P's service in keeping the books for another employer, deriving thereby a greater salary than he receives from P. P cannot recover from A the amount of salary which A receives from the other employer.

c. Whether use of principal's assets predominates. Whether or not the use of assets of the principal predominates in producing a profit is a question of fact. Where an agent conducts a business upon the principal's premises, the location and facilities of the principal or the services of the agent may predominate in the creation of profits. If a ship captain uses the ship to carry heavy packages of his own, by selling which he makes a substantial profit, the owner is entitled to it; if the captain carries a box of trinkets for personal sale at ports of call, the ivory he thereby obtains does not necessarily go to the shipowner.

Illustration:

> 3. A soldier uses his official uniform and position to smuggle forbidden goods into a friendly country and thereby makes large profits. The country by which he is employed is entitled to the profits.

Comment:

d. Other remedies of principal. In addition to the rights which the principal has under the rule stated in this Section, the principal may have a cause of action for breach of contract or for a tort by the agent, or he may be entitled to a decree declaring a constructive trust in the specific proceeds of the use of an asset. These rights may be in the alternative or they may be cumulative, in accordance with the rules stated in Section 407. Thus, if the agent improperly uses the principal's chattels, the principal is entitled to recover their value, plus any damages caused to the business by their use, if the use amounts to a conversion; or he can recover the chattels in specie together with any profit which the agent has made from them, plus any damage to them or to the business caused by their use.

§ 407. Principal's Choice of Remedies

(1) If an agent has received a benefit as a result of violating his duty of loyalty, the principal is entitled to recover from him what he has so received, its value, or its proceeds, and also the amount of damage thereby caused; except that, if the violation consists of the wrongful

disposal of the principal's property, the principal cannot recover its value and also what the agent received in exchange therefor.

(2) A principal who has recovered damages from a third person because of an agent's violation of his duty of loyalty is entitled nevertheless to obtain from the agent any profit which the agent improperly received as a result of the transaction.

Chapter 14

DUTIES AND LIABILITIES OF PRINCIPAL TO AGENT

TOPIC 1. CONTRACTUAL AND RESTITUTIONAL DUTIES AND LIABILITIES

TITLE A. INTERPRETATION OF CONTRACTS AND LIABILITIES THEREUNDER

§ 438. Duty of Indemnity; The Principle

(1) A principal is under a duty to indemnify the agent in accordance with the terms of the agreement with him.

(2) In the absence of terms to the contrary in the agreement of employment, the principal has a duty to indemnify the agent where the agent

(a) makes a payment authorized or made necessary in executing the principal's affairs or, unless he is officious, one beneficial to the principal, or

(b) suffers a loss which, because of their relation, it is fair that the principal should bear.

§ 439. When Duty of Indemnity Exists

Unless otherwise agreed, a principal is subject to a duty to exonerate an agent who is not barred by the illegality of his conduct to indemnify him for:

(a) authorized payments made by the agent on behalf of the principal;

(b) payments upon contracts upon which the agent is authorized to make himself liable, and upon obligations arising from the possession or ownership of things which he is authorized to hold on account of the principal;

(c) payments of damages to third persons which he is required to make on account of the authorized performance of an act which constitutes a tort or a breach of contract;

(d) expenses of defending actions by third persons brought because of the agent's authorized conduct, such actions being unfounded but not brought in bad faith; and

(e) payments resulting in benefit to the principal, made by the agent under such circumstances that it would be inequitable for indemnity not to be made.

§ 440. When No Duty of Indemnity

Unless otherwise agreed, the principal is not subject to a duty to indemnify an agent:

(a) for pecuniary loss or other harm, not of benefit to the principal, arising from the performance of unauthorized acts or resulting solely from the agent's negligence or other fault; or

(b) if the principal has otherwise performed his duties to the agent, for physical harm caused by the performance of authorized acts, for harm suffered as a result of torts, other than the tortious institution of suits, committed upon the agent by third persons because of his employment, or for harm suffered by the refusal of third persons to deal with him; or

(c) if the agent's loss resulted from an enterprise which he knew to be illegal.

§ 442. Period of Employment

Unless otherwise agreed, mutual promises by principal and agent to employ and to serve create obligations to employ and to serve which are terminable upon notice by either party; if neither party terminates the employment, it may terminate by lapse of time or by supervening events.

RESTATEMENT (THIRD) OF AGENCY

(2006)

TABLE OF CONTENTS

CHAPTER 1

INTRODUCTORY MATTERS

TOPIC 1. DEFINITIONS AND TERMINOLOGY

CHAPTER 2

PRINCIPLES OF ATTRIBUTION

TOPIC 1. ACTUAL AUTHORITY

TOPIC 2. APPARENT AUTHORITY

TOPIC 3. RESPONDEAT SUPERIOR

CHAPTER 3

CREATION AND TERMINATION OF AUTHORITY AND AGENCY RELATIONSHIPS

TOPIC 1. CREATING AND EVIDENCING ACTUAL AUTHORITY

TOPIC 2. CREATING APPARENT AUTHORITY

CHAPTER 1

INTRODUCTORY MATTERS

TOPIC 1. DEFINITIONS AND TERMINOLOGY

§ 1.01 Agency Defined

Agency is the fiduciary relationship that arises when one person (a "principal") manifests assent to another person (an "agent") that the agent shall act on the principal's behalf and subject to the principal's control, and the agent manifests assent or otherwise consents so to act.

§ 1.02 Parties' Labeling and Popular Usage Not Controlling

An agency relationship arises only when the elements stated in § 1.01 are present. Whether a relationship is characterized as agency in an agreement between parties or in the context of industry or popular usage is not controlling.

§ 1.03 Manifestation

A person manifests assent or intention through written or spoken words or other conduct.

§ 1.04 Terminology

(1) *Coagents.* Coagents have agency relationships with the same principal. A coagent may be appointed by the principal or by another agent actually or apparently authorized by the principal to do so.

(2) *Disclosed, undisclosed, and unidentified principals.*

(a) *Disclosed principal.* A principal is disclosed if, when an agent and a third party interact, the third party has notice that the agent is acting for a principal and has notice of the principal's identity.

(b) *Undisclosed principal.* A principal is undisclosed if, when an agent and a third party interact, the third party has no notice that the agent is acting for a principal.

(c) *Unidentified principal.* A principal is unidentified if, when an agent and a third party interact, the third party has notice that the agent is acting for a principal but does not have notice of the principal's identity.

(3) *Gratuitous agent.* A gratuitous agent acts without a right to compensation.

(4) *Notice.* A person has notice of a fact if the person knows the fact, has reason to know the fact, has received an effective notification of the fact, or should know the fact to fulfill a duty owed to another person. Notice of a fact that an agent knows or has reason to know is imputed to the principal as stated in §§ 5.03 and 5.04. A notification given to or by an agent is effective as notice to or by the principal as stated in § 5.02.

(5) *Person.* A person is (a) an individual; (b) an organization or association that has legal capacity to possess rights and incur obligations; (c) a government, political subdivision, or instrumentality or entity created by government; or (d) any other entity that has legal capacity to possess rights and incur obligations.

(6) *Power given as security.* A power given as security is a power to affect the legal relations of its creator that is created in the form of a manifestation of actual authority and held for the benefit of the holder or a third person. It is given to protect a legal or equitable title or to secure the performance of a duty apart from any duties owed the holder of the power by its creator that are incident to a relationship of agency under § 1.01.

(7) *Power of attorney.* A power of attorney is an instrument that states an agent's authority.

(8) *Subagent.* A subagent is a person appointed by an agent to perform functions that the agent has consented to perform on behalf of the agent's principal and for whose conduct the appointing agent is responsible to the principal. The relationship between an appointing agent and a subagent is one of agency, created as stated in § 1.01.

(9) *Superior and subordinate coagents.* A superior coagent has the right, conferred by the principal, to direct a subordinate coagent.

(10) *Trustee and agent-trustee.* A trustee is a holder of property who is subject to fiduciary duties to deal with the property for the benefit of charity or for one or more persons, at least one of whom is not the sole trustee. An agent-trustee is a trustee subject to the control of the settlor or of one or more beneficiaries.

CHAPTER 2

PRINCIPLES OF ATTRIBUTION

TOPIC 1. ACTUAL AUTHORITY

§ 2.01 Actual Authority

An agent acts with actual authority when, at the time of taking action that has legal consequences for the principal, the agent reasonably believes, in accordance with the principal's manifestations to the agent, that the principal wishes the agent so to act.

Comment:

a. Scope and cross-references. Section 1.03 defines manifestation. Section 2.02 covers the scope of actual authority, including criteria with which to assess the reasonableness of the agent's belief. Sections 3.01 and 3.02 state the means by which a principal creates actual authority, including circumstances in which a writing is required.

b. Terminology. As defined in this section, "actual authority" is a synonym for "true authority," a term used in some opinions. The definition in this section does not attempt to classify different types of actual authority on the basis of the degree of detail in the principal's manifestation, which may consist of written or spoken words or other conduct. See § 1.03. As commonly used, the term "express authority" often means actual authority that a principal has stated in very specific or detailed language.

The term "implied authority" has more than one meaning. "Implied authority" is often used to mean actual authority either (1) to do what is necessary, usual, and proper to accomplish or perform an agent's express responsibilities or (2) to act in a manner in which an agent believes the principal wishes the agent to act based on the agent's reasonable interpretation of the principal's manifestation in light of the principal's objectives and other facts known to the agent. These meanings are not mutually exclusive. Both fall within the definition of actual authority. Section 2.02, which delineates the scope of actual authority, subsumes the practical consequences of implied authority.

The term "inherent agency power," used in the Restatement Second of Agency and defined therein by § 8 A, is not used in this Restatement. Inherent agency power is defined as "a term used . . . to indicate the power of an agent which is derived not from authority, apparent authority or estoppel, but solely from the agency relation and exists for the protection of persons harmed by or dealing with a servant or other agent." Other doctrines stated in this Restatement encompass the justifications underpinning § 8 A, including the importance of interpretation by the agent in the agent's relationship with the principal, as well as the doctrines of apparent authority, estoppel, and restitution.

c. Rationale. Actual authority is a consequence of a principal's expressive conduct toward the agent, through which the principal manifests assent to be affected by the agent's action, and the agent's reasonable understanding of the principal's manifestation. An agent's actions establish the agent's consent to act on the principal's behalf, as does any separate manifestation of assent by the agent. When an agent acts with actual authority, the agent's power to affect the principal's legal relations with third parties is coextensive with the agent's right to do so, which actual authority creates. In contrast, although an agent who acts with only apparent authority also affects the principal's legal relations, the agent lacks the right to do so, and the agent's act is not rightful as toward the principal. Actual authority often overlaps with the presence of apparent authority. . . .

The focal point for determining whether an agent acted with actual authority is the agent's reasonable understanding at the time the agent takes action. Although it is commonly said that a principal grants or confers actual authority, the principal's initial manifestation to the agent may often be modified or supplemented by subsequent manifestations from the principal and by other developments that the agent should reasonably consider in determining what the principal wishes to be done. A principal's manifestations may reach the agent directly or indirectly. Often a principal's manifestation will state that the agent should refrain from acting in a particular way. In that situation, the agent's failure to act conforms to the principal's expressed wishes.

Illustration:

> 1. P gives A a power of attorney authorizing A to sell a piece of property owned by P. P subsequently says to A, "Don't

sell the property. Lease it instead." After P's statement, A has actual authority only to lease.

The presence of actual authority requires that an agent's belief be reasonable at the time the agent acts. It is also necessary that the agent in fact believes that the principal desires the action taken by the agent.

Illustrations:

2. Same facts as Illustration 1, except that A overhears P say to a third party that P no longer wishes to sell the property and wishes A to lease it. A has actual authority only to lease because A knows P does not wish the property to be sold.

3. Same facts as Illustration 1, except that, after telling A to lease the property instead of selling it, P tells F that P regrets making this statement and wishes that the property be sold. A is unaware of P's statement to F. A sells the property to T, showing T the power of attorney. T is unaware of P's oral statements to A and F. A did not have actual authority to sell the property. A acted with apparent authority as defined in § 2.03.

Unless a principal's manifestation expressly states that the authority is irrevocable and constitutes a power given as security or an irrevocable proxy as defined in § 3.12, the principal has power to revoke actual authority even when the principal has contracted not to do so. If a principal's revocation of actual authority breaches a contract with the agent, the agent's authority terminates but the principal is subject to liability to the agent for breach of contract.

Illustration:

4. Same facts as Illustration 1, except that the power of attorney states that A's authority to sell shall be irrevocable by P for six months, in exchange for A's promise to use best efforts to sell the property. At the end of three months, P tells A that P revokes A's authority. A's authority is terminated, but P is subject to liability for breach of contract.

A principal's manifestation to an agent often consists of an intentional act. However, a principal may also convey actual authority to the agent through unintended conduct that the agent reasonably believes to constitute an expression of the principal's intentions.

Illustrations:

5. P drafts and executes a power of attorney authorizing A to sell a piece of property. Following a change of mind, P drafts and executes a second power authorizing A only to lease the

property. P inadvertently sends the first power to A and does not otherwise communicate with A regarding the nature of A's authority. A has actual authority to sell the property.

6.   Same facts as Illustration 5, except that after A receives the power of attorney from P, P sends A a letter asking for a status report on A's efforts to lease the property. The letter also states that P is glad the property will not be sold. After receiving P's letter, A lacks actual authority to sell the property because it is not reasonable for A to believe that P wishes A to sell it. . . .

§ 2.02   Scope of Actual Authority

(1) An agent has actual authority to take action designated or implied in the principal's manifestations to the agent and acts necessary or incidental to achieving the principal's objectives, as the agent reasonably understands the principal's manifestations and objectives when the agent determines how to act.

(2) An agent's interpretation of the principal's manifestations is reasonable if it reflects any meaning known by the agent to be ascribed by the principal and, in the absence of any meaning known to the agent, as a reasonable person in the agent's position would interpret the manifestations in light of the context, including circumstances of which the agent has notice and the agent's fiduciary duty to the principal.

(3) An agent's understanding of the principal's objectives is reasonable if it accords with the principal's manifestations and the inferences that a reasonable person in the agent's position would draw from the circumstances creating the agency.

Comment . . .

e. Agent's reasonable understanding of principal's manifestation. An agent does not have actual authority to do an act if the agent does not reasonably believe that the principal has consented to its commission. Whether an agent's belief is reasonable is determined from the viewpoint of a reasonable person in the agent's situation under all of the circumstances of which the agent has notice. Lack of actual authority is established by showing either that the agent did not believe, or could not reasonably have believed, that the principal's grant of actual authority encompassed the act in question. This standard requires that the agent's belief be reasonable, an objective standard, and that the agent actually hold the belief, a subjective standard.

Illustration:

4.   P, a photographer, employs A as a business manager. P authorizes A to endorse and deposit checks P receives from

publishers of photographs taken by P. Based on P's statements to A, A believes A's authority is limited to endorsing and depositing checks and does not include entering into agreements that bind P in other respects. A endorses and deposits a check from T, a magazine publisher, made payable to P. Printed on the back of the check is a legend: "Endorsement constitutes a release of all claims." It is beyond the scope of A's actual authority to release claims that P has against T.

The context in which principal and agent interact, including the nature of the principal's business or the principal's personal situation, frames the reasonableness of an agent's understanding of the principal's objectives. An agent's actual authority encompasses acts necessary to accomplish the end the principal has directed that the agent achieve. In exigent circumstances not known to the principal, the agent may reasonably believe that the principal would wish the agent to act beyond the specifics detailed by the principal.

Illustrations:

5. P Corporation employs A as the Facilities Manager at an amusement park owned by P Corporation. A reports to B, P Corporation's Vice President for Leisure Activities. B directs A to arrange for the reseeding of the badly deteriorated lawn adjacent to the park's entrance. B also directs A to complete the reseeding by the end of the week. A purchases grass seed and directs groundskeepers to schedule time for reseeding. A then learns that the park location is in the path of a forecasted hurricane. A has actual authority to postpone the reseeding.

6. Same facts as Illustration 5, except weather conditions do not interrupt the reseeding. A knows that the lawn could be reseeded either at much higher cost to achieve turf conditions suitable for a golf course, or at lower cost to achieve conditions that are visually attractive but not suitable for use as a golf course. Absent other manifestations from B, or other knowledge of P Corporation's practices, A lacks actual authority to reseed to achieve the golf-course standard. In light of the use P Corporation will make of the lawn, it is not reasonable for A to believe that P Corporation's objectives require that the lawn be usable as a golf course.

Factors relevant to the reasonableness of an agent's understanding of the principal's manifestation include the fiduciary character of the agent's relationship with the principal and the agent's inability to react to the principal's unexpressed interests or wishes. An agent's fiduciary position obliges the agent to act loyally to serve the principal's interests and objectives that the agent knows or should know. See § 8.01. The relevant interests and objectives are those with respect to the agency and do not encompass other objectives or interests that a principal may have. A principal's situation, if known to the agent at the time the agent acts, may affect the agent's authority to do a particular act. Additionally, the principal may revoke or limit authority subsequent to granting it. An agent's understanding at the time the agent acts is controlling. If an agent knows that the principal's reason for previously authorizing the agent to do an act is no longer operative, the agent does not have actual authority to do the act. An agent's actual authority is not affected by changes in the principal's situation that are not known to the agent....

Illustrations:

7. The directors of P Corporation approve a plan to upgrade a plant that is suitable for the manufacture of one product line. P Corporation's Executive Vice President tells M, the plant manager, to contract with an engineering firm for a redesign of the production process that must precede the upgrade work. After adopting the resolution, the directors abandon the upgrade plan and so notify the Executive Vice President. No one tells M, who on behalf of P Corporation enters into a contract with T, an engineering firm, to do the redesign. P Corporation is bound by the contract. M had actual authority to make the contract.

8. Same facts as Illustration 7, except that M reads in the newspaper that P Corporation's directors have discontinued the sole product line manufactured in the plant. M no longer has actual authority to make the contract with T. M may have apparent authority as defined in § 2.03 if T reasonably believes M has authority to make the contract. T's belief will not be reasonable if T is also aware that the product line has been discontinued.

9. Same facts as Illustration 7, except that the upgrade plan depends on using a particular building technology. M is aware of this fact. After the directors adopt the resolution and M is directed to contract for the redesign work, M learns that regulatory restrictions will prevent P Corporation from using the particular technology on which the plan depends. M no longer has actual authority to make the contract with T. M may have apparent authority as defined in § 2.03 if T reasonably believes that M has authority to make the contract.

10. Same facts as Illustration 7, except that P Corporation's Chief Financial Officer tells M that the upgrade plans have been abandoned. M no longer has actual authority even though M does not report to the Chief Financial Officer.

The nature of actual authority means that the relevant inquiry always focuses on the time the agent acts. In Illustrations 8, 9, and 10, the temporal focus, which is the time the agent acts, is not the time of the principal's initial manifestation to the agent. An alternative formulation, which would reach the same outcomes on these Illustrations, is to say that M had actual authority but that subsequent developments terminated it. This formulation unnecessarily adds two elements, the initial presence of authority and its subsequent termination, to the determinative inquiry, which is the reasonableness of M's belief at the time of determining the action to take. . . .

An agent's understanding of the principal's interests and objectives is an element of the agent's reasonable interpretation of the principal's conduct. If a literal interpretation of a principal's communication to the agent would authorize an act inconsistent with the principal's interests or objectives known to the agent, it is open to question whether the agent's literal interpretation is reasonable.

Illustration:

> 11. P, a toy designer, employs A as an agent to present P's designs to toy manufacturers. P says to A, "Before you show the design, sign whatever forms the manufacturer requires." A knows that P's practice is to retain all copyright and other intellectual-property interests in P's designs. It may not be reasonable for A to interpret P's instruction to authorize A to sign a form that assigns or releases all of P's interests in the design to T, a toy manufacturer. If T, an important presence in the industry, always demands that such a release be executed, when feasible A should contact P for further instructions. When not feasible, it is a question of fact whether A acted reasonably in signing the form presented by T. A has apparent authority as defined in § 2.03 only if based on P's conduct it is reasonable for T to believe that A has authority to sign the form.

Interactions between principal and agent do not occur in a vacuum. Prior dealings between them are relevant to the reasonableness of the agent's understanding of the principal's manifestation. If a principal and an agent share an idiosyncratic understanding of what is meant by the principal's manifestation, that understanding controls the scope of the agent's actual authority, not the understanding that a reasonable person would have. Unlike a party dealing at arm's length with another, the focus for an agent is interpreting the principal's manifestations so as to further the principal's objectives.

Illustrations:

> 12. P, who owns a number of residential rental properties, retains A to manage them. P directs A, "Install smoke detectors

51

in each room." Based on A's prior dealings with P, A knows that by "each room," P means "each room in which the housing code requires a smoke detector." A also knows that P views compliance with the housing code as a business necessity. A's actual authority to install smoke detectors is limited to rooms in which the housing code requires their installation.

13. Same facts as Illustration 12, except that after P's directive to A, the housing code is amended to require the installation of smoke detectors in hallways as well as rooms. A has actual authority to install smoke detectors in hallways as well as rooms.

In determining whether an agent's action reflected a reasonable understanding of the principal's manifestations of consent, it is relevant whether the principal knew of prior similar actions by the agent and acquiesced in them.

Illustration:

14. Same facts as Illustration 12, except that P knows that, given the same directive in the past, A has installed smoke detectors in all rooms. P has not objected or complained. A has actual authority to install smoke detectors in all rooms.

The context in which principal and agent interact will often include customs and usages that are particular to a type of business or a geographic locale. A person carrying on business has reason to know of such customs and usages and thus has notice of them as defined in § 1.04(4). If an agent has notice that the principal does not know of a custom or usage, the agent is not authorized to act in accordance with it if doing so would result in a transaction different from that which the agent has notice is desired by the principal.

If a principal states the agent's authority in terms that contemplate that the agent will use substantial discretion to determine the particulars, it is ordinarily reasonable for the agent to believe that following usage and custom will be acceptable to the principal. In contrast, if a principal's express statement of authority is highly detailed, it is not reasonable for the agent to believe the principal intended that the agent should follow a custom or usage that is at odds with the terms of the principal's express authorization. When a practice is common in a particular industry, it will be difficult for the principal credibly to claim no notice of it. Cases addressing the relevance of usage and custom reflect some division whether it is necessary to show that the principal had notice of the existence of the customs, usages, or practices at issue. This issue should be treated as an aspect of a broader inquiry into the reasonableness of the agent's belief that the agent had authority.

f. Interpretation by agent. In order to determine with specificity what a principal would wish the agent to do, the agent must interpret the language the principal uses or assess the principal's conduct or the situation in which the principal has placed the agent. An agent's position requires such interpretation regardless of the circumstances under which the principal created actual authority. Thus, interpretation by the agent is necessary whether the agent has received explicit instructions from the principal, has received a general directive, or has been appointed to a position in an organization with delegated powers. The benchmark for interpretation reflects the agent's fiduciary position. If the principal gives imperative instructions using clear and precise language and the instructions do not demand illegal conduct and do not appear to have been issued in error, the agent should follow the instructions even if they conflict with industry usage or custom. A reasonable agent would understand the principal's choice of precise language, imperatively stated, as an accurate reflection of the principal's wishes. An industry custom or practice contrary to the principal's definite instructions does not excuse the agent's violation of the principal's instructions.

A principal's ability to communicate with the agent is a basic component of the principal's exercise of the right of control. In particular, a principal has the opportunity to state instructions to the agent with clarity and specificity. Moreover, much that underlies the occurrence of the risk that the agent will depart from instructions is within the principal's control. The principal's instructions may be insufficiently clear in their import to enable the agent to discern what acts the principal wishes the agent to do or to refrain from doing. The principal's instructions, albeit clear as far as they go, may be incomplete in some significant respect, or the instructions may reasonably be understood by the agent to authorize the agent to exercise discretion. Moreover, an agent may depart from instructions because the agent interprets the instructions from a perspective that differs in significant respects from the perspective from which the principal would interpret the identical language. Although not all factors that underlie such differences in perspective are always within the principal's control, in significant respects the principal makes decisions that shape the viewpoint from which the agent interprets instructions.

Occasionally, it may be open to doubt what a principal's instructions mean, even when they are interpreted literally. As a result, the agent may interpret them differently from the interpretation the principal would have preferred. The agent's fiduciary duty to the principal obliges the agent to interpret the principal's manifestations so as to infer, in a reasonable manner, what the principal desires to be done in light of facts of which the agent has notice at the time of acting. Within this basic framework, however, it is not surprising that more than one reasonable interpretation of instructions might be possible. Not all agents are equally gifted in their capacity for reasonable interpretation, especially when the instructions themselves are not specific or when the principal has not furnished the agent with a separate instruction that specifies how to resolve doubtful cases.

A principal may take steps that, by reducing ambiguity or other lack of clarity, reduce the risk that the agent's actions will deviate from the principal's wishes, interests, or objectives. Giving an agent a formal written set of instructions reduces the agent's discretion and potential to err in determining what actions to take. A principal may also reduce the risk of deviation by monitoring the agent, for example by requiring prompt checks on the agent's actions by a superior coagent or an external auditor. How an organizational principal structures itself, including titles given to individuals and habitual patterns of interaction among them, may also reduce the risk of deviation by orienting individuals to defined roles and organizationally specified constraints on action.

An organizational principal, like any principal, is at risk of misunderstanding and misinterpretation. Detailed instructions may be so complex that lapses occur because an agent's attentiveness slips. Prolix instructions may cause some agents to decide that certain instructions may be ignored as trivial or as unwittingly imposed obstacles to achieving what the agent perceives to be the principal's overriding objective. An agent is not privileged to disregard instructions unless the agent reasonably believes that the principal wishes the agent to do so. If third parties with whom the agent interacts reasonably believe the agent to be authorized, the doctrine of apparent authority, defined in § 2.03, may apply to protect the third party. It does not protect an agent who departs from instructions. See § 8.09(2) on an agent's duty to comply with all lawful instructions received from the principal.

Interactions among coagents within an organization often involve superior agents giving instructions to junior or subordinate agents. See § 1.04(9). A subordinate agent may realize correctly that the superior agent is not the principal. Whether correctly or mistakenly, the subordinate agent may believe that the principal's interests would best be served by disregarding the superior agent's instructions. Each separate occasion for the communication and interpretation of instruction downward within a sequential chain of agents enhances the likelihood of miscommunication, misunderstanding, and departure from instructions.

A principal may believe when initially giving instructions to the agent that the principal's best interests will be served by investing the agent with a large measure of discretion, a decision later regretted by the principal when reviewing the agent's actual use of discretion. Regardless of any later regret, the principal is bound by the agent's acts so long as the agent's interpretation was reasonable.

Illustrations:

15. A is the manager of a retail clothing store owned by P, who owns several such stores. P authorizes store managers to buy, from vendors specified by P, inventory of items specified by P for their stores up to limits specified in dollar amount. P identifies "men's dress shirts" as an inventory type that A has authority to buy. A knows that by "dress shirts" P means "shirts suitable for wearing with a tuxedo." A does not have actual authority to buy dress shirts not suitable for tuxedo wear.

16. Same facts as Illustration 15, except that P ascribes no unusual meaning to "men's dress shirts" that is known to A. P provides A with no directions as to the color assortment of shirts. At the time A places the order, a particular color is fashionable and A orders many shirts in that color, believing that the fashion will continue. The shirts fail to sell. A had actual authority to buy the shirts.

17. Same facts as Illustration 16, except that A believes P has set the dollar limit at an unnecessarily low level. A also believes that the limit will result in an inadequate range of selections for P's customers. A purchases men's dress shirts in a quantity that exceeds the dollar limit set by P. A does not have actual authority to exceed P's limit.

18. Same facts as Illustration 17, except that A purchases shirts in a quantity exceeding the limit set by P because A does not notice the limit, failing carefully to read the written statement that A received from P. A lacks actual authority to buy beyond the limit.

19. P Corporation, a financial firm, employs A as a trader in financial instruments on P Corporation's own account. P Corporation imposes no express limits on the type of financial instrument in which A may take trading positions. Additionally, P Corporation awards bonuses to A based on the overall profitability of the portfolio that A manages. A commits P Corporation to a series of risky and unusual investments that result in a substantial loss sustained by the portfolio as a whole. A had actual authority to make the risky and unusual investments. P Corporation imposed no explicit limits on A, and P Corpora-

tion's prior treatment of A's investment decisions would not give A a basis for inferring a limit.

An agent who knowingly contravenes or exceeds the principal's instructions may believe that to do so best serves the principal's interests. The agent may believe that circumstances have changed since the initial instructions and that, were the principal to reconsider the matter, different instructions would be given. Unless it is reasonable for the agent to believe that the principal wishes the agent to construe the instructions in light of changed circumstances, the agent lacks actual authority to violate instructions.

Illustrations:

> 20. P retains A, directing A to buy Blackacre but to offer no more than $250,000. A then learns that Blackacre has increased substantially in value and, if purchased for $300,000, would represent a bargain. As A knows, it is financially feasible for P to pay $300,000 for Blackacre. A does not have actual authority to offer more than $250,000 for Blackacre.
>
> 21. Same facts as Illustration 20, except that Blackacre is to be sold at an auction in which the successful bidder will be required to deposit a check in an amount equal to 10 percent of the bid. P gives A a blank check to use in making the deposit. A does not have actual authority to bid more than $250,000 for Blackacre.
>
> 22. Same facts as Illustration 20, except that P owns and operates a golf course on land that almost entirely surrounds Blackacre. A has notice of P's long-term business plan to enhance the aesthetic and athletic qualities of the course and thereby make it more profitable. At the auction of Blackacre, A learns for the first time that there will be one other bidder, B. A also learns that B's plan for using Blackacre is to construct a cement factory on it. A is unable to contact P to relay this information and receive further instructions. A succeeds in purchasing Blackacre for P by bidding $260,000. A acted with actual authority. . . .

It is often feasible for an agent to contact the principal to inquire what the principal now wishes to be done. In an era of rapid electronic communication, it is often cheap and easy for an agent to inquire before proceeding. The agent's inquiry gives the principal the opportunity to clarify or supplement the prior instructions. However, an agent may believe that it is infeasible to contact the principal for clarification or that the advantage promised by the transaction will be lost if the agent does not conclude it promptly.

Unless the agent has a basis reasonably to believe that the principal does not wish to resolve the question, the agent should attempt to contact the principal prior to exercising discretion to disregard prior instructions. If the principal does not respond to the agent's inquiry and viewed objectively the action then taken by the agent reasonably serves the principal's interests as the agent could best discern them, the agent acted with actual authority.

A principal's instructions may not address prior occasions on which the agent has contravened instructions. On prior occasions the principal may have affirmatively approved of the agent's unauthorized act or silently acquiesced in it by failing to voice affirmative disapproval. The history is likely to influence the agent's subsequent interpretation of instructions. If the principal's subsequent instructions do not address the history, the agent may well infer from the principal's silence that the principal will not demand compliance with the instructions to any degree greater than the principal has done in the past. It is a question of fact whether the agent is reasonable in drawing such an inference. It will probably not be reasonable if the principal has recently renewed the instructions or newly emphasized the importance of complying with them.

An agent may believe, whether correctly or erroneously, that the agent knows the principal's best interests better than the principal does. What appears to be hubris on the agent's part may be present when the agent in fact has greater expertise or knowledge than does the principal as to matters within the scope of the agency relationship. Agents are often said to depart from their instructions due to an "excess of zeal." One explanation for this phenomenon is the agent's belief in a superior understanding of the principal's best interests. Additionally, agents sometimes exhibit an "excess of zeal" because they have information about the principal's situation that differs from the principal's own information and beliefs based upon it. Matters that seem urgent or imperative to the agent may seem less so to the principal, whose knowledge will often be broader in scope and whose time horizon will often extend farther into the future than will the agent's.

The incentive structure embedded in an agent's relationship with the principal may aggravate differences in perspective. Lapses from instructions may well follow if the agent's compensation depends on the volume of transactions concluded by the agent or on their dollar value, or if the agent fears the principal will terminate the agency relationship if the agent does not achieve success. Regardless of the explanation for the lapse, the agent does not have actual authority to disregard instructions unless it is reasonable for the agent to believe that the principal wishes the agent to do so.

Illustrations:

23. VP, the vice president of P Corporation in charge of P Corporation's information technology, enters into negotiations with T Corporation to buy a new computer system. Before VP begins negotiations with T Corporation, the board of directors of P Corporation authorizes the expenditure of up to $5 million on a new computer system. The CEO of P Corporation then directs VP not to buy a computer system from T Corporation because the CEO has been told by other CEOs that T Corporation's products demand a high level of user sophistication. Believing that the CEO has underestimated the computer skills of P Corporation's work force, VP enters into a contract with T Corporation to buy a computer system for $4 million. VP did not have actual authority to enter into a transaction specifically forbidden by the CEO.

24. Same facts as Illustration 23, except that VP, additionally, has good reason to believe that the computer system is a bargain at the $4 million price. VP does not have actual authority to contract to buy it.

g. *Explicit instructions.* A principal may direct an agent to do or refrain from doing a specific act. The agent's fiduciary duty to the principal obliges the agent to interpret the principal's instructions so as to infer, in a reasonable manner, what the principal would wish the agent to do in light of the facts of which the agent has notice at the time of acting.

Although an agent's task of interpretation is often straightforward when given specific instructions, the principal's language does not interpret itself. Circumstances may require the agent to exercise discretion in ascertaining the principal's wishes. Suppose the principal (P), the owner of a menagerie, makes a statement that P believes directs the general manager of the menagerie (A) to buy no more horses. If A enters into an agreement to buy another horse for the menagerie, A did not act with actual authority unless A reasonably believed that P wished the purchase to be made.

Consider the variety of explanations for A's purchase of the horse on P's account despite what appears to be P's direction to the contrary. First, P's statement might not have expressed P's wishes clearly. Perhaps P said, "I'm not into horses anymore," which is not a categorical statement of an instruction to A. If A sought clarification from P, P might have responded, "What I meant was, buy no more horses." A's purchase of the additional horse would be unauthorized. A might, however, reasonably believe that no clarification was necessary. Perhaps A believed that P meant to discontinue P's private use of horses, separate from the menagerie business. A's belief is not reasonable, though, in the absence of some reason to ascribe that interpretation to P's statement. A might fail to seek clarification from P if logistics make it difficult or impossible to do so or if P seems too rushed or distracted to explain further. It is a question of fact whether A's failure to seek clarification is reasonable under the circumstances.

Suppose P said to A originally (or in response to A's request for clarification): "Buy no more horses." This instruction, clear on its face, might nonetheless leave A in doubt in some circumstances. P's language does not itself define the word "horse" and does not eliminate A's need to interpret P's language to determine whether P intends to prohibit A's purchase of a pony or a zebra or toy horses for sale in the menagerie's gift shop. A's interpretation will not be reasonable unless it takes into account A's prior experience with P which is likely to reveal how P uses language when referring to the menagerie.

Moreover, A might wonder how absolutely or unconditionally to interpret P's instruction. Would it contravene the instruction to buy an additional horse after the death of one of the horses on display in the menagerie? Should A understand P to mean that the value of an additional horse, relative to the sale price, is totally irrelevant? Must A pass on the opportunity to buy an especially valuable horse at a very low price? A may believe that P's best interests would be served by ignoring the literal interpretation of P's instruction. Unless A has reason to believe that P wishes A to do so, however, it is not reasonable for A to disregard the instruction rather than contacting P, if feasible, for further clarification.

A might decide to contravene P's instruction if A believes it to be a mistake from the standpoint of the business interest of the menagerie itself. Although A's departure from P's instructions may well be understandable, it is not consistent with A's duty of loyalty, which is owed to P and not to the menagerie itself. A lacks authority to depart from P's instructions to serve A's perception of what is required to further the interests of the menagerie.

Regardless of the breadth or narrowness with which a principal has conveyed authority to the agent, an agent's actual authority extends only to acts that the agent reasonably believes the principal has authorized or wishes the agent to perform. The fiduciary character of the agency relationship shapes the agent's permissible interpretation of authority, disallowing an interpretation that is inconsistent with interests of the principal that the agent knows or should know....

TOPIC 2. APPARENT AUTHORITY

§ 2.03 Apparent Authority

Apparent authority is the power held by an agent or other actor to affect a principal's legal relations with third parties when a third party reasonably believes the actor has authority to act on behalf of the principal and that belief is traceable to the principal's manifestations.

TOPIC 3. RESPONDEAT SUPERIOR

§ 2.04 Respondeat Superior

An employer is subject to liability for torts committed by employees while acting within the scope of their employment.

§ 2.05 Estoppel to Deny Existence of Agency Relationship

A person who has not made a manifestation that an actor has authority as an agent and who is not otherwise liable as a party to a transaction purportedly done by the actor on that person's account is subject to liability to a third party who justifiably is induced to make a detrimental change in position because the transaction is believed to be on the person's account, if

(1) the person intentionally or carelessly caused such belief, or

(2) having notice of such belief and that it might induce others to change their positions, the person did not take reasonable steps to notify them of the facts.

§ 2.06 Liability of Undisclosed Principal

(1) An undisclosed principal is subject to liability to a third party who is justifiably induced to make a detrimental change in position by an agent acting on the principal's behalf and without actual authority if the principal, having notice of the agent's conduct and that it might induce others to change their positions, did not take reasonable steps to notify them of the facts.

(2) An undisclosed principal may not rely on instructions given an agent that qualify or reduce the agent's authority to less than the authority a third party would reasonably believe the agent to have under the same circumstances if the principal had been disclosed.

§ 2.07 Restitution of Benefit

If a principal is unjustly enriched at the expense of another person by the action of an agent or a person who appears to be an agent, the principal is subject to a claim for restitution by that person.

CHAPTER 3

CREATION AND TERMINATION OF AUTHORITY AND AGENCY RELATIONSHIPS

TOPIC 1. CREATING AND EVIDENCING ACTUAL AUTHORITY

§ 3.01 Creation of Actual Authority

Actual authority, as defined in § 2.01, is created by a principal's manifestation to an agent that, as reasonably understood by the agent, expresses the principal's assent that the agent take action on the principal's behalf.

§ 3.02 Formal Requirements

If the law requires a writing or record signed by the principal to evidence an agent's authority to bind a principal to a contract or other transaction, the principal is not bound in the absence of such a writing or record. A principal may be estopped to assert the lack of such a writing or record when a third party has been induced to make a detrimental change in position by the reasonable belief that an agent has authority to bind the principal that is traceable to a manifestation made by the principal.

TOPIC 2. CREATING APPARENT AUTHORITY

§ 3.03 Creation of Apparent Authority

Apparent authority, as defined in § 2.03, is created by a person's manifestation that another has authority to act with legal consequences for the person who makes the manifestation, when a third party reasonably believes the actor to be authorized and the belief is traceable to the manifestation. . . .

TOPIC 4. TERMINATION OF AGENT'S POWER

TITLE A. TERMINATION OF ACTUAL AUTHORITY

§ 3.10 Manifestation Terminating Actual Authority

(1) Notwithstanding any agreement between principal and agent, an agent's actual authority terminates if the agent renounces it by a manifestation to the principal or if the principal revokes the agent's actual authority by a manifestation to the agent. A revocation or a renunciation is effective when the other party has notice of it.

(2) A principal's manifestation of revocation is, unless otherwise agreed, ineffective to terminate a power given as security or to terminate a proxy to vote securities or other membership or ownership interests that is made irrevocable in compliance with applicable legislation. See §§ 3.12–3.13.

TITLE B. TERMINATION OF APPARENT AUTHORITY

§ 3.11 Termination of Apparent Authority

(1) The termination of actual authority does not by itself end any apparent authority held by an agent.

(2) Apparent authority ends when it is no longer reasonable for the third party with whom an agent deals to believe that the agent continues to act with actual authority.

TITLE C. IRREVOCABLE POWERS

§ 3.12 Power Given as Security; Irrevocable Proxy

(1) A power given as security is a power to affect the legal relations of its creator that is created in the form of a manifestation of actual authority and held for the benefit of the holder or a third person. This power is given to protect a legal or equitable title or to secure the performance of a duty apart from any duties owed the holder of the power by its creator that are incident to a relationship of agency under § 1.01. It is given upon the creation of the duty or title or for consideration. It is distinct from actual authority that the holder may exercise if the holder is an agent of the creator of the power.

(2) A power to exercise voting rights associated with securities or a membership interest may be conferred on a proxy through a manifestation of actual authority. The power may be given as security under (1) and may be made irrevocable in compliance with applicable legislation.

Comment ...

b. Distinguished from agency and actual authority. A power given as security creates neither a relationship of agency as defined in § 1.01 nor actual authority as defined in § 2.01, although the power enables its holder to affect the legal relations of the creator of the power. The power arises from a manifestation of assent by its creator that the holder of the power may properly create liability against the creator, or dispose of property or other interests of the creator, or perfect or otherwise protect a title already held by the holder of the power or the person for whose benefit the holder is to act. If the power is given as security for the performance of a duty, it must be supported by consideration, but consideration is not necessary if the power is given to facilitate transfers of title to the power holder.

The rights created by a power given as security, or by an irrevocable proxy, entitle the holder to take specific actions. If the creator of a validly created power given as security purports to revoke the holder's authority contrary to the agreement pursuant to which the creator granted the power, specific enforcement of the holder's rights is an appropriate remedy, subject to the court's discretion in granting an equitable remedy. Likewise, specific enforcement may be warranted to protect the rights of the holder of a validly created irrevocable proxy. In both cases, it will often be difficult or impossible for the holder to prove quantifiable damages or to obtain a substitute performance. See Restatement Second, Contracts § 360, Comments *b* and *c*.

A power given as security does not create a relationship of agency as defined in § 1.01 because it is neither given for, nor exercised for, the benefit of the person who creates it. The holder is not subject to the creator's control and the holder does not owe fiduciary duties to the creator. An agent's right to act, created by actual authority, does not constitute a power given as security although the agent has an interest in earning a commission by performing services and the principal has contracted with the agent not to revoke the agent's actual authority. An agent's interest in being paid a commission is an ordinary incident of agency and its presence does not convert the agent's authority into a power held for the agent's benefit. In contrast, cases interpreting statutes applicable to irrevocable proxies hold that a proxy holder's interest in an employment agreement with the corporation suffices to support irrevocability. See Comment *d*. However, if a power holder has a distinct interest in the subject matter of an agency relationship, separate from acting as an agent, a power given to protect that interest is a power given as security, as is a power given to protect a distinct relationship, separate from the agency relationship, between the agent and the principal. A power may be granted irrevocably for the benefit of its creator as well as the holder.

A power given as security may also be created and held for the benefit of a third party, other than the holder of the power. The creator of the power and the holder have the ability to create an enforceable right in a third party to benefit from the power, just as two parties to a contract have the ability to create a right in a third-party beneficiary. See Restatement Second, Contracts § 304, Comment *b*.

Illustrations:

    1. P owns Blackacre, which is situated next to Whiteacre, on which P operates a restaurant. To finance renovations and

expansions, P borrows money from A. A written agreement between P and A provides that A shall irrevocably have P's authority to transfer ownership of Blackacre to A in the event P defaults on the loan. A has a power given as security.

2.   Same facts as Illustration 1, except that A is a corporation and the agreement with P provides that M, an officer of A, shall have P's authorization to transfer ownership of Blackacre. M has a power given as security. The power was given by P for the benefit of A.

3.   P owns a resort hotel. P engages A to manage the hotel for a term of 10 years, in an agreement that expressly provides that P may not revoke A's authority except pursuant to mutual agreement. The agreement states that P's promise not to revoke A's authority constitutes security to A for A's interest in receiving the management fee specified in the agreement, which is three percent of gross revenues for the first five years, and five percent for the second five years. A does not have a power given as security. If P revokes A's authority, A will not have a specifically enforceable right to continue to manage the hotel. A may claim that P's revocation is a breach of contract and seek money damages from P.

4.   P develops a mechanical invention and engages A to patent the invention and arrange for its commercial manufacture. P authorizes A to file patent documents on P's behalf and to enter into contracts with suitable manufacturers. P agrees to pay A's expenses and agrees to pay A half of P's profits. Even if A's authority is stated to be irrevocable, A does not hold a power given as security.

5.   Same facts as Illustration 4, except that P grants A a one-half ownership interest in the invention and P's rights in it, and A agrees to cover the expenses of A's efforts. It may be found that A has a power given as security. A will exercise the power for A's benefit as well as P's.

6.   Same facts as Illustration 5, except that P, at A's request, grants the one-half ownership interest to C, to whom A is indebted. It may be found that A has a power given as security, to be exercised for the benefit of C.

c.   *Power coupled with an interest.* Some jurisdictions follow a test narrower than that stated in this section, under which it is necessary that a power holder possess a proprietary interest in the "subject matter of the agency itself." This test also requires that the power and the proprietary interest be united in the same person. The narrower test has a distinguished lineage, beginning with Chief Justice Marshall's opinion in Hunt v. Rousmanier's Administrators, 21 U.S. (8 Wheat.) 174 (1823). Rousmanier had given Hunt a power of attorney to sell a brig and a schooner owned by Rousmanier, to be exercisable if Rousmanier defaulted in repaying loans he owed to Hunt. After Rousmanier died insolvent, following his default on the loans, the court held that the power was not enforceable. The court held that the power created only a revocable agency, which perished with Rousmanier's death, as opposed to "a power coupled with an interest" that survives its creator's death and may be exercised after it. 21 U.S. at 203. To create such a power, the holder must be vested with an interest or estate that accompanies the power. The focus of the court's opinion is the demise of Rousmanier's legal personality with his death, not the commercial function of the power, which the parties intended as a substitute for a mortgage on the ships that might not have been enforceable.

The difference between the test for irrevocability derived from *Hunt*, and that stated in this section, has practical consequences in two situations. First, under the "power coupled with an interest" approach, the power P granted to A in Illustration 1 is revocable because it does not accompany any proprietary interest of A in Blackacre itself. More generally, if a power must be coupled with a property interest to be made irrevocable, granting a power of sale as to property owned by the debtor, in which a creditor has no proprietary interest, will not effectively protect the creditor's interests. Unsurprisingly, the law applicable to loan transactions has itself evolved to overcome this obstacle. For example, a mortgage lender by statute has the right in every jurisdiction to cause the sale of the mortgaged property through judicial foreclosure. Additionally, in about 60 percent of the states, statutes authorize a mortgagee to sell pursuant to a power of sale, created by the mortgagor by conveying the property to a trustee who holds the property and the power to sell it as a fiduciary for the benefit of the mortgagee-beneficiary. The trustee exercises the power of sale. Separately, in secured financing under U.C.C. Article 9, it is irrelevant whether a lender obtains title to the collateral. A secured lender's rights concerning collateral, including the right to dispose of it after the borrower's default, are specified and regulated by the Code.

Second, the test derived from *Hunt* requires that the same person hold both the interest and the power. As a consequence, it does not recognize the irrevocability of a power created in one person when the creator transfers the requisite proprietary interest to another person, even if the holder and the transferor are closely related, such as affiliated corporations in the same group. Illustration 6 presents such a situation. The rule stated in this section permits an irrevocable power to be held for the benefit of a third party, which implies that the power holder and the interest-holder may be distinct persons.

Distinguished lineage aside, the quest for an interest to which a power has been coupled is not a useful exercise when it is clear that the power has been created for the benefit of a person other than the creator, as in *Hunt* itself. It is unnecessary to impose further limits on the creator's range of choices.

d.   Irrevocable proxies. A right to vote associated with securities may be delegated by the owner to an agent. Likewise, many organizational statutes contemplate that members of not-for-profit corporations may delegate voting rights to agents, as may members of limited-liability companies (LLCs). In such statutes, the treatment of voting by proxy is less fully developed than in business-corporation statutes.

Designating a proxy to vote creates a relationship of agency as defined in § 1.01 unless the proxy is irrevocable. Thus, the principal may revoke a proxy holder's actual authority. The principal lacks power to revoke the proxy holder's authority to vote when such authority is expressly made irrevocable and the holder receives the proxy as a power given as security as defined in § 3.12(1), or the proxy is supported by an interest that suffices to make it irrevocable under the applicable organizational statute. Revocation requires a manifestation from the principal, which may be made by conduct from which dissent to the proxy holder's authority may be inferred. See Comment *c.* The death of the proxy holder revokes a proxy that has expressly been made irrevocable only when the proxy was given to support an interest that terminates with the holder's death. See § 3.13.

An irrevocable proxy separates voting power from stock ownership; even when the proxy holder owns stock, the ability to vote stock owned by another augments the proxy holder's voting power. An irrevocable proxy thereby distorts the allocation of voting power to or among a corporation's residual economic claimants, who own its stock. The proxy holder's interests may not always be aligned with those of stockholders. For example, if the holder owns no stock but has an interest in employment by the corporation or an interest in commercial transactions with it, the proxy holder's interests may diverge from the stockholders' interests.

This potential for divergence in interests explains why, in many cases, courts refused to enforce irrevocable proxies. Courts enforced irrevocable proxies only when the holder had a proprietary interest in the shares themselves, as would a pledgee who has lent money on the security of the shares to their owner. Even when coupled with such an interest, an irrevocable proxy always operates with regard to two subjects: first, the shares; and, as a secondary subject, the corporation. The holder's vote affects the interests, but not the legal relations, of all of the corporation's shareholders. The spillover effect from the principal to the corporation and its other shareholders may also explain why irrevocable proxies attracted skepticism. An irrevocable proxy affects the interests of all shareholders because, if the holder has majority control, the holder ordinarily has power to choose the corporation's directors and holds veto power over fundamental transactions that require a shareholder vote.

Judicial skepticism lessened in some jurisdictions. Irrevocability was a practical necessity to combinations among shareholders because it enabled the coalescence of voting power in a predictable and enforceable manner. Only specific enforcement of the proxy by its terms, and not money damages, can provide control over voting. In response, some courts recast the terms of analysis to examine the grantor's motive or objective in granting the proxy. Such cases focus on whether the grantor had the pursuit of purely personal gain as an objective, as opposed to the good of all shareholders. This test has proven difficult to state or apply with precision. Business-corporation statutes also evolved to permit stockholders to form voting trusts, or to enter into specifically enforceable voting agreements, both devices that separate control over voting from stock ownership.

Most business-corporation statutes now address the question of irrevocability, albeit against the background sketched above. The statutes, and recent cases interpreting them, broaden the circumstances in which a proxy may be made irrevocable well beyond those applicable more generally to powers given as security, defined in § 3.12(1). Most business-corporation statutes provide that a proxy shall be irrevocable if it expressly so states and if the proxy is "coupled with an interest." The statutes vary in the extent to which they specify what shall suffice as an interest and in whether the statute makes the specification exclusive. Many statutes specify a nonexclusive list of relationships that suffice as an interest. The typical statement is that the appointment of a proxy is coupled with an interest when the appointee is a pledgee, a person who has purchased or agreed to purchase the shares, a creditor who extended credit to the corporation under terms requiring the appointment, an employee whose employment contract with the corporation requires the appointment, or a party to a voting agreement created pursuant to the statute. In some statutes, including those of New York and California, the list of specified interests is exclusive. Several statutes, including those of Delaware and Massachusetts, use broader language without specifying particular interests. Under the Delaware statute, "[a] duly executed proxy shall be irrevocable if it states that it is irrevocable and if, and only as long as, it is coupled with an interest sufficient in law to support an irrevocable power. A proxy may be made irrevocable regardless of whether the interest with which it is coupled is an interest in the stock itself or an interest in the corporation generally." Del. Code Ann., tit. 8, § 212(e) (2005).

Recent Delaware authority holds that an interest in employment constitutes "an interest in the corporation generally." This possibility is present as well under statutes that define interest to include an employment contract that requires the irrevocable proxy. So treating an interest in employment is at odds with the cases defining the more general doctrine of power given as security, stated in § 3.12(1). An agent's interest in receiving commissions or other compensation is insufficient to support such a power because it is an ordinary incident of the agency itself.

Competing policies apply to the treatment of interests in employment. The policy factors are especially pertinent when the relevant organizational statute authorizes voting by proxy but does not specify when a proxy may be made irrevocable. For example, some LLC statutes, like some not-for-profit corporation statutes, authorize voting by proxy but are silent on irrevocability. A proxy holder's self-interest in employment could lead to the election of directors, or to votes on fundamental transactions, that disserve the interests of most shareholders or members. This risk, however, may not warrant a stricter rule or at least not a categorically stricter rule. The risk will not materialize unless the holder's vote controls the voting outcome. Even when a proxy holder has effective control, other legal doctrines regulate how that control may be used. For example, corporate law regulates the use of voting control through doctrines specifically applicable to shareholders who use control to benefit themselves at the expense of other shareholders. See Principles of Corporate Governance: Analysis and Recommendations §§ 5.10–5.14. Moreover, a corporation's directors, regardless of how or by whom elected, owe fiduciary duties to the entire corporation, which encompasses the interests of its noncontrolling shareholders. See id. §§ 5.02–5.09. The terms of the employment contract between a proxy holder and the organization may also mitigate the risk, for example by tying the holder's compensation to performance-related criteria, and thereby aligning the holder's economic interests more closely to those of stockholders or members.

In general, irrevocable proxies to vote sufficient shares to constitute control are much more likely in closely held corporations or other business organizations than in publicly held corporations. In closely held enterprises, it is also more likely that most members will assent to, or at least be aware of, the circumstances that led to the proxy holder's irrevocable appointment.

§ 3.13 Termination of Power Given as Security or Irrevocable Proxy

(1) A power given as security or an irrevocable proxy is terminated by an event that

(a) discharges the obligation secured by the power or terminates the interest secured or supported by the proxy, or

(b) makes its execution illegal or impossible, or

(c) constitutes an effective surrender of the power or proxy by the person for whose benefit it was created or conferred.

(2) Unless otherwise agreed, neither a power given as security nor a proxy made irrevocable as provided in § 3.12(2) is terminated by:

(a) a manifestation revoking the power or proxy made by the person who created it; or

(b) surrender of the power or proxy by its holder if it is held for the benefit of another person, unless that person consents; or

(c) loss of capacity by the creator or the holder of the power or proxy; or

(d) death of the holder of the power or proxy, unless the holder's death terminates the interest secured or supported by the power or proxy; or

(e) death of the creator of the power or proxy, if the power or proxy is given as security for the performance of a duty that does not terminate with the death of its creator.

Comment . . .

b. Distinguished from revocation and renunciation of actual authority. Powers given as security and irrevocable proxies do not create relationships of agency as defined in § 1.01 and, despite their form, do not create actual authority under §§ 2.01 and 3.01. The power or proxy is held for the benefit of the holder or a third party and not solely for the benefit of its creator. A power given as security is not terminated by a manifestation of revocation by the creator of the power unless the parties have so agreed. A proxy made irrevocable in compliance with applicable legislation is not terminated by a manifestation of revocation from the owner of the securities or interest. In contrast, a manifestation of revocation by a principal terminates an agent's actual authority, notwithstanding any prior contrary agreement between principal and agent. See § 3.10.

Three basic concepts explain when powers given as security and irrevocable proxies will always terminate. Additionally, if the creator and holder of the power so agree, the power or proxy may be made subject to additional circumstances that result in termination. First, a power given as security or an irrevocable proxy is by definition tied to or supported by an interest or obligation that differentiates the power or proxy from a relationship of agency. Duration of the power or proxy is thus coterminous with such interest or obligation, with the consequence that terminating the interest or obligation terminates the power or proxy as well. For example, if the creator grants the power as security to a creditor, discharging the creator's obligation to the creditor terminates the power. If the creator grants the power to protect an ownership interest of the holder, the power terminates when the holder no longer has the ownership interest.

Second, a power given as security or an irrevocable proxy terminates when the power cannot be executed, either practically or legally, or when it is no longer possible for the proxy holder to vote because the grantor of the proxy no longer owns the securities or membership interest. For example, if the power is a power to sell property, the creator's sale of the same property to a bona fide purchaser who lacks notice of the power terminates the holder's power of sale.

Third, a power given as security or an irrevocable proxy terminates with the consent of the person for whose benefit it was created, manifested by surrendering the power or proxy. If the power was created for the benefit of a person other than the holder, the holder's surrender or renunciation does not terminate the power without the beneficiary's consent. This limit on surrender is analogous to the doctrine protecting the right of a third-party beneficiary to performance of a promise when the promisor and promisee have agreed that the third-party beneficiary shall hold a right to performance that may not be varied without the beneficiary's consent. See Restatement Second, Contracts § 311(1) and Comment *a*.

Under statutes in many states, the interests that may support an irrevocable proxy are broader than those requisite for a power granted as security. These interests include those created by an employment agreement with the corporation that requires the proxy, as well as by a voting agreement among shareholders. See § 3.12, Comment *d*. Some statutes formulate the requisite interest in nonspecific terms, such as "an interest in the corporation generally." See Del. Code Ann. tit. 8, § 212(e) (2005). The power irrevocably conferred by the proxy terminates when the holder's interest ends....

TOPIC 5.   AGENTS WITH MULTIPLE PRINCIPALS

§ 3.14 Agents with Multiple Principals

An agent acting in the same transaction or matter on behalf of more than one principal may be one or both of the following:

    (a) a subagent, as stated in § 3.15; or

    (b) an agent for coprincipals, as stated in § 3.16.

§ 3.15 Subagency

(1) A subagent is a person appointed by an agent to perform functions that the agent has consented to perform on behalf of the

agent's principal and for whose conduct the appointing agent is responsible to the principal. The relationships between a subagent and the appointing agent and between the subagent and the appointing agent's principal are relationships of agency as stated in § 1.01.

(2) An agent may appoint a subagent only if the agent has actual or apparent authority to do so.

Comment . . .

b. Subagency contrasted with coagency. Agency creates a personal relationship between principal and agent; an agent's delegation of power to another person to act on behalf of the principal is inconsistent with the undertaking made when a person consents to act as agent on behalf of a principal. However, a principal may empower an agent to appoint another agent to act on the principal's behalf. The second agent may be a subagent or a coagent. . . .

An agent who appoints a subagent delegates to the subagent power to act on behalf of the principal that the principal has conferred on the agent. A subagent acts subject to the control of the appointing agent, and the principal's legal position is affected by action taken by the subagent as if the action had been taken by the appointing agent. Thus, a subagent has two principals, the appointing agent and that agent's principal. Although an appointing agent has the right and duty to control a subagent, the interests and instructions of the appointing agent's principal are paramount. . . .

§ 3.16 Agent for Coprincipals

Two or more persons may as coprincipals appoint an agent to act for them in the same transaction or matter.

CHAPTER 4

RATIFICATION

§ 4.01 Ratification Defined

(1) Ratification is the affirmance of a prior act done by another, whereby the act is given effect as if done by an agent acting with actual authority.

(2) A person ratifies an act by

(a) manifesting assent that the act shall affect the person's legal relations, or

(b) conduct that justifies a reasonable assumption that the person so consents.

(3) Ratification does not occur unless

    (a) the act is ratifiable as stated in § 4.03,

    (b) the person ratifying has capacity as stated in § 4.04,

    (c) the ratification is timely as stated in § 4.05, and

    (d) the ratification encompasses the act in its entirety as stated in § 4.07.

§ 4.02   Effect of Ratification

(1) Subject to the exceptions stated in subsection (2), ratification retroactively creates the effects of actual authority.

(2) Ratification is not effective:

    (a) in favor of a person who causes it by misrepresentation or other conduct that would make a contract voidable;

    (b) in favor of an agent against a principal when the principal ratifies to avoid a loss; or

    (c) to diminish the rights or other interests of persons, not parties to the transaction, that were acquired in the subject matter prior to the ratification.

§ 4.03   Acts That May Be Ratified

A person may ratify an act if the actor acted or purported to act as an agent on the person's behalf.

§ 4.04   Capacity to Ratify

(1) A person may ratify an act if

    (a) the person existed at the time of the act, and

    (b) the person had capacity as defined in § 3.04 at the time of ratifying the act.

(2) At a later time, a principal may avoid a ratification made earlier when the principal lacked capacity as defined in § 3.04.

Comment ...

    b. Capacity to be a principal . . . .

Earlier statements of ratification doctrine were more stringent on this score, requiring that the principal have had capacity at the time of the original act as well as at the time of ratification. See Restatement Second, Agency § 84(1). . . .

    c. Nonexistent principals, including corporations yet to be formed. Under the rule stated in subsection (1)(a), a person not in existence at the time of an act or transaction may not subsequently ratify it. Instead, a person may elect to become bound under such circumstances by adopting what was done prior to the person's existence. Adoption operates analogously to ratification because it requires assent or affirmance on the part of the ratifier. Unlike ratification, adoption does not have a relation-back effect. Additionally, an adoption, unlike a novation, does not itself release obligors from liabilities created by the original transaction.

Illustration:

1. A, acting on behalf of P Corporation, which is not yet incorporated, enters into an oral employment contract for a term of 18 months with B. Once formed, P Corporation adopts the contract 13 months after A made the contract with B. The applicable Statute of Frauds requires that contracts not to be performed within one year of their making, including contracts of employment, be evidenced by a writing signed by the party to be charged. B's contract is enforceable notwithstanding the Statute of Frauds because P Corporation's adoption does not relate back to the time of the original contract.

This limit on ratification has a long lineage in disputes involving transactions made by promoters on behalf of corporations that have not yet been formed. Comparable questions may arise concerning promoters' transactions on behalf of not-yet-formed limited partnerships and limited-liability companies. A corporation should not be bound by the terms of a contract made prior to its existence until its own mechanisms of governance are in place and able to assess the merits of the transaction. A promoter's interests are often not identical to the interests of those who own equity in a corporation once it is formed.

If a promoter enters into a contract with a third party on behalf of a corporation that has not yet commenced legal existence, the corporation itself cannot be a party to the contract prior to its existence. This is so whether the contract purports to be made on behalf of a corporation characterized as one yet to be formed or characterizes the corporation as one presently in existence. If the contract is to bind the third party prior to the existence of the corporation, unless the relationship is structured as an option that may be exercised by the corporation when formed, either the promoter or someone else must be liable on the contract. The parties' intention must often be determined on the basis of inferences to be drawn from the circumstances, which include whether the promoter and the other party are aware that the corporation does not yet exist. A third party may agree in a contract made by a promoter to release the promoter's liability when and if the corporation adopts the contract. In the absence of an express agreement by the third party to release the promoter, some cases permit the promoter to establish that the parties intended that the promoter would not be personally liable. A corporation may adopt a contract made by a promoter by accepting its benefits with knowledge of its terms.

This doctrine has the potential to carry harsh consequences for promoters when a third party does not agree to release a promoter's individual liability when and if the corporation adopts the contract. The third party may determine that the corporation's ability to perform under the contract looks risky and decline to release the promoter or, regardless of its assessment of prospects of the corporation's performance, the third party may prefer to have more rather than fewer obligors on the contract. When a third party knows at the time of contracting with a promoter that the corporation has not yet been formed, the promoter's conduct has not deceived the third party. Moreover, even if the corporation agrees to indemnify the promoter against loss stemming from the promoter's individual liability, the indemnity will not protect the promoter if the corporation is insolvent and cannot pay when the promoter seeks to be indemnified.

Viewed in a broader perspective, the risk of individual liability may be beneficial because it encourages promoters to complete the formal requisites for incorporation sooner rather than later. The process requisite to incorporation under contemporary corporation statutes is not cumbersome. Moreover, duly completing the process of forming a corporation creates a publicly accessible document, filed with the state, that furnishes useful albeit minimal information, including the corporation's name and the name and address of the agent it has designated to receive service of process. Such a formal record provides a source of information that enables the state to enforce applicable law, as well as enabling private parties to pursue legal process.

Provisions in corporation statutes reflect different judgments about how contractual risk should be allocated as between promoter and third party when a contract purports to be made on behalf of a not-yet-formed corporation as if it had present existence. Several states have adopted verbatim the language of § 2.04 of the Model Business Corporation Act, which provides that "[a]ll persons purporting to act as or on behalf of a corporation, knowing there was no incorporation under this act, are jointly and severally liable for all liabilities created while so acting." In a few states, a promoter must have "actual knowledge" that there was no incorporation, while in several other states, the promoter is liable whether or not the promoter knows that the corporation has not yet been incorporated. A few states excuse a promoter from liability when the promoter believes in good faith that incorporation has occurred or do not permit a person "who also knew that there was no incorporation" to hold the promoter liable.

A court may determine that a third party should be estopped from seeking a promoter's personal liability. For example, if a promoter is reluctant to enter into a contract personally but a third party persuades the promoter to contract in the name of a nonexistent corporation, the third party has induced the promoter to take action the promoter would likely not have taken otherwise.

REPORTER'S NOTES ...

c. Nonexistent principals, including corporations yet to be formed. Illustration 1 is based on McArthur v. Times Printing Co., 51 N.W. 216, 217 (1892).

For the proposition that a corporation may adopt preincorporation transactions, see Illinois Controls, Inc. v. Langham, 639 N.E.2d 771, 780 (Ohio 1994). See also Madeja v. Olympic Packer, LLC, 155 F. Supp. 2d 1183, 1204 (D. Hawaii 2001), aff'd, 310 F.3d 628 (9th Cir. 2002) (holding that charter agreement was not void because made prior to incorporation of company that chartered vessel; either corporation or individual who signed charter on its behalf as president would be required to perform terms of charter).

Cases holding that a corporation once formed may "adopt" but not ratify promoters' contracts include Commissioners of Lewes v. Breakwater Fisheries Co., 117 A. 823 (Del. 1923); Davis & Rankin Bldg. & Mfg. Co. v. Hillsboro Creamery Co., 37 N.E. 549 (Ind. 1894); McCrillis v. A & W Enters., Inc., 155 S.E.2d 281 (N.C. 1967). The sole authority to the contrary appears to be Stanton v. New York & E.Ry. Co., 22 A. 300 (Conn. 1890).

Some opinions use the terms "ratification" and "adoption" interchangeably when no operative consequences follow. See Yost v. Early, 589 A.2d 1291, 1300 (Md. Ct. Spec. App. 1991); Eden Temp. Servs., Inc. v. House of Excellence, Inc., 704 N.Y.S.2d 239, 240 (App. Div. 2000); Coastal Shutters & Insulation, Inc. v. Derr, 809 S.W.2d 916, 920 (Tex. App. 1991).

Cases holding that a promoter retains individual liability despite the corporation's adoption of the contract include Allen Steel Supply Co. v. Bradley, 402 P.2d 394 (Idaho 1965); Jacobson v. Stern, 605 P.2d 198 (Nev. 1980). This gives the third party "double security." See Carle v. Corhan, 103 S.E. 699, 702 (Va. 1920); Eddie Flores, The Case for Eliminating Promoter Liability on Preincorporation Agreements, 32 Ariz. L. Rev. 405, 407 (1990).

Cases looking to the parties' intention to determine whether a promoter is personally liable include Quaker Hill, Inc. v. Parr, 364 P.2d 1056 (Colo. 1961) (no intention to hold promoters personally liable when contract signed in name of corporation and both parties knew corporation not in existence); Tin Cup Pass Ltd. P'ship v. Daniels, 553 N.E.2d 82 (Ill. App. Ct. 1990) (holding promoters not liable when lease signed in name of corporation that both parties knew had not been formed); Company Stores Dev. Corp. v. Pottery Warehouse, Inc., 733 S.W.2d 886, 887 (Tenn. Ct. App. 1987) (holding promoter not liable on lease when lessor agreed to look only to named lessee as " 'a corporation to be formed' ")....

§ 4.05 Timing of Ratification

A ratification of a transaction is not effective unless it precedes the occurrence of circumstances that would cause the ratification to have adverse and inequitable effects on the rights of third parties. These circumstances include:

(1) any manifestation of intention to withdraw from the transaction made by the third party;

(2) any material change in circumstances that would make it inequitable to bind the third party, unless the third party chooses to be bound; and

(3) a specific time that determines whether a third party is deprived of a right or subjected to a liability.

§ 4.06 Knowledge Requisite to Ratification

A person is not bound by a ratification made without knowledge of material facts involved in the original act when the person was unaware of such lack of knowledge.

§ 4.07 No Partial Ratification

A ratification is not effective unless it encompasses the entirety of an act, contract, or other single transaction.

§ 4.08 Estoppel to Deny Ratification

If a person makes a manifestation that the person has ratified another's act and the manifestation, as reasonably understood by a third party, induces the third party to make a detrimental change in position, the person may be estopped to deny the ratification.

CHAPTER 5

NOTIFICATIONS AND NOTICE

§ 5.01 Notifications and Notice—In General

(1) A notification is a manifestation that is made in the form required by agreement among parties or by applicable law, or in a reasonable manner in the absence of an agreement or an applicable law, with the intention of affecting the legal rights and duties of the notifier in relation to rights and duties of persons to whom the notification is given.

(2) A notification given to or by an agent is effective as notification to or by the principal as stated in § 5.02.

(3) A person has notice of a fact if the person knows the fact, has reason to know the fact, has received an effective notification of the fact, or should know the fact to fulfill a duty owed to another person.

(4) Notice of a fact that an agent knows or has reason to know is imputed to the principal as stated in §§ 5.03 and 5.04.

§ 5.02 Notification Given by or to an Agent

(1) A notification given to an agent is effective as notice to the principal if the agent has actual or apparent authority to receive the notification, unless the person who gives the notification knows or has reason to know that the agent is acting adversely to the principal as stated in § 5.04.

(2) A notification given by an agent is effective as notification given by the principal if the agent has actual or apparent authority to give the notification, unless the person who receives the notification knows or has reason to know that the agent is acting adversely to the principal as stated in § 5.04.

§ 5.03 Imputation of Notice of Fact to Principal

For purposes of determining a principal's legal relations with a third party, notice of a fact that an agent knows or has reason to know is imputed to the principal if knowledge of the fact is material to the agent's duties to the principal, unless the agent

(a) acts adversely to the principal as stated in § 5.04, or

(b) is subject to a duty to another not to disclose the fact to the principal.

§ 5.04 An Agent Who Acts Adversely to a Principal

For purposes of determining a principal's legal relations with a third party, notice of a fact that an agent knows or has reason to know is not imputed to the principal if the agent acts adversely to the principal in a transaction or matter, intending to act solely for the agent's own purposes or those of another person. Nevertheless, notice is imputed

(a) when necessary to protect the rights of a third party who dealt with the principal in good faith; or

(b) when the principal has ratified or knowingly retained a benefit from the agent's action.

A third party who deals with a principal through an agent, knowing or having reason to know that the agent acts adversely to the principal, does not deal in good faith for this purpose.

CHAPTER 6

CONTRACTS AND OTHER TRANSACTIONS WITH THIRD PARTIES

TOPIC 1. PARTIES TO CONTRACTS

§ 6.01   Agent for Disclosed Principal

When an agent acting with actual or apparent authority makes a contract on behalf of a disclosed principal,

(1) the principal and the third party are parties to the contract; and

(2) the agent is not a party to the contract unless the agent and third party agree otherwise.

Comment ...

b. Bases and consequences of contractual liability when agent acts on behalf of disclosed principal. An agent acts on behalf of a disclosed principal when the third party with whom the agent deals has notice that the agent acts for a principal and also has notice of the principal's identity. See § 1.04(2)(a). An agent has power to make contracts on behalf of the agent's principal when the agent acts with actual or apparent authority. . . .

Illustration:

> 1. P, a wine merchant, engages A to dispose of portions of P's inventory. P directs A to sell all of P's inventory of French wines to T, another wine merchant. A makes an offer to T on P's behalf. T replies: "I do not believe that you have authority to sell all of P's French wine, but I will chance it and accept the offer." There is a contract between P and T. A had actual authority to bind P, although T doubts whether this is so. . . .

An agent who enters into a contract on behalf of a disclosed principal does not become a party to the contract and is not subject to liability as a guarantor of the principal's performance unless the agent and the third party so agree. Thus, in the absence of such agreement, an agent for a disclosed principal who enters into a contract on the principal's behalf is not subject to liability if the principal fails to perform obligations created by the contract. As a consequence, the agent is not a necessary party to breach-of-contract litigation between a disclosed principal and the third party to a contract made by the agent on the principal's behalf.

Through ratification, a person may become a party to a contract purportedly made on that person's behalf by another who acted without actual or apparent authority. See Chapter 4.

78

[The] parties to a contract, a principal and third party, have the same rights, liabilities, and defenses against each other as if the principal had made the contract directly, subject to §§ 6.05–6.09. A disclosed principal may assert against the third party all defenses that arise out of the contract itself and all defenses that are personal to the principal. The principal may not assert defenses that would have been personal to the agent had the agent been a party to the contract. . . .

c. *Contract made on behalf of a disclosed principal.* If an agent makes a contract in the name of a principal or a description in the contract is sufficient to identify the principal, the principal is a disclosed principal and is a party to the contract. When a disclosed principal is a corporation or other organization with separate legal personality, the corporation becomes a party to contracts made on its behalf by its agents. Corporate or other organizational agents, like agents for other disclosed principals, are not parties to a corporate contract unless the agent and the third party so agree. . . .

4. P, a farmer, incorporates the farm business under the name "P Farms Corp." P operates the business of P Farms Corp. as its chief executive officer. On behalf of and in the name of P Farms Corp., P purchases supplies on credit from T. P is not a party to, and is not subject to liability on, contracts between P Farms Corp. and T. . . .

§ 6.02 Agent for Unidentified Principal

When an agent acting with actual or apparent authority makes a contract on behalf of an unidentified principal,

(1) the principal and the third party are parties to the contract; and

(2) the agent is a party to the contract unless the agent and the third party agree otherwise.

Comment . . .

b. *Bases of contractual liability when agent acts on behalf of unidentified principal.* An agent acts on behalf of an unidentified principal when the third party with whom the agent deals has notice that the agent acts on behalf of a principal but does not have notice of the principal's identity. See § 1.04(2)(c). Many cases, like Restatement Second, Agency § 4(2), refer to such a principal as a "partially disclosed principal." This Restatement instead uses the term "unidentified principal." . . .

An agent has power to make contracts on behalf of an unidentified principal when the agent acts with actual or apparent authority, just as an agent acting with actual or apparent authority has power to make contracts on behalf of a disclosed principal. See § 6.01(1). If an agent purports to act on behalf of an unidentified principal but lacks actual or apparent authority to bind the principal, the agent is subject to liability on the agent's implied warranty of authority....

Unless the third party and the agent agree otherwise, an agent who makes a contract on behalf of a disclosed principal does not become a party to the contract. See § 6.01(2). In contrast, as stated in subsection (2) of this section, an agent who makes a contract on behalf of an unidentified principal becomes a party to the contract unless the third party and the agent agree otherwise. When a third party has notice that an agent deals on behalf of a principal but does not have notice of the principal's identity, it is not likely that the third party will rely solely on the principal's solvency or ability to perform obligations arising from the contract. Without notice of a principal's identity, a third party will be unable to assess the principal's reputation, assets, and other indicia of creditworthiness and ability to perform duties under the contract. If an agent provides reassurances about the principal's soundness only generally or describes the principal, the third party will be unable to verify such claims without notice of the principal's identity....

Illustrations:

1.   P, who deals in antiques, retains A to purchase antiques on P's behalf. P directs A not to disclose P's identity to persons with whom A deals. A complies. A contracts to buy an antique clock owned by T, telling T that A is purchasing the clock on behalf of A's principal. P is A's unidentified principal. P and T are parties to the contract for the sale of the clock. A is also a party to the contract unless A and T agree otherwise.

2.   Same facts as Illustration 1, except that, prior to contracting to sell the clock, T learns from a friend that A represents P. As to T, P is A's disclosed principal. T knew P's identity when making the contract with A. P and T are parties to the contract for the sale of the clock. A is not a party unless A and T agree otherwise. See § 6.01(2)....

e. Agent's position as party to contract. In an action by a third party against an agent who has made a contract on behalf of an unidentified principal, the agent may assert all defenses that arise from the transaction itself and defenses available to the agent personally.

§ 6.03   Agent for Undisclosed Principal

When an agent acting with actual authority makes a contract on behalf of an undisclosed principal,

(1) unless excluded by the contract, the principal is a party to the contract;

(2) the agent and the third party are parties to the contract; and

(3) the principal, if a party to the contract, and the third party have the same rights, liabilities, and defenses against each other as if the principal made the contract personally, subject to §§ 6.05–6.09.

Comment ...

b. Rationales for contractual liability. ...

[W]ell-settled doctrine treats an undisclosed principal as a party to a contract that an agent makes on behalf of the principal, unless the contract excludes the principal as a party....

Illustration:

>   1. A, the sole proprietor of a construction business, deals over several years with T, who is in the building-supplies business. A maintains an account with T that requires A to pay for supplies 30 days following delivery. Without notice to T, A incorporates A's business as "A Construction Corp." and transfers to A Construction Corp. ownership of all assets used by A in operating the business. A continues to run the business as before and continues to purchase supplies on credit from T. Both A and A Construction Corp. are subject to liability for payment owed to T for supplies delivered by T to A's business after A incorporates it. A acted as the agent of A Construction Corp., A's undisclosed principal.

An agent who makes a contract on behalf of an undisclosed principal also becomes a party to the contract. The basis for treating the agent as a party to the contract is the expectation of the third party. The agent has dealt with the third party as if the agent were the sole party whose legal relations would be affected as a consequence of making the contract....

d. Circumstances that affect rights or liabilities of undisclosed principal; contract excluding undisclosed principal as party. ...

The nature of the performance that a contract requires determines whether performance by an undisclosed principal will be effective as performance under the contract and whether an undisclosed principal can require that the third party render performance to the principal. Performance by an undisclosed principal is not effective as performance under a contract if the third party has a substantial interest in receiving performance from the agent who made the contract. This limit corresponds to the limit on delegability of performance of a duty as stated in Restatement Second, Contracts § 318(2).

Illustrations:

>   6. T enters into a contract with A in which A promises to manage T's investment portfolio. A does not disclose that A

makes the contract on behalf of P. P offers to manage T's portfolio. T is free to accept or reject P's offer of performance. P's offer does not constitute an offer of performance of the contract made by A. T has a substantial interest in receiving investment-management services from A.

7. T enters into a contract to purchase a quantity of coal of a specified kind from A. A does not disclose that A makes the contract on behalf of P. P tenders coal to T of the specified kind and quantity. P's tender has the effect of a tender by A because T has no substantial interest in receiving the coal from A.

The nature of the performance that a contract requires from a third party determines whether an undisclosed principal is entitled to receive that performance. An undisclosed principal may not require that a third party render performance to the principal if rendering performance to the principal would materially change the nature of the third party's duty, materially increase the burden or risk imposed on the third party, or materially impair the third party's chance of receiving return performance. These limits correspond to the limits imposed on assignment of a contractual right. See Restatement Second, Contracts § 317(2).

Illustrations:

8. T agrees to work as a nanny for A. P, A's undisclosed principal, cannot require T to work as a nanny for P. The contract between T and A requires that T render personal services in an ongoing close association. Requiring T to render the services to P would materially change the nature of T's duties.

9. T agrees to sell Blackacre in exchange for cash to A, who acts on behalf of P, A's undisclosed principal. P may require performance from T. The contract made by A requires only the payment of money in exchange for Blackacre.

e. Position of agent as party to contract. As a party to a contract made on behalf of an undisclosed principal, an agent may sue the third party in the agent's own name. The agent is subject to liability on the contract. If sued on the contract, the agent may assert all defenses arising from the transaction and defenses personal to the agent.

Illustration:

10. P owns a farm which A manages. A makes a contract to sell a quantity of potatoes from P's farm to T, expressly warranting that they are seed potatoes. T does not have notice that A acts on behalf of P. After T takes delivery of the potatoes, pays for them, and resells them, T discovers that they

are not seed potatoes. A and P are subject to liability to T for breach of warranty. . . .

§ 6.04 Principal Does Not Exist or Lacks Capacity

Unless the third party agrees otherwise, a person who makes a contract with a third party purportedly as an agent on behalf of a principal becomes a party to the contract if the purported agent knows or has reason to know that the purported principal does not exist or lacks capacity to be a party to a contract.

Comment . . .

c. Contracts made on behalf of entities yet to be formed. The rule stated in this section is applicable when a person purports to make a contract with a third party on behalf of an entity that does not exist. If that person and the third party manifest assent that the contract shall bind the third party, the person who purports to act on behalf of the entity is personally liable on the contract.

Illustration:

2. A is the president and sole shareholder of "Marketing Designs, Inc." Wishing to do business as a wholesaler of seafood, A makes a contract to purchase salmon from T, a fish importer. A expressly makes the contract on behalf of "Boston International Seafood Exchange, Inc.," believing that the name more closely identifies A with the seafood industry. A knows that Boston International Seafood Exchange, Inc., does not exist. Payment for the salmon is not made as required by the contract. A is subject to liability on the contract with T. As A knew, the corporation on whose behalf A purportedly made the contract did not exist.

The classic instance of this situation arises when a person enters into a contract purportedly on behalf of an entity that has not yet been formed, such as a business or a not-for-profit corporation or a limited-liability company. Promoters of entities yet-to-be-formed may find it attractive and even imperative to obtain binding commitments from third parties before the formal process of organization has been completed. The statute applicable to forming the particular type of entity may address the circumstances under which a promoter will be subject to individual liability on a contract made on behalf of a not-yet-formed entity. When an entity comes into existence, it may adopt the contract made by the promoter. See § 4.04, Comment c. An entity's adoption of a contract made by a promoter does not by itself release the promoter from any individual liability that the promoter may have on the contract. See id.

If a promoter enters into a contract with a third party on behalf of an entity that has not yet commenced legal existence, the entity itself cannot be a party to the contract prior to its existence. This is so whether the contract purports to be made on behalf of an entity characterized as one yet to be formed or characterizes the entity as one presently in existence. If the contract is to bind the third party prior to the entity's existence, unless the relationship is structured as an option that may be exercised by the entity when formed, either the promoter or someone else must be liable on the contract. The parties' intention must often be determined on the basis of inferences to be drawn from the circumstances, which include whether the promoter and the other party are aware that the entity does not yet exist. A third party may agree in a contract made by a promoter to release the promoter's liability when and if the entity adopts the contract. In the absence of an express agreement by the third party to release the promoter, some cases permit the promoter to establish that the parties intended that the promoter would not be personally liable. An entity may adopt a contract made by a promoter by accepting its benefits with knowledge of its terms. For further discussion, see § 4.04, Comment *c*.

Similar questions arise when a person purports to take action on behalf of an entity when its powers have been suspended or forfeited, or when the entity has been dissolved. The organizational statute applicable to the entity may specify the circumstances under which such action will result in individual liability to third parties....

TOPIC 2. RIGHTS, LIABILITIES, AND DEFENSES
TITLE A.　IN GENERAL

§ 6.05 Contract That Is Unauthorized in Part or That Combines Orders of Several Principals

(1) If an agent makes a contract with a third party that differs from the contract that the agent had actual or apparent authority to make only in an amount or by the inclusion or exclusion of a separable part, the principal is subject to liability to the third party to the extent of the contract that the agent had actual or apparent authority to make if

(a) the third party seasonably makes a manifestation to the principal of willingness to be bound; and

(b) the principal has not changed position in reasonable reliance on the belief that no contract bound the principal and the third party.

(2) Two or more principals may authorize the same agent to make separate contracts for them. If the agent makes a single contract with a

third party on the principals' behalves that combines the principals' separate orders or interests and calls for a single performance by the third party,

(a) if the agent purports to make the combined contract on behalf of disclosed principals, the agent is subject to liability to the third party for breach of the agent's warranty of authority as stated in § 6.10, unless the separate principals are bound by the combined contract;

(b) if the principals are unidentified or undisclosed, the third party and the agent are the only parties to the combined contract; and

(c) unless the agent acted with actual or apparent authority to bind each of the principals to the combined contract,

(i) subject to (1), none of the separate principals is subject to liability on the combined contract; and

(ii) the third party is not subject to liability on the combined contract to any of the separate principals.

§ 6.06 Setoff

(1) When an agent makes a contract on behalf of a disclosed or unidentified principal, unless the principal and the third party agree otherwise,

(a) the third party may not set off any amount that the agent independently owes the third party against an amount the third party owes the principal under the contract; and

(b) the principal may not set off any amount that the third party independently owes the agent against an amount the principal owes the third party under the contract.

(2) When an agent makes a contract on behalf of an undisclosed principal,

(a) the third party may set off

(i) any amount that the agent independently owed the third party at the time the agent made the contract and

(ii) any amount that the agent thereafter independently comes to owe the third party until the third party has notice that the agent acts on behalf of a principal against an amount the third party owes the principal under the contract;

(b) after the third party has notice that the agent acts on behalf of a principal, the third party may not set off any amount that the agent thereafter independently comes to owe the third party against an amount the third party owes the principal under the contract unless the principal consents; and

85

(c) the principal may not set off any amount that the third party independently owes the agent against an amount that the principal owes the third party under the contract, unless the principal and the third party agree otherwise.

(3) Unless otherwise agreed, an agent who is a party to a contract may not set off any amount that the principal independently owes the agent against an amount that the agent owes the third party under the contract. However, with the principal's consent, the agent may set off any amount that the principal could set off against an amount that the principal owes the third party under the contract.

TITLE B.　SUBSEQUENT DEALINGS BETWEEN THIRD PARTY AND PRINCIPAL OR AGENT

§ 6.07　Settlement with Agent by Principal or Third Party

(1) A principal's payment to or settlement of accounts with an agent discharges the principal's liability to a third party with whom the agent has made a contract on the principal's behalf only when the principal acts in reasonable reliance on a manifestation by the third party, not induced by misrepresentation by the agent, that the agent has settled the account with the third party.

(2) A third party's payment to or settlement of accounts with an agent discharges the third party's liability to the principal if the agent acts with actual or apparent authority in accepting the payment or settlement.

(3) When an agent has made a contract on behalf of an undisclosed principal,

(a) until the third party has notice of the principal's existence, the third party's payment to or settlement of accounts with the agent discharges the third party's liability to the principal;

(b) after the third party has notice of the principal's existence, the third party's payment to or settlement of accounts with the agent discharges the third party's liability to the principal if the agent acts with actual or apparent authority in accepting the payment or settlement; and

(c) after receiving notice of the principal's existence, the third party may demand reasonable proof of the principal's identity and relationship to the agent. Until such proof is received, the third party's payment to or settlement of accounts in good faith with the agent discharges the third party's liability to the principal.

§ 6.08　Other Subsequent Dealings Between Third Party and Agent

(1) When an agent has made a contract with a third party on behalf of a disclosed or unidentified principal, subsequent dealings between the

agent and the third party may increase or diminish the principal's rights or liabilities to the third party if the agent acts with actual or apparent authority or the principal ratifies the agent's action.

(2) When an agent has made a contract with a third party on behalf of an undisclosed principal,

(a) until the third party has notice of the principal's existence, subsequent dealings between the third party and the agent may increase or diminish the rights or liabilities of the principal to the third party if the agent acts with actual authority, or the principal ratifies the agent's action; and

(b) after the third party has notice of the principal's existence, subsequent dealings between the third party and the agent may increase or diminish the principal's rights or liabilities to the third party if the agent acts with actual or apparent authority or the principal ratifies the agent's action.

§ 6.09 Effect of Judgment Against Agent or Principal

When an agent has made a contract with a third party on behalf of a principal, unless the contract provides otherwise,

(1) the liability, if any, of the principal or the agent to the third party is not discharged if the third party obtains a judgment against the other; and

(2) the liability, if any, of the principal or the agent to the third party is discharged to the extent a judgment against the other is satisfied.

TITLE C
AGENT'S WARRANTIES AND REPRESENTATIONS

§ 6.10 Agent's Implied Warranty of Authority

A person who purports to make a contract, representation, or conveyance to or with a third party on behalf of another person, lacking power to bind that person, gives an implied warranty of authority to the third party and is subject to liability to the third party for damages for loss caused by breach of that warranty, including loss of the benefit expected from performance by the principal, unless

(1) the principal or purported principal ratifies the act as stated in § 4.01; or

(2) the person who purports to make the contract, representation, or conveyance gives notice to the third party that no warranty of authority is given; or

(3) the third party knows that the person who purports to make the contract, representation, or conveyance acts without actual authority.

Comment . . .

   b. Agent's implied warranty of authority—in general. . . .

The measure of recovery for breach of an implied warranty of authority should reflect the fact that the third party may have been deprived of a benefit that the third party would have realized, had the principal been bound as the agent purported to have authority to do. Thus, if an agent purports to bind a principal to a contract, the third party's measure of recovery should compensate the third party for loss suffered and should include the benefit of the bargain to the third party, had the principal been bound by the contract. Some courts, in contrast, limit the third party's recovery to the damage or loss the third party suffered and exclude the third party's expected gain from the contract. Some cases explicitly characterize the third party's claim for breach of warranty as equivalent to a tort claim based on a misrepresentation.

The better rule recognizes that the function of the agent's implied warranty is to safeguard the third party's expectation that the agent in fact has power to bind the principal to the legal consequences of the agent's actions. Although the agent's implied warranty of authority is grounded in an implied representation made by the agent, the representation is that the agent's actions will bind the principal whom the agent purports to represent. When an agent purports to bind a principal to a contract but lacks power to do so, the third party has been deprived of the anticipated benefit of a bargain. The third party's recovery against the agent should include the value of this anticipated benefit. As noted above, an agent's implied representation may, separately, subject the agent to tort liability. . . .

§ 6.11 Agent's Representations

(1) When an agent for a disclosed or unidentified principal makes a false representation about the agent's authority to a third party, the principal is not subject to liability unless the agent acted with actual or apparent authority in making the representation and the third party does not have notice that the agent's representation is false.

(2) A representation by an agent made incident to a contract or conveyance is attributed to a disclosed or unidentified principal as if the principal made the representation directly when the agent had actual or apparent authority to make the contract or conveyance unless the third party knew or had reason to know that the representation was untrue or that the agent acted without actual authority in making it.

(3) A representation by an agent made incident to a contract or conveyance is attributed to an undisclosed principal as if the principal made the representation directly when

(a) the agent acted with actual authority in making the representation, or

(b) the agent acted without actual authority in making the representation but had actual authority to make true representations about the same matter.

The agent's representation is not attributed to the principal when the third party knew or had reason to know it was untrue.

(4) When an agent who makes a contract or conveyance on behalf of an undisclosed principal falsely represents to the third party that the agent does not act on behalf of a principal, the third party may avoid the contract or conveyance if the principal or agent had notice that the third party would not have dealt with the principal.

Comment . . .

b. Agent's representation concerning agent's own authority. An agent's own statements about the nature or extent of the agent's authority to act on behalf of the principal do not create apparent authority by themselves. An agent acts with apparent authority only when a third party's belief that the agent acts with authority is reasonable and is traceable to a manifestation made by the principal. . . .

Illustrations:

1. P, who owns a tree nursery, tells T, who owns a garden center, that A is authorized to sell P's trees only at prices set by P and communicated by P to T. A tells T that A now has P's authority to set the prices for P's trees. A's statement to T does not by itself create apparent authority to bind P to sell trees to T at prices set by A. . . .

CHAPTER 7

TORTS—LIABILITY OF AGENT AND PRINCIPAL

TOPIC 1. AGENT'S LIABILITY

§ 7.01 Agent's Liability to Third Party

An agent is subject to liability to a third party harmed by the agent's tortious conduct. Unless an applicable statute provides otherwise, an actor remains subject to liability although the actor acts as an agent or an employee, with actual or apparent authority, or within the scope of employment.

§ 7.02 Duty to Principal; Duty to Third Party

An agent's breach of a duty owed to the principal is not an independent basis for an agent's tort liability to a third party. An agent is subject to tort liability to a third party harmed by the agent's conduct only when the agent's conduct breaches a duty that the agent owes to the third party.

TOPIC 2

PRINCIPAL'S LIABILITY

§ 7.03   Principal's Liability—In General

(1) A principal is subject to direct liability to a third party harmed by an agent's conduct when

(a) as stated in § 7.04, the agent acts with actual authority or the principal ratifies the agent's conduct and

(i) the agent's conduct is tortious, or

(ii) the agent's conduct, if that of the principal, would subject the principal to tort liability; or

(b) as stated in § 7.05, the principal is negligent in selecting, supervising, or otherwise controlling the agent; or

(c) as stated in § 7.06, the principal delegates performance of a duty to use care to protect other persons or their property to an agent who fails to perform the duty.

(2) A principal is subject to vicarious liability to a third party harmed by an agent's conduct when

(a) as stated in § 7.07, the agent is an employee who commits a tort while acting within the scope of employment; or

(b) as stated in § 7.08, the agent commits a tort when acting with apparent authority in dealing with a third party on or purportedly on behalf of the principal.

§ 7.04   Agent Acts with Actual Authority

A principal is subject to liability to a third party harmed by an agent's conduct when the agent's conduct is within the scope of the agent's actual authority or ratified by the principal; and

(1) the agent's conduct is tortious, or

(2) the agent's conduct, if that of the principal, would subject the principal to tort liability.

Comment ...

b.   In general. When an agent acts with actual authority, the agent reasonably believes, in accordance with manifestations of the principal, that the principal wishes the agent so to act. . . .

Illustrations:

1. P, who publishes a newspaper, engages D to deliver copies of the newspaper to a neighboring community. P directs D to deliver the newspapers in the midst of an ice storm when both P and D know that driving conditions are hazardous, that the vehicle D will use is not equipped for such conditions, and that D lacks experience in driving under such conditions. In the course of making deliveries, D skids on an icy road, injuring T. P is subject to liability to T. P's instruction to D directed D to act in a negligent manner. D is also subject to liability to T. See § 7.01. . . .

c. When actor is not personally subject to liability. A person may be subject to tort liability because of an actor's conduct although the actor is not subject to liability. For example, a person who directs conduct may have notice of facts that the actor lacks.

Illustration:

5. P, in the produce business, directs A to make a delivery to a customer using a particular truck. P knows that the truck's brakes do not work properly. A does not know this and has no reason or duty to know it. T, a pedestrian, is injured when the truck's brakes fail while A is driving the truck to make the delivery and attempts to stop at a stop sign. P is subject to liability to T. A is not subject to liability to T. . . .

§ 7.05 Principal's Negligence in Conducting Activity Through Agent; Principal's Special Relationship with Another Person

(1) A principal who conducts an activity through an agent is subject to liability for harm to a third party caused by the agent's conduct if the harm was caused by the principal's negligence in selecting, training, retaining, supervising, or otherwise controlling the agent.

(2) When a principal has a special relationship with another person, the principal owes that person a duty of reasonable care with regard to risks arising out of the relationship, including the risk that agents of the principal will harm the person with whom the principal has such a special relationship.

Comment . . .

b. In general; relationship to other bases for liability. . . .

A foreseeable risk of harm may be created when one person conducts an activity through another person. For example, the actor chosen for a task may lack competence to perform it without endangering others. A task may require using an instrumentality that is dangerous to others unless the user has appropriate skill or supervision. Some tasks require performance in settings that pose a foreseeable risk of criminal or other intentional misconduct against third parties or their property unless the actor is chosen with due care in reference to that risk.

Illustrations:

1.   P, who owns an apartment building, employs A as its on-site manager. P knows that A is impatient and has a violent temper. T, one of P's tenants, complains to A about the lack of heat in T's apartment. Enraged, A assaults T. P is subject to liability to T. P hired A knowing that A's temperament was not suited to the foreseeable demands of on-site residential management. P's liability to T under this section is independent of whether P is subject to liability to T under § 7.07 on the basis that A's conduct was within the scope of A's employment by P....

3.   P, who owns a furniture store, employs A to deliver furniture to retail customers. A's duties include entering customers' homes to situate items they have purchased. Having entered T's home to deliver a sofa, A assaults T. Prior to employing A, P conducted no check of A's background. Had P done so, P would have discovered criminal convictions for assault. Had P known of A's criminal history, P would not have employed A to make deliveries. P is subject to liability to T....

§ 7.06   Failure in Performance of Principal's Duty of Protection

A principal required by contract or otherwise by law to protect another cannot avoid liability by delegating performance of the duty, whether or not the delegate is an agent.

§ 7.07   Employee Acting Within Scope of Employment

(1) An employer is subject to vicarious liability for a tort committed by its employee acting within the scope of employment.

(2) An employee acts within the scope of employment when performing work assigned by the employer or engaging in a course of conduct subject to the employer's control. An employee's act is not within the scope of employment when it occurs within an independent course of conduct not intended by the employee to serve any purpose of the employer.

(3) For purposes of this section,

(a) an employee is an agent whose principal controls or has the right to control the manner and means of the agent's performance of work, and

(b) the fact that work is performed gratuitously does not relieve a principal of liability.

Comment . . .

b. When tortious conduct is within the scope of employment—in general. An employee's conduct, although tortious, may be within the scope of employment as defined in subsection (2). If an employee commits a tort while performing work assigned by the employer or while acting within a course of conduct subject to the employer's control, the employee's conduct is within the scope of employment unless the employee was engaged in an independent course of conduct not intended to further any purpose of the employer. The formulation in subsection (2) reflects the definition of scope of employment applied in most cases and in most jurisdictions. . . .

[R]espondeat superior subjects an employer to vicarious liability for employee torts committed within the scope of employment, distinct from whether the employer is subject to direct liability. An employer's ability to exercise control over its employees' work-related conduct enables the employer to take measures to reduce the incidence of tortious conduct. It may be difficult, after the fact of an employee's tortious conduct, to identify an instance of negligence on the part of the employer. This may be so even when, before the fact of the employee's tortious conduct, steps were available to the employer that, if taken, would have prevented the tort. In contrast, when an employee's tortious conduct is outside the range of activity that an employer may control, subjecting the employer to liability would not provide incentives for the employer to take measures to reduce the incidence of such tortious conduct. Moreover, for an employer to insure against a risk of liability, whether from third-party sources or its own assets, the risk must be at least to some degree ascertainable and quantifiable.

In assessing the scope of employment limitation on respondeat superior, it is helpful to recognize that the range of tortious conduct by employees to which the doctrine is relevant is not all-encompassing. Respondeat superior is not the sole basis for liability when an employer itself is at fault, see §§ 7.04, 7.05, and 7.06, nor is it the sole basis for vicarious liability when an employee's apparent authority enables the employee to commit a tort, see § 7.08. . . .

Under subsection (2), an employee's tortious conduct is outside the scope of employment when the employee is engaged in an independent course of conduct not intended to further any purpose of the employer. An independent course of conduct represents a departure from, not an escalation of, conduct involved in performing assigned work or other conduct that an employer permits or controls. When an employee commits a tort with the sole intention of furthering the employee's own purposes, and not any purpose of the employer, it is neither fair nor true-to-life to characterize the employee's action as that of a representative of the employer. The employee's intention severs the basis for treating the employee's act as that of the employer in the employee's interaction with the third party. . . .

c. Conduct in the performance of work and scope of employment. An employee's conduct is within the scope of employment when it constitutes performance of work assigned to the employee by the employer. The fact that the employee performs the work carelessly does not take the employee's conduct outside the scope of employment, nor does the fact that the employee otherwise makes a mistake in performing the work. Likewise, conduct is not outside the scope of employment merely because an employee disregards the employer's instructions.

Illustrations:

1. P, who writes bail bonds, employs A as a bond "runner." A's assigned work is to locate persons for whom P has written bonds who jump bail and return them to custody. P directs A to search for J. A mistakenly identifies T as J, breaks down the door of T's home, and holds T at gunpoint. Under applicable law, A's conduct toward T is tortious. P is subject to liability to T. A's actions constituted performance of work P assigned to A.

2. Same facts as Illustration 1, except that P instructs its runners to contact P's office prior to attempting a forcible entry into a residence. A neglects to do this before breaking down the door of T's home. Same result.

In Illustration 2, A's conduct is within the scope of employment, despite A's disregard for P's instruction, because A is engaged in doing work assigned by P. Likewise, had A contravened an instruction not to exceed the speed limit while pursuing a bail jumper and caused an accident that injured another driver or a pedestrian, A would have been acting within the scope of employment. Thus, the fact that an employee's action violates a generally applicable law, such as a speeding limit, does not by itself place the employee's conduct outside the scope of employment. These results are not surprising. An employee may believe that the employer wishes the employee to disregard an inconvenient constraint when the employee fears that compliance would jeopardize completing the employee's assigned mission at all or completing it on or ahead of schedule. Although the employee's belief may be mistaken, it is compatible with acting in an assigned role to do an assigned task. However, the character, extreme nature, or other circumstances accompanying an employee's actions may demonstrate that the employee's course of conduct is independent of performing work assigned by the employer and intended solely to further the employee's own purposes....

e. Peregrinations. In general, travel required to perform work, such as travel from an employer's office to a job site or from one job site to another, is within the scope of an employee's employment while traveling to and from work is not. However, an employer may place an employee's travel to and from work within the scope of employment by providing the employee with a vehicle and asserting control over how the employee uses the vehicle so that the employee may more readily respond to the needs of the employer's enterprise. An employee's travel to and from work may also be within the scope of employment if the employee does more than simply travel to and from work, for example by stopping for the employer's benefit to accomplish a task assigned by the employer.

An employee's travel during the work day that is not within the scope of employment has long been termed a "frolic" of the employee's own. De minimis departures from assigned routes are not "frolics." A "frolic" may also consist of activity on an employer's premises and within working hours, as in Illustrations 10 and 11. The conventional meaning of the term "detour" is a deviation from travel on an assigned route that is still within the scope of employment.

Illustrations:

12. P, who owns a tree-maintenance service, employs A as foreman for a crew that provides tree-trimming services for utility companies and owners of commercial and residential property. P furnishes A with a pickup truck and authorizes A to use the truck to commute between A's residence and the day's job site. P also directs A to use the truck to make sales calls to prospective customers. En route from home to a utility job site, A stops to visit C, a prospective residential customer. As A turns to pull into C's driveway, A injures T, a pedestrian whom A negligently failed to notice. P is subject to liability to T. Visiting C was part of A's assigned work for P.

13. Same facts as Illustration 12, except that en route to visit C, A departs slightly from the most direct route to visit A's favorite take-out restaurant. A's departure is within the scope of employment.

14. P, who owns a nursery, employs A. A's assigned duties include caring for the nursery's lawn and keeping the nursery's lawn mower filled with gas. En route to the nursery from home, A stops at a drugstore to pick up medicine for A's spouse, then stops at a gas station across the street to buy a can of gas for the nursery's lawn mower. A next returns home to drop off the

medicine, then stops at another gas station to buy gas for A's truck. Leaving this second gas station, A drives negligently and collides with T. P is subject to liability to T. A was transporting gas to fill the nursery's lawnmower, necessary for A to perform A's assigned work. A's stop for gas was an incidental deviation from A's performance of assigned work. . . .

f. Definition of employee. For purposes of respondeat superior, an agent is an employee only when the principal controls or has the right to control the manner and means through which the agent performs work. The definition has the consequence of distinguishing between employees and agents who are not employees because they retain the right to control how they perform their work. If a person has no right to control an actor and exercises no control over the actor, the actor is not an agent. . . .

Numerous factual indicia are relevant to whether an agent is an employee. These include: the extent of control that the agent and the principal have agreed the principal may exercise over details of the work; whether the agent is engaged in a distinct occupation or business; whether the type of work done by the agent is customarily done under a principal's direction or without supervision; the skill required in the agent's occupation; whether the agent or the principal supplies the tools and other instrumentalities required for the work and the place in which to perform it; the length of time during which the agent is engaged by a principal; whether the agent is paid by the job or by the time worked; whether the agent's work is part of the principal's regular business; whether the principal and the agent believe that they are creating an employment relationship; and whether the principal is or is not in business. Also relevant is the extent of control that the principal has exercised in practice over the details of the agent's work.

In some employment relationships, an employer's right of control may be attenuated. For example, senior corporate officers, like captains of ships, may exercise great discretion in operating the enterprises entrusted to them, just as skilled professionals exercise discretion in performing their work. Nonetheless, all employers retain a right of control, however infrequently exercised. . . .

§ 7.08   Agent Acts with Apparent Authority

A principal is subject to vicarious liability for a tort committed by an agent in dealing or communicating with a third party on or purportedly on behalf of the principal when actions taken by the agent with apparent authority constitute the tort or enable the agent to conceal its commission.

Comment:

a. Scope and cross-references. The rule stated in this section applies to (1) agents, whether or not they are employees as defined in § 7.07(3); and ... agents who are employees as defined in § 7.07(3) whose tortious conduct is not within the scope of employment under § 7.07(2). The torts to which this section applies are those in which an agent appears to deal or communicate on behalf of a principal and the agent's appearance of authority enables the agent to commit a tort or conceal its commission. Such torts include fraudulent and negligent misrepresentations, defamation, tortious institution of legal proceedings, and conversion of property obtained by an agent purportedly at the principal's direction....

Illustrations:

1. P Numismatics Company urges its customers to seek investment advice from its retail salespeople, including A. T, who wishes to invest in gold coins, seeks A's advice at an office of P Numismatics Company. A encourages T to purchase a particular set of gold coins, falsely representing material facts relevant to their value. T, reasonably relying on A's representations, purchases the set of coins. P is subject to liability to T. A is also subject to liability to T. See § 7.01.

2. Same facts as Illustration 1, except that A persuades T to pay cash for the coins and to leave the coins with A so that they may be safely stored by P Numismatics Company. A then absconds with both the coins and the cash paid by T. Same results....

CHAPTER 8

DUTIES OF AGENT AND PRINCIPAL TO EACH OTHER

TOPIC 1. AGENT'S DUTIES TO PRINCIPAL

TITLE A.   GENERAL FIDUCIARY PRINCIPLE

§ 8.01   General Fiduciary Principle

An agent has a fiduciary duty to act loyally for the principal's benefit in all matters connected with the agency relationship.

Comment ...

d(1). Remedies for breach of fiduciary duty—in general. An agent's breach of fiduciary duty may create several distinct bases on which the principal may recover monetary relief or receive another remedy. Under appropriate circumstances, an agent's breach or threatened breach of fiduciary duty is a basis on which the principal may receive specific nonmonetary relief through an injunction. An agent's breach of fiduciary obligation may also furnish a basis on which the principal may avoid or rescind a contract entered into with the agent or a third party.

An agent's breach also creates distinct bases on which the principal may recover monetary relief. An agent's breach subjects the agent to liability for loss that the breach causes the principal. See Restatement Second, Torts § 874. A breach of fiduciary duty may also subject the agent to liability for punitive damages when the circumstances satisfy generally applicable standards for their imposition. For general standards applicable to awards of punitive damages, see Restatement Second, Torts § 908(2). In these respects, the consequences of a breach of fiduciary duty do not differ from those of other torts that an agent may commit against a principal.

The law of restitution and unjust enrichment also creates a basis for an agent's liability to a principal when the agent breaches a fiduciary duty, even though the principal cannot establish that the agent's breach caused loss to the principal. If through the breach the agent has realized a material benefit, the agent has a duty to account to the principal for the benefit, its value, or its proceeds. The agent is subject to liability to deliver the benefit, its proceeds, or its value to the principal. . . . An agent must also account to the principal for the value of the agent's use of property of the principal when the use violates the agent's duty to the principal, although the principal cannot establish that the use was harmful. . . . If an agent's breach of duty is in connection with a transaction as or on behalf of an adverse party, an alternate remedy that may be available to the principal is avoiding the transaction. . . .

(2). Remedies for breach of fiduciary duty—forfeiture of commissions and other compensation. An agent's breach of fiduciary duty is a basis on which the agent may be required to forfeit commissions and other compensation paid or payable to the agent during the period of the agent's disloyalty. The availability of forfeiture is not limited to its use as a defense to an agent's claim for compensation.

Forfeiture may be the only available remedy when it is difficult to prove that harm to a principal resulted from the agent's breach or when the agent realizes no profit through the breach. In many cases, forfeiture enables a remedy to be determined at a much lower cost to litigants. Forfeiture may also have a valuable deterrent effect because its availability signals agents that some adverse consequence will follow a breach of fiduciary duty.

Although forfeiture is generally available as a remedy for breach of fiduciary duty, cases are divided on how absolute a measure to apply. Some cases require forfeiture of all compensation paid or payable over the period of disloyalty, while others permit apportionment over a series of tasks or specified items of work when only some are tainted by the agent's disloyal conduct. The better rule permits the court to consider the specifics of the agent's work and the nature of the agent's breach of duty and to evaluate whether the agent's breach of fiduciary duty tainted all of the agent's work or was confined to discrete transactions for which the agent was entitled to apportioned compensation....

Illustration:

9. P Bank employs A, an advisor and facilitator, and assigns A to work on a series of transactions. P Bank agrees to compensate A by paying A an annual salary plus an amount to be determined by P Bank on the basis of P Bank's annual profitability. Without P Bank's knowledge or consent, during A's last year and a half working for P Bank, A accepts for A's personal account investment opportunities from three clients with whom A worked on transactions on P Bank's account. A also does work on a fourth transaction in which A accepts no such opportunity for A's own account. All of A's compensation for the year and a half may be forfeited to P Bank. A's agreement with P Bank did not allocate A's compensation on a transaction-specific basis. A is also subject to liability to P Bank for profits made by A, or property that A obtained, through A's receipt of material benefits from third parties. See § 8.02.

Some cases permit an agent to establish that the agent's work on balance was of benefit to the principal or require the principal to establish that on balance it was damaged by the agent's breach. The better rule does not condition the availability of forfeiture as a remedy on whether a principal can establish damage. The requirement that a principal establish damage is inconsistent with a basic premise of remedies available for breach of fiduciary duty, which is that a principal need not establish harm resulting from an agent's breach to require the agent to account. See Comments *b* and *d(1)*. The requirement may also tempt an agent to undertake conduct that breaches the agent's fiduciary duty in the hope that no harm will befall the principal or that, if it does, the principal will be unable to establish it or unable or unwilling to expend the necessary resources required to litigate the question.

Likewise, the better rule does not allow an agent to offset amounts otherwise forfeitable to the principal by showing benefits gained by the principal through the agent's work. The benefits generated by a disloyal agent may be difficult to quantify, especially when incentives created by the agent's disloyalty reshape how the agent performs assigned work.

TITLE B.   DUTIES OF LOYALTY

§ 8.02   Material Benefit Arising Out of Position

An agent has a duty not to acquire a material benefit from a third party in connection with transactions conducted or other actions taken on behalf of the principal or otherwise through the agent's use of the agent's position.

Comment ...

b.   Rationale. This rule stems from the ordinary expectation that a person who acts as an agent does so to further the interests of the principal and that it is the principal who should benefit from turns of good fortune that may occur in connection with transactions that the agent undertakes on the principal's behalf. This expectation may stem from the fact when an agent acts with actual or apparent authority, the principal risks being bound by transactions that may turn out to be disadvantageous to the principal in some respect.

An additional rationale for this rule stems from risks to a principal's interests that may arise when an agent pursues material benefits from third parties in connection with actions taken on behalf of the principal. For example, an agent's interest in acquiring a benefit from a third party may supersede the agent's commitment to obtain terms from the third party that are best from the standpoint of the principal. Although the agent may believe that no harm will befall the principal, the agent is not in a position disinterestedly to assess whether harm may occur or whether the principal's interests would be better served if the agent did not pursue or acquire the benefit from the third party. Only the principal can assess the potential impact on the principal's interests of an agent's anticipated receipt of a material benefit to be furnished by a third party. By providing a material benefit to a person known to act as an agent, a third party may become subject to liability to the principal. A third party who provides substantial assistance or encouragement to an agent in breaching the agent's duty to the principal is also subject to liability to the principal....

Illustrations:

1.   P, who owns a racehorse, Grace, engages A, a jockey, to ride Grace in an upcoming race. P agrees to pay A a fee of $500. T, who has made a large bet that Grace will win the race, promises to pay A $5000 if Grace wins the race. T asks A not to tell P about T's promise. Neither A nor T tells P about T's

promise. Grace, ridden by A, wins the race. T pays A $5000. A and T are subject to liability to P. A's receipt of $5000 from T breached A's duty to P. T knowingly provided substantial assistance and encouragement to A in A's breach of duty to P. For discussion of remedies available to P, see Comment e.

The purpose of this rule is prophylactic. To establish that the agent is subject to liability, it is not necessary that the principal show that the agent's acquisition of a material benefit harmed the principal. The benefit realized by the agent can often be calculated more readily than any harm suffered by the principal. However, when the principal can establish that the agent's conduct resulted in harm to the principal, the principal may recover compensatory damages from the agent.

Moreover, an agent's acquisition of a material benefit may breach this rule even though the agent's ability to acquire the benefit depends on achieving an outcome that may appear consistent with the principal's interests. In Illustration 1, P presumably wishes that Grace will win the race, as do T and A. However, T's promise to pay A if Grace wins the race undermines P's ability to exercise control over A and may thwart P's objectives as P understands them. T's promise may induce A to spur Grace on to assure that Grace wins the race and A receives an additional $5000. However, P, unbeknownst to A, may plan to enter Grace in another race that P views as more important and thus may wish that Grace's energies not be overtaxed. Thus, the point of the rule is to focus the agent's efforts on furthering the principal's interests as the agent reasonably understands them, taking into account manifestations made by the principal. Permitting an agent's focus to encompass additional incentives offered by a third party is inconsistent with the singleness of focus due the principal....

Illustrations:

3. P, who owns a used-car lot, employs A as its general manager. A's duties include contracting with suppliers of used cars to replenish P's inventory. One supplier, T, pays A $500 for each car that A purchases for sale on P's lot. A is subject to liability to P. The payments A received from T are material benefits that A acquired in connection with transactions A conducted on P's behalf.

4. Same facts as Illustration 3, except that T does not pay A for cars that A purchases on behalf of P. Instead, T gives A a three-year-old BMW, stating, "This is a gift from me to you in gratitude for our good relationship." Same result. A is subject to liability to P....

e.   Remedies. When an agent breaches the duty stated in this section, the principal may recover monetary relief from the agent and, in appropriate circumstances, from any third party who participated in the agent's breach. A principal may avoid a contract entered into by the agent with a third party who participated in the agent's breach of duty. The principal may recover any material benefit received by the agent through the agent's breach, the value of the benefit, or proceeds of the benefit retained by the agent. The principal may also recover damages for any harm caused by the agent's breach. If an agent's breach of duty involves a wrongful disposal of assets of the principal, the principal cannot recover both the value of the asset and what the agent received in exchange. If a principal recovers damages from a third party as a consequence of an agent's breach of fiduciary duty, the principal remains entitled to recover from the agent any benefit that the agent improperly received from the transaction. . . .

§ 8.03   Acting as or on Behalf of an Adverse Party

An agent has a duty not to deal with the principal as or on behalf of an adverse party in a transaction connected with the agency relationship.

Comment . . .

b.   Rationale. As a fiduciary, an agent has a duty to the principal to act loyally in the principal's interest in all matters in connection with the agency relationship. See § 8.01. The rule stated in this section is a specific application of this general principle. . . .

A principal may consent to conduct by an agent that would otherwise constitute a breach of the agent's duty. . . .

Illustrations:

1.   P Corporation, which sells fabric-forming systems used for purposes such as lining ditches, uses polypropylene fabric as a principal component in constructing systems. P Corporation hires A to make sales and perform marketing functions. A's duties do not involve negotiating the terms of P Corporation's purchase of polypropylene fabric. Unbeknownst to P Corporation, A owns one-half of the equity of T Corporation, the principal supplier of polypropylene to P Corporation. A has breached A's duty to P Corporation. A's ownership interest in T Corporation makes A an adverse party in P Corporation's dealings with T Corporation.

2.   Same facts as Illustration 1, except that A tells C, P Corporation's President, that A owns an interest in T Corpora-

tion. P Corporation, through C, has knowledge that in dealing with T Corporation, it deals with A as an adverse party.

A principal's knowledge that an agent deals as or on behalf of an adverse party does not relieve the agent of duties to the principal in connection with that transaction. Under the rule stated in § 8.06, the agent has a duty to deal fairly with the principal and to disclose to the principal all facts of which the agent has notice that are reasonably relevant to the principal's exercise of judgment, unless the principal has manifested that the principal already knows them or does not wish to know them. Thus, a principal's knowledge that its agent acts as or on behalf of an adverse party does not convert the relationship between principal and agent into an arm's-length relationship. Moreover, as stated in § 8.11, an agent has a duty to use reasonable effort to furnish information to the principal although the agent does not deal as or on behalf of an adverse party.

Illustration:

    3. Same facts as Illustration 2, except that A knows that T Corporation is well along in the process of developing a new line of polypropylene fabric that could be superior for P Corporation's purposes. A has a duty to disclose this fact to P Corporation. That a superior product is in the offing is a fact that a user of the current product would reasonably take into account in determining how much of the current product to purchase....

§ 8.04 Competition

Throughout the duration of an agency relationship, an agent has a duty to refrain from competing with the principal and from taking action on behalf of or otherwise assisting the principal's competitors. During that time, an agent may take action, not otherwise wrongful, to prepare for competition following termination of the agency relationship.

§ 8.05 Use of Principal's Property; Use of Confidential Information

An agent has a duty

(1) not to use property of the principal for the agent's own purposes or those of a third party; and

(2) not to use or communicate confidential information of the principal for the agent's own purposes or those of a third party.

Comment ...

    b. Use of principal's property. An agent who has possession of property of the principal has a duty to use it only on the principal's behalf, unless the principal consents to such use. See § 8.06. This rule is a specific application of an agent's basic fiduciary duty stated in § 8.01.... The rule is also a corollary of a principal's right, as an owner of property, to exclude usage by others. An agent is subject to this duty whether or not the agent uses property of the principal to compete with the principal or causes harm to the principal through the use. An agent may breach this duty even when the agent's use is beneficial in some sense to the property or to the principal. An agent is subject to liability to the principal for any profit made by the agent while using the principal's property when the use facilitates making the profit, or otherwise for the value of the use.

Illustrations:

1. P, who owns a stable of horses, employs A to take care of them. While P is absent for a month, and without P's consent, A rents the horses to persons who ride them. Although being ridden is beneficial to the horses, A is subject to liability to P for the amount A receives for the rentals.

2. Same facts as Illustration 1, except that A permits A's friends to ride P's horses for free during P's absence. A is subject to liability to P for the value of the use made of the horses....

§ 8.06 Principal's Consent

(1) Conduct by an agent that would otherwise constitute a breach of duty as stated in §§ 8.01, 8.02, 8.03, 8.04, and 8.05 does not constitute a breach of duty if the principal consents to the conduct, provided that

(a) in obtaining the principal's consent, the agent

(i) acts in good faith,

(ii) discloses all material facts that the agent knows, has reason to know, or should know would reasonably affect the principal's judgment unless the principal has manifested that such facts are already known by the principal or that the principal does not wish to know them, and

(iii) otherwise deals fairly with the principal; and

(b) the principal's consent concerns either a specific act or transaction, or acts or transactions of a specified type that could reasonably be expected to occur in the ordinary course of the agency relationship.

(2) An agent who acts for more than one principal in a transaction between or among them has a duty

(a) to deal in good faith with each principal,

(b) to disclose to each principal

(i) the fact that the agent acts for the other principal or principals, and

(ii) all other facts that the agent knows, has reason to know, or should know would reasonably affect the principal's judgment unless the principal has manifested that such facts are already known by the principal or that the principal does not wish to know them, and

(c) otherwise to deal fairly with each principal.

Comment ...

   b. In general. This section defines the circumstances under which conduct of a principal is effective as consent to conduct by an agent that would otherwise constitute a breach of the agent's duties of loyalty.

   Common-law agency does not accord effect to all manifestations of assent by a principal that eliminate or otherwise affect the fiduciary duties owed by an agent. This is so for two distinct reasons: (1) the law, and not the parties, determines whether a particular relationship is one of agency as defined in § 1.01; and (2) the law imposes restrictions on the efficacy of a principal's manifestations of assent in the interest of safeguarding the principal's intention in creating a relationship of common-law agency....

   Moreover, although a person may empower another to take action without regard to the interests of the person who grants the power, the law applicable to relationships of agency as defined in § 1.01 imposes mandatory limits on the circumstances under which an agent may be empowered to take disloyal action. These limits serve protective and cautionary purposes. Thus, an agreement that contains general or broad language purporting to release an agent in advance from the agent's general fiduciary obligation to the principal is not likely to be enforceable. This is because a broadly sweeping release of an agent's fiduciary duty may not reflect an adequately informed judgment on the part of the principal; if effective, the release would expose the principal to the risk that the agent will exploit the agent's position in ways not foreseeable by the principal at the time the principal agreed to the release.

   In contrast, when a principal consents to specific transactions or to specified types of conduct by the agent, the principal has a focused opportunity to assess risks that are more readily identifiable. Likewise, when a principal consents after-the-fact to action taken by an agent that would otherwise breach the agent's fiduciary duty to the principal, the principal has the opportunity to assess what the agent has done with a degree of specificity not available before the agent takes action....

   An agent bears the burden of establishing that the requirements stated in this section have been fulfilled....

105

TITLE C
DUTIES OF PERFORMANCE

§ 8.07　Duty Created by Contract

An agent has a duty to act in accordance with the express and implied terms of any contract between the agent and the principal.

§ 8.08　Duties of Care, Competence, and Diligence

Subject to any agreement with the principal, an agent has a duty to the principal to act with the care, competence, and diligence normally exercised by agents in similar circumstances. Special skills or knowledge possessed by an agent are circumstances to be taken into account in determining whether the agent acted with due care and diligence. If an agent claims to possess special skills or knowledge, the agent has a duty to the principal to act with the care, competence, and diligence normally exercised by agents with such skills or knowledge.

Comment . . .

c. Duty of competence. The specific skills that an agent must possess to be competent depend on the nature of the service that the agent undertakes to provide and the circumstances under which it will be provided, such as the magnitude and complexity of transactions that the agent will conduct on the principal's account. For example, an agent may be competent to lease apartments in a residential building but lack the competence required to negotiate a complex lease of commercial space.

If an agent undertakes to perform services as a practitioner of a trade or profession, the agent "is required to exercise the skill and knowledge normally possessed by members of that profession or trade in good standing in similar communities" unless the agent represents that the agent possesses greater or lesser skill. Restatement Second, Torts § 299A. An agent may reasonably be expected to know at least the basic rules and practices under which the agent's industry or profession operates. . . .

An agent's level of skill or knowledge may exceed the norm for similarly situated agents. Alternatively, an agent may falsely represent that this is so. An agent's performance should be evaluated consistently with the agent's claimed level of skill or knowledge unless the agent establishes that the principal knew the agent's claim to be false. The agent's professed level of skill or knowledge becomes the standard against which the agent's performance should be assessed. For a comparable rule applicable to trustees, see Restatement Third, Trusts § 77(3) (Tentative Draft No. 4, 2005). When an agent does not claim to possess special skills or knowledge but in fact has a level of skill or knowledge that exceeds the norm, the trier of fact may consider the agent's actual knowledge and skills in determining whether the agent acted with due care under the circumstances. See Restatement Third, Torts: Liability for Physical Harm § 12, Comment *a* (Proposed Final Draft No. 1, 2005). An actor's actual state of knowledge will always be relevant to determining whether the actor behaved with due care, regardless of the source of that knowledge. Id., Comment *a*. An actor's knowledge and skills are combined to a degree that makes it difficult to disaggregate them. Id. . . .

    d. Duty of diligence. An agent's duty of diligence requires the agent to bring the agent's competence to bear on matters undertaken on behalf of the principal. Ordinarily, the scope of an agent's duty to be diligent is limited by the scope of the services the agent undertakes to perform for the principal. The scope of an agent's duty may be expanded by contract or by the existence of a special relationship of trust and confidence between agent and principal. For example, a securities broker's duty of diligence to a client who directs trading in the client's own account (a "nondiscretionary" account) is limited to executing the client's orders to purchase and sell securities in the account and does not extend to advising the client or issuing risk warnings on an ongoing basis. In contrast, a securities broker's duty may include the provision of advice and warnings when the broker's relationship with the client is one in which the client's trust and confidence are invited by the broker and given by the client.

    Although an agent has a duty of diligence, that duty is to make reasonable efforts to achieve a result and not a duty to achieve the result regardless of the effort, risk, and cost involved. If an agent makes a reasonable effort, the agent is not subject to liability to the principal if the effort fails to accomplish the end desired by the principal. . . .

§ 8.09 Duty to Act Only Within Scope of Actual Authority and to Comply with Principal's Lawful Instructions

    (1) An agent has a duty to take action only within the scope of the agent's actual authority.

    (2) An agent has a duty to comply with all lawful instructions received from the principal and persons designated by the principal concerning the agent's actions on behalf of the principal.

Comment . . .

    b. Duty to act only within scope of actual authority. . . .

    If an agent takes action beyond the scope of the agent's actual authority, the agent is subject to liability to the principal for loss caused the principal. The principal's loss may stem from actions taken by the agent with apparent authority, on the basis of which the principal became subject to liability to third parties. . . .

§ 8.10 Duty of Good Conduct

An agent has a duty, within the scope of the agency relationship, to act reasonably and to refrain from conduct that is likely to damage the principal's enterprise.

§ 8.11 Duty to Provide Information

An agent has a duty to use reasonable effort to provide the principal with facts that the agent knows, has reason to know, or should know when

(1) subject to any manifestation by the principal, the agent knows or has reason to know that the principal would wish to have the facts or the facts are material to the agent's duties to the principal; and

(2) the facts can be provided to the principal without violating a superior duty owed by the agent to another person.

Comment . . .

b. In general. A principal's agents link the principal to the external world for purposes of acquiring information as well as for purposes of taking action. . . . An agent owes the principal a duty to provide information to the principal that the agent knows or has reason to know the principal would wish to have. An agent also owes the principal a duty, subject to any manifestation by the principal, to provide information to the principal that is material to the agent's duties to the principal. . . .

Illustrations:

1. A represents P Insurance Co. and solicits applications for insurance policies to be issued by it. A submits an application for life insurance completed by T to P Insurance Co. After submitting the application but before P Insurance Co. issues a policy to T, A learns that T's health has deteriorated substantially. As A knows, this is information that P Insurance Co. would desire to have in determining whether to issue a policy of life insurance to T. A has a duty to use reasonable effort to provide this information to P Insurance Co. . . .

3. P, who owns a house, retains A as a rental agent. A learns that T, the tenant who occupies the house, has vacated it and that the water pipes in the house have frozen and then thawed, causing damage to the house's flooring. As A knows, P would desire to have this information to determine what steps to take. A has a duty to use reasonable effort to provide this information to P.

4. P, who owns Blackacre, lists it for sale with A. T makes an offer to buy Blackacre for $100,000. Before T's offer is accepted, A learns that S is willing to pay $120,000 for Blackacre. As A knows, P would desire to have this information. A has a duty to use reasonable effort to provide the information to P....

11. P opens an account with A for the purpose of trading in a complex and unusual type of overseas commodities option contract. A provides P with a document stating that each option contract has three components: (1) a premium for the option; (2) a commission; and (3) a foreign service fee of 20 percent of the premium. A does not tell P that the "foreign service fee" does not represent any additional expense that A must incur to execute a transaction but, instead, is an additional commission to be retained by A. Few investors at the time understand the complexities of such transactions and P could not know what expenses a broker like A would incur in executing them. A has a duty to P to inform P that the "foreign service fee" represents monies that A will retain. P is uniquely dependent on A for this information, which was material to P's decision whether engaging in such transactions could be to P's advantage....

§ 8.12 Duties Regarding Principal's Property—Segregation, Record-Keeping, and Accounting

An agent has a duty, subject to any agreement with the principal,

(1) not to deal with the principal's property so that it appears to be the agent's property;

(2) not to mingle the principal's property with anyone else's; and

(3) to keep and render accounts to the principal of money or other property received or paid out on the principal's account.

TOPIC 2
PRINCIPAL'S DUTIES TO AGENT

§ 8.13 Duty Created by Contract

A principal has a duty to act in accordance with the express and implied terms of any contract between the principal and the agent.

§ 8.14 Duty to Indemnify

A principal has a duty to indemnify an agent

(1) in accordance with the terms of any contract between them; and

(2) unless otherwise agreed,

(a) when the agent makes a payment

(i) within the scope of the agent's actual authority, or

(ii) that is beneficial to the principal, unless the agent acts officiously in making the payment; or

(b) when the agent suffers a loss that fairly should be borne by the principal in light of their relationship.

Comment ...

b. Agent's right to indemnification—in general. In general, a principal's obligation to indemnify an agent arises when the agent makes a payment or incurs an expense or other loss while acting on behalf of the principal. An agent's actions on behalf of a principal may result in pecuniary loss for the agent. For example, an agent may be required to make payments to third parties to carry out the agent's work for the principal. Actions taken by an agent may also result in litigation against the agent brought by third parties with whom the agent has interacted on the principal's behalf. A contract between a principal and an agent may anticipate the possibility that the agent will incur pecuniary losses, specify when and to what extent the principal has a duty to indemnify the agent, and prescribe procedures to be followed by the agent in claiming rights to indemnity under the contract.

In the absence of such a contract, a principal has duties to indemnify the agent as stated in subsection (2). If an agent acts with actual authority in making a payment to a third party, the principal has a duty to indemnify the agent unless otherwise agreed.

Illustration:

1. P retains A, an import broker, to handle importation of a large quantity of herbicide. A learns that the amount of duty payable on the herbicide will exceed a prior estimate given by the customs service because the herbicide contains various chemicals not listed on its label. Fearing forfeiture of the security bond A has posted for the duty, A pays the additional amount under protest and seeks indemnity from P. P has a duty to indemnify A. A acted with actual authority in making the payment. . . .

d. Rights to indemnification in connection with litigation. In the absence of an express contractual provision that requires the principal to indemnify an agent in connection with litigation against the agent, a principal has a duty to indemnify the agent against expenses and other losses incurred by the agent in defending against actions brought by third parties if the agent acted with actual authority in taking the action challenged by the third party's suit. . . .

§ 8.15 Principal's Duty to Deal Fairly and in Good Faith

A principal has a duty to deal with the agent fairly and in good faith, including a duty to provide the agent with information about risks of physical harm or pecuniary loss that the principal knows, has reason to know, or should know are present in the agent's work but unknown to the agent.

Comment ...

b. Duty to deal with agent fairly and in good faith. A principal has a duty to deal fairly and in good faith with an agent. This duty does not supersede the principal's power to terminate the agent's authority as stated in § 3.10(1). This general duty encompasses more specific duties. The general duty obliges the principal to refrain from engaging in conduct that will foreseeably result in loss for the agent when the agent's own conduct is without fault.

Illustration:

1. P Corporation, wishing to do business in Taiwan, engages A as its general manager in Taiwan. P Corporation designates A as its "responsible person" or legal representative in Taiwan, which requires such a designation to conduct business in the country. As P Corporation's designated "responsible person," A affixes A's "chop" or signature-equivalent, to tax returns that P Corporation prepares and files in Taiwan. Having decided to cease doing business in Taiwan, P Corporation terminates A's engagement but does not remove its designation of A as its "responsible person," although A requests several times that P Corporation do so and tells P Corporation that A is concerned that A may be subject to liability in the event of tax-related disputes between P Corporation and Taiwan. Taiwan assesses a tax liability against P Corporation that P Corporation contests and then, following an adverse final determination, does not pay. Taiwanese authorities notify A that A is forbidden to leave the country until its tax dispute with P Corporation is resolved. P Corporation has breached its duty of good faith. P Corporation is subject to liability for loss suffered by A, including attorney's fees incurred by A to resolve A's predicament. ...

UNIFORM PARTNERSHIP ACT

PART I.   PRELIMINARY PROVISIONS

PART II.   NATURE OF PARTNERSHIP

PART III.   RELATIONS OF PARTNERS TO PERSONS DEALING WITH THE PARTNERSHIP

PART IV.   RELATIONS OF PARTNERS TO ONE ANOTHER

PART V.   PROPERTY RIGHTS OF A PARTNER

PART VI.   DISSOLUTION AND WINDING UP

PART VII. MISCELLANEOUS PROVISIONS*

PART I

PRELIMINARY PROVISIONS

§ 1. Name of Act

This act may be cited as Uniform Partnership Act.

§ 2. Definition of Terms

In this act, "Court" includes every court and judge having jurisdiction in the case.

"Business" includes every trade, occupation, or profession.

"Person" includes individuals, partnerships, corporations, and other associations.

"Bankrupt" includes bankrupt under the Federal Bankruptcy Act or insolvent under any state insolvent act.

"Conveyance" includes every assignment, lease, mortgage, or encumbrance.

"Real property" includes land and any interest or estate in land.

§ 3. Interpretation of Knowledge and Notice

(1) A person has "knowledge" of a fact within the meaning of this act not only when he has actual knowledge thereof, but also when he has knowledge of such other facts as in the circumstances shows bad faith.

* Omitted.

113

(2) A person has "notice" of a fact within the meaning of this act when the person who claims the benefit of the notice:

(a) States the fact to such person, or

(b) Delivers through the mail, or by other means of communication, a written statement of the fact to such person or to a proper person at his place of business or residence.

§ 4. Rules of Construction

(1) The rule that statutes in derogation of the common law are to be strictly construed shall have no application to this act.

(2) The law of estoppel shall apply under this act.

(3) The law of agency shall apply under this act.

(4) This act shall be so interpreted and construed as to effect its general purpose to make uniform the law of those states which enact it.

(5) This act shall not be construed so as to impair the obligations of any contract existing when the act goes into effect, nor to affect any action or proceedings begun or right accrued before this act takes effect.

§ 5. Rules for Cases Not Provided for in This Act

In any case not provided for in this act the rules of law and equity, including the law merchant, shall govern.

PART II

NATURE OF PARTNERSHIP

§ 6. Partnership Defined

(1) A partnership is an association of two or more persons to carry on as co-owners a business for profit.

(2) But any association formed under any other statute of this state, or any statute adopted by authority, other than the authority of this state, is not a partnership under this act, unless such association would have been a partnership in this state prior to the adoption of this act; but this act shall apply to limited partnerships except in so far as the statutes relating to such partnerships are inconsistent herewith.

§ 7. Rules for Determining the Existence of a Partnership

In determining whether a partnership exists, these rules shall apply:

(1) Except as provided by section 16 persons who are not partners as to each other are not partners as to third persons.

(2) Joint tenancy, tenancy in common, tenancy by the entireties, joint property, common property, or part ownership does not of itself

establish a partnership, whether such co-owners do or do not share any profits made by the use of the property.

(3) The sharing of gross returns does not of itself establish a partnership, whether or not the persons sharing them have a joint or common right or interest in any property from which the returns are derived.

(4) The receipt by a person of a share of the profits of a business is prima facie evidence that he is a partner in the business, but no such inference shall be drawn if such profits were received in payment:

(a) As a debt by installments or otherwise,

(b) As wages of an employee or rent to a landlord,

(c) As an annuity to a widow or representative of a deceased partner,

(d) As interest on a loan, though the amount of payment vary with the profits of the business,

(e) As the consideration for the sale of a good-will of a business or other property by installments or otherwise.

§ 8. Partnership Property

(1) All property originally brought into the partnership stock or subsequently acquired by purchase or otherwise, on account of the partnership, is partnership property.

(2) Unless the contrary intention appears, property acquired with partnership funds is partnership property.

(3) Any estate in real property may be acquired in the partnership name. Title so acquired can be conveyed only in the partnership name.

(4) A conveyance to a partnership in the partnership name, though without words of inheritance, passes the entire estate of the grantor unless a contrary intent appears.

PART III

RELATIONS OF PARTNERS TO PERSONS DEALING WITH THE PARTNERSHIP

§ 9. Partner Agent of Partnership as to Partnership Business

(1) Every partner is an agent of the partnership for the purpose of its business, and the act of every partner, including the execution in the partnership name of any instrument, for apparently carrying on in the usual way the business of the partnership of which he is a member binds the partnership, unless the partner so acting has in fact no authority to act for the partnership in the particular matter, and the person with

whom he is dealing has knowledge of the fact that he has no such authority.

(2) An act of a partner which is not apparently for the carrying on of the business of the partnership in the usual way does not bind the partnership unless authorized by the other partners.

(3) Unless authorized by the other partners or unless they have abandoned the business, one or more but less than all the partners have no authority to:

(a) Assign the partnership property in trust for creditors or on the assignee's promise to pay the debts of the partnership,

(b) Dispose of the good-will of the business,

(c) Do any other act which would make it impossible to carry on the ordinary business of a partnership,

(d) Confess a judgment,

(e) Submit a partnership claim or liability to arbitration or reference.

(4) No act of a partner in contravention of a restriction on authority shall bind the partnership to persons having knowledge of the restriction.

§ 10. Conveyance of Real Property of the Partnership

(1) Where title to real property is in the partnership name, any partner may convey title to such property by a conveyance executed in the partnership name; but the partnership may recover such property unless the partner's act binds the partnership under the provisions of paragraph (1) of section 9, or unless such property has been conveyed by the grantee or a person claiming through such grantee to a holder for value without knowledge that the partner, in making the conveyance, has exceeded his authority.

(2) Where title to real property is in the name of the partnership, a conveyance executed by a partner, in his own name, passes the equitable interest of the partnership, provided the act is one within the authority of the partner under the provisions of paragraph (1) of section 9.

(3) Where title to real property is in the name of one or more but not all the partners, and the record does not disclose the right of the partnership, the partners in whose name the title stands may convey title to such property, but the partnership may recover such property if the partners' act does not bind the partnership under the provisions of paragraph (1) of section 9, unless the purchaser or his assignee, is a holder for value, without knowledge.

(4) Where the title to real property is in the name of one or more or all the partners, or in a third person in trust for the partnership, a conveyance executed by a partner in the partnership name, or in his own name, passes the equitable interest of the partnership, provided the act is one within the authority of the partner under the provisions of paragraph (1) of section 9.

(5) Where the title to real property is in the names of all the partners a conveyance executed by all the partners passes all their rights in such property.

§ 11. Partnership Bound by Admission of Partner

An admission or representation made by any partner concerning partnership affairs within the scope of his authority as conferred by this act is evidence against the partnership.

§ 12. Partnership Charged With Knowledge of or Notice to Partner

Notice to any partner of any matter relating to partnership affairs, and the knowledge of the partner acting in the particular matter, acquired while a partner or then present to his mind, and the knowledge of any other partner who reasonably could and should have communicated it to the acting partner, operate as notice to or knowledge of the partnership, except in the case of a fraud on the partnership committed by or with the consent of that partner.

§ 13. Partnership Bound by Partner's Wrongful Act

Where, by any wrongful act or omission of any partner acting in the ordinary course of the business of the partnership or with the authority of his co-partners, loss or injury is caused to any person, not being a partner in the partnership, or any penalty is incurred, the partnership is liable therefor to the same extent as the partner so acting or omitting to act.

§ 14. Partnership Bound by Partner's Breach of Trust

The partnership is bound to make good the loss:

(a) Where one partner acting within the scope of his apparent authority receives money or property of a third person and misapplies it; and

(b) Where the partnership in the course of its business receives money or property of a third person and the money or property so received is misapplied by any partner while it is in the custody of the partnership.

§ 15. Nature of Partner's Liability

All partners are liable

(a) Jointly and severally for everything chargeable to the partnership under sections 13 and 14.

(b) Jointly for all other debts and obligations of the partnership; but any partner may enter into a separate obligation to perform a partnership contract.

§ 16. Partner by Estoppel

(1) When a person, by words spoken or written or by conduct, represents himself, or consents to another representing him to any one, as a partner in an existing partnership or with one or more persons not actual partners, he is liable to any such person to whom such representation has been made, who has, on the faith of such representation, given credit to the actual or apparent partnership, and if he has made such representation or consented to its being made in a public manner he is liable to such person, whether the representation has or has not been made or communicated to such person so giving credit by or with the knowledge of the apparent partner making the representation or consenting to its being made.

(a) When a partnership liability results, he is liable as though he were an actual member of the partnership.

(b) When no partnership liability results, he is liable jointly with the other persons, if any, so consenting to the contract or representation as to incur liability, otherwise separately.

(2) When a person has been thus represented to be a partner in an existing partnership, or with one or more persons not actual partners, he is an agent of the persons consenting to such representation to bind them to the same extent and in the same manner as though he were a partner in fact, with respect to persons who rely upon the representation. Where all the members of the existing partnership consent to the representation, a partnership act or obligation results; but in all other cases it is the joint act or obligation of the person acting and the persons consenting to the representation.

§ 17. Liability of Incoming Partner

A person admitted as a partner into an existing partnership is liable for all the obligations of the partnership arising before his admission as though he had been a partner when such obligations were incurred, except that this liability shall be satisfied only out of partnership property.

PART IV

RELATIONS OF PARTNERS TO ONE ANOTHER

§ 18. Rules Determining Rights and Duties of Partners

The rights and duties of the partners in relation to the partnership shall be determined, subject to any agreement between them, by the following rules:

(a) Each partner shall be repaid his contributions, whether by way of capital or advances to the partnership property and share equally in the profits and surplus remaining after all liabilities, including those to partners, are satisfied; and must contribute towards the losses, whether of capital or otherwise, sustained by the partnership according to his share in the profits.

(b) The partnership must indemnify every partner in respect of payments made and personal liabilities reasonably incurred by him in the ordinary and proper conduct of its business, or for the preservation of its business or property.

(c) A partner, who in aid of the partnership makes any payment or advance beyond the amount of capital which he agreed to contribute, shall be paid interest from the date of the payment or advance.

(d) A partner shall receive interest on the capital contributed by him only from the date when repayment should be made.

(e) All partners have equal rights in the management and conduct of the partnership business.

(f) No partner is entitled to remuneration for acting in the partnership business, except that a surviving partner is entitled to reasonable compensation for his services in winding up the partnership affairs.

(g) No person can become a member of a partnership without the consent of all the partners.

(h) Any difference arising as to ordinary matters connected with the partnership business may be decided by a majority of the partners; but no act in contravention of any agreement between the partners may be done rightfully without the consent of all the partners.

§ 19. Partnership Books

The partnership books shall be kept, subject to any agreement between the partners, at the principal place of business of the partnership, and every partner shall at all times have access to and may inspect and copy any of them.

§ 20. Duty of Partners to Render Information

Partners shall render on demand true and full information of all things affecting the partnership to any partner or the legal representative of any deceased partner or partner under legal disability.

§ 21. Partner Accountable as a Fiduciary

(1) Every partner must account to the partnership for any benefit, and hold as trustee for it any profits derived by him without the consent of the other partners from any transaction connected with the formation, conduct, or liquidation of the partnership or from any use by him of its property.

(2) This section applies also to the representatives of a deceased partner engaged in the liquidation of the affairs of the partnership as the personal representatives of the last surviving partner.

§ 22. Right to an Account

Any partner shall have the right to a formal account as to partnership affairs:

(a) If he is wrongfully excluded from the partnership business or possession of its property by his co-partners,

(b) If the right exists under the terms of any agreement,

(c) As provided by section 21,

(d) Whenever other circumstances render it just and reasonable.

§ 23. Continuation of Partnership Beyond Fixed Term

(1) When a partnership for a fixed term or particular undertaking is continued after the termination of such term or particular undertaking without any express agreement, the rights and duties of the partners remain the same as they were at such termination, so far as is consistent with a partnership at will.

(2) A continuation of the business by the partners or such of them as habitually acted therein during the term, without any settlement or liquidation of the partnership affairs, is prima facie evidence of a continuation of the partnership.

PART V

PROPERTY RIGHTS OF A PARTNER

§ 24. Extent of Property Rights of a Partner

The property rights of a partner are (1) his rights in specific partnership property, (2) his interest in the partnership, and (3) his right to participate in the management.

§ 25. Nature of a Partner's Right in Specific Partnership Property

(1) A partner is co-owner with his partners of specific partnership property holding as a tenant in partnership.

(2) The incidents of this tenancy are such that:

(a) A partner, subject to the provisions of this act and to any agreement between the partners, has an equal right with his partners to possess specific partnership property for partnership purposes; but he has no right to possess such property for any other purpose without the consent of his partners.

(b) A partner's right in specific partnership property is not assignable except in connection with the assignment of rights of all the partners in the same property.

(c) A partner's right in specific partnership property is not subject to attachment or execution, except on a claim against the partnership. When partnership property is attached for a partnership debt the partners, or any of them, or the representatives of a deceased partner, cannot claim any right under the homestead or exemption laws.

(d) On the death of a partner his right in specific partnership property vests in the surviving partner or partners, except where the deceased was the last surviving partner, when his right in such property vests in his legal representative. Such surviving partner or partners, or the legal representative of the last surviving partner, has no right to possess the partnership property for any but a partnership purpose.

(e) A partner's right in specific partnership property is not subject to dower, curtesy, or allowances to widows, heirs, or next of kin.

§ 26. Nature of Partner's Interest in the Partnership

A partner's interest in the partnership is his share of the profits and surplus, and the same is personal property.

§ 27. Assignment of Partner's Interest

(1) A conveyance by a partner of his interest in the partnership does not of itself dissolve the partnership, nor, as against the other partners in the absence of agreement, entitle the assignee, during the continuance of the partnership, to interfere in the management or administration of the partnership business or affairs, or to require any information or account of partnership transactions, or to inspect the partnership books; but it merely entitles the assignee to receive in accordance with his contract the profits to which the assigning partner would otherwise be entitled.

(2) In case of a dissolution of the partnership, the assignee is entitled to receive his assignor's interest and may require an account from the date only of the last account agreed to by all the partners.

§ 28. Partner's Interest Subject to Charging Order

(1) On due application to a competent court by any judgment creditor of a partner, the court which entered the judgment, order, or decree, or any other court, may charge the interest of the debtor partner with payment of the unsatisfied amount of such judgment debt with interest thereon; and may then or later appoint a receiver of his share of the profits, and of any other money due or to fall due to him in respect of the partnership, and make all other orders, directions, accounts and inquiries which the debtor partner might have made, or which the circumstances of the case may require.

(2) The interest charged may be redeemed at any time before foreclosure, or in case of a sale being directed by the court may be purchased without thereby causing a dissolution:

(a) With separate property, by any one or more of the partners, or

(b) With partnership property, by any one or more of the partners with the consent of all the partners whose interests are not so charged or sold.

(3) Nothing in this act shall be held to deprive a partner of his right, if any, under the exemption laws, as regards his interest in the partnership.

PART VI

DISSOLUTION AND WINDING UP

§ 29. Dissolution Defined

The dissolution of a partnership is the change in the relation of the partners caused by any partner ceasing to be associated in the carrying on as distinguished from the winding up of the business.

Official Comment

... In this act dissolution designates the point in time when the partners cease to carry on the business together; termination is the point in time when all the partnership affairs are wound up; winding up, the process of settling partnership affairs after dissolution.

§ 30. Partnership Not Terminated by Dissolution

On dissolution the partnership is not terminated, but continues until the winding up of partnership affairs is completed.

§ 31. Causes of Dissolution

Dissolution is caused:

(1) Without violation of the agreement between the partners,

(a) By the termination of the definite term or particular undertaking specified in the agreement,

(b) By the express will of any partner when no definite term or particular undertaking is specified,

(c) By the express will of all the partners who have not assigned their interests or suffered them to be charged for their separate debts, either before or after the termination of any specified term or particular undertaking,

(d) By the expulsion of any partner from the business bona fide in accordance with such a power conferred by the agreement between the partners;

(2) In contravention of the agreement between the partners, where the circumstances do not permit a dissolution under any other provision of this section, by the express will of any partner at any time;

(3) By any event which makes it unlawful for the business of the partnership to be carried on or for the members to carry it on in partnership;

(4) By the death of any partner;

(5) By the bankruptcy of any partner or the partnership;

(6) By decree of court under section 32.

Official Comment

Paragraph (2) will settle a matter on which at present considerable confusion and uncertainty exists. The paragraph as drawn allows a partner to dissolve a partnership in contravention of the agreement between the partners. . . .

The relation of partners is one of agency. The agency is such a personal one that equity cannot enforce it even where the agreement provides that the partnership shall continue for a definite time. The power of any partner to terminate the relation, even though in doing so he breaks a contract, should, it is submitted, be recognized.

The rights of the parties upon a dissolution in contravention of the agreement are safeguarded by section 38(2), infra.

§ 32. Dissolution by Decree of Court

(1) On application by or for a partner the court shall decree a dissolution whenever:

(a) A partner has been declared a lunatic in any judicial proceeding or is shown to be of unsound mind,

(b) A partner becomes in any other way incapable of performing his part of the partnership contract,

(c) A partner has been guilty of such conduct as tends to affect prejudicially the carrying on of the business,

(d) A partner wilfully or persistently commits a breach of the partnership agreement, or otherwise so conducts himself in matters relating to the partnership business that it is not reasonably practicable to carry on the business in partnership with him,

(e) The business of the partnership can only be carried on at a loss,

(f) Other circumstances render a dissolution equitable.

(2) On the application of the purchaser of a partner's interest under sections 28 or 29: [1]

(a) After the termination of the specified term or particular undertaking,

(b) At any time if the partnership was a partnership at will when the interest was assigned or when the charging order was issued.

§ 33. General Effect of Dissolution on Authority of Partner

Except so far as may be necessary to wind up partnership affairs or to complete transactions begun but not then finished, dissolution terminates all authority of any partner to act for the partnership,

(1) With respect to the partners,

(a) When the dissolution is not by the act, bankruptcy or death of a partner; or

(b) When the dissolution is by such act, bankruptcy or death of a partner, in cases where section 34 so requires.

(2) With respect to persons not partners, as declared in section 35.

§ 34. Right of Partner to Contribution From Co-partners After Dissolution

Where the dissolution is caused by the act, death or bankruptcy of a partner, each partner is liable to his co-partners for his share of any liability created by any partner acting for the partnership as if the partnership had not been dissolved unless

(a) The dissolution being by act of any partner, the partner acting for the partnership had knowledge of the dissolution, or

(b) The dissolution being by the death or bankruptcy of a partner, the partner acting for the partnership had knowledge or notice of the death or bankruptcy.

---

1. So in original. Probably should read "sections 27 or 28."

§ 35.   Power of Partner to Bind Partnership to Third Persons After Dissolution

(1) After dissolution a partner can bind the partnership except as provided in Paragraph (3)

(a) By any act appropriate for winding up partnership affairs or completing transactions unfinished at dissolution;

(b) By any transaction which would bind the partnership if dissolution had not taken place, provided the other party to the transaction

(I) Had extended credit to the partnership prior to dissolution and had no knowledge or notice of the dissolution; or

(II) Though he had not so extended credit, had nevertheless known of the partnership prior to dissolution, and, having no knowledge or notice of dissolution, the fact of dissolution had not been advertised in a newspaper of general circulation in the place (or in each place if more than one) at which the partnership business was regularly carried on.

(2) The liability of a partner under Paragraph (1b) shall be satisfied out of partnership assets alone when such partner had been prior to dissolution

(a) Unknown as a partner to the person with whom the contract is made; and

(b) So far unknown and inactive in partnership affairs that the business reputation of the partnership could not be said to have been in any degree due to his connection with it.

(3) The partnership is in no case bound by any act of a partner after dissolution

(a) Where the partnership is dissolved because it is unlawful to carry on the business, unless the act is appropriate for winding up partnership affairs; or

(b) Where the partner has become bankrupt; or

(c) Where the partner has no authority to wind up partnership affairs; except by a transaction with one who

(I) Had extended credit to the partnership prior to dissolution and had no knowledge or notice of his want of authority; or

(II) Had not extended credit to the partnership prior to dissolution, and, having no knowledge or notice of his want of authority, the fact of his want of authority has not been advertised in the manner provided for advertising the fact of dissolution in Paragraph (1bII).

(4) Nothing in this section shall affect the liability under Section 16 of any person who after dissolution represents himself or consents to another representing him as a partner in a partnership engaged in carrying on business.

§ 36. Effect of Dissolution on Partner's Existing Liability

(1) The dissolution of the partnership does not of itself discharge the existing liability of any partner.

(2) A partner is discharged from any existing liability upon dissolution of the partnership by an agreement to that effect between himself, the partnership creditor and the person or partnership continuing the business; and such agreement may be inferred from the course of dealing between the creditor having knowledge of the dissolution and the person or partnership continuing the business.

(3) Where a person agrees to assume the existing obligations of a dissolved partnership, the partners whose obligations have been assumed shall be discharged from any liability to any creditor of the partnership who, knowing of the agreement, consents to a material alteration in the nature or time of payment of such obligations.

(4) The individual property of a deceased partner shall be liable for all obligations of the partnership incurred while he was a partner but subject to the prior payment of his separate debts.

§ 37. Right to Wind Up

Unless otherwise agreed the partners who have not wrongfully dissolved the partnership or the legal representative of the last surviving partner, not bankrupt, has the right to wind up the partnership affairs; provided, however, that any partner, his legal representative or his assignee, upon cause shown, may obtain winding up by the court.

§ 38. Rights of Partners to Application of Partnership Property

(1) When dissolution is caused in any way, except in contravention of the partnership agreement, each partner, as against his co-partners and all persons claiming through them in respect of their interests in the partnership, unless otherwise agreed, may have the partnership property applied to discharge its liabilities, and the surplus applied to pay in cash the net amount owing to the respective partners. But if dissolution is caused by expulsion of a partner, bona fide under the partnership agreement and if the expelled partner is discharged from all partnership liabilities, either by payment or agreement under section 36(2), he shall receive in cash only the net amount due him from the partnership.

(2) When dissolution is caused in contravention of the partnership agreement the rights of the partners shall be as follows:

(a) Each partner who has not caused dissolution wrongfully shall have,

I. All the rights specified in paragraph (1) of this section, and

II. The right, as against each partner who has caused the dissolution wrongfully, to damages for breach of the agreement.

(b) The partners who have not caused the dissolution wrongfully, if they all desire to continue the business in the same name, either by themselves or jointly with others, may do so, during the agreed term for the partnership and for that purpose may possess the partnership property, provided they secure the payment by bond approved by the court, or pay to any partner who has caused the dissolution wrongfully, the value of his interest in the partnership at the dissolution, less any damages recoverable under clause (2aII) of this section, and in like manner indemnify him against all present or future partnership liabilities.

(c) A partner who has caused the dissolution wrongfully shall have:

I. If the business is not continued under the provisions of paragraph (2b) all the rights of a partner under paragraph (1), subject to clause (2aII), of this section,

II. If the business is continued under paragraph (2b) of this section the right as against his co-partners and all claiming through them in respect of their interests in the partnership, to have the value of his interest in the partnership, less any damages caused to his co-partners by the dissolution, ascertained and paid to him in cash, or the payment secured by bond approved by the court, and to be released from all existing liabilities of the partnership; but in ascertaining the value of the partner's interest the value of the good-will of the business shall not be considered.

Official Comment

The right given to each partner, where no agreement to the contrary has been made, to have his share of the surplus paid to him in cash makes certain an existing uncertainty. At present it is not certain whether a partner may or may not insist on a physical partition of the property remaining after third persons have been paid.

§ 39. Rights Where Partnership Is Dissolved for Fraud or Misrepresentation

Where a partnership contract is rescinded on the ground of the fraud or misrepresentation of one of the parties thereto, the party entitled to rescind is, without prejudice to any other right, entitled,

(a) To a lien on, or a right of retention of, the surplus of the partnership property after satisfying the partnership liabilities to third persons for any sum of money paid by him for the purchase of an interest in the partnership and for any capital or advances contributed by him; and

(b) To stand, after all liabilities to third persons have been satisfied, in the place of the creditors of the partnership for any payments made by him in respect of the partnership liabilities; and

(c) To be indemnified by the person guilty of the fraud or making the representation against all debts and liabilities of the partnership.

§ 40. Rules for Distribution

In settling accounts between the partners after dissolution, the following rules shall be observed, subject to any agreement to the contrary:

(a) The assets of the partnership are:

I.   The partnership property,

II.   The contributions of the partners necessary for the payment of all the liabilities specified in clause (b) of this paragraph.

(b) The liabilities of the partnership shall rank in order of payment, as follows:

I.   Those owing to creditors other than partners,

II.   Those owing to partners other than for capital and profits,

III.   Those owing to partners in respect of capital,

IV.   Those owing to partners in respect of profits.

(c) The assets shall be applied in order of their declaration in clause (a) of this paragraph to the satisfaction of the liabilities.

(d) The partners shall contribute, as provided by section 18(a) the amount necessary to satisfy the liabilities; but if any, but not all, of the partners are insolvent, or, not being subject to process, refuse to contribute, the other partners shall contribute their share of the liabilities, and, in the relative proportions in which they share the profits, the additional amount necessary to pay the liabilities.

(e) An assignee for the benefit of creditors or any person appointed by the court shall have the right to enforce the contributions specified in clause (d) of this paragraph.

(f) Any partner or his legal representative shall have the right to enforce the contributions specified in clause (d) of this paragraph, to the extent of the amount which he has paid in excess of his share of the liability.

(g) The individual property of a deceased partner shall be liable for the contributions specified in clause (d) of this paragraph.

(h) When partnership property and the individual properties of the partners are in possession of a court for distribution, partnership creditors shall have priority on partnership property and separate creditors on individual property, saving the rights of lien or secured creditors as heretofore.

(i) Where a partner has become bankrupt or his estate is insolvent the claims against his separate property shall rank in the following order:

    I. Those owing to separate creditors,

    II. Those owing to partnership creditors,

    III. Those owing to partners by way of contribution.

§ 41. Liability of Persons Continuing the Business in Certain Cases

(1) When any new partner is admitted into an existing partnership, or when any partner retires and assigns (or the representative of the deceased partner assigns) his rights in partnership property to two or more of the partners, or to one or more of the partners and one or more third persons, if the business is continued without liquidation of the partnership affairs, creditors of the first or dissolved partnership are also creditors of the partnership so continuing the business.

(2) When all but one partner retire and assign (or the representative of a deceased partner assigns) their rights in partnership property to the remaining partner, who continues the business without liquidation of partnership affairs, either alone or with others, creditors of the dissolved partnership are also creditors of the person or partnership so continuing the business.

(3) When any partner retires or dies and the business of the dissolved partnership is continued as set forth in paragraphs (1) and (2) of this section, with the consent of the retired partners or the representative of the deceased partner, but without any assignment of his right in partnership property, rights of creditors of the dissolved partnership and of the creditors of the person or partnership continuing the business shall be as if such assignment had been made.

(4) When all the partners or their representatives assign their rights in partnership property to one or more third persons who promise to pay the debts and who continue the business of the dissolved partnership, creditors of the dissolved partnership are also creditors of the person or partnership continuing the business.

(5) When any partner wrongfully causes a dissolution and the remaining partners continue the business under the provisions of section 38(2b), either alone or with others, and without liquidation of the partnership affairs, creditors of the dissolved partnership are also creditors of the person or partnership continuing the business.

(6) When a partner is expelled and the remaining partners continue the business either alone or with others, without liquidation of the partnership affairs, creditors of the dissolved partnership are also creditors of the person or partnership continuing the business.

(7) The liability of a third person becoming a partner in the partnership continuing the business, under this section, to the creditors of the dissolved partnership shall be satisfied out of partnership property only.

(8) When the business of a partnership after dissolution is continued under any conditions set forth in this section the creditors of the dissolved partnership, as against the separate creditors of the retiring or deceased partner or the representative of the deceased partner, have a prior right to any claim of the retired partner or the representative of the deceased partner against the person or partnership continuing the business, on account of the retired or deceased partner's interest in the dissolved partnership or on account of any consideration promised for such interest or for his right in partnership property.

(9) Nothing in this section shall be held to modify any right of creditors to set aside any assignment on the ground of fraud.

(10) The use by the person or partnership continuing the business of the partnership name, or the name of a deceased partner as part thereof, shall not of itself make the individual property of the deceased partner liable for any debts contracted by such person or partnership.

§ 42. Rights of Retiring or Estate of Deceased Partner When the Business Is Continued

When any partner retires or dies, and the business is continued under any of the conditions set forth in section 41(1, 2, 3, 5, 6), or section 38(2b) without any settlement of accounts as between him or his estate and the person or partnership continuing the business, unless otherwise agreed, he or his legal representative as against such persons or partnership may have the value of his interest at the date of dissolution ascertained, and shall receive as an ordinary creditor an amount equal to the value of his interest in the dissolved partnership with interest, or, at his option or at the option of his legal representative, in lieu of interest, the profits attributable to the use of his right in the property of the dissolved partnership; provided that the creditors of the dissolved partnership as against the separate creditors, or the representative of the retired or deceased partner, shall have priority on any claim arising under this section, as provided by section 41(8) of this act.

§ 43. Accrual of Actions

The right to an account of his interest shall accrue to any partner, or his legal representative, as against the winding up partners or the surviving partners or the person or partnership continuing the business, at the date of dissolution, in the absence of any agreement to the contrary.

REVISED UNIFORM PARTNERSHIP ACT (1997)

ARTICLE 1. GENERAL PROVISIONS

ARTICLE 2. NATURE OF PARTNERSHIP

ARTICLE 3. RELATIONS OF PARTNERS TO PERSONS DEALING WITH PARTNERSHIP

ARTICLE 4. RELATIONS OF PARTNERS TO EACH OTHER AND TO PARTNERSHIP

ARTICLE 5. TRANSFEREES AND CREDITORS OF PARTNER

ARTICLE 1

GENERAL PROVISIONS

Sec.
101. Definitions.
102. Knowledge and Notice.
103. Effect of Partnership Agreement; Nonwaivable Provisions.
104. Supplemental Principles of Law.
105. Execution, Filing, and Recording of Statements.
106. Governing Law.
107. Partnership Subject to Amendment or Repeal of [Act].

SECTION 101.   DEFINITIONS.

In this [Act]:

(1) "Business" includes every trade, occupation, and profession.

(2) "Debtor in bankruptcy" means a person who is the subject of:

(i) an order for relief under Title 11 of the United States Code or a comparable order under a successor statute of general application; or

(ii) a comparable order under federal, state, or foreign law governing insolvency.

(3) "Distribution" means a transfer of money or other property from a partnership to a partner in the partner's capacity as a partner or to the partner's transferee.

(4) "Foreign limited liability partnership" means a partnership that:

(i) is formed under laws other than the laws of this State; and

(ii) has the status of a limited liability partnership under those laws.

(5) "Limited liability partnership" means a partnership that has filed a statement of qualification under Section 1001 and does not have a similar statement in effect in any other jurisdiction.

133

(6) "Partnership" means an association of two or more persons to carry on as co-owners a business for profit formed under Section 202, predecessor law, or comparable law of another jurisdiction.

(7) "Partnership agreement" means the agreement, whether written, oral, or implied, among the partners concerning the partnership, including amendments to the partnership agreement.

(8) "Partnership at will" means a partnership in which the partners have not agreed to remain partners until the expiration of a definite term or the completion of a particular undertaking.

(9) "Partnership interest" or "partner's interest in the partnership" means all of a partner's interests in the partnership, including the partner's transferable interest and all management and other rights.

(10) "Person" means an individual, corporation, business trust, estate, trust, partnership, association, joint venture, government, governmental subdivision, agency, or instrumentality, or any other legal or commercial entity.

(11) "Property" means all property, real, personal, or mixed, tangible or intangible, or any interest therein.

(12) "State" means a State of the United States, the District of Columbia, the Commonwealth of Puerto Rico, or any territory or insular possession subject to the jurisdiction of the United States.

(13) "Statement" means a statement of partnership authority under Section 303, a statement of denial under Section 304, a statement of dissociation under Section 704, a statement of dissolution under Section 805, a statement of merger under Section 907, a statement of qualification under Section 1001, a statement of foreign qualification under Section 1102, or an amendment or cancellation of any of the foregoing.

(14) "Transfer" includes an assignment, conveyance, lease, mortgage, deed, and encumbrance.

Comment: . . .

The definition of a "foreign limited liability partnership" includes a partnership formed under the laws of another state, foreign country, or other jurisdiction provided it has the status of a limited liability partnership in the other jurisdiction. Since the scope and nature of foreign limited liability partnership liability shields may vary in different jurisdictions, the definition avoids reference to similar or comparable laws. Rather, the definition incorporates the concept of a limited liability partnership in the foreign jurisdiction, however defined in that jurisdiction. The reference to formation "under laws other than the laws of this State" makes clear that the definition includes partnerships formed in foreign countries as well as in another state.

The definition of a "limited liability partnership" makes clear that a partnership may adopt the special liability shield characteristics of a limited liability partnership simply by filing a statement of qualification under Section 1001. A partnership may file the statement in this State regardless of where formed. When coupled with the governing law provisions of Section 106(b), this definition simplifies the choice of law issues applicable to partnerships with multistate activities and contacts. Once a statement of qualification is filed, a partnership's internal affairs and the liability of its partners are determined by the law of the State where the statement is filed. See Section 106(b). The partnership may not vary this particular requirement. See Section 103(b)(9).

The reference to a "partnership" in the definition of a limited liability partnership makes clear that the RUPA definition of the term rather than the UPA concept controls for purposes of a limited liability partnership. Section 101(6) defines a "partnership" as "an association of two or more persons to carry on as co-owners a business for profit formed under Section 202, predecessor law, or comparable law of another jurisdiction." Section 202(b) further provides that "an association formed under a statute other than this [Act], a predecessor statute, or a comparable statute of another jurisdiction is not a partnership under this [Act]." This language was intended to clarify that a limited partnership is not a RUPA general partnership. It was not intended to preclude the application of any RUPA general partnership rules to limited partnerships where limited partnership law otherwise adopts the RUPA rules. See Comments to Section 202(b) and Prefatory Note.

The effect of these definitions leaves the scope and applicability of RUPA to limited partnerships to limited partnership law, not to sever the linkage between the two Acts in all cases. Certain provisions of RUPA will continue to govern limited partnerships by virtue of Revised Uniform Limited Partnership Act (RULPA) Section 1105 which provides that "in any case not provided for in this [Act] the provisions of the Uniform Partnership Act govern." The RUPA partnership definition includes partnerships formed under the UPA. Therefore, the limited liability partnership rules will govern limited partnerships "in any case not provided for" in RULPA. Since RULPA does not provide for any rules applicable to a limited partnership becoming a limited liability partnership, the limited liability partnership rules should apply to limited partnerships that file a statement of qualification.

Partner liability deserves special mention. RULPA Section 403(b) provides that a general partner of a limited partnership "has the liabilities of a partner in a partnership without limited partners." Thus limited partnership law expressly references general partnership law for general partner liability and does not separately consider the liability of such partners. The liability of a general partner of a limited partnership that becomes a LLLP would therefore be the liability of a general partner in an LLP and would be governed by Section 306. The liability of a limited partner in a LLLP is a more complicated matter. RULPA Section 303(a) separately considers the liability of a limited partner. Unless also a general partner, a limited partner is not liable for the obligations of a limited partnership unless the partner participates in the control of the business and then only to persons reasonably believing the limited partner is a general partner. Therefore, arguably limited partners in a LLLP will have the specific RULPA Section 303(c) liability shield while general partners will have a superior Section 306(c) liability shield. In order to clarify limited partner liability and other linkage issues, states that have adopted RUPA, these limited liability partnership rules, and RULPA may wish to consider an amendment to RULPA. A suggested form of such an amendment is:

SECTION 1107. LIMITED LIABILITY LIMITED PARTNERSHIP.

(a) A limited partnership may become a limited liability partnership by:

(1) obtaining approval of the terms and conditions of the limited partnership becoming a limited liability limited partnership by the vote necessary to amend the limited partnership agreement except, in the case of a limited partnership agreement that expressly considers contribution obligations, the vote necessary to amend those provisions;

(2) filing a statement of qualification under Section 1001(c) of the Uniform Partnership Act (1994); and

(3) complying with the name requirements of Section 1002 of the Uniform Partnership Act (1994).

(b) A limited liability limited partnership continues to be the same entity that existed before the filing of a statement of qualification under Section 1001(c) of the Uniform Partnership Act (1994).

(c) Sections 306(c) and 307(f) of the Uniform Partnership Act (1994) apply to both general and limited partners of a limited liability limited partnership. . . .

The definition of "partnership agreement" is adapted from Section 101(9) of RULPA. The RUPA definition is intended to include the agreement among the partners, including amendments, concerning either the affairs of the partnership or the conduct of its business. It does not include other agreements between some or all of the partners, such as a lease or loan agreement. The partnership agreement need not be written; it may be oral or inferred from the conduct of the parties.

Any partnership in which the partners have not agreed to remain partners until the expiration of a definite term or the completion of a particular undertaking is a "partnership at will." The distinction between an "at-will" partnership and a partnership for "a definite term or the completion of a particular undertaking" is important in determining the rights of dissociating and continuing partners following the dissociation of a partner. See Sections 601, 602, 701(b), 801(a), 802(b), and 803.

It is sometimes difficult to determine whether a partnership is at will or is for a definite term or the completion of a particular undertaking. Presumptively, every partnership is an at-will partnership. See, e.g., Stone v. Stone, 292 So.2d 686 (La.1974); Frey v. Hauke, 171 Neb. 852, 108 N.W.2d 228 (1961). To constitute a partnership for a term or a particular undertaking, the partners must agree (i) that the partnership will continue for a definite term or until a particular undertaking is completed *and* (ii) that they will remain partners until the expiration of the term or the completion of the undertaking. Both are necessary for a term partnership; if the partners have the unrestricted right, as distinguished from the power, to withdraw from a partnership formed for a term or particular undertaking, the partnership is one at will, rather than a term partnership.

To find that the partnership is formed for a definite term or a particular undertaking, there must be clear evidence of an agreement among the partners that the partnership (i) has a minimum or maximum duration or (ii) terminates at the conclusion of a particular venture whose time is indefinite but certain to occur. See, e.g., Stainton v. Tarantino, 637 F.Supp. 1051 (E.D.Pa.1986) (partnership to dissolve no later than December 30, 2020); Abel v. American Art Analog, Inc., 838 F.2d 691 (3d Cir.1988) (partnership purpose to market an art book); 68th Street Apts., Inc. v. Lauricella, 362 A.2d 78 (N.J.Super.Ct.1976) (partnership purpose to construct an apartment building). A partnership to conduct a business which may last indefinitely, however, is an at-will partnership, even though there may be an obligation of the partnership, such as a mortgage, which must be repaid by a certain date, absent a specific agreement that no partner can rightfully withdraw until the obligation is repaid. See, e.g., Page v. Page, 55 Cal.2d 192, 359 P.2d 41 (1961) (partnership purpose to operate a linen supply business); Frey v. Hauke, supra (partnership purpose to contract and operate a bowling alley); Girard Bank v. Haley, 460 Pa. 237, 332 A.2d 443 (1975) (partnership purpose to maintain and lease buildings).

"Partnership interest" or "partner's interest in the partnership" is defined to mean all of a partner's interests in the partnership, including the partner's transferable interest and all management and other rights. A partner's "transferable interest" is a more limited concept and means only his share of the profits and losses and right to receive distributions, that is, the partner's economic interests. See Section 502 and Comment. . . .

SECTION 102. KNOWLEDGE AND NOTICE.

(a) A person knows a fact if the person has actual knowledge of it.

(b) A person has notice of a fact if the person:

(1) knows of it;

(2) has received a notification of it; or

(3) has reason to know it exists from all of the facts known to the person at the time in question.

(c) A person notifies or gives a notification to another by taking steps reasonably required to inform the other person in ordinary course, whether or not the other person learns of it.

(d) A person receives a notification when the notification:

(1) comes to the person's attention; or

(2) is duly delivered at the person's place of business or at any other place held out by the person as a place for receiving communications.

(e) Except as otherwise provided in subsection (f), a person other than an individual knows, has notice, or receives a notification of a fact for purposes of a particular transaction when the individual conducting the transaction knows, has notice, or receives a notification of the fact, or in any event when the fact would have been brought to the individual's attention if the person had exercised reasonable diligence. The person exercises reasonable diligence if it maintains reasonable routines for communicating significant information to the individual conducting the transaction and there is reasonable compliance with the routines. Reasonable diligence does not require an individual acting for the person to communicate information unless the communication is part of the individual's regular duties or the individual has reason to know of the transaction and that the transaction would be materially affected by the information.

(f) A partner's knowledge, notice, or receipt of a notification of a fact relating to the partnership is effective immediately as knowledge by, notice to, or receipt of a notification by the partnership, except in the case of a fraud on the partnership committed by or with the consent of that partner.

Comment: ...

A person "knows" a fact only if that person has actual knowledge of it. Knowledge is cognitive awareness. That is solely an issue of fact. This is a change from the UPA Section 3(1) definition of "knowledge" which included the concept of "bad faith" knowledge arising from other known facts.

"Notice" is a lesser degree of awareness than "knows" and is based on a person's: (i) actual knowledge; (ii) receipt of a notification; or (iii) reason to know based on actual knowledge of other facts and the circumstances at the time. The latter is the traditional concept of inquiry notice.

Generally, under RUPA, statements filed pursuant to Section 105 [Execution, Filing, and Recording of Documents] do not constitute constructive knowledge or notice, except as expressly provided in the Act. See Section 301(1) (generally requiring knowledge of limitations on partner's apparent authority). Properly recorded statements of limitation on a partner's authority, on the other hand, generally constitute constructive knowledge with respect to the transfer of real property held in the partnership name. See Sections 303(d)(1), 303(e), 704(b), and 805(b)....

A notification is not required to be in writing. That is a change from UPA Section 3(2)(b). As under the UCC, the time and circumstances under which a notification may cease to be effective are not determined by RUPA....

SECTION 103. EFFECT OF PARTNERSHIP AGREEMENT; NONWAIVABLE PROVISIONS.

(a) Except as otherwise provided in subsection (b), relations among the partners and between the partners and the partnership are governed by the partnership agreement. To the extent the partnership agreement does not otherwise provide, this [Act] governs relations among the partners and between the partners and the partnership.

(b) The partnership agreement may not:

(1) vary the rights and duties under Section 105 except to eliminate the duty to provide copies of statements to all of the partners;

(2) unreasonably restrict the right of access to books and records under Section 403(b);

(3) eliminate the duty of loyalty under Section 404(b) or 603(b)(3), but:

(i) the partnership agreement may identify specific types or categories of activities that do not violate the duty of loyalty, if not manifestly unreasonable; or

(ii) all of the partners or a number or percentage specified in the partnership agreement may authorize or ratify, after full disclosure of all material facts, a specific act or transaction that otherwise would violate the duty of loyalty;

(4) unreasonably reduce the duty of care under Section 404(c) or 603(b)(3);

(5) eliminate the obligation of good faith and fair dealing under Section 404(d), but the partnership agreement may prescribe the standards by which the performance of the obligation is to be measured, if the standards are not manifestly unreasonable;

(6) vary the power to dissociate as a partner under Section 602(a), except to require the notice under Section 601(1) to be in writing;

(7) vary the right of a court to expel a partner in the events specified in Section 601(5);

(8) vary the requirement to wind up the partnership business in cases specified in Section 801(4), (5), or (6);

(9) vary the law applicable to a limited liability partnership under Section 106(b); or

(10) restrict rights of third parties under this [Act].

Comment:

1. The general rule under Section 103(a) is that relations among the partners and between the partners and the partnership are governed by the partnership agreement. See Section 101(5). To the extent that the partners fail to agree upon a contrary rule, RUPA provides the default rule. Only the rights and duties listed in Section 103(b), and implicitly the corresponding liabilities and remedies under Section 405, are mandatory and cannot be waived or varied by agreement beyond what is authorized. Those are the only exceptions to the general principle that the provisions of RUPA with respect to the rights of the partners *inter se* are merely default rules, subject to modification by the partners. All modifications must also, of course, satisfy the general standards of contract validity. See Section 104.

2. Under subsection (b)(1), the partnership agreement may not vary the requirements for executing, filing, and recording statements under Section 105, except the duty to provide copies to all the partners. A statement that is not executed, filed, and recorded in accordance with the statutory requirements will not be accorded the effect prescribed in the Act, except as provided in Section 303(d).

3. Subsection (b)(2) provides that the partnership agreement may not unreasonably restrict a partner or former partner's access rights to books and records under Section 403(b). It is left to the courts to determine what restrictions are reasonable. See Comment 2 to Section 403. Other information rights in Section 403 can be varied or even eliminated by agreement.

4. Subsection[s] (b)(3) through (5) are intended to ensure a fundamental core of fiduciary responsibility. Neither the fiduciary duties of loyalty or care, nor the obligation of good faith and fair dealing, may be eliminated entirely. However, the statutory requirements of each can be modified by agreement, subject to the limitation[s] stated in subsection[s] (b)(3) through (5).

There has always been a tension regarding the extent to which a partner's fiduciary duty of loyalty can be varied by agreement, as contrasted with the other partners' consent to a particular and known breach of duty. On the one hand, courts have been loathe to enforce agreements broadly "waiving" in advance a partner's fiduciary duty of loyalty, especially where there is unequal bargaining power, information, or sophistication. For this reason, a very broad provision in a partnership agreement in effect negating any duty of loyalty, such as a provision giving a managing partner complete discretion to manage the business with no liability except for acts and omissions that constitute wilful misconduct, will not likely be enforced. See, e.g., Labovitz v. Dolan, 189 Ill.App.3d 403, 136 Ill.Dec. 780, 545 N.E.2d 304 (1989). On the other hand, it is clear that the remaining partners can "consent" to a particular conflicting interest transaction or other breach of duty, after the fact, provided there is full disclosure.

RUPA attempts to provide a standard that partners can rely upon in drafting exculpatory agreements. It is not necessary that the agreement be restricted to a particular transaction. That would require bargaining over every transaction or opportunity, which would be excessively burdensome. The agreement may be drafted in terms of types or categories of activities or transactions, but it should be reasonably specific.

A provision in a real estate partnership agreement authorizing a partner who is a real estate agent to retain commissions on partnership property bought and sold by that partner would be an example of a "type or category" of activity that is not manifestly unreasonable and thus should be enforceable under the Act. Likewise, a provision authorizing that partner to buy or sell real property for his own account without prior disclosure to the other partners or without first offering it to the partnership would be enforceable as a valid category of partnership activity.

Ultimately, the courts must decide the outer limits of validity of such agreements, and context may be significant. It is intended that the risk of judicial refusal to enforce manifestly unreasonable exculpatory clauses will discourage sharp practices while accommodating the legitimate needs of the parties in structuring their relationship.

5. Subsection (b)(3)(i) permits the partners, in their partnership agreement, to identify specific types or categories of partnership activities that do not violate the duty of loyalty. A modification of the statutory standard must not, however, be manifestly unreasonable. This is intended to discourage overreaching by a partner with superior bargaining power since the courts may refuse to enforce an overly broad exculpatory clause. See, e.g., Vlases v. Montgomery Ward & Co., 377 F.2d 846, 850 (3d Cir.1967) (limitation prohibits unconscionable agreements); PPG Industries, Inc. v. Shell Oil Co., 919 F.2d 17, 19 (5th Cir.1990) (apply limitation deferentially to agreements of sophisticated parties).

Subsection (b)(3)(ii) is intended to clarify the right of partners, recognized under general law, to consent to a known past or anticipated violation of duty and to waive their legal remedies for redress of that violation. This is intended to cover situations where the conduct in question is not specifically authorized by the partnership agreement. It can also be used to validate conduct that might otherwise not satisfy the "manifestly unreasonable" standard. Clause (ii) provides that, after full disclosure of all material facts regarding a specific act or transaction that otherwise would violate the duty of loyalty, it may be authorized or ratified by the partners. That authorization or ratification must be unanimous unless a lesser number or percentage is specified for this purpose in the partnership agreement.

6. Under subsection (b)(4), the partners' duty of care may not be unreasonably reduced below the statutory standard set forth in Section 404(d), that is, to refrain from engaging in grossly negligent or reckless conduct, intentional misconduct, or a knowing violation of law.

For example, partnership agreements frequently contain provisions releasing a partner from liability for actions taken in good faith and in the honest belief that the actions are in the best interests of the partnership and indemnifying the partner against any liability incurred in connection with the business of the partnership if the partner acts in a good faith belief that he has authority to act. Many partnership agreements reach this same result by listing various activities and stating that the performance of these activities is deemed not to constitute gross negligence or wilful misconduct. These types of provisions are intended to come within the modifications authorized by subsection (b)(4). On the other hand, absolving partners of intentional misconduct is probably unreasonable. As with contractual standards of loyalty, determining the outer limit in reducing the standard of care is left to the courts.

The standard may, of course, be increased by agreement to one of ordinary care or an even higher standard of care.

7. Subsection (b)(5) authorizes the partners to determine the standards by which the performance of the obligation of good faith and fair dealing is to be measured. The language of subsection (b)(5) is based on UCC Section 1–102(3). The partners can negotiate and draft specific contract provisions tailored to their particular needs (e.g., five days notice of a partners' meeting is adequate notice), but blanket waivers of the obligation are unenforceable....

8. Section 602(a) continues the traditional UPA Section 31(2) rule that every partner has the power to withdraw from the partnership at any time, which power can not be bargained away. Section 103(b)(6) provides that the partnership agreement may not vary the power to dissociate as a partner under Section 602(a), except to require that the notice of withdrawal under Section 601(1) be in writing....

9. Under subsection (b)(7), the right of a partner to seek court expulsion of another partner under Section 601(5) can not be waived or varied (e.g., requiring a 90–day notice) by agreement. Section 601(5) refers to judicial expulsion on such grounds as misconduct, breach of duty, or impracticability.

10. Under subsection (b)(8), the partnership agreement may not vary the right of partners to have the partnership dissolved and its business wound up under Section 801(4), (5), or (6). Section 801(4) provides that the partnership must be wound up if its business is unlawful. Section 801(5) provides for judicial winding up in such circumstances as frustration of the firm's economic purpose, partner misconduct, or impracticability. Section 801(6) accords standing to transferees of an interest in the partnership to seek judicial dissolution of the partnership in specified circumstances.

11. Subsection (b)(9) makes clear that a limited liability partnership may not designate the law of a State other than the State where it filed its statement of qualification to govern its internal affairs and the liability of its partners. See Sections 101(5), 106(b), and 202(a). Therefore, the selection of a state within which to file a statement of qualification has important choice of law ramifications, particularly where the partnership was formed in another state. See Comments to Section 106(b)....

SECTION 104. SUPPLEMENTAL PRINCIPLES OF LAW.

(a) Unless displaced by particular provisions of this [Act], the principles of law and equity supplement this [Act].

(b) If an obligation to pay interest arises under this [Act] and the rate is not specified, the rate is that specified in [applicable statute].

Comment:

The principles of law and equity supplement RUPA unless displaced by a particular provision of the Act.... These supplementary principles encompass not only the law of agency and estoppel and the law merchant mentioned in the UPA, but all of the other principles listed in UCC Section 1–103: the law relative to capacity to contract, fraud, misrepresentation, duress, coercion, mistake, bankruptcy, and other common law validating or invalidating causes, such as unconscionability. No substantive change from either the UPA or the UCC is intended....

SECTION 105. EXECUTION, FILING, AND RECORDING OF STATEMENTS.

(a) A statement may be filed in the office of [the Secretary of State]. A certified copy of a statement that is filed in an office in another State may be filed in the office of [the Secretary of State]. Either filing has the effect provided in this [Act] with respect to partnership property located in or transactions that occur in this State.

(b) A certified copy of a statement that has been filed in the office of the [Secretary of State] and recorded in the office for recording transfers of real property has the effect provided for recorded statements in this [Act]. A recorded statement that is not a certified copy of a statement filed in the office of the [Secretary of State] does not have the effect provided for recorded statements in this [Act].

(c) A statement filed by a partnership must be executed by at least two partners. Other statements must be executed by a partner or other person authorized by this [Act]. An individual who executes a statement as, or on behalf of, a partner or other person named as a partner in a statement shall personally declare under penalty of perjury that the contents of the statement are accurate.

(d) A person authorized by this [Act] to file a statement may amend or cancel the statement by filing an amendment or cancellation that names the partnership, identifies the statement, and states the substance of the amendment or cancellation.

(e) A person who files a statement pursuant to this section shall promptly send a copy of the statement to every nonfiling partner and to any other person named as a partner in the statement. Failure to send a copy of a statement to a partner or other person does not limit the effectiveness of the statement as to a person not a partner.

(f) The [Secretary of State] may collect a fee for filing or providing a certified copy of a statement. The [officer responsible for] recording transfers of real property may collect a fee for recording a statement.

Comment:

1. Section 105 is new. It mandates the procedural rules for the execution, filing, and recording of the various "statements" (see Section 101(11)) authorized by RUPA....

No filings are mandatory under RUPA. In all cases, the filing of a statement is optional and voluntary. A system of mandatory filing and disclosure for partnerships, similar to that required for corporations and limited partnerships, was rejected for several reasons. First, RUPA is designed to accommodate the needs of small partnerships, which often have unwritten or sketchy agreements and limited resources. Furthermore, inadvertent partnerships are also governed by the Act, as the default form of business organization, in which case filing would be unlikely.

The RUPA filing provisions are, however, likely to encourage the voluntary use of partnership statements. There are a number of strong incentives for the partnership or the partners to file statements or for third parties, such as lenders or transferees of partnership property, to compel them to do so.

Only statements that are executed, filed, and, if appropriate (such as the authority to transfer real property), recorded in conformity with Section 105 have the legal consequences accorded statements by RUPA. The requirements of Section 105 cannot be varied in the partnership agreement, except the duty to provide copies of statements to all the partners. See Section 103(b)(1)....

SECTION 106. GOVERNING LAW.

(a) Except as otherwise provided in subsection (b), the law of the jurisdiction in which a partnership has its chief executive office governs relations among the partners and between the partners and the partnership.

(b) The law of this State governs relations among the partners and between the partners and the partnership and the liability of partners for an obligation of a limited liability partnership.

Comment:

The subsection (a) internal relations rule is new....

RUPA looks to the jurisdiction in which a partnership's chief executive office is located to provide the law governing the internal relations among the partners and between the partners and the partnership. The concept of the partnership's "chief executive office" is drawn from UCC Section 9–103(3)(d). It was chosen in lieu of the State of organization because no filing is necessary to form a general partnership, and thus the situs of its organization is not always clear, unlike a limited partnership, which is organized in the State where its certificate is filed.

The term "chief executive office" is not defined in the Act, nor is it defined in the UCC. Paragraph 5 of the Official Comment to UCC Section 9–103(3)(d) explains:

> "Chief executive office" ... means the place from which in fact the debtor manages the main part of his business operations.... Doubt may arise as to which is the "chief executive office" of a multi-state enterprise, but it would be rare that there could be more than two possibilities.... [The rule] will be simple to apply in most cases....

In the absence of any other clear rule for determining a partnership's legal situs, it seems convenient to use that rule for choice of law purposes as well.

The choice-of-law rule provided by Section 106 is only a default rule, and the partners may by agreement select the law of another State to govern their internal affairs, subject to generally applicable conflict of laws requirements. For example, where the partners may not resolve a particular issue by an explicit provision of the partnership agreement, such as the rights and duties set forth in Section 103(b), the law chosen will not be applied if the partners or the partnership have no substantial relationship to the chosen State or other reasonable basis for their choice or if application of the law of the chosen State would be contrary to a fundamental policy of a State that has a materially greater interest than the chosen State. See Restatement (Second) of Conflict of Laws § 187(2) (1971). The partners must ... select only one State to govern their internal relations. They cannot select one State for some aspects of their internal relations and another State for others.

Contrasted with the variable choice-of-law rule provided by subsection (a), the law of the State where a limited liability partnership files its statement of qualification applies to such a partnership and may not be varied by the agreement of the partners. See Section 103(b)(9). Also, a partnership that files a statement of qualification in another state is not defined as a limited liability partnership in this state. See Section 101(5). Unlike a general partnership which may be formed without any filing, a partnership may only become a limited liability partnership by filing a statement of qualification. Therefore, the situs of its organization is clear. Because it is often unclear where a general partnership is actually formed, the decision to file a statement of qualification in a particular state constitutes a choice-of-law for the partnership which cannot be altered by the partnership agreement. See Comments to Section 103(b)(9). If the partnership agreement of an existing partnership specifies the law of a particular state as its governing law, and the partnership thereafter files a statement of qualification in another state, the partnership agreement choice is no longer controlling. In such cases, the filing of a statement of qualification "amends" the partnership agreement on this limited matter. Accordingly, if a statement of qualification is revoked or canceled for a limited liability partnership, the law of the state of filing would continue to apply unless the partnership agreement thereafter altered the applicable law rule.

SECTION 107. PARTNERSHIP SUBJECT TO AMENDMENT OR REPEAL OF [ACT].

A partnership governed by this [Act] is subject to any amendment to or repeal of this [Act].

Comment:

The reservation of power provision is new. It is adapted from Section 1.02 of the Revised Model Business Corporation Act (RMBCA) and Section 1106 of RULPA.

As explained in the Official Comment to the RMBCA, the genesis of those provisions is Trustees of Dartmouth College v. Woodward, 17 U.S. (4 Wheat) 518 (1819), which held that the United States Constitution prohibits the application of newly enacted statutes to existing corporations, while suggesting the efficacy of a reservation of power provision. Its purpose is to avoid any possible argument that a legal entity created pursuant to statute or its members have a contractual or vested right in any specific statutory provision and to ensure that the State may in the future modify its enabling statute as it deems appropriate and require existing entities to comply with the statutes as modified.

ARTICLE 2

NATURE OF PARTNERSHIP

SECTION 201. PARTNERSHIP AS ENTITY.

(a) A partnership is an entity distinct from its partners.

(b) A limited liability partnership continues to be the same entity that existed before the filing of a statement of qualification under Section 1001.

Comment:

RUPA embraces the entity theory of the partnership. In light of the UPA's ambivalence on the nature of partnerships, the explicit statement provided by subsection (a) is deemed appropriate as an expression of the increased emphasis on the entity theory as the dominant model. *But see* Section 306 (partners' liability joint and several unless the partnership has filed a statement of qualification to become a limited liability partnership).

Giving clear expression to the entity nature of a partnership is intended to allay previous concerns stemming from the aggregate theory, such as the necessity of a deed to convey title from the "old" partnership to the "new" partnership every time there is a change of cast among the partners. Under RUPA, there is no "new" partnership just because of membership changes. That will avoid the result in cases such as Fairway Development Co. v. Title Insurance Co., 621 F.Supp. 120 (N.D.Ohio 1985), which held that the "new" partnership resulting from a partner's death did not have standing to enforce a title insurance policy issued to the "old" partnership.

Subsection (b) makes clear that the explicit entity theory provided by subsection (a) applies to a partnership both before and after it files a statement of qualification to become a limited liability partnership. Thus, just as there is no "new" partnership resulting from membership changes, the filing of a statement of qualification does not create a "new" partnership. The filing partnership continues to be the same partnership entity that existed before the filing. Similarly, the amendment or cancellation of a statement of qualification under Section 105(d) or the revocation of a statement of qualification under Section 1003(c) does not terminate the partnership and create a "new" partnership. See Section 1003(d). Accordingly, a partnership remains the same entity regardless of a filing, cancellation, or revocation of a statement of qualification.

SECTION 202. FORMATION OF PARTNERSHIP.

(a) Except as otherwise provided in subsection (b), the association of two or more persons to carry on as co-owners a business for profit forms a partnership, whether or not the persons intend to form a partnership.

much like §7 of Uniformed Partnership Act

(b) An association formed under a statute other than this [Act], a predecessor statute, or a comparable statute of another jurisdiction is not a partnership under this [Act].

(c) In determining whether a partnership is formed, the following rules apply:

(1) Joint tenancy, tenancy in common, tenancy by the entireties, joint property, common property, or part ownership does not by itself establish a partnership, even if the co-owners share profits made by the use of the property.

(2) The sharing of gross returns does not by itself establish a partnership, even if the persons sharing them have a joint or common right or interest in property from which the returns are derived.

(3) A person who receives a share of the profits of a business is presumed to be a partner in the business, unless the profits were received in payment:

(i) of a debt by installments or otherwise;

(ii) for services as an independent contractor or of wages or other compensation to an employee;

(iii) of rent;

(iv) of an annuity or other retirement or health benefit to a beneficiary, representative, or designee of a deceased or retired partner;

(v) of interest or other charge on a loan, even if the amount of payment varies with the profits of the business, including a direct or indirect present or future ownership of the collateral, or rights to income, proceeds, or increase in value derived from the collateral; or

(vi) for the sale of the goodwill of a business or other property by installments or otherwise.

Comment:

1. Section 202 combines UPA Sections 6 and 7. The traditional UPA Section 6(1) "definition" of a partnership is recast as an operative rule of law. No substantive change in the law is intended. The UPA "definition" has always been understood as an operative rule, as well as a definition. The addition of the phrase, "whether or not the persons intend to form a partnership," merely codifies the universal judicial construction of UPA Section 6(1) that a partnership is created by the association of persons whose intent is to carry on as co-owners a business for profit, regardless of their subjective intention to be "partners." Indeed, they may inadvertently create a

149

partnership despite their expressed subjective intention not to do so. The new language alerts readers to this possibility.

As under the UPA, the attribute of co-ownership distinguishes a partnership from a mere agency relationship. A business is a series of acts directed toward an end. Ownership involves the power of ultimate control. To state that partners are co-owners of a business is to state that they each have the power of ultimate control. See Official Comment to UPA § 6(1). On the other hand, as subsection (c)(1) makes clear, passive co-ownership of property by itself, as distinguished from the carrying on of a business, does not establish a partnership.

2. Subsection (b) provides that business associations organized under other statutes are not partnerships. Those statutory associations include corporations, limited partnerships, and limited liability companies. That continues the UPA concept that general partnership is the residual form of for profit business association, existing only if another form does not.

A limited partnership is not a partnership under this definition. Nevertheless, certain provisions of RUPA will continue to govern limited partnerships because RULPA itself, in Section 1105, so requires "in any case not provided for" in RULPA. For example, the rules applicable to a limited liability partnership will generally apply to limited partnerships. See Comment to Section 101(5) (definition of a limited liability partnership). In light of ... RULPA Section 1105, UPA Section 6(2), which provides that limited partnerships are governed by the UPA, is redundant and has not been carried over to RUPA. It is also more appropriate that the applicability of RUPA to limited partnerships be governed exclusively by RULPA. For example, a RULPA amendment may clarify certain linkage questions regarding the application of the limited liability partnership rules to limited partnerships. See Comment to Section 101(5) for a suggested form of such an amendment. . . .

Relationships that are called "joint ventures" are partnerships if they otherwise fit the definition of a partnership. An association is not classified as a partnership, however, simply because it is called a "joint venture."

An unincorporated nonprofit organization is not a partnership under RUPA, even if it qualifies as a business, because it is not a "for profit" organization.

3. Subsection (c) provides three rules of construction that apply in determining whether a partnership has been formed under subsection (a). They are largely derived from UPA Section 7, and to that extent no substantive change is intended. The sharing of profits is recast as a rebuttable presumption of a partnership, a more contemporary construction, rather than as prima facie evi-

dence thereof. The protected categories, in which receipt of a share of the profits is not presumed to create a partnership, apply whether the profit share is a single flat percentage or a ratio which varies, for example, after reaching a dollar floor or different levels of profits.

Like its predecessor, RUPA makes no attempt to answer in every case whether a partnership is formed. Whether a relationship is more properly characterized as that of borrower and lender, employer and employee, or landlord and tenant is left to the trier of fact. As under the UPA, a person may function in both partner and nonpartner capacities....

SECTION 203. PARTNERSHIP PROPERTY.

Property acquired by a partnership is property of the partnership and not of the partners individually.

Comment:

All property acquired by a partnership, by transfer or otherwise, becomes partnership property and belongs to the partnership as an entity, rather than to the individual partners. This expresses the substantive result of UPA Sections 8(1) and 25.

Neither UPA Section 8(1) nor RUPA Section 203 provides any guidance concerning when property is "acquired by" the partnership. That problem is dealt with in Section 204....

SECTION 204. WHEN PROPERTY IS PARTNERSHIP PROPERTY.

(a) Property is partnership property if acquired in the name of:

(1) the partnership; or

(2) one or more partners with an indication in the instrument transferring title to the property of the person's capacity as a partner or of the existence of a partnership but without an indication of the name of the partnership.

(b) Property is acquired in the name of the partnership by a transfer to:

(1) the partnership in its name; or

(2) one or more partners in their capacity as partners in the partnership, if the name of the partnership is indicated in the instrument transferring title to the property.

(c) Property is presumed to be partnership property if purchased with partnership assets, even if not acquired in the name of the partnership or of one or more partners with an indication in the instrument transferring title to the property of the person's capacity as a partner or of the existence of a partnership.

(d) Property acquired in the name of one or more of the partners, without an indication in the instrument transferring title to the property of the person's capacity as a partner or of the existence of a partnership and without use of partnership assets, is presumed to be separate property, even if used for partnership purposes.

Comment: ...

3.   Ultimately, it is the intention of the partners that controls whether property belongs to the partnership or to one or more of the partners in their individual capacities, at least as among the partners themselves.   RUPA sets forth two rebuttable presumptions that apply when the partners have failed to express their intent.

First, under subsection (c), property purchased with partnership funds is presumed to be partnership property, notwithstanding the name in which title is held.   The presumption is intended to apply if partnership credit is used to obtain financing, as well as the use of partnership cash or property for payment.   Unlike the rule in subsection (b), under which property is *deemed* to be partnership property if the partnership's name or the partner's capacity as a partner is disclosed in the instrument of conveyance, subsection (c) raises only a *presumption* that the property is partnership property if it is purchased with partnership assets.

That presumption is also subject to an important caveat.   Under Section 302(b), partnership property held in the name of individual partners, without an indication of their capacity as partners or of the existence of a partnership, that is transferred by the partners in whose name title is held to a purchaser without knowledge that it is partnership property is free of any claims of the partnership.

Second, under subsection (d), property acquired in the name of one or more of the partners, without an indication of their capacity as partners and without use of partnership funds or credit, is presumed to be the partners' separate property, even if used for partnership purposes.   In effect, it is presumed in that case that only the use of the property is contributed to the partnership....

ARTICLE 3

RELATIONS OF PARTNERS TO PERSONS DEALING WITH PARTNERSHIP

SECTION 301.   PARTNER AGENT OF PARTNERSHIP.

Subject to the effect of a statement of partnership authority under Section 303:

(1) Each partner is an agent of the partnership for the purpose of its business. An act of a partner, including the execution of an instrument in the partnership name, for apparently carrying on in the ordinary course the partnership business or business of the kind carried on by the partnership binds the partnership, unless the partner had no authority to act for the partnership in the particular matter and the person with whom the partner was dealing knew or had received a notification that the partner lacked authority.

(2) An act of a partner which is not apparently for carrying on in the ordinary course the partnership business or business of the kind carried on by the partnership binds the partnership only if the act was authorized by the other partners.

Comment: ...

2. Section 301(1) retains the basic principles reflected in UPA Section 9(1). It declares that each partner is an agent of the partnership and that, by virtue of partnership status, each partner has apparent authority to bind the partnership in ordinary course transactions. The effect of Section 301(1) is to characterize a partner as a general managerial agent having both actual and apparent authority co-extensive in scope with the firm's ordinary business, at least in the absence of a contrary partnership agreement.

Section 301(1) effects two changes from UPA Section 9(1). First, it clarifies that a partner's apparent authority includes acts for carrying on in the ordinary course "business of the kind carried on by the partnership," not just the business of the particular partnership in question. The UPA is ambiguous on this point, but there is some authority for an expanded construction in accordance with the so-called English rule. See, e.g., Burns v. Gonzalez, 439 S.W.2d 128, 131 (Tex.Civ.App.1969) (dictum); Commercial Hotel Co. v. Weeks, 254 S.W. 521 (Tex.Civ.App.1923). No substantive change is intended by use of the more customary phrase "carrying on in the ordinary course" in lieu of the UPA phrase "in the usual way." The UPA and the case law use both terms without apparent distinction.

The other change from the UPA concerns the allocation of risk of a partner's lack of authority. RUPA draws the line somewhat differently from the UPA.

Under UPA Section 9(1) and (4), only a person with knowledge of a restriction on a partner's authority is bound by it. Section 301(1) provides that a person who has received a notification of a partner's lack of authority is also bound. The meaning of "receives a notification" is explained in Section 102(d). Thus, the partnership may protect itself from unauthorized acts by giving a notification of a restriction on a partner's authority to a person dealing with that partner. A notification may be effective upon delivery, whether or not it actually comes to the other person's attention. To that extent, the risk of lack of authority is shifted to those dealing with partners.

On the other hand, as used in the UPA, the term "knowledge" embodies the concept of "bad faith" knowledge arising from other known facts. As used in RUPA, however, "knowledge" is limited to actual knowledge. See Section 102(a). Thus, RUPA does not expose persons dealing with a partner to the greater risk of being bound by a restriction based on their purported reason to know of the partner's lack of authority from all the facts they did know. Compare Section 102(b)(3) (notice).

With one exception, this result is not affected even if the partnership files a statement of partnership authority containing a limitation on a partner's authority. Section 303(f) makes clear that a person dealing with a partner is not deemed to know of such a limitation merely because it is contained in a filed statement of authority. Under Section 303(e), however, all persons are deemed to know of a limitation on the authority of a partner to transfer real property contained in a recorded statement. Thus, a recorded limitation on authority concerning real property constitutes constructive knowledge of the limitation to the whole world.

3. Section 301(2) is drawn directly from UPA Section 9(2), with conforming changes to mirror the new language of subsection (1). Subsection (2) makes it clear that the partnership is bound by a partner's actual authority, even if the partner has no apparent authority. Section 401(j) requires the unanimous consent of the partners for a grant of authority outside the ordinary course of business, unless the partnership agreement provides otherwise. Under general agency principles, the partners can subsequently ratify a partner's unauthorized act. See Section 104(a).

4. UPA Section 9(3) contains a list of five extraordinary acts that require unanimous consent of the partners before the partnership is bound. RUPA omits that section. That leaves it to the courts to decide the outer limits of the agency power of a partner.

Most of the acts listed in UPA Section 9(3) probably remain outside the apparent authority of a partner under RUPA, such as disposing of the goodwill of the business, but elimination of a statutory rule will afford more flexibility in some situations specified in UPA Section 9(3). In particular, it seems archaic that the submission of a partnership claim to arbitration always requires unanimous consent. See UPA § 9(3)(e). . . . .

SECTION 302. TRANSFER OF PARTNERSHIP PROPERTY.

(a) Partnership property may be transferred as follows:

(1) Subject to the effect of a statement of partnership authority under Section 303, partnership property held in the name of the partnership may be transferred by an instrument of transfer executed by a partner in the partnership name.

(2) Partnership property held in the name of one or more partners with an indication in the instrument transferring the property to them of their capacity as partners or of the existence of a partnership, but without an indication of the name of the partnership, may be transferred by an instrument of transfer executed by the persons in whose name the property is held.

(3) Partnership property held in the name of one or more persons other than the partnership, without an indication in the instrument transferring the property to them of their capacity as partners or of the existence of a partnership, may be transferred by an instrument of transfer executed by the persons in whose name the property is held.

(b) A partnership may recover partnership property from a transferee only if it proves that execution of the instrument of initial transfer did not bind the partnership under Section 301 and:

(1) as to a subsequent transferee who gave value for property transferred under subsection (a)(1) and (2), proves that the subsequent transferee knew or had received a notification that the person who executed the instrument of initial transfer lacked authority to bind the partnership; or

(2) as to a transferee who gave value for property transferred under subsection (a)(3), proves that the transferee knew or had received a notification that the property was partnership property and that the person who executed the instrument of initial transfer lacked authority to bind the partnership.

(c) A partnership may not recover partnership property from a subsequent transferee if the partnership would not have been entitled to recover the property, under subsection (b), from any earlier transferee of the property.

(d) If a person holds all of the partners' interests in the partnership, all of the partnership property vests in that person. The person may execute a document in the name of the partnership to evidence vesting of the property in that person and may file or record the document.

SECTION 303.   STATEMENT OF PARTNERSHIP AUTHORITY.

(a) A partnership may file a statement of partnership authority, which:

(1) must include:

(i) the name of the partnership;

(ii) the street address of its chief executive office and of one office in this State, if there is one;

(iii) the names and mailing addresses of all of the partners or of an agent appointed and maintained by the partnership for the purpose of subsection (b); and

(iv) the names of the partners authorized to execute an instrument transferring real property held in the name of the partnership; and

(2) may state the authority, or limitations on the authority, of some or all of the partners to enter into other transactions on behalf of the partnership and any other matter.

(b) If a statement of partnership authority names an agent, the agent shall maintain a list of the names and mailing addresses of all of the partners and make it available to any person on request for good cause shown.

(c) If a filed statement of partnership authority is executed pursuant to Section 105(c) and states the name of the partnership but does not contain all of the other information required by subsection (a), the statement nevertheless operates with respect to a person not a partner as provided in subsections (d) and (e).

(d) Except as otherwise provided in subsection (g), a filed statement of partnership authority supplements the authority of a partner to enter into transactions on behalf of the partnership as follows:

(1) Except for transfers of real property, a grant of authority contained in a filed statement of partnership authority is conclusive in favor of a person who gives value without knowledge to the contrary, so long as and to the extent that a limitation on that authority is not then contained in another filed statement. A filed cancellation of a limitation on authority revives the previous grant of authority.

(2) A grant of authority to transfer real property held in the name of the partnership contained in a certified copy of a filed statement of partnership authority recorded in the office for record-

ing transfers of that real property is conclusive in favor of a person who gives value without knowledge to the contrary, so long as and to the extent that a certified copy of a filed statement containing a limitation on that authority is not then of record in the office for recording transfers of that real property. The recording in the office for recording transfers of that real property of a certified copy of a filed cancellation of a limitation on authority revives the previous grant of authority.

(e) A person not a partner is deemed to know of a limitation on the authority of a partner to transfer real property held in the name of the partnership if a certified copy of the filed statement containing the limitation on authority is of record in the office for recording transfers of that real property.

(f) Except as otherwise provided in subsections (d) and (e) and Sections 704 and 805, a person not a partner is not deemed to know of a limitation on the authority of a partner merely because the limitation is contained in a filed statement.

(g) Unless earlier canceled, a filed statement of partnership authority is canceled by operation of law five years after the date on which the statement, or the most recent amendment, was filed with the [Secretary of State].

Comment:

1. Section 303 is new. It provides for an optional statement of partnership authority specifying the names of the partners authorized to execute instruments transferring real property held in the name of the partnership. It may also grant supplementary authority to partners, or limit their authority, to enter into other transactions on behalf of the partnership. The execution, filing, and recording of statements is governed by Section 105....

2. The most important goal of the statement of authority is to facilitate the transfer of real property held in the name of the partnership. A statement must specify the names of the partners authorized to execute an instrument transferring that property.

Under subsection (d)(2), a recorded grant of authority to transfer real property held in the name of the partnership is conclusive in favor of a transferee for value without actual knowledge to the contrary....

Under subsection (e), third parties are deemed to know of a recorded limitation on the authority of a partner to transfer real property held in the partnership name. Since transferees are bound under Section 301 by knowledge of a limitation on a partner's authority, they are bound by such a recorded limitation. Of course, a transferee with actual knowledge of a limitation on a partner's authority is bound under Section 301, whether or not there is a recorded statement of limitation.

3. A statement of partnership authority may have effect beyond the transfer of real property held in the name of the partnership. Under subsection (a)(2), a statement of authority may contain any other matter the partnership chooses, including a grant of authority, or a limitation on the authority, of some or all of the partners to enter into other transactions on behalf of the partnership. Since Section 301 confers authority on all partners to act for the partnership in ordinary matters, the real import of such a provision is to grant extraordinary authority, or to limit the ordinary authority, of some or all of the partners.

The effect given to such a provision is different from that accorded a provision regarding the transfer of real property. Under subsection (d)(1), a filed grant of authority is binding on the partnership, in favor of a person who gives value without actual knowledge to the contrary, unless limited by another filed statement. That is the same rule as for statements involving real property under subsection 301(d)(2). There is, however, no counterpart to subsection (e) regarding a filed limitation of authority. To the contrary, subsection (f) makes clear that filing a limitation of authority does not operate as constructive knowledge of a partner's lack of authority with respect to non-real property transactions.

Under Section 301, only a third party who knows or has received a notification of a partner's lack of authority in an ordinary course transaction is bound. Thus, a limitation on a partner's authority to transfer personal property or to enter into other non-real property transactions on behalf of the partnership, contained in a filed statement of partnership authority, is effective only against a third party who knows or has received a notification of it. The fact of the statement being filed has no legal significance in those transactions, although the filed statement is a potential source of actual knowledge to third parties.

4. It should be emphasized that Section 303 concerns the authority of partners to bind the partnership to third persons. As among the partners, the authority of a partner to take any action is governed by the partnership agreement, or by the provisions of RUPA governing the relations among partners, and is not affected by the filing or recording of a statement of partnership authority. . . .

SECTION 304. STATEMENT OF DENIAL.

A partner or other person named as a partner in a filed statement of partnership authority or in a list maintained by an agent pursuant to Section 303(b) may file a statement of denial stating the name of the partnership and the fact that it is being denied, which may include denial of a person's authority or status as a partner. A statement of denial is a limitation on authority as provided in Section 303(d) and (e).

SECTION 305. PARTNERSHIP LIABLE FOR PARTNER'S ACTIONABLE CONDUCT.

(a) A partnership is liable for loss or injury caused to a person, or for a penalty incurred, as a result of a wrongful act or omission, or other actionable conduct, of a partner acting in the ordinary course of business of the partnership or with authority of the partnership.

(b) If, in the course of the partnership's business or while acting with authority of the partnership, a partner receives or causes the partnership to receive money or property of a person not a partner, and the money or property is misapplied by a partner, the partnership is liable for the loss.

Comment:

Section 305(a), which is derived from UPA Section 13, imposes liability on the partnership for the wrongful acts of a partner acting in the ordinary course of the partnership's business or otherwise within the partner's authority. The scope of the section has been expanded by deleting from UPA Section 13, "not being a partner in the partnership." This is intended to permit a partner to sue the partnership on a tort or other theory during the term of the partnership, rather than being limited to the remedies of dissolution and an accounting. See also Comment 2 to Section 405.

The section has also been broadened to cover no-fault torts by the addition of the phrase, "or other actionable conduct."

The partnership is liable for the actionable conduct or omission of a partner acting in the ordinary course of its business or "with the authority of the partnership." This is intended to include a partner's apparent, as well as actual, authority....

Section 305(b).... imposes strict liability on the partnership for the misapplication of money or property received by a partner in the course of the partnership's business or otherwise within the scope of the partner's actual authority.

SECTION 306. PARTNER'S LIABILITY.

(a) Except as otherwise provided in subsection (b), all partners are liable jointly and severally for all obligations of the partnership unless otherwise agreed by the claimant or provided by law.

(b) A person admitted as a partner into an existing partnership is not personally liable for any partnership obligation incurred before the person's admission as a partner.

(c) An obligation of a partnership incurred while the partnership is a limited liability partnership, whether arising in contract, tort, or otherwise, is solely the obligation of the partnership. A partner is not personally liable, directly or indirectly, by way of contribution or otherwise, for such a partnership obligation solely by reason of being or so acting as a partner. This subsection applies notwithstanding anything inconsistent in the partnership agreement that existed immediately before the vote required to become a limited liability partnership under Section 1001(b).

Comment:

1. Section 306(a) changes the UPA rule by imposing joint and several liability on the partners for all partnership obligations where the partnership is not a limited liability partnership. Under UPA Section 15, partners' liability for torts is joint and several, while their liability for contracts is joint but not several. About ten States that have adopted the UPA already provide for joint and several liability. The UPA reference to "debts and obligations" is redundant, and no change is intended by RUPA's reference solely to "obligations."

Joint and several liability under RUPA differs, however, from the classic model, which permits a judgment creditor to proceed immediately against any of the joint and several judgment debtors. Generally, Section 307(d) requires the judgment creditor to exhaust the partnership's assets before enforcing a judgment against the separate assets of a partner. . . .

3. Subsection (c) alters classic joint and several liability of general partners for obligations of a partnership that is a limited liability partnership. Like shareholders of a corporation and members of a limited liability company, partners of a limited liability partnership are not personally liable for partnership obligations incurred while the partnership liability shield is in place solely because they are partners. As with shareholders of a corporation and members of a limited liability company, partners remain personally liable for their personal misconduct.

In cases of partner misconduct, Section 401(c) sets forth a partnership's obligation to indemnify the culpable partner where the partner's liability was incurred in the ordinary course of the partnership's business. When indemnification occurs, the assets of both the partnership and the culpable partner are available to a creditor. However, Sections 306(c), 401(b), and 807(b) make clear that a partner who is not otherwise liable under Section 306(c) is not obligated to contribute assets to the partnership in excess of agreed contributions to share the loss with the culpable partner. (See Comments to Sections 401(b) and 807(b) regarding a slight variation in the context of priority of payment of partnership obligations.)

Accordingly, Section 306(c) makes clear that an innocent partner is not personally liable for specified partnership obligations, directly or indirectly, by way of contribution or otherwise.

Although the liability shield protections of Section 306(c) may be modified in part or in full in a partnership agreement (and by way of private contractual guarantees), the modifications must constitute an intentional waiver of the liability protections. See Sections 103(b), 104(a), and 902(b). Since the mere act of filing a statement of qualification reflects the assumption that the partners intend to modify the otherwise applicable partner liability rules, the final sentence of subsection (c) makes clear that the filing negates inconsistent aspects of the partnership agreement that existed immediately before the vote to approve becoming a limited liability partnership. The negation only applies to a partner's personal liability for future partnership obligations. The filing however has no effect as to previously created partner obligations to the partnership in the form of specific capital contribution requirements.

Inter se contribution agreements may erode part or all of the effects of the liability shield. For example, Section 807(f) provides that an assignee for the benefit of creditors of a partnership or a partner may enforce a partner's obligation to contribute to the partnership. The ultimate effect of such contribution obligations may make each partner jointly and severally liable for all partnership obligations—even those incurred while the partnership is a limited liability partnership. Although the final sentence of subsection (c) negates such provisions existing before a statement of qualification is filed, it will have no effect on any amendments to the partnership agreement after the statement is filed. . . .

SECTION 307. ACTIONS BY AND AGAINST PARTNERSHIP AND PARTNERS.

(a) A partnership may sue and be sued in the name of the partnership.

(b) An action may be brought against the partnership and, to the extent not inconsistent with section 306, any or all of the partners in the same action or in separate actions.

(c) A judgment against a partnership is not by itself a judgment against a partner. A judgment against a partnership may not be satisfied from a partner's assets unless there is also a judgment against the partner.

(d) A judgment creditor of a partner may not levy execution against the assets of the partner to satisfy a judgment based on a claim against the partnership unless the partner is personally liable for the claim under Section 306 and:

(1) a judgment based on the same claim has been obtained against the partnership and a writ of execution on the judgment has been returned unsatisfied in whole or in part;

(2) the partnership is a debtor in bankruptcy;

(3) the partner has agreed that the creditor need not exhaust partnership assets;

(4) a court grants permission to the judgment creditor to levy execution against the assets of a partner based on a finding that partnership assets subject to execution are clearly insufficient to satisfy the judgment, that exhaustion of partnership assets is excessively burdensome, or that the grant of permission is an appropriate exercise of the court's equitable powers; or

(5) liability is imposed on the partner by law or contract independent of the existence of the partnership.

(e) This section applies to any partnership liability or obligation resulting from a representation by a partner or purported partner under Section 308.

Comment:

1. Section 307 is new. Subsection (a) provides that a partnership may sue and be sued in the partnership name. That entity approach is designed to simplify suits by and against a partnership.

At common law, a partnership, not being a legal entity, could not sue or be sued in the firm name. The UPA itself is silent on this point, so in the absence of another enabling statute, it is generally necessary to join all the partners in an action against the partnership.

Most States have statutes or rules authorizing partnerships to sue or be sued in the partnership name. Many of those statutes, however, are found in the state provisions dealing with civil procedure rather than in the partnership act. . . .

3. Subsection (c) provides that a judgment against the partnership is not, standing alone, a judgment against the partners, and it cannot be satisfied from a partner's personal assets unless there is a judgment against the partner. Thus, a partner must be individually named and served, either in the action against the partnership or in a later suit, before his personal assets may be subject to levy for a claim against the partnership.

RUPA leaves it to the law of judgments, as did the UPA, to determine the collateral effects to be accorded a prior judgment for or against the partnership in a subsequent action against a partner individually. . . .

SECTION 308.   LIABILITY OF PURPORTED PARTNER.

(a) If a person, by words or conduct, purports to be a partner, or consents to being represented by another as a partner, in a partnership or with one or more persons not partners, the purported partner is liable to a person to whom the representation is made, if that person, relying on the representation, enters into a transaction with the actual or purported partnership. If the representation, either by the purported partner or by a person with the purported partner's consent, is made in a public manner, the purported partner is liable to a person who relies upon the purported partnership even if the purported partner is not aware of being held out as a partner to the claimant. If partnership liability results, the purported partner is liable with respect to that liability as if the purported partner were a partner. If no partnership liability results, the purported partner is liable with respect to that liability jointly and severally with any other person consenting to the representation.

(b) If a person is thus represented to be a partner in an existing partnership, or with one or more persons not partners, the purported partner is an agent of persons consenting to the representation to bind them to the same extent and in the same manner as if the purported partner were a partner, with respect to persons who enter into transactions in reliance upon the representation. If all of the partners of the existing partnership consent to the representation, a partnership act or obligation results. If fewer than all of the partners of the existing partnership consent to the representation, the person acting and the partners consenting to the representation are jointly and severally liable.

(c) A person is not liable as a partner merely because the person is named by another in a statement of partnership authority.

(d) A person does not continue to be liable as a partner merely because of a failure to file a statement of dissociation or to amend a statement of partnership authority to indicate the partner's dissociation from the partnership.

(e) Except as otherwise provided in subsections (a) and (b), persons who are not partners as to each other are not liable as partners to other persons.

ARTICLE 4

RELATIONS OF PARTNERS TO EACH OTHER AND TO PARTNERSHIP

SECTION 401.   PARTNER'S RIGHTS AND DUTIES.

(a) Each partner is deemed to have an account that is:

(1) credited with an amount equal to the money plus the value of any other property, net of the amount of any liabilities, the partner contributes to the partnership and the partner's share of the partnership profits; and

(2) charged with an amount equal to the money plus the value of any other property, net of the amount of any liabilities, distributed by the partnership to the partner and the partner's share of the partnership losses.

(b) Each partner is entitled to an equal share of the partnership profits and is chargeable with a share of the partnership losses in proportion to the partner's share of the profits.

(c) A partnership shall reimburse a partner for payments made and indemnify a partner for liabilities incurred by the partner in the ordinary course of the business of the partnership or for the preservation of its business or property.

(d) A partnership shall reimburse a partner for an advance to the partnership beyond the amount of capital the partner agreed to contribute.

(e) A payment or advance made by a partner which gives rise to a partnership obligation under subsection (c) or (d) constitutes a loan to the partnership which accrues interest from the date of the payment or advance.

(f) Each partner has equal rights in the management and conduct of the partnership business.

(g) A partner may use or possess partnership property only on behalf of the partnership.

(h) A partner is not entitled to remuneration for services performed for the partnership, except for reasonable compensation for services rendered in winding up the business of the partnership.

(i) A person may become a partner only with the consent of all of the partners.

(j) A difference arising as to a matter in the ordinary course of business of a partnership may be decided by a majority of the partners. An act outside the ordinary course of business of a partnership and an amendment to the partnership agreement may be undertaken only with the consent of all of the partners.

(k) This section does not affect the obligations of a partnership to other persons under Section 301.

Comment: ...

3. Subsection (b) establishes the default rules for the sharing of partnership profits and losses. The UPA Section 18(a) rules that profits are shared equally and that losses, whether capital or operating, are shared in proportion to each partner's share of the profits are continued. Thus, under the default rule, partners share profits per capita and not in proportion to capital contribution as do corporate shareholders or partners in limited partnerships. Compare RULPA Section 504. With respect to losses, the qualifying phrase, "whether capital or operating," has been deleted as inconsistent with contemporary partnership accounting practice and terminology; no substantive change is intended.

If partners agree to share profits other than equally, losses will be shared similarly to profits, absent agreement to do otherwise. That rule, carried over from the UPA, is predicated on the assumption that partners would likely agree to share losses on the same basis as profits, but may fail to say so. Of course, by agreement, they may share losses on a different basis from profits.

The default rules apply, as does UPA Section 18(a), where one or more of the partners contribute no capital, although there is case law to the contrary. See, e.g., Kovacik v. Reed, 49 Cal.2d 166, 315 P.2d 314 (1957); Becker v. Killarney, 177 Ill.App.3d 793, 523 N.E.2d 467 (1988). It may seem unfair that the contributor of services, who contributes little or no capital, should be obligated to contribute toward the capital loss of the large contributor who contributed no services. In entering a partnership with such a capital structure, the partners should foresee that application of the default rule may bring about unusual results and take advantage of their power to vary by agreement the allocation of capital losses.

Subsection (b) provides that each partner "is chargeable" with a share of the losses, rather than the UPA formulation that each partner shall "contribute" to losses. Losses are charged to each partner's account as provided in subsection (a)(2). It is intended to make clear that a partner is not obligated to contribute to partnership losses before his withdrawal or the liquidation of the partnership, unless the partners agree otherwise. In effect, unless related to an obligation for which the partner is not personally liable under Section 306(c), a partner's negative account represents a debt to the partnership unless the partners agree to the contrary. Similarly, each partner's share of the profits is credited to his account under subsection (a)(1). Absent an agreement to the contrary, however, a partner does not have a right to receive a current distribution of the profits credited to his account, the interim distribution of profits being a matter arising in the ordinary course of business to be decided by majority vote of the partners.

However, where a liability to contribute at dissolution and winding up relates to a partnership obligation governed by the limited liability rule of Section 306(c), a partner is not obligated to contribute additional assets even at dissolution and winding up. See Section 807(b). In such a case, although a partner is not personally liable for the partnership obligation, that partner's interest in the partnership remains at risk. See also Comment to Section 401(c) relating to indemnification.

In the case of an operating limited liability partnership, the Section 306 liability shield may be partially eroded where the limited liability partnership incurs both shielded and unshielded liabilities. Where the limited liability partnership uses its assets to pay shielded liabilities before paying unshielded liabilities, each partner's obligation to contribute to the limited liability partnership for that partner's share of the unpaid and unshielded obligations at dissolution and winding up remains intact. The same issue is less likely to occur in the context of the termination of a limited liability partnership since a partner's contribution obligation is based only on that partner's share of unshielded obligations and the partnership will ordinarily use the contributed assets to pay unshielded claims first as they were the basis of the contribution obligations. See Comments to Section 807(b).

4. Subsection (c) is derived from UPA Section 18(b) and provides that the partnership shall reimburse partners for payments made and indemnify them for liabilities incurred in the ordinary course of the partnership's business or for the preservation of its business or property. Reimbursement and indemnification is an obligation of the partnership. Indemnification may create a loss toward which the partners must contribute. Although the right to indemnification is usually enforced in the settlement of accounts among partners upon dissolution and winding up of the partnership business, the right accrues when the liability is incurred and thus may be enforced during the term of the partnership in an appropriate case. See Section 405 and Comment. A partner's right to indemnification under this Act is not affected by the partnership becoming a limited liability partnership. Accordingly, partners continue to share partnership losses to the extent of partnership assets....

7. Under subsection (f), each partner has equal rights in the management and conduct of the business. It is based on UPA Section 18(e), which has been interpreted broadly to mean that, absent contrary agreement, each partner has a continuing right to participate in the management of the partnership and to be in-

formed about the partnership business even if his assent to partnership business decisions is not required. There are special rules regarding the partner vote necessary to approve a partnership becoming (or canceling its status as) a limited liability partnership. See Section 1001(b)....

11. Subsection (j) continues with one important clarification the UPA Section 18(h) scheme of allocating management authority among the partners. In the absence of an agreement to the contrary, matters arising in the ordinary course of the business may be decided by a majority of the partners. Amendments to the partnership agreement and matters outside the ordinary course of the partnership business require unanimous consent of the partners. Although the text of the UPA is silent regarding extraordinary matters, courts have generally required the consent of all partners for those matters. See, e.g., Paciaroni v. Crane, 408 A.2d 946 (Del.Ch.1989); Thomas v. Marvin E. Jewell & Co., 232 Neb. 261, 440 N.W.2d 437 (1989); Duell v. Hancock, 83 A.D.2d 762, 443 N.Y.S.2d 490 (1981)....

SECTION 402. DISTRIBUTIONS IN KIND.

A partner has no right to receive, and may not be required to accept, a distribution in kind.

Comment: ...

This section is complemented by Section 807(a) which provides that, in winding up the partnership business on dissolution, any surplus after the payment of partnership obligations must be applied to pay in cash the net amount distributable to each partner.

SECTION 403. PARTNER'S RIGHTS AND DUTIES WITH RE-SPECT TO INFORMATION.

(a) A partnership shall keep its books and records, if any, at its chief executive office.

(b) A partnership shall provide partners and their agents and attorneys access to its books and records. It shall provide former partners and their agents and attorneys access to books and records pertaining to the period during which they were partners. The right of access provides the opportunity to inspect and copy books and records during ordinary business hours. A partnership may impose a reasonable charge, covering the costs of labor and material, for copies of documents furnished.

(c) Each partner and the partnership shall furnish to a partner, and to the legal representative of a deceased partner or partner under legal disability:

(1) without demand, any information concerning the partnership's business and affairs reasonably required for the proper exer-

cise of the partner's rights and duties under the partnership agreement or this [Act]; and

(2) on demand, any other information concerning the partnership's business and affairs, except to the extent the demand or the information demanded is unreasonable or otherwise improper under the circumstances.

Comment: . . .

2. . . . A partner's right to inspect and copy the partnership's books and records is not conditioned on the partner's purpose or motive.   Compare RMBCA Section 16.02(c)(1) (shareholder must have proper purpose to inspect certain corporate records).   A partner's unlimited personal liability justifies an unqualified right of access to the partnership books and records.   An abuse of the right to inspect and copy might constitute a violation of the obligation of good faith and fair dealing for which the other partners would have a remedy.   See Sections 404(d) and 405.

Under Section 103(b)(2), a partner's right of access to partnership books and records may not be unreasonably restricted by the partnership agreement.   Thus, to preserve a partner's core information rights despite unequal bargaining power, an agreement limiting a partner's right to inspect and copy partnership books and records is subject to judicial review.   Nevertheless, reasonable restrictions on access to partnership books and records by agreement are authorized.   For example, a provision in a partnership agreement denying partners access to the compensation of other partners should be upheld, absent any abuse such as fraud or duress. . . .

3. . . . Paragraph (2) continues the UPA rule that partners are entitled, on demand, to any other information concerning the partnership's business and affairs.   The demand may be refused if either the demand or the information demanded is unreasonable or otherwise improper.   That qualification is new to the statutory formulation.   The burden is on the partnership or partner from whom the information is requested to show that the demand is unreasonable or improper. . . .

The Section 403(c) information rights can be waived or varied by agreement of the partners, since there is no Section 103(b) limitation on the variation of those rights as there is with respect to the Section 403(b) access rights to books and records.   See Section 103(b)(2).

SECTION 404.   GENERAL STANDARDS OF PARTNER'S CONDUCT.

(a) The only fiduciary duties a partner owes to the partnership and the other partners are the duty of loyalty and the duty of care set forth in subsections (b) and (c).

(b) A partner's duty of loyalty to the partnership and the other partners is limited to the following:

(1) to account to the partnership and hold as trustee for it any property, profit, or benefit derived by the partner in the conduct and winding up of the partnership business or derived from a use by the partner of partnership property, including the appropriation of a partnership opportunity;

(2) to refrain from dealing with the partnership in the conduct or winding up of the partnership business as or on behalf of a party having an interest adverse to the partnership; and

(3) to refrain from competing with the partnership in the conduct of the partnership business before the dissolution of the partnership.

(c) A partner's duty of care to the partnership and the other partners in the conduct and winding up of the partnership business is limited to refraining from engaging in grossly negligent or reckless conduct, intentional misconduct, or a knowing violation of law.

(d) A partner shall discharge the duties to the partnership and the other partners under this [Act] or under the partnership agreement and exercise any rights consistently with the obligation of good faith and fair dealing.

(e) A partner does not violate a duty or obligation under this [Act] or under the partnership agreement merely because the partner's conduct furthers the partner's own interest.

(f) A partner may lend money to and transact other business with the partnership, and as to each loan or transaction the rights and obligations of the partner are the same as those of a person who is not a partner, subject to other applicable law.

(g) This section applies to a person winding up the partnership business as the personal or legal representative of the last surviving partner as if the person were a partner.

Comment:

1. Section 404 is new. The title, "General Standards of Partner's Conduct," is drawn from RMBCA Section 8.30. Section 404 is both comprehensive and exclusive. In that regard, it is structurally different from the UPA which touches only sparingly on a partner's duty of loyalty and leaves any further development of the fiduciary duties of partners to the common law of agency. Compare UPA Sections 4(3) and 21.

Section 404 begins by stating that the **only** fiduciary duties a partner owes to the partnership and the other partners are the duties of loyalty and care set forth in subsections (b) and (c) of the Act. Those duties may not be waived or eliminated in the partnership agreement, but the agreement may identify activities and determine standards for measuring performance of the duties, if not manifestly unreasonable. See Sections 103(b)(3)–(5)....

[2.] Under Section 103(b)(3), the partnership agreement may not "eliminate" the duty of loyalty. Section 103(b)(3)(i) expressly empowers the partners, however, to identify specific types or categories of activities that do not violate the duty of loyalty, if not manifestly unreasonable. As under UPA Section 21, the other partners may also consent to a specific act or transaction that otherwise violates one of the rules. For the consent to be effective under Section 103(b)(3)(ii), there must be full disclosure of all material facts regarding the act or transaction and the partner's conflict of interest. See Comment 5 to Section 103.

3. Subsection (c) is new and establishes the duty of care that partners owe to the partnership and to the other partners. There is no statutory duty of care under the UPA, although a common law duty of care is recognized by some courts. See, e.g., Rosenthal v. Rosenthal, 543 A.2d 348, 352 (Me.1988) (duty of care limited to acting in a manner that does not constitute gross negligence or wilful misconduct).

The standard of care imposed by RUPA is that of gross negligence, which is the standard generally recognized by the courts. See, e.g., Rosenthal v. Rosenthal, supra. Section 103(b)(4) provides that the duty of care may not be eliminated entirely by agreement, but the standard may be reasonably reduced. See Comment 6 to Section 103.

4. Subsection (d) is also new. It provides that partners have an obligation of good faith and fair dealing in the discharge of all their duties, including those arising under the Act, such as their fiduciary duties of loyalty and care, and those arising under the partnership agreement. The exercise of any rights by a partner is also subject to the obligation of good faith and fair dealing. The obligation runs to the partnership and to the other partners in all matters related to the conduct and winding up of the partnership business.

The obligation of good faith and fair dealing is a contract concept, imposed on the partners because of the consensual nature of a partnership. See Restatement (Second) of Contracts § 205 (1981). It is not characterized, in RUPA, as a fiduciary duty arising out of the partners' special relationship. Nor is it a separate and independent obligation. It is an ancillary obligation that applies whenever a partner discharges a duty or exercises a right under the partnership agreement or the Act.

The meaning of "good faith and fair dealing" is not firmly fixed under present law. "Good faith" clearly suggests a subjective element, while "fair dealing" implies an objective component. It was decided to leave the terms undefined in the Act and allow the courts to develop their meaning based on the experience of real cases. . . .

In some situations the obligation of good faith includes a disclosure component. Depending on the circumstances, a partner may have an affirmative disclosure obligation that supplements the Section 403 duty to render information.

Under Section 103(b)(5), the obligation of good faith and fair dealing may not be eliminated by agreement, but the partners by agreement may determine the standards by which the performance of the obligation is to be measured, if the standards are not manifestly unreasonable. See Comment 7 to Section 103.

5. Subsection (e) is new and deals expressly with a very basic issue on which the UPA is silent. A partner as such is not a trustee and is not held to the same standards as a trustee. Subsection (e) makes clear that a partner's conduct is not deemed to be improper merely because it serves the partner's own individual interest.

That admonition has particular application to the duty of loyalty and the obligation of good faith and fair dealing. It underscores the partner's rights as an owner and principal in the enterprise, which must always be balanced against his duties and obligations as an agent and fiduciary. For example, a partner who, with consent, owns a shopping center may, under subsection (e), legitimately vote against a proposal by the partnership to open a competing shopping center.

6. Subsection (f) authorizes partners to lend money to and transact other business with the partnership and, in so doing, to enjoy the same rights and obligations as a nonpartner. That language is drawn from RULPA Section 107. The rights and obligations of a partner doing business with the partnership as an outsider are expressly made subject to the usual laws governing those transactions. They include, for example, rules limiting or qualifying the rights and remedies of inside creditors, such as fraudulent transfer law, equitable subordination, and the law of avoidable preferences, as well as general debtor-creditor law. The reference to "other applicable law" makes clear that subsection (f) is not intended to displace those laws, and thus they are preserved under Section 104(a).

It is unclear under the UPA whether a partner may, for the partner's own account, purchase the assets of the partnership at a foreclosure sale or upon the liquidation of the partnership. Those purchases are clearly within subsection (f)'s broad approval. It is also clear under that subsection that a partner may purchase partnership assets at a foreclosure sale, whether the partner is the mortgagee or the mortgagee is an unrelated third party. Similarly, a partner may purchase partnership property at a tax sale. The obligation of good faith requires disclosure of the partner's interest in the transaction, however. . . .

SECTION 405. ACTIONS BY PARTNERSHIP AND PARTNERS.

(a) A partnership may maintain an action against a partner for a breach of the partnership agreement, or for the violation of a duty to the partnership, causing harm to the partnership.

(b) A partner may maintain an action against the partnership or another partner for legal or equitable relief, with or without an accounting as to partnership business, to:

(1) enforce the partner's rights under the partnership agreement;

(2) enforce the partner's rights under this [Act], including:

(i) the partner's rights under Sections 401, 403, or 404;

(ii) the partner's right on dissociation to have the partner's interest in the partnership purchased pursuant to Section 701 or enforce any other right under [Article] 6 or 7; or

(iii) the partner's right to compel a dissolution and winding up of the partnership business under Section 801 or enforce any other right under [Article] 8; or

(3) enforce the rights and otherwise protect the interests of the partner, including rights and interests arising independently of the partnership relationship.

(c) The accrual of, and any time limitation on, a right of action for a remedy under this section is governed by other law. A right to an accounting upon a dissolution and winding up does not revive a claim barred by law.

Comment:

1. Section 405(a) is new and reflects the entity theory of partnership. It provides that the partnership itself may maintain an action against a partner for any breach of the partnership agreement or for the violation of any duty owed to the partnership, such as a breach of fiduciary duty.

2. Section 405(b) is the successor to UPA Section 22, but with significant changes. At common law, an accounting was generally not available before dissolution. That was modified by UPA Section 22 which specifies certain circumstances in which an accounting action is available without requiring a partner to dissolve the partnership. Section 405(b) goes far beyond the UPA rule. It provides that, during the term of the partnership, partners may

maintain a variety of legal or equitable actions, including an action for an accounting, as well as a final action for an accounting upon dissolution and winding up. It reflects a new policy choice that partners should have access to the courts during the term of the partnership to resolve claims against the partnership and the other partners, leaving broad judicial discretion to fashion appropriate remedies....

Under subsection (b), a partner may bring a direct suit against the partnership or another partner for almost any cause of action arising out of the conduct of the partnership business. That eliminates the present procedural barriers to suits between partners filed independently of an accounting action. In addition to a formal account, the court may grant any other appropriate legal or equitable remedy. Since general partners are not passive investors like limited partners, RUPA does not authorize derivative actions, as does RULPA Section 1001....

3. Generally, partners may limit or contract away their Section 405 remedies. They may not, however, eliminate entirely the remedies for breach of those duties that are mandatory under Section 103(b). See Comment 1 to Section 103....

SECTION 406. CONTINUATION OF PARTNERSHIP BEYOND DEFINITE TERM OR PARTICULAR UNDERTAKING.

(a) If a partnership for a definite term or particular undertaking is continued, without an express agreement, after the expiration of the term or completion of the undertaking, the rights and duties of the partners remain the same as they were at the expiration or completion, so far as is consistent with a partnership at will.

(b) If the partners, or those of them who habitually acted in the business during the term or undertaking, continue the business without any settlement or liquidation of the partnership, they are presumed to have agreed that the partnership will continue.

ARTICLE 5

TRANSFEREES AND CREDITORS OF PARTNER

SECTION 501.   PARTNER NOT CO–OWNER OF PARTNERSHIP PROPERTY.

A partner is not a co-owner of partnership property and has no interest in partnership property which can be transferred, either voluntarily or involuntarily.

Comment:

Section 501 provides that a partner is not a co-owner of partnership property and has no interest in partnership property that can be transferred, either voluntarily or involuntarily. Thus, the section abolishes the UPA Section 25(1) concept of tenants in partnership and reflects the adoption of the entity theory. Partnership property is owned by the entity and not by the individual partners. See also Section 203, which provides that property transferred to or otherwise acquired by the partnership is property of the partnership and not of the partners individually. . . .

Adoption of the entity theory also has the effect of protecting partnership property from execution or other process by a partner's personal creditors. That continues the result under UPA Section 25(2)(c). Those creditors may seek a charging order under Section 504 to reach the partner's transferable interest in the partnership. . . .

SECTION 502.   PARTNER'S TRANSFERABLE INTEREST IN PARTNERSHIP.

The only transferable interest of a partner in the partnership is the partner's share of the profits and losses of the partnership and the partner's right to receive distributions. The interest is personal property.

Comment:

Section 502 continues the UPA Section 26 concept that a partner's only transferable interest in the partnership is the partner's share of profits and losses and right to receive distributions, that is, the partner's financial rights. The term "distribution" is defined in Section 101(3). . . .

Under Section 503(b)(3), a transferee of a partner's transferable interest has standing to seek judicial dissolution of the partnership business.

A partner has other interests in the partnership that may not be transferred, such as the right to participate in the management of the business. Those rights are included in the broader concept of a "partner's interest in the partnership." See Section 101(9).

SECTION 503. TRANSFER OF PARTNER'S TRANSFERABLE INTEREST.

(a) A transfer, in whole or in part, of a partner's transferable interest in the partnership:

(1) is permissible;

(2) does not by itself cause the partner's dissociation or a dissolution and winding up of the partnership business; and

(3) does not, as against the other partners or the partnership, entitle the transferee, during the continuance of the partnership, to participate in the management or conduct of the partnership business, to require access to information concerning partnership transactions, or to inspect or copy the partnership books or records.

(b) A transferee of a partner's transferable interest in the partnership has a right:

(1) to receive, in accordance with the transfer, distributions to which the transferor would otherwise be entitled;

(2) to receive upon the dissolution and winding up of the partnership business, in accordance with the transfer, the net amount otherwise distributable to the transferor; and

(3) to seek under Section 801(6) a judicial determination that it is equitable to wind up the partnership business.

(c) In a dissolution and winding up, a transferee is entitled to an account of partnership transactions only from the date of the latest account agreed to by all of the partners.

(d) Upon transfer, the transferor retains the rights and duties of a partner other than the interest in distributions transferred.

(e) A partnership need not give effect to a transferee's rights under this section until it has notice of the transfer.

(f) A transfer of a partner's transferable interest in the partnership in violation of a restriction on transfer contained in the partnership agreement is ineffective as to a person having notice of the restriction at the time of transfer.

Comment:

1. ... Subsection (a)(1) states explicitly that a partner has the right to transfer his transferable interest in the partnership. The term "transfer" is used throughout RUPA in lieu of the term "assignment." See Section 101(10).

Subsection (a)(2) continues the UPA Section 27(1) rule that an assignment of a partner's interest in the partnership does not of itself cause a winding up of the partnership business. Under Section 601(4)(ii), however, a partner who has transferred substantially all of his partnership interest may be expelled by the other partners. . . .

4. Subsection (d) is new. It makes clear that unless otherwise agreed the partner whose interest is transferred retains all of the rights and duties of a partner, other than the right to receive distributions. That means the transferor is entitled to participate in the management of the partnership and remains personally liable for all partnership obligations, unless and until he withdraws as a partner, is expelled under Section 601(4)(ii), or is otherwise dissociated under Section 601. . . .

6. Subsection (f) is new and provides that a transfer of a partner's transferable interest in the partnership in violation of a restriction on transfer contained in a partnership agreement is ineffective as to a person with timely notice of the restriction. Under Section 103(a), the partners may agree among themselves to restrict the right to transfer their partnership interests. Subsection (f) makes explicit that a transfer in violation of such a restriction is ineffective as to a transferee with notice of the restriction. See Section 102(b) for the meaning of "notice." RUPA leaves to general law and the UCC the issue of whether a transfer in violation of a valid restriction is effective as to a transferee without notice of the restriction.

Whether a particular restriction will be enforceable, however, must be considered in light of other law. See 11 U.S.C. § 541(c)(1) (property owned by bankrupt passes to trustee regardless of restrictions on transfer); UCC § 9–318(4) (agreement between account debtor and assignor prohibiting creation of security interest in a general intangible or requiring account debtor's consent is ineffective); Battista v. Carlo, 57 Misc.2d 495, 293 N.Y.S.2d 227 (1968) (restriction on transfer of partnership interest subject to rules against unreasonable restraints on alienation of property) (dictum); Tupper v. Kroc, 88 Nev. 146, 494 P.2d 1275 (1972) (partnership interest subject to charging order even if partnership agreement prohibits assignments). Cf. Tu–Vu Drive–In Corp. v. Ashkins, 61 Cal.2d 283, 38 Cal.Rptr. 348, 391 P.2d 828 (1964) (restraints on transfer of corporate stock must be reasonable). Even if a restriction on the transfer of a partner's transferable interest in a partnership were held to be unenforceable, the transfer might be grounds for expelling the partner-transferor from the partnership under Section 601(5)(ii).

7. Other rules that apply in the case of transfers include Section 601(4)(ii) (expulsion of partner who transfers substantially all of partnership interest); Section 601(6) (dissociation of partner who makes an assignment for benefit of creditors); and Section 801(6) (transferee has standing to seek judicial winding up).

SECTION 504. PARTNER'S TRANSFERABLE INTEREST SUBJECT TO CHARGING ORDER.

(a) On application by a judgment creditor of a partner or of a partner's transferee, a court having jurisdiction may charge the transferable interest of the judgment debtor to satisfy the judgment. The court may appoint a receiver of the share of the distributions due or to become due to the judgment debtor in respect of the partnership and make all other orders, directions, accounts, and inquiries the judgment debtor might have made or which the circumstances of the case may require.

(b) A charging order constitutes a lien on the judgment debtor's transferable interest in the partnership. The court may order a foreclosure of the interest subject to the charging order at any time. The purchaser at the foreclosure sale has the rights of a transferee.

(c) At any time before foreclosure, an interest charged may be redeemed:

(1) by the judgment debtor;

(2) with property other than partnership property, by one or more of the other partners; or

(3) with partnership property, by one or more of the other partners with the consent of all of the partners whose interests are not so charged.

(d) This [Act] does not deprive a partner of a right under exemption laws with respect to the partner's interest in the partnership.

(e) This section provides the exclusive remedy by which a judgment creditor of a partner or partner's transferee may satisfy a judgment out of the judgment debtor's transferable interest in the partnership.

ARTICLE 6

PARTNER'S DISSOCIATION

Sec.
601.   Events Causing Partner's Dissociation.
602.   Partner's Power to Dissociate; Wrongful Dissociation.
603.   Effect of Partner's Dissociation.

SECTION 601. EVENTS CAUSING PARTNER'S DISSOCIATION.

A partner is dissociated from a partnership upon the occurrence of any of the following events:

(1) the partnership's having notice of the partner's express will to withdraw as a partner [upon the date of notice] or on a later date specified by the partner;

(2) an event agreed to in the partnership agreement as causing the partner's dissociation;

(3) the partner's expulsion pursuant to the partnership agreement;

(4) the partner's expulsion by the unanimous vote of the other partners if:

(i) it is unlawful to carry on the partnership business with that partner;

(ii) there has been a transfer of all or substantially all of that partner's transferable interest in the partnership, other than a transfer for security purposes, or a court order charging the partner's interest, which has not been foreclosed;

(iii) within 90 days after the partnership notifies a corporate partner that it will be expelled because it has filed a certificate of dissolution or the equivalent, its charter has been revoked, or its right to conduct business has been suspended by the jurisdiction of its incorporation, [and] there is no revocation of the certificate of dissolution or no reinstatement of its charter or its right to conduct business; or

(iv) a partnership that is a partner has been dissolved and its business is being wound up;

(5) on application by the partnership or another partner, the partner's expulsion by judicial determination because:

(i) the partner engaged in wrongful conduct that adversely and materially affected the partnership business;

(ii) the partner willfully or persistently committed a material breach of the partnership agreement or of a duty owed to the partnership or the other partners under Section 404; or

(iii) the partner engaged in conduct relating to the partnership business which makes it not reasonably practicable to carry on the business in partnership with the partner;

(6) the partner's:

(i) becoming a debtor in bankruptcy;

(ii) executing an assignment for the benefit of creditors;

(iii) seeking, consenting to, or acquiescing in the appointment of a trustee, receiver, or liquidator of that partner or of all or substantially all of that partner's property; or

(iv) failing, within 90 days after the appointment, to have vacated or stayed the appointment of a trustee, receiver, or liquidator of the partner or of all or substantially all of the partner's property obtained without the partner's consent or acquiescence, or failing within 90 days after the expiration of a stay to have the appointment vacated;

(7) in the case of a partner who is an individual:

(i) the partner's death;

(ii) the appointment of a guardian or general conservator for the partner; or

(iii) a judicial determination that the partner has otherwise become incapable of performing the partner's duties under the partnership agreement;

(8) in the case of a partner that is a trust or is acting as a partner by virtue of being a trustee of a trust, distribution of the trust's entire transferable interest in the partnership, but not merely by reason of the substitution of a successor trustee;

(9) in the case of a partner that is an estate or is acting as a partner by virtue of being a personal representative of an estate, distribution of the estate's entire transferable interest in the partnership, but not merely by reason of the substitution of a successor personal representative; or

(10) termination of a partner who is not an individual, partnership, corporation, trust, or estate.

Comment:

1.   RUPA dramatically changes the law governing partnership breakups and dissolution.   An entirely new concept, "dissociation," is used in lieu of the UPA term "dissolution" to denote the change in the relationship caused by a partner's ceasing to be associated in the carrying on of the business.   "Dissolution" is retained but with a different meaning.   See Section 802.   The entity theory of partnership provides a conceptual basis for continuing the firm itself despite a partner's withdrawal from the firm.

Under RUPA, unlike the UPA, the dissociation of a partner does not necessarily cause a dissolution and winding up of the business of the partnership.   Section 801 identifies the situations in which the dissociation of a partner causes a winding up of the business. Section 701 provides that in all other situations there is a buyout of the partner's interest in the partnership, rather than a windup of the partnership business.   In those other situations, the partnership entity continues, unaffected by the partner's dissociation.

A dissociated partner remains a partner for some purposes and still has some residual rights, duties, powers, and liabilities.   Although Section 601 determines when a partner is dissociated from the partnership, the consequences of the partner's dissociation do not all occur at the same time.   Thus, it is more useful to think of a dissociated partner as a partner for some purposes, but as a former partner for others.   For example, see Section 403(b) (former partner's access to partnership books and records).   The consequences of a partner's dissociation depend on whether the partnership continues or is wound up, as provided in Articles 6, 7 and 8.

Section 601 enumerates all of the events that cause a partner's dissociation....

2.   Section 601(1) provides that a partner is dissociated when the partnership has notice of the partner's express will to withdraw as a partner, unless a later date is specified by the partner. If a future date is specified by the partner, other partners may dissociate before that date; specifying a future date does not bind the others to remain as partners until that date. See also Section 801(2)(i).

Section 602(a) provides that a partner has the power to withdraw at any time. The power to withdraw is immutable under Section 103(b)(6), with the exception that the partners may agree the notice must be in writing. This continues the present rule that a partner has the power to withdraw at will, even if not the right. See UPA Section 31(2). Since no writing is required to create a partner relationship, it was felt unnecessarily formalistic, and a trap for the unwary, to require a writing to end one. If a written notification is given, Section 102(d) clarifies when it is deemed received.

RUPA continues the UPA "express will" concept, thus preserving existing case law. Section 601(1) clarifies existing law by providing that the partnership must have notice of the partner's expression of will before the dissociation is effective. See Section 102(b) for the meaning of "notice."   ...

4.   Section 601(3) provides that a partner may be expelled by the other partners pursuant to a power of expulsion contained in the partnership agreement. That continues the basic rule of UPA Section 31(1)(d). The expulsion can be with or without cause. As under existing law, the obligation of good faith under Section 404(d) does not require prior notice, specification of cause, or an opportunity to be heard. See Holman v. Coie, 11 Wash.App. 195, 522 P.2d 515, cert. denied, 420 U.S. 984 (1974).

5.   Section 601(4) empowers the partners, by unanimous vote, to expel a partner for specified causes, even if not authorized in the partnership agreement. This changes the UPA Section 31(1)(d) rule that authorizes expulsion only if provided in the partnership agreement. A partner may be expelled from a term partnership, as well as from a partnership at will. Under Section 103(a), the partnership agreement may change or abolish the partners' power of expulsion....

Subsection (4)(ii) provides that a partner may be expelled for transferring substantially all of his transferable interest in the partnership, other than as security for a loan. (He may, however, be expelled upon foreclosure.)   This rule is derived from UPA Section 31(1)(c).   To avoid the presence of an unwelcome transferee, the remaining partners may dissolve the partnership under Section 801(2)(ii), after first expelling the transferor partner. . . .

6.   . . . Subsection (5)(iii) provides for judicial expulsion of a partner who engaged in conduct relating to the partnership business that makes it not reasonably practicable to carry on the business in partnership with that partner.   Expulsion for such misconduct makes the partner's dissociation wrongful under Section 602(a)(ii) and may also support a judicial decree of dissolution under Section 801(5)(ii).

7.   Section 601(6) provides that a partner is dissociated upon becoming a debtor in bankruptcy or upon taking or suffering other action evidencing the partner's insolvency or lack of financial responsibility. . . .

Initially, upon the filing of the bankruptcy petition, the debtor partner's transferable interest in the partnership will pass to the bankruptcy trustee as property of the estate under Section 541(a)(1) of the Bankruptcy Code, notwithstanding any restrictions on transfer provided in the partnership agreement.   In most Chapter 7 cases, that will result in the eventual buyout of the partner's interest.

The application of various provisions of the federal Bankruptcy Code to Section 601(6)(i) is unclear.   In particular, there is uncertainty as to the validity of UPA Section 31(5), and thus its RUPA counterpart, under Sections 365(e) and 541(c)(1) of the Bankruptcy Code.   Those sections generally invalidate so-called *ipso facto* laws that cause a termination or modification of the debtor's contract or property rights because of the bankruptcy filing.   As a consequence, RUPA Section 601(6)(i), which provides for a partner's dissociation by operation of law upon becoming a debtor in bankruptcy, may be invalid under the Supremacy Clause. . . .

8.   UPA Section 31(4) provides for the dissolution of a partnership upon the death of any partner, although by agreement the remaining partners may continue the partnership business.   RUPA Section 601(7)(i), on the other hand, provides for dissociation upon the death of a partner who is an individual, rather than dissolution of the partnership. . . .   Normally, under RUPA, the deceased partner's transferable interest in the partnership will pass to his estate and be bought out under Article 7. . . .

SECTION 602.   PARTNER'S POWER TO DISSOCIATE; WRONGFUL DISSOCIATION.

(a) A partner has the power to dissociate at any time, rightfully or wrongfully, by express will pursuant to Section 601(1).

(b) A partner's dissociation is wrongful only if:

(1) it is in breach of an express provision of the partnership agreement; or

(2) in the case of a partnership for a definite term or particular undertaking, before the expiration of the term or the completion of the undertaking;

(i) the partner withdraws by express will, unless the withdrawal follows within 90 days after another partner's dissociation by death or otherwise under Section 601(6) through (10) or wrongful dissociation under this subsection;

(ii) the partner is expelled by judicial determination under Section 601(5);

(iii) the partner is dissociated by becoming a debtor in bankruptcy; or

(iv) in the case of a partner who is not an individual, trust other than a business trust, or estate, the partner is expelled or otherwise dissociated because it willfully dissolved or terminated.

(c) A partner who wrongfully dissociates is liable to the partnership and to the other partners for damages caused by the dissociation. The liability is in addition to any other obligation of the partner to the partnership or to the other partners.

Comment:

1. Subsection (a) states explicitly what is implicit in UPA Section 31(2) and RUPA Section 601(1)—that a partner has the power to dissociate at any time by expressing a will to withdraw, even in contravention of the partnership agreement. The phrase "rightfully or wrongfully" reflects the distinction between a partner's *power* to withdraw in contravention of the partnership agreement and a partner's *right* to do so. In this context, although a partner can not be enjoined from exercising the power to dissociate, the dissociation may be wrongful under subsection (b).

2. Subsection (b) provides that a partner's dissociation is wrongful only if it results from one of the enumerated events. The significance of a wrongful dissociation is that it may give rise to damages under subsection (c) and, if it results in the dissolution of the partnership, the wrongfully dissociating partner is not entitled to participate in winding up the business under Section 804.

Under subsection (b), a partner's dissociation is wrongful if (1) it breaches an express provision of the partnership agreement or (2), in a term partnership, before the expiration of the term or the completion of the undertaking (i) the partner voluntarily withdraws by express will, except a withdrawal following *another* partner's wrongful dissociation or dissociation by death or otherwise under Section 601(6) through (10); (ii) the partner is expelled for misconduct under Section 601(5); (iii) the partner becomes a debtor in bankruptcy (see Section 101(2)); or (iv) a partner that is an entity (other than a trust or estate) is expelled or otherwise dissociated because its dissolution or termination was willful. Since subsection (b) is merely a default rule, the partnership agreement may eliminate or expand the dissociations that are wrongful or modify the effects of wrongful dissociation.

The exception in subsection (b)(2)(i) is intended to protect a partner's reactive withdrawal from a term partnership after the premature departure of another partner, such as the partnership's rainmaker or main supplier of capital, under the same circumstances that may result in the dissolution of the partnership under Section 801(2)(i). Under that section, a term partnership is dissolved 90 days after the bankruptcy, incapacity, death (or similar dissociation of a partner that is an entity), or wrongful dissociation of any partner, unless a majority in interest (see Comment 5(i) to Section 801 for a discussion of the term "majority in interest") of the remaining partners agree to continue the partnership. Under Section 602(b)(2)(i), a partner's exercise of the right of withdrawal by express will under those circumstances is rendered "rightful," even if the partnership is continued by others, and does not expose the withdrawing partner to damages for wrongful dissociation under Section 602(c).

A partner wishing to withdraw prematurely from a term partnership for any other reason, such as another partner's misconduct, can avoid being treated as a wrongfully dissociating partner by applying to a court under Section 601(5)(iii) to have the offending partner expelled. Then, the partnership could be dissolved under Section 801(2)(i) or the remaining partners could, by unanimous vote, dissolve the partnership under Section 801(2)(ii).

3. Subsection (c) provides that a wrongfully dissociating partner is liable to the partnership and to the other partners for any damages caused by the wrongful nature of the dissociation. That liability is in addition to any other obligation of the partner to the partnership or to the other partners. For example, the partner would be liable for any damage caused by breach of the partnership agreement or other misconduct. The partnership might also incur substantial expenses resulting from a partner's premature withdrawal from a term partnership, such as replacing the partner's expertise or obtaining new financing. The wrongfully dissociating partner would be liable to the partnership for those and all other expenses and damages that are causally related to the wrongful dissociation.

Section 701(c) provides that any damages for wrongful dissociation may be offset against the amount of the buyout price due to the partner under Section 701(a), and Section 701(h) provides that a partner who wrongfully dissociates from a term partnership is not entitled to payment of the buyout price until the term expires.

Under UPA Section 38(2)(c)(II), in addition to an offset for damages, the goodwill value of the partnership is excluded in determining the value of a wrongfully dissociating partner's partnership interest. Under RUPA, however, unless the partnership's goodwill is damaged by the wrongful dissociation, the value of the wrongfully dissociating partner's interest will include any goodwill value of the partnership. If the firm's goodwill is damaged, the amount of the damages suffered by the partnership and the remaining partners will be offset against the buyout price. See Section 701 and Comments.

SECTION 603. EFFECT OF PARTNER'S DISSOCIATION.

(a) If a partner's dissociation results in a dissolution and winding up of the partnership business, [Article] 8 applies; otherwise, [Article] 7 applies.

(b) Upon a partner's dissociation:

(1) the partner's right to participate in the management and conduct of the partnership business terminates, except as otherwise provided in Section 803;

(2) the partner's duty of loyalty under Section 404(b)(3) terminates; and

(3) the partner's duty of loyalty under Section 404(b)(1) and (2) and duty of care under Section 404(c) continue only with regard to matters arising and events occurring before the partner's dissociation, unless the partner participates in winding up the partnership's business pursuant to Section 803.

Comment:

1. Section 603(a) is a "switching" provision. It provides that, after a partner's dissociation, the partner's interest in the partnership must be purchased pursuant to the buyout rules in Article 7 *unless* there is a dissolution and winding up of the partnership business under Article 8. Thus, a partner's dissociation will always result in either a buyout of the dissociated partner's interest or a dissolution and winding up of the business.

By contrast, under the UPA, every partner dissociation results in the dissolution of the partnership, most of which trigger a right to have the business wound up unless the partnership agreement provides otherwise. See UPA § 38. The only exception in which the remaining partners have a statutory right to continue the business is when a partner wrongfully dissolves the partnership in breach of the partnership agreement. See UPA § 38(2)(b).

2. Section 603(b) is new and deals with some of the internal effects of a partner's dissociation. Subsection (b)(1) makes it clear that one of the consequences of a partner's dissociation is the immediate loss of the right to participate in the management of the business, unless it results in a dissolution and winding up of the business. In that case, Section 804(a) provides that all of the partners who have not wrongfully dissociated may participate in winding up the business.

Subsection[s] (b)(2) and (3) clarify a partner's fiduciary duties upon dissociation. No change from current law is intended. With respect to the duty of loyalty, the Section 404(b)(3) duty not to compete terminates upon dissociation, and the dissociated partner is free immediately to engage in a competitive business, without any further consent. With respect to the partner's remaining loyalty duties under Section 404(b) and duty of care under Section 404(c), a withdrawing partner has a continuing duty after dissociation, but it is limited to matters that arose or events that occurred before the partner dissociated. For example, a partner who leaves a brokerage firm may immediately compete with the firm for new clients, but must exercise care in completing on-going client transactions and must account to the firm for any fees received from the old clients on account of those transactions. As the last clause makes clear, there is no contraction of a dissociated partner's duties under subsection (b)(3) if the partner thereafter participates in the dissolution and winding up the partnership's business.

ARTICLE 7

PARTNER'S DISSOCIATION WHEN BUSINESS NOT WOUND UP

Sec.
701. Purchase of Dissociated Partner's Interest.
702. Dissociated Partner's Power to Bind and Liability to Partnership.
703. Dissociated Partner's Liability to Other Persons.
704. Statement of Dissociation.
705. Continued Use of Partnership Name.

SECTION 701. PURCHASE OF DISSOCIATED PARTNER'S IN-TEREST.

(a) If a partner is dissociated from a partnership without resulting in a dissolution and winding up of the partnership business under Section 801, the partnership shall cause the dissociated partner's interest in the partnership to be purchased for a buyout price determined pursuant to subsection (b).

(b) The buyout price of a dissociated partner's interest is the amount that would have been distributable to the dissociating partner under Section 807(b) if, on the date of dissociation, the assets of the partnership were sold at a price equal to the greater of the liquidation value or the value based on a sale of the entire business as a going concern without the dissociated partner and the partnership were wound up as of that date. Interest must be paid from the date of dissociation to the date of payment.

(c) Damages for wrongful dissociation under Section 602(b), and all other amounts owing, whether or not presently due, from the dissociated partner to the partnership, must be offset against the buyout price. Interest must be paid from the date the amount owed becomes due to the date of payment.

(d) A partnership shall indemnify a dissociated partner whose interest is being purchased against all partnership liabilities, whether incurred before or after the dissociation, except liabilities incurred by an act of the dissociated partner under Section 702.

(e) If no agreement for the purchase of a dissociated partner's interest is reached within 120 days after a written demand for payment, the partnership shall pay, or cause to be paid, in cash to the dissociated partner the amount the partnership estimates to be the buyout price and accrued interest, reduced by any offsets and accrued interest under subsection (c).

(f) If a deferred payment is authorized under subsection (h), the partnership may tender a written offer to pay the amount it estimates to be the buyout price and accrued interest, reduced by any offsets under subsection (c), stating the time of payment, the amount and type of security for payment, and the other terms and conditions of the obligation.

(g) The payment or tender required by subsection (e) or (f) must be accompanied by the following:

(1) a statement of partnership assets and liabilities as of the date of dissociation;

(2) the latest available partnership balance sheet and income statement, if any;

(3) an explanation of how the estimated amount of the payment was calculated; and

(4) written notice that the payment is in full satisfaction of the obligation to purchase unless, within 120 days after the written notice, the dissociated partner commences an action to determine

the buyout price, any offsets under subsection (c), or other terms of the obligation to purchase.

(h) A partner who wrongfully dissociates before the expiration of a definite term or the completion of a particular undertaking is not entitled to payment of any portion of the buyout price until the expiration of the term or completion of the undertaking, unless the partner establishes to the satisfaction of the court that earlier payment will not cause undue hardship to the business of the partnership. A deferred payment must be adequately secured and bear interest.

(i) A dissociated partner may maintain an action against the partnership, pursuant to Section 405(b)(2)(ii), to determine the buyout price of that partner's interest, any offsets under subsection (c), or other terms of the obligation to purchase. The action must be commenced within 120 days after the partnership has tendered payment or an offer to pay or within one year after written demand for payment if no payment or offer to pay is tendered. The court shall determine the buyout price of the dissociated partner's interest, any offset due under subsection (c), and accrued interest, and enter judgment for any additional payment or refund. If deferred payment is authorized under subsection (h), the court shall also determine the security for payment and other terms of the obligation to purchase. The court may assess reasonable attorney's fees and the fees and expenses of appraisers or other experts for a party to the action, in amounts the court finds equitable, against a party that the court finds acted arbitrarily, vexatiously, or not in good faith. The finding may be based on the partnership's failure to tender payment or an offer to pay or to comply with subsection (g).

Comment:

1. Article 7 is new and provides for the buyout of a dissociated partner's interest in the partnership when the partner's dissociation does not result in a dissolution and winding up of its business under Article 8. See Section 603(a). If there is no dissolution, the remaining partners have a right to continue the business and the dissociated partner has a right to be paid the value of his partnership interest. These rights can, of course, be varied in the partnership agreement. See Section 103. A dissociated partner has a continuing relationship with the partnership and third parties as provided in Sections 603(b), 702, and 703. See also Section 403(b) (former partner's access to partnership books and records).

2. Subsection (a) provides that, if a partner's dissociation does not result in a windup of the business, the partnership shall cause the interest of the dissociating partner to be purchased for a buyout price determined pursuant to subsection (b). The buyout is mandatory. The "cause to be purchased" language is intended to accom-

modate a purchase by the partnership, one or more of the remaining partners, or a third party....

3. Subsection (b) provides how the "buyout price" is to be determined. The terms "fair market value" or "fair value" were not used because they are often considered terms of art having a special meaning depending on the context, such as in tax or corporate law. "Buyout price" is a new term. It is intended that the term be developed as an independent concept appropriate to the partnership buyout situation, while drawing on valuation principles developed elsewhere.

Under subsection (b), the buyout price is the amount that would have been distributable to the dissociating partner under Section 807(b) if, on the date of dissociation, the assets of the partnership were sold at a price equal to the greater of liquidation value or going concern value without the departing partner. Liquidation value is not intended to mean distress sale value. Under general principles of valuation, the hypothetical selling price in either case should be the price that a willing and informed buyer would pay a willing and informed seller, with neither being under any compulsion to deal. The notion of a minority discount in determining the buyout price is negated by valuing the business as a going concern. Other discounts, such as for a lack of marketability or the loss of a key partner, may be appropriate, however.

Since the buyout price is based on the value of the business at the time of dissociation, the partnership must pay interest on the amount due from the date of dissociation until payment to compensate the dissociating partner for the use of his interest in the firm. Section 104(b) provides that interest shall be at the legal rate unless otherwise provided in the partnership agreement....

UPA Section 38(2)(c)(II) provides that the good will of the business not be considered in valuing a wrongfully dissociating partner's interest. The forfeiture of good will rule is implicitly rejected by RUPA. See Section 602(c) and Comment 3.

The Section 701 rules are merely default rules. The partners may, in the partnership agreement, fix the method or formula for determining the buyout price and all of the other terms and conditions of the buyout right. Indeed, the very right to a buyout itself may be modified, although a provision providing for a complete forfeiture would probably not be enforceable. See Section 104(a).

4. Subsection (c) provides that the partnership may offset against the buyout price all amounts owing by the dissociated partner to the partnership, whether or not presently due, including any damages for wrongful dissociation under Section 602(c). This has the effect of accelerating payment of amounts not yet due from the departing partner to the partnership, including a long-term loan

by the partnership to the dissociated partner. Where appropriate, the amounts not yet due should be discounted to present value. A dissociating partner, on the other hand, is not entitled to an add-on for amounts owing to him by the partnership. Thus, a departing partner who has made a long-term loan to the partnership must wait for repayment, unless the terms of the loan agreement provide for acceleration upon dissociation.

It is not intended that the partnership's right of setoff be construed to limit the amount of the damages for the partner's wrongful dissociation and any other amounts owing to the partnership to the value of the dissociated partner's interest. Those amounts may result in a net sum due to the partnership from the dissociated partner.

5. Subsection (d) follows the UPA Section 38 rule and provides that the partnership must indemnify a dissociated partner against all partnership liabilities, whether incurred before or after the dissociation, except those incurred by the dissociated partner under Section 702.

6. Subsection (e) provides that, if no agreement for the purchase of the dissociated partner's interest is reached within 120 days after the dissociated partner's written demand for payment, the partnership must pay, or cause to be paid, in cash the amount it estimates to be the buyout price, adjusted for any offsets allowed and accrued interest. Thus, the dissociating partner will receive in cash within 120 days of dissociation the undisputed minimum value of the partner's partnership interest. If the dissociated partner claims that the buyout price should be higher, suit may thereafter be brought as provided in subsection (i) to have the amount of the buyout price determined by the court. This is similar to the procedure for determining the value of dissenting shareholders' shares under RMBCA Sections 13.20–13.28.

The "cause to be paid" language of subsection (a) is repeated here to permit either the partnership, one or more of the continuing partners, or a third-party purchaser to tender payment of the estimated amount due.

7. Subsection (f) provides that, when deferred payment is authorized in the case of a wrongfully dissociating partner, a written offer stating the amount the partnership estimates to be the purchase price should be tendered within the 120–day period, even though actual payment of the amount may be deferred, possibly for many years. . . . The dissociated partner is entitled to know at the time of dissociation what amount the remaining partners think is due, including the estimated amount of any damages allegedly caused by the partner's wrongful dissociation that may be offset against the buyout price. . . .

9.   Subsection (h) replaces UPA Section 38(2)(c) and provides a somewhat different rule for payment to a partner whose dissociation before the expiration of a definite term or the completion of a particular undertaking is wrongful under Section 602(b).   Under subsection (h), a wrongfully dissociating partner is not entitled to receive any portion of the buyout price before the expiration of the term or completion of the undertaking, unless the dissociated partner establishes to the satisfaction of the court that earlier payment will not cause undue hardship to the business of the partnership. In all other cases, there must be an immediate payment in cash.

10.   Subsection (i) provides that a dissociated partner may maintain an action against the partnership to determine the buyout price, any offsets, or other terms of the purchase obligation.   The action must be commenced within 120 days after the partnership tenders payment of the amount it estimates to be due or, if deferred payment is authorized, its written offer.   This provision creates a 120-day "cooling off" period.   It also allows the parties an opportunity to negotiate their differences after disclosure by the partnership of its financial statements and other required information.

If the partnership fails to tender payment of the estimated amount due (or a written offer, if deferred payment is authorized), the dissociated partner has one year after written demand for payment in which to commence suit.

If the parties fail to reach agreement, the court must determine the buyout price of the partner's interest, any offsets, including damages for wrongful dissociation, and the amount of interest accrued.   If payment to a wrongfully dissociated partner is deferred, the court may also require security for payment and determine the other terms of the obligation....

SECTION 702. DISSOCIATED PARTNER'S POWER TO BIND AND LIABILITY TO PARTNERSHIP.

(a) For two years after a partner dissociates without resulting in a dissolution and winding up of the partnership business, the partnership, including a surviving partnership under [Article] 9, is bound by an act of the dissociated partner which would have bound the partnership under Section 301 before dissociation only if at the time of entering into the transaction the other party:

(1) reasonably believed that the dissociated partner was then a partner;

(2) did not have notice of the partner's dissociation; and

(3) is not deemed to have had knowledge under Section 303(e) or notice under Section 704(c).

190

(b) A dissociated partner is liable to the partnership for any damage caused to the partnership arising from an obligation incurred by the dissociated partner after dissociation for which the partnership is liable under subsection (a).

Comment:

1. Section 702 deals with a dissociated partner's lingering apparent authority to bind the partnership in ordinary course partnership transactions and the partner's liability to the partnership for any loss caused thereby. It also applies to partners who withdraw incident to a merger under Article 9. See Section 906(e).

A dissociated partner has no *actual* authority to act for the partnership. See Section 603(b)(1). Nevertheless, in order to protect innocent third parties, Section 702(a) provides that the partnership remains bound, for two years after a partner's dissociation, by that partner's acts that would, before his dissociation, have bound the partnership under Section 301 if, and only if, the other party to the transaction reasonably believed that he was still a partner, did not have notice of the partner's dissociation, and is not deemed to have had knowledge of the dissociation under Section 303(e) or notice thereof under Section 704(c).

Under Section 301, every partner has *apparent* authority to bind the partnership by any act for carrying on the partnership business in the ordinary course, unless the other party knows that the partner has no actual authority to act for the partnership or has received a notification of the partner's lack of authority. Section 702(a) continues that general rule for two years after a partner's dissociation, subject to three modifications.

After a partner's dissociation, the general rule is modified, first, by requiring the other party to show reasonable reliance on the partner's status as a partner. Section 301 has no explicit reliance requirement, although the partnership is bound only if the partner purports to act on its behalf. Thus, the other party will normally be aware of the partnership and presumably the partner's status as such.

The second modification is that, under Section 702(a), the partnership is not bound if the third party has *notice* of the partner's dissociation, while under the general rule of Section 301 the partnership is bound unless the third party *knows* of the partner's lack of authority. Under Section 102(b), a person has "notice" of a fact if he knows or has reason to know it exists from all the facts that are known to him or he has received a notification of it. Thus, the partnership may protect itself by sending a notification of the dissociation to a third party, and a third party may, in any event, have a duty to inquire further based on what is known. That provides the partnership with greater protection from the unauthorized acts of a dissociated partner than from those of partners generally.

The third modification of the general apparent authority rule under Section 702(a) involves the effect of a statement of dissociation. Section 704(c) provides that, for the purposes of Sections 702(a)(3) and 703(b)(3), third parties are deemed to have notice of a partner's dissociation 90 days after the filing of a statement of dissociation. Thus, the filing of a statement operates as constructive notice of the dissociated partner's lack of authority after 90 days, conclusively terminating the dissociated partner's Section 702 apparent authority. . . .

Under RUPA, therefore, a partnership should notify all known creditors of a partner's dissociation and may, by filing a statement of dissociation, conclusively limit to 90 days a dissociated partner's lingering agency power. Moreover, under Section 703(b), a dissociated partner's lingering liability for post-dissociation partnership liabilities may be limited to 90 days by filing a statement of dissociation. These incentives should encourage both partnerships and dissociating partners to file statements routinely. Those transacting substantial business with partnerships can protect themselves from the risk of dealing with dissociated partners, or relying on their credit, by checking the partnership records at least every 90 days.

2. Section 702(b) is a corollary to subsection (a) and provides that a dissociated partner is liable to the partnership for any loss resulting from an obligation improperly incurred by the partner under subsection (a). In effect, the dissociated partner must indemnify the partnership for any loss, meaning a loss net of any gain from the transaction. The dissociated partner is also personally liable to the third party for the unauthorized obligation.

SECTION 703. DISSOCIATED PARTNER'S LIABILITY TO OTHER PERSONS.

(a) A partner's dissociation does not of itself discharge the partner's liability for a partnership obligation incurred before dissociation. A dissociated partner is not liable for a partnership obligation incurred after dissociation, except as otherwise provided in subsection (b).

(b) A partner who dissociates without resulting in a dissolution and winding up of the partnership business is liable as a partner to the other party in a transaction entered into by the partnership, or a surviving partnership under [Article] 9, within two years after the partner's dissociation, only if at the time of entering into the transaction the other party:

   (1) reasonably believed that the dissociated partner was then a partner;

(2) did not have notice of the partner's dissociation; and

(3) is not deemed to have had knowledge under Section 303(e) or notice under Section 704(c).

(c) By agreement with the partnership creditor and the partners continuing the business, a dissociated partner may be released from liability for a partnership obligation.

(d) A dissociated partner is released from liability for a partnership obligation if a partnership creditor, with notice of the partner's dissociation but without the partner's consent, agrees to a material alteration in the nature or time of payment of a partnership obligation.

SECTION 704. STATEMENT OF DISSOCIATION.

(a) A dissociated partner or the partnership may file a statement of dissociation stating the name of the partnership and that the partner is dissociated from the partnership.

(b) A statement of dissociation is a limitation on the authority of a dissociated partner for the purposes of Section 303(d) and (e).

(c) For the purposes of Sections 702(a)(3) and 703(b)(3), a person not a partner is deemed to have notice of the dissociation 90 days after the statement of dissociation is filed.

SECTION 705. CONTINUED USE OF PARTNERSHIP NAME.

Continued use of a partnership name, or a dissociated partner's name as part thereof, by partners continuing the business does not of itself make the dissociated partner liable for an obligation of the partners or the partnership continuing the business.

ARTICLE 8

WINDING UP PARTNERSHIP BUSINESS

SECTION 801. EVENTS CAUSING DISSOLUTION AND WINDING UP OF PARTNERSHIP BUSINESS.

A partnership is dissolved, and its business must be wound up, only upon the occurrence of any of the following events:

(1) in a partnership at will, the partnership's having notice from a partner, other than a partner who is dissociated under Section 601(2) through (10), of that partner's express will to withdraw as a partner [as of the time of the notice], or on a later date specified by the partner;

(2) in a partnership for a definite term or particular undertaking:

(i) within 90 days after a partner's dissociation by death or otherwise under Section 601(6) through (10) or wrongful dissociation under Section 602(b), the express will of at least half of the remaining partners to wind up the partnership business, for which purpose a partner's rightful dissociation pursuant to Section 602(b)(2)(i) constitutes the expression of that partner's will to wind up the partnership business;

(ii) the express will of all of the partners to wind up the partnership business; or

(iii) the expiration of the term or the completion of the undertaking;

(3) an event agreed to in the partnership agreement resulting in the winding up of the partnership business;

(4) an event that makes it unlawful for all or substantially all of the business of the partnership to be continued, but a cure of illegality within 90 days after notice to the partnership of the event is effective retroactively to the date of the event for purposes of this section;

(5) on application by a partner, a judicial determination that:

(i) the economic purpose of the partnership is likely to be unreasonably frustrated;

(ii) another partner has engaged in conduct relating to the partnership business which makes it not reasonably practicable to carry on the business in partnership with that partner; or

(iii) it is not otherwise reasonably practicable to carry on the partnership business in conformity with the partnership agreement; or

(6) on application by a transferee of a partner's transferable interest, a judicial determination that it is equitable to wind up the partnership business:

(i) after the expiration of the term or completion of the undertaking, if the partnership was for a definite term or particular undertaking at the time of the transfer or entry of the charging order that gave rise to the transfer; or

(ii) at any time, if the partnership was a partnership at will at the time of the transfer or entry of the charging order that gave rise to the transfer.

Comment:

1. Under UPA Section 29, a partnership is dissolved every time a partner leaves. That reflects the aggregate nature of the partnership under the UPA. Even if the business of the partnership is continued by some of the partners, it is technically a new partnership. The dissolution of the old partnership and creation of a new partnership causes many unnecessary problems....

RUPA's move to the entity theory is driven in part by the need to prevent a technical dissolution or its consequences. Under RUPA, not every partner dissociation causes a dissolution of the partnership. Only certain departures trigger a dissolution. The basic rule is that a partnership is dissolved, and its business must be wound up, only upon the occurrence of one of the events listed in Section 801. All other dissociations result in a buyout of the partner's interest under Article 7 and a continuation of the partnership entity and business by the remaining partners. See Section 603(a).

With only three exceptions, the provisions of Section 801 are merely default rules and may by agreement be varied or eliminated as grounds for dissolution. The first exception is dissolution under Section 801(4) resulting from carrying on an illegal business. The other two exceptions cover the power of a court to dissolve a partnership under Section 801(5) on application of a partner and under Section 801(6) on application of a transferee....

2. Under RUPA, "dissolution" is merely the commencement of the winding up process. The partnership continues for the limited purpose of winding up the business. In effect, that means the scope of the partnership business contracts to completing work in process and taking such other actions as may be necessary to wind up the business. Winding up the partnership business entails selling its assets, paying its debts, and distributing the net balance, if any, to the partners in cash according to their interests. The partnership entity continues, and the partners are associated in the winding up of the business until winding up is completed. When the winding up is completed, the partnership entity terminates.

3. Section 801 continues two basic rules from the UPA. First, it continues the rule that any member of an *at-will* partnership has the right to force a liquidation. Second, by negative implication, it continues the rule that the partners who wish to continue the business of a *term* partnership can not be forced to liquidate the business by a partner who withdraws prematurely in violation of the partnership agreement....

4. Section 801(1) provides that a partnership at will is dissolved and its business must be wound up upon the partnership's

having notice of a partner's express will to withdraw as a partner, unless a later effective date is specified by the partner. . . .

If, after dissolution, none of the partners wants the partnership wound up, Section 802(b) provides that, with the consent of all the partners, including the withdrawing partner, the remaining partners may continue the business. In that event, although there is a technical dissolution of the partnership and, at least in theory, a temporary contraction of the scope of the business, the partnership entity continues and the scope of its business is restored. See Section 802(b) and Comment 2.

5. Section 801(2) provides three ways in which a term partnership may be dissolved before the expiration of the term:

(i) Subsection (2)(i) provides for dissolution after a partner's dissociation by death or otherwise under Section 601(6) to (10) or wrongful dissociation under Section 602(b), if within 90 days after the dissociation at least half of the remaining partners express their will to dissolve the partnership. Thus if a term partnership had six partners and one of the partners dies or wrongfully dissociates before the end of the term, the partnership will, as a result of the dissociation, be dissolved only if three of the remaining five partners affirmatively vote in favor of dissolution within 90 days after the dissociation.* This reactive dissolution of a term partnership protects the remaining partners where the dissociating partner is crucial to the successful continuation of the business. The corresponding UPA Section 38(2)(b) rule requires unanimous consent of the remaining partners to continue the business, thus giving each partner an absolute right to a reactive liquidation. Under [the 1994 revision of RUPA], if the partnership is continued by the majority, any dissenting partner who wants to withdraw may do so rightfully under the exception to Section 602(b)(2)(i), in which case his interest in the partnership will be bought out under Article 7. By itself, however, a partner's vote not to continue the business is not necessarily an expression of the partner's will to withdraw, and a dissenting partner may still elect to remain a partner and continue in the business.

* Prior to August 1997, Section 801(2)(i) provided that upon the dissociation of a partner in a term partnership by death or otherwise under Section 601(6) through (10) or wrongful dissociation under 602(b) the partnership would dissolve unless "a majority in interest of the remaining partners (including partners who have rightfully dissociated pursuant to Section 602(b)(2)(i)) agree to continue the partnership." This language was thought to be necessary for a term partnership to lack continuity of life under the Internal Revenue Act tax classification regulations. These regulations were repealed effective January 1, 1997. The current language, approved at the 1997 annual meeting of the National Conference of Commissioners on Uniform State Laws, allows greater continuity in a term partnership than the prior version of this subsection and UPA Section 38(2)(b). (Footnote by NCCUSL).

The Section 601 dissociations giving rise to a reactive dissolution are: (6) a partner's bankruptcy or similar financial impairment; (7) a partner's death or incapacity; (8) the distribution by a trust-partner of its entire partnership interest; (9) the distribution by an estate-partner of its entire partnership interest; and (10) the termination of an entity-partner. Any dissociation during the term of the partnership that is wrongful under Section 602(b), including a partner's voluntary withdrawal, expulsion or bankruptcy, also gives rise to a reactive dissolution. Those statutory grounds may be varied by agreement or the reactive dissolution may be abolished entirely.

Under Section 601(6)(i), a partner is dissociated upon becoming a debtor in bankruptcy. The bankruptcy of a partner or of the partnership is not, however, an event of dissolution under Section 801. That is a change from UPA Section 31(5). A partner's bankruptcy does, however, cause dissolution of a term partnership under Section 801(2)(i), unless a majority in interest of the remaining partners thereafter agree to continue the partnership. Affording the other partners the option of buying out the bankrupt partner's interest avoids the necessity of winding up a term partnership every time a partner becomes a debtor in bankruptcy.

Similarly, under Section 801(2)(i), the death of any partner will result in the dissolution of a term partnership, only if at least half of the remaining partners express their will to wind up the partnership's business. If dissolution does occur, the deceased partner's transferable interest in the partnership passes to his estate and must be bought out under Article 7. See Comment 8 to Section 601.

(ii) Section 801(2)(ii) provides that a term partnership may be dissolved and wound up at any time by the express will of all the partners. That is merely an expression of the general rule that the partnership agreement may override the statutory default rules and that the partnership agreement, like any contract, can be amended at any time by unanimous consent.

UPA Section 31(1)(c) provides that a term partnership may be wound up by the express will of all the partners whose transferable interests have not been assigned or charged for a partner's separate debts. That rule reflects the belief that the remaining partners may find transferees very intrusive. This provision has been deleted, however, because the liquidation is easily accomplished under Section 801(2)(ii) by first expelling the transferor partner under Section 601(4)(ii).

(iii) Section 801(2)(iii) is based on UPA Section 31(1)(a) and provides for winding up a term partnership upon the expiration of the term or the completion of the undertaking.

Subsection (2)(iii) must be read in conjunction with Section 406. Under Section 406(a), if the partners continue the business after the expiration of the term or the completion of the undertaking, the partnership will be treated as a partnership at will. Moreover, if the partners continue the business without any settlement or liquidation of the partnership, under Section 406(b) they are presumed to have agreed that the partnership will continue, despite the lack of a formal agreement. The partners may also agree to ratify all acts taken since the end of the partnership's term.

6. Section 801(3) provides for dissolution upon the occurrence of an event specified in the partnership agreement as resulting in the winding up of the partnership business. The partners may, however, agree to continue the business and to ratify all acts taken since dissolution.

7. Section 801(4) continues the basic rule in UPA Section 31(3) and provides for dissolution if it is unlawful to continue the business of the partnership, unless cured. The "all or substantially all" proviso is intended to avoid dissolution for insubstantial or innocent regulatory violations. If the illegality is cured within 90 days after notice to the partnership, it is effective retroactively for purposes of this section. The requirement that an uncured illegal business be wound up cannot be varied in the partnership agreement. See Section 103(b)(8).

8. Section 801(5) provides for judicial dissolution on application by a partner. It is based in part on UPA Section 32(1), and the language comes in part from RULPA Section 802. A court may order a partnership dissolved upon a judicial determination that: (i) the economic purpose of the partnership is likely to be unreasonably frustrated; (ii) another partner has engaged in conduct relating to the partnership business which makes it not reasonably practicable to carry on the business in partnership with that partner; or (iii) it is not otherwise reasonably practicable to carry on the partnership business in conformity with the partnership agreement. The court's power to wind up the partnership under Section 801(5) cannot be varied in the partnership agreement. See Section 103(b)(8).

RUPA deletes UPA Section 32(1)(e) which provides for dissolution when the business can only be carried on at a loss. That provision might result in a dissolution contrary to the partners' expectations in a start-up or tax shelter situation, in which case "book" or "tax" losses do not signify business failure. Truly poor financial performance may justify dissolution under subsection (5)(i) as a frustration of the partnership's economic purpose.

RUPA also deletes UPA Section 32(1)(f) which authorizes a court to order dissolution of a partnership when "other circumstances render a dissolution equitable." That provision was regarded as too open-ended and, given RUPA's expanded remedies for partners, unnecessary. No significant change in result is intended, however, since the interpretation of UPA Section 32(1)(f) is comparable to the specific grounds expressed in subsection (5). *See, e.g., Karber v. Karber,* 145 Ariz. 293, 701 P.2d 1 (Ct.App.1985) (partnership dissolved on basis of suspicion and ill will, citing UPA §§ 32(1)(d) and (f)); *Fuller v. Brough,* 159 Colo. 147, 411 P.2d 18 (1966) (not equitable to dissolve partnership for trifling causes or temporary grievances that do not render it impracticable to carry on partnership business); *Lau v. Wong,* 1 Haw.App. 217, 616 P.2d 1031 (1980) (partnership dissolved where business operated solely for benefit of managing partner).

9. Section 801(6) provides for judicial dissolution on application by a transferee of a partner's transferable interest in the partnership, including the purchaser of a partner's interest upon foreclosure of a charging order. It is based on UPA Section 32(2) and authorizes dissolution upon a judicial determination that it is equitable to wind up the partnership business (i) after the expiration of the partnership term or completion of the undertaking or (ii) at any time, if the partnership were a partnership at will at the time of the transfer or when the charging order was issued. The requirement that the court determine that it is equitable to wind up the business is new. The rights of a transferee under this section cannot be varied in the partnership agreement. *See* Section 103(b)(8).

SECTION 802. PARTNERSHIP CONTINUES AFTER DISSOLUTION.

(a) Subject to subsection (b), a partnership continues after dissolution only for the purpose of winding up its business. The partnership is terminated when the winding up of its business is completed.

(b) At any time after the dissolution of a partnership and before the winding up of its business is completed, all of the partners, including any dissociating partner other than a wrongfully dissociating partner, may waive the right to have the partnership's business wound up and the partnership terminated. In that event:

(1) the partnership resumes carrying on its business as if dissolution had never occurred, and any liability incurred by the partnership or a partner after the dissolution and before the waiver is determined as if dissolution had never occurred; and

(2) the rights of a third party accruing under Section 804(1) or arising out of conduct in reliance on the dissolution before the third party knew or received a notification of the waiver may not be adversely affected.

Comment:

1.   Section 802(a) is derived from UPA Section 30 and provides that a partnership continues after dissolution only for the purpose of winding up its business, after which it is terminated. RUPA continues the concept of "termination" to mark the completion of the winding up process. Since no filing or other formality is required, the date will often be determined only by hindsight. No legal rights turn on the partnership's termination or the date thereof. Even after termination, if a previously unknown liability is asserted, all of the partners are still liable.

2.   Section 802(b) makes explicit the right of the remaining partners to continue the business after an event of dissolution if all of the partners, including the dissociating partner or partners, waive the right to have the business wound up and the partnership terminated. Only those "dissociating" partners whose dissociation was the immediate cause of the dissolution must waive the right to have the business wound up. The consent of wrongfully dissociating partners is not required.

3.   Upon waiver of the right to have the business wound up, paragraph (1) of the subsection provides that the partnership entity may resume carrying on its business as if dissolution had never occurred, thereby restoring the scope of its business to normal. "Resumes" is intended to mean that acts appropriate to winding up, authorized when taken, are in effect ratified, and the partnership remains liable for those acts, as provided explicitly in paragraph (2). . . .

SECTION 803. RIGHT TO WIND UP PARTNERSHIP BUSINESS.

(a) After dissolution, a partner who has not wrongfully dissociated may participate in winding up the partnership's business, but on application of any partner, partner's legal representative, or transferee, the [designate the appropriate court], for good cause shown, may order judicial supervision of the winding up.

(b) The legal representative of the last surviving partner may wind up a partnership's business.

(c) A person winding up a partnership's business may preserve the partnership business or property as a going concern for a reasonable time, prosecute and defend actions and proceedings, whether civil, criminal, or administrative, settle and close the partnership's business, dispose of and transfer the partnership's property, discharge the partnership's liabilities, distribute the assets of the partnership pursuant to Section 807, settle disputes by mediation or arbitration, and perform other necessary acts.

SECTION 804. PARTNER'S POWER TO BIND PARTNERSHIP AFTER DISSOLUTION.

Subject to Section 805, a partnership is bound by a partner's act after dissolution that:

(1) is appropriate for winding up the partnership business; or

(2) would have bound the partnership under Section 301 before dissolution, if the other party to the transaction did not have notice of the dissolution.

SECTION 805. STATEMENT OF DISSOLUTION.

(a) After dissolution, a partner who has not wrongfully dissociated may file a statement of dissolution stating the name of the partnership and that the partnership has dissolved and is winding up its business.

(b) A statement of dissolution cancels a filed statement of partnership authority for the purposes of Section 303(d) and is a limitation on authority for the purposes of Section 303(e).

(c) For the purposes of Sections 301 and 804, a person not a partner is deemed to have notice of the dissolution and the limitation on the partners' authority as a result of the statement of dissolution 90 days after it is filed.

(d) After filing and, if appropriate, recording a statement of dissolution, a dissolved partnership may file and, if appropriate, record a statement of partnership authority which will operate with respect to a person not a partner as provided in Section 303(d) and (e) in any transaction, whether or not the transaction is appropriate for winding up the partnership business.

Comment:

1. Section 805 is new. Subsection (a) provides that, after an event of dissolution, any partner who has not wrongfully dissociated may file a statement of dissolution on behalf of the partnership. The filing and recording of a statement of dissolution is optional. The execution, filing, and recording of the statement is governed by Section 105. The legal consequences of filing a statement of dissolution are similar to those of a statement of dissociation under Section 704....

SECTION 806. PARTNER'S LIABILITY TO OTHER PARTNERS AFTER DISSOLUTION.

(a) Except as otherwise provided in subsection (b) and Section 306, after dissolution a partner is liable to the other partners for the partner's share of any partnership liability incurred under Section 804.

(b) A partner who, with knowledge of the dissolution, incurs a partnership liability under Section 804(2) by an act that is not appropriate for winding up the partnership business is liable to the partnership for any damage caused to the partnership arising from the liability.

Comment: ...

Subsection (a) provides that, except as provided in Section 306(a) and subsection (b), after dissolution each partner is liable to the other partners by way of contribution for his share of any partnership liability incurred under Section 804. That includes not only obligations that are appropriate for winding up the business, but also obligations that are inappropriate if within the partner's apparent authority. Consistent with other provisions of this Act, Section 806(a) makes clear that a partner does not have a contribution obligation with regard to limited liability partnership obligations for which the partner is not liable under Section 306. See Comments to Section 401(b). ...

Section 806 is merely a default rule and may be varied in the partnership agreement. See Section 103(a).

SECTION 807. SETTLEMENT OF ACCOUNTS AND CONTRIBUTIONS AMONG PARTNERS.

(a) In winding up a partnership's business, the assets of the partnership, including the contributions of the partners required by this section, must be applied to discharge its obligations to creditors, including, to the extent permitted by law, partners who are creditors. Any surplus must be applied to pay in cash the net amount distributable to partners in accordance with their right to distributions under subsection (b).

(b) Each partner is entitled to a settlement of all partnership accounts upon winding up the partnership business. In settling accounts among the partners, the profits and losses that result from the liquidation of the partnership assets must be credited and charged to the partners' accounts. The partnership shall make a distribution to a partner in an amount equal to any excess of the credits over the charges in the partner's account. A partner shall contribute to the partnership an amount equal to any excess of the charges over the credits in the partner's account but excluding from the calculation charges attributable to an obligation for which the partner is not personally liable under Section 306.

(c) If a partner fails to contribute the full amount required under subsection (b), all of the other partners shall contribute, in the proportions in which those partners share partnership losses, the additional amount necessary to satisfy the partnership obligations for which they are personally liable under Section 306. A partner or partner's legal representative may recover from the other partners any contributions the partner makes to the extent the amount contributed exceeds that partner's share of the partnership obligations for which the partner is personally liable under Section 306.

(d) After the settlement of accounts, each partner shall contribute, in the proportion in which the partner shares partnership losses, the amount necessary to satisfy partnership obligations that were not known at the time of the settlement and for which the partner is personally liable under Section 306.

(e) The estate of a deceased partner is liable for the partner's obligation to contribute to the partnership.

(f) An assignee for the benefit of creditors of a partnership or a partner, or a person appointed by a court to represent creditors of a partnership or a partner, may enforce a partner's obligation to contribute to the partnership.

Comment:

1. Section 807 provides the default rules for the settlement of accounts and contributions among the partners in winding up the business. It is derived in part from UPA Sections 38(1) and 40.

2. Subsection (a) continues the rule in UPA Section 38(1) that, in winding up the business, the partnership assets must first be applied to discharge partnership liabilities to creditors. For this purpose, any required contribution by the partners is treated as an asset of the partnership. After the payment of all partnership liabilities, any surplus must be applied to pay in cash the net amount due the partners under subsection (b) by way of a liquidating distribution.

RUPA continues the "in-cash" rule of UPA Section 38(1) and is consistent with Section 402, which provides that a partner has no right to receive, and may not be required to accept, a distribution in kind, unless otherwise agreed. The in-cash rule avoids the valuation problems that afflict unwanted in-kind distributions.

The partnership must apply its assets to discharge the obligations of partners who are creditors on a parity with other creditors. See Section 404(f).... In effect, that abolishes the priority rules in UPA Section 40(b) and (c) which subordinate the payment of inside debt to outside debt. Both RULPA and the RMBCA do likewise. See RULPA § 804; RMBCA §§ 6.40(f), 14.05(a). Ultimately, however, a partner whose "debt" has been repaid by the partnership is personally liable, as a partner, for any outside debt remaining unsatisfied, unlike a limited partner or corporate shareholder. Accordingly, the obligation to contribute sufficient funds to satisfy the claims of outside creditors may result in the equitable subordination of inside debt when partnership assets are insufficient to satisfy all obligations to non-partners.

RUPA in effect abolishes the "dual priority" or "jingle" rule of UPA Section 40(h) and (i). Those sections gave partnership creditors priority as to partnership property and separate creditors priority as to separate property. The jingle rule has already been preempted by the Bankruptcy Code, at least as to Chapter 7 partnership liquidation proceedings. Under Section 723(c) of the Bankruptcy Code, and under RUPA, partnership creditors share pro rata with the partners' individual creditors in the assets of the partners' estates.

3. Subsection (b) provides that each partner is entitled to a settlement of all partnership accounts upon winding up. It also establishes the default rules for closing out the partners' accounts. First, the profits and losses resulting from the liquidation of the partnership assets must be credited or charged to the partners' accounts, according to their respective shares of profits and losses. Then, the partnership must make a final liquidating distribution to those partners with a positive account balance. That distribution should be in the amount of the excess of credits over the charges in the account. Any partner with a negative account balance must contribute to the partnership an amount equal to the excess of charges over the credits in the account provided the excess relates to an obligation for which the partner is personally liable under Section 306. The partners may, however, agree that a negative account does not reflect a debt to the partnership and need not be repaid in settling the partners' accounts.

Section 807(b) makes clear that a partner's contribution obligation to a partnership in dissolution only considers the partner's share of obligations for which the partner was personally liable under Section 306 ("unshielded obligations"). See Comments to Section 401(b) (partner contribution obligation to an operating partnership). Properly determined under this Section, the total required partner contributions will be sufficient to satisfy the partnership's total unshielded obligations. In special circumstances where a partnership has both shielded and unshielded obligations and the [partners] required contributions are used to first pay shielded partnership obligations, the partners may be required to make further contributions to satisfy the partnership unpaid unshielded obligations. The proper resolution of this matter is left to debtor-creditor law as well as the law governing the fiduciary obligations of the partners. See Section 104(a).

RUPA eliminates the distinction in UPA Section 40(b) between the liability owing to a partner in respect of capital and the liability owing in respect of profits. Section 807(b) speaks simply of the right of a partner to a liquidating distribution. That implements the logic of RUPA Sections 401(a) and 502 under which contributions to capital and shares in profits and losses combine to determine the right to distributions. The partners may, however, agree to share "operating" losses differently from "capital" losses, thereby continuing the UPA distinction.

4. Subsection (c) continues the UPA Section 40(d) rule that solvent partners share proportionately in the shortfall caused by insolvent partners who fail to contribute their proportionate share. The partnership may enforce a partner's obligation to contribute. See Section 405(a). A partner is entitled to recover from the other partners any contributions in excess of that partner's share of the partnership's liabilities. See Section 405(b)(iii).

5. Subsection (d) provides that, after settling the partners' accounts, each partner must contribute, in the proportion in which he shares losses, the amount necessary to satisfy partnership obligations that were not known at the time of the settlement. That continues the basic rule of UPA Section 40(d) and underscores that the obligation to contribute exists independently of the partnership's books of account. It specifically covers the situation of a partnership liability that was unknown when the partnership books were closed. . . .

ARTICLE 9

CONVERSIONS AND MERGERS

SECTION 901. DEFINITIONS.

In this [article]:

(1) "General partner" means a partner in a partnership and a general partner in a limited partnership.

(2) "Limited partner" means a limited partner in a limited partnership.

(3) "Limited partnership" means a limited partnership created under the [State Limited Partnership Act], predecessor law, or comparable law of another jurisdiction.

(4) "Partner" includes both a general partner and a limited partner.

Comment: ...

2. As Section 908 makes clear, the requirements of Article 9 are not mandatory, and a partnership may convert or merge in any other manner provided by law. Article 9 is merely a "safe harbor." If the requirements of the article are followed, the conversion or merger is legally valid. Since most States have no other established procedure for the conversion or merger of partnerships, it is likely that the Article 9 procedures will be used in virtually all cases....

SECTION 902. CONVERSION OF PARTNERSHIP TO LIMITED PARTNERSHIP.

(a) A partnership may be converted to a limited partnership pursuant to this section.

(b) The terms and conditions of a conversion of a partnership to a limited partnership must be approved by all of the partners or by a number or percentage specified for conversion in the partnership agreement.

(c) After the conversion is approved by the partners, the partnership shall file a certificate of limited partnership in the jurisdiction in which the limited partnership is to be formed. The certificate must include:

(1) a statement that the partnership was converted to a limited partnership from a partnership;

(2) its former name; and

(3) a statement of the number of votes cast by the partners for and against the conversion and, if the vote is less than unanimous, the number or percentage required to approve the conversion under the partnership agreement.

(d) The conversion takes effect when the certificate of limited partnership is filed or at any later date specified in the certificate.

(e) A general partner who becomes a limited partner as a result of the conversion remains liable as a general partner for an obligation incurred by the partnership before the conversion takes effect. If the other party to a transaction with the limited partnership reasonably believes when entering the transaction that the limited partner is a general partner, the limited partner is liable for an obligation incurred by the limited partnership within 90 days after the conversion takes effect. The limited partner's liability for all other obligations of the limited partnership incurred after the conversion takes effect is that of a limited partner as provided in the [State Limited Partnership Act].

SECTION 903. CONVERSION OF LIMITED PARTNERSHIP TO PARTNERSHIP.

(a) A limited partnership may be converted to a partnership pursuant to this section.

(b) Notwithstanding a provision to the contrary in a limited partnership agreement, the terms and conditions of a conversion of a limited partnership to a partnership must be approved by all of the partners.

(c) After the conversion is approved by the partners, the limited partnership shall cancel its certificate of limited partnership.

(d) The conversion takes effect when the certificate of limited partnership is canceled.

(e) A limited partner who becomes a general partner as a result of the conversion remains liable only as a limited partner for an obligation incurred by the limited partnership before the conversion takes effect. Except as otherwise provided in Section 306, the partner is liable as a general partner for an obligation of the partnership incurred after the conversion takes effect.

SECTION 904. EFFECT OF CONVERSION; ENTITY UNCHANGED.

(a) A partnership or limited partnership that has been converted pursuant to this [article] is for all purposes the same entity that existed before the conversion.

(b) When a conversion takes effect:

(1) all property owned by the converting partnership or limited partnership remains vested in the converted entity;

(2) all obligations of the converting partnership or limited partnership continue as obligations of the converted entity; and

(3) an action or proceeding pending against the converting partnership or limited partnership may be continued as if the conversion had not occurred.

SECTION 905. MERGER OF PARTNERSHIPS.

(a) Pursuant to a plan of merger approved as provided in subsection (c), a partnership may be merged with one or more partnerships or limited partnerships.

(b) The plan of merger must set forth:

(1) the name of each partnership or limited partnership that is a party to the merger;

(2) the name of the surviving entity into which the other partnerships or limited partnerships will merge;

(3) whether the surviving entity is a partnership or a limited partnership and the status of each partner;

(4) the terms and conditions of the merger;

(5) the manner and basis of converting the interests of each party to the merger into interests or obligations of the surviving entity, or into money or other property in whole or part; and

(6) the street address of the surviving entity's chief executive office.

(c) The plan of merger must be approved:

(1) in the case of a partnership that is a party to the merger, by all of the partners, or a number or percentage specified for merger in the partnership agreement; and

(2) in the case of a limited partnership that is a party to the merger, by the vote required for approval of a merger by the law of the State or foreign jurisdiction in which the limited partnership is organized and, in the absence of such a specifically applicable law, by all of the partners, notwithstanding a provision to the contrary in the partnership agreement.

(d) After a plan of merger is approved and before the merger takes effect, the plan may be amended or abandoned as provided in the plan.

(e) The merger takes effect on the later of:

(1) the approval of the plan of merger by all parties to the merger, as provided in subsection (c);

(2) the filing of all documents required by law to be filed as a condition to the effectiveness of the merger; or

(3) any effective date specified in the plan of merger.

Comment:

Section 905 provides a "safe harbor" for the merger of a general partnership and one or more general or limited partnerships. The surviving entity may be either a general or a limited partnership. . . .

SECTION 906. EFFECT OF MERGER.

(a) When a merger takes effect:

(1) the separate existence of every partnership or limited partnership that is a party to the merger, other than the surviving entity, ceases;

(2) all property owned by each of the merged partnerships or limited partnerships vests in the surviving entity;

(3) all obligations of every partnership or limited partnership that is a party to the merger become the obligations of the surviving entity; and

(4) an action or proceeding pending against a partnership or limited partnership that is a party to the merger may be continued

as if the merger had not occurred, or the surviving entity may be substituted as a party to the action or proceeding.

(b) The [Secretary of State] of this State is the agent for service of process in an action or proceeding against a surviving foreign partnership or limited partnership to enforce an obligation of a domestic partnership or limited partnership that is a party to a merger. The surviving entity shall promptly notify the [Secretary of State] of the mailing address of its chief executive office and of any change of address. Upon receipt of process, the [Secretary of State] shall mail a copy of the process to the surviving foreign partnership or limited partnership.

(c) A partner of the surviving partnership or limited partnership is liable for:

(1) all obligations of a party to the merger for which the partner was personally liable before the merger;

(2) all other obligations of the surviving entity incurred before the merger by a party to the merger, but those obligations may be satisfied only out of property of the entity; and

(3) except as otherwise provided in Section 306, all obligations of the surviving entity incurred after the merger takes effect, but those obligations may be satisfied only out of property of the entity if the partner is a limited partner.

(d) If the obligations incurred before the merger by a party to the merger are not satisfied out of the property of the surviving partnership or limited partnership, the general partners of that party immediately before the effective date of the merger shall contribute the amount necessary to satisfy that party's obligations to the surviving entity, in the manner provided in Section 807 or in the [Limited Partnership Act] of the jurisdiction in which the party was formed, as the case may be, as if the merged party were dissolved.

(e) A partner of a party to a merger who does not become a partner of the surviving partnership or limited partnership is dissociated from the entity, of which that partner was a partner, as of the date the merger takes effect. The surviving entity shall cause the partner's interest in the entity to be purchased under Section 701 or another statute specifically applicable to that partner's interest with respect to a merger. The surviving entity is bound under Section 702 by an act of a general partner dissociated under this subsection, and the partner is liable under Section 703 for transactions entered into by the surviving entity after the merger takes effect.

SECTION 907.   STATEMENT OF MERGER.

(a) After a merger, the surviving partnership or limited partnership may file a statement that one or more partnerships or limited partnerships have merged into the surviving entity.

(b) A statement of merger must contain:

(1) the name of each partnership or limited partnership that is a party to the merger;

(2) the name of the surviving entity into which the other partnerships or limited partnership were merged;

(3) the street address of the surviving entity's chief executive office and of an office in this State, if any; and

(4) whether the surviving entity is a partnership or a limited partnership.

(c) Except as otherwise provided in subsection (d), for the purposes of Section 302, property of the surviving partnership or limited partnership which before the merger was held in the name of another party to the merger is property held in the name of the surviving entity upon filing a statement of merger.

(d) For the purposes of Section 302, real property of the surviving partnership or limited partnership which before the merger was held in the name of another party to the merger is property held in the name of the surviving entity upon recording a certified copy of the statement of merger in the office for recording transfers of that real property.

(e) A filed and, if appropriate, recorded statement of merger, executed and declared to be accurate pursuant to Section 105(c), stating the name of a partnership or limited partnership that is a party to the merger in whose name property was held before the merger and the name of the surviving entity, but not containing all of the other information required by subsection (b), operates with respect to the partnerships or limited partnerships named to the extent provided in subsections (c) and (d).

SECTION 908.   NONEXCLUSIVE.

This [article] is not exclusive. Partnerships or limited partnerships may be converted or merged in any other manner provided by law.

[ARTICLE] 10

LIMITED LIABILITY PARTNERSHIP

Sec.
1001.   Statement of Qualification.
1002.   Name.
1003.   Annual Report.

SECTION 1001.   STATEMENT OF QUALIFICATION.

(a) A partnership may become a limited liability partnership pursuant to this section.

(b) The terms and conditions on which a partnership becomes a limited liability partnership must be approved by the vote necessary to amend the partnership agreement except, in the case of a partnership agreement that expressly considers contribution obligations, the vote necessary to amend those provisions.

(c) After the approval required by subsection (b), a partnership may become a limited liability partnership by filing a statement of qualification. The statement must contain:

(1) the name of the partnership;

(2) the street address of the partnership's chief executive office and, if different, the street address of an office in this State, if any;

(3) if there is no office in this State, the name and street address of the partnership's agent for service of process who must be an individual resident of this State or any other person authorized to do business in this State;

(4) a statement that the partnership elects to be a limited liability partnership; and

(5) a deferred effective date, if any.

(d) The status of a partnership as a limited liability partnership is effective on the later of the filing of the statement or a date specified in the statement. The status remains effective, regardless of changes in the partnership, until it is canceled pursuant to Section 105(d) or revoked pursuant to Section 1003.

(e) The status of a partnership as a limited liability partnership and the liability of its partners is not affected by errors or later changes in the information required to be contained in the statement of qualification under subsection (c).

(f) The filing of a statement of qualification establishes that a partnership has satisfied all conditions precedent to the qualification of the partnership as a limited liability partnership.

(g) An amendment or cancellation of a statement of qualification is effective when it is filed or on a deferred effective date specified in the amendment or cancellation.

Comment:

Any partnership may become a limited liability partnership by filing a statement of qualification. See Comments to Sections 101(6) and 202(b) regarding a limited partnership filing a statement of qualification to become a limited liability limited partnership. Section 1001 sets forth the required contents of a statement of qualification. The section also sets forth requirements for the approval of a statement of qualification, establishes the effective date of the filing (and any amendments) which remains effective until canceled or revoked, and provides that the liability of the partners of a limited liability partnership is not affected by errors or later changes in the statement information.

Subsection (b) provides that the terms and conditions on which a partnership becomes a limited liability partnership must ... generally be approved by the vote necessary to amend the partnership agreement. This means that the act of becoming a limited liability partnership is equivalent to an amendment of the partnership agreement. Where the partnership agreement is silent as to how it may be amended, the subsection (b) vote requires the approval of every partner. Since the limited liability partnership rules are not intended to increase the vote necessary to amend the partnership agreement, where the partnership agreement specifically sets forth an amendment process, that process may be used. Where a partnership agreement sets forth several amendment procedures depending upon the nature of the amendment, the required vote will be that necessary to amend the contribution obligations of the partners. The specific "contribution" vote is preferred because the filing of the statement directly affects partner contribution obligations. Therefore, the language "considers contribution" should be broadly interpreted to include any amendment vote that indirectly affects any partner's contribution obligation such as a partner's obligation to "indemnify" other partners.

The unanimous vote default rule reflects the significance of a partnership becoming a limited liability partnership. In general, upon such a filing each partner is released from the personal contribution obligation imposed under this Act in exchange for relinquishing the right to enforce the contribution obligations of other partners under this Act. See Comments to Sections 306(c) and 401(b). The wisdom of this bargain will depend on many factors including the relative risks of the partners' duties and the assets of the partnership.

Subsection (c) sets forth the information required in a statement of qualification. The [information] must include the name of the partnership which must comply with Section 1002 to identify the partnership as a limited liability partnership. The statement must also include the address of the partnership's chief executive office and, if different, the street address of any other office in this State. A statement must include the name and street address of an agent for service of process only if it does not have any office in this State.

As with other statements, a statement of qualification must be filed in the office of the Secretary of State. See Sections 101(13) and 105(a). Accordingly, a statement of qualification is executed, filed, and otherwise regarded as a statement under this Act. For example, a copy of a filed statement must be sent to every nonfiling partner unless otherwise provided in the partnership agreement. See Sections 105(e) and 103(b)(1). A statement of qualification must be executed by at least two partners under penalties of perjury that the contents of the statement are accurate. See Section 105(c). A person who files the statement must promptly send a copy of the statement to every nonfiling partner but failure to send the copy does not limit the effectiveness of the filed statement to a nonpartner. Section 105(e). The filing must be accompanied by the fee required by the Secretary of State. Section 105(f).

Subsection (d) makes clear that once a statement is filed and effective, the status of the partnership as a limited liability partnership remains effective until the partnership status is either canceled or revoked "regardless of changes in the partnership." Accordingly, a partnership that dissolves but whose business is continued under a business continuation agreement retains its status as a limited liability partnership without the need to refile a new statement. Also, limited liability partnership status remains even though a partnership may be dissolved, wound up, and terminated. Even after the termination of the partnership, the former partners of a terminated partnership would not be personally liable for partnership obligations incurred while the partnership was a limited liability partnership.

Subsection (d) also makes clear that limited liability partnership status remains effective until actual cancellation under Section 1003 or revocation under Section 105(d). Ordinarily the terms and conditions of becoming a limited liability partnership must be approved by the vote necessary to amend the partnership agreement. See Sections 1001(b), 306(c), and 401(j). Since the statement of cancellation may be filed by a person authorized to file the original statement of qualification, the same vote necessary to approve the filing of the statement of qualification must be obtained to file the statement of cancellation. See Section 105(d).

Subsection (f) provides that once a statement of qualification is executed and filed under subsection (c) and Section 105, the partnership assumes the status of a limited liability partnership. This status is intended to be conclusive with regard to third parties dealing with the partnership. It is not intended to affect the rights of partners. For example, a properly executed and filed statement of qualification conclusively establishes the limited liability shield described in Section 306(c). If the partners executing and filing the statement exceed their authority, the internal abuse of authority has no effect on the liability shield with regard to third parties. Partners may challenge the abuse of authority for purposes of establishing the liability of the culpable partners but may not effect the liability shield as to third parties. Likewise, third parties may not challenge the existence of the liability shield because the decision to file the statement lacked the proper vote. As a result, the filing of the statement creates the liability shield even when the required subsection (b) vote is not obtained.

SECTION 1002.   NAME.

The name of a limited liability partnership must end with "Registered Limited Liability Partnership", "Limited Liability Partnership", "R.L.L.P.", "L.L.P.", "RLLP," or "LLP".

Comment:

The name provisions are intended to alert persons dealing with a limited liability partnership of the presence of the liability shield. Because many jurisdictions have adopted the naming concept of a "registered" limited liability partnership, this aspect has been retained. These name requirements also distinguish limited partnerships and general partnerships that become limited liability partnerships because the new name must be at the end of and in addition to the general or limited partnership's regular name. See Comments to Section 101(6). Since the name identification rules of this section do not alter the regular name of the partnership, they do not disturb historic notions of apparent authority of partners in both general and limited partnerships.

SECTION 1003.   ANNUAL REPORT.

(a) A limited liability partnership, and a foreign limited liability partnership authorized to transact business in this State, shall file an annual report in the office of the [Secretary of State] which contains:

(1) the name of the limited liability partnership and the State or other jurisdiction under whose laws the foreign limited liability partnership is formed;

(2) the current street address of the partnership's chief executive office and, if different, the current street address of an office in this State, if any; and

(3) if there is no current office in this State, the name and street address of the partnership's current agent for service of process who must be an individual resident of this State or any other person authorized to do business in this State.

(b) An annual report must be filed between [January 1 and April 1] of each year following the calendar year in which a partnership files a statement of qualification or a foreign partnership becomes authorized to transact business in this State.

(c) The [Secretary of State] may administratively revoke the statement of qualification of a partnership that fails to file an annual report when due or to pay the required filing fee. The [Secretary of State] shall provide the partnership at least 60 days' written notice of intent to revoke the statement. The notice must be mailed to the partnership at its chief executive office set forth in the last filed statement of qualification or annual report. The notice must specify the annual report that has not been filed, the fee that has not been paid, and the effective date of the revocation. The revocation is not effective if the annual report is filed and the fee is paid before the effective date of the revocation.

(d) A revocation under subsection (c) only affects a partnership's status as a limited liability partnership and is not an event of dissolution of the partnership.

(e) A partnership whose statement of qualification has been administratively revoked may apply to the [Secretary of State] for reinstatement within two years after the effective date of the revocation. The application must state:

(1) the name of the partnership and the effective date of the revocation; and

(2) that the ground for revocation either did not exist or has been corrected.

(f) A reinstatement under subsection (e) relates back to and takes effect as of the effective date of the revocation, and the partnership's status as a limited liability partnership continues as if the revocation had never occurred.

Comment:

Section 1003 sets forth the requirements of an annual report that must be filed by all limited liability partnerships and any foreign limited liability partnership authorized to transact business in this State. See Sections 101(5) (definition of a limited liability partnership) and 101(4) (definition of a foreign limited liability partnership). The failure of a limited liability partnership to file an annual report is a basis for the Secretary of State to administratively revoke its statement of qualification. See Section 1003(c). A foreign limited liability partnership that fails to file an annual report may not maintain an action or proceeding in this State. See Section 1103(a).

Subsection (a) generally requires that an annual report contain the same information required in a statement of qualification. Compare Sections 1001(a) and 1003(a). The differences are that the annual report requires disclosure of the state of formation of a foreign limited liability partnership but deletes the delayed effective date and limited liability partnership election statement provisions of a statement of qualification. As such, the annual report serves to update the information required in a statement of qualification. Under subsection (b), the annual report must be filed between January 1 and April 1 of each calendar year following the year in which a statement of qualification was filed or a foreign limited liability partnership becomes authorized to transact business. This timing requirement means that a limited liability partnership must make an annual filing and may not prefile multiple annual reports in a single year.

Subsection (c) sets forth the procedure for the Secretary of State to administratively revoke a partnership's statement of qualification for the failure to file an annual report when due or pay the required filing fee. The Secretary of State must provide a partnership at least 60 days' written notice of the intent to revoke the statement. The notice must be mailed to the partnership at the address of its chief executive office set forth in the last filed statement or annual report and must state the grounds for revocation as well as the effective date of revocation. The revocation is not effective if the stated problem is cured before the stated effective date.

Under subsection (d), a revocation only terminates the partnership's status as a limited liability partnership but is not an event of dissolution of the partnership itself. Where revocation occurs, a partnership may apply for reinstatement under subsection (e) within two years after the effective date of the revocation. The application must state that the grounds for revocation either did not exist or have been corrected. The Secretary of State may grant the application on the basis of the statements alone or require proof of correction. Under subsection (f), when the application is granted, the reinstatement relates back to and takes effect as of the effective date of the revocation. The relation back doctrine prevents gaps in a reinstated partnership's liability shield. See Comments to Section 306(c).

[ARTICLE] 11

FOREIGN LIMITED LIABILITY PARTNERSHIP

Sec.
1101. Law Governing Foreign Limited Liability Partnership.
1102. Statement of Foreign Qualification.
1103. Effect of Failure to Qualify.
1104. Activities Not Constituting Transacting Business.
1105. Action By [Attorney General].

SECTION 1101. LAW GOVERNING FOREIGN LIMITED LIABILITY PARTNERSHIP.

(a) The laws under which a foreign limited liability partnership is formed govern relations among the partners and between the partners and the partnership and the liability of partners for obligations of the partnership.

(b) A foreign limited liability partnership may not be denied a statement of foreign qualification by reason of any difference between the laws under which the partnership was formed and the laws of this State.

(c) A statement of foreign qualification does not authorize a foreign limited liability partnership to engage in any business or exercise any power that a partnership may not engage in or exercise in this State as a limited liability partnership.

Comment:

Section 1101 provides that the laws where a foreign limited liability partnership is formed rather than the laws of this State govern both the internal relations of the partnership and liability of its partners for the obligations of the partnership. See Section 101(4) (definition of a foreign limited liability partnership). Section 106(b) provides that the laws of this State govern the internal relations of a domestic limited liability and the liability of its partners for the obligations of the partnership. See Sections 101(5) (definition of a domestic limited liability partnership). A partnership may therefore choose the laws of a particular jurisdiction by filing a statement of qualification in that jurisdiction. But there are limitations on this choice.

Subsections (b) and (c) together make clear that although a foreign limited liability partnership may not be denied a statement of foreign qualification simply because of a difference between the laws of its foreign jurisdiction and the laws of this State, it may not engage in any business or exercise any power in this State that a domestic limited liability partnership may not engage in or exercise. Under subsection (c), a foreign limited liability partnership that engages in a business or exercises a power in this State that a domestic may not engage in or exercise, does so only as an ordinary partnership without the benefit of the limited liability partnership liability shield set forth in Section 306(c). In this sense, a foreign limited liability partnership is treated the same as a domestic limited liability partnership. Also, the Attorney General may maintain an action to restrain a foreign limited liability partnership from transacting an unauthorized business in this State. See Section 1105.

SECTION 1102. STATEMENT OF FOREIGN QUALIFICATION.

(a) Before transacting business in this State, a foreign limited liability partnership must file a statement of foreign qualification. The statement must contain:

(1) the name of the foreign limited liability partnership which satisfies the requirements of the State or other jurisdiction under whose laws it is formed and ends with "Registered Limited Liability

Partnership", "Limited Liability Partnership", "R.L.L.P.", "L.L.P.", "RLLP," or "LLP";

(2) the street address of the partnership's chief executive office and, if different, the street address of an office in this State, if any;

(3) if there is no office in this State, the name and street address of the partnership's agent for service of process who must be an individual resident of this State or any other person authorized to do business in this State; and

(4) a deferred effective date, if any.

(b) The status of a partnership as a foreign limited liability partnership is effective on the later of the filing of the statement of foreign qualification or a date specified in the statement. The status remains effective, regardless of changes in the partnership, until it is canceled pursuant to Section 105(d) or revoked pursuant to Section 1003.

(c) An amendment or cancellation of a statement of foreign qualification is effective when it is filed or on a deferred effective date specified in the amendment or cancellation.

Comment:

Section 1102 provides that a foreign limited liability partnership must file a statement of foreign qualification before transacting business in this State. The section also sets forth the information required in the statement. As with other statements, a statement of foreign qualification must be filed in the office of the Secretary of State. See Sections 101(13), 105(a), and 1001(c). Accordingly, a statement of foreign qualification is executed, filed, and otherwise regarded as a statement under this Act. See Section 101(13) (definition of a statement includes a statement of foreign qualification).

Subsection (a) generally requires the same information in a statement of foreign qualification as is required in a statement of qualification. Compare Sections 1001(c). The statement of foreign qualification must include a name that complies with the requirements for domestic limited liability partnership under Section 1002 and must include the address of the partnership's chief executive office and, if different, the street address of any other office in this State. If a foreign limited liability partnership does not have any office in this State, the statement of foreign qualification must include the name and street address of an agent for service of process.

As with a statement of qualification, a statement of foreign qualification (and amendments) is effective when filed or at a later specified filing date. Compare Sections 1102(b) and (c) with Sections 1001(e) and (h). Likewise, a statement of foreign qualification remains effective until canceled by the partnership or revoked by the Secretary of State, regardless of changes in the partnership. See Sections 105(d) (statement cancellation) and Section 1003 (revocation for failure to file annual report or pay annual filing fee) and compare Sections 1102(b) and 1001(e). Statement of qualification provisions regarding the relationship of the status of a foreign partnership relative to its initial filing of a statement are governed by foreign law and are therefore omitted from this section. See Sections 1001(f) (effect of errors and omissions) and (g) (filing establishes all conditions precedent to qualification).

SECTION 1103. EFFECT OF FAILURE TO QUALIFY.

(a) A foreign limited liability partnership transacting business in this State may not maintain an action or proceeding in this State unless it has in effect a statement of foreign qualification.

(b) The failure of a foreign limited liability partnership to have in effect a statement of foreign qualification does not impair the validity of a contract or act of the foreign limited liability partnership or preclude it from defending an action or proceeding in this State.

(c) Limitations on personal liability of partners are not waived solely by transacting business in this State without a statement of foreign qualification.

(d) If a foreign limited liability partnership transacts business in this State without a statement of foreign qualification, the [Secretary of State] is its agent for service of process with respect to [claims for relief] arising out of the transaction of business in this State.

Comment:

Section 1103 makes clear that the only consequence of a failure to file a statement of foreign qualification is that the foreign limited liability partnership will not be able to maintain an action or proceeding in this State. The partnership's contracts remain valid, it may defend an action or proceeding, personal liability of the partners is not waived, and the Secretary of State is the agent for service of process with respect to claims arising out of transacting business in this State. Sections 1103(b)–(d). Once a statement of foreign qualification is filed, the Secretary of State may revoke the statement for failure to file an annual report but the partnership has the right to cure the failure for two years. See Section 1003(c) and (e). Since the failure to file a statement of foreign qualification has no impact on the liability shield of the partners, a revocation of a statement of foreign qualification also has no impact on the liability shield created under foreign laws. Compare Sections 1103(c) and 1003(f) (revocation of the statement of qualification of a domestic limited liability partnership removes partner liability shield unless filing problems cured within two years).

SECTION 1104. ACTIVITIES NOT CONSTITUTING TRANSACTING BUSINESS.

(a) Activities of a foreign limited liability partnership which do not constitute transacting business within the meaning of this [article] include:

(1) maintaining, defending, or settling an action or proceeding;

(2) holding meetings of its partners or carrying on any other activity concerning its internal affairs;

(3) maintaining bank accounts;

(4) maintaining offices or agencies for the transfer, exchange, and registration of the partnership's own securities or maintaining trustees or depositories with respect to those securities;

(5) selling through independent contractors;

(6) soliciting or obtaining orders, whether by mail or through employees or agents or otherwise, if the orders require acceptance outside this State before they become contracts;

(7) creating or acquiring indebtedness, mortgages, or security interests in real or personal property;

(8) securing or collecting debts or foreclosing mortgages or other security interests in property securing the debts, and holding, protecting, and maintaining property so acquired;

(9) conducting an isolated transaction that is completed within 30 days and is not one in the course of similar transactions of like nature; and

(10) transacting business in interstate commerce.

(b) For purposes of this [article], the ownership in this State of income-producing real property or tangible personal property, other than property excluded under subsection (a), constitutes transacting business in this State.

(c) This section does not apply in determining the contacts or activities that may subject a foreign limited liability partnership to service of process, taxation, or regulation under any other law of this State.

Comment:

Because the Attorney General may restrain a foreign limited liability partnership from transacting an unauthorized business in this State and a foreign partnership may not maintain an action or proceeding in this State, the concept of "transacting business" in this State is important. To provide more certainty, subsection (a) sets forth ten separate categories of activities that do not constitute transacting business. Subsection (c) makes clear that the section only considers the definition of "transacting business" and as no impact on whether a foreign limited liability partnership's activities in this State subject it to service of process, taxation, or regulation under any other law of this State.

SECTION 1105. ACTION BY [ATTORNEY GENERAL].

The [Attorney General] may maintain an action to restrain a foreign limited liability partnership from transacting business in this State in violation of this [article].

Comment:

Section 1105 makes clear that the Attorney General may restrain a foreign limited liability from transacting an unauthorized business in this State. As a threshold matter, a foreign limited liability partnership must be "transacting business" in this State within the meaning of Section 1104. Secondly, the business transacted in this State must be that which could not be engaged in by a domestic limited liability partnership. See Section 1101(c). The fact that a foreign limited liability partnership has a statement of foreign qualification does not permit it to engage in any unauthorized business in this State or impair the power of the Attorney General to restrain the foreign partnership from engaging in the unauthorized business. See Section 1101(c).

ARTICLE 12

MISCELLANEOUS PROVISIONS

SECTION 1201. UNIFORMITY OF APPLICATION AND CONSTRUCTION.

This [Act] shall be applied and construed to effectuate its general purpose to make uniform the law with respect to the subject of this [Act] among States enacting it.

SECTION 1202. SHORT TITLE.

This [Act] may be cited as the Uniform Partnership Act (1994).

SECTION 1203.   SEVERABILITY CLAUSE.

If any provision of this [Act] or its application to any person or circumstance is held invalid, the invalidity does not affect other provisions or applications of this [Act] which can be given effect without the invalid provision or application, and to this end the provisions of this [Act] are severable.

SECTION 1204.   EFFECTIVE DATE.

This [Act] takes effect _____.

SECTION 1205.   REPEALS.

Effective January 1, 199__, the following acts and parts of acts are repealed: [the State Partnership Act as amended and in effect immediately before the effective date of this Act].

SECTION 1206.   APPLICABILITY.

(a) Before January 1, 199__, this [Act] governs only a partnership formed:

(1) after the effective date of this [Act], unless that partnership is continuing the business of a dissolved partnership under [Section 41 of the prior Uniform Partnership Act]; and

(2) before the effective date of this [Act], that elects, as provided by subsection (c), to be governed by this [Act].

(b) After January 1, 199__, this [Act] governs all partnerships.

(c) Before January 1, 199__, a partnership voluntarily may elect, in the manner provided in its partnership agreement or by law for amending the partnership agreement, to be governed by this [Act]. The provisions of this [Act] relating to the liability of the partnership's partners to third parties apply to limit those partners' liability to a third party who had done business with the partnership within one year preceding the partnership's election to be governed by this [Act], only if the third party knows or has received a notification of the partnership's election to be governed by this [Act].

SECTION 1207.   SAVINGS CLAUSE.

This [Act] does not affect an action or proceeding commenced or right accrued before this [Act] takes effect.

FORM OF PARTNERSHIP AGREEMENT

by

JACK S. JOHAL, ERIK S. SCHIMMELBUSCH & HILTON S. WILLIAMS

The following Annotated Form of Partnership Agreement was drafted by Jack S. Johal, Erik S. Schimmelbusch, and Hilton S. Williams. The form was originally published in the State Bar of California's Business Law News, Summer 1997, at p. 15.

The Form was prepared with California partnerships in mind, but since the California statute is based on RUPA (although it differs from RUPA in certain respects), the Form would by and large be an appropriate starting-point for drafting a partnership agreement under most or all versions of RUPA. As originally published, the form made cross-references to the California statute. For ease of use in this Supplement, the editor of the Supplement has inserted, in place of the California cross-references, cross-references to RUPA.

General Partnership Agreement for

_____,

a California General Partnership

This Agreement of General Partnership (**"Agreement"**), dated for reference purposes only _____, 19__ (**"Effective Date"**), is entered into by and between the parties listed on the signature pages of this Agreement (collectively referred to as **"Partners"** and individually as **"Partner"**).

AGREEMENT

1. FORMATION AND ORGANIZATION.

1.1 <u>Formation</u>. The Partners hereby form a general partnership (**"Partnership"**) pursuant to the laws of the State of California, which Partnership shall be governed by and in accordance with the Uniform Partnership Act of 1994, (**"Partnership Act"**).

1.2 <u>Name</u>. The Partnership's name shall be "_____" and the Partnership's business shall continue to be conducted under said name.

1.3 <u>Principal Place of Business</u>. The Partnership's principal place of business shall be located at (i) _____, or (ii) such other place or places in California as a majority interest of the Partners may select from time to time upon written notice thereof to the other Partners.

1.4 <u>Business</u>. The Partnership's business shall be to _____

The Partnership shall have the power to do all acts and things in furtherance of and incidental to the foregoing business.

1.5 <u>Filings</u>.

    1.5.1 <u>Fictitious Business Name</u>. As soon after the Effective Date as is reasonably practicable, the Partners shall execute, file, and publish an appropriate fictitious business name statement for the Partnership in accordance with the California Business and Professions Code.

    1.5.2 <u>Statement of Partnership Authority</u>. As soon after the Effective Date as is reasonably practicable, the Partners shall (i) sign, acknowledge and verify a statement of partnership authority pursuant to RUPA § 303, (ii) file such statement in the Secretary of State's office, and (iii) cause said statement to be recorded in each county in California in which the Partnership owns or contemplates owning real property or any interest in real property. Promptly following any change in the Partners of the Partnership, the Partners shall amend such statement, file such statement with the Secretary of State's office and cause said amended statement to be recorded in each county in California in which the Partnership owns or contemplates owning real property or any interest in real property.[3]

    1.5.3 <u>Percentage Interests</u>. As used in this Agreement, a Partner's **"Percentage Interest"** shall mean the percentage set forth below opposite such Partner's name:

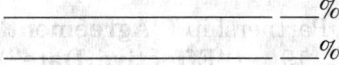

As used in this Agreement, **"Percentage Interests"** shall mean the aggregate of all such percentages, unless the context requires otherwise. **"Majority Interest"** shall mean those Partners who hold a majority of the Percentage Interests which all Partners hold.

1.6 <u>Term</u>. The Partnership shall commence upon the Effective Date and shall continue for a period of forty (40) years thereafter, unless sooner terminated in accordance with Section 10 below.

2. CAPITAL CONTRIBUTIONS.

2.1 <u>Initial Capital</u>.

    2.1.1 <u>Partner #1</u>. Upon the formation of the Partnership, Partner #1 shall contribute cash in the amount of One Hundred

---

3. *Comment:* Pursuant to RUPA § 303(a), a partnership may file a Statement of Partnership Authority with the Secretary of State. The Statement may specify the authority, or limitations on authority, of some or all of the partners to enter into transactions on behalf of the partnership. A filed Statement of Partnership Authority binds the partnership in favor of third parties who lack knowledge contrary to the statements in the document as to personal property transactions, and as to real property transactions if the Statement is recorded in the office for recording transfers of that property.

Thousand Dollars ($100,000) to the Partnership. Partner #1 shall receive a corresponding credit to its Capital Account.

    2.1.2 <u>Partner #2</u>. Upon the formation of the Partnership, Partner #2 shall contribute to the Partnership all of its right, title, and interest in and to that certain real property described on the attached Exhibit "___." The Partners agree that such property has a net fair market value of One Hundred Thousand Dollars ($100,-000). Partner #2 shall receive a credit to its Capital Account equal to such net fair market value.

    2.1.3 <u>Partner #3</u>. Upon the formation of the Partnership, Partner #3 shall contribute to the Partnership all of his or her right to acquire that certain real property described on the attached Exhibit "___" pursuant to that certain Purchase Agreement, dated April 1, 1995, by and between Partner #3 and John Doe. The Partners agree that such right has a net fair market value of One Hundred Thousand Dollars ($100,000). Partner #3 shall receive a credit to his or her Capital Account equal to such value.

    2.1.4 As used in this agreement, **"Capital Contribution"** shall mean any cash or its equivalent in property, both real and personal, contributed to the capital of the Partnership.

2.2 <u>Additional Capital</u>. No Partner shall be required to make any additional Capital Contributions. To the extent *[unanimously or by Majority Interest]* approved by the Partners, from time to time, the Partners may be permitted to make additional Capital Contributions if and to the extent they so desire, and if the Partners determine that such additional Capital Contributions are necessary or appropriate for the conduct of the Partnership's business *[including, without limitation, expansion or diversification]*. In that event, the Partners shall have the opportunity, but not the obligation, to participate in such Capital Contributions on a pro rata basis in accordance with their Percentage Interests. Each Partner shall receive a credit to its Capital Account in the amount of any additional capital which it contributes to the Partnership. Immediately following such Capital Contributions, the Percentage Interests shall be adjusted by the Partners to reflect the new relative proportions of the Capital Accounts of the Partners.

2.3 <u>Capital Accounts</u>. The Partnership shall establish and maintain an individual capital account (**"Capital Account"**) for each Partner in accordance with [Internal Revenue Code Treasury] Regulations Section 1.704–1(b)(2)(iv).[4] If a Partner transfers all or part of its

---

    4. *Comment:* For tax purposes, allocations of income, gain, loss, deduction and credit must be made in accordance with the partners' respective interests in the partnership. I.R.C. § 704. Allocations which have substantial economic effect are deemed to be in accordance with the partners' respective interests for these purposes. Allocations will have economic effect if the partnership agreement incorporates the "safe harbor" provisions, set forth in Treasury Regulations Section

Partnership Interest in accordance with this Agreement, such Partner's Capital Account attributable to the transferred Partnership Interest shall carry over to the new owner of such Partnership Interest pursuant to Regulations Section 1.704–1(b)(2)(iv)(1).

2.4 <u>No Interest</u>. No Partner shall be entitled to interest on the unreturned portion of his capital contributions.

2.5 <u>Withdrawal of Partner or Capital</u>. No Partner may withdraw as a partner of, or withdraw capital from, the Partnership without the consent of a Majority Interest of the Partners.[5]

2.6 <u>Return of Capital</u>. No Partner guarantees the return of another Partner's capital contributions.

3. DISTRIBUTIONS.

3.1 <u>Cash Available for Distribution</u>. As used in this Agreement, the term **"Cash Available for Distribution"** shall mean the amount of cash which *[all or a Majority Interest]* of the Partners deem available for distribution to the Partners, taking into account, among other factors, (i) all Partnership obligations then due and payable (including any compensation payable to the Partners in accordance with Section 5.6 below), (ii) anticipated Partnership expenditures, and (iii) those amounts which the Partners deem reasonably necessary, in [their] sole discretion, to place into reserves to satisfy customary and usual costs and claims with respect to the Partnership's business.

3.2 <u>Manner of Distribution</u>. The Partnership shall distribute Cash Available For Distribution to the Partners in the following order of priority:

    (a) First, to the Partners, pro rata, in accordance with the amount of capital which the Partners have contributed to the Partnership, until each Partner has received distributions under this subsection (a) which, in the aggregate, equal one hundred percent (100%) of the capital which such Partner has contributed to the Partnership; and

    (b) Thereafter, to the Partners, pro rata, in accordance with their respective Percentage Interests.

1.704–1(b)(2). Pursuant to such "safe harbor" provisions, (i) capital accounts must be maintained in accordance with Treasury Regulations Section 1.704–1(b)(2)(iv), (ii) liquidating distributions must be made in accordance with positive capital account balances, and (iii) each partner must be obligated to restore any deficit balance in its capital account upon liquidation of its interest in the partnership. In lieu of a deficit restoration requirement, the partnership agreement can include "qualified income offset" and corresponding "loss limitation" provisions drafted to comply with treasury Regulations Section 1.704–1(b)(2)(ii)(d). In order to ensure that allocations will be respected for tax purposes, the partnership agreement should contain a provision which requires capital accounts to be maintained in accordance with Treasury Regulations Section 1.704–1(b)(2)(iv), as well as provisions which satisfy the remaining "safe harbor" requirements.

5. *See* Section 9 of the Agreement concerning dissociation.

3.3 <u>Time of Distribution</u>. The Partnership shall distribute Cash Available For Distribution to the Partners pursuant to Section 3.2 above in such amounts and at such times as *[all or a Majority Interest]* of the Partners shall determine.

3.4 <u>Withholding</u>. The Partnership shall withhold and pay all [state] withholding taxes in accordance with the provisions [of state law].

4. PROFITS AND LOSSES.

4.1 <u>Determination of Profits and Losses</u>. Partnership profits and losses shall be determined in accordance with Internal Revenue Code Sections 703 and 704, as amended (**"Code"**), and the Treasury Regulations promulgated thereunder.

4.2 <u>Allocation of Profits and Losses</u>. *[RUPA § 401(b)]*

4.2.1 <u>Losses</u>. Subject to Section 4.3 below, Partnership losses shall be allocated to the Partners in the following order of priority:

(a) First, to the Partners in the amount of any profits previously allocated to them pursuant to Section 4.2.2(b) below (to the extent such profits have not been offset by prior loss allocations under this subsection (a));

(b) Second, to the Partners, pro rata, in proportion to their positive Capital Account balances, until no Partner has a positive Capital Account balance; and

(c) Thereafter, to the Partners, pro rata, in accordance with their respective Percentage Interests.

4.2.2 <u>Profits</u>. Subject to Section 4.3 below, Partnership profits shall be allocated to the Partners in the following order of priority:

(a) First, to the Partners in the amount of any losses previously allocated to them pursuant to Sections 4.2.1(b) and 4.2.1(c) above (to the extent such losses have not been offset by prior profit allocations under this subsection (a)); and

(b) Thereafter, to the Partners, pro rata, in accordance with their respective Percentage Interests.

4.3 <u>Special Allocations</u>.

4.3.1 <u>Minimum Gain Chargeback</u>. If there is a net decrease in "Partnership Minimum Gain" (as defined in Treasury Regulations Section 1.704–2(d)) during any fiscal year of the Partnership, each Partner shall be specially allocated items of Partnership income and gain for such fiscal year (and, if necessary, in subsequent fiscal years) in an amount equal to the portion of such Partner's share of the net decrease in Partnership Minimum Gain that is allocable to the disposition of any Partnership property which is subject to a "Nonrecourse Liability" (as defined in Treasury Regulations Section 1.752–1(a)(2)), which share of such net decrease shall be determined in accordance with Treasury Regulations Section 1.704–2(g)(2). Allocations pursuant to this Section 4.3.1 shall be made in proportion to the respective amounts required to be allocated to each Partner under this Section 4.3.1. The items to be so allocated shall be determined in accordance with Treasury Regulations Section 1.704–2(f). This Section 4.3.1 is intended to comply and shall be interpreted consistently with the minimum gain chargeback requirement contained in Treasury Regulations Section 1.704–2(f).

4.3.2 Chargeback of Minimum Gain Attributable To Partner Nonrecourse Debt. If there is a net decrease in Partnership Minimum Gain attributable to a "Partner Nonrecourse Debt" (as defined in Treasury Regulations Section 1.704–2(b)(4)) during any Partnership fiscal year, each Partner who has a share of the Partnership Minimum Gain attributable to such Partner Nonrecourse Debt (determined in accordance with Treasury Regulations Section 1.704–2(i)(5)) shall be specially allocated items of Partnership income and gain for such fiscal year (and, if necessary, in subsequent fiscal years) in an amount equal to that portion of such Partner's share of the net decrease in Partnership Minimum Gain attributable to such Partner Nonrecourse Debt that is allocable to the disposition of Partnership property subject to such Partner Nonrecourse Debt (which share of such net decrease shall be determined in accordance with Treasury Regulations Section 1.704–2(i)(5)). Allocations pursuant to this Section 4.3.2 shall be made in proportion to the respective amounts required to be allocated to each Partner under this Section 4.3.2. The items to be so allocated shall be determined in accordance with Treasury Regulations Section 1.704–2(i)(4). This Section 4.3.2 is intended to comply and shall be interpreted consistently with the minimum gain chargeback requirement contained in Treasury Regulations Section 1.704–2(i)(4).

4.3.3 Nonrecourse Deductions. Any nonrecourse deductions (as defined in Treasury Regulations Section 1.704–2(b)(1)) for any fiscal year or other period shall be specially allocated to the Partners, pro rata, in accordance with their respective Percentage Interests.

4.3.4 Partner Nonrecourse Deductions. Any items of Partnership loss, deduction, or [Internal Revenue] Code Section 705(a)(2)(B) expenditures attributable to a Partner Nonrecourse Debt for any fiscal year or other period shall be specially allocated to the Partner who bears the economic risk of loss with respect to the Partner Nonrecourse Debt to which such items of Partnership loss, deduction, or Code Section 705(a)(2)(B) expenditures are attributable in accordance with Treasury Regulations Section 1.704–2(i).

4.4 Code Section 704(c) Allocations. Notwithstanding Sections 4.2 and 4.3 above, in accordance with Code Section 704(c) and the Treasury

Regulations promulgated thereunder, income, gain, loss, and deduction with respect to any Partnership property contributed to the capital of the Partnership shall be allocated between the Partners so as to take account of any variation between the adjusted basis of such property to the Partnership for federal income tax purposes and its fair market value on the date of contribution. Allocations pursuant to this Section 4.4 are solely for purposes of federal, state, and local taxes. As such, they shall not affect or in any way be taken into account in computing a Partner's Capital Account or share of profits, losses, or other items of distributions pursuant to this Agreement.

5. MANAGEMENT AND AUTHORITY.

5.1 <u>Participation by Partners</u>. Except as expressly provided otherwise in this Agreement, (i) each Partner shall participate in the control, management and direction of the Partnership's business, and (ii) all Partnership matters shall be decided by a Majority Interest of the Partners. *[RUPA § 401(f)]* [6]

5.2 <u>Fiduciary Duties</u>. Each Partner owes to the Partnership the duty of loyalty and the duty of care. Accordingly, each Partner shall (i) account to the Partnership for any property, profit, or benefit obtained by such Partner in the conduct of the Partnership's business, and (ii) refrain from dealing with the Partnership as or on behalf of a party having an adverse interest to that of the Partnership. [7]

6. *Comment:* Under RUPA, in the absence of a contrary agreement, each partner has equal rights in the management and conduct of the partnership business, and may possess partnership property only on behalf of the partnership. A majority of the partners may resolve a difference arising as to a matter in the ordinary course of business of the partnership; however, an act outside the ordinary course of business and/or an amendment to the partnership agreement requires the consent of all of the partners. *See* Section 5.4 below, providing for decisions to be made by unanimous vote of the partners with respect to matters in the ordinary course of the partnership's business.

7. *Comment:* RUPA sets forth specific duties owed by a partner to the partnership and the other partners. The two principal duties that a partner owes to the partnership and the other partners are (i) the duty of loyalty, and (ii) the duty of care. The duty of loyalty includes (i) the duty to account to the partnership for any property, profit, or benefit obtained by the partner in the conduct of the partnership business or from the use of partnership property or information including the appropriation of a partnership opportunity; (ii) the duty to refrain from dealing with the partnership in the conduct or winding up of the partnership business as or on behalf of a party having an interest adverse to the partnership; and (iii) the duty to refrain from competing with the partnership in the conduct of the partnership business before the partnership's dissolution. A partner's duty of care to the partnership and the other partners is limited to refraining from engaging in grossly negligent or reckless conduct, intentional misconduct, or a knowing violation of law. Certain provisions of RUPA regarding fiduciary duties may not be varied by the partnership agreement. The partnership agreement may not eliminate the duty of loyalty. If not manifestly unreasonable, however, the partnership agreement may (i) identify specific types or categories of activities that do not violate the duty of loyalty; or (ii) provide that a specified percentage of the partners may authorize or ratify, after full disclosure of all material facts, a specific act or transaction that would otherwise violate the duty of loyalty. In addition, the partnership agreement may not unreasonably reduce the duty of care or eliminate the obligation of good faith and fair dealing. The partner-

5.3 Rights and Responsibilities. The Partners shall be responsible for the day-to-day management and operation of the Partnership's business. In addition, all things to be done by the Partnership shall be, except as expressly provided otherwise in this Agreement, decided by a Majority Interest of the Partners including the following *[RUPA § 401(j)]*:

(a) Execute all contracts, notes, deeds of trust, grant deeds, agreements for sale, escrow instructions, releases, easements, and other documents and instruments in connection with the Partnership's business;

(b) [Sell,] lease, exchange or otherwise dispose of all or any part of the Partnership's property;

(c) Exercise the Partnership's rights and fulfill the Partnership's obligations with respect to any partnership in which the Partnership is a partner, whether such rights and obligations are conferred by law or set forth in the governing instrument for such other partnership;

(d) Employ or discharge, at the Partnership's expense, ... agents, employees, independent contractors, attorneys, and/or accountants;

(e) Operate and maintain Partnership property;

(f) Obtain insurance necessary for the proper protection of the Partnership and the Partners; and

(g) Adjust any and all claims against the Partnership.

5.4 Unanimous Consent Required. Notwithstanding Section 5.3 above, none of the following shall be effected without the unanimous prior written consent of all Partners *[RUPA § 401(j)]*

(a) Admit an additional Partner to the Partnership;

(b) Borrow money on behalf of the Partnership in excess of _____;

(c) Prepay (in whole or in part), refinance, increase, modify, or extend any Partnership obligation;

(d) Pledge, hypothecate or otherwise encumber all or any part of the Partnership's assets;

(e) Dissolve the Partnership;

(f) Assign the Partnership's property in trust for creditors or on the assignee's promise to pay the Partnership's debts;

(g) Confess a judgment;

ship agreement may, however, prescribe the standards by which the performance of the obligation is to be measured, provided that such standards are not manifestly unreasonable.

230

(h) Do any act which would make it impossible for the Partners to carry on the ordinary business of the Partnership;

(i) Submit a Partnership claim or liability to arbitration or reference; . . .

(j) Authorize the merger *[RUPA §§ 905–907]* [8] with, or conversion *[RUPA §§ 901–904]* [9] into, a foreign or domestic other business entity[; or]

(k) Do any act in contravention of this Agreement.

8. *Comment:* RUPA provides for the merger of one or more partnerships into one partnership or any other number of business entities provided that the entities that are parties to the merger are permitted under the laws of their respective states of organization to effect the merger. Each party must approve an Agreement containing (i) terms and conditions of the merger; (ii) name and place of organization of the surviving entity; (iii) the manner of converting interests; (iv) any other details or provisions as are required by the laws under which constituent entities are organized; and (v) any other desired provisions.

A Statement of Merger may be filed pursuant to RUPA § 915 to evidence a merger in which (i) only partnerships are involved; and (ii) a domestic partnership is a party and no other party is a domestic entity. Although it is optional, a Statement of Merger should be filed whenever a constituent partnership owns real property and recorded in each county in which real property is owned.

Upon a merger, the separate existence of the non-surviving entities ceases, and the surviving entity succeeds to all rights and property of the non-surviving entities without further act or deed and is subject to the obligations of the disappearing entities.

9. *Comment:* RUPA provides that a partnership may be converted into a domestic limited partnership, limited liability company, or a foreign other business entity if each of the partners would, pursuant to the proposed conversion, receive a percentage interest in the profits and capital of the converted business entity equal to the partner's percentage interest in profits and capital of the converting partnership as of the effective time of the conversion. The conversion may be effected only if (i) the law under which the new entity will exist expressly permits the formation of such new entity pursuant to a conversion; and (ii) the partnership complies with all of the requirements of such other law that applies to the conversion of such other business entity.

The partnership must approve a plan of conversion that states (i) the terms and conditions of the conversion; (ii) the place of the organization of the converted entity and of the converting partnership; (iii) the name of the converted entity after conversion, if different from that of the converting partnership; (iv) the manner of converting the partnership interests of each of the partners into securities of or interests in the converted entity; (v) the provisions of the governing document for the converted entity to which the holders of interest in the converted entity are to be bound; (vi) any other details or provisions required by law under which the converted entity is organized; and (vii) any other details or provisions desired by the parties.

An entity that converts into another entity is for all purposes considered the same entity that existed prior to the conversion. When a conversion takes effect, all of the following apply: (i) all rights and property of the converting entity remain vested in the converted entity; (ii) all debts, liabilities and obligations of the converting entity continue as debts, liabilities and obligations of the converted entity; (iii) all rights of creditors and liens upon the property of the converting entity are preserved and remain enforceable against the converted entity; and (iv) any action or proceeding pending by or against the converting entity may be continued against the converted entity as if the conversion had never occurred.

The personal liability of a partner of a converting partnership is unchanged regarding all obligations for which the partner was personally liable prior to the conversion. Similarly, a partner of a partnership that converted from another business entity is liable for any obligations of the converting other business entity for which the partner was personally liable prior to the conversion. . . .

5.5 Time and Opportunities. The Partners shall devote to the Partnership such time as is reasonably necessary to carry out their respective obligations under this Agreement. During the term of this Partnership, each Partner may engage in any business activity for his own profit or advantage without the other Partners' consent, provided such other activity is not in competition with the Partnership's business. *[RUPA § 404(b)(3)]*

5.6 Expenses. Each Partner shall be entitled to reimbursement from the Partnership for those out-of-pocket expenses which such Partner reasonably incurs in the proper conduct of the Partnership's business. Each Partner shall itemize all such expenses in reasonable detail.

5.7 Compensation.

5.7.1 In General. Except as expressly provided otherwise in this Section, no Partner shall be entitled to receive compensation for services rendered to the Partnership, unless such compensation is approved in writing by *[all or a Majority Interest]* of the Partners. *[RUPA § 401(h)]*

5.7.2 Contracts With Partners and Affiliates. The Partnership may enter into contracts with a Partner or an affiliate of a Partner for the performance of services upon such terms and conditions as the Partners deem to be in the Partnership's best interests; provided, however, such contracts must provide for commercially reasonable fees, compensation, and/or other monetary payments.[10]

5.7.3 Tax Treatment. Any compensation which the Partnership pays to a Partner in accordance with this Section shall be treated as a payment made to one who is not a partner under Code Section 707(a) or 707(c).

5.8 Indemnification. The Partnership shall bear the cost of all expenditures and liabilities which the Partners incur in the proper conduct of the Partnership's business. The Partnership, to the extent of its assets, shall indemnify, defend and hold harmless a Partner from and against any and all liabilities of every kind, arising in any manner out of or in connection with the operation of the Partnership's business, except as to those matters arising by reason of such Partner's fraud, gross negligence, willful misconduct, or breach of fiduciary duty.

6. ACCOUNTING AND BANKING.

6.1 Fiscal Year. The fiscal year of the Partnership shall be the calendar year.

---

10. *Comment:* Partners should be advised that notwithstanding the foregoing provision, they must ensure that if they or their affiliates enter into contracts with the Partnership, that they do not violate the duties of loyalty and care discussed above with respect to Section 5.2.

6.2 Accounting Method. The Partnership's books shall be kept on the method of accounting which the Partners select, provided the Partnership is entitled under the Code to use such method of accounting. The Partnership shall prepare, or cause to be prepared, financial statements for financial reporting purposes on such method of accounting in accordance with those accounting principles used to prepare the Partnership's federal income tax returns, consistently applied.

6.3 Books and Records. The Partners shall keep, or cause to be kept, (i) accurate records of all transactions entered into with respect to the Partnership's business, and (ii) accurate books and accounts with respect to the Partnership's management and operation. The Partners shall (i) maintain the Partnership's books of account and other records at the Partnership's principal place of business, and (ii) make such documents available at ordinary business hours for inspection and copying by each Partner or its designated representative. Any copies which a Partner makes of the documents specified herein shall be at such Partner's expense. *[RUPA § 403]*

6.4 Bank Accounts. The Partners shall open and thereafter maintain a separate bank account(s) in the Partnership's name, in which all Partnership funds shall be deposited. All withdrawals from the Partnership's bank account(s) shall be made only by checks requiring the signature of such person or persons as *[all or a Majority Interest]* of the Partners shall designate.

6.5 Tax Matters.

6.5.1 Tax Returns. The Partners shall prepare and file, or cause to be prepared and filed, at the Partnership's expense, all federal and state tax returns on behalf of the Partnership in a timely manner.

6.5.2 Tax Elections. The Partners may cause the Partnership to make any tax elections available to the Partnership under the Code or any state revenue or taxation law.

7. TRANSFERS OF PARTNERSHIP INTERESTS.

7.1 General Prohibition. No Partner may sell, assign, pledge, hypothecate, or otherwise transfer or encumber all or any part of its interest in the Partnership without the other Partners' prior written consent, which consent may be withheld for any reason or for no reason at all. Any attempted sale, assignment, pledge, hypothecation, or other transfer or encumbrance of a Partner's interest in the Partnership in violation of this Section 7.1 shall be invalid. As such, it shall neither (i) relieve the transferor Partner of any of its obligations under this Agreement, nor (ii) entitle the transferee to any rights as a partner of the Partnership, as such rights are set forth in this Agreement and/or conferred by law.

7.2 Permitted Transfers. A Partner *[without the other Partners' consent]* may, transfer all or any part of his interest in the Partnership in trust for the benefit of himself, his spouse, his children, or grandchildren, or any combination thereof, provided (i) such Partner is a trustee or co-trustee of such trust, and (ii) such Partner, as trustee or co-trustee, agrees in writing to abide by the terms and conditions of this Agreement.

7.3 Transferee As Partner. Any transferee which acquires an interest in the Partnership in accordance with Sections 7.1 or 7.2 above shall satisfy each of the following conditions:

(a) The transferee must execute a written agreement whereby such transferee agrees to be bound by all of the terms, conditions, restrictions, and limitations set forth in this Agreement;

(b) The spouse of such transferee, if any, must consent in writing to be bound by all of the terms, conditions, restrictions, and limitations set forth in this Agreement; and

(c) The transferee must reimburse the Partnership for all reasonable legal and accounting fees and other costs which the Partnership must pay as a result of the transaction.

7.4 Status of Transferee. Upon the satisfaction of those conditions set forth in Section 7.3 above, the transferee shall succeed to the Partnership interest of the transferor Partner in the same capacity as the transferor Partner held in the Partnership. Accordingly, the transferee shall acquire all rights and obligations with respect to title, management, capital, allocations, and distributions which the transferor Partner held in the Partnership, as such rights and obligations are set forth in this Agreement and/or conferred by law. If any of the conditions set forth in Section 7.3 above are not satisfied or waived in writing by the Partners, then (i) the transferor Partner shall not be relieved of any of its obligations as a Partner of the Partnership (as such obligations are set forth in this Agreement and/or conferred by law), and (ii) the transferee shall not be entitled to any rights of a Partner under this Agreement, other than the right to receive as much of the transferor Partner's share of Partnership profits, losses and distributions to which the transferor Partner otherwise would be entitled under this Agreement.[11] *[RUPA § 503]*

11. *Comment:* RUPA § 502 provides that a partner's only "transferable interest" in the partnership under RUPA is the partner's share of the profits, losses, and distributions. The interest is characterized as personal property. Although a partner may transfer his or her interest in the partnership, RUPA § 503(a) provides that such transfer does not (i) by itself cause the partner's dissociation or a dissolution of the partnership; or (ii) entitle the transferee to participate in the management or conduct of the partnership business; or (iii) entitle the transferee to access to partnership information or inspect or copy the partnership books or records. Despite these limitations, a transferee has a right to (i) receive distributions to which the transferor would otherwise be entitled; (ii) receive a net amount otherwise distributable to the transferor upon the dissolution and winding up of the partnership's business; and (iii) seek a judicial determination that it is equitable to wind up the partnership business.

7.5 <u>Transfers By Operation of Law</u>. Any party who acquires any interest in the Partnership by operation of law, including by death or court decree, shall not be entitled to vote or otherwise participate in the Partnership's business.

8. ADDITIONAL PARTNERS.

8.1 <u>Admission</u>. A person or entity may be admitted as an additional Partner in the Partnership only with the written consent of all Partners, which consent may be withheld for any reason or for no reason at all. *[RUPA § 401(i)]*

8.2 <u>Amendment</u>. Upon the admission of an additional Partner pursuant to Section 8.1 above, each Partner (including the additional Partner) shall execute an amendment to this Agreement (i) evidencing the additional Partner's consent to be bound by all of the provisions contained in this Agreement, and (ii) reflecting the Partners' new Percentage Interests.

9. DISSOCIATION OF A PARTNER.

A Partner shall cease to be a Partner, and shall be deemed "dissociated" within the meaning of [RUPA §§ 601–603], upon the occurrence of any of the events described in Section 9.1 below.

9.1 <u>Events of Dissociation</u>. The following events shall result in a Partner's dissociation from the Partnership *[RUPA § 601]*:

(a) Such Partner's expulsion pursuant to the unanimous vote of the other Partners;

(b) Such Partner's expulsion pursuant to an order of a court of competent jurisdiction;

(c) Such Partner becomes a debtor in bankruptcy;

(d) In the case of a Partner who is an individual, such Partner's death or incapacity;

(e) In the case of a Partner that is a trust or an estate, the distribution of the trust's or estate's entire transferable interest in the Partnership; or

(f) The termination of a Partner who is not an individual, partnership, corporation, trust, or estate.[12]

---

12. *Comment:* Under the UPA, the death or withdrawal of a partner automatically triggered a dissolution of the partnership. Accordingly, the termination of a partner's relationship with the partnership was discussed only in the context of dissolution. In contrast, RUPA treats the dissolution of a partnership and the withdrawal of a partner as two separate concepts. The withdrawal of a partner from a partnership is referred to as "dissociation" in RUPA. RUPA § 601 lists events, which include those described above, which result in a partner's dissociation. In addition, the partnership agreement may identify other events causing a partner's dissociation.

235

9.2 Wrongful Dissociation.

9.2.1 Events Causing Wrongful Dissociation. A Partner's dissociation shall be deemed wrongful if such dissociation (i) resulted from an event described in paragraphs (b), (c), (e) or (f) of Section 9.1 above, or (ii) resulted from an event not described in Section 9.1 above.[13] *[RUPA § 602]*

9.2.2 Liability of Wrongfully Dissociated Partner. A Partner who wrongfully dissociates is liable to the Partnership and to the other Partners for any damages caused by such wrongful dissociation, and such liability is in addition to any other obligation owed by the Partner to the Partnership.[14] *[RUPA § 602(c)]*

9.3 Liability of Dissociated Partner. A dissociated Partner is liable to the Partnership for any obligation incurred prior to that Partner's dissociation. A dissociated Partner may be liable for a transaction entered into by the Partnership within two years after the Partner's dissociation, provided the requirements set forth in RUPA § 703(b) are satisfied.[15] *[RUPA § 702]*

13. *Comment:* A partner has the power to dissociate at any time by express will, irrespective of whether such dissociation is rightful or wrongful. A partner's dissociation is wrongful if it is in breach of an express provision of the partnership agreement. Dissociation is also wrongful if, in the case of a partnership for a definite term or particular undertaking, (i) the partner withdraws by express will (except as specified under limited circumstances); (ii) the partner is expelled by judicial determination; (iii) the partner is dissociated by becoming a debtor in bankruptcy; or (iv) in the case of a partner who is not an individual, trust other than a business trust, or estate, the partner is expelled or dissociated because it willfully dissolved or terminated. A partner who wrongfully dissociates is liable to the partnership and to the other partners for any damages caused by such wrongful dissociation, and such liability is in addition to any other obligation owed by the partner to the partnership. Accordingly, the partnership agreement may specify additional consequences of a partner's wrongful dissociation.

14. *Comment:* The language contained in Section 9.2.2 mirrors the language of RUPA § 602(c). Under RUPA, a partner's liability for wrongfully dissociating, as described above, is in addition to any other obligation owed by the partner to the partnership. Accordingly, a wrongfully dissociating partner will be held liable for any

other breach of the partnership agreement and the partnership agreement may specify additional consequences of a partner's wrongful dissociation.

15. *Comment:* Under RUPA, a partner is not discharged from liability for a partnership obligation incurred before dissociation merely because he or she has dissociated from the partnership. Generally, a dissociated partner is not liable for partnership obligations incurred after dissociation. A dissociated partner may, however, be liable to a third party for transactions entered into by the partnership within two years after the partner's dissociation, if (i) the other party reasonably believed that the dissociated partner was then a partner; (ii) the other party did not have notice of the partner's dissociation; and (iii) the other party is not deemed to have had knowledge or notice by reason of the filing of a Statement of Partnership Authority or Statement of Dissociation. A dissociated partner may be released from liability for a partnership obligation by agreement with the partnership creditor and the partners continuing the partnership business. In addition, a dissociated partner is released from liability for a partnership obligation if a partnership creditor, with notice of the partner's dissociation but without the partner's consent, agrees to a material alteration in the form of nature or time of payment of a partnership obligation.

10. DISSOLUTION AND TERMINATION OF PARTNERSHIP.

10.1 <u>Events of Dissolution</u>.[16] The Partnership shall dissolve upon the occurrence of any of the following events:

(a) The expiration of the Partnership's term, as set forth in Section 1.6 above; [17] *[RUPA § 801(2)(iii)]*

(b) The Partners' unanimous written consent to dissolve the Partnership;[18] *[RUPA § 801(2)(ii)]*

(c) The sale, transfer or other disposition of all or substantially all of the Partnership's assets;

(d) The occurrence of any event which makes it unlawful for the Partners to carry on the Partnership's business; *[RUPA § 801(4)]* or

(e) Whenever a court of competent jurisdiction so properly decrees.[19] *[RUPA § 801(5)]*

10.2 <u>Winding–Up</u>. Upon the Partnership's dissolution, the Partnership's business shall be wound up within a reasonable period of time, its assets liquidated, a final accounting made, and the Partnership's books closed. The Partners shall liquidate the Partnership's real prop-

---

16. *Comment:* In a partnership at will, RUPA provides that the partnership will dissolve by the express will of at least half of the partners, including partners, other than wrongfully dissociating partners, who have dissociated within the preceding 90 days and for which purpose such dissociation constitutes an expression of that partner's will to dissolve and wind up the partnership business.

Regardless of whether a partnership is at will or for a definite term or undertaking, RUPA provides that the partnership will be dissolved and must be wound up upon the occurrence of (i) an event agreed to in the partnership agreement; (ii) an event that makes it unlawful for all or substantially all of the business of the partnership to be continued, unless such illegality is cured within 90 days after notice to the partnership of such event; or (iii) on application by a partner, a judicial determination that any of the following provisions of RUPA § 801 apply: (1) the partnership's economic purpose is likely to be frustrated; (2) another partner has engaged in conduct relating to the partnership business that makes it not reasonably practicable to carry on the business in partnership with that partner, or (3) it is not otherwise reasonably practical to conduct the partnership business in conformity with the partnership agreement.

17. *Comment:* In a partnership for a definite term, dissolution is triggered by (i) the expiration of 90 days after a partner's dissociation by several specified events, including, without limitation, a partner's death, bankruptcy, or wrongful dissociation, unless before that time a majority in interest of the partners (including partners who have rightfully dissociated) agree to continue the partnership; (ii) the expiration of the term.

18. *Comment:* Where the partnership is for a definite term, RUPA § 801(2)(ii) requires the express will of all of the partners to wind up the partnership business.

19. *Comment:* To obtain a judicial decree that a partnership should be dissolved, a partner must make application for such decree, and the court must determine that one of the requirements contained in RUPA § 801 is fulfilled (See, footnote 13). In addition, a partnership is dissolved if, on application by a transferee of a partner's interest, a judicial determination is made that it is equitable to wind up the partnership business after the expiration of the term or completion of the undertaking, provided that the partnership was for a definite term or specific undertaking at the time of the transfer or entry of the charging order that gave rise to the transfer.

erty in an orderly fashion over a reasonable period of time pursuant to established real estate practices.[20] *[RUPA §§ 801–807]*

10.3 <u>Manner of Distribution</u>. Those proceeds which the Partnership derives from the liquidation of its assets shall be applied and distributed in the following order of priority:

(a) First, to the payment of expenses of liquidation and Partnership debts owing to creditors other than Partners;

(b) Second, to the payment of any Partnership debts owing to Partners; and

(c) Thereafter, to the Partners in accordance with their positive Capital Account balances, after taking into account income and loss allocations for the Partnership taxable year during which liquidation occurs. These liquidating distributions shall be made by the end of the Partnership taxable year in which the Partnership is liquidated, or, if later, within ninety (90) days after the date of such liquidation.

10.4 <u>Deficit Restoration Requirement</u>. If, upon liquidation, any Partner has a deficit balance in his Capital Account, after taking into account all Capital Account adjustments for the Partnership taxable year during which liquidation occurs, such Partner shall contribute cash to the capital of the Partnership in the amount necessary to eliminate such deficit balance by the end of the Partnership taxable year during which liquidation occurs or, if later, within ninety (90) days after the date of such liquidation. *[RUPA § 807(b)]*

---

20. *Comment:* Any partner who has not dissociated may participate in winding up the partnership's business. Upon application by any partner, however, a court may order judicial supervision of the winding up. The person winding up the partnership's business may do the following:

(i) preserve the partnership business or property as a going concern for a reasonable time; (ii) prosecute and defend actions and proceedings, whether civil, criminal, or administrative; (iii) settle and close the partnership's business; (iv) dispose of and transfer the partnership's property; (v) discharge the partnership's liabilities; (vi) distribute the partnership's assets; (vii) settle disputes by mediation or arbitration; and (viii) perform other necessary acts.

Under limited circumstances, a partnership may be bound by acts that occur during the winding up process. A partnership is bound by a partner's act after dissolution that is (i) appropriate for winding up the partnership's business; or (ii) would have bound the partnership before dissolution, if the other party to the transaction did not have notice of the dissolution.

RUPA provides that a partner who has not wrongfully dissociated may file a statement of dissolution stating, (i) the name of the partnership as filed with the Secretary of State; (ii) any identification number issued by the Secretary of State; and (iii) that the partnership has dissolved and is winding up its business. A Statement of Dissolution cancels a filed Statement of Partnership Authority, and is a limitation on authority for purposes of RUPA § 303(e). A third party is deemed to have notice of the dissolution and limitation of a partner's authority as a result of the Statement of Dissolution 90 days after it is filed.

After filing a Statement of Dissolution, a dissolved partnership may file and, if appropriate, record a Statement of Partnership Authority that will be valid with respect to any transaction, whether or not the transaction is appropriate for winding up the partnership's business.

10.5 Termination. Immediately after the application and distribution of liquidation proceeds in accordance with Section 10.3 above, the Partnership shall terminate.[21]

11. MISCELLANEOUS.

11.1 Amendment. This Agreement is subject to amendment only with the written consent of those Partners whose consent is required under this Agreement to accomplish the action reflected in such amendment.

11.2 Binding Effect. Subject to the restrictions set forth herein, this Agreement shall be binding upon the Partners and their respective successors, assigns, representatives, and beneficiaries.

11.3 Captions and Headings. Captions and headings used in this Agreement are for convenience purposes only. As such, they shall not control, affect, modify, amend or change the meaning and/or construction of any term or provision contained in this Agreement.

11.4 Counterparts and Facsimiles. The Partners may execute this Agreement simultaneously, in any number of counterparts, or on facsimile copies, each of which shall be deemed an original, but all of which together shall constitute one and the same Agreement.

11.5 Entire Agreement. This Agreement contains the Partners' entire agreement and supersedes any prior oral or written agreements among them with respect to the subject matter contained herein. There are no representations, agreements, arrangements, or understandings (oral or written) among the Partners relating to the subject matter of this Agreement which are not fully expressed herein.

11.6 Further Documents. Each party agrees to execute, with acknowledgment and affidavit if required, any and all documents in writing which may be required under this Agreement.

11.7 Governing Law. This Agreement, together with the Partners' respective rights and obligations hereunder, shall be governed by and construed in accordance with the laws of the State of California.

11.8 Notices. Any notice required or permitted hereunder shall be given in writing and shall be deemed effectively given upon (i) personal delivery, (ii) twenty-four (24) hours after deposit with Federal Express or a comparable express courier, addressed to a party at the address set forth below his signature hereto, or (iii) forty-eight (48) hours after deposit in the United States mail, by certified mail, return receipt requested, postage prepaid, addressed to a Partner at the address set forth below his signature hereto. A Partner may designate another

---

21. *Comment:* RUPA provides that a partnership continues after dissolution only for the purpose of winding up its business. The partnership is terminated when the winding [up is completed].

address for notice purposes upon written notice thereof to the Partnership.

11.9 <u>Partition—No Right</u>. No Partner shall have any right to seek or demand (i) partition of all or any part of the Partnership's assets, or (ii) any specific Partnership assets upon the liquidation of the Partnership.

11.10 <u>Prevailing Party's Fees</u>. If any party commences an action against another party to interpret or enforce any of the terms of this Agreement, or because of the other party's breach of any provision set forth in this Agreement, the losing party shall pay to the prevailing party reasonable attorneys' fees, costs and expenses, court costs and other costs of action incurred in connection with the prosecution or defense of such action, whether or not the action is prosecuted to a final judgment. For purposes of this Agreement, the terms "attorneys' fees" or "attorneys' fees and costs" shall mean the fees and expenses of counsel to the parties hereto, which may include, without limitation, printing, photostating, duplicating and other expenses, air freight charges, and fees billed for law clerks, paralegals, librarians and others not admitted to the bar but performing services under the supervision of an attorney. The terms "attorneys' fees" or "attorneys' fees and costs" shall also include, without limitation, all such fees and expenses incurred with respect to appeals, arbitrations and bankruptcy proceedings, and whether or not any action or proceeding is brought with respect to the matter for which said fees and expenses were incurred. The term "attorney" shall have the same meaning as the term "counsel."

11.11 <u>Pronouns and Gender</u>. Any pronouns or references used in this Agreement shall be deemed to include the masculine, feminine, or neuter gender, as appropriate. Any expression in the singular or plural shall, if appropriate in the context, include both the singular and the plural.

11.12 <u>Recitals and Exhibits</u>. All recitals set forth in this Agreement and all exhibits referenced in this Agreement are incorporated into this Agreement by this reference.

11.13 <u>Severability</u>. If a court of competent jurisdiction finds any provision in this Agreement to be invalid, such invalidity shall not affect the remainder of the Agreement. In such event, the invalid provision shall be deemed severed therefrom and the remainder of the Agreement shall remain enforceable in accordance with its terms and of full force and effect.

11.14 <u>Third Parties—No Interest</u>. Nothing in this Agreement (whether express or implied) is intended to or shall (i) confer any rights or remedies under or by reason of this Agreement on any persons other than the parties hereto and their respective successors and assigns, (ii) relieve or discharge the obligation or liability of any third person to any party hereto, or (iii) give any third person any right of subrogation or action against any party to this Agreement.

11.15 <u>Waiver</u>. A party's waiver of any breach of any provision contained in this Agreement shall not constitute a continuing waiver or a waiver of any subsequent breach of such provision or any other provision contained in this Agreement.

11.16 <u>Time of Essence</u>. Time is of the essence of this Agreement and all terms, covenants, conditions and provisions set forth in this Agreement.

12. EXECUTION.

IN WITNESS WHEREOF, the Partners have executed this Agreement effective as of the Effective Date as set forth in the Agreement.

Date: _____

_____
Signature

_____
Typed Name

_____
Residence Address

Date: _____

_____
Signature

_____
Typed Name

_____
Residence Address

13. CONSENT OF SPOUSES.

We certify that:

(1) We are the spouses of the persons who signed the foregoing Partnership Agreement and who constitute the members of the Partnership described in that Agreement.

(2) We have read and approve the provisions of that Partnership Agreement, including but not limited to those relating to the purchase, sale, or other disposition of the interest of a deceased, retiring, withdrawing, or terminating partner.

(3) We agree to be bound by and accept those provisions of that Partnership Agreement in lieu of all other interests we, or any of us,

may have in that Partnership, whether the interest be community property or otherwise.

(4) Our spouses shall have the full power of management of their interests in the Partnership, including any portion of those interests that are our community property, and they have the full right, without our further approval, to exercise their voting rights as partners in the Partnership, to execute any amendments to the Partnership Agreement, and to sell, transfer, encumber, and deal in any manner with those Partnership interests, including any portion of those interests that are our community property.

Executed on Date: _____, at: _____, California.

_____
Signature

_____
Typed Name

_____
Signature

_____
Typed Name

REVISED UNIFORM LIMITED PARTNERSHIP ACT (1976) WITH 1985 AMENDMENTS

ARTICLE 1. GENERAL PROVISIONS

ARTICLE 2. FORMATION; CERTIFICATE OF LIMITED PARTNERSHIP

ARTICLE 3. LIMITED PARTNERS

ARTICLE 4. GENERAL PARTNERS

ARTICLE 5. FINANCE

* Omitted.

* Omitted.

ARTICLE 1

GENERAL PROVISIONS

§ 101. Definitions

As used in this [Act], unless the context otherwise requires:

(1) "Certificate of limited partnership" means the certificate referred to in Section 201, and the certificate as amended or restated.

(2) "Contribution" means any cash, property, services rendered, or a promissory note or other binding obligation to contribute cash or property or to perform services, which a partner contributes to a limited partnership in his capacity as a partner.

(3) "Event of withdrawal of a general partner" means an event that causes a person to cease to be a general partner as provided in Section 402.

(4) "Foreign limited partnership" means a partnership formed under the laws of any state other than this State and having as partners one or more general partners and one or more limited partners.

(5) "General partner" means a person who has been admitted to a limited partnership as a general partner in accordance with the partnership agreement and named in the certificate of limited partnership as a general partner.

(6) "Limited partner" means a person who has been admitted to a limited partnership as a limited partner in accordance with the partnership agreement.

(7) "Limited partnership" and "domestic limited partnership" mean a partnership formed by two or more persons under the laws of this State and having one or more general partners and one or more limited partners.

(8) "Partner" means a limited or general partner.

(9) "Partnership agreement" means any valid agreement, written or oral, of the partners as to the affairs of a limited partnership and the conduct of its business.

(10) "Partnership interest" means a partner's share of the profits and losses of a limited partnership and the right to receive distributions of partnership assets.

(11) "Person" means a natural person, partnership, limited partnership (domestic or foreign), trust, estate, association, or corporation.

(12) "State" means a state, territory, or possession of the United States, the District of Columbia, or the Commonwealth of Puerto Rico.

§ 102. Name

The name of each limited partnership as set forth in its certificate of limited partnership:

(1) shall contain without abbreviation the words "limited partnership";

(2) may not contain the name of a limited partner unless (i) it is also the name of a general partner or the corporate name of a corporate general partner, or (ii) the business of the limited partnership had been carried on under that name before the admission of that limited partner;

(3) may not be the same as, or deceptively similar to, the name of any corporation or limited partnership organized under the laws of this State or licensed or registered as a foreign corporation or limited partnership in this State; and

(4) may not contain the following words [here insert prohibited words]....

§ 105. Records to Be Kept

(a) Each limited partnership shall keep at the office referred to in Section 104(1) the following:

(1) a current list of the full name and last known business address of each partner, separately identifying the general partners (in alphabetical order) and the limited partners (in alphabetical order);

(2) a copy of the certificate of limited partnership and all certificates of amendment thereto, together with executed copies of any powers of attorney pursuant to which any certificate has been executed;

(3) copies of the limited partnership's federal, state and local income tax returns and reports, if any, for the three most recent years;

(4) copies of any then effective written partnership agreements and of any financial statements of the limited partnership for the three most recent years; and

(5) unless contained in a written partnership agreement, a writing setting out:

(i) the amount of cash and a description and statement of the agreed value of the other property or services contributed by each partner and which each partner has agreed to contribute;

(ii) the times at which or events on the happening of which any additional contributions agreed to be made by each partner are to be made;

(iii) any right of a partner to receive, or of a general partner to make, distributions to a partner which include a return of all or any part of the partner's contribution; and

(iv) any events upon the happening of which the limited partnership is to be dissolved and its affairs wound up.

(b) Records kept under this section are subject to inspection and copying at the reasonable request and at the expense of any partner during ordinary business hours.

§ 106. Nature of Business

A limited partnership may carry on any business that a partnership without limited partners may carry on except [here designate prohibited activities].

§ 107. Business Transactions of Partner With Partnership

Except as provided in the partnership agreement, a partner may lend money to and transact other business with the limited partnership and, subject to other applicable law, has the same rights and obligations with respect thereto as a person who is not a partner.

ARTICLE 2

FORMATION; CERTIFICATE OF LIMITED PARTNERSHIP

§ 201. Certificate of Limited Partnership

(a) In order to form a limited partnership, a certificate of limited partnership must be executed and filed in the office of the Secretary of State. The certificate shall set forth:

(1) the name of the limited partnership;

(2) the address of the office and the name and address of the agent for service of process required to be maintained by Section 104;

(3) the name and the business address of each general partner;

(4) the latest date upon which the limited partnership is to dissolve; and

(5) any other matters the general partners determine to include therein.

(b) A limited partnership is formed at the time of the filing of the certificate of limited partnership in the office of the Secretary of State or at any later time specified in the certificate of limited partnership if, in either case, there has been substantial compliance with the requirements of this section.

Comment

The 1985 Act requires far fewer matters to be set forth in the certificate of limited partnership than did Section 2 of the 1916 Act and Section 201 of the 1976 Act. This is in recognition of the fact that the partnership agreement, not the certificate of limited partnership, has become the authoritative and comprehensive document for most limited partnerships, and that creditors and potential creditors of the partnership do and should refer to the partnership agreement and to other information furnished to them directly by the partnership and by others, not to the certificate of limited partnership, to obtain facts concerning the capital and finances of the partnership and other matters of concern. Subparagraph (b), which is based upon the 1916 Act, has been retained to make it clear that existence of the limited partnership depends only upon compliance with this section. Its continued existence is not dependent upon compliance with other provisions of this Act.

§ 202. Amendment to Certificate

(a) A certificate of limited partnership is amended by filing a certificate of amendment thereto in the office of the Secretary of State. The certificate shall set forth:

(1) the name of the limited partnership;

(2) the date of filing the certificate; and

(3) the amendment to the certificate.

(b) Within 30 days after the happening of any of the following events, an amendment to a certificate of limited partnership reflecting the occurrence of the event or events shall be filed:

(1) the admission of a new general partner;

(2) the withdrawal of a general partner; or

(3) the continuation of the business under Section 801 after an event of withdrawal of a general partner.

(c) A general partner who becomes aware that any statement in a certificate of limited partnership was false when made or that any arrangements or other facts described have changed, making the certificate inaccurate in any respect, shall promptly amend the certificate.

(d) A certificate of limited partnership may be amended at any time for any other proper purpose the general partners determine.

(e) No person has any liability because an amendment to a certificate of limited partnership has not been filed to reflect the occurrence of any event referred to in subsection (b) of this section if the amendment is filed within the 30–day period specified in subsection (b).

(f) A restated certificate of limited partnership may be executed and filed in the same manner as a certificate of amendment....

§ 204. Execution of Certificates

(a) Each certificate required by this Article to be filed in the office of the Secretary of State shall be executed in the following manner:

(1) an original certificate of limited partnership must be signed by all general partners;

(2) a certificate of amendment must be signed by at least one general partner and by each other general partner designated in the certificate as a new general partner; and

(3) a certificate of cancellation must be signed by all general partners.

(b) Any person may sign a certificate by an attorney-in-fact, but a power of attorney to sign a certificate relating to the admission of a general partner must specifically describe the admission.

(c) The execution of a certificate by a general partner constitutes an affirmation under the penalties of perjury that the facts stated therein are true.

§ 206. Filing in Office of Secretary of State

(a) Two signed copies of the certificate of limited partnership and of any certificates of amendment or cancellation (or of any judicial decree of amendment or cancellation) shall be delivered to the Secretary of State. A person who executes a certificate as an agent or fiduciary need not exhibit evidence of his [or her] authority as a prerequisite to filing. Unless the Secretary of State finds that any certificate does not conform to law, upon receipt of all filing fees required by law he [or she] shall:

(1) endorse on each duplicate original the word "Filed" and the day, month, and year of the filing thereof;

(2) file one duplicate original in his [or her] office; and

(3) return the other duplicate original to the person who filed it or his [or her] representative.

(b) Upon the filing of a certificate of amendment (or judicial decree of amendment) in the office of the Secretary of State, the certificate of limited partnership shall be amended as set forth therein, and upon the effective date of a certificate of cancellation (or a judicial decree thereof), the certificate of limited partnership is cancelled.

§ 207. Liability for False Statement in Certificate

If any certificate of limited partnership or certificate of amendment or cancellation contains a false statement, one who suffers loss by reliance on the statement may recover damages for the loss from:

(1) any person who executes the certificate, or causes another to execute it on his behalf, and knew, and any general partner who knew or

should have known, the statement to be false at the time the certificate was executed; and

(2) any general partner who thereafter knows or should have known that any arrangement or other fact described in the certificate has changed, making the statement inaccurate in any respect within a sufficient time before the statement was relied upon reasonably to have enabled that general partner to cancel or amend the certificate, or to file a petition for its [judicial] cancellation or amendment. . . .

§ 208. Scope of Notice

The fact that a certificate of limited partnership is on file in the office of the Secretary of State is notice that the partnership is a limited partnership and the persons designated therein as general partners are general partners, but it is not notice of any other fact.

Comment

. . . By stating that the filing of a certificate of limited partnership only results in notice of the general liability of the general partners, Section 208 obviates the concern that third parties may be held to have notice of special provisions set forth in the certificate. While this section is designed to preserve by implication the limited liability of limited partners, the implicit protection provided is not intended to change any liability of a limited partner which may be created by his action or inaction under the law of estoppel, agency, fraud or the like.

§ 209. Delivery of Certificates to Limited Partners

Upon the return by the Secretary of State pursuant to Section 206 of a certificate marked "Filed," the general partners shall promptly deliver or mail a copy of the certificate of limited partnership and each certificate of amendment or cancellation to each limited partner unless the partnership agreement provides otherwise.

ARTICLE 3

LIMITED PARTNERS

§ 301. Admission of Limited Partners

(a) A person becomes a limited partner:

(1) at the time the limited partnership is formed; or

(2) at any later time specified in the records of the limited partnership for becoming a limited partner.

(b) After the filing of a limited partnership's original certificate of limited partnership, a person may be admitted as an additional limited partner:

(1) in the case of a person acquiring a partnership interest directly from the limited partnership, upon compliance with the partnership agreement or, if the partnership agreement does not so provide, upon the written consent of all partners; and

(2) in the case of an assignee of a partnership interest of a partner who has the power, as provided in Section 704, to grant the assignee the right to become a limited partner, upon the exercise of that power and compliance with any conditions limiting the grant or exercise of the power.

§ 302. Voting

Subject to Section 303, the partnership agreement may grant to all or a specified group of the limited partners the right to vote (on a per capita or other basis) upon any matter.

Comment

Section 302 first appeared in the 1976 Act, and must be read together with subdivision (b)(6) of Section 303. Although the 1916 Act did not speak specifically of the voting powers of limited partners, it was not uncommon for partnership agreements to grant such powers to limited partners. Section 302 is designed only to make it clear that the partnership agreement may grant such power to limited partners. If such powers are granted to limited partners beyond the "safe harbor" of subdivision (6) or (8) of Section 303(b), a court may (but of course need not) hold that, under the circumstances, the limited partners have participated in "control of the business" within the meaning of Section 303(a). Section 303(c) makes clear that the exercise of powers beyond the ambit of Section 303(b) is not ipso facto to be taken as taking part in the control of the business.

§ 303. Liability to Third Parties

(a) Except as provided in subsection (d), a limited partner is not liable for the obligations of a limited partnership unless he [or she] is also a general partner or, in addition to the exercise of his [or her] rights and powers as a limited partner, he [or she] participates in the control of the business. However, if the limited partner participates in the control of the business, he [or she] is liable only to persons who transact business with the limited partnership reasonably believing, based upon the limited partner's conduct, that the limited partner is a general partner.

(b) A limited partner does not participate in the control of the business within the meaning of subsection (a) solely by doing one or more of the following:

(1) being a contractor for or an agent or employee of the limited partnership or of a general partner or being an officer, director, or shareholder of a general partner that is a corporation;

(2) consulting with and advising a general partner with respect to the business of the limited partnership;

(3) acting as surety for the limited partnership or guaranteeing or assuming one or more specific obligations of the limited partnership;

(4) taking any action required or permitted by law to bring or pursue a derivative action in the right of the limited partnership;

(5) requesting or attending a meeting of partners;

(6) proposing, approving, or disapproving, by voting or otherwise, one or more of the following matters:

(i) the dissolution and winding up of the limited partnership;

(ii) the sale, exchange, lease, mortgage, pledge, or other transfer of all or substantially all of the assets of the limited partnership;

(iii) the incurrence of indebtedness by the limited partnership other than in the ordinary course of its business;

(iv) a change in the nature of the business;

(v) the admission or removal of a general partner;

(vi) the admission or removal of a limited partner;

(vii) a transaction involving an actual or potential conflict of interest between a general partner and the limited partnership or the limited partners;

(viii) an amendment to the partnership agreement or certificate of limited partnership; or

(ix) matters related to the business of the limited partnership not otherwise enumerated in this subsection (b), which the partnership agreement states in writing may be subject to the approval or disapproval of limited partners;

(7) winding up the limited partnership pursuant to Section 803; or

(8) exercising any right or power permitted to limited partners under this [Act] and not specifically enumerated in this subsection (b).

(c) The enumeration in subsection (b) does not mean that the possession or exercise of any other powers by a limited partner constitutes participation by him [or her] in the business of the limited partnership.

(d) A limited partner who knowingly permits his [or her] name to be used in the name of the limited partnership, except under circumstances permitted by Section 102(2), is liable to creditors who extend credit to the limited partnership without actual knowledge that the limited partner is not a general partner.

Comment

... The second sentence of Section 303(a) ... was adopted partly because of the difficulty of determining when the "control" line has been overstepped, but also (and more importantly) because of a determination that it is not sound public policy to hold a limited partner who is not also a general partner liable for the obligations of the partnership except to persons who have done business with the limited partnership reasonably believing, based on the limited partner's conduct, that he is a general partner. Paragraph (b) is intended to provide a "safe harbor" by enumerating certain activities which a limited partner may carry on for the partnership without being deemed to have taken part in control of the business. This "safe harbor" list has been expanded beyond that set out in the 1976 Act to reflect case law and statutory developments and more clearly to assure that limited partners are not subjected to general liability where such liability is inappropriate. Paragraph (d) is derived from Section 5 of the 1916 Act, but adds as a condition to the limited partner's liability the requirement that a limited partner must have knowingly permitted his name to be used in the name of the limited partnership.

§ 304. Person Erroneously Believing Himself [or Herself] Limited Partner

(a) Except as provided in subsection (b), a person who makes a contribution to a business enterprise and erroneously but in good faith believes that he [or she] has become a limited partner in the enterprise is not a general partner in the enterprise and is not bound by its obligations by reason of making the contribution, receiving distributions from the enterprise, or exercising any rights of a limited partner, if, on ascertaining the mistake, he [or she]:

(1) causes an appropriate certificate of limited partnership or a certificate of amendment to be executed and filed; or

(2) withdraws from future equity participation in the enterprise by executing and filing in the office of the Secretary of State a certificate declaring withdrawal under this section.

(b) A person who makes a contribution of the kind described in subsection (a) is liable as a general partner to any third party who transacts business with the enterprise (i) before the person withdraws and an appropriate certificate is filed to show withdrawal, or (ii) before an appropriate certificate is filed to show that he [or she] is not a general partner, but in either case only if the third party actually believed in good faith that the person was a general partner at the time of the transaction.

§ 305. Information

Each limited partner has the right to:

(1) inspect and copy any of the partnership records required to be maintained by Section 105; and

(2) obtain from the general partners from time to time upon reasonable demand (i) true and full information regarding the state of the business and financial condition of the limited partnership, (ii) promptly after becoming available, a copy of the limited partnership's federal, state, and local income tax returns for each year, and (iii) other information regarding the affairs of the limited partnership as is just and reasonable.

ARTICLE 4
GENERAL PARTNERS

§ 401. Admission of Additional General Partners

After the filing of a limited partnership's original certificate of limited partnership, additional general partners may be admitted as provided in writing in the partnership agreement or, if the partnership agreement does not provide in writing for the admission of additional general partners, with the written consent of all partners.

§ 402. Events of Withdrawal

Except as approved by the specific written consent of all partners at the time, a person ceases to be a general partner of a limited partnership upon the happening of any of the following events:

(1) the general partner withdraws from the limited partnership as provided in Section 602;

(2) the general partner ceases to be a member of the limited partnership as provided in Section 702;

(3) the general partner is removed as a general partner in accordance with the partnership agreement;

(4) unless otherwise provided in writing in the partnership agreement, the general partner: (i) makes an assignment for the benefit of creditors; (ii) files a voluntary petition in bankruptcy; (iii) is adjudicated a bankrupt or insolvent; (iv) files a petition or answer seeking for himself [or herself] any reorganization, arrangement, composition, readjustment, liquidation, dissolution, or similar relief under any statute, law, or regulation; (v) files an answer or other pleading admitting or

failing to contest the material allegations of a petition filed against him [or her] in any proceeding of this nature; or (vi) seeks, consents to, or acquiesces in the appointment of a trustee, receiver, or liquidator of the general partner or of all or any substantial part of his [or her] properties;

(5) unless otherwise provided in writing in the partnership agreement, [120] days after the commencement of any proceeding against the general partner seeking reorganization, arrangement, composition, readjustment, liquidation, dissolution, or similar relief under any statute, law, or regulation, the proceeding has not been dismissed, or if within [90] days after the appointment without his [or her] consent or acquiescence of a trustee, receiver, or liquidator of the general partner or of all or any substantial part of his [or her] properties, the appointment is not vacated or stayed or within [90] days after the expiration of any such stay, the appointment is not vacated;

(6) in the case of a general partner who is a natural person,

(i) his [or her] death; or

(ii) the entry of an order by a court of competent jurisdiction adjudicating him [or her] incompetent to manage his [or her] person or his [or her] estate;

(7) in the case of a general partner who is acting as a general partner by virtue of being a trustee of a trust, the termination of the trust (but not merely the substitution of a new trustee);

(8) in the case of a general partner that is a separate partnership, the dissolution and commencement of winding up of the separate partnership;

(9) in the case of a general partner that is a corporation, the filing of a certificate of dissolution, or its equivalent, for the corporation or the revocation of its charter; or

(10) in the case of an estate, the distribution by the fiduciary of the estate's entire interest in the partnership.

Comment

Section 402 expands considerably the provisions of Section 20 of the 1916 Act, which provided for dissolution in the event of the retirement, death or insanity of a general partner. Subdivisions (1), (2) and (3) recognize that the general partner's agency relationship is terminable at will, although it may result in a breach of the partnership agreement giving rise to an action for damages. Subdivisions (4) and (5) reflect a judgment that, unless the limited partners agree otherwise, they ought to have the power to rid themselves of a general partner who is in such dire financial straits that he is the subject of proceedings under the National Bankruptcy Code or a similar provision of law. Subdivisions

(6) through (10) simply elaborate on the notion of death in the case of a general partner who is not a natural person. . . .

§ 403. General Powers and Liabilities

(a) Except as provided in this [Act] or in the partnership agreement, a general partner of a limited partnership has the rights and powers and is subject to the restrictions of a partner in a partnership without limited partners.

(b) Except as provided in this [Act], a general partner of a limited partnership has the liabilities of a partner in a partnership without limited partners to persons other than the partnership and the other partners. Except as provided in this [Act] or in the partnership agreement, a general partner of a limited partnership has the liabilities of a partner in a partnership without limited partners to the partnership and to the other partners.

§ 404. Contributions by General Partner

A general partner of a limited partnership may make contributions to the partnership and share in the profits and losses of, and in distributions from, the limited partnership as a general partner. A general partner also may make contributions to and share in profits, losses, and distributions as a limited partner. A person who is both a general partner and a limited partner has the rights and powers, and is subject to the restrictions and liabilities, of a general partner and, except as provided in the partnership agreement, also has the powers, and is subject to the restrictions, of a limited partner to the extent of his [or her] participation in the partnership as a limited partner.

§ 405. Voting

The partnership agreement may grant to all or certain identified general partners the right to vote (on a per capita or any other basis), separately or with all or any class of the limited partners, on any matter.

ARTICLE 5

FINANCE

§ 501. Form of Contribution

The contribution of a partner may be in cash, property, or services rendered, or a promissory note or other obligation to contribute cash or property or to perform services.

§ 502. Liability for Contribution

(a) A promise by a limited partner to contribute to the limited partnership is not enforceable unless set out in a writing signed by the limited partner.

(b) Except as provided in the partnership agreement, a partner is obligated to the limited partnership to perform any enforceable promise to contribute cash or property or to perform services, even if he [or she] is unable to perform because of death, disability, or any other reason. If a partner does not make the required contribution of property or services, he [or she] is obligated at the option of the limited partnership to contribute cash equal to that portion of the value, as stated in the partnership records required to be kept pursuant to Section 105, of the stated contribution which has not been made.

(c) Unless otherwise provided in the partnership agreement, the obligation of a partner to make a contribution or return money or other property paid or distributed in violation of this [Act] may be compromised only by consent of all partners. Notwithstanding the compromise, a creditor of a limited partnership who extends credit or otherwise acts in reliance on that obligation after the partner signs a writing which reflects the obligation, and before the amendment or cancellation thereof to reflect the compromise, may enforce the original obligation.

§ 503. Sharing of Profits and Losses

The profits and losses of a limited partnership shall be allocated among the partners, and among classes of partners, in the manner provided in writing in the partnership agreement. If the partnership agreement does not so provide in writing, profits and losses shall be allocated on the basis of the value, as stated in the partnership records required to be kept pursuant to Section 105, of the contributions made by each partner to the extent they have been received by the partnership and have not been returned.

§ 504. Sharing of Distributions

Distributions of cash or other assets of a limited partnership shall be allocated among the partners and among classes of partners in the manner provided in writing in the partnership agreement. If the partnership agreement does not so provide in writing, distributions shall be made on the basis of the value, as stated in the partnership records required to be kept pursuant to Section 105, of the contributions made by each partner to the extent they have been received by the partnership and have not been returned.

ARTICLE 6

DISTRIBUTIONS AND WITHDRAWAL

§ 601. Interim Distributions

Except as provided in this Article, a partner is entitled to receive distributions from a limited partnership before his [or her] withdrawal from the limited partnership and before the dissolution and winding up thereof to the extent and at the times or upon the happening of the events specified in the partnership agreement.

§ 602. Withdrawal of General Partner

A general partner may withdraw from a limited partnership at any time by giving written notice to the other partners, but if the withdrawal violates the partnership agreement, the limited partnership may recover from the withdrawing general partner damages for breach of the partnership agreement and offset the damages against the amount otherwise distributable to him [or her].

§ 603. Withdrawal of Limited Partner

A limited partner may withdraw from a limited partnership at the time or upon the happening of events specified in writing in the partnership agreement. If the agreement does not specify in writing the time or the events upon the happening of which a limited partner may withdraw or a definite time for the dissolution and winding up of the limited partnership, a limited partner may withdraw upon not less than six months' prior written notice to each general partner at his [other] address on the books of the limited partnership at its office in this State.

§ 604. Distribution Upon Withdrawal

Except as provided in this Article, upon withdrawal any withdrawing partner is entitled to receive any distribution to which he [or she] is entitled under the partnership agreement and, if not otherwise provided in the agreement, he [or she] is entitled to receive, within a reasonable time after withdrawal, the fair value of his [or her] interest in the limited partnership as of the date of withdrawal based upon his [or her] right to share in distributions from the limited partnership.

§ 605. Distribution in Kind

Except as provided in writing in the partnership agreement, a partner, regardless of the nature of his [or her] contribution, has no right to demand and receive any distribution from a limited partnership in any form other than cash. Except as provided in writing in the partnership agreement, a partner may not be compelled to accept a distribution of any asset in kind from a limited partnership to the extent that the percentage of the asset distributed to him [or her] exceeds a percentage of that asset which is equal to the percentage in which he [or she] shares in distributions from the limited partnership.

§ 606. Right to Distribution

At the time a partner becomes entitled to receive a distribution, he [or she] has the status of, and is entitled to all remedies available to, a creditor of the limited partnership with respect to the distribution.

§ 607. Limitations on Distribution

A partner may not receive a distribution from a limited partnership to the extent that, after giving effect to the distribution, all liabilities of the limited partnership, other than liabilities to partners on account of their partnership interests, exceed the fair value of the partnership assets.

§ 608. Liability Upon Return of Contribution

(a) If a partner has received the return of any part of his [or her] contribution without violation of the partnership agreement or this [Act], he [or she] is liable to the limited partnership for a period of one year thereafter for the amount of the returned contribution, but only to the extent necessary to discharge the limited partnership's liabilities to creditors who extended credit to the limited partnership during the period the contribution was held by the partnership.

(b) If a partner has received the return of any part of his [or her] contribution in violation of the partnership agreement or this [Act], he [or she] is liable to the limited partnership for a period of six years thereafter for the amount of the contribution wrongfully returned.

(c) A partner receives a return of his [or her] contribution to the extent that a distribution to him [or her] reduces his [or her] share of the fair value of the net assets of the limited partnership below the value, as set forth in the partnership records required to be kept pursuant to Section 105, of his contribution which has not been distributed to him [or her].

ARTICLE 7

ASSIGNMENT OF PARTNERSHIP INTERESTS

§ 701. Nature of Partnership Interest

A partnership interest is personal property.

§ 702. Assignment of Partnership Interest

Except as provided in the partnership agreement, a partnership interest is assignable in whole or in part. An assignment of a partnership interest does not dissolve a limited partnership or entitle the assignee to become or to exercise any rights of a partner. An assignment entitles the assignee to receive, to the extent assigned, only the distribution to which the assignor would be entitled. Except as provided in the partnership agreement, a partner ceases to be a partner upon assignment of all his [or her] partnership interest.

§ 703. Rights of Creditor

On application to a court of competent jurisdiction by any judgment creditor of a partner, the court may charge the partnership interest of the partner with payment of the unsatisfied amount of the judgment with interest. To the extent so charged, the judgment creditor has only the rights of an assignee of the partnership interest. This [Act] does not deprive any partner of the benefit of any exemption laws applicable to his [or her] partnership interest.

§ 704. Right of Assignee to Become Limited Partner

(a) An assignee of a partnership interest, including an assignee of a general partner, may become a limited partner if and to the extent that (i) the assignor gives the assignee that right in accordance with authority described in the partnership agreement, or (ii) all other partners consent.

(b) An assignee who has become a limited partner has, to the extent assigned, the rights and powers, and is subject to the restrictions and liabilities, of a limited partner under the partnership agreement and this [Act]. An assignee who becomes a limited partner also is liable for the obligations of his [or her] assignor to make and return contributions as provided in Articles 5 and 6. However, the assignee is not obligated for liabilities unknown to the assignee at the time he [or she] became a limited partner.

(c) If an assignee of a partnership interest becomes a limited partner, the assignor is not released from his [or her] liability to the limited partnership under Sections 207 and 502.

§ 705. Power of Estate of Deceased or Incompetent Partner

If a partner who is an individual dies or a court of competent jurisdiction adjudges him [or her] to be incompetent to manage his [or her] person or his [or her] property, the partner's executor, administrator, guardian, conservator, or other legal representative may exercise all of the partner's rights for the purpose of settling his [or her] estate or administering his [or her] property, including any power the partner had to give an assignee the right to become a limited partner. If a partner is a corporation, trust, or other entity and is dissolved or terminated, the powers of that partner may be exercised by its legal representative or successor.

ARTICLE 8

DISSOLUTION

§ 801. Nonjudicial Dissolution

A limited partnership is dissolved and its affairs shall be wound up upon the happening of the first to occur of the following:

(1) at the time specified in the certificate of limited partnership;

(2) upon the happening of events specified in writing in the partnership agreement;

(3) written consent of all partners;

(4) an event of withdrawal of a general partner unless at the time there is at least one other general partner and the written provisions of the partnership agreement permit the business of the limited partnership to be carried on by the remaining general partner and that partner does so, but the limited partnership is not dissolved and is not required to be wound up by reason of any event of withdrawal, if, within 90 days after the withdrawal, all partners agree in writing to continue the business of the limited partnership and to the appointment of one or more additional general partners if necessary or desired; or

(5) entry of a decree of judicial dissolution under Section 802.

§ 802. Judicial Dissolution

On application by or for a partner the [designate the appropriate court] court may decree dissolution of a limited partnership whenever it is not reasonably practicable to carry on the business in conformity with the partnership agreement.

§ 803. Winding Up

Except as provided in the partnership agreement, the general partners who have not wrongfully dissolved a limited partnership or, if none, the limited partners, may wind up the limited partnership's affairs; but the [designate the appropriate court] court may wind up the limited partnership's affairs upon application of any partner, his [or her] legal representative, or assignee.

§ 804. Distribution of Assets

Upon the winding up of a limited partnership, the assets shall be distributed as follows:

(1) to creditors, including partners who are creditors, to the extent permitted by law, in satisfaction of liabilities of the limited partnership other than liabilities for distributions to partners under Section 601 or 604;

(2) except as provided in the partnership agreement, to partners and former partners in satisfaction of liabilities for distributions under Section 601 or 604; and

(3) except as provided in the partnership agreement, to partners first for the return of their contributions and secondly respecting their partnership interests, in the proportions in which the partners share in distributions....

ARTICLE 10

DERIVATIVE ACTIONS

§ 1001. Right of Action

A limited partner may bring an action in the right of a limited partnership to recover a judgment in its favor if general partners with authority to do so have refused to bring the action or if an effort to cause those general partners to bring the action is not likely to succeed.

§ 1002. Proper Plaintiff

In a derivative action, the plaintiff must be a partner at the time of bringing the action and (i) must have been a partner at the time of the transaction of which he [or she] complains or (ii) his [or her] status as a partner must have devolved upon him [or her] by operation of law or pursuant to the terms of the partnership agreement from a person who was a partner at the time of the transaction.

§ 1003. Pleading

In a derivative action, the complaint shall set forth with particularity the effort of the plaintiff to secure initiation of the action by a general partner or the reasons for not making the effort.

§ 1004. Expenses

If a derivative action is successful, in whole or in part, or if anything is received by the plaintiff as a result of a judgment, compromise, or settlement of an action or claim, the court may award the plaintiff reasonable expenses, including reasonable attorney's fees, and shall direct him [or her] to remit to the limited partnership the remainder of those proceeds received by him [or her].

ARTICLE 11

MISCELLANEOUS

§ 1105. Rules for Cases Not Provided for in This [Act]

In any case not provided for in this [Act] the provisions of the Uniform Partnership Act govern.

UNIFORM LIMITED PARTNERSHIP
ACT 2001

TABLE OF CONTENTS

[ARTICLE] 1
GENERAL PROVISIONS

[ARTICLE] 2
FORMATION; CERTIFICATE OF
LIMITED PARTNERSHIP AND OTHER FILINGS

* Omitted.

[ARTICLE] 3
LIMITED PARTNERS

[ARTICLE] 4
GENERAL PARTNERS

[ARTICLE] 5
CONTRIBUTIONS AND DISTRIBUTIONS

[ARTICLE] 6
DISSOCIATION

[ARTICLE] 7
TRANSFERABLE INTERESTS AND RIGHTS
OF TRANSFEREES AND CREDITORS

[ARTICLE] 8
DISSOLUTION

* Omitted.

PREFATORY NOTE

The Act's Overall Approach

The new Limited Partnership Act is a "stand alone" act, "de-linked" from both the original general partnership act ("UPA") and the Revised Uniform Partnership Act ("RUPA"). To be able to stand alone, the Limited Partnership [Act] incorporates many provisions from RUPA and some from the Uniform Limited Liability Company Act ("ULLCA"). As a result, the new Act is far longer and more complex than its immediate predecessor, the Revised Uniform Limited Partnership Act ("RULPA").

The new Act has been drafted for a world in which limited liability partnerships and limited liability companies can meet many of the needs formerly met by limited partnerships. This Act therefore targets two types of enterprises that seem largely beyond the scope of LLPs and LLCs: (i) sophisticated, manager-entrenched commercial deals whose participants commit for the long term, and (ii) estate planning arrangements (family limited partnerships). This Act accordingly assumes that, more often than not, people utilizing it will want:

- strong centralized management, strongly entrenched, and

- passive investors with little control over or right to exit the entity

The Act's rules, and particularly its default rules, have been designed to reflect these assumptions....

Availability of LLLP Status

Following the example of a growing number of States, this Act provides for limited liability limited partnerships. In a limited liability limited partnership ("LLLP"), no partner—whether general or limited—is liable on account of partner status for the limited partnership's obligations. Both general and limited partners benefit from a full, status-based liability shield that is equivalent to the shield enjoyed by corporate shareholders, LLC members, and partners in an LLP.

This Act is designed to serve preexisting limited partnerships as well as limited partnerships formed after the Act's enactment. Most of those preexisting limited partnership will not be LLLPs, and accordingly the Act does not prefer or presume LLLP status. Instead, the Act makes LLLP status available through a simple statement in the certificate of limited partnership. See Sections 102(9), 201(a)(4) and 404(c).

268

Liability Shield for Limited Partners

RULPA provides only a restricted liability shield for limited partners. The shield is at risk for any limited partner who "participates in the control of the business." RULPA Section 303(a). Although this "control rule" is subject to a lengthy list of safe harbors, RULPA Section 303(b), in a world with LLPs, LLCs and, most importantly, LLLPs, the rule is an anachronism. This Act therefore eliminates the control rule and provides a full, status-based shield against limited partner liability for entity obligations. The shield applies whether or not the limited partnership is an LLLP. See Section 303.

Transition Issues

Following RUPA's example, this Act provides (i) an effective date, after which all newly formed limited partnerships are subject to this Act; (ii) an optional period, during which limited partnerships formed under a predecessor statute may elect to become subject to this Act; and (iii) a mandatory date, on which all preexisting limited partnerships become subject to this Act by operation of law.

A few provisions of this Act differ so substantially from prior law that they should not apply automatically to a preexisting limited partnership. Section 1206(c) lists these provisions and states that each remains inapplicable to a preexisting limited partnership, unless the limited partnership elects for the provision to apply.

Comparison of RULPA and this Act

The following table compares some of the major characteristics of RULPA and this Act. In most instances, the rules involved are "default" rules—i.e., subject to change by the partnership agreement.

Characteristic	RULPA	this Act
relationship to general partnership act	linked, Sections 1105, 403; UPA Section 6(2)	de-linked (but many RUPA provisions incorporated)
permitted purposes	subject to any specified exceptions, "any business that a partnership without limited partners may carry on," Section 106	any lawful purpose, Section 104(b)
constructive notice via publicly filed documents	only that limited partnership exists and that designated general partners are general partners, Section 208	RULPA constructive notice provisions carried forward, Section 103(c), plus constructive notice, 90 days after appropriate filing, of:

Characteristic	RULPA	this Act
		general partner dissociation and of limited partnership dissolution, termination, merger and conversion, Section 103(d)
duration	specified in certificate of limited partnership, Section 201(a)(4)	perpetual, Section 104(c); subject to change in partnership agreement
use of limited partner name in entity name	prohibited, except in unusual circumstances, Section 102(2)	permitted, Section 108(a)
annual report	none	required, Section 210
limited partner liability for entity debts	none unless limited partner "participates in the control of the business" and person "transact[s] business with the limited partnership reasonably believing . . . that the limited partner is a general partner," Section 303(a); safe harbor lists many activities that do not constitute participating in the control of the business, Section 303(b)	none, regardless of whether the limited partnership is an LLLP, "even if the limited partner participates in the management and control of the limited partnership," Section 303
limited partner duties	none specified	no fiduciary duties "solely by reason of being a limited partner," Section 305(a); each limited partner is obliged to "discharge duties . . . and exercise rights consistently with the obligation of good faith and fair dealing," Section 305(b)
partner access to information—required records/information	all partners have right of access; no requirement of good cause; Act does not state whether partnership agreement may limit access; Sections	list of required information expanded slightly; Act expressly states that partner does not have to show good

Characteristic	RULPA	this Act
	105(b) and 305(1)	cause; Sections 304(a), 407(a); however, the partnership agreement may set reasonable restrictions on access to and use of required information, Section 110(b)(4), and limited partnership may impose reasonable restrictions on the use of information, Sections 304(g) and 407(f)
partner access to information—other information	limited partners have the right to obtain other relevant information "upon reasonable demand," Section 305(2); general partner rights linked to general partnership act, Section 403	for limited partners, RULPA approach essentially carried forward, with procedures and standards for making a reasonable demand stated in greater detail, plus requirement that limited partnership supply known material information when limited partner consent sought, Section 304; general partner access rights made explicit, following ULLCA and RUPA, including obligation of limited partnership and general partners to volunteer certain information, Section 407; access rights provided for former partners, Sections 304 and 407
general partner liability for entity debts	complete, automatic and formally inescapable, Section 403(b) (n.b.—in practice, most modern	LLLP status available via a simple statement in the certificate of limit-

Characteristic	RULPA	this Act
	limited partnerships have used a general partner that has its own liability shield; *e.g.*, a corporation or limited liability company)	ed partnership, Sections 102(9), 201(a)(4); LLLP status provides a full liability shield to all general partners, Section 404(c); if the limited partnership is not an LLLP, general partners are liable just as under RULPA, Section 404(a)
general partner duties	linked to duties of partners in a general partnership, Section 403	RUPA general partner duties imported, Section 408; general partner's non-compete duty continues during winding up, Section 408(b)(3)
allocation of profits, losses and distributions	provides separately for sharing of profits and losses, Section 503, and for sharing of distributions, Section 504; allocates each according to contributions made and not returned	eliminates as unnecessary the allocation rule for profits and losses; allocates distributions according to contributions made, Section 503 (n.b.—in the default mode, the Act's formulation produces the same result as RULPA formulation)
partner liability for distributions	recapture liability if distribution involved "the return of . . . contribution"; one year recapture liability if distribution rightful, Section 608(a); six year recapture liability if wrongful, Section 608(b)	following ULLCA Sections 406 and 407, the Act adopts the RMBCA approach to improper distributions, Sections 508 and 509
limited partner voluntary dissociation	theoretically, limited partner may withdraw on six months notice unless partnership agreement specifies a term for	no "right to dissociate as a limited partner before the termination of the limited partner-

Characteristic	RULPA	this Act
	the limited partnership or withdrawal events for limited partner, Section 603; practically, virtually every partnership agreement specifies a term, thereby eliminating the right to withdraw (n.b.— due to estate planning concerns, several States have amended RULPA to prohibit limited partner withdrawal unless otherwise provided in the partnership agreement)	ship," Section 601(a); power to dissociate expressly recognized, Section 601(b)(1), but can be eliminated by the partnership agreement
limited partner involuntary dissociation	not addressed	lengthy list of causes, Section 601(b), taken with some modification from RUPA
limited partner dissociation—payout	"fair value . . . based upon [the partner's] right to share in distributions," Section 604	no payout; person becomes transferee of its own transferable interest, Section 602(3)
general partner voluntary dissociation	right exists unless otherwise provided in partnership agreement, Section 602; power exists regardless of partnership agreement, Section 602	RULPA rule carried forward, although phrased differently, Section 604(a); dissociation before termination of the limited partnership is defined as wrongful, Section 604(b)(2)
general partner involuntary dissociation	Section 402 lists causes	following RUPA, Section 603 expands the list of causes, including expulsion by court order, Section 603(5)
general partner dissociation—payout	"fair value . . . based upon [the partner's] right to share in distributions," Section 604, subject to offset for dam-	no payout; person becomes transferee of its own transferable interest, Section 605(5)

Characteristic	RULPA	this Act
	ages caused by wrongful withdrawal, Section 602	
transfer of partner interest—nomenclature	"Assignment of Partnership Interest," Section 702	"Transfer of Partner's Transferable Interest," Section 702
transfer of partner interest—substance	economic rights fully transferable, but management rights and partner status are not transferable, Section 702	same rule, but Sections 701 and 702 follow RUPA's more detailed and less oblique formulation
rights of creditor of partner	limited to charging order, Section 703	essentially the same rule, but, following RUPA and ULLCA, the Act has a more elaborate provision that expressly extends to creditors of transferees, Section 703
dissolution by partner consent	requires unanimous written consent, Section 801(3)	requires consent of "all general partners and of limited partners owning a majority of the rights to receive distributions as limited partners at the time the consent is to be effective," Section 801(2)
dissolution following dissociation of a general partner	occurs automatically unless all partners agree to continue the business and, if there is no remaining general partner, to appoint a replacement general partner, Section 801(4)	if at least one general partner remains, no dissolution unless "within 90 days after the dissociation . . . partners owning a majority of the rights to receive distributions as partners" consent to dissolve the limited partnership; Section 801(3)(A); if no general partner remains, disso-

274

Characteristic	RULPA	this Act
		lution occurs upon the passage of 90 days after the dissociation, unless before that deadline limited partners owning a majority of the rights to receive distributions owned by limited partners consent to continue the business and admit at least one new general partner and a new general partner is admitted, Section 801(3)(B)
filings related to entity termination	certificate of limited partnership to be cancelled when limited partnership dissolves and begins winding up, Section 203	limited partnership may amend certificate to indicate dissolution, Section 803(b)(1), and may file statement of termination indicating that winding up has been completed and the limited partnership is terminated, Section 203
procedures for barring claims against dissolved limited partnership	none	following ULLCA Sections 807 and 808, the Act adopts the RMBCA approach providing for giving notice and barring claims, Sections 806 and 807
conversions and mergers	no provision	Article 11 permits conversions to and from and mergers with any "organization," defined as "a general partnership, including a limited liability partnership; limit-

Characteristic	RULPA	this Act
		ed partnership, including a limited liability limited partnership; limited liability company; business trust; corporation; or any other entity having a governing statute . . . [including] domestic and foreign entities regardless of whether organized for profit." Section 1101(8)
writing requirements	some provisions pertain only to written understandings; *see, e.g.*, Sections 401 (partnership agreement may "provide in writing for the admission of additional general partners"; such admission also permitted "with the written consent of all partners"), 502(a) (limited partner's promise to contribute "is not enforceable unless set out in a writing signed by the limited partner"), 801(2) and (3) (dissolution occurs "upon the happening of events specified in writing in the partnership agreement" and upon "written consent of all partners"), 801(4) (dissolution avoided following withdrawal of a general partner if "all partners agree in writing")	removes virtually all writing requirements; but does require that certain information be maintained in record form, Section 111

[ARTICLE] 1

GENERAL PROVISIONS

SECTION 101.   SHORT TITLE. This [Act] may be cited as the Uniform Limited Partnership Act [year of enactment].

SECTION 102.   DEFINITIONS. In this [Act]:

(1) "Certificate of limited partnership" means the certificate required by Section 201. The term includes the certificate as amended or restated.

(2) "Contribution", except in the phrase "right of contribution," means any benefit provided by a person to a limited partnership in order to become a partner or in the person's capacity as a partner.

(3) "Debtor in bankruptcy" means a person that is the subject of:

(A) an order for relief under Title 11 of the United States Code or a comparable order under a successor statute of general application; or

(B) a comparable order under federal, state, or foreign law governing insolvency.

(4) "Designated office" means:

(A) with respect to a limited partnership, the office that the limited partnership is required to designate and maintain under Section 114; and

(B) with respect to a foreign limited partnership, its principal office.

(5) "Distribution" means a transfer of money or other property from a limited partnership to a partner in the partner's capacity as a partner or to a transferee on account of a transferable interest owned by the transferee.

(6) "Foreign limited liability limited partnership" means a foreign limited partnership whose general partners have limited liability for the obligations of the foreign limited partnership under a provision similar to Section 404(c).

(7) "Foreign limited partnership" means a partnership formed under the laws of a jurisdiction other than this State and required by those laws to have one or more general partners and one or more limited partners. The term includes a foreign limited liability limited partnership.

(8) "General partner" means:

(A) with respect to a limited partnership, a person that:

277

(i) becomes a general partner under Section 401; or

(ii) was a general partner in a limited partnership when the limited partnership became subject to this [Act] under Section 1206(a) or (b); and

(B) with respect to a foreign limited partnership, a person that has rights, powers, and obligations similar to those of a general partner in a limited partnership.

(9) "Limited liability limited partnership", except in the phrase "foreign limited liability limited partnership", means a limited partnership whose certificate of limited partnership states that the limited partnership is a limited liability limited partnership.

(10) "Limited partner" means:

(A) with respect to a limited partnership, a person that:

(i) becomes a limited partner under Section 301; or

(ii) was a limited partner in a limited partnership when the limited partnership became subject to this [Act] under Section 1206(a) or (b); and

(B) with respect to a foreign limited partnership, a person that has rights, powers, and obligations similar to those of a limited partner in a limited partnership.

(11) "Limited partnership", except in the phrases "foreign limited partnership" and "foreign limited liability limited partnership", means an entity, having one or more general partners and one or more limited partners, which is formed under this [Act] by two or more persons or becomes subject to this [Act] under [Article] 11 or Section 1206(a) or (b). The term includes a limited liability limited partnership.

(12) "Partner" means a limited partner or general partner.

(13) "Partnership agreement" means the partners' agreement, whether oral, implied, in a record, or in any combination, concerning the limited partnership. The term includes the agreement as amended.

(14) "Person" means an individual, corporation, business trust, estate, trust, partnership, limited liability company, association, joint venture, government; governmental subdivision, agency, or instrumentality; public corporation, or any other legal or commercial entity.

(15) "Person dissociated as a general partner" means a person dissociated as a general partner of a limited partnership.

(16) "Principal office" means the office where the principal executive office of a limited partnership or foreign limited partnership is located, whether or not the office is located in this State.

(17) "Record" means information that is inscribed on a tangible medium or that is stored in an electronic or other medium and is retrievable in perceivable form.

(18) "Required information" means the information that a limited partnership is required to maintain under Section 111.

(19) "Sign" means:

(A) to execute or adopt a tangible symbol with the present intent to authenticate a record; or

(B) to attach or logically associate an electronic symbol, sound, or process to or with a record with the present intent to authenticate the record.

(20) "State" means a State of the United States, the District of Columbia, Puerto Rico, the United States Virgin Islands, or any territory or insular possession subject to the jurisdiction of the United States.

(21) "Transfer" includes an assignment, conveyance, deed, bill of sale, lease, mortgage, security interest, encumbrance, gift, and transfer by operation of law.

(22) "Transferable interest" means a partner's right to receive distributions.

(23) "Transferee" means a person to which all or part of a transferable interest has been transferred, whether or not the transferor is a partner.

Comment

This section contains definitions applicable throughout the Act. Section 1101 provides additional definitions applicable within Article 11....

Paragraph (11) [Limited partnership]—This definition pertains to what is commonly termed a "domestic" limited partnership. The definition encompasses: (i) limited partnerships originally formed under this Act, including limited partnerships formed under Section 1101(11) to be the surviving organization in a merger; (ii) any entity that becomes subject to this Act by converting into a limited partnership under Article 11; (iii) any preexisting domestic limited partnership that elects pursuant to Section 1206(a) to become subject to this Act; and (iv) all other preexisting domestic limited partnerships when they become subject to this Act under Section 1206(b).

Following the approach of predecessor law, RULPA Section 101(7), this definition contains two substantive requirements. First, it is of the essence of a limited partnership to have two classes of partners. Accordingly, under Section 101(11) a limited partnership must have at least one general and one limited partner. Section 801(3)(B) and (4) provide that a limited partnership dissolves if its sole general partner or sole limited partner dissociates and the limited partnership fails to admit a replacement within 90 days of the dissociation. The 90 day limitation is a default rule, but, in light of Section 101(11), a limited partnership may not indefinitely delay "having one or more general partners and one or more limited partners."

It is also of the essence of a limited partnership to have at least two partners. Section 101(11) codifies this requirement by referring to a limited partnership as "an entity ... which is formed under this [Act] by two or more persons." Thus, while the same person may be both a general and limited partner, Section 113 (Dual Capacity), one person alone cannot be the "two persons" contemplated by this definition. However, nothing in this definition prevents two closely affiliated persons from satisfying the two person requirement.

Paragraph (13) [Partnership agreement]—Section 110 is essential to understanding the significance of the partnership agreement. See also Section 201(d) (resolving inconsistencies between the certificate of limited partnership and the partnership agreement).

Paragraph (21) [Transfer]—Following RUPA, this Act uses the words "transfer" and "transferee" rather than the words "assignment" and "assignee." See RUPA Section 503.

The reference to "transfer by operation of law" is significant in connection with Section 702 (Transfer of Partner's Transferable Interest). That section severely restricts a transferee's rights (absent the consent of the partners), and this definition makes those restrictions applicable, for example, to transfers ordered by a family court as part of a divorce proceeding and transfers resulting from the death of a partner.

Paragraph (23) [Transferee]—See comment to Paragraph 21 for an explanation of why this Act refers to "transferee" rather than "assignee."

SECTION 103.   KNOWLEDGE AND NOTICE.

(a) A person knows a fact if the person has actual knowledge of it.

(b) A person has notice of a fact if the person:

(1) knows of it;

(2) has received a notification of it;

(3) has reason to know it exists from all of the facts known to the person at the time in question; or

(4) has notice of it under subsection (c) or (d).

(c) A certificate of limited partnership on file in the [office of the Secretary of State] is notice that the partnership is a limited partnership and the persons designated in the certificate as general partners are general partners. Except as otherwise provided in subsection (d), the certificate is not notice of any other fact.

(d) A person has notice of:

(1) another person's dissociation as a general partner, 90 days after the effective date of an amendment to the certificate of limited partnership which states that the other person has dissociated or 90 days after the effective date of a statement of dissociation pertaining to the other person, whichever occurs first;

(2) a limited partnership's dissolution, 90 days after the effective date of an amendment to the certificate of limited partnership stating that the limited partnership is dissolved;

(3) a limited partnership's termination, 90 days after the effective date of a statement of termination;

(4) a limited partnership's conversion under [Article] 11, 90 days after the effective date of the articles of conversion; or

(5) a merger under [Article] 11, 90 days after the effective date of the articles of merger.

(e) A person notifies or gives a notification to another person by taking steps reasonably required to inform the other person in ordinary course, whether or not the other person learns of it.

(f) A person receives a notification when the notification:

(1) comes to the person's attention; or

(2) is delivered at the person's place of business or at any other place held out by the person as a place for receiving communications.

(g) Except as otherwise provided in subsection (h), a person other than an individual knows, has notice, or receives a notification of a fact for purposes of a particular transaction when the individual conducting the transaction for the person knows, has notice, or receives a notification of the fact, or in any event when the fact would have been brought to the individual's attention if the person had exercised reasonable diligence. A person other than an individual exercises reasonable diligence if it maintains reasonable routines for communicating significant information to the individual conducting the transaction for the person and there is reasonable compliance with the routines. Reasonable diligence does not require an individual acting for the person to communicate information unless the communication is part of the individual's regular duties or the individual has reason to know of the transaction and that the transaction would be materially affected by the information.

(h) A general partner's knowledge, notice, or receipt of a notification of a fact relating to the limited partnership is effective immediately as knowledge of, notice to, or receipt of a notification by the limited partnership, except in the case of a fraud on the limited partnership committed by or with the consent of the general partner. A limited partner's knowledge, notice, or receipt of a notification of a fact relating to the limited partnership is not effective as knowledge of, notice to, or receipt of a notification by the limited partnership.

Comment . . .

Subsection (e)—The phrase "person learns of it" in this subsection is equivalent to the phrase "knows of it" in subsection (b)(1).

Subsection (h)—Under this subsection and Section 302, information possessed by a person that is only a limited partner is not attributable to the limited partnership. However, information possessed by a person that is both a general partner and a limited partner is attributable to the limited partnership. See Section 113 (Dual Capacity)

SECTION 104. NATURE, PURPOSE, AND DURATION OF ENTITY.

(a) A limited partnership is an entity distinct from its partners. A limited partnership is the same entity regardless of whether its certificate states that the limited partnership is a limited liability limited partnership.

(b) A limited partnership may be organized under this [Act] for any lawful purpose.

(c) A limited partnership has a perpetual duration.

Comment

Subsection (a)—Acquiring or relinquishing an LLLP shield changes only the rules governing a general partner's liability for subsequently incurred obligations of the limited partnership. The underlying entity is unaffected. . . .

Subsection (c)—The partnership agreement has the power to vary this subsection, either by stating a definite term or by specifying an event or events which cause dissolution. Sections 110(a) and 801(1). Section 801 also recognizes several other occurrences that cause dissolution. . . .

SECTION 105. POWERS.
A limited partnership has the powers to do all things necessary or convenient to carry on its activities, including the power to sue, be sued, and defend in its own name and to maintain an action against a partner for harm caused to the limited partnership by a breach of the partnership agreement or violation of a duty to the partnership.

Comment

This Act omits as unnecessary any detailed list of specific powers. The power to sue and be sued is mentioned specifically so

282

that Section 110(b)(1) can prohibit the partnership agreement from varying that power. The power to maintain an action against a partner is mentioned specifically to establish that the limited partnership itself has standing to enforce the partnership agreement.

SECTION 106. GOVERNING LAW. The law of this State governs relations among the partners of a limited partnership and between the partners and the limited partnership and the liability of partners as partners for an obligation of the limited partnership.

Comment

To partially define its scope, this section uses the phrase "relations among the partners of a limited partnership and between the partners and the limited partnership." Section 110(a) uses essentially identical language in defining the proper realm of the partnership agreement: "relations among the partners and between the partners and the partnership."

Despite the similarity of language, this section has no bearing on the power of a partnership agreement to vary other provisions of this Act. It is quite possible for a provision of this Act to involve "relations among the partners of a limited partnership and between the partners and the limited partnership" and thus come within this section, and yet not be subject to variation by the partnership agreement. Although Section 110(a) grants plenary authority to the partnership agreement to regulate "relations among the partners and between the partners and the partnership," that authority is subject to Section 110(b).

For example, Section 408 (General Standards of General Partners's Conduct) certainly involves "relations among the partners of a limited partnership and between the partners and the limited partnership." Therefore, according to this section, Section 408 applies to a limited partnership formed or otherwise subject to this Act. Just as certainly, Section 408 pertains to "relations among the partners and between the partners and the partnership" for the purposes of Section 110(a), and therefore the partnership agreement may properly address matters covered by Section 408. However, Section 110(b)(5), (6), and (7) limit the power of the partnership agreement to vary the rules stated in Section 408. See also, e.g., Section 502(c) (stating creditor's rights, which are protected under Section 110(b)(13) from being restricted by the partnership agreement) and Comment to Section 509.

This section also applies to "the liability of partners as partners for an obligation of a limited partnership." The phrase "as partners" contemplates the liability shield for limited partners under Section 303 and the rules for general partner liability stated in

Section 404. Other grounds for liability can be supplied by other law, including the law of some other jurisdiction. For example, a partner's contractual guaranty of a limited partnership obligation might well be governed by the law of some other jurisdiction.

Transferees derive their rights and status under this Act from partners and accordingly this section applies to the relations of a transferee to the limited partnership.

The partnership agreement may not vary the rule stated in this section. See Section 110(b)(2).

SECTION 107. SUPPLEMENTAL PRINCIPLES OF LAW; RATE OF INTEREST.

(a) Unless displaced by particular provisions of this [Act], the principles of law and equity supplement this [Act].

(b) If an obligation to pay interest arises under this [Act] and the rate is not specified, the rate is that specified in [applicable statute].

Comment

Subsection (a)—This language comes from RUPA Section 104 and does not address an important question raised by the de-linking of this Act from the UPA and RUPA—namely, to what extent is the case law of general partnerships relevant to limited partnerships governed by this Act?

Predecessor law, RULPA Section 403, expressly equated the rights, powers, restrictions, and liabilities of a general partner in a limited partnership with the rights, powers, restrictions, and liabilities of a partner in a general partnership. This Act has no comparable provision. See Prefatory Note. Therefore, a court should not assume that a case concerning a general partnership is automatically relevant to a limited partnership governed by this Act. A general partnership case may be relevant by analogy, especially if (1) the issue in dispute involves a provision of this Act for which a comparable provision exists under the law of general partnerships; and (2) the fundamental differences between a general partnership and limited partnership are immaterial to the disputed issue.

SECTION 108. NAME.

(a) The name of a limited partnership may contain the name of any partner.

(b) The name of a limited partnership that is not a limited liability limited partnership must contain the phrase "limited partnership" or the abbreviation "L.P." or "LP" and may not contain the phrase "limited liability limited partnership" or the abbreviation "LLLP" or "L.L.L.P.".

(c) The name of a limited liability limited partnership must contain the phrase "limited liability limited partnership" or the abbreviation "LLLP" or "L.L.L.P." and must not contain the abbreviation "L.P."or "LP." ...

SECTION 110. EFFECT OF PARTNERSHIP AGREEMENT; NONWAIVABLE PROVISIONS.

(a) Except as otherwise provided in subsection (b), the partnership agreement governs relations among the partners and between the partners and the partnership. To the extent the partnership agreement does not otherwise provide, this [Act] governs relations among the partners and between the partners and the partnership.

(b) A partnership agreement may not:

(1) vary a limited partnership's power under Section 105 to sue, be sued, and defend in its own name;

(2) vary the law applicable to a limited partnership under Section 106;

(3) vary the requirements of Section 204;

(4) vary the information required under Section 111 or unreasonably restrict the right to information under Sections 304 or 407, but the partnership agreement may impose reasonable restrictions on the availability and use of information obtained under those sections and may define appropriate remedies, including liquidated damages, for a breach of any reasonable restriction on use;

(5) eliminate the duty of loyalty under Section 408, but the partnership agreement may:

(A) identify specific types or categories of activities that do not violate the duty of loyalty, if not manifestly unreasonable; and

(B) specify the number or percentage of partners which may authorize or ratify, after full disclosure to all partners of all material facts, a specific act or transaction that otherwise would violate the duty of loyalty;

(6) unreasonably reduce the duty of care under Section 408(c);

(7) eliminate the obligation of good faith and fair dealing under Sections 305(b) and 408(d), but the partnership agreement may prescribe the standards by which the performance of the obligation is to be measured, if the standards are not manifestly unreasonable;

(8) vary the power of a person to dissociate as a general partner under Section 604(a) except to require that the notice under Section 603(1) be in a record;

(9) vary the power of a court to decree dissolution in the circumstances specified in Section 802;

(10) vary the requirement to wind up the partnership's business as specified in Section 803;

(11) unreasonably restrict the right to maintain an action under [Article] 10;

(12) restrict the right of a partner under Section 1110(a) to approve a conversion or merger or the right of a general partner under Section 1110(b) to consent to an amendment to the certificate of limited partnership which deletes a statement that the limited partnership is a limited liability limited partnership; or

(13) restrict rights under this [Act] of a person other than a partner or a transferee.

Comment . . .

Subject only to subsection (b), the partnership agreement has plenary power to structure and regulate the relations of the partners *inter se*. Although the certificate of limited partnership is a limited partnership's foundational document, among the partners the partnership agreement controls. See Section 201(d).

The partnership agreement has the power to control the manner of its own amendment. In particular, a provision of the agreement prohibiting oral modifications is enforceable, despite any common law antagonism to "no oral modification" provisions. Likewise, a partnership agreement can impose "made in a record" requirements on other aspects of the partners' relationship, such as requiring consents to be made in a record and signed, or rendering unenforceable oral promises to make contributions or oral understandings as to "events upon the happening of which the limited partnership is to be dissolved," Section 111(9)(D). See also Section 801(1).

Subsection (b)(3)—The referenced section states who must sign various documents.

Subsection (b)(4)—In determining whether a restriction is reasonable, a court might consider: (i) the danger or other problem the restriction seeks to avoid; (ii) the purpose for which the information is sought; and (iii) whether, in light of both the problem and the purpose, the restriction is reasonably tailored. Restricting access to or use of the names and addresses of limited partners is not per se unreasonable.

Under this Act, general and limited partners have sharply different roles. A restriction that is reasonable as to a limited partner is not necessarily reasonable as to a general partner.

Sections 304(g) and 407(f) authorize the limited partnership (as distinguished from the partnership agreement) to impose restrictions on the use of information. For a comparison of restrictions contained in the partnership agreement and restrictions imposed unilaterally by the limited partnership, see the Comment to Section 304(g).

Subsection (b)(5)(A)—It is not per se manifestly unreasonable for the partnership agreement to permit a general partner to compete with the limited partnership.

Subsection (b)(5)(B)—The Act does not require that the authorization or ratification be by **disinterested** partners, although the partnership agreement may so provide. The Act does require that the disclosure be made to all partners, even if the partnership agreement excludes some partners from the authorization or ratification process. An interested partner that participates in the authorization or ratification process is subject to the obligation of good faith and fair dealing. Sections 305(b) and 408(d).

Subsection (b)(8)—This restriction applies only to the power of a person to dissociate as a general partner. The partnership agreement may eliminate the power of a person to dissociate as a limited partner.

Subsection (b)(9)—This provision should not be read to limit a partnership agreement's power to provide for arbitration. For example, an agreement to arbitrate all disputes—including dissolution disputes—is enforceable. Any other interpretation would put this Act at odds with federal law. *See Southland Corp. v. Keating*, 465 U.S. 1 (1984) (holding that the Federal Arbitration Act preempts state statutes that seek to invalidate agreements to arbitrate) and *Allied-Bruce Terminix Cos., Inc. v. Dobson*, 513 U.S. 265 (1995) (same). This provision does prohibit any narrowing of the substantive grounds for judicial dissolution as stated in Section 802.

> **Example:** A provision of a partnership agreement states that no partner may obtain judicial dissolution without showing that a general partner is in material breach of the partnership agreement. The provision is ineffective to prevent a court from ordering dissolution under Section 802.

Subsection (b)(11)—Section 1001 codifies a partner's right to bring a direct action, and the rest of Article 10 provides for derivative actions. The partnership agreement may not restrict a partner's right to bring either type of action if the effect is to undercut or frustrate the duties and rights protected by Section 110(b).

The reasonableness of a restriction on derivative actions should be judged in light of the history and purpose of derivative actions. They originated as an equitable remedy, intended to protect passive owners against management abuses. A partnership agreement may not provide that all derivative claims will be subject to final determination by a special litigation committee appointed by the limited partnership, because that provision would eliminate, not merely restrict, a partner's right to bring a derivative *action*.

Subsection (b)(12)—Section 1110 imposes special consent requirements with regard to transactions that might make a partner personally liable for entity debts.

Subsection (b)(13)—The partnership agreement is a contract, and this provision reflects a basic notion of contract law—namely, that a contract can **directly** restrict rights only of parties to the contract and of persons who derive their rights from the contract. A provision of a partnership agreement can be determined to be unenforceable against third parties under paragraph (b)(13) without therefore and automatically being unenforceable *inter se* the partners and any transferees. How the former determination affects the latter question is a matter of other law.

SECTION 111. REQUIRED INFORMATION. A limited partnership shall maintain at its designated office the following information:

(1) a current list showing the full name and last known street and mailing address of each partner, separately identifying the general partners, in alphabetical order, and the limited partners, in alphabetical order;

(2) a copy of the initial certificate of limited partnership and all amendments to and restatements of the certificate, together with signed copies of any powers of attorney under which any certificate, amendment, or restatement has been signed;

(3) a copy of any filed articles of conversion or merger;

(4) a copy of the limited partnership's federal, state, and local income tax returns and reports, if any, for the three most recent years;

(5) a copy of any partnership agreement made in a record and any amendment made in a record to any partnership agreement;

(6) a copy of any financial statement of the limited partnership for the three most recent years;

(7) a copy of the three most recent annual reports delivered by the limited partnership to the [Secretary of State] pursuant to Section 210;

(8) a copy of any record made by the limited partnership during the past three years of any consent given by or vote taken of any partner pursuant to this [Act] or the partnership agreement; and

(9) unless contained in a partnership agreement made in a record, a record stating:

(A) the amount of cash, and a description and statement of the agreed value of the other benefits, contributed and agreed to be contributed by each partner;

(B) the times at which, or events on the happening of which, any additional contributions agreed to be made by each partner are to be made;

(C) for any person that is both a general partner and a limited partner, a specification of what transferable interest the person owns in each capacity; and

(D) any events upon the happening of which the limited partnership is to be dissolved and its activities wound up.

Comment ...

Sections 304 and 407 govern access to the information required by this section, as well as to other information pertaining to a limited partnership. . . .

SECTION 112. BUSINESS TRANSACTIONS OF PARTNER WITH PARTNERSHIP.

A partner may lend money to and transact other business with the limited partnership and has the same rights and obligations with respect to the loan or other transaction as a person that is not a partner.

Comment ...

This section has no impact on a general partner's duty under Section 408(b)(2) (duty of loyalty includes refraining from acting as or for an adverse party) and means rather that this Act does not discriminate against a creditor of a limited partnership that happens also to be a partner. *See, e.g., BT–I v. Equitable Life Assurance Society of the United States,* 75 Cal.App.4th 1406, 1415, 89 Cal. Rptr.2d 811, 814 (Cal.App. 4 Dist.1999). and *SEC v. DuPont, Homsey & Co.,* 204 F. Supp. 944, 946 (D. Mass. 1962), vacated and remanded on other grounds, 334 F2d 704 (1st Cir. 1964). This section does not, however, override other law, such as fraudulent transfer or conveyance acts.

SECTION 113. DUAL CAPACITY.

A person may be both a general partner and a limited partner. A person that is both a general and limited partner has the rights, powers, duties, and obligations provided by this [Act] and the partnership agreement in each of those capacities. When the person acts as a general partner, the person is subject to the obligations, duties and restrictions under this [Act] and the partnership agreement for general partners. When the person acts as a limited partner, the person is subject to the obligations, duties and restrictions under this [Act] and the partnership agreement for limited partners.

289

SECTION 114. OFFICE AND AGENT FOR SERVICE OF PROCESS.

(a) A limited partnership shall designate and continuously maintain in this State:

(1) an office, which need not be a place of its activity in this State; and

(2) an agent for service of process.

(b) A foreign limited partnership shall designate and continuously maintain in this State an agent for service of process.

(c) An agent for service of process of a limited partnership or foreign limited partnership must be an individual who is a resident of this State or other person authorized to do business in this State.

SECTION 118. CONSENT AND PROXIES OF PARTNERS.

Action requiring the consent of partners under this [Act] may be taken without a meeting, and a partner may appoint a proxy to consent or otherwise act for the partner by signing an appointment record, either personally or by the partner's attorney in fact.

[ARTICLE] 2

FORMATION; CERTIFICATE OF LIMITED PARTNERSHIP AND OTHER FILINGS

SECTION 201. FORMATION OF LIMITED PARTNERSHIP; CERTIFICATE OF LIMITED PARTNERSHIP.

(a) In order for a limited partnership to be formed, a certificate of limited partnership must be delivered to the [Secretary of State] for filing. The certificate must state:

(1) the name of the limited partnership, which must comply with Section 108;

(2) the street and mailing address of the initial designated office and the name and street and mailing address of the initial agent for service of process;

(3) the name and the street and mailing address of each general partner;

(4) whether the limited partnership is a limited liability limited partnership; and

(5) any additional information required by [Article] 11.

(b) A certificate of limited partnership may also contain any other matters but may not vary or otherwise affect the provisions specified in Section 110(b) in a manner inconsistent with that section.

(c) If there has been substantial compliance with subsection (a), subject to Section 206(c) a limited partnership is formed when the [Secretary of State] files the certificate of limited partnership.

(d) Subject to subsection (b), if any provision of a partnership agreement is inconsistent with the filed certificate of limited partnership or with a filed statement of dissociation, termination, or change or filed articles of conversion or merger:

(1) the partnership agreement prevails as to partners and transferees; and

(2) the filed certificate of limited partnership, statement of dissociation, termination, or change or articles of conversion or merger prevail as to persons, other than partners and transferees, that reasonably rely on the filed record to their detriment.

Comment . . .

A limited partnership is a creature of statute, and this section governs how a limited partnership comes into existence. A limited partnership is formed only if (i) a certificate of limited partnership is prepared and delivered to the specified public official for filing, (ii) the public official files the certificate, and (iii) the certificate, delivery and filing are in "substantial compliance" with the requirements of subsection (a). Section 206(c) governs when a limited partnership comes into existence.

Despite its foundational importance, a certificate of limited partnership is far less powerful than a corporation's articles of incorporation. Among partners and transferees, for example, the partnership agreement is paramount. See Section 201(d). . . .

Subsection (a)(4)—This Act permits a limited partnership to be a limited liability limited partnership ("LLLP"), and this provision requires the certificate of limited partnership to state whether the limited partnership is an LLLP. The requirement is intended to force the organizers of a limited partnership to decide whether the limited partnership is to be an LLLP.

Subject to Sections 406(b)(2) and 1110, a limited partnership may amend its certificate of limited partnership to add or delete a statement that the limited partnership is a limited liability limited partnership. An amendment deleting such a statement must be accompanied by an amendment stating that the limited partnership is **not** a limited liability limited partnership. Section 201(a)(4) does not permit a certificate of limited partnership to be silent on this point, except for pre-existing partnerships that become subject to this Act under Section 1206. See Section 1206(c)(2). . . .

A limited partnership is a creature of contract as well as a creature of statute. It will be possible, albeit improper, for the partnership agreement to be inconsistent with the certificate of limited partnership or other specified public filings relating to the limited partnership. For those circumstances, this subsection provides the rule for determining which source of information prevails.

For partners and transferees, the partnership agreement is paramount. For third parties seeking to invoke the public record, actual knowledge of that record is necessary and notice under Section 103(c) or (d) is irrelevant. A third party wishing to enforce the public record over the partnership agreement must show reasonable reliance on the public record, and reliance presupposes knowledge. . . .

SECTION 202.   AMENDMENT OR RESTATEMENT OF CERTIFICATE.

(a) In order to amend its certificate of limited partnership, a limited partnership must deliver to the [Secretary of State] for filing an amendment or, pursuant to [Article] 11, articles of merger stating:

(1) the name of the limited partnership;

(2) the date of filing of its initial certificate; and

(3) the changes the amendment makes to the certificate as most recently amended or restated.

(b) A limited partnership shall promptly deliver to the [Secretary of State] for filing an amendment to a certificate of limited partnership to reflect:

(1) the admission of a new general partner;

(2) the dissociation of a person as a general partner; or

(3) the appointment of a person to wind up the limited partnership's activities under Section 803(c) or (d).

(c) A general partner that knows that any information in a filed certificate of limited partnership was false when the certificate was filed or has become false due to changed circumstances shall promptly:

(1) cause the certificate to be amended; or

(2) if appropriate, deliver to the [Secretary of State] for filing a statement of change pursuant to Section 115 or a statement of correction pursuant to Section 207.

(d) A certificate of limited partnership may be amended at any time for any other proper purpose as determined by the limited partnership.

(e) A restated certificate of limited partnership may be delivered to the [Secretary of State] for filing in the same manner as an amendment.

(f) Subject to Section 206(c), an amendment or restated certificate is effective when filed by the [Secretary of State].

SECTION 203. STATEMENT OF TERMINATION. A dissolved limited partnership that has completed winding up may deliver to the [Secretary of State] for filing a statement of termination that states:

(1) the name of the limited partnership;

(2) the date of filing of its initial certificate of limited partnership; and

(3) any other information as determined by the general partners filing the statement or by a person appointed pursuant to Section 803(c) or (d).

SECTION 209. CERTIFICATE OF EXISTENCE OR AUTHORIZATION.

(a) The [Secretary of State], upon request and payment of the requisite fee, shall furnish a certificate of existence for a limited partnership if the records filed in the [office of the Secretary of State] show that the [Secretary of State] has filed a certificate of limited partnership and has not filed a statement of termination....

SECTION 210. ANNUAL REPORT FOR [SECRETARY OF STATE].

(a) A limited partnership or a foreign limited partnership authorized to transact business in this State shall deliver to the [Secretary of State] for filing an annual report that states:

(1) the name of the limited partnership or foreign limited partnership;

(2) the street and mailing address of its designated office and the name and street and mailing address of its agent for service of process in this State;

(3) in the case of a limited partnership, the street and mailing address of its principal office; and

(4) in the case of a foreign limited partnership, the State or other jurisdiction under whose law the foreign limited partnership is formed and any alternate name adopted under Section 905(a).

(b) Information in an annual report must be current as of the date the annual report is delivered to the [Secretary of State] for filing.

(c) The first annual report must be delivered to the [Secretary of State] between [January 1 and April 1] of the year following the calendar year in which a limited partnership was formed or a foreign limited partnership was authorized to transact business. An annual report must be delivered to the [Secretary of State] between [January 1 and April 1] of each subsequent calendar year.

(d) If an annual report does not contain the information required in subsection (a), the [Secretary of State] shall promptly notify the reporting limited partnership or foreign limited partnership and return the report to it for correction. If the report is corrected to contain the information required in subsection (a) and delivered to the [Secretary of State] within 30 days after the effective date of the notice, it is timely delivered. . . .

[ARTICLE]   3

LIMITED PARTNERS

SECTION 301. BECOMING LIMITED PARTNER. A person becomes a limited partner:

(1) as provided in the partnership agreement;

(2) as the result of a conversion or merger under [Article] 11; or

(3) with the consent of all the partners.

SECTION 302. NO RIGHT OR POWER AS LIMITED PARTNER TO BIND LIMITED PARTNERSHIP. A limited partner does not have the right or the power as a limited partner to act for or bind the limited partnership.

Comment

In this respect a limited partner is analogous to a shareholder in a corporation; status as owner provides neither the right to manage nor a reasonable appearance of that right.

The phrase "as a limited partner" is intended to recognize that: (i) this section does not disable a general partner that also owns a limited partner interest, (ii) the partnership agreement may as a matter of contract allocate managerial rights to one or more limited partners; and (iii) a separate agreement can empower and entitle a person that is a limited partner to act for the limited partnership in another capacity; *e.g.*, as an agent. See Comment to Section 305.

The fact that a limited partner *qua* limited partner has no power to bind the limited partnership means that, subject to Section 113 (Dual Capacity), information possessed by a limited partner is not attributed to the limited partnership. See Section 103(h).

This Act specifies various circumstances in which limited partners have consent rights, including:

• admission of a limited partner, Section 301(3)

- admission of a general partner, Section 401(4)
- amendment of the partnership agreement, Section 406(b)(1)
- the decision to amend the certificate of limited partnership so as to obtain or relinquish LLLP status, Section 406(b)(2)
- the disposition of all or substantially all of the limited partnership's property, outside the ordinary course, Section 406(b)(3)
- the compromise of a partner's obligation to make a contribution or return an improper distribution, Section 502(c)
- expulsion of a limited partner by consent of the other partners, Section 601(b)(4)
- expulsion of a general partner by consent of the other partners, Section 603(4)
- redemption of a transferable interest subject to charging order, using limited partnership property, Section 703(c)(3)
- causing dissolution by consent, Section 801(2)
- causing dissolution by consent following the dissociation of a general partner, when at least one general partner remains, Section 801(3)(A)
- avoiding dissolution and appointing a successor general partner, following the dissociation of the sole general partner, Section 801(3)(B)
- appointing a person to wind up the limited partnership when there is no general partner, Section 803(C)
- approving, amending or abandoning a plan of conversion, Section 1103(a) and (b)(2)
- approving, amending or abandoning a plan of merger, Section 1107(a) and (b)(2).

SECTION 303.   NO LIABILITY AS LIMITED PARTNER FOR LIMITED PARTNERSHIP OBLIGATIONS. An obligation of a limited partnership, whether arising in contract, tort, or otherwise, is not the obligation of a limited partner. A limited partner is not personally liable, directly or indirectly, by way of contribution or otherwise, for an obligation of the limited partnership solely by reason of being a limited partner, even if the limited partner participates in the management and control of the limited partnership.

Comment

This section provides a full, status-based liability shield for each limited partner, "even if the limited partner participates in the management and control of the limited partnership." The section thus eliminates the so-called "control rule" with respect to personal liability for entity obligations and brings limited partners into parity with LLC members, LLP partners and corporate shareholders.

The "control rule" first appeared in an uniform act in 1916, although the concept is much older. Section 7 of the original Uniform Limited Partnership Act provided that "A limited partner shall not become liable as a general partner [i.e., for the obligations of the limited partnership] unless ... he takes part in the control of the business." The 1976 Uniform Limited Partnership Act (ULPA—1976) "carrie[d] over the basic test from former Section 7," but recognized "the difficulty of determining when the 'control' line has been overstepped." Comment to ULPA–1976, Section 303. Accordingly, ULPA–1976 tried to buttress the limited partner's shield by (i) providing a safe harbor for a lengthy list of activities deemed not to constitute participating in control, ULPA–1976, Section 303(b), and (ii) limiting a limited partner's "control rule" liability "only to persons who transact business with the limited partnership with actual knowledge of [the limited partner's] participation in control." ULPA–1976, Section 303(a). However, these protections were complicated by a countervailing rule which made a limited partner generally liable for the limited partnership's obligations "if the limited partner's participation in the control of the business is ... substantially the same as the exercise of the powers of a general partner." ULPA–1976, Section 303(a).

The 1985 amendments to ULPA–1976 (i.e., RULPA) further buttressed the limited partner's shield, removing the "substantially the same" rule, expanding the list of safe harbor activities and limiting "control rule" liability "only to persons who transact business with the limited partnership reasonably believing, based upon the limited partner's conduct, that the limited partner is a general partner."

In a world with LLPs, LLCs and, most importantly, LLLPs, the control rule has become an anachronism. This Act therefore takes the next logical step in the evolution of the limited partner's liability shield and renders the control rule extinct.

The shield established by this section protects only against liability for the limited partnership's obligations and only to the extent that the limited partner is claimed to be liable on account of being a limited partner. Thus, a person that is both a general and limited partner will be liable as a general partner for the limited partnership's obligations. Moreover, this section does not prevent a limited partner from being liable as a result of the limited partner's own conduct and is therefore inapplicable when a third party asserts that a limited partner's own wrongful conduct has injured the third party. This section is likewise inapplicable to claims by the limited partnership or another partner that a limited partner has breached a duty under this Act or the partnership agreement.

This section does not eliminate a limited partner's liability for promised contributions, Section 502 or improper distributions[,] Section 509. That liability pertains to a person's status as a limited partner but is **not** liability for an obligation of the limited partnership.

The shield provided by this section applies whether or not a limited partnership is a limited liability limited partnership.

SECTION 304. RIGHT OF LIMITED PARTNER AND FORMER LIMITED PARTNER TO INFORMATION.

(a) On 10 days' demand, made in a record received by the limited partnership, a limited partner may inspect and copy required information during regular business hours in the limited partnership's designated office. The limited partner need not have any particular purpose for seeking the information.

(b) During regular business hours and at a reasonable location specified by the limited partnership, a limited partner may obtain from the limited partnership and inspect and copy true and full information regarding the state of the activities and financial condition of the limited partnership and other information regarding the activities of the limited partnership as is just and reasonable if:

(1) the limited partner seeks the information for a purpose reasonably related to the partner's interest as a limited partner;

(2) the limited partner makes a demand in a record received by the limited partnership, describing with reasonable particularity the information sought and the purpose for seeking the information; and

(3) the information sought is directly connected to the limited partner's purpose.

(c) Within 10 days after receiving a demand pursuant to subsection (b), the limited partnership in a record shall inform the limited partner that made the demand:

(1) what information the limited partnership will provide in response to the demand;

(2) when and where the limited partnership will provide the information; and

(3) if the limited partnership declines to provide any demanded information, the limited partnership's reasons for declining.

(d) Subject to subsection (f), a person dissociated as a limited partner may inspect and copy required information during regular business hours in the limited partnership's designated office if:

(1) the information pertains to the period during which the person was a limited partner;

(2) the person seeks the information in good faith; and

(3) the person meets the requirements of subsection (b).

(e) The limited partnership shall respond to a demand made pursuant to subsection (d) in the same manner as provided in subsection (c).

(f) If a limited partner dies, Section 704 applies.

(g) The limited partnership may impose reasonable restrictions on the use of information obtained under this section. In a dispute concerning the reasonableness of a restriction under this subsection, the limited partnership has the burden of proving reasonableness.

(h) A limited partnership may charge a person that makes a demand under this section reasonable costs of copying, limited to the costs of labor and material.

(i) Whenever this [Act] or a partnership agreement provides for a limited partner to give or withhold consent to a matter, before the consent is given or withheld, the limited partnership shall, without demand, provide the limited partner with all information material to the limited partner's decision that the limited partnership knows.

(j) A limited partner or person dissociated as a limited partner may exercise the rights under this section through an attorney or other agent. Any restriction imposed under subsection (g) or by the partnership agreement applies both to the attorney or other agent and to the limited partner or person dissociated as a limited partner.

(k) The rights stated in this section do not extend to a person as transferee, but may be exercised by the legal representative of an individual under legal disability who is a limited partner or person dissociated as a limited partner.

Comment

This section balances two countervailing concerns relating to information: the need of limited partners and former limited partners for access versus the limited partnership's need to protect confidential business data and other intellectual property. The balance must be understood in the context of fiduciary duties. The general partners are obliged through their duties of care and loyalty to protect information whose confidentiality is important to the limited partnership or otherwise inappropriate for dissemination. See Section 408 (general standards of general partner conduct). A limited partner, in contrast, "does not have any fiduciary duty to the limited partnership or to any other partner solely by reason of being a limited partner." Section 305(a). (Both general partners and limited partners are subject to a duty of good faith and fair dealing. Section 305(b) and 408(d).)

Like predecessor law, this Act divides limited partner access rights into two categories—required information and other information. However, this Act builds on predecessor law by:

- expanding slightly the category of required information and stating explicitly that a limited partner may have access to that information without having to show cause

- specifying a procedure for limited partners to follow when demanding access to other information

- specifying how a limited partnership must respond to such a demand and setting a time limit for the response

- retaining predecessor law's "just and reasonable" standard for determining a limited partner's right to other information, while recognizing that, to be "just and reasonable," a limited partner's demand for other information must meet at minimum standards of relatedness and particularity

- expressly requiring the limited partnership to volunteer known, material information when seeking or obtaining consent from limited partners

- codifying (while limiting) the power of the partnership agreement to vary limited partner access rights

- permitting the limited partnership to establish other reasonable limits on access

- providing access rights for former limited partners.

The access rights stated in this section are personal to each limited partner and are enforceable through a direct action under Section 1001(a). These access rights are in addition to whatever discovery rights a party has in a civil suit.

Subsection (a)—The phrase "required information" is a defined term. See Sections 102(18) and 111. This subsection's broad right of access is subject not only to reasonable limitations in the partnership agreement, Section 110(b)(4), but also to the power of the limited partnership to impose reasonable limitations on use. Unless the partnership agreement provides otherwise, it will be the general partner or partners that have the authority to use that power. See Section 406(a).

Subsection (b)—The language describing the information to be provided comes essentially verbatim from RULPA Section 305(a)(2)(i) and (iii). The procedural requirements derive from RMBCA Section 16.02(c). This subsection does not impose a requirement of good faith, because Section 305(b) contains a generally applicable obligation of good faith and fair dealing for limited partners.

Subsection (d)—The notion that former owners should have information rights comes from RUPA Section 403(b) and ULLCA Section 408(a). The access is limited to the required information and is subject to certain conditions.

> **Example:** A person dissociated as a limited partner seeks data which the limited partnership has compiled, which relates to the period when the person was a limited partner, but which is beyond the scope of the information required by Section 111. No matter how reasonable the person's purpose and how well drafted the person's demand, the limited partnership is not obliged to provide the data.

> **Example:** A person dissociated as a limited partner seeks access to required information pertaining to the period during which the person was a limited partner. The person makes a bald demand, merely stating a desire to review the required information at the limited partnership's designated office. In particular, the demand does not describe "with reasonable particularity the information sought and the purpose for seeking the information." See subsection (b)(2). The limited partnership is not obliged to allow access. The person must first comply with subsection (d), which incorporates by reference the requirements of subsection (b).

Subsection (f) and Section 704 provide greater access rights for the estate of a deceased limited partner.

Subsection (d)(2)—A duty of good faith is needed here, because a person claiming access under this subsection is no longer a limited partner and is no longer subject to Section 305(b). See Section 602(a)(2) (dissociation as a limited partner terminates duty of good faith as to subsequent events).

Subsection (g)—This subsection permits the limited partnership—as distinguished from the partnership agreement—to impose use limitations. Contrast Section 110(b)(4). Under Section 406(a), it will be the general partner or partners that decide whether the limited partnership will impose use restrictions.

The limited partnership bears the burden of proving the reasonableness of any restriction imposed under this subsection. In determining whether a restriction is reasonable, a court might consider: (i) the danger or other problem the restriction seeks to avoid; (ii) the purpose for which the information is sought; and (iii) whether, in light of both the problem and the purpose, the restriction is reasonably tailored. Restricting use of the names and addresses of limited partners is not per se unreasonable.

The following table compares the limitations available through the partnership agreement with those available under this subsection.

	partnership agreement	Section 304(g)
how restrictions adopted	by the consent of partners when they adopt or amend the partnership agreement, unless the partnership agreement provides another method of amendment	by the general partners, acting under Section 406(a)
what restrictions may be imposed	"reasonable restrictions on the availability and use of information obtained," Section 110(b)(4)	"reasonable restrictions on the use of information obtained"
burden of proof	the person challenging the restriction must prove that the restriction will "unreasonably restrict the right of information," Section 110(b)(4) …	"the limited partnership has the burden of proving reasonableness"

Subsection (i)—The duty stated in this subsection is at the core of the duties owed the limited partners by a limited partnership and its general partners. This subsection imposes an affirmative duty to volunteer information, but that obligation is limited to information which is both material and known by the limited partnership. The duty applies to known, material information, even if the limited partnership does not know that the information is material.

A limited partnership will "know" what its general partners know. Section 103(h). A limited partnership may also know information known by the "individual conducting the transaction for the [limited partnership]." Section 103(g).

A limited partner's right to information under this subsection is enforceable through the full panoply of "legal or equitable relief" provided by Section 1001(a), including in appropriate circumstances the withdrawal or invalidation of improperly obtained consent and the invalidation or [rescission] of action taken pursuant to that consent.

Subsection (k)—Section 304 provides no information rights to a transferee as transferee. Transferee status brings only the very limited information rights stated in Section 702(c).

It is nonetheless possible for a person that happens to be a transferee to have rights under this section. For example, under Section 602(a)(3) a person dissociated as a limited partner becomes a "mere transferee" of its own transferable interest. While that status provides the person no rights under this section, the status of person dissociated as a limited partner triggers rights under subsection (d).

SECTION 305. LIMITED DUTIES OF LIMITED PARTNERS.

(a) A limited partner does not have any fiduciary duty to the limited partnership or to any other partner solely by reason of being a limited partner.

(b) A limited partner shall discharge the duties to the partnership and the other partners under this [Act] or under the partnership agreement and exercise any rights consistently with the obligation of good faith and fair dealing.

(c) A limited partner does not violate a duty or obligation under this [Act] or under the partnership agreement merely because the limited partner's conduct furthers the limited partner's own interest.

Comment

Subsection (a)—Fiduciary duty typically attaches to a person whose status or role creates significant power for that person over the interests of another person. Under this Act, limited partners have very limited power of any sort in the regular activities of the limited partnership and no power whatsoever justifying the imposition of fiduciary duties either to the limited partnership or fellow partners. It is possible for a partnership agreement to allocate significant managerial authority and power to a limited partner, but in that case the power exists not as a matter of status or role but rather as a matter of contract. The proper limit on such contract-based power is the obligation of good faith and fair dealing, not fiduciary duty, unless the partnership agreement itself expressly imposes a fiduciary duty or creates a role for a limited partner which, as a matter of other law, gives rise to a fiduciary duty. For example, if the partnership agreement makes a limited partner an agent for the limited partnership as to particular matters, the law of agency will impose fiduciary duties on the limited partner with respect to the limited partner's role as agent.

Subsection (b) . . .

The obligation of good faith and fair dealing is *not* a fiduciary duty, does not command altruism or self-abnegation, and does not prevent a partner from acting in the partner's own self-interest. Courts should not use the obligation to change *ex post facto* the parties' or this Act's allocation of risk and power. To the contrary, in light of the nature of a limited partnership, the obligation should be used only to protect agreed-upon arrangements from conduct that is manifestly beyond what a reasonable person could have contemplated when the arrangements were made.

The partnership agreement or this Act may grant discretion to a partner, and that partner may properly exercise that discretion even though another partner suffers as a consequence. Conduct does not violate the obligation of good faith and fair dealing merely because that conduct substantially prejudices a party. Indeed, parties allocate risk precisely because prejudice may occur. The exercise of discretion constitutes a breach of the obligation of good faith and fair dealing only when the party claiming breach shows that the conduct has no honestly-held purpose that legitimately comports with the parties' agreed-upon arrangements. Once such a purpose appears, courts should not second guess a party's choice of method in serving that purpose, unless the party invoking the obligation of good faith and fair dealing shows that the choice of method itself lacks any honestly-held purpose that legitimately comports with the parties' agreed-upon arrangements.

In sum, the purpose of the obligation of good faith and fair dealing is to protect the arrangement the partners have chosen for themselves, not to restructure that arrangement under the guise of safeguarding it.

SECTION 306. PERSON ERRONEOUSLY BELIEVING SELF TO BE LIMITED PARTNER.

(a) Except as otherwise provided in subsection (b), a person that makes an investment in a business enterprise and erroneously but in good faith believes that the person has become a limited partner in the enterprise is not liable for the enterprise's obligations by reason of making the investment, receiving distributions from the enterprise, or exercising any rights of or appropriate to a limited partner, if, on ascertaining the mistake, the person:

(1) causes an appropriate certificate of limited partnership, amendment, or statement of correction to be signed and delivered to the [Secretary of State] for filing; or

(2) withdraws from future participation as an owner in the enterprise by signing and delivering to the [Secretary of State] for filing a statement of withdrawal under this section.

(b) A person that makes an investment described in subsection (a) is liable to the same extent as a general partner to any third party that enters into a transaction with the enterprise, believing in good faith that the person is a general partner, before the [Secretary of State] files a statement of withdrawal, certificate of limited partnership, amendment, or statement of correction to show that the person is not a general partner.

(c) If a person makes a diligent effort in good faith to comply with subsection (a)(1) and is unable to cause the appropriate certificate of limited partnership, amendment, or statement of correction to be signed and delivered to the [Secretary of State] for filing, the person has the right to withdraw from the enterprise pursuant to subsection (a)(2) even if the withdrawal would otherwise breach an agreement with others that are or have agreed to become co-owners of the enterprise.

[ARTICLE]　4

GENERAL PARTNERS

SECTION 401.　BECOMING GENERAL PARTNER. A person becomes a general partner:

(1) as provided in the partnership agreement:

(2) under Section 801(3)(B) following the dissociation of a limited partnership's last general partner;

(3) as the result of a conversion or merger under [Article] 11; or

(4) with the consent of all the partners.

SECTION 402.　GENERAL PARTNER AGENT OF LIMITED PARTNERSHIP.

(a) Each general partner is an agent of the limited partnership for the purposes of its activities. An act of a general partner, including the signing of a record in the partnership's name, for apparently carrying on in the ordinary course the limited partnership's activities or activities of the kind carried on by the limited partnership binds the limited partnership, unless the general partner did not have authority to act for the limited partnership in the particular matter and the person with which the general partner was dealing knew, had received a notification, or had notice under Section 103(d) that the general partner lacked authority.

(b) An act of a general partner which is not apparently for carrying on in the ordinary course the limited partnership's activities or activities of the kind carried on by the limited partnership binds the limited partnership only if the act was actually authorized by all the other partners.

SECTION 403. LIMITED PARTNERSHIP LIABLE FOR GENERAL PARTNER'S ACTIONABLE CONDUCT.

(a) A limited partnership is liable for loss or injury caused to a person, or for a penalty incurred, as a result of a wrongful act or omission, or other actionable conduct, of a general partner acting in the ordinary course of activities of the limited partnership or with authority of the limited partnership.

(b) If, in the course of the limited partnership's activities or while acting with authority of the limited partnership, a general partner receives or causes the limited partnership to receive money or property of a person not a partner, and the money or property is misapplied by a general partner, the limited partnership is liable for the loss.

SECTION 404.   GENERAL PARTNER'S LIABILITY.

(a) Except as otherwise provided in subsections (b) and (c), all general partners are liable jointly and severally for all obligations of the limited partnership unless otherwise agreed by the claimant or provided by law.

(b) A person that becomes a general partner of an existing limited partnership is not personally liable for an obligation of a limited partnership incurred before the person became a general partner.

(c) An obligation of a limited partnership incurred while the limited partnership is a limited liability limited partnership, whether arising in contract, tort, or otherwise, is solely the obligation of the limited partnership. A general partner is not personally liable, directly or indirectly, by way of contribution or otherwise, for such an obligation solely by reason of being or acting as a general partner. This subsection applies despite anything inconsistent in the partnership agreement that existed immediately before the consent required to become a limited liability limited partnership under Section 406(b)(2).

SECTION 405. ACTIONS BY AND AGAINST PARTNER-SHIP AND PARTNERS.

(a) To the extent not inconsistent with Section 404, a general partner may be joined in an action against the limited partnership or named in a separate action.

(b) A judgment against a limited partnership is not by itself a judgment against a general partner. A judgment against a limited partnership may not be satisfied from a general partner's assets unless there is also a judgment against the general partner.

(c) A judgment creditor of a general partner may not levy execution against the assets of the general partner to satisfy a judgment based on a claim against the limited partnership, unless the partner is personally liable for the claim under Section 404 and:

(1) a judgment based on the same claim has been obtained against the limited partnership and a writ of execution on the judgment has been returned unsatisfied in whole or in part;

(2) the limited partnership is a debtor in bankruptcy;

(3) the general partner has agreed that the creditor need not exhaust limited partnership assets;

(4) a court grants permission to the judgment creditor to levy execution against the assets of a general partner based on a finding that limited partnership assets subject to execution are clearly insufficient to satisfy the judgment, that exhaustion of limited partnership assets is excessively burdensome, or that the grant of permission is an appropriate exercise of the court's equitable powers; or

(5) liability is imposed on the general partner by law or contract independent of the existence of the limited partnership.

SECTION 406. MANAGEMENT RIGHTS OF GENERAL PARTNER.

(a) Each general partner has equal rights in the management and conduct of the limited partnership's activities. Except as expressly provided in this [Act], any matter relating to the activities of the limited partnership may be exclusively decided by the general partner or, if there is more than one general partner, by a majority of the general partners.

(b) The consent of each partner is necessary to:

(1) amend the partnership agreement;

(2) amend the certificate of limited partnership to add or, subject to Section 1110, delete a statement that the limited partnership is a limited liability limited partnership; and

(3) sell, lease, exchange, or otherwise dispose of all, or substantially all, of the limited partnership's property, with or without the good will, other than in the usual and regular course of the limited partnership's activities.

(c) A limited partnership shall reimburse a general partner for payments made and indemnify a general partner for liabilities incurred by the general partner in the ordinary course of the activities of the partnership or for the preservation of its activities or property.

(d) A limited partnership shall reimburse a general partner for an advance to the limited partnership beyond the amount of capital the general partner agreed to contribute.

(e) A payment or advance made by a general partner which gives rise to an obligation of the limited partnership under subsection (c) or (d) constitutes a loan to the limited partnership which accrues interest from the date of the payment or advance.

(f) A general partner is not entitled to remuneration for services performed for the partnership.

Comment . . .

Subsection (a)—As explained in the Prefatory Note, this Act assumes that, more often than not, people utilizing the Act will want (i) strong centralized management, strongly entrenched, and (ii) passive investors with little control over the entity. Section 302 essentially excludes limited partners from the ordinary management of a limited partnership's activities. This subsection states affirmatively the general partners' commanding role. Only the partnership agreement and the express provisions of this Act can limit that role.

The authority granted by this subsection includes the authority to delegate. Delegation does not relieve the delegating general partner or partners of their duties under Section 408. However, the fact of delegation is a fact relevant to any breach of duty analysis.

> **Example:** A sole general partner personally handles all "important paperwork" for a limited partnership. The general partner neglects to renew the fire insurance coverage on the a building owned by the limited partnership, despite having received and read a warning notice from the insurance company. The building subsequently burns to the ground and is a total loss. The general partner might be liable for breach of the duty of care under Section 408(c) (gross negligence).

> **Example:** A sole general partner delegates responsibility for insurance renewals to the limited partnership's office manager, and that manager neglects to renew the fire insurance coverage on the building. Even assuming that the office manager has been grossly negligent, the general partner is not necessarily liable under Section 408(c). The office manager's gross negligence is not automatically attributed to the general partner. Under Section 408(c), the question is whether the general partner was grossly negligent (or worse) in selecting the general manager, delegating insurance renewal matters to the general manager and supervising the general manager after the delegation. . . .

Subsection (b)—This subsection limits the managerial rights of the general partners, requiring the consent of each general and limited partner for the specified actions. The subsection is subject to change by the partnership agreement, except as provided in Section

110(b)(12) (pertaining to consent rights established by Section 1110)....

SECTION 407. RIGHT OF GENERAL PARTNER AND FORMER GENERAL PARTNER TO INFORMATION.

(a) A general partner, without having any particular purpose for seeking the information, may inspect and copy during regular business hours:

(1) in the limited partnership's designated office, required information; and

(2) at a reasonable location specified by the limited partnership, any other records maintained by the limited partnership regarding the limited partnership's activities and financial condition.

(b) Each general partner and the limited partnership shall furnish to a general partner:

(1) without demand, any information concerning the limited partnership's activities and activities reasonably required for the proper exercise of the general partner's rights and duties under the partnership agreement or this [Act]; and

(2) on demand, any other information concerning the limited partnership's activities, except to the extent the demand or the information demanded is unreasonable or otherwise improper under the circumstances.

(c) Subject to subsection (e), on 10 days' demand made in a record received by the limited partnership, a person dissociated as a general partner may have access to the information and records described in subsection (a) at the location specified in subsection (a) if:

(1) the information or record pertains to the period during which the person was a general partner;

(2) the person seeks the information or record in good faith; and

(3) the person satisfies the requirements imposed on a limited partner by Section 304(b).

(d) The limited partnership shall respond to a demand made pursuant to subsection (c) in the same manner as provided in Section 304(c).

(e) If a general partner dies, Section 704 applies.

(f) The limited partnership may impose reasonable restrictions on the use of information under this section. In any dispute concerning the reasonableness of a restriction under this subsection, the limited partnership has the burden of proving reasonableness.

(g) A limited partnership may charge a person dissociated as a general partner that makes a demand under this section reasonable costs of copying, limited to the costs of labor and material.

(h) A general partner or person dissociated as a general partner may exercise the rights under this section through an attorney or other agent. Any restriction imposed under subsection (f) or by the partnership agreement applies both to the attorney or other agent and to the general partner or person dissociated as a general partner.

(i) The rights under this section do not extend to a person as transferee, but the rights under subsection (c) of a person dissociated as a general [partner] may be exercised by the legal representative of an individual who dissociated as a general partner under Section 603(7)(B) or (C).

SECTION 408. GENERAL STANDARDS OF GENERAL PARTNER'S CONDUCT.

(a) The only fiduciary duties that a general partner has to the limited partnership and the other partners are the duties of loyalty and care under subsections (b) and (c).

(b) A general partner's duty of loyalty to the limited partnership and the other partners is limited to the following:

(1) to account to the limited partnership and hold as trustee for it any property, profit, or benefit derived by the general partner in the conduct and winding up of the limited partnership's activities or derived from a use by the general partner of limited partnership property, including the appropriation of a limited partnership opportunity;

(2) to refrain from dealing with the limited partnership in the conduct or winding up of the limited partnership's activities as or on behalf of a party having an interest adverse to the limited partnership; and

(3) to refrain from competing with the limited partnership in the conduct or winding up of the limited partnership's activities.

(c) A general partner's duty of care to the limited partnership and the other partners in the conduct and winding up of the limited partnership's activities is limited to refraining from engaging in grossly negligent or reckless conduct, intentional misconduct, or a knowing violation of law.

(d) A general partner shall discharge the duties to the partnership and the other partners under this [Act] or under the partnership agreement and exercise any rights consistently with the obligation of good faith and fair dealing.

(e) A general partner does not violate a duty or obligation under this [Act] or under the partnership agreement merely because the general partner's conduct furthers the general partner's own interest.

Comment ...

This section does not prevent a general partner from delegating one or more duties, but delegation does not discharge the duty. For further discussion, see the Comment to Section 406(a). . . .

For the partnership agreement's power directly to circumscribe a general partner's fiduciary duty, see Section 110(b)(5) and (6).

Subsection (b)—A general partner's duty under this subsection continues through winding up, since the limited partners' dependence on the general partner does not end at dissolution. . . .

[ARTICLE] 5

CONTRIBUTIONS AND DISTRIBUTIONS

SECTION 501.   FORM OF CONTRIBUTION. A contribution of a partner may consist of tangible or intangible property or other benefit to the limited partnership, including money, services performed, promissory notes, other agreements to contribute cash or property, and contracts for services to be performed.

SECTION 502.   LIABILITY FOR CONTRIBUTION.

(a) A partner's obligation to contribute money or other property or other benefit to, or to perform services for, a limited partnership is not excused by the partner's death, disability, or other inability to perform personally.

(b) If a partner does not make a promised non-monetary contribution, the partner is obligated at the option of the limited partnership to contribute money equal to that portion of the value, as stated in the required information, of the stated contribution which has not been made.

(c) The obligation of a partner to make a contribution or return money or other property paid or distributed in violation of this [Act] may be compromised only by consent of all partners. A creditor of a limited partnership which extends credit or otherwise acts in reliance on an obligation described in subsection (a), without notice of any compromise under this subsection, may enforce the original obligation.

SECTION 503.   SHARING OF DISTRIBUTIONS. A distribution by a limited partnership must be shared among the partners on the basis of the value, as stated in the required records when the limited partnership decides to make the distribution, of the contributions the limited partnership has received from each partner.

Comment

This Act has no provision allocating profits and losses among the partners. Instead, the Act directly apportions the right to receive distributions. . . .

SECTION 504. INTERIM DISTRIBUTIONS. A partner does not have a right to any distribution before the dissolution and winding up of the limited partnership unless the limited partnership decides to make an interim distribution.

Comment

Under Section 406(a), the general partner or partners make this decision for the limited partnership.

SECTION 505. NO DISTRIBUTION ON ACCOUNT OF DISSOCIATION. A person does not have a right to receive a distribution on account of dissociation.

Comment

This section varies substantially from predecessor law. RULPA Sections 603 and 604 permitted a limited partner to withdraw on six months notice and receive the fair value of the limited partnership interest, unless the partnership agreement provided the limited partner with some exit right or stated a definite duration for the limited partnership.

Under this Act, a partner that dissociates becomes a transferee of its own transferable interest. See Sections 602(a)(3) (person dissociated as a limited partner) and 605(a)(5) (person dissociated as a general partner).

SECTION 506. DISTRIBUTION IN KIND. A partner does not have a right to demand or receive any distribution from a limited partnership in any form other than cash. Subject to Section 812(b), a limited partnership may distribute an asset in kind to the extent each partner receives a percentage of the asset equal to the partner's share of distributions.

SECTION 507.   RIGHT TO DISTRIBUTION. When a partner or transferee becomes entitled to receive a distribution, the partner or transferee has the status of, and is entitled to all remedies available to, a creditor of the limited partnership with respect to the distribution. However, the limited partnership's obligation to make a distribution is subject to offset for any amount owed to the limited partnership by the partner or dissociated partner on whose account the distribution is made.

SECTION 508.   LIMITATIONS ON DISTRIBUTION.

(a) A limited partnership may not make a distribution in violation of the partnership agreement.

(b) A limited partnership may not make a distribution if after the distribution:

(1) the limited partnership would not be able to pay its debts as they become due in the ordinary course of the limited partnership's activities; or

(2) the limited partnership's total assets would be less than the sum of its total liabilities plus the amount that would be needed, if the limited partnership were to be dissolved, wound up, and terminated at the time of the distribution, to satisfy the preferential rights upon dissolution, winding up, and termination of partners whose preferential rights are superior to those of persons receiving the distribution.

(c) A limited partnership may base a determination that a distribution is not prohibited under subsection (b) on financial statements prepared on the basis of accounting practices and principles that are reasonable in the circumstances or on a fair valuation or other method that is reasonable in the circumstances.

(d) Except as otherwise provided in subsection (g), the effect of a distribution under subsection (b) is measured:

(1) in the case of distribution by purchase, redemption, or other acquisition of a transferable interest in the limited partnership, as of the date money or other property is transferred or debt incurred by the limited partnership; and

(2) in all other cases, as of the date:

(A) the distribution is authorized, if the payment occurs within 120 days after that date; or

(B) the payment is made, if payment occurs more than 120 days after the distribution is authorized.

(e) A limited partnership's indebtedness to a partner incurred by reason of a distribution made in accordance with this section is at parity with the limited partnership's indebtedness to its general, unsecured creditors.

(f) A limited partnership's indebtedness, including indebtedness issued in connection with or as part of a distribution, is not considered a liability for purposes of subsection (b) if the terms of the indebtedness provide that payment of principal and interest are made only to the extent that a distribution could then be made to partners under this section.

(g) If indebtedness is issued as a distribution, each payment of principal or interest on the indebtedness is treated as a distribution, the effect of which is measured on the date the payment is made.

SECTION 509. LIABILITY FOR IMPROPER DISTRIBUTIONS.

(a) A general partner that consents to a distribution made in violation of Section 508 is personally liable to the limited partnership for the amount of the distribution which exceeds the amount that could have been distributed without the violation if it is established that in consenting to the distribution the general partner failed to comply with Section 408.

(b) A partner or transferee that received a distribution knowing that the distribution to that partner or transferee was made in violation of Section 508 is personally liable to the limited partnership but only to the extent that the distribution received by the partner or transferee exceeded the amount that could have been properly paid under Section 508.

(c) A general partner against which an action is commenced under subsection (a) may:

(1) implead in the action any other person that is liable under subsection (a) and compel contribution from the person; and

(2) implead in the action any person that received a distribution in violation of subsection (b) and compel contribution from the person in the amount the person received in violation of subsection (b).

(d) An action under this section is barred if it is not commenced within two years after the distribution.

Comment ...

In substance and effect this section protects the interests of creditors of the limited partnership. Therefore, according to Section 110(b)(13), the partnership agreement may not change this section in a way that restricts the rights of those creditors. As for a limited partnership's power to compromise a claim under this section, see Section 502(c).

Subsection (a)—This subsection refers both to Section 508, which includes in its subsection (c) a standard of ordinary care ("reasonable in the circumstances"), and to Section 408, which includes in its subsection (c) a general duty of care that is limited to "refraining from engaging in grossly negligent or reckless conduct, intentional misconduct, or a knowing violation of law."

A limited partnership's failure to meet the standard of Section 508(c) cannot by itself cause a general partner to be liable under Section 509(a). *Both* of the following would have to occur before a failure to satisfy Section 508(c) could occasion personal liability for a general partner under Section 509(a):

- the limited partnership "base[s] a determination that a distribution is not prohibited . . . on financial statements prepared on the basis of accounting practices and principles that are [not] reasonable in the circumstances or on a [not] fair valuation or other method that is [not] reasonable in the circumstances" [Section 508(c)]

    AND

- the general partner's decision to rely on the improper methodology in consenting to the distribution constitutes "grossly negligent or reckless conduct, intentional misconduct, or a knowing violation of law" [Section 408(c)] or breaches some other duty under Section 408.

To serve the protective purpose of Sections 508 and 509, in this subsection "consent" must be understood as encompassing any form of approval, assent or acquiescence, whether formal or informal, express or tacit.

Subsection (d)—The subsection's limitation applies to the commencement of an action under subsection (a) or (b) and not to subsection (c), under which a general partner may implead other persons.

[ARTICLE] 6

DISSOCIATION

SECTION 601. DISSOCIATION AS LIMITED PARTNER.

(a) A person does not have a right to dissociate as a limited partner before the termination of the limited partnership.

(b) A person is dissociated from a limited partnership as a limited partner upon the occurrence of any of the following events:

(1) the limited partnership's having notice of the person's express will to withdraw as a limited partner or on a later date specified by the person;

(2) an event agreed to in the partnership agreement as causing the person's dissociation as a limited partner;

(3) the person's expulsion as a limited partner pursuant to the partnership agreement;

(4) the person's expulsion as a limited partner by the unanimous consent of the other partners if:

(A) it is unlawful to carry on the limited partnership's activities with the person as a limited partner;

(B) there has been a transfer of all of the person's transferable interest in the limited partnership, other than a transfer for security purposes, or a court order charging the person's interest, which has not been foreclosed;

(C) the person is a corporation and, within 90 days after the limited partnership notifies the person that it will be expelled as a limited partner because it has filed a certificate of dissolution or the equivalent, its charter has been revoked, or its right to conduct business has been suspended by the jurisdiction of its incorporation, there is no revocation of the certificate of dissolution or no reinstatement of its charter or its right to conduct business; or

(D) the person is a limited liability company or partnership that has been dissolved and whose business is being wound up;

(5) on application by the limited partnership, the person's expulsion as a limited partner by judicial order because:

(A) the person engaged in wrongful conduct that adversely and materially affected the limited partnership's activities;

(B) the person willfully or persistently committed a material breach of the partnership agreement or of the obligation of good faith and fair dealing under Section 305(b); or

(C) the person engaged in conduct relating to the limited partnership's activities which makes it not reasonably practicable to carry on the activities with the person as limited partner;

(6) in the case of a person who is an individual, the person's death;

(7) in the case of a person that is a trust or is acting as a limited partner by virtue of being a trustee of a trust, distribution of the trust's entire transferable interest in the limited partnership, but not merely by reason of the substitution of a successor trustee;

(8) in the case of a person that is an estate or is acting as a limited partner by virtue of being a personal representative of an estate, distribution of the estate's entire transferable interest in the limited partnership, but not merely by reason of the substitution of a successor personal representative;

(9) termination of a limited partner that is not an individual, partnership, limited liability company, corporation, trust, or estate;

(10) the limited partnership's participation in a conversion or merger under [Article] 11, if the limited partnership:

(A) is not the converted or surviving entity; or

(B) is the converted or surviving entity but, as a result of the conversion or merger, the person ceases to be a limited partner.

Comment ...

This section adopts RUPA's dissociation provision essentially verbatim, except for provisions inappropriate to limited partners. For example, this section does not provide for the dissociation of a person as a limited partner on account of bankruptcy, insolvency or incompetency....

Subsection (b)(1)—This provision gives a person the power to dissociate as a limited partner even though the dissociation is wrongful under subsection (a). See, however, Section 110(b)(8) (prohibiting the partnership agreement from eliminating the power of a person to dissociate as a *general* partner but imposing no comparable restriction with regard to a person's dissociation as a *limited* partner).

Subsection (b)(5)—In contrast to RUPA, this provision may be varied or even eliminated by the partnership agreement.

SECTION 602. EFFECT OF DISSOCIATION AS LIMITED PARTNER.

(a) Upon a person's dissociation as a limited partner:

(1) subject to Section 704, the person does not have further rights as a limited partner;

(2) the person's obligation of good faith and fair dealing as a limited partner under Section 305(b) continues only as to matters arising and events occurring before the dissociation; and

(3) subject to Section 704 and [Article] 11, any transferable interest owned by the person in the person's capacity as a limited partner immediately before dissociation is owned by the person as a mere transferee.

(b) A person's dissociation as a limited partner does not of itself discharge the person from any obligation to the limited partnership or the other partners which the person incurred while a limited partner.

Comment . . .

Subsection (a)(1)—In general, when a person dissociates as a limited partner, the person's rights as a limited partner disappear and, subject to Section 113 (Dual Status), the person's status degrades to that of a mere transferee. However, Section 704 provides some special rights when dissociation is caused by an individual's death. . . .

Subsection (a)(3)—For any person that is both a general partner and a limited partner, the required records must state which transferable interest is owned in which capacity. Section 111(9)(C). . . .

SECTION 603. DISSOCIATION AS GENERAL PARTNER. A person is dissociated from a limited partnership as a general partner upon the occurrence of any of the following events:

(1) the limited partnership's having notice of the person's express will to withdraw as a general partner or on a later date specified by the person;

(2) an event agreed to in the partnership agreement as causing the person's dissociation as a general partner;

(3) the person's expulsion as a general partner pursuant to the partnership agreement;

(4) the person's expulsion as a general partner by the unanimous consent of the other partners if:

(A) it is unlawful to carry on the limited partnership's activities with the person as a general partner;

(B) there has been a transfer of all or substantially all of the person's transferable interest in the limited partnership, other than a transfer for security purposes, or a court order charging the person's interest, which has not been foreclosed;

(C) the person is a corporation and, within 90 days after the limited partnership notifies the person that it will be expelled as a general partner because it has filed a certificate of dissolution or the equivalent, its charter has been revoked, or its right to conduct business has been suspended by the jurisdiction of its incorporation, there is no revocation of the certificate of dissolution or no reinstatement of its charter or its right to conduct business; or

(D) the person is a limited liability company or partnership that has been dissolved and whose business is being wound up;

(5) on application by the limited partnership, the person's expulsion as a general partner by judicial determination because:

(A) the person engaged in wrongful conduct that adversely and materially affected the limited partnership activities;

(B) the person willfully or persistently committed a material breach of the partnership agreement or of a duty owed to the partnership or the other partners under Section 408; or

(C) the person engaged in conduct relating to the limited partnership's activities which makes it not reasonably practicable to carry on the activities of the limited partnership with the person as a general partner;

(6) the person's:

(A) becoming a debtor in bankruptcy;

(B) execution of an assignment for the benefit of creditors;

(C) seeking, consenting to, or acquiescing in the appointment of a trustee, receiver, or liquidator of the person or of all or substantially all of the person's property; or

(D) failure, within 90 days after the appointment, to have vacated or stayed the appointment of a trustee, receiver, or liquidator of the general partner or of all or substantially all of the person's property obtained without the person's consent or acquiescence, or failing within 90 days after the expiration of a stay to have the appointment vacated;

(7) in the case of a person who is an individual:

(A) the person's death;

(B) the appointment of a guardian or general conservator for the person; or

(C) a judicial determination that the person has otherwise become incapable of performing the person's duties as a general partner under the partnership agreement;

(8) in the case of a person that is a trust or is acting as a general partner by virtue of being a trustee of a trust, distribution of the trust's entire transferable interest in the limited partnership, but not merely by reason of the substitution of a successor trustee;

(9) in the case of a person that is an estate or is acting as a general partner by virtue of being a personal representative of an estate, distribution of the estate's entire transferable interest in the limited partnership, but not merely by reason of the substitution of a successor personal representative;

(10) termination of a general partner that is not an individual, partnership, limited liability company, corporation, trust, or estate; or

(11) the limited partnership's participation in a conversion or merger under [Article] 11, if the limited partnership:

(A) is not the converted or surviving entity; or

(B) is the converted or surviving entity but, as a result of the conversion or merger, the person ceases to be a general partner.

Comment . . .

This section adopts RUPA's dissociation provision essentially verbatim. . . .

Paragraph (1)—The partnership agreement may not eliminate this power to dissociate. See Section 110(b)(8).

Paragraph (5)—In contrast to RUPA, this provision may be varied or even eliminated by the partnership agreement.

SECTION 604. PERSON'S POWER TO DISSOCIATE AS GENERAL PARTNER; WRONGFUL DISSOCIATION.

(a) A person has the power to dissociate as a general partner at any time, rightfully or wrongfully, by express will pursuant to Section 603(1).

(b) A person's dissociation as a general partner is wrongful only if:

(1) it is in breach of an express provision of the partnership agreement; or

(2) it occurs before the termination of the limited partnership, and:

(A) the person withdraws as a general partner by express will;

(B) the person is expelled as a general partner by judicial determination under Section 603(5);

(C) the person is dissociated as a general partner by becoming a debtor in bankruptcy; or

(D) in the case of a person that is not an individual, trust other than a business trust, or estate, the person is expelled or otherwise dissociated as a general partner because it willfully dissolved or terminated.

(c) A person that wrongfully dissociates as a general partner is liable to the limited partnership and, subject to Section 1001, to the other partners for damages caused by the dissociation. The liability is in addition to any other obligation of the general partner to the limited partnership or to the other partners.

Comment ...

Subsection (a)—The partnership agreement may not elimi-nate this power. See Section 110(b)(8).

Subsection (b)(1)—The reference to "an express provision of the partnership agreement" means that a person's dissociation as a general partner in breach of the obligation of good faith and fair dealing is not wrongful dissociation for the purposes of this section. The breach might be actionable on other grounds.

Subsection (b)(2)—The reference to "before the termination of the limited partnership" reflects the expectation that each gener-al partner will shepherd the limited partnership through winding up. See Comment to Section 406(f). A person's obligation to remain as general partner through winding up continues even if another general partner dissociates and even if that dissociation leads to the limited partnership's premature dissolution under Section 801(3)(A).

Subsection (c)—The language "subject to Section 1001" is intended to preserve the distinction between direct and derivative claims.

SECTION 605. EFFECT OF DISSOCIATION AS GENERAL PARTNER.

(a) Upon a person's dissociation as a general partner:

(1) the person's right to participate as a general partner in the management and conduct of the partnership's activities terminates;

(2) the person's duty of loyalty as a general partner under Section 408(b)(3) terminates;

(3) the person's duty of loyalty as a general partner under Section 408(b)(1) and (2) and duty of care under Section 408(c) continue only with regard to matters arising and events occurring before the person's dissociation as a general partner;

(4) the person may sign and deliver to the [Secretary of State] for filing a statement of dissociation pertaining to the person and, at the request of the limited partnership, shall sign an amendment to the certificate of limited partnership which states that the person has dissociated; and

(5) subject to Section 704 and [Article] 11, any transferable interest owned by the person immediately before dissociation in the person's capacity as a general partner is owned by the person as a mere transferee.

(b) A person's dissociation as a general partner does not of itself discharge the person from any obligation to the limited partnership or the other partners which the person incurred while a general partner.

Comment ...

Subsection (a)(1)—Once a person dissociates as a general partner, the person loses all management rights as a general partner regardless of what happens to the limited partnership....

Subsection (a)(5)—In general, when a person dissociates as a general partner, the person's rights as a general partner disappear and, subject to Section 113 (Dual Status), the person's status degrades to that of a mere transferee....

SECTION 606. POWER TO BIND AND LIABILITY TO LIMITED PARTNERSHIP BEFORE DISSOLUTION OF PARTNERSHIP OF PERSON DISSOCIATED AS GENERAL PARTNER.

(a) After a person is dissociated as a general partner and before the limited partnership is dissolved, converted under [Article] 11, or merged out of existence under [Article 11], the limited partnership is bound by an act of the person only if:

(1) the act would have bound the limited partnership under Section 402 before the dissociation; and

(2) at the time the other party enters into the transaction:

(A) less than two years has passed since the dissociation; and

(B) the other party does not have notice of the dissociation and reasonably believes that the person is a general partner.

(b) If a limited partnership is bound under subsection (a), the person dissociated as a general partner which caused the limited partnership to be bound is liable:

(1) to the limited partnership for any damage caused to the limited partnership arising from the obligation incurred under subsection (a); and

(2) if a general partner or another person dissociated as a general partner is liable for the obligation, to the general partner or other person for any damage caused to the general partner or other person arising from the liability.

Comment ...

This Act contains three sections pertaining to the lingering power to bind of a person dissociated as a general partner:

* this section, which applies until the limited partnership dissolves, converts to another form of organization under Article 11, or is merged out of existence under Article 11;

* Section 804(b), which applies after a limited partnership dissolves; and

321

• Section 1112(b), which applies after a conversion or merger....

Subsection (b)—The liability provided by this subsection is not exhaustive. For example, if a person dissociated as a general partner causes a limited partnership to be bound under subsection (a) and, due to a guaranty, some other person is liable on the resulting obligation, that other person may have a claim under other law against the person dissociated as a general partner.

SECTION 607. LIABILITY TO OTHER PERSONS OF PERSON DISSOCIATED AS GENERAL PARTNER.

(a) A person's dissociation as a general partner does not of itself discharge the person's liability as a general partner for an obligation of the limited partnership incurred before dissociation. Except as otherwise provided in subsections (b) and (c), the person is not liable for a limited partnership's obligation incurred after dissociation.

(b) A person whose dissociation as a general partner resulted in a dissolution and winding up of the limited partnership's activities is liable to the same extent as a general partner under Section 404 on an obligation incurred by the limited partnership under Section 804.

(c) A person that has dissociated as a general partner but whose dissociation did not result in a dissolution and winding up of the limited partnership's activities is liable on a transaction entered into by the limited partnership after the dissociation only if:

(1) a general partner would be liable on the transaction; and

(2) at the time the other party enters into the transaction:

(A) less than two years has passed since the dissociation; and

(B) the other party does not have notice of the dissociation and reasonably believes that the person is a general partner.

(d) By agreement with a creditor of a limited partnership and the limited partnership, a person dissociated as a general partner may be released from liability for an obligation of the limited partnership.

(e) A person dissociated as a general partner is released from liability for an obligation of the limited partnership if the limited partnership's creditor, with notice of the person's dissociation as a general partner but without the person's consent, agrees to a material alteration in the nature or time of payment of the obligation.

Comment ...

A person's dissociation as a general partner does not categorically prevent the person from being liable as a general partner for subsequently incurred obligations of the limited partnership. If the dissociation results in dissolution, subsection (b) applies and the person will be liable as a general partner on any partnership obligation incurred under Section 804. In these circumstances, neither filing a statement of dissociation nor amending the certificate of limited partnership to state that the person has dissociated as a general partner will curtail the person's lingering exposure to liability....

Subsection (a)—The phrase "liability as a general partner for an obligation of the limited partnership" refers to liability under Section 404. Following RUPA and the UPA, this Act leaves to other law the question of when a limited partnership obligation is incurred....

[ARTICLE] 7

TRANSFERABLE INTERESTS AND RIGHTS OF TRANSFEREES AND CREDITORS

SECTION 701. PARTNER'S TRANSFERABLE INTEREST.
The only interest of a partner which is transferable is the partner's transferable interest. A transferable interest is personal property.

Comment ...

Like all other partnership statutes, this Act dichotomizes each partner's rights into economic rights and other rights. The former are freely transferable, as provided in Section 702. The latter are not transferable at all, unless the partnership agreement so provides....

Although a partner or transferee owns a transferable interest as a present right, that right only entitles the owner to distributions if and when made. See Sections 504 (subject to any contrary provision in the partnership agreement, no right to interim distribution unless the limited partnership decides to make an interim distribution) and the Comment to Section 812 (subject to any contrary provision in the partnership agreement, no partner obligated to contribute for the purpose of equalizing or otherwise allocating capital losses).

SECTION 702. TRANSFER OF PARTNER'S TRANSFERABLE INTEREST.

(a) A transfer, in whole or in part, of a partner's transferable interest:

(1) is permissible;

(2) does not by itself cause the partner's dissociation or a dissolution and winding up of the limited partnership's activities; and

(3) does not, as against the other partners or the limited partnership, entitle the transferee to participate in the management or conduct of the limited partnership's activities, to require access to information concerning the limited partnership's transactions except as otherwise provided in subsection (c), or to inspect or copy the required information or the limited partnership's other records.

(b) A transferee has a right to receive, in accordance with the transfer:

(1) distributions to which the transferor would otherwise be entitled; and

(2) upon the dissolution and winding up of the limited partnership's activities the net amount otherwise distributable to the transferor.

(c) In a dissolution and winding up, a transferee is entitled to an account of the limited partnership's transactions only from the date of dissolution.

(d) Upon transfer, the transferor retains the rights of a partner other than the interest in distributions transferred and retains all duties and obligations of a partner.

(e) A limited partnership need not give effect to a transferee's rights under this section until the limited partnership has notice of the transfer.

(f) A transfer of a partner's transferable interest in the limited partnership in violation of a restriction on transfer contained in the partnership agreement is ineffective as to a person having notice of the restriction at the time of transfer.

(g) A transferee that becomes a partner with respect to a transferable interest is liable for the transferor's obligations under Sections 502 and 509. However, the transferee is not obligated for liabilities unknown to the transferee at the time the transferee became a partner.

Comment ...

Subsection (a)(2)—The phrase "by itself" is significant. A transfer of all of a person's transferable interest could lead to dissociation via expulsion, Sections 601(b)(4)(B) and 603(4)(B).

Subsection (a)(3)—Mere transferees have no right to intrude as the partners carry on their activities as partners. Moreover, a partner's obligation of good faith and fair dealing under Sections 305(b) and 408(d) is framed in reference to "the limited partnership and the other partners." ...

SECTION 703. RIGHTS OF CREDITOR OF PARTNER OR TRANSFEREE.

(a) On application to a court of competent jurisdiction by any judgment creditor of a partner or transferee, the court may charge the transferable interest of the judgment debtor with payment of the unsatisfied amount of the judgment with interest. To the extent so charged, the judgment creditor has only the rights of a transferee. The court may appoint a receiver of the share of the distributions due or to become due to the judgment debtor in respect of the partnership and make all other orders, directions, accounts, and inquiries the judgment debtor might have made or which the circumstances of the case may require to give effect to the charging order.

(b) A charging order constitutes a lien on the judgment debtor's transferable interest. The court may order a foreclosure upon the interest subject to the charging order at any time. The purchaser at the foreclosure sale has the rights of a transferee.

(c) At any time before foreclosure, an interest charged may be redeemed:

(1) by the judgment debtor;

(2) with property other than limited partnership property, by one or more of the other partners; or

(3) with limited partnership property, by the limited partnership with the consent of all partners whose interests are not so charged.

(d) This [Act] does not deprive any partner or transferee of the benefit of any exemption laws applicable to the partner's or transferee's transferable interest.

(e) This section provides the exclusive remedy by which a judgment creditor of a partner or transferee may satisfy a judgment out of the judgment debtor's transferable interest.

Comment ...

This section balances the needs of a judgment creditor of a partner or transferee with the needs of the limited partnership and non-debtor partners and transferees. The section achieves that balance by allowing the judgment creditor to collect on the judgment through the transferable interest of the judgment debtor while prohibiting interference in the management and activities of the limited partnership.

Under this section, the judgment creditor of a partner or transferee is entitled to a charging order against the relevant transferable interest. While in effect, that order entitles the judgment creditor to whatever distributions would otherwise be due to the partner or transferee whose interest is subject to the order. The creditor has no say in the timing or amount of those distributions. The charging order does not entitle the creditor to accelerate any distributions or to otherwise interfere with the management and activities of the limited partnership.

Foreclosure of a charging order effects a permanent transfer of the charged transferable interest to the purchaser. The foreclosure does not, however, create any rights to participate in the management and conduct of the limited partnership's activities. The purchaser obtains nothing more than the status of a transferee.

Subsection (a)—The court's power to appoint a receiver and "make all other orders, directions, accounts, and inquiries the judgment debtor might have made or which the circumstances of the case may require" must be understood in the context of the balance described above. In particular, the court's power to make orders "which the circumstances may require" is limited to "giv[ing] effect to the charging order."

> **Example:** A judgment creditor with a charging order believes that the limited partnership should invest less of its surplus in operations, leaving more funds for distributions. The creditor moves the court for an order directing the general partners to restrict re-investment. This section does not authorize the court to grant the motion.

> **Example:** A judgment creditor with a judgment for $10,000 against a partner obtains a charging order against the partner's transferable interest. The limited partnership is duly served with the order. However, the limited partnership subsequently fails to comply with the order and makes a $3000 distribution to the partner. The court has the power to order the limited partnership to turn over $3000 to the judgment creditor to "give effect to the charging order."

The court also has the power to decide whether a particular payment is a distribution, because this decision determines whether the payment is part of a transferable interest subject to a charging order. (To the extent a payment is not a distribution, it is not part of the transferable interest and is not subject to subsection (e). The payment is therefore subject to whatever other creditor remedies may apply.)

Subsection (c)(3)—This provision requires the consent of all the limited as well as general partners.

SECTION 704. POWER OF ESTATE OF DECEASED PARTNER. If a partner dies, the deceased partner's personal representative or other legal representative may exercise the rights of a transferee as provided in Section 702 and, for the purposes of settling the estate, may exercise the rights of a current limited partner under Section 304.

[ARTICLE] 8

DISSOLUTION

SECTION 801. NONJUDICIAL DISSOLUTION. Except as otherwise provided in Section 802, a limited partnership is dissolved, and its activities must be wound up, only upon the occurrence of any of the following:

(1) the happening of an event specified in the partnership agreement;

(2) the consent of all general partners and of limited partners owning a majority of the rights to receive distributions as limited partners at the time the consent is to be effective;

(3) after the dissociation of a person as a general partner:

(A) if the limited partnership has at least one remaining general partner, the consent to dissolve the limited partnership given within 90 days after the dissociation by partners owning a majority of the rights to receive distributions as partners at the time the consent is to be effective; or

(B) if the limited partnership does not have a remaining general partner, the passage of 90 days after the dissociation, unless before the end of the period:

(i) consent to continue the activities of the limited partnership and admit at least one general partner is given by limited partners owning a majority of the rights to receive distributions as limited partners at the time the consent is to be effective; and

(ii) at least one person is admitted as a general partner in accordance with the consent;

(4) the passage of 90 days after the dissociation of the limited partnership's last limited partner, unless before the end of the period the limited partnership admits at least one limited partner; or

(5) the signing and filing of a declaration of dissolution by the [Secretary of State] under Section 809(c).

Comment

In several provisions, this section provides for consent in terms of rights to receive distributions. Distribution rights of non-partner transferees are not relevant. Mere transferees have no consent rights, and their distribution rights are not counted in determining whether majority consent has been obtained....

Paragraph (2)—Rights to receive distributions owed by a person that is both a general and a limited partner figure into the limited partner determination only to the extent those rights are owned in the person's capacity as a limited partner. See Section 111(9)(C).

Example: XYZ is a limited partnership with three general partners, each of whom is also a limited partner, and 5 other limited partners. Rights to receive distributions are allocated as follows:

Partner #1 as general partner—3%

Partner #2 as general partner—2%

Partner #3 as general partner—1%

Partner #1 as limited partner—7%

Partner #2 as limited partner—3%

Partner #3 as limited partner—4%

Partner #4 as limited partner—5%

Partner #5 as limited partner—5%

Partner #6 as limited partner—5%

Partner #7 as limited partner—5%

Partner #8 as limited partner—5%

Several non-partner transferees, in the aggregate—55%

Distribution rights owned by persons as limited partners amount to 39% of total distribution rights. A majority is therefore anything greater than 19.5%. If only Partners 1,2, 3 and 4 consent to dissolve, the limited partnership is not dissolved. Together these partners own as limited partners 19% of the distribution rights owned by persons as limited partners—just short of the necessary majority. For purposes of this calculation, distribution rights owned by non-partner transferees are irrelevant. So, too, are distribution rights owned by persons as general partners. (However, dissolution under this provision requires "the consent of all general partners.")

Paragraph (3)(A)—Unlike paragraph (2), this paragraph makes no distinction between distribution rights owned by persons as general partners and distribution rights owned by persons as limited partners. Distribution rights owned by non-partner transferees are irrelevant.

SECTION 802. JUDICIAL DISSOLUTION. On application by a partner the [appropriate court] may order dissolution of a limited partnership if it is not reasonably practicable to carry on the activities of the limited partnership in conformity with the partnership agreement.

Comment ...

Section 110(b)(9) limits the power of the partnership agreement with regard to this section.

SECTION 803. WINDING UP.

(a) A limited partnership continues after dissolution only for the purpose of winding up its activities.

(b) In winding up its activities, the limited partnership:

(1) may amend its certificate of limited partnership to state that the limited partnership is dissolved, preserve the limited partnership business or property as a going concern for a reasonable time, prosecute and defend actions and proceedings, whether civil, criminal, or administrative, transfer the limited partnership's property, settle disputes by mediation or arbitration, file a statement of termination as provided in Section 203, and perform other necessary acts; and

(2) shall discharge the limited partnership's liabilities, settle and close the limited partnership's activities, and marshal and distribute the assets of the partnership.

(c) If a dissolved limited partnership does not have a general partner, a person to wind up the dissolved limited partnership's activities may be appointed by the consent of limited partners owning a majority of the rights to receive distributions as limited partners at the time the consent is to be effective. A person appointed under this subsection:

(1) has the powers of a general partner under Section 804; and

(2) shall promptly amend the certificate of limited partnership to state:

(A) that the limited partnership does not have a general partner;

(B) the name of the person that has been appointed to wind up the limited partnership; and

(C) the street and mailing address of the person.

(d) On the application of any partner, the [appropriate court] may order judicial supervision of the winding up, including the appointment of a person to wind up the dissolved limited partnership's activities, if:

(1) a limited partnership does not have a general partner and within a reasonable time following the dissolution no person has been appointed pursuant to subsection (c); or

(2) the applicant establishes other good cause.

SECTION 804. POWER OF GENERAL PARTNER AND PERSON DISSOCIATED AS GENERAL PARTNER TO BIND PARTNERSHIP AFTER DISSOLUTION.

(a) A limited partnership is bound by a general partner's act after dissolution which:

(1) is appropriate for winding up the limited partnership's activities; or

(2) would have bound the limited partnership under Section 402 before dissolution, if, at the time the other party enters into the transaction, the other party does not have notice of the dissolution.

(b) A person dissociated as a general partner binds a limited partnership through an act occurring after dissolution if:

(1) at the time the other party enters into the transaction:

(A) less than two years has passed since the dissociation; and

(B) the other party does not have notice of the dissociation and reasonably believes that the person is a general partner; and

(2) the act:

(A) is appropriate for winding up the limited partnership's activities; or

(B) would have bound the limited partnership under Section 402 before dissolution and at the time the other party enters into the transaction the other party does not have notice of the dissolution.

SECTION 805. LIABILITY AFTER DISSOLUTION OF GENERAL PARTNER AND PERSON DISSOCIATED AS GENERAL PARTNER TO LIMITED PARTNERSHIP, OTHER GENERAL PARTNERS, AND PERSONS DISSOCIATED AS GENERAL PARTNER.

(a) If a general partner having knowledge of the dissolution causes a limited partnership to incur an obligation under Section 804(a) by an act that is not appropriate for winding up the partnership's activities, the general partner is liable:

(1) to the limited partnership for any damage caused to the limited partnership arising from the obligation; and

(2) if another general partner or a person dissociated as a general partner is liable for the obligation, to that other general partner or person for any damage caused to that other general partner or person arising from the liability.

(b) If a person dissociated as a general partner causes a limited partnership to incur an obligation under Section 804(b), the person is liable:

(1) to the limited partnership for any damage caused to the limited partnership arising from the obligation; and

(2) if a general partner or another person dissociated as a general partner is liable for the obligation, to the general partner or other person for any damage caused to the general partner or other person arising from the liability.

SECTION 806. KNOWN CLAIMS AGAINST DISSOLVED LIMITED PARTNERSHIP.

(a) A dissolved limited partnership may dispose of the known claims against it by following the procedure described in subsection (b).

(b) A dissolved limited partnership may notify its known claimants of the dissolution in a record. The notice must:

(1) specify the information required to be included in a claim;

(2) provide a mailing address to which the claim is to be sent;

(3) state the deadline for receipt of the claim, which may not be less than 120 days after the date the notice is received by the claimant;

(4) state that the claim will be barred if not received by the deadline; and

(5) unless the limited partnership has been throughout its existence a limited liability limited partnership, state that the barring of a claim against the limited partnership will also bar any corresponding claim against any general partner or person dissociated as a general partner which is based on Section 404.

(c) A claim against a dissolved limited partnership is barred if the requirements of subsection (b) are met and:

(1) the claim is not received by the specified deadline; or

(2) in the case of a claim that is timely received but rejected by the dissolved limited partnership, the claimant does not commence an action to enforce the claim against the limited partnership within 90 days after the receipt of the notice of the rejection.

(d) This section does not apply to a claim based on an event occurring after the effective date of dissolution or a liability that is contingent on that date.

Comment . . .

Paragraph (b)(5)—If the limited partnership has always been a limited liability limited partnership, there can be no liability under Section 404 for any general partner or person dissociated as a general partner.

SECTION 807. OTHER CLAIMS AGAINST DISSOLVED LIMITED PARTNERSHIP.

(a) A dissolved limited partnership may publish notice of its dissolution and request persons having claims against the limited partnership to present them in accordance with the notice.

(b) The notice must:

(1) be published at least once in a newspaper of general circulation in the [county] in which the dissolved limited partnership's principal office is located or, if it has none in this State, in the [county] in which the limited partnership's designated office is or was last located;

(2) describe the information required to be contained in a claim and provide a mailing address to which the claim is to be sent;

(3) state that a claim against the limited partnership is barred unless an action to enforce the claim is commenced within five years after publication of the notice; and

(4) unless the limited partnership has been throughout its existence a limited liability limited partnership, state that the barring of a claim against the limited partnership will also bar any corresponding claim against any general partner or person dissociated as a general partner which is based on Section 404.

(c) If a dissolved limited partnership publishes a notice in accordance with subsection (b), the claim of each of the following claimants is barred unless the claimant commences an action to enforce the claim against the dissolved limited partnership within five years after the publication date of the notice:

(1) a claimant that did not receive notice in a record under Section 806;

(2) a claimant whose claim was timely sent to the dissolved limited partnership but not acted on; and

(3) a claimant whose claim is contingent or based on an event occurring after the effective date of dissolution.

(d) A claim not barred under this section may be enforced:

(1) against the dissolved limited partnership, to the extent of its undistributed assets;

(2) if the assets have been distributed in liquidation, against a partner or transferee to the extent of that person's proportionate share of the claim or the limited partnership's assets distributed to the partner or transferee in liquidation, whichever is less, but a person's total liability for all claims under this paragraph does not exceed the total amount of assets distributed to the person as part of the winding up of the dissolved limited partnership; or

(3) against any person liable on the claim under Section 404.

Comment ...

Paragraph (b)(4)—If the limited partnership has always been a limited liability limited partnership, there can be no liability under Section 404 for any general partner or person dissociated as a general partner.

SECTION 808. LIABILITY OF GENERAL PARTNER AND PERSON DISSOCIATED AS GENERAL PARTNER WHEN CLAIM AGAINST LIMITED PARTNERSHIP BARRED. If a claim against a dissolved limited partnership is barred under Section 806 or 807, any corresponding claim under Section 404 is also barred.

Comment

The liability under Section 404 of a general partner or person dissociated as a general partner is merely liability for the obligations of the limited partnership.

SECTION 809. ADMINISTRATIVE DISSOLUTION.

(a) The [Secretary of State] may dissolve a limited partnership administratively if the limited partnership does not, within 60 days after the due date:

(1) pay any fee, tax, or penalty due to the [Secretary of State] under this [Act] or other law; or

(2) deliver its annual report to the [Secretary of State].

(b) If the [Secretary of State] determines that a ground exists for administratively dissolving a limited partnership, the [Secretary of State] shall file a record of the determination and serve the limited partnership with a copy of the filed record.

(c) If within 60 days after service of the copy the limited partnership does not correct each ground for dissolution or demonstrate to the reasonable satisfaction of the [Secretary of State] that each ground determined by the [Secretary of State] does not exist, the [Secretary of State] shall administratively dissolve the limited partnership by preparing, signing and filing a declaration of dissolution that states the grounds for dissolution. The [Secretary of State] shall serve the limited partnership with a copy of the filed declaration.

(d) A limited partnership administratively dissolved continues its existence but may carry on only activities necessary to wind up its activities and liquidate its assets under Sections 803 and 812 and to notify claimants under Sections 806 and 807.

(e) The administrative dissolution of a limited partnership does not terminate the authority of its agent for service of process.

SECTION 812.   DISPOSITION OF ASSETS; WHEN CONTRIBUTIONS REQUIRED.

(a) In winding up a limited partnership's activities, the assets of the limited partnership, including the contributions required by this section, must be applied to satisfy the limited partnership's obligations to creditors, including, to the extent permitted by law, partners that are creditors.

(b) Any surplus remaining after the limited partnership complies with subsection (a) must be paid in cash as a distribution.

(c) If a limited partnership's assets are insufficient to satisfy all of its obligations under subsection (a), with respect to each unsatisfied obligation incurred when the limited partnership was not a limited liability limited partnership, the following rules apply:

(1) Each person that was a general partner when the obligation was incurred and that has not been released from the obligation under Section 607 shall contribute to the limited partnership for the purpose of enabling the limited partnership to satisfy the obligation. The contribution due from each of those persons is in proportion to the right to receive distributions in the capacity of general partner in effect for each of those persons when the obligation was incurred.

(2) If a person does not contribute the full amount required under paragraph (1) with respect to an unsatisfied obligation of the limited partnership, the other persons required to contribute by paragraph (1) on account of the obligation shall contribute the additional amount necessary to discharge the obligation. The additional contribution due from each of those other persons is in proportion to the right to receive distributions in the capacity of general partner in effect for each of those other persons when the obligation was incurred.

(3) If a person does not make the additional contribution required by paragraph (2), further additional contributions are determined and due in the same manner as provided in that paragraph.

(d) A person that makes an additional contribution under subsection (c)(2) or (3) may recover from any person whose failure to contribute under subsection (c)(1) or (2) necessitated the additional contribution. A person may not recover under this subsection more than the amount additionally contributed. A person's liability under this subsection may not exceed the amount the person failed to contribute.

(e) The estate of a deceased individual is liable for the person's obligations under this section.

(f) An assignee for the benefit of creditors of a limited partnership or a partner, or a person appointed by a court to represent creditors of a limited partnership or a partner, may enforce a person's obligation to contribute under subsection (c).

Comment

In some circumstances, this Act requires a partner to make payments to the limited partnership. See, e.g., Sections 502(b), 509(a), 509(b), and 812(c). In other circumstances, this Act requires a partner to make payments to other partners. See, e.g., Sections 509(c) and 812(d). In no circumstances does this Act require a partner to make a payment for the purpose of equalizing or otherwise reallocating capital losses incurred by partners.

> **Example:** XYZ Limited Partnership ("XYZ") has one general partner and four limited partners. According to XYZ's required information, the value of each partner's contributions to XYZ are:
>
> General partner—$5,000
>
> Limited partner #1—$10,000
>
> Limited partner #2—$15,000
>
> Limited partner #3—$20,000
>
> Limited partner #4—$25,000

XYZ is unsuccessful and eventually dissolves without ever having made a distribution to its partners. XYZ lacks any assets with which to return to the partners the value of their respective contributions. No partner is obliged to make any payment either to the limited partnership or to fellow partners to adjust these capital losses. These losses are not part of "the limited partnership's obligations to creditors." Section 812(a).

> **Example:** Same facts, except that Limited Partner #4 loaned $25,000 to XYZ when XYZ was not a limited liability limited partnership, and XYZ lacks the assets to repay the

loan. The general partner must contribute to the limited partnership whatever funds are necessary to enable XYZ to satisfy the obligation owned to Limited Partner #4 on account of the loan. Section 812(a) and (c).

Subsection (c)—Following RUPA and the UPA, this Act leaves to other law the question of when a limited partnership obligation is incurred.

[ARTICLE] 9

FOREIGN LIMITED PARTNERSHIPS

SECTION 901.   GOVERNING LAW.

(a) The laws of the State or other jurisdiction under which a foreign limited partnership is organized govern relations among the partners of the foreign limited partnership and between the partners and the foreign limited partnership and the liability of partners as partners for an obligation of the foreign limited partnership.

(b) A foreign limited partnership may not be denied a certificate of authority by reason of any difference between the laws of the jurisdiction under which the foreign limited partnership is organized and the laws of this State.

(c) A certificate of authority does not authorize a foreign limited partnership to engage in any business or exercise any power that a limited partnership may not engage in or exercise in this State.

[ARTICLE] 10

ACTIONS BY PARTNERS

SECTION 1001.   DIRECT ACTION BY PARTNER.

(a) Subject to subsection (b), a partner may maintain a direct action against the limited partnership or another partner for legal or equitable relief, with or without an accounting as to the partnership's activities, to enforce the rights and otherwise protect the interests of the partner, including rights and interests under the partnership agreement or this [Act] or arising independently of the partnership relationship.

(b) A partner commencing a direct action under this section is required to plead and prove an actual or threatened injury that is not solely the result of an injury suffered or threatened to be suffered by the limited partnership.

(c) The accrual of, and any time limitation on, a right of action for a remedy under this section is governed by other law. A right to an accounting upon a dissolution and winding up does not revive a claim barred by law.

Comment

Subsection (b)—In ordinary contractual situations it is axiomatic that each party to a contract has standing to sue for breach of that contract. Within a limited partnership, however, different circumstances may exist. A partner does not have a direct claim against another partner merely because the other partner has breached the partnership agreement. Likewise a partner's violation of this Act does not automatically create a direct claim for every other partner. To have standing in his, her, or its own right, a partner plaintiff must be able to show a harm that occurs independently of the harm caused or threatened to be caused to the limited partnership.

The reference to "threatened" harm is intended to encompass claims for injunctive relief and does not relax standards for proving injury.

SECTION 1002. DERIVATIVE ACTION. A partner may maintain a derivative action to enforce a right of a limited partnership if:

(1) the partner first makes a demand on the general partners, requesting that they cause the limited partnership to bring an action to enforce the right, and the general partners do not bring the action within a reasonable time; or

(2) a demand would be futile.

SECTION 1003. PROPER PLAINTIFF. A derivative action may be maintained only by a person that is a partner at the time the action is commenced and:

(1) that was a partner when the conduct giving rise to the action occurred; or

(2) whose status as a partner devolved upon the person by operation of law or pursuant to the terms of the partnership agreement from a person that was a partner at the time of the conduct.

SECTION 1004. PLEADING. In a derivative action, the complaint must state with particularity:

(1) the date and content of plaintiff's demand and the general partners' response to the demand; or

(2) why demand should be excused as futile.

337

SECTION 1005. PROCEEDS AND EXPENSES.

(a) Except as otherwise provided in subsection (b):

(1) any proceeds or other benefits of a derivative action, whether by judgment, compromise, or settlement, belong to the limited partnership and not to the derivative plaintiff;

(2) if the derivative plaintiff receives any proceeds, the derivative plaintiff shall immediately remit them to the limited partnership.

(b) If a derivative action is successful in whole or in part, the court may award the plaintiff reasonable expenses, including reasonable attorney's fees, from the recovery of the limited partnership.

[ARTICLE] 11

CONVERSION AND MERGER

SECTION 1101. DEFINITIONS.

In this [article]:

(1) "Constituent limited partnership" means a constituent organization that is a limited partnership.

(2) "Constituent organization" means an organization that is party to a merger.

(3) "Converted organization" means the organization into which a converting organization converts pursuant to Sections 1102 through 1105.

(4) "Converting limited partnership" means a converting organization that is a limited partnership.

(5) "Converting organization" means an organization that converts into another organization pursuant to Section 1102.

(6) "General partner" means a general partner of a limited partnership.

(7) "Governing statute" of an organization means the statute that governs the organization's internal affairs.

(8) "Organization" means a general partnership, including a limited liability partnership; limited partnership, including a limited liability limited partnership; limited liability company; business trust; corporation; or any other person having a governing statute. The term includes domestic and foreign organizations whether or not organized for profit.

(9) "Organizational documents" means:

(A) for a domestic or foreign general partnership, its partnership agreement;

(B) for a limited partnership or foreign limited partnership, its certificate of limited partnership and partnership agreement;

(C) for a domestic or foreign limited liability company, its articles of organization and operating agreement, or comparable records as provided in its governing statute;

(D) for a business trust, its agreement of trust and declaration of trust;

(E) for a domestic or foreign corporation for profit, its articles of incorporation, bylaws, and other agreements among its shareholders which are authorized by its governing statute, or comparable records as provided in its governing statute; and

(F) for any other organization, the basic records that create the organization and determine its internal governance and the relations among the persons that own it, have an interest in it, or are members of it.

(10) "Personal liability" means personal liability for a debt, liability, or other obligation of an organization which is imposed on a person that co-owns, has an interest in, or is a member of the organization:

(A) by the organization's governing statute solely by reason of the person co-owning, having an interest in, or being a member of the organization; or

(B) by the organization's organizational documents under a provision of the organization's governing statute authorizing those documents to make one or more specified persons liable for all or specified debts, liabilities, and other obligations of the organization solely by reason of the person or persons co-owning, having an interest in, or being a member of the organization.

(11) "Surviving organization" means an organization into which one or more other organizations are merged. A surviving organization may preexist the merger or be created by the merger.

SECTION 1102. CONVERSION.

(a) An organization other than a limited partnership may convert to a limited partnership, and a limited partnership may convert to another organization pursuant to this section and Sections 1103 through 1105 and a plan of conversion, if:

(1) the other organization's governing statute authorizes the conversion;

(2) the conversion is not prohibited by the law of the jurisdiction that enacted the governing statute; and

(3) the other organization complies with its governing statute in effecting the conversion.

(b) A plan of conversion must be in a record and must include:

(1) the name and form of the organization before conversion;

(2) the name and form of the organization after conversion; and

(3) the terms and conditions of the conversion, including the manner and basis for converting interests in the converting organization into any combination of money, interests in the converted organization, and other consideration; and

(4) the organizational documents of the converted organization.

Comment

In a statutory conversion an existing entity changes its form, the jurisdiction of its governing statute or both. For example, a limited partnership organized under the laws of one jurisdiction might convert to:

- a limited liability company (or other form of entity) organized under the laws of the same jurisdiction,

- a limited liability company (or other form of entity) organized under the laws of another jurisdiction, or

- a limited partnership organized under the laws of another jurisdiction (referred to in some statutes as "domestication").

In contrast to a merger, which involves at least two entities, a conversion involves only one. The converting and converted organization are the same entity. See Section 1105(a). For this Act to apply to a conversion, either the converting or converted organization must be a limited partnership subject to this Act. If the converting organization is a limited partnership subject to this Act, the partners of the converting organization are subject to the duties and obligations stated in this Act, including Sections 304 (informational rights of limited partners), 305(b) (limited partner's obligation of good faith and fair dealing), 407 (informational rights of general partners), and 408 (general partner duties).

Subsection (a)(2)—Given the very broad definition of "organization," Section 1101(8), this Act authorizes conversions involving non-profit organizations. This provision is intended as an additional safeguard for that context.

Subsection (b)(3)—A plan of conversion may provide that some persons with interests in the converting organization will receive interests in the converted organization while other persons with interests in the converting organization will receive some other form of consideration. Thus, a "squeeze out" conversion is possible. As noted above, if the converting organization is a limited partnership subject to this Act, the partners of the converting organization are subject to the duties and obligations stated in this Act. Those duties would apply to the process and terms under which a squeeze out conversion occurs.

If the converting organization is a limited partnership, the plan of conversion will determine the fate of any interests held by mere transferees. This Act does not state any duty or obligation owed by a converting limited partnership or its partners to mere transferees. That issue is a matter for other law.

SECTION 1103. ACTION ON PLAN OF CONVERSION BY CONVERTING LIMITED PARTNERSHIP.

(a) Subject to Section 1110, a plan of conversion must be consented to by all the partners of a converting limited partnership.

(b) Subject to Section 1110 and any contractual rights, after a conversion is approved, and at any time before a filing is made under Section 1104, a converting limited partnership may amend the plan or abandon the planned conversion:

(1) as provided in the plan; and

(2) except as prohibited by the plan, by the same consent as was required to approve the plan.

Comment

Section 1110 imposes special consent requirements for transactions which might cause a partner to have "personal liability," as defined in Section 1101(10)[,] for entity debts. The partnership agreement may not restrict the rights provided by Section 1110. See Section 110(b)(12).

Subsection (a)—Like many of the rules stated in this Act, this subsection's requirement of unanimous consent is a default rule. Subject only to Section 1110, the partnership agreement may state a different quantum of consent or provide a completely different approval mechanism. Varying this subsection's rule means that a partner might be subject to a conversion (including a "squeeze out" conversion) without consent and with no appraisal remedy. If the converting organization is a limited partnership subject to this Act, the partners of the converting organization are subject to the duties and obligations stated in this Act. Those duties would apply to the process and terms under which the conversion occurs. However, if the partnership agreement allows for a conversion with less than unanimous consent, the mere fact a partner objects to a conversion does not mean that the partners favoring, arranging, consenting to or effecting the conversation have breached a duty under this Act.

SECTION 1105. EFFECT OF CONVERSION.

(a) An organization that has been converted pursuant to this [article] is for all purposes the same entity that existed before the conversion.

(b) When a conversion takes effect:

(1) all property owned by the converting organization remains vested in the converted organization;

(2) all debts, liabilities, and other obligations of the converting organization continue as obligations of the converted organization;

(3) an action or proceeding pending by or against the converting organization may be continued as if the conversion had not occurred;

(4) except as prohibited by other law, all of the rights, privileges, immunities, powers, and purposes of the converting organization remain vested in the converted organization;

(5) except as otherwise provided in the plan of conversion, the terms and conditions of the plan of conversion take effect; and

(6) except as otherwise agreed, the conversion does not dissolve a converting limited partnership for the purposes of [Article] 8.

(c) A converted organization that is a foreign organization consents to the jurisdiction of the courts of this State to enforce any obligation owed by the converting limited partnership, if before the conversion the converting limited partnership was subject to suit in this State on the obligation. A converted organization that is a foreign organization and not authorized to transact business in this State appoints the [Secretary of State] as its agent for service of process for purposes of enforcing an obligation under this subsection. Service on the [Secretary of State] under this subsection is made in the same manner and with the same consequences as in Section 117(c) and (d).

Comment

Subsection (a)—A conversion changes an entity's legal type, but does not create a new entity.

Subsection (b)—Unlike a merger, a conversion involves a single entity, and the conversion therefore does not transfer any of the entity's rights or obligations.

SECTION 1106. MERGER.

(a) A limited partnership may merge with one or more other constituent organizations pursuant to this section and Sections 1107 through 1109 and a plan of merger, if:

(1) the governing statute of each the other organizations authorizes the merger;

(2) the merger is not prohibited by the law of a jurisdiction that enacted any of those governing statutes; and

(3) each of the other organizations complies with its governing statute in effecting the merger.

(b) A plan of merger must be in a record and must include:

(1) the name and form of each constituent organization;

(2) the name and form of the surviving organization and, if the surviving organization is to be created by the merger, a statement to that effect;

(3) the terms and conditions of the merger, including the manner and basis for converting the interests in each constituent organization into any combination of money, interests in the surviving organization, and other consideration;

(4) if the surviving organization is to be created by the merger, the surviving organization's organizational documents; and

(5) if the surviving organization is not to be created by the merger, any amendments to be made by the merger to the surviving organization's organizational documents.

Comment

For this Act to apply to a merger, at least one of the constituent organizations must be a limited partnership subject to this Act. The partners of any such limited partnership are subject to the duties and obligations stated in this Act, including Sections 304 (informational rights of limited partners), 305(b) (limited partner's obligation of good faith and fair dealing), 407 (informational rights of general partners), and 408 (general partner duties).

Subsection (a)(2)—Given the very broad definition of "organization," Section 1101(8), this Act authorizes mergers involving non-profit organizations. This provision is intended as an additional safeguard for that context.

Subsection (b)(3)—A plan of merger may provide that some persons with interests in a constituent organization will receive interests in the surviving organization, while other persons with interests in the same constituent organization will receive some other form of consideration. Thus, a "squeeze out" merger is possible. As noted above, the duties and obligations stated in this Act apply to the partners of a constituent organization that is a limited partnership subject to this Act. Those duties would apply to the process and terms under which a squeeze out merger occurs.

If a constituent organization is a limited partnership, the plan of merger will determine the fate of any interests held by mere transferees. This Act does not state any duty or obligation owed by a constituent limited partnership or its partners to mere transferees. That issue is a matter for other law.

SECTION 1107.   ACTION ON PLAN OF MERGER BY CONSTITUENT LIMITED PARTNERSHIP.

(a) Subject to Section 1110, a plan of merger must be consented to by all the partners of a constituent limited partnership.

(b) Subject to Section 1110 and any contractual rights, after a merger is approved, and at any time before a filing is made under Section 1108, a constituent limited partnership may amend the plan or abandon the planned merger:

(1) as provided in the plan; and

(2) except as prohibited by the plan, with the same consent as was required to approve the plan.

Comment

Section 1110 imposes special consent requirements for transactions which might make a partner personally liable for entity debts. The partnership agreement may not restrict the rights provided by Section 1110. See Section 110(b)(12).

Subsection (a)—Like many of the rules stated in this Act, this subsection's requirement of unanimous consent is a default rule. Subject only to Section 1110, the partnership agreement may state a different quantum of consent or provide a completely different approval mechanism. Varying this subsection's rule means that a partner might be subject to a merger (including a "squeeze out" merger) without consent and with no appraisal remedy. The partners of a constituent limited partnership are subject to the duties and obligations stated in this Act, and those duties would apply to the process and terms under which the merger occurs. However, if the partnership agreement allows for a merger with less than unanimous consent, the mere fact a partner objects to a merger does not mean that the partners favoring, arranging, consenting to or effecting the merger have breached a duty under this Act.

SECTION 1109.   EFFECT OF MERGER.

(a) When a merger becomes effective:

(1) the surviving organization continues or comes into existence;

(2) each constituent organization that merges into the surviving organization ceases to exist as a separate entity;

(3) all property owned by each constituent organization that ceases to exist vests in the surviving organization;

(4) all debts, liabilities, and other obligations of each constituent organization that ceases to exist continue as obligations of the surviving organization;

(5) an action or proceeding pending by or against any constituent organization that ceases to exist may be continued as if the merger had not occurred;

(6) except as prohibited by other law, all of the rights, privileges, immunities, powers, and purposes of each constituent organization that ceases to exist vest in the surviving organization;

(7) except as otherwise provided in the plan of merger, the terms and conditions of the plan of merger take effect; and

(8) except as otherwise agreed, if a constituent limited partnership ceases to exist, the merger does not dissolve the limited partnership for the purposes of [Article] 8;

(9) if the surviving organization is created by the merger:

(A) if it is a limited partnership, the certificate of limited partnership becomes effective; or

(B) if it is an organization other than a limited partnership, the organizational document that creates the organization becomes effective; and

(10) if the surviving organization preexists the merger, any amendments provided for in the articles of merger for the organizational document that created the organization become effective.

SECTION 1110. RESTRICTIONS ON APPROVAL OF CONVERSIONS AND MERGERS AND ON RELINQUISHING LLLP STATUS.

(a) If a partner of a converting or constituent limited partnership will have personal liability with respect to a converted or surviving organization, approval and amendment of a plan of conversion or merger are ineffective without the consent of the partner, unless:

(1) the limited partnership's partnership agreement provides for the approval of the conversion or merger with the consent of fewer than all the partners; and

(2) the partner has consented to the provision of the partnership agreement.

(b) An amendment to a certificate of limited partnership which deletes a statement that the limited partnership is a limited liability limited partnership is ineffective without the consent of each general partner unless:

(1) the limited partnership's partnership agreement provides for the amendment with the consent of less than all the general partners; and

(2) each general partner that does not consent to the amendment has consented to the provision of the partnership agreement.

(c) A partner does not give the consent required by subsection (a) or (b) merely by consenting to a provision of the partnership agreement which permits the partnership agreement to be amended with the consent of fewer than all the partners.

Comment

This section imposes special consent requirements for transactions that might make a partner personally liable for entity debts. The partnership agreement may not restrict the rights provided by this section. See Section 110(b)(12).

Subsection (c)—This subsection prevents circumvention of the consent requirements of subsections (a) and (b).

> **Example:** As initially consented to, the partnership agreement of a limited partnership leaves in place the Act's rule requiring unanimous consent for a conversion or merger. The partnership agreement does provide, however, that the agreement may be amended with the affirmative vote of general partners owning 2/3 of the rights to receive distributions as general partners and of limited partners owning 2/3 of the rights to receive distributions as limited partners. The required vote is obtained for an amendment that permits approval of a conversion or merger by the same vote necessary to amend the partnership agreement. Partner X votes for the amendment. Partner Y votes against. Partner Z does not vote.
>
> Subsequently the limited partnership proposes to convert to a limited partnership (not an LLLP) organized under the laws of another state, with Partners X, Y and Z each receiving interests as general partners. Under the amended partnership agreement, approval of the conversion does not require unanimous consent. However, since after the conversion, Partners X, Y and Z will each have "personal liability with respect to [the] converted ... organization," Section 1110(a) applies.
>
> As a result, the approval of the plan of conversion will require the consent of Partner Y and Partner Z. They did not consent to the amendment that provided for non-unanimous approval of a conversion or merger. Their initial consent to the partnership agreement, with its provision permitting non-unanimous consent for amendments, does

not satisfy the consent requirement of Subsection 1110(a)(2).

In contrast, Partner X's consent is not required. Partner X lost its Section 1110(a) veto right by consenting directly to the amendment to the partnership agreement which permitted non-unanimous consent to a conversion or merger.

SECTION 1111. LIABILITY OF GENERAL PARTNER AFTER CONVERSION OR MERGER.

(a) A conversion or merger under this [article] does not discharge any liability under Sections 404 and 607 of a person that was a general partner in or dissociated as a general partner from a converting or constituent limited partnership, but:

(1) the provisions of this [Act] pertaining to the collection or discharge of the liability continue to apply to the liability;

(2) for the purposes of applying those provisions, the converted or surviving organization is deemed to be the converting or constituent limited partnership; and

(3) if a person is required to pay any amount under this subsection:

(A) the person has a right of contribution from each other person that was liable as a general partner under Section 404 when the obligation was incurred and has not been released from the obligation under Section 607; and

(B) the contribution due from each of those persons is in proportion to the right to receive distributions in the capacity of general partner in effect for each of those persons when the obligation was incurred.

(b) In addition to any other liability provided by law:

(1) a person that immediately before a conversion or merger became effective was a general partner in a converting or constituent limited partnership that was not a limited liability limited partnership is personally liable for each obligation of the converted or surviving organization arising from a transaction with a third party after the conversion or merger becomes effective, if, at the time the third party enters into the transaction, the third party:

(A) does not have notice of the conversion or merger; and

(B) reasonably believes that:

(i) the converted or surviving business is the converting or constituent limited partnership;

(ii) the converting or constituent limited partnership is not a limited liability limited partnership; and

(iii) the person is a general partner in the converting or constituent limited partnership; and

(2) a person that was dissociated as a general partner from a converting or constituent limited partnership before the conversion or merger became effective is personally liable for each obligation of the converted or surviving organization arising from a transaction with a third party after the conversion or merger becomes effective, if:

(A) immediately before the conversion or merger became effective the converting or surviving limited partnership was a not a limited liability limited partnership; and

(B) at the time the third party enters into the transaction less than two years have passed since the person dissociated as a general partner and the third party:

(i) does not have notice of the dissociation;

(ii) does not have notice of the conversion or merger; and

(iii) reasonably believes that the converted or surviving organization is the converting or constituent limited partnership, the converting or constituent limited partnership is not a limited liability limited partnership, and the person is a general partner in the converting or constituent limited partnership.

Comment

This section extrapolates the approach of Section 607 into the context of a conversion or merger involving a limited partnership.

Subsection (a)—This subsection pertains to general partner liability for obligations which a limited partnership incurred before a conversion or merger. Following RUPA and the UPA, this Act leaves to other law the question of when a limited partnership obligation is incurred.

If the converting or constituent limited partnership was a limited liability limited partnership at all times before the conversion or merger, this subsection will not apply because no person will have any liability under Section 404 or 607.

Subsection (b)—This subsection pertains to entity obligations incurred after a conversion or merger and creates lingering exposure to personal liability for general partners and persons previously dissociated as general partners. In contrast to subsection (a)(3), this subsection does not provide for contribution among persons personally liable under this section for the same entity obligation. That issue is left for other law.

348

Subsection (b)(1)—If the converting or constituent limited partnership was a limited liability limited partnership immediately before the conversion or merger, there is no lingering exposure to personal liability under this subsection....

SECTION 1112. POWER OF GENERAL PARTNERS AND PERSONS DISSOCIATED AS GENERAL PARTNERS TO BIND ORGANIZATION AFTER CONVERSION OR MERGER.

(a) An act of a person that immediately before a conversion or merger became effective was a general partner in a converting or constituent limited partnership binds the converted or surviving organization after the conversion or merger becomes effective, if:

(1) before the conversion or merger became effective, the act would have bound the converting or constituent limited partnership under Section 402; and

(2) at the time the third party enters into the transaction, the third party:

(A) does not have notice of the conversion or merger; and

(B) reasonably believes that the converted or surviving business is the converting or constituent limited partnership and that the person is a general partner in the converting or constituent limited partnership.

(b) An act of a person that before a conversion or merger became effective was dissociated as a general partner from a converting or constituent limited partnership binds the converted or surviving organization after the conversion or merger becomes effective, if:

(1) before the conversion or merger became effective, the act would have bound the converting or constituent limited partnership under Section 402 if the person had been a general partner; and

(2) at the time the third party enters into the transaction, less than two years have passed since the person dissociated as a general partner and the third party:

(A) does not have notice of the dissociation;

(B) does not have notice of the conversion or merger; and

(C) reasonably believes that the converted or surviving organization is the converting or constituent limited partnership and that the person is a general partner in the converting or constituent limited partnership.

(c) If a person having knowledge of the conversion or merger causes a converted or surviving organization to incur an obligation under subsection (a) or (b), the person is liable:

349

(1) to the converted or surviving organization for any damage caused to the organization arising from the obligation; and

(2) if another person is liable for the obligation, to that other person for any damage caused to that other person arising from the liability.

Comment

This section extrapolates the approach of Section 606 into the context of a conversion or merger involving a limited partnership.

Subsection (a)(2)(A)—A person might have notice under Section 103(d)(4) or (5) as well as under Section 103(b).

Subsection (b)(2)(A)—A person might have notice under Section 103(d)(1) as well as under Section 103(b).

Subsection (b)(2)(B)—A person might have notice under Section 103(d)(4) or (5) as well as under Section 103(b).

SECTION 1113. [ARTICLE] NOT EXCLUSIVE. This [article] does not preclude an entity from being converted or merged under other law.

[ARTICLE] 12

MISCELLANEOUS PROVISIONS

SECTION 1206. APPLICATION TO EXISTING RELATION-SHIPS.

(a) Before [all-inclusive date], this [Act] governs only:

(1) a limited partnership formed on or after [the effective date of this [Act]]; and

(2) except as otherwise provided in subsections (c) and (d), a limited partnership formed before [the effective date of this [Act]] which elects, in the manner provided in its partnership agreement or by law for amending the partnership agreement, to be subject to this [Act].

(b) Except as otherwise provided in subsection (c), on and after [all-inclusive date] this [Act] governs all limited partnerships.

(c) With respect to a limited partnership formed before [the effective date of this [Act]], the following rules apply except as the partners otherwise elect in the manner provided in the partnership agreement or by law for amending the partnership agreement:

(1) Section 104(c) does not apply and the limited partnership has whatever duration it had under the law applicable immediately before [the effective date of this [Act]].

(2) the limited partnership is not required to amend its certificate of limited partnership to comply with Section 201(a)(4).

(3) Sections 601 and 602 do not apply and a limited partner has the same right and power to dissociate from the limited partnership, with the same consequences, as existed immediately before [the effective date of this [Act]].

(4) Section 603(4) does not apply.

(5) Section 603(5) does not apply and a court has the same power to expel a general partner as the court had immediately before [the effective date of this [Act]].

(6) Section 801(3) does not apply and the connection between a person's dissociation as a general partner and the dissolution of the limited partnership is the same as existed immediately before [the effective date of this [Act]].

(d) With respect to a limited partnership that elects pursuant to subsection (a)(2) to be subject to this [Act], after the election takes effect the provisions of this [Act] relating to the liability of the limited partnership's general partners to third parties apply:

(1) before [all-inclusive date], to:

(A) a third party that had not done business with the limited partnership in the year before the election took effect; and

(B) a third party that had done business with the limited partnership in the year before the election took effect only if the third party knows or has received a notification of the election; and

(2) on and after [all-inclusive date], to all third parties, but those provisions remain inapplicable to any obligation incurred while those provisions were inapplicable under paragraph (1)(B).

Comment ...

This section pertains exclusively to domestic limited partnerships—i.e., to limited partnerships formed under this Act or a predecessor statute enacted by the same jurisdiction. For foreign limited partnerships, see the Comment to Section 1204.

This Act governs all limited partnerships formed on or after the Act's effective date. As for pre-existing limited partnerships, this section establishes an optional "elect in" period and a mandatory, all-inclusive date. The "elect in" period runs from the effective date, stated in Section 1204, until the all-inclusive date, stated in both subsection(a) and (b).

During the "elect in" period, a pre-existing limited partnership may elect to become subject to this Act. Subsection (d) states certain important consequences for a limited partnership that elects in. Beginning on the all-inclusive date, each pre-existing limited partnership that has not previously elected in becomes subject to this Act by operation of law.

Subsection (c)—This subsection specifies six provisions of this Act which never automatically apply to any pre-existing limited partnership. Except for subsection (c)(2), the list refers to provisions governing the relationship of the partners *inter se* and considered too different than predecessor law to be fairly applied to a preexisting limited partnership without the consent of its partners. Each of these *inter se* provisions is subject to change in the partnership agreement. However, many pre-existing limited partnerships may have taken for granted the analogous provisions of predecessor law and may therefore not have addressed the issues in their partnership agreements.

Subsection (c)(1)—Section 104(c) provides that a limited partnership has a perpetual duration.

Subsection (c)(2)—Section 201(a)(4) requires the certificate of limited partnership to state "whether the limited partnership is a limited liability limited partnership." The requirement is intended to force the organizers of a limited partnership to decide whether the limited partnership is to be an LLLP and therefore is inapposite to pre-existing limited partnerships. Moreover, applying the requirement to pre-existing limited partnerships would create a significant administrative burden both for limited partnerships and the filing officer and probably would result in many pre-existing limited partnerships being in violation of the requirement.

Subsection (c)(3)—Section 601 and 602 concern a person's dissociation as a limited partner.

Subsection (c)(4)—Section 603(4) provides for the expulsion of a general partner by the unanimous consent of the other partners in specified circumstances.

Subsection (c)(5)—Section 603(5) provides for the expulsion of a general partner by a court in specified circumstances.

Subsection (c)(6)—Section 801(3) concerns the continuance or dissolution of a limited partnership following a person's dissociation as a general partner.

Subsection (d)—Following RUPA Section 1206(c), this subsection limits the efficacy of the Act's liability protections for partners of an "electing in" limited partnership. The limitation:

- applies only to the benefit of "a third party that had done business with the limited partnership in the year before the election took effect," and

• ceases to apply when "the third party knows or has received a notification of the election" or on the "all-inclusive" date, whichever occurs first.

If the limitation causes a provision of this Act to be inapplicable with regard to a third party, the comparable provision of predecessor law applies.

Example: A pre-existing limited partnership elects to be governed by this Act before the "all-inclusive" date. Two months before the election, Third Party provided services to the limited partnership. Third Party neither knows nor has received a notification of the election. Until the "all inclusive" date, with regard to Third Party, Section 303's full liability shield does not apply to each limited partner. Instead, each limited partner has the liability shield applicable under predecessor law.

Subsection (d)(2)—To the extent subsection (d) causes a provision of this Act to be inapplicable when an obligation is incurred, the inapplicability continues as to that obligation even after the "all inclusive" date. . . .

DELAWARE LIMITED LIABILITY COMPANY ACT
DEL.CODE ANN. TITLE 6, CHAPTER 18

SUBCHAPTER I. GENERAL PROVISIONS

* Omitted.

SUBCHAPTER I. GENERAL PROVISIONS

§ 18–101. Definitions.

As used in this chapter unless the context otherwise requires:

(1) "Bankruptcy" means an event that causes a person to cease to be a member as provided in § 18–304 of this title.

---

* Omitted.

(2) "Certificate of formation" means the certificate referred to in § 18–201 of this title, and the certificate as amended.

(3) "Contribution" means any cash, property, services rendered or a promissory note or other obligation to contribute cash or property or to perform services, which a person contributes to a limited liability company in his capacity as a member.

(4) "Foreign limited liability company" means a limited liability company formed under the laws of any state or under the laws of any foreign country or other foreign jurisdiction and denominated as such under the laws of such state or foreign country or other foreign jurisdiction.

(5) "Knowledge" means a person's actual knowledge of a fact, rather than the person's constructive knowledge of the fact.

(6) "Limited liability company" and "domestic limited liability company" means a limited liability company formed under the laws of the State of Delaware and having 1 or more members.

(7) "Limited liability company agreement" means any agreement (whether referred to as a limited liability company agreement, an operating agreement, or otherwise), written or oral, of the member or members as to the affairs of a limited liability company and the conduct of its business. A member or manager of a limited liability company or an assignee of a limited liability company interest is bound by the limited liability company agreement whether or not the member or manager or assignee executes the limited liability company agreement. A limited liability company is not required to execute its limited liability company agreement. A limited liability company is bound by its limited liability company agreement whether or not the limited liability company executes the limited liability company agreement. A limited liability company agreement of a limited liability company having only one member shall not be unenforceable by reason of there being only one person who is a party to the limited liability company agreement. A limited liability company agreement may provide rights to any person, including a person who is not a party to the limited liability company agreement, to the extent set forth therein. A written limited liability company agreement or another written agreement or writing:

    a. May provide that a person shall be admitted as a member of a limited liability company, or shall become an assignee of a limited liability company interest or other rights or powers of a member to the extent assigned:

        1. If such person (or a representative authorized by such person orally, in writing or by other action such as payment for a limited liability company interest) executes

the limited liability company agreement or any other writing evidencing the intent of such person to become a member or assignee; or

2. Without such execution, if such person (or a representative authorized by such person orally, in writing or by other action such as payment for a limited liability company interest) complies with the conditions for becoming a member or assignee as set forth in the limited liability company agreement or any other writing; and

b. Shall not be unenforceable by reason of its not having been signed by a person being admitted as a member or becoming an assignee as provided in subparagraph a. of this paragraph, or by reason of its having been signed by a representative as provided in this chapter.

(8) "Limited liability company interest" means a member's share of the profits and losses of a limited liability company and a member's right to receive distributions of the limited liability company's assets.

(9) "Liquidating trustee" means a person carrying out the winding up of a limited liability company.

(10) "Manager" means a person who is named as a manager of a limited liability company in, or designated as a manager of a limited liability company pursuant to, a limited liability company agreement or similar instrument under which the limited liability company is formed.

(11) "Member" means a person who has been admitted to a limited liability company as a member as provided in § 18–301 of this title or, in the case of a foreign limited liability company, in accordance with the laws of the state or foreign country or other foreign jurisdiction under which the foreign limited liability company is organized.

(12) "Person" means a natural person, partnership (whether general or limited), trust, estate, association, corporation, custodian, nominee or any other individual or entity in its own or any representative capacity, in each case, whether domestic or foreign, and a limited liability company or foreign limited liability company.

(13) "Personal representative" means, as to a natural person, the executor, administrator, guardian, conservator or other legal representative thereof and, as to a person other than a natural person, the legal representative or successor thereof.

(14) "State" means the District of Columbia or the Commonwealth of Puerto Rico or any state, territory, possession or other jurisdiction of the United States other than the State of Delaware.

§ 18–102. Name Set Forth in Certificate

The name of each limited liability company as set forth in its certificate of formation:

(1) Shall contain the words "Limited Liability Company" or the abbreviation "L.L.C." or the designation LLC;

(2) May contain the name of a member or manager;

(3) Must be such as to distinguish it upon the records in the office of the Secretary of State from the name on such records of any corporation, partnership, limited partnership, statutory trust or limited liability company reserved, registered, formed or organized under the laws of the State of Delaware or qualified to do business or registered as a foreign corporation, foreign limited partnership, foreign statutory trust, foreign partnership or foreign limited liability company in the State of Delaware; provided however, that a limited liability company may register under any name which is not such as to distinguish it upon the records in the office of the Secretary of State from the name on such records of any domestic or foreign corporation, partnership, limited partnership, statutory trust or limited liability company reserved, registered, formed or organized under the laws of the State of Delaware with the written consent of the other corporation, partnership, limited partnership, statutory trust or limited liability company, which written consent shall be filed with the Secretary of State; and

(4) May contain the following words: "Company," "Association," "Club," "Foundation," "Fund," "Institute," "Society," "Union," "Syndicate," "Limited" or "Trust" (or abbreviations of like import).

§ 18–104. Registered Office; Registered Agent

(a) Each limited liability company shall have and maintain in the State of Delaware:

(1) A registered office, which may but need not be a place of its business in the State of Delaware; and

(2) A registered agent for service of process on the limited liability company, which agent may be either an individual resident of the State of Delaware whose business office is identical with the limited liability company's registered office, or a domestic corporation, or a domestic limited partnership, or a domestic limited liability company, or a domestic statutory trust, or a foreign corporation, or a foreign limited partnership, or a foreign limited liability company authorized to do business in the State of Delaware having a business office identical with such registered office, which is generally open during normal business hours to accept service of process

and otherwise perform the functions of a registered agent, or the limited liability company itself. . . .

§ 18–105. Service of Process on Domestic Limited Liability Companies

(a) Service of legal process upon any domestic limited liability company shall be made by delivering a copy personally to any manager of the limited liability company in the State of Delaware or the registered agent of the limited liability company in the State of Delaware, or by leaving it at the dwelling house or usual place of abode in the State of Delaware of any such manager or registered agent (if the registered agent be an individual), or at the registered office or other place of business of the limited liability company in the State of Delaware. If the registered agent be a corporation, service of process upon it as such may be made by serving, in the State of Delaware, a copy thereof on the president, vice-president, secretary, assistant secretary or any director of the corporate registered agent. Service by copy left at the dwelling house or usual place of abode of a manager or registered agent, or at the registered office or other place of business of the limited liability company in the State of Delaware, to be effective, must be delivered thereat at least 6 days before the return date of the process, and in the presence of an adult person, and the officer serving the process shall distinctly state the manner of service in his return thereto. Process returnable forthwith must be delivered personally to the manager or registered agent.

(b) In case the officer whose duty it is to serve legal process cannot by due diligence serve the process in any manner provided for by subsection (a) of this section, it shall be lawful to serve the process against the limited liability company upon the Secretary of State, and such service shall be as effectual for all intents and purposes as if made in any of the ways provided for in subsection (a) of this section. In the event that service is effected through the Secretary of State in accordance with this subsection, the Secretary of State shall forthwith notify the limited liability company by letter, certified mail, return receipt requested, directed to the limited liability company at its address as it appears on the records relating to such limited liability company on file with the Secretary of State or, if no such address appears, at its last registered office. Such letter shall enclose a copy of the process and any other papers served on the Secretary of State pursuant to this subsection. It shall be the duty of the plaintiff in the event of such service to serve process and any other papers in duplicate, to notify the Secretary of State that service is being effected pursuant to this subsection, and to pay the Secretary of State the sum of $50 for the use of the State of Delaware, which sum shall be taxed as part of the costs in the proceeding if the plaintiff shall prevail therein. The Secretary of State shall maintain an alphabetical record of any such service setting forth the name of the plaintiff and defendant, the title, docket number and nature of the proceeding in which process has been served upon the Secretary, the fact that service has been effected pursuant to this subsection, the return date thereof, and the day and hour when the service was made. The Secretary of State shall not be required to retain such information for a period longer than 5 years from the Secretary's receipt of the service of process.

§ 18–106. Nature of Business Permitted; Powers

(a) A limited liability company may carry on any lawful business, purpose or activity, whether or not for profit, with the exception of the business of banking as defined in § 126 of Title 8.

(b) A limited liability company shall possess and may exercise all the powers and privileges granted by this chapter or by any other law or by its limited liability company agreement, together with any powers incidental thereto, including such powers and privileges as are necessary or convenient to the conduct, promotion or attainment of the business, purposes or activities of the limited liability company.

(c) Notwithstanding any provision of this chapter to the contrary, without limiting the general powers enumerated in subsection (b) above, a limited liability company shall, subject to such standards and restrictions, if any, as are set forth in its limited liability company agreement, have the power and authority to make contracts of guaranty and suretyship, and enter into interest rate, basis, currency, hedge or other swap agreements, or cap, floor, put, call, option, exchange or collar agreements, derivative agreements or other agreements similar to any of the foregoing.

§ 18–107. Business Transactions of Member or Manager With the Limited Liability Company

Except as provided in a limited liability company agreement, a member or manager may lend money to, borrow money from, act as a surety, guarantor or endorser for, guarantee or assume 1 or more obligations of, provide collateral for, and transact other business with, a limited liability company and, subject to other applicable law, has the same rights and obligations with respect to any such matter as a person who is not a member or manager.

§ 18–108. Indemnification

Subject to such standards and restrictions, if any, as are set forth in its limited liability company agreement, a limited liability company may, and shall have the power to, indemnify and hold harmless any member or manager or other person from and against any and all claims and demands whatsoever.

§ 18–109. Service of Process on Managers and Liquidating Trustees

(a) A manager or a liquidating trustee of a limited liability company may be served with process in the manner prescribed in this section in all civil actions or proceedings brought in the State of Delaware involving or relating to the business of the limited liability company or a violation by the manager or the liquidating trustee of a duty to the limited liability company, or any member of the limited liability company, whether or not the manager or the liquidating trustee is a manager or a liquidating trustee at the time suit is commenced. A manager's or a liquidating trustee's serving as such constitutes such person's consent to the appointment of the registered agent of the limited liability company (or, if there is none, the Secretary of State) as such person's agent upon whom service of process may be made as provided in this section. Such service as a manager or a liquidating trustee shall signify the consent of such manager or liquidating trustee that any process when so served shall be of the same legal force and validity as if served upon such manager or liquidating trustee within the State of Delaware and such appointment of the registered agent (or, if there is none, the Secretary of State) shall be irrevocable. As used in this subsection (a) and in subsection (b), (c), and (d) of this § 18–109, the term "manager" refers (i) to a person who is a manager as defined in § 18–101(10) of this chapter and (ii) to a person, whether or not a member of a limited liability company, who, although not a manager as defined in § 18–101(10) of this chapter, participates materially in the management of the limited liability company, provided, however, that the power to elect or otherwise select or to participate in the election or selection of a person to be a manager as defined in § 18–101(10) of this chapter shall not, by itself, constitute participation in the management of the limited liability company.

(b) Service of process shall be effected by serving the registered agent (or, if there is none, the Secretary of State) with 1 copy of such process in the manner provided by law for service of writs of summons. In the event service is made under this subsection upon the Secretary of State, the plaintiff shall pay to the Secretary of State the sum of $50 for the use of the State of Delaware, which sum shall be taxed as part of the costs of the proceeding if the plaintiff shall prevail therein. In addition, the Prothonotary or the Register in Chancery of the court in which the civil action or proceeding is pending shall, within 7 days of such service, deposit in the United States mails, by registered mail, postage prepaid, true and attested copies of the process, together with a statement that service is being made pursuant to this section, addressed to such manager or liquidating trustee at the registered office of the limited liability company and at his address last known to the party desiring to make such service.

(c) In any action in which any such manager or liquidating trustee has been served with process as hereinabove provided, the time in which a defendant shall be required to appear and file a responsive pleading shall be computed from the date of mailing by the Prothonotary or the Register in Chancery as provided in subsection (b) of this section; however, the court in which such action has been commenced may order such continuance or continuances as may be necessary to afford such manager or liquidating trustee reasonable opportunity to defend the action.

(d) In a written limited liability company agreement or other writing, a manager or member may consent to be subject to the nonexclusive jurisdiction of the courts of, or arbitration in, a specified jurisdiction, or the exclusive jurisdiction of the courts of the State of Delaware, or the exclusivity of arbitration in a specified jurisdiction or the State of Delaware, and to be served with legal process in the manner prescribed in such limited liability company agreement or other writing. Except by agreeing to arbitrate any arbitrable matter in a specified jurisdiction or in the State of Delaware, a member who is not a manager may not waive its right to maintain a legal action or proceeding in the courts of the State of Delaware with respect to matters relating to the organization or internal affairs of a limited liability company.

(e) Nothing herein contained limits or affects the right to serve process in any other manner now or hereafter provided by law. This section is an extension of and not a limitation upon the right otherwise existing of service of legal process upon nonresidents.

(f) The Court of Chancery and the Superior Court may make all necessary rules respecting the form of process, the manner of issuance and return thereof and such other rules which may be necessary to implement this section and are not inconsistent with this section.

§ 18–110. Contested Matters Relating to Managers; Contested Votes

(a) Upon application of any member or manager, the Court of Chancery may hear and determine the validity of any admission, election, appointment, removal or resignation of a manager of a limited liability company, and the right of any person to become or continue to be a manager of a limited liability company, and, in case the right to serve as a manager is claimed by more than 1 person, may determine the person or persons entitled to serve as managers; and to that end make such order or decree in any such case as may be just and proper, with power to enforce the production of any books, papers and records of the limited liability company relating to the issue. In any such application the limited liability company shall be named as a party and service of copies of the application upon the registered agent of the limited liability company shall be deemed to be service upon the limited liability company and upon the person or persons whose right to serve as a manager is contested and upon the person or persons, if any, claiming to be a manager or claiming the right to be a manager; and the registered agent shall forward immediately a copy of the application to the limited liability company and to the person or persons whose right to serve as a manager is contested and to the person or persons, if any, claiming to be a manager or the right to be a manager, in a postpaid, sealed, registered letter addressed to such limited liability company and such person or persons at their post-office addresses last known to the registered agent or furnished to the registered agent by the applicant member or manager. The Court may make such order respecting further or other notice of such application as it deems proper under [the] circumstances.

(b) Upon application of any member or manager, the Court of Chancery may hear and determine the result of any vote of members or managers upon matters as to which the members or managers of the limited liability company, or any class or group of members or managers, have the right to vote pursuant to the limited liability company agreement or other agreement or this chapter (other than the admission, election, appointment, removal or resignation of managers). In any such application, the limited liability company shall be named as a party and service of the application upon the registered agent of the limited liability company shall be deemed to be service upon the limited liability company, and no other party need be joined in order for the Court to adjudicate the result of the vote. The Court may make such order respecting further or other notice of such application as it deems proper under [the] circumstances.

(c) Nothing herein contained limits or affects the right to serve process in any other manner now or hereafter provided by law. This section is an extension of and not a limitation upon the right otherwise existing of service of legal process upon nonresidents.

§ 18–111. Interpretation and Enforcement of Limited Liability Company Agreement

Any action to interpret, apply or enforce the provisions of a limited liability company agreement, or the duties, obligations or liabilities of a limited liability company to the members or managers of the limited liability company, or the duties, obligations or liabilities among members or managers and of members or managers to the limited liability company, or the rights or powers of, or restrictions on, the limited liability company, members or managers, may be brought in the Court of Chancery.

SUBCHAPTER II. FORMATION; CERTIFICATE OF FORMATION

§ 18–201. Certificate of Formation

(a) In order to form a limited liability company, 1 or more authorized persons must execute a certificate of formation. The certificate of formation shall be filed in the office of the Secretary of State and set forth:

(1) The name of the limited liability company;

(2) The address of the registered office and the name and address of the registered agent for service of process required to be maintained by § 18–104 of this title; and

(3) Any other matters the members determine to include therein.

(b) A limited liability company is formed at the time of the filing of the initial certificate of formation in the office of the Secretary of State or at any later date or time specified in the certificate of formation if, in either case, there has been substantial compliance with the requirements of this section. A limited liability company formed under this chapter shall be a separate legal entity, the existence of which as a separate legal entity shall continue until cancellation of the limited liability company's certificate of formation.

(c) The filing of the certificate of formation in the office of the Secretary of State shall make it unnecessary to file any other documents under Chapter 31 of this title.

(d) A limited liability company agreement may be entered into either before, after or at the time of the filing of a certificate of formation and, whether entered into before, after or at the time of such filing, may be made effective as of the formation of the limited liability company or at such other time or date as provided in the limited liability company agreement.

§ 18–202. Amendment to Certificate of Formation

(a) A certificate of formation is amended by filing a certificate of amendment thereto in the office of the Secretary of State. The certificate of amendment shall set forth:

(1) The name of the limited liability company; and

(2) The amendment to the certificate of formation.

(b) A manager or, if there is no manager, then any member who becomes aware that any statement in a certificate of formation was false when made, or that any matter described has changed making the certificate of formation false in any material respect, shall promptly amend the certificate of formation.

(c) A certificate of formation may be amended at any time for any other proper purpose.

(d) Unless otherwise provided in this chapter or unless a later effective date or time (which shall be a date or time certain) is provided for in the certificate of amendment, a certificate of amendment shall be effective at the time of its filing with the Secretary of State.

§ 18–203. Cancellation of Certificate

A certificate of formation shall be cancelled upon the dissolution and the completion of winding up of a limited liability company, or as provided in § 18–104(d) or § 18–1108 [cancellation of certificate of formation for failure to pay taxes] of this chapter, or upon the filing of a certificate of merger or consolidation if the limited liability company is not the surviving or resulting entity in a merger or consolidation, or upon the filing of a certificate of transfer, or upon the filing of a certificate of conversion to a non-Delaware entity. A certificate of cancellation shall be filed in the office of the Secretary of State to accomplish the cancellation of a certificate of formation upon the dissolution and the completion of winding up of a limited liability company and shall set forth:

(1) The name of the limited liability company;

(2) The date of filing of its certificate of formation;

(3) The future effective date or time (which shall be a date or time certain) of cancellation if it is not to be effective upon the filing of the certificate; and

(4) Any other information the person filing the certificate of cancellation determines.

§ 18–204. Execution

(a) Each certificate required by this subchapter to be filed in the office of the Secretary of State shall be executed by 1 or more authorized persons.

(b) Unless otherwise provided in a limited liability company agreement, any person may sign any certificate or amendment thereof or enter into a limited liability company agreement or amendment thereof by an agent, including an attorney-in-fact. An authorization, including a power of attorney, to sign any certificate or amendment thereof or to enter into a limited liability company agreement or amendment thereof need not be in writing, need not be sworn to, verified or acknowledged, and need not be filed in the office of the Secretary of State, but if in writing, must be retained by the limited liability company.

(c) The execution of a certificate by an authorized person constitutes an oath or affirmation, under the penalties of perjury in the third degree, that, to the best of the authorized person's knowledge and belief, the facts stated therein are true.

§ 18–205. Execution, Amendment or Cancellation by Judicial Order

(a) If a person required to execute a certificate required by this subchapter fails or refuses to do so, any other person who is adversely affected by the failure or refusal may petition the Court of Chancery to direct the execution of the certificate. If the Court finds that the execution of the certificate is proper and that any person so designated has failed or refused to execute the certificate, it shall order the Secretary of State to record an appropriate certificate.

(b) If a person required to execute a limited liability company agreement or amendment thereof fails or refuses to do so, any other person who is adversely affected by the failure or refusal may petition the Court of Chancery to direct the execution of the limited liability company agreement or amendment thereof. If the Court finds that the limited liability company agreement or amendment thereof should be executed and that any person required to execute the limited liability company agreement or amendment thereof has failed or refused to do so, it shall enter an order granting appropriate relief.

§ 18–206. Filing

(a) The signed copy of the certificate of formation and of any certificates of amendment, correction, amendment of a certificate with a future effective date or time, termination of a certificate with a future date or time or cancellation (or of any judicial decree of amendment or cancellation), and of any certificate of merger or consolidation, any restated certificate, any corrected certificate, any certificate of conversion to limited liability company, any certificate of conversion to a non-Delaware entity, any certificate of transfer, any certificate of transfer and continuance, any certificate of limited liability company domestication, and of any certificate of revival shall be delivered to the Secretary of State. A person who executes a certificate as an agent or fiduciary need not exhibit evidence of his authority as a prerequisite to filing. Any signature on any certificate authorized to be filed with the Secretary of State under any provision of this chapter may be a facsimile, a conformed signature or an electronically transmitted signature. Upon delivery of any certificate, the Secretary of State shall record the date and time of its delivery. Unless the Secretary of State finds that any certificate does not conform to law, upon receipt of all filing fees required by law he shall:

(1) Certify that the certificate of formation, the certificate of amendment, the certificate of correction, the certificate of amendment of a certificate with a future effective date or time, the certificate of termination of a certificate with a future effective date or time, the certificate of cancellation (or of any judicial decree of amendment or cancellation), the certificate of merger or consolidation, the restated certificate, the corrected certificate, the certificate of conversion to [a] limited liability company, the certificate of conversion to a non-Delaware entity, the certificate of transfer, the certificate of transfer and continuance, the certificate of limited liability company domestication or the certificate of revival has been filed in his office by endorsing upon the signed certificate the word

"Filed", and the date and time of the filing. This endorsement is conclusive of the date and time of its filing in the absence of actual fraud. Except as provided in subsection (a)(5) or (a)(6) of this section, such date and time of filing of a certificate shall be the date and time of delivery of the certificate;

(2) File and index the endorsed certificate;

(3) Prepare and return to the person who filed it or his representative a copy of the signed certificate, similarly endorsed, and shall certify such copy as a true copy of the signed certificate; and

(4) Cause to be entered such information from the certificate as the Secretary of State deems appropriate into the Delaware Corporation Information System or any system which is a successor thereto in the office of the Secretary of State, and such information and a copy of such certificate shall be permanently maintained as a public record on a suitable medium. The Secretary of State is authorized to grant direct access to such system to registered agents subject to the execution of an operating agreement between the Secretary of State and such registered agent. Any registered agent granted such access shall demonstrate the existence of policies to ensure that information entered into the system accurately reflects the content of certificates in the possession of the registered agent at the time of entry.

(5) Upon request made upon or prior to delivery, the Secretary of State may, to the extent deemed practicable, establish as the date and time of filing of a certificate a date and time after its delivery. If the Secretary of State refuses to file any certificate due to an error, omission or other imperfection, the Secretary of State may hold such certificate in suspension, and in such event, upon delivery of a replacement certificate in proper form for filing and tender of the required fees within 5 business days after notice of such suspension is given to the filer, the Secretary of State shall establish as the date and time of filing of such certificate the date and time that would have been the date and time of filing of the rejected certificate had it been accepted for filing. The Secretary of State shall not issue a certificate of good standing with respect to any limited liability company with a certificate held in suspension pursuant to this subsection. The Secretary of State may establish as the date and time of filing of a certificate the date and time at which information from such certificate is entered pursuant to subdivision (a)(4) of this section if such certificate is delivered on the same date and within 4 hours after such information is entered.

(6) If:

a. Together with the actual delivery of a certificate and tender of the required fees, there is delivered to the Secretary of State a separate affidavit (which in its heading shall be designated as an affidavit of extraordinary condition) attesting, on the basis of personal knowledge of the affiant or a reliable source of knowledge identified in the affidavit, that an earlier effort to deliver such certificate and tender such fees was made in good faith, specifying the nature, date and time of such good faith effort and requesting that the Secretary of State establish such date and time as the date and time of filing of such certificate; or

b. Upon the actual delivery of a certificate and tender of the required fees, the Secretary of State in his or her discretion provides a written waiver of the requirement for such an affidavit stating that it appears to the Secretary of State that an earlier effort to deliver such certificate and tender such fees was made in good faith and specifying the date and time of such effort; and

c. The Secretary of State determines that an extraordinary condition existed at such date and time, that such earlier effort was unsuccessful as a result of the existence of such extraordinary condition, and that such actual delivery and tender were made within a reasonable period (not to exceed 2 business days) after the cessation of such extraordinary condition,

then the Secretary of State may establish such date and time as the date and time of filing of such certificate. No fee shall be paid to the Secretary of State for receiving an affidavit of extraordinary condition. For purposes of this subsection, an extraordinary condition means: any emergency resulting from an attack on, invasion or occupation by foreign military forces of, or disaster, catastrophe, war or other armed conflict, revolution or insurrection or rioting or civil commotion in, the United States or a locality in which the Secretary of State conducts its business or in which the good faith effort to deliver the certificate and tender the required fees is made, or the immediate threat of any of the foregoing; or any malfunction or outage of the electrical or telephone service to the Secretary of State's office, or weather or other condition in or about a locality in which the Secretary of State conducts its business, as a result of which the Secretary of State's office is not open for the purpose of the filing of certificates under this chapter or such filing cannot be effected without extraordinary effort. The Secretary of State may require such proof as it deems necessary to make the determination required under this subparagraph of subdivision (a)(6), and any such determination shall be conclusive in the absence of actual fraud. If the Secretary of State establishes the date and time of filing of a certificate pursuant to this subsection, the date and time of delivery of the affidavit of extraordinary condition or the date and time of the Secretary of State's written waiver of such affidavit shall be endorsed on such affidavit or waiver and such affidavit or waiver, so endorsed, shall be attached to the filed certificate to which it relates. Such filed certificate shall be effective as of the date and time established as the date and time of filing by the Secretary of State pursuant to this subsection, except as to those persons who are substantially and adversely affected by such establishment and, as to those persons, the certificate shall be effective from the date and time endorsed on the affidavit of extraordinary condition or written waiver attached thereto.

(b) Upon the filing of a certificate of amendment (or judicial decree of amendment), certificate of correction, corrected certificate or restated certificate in the office of the Secretary of State, or upon the future effective date or time of a certificate of amendment (or judicial decree thereof) or restated certificate, as provided for therein, the certificate of formation shall be amended, corrected or restated as set forth therein. Upon the filing of a certificate of cancellation (or a judicial decree thereof), or a certificate of merger or consolidation which acts as a certificate of cancellation, or a certificate of transfer or a certificate of conversion to a non-Delaware entity, or upon the future effective date or time of a certificate of cancellation (or a judicial decree thereof) or of a certificate of merger or consolidation which acts as a certificate of cancellation, or a certificate of transfer or a certificate of conversion to a non-Delaware entity, as provided for therein, or as specified in § 18–104(d) of this title, the certificate of formation is cancelled. Upon the filing of a certificate of limited liability company domestication, or upon the future effective date or time of a certificate of limited liability company domestication, the entity filing the certificate of limited liability company domestication is domesticated as a limited liability company with the effect provided in § 18–212 of this title. Upon the filing of a certificate of conversion to limited liability company, or upon the future effective date or time of a certificate of conversion to limited liability company, the entity filing the certificate of conversion to limited liability company is converted to a limited liability company with the effect provided in § 18–214 of this title.... Upon the filing of a certificate of transfer and continuance, or upon the future effective date or time of a certificate of transfer and continuance, as provided for therein, the limited liability company filing the certificate of transfer and continuance shall continue to exist as a limited liability company of the State of Delaware with the effect provided in Section 18–213 of this title.

(c) If any certificate filed in accordance with this chapter provides for a future effective date or time and if, prior to such future effective date or time set forth in such certificate, the transaction is terminated or its terms are amended to change the future effective date or time or any other matter described in such certificate so as to make such certificate false or inaccurate in any respect, such certificate shall, prior to the future effective date or time set forth in such certificate, be terminated or amended by the filing of a certificate of termination or certificate of amendment of such certificate, executed in accordance with § 18–204 of this title, which shall identify the certificate which has been terminated or amended and shall state that the certificate has been terminated or the manner in which it has been amended. Upon the filing of a certificate of amendment of a certificate with a future effective date or time, the certificate identified in such certificate of amendment is amended. Upon the filing of a certificate of termination of a certificate with a future effective date or time, the certificate identified in such certificate of termination is terminated. . . .

§ 18–207. Notice

The fact that a certificate of formation is on file in the office of the Secretary of State is notice that the entity formed in connection with the filing of the certificate of formation is a limited liability company formed under the laws of the State of Delaware and is notice of all other facts set forth therein which are required to be set forth in a certificate of formation by § 18–201(a)(1) and (2) of this title and which are permitted to be set forth in a certificate of formation by § 18–215(b) of this chapter.

§ 18–209. Merger and Consolidation

(a) As used in this section, "other business entity" means a corporation, a statutory trust, or a business trust or association, a real estate investment trust, a common-law trust, or any other unincorporated business, including a partnership (whether general (including a limited liability partnership) or limited (including a limited liability partnership)), and a foreign limited liability company, but excluding a domestic limited liability company.

(b) Pursuant to an agreement of merger or consolidation, 1 or more domestic limited liability companies may merge or consolidate with or into 1 or more domestic limited liability companies or 1 or more other business entities formed or organized under the laws of the State of Delaware or any other state or the United States or any foreign country or other foreign jurisdiction, or any combination thereof, with such domestic limited liability companies or other business entity as the agreement shall provide being the surviving or resulting domestic limited liability companies or other business entity. Unless otherwise provided in the limited liability company agreement, a merger or consolidation shall be approved by each domestic limited liability company which is to merge or consolidate by the members or, if there is more than one class or group of members, then by each class or group of members, in either case, by members who own more than 50 percent of the then current percentage or other interest in the profits of the domestic limited liability company owned by all of the members or by the members in each class or group, as appropriate. In connection with a merger or consolidation hereunder, rights or securities of, or interests in, a domestic limited liability company or other business entity which is a constituent party to the merger or consolidation may be exchanged for or converted into cash, property, rights or securities of, or interests in, the surviving or resulting domestic limited liability company or other business entity or, in addition to or in lieu thereof, may be exchanged for or converted into cash, property, rights or securities of, or interests in, a domestic limited liability company or other business entity which is not the surviving or resulting limited liability company or other business entity in the merger or consolidation or may be cancelled. Notwithstanding prior approval, an agreement of merger or consolidation may be terminated or amended pursuant to a provision for such termination or amendment contained in the agreement of merger or consolidation.

(c) If a domestic limited liability company is merging or consolidating under this section, the domestic limited liability company or other business entity surviving or resulting in or from the merger or consolidation shall file a certificate of merger or consolidation executed by one or more persons on behalf of the domestic limited liability company when it is the surviving or resulting entity in the office of the Secretary of State. The certificate of merger or consolidation shall state:

(1) The name and jurisdiction of formation or organization of each of the domestic limited liability companies and other business entities which is to merge or consolidate;

(2) That an agreement of merger or consolidation has been approved and executed by each of the domestic limited liability companies and other business entities which is to merge or consolidate;

(3) The name of the surviving or resulting domestic limited liability company or other business entity;

(4) In the case of a merger in which a domestic limited liability company is the surviving entity, such amendments, if any, to the certificate of formation of the surviving domestic limited liability company to change its name as are desired to be effected by the merger;

(5) The future effective date or time (which shall be a date or time certain) of the merger or consolidation if it is not to be effective upon the filing of the certificate of merger or consolidation;

(6) That the agreement of merger or consolidation is on file at a place of business of the surviving or resulting domestic limited liability company or other business entity, and shall state the address thereof;

(7) That a copy of the agreement of merger or consolidation will be furnished by the surviving or resulting domestic limited liability company or other business entity, on request and without cost, to

any member of any domestic limited liability company or any person holding an interest in any other business entity which is to merge or consolidate; and

(8) If the surviving or resulting entity is not a domestic limited liability company, or a corporation or limited partnership organized under the laws of the State of Delaware, or a statutory trust organized under Chapter 38 of Title 12, a statement that such surviving or resulting other business entity agrees that it may be served with process in the State of Delaware in any action, suit or proceeding for the enforcement of any obligation of any domestic limited liability company which is to merge or consolidate, irrevocably appointing the Secretary of State as its agent to accept service of process in any such action, suit or proceeding and specifying the address to which a copy of such process shall be mailed to it by the Secretary of State. In the event of service hereunder upon the Secretary of State, the procedures set forth in § 18–911(c) of this title shall be applicable, except that the plaintiff in any such action, suit or proceeding shall furnish the Secretary of State with the address specified in the certificate of merger or consolidation provided for in this section and any other address which the plaintiff may elect to furnish, together with copies of such process as required by the Secretary of State, and the Secretary of State shall notify such surviving or resulting other business entity at all such addresses furnished by the plaintiff in accordance with the procedures set forth in § 18–911(c) of this title.

(d) Unless a future effective date or time is provided in a certificate of merger or consolidation, in which event a merger or consolidation shall be effective at any such future effective date or time, a merger or consolidation shall be effective upon the filing in the office of the Secretary of State of a certificate of merger or consolidation.

(e) A certificate of merger or consolidation shall act as a certificate of cancellation for a domestic limited liability company which is not the surviving or resulting entity in the merger or consolidation. A certificate of merger that sets forth any amendment in accordance with Subsection (c)(4) of this Section shall be deemed to be an amendment to the certificate of formation of the limited liability company, and the limited liability company shall not be required to take any further action to amend its certificate of formation under § 18–202 of this Title with respect to such amendments set forth in the certificate of merger. Whenever this section requires the filing of a certificate of merger or consolidation, such requirement shall be deemed satisfied by the filing of an agreement of merger or consolidation containing the information required by this section to be set forth in the certificate of merger or consolidation.

(f) An agreement of merger or consolidation approved in accordance with subsection (b) of this section may:

    (1) Effect any amendment to the limited liability company agreement; or

    (2) Effect the adoption of a new limited liability company agreement ... for a limited liability company if it is the surviving or resulting limited liability company in the merger or consolidation.

Any amendment to a limited liability company agreement or adoption of a new limited liability company agreement made pursuant to the foregoing sentence shall be effective at the effective time or date of the merger or consolidation. The provisions of this subsection shall not be construed to limit the accomplishment of a merger or of any of the matters referred to herein by any other means provided for in a limited liability company agreement or other agreement or as otherwise permitted by law, including that the limited liability company agreement of any constituent limited liability company to the merger or consolidation (including a limited liability company formed for the purpose of consummating a merger or consolidation) shall be the limited liability company agreement of the surviving or resulting limited liability company.

(g) When any merger or consolidation shall have become effective under this section, for all purposes of the laws of the State of Delaware, all of the rights, privileges and powers of each of the domestic limited liability companies and other business entities that have merged or consolidated, and all property, real, personal and mixed, and all debts due to any of said domestic limited liability companies and other business entities, as well as all other things and causes of action belonging to each of such domestic limited liability companies and other business entities, shall be vested in the surviving or resulting domestic limited liability company or other business entity, and shall thereafter be the property of the surviving or resulting domestic limited liability company or other business entity as they were of each of the domestic limited liability companies and other business entities that have merged or consolidated, and the title to any real property vested by deed or otherwise, under the laws of the State of Delaware, in any of such domestic limited liability companies and other business entities, shall not revert or be in any way impaired by reason of this chapter; but all rights of creditors and all liens upon any property of any of said domestic limited liability companies and other business entities shall be preserved unimpaired, and all debts, liabilities and duties of each of the said domestic limited liability companies and other business entities that have merged or consolidated shall thenceforth attach to the surviving or resulting domestic limited liability company or other business entity, and may be enforced against it to the same extent as if said debts, liabilities and duties had been incurred or contracted by it. Unless otherwise agreed, a merger or consolidation of a domestic limited liability company, including a domestic limited liability company which is not the surviving or resulting entity in the merger or consolidation, shall not require such domestic limited liability company to wind up its affairs under § 18–803 of this title or pay its liabilities and distribute its assets under § 18–804 of this title.

§ 18–210. Contractual Appraisal Rights

A limited liability company agreement or an agreement of merger or consolidation may provide that contractual appraisal rights with respect to a limited liability company shall be available for any class or group of members or limited liability company interests in connection with any amendment of a limited liability company agreement, any merger or consolidation in which the limited liability company is a constituent party to the merger or consolidation, any conversion of the limited liability company to another business form, any transfer to or domestication in any jurisdiction by the limited liability company, or the sale of all or substantially all of the limited liability company's assets. The Court of Chancery shall have jurisdiction to hear and determine any matter relating to any such appraisal rights.

§ 18–211. Certificate of Correction

(a) Whenever any certificate authorized to be filed with the office of the Secretary of State under any provision of this chapter has been so filed and is an inaccurate record of the action therein referred to, or was defectively or erroneously executed, such certificate may be corrected by filing with the office of the Secretary of State a certificate of correction of such certificate. The certificate of correction shall specify the inaccuracy or defect to be corrected, shall set forth the portion of the certificate in corrected form and shall be executed and filed as required by this chapter. The certificate of correction shall be effective as of the date the original certificate was filed, except as to those persons who are substantially and adversely affected by the correction, and as to those persons the certificate of correction shall be effective from the filing date.

(b) In lieu of filing a certificate of correction, a certificate may be corrected by filing with the Secretary of State a corrected certificate which shall be executed and filed as if the corrected certificate were the certificate being corrected, and a fee equal to the fee payable to the Secretary of State if the certificate being corrected were then being filed shall be paid and collected by the Secretary of State for the use of the State of Delaware in connection with the filing of the corrected certificate. The corrected certificate shall be specifically designated as such in its heading, shall specify the inaccuracy or defect to be corrected, and shall set forth the entire certificate in corrected form. A certificate corrected in accordance with this section shall be effective as of the date the original certificate was filed, except as to those persons who are substantially and adversely affected by the correction and as to those persons the certificate as corrected shall be effective from the filing date.

§ 18–212. Domestication of Non–United States Entities

(a) As used in this section, "non-United States entity" means a foreign limited liability company (other than one formed under the laws of a state) or a corporation, a business trust or association, a real estate investment trust, a common-law trust or any other unincorporated business, including a partnership (whether general (including a limited liability partnership) or limited (including a limited liability limited partnership)) formed, incorporated, created or that otherwise came into being under the laws of any foreign country or other foreign jurisdiction (other than any state).

(b) Any non-United States entity may become domesticated as a limited liability company in the State of Delaware by complying with subsection (g) of this section and filing in the office of the Secretary of State in accordance with § 18–206 of this title:

(1) A certificate of limited liability company domestication that has been executed by 1 or more authorized persons in accordance with § 18–204 of this title; and

(2) A certificate of formation that complies with § 18–201 of this title and has been executed by 1 or more authorized persons in accordance with § 18–204 of this title.

(c) The certificate of limited liability company domestication shall state:

(1) The date on which and jurisdiction where the non-United States entity was first formed, incorporated, created or otherwise came into being;

(2) The name of the non-United States entity immediately prior to the filing of the certificate of limited liability company domestication;

(3) The name of the limited liability company as set forth in the certificate of formation filed in accordance with subsection (b) of this section;

(4) The future effective date or time (which shall be a date or time certain) of the domestication as a limited liability company if it is not to be effective upon the filing of the certificate of limited liability company domestication and the certificate of formation; and

(5) The jurisdiction that constituted the seat, siege social, or principal place of business or central administration of the non-United States entity, or any other equivalent thereto under applica-

ble law, immediately prior to the filing of the certificate of limited liability company domestication.

(d) Upon the filing in the office of the Secretary of State of the certificate of limited liability company domestication and the certificate of formation or upon the future effective date or time of the certificate of limited liability company domestication and the certificate of formation, the non-United States entity shall be domesticated as a limited liability company in the State of Delaware and the limited liability company shall thereafter be subject to all of the provisions of this chapter, except that notwithstanding § 18–201 of this title, the existence of the limited liability company shall be deemed to have commenced on the date the non-United States entity commenced its existence in the jurisdiction in which the non-United States entity was first formed, incorporated, created or otherwise came into being.

(e) The domestication of any non-United States entity as a limited liability company in the State of Delaware shall not be deemed to affect any obligations or liabilities of the non-United States entity incurred prior to its domestication as a limited liability company in the State of Delaware, or the personal liability of any person therefor.

(f) The filing of a certificate of limited liability company domestication shall not affect the choice of law applicable to the non-United States entity, except that from the effective date or time of the domestication, the law of the State of Delaware, including the provisions of this chapter, shall apply to the non-United States entity to the same extent as if the non-United States entity had been formed as a limited liability company on that date.

(g) Prior to filing a certificate of limited liability company domestication with the Office of the Secretary of State, the domestication shall be approved in the manner provided for by the document, instrument, agreement or other writing, as the case may be, governing the internal affairs of the non-United States entity and the conduct of its business or by applicable non-Delaware law, as appropriate, and a limited liability company agreement shall be approved by the same authorization required to approve the domestication.

(h) When any domestication shall have become effective under this section, for all purposes of the laws of the State of Delaware, all of the rights, privileges and powers of the non-United States entity that has been domesticated, and all property, real, personal and mixed, and all debts due to such non-United States entity, as well as all other things and causes of action belonging to such non-United States entity, shall remain vested in the domestic limited liability company to which such non-United States entity has been domesticated and shall be the property of such domestic limited liability company, and the title to any real property vested by deed or otherwise in such non-United States entity shall not revert or be in any way impaired by reason of this chapter; but all rights of creditors and all liens upon any property of such non-United States entity shall be preserved unimpaired, and all debts, liabilities and duties of the non-United States entity that has been domesticated shall remain attached to the domestic limited liability company to which such non-United States entity has been domesticated, and may be enforced against it to the same extent as if said debts, liabilities and duties had originally been incurred or contracted by it in its capacity as a domestic limited liability company. The rights, privileges, powers and interests in property of the non-United States entity, as well as the debts, liabilities and duties of the non-United States entity, shall not be deemed, as a consequence of the domestication, to have been transferred to the domestic limited liability company to which such non-United States entity has domesticated for any purpose of the laws of the State of Delaware.

(i) When a non-United States entity has become domesticated as a limited liability company pursuant to this section, the limited liability company shall, for all purposes of the laws of the State of Delaware, be deemed to be the same entity as the domesticating non-United States entity. Unless otherwise agreed, for all purposes of the laws of the State of Delaware, the domesticating non-United States entity shall not be required to wind up its affairs or pay its liabilities and distribute its assets, the domestication shall not be deemed to constitute a dissolution of such non-United States entity, and the domestication shall constitute a continuation of the existence of the domesticating non-United States entity in the form of a domestic limited liability company. If, following domestication, a non-United States entity that has become domesticated as a limited liability company continues its existence in the foreign country or other foreign jurisdiction in which it was existing immediately prior to domestication, the limited liability company and such non-United States entity shall, for all purposes of the laws of the State of Delaware, constitute a single entity formed, incorporated, created or otherwise having come into being, as applicable, and existing under the laws of the State of Delaware and the laws of such foreign country or other foreign jurisdiction.

(j) In connection with a domestication hereunder, rights or securities of, or interests in, the non-United States entity that is to be domesticated as a domestic limited liability company may be exchanged for or converted into cash, property, rights or securities of, or interests in, such domestic limited liability company or, in addition to or in lieu thereof, may be exchanged for or converted into cash, property, rights or securities of, or interests in, another domestic liability company or entity or may be cancelled.

§ 18–213. Transfer or Continuance of Domestic Limited Liability Companies

(a) Upon compliance with the provisions of this section, any limited liability company may transfer to or domesticate in any jurisdiction, other than any state, and, in connection therewith, may elect to continue its existence as a limited liability company in the State of Delaware.

(b) If the limited liability company agreement specifies the manner of authorizing a transfer or domestication described in subsection (a) of this section, the transfer or domestication shall be authorized as specified in the limited liability company agreement. If the limited liability company agreement does not specify the manner of authorizing a transfer or domestication described in subsection (a) of this section and does not prohibit such a transfer or domestication, the transfer or domestication shall be authorized in the same manner as is specified in the limited liability company agreement for authorizing a merger or consolidation that involves the limited liability company as a constituent party to the merger or consolidation. If the limited liability company agreement does not specify the manner of authorizing a transfer or domestication described in subsection (a) of this section or a merger or consolidation that involves the limited liability company as a constituent party and does not prohibit such a transfer or domestication, the transfer or domestication shall be authorized by the approval by the members or, if there is more than 1 class or group of members, then by each class or group of members, in either case, by the members who own more than 50% of the then current percentage or other interest in the profits of the domestic limited liability company owned by all of the members or by the members in each class or group, as appropriate. If a transfer or domestication described in subsection (a) of this section shall be authorized as provided in this subsection (b), a certificate of transfer if the limited liability company's existence as a limited liability company of the State of Delaware is to cease, or a certificate of transfer and continuance if the limited liability company's existence as a limited liability company in the State of Delaware is to continue, executed in accordance with § 18–204 of this title, shall be filed in the Office of the Secretary of State in accordance with § 18–206 of this title. The certificate of transfer or the certificate of transfer and continuance shall state:

(1) The name of the limited liability company and, if it has been changed, the name under which its certificate of formation was originally filed;

(2) The date of the filing of its original certificate of formation with the Secretary of State;

(3) The jurisdiction to which the limited liability company shall be transferred or in which it shall be domesticated;

(4) The future effective date or time (which shall be a date or time certain) of the transfer or domestication to the jurisdiction specified in subsection (b)(3) of this section if it is not to be effective upon the filing of the certificate of transfer or the certificate of transfer and continuance;

(5) That the transfer or domestication or continuance of the limited liability company has been approved in accordance with the provisions of this section;

(6) In the case of a certificate of transfer, (i) that the existence of the limited liability company as a limited liability company of the State of Delaware shall cease when the certificate of transfer becomes effective, and (ii) the agreement of the limited liability company that it may be served with process in the State of Delaware in any action, suit or proceeding for enforcement of any obligation of the limited liability company arising while it was a limited liability company of the State of Delaware, and that it irrevocably appoints the Secretary of State as its agent to accept service of process in any such action, suit or proceeding;

(7) The address to which a copy of the process referred to in subsection (b)(6) of this section shall be mailed to it by the Secretary of State. In the event of service hereunder upon the Secretary of State, the procedures set forth in § 18–911(c) of this title shall be applicable, except that the plaintiff in any such action, suit or proceeding shall furnish the Secretary of State with the address specified in this subsection and any other address that the plaintiff may elect to furnish, together with copies of such process as required by the Secretary of State, and the Secretary of State shall notify the limited liability company that has transferred or domesticated out of the State of Delaware at all such addresses furnished by the plaintiff in accordance with the procedures set forth in § 18–911(c) of this title; and

(8) In the case of a certificate of transfer and continuance, that the limited liability company will continue to exist as a limited liability company of the State of Delaware after the certificate of transfer and continuance becomes effective.

(c) Upon the filing in the Office of the Secretary of State of the certificate of transfer or upon the future effective date or time of the certificate of transfer and payment to the Secretary of State of all fees prescribed in this chapter, the Secretary of State shall certify that the limited liability company has filed all documents and paid all fees required by this chapter, and thereupon the limited liability company shall cease to exist as a limited liability company of the State of Delaware. Such certificate of the Secretary of State shall be *prima facie* evidence of the transfer or domestication by such limited liability company out of the State of Delaware.

(d) The transfer or domestication of a limited liability company out of the State of Delaware in accordance with this section and the resulting cessation of its existence as a limited liability company of the State of Delaware pursuant to a certificate of transfer shall not be deemed to affect any obligations or liabilities of the limited liability company incurred prior to such transfer or domestication or the personal liability of any person incurred prior to such transfer or domestication, nor shall it be deemed to affect the choice of law applicable to the limited liability company with respect to matters arising prior to such transfer or domestication. Unless otherwise agreed, the transfer or domestication of a limited liability company out of the State of Delaware in accordance with this section shall not require such limited liability company to wind up its affairs under § 18–803 of this title or pay its liabilities and distribute its assets under § 18–804 of this title.

(e) If a limited liability company files a certificate of transfer and continuance, after the time the certificate of transfer and continuance becomes effective, the limited liability company shall continue to exist as a limited liability company of the State of Delaware, and the laws of the State of Delaware, including the provisions of this chapter, shall apply to the limited liability company, to the same extent as prior to such time. So long as a limited liability company continues to exist as a limited liability company of the State of Delaware following the filing of a certificate of transfer and continuance, the continuing domestic limited liability company and the entity formed, incorporated, created or that otherwise came into being as a consequence of the transfer of the limited liability company to, or its domestication in, a foreign country or other foreign jurisdiction shall, for all purposes of the laws of the State of Delaware, constitute a single entity formed, incorporated, created or otherwise having come into being, as applicable, and existing under the laws of the State of Delaware and the laws of such foreign country or other foreign jurisdiction.

(f) In connection with a transfer or domestication of a domestic limited liability company to or in another jurisdiction pursuant to subsection (a) of this section, rights or securities of, or interests in, such limited liability company may be exchanged for or converted into cash, property, rights or securities of, or interests in, the business form in which the limited liability company will exist in such other jurisdiction as a consequence of the transfer or domestication or, in addition to or in lieu thereof, may be exchanged for or converted into cash, property, rights or securities of, or interests in, another business form or may be cancelled.

(g) When a limited liability company has transferred or domesticated out of the State of Delaware pursuant to this Section, the transferred or domesticated business form shall, for all purposes of the laws of the State of Delaware, be deemed to be the same entity as the limited liability company. When any transfer or domestication of a limited liability company out of the State of Delaware shall have become effective under this Section, for all purposes of the laws of the State of Delaware, all of the rights, privileges and powers of the limited liability company that has transferred or domesticated, and all property, real, personal and mixed, and all debts due to such limited liability company, as well as all other things and causes of action belonging to such limited liability company, shall remain vested in the transferred or domesticated business form and shall be the property of such transferred or domesticated business form, and the title to any real property vested by deed or otherwise in such limited liability company shall not revert or be in any way impaired by reason of this Chapter; but all rights of creditors and all liens upon any property of such limited liability company shall be preserved unimpaired, and all debts, liabilities and duties of the limited liability company that has transferred or domesticated shall remain attached to the transferred or domesticated business form, and may be enforced against it to the same extent as if said debts, liabilities and duties had originally been incurred or contracted by it in its capacity as the transferred or domesticated business form. The rights, privileges, powers and interests in property of the limited liability company that has transferred or domesticated, as well as the debts, liabilities and duties of such limited liability company, shall not be deemed, as a consequence of the transfer or domestication out of the State of Delaware, to have been transferred to the transferred or domesticated business form for any purpose of the laws of the State of Delaware.

§ 18–214. Conversion of Certain Entities to a Limited Liability Company

(a) As used in this section, the term "other entity" means a corporation, statutory trust, business trust or association, a real estate investment trust, a common-law trust or any other unincorporated business, including a partnership (whether general (including a limited liability partnership) or limited (including a limited liability limited partnership)) or a foreign limited liability company.

(b) Any other entity may convert to a domestic limited liability company by complying with subsection (h) of this section and filing in the office of the Secretary of State in accordance with § 18–206 of this title:

(1) A certificate of conversion to limited liability company that has been executed by 1 or more authorized persons in accordance with § 18–204 of this title; and

(2) A certificate of formation that complies with § 18–201 of this title and has been executed by 1 or more authorized persons in accordance with § 18–204 of this title.

(c) The certificate of conversion to limited liability company shall state:

(1) The date on which and jurisdiction where the other entity was first created, incorporated, formed or otherwise came into being and, if it has changed, its jurisdiction immediately prior to its conversion to a domestic limited liability company;

(2) The name of the other entity immediately prior to the filing of the certificate of conversion to limited liability company;

(3) The name of the limited liability company as set forth in its certificate of formation filed in accordance with subsection (b) of this section; and

(4) The future effective date or time (which shall be a date or time certain) of the conversion to a limited liability company if it is not to be effective upon the filing of the certificate of conversion to limited liability company and the certificate of formation.

(d) Upon the filing in the office of the Secretary of State of the certificate of conversion to limited liability company and the certificate of formation or upon the future effective date or time of the certificate of conversion to limited liability company and the certificate of formation, the other entity shall be converted into a domestic limited liability company and the limited liability company shall thereafter be subject to all of the provisions of this chapter, except that notwithstanding § 18–201 of this title, the existence of the limited liability company shall be deemed to have commenced on the date the other entity commenced its existence in the jurisdiction in which the other entity was first created, formed, incorporated or otherwise came into being.

(e) The conversion of any other entity into a domestic limited liability company shall not be deemed to affect any obligations or liabilities of the other entity incurred prior to its conversion to a domestic limited liability company or the personal liability of any person incurred prior to such conversion.

(f) When any conversion shall have become effective under this section, for all purposes of the laws of the State of Delaware, all of the rights, privileges and powers of the other entity that has converted, and all property, real, personal and mixed, and all debts due to such other entity, as well as all other things and causes of action belonging to such other entity, shall remain vested in the domestic limited liability company to which such other entity has converted and shall be the property of such domestic limited liability company, and the title to any real property vested by deed or otherwise in such other entity shall not revert or be in any way impaired by reason of this chapter; but all rights of creditors and all liens upon any property of such other entity shall be preserved unimpaired, and all debts, liabilities and duties of the other entity that has converted shall remain attached to the domestic limited liability company to which such other entity has converted, and may be enforced against it to the same extent as if said debts, liabilities and duties had originally been incurred or contracted by it in its capacity as a domestic limited liability company. The rights, privileges, powers and interests in property of the other entity, as well as the debts, liabilities and duties of the other entity, shall not be deemed, as a consequence of the conversion, to have been transferred to the domestic limited liability company to which such other entity has converted for any purpose of the laws of the State of Delaware.

(g) Unless otherwise agreed, for all purposes of the law of the State of Delaware, the converting other entity shall not be required to wind up its affairs or pay its liabilities and distribute its assets, the conversion shall not be deemed to constitute a dissolution of such other entity, and the conversion shall constitute a continuation of the existence of the converting other entity in the form of a domestic limited liability company. When an other entity has been converted to a limited liability company pursuant to this section, the limited liability company shall, for all purposes of the laws of the State of Delaware, be deemed to be the same entity as the converting other entity.

(h) Prior to filing a certificate of conversion to limited liability company with the office of the Secretary of State, the conversion shall be approved in the manner provided for by the document, instrument, agreement or other writing, as the case may be, governing the internal affairs of the other entity and the conduct of its business or by applicable law, as appropriate and a limited liability company agreement shall be approved by the same authorization required to approve the conversion.

(i) In connection with a conversion hereunder, rights or securities of, or interests in, the other entity which is to be converted to a domestic limited liability company may be exchanged for or converted into cash, property, rights or securities or, or interests in, such domestic limited liability company or, in addition to or in lieu thereof, may be exchanged for or converted into cash, property, rights or securities or,or interests in, another domestic limited liability company or other entity or may be cancelled.

(j) The provisions of this section shall not be construed to limit the accomplishment of a change in the law governing, or the domicile of, an other entity to the State of Delaware by any other means provided for in a limited liability company agreement or other agreement or as other-wise permitted by law, including by the amendment of a limited liability company agreement or other agreement.

§ 18–215. Series of Members, Managers or Limited Liability Company Interests

(a) A limited liability company agreement may establish or provide for the establishment of 1 or more designated series of members, managers or limited liability company interests having separate rights, powers or duties with respect to specified property or obligations of the limited liability company or profits and losses associated with specified property or obligations, and any such series may have a separate business purpose or investment objective.

(b) Notwithstanding anything to the contrary set forth in this chapter or under other applicable law, in the event that a limited liability company agreement establishes or provides for the establishment of 1 or more series, and if separate and distinct records are maintained for any such series and the assets associated with any such series are held in such separate and distinct records (directly or indirectly, including through a nominee or otherwise) and accounted for in such separate and distinct records separately from the other assets of the limited liability company, or any other series thereof, and if the limited liability company agreement so provides, and if notice of the limitation on liabilities of a series as referenced in this subsection is set forth in the certificate of formation of the limited liability company, then the debts, liabilities, and obligations and expenses incurred, contracted for or otherwise existing with respect to a particular series shall be enforceable against the assets of such series only, and not against the assets of the limited liability company generally or any other series thereof, and, unless otherwise provided in the limited liability company agreement, none of the debts, liabilities, obligations and expenses incurred, contracted for or otherwise existing with respect to the limited liability company generally or any other series thereof shall be enforceable against the assets of such series. Notice in a certificate of formation of the limitation on liabilities of a series as referenced in this subsection shall be sufficient for all purposes of this subsection whether or not the limited liability company has established any series when such notice is included in the certificate of formation, and there shall be no requirement that any specific series of the limited liability company be referenced in such notice. The fact that a certificate of formation that contains the foregoing notice of the limitation on liabilities of a series is on file in the office of the Secretary of State shall constitute notice of such limitation on liabilities of a series.

(c) Notwithstanding § 18–303(a) of this title, under a limited liability company agreement or under another agreement, a member or manager may agree to be obligated personally for any or all of the debts, obligations and liabilities of one or more series.

(d) A limited liability company agreement may provide for classes or groups of members or managers associated with a series having such relative rights, powers and duties as the limited liability company agreement may provide, and may make provision for the future creation in the manner provided in the limited liability company agreement of additional classes or groups of members or managers associated with the series having such relative rights, powers and duties as may from time to time be established, including rights, powers and duties senior to existing classes and groups of members or managers associated with the series. A limited liability company agreement may provide for the taking of an action, including the amendment of the limited liability company agreement, without the vote or approval of any member or manager or class or group of members or managers, including an action to create under the provisions of the limited liability company agreement a class or group of [a] series of limited liability company interests that was not previously outstanding. A limited liability company agreement may provide that any member or class or group of members associated with a series shall have no voting rights.

(e) A limited liability company agreement may grant to all or certain identified members or managers or a specified class or group of the members or managers associated with a series the right to vote separately or with all or any class or group of the members or managers associated with the series, on any matter. Voting by members or managers associated with a series may be on a per capita, number, financial interest, class, group or any other basis.

(f) Unless otherwise provided in a limited liability company agreement, the management of a series shall be vested in the members associated with such series in proportion to the then current percentage or other interest of members in the profits of the series owned by all of the members associated with such series, the decision of members owning more than 50 percent of the said percentage or other interest in the profits controlling; provided, however, that if a limited liability company agreement provides for the management of the series, in whole or in part, by a manager, the management of the series, to the extent so provided, shall be vested in the manager who shall be chosen in the manner provided in the limited liability company agreement. The manager of the series shall also hold the offices and have the responsibilities accorded to the manager as set forth in a limited liability company agreement. A series may have more than 1 manager. Subject to § 18–602 of this title, a manager shall cease to be a manager with respect to a series as provided in a limited liability company agreement. Except as otherwise provided in a limited liability company agreement, any event under this chapter or in a limited liability company agreement that causes a manager to cease to be a manager with respect to a series shall not, in itself, cause such manager to cease to be a manager of the limited liability company or with respect to any other series thereof.

(g) Notwithstanding § 18–606 of this title, but subject to subsections (h) and (k) of this section, and unless otherwise provided in a limited liability company agreement, at the time a member associated with a series that has been established in accordance with subsection (b) of this section becomes entitled to receive a distribution with respect to such series, the member has the status of, and is entitled to all remedies available to, a creditor of the series, with respect to the distribution. A limited liability company agreement may provide for the establishment of a record date with respect to allocations and distributions with respect to a series.

(h) Notwithstanding § 18–607(a) of this title, a limited liability company may make a distribution with respect to a series that has been established in accordance with subsection (b) of this section. A limited liability company shall not make a distribution with respect to a series that has been established in accordance with subsection (b) of this section to a member to the extent that at the time of the distribution, after giving effect to the distribution, all liabilities of such series, other than liabilities to members on account of their limited liability company interests with respect to such series and liabilities for which the recourse of creditors is limited to specified property of such series, exceed the fair value of the assets associated with such series, except that the fair value of property of the series that is subject to a liability for which the recourse of creditors is limited shall be included in the assets associated with such series only to the extent that the fair value of that property exceeds that liability. For purposes of the immediate preceding sentence, the term "distribution" shall not include amounts constituting reasonable compensation for present or past services or reasonable payments made in the ordinary course of business pursuant to a bona fide retirement plan or other benefits program. A member who receives a distribution in violation of this subsection, and who knew at the time of the distribution that the distribution violated this subsection, shall be liable to a series for the amount of the distribution. A member who receives a distribution in violation of this subsection, and who did not know at the time of the distribution that the distribution violated this subsection, shall not be liable for the amount of the distribution. Subject to § 18–607(c) of this title, which shall apply to any distribution made with respect to a series under this subsection, this subsection shall not affect any obligation or liability of a member under an agreement or other applicable law for the amount of a distribution.

(i) Unless otherwise provided in the limited liability company agreement, a member shall cease to be associated with a series and to have the power to exercise any rights or powers of a member with respect to such series upon the assignment of all of the member's limited liability company interest with respect to such series. Except as otherwise provided in a limited liability company agreement, any event under this chapter or a limited liability company agreement that causes a member to cease to be associated with a series shall not, in itself, cause such member to cease to be associated with any other series or terminate the continued membership of a member in the limited liability company or cause the termination of the series, regardless of whether such member was the last remaining member associated with such series.

(j) Subject to § 18–801 of this title, except to the extent otherwise provided in the limited liability company agreement, a series may be terminated and its affairs wound up without causing the dissolution of the limited liability company. The termination of a series established in accordance with subsection (b) of this section shall not affect the limitation on liabilities of such series provided by subsection (b) of this section. A series is terminated and its affairs shall be wound up upon the dissolution of the limited liability company under § 18–801 of this title or otherwise upon the first to occur of the following:

(1) At the time specified in the limited liability company agreement;

(2) Upon the happening of events specified in the limited liability company agreement;

(3) Unless otherwise provided in the limited liability company agreement, upon the affirmative vote or written consent of the members of the limited liability company associated with such series or, if there is more than one class or group of members associated with such series, then by each class or group of members associated with such series, in either case, by members associated with such series who own more than two-thirds of the then-current percentage or other interest in the profits of the series of the limited liability company owned by all of the members associated with such series or by the members in each class or group of such series, as appropriate; or

(4) The termination of such series under subsection (*l*) of this section.

(k) Notwithstanding § 18–803(a) of this title, unless otherwise provided in the limited liability company agreement, a manager associated with a series who has not wrongfully terminated the series or, if none, the members associated with the series or a person approved by the members associated with the series or, if there is more than 1 class or group of members associated with the series, then by each class or group of members associated with the series, in either case, by members who own more than 50 percent of the then current percentage or other interest in the profits of the series owned by all of the members associated with the series or by the members in each class or group associated with the series, as appropriate, may wind up the affairs of the series; but, if the series has been established in accordance with subsection (b) of this section, the Court of Chancery, upon cause shown, may wind up the affairs of the series upon application of any member associated with the series, the member's personal representative or assignee, and in connection therewith, may appoint a liquidating trustee. The persons winding up the affairs of a series may, in the name of the limited liability company and for and on behalf of the limited liability company and such series, take all actions with respect to the series as are permitted under § 18–803(b) of this title, which section shall apply to the winding up and distribution of assets of a series. The persons winding up the affairs of a series shall provide for the claims and obligations of the series as provided in § 18–804(b) of this title and distribute the assets of the series as provided in § 18–804(a) of this title. Actions taken in accordance with this subsection shall not affect the liability of members and shall not impose liability on a liquidating trustee.

(*l*) On application by or for a member or manager associated with a series established in accordance with subsection (b) of this section, the Court of Chancery may decree termination of such series whenever it is not reasonably practicable to carry on the business of the series in conformity with a limited liability company agreement.

(m) If a foreign limited liability company that is registering to do business in the State of Delaware in accordance with § 18–902 of this title is governed by a limited liability company agreement that establishes or provides for the establishment of designated series of members, managers or limited liability company interests having separate rights, powers or duties with respect to specified property or obligations of the foreign limited liability company or profits and losses associated with specified property or obligations, that fact shall be so stated on the application for registration as a foreign limited liability company. In addition, the foreign limited liability company shall state on such application whether the debts, liabilities and obligations incurred, contracted for or otherwise existing with respect to a particular series, if any, shall be enforceable against the assets of such series only, and not against the assets of the foreign limited liability company generally or any other series thereof, and, unless otherwise provided in the limited liability company agreement, none of the debts, liabilities, obligations and expenses incurred, contracted for or otherwise existing with respect to the foreign limited liability company generally or any other series thereof shall be enforceable against the assets of such series.

§ 18–216. Approval of Conversion of a Limited Liability Company

(a) Upon compliance with this section, a domestic limited liability company may convert to a corporation, statutory trust, business trust or association, a real estate investment trust, a common-law trust or any other unincorporated business, including a partnership (whether general (including a limited liability partnership) or limited (including a limited liability limited partnership)) or a foreign limited liability company.

(b) If the limited liability company agreement specifies the manner of authorizing a conversion of the limited liability company, the conversion shall be authorized as specified in the limited liability company agreement. If the limited liability company agreement does not specify the manner of authorizing a conversion of the limited liability company and does not prohibit a conversion of the limited liability company, the conversion shall be authorized in the same manner as is specified in the limited liability company agreement for authorizing a merger or consolidation that involves the limited liability company as a constituent party to the merger or consolidation. If the limited liability company agreement does not specify the manner of authorizing a conversion of the limited liability company or a merger or consolidation that involves the limited liability company as a constituent party and does not prohibit a conversion of the limited liability company, the conversion shall be authorized by the approval by the members or, if there is more than 1 class or group of members, then by each class or group of members, in either case, by members who own more than 50 percent of the then current percentage or other interest in the profits of the domestic limited liability company owned by all of the members or by the members in each class or group, as appropriate.

(c) Unless otherwise agreed, the conversion of a domestic limited liability company to another business form pursuant to this section shall not require such limited liability company to wind up its affairs under § 18–803 of this title or pay its liabilities and distribute its assets under § 18–804 of this title.

(d) In connection with a conversion of a domestic limited liability company to another business form pursuant to this section, rights or securities of or interests in the domestic limited liability company which is to be converted may be exchanged for or converted into cash, property, rights or securities of or interests in the business form into which the domestic limited liability company is being converted or, in addition to or in lieu thereof, may be exchanged for or converted into cash, property, rights or securities of or interests in another business form or may be cancelled.

(e) If a limited liability company shall convert in accordance with this section to another business form organized, formed or created under the laws of a jurisdiction other than the State of Delaware, a certificate of conversion to non-Delaware entity executed in accordance with § 18–204 of this title, shall be filed in the office of the Secretary of State in accordance with § 18–206 of this title. The certificate of conversion to non-Delaware entity shall state:

(1) The name of the limited liability company and, if it has been changed, the name under which its certificate of formation was originally filed;

(2) The date of filing of its original certificate of formation with the Secretary of State;

(3) The jurisdiction in which the business form, to which the limited liability company shall be converted, is organized, formed or created;

(4) The future effective date or time (which shall be a date or time certain) of the conversion if it is not to be effective upon the filing of the certificate of conversion to non-Delaware entity;

(5) That the conversion has been approved in accordance with this section;

(6) The agreement of the limited liability company that it may be served with process in the State of Delaware in any action, suit or proceeding for enforcement of any obligation of the limited liability company arising while it was a limited liability company of the State of Delaware, and that it irrevocably appoints the Secretary of State as its agent to accept service of process in any such action, suit or proceeding;

(7) The address to which a copy of the process referred to in paragraph (6) of this subsection shall be mailed to it by the Secretary of State. In the event of service hereunder upon the Secretary of State, the procedures set forth in § 18–911(c) of this title shall be applicable, except that the plaintiff in any such action, suit or proceeding shall furnish the Secretary of State with the address specified in this subdivision and any other address that the plaintiff may elect to furnish, together with copies of such process as required by the Secretary of State, and the Secretary of State shall notify the limited liability company that has converted out of the State of Delaware at all such addresses furnished by the plaintiff in accordance with the procedures set forth in § 18–911(c) of this title.

(f) Upon the filing in the office of the Secretary of State of the certificate of conversion to non-Delaware entity or upon the future effective date or time of the certificate of conversion to [a] non-Delaware entity and payment to the Secretary of State of all fees prescribed in this chapter, the Secretary of State shall certify that the limited liability company has filed all documents and paid all fees required by this chapter, and thereupon the limited liability company shall cease to exist as a limited liability company of the State of Delaware. Such certificate of the Secretary of State shall be prima facie evidence of the conversion by such limited liability company out of the State of Delaware.

(g) The conversion of a limited liability company out of the State of Delaware in accordance with this section and the resulting cessation of its existence as a limited liability company of the State of Delaware pursuant to a certificate of conversion to non-Delaware entity shall not be deemed to affect any obligations or liabilities of the limited liability company incurred prior to such conversion or the personal liability of any person incurred prior to such conversion, nor shall it be deemed to affect the choice of law applicable to the limited liability company with respect to matters arising prior to such conversion.

(h) When a limited liability company has been converted to another business form pursuant to this Section the other business form shall, for all purposes of the laws of the State of Delaware, be deemed to be the same entity as the limited liability company. When any conversion shall have become effective under this Section for all purposes of the laws of the State of Delaware, all of the rights, privileges and powers of the limited liability company that has converted, and all property, real, personal and mixed, and all debts due to such limited liability company, as well as all other things and causes of action belonging to such limited liability company, shall remain vested in the other business form to which such limited liability company has converted and shall be the property of such other business form, and the title to any real property vested deed or otherwise in such limited liability company shall not revert or be in any way impaired by reason of this Chapter; but all rights of creditors and all liens upon any property of such limited liability company shall be preserved unimpaired, and all debts, liabilities and duties of the limited liability company that has converted shall remain attached to the other business form to which such limited liability company has converted, and may be enforced against it to the same extent as if said debts, liabilities and duties had originally been incurred or contracted by it in its capacity as such other business form. The rights, privileges, powers and interest in property of the limited liability company that has converted, as well as the debts, liabilities and duties of such limited liability company, shall not be deemed, as a consequence of the conversion, to have been transferred to the other business form to which such limited liability company has converted for any purpose of the laws of the State of Delaware.

SUBCHAPTER III. MEMBERS

§ 18–301. Admission of Members

(a) In connection with the formation of a limited liability company, a person is admitted as a member of the limited liability company upon the later to occur of:

(1) The formation of the limited liability company; or

(2) The time provided in and upon compliance with the limited liability company agreement or, if the limited liability company agreement does not so provide, when the person's admission is reflected in the records of the limited liability company.

(b) After the formation of a limited liability company, a person is admitted as a member of the limited liability company:

(1) In the case of a person who is not an assignee of a limited liability company interest, including a person acquiring a limited liability company interest directly from the limited liability company and a person to be admitted as a member of the limited liability company without acquiring a limited liability company interest in the limited liability company, at the time provided in and upon compliance with the limited liability company agreement or, if the limited liability company agreement does not so provide, upon the consent of all members and when the person's admission is reflected in the records of the limited liability company;

(2) In the case of an assignee of a limited liability company interest, as provided in § 18–704(a) of this title and at the time provided in and upon compliance with the limited liability company agreement or, if the limited liability company agreement does not so provide, when any such person's permitted admission is reflected in the records of the limited liability company; or

(3) In the case of a person being admitted as a member of a surviving or resulting limited liability company pursuant to a merger or consolidation approved in accordance with § 18–209(b) of this title, as provided in the limited liability company agreement of the surviving or resulting limited liability company or in the agreement of merger or consolidation, and in the event of any inconsistency, the terms of the agreement of merger or consolidation shall control; and in the case of a person being admitted as a member of a limited liability company pursuant to a merger or consolidation in which such limited liability company is not the surviving or resulting limited liability company in the merger or consolidation, as provided in the limited liability company agreement of such limited liability company.

(c) In connection with the domestication of a non-United States entity (as defined in § 18–212 of this title) as a limited liability company in the State of Delaware in accordance with § 18–212 of this title or the conversion of an other entity (as defined in § 18–214 of this title) to a domestic limited liability company in accordance with § 18–214 of this title, a person is admitted as a member of the limited liability company as provided in the limited liability company agreement.

(d) A person may be admitted to a limited liability company as a member of the limited liability company and may receive a limited liability company interest in the limited liability company without making a contribution or being obligated to make a contribution to the limited liability company. Unless otherwise provided in a limited liability company agreement, a person may be admitted to a limited liability company as a member of the limited liability company without acquiring a limited liability company interest in the limited liability company. Unless otherwise provided in a limited liability company agreement, a person may be admitted as the sole member of a limited liability company without making a contribution or being obligated to make a contribution to the limited liability company or without acquiring a limited liability company interest in the limited liability company.

(e) Unless otherwise provided in a limited liability company agreement or another agreement, a member shall have no preemptive right to subscribe to any additional issue of limited liability company interests or another interest in a limited liability company.

§ 18–302. Classes and Voting

(a) A limited liability company agreement may provide for classes or groups of members having such relative rights, powers and duties as the limited liability company agreement may provide, and may make provision for the future creation in the manner provided in the limited liability company agreement of additional classes or groups of members having such relative rights, powers and duties as may from time to time be established, including rights, powers and duties senior to existing classes and groups of members. A limited liability company agreement may provide for the taking of an action, including the amendment of the limited liability company agreement, without the vote or approval of any member or class or group of members, including an action to create under the provisions of the limited liability company agreement a class or group of limited liability company interests that was not previously outstanding. A limited liability company agreement may provide that any member or class or group of members shall have no voting rights.

(b) A limited liability company agreement may grant to all or certain identified members or a specified class or group of the members the right to vote separately or with all or any class or group of the members or managers, on any matter. Voting by members may be on a per capita, number, financial interest, class, group or any other basis.

(c) A limited liability company agreement may set forth provisions relating to notice of the time, place or purpose of any meeting at which any matter is to be voted on by any members, waiver of any such notice, action by consent without a meeting, the establishment of a record date, quorum requirements, voting in person or by proxy, or any other matter with respect to the exercise of any such right to vote.

(d) Unless otherwise provided in a limited liability company agreement, on any matter that is to be voted on, consented to or approved by members, the members may take such action without a meeting, without prior notice and without a vote, if a consent or consents in writing, setting forth the action so taken, shall be signed by the members having not not less than the minimum number of votes that would be necessary to authorize or take such action at a meeting at which all members entitled to vote thereon were present and voted. Unless otherwise provided in a limited liability company agreement, on any matter that is to be voted on by members, the members may vote in person or by proxy, and such proxy may be granted in writing, by means of electronic transmission or as otherwise permitted by applicable law. Unless otherwise provided in a limited liability company agreement, a consent transmitted by electronic transmission by a member or by a person or persons authorized to act for a member shall be deemed to be written and signed for purposes of this subsection (d). For purposes of this subsection (d), the term "electronic transmission" means any form of communication not directly involving the physical transmission of paper that creates a record that may be retained, retrieved and reviewed by a recipient thereof and that may be directly reproduced in paper form by such a recipient through an automated process.

(e) If a limited liability company agreement provides for the manner in which it may be amended, including by requiring the approval of a person who is not a party to the limited liability company agreement or the satisfaction of conditions, it may be amended only in that manner or as otherwise permitted by law (provided that the approval of any person may be waived by such person and that any such conditions may be waived by all persons for whose benefit such conditions were intended).

§ 18–303. Liability to Third Parties

(a) Except as otherwise provided by this chapter, the debts, obligations and liabilities of a limited liability company, whether arising in contract, tort or otherwise, shall be solely the debts, obligations and liabilities of the limited liability company, and no member or manager of a limited liability company shall be obligated personally for any such debt, obligation or liability of the limited liability company solely by reason of being a member or acting as a manager of the limited liability company.

(b) Notwithstanding the provisions of Section 18–303(a) of this chapter, under a limited liability company agreement or under another agreement, a member or manager may agree to be obligated personally for any or all of the debts, obligations and liabilities of the limited liability company.

§ 18–304. Events of Bankruptcy

A person ceases to be a member of a limited liability company upon the happening of any of the following events:

(1) Unless otherwise provided in a limited liability company agreement, or with the written consent of all members, a member:

a.   Makes an assignment for the benefit of creditors;

b.   Files a voluntary petition in bankruptcy;

c.   Is adjudged a bankrupt or insolvent, or has entered against him an order for relief, in any bankruptcy or insolvency proceeding;

d.   Files a petition or answer seeking for himself any reorganization, arrangement, composition, readjustment, liquidation, dissolution or similar relief under any statute, law or regulation;

e.   Files an answer or other pleading admitting or failing to contest the material allegations of a petition filed against him in any proceeding of this nature;

f.   Seeks, consents to or acquiesces in the appointment of a trustee, receiver or liquidator of the member or of all or any substantial part of his properties; or

(2) Unless otherwise provided in a limited liability company agreement, or with the written consent of all members, 120 days after the commencement of any proceeding against the member seeking reorganization, arrangement, composition, readjustment, liquidation, dissolution or similar relief under any statute, law or regulation, if the proceeding has not been dismissed, or if within 90 days after the appointment without his consent or acquiescence of a trustee, receiver or liquidator of the member or of all or any substantial part of his properties, the appointment is not vacated or stayed, or within 90 days after the expiration of any such stay, the appointment is not vacated.

§ 18–305. Access to and Confidentiality of Information; Records

(a) Each member of a limited liability company has the right, subject to such reasonable standards (including standards governing what information and documents are to be furnished at what time and location and at whose expense) as may be set forth in a limited liability company agreement or otherwise established by the manager or, if there is no manager, then by the members, to obtain from the limited liability company from time to time upon reasonable demand for any purpose reasonably related to the member's interest as a member of the limited liability company:

(1) True and full information regarding the status of the business and financial condition of the limited liability company;

(2) Promptly after becoming available, a copy of the limited liability company's federal, state and local income tax returns for each year;

(3) A current list of the name and last known business, residence or mailing address of each member and manager;

(4) A copy of any written limited liability company agreement and certificate of formation and all amendments thereto, together with executed copies of any written powers of attorney pursuant to which the limited liability company agreement and any certificate and all amendments thereto have been executed;

(5) True and full information regarding the amount of cash and a description and statement of the agreed value of any other property or services contributed by each member and which each member has agreed to contribute in the future, and the date on which each became a member; and

(6) Other information regarding the affairs of the limited liability company as is just and reasonable.

(b) Each manager shall have the right to examine all of the information described in subsection (a) of this section for a purpose reasonably related to his position as a manager.

(c) The manager of a limited liability company shall have the right to keep confidential from the members, for such period of time as the manager deems reasonable, any information which the manager reasonably believes to be in the nature of trade secrets or other information the disclosure of which the manager in good faith believes is not in the best interest of the limited liability company or could damage the limited liability company or its business or which the limited liability company is required by law or by agreement with a third party to keep confidential.

(d) A limited liability company may maintain its records in other than a written form if such form is capable of conversion into written form within a reasonable time.

(e) Any demand by a member under this section shall be in writing and shall state the purpose of such demand.

(f) Any action to enforce any right arising under this section shall be brought in the Court of Chancery. If the limited liability company refuses to permit a member to obtain or a manager to examine the information described in subsection (a)(3) of this section or does not reply to the demand that has been made within 5 business days after the demand has been made, the demanding member or manager may apply to the Court of Chancery for an order to compel such disclosure. The Court of Chancery is hereby vested with exclusive jurisdiction to determine whether or not the person seeking such information is entitled to the information sought. The Court of Chancery may summarily order the limited liability company to permit the demanding member to obtain or manager to examine the information described in subsection (a)(3) of this section and to make copies or abstracts therefrom; or the Court of Chancery may summarily order the limited liability company to furnish to the demanding member or manager the information described in subsection (a)(3) of this section on the condition that the demanding member or manager first pay to the limited liability company the reasonable cost of obtaining and furnishing such information and on such other conditions as the Court of Chancery deems appropriate. When a demanding member seeks to obtain or a manager seeks to examine the information described in subsection (a)(3) of this section, the demanding member or manager shall first establish (1) that the demanding member or manager has complied with the provisions of this section respecting the form and manner of making demand for obtaining or examining of such information, and (2) that the information the demanding member or manager seeks is reasonably related to the member's interest as a member or the manager's position as a manager, as the case may be. The Court of Chancery may, in its discretion, prescribe any limitations or conditions with reference to the obtaining or examining of information, or award such other or further relief as the Court of Chancery may deem just and proper. The Court of Chancery may order books, documents and records, pertinent extracts therefrom, or duly authenticated copies thereof, to be brought within the State of Delaware and kept in the State of Delaware upon such terms and conditions as the order may prescribe.

(g) The rights of a member or manager to obtain information as provided in this section may be restricted in an original limited liability company agreement or in any subsequent amendment approved or adopted by all of the members and in compliance with any applicable requirements of the limited liability company agreement. The provisions of this subsection shall not be construed to limit the ability to impose restrictions on the rights of a member or manager to obtain information by any other means permitted under this section.

§ 18–306. Remedies for Breach of Limited Liability Company Agreement by Member

A limited liability company agreement may provide that:

(1) A member who fails to perform in accordance with, or to comply with the terms and conditions of, the limited liability company agreement shall be subject to specified penalties or specified consequences; and

(2) At the time or upon the happening of events specified in the limited liability company agreement, a member shall be subject to specified penalties or specified consequences.

Such specified penalties or specified consequences may include and take the form of any penalty or consequence set forth in § 18–502(c) of this chapter.

SUBCHAPTER IV. MANAGERS

§ 18–401. Admission of Managers

A person may be named or designated as a manager of the limited liability company as provided in § 18–101(10) of this title.

§ 18–402. Management of Limited Liability Company

Unless otherwise provided in a limited liability company agreement, the management of a limited liability company shall be vested in its members in proportion to the then current percentage or other interest of members in the profits of the limited liability company owned by all of the members, the decision of members owning more than 50 percent of the said percentage or other interest in the profits controlling; provided however, that if a limited liability company agreement provides for the management, in whole or in part, of a limited liability company by a manager, the management of the limited liability company, to the extent so provided, shall be vested in the manager who shall be chosen in the manner provided in the limited liability company agreement. The manager shall also hold the offices and have the responsibilities accorded to the manager by or in the manner provided in a limited liability company agreement. Subject to § 18–602 of this title, a manager shall cease to be a manager as provided in a limited liability company agreement. A limited liability company may have more than 1 manager. Unless otherwise provided in a limited liability company agreement, each member and manager has the authority to bind the limited liability company.

§ 18–403. Contributions by a Manager

A manager of a limited liability company may make contributions to the limited liability company and share in the profits and losses of, and in distributions from, the limited liability company as a member. A person who is both a manager and a member has the rights and powers, and is subject to the restrictions and liabilities, of a manager and, except as provided in a limited liability company agreement, also has the rights and powers, and is subject to the restrictions and liabilities, of a member to the extent of his participation in the limited liability company as a member.

§ 18–404. Classes and Voting

(a) A limited liability company agreement may provide for classes or groups of managers having such relative rights, powers and duties as the limited liability company agreement may provide, and may make provision for the future creation in the manner provided in the limited liability company agreement of additional classes or groups of managers having such relative rights, powers and duties as may from time to time be established, including rights, powers and duties senior to existing classes and groups of managers. A limited liability company agreement may provide for the taking of an action, including the amendment of the limited liability company agreement, without the vote or approval of any manager or class or group of managers, including an action to create under the provisions of the limited liability company agreement a class or group of limited liability company interests that was not previously outstanding.

(b) A limited liability company agreement may grant to all or certain identified managers or a specified class or group of the managers the right to vote, separately or with all or any class or group of managers or members, on any matter. Voting by managers may be on a per capita, number, financial interest, class, group or any other basis.

(c) A limited liability company agreement may set forth provisions relating to notice of the time, place or purpose of any meeting at which any matter is to be voted on by any manager or class or group of managers, waiver of any such notice, action by consent without a meeting, the establishment of a record date, quorum requirements, voting in person or by proxy, or any other matter with respect to the exercise of any such right to vote.

(d) Unless otherwise provided in a limited liability company agreement, on any matter that is to be voted on, consented to or approved by managers, the managers may take such action without a meeting, without prior notice and without a vote, if a consent or consents in writing, setting forth the action so taken, shall be signed by the managers having not less than the minimum number of votes that would be necessary to authorize or take such action at a meeting at which all managers entitled to vote thereon were present and voted. Unless otherwise provided in a limited liability company agreement, on any matter that is to be voted on by managers, the managers may vote in person or by proxy, and such proxy may be granted in writing, by means of electronic transmission or as otherwise permitted by applicable law. Unless otherwise provided in a limited liability company agreement, a consent transmitted by electronic transmission by a manager or by a person or persons authorized to act for a manager shall be deemed to be written and signed for purposes of this subsection (d). For purposes of this subsection (d), the term "electronic transmission" means any form of communication not directly involving the physical transmission of paper that creates a record that may be retained, retrieved and reviewed by a recipient thereof and that may be directly reproduced in paper form by such a recipient through an automated process.

§ 18–405. Remedies for Breach of Limited Liability Company Agreement by Manager

A limited liability company agreement may provide that:

(1) A manager who fails to perform in accordance with, or to comply with the terms and conditions of, the limited liability company agreement shall be subject to specified penalties or specified consequences; and

(2) At the time or upon the happening of events specified in the limited liability company agreement, a manager shall be subject to specified penalties or specified consequences.

§ 18–406. Reliance on Reports and Information by Member or Manager

A member, manager or liquidating trustee of a limited liability company shall be fully protected in relying in good faith upon the records of the limited liability company and upon information, opinions,

reports or statements presented by another manager, member or liquidating trustee, an officer or employee of the limited liability company, or
committees of the limited liability company, members or managers, or by
any other person as to matters the member, manager or liquidating
trustees reasonably believes are within such other person's professional
or expert competence, including information, opinions, reports or statements as to the value and amount of the assets, liabilities, profits or
losses of the limited liability company, or the value and amount of assets
or reserves or contracts, agreements or other undertakings that would be
sufficient to pay claims and obligations of the limited liability company
or to make reasonable provision to pay such claims and obligations, or
any other facts pertinent to the existence and amount of assets from
which distributions to members or creditors might properly be paid.

§ 18–407. Delegation of Rights and Powers to Manage

Unless otherwise provided in the limited liability company agreement, a member or manager of limited liability company has the power
and authority to delegate to one or more other persons the member's or
manager's, as the case may be, rights and powers to manage and control
the business and affairs of the limited liability company, including to
delegate to agents, officers and employees of a member or manager [of]
the limited liability company, and to delegate by a management agreement or another agreement with, or otherwise to, other persons. Unless
otherwise provided in the limited liability company agreement, such
delegation by a member or manager of a limited liability company shall
not cause the member or manager to cease to be a member or manager,
as the case may be, of the limited liability company or cause the person
to whom any such rights and powers have been delegated to be a
member or manager, as the case may be, of the limited liability company.

SUBCHAPTER V. FINANCE

§ 18–501. Form of Contribution

The contribution of a member to a limited liability company may be
in cash, property or services rendered, or a promissory note or other
obligation to contribute cash or property or to perform services.

§ 18–502. Liability for Contribution

(a) Except as provided in a limited liability company agreement, a
member is obligated to a limited liability company to perform any
promise to contribute cash or property or to perform services, even if he
is unable to perform because of death, disability or any other reason. If
a member does not make the required contribution of property or
services, he is obligated at the option of the limited liability company to
contribute cash equal to that portion of the agreed value (as stated in the

records of the limited liability company) of the contribution that has not been made. The foregoing option shall be in addition to, and not in lieu of, any other rights, including the right to specific performance, that the limited liability company may have against such member under the limited liability company agreement or applicable law.

(b) Unless otherwise provided in a limited liability company agreement, the obligation of a member to make a contribution or return money or other property paid or distributed in violation of this chapter may be compromised only by consent of all the members. Notwithstanding the compromise, a creditor of a limited liability company who extends credit, after the entering into of a limited liability company agreement or an amendment thereto which, in either case, reflects the obligation, and before the amendment thereof to reflect the compromise, may enforce the original obligation to the extent that, in extending credit, the creditor reasonably relied on the obligation of a member to make a contribution or return. A conditional obligation of a member to make a contribution or return money or other property to a limited liability company may not be enforced unless the conditions of the obligation have been satisfied or waived as to or by such member. Conditional obligations include contributions payable upon a discretionary call of a limited liability company prior to the time the call occurs.

(c) A limited liability company agreement may provide that the interest of any member who fails to make any contribution that he is obligated to make shall be subject to specified penalties for, or specified consequences of, such failure. Such penalty or consequence may take the form of reducing or eliminating the defaulting member's proportionate interest in a limited liability company, subordinating his limited liability company interest to that of nondefaulting members, a forced sale of his limited liability company interest, forfeiture of his limited liability company interest, the lending by other members of the amount necessary to meet his commitment, a fixing of the value of his limited liability company interest by appraisal or by formula and redemption or sale of his limited liability company interest at such value, or other penalty or consequence.

§ 18–503. Allocation of Profits and Losses

The profits and losses of a limited liability company shall be allocated among the members, and among classes or groups of members, in the manner provided in a limited liability company agreement. If the limited liability company agreement does not so provide, profits and losses shall be allocated on the basis of the agreed value (as stated in the records of the limited liability company) of the contributions made by each member to the extent they have been received by the limited liability company and have not been returned.

§ 18–504. Allocation of Distributions

Distributions of cash or other assets of a limited liability company shall be allocated among the members, and among classes or groups of members, in the manner provided in a limited liability company agreement. If the limited liability company agreement does not so provide, distributions shall be made on the basis of the agreed value (as stated in the records of the limited liability company) of the contributions made by each member to the extent they have been received by the limited liability company and have not been returned.

SUBCHAPTER VI. DISTRIBUTIONS AND RESIGNATION

§ 18–601. Interim Distributions

Except as provided in this subchapter, to the extent and at the times or upon the happening of the events specified in a limited liability company agreement, a member is entitled to receive from a limited liability company distributions before his resignation from the limited liability company and before the dissolution and winding up thereof.

§ 18–602. Resignation of Manager

A manager may resign as a manager of a limited liability company at the time or upon the happening of events specified in a limited liability company agreement and in accordance with the limited liability company agreement. A limited liability company agreement may provide that a manager shall not have the right to resign as a manager of a limited liability company. Notwithstanding that a limited liability company agreement provides that a manager does not have the right to resign as a manager of a limited liability company, a manager may resign as a manager of a limited liability company at any time by giving written notice to the members and other managers. If the resignation of a manager violates a limited liability company agreement, in addition to any remedies otherwise available under applicable law, a limited liability company may recover from the resigning manager damages for breach of the limited liability company agreement and offset the damages against the amount otherwise distributable to the resigning manager.

§ 18–603. Resignation of Member

A member may resign from a limited liability company only at the time or upon the happening of events specified in a limited liability company agreement and in accordance with the limited liability company agreement. Notwithstanding anything to the contrary under applicable law, unless a limited liability company agreement provides otherwise, a member may not resign from a limited liability company prior to the dissolution and winding up of the limited liability company. Notwithstanding anything to the contrary under applicable law, a limited liability company agreement may provide that a limited liability company interest may not be assigned prior to the dissolution and winding up of the limited liability company. . . .

§ 18–604. Distribution Upon Resignation

Except as provided in this subchapter, upon resignation any resigning member is entitled to receive any distribution to which such member is entitled under a limited liability company agreement and, if not otherwise provided in a limited liability company agreement, such member is entitled to receive, within a reasonable time after resignation, the fair value of such member's limited liability company interest as of the date of resignation based upon such member's right to share in distributions from the limited liability company.

§ 18–605. Distribution in Kind

Except as provided in a limited liability company agreement, a member, regardless of the nature of the member's contribution, has no right to demand and receive any distribution from a limited liability company in any form other than cash. Except as provided in a limited liability company agreement, a member may not be compelled to accept a distribution of any asset in kind from a limited liability company to the extent that the percentage of the asset distributed exceeds a percentage of that asset which is equal to the percentage in which the member shares in distributions from the limited liability company. Except as provided in the limited liability company agreement, a member may be compelled to accept a distribution of any asset in kind from a limited liability company to the extent that the percentage of the asset distributed to him is equal to a percentage of that asset which is equal to the percentage in which the member shares in distributions from the limited liability company.

§ 18–606. Right to Distribution

Subject to §§ 18–607 and 18–804 of this title, and unless otherwise provided in a limited liability company agreement, at the time a member becomes entitled to receive a distribution, he has the status of, and is entitled to all remedies available to, a creditor of a limited liability company with respect to the distribution. A limited liability company agreement may provide for the establishment of a record date with respect to allocations and distributions by a limited liability company.

§ 18–607. Limitations on Distribution

(a) A limited liability company shall not make a distribution to a member to the extent that at the time of the distribution, after giving effect to the distribution, all liabilities of the limited liability company, other than liabilities to members on account of their limited liability company interests and liabilities for which the recourse of creditors is limited to specified property of the limited liability company, exceed the fair value of the assets of the limited liability company, except that the fair value of property that is subject to a liability for which the recourse of creditors is limited shall be included in the assets of the limited liability company only to the extent that the fair value of that property exceeds that liability. For purposes of this subsection (a), the term "distribution" shall not include amounts constituting reasonable compensation for present or past services or reasonable payments made in the ordinary course of business pursuant to a bona fide retirement plan or other benefits program.

(b) A member who receives a distribution in violation of subsection (a) of this section, and who knew at the time of the distribution that the distribution violated subsection (a) of this section, shall be liable to a limited liability company for the amount of the distribution. A member who receives a distribution in violation of subsection (a) of this section, and who did not know at the time of the distribution that the distribution violated subsection (a) of this section, shall not be liable for the amount of the distribution. Subject to subsection (c) of this section, this subsection shall not affect any obligation or liability of a member under agreement or other applicable law for the amount of a distribution.

(c) Unless otherwise agreed, a member who receives a distribution from a limited liability company shall have no liability under this chapter or other applicable law for the amount of the distribution after the expiration of 3 years from the date of the distribution unless an action to recover the distribution from such member is commenced prior to the expiration of the said 3–year period and an adjudication of liability against such member is made in the said action.

SUBCHAPTER VII. ASSIGNMENT OF LIMITED LIABILITY COMPANY INTERESTS

§ 18–701. Nature of Limited Liability Company Interest

A limited liability company interest is personal property. A member has no interest in specific limited liability company property.

§ 18–702. Assignment of Limited Liability Company Interest

(a) A limited liability company interest is assignable in whole or in part except as provided in a limited liability company agreement. The assignee of a member's limited liability company interest shall have no right to participate in the management of the business and affairs of a limited liability company except as provided in a limited liability company agreement and upon:

(1) The approval of all of the members of the limited liability company other than the member assigning his limited liability company interest; or

(2) Compliance with any procedure provided for in the limited liability company agreement.

(b) Unless otherwise provided in a limited liability company agreement:

(1) An assignment of a limited liability company interest does not entitle the assignee to become or to exercise any rights or powers of a member;

(2) An assignment of a limited liability company interest entitles the assignee to share in such profits and losses, to receive such distribution or distributions, and to receive such allocation of income, gain, loss, deduction, or credit or similar item to which the assignor was entitled, to the extent assigned; and

(3) A member ceases to be a member and to have the power to exercise any rights or powers of a member upon assignment of all of his limited liability company interest. Unless otherwise provided in a limited liability company agreement, the pledge of, or granting of a security interest, lien or other encumbrance in or against, any or all of the limited liability company interest of a member shall not cause the member to cease to be a member or to have the power to exercise any rights or powers of a member.

(c) Unless otherwise provided in a limited liability company agreement, a member's interest in a limited liability company may be evidenced by a certificate of limited liability company interest issued by the limited liability company. A limited liability company agreement may provide for the assignment or transfer of any limited liability company interest represented by such a certificate and make other provisions with respect to such certificates.

(d) Unless otherwise provided in a limited liability company agreement and except to the extent assumed by agreement, until an assignee of a limited liability company interest becomes a member, the assignee shall have no liability as a member solely as a result of the assignment.

(e) Unless otherwise provided in the limited liability company agreement, a limited liability company may acquire, by purchase, redemption or otherwise, any limited liability company interest or other interest of a member or manager in the limited liability company. Unless otherwise provided in the limited liability company agreement, any such interest so acquired by the limited liability company shall be deemed canceled.

§ 18–703. Member's Limited Liability Company Interest Subject to Charging Order.

(a) On application by a judgment creditor of a member or of a member's assignee, a court having jurisdiction may charge the limited liability company interest of the judgment debtor to satisfy the judgment. To the extent so charged, the judgment creditor has only the right to receive any distribution or distributions to which the judgment debtor would otherwise have been entitled in respect of such limited liability company interest.

(b) A charging order constitutes a lien on the judgment debtor's limited liability company interest.

(c) This chapter does not deprive a member or member's assignee of a right under exemption laws with respect to the judgment debtor's limited liability company interest.

(d) The entry of a charging order is the exclusive remedy by which a judgment creditor of a member or of a member's assignee may satisfy a judgment out of the judgment debtor's limited liability company interest.

(e) No creditor of a member or of a member's assignee shall have any right to obtain possession of, or otherwise exercise legal or equitable remedies with respect to,the property of the limited liability company.

(f) The Court of Chancery shall have jurisdiction to hear and determine any matter relating to any such charging order.

§ 18–704. Right of Assignee to Become Member

(a) An assignee of a limited liability company interest may become a member as provided in a limited liability company agreement and upon:

(1) The approval of all of the members of the limited liability company other than the member assigning his limited liability company interest; or

(2) Compliance with any procedure provided for in the limited liability company agreement.

(b) An assignee who has become a member has, to the extent assigned, the rights and powers, and is subject to the restrictions and liabilities, of a member under a limited liability company agreement and this chapter. Notwithstanding the foregoing, unless otherwise provided in a limited liability company agreement, an assignee who becomes a member is liable for the obligations of his assignor to make contributions as provided in § 18–502 of this title, but shall not be liable for the obligations of his assignor under subchapter VI of this chapter. However, the assignee is not obligated for liabilities, including the obligations of his assignor to make contributions as provided in § 18–502 of this title, unknown to the assignee at the time he became a member and which could not be ascertained from a limited liability company agreement.

(c) Whether or not an assignee of a limited liability company interest becomes a member, the assignor is not released from his liability to a limited liability company under subchapters V and VI of this chapter.

§ 18–705. Powers of Estate of Deceased or Incompetent Member

If a member who is an individual dies or a court of competent jurisdiction adjudges him to be incompetent to manage his person or his property, the member's personal representative may exercise all of the member's rights for the purpose of settling his estate or administering his property, including any power under a limited liability company agreement of an assignee to become a member. If a member is a corporation, trust or other entity and is dissolved or terminated, the powers of that member may be exercised by its personal representative.

SUBCHAPTER VIII. DISSOLUTION

§ 18–801. Dissolution

(a) A limited liability company is dissolved and its affairs shall be wound up upon the first to occur of the following:

(1) At the time specified in a limited liability company agreement, but if no such time is set forth in the limited liability company agreement, then the limited liability company shall have a perpetual existence;

(2) Upon the happening of events specified in a limited liability company agreement;

(3) Unless otherwise provided in the limited liability company agreement, upon the affirmative vote or written consent of the members of the limited liability company or, if there is more than one class or group of members, then by each class or group of members, in either case, by members who own more than two-thirds of the then-current percentage or other interest in the profits of the limited liability company owned by all of the members or by the members in each class or group, as appropriate;

(4) At any time there are no members; provided that the limited liability company is not dissolved and is not required to be wound up if, (i) unless otherwise provided in a limited liability company agreement, within 90 days or such other period as is provided for in the limited liability company agreement after the occurrence of the event that terminated the continued membership of the last remaining member, the personal representative of the last remaining member agrees in writing to continue the limited liability company and to the admission of the personal representative of such member or its nominee or designee to the limited liability company as a member, effective as of the occurrence of the event that terminated the continued membership of the last remaining member; provided that a limited liability company agreement may provide that the personal representative of the last remaining member shall be obligated to agree in writing to continue the limited liability compa-

ny and to the admission of the personal representative of such member or its nominee or designee to the limited liability company as a member, effective as of the occurrence of the event that terminated the continued membership of the last remaining member, or, (ii) a member is admitted to the limited liability company in the manner provided for in the limited liability company agreement, effective as of the occurrence of the event that terminated the continued membership of the last remaining member, within 90 days or such other period as is provided for in the limited liability company agreement after the occurrence of the event that terminated the continued membership of the last remaining member, pursuant to a provision of the limited liability company agreement that specifically provides for the admission of a member to the limited liability company after there is no longer a remaining member of the limited liability company.

(5) The entry of a decree of judicial dissolution under § 18–802 of this title.

(b) Unless otherwise provided in a limited liability company agreement, the death, retirement, resignation, expulsion, bankruptcy or dissolution of any member or the occurrence of any other event that terminates the continued membership of any member shall not cause the limited liability company to be dissolved or its affairs to be wound up, and upon the occurrence of any such event, the limited liability company shall be continued without dissolution.

§ 18–802. Judicial Dissolution

On application by or for a member or manager the Court of Chancery may decree dissolution of a limited liability company whenever it is not reasonably practicable to carry on the business in conformity with a limited liability company agreement.

§ 18–803. Winding Up

(a) Unless otherwise provided in a limited liability company agreement, a manager who has not wrongfully dissolved a limited liability company or, if none, the members or a person approved by the members or, if there is more than 1 class or group of members, then by each class or group of members, in either case, by members who own more than 50 percent of the then current percentage or other interest in the profits of the limited liability company owned by all of the members or by the members in each class or group, as appropriate, may wind up the limited liability company's affairs; but the Court of Chancery, upon cause shown, may wind up the limited liability company's affairs upon application of any member or manager, his personal representative or assignee, and in connection therewith, may appoint a liquidating trustee.

(b) Upon dissolution of a limited liability company and until the filing of a certificate of cancellation as provided in § 18–203 of this title, the persons winding up the limited liability company's affairs may, in the name of, and for and on behalf of, the limited liability company, prosecute and defend suits, whether civil, criminal or administrative, gradually settle and close the limited liability company's business, dispose of and convey the limited liability company's property, discharge or make reasonable provision for the limited liability company's liabilities, and distribute to the members any remaining assets of the limited liability company, all without affecting the liability of members and managers and without imposing liability on a liquidating trustee.

§ 18–804. Distribution of Assets

(a) Upon the winding up of a limited liability company, the assets shall be distributed as follows:

(1) To creditors, including members and managers who are creditors, to the extent otherwise permitted by law, in satisfaction of liabilities of the limited liability company (whether by payment or the making of reasonable provision for payment thereof) other than liabilities for which reasonable provision for payment has been made and liabilities for distributions to members and former members under § 18–601 or § 18–604 of this title;

(2) Unless otherwise provided in a limited liability company agreement, to members and former members in satisfaction of liabilities for distributions under § 18–601 or § 18–604 of this title; and

(3) Unless otherwise provided in a limited liability company agreement, to members first for the return of their contributions and second respecting their limited liability company interests, in the proportions in which the members share in distributions.

(b) A limited liability company which has dissolved (i) shall pay or make reasonable provision to pay all claims and obligations, including all contingent, conditional or unmatured contractual claims, known to the limited liability company, (ii) shall make such provision as will be reasonably likely to be sufficient to provide compensation for any claim against the limited liability company which is the subject of a pending action, suit or proceeding to which the limited liability company is a party and (iii) shall make such provision as will be reasonably likely to be sufficient to provide compensation for claims that have not been made known to the limited liability company or that have not arisen but that, based on facts known to the limited liability company, are likely to arise or to become known to the limited liability company within 10 years after the date of dissolution. If there are sufficient assets, such claims and obligations shall be paid in full and any such provision for payment made shall be made in full. If there are insufficient assets, such claims and obligations shall be paid or provided for according to their priority and, among claims of equal priority, ratably to the extent of assets available therefor. Unless otherwise provided in the limited liability company agreement, any remaining assets shall be distributed as provided in this chapter. Any liquidating trustee winding up a limited liability company's affairs who has complied with this section shall not be personally liable to the claimants of the dissolved limited liability company by reason of such person's actions in winding up the limited liability company.

(c) A member who receives a distribution in violation of subsection (a) of this section, and who knew at the time of the distribution that the distribution violated subsection (a) of this section, shall be liable to the limited liability company for the amount of the distribution. For purposes of the immediately preceding sentence, the term "distribution" shall not include amounts constituting reasonable compensation for present or past services or reasonable payments made in the ordinary course of business pursuant to a bona fide retirement plan or other benefits program. A member who receives a distribution in violation of subsection (a) of this section, and who did not know at the time of the distribution that the distribution violated subsection (a) of this section, shall not be liable for the amount of the distribution. Subject to subsection (d) of this section, this subsection shall not affect any obligation or liability of a member under an agreement or other applicable law for the amount of a distribution.

(d) Unless otherwise agreed, a member who receives a distribution from a limited liability company to which this section applies shall have no liability under this chapter or other applicable law for the amount of the distribution after the expiration of 3 years from the date of the distribution unless an action to recover the distribution from such member is commenced prior to the expiration of the said 3–year period and an adjudication of liability against such member is made in the said action.

(e) Section 18–607 of this title shall not apply to a distribution to which this section applies.

§ 18–806. Revocation of Dissolution.

Notwithstanding the occurrence of an event set forth in § 18–801(a)(1), (2), (3) or (4) of this title, the limited liability company shall not be dissolved and its affairs shall not be wound up if, prior to the filing of a certificate of cancellation in the office of the Secretary of State, the limited liability company is continued, effective as of the occurrence of such event, pursuant to the affirmative vote or written consent of all remaining members of the limited liability company or the personal representative of the last remaining member of the limited liability company if there is no remaining member (and any other person whose approval is required under the limited liability company agreement to revoke a dissolution pursuant to this section); provided, however, if the dissolution was caused by a vote or written consent, the dissolution shall not be revoked unless each member and other person (or their respective personal representatives) who voted in favor of, or consented to, the dissolution has voted or consented in writing to continue the limited liability company. If there is no remaining member of the limited liability company and the personal representative of the last remaining member votes in favor of or consents to the continuation of the limited liability company, such personal representative shall be required to agree in writing to the admission of the personal representative of such member or its nominee or designee to the limited liability company as a member, effective as of the occurrence of the event that terminated the continued membership of the last remaining member.

SUBCHAPTER IX.   FOREIGN LIMITED LIABILITY COMPANIES

§ 18–901.   Law Governing

(a) Subject to the Constitution of the State of Delaware:

(1) The laws of the state, territory, possession, or other jurisdiction or country under which a foreign limited liability company is organized govern its organization and internal affairs and the liability of its members and managers; and

(2) A foreign limited liability company may not be denied registration by reason of any difference between those laws and the laws of the State of Delaware.

(b) A foreign limited liability company shall be subject to § 18–106 of this title.

§ 18–902.   Registration Required; Application

Before doing business in the State of Delaware, a foreign limited liability company shall register with the Secretary of State....

§ 18–912. Activities Not Constituting Doing Business.

(a) Activities of a foreign limited liability company in the State of Delaware that do not constitute doing business for the purpose of this subchapter include:

(1) Maintaining, defending or settling an action or proceeding;

(2) Holding meetings of its members or managers or carrying on any other activity concerning its internal affairs;

(3) Maintaining bank accounts;

(4) Maintaining offices or agencies for the transfer, exchange or registration of the limited liability company's own securities or maintaining trustees or depositories with respect to those securities;

(5) Selling through independent contractors;

(6) Soliciting or obtaining orders, whether by mail or through employees or agents or otherwise, if the orders require acceptance outside the State of Delaware before they become contracts;

(7) Selling, by contract consummated outside the State of Delaware, and agreeing, by the contract, to deliver into the State of Delaware, machinery, plants or equipment, the construction, erection or installation of which within the State of Delaware requires the supervision of technical engineers or skilled employees performing services not generally available, and as part of the contract of sale agreeing to furnish such services, and such services only, to the vendee at the time of construction, erection or installation;

(8) Creating, as borrower or lender, or acquiring indebtedness with or without a mortgage or other security interest in property;

(9) Collecting debts or foreclosing mortgages or other security interests in property securing the debts, and holding, protecting and maintaining property so acquired;

(10) Conducting an isolated transaction that is not one in the course of similar transactions;

(11) Doing business in interstate commerce; and

(12) Doing business in the State of Delaware as an insurance company.

(b) A person shall not be deemed to be doing business in the State of Delaware solely by reason of being a member or manager of a domestic limited liability company or a foreign limited liability company.

(c) This section does not apply in determining whether a foreign limited liability company is subject to service of process, taxation or regulation under any other law of the State of Delaware.

SUBCHAPTER X. DERIVATIVE ACTIONS

§ 18–1001. Right to Bring Action

A member or an assignee of a limited liability company interest may bring an action in the Court of Chancery in the right of a limited liability company to recover a judgment in its favor if managers or members with authority to do so have refused to bring the action or if an effort to cause those managers or members to bring the action is not likely to succeed.

§ 18–1002. Proper Plaintiff

In a derivative action, the plaintiff must be a member or an assignee of a limited liability company interest at the time of bringing the action and:

(1) At the time of the transaction of which he complains; or

(2) His status as a member or an assignee of a limited liability company interest had devolved upon him by operation of law or pursuant to the terms of a limited liability company agreement from a person who was a member or an assignee of a limited liability company interest at the time of the transaction.

§ 18–1003. Complaint

In a derivative action, the complaint shall set forth with particularity the effort, if any, of the plaintiff to secure initiation of the action by a manager or member or the reasons for not making the effort.

§ 18–1004. Expenses

If a derivative action is successful, in whole or in part, as a result of a judgment, compromise or settlement of any such action, the court may award the plaintiff reasonable expenses, including reasonable attorney's fees, from any recovery in any such action or from a limited liability company.

SUBCHAPTER XI.   MISCELLANEOUS

§ 18–1101. Construction and Application of Chapter and Limited Liability Company Agreement

(a) The rule that statutes in derogation of the common law are to be strictly construed shall have no application to this chapter.

(b) It is the policy of this chapter to give the maximum effect to the principle of freedom of contract and to the enforceability of limited liability company agreements.

(c) To the extent that, at law or in equity, a member or manager or other person has duties (including fiduciary duties) to a limited liability company or to another member or manager or to another person that is a party to or is otherwise bound by a limited liability company agreement, the member's or manager's or other person's duties may be expanded or restricted or eliminated by provisions in the limited liability company agreement; provided that the limited liability company agreement may not eliminate the implied contractual covenant of good faith and fair dealing.

(d) Unless otherwise provided in a limited liability company agreement, a member or manager or other person shall not be liable to a limited liability company or to another member or manager or to another person that is a party to or is otherwise bound by a limited liability company agreement for breach of fiduciary duty for the member's or manager's or other person's good faith reliance on the provisions of the limited liability company agreement.

(e) A limited liability company agreement may provide for the limitation or elimination of any and all liabilities for breach of contract and breach of duties (including fiduciary duties) of a member, manager or other person to a limited liability company or to another member or manager or to another person that is a party to or is otherwise bound by a limited liability company agreement; provided that a limited liability company agreement may not limit or eliminate liability for any act or omission that constitutes a bad faith violation of the implied contractual covenant of good faith and fair dealing.

(f) Unless the context otherwise requires, as used herein, the singular shall include the plural and the plural may refer to only the singular. The use of any gender shall be applicable to all genders. The captions contained herein are for purposes of convenience only and shall not control or affect the construction of this chapter . . . .

§ 18–1102. Short Title

This chapter may be cited as the "Delaware Limited Liability Company Act."

§ 18–1104. Cases Not Provided for in This Chapter

In any case not provided for in this chapter, the rules of law and equity, including the law merchant, shall govern.

§ 18–1106. Reserved Power of State of Delaware to Alter or Repeal Chapter

All provisions of this chapter may be altered from time to time or repealed and all rights of members and managers are subject to this reservation. Unless expressly stated to the contrary in this chapter, all amendments of this chapter shall apply to limited liability companies and members and managers whether or not existing as such at the time of the enactment of any such amendment.

§ 18–1107. Taxation of Limited Liability Companies

(a) For purposes of any tax imposed by the State of Delaware or any instrumentality, agency or political subdivision of the State of Delaware, a limited liability company formed under this chapter or qualified to do business in the State of Delaware as a foreign limited liability company shall be classified as a partnership unless classified otherwise for federal income tax purposes, in which case the limited liability company shall be classified in the same manner as it is classified for federal income tax purposes . . . .

UNIFORM LIMITED LIABILITY
COMPANY ACT (1996)

TABLE OF CONTENTS

Prefatory Note *

* Omitted.

[ARTICLE] 1

GENERAL PROVISIONS

Section 101. Definitions.

In this [Act]:

(1) "Articles of organization" means initial, amended, and re-stated articles of organization and articles of merger. In the case of a foreign limited liability company, the term includes all records serving a similar function required to be filed in the office of the [Secretary of State] or other official having custody of company records in the State or country under whose law it is organized.

(2) "At-will company" means a limited liability company other than a term company.

(3) "Business" includes every trade, occupation, profession, and other lawful purpose, whether or not carried on for profit.

(4) "Debtor in bankruptcy" means a person who is the subject of an order for relief under Title 11 of the United States Code or a comparable order under a successor statute of general application or a comparable order under federal, state, or foreign law governing insolvency.

(5) "Distribution" means a transfer of money, property, or other benefit from a limited liability company to a member in the member's capacity as a member or to a transferee of the member's distributional interest.

(6) "Distributional interest" means all of a member's interest in distributions by the limited liability company.

(7) "Entity" means a person other than an individual.

(8) "Foreign limited liability company" means an unincorporated entity organized under laws other than the laws of this State which afford limited liability to its owners comparable to the liability under Section 303 and is not required to obtain a certificate of authority to transact business under any law of this State other than this [Act].

(9) "Limited liability company" means a limited liability company organized under this [Act].

(10) "Manager" means a person, whether or not a member of a manager-managed company, who is vested with authority under Section 301.

(11) "Manager-managed company" means a limited liability company which is so designated in its articles of organization.

(12) "Member-managed company" means a limited liability company other than a manager-managed company.

(13) "Operating agreement" means the agreement under Section 103 concerning the relations among the members, managers, and limited liability company. The term includes amendments to the agreement.

(14) "Person" means an individual, corporation, business trust, estate, trust, partnership, limited liability company, association, joint venture, government, governmental subdivision, agency, or instrumentality, or any other legal or commercial entity.

(15) "Principal office" means the office, whether or not in this State, where the principal executive office of a domestic or foreign limited liability company is located.

(16) "Record" means information that is inscribed on a tangible medium or that is stored in an electronic or other medium and is retrievable in perceivable form.

(17) "Sign" means to identify a record by means of a signature, mark, or other symbol, with intent to authenticate it.

(18) "State" means a State of the United States, the District of Columbia, the Commonwealth of Puerto Rico, or any territory or insular possession subject to the jurisdiction of the United States.

(19) "Term company" means a limited liability company in which its members have agreed to remain members until the expiration of a term specified in the articles of organization.

(20) "Transfer" includes an assignment, conveyance, deed, bill of sale, lease, mortgage, security interest, encumbrance, and gift.

Comment:

Uniform Limited Liability Company Act ("ULLCA") definitions, like the rest of the Act, are a blend of terms and concepts derived from the Uniform Partnership Act ("UPA"), the Uniform Partnership Act (1994) ("UPA 1994", also previously known as the Revised Uniform Partnership Act or "RUPA"), the Revised Uniform Limited Partnership Act ("RULPA"), the Uniform Commercial Code ("UCC"), and the Model Business Corporation Act ("MBCA"), or their revisions from time to time; some are tailored specially for this Act.

"Business." A limited liability company may be organized to engage in an activity either for or not for profit. The extent to which contributions to a nonprofit company may be deductible for Federal income tax purposes is determined by federal law. Other state law determines the extent of exemptions from state and local income and property taxes.

"Debtor in bankruptcy." The filing of a voluntary petition operates immediately as an "order for relief." See Sections 601(7)(i) and 602(b)(2)(iii).

"Distribution." This term includes all sources of a member's distributions including the member's capital contributions, undistributed profits, and residual interest in the assets of the company after all claims, including those of third parties and debts to members, have been paid.

"Distributional interest." The term does not include a member's broader rights to participate in the management of the company. See Comments to Article 5.

"Foreign limited liability company." The term is not restricted to companies formed in the United States.

"Manager." The rules of agency apply to limited liability companies. Therefore, managers may designate agents with whatever titles, qualifications, and responsibilities they desire. For example, managers may designate an agent as "President."

"Manager-managed company." The term includes only a company designated as such in the articles of organization. In a manager-managed company agency authority is vested exclusively in one or more managers and not in the members. See Sections 101(10) (manager), 203(a)(6) (articles designation), and 301(b) (agency authority of members and managers).

"Member-managed limited liability company." The term includes every company not designated as "manager-managed" under Section 203(a)(6) in its articles of organization.

"Operating agreement." This agreement may be oral. Members may agree upon the extent to which their relationships are to be governed by writings.

"Principal office." The address of the principal office must be set forth in the annual report required under Section 211(a)(3).

"Record." This Act is the first Uniform Act promulgated with a definition of this term. The definition brings this Act in conformity with the present state of technology and accommodates prospective future technology in the communication and storage of information other than by human memory. Modern methods of communicating and storing information employed in commercial practices are no longer confined to physical documents.

The term includes any writing. A record need not be permanent or indestructible, but an oral or other unwritten communication must be stored or preserved on some medium to qualify as a record. Information that has not been retained other than through human memory does not qualify as a record. A record may be signed or may be created without the knowledge or intent of a particular person. Other law must be consulted to determine admissibility in evidence, the applicability of statute of frauds, and other questions regarding the use of records. Under Section 206(a), electronic filings may be permitted and even encouraged.

Section 102. Knowledge and Notice.

(a) A person knows a fact if the person has actual knowledge of it.

(b) A person has notice of a fact if the person:

(1) knows the fact;

(2) has received a notification of the fact; or

(3) has reason to know the fact exists from all of the facts known to the person at the time in question.

(c) A person notifies or gives a notification of a fact to another by taking steps reasonably required to inform the other person in ordinary course, whether or not the other person knows the fact.

(d) A person receives a notification when the notification:

(1) comes to the person's attention; or

(2) is duly delivered at the person's place of business or at any other place held out by the person as a place for receiving communications.

(e) An entity knows, has notice, or receives a notification of a fact for purposes of a particular transaction when the individual conducting the transaction for the entity knows, has notice, or receives a notification of the fact, or in any event when the fact would have been brought to the individual's attention had the entity exercised reasonable diligence. An entity exercises reasonable diligence if it maintains reasonable routines for communicating significant information to the individual conducting the transaction for the entity and there is reasonable compliance with the routines. Reasonable diligence does not require an individual acting for the entity to communicate information unless the communication is part of the individual's regular duties or the individual has reason to know of the transaction and that the transaction would be materially affected by the information.

Comment:

Knowledge requires cognitive awareness of a fact, whereas notice is based on a lesser degree of awareness. The Act imposes constructive knowledge under limited circumstances. See Comments to Sections 301(c), 703, and 704.

Section 103. Effect of Operating Agreement; Nonwaivable Provisions.

(a) Except as otherwise provided in subsection (b), all members of a limited liability company may enter into an operating agreement, which need not be in writing, to regulate the affairs of the company and the conduct of its business, and to govern relations among the members, managers, and company. To the extent the operating agreement does not otherwise provide, this [Act] governs relations among the members, managers, and company.

(b) The operating agreement may not:

(1) unreasonably restrict a right to information or access to records under Section 408;

(2) eliminate the duty of loyalty under Section 409(b) or 603(b)(3), but the agreement may:

(i) identify specific types or categories of activities that do not violate the duty of loyalty, if not manifestly unreasonable; and

(ii) specify the number or percentage of members or disinterested managers that may authorize or ratify, after full disclosure of all material facts, a specific act or transaction that otherwise would violate the duty of loyalty;

(3) unreasonably reduce the duty of care under Section 409(c) or 603(b)(3);

(4) eliminate the obligation of good faith and fair dealing under Section 409(d), but the operating agreement may determine the standards by which the performance of the obligation is to be measured, if the standards are not manifestly unreasonable;

(5) vary the right to expel a member in an event specified in Section 601(6);

(6) vary the requirement to wind up the limited liability company's business in a case specified in Section 801(3); or

(7) restrict rights of a person, other than a manager, member, and transferee of a member's distributional interest, under this [Act].

Comment:

The operating agreement is the essential contract that governs the affairs of a limited liability company. Since it is binding on all members, amendments must be approved by all members unless otherwise provided in the agreement. Although many agreements will be in writing, the agreement and any amendments may be oral or may be in the form of a record. Course of dealing, course of performance and usage of trade are relevant to determine the meaning of the agreement unless the agreement provides that all amendments must be in writing.

This section makes clear that the only matters an operating agreement may not control are specified in subsection (b). Accordingly, an operating agreement may modify or eliminate any rule specified in any section of this Act except matters specified in subsection (b). To the extent not otherwise mentioned in subsection (b), every section of this Act is simply a default rule, regardless of whether the language of the section appears to be otherwise mandatory. This approach eliminates the necessity of repeating the phrase "unless otherwise agreed" in each section and its commentary.

Under subsection (b)(1), an operating agreement may not unreasonably restrict the right to information or access to any records under Section 408. This does not create an independent obligation beyond Section 408 to maintain any specific records. Under subsections (b)(2) to (4), an irreducible core of fiduciary responsibilities survive any contrary provision in the operating agreement. Subsection (b)(2)(i) authorizes an operating agreement to modify, but not eliminate, the three specific duties of loyalty set forth in Section 409(b)(1) to (3) provided the modification itself is not manifestly unreasonable, a question of fact. Subsection (b)(2)(ii) preserves the common law right of the members to authorize future or ratify past violations of the duty of loyalty provided there has been a full disclosure of all material facts. The authorization or ratification must be unanimous unless otherwise provided in an operating agreement, because the authorization or ratification itself constitutes an amendment to the agreement. The authorization or ratification of specific past or future conduct may sanction conduct that would have been manifestly unreasonable under subsection (b)(2)(i).

Section 104. Supplemental Principles of Law.

(a) Unless displaced by particular provisions of this [Act], the principles of law and equity supplement this [Act].

(b) If an obligation to pay interest arises under this [Act] and the rate is not specified, the rate is that specified in [applicable statute].

Comment:

Supplementary principles include, but are not limited to, the law of agency, estoppel, law merchant, and all other principles listed in UCC Section 1–103, including the law relative to the capacity to contract, fraud, misrepresentation, duress, coercion, mistake, bankruptcy, and other validating and invalidating clauses. Other principles such as those mentioned in UCC Section 1–205 (Course of Dealing and Usage of Trade) apply as well as course of performance. As with UPA 1994 Section 104, upon which this provision is based, no substantive change from either the UPA or the UCC is intended. Section 104(b) establishes the applicable rate of interest in the absence of an agreement among the members.

Section 105. Name.

(a) The name of a limited liability company must contain "limited liability company" or "limited company" or the abbreviation "L.L.C.", "LLC", "L.C.", or "LC". "Limited" may be abbreviated as "Ltd.", and "company" may be abbreviated as "Co.".

(b) Except as authorized by subsections (c) and (d), the name of a limited liability company must be distinguishable upon the records of the [Secretary of State] from:

(1) the name of any corporation, limited partnership, or company incorporated, organized or authorized to transact business, in this State;

(2) a name reserved or registered under Section 106 or 107;

(3) a fictitious name approved under Section 1005 for a foreign company authorized to transact business in this State because its real name is unavailable.

(c) A limited liability company may apply to the [Secretary of State] for authorization to use a name that is not distinguishable upon the records of the [Secretary of State] from one or more of the names described in subsection (b). The [Secretary of State] shall authorize use of the name applied for if:

(1) the present user, registrant, or owner of a reserved name consents to the use in a record and submits an undertaking in form satisfactory to the [Secretary of State] to change the name to a name that is distinguishable upon the records of the [Secretary of State] from the name applied for; or

(2) the applicant delivers to the [Secretary of State] a certified copy of the final judgment of a court of competent jurisdiction

establishing the applicant's right to use the name applied for in this State.

(d) A limited liability company may use the name, including a fictitious name, of another domestic or foreign company which is used in this State if the other company is organized or authorized to transact business in this State and the company proposing to use the name has:

(1) merged with the other company;

(2) been formed by reorganization with the other company; or

(3) acquired substantially all of the assets, including the name, of the other company.

Section 106.   Reserved Name.

(a) A person may reserve the exclusive use of the name of a limited liability company, including a fictitious name for a foreign company whose name is not available, by delivering an application to the [Secretary of State] for filing.   The application must set forth the name and address of the applicant and the name proposed to be reserved.   If the [Secretary of State] finds that the name applied for is available, it must be reserved for the applicant's exclusive use for a nonrenewable 120–day period.

(b) The owner of a name reserved for a limited liability company may transfer the reservation to another person by delivering to the [Secretary of State] a signed notice of the transfer which states the name and address of the transferee.

Comment:

A foreign limited liability company that is not presently authorized to transact business in the State may reserve a fictitious name for a nonrenewable 120–day period.   When its actual name is available, a company will generally register that name under Section 107 because the registration is valid for a year and may be extended indefinitely.

Section 107.   Registered Name.

(a) A foreign limited liability company may register its name subject to the requirements of Section 1005, if the name is distinguishable upon the records of the [Secretary of State] from names that are not available under Section 105(b).

(b) A foreign limited liability company registers its name, or its name with any addition required by Section 1005, by delivering to the [Secretary of State] for filing an application:

(1) setting forth its name, or its name with any addition required by Section 1005, the State or country and date of its organi-

zation, and a brief description of the nature of the business in which it is engaged; and

(2) accompanied by a certificate of existence, or a record of similar import, from the State or country of organization.

(c) A foreign limited liability company whose registration is effective may renew it for successive years by delivering for filing in the office of the [Secretary of State] a renewal application complying with subsection (b) between October 1 and December 31 of the preceding year. The renewal application renews the registration for the following calendar year.

(d) A foreign limited liability company whose registration is effective may qualify as a foreign company under its name or consent in writing to the use of its name by a limited liability company later organized under this [Act] or by another foreign company later authorized to transact business in this State. The registered name terminates when the limited liability company is organized or the foreign company qualifies or consents to the qualification of another foreign company under the registered name.

Section 108. Designated Office and Agent for Service of Process.

(a) A limited liability company and a foreign limited liability company authorized to do business in this State shall designate and continuously maintain in this State:

(1) an office, which need not be a place of its business in this State; and

(2) an agent and street address of the agent for service of process on the company.

(b) An agent must be an individual resident of this State, a domestic corporation, another limited liability company, or a foreign corporation or foreign company authorized to do business in this State.

Comment:

Limited liability companies organized under Section 202 or authorized to transact business under Section 1004 are required to designate and continuously maintain an office in the State. Although the designated office need not be a place of business, it most often will be the only place of business of the company. The company must also designate an agent for service of process within the State and the agent's street address. The agent's address need not be the same as the company's designated office address. The initial office and agent designations must be set forth in the articles of organization, including the address of the designated office. See Section 203(a)(2) to (3). The current office and agent designations must be set forth in the company's annual report. See Section 211(a)(2). See also Section 109 (procedure for changing the office or agent designations), Section 110 (procedure for an agent to resign), and Section 111(b) (the filing officer is the service agent for the company if it fails to maintain its own service agent).

Section 109. Change of Designated Office or Agent for Service of Process.

A limited liability company may change its designated office or agent for service of process by delivering to the [Secretary of State] for filing a statement of change which sets forth:

(1) the name of the company;

(2) the street address of its current designated office;

(3) if the current designated office is to be changed, the street address of the new designated office;

(4) the name and address of its current agent for service of process; and

(5) if the current agent for service of process or street address of that agent is to be changed, the new address or the name and street address of the new agent for service of process.

Section 110. Resignation of Agent for Service of Process.

(a) An agent for service of process of a limited liability company may resign by delivering to the [Secretary of State] for filing a record of the statement of resignation.

(b) After filing a statement of resignation, the [Secretary of State] shall mail a copy to the designated office and another copy to the limited liability company at its principal office.

(c) An agency is terminated on the 31st day after the statement is filed in the office of the [Secretary of State].

Section 111. Service of Process.

(a) An agent for service of process appointed by a limited liability company or a foreign limited liability company is an agent of the company for service of any process, notice, or demand required or permitted by law to be served upon the company.

(b) If a limited liability company or foreign limited liability company fails to appoint or maintain an agent for service of process in this State or the agent for service of process cannot with reasonable diligence be found at the agent's address, the [Secretary of State] is an agent of the company upon whom process, notice, or demand may be served.

(c) Service of any process, notice, or demand on the [Secretary of State] may be made by delivering to and leaving with the [Secretary of

State], the [Assistant Secretary of State], or clerk having charge of the limited liability company department of the [Secretary of State's] office duplicate copies of the process, notice, or demand. If the process, notice, or demand is served on the [Secretary of State], the [Secretary of State] shall forward one of the copies by registered or certified mail, return receipt requested, to the company at its designated office. Service is effected under this subsection at the earliest of:

(1) the date the company receives the process, notice, or demand;

(2) the date shown on the return receipt, if signed on behalf of the company; or

(3) five days after its deposit in the mail, if mailed postpaid and correctly addressed.

(d) The [Secretary of State] shall keep a record of all processes, notices, and demands served pursuant to this section and record the time of and the action taken regarding the service.

(e) This section does not affect the right to serve process, notice, or demand in any manner otherwise provided by law.

Comment:

Service of process on a limited liability company and a foreign company authorized to transact business in the State must be made on the company's agent for service of process whose name and address should be on file with the filing office. If for any reason a company fails to appoint or maintain an agent for service of process or the agent cannot be found with reasonable diligence at the agent's address, the filing officer will be deemed the proper agent.

Section 112. Nature of Business and Powers.

(a) A limited liability company may be organized under this [Act] for any lawful purpose, subject to any law of this State governing or regulating business.

(b) Unless its articles of organization provide otherwise, a limited liability company has the same powers as an individual to do all things necessary or convenient to carry on its business or affairs, including power to:

(1) sue and be sued, and defend in its name;

(2) purchase, receive, lease, or otherwise acquire, and own, hold, improve, use, and otherwise deal with real or personal property, or any legal or equitable interest in property, wherever located;

(3) sell, convey, mortgage, grant a security interest in, lease, exchange, and otherwise encumber or dispose of all or any part of its property;

(4) purchase, receive, subscribe for, or otherwise acquire, own, hold, vote, use, sell, mortgage, lend, grant a security interest in, or otherwise dispose of and deal in and with, shares or other interests in or obligations of any other entity;

(5) make contracts and guarantees, incur liabilities, borrow money, issue its notes, bonds, and other obligations, which may be convertible into or include the option to purchase other securities of the limited liability company, and secure any of its obligations by a mortgage on or a security interest in any of its property, franchises, or income;

(6) lend money, invest and reinvest its funds, and receive and hold real and personal property as security for repayment;

(7) be a promoter, partner, member, associate, or manager of any partnership, joint venture, trust, or other entity;

(8) conduct its business, locate offices, and exercise the powers granted by this [Act] within or without this State;

(9) elect managers and appoint officers, employees, and agents of the limited liability company, define their duties, fix their compensation, and lend them money and credit;

(10) pay pensions and establish pension plans, pension trusts, profit sharing plans, bonus plans, option plans, and benefit or incentive plans for any or all of its current or former members, managers, officers, employees, and agents;

(11) make donations for the public welfare or for charitable, scientific, or educational purposes; and

(12) make payments or donations, or do any other act, not inconsistent with law, that furthers the business of the limited liability company.

Comment:

A limited liability company may be organized for any lawful purpose unless the State has specifically prohibited a company from engaging in a specific activity. For example, many States require that certain regulated industries, such as banking and insurance, be conducted only by organizations that meet the special requirements. Also, many States impose restrictions on activities in which a limited liability company may engage. For example, the practice of certain professionals is often subject to special conditions.

A limited liability company has the power to engage in and perform important and necessary acts related to its operation and function. A company's power to enter into a transaction is distinguishable from the authority of an agent to enter into the transaction. See Section 301 (agency rules).

[ARTICLE] 2

ORGANIZATION

Section 201. Limited Liability Company as Legal Entity.

A limited liability company is a legal entity distinct from its members.

Comment:

A limited liability company is legally distinct from its members who are not normally liable for the debts, obligations, and liabilities of the company. See Section 303. Accordingly, members are not proper parties to suits against the company unless an object of the proceeding is to enforce members' rights against the company or to enforce their liability to the company.

Section 202. Organization.

(a) One or more persons may organize a limited liability company, consisting of one or more members, by delivering articles of organization to the office of the [Secretary of State] for filing.

(b) Unless a delayed effective date is specified, the existence of a limited liability company begins when the articles of organization are filed.

(c) The filing of the articles of organization by the [Secretary of State] is conclusive proof that the organizers satisfied all conditions precedent to the creation of a limited liability company.

Comment:

Any person may organize a limited liability company by performing the ministerial act of signing and filing the articles of organization. The person need not be a member. As a matter of flexibility, a company may be organized and operated with only one member to enable sole proprietors to obtain the benefit of a liability shield. The effect of organizing or operating a company with one member on the Federal tax classification of the company is determined by federal law.

The existence of a company begins when the articles are filed. Therefore, the filing of the articles of organization is conclusive as to the existence of the limited liability shield for persons who enter into transactions on behalf of the company. Until the articles are filed, a firm is not organized under this Act and is not a "limited liability company" as defined in Section 101(9). In that case, the parties' relationships are not governed by this Act unless they have expressed a contractual intent to be bound by the provisions of the Act. Third parties would also not be governed by the provisions of this Act unless they have expressed a contractual intent to extend a limited liability shield to the members of the would-be limited liability company.

Section 203. Articles of Organization.

(a) Articles of organization of a limited liability company must set forth:

(1) the name of the company;

(2) the address of the initial designated office;

(3) the name and street address of the initial agent for service of process;

(4) the name and address of each organizer;

(5) whether the company is to be a term company and, if so, the term specified;

(6) whether the company is to be manager-managed, and, if so, the name and address of each initial manager; and

(7) whether one or more of the members of the company are to be liable for its debts and obligations under Section 303(c).

(b) Articles of organization of a limited liability company may set forth:

(1) provisions permitted to be set forth in an operating agreement; or

(2) other matters not inconsistent with law.

(c) Articles of organization of a limited liability company may not vary the nonwaivable provisions of Section 103(b). As to all other matters, if any provision of an operating agreement is inconsistent with the articles of organization:

(1) the operating agreement controls as to managers, members, and members' transferees; and

(2) the articles of organization control as to persons, other than managers, members and their transferees, who reasonably rely on the articles to their detriment.

Comment:

The articles serve primarily a notice function and generally do not reflect the substantive agreement of the members regarding the business affairs of the company. Those matters are generally reserved for an operating agreement which may be unwritten. Under Section 203(b), the articles may contain provisions permitted to be set forth in an operating agreement. Where the articles and operating agreement conflict, the operating agreement controls as to members but the articles control as to third parties. The articles may also contain any other matter not inconsistent with law. The most important is a Section 301(c) limitation on the authority of a member or manager to transfer interests in the company's real property.

A company will be at-will unless it is designated as a term company and the duration of its term is specified in its articles under Section 203(a)(5). The duration of a term company may be specified in any manner which sets forth a specific and final date for the dissolution of the company. For example, the period specified may be in the form of "50 years from the date of filing of the articles" or "the period ending on January 1, 2020." Mere specification of a particular undertaking of an uncertain business duration is not sufficient unless the particular undertaking is within a longer fixed period. An example of this type of designation would include "2020 or until the building is completed, whichever occurs first." When the specified period is incorrectly specified, the company will be an at-will company. Notwithstanding the correct specification of a term in the articles, a company will be an at-will company among the members under Section 203(c)(1) if an operating agreement so provides. A term company that continues after the expiration of its term specified in its articles will also be an at-will company.

A term company possesses several important default rule characteristics that differentiate it dramatically from an at-will company. An operating agreement may alter any of these rules. Any dissociation of an at-will member dissolves a member-managed company unless a specified percentage of the remaining members agree to continue the business of the company. Before the expiration of its term, only specified dissociation events (excluding voluntary withdrawal) of a term member will dissolve a member-managed company unless a specified percentage of the remaining members agree to continue the business of the company. See Comments to Sections

601 and 801(b)(3). Also, even if the dissociation of an at-will member does not result in a dissolution of a member-managed company, the dissociated member is entitled to have the company purchase that member's interest for its fair value. Unless the company earlier dissolves, a term member must generally await the expiration of the agreed term to withdraw the fair value of the interest. See Comments to Section 701(a).

A company will be member-managed unless it is designated as manager-managed under Section 203(a)(6). Absent further designation in the articles, a company will be a member-managed at-will company. The designation of a limited liability company as either member- or manager-managed is important because it defines who are agents and have the apparent authority to bind the company under Section 301 and determines whether the dissociation of members who are not managers will threaten dissolution of the company. In a member-managed company, the members have the agency authority to bind the company. In a manager-managed company only the managers have that authority. The effect of the agency structure of a company on the Federal tax classification of the company is determined by federal law. The agency designation relates only to agency and does not preclude members of a manager-managed company from participating in the actual management of company business. See Comments to Section 404(b).

In a member-managed company, the dissociation of any member will cause the company to dissolve unless a specified percentage of the remaining members agree to continue the business of the company. In a manager-managed company, only the dissociation of any member who is also a manager threatens dissolution of the company. Only where there are no members who are also managers will the dissociation of members who are not managers threaten dissolution of a manager-managed company. See Comments to Section 801.

Section 204. Amendment or Restatement of Articles of Organization.

(a) Articles of organization of a limited liability company may be amended at any time by delivering articles of amendment to the [Secretary of State] for filing. The articles of amendment must set forth the:

    (1) name of the limited liability company;

    (2) date of filing of the articles of organization; and

    (3) amendment to the articles.

(b) A limited liability company may restate its articles of organization at any time. Restated articles of organization must be signed and filed in the same manner as articles of amendment. Restated articles of organization must be designated as such in the heading and state in the heading or in an introductory paragraph the limited liability company's present name and, if it has been changed, all of its former names and the date of the filing of its initial articles of organization.

Comment:

An amendment to the articles requires the consent of all the members unless an operating agreement provides for a lesser number. See Section 404(c)(3).

Section 205.   Signing of Records.

(a) Except as otherwise provided in this [Act], a record to be filed by or on behalf of a limited liability company in the office of the [Secretary of State] must be signed in the name of the company by a:

(1) manager of a manager-managed company;

(2) member of a member-managed company;

(3) person organizing the company, if the company has not been formed; or

(4) fiduciary, if the company is in the hands of a receiver, trustee, or other court-appointed fiduciary.

(b) A record signed under subsection (a) must state adjacent to the signature the name and capacity of the signer.

(c) Any person may sign a record to be filed under subsection (a) by an attorney-in-fact. Powers of attorney relating to the signing of records to be filed under subsection (a) by an attorney-in-fact need not be filed in the office of the [Secretary of State] as evidence of authority by the person filing but must be retained by the company.

Comment:

Both a writing and a record may be signed. An electronic record is signed when a person adds a name to the record with the intention to authenticate the record. See Sections 101(16) ("record" definition) and 101(17) ("signed" definition).

Other provisions of this Act also provide for the filing of records with the filing office but do not require signing by the persons specified in clauses (1) to (3). Those specific sections prevail.

Section 206.   Filing in Office of [Secretary of State].

(a) Articles of organization or any other record authorized to be filed under this [Act] must be in a medium permitted by the [Secretary of State] and must be delivered to the office of the [Secretary of State]. Unless the [Secretary of State] determines that a record fails to comply as to form with the filing requirements of this [Act], and if all filing fees have been paid, the [Secretary of State] shall file the record and send a receipt for the record and the fees to the limited liability company or its representative.

(b) Upon request and payment of a fee, the [Secretary of State] shall send to the requester a certified copy of the requested record.

(c) Except as otherwise provided in subsection (d) and Section 207(c), a record accepted for filing by the [Secretary of State] is effective:

(1) at the time of filing on the date it is filed, as evidenced by the [Secretary of State's] date and time endorsement on the original record; or

(2) at the time specified in the record as its effective time on the date it is filed.

(d) A record may specify a delayed effective time and date, and if it does so the record becomes effective at the time and date specified. If a delayed effective date but no time is specified, the record is effective at the close of business on that date. If a delayed effective date is later than the 90th day after the record is filed, the record is effective on the 90th day.

Comment:

The definition and use of the term "record" permits filings with the filing office under this Act to conform to technological advances that have been adopted by the filing office. However, since Section 206(a) provides that the filing "must be in a medium permitted by the [Secretary of State]", the Act simply conforms to filing changes as they are adopted.

Section 207.   Correcting Filed Record.

(a) A limited liability company or foreign limited liability company may correct a record filed by the [Secretary of State] if the record contains a false or erroneous statement or was defectively signed.

(b) A record is corrected:

(1) by preparing articles of correction that:

(i) describe the record, including its filing date, or attach a copy of it to the articles of correction;

(ii) specify the incorrect statement and the reason it is incorrect or the manner in which the signing was defective; and

(iii) correct the incorrect statement or defective signing; and

(2) by delivering the corrected record to the [Secretary of State] for filing.

(c) Articles of correction are effective retroactively on the effective date of the record they correct except as to persons relying on the uncorrected record and adversely affected by the correction. As to those persons, articles of correction are effective when filed.

Section 208. Certificate of Existence or Authorization.

(a) A person may request the [Secretary of State] to furnish a certificate of existence for a limited liability company or a certificate of authorization for a foreign limited liability company.

(b) A certificate of existence for a limited liability company must set forth:

(1) the company's name;

(2) that it is duly organized under the laws of this State, the date of organization, whether its duration is at-will or for a specified term, and, if the latter, the period specified;

(3) if payment is reflected in the records of the [Secretary of State] and if nonpayment affects the existence of the company, that all fees, taxes, and penalties owed to this State have been paid;

(4) whether its most recent annual report required by Section 211 has been filed with the [Secretary of State];

(5) that articles of termination have not been filed; and

(6) other facts of record in the office of the [Secretary of State] which may be requested by the applicant.

(c) A certificate of authorization for a foreign limited liability company must set forth:

(1) the company's name used in this State;

(2) that it is authorized to transact business in this State;

(3) if payment is reflected in the records of the [Secretary of State] and if nonpayment affects the authorization of the company, that all fees, taxes, and penalties owed to this State have been paid;

(4) whether its most recent annual report required by Section 211 has been filed with the [Secretary of State];

(5) that a certificate of cancellation has not been filed; and

(6) other facts of record in the office of the [Secretary of State] which may be requested by the applicant.

(d) Subject to any qualification stated in the certificate, a certificate of existence or authorization issued by the [Secretary of State] may be relied upon as conclusive evidence that the domestic or foreign limited liability company is in existence or is authorized to transact business in this State.

Section 209.   Liability for False Statement in Filed Record.

If a record authorized or required to be filed under this [Act] contains a false statement, one who suffers loss by reliance on the statement may recover damages for the loss from a person who signed the record or caused another to sign it on the person's behalf and knew the statement to be false at the time the record was signed.

Section 210.   Filing by Judicial Act.

If a person required by Section 205 to sign any record fails or refuses to do so, any other person who is adversely affected by the failure or refusal may petition the [designate the appropriate court] to direct the signing of the record.   If the court finds that it is proper for the record to be signed and that a person so designated has failed or refused to sign the record, it shall order the [Secretary of State] to sign and file an appropriate record.

Section 211.   Annual Report for [Secretary of State].

(a) A limited liability company, and a foreign limited liability company authorized to transact business in this State, shall deliver to the [Secretary of State] for filing an annual report that sets forth:

(1) the name of the company and the State or country under whose law it is organized;

(2) the address of its designated office and the name and address of its agent for service of process in this State;

(3) the address of its principal office; and

(4) the names and business addresses of any managers.

(b) Information in an annual report must be current as of the date the annual report is signed on behalf of the limited liability company.

(c) The first annual report must be delivered to the [Secretary of State] between [January 1 and April 1] of the year following the calendar year in which a limited liability company was organized or a foreign company was authorized to transact business. Subsequent annual reports must be delivered to the [Secretary of State] between [January 1 and April 1] of the ensuing calendar years.

(d) If an annual report does not contain the information required in subsection (a), the [Secretary of State] shall promptly notify the reporting limited liability company or foreign limited liability company and return the report to it for correction. If the report is corrected to contain the information required in subsection (a) and delivered to the [Secretary of State] within 30 days after the effective date of the notice, it is timely filed.

Comment:

Failure to deliver the annual report within 60 days after its due date is a primary ground for administrative dissolution of the company under Section 809. See Comments to Sections 809 to 812.

[ARTICLE] 3

RELATIONS OF MEMBERS AND MANAGERS TO PERSONS DEALING WITH LIMITED LIABILITY COMPANY

Sec.
301. Agency of Members and Managers.
302. Limited Liability Company Liable for Member's or Manager's Actionable Conduct.
303. Liability of Members and Managers.

Section 301. Agency of Members and Managers.

(a) Subject to subsections (b) and (c):

(1) Each member is an agent of the limited liability company for the purpose of its business, and an act of a member, including the signing of an instrument in the company's name, for apparently carrying on in the ordinary course the company's business or business of the kind carried on by the company binds the company, unless the member had no authority to act for the company in the particular matter and the person with whom the member was dealing knew or had notice that the member lacked authority.

(2) An act of a member which is not apparently for carrying on in the ordinary course the company's business or business of the kind carried on by the company binds the company only if the act was authorized by the other members.

(b) Subject to subsection (c), in a manager-managed company:

(1) A member is not an agent of the company for the purpose of its business solely by reason of being a member. Each manager is an agent of the company for the purpose of its business, and an act of a manager, including the signing of an instrument in the company's name, for apparently carrying on in the ordinary course the company's business or business of the kind carried on by the company binds the company, unless the manager had no authority to act for the company in the particular matter and the person with whom the manager was dealing knew or had notice that the manager lacked authority.

(2) An act of a manager which is not apparently for carrying on in the ordinary course the company's business or business of the

439

kind carried on by the company binds the company only if the act was authorized under Section 404.

(c) Unless the articles of organization limit their authority, any member of a member-managed company or manager of a manager-managed company may sign and deliver any instrument transferring or affecting the company's interest in real property. The instrument is conclusive in favor of a person who gives value without knowledge of the lack of the authority of the person signing and delivering the instrument.

Comment:

Members of a member-managed and managers of manager-managed company, as agents of the firm, have the apparent authority to bind a company to third parties. Members of a manager-managed company are not as such agents of the firm and do not have the apparent authority, as members, to bind a company. Members and managers with apparent authority possess actual authority by implication unless the actual authority is restricted in an operating agreement. Apparent authority extends to acts for carrying on in the ordinary course the company's business and business of the kind carried on by the company. Acts beyond this scope bind the company only where supported by actual authority created before the act or ratified after the act.

Ordinarily, restrictions on authority in an operating agreement do not affect the apparent authority of members and managers to bind the company to third parties without notice of the restriction. However, the restriction may make a member or manager's conduct wrongful and create liability to the company for the breach. This rule is subject to three important exceptions. First, under Section 301(c), a limitation reflected in the articles of organization on the authority of any member or manager to sign and deliver an instrument affecting an interest in company real property is effective when filed, even to persons without knowledge of the agent's lack of authority. The effect of such a limitation on authority on the Federal tax classification of the company is determined by federal law. Secondly, under Section 703, a dissociated member's apparent authority terminates two years after dissociation, even to persons without knowledge of the dissociation. Thirdly, under Section 704, a dissociated member's apparent authority may be terminated earlier than the two years by filing a statement of dissociation. The statement is effective 90 days after filing, even to persons without knowledge of the filing. Together, these three provisions provide constructive knowledge to the world of the lack of apparent authority of an agent to bind the company.

440

Section 302. Limited Liability Company Liable for Member's or Manager's Actionable Conduct.

A limited liability company is liable for loss or injury caused to a person, or for a penalty incurred, as a result of a wrongful act or omission, or other actionable conduct, of a member or manager acting in the ordinary course of business of the company or with authority of the company.

Comment:

Since a member of a manager-managed company is not as such an agent, the acts of the member are not imputed to the company unless the member is acting under actual or apparent authority created by circumstances other than membership status.

Section 303. Liability of Members and Managers.

(a) Except as otherwise provided in subsection (c), the debts, obligations, and liabilities of a limited liability company, whether arising in contract, tort, or otherwise, are solely the debts, obligations, and liabilities of the company. A member or manager is not personally liable for a debt, obligation, or liability of the company solely by reason of being or acting as a member or manager.

(b) The failure of a limited liability company to observe the usual company formalities or requirements relating to the exercise of its company powers or management of its business is not a ground for imposing personal liability on the members or managers for liabilities of the company.

(c) All or specified members of a limited liability company are liable in their capacity as members for all or specified debts, obligations, or liabilities of the company if:

(1) a provision to that effect is contained in the articles of organization; and

(2) a member so liable has consented in writing to the adoption of the provision or to be bound by the provision.

Comment:

A member or manager, as an agent of the company, is not liable for the debts, obligations, and liabilities of the company simply because of the agency. A member or manager is responsible for acts or omissions to the extent those acts or omissions would be actionable in contract or tort against the member or manager if that person were acting in an individual capacity. Where a member or manager delegates or assigns the authority or duty to exercise appropriate company functions, the member or manager is ordinarily not personally liable for the acts or omissions of the officer, employee, or agent if the member or manager has complied with the duty of care set forth in Section 409(c).

Under Section 303(c), the usual liability shield may be waived, in whole or in part, provided the waiver is reflected in the articles of organization and the member has consented in writing to be bound by the waiver. The importance and unusual nature of the waiver consent requires that the consent be evidenced by a writing and not merely an unwritten record. See Comments to Section 205. The effect of a waiver on the Federal tax classification of the company is determined by federal law.

[ARTICLE] 4

RELATIONS OF MEMBERS TO EACH OTHER AND TO LIMITED LIABILITY COMPANY

Section 401. Form of Contribution.

A contribution of a member of a limited liability company may consist of tangible or intangible property or other benefit to the company, including money, promissory notes, services performed, or other agreements to contribute cash or property, or contracts for services to be performed.

Comment:

Unless otherwise provided in an operating agreement, admission of a member and the nature and valuation of a would-be member's contribution are matters requiring the consent of all of the other members. See Section 404(c)(7). An agreement to contribute to a company is controlled by the operating agreement and therefore may not be created or modified without amending that agreement through the unanimous consent of all the members, including the member to be bound by the new contribution terms. See 404(c)(1).

Section 402. Member's Liability for Contributions.

(a) A member's obligation to contribute money, property, or other benefit to, or to perform services for, a limited liability company is not excused by the member's death, disability, or other inability to perform personally. If a member does not make the required contribution of property or services, the member is obligated at the option of the company to contribute money equal to the value of that portion of the stated contribution which has not been made.

(b) A creditor of a limited liability company who extends credit or otherwise acts in reliance on an obligation described in subsection (a), and without notice of any compromise under Section 404(c)(5), may enforce the original obligation.

Comment:

An obligation need not be in writing to be enforceable. Given the informality of some companies, a writing requirement may frustrate reasonable expectations of members based on a clear oral agreement. Obligations may be compromised with the consent of all of the members under Section 404(c)(5), but the compromise is generally effective only among the consenting members. Company creditors are bound by the compromise only as provided in Section 402(b).

Section 403. Member's and Manager's Rights to Payments and Reimbursement.

(a) A limited liability company shall reimburse a member or manager for payments made and indemnify a member or manager for liabilities incurred by the member or manager in the ordinary course of the business of the company or for the preservation of its business or property.

(b) A limited liability company shall reimburse a member for an advance to the company beyond the amount of contribution the member agreed to make.

(c) A payment or advance made by a member which gives rise to an obligation of a limited liability company under subsection (a) or (b) constitutes a loan to the company upon which interest accrues from the date of the payment or advance.

(d) A member is not entitled to remuneration for services performed for a limited liability company, except for reasonable compensation for services rendered in winding up the business of the company.

Comment:

The presence of a liability shield will ordinarily prevent a member or manager from incurring personal liability on behalf of the company in the ordinary course of the company's business. Where a member of a member-managed or a manager of a manager-managed company incurs such liabilities, Section 403(a) provides that the company must indemnify the member or manager where that person acted in the ordinary course of the company's business or the preservation of its property. A member or manager is therefore entitled to indemnification only if the act was within the member or manager's actual authority. A member or manager is therefore not entitled to indemnification for conduct that violates the duty of care set forth in Section 409(c) or for tortious conduct against a third party. Since members of a manager-managed company do not possess the apparent authority to bind the company, it would be more unusual for such a member to incur a liability for indemnification in the ordinary course of the company's business.

Section 404. Management of Limited Liability Company.

(a) In a member-managed company:

(1) each member has equal rights in the management and conduct of the company's business; and

(2) except as otherwise provided in subsection (c), any matter relating to the business of the company may be decided by a majority of the members.

(b) In a manager-managed company:

(1) each manager has equal rights in the management and conduct of the company's business;

(2) except as otherwise provided in subsection (c), any matter relating to the business of the company may be exclusively decided by the manager or, if there is more than one manager, by a majority of the managers; and

(3) a manager:

(i) must be designated, appointed, elected, removed, or replaced by a vote, approval, or consent of a majority of the members; and

(ii) holds office until a successor has been elected and qualified, unless the manager sooner resigns or is removed.

(c) The only matters of a member or manager-managed company's business requiring the consent of all of the members are:

(1) the amendment of the operating agreement under Section 103;

(2) the authorization or ratification of acts or transactions under Section 103(b)(2)(ii) which would otherwise violate the duty of loyalty;

(3) an amendment to the articles of organization under Section 204;

(4) the compromise of an obligation to make a contribution under Section 402(b);

(5) the compromise, as among members, of an obligation of a member to make a contribution or return money or other property paid or distributed in violation of this [Act];

(6) the making of interim distributions under Section 405(a), including the redemption of an interest;

(7) the admission of a new member;

(8) the use of the company's property to redeem an interest subject to a charging order;

(9) the consent to dissolve the company under Section 801(b)(2);

(10) a waiver of the right to have the company's business wound up and the company terminated under Section 802(b);

(11) the consent of members to merge with another entity under Section 904(c)(1); and

(12) the sale, lease, exchange, or other disposal of all, or substantially all, of the company's property with or without goodwill.

(d) Action requiring the consent of members or managers under this [Act] may be taken without a meeting.

(e) A member or manager may appoint a proxy to vote or otherwise act for the member or manager by signing an appointment instrument, either personally or by the member's or manager's attorney-in-fact.

Comment:

In a member-managed company, each member has equal rights in the management and conduct of the company's business unless otherwise provided in an operating agreement. For example, an operating agreement may allocate voting rights based upon capital contributions rather than the subsection (a) per capita rule. Also, member disputes as to any matter relating to the company's business may be resolved by a majority of the members unless the matter relates to a matter specified either in subsection (c) (unanimous consent required) or in Section 801(b)(3)(i) (special consent required). Regardless of how the members allocate management rights, each member is an agent of the company with the apparent authority to bind the company in the ordinary course of its business.

See Comments to Section 301(a). A member's right to participate in management terminates upon dissociation. See Section 603(b)(1).

In a manager-managed company, the members, unless also managers, have no rights in the management and conduct of the company's business unless otherwise provided in an operating agreement. If there is more than one manager, manager disputes as to any matter relating to the company's business may be resolved by a majority of the managers unless the matter relates to a matter specified either in subsection (c) (unanimous member consent required) or Section 801(b)(3)(i) (special consent required). Managers must be designated, appointed, or elected by a majority of the members. A manager need not be a member and is an agent of the company with the apparent authority to bind the company in the ordinary course of its business. See Sections 101(10) and 301(b).

To promote clarity and certainty, subsection (c) specifies those exclusive matters requiring the unanimous consent of the members, whether the company is member- or manager-managed. For example, interim distributions, including redemptions, may not be made without the unanimous consent of all the members. Unless otherwise agreed, all other company matters are to be determined under the majority of members or managers rules of subsections (a) and (b).

Section 405.   Sharing of and Right to Distributions.

(a) Any distributions made by a limited liability company before its dissolution and winding up must be in equal shares.

(b) A member has no right to receive, and may not be required to accept, a distribution in kind.

(c) If a member becomes entitled to receive a distribution, the member has the status of, and is entitled to all remedies available to, a creditor of the limited liability company with respect to the distribution.

Comment:

Recognizing the informality of many limited liability companies, this section creates a simple default rule regarding interim distributions. Any interim distributions made must be in equal shares and approved by all members. See Section 404(c)(6). The rule assumes that: profits will be shared equally; some distributions will constitute a return of contributions that should be shared equally rather than a distribution of profits; and property contributors should have the right to veto any distribution that threatens their return of contributions on liquidation. In the simple case where the members make equal contributions of property or equal contributions of services, those assumptions avoid the necessity of maintaining a complex capital account or determining profits. Where some members contribute services and others property, the unanimous vote necessary to approve interim distributions protects against unwanted distributions of contributions to service contributors. Consistently, Section 408(a) does not require the company to maintain a separate account for each member, the Act does not contain a default rule for allocating profits and losses, and Section 806(b) requires that liquidating distributions to members be made in equal shares after the return of contributions not previously returned. See Comments to Section 806(b).

Section 405(c) governs distributions declared or made when the company was solvent. Section 406 governs distributions declared or made when the company is insolvent.

Section 406. Limitations on Distributions.

(a) A distribution may not be made if:

(1) the limited liability company would not be able to pay its debts as they become due in the ordinary course of business; or

(2) the company's total assets would be less than the sum of its total liabilities plus the amount that would be needed, if the company were to be dissolved, wound up, and terminated at the time of the distribution, to satisfy the preferential rights upon dissolution, winding up, and termination of members whose preferential rights are superior to those receiving the distribution.

(b) A limited liability company may base a determination that a distribution is not prohibited under subsection (a) on financial statements prepared on the basis of accounting practices and principles that are reasonable in the circumstances or on a fair valuation or other method that is reasonable in the circumstances.

(c) Except as otherwise provided in subsection (e), the effect of a distribution under subsection (a) is measured:

(1) in the case of distribution by purchase, redemption, or other acquisition of a distributional interest in a limited liability company, as of the date money or other property is transferred or debt incurred by the company; and

(2) in all other cases, as of the date the:

(i) distribution is authorized if the payment occurs within 120 days after the date of authorization; or

(ii) payment is made if it occurs more than 120 days after the date of authorization.

(d) A limited liability company's indebtedness to a member incurred by reason of a distribution made in accordance with this section is at parity with the company's indebtedness to its general, unsecured creditors.

447

(e) Indebtedness of a limited liability company, including indebtedness issued in connection with or as part of a distribution, is not considered a liability for purposes of determinations under subsection (a) if its terms provide that payment of principal and interest are made only if and to the extent that payment of a distribution to members could then be made under this section. If the indebtedness is issued as a distribution, each payment of principal or interest on the indebtedness is treated as a distribution, the effect of which is measured on the date the payment is made.

Comment:

This section establishes the validity of company distributions, which in turn determines the potential liability of members and managers for improper distributions under Section 407. Distributions are improper if the company is insolvent under subsection (a) at the time the distribution is measured under subsection (c). In recognition of the informality of many limited liability companies, the solvency determination under subsection (b) may be made on the basis of a fair valuation or other method reasonable under the circumstances.

The application of the equity insolvency and balance sheet tests present special problems in the context of the purchase, redemption, or other acquisition of a company's distributional interests. Special rules establish the time of measurement of such transfers. Under Section 406(c)(1), the time for measuring the effect of a distribution to purchase a distributional interest is the date of payment. The company may make payment either by transferring property or incurring a debt to transfer property in the future. In the latter case, subsection (c)(1) establishes a clear rule that the legality of the distribution is tested when the debt is actually incurred, not later when the debt is actually paid. Under Section 406(e), indebtedness is not considered a liability for purposes of subsection (a) if the terms of the indebtedness itself provide that payments can be made only if and to the extent that a payment of a distribution could then be made under this section. The effect makes the holder of the indebtedness junior to all other creditors but senior to members in their capacity as members.

Section 407. Liability for Unlawful Distributions.

(a) A member of a member-managed company or a member or manager of a manager-managed company who votes for or assents to a distribution made in violation of Section 406, the articles of organization, or the operating agreement is personally liable to the company for the amount of the distribution which exceeds the amount that could have been distributed without violating Section 406, the articles of organization, or the operating agreement if it is established that the member or manager did not perform the member's or manager's duties in compliance with Section 409.

(b) A member of a manager-managed company who knew a distribution was made in violation of Section 406, the articles of organization, or the operating agreement is personally liable to the company, but only to the extent that the distribution received by the member exceeded the amount that could have been properly paid under Section 406.

(c) A member or manager against whom an action is brought under this section may implead in the action all:

(1) other members or managers who voted for or assented to the distribution in violation of subsection (a) and may compel contribution from them; and

(2) members who received a distribution in violation of subsection (b) and may compel contribution from the member in the amount received in violation of subsection (b).

(d) A proceeding under this section is barred unless it is commenced within two years after the distribution.

Comment:

Whenever members or managers fail to meet the standards of conduct of Section 409 and vote for or assent to an unlawful distribution, they are personally liable to the company for the portion of the distribution that exceeds the maximum amount that could have been lawfully distributed. The recovery remedy under this section extends only to the company, not the company's creditors. Under subsection (a), members and managers are not liable for an unlawful distribution provided their vote in favor of the distribution satisfies the duty of care of Section 409(c).

Subsection (a) creates personal liability in favor of the company against members or managers who approve an unlawful distribution for the entire amount of a distribution that could not be lawfully distributed. Subsection (b) creates personal liability against only members who knowingly received the unlawful distribution, but only in the amount measured by the portion of the actual distribution received that was not lawfully made. Members who both vote for or assent to an unlawful distribution and receive a portion or all of the distribution will be liable, at the election of the company, under either but not both subsections.

A member or manager who is liable under subsection (a) may seek contribution under subsection (c)(1) from other members and managers who also voted for or assented to the same distribution and may also seek recoupment under subsection (c)(2) from members who received the distribution, but only if they accepted the payments knowing they were unlawful.

The two-year statute of limitations of subsection (d) is measured from the date of the distribution. The date of the distribution is determined under Section 406(c).

Section 408.   Member's Right to Information.

(a) A limited liability company shall provide members and their agents and attorneys access to its records, if any, at the company's principal office or other reasonable locations specified in the operating agreement. The company shall provide former members and their agents and attorneys access for proper purposes to records pertaining to the period during which they were members. The right of access provides the opportunity to inspect and copy records during ordinary business hours. The company may impose a reasonable charge, limited to the costs of labor and material, for copies of records furnished.

(b) A limited liability company shall furnish to a member, and to the legal representative of a deceased member or member under legal disability:

(1) without demand, information concerning the company's business or affairs reasonably required for the proper exercise of the member's rights and performance of the member's duties under the operating agreement or this [Act]; and

(2) on demand, other information concerning the company's business or affairs, except to the extent the demand or the information demanded is unreasonable or otherwise improper under the circumstances.

(c) A member has the right upon written demand given to the limited liability company to obtain at the company's expense a copy of any written operating agreement.

Comment:

Recognizing the informality of many limited liability companies, subsection (a) does not require a company to maintain any records. In general, a company should maintain records necessary to enable members to determine their share of profits and losses and their rights on dissociation. If inadequate records are maintained to determine those and other critical rights, a member may maintain an action for an accounting under Section 410(a). Normally, a company will maintain at least records required by state or federal authorities regarding tax and other filings.

The obligation to furnish access includes the obligation to insure that all records, if any, are accessible in intelligible form. For example, a company that switches computer systems has an obligation either to convert the records from the old system or retain at least one computer capable of accessing the records from the old system.

The right to inspect and copy records maintained is not conditioned on a member or former member's purpose or motive. However, an abuse of the access and copy right may create a remedy in favor of the other members as a violation of the requesting member or former member's obligation of good faith and fair dealing. See Section 409(d).

Although a company is not required to maintain any records under subsection (a), it is nevertheless subject to a disclosure duty to furnish specified information under subsection (b)(1). A company must therefore furnish to members, without demand, information reasonably needed for members to exercise their rights and duties as members. A member's exercise of these duties justifies an unqualified right of access to the company's records. The member's right to company records may not be unreasonably restricted by the operating agreement. See Section 103(b)(1).

Section 409. General Standards of Member's and Manager's Conduct.

(a) The only fiduciary duties a member owes to a member-managed company and its other members are the duty of loyalty and the duty of care imposed by subsections (b) and (c).

(b) A member's duty of loyalty to a member-managed company and its other members is limited to the following:

(1) to account to the company and to hold as trustee for it any property, profit, or benefit derived by the member in the conduct or winding up of the company's business or derived from a use by the member of the company's property, including the appropriation of a company's opportunity;

(2) to refrain from dealing with the company in the conduct or winding up of the company's business as or on behalf of a party having an interest adverse to the company; and

(3) to refrain from competing with the company in the conduct of the company's business before the dissolution of the company.

(c) A member's duty of care to a member-managed company and its other members in the conduct of and winding up of the company's business is limited to refraining from engaging in grossly negligent or reckless conduct, intentional misconduct, or a knowing violation of law.

(d) A member shall discharge the duties to a member-managed company and its other members under this [Act] or under the operating agreement and exercise any rights consistently with the obligation of good faith and fair dealing.

(e) A member of a member-managed company does not violate a duty or obligation under this [Act] or under the operating agreement merely because the member's conduct furthers the member's own inter-est.

(f) A member of a member-managed company may lend money to and transact other business with the company. As to each loan or transaction, the rights and obligations of the member are the same as those of a person who is not a member, subject to other applicable law.

(g) This section applies to a person winding up the limited liability company's business as the personal or legal representative of the last surviving member as if the person were a member.

(h) In a manager-managed company:

(1) a member who is not also a manager owes no duties to the company or to the other members solely by reason of being a member;

(2) a manager is held to the same standards of conduct pre-scribed for members in subsections (b) through (f);

(3) a member who pursuant to the operating agreement exercis-es some or all of the rights of a manager in the management and conduct of the company's business is held to the standards of conduct in subsections (b) through (f) to the extent that the member exercises the managerial authority vested in a manager by this [Act]; and

(4) a manager is relieved of liability imposed by law for viola-tion of the standards prescribed by subsections (b) through (f) to the extent of the managerial authority delegated to the members by the operating agreement.

Comment:

Under subsections (a), (c), and (h), members and managers, and their delegatees, owe to the company and to the other members and managers only the fiduciary duties of loyalty and care set forth in subsections (b) and (c) and the obligation of good faith and fair dealing set forth in subsection (d). An operating agreement may not waive or eliminate the duties or obligation, but may, if not manifestly unreasonable, identify activities and determine standards for measuring the performance of them. See Section 103(b)(2) to (4).

Upon a member's dissociation, the duty to account for personal profits under subsection (b)(1), the duty to refrain from acting as or representing adverse interests under subsection (b)(2), and the duty of care under subsection (c) are limited to those derived from matters arising or events occurring before the dissociation unless the member participates in winding up the company's business. Also, the duty not to compete terminates upon dissociation. See Section 603(b)(3) and (b)(2). However, a dissociated member is not free to use confidential company information after dissociation. For example, a dissociated member of a company may immediately compete with the company for new clients but must exercise care in completing on-going client transactions and must account to the company for any fees from the old clients on account of those transactions. Subsection (c) adopts a gross negligence standard for the duty of care, the standard actually used in most partnerships and corporations.

Subsection (b)(2) prohibits a member from acting adversely or representing an adverse party to the company. The rule is based on agency principles and seeks to avoid the conflict of opposing interests in the mind of the member agent whose duty is to act for the benefit of the principal company. As reflected in subsection (f), the rule does not prohibit the member from dealing with the company other than as an adversary. A member may generally deal with the company under subsection (f) when the transaction is approved by the company.

Subsection (e) makes clear that a member does not violate the obligation of good faith under subsection (d) merely because the member's conduct furthers that member's own interest. For example, a member's refusal to vote for an interim distribution because of negative tax implications to that member does not violate that member's obligation of good faith to the other members. Likewise, a member may vote against a proposal by the company to open a shopping center that would directly compete with another shopping center in which the member owns an interest.

Section 410.   Actions by Members.

(a) A member may maintain an action against a limited liability company or another member for legal or equitable relief, with or without an accounting as to the company's business, to enforce:

(1) the member's rights under the operating agreement;

(2) the member's rights under this [Act]; and

(3) the rights and otherwise protect the interests of the member, including rights and interests arising independently of the member's relationship to the company.

(b) The accrual, and any time limited for the assertion, of a right of action for a remedy under this section is governed by other law. A right to an accounting upon a dissolution and winding up does not revive a claim barred by law.

Comment:

During the existence of the company, members have under this section access to the courts to resolve claims against the company and other members, leaving broad judicial discretion to fashion appropriate legal remedies. A member pursues only that member's claim against the company or another member under this section. Article 11 governs a member's derivative pursuit of a claim on behalf of the company.

A member may recover against the company and the other members under subsection (a)(3) for personal injuries or damage to the member's property caused by another member. One member's negligence is therefore not imputed to bar another member's action.

Section 411. Continuation of Term Company After Expiration of Specified Term.

(a) If a term company is continued after the expiration of the specified term, the rights and duties of the members and managers remain the same as they were at the expiration of the term except to the extent inconsistent with rights and duties of members and managers of an at-will company.

(b) If the members in a member-managed company or the managers in a manager-managed company continue the business without any winding up of the business of the company, it continues as an at-will company.

Comment:

A term company will generally dissolve upon the expiration of its term unless either its articles are amended before the expiration of the original specified term to provide for an additional specified term or the members or managers simply continue the company as an at-will company under this section. Amendment of the articles specifying an additional term requires the unanimous consent of the members. See Section 404(c)(3). Therefore, any member has the right to block the amendment. Absent an amendment to the articles, a company may only be continued under subsection (b) as an at-will company. The decision to continue a term company as an at-will company does not require the unanimous consent of the members and is treated as an ordinary business matter with disputes resolved by a simple majority vote of either the members or managers. See Section 404. In that case, subsection (b) provides that the members' conduct amends or becomes part of an operating agreement to "continue" the company as an at-will company. The amendment to the operating agreement does not alter the rights of creditors who suffer detrimental reliance because the company does not liquidate after the expiration of its specified term. See Section 203(c)(2).

Preexisting operating-agreement provisions continue to control the relationship of the members under subsection (a) except to the extent inconsistent with the rights and duties of members of an at-will company with an operating agreement containing the same provisions. However, the members could agree in advance that, if the company's business continues after the expiration of its specified term, the company continues as a company with a new specified term or that the provisions of its operating agreement survive the expiration of the specified term.

[ARTICLE] 5

TRANSFEREES AND CREDITORS OF MEMBER

Sec.
501. Member's Distributional Interest.
502. Transfer of Distributional Interest.
503. Rights of Transferee.
504. Rights of Creditor.

Section 501.   Member's Distributional Interest.

(a) A member is not a co-owner of, and has no transferable interest in, property of a limited liability company.

(b) A distributional interest in a limited liability company is personal property and, subject to Sections 502 and 503, may be transferred in whole or in part.

(c) An operating agreement may provide that a distributional interest may be evidenced by a certificate of the interest issued by the limited liability company and, subject to Section 503, may also provide for the transfer of any interest represented by the certificate.

Comment:

Members have no property interest in property owned by a limited liability company. A distributional interest is personal property and is defined under Section 101(6) as a member's interest in distributions only and does not include the member's broader rights to participate in management under Section 404 and to inspect company records under Section 408.

Under Section 405(a), distributions are allocated in equal shares unless otherwise provided in an operating agreement. Whenever it is desirable to allocate distributions in proportion to contributions rather than per capita, certification may be useful to reduce valuation issues. The effect of certification on the Federal tax classification of the company is determined by federal law.

Section 502.   Transfer of Distributional Interest.

A transfer of a distributional interest does not entitle the transferee to become or to exercise any rights of a member. A transfer entitles the transferee to receive, to the extent transferred, only the distributions to which the transferor would be entitled.

Comment:

Under Sections 501(b) and 502, the only interest a member may freely transfer is that member's distributional interest. A member's transfer of part, all, or substantially all of a distributional interest will threaten the dissolution of the company under Section 801(b)(3)(i) only if the transfer constitutes an event of dissociation. See Section 601(3). Member dissociation has defined dissolution consequences under Section 801(b)(3)(i) depending upon whether the company is an at-will or term company and whether it is member- or manager-managed. Only the transfer of all or substantially all of a member's distributional interest constitutes or may constitute a member dissociation. A transfer of less than substantially all of a member's distributional interest is not an event of dissociation. A member ceases to be a member upon the transfer of all that member's distributional interest and that transfer is also an event of dissociation under Section 601(3). Relating the event of dissociation to the member's transfer of all of the member's distributional interest avoids the need for the company to track potential future dissociation events associated with a member no longer financially interested in the company. Also, all the remaining members may expel a member upon the transfer of "substantially all" the member's distributional interest. The expulsion is an event of dissociation under Section 601(5)(ii).

Section 503.   Rights of Transferee.

(a) A transferee of a distributional interest may become a member of a limited liability company if and to the extent that the transferor gives the transferee the right in accordance with authority described in the operating agreement or all other members consent.

(b) A transferee who has become a member, to the extent transferred, has the rights and powers, and is subject to the restrictions and liabilities, of a member under the operating agreement of a limited liability company and this [Act]. A transferee who becomes a member also is liable for the transferor member's obligations to make contributions under Section 402 and for obligations under Section 407 to return unlawful distributions, but the transferee is not obligated for the transferor member's liabilities unknown to the transferee at the time the transferee becomes a member.

(c) Whether or not a transferee of a distributional interest becomes a member under subsection (a), the transferor is not released from liability to the limited liability company under the operating agreement or this [Act].

(d) A transferee who does not become a member is not entitled to participate in the management or conduct of the limited liability company's business, require access to information concerning the company's transactions, or inspect or copy any of the company's records.

(e) A transferee who does not become a member is entitled to:

(1) receive, in accordance with the transfer, distributions to which the transferor would otherwise be entitled;

(2) receive, upon dissolution and winding up of the limited liability company's business:

(i) in accordance with the transfer, the net amount otherwise distributable to the transferor;

(ii) a statement of account only from the date of the latest statement of account agreed to by all the members;

(3) seek under Section 801(5) a judicial determination that it is equitable to dissolve and wind up the company's business.

(f) A limited liability company need not give effect to a transfer until it has notice of the transfer.

Comment:

The only interest a member may freely transfer is the member's distributional interest. A transferee may acquire the remaining rights of a member only by being admitted as a member of the company by all of the remaining members. The effect of these default rules and any modifications on the Federal tax classification of the company is determined by federal law.

A transferee not admitted as a member is not entitled to participate in management, require access to information, or inspect or copy company records. The only rights of a transferee are to receive the distributions the transferor would otherwise be entitled, receive a limited statement of account, and seek a judicial dissolution under Section 801(b)(6).

Subsection (e) sets forth the rights of a transferee of an existing member. Although the rights of a dissociated member to participate in the future management of the company parallel the rights of a transferee, a dissociated member retains additional rights that accrued from that person's membership such as the right to enforce Article 7 purchase rights. See and compare Sections 603(b)(1) and 801(b)(5) and Comments.

Section 504. Rights of Creditor.

(a) On application by a judgment creditor of a member of a limited liability company or of a member's transferee, a court having jurisdiction may charge the distributional interest of the judgment debtor to satisfy the judgment. The court may appoint a receiver of the share of the distributions due or to become due to the judgment debtor and make all other orders, directions, accounts, and inquiries the judgment debtor might have made or which the circumstances may require to give effect to the charging order.

(b) A charging order constitutes a lien on the judgment debtor's distributional interest. The court may order a foreclosure of a lien on a distributional interest subject to the charging order at any time. A purchaser at the foreclosure sale has the rights of a transferee.

(c) At any time before foreclosure, a distributional interest in a limited liability company which is charged may be redeemed:

(1) by the judgment debtor;

(2) with property other than the company's property, by one or more of the other members; or

(3) with the company's property, but only if permitted by the operating agreement.

(d) This [Act] does not affect a member's right under exemption laws with respect to the member's distributional interest in a limited liability company.

(e) This section provides the exclusive remedy by which a judgment creditor of a member or a transferee may satisfy a judgment out of the judgment debtor's distributional interest in a limited liability company.

Comment:

A charging order is the only remedy by which a judgment creditor of a member or a member's transferee may reach the distributional interest of a member or member's transferee. Under Section 503(e), the distributional interest of a member or transferee is limited to the member's right to receive distributions from the company and to seek judicial liquidation of the company.

[ARTICLE] 6

MEMBER'S DISSOCIATION

Sec.
601. Events Causing Member's Dissociation.
602. Member's Power to Dissociate; Wrongful Dissociation.
603. Effect of Member's Dissociation.

Section 601. Events Causing Member's Dissociation.

A member is dissociated from a limited liability company upon the occurrence of any of the following events:

(1) the company's having notice of the member's express will to withdraw upon the date of notice or on a later date specified by the member;

(2) an event agreed to in the operating agreement as causing the member's dissociation;

(3) upon transfer of all of a member's distributional interest, other than a transfer for security purposes or a court order charging the member's distributional interest which has not been foreclosed;

(4) the member's expulsion pursuant to the operating agreement;

(5) the member's expulsion by unanimous vote of the other members if:

(i) it is unlawful to carry on the company's business with the member;

(ii) there has been a transfer of substantially all of the member's distributional interest, other than a transfer for security purposes or a court order charging the member's distributional interest which has not been foreclosed;

(iii) within 90 days after the company notifies a corporate member that it will be expelled because it has filed a certificate of dissolution or the equivalent, its charter has been revoked, or its right to conduct business has been suspended by the jurisdiction of its incorporation, the member fails to obtain a revocation of the certificate of dissolution or a reinstatement of its charter or its right to conduct business; or

(iv) a partnership or a limited liability company that is a member has been dissolved and its business is being wound up;

(6) on application by the company or another member, the member's expulsion by judicial determination because the member:

(i) engaged in wrongful conduct that adversely and materially affected the company's business;

(ii) willfully or persistently committed a material breach of the operating agreement or of a duty owed to the company or the other members under Section 409; or

(iii) engaged in conduct relating to the company's business which makes it not reasonably practicable to carry on the business with the member;

(7) the member's:

(i) becoming a debtor in bankruptcy;

(ii) executing an assignment for the benefit of creditors;

(iii) seeking, consenting to, or acquiescing in the appointment of a trustee, receiver, or liquidator of the member or of all or substantially all of the member's property; or

(iv) failing, within 90 days after the appointment, to have vacated or stayed the appointment of a trustee, receiver, or liquidator of the member or of all or substantially all of the member's property obtained without the member's consent or acquiescence, or failing within 90 days after the expiration of a stay to have the appointment vacated;

(8) in the case of a member who is an individual:

(i) the member's death;

(ii) the appointment of a guardian or general conservator for the member; or

(iii) a judicial determination that the member has otherwise become incapable of performing the member's duties under the operating agreement;

(9) in the case of a member that is a trust or is acting as a member by virtue of being a trustee of a trust, distribution of the trust's entire rights to receive distributions from the company, but not merely by reason of the substitution of a successor trustee;

(10) in the case of a member that is an estate or is acting as a member by virtue of being a personal representative of an estate, distribution of the estate's entire rights to receive distributions from the company, but not merely the substitution of a successor personal representative; or

(11) termination of the existence of a member if the member is not an individual, estate, or trust other than a business trust.

Comment:

The term "dissociation" refers to the change in the relationships among the dissociated member, the company and the other members caused by a member's ceasing to be associated in the carrying on of the company's business. Member dissociation for any reason from a member-managed at-will company will cause a dissolution of the company under Section 801(b)(3) unless a specified percentage of the remaining members agree to continue the business of the company. If the dissociation does not dissolve the company, the dissociated member's distributional interest must be immediately purchased by the company under Article 7. Member dissociation from a member-managed term company, but only for the reasons specified in paragraphs (7) to (11), will cause a dissolution of the company under Section 801(b)(3) unless a specified percentage of the remaining members agree to continue the business of the company. Member dissociations specified in paragraphs (1) to (6) do not threaten dissolution under Section 801(b)(3) of a member-managed term company. If the dissociation does not dissolve the company, it is not required to purchase the dissociated member's distributional interest until the expiration of the specified term that existed on the date of the member's dissociation. If an at-will company or a term company is manager-managed, only the dissociation of a member who is also a manager or, if there is none, any member specified above threatens dissolution. The effect on the Federal tax classification of the company creating a member-manager with a minimal interest in the company is determined by federal law.

A member may be expelled from the company under paragraph (5)(ii) by the unanimous vote of the other members upon a transfer of "substantially all" of the member's distributional interest other than for a transfer as security for a loan. A transfer of "all" of the member's distributional interest is an event of dissociation under paragraph (3).

Although a member is dissociated upon death, the effect of the dissociation where the company does not dissolve depends upon whether the company is at-will or term and whether manager-managed. Only the decedent's distributional interest transfers to the decedent's estate which does not acquire the decedent member's management rights. See Section 603(b)(1). Unless otherwise agreed, if the company was at-will, the estate's distributional interest must be purchased by the company at fair value determined at the date of death. However, if a term company, the estate and its transferees continue only as the owner of the distributional interest with no management rights until the expiration of the specified term that existed on the date of death. At the expiration of that term, the company must purchase the interest of a dissociated member if the company continues for an additional term by amending its articles or simply continues as an at-will company. See Sections 411 and 701(a)(2) and Comments. Before that time, the estate and its transferees have the right to make application for a judicial dissolution of the company under Section 801(b)(5) as successors in interest to a dissociated member. See Comments to Sections 801, 411, and 701. Where the members have allocated management rights on the basis of contributions rather than simply the number of members, a member's death will result in a transfer of management rights to the remaining members on a proportionate basis. This transfer of rights may be avoided by a provision in an operating agreement extending the Section 701(a)(1) at-will purchase right to a decedent member of a term company.

Section 602. Member's Power to Dissociate; Wrongful Dissociation.

(a) Unless otherwise provided in the operating agreement, a member has the power to dissociate from a limited liability company at any time, rightfully or wrongfully, by express will pursuant to Section 601(1).

(b) If the operating agreement has not eliminated a member's power to dissociate, the member's dissociation from a limited liability company is wrongful only if:

(1) it is in breach of an express provision of the agreement; or

(2) before the expiration of the specified term of a term company:

(i) the member withdraws by express will;

(ii) the member is expelled by judicial determination under Section 601(6);

(iii) the member is dissociated by becoming a debtor in bankruptcy; or

(iv) in the case of a member who is not an individual, trust other than a business trust, or estate, the member is expelled or otherwise dissociated because it willfully dissolved or terminated its existence.

(c) A member who wrongfully dissociates from a limited liability company is liable to the company and to the other members for damages caused by the dissociation. The liability is in addition to any other obligation of the member to the company or to the other members.

(d) If a limited liability company does not dissolve and wind up its business as a result of a member's wrongful dissociation under subsection (b), damages sustained by the company for the wrongful dissociation must be offset against distributions otherwise due the member after the dissociation.

Comment:

A member has the power to withdraw from both an at-will company and a term company although the effects of the withdrawal are remarkably different. See Comments to Section 601. At a minimum, the exercise of a power to withdraw enables members to terminate their continuing duties of loyalty and care. See Section 603(b)(2) to (3).

A member's power to withdraw by express will may be eliminated by an operating agreement. The effect of such a provision on the Federal tax classification of the company is determined by federal law. An operating agreement may eliminate a member's power to withdraw by express will to promote the business continuity of an at-will company by removing the threat of dissolution and to eliminate the member's right to force the company to purchase the member's distributional interest. See Sections 801(b)(3) and 701(a)(1). However, such a member retains the ability to seek a judicial dissolution of the company. See Section 801(b)(5).

If a member's power to withdraw by express will is not eliminated in an operating agreement, the withdrawal may nevertheless be made wrongful under subsection (b). All dissociations, including withdrawal by express will, may be made wrongful under subsection (b)(1) in both an at-will and term company by the inclusion of a provision in an operating agreement. Even where an operating agreement does not eliminate the power to withdraw by express will or make any dissociation wrongful, the dissociation of a member of a term company for the reasons specified under subsection (b)(2) is wrongful. The member is liable to the company and other members for damages caused by a wrongful dissociation under subsection (c) and, under subsection (d), the damages may be offset against all distributions otherwise due the member after the dissociation. Section 701(f) provides a similar rule permitting damages for wrongful dissociation to be offset against any company purchase of the member's distributional interest.

Section 603.   Effect of Member's Dissociation.

(a) Upon a member's dissociation;

   (1) in an at-will company, the company must cause the dissociated member's distributional interest to be purchased under [Article] 7; and

   (2) in a term company:

      (i) if the company dissolves and winds up its business on or before the expiration of its specified term, [Article] 8 applies to determine the dissociated member's rights to distributions; and

      (ii) if the company does not dissolve and wind up its business on or before the expiration of its specified term, the company must cause the dissociated member's distributional interest to be purchased under [Article] 7 on the date of the expiration of the term specified at the time of the member's dissociation.

(b) Upon a member's dissociation from a limited liability company:

   (1) the member's right to participate in the management and conduct of the company's business terminates, except as otherwise provided in Section 803, and the member ceases to be a member and is treated the same as a transferee of a member;

   (2) the member's duty of loyalty under Section 409(b)(3) terminates; and

   (3) the member's duty of loyalty under Section 409(b)(1) and (2) and duty of care under Section 409(c) continue only with regard to matters arising and events occurring before the member's dissociation, unless the member participates in winding up the company's business pursuant to Section 803.

Comment:

Dissociation from an at-will company that does not dissolve the company causes the dissociated member's distributional interest to be immediately purchased under Article 7. See Comments to Sections 602 and 603. Dissociation from a term company that does not dissolve the company does not cause the dissociated member's distributional interest to be purchased under Article 7 until the expiration of the specified term that existed on the date of dissociation.

Subsection (b)(1) provides that a dissociated member forfeits the right to participate in the future conduct of the company's business. Dissociation does not however forfeit that member's right to enforce the Article 7 rights that accrue by reason of the dissociation. Similarly, where dissociation occurs by death, the decedent member's successors in interest may enforce that member's Article 7 rights. See and compare Comments to Section 503(e).

Dissociation terminates the member's right to participate in management, including the member's actual authority to act for the company under Section 301, and begins the two-year period after which a member's apparent authority conclusively ends. See Comments to Section 703. Dissociation also terminates a member's continuing duties of loyalty and care, except with regard to continuing transactions, to the company and other members unless the member participates in winding up the company's business. See Comments to Section 409.

[ARTICLE] 7

MEMBER'S DISSOCIATION WHEN BUSINESS NOT WOUND UP

Sec.
701. Company Purchase of Distributional Interest.
702. Court Action to Determine Fair Value of Distributional Interest.
703. Dissociated Member's Power to Bind Limited Liability Company.
704. Statement of Dissociation.

Section 701. Company Purchase of Distributional Interest.

(a) A limited liability company shall purchase a distributional interest of a:

(1) member of an at-will company for its fair value determined as of the date of the member's dissociation if the member's dissociation does not result in a dissolution and winding up of the company's business under Section 801; or

(2) member of a term company for its fair value determined as of the date of the expiration of the specified term that existed on the

date of the member's dissociation if the expiration of the specified term does not result in a dissolution and winding up of the company's business under Section 801.

(b) A limited liability company must deliver a purchase offer to the dissociated member whose distributional interest is entitled to be purchased not later than 30 days after the date determined under subsection (a). The purchase offer must be accompanied by:

   (1) a statement of the company's assets and liabilities as of the date determined under subsection (a);

   (2) the latest available balance sheet and income statement, if any; and

   (3) an explanation of how the estimated amount of the payment was calculated.

(c) If the price and other terms of a purchase of a distributional interest are fixed or are to be determined by the operating agreement, the price and terms so fixed or determined govern the purchase unless the purchaser defaults. If a default occurs, the dissociated member is entitled to commence a proceeding to have the company dissolved under Section 801(4)(iv).

(d) If an agreement to purchase the distributional interest is not made within 120 days after the date determined under subsection (a), the dissociated member, within another 120 days, may commence a proceeding against the limited liability company to enforce the purchase. The company at its expense shall notify in writing all of the remaining members, and any other person the court directs, of the commencement of the proceeding. The jurisdiction of the court in which the proceeding is commenced under this subsection is plenary and exclusive.

(e) The court shall determine the fair value of the distributional interest in accordance with the standards set forth in Section 702 together with the terms for the purchase. Upon making these determinations, the court shall order the limited liability company to purchase or cause the purchase of the interest.

(f) Damages for wrongful dissociation under Section 602(b), and all other amounts owing, whether or not currently due, from the dissociated member to a limited liability company, must be offset against the purchase price.

Comment:

This section sets forth default rules regarding an otherwise mandatory company purchase of a distributional interest. Even though a dissociated member's rights to participate in the future management of the company are equivalent to those of a transferee of a member, the dissociation does not forfeit that member's right to enforce the Article 7 purchase right. Similarly, if the dissociation occurs by reason of death, the decedent member's successors in interest may enforce the Article 7 rights. See Comments to Sections 503(e) and 603(b)(1).

An at-will company must purchase a dissociated member's distributional interest under subsection (a)(1) when that member's dissociation does not result in a dissolution of the company. The purchase price is equal to the fair value of the interest determined as of the date of dissociation. Any damages for wrongful dissociation must be offset against the purchase price.

Dissociation from a term company does not require an immediate purchase of the member's interest but certain types of dissociation may cause the dissolution of the company. See Section 801(b)(3). A term company must only purchase the dissociated member's distributional interest under subsection (a)(2) on the expiration of the specified term that existed on the date of the member's dissociation. The purchase price is equal to the fair value of the interest determined as of the date of the expiration of that specified term. Any damages for wrongful dissociation must be offset against the purchase price.

The valuation dates differ between subsections (a)(1) and (a)(2) purchases. The former is valued on the date of member dissociation whereas the latter is valued on the date of the expiration of the specified term that existed on the date of dissociation. A subsection (a)(2) dissociated member therefore assumes the risk of loss between the date of dissociation and the expiration of the then stated specified term. See Comments to Section 801 (dissociated member may file application to dissolve company under Section 801(b)(6)).

The default valuation standard is fair value. See Comments to Section 702. An operating agreement may fix a method or formula for determining the purchase price and the terms of payment. The purchase right may be modified. For example, an operating agreement may eliminate a member's power to withdraw from an at-will company which narrows the dissociation events contemplated under subsection (a)(1). See Comments to Section 602(a). However, a provision in an operating agreement providing for complete forfeiture of the purchase right be unenforceable where the power to dissociate has not also been eliminated. See Section 104(a).

The company must deliver a purchase offer to the dissociated member within 30 days after the date determined under subsection (a). The offer must be accompanied by information designed to enable the dissociated member to evaluate the fairness of the offer. The subsection (b)(3) explanation of how the offer price was calculated need not be elaborate. For example, a mere statement of the basis of the calculation, such as "book value," may be sufficient.

The company and the dissociated member must reach an agreement on the purchase price and terms within 120 days after the date determined under subsection (a). Otherwise, the dissociated member may file suit within another 120 days to enforce the purchase under subsection (d). The court will then determine the fair value and terms of purchase under subsection (e). See Section 702. The member's lawsuit is not available under subsection (c) if the parties have previously agreed to price and terms in an operating agreement.

Section 702. Court Action to Determine Fair Value of Distributional Interest.

(a) In an action brought to determine the fair value of a distributional interest in a limited liability company, the court shall:

(1) determine the fair value of the interest, considering among other relevant evidence the going concern value of the company, any agreement among some or all of the members fixing the price or specifying a formula for determining value of distributional interests for any other purpose, the recommendations of any appraiser appointed by the court, and any legal constraints on the company's ability to purchase the interest;

(2) specify the terms of the purchase, including, if appropriate, terms for installment payments, subordination of the purchase obligation to the rights of the company's other creditors, security for a deferred purchase price, and a covenant not to compete or other restriction on a dissociated member; and

(3) require the dissociated member to deliver an assignment of the interest to the purchaser upon receipt of the purchase price or the first installment of the purchase price.

(b) After the dissociated member delivers the assignment, the dissociated member has no further claim against the company, its members, officers, or managers, if any, other than a claim to any unpaid balance of the purchase price and a claim under any agreement with the company or the remaining members that is not terminated by the court.

(c) If the purchase is not completed in accordance with the specified terms, the company is to be dissolved upon application under Section 801(b)(5)(iv). If a limited liability company is so dissolved, the dissociated member has the same rights and priorities in the company's assets as if the sale had not been ordered.

(d) If the court finds that a party to the proceeding acted arbitrarily, vexatiously, or not in good faith, it may award one or more other parties their reasonable expenses, including attorney's fees and the expenses of appraisers or other experts, incurred in the proceeding. The finding may be based on the company's failure to make an offer to pay or to comply with Section 701(b).

(e) Interest must be paid on the amount awarded from the date determined under Section 701(a) to the date of payment.

Comment:

The default valuation standard is fair value. Under this broad standard, a court is free to determine the fair value of a distributional interest on a fair market, liquidation, or any other method deemed appropriate under the circumstances. A fair market value standard is not used because it is too narrow, often inappropriate, and assumes a fact not contemplated by this section—a willing buyer and a willing seller.

The court has discretion under subsection (a)(2) to include in its order any conditions the court deems necessary to safeguard the interests of the company and the dissociated member or transferee. The discretion may be based on the financial and other needs of the parties.

If the purchase is not consummated or the purchaser defaults, the dissociated member or transferee may make application for dissolution of the company under subsection (c). The court may deny the petition for good cause but the proceeding affords the company an opportunity to be heard on the matter and avoid dissolution. See Comments to Section 801(b)(5).

The power of the court to award all costs and attorney's fees incurred in the suit under subsection (d) is an incentive for both parties to act in good faith. See Section 701(c).

Section 703. Dissociated Member's Power to Bind Limited Liability Company.

For two years after a member dissociates without the dissociation resulting in a dissolution and winding up of a limited liability company's business, the company, including a surviving company under [Article] 9, is bound by an act of the dissociated member which would have bound the company under Section 301 before dissociation only if at the time of entering into the transaction the other party:

(1) reasonably believed that the dissociated member was then a member;

(2) did not have notice of the member's dissociation; and

(3) is not deemed to have had notice under Section 704.

Comment:

A dissociated member of a member-managed company does not have actual authority to act for the company. See Section 603(b)(1). Under Section 301(a), a dissociated member of a member-managed company has apparent authority to bind the company in ordinary course transactions except as to persons who knew or had notice of the dissociation. This section modifies that rule by requiring the person to show reasonable reliance on the member's status as a member provided a Section 704 statement has not been filed within the previous 90 days. See also Section 804 (power to bind after dissolution).

Section 704. Statement of Dissociation.

(a) A dissociated member or a limited liability company may file in the office of the [Secretary of State] a statement of dissociation stating the name of the company and that the member is dissociated from the company.

(b) For the purposes of Sections 301 and 703, a person not a member is deemed to have notice of the dissociation 90 days after the statement of dissociation is filed.

[ARTICLE] 8

WINDING UP COMPANY'S BUSINESS

Section 801. Events Causing Dissolution and Winding Up of Company's Business.

A limited liability company is dissolved, and its business must be wound up, upon the occurrence of any of the following events:

(1) an event specified in the operating agreement;

(2) consent of the number or percentage of members specified in the operating agreement;

(3) an event that makes it unlawful for all or substantially all of the business of the company to be continued, but any cure of

illegality within 90 days after notice to the company of the event is effective retroactively to the date of the event for purposes of this section;

(4) on application by a member or a dissociated member, upon entry of a judicial decree that:

(i) the economic purpose of the company is likely to be unreasonably frustrated;

(ii) another member has engaged in conduct relating to the company's business that makes it not reasonably practicable to carry on the company's business with that member;

(iii) it is not otherwise reasonably practicable to carry on the company's business in conformity with the articles of organization and the operating agreement;

(iv) the company failed to purchase the petitioner's distributional interest as required by Section 701; or

(v) the managers or members in control of the company have acted, are acting, or will act in a manner that is illegal, oppressive, fraudulent, or unfairly prejudicial to the petitioner; or

(5) on application by a transferee of a member's interest, a judicial determination that it is equitable to wind up the company's business:

(i) after the expiration of the specified term, if the company was for a specified term at the time the applicant became a transferee by member dissociation, transfer, or entry of a charging order that gave rise to the transfer; or

(ii) at any time, if the company was at will at the time the applicant became a transferee by member dissociation, transfer, or entry of a charging order that gave rise to the transfer.

Section 802.   Limited Liability Company Continues After Dissolution.

(a) Subject to subsection (b), a limited liability company continues after dissolution only for the purpose of winding up its business.

(b) At any time after the dissolution of a limited liability company and before the winding up of its business is completed, the members, including a dissociated member whose dissociation caused the dissolution, may unanimously waive the right to have the company's business wound up and the company terminated. In that case:

(1) the limited liability company resumes carrying on its business as if dissolution had never occurred and any liability incurred by the company or a member after the dissolution and before the waiver is determined as if the dissolution had never occurred; and

(2) the rights of a third party accruing under Section 804(a) or arising out of conduct in reliance on the dissolution before the third party knew or received a notification of the waiver are not adversely affected.

Comment:

The liability shield continues in effect for the winding up period because the legal existence of the company continues under subsection (a). The company is terminated on the filing of articles of termination. See Section 805.

Section 803. Right to Wind Up Limited Liability Company's Business.

(a) After dissolution, a member who has not wrongfully dissociated may participate in winding up a limited liability company's business, but on application of any member, member's legal representative, or transferee, the [designate the appropriate court], for good cause shown, may order judicial supervision of the winding up.

(b) A legal representative of the last surviving member may wind up a limited liability company's business.

(c) A person winding up a limited liability company's business may preserve the company's business or property as a going concern for a reasonable time, prosecute and defend actions and proceedings, whether civil, criminal, or administrative, settle and close the company's business, dispose of and transfer the company's property, discharge the company's liabilities, distribute the assets of the company pursuant to Section 806, settle disputes by mediation or arbitration, and perform other necessary acts.

Section 804. Member's or Manager's Power and Liability as Agent After Dissolution.

(a) A limited liability company is bound by a member's or manager's act after dissolution that:

(1) is appropriate for winding up the company's business; or

(2) would have bound the company under Section 301 before dissolution, if the other party to the transaction did not have notice of the dissolution.

(b) A member or manager who, with knowledge of the dissolution, subjects a limited liability company to liability by an act that is not appropriate for winding up the company's business is liable to the company for any damage caused to the company arising from the liability.

471

Comment:

After dissolution, members and managers continue to have the authority to bind the company that they had prior to dissolution provided that the third party did not have notice of the dissolution. See Section 102(b) (notice defined). Otherwise, they have only the authority appropriate for winding up the company's business. See Section 703 (agency power of member after dissociation).

Section 805. Articles of Termination.

(a) At any time after dissolution and winding up, a limited liability company may terminate its existence by filing with the [Secretary of State] articles of termination stating:

(1) the name of the company;

(2) the date of the dissolution; and

(3) that the company's business has been wound up and the legal existence of the company has been terminated.

(b) The existence of a limited liability company is terminated upon the filing of the articles of termination, or upon a later effective date, if specified in the articles of termination.

Comment:

The termination of legal existence also terminates the company's liability shield. See Comments to Section 802 (liability shield continues in effect during winding up). It also ends the company's responsibility to file an annual report. See Section 211.

Section 806. Distribution of Assets in Winding Up Limited Liability Company's Business.

(a) In winding up a limited liability company's business, the assets of the company must be applied to discharge its obligations to creditors, including members who are creditors. Any surplus must be applied to pay in money the net amount distributable to members in accordance with their right to distributions under subsection (b).

(b) Each member is entitled to a distribution upon the winding up of the limited liability company's business consisting of a return of all contributions which have not previously been returned and a distribution of any remainder in equal shares.

Section 807. Known Claims Against Dissolved Limited Liability Company.

(a) A dissolved limited liability company may dispose of the known claims against it by following the procedure described in this section.

(b) A dissolved limited liability company shall notify its known claimants in writing of the dissolution. The notice must:

(1) specify the information required to be included in a claim;

(2) provide a mailing address where the claim is to be sent;

(3) state the deadline for receipt of the claim, which may not be less than 120 days after the date the written notice is received by the claimant; and

(4) state that the claim will be barred if not received by the deadline.

(c) A claim against a dissolved limited liability company is barred if the requirements of subsection (b) are met, and:

(1) the claim is not received by the specified deadline; or

(2) in the case of a claim that is timely received but rejected by the dissolved company, the claimant does not commence a proceeding to enforce the claim within 90 days after the receipt of the notice of the rejection.

(d) For purposes of this section, "claim" does not include a contingent liability or a claim based on an event occurring after the effective date of dissolution.

Comment:

A known claim will be barred when the company provides written notice to a claimant that a claim must be filed with the company no later than at least 120 days after receipt of the written notice and the claimant fails to file the claim. If the claim is timely received but is rejected by the company, the claim is nevertheless barred unless the claimant files suit to enforce the claim within 90 days after the receipt of the notice of rejection. A claim described in subsection (d) is not a "known" claim and is governed by Section 808. This section does not extend any other applicable statutes of limitation. See Section 104. Depending on the management of the company, members or managers must discharge or make provision for discharging all of the company's known liabilities before distributing the remaining assets to the members. See Sections 806(a), 406, and 407.

Section 808. Other Claims Against Dissolved Limited Liability Company.

(a) A dissolved limited liability company may publish notice of its dissolution and request persons having claims against the company to present them in accordance with the notice.

(b) The notice must:

(1) be published at least once in a newspaper of general circulation in the [county] in which the dissolved limited liability compa-

ny's principal office is located or, if none in this State, in which its designated office is or was last located;

(2) describe the information required to be contained in a claim and provide a mailing address where the claim is to be sent; and

(3) state that a claim against the limited liability company is barred unless a proceeding to enforce the claim is commenced within five years after publication of the notice.

(c) If a dissolved limited liability company publishes a notice in accordance with subsection (b), the claim of each of the following claimants is barred unless the claimant commences a proceeding to enforce the claim against the dissolved company within five years after the publication date of the notice:

(1) a claimant who did not receive written notice under Section 807;

(2) a claimant whose claim was timely sent to the dissolved company but not acted on; and

(3) a claimant whose claim is contingent or based on an event occurring after the effective date of dissolution.

(d) A claim not barred under this section may be enforced:

(1) against the dissolved limited liability company, to the extent of its undistributed assets; or

(2) if the assets have been distributed in liquidation, against a member of the dissolved company to the extent of the member's proportionate share of the claim or the company's assets distributed to the member in liquidation, whichever is less, but a member's total liability for all claims under this section may not exceed the total amount of assets distributed to the member.

Comment:

An unknown claim will be barred when the company publishes notice requesting claimants to file claims with the company and stating that claims will be barred unless the claimant files suit to enforce the claim within five years after the date of publication. The procedure also bars known claims where the claimant either did not receive written notice described in Section 807 or received notice [and] mailed a claim, but the company did not act on the claim.

Depending on the management of the company, members or managers must discharge or make provision for discharging all of the company's known liabilities before distributing the remaining assets to the members. See Comment to Section 807. This section does not contemplate that a company will postpone member distributions until all unknown claims are barred under this section. In appropriate cases, the company may purchase insurance or set aside funds permitting a distribution of the remaining assets. Where winding up distributions have been made to members, subsection (d)(2) authorizes recovery against those members. However, a claimant's recovery against a member is limited to the lesser of the member's proportionate share of the claim or the amount received in the distribution. This section does not extend any other applicable statutes of limitation. See Section 104.

Section 809.   Grounds for Administrative Dissolution.

The [Secretary of State] may commence a proceeding to dissolve a limited liability company administratively if the company does not:

(1) pay any fees, taxes, or penalties imposed by this [Act] or other law within 60 days after they are due; or

(2) deliver its annual report to the [Secretary of State] within 60 days after it is due.

Comment:

Administrative dissolution is an effective enforcement mechanism for a variety of statutory obligations under this Act and it avoids the more expensive judicial dissolution process. When applicable, administrative dissolution avoids wasteful attempts to compel compliance by a company abandoned by its members.

Section 810.   Procedure for and Effect of Administrative Dissolution.

(a) If the [Secretary of State] determines that a ground exists for administratively dissolving a limited liability company, the [Secretary of State] shall enter a record of the determination and serve the company with a copy of the record.

(b) If the company does not correct each ground for dissolution or demonstrate to the reasonable satisfaction of the [Secretary of State] that each ground determined by the [Secretary of State] does not exist within 60 days after service of the notice, the [Secretary of State] shall administratively dissolve the company by signing a certification of the dissolution that recites the ground for dissolution and its effective date. The [Secretary of State] shall file the original of the certificate and serve the company with a copy of the certificate.

(c) A company administratively dissolved continues its existence but may carry on only business necessary to wind up and liquidate its business and affairs under Section 802 and to notify claimants under Sections 807 and 808.

(d) The administrative dissolution of a company does not terminate the authority of its agent for service of process.

Comment:

A company's failure to comply with a ground for administrative dissolution may simply occur because of oversight. Therefore, subsections (a) and (b) set forth a mandatory notice by the filing officer to the company of the ground for dissolution and a 60 day grace period for correcting the ground.

Section 811. Reinstatement Following Administrative Dissolution.

(a) A limited liability company administratively dissolved may apply to the [Secretary of State] for reinstatement within two years after the effective date of dissolution. The application must:

(1) recite the name of the company and the effective date of its administrative dissolution;

(2) state that the ground for dissolution either did not exist or have been eliminated;

(3) state that the company's name satisfies the requirements of Section 105; and

(4) contain a certificate from the [taxing authority] reciting that all taxes owed by the company have been paid.

(b) If the [Secretary of State] determines that the application contains the information required by subsection (a) and that the information is correct, the [Secretary of State] shall cancel the certificate of dissolution and prepare a certificate of reinstatement that recites this determination and the effective date of reinstatement, file the original of the certificate, and serve the company with a copy of the certificate.

(c) When reinstatement is effective, it relates back to and takes effect as of the effective date of the administrative dissolution and the company may resume its business as if the administrative dissolution had never occurred.

Section 812. Appeal From Denial of Reinstatement.

(a) If the [Secretary of State] denies a limited liability company's application for reinstatement following administrative dissolution, the [Secretary of State] shall serve the company with a record that explains the reason or reasons for denial.

(b) The company may appeal the denial of reinstatement to the [name appropriate] court within 30 days after service of the notice of denial is perfected. The company appeals by petitioning the court to set aside the dissolution and attaching to the petition copies of the [Secretary of State's] certificate of dissolution, the company's application for reinstatement, and the [Secretary of State's] notice of denial.

(c) The court may summarily order the [Secretary of State] to reinstate the dissolved company or may take other action the court considers appropriate.

(d) The court's final decision may be appealed as in other civil proceedings.

[ARTICLE] 9

CONVERSIONS AND MERGERS

Sec.
901. Definitions.
902. Conversion of Partnership or Limited Partnership To Limited Liability Company.
903. Effect of Conversion; Entity Unchanged.
904. Merger of Entities.
905. Articles of Merger.
906. Effect of Merger.
907. [Article] Not Exclusive.

Section 901. Definitions.

In this [article]:

(1) "Corporation" means a corporation under [the State Corporation Act], a predecessor law, or comparable law of another jurisdiction.

(2) "General partner" means a partner in a partnership and a general partner in a limited partnership.

(3) "Limited partner" means a limited partner in a limited partnership.

(4) "Limited partnership" means a limited partnership created under [the State Limited Partnership Act], a predecessor law, or comparable law of another jurisdiction.

(5) "Partner" includes a general partner and a limited partner.

(6) "Partnership" means a general partnership under [the State Partnership Act], a predecessor law, or comparable law of another jurisdiction.

(7) "Partnership agreement" means an agreement among the partners concerning the partnership or limited partnership.

(8) "Shareholder" means a shareholder in a corporation.

Comment:

Section 907 makes clear that the provisions of Article 9 are not mandatory. Therefore, a partnership or a limited liability company

477

may convert or merge in any other manner provided by law. However, if the requirements of Article 9 are followed, the conversion or merger is legally valid. Article 9 is not restricted to domestic business entities.

Section 902. Conversion of Partnership or Limited Partnership to Limited Liability Company.

(a) A partnership or limited partnership may be converted to a limited liability company pursuant to this section.

(b) The terms and conditions of a conversion of a partnership or limited partnership to a limited liability company must be approved by all of the partners or by a number or percentage of the partners required for conversion in the partnership agreement.

(c) An agreement of conversion must set forth the terms and conditions of the conversion of the interests of partners of a partnership or of a limited partnership, as the case may be, into interests in the converted limited liability company or the cash or other consideration to be paid or delivered as a result of the conversion of the interests of the partners, or a combination thereof.

(d) After a conversion is approved under subsection (b), the partnership or limited partnership shall file articles of organization in the office of the [Secretary of State] which satisfy the requirements of Section 203 and contain:

(1) a statement that the partnership or limited partnership was converted to a limited liability company from a partnership or limited partnership, as the case may be;

(2) its former name;

(3) a statement of the number of votes cast by the partners entitled to vote for and against the conversion and, if the vote is less than unanimous, the number or percentage required to approve the conversion under subsection (b); and

(4) in the case of a limited partnership, a statement that the certificate of limited partnership is to be canceled as of the date the conversion took effect.

(e) In the case of a limited partnership, the filing of articles of organization under subsection (d) cancels its certificate of limited partnership as of the date the conversion took effect.

(f) A conversion takes effect when the articles of organization are filed in the office of the [Secretary of State] or at any later date specified in the articles of organization.

(g) A general partner who becomes a member of a limited liability company as a result of a conversion remains liable as a partner for an obligation incurred by the partnership or limited partnership before the conversion takes effect.

(h) A general partner's liability for all obligations of the limited liability company incurred after the conversion takes effect is that of a member of the company. A limited partner who becomes a member as a result of a conversion remains liable only to the extent the limited partner was liable for an obligation incurred by the limited partnership before the conversion takes effect.

Comment:

Subsection (b) makes clear that the terms and conditions of the conversion of a general or limited partnership to a limited liability company must be approved by all of the partners unless the partnership agreement specifies otherwise.

Section 903. Effect of Conversion; Entity Unchanged.

(a) A partnership or limited partnership that has been converted pursuant to this [article] is for all purposes the same entity that existed before the conversion.

(b) When a conversion takes effect:

(1) all property owned by the converting partnership or limited partnership vests in the limited liability company;

(2) all debts, liabilities, and other obligations of the converting partnership or limited partnership continue as obligations of the limited liability company;

(3) an action or proceeding pending by or against the converting partnership or limited partnership may be continued as if the conversion had not occurred;

(4) except as prohibited by other law, all of the rights, privileges, immunities, powers, and purposes of the converting partnership or limited partnership vest in the limited liability company; and

(5) except as otherwise provided in the agreement of conversion under Section 902(c), all of the partners of the converting partnership continue as members of the limited liability company.

Comment:

A conversion is not a conveyance or transfer and does not give rise to claims of reverter or impairment of title based on a prohibited conveyance or transfer. Under subsection (b)(1), title to all partnership property, including real estate, vests in the limited liability company as a matter of law without reversion or impairment.

Section 904.   Merger of Entities.

(a) Pursuant to a plan of merger approved under subsection (c), a limited liability company may be merged with or into one or more limited liability companies, foreign limited liability companies, corporations, foreign corporations, partnerships, foreign partnerships, limited partnerships, foreign limited partnerships, or other domestic or foreign entities.

(b) A plan of merger must set forth:

(1) the name of each entity that is a party to the merger;

(2) the name of the surviving entity into which the other entities will merge;

(3) the type of organization of the surviving entity;

(4) the terms and conditions of the merger;

(5) the manner and basis for converting the interests of each party to the merger into interests or obligations of the surviving entity, or into money or other property in whole or in part; and

(6) the street address of the surviving entity's principal place of business.

(c) A plan of merger must be approved:

(1) in the case of a limited liability company that is a party to the merger, by all of the members or by a number or percentage of members specified in the operating agreement;

(2) in the case of a foreign limited liability company that is a party to the merger, by the vote required for approval of a merger by the law of the State or foreign jurisdiction in which the foreign limited liability company is organized;

(3) in the case of a partnership or domestic limited partnership that is a party to the merger, by the vote required for approval of a conversion under Section 902(b); and

(4) in the case of any other entities that are parties to the merger, by the vote required for approval of a merger by the law of this State or of the State or foreign jurisdiction in which the entity is organized and, in the absence of such a requirement, by all the owners of interests in the entity.

(d) After a plan of merger is approved and before the merger takes effect, the plan may be amended or abandoned as provided in the plan.

(e) The merger is effective upon the filing of the articles of merger with the [Secretary of State], or at such later date as the articles may provide.

Comment:

This section sets forth a "safe harbor" for cross-entity mergers of limited liability companies with both domestic and foreign: corporations, general and limited partnerships, and other limited liability companies. Subsection (c) makes clear that the terms and conditions of the plan of merger must be approved by all of the partners unless applicable state law specifies otherwise for the merger.

Section 905. Articles of Merger.

(a) After approval of the plan of merger under Section 904(c), unless the merger is abandoned under Section 904(d), articles of merger must be signed on behalf of each limited liability company and other entity that is a party to the merger and delivered to the [Secretary of State] for filing. The articles must set forth:

(1) the name and jurisdiction of formation or organization of each of the limited liability companies and other entities that are parties to the merger;

(2) for each limited liability company that is to merge, the date its articles of organization were filed with the [Secretary of State];

(3) that a plan of merger has been approved and signed by each limited liability company and other entity that is to merge;

(4) the name and address of the surviving limited liability company or other surviving entity;

(5) the effective date of the merger;

(6) if a limited liability company is the surviving entity, such changes in its articles of organization as are necessary by reason of the merger;

(7) if a party to a merger is a foreign limited liability company, the jurisdiction and date of filing of its initial articles of organization and the date when its application for authority was filed by the [Secretary of State] or, if an application has not been filed, a statement to that effect; and

(8) if the surviving entity is not a limited liability company, an agreement that the surviving entity may be served with process in this State and is subject to liability in any action or proceeding for the enforcement of any liability or obligation of any limited liability company previously subject to suit in this State which is to merge, and for the enforcement, as provided in this [Act], of the right of members of any limited liability company to receive payment for their interest against the surviving entity.

(b) If a foreign limited liability company is the surviving entity of a merger, it may not do business in this State until an application for that authority is filed with the [Secretary of State].

(c) The surviving limited liability company or other entity shall furnish a copy of the plan of merger, on request and without cost, to any member of any limited liability company or any person holding an interest in any other entity that is to merge.

(d) Articles of merger operate as an amendment to the limited liability company's articles of organization.

Section 906.   Effect of Merger.

(a) When a merger takes effect:

(1) the separate existence of each limited liability company and other entity that is a party to the merger, other than the surviving entity, terminates;

(2) all property owned by each of the limited liability companies and other entities that are party to the merger vests in the surviving entity;

(3) all debts, liabilities, and other obligations of each limited liability company and other entity that is party to the merger become the obligations of the surviving entity;

(4) an action or proceeding pending by or against a limited liability company or other party to a merger may be continued as if the merger had not occurred or the surviving entity may be substituted as a party to the action or proceeding; and

(5) except as prohibited by other law, all the rights, privileges, immunities, powers, and purposes of every limited liability company and other entity that is a party to a merger vest in the surviving entity.

(b) The [Secretary of State] is an agent for service of process in an action or proceeding against the surviving foreign entity to enforce an obligation of any party to a merger if the surviving foreign entity fails to appoint or maintain an agent designated for service of process in this State or the agent for service of process cannot with reasonable diligence be found at the designated office.   Upon receipt of process, the [Secretary of State] shall send a copy of the process by registered or certified mail, return receipt requested, to the surviving entity at the address set forth in the articles of merger.   Service is effected under this subsection at the earliest of:

(1) the date the company receives the process, notice, or demand;

(2) the date shown on the return receipt, if signed on behalf of the company; or

(3) five days after its deposit in the mail, if mailed postpaid and correctly addressed.

(c) A member of the surviving limited liability company is liable for all obligations of a party to the merger for which the member was personally liable before the merger.

(d) Unless otherwise agreed, a merger of a limited liability company that is not the surviving entity in the merger does not require the limited liability company to wind up its business under this [Act] or pay its liabilities and distribute its assets pursuant to this [Act].

(e) Articles of merger serve as articles of dissolution for a limited liability company that is not the surviving entity in the merger.

Section 907. [Article] Not Exclusive.

This [article] does not preclude an entity from being converted or merged under other law.

[ARTICLE] 10

FOREIGN LIMITED LIABILITY COMPANIES

Sec.

1001. Law Governing Foreign Limited Liability Companies.
1002. Application for Certificate of Authority.
1003. Activities Not Constituting Transacting Business.
1004. Issuance of Certificate of Authority.
1005. Name of Foreign Limited Liability Company.
1006. Revocation of Certificate of Authority.
1007. Cancellation of Authority.
1008. Effect of Failure to Obtain Certificate of Authority.
1009. Action by [Attorney General].

Section 1001. Law Governing Foreign Limited Liability Companies.

(a) The laws of the State or other jurisdiction under which a foreign limited liability company is organized govern its organization and internal affairs and the liability of its managers, members, and their transferees.

(b) A foreign limited liability company may not be denied a certificate of authority by reason of any difference between the laws of another jurisdiction under which the foreign company is organized and the laws of this State.

(c) A certificate of authority does not authorize a foreign limited liability company to engage in any business or exercise any power that a limited liability company may not engage in or exercise in this State.

Comment:

The law where a foreign limited liability company is organized, rather than this Act, governs that company's internal affairs and the

483

liability of its owners. Accordingly, any difference between the laws of the foreign jurisdiction and this Act will not constitute grounds for denial of a certificate of authority to transact business in this State. However, a foreign limited liability company transacting business in this State by virtue of a certificate of authority is limited to the business and powers that a limited liability company may lawfully pursue and exercise under Section 112.

Section 1002. Application for Certificate of Authority.

(a) A foreign limited liability company may apply for a certificate of authority to transact business in this State by delivering an application to the [Secretary of State] for filing. The application must set forth:

(1) the name of the foreign company or, if its name is unavailable for use in this State, a name that satisfies the requirements of Section 1005;

(2) the name of the State or country under whose law it is organized;

(3) the street address of its principal office;

(4) the address of its initial designated office in this State;

(5) the name and street address of its initial agent for service of process in this State;

(6) whether the duration of the company is for a specified term and, if so, the period specified;

(7) whether the company is manager-managed, and, if so, the name and address of each initial manager; and

(8) whether the members of the company are to be liable for its debts and obligations under a provision similar to Section 303(c).

(b) A foreign limited liability company shall deliver with the completed application a certificate of existence or a record of similar import authenticated by the secretary of state or other official having custody of company records in the State or country under whose law it is organized.

Comment:

As with articles of organization, the application must be signed and filed with the filing office. See Sections 105, 107 (name registration), 205, 206, 209 (liability for false statements), and 1005.

Section 1003. Activities Not Constituting Transacting Business.

(a) Activities of a foreign limited liability company that do not constitute transacting business in this State within the meaning of this [article] include:

(1) maintaining, defending, or settling an action or proceeding;

(2) holding meetings of its members or managers or carrying on any other activity concerning its internal affairs;

(3) maintaining bank accounts;

(4) maintaining offices or agencies for the transfer, exchange, and registration of the foreign company's own securities or maintaining trustees or depositories with respect to those securities;

(5) selling through independent contractors;

(6) soliciting or obtaining orders, whether by mail or through employees or agents or otherwise, if the orders require acceptance outside this State before they become contracts;

(7) creating or acquiring indebtedness, mortgages, or security interests in real or personal property;

(8) securing or collecting debts or enforcing mortgages or other security interests in property securing the debts, and holding, protecting, and maintaining property so acquired;

(9) conducting an isolated transaction that is completed within 30 days and is not one in the course of similar transactions of a like manner; and

(10) transacting business in interstate commerce.

(b) For purposes of this [article], the ownership in this State of income-producing real property or tangible personal property, other than property excluded under subsection (a), constitutes transacting business in this State.

(c) This section does not apply in determining the contacts or activities that may subject a foreign limited liability company to service of process, taxation, or regulation under any other law of this State.

Section 1004. Issuance of Certificate of Authority.

Unless the [Secretary of State] determines that an application for a certificate of authority fails to comply as to form with the filing requirements of this [Act], the [Secretary of State], upon payment of all filing fees, shall file the application and send a receipt for it and the fees to the limited liability company or its representative.

Section 1005. Name of Foreign Limited Liability Company.

(a) If the name of a foreign limited liability company does not satisfy the requirements of Section 105, the company, to obtain or maintain a certificate of authority to transact business in this State, must use a fictitious name to transact business in this State if its real name is unavailable and it delivers to the [Secretary of State] for filing a copy of the resolution of its managers, in the case of a manager-managed company, or of its members, in the case of a member-managed company, adopting the fictitious name.

(b) Except as authorized by subsections (c) and (d), the name, including a fictitious name to be used to transact business in this State, of a foreign limited liability company must be distinguishable upon the records of the [Secretary of State] from:

(1) the name of any corporation, limited partnership, or company incorporated, organized, or authorized to transact business in this State;

(2) a name reserved or registered under Section 106 or 107; and

(3) the fictitious name of another foreign limited liability company authorized to transact business in this State.

(c) A foreign limited liability company may apply to the [Secretary of State] for authority to use in this State a name that is not distinguishable upon the records of the [Secretary of State] from a name described in subsection (b). The [Secretary of State] shall authorize use of the name applied for if:

(1) the present user, registrant, or owner of a reserved name consents to the use in a record and submits an undertaking in form satisfactory to the [Secretary of State] to change its name to a name that is distinguishable upon the records of the [Secretary of State] from the name of the foreign applying limited liability company; or

(2) the applicant delivers to the [Secretary of State] a certified copy of a final judgment of a court establishing the applicant's right to use the name applied for in this State.

(d) A foreign limited liability company may use in this State the name, including the fictitious name, of another domestic or foreign entity that is used in this State if the other entity is incorporated, organized, or authorized to transact business in this State and the foreign limited liability company:

(1) has merged with the other entity;

(2) has been formed by reorganization of the other entity; or

(3) has acquired all or substantially all of the assets, including the name, of the other entity.

(e) If a foreign limited liability company authorized to transact business in this State changes its name to one that does not satisfy the requirements of Section 105, it may not transact business in this State under the name as changed until it adopts a name satisfying the requirements of Section 105 and obtains an amended certificate of authority.

Section 1006. Revocation of Certificate of Authority.

(a) A certificate of authority of a foreign limited liability company to transact business in this State may be revoked by the [Secretary of State] in the manner provided in subsection (b) if:

(1) the company fails to:

    (i) pay any fees, taxes, and penalties owed to this State;

    (ii) deliver its annual report required under Section 211 to the [Secretary of State] within 60 days after it is due;

    (iii) appoint and maintain an agent for service of process as required by this [article]; or

    (iv) file a statement of a change in the name or business address of the agent as required by this [article]; or

(2) a misrepresentation has been made of any material matter in any application, report, affidavit, or other record submitted by the company pursuant to this [article].

(b) The [Secretary of State] may not revoke a certificate of authority of a foreign limited liability company unless the [Secretary of State] sends the company notice of the revocation, at least 60 days before its effective date, by a record addressed to its agent for service of process in this State, or if the company fails to appoint and maintain a proper agent in this State, addressed to the office required to be maintained by Section 108. The notice must specify the cause for the revocation of the certificate of authority. The authority of the company to transact business in this State ceases on the effective date of the revocation unless the foreign limited liability company cures the failure before that date.

Section 1007. Cancellation of Authority.

A foreign limited liability company may cancel its authority to transact business in this State by filing in the office of the [Secretary of State] a certificate of cancellation. Cancellation does not terminate the authority of the [Secretary of State] to accept service of process on the company for [claims for relief] arising out of the transactions of business in this State.

Section 1008. Effect of Failure to Obtain Certificate of Authority.

(a) A foreign limited liability company transacting business in this State may not maintain an action or proceeding in this State unless it has a certificate of authority to transact business in this State.

(b) The failure of a foreign limited liability company to have a certificate of authority to transact business in this State does not impair the validity of a contract or act of the company or prevent the foreign limited liability company from defending an action or proceeding in this State.

(c) Limitations on personal liability of managers, members, and their transferees are not waived solely by transacting business in this State without a certificate of authority.

(d) If a foreign limited liability company transacts business in this State without a certificate of authority, it appoints the [Secretary of State] as its agent for service of process for [claims for relief] arising out of the transaction of business in this State.

Section 1009. Action by [Attorney General].

The [Attorney General] may maintain an action to restrain a foreign limited liability company from transacting business in this State in violation of this [article].

[ARTICLE] 11

DERIVATIVE ACTIONS

Sec.
1101. Right of Action.
1102. Proper Plaintiff.
1103. Pleading.
1104. Expenses.

Section 1101. Right of Action.

A member of a limited liability company may maintain an action in the right of the company if the members or managers having authority to do so have refused to commence the action or an effort to cause those members or managers to commence the action is not likely to succeed.

Comment:

A member may bring an action on behalf of the company when the members or managers having the authority to pursue the company recovery refuse to do so or an effort to cause them to pursue the recovery is not likely to succeed. See Comments to Section 411(a) (personal action of member against company or another member).

Section 1102. Proper Plaintiff.

In a derivative action for a limited liability company, the plaintiff must be a member of the company when the action is commenced; and:

(1) must have been a member at the time of the transaction of which the plaintiff complains; or

(2) the plaintiff's status as a member must have devolved upon the plaintiff by operation of law or pursuant to the terms of the operating agreement from a person who was a member at the time of the transaction.

Section 1103. Pleading.

In a derivative action for a limited liability company, the complaint must set forth with particularity the effort of the plaintiff to secure initiation of the action by a member or manager or the reasons for not making the effort.

Comment:

There is no obligation of the company or its members or managers to respond to a member demand to bring an action to pursue a company recovery. However, if a company later decides to commence the demanded action or assume control of the derivative litigation, the member's right to commence or control the proceeding ordinarily ends.

Section 1104. Expenses.

If a derivative action for a limited liability company is successful, in whole or in part, or if anything is received by the plaintiff as a result of a judgment, compromise, or settlement of an action or claim, the court may award the plaintiff reasonable expenses, including reasonable attorney's fees, and shall direct the plaintiff to remit to the limited liability company the remainder of the proceeds received.

[ARTICLE] 12

MISCELLANEOUS PROVISIONS

Section 1201. Uniformity of Application and Construction.

This [Act] shall be applied and construed to effectuate its general purpose to make uniform the law with respect to the subject of this [Act] among States enacting it.

Section 1202. Short Title.

This [Act] may be cited as the Uniform Limited Liability Company Act (1995).

Section 1203. Severability Clause.

If any provision of this [Act] or its application to any person or circumstance is held invalid, the invalidity does not affect other provisions or applications of this [Act] which can be given effect without the invalid provision or application, and to this end the provisions of this [Act] are severable ...

Section 1204.   Effective Date.

This [Act] takes effect [_____].

FORM OF LIMITED LIABILITY COMPANY OPERATING AGREEMENT*

BY

ROBERT R. KEATINGE

MANAGER–MANAGED[1] [LONG FORM]

[OPERATING/LIMITED LIABILITY COMPANY] AGREEMENT[2]

OF

_____, LLC

A [STATE] LIMITED LIABILITY COMPANY

EFFECTIVE AS OF _____, ___

THE INTERESTS DESCRIBED AND REPRESENTED BY THIS [OPERATING/LIMITED LIABILITY COMPANY] AGREEMENT HAVE NOT BEEN REGISTERED UNDER THE SECURITIES ACT OF 1933 OR ANY APPLICABLE STATE SECURITIES LAWS (THE "SECURITIES LAWS") AND MAY BE RESTRICTED SECURITIES AS THAT TERM IS DEFINED IN RULE 144 UNDER THE SECURITIES LAWS. TO THE EXTENT THE INTERESTS CONSTITUTE SECURITIES UNDER THE SECURITIES LAWS, THE SECURITIES MAY NOT BE OFFERED FOR SALE, SOLD, OR OTHERWISE TRANSFERRED EXCEPT PURSUANT TO AN EFFECTIVE REGISTRATION STATEMENT OR QUALIFICATION UNDER THE SECURITIES LAWS OR PURSUANT TO AN EXEMPTION FROM REGISTRATION UNDER THE SECURITIES LAWS, THE AVAILABILITY OF WHICH IS TO BE ESTABLISHED TO THE SATISFACTION OF THE COMPANY.[3]

---

* © Holland & Hart LLP 2006. Reproduced by permission.

1. In most states, LLCs can be organized either as "member-managed" LLCs or "manager-managed" LLC. In a member-managed LLC, each member is an agent of the LLC for carrying on the business of the LLC in the usual course. On the other hand, in a manager-managed LLC, members do not have agency authority, and managers do. This is a manager-managed LLC. Some states, such as Colorado, permit an LLC to be manager-managed (i.e., to provide that members do not have agency authority) but do not require that the LLC have a manager. In such case, the members will determine who will exercise authority on behalf of the LLC.

This operating agreement is for a manager-managed LLC with a manager.

2. The agreement is referred to in different ways in different statutes. The predominant nomenclature is "operating agreement," but it is known in Delaware as a "limited liability company agreement," and elsewhere as "regulations" or a "member control agreement." Delaware acknowledges that an agreement will still constitute a limited liability company agreement under its act even if it is referred to as an "operating agreement" 6 Del. C. § 18–101(7)(" 'Limited liability company agreement' means any agreement (whether referred to as a limited liability company agreement, operating agreement or otherwise) .. ").

3. Many interests in LLCs will be considered securities. If they are considered

TABLE OF CONTENTS

ARTICLE 1. DEFINITIONS

securities and are intended to be sold pursuant to an exemption from registration based on sales of securities not acquired for resale, the issuer will want to assure itself that the securities are not being sold to "Underwriters" (i.e., persons acquiring the securities for resale). Among the actions that the Company may take to assure that the securities are not being acquired for resale are:

(1) Reasonable inquiry to determine if the purchaser is acquiring the securities for himself or for other persons;

(2) Written disclosure to each purchaser prior to sale that the securities have not been registered under the Act and, therefore, cannot be resold unless they are registered under the Act or unless an exemption from registration is available; and

(3) Placement of a legend on the certificate or other document that evidences the securities stating that the securities have not been registered under the Act and setting forth or referring to the restrictions on transferability and sale of the securities.

See Regulation D, Rule 502(d), 17 CFR 230.502(d).

ARTICLE 2. FORMATION OF COMPANY

ARTICLE 3. BUSINESS OF COMPANY

ARTICLE 4. NAMES AND ADDRESSES OF EQUITY OWNERS

ARTICLE 5. RIGHTS AND DUTIES OF MANAGERS

ARTICLE 6. RIGHTS AND OBLIGATIONS
OF EQUITY OWNERS

ARTICLE 7. ACTIONS OF MEMBERS

This Agreement[4] is made and entered into this [___] day of [_____], 200[__], by and among *[the Company and]*[5] each of the Members whose signatures appear on the signature page hereof (the "Initial Members"). In consideration of the mutual covenants contained

4. Under most statutes an organization does not qualify as a limited liability company until it has at least one member (see, e.g., 6 Del. C § 18–101(6)) (" 'Limited liability company' and 'domestic limited liability company' means a limited liability company formed under the laws of the State of Delaware and having 1 or more members."), but is formed by filing articles of organization or a certificate of formation (see, e.g., 6 Del. C. § 18–201(b) ("A limited liability company is formed at the time of the filing of the initial certificate of formation in the office of the Secretary of State or at any later date or time specified in the certificate of formation if, in either case, there has been substantial compliance with the requirements of this section. A limited liability company formed under this chapter shall be a separate legal entity, the existence of which as a separate legal entity shall continue until cancellation of the limited liability company's certificate of formation.") As such the effective date of the agreement should be as of or after the effective date of the filed articles. See, e.g., 6 Del. C. § 18–

5. Bracketed and italicized language in this agreement represents optional or alternative provisions that a drafter may want to consider including.

There has been a concern about whether the LLC itself should be a party to the operating agreement (or at least be bound by the operating agreement). Compare Bubbles & Bleach, LLC v. Becker, No. 97 C 1320, 1997 WL 285938 (N.D. Ill. May 23, 1997) (holding an arbitration agreement not binding on an LLC because it was not a party to it) with Elf Atochem North America, Inc. v. Jaffari, 727 A.2d 286 (Del. 1999). (to the contrary). The Delaware LLC act has addressed this issue in 6 Del. C. § 18–101(7) ("A limited liability company is not required to execute its limited liability company agreement. A limited liability company is bound by its limited liability company agreement whether or not the limited liability company executes the limited liability company agreement.")

herein and for other good and valuable consideration, the Members and the Company (and each person who subsequently becomes an Equity Owner) hereby agree as follows:

ARTICLE 1

DEFINITIONS

The following terms used in this Agreement shall have the following meanings (unless otherwise expressly provided herein); certain other capitalized terms have the meanings ascribed to them throughout this Agreement.

1.1 <u>Act</u>. The [*State*] Limited Liability Company Act [*, as amended from time to time*].[6]

1.2 <u>Adjusted Capital Contributions</u>. An amount equal to the excess of such Equity Owner's Capital Contributions, if any, pursuant to Section 8.1 and Section 8.2, over any Distributions made to such Equity Owner pursuant to Section 9.4(b)(ii).[7]

1.3 <u>Affiliate</u>. In the case of an individual, the spouse, estate, heirs, devisees, lineal descendants (including adopted children) or the spouse of a lineal descendant of that individual, or a trust or other Entity formed by the individual for the benefit of the individual or his spouse or lineal descendants or the spouse of a lineal descendant of that individual and in which day-to-day voting control is directly or indirectly held by the individual, and in the case of a Person other than an individual, (a) any Person directly or indirectly controlling, controlled by, or under common control with such Person, (b) any Person owning or controlling ten percent (10%) or more of the outstanding voting interests of such Person, (c) any officer, director, manager, or general partner of such Person, or (d) any Person who is an officer, director, manager, general partner, trustee, or holder of ten percent (10%) or more of the voting interests of any Person described in clauses (a) through (c) of this sentence. For purposes of this definition, the term "control," "controls," "controlling," "controlled by," or "under common control with" shall mean the possession, direct or indirect, of the power to direct or cause

---

6. This operating agreement is intended to as a generic example. It will need to be adapted to the particular language and limitations of the act under which the LLC is organized. Some amendments to the LLC statute will not be effective as to existing LLCs in order to avoid disturbing contractual relationships. It may be appropriate to include the express reference to the act "as amended" to ensure that such amendments will be used in interpreting the agreement.

7. This definition is intended to be used when alternative 2 in section 9.4 is used. The "adjusted capital contributions" represents the total value of the contributions by a member reduced by the actual amount of cash distributed to the member (not counting any cash distributed on account of a preferred accrual). Allocations of profits and losses are disregarded in determining the adjusted capital contributions.

the direction of the management and policies of a Person, whether through the ownership of voting securities, by contract or otherwise.[8]

1.4 Agreement. This *[Operating/Limited Liability Company]* Agreement as originally executed and as amended from time to time.

1.5 Annual Operating Plan. The business plan designated as such pursuant to Section 5.12.[9]

1.6 Approve or Approval.

(a) With respect to Members, such Members' approval expressed by the Members holding the required number of Voting Interests at a meeting of the Members or expressed by written consent by Members holding the required number of Voting Interests as provided for in Article 7 of this Agreement; and

(b) With respect to Managers, such Managers' approval as required pursuant to Section 5.1.

1.7 [Articles of Organization/Certificate of Formation.] The *[articles of organization/certificate of formation]* of the Company as filed with the Secretary of State as the same may be amended from time to time.

1.8 Available Ownership Interest. The Ownership Interest designated as such in Section 8.5(b)(i).

1.9 Bankruptcy. With respect to a Person, the occurrence of any of the following events:

(a) Such Person makes an assignment for the benefit of creditors;

(b) Such Person files a voluntary petition in bankruptcy;

(c) Such Person is adjudged a bankrupt or insolvent, or has entered against it an order for relief, in any bankruptcy or insolvency proceeding;

(d) Such Person files a petition or answer seeking for itself any reorganization, arrangement, composition, readjustment, liquidation, dissolution, or similar relief under any statute, law or regulation;

(e) Such Person files an answer or other pleading admitting or failing to contest the material allegations of a petition filed against it in any proceeding of this nature;

---

8. This definition should be used when there are restrictions (or approval requirements) with respect to certain transactions with Equity Owners, Managers, or any of their Affiliates.

9. This agreement provides for a business plan as a way of anticipating expenditures and other issues which might otherwise require approval. If the Members are willing to expend the effort to maintain an operating plan it can be a useful vehicle for operating the business of the Company.

(f) Such Person seeks, consents to, or acquiesces in the appointment of a trustee, receiver, or liquidator of such Person or of all or any substantial part of its properties; or

(g) One hundred twenty (120) days after the commencement of any proceeding against such Person seeking reorganization, arrangement, composition, readjustment, liquidation, dissolution, or similar relief under any statute, law, or regulation, if the proceeding has not been dismissed, or if within ninety (90) days after the appointment without its consent or acquiescence of a trustee, receiver, or liquidator of such Person or of all or any substantial part of its properties, the appointment is not vacated or stayed, or within ninety (90) days after the expiration of any such stay, the appointment is not vacated.

1.10 <u>Buying Member</u>. A Member exercising the option granted pursuant to Section 10.2(b).

1.11 <u>Buy Notice</u>. The notice given pursuant to Section 10.2(b).

1.12 <u>Buy Option</u>. The option granted pursuant to Section 10.2(b).

1.13 <u>Capital Account</u>. As of any given date, the capital account of each Equity Owner as described in Section 8.3 and maintained to such date in accordance with this Agreement.[10]

1.14 <u>Capital Contribution</u>. Any contribution to the capital of the Company in cash or property by an Equity Owner whenever made. "Initial Capital Contribution" shall mean the initial contribution to the capital of the Company pursuant to this Agreement.

1.15 <u>Code</u>. The Internal Revenue Code of 1986, as amended from time to time.

1.16 <u>Company</u>. [_____] LLC.

1.17 <u>Company Minimum Gain</u>. Partnership minimum gain as determined in accordance with Section 1.704–2(d) of the Regulations.

1.18 <u>Company Property</u>. All assets (real or personal, tangible or intangible, including cash) of the Company.

1.19 <u>CPI Index</u>. The Consumer Price Index for All Items All Urban Consumers (DPI–U) (1982–84 = 100) for the United States, as published by the United States Department of Labor's Bureau of Labor Statistics.

1.20 <u>Default Buyout Price</u>. The price established by Section 8.5(b)(v).

1.21 <u>Defaulting Equity Owner</u>. An Equity Owner designated as such in Section 8.5.

1.22 <u>Default Notice</u>. The notice required by Section 8.5.

---

10. The Capital Account is where the allocation of profits and losses are turned into cash distributions. On the liquidation of the Company, the Capital Accounts will dictate the amounts distributed to each of the Equity Owners.

1.23 <u>Default Purchase Option</u>. The option granted pursuant to Section 8.5(b).

1.24 <u>Default Purchase Option Notice</u>. The notice required by Section 8.5(b).

1.25 <u>Deficit Capital Account</u>. With respect to any Equity Owner, the deficit balance, if any, in such Equity Owner's Capital Account as of the end of the Fiscal Year, after giving effect to the following adjustments:

(a) Credit to such Capital Account the amount, if any, which such Equity Owner is obligated to restore under Section 1.704–1(b)(2)(ii)(c) of the Regulations, as well as any addition thereto pursuant to the next to last sentence of Sections 1.704–2(g)(1) and (i)(5) of the Regulations, after taking into account thereunder any changes during such year in Company Minimum Gain and in any Equity Owner Minimum Gain; and

(b) Debit to such Capital Account the items described in Sections 1.704–1(b)(2)(ii)(d)(4), (5) and (6) of the Regulations.

This definition of Deficit Capital Account is intended to comply with the provisions of Sections 1.704–1(b)(2)(ii)(d) and 1.704–2 of the Regulations, and shall be interpreted consistently with those provisions.

1.26 <u>Depreciation</u>. For each Fiscal Year, an amount equal to the depreciation, amortization, or other cost recovery deduction allowable with respect to an asset for such Fiscal Year, except that if the Gross Asset Value of an asset differs from its adjusted basis for federal income tax purposes at the beginning of such Fiscal Year, Depreciation shall be an amount which bears the same ratio to such beginning Gross Asset Value as the federal income tax depreciation, amortization, or other cost recovery deduction for such Fiscal Year bears to such beginning adjusted tax basis; provided, however, that if the adjusted basis for federal income tax purposes of an asset at the beginning of such Fiscal Year is zero, Depreciation shall be determined with reference to such beginning Gross Asset Value using any reasonable method selected by the Managers. Notwithstanding the foregoing, if the Company uses the remedial method pursuant to Section 1.704–3(d) of the Regulations with respect to one or more of the Company's assets, Depreciation with respect to such assets shall not be determined in accordance with the preceding sentence of this definition, but shall instead be determined in a manner consistent with tax capital accounting principles and consistent with the treatment of such assets under the remedial method, as determined by the Managers in consultation with the Company's tax advisors.

1.27 <u>Disability or Disabled</u>. With respect to any individual a permanent disability as determined by *[two]* physicians, *[one selected by the Company and one by the authorized agent of such Person,]* who has examined such Person and concluded that such Person is incapable of performing his usual duties for a continuous period of *[two]* months or more.[11]

1.28 <u>Distributable Cash</u>. All cash, whether revenues or other funds received by the Company, less the sum of the following to the extent paid or set aside by the Company: (i) all principal and interest payments on indebtedness of the Company and all other sums paid to lenders; (ii) all cash expenditures incurred incident to the normal operation of the Company's business; and (iii) Reserves. Any funds released from a Reserve shall be considered a cash receipt by the Company for purposes of this definition.

1.29 <u>Distribution</u>. Any Transfer of Company Property from the Company to or for the benefit of an Equity Owner by reason of such Equity Owner's ownership of an Economic Interest.

1.30 <u>Donee</u>. A Person designated as such in Section 10.5.

1.31 <u>Economic Interest</u>. An Equity Owner's share of one or more of the Profits, Losses, and Distributions pursuant to this Agreement and the Act, but not including any right to participate in the management or affairs of the Company, such as the right to Approve or otherwise participate in any decision of the Members or Managers.[12]

1.32 <u>Economic Interest Owner</u>. The owner of an Economic Interest who is not a Member.

1.33 <u>Electing Equity Owner</u>. An Equity Owner designated as such in Section 8.5(b)(iii).

1.34 <u>Entity</u>. Any general partnership (including a limited liability partnership), limited partnership (including a limited liability limited partnership), limited liability company, corporation, joint venture, trust, business trust, cooperative, association, foreign trust, or foreign business organization.

1.35 <u>Equity Owner</u>. An Economic Interest Owner or a Member.

1.36 <u>Equity Owner Minimum Gain</u>. Partner nonrecourse debt minimum gain as determined under Section 1.704–2(i)(3) of the Regulations.

1.37 <u>Equity Owner Nonrecourse Debt</u>. Partner nonrecourse debt as defined under Section 1.704–2(b)(4) of the Regulations.

1.38 <u>Exercise Notice</u>. The notice required by Section 8.5(b)(ii).

---

11. The definition of "Disability" is used in conjunction with removal of Managers or withdrawals/transfers of Ownership Interests.

12. Definitions such as "Economic Interest," "Economic Interest Owner," and "Equity Owner" are intended to facilitate the distinction between "Members" who are admitted to the LLC either at the outset or by the consent of the other Members and who have both economic rights and rights to participate in management of the Company and "Economic Interest Owners" who are assignees or transferees of an interest but who are not admitted as Members and therefore do not have the right to participate in management or to receive information from the Company.

1.39 <u>Fiscal Year</u>. The taxable year of the Company as determined under the Code.

1.40 <u>Gift</u>. A gift, devise, bequest, or other transfer for no consideration, whether or not by operation of law, except in the case of Bankruptcy.

1.41 <u>Gifting Equity Owner</u>. Any Equity Owner who Gifts all or any part of its Ownership Interest.

1.42 <u>Gross Asset Value</u>.[13] With respect to any asset, the asset's adjusted basis for federal income tax purposes, except as follows:

(a)   The initial Gross Asset Value of any asset contributed by an Equity Owner to the Company shall be the gross fair market value of such asset on the date of contribution, *[as determined by the contributing Member and the Managers]*, provided that the initial Gross Asset Values of the assets contributed to the Company pursuant to Section 8.1 hereof shall be as set forth in <u>Exhibit 8.1</u>, and provided further that, if the contributing Member is a Manager, the determination of the fair market value of any other contributed asset shall require the Approval of the other Members owning a Majority Interest (determined without regard to the Voting Interest of such contributing Member);

(b)   The Gross Asset Values of all Company assets shall be adjusted to equal their respective gross fair market values (taking into account Section 7701(g) of the Code), as *[reasonably]* determined by the Managers[14] as of the following times: (i) the acquisition of an interest by any new Equity Owner or an additional interest by an existing Equity Owner in exchange for more than a *de minimis* contribution of property (including money); (ii) the Distribution by the Company to an Equity Owner of more than a *de minimis* amount of property as consideration for an Ownership Interest; *[and]* (iii) the liquidation of the Company within the meaning of Section 1.704–1(b)(2)(ii)(g) of the Regulations; *[and (iv) the grant of an Ownership Interest in the Company (other than a de minimis interest) as consideration for the provision of services to or for the benefit of the Company by an existing Equity Owner acting in the capacity of an Equity Owner or by a new Equity Owner acting in*

---

13. As noted in definitions set forth below, the definition of "Gross Asset Value" facilitates several economic transactions, not the least of which is to provide for "book-ups" by which the economic interests of the Equity Owners is adjusted on the admission or redemption of an Equity Owner.

14. This provision sets forth the rules for a "book-up" of the assets of the Company on certain events. The effect of the book-up is to adjust the value of the Capital Accounts to fair market value on these events by treating the Company as if the assets were sold for fair market value and the resulting profits and losses were allocated in accordance the provisions for sharing profits and losses within the agreement. It is ordinarily done to ensure that on the admission or departure of a member, the historic members get the benefit of unrealized appreciation of the assets that has not yet been allocated to the owners.

the capacity of an Equity Owner or in anticipation of being an Equity Owner;][15] provided, however, that adjustments pursuant to clauses (i) and (ii) above shall be made only if the Managers *[reasonably]* determine that such adjustments are necessary or appropriate to reflect the relative economic interests of the Equity Owners in the Company;

(c) The Gross Asset Value of any Company asset Distributed to any Equity Owner shall be adjusted to equal the gross fair market value of such asset on the date of Distribution as *[reasonably]* determined by the distributee and the Managers, provided that, if the distributee is a Manager, the determination of the fair market value of the Distributed asset shall require the Approval of the other Members owning a Majority Interest (determined without regard to the Voting Interest of the distributee Member); and

(d) The Gross Asset Values of Company assets shall be increased (or decreased) to reflect any adjustments to the adjusted basis of such assets pursuant to Section 734(b) or Section 743(b) of the Code, but only to the extent that such adjustments are taken into account in determining Capital Accounts pursuant to Section 1.704–1(b)(2)(iv)(m) of the Regulations and Section 9.2(g) and subparagraph (g) under the definition of Profits and Losses; provided, however, that Gross Asset Values shall not be adjusted pursuant to this subparagraph (d) of this definition to the extent that the Managers *[reasonably]* determine that an adjustment pursuant to subparagraph (b) of this definition is necessary or appropriate in connection with a transaction that would otherwise result in an adjustment pursuant to this subparagraph (d).

If the Gross Asset Value of an asset has been determined or adjusted pursuant to subparagraph (a), (b), or (d) of this definition, then such Gross Asset Value shall thereafter be adjusted by the Depreciation taken into account with respect to such asset for purposes of computing Profits and Losses.

1.43 Hypothecation. A lien, pledge, hypothecation, mortgage, grant of a security interest, or effecting an encumbrance either as security for repayment of a liability or for any other purpose.

1.44 Issuance Items. Any income, gain, loss or deduction realized by the Company as a direct or indirect result of the issuance of an interest in the Company by the Company to an Equity Owner.

1.45 Loan Decision Period. The time period specified in Section 8.5(a).

1.46 Liquidators. The Persons specified as such in Section 12.3(a).

---

15. This provision allows for a book-up on the grant of a "profits interest." In order for a compensatory interest to constitute a "profits interest" under Rev. Proc. 93–27, it must entitle it holder to an interest that would yield nothing if the LLC were liquidated immediately after it is granted.

1.47 <u>Majority Interest</u>. One or more Voting Interests of Members which taken together exceed fifty percent (50%) of the aggregate of all Voting Interests.

1.48 <u>Managers</u>. One or more managers designated as provided in Section 5.2.

1.49 <u>Member</u>. Each of the parties who executes a counterpart of this Agreement as a Member (an "Initial Member") and each Person who may hereafter become a Member. If a Person is a Member immediately prior to the purchase or other acquisition by such Person of an Economic Interest, such Person shall have all of the rights of a Member with respect to such purchased or otherwise acquired Economic Interest, as the case may be.

1.50 <u>Membership Interest</u>. A Member's entire interest in the Company, including such Member's Economic Interest and such other rights and privileges that the Member may enjoy by being a Member.

1.51 <u>Non–Cash Consideration</u>. The consideration designated as such pursuant to Section 10.2(a).

1.52 <u>Non–Defaulting Equity Owners</u>. The Equity Owners designated as such pursuant to Section 8.5.

1.53 <u>Notice of Sale</u>. The notice provided pursuant to Section 10.2(a).

1.54 <u>Offered Interest</u>. The Ownership Interest offered pursuant to Section 10.2(a).

1.55 <u>Option Period</u>. The period of time provided for pursuant to Section 10.2(b).

1.56 <u>Ownership Interest</u>. In the case of a Member, the Member's Membership Interest; and in the case of an Economic Interest Owner, the Economic Interest Owner's Economic Interest.

1.57 <u>Person</u>. Any individual or Entity, and the heirs, executors, administrators, legal representatives, successors, and assigns of such "Person" where the context so permits.

1.58 <u>Preferred Accrual</u>. The mathematical equivalent of interest at the rate of ten percent simple interest per annum on the balance from time to time of their respective Adjusted Capital Contributions.[16]

1.59 <u>Prime Rate</u>. The prime commercial lending rate in effect from time to time at the principal bank used by the Company for banking and borrowing purposes.

1.60 <u>Profits and Losses</u>. For each Fiscal Year of the Company an amount equal to the Company's net taxable income or loss for such year as determined for federal income tax purposes (including separately

---

16. This definition is intended to be used when alternative 2 in section 9.4 and, in particular section 9.4(b)(i), is used. The Preferred Accrual sometimes described as a "Preferred Return" is an interest-like amount paid on, and returned in addition to, Adjusted Capital Contributions.

stated items) in accordance with the accounting method and rules used by the Company and in accordance with Section 703 of the Code with the following adjustments:

(a) Any items of income, gain, loss and deduction allocated to Equity Owners pursuant to Sections 9.2, 9.3, or 9.12 shall not be taken into account in computing Profits or Losses;

(b) Any income of the Company that is exempt from federal income tax and not otherwise taken into account in computing Profits and Losses (pursuant to this definition) shall be added to such taxable income or loss;

(c) Any expenditure of the Company described in Section 705(a)(2)(B) of the Code or treated as such in Section 1.704–1(b)(2)(iv)(*i*) of the Regulations and not otherwise taken into account in computing Profits and Losses (pursuant to this definition) shall be subtracted from such taxable income or loss;

(d) In the event the Gross Asset Value of any Company asset is adjusted pursuant to subparagraphs (b) or (c) of the definition of Gross Asset Value, the amount of such adjustment shall be taken into account as gain or loss from the disposition of such asset for purposes of computing Profits and Losses;[17]

(e) Gain or loss resulting from any disposition of any Company asset with respect to which gain or loss is recognized for federal income tax purposes shall be computed with reference to the Gross Asset Value of the asset disposed of, notwithstanding that the adjusted tax basis of such asset differs from its Gross Asset Value;

(f) In lieu of the depreciation, amortization, and other cost recovery deductions taken into account in computing such taxable income or loss, there shall be taken into account Depreciation for such Fiscal Year; and

(g) To the extent an adjustment to the adjusted tax basis of any asset pursuant to Section 734(b) or Section 743(b) of the Code is required pursuant to Section 1.704–1(b)(2)(iv)(*m*) of the Regulations in determining Capital Accounts, the amount of such adjustment shall be treated as an item of gain (if the adjustment increases the basis of the asset) or loss (if the adjustment decreases the basis of the asset) from the disposition of the asset and shall be taken into account for purposes of computing Profits or Losses.

1.61 Purchase Price. The price determined pursuant to Section 10.2(a).

1.62 Regulations. The proposed, temporary, and final regulations promulgated under the Code in effect as of the date of filing the *[Articles*

---

17. This provision works together with the definition of Gross Asset Value to cause the amount of the adjustment to be credited to, or debited from Capital Accounts in the event of a book-up.

of Organization/Certificate of Formation] and the corresponding sections of any regulations subsequently issued that amend or supersede such regulations.

1.63 <u>Regulatory Allocations</u>. The allocations made pursuant to Sections 9.2(a), 9.2(b), 9.2(c), 9.2(d), 9.2(e), 9.2(f), and 9.2(g).

1.64 <u>Remaining Members</u>. The members designated as such pursuant to Section 10.2(a).

1.64 <u>Reorganization</u>. The merger or conversion of the Company, the sale or other disposition of all or substantially all of the assets of the Company, the sale or other disposition of all or substantially all of the Ownership Interests, or any other transaction pursuant to which one or more Persons acquire all or substantially all of the assets of, or Ownership Interests in, the Company in a single or series of related transactions, including a merger or conversion of the Company into a corporation or other Entity, whether or not such corporation or other Entity has the same owners as the Company and whether or not additional capital is contributed to such corporation or other Entity; provided, however, that a Reorganization in no event shall include the merger or conversion of the Company into a general partnership which is not a limited liability partnership or a limited partnership that is not a limited liability limited partnership.[18]

1.66 <u>Reserves</u>. With respect to any fiscal period, funds set aside or amounts allocated during such period to reserves which shall be maintained in amounts *[reasonably]* deemed sufficient by the Managers for working capital and for payment of taxes, insurance, debt service, or other costs or expenses incident to the ownership or operation of the Company's business.[19]

1.67 <u>Sale or Sell</u>. A sale, assignment, exchange, Hypothecation, assignment by reason of Bankruptcy, *[or]* other transfer for consideration, *[or change in ownership by reason of the Reorganization or other transformation in the identity or form of business organization of the owner, regardless of whether such change or transformation is characterized by state law as not changing the identity of the owner].*

1.68 <u>Secretary of State</u>. The Secretary of State of *[State]*.

1.69 <u>Securities Laws</u>. Any Federal securities acts and laws as well as the securities acts and laws of any state, including the Securities Act of 1933.

---

18. This last clause is intended to exclude the conversion of the Company into an organization in which one or more Equity Owners will undertake liability for the obligations of organization.

19. Reserves, and the determination of Reserves, is important in establishing the amount of Distributable Cash. While the determination of Reserves may be less important where the Managers have discretion in making Distributions, if the Managers are required to Distribute Distributable Cash, "Reserves" provide the one basis on which Managers can retain cash for operations.

1.70 <u>Seller's Estimate</u>. The estimate made pursuant to Section 10.2(a).

1.71 <u>Selling Equity Owner</u>. Any Equity Owner that Sells all or any portion of its Ownership Interest.

1.72 <u>Sharing Ratio</u>. The percentages in which the Equity Owners share those items making specific references to "Sharing Ratios" in this Agreement.[20] The initial[21] Sharing Ratio shall be:

Equity Owners	**Sharing Ratio**

The Sharing Ratio shall be adjusted from time to time as provided in this Agreement.[22]

1.73 <u>Tax Profits</u>. The amounts designated as such pursuant to Section 9.4(a).

1.74 <u>Tax Rate</u>. The highest marginal federal and [State] income tax rate for individuals then in effect (after taking into account the assumed deductibility of the amount of *[State]* income tax from federal taxable income).

1.75 <u>Third Party Offer</u>. An offer designated as such pursuant to Section 10.2(a).

1.76 <u>Third Party Purchaser</u>. A Person designated as such pursuant to Section 10.2(a).

1.77 <u>TMP</u>. The Tax Matters Partner designated in Section 9.11.

1.78 <u>Transfer</u>. Any Sale or Gift.

1.79 <u>Transferring Equity Owner</u>. Selling Equity Owner or a Gifting Equity Owner.

20. Sharing Ratio serves to define the manner in which voting is conducted and the percentages in which Profits and Losses are shared.

21. Upon transfer of a partial interest or the admission or redemption of Equity Owners the Sharing Ratio will need to be adjusted. If there are to be a lot of transactions of that sort, it may be more efficient to use "Units" to determine the manner in which management and economic results are to be shared. The concern with the use of Units is that it is easy for people to confuse "Units" with shares of stock in a corporation. Like "Sharing Ratios," "Units" serve only as a measure of sharing management and profits, but do not include Capital Accounts, which are determined in the first instance by the initial contributions.

22. The events that may require the adjustment of the Sharing Ratio include: (1) the admission of a new Member; (2) disproportionate contributions of capital, if the agreement so provides, (3) the redemption of an Equity Owner; (4) disproportionate distributions of capital; or (5) as a consequence of a default under the agreement if the agreement so provides.

1.80 <u>Two–Thirds Interest</u>. One or more Voting Interests of Members which taken together exceed 66.67% of the aggregate of all Voting Interests.

1.81 <u>Unrecovered Losses</u>. Amounts designated as such pursuant to Section 9.1(b)(i).

1.82 <u>Voting Interest</u>. The percentages in which the Members are entitled to vote for purposes of those provisions making specific references to "Voting Interest" in this Agreement.[23] The initial Voting Interests shall be:

Members	Voting Interest

The Voting Interest shall be adjusted from time to time as provided in this Agreement.[24]

ARTICLE 2

FORMATION OF COMPANY

2.1 <u>Formation</u>. On [_____], 20[_], [_____] organized a limited liability company pursuant to the Act by *[executing and delivering the Certificate of Formation][causing the Articles of Organization to be delivered]*[25] to the Secretary of State in accordance with and pursuant to the Act. The Company and the Members hereby forever discharge the organizer, and the organizer shall be indemnified by the Company and the Members from and against any expense or liability actually incurred by the organizer by reason of having been the organizer of the Company.

2.2 <u>Name</u>. The name of the Company is [_____] LLC.

2.3 <u>Principal Place of Business</u>. The principal place of business of the Company shall be *[_____][as set forth in the Articles of Organization.]*[26] The principal place of business may be changed from

---

23. Often the "Voting Interest" is simply the Sharing Ratio adjusted to exclude Economic Interest Owners from the computation.

24. The events that may require the adjustment of the Voting Interest include: (1) the admission of a new Member; (2) disproportionate contributions of capital, if the agreement so provides, (3) the redemption of an Equity Owner; (4) disproportionate distributions of capital; (5) as a conse-

quence of a default under the agreement if the agreement so provides; or (6) the transfer of an interest to a transferee who is not admitted as a Member.

25. This language should conform to the language used in the state LLC statute with respect to filing.

26. Some state statutes require that a principal office or principal place of business [often a mailing address that does not

time to time by filing a notice of change of the address of the principal office with the Secretary of State pursuant to the Act. The Company may locate its places of business and registered office at any other place or places as the Managers may from time to time deem advisable.

2.4 <u>Registered Office and Registered Agent</u>. The Company's initial registered office and the name of the registered agent at such address shall be as set forth in the *[Articles of Organization/Certificate of Formation]*. The registered office and registered agent may be changed from time to time by filing a notice of change in the address of the new registered office or the name of the new registered agent with the Secretary of State pursuant to the Act.

2.5 <u>Term</u>. The Company shall continue in existence until it terminates in accordance with the provisions of this Agreement or the Act.

ARTICLE 3
BUSINESS OF COMPANY

The business of the Company shall be:

(a) *[To acquire, improve, manage, operate and dispose of real property and to accomplish any lawful business whatsoever, or which shall at any time appear conducive to or expedient for the protection or benefit of the Company and its assets.]*[27]

(b) To exercise all other powers necessary to or reasonably connected with the Company's business that may be legally exercised by limited liability companies under the Act.

(c) To engage in all activities necessary, customary, convenient, or incident to any of the foregoing.

ARTICLE 4
NAMES AND ADDRESSES OF EQUITY OWNERS

4.1 <u>Initial Members</u>. The names and addresses of the Initial Members are as set forth on the attached <u>Exhibit 8.1</u>.[28]

need to be in the state] be listed in the articles of organization. This is an address that may be used to mail notice to the Company if the registered agent cannot be found. If the principal place of business is required to be set forth in the articles, it reduces the possibility of error to refer to that address rather than set it forth again here.

27. The business of the Company is important for several reasons. First, what constitutes decisions in the ordinary course of the Company's business will be dictated by what that business is. Second, the business of the company may serve as a limitation on the ability of managers to take the Company in a dramatically different direction without whatever consent is necessary to amend this provision. Third, the business of the Company will be important in determining what constitute opportunities of the Company which need to be offered to it by those who owe fiduciary duties to the Company.

28. Most statutes require a record of the names and addresses of members as

4.2 <u>Other Equity Owners</u>. The names and addresses of other Equity Owners shall be maintained as provided under Sections 13.1 and 13.2.

ARTICLE 5

RIGHTS AND DUTIES OF MANAGERS

5.1 <u>Management</u>. The business and affairs of the Company shall be managed by its Managers. Except for situations in which the Approval of the Members is expressly required by this Agreement or by non-waivable provisions of applicable law, the Managers shall have full and complete authority, power, and discretion to manage and control the business, affairs and Properties of the Company, to make all decisions regarding those matters and to perform any and all other acts and activities customary or incident to the management of the Company's business. At any time when there is more than one Manager, *[any one Manager may take any action permitted to be taken by the Managers, unless the Approval of more than one of the Managers is expressly required pursuant to this Agreement or the Act or unless a majority of the Managers determine in a writing provided to the remaining Managers prior to such Managers taking a specified action that the Approval of more than one of the Managers is required in order to take such action].*[29] Unless authorized to do so by this Agreement or by the Managers, no attorney-in-fact, employee, or other agent of the Company shall have any power or authority to bind the Company in any way, to pledge its credit, or to render it liable pecuniarily for any purpose.

5.2 <u>Number, Tenure and Qualifications</u>. The number of Managers shall be fixed from time to time by the Approval of Members holding at least a *[Two–Thirds]* Interest,[30] but in no instance shall there be less than one Manager.[31] The Members hereby set the number of Managers

---

well as the amount of cash and agreed value of contributions. This may be done in the text of the agreement, in an appendix or in a separate record (particularly with respect to the contribution). Because the initial Members need to be parties to the Operating Agreement, it is a good idea to identify them in it and have them sign it.

29. This provision enables Managers in a multi-Manager Company to take action without having to meet. An alternative to this is to have a "managing Manager" or other officer who is subject to the control of the Managers but may take day-to-day decisions.

30. In some circumstances, the Members may want the ability for each Member to appoint and remove a Manager. If Managers are effectively serving in representative capacities with their principal obligations to the Member appointing the Manager, that consequences of that should be clear. That arrangement may have a significant impact on the duties of the Managers and a consequence of a Member's default may be the removal or suspension of voting rights of the Manager appointed by that Member.

31. As noted above, some states permit a Manager-managed Company to operate without a Manager and no statute states

at [_____], and the Managers shall be [_____], [_____], and [_____]. Each Manager shall hold office until such Manager resigns pursuant to Section 5.8 or is removed pursuant to Section 5.9. Managers need not be residents of *[State]* or Members.

5.3 <u>Certain Powers of Managers</u>. Without limiting the generality of Section 5.1 but subject to the limitations of Section 5.4, the Managers shall have power and authority, on behalf of the Company, to:[32]

(a) Acquire property from any Person as the Managers may determine (the fact that a Manager or an Equity Owner is directly or indirectly affiliated or connected with any such Person shall not prohibit the Managers from dealing with that Person);

(b) Borrow money for the Company from banks, other lending institutions, the Managers, Equity Owners, or Affiliates of the Managers or Equity Owners on such terms as the Managers deem appropriate and, in connection therewith, to Hypothecate Company Property to secure repayment of the borrowed sums;

(c) Purchase liability and other insurance to protect the Company's property and business;

(d) Hold and own any Company real or personal properties in the name of the Company;

(e) Invest any Company funds (by way of example but not limitation) in time deposits, short-term governmental obligations, commercial paper, or other investments;

(f) Execute on behalf of the Company all instruments and documents, including checks, drafts, notes and other negotiable instruments; mortgages or deeds of trust; security agreements; financing statements; documents providing for the acquisition, mortgage, or disposition of Company Property; assignments; bills of sale; leases; partnership agreements; operating (or limited liability company) agreements of other limited liability companies; and any other instruments or documents necessary, in the *[reasonable]* opinion of the Managers, to the conduct of the business of the Company;

(g) Employ accountants, legal counsel, managing agents, or other experts to perform services for the Company and to compensate them from Company funds;

(h) Enter into any and all other agreements on behalf of the Company, with any other Person for any purpose and in such forms as the Managers may approve;

---

what the penalty for failing to maintain a Manager is.

32. The matters set forth in this and subsequent sections should be reviewed so that each decision gets a level of approval that the Members believe to be appropriate in light of the deal and the Members' desires.

(i) Execute and file such other instruments, documents, and certificates which may from time to time be required by the laws of *[State]* or any other jurisdiction in which the Company shall determine to do business, or any political subdivision or agency thereof, to effectuate, implement, continue, and defend the valid existence of the Company;

(j) Open bank accounts in the name of the Company and to be the sole signatory thereon unless the Managers determine otherwise;

(k) Cause the Company to be a party to a Reorganization; and

(*l*) Do and perform all other acts as may be necessary or appropriate to the conduct of the Company's business.

5.4 <u>Limitations on Authority</u>. Notwithstanding any other provision of this Agreement, the Managers shall not cause or commit the Company to do any of the following without the Approval of Members holding a *[Two–Thirds Interest]*:

(a) Sell or otherwise dispose all or substantially all of the Company Property or any Company Property other than in the ordinary course of business;

(b) Hypothecate any Company Property to the extent that the secured indebtedness from such Hypothecation would exceed $__ ; [33]

(c) Incur or refinance any indebtedness for money borrowed by the Company, whether secured or unsecured and including any indebtedness for money borrowed from a Member if, after such financing, the aggregate indebtedness of the Company would exceed $___ ; [34]

(d) Incur any liability or make any single expenditure or series of related expenditures in an amount exceeding $____ ; [35]

(e) Construct any capital improvements, repairs, alterations or changes involving an amount in excess of $____ ; [36]

---

33. If the Company maintains an Annual Operating Plan, these should be tied to that Plan *e.g.* exceeding the amount specified in the Annual Operating Plan by more than $_____ or may not be in excess of _____ % of the amount specified in the Annual Operating Plan.

34. If the Company maintains an Annual Operating Plan, these should be tied to that Plan *e.g.* exceeding the amount specified in the Annual Operating Plan by more than $_____ or may not be in excess of _____ % of the amount specified in the Annual Operating Plan.

35. If the Company maintains an Annual Operating Plan, these should be tied to that Plan *e.g.* exceeding the amount specified in the Annual Operating Plan by more than $_____ or may not be in excess of _____ % of the amount specified in the Annual Operating Plan.

36. If the Company maintains an Annual Operating Plan, these should be tied to that Plan *e.g.* exceeding the amount specified in the Annual Operating Plan by more than $_____ or may not be in excess of _____ % of the amount specified in the Annual Operating Plan.

(f) Lend money to or guaranty or become surety for the obligations of any Person;

(g) Compromise or settle any claim against or inuring to the benefit of the Company involving an amount in controversy in excess of $_____ ; or

(h) Cause the Company to commence a voluntary case as debtor under the United States Bankruptcy Code.

5.5 Liability for Certain Acts.

(a) The Managers do not, in any way, guarantee the return of the Equity Owners' Capital Contributions or a profit for the Equity Owners from the operations of the Company.

(b) No Manager *[and no Affiliate of a Manager]* shall be liable to the Company or to any Equity Owner for any loss or damage sustained by the Company or any Equity Owner (or successor thereto), except to the extent, if any, that the loss or damage shall have been the result of *[negligence,]* *[gross negligence,]*[37] fraud, deceit, willful misconduct, or *[intentional]*[38] breach of this Agreement by such Manager *[or by such Affiliate of a Manager]*.

5.6 Managers and Members Have No Exclusive Duty to Company. The Managers, Members, *[and their Affiliates]* shall have no exclusive duty to act on behalf of the Company. Each Manager, Member, *[and their Affiliates]* may have other business interests and may engage in other activities in addition to those relating to the Company. Neither the Company nor any Member shall have any right, by virtue of this Agreement, to share or participate in any other investments or activities of any other Member, the Manager, *[or any of their Affiliates]*. Neither any Manager, Member, *[or any of their Affiliates]* shall incur any liability to the Company or to any of the Equity Owners as a result of engaging in any other business or venture.[39]

---

37. The default standard of care under the uniform partnership and LLC statutes is gross negligence.

38. Consider as alternatives or in addition, "material" and "repeated."

39. This provision should be carefully considered in a couple of respects. First, the more specific the waiver of a duty of loyalty is, the more likely it is to be enforced by a court. If there are particular types of transactions that can be anticipated, it may be advisable to list them in particular, perhaps using language above followed by something like "Without limiting the generality of the foregoing, the Member expressly agree that a Member or Manager may _____." Second, states differ in the ability to modify duties, particularly the duty of loyalty. The state statute should be carefully reviewed. Finally, the Members should consider whether they want the duty of loyalty reduced to the maximum extent possible. This is one section where the agreement should accurately reflect the expectations of the parties. See, e.g., *McConnell v. Hunt Sport Enterprises*, 725 N.E.2d 1193 (Ohio App. 1999) upholding a provision stating that "Members shall not in any way be prohibited from or restricted in engaging or owning an interest in any other business venture of any nature, including any venture which might be competitive with the business of the Company . . ."

5.7 <u>Indemnity of the Managers, Employees and Other Agents</u>.

(a)   The Company shall indemnify each Manager *[and its Affiliates]* for any loss in connection with its activities (other than solely in its capacity as an Equity Owner, if applicable) in connection with the establishment, management or operations of the Company and make advances for expenses to the maximum extent permitted under the Act, except to the extent the claim for which indemnification is sought results from an act or omission for which the Manager *[or the Affiliates of such Manager] [may be] [is]* held liable to the Company or to a Member under Section 5.5(b).[40] The Company shall indemnify its employees and other agents who are not Managers to the fullest extent permitted by law, *[provided that such indemnification in any given situation is Approved by Members owning a Majority Interest]*.

(b)   Expenses (including legal fees and expenses) incurred by a Manager *[or by one of its Affiliates]* in defending any claim, demand, action, suit or proceeding subject to subsection (a) above shall be paid by the Company in advance of the final disposition of such claim, demand, action, suit, or proceeding upon receipt of an undertaking (which need not be secured) by or on behalf of the Manager to repay such amount if it shall ultimately be finally determined by a court of competent jurisdiction and not subject to appeal, that the Manager *[or such Affiliate]* is not entitled to be indemnified by the Company as authorized hereunder.

5.8 <u>Resignation</u>. Any Manager may resign at any time by giving written notice to the Members. The resignation of any Manager shall take effect upon receipt of notice thereof or at such later time as shall be specified in such notice; and, unless otherwise specified therein, the acceptance of such resignation shall not be necessary to make it effective. The resignation of a Manager who is also an Equity Owner shall not affect the Manager's rights as an Equity Owner and shall not constitute a withdrawal of an Equity Owner.

5.9 <u>Removal</u>. At a meeting called expressly for that purpose, all or any lesser number of Managers may be removed at any time by Approval of the Members holding a *[Majority Interest] [Two–Thirds Interest]* (determined without regard to any Voting Interest held by the Manager who is to be removed and who is also a Member) for *[gross negligence, fraud, deceit or intentional misconduct which had a material adverse effect on the Company, or if the Manager is adjudicated incompetent by a Court of competent jurisdiction] is Disabled] [with or without cause]*. The removal of a Manager who is also an Equity Owner shall not affect the

---

40.   Regardless of how the previous sections address the duty of care and loyalty, the indemnification section should provide for indemnification to the extent that the actions do not violate the standards set forth in those sections so that in the event of any loss, if the loss does not result from the violation of the agreed-upon standard, the Company bears the loss and if it does, the Member or Manager violating the standard bears the loss.

Manager's rights as an Equity Owner and shall not constitute a withdrawal of an Equity Owner.[41]

5.10 <u>Vacancies</u>. Any vacancy occurring for any reason in the number of Managers shall be filled by the Approval of Members holding a *[Majority Interest]* (determined without regard to any Voting Interest owned by a Manager who was removed pursuant to Section 5.9 during the preceding 24–month period). Any Manager's position to be filled by reason of an increase in the number of Managers shall be filled by the Approval of Members holding a Majority Interest.

5.11 <u>Compensation, Reimbursement, Organization Expenses</u>.

(a) *[The compensation of the Managers shall be fixed from time to time by Approval of Members holding at least a Majority Interest, and no Manager shall be prevented from receiving such compensation by reason of the fact that he is also a Member.] [No Member shall be entitled to compensation from the Company for services rendered to the Company as such.]* Upon the submission of appropriate documentation, each Manager shall be reimbursed by the Company for reasonable out-of-pocket expenses incurred on behalf, or at the request, of the Company.

(b) The Company shall reimburse ____ and ____ for the legal expenses reasonably incurred by them in connection with the formation, organization and capitalization of the Company, including the legal fees incurred in connection with negotiating and drafting this Agreement and ____ .

(c) The Managers shall cause the Company to make an appropriate election to treat the expenses incurred by the Company in connection with the formation and organization of the Company to be amortized over the period allowed by Code Section 709 to the extent that such expenses constitute "organizational expenses" of the Company within the meaning of Code Section 709(b)(2).

(d) *[The Company shall reimburse each Manager for the costs it incurs for legal advice from that Manager's own attorney with respect to the Manager's rights and duties under this Agreement and the Act. The Company and the Members expressly agree that notwithstanding the reimbursement of the Manager's legal expenses, the Manager's attorney shall not be attorney for, nor have an attorney-client relationship with, the Company or for any other Person other than the Manager by reason of the reimbursement.]*[42]

41. Consider the advisability of including an option in favor of the Company or the other members to purchase the Ownership Interest of a Manager (assuming the Manager has an Ownership Interest) in the event that the Manager is removed for cause pursuant to this Section 5.9. For example, if the Manager commits fraud, the Company will presumably wish it had an option to buy out any Membership Interest owned by the offending Member.

42. In a particularly contentious situation a Manager may want the Company to defer the costs of the Manager's attorney, while affording the Manager the benefit of

5.12 <u>Annual Operating Plan</u>.[43] The Members have approved the Company's construction budget. The Managers shall prepare for the Approval of the Members each Fiscal Year (no later than thirty (30) days prior to the end of the then current Fiscal Year) a business plan (the "<u>Annual Operating Plan</u>") for the next Fiscal Year, setting forth at a minimum the estimated receipts (including capital calls) and expenditures (capital, operating and other) of the Company in sufficient detail to provide an estimate of cash flow, capital proceeds, and other financial requirements of the Company for such year. Any such Annual Operating Plan shall also include such other information or other matters necessary in order to inform the Members of the Company's business and to enable the Members to make an informed decision with respect to their Approval of such Annual Operating Plan. The Members shall review the proposed Annual Operating Plan and shall offer any revisions thereto within *[30]* days. After the final Annual Operating Plan has been approved by the Members, the Managers shall implement the Annual Operating Plan and shall be authorized to make only the expenditures and incur only the obligations provided for therein (subject to Section 5.4(b)). Notwithstanding the foregoing, the Managers may make any expenditure or incur any obligation, whether or not such expenditure or obligation is provided for in an Annual Operating Plan, which is the legal obligation of the Company and not within the reasonable control of the Managers (*e.g.*, real or personal property taxes). If the Members are not able to agree on an Annual Operating Plan for any year, each line item in the Annual Operating Plan for the prior year shall be increased by the percentage increase in the CPI Index from the first day for which the previous Annual Operating Plan was in effect to the first day for which the new Annual Operating Plan is to be in effect. If the CPI Index is no longer published, published less frequently, or altered in some other manner, then the Managers shall, from time to time, adopt a substitute index or substitute procedure which reasonably reflects and monitors consumer prices, and the resulting plan shall be the Annual Operating Plan for the current year.

5.13 <u>Right to Rely on the Managers</u>. Any Person dealing with the Company may rely (without duty of further inquiry) upon a certificate signed by any Manager as to:

    (a)   The identity of any Manager or Equity Owner;

    (b)   The existence or nonexistence of any fact or facts which constitute a condition precedent to acts on behalf of the Company by any Manager or which are in any other manner germane to the affairs of the Company;

---

its own counsel. This provision, if desired, needs to be carefully considered as do the ethical considerations for the attorney for the Manager.

43. As noted above, if his provision is included. Sections 5.3 and 5.4 should be conformed with the Annual Operating Plan.

(c)   The Persons who are authorized to execute and deliver any instrument or document of the Company; or

(d)   Any act or failure to act by the Company or any other matter whatsoever involving the Company or any Equity Owner.

ARTICLE 6

RIGHTS AND OBLIGATIONS OF EQUITY OWNERS

6.1 <u>Limitation of Liability</u>. Except as otherwise provided by this Agreement and the non-waivable provisions of the Act, no Equity Owner shall be liable for an obligation of the Company solely by reason of being or acting as an Equity Owner.

6.2 <u>List of Equity Owners</u>. Upon written request of any Member made in good faith and for a purpose reasonably related to the Member's rights as a Member under this Agreement (which reason shall be set forth in the written request), a Manager shall provide a list showing the names, addresses and Ownership Interests of all Equity Owners. Economic Interest Owners shall have no rights to information under this Section 6.2.

6.3 <u>Equity Owners Have No Agency Authority</u>. Except as expressly provided in this Agreement, the Equity Owners (in their capacity as Equity Owners) shall have no agency authority on behalf of the Company.

6.4 <u>Priority and Return of Capital</u>. Except as may be expressly provided in Article 9, no Equity Owner shall have priority over any other Equity Owner, either as to the return of Capital Contributions or as to Profits, Losses or Distributions; provided, however, that this Section 6.4 shall not apply to loans (as distinguished from Capital Contributions) which an Equity Owner has made to the Company.

6.5 <u>Non-Colorado Resident Equity Owners</u>. Equity Owners that are not residents of Colorado agree to sign a completed Colorado Department of Revenue form DR0107 and agree to return the completed form to the Company. Such Equity Owners also agree to file a Colorado income tax return and pay all Colorado taxes with respect to their allocable share of the taxable earnings of the Company each year. All Equity Owners agree to comply with similar provisions imposed on non-resident Equity Owners in any other state in which the Company does business and which imposes similar requirements on non-resident Equity Owners.

ARTICLE 7

ACTIONS OF MEMBERS

7.1 <u>Approval of Members</u>. Unless otherwise required in this Agreement, Approvals of the Members may be communicated or reflected [orally,] electronically[,] or in writing, and no action need be taken at a formal meeting. If, however, any Approval is required to be in writing, such Approval shall be evidenced (i) by a written consent, which may be executed in separate written counterparts or (ii) by the Approval of the Members at a meeting, in each case by Members holding the requisite number of Voting Interests required for such Approval. If not done in writing, then (unless such Approval is required to be in writing) any Approval of the Members shall be effective when a sufficient number of Members holding the requisite threshold of Voting Interests required to give such Approval communicate their Approval to the Managers.

7.2 <u>Members' Meetings</u>. Members may, but are not required to, meet from time to time on at least five days' written notice which may be given by a Manager or by any Member [holding at least a Majority Interest]. Members holding at least a [Majority Interest], represented in person or by proxy, shall constitute a quorum at any meeting of the Members. The foregoing shall constitute the procedure for all meetings of the Members.

7.3 <u>No Required Meetings</u>. The Members may, but shall not be required to, hold any annual, periodic, or other formal meetings. However, meetings of the Members may be called by any Manager *[who is also a Member]* or by any Member or Members holding at least [＿＿] percent of the Voting Interests.[46]

7.4 <u>Place of Meetings</u>. The Member or Members calling the meeting may designate any place within *[State]* as the place of meeting for any meeting of the Members; Members holding a Two–Thirds Interest may designate any place outside *[State]* as the place of meeting for any meeting of the Members. If no designation is made, or if a special meeting be otherwise called, the place of meeting shall be the principal executive office of the Company in *[State]*.

7.5 <u>Notice of Meetings</u>. Except as provided in Section 7.6, written notice stating the place, day and hour of the meeting and the purpose or purposes for which the meeting is called shall be delivered not less than ten nor more than 50 days before the date of the meeting, either personally or by mail, by or at the direction of the Member or Members calling the meeting, to each Member entitled to vote at such meeting.

7.6 <u>Meeting of all Members</u>. If all of the Members shall meet at any time and place, either within or outside of *[State]*, and Approve to the

---

46. In some circumstances, such as two-member LLCs, the complex meeting provisions set forth in this and the following sections will be unnecessary and can be dispensed with.

holding of a meeting at such time and place, such meeting shall be valid without call or notice, and at such meeting lawful action may be taken.

7.7 <u>Record Date</u>. For the purpose of determining Members entitled to notice of or to vote at any meeting of Members or any adjournment thereof, or Members entitled to receive payment of any Distribution, or in order to make a determination of Members for any other purpose, the date on which notice of the meeting is mailed or the date on which the resolution declaring such Distribution is adopted, as the case may be, shall be the record date for such determination of Members. When a determination of Members entitled to vote at any meeting of Members has been made as provided in this Section 7.7, such determination shall apply to any adjournment thereof.

7.8 <u>Quorum</u>. Members holding at least a *[Two–Thirds Interest]*, represented in person or by proxy, shall constitute a quorum at any meeting of Members. In the absence of a quorum at any such meeting, a majority of the Voting Interests so represented may adjourn the meeting from time to time for a period not to exceed 60 days without further notice. However, if the adjournment is for more than 60 days, or if after the adjournment a new record date is fixed for the adjourned meeting, a notice of the adjourned meeting shall be given to each Member of record entitled to vote at the meeting. At such adjourned meeting at which a quorum shall be present or represented, any business may be transacted which might have been transacted at the meeting as originally noticed. The Members present at a duly organized meeting may continue to transact business until adjournment, notwithstanding the withdrawal during such meeting of that number of Voting Interests whose absence would cause less than a quorum.

7.9 <u>Manner of Acting</u>. If a quorum is present, the affirmative vote of Members holding a Majority Interest shall be the act of the Members, unless the vote of a greater or lesser proportion or number is otherwise required by the Act, by the *[Articles of Organization/Certificate of Formation]*, or by this Agreement. Unless otherwise expressly provided herein, Members, who have an interest (economic or otherwise) in the outcome of any particular matter upon which the Members vote, may vote upon any such matter, and their Voting Interest shall be counted in the determination of whether the requisite matter is approved by the Members.

7.10 <u>Proxies</u>. At all meetings of Members, a Member who is qualified to vote may vote in person or by proxy executed in writing by the Member or by a duly authorized attorney-in-fact. Such proxy shall be filed with the Managers before or at the time of the meeting. Such proxy shall expire eleven months from the date of its execution or the date indicated in such proxy, whichever occurs first.

7.11 <u>Action by Members Without a Meeting</u>. Action required or permitted to be taken at a meeting of Members may be taken without a meeting if the action is evidenced by one or more written consents describing the action taken and signed by Members holding sufficient Voting Interests, as the case may be, to Approve such action had such action been properly voted on at a duly called meeting of the Members. Action taken under this Section 7.11 is effective when Members with the requisite Voting Interests have signed the consent, unless the consent specifies a different effective date. The record date for determining the Members who are entitled to take action without a meeting shall be the date the first Member signs a consent.

7.12 <u>Waiver of Notice</u>. When any notice is required to be given to any Member, a waiver thereof in writing signed by the person entitled to such notice, whether before, at, or after the time stated therein, shall be equivalent to the giving of such notice.

ARTICLE 8

CONTRIBUTIONS TO THE COMPANY
AND CAPITAL ACCOUNTS

8.1 <u>Members' Capital Contributions</u>. Not later than *[ten days after each of the parties has executed this Agreement and delivered an executed copy of same to the Managers]*, each Equity Owner shall contribute such amount as is set forth in <u>Exhibit 8.1</u> hereto as its share of the Initial Capital Contribution.

8.2 <u>Additional Contributions</u>. *[Each Equity Owner shall be required to make such additional Capital Contributions as shall be determined by the Managers from time to time to be necessary to meet the expenses of the Company; provided, however, that the maximum amount which an Equity Owner shall be required to contribute to the Company pursuant to this Section 8.2 (i.e., in addition to the amount contributed by such Equity Owner pursuant to Section 8.1) shall not exceed the amount set forth corresponding to such Equity Owner's name on <u>Exhibit 8.2</u>. Upon the making of any such determination, the Managers shall give written notice to each Equity Owner of the amount of required additional contribution, and each Equity Owner shall deliver to the Company its pro rata share thereof (in proportion to [Sharing Ratios/other?] of the Member on the date such notice is given) no later than 30 days following the date such notice is given. None of the terms, covenants, obligations or rights contained in this Section 8.2 is or shall be deemed to be for the benefit of any Person other than the Equity Owners and the Company, and no such third person shall under any circumstances have any right to compel any actions or payments by the Managers or the Equity Owners.]*

OR

[Except as set forth in Section 8.1, no Equity Owner shall be required to make any Capital Contributions. To the extent unanimously Approved

by the Managers, from time to time, the Equity Owners may be permitted to make additional Capital Contributions if and to the extent that both (i) they so desire and (ii) the Managers determine that such additional Capital Contributions are necessary or appropriate in connection with the conduct of the Company's business (including expansion or diversification). In such event, the Equity Owners shall have the opportunity (but not the obligation) to participate in such additional Capital Contributions proportionate to [their Sharing Ratios]. [At the time such Capital Contributions are made, the Sharing Ratios of the Equity Owners [and Voting Interests of the Members] shall be adjusted in an equitable manner determined by the Managers and the Members in their reasonable discretion.]

8.3 Capital Accounts.

(a) A separate Capital Account shall be maintained for each Equity Owner. Each Equity Owner's Capital Account shall be increased by (i) the amount of money contributed by such Equity Owner to the Company; (ii) the Gross Asset Value of property contributed by such Equity Owner to the Company (net of liabilities secured by such contributed property that the Company is considered to assume or take subject to under Section 752 of the Code); (iii) allocations to such Equity Owner of Profits; and (iv) any items in the nature of income and gain which are specially allocated to the Equity Owner pursuant to Sections 9.2 and 9.3. Each Equity Owner's Capital Account shall be decreased by (1) the amount of money Distributed to such Equity Owner by the Company; (2) the Gross Asset Value of property Distributed to such Equity Owner by the Company (net of liabilities secured by such Distributed property that such Equity Owner is considered to assume or take subject to under Section 752 of the Code); (3) any items in the nature of deduction and loss that are specially allocated to the Equity Owner pursuant to Sections 9.2 and 9.3; and (4) allocations to such Equity Owner of Losses.

(b) Without limiting the other rights and duties of a transferee of an Ownership Interest pursuant to this Agreement, in the event of a permitted sale or exchange of an Ownership Interest in the Company, (i) the Capital Account of the transferor shall become the Capital Account of the transferee to the extent it relates to the transferred Ownership Interest in accordance with Section 1.704–1(b)(2)(iv) of the Regulations, and (ii) the transferee shall be treated as the transferor for purposes of allocations and distributions pursuant to Article 9 to the extent that such allocations and distributions relate to the transferred Ownership Interest.

(c) The manner in which Capital Accounts are to be maintained pursuant to this Section 8.3 is intended to comply with the requirements of Section 704(b) of the Code and the Regulations

521

thereunder. If in the opinion of the Company's accountants the manner in which Capital Accounts are to be maintained pursuant to the preceding provisions of this Section 8.3 should be modified in order to comply with Section 704(b) of the Code and the Regulations thereunder, then, notwithstanding anything to the contrary contained in the preceding provisions of this Section 8.3, the method in which Capital Accounts are maintained shall be so modified; provided, however, that any change in the manner of maintaining Capital Accounts shall not materially alter the economic agreement between or among the Equity Owners.

(d)   Upon liquidation of the Company, liquidating Distributions shall be made in accordance with the positive Capital Account balances of the Equity Owners, as determined after taking into account all Capital Account adjustments for the Company's taxable year during which the liquidation occurs. Liquidation proceeds shall be paid in accordance with Section 12.3. The Company may offset damages for breach of this Agreement by any Equity Owner whose interest is liquidated (either upon the withdrawal of the Equity Owner or the liquidation of the Company) against the amount otherwise Distributable to such Equity Owner. No Equity Owner shall have any obligation to restore all or any portion of a deficit balance in such Equity Owner's Capital Account.

(e)   The Managers shall also: (i) make any adjustments that are necessary or appropriate to maintain equality between the Capital Accounts of the Equity Owners and the amount of capital reflected on the Company's balance sheet, as computed for book purposes, in accordance with Section 1.704–1(b)(2)(iv)(q) of the Regulations, and (ii) make any appropriate modifications in the event unanticipated events might otherwise cause this Agreement not to comply with Section 1.704–1(b) of the Regulations; provided that, to the extent that any such adjustment is inconsistent with other provisions of this Agreement and would have a material adverse effect on any Equity Owner, such adjustment shall require the consent of such Equity Owner.

8.4 Withdrawal or Reduction of Equity Owners' Contributions to Capital.

(a)   A Member may withdraw as a Member at any time. A Member's withdrawal shall cause the Member's Membership Interest to become an Economic Interest, but shall not entitle the former Member or his or her successor to demand that the Economic Interest be liquidated.

(b)   An Equity Owner shall not receive a Distribution of any part of its Capital Contribution to the extent such Distribution would violate Section 9.5.

(c) An Equity Owner, irrespective of the nature of its Capital Contribution, does not have the right to demand and receive property other than cash in return for its Capital Contribution.

8.5 Remedies for Non–Payment of Capital Contributions. Failure of any Equity Owner to make full and timely payment to the Company of any additional Capital Contribution properly assessed hereunder shall constitute a breach of this Agreement (and any such Equity Owner shall be hereinafter referred to as a "Defaulting Equity Owner"). Upon such a breach, the Managers shall promptly give notice (the "Default Notice") to all Equity Owners of: (a) the breach and (b) a Special Meeting to discuss the appropriate course of action. The Equity Owners who timely satisfied their obligation to make the required Additional Capital Contributions (the "Non–Defaulting Equity Owners") may, upon the Approval of those Non–Defaulting Equity Owners which are Members holding a majority of the Voting Interests owned by all Non–Defaulting Equity Owners which are Members, pursue the following courses of action:

(a) The Non–Defaulting Equity Owners, shall have an option, but no obligation, to loan to the Company within sixty (60) days after the Default Notice is given (the "Loan Decision Period") the amount which the Defaulting Equity Owners have failed to contribute to the Company (proportionate to the ratio of the interest in Profits held by each respective Equity Owner electing to loan funds, to the interest in Profits Interests held by all Equity Owners electing to advance funds). The amount that is loaned by any Non–Defaulting Equity Owner shall, at the election of each such Equity Owner (exercised by written notice to the Defaulting Equity Owner and the Company at the time the loan is made), be treated in either of the following manners:

(i) The loan may be treated as a loan to the Company, bearing interest at a floating rate equal to five (5) percentage points higher than the prime commercial lending rate in effect from time to time at the principal bank used by the Company for banking and borrowing purposes..., payable out of any funds paid by, or withheld by the Company from, the Defaulting Equity Owner to cure the breach, or at such other time as the Company and the lending Equity Owners may agree. Payments shall be credited first to accrued interest. The promissory note or other loan documentation shall contain such other terms and conditions as mutually agreed by the Company and the lending Equity Owners.

(ii) The loan may be treated as a loan to the Defaulting Equity Owner, followed by a contribution of the borrowed funds to the Company by the Defaulting Equity Owner curing the breach in whole or in part. Such a loan shall be payable on demand and bear interest at the default rate provided above.

Until the Defaulting Equity Owner's debt to any Non–Defaulting Equity Owners, together with interest thereon, is paid in full, any funds or property which would otherwise be Distributed to the Defaulting Equity Owner from time to time hereunder shall be paid to such Non–Defaulting Equity Owners, according to their respective shares of loans (which are treated as loans to the Defaulting Equity Owner). Any such payments shall be deemed to be Distributions to the Defaulting Equity Owner by the Company, followed by appropriate payments by the Defaulting Equity Owner to the respective Non–Defaulting Equity Owners. Payments shall be credited first to accrued interest. Payments to Non–Defaulting Equity Owners of loans by them pursuant to either Section 8.5(a)(1) or 8.5(a)(2) shall be made *pari passu.*

(b) If the Non–Defaulting Equity Owners do not make loans pursuant to Section 8.5(a) in an amount at least equal to the amount which the Defaulting Equity Owner failed to contribute (and the Defaulting Equity Owner has not cured said breach prior to the expiration of the Loan Decision Period), then promptly upon the expiration of the Loan Decision Period, the Managers shall give notice (the "Default Purchase Option Notice" as more fully described below) to all of the Equity Owners. The Non–Defaulting Equity Owners shall have the option (but no obligation) for the sixty (60) day period commencing upon the date of the Default Purchase Option Notice to purchase all, but not less than all, of a Defaulting Equity Owner's Interest as provided in this Section 8.5(b). The option granted in this Section 8.5(b) (the "Default Purchase Option") shall be exercisable in the following manner and in accordance with the following terms:

(i) The Default Purchase Option Notice shall notify the Non–Defaulting Equity Owners that they have the opportunity to purchase all, but not less than all, of the Ownership Interest owned by the Defaulting Equity Owner ("Available Ownership Interest").

(ii) A Non–Defaulting Equity Owner wishing to exercise the Default Purchase Option shall so notify (the "Exercise Notice") the Defaulting Equity Owner and the Company within forty-five (45) days after the date that the Default Purchase Option Notice is given.

(iii) Each Non–Defaulting Equity Owner electing to exercise the Default Purchase Option (each an "Electing Equity Owner" and collectively the "Electing Equity Owners") shall be entitled to purchase a portion of the Available Ownership Interest proportionate to the Electing Equity Owner's sharing ratio.

(iv)   The closing for any purchase and sale of the Available Ownership Interest pursuant to this Section 8.5(b) shall take place within ninety (90) days after the date that the Default Purchase Option Notice is given. The specific time and place of closing shall be as agreed by the Electing Equity Owners and the Defaulting Member; provided, however, that in the absence of agreement, the closing shall take place at the Company's principal office.

(v)   The price for the Defaulting Equity Owner's Ownership Interest (the "Default Buyout Price") shall be equal to *[fifty percent (50%)]* of the Defaulting Equity Owner's Capital Account balance as of the last day of the month preceding the month in which the Exercise Notice is given. For purposes of this Section 8.5(b), the Company's independent certified public accountant shall determine the balance in the Defaulting Equity Owner's Capital Account (without regard to any optional adjustments which may, but are not required, to be made for any purpose, including any optional adjustments that may be made in order to reflect the fair market value of Company Property), and such determination shall be final for purposes of this Agreement.

(vi)   Upon any purchase of a Defaulting Equity Owner's Ownership Interest pursuant to this Section 8.5(b), the Default Buyout Price may be paid at closing in immediately available funds, or, in the sole discretion of each Electing Equity Owner, by delivering at closing a note issued by the Electing Members as payment for the portion of the Buyout Price attributable to the portion of the Ownership Interest to be purchased by the Electing Equity Owner. The notes issued as payment for the Default Buyout Price shall be negotiable promissory notes of the Company or of the Electing Equity Owner, as appropriate, bearing interest per annum at a floating rate one percentage point over the prime commercial lending rate in effect from time to time at the principal bank used by the Company for banking and borrowing purposes. Any such notes shall provide for payments of principal and interest in equal consecutive monthly installments over a period of not more than five years from the date of issuance of such note, commencing from the date of issuance of such note. Any such notes shall be prepayable without penalty, in whole or in part, with prepayments applied to the last installment or installments coming due. Such notes shall provide that if any installment of principal or interest is not paid when due or if suit is brought thereon, the maker will pay all costs of collection, including reasonable attorneys' fees.

(vii) After purchasing an Available Ownership Interest, each Electing Equity Owner shall make an additional Capital Contribution to the Company in an amount equal to the proportionate share of the Defaulted Capital Contribution attributable to the portion of the Available Ownership Interest purchased by the Electing Equity Owner.

ARTICLE 9

ALLOCATIONS, INCOME TAX, DISTRIBUTIONS, ELECTIONS AND REPORTS

9.1 <u>Allocations of Profits and Losses from Operations</u>. Except as provided in Sections 9.2 and 9.3, the Profits and Losses for each Fiscal Year shall be allocated as follows:

(a) *[Losses shall be allocated among the Equity Owners in accordance with their relative Sharing Ratios.*

(b) *Profits shall be allocated as follows:*

(i) *First, to each Equity Owner which previously has been allocated Losses pursuant to Section 9.1(a) which have not been fully offset by allocations of Profits pursuant to this Section 9.1(b)(i) ("Unrecovered Losses") until the total amount of Profits allocated to each such Equity Owner pursuant to this Section 9.1(b)(i) is equal to the total amount of Losses which have been allocated to such Equity Owner pursuant to Section 9.1(a). Profits allocated pursuant to this Section 9.1(b)(i) shall be allocated to the Equity Owners in proportion to their respective Unrecovered Losses;*

(ii) *Second, to each Equity Owner an amount equal to the total amount of the Preferred Accrual proportionate with the Preferred Accruals of all Equity Owners until the aggregate amount allocated pursuant to this Section 9.1(b)(ii) equals its Preferred Accrual;*[47]

(iii) *Third, to the Equity Owners in proportion to their Sharing Ratios.]*

Notwithstanding the provisions of this Section 9.1, it is the intent of the Equity Owners that Profits and Losses will be allocated in a manner that causes the Capital Accounts of the Equity Owners, in conjunction with all Distributions made in accordance with Section 9.4, to have balances such that the Equity Owners would receive amounts equal to that called for in Section 9.4 on a liquidation pursuant to Article 12 and this Section 9.1 shall be interpreted in a manner to accomplish this

---

47. *This section 9.1(b) should be used when section 9.4(b)(i) is used [consider drafting so that allocations follow cash flow if cash situation may create phantom income problem, but consider risk that income may not be sufficient to follow cash.]*

result, including special allocations of gross income and gross deductions, by the Managers.

9.2 <u>Special Allocations to Capital Accounts</u>. Notwithstanding Section 9.1 hereof:

(a) In the event that any Equity Owner unexpectedly receives any adjustments, allocations or Distributions described in Sections 1.704–1(b)(2)(ii)(d)(4), (5), or (6) of the Regulations, which create or increase a Deficit Capital Account of such Equity Owner, then items of Company income and gain (consisting of a *pro rata* portion of each item of Company income, including gross income, and gain for such year and, if necessary, for subsequent years) shall be specially allocated to such Equity Owner in an amount and manner sufficient to eliminate, to the extent required by the Regulations, the Deficit Capital Account so created as quickly as possible. It is the intent that this Section 9.2(a) be interpreted to comply with the alternate test for economic effect set forth in Section 1.704–1(b)(2)(ii)(d) of the Regulations.

(b) The Losses allocated pursuant to Section 9.1 hereof shall not exceed the maximum amount of Losses that can be so allocated without causing any Equity Owner to have a Deficit Capital Account at the end of any Fiscal Year. In the event that some, but not all, of the Equity Owners would have Deficit Capital Accounts as a consequence of an allocation of Losses pursuant to Section 9.1 hereof, the limitation set forth in the preceding sentence shall be applied on a Equity Owner by Equity Owner basis so as to allocate the maximum permissible Losses to each Equity Owner under Section 1.704–1(b)(2)(ii)(d) of the Regulations. All Losses in excess of the limitation set forth in this Section 9.2(b) shall be allocated to the Equity Owners in proportion to their respective positive Capital Account balances, if any, and thereafter to the Equity Owners in accordance with their interests in the Company as determined by the Managers in their reasonable discretion. In the event that any Equity Owner would have a Deficit Capital Account at the end of any Fiscal Year, the Capital Account of such Equity Owner shall be specially credited with items of Company income (including gross income) and gain in the amount of such excess as quickly as possible.

(c) Notwithstanding any other provision of this Section 9.2, if there is a net decrease in the Company Minimum Gain during any Fiscal Year, then the Capital Accounts of each Equity Owner shall be specially allocated items of income (including gross income) and gain for such Fiscal Year (and if necessary for subsequent Fiscal Years) equal to that Equity Owner's share of the net decrease in Company Minimum Gain, determined in accordance with Section 1.704–2(g) of the Regulations. Allocations pursuant to the previous sentence shall be made in proportion to the respective amounts required to be allocated to each Equity Owner pursuant thereto. The items to be so allocated shall be determined in accordance with Sections 1.704–2(f)(6) and 1.704–2(j)(2) of the Regulations. If in any Fiscal Year that the Company has a net decrease in the Company Minimum Gain, if the minimum gain chargeback requirement would cause a distortion in the economic arrangement among the Equity Owners and it is not expected that the Company will have sufficient other income to correct that distortion, the Managers may in their discretion (and shall, if requested to do so by a Equity Owner) seek to have the Internal Revenue Service waive the minimum gain chargeback requirement in accordance with Section 1.704–2(f)(4) of the Regulations.

(d) Notwithstanding any other provision of this Section 9.2 except Section 9.2(c), if there is a net decrease in Equity Owner Minimum Gain attributable to a Equity Owner Nonrecourse Debt during any Fiscal Year, each Equity Owner who has a share of the Equity Owner Minimum Gain as of the beginning of the Fiscal Year shall be specially allocated items of Company income and gain for such Fiscal Year (and, if necessary, subsequent Fiscal Years) equal to such Equity Owner's share of the net decrease in Equity Owner Minimum Gain attributable to such Equity Owner Nonrecourse Debt, determined in accordance with Section 1.704–2(i)(4) of the Regulations. An Equity Owner shall not be subject to this provision to the extent that an exception is provided by Section 1.704–2(i)(4) of the Regulations and any administrative guidance issued by the Internal Revenue Service with respect thereto. Allocations pursuant to the previous sentence shall be made in proportion to the respective amounts required to be allocated to each Equity Owner pursuant thereto. The items to be so allocated shall be determined in accordance with Sections 1.704–2(i)(4) and 1.704–2(j)(2) of the Regulations. Any Equity Owner Minimum Gain allocated pursuant to this provision shall consist of first, gains recognized from the disposition of Company property subject to the Equity Owner Nonrecourse Debt, and, second, if necessary, a *pro rata* portion of the Company's other items of income or gain (including gross income) for that Fiscal Year. This Section 9.2(d) is intended to comply with the minimum gain chargeback requirement in Section 1.704–2(i)(4) of the Regulations and shall be interpreted consistently therewith.

(e) Items of Company loss, deduction and expenditures described in Section 705(a)(2)(B) of the Code which are attributable to any nonrecourse debt of the Company and are characterized as partner nonrecourse deductions under Section 1.704–2(i) of the Regulations shall be allocated to the Equity Owners' Capital Accounts in accordance with said Section 1.704–2(i) of the Regulations.

(f) Beginning in the first taxable year in which there are allocations of "nonrecourse deductions" (as described in Section

1.704–2(b) of the Regulations), such deductions shall be allocated to the Equity Owners in the same manner as Loss is allocated for such period.

(g) To the extent that an adjustment to the adjusted tax basis of any Company asset pursuant to Section 734(b) or 743(b) of the Code is required pursuant to Section 1.704–1(b)(2)(iv)(m)(2) or 1.704–1(b)(2)(iv)(m)(4) of the Regulations, to be taken into account in determining Capital Accounts as the result of a Distribution to an Equity Owner in complete liquidation of its Ownership Interest, the amount of such adjustment to Capital Accounts shall be treated as an item of gain (if the adjustment increases the basis of the asset) or loss (if the adjustment decreases such basis), and such gain or loss shall be specially allocated to the Equity Owners in accordance with their interests in the Company in the event Section 1.704–1(b)(2)(iv)(m)(2) of the Regulations applies, or to the Equity Owner to whom such Distribution was made in the event Section 1.704–1(b)(2)(iv)(m)(4) of the Regulations applies.

(h) The Issuance Items shall be allocated among the Equity Owners so that, to the extent possible, the net amount of such Issuance Items, together with all other allocations under this Agreement to each Equity Owner, shall be equal to the net amount that would have been allocated to each such Equity Owner if the Issuance Items had not been realized.

9.3 Credit or Charge to Capital Accounts. Any credit or charge to the Capital Accounts of the Equity Owners pursuant to the Regulatory Allocations shall be taken into account in computing subsequent allocations of Profits and Losses pursuant to Section 9.1, so that the net amount of any items charged or credited to Capital Accounts pursuant to Section 9.1 and the Regulatory Allocations hereof and this Section 9.3 shall to the extent possible, be equal to the net amount that would have been allocated to the Capital Account of each Equity Owner pursuant to the provisions of this Article 9 if the special allocations required by the Regulatory Allocations hereof had not occurred; provided, however, that no such allocation will be made pursuant to this Section 9.3 if (i) the Regulatory Allocation had the effect of offsetting a prior Regulatory Allocation or (ii) the Regulatory Allocation likely (in the opinion of the Company's accountants) will be offset by another Regulatory Allocation in the future (*e.g.*, Regulatory Allocation of "nonrecourse deductions" under Section 9.2(e) that likely will be subject to a subsequent "minimum gain chargeback" under Section 9.2(c)).

9.4 Distributions. *[ALTERNATIVE 1 Except as provided in Sections 8.3(d) (with respect to liquidating Distributions) and 9.5 (with respect to limitations on Distributions), the Company shall Distribute Distributable Cash [not less frequently than quarterly] to the Equity Owners in accordance with their [Sharing Ratios]. All Distributions which, when made, exceed the recipient Equity Owner's basis in that Equity Owner's Owner-ship Interest shall be considered advances or drawings against the Equity Owner's distributive share of taxable income or gain. To the extent it is determined at the end of the Fiscal Year that the recipient Equity Owner has not been allocated taxable income or gain that equals or exceeds the total of such advances or drawings for such Fiscal Year, such Equity Owner shall be obligated to recontribute any such excess advances or drawings to the Company. Notwithstanding the foregoing sentence, an Equity Owner will not be required to recontribute such advances or drawings to the extent that, on the last day of the Fiscal Year, such Equity Owner's basis in its Ownership Interest in the Company has increased from the time of such advance or drawing. Any advance or drawings which are recontributed by a Equity Owner pursuant to this Section 9.4, shall be redistributed to such Equity Owner either at the option of such Equity Owner or at such time that such distribution will not exceed such Equity Owner's basis in its Ownership Interest.]*

[Alternative 2/for illustrative purposes only: Except as provided in Sections 8.3(d) (with respect to liquidating Distributions) and 9.5 (with respect to limitations on Distributions):

(a)   The Company shall Distribute Distributable Cash [not less frequently than quarterly] to each Equity Owner in proportion to the federal taxable income of the Company which will be [and has been] allocated to such Equity Owner ("Tax Profits") for the current [and all prior] Fiscal Year[s] as reasonably estimated by the Managers no later than 10 days prior to the dates that federal estimated quarterly taxes are due for individuals an amount equal to the remainder, if any, of: (i) the product of [40%] [the Tax Rate] multiplied times the estimated Tax Profits allocable to such Equity Owner [for the prior years and the] portion of the year ending on the last day of the most recent quarter, minus (ii) the sum of all Distributions made to each such Equity Owner pursuant to this Section 9.4(a) with respect to such Fiscal Year[s], plus the product of [40%] [the Tax Rate] multiplied times any Unrecovered Tax Losses attributable to such Equity Owner as of the first day of the current Fiscal Year. The Unrecovered Tax Losses attributable to an Equity Owner shall mean the positive remainder, if any, of such Equity Owner's share of the Company's federal tax losses for all prior Fiscal Years minus the Equity Owner's share of Tax Profits for all prior Fiscal Years. The objective of this Section 9.4(a) is to make distributions with reference to each Equity Owner's (and such Equity Owner's predecessor's) share of cumula-tive Company taxable income or loss. Without limiting this objective, for purposes of this Section 9.4(a), an Equity Owner's share of Tax Profits and Unrecovered Tax Losses shall be determined with refer-ence to Sections 704(c), 734, and 743 of the Code. Discretionary Distributions actually made during the calendar year pursuant to Section 9.4(b) shall reduce the Distributions otherwise contemplated

by this Section 9.4(a). Distributions made pursuant to this Section 9.4(a) shall be treated as draws upon Distributions to be made pursuant to Sections 9.4(b) and 12.3 such that future Distributions otherwise contemplated by Sections 9.4(b) and 12.3 shall be reduced by Distributions made pursuant to this Section 9.4(a).[48]

(b)   The Company may Distribute Distributable Cash subject to the Approval in accordance with Section 5.4. All such Distributions shall be made as follows:

(i)   First, to the Equity Owners in proportion to the Preferred Accruals of all Equity Owners until they have received aggregate Distributions under this Section 9.4(b)(i) equal to Preferred Accrual.

(ii)   Second, to the Equity Owners proportionate with their Adjusted Capital Contributions until the amount of their respective Adjusted Capital Contributions equals zero.

(iii)   Third, to the Equity Owners in accordance with their Sharing Ratios.]

All Distributions which, when made, exceed the recipient Equity Owner's basis in that Equity Owner's Ownership Interest shall be considered advances or drawings against the Equity Owner's distributive share of Profits, or other items of net income or gain. To the extent it is determined at the end of the Fiscal Year that the recipient Equity Owner has not been allocated Profits, or other items of net income or gain, that equals or exceeds the total of such advances or drawings for such year, such Equity Owner shall be obligated to recontribute any such excess advances or drawings to the Company. Notwithstanding the foregoing sentence, an Equity Owner will not be required to recontribute such advances or drawings to the extent that, on the last day of the Fiscal Year, such Equity Owner's basis in its Ownership Interest in the Company has increased from the time of such advance or drawing. Any advance or drawings which are recontributed by a Member pursuant to this Section 9.4, shall be redistributed to such Member either at the option of such Member or at such time that such distribution will not exceed such Member's basis in its Ownership Interest.][49]

All Distributions to Equity Owners will be subject to withholding if required by the Code or other applicable law. All amounts so withheld nonetheless will be deemed to have been distributed to such Equity Owner.

---

48. Normally where there is a preferred return it is advisable to have a provision mandating tax distributions. Otherwise, the Member not receiving the preferred return will have taxable income without any distribution to pay the taxes.

49. Distribution arrangements need to be carefully evaluated (in light of the particular facts of the transaction) under the disguised sale rules. (IRC § 707(a)(2)(b) and Treas. Reg. § 1.707–4 and 1.707–5).

9.5 <u>Limitation Upon Distributions</u>. No Distribution shall be made if such Distribution would violate the Act.[50]

9.6 <u>Interest on and Return of Capital Contributions</u>. No Member shall be entitled to interest on its Capital Contribution or to return of its Capital Contribution, except as otherwise specifically provided for herein.

9.7 <u>Accounting Period</u>. The Company's accounting period shall be the Fiscal Year.

9.8 <u>Accounting Principles</u>. For financial reporting purposes, the Company shall use accounting principles applied on a consistent basis using the accrual method of accounting determined by the Managers, unless the Company is required to use a different method of accounting for federal income tax purposes, in which case that method of accounting shall be the Company's method of accounting.

9.9 <u>Loans to Company</u>. Nothing in this Agreement shall prevent any Member from making secured or unsecured loans to the Company by agreement with the Company.

9.10 <u>Returns and Other Elections</u>. The Managers shall cause the preparation and timely filing of all tax returns required to be filed by the Company pursuant to the Code and all other tax returns deemed necessary and required in each jurisdiction in which the Company does business. Copies of such returns, or pertinent information therefrom, shall be furnished to the Equity Owners within a reasonable amount of time after the end of the Fiscal Year. All elections permitted to be made by the Company under federal or state laws shall be made by the Managers in their sole discretion; provided, however, that the Managers shall make any tax election requested by Members owning a Majority Interest.

9.11 <u>Tax Matters Partner</u>. Any Manager selected by a vote of the Managers, so long as the Manager so selected is also a Member, is hereby designated the Tax Matters Partner ("<u>TMP</u>") as defined in Section 6231(a)(7) of the Code. The TMP and the other Members shall use their reasonable efforts to comply with the responsibilities outlined in Sections 6221 through 6233 of the Code (including any Regulations promulgated thereunder), and in doing so shall incur no liability to any other Member.

9.12 <u>Certain Allocations for Income Tax (But Not Book Capital Account) Purposes</u>.

(a) In accordance with Section 704(c)(1)(A) of the Code and Section 1.704–1(b)(2)(iv)(d) of the Regulations, if an Equity Owner contributes property with an initial Gross Asset Value that differs

---

50. It may be necessary or advisable from a tax standpoint to add special limitations on distributions of appreciated property (or to restrict certain distribution to a member that has contributed appreciated property). See IRC §§ 704(c)(1)(b) and 737.

from its adjusted basis at the time of contribution, income, gain, loss and deductions with respect to the property shall, <u>solely for federal income tax purposes</u> (and not for Capital Account purposes), be allocated among the Equity Owners so as to take account of any variation between the adjusted basis of such property to the Company and its Gross Asset Value at the time of contribution *[pursuant to the traditional method under Section 1.704–3(b) of the Regulations] [in accordance with Section 704(c)(1)(A) of the Code and Section 1.704–1(b)(2)(i)(iv) of the Regulations, if an Equity Owner contributes property with an initial Gross Asset Value that differs from its adjusted basis at the time of contribution, income, gain, loss and deductions with respect to the property shall, <u>solely for federal income tax purposes</u> (and not for Capital Account purposes), be allocated among the Equity Owners so as to take account of any variation between the adjusted basis of such property to the Company and its Gross Asset Value at the time of contribution. Notwithstanding the foregoing sentence, in the event any Equity Owner is limited in recognizing any tax allocations cost recovery deductions or loss with respect to contributed property by the "ceiling rule" as described in Regulation Section 1.704–3(b), then, in addition to the allocation of items with respect to the contributed property allocated pursuant to the previous sentence, all items _____ [51] of the Company other than with respect to the property shall, <u>solely for federal income tax purposes</u> (and not for Capital Account purposes), be allocated among the Equity Owners pursuant to [the traditional method with curative allocations described in Regulation Section 1.704–3(c) so as to offset the effect of the ceiling rule. The allocations described in the previous sentence shall be limited to items of ordinary loss and deduction of the Company other than with respect to the property even if such items do not offset fully the effect of the ceiling rule.] [in accordance with the remedial allocation method under Regulation Section 1.704–3(d)].*[52] In the event the Gross Asset Value of any Company asset is adjusted pursuant to Section 1.42(b), subsequent allocations of income, gain, loss, and deduction with respect to such asset shall take account of any variation between the adjusted basis of such asset for federal income tax purposes and its Gross Asset Value in the same manner as under Code Section 704(c) and the Regulations thereunder.

(b) All recapture of income tax deductions resulting from sale or disposition of Company Property shall be allocated to the Equity

---

51. Under the traditional method with curative allocations you can designate the items of income or loss of the Company (other than from the property giving rise to the variation) that will be adjusted, so long as the tax characterization of the item is the same as the property giving rise to the variation.

52. The selection of the manner in which book-tax differences are recognized can have significant tax consequences and should be considered carefully with the client.

Owners to whom the deduction that gave rise to such recapture was allocated hereunder to the extent that such Equity Owner is allocated any gain from the sale or other disposition of such property.

ARTICLE 10

TRANSFERABILITY

10.1 <u>General</u>.

(a)   An Equity Owner shall only have the right to Transfer all or any portion of the Equity Owner's Ownership Interests if such Transfer is in full compliance with the provisions herein.

(b)   Each Equity Owner hereby acknowledges the reasonableness of the restrictions on Transfer of Ownership Interests imposed by this Agreement in view of the Company's purposes and the relationship of the Equity Owners. Accordingly, the restrictions on Transfer contained herein shall be specifically enforceable.

(c)   *[In the event that any Equity Owner Hypothecates any of its Ownership Interest, any such Hypothecation shall be made pursuant to a pledge or hypothecation agreement that requires the pledgee or secured party to be bound by all the terms and conditions of this Article 10, and the pledging Equity Owner shall provide notice of such pledge or encumbrance to the Managers at such time that the Equity Owner first contemplates such Hypothecation.]*

10.2 <u>Right of First Refusal</u>.

(a)   A Selling Equity Owner that desires to Sell all or any portion of its Ownership Interest to a third party purchaser *[other than a Member/including a Member (or the Company)]* shall obtain from such third party purchaser ("Third Party Purchaser") a *bona fide* written offer to purchase such interest, stating the terms and conditions upon which the Sale is to be made and the consideration offered therefor ("Third Party Offer"). The Selling Equity Owner shall give written notification ("Notice of Sale") to the Company and the other Equity Owners who are Members (the "Remaining Members"), by certified mail or personal delivery, of its intention to so Sell such Ownership Interest (the "Offered Interest"). The Notice of Sale shall be accompanied by a copy of the Third Party Offer. For purposes of paragraph 10.2(b) and 10.2(c), the purchase price of the Offered Interest (the "Purchase Price") shall be equal to the purchase price offered by such Third Party Purchaser, to the extent such offer consists of cash or a promissory note, plus the fair market value of any consideration other than cash or a promissory note ("Non-cash Consideration"). If any portion of the Purchase Price depends on the value of Non-cash Consideration, then: (i) the Notice of Sale also shall be accompanied by a good faith estimate by the

Selling Equity Owner of the fair market value of the Non-cash Consideration ("Seller's Estimate"), and (ii) the fair market value of the Non-cash Consideration shall be equal to either (x) the Seller's Estimate or (y) in the discretion of the Managers, the appraised fair market value of the Non-cash Consideration determined by an independent appraiser selected by the Managers in their sole discretion. The Managers shall have the sole discretion to choose between the amount determined pursuant to clauses (x) and (y) of this subsection 10.2(a). If the appraised fair market value of the Non-cash Consideration is not determined within twenty (20) days after the Notice of Sale, then such fair market value shall be equal to the amount of the Seller's Estimate.

(b) The Remaining Members shall have the option ("Buy Option") to purchase all, but not less than all, of the Offered Interest, on a basis *pro rata* to the Sharing Ratios of the Remaining Members exercising such option pursuant to this Section 10.2(b). The Buy Option may be exercised by one or more of the Remaining Members by giving written notification ("Buy Notice") to the Selling Equity Owner within thirty (30) days after receiving the Notice of Sale (the "Option Period"). Each Remaining Member who timely gives a Buy Notice ("Buying Member") shall purchase such portion of the Offered Interest which is equal to the relative Sharing Ratios of all of the Buying Members. If there are no Buying Members, the Buy Option shall terminate and at any time within ninety (90) days following the expiration of the Option Period, the Selling Equity Owner shall be entitled to consummate the Sale of the Offered Interest to the Third Party Purchaser or one or more of its Affiliates upon terms no less favorable than are set forth in the Third Party Offer.

(c) If there is at least one Buying Member (i) the Buying Members shall designate the time, date and place of closing, provided that the date of closing shall be within thirty (30) days after the receipt of the Buy Notice, and (ii) at the closing, the Buying Members shall purchase, and the Selling Equity Owner shall Sell, the Offered Interest for an amount equal to the Purchase Price and in accordance with such other terms and conditions set forth in the Third Party Offer.

(d) A Sale of an Offered Interest pursuant to this Section 10.2, shall be subject to Sections 10.3 and 10.4.

10.3 Transferee Not Member in Absence of Consent.

(a) Except as provided in this Section 10.3(a), if *[all of the remaining Members/Members holding a Majority Interest/Members Holding a Two–Thirds Interest (inclusive of the Members proposing to sell)]* do not unanimously Approve the proposed Transfer of the Transferring Equity Owner's Ownership Interest to a transferee which is not a Member immediately prior to the Transfer, then the proposed transferee shall have no right to participate in the management of the business and affairs of the Company or to become a Member. Such transferee shall be merely an Economic Interest Owner. No Transfer of a Member's Membership Interest (including any Transfer of the Economic Interest or any other Transfer which has not been approved as provided herein) shall be effective unless and until written notice (including the name and address of the proposed transferee and the date of such Transfer) has been provided to the Company and the non-transferring Members. *[Notwithstanding anything to the contrary herein, any Gift by a Member which is permitted under Section 10.5 and made in accordance with this Section 10.3(a) shall automatically constitute the transferee as a Member.]*

(b) Upon and contemporaneously with any Transfer of an Equity Owner's Ownership Interest, the Transferring Equity Owner shall cease to have any residual rights associated with the Ownership Interest Transferred to the transferee.

10.4 Additional Conditions to Recognition of Transferee.

(a) If a Transferring Equity Owner Transfers an Ownership Interest to a Person who is not already a Member, as a condition to recognizing the effectiveness and binding nature of such Transfer (subject to Section 10.3 above), the remaining Members may require the Transferring Equity Owner and the proposed successor-in-interest to execute, acknowledge and deliver to the Managers such instruments of transfer, assignment and assumption and such other certificates, representations and documents, and to perform all such other acts which the Managers may deem necessary or desirable to accomplish any one or more of the following:

(i) Constitute such successor-in-interest as an Equity Owner;

(ii) Confirm that the proposed successor-in-interest as an Economic Interest Owner, or to be admitted as a Member, has accepted, assumed and agreed to be subject to and bound by all of the terms, obligations and conditions of this Agreement, as the same may have been further amended (whether such Person is to be admitted as a new Member or will merely be an Economic Interest Owner);

(iii) Preserve the Company after the completion of such Transfer under the laws of each jurisdiction in which the Company is qualified, organized or does business;

(iv) *[Prevent a termination of the Company for tax purposes under Section 708(b)(1)(B) of the Code;]*

(v) Maintain the status of the Company as a partnership for federal tax purposes; and

(vi) Assure compliance with any applicable state and federal laws, including Securities Laws and regulations.

(b) Any Transfer of an Ownership Interest and admission of a Member in compliance with this Article 10 shall be deemed effective as of the last day of the calendar month in which the remaining Members' Approval thereto was given *[or, if no such Approval was required pursuant to Section 10.3, then on such date that the successor in interest complies with Section 10.4(a).]*[53] The Transferring Equity Owner hereby indemnifies the Company and the remaining Members against any and all loss, damage, or expense (including tax liabilities or loss of tax benefits) arising directly or indirectly as a result of any Transfer or purported Transfer in violation of this Article 10.

(c) Any Equity Owner that Transfers an Ownership Interest shall notify the Company of the Transfer in writing within thirty (30) days of the Transfer, or, if earlier, by March 31 following the Transfer, and must include the names and addresses of the transferor and transferee, the taxpayer identification numbers of the transferor and transferee, if known, and the date of the Transfer.

10.5 <u>Gifts of Ownership Interests</u>. *[A Gifting Equity Owner may Gift all or any portion of its Ownership Interest (without regard to Sections 10.2(a) and 10.2(b)); provided, however, that the successor-in-interest ("*<u>Donee</u>*") complies with Section 10.4(a) and further provided that the Donee is either the Gifting Equity Owner's spouse, former spouse, lineal descendant (including adopted children) or . . . an Entity in which day-to-day voting control is directly or indirectly held by one or more of the Gifting Equity Owners, or the Gifting Equity Owner's spouse, former spouse, or lineal descendant (including adopted children). In the event of the Gift of all or any portion of a Gifting Equity Owner's Ownership Interest to one or more Donees who are under twenty-five (25) years of age, one or more trusts shall be established to hold the Gifted Ownership Interests for the benefit of such Donees until the respective Donees reach the age of at least twenty-five (25) years.]*

10.6 <u>Buy-Sell Agreement</u>.[54]

(a) Upon _____[55] any Member (the "Offeror")[56] may make a buy-sell offer (the "Offer") to any other Equity Owner, (the "Offer-

---

53. This provision should be deleted if last sentence of 10.3 is deleted.

54. While the entire agreement is merely intended to assist the drafter in considering issues, this provision merits a great deal of consideration taking into account the ability of parties to pay for the interest, the ability to obtain releases of guarantees, and the viability of the business of the Company on the dissociation of a Member. It may be that on a serious disagreement the only alternative is to dissolve and wind up the Company.

55. It may be appropriate to condition the buy-sell option on the passage of time or a specific event.

56. Under this arrangement only Members can be Offerors initiating this process,

ee") holding an Ownership Interest by notifying the Offeree and all other Members in writing of the exercise of this right and stating in such notice the Deemed Value and Purchase Price as defined below. The "Deemed Value" is an amount designated by the Offeror to be the value of the Company Property of the Company net of any obligations and liabilities of the Company that would need to be paid or satisfied before a Distribution could be made under Section 12.3(b)(iii). The "Purchase Price" with respect to either the Offeree's Ownership Interest or Offeror's Membership Interest[57] in the Company shall be equal to the amount that would have been Distributed to either the Offeror or the Offereee, as the case may be under Section 12.3(b)(iv) on the assumption that the fair market value of the Company's assets available for Distribution under Section 12.3(b)(iv) is the Deemed Value.

(b) Within thirty (30) days after receipt by the Offeree of the Offeror's written notice of the Offer, the Offeree shall send to the Offeror a written notice stating whether the Offeree elects (i) to purchase from the Offeror the Offeror's entire Membership Interest for the Purchase Price of such Interest as provided below (in which case the Offeree shall be the "Purchaser" and the Offeror shall be the "Seller" for purposes of this Section 10.6), or (ii) to sell to the Offeror the Offeror's entire Membership Interest for the Purchase Price of such Interest as provided below (in which case the Offeror shall be the "Purchaser" and the Offeree shall be the "Seller" for purposes of this Section 10.6).

(c) The closing of the sale shall be held at the Company's principal office (or at such other place as the Offeror and the Offeree may in writing agree) no later than fifteen (15) days after the expiration of the notice period specified in subsection (b) above. At the closing the Purchaser shall deliver to the Seller: (i) confirmation of payment of, or a release of the Seller and all Seller's Affiliates from all liabilities of the Company for which the Seller or any Affiliate of the Seller is liable either directly or as a guarantor or with respect to which any asset of the Seller or any Affiliate of the Seller is secured;[58] (ii) payment in cash or immediately available funds of (x) any amount to which the Seller would have been entitled under Section 12.3(b)(iii) on winding up of the Company and (y) the Purchase Price for the Seller's Interest. The Purchaser

---

although the Offeree, who is not necessarily a Member, does have the right to elect to be a purchaser.

57. Note that what is purchased is a Membership Interest not Units, which are just one component of a Membership Interest.

58. This will require the discharge or release of the Seller from guarantees. This may be difficult and the drafter may want to consider an alternative direct indemnification with respect to guarantees. This can be a particular problem with respect to guarantees with respect to ongoing liabilities such as leases.

may reduce the amount due under the foregoing clause by any liquidated and undisputed amounts owed by the Seller to either the Purchaser or the Company.[59] The Purchaser may use assets of the Company to provide some or all of the consideration to be paid to the Seller provided that such use does not violate the Act or otherwise subject the Seller to additional liability to any Person. At the closing Seller shall execute and deliver to the Purchaser a document assigning the Membership Interest to the Purchaser or such other Person as the Purchaser may designate, representing and warranting to the Purchaser, its Affiliates, the Company and the Person to whom the Membership Interest is transferred that the Seller is the sole owner of the Membership Interest being sold, providing for reasonable noncompetition, trade secret, and nondisparagement protection for the Purchaser, its Affiliates, the Company and the Person to whom the Membership Interest is transferred, and agreeing to indemnify the Purchaser, the Company and the Person to whom the Membership Interest is transferred against any liabilities of the Company that were incurred by the Seller or its Affiliate but only if at the time of closing the Purchaser is not aware and has no reason to be aware of such liability. At the closing Purchaser shall execute and deliver to the Seller a document providing reasonable nondisparagement protection for the Seller and its Affiliates and agreeing to indemnify the Seller and its Affiliates against any liabilities of the Company excepting only liabilities that were incurred by the Seller or its Affiliate with respect to which at the time of closing the Purchaser is not aware and has no reason to be aware of such liability.

(d) Each of the Equity Owners agrees that in connection with the exercise of that Member's rights under this Section 10.6, that Member will act in good faith and that in connection with the Offer and the response each Equity Owner shall have the obligation to disclose to the other Member all material facts with respect to the Company and its business. Further the Purchaser shall act in good faith in the preparation of all tax returns and reports of the Company affecting the rights of the Seller or any of its Affiliates.[60]

Except with respect to the obligations of the Members set forth in this Paragraph 10.6, upon the closing described herein, the Seller and its

---

59. The amount owed to the Company may serve as a reduction to the extent that the Purchaser will succeed to the Seller's obligation to the Company.

60. This clause should be considered carefully. On the one hand it will make the process fairer. On the other, it will give an Equity Owner who feels misused by the process an easier access to court, particularly where there is the allegation that either

the price was not suggested in good faith or that there was information not made available to the Offeree. It should further be noted that many believe that no fiduciary duties are owed to Economic Interest owners who are not Members and such persons are certainly not entitled to the information rights owed to Members. This section would entitle such a person a right to information in connection with the Offer.

Affiliates shall be released from all obligations of any sort to the Purchaser or the Company by reason of the Seller's having been a Member of the Company or a Party to this LLC Agreement; and the Purchaser, its Affiliates, the Company, and the Person to whom the Interest is Transferred shall be released from all obligations of any sort to the Seller or its Affiliates by reason of Seller's having been a Member of the Company or a Party to this Agreement.

ARTICLE 11

ISSUANCE OF MEMBERSHIP INTERESTS

11.1 Issuance of Additional Membership Interests to New Members. From the date of the formation of the Company, any Person acceptable to [_____][61] may become a Member in the Company by the issuance by the Company of Membership Interests for such consideration as the Members *[by their unanimous Approval/holding a Two–Thirds Interest]* shall determine, subject to the terms and conditions of this Agreement.

11.2 Issuance of Additional Membership Interests to Existing Members. From the date of the formation of the Company, the Company may issue additional Ownership Interests to one or more existing Members for such consideration as the Members *[by their unanimous Approval/holding a Two–Thirds Interest]* shall determine, subject to the terms and conditions of this Agreement.

11.3 Part Year Allocations With Respect to New Members. No new Members shall be entitled to any retroactive allocation of losses, income, or expense deductions incurred by the Company. At the time a Member is admitted and in accordance with the provisions of Section 706(d) of the Code and the Regulations thereunder, the Managers may, at their option, close the Company books (as though the Company's Fiscal Year had ended) or make *pro rata* allocations of loss, income, and expense deductions to a new Equity Owner for that portion of the Company's Fiscal Year in which a Person became an Equity Owner.

ARTICLE 12

DISSOLUTION AND TERMINATION

12.1 Dissolution.

(a) The Company shall be dissolved only upon the occurrence of any of the following events:

(i) by the *[unanimous Approval of the Members]/[the Approval of Members holding a Two–Thirds Interest]*[62];

---

61. Presumably the same Member or Members entitled to approve the admission of a transferee as a Member must approve this [issuance].

62. In a family LLC carefully consider the potential impact of IRC § 2704(a).

(ii) *[by an order of a court of competent jurisdiction in an action commenced by any Member in which the Member can show that:*

(1) The Members are deadlocked in the management of the Company's affairs with respect to material matters over which they have a vote, and irreparable injury to the Company is threatened or being suffered, or the business and affairs of the Company can no longer be conducted, because of the deadlock;

(2) The Managers or other Members in control of the Company have acted, are acting, or will act in a manner that is illegal, oppressive, or fraudulent;

(3) There have been repeated, material breaches of the Agreement by the Company or by other Members or Managers; or

(4) The assets of the Company are being misapplied or wasted,][63] *or*

(iii) *[upon the expiration of the term, if any, specified in Section 2.5 of this Agreement].*

Notwithstanding anything to the contrary in the Act, the Company shall not be dissolved upon the death, retirement, resignation, expulsion, Bankruptcy or dissolution of an Equity Owner.[64]

(b) As soon as possible following the occurrence of any of the events specified in Section 12.1(a) effecting the dissolution of the Company, the appropriate representative of the Company shall execute all documents required by the Act at the time of dissolution and file or record such statements with the appropriate officials.[65]

12.2 <u>Effect of Dissolution</u>. Upon dissolution, the Company shall cease to carry on its business, except insofar as may be necessary for the winding up of its business, but its separate existence shall continue until winding up and Distribution is completed.

63. Under some LLC statutes there is not a provision for judicial dissolution even for breach of the agreement, fraud, or conversion. It may be worth considering a provision of this sort in an agreement to protect minority members.

64. Some statutes still have a default rule under which the LLC will dissolve on the dissociation of a member but allow the modification of that rules in the operating agreement. This language is intended to make clear that such an amendment is appropriate.

65. If the LLC is not a Colorado LLC, the resignation of a member may need to be specifically addressed. In Colorado, the default rule under the Colorado LLC act is that the resigning member has no right to demand the liquidation of his interest by the LLC and that after resigning he becomes a mere economic interest owner.

12.3 <u>Winding Up, Liquidation and Distribution of Assets</u>.

(a) Upon dissolution, an accounting shall be made by the Company's *[Managers] [independent accountants (the "<u>Liquidators</u>")]* of the accounts of the Company and of the Company's assets, liabilities, and results of operations from the date of the last previous accounting until the date of dissolution. The *[Managers] [Liquidators]* shall immediately proceed to wind up the affairs of the Company.

(b) If the Company is dissolved and its affairs are to be wound up, the *[Managers] [Liquidators]* shall:

(i) Sell or otherwise liquidate all of the Company Property as promptly as practicable (except to the extent that the *[Managers] [Liquidators]* may determine to Distribute in kind any assets to the Equity Owners);

(ii) Allocate any Profit or Loss resulting from such sales to the Equity Owners' Capital Accounts in accordance with Article 9 hereof;

(iii) Discharge all liabilities of the Company, including liabilities to Equity Owners who are also creditors, to the extent otherwise permitted by law, other than liabilities to Equity Owners for Distributions and the return of capital, and establish such Reserves as may be reasonably necessary to provide for contingent liabilities of the Company (for purposes of determining the Capital Accounts of the Equity Owners, the amounts of such Reserves shall be deemed to be an expense of the Company); and

(iv) Distribute the remaining assets to the Equity Owners in accordance with their positive Capital Account balances, as follows:

(1) The positive balance (if any) of each Equity Owner's Capital Account (as determined after taking into account all Capital Account adjustments for the Company's Fiscal Year during which the liquidation occurs) shall be Distributed to the Equity Owners, either in cash or in kind, as determined by the *[Managers] [Liquidators]*, with any Company Property Distributed in kind being valued for this purpose at their fair market value. Any such Distributions to the Equity Owners in respect of their Capital Accounts shall be made in accordance with the time requirements set forth in Section 1.704–1(b)(2)(ii)(b)(2) of the Regulations; and

(2) If any Company Property is to be Distributed in kind, the net fair market value of such Company Property as of the date of dissolution shall be determined by agreement of the Members, or, if the Members do not agree, by

an appraiser selected by the *[Managers] [Liquidators]*. Such Company Property shall be deemed to have been sold as of the date of dissolution for their fair market value, and the Capital Accounts of the Equity Owners shall be adjusted pursuant to the provisions of Article 9 and Section 8.3 of this Agreement to reflect such deemed sale.

It is intended that the amount to be Distributed to each Equity Owner pursuant to Section 12.3(b)(iv) (the "Liquidating Distribution") would equal the amount such Equity Owner would receive if liquidation proceeds were instead Distributed in accordance with the provisions set forth in Section 9.4 (the "Targeted Distribution Amounts"). Notwithstanding any provision of this Agreement to the contrary, if any Equity Owner's ending Capital Account balance immediately prior to the Liquidating Distribution otherwise would be less than the balance required to ensure that such Equity Owner receives its Targeted Distribution Amount, then, for such Fiscal Year of liquidation and dissolution and, to the extent amended tax returns can be filed, for prior Fiscal Years of the Company (if necessary), such Equity Owner shall be specially allocated items of income or gain for such current or prior years, and items of loss or deduction for such current or prior years shall be specially allocated to the other Equity Owners, until Profits or Losses for the year of liquidation and dissolution of the Company can be allocated so as to cause such Equity Owner's Liquidating Distribution to equal (or, if not equal to, as close as possible to) the Targeted Distribution Amount for such Equity Owner.[66]

(c) Notwithstanding anything to the contrary in this Agreement, upon a liquidation within the meaning of Section 1.704–1(b)(2)(ii)(g) of the Regulations, if any Equity Owner has a Deficit Capital Account (after giving effect to all contributions, Distributions, allocations and other Capital Account adjustments for all Fiscal Years, including the year during which such liquidation occurs), such Equity Owner shall have no obligation to make any Capital Contribution so as to restore its Capital Account to zero, and the negative balance of such Equity Owner's Capital Account shall not be considered a debt owed by such Equity Owner to the Company, to the other Equity Owners, or to any other Person for any purpose whatsoever.

66. In the context of the particular deal, think about the possible need for distributions of certain LLC assets to certain members. For example, in strategic ventures, it is often important to carefully address the exit strategy (*i.e.*, and who gets what if the LLC dissolves). The ability of one or more of the members to receive or have the option to receive (or by distribution or purchase) specified assets may be important. It also may be advisable for the operating agreement to require the LLC or members who receive intellectual property assets from the LLC to license those assets to the other members. Also, remember to conform this provision to 8.4.

(d) Upon completion of the winding up, liquidation, and Distribution of the assets, the Company shall be deemed terminated.

(e) The *[Managers] [Liquidators]* shall comply with any requirements of applicable law pertaining to the winding up of the affairs of the Company and the final Distribution of its assets.

12.4 Filing or Recording Statements. Upon the conclusion of winding up, the appropriate representative of the Company shall execute all documents required by the Act at the time of completion of winding up and file or record such documents with the appropriate officials.

12.5 Return of Contribution Nonrecourse to Other Equity Owners. Except as provided by law or as expressly provided in this Agreement, upon dissolution, each Equity Owner shall look solely to the assets of the Company for the return of its Capital Contribution. If the Company Property remaining after the payment or discharge of the debts and liabilities of the Company is insufficient to return the cash contribution of one or more Equity Owners, such Equity Owners shall have no recourse against any other Equity Owner.

ARTICLE 13

MISCELLANEOUS PROVISIONS

13.1 Notices. Any notice, demand, or communication required or permitted to be given by any provision of this Agreement shall be deemed to have been sufficiently given or served if sent by facsimile or electronic mail transmission, delivered by messenger, overnight courier, or mailed, certified first class mail, postage prepaid, return receipt requested, and addressed or sent to the Equity Owner's or the Company's address, as set forth on Exhibit 8.1 and, if applicable, Exhibit 13.1. Such notice shall be effective, (a) if delivered by messenger or by overnight courier, upon actual receipt (or if the date of actual receipt is not a business day, upon the next business day); (b) if sent by facsimile or electronic mail transmission, upon electronic confirmation of receipt (or if the date of such electronic confirmation of receipt is not a business day, upon the next business day); or (c) if mailed, upon the earlier of (i) three (3) business days after deposit in the mail and (ii) the delivery as shown by return receipt therefor. Any Equity Owner or the Company may change its address by giving notice in writing to the Company and the other Equity Owners of its new address.

13.2 Liquidation Safe Harbor Valuation.[67] This Section 13.2 shall apply after the effective date of any final Regulations or of final guidance

---

67. As should be clear from the explanation, this section is intended to anticipate the proposed tax guidance on the issuance of an interest for services. This election will facilitate the issuance of profits interests but will generally be disadvantageous to recipients of capital interests.

by the Internal Revenue Service with respect to the Transfer of a Membership Interest to a new or existing Member of the Company in connection with the performance of services for the Company or otherwise under which the Company may make an election (a *"Safe Harbor Election"*) to treat the liquidation value of [a] Membership Interest so Transferred as being the fair market value of [the] Membership Interest for purposes of Section 83 of the Code. From and after the effective date of any final Regulations or of final guidance by the Internal Revenue Service, each Member and each Person (including any Person to whom any Units are Transferred in connection with the performance of services for the Company or otherwise) and each assignee and Transferee of a Member who acquires Units agrees that that (a) the Company is authorized and directed to make the Safe Harbor Election, and (b) each such Person agrees to comply with all requirements of such Regulations or guidance with respect to all Units so Transferred while the Safe Harbor Election remains effective. The Safe Harbor Election may be revoked by the consent of *[Members holding a Majority Interest] [all of the Members]*.

13.3 Books of Account and Records. At the expense of the Company, proper and complete records, books of account and other relevant Company documents shall be maintained and preserved, during the term of the Company, and for five years *[thereafter] [after dissolution]*, by the Managers, in which shall be entered fully and accurately all transactions and other matters relating to the Company's business in such detail and completeness as is customary and usual for businesses of the type engaged in by the Company. The books and records shall be open to the reasonable inspection and examination of the Equity Owners or their duly authorized representatives, upon reasonable request, during ordinary business hours at the requesting Member's expense. At a minimum the Company shall keep at its principal place of business the following records:

(a) A current list of the full name and last known business, residence, or mailing address of each Equity Owner and Manager, both past and present;

(b) A copy of the Articles of Organization and all amendments thereto, together with executed copies of any powers of attorney pursuant to which any amendment has been executed;

(c) Copies of the Company's federal, state, and local income tax returns and reports, if any, for the four most recent Fiscal Years;

(d) Copies of the Company's currently effective written Agreement, copies of any writings permitted or required with respect to an Equity Owner's obligation to contribute cash, property or services, and copies of any financial statements of the Company for the three most recent Fiscal Years;

(e) Minutes of every annual, special, and court-ordered meeting of the Members and Managers, if any; and

(f) Any written Approvals obtained from Members for actions taken by Members without a meeting.

13.4 Application of [State] Law. This agreement shall be construed and enforced in accordance with and governed by the laws of the state of *[State]* applicable to agreements made and to be performed entirely within such state other than such laws, rules, regulations and case law that would result in the application of the laws of a jurisdiction other than the state of *[State]*.

13.5 Waiver of Action for Partition. During the term of the Company, each Equity Owner irrevocably waives any right that it may have to maintain any action for partition with respect to the Company Property.

13.6 Amendments. *[This Agreement may not be amended except by the unanimous Approval of all of the Members.]*

OR

[This Agreement may be amended only with the Approval of Members holding a [Two–Thirds Interest]. No amendment which has been agreed to in accordance with the preceding sentence shall be effective to the extent that such amendment has a Material Adverse Effect upon one or more Equity Owners who did not agree in writing to such amendment. For purposes of the preceding sentence, "Material Adverse Effect" shall mean any modification of the relative rights to Distributions by the Company (including allocations of Profits and Losses which are reflected in the Capital Accounts). Without limiting the generality of the foregoing, an amendment which has a proportionate effect on all Equity Owners (or in the case of a redemption of Ownership Interests or issuance of additional Ownership Interests, an amendment which has a proportionate effect on all Equity Owners immediately after such redemption or issuance) with respect to their rights to Distributions shall be deemed to not have a Material Adverse Effect on Equity Owners who do not agree in writing to such amendment. In addition, an amendment made to ensure that Distributions are made in accordance with Section 9.4 shall be deemed to not have a Material Adverse Effect on Equity Owners who do not agree in writing to such amendment. Notwithstanding the foregoing provisions of this Section 13.6, no amendment shall be made to a provision herein which requires the Approval of the Members holding more than a [Two–Thirds Interest], unless Members holding such greater Voting Interests Approve of such amendment.][68]

68. In many respects the amendment provision is the most important provision in the agreement. As a result of the flexibility of LLC statutes, an amendment can make profound changes in the LLC. If fewer than all of the members are needed to amend an agreement, minority members should consider appropriate protections in the event of an unacceptable amendment. Such a provision might include a right to withdraw or a limitation on the ability to amend some provisions of the agreement. Unanimous

13.7 Execution of Additional Instruments. Each Equity Owner hereby agrees to execute such other and further statements of interest and holdings, designations, powers of attorney, and other instruments necessary to comply with any laws, rules, or regulations.

13.8 Construction. Whenever the singular number is used in this Agreement and when required by the context, the same shall include the plural and *vice versa*, and the masculine gender shall include the feminine and neuter genders and *vice versa*. The words "including" and "or" shall be ascribed non-exclusive meanings unless the context clearly requires otherwise.

13.9 Effect of Inconsistencies with the Act. It is the express intention of the Equity Owners and the Company that this Agreement shall be the sole source of agreement among them, and, except to the extent that a provision of this Agreement expressly incorporates federal income tax rules by reference to sections of the Code or Regulations or is expressly prohibited or ineffective under the Act, this Agreement shall govern, even when inconsistent with, or different than, the provisions of the Act or any other law or rule. In the event that the Act is subsequently amended or interpreted in such a way to make valid any provision of this Agreement that was formerly invalid, such provision shall be considered to be valid from the effective date of such interpretation or amendment. The Members and the Company hereby agree that the duties and obligations imposed on the Members as such shall be those set forth in this Agreement, which is intended to govern the relationship among the Company and the Equity Owners, notwithstanding any provision of the Act or common law to the contrary.

13.10 Waivers. The failure of any party to seek redress for violation of or to insist upon the strict performance of any covenant or condition of this Agreement shall not prevent a subsequent act, which would have originally constituted a violation, from having the effect of an original violation.

13.11 Rights and Remedies Cumulative. The rights and remedies provided by this Agreement are cumulative and the use of any one right or remedy by any party shall not preclude or waive the right to use any or all other remedies. Said rights and remedies are given in addition to any other rights the parties may have by law, statute, ordinance, or otherwise.

13.12 Attorneys' Fees. Should the Company or any party to this Agreement reasonably retain counsel for the purpose of enforcing or preventing breach of any provision of this Agreement, including instituting any action or proceeding to enforce any provision of this Agreement, for damages by reason of any alleged breach of any provision of this

consent should be required to amend any
provision of the agreement which requires a
unanimous vote to approve an action.

Agreement, for a declaration of such party's rights or obligations under this Agreement, or for any other judicial remedy, then, if the matter is settled by judicial determination or arbitration, the prevailing party (whether at trial, on appeal, or arbitration) shall be entitled, in addition to such other relief as may be granted, to be reimbursed by the losing party for all costs and expenses incurred, including reasonable attorneys' fees and costs for services rendered to the prevailing party or parties.

13.13 Severability. If any provision of this Agreement or the application thereof to any person or circumstance shall be invalid, illegal, or unenforceable to any extent, the remainder of this Agreement and the application thereof shall not be affected and shall be enforceable to the fullest extent permitted by law. Without limiting the generality of the foregoing sentence, to the extent that any provision of this Agreement is prohibited or ineffective under the Act or common law, this Agreement shall be considered amended to the smallest degree possible in order to make the Agreement effective under the Act or common law.

13.14 Heirs, Successors, and Assigns. Each and all of the covenants, terms, provisions, and agreements herein contained shall be binding upon and inure to the benefit of the parties hereto and, to the extent permitted by this Agreement, their respective heirs, legal representatives, successors, and assigns.

13.15 Creditors. None of the provisions of this Agreement shall be for the benefit of or enforceable by any creditors of the Company.

13.16 Counterparts; Facsimile. This Agreement may be delivered by facsimile and executed in counterparts, each of which shall be deemed an original but all of which shall constitute one and the same instrument.

13.17 Entire Agreement. This Agreement contains the entire agreement of the Company and the Equity Owners relating to the rights granted and obligations assumed under this Agreement. Any oral representations or modifications concerning this Agreement shall be of no force or effect unless contained in a subsequent written modification signed by the Equity Owner to be charged.

13.18 Rule Against Perpetuities. The parties hereto intend that the Rule Against Perpetuities (and any similar rule of law) not be applicable to any provisions of this Agreement. However, notwithstanding anything to the contrary in this Agreement, if any provision in this Agreement would be invalid or unenforceable because of the Rule Against Perpetuities or any similar rule of law but for this Section 13.18, the parties hereto hereby agree that any future interest which is created pursuant to said provision shall cease if it is not vested within twenty-one (21) years after the death of the survivor of the group composed of *[the undersigned individuals]* and their issue who are living on the effective date of this Agreement.[69]

---

69. While this seems an unnecessary provision, it is included as a protective measure.

13.19 <u>Power of Attorney</u>.[70] Each Equity Owner hereby irrevocably makes, constitutes, and appoints the Managers, with full power of substitution, so long as such Managers are acting in such a capacity (and any successor Manager thereof so long as such Manager is acting in such capacity), its true and lawful attorney, in such Equity Owner's name, place, and stead (it being expressly understood and intended that the grant of such power of attorney is coupled with an interest) to make, execute, sign, acknowledge, swear, and file with respect to the Company:

(a) *[All amendments of this Agreement adopted in accordance with the terms of Section 13.6]*;

(b) All documents which the Managers deem necessary or desirable to effect the dissolution and termination of the Company;

(c) All bills of sale, assignment forms or other appropriate transfer documents necessary to effectuate Transfers of an Equity Owner's Ownership Interest pursuant to Article 10;

(d) All such other instruments, documents, and certificates which may from time to time be required by the laws of *[State]* or any other jurisdiction in which the Company shall determine to do business, or any political subdivision or agency thereof, to effectuate, implement, continue, and defend the valid existence of the Company; and

(e) All instruments, documents, and certificates which the Managers deem necessary or desirable in connection with a Reorganization or the dissolution and termination of the Company, either of which has been authorized in accordance with the terms of this Agreement.[71]

This power of attorney shall not be affected by and shall survive the Bankruptcy, insolvency, death, incompetency, or dissolution of an Equity Owner and shall survive the delivery of any assignment by the Equity Owner of the whole or any portion of its Ownership Interest. Each Equity Owner hereby releases each Manager from any liability or claim in connection with the exercise of the authority granted pursuant to this power of attorney, and in connection with any other action taken by such Manager pursuant to which such Manager purports to act as the attorney-in-fact for one or more Equity Owners, if the Manager believed in good faith that such action taken was consistent with the authority granted to it pursuant to this Section 13.19.

---

70. It is not clear that this section is necessary or even helpful. To some extent it is a vestige of the Uniform Limited Partnership Act (1916) which required all the limited partners to sign the certificate of limited partnership.

71. The drafter should consider other provisions. For example, if the agreement provides for a forfeiture of equity interest in the event of certain events (*e.g.* termination of employment, breach of the agreement, etc.), then you may want to give the Managers a Power of Attorney to effectuate any forfeiture of the ownership interest of the likely uncooperative departing Equity Owner.

13.20 <u>Investment Representations</u>. The undersigned Equity Owners understand (a) that the Ownership Interests evidenced by this Agreement have not been registered under the Securities Laws because the Company is issuing these Ownership Interests in reliance upon the exemptions from the registration requirements of the Securities Laws providing for issuance of securities not involving a public offering, (b) that the Company has relied upon the fact that the Ownership Interests are to be held by each Equity Owner for investment, and (c) that exemption from registrations under the Securities Laws would not be available if the Ownership Interests were acquired by an Equity Owner with a view to distribution.

Accordingly, each Equity Owner hereby confirms to the Company that such Equity Owner is acquiring the Ownership Interests for such own Equity Owner's account, for investment, and not with a view to the resale or distribution thereof. Each Equity Owner agrees not to transfer, sell, or offer for sale any portion of the Ownership Interests unless there is an effective registration relating thereto under the Securities Laws or unless the holder of Ownership Interests delivers to the Company an opinion of counsel, satisfactory to the Company, that such registration or other qualification under applicable Securities Laws is not required in connection with such transfer, offer, or sale. Each Equity Owner understands that the Company is under no obligation to register the Ownership Interests or to assist such Equity Owner in complying with any exemption from registration under the Securities Laws if such Equity Owner should, at a later date, wish to dispose of the Ownership Interest. Furthermore, each Equity Owner realizes that the Ownership Interests are unlikely to qualify for disposition under Rule 144 of the Securities and Exchange Commission unless such Equity Owner is not an "affiliate" of the Company and the Ownership Interest has been beneficially owned and fully paid for by such Equity Owner for at least two years.

Each Equity Owner, prior to acquiring an Ownership Interest, has made an investigation of the Company and its business, and the Company has made available to each Equity Owner all information with respect to the Company which such Equity Owner needs in order to make an informed decision to acquire the Ownership Interest. Each Equity Owner has relied on its own tax and legal advisors in connection with such Equity Owner's decision to acquire an Ownership Interest. Each Equity Owner considers itself to be a Person possessing experience and sophistication as an investor which are adequate for the evaluation of the merits and risks of such Equity Owner's investment in the Ownership Interest.[72]

---

72. As noted with respect to the legend on the cover of the agreement, many Membership Interests may be "securities" under the federal and state securities laws. It is probably not a good idea to include this provision unless you conclude, after consulting a securities lawyer, that the Membership Interests are securities and therefore that steps will have to be taken to comply with the securities laws. If a sub-

13.21 Representations and Warranties.

(a) In General. As of the date hereof, each of the Equity Owners hereby makes each of the representations and warranties applicable to such Equity Owner as set forth in Section 13.20 hereof, and such warranties and representations shall survive the execution of this Agreement.

(b) Representations and Warranties. Each Equity Owner represents and warrants that:

(i) Due Incorporation or Formation; Authorization of Agreement. Such Equity Owner, if an Entity, is duly organized (if a corporation) or duly formed (if a partnership or limited liability company), validly existing, and in good standing under the laws of the jurisdiction of its incorporation or formation and has the corporate, partnership, or limited liability company power and authority to own its property and carry on its business as owned and carried on at the date hereof and as contemplated hereby. Such Equity Owner is duly licensed or qualified to do business and in good standing in each of the jurisdictions in which the failure to be so licensed or qualified would have a material adverse effect on its financial condition or its ability to perform its obligations hereunder. Such Equity Owner has the corporate, partnership, or limited liability company power and authority to execute and deliver this Agreement and to perform its obligations hereunder and the execution, delivery, and performance of this Agreement has been duly authorized by all necessary corporate, partnership or limited liability company action. This Agreement constitutes the legal, valid, and binding obligation of such Equity Owner.

(ii) No Conflict with Restrictions; No Default. Neither the execution, delivery, and performance of this Agreement nor the consummation by such Equity Owner of the transactions contemplated hereby (1) will conflict with, violate, or result in a breach of any of the terms, conditions, or provisions of any law, regulation, order, writ, injunction, decree, determination, or award of any court, any governmental department, board, agency, or instrumentality, domestic or foreign, or any arbitrator, applicable to such Equity Owner or any of its Affiliates, (2) if such Equity Owner is an Entity, will conflict with, violate, result in a breach of, or constitute a default under any of the terms, conditions, or provisions of the articles of incorporation, bylaws, partnership agreement, limited liability company agreement, or operating agreement of such Equity Owner or any of

scription agreement is used and a provision like the foregoing is used in the operating agreement, make sure that the securities lawyer on the deal conforms this provision to the language in the subscription agreement.

its Affiliates or of any material agreement or instrument to which such Equity Owner or any of its Affiliates is a party or by which such Equity Owner, or any of its Affiliates is or may be bound or to which any of its material properties or assets is subject, (3) will conflict with, violate, result in a breach of, constitute a default under (whether with notice or lapse of time or both), accelerate or permit the acceleration of the performance required by, give to others any material interests or rights, or require any approval under any indenture, mortgage, lease agreement, or instrument to which such Equity Owner or any of its Affiliates is a party or by which such Equity Owner or any of its Affiliates is or may be bound, or (4) will result in the creation or imposition of any lien upon any of the material properties or assets of such Equity Owner or any of its Affiliates.

(iii) <u>Government Authorizations</u>. Any registration, declaration, or filing with, or consent, approval, license, permit, or other authorization or order by, any government or regulatory authority, domestic or foreign, that is required in connection with the valid execution, delivery, acceptance, and performance by such Equity Owner under this Agreement or the consummation by such Equity Owner of any transaction contemplated hereby has been completed, made, or obtained on or before the effective date of this Agreement.

(iv) <u>Litigation</u>. There are no actions, suits, proceedings, or investigations pending or, to the knowledge of such Equity Owner or any of its Affiliates, threatened against or affecting such Equity Owner or any of its Affiliates or any of their properties, assets, or businesses in any court or before or by any governmental department, board, agency, or instrumentality, domestic or foreign, or any arbitrator which could, if adversely determined (or, in the case of an investigation could lead to any action, suit, or proceeding, which if adversely determined could) reasonably be expected to materially impair such Equity Owner's ability to perform its obligations under this Agreement or to have a material adverse effect on the consolidated financial condition of such member; and such Equity Owner or any of its Affiliates has not received any currently effective notice of any default, and such Equity Owner or any of its Affiliates is not in default, under any applicable order, writ, injunction, decree, permit, determination, or award of any court, any governmental department, board, agency, or instrumentality, domestic or foreign, or any arbitrator which could reasonably be expected to materially impair such Equity Owner's ability to perform its obligations under this Agreement or to have a material adverse effect on the consolidated financial condition of such Equity Owner.

(v) <u>Investment Company Act; Public Utility Holding Company Act</u>. Neither such Equity Owner nor any of its Affiliates is, nor will the Company as a result of such Equity Owner holding an Ownership Interest be, an "investment company" as defined in, or subject to regulation under, the Investment Company Act of 1940. Neither such Equity Owner nor any of its Affiliates is, nor will the Company as a result of such Equity Owner holding an Ownership Interest be, a "holding company," "an affiliate of a holding company," or a "subsidiary of a holding company," as defined in, or subject to regulation under, the Public Utility Holding Company Act of 1935.

(vi) <u>Subsidiary</u>. All of the outstanding capital stock or ownership interests in the capital and profits of such Equity Owner is owned, directly or indirectly, by [___].

(c) <u>Confidentiality</u>. Except as contemplated hereby or required by a court of competent authority, each Equity Owner shall keep confidential and shall not disclose to others and shall use its reasonable efforts to prevent its Affiliates and any of its, or its Affiliates' present or former employees, agents, and representatives from disclosing to others without the prior written Approval of the Managers any information which (x) pertains to this Agreement, any negotiations pertaining thereto, any of the transactions contemplated hereby, or the business of the Company, or (y) pertains to confidential or proprietary information of any Member or the Company or which any Equity Owner has labeled in writing as confidential or proprietary; provided that any Equity Owner may disclose to its and its Affiliates' employees, agents, and representatives any information made available to such Equity Owner. No Equity Owner shall use, and each Equity Owner shall use its best efforts to prevent any Affiliate of such Equity Owner from using, any information which (1) pertains to this Agreement, any negotiations pertaining hereto, any of the transactions contemplated hereby, or the business of the Company, or (2) pertains to the confidential or proprietary information of any Equity Owner or the Company or which any Equity Owner has labeled in writing as confidential or proprietary, except in connection with the transactions contemplated hereby. Notwithstanding the foregoing provisions of this Section 13.21(c), the Equity Owners (and each employee, representative, or other agent of the Equity Owners) may disclose to any and all Persons, without limitation of any kind, the tax treatment and tax structure of the transactions contemplated hereby and all materials of any kind (including opinions or other tax analyses) that are provided to the Equity Owners relating to such tax treatment and tax structure.

CERTIFICATE

The undersigned hereby agree, acknowledge, and certify that the foregoing Agreement, consisting of 66 pages, excluding the Table of Contents and attached Exhibits, constitutes the Agreement of [_____] LLC adopted by the Equity Owners as of [_____].

[_____], LLC

By: _____

Its: _____

MEMBERS:

_____

_____

_____

_____

_____

_____

Exhibit 8.1
TO
[Operating/Limited liability Company] Agreement of [_____]
dated effective as of [_____]
Initial Capital Contributions

Name, Address and Facsimile Number of Initial Member	Initial Capital Contribution

Exhibit 8.2
TO
[Operating/Limited liability Company] Agreement of [_____]
dated effective as of [_____]
Additional Capital Contributions

Member	Maximum Additional Capital Contribution

EXHIBIT 13.1
TO
[OPERATING/LIMITED LIABILITY COMPANY] AGREEMENT OF [_____]
DATED EFFECTIVE AS OF [_____]

NAME, ADDRESS AND FACSIMILE NUMBER OF OTHER EQUITY OWNERS

Name/Address	Facsimile Number

INTERNAL REVENUE CODE 26 U.S.C.
§ 7701 AND REGULATIONS
THEREUNDER

IRC § 7701

Sec. 7701. (a) When used in this title, where not otherwise distinctly expressed or manifestly incompatible with the intent thereof—

(1) PERSON.—The term "person" shall be construed to mean and include an individual, a trust, estate, partnership, association, company or corporation.

(2) PARTNERSHIP AND PARTNER.—The term "partnership" includes a syndicate, group, pool, joint venture, or other unincorporated organization, through or by means of which any business, financial operation, or venture is carried on, and which is not, within the meaning of this title, a trust or estate or a corporation; and the term "partner" includes a member in such a syndicate, group, pool, joint venture, or organization.

(3) CORPORATION.—The term "corporation" includes associations, joint-stock companies, and insurance companies....

REGULATIONS UNDER IRC § 7701

Regulation 301.7701-1. **Classification of organizations for federal tax purposes.**—(a) *Organizations for federal tax purposes*— (1) *In general.* The Internal Revenue Code prescribes the classification of various organizations for federal tax purposes. Whether an organization is an entity separate from its owners for federal tax purposes is a matter of federal tax law and does not depend on whether the organization is recognized as an entity under local law.

(2) *Certain joint undertakings give rise to entities for federal tax purposes.* A joint venture or other contractual arrangement may create a separate entity for federal tax purposes if the participants carry on a trade, business, financial operation, or venture and divide the profits therefrom. For example, a separate entity exists for federal tax purposes if co-owners of an apartment building lease space and in addition provide services to the occupants either directly or through an agent. Nevertheless, a joint undertaking merely to share expenses does not create a separate entity for federal tax purposes. For example, if two or more persons jointly construct a ditch merely to drain surface water from their proper-

ties, they have not created a separate entity for federal tax purposes. Similarly, mere co-ownership of property that is maintained, kept in repair, and rented or leased does not constitute a separate entity for federal tax purposes. For example, if an individual owner, or tenants in common, of farm property lease it to a farmer for a cash rental or a share of the crops, they do not necessarily create a separate entity for federal tax purposes. . . .

(4) *Single owner organizations.* Under Regulations 7701–2 and 7701–3, certain organizations that have a single owner can choose to be recognized or disregarded as entities separate from their owners.

(b) *Classification of organizations.* The classification of organizations that are recognized as separate entities is determined under Regulations 7701–2, 7701–3, and 7701–4. . . .

Regulation 301.7701–2. **Business entities; definitions.**—(a) *Business entities.* For purposes of this section and Regulation 7701–3, a *business entity* is any entity recognized for federal tax purposes (including an entity with a single owner that may be disregarded as an entity separate from its owner under Regulation 7701–3) that is not properly classified as a trust under Regulation 7701–4 or otherwise subject to special treatment under the Internal Revenue Code. A business entity with two or more members is classified for federal tax purposes as either a corporation or a partnership. A business entity with only one owner is classified as a corporation or is disregarded; if the entity is disregarded, its activities are treated in the same manner as a sole proprietorship, branch, or division of the owner.

(b) *Corporations.* For federal tax purposes, the term *corporation* means—

(1) A business entity organized under a Federal or State statute, or under a statute of a federally recognized Indian tribe, if the statute describes or refers to the entity as incorporated or as a corporation, body corporate, or body politic;

(2) An association (as determined under Regulation 7701–3);

(3) A business entity organized under a State statute, if the statute describes or refers to the entity as a joint-stock company or joint-stock association;

(4) An insurance company;

(5) A State-chartered business entity conducting banking activities, if any of its deposits are insured under the Federal Deposit Insurance Act, as amended, 12 U.S.C. 1811 et seq., or a similar federal statute;

(6) A business entity wholly owned by a State or any political subdivision thereof, or a business entity owned by a foreign government . . .;

(7) A business entity that is taxable as a corporation under a provision of the Internal Revenue Code other than section 7701(a)(3); and

(8) *Certain foreign entities—* . . .

Regulation 7701–3. **Classification of certain business entities.**—(a) *In general.* A business entity that is not classified as a corporation under Regulations 7701–2(b)(1), (3), (4), (5), (6), (7), or (8) (an *eligible entity*) can elect its classification for federal tax purposes as provided in this section. An eligible entity with at least two members can elect to be classified as either an association (and thus a corporation under Regulation 7701–2(b)(2)) or a partnership, and an eligible entity with a single owner can elect to be classified as an association or to be disregarded as an entity separate from its owner. Paragraph (b) of this section provides a default classification for an eligible entity that does not make an election. Thus, elections are necessary only when an eligible entity chooses to be classified initially as other than the default classification or when an eligible entity chooses to change its classification. An entity whose classification is determined under the default classification retains that classification . . . until the entity makes an election to change that classification. . . .

(b) *Classification of eligible entities that do not file an election—*(1) *Domestic eligible entities.* Except as provided in paragraph (b)(3) of this section, unless the entity elects otherwise, a domestic eligible entity is—

(i) A partnership if it has two or more members; or

(ii) Disregarded as an entity separate from its owner if it has a single owner. . . .

(3) *Existing eligible entities—*(i) *In general.* Unless the entity elects otherwise, an eligible entity in existence prior to the effective date of this section will have the same classification that the entity claimed under Regulations 7701–1 through 7701–3 as in effect on the date prior to the effective date of this section; except that if an eligible entity with a single owner claimed to be a partnership under those regulations, the entity will be disregarded as an entity separate from its owner under this paragraph (b)(3)(i). . . .

(c)(1)(iv) *Limitation.* If an eligible entity makes an election . . . to change its classification (other than an election made by an existing entity to change its classification as of the effective date of this section), the entity cannot change its classification by election again during the sixty months succeeding the effective date of the election. However, the Commissioner may permit the entity to change its classification by election within the sixty months if more than fifty percent of the ownership interests in the entity as of the effective date of the subsequent election are owned by person that did not own any interests in the entity on the filing date or on the effective date of the entity's prior election. . . .

DELAWARE GENERAL CORPORATION LAW

SUBCHAPTER I. FORMATION

SUBCHAPTER II. POWERS

SUBCHAPTER III. REGISTERED OFFICE AND REGISTERED AGENT

* Omitted.

* Omitted.

* Omitted.

SUBCHAPTER XI.   INSOLVENCY;
RECEIVERS AND TRUSTEES*

SUBCHAPTER XII.   RENEWAL, REVIVAL, EXTENSION
AND RESTORATION OF CERTIFICATE OF
INCORPORATION OR CHARTER*

SUBCHAPTER XIII.   SUITS AGAINST CORPORATIONS,
DIRECTORS, OFFICERS OR STOCKHOLDERS

* Omitted.

* Omitted.

SUBCHAPTER I. FORMATION

§ 101. Incorporators; How Corporation Formed; Purposes

(a) Any person, partnership, association or corporation, singly or jointly with others, and without regard to such person or entity's residence, domicile or state of incorporation, may incorporate or organize a corporation under this chapter by filing with the Secretary of State a certificate of incorporation which shall be executed, acknowledged and filed in accordance with section 103 of this title.

(b) A corporation may be incorporated or organized under this chapter to conduct or promote any lawful business or purposes, except as may otherwise be provided by the constitution or other law of this State.

* Omitted.

(c) Corporations for constructing, maintaining and operating public utilities, whether in or outside of this State, may be organized under this chapter, but corporations for constructing, maintaining and operating public utilities within this State shall be subject to, in addition to the provisions of this chapter, the special provisions and requirements of Title 26 applicable to such corporations.

(d) Except for provisions included pursuant to sections 102(a)(1), 102(a)(2), 102(a)(5), 102(a)(6), 102(b)(2), 102(b)(5), 102(b)(7) of this chapter, and provisions included pursuant to section 102(a)(4) specifying the classes, number of shares, and par value of shares the corporation is authorized to issue, any provision of the certificate of incorporation may be made dependent upon facts ascertainable outside such instrument, provided that the manner in which such facts shall operate upon the provision is clearly and explicitly set forth therein. The term "facts," as used in this subsection, includes, but is not limited to, the occurrence of any event, including a determination or action by any person or body, including the corporation.

§ 102. Certificate of Incorporation; Contents

(a) The certificate of incorporation shall set forth—

(1) The name of the corporation which (i) shall contain one of the words "association", "company", "corporation", "club", "foundation", "fund", "incorporated", "institute", "society", "union", "syndicate", or "limited" (or abbreviations thereof, with or without punctuation), or words (or abbreviations thereof, with or without punctuation) of like import of foreign countries or jurisdictions (provided they are written in Roman characters or letters); provided, however, that the Division of Corporations in the Department of State may waive such requirement (unless it determines that such name is, or might otherwise appear to be, that of a natural person) if such corporation executes, acknowledges and files with the Secretary of State in accordance with § 103 of this title a certificate stating that its total assets, as defined in subsection (ii) of § 503 of this title, are not less than 10 million dollars, (ii) shall be such as to distinguish it upon the records in the office of the Division of Corporations in the Department of State from the names on such records of other corporations, partnerships, limited partnerships, limited liability companies or statutory trusts organized, reserved or registered as a foreign corporation, partnership, limited partnership, limited liability company or statutory trust under the laws of this State, except with the written consent of such other foreign corporation or domestic or foreign partnership, limited partnership, limited liability company or statutory trust executed, acknowledged and filed with the Secretary of State in accordance with § 103 of this title and (iii) shall not contain the word "bank", or any variation thereof, except for the name of a bank reporting to and under the supervision of the State Bank Commissioner of this State, or a subsidiary of a bank or savings association (as those terms are

defined in the Federal Deposit Insurance Act, as amended, at 12 U.S.C. § 1813), or a corporation regulated under the Bank Holding Company Act of 1956, as amended, 12 U.S.C. § 1841 et seq., or the Home Owners' Loan Act, as amended, 12 U.S.C. § 1461 et seq., provided, however, that this section shall not be consumed to prevent the use of the word "bank", or any variation thereof, in a context clearly not purporting to refer to a banking business or otherwise likely to mislead the public about the nature of the business of the corporation or to lead to a pattern and practice of abuse that might cause harm to the interests of the public or the State as determined by the Division of Corporations in the Department of State;

(2) The address (which shall include the street, number, city and county) of the corporation's registered office in this State, and the name of its registered agent at such address;

(3) The nature of the business or purposes to be conducted or promoted. It shall be sufficient to state, either alone or with other businesses or purposes, that the purpose of the corporation is to engage in any lawful act or activity for which corporations may be organized under the General Corporation Law of Delaware, and by such statement all lawful acts and activities shall be within the purposes of the corporation, except for express limitations, if any;

(4) If the corporation is to be authorized to issue only one class of stock, the total number of shares of stock which the corporation shall have authority to issue and the par value of each of such shares, or a statement that all such shares are to be without par value. If the corporation is to be authorized to issue more than one class of stock, the certificate of incorporation shall set forth the total number of shares of all classes of stock which the corporation shall have authority to issue and the number of shares of each class, and shall specify each class the shares of which are to be without par value and each class the shares of which are to have par value and the par value of the shares of each such class. The certificate of incorporation shall also set forth a statement of the designations and the powers, preferences and rights, and the qualifications, limitations or restrictions thereof, which are permitted by § 151 of this Title in respect of any class or classes of stock or any series of any class of stock of the corporation and the fixing of which by the certificate of incorporation is desired, and an express grant of such authority as it may then be desired to grant to the board of directors to fix by resolution or resolutions any thereof that may be desired but which shall not be fixed by the certificate of incorporation. ...;

(5) The name and mailing address of the incorporator or incorporators;

(6) If the powers of the incorporator or incorporators are to terminate upon the filing of the certificate of incorporation, the names and mailing addresses of the persons who are to serve as directors until the

first annual meeting of stockholders or until their successors are elected and qualify.

(b) In addition to the matters required to be set forth in the certificate of incorporation by subsection (a) of this section the certificate of incorporation may also contain any or all of the following matters—

(1) Any provision for the management of the business and for the conduct of the affairs of the corporation, and any provision creating, defining, limiting and regulating the powers of the corporation, the directors, and the stockholders, or any class of the stockholders, or the members of a non-stock corporation; if such provisions are not contrary to the laws of this State. Any provision which is required or permitted by any section of this chapter to be stated in the by-laws may instead be stated in the certificate of incorporation;

(2) The following provisions, in haec verba, viz.—

"Whenever a compromise or arrangement is proposed between this corporation and its creditors or any class of them and/or between this corporation and its stockholders or any class of them, any court of equitable jurisdiction within the State of Delaware may, on the application in a summary way of this corporation or of any creditor or stockholder thereof or on the application of any receiver or receivers appointed for this corporation under the provisions of section 291 of Title 8 of the Delaware Code or on the application of trustees in dissolution or of any receiver or receivers appointed for this corporation under the provisions of section 279 of Title 8 of the Delaware Code order a meeting of the creditors or class of creditors, and/or of the stockholders or class of stockholders of this corporation, as the case may be, to be summoned in such manner as the said court directs. If a majority in number representing three-fourths in value of the creditors or class of creditors, and/or of the stockholders or class of stockholders of this corporation, as the case may be, agree to any compromise or arrangement and to any reorganization of this corporation as consequence of such compromise or arrangement, the said compromise or arrangement and the said reorganization shall, if sanctioned by the court to which the said application has been made, be binding on all the creditors or class of creditors, and/or on all the stockholders or class of stockholders, of this corporation, as the case may be, and also on this corporation";

(3) Such provisions as may be desired granting to the holders of the stock of the corporation, or the holders of any class or series of a class thereof, the preemptive right to subscribe to any or all additional issues of stock of the corporation of any or all classes or series thereof, or to any securities of the corporation convertible into such stock. No stockholder shall have any preemptive right to subscribe to an additional issue of stock or to any security convertible into such stock unless, and except to the extent that, such right is expressly granted to such stockholder in the certificate of incorporation. All such rights in exis-

tence on July 3, 1967, shall remain in existence unaffected by this paragraph (3) unless and until changed or terminated by appropriate action which expressly provides for such change or termination;

(4) Provisions requiring for any corporate action, the vote of a larger portion of the stock or of any class or series thereof, or of any other securities having voting power, or a larger number of the directors, that is required by this chapter;

(5) A provision limiting the duration of the corporation's existence to a specified date; otherwise, the corporation shall have perpetual existence;

(6) A provision imposing personal liability for the debts of the corporation on its stockholders or members to a specified extent and upon specified conditions; otherwise, the stockholders or members of a corporation shall not be personally liable for the payment of the corporation's debts except as they may be liable by reason of their own conduct or acts;

(7) A provision eliminating or limiting the personal liability of a director to the corporation or its stockholders for monetary damages for breach of fiduciary duty as a director, provided that such provision shall not eliminate or limit the liability of a director (i) for any breach of the director's duty of loyalty to the corporation or its stockholders, (ii) for acts or omissions not in good faith or which involve intentional misconduct or a knowing violation of law, (iii) under section 174 of this Title, or (iv) for any transaction from which the director derived an improper personal benefit. No such provision shall eliminate or limit the liability of a director for any act or omission occurring prior to the date when such provision becomes effective. All references in this paragraph to a director shall also be deemed to refer (x) to a member of the governing body of a corporation which is not authorized to issue capital stock, and (y) to such other person or persons, if any, who, pursuant to a provision of the certificate of incorporation in accordance with § 141(a) of this title, exercise or perform any of the powers or duties otherwise conferred or imposed upon the board of directors by this title.

(c) It shall not be necessary to set forth in the certificate of incorporation any of the powers conferred on corporations by this chapter.

§ 103. Execution, Acknowledgment, Filing, Recording and Effective Date of Original Certificate of Incorporation and Other Instruments; Exceptions

(a) Whenever any provision of this chapter requires any instrument to be filed with the Secretary of State or in accordance with this section or chapter, such instrument shall be executed as follows:

(1) The certificate of incorporation, and any other instrument to be filed before the election of the initial board of directors if the initial directors were not named in the certificate of incorporation, shall be signed by the incorporator or incorporators (or, in the case of any such other instrument, such incorporator's or incorporators' successors and assigns). If any incorporator is not available by reason of death, incapacity, unknown address, or refusal or neglect to act, then any such other instrument may be signed, with the same effect as if such incorporator had signed it, by any person for whom or on whose behalf such incorporator, in executing the certificate of incorporation, was acting directly or indirectly as employee or agent, provided that such other instrument shall state that such incorporator is not available and the reason therefor, that such incorporator in executing the certificate of incorporation was acting directly or indirectly as employee or agent for or on behalf of such person, and that such person's signature on such instrument is otherwise authorized and not wrongful.

(2) All other instruments shall be signed:

    a.   By any authorized officer of the corporation; or

    b.   If it shall appear from the instrument that there are no such officers, then by a majority of the directors or by such directors as may be designated by the board; or

    c.   If it shall appear from the instrument that there are no such officers or directors, then by the holders of record, or such of them as may be designated by the holders of record, of a majority of all outstanding shares of stock; or

    d.   By the holders of record of all outstanding shares of stock.

(b) Whenever any provision of this chapter requires any instrument to be acknowledged, such requirement is satisfied by either:

(1) The formal acknowledgment by the person or one of the persons signing the instrument that it is such person's act and deed or the act and deed of the corporation, as the case may be, and that the facts stated therein are true. Such acknowledgment shall be made before a person who is authorized by the law of the place of execution to take acknowledgments of deeds. If such person has a seal of office, such person shall affix it to the instrument.

(2) The signature, without more, of the person or persons signing the instrument, in which case such signature or signatures shall constitute the affirmation or acknowledgment of the signatory, under penalties of perjury, that the instrument is such person's act and deed or the act and deed of the corporation, as the case may be, and that the facts stated therein are true.

(c) Whenever any provision of this chapter requires any instrument to be filed with the Secretary of State or in accordance with this section or chapter, such requirement means that:

(1) The signed instrument shall be delivered to the office of the Secretary of State;

(2) All taxes and fees authorized by law to be collected by the Secretary of State in connection with the filing of the instrument shall be tendered to the Secretary of State; and

(3) Upon delivery of the instrument, the Secretary of State shall record the date and time of its delivery. Upon such delivery and tender of the required taxes and fees, the Secretary of State shall certify that the instrument has been filed in the Secretary of State's office by endorsing upon the signed instrument the word "Filed", and the date and time of its filing. This endorsement is the "filing date" of the instrument, and is conclusive of the date and time of its filing in the absence of actual fraud. The Secretary of State shall file and index the endorsed instrument. Except as provided in paragraph (4) of this subsection and in subsection (i) of this section, such filing date of an instrument shall be the date and time of delivery of the instrument.

(4) Upon request made upon or prior to delivery, the Secretary of State may, to the extent deemed practicable, establish as the filing date of an instrument a date and time after its delivery. If the Secretary of State refuses to file any instrument due to an error, omission or other imperfection, the Secretary of State may hold such instrument in suspension, and in such event, upon delivery of a replacement instrument in proper form for filing and tender of the required taxes and fees within 5 business days after notice of such suspension is given to the filer, the Secretary of State shall establish as the filing date of such instrument the date and time that would have been the filing date of the rejected instrument had it been accepted for filing. The Secretary of State shall not issue a certificate of good standing with respect to any corporation with an instrument held in suspension pursuant to this subsection. The Secretary of State may establish as the filing date of an instrument the date and time at which information from such instrument is entered pursuant to subdivision (c)(7) of this section [municipality fees] if such instrument is delivered on the same date and within 4 hours after such information is entered.

(5) The Secretary of State, acting as agent for the recorders of each of the counties, shall collect and deposit in a separate account established exclusively for that purpose a county assessment fee with respect to each filed instrument, and shall thereafter weekly remit from such account to the recorder of each of the said counties the amount or amounts of such fees as provided for in paragraph (c)(6) of this section or as elsewhere provided by law. Said fees shall be for the purposes of defraying certain costs incurred by the counties in merging the information and images of such filed documents with the document information systems of each of the recorder's offices in the counties, and in retrieving, maintaining and displaying such information and images in the

offices of the recorders and at remote locations in each of such counties. In consideration for its acting as the agent for the recorders with respect to the collection and payment of the county assessment fees, the Secretary of State shall retain and pay over to the general fund of the State an administrative charge of one percent of the total fees collected.

(6) The assessment fee to the counties shall be $24 for each one-page instrument filed with the Secretary of State in accordance with this section and $9 for each additional page for instruments with more than one page. The recorder's office to receive the assessment fee shall be the recorder's office in the county in which the corporation's registered office in this State is, or is to be, located, except that an assessment fee shall not be charged for either a certificate of dissolution qualifying for treatment under § 391(a)(5)(b) ... [short-form dissolution], or a document filed in accordance with subchapter XV of this title....

(8) The Secretary of State shall cause to be entered such information from each instrument as the Secretary of State deems appropriate into the Delaware Corporation Information System or any system which is a successor thereto in the office of the Secretary of State, and such information and a copy of each such instrument shall be permanently maintained as a public record on a suitable medium. The Secretary of State is authorized to grant direct access to such system to registered agents subject to the execution of an operating agreement between the Secretary of State and such registered agent. Any registered agent granted such access shall demonstrate the existence of policies to ensure that information entered into the system accurately reflects the content of instruments in the possession of the registered agent at the time of entry.

(d) Any instrument filed in accordance with subsection (c) of this section shall be effective upon its filing date. Any instrument may provide that it is not to become effective until a specified time subsequent to the time it is filed, but such time shall not be later than a time on the 90th day after the date of its filing. ...

(f) Whenever any instrument authorized to be filed with the Secretary of State under any provision of this title has been so filed and is an inaccurate record of the corporate action therein referred to, or was defectively or erroneously executed, sealed or acknowledged, such instrument may be corrected by filing with the Secretary of State a certificate of correction of such instrument which shall be executed, acknowledged and filed in accordance with this section. The certificate of correction shall specify the inaccuracy or defect to be corrected and shall set forth the portion of the instrument in corrected form. In lieu of filing a certificate of correction the instrument may be corrected by filing with the Secretary of State a corrected instrument which shall be executed, acknowledged and filed in accordance with this section. The corrected instrument shall be specifically designated as such in its heading, shall specify the inaccuracy or defect to be corrected, and shall set forth the entire instrument in corrected form. An instrument corrected in accordance with this section shall be effective as of the date the original instrument was filed, except as to those persons who are substantially and adversely affected by the correction and as to those persons the instrument as corrected shall be effective from the filing date.

(g) Notwithstanding that any instrument authorized to be filed with the Secretary of State under any provision of this title is when filed inaccurately, defectively or erroneously executed, sealed or acknowledged, or otherwise defective in any respect, the Secretary of State shall have no liability to any person for the preclearance for filing, the acceptance for filing, or the filing and indexing of such instrument by the Secretary of State.

(h) Any signature or any instrument authorized to be filed with the Secretary of State under any provision of this title may be a facsimile, a conformed signature or an electronically transmitted signature....

§ 104. Certificate of Incorporation: Definition

The term "certificate of incorporation", is used in this chapter, unless the context requires otherwise, includes not lonely the original certificate of incorporation filed to create a corporation but also all other certificates, agreements of merger or consolidation, plans of reorganization, or other instruments, howsoever designated, which are filed pursuant to §§ 102, 133–136, 151, 241–243, 245, 251–258, 263–264, 303, or any other section of this title, and which have the effect of amending or supplementing in some respect a corporation's original certificate of incorporation.

§ 105. Certificate of Incorporation and Other Certificates; Evidence

A copy of a certificate of incorporation, or a restated certificate of incorporation, or of any other certificate which has been filed in the office of the Secretary of State as required by any provision of this title shall, when duly certified by the Secretary of State, be received in all courts, public offices, and official bodies as prima facie evidence of:

(1) Due execution, acknowledgment and filing of the instrument;

(2) Observance and performance of all acts and conditions necessary to have been observed and performed precedent to the instrument becoming effective; and of

(3) Any other facts required or permitted by law to be stated in the instrument.

§ 106. Commencement of Corporate Existence

Upon the filing with the Secretary of State of the certificate of incorporation, executed and acknowledged in accordance with section 103, the incorporator or incorporators who signed the certificate, and such incorporator's or incorporators' successors and assigns, shall, from the date of such filing, be and constitute a body corporate, by the name set forth in the certificate, subject to the provisions of section 103(d) of this title and subject to dissolution or other termination of its existence as provided in this chapter.

§ 107. Powers of Incorporators

If the persons who are to serve as directors until the first annual meeting of stockholders have not been named in the certificate of incorporation, the incorporator or incorporators, until the directors are elected, shall manage the affairs of the corporation and may do whatever is necessary and proper to perfect the organization of the corporation, including the adoption of the original by-laws of the corporation and the election of directors.

§ 108. Organization Meeting of Incorporators or Directors Named in Certificate of Incorporation

(a) After the filing of the certificate of incorporation an organization meeting of the incorporator or incorporators, or of the board of directors if the initial directors were named in the certificate of incorporation, shall be held, either within or without this State, at the call of a majority of the incorporators or directors, as the case may be, for the purposes of adopting by-laws, electing directors (if the meeting is of the incorporators) to serve or hold office until the first annual meeting of stockholders or until their successors are elected and qualify, electing officers if the meeting is of the directors, doing any other or further acts to perfect the organization of the corporation, and transacting such other business as may come before the meeting.

(b) The persons calling the meeting shall give to each other incorporator or director, as the case may be, at least 2 days written notice thereof by any usual means of communication, which notice shall state the time, place and purposes of the meeting as fixed by the persons calling it. Notice of the meeting need not be given to anyone who attends the meeting or who signs a waiver of notice either before or after the meeting.

(c) Any action permitted to be taken at the organization meeting of the incorporators or directors, as the case may be, may be taken without a meeting if each incorporator or director, where there is more than one, or the sole incorporator or director where there is only one, signs an instrument which states the action so taken.

§ 109. By–Laws

(a) The original or other by-laws of a corporation may be adopted, amended, or repealed by the incorporators, by the initial directors if they were named in the certificate of incorporation, or, before a corporation has received any payment for any of its stock, by its board of directors. After a corporation has received any payment for any of its stock, the power to adopt, amend or repeal by-laws shall be in the stockholders entitled to vote, or, in the case of a non-stock corporation, in its members entitled to vote; provided, however, any corporation may, in its certificate of incorporation, confer the power to adopt, amend, or repeal by-laws upon the directors or, in the case of a non-stock corporation, upon its governing body by whatever name designated. The fact that such power has been so conferred upon the directors or governing body, as the case may be, shall not divest the stockholders or members of the power, nor limit their power to adopt, amend or repeal by-laws.

(b) The by-laws may contain any provision, not inconsistent with law or with the certificate of incorporation, relating to the business of the corporation, the conduct of its affairs, and its rights or powers or the rights or powers of its stockholders, directors, officers or employees.

§ 110. Emergency By–Laws and Other Powers in Emergency

The board of directors of any corporation may adopt emergency by-laws, subject to repeal or change by action of the stockholders, which shall notwithstanding any different provision elsewhere in this chapter or in Chapters 3 and 5 of Title 26, or in Chapter 7 of Title 5, or in the certificate of incorporation or by-laws, be operative during any emergency resulting from an attack on the United States or on a locality in which the corporation conducts its business or customarily holds meetings of its board of directors or its stockholders, or during any nuclear or atomic disaster, or during the existence of any catastrophe, or other similar emergency condition, as a result of which a quorum of the board of directors or a standing committee thereof cannot readily be convened for action. The emergency by-laws may make any provision that may be practical and necessary for the circumstances of the emergency.

§ 111. Interpretation and Enforcement of the Certificate of Incorporation and Bylaws

(a) Any civil action to interpret, apply, enforce or determine the validity of the provisions of:

(1) The certificate of incorporation or the bylaws of a corporation;

(2) Any instrument, document or agreement by which a corporation creates or sells, or offers to create or sell, any of its stock, or any rights or options respecting its stock;

(3) Any written restrictions on the transfer, registration of transfer or ownership of securities under § 202 of this title;

(4) Any proxy under § 212 or 215 of this title;

(5) Any voting trust or other voting agreement under § 218 of this title;

(6) Any agreement or certificate of merger or consolidation governed by § 251–253, 255–258, 263 or 264 of this title;

(7) Any certificate of conversion under § 265 or 266 of this title;

(8) Any certificate of domestication, transfer or continuance under § 388, 389 or 390 of this title; or

(9) Any other instrument, document, agreement, or certificate required by any provision of this title;

May be brought in the Court of Chancery, except to the extent that a statute confers exclusive jurisdiction on a court, agency or tribunal other than the Court of Chancery.

(b) Any civil action to interpret, apply or enforce any provision of this title may be brought in the Court of Chancery.

SUBCHAPTER II. POWERS

§ 121. General Powers

(a) In addition to the powers enumerated in Section 122 of this title, every corporation, its officers, directors, and stockholders shall possess and may exercise all the powers and privileges granted by this chapter or by any other law or by its certificate of incorporation, together with any powers incidental thereto, so far as such powers and privileges are necessary or convenient to the conduct, promotion or attainment of the business or purposes set forth in its certificate of incorporation.

(b) Every corporation shall be governed by the provisions and be subject to the restrictions and liabilities contained in this chapter.

§ 122. Specific Powers

Every corporation created under this chapter shall have power to—

(1) Have perpetual succession by its corporate name, unless a limited period of duration is stated in its certificate of incorporation;

(2) Sue and be sued in all courts and participate, as a party or otherwise, in any judicial, administrative, arbitrative or other proceeding, in its corporate name;

(3) Have a corporate seal, which may be altered at pleasure, and use the same by causing it or a facsimile thereof, to be impressed or affixed or in any other manner reproduced;

(4) Purchase, receive, take by grant, gift, devise, bequest or otherwise, lease, or otherwise acquire, own, hold, improve, employ, use and otherwise deal in and with real or personal property, or any interest therein, wherever situated, and to sell, convey, lease, exchange, transfer or otherwise dispose of, or mortgage or pledge, all or any of its property and assets, or any interest therein, wherever situated;

(5) Appoint such officers and agents as the business of the corporation requires and to pay or otherwise provide for them suitable compensation;

(6) Adopt, amend and repeal by-laws;

(7) Wind up and dissolve itself in the manner provided in this chapter;

(8) Conduct its business, carry on its operations, and have offices and exercise its powers within or without this State;

(9) Make donations for the public welfare or for charitable, scientific or educational purposes, and in time of war or other national emergency in aid thereof;

(10) Be an incorporator, promoter, or manager of other corporations of any type or kind;

(11) Participate with others in any corporation, partnership, limited partnership, joint venture, or other association of any kind, or in any transaction, undertaking or arrangement which the participating corporation would have power to conduct by itself, whether or not such participation involves sharing or delegation of control with or to others;

(12) Transact any lawful business which the corporation's board of directors shall find to be in aid of governmental authority;

(13) Make contracts, including contracts of guaranty and suretyship, incur liabilities, borrow money at such rates of interest as the corporation may determine, issue its notes, bonds and other obligations, and secure any of its obligations by mortgage, pledge or other encumbrance of all or any of its property, franchises and income, and make contracts of guaranty and suretyship which are necessary or convenient to the conduct, promotion or attainment of the business of (a) a corporation all of the outstanding stock of which is owned, directly or indirectly, by the contracting corporation, or (b) a corporation which owns, directly or indirectly, all of the outstanding stock of the contracting corporation, or (c) a corporation all of the outstanding stock of which is owned, directly or indirectly, by a corporation which owns, directly or indirectly, all of the outstanding stock of the contracting corporation, which contracts of guaranty and suretyship shall be deemed to be necessary or convenient to the conduct, promotion or attainment of the business of the contracting corporation, and make other contracts of guaranty and suretyship which are necessary or convenient to the conduct, promotion or attainment of the business of the contracting corporation;

(14) Lend money for its corporate purposes, invest and reinvest its funds, and take, hold and deal with real and personal property as security for the payment of funds so loaned or invested;

(15) Pay pensions and establish and carry out pension, profit sharing, stock option, stock purchase, stock bonus, retirement, benefit, incentive and compensation plans, trusts and provisions for any or all of its directors, officers, and employees, and for any or all of the directors, officers, and employees of its subsidiaries;

(16) Provide insurance for its benefit on the life of any of its directors, officers, or employees, or on the life of any stockholder for the purpose of acquiring at such stockholder's death shares of its stock owned by such stockholder.

(17) Renounce, in its certificate of incorporation or by action of its board of directors, any interest or expectancy of the corporation in, or in being offered an opportunity to participate in, specified business opportunities or specified classes or categories of business opportunities that are presented to the corporation or one or more of its officers, directors or stockholders.

§ 123. Powers Respecting Securities of Other Corporations or Entities

Any corporation organized under the laws of this State may guarantee, purchase, take, receive, subscribe for or otherwise acquire; own, hold, use or otherwise employ; sell, lease, exchange, transfer, or otherwise dispose of; mortgage, lend, pledge or otherwise deal in and with, bonds and other obligations of, or shares or other securities or interests in, or issued by, any other domestic or foreign corporation, partnership, association, or individual, or by any government or agency or instrumentality thereof. A corporation while owner of any such securities may exercise all the rights, powers and privileges of ownership, including the right to vote.

§ 124. Lack of Corporate Capacity or Power; Effect; Ultra Vires

No act of a corporation and no conveyance or transfer of real or personal property to or by a corporation shall be invalid by reason of the fact that the corporation was without capacity or power to do such act or to make or receive such conveyance or transfer, but such lack of capacity or power may be asserted:

(1) In a proceeding by a stockholder against the corporation to enjoin the doing of any act or acts or the transfer of real or personal property by or to the corporation. If the unauthorized acts or transfer sought to be enjoined are being, or are to be, performed or made pursuant to any contract to which the corporation is a party, the court may, if all of the parties to the contract are parties to the proceeding and

if it deems the same to be equitable, set aside and enjoin the performance of such contract, and in so doing may allow to the corporation or to the other parties to the contract, as the case may be, such compensation as may be equitable for the loss or damage sustained by any of them which may result from the action of the court in setting aside and enjoining the performance of such contract, but anticipated profits to be derived from the performance of the contract shall not be awarded by the court as a loss or damage sustained.

(2) In a proceeding by the corporation, whether acting directly or through a receiver, trustee, or other legal representative, or through stockholders in a representative suit, against an incumbent or former officer or director of the corporation, for loss or damage due to such incumbent or former officer's or director's unauthorized act.

(3) In a proceeding by the Attorney General to dissolve the corporation, or to enjoin the corporation from the transaction of unauthorized business.

SUBCHAPTER III.   REGISTERED OFFICE AND REGISTERED AGENT

§ 131.   Registered Office in State; Principal Office or Place of Business in State

(a) Every corporation shall have and maintain in this State a registered office which may, but need not be, the same as its place of business.

(b) Whenever the term "corporation's principal office or place of business in this State" or "principal office or place of business of the corporation in this State", or other term of like import, is or has been used in a corporation's certificate of incorporation, or in any other document, or in any statute, it shall be deemed to mean and refer to, unless the context indicates otherwise, the corporation's registered office required by this section; and it shall not be necessary for any corporation to amend its certificate of incorporation or any other document to comply with this section.

§ 132.   Registered Agent in State; Resident Agent

(a) Every corporation shall have and maintain in this State a registered agent, which agent may be any of (i) the corporation itself, (ii) an individual resident in this State, (iii) a domestic corporation (other than the corporation itself), a domestic limited partnership, a domestic limited liability company or a domestic statutory trust or (iv) a foreign corporation, a foreign limited partnership or a foreign limited liability company authorized to transact business in this State, in each case, having a business office identical with the office of such registered agent which generally is open during normal business hours to accept service of process and otherwise perform the functions of a registered agent.

(b) Whenever the term "resident agent" or "resident agent in charge of a corporation's principal office or place of business in this State", or other term of like import which refers to a corporation's agent required by statute to be located in this State, is or has been used in a corporation's certificate of incorporation, or in any other document, or in any statute, it shall be deemed to mean and refer to, unless the context indicates otherwise, the corporation's registered agent required by this section; and it shall not be necessary for any corporation to amend its certificate of incorporation or any other document to comply with this section.

SUBCHAPTER IV.   DIRECTORS AND OFFICERS

§ 141. Board of Directors; Powers; Number, Qualifications, Terms and Quorum; Committees; Classes of Directors; ... Reliance Upon Books; Action Without Meeting, etc.

(a) The business and affairs of every corporation organized under this chapter shall be managed by or under the direction of a board of directors, except as may be otherwise provided in this chapter or in its certificate of incorporation. If any such provision is made in the certificate of incorporation, the powers and duties conferred or imposed upon the board of directors by this chapter shall be exercised or performed to such extent and by such person or persons as shall be provided in the certificate of incorporation.

(b) The board of directors of a corporation shall consist of one or more members, each of whom shall be a natural person. The number of directors shall be fixed by, or in the manner provided in, the by-laws, unless the certificate of incorporation fixes the number of directors, in which case a change in the number of directors shall be made only by amendment of the certificate. Directors need not be stockholders unless so required by the certificate of incorporation or the by-laws. The certificate of incorporation or by-laws may prescribe other qualifications for directors. Each director shall hold office until such director's successor is elected and qualified or until such director's earlier resignation or removal. Any director may resign at any time upon notice given in writing or by electronic transmission to the corporation. A majority of the total number of directors shall constitute a quorum for the transaction of business unless the certificate of incorporation or the by-laws require a greater number. Unless the certificate of incorporation provides otherwise, the by-laws may provide that a number less than a majority shall constitute a quorum which in no case shall be less than one-third of the total number of directors except that when a board of one director is authorized under the provisions of this section, then one director shall constitute a quorum. The vote of the majority of the directors present at a meeting at which a quorum is present shall be the act of the board of directors unless the certificate of incorporation or the by-laws shall require a vote of a greater number.

(c)(1) All corporations incorporated prior to July 1, 1996, shall be governed by subsection (1) of this section, provided that any such corporation may by a resolution adopted by a majority of the whole board elect to be governed by subsection (2) of this section, in which case subsection (1) of this section shall not apply to such corporation. All corporations incorporated on or after July 1, 1996, shall be governed by subsection (2) of this section. The board of directors may, by resolution passed by a majority of the whole board, designate one or more committees, each committee to consist of one or more of the directors of the corporation. The board may designate one or more directors as alternate members of any committee, who may replace any absent or disqualified member at any meeting of the committee. The by-laws may provide that in the absence or disqualification of a member of a committee, the member or members thereof present at any meeting and not disqualified from voting, whether or not he or they constitute a quorum, may unanimously appoint another member of the board of directors to act at the meeting in the place of any such absent or disqualified member. Any such committee, to the extent provided in the resolution of the board of directors, or in the by-laws of the corporation, shall have and may exercise all the powers and authority of the board of directors in the management of the business and affairs of the corporation, and may authorize the seal of the corporation to be affixed to all papers which may require it; but no such committee shall have the power or authority in reference to amending the certificate of incorporation (except that a committee may, to the extent authorized in the resolution or resolutions providing for the issuance of shares of stock adopted by the board of directors as provided in Section 151(a) of this title, fix the designations and any of the preferences or rights of such shares relating to dividends, redemption, dissolution, any distribution of assets of the corporation or the conversion into, or the exchange of such shares for, shares of any other class or classes or any other series of the same or any other class or classes of stock of the corporation or fix the number of shares of any series of stock or authorize the increase or decrease of the shares of any series), adopting an agreement of merger or consolidation under Sections 251, 252, 254, 255, 256, 257, 258, 263 or 264 of this title, recommending to the stockholders the sale, lease or exchange of all or substantially all of the corporation's property and assets, recommending to the stockholders a dissolution of the corporation or a revocation of a dissolution, or amending the by-laws of the corporation; and, unless the resolution, by-laws, or certificate of incorporation expressly so provide, no such committee shall have the power or authority to declare a dividend, to authorize the issuance of stock, or to adopt a certificate of ownership and merger pursuant to Section 253 of this title.

(2) The board of directors may designate 1 or more committees, each committee to consist of 1 or more of the directors of the corporation. The board may designate one or more directors as alternate members of any committee, who may replace any absent or disqualified member at any meeting of the committee. The bylaws may provide that in the absence or disqualification of a member of a committee, the member or members present at any meeting and not disqualified from voting, whether or not such member or members constitute a quorum, may unanimously appoint another member of the board of directors to act at the meeting in the place of any such absent or disqualified member. Any such committee, to the extent provided in the resolution of the board of directors, or in the bylaws of the corporation, shall have and may exercise all the powers and authority of the board of directors in the management of the business and affairs of the corporation, and may authorize the seal of the corporation to be affixed to all papers which may require it; but no such committee shall have the power or authority in reference to the following matters: (i) approving or adopting, or recommending to the stockholders, any action or matter (other than the election or removal of directors) expressly required by this chapter to be submitted to stockholders for approval or (ii) adopting, amending or repealing any bylaw of the corporation.

(3) Unless otherwise provided in the certificate of incorporation, the bylaws or the resolution of the board of directors designating the committee, a committee may create one or more subcommittees, each subcommittee to consist of one or more members of the committee, and delegate to a subcommittee any or all of the powers and authority of the committee.

(d) The directors of any corporation organized under this chapter may, by the certificate of incorporation or by an initial bylaw, or by a bylaw adopted by a vote of the stockholders, be divided into 1, 2 or 3 classes; the term of office of those of the first class to expire at the annual meeting next ensuing; of the second class 1 year thereafter; of the third class 2 years thereafter; and at each annual election held after such classification and election, directors shall be chosen for a full term, as the case may be, to succeed those whose terms expire. The certificate of incorporation may confer upon holders of any class or series of stock the right to elect 1 or more directors who shall serve for such term, and have such voting powers as shall be stated in the certificate of incorporation. The terms of office and voting powers of the directors elected separately by the holders of any class or series of stock may be greater than or less than those of any other director or class of directors. In addition, the certificate of incorporation may confer upon one or more directors, whether or not elected separately by the holders of any class or series of stock, voting powers greater than or less than those of other directors. If the certificate of incorporation provides that one or more directors shall have more or less than 1 vote per director on any matter, every reference in this chapter to a majority or other proportion of the directors shall refer to a majority or other proportion of the votes of the directors.

(e) A member of the board of directors, or a member of any committee designated by the board of directors, shall, in the performance of such member's duties, be fully protected in relying in good faith upon the records of the corporation and upon such information, opinions, reports or statements presented to the corporation by any of the corporation's officers or employees, or committees of the board of directors, or by any other person as to matters the member reasonably believes are within such other person's professional or expert competence and who has been selected with reasonable care by or on behalf of the corporation.

(f) Unless otherwise restricted by the certificate of incorporation or by-laws, any action required or permitted to be taken at any meeting of the board of directors, or of any committee thereof may be taken without a meeting if all members of the board or committee, as the case may be, consent thereto in writing or by electronic transmission, and the writing or writings or electronic transmission or transmissions are filed with the minutes of proceedings of the board or committee. Such filing shall be in paper form if the minutes are maintained in paper form and shall be in electronic form if the minutes are maintained in electronic form.

(g) Unless otherwise restricted by the certificate of incorporation or by-laws, the board of directors of any corporation organized under this chapter may hold its meetings, and have an office or offices, outside of this State.

(h) Unless otherwise restricted by the certificate of incorporation or by-laws, the board of directors shall have the authority to fix the compensation of directors.

(i) Unless otherwise restricted by the certificate of incorporation or by-laws, members of the board of directors of any corporation, or any committee designated by such board, may participate in a meeting of such board or committee by means of conference telephone or other communications equipment by means of which all persons participating in the meeting can hear each other, and participation in a meeting pursuant to this subsection shall constitute presence in person at such meeting. ...

(k) Any director or the entire board of directors may be removed, with or without cause, by the holders of a majority of the shares then entitled to vote at an election of directors, except as follows:

(i) Unless the certificate of incorporation otherwise provides, in the case of a corporation whose board is classified as provided in subsection (d) of this section, shareholders may effect such removal only for cause; or

(ii) In the case of a corporation having cumulative voting, if less than the entire board is to be removed, no director may be removed without cause if the votes cast against such director's removal would be sufficient to elect such director if then cumulatively voted at an election of the entire board of directors, or, if there be classes of directors, at an election of the class of directors of which such director is a part.

Whenever the holders of any class or series are entitled to elect one or more directors by the provisions of the certificate of incorporation, the provisions of this subsection shall apply, in respect to the removal without cause of a director or directors so elected, to the vote of the holders of the outstanding shares of that class or series and not to the vote of the outstanding shares as a whole.

§ 142. Officers; Titles, Duties, Selection, Term; Failure to Elect; Vacancies

(a) Every corporation organized under this chapter shall have such officers with such titles and duties as shall be stated in the by-laws or in a resolution of the board of directors which is not inconsistent with the by-laws and as may be necessary to enable it to sign instruments and stock certificates which comply with sections 103(a)(2) and 158 of this chapter. One of the officers shall have the duty to record the proceedings of the meetings of the stockholders and directors in a book to be kept for that purpose. Any number of offices may be held by the same person unless the certificate of incorporation or bylaws otherwise provide.

(b) Officers shall be chosen in such manner and shall hold their offices for such terms as are prescribed by the by-laws or determined by the board of directors or other governing body. Each officer shall hold office until such officer's successor is elected and qualified or until such officer's earlier resignation or removal. Each officer shall hold office until such officer's successor is elected and qualified or until such officer's earlier resignation or removal.

(c) The corporation may secure the fidelity of any or all of its officers or agents by bond or otherwise.

(d) A failure to elect officers shall not dissolve or otherwise affect the corporation.

(e) Any vacancy occurring in any office of the corporation by death, resignation, removal or otherwise, shall be filled as the by-laws provide. In the absence of such provision, the vacancy shall be filled by the board of directors or other governing body.

§ 143. Loans to Employees and Officers; Guaranty of Obligations of Employees and Officers

Any corporation may lend money to, or guarantee any obligation of, or otherwise assist any officer or other employee of the corporation or of its subsidiary, including any officer or employee who is a director of the corporation or its subsidiary, whenever, in the judgment of the directors, such loan, guaranty or assistance may reasonably be expected to benefit the corporation. The loan, guaranty or other assistance may be with or without interest, and may be unsecured, or secured in such manner as the board of directors shall approve, including, without limitation, a pledge of shares of stock of the corporation. Nothing in this section contained shall be deemed to deny, limit or restrict the powers of guaranty or warranty of any corporation at common law or under any statute.

§ 144. Interested Directors; Quorum

(a) No contract or transaction between a corporation and one or more of its directors or officers, or between a corporation and any other corporation, partnership, association, or other organization in which one or more of its directors or officers are directors or officers, or have a financial interest, shall be void or voidable solely for this reason, or solely because the director or officer is present at or participates in the meeting of the board or committee thereof which authorizes the contract or transaction, or solely because any such director's or officer's votes are counted for such purpose, if:

(1) The material facts as to the director's or officer's relationship or interest and as to the contract or transaction are disclosed or are known to the board of directors or the committee, and the board or committee in good faith authorizes the contract or transaction by the affirmative votes of a majority of the disinterested directors, even though the disinterested directors be less than a quorum; or

(2) The material facts as to the director's or officer's relationship or interest and as to the contract or transaction are disclosed or are known to the shareholders entitled to vote thereon, and the contract or transaction is specifically approved in good faith by vote of the shareholders; or

(3) The contract or transaction is fair as to the corporation as of the time it is authorized, approved or ratified, by the board of directors, a committee thereof, or the shareholders.

(b) Common or interested directors may be counted in determining the presence of a quorum at a meeting of the board of directors or of a committee which authorizes the contract or transaction.

§ 145. Indemnification of Officers, Directors, Employees and Agents; Insurance

(a) A corporation shall have power to indemnify any person who was or is a party or is threatened to be made a party to any threatened, pending or completed action, suit or proceeding, whether civil, criminal, administrative or investigative (other than an action by or in the right of the corporation) by reason of the fact that such person is or was a director, officer, employee or agent of the corporation, or is or was serving at the request of the corporation as a director, officer, employee or agent of another corporation, partnership, joint venture, trust or other enterprise, against expenses (including attorneys' fees), judgments, fines and amounts paid in settlement actually and reasonably incurred by such person in connection with such action, suit or proceeding if such person acted in good faith and in a manner such person reasonably believed to be in or not opposed to the best interests of the corporation, and, with respect to any criminal action or proceeding, had no reasonable cause to believe such person's conduct was unlawful. The termination of any action, suit or proceeding by judgment, order, settlement, conviction, or upon a plea of *nolo contendere* or its equivalent, shall not, of itself, create a presumption that the person did not act in good faith and in a manner which such person reasonably believed to be in or not opposed to the best interests of the corporation, and, with respect to any criminal action or proceeding, had reasonable cause to believe that such person's conduct was unlawful.

(b) A corporation shall have power to indemnify any person who was or is a party or is threatened to be made a party to any threatened, pending or completed action or suit by or in the right of the corporation to procure a judgment in its favor by reason of the fact that such person is or was a director, officer, employee or agent of the corporation, or is or was serving at the request of the corporation as a director, officer, employee or agent of another corporation, partnership, joint venture, trust or other enterprise against expenses (including attorneys' fees) actually and reasonably incurred by such person in connection with the defense or settlement of such action or suit if such person acted in good faith and in a manner such person reasonably believed to be in or not opposed to the best interests of the corporation and except that no indemnification shall be made in respect of any claim, issue or matter as to which such person shall have been adjudged to be liable to the corporation unless and only to the extent that the Court of Chancery or the court in which such action or suit was brought shall determine upon application that, despite the adjudication of liability but in view of all the circumstances of the case, such person is fairly and reasonably entitled to indemnity for such expenses which the Court of Chancery or such other court shall deem proper.

(c) To the extent that a present or former director or officer of a corporation has been successful on the merits or otherwise in defense of any action, suit or proceeding referred to in subsections (a) and (b), or in defense of any claim, issue or matter therein, such person shall be indemnified against expenses (including attorneys' fees) actually and reasonably incurred by such person in connection therewith.

(d) Any indemnification under subsections (a) and (b) of this section (unless ordered by a court) shall be made by the corporation only as authorized in the specific case upon a determination that indemnification of the present or former director, officer, employee or agent is proper in the circumstances because such person has met the applicable standard of conduct set forth in subsections (a) and (b) of this section. Such determination shall be made, with respect to a person who is a director or officer at the time of such determination, (1) by a majority vote of the directors who are not parties to such action, suit or proceeding, even though less than a quorum, or (2) by a committee of such directors designated by majority vote of such directors, even though less than a quorum, or (3) if there are no such directors, or if such directors so direct, by independent legal counsel in a written opinion, or (4) by the stockholders.

(e) Expenses (including attorneys' fees) incurred by an officer or director in defending any civil, criminal, administrative, or investigative action, suit or proceeding may be paid by the corporation in advance of the final disposition of such action, suit or proceeding upon receipt of an undertaking by or on behalf of such director or officer to repay such amount if it shall ultimately be determined that such person is not entitled to be indemnified by the corporation as authorized in this Section. Such expenses (including attorneys' fees) incurred by former directors and officers or other employees and agents may be so paid upon such terms and conditions, if any, as the corporation deems appropriate.

(f) The indemnification and advancement of expenses provided by, or granted pursuant to, the other subsections of this section shall not be deemed exclusive of any other rights to which those seeking indemnification or advancement of expenses may be entitled under any by-law, agreement, vote of stockholders or disinterested directors or otherwise, both as to action in such person's official capacity and as to action in another capacity while holding such office.

(g) A corporation shall have power to purchase and maintain insurance on behalf of any person who is or was a director, officer, employee or agent of the corporation, or is or was serving at the request of the corporation as a director, officer, employee or agent of another corporation, partnership, joint venture, trust or other enterprise against any liability asserted against such person and incurred by such person in any such capacity, or arising out of such person's status as such, whether or not the corporation would have the power to indemnify such person against such liability under the provisions of this section.

(h) For purposes of this Section, references to "the corporation" shall include, in addition to the resulting corporation, any constituent corporation (including any constituent of a constituent) absorbed in a consolidation or merger which, if its separate existence had continued, would have had power and authority to indemnify its directors, officers, and employees or agents, so that any person who is or was a director, officer, employee or agent of such constituent corporation, or is or was serving at the request of such constituent corporation as a director, officer, employee or agent of another corporation, partnership, joint venture, trust or other enterprise, shall stand in the same position under the provisions of this Section with respect to the resulting or surviving corporation as such person would have with respect to such constituent corporation if its separate existence had continued.

(i) For purposes of this Section, references to "other enterprises" shall include employee benefit plans; references to "fines" shall include any excise taxes assessed on a person with respect to an employee benefit plan; and references to "serving at the request of the corporation" shall include any service as a director, officer, employee or agent of the corporation which imposes duties on, or involves services by, such director, officer, employee, or agent with respect to an employee benefit plan, its participants, or beneficiaries; and a person who acted in good faith and in a manner such person reasonably believed to be in the interest of the participants and beneficiaries of an employee benefit plan shall be deemed to have acted in a manner "not opposed to the best interests of the corporation" as referred to in this Section.

(j) The indemnification and advancement of expenses provided by, or granted pursuant to, this section shall, unless otherwise provided when authorized or ratified, continue as to a person who has ceased to be a director, officer, employee or agent and shall inure to the benefit of the heirs, executors and administrators of such a person.

(k) The Court of Chancery is hereby vested with exclusive jurisdiction to hear and determine all actions for advancement of expenses or indemnification brought under this section or under any bylaw, agreement, vote of stockholders or disinterested directors, or otherwise. The Court of Chancery may summarily determine a corporation's obligation to advance expenses (including attorneys' fees).

§ 146. [Submitting Matters to a Vote]

A corporation may agree to submit a matter to a vote of its stockholders whether or not the board of directors determines at any time subsequent to approving such matter that such matter is no longer advisable and recommends that the stockholders reject or vote against the matter.

SUBCHAPTER V. STOCK AND DIVIDENDS

§ 151. Classes and Series of Stock; Rights, etc.

(a) Every corporation may issue one or more classes of stock or one or more series of stock within any class thereof, any or all of which classes may be of stock with par value or stock without par value and which classes or series may have such voting powers, full or limited, or no voting powers, and such designations, preferences and relative, participating, optional or other special rights, and qualifications, limitations or restrictions thereof, as shall be stated and expressed in the certificate of incorporation or of any amendment thereto, or in the resolution or resolutions providing for the issue of such stock adopted by the board of directors pursuant to authority expressly vested in it by the provisions of its certificate of incorporation. Any of the voting powers, designations, preferences, rights and qualifications, limitations or restrictions of any such class or series of stock may be made dependent upon facts ascertainable outside the certificate of incorporation or of any amendment thereto, or outside the resolution or resolutions providing for the issue of such stock adopted by the board of directors pursuant to authority expressly vested in it by the provisions of its certificate of incorporation, provided that the manner in which such facts shall operate upon the voting powers, designations, preferences, rights and qualifications, limitations or restrictions of such class or series of stock is clearly and expressly set forth in the certificate of incorporation or in the resolution or resolutions providing for the issue of such stock adopted by the board of directors. The term "facts," as used in this subsection, includes, but is not limited to, the occurrence of any event, including a determination or action by any person or body, including the corporation. The power to increase or decrease or otherwise adjust the capital stock as provided in this chapter shall apply to all or any such classes of stock.

(b) Any stock of any class or series may be made subject to redemption by the corporation at its option or at the option of the holders of such stock or upon the happening of a specified event; provided, however, that immediately following any such redemption the corporation shall have outstanding 1 or more shares of 1 or more classes or series of stock, which share, or shares together, shall have full voting powers. Notwithstanding the limitation stated in the foregoing proviso:

(1) Any stock of a regulated investment company registered under the Investment Company Act of 1940, as heretofore or hereafter amended, may be made subject to redemption by the corporation at its option or at the option of the holders of such stock.

(2) Any stock of a corporation which holds (directly or indirectly) a license or franchise from a governmental agency to conduct its business or is a member of a national securities exchange, which license, franchise or membership is conditioned upon some or all of the holders of its stock possessing prescribed qualifications, may be made subject to redemption by the corporation to the extent necessary to prevent the loss of such license, franchise or membership or to reinstate it.

Any stock which may be made redeemable under this section may be redeemed for cash, property or rights, including securities of the same or another corporation, at such time or times, price or prices, or rate or rates, and with such adjustments, as shall be stated in the certificate of incorporation or in the resolution or resolutions providing for the issue of such stock adopted by the board of directors pursuant to subsection (a) of this section.

(c) The holders of preferred or special stock of any class or of any series thereof shall be entitled to receive dividends at such rates, on such conditions and at such times as shall be stated in the certificate of incorporation or in the resolution or resolutions providing for the issue of such stock adopted by the board of directors as hereinabove provided, payable in preference to, or in such relation to, the dividends payable on any other class or classes or of any other series of stock, and cumulative or non-cumulative as shall be so stated and expressed. When dividends upon the preferred and special stocks, if any, to the extent of the preference to which such stocks are entitled, shall have been paid or declared and set apart for payment, a dividend on the remaining class or classes or series of stock may then be paid out of the remaining assets of the corporation available for dividends as elsewhere in this chapter provided.

(d) The holders of the preferred or special stock of any class or of any series thereof shall be entitled to such rights upon the dissolution of, or upon any distribution of the assets of, the corporation as shall be stated in the certificate of incorporation or in the resolution or resolutions providing for the issue of such stock adopted by the board of directors as hereinabove provided.

(e) Any stock of any class or of any series thereof may be made convertible into, or exchangeable for, at the option of either the holder or the corporation or upon the happening of a specified event, shares of any other class or classes or any other series of the same or any other class or classes of stock of the corporation, at such price or prices or at such rate or rates of exchange and with such adjustments as shall be stated in the certificate of incorporation or in the resolution or resolutions providing for the issue of such stock adopted by the board of directors as hereinabove provided.

(f) If any corporation shall be authorized to issue more than one class of stock or more than one series of any class, the powers, designations, preferences and relative, participating, optional or other special rights of each class of stock or series thereof and the qualifications, limitations or restrictions of such preferences and/or rights shall be set forth in full or summarized on the face or back of the certificate which the corporation shall issue to represent such class or series of stock, provided that, except as otherwise provided in section 202 of this title, in lieu of the foregoing requirements, there may be set forth on the face or back of the certificate which the corporation shall issue to represent such class or series of stock, a statement that the corporation will furnish without charge to each stockholder who so requests the powers, designations, preferences and relative, participating, optional or other special rights of each class of stock or series thereof and the qualifications, limitations or restrictions of such preferences and/or rights. Within a reasonable time after the issuance or transfer of uncertificated stock, the corporation shall send to the registered owner thereof a written notice containing the information required to be set forth or stated on certificates pursuant to this Section or Sections 156, 202(a) or 218(a) or with respect to this Section a statement that the corporation will furnish without charge to each stockholder who so requests the powers, designations, preferences and relative participating, optional or other special rights of each class of stock or series thereof and the qualifications, limitations or restrictions of such preferences and/or rights. Except as otherwise expressly provided by law, the rights and obligations of the holders of uncertificated stock and the rights and obligations of the holders of certificates representing stock of the same class and series shall be identical.

(g) When any corporation desires to issue any shares of stock of any class or of any series of any class of which the powers, designations, preferences and relative, participating, optional or other rights, if any, or the qualifications, limitations or restrictions thereof, if any, shall not have been set forth in the certificate of incorporation or in any amendment thereto but shall be provided for in a resolution or resolutions adopted by the board of directors pursuant to authority expressly vested in it by the provisions of the certificate of incorporation or any amendment thereto, a certificate of designations setting forth a copy of such resolution or resolutions and the number of shares of stock of such class or series as to which the resolution or resolutions apply shall be executed, acknowledged, filed, and shall become effective, in accordance with § 103 of this Title. Unless otherwise provided in any such resolution or resolutions, the number of shares of stock of any such series to which such resolution or resolutions apply may be increased (but not above the total number of authorized shares of the class) or decreased (but not below the number of shares thereof then outstanding) by a certificate likewise executed, acknowledged and filed setting forth a statement that a specified increase or decrease therein had been authorized and directed by a resolution or resolutions likewise adopted by the board of directors. In case the number of such shares shall be decreased the number of shares so specified in the certificate shall resume the status which they had prior to the adoption of the first resolution or resolutions. When no shares of any such class or series are outstanding, either because none were issued or because no issued shares of any such class or series remain outstanding, a certificate setting forth a resolution or resolutions adopted by the board of directors that none of the authorized shares of such class or series are outstanding, and that none will be issued subject to the certificate of designations previously filed with respect to such class or series, may be executed, acknowledged and filed in accordance with § 103 of this Title and, when such certificate becomes effective, it shall have the effect of eliminating from the certificate of incorporation all matters set forth in the certificate of designations with respect to such class or series of stock. Unless otherwise provided in the certificate of incorporation, if no shares of stock have been issued of a class or series of stock established by a resolution of the board of directors, the voting powers, designations, preferences and relative, participating, optional or other rights, if any, or the qualifications, limitations or restrictions thereof, may be amended by a resolution or resolutions adopted by the board of directors. A certificate which (1) states that no shares of the class or series have been issued, (2) sets forth a copy of the resolution or resolutions and (3) if the designation of the class or series is being changed, indicates the original designation and the new designation, shall be executed, acknowledged and filed, and shall become effective, in accordance with § 103 of this title. When any certificate filed under this subsection becomes effective, it shall have the effect of amending the certificate of incorporation; except that neither the filing of such certificate nor the filing of a restated certificate of incorporation pursuant to § 245 of this title shall prohibit the board of directors from subsequently adopting such resolutions as authorized by this subsection.

§ 152. Issuance of Stock, Lawful Consideration; Fully Paid Stock

The consideration, as determined pursuant to subsections (a) and (b) of § 153 of this title, for subscriptions to, or the purchase of, the capital stock to be issued by a corporation shall be paid in such form and in such manner as the board of directors shall determine. The board of directors may authorize capital stock to be issued for consideration consisting of cash, any tangible or intangible property or any benefit to the corporation, or any combination thereof. In the absence of actual fraud in the transaction, the judgment of the directors as to the value of such consideration shall be conclusive. The capital stock so issued shall be deemed to be fully paid and nonassessable stock upon receipt by the corporation of such consideration; provided, however, nothing contained herein shall prevent the board of directors from issuing partly paid shares under § 156 of this title.

§ 153. Consideration for Stock

(a) Shares of stock with par value may be issued for such consideration, having a value not less than the par value thereof, as is determined from time to time by the board of directors, or by the stockholders if the certificate of incorporation so provides.

(b) Shares of stock without par value may be issued for such consideration as is determined from time to time by the board of directors, or by the stockholders if the certificate of incorporation so provides.

(c) Treasury shares may be disposed of by the corporation for such consideration as may be determined from time to time by the board of directors, or by the stockholders if the certificate of incorporation so provides.

(d) If the certificate of incorporation reserves to the stockholders the right to determine the consideration for the issue of any shares, the stockholders shall, unless the certificate requires a greater vote, do so by a vote of a majority of the outstanding stock entitled to vote thereon.

§ 154. Determination of Amount of Capital; Capital, Surplus and Net Assets Defined

Any corporation may, by resolution of its board of directors, determine that only a part of the consideration which shall be received by the corporation for any of the shares of its capital stock which it shall issue from time to time shall be capital; but, in case any of the shares issued shall be shares having a par value, the amount of the part of such consideration so determined to be capital shall be in excess of the aggregate par value of the shares issued for such consideration having a par value, unless all the shares issued shall be shares having a par value, in which case the amount of the part of such consideration so determined to be capital need be only equal to the aggregate par value of such shares. In each such case the board of directors shall specify in dollars the part of such consideration which shall be capital. If the board of directors shall not have determined (1) at the time of issue of any shares of the capital stock of the corporation issued for cash or (2) within 60 days after the issue of any shares of the capital stock of the corporation issued for consideration other than cash what part of the consideration for such shares shall be capital, the capital of the corporation in respect of such shares shall be an amount equal to the aggregate par value of such shares having a par value, plus the amount of the consideration for such shares without par value. The amount of the consideration so determined to be capital in respect of any shares without par value shall be the stated capital of such shares. The capital of the corporation may be increased from time to time by resolution of the board of directors directing that a portion of the net assets of the corporation in excess of the amount so determined to be capital be transferred to the capital account. The board of directors may direct that the portion of such net assets so transferred shall be treated as capital in respect of any shares of the corporation of any designated class or classes. The excess, if any, at any given time, of the net assets of the corporation over the amount so determined to be capital shall be surplus. Net assets means the amount by which total assets exceed total liabilities. Capital and surplus are not liabilities for this purpose.

§ 155. Fractions of Shares

A corporation may, but shall not be required to, issue fractions of a share. If it does not issue fractions of a share, it shall (1) arrange for the disposition of fractional interests by those entitled thereto, (2) pay in cash the fair value of fractions of a share as of the time when those entitled to receive such fractions are determined or (3) issue scrip or warrants in registered form (either represented by a certificate or uncertificated) or in bearer form (represented by a certificate) which shall entitle the holder to receive a full share upon the surrender of such scrip or warrants aggregating a full share. A certificate for a fractional share or an uncertificated fractional share shall, but scrip or warrants shall not unless otherwise provided therein, entitle the holder to exercise voting rights, to receive dividends thereon, and to participate in any of the assets of the corporation in the event of liquidation. The board of directors may cause scrip or warrants to be issued subject to the conditions that they shall become void if not exchanged for certificates representing the full shares or uncertificated full shares before a specified date, or subject to the conditions that the shares for which scrip or warrants are exchangeable may be sold by the corporation and the proceeds thereof distributed to the holders of scrip or warrants, or subject to any other conditions which the board of directors may impose.

§ 156. Partly Paid Shares

Any corporation may issue the whole or any part of its shares as partly paid and subject to call for the remainder of the consideration to be paid therefor. Upon the face or back of each stock certificate issued to represent any such partly paid shares, or upon the books and records of the corporation in the case of uncertificated partly paid shares, the total amount of the consideration to be paid therefor and the amount paid thereon shall be stated. Upon the declaration of any dividend on fully paid shares, the corporation shall declare a dividend upon partly paid shares of the same class, but only upon the basis of the percentage of the consideration actually paid thereon.

§ 157. Rights and Options Respecting Stock

(a) Subject to any provisions in the certificate of incorporation, every corporation may create and issue, whether or not in connection with the issue and sale of any shares of stock or other securities of the corporation, rights or options entitling the holders thereof to acquire from the corporation any shares of its capital stock of any class or classes, such rights or options to be evidenced by or in such instrument or instruments as shall be approved by the board of directors.

(b) The terms upon which, including the time or times which may be limited or unlimited in duration, at or within which, and the consideration (including a formula by which such consideration may be determined) for which any such shares may be acquired from the corporation upon the exercise of any such right or option, shall be such as shall be stated in the certificate of incorporation, or in a resolution adopted by the board of directors providing for the creation and issue of such rights or options, and, in every case, shall be set forth or incorporated by reference in the instrument or instruments evidencing such rights or options. In the absence of actual fraud in the transaction, the judgment of the directors as to the consideration for the issuance of such rights or options and the sufficiency thereof shall be conclusive.

(c) The board of directors may, by a resolution adopted by the board, authorize one or more officers of the corporation to do one or both of the following: (i) designate officers and employees of the corporation or of any of its subsidiaries to be recipients of such rights or options created by the corporation and (ii) determine the number of such rights or options to be received by such officers and employees; provided, however, that the resolution so authorizing such officer or officers shall specify the total number of rights or options such officer or officers may so award. The board of directors may not authorize an officer to designate himself or herself as a recipient of any such rights or options.

(d) In case the shares of stock of the corporation to be issued upon the exercise of such rights or options shall be shares having a par value, the consideration so to be received therefor shall have a value not less than the par value thereof. In case the shares of stock so to be issued shall be shares of stock without par value, the consideration therefor shall be determined in the manner provided in section 153 of this title.

§ 158. Stock Certificates; Uncertificated Shares

The shares of a corporation shall be represented by certificates, provided that the board of directors of the corporation may provide by resolution or resolutions that some or all of any or all classes or series of its stock shall be uncertificated shares. Any such resolution shall not apply to shares represented by a certificate until such certificate is surrendered to the corporation. Every holder of stock represented by certificates shall be entitled to have a certificate signed by, or in the name of the corporation by the chairperson or vice-chairperson of the board or directors, or the president or vice president, and by the treasurer or an assistant treasurer, or the secretary or an assistant secretary of such corporation representing the number of shares registered in certificate form. Any or all the signatures on the certificate may be a facsimile. In case any officer, transfer agent, or registrar who has signed or whose facsimile signature has been placed upon a certificate shall have ceased to be such officer, transfer agent or registrar before such certificate is issued, it may be issued by the corporation with the same effect as if such person were such officer, transfer agent or registrar at the date of issue. A corporation shall not have power to issue a certificate in bearer form.

§ 160. Corporation's Powers Respecting Ownership, Voting, etc. of Its Own Stock; Rights of Stock Called for Redemption

(a) Every corporation may purchase, redeem, receive, take or otherwise acquire, own and hold, sell, lend, exchange, transfer or otherwise dispose of, pledge, use and otherwise deal in and with its own shares; provided, however, that no corporation shall—

1. Purchase or redeem its own shares of capital stock for cash or other property when the capital of the corporation is impaired or when such purchase or redemption would cause any impairment of the capital of the corporation, except that a corporation may purchase or redeem out of capital any of its own shares which are entitled upon any distribution of its assets, whether by dividend or in liquidation, to a preference over another class or series of its stock or, if no shares entitled to such a preference are outstanding, any of its own shares, if such shares will be retired upon their acquisition and the capital of the corporation reduced in accordance with Sections 243 and 244 of this title. Nothing in this subsection shall invalidate or otherwise affect a note, debenture or other obligation of a corporation given by it as consideration for its acquisition by purchase, redemption or exchange of its shares of stock if at the time such note, debenture or obligation was delivered by the corporation its capital was not then impaired or did not thereby become impaired;

2. Purchase, for more than the price at which they may then be redeemed, any of its shares which are redeemable at the option of the corporation; or,

3. Redeem any of its shares unless their redemption is authorized by Section 151(b) of this title and then only in accordance with such Section and the certificate of incorporation.

(b) Nothing in this section limits or affects a corporation's right to resell any of its shares theretofore purchased or redeemed out of surplus and which have not been retired, for such consideration as shall be fixed by the board of directors.

(c) Shares of its own capital stock belonging to the corporation or to another corporation, if a majority of the shares entitled to vote in the election of directors of such other corporation is held, directly or indirectly, by the corporation, shall neither be entitled to vote nor be counted for quorum purposes. Nothing in this section shall be construed as limiting the right of any corporation to vote stock, including but not limited to its own stock, held by it in a fiduciary capacity.

(d) Shares which have been called for redemption shall not be deemed to be outstanding shares for the purpose of voting or determining the total number of shares entitled to vote on any matter on and after the date on which written notice of redemption has been sent to holders thereof and a sum sufficient to redeem such shares has been irrevocably deposited or set aside to pay the redemption price to the holders of the shares upon surrender of certificates therefor.

§ 161. Issuance of Additional Stock; When and by Whom

The directors may, at any time and from time to time, if all of the shares of capital stock which the corporation is authorized by its certificate of incorporation to issue have not been issued, subscribed for, or otherwise committed to be issued, issue or take subscriptions for additional shares of its capital stock up to the amount authorized in its certificate of incorporation.

§ 162. Liability of Stockholder or Subscriber for Stock Not Paid in Full

(a) When the whole of the consideration payable for shares of a corporation has not been paid in, and the assets shall be insufficient to satisfy the claims of its creditors, each holder of or subscriber for such shares shall be bound to pay on each share held or subscribed for by such holder or subscriber the sum necessary to complete the amount of the unpaid balance of the consideration for which such shares were issued or to be issued by the corporation.

(b) The amounts which shall be payable as provided in subsection (a) of this section may be recovered as provided in section 325 of this title, after a writ of execution against the corporation has been returned unsatisfied as provided in that section.

(c) Any person becoming an assignee or transferee of shares or of a subscription for shares in good faith and without knowledge or notice that the full consideration therefor has not been paid shall not be personally liable for any unpaid portion of such consideration, but the transferor shall remain liable therefor.

(d) No person holding shares in any corporation as collateral security shall be personally liable as a stockholder but the person pledging such shares shall be considered the holder thereof and shall be so liable. No executor, administrator, guardian, trustee or other fiduciary shall be personally liable as a stockholder, but the estate or funds held by such executor, administrator, guardian, trustee or other fiduciary in such fiduciary capacity shall be liable.

(e) No liability under this section or under section 325 of this title shall be asserted more than six years after the issuance of the stock or the date of the subscription upon which the assessment is sought.

(f) In any action by a receiver or trustee of an insolvent corporation or by a judgment creditor to obtain an assessment under this section, any stockholder or subscriber for stock of the insolvent corporation may appear and contest the claim or claims of such receiver or trustee.

§ 163.　Payment for Stock Not Paid in Full

The capital stock of a corporation shall be paid for in such amounts and at such times as the directors may require.　The directors may, from time to time, demand payment, in respect of each share of stock not fully paid, of such sum of money as the necessities of the business may, in the judgment of the board of directors, require, not exceeding in the whole the balance remaining unpaid on said stock, and such sum so demanded shall be paid to the corporation at such times and by such installments as the directors shall direct.　The directors shall give written notice of the time and place of such payments, which notice shall be mailed at least 30 days before the time for such payment, to each holder of or subscriber for stock which is not fully paid at such holder's or subscriber's last known post-office address.

§ 164.　Failure to Pay for Stock;　Remedies

When any stockholder fails to pay any installment or call upon such stockholder's stock which may have been properly demanded by the directors, at the time when such payment is due, the directors may collect the amount of any such installment or call or any balance thereof remaining unpaid, from the said stockholder by an action at law, or they shall sell at public sale such part of the shares of such delinquent stockholder as will pay all demands then due from such stockholder with interest and all incidental expenses, and shall transfer the shares so sold to the purchaser, who shall be entitled to a certificate therefor.

Notice of the time and place of such sale and of the sum due on each share shall be given by advertisement at least one week before the sale, in a newspaper of the county in this State where such corporation's registered office is located, and such notice shall be mailed by the corporation to such delinquent stockholder at such stockholder's last known postoffice address, at least 20 days before such sale.

If no bidder can be had to pay the amount due on the stock, and if the amount is not collected by an action at law, which may be brought within the county where the corporation has its registered office, within one year from the date of the bringing of such action at law, the said stock and the amount previously paid in by the delinquent stockholder on the stock shall be forfeited to the corporation.

§ 165.　Revocability of Pre-incorporation Subscriptions

Unless otherwise provided by the terms of the subscription, a subscription for stock of a corporation to be formed shall be irrevocable, except with the consent of all other subscribers or the corporation, for a period of six months from its date.

§ 166. Formalities Required of Stock Subscriptions

A subscription for stock of a corporation, whether made before or after the formation of a corporation, shall not be enforceable against a subscriber, unless in writing and signed by the subscriber or by such subscriber's agent.

§ 169. Situs of Ownership of Stock

For all purposes of title, action, attachment, garnishment and jurisdiction of all courts held in this State, but not for the purpose of taxation, the situs of the ownership of the capital stock of all corporations existing under the laws of this State, whether organized under this chapter or otherwise, shall be regarded as in this State.

§ 170. Dividends; Payment; Wasting Asset Corporations

(a) The directors of every corporation, subject to any restrictions contained in its certificate of incorporation, may declare and pay dividends upon the shares of its capital stock ... either (1) out of its surplus, as defined in and computed in accordance with sections 154 and 244 of this title, or (2) in case there shall be no such surplus, out of its net profits for the fiscal year in which the dividend is declared and/or the preceding fiscal year. If the capital of the corporation, computed in accordance with sections 154 and 244 of this title, shall have been diminished by depreciation in the value of its property, or by losses, or otherwise, to an amount less than the aggregate amount of the capital represented by the issued and outstanding stock of all classes having a preference upon the distribution of assets, the directors of such corporation shall not declare and pay out of such net profits any dividends upon any shares of any classes of its capital stock until the deficiency in the amount of capital represented by the issued and outstanding stock of all classes having a preference upon the distribution of assets shall have been repaired. Nothing in this subsection shall invalidate or otherwise affect a note, debenture or other obligation of the corporation paid by it as a dividend on shares of its stock, or any payment made thereon, if at the time such note, debenture or obligation was delivered by the corporation, the corporation had either surplus or net profits as provided in clause (1) or (2) of this subsection from which the dividend could lawfully have been paid.

(b) Subject to any restrictions contained in its certificate of incorporation, the directors of any corporation engaged in the exploitation of wasting assets (including but not limited to a corporation engaged in the exploitation of natural resources or other wasting assets, including patents, or engaged primarily in the liquidation of specific assets) may determine the net profits derived from the exploitation of such wasting assets or the net proceeds derived from such liquidation without taking into consideration the depletion of such assets resulting from lapse of time, consumption, liquidation or exploitation of such assets.

§ 171. Special Purpose Reserves

The directors of a corporation may set apart out of any of the funds of the corporation available for dividends a reserve or reserves for any proper purpose and may abolish any such reserve.

§ 172. Liability of Directors as to Dividends or Stock Redemption

A member of the board of directors, or a member of any committee designated by the board of directors, shall be fully protected in relying in good faith upon the records of the corporation and upon such information, opinions, reports or statements presented to the corporation by any of its officers or employees, or committees of the board of directors, or by any other person as to matters the director reasonably believes are within such other person's professional or expert competence and who has been selected with reasonable care by or on behalf of the corporation, as to the value and amount of the assets, liabilities and/or net profits of the corporation, or any other facts pertinent to the existence and amount of surplus or other funds from which dividends might properly be declared and paid, or with which the corporation's stock might properly be purchased or redeemed.

§ 173. Declaration and Payment of Dividends

No corporation shall pay dividends except in accordance with the provisions of this chapter. Dividends may be paid in cash, in property, or in shares of the corporation's capital stock. If the dividend is to be paid in shares of the corporation's theretofore unissued capital stock the board of directors shall, by resolution, direct that there be designated as capital in respect of such shares an amount which is not less than the aggregate par value of par value shares being declared as a dividend and, in the case of shares without par value being declared as a dividend, such amount as shall be determined by the board of directors. No such designation as capital shall be necessary if shares are being distributed by a corporation pursuant to a split-up or division of its stock rather than as payment of a dividend declared payable in stock of the corporation.

§ 174. Liability of Directors for Unlawful Payment of Dividend or Unlawful Stock Purchase or Redemption; Exoneration From Liability; Contribution Among Directors; Subrogation

(a) In case of any willful or negligent violation of the provisions of sections 160 or 173 of this title, the directors under whose administration the same may happen shall be jointly and severally liable, at any time within six years after paying such unlawful dividend or after such unlawful stock purchase or redemption, to the corporation, and to its creditors in the event of its dissolution or insolvency, to the full amount of the dividend unlawfully paid, or to the full amount unlawfully paid for the purchase or redemption of the corporation's stock, with interest from the time such liability accrued. Any director who may have been absent when the same was done, or who may have dissented from the act or resolution by which the same was done, may be exonerated from such liability by causing his or her dissent to be entered on the books containing the minutes of the proceedings of the directors at the time the same was done, or immediately after such director has notice of the same.

(b) Any director against whom a claim is successfully asserted under this section shall be entitled to contribution from the other directors who voted for or concurred in the unlawful dividend, stock purchase or stock redemption.

(c) Any director against whom a claim is successfully asserted under this section shall be entitled, to the extent of the amount paid by such director as a result of such claim, to be subrogated to the rights of the corporation against stockholders who received the dividend on, or assets for the sale or redemption of, their stock with knowledge of facts indicating that such dividend, stock purchase or redemption was unlawful under this chapter, in proportion to the amounts received by such stockholders respectively.

SUBCHAPTER VI. STOCK TRANSFERS

§ 201. Transfer of Stock, Stock Certificates and Uncertificated Stock

Except as otherwise provided in this Chapter, the transfer of stock and the certificates of stock which represent the stock or uncertificated stock shall be governed by Article 8 of Subtitle I of Title 6.* To the extent that any provision of this Chapter is inconsistent with any provision of Subtitle I of Title 6, the provisions of this Chapter shall be controlling.

§ 202. Restriction on Transfer and Ownership of Securities

(a) A written restriction or restrictions on the transfer or registration of transfer of a security of a corporation, or on the amount of the corporation's securities that may be owned by any person or group of persons, if permitted by this section and noted conspicuously on the certificate or certificates representing the security or securities so restricted or, in the case of uncertificated shares, contained in the notice

---

* The Article referred to is UCC Article 8.
[Footnote by ed.]

sent pursuant to subsection (f) of § 151 of this title, may be enforced against the holder of the restricted security or securities or any successor or transferee of the holder including an executor, administrator, trustee, guardian or other fiduciary entrusted with like responsibility for the person or estate of the holder. Unless noted conspicuously on the certificate or certificates representing the security securities so restricted or, in the case of uncertificated shares, contained in the notice sent pursuant to subsection (f) of § 151 of this title, a restriction, even though permitted by this section, is ineffective except against a person with actual knowledge of the restriction.

(b) A restriction on the transfer or registration of transfer of securities of a corporation, or on the amount of a corporation's securities that may be owned by any person or group of persons, may be imposed by the certificate of incorporation or by the bylaws or by an agreement among any number of security holders or among such holders and the corporation. No restrictions so imposed shall be binding with respect to securities issued prior to the adoption of the restriction unless the holders of the securities are parties to an agreement or voted in favor of the restriction.

(c) A restriction on the transfer or registration of transfer of securities of a corporation or on the amount of such securities that may be owned by any person or group of persons is permitted by this section if it:

(1) Obligates the holder of the restricted securities to offer to the corporation or to any other holders of securities of the corporation or to any other person or to any combination of the foregoing, a prior opportunity, to be exercised within a reasonable time, to acquire the restricted securities; or

(2) Obligates the corporation or any holder of securities of the corporation or any other person or any combination of the foregoing, to purchase the securities which are the subject of an agreement respecting the purchase and sale of the restricted securities; or

(3) Requires the corporation or the holders of any class or series of securities of the corporation to consent to any proposed transfer of the restricted securities or to approve the proposed transferee of the restricted securities, or to approve the amount of securities of the corporation that may be owned by an person or group of persons; or

(4) Obligates the holder of the restricted securities to sell or transfer an amount of restricted securities to the corporation or to any other holders of securities of the corporation or to any other person or to any combination of the foregoing, or causes or results in the automatic sale or transfer of an amount of restricted securities to the corporation or to any other holders of securities of the corporation or to any other person or to any combination of the foregoing; or

(5) Prohibits or restricts the transfer of the restricted securities to, or the ownership of restricted securities by, designated persons or classes of persons or groups of persons, and such designation is not manifestly unreasonable.

(d) Any restriction on the transfer or the registration of transfer of the securities of a corporation, or on the amount of securities of a corporation that may be owned by a person or group of persons, for any of the following purposes shall be conclusively presumed to be for a reasonable purpose:

(1) maintaining any local, state, federal, or foreign tax advantage to the corporation or its stockholders, including without limitation (i) maintaining the corporation's status as an electing small business corporation under subchapter S of the United States Internal Revenue Code [26 U.S.C.A. § 1371 et seq.], or (ii) maintaining or preserving any tax attribute (including without limitation net operating losses), or (iii) qualifying or maintaining the qualification of the corporation as a real estate investment trust pursuant to the United States Internal Revenue Code or regulations adopted pursuant to the United States Internal Revenue Code, or

(2) maintaining any statutory or regulatory advantage or complying with any statutory or regulatory requirements under applicable local, state, federal, or foreign law.

(e) Any other lawful restriction on transfer or registration of transfer of securities, or on the amount of securities that may be owned by any person or group of persons, is permitted by this section.

§ 203. Business Combinations With Interested Stockholders

(a) Notwithstanding any other provisions of this chapter, a corporation shall not engage in any business combination with any interested stockholder for a period of 3 years following the time that such stockholder became an interested stockholder, unless (1) prior to such time the board of directors of the corporation approved either the business combination or the transaction which resulted in the stockholder becoming an interested stockholder, or (2) upon consummation of the transaction which resulted in the stockholder becoming an interested stockholder, the interested stockholder owned at least 85% of the voting stock of the corporation outstanding at the time the transaction commenced, excluding for purposes of determining the voting stock outstanding (but not the outstanding voting stock owned by the interested stockholder) those shares owned (i) by persons who are directors and also officers and (ii) employee stock plans in which employee participants do not have the right to determine confidentially whether shares held subject to the plan will be tendered in a tender or exchange offer, or (3) at or subsequent to such time the business combination is approved by the board of directors and authorized at an annual or special meeting of stockholders, and not by written consent, by the affirmative vote of at least 66⅔% of the outstanding voting stock which is not owned by the interested stockholder.

(b) The restrictions contained in this section shall not apply if:

(1) the corporation's original certificate of incorporation contains a provision expressly electing not to be governed by this section;

(2) the corporation, by action of its board of directors, adopts an amendment to its bylaws within 90 days of the effective date of this section, expressly electing not to be governed by this section, which amendment shall not be further amended by the board of directors;

(3) the corporation, by action of its stockholders, adopts an amendment to its certificate of incorporation or bylaws expressly electing not to be governed by this section, provided that, in addition to any other vote required by law, such amendment to the certificate of incorporation or bylaws must be approved by the affirmative vote of a majority of the shares entitled to vote. An amendment adopted pursuant to this paragraph shall be effective immediately in the case of a corporation that both (i) has never had a class of voting stock that falls within any of the three categories set out in subsection (b)(4) hereof, and (ii) has not elected by a provision in its original certificate of incorporation or any amendment thereto to be governed by this section. In all other cases, an amendment adopted pursuant to this paragraph shall not be effective until 12 months after the adoption of such amendment and shall not apply to any business combination between such corporation and any person who became an interested stockholder of such corporation on or prior to such adoption. A bylaw amendment adopted pursuant to this paragraph shall not be further amended by the board of directors;

(4) the corporation does not have a class of voting stock that is (i) listed on a national securities exchange, (ii) authorized for quotation on The NASDAQ Stock Market or (iii) held of record by more than 2,000 stockholders, unless any of the foregoing results from action taken, directly or indirectly, by an interested stockholder or from a transaction in which a person becomes an interested stockholder;

(5) a stockholder becomes an interested stockholder inadvertently and (i) as soon as practicable divests itself of ownership of sufficient shares so that the stockholder ceases to be an interested stockholder and (ii) would not, at any time within the 3 year period immediately prior to a business combination between the corporation and such stockholder, have been an interested stockholder but for the inadvertent acquisition of ownership;

(6) the business combination is proposed prior to the consummation or abandonment of and subsequent to the earlier of the public announcement or the notice required hereunder of a proposed transaction which (i) constitutes one of the transactions described in the second sentence of

this paragraph; (ii) is with or by a person who either was not an interested stockholder during the previous 3 years or who became an interested stockholder with the approval of the corporation's board of directors or during the period described in paragraph (7) of this subsection (b); and (iii) is approved or not opposed by a majority of the members of the board of directors then in office (but not less than 1) who were directors prior to any person becoming an interested stockholder during the previous 3 years or were recommended for election or elected to succeed such directors by a majority of such directors. The proposed transactions referred to in the preceding sentence are limited to (x) a merger or consolidation of the corporation (except for a merger in respect of which, pursuant to section 251(f) of the chapter, no vote of the stockholders of the corporation is required); (y) a sale, lease, exchange, mortgage, pledge, transfer or other disposition (in one transaction or a series of transactions), whether as part of a dissolution or otherwise, of assets of the corporation or of any direct or indirect majority-owned subsidiary of the corporation (other than to any direct or indirect wholly-owned subsidiary or to the corporation) having an aggregate market value equal to 50% or more of either [the] aggregate market value of all of the assets of the corporation determined on a consolidated basis or the aggregate market value of all the outstanding stock of the corporation; or (z) a proposed tender or exchange offer for 50% or more of the outstanding voting stock of the corporation. The corporation shall give not less then 20 days notice to all interested stockholders prior to the consummation of any of the transactions described in clauses (x) or (y) of the second sentence of this paragraph; or

(7) The business combination is with an interested stockholder who became an interested stockholder at a time when the restrictions contained in this section did not apply by reason of any of paragraphs (1) through (4) of this subsection (b), provided, however, that this paragraph (7) shall not apply if, at the time such interested stockholder became an interested stockholder, the corporation's certificate of incorporation contained a provision authorized by the last sentence of this subsection (b).

Notwithstanding paragraphs (1), (2), (3) and (4) of this subsection, a corporation may elect by a provision of its original certificate of incorporation or any amendment thereto to be governed by this section; provided that any such amendment to the certificate of incorporation shall not apply to restrict a business combination between the corporation and an interested stockholder of the corporation if the interested stockholder became such prior to the effective date of the amendment.

(c) As used in this section only, the term:

(1) "affiliate" means a person that directly, or indirectly through one or more intermediaries, controls, or is controlled by, or is under common control with, another person.

(2) "associate," when used to indicate a relationship with any person, means (i) any corporation, partnership, unincorporated association or other entity of which such person is a director, officer or partner or is, directly or indirectly, the owner of 20% or more of any class of voting stock, (ii) any trust or other estate in which such person has at least a 20% beneficial interest or as to which such person serves as trustee or in a similar fiduciary capacity, and (iii) any relative or spouse of such person, or any relative of such spouse, who has the same residence as such person.

(3) "business combination," when used in reference to any corporation and any interested stockholder of such corporation, means:

(i) any merger or consolidation of the corporation or any direct or indirect majority-owned subsidiary of the corporation with (A) the interested stockholder, or (B) with any other corporation, partnership, unincorporated association or other entity if the merger or consolidation is caused by the interested stockholder and as a result of such merger or consolidation subsection (a) of this section is not applicable to the surviving entity;

(ii) any sale, lease, exchange, mortgage, pledge, transfer or other disposition (in one transaction or a series of transactions), except proportionately as a stockholder of such corporation, to or with the interested stockholder, whether as part of a dissolution or otherwise, of assets of the corporation or of any direct or indirect majority-owned subsidiary of the corporation which assets have an aggregate market value equal to 10% or more of either the aggregate market value of all the assets of the corporation determined on a consolidated basis or the aggregate market value of all the outstanding stock of the corporation;

(iii) any transaction which results in the issuance or transfer by the corporation or by any direct or indirect majority-owned subsidiary of the corporation of any stock of the corporation or of such subsidiary to the interested stockholder, except (A) pursuant to the exercise, exchange or conversion of securities exercisable for, exchangeable for or convertible into stock of such corporation or any such subsidiary which securities were outstanding prior to the time that the interested stockholder became such, (B) pursuant to a merger under Section 251(g) of this title, (C) pursuant to a dividend or distribution paid or made, or the exercise, exchange or conversion of securities exercisable for, exchangeable for or convertible into stock of such corporation or any such subsidiary which security is distributed, pro rata to all holders of a class or series of stock of such corporation subsequent to the time the interested stockholder became such, (D) pursuant to an exchange offer by the corporation to purchase stock made on the same terms to all holders of said stock, or (E) any issuance or transfer of stock by the corporation, provided however, that in no case under (C)–(E) above shall there be an increase in the interested stockholder's proportionate share of the stock of any class or series of the corporation or of the voting stock of the corporation;

(iv) any transaction involving the corporation or any direct or indirect majority-owned subsidiary of the corporation which has the effect, directly or indirectly, of increasing the proportionate share of the stock of any class or series, or securities convertible into the stock of any class or series, of the corporation or of any such subsidiary which is owned by the interested stockholder, except as a result of immaterial changes due to fractional share adjustments or as a result of any purchase or redemption of any shares of stock not caused, directly or indirectly, by the interested stockholder; or

(v) any receipt by the interested stockholder of the benefit, directly or indirectly (except proportionately as a stockholder of such corporation) of any loans, advances, guarantees, pledges or other financial benefits (other than those expressly permitted in subparagraphs (i)–(iv) above) provided by or through the corporation or any direct or indirect majority-owned subsidiary.

(4) "control," including the term "controlling," "controlled by" and "under common control with," means the possession, directly or indirectly, of the power to direct or cause the direction of the management and policies of a person, whether through the ownership of voting stock, by contract, or otherwise. A person who is the owner of 20% or more of the outstanding voting stock of any corporation, partnership, unincorporated association or other entity shall be presumed to have control of such entity, in the absence of proof by a preponderance of the evidence to the contrary. Notwithstanding the foregoing, a presumption of control shall not apply where such person holds voting stock, in good faith and not for the purpose of circumventing this section, as an agent, bank, broker, nominee, custodian or trustee for one or more owners who do not individually or as a group have control of such entity.

(5) "interested stockholder" means any person (other than the corporation and any direct or indirect majority-owned subsidiary of the corporation) that (i) is the owner of 15% or more of the outstanding voting stock of the corporation, or (ii) is an affiliate or associate of the corporation and was the owner of 15% or more of the outstanding voting stock of the corporation at any time within the 3–year period immediately prior to the date on which it is sought to be determined whether such person is an interested stockholder; and the affiliates and associates of such person; provided, however, that the term "interested stockholder" shall not include (x) any person who (A) owned shares in excess of the 15% limitation set forth herein as of, or acquired such shares pursuant to a tender offer commenced prior to, December 23, 1987 or pursuant to an exchange offer announced prior to the aforesaid date and commenced

within 90 days thereafter and either (I) continued to own shares in excess of such 15% limitation or would have but for action by the corporation or (II) is an affiliate or associate of the corporation and so continued (or so would have continued but for action by the corporation) to be the owner of 15% or more of the outstanding voting stock of the corporation at any time within the 3–year period immediately prior to the date on which it is sought to be determined whether such a person is an interested stockholder or (B) acquired said shares from a person described in (A) above by gift, inheritance or in a transaction in which no consideration was exchanged; or (y) any person whose ownership of shares in excess of the 15% limitation set forth herein [is] the result of action taken solely by the corporation provided that such person shall be an interested stockholder if thereafter such person acquires additional shares of voting stock of the corporation, except as a result of further corporate action not caused, directly or indirectly, by such person. For the purpose of determining whether a person is an interested stockholder, the voting stock of the corporation deemed to be outstanding shall include stock deemed to be owned by the person through application of paragraph (9) of this subsection but shall not include any other unissued stock of such corporation which may be issuable pursuant to any agreement, arrangement or understanding, or upon exercise of conversion rights, warrants or options, or otherwise.

(6) "person" means any individual, corporation, partnership, unincorporated association or other entity.

(7) "stock" means, with respect to any corporation, capital stock and, with respect to any other entity, any equity interest.

(8) "voting stock" means, with respect to any corporation, stock of any class or series entitled to vote generally in the election of directors and, with respect to any entity that is not a corporation, any equity interest entitled to vote generally in the election of the governing body of such entity. Every reference to a percentage of voting stock shall refer to such percentage of the votes of such voting stock.

(9) "owner" including the terms "own" and "owned" when used with respect to any stock means a person that individually or with or through any of its affiliates or associates:

    (i) beneficially owns such stock, directly or indirectly; or

    (ii) has (A) the right to acquire such stock (whether such right is exercisable immediately or only after the passage of time) pursuant to any agreement, arrangement or understanding, or upon the exercise of conversion rights, exchange rights, warrants or options, or otherwise; provided, however, that a person shall not be deemed the owner of stock tendered pursuant to a tender or exchange offer made by such person or any of such person's affiliates or associates until such tendered stock is accepted for purchase or exchange; or (B) the right to vote such stock pursuant to any agreement, arrangement or understanding; provided, however, that a person shall not be deemed the owner of any stock because of such person's right to vote such stock if the agreement, arrangement or understanding to vote such stock arises solely from a revocable proxy or consent given in response to a proxy or consent solicitation made to 10 or more persons; or

(iii) has any agreement, arrangement or understanding for the purpose of acquiring, holding, voting (except voting pursuant to a revocable proxy or consent as described in item (B) of clause (ii) of this paragraph), or disposing of such stock with any other person that beneficially owns, or whose affiliates or associates beneficially own, directly or indirectly, such stock.

(d) No provision of a certificate of incorporation or bylaw shall require, for any vote of stockholders required by this section a greater vote of stockholders than that specified in this section.

(e) The Court of Chancery is hereby vested with exclusive jurisdiction to hear and determine all matters with respect to this section.

SUBCHAPTER VII. MEETINGS, ELECTIONS, VOTING AND NOTICE

§ 211. Meetings of Stockholders

(a)(1) Meetings of stockholders may be held at such place, either within or without this State, as may be designated by or in the manner provided in the certificate or incorporation or by-laws or, if not so designated, as determined by the board of directors. If, pursuant to this paragraph (a)(1) or the certificate of incorporation or the bylaws of the corporation, the board of directors is authorized to determine the place of a meeting of stockholders, the board of directors may, in its sole discretion, determine that the meeting shall not be held at any place, but may instead be held solely by means of remote communication as authorized by paragraph (a)(2) of this Section 211.

(2) If authorized by the board of directors in its sole discretion, and subject to such guidelines and procedures as the board of directors may adopt, stockholders and proxyholders not physically present at a meeting of stockholders may, by means of remote communication:

(A) participate in a meeting of stockholders; and

(B) be deemed present in person and vote at a meeting of stockholders whether such meeting is to be held at a designated place or solely by means of remote communication, provided that (i) the corporation shall implement reasonable measures to verify that each person deemed present and permitted to vote at the meeting by means of remote communication is a stockholder or proxyholder, (ii) the corporation shall implement reasonable measures to provide such stockholders and proxyholders a reasonable opportunity to participate in the meeting and to vote on matters submitted to the stockholders, including an opportunity to read or hear the proceedings of the meeting substantially concurrently with such proceedings, and (iii) if any stockholder or proxyholder votes or takes other action at the meeting by means of remote communication, a record of such vote or other action shall be maintained by the corporation.

(b) Unless directors are elected by written consent in lieu of an annual meeting as permitted by this subsection, an annual meeting of stockholders shall be held for the election of directors on a date and at a time designated by or in the manner provided in the by-laws. Stockholders may, unless the certificate of incorporation otherwise provides, act by written consent to elect directors; provided, however, that, if such consent is less than unanimous, such action by written consent may be in lieu of holding an annual meeting only if all of the directorships to which directors could be elected at an annual meeting held at the effective time of such action are vacant and are filled by such action. Any other proper business may be transacted at the annual meeting.

(c) A failure to hold the annual meeting at the designated time or to elect a sufficient number of directors to conduct the business of the corporation shall not affect otherwise valid corporate acts or work a forfeiture or dissolution of the corporation except as may be otherwise specifically provided in this chapter. If the annual meeting for election of directors is not held on the date designated therefor or action by written consent to elect directors in lieu of an annual meeting has not been taken, the directors shall cause the meeting to be held as soon as is convenient. If there be a failure to hold the annual meeting or to take action by written consent to elect directors in lieu of an annual meeting for a period of 30 days after the date designated for the annual meeting, or if no date has been designated, for a period of 13 months after the latest to occur of the organization of the corporation, its last annual meeting or the last action by written consent to elect directors in lieu of an annual meeting, the Court of Chancery may summarily order a meeting to be held upon the application of any stockholder or director. The shares of stock represented at such meeting, either in person or by proxy, and entitled to vote thereat, shall constitute a quorum for the purpose of such meeting, notwithstanding any provision of the certificate of incorporation or by-laws to the contrary. The Court of Chancery may issue such orders as may be appropriate, including, without limitation, orders designating the time and place of such meeting, the record date for determination of stockholders entitled to vote, and the form of notice of such meeting.

(d) Special meetings of the stockholders may be called by the board of directors or by such person or persons as may be authorized by the certificate of incorporation or by the by-laws.

(e) All elections of directors shall be by written ballot, unless otherwise provided in the certificate of incorporation; if authorized by the board of directors, such requirement of a written ballot shall be satisfied by a ballot submitted by electronic transmission, provided that any such electronic transmission must either set forth or be submitted with information from which it can be determined that the electronic transmission was authorized by the stockholder or proxyholder.

§ 212. Voting Rights of Stockholders; Proxies; Limitations

(a) Unless otherwise provided in the certificate of incorporation and subject to the provisions of section 213 of this title, each stockholder shall be entitled to one vote for each share of capital stock held by such stockholder. If the certificate of incorporation provides for more or less than one vote for any share on any matter, every reference in this chapter to a majority or other proportion of stock, voting stock or shares shall refer to such majority or other proportion of the votes of such stock, voting stock or shares.

(b) Each stockholder entitled to vote at a meeting of stockholders or to express consent or dissent to corporate action in writing without a meeting may authorize another person or persons to act for such stockholder by proxy, but no such proxy shall be voted or acted upon after three years from its date, unless the proxy provides for a longer period.

(c) Without limiting the manner in which a stockholder may authorize another person or persons to act for such stockholder as proxy pursuant to subsection (b) of this section, the following shall constitute a valid means by which a stockholder may grant such authority:

(1) A stockholder may execute a writing authorizing another person or persons to act for such stockholder as proxy. Execution may be accomplished by the stockholder or such stockholder's authorized officer, director, employee or agent signing such writing or causing such person's signature to be affixed to such writing by any reasonable means including, but not limited to, by facsimile signature.

(2) A stockholder may authorize another person or persons to act for such stockholder as proxy by transmitting or authorizing the transmission of a telegram, cablegram, or other means of electronic transmission to the person who will be the holder of the proxy or to a proxy solicitation firm, proxy support service organization or like agent duly authorized by the person who will be the holder of the proxy to receive such transmission, provided that any such telegram, cablegram or other means of electronic transmission must either set

forth or be submitted with information from which it can be determined that the telegram, cablegram or other electronic transmission was authorized by the stockholder. If it is determined that such telegrams, cablegrams or other electronic transmissions are valid, the inspectors or, if there are no inspectors, such other persons making that determination shall specify the information upon which they relied.

(d) Any copy, facsimile telecommunication or other reliable reproduction of the writing or transmission created pursuant to subsection (c) of this section may be substituted or used in lieu of the original writing or transmission for any and all purposes for which the original writing or transmission could be used, provided that such copy, facsimile telecommunication or other reproduction shall be a complete reproduction of the entire original writing or transmission.

(e) A duly executed proxy shall be irrevocable if it states that it is irrevocable and if, and only as long as, it is coupled with an interest sufficient in law to support an irrevocable power. A proxy may be made irrevocable regardless of whether the interest with which it is coupled is an interest in the stock itself or an interest in the corporation generally.

§ 213. Fixing Date for Determination of Stockholders of Record

(a) In order that the corporation may determine the stockholders entitled to notice of or to vote at any meeting of stockholders or any adjournment thereof, the board of directors may fix a record date, which record date shall not precede the date upon which the resolution fixing the record date is adopted by the board of directors, and which record date shall not be more than sixty nor less than ten days before the date of such meeting. If no record date is fixed by the board of directors, the record date for determining stockholders entitled to notice of or to vote at a meeting of stockholders shall be at the close of business on the day next preceding the day on which notice is given, or, if notice is waived, at the close of business on the day next preceding the day on which the meeting is held. A determination of stockholders of record entitled to notice of or to vote at a meeting of stockholders shall apply to any adjournment of the meeting; provided, however, that the board of directors may fix a new record date for the adjourned meeting.

(b) In order that the corporation may determine the stockholders entitled to consent to corporate action in writing without a meeting, the board of directors may fix a record date, which record date shall not precede the date upon which the resolution fixing the record date is adopted by the board of directors, and which date shall not be more than ten days after the date upon which the resolution fixing the record date is adopted by the board of directors. If no record date has been fixed by the board of directors, the record date for determining stockholders entitled to consent to corporate action in writing without a meeting, when no prior action by the board of directors is required by this chapter, shall be the first date on which a signed written consent setting forth the action taken or proposed to be taken is delivered to the corporation by delivery to its registered office in this State, its principal place of business, or an officer or agent of the corporation having custody of the book in which proceedings of meetings of stockholders are recorded. Delivery made to a corporation's registered office shall be by hand or by certified or registered mail, return receipt requested. If no record date has been fixed by the board of directors and prior action by the board of directors is required by this chapter, the record date for determining stockholders entitled to consent to corporate action in writing without a meeting shall be at the close of business on the day on which the board of directors adopts the resolution taking such prior action.

(c) In order that the corporation may determine the stockholders entitled to receive payment of any dividend or other distribution or allotment of any rights or the stockholders entitled to exercise any rights in respect of any change, conversion or exchange of stock, or for the purpose of any other lawful action, the board of directors may fix a record date, which record date shall not precede the date upon which the resolution fixing the record date is adopted, and which record date shall be not more than sixty days prior to such action. If no record date is fixed, the record date for determining stockholders for any such purpose shall be at the close of business on the day on which the board of directors adopts the resolution relating thereto.

§ 214. Cumulative Voting

The certificate of incorporation of any corporation may provide that at all elections of directors of the corporation, or at elections held under specified circumstances, each holder of stock or of any class or classes or of a series or series thereof shall be entitled to as many votes as shall equal the number of votes which (except for such provision as to cumulative voting) such holder would be entitled to cast for the election of directors with respect to such holder's shares of stock multiplied by the number of directors to be elected by such holder, and that such holder may cast all of such votes for a single director or may distribute them among the number to be voted for, or for any two or more of them as such holder may see fit.

§ 216. Quorum and Required Vote for Stock Corporations

Subject to this chapter in respect of the vote that shall be required for a specified action, the certificate of incorporation or by-laws of any corporation authorized to issue stock may specify the number of shares and/or the amount of other securities having voting power the holders of which shall be present or represented by proxy at any meeting in order to constitute a quorum for, and the votes that shall be necessary for, the transaction of any business, but in no event shall a quorum consist of less than one-third of the shares entitled to vote at the meeting, except that, where a separate vote by a class or series or classes or series is required, a quorum shall consist of no less than one-third of the shares of such class or series or classes or series. In the absence of such specification in the certificate of incorporation or by-laws of the corporation, (i) a majority of the shares entitled to vote, present in person or represented by proxy, shall constitute a quorum at a meeting of stockholders; (ii) In all matters other than the election of directors, the affirmative vote of the majority of shares present in person or represented by proxy at the meeting and entitled to vote on the subject matter shall be the act of the stockholders; (iii) Directors shall be elected by a plurality of the votes of the shares present in person or represented by proxy at the meeting and entitled to vote on the election of directors; and (iv) Where a separate vote by a class or series or classes or series is required, a majority of the outstanding shares of such class or series or classes or series, present in person or represented by proxy, shall constitute a quorum entitled to take action with respect to that vote on that matter and the affirmative vote of the majority of shares of such class or series or classes or series present in person or represented by proxy at the meeting shall be the act of such class or series or classes or series.

§ 217. Voting Rights of Fiduciaries, Pledgors and Joint Owners of Stock

(a) Persons holding stock in a fiduciary capacity shall be entitled to vote the shares so held. Persons whose stock is pledged shall be entitled to vote, unless in the transfer by the pledgor on the books of the corporation such person has expressly empowered the pledgee to vote thereon, in which case only the pledgee, or such pledgee's proxy, may represent such stock and vote thereon.

(b) If shares or other securities having voting power stand of record in the names of two or more persons, whether fiduciaries, members of a partnership, joint tenants, tenants in common, tenants by the entirety or otherwise, or if two or more persons have the same fiduciary relationship respecting the same shares, unless the secretary of the corporation is given written notice to the contrary and is furnished with a copy of the instrument or order appointing them or creating the relationship wherein it is so provided, their acts with respect to voting shall have the following effect:

(1) If only one votes, such person's act binds all;

(2) If more than one vote, the act of the majority so voting binds all;

(3) If more than one vote, but the vote is evenly split on any particular matter, each faction may vote the securities in question

proportionally, or any person voting the shares, or a beneficiary, if any, may apply to the Court of Chancery or such other court as may have jurisdiction to appoint an additional person to act with the persons so voting the shares, which shall then be voted as determined by a majority of such persons and the person appointed by the Court. If the instrument so filed shows that any such tenancy is held in unequal interests, a majority or even-split for the purpose of this subsection shall be a majority or even-split in interest.

§ 218. Voting Trusts and Other Voting Agreements

(a) One stockholder or 2 or more stockholders may by agreement in writing deposit capital stock of an original issue with or transfer capital stock to any person or persons, or entity or entities authorized to act as trustee, for the purpose of vesting in such person or persons, entity or entities, who may be designated voting trustee, or voting trustees, the right to vote thereon for any period of time determined by such agreement, upon the terms and conditions stated in such agreement. The agreement may contain any other lawful provisions not inconsistent with such purpose. After the filing of a copy of the agreement in the registered office of the corporation in this State, which copy shall be open to the inspection of any stockholder of the corporation or any beneficiary of the trust under the agreement daily during business hours, certificates of stock or uncertificated stock shall be issued to the voting trustee or trustees to represent any stock of an original issue so deposited with such voting trustee or trustees, and any certificates of stock or uncertificated stock so transferred to the voting trustee or trustees shall be surrendered and cancelled and new certificates or uncertificated stock shall be issued therefore to the voting trustee or trustees. In the certificate so issued, if any, it shall be stated that it is issued pursuant to such agreement, and that fact shall also be stated in the stock ledger of the corporation. The voting trustee or trustees may vote the stock so issued or transferred during the period specified in the agreement. Stock standing in the name of the voting trustee or trustees may be voted either in person or by proxy, and in voting the stock, the voting trustee or trustees shall incur no responsibility as stockholder, trustee or otherwise, except for their own individual malfeasance. In any case where two or more persons or entities are designated as voting trustees, and the right and method of voting any stock standing in their names at any meeting of the corporation are not fixed by the agreement appointing the trustees, the right to vote the stock and the manner of voting it at the meeting shall be determined by a majority of the trustees, or if they be equally divided as to the right and manner of voting the stock in any particular case, the vote of the stock in such case shall be divided equally among the trustees.

(b) Any amendment to a voting trust agreement shall be made by a written agreement, a copy of which shall be filed in the registered office of the corporation in this State.

(c) An agreement between two or more stockholders, if in writing and signed by the parties thereto, may provide that in exercising any voting rights, the shares held by them shall be voted as provided by the agreement, or as the parties may agree, or as determined in accordance with a procedure agreed upon by them.

(d) This section shall not be deemed to invalidate any voting or other agreement among stockholders or any irrevocable proxy which is not otherwise illegal.

§ 219. List of Stockholders Entitled to Vote; Penalty for Refusal to Produce; Stock Ledger

(a) The officer who has charge of the stock ledger of a corporation shall prepare and make, at least ten days before every meeting of stockholders, a complete list of the stockholders entitled to vote at the meeting, arranged in alphabetical order, and showing the address of each stockholder and the number of shares registered in the name of each stockholder. Nothing contained in this Section shall require the corporation to include electronic mail addresses or other electronic contact information on such list. Such list shall be open to the examination of any stockholder, for any purpose germane to the meeting for a period of at least 10 days prior to the meeting: (i) on a reasonably accessible electronic network, provided that the information required to gain access to such list is provided with the notice of the meeting, or (ii) during ordinary business hours, at the principal place of business of the corporation. In the event that the corporation determines to make the list available on an electronic network, the corporation may take reasonable steps to ensure that such information is available only to stockholders of the corporation. If the meeting is to be held at a place, then the list shall be produced and kept at the time and place of the meeting during the whole time thereof, and may be inspected by any stockholder who is present. If the meeting is to be held solely by means of remote communication, then the list shall also be open to the examination of any stockholder during the whole time of the meeting on a reasonably accessible electronic network, and the information required to access such list shall be provided with the notice of the meeting.

(b) Upon the willful neglect or refusal of the directors to produce such a list at any meeting for the election of directors held at a place, or to open such a list to examination on a reasonably accessible electronic network during any meeting for the election of directors held solely by means of remote communication, they shall be ineligible for election to any office at such meeting.

(c) The stock ledger shall be the only evidence as to who are the stockholders entitled by this section to examine the list required by this section or to vote in person or by proxy at any meeting of stockholders.

§ 220. Inspection of Books and Records

(a) As used in this section:

(1) "List of stockholders" includes lists of members in a non-stock corporation.

(2) "Stockholder" means a holder of record of stock in a stock corporation, or a person who is the beneficial owner of shares of such stock held either in a voting trust or by a nominee on behalf of such person, and also a member of a nonstock corporation as reflected on the records of the nonstock corporation.

(3) "Subsidiary" means any entity directly or indirectly owned, in whole or in part, by the corporation of which the stockholder is a stockholder and over the affairs of which the corporation directly or indirectly exercises control, and includes, without limitation, corporations, partnerships, limited partnerships, limited liability partnerships, limited liability companies, statutory trusts and/or joint ventures.

(4) "Under oath" includes statements the declarant affirms to be true under penalty of perjury under the laws of the United States or any state.

(b) Any stockholder, in person or by attorney or other agent, shall, upon written demand under oath stating the purpose thereof, have the right during the usual hours for business to inspect for any proper purpose, and to make copies and extracts from:

(1) The corporation's stock ledger, a list of its stockholders, and its other books and records; and

(2) A subsidiary's books and records, to the extent that:

(i) The corporation has actual possession and control of such records of such subsidiary; or

(ii) The corporation could obtain such records through the exercise of control over such subsidiary, provided that as of the date of the making of the demand:

(A) The stockholder inspection of such books and records of the subsidiary would not constitute a breach of an agreement between the corporation or the subsidiary and a person or persons not affiliated with the corporation; and

(B) The subsidiary would not have the right under the law applicable to it to deny the corporation access to such books and records upon demand by the corporation.

In every instance where the stockholder is other than a record holder of stock in a stock corporation or a member of a nonstock corporation, the demand under oath shall state the person's status as a stockholder, be accompanied by documentary evidence of beneficial ownership of the stock, and state that such documentary evidence is a true and correct copy of what it purports to be. A proper purpose shall mean a purpose reasonably related to such person's interest as a stockholder. In every instance where an attorney or other agent shall be the person who seeks the right to inspection, the demand under oath shall be accompanied by a power of attorney or such other writing which authorizes the attorney or other agent to so act on behalf of the stockholder. The demand under oath shall be directed to the corporation at its registered office in this State or at its principal place of business.

(c) If the corporation, or an officer or agent thereof, refuses to permit an inspection sought by a stockholder or attorney or other agent acting for the stockholder pursuant to sub-section (b) or does not reply to the demand within five business days after the demand has been made, the stockholder may apply to the Court of Chancery for an order to compel such inspection. The Court of Chancery is hereby vested with exclusive jurisdiction to determine whether or not the person seeking inspection is entitled to the inspection sought. The court may summarily order the corporation to permit the stockholder to inspect the corporation's stock ledger, an existing list of stockholders, and its other books and records, and to make copies or extracts therefrom; or the Court may order the corporation to furnish to the stockholder a list of its stockholders as of a specific date on condition that the stockholder first pay to the corporation the reasonable cost of obtaining and furnishing such list and on such other conditions as the Court deems appropriate. Where the stockholder seeks to inspect the corporation's books and records, other than its stock ledger or list of stockholders, such stockholder shall first establish that: (1) Such stockholder is a stockholder; (2) Such stockholder has complied with this section respecting the form and manner of making demand for inspection of such documents; and (3) The inspection such stockholder seeks is for a proper purpose. Where the stockholder seeks to inspect the corporation's stock ledger or list of stockholders and establishes that he, she or it is a stockholder and has complied with this section respecting the form and manner of making demand for inspection of such documents, the burden of proof shall be upon the corporation to establish that the inspection such stockholder seeks is for an improper purpose. The court may, in its discretion, prescribe any limitations or conditions with reference to the inspection, or award such other or further relief as the court may deem just and proper. The court may order books, documents and records, pertinent extracts therefrom, or duly authenticated copies thereof, to be brought within this State and kept in this State upon such terms and conditions as the order may prescribe.

(d) Any director ... shall have the right to examine the corporation's stock ledger, a list of its stockholders and its other books and records for a purpose reasonably related to his position as a director. The Court of Chancery is hereby vested with the exclusive jurisdiction to determine whether a director is entitled to the inspection sought. The court may summarily order the corporation to permit the director to inspect any and all books and records, the stock ledger and the list of stockholders and to make copies or extracts therefrom. The burden of proof shall be upon the corporation to establish that the inspection such director seeks is for an improper purpose. The court may, in its discretion, prescribe any limitations or conditions with reference to the inspection, or award such other and further relief as the court may deem just and proper.

§ 221. Voting, Inspection and Other Rights of Bondholders and Debenture Holders

Every corporation may in its certificate of incorporation confer upon the holders of any bonds, debentures, or other obligations issued or to be issued by the corporation the power to vote in respect to the corporate affairs and management of the corporation to the extent and in the manner provided in the certificate of incorporation, and may confer upon such holders of bonds, debentures or other obligations the same right of inspection of its books, accounts and other records, and also any other rights, which the stockholders of the corporation have or may have by reason of the provisions of this chapter or of its certificate of incorporation. If the certificate of incorporation so provides, such holders of bonds, debentures or other obligations shall be deemed to be stockholders, and their bonds, debentures or other obligations shall be deemed to be shares of stock, for the purpose of any provision of this chapter which requires the vote of stockholders as a prerequisite to any corporate action and the certificate of incorporation may divest the holders of capital stock, in whole or in part, of their right to vote on any corporate matter whatsoever, except as set forth in § 242(b)(2) of this chapter.

§ 222. Notice of Meetings and Adjourned Meetings

(a) Whenever stockholders are required or permitted to take any action at a meeting, a written notice of the meeting shall be given which shall state the place, if any, date and hour of the meeting, the means of remote communications, if any, by which stockholders and proxy holders may be deemed to be present in person and vote at such meeting, and, in the case of a special meeting, the purpose or purposes for which the meeting is called.

(b) Unless otherwise provided in this chapter, the written notice of any meeting shall be given not less than ten nor more than sixty days before the date of the meeting to each stockholder entitled to vote at such meeting. If mailed, notice is given when deposited in the United

States mail, postage prepaid, directed to the stockholder at such stockholder's address as it appears on the records of the corporation. An affidavit of the secretary or an assistant secretary or of the transfer agent or other agent of the corporation that the notice has been given shall, in the absence of fraud, be prima facie evidence of the facts stated therein.

(c) When a meeting is adjourned to another time or place, unless the by-laws otherwise require, notice need not be given of the adjourned meeting if the time, place, if any, thereof, and the means of remote communication, if any, by which stockholders and proxyholders may be deemed to be present in person and vote at such adjourned meeting are announced at the meeting at which the adjournment is taken. At the adjourned meeting the corporation may transact any business which might have been transacted at the original meeting. If the adjournment is for more than thirty days, or if after the adjournment a new record date is fixed for the adjourned meeting, a notice of the adjourned meeting shall be given to each stockholder of record entitled to vote at the meeting.

§ 223. Vacancies and Newly Created Directorships

(a) Unless otherwise provided in the certificate of incorporation or by-laws:

(1) vacancies and newly created directorships resulting from any increase in the authorized number of directors elected by all of the stockholders having the right to vote as a single class may be filled by a majority of the directors then in office, although less than a quorum, or by a sole remaining director;

(2) whenever the holders of any class or classes of stock or series thereof are entitled to elect one or more directors by the provisions of the certificate of incorporation, vacancies and newly created directorships of such class or classes or series may be filled by a majority of the directors elected by such class or classes or series thereof then in office, or by a sole remaining director so elected.

If at any time, by reason of death or resignation or other cause, a corporation should have no directors in office, then any officer or any stockholder or an executor, administrator, trustee or guardian of a stockholder, or other fiduciary entrusted with like responsibility for the person or estate of a stockholder, may call a special meeting of stockholders in accordance with the provisions of the certificate of incorporation or the by-laws, or may apply to the Court of Chancery for a decree summarily ordering an election as provided in section 211 of this title.

(b) In the case of a corporation the directors of which are divided into classes, any directors chosen under subsection (a) of this section shall hold office until the next election of the class for which such directors shall have been chosen, and until their successors shall be elected and qualified.

(c) If, at the time of filling any vacancy or any newly created directorship, the directors then in office shall constitute less than a majority of the whole board (as constituted immediately prior to any such increase), the Court of Chancery may, upon application of any stockholder or stockholders holding at least ten percent of the voting stock at the time outstanding having the right to vote for such directors, summarily order an election to be held to fill any such vacancies or newly created directorships, or to replace the directors chosen by the directors then in office as aforesaid, which election shall be governed by the provisions of section 211 of this title as far as applicable.

(d) Unless otherwise provided in the certificate of incorporation or by-laws, when one or more directors shall resign from the board, effective at a future date, a majority of the directors then in office, including those who have so resigned, shall have power to fill such vacancy or vacancies, the vote thereon to take effect when such resignation or resignations shall become effective, and each director so chosen shall hold office as provided in this section in the filling of other vacancies.

§ 225. Contested Election of Directors; Proceedings to Determine Validity

(a) Upon application of any stockholder or director, or any officer whose title to office is contested, or any member of a corporation without capital stock, the Court of Chancery may hear and determine the validity of any election, appointment, removal or resignation of any director, member of the governing body, or officer of any corporation, and the right of any person to hold or continue to hold such office, and, in case any such office is claimed by more than one person, may determine the person entitled thereto; and to that end make such order or decree in any such case as may be just and proper, with power to enforce the production of any books, papers and records of the corporation relating to the issue. In case it should be determined that no valid election has been held, the Court of Chancery may order an election to be held in accordance with sections 211 or 215 of this title. In any such application, service of copies of the application upon the registered agent of the corporation shall be deemed to be service upon the corporation and upon the person whose title to office is contested and upon the person, if any, claiming such office; and the registered agent shall forward immediately a copy of the application to the corporation and to the person whose title to office is contested and to the person, if any, claiming such office, in a postpaid, sealed, registered letter addressed to such corporation and such person at their post-office addresses last known to the registered agent or furnished to the registered agent by the applicant stockholder. The

Court may make such order respecting further or other notice of such application as it deems proper under the circumstances.

(b) Upon application of any stockholder or any member of a corporation without capital stock, the Court of Chancery may hear and determine the result of any vote of stockholders or members, as the case may be, upon matters other than the election of directors, officers or members of the governing body. Service of the application upon the registered agent of the corporation shall be deemed to be service upon the corporation, and no other party need be joined in order for the Court to adjudicate the result of the vote. The Court may make such order respecting notice of the application as it deems proper under the circumstances.

§ 226. Appointment of Custodian or Receiver of Corporation on Deadlock or for Other Cause

(a) The Court of Chancery, upon application of any stockholder, may appoint one or more persons to be custodians, and, if the corporation is insolvent, to be receivers, of and for any corporation when:

(1) At any meeting held for the election of directors the stockholders are so divided that they have failed to elect successors to directors whose terms have expired or would have expired upon qualification of their successors; or

(2) The business of the corporation is suffering or is threatened with irreparable injury because the directors are so divided respecting the management of the affairs of the corporation that the required vote for action by the board of directors cannot be obtained and the stockholders are unable to terminate this division; or

(3) The corporation has abandoned its business and has failed within a reasonable time to take steps to dissolve, liquidate or distribute its assets.

(b) A custodian appointed under this section shall have all the powers and title of a receiver appointed under section 291 of this title, but the authority of the custodian is to continue the business of the corporation and not to liquidate its affairs and distribute its assets, except when the Court shall otherwise order and except in cases arising under subparagraph (a)(3) of this section or section 352(a)(2) of this title.

§ 227. Powers of Court in Elections of Directors

(a) The Court of Chancery, in any proceeding instituted under sections 211, 215 or 225 of this title may determine the right and power of persons claiming to own stock, or in the case of a corporation without capital stock, of the persons claiming to be members, to vote at any meeting of the stockholders or members.

(b) The Court of Chancery may appoint a master to hold any election provided for in sections 211, 215 or 225 of this title under such orders and powers as it deems proper; and it may punish any officer or director for contempt in case of disobedience of any order made by the Court; and, in case of disobedience by a corporation of any order made by the Court, may enter a decree against such corporation for a penalty of not more than $5,000.

§ 228. Consent of Stockholders in Lieu of Meeting

(a) Unless otherwise provided in the certificate of incorporation, any action required by this chapter to be taken at any annual or special meeting of stockholders of a corporation, or any action which may be taken at any annual or special meeting of such stockholders, may be taken without a meeting, without prior notice and without a vote, if a consent or consents in writing, setting forth the action so taken, shall be signed by the holders of outstanding stock having not less than the minimum number of votes that would be necessary to authorize or take such action at a meeting at which all shares entitled to vote thereon were present and voted and shall be delivered to the corporation by delivery to its registered office in this State, its principal place of business, or an officer or agent of the corporation having custody of the book in which proceedings of meetings of stockholders are recorded. Delivery made to a corporation's registered office shall be by hand or by certified or registered mail, return receipt requested. . . .

(c) Every written consent shall bear the date of signature of each stockholder . . . who signs the consent and no written consent shall be effective to take the corporate action referred to therein unless, within sixty days of the earliest dated consent delivered in the manner required by this Section to the corporation, written consents signed by a sufficient number of holders . . . to take action are delivered to the corporation by delivery to its registered office in this State, its principal place of business, or an officer or agent of the corporation having custody of the book in which proceedings of meetings of stockholders . . . are recorded. Delivery made to a corporation's registered office shall be by hand or by certified or registered mail, return receipt requested.

(d)(1) A telegram, cablegram or other electronic transmission consenting to an action to be taken and transmitted by a stockholder, member or proxyholder, or by a person or persons authorized to act for a stockholder, member or proxyholder, shall be deemed to be written, signed and dated for the purposes of this section, provided that any such telegram, cablegram or other electronic transmission sets forth or is delivered with information from which the corporation can determine (A) that the telegram, cablegram or other electronic transmission was transmitted by the stockholder, member or proxyholder or by a person or persons authorized to act for the stockholder, member or proxyholder and (B) the date on which such stockholder, member or proxyholder or authorized person or persons transmitted such telegram, cablegram or electronic transmission. The date on which such telegram, cablegram or electronic transmission is transmitted shall be deemed to be the date on which such consent was signed. No consent given by telegram, cablegram or other electronic transmission shall be deemed to have been delivered until such consent is reproduced in paper form and until such paper form shall be delivered to the corporation by delivery to its registered office in this State, its principal place of business or an officer or agent of the corporation having custody of the book in which proceedings of meetings of stockholders or members are recorded. Delivery made to a corporation's registered office shall be made by hand or by certified or registered mail, return receipt requested. Notwithstanding the foregoing limitations on delivery, consents given by telegram, cablegram or other electronic transmission may be otherwise delivered to the principal place of business of the corporation or to an officer or agent of the corporation having custody of the book in which the proceedings of meetings of stockholders or members are recorded if, to the extent and in the manner provided by resolution of the board of directors or governing body of the corporation.

(d)(2) Any copy, facsimile or other reliable reproduction of a consent in writing may be substituted or used in lieu of the original writing for any and all purposes for which the original writing could be used, provided that such copy, facsimile or other reproduction shall be a complete reproduction of the entire original writing.

(e) Prompt notice of the taking of the corporate action without a meeting by less than unanimous written consent shall be given to those stockholders ... who have not consented in writing and who, if the action had been taken at a meeting, would have been entitled to notice of the meeting if the record date for such meeting had been the date that written consents signed by a sufficient number of holders or members to take the action were delivered to the corporation as provided in subsection (c) of this section. In the event that the action which is consented to is such as would have required the filing of a certificate under any other section of this title, if such action had been voted on by stockholders ... at a meeting thereof, the certificate filed under such other section shall state, in lieu of any statement required by such section concerning any vote of stockholders ..., that written consent has been given in accordance with the provisions of this section.

§ 229. Waiver of Notice

Whenever notice is required to be given under any provision of this chapter or of the certificate of incorporation or by-laws, a written waiver thereof, signed by the person entitled to notice, or a waiver by electronic transmission by the person entitled to notice, whether before or after the time stated therein, shall be deemed equivalent to notice. Attendance of a person at a meeting shall constitute a waiver of notice of such meeting, except when the person attends a meeting for the express purpose of objecting, at the beginning of the meeting, to the transaction of any business because the meeting is not lawfully called or convened. Neither the business to be transacted at, nor the purpose of, any regular or special meeting of the stockholders, directors, or members of a committee of directors need be specified in any written waiver of notice or any waiver by electronic transmission unless so required by the certificate of incorporation or the by-laws.

§ 231. Voting Procedures and Inspectors of Elections

(a) The corporation shall, in advance of any meeting of stockholders, appoint 1 or more inspectors to act at the meeting and make a written report thereof. The corporation may designate 1 or more persons as alternate inspectors to replace any inspector who fails to act. If no inspector or alternate is able to act at a meeting of stockholders, the person presiding at the meeting shall appoint 1 or more inspectors to act at the meeting. Each inspector, before entering upon the discharge of the duties of inspector, shall take and sign an oath faithfully to execute the duties of inspector with strict impartiality and according to the best of such inspector's ability.

(b) The inspectors shall:

(1) Ascertain the number of shares outstanding and the voting power of each;

(2) Determine the shares represented at a meeting and the validity of proxies and ballots;

(3) Count all votes and ballots;

(4) Determine and retain for a reasonable period a record of the disposition of any challenges made to any determination by the inspectors; and

(5) Certify their determination of the number of shares represented at the meeting, and their count of all votes and ballots.

The inspectors may appoint or retain other persons or entities to assist the inspectors in the performance of the duties of the inspectors.

(c) The date and time of the opening and the closing of the polls for each matter upon which the stockholders will vote at a meeting shall be announced at the meeting. No ballot, proxies or votes, nor any revocations thereof or changes thereto, shall be accepted by the inspectors after the closing of the polls unless the Court of Chancery upon application by a stockholder shall determine otherwise.

(d) In determining the validity and counting of proxies and ballots, the inspectors shall be limited to an examination of the proxies, any envelopes submitted with those proxies, any information provided in accordance with Section 211(e) or Section 212(c)(2) of this title, or any information provided pursuant to Section 211(a)(2)(B)(i) or (iii) of this title, ballots and the regular books and records of the corporation, except that the inspectors may consider other reliable information for the limited purpose of reconciling proxies and ballots submitted by or on behalf of banks, brokers, their nominees or similar persons which represent more votes than the holder of a proxy is authorized by the record owner to cast or more votes than the stockholder holds of record. If the inspectors consider other reliable information for the limited purpose permitted herein, the inspectors at the time they make their certification pursuant to subsection (b)(5) of this section shall specify the precise information considered by them including the person or persons from whom they obtained the information, when the information was obtained, the means by which the information was obtained and the basis for the inspectors' belief that such information is accurate and reliable.

(e) Unless otherwise provided in the certificate of incorporation or bylaws, this section shall not apply to a corporation that does not have a class of voting stock that is:

(1) Listed on a national securities exchange;

(2) Authorized for quotation on an interdealer quotation system of a registered national securities association; or

(3) Held of record by more than 2,000 stockholders.

§ 232. Notice by Electronic Transmission

(a) Without limiting the manner by which notice otherwise may be given effectively to stockholders, any notice to stockholders given by the corporation under any provision of this chapter, the certificate of incorporation, or the bylaws shall be effective if given by a form of electronic transmission consented to by the stockholder to whom the notice is given. Any such consent shall be revocable by the stockholder by written notice to the corporation. Any such consent shall be deemed revoked if (1) the corporation is unable to deliver by electronic transmission two consecutive notices given by the corporation in accordance with such consent and (2) such inability becomes known to the secretary or an assistant secretary of the corporation or to the transfer agent, or other person responsible for the giving of notice; provided, however, the inadvertent failure to treat such inability as a revocation shall not invalidate any meeting or other action.

(b) Notice given pursuant to subsection (a) of this section shall be deemed given: (1) if by facsimile telecommunication, when directed to a number at which the stockholder has consented to receive notice; (2) if by electronic mail, when directed to an electronic mail address at which the stockholder has consented to receive notice; (3) if by a posting on an electronic network together with separate notice to the stockholder of such specific posting, upon the later of (A) such posting and (B) the giving of such separate notice; and (4) if by any other form of electronic transmission, when directed to the stockholder. An affidavit of the secretary or an assistant secretary or of the transfer agent or other agent of the corporation that the notice has been given by a form of electronic transmission shall, in the absence of fraud, be prima facie evidence of the facts stated therein.

(c) For purposes of this chapter, "electronic transmission" means any form of communication, not directly involving the physical transmission of paper, that creates a record that may be retained, retrieved, and reviewed by a recipient thereof, and that may be directly reproduced in paper form by such a recipient through an automated process.

(d) This section shall apply to a corporation organized under this chapter that is not authorized to issue capital stock, and when so applied, all references to stockholders shall be deemed to refer to members of such a corporation.

(e) This section shall not apply to §§ 164, 296, 311, 312, or 324 of this chapter.

§ 233. Notice to Stockholders Sharing an Address

(a) Without limiting the manner by which notice otherwise may be given effectively to stockholders, any notice to stockholders given by the corporation under any provision of this chapter, the certificate of incorporation or the bylaws shall be effective if given by a single written notice to stockholders who share an address if consented to by the stockholders at that address to whom such notice is given. Any such consent shall be revocable by the stockholder by written notice to the corporation.

(b) Any stockholder who fails to object in writing to the corporation, within 60 days of having been given written notice by the corporation of its intention to send the single notice permitted under subsection (a) of this section, shall be deemed to have consented to receiving such single written notice.

(c) This section shall apply to a corporation organized under this chapter that is not authorized to issue capital stock, and when so applied, all references to stockholders shall be deemed to refer to members of such a corporation.

(d) This section shall not apply to §§ 164, 296, 311, 312 or 324 of this chapter.

SUBCHAPTER VIII. AMENDMENT OF CERTIFICATE OF INCORPORATION; CHANGES IN CAPITAL AND CAPITAL STOCK

§ 241. Amendment of Certificate of Incorporation Before Receipt of Payment for Stock

(a) Before a corporation has received any payment for any of its stock, it may amend its certificate of incorporation at any time or times, in any and as many respects as may be desired, so long as its certificate of incorporation as amended would contain only such provisions as it would be lawful and proper to insert in an original certificate of incorporation filed at the time of filing the amendment.

(b) The amendment of a certificate of incorporation authorized by this section shall be adopted by a majority of the incorporators, if directors were not named in the original certificate of incorporation or have not yet been elected, or, if directors were named in the original certificate of incorporation or have been elected and have qualified, by a majority of the directors. A certificate setting forth the amendment and certifying that the corporation has not received any payment for any of its stock and that the amendment has been duly adopted in accordance with the provisions of this section shall be executed, acknowledged and filed in accordance with section 103 of this title. Upon such filing, the corporation's certificate of incorporation shall be deemed to be amended accordingly as of the date on which the original certificate of incorporation became effective, except as to those persons who are substantially and adversely affected by the amendment and as to those persons the amendment shall be effective from the filing date.

§ 242. Amendment of Certificate of Incorporation After Receipt of Payment for Stock ...

(a) After a corporation has received payment for any of its capital stock, it may amend its certificate of incorporation, from time to time, in any and as many respects as may be desired, so long as its certificate of incorporation as amended would contain only such provisions as it would be lawful and proper to insert in an original certificate of incorporation filed at the time of the filing of the amendment; and, if a change in stock or the rights of stockholders, or an exchange, reclassification, subdivision, combination or cancellation of stock or rights of stockholders is to be made, such provisions as may be necessary to effect such change, exchange, reclassification, subdivision, combination or cancellation. In particular, and without limitation upon such general power of amendment, a corporation may amend its certificate of incorporation, from time to time, so as:

(1) To change its corporate name; or

(2) To change, substitute, enlarge or diminish the nature of its business or its corporate powers and purposes; or

(3) To increase or decrease its authorized capital stock or to reclassify the same, by changing the number, par value, designations, preferences, or relative, participating, optional, or other special rights of the shares, or the qualifications, limitations or restrictions of such rights, or by changing shares with par value into shares without par value, or shares without par value into shares with par value either with or without increasing or decreasing the number of shares, or by subdividing or combining the outstanding shares of any class or series of a class of shares into a greater or lesser number of outstanding shares; or

(4) To cancel or otherwise affect the right of the holders of the shares of any class to receive dividends which have accrued but have not been declared; or

(5) To create new classes of stock having rights and preferences either prior and superior or subordinate and inferior to the stock of any class then authorized, whether issued or unissued; or

(6) To change the period of its duration.

Any or all such changes or alterations may be effected by one certificate of amendment.

(b) Every amendment authorized by subsection (a) of this section shall be made and effected in the following manner—

(1) If the corporation has capital stock, its board of directors shall adopt a resolution setting forth the amendment proposed, declaring its advisability, and either calling a special meeting of the stockholders entitled to vote in respect thereof for the consideration of such amendment or directing that the amendment proposed be considered at the next annual meeting of the stockholders. Such special or annual meeting shall be called and held upon notice in accordance with section 222 of this title. The notice shall set forth such amendment in full or a brief summary of the changes to be effected thereby, as the directors shall deem advisable. At the meeting a vote of the stockholders entitled to vote thereon shall be taken for and against the proposed amendment. If a majority of the outstanding stock entitled to vote thereon, and a majority of the outstanding stock of each class entitled to vote thereon as a class has been voted in favor of the amendment, a certificate setting forth the amendment and certifying that such amendment has been duly adopted in accordance with the provisions of this section shall be executed, acknowledged and filed, and shall become effective in accordance with section 103 of this title.

(2) The holders of the outstanding shares of a class shall be entitled to vote as a class upon a proposed amendment, whether or not entitled to vote thereon by the provisions of the certificate of incorporation, if the

amendment would increase or decrease the aggregate number of authorized shares of such class, increase or decrease the par value of the shares of such class, or alter or change the powers, preferences or special rights of the shares of such class so as to affect them adversely. If any proposed amendment would alter or change the powers, preferences, or special rights of one or more series of any class so as to affect them adversely, but shall not so affect the entire class, then only the shares of the series so affected by the amendment shall be considered a separate class for the purposes of this paragraph. The number of authorized shares of any such class or classes of stock may be increased or decreased (but not below the number of shares thereof then outstanding) by the affirmative vote of the holders of a majority of the stock of the corporation entitled to vote irrespective of the provisions of this paragraph (b)(2), if so provided in the original certificate of incorporation, in any amendment thereto which created such class or classes of stock or which was adopted prior to the issuance of any shares of such class or classes of stock, or in any amendment thereto which was authorized by a resolution or resolutions adopted by the affirmative vote of the holders of a majority of such class or classes of stock. . . .

(4) Whenever the certificate of incorporation shall require for action by the board of directors, by the holders of any class or series of shares or by the holders of any other securities having voting power the vote of a greater number or proportion than is required by any section of this title, the provision of the certificate of incorporation requiring such greater vote shall not be altered, amended or repealed except by such greater vote.

(c) The resolution authorizing a proposed amendment to the certificate of incorporation may provide that at any time prior to the effectiveness of the filing of the amendment with the Secretary of State, notwithstanding authorization of the proposed amendment by the stockholders of the corporation ..., the board of directors ... may abandon such proposed amendment without further action by the stockholders. . . .

§ 243. Retirement of Stock

(a) A corporation, by resolution of its board of directors, may retire any shares of its capital stock that are issued but are not outstanding.

(b) Whenever any shares of the capital stock of a corporation are retired, they shall resume the status of authorized and unissued shares of the class or series to which they belong unless the certificate of incorporation otherwise provides. If the certificate of incorporation prohibits the reissuance of such shares, or prohibits the reissuance of such shares as a part of a specific series only, a certificate stating that reissuance of the shares (as part of the class or series) is prohibited[,] identifying the shares and reciting their retirement shall be executed, acknowledged and filed and shall become effective in accordance with

§ 103 of this Title. When such certificate becomes effective, it shall have the effect of amending the certificate of incorporation so as to reduce accordingly the number of authorized shares of the class or series to which such shares belong or, if such retired shares constitute all of the authorized shares of the class or series to which they belong, of eliminating from the certificate of incorporation all reference to such class or series of stock.

(c) If the capital of the corporation will be reduced by or in connection with the retirement of shares, the reduction of capital shall be effected pursuant to Section 244 of this title.

§ 244. Reduction of Capital

(a) A corporation, by resolution of its board of directors, may reduce its capital in any of the following ways:

1. By reducing or eliminating the capital represented by shares of capital stock which have been retired;

2. By applying to an otherwise authorized purchase or redemption of outstanding shares of its capital stock some or all of the capital represented by the shares being purchased or redeemed, or any capital that has not been allocated to any particular class of its capital stock;

3. By applying to an otherwise authorized conversion or exchange of outstanding shares of its capital stock some or all of the capital represented by the shares being converted or exchanged, or some or all of any capital that has not been allocated to any particular class of its capital stock, or both, to the extent that such capital in the aggregate exceeds the total aggregate par value or the stated capital of any previously unissued shares issuable upon such conversion or exchange; or,

4. By transferring to surplus (i) some or all of the capital not represented by any particular class of its capital stock; (ii) some or all of the capital represented by issued shares of its par value capital stock, which capital is in excess of the aggregate par value of such shares; or (iii) some of the capital represented by issued shares of its capital stock without par value.

(b) Notwithstanding the other provisions of this section, no reduction of capital shall be made or effected unless the assets of the corporation remaining after such reduction shall be sufficient to pay any debts of the corporation for which payment has not been otherwise provided. No reduction of capital shall release any liability of any stockholder whose shares have not been fully paid.

SUBCHAPTER IX. MERGER, CONSOLIDATION, OR CONVERSION

§ 251. Merger or Consolidation of Domestic Corporations

(a) Any two or more corporations existing under the laws of this State may merge into a single corporation, which may be any one of the constituent corporations or may consolidate into a new corporation formed by the consolidation, pursuant to an agreement of merger or consolidation, as the case may be, complying and approved in accordance with this section.

(b) The board of directors of each corporation which desires to merge or consolidate shall adopt a resolution approving an agreement of merger or consolidation and declaring its advisability. The agreement shall state: (1) the terms and conditions of the merger or consolidation; (2) the mode of carrying the same into effect; (3) in the case of a merger, such amendments or changes in the certificate of incorporation of the surviving corporation as are desired to be effected by the merger, or, if no such amendments or changes are desired, a statement that the certificate of incorporation of the surviving corporation shall be its certificate of incorporation; (4) in the case of a consolidation, that the certificate of incorporation of the resulting corporation shall be as is set forth in an attachment to the agreement; (5) the manner, if any, of converting the shares of each of the constituent corporations into shares or other securities of the corporation surviving or resulting from the merger or consolidation, or of canceling some or all of such shares, and, if any shares of any of the constituent corporations are not to remain outstanding, to be converted solely into shares or other securities of the surviving or resulting corporation or to be cancelled, the cash, property, rights or securities of any other corporation or entity which the holders of such shares are to receive in exchange for, or upon conversion of such shares and the surrender of any certificates evidencing them, which cash, property, rights or securities of any other corporation or entity may be in addition to or in lieu of shares or other securities of the surviving or resulting corporation; and (6) such other details or provisions as are deemed desirable, including, without limiting the generality of the foregoing, a provision for the payment of cash in lieu of the issuance or recognition of fractional shares, interests or rights, or for any other arrangement with respect thereto, consistent with the provisions of section 155 of this title. The agreement so adopted shall be executed and acknowledged in accordance with section 103 of this title. Any of the terms of the agreement of merger or consolidation may be made dependent upon facts ascertainable outside of such agreement, provided that the manner in which such facts shall operate upon the terms of the agreement is clearly and expressly set forth in the agreement of merger or consolidation. The term "facts," as used in the preceding sentence, includes, but is not limited to, the occurrence of any event, including a determination or action by any person or body, including the corporation.

(c) The agreement required by subsection (b) shall be submitted to the stockholders of each constituent corporation at an annual or special meeting thereof for the purpose of acting on the agreement. Due notice of the time, place and purpose of the meeting shall be mailed to each holder of stock, whether voting or non-voting, of the corporation at his address as it appears on the records of the corporation, at least 20 days prior to the date of the meeting. The notice shall contain a copy of the agreement or a brief summary thereof, as the directors shall deem advisable. At the meeting the agreement shall be considered and a vote taken for its adoption or rejection. If a majority of the outstanding stock of the corporation entitled to vote thereon shall be voted for the adoption of the agreement, that fact shall be certified on the agreement by the secretary or assistant secretary of the corporation. If the agreement shall be so adopted and certified by each constituent corporation, it shall then be filed, and shall become effective, in accordance with section 103 of this title. In lieu of filing the agreement of merger or consolidation required by this Section, the surviving or resulting corporation may file a certificate of merger or consolidation, executed in accordance with section 103 of this title, which states:

(1) The name and state of incorporation of each of the constituent corporations;

(2) That an agreement of merger or consolidation has been approved, adopted, certified, executed and acknowledged by each of the constituent corporations in accordance with this section;

(3) The name of the surviving or resulting corporation;

(4) In the case of a merger, such amendments or changes in the certificate of incorporation of the surviving corporation as are desired to be effected by the merger, or, if no such amendments or changes are desired, a statement that the certificate of incorporation of the surviving corporation shall be its certificate of incorporation;

(5) In the case of a consolidation, that the certificate of incorporation of the resulting corporation shall be as set forth in an attachment to the certificate;

(6) That the executed agreement of consolidation or merger is on file at an office of the surviving corporation, stating the address thereof; and

(7) That a copy of the agreement of consolidation or merger will be furnished by the surviving corporation, on request and without cost, to any stockholder of any constituent corporation.

(d) Any agreement of merger or consolidation may contain a provision that at any time prior to the time that the agreement (or a certificate in lieu thereof) filed with the Secretary of State becomes effective in accordance with § 103 of this title, the agreement may be terminated by the board of directors of any constituent corporation notwithstanding approval of the agreement by the stockholders of all or any of the constituent corporations; in the event the agreement of merger or consolidation is terminated after the filing of the agreement (or a certificate in lieu thereof) with the Secretary of State but before the agreement (or a certificate in lieu thereof) has become effective, a certificate of termination or merger or consolidation shall be filed in accordance with § 103 of this title. Any agreement of merger or consolidation may contain a provision that the boards of directors of the constituent corporations may amend the agreement at any time prior to the time that the agreement (or a certificate in lieu thereof) filed with the Secretary of State becomes effective in accordance with § 103 of this title, provided that an amendment made subsequent to the adoption of the agreement by the stockholders of any constituent corporation shall not (1) alter or change the amount or kind of shares, securities, cash, property and/or rights to be received in exchange for or on conversion of all or any of the shares of any class or or series thereof of such constituent corporation, (2) alter or change any term of the certificate of incorporation of the surviving corporation to be effected by the merger or consolidation, or (3) alter or change any of the terms and conditions of the agreement if such alteration or change would adversely affect the holder of any class or series thereof of such constituent corporation; in the event the agreement of merger or consolidation is amended after the filing thereof with the Secretary of State but before the agreement has become effective, a certificate of amendment of merger or consolidation shall be filed in accordance with § 103 of this title.

(e) In the case of a merger, the certificate of incorporation of the surviving corporation shall automatically be amended to the extent, if any, that changes in the certificate of incorporation are set forth in the agreement of merger.

(f) Notwithstanding the requirements of subsection (c), unless required by its certificate of incorporation, no vote of stockholders of a constituent corporation surviving a merger shall be necessary to authorize a merger if (1) the agreement of merger does not amend in any respect the certificate of incorporation of such constituent corporation, (2) each share of stock of such constituent corporation outstanding immediately prior to the effective date of the merger is to be an identical outstanding or treasury share of the surviving corporation after the effective date of the merger, and (3) either no shares of common stock of the surviving corporation and no shares, securities or obligations convertible into such stock are to be issued or delivered under the plan of merger, or the authorized unissued shares or the treasury shares of common stock of the surviving corporation to be issued or delivered under the plan of merger plus those initially issuable upon conversion of any other shares, securities or obligations to be issued or delivered under such plan do not exceed 20 percent of the shares of common stock of such constituent corporation outstanding immediately prior to the effective date of the merger. No vote of stockholders of a constituent corporation shall be necessary to authorize a merger or consolidation if no shares of the stock of such corporation shall have been issued prior to the adoption by the board of directors of the resolution approving the agreement of merger or consolidation. If an agreement of merger is adopted by the constituent corporation surviving the merger, by action of its board of directors and without any vote of its stockholders pursuant to this subsection, the secretary or assistant secretary of that corporation shall certify on the agreement that the agreement has been adopted pursuant to this subsection and, (1) if it has been adopted pursuant to the first sentence of this subsection, that the conditions specified in that sentence have been satisfied, or (2) if it has been adopted pursuant to the second sentence of this subsection, that no shares of stock of such corporation were issued prior to the adoption by the board of directors of the resolution approving the agreement of merger or consolidation. The agreement so adopted and certified shall then be filed and shall become effective, in accordance with section 103 of this title. Such filing shall constitute a representation by the person who executes the agreement that the facts stated in the certificate remain true immediately prior to such filing.

(g) Notwithstanding the requirements of subsection (c) of this section, unless expressly required by its certificate of incorporation, no vote of stockholders of a constituent corporation shall be necessary to authorize a merger with or into a single direct or indirect wholly-owned subsidiary of such constituent corporation if: (1) such constituent corporation and the direct or indirect wholly-owned subsidiary of such constituent corporation are the only constituent entities to the merger; (2) each share or fraction of a share of the capital stock of the constituent corporation outstanding immediately prior to the effective time of the merger is converted in the merger into a share or equal fraction of [a] share of capital stock of a holding company having the same designations, rights, powers and preferences, and the qualifications, limitations and restrictions thereof, as the share of stock of the constituent corporation being converted in the merger; (3) the holding company and the constituent corporation are corporations of this State and the direct or indirect wholly-owned subsidiary that is the other constituent entity to the merger is a corporation or limited liability company of this State; (4) the certificate of incorporation and by-laws of the holding company immediately following the effective time of the merger contain provisions identical to the certificate of incorporation and by-laws of the constituent corporation immediately prior to the effective time of the merger (other than provisions, if any, regarding the incorporator or incorporators, the corporate name, the registered office and agent, the initial board of directors and the initial subscribers for shares and such provisions contained in any amendment to the certificate of incorporation as were necessary to effect a change, exchange, reclassification, subdivision, combination or cancellation of stock, if such change, exchange, reclassification or cancellation has become effective); (5) as a result of the merger the constituent corporation or its successor becomes or remains a direct or indirect wholly-owned subsidiary of the holding company; (6) the directors of the constituent corporation become or remain the directors of the holding company upon the effective time of the merger; (7) the organizational documents of the surviving entity immediately following the effective time of the merger contain provisions identical to the certificate of incorporation of the constituent corporation immediately prior to the effective time of the merger (other than provisions, if any, regarding the incorporator or incorporators, the corporate or entity name, the registered office and agent, the initial board of directors and the initial subscribers for shares, references to members rather than stockholders or shareholders, references to interests, units or the like rather than stock or shares, references to managers, managing members or other members of the governing body rather than directors and such provisions contained in any amendment to the certificate of incorporation as were necessary to effect a change, exchange, reclassification, subdivision, combination or cancellation of stock, if such change, exchange, reclassification, subdivision, combination or cancellation has become effective); provided, however, that (i) if the organizational documents of the surviving entity do not contain the following provisions, they shall be amended in the merger to contain provisions requiring that (A) any act or transaction by or involving the surviving entity, other than the election or removal of directors or managers, managing members or other members of the governing body of the surviving entity, that requires for its adoption under this chapter or its organizational documents the approval of the stockholders or members of the surviving entity shall, by specific reference to this subsection, require, in addition, the approval of the stockholders of the holding company (or any successor by merger), by the same vote as is required by this chapter and/or by the organizational documents of the surviving entity; provided, however, that for purposes of this clause (i)(A), any surviving entity that is not a corporation shall include in such amendment a requirement that the approval of the stockholders of the holding company be obtained for any act or transaction by or involving the surviving entity, other than the election or removal of directors or managers, managing members or other members of the governing body of the surviving entity, which would require the approval of the stockholders of the surviving entity if the surviving entity were a corporation subject to this chapter; (B) any amendment of the organizational documents of a surviving entity that is not a corporation, which amendment would, if adopted by a corporation subject to this chapter, be required to be included in the certificate of incorporation of such corporation, shall, by specific reference to this subsection, require, in addition, the approval of the stockholders of the holding company (or any successor by merger), by the same vote as is required by this chapter and/or by the organizational documents of the surviving entity, and (C) the business and affairs of a surviving entity that is not a corporation shall be managed by or under the direction of a board of directors, board of managers or other governing body consisting of individuals who are subject to the same fiduciary duties applicable to, and who are liable for breach of such duties to the same extent as, directors of a corporation subject to this chapter; and (ii) the organizational documents of the surviving entity may be amended in the merger (A) to reduce the number of classes and shares of capital stock or other equity interests or units that the surviving entity is authorized to issue and (B) to eliminate any provision authorized by subsection (d) of § 141 of this title; and (8) the stockholders of the constituent corporation do not recognize gain or loss for United States federal income tax purposes as determined by the board of directors of the constituent corporation. Neither subsection (g)(7)(i) of this section nor any provision of a surviving entity's organizational documents required by subsection (g)(7)(i) shall be deemed or construed to require approval of the stockholders of the holding company to elect or remove directors or managers, managing members or other members of the governing body of the surviving entity. The term "organizational documents", as used in subsection (g)(7) and in the preceding sentence, shall, when used in reference to a corporation, mean the certificate of incorporation of such corporation and, when used in reference to a limited liability company, mean the limited liability company agreement of such limited liability company.

As used in this subsection only, the term "holding company" means a corporation which, from its incorporation until consummation of a merger governed by this subsection, was at all times a direct or indirect wholly-owned subsidiary of the constituent corporation and whose capital stock is issued in such merger. From and after the effective time of a merger adopted by a constituent corporation by action of its board of directors and without any vote of stockholders pursuant to this subsection: (i) to the extent the restrictions of § 203 of this Chapter applied to the constituent corporation and its stockholders at the effective time of the merger, such restrictions shall apply to the holding company and its stockholders immediately after the effective time of the merger as though it were the constituent corporation, and all shares of stock of the holding company acquired in the merger shall for purposes of § 203 be deemed to have been acquired at the time that the shares of stock of the constituent corporation converted in the merger were acquired, and provided further that any stockholder who immediately prior to the effective time of the merger was not an interested stockholder within the meaning of § 203 shall not solely by reason of the merger become an interested stockholder of the holding company, (ii) if the corporate name of the holding company immediately following the effective time of the merger is the same as the corporate name of the constituent corporation immediately prior to the effective time of the merger, the shares of capital stock of the holding company into which the shares of capital stock of the constituent corporation are converted in the merger shall be represented by the stock certificates that previously represented shares of capital stock of the constituent corporation and (iii) to the extent a stockholder of the constituent corporation immediately prior to the merger had standing to institute or maintain derivative litigation on behalf of the constituent corporation, nothing in this section shall be deemed to limit or extinguish such standing. If an agreement of merger is adopted by a constituent corporation by action of its board of directors and without any vote of stockholders pursuant to this subsection, the secretary or assistant secretary of the constituent corporation shall certify on the agreement that the agreement has been adopted pursuant to this subsection and that the conditions specified in the first sentence of this subsection have been satisfied. The agreement so adopted and certified shall then be filed and become effective, in accordance with § 103 of this title. Such filing shall constitute a representation by the person who executes the agreement that the facts stated in the certificate remain true immediately prior to such filing. Neither subsection (g)(7)(i) hereof nor any provision of a surviving corporation's certificate of incorporation required by subsection (g)(7)(i) shall be deemed or construed to require approval of the stockholders of the holding company to elect or remove directors of the surviving corporation.

§ 253. Merger of Parent Corporation and Subsidiary or Subsidiaries

(a) In any case in which at least 90 percent of the outstanding shares of each class of the stock of a corporation or corporations (other than a corporation which has in its certificate of incorporation the provision required by subsection (g)(7)(i) of Section 251 of this title), of which class there are outstanding shares that, absent this subsection, would be entitled to vote on such merger, is owned by another corporation and one of such corporations is a corporation of this State and the other or others are corporations of this State or of any other state or states or of the District of Columbia and the laws of such other state or states or of the District permit a corporation of such jurisdiction to merge with a corporation of another jurisdiction, the corporation having such stock ownership may either merge such other corporation or corporations into itself and assume all of its or their obligations, or merge itself, or itself and one or more of such other corporations, into one of such other corporations by executing, acknowledging and filing, in accordance with section 103 of this title, a certificate of such ownership and merger setting forth a copy of the resolution of its board of directors to so merge and the date of the adoption thereof; provided, however, that in case the parent corporation shall not own all the outstanding stock of all the subsidiary corporations, parties to a merger as aforesaid, the resolution of the board of directors of the parent corporation shall state the terms and conditions of the merger, including the securities, cash, property, or rights to be issued, paid, delivered or granted by the surviving corporation upon surrender of each share of the subsidiary corporation or corporations not owned by the parent corporation, or the cancellation of some or all of such shares. Any of the terms of the resolution of the board of directors to so merge may be made dependent upon facts ascertainable outside of such resolution, provided that the manner in which such facts shall operate upon the terms of the resolution is clearly and expressly set forth in the resolution. The term "facts", as used in the preceding sentence, includes, but is not limited to, the occurrence of any event, including a determination or action by any person or body, including the corporation. If the parent corporation be not the surviving corporation, the resolution shall include provision for the pro rata issuance of stock of the surviving corporation to the holders of the stock of the parent corporation on surrender of any certificates therefor, and the certificate of ownership and merger shall state that the proposed merger has been approved by a majority of the outstanding stock of the parent corporation entitled to vote thereon at a meeting thereof duly called and held after 20 days' notice of the purpose of the meeting mailed to each such stockholder at his address as it appears on the records of the corporation if the parent corporation is a corporation of this State or state that the proposed merger has been adopted, approved, certified, executed and acknowledged by the parent corporation in accordance with the laws under which it is organized if the parent corporation is not a corporation of this State. If the surviving corporation exists under the laws of the District of Columbia or any state or jurisdiction other than this State, the provisions of section 252(d) of this title shall also apply to a merger under this section.

(b) If the surviving corporation is a Delaware corporation, it may change its corporate name by the inclusion of a provision to that effect in the resolution of merger adopted by the directors of the parent corporation and set forth in the certificate of ownership and merger, and upon the effective date of the merger, the name of the corporation shall be so changed.

(c) The provisions of Section 251(d) of this title shall apply to a merger under this section, and the provisions of Section 251(e) shall apply to a merger under this section in which the surviving corporation is the subsidiary corporation and is a corporation of this State. References to "agreement of merger" in Sections 251(d) and 251(e) of this title shall mean for purposes of this Section 253(c) the resolution of merger adopted by the board of directors of the parent corporation. Any merger which effects any changes other than those authorized by this section or made applicable by this subsection shall be accomplished under the provisions of Section 251 or Section 252 of this title. The provisions of Section 262 of this title shall not apply to any merger effected under this section, except as provided in subsection (d) of this section.

(d) In the event all of the stock of a subsidiary Delaware corporation party to a merger effected under this Section is not owned by the parent corporation immediately prior to the merger, the stockholders of the subsidiary Delaware corporation party to the merger shall have appraisal rights as set forth in Section 262 of this Title.

(e) A merger may be effected under this section although one or more of the corporations parties to the merger is a corporation organized under the laws of a jurisdiction other than one of the United States; provided that the laws of such jurisdiction permit a corporation of such jurisdiction to merge with a corporation of another jurisdiction.

§ 259. Status, Rights, Liabilities, etc. of Constituent and Surviving or Resulting Corporations Following Merger or Consolidation

(a) When any merger or consolidation shall have become effective under this chapter, for all purposes of the laws of this State the separate existence of all the constituent corporations, or of all such constituent corporations except the one into which the other or others of such constituent corporations have been merged, as the case may be, shall cease and the constituent corporations shall become a new corporation, or be merged into one of such corporations, as the case may be, possessing all the rights, privileges, powers and franchises as well of a public as of a private nature, and being subject to all the restrictions, disabilities and duties of each of such corporations so merged or consolidated; and all and singular, the rights, privileges, powers and franchises of each of said corporations, and all property, real, personal and mixed, and all debts due to any of said constituent corporations on whatever account, as well for stock subscriptions as all other things in action or belonging to each of such corporations shall be vested in the corporation surviving or resulting from such merger or consolidation; and all property, rights, privileges, powers and franchises, and all and every other interest shall be thereafter as effectually the property of the surviving or resulting corporation as they were of the several and respective constituent corporations, and the title to any real estate vested by deed or otherwise, under the laws of this State, in any of such constituent corporations, shall not revert or be in any way impaired by reason of this chapter; but all rights of creditors and all liens upon any property of any of said constituent corporations shall be preserved unimpaired, and all debts, liabilities and duties of the respective constituent corporations shall thenceforth attach to said surviving or resulting corporation, and may be enforced against it to the same extent as if said debts, liabilities and duties had been incurred or contracted by it. . . .

§ 260. Powers of Corporation Surviving or Resulting From Merger or Consolidation; Issuance of Stock, Bonds or Other Indebtedness

When two or more corporations are merged or consolidated, the corporation surviving or resulting from the merger may issue bonds or other obligations, negotiable or otherwise, and with or without coupons or interest certificates thereto attached, to an amount sufficient with its capital stock to provide for all the payments it will be required to make, or obligations it will be required to assume, in order to effect the merger or consolidation. For the purpose of securing the payment of any such bonds and obligations, it shall be lawful for the surviving or resulting corporation to mortgage its corporate franchise, rights, privileges and property, real, personal or mixed. The surviving or resulting corporation may issue certificates of its capital stock or uncertificated stock if authorized to do so and other securities to the stockholders of the constituent corporations in exchange or payment for the original shares, in such amount as shall be necessary in accordance with the terms of the agreement of merger or consolidation in order to effect such merger or consolidation in the manner and on the terms specified in the agreement.

§ 261. Effect of Merger Upon Pending Actions

Any action or proceeding, whether civil, criminal or administrative, pending by or against any corporation which is a party to a merger or consolidation shall be prosecuted as if such merger or consolidation had not taken place, or the corporation surviving or resulting from such merger or consolidation may be substituted in such action or proceeding.

§ 262. Appraisal Rights

(a) Any stockholder of a corporation of this State who holds shares of stock on the date of the making of a demand pursuant to subsection (d) of this section with respect to such shares, who continuously holds such shares through the effective date of the merger or consolidation, who has otherwise complied with subsection (d) of this section and who has neither voted in favor of the merger or consolidation nor consented thereto in writing pursuant to § 228 of this title shall be entitled to an appraisal by the Court of Chancery of the fair value of his shares of stock under the circumstances described in subsections (b) and (c) of this section. As used in this section, the word "stockholder" means a holder of record of stock in a stock corporation and also a member of record of a nonstock corporation; the words "stock" and "share" mean and include what is ordinarily meant by those words and also membership or membership interest of a member of a nonstock corporation; and the words "depository receipt" mean a receipt or other instrument issued by a depository representing an interest in one or more shares, or fractions thereof, solely of stock of a corporation, which stock is deposited with the depository.

(b) Appraisal rights shall be available for the shares of any class or series of stock of a constituent corporation in a merger or consolidation to be effected pursuant to § 251 (other than a merger effected pursuant to subsection (g) of § 251), § 252, § 254, § 257, § 258, § 263 or § 264 of this title:

(1) Provided, however, that no appraisal rights under this section shall be available for the shares of any class or series of stock, which stock, or depository receipts in respect thereof, at the record date fixed to determine the stockholders entitled to receive notice of and to vote at the meeting of stockholders to act upon the agreement of merger or consolidation, were either (i) listed on a national securities exchange or designated as a national market system security on an interdealer quotation system by the National Association of Securities Dealers, Inc. or (ii) held of record by more than 2,000 holders; and further provided that no appraisal rights shall be available for any shares of stock of the constituent corporation surviving a merger if the merger did not require for its approval the vote of the stockholders of the surviving corporation as provided in subsection (f) of § 251 of this title.

(2) Notwithstanding paragraph (1) of this subsection, appraisal rights under this section shall be available for the shares of any class or series of stock of a constituent corporation if the holders thereof are required by the terms of an agreement of merger or consolidation pursuant to §§ 251, 252, 254, 257, 258, 263 and 264 of this title to accept for such stock anything except:

a. Shares of stock of the corporation surviving or resulting from such merger or consolidation, or depository receipts in respect thereof;

b. Shares of stock of any other corporation, or depository receipts in respect thereof, which shares of stock (or depository receipts in respect thereof) or depository receipts at the effective date of the merger or consolidation will be either listed on a national securities exchange or designated as a national market system security on an interdealer quotation system by the National Association of Securities Dealers, Inc. or held of record by more than 2,000 holders;

c. Cash in lieu of fractional shares or fractional depository receipts described in the foregoing subparagraphs a. and b. of this paragraph; or

d. Any combination of the shares of stock, depository receipts and cash in lieu of fractional shares or fractional depository receipts described in the foregoing subparagraphs a., b. and c. of this paragraph.

(3) In the event all of the stock of a subsidiary Delaware corporation party to a merger effected under Section 253 of this chapter is not owned by the parent corporation immediately prior to the merger, appraisal rights shall be available for the shares of the subsidiary Delaware corporation.

(c) Any corporation may provide in its certificate of incorporation that appraisal rights under this Section shall be available for the shares of any class or series of its stock as a result of an amendment to its certificate of incorporation, any merger or consolidation in which the corporation is a constituent corporation or the sale of all or substantially all of the assets of the corporation. If the certificate of incorporation contains such a provision, the procedures of this Section, including those set forth in subsections (d) and (e), shall apply as nearly as is practicable.

(d) Appraisal rights shall be perfected as follows:

(1) If a proposed merger or consolidation for which appraisal rights are provided under this Section is to be submitted for approval at a meeting of stockholders, the corporation, not less than 20 days prior to the meeting, shall notify each of its stockholders who was such on the record date for such meeting with respect to shares for which appraisal rights are available pursuant to subsections (b) or (c) hereof that appraisal rights are available for any or all of the shares of the constituent corporations, and shall include in such notice a copy of this Section. Each stockholder electing to demand the appraisal of such stockholder's shares shall deliver to the corporation, before the taking of the vote on the merger or consolidation, a written demand for appraisal of such stockholder's shares. Such demand will be sufficient if it reasonably informs the corporation of the identify of the stockholder and that the stockholder intends thereby to demand the appraisal of such stockholder's shares. A proxy or vote against the merger or consolidation shall not constitute such a demand. A stockholder electing to take such action must do so by a separate written demand as herein provided. Within 10 days after the effective date of such merger or consolidation, the surviving or resulting corporation shall notify each stockholder of each constituent corporation who has complied with the provisions of this subsection and has not voted in favor of or consented to the merger or consolidation of the date that the merger or consolidation has become effective; or

(2) If the merger or consolidation was approved pursuant to § 228 or § 253 of this title, then, either a constituent corporation before the effective date of the merger or consolidation, or the surviving or resulting corporation within ten days thereafter, shall notify each of the holders of any class or series of stock of such constituent corporation who are entitled to appraisal rights of the approval of the merger or consolidation and that appraisal rights are available for any or all shares of such class or series of stock of such constituent corporation, and shall

include in such notice a copy of this section. Such notice may, and, if given on or after the effective date of the merger or consolidation, shall, also notify such stockholders of the effective date of the merger or consolidation. Any stockholder entitled to appraisal rights may, within twenty days after the date of mailing of such notice, demand in writing from the surviving or resulting corporation the appraisal of such holder's shares. Such demand will be sufficient if it reasonably informs the corporation of the identity of the stockholder and that the stockholder intends thereby to demand the appraisal of such holder's shares. If such notice did not notify stockholders of the effective date of the merger or consolidation, either (i) each such constituent corporation shall send a second notice before the effective date of the merger or consolidation notifying each of the holders of any class or series of stock of such constituent corporation that are entitled to appraisal rights of the effective date of the merger or consolidation or (ii) the surviving or resulting corporation shall send such a second notice to all such holders on or within 10 days after such effective date; provided, however, that if such second notice is sent more than 20 days following the sending of the first notice, such second notice need only be sent to each stockholder who is entitled to appraisal rights and who has demanded appraisal of such holder's shares in accordance with this subsection. An affidavit of the secretary or assistant secretary or of the transfer agent of the corporation that is required to give either notice that such notice has been given shall, in the absence of fraud, be prima facie evidence of the facts stated therein. For purposes of determining the stockholders entitled to receive either notice, each constituent corporation may fix, in advance, a record date that shall be not more than 10 days prior to the date the notice is given; provided that, if the notice is given on or after the effective date of the merger or consolidation, the record date shall be such effective date. If no record date is fixed and the notice is given prior to the effective date, the record date shall be the close of business on the day next preceding the day on which the notice is given.

(e) Within 120 days after the effective date of the merger or consolidation, the surviving or resulting corporation or any stockholder who has complied with the provisions of subsections (a) and (d) hereof and who is otherwise entitled to appraisal rights, may file a petition in the Court of Chancery demanding a determination of the value of the stock of all such stockholders. Notwithstanding the foregoing, at any time within 60 days after the effective date of the merger or consolidation, any stockholder shall have the right to withdraw such stockholder's demand for appraisal and to accept the terms offered upon the merger or consolidation. Within 120 days after the effective date of the merger or consolidation, any stockholder who has complied with the requirements of subsections (a) and (d) hereof, upon written request, shall be entitled to receive from the corporation surviving the merger or resulting from the consolidation a statement setting forth the aggregate number of shares not voted in favor of the merger or consolidation and with respect to which demands for appraisal have been received and the aggregate number of holders of such shares. Such written statement shall be mailed to the stockholder within 10 days after such stockholder's written request for such a statement is received by the surviving or resulting corporation or within 10 days after expiration of the period for delivery of demands for appraisal under subsection (d) hereof, whichever is later.

(f) Upon the filing of any such petition by a stockholder, service of a copy thereof shall be made upon the surviving or resulting corporation, which shall within 20 days after such service file in the office of the Register in Chancery in which the petition was filed a duly verified list containing the names and addresses of all stockholders who have demanded payment for their shares and with whom agreements as to the value of their shares have not been reached by the surviving or resulting corporation. If the petition shall be filed by the surviving or resulting corporation, the petition shall be accompanied by such a duly verified list. The Register in Chancery, if so ordered by the Court, shall give notice of the time and place fixed for the hearing of such petition by registered or certified mail to the surviving or resulting corporation and to the stockholders shown on the list at the addresses therein stated. Such notice shall also be given by one or more publications at least one week before the day of the hearing, in a newspaper of general circulation published in the City of Wilmington, Delaware or such publication as the Court deems advisable. The forms of the notices by mail and by publication shall be approved by the Court, and the costs thereof shall be borne by the surviving or resulting corporation.

(g) At the hearing on such petition, the Court shall determine the stockholders who have complied with the provisions of this Section and who have become entitled to appraisal rights. The Court may require the stockholders who have demanded an appraisal for their shares and who hold stock represented by certificates to submit their certificates of stock to the Register in Chancery for notation thereon of the pendency of the appraisal proceedings; and if any stockholder fails to comply with such direction, the Court may dismiss the proceedings as to such stockholder.

(h) After determining the stockholders entitled to an appraisal, the Court shall appraise the shares, determining their fair value exclusive of any element of value arising from the accomplishment or expectation of the merger or consolidation, together with a fair rate of interest, if any, to be paid upon the amount determined to be the fair value. In determining such fair value, the Court shall take into account all relevant factors. In determining the fair rate of interest, the Court may consider all relevant factors, including the rate of interest which the surviving or resulting corporation would have had to pay to borrow money during the pendency of the proceeding. Upon application by the surviving or resulting corporation or by any stockholder entitled to participate in the appraisal proceeding, the Court may, in its discretion, permit discovery or other pretrial proceedings and may proceed to trial upon the appraisal prior to the final determination of the stockholder entitled to an appraisal. Any stockholder whose name appears on the list filed by the surviving or resulting corporation pursuant to subsection (f) of this Section and who has submitted such stockholder's certificates of stock to the Register in Chancery, if such is required, may participate fully in all proceedings until it is finally determined that such stockholder is not entitled to appraisal rights under this Section.

(i) The Court shall direct the payment of the fair value of the shares, together with interest, if any, by the surviving or resulting corporation to the stockholders entitled thereto. Interest may be simple or compound, as the Court may direct. Payment shall be so made to each such stockholder, in the case of holders of uncertificated stock forthwith, and in the case of holders of shares represented by certificates upon the surrender to the corporation of the certificates representing such stock. The Court's decree may be enforced as other decrees in the Court of Chancery may be enforced, whether such surviving or resulting corporation be a corporation of this State or of any other state.

(j) The costs of the proceeding may be determined by the Court and taxed upon the parties as the Court deems equitable in the circumstances. Upon application of a stockholder, the Court may order all or a portion of the expenses incurred by any stockholder in connection with the appraisal proceeding, including, without limitation, reasonable attorney's fees and the fees and expenses of experts, to be charged pro rata against the value of all of the shares entitled to an appraisal.

(k) From and after the effective date of the merger or consolidation, no stockholder who has demanded his appraisal rights as provided in subsection (d) of this Section shall be entitled to vote such stock for any purpose or to receive payment of dividends or other distributions on the stock (except dividends or other distributions payable to stockholders of record at a date which is prior to the effective date of the merger or consolidation); provided, however, that if no petition for an appraisal shall be filed within the time provided in subsection (e) of this Section, or if such stockholder shall deliver to the surviving or resulting corporation a written withdrawal of such stockholder's demand for an appraisal and an acceptance of the merger or consolidation, either within 60 days after the effective date of the merger or consolidation as provided in subsection (e) of this Section or thereafter with the written approval of the corporation, then the right of such stockholder to an appraisal shall cease. Notwithstanding the foregoing, no appraisal proceeding in the Court of Chancery shall be dismissed as to any stockholder without the approval of the Court, and such approval may be conditioned upon such terms as the Court deems just.

(*l*) The shares of the surviving or resulting corporation into which the shares of such objecting stockholders would have been converted had they assented to the merger or consolidation shall have the status of authorized and unissued shares of the surviving or resulting corporation.

§ 263. Merger or Consolidation of Domestic Corporation and Partnership

(a) Any 1 or more corporations of this State may merge or consolidate with 1 or more partnerships (whether general (including a limited liability partnership) or limited (including a limited liability partnership)), of this State or of any other state or states of the United States, or of the District of Columbia, unless the laws of such other state or states or the District of Columbia forbid such merger or consolidation. Such corporation or corporations and such one or more partnerships may merge with or into a corporation, which may be any one of such corporations, or they may merge with or into a partnership, which may be any one of such partnerships, or they may consolidate into a new corporation or partnership formed by the consolidation, which shall be a corporation or limited partnership of this State or any other state of the United States, or the District of Columbia, which permits such merger or consolidation, pursuant to an agreement of merger or consolidation, as the case may be, complying and approved in accordance with this section.

(b) Each such corporation and partnership shall enter into a written agreement of merger or consolidation. The agreement shall state: (1) The terms and conditions of the merger or consolidation; (2) the mode of carrying the same into effect; (3) the manner, if any, of converting the shares of stock of each such corporation and the partnership interests of each such partnership into shares, partnership interests or other securities of the entity surviving or resulting from such merger or consolidation or of cancelling some or all of such shares or interests, and if any shares of any such corporation or any partnership interests of any such partnership are not to remain outstanding, to be converted solely into shares, partnership interests or other securities of the entity surviving or resulting from such merger or consolidation or to be cancelled, the cash, property, rights or securities of any other corporation or entity which the holders of such shares or partnership interests are to receive in exchange for, or upon conversion of such shares or partnership interests and the surrender of any certificates evidencing them, which cash, property, rights or securities of any other corporation or entity may be in addition to or in lieu of shares, partnership interests or other securities of the entity surviving or resulting from such merger or consolidation; and (4) such other details or provisions as are deemed desirable, including, without limiting the generality of the foregoing, a provision for the payment of cash in lieu of the issuance of fractional shares or interests of the surviving or resulting corporation or limited partnership. Any of the terms of the agreement of merger or consolidation may be made dependent upon facts ascertainable outside of such agreement, provided that the manner in which such facts shall operate upon the terms of the agreement is clearly and expressly set forth in the agreement of merger or consolidation. The term "facts," as used in the preceding sentence, includes, but is not limited to, the occurrence of any event, including a determination or action by any person or body, including the corporation.

(c) The agreement required by subsection (b) of this section shall be adopted, approved, certified, executed and acknowledged by each of the corporations in the same manner as is provided in § 251 of this title and, in the case of the partnerships, in accordance with their partnership agreements and in accordance with the laws of the state under which they are formed, as the case may be. If the surviving or resulting entity is a partnership, in addition to any other approvals, each stockholder of a merging corporation who will become a general partner of the surviving or resulting partnership must approve the agreement of merger or consolidation. The agreement shall be filed and shall become effective for all purposes of the laws of this State when and as provided in § 251 of this title with respect to the merger or consolidation of corporations of this State. In lieu of filing the agreement of merger or consolidation, the surviving or resulting corporation or partnership may file a certificate of merger or consolidation, executed in accordance with § 103 of this title, if the surviving or resulting entity is a corporation, or by a general partner, if the surviving or resulting entity is a partnership, which states: (1) The name and state of domicile of each of the constituent entities; (2) that an agreement of merger or consolidation has been approved, adopted, certified, executed and acknowledged by each of the constituent entities in accordance with this subsection; (3) the name of the surviving or resulting corporation or partnership; (4) in the case of a merger in which a corporation is the surviving entity, such amendments or changes in the certificate of incorporation of the surviving corporation as are desired to be effected by the merger, or, if no such amendments or changes are desired, a statement that the certificate of incorporation of the surviving corporation shall be its certificate of incorporation; (5) in the case of a consolidation in which a corporation is the resulting entity, that the certificate of incorporation of the resulting corporation shall be as is set forth in an attachment to the certificate; (6) that the executed agreement of consolidation or merger is on file at an office of the surviving corporation or partnership and the address thereof; (7) that a copy of the agreement of consolidation or merger will be furnished by the surviving or resulting entity, on request and without cost, to any stockholder of any constituent corporation or any partner of any constituent partnership; and (8) the agreement, if any, required by subsection (d) of this section.

(d) If the entity surviving or resulting from the merger or consolidation is to be governed by the laws of the District of Columbia or any state other than this State, it shall agree that it may be served with process in this State in any proceeding for enforcement of any obligation of any constituent corporation or partnership of this State, as well as for enforcement of any obligation of the surviving or resulting corporation or partnership arising from the merger or consolidation, including any suit or other proceeding to enforce the right of any stockholders as determined in appraisal proceedings pursuant to § 262 of this title, and shall irrevocably appoint the Secretary of State as its agent to accept service of process in any such suit or other proceedings and shall specify the address to which a copy of such process shall be mailed by the Secretary of State. In the event of such service upon the Secretary of State in accordance with this subsection, the Secretary of State shall forthwith notify such surviving or resulting corporation or partnership thereof by letter, certified mail, return receipt requested, directed to such surviving or resulting corporation or partnership at its address so specified, unless such surviving or resulting corporation or partnership shall have designated in writing to the Secretary of State a different address for such purpose, in which case it shall be mailed to the last address so designated. Such letter shall enclose a copy of the process and any other papers served on the Secretary of State pursuant to this subsection. It shall be the duty of the plaintiff in the event of such service to serve process and any other papers in duplicate, to notify the Secretary of State that service is being effected pursuant to this subsection and to pay the Secretary of State the sum of $50 for the use of the State, which sum shall be taxed as part of the costs in the proceeding, if the plaintiff shall prevail therein. The Secretary of State shall maintain an alphabetical record of any such service setting forth the name of the plaintiff and the defendant, the title, docket number and nature of the proceeding in which process has been served upon the Secretary of State, the fact that service has been effected pursuant to this subsection, the return date thereof, and the day and hour service was made. The Secretary of State shall not be required to retain such information longer than 5 years from receipt of the service of process.

(e) Sections 251(c) (second sentence) and (d)–(f), 259–261 and 328 of this title shall, insofar as they are applicable, apply to mergers or consolidations between corporations and partnerships.

§ 264. Merger or Consolidation of Domestic Corporation and Limited Liability Company

(a) Any one or more corporations of this State may merge or consolidate with one or more limited liability companies, of this State or of any other state or states of the United States, or of the District of Columbia, unless the laws of such other state or states or the District of Columbia forbid such merger or consolidation. Such corporation or corporations and such one or more limited liability companies may merge with or into a corporation, which may be any one of such corporations, or they may merge with or into a limited liability company, which may be any one of such limited liability companies, or they may consolidate into a new corporation or limited liability company formed by the consolidation, which shall be a corporation or limited liability company of this State or any other state of the United States, or the District of Columbia, which permits such merger or consolidation, pursuant to an agreement of merger or consolidation, as the case may be, complying and approved in accordance with this section.

(b) Each such corporation and limited liability company shall enter into a written agreement of merger or consolidation. The agreement shall state:

(1) The terms and conditions of the merger or consolidation;

(2) The mode of carrying the same into effect;

(3) The manner, if any, of converting the shares of stock of each such corporation and the limited liability company interests of each such limited liability company into shares, limited liability company interests or other securities of the entity surviving or resulting from such merger or consolidation or of cancelling some or all of such shares or interests, and if any shares of any such corporation or any limited liability company interests of any such limited liability company are not to remain outstanding, to be converted solely into shares, limited liability company interests or other securities of the entity surviving or resulting from such merger or consolidation or to be cancelled, the cash, property, rights or securities of any other corporation or entity which the holders of such shares or limited liability company interests are to receive in exchange for, or upon conversion of such shares or limited liability company interests and the surrender of any certificates evidencing them, which cash, property, rights or securities of any other corporation or entity may be in addition to or in lieu of shares, limited liability company interests or other securities of the entity surviving or resulting from such merger or consolidation; and

(4) Such other details or provisions as are deemed desirable, including, without limiting the generality of the foregoing, a provision for the payment of cash in lieu of the issuance of fractional shares or interests of the surviving or resulting corporation or limited liability company. Any of the terms of the agreement of merger or consolidation may be made dependent upon facts ascertainable outside of such agreement, provided that the manner in which such facts shall operate upon the terms of the agreement is clearly and expressly set forth in the agreement of merger or consolidation. The term "facts," as used in the preceding sentence, includes, but is not limited to, the occurrence of any event, including

a determination or action by any person or body, including the corporation.

(c) The agreement required by subsection (b) shall be adopted, approved, certified, executed and acknowledged by each of the corporations in the same manner as is provided in § 251 of this title and, in the case of the limited liability companies, in accordance with their limited liability company agreements and in accordance with the laws of the state under which they are formed, as the case may be. The agreement shall be filed and shall become effective for all purposes of the laws of this State when and as provided in § 251 of this title with respect to the merger or consolidation of corporations of this State. In lieu of filing the agreement of merger or consolidation, the surviving or resulting corporation or limited liability company may file a certificate of merger or consolidation, executed in accordance with § 103 of this title, if the surviving or resulting entity is a corporation, or by an authorized person, if the surviving or resulting entity is a limited liability company, which states:

(1) The name and state of domicile of each of the constituent entities;

(2) That an agreement of merger or consolidation has been approved, adopted, certified, executed and acknowledged by each of the constituent entities in accordance with this subsection;

(3) The name of the surviving or resulting corporation or limited liability company;

(4) In the case of a merger in which a corporation is the surviving entity, such amendments or changes in the certificate of incorporation of the surviving corporation as are desired to be effected by the merger, or, if no such amendments or changes are desired, a statement that the certificate of incorporation of the surviving corporation shall be its certificate of incorporation;

(5) In the case of a consolidation in which a corporation is the resulting entity, that the certificate of incorporation of the resulting corporation shall be as is set forth in an attachment to the certificate;

(6) That the executed agreement of consolidation or merger is on file at an office of the surviving corporation or limited liability company and the address thereof;

(7) That a copy of the agreement of consolidation or merger will be furnished by the surviving or resulting entity, on request and without cost, to any stockholder of any constituent corporation or any member of any constituent limited liability company; and

(8) The agreement, if any, required by subsection (d) of this section.

651

(d) If the entity surviving or resulting from the merger or consolidation is to be governed by the laws of the District of Columbia or any state other than this State, it shall agree that it may be served with process in this State in any proceeding for enforcement of any obligation of any constituent corporation or limited liability company of this State, as well as for enforcement of any obligation of the surviving or resulting corporation or limited liability company arising from the merger or consolidation, including any suit or other proceeding to enforce the right of any stockholders as determined in appraisal proceedings pursuant to the provisions of § 262 of this title, and shall irrevocably appoint the Secretary of State as its agent to accept service of process in any such suit or other proceedings and shall specify the address to which a copy of such process shall be mailed by the Secretary of State. In the event of such service upon the Secretary of State in accordance with this subsection, the Secretary of State shall forthwith notify such surviving or resulting corporation or limited liability company thereof by letter, certified mail, return receipt requested, directed to such surviving or resulting corporation or limited liability company at its address so specified, unless such surviving or resulting corporation or limited liability company shall have designated in writing to the Secretary of State a different address for such purpose, in which case it shall be mailed to the last address so designated. Such letter shall enclose a copy of the process and any other papers served on the Secretary of State pursuant to this subsection. It shall be the duty of the plaintiff in the event of such service to serve process and any other papers in duplicate, to notify the Secretary of State that service is being effected pursuant to this subsection and to pay the Secretary of State the sum of $50 for the use of the State, which sum shall be taxed as part of the costs in the proceeding, if the plaintiff shall prevail therein. The Secretary of State shall maintain an alphabetical record of any such service setting forth the name of the plaintiff and the defendant, the title, docket number and nature of the proceeding in which process has been served upon the Secretary of State, the fact that service has been effected pursuant to this subsection, the return date thereof, and the day and hour service was made. The Secretary of State shall not be required to retain such information longer than 5 years from receipt of the service of process.

(e) Sections 251(c) (second sentence) and (d)–(f), 259–261 and 328 of this title shall, insofar as they are applicable, apply to mergers or consolidations between corporations and limited liability companies.

§ 265. Conversion of Other Entities to a Domestic Corporation

(a) As used in this section, the term "other entity" means a limited liability company, statutory trust, business trust or association, real estate investment trust, common-law trust or any other unincorporated business including a partnership (whether general (including a limited liability partnership) or limited (including a limited liability partnership)), or a foreign corporation.

(b) Any other entity may convert to a corporation of this State by complying with subsection (h) of this section and filing in the office of the Secretary of State:

(1) A certificate of conversion to corporation that has been executed in accordance with subsection (i) of this section and filed in accordance with § 103 of this title; and

(2) A certificate of incorporation that has been executed, acknowledged and filed in accordance with § 103 of this title.

(c) The certificate of conversion to corporation shall state:

(1) The date on which and jurisdiction where the other entity was first created, incorporated, formed or otherwise came into being and, if it has changed, its jurisdiction immediately prior to its conversion to a domestic corporation;

(2) The name of the other entity immediately prior to the filing of the certificate of conversion to corporation; and

(3) The name of the corporation as set forth in its certificate of incorporation filed in accordance with subsection (b) of this section.

(d) Upon the effective time of the certificate of conversion to corporation and the certificate of incorporation, the other entity shall be converted to a corporation of this State and the corporation shall thereafter be subject to all of the provisions of this title, except that notwithstanding § 106 of this title, the existence of the corporation shall be deemed to have commenced on the date the other entity commenced its existence in the jurisdiction in which the other entity was first created, formed, incorporated or otherwise came into being.

(e) The conversion of any other entity to a corporation of this State shall not be deemed to affect any obligations or liabilities of the other entity incurred prior to its conversion to a corporation of this State or the personal liability of any person incurred prior to such conversion.

(f) When an other entity has been converted to a corporation of this State pursuant to this section, the corporation of this State shall, for all purposes of the laws of the State of Delaware, be deemed to be the same entity as the converting other entity. When any conversion shall have become effective under this section, for all purposes of the laws of the State of Delaware, all of the rights, privileges and powers of the other entity that has converted, and all property, real, personal and mixed, and all debts due to such other entity, as well as all other things and causes of action belonging to such other entity, shall remain vested in the domestic corporation to which such other entity has converted and shall be the property of such domestic corporation and the title to any real property vested by deed or otherwise in such other entity shall not revert or be in any way impaired by reason of this chapter; but all rights of creditors and all liens upon any property of such other entity shall be preserved unimpaired, and all debts, liabilities and duties of the other entity that has converted shall remain attached to the corporation of this State to which such other entity has converted, and may be enforced against it to the same extent as if said debts, liabilities and duties had originally been incurred or contracted by it in its capacity as a corporation of this State. The rights, privileges, powers and interests in property of the other entity, as well as the debts, liabilities and duties of the other entity, shall not be deemed, as a consequence of the conversion, to have been transferred to the domestic corporation to which such other entity has converted for any purpose of the laws of the State of Delaware.

(g) Unless otherwise agreed for all purposes of the laws of the State of Delaware or as required under applicable non-Delaware law, the converting other entity shall not be required to wind up its affairs or pay its liabilities and distribute its assets, and the conversion shall not be deemed to constitute a dissolution of such other entity and shall constitute a continuation of the existence of the converting other entity in the form of a corporation of this State.

(h) Prior to filing a certificate of conversion to corporation with the office of the Secretary of State, the conversion shall be approved in the manner provided for by the document, instrument, agreement or other writing, as the case may be, governing the internal affairs of the other entity and the conduct of its business or by applicable law, as appropriate, and a certificate of incorporation shall be approved by the same authorization required to approve the conversion.

(i) The certificate of conversion to corporation shall be signed by any person who is authorized to sign the certificate of conversion to corporation on behalf of the other entity.

(j) In connection with a conversion hereunder, rights or securities of, or interests in, the other entity which is to be converted to a corporation of this State may be exchanged for or converted into cash, property, or shares of stock, rights or securities of such corporation of this State or, in addition to or in lieu thereof, may be exchanged for or converted into cash, property, or shares of stock, rights or securities of or interests in another domestic corporation or other entity or may be cancelled.

§ 266. Conversion of a Domestic Corporation to Other Entities

(a) A corporation of this State may, upon the authorization of such conversion in accordance with this section, convert to a limited liability company, statutory trust, business trust or association, real estate investment trust, common-law trust or any other unincorporated business including a partnership (whether general (including a limited liability partnership) or limited (including a limited liability limited partnership)) or a foreign corporation.

(b) The board of directors of the corporation which desires to convert under this section shall adopt a resolution approving such conversion, specifying the type of entity into which the corporation shall be converted and recommending the approval of such conversion by the stockholders of the corporation. Such resolution shall be submitted to the stockholders of the corporation at an annual or special meeting. Due notice of the time, and purpose of the meeting shall be mailed to each holder of stock, whether voting or nonvoting, of the corporation at the address of the stockholder as it appears on the records of the corporation, at least 20 days prior to the date of the meeting. At the meeting, the resolution shall be considered and a vote taken for its adoption or rejection. If all outstanding shares of stock of the corporation, whether voting or nonvoting, shall be voted for the adoption of the resolution, the conversion shall be authorized.

(c) If a corporation shall convert in accordance with this section to another entity organized, formed or created under the laws of a jurisdiction other than the State of Delaware, the corporation shall file with the Secretary of State a certificate of conversion executed in accordance with § 103 of this title, which certifies:

(1) The name of the corporation, and if it has been changed, the name under which it was originally incorporated;

(2) The date of filing of its original certificate of incorporation with the Secretary of State;

(3) The name and jurisdiction of the entity to which the corporation shall be converted;

(4) That the conversion has been approved in accordance with the provisions of this section;

(5) The agreement of the corporation that it may be served with process in the State of Delaware in any action, suit or proceeding for enforcement of any obligation of the corporation arising while it was a corporation of this State, and that it irrevocably appoints the Secretary of State as its agent to accept service of process in any such action, suit or proceeding; and

(6) The address to which a copy of the process referred to in subsection (c)(5) of this section shall be mailed to it by the Secretary of State. In the event of such service upon the Secretary of State in accordance with subsection (c)(5) of this section, the Secretary of State shall forthwith notify such corporation that has converted out of the State of Delaware by letter, certified mail, return receipt requested, directed to such corporation that has converted out of the State of Delaware at the address so specified, unless such corporation shall have designated in writing to the Secretary of State a

different address for such purpose, in which case it shall be mailed to the last address designated. Such letter shall enclose a copy of the process and any other papers served on the Secretary of State pursuant to this subsection. It shall be the duty of the plaintiff in the event of such service to serve process and any other papers in duplicate, to notify the Secretary of State that service is being effected pursuant to this subsection and to pay the Secretary of State the sum of $50 for the use of the State, which sum shall be taxed as part of the costs in the proceeding, if the plaintiff shall prevail therein. The Secretary of State shall maintain an alphabetical record of any such service setting forth the name of the plaintiff and the defendant, the title, docket number and nature of the proceeding in which process has been served, the fact that service has been effected pursuant to this subsection, the return date thereof, and the day and hour service was made. The Secretary of State shall not be required to retain such information longer than 5 years from receipt of the service of process.

(d) Upon the filing in the Office of the Secretary of State of a certificate of conversion to non-Delaware entity in accordance with subsection (c) of this section or upon the future effective date or time of the certificate of conversion to non-Delaware entity and payment to the Secretary of State of all fees prescribed under this title, the Secretary of State shall certify that the corporation has filed all documents and paid all fees required by this title, and thereupon the corporation shall cease to exist as a corporation of this State at the time the certificate of conversion becomes effective in accordance with § 103 of this title. Such certificate of the Secretary of State shall be prima facie evidence of the conversion by such corporation out of the State of Delaware.

(e) The conversion of a corporation out of the State of Delaware in accordance with this section and the resulting cessation of its existence as a corporation of this State pursuant to a certificate of conversion to non-Delaware entity shall not be deemed to affect any obligations or liabilities of the corporation incurred prior to such conversion or the personal liability of any person incurred prior to such conversion, nor shall it be deemed to affect the choice of law applicable to the corporation with respect to matters arising prior to such conversion.

(f) Unless otherwise provided in a resolution of conversion adopted in accordance with this section, the converting corporation shall not be required to wind up its affairs or pay its liabilities and distribute its assets, and the conversion shall not constitute a dissolution of such corporation.

(g) In connection with a conversion of a domestic corporation to another entity pursuant to this section, shares of stock, of the corporation of this State which is to be converted may be exchanged for or converted into cash, property, rights or securities of, or interests in, the entity to which the corporation of this State is being converted or, in addition to or in lieu thereof, may be exchanged for or converted into cash, property, shares of stock, rights or securities of, or interests in, another domestic corporation or other entity or may be cancelled.

(h) When a corporation has been converted to another entity or business form pursuant to this section, the other entity or business form shall, for all purposes of the laws of the State of Delaware, be deemed to be the same entity as the corporation. When any conversion shall have become effective under this section, for all purposes of the laws of the State of Delaware, all of the rights, privileges and powers of the corporation that has converted, and all property, real, personal and mixed, and all debts due to such corporation, as well as all other things and causes of action belonging to such corporation, shall remain vested in the other entity or business form to which such corporation has converted and shall be the property of such other entity or business form, and the title to any real property vested by deed or otherwise in such corporation shall not revert or be in any way impaired by reason of this chapter; but all rights of creditors and all liens upon any property of such corporation shall be preserved unimpaired, and all debts, liabilities and duties of the corporation that has converted shall remain attached to the other entity or business form to which such corporation has converted, and may be enforced against it to the same extent as if said debts, liabilities and duties had originally been incurred or contracted by it in its capacity as such other entity or business form. The rights, privileges, powers and interest in property of the corporation that has converted, as well as the debts, liabilities and duties of such corporation, shall not be deemed, as a consequence of the conversion, to have been transferred to the other entity or business form to which such corporation has converted for any purpose of the laws of the State of Delaware.

(i) No vote of stockholders of a corporation shall be necessary to authorize a conversion if no shares of the stock of such corporation shall have been issued prior to the adoption by the board of directors of the resolution approving the conversion.

SUBCHAPTER X. SALE OF ASSETS, DISSOLUTION AND WINDING UP

§ 271. Sale, Lease or Exchange of Assets; Consideration; Procedure

(a) Every corporation may at any meeting of its board of directors or governing body sell, lease, or exchange all or substantially all of its property and assets, including its goodwill and its corporate franchises, upon such terms and conditions and for such consideration, which may consist in whole or in part of money or other property, including shares of stock in, and/or other securities of, any other corporation or corporations, as its board of directors or governing body deems expedient and for the best interests of the corporation, when and as authorized by a resolution adopted by the holders of a majority of the outstanding stock of the corporation entitled to vote thereon or, if the corporation is a non-stock corporation, by a majority of the members having the right to vote for the election of the members of the governing body, at a meeting duly called upon at least 20 days notice. The notice of the meeting shall state that such a resolution will be considered.

(b) Notwithstanding authorization or consent to a proposed sale, lease or exchange of a corporation's property and assets by the stockholders or members, the board of directors or governing body may abandon such proposed sale, lease or exchange without further action by the stockholders or members, subject to the rights, if any, of third parties under any contract relating thereto.

(c) For purposes of this section only, the property and assets of the corporation include the property and assets of any subsidiary of the corporation. As used in this subsection, "subsidiary" means any entity wholly-owned and controlled, directly or indirectly, by the corporation and includes, without limitation, corporations, partnerships, limited partnerships, limited liability partnerships, limited liability companies, and/or statutory trusts. Notwithstanding subsection (a) of this section, except to the extent the certificate of incorporation otherwise provides, no resolution by stockholders or members shall be required for a sale, lease or exchange of property and assets of the corporation to a subsidiary.

§ 272. Mortgage or Pledge of Assets

The authorization or consent of stockholders to the mortgage or pledge of a corporation's property and assets shall not be necessary, except to the extent that the certificate of incorporation otherwise provides.

§ 273. Dissolution of Joint Venture Corporation Having Two Stockholders

(a) If the stockholders of a corporation of this State, having only two stockholders each of which owns 50% of the stock therein, shall be engaged in the prosecution of a joint venture and if such stockholders shall be unable to agree upon the desirability of discontinuing such joint venture and disposing of the assets used in such venture, either stockholder may, unless otherwise provided in the certificate of incorporation of the corporation or in a written agreement between the stockholders, file with the Court of Chancery a petition stating that it desires to discontinue such joint venture and to dispose of the assets used in such venture in accordance with a plan to be agreed upon by both stockholders or that, if no such plan shall be agreed upon by both stockholders, the corporation be dissolved. Such petition shall have attached thereto a copy of the proposed plan of discontinuance and distribution and a certificate stating that copies of such petition and plan have been transmitted in writing to the other stockholder and to the directors and officers of such corporation. The petition and certificate shall be executed and acknowledged in accordance with section 103 of this title.

(b) Unless both stockholders file with the Court of Chancery (i) within three months of the date of the filing of such petition, a certificate similarly executed and acknowledged stating that they have agreed on such plan, or a modification thereof, and (ii) within one year from the date of the filing of such petition, a certificate similarly executed and acknowledged stating that the distribution provided by such plan has been completed, the Court of Chancery may dissolve such corporation and may by appointment of one or more trustees or receivers with all the powers and title of a trustee or receiver appointed under section 279 of this title, administer and wind up its affairs. Either or both of the above periods may be extended by agreement of the stockholders, evidenced by a certificate similarly executed, acknowledged and filed with the Court of Chancery prior to the expiration of such period.

§ 275. Dissolution; Procedure

(a) If it should be deemed advisable in the judgment of the board of directors of any corporation that it should be dissolved, the board, after the adoption of a resolution to that effect by a majority of the whole board at any meeting called for that purpose, shall cause notice to be mailed to each stockholder entitled to vote thereon of the adoption of the resolution and of a meeting of stockholders to take action upon the resolution.

(b) At the meeting a vote shall be taken upon the proposed dissolution. If a majority of the outstanding stock of the corporation entitled to vote thereon shall vote for the proposed dissolution, a certification of dissolution shall be filed with the Secretary of State pursuant to subsection (d) of this Section.

(c) Dissolution of a corporation may also be authorized without action of the directors if all the stockholders entitled to vote thereon shall consent in writing and a certificate of dissolution shall be filed with the Secretary of State pursuant to subsection (d) of this Section.

(d) If dissolution is authorized in accordance with this Section, a certificate of dissolution shall be executed, acknowledged and filed, and shall become effective, in accordance with § 103 of this Title. Such certificate of dissolution shall set forth:

(i) the name of the corporation;

(ii) the date dissolution was authorized;

(iii) that the dissolution has been authorized by the board of directors and stockholders of the corporation, in accordance with subsections (a) and (b) of this Section, or that the dissolution has been authorized by all of the stockholders of the corporation entitled to vote on a dissolution, in accordance with subsection (c) of this section; and

(iv) the names and addresses of the directors and officers of the corporation.

(e) The resolution authorizing a proposed dissolution may provide that notwithstanding authorization or consent to the proposed dissolution by the stockholders ... the board of directors or governing body may abandon such proposed dissolution without further action by the stockholders or members.

(f) Upon a certificate of dissolution becoming effective in accordance with § 103 of this title, the corporation shall be dissolved.

§ 278. Continuation of Corporation After Dissolution for Purposes of Suit and Winding Up Affairs

All corporations, whether they expire by their own limitation or are otherwise dissolved, shall nevertheless be continued, for the term of three years from such expiration or dissolution or for such longer period as the Court of Chancery shall in its discretion direct, bodies corporate for the purpose of prosecuting and defending suits, whether civil, criminal or administrative, by or against them, and of enabling them gradually to settle and close their business, to dispose of and convey their property, to discharge their liabilities, and to distribute to their stockholders any remaining assets, but not for the purpose of continuing the business for which the corporation was organized. With respect to any action, suit or proceeding begun by or against the corporation either prior to or within 3 years after the date of its expiration or dissolution the action shall not abate by reason of the dissolution of the corporation; the corporation shall, solely for the purpose of such action, suit or proceeding, be continued as a body corporate beyond the 3–year period and until any judgments, orders or decrees therein shall be fully executed, without the necessity for any special direction to that effect by the Court of Chancery.

§ 279. Trustees or Receivers for Dissolved Corporations; Appointment; Powers; Duties

When any corporation organized under this chapter shall be dissolved in any manner whatever, the Court of Chancery, on application of any creditor, stockholder or director of the corporation, or any other person who shows good cause therefor, at any time, may either appoint one or more of the directors of the corporation to be trustees, or appoint one or more persons to be receivers, of and for the corporation, to take charge of the corporation's property, and to collect the debts and property due and belonging to the corporation, with power to prosecute and defend, in the name of the corporation, or otherwise, all such suits as may be necessary or proper for the purposes aforesaid, and to appoint an agent or agents under them, and to do all other acts which might be done by the corporation, if in being, that may be necessary for the final settlement of the unfinished business of the corporation. The powers of the trustees or receivers may be continued as long as the Court of Chancery shall think necessary for the purposes aforesaid.

§ 280. Notice of Claimants; Filing of Claims

(a)(1) After a corporation has been dissolved in accordance with the procedures set forth in this chapter, the corporation or any successor entity may give notice of the dissolution, requiring all persons having a claim against the corporation other than a claim against the corporation in a pending action, suit or proceeding to which the corporation is a party to present their claims against the corporation in accordance with such notice. Such notice shall state:

a. That all such claims must be presented in writing and must contain sufficient information reasonably to inform the corporation or successor entity of the identity of the claimant and the substance of the claim;

b. The mailing address to which such a claim must be sent;

c. The date by which such a claim must be received by the corporation or successor entity, which date shall be no earlier than 60 days from the date thereof; and

d. That such claim will be barred if not received by the date referred to in subparagraph c. of this subsection; and

e. That the corporation or a successor entity may make distributions to other claimants and the corporation's stockholders or persons interested as having been such without further notice to the claimant; and

f. The aggregate amount, on an annual basis, of all distributions made by the corporation to its stockholders for each of the 3 years prior to the date the corporation dissolved.

Such notice shall also be published at least once a week for 2 consecutive weeks in a newspaper of general circulation in the county in which the office of the corporation's last registered agent in this State is located and in the corporation's principal place of business and, in the case of a corporation having $10,000,000 or more in total assets at the time of its dissolution, at least once in all editions of a daily newspaper with a national circulation. On or before the date of the first publication of such notice, the corporation or successor entity shall mail a copy of such notice by certified or registered mail, return receipt requested, to each known claimant of the corporation including persons with claims asserted against the corporation in a pending action, suit or proceeding to which the corporation is a party.

(2) Any claim against the corporation required to be presented pursuant to this subsection is barred if a claimant who was given actual notice under this subsection does not present the claim to the dissolved corporation or successor entity by the date referred to in subparagraph (1)c. of this subsection.

(3) A corporation or successor entity may reject, in whole or in part, any claim made by a claimant pursuant to this subsection by mailing notice of such rejection by certified or registered mail, return receipt requested, to the claimant within 90 days after receipt of such claim and, in all events, at least 150 days before the expiration of the period described in § 278 of this title; provided however, that in the case of a claim filed pursuant to § 295 of this title against a corporation or successor entity for which a receiver or trustee has been appointed by the Court of Chancery the time period shall be as provided in § 296 of this title, and the 30–day appeal period provided for in § 296 of this title shall be applicable. A notice sent by a corporation or successor entity pursuant to this subsection shall state that any claim rejected therein will be barred if an action, suit or proceeding with respect to the claim is not commenced within 120 days of the date thereof, and shall be accompanied by a copy of §§ 278–283 of this title and, in the case of a notice sent by a court-appointed receiver or trustee and as to which a claim has been filed pursuant to § 295 of this title, copies of §§ 295 and 296 of this title.

(4) A claim against a corporation is barred if a claimant whose claim is rejected pursuant to paragraph (3) of this subsection does not commence an action, suit or proceeding with respect to the claim no later than 120 days after the mailing of the rejection notice.

(b)(1) A corporation or successor entity electing to follow the procedures described in subsection (a) of this section shall also give notice of the dissolution of the corporation to persons with contractual claims contingent upon the occurrence or nonoccurrence of future events or otherwise conditional or unmatured, and request that such persons present such claims in accordance with the terms of such notice. Provided however, that as used in this section and in § 281 of this title, the term "contractual claims" shall not include any implied warranty as to any product manufactured, sold, distributed or handled by the dissolved corporation. Such notice shall be in substantially the form, and sent and published in the same manner, as described in subsection (a)(1) of this section.

(2) The corporation or successor entity shall offer any claimant on a contract whose claim is contingent, conditional or unmatured such security as the corporation or successor entity determines is sufficient to

provide compensation to the claimant if the claim matures. The corporation or successor entity shall mail such offer to the claimant by certified or registered mail, return receipt requested, within 90 days of receipt of such claim and, in all events, at least 150 days before the expiration of the period described in § 278 of this title. If the claimant offered such security does not deliver in writing to the corporation or successor entity a notice rejecting the offer within 120 days after receipt of such offer for security, the claimant shall be deemed to have accepted such security as the sole source from which to satisfy his claim against the corporation.

(c)(1) A corporation or successor entity which has given notice in accordance with subsection (a) of this section shall petition the Court of Chancery to determine the amount and form of security that will be reasonably likely to be sufficient to provide compensation for any claim against the corporation which is the subject of a pending action, suit or proceeding to which the corporation is a party other than a claim barred pursuant to subsection (a) of this section.

(2) A corporation or successor entity which has given notice in accordance with subsections (a) and (b) of this section shall petition the Court of Chancery to determine the amount and form of security that will be sufficient to provide compensation to any claimant who has rejected the offer for security made pursuant to subsection (b)(2) of this section.

(3) A corporation or successor entity which has given notice in accordance with subsection (a) of this section shall petition the Court of Chancery to determine the amount and form of security which will be reasonably likely to be sufficient to provide compensation for claims that have not been made known to the corporation or that have not arisen but that, based on facts known to the corporation or successor entity, are likely to arise or to become known to the corporation or successor entity within 5 years after the date of dissolution or such longer period of time as the Court of Chancery may determine not to exceed 10 years after the date of dissolution. The Court of Chancery may appoint a guardian ad litem in respect of any such proceeding brought under this subsection. The reasonable fees and expenses of such guardian, including all reasonable expert witness fees, shall be paid by the petitioner in such proceeding.

(d) The giving of any notice or making of any offer pursuant to the provisions of this section shall not revive any claim then barred or constitute acknowledgment by the corporation or successor entity that any person to whom such notice is sent is a proper claimant and shall not operate as a waiver of any defense or counterclaim in respect of any claim asserted by any person to whom such notice is sent.

(e) As used in this section, the term "successor entity" shall include any trust, receivership or other legal entity governed by the laws of this

State to which the remaining assets and liabilities of a dissolved corporation are transferred and which exists solely for the purposes of prosecuting and defending suits, by or against the dissolved corporation, enabling the dissolved corporation to settle and close the business of the dissolved corporation, to dispose of and convey the property of the dissolved corporation, to discharge the liabilities of the dissolved corporation, and to distribute to the dissolved corporation's stockholders any remaining assets, but not for the purpose of continuing the business for which the dissolved corporation was organized.

(f) The time periods and notice requirements of this section shall, in the case of a corporation or successor entity for which a receiver or trustee has been appointed by the Court of Chancery, be subject to variation by, or in the manner provided in, the Rules of the Court of Chancery.

§ 281. Payment and Distribution to Claimants and Stockholders

(a) A dissolved corporation or successor entity which has followed the procedures described in § 280 of this title (i) shall pay the claims made and not rejected in accordance with § 280(a) of this title, (ii) shall post the security offered and not rejected pursuant to § 280(b)(2) of this title, (iii) shall post any security ordered by the Court of Chancery in any proceeding under § 280(c) of this title and (iv) shall pay or make provision for all other claims that are mature, known and uncontested or that have been finally determined to be owing by the corporation or such successor entity. Such claims or obligations shall be paid in full and any such provision for payment shall be made in full if there are sufficient assets. If there are insufficient assets, such claims and obligations shall be paid or provided for according to their priority, and, among claims of equal priority, ratably to the extent of assets legally available therefor. Any remaining assets shall be distributed to the stockholders of the dissolved corporation; provided, however, that such distribution shall not be made before the expiration of 150 days from the date of the last notice of rejections given pursuant to § 280(a)(3) of this title. In the absence of actual fraud, the judgment of the directors of the dissolved corporation or the governing persons of such successor entity as to the provision made for the payment of all obligations under (iv) above shall be conclusive.

(b) A dissolved corporation or successor entity which has not followed the procedures described in § 280 of this title shall, prior to the expiration of the period described in § 278 of this title, adopt a plan of distribution pursuant to which the dissolved corporation or successor entity (i) shall pay or make reasonable provision to pay all claims and obligations, including all contingent, conditional or unmatured contractual claims known to the corporation or such successor entity, (ii) shall make such provision as will be reasonably likely to be sufficient to provide compensation for any claim against the corporation which is the subject of a pending action, suit or proceeding to which the corporation is a party and (iii) shall make such provision as will be reasonably likely to be sufficient to provide compensation for claims that have not been made known to the corporation or that have not arisen but that, based on facts known to the corporation or successor entity, are likely to arise or to become known to the corporation or successor entity within 10 years after the date of dissolution. The plan of distribution shall provide that such claims shall be paid in full and any such provision for payment made shall be made in full if there are sufficient assets. If there are insufficient assets, such plan shall provide that such claims and obligations shall be paid or provided for according to their priority and, among claims of equal priority, ratably to the extent of assets legally available therefor. Any remaining assets shall be distributed to the stockholders of the dissolved corporation.

(c) Directors of a dissolved corporation or governing persons of a successor entity which has complied with subsections (a) or (b) of this section shall not be personally liable to the claimants of the dissolved corporation.

(d) As used in this section, the term "successor entity" has the meaning set forth in § 280(e) of this title.

(e) The term "priority", as used in this section, does not refer either to the order of payments set forth in subsection (a)(1)–(4) of this section or to the relative times at which any claims mature or are reduced to judgment.

§ 282. Liability of Stockholders of Dissolved Corporations

(a) A stockholder of a dissolved corporation the assets of which were distributed pursuant to § 281(a) or (b) of this title shall not be liable for any claim against the corporation in an amount in excess of such stockholder's pro rata share of the claim or the amount so distributed to such stockholder, whichever is less.

(b) A stockholder of a dissolved corporation the assets of which were distributed pursuant to § 281(a) of this title shall not be liable for any claim against the corporation on which an action, suit or proceeding is not begun prior to the expiration of the period described in § 278 of this title.

(c) The aggregate liability of any stockholder of a dissolved corporation for claims against the dissolved corporation shall not exceed the amount distributed to such stockholder in dissolution.

§ 283. Jurisdiction of the Court

The Court of the Chancery shall have jurisdiction of any application prescribed in this subchapter and of all questions arising in the proceedings thereon, and may make such orders and decrees and issue injunctions therein as justice and equity shall require.

§ 284. Revocation or Forfeiture of Charter; Proceedings

(a) The Court of Chancery shall have jurisdiction to revoke or forfeit the charter of any corporation for abuse, misuse or nonuse of its corporate powers, privileges or franchises. The Attorney General shall, upon the Attorney General's own motion or upon the relation of a proper party, proceed for this purpose by complaint in the County in which the registered office of the corporation is located.

(b) The Court of Chancery shall have power, by appointment of receivers or otherwise, to administer and wind up the affairs of any corporation whose charter shall be revoked or forfeited by any court under any section of this title or otherwise, and to make such orders and decrees with respect thereto as shall be just and equitable respecting its affairs and assets and the rights of its stockholders and creditors.

(c) No proceeding shall be instituted under this section for non-use of any corporation's powers, privileges or franchises during the first two years after its incorporation.

SUBCHAPTER XIII. SUITS AGAINST COR-PORATIONS, DIRECTORS, OFFICERS OR STOCKHOLDERS

§ 325. Actions Against Officers, Directors or Stockholders to Enforce Liability of Corporation; Unsatisfied Judgment Against Corporation

(a) When the officers, directors or stockholders of any corporation shall be liable by the provisions of this chapter to pay the debts of the corporation, or any part thereof, any person to whom they are liable may have an action, at law or in equity, against any one or more of them, and the complaint shall state the claim against the corporation, and the ground on which the plaintiff expects to charge the defendants personally.

(b) No suit shall be brought against any officer, director, or stockholder for any debt of a corporation of which such person is an officer, director or stockholder, until judgment be obtained therefor against the corporation and execution thereon returned unsatisfied.

§ 327. Stockholder's Derivative Action; Allegation of Stock Ownership

In any derivative suit instituted by a stockholder of a corporation, it shall be averred in the complaint that the plaintiff was a stockholder of the corporation at the time of the transaction of which such stockholder complains or that such stockholder's stock thereafter devolved upon such stockholder by operation of law.

§ 328. Liability of Corporation, etc., Impairment by Certain Transactions

The liability of a corporation of this State, or the stockholders, directors or officers thereof, or the rights or remedies of the creditors thereof, or of persons doing or transacting business with the corporation, shall not in any way be lessened or impaired by the sale of its assets, or by the increase or decrease in the capital stock of the corporation, or by its merger or consolidation with one or more corporations or by any change or amendment in its certificate of incorporation.

§ 329. Defective Organization of Corporation as Defense

(a) No corporation of this State and no person sued by any such corporation shall be permitted to assert the want of legal organization as a defense to any claim.

(b) This section shall not be construed to prevent judicial inquiry into the regularity or validity of the organization of a corporation, or its lawful possession of any corporate power it may assert in any other suit or proceeding where its corporate existence or the power to exercise the corporate rights it asserts is challenged, and evidence tending to sustain the challenge shall be admissible in any such suit or proceeding....

SUBCHAPTER XIV. CLOSE CORPORATIONS; SPECIAL PROVISIONS

§ 341. Law Applicable to Close Corporation

(a) This subchapter applies to all close corporations, as defined in section 342 of this title. Unless a corporation elects to become a close corporation under this subchapter in the manner prescribed in this subchapter, it shall be subject in all respects to the provisions of this chapter, except the provisions of this subchapter.

(b) All provisions of this chapter shall be applicable to all close corporations, as defined in section 342 of this title, except insofar as this subchapter otherwise provides.

§ 342. Close Corporation Defined; Contents of Certificate of Incorporation

(a) A close corporation is a corporation organized under this chapter whose certificate of incorporation contains the provisions required by section 102 of this title and, in addition, provides that:

(1) All of the corporation's issued stock of all classes, exclusive of treasury shares, shall be represented by certificates and shall be held of

record by not more than a specified number of persons, not exceeding thirty; and

(2) All of the issued stock of all classes shall be subject to one or more of the restrictions on transfer permitted by section 202 of this title; and

(3) The corporation shall make no offering of any of its stock of any class which would constitute a "public offering" within the meaning of the United States Securities Act of 1933, as it may be amended from time to time.

(b) The certificate of incorporation of a close corporation may set forth the qualifications of stockholders, either by specifying classes of persons who shall be entitled to be holders of record of stock of any class, or by specifying classes of persons who shall not be entitled to be holders of stock of any class or both.

(c) For purposes of determining the number of holders of record of the stock of a close corporation, stock which is held in joint or common tenancy or by the entireties shall be treated as held by one stockholder.

§ 343. Formation of a Close Corporation

A close corporation shall be formed in accordance with sections 101, 102 and 103 of this title, except that:

(a) Its certificate of incorporation shall contain a heading stating the name of the corporation and that it is a close corporation, and

(b) Its certificate of incorporation shall contain the provisions required by section 342 of this title.

§ 344. Election of Existing Corporation to Become a Close Corporation

Any corporation organized under this chapter may become a close corporation under this subchapter by executing, acknowledging and filing in accordance with section 103 of this title, a certificate of amendment of its certificate of incorporation which shall contain a statement that it elects to become a close corporation, the provisions required by section 342 of this title to appear in the certificate of incorporation of a close corporation, and a heading stating the name of the corporation and that it is a close corporation. Such amendment shall be adopted in accordance with the requirements of section 241 or 242 of this title, except that it must be approved by a vote of the holders of record of at least two-thirds of the shares of each class of stock of the corporation which are outstanding.

§ 345. Limitations on Continuation of Close Corporation Status

A close corporation continues to be such and to be subject to this subchapter until:

(a) It files with the Secretary of State a certificate of amendment deleting from its certificate of incorporation the provisions required or permitted by section 342 of this title to be stated in the certificate of incorporation to qualify it as a close corporation, or

(b) Any one of the provisions or conditions required or permitted by section 342 of this title to be stated in a certificate of incorporation to qualify a corporation as a close corporation has in fact been breached and neither the corporation nor any of its stockholders takes the steps required by section 348 of this title to prevent such loss of status or to remedy such breach.

§ 346. Voluntary Termination of Close Corporation Status by Amendment of Certificate of Incorporation; Vote Required

(a) A corporation may voluntarily terminate its status as a close corporation and cease to be subject to this subchapter by amending its certificate of incorporation to delete therefrom the additional provisions required or permitted by section 342 of this title to be stated in the certificate of incorporation of a close corporation. Any such amendment shall be adopted and shall become effective in accordance with section 242 of this title, except that it must be approved by a vote of the holders of record of at least two-thirds of the shares of each class of stock of the corporation which are outstanding.

(b) The certificate of incorporation of a close corporation may provide that on any amendment to terminate its status as a close corporation, a vote greater than two-thirds or a vote of all shares of any class shall be required; and if the certificate of incorporation contains such a provision, that provision shall not be amended, repealed or modified by any vote less than that required to terminate the corporation's status as a close corporation.

§ 347. Issuance or Transfer of Stock of a Close Corporation in Breach of Qualifying Conditions

(a) If stock of a close corporation is issued or transferred to any person who is not entitled under any provision of the certificate of incorporation permitted by section 342(b) of this title to be a holder of record of stock of such corporation, and if the certificate for such stock conspicuously notes the qualifications of the persons entitled to be holders of record thereof, such person is conclusively presumed to have notice of the fact of such person's ineligibility to be a stockholder.

(b) If the certificate of incorporation of a close corporation states the number of persons, not in excess of thirty, who are entitled to be holders of record of its stock, and if the certificate for such stock conspicuously states such number, and if the issuance or transfer of stock to any person would cause the stock to be held by more than such number of persons, the person to whom such stock is issued or transferred is conclusively presumed to have notice of this fact.

(c) If a stock certificate of any close corporation conspicuously notes the fact of a restriction on transfer of stock of the corporation, and the restriction is one which is permitted by section 202 of this title, the transferee of the stock is conclusively presumed to have notice of the fact that such person has acquired stock in violation of the restriction, if such acquisition violates the restriction.

(d) Whenever any person to whom stock of a close corporation has been issued or transferred has, or is conclusively presumed under this section to have, notice either (i) that such person is a person not eligible to be a holder of stock of the corporation, or (ii) that transfer of stock to such person would cause the stock of the corporation to be held by more than the number of persons permitted by its certificate of incorporation to hold stock of the corporation, or (iii) that the transfer of stock is in violation of a restriction on transfer of stock, the corporation may, at its option, refuse to register transfer of the stock into the name of the transferee.

(e) The provisions of subsection (d) shall not be applicable if the transfer of stock, even though otherwise contrary to subsections (a), (b) or (c), has been consented to by all the stockholders of the close corporation, or if the close corporation has amended its certificate of incorporation in accordance with section 346 of this title.

(f) The term "transfer", as used in this section, is not limited to a transfer for value.

(g) The provisions of this section do not in any way impair any rights of a transferee regarding any right to rescind the transaction or to recover under any applicable warranty express or implied.

§ 348. Involuntary Termination of Close Corporation Status; Proceeding to Prevent Loss of Status

(a) If any event occurs as a result of which one or more of the provisions or conditions included in a close corporation's certificate of incorporation pursuant to section 342 of this title to qualify it as a close corporation has been breached, the corporation's status as a close corporation under this subchapter shall terminate unless

(1) within thirty days after the occurrence of the event, or within thirty days after the event has been discovered, whichever is later, the corporation files with the Secretary of State a certificate, executed and acknowledged in accordance with section 103 of this title, stating that a specified provision or condition included in its certificate of incorporation pursuant to section 342 of this title to qualify it as a close corporation has ceased to be applicable, and furnishes a copy of such certificate to each stockholder, and

(2) the corporation concurrently with the filing of such certificate takes such steps as are necessary to correct the situation which threatens its status as a close corporation, including, without limitation, the refusal to register the transfer of stock which has been wrongfully transferred as provided by section 347 of this title, or a proceeding under subsection (b) of this section.

(b) The Court of Chancery, upon the suit of the corporation or any stockholder, shall have jurisdiction to issue all orders necessary to prevent the corporation from losing its status as a close corporation, or to restore its status as a close corporation by enjoining or setting aside any act or threatened act on the part of the corporation or a stockholder which would be inconsistent with any of the provisions or conditions required or permitted by section 342 of this title to be stated in the certificate of incorporation of a close corporation, unless it is an act approved in accordance with section 346 of this title. The Court of Chancery may enjoin or set aside any transfer or threatened transfer of stock of a close corporation which is contrary to the terms of its certificate of incorporation or of any transfer restriction permitted by section 202 of this title, and may enjoin any public offering, as defined in section 342 of this title, or threatened public offering of stock of the close corporation.

§ 349. Corporate Option Where a Restriction on Transfer of a Security Is Held Invalid

If a restriction on transfer of a security of a close corporation is held not to be authorized by section 202 of this title, the corporation shall nevertheless have an option, for a period of thirty days after the judgment setting aside the restriction becomes final, to acquire the restricted security at a price which is agreed upon by the parties, or if no agreement is reached as to price, then at the fair value as determined by the Court of Chancery. In order to determine fair value, the Court may appoint an appraiser to receive evidence and report to the Court such appraiser's findings and recommendation as to fair value.

§ 350. Agreements Restricting Discretion of Directors

A written agreement among the stockholders of a close corporation holding a majority of the outstanding stock entitled to vote, whether solely among themselves or with a party not a stockholder, is not invalid, as between the parties to the agreement, on the ground that it so relates to the conduct of the business and affairs of the corporation as to restrict or interfere with the discretion or powers of the board of directors. The effect of any such agreement shall be to relieve the directors and impose upon the stockholders who are parties to the agreement the liability for managerial acts or omissions which is imposed on directors to the extent and so long as the discretion or powers of the board in its management of corporate affairs is controlled by such agreement.

§ 351. Management by Stockholders

The certificate of incorporation of a close corporation may provide that the business of the corporation shall be managed by the stockholders of the corporation rather than by a board of directors. So long as this provision continues in effect,

(1) No meeting of stockholders need be called to elect directors;

(2) Unless the context clearly requires otherwise, the stockholders of the corporation shall be deemed to be directors for purposes of applying provisions of this chapter; and

(3) The stockholders of the corporation shall be subject to all liabilities of directors.

Such a provision may be inserted in the certificate of incorporation by amendment if all incorporators and subscribers or all holders of record of all of the outstanding stock, whether or not having voting power, authorize such a provision. An amendment to the certificate of incorporation to delete such a provision shall be adopted by a vote of the holders of a majority of all outstanding stock of the corporation, whether or not otherwise entitled to vote. If the certificate of incorporation contains a provision authorized by this section, the existence of such provision shall be noted conspicuously on the face or back of every stock certificate issued by such corporation.

§ 352. Appointment of Custodian for Close Corporation

(a) In addition to the provisions of section 226 of this title respecting the appointment of a custodian for any corporation, the Court of Chancery, upon application of any stockholder, may appoint one or more persons to be custodians, and, if the corporation is insolvent, to be receivers, of any close corporation when:

(1) Pursuant to section 351 of this title the business and affairs of the corporation are managed by the stockholders and they are so divided that the business of the corporation is suffering or is threatened with irreparable injury and any remedy with respect to such deadlock provided in the certificate of incorporation or by-laws or in any written agreement of the stockholders has failed; or

(2) The petitioning stockholder has the right to the dissolution of the corporation under a provision of the certificate of incorporation permitted by section 355 of this title.

(b) In lieu of appointing a custodian for a close corporation under this section or section 226 of this title the Court of Chancery may appoint a provisional director, whose powers and status shall be as provided in section 353 of this title if the Court determines that it would be in the best interest of the corporation. Such appointment shall not preclude any subsequent order of the Court appointing a custodian for such corporation.

§ 353. Appointment of a Provisional Director in Certain Cases

(a) Notwithstanding any contrary provision of the certificate of incorporation or the by-laws or agreement of the stockholders, the Court of Chancery may appoint a provisional director for a close corporation if the directors are so divided respecting the management of the corporation's business and affairs that the votes required for action by the board of directors cannot be obtained with the consequence that the business and affairs of the corporation can no longer be conducted to the advantage of the stockholders generally.

(b) An application for relief under this section must be filed (1) by at least one-half of the number of directors then in office, (2) by the holders of at least one-third of all stock then entitled to elect directors, or, (3) if there be more than one class of stock then entitled to elect one or more directors, by the holders of two-thirds of the stock of any such class; but the certificate of incorporation of a close corporation may provide that a lesser proportion of the directors or of the stockholders or of a class of stockholders may apply for relief under this section.

(c) A provisional director shall be an impartial person who is neither a stockholder nor a creditor of the corporation or of any subsidiary or affiliate of the corporation, and whose further qualifications, if any, may be determined by the Court of Chancery. A provisional director is not a receiver of the corporation and does not have the title and powers of a custodian or receiver appointed under sections 226 and 291 of this title. A provisional director shall have all the rights and powers of a duly elected director of the corporation, including the right to notice of and to vote at meetings of directors, until such time as such person shall be removed by order of the Court of Chancery or by the holders of a majority of all shares then entitled to vote to elect directors or by the holders of two-thirds of the shares of that class of voting shares which filed the application for appointment of a provisional director. A provisional director's compensation shall be determined by agreement between such person and the corporation subject to approval of the Court of Chancery, which may fix such person's compensation in the absence of agreement or in the event of disagreement between the provisional director and the corporation.

(d) Even though the requirements of subsection (b) of this section relating to the number of directors or stockholders who may petition for appointment of a provisional director are not satisfied, the Court of Chancery may nevertheless appoint a provisional director if permitted by subsection (b) of section 352 of this title.

§ 354. Operating Corporation as Partnership

No written agreement among stockholders of a close corporation, nor any provision of the certificate of incorporation or of the by-laws of the corporation, which agreement or provision relates to any phase of the affairs of such corporation, including but not limited to the management of its business or declaration and payment of dividends or other division of profits or the election of directors or officers or the employment of stockholders by the corporation or the arbitration of disputes, shall be invalid on the ground that it is an attempt by the parties to the agreement or by the stockholders of the corporation to treat the corporation as if it were a partnership or to arrange relations among the stockholders or between the stockholders and the corporation in a manner that would be appropriate only among partners.

§ 355. Stockholders' Option to Dissolve Corporation

(a) The certificate of incorporation of any close corporation may include a provision granting to any stockholder, or to the holders of any specified number or percentage of shares of any class of stock, an option to have the corporation dissolved at will or upon the occurrence of any specified event or contingency. Whenever any such option to dissolve is exercised, the stockholders exercising such option shall give written notice thereof to all other stockholders. After the expiration of 30 days following the sending of such notice, the dissolution of the corporation shall proceed as if the required number of stockholders having voting power had consented in writing to dissolution of the corporation as provided by section 228 of this title.

(b) If the certificate of incorporation as originally filed does not contain a provision authorized by subsection (a), the certificate may be amended to include such provision if adopted by the affirmative vote of the holders of all the outstanding stock, whether or not entitled to vote, unless the certificate of incorporation specifically authorizes such an amendment by a vote which shall be not less than two-thirds of all the outstanding stock whether or not entitled to vote.

(c) Each stock certificate in any corporation whose certificate of incorporation authorizes dissolution as permitted by this section shall conspicuously note on the face thereof the existence of the provision. Unless noted conspicuously on the face of the stock certificate, the provision is ineffective.

§ 356. Effect of This Subchapter on Other Laws

The provisions of this subchapter shall not be deemed to repeal any statute or rule of law which is or would be applicable to any corporation which is organized under the provisions of this chapter but is not a close corporation.

SUBCHAPTER XV. FOREIGN CORPORATIONS

§ 371. Definition; Qualification to Do Business in State; Procedure

(a) As used in this chapter, the words "foreign corporation" mean a corporation organized under the laws of any jurisdiction other than this State.

(b) No foreign corporation shall do any business in this State, through or by branch offices, agents or representatives located in this State, until it shall have paid to the Secretary of State of this State for the use of the State, $80, and shall have filed in the Office of the Secretary of State:

(1) A certificate issued by an authorized officer of the jurisdiction of its incorporation evidencing its corporate existence. If such certificate is in a foreign language, a translation thereof, under oath of the translator, shall be attached thereto.

(2) A statement executed by an authorized officer of each corporation setting forth (i) the name and address of its registered agent in this State, which agent shall be either an individual resident in this State when appointed or another corporation authorized to transact business in this State, (ii) a statement, as of a date not earlier than six months prior to the filing date, of the assets and liabilities of the corporation, and (iii) the business it proposes to do in this State and a statement that it is authorized to do that business in the jurisdiction of its incorporation. The statement shall be acknowledged in accordance with § 103 of this Title.

(c) The certificate of the Secretary of State, under his seal of office, of the filing of the certificates required by subsection (b) of this section, shall be delivered to the registered agent upon the payment to the Secretary of State of the fee prescribed for his certificates and the certificate shall be prima facie evidence of the right of the corporation to do business in this State; provided that the Secretary of State shall not issue such certificate unless the name of the corporation is such as to distinguish it upon the records of the office of the Secretary of State from the names of other corporations or limited partnerships organized under the laws of this State or reserved or registered as a foreign corporation or foreign limited partnership under the laws of this State except with the written consent of such other corporation or limited partnership, executed, acknowledged, and filed with the Secretary of State in accordance with section 103 of this title. If the name of the foreign corporation conflicts with the name of a corporation, limited partnership, limited liability company, registered limited liability partnership or statutory trust organized under the laws of this State, or a name reserved for a corporation, limited partnership, limited liability company, registered limited liability partnership or statutory trust to be organized under the laws of this State, or a name reserved or registered as that of a foreign corporation, foreign limited partnership or foreign limited liability company under the laws of this State, the foreign corporation may qualify to do business if it adopts an assumed name which shall be used when doing business in this State as long as the assumed name is authorized for use by this section.

§ 383. Actions by and Against Unqualified Foreign Corporations

(a) A foreign corporation which is required to comply with the provisions of sections 371 and 372 of this title and which has done business in this State without authority shall not maintain any action or special proceeding in this State unless and until such corporation has been authorized to do business in this State and has paid to the State all fees, penalties and franchise taxes for the years or parts thereof during which it did business in this State without authority. This prohibition shall not apply to any successor in interest of such foreign corporation.

(b) The failure of a foreign corporation to obtain authority to do business in this State shall not impair the validity of any contract or act of the foreign corporation or the right of any other party to the contract to maintain any action or special proceeding thereon, and shall not prevent the foreign corporation from defending any action or special proceeding in this State.

SUBCHAPTER XVI. TRANSFER AND CONTINUANCE OF CORPORATIONS

§ 390. Transfer, Domestication or Continuance of Domestic Corporations.

(a) Upon compliance with the provisions of this section, any corporation existing under the laws of this State may transfer to or domesticate or continue in any foreign jurisdiction and, in connection therewith, may elect to continue its existence as a corporation of this State. As used in this section, the term:

(1) "Foreign jurisdiction" means any foreign country, or other foreign jurisdiction (other than the United States, any state, the District of Columbia, or any possession or territory of the United States); and

(2) "Resulting entity" means the entity formed, incorporated, created or otherwise coming into being as a consequence of the transfer of the corporation to, or its domestication or continuance in, a foreign jurisdiction pursuant to this section.

(b) The board of directors of the corporation which desires to transfer to or domesticate or continue in a foreign jurisdiction shall adopt a resolution approving such transfer, domestication or continuance specifying the foreign jurisdiction to which the corporation shall be transferred or in which the corporation shall be domesticated or continued and, if applicable, that in connection with such transfer, domestication or continuance the corporation's existence as a corporation of this State is to continue and recommending the approval of such transfer or domestication or continuance by the stockholders of the corporation. Such resolution shall be submitted to the stockholders of the corporation at an annual or special meeting. Due notice of the time, place and purpose of the meeting shall be mailed to each holder of stock, whether voting or nonvoting, of the corporation at the address of the stockholder as it appears on the records of the corporation, at least 20 days prior to the date of the meeting. At the meeting, the resolution shall be considered and a vote taken for its adoption or rejection. If all outstanding shares of stock of the corporation, whether voting or nonvoting, shall be voted for the adoption of the resolution, the corporation shall file with the Secretary of State a certificate of transfer if its existence as a corporation of this State is to cease or a certificate of transfer and domestic continuance if its existence as a corporation of this State is to continue, executed in accordance with § 103 of this title, which certifies:

(1) The name of the corporation, and if it has been changed, the name under which it was originally incorporated.

(2) The date of filing of its original certificate of incorporation with the Secretary of State.

(3) The foreign jurisdiction to which the corporation shall be transferred or in which it shall be domesticated or continued and the name of the resulting entity.

(4) That the transfer, domestication or continuance of the corporation has been approved in accordance with the provisions of this section.

(5) In the case of a certificate of transfer, (i) that the existence of the corporation as a corporation of this State shall cease when the certificate of transfer becomes effective, and (ii) the agreement of the corporation that it may be served with process in this State in any proceeding for enforcement of any obligation of the corporation arising while it was a corporation of this State which shall also irrevocably appoint the Secretary of State as its agent to accept service of process in any such proceeding and specify the address to which a copy of such process shall be mailed by the Secretary of State.

(6) In the case of a certificate of transfer and domestic continuance, that the corporation will continue to exist as a corporation of

this State after the certificate of transfer and domestic continuance becomes effective.

(c) Upon the filing of a certificate of transfer in accordance with subsection (b) of this section and payment to the Secretary of State of all fees prescribed under this title, the Secretary of State shall certify that the corporation has filed all documents and paid all fees required by this title, and thereupon the corporation shall cease to exist as a corporation of this State at the time the certificate of transfer becomes effective in accordance with § 103 of this title. Such certificate of the Secretary of State shall be prima facie evidence of the transfer, domestication or continuance by such corporation out of this State.

(d) The transfer, domestication or continuance of a corporation out of this State in accordance with this section and the resulting cessation of its existence as a corporation of this State pursuant to a certificate of transfer shall not be deemed to affect any obligations or liabilities of the corporation incurred prior to such transfer, domestication or continuance, the personal liability of any person incurred prior to such transfer, domestication or continuance, or the choice of law applicable to the corporation with respect to matters arising prior to such transfer, domestication or continuance. Unless otherwise agreed or otherwise provided in the certificate of incorporation, the transfer, domestication or continuance of a corporation out of the State of Delaware in accordance with this section shall not require such corporation to wind up its affairs or pay its liabilities and distribute its assets under this title and shall not be deemed to constitute a dissolution of such corporation.

(e) If a corporation files a certificate of transfer and domestic continuance, after the time the certificate of transfer and domestic continuance becomes effective, the corporation shall continue to exist as a corporation of this State, and the law of the State of Delaware, including this title, shall apply to the corporation to the same extent as prior to such time. So long as a corporation continues to exist as a corporation of the State of Delaware following the filing of a certificate of transfer and domestic continuance, the continuing corporation and the resulting entity shall, for all purposes of the laws of the State of Delaware, constitute a single entity formed, incorporated, created or otherwise having come into being, as applicable, and existing under the laws of the State of Delaware and the laws of the foreign jurisdiction.

(f) When a corporation has transferred, domesticated or continued pursuant to this section, for all purposes of the laws of the State of Delaware, the resulting entity shall be deemed to be the same entity as the transferring, domesticating or continuing corporation and shall constitute a continuation of the existence of such corporation in the form of the resulting entity. When any transfer, domestication or continuance shall have become effective under this section, for all purposes of the laws of the State of Delaware, all of the rights, privileges and powers of the corporation that has transferred, domesticated or continued, and all property, real, personal and mixed, and all debts due to such corporation, as well as all other things and causes of action belonging to such corporation, shall remain vested in the resulting entity (and also in the corporation that has transferred, domesticated or continued, if and for so long as such corporation continues its existence as a corporation of this State) and shall be the property of such resulting entity (and also of the corporation that has transferred, domesticated or continued, if and for so long as such corporation continues its existence as a corporation of this State), and the title to any real property vested by deed or otherwise in such corporation shall not revert or be in any way impaired by reason of this title; but all rights of creditors and all liens upon any property of such corporation shall be preserved unimpaired, and all debts, liabilities and duties of such corporation shall remain attached to the resulting entity (and also to the corporation that has transferred, domesticated or continued, if and for so long as such corporation continues its existence as a corporation of this State), and may be enforced against it to the same extent as if said debts, liabilities and duties had originally been incurred or contracted by it in its capacity as such resulting entity. The rights, privileges, powers and interests in property of the corporation, as well as the debts, liabilities and duties of the corporation, shall not be deemed, as a consequence of the transfer, domestication or continuance, to have been transferred to the resulting entity for any purpose of the laws of the State of Delaware.

(g) In connection with a transfer, domestication or continuance under this section, shares of stock of the transferring, domesticating or continuing corporation may be exchanged for or converted into cash, property, or shares of stock, rights or securities of, or interests in, the resulting entity or, in addition to or in lieu thereof, may be exchanged for or converted into cash, property, or shares of stock, rights or securities of, or interests in, another corporation or other entity or may be cancelled.

(h) No vote of the stockholders of a corporation shall be necessary to authorize a transfer, domestication or continuance if no shares of the stock of such corporation shall have been issued prior to the adoption by the board of directors of the resolution approving the transfer, domestication or continuance.

SUBCHAPTER XVII. MISCELLANEOUS PROVISIONS

§ 394. Reserved Power of State to Amend or Repeal Chapter; Chapter Part of Corporation's Charter or Certificate of Incorporation

This chapter may be amended or repealed, at the pleasure of the Legislature, but any amendment or repeal shall not take away or impair any remedy under this chapter against any corporation or its officers for any liability which shall have been previously incurred. This chapter and all amendments thereof shall be a part of the charter or certificate of incorporation of every corporation except so far as the same are inapplicable and inappropriate to the objects of the corporation.

REVISED MODEL BUSINESS CORPORATION ACT

CHAPTER 1. GENERAL PROVISIONS

Subchapter A. Short Title and Reservation of Power

Subchapter B. Filing Documents

Subchapter C. Secretary of State*

Subchapter D. Act Definitions and Other Provisions of General Applicability

CHAPTER 2. INCORPORATION

* Omitted.

* Omitted.

* Omitted.

EDITOR'S APPENDIX—PRIOR VERSIONS OF
SELECTED MODEL ACT SECTIONS

CHAPTER 10.   AMENDMENT OF ARTICLES
OF INCORPORATION AND BYLAWS
[PRIOR VERSION]

Subchapter A.   Amendment of Articles of Incorporation

Subchapter B.   Amendment of Bylaws

CHAPTER 11.   MERGER AND SHARE
EXCHANGE [PRIOR VERSION]

* Omitted.

Chapter 1

GENERAL PROVISIONS

Subchapter A

Short Title and Reservation of Power

§ 1.01 Short Title

This Act shall be known and may be cited as the "[name of state] Business Corporation Act."

* Omitted.

§ 1.02   Reservation of Power to Amend or Repeal

The [name of state legislature] has power to amend or repeal all or part of this Act at any time and all domestic and foreign corporations subject to this Act are governed by the amendment or repeal.

Subchapter B

Filing Documents

§ 1.20   Filing Requirements

(a) A document must satisfy the requirements of this section, and of any other section that adds to or varies these requirements, to be entitled to filing by the secretary of state.

(b) This Act must require or permit filing the document in the office of the secretary of state.

(c) The document must contain the information required by this Act. It may contain other information as well.

(d) The document must be typewritten or printed or, if electronically transmitted, it must be in a format that can be retrieved or reproduced in typewritten or printed form.

(e) The document must be in the English language. A corporate name need not be in English if written in English letters or Arabic or Roman numerals, and the certificate of existence required of foreign corporations need not be in English if accompanied by a reasonably authenticated English translation.

(f) The document must be executed:

   (1) by the chairman of the board of directors of a domestic or foreign corporation, by its president, or by another of its officers;

   (2) if directors have not been selected or the corporation has not been formed, by an incorporator; or

   (3) if the corporation is in the hands of a receiver, trustee, or other court-appointed fiduciary, by that fiduciary.

(g) The person executing the document shall sign it and state beneath or opposite his signature his name and the capacity in which he signs. The document may but need not contain a corporate seal, attestation, acknowledgement, or verification.

(h) If the secretary of state has prescribed a mandatory form for the document under section 1.21, the document must be in or on the prescribed form.

(i) The document must be delivered to the office of the secretary of state for filing. Delivery may be made by electronic transmission if and to the extent permitted by the secretary of state. If it is filed in typewritten or printed form and not transmitted electronically, the secretary of state may require one exact or conformed copy to be delivered with the document (except as provided in sections 5.03 and 15.09).

(j) When the document is delivered to the office of the secretary of state for filing, the correct filing fee, and any franchise tax, license fee, or penalty required to be paid therewith by this Act or other law must be paid or provision for payment made in a manner permitted by the secretary of state.

(k) Whenever a provision of this Act permits any of the terms of a plan or a filed document to be dependent on facts objectively ascertainable outside the plan or filed document, the following provisions apply:

    (1) The manner in which the facts will operate upon the terms of the plan or filed document shall be set forth in the plan or filed document.

    (2) The facts may include, but are not limited to:

        (i) any of the following that is available in a nationally recognized news or information medium either in print or electronically: statistical or market indices, market prices of any security or group of securities, interest rates, currency exchange rates, or similar economic or financial data;

        (ii) a determination or action by any person or body, including the corporation or any other party to a plan or filed document; or

        (iii) the terms of, or actions taken under, an agreement to which the corporation is a party, or any other agreement or document.

    (3) As used in this subsection:

        (i) "filed document" means a document filed with the secretary of state under any provision of this Act except chapter 15 or section 16.21; and

        (ii) "plan" means a plan of domestication, nonprofit conversion, entity conversion, merger or share exchange.

    (4) The following provisions of a plan or filed document may not be made dependent on facts outside the plan or filed document:

        (i) The name and address of any person required in a filed document.

        (ii) The registered office of any entity required in a filed document.

        (iii) The registered agent of any entity required in a filed document.

        (iv) The number of authorized shares and designation of each class or series of shares.

(v)   The effective date of a filed document.

(vi)   Any required statement in a filed document of the date on which the underlying transaction was approved or the manner in which that approval was given.

(5) If a provision of a filed document is made dependent on a fact ascertainable outside of the filed document, and that fact is not ascertainable by reference to a source described in subsection (k)(2)(i) or a document that is a matter of public record, or the affected shareholders have not received notice of the fact from the corporation, then the corporation shall file with the secretary of state articles of amendment setting forth the fact promptly after the time when the fact referred to is first ascertainable or thereafter changes. Articles of amendment under this subsection (k)(5) are deemed to be authorized by the authorization of the original filed document or plan to which they relate and may be filed by the corporation without further action by the board of directors or the shareholders.

§ 1.21   Forms

(a) The secretary of state may prescribe and furnish on request forms for: (1) an application for a certificate of existence, (2) a foreign corporation's application for a certificate of authority to transact business in this state, (3) a foreign corporation's application for a certificate of withdrawal, and (4) the annual report. If the secretary of state so requires, use of these forms is mandatory.

(b) The secretary of state may prescribe and furnish on request forms for other documents required or permitted to be filed by this Act but their use is not mandatory.

§ 1.23   Effective Time and Date of Document

(a) Except as provided in subsection (b) and section 1.24(c), a document accepted for filing is effective:

(1) at the date and time of filing, as evidenced by such means as the secretary of state may use for the purpose of recording the date and time of filing; or

(2) at the time specified in the document as its effective time on the date it is filed.

(b) A document may specify a delayed effective time and date, and if it does so the document becomes effective at the time and date specified. If a delayed effective date but no time is specified, the document is effective at the close of business on that date. A delayed effective date for a document may not be later than the 90th day after the date it is filed.

§ 1.24 Correcting Filed Document

(a) A domestic or foreign corporation may correct a document filed by the secretary of state if (1) the document contains an inaccuracy, or (2) the document was defectively executed, attested, sealed, verified, or acknowledged, or (3) the electronic transmission was defective.

(b) A document is corrected:

    (1) by preparing articles of correction that

        (i)   describe the document (including its filing date) or attach a copy of it to the articles,

        (ii) specify the inaccuracy or defect to be corrected, and

        (iii) correct the inaccuracy or defect; and

    (2) by delivering the articles to the secretary of state for filing.

(c) Articles of correction are effective on the effective date of the document they correct except as to persons relying on the uncorrected document and adversely affected by the correction. As to those persons, articles of correction are effective when filed.

§ 1.25 Filing Duty of Secretary of State

(a) If a document delivered to the office of the secretary of state for filing satisfies the requirements of section 1.20, the secretary of state shall file it.

(b) The secretary of state files a document by recording it as filed on the date and time of receipt. After filing a document, except as provided in sections 5.03 and 15.10, the secretary of state shall deliver to the domestic or foreign corporation or its representative a copy of the document with an acknowledgement of the date and time of filing.

(c) If the secretary of state refuses to file a document, he shall return it to the domestic or foreign corporation or its representative within five days after the document was delivered, together with a brief, written explanation of the reason for his refusal.

(d) The secretary of state's duty to file documents under this section is ministerial. His filing or refusing to file a document does not:

    (1) affect the validity or invalidity of the document in whole or part;

    (2) relate to the correctness or incorrectness of information contained in the document;

    (3) create a presumption that the document is valid or invalid or that information contained in the document is correct or incorrect.

§ 1.27 Evidentiary Effect of Copy of Filed Document

A certificate from the secretary of state delivered with a copy of a document filed by the secretary of state is conclusive evidence that the original document is on file with the secretary of state.

Subchapter D

Act Definitions and Other Provisions
of General Applicability

§ 1.40   Act Definitions

In this Act:

(1)   "Articles of incorporation" means the original articles of incorporation, all amendments thereof, and any other documents filed with the secretary of state with respect to a domestic business corporation under any provision of this Act except section 16.21. If any document filed under this Act restates the articles in their entirety, thenceforth the articles shall not include any prior documents.

(2)   "Authorized shares" means the shares of all classes a domestic or foreign corporation is authorized to issue.

(3)   "Conspicuous" means so written that a reasonable person against whom the writing is to operate should have noticed it. For example, printing in italics or boldface or contrasting color, or typing in capitals or underlined, is conspicuous.

(4)   "Corporation," "domestic corporation" or "domestic business corporation" means a corporation for profit, which is not a foreign corporation, incorporated under or subject to the provisions of this Act.

(5)   "Deliver" or "delivery" means any method of delivery used in conventional commercial practice, including delivery by hand, mail, commercial delivery, and electronic transmission.

(6)   "Distribution" means a direct or indirect transfer of money or other property (except its own shares) or incurrence of indebtedness by a corporation to or for the benefit of its shareholders in respect of any of its shares. A distribution may be in the form of a declaration or payment of a dividend; a purchase, redemption, or other acquisition of shares; a distribution of indebtedness; or otherwise.

(6A)   "Domestic unincorporated entity" means an unincorporated entity whose internal affairs are governed by the laws of this state.

(7)   "Effective date of notice" is defined in section 1.41.

(7A)   "Electronic transmission" or "electronically transmitted" means any process of communication not directly involving the physical transfer of paper that is suitable for the retention, retrieval, and reproduction of information by the recipient.

(7B)   "Eligible entity" means a domestic or foreign unincorporated entity or a domestic or foreign nonprofit corporation.

(7C) "Eligible interests" means interests or memberships.

(8) "Employee" includes an officer but not a director. A director may accept duties that make him also an employee.

(9) "Entity" includes a domestic and foreign business corporation; domestic and foreign nonprofit corporation; estate; trust; domestic and foreign unincorporated entity; and state, United States, and foreign government.

(9A) The phrase "facts objectively ascertainable" outside of a filed document or plan is defined in section 1.20(k).

(9AA) "Expenses" means reasonable expenses of any kind that are incurred in connection with a matter.

(9B) "Filing entity" means an unincorporated entity that is created by filing a public organic document.

(10) "Foreign corporation" or "foreign business corporation" means a corporation incorporated under a law other than the law of this state, which would be a business corporation if incorporated under the laws of this state.

(10A) "Foreign nonprofit corporation" means a corporation incorporated under a law other than the law of this state, which would be a nonprofit corporation if incorporated under the laws of this state.

(10B) "Foreign unincorporated entity" means an unincorporated entity whose internal affairs are governed by an organic law of a jurisdiction other than this state.

(11) "Governmental subdivision" includes an authority, county, district, and municipality.

(12) "Includes" denotes a partial definition.

(13) "Individual" means a natural person.

(13A) "Interest" means either or both of the following rights under the organic law of an unincorporated entity:
  (i) the right to receive distributions from the entity either in the ordinary course or upon liquidation; or
  (ii) the right to receive notice or vote on issues involving its internal affairs, other than as an agent, assignee, proxy or person responsible for managing its business and affairs.

(13B) "Interest holder" means a person who holds of record an interest.

(14) "Means" denotes an exhaustive definition.

(14A) "Membership" means the rights of a member in a domestic or foreign nonprofit corporation.

(14B) "Nonfiling entity" means an unincorporated entity that is not created by filing a public organic document.

(14C) "Nonprofit corporation" or "domestic nonprofit corporation" means a corporation incorporated under the laws of this state and subject to the provisions of the [*Model Nonprofit Corporation Act*].

(15)   "Notice" is defined in section 1.41.

(15A) "Organic document" means a public organic document or a private organic document.

(15B) "Organic law" means the statute governing the internal affairs of a domestic or foreign business or nonprofit corporation or unincorporated entity.

(15C) "Owner liability" means personal liability for a debt, obligation or liability of a domestic or foreign business or nonprofit corporation or unincorporated entity that is imposed on a person:

   (i) solely by reason of the person's status as a shareholder, member or interest holder; or

   (ii) by the articles of incorporation, bylaws or an organic document pursuant to a provision of the organic law authorizing the articles of incorporation, bylaws or an organic document to make one or more specified shareholders, members or interest holders liable in their capacity as shareholders, members or interest holders for all or specified debts, obligations or liabilities of the entity.

(16)   "Person" includes an individual and an entity.

(17)   "Principal office" means the office (in or out of this state) so designated in the annual report where the principal executive offices of a domestic or foreign corporation are located.

(17A) "Private organic document" means any document (other than the public organic document, if any) that determines the internal governance of an unincorporated entity. Where a private organic document has been amended or restated, the term means the private organic document as last amended or restated.

(17B) "Public organic document" means the document, if any, that is filed of public record to create an unincorporated entity. Where a public organic document has been amended or restated, the term means the public organic document as last amended or restated.

(18)   "Proceeding" includes civil suit and criminal, administrative, and investigatory action.

(18A) "Public corporation" means a corporation that has shares listed on a national securities exchange or regularly traded in a market maintained by one or more members of a national or affiliated securities association.

(18B) "Qualified director" is defined in section 1.43.

(19)   "Record date" means the date established under chapter 6 or 7 on which a corporation determines the identity of its shareholders and their shareholdings for purposes of this Act. The determinations shall be made as of the close of business on the record date unless another time for doing so is specified when the record date is fixed.

(20) "Secretary" means the corporate officer to whom the board of directors has delegated responsibility under section 8.40(c) for custody of the minutes of the meetings of the board of directors and of the shareholders and for authenticating records of the corporation.

(21) "Shares" means the units into which the proprietary interests in a corporation are divided.

(22) "Shareholder" means the person in whose name shares are registered in the records of a corporation or the beneficial owner of shares to the extent of the rights granted by a nominee certificate on file with a corporation.

(22A) "Sign" or "signature" includes any manual, facsimile, conformed or electronic signature.

(23) "State," when referring to a part of the United States, includes a state and commonwealth (and their agencies and governmental subdivisions) and a territory and insular possession (and their agencies and governmental subdivisions) of the United States.

(24) "Subscriber" means a person who subscribes for shares in a corporation, whether before or after incorporation.

(24A) "Unincorporated entity" means an organization or artificial legal person that either has a separate legal existence or has the power to acquire an estate in real property in its own name and that is not any of the following: a domestic or foreign business or non-profit corporation, an estate, a trust, a state, the United States, or a foreign government. The term includes a general partnership, limited liability company, limited partnership, business trust, joint stock association and unincorporated nonprofit association.

(25) "United States" includes a district, authority, bureau, commission, department, and any other agency of the United States.

(26) "Voting group" means all shares of one or more classes or series that under the articles of incorporation or this Act are entitled to vote and be counted together collectively on a matter at a meeting of shareholders. All shares entitled by the articles of incorporation or this Act to vote generally on the matter are for that purpose a single voting group.

(27) "Voting power" means the current power to vote in the election of directors.

Official Comment ...

2. Corporation, Domestic Corporation, Domestic Business Corporation, Foreign Corporation and Foreign Business Corporation.

"Corporation," "domestic corporation," "domestic business corporation," "foreign corporation" and "foreign business corporation" are defined in sections 1.40(4) and (10). The word "corporation," when used alone, refers only to domestic corporations. In a few instances, the phrase "domestic corporation" has been used in order to contrast it with a foreign corporation. The phrase "domestic business corporation" has been used on occasion to contrast it with a domestic nonprofit corporation.

3. Distribution

The term "distribution" defined in section 1.40(6) is a fundamental element of the financial provisions of the Model Act as amended in 1980. Section 6.40 sets forth a single, unitary test for the validity of any "distribution." Section 1.40(6) in turn defines "distribution" to include all transfers of money or other property made by a corporation to any shareholder in respect of the corporation's shares, except mere changes in the unit of interest such as share dividends and share splits. Thus, a "distribution" includes the declaration or payment of a dividend, a purchase by a corporation of its own shares, a distribution of evidences of indebtedness or promissory notes of the corporation, and a distribution in voluntary or involuntary liquidation. If a corporation incurs indebtedness in connection with a distribution (as in the case of a distribution of a debt instrument or an installment purchase of shares), the creation, incurrence, or distribution of the indebtedness is the event which constitutes the distribution rather than the subsequent payment of the debt by the corporation.

The term "indirect" in the definition of "distribution" is intended to include transactions like the repurchase of parent company shares by a subsidiary whose actions are controlled by the parent. It also is intended to include any other transaction in which the substance is clearly the same as a typical dividend or share repurchase, no matter how structured or labeled.....

5. Entity

The term "entity," defined in section 1.40(9), appears in the definition of "person" in section 1.40(16) and is included to cover all types of artificial persons. Estates and trusts and general partnerships are included even though they may not, in some jurisdictions, be considered artificial persons. "Trust," by itself, means a non-business trust, such as a traditional testamentary or inter vivos trust.

The term "entity" is broader than the term "unincorporated entity" which is defined in section 1.40(24A). See also the definitions of "governmental subdivision" in section 1.40(11), "state" in section 1.40(23), and "United States" in section 1.40(25).

A form of co-ownership of property or sharing of returns from property that is not a partnership under the Uniform Partnership Act (1997) will not be an "unincorporated entity." In that connection,

Section 202(c) of the Uniform Partnership Act (1997) provides, among other things, that:

> In determining whether a partnership is formed, the following rules apply:
>
> (1) Joint tenancy, tenancy in common, tenancy by the entireties, joint property, common property, or part ownership does not by itself establish a partnership, even if the co-owners share profits made by the use of the property.
>
> (2) The sharing of gross returns does not by itself establish a partnership, even if the persons sharing them have a joint or common right or interest in property from which the returns are derived. . . .

5.2 Membership

"Membership" is defined in section 1.40(14A) for purposes of this Act to refer only to the rights of a member in a nonprofit corporation. Although the owners of a limited liability company are generally referred to as "members," for purposes of this Act they are referred to as "interest holders" and what they own in the limited liability company is referred to in this Act as an "interest."

5.3 Organic Documents, Public Organic Documents and Private Organic Documents

The term "organic documents" in section 1.40(15A) includes both public organic documents and private organic documents. The term "public organic document" includes such documents as the certificate of limited partnership of a limited partnership, the articles of organization or certificate of formation of a limited liability company, the deed of trust of a business trust and comparable documents, however denominated, that are publicly filed to create other types of unincorporated entities. An election of limited liability partnership status is not of itself a public organic document because it does not create the underlying general or limited partnership filing the election, although the election may be made part of the public organic document of the partnership by its organic law. The term "private organic document" includes such documents as a partnership agreement of a general or limited partnership, an operating agreement of a limited liability company and comparable documents, however denominated, of other types of unincorporated entities.

5.4 Owner Liability

The term "owner liability" is used in the context of provisions in Chapters 9 and 11 that preserve the personal liability of shareholders, members and interest holders when the entity in which they hold shares, memberships or interests is the subject of a transaction under those chapters. The term includes only liabilities that are imposed pursuant to statute on shareholders, members or interest holders. Liabilities that a shareholder, member or interest holder incurs by contract are not included. Thus, for example, if a state's business corporation law were to make shareholders personally liable for unpaid wages, that liability would be an "owner liability." If, on the other hand, a shareholder were to guarantee payment of an obligation of a corporation, that liability would not be an "owner liability." The reason for excluding contractual liabilities from the definition of "owner liability" is because those liabilities are constitutionally protected from impairment and thus do not need to be separately protected in Chapters 9 and 11.

5.5 Unincorporated Entity

The term "unincorporated entity" is a subset of the broader term "entity."

There is some question as to whether a partnership subject to the Uniform Partnership Act (1914) is an entity or merely an aggregation of its partners. That question has been resolved by Section 201 of the Uniform Partnership Act (1997), which makes clear that a general partnership is an entity with its own separate legal existence. Section 8 of the Uniform Partnership Act (1914) gives partnerships subject to it the power to acquire estates in real property and thus such a partnership will be an "unincorporated entity." As a result, all general partnerships will be "unincorporated entities" regardless of whether the state in which they are organized has adopted the new Uniform Partnership Act (1997).

The term "unincorporated entity" includes limited liability partnerships and limited liability limited partnerships because those entities are forms of general partnerships and limited partnerships, respectively, that have made the additional required election claiming that status.

Section 4 of the Uniform Unincorporated Nonprofit Association Act gives an unincorporated nonprofit association the power to acquire an estate in real property and thus an unincorporated nonprofit association organized in a state that has adopted that act will be an "unincorporated entity." At common law, an unincorporated nonprofit association was not a legal entity and did not have the power to acquire real property. Most states that have not adopted the Uniform Act have nonetheless modified the common law rule, but states that have not adopted the Uniform Act should analyze whether they should modify the definition of "unincorporated entity" to add an express reference to unincorporated nonprofit associations.

"Business trust" includes any trust carrying on a business, such as a Massachusetts trust, real estate investment trust, or other common law or statutory business trust. The term "unincorporated entity" expressly excludes estates and trusts (i.e., trusts that are not business trusts), whether or not they would be considered artificial persons under the governing jurisdiction's law, to make it clear that they are not eligible to participate in a conversion under subchapter E of chapter 9 or a merger or share exchange under chapter 11....

6.1. Public Corporation

The term "public corporation" defined in section 1.40(18A) is used in sections 7.32, 8.01, 14.31 and 14.34 to distinguish publicly held corporations from other corporations. The definition establishes that distinction by reference to the existence of an organized trading market in the corporation's shares as an indication of broad share ownership. The reference to markets comes from the securities law governing regulation of securities trading markets.

9. Voting Group

Section 1.40(26) defines "voting group" for purposes of the Act as a matter of convenient reference. A "voting group" consists of all shares of one or more classes or series that under the articles of incorporation or the revised Model Act are entitled to vote and be counted together collectively on a matter. Shares entitled to vote "generally" on a matter under the articles of incorporation or this Act are for that purpose a single voting group. The word "generally" signifies all shares entitled to vote on the matter by the articles of incorporation or this Act that do not expressly have the right to be counted or tabulated separately. "Voting groups" are thus the basic units of collective voting at a shareholders' meeting, and voting by voting groups may provide essential protection to one or more classes or series of shares against actions that are detrimental to the rights or interests of that class or series.

The determination of which shares form part of a single voting group must be made from the provisions of the articles of incorporation and of this Act. In a few instances under the Model Act, the board of directors may establish the right to vote by voting groups. On most matters coming before shareholders' meetings, only a single voting group, consisting of a class of voting or common shares, will be involved, and action on such a matter is effective when approved by that voting group pursuant to section 7.25. See section 7.26(a). If a second class of shares is also entitled to vote on the matter, then a further determination must be made as to whether that class is to vote as a separate voting group or whether it is to vote along with the other voting shares as part of a single voting group.

Members of the board of directors are usually elected by the single voting group of shares entitled to vote generally; in some circumstances, however, some members of the board may be selected by one voting group and other members by one or more different voting groups. See section 8.03.

The definition of a voting group permits the establishment by statute of quorum and voting requirements for a variety of matters considered at shareholders' meetings in corporations with multiple classes of shares. See sections 7.25 and 7.26. Depending on the circumstances, two classes or series of shares may vote together collectively on a matter as a single voting group, they may be entitled to vote on the matter separately as two voting groups, or one or both of them may not be entitled to vote on the matter at all.

12. Voting Power

Under section 1.40(27) the term "voting power" means the current power to vote in the election of directors. Application of this definition turns on whether the relevant shares carry the power to vote in the election of directors as of the time for voting on the relevant transaction. If shares carry the power to vote in the election of directors only under a certain contingency, as is often the case with preferred stock, the shares would not carry voting power within the meaning of section 1.40(27) unless the contingency has occurred, and only during the period when the voting rights are in effect. Shares that carry the power to vote for any directors as of the time to vote on the relevant transaction have the current power to vote in the election of directors within the meaning of section 1.40(27) even if the shares do not carry the power to vote for all directors.

§ 1.41 Notice

(a) Notice under this Act must be in writing unless oral notice is reasonable under the circumstances. Notice by electronic transmission is written notice.

(b) Notice may be communicated in person; by mail or other method of delivery; or by telephone, voice mail or other electronic means. If these forms of personal notice are impracticable, notice may be communicated by a newspaper of general circulation in the area where published, or by radio, television, or other form of public broadcast communication.

(c) Written notice by a domestic or foreign corporation to its shareholder, if in a comprehensible form, is effective (i) upon deposit in the United States mail, if mailed postpaid and correctly addressed to the shareholder's address shown in the corporation's current record of shareholders, or (ii) when electronically transmitted to the shareholder in a manner authorized by the shareholder.

(d) Written notice to a domestic or foreign corporation (authorized to transact business in this state) may be addressed to its registered agent at its registered office or to the secretary of the corporation at its principal office shown in its most recent annual report or, in the case of a foreign corporation that has not yet delivered an annual report, in its application for a certificate of authority.

(e) Except as provided in subsection (c), written notice, if in a comprehensible form, is effective at the earliest of the following:

    (1) when received;

    (2) five days after its deposit in the United States Mail if mailed postpaid and correctly addressed;

    (3) On the date shown on the return receipt, if sent by registered or certified mail, return receipt requested, and the receipt is signed by or on behalf of the addressee.

(f) Oral notice is effective when communicated if communicated in a comprehensible manner.

(g) If this Act prescribes notice requirements for particular circumstances, those requirements govern. If articles of incorporation or bylaws prescribe notice requirements, not inconsistent with this section or other provisions of this Act, those requirements govern.

§ 1.42 Number of Shareholders

(a) For purposes of this Act, the following identified as a shareholder in a corporation's current record of shareholders constitutes one shareholder:

    (1) three or fewer coowners;

    (2) a corporation, partnership, trust, estate, or other entity;

    (3) the trustees, guardians, custodians, or other fiduciaries of a single trust, estate, or account.

(b) For purposes of this Act, shareholdings registered in substantially similar names constitute one shareholder if it is reasonable to believe that the names represent the same person.

§ 1.43 Qualified Director

(a) A "qualified director" is a director who, at the time action is to be taken under:

    (1) section 7.44, does not have (i) a material interest in the outcome of the proceeding, or (ii) a material relationship with a person who has such an interest;

    (2) section 8.53 or 8.55, (i) is not a party to the proceeding, (ii) is not a director as to whom a transaction is a director's conflicting interest transaction or who sought a disclaimer of the corporation's interest in a business opportunity under section 8.70, which transaction or disclaimer is challenged in the proceeding, and (iii) does not have a material relationship with a director described in either clause (i) or clause (ii) of this subsection (a)(2);

(3) section 8.62, is not a director (i) as to whom the transaction is a director's conflicting interest transaction, or (ii) who has a material relationship with another director as to whom the transaction is a director's conflicting interest transaction; or

(4) section 8.70, would be a qualified director under subsection (a)(3) if the business opportunity were a director's conflicting interest transaction.

(b) For purposes of this section,

(1) "material relationship" means a familial, financial, professional, employment or other relationship that would reasonably be expected to impair the objectivity of the director's judgment when participating in the action to be taken; and

(2) "material interest" means an actual or potential benefit or detriment (other than one which would devolve on the corporation or the shareholders generally) that would reasonably be expected to impair the objectivity of the director's judgment when participating in the action to be taken.

(c) The presence of one or more of the following circumstances shall not automatically prevent a director from being a qualified director:

(1) nomination or election of the director to the current board by any director who is not a qualified director with respect to the matter (or by any person that has a material relationship with that director), acting alone or participating with others;

(2) service as a director of another corporation of which a director who is not a qualified director with respect to the matter (or any individual who has a material relationship with that director), is or was also a director; or

(3) with respect to action to be taken under section 7.44, status as a named defendant, as a director against whom action is demanded, or as a director who approved the conduct being challenged.

Official Comment

The definition of the term "qualified director" identifies those directors: (i) who may take action on the dismissal of a derivative proceeding (section 7.44); (ii) who are eligible to make, in the first instance, the authorization and determination required in connection with the decision on a request for advance for expenses (section 8.53(c)) or for indemnification (sections 8.55(b) and (c)); (iii) who may authorize a director's conflicting interest transactions (section 8.62); and (iv) who may disclaim the corporation's interest in a business opportunity (section 8.70(a)).

The judicial decisions that have examined the qualifications of directors for such purposes have generally required that directors be both *disinterested,* in the sense of not having exposure to an actual or potential benefit or detriment arising out of the action being taken (as opposed to an actual or potential benefit or detriment to the corporation or all shareholders generally), and *independent*, in the sense of having no personal or other relationship with an interested director (*e.g.*, a director who is a party to a transaction with the corporation) that presents a reasonable likelihood that the director's objectivity will be impaired. The "qualified director" concept embraces both of those requirements, and its application is situation-specific; that is, "qualified director" determinations will depend upon the directly relevant facts and circumstances, and the disqualification of a director to act arises from factors that would reasonably be expected to impair the objectivity of the director's judgment. On the other hand, the concept does not suggest that a "qualified director" has or should have special expertise to act on the matter in question.

1. Disqualification Due to Conflicting Interest

The "qualified director" concept prescribes significant disqualifications, depending upon the purpose for which a director might be considered eligible to participate in the action to be taken. In each context in which the definition applies, it excludes directors who should not be considered disinterested:

- In the case of action on dismissal of a derivative proceeding under section 7.44, the definition excludes directors who have a material interest in the outcome of the proceeding, such as where the proceeding involves a challenge to the validity of a transaction in which the director has a material financial interest. As defined in subsection (b)(2), a "material interest" in the outcome of the proceeding involves an actual or potential benefit (other than one that would devolve on the corporation of the shareholders generally) that would arise from dismissal of the proceeding and would reasonably be expected to impair the objectivity of the director's judgment in acting on dismissal of the proceeding.

- In the case of action to approve indemnification or advance of funds for expenses, the definition excludes directors who are parties to the proceeding (see section 8.50(6) for the definition of "party" and section 8.50(7) for the definition of "proceeding"). It also excludes a director who is not a party to the proceeding but as to whom a transaction is a director's conflicting interest transaction or who sought a disclaimer of the corporation's interest in a business opportunity, where that transaction or disclaimer is challenged in the proceeding.

- In the case of action to approve a director's conflicting interest transaction, the definition excludes any director whose interest, knowledge or status results in the transaction being treated as a "director's conflicting interest transaction." See section 8.60(1) for the definition of "director's conflicting interest transaction."

• Finally, in the case of action under section 8.70(a) to disclaim corporate interest in a business opportunity, the definition excludes any director who would not be considered a "qualified director" if the business opportunity were a "director's conflicting interest transaction."

Whether a director has a material interest in the outcome of a proceeding in which the director does not have a conflicting personal interest is heavily fact-dependent. Such cases lie along a spectrum. At one end of the spectrum, if a claim against a director is clearly frivolous or is not supported by particularized and well-pleaded facts, the director should not be deemed to have a "material interest in the outcome of the proceeding" within the meaning of subsection (a)(1), even though the director is named as a defendant. At the other end of the spectrum, a director normally should be deemed to have a "material interest in the outcome of the proceeding" within the meaning of subsection (a)(1) if a claim against the director is supported by particularized and well-pleaded facts which, if true, would be likely to give rise to a significant adverse outcome against the director. Whether a director should be deemed to have a "material interest in the outcome of the proceeding" based on a claim that lies between these two ends of the spectrum will depend on the application of that test to the claim, given all the facts and circumstances.

2. Disqualification Due to Relationships with Interested Persons

In each context in which the "qualified director" definition applies, it also excludes a director who has a "material relationship" with another director who is not disinterested for one or more of the reasons outlined in the preceding paragraph. Any relationship with such a director, whether the relationship is familial, financial, professional, employment or otherwise, is a "material relationship," as that term is defined in subsection (b)(1), where it would reasonably be expected to impair the objectivity of the director's judgment when voting or otherwise participating in action to be taken on a matter referred to in subsection (a). The determination of whether there is a "material relationship" should be based on the practicalities of the situation rather than on formalistic considerations. For example, a director employed by a corporation controlled by a director should be regarded as having an employment relationship with that director. On the other hand, a casual social acquaintance with another director should not be regarded as a disqualifying relationship. See *Beam ex rel. Martha Stewart Living Omnimedia, Inc. v. Stewart*, 845 A.2d 1040, 1050 (Del. 2004).

Although the term "qualified director" embraces the concept of independence, it does so only in relation to the director's interest or involvement in the specific situations to which the definition applies. Thus, the term "qualified director" is distinct from the generic term "independent director" used in section 8.01(c) of the Act to describe a director's general status. As a result, an "independent director" may in some circumstances not be a "qualified director," and vice versa. For example, in action being taken under section 8.70 concerning a business opportunity, an "independent" director who has a material interest in the business opportunity would not be a "qualified director" eligible to vote on the matter. Conversely, a director who does not have "independent" status may be a "qualified director" for purposes of voting on that action. See also the Official Comment to section 8.01(c).

3. Elimination of Automatic Disqualification in Certain Circumstances

Subsection (c) of the definition of "qualified director" addresses three categories of circumstances that, if present alone or together, do not automatically prevent a director from being a qualified director.

- Subsection (c)(1) makes it clear that the participation of non-qualified directors (or interested shareholders or other interested persons) in the nomination or election of a director does not automatically prevent the director so nominated or elected from being qualified. Special litigation committees acting upon the dismissal of derivative litigation often consist of directors elected (after the alleged wrongful acts) by directors named as defendants in the action. In other settings, directors who are seeking indemnification, or who are interested in a director's conflicting interest transaction, may have participated in the nomination or election of an individual director who is otherwise a "qualified director."

- Subsection (c)(2) provides, in a similar fashion, that the mere fact that an individual director is or was a director of another corporation—on the board of which a director who is not a "qualified director" also serves or has served—does not automatically prevent qualification to act.

- Subsection (c)(3) confirms a number of decisions, involving dismissal of derivative proceedings, in which the court rejected a disqualification claim predicated on the mere fact that a director had been named as a defendant, was an individual against whom action has been demanded, or had approved the action being challenged. These cases have held that, where a director's approval of the challenged action is at issue, approval does not automatically make the director ineligible to act. See *Aronson v. Lewis*, 473 A. 2d 805, 816 (Del. 1984); *Lewis v. Graves*, 701 F.2d 245 (2d Cir.1983). On the other hand, for example, director approval of a challenged transaction, in combination with other particularized facts showing that the director's ability to act objectively on a proposal to dismiss a derivative proceeding is impaired by a material conflicting personal interest in the transaction, disqualifies a director from acting on the proposal to dismiss the proceeding.

Where status as a qualified director is challenged in a litigation context, the court must assess the likelihood that an interest or relationship has impaired a director's objectivity, without the need for any presumption arising from the presence of one or more of the three specified circumstances. Thus, the effect of subsection (c) of the definition, while significant, is limited. It merely precludes an automatic inference of director disqualification from the circumstances specified in clauses (1), (2) and (3) of subsection (c).

§ 1.44 Householding

(a) A corporation has delivered written notice or any other report or statement under this Act, the articles of incorporation or the bylaws to all shareholders who share a common address if:

    (1) The corporation delivers one copy of the notice, report or statement to the common address;

    (2) The corporation addresses the notice, report or statement to those shareholders either as a group or to each of those shareholders individually or to the shareholders in a form to which each of those shareholders has consented; and

    (3) Each of those shareholders consents to delivery of a single copy of such notice, report or statement to the shareholders' common address. Any such consent shall be revocable by any of such shareholders who deliver written notice of revocation to the corporation. If such written notice of revocation is delivered, the corporation shall begin providing individual notices, reports or other statements to the revoking shareholder no later than 30 days after delivery of the written notice of revocation.

(b) Any shareholder who fails to object by written notice to the corporation, within 60 days of written notice by the corporation of its intention to send single copies of notices, reports or statements to shareholders who share a common address as permitted by subsection (a), shall be deemed to have consented to receiving such single copy at the common address.

Official Comment

The proxy rules under the Securities Exchange Act of 1934 permit publicly held corporations to meet their obligation to deliver proxy statements and annual reports to shareholders who share a common address by delivery of a single copy of such materials to the common address under certain conditions. See 17 C.F.R. § 240.14a–3(e). This practice is known as "householding." This section permits a corporation comparable flexibility to household the written notice of shareholder meetings as well as any other written notices, reports or statements required to be delivered to shareholders under the Act, the corporation's articles of incorporation or the corporation's bylaws. Ability to household such notices, reports or statements would not, of course, eliminate the practical necessity of delivering to a common address sufficient copies of any accompanying document requiring individual shareholder signature or other action, such as a proxy card or consent.

In order to meet the conditions of subsection (a), the written notice, report or statement must be delivered to the common address. Address means a street address, a post office box number, an electronic mail address, a facsimile telephone number or another similar destination to which paper or electronic transmission may be sent. The written notice, report or statement must also be addressed to the shareholders who share that address either as a group (*e.g.*, "ABC Corporation Shareholders," "Jane Doe and Household," or "the Smith Family") or to each of the shareholders individually (*e.g.*, "John Doe and Richard Jones"). Such shareholders must consent specifically to being addressed in any other way than as a group or individually. Finally, each shareholder at the common address must have consented to household delivery either affirmatively or implicitly by failure to object to the notice by the corporation permitted in subsection (b). Affirmative consent may be by any reasonable means of written or oral communication to the corporation or its agent. Implicit consent may only be given by means of the notice permitted in subsection (b).

Whether consent is explicit or implicit, it is revocable at any time by a shareholder by written notice delivered to the corporation. If such written notice of revocation is delivered, the corporation shall provide individual notices, reports or other statements to the revoking shareholder beginning no later than 30 days after delivery of the written revocation to the corporation.

In order to be effective, the written notice of intention to household notices, reports or other statements permitted by subsection (b) must explain that affirmative or implied consent may be revoked and the method for revoking.

Chapter 2

INCORPORATION

§ 2.01 Incorporators

One or more persons may act as the incorporator or incorporators of a corporation by delivering articles of incorporation to the secretary of state for filing.

§ 2.02 Articles of Incorporation

(a) The articles of incorporation must set forth:

    (1) a corporate name for the corporation that satisfies the requirements of section 4.01;

(2) the number of shares the corporation is authorized to issue;

(3) the street address of the corporation's initial registered office and the name of its initial registered agent at that office; and

(4) the name and address of each incorporator.

(b) The articles of incorporation may set forth:

(1) the names and addresses of the individuals who are to serve as the initial directors;

(2) provisions not inconsistent with law regarding:

    (i) the purpose or purposes for which the corporation is organized;

    (ii) managing the business and regulating the affairs of the corporation;

    (iii) defining, limiting, and regulating the powers of the corporation, its board of directors, and shareholders;

    (iv) a par value for authorized shares or classes of shares;

    (v) the imposition of personal liability on shareholders for the debts of the corporation to a specified extent and upon specified conditions;

(3) any provision that under this Act is required or permitted to be set forth in the bylaws;

(4) a provision eliminating or limiting the liability of a director to the corporation or its shareholders for money damages for any action taken, or any failure to take any action, as a director, except liability for (A) the amount of a financial benefit received by a director to which he is not entitled; (B) an intentional infliction of harm on the corporation or the shareholders; (C) a violation of section 8.33; or (D) an intentional violation of criminal law; and

(5) a provision permitting or making obligatory indemnification of a director for liability (as defined in section 8.50(5)) to any person for any action taken, or any failure to take any action, as a director, except liability for (A) receipt of a financial benefit to which he is not entitled, (B) an intentional infliction of harm on the corporation or its shareholders, (C) a violation of section 8.33, or (D) an intentional violation of criminal law.

(c) The articles of incorporation need not set forth any of the corporate powers enumerated in this Act.

(d) Provisions of the articles of incorporation may be made dependent upon facts objectively ascertainable outside the articles of incorporation in accordance with section 1.20(k).

Official Comment

1. Introduction

Section 2.02(a) sets forth the minimum mandatory requirements for all articles of incorporation while section 2.02(b) describes optional provisions that may be included. A corporation that is formed solely pursuant to the mandatory requirements will generally have the broadest powers and least restrictions on activities permitted by the Model Act. The Model Act thus permits the creation of a "standard" corporation by a simple and easily prepared one-page document.

No reference is made in section 2.02(a) either to the period of duration of the corporation or to its purposes. A corporation formed under these provisions will automatically have perpetual duration under section 3.02(1) unless a special provision is included providing a shorter period. Similarly, a corporation formed without reference to a purpose clause will automatically have the purpose of engaging in any lawful business under section 3.01(a). The option of providing a narrower purpose clause is also preserved in sections 2.02(b)(2) and 3.01, with the effect described in the Official Comment to section 3.01....

2. Optional Provisions ...

e. *Shareholder liability*

The basic tenet of modern corporation law is that shareholders are not liable for the corporation's debts by reason of their status as shareholders. Section 2.02(b)(2)(v) nevertheless permits a corporation to impose that liability under specified circumstances if that is desirable. If no provision of this type is included shareholders have no liability for corporate debts except to the extent they become liable by reason of their own conduct or acts. See section 6.22(b). ...

i. *Director liability*

Section 2.02(b)(4) authorizes the inclusion of a provision in the articles of incorporation eliminating or limiting, with certain exceptions, the liability of the directors to the corporation or its shareholders for money damages. This grant of authority to the shareholders is consistent with the more general authorization of section 2.02(b)(2) for the articles to include a wide range of provisions regulating various matters affecting the corporation, including allocating power between the directors and the shareholders. Developments in the mid- and late 1980s highlighted the need to permit reasonable protection of directors from exposure to personal liability, in addition to indemnification, so that directors would not be discouraged from fully and freely carrying out their duties, including responsible entrepreneurial risk-taking. These developments included increased costs and reduced availability of director and officer liability insurance, the decision of the Delaware

Supreme Court in Smith v. Van Gorkom, 488 A.2d 858 (1985), and the resulting reluctance of qualified individuals to serve as directors.

... [S]ection 2.02(b)(4) is optional rather than self-executing. In addition, it follows the path of virtually all the states that have adopted charter option statutes and is applicable only to money damages and not to equitable relief. Likewise, nothing in section 2.02(b)(4) in any way affects the right of the shareholders to remove directors, under section 8.08(a), with or without cause.

The language "any action taken, or any failure to take any action, as a director" parallels section 8.30(d). It is recognized that in the case of individuals who are both directors and officers it will often not be clear in which capacity the individual is acting. The phrase "as a director" emphasizes that section 2.02(b)(4) applies to a director's actions or failures to take action in his capacity as a director and not in any other capacity, such as officer, employee, or controlling shareholder. However, it is not intended to exclude coverage of conduct by individuals, even though they are officers, when they are acting in their capacity as directors.

§ 2.03 Incorporation

(a) Unless a delayed effective date is specified, the corporate existence begins when the articles of incorporation are filed.

(b) The secretary of state's filing of the articles of incorporation is conclusive proof that the incorporators satisfied all conditions precedent to incorporation except in a proceeding by the state to cancel or revoke the incorporation or involuntarily dissolve the corporation.

Official Comment

5. Conclusiveness of Secretary of State's Action on Question of Individual Liability for Corporate Actions

Under section 2.03(b) the filing of the articles of incorporation as evidenced by return of the stamped copy of the articles with the fee receipt is conclusive proof that all conditions precedent to incorporation have been met, except in proceedings brought by the state. Thus the filing of the articles of incorporation is conclusive as to the existence of limited liability for persons who enter into transactions on behalf of the corporation. If articles of incorporation have not been filed, section 2.04 generally imposes personal liability on all persons who prematurely act as or on behalf of a "corporation" knowing that articles have not been filed. Section 2.04 may protect some of these persons to a limited extent, however; see the Official Comment to that section.

§ 2.04 Liability for Preincorporation Transactions

All persons purporting to act as or on behalf of a corporation, knowing there was no incorporation under this Act, are jointly and severally liable for all liabilities created while so acting.

Official Comment

Earlier versions of the Model Act, and the statutes of many states, have long provided that corporate existence begins only with the acceptance of articles of incorporation by the secretary of state. Many states also have statutes that provide expressly that those who prematurely act as or on behalf of a corporation are personally liable on all transactions entered into or liabilities incurred before incorporation. A review of recent case law indicates, however, that even in states with such statutes courts have continued to rely on common law concepts of de facto corporations, de jure corporations, and corporations by estoppel that provide uncertain protection against liability for preincorporation transactions. These cases caused a review of the underlying policies represented in earlier versions of the Model Act and the adoption of a slightly more flexible or relaxed standard.

Incorporation under modern statutes is so simple and inexpensive that a strong argument may be made that nothing short of filing articles of incorporation should create the privilege of limited liability. A number of situations have arisen, however, in which the protection of limited liability arguably should be recognized even though the simple incorporation process established by modern statutes has not been completed.

(1) The strongest factual pattern for immunizing participants from personal liability occurs in cases in which the participant honestly and reasonably but erroneously believed the articles had been filed. In Cranson v. International Business Machines Corp., 234 Md. 477, 200 A.2d 33 (1964), for example, the defendant had been shown executed articles of incorporation some months earlier before he invested in the corporation and became an officer and director. He was also told by the corporation's attorney that the articles had been filed, but in fact they had not been filed because of a mix-up in the attorney's office. The defendant was held not liable on the "corporate" obligation.

(2) Another class of cases, which is less compelling but in which the participants sometimes have escaped personal liability, involves the defendant who mails in articles of incorporation and then enters into a transaction in the corporate name; the letter is either delayed or the secretary of state's office refuses to file the articles after receiving them or returns them for correction. E.g., Cantor v. Sunshine Greenery, Inc., 165 N.J.Super. 411, 398 A.2d 571 (1979). Many state filing agencies adopt the practice of treating the date of receipt as the date of issuance of the certificate even though delays and the review process may result in the certificate being backdated. The finding of nonliability in cases of this second type can be considered an extension of this principle by treating the date of original mailing or original filing as the date of incorporation.

(3) A third class of cases in which the participants sometimes have escaped personal liability involves situations where the third person has urged immediate execution of the contract in the corporate name even though he knows that the other party has not taken any steps toward incorporating. E.g., Quaker Hill v. Parr, 148 Colo. 45, 364 P.2d 1056 (1961).

(4) In another class of cases the defendant has represented that a corporation exists and entered into a contract in the corporate name when he knows that no corporation has been formed, either because no attempt has been made to file articles of incorporation or because he has already received rejected articles of incorporation from the filing agency. In these cases, the third person has dealt solely with the "corporation" and has not relied on the personal assets of the defendant. The imposition of personal liability in this class of case, it has sometimes been argued, gives the plaintiff more than he originally bargained for. On the other hand, to recognize limited liability in this situation threatens to undermine the incorporation process, since one then may obtain limited liability by consistently conducting business in the corporate name. Most courts have imposed personal liability in this situation. E.g., Robertson v. Levy, 197 A.2d 443 (D.C.App.1964).

(5) A final class of cases involves inactive investors who provide funds to a promoter with the instruction, "Don't start doing business until you incorporate." After the promoter does start business without incorporating, attempts have been made, sometimes unsuccessfully, to hold the investors liable as partners. E.g., Frontier Refining Co. v. Kunkels, Inc., 407 P.2d 880 (Wyo.1965). One case held that the language of section 146 of the 1969 Model Act ["*persons who assume to act* as a corporation are liable for preincorporation transactions"] creates a distinction between active and inactive participants, makes only the former liable as partners, and therefore relieves the latter of personal liability. Nevertheless, "active" participation was defined to include all investors who actively participate in the policy and operational decisions of the organization and is, therefore, a larger group than merely the persons who incurred the obligation in question on behalf of the "corporation." Timberline Equipment Co. v. Davenport, 267 Or. 64, 72–76, 514 P.2d 1109, 1113–14 (1973).

After a review of these situations, it seemed appropriate to impose liability only on persons who act as or on behalf of corporations "knowing" that no corporation exists. Analogous protection has long been accorded under the uniform limited partnership acts to limited partners who contribute capital to a partnership in the erroneous belief that a limited partnership certificate has been filed. Uniform Limited Partnership Act § 12 (1916); Revised Uniform Limited Partnership Act § 3.04 (1976). Persons protected under § 3.04 of the latter are persons who "erroneously but in good faith" believe that a limited partnership certificate has been filed. The language of section 2.04 has essentially the same meaning.

While no special provision is made in section 2.04, the section does not foreclose the possibility that persons who urge defendants to execute contracts in the corporate name knowing that no steps to incorporate have been taken may be estopped to impose personal liability on individual defendants. This estoppel may be based on the inequity perceived when persons, unwilling or reluctant to enter into a commitment under their own name, are persuaded to use the name of a nonexistent corporation, and then are sought to be held personally liable under section 2.04 by the party advocating that form of execution. By contrast, persons who knowingly participate in a business under a corporate name are jointly and severally liable on "corporate" obligations under section 2.04 and may not argue that plaintiffs are "estopped" from holding them personally liable because all transactions were conducted on a corporate basis.

§ 2.05   Organization of Corporation

(a) After incorporation:

   (1) if initial directors are named in the articles of incorporation, the initial directors shall hold an organizational meeting, at the call of a majority of the directors, to complete the organization of the corporation by appointing officers, adopting bylaws, and carrying on any other business brought before the meeting;

   (2) if initial directors are not named in the articles, the incorporator or incorporators shall hold an organizational meeting at the call of a majority of the incorporators:

   (i)   to elect directors and complete the organization of the corporation; or

   (ii)   to elect a board of directors who shall complete the organization of the corporation.

(b) Action required or permitted by this Act to be taken by incorporators at an organizational meeting may be taken without a meeting if the action taken is evidenced by one or more written consents describing the action taken and signed by each incorporator.

(c) An organizational meeting may be held in or out of this state.

§ 2.06   Bylaws

(a) The incorporators or board of directors of a corporation shall adopt initial bylaws for the corporation.

(b) The bylaws of a corporation may contain any provision for managing the business and regulating the affairs of the corporation that is not inconsistent with law or the articles of incorporation.

Chapter 3

PURPOSES AND POWERS

§ 3.01 Purposes

(a) Every corporation incorporated under this Act has the purpose of engaging in any lawful business unless a more limited purpose is set forth in the articles of incorporation.

(b) A corporation engaging in a business that is subject to regulation under another statute of this state may incorporate under this Act only if permitted by, and subject to all limitations of, the other statute.

§ 3.02 General Powers

Unless its articles of incorporation provide otherwise, every corporation has perpetual duration and succession in its corporate name and has the same powers as an individual to do all things necessary or convenient to carry out its business and affairs, including without limitation power:

(1) to sue and be sued, complain and defend in its corporate name;

(2) to have a corporate seal, which may be altered at will, and to use it, or a facsimile of it, by impressing or affixing it or in any other manner reproducing it;

(3) to make and amend bylaws, not inconsistent with its articles of incorporation or with the laws of this state, for managing the business and regulating the affairs of the corporation;

(4) to purchase, receive, lease, or otherwise acquire, and own, hold, improve, use, and otherwise deal with, real or personal property, or any legal or equitable interest in property, wherever located;

(5) to sell, convey, mortgage, pledge, lease, exchange, and otherwise dispose of all or any part of its property;

(6) to purchase, receive, subscribe for, or otherwise acquire; own, hold, vote, use, sell, mortgage, lend, pledge, or otherwise dispose of; and deal in and with shares or other interests in, or obligations of, any other entity;

(7) to make contracts and guarantees, incur liabilities, borrow money, issue its notes, bonds, and other obligations (which may be convertible into or include the option to purchase other securities of the corporation), and secure any of its obligations by mortgage or pledge of any of its property, franchises, or income;

(8) to lend money, invest and reinvest its funds, and receive and hold real and personal property as security for repayment;

(9) to be a promoter, partner, member, associate, or manager of any partnership, joint venture, trust, or other entity;

(10) to conduct its business, locate offices, and exercise the powers granted by this Act within or without this state;

(11) to elect directors and appoint officers, employees, and agents of the corporation, define their duties, fix their compensation, and lend them money and credit;

(12) to pay pensions and establish pension plans, pension trusts, profit sharing plans, share bonus plans, share option plans, and benefit or incentive plans for any or all of its current or former directors, officers, employees, and agents;

(13) to make donations for the public welfare or for charitable, scientific, or educational purposes;

(14) to transact any lawful business that will aid governmental policy;

(15) to make payments or donations, or do any other act, not inconsistent with law, that furthers the business and affairs of the corporation.

Official Comment

Section 3.02(15) permits payments or donations or other acts "that further the business and affairs of the corporation." This clause, which is in addition to and independent of the power to make charitable and similar donations under section 3.02(13), permits contributions for purposes that may not be charitable, such as for political purposes or to influence elections. This power exists only to the extent consistent with law other than the Model Act. It is the purpose of this section to authorize all corporate actions that are lawful or not against public policy....

§ 3.04   Ultra Vires

(a) Except as provided in subsection (b), the validity of corporate action may not be challenged on the ground that the corporation lacks or lacked power to act.

(b) A corporation's power to act may be challenged:

   (1) in a proceeding by a shareholder against the corporation to enjoin the act;

   (2) in a proceeding by the corporation, directly, derivatively, or through a receiver, trustee, or other legal representative, against an incumbent or former director, officer, employee, or agent of the corporation; or

   (3) in a proceeding by the Attorney General under section 14.30.

(c) In a shareholder's proceeding under subsection (b)(1) to enjoin an unauthorized corporate act, the court may enjoin or set aside the act, if equitable and if all affected persons are parties to the proceeding, and may award damages for loss (other than anticipated profits) suffered by the corporation or another party because of enjoining the unauthorized act.

Official Comment

The basic purpose of section 3.04—as has been the purpose of all similar statutes during the 20th century—is to eliminate all vestiges of the doctrine of inherent incapacity of corporations. ... Under this section it is unnecessary for persons dealing with a corporation to inquire into limitations on its purposes or powers that may appear in its articles of incorporation. A person who is unaware of these limitations when dealing with the corporation is not bound by them. The phrase in section 3.04(a) that the "validity of corporate action may not be challenged on the ground that the corporation lacks or lacked power to act" applies equally to the use of the doctrine as a sword or as a shield: a third person may no more avoid an undesired contract with a corporation on the ground the corporation was without authority to make the contract than a corporation may defend a suit on a contract on the ground that the contract is ultra vires.

The language of section 3.04 extends beyond contracts and conveyances of property; "corporate action" of any kind cannot be challenged on the ground of ultra vires. For this reason it makes no difference whether a limitation in articles of incorporation is considered to be a limitation on a purpose or a limitation on a power; both are equally subject to section 3.04. Corporate action also includes inaction or refusal to act. The common law of ultra vires distinguished between executory contracts, partially executed contracts, and fully executed ones; section 3.04 treats all corporate action the same—except to the extent described in section 3.04(b)—and the same rules apply to all contracts no matter at what stage of performance.

Section 3.04, however, does not validate corporate conduct that is made illegal or unlawful by statute or common law decision. This conduct is subject to whatever sanction, criminal or civil, that is provided by the statute or decision. Whether or not illegal corporate conduct is voidable or rescindable depends on the applicable statute or substantive law and is not affected by section 3.04. ...

... [Under subsection (c)] an ultra vires act may be enjoined only if all "affected parties" are parties to the suit. The requirement that the action be "equitable" generally means that only third persons dealing with a corporation while specifically aware that the corporation's action was ultra vires will be enjoined. The general phrase "if equitable" was retained because of the possibility that other circumstances may exist in which it may be equitable to refuse to enforce an ultra vires contract. ...

Chapter 4

NAME

§ 4.01 Corporate Name

(a) A corporate name:

(1) must contain the word "corporation," "incorporated," "company," or "limited," or the abbreviation "corp.," "inc.," "co.," or "ltd.," or words or abbreviations of like import in another language; and

(2) may not contain language stating or implying that the corporation is organized for a purpose other than that permitted by section 3.01 and its articles of incorporation....

Chapter 5

OFFICE AND AGENT

§ 5.01 Registered Office and Registered Agent

Each corporation must continuously maintain in this state:

(1) a registered office that may be the same as any of its places of business; and

(2) a registered agent, who may be:

   (i) an individual who resides in this state and whose business office is identical with the registered office;

   (ii) a domestic corporation or not-for-profit domestic corporation whose business office is identical with the registered office; or

   (iii) a foreign corporation or not-for-profit foreign corporation authorized to transact business in this state whose business office is identical with the registered office.

Chapter 6

SHARES AND DISTRIBUTIONS

Subchapter A

Shares

§ 6.01 Authorized Shares

(a) The articles of incorporation must set forth any classes of shares and series of shares within a class, and the number of shares of each class and series, that the corporation is authorized to issue. If more than one class or series of shares is authorized, the articles of incorporation must prescribe a distinguishing designation for each class or series and must describe, prior to the issuance of shares of a class or series, the terms, including the preferences, rights, and limitations, of that class or series. Except to the extent varied as permitted by this section, all shares of a class or series must have terms, including preferences, rights and limitations, that are identical with those of other shares of the same class or series.

(b) The articles of incorporation must authorize:

   (1) one or more classes or series of shares that together have unlimited voting rights, and

   (2) one or more classes or series of shares (which may be the same class or classes as those with voting rights) that together are entitled to receive the net assets of the corporation upon dissolution.

(c) The articles of incorporation may authorize one or more classes or series of shares that:

   (1) have special, conditional, or limited voting rights, or no right to vote, except to the extent otherwise provided by this Act;

   (2) are redeemable or convertible as specified in the articles of incorporation:

      (i) at the option of the corporation, the shareholder, or another person or upon the occurrence of a specified event;

      (ii) for cash, indebtedness, securities, or other property; and

      (iii) at prices and in amounts specified, or determined in accordance with a formula;

   (3) entitle the holders to distributions calculated in any manner, including dividends that may be cumulative, noncumulative, or partially cumulative; or

   (4) have preference over any other class or series of shares with respect to distributions, including distributions upon the dissolution of the corporation.

(d) Terms of shares may be made dependent upon facts objectively ascertainable outside the articles of incorporation in accordance with section 1.20(k).

(e) Any of the terms of shares may vary among holders of the same class or series so long as such variations are expressly set forth in the articles of incorporation.

(f) The description of the preferences, rights and limitations of classes or series of shares in subsection (c) is not exhaustive.

Official Comment

Section 6.01 adopts a new terminology from that traditionally used in corporation statutes to describe classes and series of shares that may be created, but makes only limited substantive changes from earlier versions of the Model Act. Traditional corporation statutes work from a perceived inheritance of concepts of "common shares" and "preferred shares" that at one time may have had considerable meaning but that today often do not involve significant distinctions. It is possible under modern corporation statutes to create classes of "common" shares that have important preferential rights and classes of "preferred" shares that are subordinate in all important economic aspects or that are indistinguishable from common shares in either voting rights or entitlement to participate in the assets of the corporation upon dissolution. The Model Act breaks away from the inherited concepts of "common" and "preferred" shares and develops more general language to reflect the actual flexibility in the creation of classes and series of shares that exists in modern corporate practice.

1. Section 6.01(a)

Section 6.01(a) requires that the articles of incorporation prescribe the classes and series of shares and the number of shares of each class and series that the corporation is authorized to issue. If the articles authorize the issue of only one class of shares, no designation or description of the shares is required, it being understood that these shares have both the power to vote and the power to receive the net assets of the corporation upon dissolution. See section 6.01(b). Shares with both of these characteristics are usually referred to as "common shares" or "common stock," but no specific designation is required by the Model Act. The articles of incorporation may set forth the number of shares authorized and permit the board of directors under section 6.02 to allocate the authorized shares among designated classes or series of shares.

If more than one class or series of shares is authorized, the terms, including the preferences, rights and limitations, of each class or series of shares must be described in the articles of incorporation before any shares of that class or series are issued, or the board of directors may be given authority to establish them under section 6.02. These descriptions constitute the "contract" of the holders of those classes and series of shares with respect to their interest in the corporation and must be set forth in sufficient detail reasonably to define their interest. The terms, including the preferences, rights and limitations, of shares with one or more special or preferential rights which may be authorized are further described in section 6.01(c).

If more than one class or series is authorized (or if only one class or series is originally authorized but at some future time one or more other classes or series of shares are added by amendment), the terms, including the preferences, rights and limitations of each class, classes or series of shares, including the class, classes or series that possess the fundamental characteristics of voting and residual equity financial interests, must be described before shares of those classes or series are issued. If both fundamental characteristics are placed exclusively in a single class of shares, that class may be described simply as "common shares" or by statements such as the "shares have the general distribution and voting rights," the "shares have all the rights of common shares," or the "shares have all rights not granted to the class A shares."

If the articles of incorporation create classes or series of shares that divide these fundamental rights among two or more classes or series of shares, it is necessary that the rights be clearly allocated among the classes and series. Specificity is required only to the extent necessary to differentiate the relative rights of the respective classes and series. For example, where one class or series has a liquidation preference over another, it is necessary to specify only the preferential liquidation right of that class or series; in the absence of a contrary provision in the articles, the remaining class or series would be entitled to receive the net assets remaining after the liquidation preference has been satisfied.

More than one class or series of shares may be designated as "common shares"; however, each must have a "distinguishing designation" under section 6.01(a), e.g., "nonvoting common shares" or "class A common shares", and the rights of the classes and series must be described. For example, if a corporation authorizes two classes of shares with equal rights to share in all distributions and with identical voting rights except that one class is entitled exclusively to elect one director and the second class is entitled exclusively to elect a second director, the two classes may be designated, e.g., as "Class A common" and "Class B common." What is required is language that makes the allocation of these rights clear.

Rather than describing the terms of each class or series of shares in the articles of incorporation, the corporation may delegate to the board of directors under section 6.02 the power to establish the terms of a class of shares (or of series within a class of shares) if no shares of that class or series have previously been issued. Those terms, however, must be set forth in an amendment to the articles of incorporation that is effective before the shares are issued.

2. Section 6.01(b)

Section 6.01(b) requires that every corporation authorize one or more classes or series of shares that have the two fundamental characteristics of unlimited voting rights and the right to receive the net assets of the corporation upon its dissolution. These two fundamental characteristics need not be placed in a single class or series of shares but may be divided as desired. It is nevertheless essential that the corporation always have authorized shares with these two characteristics, and section 6.03 requires that shares having in the aggregate these characteristics always be outstanding.

Section 6.01(b) ensures that there is always in existence one or more classes or series of shares which share in the ultimate residual interest in the corporation and which are entitled to elect a board of directors and make other fundamental decisions with respect to the corporation.

3.   Section 6.01(c)

Section 6.01(c) lists the principal features that are customarily incorporated into classes or series of shares. Section 6.01(f) makes clear that this listing is not exhaustive.

a.   In general

Section 6.01(c) authorizes creation of classes or series of shares with a virtually unlimited range of preferences, rights and limitations. In earlier versions of the Model Act and in the statutes of many states, certain types of rights or privileges were not permitted. Many such statutes, for example, prohibited the creation of a class of voting shares without preferential financial rights that is callable at the discretion of the corporation ("callable common shares"). Another common prohibition was against shares that have the power to be converted at the option of the shareholder into other classes of shares that have preferential financial rights, or into debt securities of the corporation ("upstream" conversion privileges). For the reasons set forth below, these restrictions are not preserved in the Model Act.

b.   Voting of shares

Any class or series of shares may be granted multiple or fractional votes per share without limitation. See section 7.21. Shares of any class or series may also be made nonvoting "except to the extent otherwise provided by this Act." This "except" clause refers to the provisions in the Model Act that permit shares that are designated to be nonvoting to vote as separate voting groups on amendments to articles of incorporation and other organic changes in the corporation that directly affect that class (sections 7.26 and 10.04). In addition, shares may be given voting rights that are limited or conditional (e.g., on the passing of a specified number of dividends). Section 6.01(b), however, requires that there always be one or more classes or series of shares that together have unlimited voting rights.

c.   Redemption of shares

Section 6.01(c)(2) permits classes or series of shares to be made redeemable on the terms set forth in the articles of incorporation. Under this section, shares may be made "redeemable" at the option of the holder, the corporation, or another person; shares redeemable at the option of the corporation are sometimes called "callable shares," while shares redeemable at the option of the shareholder are sometimes described as involving a "put". The Model Act permits either type of redemption for any class or series of shares and thereby permits the creation of redeemable or callable shares without limitation (subject only to the provisions that the class, classes or series of shares described in section 6.01(b) must always exist and that at least one share of each class or series with those rights must be outstanding under section 6.03).

Earlier versions of the Model Act and the statutes of many states contained a direct or indirect prohibition against callable voting shares or callable common shares. Even where such a prohibition exists, however, the same effect can be obtained by the use of consensual share transfer restrictions (see section 6.27). If it is possible to create what is essentially a callable voting share by agreement, there is no reason why such provisions should not be built directly and publicly into the capital structure of the corporation if that is desired.

The recognition of a redemption that is a "put" exercisable by the holders of the shares (or a third person such as holders of other classes of shares) is also new to the Model Act and is not permitted in many states. However, consensual share transfer restrictions may create a right that is indistinguishable from such a right of redemption, and a right of redemption is expressly recognized by many states in connection with certain specialized types of corporations such as open-end investment companies. As described below, if a right of redemption is recognized, prohibitions in earlier versions of the Model Act and many state statutes against "upstream" conversions serve no purpose.

The prices to be paid upon the redemption of shares under section 6.01(c)(2) and the amounts to be redeemed may be fixed in the articles of incorporation or "determined in accordance with a formula." The formula could be self contained, or, pursuant to the provisions of Section 6.01(d), could be determined by reference to extrinsic data or events. This is intended to permit the redemption price and the amounts to be redeemed to be established on the basis of matters external to the corporation, such as the purchase price of other shares, the level of the prime rate, the effective interest rate at which the corporation may obtain short or long-term financing, the consumer price index or a designated currency ratio.

All redemptions of shares are subject to the restrictions on distributions set forth in section 6.40. See section 6.03(b).

d.   Convertibility of shares

Section 6.01(c)(2) also permits shares of any class or series to be made convertible into shares of any other class or series or into cash, indebtedness, securities, or other property of the corporation or another person.

As described above, earlier versions of the Model Act and the statutes of many states prohibited so-called "upstream" conversions, that is, shares convertible into debt securities or into a class of shares having prior or superior preference rights. This restriction was eliminated from the Model Act since it was recognized that the power to make shares redeemable at the option of the shareholder for cash (see section 6.01(c)(2)(ii)) should logically permit the shares to be redeemable or convertible at the option of the shareholder into other shares with senior preferential rights. Creditors of the corporation and holders of shares with preferential rights are less seriously affected by a conversion of shares into debt or into shares with preferential rights than they would be by the redemption of the shares for money, which is permitted by the Model Act, subject to the limitations of section 6.40. Shares made "redeemable" for debt under section 6.01(c)(2)(ii), achieve the same effect as a right to "convert" shares into debt securities. The authorization by the board of directors of the issuance of shares of one class or series convertible into shares of another class or series constitutes authorization of the issuance of the latter shares.

e. Extrinsic Facts

Subsection 6.01(d) permits the creation of classes of shares or series with terms that are dependent upon facts objectively ascertainable outside the articles of incorporation. See Section 1.20 and the related Official Comment for an explanation of the meaning of the phrase "facts objectively ascertainable" and the requirement for the filing of articles of amendment under the circumstances set forth in that section. Terms that depend upon reference to extrinsic facts may include dividend rates that vary according to some external index or event. Because such "variable rate" stock would be intended to respond to current market conditions, it is most often employed with "blank check" stock having terms set by the board of directors immediately before issuance. See the Official Comment to Section 6.02. Note that Section 6.21 requires the board to determine the adequacy of consideration received or to be received by the corporation before issuing shares. If shares with terms to be determined by reference to extrinsic facts are to be authorized for issuance, the board should take care to establish appropriately defined parameters for such terms in order to discharge its duties under Section 6.21.

f. Variation among holders.

Subsection 6.01(e) permits the creation of classes of shares or series with terms that may vary among holders of the same class or series of shares so long as such variations are expressly set forth in the articles of incorporation. An example of the authority to vary terms among holders would be a provision that shares held by a bank or bank holding company in excess of a certain percentage would not have voting rights.

g. Nonexclusivity.

Section 6.01(f) also recognizes that the description of the preferences, rights and limitations of classes or series of shares in subsection 6.01(c) is not exhaustive.

4. Examples of Classes or Series of Shares Permitted by Section 6.01

Section 6.01 authorizes the creation of new or innovative classes or series of shares without limitation or restriction. The section is basically enabling rather than restrictive since corporations often find it necessary to create new and innovative classes or series of shares for a variety of reasons, and with the disclosure of the terms of the new classes and series in the articles of incorporation that are a matter of public record there is no reason to restrict the power to create these classes and series. Innovative classes or series of shares may be created in connection with raising debt or equity capital.

Securities with novel provisions are often created to meet perceived corporate needs in specific circumstances or because of financial problems generated by market conditions for capital. Classes or series of shares may also be created in order to effectuate desired control relationships among the participants in a venture. Classes or series of shares are likely to be used for this purpose in closely held corporations, whether or not statutory close corporation status is elected, but may also be used for this purpose by publicly held corporations.

Examples of such classes and series of shares are the following:

(1) Shares of one class or series may be authorized to elect a specified number of directors while shares of a second class or series may be authorized to elect the same or a different number of directors.

(2) Shares of one class or series may be entitled to vote as a separate voting group on certain transactions, but shares of two or more classes or series may be only entitled to vote together as a single voting group on the election of directors and other matters.

(3) Shares of one class or series may be nonvoting or may be given multiple or fractional votes per share.

(4) Shares of one class or series may be entitled to different dividend rights or rights on dissolution than shares of another class or series.

These examples are intended to be illustrative only and not to exhaust the variations permissible under the Model Act.

A corporation has power to issue debt securities under section 3.02(7). Although 6.01 authorizes the creation of interests that usually will be classed as "equity" rather than "debt", it is permissible to create classes or series of securities under section 6.01 that have some of the characteristics of debt securities. These securities are often referred to as "hybrid securities".

Section 6.01 of the Model Act does not limit the development of hybrid securities, and equity securities may be created under the Model Act that embody any characteristics of debt that may be desired. Unlike some state statutes, however, the Model Act restricts the power to vote to securities classed as "shares" in the articles of incorporation.

§ 6.02 Terms of Class or Series Determined by Board of Directors

(a) If the articles of incorporation so provide, the board of directors is authorized, without shareholder approval, to:

    (1) classify any unissued shares into one or more classes or into one or more series within a class,

    (2) reclassify any unissued shares of any class into one or more classes or into one or more series within one or more classes, or

    (3) reclassify any unissued shares of any series of any class into one or more classes or into one or more series within a class.

(b) If the board of directors acts pursuant to subsection (a), it must determine the terms, including the preferences, rights and limitations, to the same extent permitted under section 6.01, of:

    (1) any class of shares before the issuance of any shares of that class, or

    (2) any series within a class before the issuance of any shares of that series.

(c) Before issuing any shares of a class or series created under this section, the corporation must deliver to the secretary of state for filing articles of amendment setting forth the terms determined under subsection (a).

Official Comment

Section 6.02 permits the board of directors, if authority to do so is contained in the articles, to fix the terms of a class or series of shares or of a series of shares within a class to meet corporate needs, including current requirements of the securities markets or the exigencies of negotiations for acquisition of other corporations or properties, without the necessity of holding a shareholders' meeting to amend the articles. This section therefore permits prompt action and gives desirable flexibility. The articles of incorporation may also create "series" of shares within a class (rather than designating that "series" as a separate class).

The board of directors may create new series within a class. The board may also set the terms of a class or series if there are no outstanding shares of that class or series. In some contexts there is no substantive difference between a "class" and a "series within a class". Labels are often a matter of convenience.

Shares that are authorized by the articles to be issued in different classes or series with terms to be set by the board of directors are sometimes referred to as "blank check stock". The power to make the terms of "blank check stock" dependent on facts objectively ascertainable outside the articles and to vary the terms of "blank check stock" among holders of the same class or series extends to all the permitted variables set forth in section 6.01(c).

The granting of authority to create and set the terms for new classes and series of shares permits the board of directors to adjust the capital structure of the corporation without the time and expense of shareholder approval. This power is often used to create classes or series of preferred shares with fixed terms established in light of current market conditions or transactional needs. It is also used in connection with the issuance of so-called variable-rate or auction-rate preferred stock, i.e., stock with a dividend rate that varies according to an extrinsic referent such as the London Interbank Offered Rate, the prime commercial rate established by a bank or even the bids of prospective buyers of the stock as submitted from time to time and accepted by the corporation. This flexibility permits the corporation to respond to evolving market conditions and other time-sensitive developments.

Subsections (a) and (b) make it clear that the board has the same broad flexibility with regard to setting the terms of a class or series under this section as is permitted under 6.01(c).

Subsection (c) requires a simple filing to amend the articles so there will be a public record of the class or series which the corporation intends to issue. The amendment does not require shareholder action. See section 10.05(8).

§ 6.03 Issued and Outstanding Shares

(a) A corporation may issue the number of shares of each class or series authorized by the articles of incorporation. Shares that are issued are outstanding shares until they are reacquired, redeemed, converted, or cancelled.

(b) The reacquisition, redemption, or conversion of outstanding shares is subject to the limitations of subsection (c) of this section and to section 6.40.

(c) At all times that shares of the corporation are outstanding, one or more shares that together have unlimited voting rights and one or more shares that together are entitled to receive the net assets of the corporation upon dissolution must be outstanding.

§ 6.04 Fractional Shares

(a) A corporation may:

(1) issue fractions of a share or pay in money the value of fractions of a share;

(2) arrange for disposition of fractional shares by the shareholders;

(3) issue scrip in registered or bearer form entitling the holder to receive a full share upon surrendering enough scrip to equal a full share.

(b) Each certificate representing scrip must be conspicuously labeled "scrip" and must contain the information required by section 6.25(b).

(c) The holder of a fractional share is entitled to exercise the rights of a shareholder, including the right to vote, to receive dividends, and to participate in the assets of the corporation upon liquidation. The holder of scrip is not entitled to any of these rights unless the scrip provides for them.

(d) The board of directors may authorize the issuance of scrip subject to any condition considered desirable, including:

(1) that the scrip will become void if not exchanged for full shares before a specified date; and

(2) that the shares for which the scrip is exchangeable may be sold and the proceeds paid to the scripholders.

Subchapter B

Issuance of Shares

§ 6.20 Subscription for Shares Before Incorporation

(a) A subscription for shares entered into before incorporation is irrevocable for six months unless the subscription agreement provides a longer or shorter period or all the subscribers agree to revocation.

(b) The board of directors may determine the payment terms of subscriptions for shares that were entered into before incorporation, unless the subscription agreement specifies them. A call for payment by the board of directors must be uniform so far as practicable as to all shares of the same class or series, unless the subscription agreement specifies otherwise.

(c) Shares issued pursuant to subscriptions entered into before incorporation are fully paid and nonassessable when the corporation receives the consideration specified in the subscription agreement.

(d) If a subscriber defaults in payment of money or property under a subscription agreement entered into before incorporation, the corporation may collect the amount owed as any other debt. Alternatively, unless the subscription agreement provides otherwise, the corporation may rescind the agreement and may sell the shares if the debt remains unpaid more than 20 days after the corporation sends written demand for payment to the subscriber.

(e) A subscription agreement entered into after incorporation is a contract between the subscriber and the corporation subject to section 6.21.

Official Comment

Agreements for the purchase of shares to be issued by a corporation are typically referred to as "subscriptions" or "subscription agreements." Section 6.20 deals exclusively with preincorporation subscriptions, that is, subscriptions entered into before the corporation was formed. Preincorporation subscriptions have often been considered to be revocable offers rather than binding contracts. Since the corporation is not in existence, it cannot be a party to the agreement and the consideration established for the shares is not determined by the board of directors. While preincorporation subscriptions entered into simultaneously by several subscribers may be considered a binding contract between or among the subscribers, not all factual situations lend themselves to contractual analysis. Because of the uncertainty of the legal enforceability of these transactions, section 6.20 provides a simple set of legal rules applicable to the enforcement of preincorporation subscriptions by the corporation after its formation. It does not address the extent to which preincorporation subscriptions may constitute a contract between or among subscribers, and other subscribers may enforce whatever contract rights they have without regard to section 6.20.

Section 6.20(a) provides that preincorporation subscriptions are irrevocable for six months unless the subscription agreement provides that they are revocable or that they are irrevocable for some other period. Nevertheless, all the subscribers to shares may agree at any time that a subscriber may withdraw in part from his commitment to subscribe for shares, that a subscriber may revoke his subscription entirely, or that the period of irrevocability may continue for an additional stated period. If the corporation accepts the subscription during the period of irrevocability, the subscription becomes a contract binding on both the subscribers and the corporation. The terms of this contract are set forth in sections 6.20(b) and (d). . . .

Postincorporation subscriptions are contracts between the corporation and the investor by which the corporation agrees to issue shares for a stated consideration and the investor agrees to purchase the shares for that consideration. Postincorporation subscriptions are simple contracts subject to the power of the board of directors and they may contain any mutually acceptable provisions subject to section 6.21. Section 6.20(e) states, for completeness, that postincorporation subscriptions are contracts between the corporation and the subscriber subject to section 6.21.

§ 6.21 Issuance of Shares

(a) The powers granted in this section to the board of directors may be reserved to the shareholders by the articles of incorporation.

(b) The board of directors may authorize shares to be issued for consideration consisting of any tangible or intangible property or benefit to the corporation, including cash, promissory notes, services performed, contracts for services to be performed, or other securities of the corporation.

(c) Before the corporation issues shares, the board of directors must determine that the consideration received or to be received for shares to be issued is adequate. That determination by the board of directors is conclusive insofar as the adequacy of consideration for the issuance of shares relates to whether the shares are validly issued, fully paid, and nonassessable.

(d) When the corporation receives the consideration for which the board of directors authorized the issuance of shares, the shares issued therefor are fully paid and nonassessable.

(e) The corporation may place in escrow shares issued for a contract for future services or benefits or a promissory note, or make other arrangements to restrict the transfer of the shares, and may credit distributions in respect of the shares against their purchase price, until the services are performed, the note is paid, or the benefits received. If the services are not performed, the note is not paid, or the benefits are not received, the shares escrowed or restricted and the distributions credited may be cancelled in whole or part.

(f) (1) An issuance of shares or other securities convertible into or rights exercisable for shares, in a transaction or a series of integrated transactions, requires approval of the shareholders, at a meeting at which a quorum consisting of at least a majority of the votes entitled to be cast on the matter exists, if:

   (i) the shares, other securities, or rights are issued for consideration other than cash or cash equivalents, and

   (ii) the voting power of shares that are issued and issuable as a result of the transaction or series of integrated transactions will comprise more than 20 percent of the voting power of the shares of the corporation that were outstanding immediately before the transaction.

(2) In this subsection:

   (i) For purposes of determining the voting power of shares issued and issuable as a result of a transaction or series of integrated transactions, the voting power of shares shall be the greater of (A) the voting power of the shares to be issued, or (B) the voting power of the shares that would be outstanding after giving effect to the conversion of convertible shares and other securities and the exercise of rights to be issued.

   (ii) A series of transactions is integrated if consummation of one transaction is made contingent on consummation of one or more of the other transactions.

Official Comment

The financial provisions of the Model Act reflect a modernization of the concepts underlying the capital structure and limitations on distributions of corporations. This process of modernization began with amendments in 1980 to the 1969 Model Act that eliminated the concepts of "par value" and "stated capital," and further modernization occurred in connection with the development of the revised Act in 1984. Practitioners and legal scholars have long recognized that the statutory structure embodying "par value" and "legal capital" concepts is not only complex and confusing but also fails to serve the original purpose of protecting creditors and senior security holders from payments to junior security holders. Indeed, to the extent security holders are led to believe that it provides this protection, these provisions may be affirmatively misleading. The Model Act has therefore eliminated these concepts entirely and substituted a simpler and more flexible structure that provides more realistic protection to these interests. Major aspects of this new structure are:

(1) the provisions relating to the issuance of shares set forth in this and the following sections;

(2) the provisions limiting distributions by corporations set forth in section 6.40 and discussed in the Official Comment to that section; and

(3) the elimination of the concept of treasury shares described in the Official Comment to section 6.31.

Section 6.21 incorporates not only the elimination of the concepts of par value and stated capital from the Model Act in 1980 but also eliminates the earlier rule declaring certain kinds of property ineligible as consideration for shares. . . .

1. Consideration

Since shares need not have a par value, under section 6.21 there is no minimum price at which specific shares must be issued and therefore there can be no "watered stock" liability for issuing shares below an arbitrarily fixed price. The price at which shares are issued is primarily a matter of concern to other shareholders whose interests may be diluted if shares are issued at unreasonably low prices or for overvalued property. This problem of equality of treatment essentially involves honest and fair judgments by directors and cannot be effectively addressed by an arbitrary doctrine establishing a minimum price for shares such as "par value" provided under older statutes.

Section 6.21(b) specifically validates contracts for future services (including promoters' services), promissory notes, or "any tangible or intangible property or benefit to the corporation," as consideration for the present issue of shares. The term "benefit" should be broadly construed to include, for example, a reduction of a liability, a release of a claim, or benefits obtained by a corporation by contribution of its shares to a charitable organization or as a prize in a promotion. In the realities of commercial life, there is sometimes a need for the issuance of shares for contract rights or such intangible property or benefits. And, as a matter of business economics, contracts for future services, promissory notes, and intangible property or benefits often have value that is as real as the value of tangible property or past services, the only types of property that many older statutes permit as consideration for shares. Thus, only business judgment should determine what kind of property should be obtained for shares, and a determination by the directors meeting the requirements of section 8.30 to accept a specific kind of valuable property for shares should be accepted and not circumscribed by artificial or arbitrary rules.

2. Board Determination of Adequacy

The issuance of some shares for cash and other shares for promissory notes, contracts for past or future services, or for tangible or intangible property or benefits, like the issuance of shares for an inadequate consideration, opens the possibility of dilution of the interests of other shareholders. For example, persons acquiring shares for cash may be unfairly treated if optimistic values are placed on past or future services or intangible benefits being provided by other persons. The problem is particularly acute if the persons providing services, promissory notes, or property or benefits of debatable value are themselves connected with the promoters of the corporation or with its directors. Protection of shareholders against abuse of the power granted to the board of directors to determine that shares should be issued for intangible property or benefits is provided in part by the requirement that the board must act in accordance with the requirements of section 8.30, and, if applicable, section 8.31, in determining that the consideration received for shares is adequate, and in part by the requirement of section 16.21 that the corporation must inform all shareholders annually of all shares issued during the previous year for promissory notes or promises of future services.

Accounting principles are not specified in the Model Act, and the board of directors is not required by the statute to determine the "value" of noncash consideration received by the corporation (as was the case in earlier versions of the Model Act). In many instances, property or benefit received by the corporation will be of uncertain value; if the board of directors determines that the issuance of shares for the property or benefit is an appropriate transaction that protects the shareholders from dilution, that is sufficient under section 6.21. The board of directors does not have to make an explicit "adequacy" determination by formal resolution; that determination may be inferred from a determination to authorize the issuance of shares for a specified consideration.

Section 6.21 also does not require that the board of directors determine the value of the consideration to be entered on the books of the corporation, though the board of directors may do so if it wishes. Of course, a specific value must be placed on the consideration received for the shares for bookkeeping purposes, but bookkeeping details are not the statutory responsibility of the board of directors. The statute also does not require the board of directors to determine the corresponding entry on the right-hand side of the balance sheet under owner's equity to be designated as "stated capital" or be allocated among "stated capital" and other surplus accounts. The corporation, however, may determine that the shareholders' equity accounts should be divided into these traditional categories if it wishes.

The second sentence of section 6.21(c) describes the effect of the determination by the board of directors that consideration is adequate for the issuance of shares. That determination, without more, is conclusive to the extent that adequacy is relevant to the question whether the shares are validly issued, fully paid, and nonassessable. Section 6.21(c) provides that shares are fully paid and nonassessable when the corporation receives the consideration for which the board of directors authorized their issuance. Whether shares are validly issued may depend on compliance with corporate procedural requirements, such as issuance within the amount authorized in the articles of incorporation or holding a directors' meeting upon proper notice and with a quorum present. The Model Act does not address the remedies that may be available for issuances that are subject to challenge. . . .

The revised Model Act does not address the question whether validly issued shares may thereafter be cancelled on the grounds of fraud or bad faith if the shares are in the hands of the original shareholder or other persons who were aware of the circumstances under which they were issued when they acquired the shares. It also leaves to the Uniform Commercial Code other questions relating to the rights of persons other than the person acquiring the shares from the corporation. . . .

3.   Shareholder Approval Requirement for Certain Issuances

Section 6.21(f) provides that an issuance of shares or other securities convertible into or rights exercisable for shares, in a transaction or a series of integrated transactions, for consideration other than cash or cash equivalents, requires shareholder approval if either the voting power of the shares to be issued, or the voting power of the shares into which those shares and other securities are convertible and for which any rights to be issued are exercisable, will comprise more than 20 percent of the voting power outstanding immediately before the issuance. Section 6.21(f) is generally patterned on New York Stock Exchange Listed Company Manual Rule 312.03, American Stock Exchange Company Guide Rule 712(b), and NASDAQ Stock Market Rule 4310(c)(25)(H)(i). The calculation of the 20 percent compares the maximum number of votes entitled to be cast by the shares to be issued or that could be outstanding after giving effect to the conversion of convertible securities and the exercise of rights being issued, with the actual number of votes entitled to be cast by outstanding shares before the transaction. The test tends to be conservative: The calculation of one part of the equation, voting power outstanding immediately before the transaction, is based on actual voting power of the shares then outstanding, without giving effect to the possible conversion of existing convertible shares and securities and the exercise of existing rights. In contrast, the calculation of the other part of the equation—voting power that is or may be outstanding as a result of the issuance—takes into account the possible future conversion of shares and securities and the exercise of rights to be issued as part of the transaction.

In making the 20 percent determination under this subsection, shares that are issuable in a business combination of any kind, including a merger, share exchange, acquisition of assets, or otherwise, on a contingent basis are counted as shares or securities to be issued as a result of the transaction. On the other hand, shares that are issuable under antidilution clauses, such as those designed to take account of future share splits or share dividends, are not counted as shares or securities to be issued as a result of the transaction, because they are issuable only as a result of a later corporate action authorizing the split or dividend. If a transaction involves an earn-out provision, under which the total amount of shares or securities to be issued will depend on future earnings or other performance measures, the maximum amount of shares or securities that can be issued under the earn-out shall be included in the determination.

If the number of shares to be issued or issuable is not fixed, but is subject to a formula, the application of the test in section 6.21(f)(2)(i) requires a calculation of the maximum amount that could be issued under the formula, whether stated as a range or otherwise, in the governing agreement. Even if ultimate issuance of the maximum amount is unlikely, a vote will be required if the maximum amount would result in an issuance of more than 20 percent of the voting power of shares outstanding immediately before the transaction.

Shares that have or would have only contingent voting rights when issued or issuable are not shares that carry voting power for purposes of the calculation under section 6.21(f).

The vote required to approve issuances that fall within section 6.21(f) is the basic voting rule under the Act, set forth in section 7.25, that more shares must be voted in favor of the issuance than are voted against. This is the same voting rule that applies under chapter 10 for amendments of the articles of incorporation, under chapter 11 for mergers and share exchanges, under chapter 12 for a disposition of assets that requires shareholder approval, and under chapter 14 for voluntary dissolution. The quorum rule under section 6.21(f) is also the same as the quorum rule under chapters 10, 11, 12, and 14: there must be present at the meeting at least a majority of the votes entitled to be cast on the matter.

Section 6.21(f) does not apply to an issuance for cash or cash equivalents, whether or not in connection with a public offering. "Cash equivalents," within the meaning of section 6.21(f), are short-term investments that are both readily convertible to known amounts of cash and present insignificant risk of changes in interest rates. Generally, only investments with original maturities of three months or less or investments that are highly liquid and can be cashed in at any time on short notice could qualify under these definitions. Examples of cash equivalents are types of Treasury Bills, investment grade commercial paper, and money-market funds. Shares that are issued partly for cash or cash equivalents and partly for other consideration are "issued for consideration other than cash or cash equivalents" within the meaning of section 6.21(f).

The term "rights" in section 6.21(f) includes warrants, options, and rights of exchange, whether at the option of the holder, the corporation, or another person. The term "voting power" is defined in section 1.40(27) as the current power to vote in the election of directors. See also the Comment to that subsection. Transactions are integrated within the meaning of section 6.21(f) where consummation of one transaction is made contingent on consummation of one or more of the other transactions. If this test is not satisfied, transactions are not integrated for purposes of section 6.21(f) merely because they are proximate in time or because the kind of consideration for which the corporation issues shares is similar in each transaction.

Section 6.21(f) only applies to issuances for consideration. Accordingly, like the Stock Exchange and NASDAQ rules on which section 6.21(f) is based, section 6.21(f) does not require shareholder approval for share dividends (which includes "splits") or for shareholder rights plans. See section 6.23 and the official Comment thereto.

Illustrations of the application of section 6.21(f) follow:

1.   C corporation, which has 2 million shares of Class A voting common stock outstanding (carrying one vote per share), proposes to issue 600,000 shares of authorized but unissued shares of Class B nonvoting common stock in exchange for a business owned by D Corporation. The proposed issuance does not require shareholder approval under section 6.21(f), because the Class B shares do not carry voting power.

2.   The facts being otherwise as stated in Illustration 1, C proposes to issue 600,000 additional shares of its Class A voting common stock. The proposed issuance requires shareholder approval under section 6.21(f), because the voting power carried by the shares to be issued will comprise more than 20 percent of the voting power of C's shares outstanding immediately before the issuance.

3.   The facts being otherwise as stated in Illustration 1, C proposes to issue 400,000 shares of authorized but unissued voting preferred, each

share of which carries one vote and is convertible into 1.5 shares of Class A voting common. The proposed issuance requires shareholder approval under section 6.21(f). Although the voting power of the preferred shares to be issued will not comprise more than 20 percent of the voting power of C's shares outstanding immediately before the issuance, the voting power of the shares issuable upon conversion of the preferred will carry more than 20 percent of such voting power.

4. The facts being otherwise as stated in Illustration 1, C proposes to issue 200,000 shares of its Class A voting common stock, and 100,000 shares of authorized but unissued nonvoting preferred stock, each share of which is convertible into 2.5 shares of C's Class A voting common stock. The proposed issuance requires shareholder approval under section 6.21(f), because the voting power of the Class A shares to be issued, after giving effect to the common stock that is issuable upon conversion of the preferred, would comprise more than 20 percent of the voting power of C's outstanding shares immediately before the issuance.

5. The facts being otherwise as stated in Illustration 4, each share of the preferred stock is convertible into 1.2 shares of the Class A voting common stock. The proposed issuance does not require shareholder approval under section 6.21(f), because neither the voting power of the shares to be issued at the outset (200,000) nor the voting power of the shares that would be outstanding after giving effect to the common issuable upon conversion of the preferred (a total of 320,000) constitutes more than 20 percent of the voting power of C's outstanding shares immediately before the issuance.

6. The facts being otherwise as stated in Illustration 1, C proposes to acquire businesses from Corporations G, H, and I, for 200,000, 300,000, and 400,000 shares of Class A voting common stock, respectively, within a short period of time. None of the transactions is conditioned on the negotiation or completion of the other transactions. The proposed issuance of voting shares does not require shareholder approval, because the three transactions are not integrated within the meaning of section 6.21(f), and none of the transactions individually involves the issuance of more than 20 percent of the voting power of C's outstanding shares immediately before each issuance.

§ 6.22 Liability of Shareholders

(a) A purchaser from a corporation of its own shares is not liable to the corporation or its creditors with respect to the shares except to pay the consideration for which the shares were authorized to be issued (section 6.21) or specified in the subscription agreement (section 6.20).

(b) Unless otherwise provided in the articles of incorporation, a shareholder of a corporation is not personally liable for the acts or debts of the corporation except that he may become personally liable by reason of his own acts or conduct.

§ 6.23 Share Dividends

(a) Unless the articles of incorporation provide otherwise, shares may be issued pro rata and without consideration to the corporation's shareholders or to the shareholders of one or more classes or series. An issuance of shares under this subsection is a share dividend.

(b) Shares of one class or series may not be issued as a share dividend in respect of shares of another class or series unless (1) the articles of incorporation so authorize, (2) a majority of the votes entitled to be cast by the class or series to be issued approve the issue, or (3) there are no outstanding shares of the class or series to be issued.

(c) If the board of directors does not fix the record date for determining shareholders entitled to a share dividend, it is the date the board of directors authorizes the share dividend.

Official Comment

A share dividend is solely a paper transaction: No assets are received by the corporation for the shares and any "dividend" paid in shares does not involve the distribution of property by the corporation to its shareholders. Section 6.23 therefore recognizes that such a transaction involves the issuance of shares "without consideration," and section 1.40(6) excludes it from the definition of a "distribution." Such transactions were treated in a fictional way under the old "par value" and "stated capital" statutes, which treated a share dividend as involving transfers from a surplus account to stated capital and assumed that par value shares could be issued without receiving any consideration by reason of that transfer of surplus.

The par value statutory treatment of share dividend transactions distinguished a share "split" from a dividend. In a share "split" the par value of the former shares was divided among the new shares and there was no transfer of surplus into the stated capital account as in the case of a share "dividend." Since the Model Act has eliminated the concept of par value, the distinction between a "split" and a "dividend" has not been retained and both types of transactions are referred to simply as "share dividends." A distinction between "share dividends" and "share splits," however, continues to exist in other contexts—for example, in connection with transactions by publicly held corporations, see N.Y.S.E. Listed Company Manual § 703.02(a), or corporations that have optionally retained par value for their shares. The change made in the Model Act is not intended to affect the manner in which transactions by these corporations are handled or described but simply reflects the elimination of artificial legal distinctions based on the par value statutes....

§ 6.24 Share Options

(a) A corporation may issue rights, options, or warrants for the purchase of shares or other securities of the corporation. The board of directors shall determine (i) the terms upon which the rights, options, or warrants are issued and (ii) the terms, including the consideration for which the shares or other securities are to be issued. The authorization by the board of directors for the corporation to issue such rights, options, or warrants constitutes authorization of the issuance of the shares or other securities for which the rights, options or warrants are exercisable.

(b) The terms and conditions of such rights, options or warrants, including those outstanding on the effective date of this section, may include, without limitation, restrictions or conditions that:

(1) preclude or limit the exercise, transfer or receipt of such rights, options or warrants by any person or persons owning or offering to acquire a specified number or percentage of the outstanding shares or other securities of the corporation or by any transferee or transferees of any such person or persons, or

(2) invalidate or void such rights, options or warrants held by any such person or persons or any such transferee or transferees.

Official Comment

A specific provision authorizing the creation of rights, options and warrants appears in many state business corporation statutes. Even though corporations doubtless have the inherent power to issue these instruments, specific authorization is desirable because of the economic importance of rights, options and warrants, and because it is desirable to confirm the broad discretion of the board of directors in determining the consideration to be received by the corporation for their issuance. The creation of incentive compensation plans for directors, officers, agents, and employees is basically a matter of business judgment. This is equally true for incentive plans that involve the issuance of rights, options or warrants and for those that involve the payment of cash. In appropriate cases incentive plans may provide for exercise prices that are below the current market prices of the underlying shares or other securities.

Section 6.24(a) does not require shareholder approval of rights, options or warrants. Of course, prior shareholder approval may be sought as a discretionary matter, or required in order to comply with the rules of national securities markets (see N.Y.S.E. Listed Company Manual section 309.00), or to acquire the federal income tax benefits conditioned upon shareholder approval of such plans (see section 422(b)(1) of the Internal Revenue Code of 1986, as amended).

Under section 6.24(a), the board of directors may designate the interests issued as options, warrants, rights, or by some other name.

These interests may be evidenced by certificates, contracts, letter agreements, or in other forms that are appropriate under the circumstances. Rights, options, or warrants may be issued together with or independently of the corporation's issuance and sale of its shares or other securities.

Some publicly held corporations have delegated administration of programs involving incentive compensation in the form of share rights or options to compensation committees composed of nonmanagement directors, subject to the general oversight of the board of directors.

Section 6.24(b) is intended to clarify that the issuance of rights, options, or warrants as part of a shareholder rights plan is permitted. A number of courts have addressed whether shareholder rights plans are permitted under statutes similar to prior sections 6.01, 6.02, and 6.24. These courts have not agreed on whether provisions similar in language in sections 6.01, 6.02, and 6.24 permit such plans to distinguish between holders of the same class of shares based on the identity of the holder of the shares. However, in each of the states in which a court has interpreted a statute of that state as prohibiting such shareholder rights plans, the legislature has subsequently adopted legislation validating such plans. Section 6.24(b) clarifies that such plans are permitted.

The permissible scope of shareholder rights plans may, however, be limited by the courts. For example, courts have been sensitive to plans containing provisions which the courts perceive as infringing upon the power of the board of directors.

§ 6.25   Form and Content of Certificates

(a) Shares may but need not be represented by certificates. Unless this Act or another statute expressly provides otherwise, the rights and obligations of shareholders are identical whether or not their shares are represented by certificates.

(b) At a minimum each share certificate must state on its face:

    (1) the name of the issuing corporation and that it is organized under the law of this state;

    (2) the name of the person to whom issued; and

    (3) the number and class of shares and the designation of the series, if any, the certificate represents.

(c) If the issuing corporation is authorized to issue different classes of shares or different series within a class, the designations, relative rights, preferences, and limitations applicable to each class and the variations in rights, preferences, and limitations determined for each series (and the authority of the board of directors to determine variations for future series) must be summarized on the front or back of each certificate. Alternatively, each certificate may state conspicuously on its front or back that the corporation will furnish the shareholder this information on request in writing and without charge.

(d) Each share certificate (1) must be signed (either manually or in facsimile) by two officers designated in the bylaws or by the board of directors and (2) may bear the corporate seal or its facsimile.

(e) If the person who signed (either manually or in facsimile) a share certificate no longer holds office when the certificate is issued, the certificate is nevertheless valid.

§ 6.26   Shares Without Certificates

(a) Unless the articles of incorporation or bylaws provide otherwise, the board of directors of a corporation may authorize the issue of some or all of the shares of any or all of its classes or series without certificates. The authorization does not affect shares already represented by certificates until they are surrendered to the corporation.

(b) Within a reasonable time after the issue or transfer of shares without certificates, the corporation shall send the shareholder a written statement of the information required on certificates by section 6.25(b) and (c), and, if applicable, section 6.27.

§ 6.27   Restriction on Transfer of Shares and Other Securities

(a) The articles of incorporation, bylaws, an agreement among shareholders, or an agreement between shareholders and the corporation may impose restrictions on the transfer or registration of transfer of shares of the corporation. A restriction does not affect shares issued before the restriction was adopted unless the holders of the shares are parties to the restriction agreement or voted in favor of the restriction.

(b) A restriction on the transfer or registration of transfer of shares is valid and enforceable against the holder or a transferee of the holder if the restriction is authorized by this section and its existence is noted conspicuously on the front or back of the certificate or is contained in the information statement required by section 6.26(b). Unless so noted, a restriction is not enforceable against a person without knowledge of the restriction.

(c) A restriction on the transfer or registration of transfer of shares is authorized:

   (1) to maintain the corporation's status when it is dependent on the number or identity of its shareholders;

   (2) to preserve exemptions under federal or state securities law;

   (3) for any other reasonable purpose.

(d) A restriction on the transfer or registration of transfer of shares may:

(1) obligate the shareholder first to offer the corporation or other persons (separately, consecutively, or simultaneously) an opportunity to acquire the restricted shares;

(2) obligate the corporation or other persons (separately, consecutively, or simultaneously) to acquire the restricted shares;

(3) require the corporation, the holders of any class of its shares, or another person to approve the transfer of the restricted shares, if the requirement is not manifestly unreasonable;

(4) prohibit the transfer of the restricted shares to designated persons or classes of persons, if the prohibition is not manifestly unreasonable.

(e) For purposes of this section, "shares" includes a security convertible into or carrying a right to subscribe for or acquire shares.

§ 6.28 Expense of Issue

A corporation may pay the expenses of selling or underwriting its shares, and of organizing or reorganizing the corporation, from the consideration received for shares.

Subchapter C

Subsequent Acquisition of Shares by Shareholders and Corporation

§ 6.30 Shareholders' Preemptive Rights

(a) The shareholders of a corporation do not have a preemptive right to acquire the corporation's unissued shares except to the extent the articles of incorporation so provide.

(b) A statement included in the articles of incorporation that "the corporation elects to have preemptive rights" (or words of similar import) means that the following principles apply except to the extent the articles of incorporation expressly provide otherwise:

(1) The shareholders of the corporation have a preemptive right, granted on uniform terms and conditions prescribed by the board of directors to provide a fair and reasonable opportunity to exercise the right, to acquire proportional amounts of the corporation's unissued shares upon the decision of the board of directors to issue them.

(2) A shareholder may waive his preemptive right. A waiver evidenced by a writing is irrevocable even though it is not supported by consideration.

(3) There is no preemptive right with respect to:

    (i) shares issued as compensation to directors, officers, agents, or employees of the corporation, its subsidiaries or affiliates;

    (ii) shares issued to satisfy conversion or option rights created to provide compensation to directors, officers, agents, or employees of the corporation, its subsidiaries or affiliates;

    (iii) shares authorized in articles of incorporation that are issued within six months from the effective date of incorporation;

    (iv) shares sold otherwise than for money.

(4) Holders of shares of any class without general voting rights but with preferential rights to distributions or assets have no preemptive rights with respect to shares of any class.

(5) Holders of shares of any class with general voting rights but without preferential rights to distributions or assets have no preemptive rights with respect to shares of any class with preferential rights to distributions or assets unless the shares with preferential rights are convertible into or carry a right to subscribe for or acquire shares without preferential rights.

(6) Shares subject to preemptive rights that are not acquired by shareholders may be issued to any person for a period of one year after being offered to shareholders at a consideration set by the board of directors that is not lower than the consideration set for the exercise of preemptive rights. An offer at a lower consideration or after the expiration of one year is subject to the shareholders' preemptive rights.

(c) For purposes of this section, "shares" includes a security convertible into or carrying a right to subscribe for or acquire shares.

Official Comment

Section 6.30(a) adopts an "opt in" provision for preemptive rights: Unless an affirmative reference to these rights appears in the articles of incorporation, no preemptive rights exist. Whether or not preemptive rights are elected, however, the directors' fiduciary duties extend to the issuance of shares. Issuance of shares at favorable prices to directors (but excluding other shareholders) or the issuance of shares on a nonproportional basis for the purpose of affecting control rather than raising capital may violate that duty. These duties, it is believed, form a more rational structure of regulation than the technical principles of traditional preemptive rights.

Section 6.30(b) provides a standard model for preemptive rights if the corporation desires to exercise the "opt in" alternative of section 6.30(a). The simple phrase, "the corporation elects to have preemptive rights," or words of similar import, results in the rest of subsection (b) becoming applicable to the corporation. But a corporation may qualify or limit any of the rules set forth in subsection (b) by express provisions in the articles of incorporation if the rules are felt to be undesirable or inappropriate for the specific corporation. The purposes of this standard model for preemptive rights are (1) to simplify drafting articles of incorporation and (2) to provide a simple checklist of business considerations for the benefit of attorneys who are considering the inclusion of preemptive rights in articles of incorporation. . . .

§ 6.31   Corporation's Acquisition of Its Own Shares

(a) A corporation may acquire its own shares, and shares so acquired constitute authorized but unissued shares.

(b) if the articles of incorporation prohibit the reissue of the acquired shares, the number of authorized shares is reduced by the number of shares acquired.

Official Comment

Section 6.31 applies only to shares that a corporation acquires for its own account. Shares that a corporation acquires in a fiduciary capacity for the account of others are not considered to be acquired by the corporation for purposes of this section.

Shares that are reacquired by the corporation become authorized but unissued shares under section 6.31(a) unless the articles prohibit reissue, in which event the shares are canceled and the number of authorized shares is reduced as required by section 6.31(b).

If the number of authorized shares of a class is reduced as a result of the operation of section 6.31(b), the board should amend the articles of incorporation under section 10.05(6) to reflect that reduction. If there are no remaining authorized shares in a class as a result of the operation of section 6.31, the board should amend the articles of incorporation under section 10.05(7) to delete the class from the classes of shares authorized by articles of incorporation.

Subchapter D

Distributions

§ 6.40   Distributions to Shareholders

(a) A board of directors may authorize and the corporation may make distributions to its shareholders subject to restriction by the articles of incorporation and the limitation in subsection (c).

(b) If the board of directors does not fix the record date for determining shareholders entitled to a distribution (other than one involving a purchase, redemption, or other acquisition of the corporation's shares), it is the date the board of directors authorizes the distribution.

(c) No distribution may be made if, after giving it effect:

(1) the corporation would not be able to pay its debts as they become due in the usual course of business; or

(2) the corporation's total assets would be less than the sum of its total liabilities plus (unless the articles of incorporation permit otherwise) the amount that would be needed, if the corporation were to be dissolved at the time of the distribution, to satisfy the preferential rights upon dissolution of shareholders whose preferential rights are superior to those receiving the distribution.

(d) The board of directors may base a determination that a distribution is not prohibited under subsection (c) either on financial statements prepared on the basis of accounting practices and principles that are reasonable in the circumstances or on a fair valuation or other method that is reasonable in the circumstances.

(e) Except as provided in subsection (g), the effect of a distribution under subsection (c) is measured:

(1) in the case of distribution by purchase, redemption, or other acquisition of the corporation's shares, as of the earlier of (i) the date money or other property is transferred or debt incurred by the corporation or (ii) the date the shareholder ceases to be a shareholder with respect to the acquired shares;

(2) in the case of any other distribution of indebtedness, as of the date the indebtedness is distributed; and

(3) in all other cases, as of (i) the date the distribution is authorized if the payment occurs within 120 days after the date of authorization or (ii) the date the payment is made if it occurs more than 120 days after the date of authorization.

(f) A corporation's indebtedness to a shareholder incurred by reason of a distribution made in accordance with this section is at parity with the corporation's indebtedness to its general, unsecured creditors except to the extent subordinated by agreement.

(g) Indebtedness of a corporation, including indebtedness issued as a distribution, is not considered a liability for purposes of determinations under subsection (c) if its terms provide that payment of principal and interest are made only if and to the extent that payment of a distribution to shareholders could then be made under this section. If the indebtedness is issued as a distribution, each payment of principal or interest is treated as a distribution, the effect of which is measured on the date the payment is actually made.

(h) This section shall not apply to distributions in liquidation under chapter 14.

Official Comment

The reformulation of the statutory standards governing distributions is another important change made by the 1980 revisions to the financial provisions of the Model Act. It has long been recognized that the traditional "par value" and "stated capital" statutes do not provide significant protection against distributions of capital to shareholders. While most of these statutes contained elaborate provisions establishing "stated capital," "capital surplus," and "earned surplus" (and often other types of surplus as well), the net effect of most statutes was to permit the distribution to shareholders of most or all of the corporation's net assets—its capital along with its earnings—if the shareholders wished this to be done. However, statutes also generally imposed an equity insolvency test on distributions that prohibited distributions of assets if the corporation was insolvent or if the distribution had the effect of making the corporation insolvent or unable to meet its obligations as they were projected to arise.

The financial provisions of the revised Model Act, which are based on the 1980 amendments, sweep away all the distinctions among the various types of surplus but retain restrictions on distributions built around both the traditional equity insolvency and balance sheet tests of earlier statutes.

1. The Scope of Section 6.40

Section 1.40 defines "distribution" to include virtually all transfers of money, indebtedness of the corporation or other property to a shareholder in respect of the corporation's shares. It thus includes cash or property dividends, payments by a corporation to purchase its own shares, distributions of promissory notes or indebtedness, and distributions in partial or complete liquidation or voluntary or involuntary dissolution. Section 1.40 excludes from the definition of "distribution" transactions by the corporation in which only its own shares are distributed to its shareholders. These transactions are called "share dividends" in the revised Model Business Corporation Act. See section 6.23.

Section 6.40 imposes a single, uniform test on all distributions. Many of the old "par value" and "stated capital" statutes provided tests that varied with the type of distribution under consideration or did not cover certain types of distributions at all.

2. Equity Insolvency Test

As noted above, older statutes prohibited payments of dividends if the corporation was, or as a result of the payment would be, insolvent in the equity sense. This test is retained, appearing in section 6.40(c)(1).

In most cases involving a corporation operating as a going concern in the normal course, information generally available will make it quite apparent that no particular inquiry concerning the equity insolvency test is needed. While neither a balance sheet nor an income statement can be conclusive as to this test, the existence of significant shareholders' equity and normal operating conditions are of themselves a strong indication that no issue should arise under that test. Indeed, in the case of a corporation having regularly audited financial statements, the absence of any qualification in the most recent auditor's opinion as to the corporation's status as a "going concern," coupled with a lack of subsequent adverse events, would normally be decisive.

It is only when circumstances indicate that the corporation is encountering difficulties or is in an uncertain position concerning its liquidity and operations that the board of directors or, more commonly, the officers or others upon whom they may place reliance under section 8.30(b), may need to address the issue. Because of the overall judgment required in evaluating the equity insolvency test, no one or more "bright line" tests can be employed. However, in determining whether the equity insolvency test has been met, certain judgments or assumptions as to the future course of the corporation's business are customarily justified, absent clear evidence to the contrary. These include the likelihood that (a) based on existing and contemplated demand for the corporation's products or services, it will be able to generate funds over a period of time sufficient to satisfy its existing and reasonably anticipated obligations as they mature, and (b) indebtedness which matures in the near-term will be refinanced where, on the basis of the corporation's financial condition and future prospects and the general availability of credit to businesses similarly situated, it is reasonable to assume that such refinancing may be accomplished. To the extent that the corporation may be subject to asserted or unasserted contingent liabilities, reasonable judgments as to the likelihood, amount, and time of any recovery against the corporation, after giving consideration to the extent to which the corporation is insured or otherwise protected against loss, may be utilized. There may be occasions when it would be useful to consider a cash flow analysis, based on a business forecast and budget, covering a sufficient period of time to permit a conclusion that known obligations of the corporation can reasonably be expected to be satisfied over the period of time that they will mature.

In exercising their judgment, the directors are entitled to rely, under section 8.30(b) as noted above, on information, opinions, reports, and statements prepared by others. Ordinarily, they should not be expected to become involved in the details of the various analyses or market or economic projections that may be relevant. Judgments must of necessity be made on the basis of information in the hands of the directors when a distribution is authorized. They should not, of course, be held responsible as a matter of hindsight for unforeseen developments. This is particularly true with respect to assumptions as to the ability of the corporation's business to repay long-term obligations which do not mature for several years, since the primary focus of the directors' decision to make a distribution should normally be on the corporation's prospects and obligations in the shorter term, unless special factors concerning the corporation's prospects require the taking of a longer term perspective.

3. Relationship to the Federal Bankruptcy Act and Other Fraudulent Conveyance Statutes

The revised Model Business Corporation Act establishes the validity of distributions from the corporate law standpoint under section 6.40 and determines the potential liability of directors for improper distributions under sections 8.30 and 8.33. The federal Bankruptcy Act and state fraudulent conveyance statutes, on the other hand, are designed to enable the trustee or other representative to recapture for the benefit of creditors funds distributed to others in some circumstances. In light of these diverse purposes, it was not thought necessary to make the tests of section 6.40 identical to the tests for insolvency under these various statutes.

4. Balance Sheet Test

Section 6.40(c)(2) requires that, after giving effect to any distribution, the corporation's assets equal or exceed its liabilities plus (with some exceptions) the dissolution preferences of senior equity securities. Section 6.40(d) authorizes asset and liability determinations to be made for this purpose on the basis of either (1) financial statements prepared on the basis of accounting practices and principles that are reasonable in the circumstances or (2) a fair valuation or other method that is reasonable in the circumstances. The determination of a corporation's assets and liabilities and the choice of the permissible basis on which to do so are left to the judgment of its board of directors. In making a judgment under section 6.40(d), the board may rely under section 8.30 upon opinions, reports, or statements, including financial statements and other financial data prepared or presented by public accountants or others.

Section 6.40 does not utilize particular accounting terminology of a technical nature or specify accounting concepts. In making determinations under this section, the board of directors may make judgments about accounting matters, giving full effect to its right to rely upon professional or expert opinion.

In a corporation with subsidiaries, the board of directors may rely on unconsolidated statements prepared on the basis of the equity method of accounting (see American Institute of Certified Public Accountants, APB Opinion No. 18 (1971)) as to the corporation's investee corporations, including corporate joint ventures and subsidiaries, although other evidence would be relevant in the total determination.

a. *Generally Accepted Accounting Principles*

The board of directors should in all circumstances be entitled to rely upon reasonably current financial statements prepared on the basis of generally accepted accounting principles in determining whether or not the balance sheet test of section 6.40(c)(2) has been met, unless the board is then aware that it would be unreasonable to rely on the financial statements because of newly-discovered or subsequently arising facts or circumstances. But section 6.40 does not mandate the use of generally accepted accounting principles; it only requires the use of accounting practices and principles that are reasonable in the circumstances. While publicly-owned corporations subject to registration under the Securities Exchange Act of 1934 must, and many other corporations in fact do, utilize financial statements prepared on the basis of generally accepted accounting principles, a great number of smaller or closely-held corporations do not. Some of these corporations maintain records solely on a tax accounting basis and their financial statements are of necessity prepared on that basis. Others prepare financial statements that substantially reflect generally accepted accounting principles but may depart from them in some respects (e.g., footnote disclosure). These facts of corporate life indicate that a statutory standard of reasonableness, rather than stipulating generally accepted accounting principles as the normative standard, is appropriate in order to achieve a reasonable degree of flexibility and to accommodate the needs of the many different types of business corporations which might be subject to these provisions, including in particular closely-held corporations. Accordingly, the revised Model Business Corporation Act contemplates that generally acceptable accounting principles are always "reasonable in the circumstances" and that other accounting principles may be perfectly acceptable, under a general standard of reasonableness, even if they do not involve the "fair value" or "current value" concepts that are also contemplated by section 6.40(d).

b. Other Principles

Section 6.40(d) specifically permits determinations to be made under section 6.40(c)(2) on the basis of a fair valuation or other method that is reasonable in the circumstances. Thus the statute authorizes departures from historical cost accounting and sanctions the use of appraisal and current value methods to determine the amount available for distribution. No particular method of valuation is prescribed in the statute, since different methods may have validity depending upon the circumstances, including the type of enterprise and the purpose for which the determination is made. For example, it is inappropriate in most cases to apply a "quick-sale liquidation" method to value an enterprise, particularly with respect to the payment of normal dividends. On the other hand, a "quick-sale liquidation" valuation method might be appropriate in certain circumstances for an enterprise in the course of reducing its asset or business base by a material degree. In most cases, a fair valuation method or a going-concern basis would be appropriate if it is believed that the enterprise will continue as a going concern.

Ordinarily a corporation should not selectively revalue assets. It should consider the value of all its material assets, whether or not reflected in the financial statements (e.g., a valuable executory contract). Likewise, all of a corporation's material obligations should be considered and revalued to the extent appropriate and possible. In any event, section 6.40(d) calls for the application under section 6.40(c)(2) of a method of determining the aggregate amount of assets and liabilities that is reasonable in the circumstances.

Section 6.40(d) also refers to some "other method that is reasonable in the circumstances." This phrase is intended to comprehend within section 6.40(c)(2) the wide variety of possibilities that might not be considered to fall under a "fair valuation" or "current value" but might be reasonable in the circumstances of a particular case.

5. Preferential Dissolution Rights and the Balance Sheet Test

Section 6.40(c)(2) provides that a distribution may not be made unless the total assets of the corporation exceed its liabilities plus the amount that would be needed to satisfy any shareholders' superior preferential rights upon dissolution if the corporation were to be dissolved at the time of the distribution. This requirement in effect treats preferential dissolution rights of shares for distribution purposes as if they were liabilities for the sole purpose of determining the amount available for distributions, and carries forward analogous treatment of shares having preferential dissolution rights from earlier versions of the Model Act. In making the calculation of the amount that must be added to the liabilities of the corporation to reflect the preferential dissolution rights, the assumption should be made that the preferential dissolution rights are to be established pursuant to the articles of incorporation, as of the date of the distribution or proposed distribution. The amount so determined must include arrearages in preferential dividends if the articles of incorporation or resolution require that they be paid upon the dissolution of the corporation. In the case of shares having both a preferential right upon dissolution and other nonpreferential rights, only the preferential right should be taken into account. The treatment of preferential dissolution rights of classes of shares set forth in section 6.40(c)(2) is applicable only to the balance sheet test and is not applicable to the equity insolvency test of section 6.40(c)(1). The treatment of preferential rights mandated by this section may always be eliminated by an appropriate provision in the articles of incorporation.

6. Time of Measurement

Section 6.40(e)(3) provides that the time for measuring the effect of a distribution for compliance with the equity insolvency and balance sheet tests for all distributions not involving the reacquisition of shares or the distribution of indebtedness is the date of authorization, if the payment occurs within 120 days following the authorization; if the payment occurs more than 120 days after the authorization, however, the date of payment must be used. If the corporation elects to make a distribution in the form of its own indebtedness under section 6.40(e)(2) the validity of that distribution must be measured as of the time of distribution, unless the indebtedness qualifies under section 6.40(g).

Section 6.40(e)(1) provides a different rule for the time of measurement when the distribution involves a reacquisition of shares. See below, Application to Reacquisition of Shares—Time of Measurement.

7. Record Date

Section 6.40(b) fixes the record date (if the board of directors does not otherwise fix it) for distributions other than those involving a reacquisition of shares as the date the board of directors authorizes the distribution. No record date is necessary for a reacquisition of shares from one or more specific shareholders. The board of directors has discretion to set a record date for a reacquisition if it is to be pro rata and to be offered to all shareholders as of a specified date.

8. Application to Reacquisition of Shares

The application of the equity insolvency and balance sheet tests to distributions that involve the purchase, redemption, or other acquisition of the corporation's shares creates unique problems; section 6.40 provides a specific rule for the resolution of these problems as described below.

a. *Time of Measurement*

Section 6.40(e)(1) provides that the time for measuring the effect of a distribution under section 6.40(c), if shares of the corporation are reacquired, is the earlier of (i) the payment date, or (ii) the date the shareholder ceased to be a shareholder with respect to the shares, except as provided in section 6.40(g).

b. *When Tests Are Applied to Redemption–Related Debt*

In an acquisition of its shares, a corporation may transfer property or incur debt to the former holder of the shares. The case law on the status of this debt is conflicting. However, share repurchase agreements involving payment for shares over a period of time are of special importance in closely-held corporate enterprises. Section 6.40(e) provides a clear rule for this situation: the legality of the distribution must be measured at the time of the issuance [or] incurrence of the debt, not at a later date when the debt is actually paid, except as provided in section 6.40(g). Of course, this does not preclude a later challenge of a payment on account of redemption-related debt by a bankruptcy trustee on the ground that it constitutes a preferential payment to a creditor.

*c. Priority of Debt Distributed Directly or Incurred in Connection
     With a Reacquisition of Shares*

Section 6.40(f) provides that indebtedness created to acquire the
corporation's shares or issued as a distribution is on a parity with the
indebtedness of the corporation to its general, unsecured creditors,
except to the extent subordinated by agreement. General creditors are
better off in these situations than they would have been if cash or other
property had been paid out for the shares or distributed (which is proper
under the statute), and no worse off than if cash had been paid or
distributed and then lent back to the corporation, making the shareholders (or former shareholders) creditors. The parity created by section
6.40(f) therefore is logically consistent with the rule established by
section 6.40(e) that these transactions should be judged at the time of
the issuance of the debt.

9. Distributions in Liquidation

Subsection (h) provides that distributions in liquidation under chap-
ter14 are not subject to the distribution limitations of section 6.40.Chap-
ter 14 provides specifically for payment of creditor claims and distributions to shareholders in liquidation upon dissolution of the corporation.
See section 14.09.

Chapter 7

SHAREHOLDERS

Subchapter A

Meetings

§ 7.01 Annual Meeting

(a) Unless directors are elected by written consent in lieu of an annual
    meeting as permitted by section 7.04, a corporation shall hold a
    meeting of shareholders annually at a time stated in or fixed in
    accordance with the bylaws; provided, however, that if a corpora-
    tion's articles of incorporation authorize shareholders to cumulate
    their votes when electing directors pursuant to section 7.28, directors
    may not be elected by less than unanimous written consent.

(b) Annual shareholders' meetings may be held in or out of this state at
    the place stated in or fixed in accordance with the bylaws. If no place
    is stated in or fixed in accordance with the bylaws, annual meetings
    shall be held at the corporation's principal office.

(c) The failure to hold an annual meeting at the time stated in or fixed
    in accordance with a corporation's bylaws does not affect the validity
    of any corporate action.

Official Comment

Section 7.01(a) requires every corporation to hold an annual meeting of shareholders entitled to participate in the election of directors unless directors are elected by written consent as provided for in section 7.04. The principal action to be taken at the annual meeting is the election of directors pursuant to section 8.03, but the purposes of the annual meeting are not limited and all matters appropriate for shareholder action may be considered at that meeting. An annual meeting is also an appropriate forum for a shareholder to raise any relevant question about the corporation's operations.

The requirement of section 7.01(a) that an annual meeting be held is phrased in mandatory terms to ensure that every shareholder entitled to participate in an annual meeting has the unqualified rights to (1) demand that an annual meeting be held and (2) compel the holding of the meeting under section 7.03 if the corporation does not promptly hold the meeting and if the shareholders have not elected directors by written consent.

Many corporations, such as non-public subsidiaries and closely held corporations, do not regularly hold annual meetings and, if no shareholder objects or action has been taken by written consent, that practice creates no problem under section 7.01, since section 7.01(c) provides that failure to hold an annual meeting does not affect the validity of any corporate action. The shareholders may act by consent under section 7.04. Directors, once duly elected, remain in office until their successors are elected or they resign or are removed. See section 8.05. Where the articles of incorporation permit the election of directors by less than unanimous written consent, however, such action could result in the replacement of directors, through the election of new directors, even if the vote in favor of such election were less than the vote necessary to satisfy a provision in the corporation's articles of incorporation or bylaws requiring a higher vote to remove directors.

Where a corporation's articles of incorporation permit cumulative voting in the election of directors, directors may not be elected by less than unanimous written consent.

The time and place of the annual meeting may be "stated in or fixed in accordance with the bylaws." If the bylaws do not themselves fix a time and place for the annual meeting, authority to fix them may be delegated to the board of directors or to a specified corporate officer. This section thus gives corporations the flexibility to hold annual meetings in varying places at varying times as convenience may dictate.

The annual meeting may be held either inside or outside the state or in a foreign country, but if the bylaws do not fix, or state the method of fixing, the place of the meeting, the meeting must be held at the "principal office" of the corporation. The principal office is defined in section 1.40 as the location of the principal executive office of the corporation and may or may not be its registered or official office under section 5.01. Section 16.21 requires that the address of the principal office be specified in the corporation's annual report.

Authority granted to the board of directors or some individual to fix the time and place of the annual meeting must be exercised in good faith. See *Schnell v. Chris–Craft Industries, Inc.*, 285 A.2d 437 (Del. 1971).

§ 7.02   Special Meeting

(a) A corporation shall hold a special meeting of shareholders:

    (1) on call of its board of directors or the person or persons authorized to do so by the articles of incorporation or bylaws; or

    (2) if the holders of at least 10 percent of all the votes entitled to be cast on any issue proposed to be considered at the proposed special meeting sign, date, and deliver to the corporation's secretary one or more written demands for the meeting describing the purpose or purposes for which it is to be held, provided that the articles of incorporation may fix a lower percentage or a higher percentage not exceeding 25 percent of all the votes entitled to be cast on any issue proposed to be considered. Unless otherwise provided in the articles of incorporation, a written demand for a special meeting may be revoked by a writing to that effect received by the corporation prior to the receipt by the corporation of demands sufficient in number to require the holding of a special meeting.

(b) If not otherwise fixed under section 7.03 or 7.07, the record date for determining shareholders entitled to demand a special meeting is the date the first shareholder signs the demand.

(c) Special shareholders' meetings may be held in or out of this state at the place stated in or fixed in accordance with the bylaws. If no place is stated or fixed in accordance with the bylaws, special meetings shall be held at the corporation's principal office.

(d) Only business within the purpose or purposes described in the meeting notice required by section 7.05(c) may be conducted at a special shareholders' meeting.

§ 7.03   Court–Ordered Meeting

(a) The [name or describe] court of the county where a corporation's principal office (or, if none in this state, its registered office) is located may summarily order a meeting to be held:

    (1) on application of any shareholder of the corporation entitled to participate in an annual meeting if an annual meeting was not held or action by written consent in lieu thereof did not become

effective within the earlier of 6 months after the end of the corporation's fiscal year or 15 months after its last annual meeting; or

(2) on application of a shareholder who signed a demand for a special meeting valid under section 7.02, if:

    (i) notice of the special meeting was not given within 30 days after the date the demand was delivered to the corporation's secretary; or

    (ii) the special meeting was not held in accordance with the notice.

(b) The court may fix the time and place of the meeting, determine the shares entitled to participate in the meeting, specify a record date for determining shareholders entitled to notice of and to vote at the meeting, prescribe the form and content of the meeting notice, fix the quorum required for specific matters to be considered at the meeting (or direct that the votes represented at the meeting constitute a quorum for action on those matters), and enter other orders necessary to accomplish the purpose or purposes of the meeting.

§ 7.04 Action Without Meeting

(a) Action required or permitted by this Act to be taken at a shareholders' meeting may be taken without a meeting if the action is taken by all the shareholders entitled to vote on the action. The action must be evidenced by one or more written consents bearing the date of signature and describing the action taken, signed by all the shareholders entitled to vote on the action and delivered to the corporation for inclusion in the minutes or filing with the corporate records.

(b) The articles of incorporation may provide that any action required or permitted by this Act to be taken at a shareholders' meeting may be taken without a meeting, and without prior notice, if consents in writing setting forth the action so taken are signed by the holders of outstanding shares having not less than the minimum number of votes that would be required to authorize or take the action at a meeting at which all shares entitled to vote on the action were present and voted. The written consent shall bear the date of signature of the shareholder who signs the consent and be delivered to the corporation for inclusion in the minutes or filing with the corporate records.

(c) If not otherwise fixed under section 7.07 and if prior board action is not required respecting the action to be taken without a meeting, the record date for determining the shareholders entitled to take action without a meeting shall be the first date on which a signed written consent is delivered to the corporation. If not otherwise fixed under section 7.07 and if prior board action is required respecting the action to be taken without a meeting, the record date shall be the close of business on the day the resolution of the board taking such prior action is adopted. No written consent shall be effective to take the corporate action referred to therein unless, within 60 days of the earliest date on which a consent delivered to the corporation as required by this section was signed, written consents signed by the holders of shares having sufficient votes to take the action have been delivered to the corporation. A written consent may be revoked by a writing to that effect delivered to the corporation before unrevoked written consents sufficient in number to take the corporate action are delivered to the corporation.

(d) A consent signed pursuant to the provisions of this section has the effect of a vote taken at a meeting and may be described as such in any document. Unless the articles of incorporation, bylaws or a resolution of the board of directors provides for a reasonable delay to permit tabulation of written consents, the action taken by written consent shall be effective when written consents signed by the holders of shares having sufficient votes to take the action are delivered to the corporation.

(e) If this Act requires that notice of a proposed action be given to nonvoting shareholders and the action is to be taken by written consent of the voting shareholders, the corporation must give its nonvoting shareholders written notice of the action not more than 10 days after (i) written consents sufficient to take the action have been delivered to the corporation, or (ii) such later date that tabulation of consents is completed pursuant to an authorization under subsection (d). The notice must reasonably describe the action taken and contain or be accompanied by the same material that, under any provision of this Act, would have been required to be sent to nonvoting shareholders in a notice of a meeting at which the pro- posed action would have been submitted to the shareholders for action.

(f) If action is taken by less than unanimous written consent of the voting shareholders, the corporation must give its nonconsenting voting shareholders written notice of the action not more than 10 days after (i) written consents sufficient to take the action have been delivered to the corporation, or (ii) such later date that tabulation of consents is completed pursuant to an authorization under subsection (d). The notice must reasonably describe the action taken and contain or be accompanied by the same material that, under any provision of this Act, would have been required to be sent to voting shareholders in a notice of a meeting at which the action would have been submitted to the shareholders for action.

(g) The notice requirements in subsections (e) and (f) shall not delay the effectiveness of actions taken by written consent, and a failure to comply with such notice requirements shall not invalidate actions taken by written consent, provided that this subsection shall not be deemed to limit judicial power to fashion any appropriate remedy in favor of a shareholder adversely affected by a failure to give such notice within the required time period.

(h) An electronic transmission may be used to consent to an action, if the electronic transmission contains or is accompanied by information from which the corporation can determine the date on which the electronic transmission was signed and that the electronic transmission was authorized by the shareholder, the shareholder's agent or the shareholder's attorney-in-fact.

(i) Delivery of a written consent to the corporation under this section is delivery to the corporation's registered agent at its registered office or to the secretary of the corporation at its principal office.

Official Comment

Section 7.04 permits shareholders to act by written consent without holding a meeting. Section 7.04(a) permits shareholders to take action by unanimous written consent and is applicable to all corporations. As a practical matter, unanimous written consent is obtainable only for matters on which there are relatively few shareholders entitled to vote, and is thus generally not used by public corporations. Under section 7.04(b) a corporation may include in its articles of incorporation a provision that permits shareholder action by less than unanimous written consent. For closely held corporations, this provision provides an opportunity to eliminate formalities that the owners may consider unnecessary. In considering whether to include this provision, one should take into account that some shareholders may oppose the elimination of the annual meeting because of their desire to meet with the corporation's management and directors at that meeting. The availability of shareholder action by less than unanimous consent may also facilitate a sudden change in control.

The unanimous written consent permitted in section 7.04(a) is applicable to any shareholder action, including, without limitation, election of directors, approval of mergers or sales of substantially all the corporate property not in the ordinary course of business, amendments of articles of incorporation, and dissolution. If the articles of incorporation permit action by less than unanimous written consent, they may also limit or otherwise specify the shareholder actions that may be approved by less than unanimous consent. If a corporation has determined to elect directors by cumulative voting, such directors may not be elected by less than unanimous written consent. See sections 7.01(a) and 7.28. Action by written consent has the same effect as a meeting vote and may be described as such in any document, including documents delivered to the secretary of state for filing.

1. Form of Written Consent

To be effective, a consent must be in writing, dated and delivered to the corporation's registered agent at its registered office or to its secretary at its principal office. A written consent may be delivered by means of an electronic transmission. See section 1.40(5).

A shareholder or proxy may use an electronic transmission to consent to an action. If an electronic transmission is used to consent to an action, the corporation must be able to determine from the transmission the date of the signature and that the consent was authorized by the shareholder or a person authorized to act for the shareholder. See sections 1.40(7A), 1.40(22A) and 7.22(b).

A unanimous written consent must be signed by all the shareholders entitled to vote on the action. A less than unanimous written consent must be signed by those shareholders entitled to cast not less than the minimum number of votes necessary to take the action if all shares entitled to vote on the action were present and voted at a meeting of shareholders. In some cases, more votes may be required to approve an action by less than unanimous written consent than would be required to approve the same action at a meeting that is not attended by all shareholders. For example, if an action requires the approval of a majority of shares represented at a meeting where a quorum (a majority of the votes entitled to be cast) is present, a corporation with 1,000 shares eligible to vote on the action will need 501 votes to approve the action by less than unanimous written consent; at a meeting at which only a quorum is present the same action will be approved if the votes cast in favor of the proposed action exceed the votes cast opposing the action, resulting in approval by as few as 251 votes (assuming no abstentions). Where the corporation's articles of incorporation provide for a greater voting requirement, however, the number of shares required to consent to an action may be the same as the number of shares required to approve the action at a meeting of shareholders.

The phrase "one or more written consents" is included in section 7.04 to make it clear that shareholders do not need to sign the same piece of paper. For actions that do not require prior board action, the record date for determining who is entitled to vote, if not otherwise fixed by or in accordance with the bylaws, is the date the first signed consent is delivered to the corporation. For actions that require prior board action, if not otherwise fixed by the board, the record date is the date the board's prior action is adopted. To minimize the possibility that action by written consent will be authorized by action of persons who may no longer be shareholders at the time the action is taken, section 7.04(c) requires that all consents be signed within 60 days of the earliest signature date of the consents delivered to the corporation.

2. Notice to Nonconsenting Shareholders

When action is taken by less than unanimous written consent, the Model Act requires that notice be given to nonconsenting shareholders not more than 10 days after the later of the date (a) written consents sufficient for the action to be valid are delivered to the corporation and (b) tabulation of consents is completed. The notice must describe the action that was taken and be accompanied by any materials required to be given to shareholders in a notice of a meeting at which the action was to be considered. The failure to give notice within the required time period will not invalidate or delay the effectiveness of a shareholder action, although a shareholder may seek other remedies. By requiring notice only after shareholder action has been taken, the Model Act preserves the practical utility of the less than unanimous written consent when action needs to be taken quickly, without the delay that would result from a mandatory prior notice requirement. Of course a corporation may provide for advance notice in its articles of incorporation.

3. Effectiveness and Revocation of Consent

Shareholder approval in the form of action by written consent is effective only when the last shareholder required to validly take action by written consent has signed the written consent and all consents have been delivered to the corporation. Before that time, a shareholder may withdraw a consent simply by delivering a written revocation of the consent to the corporation. *Cf. Calumet Industries, Inc. v. McClure*, 464 F. Supp. 19 (N.D. Ill. 1978). The withdrawal of a single consent, of course, destroys the unanimous written consent but may not impact a less than unanimous written consent. If a shareholder seeks to withdraw a consent after the requisite number of shareholders to validly take an action by written consent have signed written consents and filed them with the corporation, such withdrawal will be a nullity and shall be given no effect.

4. Consent to Fundamental Corporate Changes

Section 7.04(a) is applicable to all shareholder actions, including the approval of fundamental corporate changes described in chapters 10, 11, 12 and 14. If permitted by a corporation's articles of incorporation, shareholders may also approve fundamental corporate changes by less than unanimous written consent. If action approving fundamental corporate changes were taken at an annual or special meeting, shareholders who were not entitled to vote on the matter would nevertheless be entitled to receive notice of the meeting, including a description of the transaction proposed to be considered at the meeting. See, e.g., sections 10.03 (notice of proposed amendment), 11.04 (notice of proposed merger). If action is taken by written consent rather than at a meeting, section 7.04(e) provides that nonvoting shareholders must be given the same written notice of the action not more than 10 days after the later of the date (a) written consents sufficient for the action to be valid are delivered to the corporation and (b) tabulation of consents is completed. The notice must be accompanied by the same materials required by the Model Act to be given to nonvoting shareholders in a notice of meeting at which the action was to be considered.

§ 7.05   Notice of Meeting

(a) A corporation shall notify shareholders of the date, time, and place of each annual and special shareholders' meeting no fewer than 10 nor more than 60 days before the meeting date. Unless this Act or the articles of incorporation require otherwise, the corporation is required to give notice only to shareholders entitled to vote at the meeting.

(b) Unless this Act or the articles of incorporation require otherwise, notice of an annual meeting need not include a description of the purpose or purposes for which the meeting is called.

(c) Notice of a special meeting must include a description of the purpose or purposes for which the meeting is called.

(d) If not otherwise fixed under section 7.03 or 7.07, the record date for determining shareholders entitled to notice of and to vote at an annual or special shareholders' meeting is the day before the first notice is delivered to shareholders.

(e) Unless the bylaws require otherwise, if an annual or special shareholders' meeting is adjourned to a different date, time, or place, notice need not be given of the new date, time, or place if the new date, time, or place is announced at the meeting before adjournment. If a new record date for the adjourned meeting is or must be fixed under section 7.07, however, notice of the adjourned meeting must be given under this section to persons who are shareholders as of the new record date.

Official Comment ...

2. Statement of Matters to Be Considered at an Annual Meeting

Notice of all special meetings must include a description of the purpose or purposes for which the meeting is called and the matters acted upon at the meeting are limited to those within the notice of meeting. By contrast, the Model Act does not require that the notice of an annual meeting refer to any specific purpose or purposes, and any matter appropriate for shareholder action may be considered. As recognized in subsection (b), however, other provisions of the Model Act provide that certain types of fundamental corporate changes may be considered at an annual meeting only if specific reference to the proposed action appears in the notice of meeting. See sections 10.03, 11.03, 12.02, and 14.02. In addition, as a condition to relying upon shareholder action to establish the safe harbor protection of section 8.61(b), section

8.63 requires notice to shareholders providing information regarding any director's conflicting interest in a transaction. If the board of directors chooses, a notice of an annual meeting may also contain references to purposes or proposals not required by statute. In the event that management intends to present non-routine proposals for a shareholder vote and shareholders have not otherwise been informed of such proposals, good corporate practice suggests that references to such proposals be made in the notice. In any event, if a notice of an annual meeting refers specifically to one or more purposes, the meeting is not limited to those purposes. . . .

§ 7.06 Waiver of Notice

(a) A shareholder may waive any notice required by this Act, the articles of incorporation, or bylaws before or after the date and time stated in the notice. The waiver must be in writing, be signed by the shareholder entitled to the notice, and be delivered to the corporation for inclusion in the minutes or filing with the corporate records.

(b) A shareholder's attendance at a meeting:

(1) waives objection to lack of notice or defective notice of the meeting, unless the shareholder at the beginning of the meeting objects to holding the meeting or transacting business at the meeting;

(2) waives objection to consideration of a particular matter at the meeting that is not within the purpose or purposes described in the meeting notice, unless the shareholder objects to considering the matter when it is presented.

§ 7.07 Record Date

(a) The bylaws may fix or provide the manner of fixing the record date for one or more voting groups in order to determine the shareholders entitled to notice of a shareholders' meeting, to demand a special meeting, to vote, or to take any other action. If the bylaws do not fix or provide for fixing a record date, the board of directors of the corporation may fix a future date as the record date.

(b) A record date fixed under this section may not be more than 70 days before the meeting or action requiring a determination of shareholders.

(c) A determination of shareholders entitled to notice of or to vote at a shareholders' meeting is effective for any adjournment of the meeting unless the board of directors fixes a new record date, which it must do if the meeting is adjourned to a date more than 120 days after the date fixed for the original meeting.

(d) If a court orders a meeting adjourned to a date more than 120 days after the date fixed for the original meeting, it may provide that the original record date continues in effect or it may fix a new record date.

§ 7.08 Conduct of the Meeting

(a) At each meeting of shareholders, a chair shall preside. The chair shall be appointed as provided in the bylaws or, in the absence of such provision, by the board.

(b) The chair, unless the articles of incorporation or bylaws provide otherwise, shall have the authority to determine the order of business and shall establish rules for the conduct of the meeting.

(c) Any rules adopted for, and the conduct of, the meeting shall be fair to shareholders.

(d) The chair of the meeting shall announce at the meeting when the polls close for each matter voted upon. If no announcement is made, the polls shall be deemed to have closed upon the final adjournment of the meeting. After the polls close, no ballots, proxies or votes nor any revocations or changes thereto may be accepted.

Official Comment ...

The Act provides that only business within the purpose or purposes described in the meeting notice may be conducted at a special shareholders' meeting. See sections 7.02(d) and 7.05(c). In addition, a corporation's articles of incorporation or, more typically, its bylaws, may contain advance notice provisions requiring that shareholder nominations for election to the board of directors or resolutions intended to be voted on at the annual meeting must be made in writing and received by the corporation a prescribed number of days in advance of the meeting. Such advance notice bylaws are permitted provided (1) there is reasonable opportunity for shareholders to comply with them in a timely fashion, and (2) the requirements of the bylaws are reasonable in relationship to corporate needs. . . .

Among the considerations to be taken into account in determining reasonableness are (a) how and with what frequency shareholders are advised of the specific bylaw provisions, and (b) whether the time frame within which director nominations or shareholder resolutions must be submitted is consistent with the corporation's need, if any, (i) to prepare and publish a proxy statement, (ii) to verify that the director nominee meets any established qualifications for director and is willing to serve, (iii) to determine that a proposed resolution is a proper subject for shareholder action under the Act or other state law, or (iv) to give interested parties adequate opportunity to communicate a recommendation or response with respect to such matters, or to solicit proxies. Whether or not an advance notice provision has been adopted, if a public company receives advance notice of a matter to be raised for a vote at an annual meeting, management may exercise its discretionary proxy authority only in compliance with SEC Rule 14a–4(c)(1) adopted under the Securities Exchange Act of 1934....

Subchapter B

Voting

§ 7.20 Shareholders' List for Meeting

(a) After fixing a record date for a meeting, a corporation shall prepare an alphabetical list of the names of all its shareholders who are entitled to notice of a shareholders' meeting. The list must be arranged by voting group (and within each voting group by class or series of shares) and show the address of and number of shares held by each shareholder.

(b) The shareholders' list must be available for inspection by any shareholder, beginning two business days after notice of the meeting is given for which the list was prepared and continuing through the meeting, at the corporation's principal office or at a place identified in the meeting notice in the city where the meeting will be held. A shareholder, his agent, or attorney is entitled on written demand to inspect and, subject to the requirements of section 16.02(c), to copy the list, during regular business hours and at his expense, during the period it is available for inspection.

(c) The corporation shall make the shareholders' list available at the meeting, and any shareholder, his agent, or attorney is entitled to inspect the list at any time during the meeting or any adjournment.

(d) If the corporation refuses to allow a shareholder, his agent, or attorney to inspect the shareholders' list before or at the meeting (or copy the list as permitted by subsection (b)), the [name or describe] court of the county where a corporation's principal office (or, if none in this state, its registered office) is located, on application of the shareholder, may summarily order the inspection or copying at the corporation's expense and may postpone the meeting for which the list was prepared until the inspection or copying is complete.

(e) Refusal or failure to prepare or make available the shareholders' list does not affect the validity of action taken at the meeting.

Official Comment ...

5. The Right to Obtain a Copy of the List

Section 7.20(b) permits shareholders to "inspect" the list without limitation, but permits the shareholder to "copy" the list only if the shareholder complies with the requirement of section 16.02(c), that the demand be "made in good faith and for a proper purpose." The right to copy the list includes, if reasonable, the right to receive a copy of the list upon payment of a reasonable charge. See sections 16.03(b) and (c). The distinction between "inspection" and "copying" set forth in section 7.20(b) reflects an accommodation between competing considerations of permitting shareholders access to the list before a meeting and possible misuse of the list.

6. Relationship to Right to Inspect Corporate Records Generally

Section 7.20 creates a right of shareholders to inspect a list of shareholders in advance of and at a meeting that is independent of the rights of shareholders to inspect corporate records under chapter 16A. A shareholder may obtain the right to inspect the list of shareholders as provided in chapter 16A without regard to the provisions relating to the pendency of a meeting in section 7.20, and similarly the limitations of chapter 16A are not applicable to the right of inspection created by section 7.20 except to the extent the shareholder seeks to copy the list in advance of the meeting.

The right to inspect under chapter 16A is also broader in the sense that in some circumstances the shareholder may be entitled to receive copies of the documents he may inspect. See section 16.03.

§ 7.21 Voting Entitlement of Shares

(a) Except as provided in subsections (b) and (c) or unless the articles of incorporation provide otherwise, each outstanding share, regardless of class, is entitled to one vote on each matter voted on at a shareholders' meeting. Only shares are entitled to vote.

(b) Absent special circumstances, the shares of a corporation are not entitled to vote if they are owned, directly or indirectly, by a second corporation, domestic or foreign, and the first corporation owns, directly or indirectly, a majority of the shares entitled to vote for directors of the second corporation.

(c) Subsection (b) does not limit the power of a corporation to vote any shares, including its own shares, held by it in a fiduciary capacity.

(d) Redeemable shares are not entitled to vote after notice of redemption is mailed to the holders and a sum sufficient to redeem the shares has been deposited with a bank, trust company, or other financial institution under an irrevocable obligation to pay the holders the redemption price on surrender of the shares.

Official Comment

Section 7.21 deals with the entitlement of shareholders to vote, while section 7.22 deals with voting by proxy and section 7.24 establishes rules for the corporation's acceptance or rejection of proxy votes.

1. Voting Power of Shares

Section 7.21(a) provides that each outstanding share, regardless of class, is entitled to one vote per share unless otherwise provided in the articles of incorporation. See section 6.01 and its Official Comment. The articles of incorporation may provide for multiple or fractional votes per share, and may provide that some classes of shares are nonvoting on some or all matters, or that some classes have multiple or fractional votes per share while other classes have a single vote per share or different multiple or fractional votes per share, or that some classes constitute one or more separate voting groups and are entitled to vote separately on the matter.

The articles of incorporation may also authorize the board of directors to create classes or series of shares with preferential rights, which may be voting or nonvoting in whole or in part. See section 6.02 and its Official Comment.

Fractional or multiple votes per share, or nonvoting shares, are often used in the planning of business ventures, particularly closely held ventures, when the contributions of participants vary in kind or quality. It is possible through these devices, for example, to give persons with relatively small financial contributions a relatively large voting power within the corporation.

The power to vary or condition voting power is also often used to give increased protection to financial interests in the corporation. It is customary, for example, to make classes of shares with preferential rights nonvoting, but the power to vote may be granted to those classes if distributions are omitted for a specified period. This conditional right to vote may permit the class of shares with preferential rights to vote separately as a voting group to elect one or more directors or to vote with the shares having general voting rights in the election of the directors.

In order to reflect the possibility that shares may have multiple or fractional votes per share, all provisions relating to quorums, voting, and similar matters in the Model Act are phrased in terms of "votes" rather than "shares."

2. Voting Power of Nonshareholders

Under the last sentence of section 7.21(a), the power to vote cannot be granted generally to nonshareholders. The statutes of some states permit bondholders to be given the power to vote under certain specified circumstances; this option is not available under the Model Act. But creditors may in effect be given the power to vote, e.g., by creating a special class of redeemable voting shares for them, by creating a voting trust at the time the credit is extended with power in the creditors to name the voting trustees, by registering the shares in the name of the creditors as pledgees with power to vote, or by granting the creditors a revocable or irrevocable proxy to vote some or all of the outstanding shares. See the Official Comment to section 7.22.

3. Circular Holdings

Section 7.21(b) prohibits the voting of shares held by a domestic or foreign corporation that is itself a majority-owned subsidiary of the corporation issuing the shares. The purpose of this prohibition is to prevent management from using a corporate investment to perpetuate itself in power. Similar public policy considerations may be present in situations where the issuing corporation owns a large but not a majority interest in the corporation voting the shares. The inclusion of section 7.21(b) is not intended to affect the possible application of common law principles that may invalidate circular holding situations not within its literal prohibition. As to the possible existence of these common law principles, see, e.g., Cleveland Trust Co. v. Eaton, 11 Ohio Misc. 151, 229 N.E.2d 850 (1967), rev'd on the basis of statutory amendment, 21 Ohio St.2d 129, 256 N.E.2d 198 (1970). The phrase "absent special circumstances" is included to enable a court to permit the voting of shares where it deems that the purpose of the section is not violated.

4. Shares Held in a Fiduciary Capacity

Section 7.21(c) makes the prohibition against voting of circularly-owned shares of section 7.21(b) inapplicable to shares held in a fiduciary capacity. Compare Del.Gen.Corp.Law § 160(c). The Ohio statute involved in the *Eaton* case authorized a bank to vote its own shares that were held by it in a fiduciary capacity. A state may grant or prohibit such voting by another statute; section 7.21(c) provides only that such voting is not prohibited by the Model Act....

§ 7.22 Proxies

(a) A shareholder may vote his shares in person or by proxy.

(b) A shareholder or his agent or attorney-in-fact may appoint a proxy to vote or otherwise act for the shareholder by signing an appointment form, or by an electronic transmission. An electronic transmission must contain or be accompanied by information from which one can determine that the shareholder, the shareholder's agent, or the shareholder's attorney-in-fact authorized the electronic transmission.

(c) An appointment of a proxy is effective when a signed appointment form or an electronic transmission of the appointment is received by the inspector of election or the officer or agent of the corporation authorized to tabulate votes. An appointment is valid for 11 months unless a longer period is expressly provided in the appointment.

(d) An appointment of a proxy is revocable unless the appointment form or electronic transmission conspicuously states that it is irrevocable and the appointment is coupled with an interest. Appointments coupled with an interest include the appointment of:

(1) a pledgee;

(2) a person who purchased or agreed to purchase the shares;

(3) a creditor of the corporation who extended it credit under terms requiring the appointment;

(4) an employee of the corporation whose employment contract requires the appointment; or

(5) a party to a voting agreement created under section 7.31.

(e) The death or incapacity of the shareholder appointing a proxy does not affect the right of the corporation to accept the proxy's authority unless notice of the death or incapacity is received by the secretary or other officer or agent authorized to tabulate votes before the proxy exercises his authority under the appointment.

(f) An appointment made irrevocable under subsection (d) is revoked when the interest with which it is coupled is extinguished.

(g) A transferee for value of shares subject to an irrevocable appointment may revoke the appointment if he did not know of its existence when he acquired the shares and the existence of the irrevocable appointment was not noted conspicuously on the certificate representing the shares or on the information statement for shares without certificates.

(h) Subject to section 7.24 and to any express limitation on the proxy's authority stated in the appointment form or electronic transmission, a corporation is entitled to accept the proxy's vote or other action as that of the shareholder making the appointment.

Official Comment ...

1. Nomenclature

The word "proxy" is often used ambiguously, sometimes referring to the grant of authority to vote, sometimes to the document granting the authority, and sometimes to the person to whom the authority is granted. In the Model Act the word "proxy" is used only in the last sense; the terms "appointment form" and "electronic transmission" are used to describe the document or communication appointing the proxy; and the word "appointment" is used to describe the grant of authority to vote....

§ 7.23 Shares Held by Nominees

(a) A corporation may establish a procedure by which the beneficial owner of shares that are registered in the name of a nominee is recognized by the corporation as the shareholder. The extent of this recognition may be determined in the procedure.

(b) The procedure may set forth:

(1) the types of nominees to which it applies;

(2) the rights or privileges that the corporation recognizes in a beneficial owner;

(3) the manner in which the procedure is selected by the nominee;

(4) the information that must be provided when the procedure is selected;

(5) the period for which selection of the procedure is effective; and

(6) other aspects of the rights and duties created.

§ 7.24 Corporation's Acceptance of Votes

(a) If the name signed on a vote, consent, waiver, or proxy appointment corresponds to the name of a shareholder, the corporation if acting in good faith is entitled to accept the vote, consent, waiver, or proxy appointment and give it effect as the act of the shareholder.

(b) If the name signed on a vote, consent, waiver, or proxy appointment does not correspond to the name of its shareholder, the corporation if acting in good faith is nevertheless entitled to accept the vote, consent, waiver, or proxy appointment and give it effect as the act of the shareholder if:

(1) the shareholder is an entity and the name signed purports to be that of an officer or agent of the entity;

(2) the name signed purports to be that of an administrator, executor, guardian, or conservator representing the shareholder and, if the corporation requests, evidence of fiduciary status acceptable to the corporation has been presented with respect to the vote, consent, waiver, or proxy appointment;

(3) the name signed purports to be that of a receiver or trustee in bankruptcy of the shareholder and, if the corporation requests, evidence of this status acceptable to the corporation has been presented with respect to the vote, consent, waiver, or proxy appointment;

(4) the name signed purports to be that of a pledgee, beneficial owner, or attorney-in-fact of the shareholder and, if the corporation requests, evidence acceptable to the corporation of the signatory's authority to sign for the shareholder has been presented with respect to the vote, consent, waiver, or proxy appointment;

(5) two or more persons are the shareholder as cotenants or fiduciaries and the name signed purports to be the name of at least one of the coowners and the person signing appears to be acting on behalf of all the coowners.

(c) The corporation is entitled to reject a vote, consent, waiver, or proxy appointment if the secretary or other officer or agent authorized to tabulate votes, acting in good faith, has reasonable basis for doubt about the validity of the signature on it or about the signatory's authority to sign for the shareholder.

(d) The corporation and its officer or agent who accepts or rejects a vote, consent, waiver, or proxy appointment in good faith and in accordance with the standards of this section or section 7.22(b) are not liable in damages to the shareholder for the consequences of the acceptance or rejection.

(e) Corporate action based on the acceptance or rejection of a vote, consent, waiver, or proxy appointment under this section or section 7.22(b) is valid unless a court of competent jurisdiction determines otherwise.

§ 7.25 Quorum and Voting Requirements for Voting Groups

(a) Shares entitled to vote as a separate voting group may take action on a matter at a meeting only if a quorum of those shares exists with respect to that matter. Unless the articles of incorporation or this Act provide otherwise, a majority of the votes entitled to be cast on the matter by the voting group constitutes a quorum of that voting group for action on that matter.

(b) Once a share is represented for any purpose at a meeting, it is deemed present for quorum purposes for the remainder of the meeting and for any adjournment of that meeting unless a new record date is or must be set for that adjourned meeting.

(c) If a quorum exists, action on a matter (other than the election of directors) by a voting group is approved if the votes cast within the voting group favoring the action exceed the votes cast opposing the action, unless the articles of incorporation or this Act require a greater number of affirmative votes.

(d) An amendment of articles of incorporation adding, changing, or deleting a quorum or voting requirement for a voting group greater than specified in subsection (a) or (c) is governed by section 7.27.

(e) The election of directors is governed by section 7.28.

Official Comment ...

3. Quorum Requirements for Action by Voting Group....

Section 7.25(b) retains the common law view that once a share is present at a meeting, it is deemed present for quorum purposes throughout the meeting. Thus, a voting group may continue to act despite the withdrawal of persons having the power to vote one or more shares in an effort "to break the quorum." In this respect, a meeting of shareholders is governed by a different rule than a meeting of directors, where a sufficient number of directors must be present to constitute a quorum at the time action is taken. See section 8.24 and its Official Comment.

Once a share is present at a meeting it is also deemed to be present at any adjourned meeting unless a new record date is or must be set for that adjourned meeting. See section 7.07. If a new record date is set, new notice must be given to holders of shares of a voting group and a quorum must be established from within the holders of shares of that voting group on the new record date.

The shares owned by a shareholder who comes to the meeting to object on grounds of lack of notice may be counted toward the presence of a quorum. Similarly, the holdings of a shareholder who attends a meeting solely for purposes of raising the objection that a quorum is not present is counted toward the presence of a quorum. Attendance at a meeting, however, does not constitute a waiver of other objections to the meeting such as the lack of notice. Such waivers are governed by section 7.06(b).

As used in sections 7.25 and 7.26, "represented at the meeting" means the physical presence of the shareholder (whether in person or by his written authorization) in the meeting room after the meeting has been called to order or the presiding officer has commenced consideration of the business of the meeting, and before the final adjournment of the meeting. . . .

4.   Voting Requirements for Approval by Voting Group

Section 7.25(c) provides that an action (other than the election of directors, which is governed by section 7.28) is approved by a voting group at a meeting at which a quorum is present if the votes cast in favor of the action exceed the votes cast opposing the action. This section changes the traditional rule appearing in earlier versions of the Model Act and many state statutes that an action is approved at a meeting at which a quorum is present if it receives the affirmative vote "of a majority of the shares represented at that meeting." The traditional rule in effect treated abstentions as negative votes; the Revised Model Act treats them truly as abstentions. . . .

5.   Modification of Standard Requirements

. . . The articles of incorporation may increase the quorum and voting requirements to any extent desired up to and including unanimity upon compliance with section 7.27 . . . . The articles may also decrease the quorum requirement as desired. Earlier versions of the Model Act limited the power to reduce the quorum to a minimum of one-third; this restriction, was eliminated from the Revised Model Act because it was thought to be unreasonably confining in certain situations, such as where a class of shares with preferential rights is given a limited right to vote that may be exercisable only rarely. . . .

§ 7.26   Action by Single and Multiple Voting Groups

(a) If the articles of incorporation or this Act provide for voting by a single voting group on a matter, action on that matter is taken when voted upon by that voting group as provided in section 7.25.

(b) If the articles of incorporation or this Act provide for voting by two or more voting groups on a matter, action on that matter is taken only when voted upon by each of those voting groups counted separately as provided in section 7.25. Action may be taken by one voting group on a matter even though no action is taken by another voting group entitled to vote on the matter.

Official Comment

Section 7.26(a) provides that when a matter is to be voted upon by a single voting group, action is taken when the voting group votes upon the action as provided in section 7.25. In most instances the single voting group will consist of all the shares of the class or classes entitled to vote by the articles of incorporation; voting by two or more voting groups as contemplated by section 7.26(b) is the exceptional case.

Section 7.26(b) basically requires that if more than one voting group is entitled to vote on a matter, favorable action on a matter is taken only when it is voted upon favorably by each voting group, counted separately. Implicit in this section are the concepts that (1) different quorum and voting requirements may be applicable to different matters considered at a single meeting and (2) different quorum and voting requirements may be applicable to different voting groups voting on the same matter. See the Official Comment to section 7.25. Thus, each group entitled to vote must independently meet the quorum and voting requirements established by section 7.25....

2.   Participation of Shares in Multiple Voting Groups

As described in section 7.26(b), if voting by multiple voting groups is required, the votes of members of each voting group must be separately tabulated. Normally, each class or series of shares will participate in only a single voting group. But since holders of shares entitled by the articles of incorporation to vote generally on a matter are always entitled to vote in the voting group consisting of the general voting shares, in some instances classes or series of shares may be entitled to be counted simultaneously in two voting groups. This will occur whenever a class or series of shares entitled to vote generally on a matter under the articles of incorporation is affected by the matter in a way that gives rise to the right to have its vote counted separately as an independent voting group under the Act. For example, assume that corporation Y has outstanding one class of general voting shares without preferential rights ("common shares"), 500 shares issued, and one class of shares with preferential rights ("preferred shares"), 100 shares issued, that also

771

have full voting rights under the articles of incorporation, i.e., the preferred may vote for election of directors and on all other matters on which common may vote. The preferred and the common therefore are part of the general voting group. The directors propose to amend the articles of incorporation to change the preferential dividend rights of the preferred from cumulative to noncumulative. All shares are present at the meeting and they divide as follows on the proposal to adopt the amendment:

> Yes — Common   230
> — Preferred   80
> No — Common   270
> — Preferred   20

Both the preferred and the common are entitled to vote on the amendment to the articles of incorporation since they are part of a general voting group pursuant to the articles. But the vote of the preferred is also entitled to be counted separately on the proposal by section 10.04(a)(4) of the Model Act. The result is that the proposal passes by a vote of 310 to 290 in the voting group consisting of the shares entitled to vote generally and 80 to 20 in the voting group consisting solely of the preferred shares:

(a) First voting group

> Yes: Common   230
> Preferred   <u>80</u>
> 310
> No: Common   270
> Preferred   <u>20</u>
> 290

(b) Second voting group (preferred)

> Yes: Preferred   80
> No: Preferred   20

In this situation, in the absence of a special quorum requirement, a meeting could approve the proposal to amend the articles of incorporation if—and only if—a quorum of each voting group is present, i.e., at least 51 shares of preferred and 301 shares of common and preferred were represented at the meeting. . . .

§ 7.27 Greater Quorum or Voting Requirements

(a) The articles of incorporation may provide for a greater quorum or voting requirement for shareholders (or voting groups of shareholders) than is provided for by this Act.

(b) An amendment to the articles of incorporation that adds, changes, or deletes a greater quorum or voting requirement must meet the same quorum requirement and be adopted by the same vote and voting groups required to take action under the quorum and voting requirements then in effect or proposed to be adopted, whichever is greater.

Official Comment

Section 7.27(a) permits the articles of incorporation to increase the quorum or voting requirements for approval of an action by shareholders up to any desired amount including unanimity. These provisions may relate to ordinary or routine actions by the general voting group ... or to one or more other voting groups or to actions for which the Model Act provides a greater voting requirement—for example, changes of a fundamental nature in the corporation like certain amendments to articles of incorporation (Section 10.03)....

A provision that increases the requirement for approval of an ordinary matter or a fundamental change is usually referred to as a "supermajority" provision.

Section 7.27(b) requires any amendment of the articles of incorporation that adds, modifies, or repeals any supermajority provision to be approved by the greater of the proposed quorum and vote requirement or by the quorum and vote required by the articles before their amendment. Thus, a supermajority provision that requires an 80 percent affirmative vote of all eligible votes of a voting group present at the meeting may not be removed from the articles of incorporation or reduced in any way except by an 80 percent affirmative vote. If the 80 percent requirement is coupled with a quorum requirement for a voting group that shares representing two-thirds of the total votes must be present in person or by proxy, both the 80 percent voting requirement and the two-thirds quorum requirement are immune from reduction except at a meeting of the voting group at which the two-thirds quorum requirement is met and the reduction is approved by an 80 percent affirmative vote. If the proposal is to increase the 80 percent voting requirement to 90 percent, that proposal must be approved by a 90 percent affirmative vote at a meeting of the voting group at which the two-thirds quorum requirement is met; if the proposal is to increase the two-thirds quorum requirement to three-fourths without changing the 80 percent voting requirement, that proposal must be approved by an 80 percent affirmative vote at a meeting of the voting group at which a three-fourths quorum requirement is met.

§ 7.28 Voting for Directors; Cumulative Voting

(a) Unless otherwise provided in the articles of incorporation, directors are elected by a plurality of the votes cast by the shares entitled to vote in the election at a meeting at which a quorum is present.

(b) Shareholders do not have a right to cumulate their votes for directors unless the articles of incorporation so provide.

(c) A statement included in the articles of incorporation that "[all] [a designated voting group of] shareholders are entitled to cumulate their votes for directors" (or words of similar import) means that the shareholders designated are entitled to multiply the number of votes they are entitled to cast by the number of directors for whom they are entitled to vote and cast the product for a single candidate or distribute the product among two or more candidates.

(d) Shares otherwise entitled to vote cumulatively may not be voted cumulatively at a particular meeting unless:

(1) the meeting notice or proxy statement accompanying the notice states conspicuously that cumulative voting is authorized; or

(2) a shareholder who has the right to cumulate his votes gives notice to the corporation not less than 48 hours before the time set for the meeting of the shareholder's intent to cumulate his votes during the meeting, and if one shareholder gives this notice all other shareholders in the same voting group participating in the election are entitled to cumulate their votes without giving further notice.

§ 7.29 Inspectors of Election

(a) A corporation having any shares listed on a national securities exchange or regularly traded in a market maintained by one or more members of a national or affiliated securities association shall, and any other corporation may, appoint one or more inspectors to act at a meeting of shareholders and make a written report of the inspectors' determinations. Each inspector shall take and sign an oath faithfully to execute the duties of inspector with strict impartiality and according to the best of the inspector's ability.

(b) The inspectors shall
(1) ascertain the number of shares outstanding and the voting power of each;
(2) determine the shares represented at a meeting;
(3) determine the validity of proxies and ballots;
(4) count all votes; and
(5) determine the result.

(c) An inspector may be an officer or employee of the corporation.

Official Comment

Section 7.29(a) requires that, if a corporation has shares which are listed on a national securities exchange or regularly traded in a market maintained by one or more members of a national or affiliated securities association, one or more inspectors of election must be appointed to act at each meeting of shareholders and make a written report of the determinations made pursuant to section 7.29(b). It is contemplated that the selection of inspectors would be made by responsible officers or by the directors, as authorized either generally or specifically in the corporation's bylaws. Alternate inspectors could also be designated to replace any inspector who fails to act. The requirement of a written report is to facilitate judicial review of determinations made by inspectors.

Section 7.29(b) specifies the duties of inspectors of election. If no challenge of a determination by the inspectors within the authority given them under this section is timely made, such determination shall be conclusive. In the event of a challenge of any determination by the inspectors in a court of competent jurisdiction, the court should give such weight to determinations of fact by the inspectors as it shall deem appropriate, taking into account the relationship of the inspectors, if any, to the management of the company and other persons interested in the outcome of the vote, the evidence available to the inspectors, whether their determinations appear to be reasonable, and such other circumstances as the court shall regard as relevant. The court should review de novo all determinations of law made implicitly or explicitly by the inspectors. . . .

Section 7.29(c) provides that an inspector may be an officer or employee of the corporation. However, in the case of publicly-held corporations, good corporate practice suggests that such inspectors should be independent persons who are neither employees nor officers if there is a contested matter or a shareholder proposal to be considered. Not only will the issue of independent inspectors enhance investor perception as to the fairness of the voting process, but also the report of independent inspectors can be expected to be given greater evidentiary weight by any court reviewing a contested vote.

Subchapter C

Voting Trusts and Agreements

§ 7.30 Voting Trusts

(a) One or more shareholders may create a voting trust, conferring on a trustee the right to vote or otherwise act for them, by signing an agreement setting out the provisions of the trust (which may include anything consistent with its purpose) and transferring their shares to the trustee. When a voting trust agreement is signed, the trustee shall prepare a list of the names and addresses of all owners of beneficial interests in the trust, together with the number and class of shares each transferred to the trust, and deliver copies of the list and agreement to the corporation's principal office.

(b) A voting trust becomes effective on the date the first shares subject to the trust are registered in the trustee's name. A voting trust is valid for not more than 10 years after its effective date unless extended under subsection (c).

(c) All or some of the parties to a voting trust may extend it for additional terms of not more than 10 years each by signing an extension agreement and obtaining the voting trustee's written consent to the extension. An extension is valid for 10 years from the date the first shareholder signs the extension agreement. The voting trustee must deliver copies of the extension agreement and list of beneficial owners to the corporation's principal office. An extension agreement binds only those parties signing it.

§ 7.31 Voting Agreements

(a) Two or more shareholders may provide for the manner in which they will vote their shares by signing an agreement for that purpose. A voting agreement created under this section is not subject to the provisions of section 7.30.

(b) A voting agreement created under this section is specifically enforceable. *because of Ringling Bros. p 257*

Official Comment

Section 7.31(a) explicitly recognizes agreements among two or more shareholders as to the voting of shares and makes clear that these agreements are not subject to the rules relating to a voting trust. These agreements are often referred to as "pooling agreements." The only formal requirements are that they be in writing and signed by all the participating shareholders; in other respects their validity is to be judged as any other contract. They are not subject to the 10–year limitation applicable to voting trusts.

Section 7.31(b) provides that voting agreements may be specifically enforceable. A voting agreement may provide its own enforcement mechanism, as by the appointment of a proxy to vote all shares subject to the agreement; the appointment may be made irrevocable under section 7.22. If no enforcement mechanism is provided, a court may order specific enforcement of the agreement and order the votes cast as the agreement contemplates. This section recognizes that damages are not likely to be an appropriate remedy for breach of a voting agreement, and also avoids the result reached in Ringling Bros. Barnum & Bailey Combined Shows v. Ringling, 53 A.2d 441 (Del.1947), where the court held that the appropriate remedy to enforce a pooling agreement was to refuse to permit any voting of the breaching party's shares.

§ 7.32 Shareholder Agreements

(a) An agreement among the shareholders of a corporation that complies with this section is effective among the shareholders and the corporation even though it is inconsistent with one or more other provisions of this Act in that it:

　　(1) eliminates the board of directors or restricts the discretion or powers of the board of directors;

(2) governs the authorization or making of distributions whether or not in proportion to ownership of shares, subject to the limitations in section 6.40;

(3) establishes who shall be directors or officers of the corporation, or their terms of office or manner of selection or removal;

(4) governs, in general or in regard to specific matters, the exercise or division of voting power by or between the shareholders and directors or by or among any of them, including use of weighted voting rights or director proxies;

(5) establishes the terms and conditions of any agreement for the transfer or use of property or the provision of services between the corporation and any shareholder, director, officer or employee of the corporation or among any of them;

(6) transfers to one or more shareholders or other persons all or part of the authority to exercise the corporate powers or to manage the business and affairs of the corporation, including the resolution of any issue about which there exists a deadlock among directors or shareholders;

(7) requires dissolution of the corporation at the request of one or more of the shareholders or upon the occurrence of a specified event or contingency; or

(8) otherwise governs the exercise of the corporate powers or the management of the business and affairs of the corporation or the relationship among the shareholders, the directors and the corporation, or among any of them, and is not contrary to public policy.

(b) An agreement authorized by this section shall be:

(1) set forth (A) in the articles of incorporation or bylaws and approved by all persons who are shareholders at the time of the agreement or (B) in a written agreement that is signed by all persons who are shareholders at the time of the agreement and is made known to the corporation;

(2) subject to amendment only by all persons who are shareholders at the time of the amendment, unless the agreement provides otherwise; and

(3) valid for 10 years, unless the agreement provides otherwise.

(c) The existence of an agreement authorized by this section shall be noted conspicuously on the front or back of each certificate for outstanding shares or on the information statement required by section 6.26(b). If at the time of the agreement the corporation has shares outstanding represented by certificates, the corporation shall recall the outstanding certificates and issue substitute certificates that comply with this subsection. The failure to note the existence of the agreement on the certificate or information statement shall not affect the validity of the agreement or any action taken pursuant to it. Any purchaser of shares who, at the time of purchase, did not have knowledge of the existence of the agreement shall be entitled to rescission of the purchase. A purchaser shall be deemed to have knowledge of the existence of the agreement if its existence is noted on the certificate or information statement for the shares in compliance with this subsection and, if the shares are not represented by a certificate, the information statement is delivered to the purchaser at or prior to the time of purchase of the shares. An action to enforce the right of rescission authorized by this subsection must be commenced within the earlier of 90 days after discovery of the existence of the agreement or two years after the time of purchase of the shares.

(d) An agreement authorized by this section shall cease to be effective when the corporation becomes a public corporation. If the agreement ceases to be effective for any reason, the board of directors may, if the agreement is contained or referred to in the corporation's articles of incorporation or bylaws, adopt an amendment to the articles of incorporation or bylaws, without shareholder action, to delete the agreement and any references to it.

(e) An agreement authorized by this section that limits the discretion or powers of the board of directors shall relieve the directors of, and impose upon the person or persons in whom such discretion or powers are vested, liability for acts or omissions imposed by law on directors to the extent that the discretion or powers of the directors are limited by the agreement.

(f) The existence or performance of an agreement authorized by this section shall not be a ground for imposing personal liability on any shareholder for the acts or debts of the corporation even if the agreement or its performance treats the corporation as if it were a partnership or results in failure to observe the corporate formalities otherwise applicable to the matters governed by the agreement.

(g) Incorporators or subscribers for shares may act as shareholders with respect to an agreement authorized by this section if no shares have been issued when the agreement is made.

Official Comment

Shareholders of closely-held corporations, ranging from family businesses to joint ventures owned by large public corporations, frequently enter into agreements that govern the operation of the enterprise. In the past, various types of shareholder agreements were invalidated by courts for a variety of reasons, including so-called "sterilization" of the board of directors and failure to follow the statutory norms of the applicable corporation act. See, e.g., Long Park, Inc. v. Trenton–New Brunswick Theatres Co., 297 N.Y. 174, 77 N.E.2d 633 (1948). The more modern decisions reflect a greater willingness to uphold shareholder agreements. See, e.g., Galler v. Galler, 32 Ill.2d 16, 203 N.E.2d 577 (1964)....

Rather than relying on further uncertain and sporadic development of the law in the courts, section 7.32 rejects the older line of cases. It adds an important element of predictability currently absent from the Model Act and affords participants in closely-held corporations greater contractual freedom to tailor the rules of their enterprise.

Section 7.32 is not intended to establish or legitimize an alternative form of corporation. Instead, it is intended to add, within the context of the traditional corporate structure, legal certainty to shareholder agreements that embody various aspects of the business arrangement established by the shareholders to meet their business and personal needs. The subject matter of these arrangements includes governance of the entity, allocation of the economic return from the business, and other aspects of the relationships among shareholders, directors, and the corporation which are part of the business arrangement. Section 7.32 also recognizes that many of the corporate norms contained in the Model Act, as well as the corporation statutes of most states, were designed with an eye towards public companies, where management and share ownership are quite distinct. *Cf.* 1 O'Neal & Thompson, O'Neal's Close Corporations, section 5.06 (3d ed.). These functions are often conjoined in the close corporation. Thus, section 7.32 validates for nonpublic corporations various types of agreements among shareholders even when the agreements are inconsistent with the statutory norms contained in the Act.

Importantly, section 7.32 only addresses the parties to the shareholder agreement, their transferees, and the corporation, and does not have any binding legal effect on the state, creditors, or other third persons....

The types of provisions validated by section 7.32 are many and varied. Section 7.32(a) defines the range of permissible subject matter for shareholder agreements largely by illustration, enumerating seven types of agreements that are expressly validated to the extent they would not be valid absent section 7.32. The enumeration of these types of agreements is not exclusive; nor should it give rise to a negative inference that an agreement of a type that is or might be embraced by one of the categories of section 7.32(a) is, ipso facto, a type of agreement that is not valid unless it complies with section 7.32. Section 7.32(a) also contains a "catch all" which adds a measure of flexibility to the seven enumerated categories. ...

1. Section 7.32(a)

Subsection (a) is the heart of section 7.32. It states that certain types of agreements are effective among the shareholders and the corporation even if inconsistent with another provision of the Model Act. Thus, an agreement authorized by section 7.32 is, by virtue of that section, "not inconsistent with law" within the meaning of sections 2.02(b)(2) and 2.06(b) of the Act. In contrast, a shareholder agreement that is not inconsistent with any provisions of the Model Act is not subject to the requirements of section 7.32.

The range of agreements validated by section 7.32(a) is expansive though not unlimited. The most difficult problem encountered in crafting a shareholder agreement validation provision is to determine the reach of the provision. Some states have tried to articulate the limits of a shareholder agreement validation provision in terms of negative grounds, stating that no shareholder agreement shall be invalid on certain specified grounds. See, e.g., Del.Code Ann. tit. 8, sections 350, 354 (1983); N.C.Gen.Stat. section 55–73(b) (1982). The deficiency in this type of statute is the uncertainty introduced by the ever present possibility of articulating another ground on which to challenge the validity of the agreement. Other states have provided that shareholder agreements may waive or alter all provisions in the corporation act except certain enumerated provisions that cannot be varied. See, e.g., Cal.Corp.Code section 300(b)–(c) (West 1989 and Supp.1990). The difficulty with this approach is that any enumeration of the provisions that can never be varied will almost inevitably be subjective, arbitrary, and incomplete.

The approach chosen in section 7.32 is more pragmatic. It defines the types of agreements that can be validated largely by illustration. The seven specific categories that are listed are designed to cover the most frequently used arrangements. The outer boundary is provided by section 7.32(a)(8), which provides an additional "catch all" for any provisions that, in a manner inconsistent with any other provision of the Model Act, otherwise govern the exercise of the corporate powers, the management of the business and affairs of the corporation, or the relationship between and among the shareholders, the directors, and the corporation or any of them. Section 7.32(a) validates virtually all types of shareholder agreements that, in practice, normally concern shareholders and their advisors.

Given the breadth of section 7.32(a), any provision that may be contained in the articles of incorporation with a majority vote under sections 2.02(b)(2)(ii) and (iii), as well as under section 2.02(b)(4), may also be effective if contained in a shareholder agreement that complies with section 7.32.

The provisions of a shareholder agreement authorized by section 7.32(a) will often, in operation, conflict with the literal language of more than one section of the Act, and courts should in such cases construe all related sections of the Act flexibly and in a manner consistent with the underlying intent of the shareholder agreement. Thus, for example, in the case of an agreement that provides for weighted voting by directors, every reference in the Act to a majority or other proportion of directors should be construed to refer to a majority or other proportion of the votes of the directors.

While the outer limits of the catch-all provision of subsection 7.32(a)(8) are left uncertain, there are provisions of the Model Act that cannot be overridden by resort to the catch-all. Subsection (a)(8), introduced by the term "otherwise," is intended to be read in context with the preceding seven subsections and to be subject to a *ejusdem generis* rule of construction. Thus, in defining the outer limits, courts should consider whether the variation from the Model Act under consideration is similar to the variations permitted by the first seven subsections. Subsection (a)(8) is also subject to a public policy limitation, intended to give courts express authority to restrict the scope of the catch-all where there are substantial issues of public policy at stake. For example, a shareholder agreement that provides that the directors of the corporation have no duties of care or loyalty to the corporation or the shareholders would not be within the purview of section 7.32(a)(8), because it is not sufficiently similar to the types of arrangements suggested by the first seven subsections of section 7.32(a) and because such a provision could be viewed as contrary to a public policy of substantial importance. Similarly, a provision that exculpates directors from liability more broadly than permitted by section 2.02(b)(4) likely would not be validated under section 7.32, because, as the Official Comment to section 2.02(b)(4) states, there are serious public policy reasons which support the few limitations that remain on the right to exculpate directors from liability. Further development of the outer limits is left, however, for the courts.

As noted above, shareholder agreements otherwise validated by section 7.32 are not legally binding on the state, on creditors, or on other third parties. For example, an agreement that dispenses with the need to make corporate filings required by the Act would be ineffective. Similarly, an agreement among shareholders that provides that only the president has authority to enter into contracts for the corporation would not, without more, be binding against third parties, and ordinary principles of agency, including the concept of apparent authority, would continue to apply.

2. Section 7.32(b) ...

Section 7.32(b) requires unanimous shareholder approval regardless of entitlement to vote. Unanimity is required because an agreement authorized by section 7.32 can effect material organic changes in the corporation's operation and structure, and in the rights and obligations of shareholders....

3. Section 7.32(c)

Section 7.32(c) addresses the effect of a shareholder agreement on subsequent purchasers or transferees of shares. Typically, corporations with shareholder agreements also have restrictions on the transferability of the shares as authorized by section 6.27 of the Model Act, thus lessening the practical effects of the problem in the context of voluntary transferees. Transferees of shares without knowledge of the agreement or those acquiring shares upon the death of an original participant in a close corporation may, however, be heavily impacted. Weighing the burdens on transferees against the burdens on the remaining shareholders in the enterprise, section 7.32(c) affirms the continued validity of the shareholder agreement on all transferees, whether by purchase, gift, operation of law, or otherwise. Unlike restrictions on transfer, it may be impossible to enforce a shareholder agreement against less than all of the shareholders. Thus, under section 7.32, one who inherits shares subject to a shareholder agreement must continue to abide by the agreement. If that is not the desired result, care must be exercised at the initiation of the shareholder agreement to ensure a different outcome, such as providing for a buy-back upon death.

Where shares are transferred to a purchaser without knowledge of a shareholder agreement, the validity of the agreement is similarly unaffected, but the purchaser is afforded a rescission remedy against the seller. . . .

Section 7.32(c) contains an affirmative requirement that the share certificate or information statement for the shares be legended to note the existence of a shareholder agreement. No specified form of legend is required, and a simple statement that "[t]he shares represented by this certificate are subject to a shareholder agreement" is sufficient. At that point a purchaser must obtain a copy of the shareholder agreement from his transferor or proceed at his peril. In the event a corporation fails to legend share certificates or information statements, a court may, in an appropriate case, imply a cause of action against the corporation in favor of an injured purchaser without knowledge of a shareholder agreement. The circumstances under which such a remedy would be implied, the proper measure of damages, and other attributes of and limitations on such an implied remedy are left to development in the courts.

If the purchaser has no actual knowledge of a shareholder agreement, and is not charged with knowledge by virtue of a legend on the certificate or information statement, he has a rescission remedy against his transferor (which would be the corporation in the case of a new issue of shares). While the statutory rescission remedy provided in subsection (c) is nonexclusive, it is intended to be a purchaser's primary remedy. . . .

4. Section 7.32(d)

Section 7.32(d) contains a self-executing termination provision for a shareholder agreement when the shares of the corporation become publicly traded, and the corporation thereby becomes a public corporation as defined in section 1.40(18A). The statutory norms in the Model Act become more appropriate as the number of shareholders increases, as there is greater opportunity to acquire or dispose of an investment in the corporation, and as there is less opportunity for negotiation over the terms under which the enterprise will be conducted. Given that section 7.32 requires unanimity, however, in most cases a practical limit will be reached before a public market develops. Subsection (d) rejects the use of an absolute number of shareholders in determining when the shelter of section 7.32 is lost.

Subchapter D

Derivative Proceedings ...

§ 7.40 Subchapter Definitions

In this subchapter:

(1) "Derivative proceeding" means a civil suit in the right of a domestic corporation or, to the extent provided in section 7.47, in the right of a foreign corporation.

(2) "Shareholder" includes a beneficial owner whose shares are held in a voting trust or held by a nominee on the beneficial owner's behalf.

Official Comment

The definition of "derivative proceeding" makes it clear that the subchapter applies to foreign corporations only to the extent provided in section 7.47. Section 7.47 provides that the law of the jurisdiction of incorporation governs except for sections 7.43 (stay of proceedings), 7.45 (discontinuance or settlement) and 7.46 (payment of expenses). See the Official Comment to section 7.47.

The definition of "shareholder", which applies only to subchapter D, includes all beneficial owners and therefore goes beyond the definition in section 1.40(22) which includes only record holders and beneficial owners who are certified by a nominee pursuant to the procedure specified in section 7.23. Similar definitions are found in section 13.01 (dissenters' rights) and section 16.02(f) (inspection of records by a shareholder). In the context of subchapter D, beneficial owner means a person having a direct economic interest in the shares. The definition is not intended to adopt the broad definition of beneficial ownership in SEC rule 13d–2 under the Securities Exchange Act of 1934 which includes persons with the right to vote or dispose of the shares even though they have no economic interest in them.

§ 7.41 Standing

A shareholder may not commence or maintain a derivative proceeding unless the shareholder:

(1) was a shareholder of the corporation at the time of the act or omission complained of or became a shareholder through transfer by operation of law from one who was a shareholder at that time; and

(2) fairly and adequately represents the interests of the corporation in enforcing the right of the corporation.

Official Comment . . .

Section 7.41 requires the plaintiff to be a shareholder and therefore does not permit creditors or holders of options, warrants, or conversion rights to commence a derivative proceeding.

Section 7.41(2) follows the requirement of Federal Rule of Civil Procedure 23.1 with the exception that the plaintiff must fairly and adequately represent the interests of *the corporation* rather than *shareholders similarly situated* as provided in the rule. The clarity of the rule's language in this regard has been questioned by the courts. See Nolen v. Shaw–Walker Company, 449 F.2d 506, 508 n. 4 (6th Cir.1971). Furthermore, it is believed that the reference to the corporation in section 7.41(2) more properly reflects the nature of the derivative suit.

The introductory language of section 7.41 refers both to the commencement and maintenance of the proceeding to make it clear that the proceeding should be dismissed if, after commencement, the plaintiff ceases to be a shareholder or a fair and adequate representative. The latter would occur, for example, if the plaintiff were using the proceeding for personal advantage. If a plaintiff no longer has standing, courts have in a number of instances provided an opportunity for one or more other shareholders to intervene.

§ 7.42 Demand

No shareholder may commence a derivative proceeding until:

(1) a written demand has been made upon the corporation to take suitable action; and

(2) 90 days have expired from the date the demand was made unless the shareholder has earlier been notified that the demand has been rejected by the corporation or unless irreparable injury to the corporation would result by waiting for the expiration of the 90 day period.

Official Comment

Section 7.42 requires a written demand on the corporation in all cases. The demand must be made at least 90 days before commencement of suit unless irreparable injury to the corporation would result. This approach has been adopted for two reasons. First, even though no director may be independent, the demand will give the board of directors the opportunity to reexamine the act complained of in the light of a potential lawsuit and take corrective action. Secondly, the provision eliminates the time and expense of the litigants and the court involved in litigating the question whether demand is required. It is believed that requiring a demand in all cases does not impose an onerous burden since a relatively short waiting period of 90 days is provided and this period may be shortened if irreparable injury to the corporation would result by waiting for the expiration of the 90-day period. Moreover, the cases in which demand is excused are relatively rare. Many plaintiffs' counsel as a matter of practice make a demand in all cases rather than litigate the issue whether demand is excused.

1. Form of Demand

Section 7.42 specifies only that the demand shall be in writing. The demand should, however, set forth the facts concerning share ownership and be sufficiently specific to apprise the corporation of the action sought to be taken and the grounds for that action so that the demand can be evaluated. See Allison v. General Motors Corp., 604 F.Supp. 1106, 1117 (D. Del.1985). Detailed pleading is not required since the corporation can contact the shareholder for clarification if there are any questions. In keeping with the spirit of this section, the specificity of the demand should not become a new source of dilatory motions.

2. Upon Whom Demand Should Be Made

Section 7.42 states that demand shall be made upon the corporation. Reference is not made specifically to the board of directors as in previous section 7.40(b) since there may be instances, such as a decision to sue a third party for an injury to the corporation, in which the taking of, or refusal to take, action would fall within the authority of an officer of the corporation. Nevertheless, it is expected that in most cases the board of directors will be the appropriate body to review the demand.

To ensure that the demand reaches the appropriate person for review, it should be addressed to the board of directors, chief executive officer or corporate secretary of the corporation at its principal office.

3. The 90–Day Period...

Two exceptions are provided to the 90-day waiting period. The first exception is the situation where the shareholder has been notified of the rejection of the demand prior to the end of the 90 days. The second exception is where irreparable injury to the corporation would otherwise result if the commencement of the proceeding is delayed for the 90-day period. The standard to be applied is intended to be the same as that governing the entry of a preliminary injunction. Compare Gimbel v. Signal Cos., 316 A.2d 599 (Del. Ch.1974) with Gelco Corp. v. Coniston Partners, 811 F.2d 414 (8th Cir.1987). Other factors may also be considered such as the possible expiration of the statute of limitations although this would depend on the period of time during which the shareholder was aware of the grounds for the proceeding.

It should be noted that the shareholder bringing suit does not necessarily have to be the person making the demand. Only one demand need be made in order for the corporation to consider whether to take corrective action.

4. Response by the Corporation

There is no obligation on the part of the corporation to respond to the demand. However, if the corporation, after receiving the demand, decides to institute litigation or, after a derivative proceeding has commenced, decides to assume control of the litigation, the shareholder's right to commence or control the proceeding ends unless it can be shown that the corporation will not adequately pursue the matter....

§ 7.43 Stay of Proceedings

If the corporation commences an inquiry into the allegations made in the demand or complaint, the court may stay any derivative proceeding for such period as the court deems appropriate.

Official Comment

Section 7.43 provides that if the corporation undertakes an inquiry, the court may in its discretion stay the proceeding for such period as the court deems appropriate. This might occur where the complaint is filed 90 days after demand but the inquiry into the matters raised by the demand has not been completed or where a demand has not been investigated but the corporation commences the inquiry after the complaint has been filed. In either case, it is expected that the court will monitor the course of the inquiry to ensure that it is proceeding expeditiously and in good faith.

§ 7.44 Dismissal

(a) A derivative proceeding shall be dismissed by the court on motion by the corporation if one of the groups specified in subsection (b) or subsection (e) has determined in good faith, after conducting a reasonable inquiry upon which its conclusions are based, that the maintenance of the derivative proceeding is not in the best interests of the corporation.

(b) Unless a panel is appointed pursuant to subsection (e), the determination in subsection (a) shall be made by:

    (1) a majority vote of qualified directors present at a meeting of the board of directors if the qualified directors constitute a quorum; or

(2) a majority vote of a committee consisting of two or more qualified directors appointed by majority vote of qualified directors present at a meeting of the board of directors, regardless of whether such qualified directors constitute a quorum.

(c) If a derivative proceeding is commenced after a determination has been made rejecting a demand by a shareholder, the complaint shall allege with particularity facts establishing either (1) that a majority of the board of directors did not consist of qualified directors at the time the determination was made or (2) that the requirements of subsection (a) have not been met.

(d) If a majority of the board of directors consisted of qualified directors at the time the determination was made, the plaintiff shall have the burden of proving that the requirements of subsection (a) have not been met; if not, the corporation shall have the burden of proving that the requirements of subsection (a) have been met.

(e) Upon motion by the corporation, the court may appoint a panel of one or more individuals to make a determination whether the maintenance of the derivative proceeding is in the best interests of the corporation. In such case, the plaintiff shall have the burden of proving that the requirements of subsection (a) have not been met.

Official Comment

At one time the Model Act did not expressly provide what happens when a board of directors properly rejects a demand to bring an action. In such event, judicial decisions indicate that the rejection should be honored and any ensuing derivative action should be dismissed. See *Aronson v. Lewis*, 473 A.2d 805, 813 (Del. 1984). The Model Act was also silent on the effect of a determination by a special litigation committee of qualified directors that a previously commenced derivative action should be dismissed. Section 7.44(a) specifically provides that the proceeding shall be dismissed if there is a proper determination that the maintenance of the proceeding is not in the best interests of the corporation. That determination can be made prior to commencement of the derivative action in response to a demand or after commencement of the action upon examination of the allegations of the complaint.

The procedures set forth in section 7.44 are not intended to be exclusive. As noted in the comment to section 7.42, there may be instances where a decision to commence an action falls within the authority of an officer of the corporation, depending upon the amount of the claim and the identity of the potential defendants.

1. The Persons Making the Determination

Section 7.44(b) prescribes the persons by whom the determination in subsection (a) may be made. Subsection (b) provides that the determination may be made (1) at a board meeting by a majority vote of qualified directors if the qualified directors constitute a quorum, or (2) by a majority vote of a committee consisting of two or more qualified directors appointed at a board meeting by a vote of the qualified directors in attendance, regardless of whether they constitute a quorum. (For the definition of "qualified director," see section 1.43 and the related official comment.) These provisions parallel the mechanics for determining entitlement to indemnification (section 8.55) and for authorizing directors' conflicting interest transactions (section 8.62). Subsection (b)(2) is an exception to section 8.25 of the Model Act, which requires the approval of at least a majority of all the directors in office to create a committee and appoint members. This approach has been taken to respond to the criticism expressed in a few cases that special litigation committees suffer from a structural bias because of their appointment by vote of directors who at that time are not qualified directors. See *Hasan v. Trust Realty Investors*, 729 F.2d 372, 376–77 (6th Cir. 1984).

Subsection (e) provides, as an alternative, for a determination by a panel of one or more individuals appointed by the court. The subsection provides for the appointment only upon motion by the corporation. This would not, however, prevent the court on its own initiative from appointing a special master pursuant to applicable state rules of procedure. (Although subsection (b)(2) requires a committee of at least two qualified directors, subsection (e) permits the appointment by the court of only one person in recognition of the potentially increased costs to the corporation for the fees and expenses of an outside person.)

This panel procedure may be desirable in a number of circumstances. If there are no qualified directors available, the corporation may not wish to enlarge the board to add qualified directors or may be unable to find persons willing to serve as qualified directors. In addition, even if there are directors who are qualified, they may not be in a position to conduct the inquiry in an expeditious manner.

Appointment by the court should also eliminate any question about the qualifications of the individual or individuals constituting the panel making the determination. Although the corporation may wish to suggest to the court possible appointees, the court will not be bound by those suggestions and, in any case, will want to satisfy itself with respect to each candidate's impartiality. When the court appoints a panel, subsection (e) places the burden on the plaintiff to prove that the requirements of subsection (a) have not been met.

2. Standards to be Applied

Section 7.44(a) requires that the determination, by the appropriate person or persons, be made "in good faith, after conducting a reasonable inquiry upon which their conclusions are based." The phrase "in good faith" modifies both the determination and the inquiry. This standard, which is also found in sections 8.30 (general standards of conduct for directors) and 8.51 (authority to indemnify) of the Model Act, is a subjective one, meaning "honestly or in an honest manner." *See also*

"Corporate Director's Guidebook (Fourth Edition)," 59 BUS.LAW. 1057, 1068 (2004). As stated in *Abella v. Universal Leaf Tobacco Co.*, 546 F. Supp. 795, 800 (E.D. Va. 1982), "the inquiry intended by this phrase goes to the spirit and sincerity with which the investigation was conducted, rather than the reasonableness of its procedures or basis for conclusions."

The word "inquiry"—rather than "investigation"—has been used to make it clear that the scope of the inquiry will depend upon the issues raised and the knowledge of the group making the determination with respect to those issues. In some cases, the issues may be so simple or the knowledge of the group so extensive that little additional inquiry is required. In other cases, the group may need to engage counsel and possibly other professionals to make an investigation and assist the group in its evaluation of the issues.

The phrase "upon which its conclusions are based" requires that the inquiry and the conclusions follow logically. This standard authorizes the court to examine the determination to ensure that it has some support in the findings of the inquiry. The burden of convincing the court about this issue lies with whichever party has the burden under subsection (d). This phrase does not require the persons making the determination to prepare a written report that sets forth their determination and the bases therefor, since circumstances will vary as to the need for such a report. There will be, in all likelihood, many instances where good corporate practice will commend such a procedure.

Section 7.44 is not intended to modify the general standards of conduct for directors set forth in section 8.30 of the Model Act, but rather to make those standards somewhat more explicit in the derivative proceeding context. In this regard, the qualified directors making the determination would be entitled to rely on information and reports from other persons in accordance with section 8.30(d).

Section 7.44 is similar in several respects and differs in certain other respects from the law as it has developed in Delaware and been followed in a number of other states. Under the Delaware cases, the role of the court in reviewing the directors' determination varies depending upon whether the plaintiff is in a demand-required or demand-excused situation.

Since section 7.42 requires demand in all cases, the distinction between demand-excused and demand-required cases does not apply. Subsections (c) and (d) carry forward that distinction, however, by establishing pleading rules and allocating the burden of proof depending on whether there is a majority of qualified directors on the board. Subsection (c), like Delaware law, assigns to the plaintiff the threshold burden of alleging facts establishing that the majority of the directors on the board are not qualified. If there is a majority, then the burden remains with the plaintiff to plead and establish that the requirements of subsection (a) section 7.44(a) have not been met. If there is not a majority of qualified directors on the board, then the burden is on the corporation to prove that the issues delineated in subsection (a) have been satisfied; that is, the corporation must prove both the eligibility of the decision makers to act on the matter and the propriety of their inquiry and determination.

Thus, the burden of proving that the requirements of subsection (a) have not been met will remain with the plaintiff in several situations. First, where the determination to dismiss the derivative proceeding is made in accordance with subsection (b)(1), the burden of proof will generally remain with the plaintiff since the subsection requires a quorum of qualified directors and a quorum is normally a majority. See section 8.24. The burden will also remain with the plaintiff if a majority of qualified directors has appointed a committee under subsection (b)(2), and the qualified directors constitute a majority of the board. Under subsection (e), the burden of proof also remains with the plaintiff in the case of a determination by a panel appointed by the court.

The burden of proof will shift to the corporation, however, where a majority of the board members are not qualified, and the determination is made by a committee under subsection (b)(2). It can be argued that, if the directors making the determination under subsection (b)(2) are qualified and have been delegated full responsibility for making the decision, the composition of the entire board is irrelevant. This argument is buttressed by the section's method of appointing the group specified in subsection (b)(2), since it departs from the general method of appointing committees and allows only qualified directors, rather than a majority of the entire board, to appoint the committee that will make the determination. Subsection (d)'s response to objections suggesting structural bias is to place the burden of proof on the corporation (despite the fact that the committee making the determination is composed exclusively of qualified directors).

Finally, section 7.44 does not authorize the court to review the reasonableness of the determination to reject a demand or seek dismissal. This contrasts with the approach in some states that permits a court, at least in some circumstances, to review the merits of the determination (*see Zapata Corp. v. Maldonado*, 430 A. 2d 779, 789 (Del. 1981)) and is similar to the approach taken in other states (*see Auerbach v. Bennett*, 393 N.E. 2d 994, 1002–03 (N.Y.1979)).

3. Pleading

The Model Act previously provided that the complaint in a derivative proceeding must allege with particularity either that demand had been made on the board of directors, together with the board's response, or why demand was excused. This requirement is similar to rule 23.1 of the Federal Rules of Civil Procedure. Since demand is now required in all cases, this provision is no longer necessary.

Subsection (c) sets forth a modified pleading rule to cover the typical situation where the plaintiff makes demand on the board, the board rejects that demand, and the plaintiff commences an action. In that scenario, in order to state a cause of action, subsection (c) requires the complaint to allege with particularity facts demonstrating either (1) that no majority of qualified directors exists or (2) why the determination made by qualified directors does not meet the standards in subsection (a).

§ 7.45 Discontinuance or Settlement

A derivative proceeding may not be discontinued or settled without the court's approval. If the court determines that a proposed discontinuance or settlement will substantially affect the interests of the corporation's shareholders or a class of shareholders, the court shall direct that notice be given to the shareholders affected.

Official Comment

Unlike the statutes of some states, section 7.45 does not address the issue of which party should bear the cost of giving this notice. That is a matter left to the discretion of the court reviewing the proposed settlement.

§ 7.46 Payment of Expenses

On termination of the derivative proceeding the court may:

(1) order the corporation to pay the plaintiff's expenses incurred in the proceeding if it finds that the proceeding has resulted in a substantial benefit to the corporation;

(2) order the plaintiff to pay any defendant's expenses incurred in defending the proceeding if it finds that the proceeding was commenced or maintained without reasonable cause or for an improper purpose; or

(3) order a party to pay an opposing party's expenses incurred because of the filing of a pleading, motion or other paper, if it finds that the pleading, motion or other paper was not well grounded in fact, after reasonable inquiry, or warranted by existing law or a good faith argument for the extension, modification or reversal of existing law and was interposed for an improper purpose, such as to harass or to cause unnecessary delay or needless increase in the cost of litigation.

§ 7.47 Applicability to Foreign Corporations

In any derivative proceeding in the right of a foreign corporation, the matters covered by this subchapter shall be governed by the laws of the jurisdiction of incorporation of the foreign corporation except for sections 7.43, 7.45, and 7.46.

§ 7.48.   **Shareholder Action to Appoint Custodian or Receiver**

(a) The [name or describe court or courts] may appoint one or more persons to be custodians, or, if the corporation is insolvent, to be receivers, of and for a corporation in a proceeding by a shareholder where it is established that:

 (1) The directors are deadlocked in the management of the corporate affairs, the shareholders are unable to break the deadlock, and irreparable injury to the corporation is threatened or being suffered; or

 (2) the directors or those in control of the corporation are acting fraudulently and irreparable injury to the corporation is threatened or being suffered.

(b) The court

 (1) may issue injunctions, appoint a temporary custodian or temporary receiver with all the powers and duties the court directs, take other action to preserve the corporate assets wherever located, and carry on the business of the corporation until a full hearing is held;

 (2) shall hold a full hearing, after notifying all parties to the proceeding and any interested persons designated by the court, before appointing a custodian or receiver; and

 (3) has jurisdiction over the corporation and all of its property, wherever located.

(c) The court may appoint an individual or domestic or foreign corporation (authorized to transact business in this state) as a custodian or receiver and may require the custodian or receiver to post bond, with or without sureties, in an amount the court directs.

(d) The court shall describe the powers and duties of the custodian or receiver in its appointing order, which may be amended from time to time. Among other powers,

 (1) a custodian may exercise all of the powers of the corporation, through or in place of its board of directors, to the extent necessary to manage the business and affairs of the corporation; and

 (2) a receiver (i) may dispose of all or any part of the assets of the corporation wherever located, at a public or private sale, if authorized by the court; and (ii) may sue and defend in the receiver's own name as receiver in all courts of this state.

(e) The court during a custodianship may redesignate the custodian a receiver, and during a receivership may redesignate the receiver a custodian, if doing so is in the best interests of the corporation.

(f) The court from time to time during the custodianship or receivership may order compensation paid and expense disbursements or reimbursements made to the custodian or receiver from the assets of the corporation or proceeds from the sale of its assets.

Official Comment

Previously, the Model Act's procedures for the appointment of a receiver or custodian were ancillary to an action for judicial dissolution under section 14.30. Section 7.48 has been added to provide a basis for relief for shareholders of any corporation, regardless of whether it is or is not a public corporation, in the two situations, both requiring a showing of actual or threatened irreparable injury, specified in (1) and (2) of section 7.48(a). These two grounds are narrower than those found in a shareholder's action for judicial dissolution of a non-public corporation under section 14.30(2). See the Official Comment to Section 14.30(2). Section 7.48 is in addition to other shareholder remedies provided by the Act and could, for example, be sought by a shareholder of a non-public corporation in lieu of involuntary dissolution under section 14.30(2).

Chapter 8

DIRECTORS AND OFFICERS

Subchapter A

Board of Directors

§ 8.01 Requirements for and Functions of Board of Directors

(a) Except as provided in section 7.32, each corporation must have a board of directors.

(b) All corporate powers shall be exercised by or under the authority of the board of directors of the corporation, and the business and affairs of the corporation shall be managed by or under the direction, and subject to the oversight, of its board of directors, subject to any limitation set forth in the articles of incorporation or in an agreement authorized under section 7.32.

(c) In the case of a public corporation, the board's oversight responsibilities include attention to:

    (i)   business performance and plans;

    (ii) major risks to which the corporation is or may be exposed;

    (iii) the performance and compensation of senior officers;

    (iv) policies and practices to foster the corporation's compliance with law and ethical conduct;

    (v) preparation of the corporation's financial statements;

    (vi) the effectiveness of the corporation's internal controls;

    (vii) arrangements for providing adequate and timely information to directors; and

(viii) the composition of the board and its committees, taking into account the important role of independent directors.

Official Comment

Section 8.01(a) requires that every corporation have a board of directors except that a shareholder agreement authorized by section 7.32 may dispense with the board of directors. Section 8.01(b) also recognizes that the powers of the board of directors may be limited by express provisions in the articles of incorporation or by an agreement among all shareholders under section 7.32.

Obviously, some form of governance is necessary for every corporation. The board of directors is the traditional form of governance but it need not be the exclusive form. Patterns of management may also be tailored to specific needs in connection with family-controlled enterprises, wholly or partially owned subsidiaries, or corporate joint ventures through a shareholder agreement under section 7.32.

Under section 7.32, an agreement among all shareholders can provide for a nontraditional form of governance until there is a regular market for the corporation's shares, a change from the 50 or fewer shareholder test in place in section 8.01 prior to 1990. As the number of shareholders increases and a market for the shares develops, there is (i) an opportunity for unhappy shareholders to dispose of shares—a "market out," (ii) a correlative opportunity for others to acquire shares with related expectations regarding the applicability of the statutory norms of governance, and (iii) no real opportunity to negotiate over the terms upon which the enterprise will be conducted. Moreover, tying the availability of nontraditional governance structures to an absolute number of shareholders at the time of adoption took no account of subsequent events, was overly mechanical, and was subject to circumvention. If a corporation does not have a shareholder agreement that satisfies the requirements of section 7.32 or if it is a public corporation, it must adopt the traditional board of directors as its governing body.

Section 8.01(b) states that if a corporation has a board of directors "its business and affairs shall be managed by or under the direction, and subject to the oversight, of its board of directors." The phrase "by or under the direction, and subject to the oversight, of," encompasses the varying functions of boards of directors of different corporations. In some closely held corporations, the board of directors may be involved in the day-to-day business and affairs and it may be reasonable to describe management as being "by" the board of directors. But in many other corporations, the business and affairs are managed "under the direction, and subject to the oversight, of" the board of directors, since operational management is delegated to executive officers and other professional managers.

While section 8.01(b), in providing for corporate powers to be exercised under the authority of the board of directors, allows the board of directors to delegate to appropriate officers, employees or agents of the corporation authority to exercise powers and perform functions not required by law to be exercised or performed by the board of directors itself, responsibility to oversee the exercise of that delegated authority nonetheless remains with the board of directors. The scope of that oversight responsibility will vary depending on the nature of the corporation's business. For public corporations, subsection (c) provides that the scope of the directors' oversight responsibility includes the matters identified in that subsection. For other corporations, that responsibility may, depending on the circumstances, include some or all of those matters as well. At least for public corporations, subsections (c)(iii) and (iv) encompass oversight of the corporation's dealings and relationships with its directors and officers, including processes designed to prevent improper related party transactions. See also, chapter 8, subchapter F, sections 8.60 *et seq.* Subsection (c)(v) encompasses the corporation's compliance with the requirements of sections 16.01 and 16.20, while subsection (c)(vi) extends also to the internal control processes in place to provide reasonable assurance regarding the reliability of financial reporting, effectiveness and efficiency of operations and compliance with applicable laws and regulations. Subsection (c)(vii) reflects that the board of directors should devote attention to whether the corporation has information and reporting systems in place to provide directors with appropriate information in a timely manner in order to permit them to discharge their responsibilities. *See In re Caremark Int'l Derivative Litig.*, 698 A.2d 959 (Del. Ch. 1996).

Subsection (c) (viii) calls for the board of a public corporation, in giving attention to the composition of the board and its committees, to take into account the important role of independent directors. It is commonly accepted that where ownership is separated from management, as is the case with public corporations, having non-management independent directors who participate actively in the board's oversight functions increases the likelihood that actions taken by the board will serve the best interests of the corporation and its shareholders and generally will be given deference in judicial proceedings. The listing standards of most public securities markets have requirements for independent directors to serve on boards; in many cases, they must constitute a majority of the board, and certain board committees must be composed entirely of independent directors. The listing standards have differing rules as to what constitutes an independent director. The Act does not attempt to define "independent director." Ordinarily, an independent director may not be a present or recent member of senior management. Also, to be considered independent, the individual usually must be free of significant professional, financial or similar relationships with the corporation—directly or as a partner, major shareholder or officer of an organization with such a relationship—and the director and members of the director's immediate family must be free of similar relationships with the corporation's senior management. Judgment is required to determine independence in light of the particular circumstances, subject to any specific requirements of a listing standard. The qualities of disinterestedness required of directors under the Act for specific purposes are similar but not necessarily identical. For the requirements for a director to be eligible to act in those situations, see section 1.43. An individual who is generally an independent director for purposes of subsection (c) may not be eligible to act in a particular case under those other provisions of the Act. Conversely, a director who is not independent for purposes of subsection (c) (for example, a member of management) may be so eligible in a particular case.

Although delegation does not relieve the board of directors from its responsibilities of oversight, directors should not be held personally responsible for actions or omissions of officers, employees, or agents of the corporation so long as the directors have relied reasonably and in good faith upon these officers, employees, or agents. See sections 8.30 and 8.31 and their Official Comments. Directors generally have the power to probe into day-to-day management to any depth they choose, but they have the obligation to do so only to the extent that the directors' oversight responsibilities may require, or, for example, when they become aware of matters which make reliance on management or other persons unwarranted.

§ 8.02   Qualifications of Directors

The articles of incorporation or bylaws may prescribe qualifications for directors. A director need not be a resident of this state or a shareholder of the corporation unless the articles of incorporation or bylaws so prescribe.

§ 8.03   Number and Election of Directors

(a) A board of directors must consist of one or more individuals, with the number specified in or fixed in accordance with the articles of incorporation or bylaws.

(b) The number of directors may be increased or decreased from time to time by amendment to, or in the manner provided in, the articles of incorporation or the bylaws.

(c) Directors are elected at the first annual shareholders' meeting and at each annual meeting thereafter unless their terms are staggered under section 8.06.

Official Comment

Section 8.03 prescribes rules for (i) the determination of the size of the board of directors of corporations that have not dispensed with a board of directors under section 7.32(a)(1), and (ii) changes in the number of directors once the board's size has been established.

1. Minimum Number of Directors

Section 8.03(a) provides that the size of the initial board of directors may be "specified in or fixed in accordance with" the articles of incorporation or bylaws. The size of the board of directors may thus be fixed initially in one or more of the fundamental corporate documents, or the decision as to the size of the initial board of directors may be made thereafter in the manner authorized in those documents.

Before 1969 the Model Act required a board of directors to consist of at least three directors. Since then, the Model Act (as well as the corporation statutes of an increasing number of states) has provided that the board of directors may consist of one or more members. A board of directors consisting of one or two individuals may be appropriate for corporations with one or two shareholders, or for corporations with more than two shareholders where in fact the full power of management is vested in only one or two persons. The requirement that every corporation have a board of directors of at least three directors may require the introduction into these closely held corporations of persons with no financial interest in the corporation.

2. Changes in the Size of the Board of Directors

Section 8.03(b) provides a corporation with the freedom to design its articles of incorporation and bylaw provisions relating to the size of the board with a view to achieving the combination of flexibility for the board of directors and protection for shareholders that it deems appropriate. The articles of incorporation could provide for a specified number of directors or a variable-range board, thereby requiring shareholder action to change the fixed size of the board, to change the limits established for the size of the variable-range board or to change from a variable-range board to a fixed board or vice versa. An alternative would be to have the bylaws provide for a specified number of directors or a variable range for the board of directors. Any change would be made in the manner provided by the bylaws. The bylaws could permit amendment by the board of directors or the bylaws could require that any amendment, in whole or in part, be made only by the shareholders in accordance with section 10.20(a). Typically the board of directors would be permitted to change the board size within the established variable range. If a corporation wishes to ensure that any change in the number of directors be approved by shareholders, then an appropriate restriction would have to be included in the articles or bylaws.

The board's power to change the number of directors, like all other board powers, is subject to compliance with applicable standards governing director conduct. In particular, it may be inappropriate to change the size of the board for the primary purpose of maintaining control or defeating particular candidates for the board. See *Blasius Industries, Inc. v. Atlas Corp.*, 564 A.2d 651 (Del. Ch. 1988).

Experience has shown, particularly in larger corporations, that it is desirable to grant the board of directors authority to change its size without incurring the expense of obtaining shareholder approval. In closely held corporations, shareholder approval for a change in the size of the board of directors may be readily accomplished if that is desired. In many closely held corporations a board of directors of a fixed size may be an essential part of a control arrangement. In these situations, an increase or decrease in the size of the board of directors by even a single member may significantly affect control. In order to maintain control arrangements dependent on a board of directors of a fixed size, the power of the board of directors to change its own size must be negated. This may be accomplished by fixing the size of the board of directors in the articles of incorporation or by expressly negating the power of the board of directors to change the size of the board, whether by amendment of the bylaws or otherwise. See section 10.20(a).

3. Annual Elections of Directors

Section 8.03(c) makes it clear that all directors are elected annually unless the board is staggered. See section 8.05 and its Official Comment.

§ 8.04 Election of Directors by Certain Classes of Shareholders

If the articles of incorporation authorize dividing the shares into classes, the articles may also authorize the election of all or a specified number of directors by the holders of one or more authorized classes of shares. A class (or classes) of shares entitled to elect one or more directors is a separate voting group for purposes of the election of directors.

Official Comment

Section 8.04 makes explicit that the articles of incorporation may provide that a specified number (or all) of the directors may be elected by the holders of one or more classes of shares. This approach is widely used in closely held corporations to effect an agreed upon allocation of control, for example, to ensure minority representation on the board of directors by issuing to that minority a class of shares entitled to elect one or more directors. A class (or classes) of shares entitled to elect separately one or more directors constitutes a separate voting group for purposes of the election of directors; within each voting group directors are elected by a plurality of votes and quorum and voting requirements must be separately met by each voting group. See sections 7.25, 7.26, and 7.28.

§ 8.05 Terms of Directors Generally

(a) The terms of the initial directors of a corporation expire at the first shareholders' meeting at which directors are elected.

(b) The terms of all other directors expire at the next annual shareholders' meeting following their election unless their terms are staggered under section 8.06.

(c) A decrease in the number of directors does not shorten an incumbent director's term.

(d) The term of a director elected to fill a vacancy expires at the next shareholders' meeting at which directors are elected.

(e) Despite the expiration of a director's term, he continues to serve until his successor is elected and qualifies or until there is a decrease in the number of directors.

§ 8.06 Staggered Terms for Directors

The articles of incorporation may provide for staggering the terms of directors by dividing the total number of directors into two or three groups, with each group containing one-half or one-third of the total, as near as may be. In that event, the terms of directors in the first group expire at the first annual shareholders' meeting after their election, the terms of the second group expire at the second annual shareholders' meeting after their election, and the terms of the third group, if any, expire at the third annual shareholders' meeting after their election. At each annual shareholders' meeting held thereafter, directors shall be chosen for a term of two years or three years, as the case may be, to succeed those whose terms expire.

Official Comment

Section 8.06 recognizes the practice of "classifying" the board or "staggering" the terms of directors so that only one-half or one-third of them are elected at each annual shareholders' meeting and directors are elected for two- or three-year terms rather than one-year terms.

The traditional purpose of a staggered board has been to assure the continuity and stability of the corporation's business strategies and policies as determined by the board. In recent years the practice has been employed with increasing frequency to ensure that a majority of the board of directors remains in place following a sudden change in shareholdings or a proxy contest. It also reduces the impact of cumulative voting since a greater number of votes is required to elect a director if the board is staggered than is required if the entire board is elected at each annual meeting. A staggered board of directors also can have the effect of making unwanted takeover attempts more difficult, particularly where the articles of incorporation provide that the shareholders may remove directors only with cause or by a supermajority vote, or both.

§ 8.07   Resignation of Directors

(a) A director may resign at any time by delivering written notice to the board of directors, its chairman, or to the corporation.

(b) A resignation is effective when the notice is delivered unless the notice specifies a later effective date.

§ 8.08   Removal of Directors by Shareholders

(a) The shareholders may remove one or more directors with or without cause unless the articles of incorporation provide that directors may be removed only for cause.

(b) If a director is elected by a voting group of shareholders, only the shareholders of that voting group may participate in the vote to remove him.

(c) If cumulative voting is authorized, a director may not be removed if the number of votes sufficient to elect him under cumulative voting is voted against his removal. If cumulative voting is not authorized, a director may be removed only if the number of votes cast to remove him exceeds the number of votes cast not to remove him.

(d) A director may be removed by the shareholders only at a meeting called for the purpose of removing him and the meeting notice must state that the purpose, or one of the purposes, of the meeting is removal of the director.

§ 8.09   Removal of Directors by Judicial Proceeding

(a) The [name or describe] court of the county where a corporation's principal office (or, if none in this state, its registered office) is located may remove a director of the corporation from office in a proceeding commenced by or in the right of the corporation if the court finds that (1) the director engaged in fraudulent conduct with respect to the corporation or its shareholders, grossly abused the position of director, or intentionally inflicted harm on the corporation; and (2) considering the director's course of conduct and the inadequacy of other available remedies, removal would be in the best interest of the corporation.

(b) A shareholder proceeding on behalf of the corporation under subsection (a) shall comply with all of the requirements of subchapter 7D, except section 7.41(1).

(c) The court, in addition to removing the director, may bar the director from reelection for a period prescribed by the court.

(d) Nothing in this section limits the equitable powers of the court to order other relief.

Official Comment

Section 8.09 is designed to operate in the limited circumstance where other remedies are inadequate to address serious misconduct by a director and it is impracticable for shareholders to invoke the usual remedy of removal under section 8.08. In recognition that director election and removal are principal prerogatives of shareholders, section 8.09 authorizes judicial removal of a director who is found to have engaged in serious misconduct as described in subsection (a)(1) if the court also finds that, taking into consideration the director's course of conduct and the inadequacy of other available remedies, removal of the director would be in the best interest of the corporation. Misconduct serious enough to justify the extraordinary remedy of judicial removal does not involve any matter falling within an individual director's lawful exercise of business judgment, no matter how unpopular the director's views may be with the other members of the board. Policy and personal differences among the members of the board of directors should be left to be resolved by the shareholders.

Section 8.09(d) makes it clear that the court is not restricted to the removal remedy in actions under this section but may order any other equitable relief. Where, for example, the complaint concerns an ongoing course of conduct that is harmful to the corporation, the court may enjoin the director from continuing that conduct. In another instance, the court may determine that the director's continuation in office is inimical to the best interest of the corporation. Judicial removal might be the most appropriate remedy in that case if shareholder removal under section 8.08 is impracticable because of situations like the following:

(1) The director charged with serious misconduct personally owns or controls sufficient shares to block removal.

(2) The director was elected by voting group or cumulative voting, and the shareholders with voting power to prevent his removal will exercise that power despite the director's serious misconduct and without regard to what the court deems to be the best interest of the corporation.

(3) A shareholders' meeting to consider removal under section 8.08 will entail considerable expense and a period of delay that will be contrary to the corporation's best interest.

A proceeding under this section may be brought by the board of directors or by a shareholder suing derivatively. If an action is brought derivatively, all of the provisions of subchapter 7D, including dismissal under section 7.44, are applicable to the action with the exception of the contemporaneous ownership requirement of section 7.41(1).

Section 8.09 is designed to interfere as little as possible with the usual mechanisms of corporate governance. Accordingly, except for limited circumstances such as those described above, where shareholders have reelected or declined to remove a director with full knowledge of the director's misbehavior, the court should decline to entertain an action for removal under section 8.09. It is not intended to permit judicial resolution of internal corporate disputes involving issues other than those specified in subsection (a)(1).

§ 8.10 Vacancy on Board

(a) Unless the articles of incorporation provide otherwise, if a vacancy occurs on a board of directors, including a vacancy resulting from an increase in the number of directors:

    (1) the shareholders may fill the vacancy;

    (2) the board of directors may fill the vacancy; or

    (3) if the directors remaining in office constitute fewer than a quorum of the board, they may fill the vacancy by the affirmative vote of a majority of all the directors remaining in office.

(b) If the vacant office was held by a director elected by a voting group of shareholders, only the holders of shares of that voting group are entitled to vote to fill the vacancy if it is filled by the shareholders.

(c) A vacancy that will occur at a specific later date (by reason of a resignation effective at a later date under section 8.07(b) or otherwise) may be filled before the vacancy occurs but the new director may not take office until the vacancy occurs.

Official Comment

Section 8.10(a)(3) allows the directors remaining in office to fill vacancies even though they are fewer than a quorum. The test for the exercise of this power is whether the directors remaining in office are fewer than a quorum, not whether the directors seeking to act are fewer than a quorum. For example, on a board of six directors where a quorum is four, if there are two vacancies, they may not be filled under section 8.10(a)(3) at a "meeting" attended by only three directors. Even though the three directors are fewer than a quorum, section 8.10(a)(3) is not applicable because the number of directors remaining in office— four—is not fewer than a quorum....

§ 8.11 Compensation of Directors

Unless the articles of incorporation or bylaws provide otherwise, the board of directors may fix the compensation of directors.

Subchapter B

Meetings and Action of the Board

§ 8.20 Meetings

(a) The board of directors may hold regular or special meetings in or out of this state.

(b) Unless the articles of incorporation or bylaws provide otherwise, the board of directors may permit any or all directors to participate in a regular or special meeting by, or conduct the meeting through the use of, any means of communication by which all directors participating may simultaneously hear each other during the meeting. A director participating in a meeting by this means is deemed to be present in person at the meeting.

§ 8.21 Action Without Meeting

(a) Except to the extent that the articles of incorporation or bylaws require that action by the board of directors be taken at a meeting, action required or permitted by this Act to be taken by the board of directors may be taken without a meeting if each director signs a consent describing the action to be taken and delivers it to the corporation.

(b) Action taken under this section is the act of the board of directors when one or more consents signed by all the directors are delivered to the corporation. The consent may specify the time at which the action taken thereunder is to be effective. A director's consent may be withdrawn by a revocation signed by the director and delivered to the corporation prior to delivery to the corporation of unrevoked written consents signed by all the directors.

(c) A consent signed under this section has the effect of action taken at a meeting of the board of directors and may be described as such in any document.

Official Comment

The power of the board of directors to act unanimously without a meeting is based on the pragmatic consideration that in many situations a formal meeting is a waste of time. For example, in a closely held corporation there will often be informal discussion by the manager-owners of the venture before a decision is made. And, of course, if there is only a single director (as is permitted by section 8.03), a written consent is the natural method of signifying director action. Consent may be signified on one or more documents if desirable. The consent document may specify the time at which the action taken thereunder is to become effective.

In publicly held corporations, formal meetings of the board of directors may be appropriate for many actions. But there will always be situations where prompt action is necessary and the decision noncontroversial, so that approval without a formal meeting may be appropriate.

Under section 8.21 the requirement of unanimous consent precludes the possibility of stifling or ignoring opposing argument. A director opposed to an action that is proposed to be taken by unanimous written consent, or uncertain about the desirability of that action, may compel the holding of a directors' meeting to discuss the matter simply by withholding consent.

§ 8.22   Notice of Meeting

(a) Unless the articles of incorporation or bylaws provide otherwise, regular meetings of the board of directors may be held without notice of the date, time, place, or purpose of the meeting.

(b) Unless the articles of incorporation or bylaws provide for a longer or shorter period, special meetings of the board of directors must be preceded by at least two days' notice of the date, time, and place of the meeting. The notice need not describe the purpose of the special meeting unless required by the articles of incorporation or bylaws.

§ 8.23   Waiver of Notice

(a) A director may waive any notice required by this Act, the articles of incorporation, or bylaws before or after the date and time stated in the notice. Except as provided by subsection (b), the waiver must be in writing, signed by the director entitled to the notice, and filed with the minutes or corporate records.

(b) A director's attendance at or participation in a meeting waives any required notice to him of the meeting unless the director at the beginning of the meeting (or promptly upon his arrival) objects to holding the meeting or transacting business at the meeting and does not thereafter vote for or assent to action taken at the meeting.

§ 8.24   Quorum and Voting

(a) Unless the articles of incorporation or bylaws require a greater number or unless otherwise specifically provided in this Act, a quorum of a board of directors consists of:

    (1) a majority of the fixed number of directors if the corporation has a fixed board size; or

    (2) a majority of the number of directors prescribed, or if no number is prescribed the number in office immediately before the meeting begins, if the corporation has a variable-range size board.

(b) The articles of incorporation or bylaws may authorize a quorum of a board of directors to consist of no fewer than one-third of the fixed or prescribed number of directors determined under subsection (a).

(c) If a quorum is present when a vote is taken, the affirmative vote of a majority of directors present is the act of the board of directors unless the articles of incorporation or bylaws require the vote of a greater number of directors.

(d) A director who is present at a meeting of the board of directors or a committee of the board of directors when corporate action is taken is deemed to have assented to the action taken unless: (1) he objects at the beginning of the meeting (or promptly upon his arrival) to holding it or transacting business at the meeting; (2) his dissent or abstention from the action taken is entered in the minutes of the meeting; or (3) he delivers written notice of his dissent or abstention to the presiding officer of the meeting before its adjournment or to the corporation immediately after adjournment of the meeting. The right of dissent or abstention is not available to a director who votes in favor of the action taken.

§ 8.25 Committees

(a) Unless this Act, the articles of incorporation or the bylaws provide otherwise, a board of directors may create one or more committees and appoint one or more members of the board of directors to serve on any such committee.

(b) Unless this Act otherwise provides, the creation of a committee and appointment of members to it must be approved by the greater of (1) a majority of all the directors in office when the action is taken or (2) the number of directors required by the articles of incorporation or bylaws to take action under section 8.24.

(c) Sections 8.20 through 8.24 apply both to committees of the board and to their members.

(d) To the extent specified by the board of directors or in the articles of incorporation or bylaws, each committee may exercise the powers of the board of directors under section 8.01.

(e) A committee may not, however:

    (1) authorize or approve distributions, except according to a formula or method, or within limits, prescribed by the board of directors;

    (2) approve or propose to shareholders action that this Act requires be approved by shareholders;

    (3) fill vacancies on the board of directors or, subject to subsection (g), on any of its committees; or

    (4) adopt, amend, or repeal bylaws.

(f) The creation of, delegation of authority to, or action by a committee does not alone constitute compliance by a director with the standards of conduct described in section 8.30.

(g) The board of directors may appoint one or more directors as alternate members of any committee to replace any absent or disqualified member during the member's absence or disqualification. Unless the articles of incorporation or the bylaws or the resolution creating the committee provide otherwise, in the event of the absence or disqualification of a member of a committee, the member or members present at any meeting and not disqualified from voting, unanimously, may appoint another director to act in place of the absent or disqualified member.

Official Comment

Section 8.25 makes explicit the common law power of a board of directors to act through committees of directors and specifies the powers of the board of directors that are nondelegable, that is, powers that only the full board of directors may exercise. Section 8.25 deals only with board committees exercising the powers or performing the functions of the board of directors; the board of directors or management, independently of section 8.25, may establish non-board committees composed of directors, employees, or others to exercise corporate powers not required to be exercised by the board of directors.

Section 8.25(b) states that, unless this Act otherwise provides, a committee of the board of directors may be created only by the affirmative vote of a majority of the board of directors then in office, or, if greater, by the number of directors required to take action by the articles of incorporation or the bylaws. This supermajority requirement reflects the importance of the decision to invest board committees with power to act under section 8.25. Section 7.44(b) requires that a special litigation committee, to consider whether the maintenance of a derivative action is in the corporation's best interest, be appointed by a majority vote of independent directors present at a meeting of the board. Sections 8.55(b) and 8.62(a), respectively, contain a generally similar requirement with regard to the appointment of a committee to consider whether indemnification is permissible and the appointment of a committee to consider approval of a director conflicting interest transaction.

Committees of the board of directors are assuming increasingly important roles in the governance of public corporations. *See* THE COMMITTEE ON CORPORATE LAWS,CORPORATE DIRECTOR'S GUIDEBOOK, (4th ed. 2004). Nominating and compensation committees, composed primarily or entirely of independent directors, are widely used by public corporations and may be required by listing standards adopted by public securities markets. Such standards, including those mandated by law, also require the appointment of audit committees, composed entirely of independent directors, to perform important functions including the selection and retention of the corporation's external auditors.

Section 8.25(a) permits a committee to consist of a single director. This accommodates situations in which only one director may be present or available to make a decision on short notice, as well as situations in which it is unnecessary or inconvenient to have more than one member on a committee. Committees also are often employed to decide matters in which other members of the board have a conflict of interest; in such a case, a court will typically scrutinize with care the committee's decision when it is the product of a lone director. *See, e.g., Lewis v. Fuqua*, 502 A.2d 962, 967 (Del. Ch. 1985). Additionally, various sections of the Model Act require the participation or approval of at least two qualified directors in order for the decision of the board or committee to have effect. (For the definition of "qualified director," see section 1.43.) These include a determination that maintenance of a derivative suit is not in the corporation's best interests (section 7.44(b)(3)), a determination that indemnification is permissible (section 8.55(b)(1)), an approval of a director conflicting interest transaction (section 8.62(a)), and a disclaimer of the corporation's interest in a business opportunity (section 8.70(a)).

Section 8.25 limits the role of board committees in light of competing policies: on the one hand, it seems clear that appropriate committee action is not only desirable but is also likely to improve the functioning of larger and more diffuse boards of directors; on the other hand, wholesale delegation of authority to a board committee, to the point of abdication of director responsibility as a board of directors, is manifestly inappropriate and undesirable. Overbroad delegation also increases the potential, where the board of directors is divided, for usurpation of basic board functions by means of delegation to a committee dominated by one faction.

The statement of nondelegable functions set out in section 8.25(e) is based on the principle that prohibitions against delegation to board committees should be limited generally to actions that substantially affect the rights of shareholders or are fundamental to the governance of the corporation. As a result, delegation of authority to committees under section 8.25(e) may be broader than mere authority to act with respect to matters arising within the ordinary course of business.

Section 8.25(e) prohibits delegation of authority with respect to most mergers, sales of substantially all the assets, amendments to articles of incorporation and voluntary dissolution since these require shareholder action. In addition, section 8.25(e) prohibits delegation to a board committee of authority to fill board vacancies, subject to subsection (g), or to amend the bylaws. On the other hand, under section 8.25(e) many actions of a material nature, such as the authorization of long-term debt and capital investment or the issuance of shares, may properly be made the subject of committee delegation. In fact, the list of nondelegable powers has been reduced from the prior formulation of section 8.25(e).

Although section 8.25(e)(1) generally makes nondelegable the decision whether to authorize or approve distributions, including dividends, it does permit the delegation to a committee of power to approve a distribution pursuant to a formula or method or within limits prescribed by the board of directors. Therefore, the board could set a dollar range and timeframe for a prospective dividend and delegate to a committee the authority to determine the exact amount and record and payment dates of the dividend. The board also could establish certain conditions to the payment of a distribution and delegate to a committee the power to determine whether the conditions have been satisfied.

The statutes of several states make nondelegable certain powers not listed in section 8.25(e)—for example, the power to change the principal corporate office, to appoint or remove officers, to fix director compensation, or to remove agents. These are not prohibited by section 8.25(e) since the whole board of directors may reverse or rescind the committee action taken, if it should wish to do so, without undue risk that implementation of the committee action might be irrevocable or irreversible.

Section 8.25(f) makes clear that although the board of directors may delegate to a committee the authority to take action, the designation of the committee, the delegation of authority to it, and action by the committee does not alone constitute compliance by a noncommittee board member with the director's responsibility under section 8.30. On the other hand, a noncommittee director also does not automatically incur personal risk should the action of the particular committee fail to meet the standard of conduct set out in section 8.30. The noncommittee member's liability in these cases will depend upon whether the director's conduct was actionable under section 8.31. Factors to be considered in this regard will include the care used in the delegation to and supervision over the committee, the extent to which the delegation was required by applicable law or listing standards, and the amount of knowledge regarding the actions being taken by the committee which is available to the noncommittee director. Care in delegation and supervision may be facilitated, in the usual case, by review of minutes and receipt of other reports concerning committee activities. The enumeration of these factors is intended to emphasize that directors may not abdicate their responsibilities and avoid liability simply by delegating authority to board committees. Rather, a director against whom liability is asserted based upon acts of a committee of which the director is not a member avoids liability under section 8.31 by an appropriate measure of monitoring—particularly if the director met the standards contained in section 8.30 with respect to the creation and supervision of the committee.

Section 8.25(f) has no application to a member of the committee itself. The standards of conduct applicable to a committee member are set forth in section 8.30.

Section 8.25(g) is a rule of convenience that permits the board or the other committee members to replace an absent or disqualified member during the time that the member is absent or disqualified. Unless otherwise provided, replacement of an absent or disqualified member is not necessary to permit the other committee members to continue to perform their duties.

Subchapter C

Standards of Conduct

§ 8.30   Standards of Conduct for Directors

(a) Each member of the board of directors, when discharging the duties of a director, shall act: (1) in good faith, and (2) in a manner the director reasonably believes to be in the best interests of the corporation.

(b) The members of the board of directors or a committee of the board, when becoming informed in connection with their decision-making function or devoting attention to their oversight function, shall discharge their duties with the care that a person in a like position would reasonably believe appropriate under similar circumstances.

(c) In discharging board or committee duties a director shall disclose, or cause to be disclosed, to the other board or committee members information not already known by them but known by the director to be material to the discharge of their decision-making or oversight functions, except that disclosure is not required to the extent that the director reasonably believes that doing so would violate a duty imposed under law, a legally enforceable obligation of confidentiality, or a professional ethics rule.

(d) In discharging board or committee duties a director who does not have knowledge that makes reliance unwarranted is entitled to rely on the performance by any of the persons specified in subsection (f)(1) or subsection (f)(3) to whom the board may have delegated, formally or informally by course of conduct, the authority or duty to perform one or more of the board's functions that are delegable under applicable law.

(e) In discharging board or committee duties a director who does not have knowledge that makes reliance unwarranted is entitled to rely on information, opinions, reports or statements, including financial statements and other financial data, prepared or presented by any of the persons specified in subsection (f).

(f) A director is entitled to rely, in accordance with subsection (d) or (e), on:

> (1) one or more officers or employees of the corporation whom the director reasonably believes to be reliable and competent in the

functions performed or the information, opinions, reports or statements provided;

(2) legal counsel, public accountants, or other persons retained by the corporation as to matters involving skills or expertise the director reasonably believes are matters (i) within the particular person's professional or expert competence or (ii) as to which the particular person merits confidence; or

(3) a committee of the board of directors of which the director is not a member if the director reasonably believes the committee merits confidence.

Official Comment

Section 8.30 defines the general standards of conduct for directors. Under subsection (a), each board member must always perform a director's duties in good faith and in a manner reasonably believed to be in the best interests of the corporation. Although each director also has a duty to comply with its requirements, the focus of subsection (b) is on the discharge of those duties by the board as a collegial body. Under subsection (b), the members of the board or a board committee are to perform their duties with the care that a person in a like position would reasonably believe appropriate under similar circumstances. This standard of conduct is often characterized as a duty of care. Subsection (c) sets out the responsibility of each director, in discharging board or committee duties, to disclose or cause to be disclosed to the other members of the board or board committee information, of which they are unaware, known by the director to be material to their decision-making or oversight responsibilities, subject to countervailing confidentiality duties and appropriate action with respect thereto.

Section 8.30 sets forth the standards of conduct for directors by focusing on the manner in which directors perform their duties, not the correctness of the decisions made. These standards of conduct are based on former section 35 of the 1969 Model Act, a number of state statutes and on judicial formulations of the standards of conduct applicable to directors. Section 8.30 should be read in light of the basic role of directors set forth in section 8.01(b), which provides that the "business and affairs of a corporation shall be managed by or under the direction and subject to the oversight of" the board, as supplemented by various provisions of the Act assigning specific powers or responsibilities to the board. Relevant thereto, directors often act collegially in performing their functions and discharging their duties. If the observance of the directors' conduct is called into question, courts will typically evaluate the conduct of the entire board (or committee). Deficient performance of section 8.30 duties on the part of a particular director may be overcome, absent unusual circumstances, by acceptable conduct (meeting, for example, subsection (b)'s standard of care) on the part of other directors sufficient in number to perform the function or discharge the duty in question. While not thereby remedied, the deficient performance becomes irrelevant in any evaluation of the action taken. (This contrasts with a director's duties of loyalty, fair dealing and disclosure which will be evaluated on an individual basis and will also implicate discharge of the director's duties under subsection (a).) Further relevant thereto, the board may delegate or assign to appropriate officers, employees or agents of the corporation the authority or duty to exercise powers that the law does not require it to retain. Since the directors are entitled to rely thereon absent knowledge making reliance unwarranted, deficient performance of the directors' section 8.30 duties will not result from their delegatees' actions or omissions so long as the board acted in good faith and complied with the other standards of conduct set forth in section 8.30 in delegating responsibility and, where appropriate, monitoring performance of the duties delegated.

In earlier versions of the Model Act the duty of care element was included in subsection (a), with the text reading: "[a] director shall discharge his duties . . . with the care an ordinarily prudent person in a like position would exercise under similar circumstances." The use of the phrase "ordinarily prudent person" in a basic guideline for director conduct, suggesting caution or circumspection vis-avis danger or risk, has long been problematic given the fact that risk-taking decisions are central to the directors' role. When coupled with the exercise of "care," the prior text had a familiar resonance long associated with the field of tort law. See the Official Comment to section 8.31. The further coupling with the phrasal verb "shall discharge" added to the inference that former section 8.30(a)'s standard of conduct involved a negligence standard, with resultant confusion. In order to facilitate its understanding, and analysis, independent of the other general standards of conduct for directors, the duty of care element has been set forth as a separate standard of conduct in subsection (b).

Long before statutory formulations of directors' standards of conduct, courts would invoke the business judgment rule in evaluating directors' conduct and determining whether to impose liability in a particular case. The elements of the business judgment rule and the circumstances for its application are continuing to be developed by the courts. Section 8.30 does not try to codify the business judgment rule or to delineate the differences between that defensive rule and the section's standards of director conduct. Section 8.30 deals only with standards of conduct—the level of performance expected of every director entering into the service of a corporation and undertaking the role and responsibilities of the office of director. The section does not deal directly with the liability of a director—although exposure to liability will usually result from a failure to honor the standards of conduct required to be observed by subsection (a). See section 8.31(a)(1) and clauses (i) and (ii)(A) of section 8.31(a)(2). The issue of directors' liability is addressed in sections 8.31 and 8.33 of this subchapter. Section 8.30 does, however, play an important role in evaluating a director's conduct and the effectiveness of board action. It has relevance in assessing, under section 8.31, the reasonableness of a director's belief. Similarly, it has relevance in assessing a director's timely attention to appropriate inquiry when particular facts and circumstances of significant concern materialize. It serves as a frame of reference for determining, under section 8.33(a), liability for an unlawful distribution. Finally, section 8.30 compliance may have a direct bearing on a court's analysis where transactional justification (*e.g.*, a suit to enjoin a pending merger) is at issue.

A director complying with the standard of care expressed in subsection (b) is entitled to rely (under subsection (d)) upon board functions performed pursuant to delegated authority by, and to rely (under subsection (e)) upon information, opinions, reports or statements, including financial statements and other financial data, provided by, the persons or committees specified in the relevant parts of subsection (f). Within this authorization, the right to rely applies to the entire range of matters for which the board of directors is responsible. However, a director so relying must be without knowledge that would cause that reliance to be unwarranted. Section 8.30 expressly prevents a director from "hiding his or her head in the sand" and relying on the delegation of board functions, or on information, opinions reports or statements, when the director has actual knowledge that makes (or has a measure of knowledge that would cause a person, in a like position under similar circumstances, to undertake reasonable inquiry that would lead to information making) reliance unwarranted. Subsection (a)'s standards of good faith and reasonable belief in the best interests of the corporation also apply to a director's reliance under subsections (d), (e) and (f).

1. Section 8.30(a)

Section 8.30(a) establishes the basic standards of conduct for all directors. Its command is to be understood as peremptory—its obligations are to be observed by every director—and at the core of the subsection's mandate is the requirement that, when performing directors' duties, a director shall act in good faith coupled with conduct reasonably believed to be in the best interests of the corporation. This mandate governs all aspects of directors' duties: the duty of care, the duty to become informed, the duty of inquiry, the duty of informed judgment, the duty of attention, the duty of disclosure, the duty of loyalty, the duty of fair dealing and, finally, the broad concept of fiduciary duty that the courts often use as a frame of reference when evaluating a director's conduct. These duties do not necessarily compartmentalize and, in fact, tend to overlap. For example, the duties of care, inquiry, becoming informed, attention, disclosure and informed judgment all relate to the board's decision-making function, whereas the duties of attention, disclosure, becoming informed and inquiry relate to the board's oversight function.

Two of the phrases chosen to specify the manner in which a director's duties are to be discharged deserve further comment:

(1) The phrase "reasonably believes" is both subjective and objective in character. Its first level of analysis is geared to what the particular director, acting in good faith, actually believes—not what objective analysis would lead another director (in a like position and acting in similar circumstances) to conclude. The second level of analysis is focused specifically on "reasonably." While a director has wide discretion in marshalling the evidence and reaching conclusions, whether a director's belief is reasonable (*i.e.,* could—not would—a reasonable person in a like position and acting in similar circumstances have arrived at that belief) ultimately involves an overview that is objective in character.

(2) The phrase "best interests of the corporation" is key to an explication of a director's duties. The term "corporation" is a surrogate for the business enterprise as well as a frame of reference encompassing the shareholder body. In determining the corporation's "best interests," the director has wide discretion in deciding how to weigh near-term opportunities versus long-term benefits as well as in making judgments where the interests of various groups within the shareholder body or having other cognizable interests in the enterprise may differ.

As a generalization, section 8.30 operates as a "baseline" principle governing director conduct "when discharging the [ongoing] duties of a director" in circumstances uncomplicated by self-interest taint. The Model Act recognizes, however, that directors' personal interests may not always align with the corporation's best interests and provides procedures by which interest-conflict transactions can be processed. See subchapter D (derivative proceedings) of chapter 7 and subchapter E (indemnification) and subchapter F (directors' conflicting interest transactions) of this chapter 8. Those procedures generally contemplate that the interested director will not be involved in taking action on the interest-conflict transaction. And the common law has recognized that other interest-conflict situations may arise which do not entail a "transaction" by or with the corporation. See subchapter G of this chapter 8 (discussing the corporate opportunity doctrine). The interested director is relieved of the duty to act in connection with the matter on behalf of the corporation (specifically, the traditional mandate to act in the corporation's best interests), given the inherent conflict. However, the interested director is still expected to act in good faith, and that duty is normally discharged by observing the obligation of fair dealing. In the case of interest-conflict transactions, where there is a conflicting interest with respect to the corporation under section 8.60(1), the interested director's conduct is governed by subchapter F of this chapter 8. The duty of fair dealing is embedded in the subsection 8.60(7) provision calling for the interested director to make the required disclosure as to the conflicting interest and the transaction and, if one of the two safe harbor procedures is not properly observed, the interested director must prove the fairness (*i.e.*, procedure, involving good faith among other aspects, as well as price) of the transaction to the corporation. In other cases, Section 8.30's standards of conduct are overlaid by various components of the duty to act fairly, the particular thrusts of which will depend upon the kind of interested director's conduct at issue and the circumstances of the case. As a general rule, the duty of fair dealing is normally discharged by the interested director through appropriate disclosure to the other directors considering the matter followed by abstention from participation in any decision-making relevant thereto. If and to the extent that the interested director's action respecting the matter goes further, the reasonableness of the director's belief as to the corporation's best interests, in respect of the action taken, should be evaluated on the basis of not only the director's honest and good faith belief but also on considerations bearing on the fairness of the transaction or conduct to the corporation.

2. Section 8.30(b)

Section 8.30(b) establishes a general standard of care for directors in the context of their dealing with the board's decision-making and oversight functions. While certain aspects will involve individual conduct (e.g., preparation for meetings), these functions are generally performed by the board through collegial action, as recognized by the reference in subsection (b) to board and committee "members" and "their duties." In contrast with subsection (a)'s individual conduct mandate, section 8.30(b) has a two-fold thrust: it provides a standard of conduct for individual action and, more broadly, it states a conduct obligation— "shall discharge their duties"—concerning the degree of care to be collegially used by the directors when performing those functions. It provides that directors have a duty to exercise "the care that a person in a like position would reasonably believe appropriate under similar circumstances."

The traditional formulation for a director's standard (or duty) of care has been geared to the "ordinarily prudent person." For example, the Model Act's prior formulation (in former section 8.30(a)(2)) referred to "the care an ordinarily prudent person in a like position would exercise under similar circumstances," and almost all state statutes that include a standard of care reflect parallel language. The phrase "ordinarily prudent person" constitutes a basic frame of reference grounded in the field of tort law and provides a primary benchmark for determining negligence. For this reason, its use in the standard of care for directors, suggesting that negligence is the proper determinant for measuring deficient (and thus actionable) conduct, has caused confusion and misunderstanding. Accordingly, the phrase "ordinarily prudent person" has been removed from the Model Act's standard of care and in its place "a person in a like position" has been substituted. The standard is not what care a particular director might believe appropriate in the circumstances but what a person—in a like position and acting under similar circumstances—would reasonably believe to be appropriate. Thus, the degree of care that directors should employ, under subsection (b), involves an objective standard.

Some state statutes have used the words "diligence," "care," and "skill" to define the duty of care. There is very little authority as to what "skill" and "diligence," as distinguished from "care," can be required or properly expected of corporate directors in the performance of their duties. "Skill," in the sense of technical competence in a particular field, should not be a qualification for the office of director. The concept of "diligence" is sufficiently subsumed within the concept of "care." Accordingly, the words "diligence" and "skill" are not used in section 8.30's standard of care.

The process by which a director becomes informed, in carrying out the decision-making and oversight functions, will vary. Relevant thereto, the directors' decision-making function is established in large part by various sections of the Act: the issuance of shares (6.21); distributions (6.40); dismissal of derivative proceedings (7.44); indemnification (8.55); interested-transaction authorization (8.62); articles of incorporation amendments (10.02 and 10.03); bylaw amendments (10.20); mergers (11.01); share exchanges (11.02); asset sales and mortgages (12.01 and 12.02); and dissolution (14.02). The directors' oversight function is established under section 8.01. In relying on the performance by management of delegated or assigned section 8.01 duties (including, for example, matters of law and legal compliance), as authorized by subsection (d), directors may depend upon the presumption of regularity absent knowledge or notice to the contrary. In discharging the section 8.01 duties associated with the board's oversight function, the standard of care entails primarily a duty of attention. In contrast with the board's decision-making function, which generally involves informed action at a point in time, the oversight function is concerned with a continuum and the duty of attention accordingly involves participatory performance over a period of time.

Several of the phrases chosen to define the standard of conduct in section 8.30(b) deserve specific mention:

(1) The phrase "becoming informed," in the context of the decision-making function, refers to the process of gaining sufficient familiarity with the background facts and circumstances in order to make an informed judgment. Unless the circumstances would permit a reasonable director to conclude that he or she is already sufficiently informed, the standard of care requires every director to take steps to become informed about the background facts and circumstances before taking action on the matter at hand. The process typically involves review of written materials provided before or at the meet-

ing and attention to/participation in the deliberations leading up to a vote. It can involve consideration of information and data generated by persons other than legal counsel, public accountants, etc., retained by the corporation, as contemplated by subsection (f)(2); for example, review of industry studies or research articles prepared by unrelated parties could be very useful. It can also involve direct communications, outside of the boardroom, with members of management or other directors. There is no one way for "becoming informed," and both the method and measure—"how to" and "how much"—are matters of reasonable judgment for the director to exercise.

(2) The phrase "devoting attention," in the context of the oversight function, refers to concern with the corporation's information and reporting systems and not to proactive inquiry searching out system inadequacies or noncompliance. While directors typically give attention to future plans and trends as well as current activities, they should not be expected to anticipate the problems which the corporation may face except in those circumstances where something has occurred to make it obvious to the board that the corporation should be addressing a particular problem. The standard of care associated with the oversight function involves gaining assurances from management and advisers that systems believed appropriate have been established, coupled with ongoing monitoring of the systems in place, such as those concerned with legal compliance or internal controls—followed up with a proactive response when alerted to the need for inquiry.

(3) The reference to "person," without embellishment, is intended to avoid implying any qualifications, such as specialized expertise or experience requirements, beyond the basic director attributes of common sense, practical wisdom, and informed judgment.

(4) The phrase "reasonably believe appropriate" refers to the array of possible options that a person possessing the basic director attributes of common sense, practical wisdom and informed judgment would recognize to be available, in terms of the degree of care that might be appropriate, and from which a choice by such person would be made. The measure of care that such person might determine to be appropriate, in a given instance, would normally involve a selection from the range of options and any choice within the realm of reason would be an appropriate decision under the standard of care called for under subsection (b). However, a decision that is so removed from the realm of reason, or is so unreasonable, that it falls outside the permissible bounds of sound discretion, and thus an abuse of discretion, will not satisfy the standard.

(5) The phrase "in a like position" recognizes that the "care" under consideration is that which would be used by the "person" if he or she were a director of the particular corporation.

(6) The combined phrase "in a like position ... under similar circumstances" is intended to recognize that (a) the nature and extent of responsibilities will vary, depending upon such factors as the size, complexity, urgency, and location of activities carried on by the particular corporation, (b) decisions must be made on the basis of the information known to the directors without the benefit of hindsight, and (c) the special background, qualifications, and management responsibilities of a particular director may be relevant in evaluating that director's compliance with the standard of care. Even though the combined phrase is intended to take into account the special background, qualifications and management responsibilities of a particular director, it does not excuse a director lacking business experience or particular expertise from exercising the basic director attributes of common sense, practical wisdom, and informed judgment.

3. Section 8.30(c)

A duty to disclose information that a director knows to be material to the oversight or decision-making functions of the board or committee has always been embraced in the standards of conduct set forth in subsections (a) and (b). Subsection (c) makes explicit this existing duty of disclosure among directors. Thus, for example, when a member of the board knows information that the director recognizes is material to a decision by the board to approve financial statements of the corporation, the director is obligated to see to it that such information is provided to the other members of the board. So long as that disclosure is accomplished, the action required of the director can occur through direct statements in meetings of the board, or by any other timely means, including, for example, communicating the information to the chairman of the board or the chairman of a committee, or to the corporation's general counsel, and requesting that the recipient inform the other board or committee members of the disclosed information.

Subsection (c) recognizes that a duty of confidentiality can override a director's obligation to share with other directors information pertaining to a current corporate matter, and that a director is not required to make such disclosure to the extent the director reasonably believes that such a duty of confidentiality prohibits it. In some circumstances, a duty of confidentiality may even prohibit disclosure of the nature or the existence of the duty itself. Ordinarily, however, a director who withholds material information based on a reasonable belief that a duty of confidentiality prohibits disclosure should advise the other directors of the existence and nature of that duty. Under the standards of conduct set forth in section 8.30(a), the director may also be required to take other action in light of the confidentiality restraint. The precise nature of that action must, of necessity, depend on the specific circumstances. Depending on the nature of the material information and of the matter before the board of directors or committee of the board, such action may include abstention or absence from all or a portion of the other directors' deliberation or vote on the matter to which the undisclosed information is material, or even resignation as a director. See Official Comment to section 8.62. Finally, a duty of confidentiality may not form the basis for the limitation on disclosure unless it is entered into and relied upon in good faith.

The required disclosure (as defined in section 8.60(7)) that must be made under section 8.62(a) in connection with a director's conflicting interest transaction, and the exceptions to the required disclosure in that context under section 8.62(b), have elements that parallel the disclosure obligation of directors under section 8.30(c). The demands of section 8.62, however, are more detailed and specific. They apply to just one situation—a director's conflict of interest transaction—while the requirements of section 8.30(c) apply generally to all other decision-making and oversight functions. For example, the specific requirements of section 8.62(a)(1) for a deliberation and vote outside the presence of the conflicted director are not imposed universally for all decision-making matters or for oversight matters that do not involve a decision. To the extent they may be different from the generally applicable provisions of section 8.30(c), the specific provisions of subchapter F control and are exclusive with respect to director conflicting interest transactions.

4.   Section 8.30(d)

The delegation of authority and responsibility under subsection (d) may take the form of (i) formal action through a board resolution, (ii) implicit action through the election of corporate officers (*e.g.*, chief financial officer or controller) or the appointment of corporate managers (e.g., credit manager), or (iii) informal action through a course of conduct (*e.g.*, involvement through corporate officers and managers in the management of a significant 50%-owned joint venture). A director may properly rely on those to whom authority has been delegated pursuant to subsection (d) respecting particular matters calling for specific action or attention in connection with the directors' decision-making function as well as matters on the board's continuing agenda, such as legal compliance and internal control, in connection with the directors' oversight function. Delegation should be carried out in accordance with the standard of care set forth in section 8.30(b).

By identifying those upon whom a director may rely in connection with the discharge of duties, section 8.30(d) does not limit the ability of directors to delegate their powers under section 8.01(b) except where delegation is expressly prohibited by the Act or otherwise by applicable law (see, *e.g.*, section 8.25(e) and § 11 of the Securities Act of 1933). See section 8.25 and its Official Comment for detailed consideration of delegation to board committees of the authority of the board under section 8.01 and the duty to perform one or more of the board's functions. And by employing the concept of delegation, section 8.30(d) does not limit the ability of directors to establish baseline principles as to management responsibilities. Specifically, section 8.01(b) provides that "all corporate powers shall be exercised by or under the authority of" the board, and a basic board function involves the allocation of management responsibilities and the related assignment (or delegation) of corporate powers. For example, a board can properly decide to retain a third party to assume responsibility for the administration of designated aspects of risk management for the corporation (*e.g.*, health insurance or disability claims). This would involve the directors in the exercise of judgment in connection with the decision-making function pursuant to subsection (b) (*i.e.*, the assignment of authority to exercise corporate powers to an agent). See the Official Comment to section 8.01. It would not entail impermissible delegation—to a person specified in subsection (f)(2) pursuant to subsection (d)—of a board function for which the directors by law have a duty to perform. They have the corporate power (under section 8.01(b)) to perform the task but administration of risk management is not a board function coming within the ambit of directors' duties; together with many similar management responsibilities, they may assign the task in the context of the allocation of corporate powers exercised under the authority of the board. This illustration highlights the distinction between delegation of a board function and assignment of authority to exercise corporate powers.

Although the board may delegate the authority or duty to perform one or more of its functions, reliance on delegation under subsection (d) may not alone constitute compliance with section 8.30 and reliance on the action taken by the delegatee may not alone constitute compliance by the directors or a noncommittee board member with section 8.01 responsibilities. On the other hand, should the board committee or the corporate officer or employee performing the function delegated fail to meet section 8.30's standard of care, noncompliance by the board with section 8.01 will not automatically result. Factors to be considered, in this regard, will include the care used in the delegation to and supervision over the delegatee, and the amount of knowledge regarding the particular matter which is available to the particular director. Care in delegation and supervision includes appraisal of the capabilities and diligence of the delegatee in light of the subject and its relative importance and may be facilitated, in the usual case, by receipt of reports concerning the delegatee's activities. The enumeration of these factors is intended to emphasize that directors may not abdicate their responsibilities and avoid accountability simply by delegating authority to others. Rather, a director charged with accountability based upon acts of others will fulfill the director's duties if the standards contained in section 8.30 are met.

5. Section 8.30(e)

Reliance under subsection (e) on a report, statement, opinion, or other information is permitted only if the director has read the information, opinion, report or statement in question, or was present at a meeting at which it was orally presented, or took other steps to become generally familiar with it. A director must comply with the general standard of care of section 8.30(b) in making a judgment as to the reliability and competence of the source of information upon which the director proposes to rely or, as appropriate, that it otherwise merits confidence.

6. Section 8.30(f)

Reliance on one or more of the corporation's officers or employees, pursuant to the intracorporate frame of reference of subsection (f)(1), is conditioned upon a reasonable belief as to the reliability and competence of those who have undertaken the functions performed or who prepared or communicated the information, opinions, reports or statements presented. In determining whether a person is "reliable," the director would typically consider (i) the individual's background experience and scope of responsibility within the corporation in gauging the individual's familiarity and knowledge respecting the subject matter and (ii) the individual's record and reputation for honesty, care and ability in discharging responsibilities which he or she undertakes. In determining whether a person is "competent," the director would normally take into account the same considerations and, if expertise should be relevant, the director would consider the individual's technical skills as well. Recognition in the statute of the right of one director to rely on the expertise and experience of another director, in the context of board or committee deliberations, is unnecessary, for the group's reliance on shared experience and wisdom is an implicit underpinning of director conduct. In relying on another member of the board, a director would quite properly take advantage of the colleague's knowledge and experience in becoming informed about the matter at hand before taking action; however, the director would be expected to exercise independent judgment when it comes time to vote.

Subsection (f)(2), which has an extracorporate frame of reference, permits reliance on outside advisers retained by the corporation, including persons specifically engaged to advise the board or a board committee. Possible advisers include not only those in the professional disciplines customarily supervised by state authorities, such as lawyers, accountants, and engineers, but also those in other fields involving special experience and skills, such as investment bankers, geologists, management consultants, actuaries, and real estate appraisers. The adviser could be an individual or an organization, such as a law firm. Reliance on a nonmanagement director, who is specifically engaged (and, normally, additionally compensated) to undertake a special assignment or a particular consulting role, would fall within this outside adviser frame of reference. The concept of "expert competence" embraces a wide variety of qualifications and is not limited to the more precise and narrower recognition of experts under the Securities Act of 1933. In this respect, subsection (f)(2) goes beyond the reliance provision found in many existing state business corporation acts. In addition, a director may also rely on outside advisers where skills or expertise of a technical nature is not a prerequisite, or where the person's professional or expert competence has not been established, so long as the director reasonably believes the person merits confidence. For example, a board might choose to assign to a private investigator the duty of inquiry (*e.g.*, follow upon rumors about a senior executive's "grand lifestyle") and properly rely on the private investigator's report. And it would be entirely appropriate for a director to rely on advice concerning highly technical aspects of environmental compliance from a corporate lawyer in the corporation's outside law firm, without due inquiry concerning that particular lawyer's technical competence, where the director reasonably believes the lawyer giving the advice is appropriately informed—by reason of resources known to be available from that adviser's legal organization or through other means—and therefore merits confidence.

Subsection (f)(3) permits reliance on a board committee when it is submitting recommendations for action by the full board of directors as well as when it is performing supervisory or other functions in instances where neither the full board of directors nor the committee takes dispositive action. For example, the compensation committee typically reviews proposals and makes recommendations for action by the full board of directors. In contrast, there may be reliance upon an investigation undertaken by a board committee and reported to the full board, which form the basis for a decision by the board of directors not to take dispositive action. Another example is reliance on a committee of the board of directors, such as a corporate audit committee with respect to the board's ongoing role of oversight of the accounting and auditing functions of the corporation. In addition where reliance on information or materials prepared or presented by a board committee is not involved, in connection with board action, a director may properly rely on oversight monitoring or dispositive action by a board committee (of which the director is not a member) empowered to act pursuant to authority delegated under section 8.25 or acting with the acquiescence of the board of directors. See the Official Comment to section 8.25. A director may similarly rely on committees not created under section 8.25 which have nondirector members. In parallel with subsection (f)(2)(ii), the concept of "confidence" is substituted for "competence" in order to avoid any inference that technical skills are a prerequisite. In the usual case, the appointment of committee members or the reconstitution of the membership of a standing committee (*e.g.*, the audit committee), following an annual shareholders' meeting, would alone manifest the noncommittee members' belief that the committee "merits confidence." However, the reliance contemplated by subsection (f)(3) is geared to the point in time when the board takes action or the period of time over which a committee is engaged in an oversight function; consequently, the judgment to be made (*i.e.*, whether a committee "merits confidence") will arise at varying points in time. After making an initial judgment that a committee (of which a director is not a member) merits confidence, the director may depend upon the presumption of regularity absent knowledge or notice to the contrary.

7. Application to Officers

Section 8.30 generally deals only with directors. Section 8.42 and its Official Comment explain the extent to which the provisions of section 8.30 apply to officers.

§ 8.31 Standards of Liability for Directors

(a) A director shall not be liable to the corporation or its shareholders for any decision to take or not to take action, or any failure to take any action, as a director, unless the party asserting liability in a proceeding establishes that:

    (1) no defense interposed by the director based on (i) any provision in the articles of incorporation authorized by section 2.02(b)(4), (ii) the protection afforded by section 8.61 (for action taken in compliance with section 8.62 or section 8.63), or (iii) the protection afforded by section 8.70, if interposed as a bar to the proceeding by the director, precludes liability; and

    (2) the challenged conduct consisted or was the result of:

        (i) action not in good faith; or

        (ii) a decision

            (A) which the director did not reasonably believe to be in the best interests of the corporation, or

            (B) as to which the director was not informed to an extent the director reasonably believed appropriate in the circumstances; or

        (iii) a lack of objectivity due to the director's familial, financial or business relationship with, or a lack of independence due to the director's domination or control by, another person having a material interest in the challenged conduct

            (A) which relationship or which domination or control could reasonably be expected to have affected the director's judgment respecting the challenged conduct in a manner adverse to the corporation, and

            (B) after a reasonable expectation to such effect has been established, the director shall not have established that the challenged conduct was reasonably believed by the director to be in the best interests of the corporation; or

        (iv) a sustained failure of the director to devote attention to ongoing oversight of the business and affairs of the corporation, or a failure to devote timely attention, by making (or causing to be made) appropriate inquiry, when particular facts and circumstances of significant concern materialize that would alert a reasonably attentive director to the need therefor; or

    (v) receipt of a financial benefit to which the director was not entitled or other breach of the director's duties to deal fairly with the corporation and its shareholders that is actionable under applicable law.

(b) The party seeking to hold the director liable:

    (1) for money damages, shall also have the burden of establishing that:

        (i) harm to the corporation or its shareholders has been suffered, and

        (ii) the harm suffered was proximately caused by the director's challenged conduct; or

    (2) for other money payment under a legal remedy, such as compensation for the unauthorized use of corporate assets, shall also have whatever persuasion burden may be called for to establish that the payment sought is appropriate in the circumstances; or

    (3) for other money payment under an equitable remedy, such as profit recovery by or disgorgement to the corporation, shall also have whatever persuasion burden may be called for to establish that the equitable remedy sought is appropriate in the circumstances.

(c) Nothing contained in this section shall (1) in any instance where fairness is at issue, such as consideration of the fairness of a transaction to the corporation under section 8.61(b)(3), alter the burden of proving the fact or lack of fairness otherwise applicable, (2) alter the fact or lack of liability of a director under another section of this Act, such as the provisions governing the consequences of an unlawful distribution under section 8.33 or a transactional interest under section 8.61, or (3) affect any rights to which the corporation or a shareholder may be entitled under another statute of this state or the United States.

Official Comment

Subsections (a) and (b) of section 8.30 establish standards of conduct that are central to the role of directors. Section 8.30(b)'s standard of conduct is frequently referred to as a director's duty of care. The employment of the concept of "care," if considered in the abstract, suggests a tort-law/negligence-based analysis looking toward a finding of fault and damage recovery where the duty of care has not been properly observed and loss has been suffered. But the Model Act's desired level of director performance, with its objectively-based standard of conduct ("the care that a person in a like position would reasonably believe appropriate under similar circumstances"), does not carry with it the same type of result-oriented liability analysis. The courts recognize that boards of directors and corporate managers make numerous decisions that involve the balancing of risks and benefits for the enterprise.

Although some decisions turn out to be unwise or the result of a mistake of judgment, it is not reasonable to reexamine an unsuccessful decision with the benefit of hindsight. As observed in *Joy v. North,* 692 F.2d 880, 885 (2d Cir.1982): "Whereas an automobile driver who makes a mistake in judgment as to speed or distance injuring a pedestrian will likely be called upon to respond in damages, a corporate [director or] officer who makes a mistake in judgment as to economic conditions, consumer tastes or production line efficiency will rarely, if ever, be found liable for damages suffered by the corporation." Therefore, as a general rule, a director is not exposed to personal liability for injury or damage caused by an unwise decision. While a director is not personally responsible for unwise decisions or mistakes of judgment—and conduct conforming with the standards of section 8.30 will almost always be protected—a director can be held liable for misfeasance or nonfeasance in performing the duties of a director. And while a director whose performance meets the standards of section 8.30 should have no liability, the fact that a director's performance fails to reach that level does not automatically establish personal liability for damages that the corporation may have suffered as a consequence.

* * *

Note on Directors' Liability

A director's financial risk exposure *(e.g.,* in a lawsuit for money damages suffered by the corporation or its shareholders claimed to have resulted from misfeasance or nonfeasance in connection with the performance of the director's duties) can be analyzed as follows:

1. *Articles of incorporation limitation.* If the corporation's articles of incorporation contain a provision eliminating its directors' liability to the corporation or its shareholders for money damages, adopted pursuant to section 2.02(b)(4), there is no liability unless the director's conduct involves one of the prescribed exceptions that preclude the elimination of liability See section 2.02 and its Official Comment.

2. *Director's conflicting interest transaction safe harbor.* If the matter at issue involves a director's conflicting interest transaction (as defined in section 8.60(2)) and a safe harbor procedure under section 8.61 involving action taken in compliance with section 8.62 or 8.63 has been properly implemented, there is no liability for the interested director arising out of the transaction. See subchapter F of this chapter 8.

3. *Business opportunities safe harbor.* Similarly, if the matter involves a director's taking of a business opportunity and a safe harbor procedure under section 8.70 has been properly implemented, there is no liability for the director arising out of the taking of the business opportunity. See subchapter G of this chapter 8.

4. *Business judgment rule.* If an articles of incorporation provision adopted pursuant to section 2.02 or a safe harbor procedure under section 8.61 or section 8.70 does not shield the director's conduct from liability, this standard of judicial review for director conduct—deeply rooted in the case law—presumes that, absent self-dealing or other breach of the duty of loyalty, directors' decision-making satisfies the applicable legal requirements. A plaintiff challenging the director's conduct in connection with a corporate decision, and asserting liability by reason thereof, encounters certain procedural barriers. In the first instance, many jurisdictions have special pleading requirements that condition the ability to pursue the challenge on the plaintiff's bringing forward specific factual allegations that put in question the availability of the business judgment presumption. Assuming the suit survives a motion to dismiss for failure to state (in satisfaction of such a condition) an actionable claim, the plaintiff has the burden of overcoming that presumption of regularity.

5. *Damages and proximate cause.* If the business judgment rule does not shield the directors' decision-making from liability, as a general rule it must be established that money damages were suffered by the corporation or its shareholders and those damages resulted from and were legally caused by the challenged act or omission of the director.

6. *Other liability for money payment.* Aside from a claim for damages, the director may be liable to reimburse the corporation pursuant to a claim under *quantum meruit* (the reasonable value of services) or *quantum valebant* (the reasonable value of goods and materials) if corporate resources have been used without proper authorization. In addition, the corporation may be entitled to short-swing profit recovery, stemming from the director's trading in its securities, under § 16(b) of the Securities Exchange Act of 1934.

7. *Equitable profit recovery or disgorgement.* An equitable remedy compelling the disgorgement of the director's improper financial gain or entitling the corporation to profit recovery, where directors' duties have been breached, may require the payment of money by the director to the corporation.

8. *Corporate indemnification.* If the court determines that the director is liable, the director may be indemnified by the corporation for any payments made and expenses incurred, depending upon the circumstances, if a third-party suit is involved. If the proceeding is by or in the right of the corporation, the director may be reimbursed for reasonable expenses incurred in connection with the proceeding if ordered by a court under section 8.54(a)(3).

9. *Insurance.* To the extent that corporate indemnification is not available, the director may be reimbursed for the money damages for which the director is accountable, together with proceeding-related expenses, if the claim/grounds for liability come within the coverage under

directors' and officers' liability insurance that has been purchased by the corporation pursuant to section 8.57.

* * *

Section 8.31 includes steps (1) through (6) in the analysis of a director's liability exposure set forth in the above Note. In establishing general standards of director liability under the Model Act, the section also serves the important purpose of providing clarification that the general standards of conduct set forth in section 8.30 are not intended to codify the business judgment rule—a point as to which there has been confusion on the part of some courts (notwithstanding a disclaimer of that purpose and effect in the prior Official Comment to section 8.30). For example, one court viewed the standard of care set forth in Washington's business corporation act (a provision based upon and almost identical to the prior section 8.30(a)—which read "A director shall discharge his duties as a director . . .: (1) in good faith; (2) with the care an ordinarily prudent person in a like position would exercise under similar circumstances; and (3) in a manner he reasonably believes to be in the best interests of the corporation") as having codified the business judgment rule. See *Seafirst Corp. v. Jenkins*, 644 F. Supp. 1152, 1159 (W.D.Wash.1986). (A later court characterized this view as a mistaken assumption and recognized the disclaimer made in section 8.30's Official Comment. See *Shinn v. Thrust IV Inc.*, 786 P.2d 285, 290 n. 1 (Wash. App.1990).) Another court declared "Section 309 *[a standard of conduct almost identical to the prior section 8.30(a)]* codifies California's business judgment rule." See *Gaillard v. Natomas Co.*, 208 Cal.App.3d 1250, 1264 (1989). The Court of Appeals of New York referred to that state's statutory standard of care for directors, a formulation set forth in NYBCL § 717 that is similar to the prior section 8.30(a), as "New York's business judgment rule." See *Lindner Fund, Inc. v. Waldbaum, Inc.*, 624 N.E.2d 160, 161 (1993). In contrast, another court considering New York's conduct standard observed:

> A board member's obligation to a corporation and its shareholders has two prongs, generally characterized as the duty of care and the duty of loyalty. The duty of care refers to the responsibility of a corporate fiduciary to exercise, in the performance of his tasks, the care that a reasonably prudent person in a similar position would use under similar circumstances. See NYBCL § 717. In evaluating a manager's compliance with the duty of care, New York courts adhere to the business judgment rule, which "bars judicial inquiry into actions of corporate directors taken in good faith and in the exercise of honest judgment in the lawful and legitimate furtherance of corporate purposes." *Norlin Corp. v. Rooney, Pace Inc.*, 744 F.2d 255, 264 (2d Cir. 1984) [quoting *Auerbach v. Bennett*, 47 N.Y.2d 619, 629 (1979)].

Sections 8.30 and 8.31 adopt the approach to director conduct and director liability taken in the *Norlin* decision. See section 8.30 and its Official Comment with respect to the standards of conduct for directors. For a detailed analysis of how and why standards of conduct and standards of liability diverge in corporate law, see Melvin A. Eisenberg, *The Divergence of Standards of Conduct and Standards of Review in Corporate Law,* 62 Fordham L. Rev. 437 (1993)....

1. Section 8.31(a)

If a provision in the corporation's articles of incorporation (adopted pursuant to section 2.02(b)(4)) shelters the director from liability for money damages, or if a safe harbor provision, under subsection (b)(1) or (b)(2) of section 8.61 or section 8.70, shelters the director's conduct in connection with a conflicting interest transaction or the taking of a business opportunity, and such defense applies to all claims in plaintiff's complaint, there is no need to consider further the application of section 8.31's standards of liability. In that event, the court would presumably grant the defendant director's motion for dismissal or summary judgment (or the equivalent) and the proceeding would be ended. If the defense applies to some but not all of plaintiff's claims, defendant is entitled to dismissal or summary judgment with respect to those claims. Termination of the proceeding or dismissal of claims on the basis of an articles of incorporation provision or safe harbor will not automatically follow, however, if the party challenging the director's conduct can assert any of the valid bases for contesting the availability of the liability shelter. Absent such a challenge, the relevant shelter provision is self-executing and the individual director's exoneration from liability is automatic. Further, under both section 8.61 and section 8.70, the directors approving the conflicting interest transaction or the director's taking of the business opportunity will presumably be protected as well, for compliance with the relevant standards of conduct under section 8.30 is important for their action to be effective and, as noted above, conduct meeting section 8.30's standards will almost always be protected.

If a claim of liability arising out of a challenged act or omission of a director is not resolved and disposed of under subsection (a)(1), subsection (a)(2) provides the basis for evaluating whether the conduct in question can be challenged.

* * *

Note on the Business Judgment Rule

Over the years, the courts have developed a broad common law concept geared to business judgment. In basic principle, a board of directors enjoys a presumption of sound business judgment and its decisions will not be disturbed (by a court substituting its own notions of what is or is not sound business judgment) if they can be attributed to any rational business purpose. See *Sinclair Oil Corp. v. Levien,* 280 A.2d 717, 720 (Del.1971). Relatedly, it is presumed that, in making a business decision, directors act in good faith, on an informed basis, and in the honest belief that the action taken is in the best interests of the corporation. See *Aronson v. Lewis,* 473 A.2d 805, 812 (Del.1983). When applied, this principle operates both as a procedural rule of evidence and a substantive rule of law, in that if the plaintiff fails to rebut the presumption that the directors acted in good faith, in the corporation's best interest and on an informed basis, the business judgment standard protects both the directors and the decisions they make. See *Citron v. Fairchild Camera & Instrument Corp.,* 569 A.2d 53, 64 (Del.1989).

Some have suggested that, within the business judgment standard's broad ambit, a distinction might usefully be drawn between that part which protects directors from personal liability for the decision they make and the part which protects the decision itself from attack. See *Revlon, Inc. v. MacAndrews & Forbes Holdings, Inc.,* 506 A.2d 173, 180 n.10 (Del.1986). While these two objects of the business judgment standard's protection are different, and judicial review might result in the decision being enjoined but no personal liability (or vice versa), their operative elements are identical (*i.e.,* good faith, disinterest, informed judgment and "best interests"). As a consequence, the courts have not observed any distinction in terminology and have generally followed the practice of referring only to the business judgment rule, whether dealing with personal liability issues or transactional justification matters.

While, in substance, the operative elements of the standard of judicial review commonly referred to as the business judgment rule have been widely recognized, courts have used a number of different word formulations to articulate the concept. The formulation adopted in § 4.01(c) of The American Law Institute's PRINCIPLES OF CORPORATE GOVERNANCE: ANALYSIS AND RECOMMENDATIONS (1994) provides that a director who makes a business judgment **in good faith** (an obvious prerequisite) fulfills the duty of care standard if the director:

(1) is not interested *[as defined]* in the subject of the business judgment;

(2) is informed with respect to the subject of the business judgment to the extent the director ... reasonably believes to be appropriate under the circumstances; and

(3) rationally believes that the business judgment is in the best interests of the corporation.

Referring to clause (2) above, the decision-making process is to be reviewed on a basis that is to a large extent individualized in nature ("informed ... to the extent the director ... reasonably believes to be appropriate under the circumstances") as contrasted with the traditional objectively-based duty-of-care standard (*e.g.,* the prior section 8.30(a)'s "care ... an ordinarily prudent person ... would exercise"). An "ordinarily prudent person" might do more to become better informed, but if a director believes, in good faith, that the director can make a sufficiently informed business judgment, the director will be protected so long as that belief is within the bounds of reason. Referring to clause (3) above, the phrase "rationally believes" is stated in the PRINCIPLES to be a term having "both an objective and subjective content. A director ... must actually believe that the business judgment is in the best interests of the corporation and that belief must be rational," 1 PRINCIPLES, at 179. Others see that aspect to be primarily geared to the process employed by a director in making the decision as opposed to the substantive content of the board decision made. See *Aronson v. Lewis, supra,* at 812 ("The business judgment rule is ... a presumption that in making a business decision the directors of a corporation acted on an informed basis, in good faith and in the honest belief that the action taken was in the best interests of the company. ... Absent an abuse of discretion, that judgment will be respected by the courts.") In practical application, an irrational belief would in all likelihood constitute an abuse of discretion. *Compare In Re Caremark International Inc. Derivative Litigation* (September 25, 1996) (1996 Del.Ch. LEXIS 125 at p. 27: "whether a judge or jury considering the matter after the fact ... believes a decision substantively wrong, or degrees of wrong extending through 'stupid' to 'egregious' or 'irrational', provides no ground for director liability, so long as the court determines that the process employed was either rational or employed in a good faith effort to advance corporate interests ... the business judgment rule is process oriented and informed by a deep respect for all good faith board decisions.")....

(a) Good faith

The expectation that a director's conduct will be in good faith is an overarching element of his or her baseline duties. Relevant thereto, it has been stated that a lack of good faith is presented where a board "lacked an actual intention to advance corporate welfare" and "bad faith" is presented where "a transaction ... is authorized for some purpose other than a genuine attempt to advance corporate welfare or is known to constitute a violation of applicable positive law." See *Gagliardi v. TriFoods Int'l Inc.,* 683 A.2d 1049 (Del.Ch.1996). If a director's conduct can be successfully challenged pursuant to other clauses of subsection (a)(2), there is a substantial likelihood that the conduct in question will also present an issue of good faith implicating clause 2(i). Conduct involving knowingly illegal conduct that exposes the corporation to harm will constitute action not in good faith, and belief that decisions made (in connection with such conduct) were in the best interests of the corporation will be subject to challenge as well. If subsection (a)(2) included only clause 2(i), much of the conduct with which the other clauses are concerned could still be considered pursuant to the subsection, on the basis that such conduct evidenced the actor's lack of good faith. Accordingly, the canon of construction known as *ejusdem generis* has substantial relevance in understanding the broad overlap of the good faith element with the various other subsection (a)(2) clauses. Where conduct has not been found deficient on other grounds, decision-making outside the bounds of reasonable judgment—an abuse of discretion perhaps explicable on no other basis—can give rise to an inference of bad faith. That form of conduct (characterized by the court as "constructive fraud" or "reckless indifference" or "deliberate disregard" in the relatively few case precedents) giving rise to an inference of bad faith will also raise a serious question whether the director could have reasonably believed that the best interests of the corporation would be served. If a director's conflicting interest transaction is determined to be manifestly unfavorable to the corporation, giving rise to an inference of bad faith tainting the directors' action approving the transaction under section 8.62, the safe harbor protection afforded by section 8.61 for both the transaction and the conflicted director would be in jeopardy. See the Official Comment to section 8.61. Depending on the facts and circumstances, the directors who approve a director's conflicting interest transaction that is manifestly unfavorable to the corporation may be at risk under clause (2)(i).

(b) Reasonable belief

A director should reasonably believe that his or her decision will be in the best interests of the corporation and a director should become sufficiently informed, with respect to any action taken or not taken, to the extent he or she reasonably believes appropriate in the circumstances. In each case, the director's reasonable belief calls for a subjective belief and, so long as it is his or her honest and good faith belief, a director has wide discretion. However, in the rare case where a decision respecting the corporation's best interests is so removed from the realm of reason (*e.g.*, corporate waste), or a belief as to the sufficiency of the director's preparation to make an informed judgment is so unreasonable as to fall outside the permissible bounds of sound discretion (*e.g.*, a clear case is presented if the director has undertaken no preparation and is woefully uninformed), the director's judgment will not be sustained.

(c) Lack of objectivity or independence

If a director has a familial, financial or business relationship with another person having a material interest in a transaction or other conduct involving the corporation, or if the director is dominated or controlled by another person having such a material interest, there is a potential for that conflicted interest or divided loyalty to affect the director's judgment. If the matter at issue involves a director's transactional interest, such as a "director's conflicting interest transaction" (see section 8.60(2)) in which a "related person" (see section 8.60(3)) is involved, it will be governed by section 8.61; otherwise, the lack of objectivity due to a relationship's influence on the director's judgment will be evaluated, in the context of the pending conduct challenge, under section 8.31. If the matter at issue involves lack of independence, the proof of domination or control and its influence on the director's judgment will typically entail different (and perhaps more convincing) evidence than what may be involved in a lack of objectivity case. The variables are manifold, and the facts must be sorted out and weighed on a case-by-case basis. If that other person is the director's spouse or employer, the concern that the director's judgment might be improperly influenced would be substantially greater than if that person is the spouse of the director's step-grandchild or the director's partner in a vacation time-share. When the party challenging the director's conduct can establish that the relationship or the domination or control in question could reasonably be expected to affect the director's judgment respecting the matter at issue in a manner adverse to the corporation, the director will then have the opportunity to establish that the action taken by him or her was reasonably believed to be in the best interests of the corporation. The reasonableness of the director's belief as to the corporation's best interests, in respect of the action taken, should be evaluated on the basis of not only the director's honest and good faith belief but also on considerations bearing on the fairness to the corporation of the transaction or other conduct involving the corporation that is at issue.

(d) Improper financial benefit

Subchapter F of chapter 8 of the Model Act deals in detail with directors' transactional interests. Its coverage of those interests is exclusive and its safe harbor procedures for directors' conflicting interest transactions (as defined)—providing shelter from legal challenges based on interest conflicts, when properly observed—will establish a director's entitlement to any financial benefit gained from the transactional event. A director's conflicting interest transaction that is not protected by the fairness standard set forth in section 8.61(b)(3), pursuant to which the conflicted director may establish the transaction to have been fair to the corporation, would often involve receipt of a financial benefit to which the director was not entitled (*i.e.*, the transaction was not "fair" to the corporation). Unauthorized use of corporate assets, such as aircraft or hotel suites, would also provide a basis for the proper challenge of a director's conduct. There can be other forms of improper financial benefit not involving a transaction with the corporation or use of its facilities, such as where a director profits from unauthorized use of proprietary information. . . .

(f) Sustained inattention

The director's role involves two fundamental components: the decision-making function and the oversight function. In contrast with the decision-making function, which generally involves action taken at a point in time, the oversight function under section 8.01(b) involves ongoing monitoring of the corporation's business and affairs over a period of time. This involves the duty of ongoing attention, when actual knowledge of particular facts and circumstances arouse suspicions which indicate a need to make inquiry. As observed by the Supreme Court of New Jersey in *Francis v. United Jersey Bank,* 432 A.2d 814, 822 (Sup. Ct. 1981):

> Directors are under a continuing obligation to keep informed about the activities of the corporation.... Directors may not shut their eyes to corporate misconduct and then claim that because they did not see the misconduct, they did not have a duty to look. The sentinel asleep at his post contributes nothing to the enterprise he is charged to protect.... Directorial management does not require a detailed inspection of day-to-day activities, but rather a general monitoring of corporate affairs and policies.

While the facts will be outcome-determinative, deficient conduct involving a sustained failure to exercise oversight—where found actionable—has typically been characterized by the courts in terms of abdication and continued neglect of a director's duty of attention, not a brief distraction or temporary interruption. However, embedded in the oversight function is the need to inquire when suspicions are aroused. This duty is not a component of ongoing oversight, and does not entail proactive vigilance, but arises when, and only when, particular facts and circumstances of material concern (*e.g.,* evidence of embezzlement at a high level or the discovery of significant inventory shortages) suddenly surface.

(g) Other breaches of a director's duties

Subsection (a)(2)(v) is, in part, a catchall provision that implements the intention to make section 8.31 a generally inclusive provision but, at the same time, to recognize the existence of other breaches of common-law duties that can give rise to liability for directors. As developed in the case law, these actionable breaches include unauthorized use of corporate property or information, unfair competition with the corporation and taking of a corporate opportunity. In the latter case, the director is alleged to have wrongfully diverted a business opportunity as to which the corporation had a prior right. Section 8.70 provides a safe harbor mechanism for a director who wishes to take advantage of a business opportunity, regardless of whether such opportunity would be characterized as a "corporate opportunity" under existing case law. Note that section 8.70(b) provides that the fact that a director did not employ the safe harbor provisions of section 8.70 does not create an inference that the opportunity should have first been presented to the corporation or alter the burden of proof otherwise applicable to establish a breach of the director's duty to the corporation.

(h) Fairness

Pursuant to section 8.61(b)(3), an interested director (or the corporation, if it chooses) can gain protection for a director's conflicting interest transaction by establishing that it was fair to the corporation. (The concept of "fair" and "fairness," in this and various other contexts, can take into account both fair price and fair dealing on the part of the interested director. See the Official Comment to section 8.61.) Under case law, personal liability as well as transactional justification issues will be subject to a fairness standard of judicial review if the plaintiff makes out a credible claim of breach of the duty of loyalty or if the presumptions of the business judgment standard (*e.g.,* an informed judgment) are overcome, with the burden of proof shifting from the plaintiff to the defendant. In this respect, the issue of fairness is relevant to both subsection (a) and subsection (b). Within the ambit of subsection (a)(2), a director can often respond to the challenge that his or her conduct was deficient by establishing that the transaction or conduct at issue was fair to the corporation. See *Kahn v. Lynch Communications Systems, Inc.* 669 A.2d 79 (Del.1995). *Cf. Cede & Co. v. Technicolor Inc.,* 634 A.2d 345 (Del.1993) (when the business judgment rule is rebutted procedurally the burden shifts to the defendant directors to prove the "entire fairness" of the challenged transaction). It is to be noted, however, that fairness may not be relevant to the matter at issue (see, e.g., clause (iv) of subsection (a)(2)). If the director is successful in establishing fairness, where the issue of fairness is relevant, then it is unlikely that the complainant can establish legal liability or the appropriateness of an equitable remedy under subsection (b).

(i) Director conduct

Subsection (a)(2) deals, throughout, with a director's action that is taken or not taken. To the extent that the director's conduct involves a breach of his or her duty of care or duty of attention within the context of collegial action by the board or one of its committees, proper performance of the relevant duty through the action taken by the director's colleagues can overcome the consequences of his or her deficient conduct. For example, where a director's conduct can be challenged under subsection (a)(2)(ii)(B) by reason of having been uninformed about the decision—he or she did not read the merger materials distributed prior to the meeting, arrived late at the board meeting just in time for the vote but, nonetheless, voted for the merger solely because the others were in favor—the favorable action by a quorum of properly informed directors would ordinarily protect the director against liability. When the director's conduct involves the duty of fair dealing within the context of action taken by the board or one of its committees, the wiser choice will usually be for the director not to participate in the collegial action. That is to say, where a director may have a conflicting interest or a divided loyalty, or even where there may be grounds for the issue to be raised, the better course to follow is usually for the director to disclose the conduct-related facts and circumstances posing the possible compromise of his or her independence or objectivity, and then to withdraw from the meeting (or, in the alternative, to abstain from the deliberations and voting). The board members free of any possible taint can then take appropriate action as contemplated by section 8.30. (If a director's conflicting interest transaction is involved, it will be governed by sub-chapter F of this chapter and the directors' action will be taken pursuant to section 8.62 (or the board can refer the matter for shareholders' action respecting the transaction under section 8.63). In this connection, particular reference is made to the definition of "qualified director" in section 1.43.) If this course is followed, the director's conduct respecting the matter in question will in all likelihood be beyond challenge. ...

§ 8.33 Directors' Liability for Unlawful Distributions

(a) A director who votes for or assents to a distribution in excess of what may be authorized and made pursuant to section 6.40(a) or 14.09(a) is personally liable to the corporation for the amount of the distribution that exceeds what could have been distributed without violating section 6.40(a) or 14.09(a) if the party asserting liability establishes that when taking the action the director did not comply with section 8.30.

(b) A director held liable under subsection (a) for an unlawful distribution is entitled to:

  (1) contribution from every other director who could be held liable under subsection (a) for the unlawful distribution; and

  (2) recoupment from each shareholder of the pro-rata portion of the amount of the unlawful distribution the shareholder accepted, knowing the distribution was made in violation of section 6.40(a) or 14.09(a).

(c) A proceeding to enforce:

  (1) the liability of a director under subsection (a) is barred unless it is commenced within two years after the date (i) on which the effect of the distribution was measured under section 6.40(e) or (g), (ii) or as of which the violation of section 6.40(a) occurred as the consequence of disregard of a restriction in the articles of incorporation, or (iii) on which the distribution of assets to shareholders under section 14.09 was made; or

  (2) contribution or recoupment under subsection (b) is barred unless it is commenced within one year after the liability of the claimant has been finally adjudicated under subsection (a).

Official Comment

Although the revisions to the financial provisions of the Model Act have simplified and rationalized the rules for determining the validity of distributions (see sections 6.40 and 14.09), the possibility remains that a distribution may be made in violation of these rules. Section 8.33

provides that if it is established a director failed to meet the relevant standards of conduct of section 8.30 *(e.g.,* good faith, reasonable care, warranted reliance) and voted for or assented to an unlawful distribution, the director is personally liable for the portion of the distribution that exceeds the maximum amount that could have been lawfully distributed.

A director whose conduct, in voting for or assenting to a distribution, is challenged under section 8.33 will have all defenses which would ordinarily be available, including the common law business judgment rule. Relevant thereto, however, there would be common issues posed by (i) a defense geared to compliance with section 8.30 (e.g., reasonable care under subsection (b) and warranted reliance under subsections (d) and (e)) and, in the alternative, (ii) a defense relying on the business judgment rule's shield *(e.g.,* informed judgment). Thus, section 8.30 compliance will in most cases make resort to the business judgment rule's shield unnecessary.

A director who is compelled to restore the amount of an unlawful distribution to the corporation is entitled to contribution from every other director who could have been held liable for the unlawful distribution. The director may also recover the pro-rata portion of the amount of the unlawful distribution from any shareholder who accepted the distribution knowing that its payment was in violation of the statute. A shareholder (other than a director) who receives a payment not knowing of its invalidity is not subject to recoupment under subsection (b)(2). Although no attempt has been made in the Model Act to work out in detail the relationship between the right of recoupment from shareholders and the right of contribution from directors, it is expected that a court will equitably apportion the obligations and benefits arising from the application of the principles set forth in this section.

Section 8.33(c) limits the time within which a proceeding may be commenced against a director for an unlawful distribution to two years after the date on which the effect of the distribution was measured or breach of a restriction in the articles of incorporation occurred. Although a statute of limitations provision is a novel concept for the Model Act, a substantial minority of jurisdictions have provisions limiting the time within which an action may be brought on account of an unlawful distribution. Section 8.33(c) also limits the time within which a proceeding for contribution or recoupment may be made to one year after the date on which the liability of the claimant has been finally determined and adjudicated. This one-year period specified in clause (2) may end within or extend beyond the two-year period specified in clause (1).

Subchapter D

Officers

§ 8.40 Officers

(a) A corporation has the offices described in its bylaws or designated by the board of directors in accordance with the bylaws.

(b) The board of directors may elect individuals to fill one or more offices of the corporation. An officer may appoint one or more officers if authorized by the bylaws or the board of directors.

(c) The bylaws or the board of directors shall assign to one of the officers responsibility for preparing minutes of the directors' and shareholders' meetings and for maintaining and authenticating the records of the corporation required to be kept under sections 16.01(a) and 16.01(e).

(d) The same individual may simultaneously hold more than one office in a corporation.

Official Comment

Section 8.40 permits every corporation to designate the offices it wants. The designation may be made in the bylaws or by the board of directors consistently with the bylaws. This is a departure from earlier versions of the Model Act and most state corporation acts, which require certain offices, usually the president, the secretary, and the treasurer, and generally authorize the corporation to designate additional offices. Experience has shown, however, that little purpose is served by a statutory requirement that there be certain offices, and statutory requirements may sometimes create problems of apparent authority or confusion with non-statutory offices the corporation desires to create.

Section 8.40(b) indicates that, while it is generally the responsibility of the board of directors to elect officers, an officer may appoint one or more officers if authorized by the bylaws or the board of directors.

The board of directors, as well as duly authorized corporate officers or other agents, may also appoint agents for the corporation. Nothing in this section is intended to limit the authority of a board of directors to organize its own internal affairs, including designating officers of the board.

The bylaws or the board of directors also must assign to an officer the responsibility to prepare minutes and authenticate the corporate records referred to in sections 16.01(a) and (e); the person performing this function is referred to as the "secretary" of the corporation throughout the Model Act. See section 1.40. Under the Act, a corporation may have this and all other corporate functions performed by a single individual.

The person who is designated by the bylaws or the board to have responsibility for preparing minutes of meetings and maintaining the corporate records has authority to bind the corporation by that officer's authentication under this section. This assignment of authority, traditionally vested in the corporate "secretary," allows third persons to rely on authenticated records without inquiry as to their truth or accuracy.

PART IV

FUNCTIONS OF OFFICERS

§ 8.41 Functions of Officers

Each officer has the authority and shall perform the functions set forth in the bylaws or, to the extent consistent with the bylaws, the functions prescribed by the board of directors or by direction of an officer authorized by the board of directors to prescribe the functions of other officers.

Official Comment

Section 8.41 recognizes that persons designated as officers have the formal authority set forth for that position (1) by its description in the bylaws, (2) by specific resolution of the board of directors, or (3) by direction of another officer authorized by the board of directors to prescribe the functions of other officers.

These methods of investing officers with formal authority do not exhaust the sources of an officer's actual or apparent authority. Many cases state that specific corporate officers, particularly the chief executive officer, may have implied authority merely by virtue of their positions. This authority, which may overlap the express authority granted by the bylaws, generally has been viewed as extending only to ordinary business transactions, though some cases have recognized unusually broad implied authority of the chief executive officer or have created a presumption that corporate officers have broad authority, thereby placing on the corporation the burden of showing lack of authority. Corporate officers may also be vested with apparent (or ostensible) authority by reason of corporate conduct on which third persons reasonably rely.

In addition to express, implied, or apparent authority, a corporation is normally bound by unauthorized acts of officers if they are ratified by the board of directors. Generally, ratification extends only to acts that could have been authorized as an original matter. Ratification may itself be express or implied and may in some cases serve as the basis of apparent (or ostensible) authority.

§ 8.42 Standards of Conduct for Officers

(a) An officer, when performing in such capacity, has the duty to act:

   (1) in good faith;

   (2) with the care that a person in a like position would reasonably exercise under similar circumstances; and

   (3) in a manner the officer reasonably believes to be in the best interests of the corporation.

(b) The duty of an officer includes the obligation:

   (1) to inform the superior officer to whom, or the board of directors or the committee thereof to which, the officer reports of information about the affairs of the corporation known to the officer, within the scope of the officer's functions, and known to the officer to be material to such superior officer, board or committee; and

   (2) to inform his or her superior officer, or another appropriate person within the corporation, or the board of directors, or a committee thereof, of any actual or probable material violation of law involving the corporation or material breach of duty to the corporation by an officer, employee, or agent of the corporation, that the officer believes has occurred or is likely to occur.

(c) In discharging his or her duties, an officer who does not have knowledge that makes reliance unwarranted is entitled to rely on:

   (1) the performance of properly delegated responsibilities by one or more employees of the corporation whom the officer reasonably believes to be reliable and competent in performing the responsibilities delegated; or

   (2) information, opinions, reports or statements, including financial statements and other financial data, prepared or presented by one or more employees of the corporation whom the officer reasonably believes to be reliable and competent in the matters presented or by legal counsel, public accountants, or other persons retained by the corporation as to matters involving skills or expertise the officer reasonably believes are matters (i) within the particular person's professional or expert competence or (ii) as to which the particular person merits confidence.

(d) An officer shall not be liable to the corporation or its shareholders for any decision to take or not to take action, or any failure to take any action, as an officer, if the duties of the office are performed in compliance with this section. Whether an officer who does not comply with this section shall have liability will depend in such instance on applicable law, including those principles of section 8.31 that have relevance.

Official Comment

Subsection (a) provides that an officer, when performing in such officer's official capacity, shall meet standards of conduct generally similar to those expected of directors under section 8.30. Consistent with the principles of agency, which generally govern the conduct of corporate employees, an officer is expected to observe the duties of obedience and loyalty and to act with the care that a person in a like position would reasonably exercise under similar circumstances. *See* RESTATEMENT (SECOND) OF AGENCY § 379(1) (1958) ("Unless otherwise agreed, a paid agent is subject to a duty to the principal to act with standard care and with the skill which is standard in the locality for the kind of work which he is employed to perform and, in addition, to exercise any special skill that he has"). This section is not intended to modify, diminish or qualify the duties or standards of conduct that may be imposed upon specific officers by other law or regulation.

The common law, including the law of agency, has recognized a duty on the part of officers and key employees to disclose to their superiors material information relevant to the affairs of the agency entrusted to them. *See* RESTATEMENT (SECOND) OF AGENCY § 381; A. Gilchrist Sparks, III & Lawrence A. Hamermesh, *Common Law Duties of Non-Director Corporate Officers*, 48 BUS. LAW. 215, 226–29 (1992). This duty is implicit in, and embraced under, the broader standard of subsection (a). New subsection (b) sets forth explicitly this disclosure obligation by confirming that the officer's duty includes the obligation (i) to keep superior corporate authorities informed of material information within the officer's sphere of functional responsibilities, and (ii) to inform the relevant superior authority, or other appropriate person within the corporation, of violations of law or breaches of duty that the officer believes have occurred or are likely to occur (i.e., more likely than not to occur) and are or would be material to the corporation. Subsection (b)(1) specifies that business information shall be transmitted through the officer's regular reporting channels. Subsection (b)(2) specifies the reporting responsibility differently with respect to actual or probable material violations of law or material breaches of duty. The use of the term "appropriate" in subsection (b)(2) is intended to accommodate both the normative standard that may have been set up by the corporation for reporting potential violations of law or duty to a specified person, such as an ombudsperson, ethics officer, internal auditor, general counsel or the like, and situations where there is no designated person but the officer's immediate superior is not appropriate (for example, because the officer believes that individual is complicit in the unlawful activity or breach of duty).

Subsection (b)(1) should not be interpreted so broadly as to discourage efficient delegation of functions. It addresses the flow of information to the board of directors and to superior officers necessary to enable them to perform their decision-making and oversight functions. See the

Official Comment to section 8.31. The officer's duties under subsection (b) may not be negated by agreement; however, their scope under subsection (b)(1) may be shaped by prescribing the scope of an officer's functional responsibilities.

With respect to the duties under subsection (b)(2), codes of conduct or codes of ethics, such as those adopted by many large corporations, may prescribe the circumstances in which and mechanisms by which officers and employees may discharge their duty to report material information to superior officers or the board of directors, or to other designated persons.

The term "material" modifying violations of law or breaches of duty in subsection (b)(2) denotes a qualitative as well as quantitative standard. It relates not only to the potential direct financial impact on the corporation, but also to the nature of the violation or breach. For example, an embezzlement of $10,000, or even less, would be material because of the seriousness of the offense, even though the amount involved would not be material to the financial position or results of operations of the corporation.

The duty under subsection (b)(2) is triggered by an officer's subjective belief that a material violation of law or breach of duty actually or probably has occurred or is likely to occur. This duty is not triggered by objective knowledge concepts, such as whether the officer should have concluded that such misconduct was occurring. The subjectivity of the trigger under subsection (b)(2), however, does not excuse officers from their obligations under subsection (a) to act in good faith and with due care in the performance of the functions assigned to them, including oversight duties within their respective areas of responsibility. There may be occasions when the principles applicable under section 8.30(c) limiting the duty of disclosure by directors where a duty of confidentiality is overriding may also apply to officers. See the Official Comment to section 8.30(c).

An officer's ability to rely on others in meeting the standards prescribed in section 8.42 may be more limited, depending upon the circumstances of the particular case, than the measure and scope of reliance permitted a director under section 8.30, in view of the greater obligation the officer may have to be familiar with the affairs of the corporation. The proper delegation of responsibilities by an officer, separate and apart from the exercise of judgment as to the delegatee's reliability and competence, is concerned with the procedure employed. This will involve, in the usual case, sufficient communication to the end that the delegatee understands the scope of the assignment and, in turn, manifests to the officer a willingness and commitment to undertake its performance. The entitlement to rely upon employees assumes that a delegating officer will maintain a sufficient level of communication with the officer's subordinates to fulfill his or her supervisory responsibilities.

The definition of "employee" in section 1.40(8) includes an officer; accordingly, section 8.42 contemplates the delegation of responsibilities to other officers as well as to non-officer employees.

It is made clear, in subsection (d), that performance meeting the section's standards of conduct will eliminate an officer's exposure to any liability to the corporation or its shareholders. In contrast, an officer failing to meet its standards will not automatically face liability. Deficient performance of duties by an officer, depending upon the facts and circumstances, will normally be dealt with through intracorporate disciplinary procedures, such as reprimand, compensation adjustment, delayed promotion, demotion or discharge. These procedures may be subject to (and limited by) the terms of an officer's employment agreement. See section 8.44.

In some cases, failure to observe relevant standards of conduct can give rise to an officer's liability to the corporation or its shareholders. A court review of challenged conduct will involve an evaluation of the particular facts and circumstances in light of applicable law. In this connection, subsection (d) recognizes that relevant principles of section 8.31, such as duties to deal fairly with the corporation and its shareholders and the challenger's burden of establishing proximately caused harm, should be taken into account. In addition, the business judgment rule will normally apply to decisions within an officer's discretionary authority. Liability to others can also arise from an officer's own acts or omissions (e.g., violations of law or tort claims) and, in some cases, an officer with supervisory responsibilities can have risk exposure in connection with the acts or omissions of others.

The Official Comment to section 8.30 supplements this Official Comment to the extent that it can be appropriately viewed as generally applicable to officers as well as directors.

§ 8.43 Resignation and Removal of Officers

(a) An officer may resign at any time by delivering notice to the corporation. A resignation is effective when the notice is delivered unless the notice specifies a later effective time. If a resignation is made effective at a later time and the board or the appointing officer accepts the future effective time, the board or the appointing officer may fill the pending vacancy before the effective time if the board or the appointing officer provides that the successor does not take office until the effective time.

(b) An officer may be removed at any time with or without cause by: (i) the board of directors; or (ii) the officer who appointed such officer, unless the bylaws or the board of directors provide otherwise; or (iii) any other officer if authorized by the bylaws or the board of directors.

(c) In this section, "appointing officer" means the officer (including any successor to that officer) who appointed the officer resigning or being removed.

Official Comment

Section 8.43(a) is consistent with current practice and declaratory of current law. It recognizes that corporate officers may resign; that, with the consent of the board of directors or the appointing officer, they may resign effective at a later date; and that a future vacancy may be filled to become effective as of the effective date of the resignation.

In part because of the unlimited power of removal confirmed by section 8.43(b), a board of directors may enter into an employment agreement with the holder of an office that extends beyond the term of the board of directors. This type of contract is binding on the corporation even if the articles of incorporation or bylaws provide that officers are elected for a term shorter than the period of the employment contract. If a later board of directors refuses to reelect that person as an officer, the person has the right to sue for damages but not for specific performance of the contract.

Section 8.43(b) is consistent with current practice and declaratory of current law. It recognizes that the officers of the corporation are subject to removal by the board of directors and, in certain instances, by other officers. It provides the corporation with the flexibility to determine when, if ever, an officer will be permitted to remove another officer. To the extent that the corporation wishes to permit an officer, other than the appointing officer, to remove another officer, the bylaws or a board resolution should set forth clearly the persons having removal authority.

A person may be removed from office irrespective of contract rights or the presence or absence of "cause" in a legal sense. Section 8.44 provides that removal from office of a holder who has contract rights is without prejudice to whatever rights the former officer may assert in a suit for damages for breach of contract.

§ 8.44 Contract Rights of Officers

(a) The appointment of an officer does not itself create contract rights.

(b) An officer's removal does not affect the officer's contract rights, if any, with the corporation. An officer's resignation does not affect the corporation's contract rights, if any, with the officer.

Subchapter E

Indemnification

Introductory Comment

The provisions for indemnification and advance for expenses of the Model Act are among the most complex and important in the entire Act.

Subchapter E of chapter 8 is an integrated treatment of this subject and strikes a balance among important social policies. Its substance is based almost entirely on an amendment to the 1969 Model Act adopted in 1980 and substantially revised in 1994.

1. Policy Issues Raised by Indemnification and Advance for Expenses

Indemnification (including advance for expenses) provides financial protection by the corporation for its directors against exposure to expenses and liabilities that may be incurred by them in connection with legal proceedings based on an alleged breach of duty in their service to or on behalf of the corporation. Today, when both the volume and the cost of litigation have increased dramatically, it would be difficult to persuade responsible persons to serve as directors if they were compelled to bear personally the cost of vindicating the propriety of their conduct in every instance in which it might be challenged. While reasonable people may differ as to what constitutes a meritorious case, almost all would agree that corporate directors should have appropriate protection against personal risk and that the rule of New York Dock Co. v. McCollom, 173 Misc. 106, 16 N.Y.S.2d 844 (Sup.Ct.1939), which denied reimbursement to directors who successfully defended their case on the merits, should as a matter of policy be overruled by statute.

The concept of indemnification recognizes that there will be situations in which the director does not satisfy all of the elements of the standard of conduct set forth in section 8.30(a) or the requirements of some other applicable law but where the corporation should nevertheless be permitted (or required) to absorb the economic costs of any ensuing litigation. A carefully constructed indemnification statute should identify these situations.

If permitted too broadly, however, indemnification may violate equally basic tenets of public policy. It is inappropriate to permit management to use corporate funds to avoid the consequences of certain conduct. For example, a director who intentionally inflicts harm on the corporation should not expect to receive assistance from the corporation for legal or other expenses and should be required to satisfy from his personal assets not only any adverse judgment but also expenses incurred in connection with the proceeding. Any other rule would tend to encourage socially undesirable conduct.

A further policy issue is raised in connection with indemnification against liabilities or sanctions imposed under state or federal civil or criminal statutes. A shift of the economic cost of these liabilities from the individual director to the corporation by way of indemnification may in some instances frustrate the public policy of those statutes.

The fundamental issue that must be addressed by an indemnification statute is the establishment of policies consistent with these broad principles: to ensure that indemnification is permitted only where it will further sound corporate policies and to prohibit indemnification where it might protect or encourage wrongful or improper conduct. As phrased by one commentator, the goal of indemnification is to "seek the middle ground between encouraging fiduciaries to violate their trust, and discouraging them from serving at all." Johnston, "Corporate Indemnification and Liability Insurance for Directors and Officers," 33 BUS.LAW. 1993, 1994 (1978). The increasing number of suits against directors, the increasing cost of defense, and the increasing emphasis on diversifying the membership of boards of directors all militate in favor of workable arrangements to protect directors against liability to the extent consistent with established principles.

Some of the same policy considerations apply to the indemnification of officers and, in many cases, employees and agents. The indemnification of officers, whose duties are specified in section 8.42, is dealt with separately in section 8.56. However, other considerations apply to employees and agents, who have significantly different roles and responsibilities and as to whom the spectre of structural bias (sympathetic directors approving indemnification for themselves or for colleagues on the board or for officers, who may work closely with board members) is not present. The indemnification of employees and agents, whose duties are prescribed by sources of law other than corporation law (e.g., contract and agency law), is beyond the scope of this subchapter. Section 8.58(d), however, makes clear that the absence in subchapter E of provisions concerning employees and agents is not intended to limit a corporation's power to indemnify or advance expenses to them in accordance with applicable law.

2. Relationship of Indemnification to Other Policies Established in the Model Act

Indemnification is closely related to the standards of conduct for directors and officers established elsewhere in chapter 8. The structure of the Model Act is based on the assumption that if a director acts consistently with the standards of conduct described in section 8.30 or with the standards of a liability-limitation provision in the articles of incorporation (as authorized by section 2.02(b)(4)), he will not have exposure to liability to the corporation or to shareholders and any expenses necessary to establish his defense will be borne by the corporation (under section 8.52). But the converse is not necessarily true. The basic standards for indemnification set forth in this subchapter for a civil action, in the absence of an indemnification provision in the corporation's articles (as authorized by section 2.02(b)(5)), are good faith and reasonable belief that the conduct was in or not opposed to the best interests of the corporation. See section 8.51. In some circumstances, a director or officer may be found to have violated a statutory or common law duty and yet be able to establish eligibility for indemnification under these standards of conduct. In addition, this subchapter permits a director or officer who is held liable for violating a statutory or common law duty, but who does not meet the relevant standard of conduct, to petition a court to order indemnification under section 8.54(a)(3) on the ground that it would be fair and reasonable to do so. . . .

§ 8.50 Subchapter Definitions

In this subchapter:

(1) "Corporation" includes any domestic or foreign predecessor entity of a corporation in a merger.

(2) "Director" or "officer" means an individual who is or was a director or officer, respectively, of a corporation or who, while a director or officer of the corporation, is or was serving at the corporation's request as a director, officer, partner, trustee, employee, or agent of another domestic or foreign corporation, partnership, joint venture, trust, employee benefit plan, or other entity. A director or officer is considered to be serving an employee benefit plan at the corporation's request if the individual's duties to the corporation also impose duties on, or otherwise involve services by, the individual to the plan or to participants in or beneficiaries of the plan. "Director" or "officer" includes, unless the context requires otherwise, the estate or personal representative of a director or officer.

(3) "Liability" means the obligation to pay a judgment, settlement, penalty, fine (including an excise tax assessed with respect to an employee benefit plan), or expenses incurred with respect to a proceeding.

(4) "Official capacity" means: (i) when used with respect to a director, the office of director in a corporation; and (ii) when used with respect to an officer, as contemplated in section 8.56, the office in a corporation held by the officer. "Official capacity" does not include service for any other domestic or foreign corporation or any partnership, joint venture, trust, employee benefit plan, or other entity.

(5) "Party" means an individual who was, is, or is threatened to be made, a defendant or respondent in a proceeding.

(6) "Proceeding" means any threatened, pending, or completed action, suit, or proceeding, whether civil, criminal, administrative, arbitrative, or investigative and whether formal or informal.

Official Comment

The definitions set forth in section 8.50 apply only to subchapter E and have no application elsewhere in the Model Act (except as set forth in section 2.02(b)(5)). The term "qualified director," which is used in section 8.53 and 8.55, is defined in section 1.43.

1. Corporation

A special definition of "corporation" is included in subchapter E to make it clear that predecessor entities that have been absorbed in mergers are included within the definition. It is probable that the same result would be reached for many transactions under section 11.07(a) (effect of merger), which provides for the assumption of liabilities by operation of law upon a merger. The express responsibility of successor entities for the liabilities of their predecessors under this subchapter is broader than under section 11.07(a) and may impose liability on a successor although section 11.07(a) does not. Section 8.50(1) is thus an essential aspect of the protection provided by this subchapter for persons eligible for indemnification.

2. Director and Officer

A special definition of "director" and "officer" is included in subchapter E to cover individuals who are made parties to proceedings because they are or were directors or officers or, while serving as directors or officers, also serve or served at the corporation's request in another capacity for another entity. The purpose of the latter part of this definition is to give directors and officers the benefits of the protection of this subchapter while serving at the corporation's request in a responsible position for employee benefit plans, trade associations, nonprofit or charitable entities, domestic or foreign entities, or other kinds of profit or nonprofit ventures. To avoid misunderstanding, it is good practice from both the corporation's and director's or officer's viewpoint for this type of request to be evidenced by resolution, memorandum or other writing. The definition covers an individual who is or was either a director or officer so that further references in the remainder of subchapter E to an individual who is a director or officer necessarily include former directors or officers.

The second sentence of section 8.50(2) addresses the question of liabilities arising under the Employee Retirement Income Security Act of 1974 (ERISA). It makes clear that a director or officer who is serving as a fiduciary of an employee benefit plan is automatically viewed for purposes of this subchapter as having been requested by the corporation to act in that capacity. Special treatment is believed necessary because of the broad definition of "fiduciary" in ERISA, and the requirement that a "fiduciary" must discharge his or her duties "solely in the interest" of the participants and beneficiaries of the employee benefit plan. Decisions by a director or officer, who is serving as a fiduciary under the plan, on questions regarding (a) eligibility for benefits, (b) investment decisions, or (c) interpretation of plan provisions respecting (i) qualifying service, (ii) years of service, or (iii) retroactivity, are all subject to the protections of this subchapter. See also sections 8.50(4) and 8.51(b) of this subchapter.

The last sentence of section 8.50(2) provides that the estate or personal representative of a director or officer is entitled to the rights of indemnification possessed by that director or officer. The phrase "unless the context requires otherwise" was added to make clear that the estate or personal representative does not have the right to participate in directorial decisions authorized in this subchapter.

3. Expenses

"Expenses" is defined to include counsel fees in order to avoid repeated references to such fees every time "expenses" appears throughout the subchapter. "Expenses" does not include the other items listed in the definition of "liability," such as judgments or amounts paid in settlement.

4. Liability

"Liability" is defined for convenience in order to avoid repeated references to recoverable items throughout the subchapter. Even though the definition of "liability" includes amounts paid in settlement or to satisfy a judgment, indemnification against certain types of settlements and judgments is not allowed under several provisions of subchapter E. For example, indemnification in suits brought by or in the right of the corporation is limited to expenses (see section 8.51(d)(1)), unless indemnification for a settlement is ordered by a court under section 8.54(a)(3).

The definition of "liability" permits the indemnification of expenses. The definition of "expenses" in section 1.40(9AA) limits expenses to those that are reasonable. The result is that any portion of expenses falling outside the perimeter of reasonableness should not be advanced or indemnified. In contrast, unlike earlier versions of the Model Act and statutes of many states, section 8.50(4) provides that amounts paid to settle or satisfy substantive claims are not subject to a reasonableness test. Since payment of these amounts is permissive—mandatory indemnification is available under section 8.52 only where the defendant is "wholly successful"—a special limitation of "reasonableness" for settlements is inappropriate.

"Penalties" and "fines" are expressly included within the definition of "liability" so that, in appropriate cases, these items may also be indemnified. The purpose of this definition is to cover every type of monetary obligation that may be imposed upon a director, including civil penalties, restitution, and obligations to give notice. This definition also expressly includes as a "fine" the levy of excise taxes under the Internal Revenue Code pursuant to ERISA.

5. Official Capacity

The definition of "official capacity" is necessary because the term determines which of the two alternative standards of conduct set forth in section 8.51(a)(1)(ii) applies. If the action was taken in an "official capacity," the individual to be indemnified must have reasonably believed that he or she was acting in the best interests of the corporation. In contrast, if the action in question was not taken in an "official capacity," the individual need only have reasonably believed that the conduct was not opposed to the best interests of the corporation. See also the Official Comment to section 8.51(a).

6. Party

The definition of "party" includes every "individual who was, is, or is threatened to be made, a defendant or respondent in a proceeding." Thus, the definition includes present and former parties in addition to individuals currently or formerly threatened with being made a party. An individual who is only called as a witness is not a "party" within this definition and, as specifically provided in section 8.58(d), payment or reimbursement of the individual's expenses is not limited by this subchapter.

7. Proceeding

The broad definition of "proceeding" ensures that the benefits of this subchapter will be available to directors in new and unexpected, as well as traditional, types of litigation or other adversarial matters, whether civil, criminal, administrative, or investigative. It also includes arbitration and other dispute resolution proceedings, lawsuit appeals and petitions to review administrative actions.

§ 8.51 Permissible Indemnification

(a) Except as otherwise provided in this section, a corporation may indemnify an individual who is a party to a proceeding because he is a director against liability incurred in the proceeding if:

    (1) (i) he conducted himself in good faith; and

        (ii) he reasonably believed:

            (A) in the case of conduct in his official capacity, that his conduct was in the best interests of the corporation; and

            (B) in all other cases, that his conduct was at least not opposed to the best interests of the corporation; and

        (iii) in the case of any criminal proceeding, he had no reasonable cause to believe his conduct was unlawful; or

    (2) he engaged in conduct for which broader indemnification has been made permissible or obligatory under a provision of the articles of incorporation (as authorized by section 2.02(b)(5)).

(b) A director's conduct with respect to an employee benefit plan for a purpose he reasonably believed to be in the interests of the participants in, and the beneficiaries of, the plan is conduct that satisfies the requirement of subsection (a)(1)(ii)(B).

(c) The termination of a proceeding by judgment, order, settlement, or conviction, or upon a plea of nolo contendere or its equivalent, is not, of itself, determinative that the director did not meet the relevant standard of conduct described in this section.

(d) Unless ordered by a court under section 8.54(a)(3), a corporation may not indemnify a director:

    (1) in connection with a proceeding by or in the right of the corporation, except for reasonable expenses incurred in connection with the proceeding if it is determined that the director has met the relevant standard of conduct under subsection (a); or

    (2) in connection with any proceeding with respect to conduct for which he was adjudged liable on the basis that he received a financial benefit to which he was not entitled, whether or not involving action in his official capacity.

Official Comment

1. Section 8.51(a)

Subsection 8.51(a) permits, but does not require, a corporation to indemnify directors if the standards of subsection (a)(1) or of a provision of the articles referred to in subsection (a)(2) are met. This authorization is subject to any limitations set forth in the articles of incorporation pursuant to section 8.58(c). Absent any such limitation, the standards for indemnification of directors contained in this subsection define the outer limits for which discretionary indemnification is permitted under the Model Act. Conduct which does not meet one of these standards is not eligible for permissible indemnification under the Model Act, although court-ordered indemnification may be available under section 8.54(a)(3). Conduct that falls within these outer limits does not automatically entitle directors to indemnification, although a corporation may obligate itself to indemnify directors to the maximum extent permitted by applicable law. See section 8.58(a). No such obligation, however, may exceed these outer limits. Absent such an obligatory provision, section 8.52 defines much narrower circumstances in which directors are entitled as a matter of right to indemnification.

Some state statutes provide separate, but usually similarly worded, standards for indemnification in third-party suits and indemnification in suits brought by or in the right of the corporation. Section 8.51 makes clear that the outer limits of conduct for which indemnification is permitted should not be dependent on the type of proceeding in which the claim arises. To prevent circularity in recovery, however, section 8.51(d)(1) limits indemnification in connection with suits brought by or in the right of the corporation to expenses incurred and excludes amounts paid to settle such suits or to satisfy judgments. In addition, to discourage wrongdoing, section 8.51(d)(2) bars indemnification where the director has been adjudged to have received a financial benefit to which he is not entitled. Nevertheless, a court may order certain relief from these limitations under section 8.54(a)(3).

The standards of conduct described in subsections (a)(1)(i) and (a)(1)(ii)(A) that must be met in order to permit the corporation to indemnify a director are closely related, but not identical, to the standards of conduct imposed on directors by section 8.30. Section 8.30(a) requires a director acting in his official capacity to discharge his duties in good faith, with due care (i.e., that which an ordinarily prudent person in a like position would exercise under similar circumstances) and in a manner he reasonably believes to be in the corporation's best interests. Unless authorized by a charter provision adopted pursuant to subsection (a)(2), it would be difficult to justify indemnifying a director who has not met any of these standards. It would not, however, make sense to require a director to meet all these standards in order to be indemnified because a director who meets all three of these standards would have no liability, at least to the corporation, under the terms of section 8.30(d).

Section 8.51(a) adopts a middle ground by authorizing discretionary indemnification in the case of a failure to meet the due care standard of section 8.30(a) because public policy would not be well served by an absolute bar. A director's potential liability for conduct which does not on each and every occasion satisfy the due care requirement of section 8.30(a), or which with the benefit of hindsight could be so viewed, would in all likelihood deter qualified individuals from serving as directors and inhibit some who serve from taking risks. Permitting indemnification against such liability tends to counter these undesirable consequences. Accordingly, section 8.51(a) authorizes indemnification at the corporation's option even though section 8.30's due care requirement is not met, but only if the director satisfies the "good faith" and "corporation's best interests" standards. This reflects a judgment that, balancing public policy considerations, the corporation may indemnify a director who does not satisfy the due care test but not one who fails either of the other two standards.

As in the case of section 8.30, where the concept of good faith is also used, no attempt is made in section 8.51 to provide a definition. The concept involves a subjective test, which would permit indemnification for "a mistake of judgment," in the words of the Official Comment to section 8.30, even though made unwisely or negligently by objective standards. Section 8.51 also requires, as does section 8.30, a "reasonable" belief by a director acting in his official capacity that his conduct was in the corporation's best interests. It then adds a provision, not found in section 8.30, relating to criminal proceedings that requires the director to have had no "reasonable cause" to believe that his conduct was unlawful. These both involve objective standards applicable to the director's belief concerning the effect of his conduct. Conduct includes both acts and omissions.

Section 8.51(a)(1)(ii)(B) requires, if a director is not acting in his official capacity, that his action be "at least not opposed to" the corporation's best interests. This standard is applicable to the director when serving another entity at the request of the corporation or when sued simply because of his status as a director. The words "at least" qualify "not opposed to" in order to make it clear that this standard is an outer limit for conduct other than in an official capacity. While this subsection is directed at the interests of the indemnifying (i.e., requesting) corporation, a director serving another entity by request remains subject to the provisions of the law governing his service to that entity, including provisions dealing with conflicts of interest. Compare sections 8.60–8.63. Should indemnification from the requesting corporation be sought by a director for acts done while serving another entity, which acts involved breach of the duty of loyalty owed to that entity, nothing in section 8.51(a)(1)(ii)(B) would preclude the requesting corporation from considering, in assessing its own best interests, whether the fact that its director had engaged in a violation of the duty owed to the other entity was in fact "opposed to" the interests of the indemnifying corporation. Receipt of an improper financial benefit from a subsidiary would normally be opposed to the best interests of the parent.

Section 8.51 also permits indemnification in connection with a proceeding involving an alleged failure to satisfy legal standards other than the standards of conduct in section 8.30, e.g., violations of federal securities laws and environmental laws. It should be noted, however, that the Securities and Exchange Commission takes the position that indemnification against liabilities under the Securities Act of 1933 is against public policy and requires that, as a condition for accelerating the effectiveness of a registration statement under the Act, the issuer must undertake that, unless in the opinion of its counsel the matter has been settled by controlling precedent, it will submit to a court the question whether such indemnification is against public policy as expressed in the Act. 17 C.F.R. § 229.512(h) (1993).

In addition to indemnification under section 8.51(a)(1), section 8.51(a)(2) permits indemnification under the standard of conduct set forth in a charter provision adopted pursuant to section 2.02(b)(5). Based on such a charter provision, section 8.51(a)(2) permits indemnification in connection with claims by third parties and, through section 8.56, applies to officers as well as directors. (This goes beyond the scope of a charter provision adopted pursuant to section 2.02(b)(4), which can only limit liability of directors against claims by the corporation or its shareholders.) Section 8.51(a)(2) is subject to the prohibition of subsection (d)(1) against indemnification of settlements and judgments in derivative suits. It is also subject to the prohibition of subsection (d)(2) against indemnification for receipt of an improper financial benefit;

however, this prohibition is already subsumed in the exception contained in section 2.02(b)(5)(A).

Notice of any indemnification under this section (or sections 8.52, 8.53 or 8.54) in a derivative proceeding must be given to the shareholders pursuant to section 16.21(a).

2.   Section 8.51(b)

As discussed in the Official Comment to Section 8.50(2), ERISA requires that a "fiduciary" (as defined in ERISA) discharge his duties "solely in the interest" of the participants in and beneficiaries of an employee benefit plan. Section 8.51(b) makes clear that a director who is serving as a trustee or fiduciary for an employee benefit plan under ERISA meets the standard for indemnification under section 8.51(a) if he reasonably believes his conduct was in the best interests of the participants in and beneficiaries of the plan.

This standard is arguably an exception to the more general standard that conduct not in an official corporate capacity is indemnifiable if it is "at least not opposed to" the best interests of the corporation. However, a corporation that causes a director to undertake fiduciary duties in connection with an employee benefit plan should expect the director to act in the best interests of the plan's beneficiaries or participants. Thus, subsection (b) establishes and provides a standard for indemnification that is consistent with the statutory policies embodied in ERISA. See Official Comment to section 8.50(2).

3.   Section 8.51(c)

The purpose of section 8.51(c) is to reject the argument that indemnification is automatically improper whenever a proceeding has been concluded on a basis that does not exonerate the director claiming indemnification. Even though a final judgment or conviction is not automatically determinative of the issue of whether the minimum standard of conduct was met, any judicial determination of substantive liability would in most instances be entitled to considerable weight. By the same token, it is clear that the termination of a proceeding by settlement or plea of nolo contendere should not of itself create a presumption either that conduct met or did not meet the relevant standard of subsection (a) since a settlement or nolo plea may be agreed to for many reasons unrelated to the merits of the claim. On the other hand, a final determination of non-liability (including one based on a liability-limitation provision adopted under section 2.02(b)(4)) or an acquittal in a criminal case automatically entitles the director to indemnification of expenses under section 8.52.

Section 8.51(c) applies to the indemnification of expenses in derivative proceedings (as well as to indemnification in third party suits). The most likely application of this subsection in connection with a derivative proceeding will be to a settlement since a judgment or order would normally result in liability to the corporation and thereby preclude indemnification for expenses under section 8.51(d)(1), unless ordered by a court under section 8.54(a)(3). In the rare event that a judgment or order entered against the director did not include a determination of liability to the corporation, the entry of the judgment or order would not be determinative that the director failed to meet the relevant standard of conduct.

4. Section 8.51(d)

This subsection makes clear that indemnification is not permissible under section 8.51 in two situations: (i) a proceeding brought by or in the right of a corporation that results in a settlement or a judgment against the director and (ii) a proceeding that results in a judgment that the director received an improper financial benefit as a result of his conduct.

Permitting indemnification of settlements and judgments in derivative proceedings would give rise to a circularity in which the corporation receiving payment of damages by the director in the settlement or judgment (less attorneys' fees) would then immediately return the same amount to the director (including attorneys' fees) as indemnification. Thus, the corporation would be in a poorer economic position than if there had been no proceeding. This situation is most egregious in the case of a judgment against the director. Even in the case of a settlement, however, prohibiting indemnification is not unfair. Under the revised procedures of section 7.44, upon motion by the corporation, the court must dismiss any derivative proceeding which independent directors (or a court-appointed panel) determine in good faith, after a reasonable inquiry, is not in the best interests of the corporation. Furthermore, under section 2.02(b)(4), the directors have the opportunity to propose to shareholders adoption of a provision limiting the liability of directors in derivative proceedings. In view of these considerations, it is unlikely that directors will be unnecessarily exposed to meritless actions. In addition, if directors were to be indemnified for amounts paid in settlement, the dismissal procedures in section 7.44 might not be fully employed since it could be less expensive for the corporation to indemnify the directors immediately for the amount of the claimed damages rather than bear the expense of the inquiry required by section 7.44. The result could increase the filing of meritless derivative proceedings in order to generate small but immediately paid attorneys' fees. Despite the prohibition on indemnification of a settlement or a judgment in a derivative proceeding, subsection (d)(1) permits indemnification of the related reasonable expenses incurred in the proceeding so long as the director meets the relevant standard of conduct set forth in section 8.51(a). In addition, indemnification of derivative proceeding expenses and amounts paid in settlement where the relevant standard was not met may be ordered by a court under section 8.54(a)(3).

If a corporation indemnifies a director in connection with a derivative proceeding, the corporation must report that fact to the shareholders prior to their next meeting. See section 16.21(a).

Indemnification under section 8.51 is also prohibited if there has been an adjudication that a director received an improper financial benefit (i.e., a benefit to which he is not entitled), even if, for example, he acted in a manner not opposed to the best interests of the corporation. For example, improper use of inside information for financial benefit should not be an action for which the corporation may elect to provide indemnification, even if the corporation was not thereby harmed. Given the express language of section 2.02(b)(5) establishing the outer limit of an indemnification provision contained in the articles of incorporation, a director found to have received an improper financial benefit would not be permitted indemnification under subsection (a)(2). Although it is unlikely that a director found to have received an improper financial benefit could meet the standard in subsection (a)(1)(ii)(B), this limitation is made explicit in section 8.51(d)(2). Section 8.54(a)(3) permits a director found liable in a proceeding referred to in subsection (d)(2) to petition a court for a judicial determination of entitlement to indemnification for reasonable expenses. The language of section 8.51(d)(2) is based on section 2.02(b)(4)(A) and, thus, the same standards should be used in interpreting the application of both provisions. Although a settlement may create an obligation to pay money, it should not be construed for purposes of this subchapter as an adjudication of liability.

§ 8.52 Mandatory Indemnification

A corporation shall indemnify a director who was <u>wholly successful, on the merits or otherwise,</u> in the defense of any proceeding to which he was a party because he was a director of the corporation against reasonable expenses incurred by him in connection with the proceeding.

Official Comment

Section 8.51 determines whether indemnification may be made voluntarily by a corporation if it elects to do so. Section 8.52 determines whether a corporation must indemnify a director for his expenses; in other words, section 8.52 creates a statutory right of indemnification in favor of the director who meets the requirements of that section. Enforcement of this right by judicial proceeding is specifically contemplated by section 8.54(a)(1). Section 8.54(b) gives the director a statutory right to recover expenses incurred by him in enforcing his statutory right to indemnification under section 8.52.

The basic standard for mandatory indemnification is that the director has been "wholly successful, on the merits or otherwise," in the defense of the proceeding. The word "wholly" is added to avoid the argument accepted in Merritt–Chapman & Scott Corp. v. Wolfson, 321 A.2d 138 (Del.1974), that a defendant may be entitled to partial mandatory indemnification if, by plea bargaining or otherwise, he was able to obtain the dismissal of some but not all counts of an indictment. A defendant is "wholly successful" only if the entire proceeding is disposed of on a basis which does not involve a finding of liability. A director who is precluded from mandatory indemnification by this requirement may still be entitled to permissible indemnification under section 8.51(a) or court-ordered indemnification under section 8.54(a)(3).

The language in earlier versions of the Model Act and in many other state statutes that the basis of success may be "on the merits or otherwise" is retained. While this standard may result in an occasional defendant becoming entitled to indemnification because of procedural defenses not related to the merits, e.g., the statute of limitations or disqualification of the plaintiff, it is unreasonable to require a defendant with a valid procedural defense to undergo a possibly prolonged and expensive trial on the merits in order to establish eligibility for mandatory indemnification.

If the corporation indemnifies or advances expenses to a director in connection with a derivative proceeding, the corporation must report that fact to the shareholders prior to their next meeting. See section 16.21(a).

§ 8.53   Advance for Expenses

(a) A corporation may, before final disposition of a proceeding, advance funds to pay for or reimburse the reasonable expenses incurred in connection with the proceeding by an individual who is a party to the proceeding because that individual is a member of the board of directors if the director delivers to the corporation:

   (1) a written affirmation of the director's good faith belief that the relevant standard of conduct described in section 8.51 has been met by the director or that the proceeding involves conduct for which liability has been eliminated under a provision of the articles of incorporation as authorized by section 2.02(b)(4); and

   (2) a written undertaking of the director to repay any funds advanced if the director is not entitled to mandatory indemnification under section 8.52 and it is ultimately determined under section 8.54 or section 8.55 that the director has not met the relevant standard of conduct described in section 8.51.

(b) The undertaking required by subsection (a)(2) must be an unlimited general obligation of the director but need not be secured and may be accepted without reference to the financial ability of the director to make repayment.

(c) Authorizations under this section shall be made:

    (1) by the board of directors:

        (i) if there are two or more qualified directors, by a majority vote of all the qualified directors (a majority of whom shall for such purpose constitute a quorum) or by a majority of the members of a committee of two or more qualified directors appointed by such a vote; or

        (ii) if there are fewer than two qualified directors, by the vote necessary for action by the board in accordance with section 8.24(c), in which authorization directors who are not qualified directors may participate; or

    (2) by the shareholders, but shares owned by or voted under the control of a director who at the time is not a qualified director may not be voted on the authorization.

Official Comment

Section 8.53 authorizes, but does not require, a corporation to pay for or reimburse, in advance, a director's reasonable expenses if two conditions are met. This authorization is subject to any limitations set forth in the articles of incorporation pursuant to section 8.58(c).

Section 8.53 recognizes an important difference between indemnification and an advance for expenses: indemnification is retrospective and, therefore, enables the persons determining whether to indemnify to do so on the basis of known facts, including the outcome of the proceeding. Advance for expenses is necessarily prospective and the individuals making the decision whether to advance expenses generally have fewer known facts on which to base their decision. Indemnification may include reimbursement for non-advanced expenses.

Section 8.53 reflects a determination that it is sound public policy to permit the corporation to advance (by direct payment or by reimbursement) the defense expenses of a director so long as the director (i) believes in good faith that the director was acting in accordance with the relevant standard for indemnification set forth in section 8.51 or that the proceeding involves conduct for which liability has been eliminated pursuant to section 2.02(b)(4) and (ii) agrees to repay any amounts advanced if it is ultimately determined that the director is not entitled to indemnification. This policy is based upon the view that a person who serves an entity in a representative capacity should not be required to finance his or her own defense. Moreover, adequate legal representation often involves substantial expenses during the course of the proceeding and many individuals are willing to serve as directors only if they have the assurance that the corporation has the power to advance funds to pay those expenses. In fact, many corporations enter into contractual obligations (*e.g.*, by a provision in the articles or bylaws or by individual agreements) to advance funds for directors' expenses. See section 8.58(a).

Section 8.53(a) requires the director's written affirmation as to the good faith belief that the director has met the relevant standard of conduct necessary for indemnification by the corporation and a written undertaking by the director to repay any funds advanced if it is ultimately determined that such standard of conduct has not been met. A single undertaking may cover all funds advanced from time to time in connection with the proceeding. Under subsection (b), the undertaking need not be secured and financial ability to repay is not a prerequisite. The theory underlying this subsection is that wealthy directors should not be favored over directors whose financial resources are modest. The undertaking must be made by the director and not by a third party. If the director or the corporation wishes some third party to be responsible for the director's obligation in this regard, either is free to make those arrangements separately with the third party.

In the absence of an obligatory provision established pursuant to section 8.58(a), the decision to advance expenses must be made in accordance with subsection (c). Section 8.53 does not address the question of the standard by which the decision to advance expenses is to be made. Accordingly, the standards of section 8.30 should, in general, govern. The conditions for advance for expenses are different from the conditions for indemnification. Directors normally meet the standards of section 8.30 in approving an advance for expenses if they limit their consideration to the financial ability of the corporation to pay the amount in question and do not have actual knowledge of facts sufficient to cause them to believe that the subsection (a)(1) affirmation was not made in good faith. The directors are not required by section 8.30 to make any inquiry into the merits of the proceeding or the good faith of the belief stated in that affirmation. Thus, in the great majority of cases, no special inquiry will be required. The directors acting on a decision to advance expenses may, but are not required to, consider any additional matters they deem appropriate and may condition the advance of expenses upon compliance with any additional requirements they desire to impose.

A corporation may obligate itself pursuant to section 8.58(a) to advance for expenses under section 8.53 by means of a provision set forth in its articles of incorporation or bylaws, by a resolution of its shareholders or board of directors, by a contract or otherwise. However, any such obligatory arrangement must comply with the requirements of subsection (a) regarding furnishing of an affirmation and undertaking. No other procedures are contemplated, although obligatory arrangements may include notice and other procedures in connection with advancement of expenses and indemnification requests.

At least one court has held that a general obligatory provision requiring indemnification to the extent permitted by law does not include advance for expenses if not specifically mentioned. See *Advanced Mining Systems, Inc. v. Fricke,* 623 A.2d 82 (Del. 1992). Unless provided otherwise, section 8.58(a) requires the opposite result.

The decision to advance expenses is required to be made only one time with respect to each proceeding rather than each time a request for payment of expenses is received by the corporation. However, the directors are free to reconsider the decision at any time (*e.g.,* upon a change in the financial ability of the corporation to pay the amount in question). The decision as to the reasonableness of any expenses may be made by any officer or agent of the corporation duly authorized to do so.

The procedures set forth in subsection (c) for authorizing an advance for expenses parallel the procedures set forth in section 8.55(b) for selecting the person or persons to make the determination that indemnification is permissible. If the advance for expenses is not authorized by the shareholders under subsection (c)(2), the procedure specified in subsection (c)(1)(i) must be used. If it is unavailable, then the procedure under subsection (c)(1)(ii) may be used.

Under subsection (c)(1)(i), the vote required when the qualified directors act as a group is an absolute majority of their number. A majority of the qualified directors constitutes a quorum for board action for this purpose.

The committee of two or more qualified directors referred to in subsection (c)(1)(i) may be a committee of the board of directors to which the power to authorize advances for expenses from time to time has been delegated, so long as (1) the committee was appointed by a majority vote of directors who were, at the time of appointment of the committee, qualified directors and (2) each advance is authorized by a majority vote of members of the committee who, at the time of the vote, are qualified directors.

Under subsection (c)(1)(ii), which is available only if subsection (c)(1)(i) is not available, the board's action must be taken in accordance with section 8.20 or section 8.21, as the case may be, and directors who are not qualified directors may participate in the vote. Allowing directors who at the time are not qualified directors to participate in the authorization decision, if there is no or only one qualified director, is a principle of prudence that is based on the concept that, if there are not at least two qualified directors, then it is preferable to return the power to make the decision to the full board (even though it includes non-qualified directors) than to leave it with one qualified director.

Illustration 1: The board consists of 15 directors, four of whom are non-qualified directors. Of the eleven qualified directors, nine are present at the meeting at which the authorization is to be made (or the committee is to be appointed). Under subsection (c)(1)(i), a quorum is present and at least six of the nine qualified directors present at the board meeting must authorize any advance for expenses because six is an absolute majority of the eleven qualified directors. Alternatively, six of the nine qualified directors present at the board meeting may appoint a committee of two or more of the qualified directors (up to all eleven) to decide whether to authorize the advance. Action by the committee would require an absolute majority of the qualified directors appointed as members.

Illustration 2: The board consists of 15 directors, only one of whom is a qualified director. Subsection (c)(1)(i) is not available because the number of qualified directors is less than two. Accordingly, the decision must be made by the board under subsection (c)(1)(ii) (or, as is always permitted, by the shareholders under subsection (c)(2)).

Authorizations by shareholders rather than by directors are permitted by subsection (c)(2), but shares owned by or voted under the control of directors who at the time are not qualified directors may not be voted on the authorizations. This does not affect general rules, as to the required presence of a quorum at the meeting, otherwise governing the authorization.

The fact that there has been an advance for expenses does not determine whether a director is entitled to indemnification. Repayment of any advance is required only if it is ultimately determined that the director did not meet the relevant standard of conduct in section 8.51. A proceeding will often terminate without a judicial or other determination as to whether the director's conduct met that standard. Nevertheless, the board of directors should make, or cause to be made, an affirmative determination of entitlement to indemnification at the conclusion of the proceeding. This decision should be made in accordance with the procedures set forth in section 8.55.

Judicial enforcement of rights granted by or pursuant to section 8.53 is specifically contemplated by section 8.54.

§ 8.54 Court–Ordered Indemnification and Advance for Expenses

(a) A director who is a party to a proceeding because he is a director may apply for indemnification or an advance for expenses to the court conducting the proceeding or to another court of competent jurisdiction. After receipt of an application and after giving any notice it considers necessary, the court shall:

(1) order indemnification if the court determines that the director is entitled to mandatory indemnification under section 8.52;

(2) order indemnification or advance for expenses if the court determines that the director is entitled to indemnification or advance for expenses pursuant to a provision authorized by section 8.58(a); or

(3) order indemnification or advance for expenses if the court determines, in view of all the relevant circumstances, that it is fair and reasonable

(i) to indemnify the director, or

(ii) to advance expenses to the director,

even if he has not met the relevant standard of conduct set forth in section 8.51(a), failed to comply with section 8.53 or was adjudged liable in a proceeding referred to in subsection 8.51(d)(1) or (d)(2), but if he was adjudged so liable his indemnification shall be limited to reasonable expenses incurred in connection with the proceeding.

(b) If the court determines that the director is entitled to indemnification under subsection (a)(1) or to indemnification or advance for expenses under subsection (a)(2), it shall also order the corporation to pay the director's reasonable expenses incurred in connection with obtaining court-ordered indemnification or advance for expenses. If the court determines that the director is entitled to indemnification or advance for expenses under subsection (a)(3), it may also order the corporation to pay the director's reasonable expenses to obtain court-ordered indemnification or advance for expenses.

Official Comment

Section 8.54(a) provides for court-ordered indemnification in three situations:

(1) A director is entitled to mandatory indemnification under section 8.52. If so, the director may enforce that right by judicial proceeding.

(2) A director is entitled to indemnification or advance for expenses pursuant to a provision in the articles or bylaws, board or shareholder resolution or contract. If so, the director may enforce that right by judicial proceeding. To the extent that these rights are contractual, the corporation may have contractual defenses. If the corporation has contracted to indemnify a director to the fullest extent permitted by law, a court may, nevertheless, deny an advance for expenses if it determines that the director did not have, at the time he delivered the affirmation required by section 8.53(a)(1), a good faith belief that he met the relevant standard of conduct.

(3) A court in its discretion determines that it is fair and reasonable under all the relevant circumstances to order an advance for expenses or indemnification for the amount of a settlement or judgment (in addition to expenses), whether or not the director met the relevant standard of conduct in section 8.51 or is otherwise ineligible for indemnification. However, there are two exceptions: an adverse judgment in a derivative proceeding (section 8.51(d)(1)) and an adverse judgment in a proceeding

charging receipt of an improper financial benefit (section 8.51(d)(2)), although in either case the court may order payment of expenses. Thus, with these exceptions, section 8.54(a)(3) permits a court to order indemnification for amounts paid in settlement of and expenses incurred in connection with a derivative proceeding or a proceeding charging receipt of an improper financial benefit. Section 8.54(a)(3) applies to (a) a situation in which a provision in the articles of incorporation, bylaws, resolution or contract obligates the corporation to indemnify or to advance expenses but the relevant standard of conduct has not been met and (b) a situation involving a permissive provision pursuant to which the board declines to exercise its authority to indemnify or to advance expenses. However, in determining whether indemnification or expense advance would be "fair and reasonable," a court should give appropriate deference to an informed decision of a board or committee made in good faith and based upon full information. Ordinarily, a court should not determine that it is "fair and reasonable" to order indemnification or expense advance where the director has not met conditions and procedures to which he agreed.

The discretionary authority of the court to order indemnification of a derivative proceeding settlement under section 8.54(a)(3) contrasts with the denial of similar authority under section 145(b) of the Delaware General Corporation Law. A director seeking court-ordered indemnification or expense advance under section 8.54(a)(3) must show that there are facts peculiar to his situation that make it fair and reasonable to both the corporation and to the director to override an intra-corporate declination or any otherwise applicable statutory prohibition against indemnification, e.g., sections 8.51(a) or (d).

Aside from the two exceptions noted above and other than the fairness and reasonableness requirement, there are no statutory outer limits on the court's power to order indemnification under section 8.54(a)(3). In an appropriate case, a court may wish to refer to the provisions of section 2.02(b)(4) establishing the outer limits of a liability-limiting charter provision. It would be an extraordinary situation in which a court would want to provide indemnification going beyond the limits of section 2.02(b)(4), but if the court, as the independent decision-maker, finds that it is "fair and reasonable," then the court is permitted to do so. It should be emphasized again, however, that the director seeking indemnification must make a showing of fairness and reasonableness and that exercise of the power granted by section 8.54(a)(3) is committed to the court's discretion.

Among the factors a court may want to consider are the gravity of the offense, the financial impact upon the corporation, the occurrence of a change in control or, in the case of an advance for expenses, the inability of the director to finance his defense. A court may want to give special attention to certain other issues. First, has the corporation joined in the application to the court for indemnification or an advance for expenses? This factor may be particularly important where under section 8.51(d) indemnification is not permitted for an amount paid in settlement of a proceeding brought by or in the right of the corporation. Second, in a case where indemnification would have been available under section 8.51(a)(2) if the corporation had adopted a provision authorized by section 2.02(b)(5), was the decision to adopt such a provision presented to and rejected by the shareholders and, if not, would exculpation of the director's conduct have resulted under a section 2.02(b)(4) provision? Third, in connection with considering indemnification for expenses under section 8.51(d)(2) in a proceeding in which a director was adjudged liable for receiving a financial benefit to which he was not entitled, was such financial benefit insubstantial—particularly in relation to the other aspects of the transaction involved—and what was the degree of the director's involvement in the transaction and the decision to participate?

Under section 8.54(b), if a director successfully sues to enforce his right to indemnification of expenses under subsection (a)(1) or to indemnification or advance for expenses under subsection (a)(2), then the court must order the corporation to pay the director's expenses in the enforcement proceeding. However, if a director successfully sues for indemnification or advance for expenses under subsection (a)(3), then the court may (but is not required to) order the corporation to pay the director's expenses in the proceeding under subsection (a)(3). The basis for the distinction is that the corporation breached its obligation in the first two cases but not in the third.

Application for indemnification under section 8.54 may be made either to the court in which the proceeding was heard or to another court of appropriate jurisdiction. For example, a defendant in a criminal proceeding who has been convicted but believes that indemnification would be proper could apply either to the court which heard the criminal proceeding or bring an action against the corporation in another forum.

A decision by the board of directors not to oppose the request for indemnification is governed by the general standards of conduct of section 8.30. Even if the corporation decided not to oppose the request, the court must satisfy itself that the person seeking indemnification is deserving of receiving it under section 8.54.

As provided in section 8.58(c), a corporation may limit the rights of a director under section 8.54 by a provision in its articles of incorporation. In the absence of such a provision, the court has general power to exercise the authority granted under this section.

If the corporation provides indemnification or advances expenses to a director in connection with a derivative proceeding, the corporation must report that fact to the shareholders prior to their next meeting. See section 16.21(a).

§ 8.55 Determination and Authorization of Indemnification

(a) A corporation may not indemnify a director under section 8.51 unless authorized for a specific proceeding after a determination has been made that indemnification is permissible because the director has met the relevant standard of conduct set forth in section 8.51.

(b) The determination shall be made:

(1) if there are two or more qualified directors, by the board of directors by a majority vote of all the qualified directors (a majority of whom shall for such purpose constitute a quorum), or by a majority of the members of a committee of two or more qualified directors appointed by such a vote;

(2) by special legal counsel:

(i) selected in the manner prescribed in subdivision (1); or

(ii) if there are fewer than two qualified directors, selected by the board of directors (in which selection directors who are not qualified directors may participate); or

(3) by the shareholders, but shares owned by or voted under the control of a director who at the time is not a qualified director may not be voted on the determination.

(c) Authorization of indemnification shall be made in the same manner as the determination that indemnification is permissible, except that if there are fewer than two qualified directors, or if the determination is made by special legal counsel, authorization of indemnification shall be made by those entitled to select special legal counsel under subsection (b)(2)(ii).

Official Comment

Section 8.55 provides the method for determining whether a corporation should indemnify a director under section 8.51. In this section a distinction is made between a "determination" and an "authorization." A "determination" involves a decision whether under the circumstances the person seeking indemnification has met the relevant standard of conduct under section 8.51 and is therefore eligible for indemnification. This decision may be made by the individuals or groups described in section 8.55(b). In addition, after a favorable "determination" has been made, the corporation must decide whether to "authorize" indemnification except to the extent that an obligatory provision under section 8.58(a) is applicable. This decision includes a review of the reasonableness of the expenses, the financial ability of the corporation to make the payment, and the judgment whether the limited financial resources of the corporation should be devoted to this or some other use. While special legal counsel may make the "determination" of eligibility for indemnification, counsel may not "authorize" the indemnification. A pre-existing obligation under section 8.58(a) to indemnify if the director is eligible for indemnification dispenses with the second-step decision to "authorize" indemnification.

Section 8.55(b) establishes procedures for selecting the person or persons who will make the determination of permissibility of indemnification. As indicated in the Official Comment to section 8.53(c), the committee of qualified directors referred to in subsection (b)(1) may include a committee of the board to which has been delegated the power to determine whether to indemnify a director so long as the appointment and composition of the committee members comply with subsection (b)(1). In selecting special legal counsel under subsection (b)(2), directors who are parties to the proceeding may participate in the decision if there are insufficient qualified directors to satisfy subsection (b)(1). Directors who are not eligible to act as qualified directors may also participate in the decision to "authorize" indemnification on the basis of a favorable "determination" if necessary to permit action by the board of directors. The authorization of indemnification is the decision that results in payment of any amounts to be indemnified. This limited participation of interested directors in the authorization decision is justified by the principle of necessity.

Under subsection (b)(1), the vote required when the qualified directors act as a group is an absolute majority of their number. A majority of the qualified directors constitutes a quorum for board action for this purpose. If there are not at least two qualified directors, then the determination of entitlement to indemnification must be made by special legal counsel or by the shareholders.

Legal counsel authorized to make the required determination is referred to as "special legal counsel." In earlier versions of the Model Act, and in the statutes of many states, reference is made to "independent" legal counsel. The word "special" is felt to be more descriptive of the role to be performed; it is intended that the counsel selected should be independent in accordance with governing legal precepts. "Special legal counsel" normally should be counsel having no prior professional relationship with those seeking indemnification, should be retained for the specific purpose, and should not be or have been either inside counsel or regular outside counsel to the corporation. Special legal counsel also should not have any familial, financial or other relationship with any of those seeking indemnification that would, in the circumstances, reasonably be expected to exert an influence on counsel in making the determination. It is important that the process be sufficiently flexible to permit selection of counsel in light of the particular circumstances and so that unnecessary expense may be avoided. Hence the phrase "special legal counsel" is not defined in the statute.

Determinations by shareholders, rather than by directors or special legal counsel, are permitted by subsection (b)(3), but shares owned by or voted under the control of directors who at the time are not qualified directors may not be voted on the determination of eligibility for indemnification. This does not affect general rules as to the required presence of a quorum at the meeting in order for the determination to be made.

Section 8.55 is subject to section 8.58(a), which authorizes an arrangement obligating the corporation in advance to provide indemnification or to advance expenses.

§ 8.56 Officers

(a) A corporation may indemnify and advance expenses under this subchapter to an officer of the corporation who is a party to a proceeding because he is an officer of the corporation.

  (1) to the same extent as a director; and

  (2) if he is an officer but not a director, to such further extent as may be provided by the articles of incorporation, the bylaws, a resolution of the board of directors, or contract except for (A) liability in connection with a proceeding by or in the right of the corporation other than for reasonable expenses incurred in connection with the proceeding or (B) liability arising out of conduct that constitutes (i) receipt by him of a financial benefit to which he is not entitled, (ii) an intentional infliction of harm on the corporation or the shareholders, or (iii) an intentional violation of criminal law.

(b) The provisions of subsection (a)(2) shall apply to an officer who is also a director if the basis on which he is made a party to the proceeding is an act or omission solely as an officer.

(c) An officer of a corporation who is not a director is entitled to mandatory indemnification under section 8.52, and may apply to a court under section 8.54 for indemnification or an advance for expenses, in each case to the same extent to which a director may be entitled to indemnification or advance for expenses under those provisions.

Official Comment

Section 8.56 correlates the general legal principles relating to the indemnification of officers of the corporation with the limitations on indemnification in subchapter E. This correlation may be summarized in general terms as follows:

  (1) An officer of a corporation who is *not* a director may be indemnified by the corporation on a discretionary basis to the same extent as though he were a director, and, in addition, may have additional indemnification rights apart from subchapter E, but the outer limits of such rights are specified. (See section 8.56(a)(2) and (c).)

(2) An officer who is *also* a director of the corporation is entitled to the indemnification rights of a director and of an officer who is not a director (see preceding paragraph) if his conduct that is the subject of the proceeding was solely in his capacity as an officer. (See section 8.56(b).)

(3) An *officer* of a corporation who is not a director has the right of mandatory indemnification granted to directors under section 8.52 and the right to apply for court-ordered indemnification under section 8.54. (See section 8.56(c).)

Section 8.56 does not deal with indemnification of employees and agents because the concerns of self-dealing that arise when directors provide for their own indemnification and expense advance (and sometimes for senior executive officers) are not present when directors (or officers) provide for indemnification and expense advance for employees and agents who are not directors or officers. Moreover, the rights of employees and agents to indemnification and advance for expenses derive from principles of agency, the doctrine of respondeat superior, collective bargaining or other contractual arrangements rather than from a corporation statute. It would be presumptuous for a corporation statute to seek to limit the indemnification bargain that a corporation may wish to make with those it hires or retains. The same standard applicable to directors and officers may not be appropriate for office workers and hazardous waste workers, brokers and custodians, engineers and farm workers. None of their roles or responsibilities are prescribed by the Model Act.

Section 3.02 grants broad powers to corporations, including powers to make contracts, appoint and fix the compensation of employees and agents and to make payments furthering the business and affairs of the corporation. Many corporations provide for the exercise of these powers in the same provisions in the articles, bylaws or otherwise in which they provide for expense advance and indemnification for directors and officers.

Indemnification may also be provided to protect employees or agents from liabilities incurred while serving at a corporation's request as a director, officer, partner, trustee, or agent of another commercial, charitable, or nonprofit venture.

Although employees and agents are not covered by subchapter E, the principles and procedures set forth in the subchapter for indemnification and advance for expenses for directors and officers may be helpful to counsel and courts in dealing with indemnification and expense advance for employees and agents.

Careful consideration should be given to extending mandatory maximum indemnification and expense advance to employees and agents. The same considerations that may favor mandatory maximum indemnification for directors and officers—e.g., encouraging qualified individuals to serve—may not be present in the cases of employees and agents. Many corporations may prefer to retain the discretion to decide, on a case-by-case basis, whether to indemnify and advance expenses to employees and agents (and perhaps even officers, especially non-executive officers) rather than binding themselves in advance to do so.

1. Officers Who Are Not Directors

While Section 8.56 does not prescribe the standards governing the rights of officers to indemnification, subsection (a) does set outer limits beyond which the corporation may not indemnify. These outer limits for officers (see subsection (a)(2)) are substantially the same as the outer limits on the corporation's power to indemnify directors: (i) in a proceeding by or in the right of the corporation, indemnification is not allowed other than for reasonable expenses incurred in connection therewith and (ii) in any proceeding, indemnification is not allowed in those situations in which directors' liability to the corporation or its shareholders could not be eliminated by a provision included in the articles pursuant to section 2.02(b)(4), i.e., where there has been receipt of a financial benefit to which he is not entitled, intentional infliction of harm on the corporation or shareholders or intentional violation of criminal law. Since officers are held to substantially the same standards of conduct as directors (see section 8.42), there does not appear to be any reasoned basis for granting officers greater indemnification rights as a substantive matter. Procedurally, however, there is an important difference. To permit greater flexibility, officers may be indemnified (within the above-mentioned outer limits) with respect to conduct that does not meet the standards set by section 8.51(a)(1) simply by authorization of the board of directors, whereas directors' indemnification can reach beyond those standards, as contemplated by section 8.51(a)(2), only with a shareholder-approved provision included in the articles pursuant to section 2.02(b)(5). This procedural difference reflects the reduced risk of self-dealing as to officers.

Section 8.56(c) grants non-director officers the same rights to mandatory indemnification under section 8.52 and to apply to a court for indemnification under section 8.54 as are granted to directors. Since their substantive rights to indemnification are essentially the same as those of directors, it is appropriate to grant officers the same affirmative procedural rights to judicial relief as are provided to directors.

The broad authority in section 8.56(a)(2) to grant indemnification may be limited by appropriate provisions in the articles of incorporation. See section 8.58(c).

2. Officers Who Are Also Directors

Subsection (b) provides, in effect, that an officer of the corporation who is also a director is subject to the same standards of indemnification as other directors and cannot avail himself of the provisions of subsection (a) unless he can establish that the act or omission that is the subject of the proceeding was committed solely in his capacity as officer. Thus, a vice president for sales who is also a director and whose actions failed to meet section 8.51(a) standards could be indemnified provided that his conduct was within the outer limits of subsection (a)(2) and involved only his officer capacity.

This more flexible approach for situations where the individual is not acting as a director seems appropriate as a matter of fairness. There are many instances where officers who also serve as directors assume responsibilities and take actions in their non-director capacities. It is hard to justify a denial of indemnification to an officer who failed to meet a standard applicable only to directors when the officer can establish that he did not act as a director. Nor are there likely to be complications or difficulties because some directors are treated differently than others where the high burden of proof—solely as officer—is met. Obviously, the burden will be especially difficult to meet where the roles of officer and director are closely intertwined, as is often the case with a chief executive officer.

For a director-officer to be indemnified under section 8.51 for conduct in his capacity as a director when he has not satisfied the standards of section 8.51(a), a provision in the articles under section 2.02(b)(5) is required. If such a provision is included in the articles, the standards for indemnification are those specified in section 2.02(b)(5). For a director-officer to be indemnified for conduct solely in his capacity as an officer, even though the director-officer has not satisfied the standards of section 8.56(a), only a resolution of the board authorizing such indemnification is required, rather than a provision in the articles. If such a resolution is adopted, the standards for indemnification are those specified in subsection (a)(2). However, when a director-officer seeks indemnification or expense advance under subsections (b) and (a)(2) on the basis of having acted solely in his capacity as an officer, indemnification or expense advance must be approved through the same procedures as set forth in sections 8.55 or 8.53(c), as the case may be, for approval of indemnification or expense advance for a director when acting in his capacity as a director.

§ 8.57 Insurance

A corporation may purchase and maintain insurance on behalf of an individual who is a director or officer of the corporation, or who, while a director or officer of the corporation, serves at the corporation's request as a director, officer, partner, trustee, employee, or agent of another domestic or foreign corporation, partnership, joint venture, trust, employee benefit plan, or other entity, against liability asserted against or incurred by him in that capacity or arising from his status as a director or officer, whether or not the corporation would have power to indemnify or advance expenses to him against the same liability under this subchapter.

Official Comment

Section 8.57 authorizes a corporation to purchase and maintain insurance on behalf of directors and officers against liabilities imposed on them by reason of actions in their official capacity, or their status as such, or arising from their service to the corporation or another entity at the corporation's request. Insurance is not limited to claims against which a corporation is entitled to indemnify under this subchapter. This insurance, usually referred to as "D & O Liability Insurance," provides protection to directors and officers in addition to the rights of indemnification created by or pursuant to this subchapter (as well as typically protecting the individual insureds against the corporation's failure to pay indemnification required or permitted by this subchapter) and provides a source of reimbursement for corporations which indemnify directors and others for conduct covered by the insurance. On the other hand, policies typically do not cover uninsurable matters, such as actions involving dishonesty, self-dealing, bad faith, knowing violations of the securities acts, or other willful misconduct. Johnston, "Corporate Indemnification and Liability Insurance for Directors and Officers," 33 Bus.Law. 1993, 2024–29 (1978). See also Knepper & Bailey, Liability of Corporate Officers and Directors § 21.07 (4th ed. 1988).

Although this section does not include employees and agents for the reasons stated in the Official Comment to section 8.56, the corporation has the power under section 3.02 to purchase and maintain insurance on their behalf. This power is confirmed in section 8.58(d).

This section is not intended to set the outer limits on the type of insurance which a corporation may maintain or the persons to be covered. Rather, it is included to remove "any doubt as to the power to carry insurance and to maintain it on behalf of directors, officers, employees and agents." Sebring, "Recent Legislative Changes in the Law of Indemnification of Directors, Officers and Others," 23 Bus.Law. 95, 106 (1967).

§ 8.58 Variation by Corporate Action; Application of Subchapter

(a) A corporation may, by a provision in its articles of incorporation or bylaws or in a resolution adopted or a contract approved by its board of directors or shareholders, obligate itself in advance of the act or omission giving rise to a proceeding to provide indemnification in accordance with section 8.51 or advance funds to pay for or reimburse expenses in accordance with section 8.53. Any such obligatory provision shall be deemed to satisfy the requirements for authorization referred to in section 8.53(c) and in section 8.55(c). Any such provision that obligates the corporation to provide indemnification to the fullest extent permitted by law shall be deemed to obligate the corporation to advance funds to pay for or reimburse expenses in accordance with section 8.53 to the fullest extent permitted by law, unless the provision specifically provides otherwise.

(b) Any provision pursuant to subsection (a) shall not obligate the corporation to indemnify or advance expenses to a director of a predecessor of the corporation, pertaining to conduct with respect to the predecessor, unless otherwise specifically provided. Any provision for indemnification or advance for expenses in the articles of incorporation, bylaws, or a resolution of the board of directors or shareholders of a predecessor of the corporation in a merger or in a contract to which the predecessor is a party, existing at the time the merger takes effect, shall be governed by section 11.06(a)(3).

(c) A corporation may, by a provision in its articles of incorporation, limit any of the rights to indemnification or advance for expenses created by or pursuant to this subchapter.

(d) This subchapter does not limit a corporation's power to pay or reimburse expenses incurred by a director or an officer in connection with his appearance as a witness in a proceeding at a time when he is not a party.

(e) This subchapter does not limit a corporation's power to indemnify, advance expenses to or provide or maintain insurance on behalf of an employee or agent.

Official Comment

Section 8.58(a) authorizes a corporation to make obligatory the permissive provisions of subchapter E in advance of the conduct giving rise to the request for assistance. Many corporations have adopted such provisions, often with shareholder approval. An obligatory provision satisfies the requirements for authorization in subsection (c) of sections 8.53 and 8.55, but compliance would still be required with subsections (a) and (b) of these sections.

Section 8.58(a) further provides that a provision requiring indemnification to the fullest extent permitted by law shall be deemed, absent an express statement to the contrary, to include an obligation to advance expenses under section 8.53. This provision of the statute is intended to avoid a decision such as that of the Delaware Supreme Court in Advanced Mining Systems, Inc. v. Fricke, 623 A.2d 82 (Del.1992). If a corporation provides for obligatory indemnification and not for obligatory advance for expenses, the provision should be reviewed to ensure that it properly reflects the intent in light of the second sentence of section 8.58(a). Also, a corporation should consider whether obligatory expense advance is intended for direct suits by the corporation as well as for derivative suits by shareholders in the right of the corporation. In the former case, assuming compliance with subsections (a) and (b) of section

8.53, the corporation could be required to fund the defense of a defendant director even where the board of directors has already concluded that he has engaged in significant wrongdoing. See Official Comment to section 8.53.

Section 8.58(b) provides that an obligatory indemnification provision as authorized by subsection (a) does not, unless specific provision is made to the contrary, bind the corporation with respect to a predecessor. An obligatory indemnification provision of a predecessor is treated as a liability (to the extent it is one) under section 11.06(a)(3), which governs the effect of a merger.

Section 8.58(c) permits a corporation to limit the right of the corporation to indemnify or advance expenses by a provision in its articles of incorporation. As provided in section 10.09, no such limitation will affect rights in existence when the provision becomes effective pursuant to section 1.23.

Section 8.58(d) makes clear that subchapter E deals only with actual or threatened defendants or respondents in a proceeding, and that expenses incurred by a director in connection with appearance as a witness may be indemnified without regard to the limitations of subchapter E. Indeed, most of the standards described in sections 8.51 and 8.54(a) by their own terms can have no meaningful application to a director whose only connection with a proceeding is that he has been called as a witness.

Subchapter E does not regulate the power of the corporation to indemnify or advance expenses to employees and agents. That subject is governed by the law of agency and related principles and frequently by contractual arrangements between the corporation and the employee or agent. Section 8.58(e) makes clear that, while indemnification, advance for expenses and insurance for employees and agents are beyond the scope of this subchapter, the elaboration in subchapter E of standards and procedures for indemnification, expense advance and insurance for directors and officers is not in any way intended to cast doubt on the power of the corporation to indemnify or advance expenses to or purchase and maintain insurance for employees and agents under section 3.02 or otherwise.

§ 8.59 Exclusivity of Subchapter

A corporation may provide indemnification or advance expenses to a director or an officer only as permitted by this subchapter.

Official Comment

This subchapter is the exclusive source for the power of a corporation to indemnify or advance expenses to a director or an officer.

Section 8.59 does not preclude provisions in articles of incorporation, bylaws, resolutions, or contracts designed to provide procedural machinery in addition to (but not inconsistent with) that provided by this subchapter. For example, a corporation may properly obligate the board of directors to consider and act expeditiously on an application for indemnification or advance for expenses or to cooperate in the procedural steps required to obtain a judicial determination under section 8.54.

Subchapter F*

Directors' Conflicting Interest Transactions

INTRODUCTORY COMMENT

1. Purposes and Special Characteristics of Subchapter F

The common law, drawing by analogy on the fiduciary principles of the law of trusts, initially took the position that any transaction between a corporation and a director of that corporation was contaminated by the director's conflicting interest, that the transaction was null and void or at least voidable and, suggesting by implication, that the interested director who benefitted from the transaction could be required to disgorge any profits and be held liable for any damages.

Eventually, it was perceived that a flat void/voidable rule could work against a corporation's best interests. Although self-interested transactions carry a potential for injury to the corporation, they also carry a potential for benefit. A director who is self-interested may nevertheless act fairly, and there may be cases where a director either owns a unique asset that the corporation needs or is willing to offer the corporation more favorable terms than are available on the market (for example, where the director is more confident of the corporation's financial ability to perform than a third person would be). Accordingly, the courts dropped the flat void/voidable rule, and substituted in its stead the rule that a self-interested transaction will be upheld if the director shoulders the burden of showing that the transaction was fair.

Later still, the Model Act and the state legislatures entered the picture by adopting statutory provisions that sheltered the transaction from any challenge that the transaction was void or voidable where it was approved by disinterested directors or shareholders. Until 1989, the successive Model Act provisions concerning director conflict-of-interest transactions and the statutory provisions in force in most states reflected basically the same objective; that is, their safe-harbor procedures concentrated on protection for the transaction, with no attention given to the possible vulnerability of the director whose conflicting interest would give rise to the transaction's potential challenge. However, in 1989 the

---

* Subchapter F, sections 8.60–8.63, replaces former section 8.31 of the Revised Model Business Corporation Act. Section 8.31 is nevertheless included as an Appendix in this Supplement, at the end of the Model Act, because many states that had adopted section 8.31 as part of their corporation statutes did not decide to adopt Subchapter F in its stead.

relevant provisions were significantly reworked in subchapter F of Chapter 8. Four basic elements in the architecture of the 1989 version of subchapter F distinguished the approach of the subchapter from most other statutory provisions of the time.

First, most other statutory provisions did not define what constituted a director's conflict-of-interest transaction. In contrast, subchapter F defined, with bright-line rules, the transactions that were to be treated as director's conflict-of-interest transactions.

Second, because most other statutory provisions did not define what constitutes a director's conflict-of-interest transaction, they left open how to deal with transactions that involved only a relatively minor conflict. In contrast, subchapter F explicitly provided that a director's transaction that was not within the statutory definition of a director's conflict of interest transaction was not subject to judicial review for fairness on the ground that it involved a conflict of interest (although circumstances that fall outside the statutory definition could, of course, afford the basis for a legal attack on the transaction on some other ground), even if the transaction involved some sort of conflict lying outside the statutory definition, such as a remote familial relationship.

Third, subchapter F made explicit, as many other statutory provisions did not, that if a director's conflict-of-interest transaction, as defined, was properly approved by disinterested (or "qualified") directors or shareholders, the transaction was thereby insulated from judicial review for fairness (although, again, it might be open to attack on some basis other than the conflict).

Fourth, subchapter F also made explicit, as no other statutory provisions had done, that if a director's conflict-of-interest transaction, as defined, was properly approved by disinterested (or "qualified") directors or shareholders, the conflicted director could not be subject to an award of damages or other sanctions with respect thereto (although the director could be subject to claims on some basis other than the conflict).

Bright-line provisions of any kind represent a trade-off between the benefits of certainty, and the danger that some transactions or conduct that fall outside the area circumscribed by the bright-lines may be so similar to the transactions and conduct that fall within the area that different treatment may seem anomalous. Subchapter F reflected the considered judgment that in corporate matters, where planning is critical, the clear and important efficiency gains that result from certainty through defining director's conflict-of-interest transactions clearly exceeded any potential and uncertain efficiency losses that might occasionally follow from excluding other director's transactions from judicial review for fairness on conflict-of-interest grounds.

The 2004 revisions of subchapter F rest on the same basic judgment that animated the original subchapter. Accordingly, the revisions made do not alter the fundamental elements and approach of the subchapter. However, the revisions refine the definition of director's conflict-of-interest transactions, simplify the text of the statute, and, within the basic approach of the original subchapter, make various clarifying and substantive changes throughout the text and comments. One of these substantive changes expands the category of persons whose interest in a transaction will be attributed to the director for purposes of subchapter F. At the same time, the revisions delete coverage of a director's interest that lies outside the transaction itself but might be deemed to be "closely related to the transaction." The latter phraseology was determined to be excessively vague and unhelpful. In combination, these revisions clarify the coverage of subchapter F, while ensuring that a transaction that poses a significant risk of adversely affecting a director's judgment will not escape statutory coverage.

2. Scope of Subchapter F

The focus of subchapter F is sharply defined and limited.

First, the subchapter is targeted on legal challenges based on interest conflicts only. Subchapter F does not undertake to define, regulate, or provide any form of procedure regarding other possible claims. For example, subchapter F does not address a claim that a controlling shareholder has violated a duty owed to the corporation or minority shareholders.

Second, subchapter F does not shield misbehavior by a director or other person that is actionable under other provisions of the Model Act, such as section 8.31, or under other legal rules, regardless of whether the misbehavior is incident to a transaction with the corporation and regardless of whether the rule is one of corporate law.

Third, subchapter F does not preclude the assertion of defenses, such as statute of limitations or failure of a condition precedent, that are based on grounds other than a director's conflicting interest in the transaction.

Fourth, the subchapter is applicable only when there is a "transaction" by or with the corporation. For purposes of subchapter F, "transaction" generally connotes negotiations or consensual arrangements between the corporation and another party or parties that concern their respective and differing economic rights or interests—not simply a unilateral action by the corporation or a director, but rather a "deal." Whether safe harbor procedures of some kind might be available to the director and the corporation with respect to non-transactional matters is discussed in numbered paragraph 4 of this Introductory Comment.

Fifth, subchapter F deals with directors only. Correspondingly, subchapter F does not deal with controlling shareholders in their capacity as such. If a corporation is wholly owned by a parent corporation or other person, there are no outside shareholders who might be injured as a result of transactions entered into between the corporation and the owner of its shares. However, transactions between a corporation and a parent corporation or other controlling shareholder who owns less than all of its shares may give rise to the possibility of abuse of power by the controlling shareholder. Subchapter F does not speak to proceedings brought on that basis because section 8.61 concerns only proceedings that are brought on the ground that a "director has an interest respecting the transaction."

Sixth, it is important to stress that the voting procedures and conduct standards prescribed in subchapter F deal solely with the complicating element presented by the director's conflicting interest. A transaction that receives favorable directors' or shareholders' action complying with subchapter F may still fail to satisfy a different quorum requirement or to achieve a different vote that may be needed for substantive approval of the transaction under other applicable statutory provisions or under the articles of incorporation, and vice versa. (Under the Model Act, latitude is granted for setting higher voting requirements and different quorum requirements in the articles of incorporation. See sections 2.02(b)(2) and 7.27.)

Seventh, a few corporate transactions or arrangements in which directors inherently have a special personal interest are of a unique character and are regulated by special procedural provisions of the Model Act. See sections 8.51 and 8.52 dealing with indemnification arrangements, section 7.44 dealing with termination of derivative proceedings by board action and section 8.11 dealing with directors' compensation. Any corporate transactions or arrangements affecting directors that are governed by such regulatory sections of the Act are not governed by subchapter F.

3. Structure of Subchapter F

Subchapter F has only four parts. Definitions are in section 8.60. Section 8.61 prescribes what a court may or may not do in various situations. Section 8.62 prescribes procedures for action by boards of directors or duly authorized committees regarding a director's conflicting interest transaction. Section 8.63 prescribes corresponding procedures for shareholders. Thus, the most important operative section of the subchapter is section 8.61.

4. Non–Transactional Situations Involving Interest Conflicts

Many situations arise in which a director's personal economic interest is or may be adverse to the economic interest of the corporation, but which do not entail a "transaction" by or with the corporation. How does the subchapter bear upon those situations?

Corporate opportunity

The corporate opportunity doctrine is anchored in a significant body of case law clustering around the core question whether the corporation has a legitimate interest in a business opportunity, either because of the nature of the opportunity or the way in which the opportunity came to the director, of such a nature that the corporation should be afforded prior access to the opportunity before it is pursued (or, to use the case law's phrase, "usurped") by a director. Because judicial determinations in this area often seem to be driven by the particular facts of a case, outcomes are often difficult to predict.

The subchapter, as such, does not apply by its terms to corporate or business opportunities since no transaction between the corporation and the director is involved in the taking of an opportunity. However, new subchapter G of chapter 8 of the Model Act provides, in effect, that the safe harbor procedures of section 8.62 or 8.63 may be employed, at the interested director's election, to protect the taking of a business opportunity that might be challenged under the doctrine. Otherwise, subchapter F has no bearing on enterprise rights or director obligations under the corporate opportunity doctrine.

Other situations

Many other kinds of situations can give rise to a clash of economic interests between a director and the corporation. For example, a director's personal financial interests can be impacted by a non-transactional policy decision of the board, such as where it decides to establish a divisional headquarters in the director's small hometown. In other situations, simple inaction by a board might work to a director's personal advantage, or a flow of ongoing business relationships between a director and that director's corporation may, without centering upon any discrete "transaction," raise questions of possible favoritism, unfair dealing, or undue influence. If a director decides to engage in business activity that directly competes with the corporation's own business, the economic interest in that competing activity ordinarily will conflict with the best interests of the corporation and put in issue the breach of the director's duties to the corporation. Basic conflicts and improprieties can also arise out of a director's personal appropriation of corporate assets or improper use of corporate proprietary or inside information.

The circumstances in which such non-transactional conflict situations should be brought to the board or shareholders for clearance, and the legal effect, if any, of such clearance, are matters for development under the common law and lie outside the ambit of subchapter F. While these non-transactional situations are unaffected one way or the other by the provisions of subchapter F, a court may well recognize that the subchapter F procedures provide a useful analogy for dealing with such situations. Where similar procedures are followed, the court may, in its discretion, accord to them an effect similar to that provided by subchapter F.

* * *

Note on Terms Used in Comments

In the Official Comments to subchapter F sections, the director who has a conflicting interest is for convenience referred to as "the director" or "*D*," and the corporation of which he or she is a director is referred to as "the corporation" or "*X* Co." A subsidiary of the corporation is referred to as "*S* Co." Another corporation dealing with *X* Co. is referred to as "*Y* Co."

§ 8.60 Subchapter Definitions

In this subchapter:

(1) "Director's conflicting interest transaction" means a transaction effected or proposed to be effected by the corporation (or by an entity controlled by the corporation)

   (i) to which, at the relevant time, the director is a party; or

   (ii) respecting which, at the relevant time, the director had knowledge and a material financial interest known to the director; or

   (iii) respecting which, at the relevant time, the director knew that a related person was a party or had a material financial interest.

(2) "Control" (including the term "controlled by") means (i) having the power, directly or indirectly, to elect or remove a majority of the members of the board of directors or other governing body of an entity, whether through the ownership of voting shares or interests, by contract, or otherwise, or (ii) being subject to a majority of the risk of loss from the entity's activities or entitled to receive a majority of the entity's residual returns.

(3) "Relevant time" means (i) the time at which directors' action respecting the transaction is taken in compliance with section 8.62, or (ii) if the transaction is not brought before the board of directors of the corporation (or its committee) for action under section 8.62, at the time the corporation (or an entity controlled by the corporation) becomes legally obligated to consummate the transaction.

(4) "Material financial interest" means a financial interest in a transaction that would reasonably be expected to impair the objectivity of the director's judgment when participating in action on the authorization of the transaction.

(5) "Related person" means:

   (i) the director's spouse;

   (ii) a child, stepchild, grandchild, parent, step parent, grandparent, sibling, step sibling, half sibling, aunt, uncle, niece or nephew (or spouse of any thereof) of the director or of the director's spouse;

   (iii) an individual living in the same home as the director;

(iv) an entity (other than the corporation or an entity controlled by the corporation) controlled by the director or any person specified above in this subdivision (5);

(v) a domestic or foreign (A) business or nonprofit corporation (other than the corporation or an entity controlled by the corporation) of which the director is a director, (B) unincorporated entity of which the director is a general partner or a member of the governing body, or (C) individual, trust or estate for whom or of which the director is a trustee, guardian, personal representative or like fiduciary; or

(vi) a person that is, or an entity that is controlled by, an employer of the director.

(6) "Fair to the corporation" means, for purposes of section 8.61(b)(3), that the transaction as a whole was beneficial to the corporation, taking into appropriate account whether it was (i) fair in terms of the director's dealings with the corporation, and (ii) comparable to what might have been obtainable in an arm's length transaction, given the consideration paid or received by the corporation.

(7) "Required disclosure" means disclosure of (i) the existence and nature of the director's conflicting interest, and (ii) all facts known to the director respecting the subject matter of the transaction that a director free of such conflicting interest would reasonably believe to be material in deciding whether to proceed with the transaction.

Official Comment

The definitions set forth in section 8.60 apply only to subchapter F's provisions and, except to the extent relevant to subchapter G, have no application elsewhere in the Model Act. (For the meaning and use of certain terms used below, such as "D," "X Co." and "Y Co.", see the Note at the end of the Introductory Comment of subchapter F.)

1. Director's Conflicting Interest Transaction

The definition of "director's conflicting interest transaction" in subdivision (1) is the core concept underlying subchapter F, demarcating the transactional area that lies within—and without—the scope of the subchapter's provisions. The definition operates preclusively in that, as used in section 8.61, it denies the power of a court to invalidate transactions or otherwise to remedy conduct that falls outside the statutory definition of "director's conflicting interest transaction" solely on the ground that the director has a conflict of interest in the transaction. (Nevertheless, as stated in the Introductory Comment, the transaction might be open to attack under rules of law concerning director misbehavior other than rules based solely on the existence of a conflict of interest transaction, as to which subchapter F is preclusive).

a. Transaction

For a director's conflicting interest transaction to arise, there must first be a transaction effected or proposed to be effected by the corporation or an entity controlled by the corporation to which the director or a related person is a party or in which the director or a related person has a material financial interest. As discussed in the Introductory Comment, the provisions of subchapter F do not apply where there is no "transaction" by the corporation—no matter how conflicting the director's interest may be. For example, a corporate opportunity usurped by a director by definition does not involve a transaction by the corporation, and thus is not covered by subchapter F, even though it may be proscribed under fiduciary duty principles.

Moreover, for purposes of subchapter F, "transaction" means (and requires) a bilateral (or multilateral) arrangement to which the corporation or an entity controlled by the corporation is a party. Subchapter F does not apply to transactions to which the corporation is not a party. Thus, a purchase or sale by the director of the corporation's shares on the open market or from or to a third party is not a "director's conflicting interest transaction" within the meaning of subchapter F because the corporation is not a party to the transaction.

b. Party to the transaction—the corporation

In the usual case, the transaction would be effected by X Co. Assume, however, that X Co. controls the vote for directors of S Co. D wishes to sell a building D owns to X Co. and X Co. is willing to buy it. As a business matter, it makes no difference to X Co. whether it takes the title directly or indirectly through its subsidiary S Co. or some other entity that X Co. controls. The applicability of subchapter F does not depend upon that formal distinction, because the subchapter includes within its operative framework transactions by entities controlled by X Co. Thus, subchapter F would apply to a sale of the building by D to S Co.

c. Party to the transaction—the director or a related person

To constitute a director's conflicting interest transaction, D (the director identified in this subchapter from time to time as a "conflicted director") must, at the relevant time, (i) be a party to the transaction, or (ii) know of the transaction and D's material financial interest in it, or (iii) know that a related person of D was a party to the transaction or (iv) know that a related person of D has a material financial interest (as defined in subdivision that would reasonably be expected to impair the objectivity of the director's judgment if D were to participate in action by the directors (or by a committee thereof) on the authorization of the transaction.

Routine business transactions frequently occur between companies with overlapping directors. If X Co. and Y Co. have routine, frequent business dealings whose terms are dictated by competitive market forces, then even if a director of *X* Co. has a relevant relationship with *Y* Co., the transactions would almost always be defensible, regardless of approval by disinterested directors or shareholders, on the ground that they are "fair." For example, a common transaction involves a purchase of the corporation's product line by *Y* Co., or perhaps by *D* or a related person, at prices normally charged by the corporation. In such circumstances, it usually will not be difficult for *D* to show that the transaction was on arms-length terms and was fair. Even a purchase by *D* of a product of *X* Co. at a usual "employee's discount," while technically assailable as a conflicting interest transaction, would customarily be viewed as a routine incident of the office of director and, thus, "fair" to the corporation.

D can have a conflicting interest in only two ways.

First, a conflicting interest can arise under either subdivision (1)(i) or (ii). This will be the case if, under clause (i), the transaction is between *D* and *X* Co. A conflicting interest also will arise under clause (ii) if *D* is not a party to the transaction, but knows about it and knows that he or she has a material financial interest in it. The personal economic stake of the director must be in the transaction itself—that is, the director's gain must flow directly from the transaction. A remote gain (for example, a future reduction in tax rates in the local community) is not enough to give rise to a conflicting interest under subdivision (1)(ii).

Second, a conflicting interest for *D* can arise under subdivision (1)(iii) from the involvement in the transaction of a "related person" of *D* that is either a party to the transaction or has a "material financial interest" in it. "Related person" is defined in subdivision (5).

Circumstances may arise where a director could have a conflicting interest under more than one clause of subdivision (1). For example, if *Y* Co. is a party to or interested in the transaction with *X* Co. and *Y* Co. is a related person of *D*, the matter would be governed by subdivision (1)(iii), but *D* also may have a conflicting interest under subdivision (1)(ii) if *D*'s economic interest in *Y* Co. is sufficiently material and if the importance of the transaction to *Y* Co. is sufficiently material.

A director may have relationships and linkages to persons and institutions that are not specified in subdivision (1)(iii). Such relationships and linkages fall outside subchapter F because the categories of persons described in subdivision (1)(iii) constitute the exclusive universe for purposes of subchapter F. For example, in a challenged transaction between *X* Co. and *Y* Co., suppose the court confronts the argument that *D* also is a major creditor of *Y* Co. and that creditor status in *Y* Co. gives D a conflicting interest. The court should rule that *D*'s creditor status in *Y* Co. does not fit any category of subdivision (1); and therefore, the conflict of interest claim must be rejected by reason of section 8.61(a). The result would be different if *Y* Co.'s debt to *D* were of such economic significance to *D* that it would either fall under subdivision (1)(ii) or, if it placed D in control of Y Co., it would fall under subdivision (1)(iii) (because Y Co. is a related person of D under subdivision (5)(iv)). To explore the example further, if D is also a shareholder of Y Co., but D does not have a material financial interest in the transaction and does not control Y Co., no director's conflicting interest transaction arises and the transaction cannot be challenged on conflict of interest grounds. To avoid any appearance of impropriety, D, nonetheless, should consider recusal from the other directors' deliberations and voting on the transaction between X Co. and Y Co.

It should be noted that any director's interest in a transaction that meets the criteria of section 8.60(1) is considered a "director's conflicting interest transaction." If the director's interest satisfies those criteria, subchapter F draws no distinction between a director's interest that clashes with the interests of the corporation and a director's interest that coincides with, or is parallel to, or even furthers the interests of the corporation. In any of these cases, if the director's "interest" is present, a "conflict" will exist.

2. Control

The definition of "control" in subdivision (2) contains two independent clauses. The first clause addresses possession of the voting or other power, directly or indirectly, to elect or remove a majority of the members of an entity's governing body. That power can arise, for example, from articles of incorporation or a shareholders' agreement. The second clause addresses the circumstances where a person is (i) subject to a majority of the risk of loss from the entity's activities, or (ii) entitled to receive a majority of the entity's residual returns. The second clause of the definition includes, among other circumstances, complex financial structures that do not have voting interests or a governing body in the traditional sense, such as special purpose entities. Although the definition of "control" operates independently of the accounting rules adopted by the U.S. accounting profession, it is consistent with the relevant generally accepted accounting principle (made effective in 2003) that governs when an entity must be included in consolidated financial statements.

3. Relevant Time

The definition of director's conflicting interest transaction requires that, except where he or she is a party, the director know of the transaction. It also requires that where not a party, the director know of the transaction either at the time it is brought before the corporation's board of directors or, if it is not brought before the corporation's board of directors (or a committee thereof), at the time the corporation (or an entity controlled by the corporation) becomes legally bound to consummate the transaction. Where the director lacks such knowledge, the risk to the corporation that the director's judgment might be improperly influenced, or the risk of unfair dealing by the director, is not present. In a corporation of significant size, routine transactions in the ordinary course of business, which typically involve decision making at lower management levels, normally will not be known to the director and, if that is the case, will be excluded from the "knowledge" requirement of the definition in subdivision (1)(ii) or (iii).

4. Material Financial Interest

The "interest" of a director or a related person in a transaction can be direct or indirect (*e.g.*, as an owner of an entity or a beneficiary of a trust or estate), but it must be financial for there to exist a "director's conflicting interest transaction." Thus, for example, an interest in a transaction between X Co. and a director's alma mater, or any other transaction involving X Co. and a party with which D might have emotional involvement but no financial interest, would not give rise to a director's conflicting interest transaction. Moreover, whether a financial interest is material does not turn on any assertion by the possibly conflicted director that the interest in question would not impair his or her objectivity if called upon to act on the authorization of the transaction. Instead, assuming a court challenge asserting the materiality of the financial interest, the standard calls upon the trier of fact to determine whether the objectivity of a reasonable director in similar circumstances would reasonably be expected to have been impaired by the financial interest when acting on the matter. Thus, the standard is objective, not subjective.

Under subdivision (1)(ii), at the relevant time a director must have knowledge of his or her financial interest in the transaction in addition to knowing about the transaction itself. As a practical matter, a director could not be influenced by a financial interest about which that director had no knowledge. For example, the possibly conflicted director might know about X Co.'s transaction with Y Co., but might not know that his or her money manager recently established a significant position in Y Co. stock for the director's portfolio. In such circumstances, the transaction with Y Co. would not give the director a "material financial interest", notwithstanding the portfolio investment's significance. Analytically, if the director did not know about the Y Co. portfolio investment, it could not reasonably be expected to impair the objectivity of that director's judgment.

Similarly, under subdivision (1)(iii), a director must know about his or her related person's financial interest in the transaction for the matter to give rise to a "material financial interest" under subdivision (4). If there is such knowledge and "interest" (*i.e.*, the financial interest could be expected to influence the director's judgment), then the matter involves a director's conflicting interest transaction under subdivision (1).

5. Related Person

Six categories of "related person" of the director are set out in subdivision (5). These categories are specific, exclusive and preemptive.

The first three categories involve closely related family, or near-family, individuals as specified in clauses (i) through (iii). The clauses are exclusive insofar as family relationships are concerned and include adoptive relationships. The references to a "spouse" include a common law spouse. Clause (iii) covers personal, as opposed to business, relationships; for example, clause (iii) does not cover a lessee.

Regarding the subcategories of persons described in clause (v) from the perspective of *X* Co., certain of *D*'s relationships with other entities and *D*'s fiduciary relationships are always a sensitive concern, separate and apart from whether *D* has a financial interest in the transaction. Clause (v) reflects the policy judgment that *D* cannot escape *D*'s legal obligation to act in the best interests of another person for whom *D* has such a relationship and, accordingly, that such a relationship (without regard to any financial interest on *D*'s part) should cause the relevant entity to have "related person" status.

The term "employer" as used in subdivision (5)(vi) is not separately defined but should be interpreted sensibly in light of the purpose of the subdivision. The relevant inquiry is whether *D*, because of an employment relationship with an employer who has a significant stake in the outcome of the transaction, is likely to be influenced to act in the interest of that employer rather than in the interest of *X* Co.

6. Fair to the Corporation

The term "fair" accords with traditional language in the case law, but for purposes of subchapter F it also has a special meaning. The transaction, viewed as a whole, must have been beneficial to the corporation, in addition to satisfying the traditional "fair price" and "fair dealing" concepts. In determining whether the transaction was beneficial, the consideration and other terms of the transaction and the process (including the conflicted director's dealings with the corporation) are relevant, but whether the transaction advanced the corporation's commercial interests is to be viewed "as a whole."

In considering the "fairness" of the transaction, the court will be required to consider not only the market fairness of the terms of the deal—whether it is comparable to what might have been obtainable in an arm's length transaction—but also (as the board would have been required to do) whether the transaction was one that was reasonably likely to yield favorable results (or reduce detrimental results). Thus, if a manufacturing company that lacks sufficient working capital allocates some of its scarce funds to purchase a sailing yacht owned by one of its directors, it will not be easy to persuade the court that the transaction was "fair" in the sense that it was reasonably made to further the business interests of the corporation. The facts that the price paid for the yacht was a "fair" market price, and that the full measure of disclosures made by the director is beyond challenge, may still not be enough to defend and uphold the transaction.

a. Consideration and other terms of the transaction

The fairness of the consideration and other transaction terms are to be judged at the relevant time. The relevant inquiry is whether the consideration paid or received by the corporation or the benefit expected to be realized by the corporation was adequate in relation to the obligations assumed or received or other consideration provided by or to the corporation. If the issue in a transaction is the "fairness" of a price, "fair" is not to be taken to imply that there is one single "fair" price, all others being "unfair." It is settled law that a "fair" price is any price within a range that an unrelated party might have been willing to pay or willing to accept, as the case may be, for the relevant property, asset, service or commitment, following a normal arm's-length business negotiation. The same approach applies not only to gauging the fairness of price, but also to the fairness evaluation of any other key term of the deal.

Although the "fair" criterion used to assess the consideration under section 8.61(b)(3) is also a range rather than a point, the width of that range may be narrower than would be the case in an arm's-length transaction. For example, the quality and completeness of disclosures, if any, made by the conflicted director that bear upon the consideration in question are relevant in determining whether the consideration paid or received by the corporation, although otherwise commercially reasonable, was "fair" for purposes of section 8.61(b)(3).

b. Process of decision and the director's conduct

In some circumstances, the behavior of the director having the conflicting interest may affect the finding and content of "fairness." Fair dealing requires that the director make required disclosure (per subdivision (7)) at the relevant time (per subdivision (3)) even if the director plays no role in arranging or negotiating the terms of the transaction. One illustration of unfair dealing is the director's failure to disclose fully the director's interest or hidden defects known to the director regarding the transaction. Another illustration would be the exertion by the director of improper pressure upon the other directors or other parties that might be involved with the transaction. Whether a transaction can be successfully challenged by reason of deficient or improper conduct, notwithstanding the fairness of the economic terms, will turn on the court's evaluation of the conduct and its impact on the transaction.

7. Required Disclosure

A critically important element of subchapter F's safe harbor procedures is that those acting for the corporation be able to make an informed judgment. In view of this requirement, subdivision (7) defines "required disclosure" to mean disclosure of all facts known to *D* about the subject of the transaction that a director free of the conflicting interest would reasonably believe to be material to the decision whether to proceed with the transaction. For example, if D knows that the land the corporation is proposing to buy from D is sinking into an abandoned coal mine, D must disclose not only D's interest in the transaction but also that the land is subsiding. As a director of X Co., D may not invoke caveat emptor. On the other hand, D does not have any obligation to reveal the price that D paid for the property ten years ago, or the fact that D inherited the property, because that information is not material to the board's evaluation of the property and its business decision whether to proceed with the transaction. Further, while material facts respecting the subject of the transaction must be disclosed, D is not required to reveal personal or subjective information that bears upon D's negotiating position (such as, for example, D's urgent need for cash, or the lowest price D would be willing to accept). This is true even though such information would be highly relevant to the corporation's decision making in the sense that, if the information were known to the corporation, it could enable the corporation to hold out for more favorable terms.

§ 8.61 Judicial Action

(a) A transaction effected or proposed to be effected by the corporation (or by an entity controlled by the corporation) may not be the subject of equitable relief, or give rise to an award of damages or other sanctions against a director of the corporation, in a proceeding by a shareholder or by or in the right of the corporation, on the ground that the director has an interest respecting the transaction, if it is not a director's conflicting interest transaction.

(b) A director's conflicting interest transaction may not be the subject of equitable relief, or give rise to an award of damages or other sanctions against a director of the corporation, in a proceeding by a shareholder or by or in the right of the corporation, on the ground that the director has an interest respecting the transaction, if:

   (1) directors' action respecting the transaction was taken in compliance with section 8.62 at any time; or

   (2) shareholders' action respecting the transaction was taken in compliance with section 8.63 at any time; or

   (3) the transaction, judged according to the circumstances at the relevant time, is established to have been fair to the corporation.

Official Comment

Section 8.61 is the operational section of subchapter F, as it prescribes the judicial consequences of the other sections.

Speaking generally:

(i) If the section 8.62 or section 8.63 procedures are complied with, or if it is established that at the relevant time a director's conflicting interest transaction was fair to the corporation, then a director's conflicting interest transaction is immune from attack on the ground of an interest of the director. However, the narrow scope of subchapter F must again be strongly emphasized; if the transaction is vulnerable to attack on some other ground, observance of subchapter F's procedures does not make it less so.

(ii) If a transaction is not a director's conflicting interest transaction, as defined in section 8.60(1), then the transaction may not be the subject of equitable relief or give rise to an award of damages or be made the basis of other sanction on the ground of an interest of a director, regardless of whether the transaction was approved under section 8.62 or 8.63. In that sense, subchapter F is specifically intended to be both comprehensive and exclusive.

(iii) If a director's conflicting interest transaction that was not at any time the subject of action taken in compliance with section 8.62 or section 8.63 is challenged on grounds of the director's conflicting interest, and is not shown to be fair to the corporation, then the court may take such remedial action as it considers appropriate under the applicable law of the jurisdiction.

1. Section 8.61(a)

As previously noted, section 8.61(a) makes clear that a transaction between a corporation and another person cannot be the subject of equitable relief, or give rise to an award of damages or other sanctions against a director, on the ground that the director has an interest respecting the transaction, unless the transaction falls within the bright-line definition of "director's conflicting interest transaction" in section 8.60. So, for example, a transaction will not constitute a director's conflicting interest transaction and, therefore, will not be subject to judicial review on the ground that a director had an interest in the transaction, where the transaction is made with a relative of a director who is not one of the relatives specified in section 8.60(5), or on the ground of an alleged interest other than a material financial interest, such as a financial interest of the director that is not material, as defined in section 8.60(4), or a nonfinancial interest. (As noted in the Introductory Comment, however, subchapter F does not apply to, and therefore does not preclude, a challenge to such a transaction based on grounds other than the director's interest.)

If there is reason to believe that the fairness of a transaction involving D could be questioned, D is well advised to subject the transaction to the safe harbor procedures of subchapter F. Sometimes, a director may be uncertain whether a particular person would be held to fall within a related person category, or whether the scale of the financial interest is material as defined in Section 8.60. In such circumstances, the obvious avenue to follow is to clear the matter with qualified directors under section 8.62 or with the holders of qualified shares under section 8.63. If it is later judicially determined that a conflicting interest in the challenged transaction did exist, the director will have safe harbor protection. It may be expected, therefore, that the procedures of section 8.62 (and, to a lesser extent, section 8.63) will probably be used for many transactions that may lie outside the sharp definitions of section 8.60—a result that is healthy and constructive.

It is important to stress that subchapter F deals only with "transactions." If a non-transactional corporate decision is challenged on the ground that *D* has a conflicting personal stake in it, subsection 8.61(a) is irrelevant.

2. Section 8.61(b)

Clause (1) of subsection (b) provides that if a director has a conflicting interest respecting a transaction, neither the transaction nor the director is legally vulnerable on the ground of the director's conflict if the procedures of section 8.62 have been properly followed. If board action under section 8.62(b)(1) is interposed as a defense in a proceeding challenging a director's conflicting interest transaction, the plaintiff then bears the burden of overcoming that defense under section 8.31.

Challenges to that board action may be based on a failure to meet the specific requirements of section 8.62 or to conform with general standards of director conduct. For example, a challenge addressed to section 8.62 compliance might question whether the acting directors were "qualified directors" or might dispute the quality and completeness of the disclosures made by *D* to the qualified directors. If such a challenge is successful, the board action is ineffective for purposes of subsection (b)(1) and both *D* and the transaction may be subject to the full range of remedies that might apply, absent the safe harbor, unless the fairness of the transaction can be established under subsection (b)(3). The fact that a transaction has been nominally passed through safe harbor procedures does not preclude a subsequent challenge based on any failure to meet the requirements of section 8.62. Recognizing the importance of traditional corporate procedures where the economic interests of a fellow director are concerned, a challenge to the effectiveness of board action for purposes of subsection (b)(1) might also assert that, while the conflicted director's conduct in connection with the process of approval by qualified directors may have been consistent with the statute's expectations, the qualified directors dealing with the matter did not act in good faith or on reasonable inquiry. The kind of relief that may be appropriate when qualified directors have approved a transaction but have not acted in good faith or have failed to become reasonably informed—and, again, where the fairness of the transaction has not been established under subsection (b)(3)—will depend heavily on the facts of the individual case; therefore, it must be largely a matter of sound judicial discretion.

Clause (2) of subsection (b) regarding shareholders' approval of the transaction is the matching piece to clause (1) regarding directors' approval.

The language "at any time" in clauses (1) and (2) of subsection (b) permits the directors or the shareholders to ratify a director's conflicting interest transaction after the fact for purposes of subchapter F. However, good corporate practice is to obtain appropriate approval prior to consummation of a director's conflicting interest transaction.

Clause (3) of subsection (b) provides that a director's conflicting interest transaction will be secure against the imposition of legal or equitable relief if it is established that, although neither directors' nor shareholders' action was taken in compliance with section 8.62 or 8.63, the transaction was fair to the corporation within the meaning of section 8.60(6). Under section 8.61(b)(3) the interested director has the burden of establishing that the transaction was fair.

* * *

Note on Directors' Compensation

Directors' fees and other forms of director compensation are typically set by the board and are specially authorized (though not regulated) by sections 8.11 and 8.57 of the Model Act. Although in the usual case a corporation's directors' compensation practices fall within normal patterns and their fairness can be readily established, they do involve a conflicting interest on the part of most if not all of the directors and, in a given case, may be abused. Therefore, while as a matter of practical necessity these practices will normally be generally accepted in principle, it must be kept in mind that board action on directors' compensation and benefits would be subject to judicial sanction if they are not favorably acted upon by shareholders pursuant to section 8.63 or if they are not in the circumstances fair to the corporation pursuant to section 8.61(b)(3).

§ 8.62 Directors' Action

(a) Directors' action respecting a director's conflicting interest transaction is effective for purposes of section 8.61(b)(1) if the transaction has been authorized by the affirmative vote of a majority (but no fewer than two) of the qualified directors who voted on the transaction, after required disclosure by the conflicted director to those qualified directors of information not already known by such qualified directors, or after modified disclosure in compliance with subsection (b), provided that:

(1) the qualified directors have deliberated and voted outside the presence of and without the participation by any other director; and

(2) where the action has been taken by a committee, all members of the committee were qualified directors, and either (i) the committee was composed of all the qualified directors on the board of directors or (ii) the members of the committee were appointed by the affirmative vote of a majority of the qualified directors on the board.

(b) Notwithstanding subsection (a), when a transaction is a director's conflicting interest transaction only because a related person described in clause (v) or clause (vi) of section 8.60(5) is a party to or has a material financial interest in the transaction, the conflicted director is not obligated to make required disclosure to the extent that the director reasonably believes that doing so would violate a duty imposed under law, a legally enforceable obligation of confidentiality, or a professional ethics rule, provided that the conflicted director discloses to the qualified directors voting on the transaction:

(1) all information required to be disclosed that is not so violative,

(2) the existence and nature of the director's conflicting interest, and

(3) the nature of the conflicted director's duty not to disclose the confidential information.

(c) A majority (but no fewer than two) of all the qualified directors on the board of directors, or on the committee, constitutes a quorum for purposes of action that complies with this section.

(d) Where directors' action under this section does not satisfy a quorum or voting requirement applicable to the authorization of the transaction by reason of the articles of incorporation, the bylaws or a provision of law, independent action to satisfy those authorization requirements must be taken by the board of directors or a committee, in which action directors who are not qualified directors may participate.

Official Comment

Section 8.62 provides the procedure for action by the board of directors or by a board committee under subchapter F. In the normal course this section, together with section 8.61(b), will be the key method for addressing directors' conflicting interest transactions. Any discussion of section 8.62 must be conducted in light of the overarching requirements that directors act in good faith and on reasonable inquiry. Director action that does not comply with those requirements, even if otherwise in compliance with section 8.62, will be subject to challenge and not be given effect under section 8.62. See the Official Comment to section 8.61(b).

1.   Section 8.62(a)

The safe harbor for directors' conflicting interest transactions will be effective under section 8.62 if and only if authorized by qualified directors. (For the definition of "qualified director," see section 1.43 and the related Official Comment.) Obviously safe harbor protection cannot be provided by fellow directors who themselves are not qualified directors; only qualified directors can do so under subsection (a). The definition of "qualified director" in section 1.43 excludes a conflicted director but its exclusions go significantly further, i.e., beyond the persons specified in the categories of section 8.60(5) for purposes of the "related person" definition. For example, if any familial or financial connection or employment or professional relationship with *D* would be likely to impair the objectivity of the director's judgment when participating in a vote on the transaction, that director would not be a qualified director.

Action by the board of directors is effective for purposes of section 8.62 if the transaction is approved by the affirmative vote of a majority (but not less than two) of the qualified directors on the board. Action may also be taken by a duly authorized committee of the board but, for the action to be effective, all members of the committee must be qualified directors and the committee must either be composed of all of the qualified directors on the board or must have been appointed by the affirmative vote of a majority of the qualified directors on the board. This requirement for effective committee action is intended to preclude the appointment as committee members of a favorably inclined minority from among all the qualified directors. Except to the limited extent found in subsection (b), authorization by the qualified directors acting on this matter must be preceded by required disclosure pursuant to subsection (a) followed by deliberation and voting outside the presence of, and without the participation by, any other director. Should there be more than one conflicted director interested in the transaction, the need for required disclosure would apply to each. After the qualified directors have had the opportunity to question a conflicted director about the material facts communicated about the transaction, action complying with subsection (a) may be taken at any time before or after the time it becomes a legal obligation. A written record of the qualified directors' deliberations and action is strongly encouraged.

2.   Section 8.62(b)

Subsection (b) is a special provision designed to accommodate, in a practical way, situations where a director who has a conflicting interest is not able to comply fully with the disclosure requirement of subsection (a) because of an extrinsic duty of confidentiality that such director reasonably believes to exist. The director may, for example, be prohibited from making full disclosure because of legal restrictions that happen to apply to the transaction (*e.g.*, grand jury seal or national security statute) or professional canon (*e.g.*, attorney-client privilege). The most frequent use of subsection (b), however, will likely involve common directors who find themselves in a position of dual fiduciary obligations that clash. If *D* is also a director of *Y Co.*, *D* may have acquired privileged information from one or both directorships relevant to a transaction between *X Co.* and *Y Co.*, that *D* cannot reveal to one without violating a fiduciary duty owed to the other. In such circumstances, subsection (b) enables the conflicting interest complication to be presented for consideration under subsection (a), and thereby enables *X Co.* (and *Y Co.*) and *D* to secure for the transaction the protection afforded by subchapter F even though *D* cannot, by reason of applicable law, confidentiality strictures or a professional ethics rule, make the full disclosure otherwise required.

To comply with subsection (b), *D* must (i) notify the qualified directors who are to vote on the transaction respecting the conflicting interest, (ii) disclose to them all information required to be disclosed that does not violate the duty not to disclose, as the case may be, to which *D* reasonably believes he or she is subject, and (iii) inform them of the nature of the duty (*e.g.*, that the duty arises out of an attorney-client privilege or out of a duty as a director of *Y Co.* that prevents *D* from making required disclosure as otherwise mandated by clause (ii) of section 8.60(7)). *D* must then play no personal role in the board's (or committee's) ultimate deliberations or action. The purpose of subsection (b) is to make it clear that the provisions of subchapter F may be employed to "safe harbor" a transaction in circumstances where a conflicted director cannot, because of enforced fiduciary silence, disclose all the known facts.* Of course, if *D* invokes subsection (b) and does not make required disclosure before leaving the meeting, the qualified directors may decline to act on the transaction out of concern that *D* knows (or may know) something they do not. On the other hand, if *D* is subject to an extrinsic duty of confidentiality but has no knowledge of material facts that should otherwise be disclosed, *D* would normally state just that and subsection (b) would be irrelevant. Having disclosed the existence and nature of the conflicting interest, *D* would thereby comply with section 8.60(7).

---

* A director could, of course, encounter the same problem of mandated silence with regard to any matter that comes before the board; that is, the problem of forced silence can arise in situations other than transactions involving a conflicting interest of a director. It could happen that at the same board meeting of *X Co.* at which *D* invokes § 8.62(b), another director who has absolutely no financial interest in the transaction might conclude that under local law he or she is bound to silence (because of attorney-client privilege, for example) and under general principles of sound director conduct would withdraw from participation in the board's deliberations and action.

While subchapter F explicitly contemplates that subsection (b) will apply to the frequently recurring situation where transacting corporations have common directors (or where a director of one party is an officer of the other), it should not otherwise be read as attempting to address the scope, or mandate the consequences, of various silence-privileges. That is a topic reserved for local law.

Subsection (b) is available to *D* if a transaction is a director's conflicting interest transaction only because a related person described in section 8.60(5)(v) or (vi) is a party to or has a material financial interest in the transaction. Its availability is so limited because in those instances a director owes a fiduciary duty to such a related person. If *D* or a related person of *D* other than a related person described in section 8.60(5)(v) or (vi) is a party to or has a material financial interest in the transaction, *D*'s only options are satisfying the required disclosure obligation on an unrestricted basis, abandoning the transaction, or accepting the risk of establishing fairness, under section 8.61(b)(3), if the transaction is challenged in a court proceeding.

Whenever a conflicted director proceeds in the manner provided in subsection (b), the other directors should recognize that the conflicted director may have information that in usual circumstances *D* would be required to reveal to the qualified directors who are acting on the transaction—information that could well indicate that the transaction would be either favorable or unfavorable for *X Co.*

3. Section 8.62(c)

Subsection (c) states the special quorum requirement for action by qualified directors to be effective under section 8.62. Obviously, conflicted directors are excluded. Also excluded are board members who, while not conflicted directors, are not eligible to be qualified directors. As stated in subsection (a), the qualified directors taking action respecting a director's conflicting interest transaction are to deliberate and vote outside the presence of, and without participation by, any other member of the board.

4. Section 8.62(d)

This subsection underscores the fact that the directors' voting procedures and requirements set forth in subsections (a) through (c) treat only the director's conflicting interest. A transaction authorized by qualified directors in accordance with subchapter F may still need to satisfy different voting or quorum requirements in order to achieve substantive approval of the transaction under other applicable statutory provisions or provisions contained in *X Co.*'s articles of incorporation or bylaws, and vice versa. Thus, in any case where the quorum and/or voting requirements for substantive approval of a transaction differ from the quorum and/or voting requirements for "safe harbor" protection under section 8.62, the directors may find it necessary to conduct (and record in the minutes of the proceedings) two separate votes—one for section 8.62 purposes and the other for substantive approval purposes.

§ 8.63 Shareholders' Action

(a) Shareholders' action respecting a director's conflicting interest transaction is effective for purposes of section 8.61(b)(2) if a majority of the votes cast by the holders of all qualified shares are in favor of the transaction after (1) notice to shareholders describing the action to be taken respecting the transaction, (2) provision to the corporation of the information referred to in subsection (b), and (3) communication to the shareholders entitled to vote on the transaction of the information that is the subject of required disclosure, to the extent the information is not known by them.

(b) A director who has a conflicting interest respecting the transaction shall, before the shareholders' vote, inform the secretary or other officer or agent of the corporation authorized to tabulate votes, in writing, of the number of shares that the director knows are not qualified shares under subsection (c), and the identity of the holders of those shares.

(c) For purposes of this section: (1) "holder" means and "held by" refers to shares held by both a record shareholder (as defined in section 13.01(7)) and a beneficial shareholder (as defined in section 13.01(2)); and (2) "qualified shares" means all shares entitled to be voted with respect to the transaction except for shares that the secretary or other officer or agent of the corporation authorized to tabulate votes either knows, or under subsection (b) is notified, are held by (A) a director who has a conflicting interest respecting the transaction or (B) a related person of the director (excluding a person described in clause (vi) of Section 8.60(5)).

(d) A majority of the votes entitled to be cast by the holders of all qualified shares constitutes a quorum for purposes of compliance with this section. Subject to the provisions of subsection (e), shareholders' action that otherwise complies with this section is not affected by the presence of holders, or by the voting, of shares that are not qualified shares.

(e) If a shareholders' vote does not comply with subsection (a) solely because of a director's failure to comply with subsection (b), and if the director establishes that the failure was not intended to influence and did not in fact determine the outcome of the vote, the court may take such action respecting the transaction and the director, and may give such effect, if any, to the shareholders' vote, as the court considers appropriate in the circumstances.

(f) Where shareholders' action under this section does not satisfy a quorum or voting requirement applicable to the authorization of the transaction by reason of the articles of incorporation, the bylaws or a provision of law, independent action to satisfy those authorization requirements must be taken by the shareholders, in which action shares that are not qualified shares may participate.

Official Comment

Section 8.63 provides the machinery for shareholders' action that confers safe harbor protection for a director's conflicting interest transaction, just as section 8.62 provides the machinery for directors' action that confers subchapter F safe harbor protection for such a transaction.

1. Section 8.63(a)

Subsection (a) specifies the procedure required to confer effective safe harbor protection for a director's conflicting interest transaction through a vote of shareholders. In advance of the vote, three steps must be taken: (1) shareholders must be given timely and adequate notice describing the transaction; (2) D must disclose the information called for in subsection (b); and (3) disclosure must be made to the shareholders entitled to vote, as required by section 8.60(7). In the case of smaller closely-held corporations, this disclosure shall be presented by the director directly to the shareholders gathered at the meeting place where the vote is to be held, or provided in writing to the secretary of the corporation for transmittal with the notice of the meeting. In the case of larger publicly held corporations where proxies are being solicited, the disclosure is to be made by the director to those responsible for preparing the proxy materials, for inclusion therein. If the holders of a majority of all qualified shares (as defined in subsection (b)) entitled to vote on the matter vote favorably, the safe harbor provision of section 8.61(b)(2) becomes effective. Action that complies with subsection (a) may be taken at any time, before or after the time when the corporation becomes legally obligated to complete the transaction.

Section 8.63 does not contain a "limited disclosure" provision that is comparable to section 8.62(b). Thus, the safe harbor protection of subchapter F is not available through shareholder action under section 8.63 in a case where D either remains silent or makes less than required disclosure because of an extrinsic duty of confidentiality. This omission is intentional. While the section 8.62(b) procedure is workable in the collegial setting of the boardroom, that is far less likely in the case of action by the shareholder body, especially in large corporations where there is heavy reliance upon the proxy mechanic. Unlike the dynamic that would normally occur in the boardroom, in most situations no opportunity exists for shareholders to quiz D about the confidentiality duty and to discuss the implications of acting without the full benefit of D's knowledge about the conflict transaction. In a case of a closely held corporation where section 8.63 procedures are followed, but with D acting in a way that would be permitted by section 8.62(b), a court could attach significance to a favorable shareholder vote in evaluating the fairness of the transaction to the corporation.

2. Section 8.63(b)

In many circumstances, the secretary or other vote tabulator of *XCo.* will have no way to know which of *XCo.'s* outstanding shares should be excluded from the tabulation. Subsection (b) (together with subsection (c)) therefore obligates a director who has a conflicting interest respecting the transaction, as a prerequisite to safe harbor protection by shareholder action, to inform the secretary, or other officer or agent authorized to tabulate votes, of the number and holders of shares known to be held by the director or by a related person described in clauses (i) through (v) of section 8.60(5).

If the tabulator of votes knows, or is notified under subsection (b), that particular shares should be excluded but for some reason fails to exclude them from the count and their inclusion in the vote does not affect its outcome, the shareholders' vote will stand. If the improper inclusion determines the outcome, the shareholders' vote fails because it does not comply with subsection (a). But see subsection (e) as to cases where the notification under subsection (b) is defective but not determinative of the outcome of the vote.

3. Section 8.63(c)

Under subsection (a), only "qualified shares" may be counted in the vote for purposes of safe harbor action under section 8.61(b)(2). Subsection (b) defines "qualified shares" to exclude all shares that, before the vote, the secretary or other tabulator of the vote knows, or is notified under subsection (b), are held by the director who has the conflicting interest, or by any specified related person of that director.

The definition of "qualified shares" excludes shares held by *D* or a "related person" as defined in the first five categories of section 8.60(5). That definition does not exclude shares held by entities or persons described in clause (vi) of section 8.60(5), i.e., a person that is, or is an entity that is controlled by, an employer of *D*. If *D* is an employee of *YCo.*, that fact does not prevent *YCo.* from exercising its usual rights to vote any shares it may hold in *XCo.* *D* may be unaware of, and would not necessarily monitor, whether his or her employer holds *XCo.* shares. Moreover, *D* will typically have no control over his or her employer and how it may vote its *XCo.* shares.

4. Section 8.63(e)

If *D* did not provide the information required under subsection (d), on its face the shareholders' action is not in compliance with subsection (a) and *D* has no safe harbor under subsection (a). In the absence of that safe harbor, *D* can be put to the burden of establishing the fairness of the transaction under section 8.61(b)(3).

That result is proper where *D's* failure to inform was determinative of the vote results or, worse, was part of a deliberate effort on *D's* part to influence the outcome. But if *D's* omission was essentially an act of negligence, if the number of unreported shares if voted would not have been determinative of the outcome of the vote, and if the omission was not motivated by *D's* effort to influence the integrity of the voting process, then the court should be free to fashion an appropriate response to the situation in light of all the considerations at the time of its decision. The court should not, in the circumstances, be automatically forced by the mechanics of subchapter F to a lengthy and retrospective trial on "fairness." Subsection (e) grants the court that discretion in those circumstances and permits it to accord such effect, if any, to the shareholders' vote, or to grant such relief respecting the transaction or *D*, as the court may find appropriate.

Despite the presumption of regularity customarily accorded the secretary's record, a plaintiff may go behind the secretary's record for purposes of subsection (e).

5.   Section 8.63(f)

This subsection underscores that the shareholders' voting procedures and requirements set forth in subsections (a) through (e) treat only the director's conflicting interest. A transaction that receives a shareholders' vote that complies with subchapter F may well fail to achieve a different vote or quorum that may be required for substantive approval of the transaction under other applicable statutory provisions or provisions contained in *XCo.*'s articles of incorporation or bylaws, and vice versa. Thus, in any case where the quorum and/or voting requirements for substantive approval of a transaction differ from the quorum and/ or voting requirements for "safe harbor" protection under section 8.63, the corporation may find it necessary to conduct (and record in the minutes of the proceedings) two separate shareholder votes—one for section 8.63 purposes and the other for substantive approval purposes (or, if appropriate, conduct two separate tabulations of one vote).

§ 8.70   Business Opportunities

(a) A director's taking advantage, directly or indirectly, of a business opportunity may not be the subject of equitable relief, or give rise to an award of damages or other sanctions against the director, in a proceeding by or in the right of the corporation on the ground that such opportunity should have first been offered to the corporation, if before becoming legally obligated respecting the opportunity the director brings it to the attention of the corporation and:

(1) action by qualified directors disclaiming the corporation's interest in the opportunity is taken in compliance with the procedures set forth in section 8.62, as if the decision being made concerned a director's conflicting interest transaction, or

(2) shareholders' action disclaiming the corporation's interest in the opportunity is taken in compliance with the procedures set forth in section 8.63, as if the decision being made concerned a director's conflicting interest transaction; except that, rather than making "required disclosure" as defined in section 8.60, in each case the director shall have made prior disclosure to those acting on behalf of the corporation of all material facts concerning the business opportunity that are then known to the director.

(b) In any proceeding seeking equitable relief or other remedies, based upon an alleged improper taking advantage of a business opportunity by a director, the fact that the director did not employ the procedure described in subsection (a) before taking advantage of the opportunity shall not create an inference that the opportunity should have been first presented to the corporation or alter the burden of proof otherwise applicable to establish that the director breached a duty to the corporation in the circumstances.

Official Comment

Section 8.70 provides a safe harbor for a director weighing possible involvement with a prospective business opportunity that might constitute a "corporate opportunity." By action of the Board of Directors or shareholders of the corporation under section 8.70, the director can receive a disclaimer of the corporation's interest in the matter before proceeding with such involvement. In the alternative, the corporation may (i) decline to disclaim its interest, (ii) delay a decision respecting granting a disclaimer pending receipt from the director of additional information (or for any other reason), or (iii) attach conditions to the disclaimer it grants under section 8.70(a). The safe harbor granted to the director pertains only to the specific opportunity and does not have broader application, such as to a line of business or a geographic area.

The common law doctrine of "corporate opportunity" has long been recognized as a core part of the director's duty of loyalty. The doctrine stands for the proposition that the corporation has a right prior to that of its director to act on certain business opportunities that come to the attention of the director. In such situations, a director who acts on the opportunity for the benefit of the director or another without having first presented it to the corporation can be held to have "usurped" or "intercepted" a right of the corporation. A defendant director who is found by a court to have violated the duty of loyalty in this regard is subject to damages or an array of equitable remedies, including injunction, disgorgement or the imposition of a constructive trust in favor of the corporation. While the doctrine's concept is easily described, whether it will be found to apply in a given case depends on the facts and circumstances of the particular situation and is thus frequently unpredictable. Ultimately, the doctrine requires the court to balance the corporation's legitimate expectations that its directors will faithfully promote its best interests against the legitimate right of individual directors to pursue their own economic interests in other contexts and venues.

In response to this difficult balancing task, courts have developed several (sometimes overlapping) principles to cabin the doctrine. Although the principles applied have varied from state to state, courts have sought to determine, for example, whether a disputed opportunity presented a business opportunity that was:

—the same as, or similar to, the corporation's current or planned business activities ("line of business" test);

—one that the corporation had already formulated plans or taken steps to acquire for its own use ("expectancy" test);

—developed by the director through the use of the corporation's property, personnel or proprietary information ("appropriation" test); or

—presented to the director with the explicit or implicit expectation that the director would present it to the corporation for its consideration—or—in contrast, one that initially came to the director's attention in the director's individual capacity unrelated to the director's corporate role ("capacity" test).

Finally, in recognition that the corporation need not pursue every business opportunity of which it becomes aware, an opportunity coming within the doctrine's criteria that has been properly presented to and declined by the corporation may then be pursued by the presenting director without breach of the director's duty of loyalty.

The fact intensive nature of the corporate opportunity doctrine resists statutory definition. Instead, subchapter G employs the broader notion of "business opportunity" that encompasses any opportunity, without regard to whether it would come within the judicial definition of a "corporate opportunity" as it may have been developed by courts in a jurisdiction. When properly employed, it provides a safe-harbor mechanism enabling a director to pursue an opportunity for his or her own account or for the benefit of another free of possible challenge claiming conflict with the director's duty of loyalty on the ground that the opportunity should first have been offered to the corporation. Section 8.70 is modeled on the safe-harbor and approval procedures of subchapter F pertaining to directors' conflicting interest transactions with, however, some modifications necessary to accommodate differences in the two topics.

1. Section 8.70(a)

Subsection (a) describes the safe harbor available to a director who elects to subject a business opportunity, regardless of whether the opportunity would be classified as a "corporate opportunity," to the disclosure and approval procedures set forth therein. The safe harbor provided is as broad as that provided for a director's conflicting interest transaction in section 8.61: if the director makes required disclosure of the facts specified and the corporation's interest in the opportunity is disclaimed by action by qualified directors under subsection (a)(1) or shareholder action under subsection (a)(2), the director has foreclosed any claimed breach of the duty of loyalty and may not be subject to equitable relief, damages or other sanctions if the director thereafter takes the opportunity for his or her own account or for the benefit of another person. As a general proposition, disclaimer by action by qualified directors under subsection (a)(1) must meet all of the requirements provided in section 8.62 with respect to a director's conflicting interest transaction and disclaimer by shareholder action under subsection (a)(2) must likewise comply with all of the requirements for shareholder action under section 8.63. Note, however, two important differences.

In contrast to director or shareholder action under sections 8.62 and 8.63, which may be taken at any time, section 8.70(a) requires that the director must present the opportunity and secure action by qualified directors or shareholder action disclaiming it *before* acting on the opportunity. The safe-harbor concept contemplates that the corporation's decision maker will have full freedom of action in deciding whether the corporation should take over a proffered opportunity or elect to disclaim the corporation's interest in it. If the interested director could seek ratification after acting on the opportunity, the option of taking over the opportunity would, in most cases, in reality be foreclosed and the corporation's decision maker would be limited to denying ratification or blessing the interested director's past conduct with a disclaimer. In sum, the safe harbor's benefit is available only when the corporation can entertain the opportunity in a fully objective way.

The second difference also involves procedure. Instead of employing section 8.60(7)'s definition of "required disclosure" that is incorporated in sections 8.62 and 8.63, section 8.70(a) requires the alternative disclosure to those acting for the corporation of "all material facts concerning the business opportunity that are then known to the director." As a technical matter, section 8.60(7) calls for, in part, disclosure of "the existence and nature of the director's conflicting interest"—that information is not only non-existent but irrelevant for purposes of subsection (a). But there is another consideration justifying replacement of the section 8.60(7) definition. In the case of the director's conflicting interest transaction, the director proposing to enter into a transaction with the corporation has presumably completed due diligence and made an in-

899

formed judgment respecting the matter; accordingly, that interested director is in a position to disclose "all facts known to the director respecting the subject matter of the transaction that a director free of such conflicting interest would reasonably believe to be material in deciding whether to proceed with the transaction." The interested director, placing himself or herself in the independent director's position, should be able to deal comfortably with the objective materiality standard. In contrast, the director proffering a business opportunity will often not have undertaken due diligence and made an informed judgment to pursue the opportunity following a corporate disclaimer. Thus, the disclosure obligation of subsection (a) requires only that the director reveal all material facts concerning the business opportunity that, at the time when disclosure is made, are known to the director. The safe-harbor procedure shields the director even if a material fact regarding the business opportunity is not disclosed, so long as the proffering director had no knowledge of such fact. In sum, the disclosure requirement for subsection (a) must be and should be different from that called for by subchapter F's provisions.

2. Section 8.70(b)

Subsection (b) reflects a fundamental difference between the coverage of subchapters F and G. Because subchapter F provides an exclusive definition of "director's conflicting interest transaction," any transaction meeting the definition that is not approved in accordance with the provisions of subchapter F is not entitled to its safe harbor. Unless the interested director can, upon challenge, establish the transaction's fairness, the director's conduct is presumptively actionable and subject to the full range of remedies that might otherwise be awarded by a court. In contrast, the concept of "business opportunity" under section 8.70 is not defined but is intended to be broader than what might be regarded as an actionable "corporate opportunity." This approach recognizes that, given the vagueness of the corporate opportunity doctrine, a director might be inclined to seek safe-harbor protection under section 8.70 before pursuing an opportunity that might or might not at a later point be subject to challenge as a "corporate opportunity." By the same token, a director might conclude that a business opportunity is not a "corporate opportunity" under applicable law and choose to pursue it without seeking a disclaimer by the corporation under section 8.70. Accordingly, subsection (b) provides that a director's decision not to employ the procedures of section 8.70(a) neither creates a negative inference nor alters the burden of proof in any subsequent proceeding seeking damages or equitable relief based upon an alleged improper taking of a "corporate opportunity."

Chapter 9

DOMESTICATION AND CONVERSION

INTRODUCTORY OFFICIAL COMMENT TO CHAPTER 9

This chapter provides a series of procedures by which a domestic business corporation may become a different form of entity or, conversely, an entity that is not a domestic business corporation may become a domestic business corporation. These various types of procedures are as follows:

- Domestication. The procedures in subchapter 9B permit a corporation to change its state of incorporation, thus allowing a domestic business corporation to become a foreign business corporation or a foreign business corporation to become a domestic business corporation.

- Nonprofit Conversion. The procedures in subchapter 9C permit a domestic business corporation to become either a domestic nonprofit corporation or a foreign nonprofit corporation.

- Foreign Nonprofit Domestication and Conversion. The procedures in subchapter 9D permit a foreign nonprofit corporation to become a domestic business corporation.

- Entity Conversion. The procedures in subchapter 9E permit a domestic business corporation to become a domestic or foreign unincorporated entity, and also permit a domestic or foreign unincorporated entity to become a domestic business corporation.

Each of the foregoing transactions could previously be accomplished by a merger under chapter 11 with a wholly owned subsidiary of the appropriate type. An important purpose of this chapter is to permit the transactions to be accomplished directly.

The provisions of this chapter apply only if a domestic business corporation is present either immediately before or immediately after a transaction. Some states may wish to generalize the provisions of this chapter so that they are not limited to transactions involving a domestic business corporation, for example, to permit a domestic limited partnership to become a domestic limited liability company. The Model Entity Transactions Act prepared by the Ad Hoc Committee on Entity Rationalization of the Section of Business Law is such a generalized statute.

The procedures of this chapter do not permit the combination of two or more entities into a single entity. Transactions of that type must continue to be conducted under chapters 11 and 12.

Subchapter A

PRELIMINARY PROVISIONS

§ 9.01   Excluded Transactions

This chapter may not be used to effect a transaction that:

(1) [*converts an insurance company organized on the mutual principle to one organized on a stock-share basis*];

(2)

(3)

Official Comment

The purpose of this section is to prohibit certain transactions from being effectuated under chapter 9. A state should use this section to list all the situations in which the state has enacted specific legislation governing the conversion of domestic business corporations that are of a particular type or that do business in a regulated industry to any other form of corporation or to an unincorporated entity. A mutual to stock conversion of an insurance company has been listed in section 9.01(1) as one example of such a transaction.

The Official Comment to section 9.30 notes that subchapter 9C has been limited to transactions in which a domestic business corporation converts to a domestic or foreign nonprofit corporation, but suggests that a state may wish to consider broadening the scope of subchapter 9C to authorize conversions of nonprofit corporations to business corporations if it does not have a separate nonprofit corporation law. If a state chooses to include conversions of nonprofit corporations, consideration should be given to also listing in this section sensitive or controversial transactions where the entity involved is not-for-profit corporation before the transaction, such as the conversion of Blue Cross and Blue Shield plans to for-profit status.

§ 9.02   Required Approvals [*Optional*]

(a) If a domestic or foreign business corporation or eligible entity may not be a party to a merger without the approval of the [*attorney general*], the [*department of banking*], the [*department of insurance*] or the [*public utility commission*], the corporation or eligible entity shall not be a party to a transaction under this chapter without the prior written approval of that agency.

(b) Property held in trust or for charitable purposes under the laws of this state by a domestic or foreign eligible entity shall not, by any transaction under this chapter, be diverted from the objects for which it was donated, granted or devised, unless and until the eligible entity obtains an order of [*court*] [*the attorney general*] specifying the disposition of the property to the extent required by and pursuant to [*cite state statutory cy pres or other nondiversion statute*].

Official Comment

Section 9.02(a) is an optional provision that should be considered in states where corporations or other entities that conduct regulated activities such as banking, insurance or the provision of public utility services are incorporated or organized under general laws instead of under special laws applicable only to entities conducting the regulated activity. Because the provisions of chapter 9 are new, there is a possibility that existing state laws that require regulatory approval of mergers by those types of entities may not be worded in a fashion that will include the transactions authorized by this chapter. If this section is used, the list of agencies should be conformed to the laws of the enacting state.

The purpose of section 9.02(a) is to ensure that transactions under chapter 9 will be subject to the same regulatory approval as mergers, in contrast to section 9.01 which is an outright prohibition on conducting certain transactions under chapter 9. This section is based on whether a merger by a regulated entity requires prior approval because the transactions authorized by this chapter may be effectuated indirectly under chapter 11 by just establishing a wholly-owned subsidiary of the desired type and then merging into it. The list of agencies in subsection (a) should be conformed to the laws of the enacting state. The consequences of violating subsection (a) will be the same as in the case of a merger consummated without the required approval.

Nonprofit corporations and unincorporated entities may participate in transactions under this chapter. As in the case of laws regulating particular industries, a state's laws governing the nondiversion of charitable and trust property to other uses may not be worded in a fashion that will include all of the transactions authorized by this chapter. To prevent the procedures in this chapter from being used to avoid restrictions on the use of property held by nonprofit entities, section 9.02(b) requires approval of the effect of transactions under this chapter by the appropriate arm of government having supervision of nonprofit entities.

Subchapter B

DOMESTICATION

§ 9.20 Domestication

(a) A foreign business corporation may become a domestic business corporation only if the domestication is permitted by the organic law of the foreign corporation.

(b) A domestic business corporation may become a foreign business corporation if the domestication is permitted by the laws of the foreign jurisdiction. Regardless of whether the laws of the foreign jurisdiction require the adoption of a plan of domestication, the domestication shall be approved by the adoption by the corporation of a plan of domestication in the manner provided in this subchapter.

(c) The plan of domestication must include:

  (1) a statement of the jurisdiction in which the corporation is to be domesticated;

(2) the terms and conditions of the domestication;

(3) the manner and basis of reclassifying the shares of the corporation following its domestication into shares or other securities, obligations, rights to acquire shares or other securities, cash, other property, or any combination of the foregoing; and

(4) any desired amendments to the articles of incorporation of the corporation following its domestication.

(d) The plan of domestication may also include a provision that the plan may be amended prior to filing the document required by the laws of this state or the other jurisdiction to consummate the domestication, except that subsequent to approval of the plan by the shareholders the plan may not be amended to change:

(1) the amount or kind of shares or other securities, obligations, rights to acquire shares or other securities, cash, or other property to be received by the shareholders under the plan;

(2) the articles of incorporation as they will be in effect immediately following the domestication, except for changes permitted by section 10.05 or by comparable provisions of the laws of the other jurisdiction; or

(3) any of the other terms or conditions of the plan if the change would adversely affect any of the shareholders in any material respect.

(e) Terms of a plan of domestication may be made dependent upon facts objectively ascertainable outside the plan in accordance with section 1.20(k).

(f) If any debt security, note or similar evidence of indebtedness for money borrowed, whether secured or unsecured, or a contract of any kind, issued, incurred or executed by a domestic business corporation before [*the effective date of this subchapter*] contains a provision applying to a merger of the corporation and the document does not refer to a domestication of the corporation, the provision shall be deemed to apply to a domestication of the corporation until such time as the provision is amended subsequent to that date.

Official Comment

1. Applicability

This subchapter authorizes a foreign business corporation to become a domestic business corporation. It also authorizes a domestic business corporation to become a foreign business corporation. In each case, the domestication is authorized only if the laws of the foreign jurisdiction permit the domestication. Whether and on what terms a foreign business corporation is authorized to domesticate in this state are issues governed by the laws of the foreign jurisdiction, not by this subchapter.

A foreign corporation is not required to have in effect a valid certificate of authority under chapter 15 in order to domesticate in this state.

2. Terms and Conditions of Domestication

This subchapter imposes virtually no restrictions or limitations on the terms and conditions of a domestication, except for those set forth in section 9.20(d) concerning provisions in a plan of domestication for amendment of the plan after it has been approved by the shareholders. Shares of a domestic business corporation that domesticates in another jurisdiction may be reclassified into shares or other securities, obligations, rights to acquire shares or other securities, cash or other property. The capitalization of the corporation may be restructured in the domestication, and its articles of incorporation may be amended by the articles of domestication in any way deemed appropriate. When a foreign business corporation domesticates in this state, the laws of the foreign jurisdiction determine which of the foregoing actions may be taken.

Although this subchapter imposes virtually no restrictions or limitations on the terms and conditions of a domestication, section 9.20(c) requires that the terms and conditions be set forth in the plan of domestication. The plan of domestication is not required to be publicly filed, and the articles of domestication that are filed with the secretary of state by a foreign corporation domesticating in this state are not required to include a plan of domestication. See section 9.22. Similarly, articles of charter surrender that are filed with the secretary of state by a domestic business corporation domesticating in another jurisdiction are not required to include a plan of domestication. See section 9.23.

The list in section 9.20(c) of required provisions in a plan of domestication is not exhaustive and the plan may include any other provisions that may be desired.

3. Amendments of Articles of Incorporation

A corporation's articles of incorporation may be amended in a domestication. Under section 9.20(c)(4), a plan of domestication of a domestic business corporation proposing to domesticate in a foreign jurisdiction may include amendments to the articles of incorporation and should include, at a minimum, any amendments required to conform the articles of incorporation to the requirements for articles of incorporation of a corporation incorporated in the foreign jurisdiction. It is assumed that the foreign jurisdiction will give effect to the articles of incorporation as amended to the same extent that it would if the articles had been independently amended before the domestication.

The laws of the foreign jurisdiction determine whether and to what extent a foreign corporation may amend its articles of incorporation when domesticating in this state. Following the domestication of a foreign corporation in this state, of course, its articles of incorporation may be amended under Chapter 10.

4. Adoption and Approval; Abandonment

The domestication of a domestic business corporation in a foreign jurisdiction must be adopted and approved as provided in section 9.21. Under section 9.25, the board of directors of a domestic business corporation may abandon a domestication before its effective date even if the plan of domestication has already been approved by the corporation's shareholders.

5. Appraisal Rights

A shareholder of a domestic business corporation that adopts and approves a plan of domestication has appraisal rights if the shareholder does not receive shares in the foreign corporation resulting from the domestication that have terms as favorable to the shareholder in all material respects, and represent at least the same percentage interest of the total voting rights of the outstanding shares of the corporation, as the shares held by the shareholder before the domestication. See sections 9.24(b) and 13.02(a)(6).

6. Transitional rule

Because the concept of domestication is new, a person contracting with a corporation or loaning it money who drafted and negotiated special rights relating to the transaction before the enactment of this subchapter should not be charged with the consequences of not having dealt with the concept of domestication in the context of those special rights. Section 9.20(e) accordingly provides a transitional rule that is intended to such special rights. If, for example, a corporation is a party to a contract that provides that the corporation cannot participate in a merger without the consent of the other party to the contract, the requirement to obtain the consent of the other party will also apply to the domestication of the corporation in another jurisdiction. If the corporation fails to obtain the consent, the result will be that the other party will have the same rights it would have if the corporation were to participate in a merger without the required consent.

The purpose of section 9.20(e) is to protect the third party to a contract with the corporation, and section 9.20(e) should not be applied in such a way as to impair unconstitutionally the third party's contract. As applied to the corporation, section 9.20(e) is an exercise of the reserved power of the state legislature set forth in section 1.02.

The transitional rule in section 9.20(e) ceases to apply at such time as the provision of the agreement or debt instrument giving rise to the special rights is first amended after the effective date of this subchapter because at that time the provision may be amended to address expressly a domestication of the corporation.

A similar transitional rule governing the application to a domestication of special voting rights of directors and shareholders and other internal corporate procedures is found in section 9.21(7).

§ 9.21 Action on a Plan of Domestication

In the case of a domestication of a domestic business corporation in a foreign jurisdiction:

(1) The plan of domestication must be adopted by the board of directors.

(2) After adopting the plan of domestication the board of directors must submit the plan to the shareholders for their approval. The board of directors must also transmit to the shareholders a recommendation that the shareholders approve the plan, unless the board of directors makes a determination that because of conflicts of interest or other special circumstances it should not make such a recommendation, in which case the board of directors must transmit to the shareholders the basis for that determination.

(3) The board of directors may condition its submission of the plan of domestication to the shareholders on any basis.

(4) If the approval of the shareholders is to be given at a meeting, the corporation must notify each shareholder, whether or not entitled to vote, of the meeting of shareholders at which the plan of domestication is to be submitted for approval. The notice must state that the purpose, or one of the purposes, of the meeting is to consider the plan and must contain or be accompanied by a copy or summary of the plan. The notice shall include or be accompanied by a copy of the articles of incorporation as they will be in effect immediately after the domestication.

(5) Unless the articles of incorporation, or the board of directors acting pursuant to paragraph (3), requires a greater vote or a greater number of votes to be present, approval of the plan of domestication requires the approval of the shareholders at a meeting at which a quorum exists consisting of at least a majority of the votes entitled to be cast on the plan, and, if any class or series of shares is entitled to vote as a separate group on the plan, the approval of each such separate voting group at a meeting at which a quorum of the voting group exists consisting of at least a majority of the votes entitled to be cast on the domestication by that voting group.

(6) Separate voting by voting groups is required by each class or series of shares that:

(i) are to be reclassified under the plan of domestication into other securities, obligations, rights to acquire shares or other securities, cash, other property, or any combination of the foregoing;

(ii) would be entitled to vote as a separate group on a provision of the plan that, if contained in a proposed amendment to articles of incorporation, would require action by separate voting groups under section 10.04; or

(iii) is entitled under the articles of incorporation to vote as a voting group to approve an amendment of the articles.

(7) If any provision of the articles of incorporation, bylaws or an agreement to which any of the directors or shareholders are parties, adopted or entered into before [*the effective date of this subchapter*], applies to a merger of the corporation and that document does not refer to a domestication of the corporation, the provision shall be deemed to apply to a domestication of the corporation until such time as the provision is amended subsequent to that date.

Official Comment

1. In General

This section sets forth the rules for adoption and approval of a plan of domestication of a domestic business corporation in a foreign jurisdiction. The manner in which the domestication of a foreign business corporation in this state must be adopted and approved will be controlled by the laws of the foreign jurisdiction. The provisions of this section follow generally the rules in chapter 11 for adoption and approval of a plan of merger or share exchange.

A plan of domestication must be adopted by the board of directors. Although section 9.21(2) permits the board to refrain from making a recommendation to the shareholders that they approve the plan, that does not change the underlying requirement that the board first adopt the plan before it is submitted to the shareholders. Approval by the shareholders of a plan of domestication is always required.

2. Voting by Separate Groups

Section 9.21(6) provides that a class or series has a right to vote on a plan of domestication as a separate voting group if, as part of the domestication, the class or series would be reclassified into other securities, interests, obligations, rights to acquire shares or other securities, cash or other property. A class or series also is entitled to vote as a separate voting group if the class or series would be entitled to vote as a separate group on a provision in the plan that, if contained in an amendment to the articles of incorporation, would require approval by that class or series under section 10.04. In this latter case, a class or series will be entitled to vote as a separate voting group if the terms of that class or series are being changed, or if the shares of that class or series are being reclassified into shares of any other class or series. It is not intended that immaterial changes in the language of the articles of incorporation made to conform to the usage of the laws of the foreign jurisdiction will alone create an entitlement to vote as a separate group.

Under section 10.04, and therefore under section 9.21(6), if a change that requires voting by separate voting groups affects two or more classes or two or more series in the same or a substantially similar way, the relevant classes or series will vote together, rather than separately, on the change. For the mechanics of voting where voting by voting groups is required under section 9.21(6), see sections 7.25 and 7.26.

If a domestication would amend the articles of incorporation to change the voting requirements on future amendments of the articles, the transaction must also be approved by the vote required by section 7.27.

3. Quorum and Voting

Section 9.21(5) provides that approval of a plan of domestication requires approval of the shareholders at a meeting at which there exists a quorum consisting of a majority of the votes entitled to be cast on the plan. Section 9.21(5) also provides that if any class or series of shares are entitled to vote as a separate group on the plan, the approval of each such separate group must be given at a meeting at which there exists a quorum consisting of at least a majority of the votes entitled to be cast on the plan by that class or series. If a quorum is present, then under sections 7.25 and 7.26 the plan will be approved if more votes are cast in favor of the plan than against it by each voting group entitled to vote on the plan.

In lieu of approval at a shareholders' meeting, approval can be given by the consent of all the shareholders entitled to vote on the domestication, under the procedures set forth in section 7.04.

4. Transitional rule

Because the concept of domestication is new, persons who drafted and negotiated special rights for directors or shareholders before the enactment of this subchapter should not be charged with the consequences of not having dealt with the concept of domestication in the context of those special rights. Section 9.21(7) accordingly provides a transitional rule that is intended to protect such special rights. Other documents, in addition to the articles of incorporation and bylaws, that may contain such special rights include shareholders agreements, voting trust agreements, vote pooling agreements or other similar arrangements. If, for example, the articles of incorporation provide that the corporation cannot participate in a merger without a supermajority vote of the shareholders, that supermajority requirement will also apply to the domestication of the corporation in another jurisdiction.

The purpose of section 9.21(7) is to protect persons who negotiated special rights for directors or shareholders whether in a contract with the corporation or in the articles of incorporation or bylaws, and section 9.21(7) should not be applied in such a way as to impair unconstitutionally the rights of any party to a contract with the corporation. As applied to the corporation, section 9.21(7) is an exercise of the reserved power of the state legislature set forth in section 1.02.

The transitional rule in section 9.21(7) ceases to apply at such time as the provision of the articles of incorporation, bylaws or agreement giving rise to the special rights is first amended after the effective date of this subchapter because at that time the provision may be amended to address expressly a domestication of the corporation.

A similar transitional rule with regard to the application to a domestication of special contractual rights of third parties is found in section 9.20(e).

§ 9.22   Articles of Domestication

(a) After the domestication of a foreign business corporation has been authorized as required by the laws of the foreign jurisdiction, articles of domestication shall be executed by any officer or other duly authorized representative. The articles shall set forth:

    (1) the name of the corporation immediately before the filing of the articles of domestication and, if that name is unavailable for use in this state or the corporation desires to change its name in connection with the domestication, a name that satisfies the requirements of section 4.01;

    (2) the jurisdiction of incorporation of the corporation immediately before the filing of the articles of domestication and the date the corporation was incorporated in that jurisdiction; and

    (3) a statement that the domestication of the corporation in this state was duly authorized as required by the laws of the jurisdiction in which the corporation was incorporated immediately before its domestication in this state.

(b) The articles of domestication shall either contain all of the provisions that section 2.02(a) requires to be set forth in articles of incorporation and any other desired provisions that section 2.02(b) permits to be included in articles of incorporation, or shall have attached articles of incorporation. In either case, provisions that would not be required to be included in restated articles of incorporation may be omitted.

(c) The articles of domestication shall be delivered to the secretary of state for filing, and shall take effect at the effective time provided in section 1.23.

(d) If the foreign corporation is authorized to transact business in this state under chapter 15, its certificate of authority shall be cancelled automatically on the effective date of its domestication.

Official Comment

The filing of articles of domestication under this section makes the domestication of a foreign corporation in this state a matter of public record. It also makes of public record the articles of incorporation of the corporation as a corporation of this state. If the foreign corporation is authorized to transact business in this state, section 9.22(d) automatically cancels its certificate of authority.

This section applies only when a foreign corporation is domesticating in this state. When a domestic business corporation is domesticating in a foreign jurisdiction, the filing required in the foreign jurisdiction is determined by the laws of that jurisdiction. When a domestic business corporation domesticates in a foreign jurisdiction, the filing required in this state is described in section 9.23.

The filing requirements for articles of domestication are set forth in section 1.20. Under section 1.23, a document may specify a delayed effective time and date, and if it does so the document becomes effective at the time and date specified, except that a delayed effective date may not be later than the 90th day after the date the document is filed. To avoid any question about a gap in the continuity of its existence, it is recommended that a corporation use a delayed effective date provision in its domestication filings in both this state and the foreign jurisdiction, or otherwise coordinate those filings, so that the filings become effective at the same time.

As section 9.20(c)(4) makes clear, a corporation may amend its articles of incorporation in connection with a domestication. Because the articles of domestication will either contain or have attached to them an integrated set of articles of incorporation, the articles of domestication will have the effect of restating the articles of incorporation.

§ 9.23 Surrender of Charter Upon Domestication

(a) Whenever a domestic business corporation has adopted and approved, in the manner required by this subchapter, a plan of domestication providing for the corporation to be domesticated in a foreign jurisdiction, articles of charter surrender shall be executed on behalf of the corporation by any officer or other duly authorized representative. The articles of charter surrender shall set forth:

(1) the name of the corporation;

   (2) a statement that the articles of charter surrender are being filed in connection with the domestication of the corporation in a foreign jurisdiction;

   (3) a statement that the domestication was duly approved by the shareholders and, if voting by any separate voting group was required, by each such separate voting group, in the manner required by this Act and the articles of incorporation;

   (4) the corporation's new jurisdiction of incorporation.

(b) The articles of charter surrender shall be delivered by the corporation to the secretary of state for filing. The articles of charter surrender shall take effect on the effective time provided in section 1.23.

Official Comment

The filing of articles of charter surrender makes the domestication of the corporation in its new jurisdiction of incorporation a matter of public record in this state. It also terminates the status of the corporation as a corporation incorporated under the laws of this state. Once the articles of charter surrender have become effective, the corporation will no longer be in good standing in this state. The corporation may, however, apply for a certificate of authority as a foreign corporation under subchapter 15A.

Where a foreign corporation domesticates in this state, the filing required to terminate its status as a corporation incorporated under the laws of the foreign jurisdiction is determined by the laws of that jurisdiction.

The filing requirements for articles of charter surrender are set forth in sections 1.20 and 1.23. Under section 1.23, a document may specify a delayed effective time and date, and if it does so the document becomes effective at the time and date specified, except that a delayed effective date may not be later than the 90th day after the date the document is filed. To avoid any question about a gap in the continuity of its existence, it is recommended that a corporation use a delayed effective date provision in its domestication filings in both this state and the foreign jurisdiction, or otherwise coordinate those filings, so that the filings become effective at the same time.

§ 9.24 Effect of Domestication

(a) When a domestication becomes effective:

   (1) the title to all real and personal property, both tangible and intangible, of the corporation remains in the corporation without reversion or impairment;

   (2) the liabilities of the corporation remain the liabilities of the corporation;

(3) an action or proceeding pending against the corporation continues against the corporation as if the domestication had not occurred;

(4) the articles of domestication, or the articles of incorporation attached to the articles of domestication, constitute the articles of incorporation of a foreign corporation domesticating in this state;

(5) the shares of the corporation are reclassified into shares, other securities, obligations, rights to acquire shares or other securities, or into cash or other property in accordance with the terms of the domestication, and the shareholders are entitled only to the rights provided by those terms and to any appraisal rights they may have under the organic law of the domesticating corporation; and

(6) the corporation is deemed to:

(i) be incorporated under and subject to the organic law of the domesticated corporation for all purposes;

(ii) be the same corporation without interruption as the domesticating corporation; and

(iii) have been incorporated on the date the domesticating corporation was originally incorporated.

(b) When a domestication of a domestic business corporation in a foreign jurisdiction becomes effective, the foreign business corporation is deemed to:

(1) appoint the secretary of state as its agent for service of process in a proceeding to enforce the rights of shareholders who exercise appraisal rights in connection with the domestication; and

(2) agree that it will promptly pay the amount, if any, to which such shareholders are entitled under chapter 13.

(c) The owner liability of a shareholder in a foreign corporation that is domesticated in this state shall be as follows:

(1) The domestication does not discharge any owner liability under the laws of the foreign jurisdiction to the extent any such owner liability arose before the effective time of the articles of domestication.

(2) The shareholder shall not have owner liability under the laws of the foreign jurisdiction for any debt, obligation or liability of the corporation that arises after the effective time of the articles of domestication.

(3) The provisions of the laws of the foreign jurisdiction shall continue to apply to the collection or discharge of any owner

liability preserved by paragraph (1), as if the domestication had not occurred.

(4) The shareholder shall have whatever rights of contribution from other shareholders are provided by the laws of the foreign jurisdiction with respect to any owner liability preserved by paragraph (1), as if the domestication had not occurred.

[*(d) A shareholder who becomes subject to owner liability for some or all of the debts, obligations or liabilities of the corporation as a result of its domestication in this state shall have owner liability only for those debts, obligations or liabilities of the corporation that arise after the effective time of the articles of domestication.*]

Official Comment

When a corporation is domesticated in this state under this subchapter, the corporation becomes a domestic business corporation with the same status as if it had been originally incorporated under this Act. Thus, the domesticated corporation will have all of the powers, privileges and rights granted to corporations originally incorporated in this state and will be subject to all of the duties, liabilities and limitations imposed on domestic business corporations. Except as provided in section 9.24(b), the effect of domesticating a corporation of this state in a foreign jurisdiction is governed by the laws of the foreign jurisdiction. See section 9.20(b).

A domestication is not a conveyance, transfer or assignment. It does not give rise to claims of reverter or impairment of title based on a prohibited conveyance, transfer or assignment. Nor does it give rise to a claim that a contract with the corporation is no longer in effect on the ground of nonassignability, unless the contract specifically provides that it does not survive a domestication.

Section 9.24(a)(1)–(3) and (b) are similar to section 11.07(a)(3)–(5) and (c) with respect to the effects of a merger. Although section 9.24(a)(1)–(3) would be implied by the general rule stated in section 9.24(a)(6) even if not stated expressly, those rules have been included to avoid any question as to whether a different result was intended.

The rule in section 9.24(a)(6)(iii) that the date of incorporation of the foreign corporation remains its date of incorporation after the corporation has been domesticated in this state is a specific application of the general rule in section 9.24(a)(6)(ii). The date of incorporation is required by section 9.22(a)(2) to be set forth in the articles of domestication.

One of the continuing liabilities of the corporation following its domestication in a foreign jurisdiction is the obligation to its shareholders who exercise appraisal rights to pay them the amount, if any, to which they are entitled under chapter 13.

Section 9.24(c) preserves liability only for owner liabilities to the extent they arise before the domestication. Owner liability is not preserved for subsequent changes in an underlying liability, regardless of whether a change is voluntary or involuntary.

Section 9.24(d) is an optional provision that will not be needed in most states. It should be included only when the statutory laws of a state impose personal liability on the shareholders of a corporation, for example, for unpaid wages owed to employees of the corporation.

§ 9.25 Abandonment of a Domestication

(a) Unless otherwise provided in a plan of domestication of a domestic business corporation, after the plan has been adopted and approved as required by this subchapter, and at any time before the domestication has become effective, it may be abandoned by the board of directors without action by the shareholders.

(b) If a domestication is abandoned under subsection (a) after articles of charter surrender have been filed with the secretary of state but before the domestication has become effective, a statement that the domestication has been abandoned in accordance with this section, executed by an officer or other duly authorized representative, shall be delivered to the secretary of state for filing prior to the effective date of the domestication. The statement shall take effect upon filing and the domestication shall be deemed abandoned and shall not become effective.

(c) If the domestication of a foreign business corporation in this state is abandoned in accordance with the laws of the foreign jurisdiction after articles of domestication have been filed with the secretary of state, a statement that the domestication has been abandoned, executed by an officer or other duly authorized representative, shall be delivered to the secretary of state for filing. The statement shall take effect upon filing and the domestication shall be deemed abandoned and shall not become effective.

Official Comment

Unless otherwise provided in a plan of domestication, a domestic business corporation proposing to domesticate in another jurisdiction may abandon the transaction without shareholder approval, even though the domestication has been previously approved by the shareholders. Whether or not the domestication of a foreign business corporation in this state may be abandoned is determined by the laws of the foreign jurisdiction.

Subchapter C

NONPROFIT CONVERSION

§ 9.30   Nonprofit Conversion

(a) A domestic business corporation may become a domestic nonprofit corporation pursuant to a plan of nonprofit conversion.

(b) A domestic business corporation may become a foreign nonprofit corporation if the nonprofit conversion is permitted by the laws of the foreign jurisdiction. Regardless of whether the laws of the foreign jurisdiction require the adoption of a plan of nonprofit conversion, the foreign nonprofit conversion shall be approved by the adoption by the domestic business corporation of a plan of nonprofit conversion in the manner provided in this subchapter.

(c) The plan of nonprofit conversion must include:

   (1) the terms and conditions of the conversion;

   (2) the manner and basis of reclassifying the shares of the corporation following its conversion into memberships, if any, or securities, obligations, rights to acquire memberships or securities, cash, other property, or any combination of the foregoing;

   (3) any desired amendments to the articles of incorporation of the corporation following its conversion; and

   (4) if the domestic business corporation is to be converted to a foreign nonprofit corporation, a statement of the jurisdiction in which the corporation will be incorporated after the conversion.

(d) The plan of nonprofit conversion may also include a provision that the plan may be amended prior to filing articles of nonprofit conversion, except that subsequent to approval of the plan by the shareholders the plan may not be amended to change:

   (1) the amount or kind of memberships or securities, obligations, rights to acquire memberships or securities, cash, or other property to be received by the shareholders under the plan;

   (2) the articles of incorporation as they will be in effect immediately following the conversion, except for changes permitted by section 10.05; or

   (3) any of the other terms or conditions of the plan if the change would adversely affect any of the shareholders in any material respect.

(e) Terms of a plan of nonprofit conversion may be made dependent upon facts objectively ascertainable outside the plan in accordance with section 1.20(k).

(f) If any debt security, note or similar evidence of indebtedness for money borrowed, whether secured or unsecured, or a contract of any kind, issued, incurred or executed by a domestic business corporation before [*the effective date of this subchapter*] contains a provision applying to a merger of the corporation and the document does not refer to a nonprofit conversion of the corporation, the provision shall be deemed to apply to a nonprofit conversion of the corporation until such time as the provision is amended subsequent to that date.

Official Comment

1. Applicability

This subchapter provides a procedure for a domestic business corporation to change its status from for-profit to not-for-profit and thus become a domestic nonprofit corporation. It is anticipated that a counterpart to this subchapter will be added to the Model Nonprofit Corporation Act which will provide a similar procedure for a nonprofit corporation to become a domestic business corporation subject to this Act by changing its status from not-for-profit to for-profit. In states that do not have a separate nonprofit corporation law, the provisions of this subchapter may be generalized to also permit nonprofit corporations (often referred to in such states as nonstock corporations) to acquire for-profit status.

This subchapter also provides a procedure for a domestic business corporation to become a foreign nonprofit corporation, which is in effect a combination of a domestication and a nonprofit conversion. However, section 9.30(b) permits a domestic business corporation to become a foreign nonprofit corporation only if the laws of the foreign jurisdiction permit the transaction.

This subchapter does not provide a procedure for a foreign business corporation to become a domestic nonprofit corporation because it is anticipated that such a procedure will be added to the Model Nonprofit Corporation Act. However, a foreign business corporation can achieve the same result by first domesticating in this state pursuant to subchapter 9B and then converting to a nonprofit corporation under this subchapter.

A separate procedure is provided in Subchapter 9D for a foreign nonprofit corporation to become a domestic business corporation.

2. Terms and Conditions of Nonprofit Conversion

This subchapter imposes virtually no restrictions or limitations on the terms and conditions of a nonprofit conversion, except for those set forth in section 9.30(d) concerning provisions in a plan of nonprofit conversion for amendment of the plan after it has been approved by the shareholders. Shares of a domestic business corporation that converts to a nonprofit corporation may be reclassified into memberships or securities, obligations, rights to acquire memberships or securities, cash or other property. The articles of incorporation of the converting business corporation will need to be amended to eliminate the provisions on its capital stock, and may be amended by the articles of nonprofit conversion in any other way deemed appropriate so long as the amended articles satisfy the requirements for articles of incorporation of a nonprofit corporation.

Although this subchapter imposes virtually no restrictions or limitations on the terms and conditions of a nonprofit conversion, section 9.30(c) requires that the terms and conditions be set forth in the plan of nonprofit conversion. The plan of nonprofit conversion is not required to be publicly filed, and the articles of nonprofit conversion that are filed with the secretary of state when a domestic business corporation converts to a domestic nonprofit corporation are not required to include a plan of nonprofit conversion. See section 9.32. Similarly, articles of charter surrender that are filed with the secretary of state by a domestic business corporation converting to a foreign nonprofit corporation are not required to include a plan of nonprofit conversion. See section 9.33.

The list in section 9.30(c) of required provisions in a plan of nonprofit conversion is not exhaustive and the plan may include any other provisions that may be desired.

3. Amendments of Articles of Incorporation

A corporation's articles of incorporation will need to be amended in its conversion to a nonprofit corporation so that the articles satisfy the requirements for articles of a nonprofit corporation. See section 9.32(b). Similarly, where a domestic business corporation converts to a foreign nonprofit corporation, the articles of incorporation will need to be amended to conform to the law of the foreign jurisdiction on the contents of articles of incorporation for a nonprofit corporation.

4. Adoption and Approval; Abandonment

The conversion of a domestic business corporation to a nonprofit corporation must be adopted and approved as provided in section 9.31. Under section 9.35, the board of directors of a domestic business corporation may abandon a conversion to nonprofit status before its effective date even if the plan of nonprofit conversion has already been approved by the corporation's shareholders.

5. Appraisal Rights

Shareholders of a domestic business corporation that adopts and approves a plan of nonprofit conversion have appraisal rights. See sections 9.34(b) and 13.02(a)(7).

6. Transitional rule

Because the concept of nonprofit conversion is new, a person contracting with a corporation or loaning it money who drafted and negotiated special rights relating to the transaction before the enactment of this subchapter should not be charged with the consequences of not having dealt with the concept of nonprofit conversion in the context of those special rights. Section 9.30(e) accordingly provides a transitional rule that is intended to protect such special rights. If, for example, a corporation is a party to a contract that provides that the corporation cannot participate in a merger without the consent of the other party to the contract, the requirement to obtain the consent of the other party will also apply to the conversion of the corporation to a domestic or foreign nonprofit corporation. If the corporation fails to obtain the consent, the result will be that the other party will have the same rights it would have if the corporation were to participate in a merger without the required consent.

The purpose of section 9.30(e) is to protect the third party to a contract with the corporation, and section 9.30(e) should not be applied in such a way as to impair unconstitutionally the third party's contract. As applied to the corporation, section 9.30(e) is an exercise of the reserved power of the state legislature set forth in section 1.02.

The transitional rule in section 9.30(e) ceases to apply at such time as the provision of the agreement or debt instrument giving rise to the special rights is first amended after the effective date of this subchapter because at that time the provision may be amended to address expressly a nonprofit conversion of the corporation.

A similar transitional rule governing the application to a nonprofit conversion of special voting rights of directors and shareholders and other internal corporate procedures is found in section 9.31(6).

§ 9.31 Action on a Plan of Nonprofit Conversion

In the case of a conversion of a domestic business corporation to a domestic or foreign nonprofit corporation:

(1) The plan of nonprofit conversion must be adopted by the board of directors.

(2) After adopting the plan of nonprofit conversion, the board of directors must submit the plan to the shareholders for their approval. The board of directors must also transmit to the shareholders a recommendation that the shareholders approve the plan, unless the board of directors makes a determination that because of conflicts of interest or other special circumstances it should not make such a recommendation, in which case the board of directors must transmit to the shareholders the basis for that determination.

(3) The board of directors may condition its submission of the plan of nonprofit conversion to the shareholders on any basis.

(4) If the approval of the shareholders is to be given at a meeting, the corporation must notify each shareholder of the meeting of shareholders at which the plan of nonprofit conversion is to be submitted for approval. The notice must state that the purpose, or one of the purposes, of the meeting is to consider the plan and must contain or be accompanied by a copy or summary of the plan. The notice shall include or be accompanied by a copy of the articles of incorporation as they will be in effect immediately after the nonprofit conversion.

(5) Unless the articles of incorporation, or the board of directors acting pursuant to paragraph (3), require a greater vote or a greater number of votes to be present, approval of the plan of nonprofit conversion requires the approval of each class or series of shares of the corporation voting as a separate voting group at a meeting at which a quorum of the voting group exists consisting of at least a majority of the votes entitled to be cast on the nonprofit conversion by that voting group.

(6) If any provision of the articles of incorporation, bylaws or an agreement to which any of the directors or shareholders are parties, adopted or entered into before [*the effective date of this subchapter*], applies to a merger of the corporation and the document does not refer to a nonprofit conversion of the corporation, the provision shall be deemed to apply to a nonprofit conversion of the corporation until such time as the provision is amended subsequent to that date.

Official Comment

1. In General

This section sets forth the rules for adoption and approval of a plan of nonprofit conversion of a domestic business corporation to a domestic or foreign nonprofit corporation.

A plan of nonprofit conversion must be adopted by the board of directors. Although section 9.31(2) permits the board to refrain from making a recommendation to the shareholders that they approve the plan, that does not change the underlying requirement that the board first adopt the plan before it is submitted to the shareholders. Approval by the shareholders of a plan of nonprofit conversion is always required.

2. Quorum and Voting

Section 9.31(5) provides that if the corporation has more than one class or series of shares, approval of a nonprofit conversion requires the approval of each class or series voting as a separate voting group at a meeting at which there exists a quorum consisting of at least a majority of the votes entitled to be cast on the plan by that class or series. If a quorum is present, then under sections 7.25 and 7.26 the plan will be approved if more votes are cast in favor of the plan than against it by each voting group entitled to vote on the plan. If the shares of a corporation are not divided into two or more classes or series, all of the shares together will constitute a single class for purposes of section 9.31(5).

In lieu of approval at a shareholders' meeting, approval can be given by the consent of all the shareholders entitled to vote on the conversion, under the procedures set forth in section 7.04.

3. Transitional rule

Because the concept of nonprofit conversion is new, persons who drafted and negotiated special rights for directors or shareholders before the enactment of this subchapter should not be charged with the consequences of not having dealt with the concept of nonprofit conversion in the context of those special rights. Section 9.31(6) accordingly provides a transitional rule that is intended to protect such special rights. Other documents, in addition to the articles of incorporation and bylaws, that may contain such special rights include shareholders agreements, voting trust agreements, vote pooling agreements or other similar arrangements. If, for example, the articles of incorporation provide that the corporation cannot participate in a merger without a supermajority vote of the shareholders, that supermajority requirement will also apply to the conversion of the corporation to a domestic or foreign nonprofit corporation.

The purpose of section 9.31(6) is to protect persons who negotiated special rights for directors or shareholders whether in a contract with the corporation or in the articles of incorporation or bylaws, and section 9.31(6) should not be applied in such a way as to impair unconstitutionally the rights of any party to a contract with the corporation. As applied to the corporation, section 9.31(6) is an exercise of the reserved power of the state legislature set forth in section 1.02.

The transitional rule in section 9.31(6) ceases to apply at such time as the provision of the articles of incorporation, bylaws or agreement giving rise to the special rights is first amended after the effective date of this subchapter because at that time the provision may be amended to address expressly a nonprofit conversion of the corporation.

A similar transitional rule with regard to the application to a nonprofit conversion of special contractual rights of third parties is found in section 9.30(e).

§ 9.32 Articles of Nonprofit Conversion

(a) After a plan of nonprofit conversion providing for the conversion of a domestic business corporation to a domestic nonprofit corporation has been adopted and approved as required by this Act, articles of nonprofit conversion shall be executed on behalf of the corporation by any officer or other duly authorized representative. The articles shall set forth:

(1) the name of the corporation immediately before the filing of the articles of nonprofit conversion and if that name does not satisfy the requirements of [*the Model Nonprofit Corporation Act*], or the corporation desires to change its name in connection with the conversion, a name that satisfies the requirements of [*the Model Nonprofit Corporation Act*];

(2) a statement that the plan of nonprofit conversion was duly approved by the shareholders in the manner required by this Act and the articles of incorporation.

(b) The articles of nonprofit conversion shall either contain all of the provisions that [*the Model Nonprofit Corporation Act*] requires to be set forth in articles of incorporation of a domestic nonprofit corporation and any other desired provisions permitted by [*the Model Nonprofit Corporation Act*], or shall have attached articles of incorporation that satisfy the requirements of [*the Model Nonprofit Corporation Act*]. In either case, provisions that would not be required to be included in restated articles of incorporation of a domestic nonprofit corporation may be omitted.

(c) The articles of nonprofit conversion shall be delivered to the secretary of state for filing, and shall take effect at the effective time provided in section 1.23.

Official Comment

The filing of articles of nonprofit conversion makes the conversion of a domestic business corporation to a domestic nonprofit corporation a matter of public record. Where a domestic business corporation is converting to a foreign nonprofit corporation, the filing required in the foreign jurisdiction is determined by the laws of that jurisdiction. The filing required in this state when a domestic business corporation converts to a foreign nonprofit corporation is described in section 9.33.

The filing requirements for articles of nonprofit conversion are set forth in section 1.20. Under section 1.23, a document may specify a delayed effective time and date, and if it does so the document becomes effective at the time and date specified, except that a delayed effective date may not be later than the 90th day after the date the document is filed.

The articles of incorporation that must be included in or attached to the articles of nonprofit conversion will satisfy the requirements of [*the Model Nonprofit Corporation Act*] for incorporating a nonprofit corporation.

This section and section 9.34(a)(6) assume that all nonprofit corporations are incorporated under the same law. If that is not the case, appropriate changes must be made to this section and section 9.34(a)(6) so that the type of nonprofit corporation that will result from the conversion is made clear.

§ 9.33 Surrender of Charter Upon Foreign Nonprofit Conversion

(a) Whenever a domestic business corporation has adopted and approved, in the manner required by this subchapter, a plan of nonprofit conversion providing for the corporation to be converted to a foreign nonprofit corporation, articles of charter surrender shall be executed on behalf of the corporation by any officer or other duly authorized representative. The articles of charter surrender shall set forth:

   (1) the name of the corporation;

   (2) a statement that the articles of charter surrender are being filed in connection with the conversion of the corporation to a foreign nonprofit corporation;

   (3) a statement that the foreign nonprofit conversion was duly approved by the shareholders in the manner required by this Act and the articles of incorporation;

   (4) the corporation's new jurisdiction of incorporation.

(b) The articles of charter surrender shall be delivered by the corporation to the secretary of state for filing. The articles of charter surrender shall take effect on the effective time provided in section 1.23.

Official Comment

The filing of articles of charter surrender makes the conversion of the domestic business corporation to a foreign nonprofit corporation in its new jurisdiction of incorporation a matter of public record in this state. It also terminates the status of the corporation as a corporation incorporated under the laws of this state. Once the articles of charter surrender have become effective, the corporation will no longer be in good standing in this state. The corporation may, however, apply for a certificate of authority as a foreign nonprofit corporation under [*subchapter 15A of the Model Nonprofit Corporation Act*].

The filing requirements for articles of charter surrender are set forth in sections 1.20 and 1.23. Under section 1.23, a document may specify a delayed effective time and date, and if it does so the document becomes effective at the time and date specified, except that a delayed effective date may not be later than the 90th day after the date the document is filed. To avoid any question about a gap in the continuity of its existence, it is recommended that a corporation use a delayed effective date provision in its nonprofit conversion filings in both this state and the foreign jurisdiction, or otherwise coordinate those filings, so that the filings become effective at the same time.

§ 9.34   Effect of Nonprofit Conversion

(a) When a conversion of a domestic business corporation to a domestic or foreign nonprofit corporation becomes effective:

   (1) the title to all real and personal property, both tangible and intangible, of the corporation remains in the corporation without reversion or impairment;

   (2) the liabilities of the corporation remain the liabilities of the corporation;

   (3) an action or proceeding pending against the corporation continues against the corporation as if the conversion had not occurred;

   (4) the articles of incorporation of the domestic or foreign nonprofit corporation become effective;

   (5) the shares of the corporation are reclassified into memberships, securities, obligations, rights to acquire memberships or securities, or into cash or other property in accordance with the plan of conversion, and the shareholders are entitled only to the rights provided in the plan of nonprofit conversion or to any rights they may have under chapter 13; and

   (6) the corporation is deemed to:

      (i) be a domestic or foreign nonprofit corporation for all purposes;

      (ii) be the same corporation without interruption as the business corporation; and

      (iii) have been incorporated on the date that it was originally incorporated as a domestic business corporation.

(b) When a conversion of a domestic business corporation to a foreign nonprofit corporation becomes effective, the foreign nonprofit corporation is deemed to:

   (1) appoint the secretary of state as its agent for service of process in a proceeding to enforce the rights of shareholders who exercise appraisal rights in connection with the conversion; and

   (2) agree that it will promptly pay the amount, if any, to which such shareholders are entitled under chapter 13.

[(c) *The owner liability of a shareholder in a domestic business corporation that converts to a domestic nonprofit corporation shall be as follows:*

(1) *The conversion does not discharge any owner liability of the shareholder as a shareholder of the business corporation to the extent any such owner liability arose before the effective time of the articles of nonprofit conversion.*

(2) *The shareholder shall not have owner liability for any debt, obligation or liability of the nonprofit corporation that arises after the effective time of the articles of nonprofit conversion.*

(3) *The laws of this state shall continue to apply to the collection or discharge of any owner liability preserved by paragraph (1), as if the conversion had not occurred.*

(4) *The shareholder shall have whatever rights of contribution from other shareholders are provided by the laws of this state with respect to any owner liability preserved by paragraph (1), as if the conversion had not occurred.*

(d) *A shareholder who becomes subject to owner liability for some or all of the debts, obligations or liabilities of the nonprofit corporation shall have owner liability only for those debts, obligations or liabilities of the nonprofit corporation that arise after the effective time of the articles of nonprofit conversion.]*

Official Comment

When a corporation is converted under this subchapter, the corporation becomes a domestic nonprofit corporation with the same status as if it had been originally incorporated under [*the Model Nonprofit Corporation Act*]. Thus, the converted corporation will have all of the powers, privileges and rights granted to nonprofit corporations originally incorporated as such in this state and will be subject to all of the duties, liabilities and limitations imposed on domestic nonprofit corporations.

A nonprofit conversion is not a conveyance, transfer or assignment. It does not give rise to claims of reverter or impairment of title based on a prohibited conveyance, transfer or assignment. Nor does it give rise to a claim that a contract with the corporation is no longer in effect on the ground of nonassignability, unless the contract specifically provides that it does not survive a conversion.

Section 9.34(a)(1)–(3) are similar to section 11.07(a)(3)–(5) with respect to the effects of a merger. Although section 9.34(a)(1)–(3) would be implied by the general rule stated in section 9.34(a)(6) even if not stated expressly, those rules have been included to avoid any question as to whether a different result was intended.

The rule in section 9.34(a)(6)(iii) that the date of incorporation of the corporation remains its date of incorporation after the corporation has been converted is a specific application of the general rule in section 9.34(a)(6)(ii). The date of incorporation is already a matter of public record in this state as a result of the original incorporation of the corporation.

One of the continuing liabilities of the corporation following its conversion to nonprofit status is the obligation to its shareholders who exercise appraisal rights to pay them the amount, if any, to which they are entitled under chapter 13.

Section 9.34(c) and (d) are optional provisions that will not be needed in most states. Those provisions should be included only when the statutory laws of a state impose some form of personal liability on the members of a nonprofit corporation that is not imposed on shareholders of a business corporation, or the reverse. Section 9.34(c) preserves liability only for owner liabilities to the extent they arise before the conversion. Owner liability is not preserved for subsequent changes in an underlying liability, regardless of whether a change is voluntary or involuntary.

§ 9.35 Abandonment of a Nonprofit Conversion

(a) Unless otherwise provided in a plan of nonprofit conversion of a domestic business corporation, after the plan has been adopted and approved as required by this subchapter, and at any time before the nonprofit conversion has become effective, it may be abandoned by the board of directors without action by the shareholders.

(b) If a nonprofit conversion is abandoned under subsection (a) after articles of nonprofit conversion or articles of charter surrender have been filed with the secretary of state but before the nonprofit conversion has become effective, a statement that the nonprofit conversion has been abandoned in accordance with this section, executed by an officer or other duly authorized representative, shall be delivered to the secretary of state for filing prior to the effective date of the nonprofit conversion. The statement shall take effect upon filing and the nonprofit conversion shall be deemed abandoned and shall not become effective.

Official Comment

Unless otherwise provided in a plan of nonprofit conversion, a domestic business corporation proposing to convert to nonprofit status may abandon the transaction without shareholder approval, even though the conversion has been previously approved by the shareholders.

Subchapter E

ENTITY CONVERSION

§ 9.50 Entity Conversion Authorized; Definitions

(a) A domestic business corporation may become a domestic unincorporated entity pursuant to a plan of entity conversion.

(b) A domestic business corporation may become a foreign unincorporated entity if the entity conversion is permitted by the laws of the foreign jurisdiction.

(c) A domestic unincorporated entity may become a domestic business corporation. If the organic law of a domestic unincorporated entity does not provide procedures for the approval of an entity conversion, the conversion shall be adopted and approved, and the entity conversion effectuated, in the same manner as a merger of the unincorporated entity, and its interest holders shall be entitled to appraisal rights if appraisal rights are available upon any type of merger under the organic law of the unincorporated entity. If the organic law of a domestic unincorporated entity does not provide procedures for the approval of either an entity conversion or a merger, a plan of entity conversion shall be adopted and approved, the entity conversion effectuated, and appraisal rights exercised, in accordance with the procedures in this subchapter and chapter 13. Without limiting the provisions of this subsection, a domestic unincorporated entity whose organic law does not provide procedures for the approval of an entity conversion shall be subject to subsection (e) and section 9.52(7). For purposes of applying this subchapter and chapter 13:

   (1) the unincorporated entity, its interest holders, interests and organic documents taken together, shall be deemed to be a domestic business corporation, shareholders, shares and articles of incorporation, respectively and vice versa, as the context may require; and

   (2) if the business and affairs of the unincorporated entity are managed by a group of persons that is not identical to the interest holders, that group shall be deemed to be the board of directors.

(d) A foreign unincorporated entity may become a domestic business corporation if the organic law of the foreign unincorporated entity authorizes it to become a corporation in another jurisdiction.

(e) If any debt security, note or similar evidence of indebtedness for money borrowed, whether secured or unsecured, or a contract of any kind, issued, incurred or executed by a domestic business corporation before [*the effective date of this subchapter*], applies to a merger of the corporation and the document does not refer to an entity conversion of the corporation, the provision shall be deemed to apply to an entity conversion of the corporation until such time as the provision is amended subsequent to that date.

(f) As used in this subchapter:

   (1) "Converting entity" means the domestic business corporation or domestic unincorporated entity that adopts a plan of entity

927

conversion or the foreign unincorporated entity converting to a domestic business corporation.

(2) "Surviving entity" means the corporation or unincorporated entity as it continues in existence immediately after consummation of an entity conversion pursuant to this subchapter.

Official Comment

1. Scope of subchapter

Subject to certain restrictions which are discussed below, this subchapter authorizes the following types of conversion:

1. a domestic business corporation to a domestic unincorporated entity,

2. a domestic business corporation to a foreign unincorporated entity,

3. a domestic unincorporated entity to a domestic business corporation,

4. a foreign unincorporated entity to a domestic business corporation.

This subchapter provides for the conversion of a domestic unincorporated entity only to a domestic business corporation because the conversion of a domestic unincorporated entity to another form of unincorporated entity or to a foreign business corporation would be outside of the scope of this Act. This subchapter similarly does not provide for the conversion of a foreign corporation or unincorporated entity to a domestic unincorporated entity. States may nonetheless wish to consider generalizing the provisions of this subchapter to authorize those types of conversions.

2. Procedural requirements

The concept of entity conversion as authorized by this subchapter is not found in many laws governing the incorporation or organization of corporations and unincorporated entities. In recognition of that fact, the rules in this section vary depending on whether the corporation or unincorporated entity desiring to convert pursuant to this subchapter is incorporated or organized under the laws of this state or of some other jurisdiction.

If the organic law of a domestic unincorporated entity does not expressly authorize it to convert to a domestic business corporation, it is intended that the first sentence of subsection (c) will provide the necessary authority. Until such time as the various organic laws of each form of unincorporated entity have been amended to provide procedures for adopting and approving a plan of entity conversion, subsection (c) provides those procedures by reference to the procedures for mergers under the organic law of the unincorporated entity or, if there are no such merger provisions, by reference to the provisions of this subchapter applicable to domestic business corporations.

Subsection (d) provides that a foreign unincorporated entity may convert to a domestic business corporation pursuant to this subchapter only if the law under which the foreign unincorporated entity is organized permits the conversion. This rule avoids issues that could arise if this state authorized a foreign unincorporated entity to participate in a transaction in this state that its home jurisdiction did not authorize. This subchapter does not specify the procedures that a foreign unincorporated entity must follow to authorize a conversion under this subchapter on the assumption that if the organic law of the foreign unincorporated entity authorizes the conversion that law will also provide the applicable procedures and any safeguards considered necessary to protect the interest holders of the unincorporated entity.

3. Transitional rule

Because the concept of entity conversion is new, a person contracting with a corporation or loaning it money who drafted and negotiated special rights relating to the transaction before the enactment of this subchapter should not be charged with the consequences of not having dealt with the concept of entity conversion in the context of those special rights. Section 9.50(e) accordingly provides a transitional rule that is intended to protect such special rights. If, for example, a corporation is a party to a contract that provides that the corporation cannot participate in a merger without the consent of the other party to the contract, the requirement to obtain the consent of the other party will also apply to the conversion of the corporation to a domestic or foreign unincorporated entity. If the corporation fails to obtain the consent, the result will be that the other party will have the same rights it would have if the corporation were to participate in a merger without the required consent.

The purpose of section 9.50(e) is to protect the third party to a contract with the corporation, and section 9.50(e) should not be applied in such a way as to impair unconstitutionally the third party's contract. As applied to the corporation, section 9.50(e) is an exercise of the reserved power of the state legislature set forth in section 1.02.

The transitional rule in section 9.50(e) ceases to apply at such time as the provision of the agreement or debt instrument giving rise to the special rights is first amended after the effective date of this subchapter because at that time the provision may be amended to address expressly an entity conversion of the corporation.

Section 9.50(e) will also apply in the case of an unincorporated entity whose organic law does not provide procedures for the approval of an entity conversion because section 9.50(c) treats such an unincorporated entity as a business corporation for purposes of section 9.50(e).

A similar transitional rule governing the application to an entity conversion of special voting rights of directors and shareholders and other internal corporate procedures is found in section 9.52(6).

§ 9.51   Plan of Entity Conversion

(a) A plan of entity conversion must include:

(1) a statement of the type of unincorporated entity the surviving entity will be and, if it will be a foreign unincorporated entity, its jurisdiction of organization;

(2) the terms and conditions of the conversion;

(3) the manner and basis of converting the shares of the domestic business corporation following its conversion into interests or other securities, obligations, rights to acquire interests or other securities, cash, other property, or any combination of the foregoing; and

(4) the full text, as they will be in effect immediately following the conversion, of the organic documents of the surviving entity.

(b) The plan of entity conversion may also include a provision that the plan may be amended prior to filing articles of entity conversion, except that subsequent to approval of the plan by the shareholders the plan may not be amended to change:

(1) the amount or kind of shares or other securities, interests, obligations, rights to acquire shares, other securities or interests, cash, or other property to be received under the plan by the shareholders;

(2) the organic documents that will be in effect immediately following the conversion, except for changes permitted by a provision of the organic law of the surviving entity comparable to section 10.05; or

(3) any of the other terms or conditions of the plan if the change would adversely affect any of the shareholders in any material respect.

(c) Terms of a plan of entity conversion may be made dependent upon facts objectively ascertainable outside the plan in accordance with section 1.20(k).

Official Comment

1.   Terms and Conditions of Entity Conversion

This subchapter imposes virtually no restrictions or limitations on the terms and conditions of an entity conversion, except for those set forth in section 9.51(b) concerning provisions in a plan of entity conversion for amendment of the plan after it has been approved by the shareholders. Shares of a domestic business corporation that converts to an unincorporated entity may be reclassified into interests or other securities, obligations, rights to acquire interests or other securities, cash or other property. The capitalization of the entity will need to be restructured in the conversion and its organic documents or articles of incorporation may be amended by the articles of entity conversion in any way deemed appropriate. When a foreign unincorporated entity converts to a domestic business corporation, the laws of the foreign jurisdiction determine which of the foregoing actions may be taken.

Although this subchapter imposes virtually no restrictions or limitations on the terms and conditions of an entity conversion, section 9.51(a) requires that the terms and conditions be set forth in the plan of entity conversion. The plan of entity conversion is not required to be publicly filed, and the articles of entity conversion that are filed with the secretary of state are not required to include a plan of entity conversion. See section 9.53. Similarly, articles of charter surrender that are filed with the secretary of state by a domestic business corporation converting to a foreign unincorporated entity are not required to include the plan of entity conversion. See section 9.54.

The list in section 9.51(a) of required provisions in a plan of entity conversion is not exhaustive and the plan may include any other provisions that may be desired.

2. Adoption and Approval; Abandonment

The conversion of a domestic business corporation to a foreign unincorporated entity must be adopted and approved as provided in section 9.52. Shareholders of a domestic business corporation that adopts and approves a plan of entity conversion have appraisal rights. See chapter 13. Under section 9.55, the board of directors of a domestic business corporation may abandon an entity conversion before its effective date even if the plan of entity conversion has already been approved by the corporation's shareholders.

§ 9.52   Action on a Plan of Entity Conversion

In the case of an entity conversion of a domestic business corporation to a domestic or foreign unincorporated entity:

(1) The plan of entity conversion must be adopted by the board of directors.

(2) After adopting the plan of entity conversion, the board of directors must submit the plan to the shareholders for their approval. The board of directors must also transmit to the shareholders a recommendation that the shareholders approve the plan, unless the board of directors makes a determination

that because of conflicts of interest or other special circumstances it should not make such a recommendation, in which case the board of directors must transmit to the shareholders the basis for that determination.

(3) The board of directors may condition its submission of the plan of entity conversion to the shareholders on any basis.

(4) If the approval of the shareholders is to be given at a meeting, the corporation must notify each shareholder, whether or not entitled to vote, of the meeting of shareholders at which the plan of entity conversion is to be submitted for approval. The notice must state that the purpose, or one of the purposes, of the meeting is to consider the plan and must contain or be accompanied by a copy or summary of the plan. The notice shall include or be accompanied by a copy of the organic documents as they will be in effect immediately after the entity conversion.

(5) Unless the articles of incorporation, or the board of directors acting pursuant to paragraph (3), requires a greater vote or a greater number of votes to be present, approval of the plan of entity conversion requires the approval of each class or series of shares of the corporation voting as a separate voting group at a meeting at which a quorum of the voting group exists consisting of at least a majority of the votes entitled to be cast on the conversion by that voting group.

(6) If any provision of the articles of incorporation, bylaws or an agreement to which any of the directors or shareholders are parties, adopted or entered into before [*the effective date of this subchapter*], applies to a merger of the corporation and the document does not refer to an entity conversion of the corporation, the provision shall be deemed to apply to an entity conversion of the corporation until such time as the provision is subsequently amended.

(7) If as a result of the conversion one or more shareholders of the corporation would become subject to owner liability for the debts, obligations or liabilities of any other person or entity, approval of the plan of conversion shall require the execution, by each such shareholder, of a separate written consent to become subject to such owner liability.

Official Comment

1. In General

This section sets forth the rules for adoption and approval of a plan of entity conversion by a domestic business corporation. The manner in which the conversion of a foreign unincorporated entity to a domestic business corporation must be adopted and approved will be controlled by the laws of the foreign jurisdiction. The provisions of this section follow generally the rules in Chapter 11 for adoption and approval of a plan of merger or share exchange.

A plan of entity conversion must be adopted by the board of directors. Although section 9.52(2) permits the board to refrain from making a recommendation to the shareholders that they approve the plan, that does not change the underlying requirement that the board adopt the plan before it is submitted to the shareholders. Approval by the shareholders of a plan of entity conversion is always required.

2. Quorum and Voting

Section 9.52(5) provides that if the corporation has more than one class or series of shares, approval of an entity conversion requires the approval of each class or series voting as a separate voting group at a meeting at which there exists a quorum consisting of at least a majority of the votes entitled to be cast on the plan by that class or series. If a quorum is present, then under sections 7.25 and 7.26 the plan will be approved if more votes are cast in favor of the plan than against it by each voting group entitled to vote on the plan. If the shares of a corporation are not divided into two or more classes or series, all of the shares together will constitute a single class for purposes of section 9.52(5).

In lieu of approval at a shareholders' meeting, approval can be given by the consent of all the shareholders entitled to vote on the domestication, under the procedures set forth in section 7.04.

3. Transitional rule

Because the concept of entity conversion is new, persons who drafted and negotiated special rights for directors or shareholders before the enactment of this subchapter should not be charged with the consequences of not having dealt with the concept of entity conversion in the context of those special rights. Section 9.52(7) accordingly provides a transitional rule that is intended to protect such special rights. Other documents, in addition to the articles of incorporation and bylaws, that may contain such special rights include shareholders agreements, voting trust agreements, vote pooling agreements or other similar arrangements. If, for example, the articles of incorporation provide that the corporation cannot participate in a merger without a supermajority vote of the shareholders, that supermajority requirement will also apply to the conversion of the corporation to a domestic or foreign unincorporated entity.

The purpose of section 9.52(6) is to protect persons who negotiated special rights for directors or shareholders whether in a contract with the corporation or in the articles of incorporation or bylaws, and section 9.52(6) should not be applied in such a way as to impair unconstitutionally the rights of any party to a contract with the corporation. As applied to the corporation, section 9.52(6) is an exercise of the reserved power of the state legislature set forth in section 1.02.

The transitional rule in section 9.52(6) ceases to apply at such time as the provision of the articles of incorporation, bylaws or agreement giving rise to the special rights is first amended after the effective date of this subchapter because at that time the provision may be amended to address expressly an entity conversion of the corporation.

Section 9.52(6) will also apply in the case of an unincorporated entity whose organic law does not provide procedures for the approval of an entity conversion because section 9.50(c) treats such an unincorporated entity as a business corporation for purposes of section 9.52(6).

A similar transitional rule with regard to the application to an entity conversion of special contractual rights of third parties is found in section 9.50(e).

§ 9.53   Articles of Entity Conversion

(a) After the conversion of a domestic business corporation to a domestic unincorporated entity has been adopted and approved as required by this Act, articles of entity conversion shall be executed on behalf of the corporation by any officer or other duly authorized representative. The articles shall:

    (1) set forth the name of the corporation immediately before the filing of the articles of entity conversion and the name to which the name of the corporation is to be changed, which shall be a name that satisfies the organic law of the surviving entity;

    (2) state the type of unincorporated entity that the surviving entity will be;

    (3) set forth a statement that the plan of entity conversion was duly approved by the shareholders in the manner required by this Act and the articles of incorporation;

    (4) if the surviving entity is a filing entity, either contain all of the provisions required to be set forth in its public organic document and any other desired provisions that are permitted, or have attached a public organic document; except that, in either case, provisions that would not be required to be included in a restated public organic document may be omitted.

(b) After the conversion of a domestic unincorporated entity to a domestic business corporation has been adopted and approved as required by the organic law of the unincorporated entity, articles of entity conversion shall be executed on behalf of the unincorporated entity by any officer or other duly authorized representative. The articles shall:

(1) set forth the name of the unincorporated entity immediately before the filing of the articles of entity conversion and the name to which the name of the unincorporated entity is to be changed, which shall be a name that satisfies the requirements of section 4.01;

(2) set forth a statement that the plan of entity conversion was duly approved in accordance with the organic law of the unincorporated entity;

(3) either contain all of the provisions that section 2.02(a) requires to be set forth in articles of incorporation and any other desired provisions that section 2.02(b) permits to be included in articles of incorporation, or have attached articles of incorporation; except that, in either case, provisions that would not be required to be included in restated articles of incorporation of a domestic business corporation may be omitted.

(c) After the conversion of a foreign unincorporated entity to a domestic business corporation has been authorized as required by the laws of the foreign jurisdiction, articles of entity conversion shall be executed on behalf of the foreign unincorporated entity by any officer or other duly authorized representative. The articles shall:

(1) set forth the name of the unincorporated entity immediately before the filing of the articles of entity conversion and the name to which the name of the unincorporated entity is to be changed, which shall be a name that satisfies the requirements of section 4.01;

(2) set forth the jurisdiction under the laws of which the unincorporated entity was organized immediately before the filing of the articles of entity conversion and the date on which the unincorporated entity was organized in that jurisdiction;

(3) set forth a statement that the conversion of the unincorporated entity was duly approved in the manner required by its organic law; and

(4) either contain all of the provisions that section 2.02(a) requires to be set forth in articles of incorporation and any other desired provisions that section 2.02(b) permits to be included in articles of incorporation, or have attached articles of incorporation; except that, in either case, provisions that would not be required to be included in restated articles of incorporation of a domestic business corporation may be omitted.

(d) The articles of entity conversion shall be delivered to the secretary of state for filing, and shall take effect at the effective time provided in section 1.23. Articles of entity conversion filed under section 9.53(a) or (b) may be combined with any required conversion filing under the organic law of the domestic unincorporated entity if the combined filing satisfies the requirements of both this section and the other organic law.

(e) If the converting entity is a foreign unincorporated entity that is authorized to transact business in this state under a provision of law similar to chapter 15, its certificate of authority or other type of foreign qualification shall be cancelled automatically on the effective date of its conversion.

Official Comment

The filing of articles of entity conversion makes the conversion a matter of public record. Where the surviving entity is organized under the laws of this state, the filing also makes of public record its articles of incorporation or public organic document. If the converting entity is a foreign unincorporated entity that is authorized to transact business in this state, section 9.53(e) automatically cancels its certificate of authority.

The filing requirements for articles of entity conversion are set forth in section 1.20. Under section 1.23, a document may specify a delayed effective time and date, and if it does so the document becomes effective at the time and date specified, except that a delayed effective date may not be later than the 90th day after the date the document is filed. In cases where an entity is changing the jurisdiction in which it is incorporated or otherwise organized, it is recommended that the entity use a delayed effective date provision in its entity conversion filings in both this state and the foreign jurisdiction, or otherwise coordinate those filings, so that the filings becoming effective at the same time. This will avoid any question about a gap in the continuity of its existence that might otherwise arise as a result of those filings taking effect at different times.

If a conversion involves a domestic unincorporated entity whose organic law also requires a filing to effectuate the conversion, section 9.53(d) permits the filings under that organic law and this Act to be combined so that only one document need be filed with the secretary of state.

§ 9.54   Surrender of Charter Upon Conversion

(a) Whenever a domestic business corporation has adopted and approved, in the manner required by this subchapter, a plan of entity conversion providing for the corporation to be converted to a foreign unincorporated entity, articles of charter surrender shall be executed on behalf of the corporation by any officer or other duly authorized representative. The articles of charter surrender shall set forth:

    (1) the name of the corporation;

    (2) a statement that the articles of charter surrender are being filed in connection with the conversion of the corporation to a foreign unincorporated entity;

    (3) a statement that the conversion was duly approved by the shareholders in the manner required by this Act and the articles of incorporation;

    (4) the jurisdiction under the laws of which the surviving entity will be organized;

    (5) if the surviving entity will be a nonfiling entity, the address of its executive office immediately after the conversion.

(b) The articles of charter surrender shall be delivered by the corporation to the secretary of state for filing. The articles of charter surrender shall take effect on the effective time provided in section 1.23.

Official Comment

The filing of articles of charter surrender makes the conversion of the domestic business corporation to a foreign unincorporated entity a matter of public record in this state. It also terminates the status of the corporation as a corporation incorporated under the laws of this state. Once the articles of charter surrender have become effective, the corporation will no longer be in good standing in this state.

The filing requirements for articles of charter surrender are set forth in section 1.20. Under section 1.23, a document may specify a delayed effective time and date, and if it does so the document becomes effective at the time and date specified, except that a delayed effective date may not be later than the 90th day after the date the document is filed. To avoid any question about a gap in the continuity of its existence, it is recommended that a corporation use a delayed effective date provision in its entity conversion filings in both this state and the foreign jurisdiction, or otherwise coordinate those filings, so that the filings becoming effective at the same time.

§ 9.55 Effect of Entity Conversion

(a) When a conversion under this subchapter becomes effective:

    (1) the title to all real and personal property, both tangible and intangible, of the converting entity remains in the surviving entity without reversion or impairment;

    (2) the liabilities of the converting entity remain the liabilities of the surviving entity;

(3) an action or proceeding pending against the converting entity continues against the surviving entity as if the conversion had not occurred;

(4) in the case of a surviving entity that is a filing entity, its articles of incorporation or public organic document and its private organic document become effective;

(5) in the case of a surviving entity that is a nonfiling entity, its private organic document becomes effective;

(6) the shares or interests of the converting entity are reclassified into shares, interests, other securities, obligations, rights to acquire shares, interests or other securities, or into cash or other property in accordance with the plan of conversion; and the shareholders or interest holders of the converting entity are entitled only to the rights provided to them under the terms of the conversion and to any appraisal rights they may have under the organic law of the converting entity; and

(7) the surviving entity is deemed to:

  (i) be incorporated or organized under and subject to the organic law of the converting entity for all purposes;

  (ii) be the same corporation or unincorporated entity without interruption as the converting entity; and

  (iii) have been incorporated or otherwise organized on the date that the converting entity was originally incorporated or organized.

(b) When a conversion of a domestic business corporation to a foreign unincorporated entity becomes effective, the surviving entity is deemed to:

  (1) appoint the secretary of state as its agent for service of process in a proceeding to enforce the rights of shareholders who exercise appraisal rights in connection with the conversion; and

  (2) agree that it will promptly pay the amount, if any, to which such shareholders are entitled under chapter 13.

(c) A shareholder who becomes subject to owner liability for some or all of the debts, obligations or liabilities of the surviving entity shall have owner liability only for those debts, obligations or liabilities of the surviving entity that arise after the effective time of the articles of entity conversion.

(d) The owner liability of an interest holder in an unincorporated entity that converts to a domestic business corporation shall be as follows:

  (1) The conversion does not discharge any owner liability under the organic law of the unincorporated entity to the extent any such

owner liability arose before the effective time of the articles of entity conversion.

(2) The interest holder shall not have owner liability under the organic law of the unincorporated entity for any debt, obligation or liability of the corporation that arises after the effective time of the articles of entity conversion.

(3) The provisions of the organic law of the unincorporated entity shall continue to apply to the collection or discharge of any owner liability preserved by paragraph (1), as if the conversion had not occurred.

(4) The interest holder shall have whatever rights of contribution from other interest holders are provided by the organic law of the unincorporated entity with respect to any owner liability preserved by paragraph (1), as if the conversion had not occurred.

Official Comment

This section provides for the effect of an entity conversion. An entity conversion is not a conveyance, transfer or assignment. It does not give rise to claims of reverter or impairment of title based on a prohibited conveyance, transfer or assignment. Nor does it give rise to a claim that a contract with the converting entity is no longer in effect on the ground of nonassignability, unless the contract specifically provides that it does not survive an entity conversion.

Section 9.55(a)(1)–(3) and (b) are similar to section 11.07(a)(3)–(5) and (c) with respect to the effects of a merger. Although section 9.55(a)(1)–(3) would be implied by the general rule stated in section 9.55(a)(7) even if not stated expressly, those rules have been included to avoid any question as to whether a different result was intended.

The rule in section 9.55(a)(7)(iii) that the date of incorporation or organization of the converting entity remains its date of incorporation or organization after the entity conversion is a specific application of the general rule in section 9.55(a)(7)(ii). The date of incorporation or organization of a foreign converting unincorporated entity is required by section 9.53(c)(2) to be set forth in the articles of entity conversion.

One of the continuing liabilities of a foreign unincorporated entity to which a domestic business corporation has been converted is the obligation to the shareholders of the converting corporation who exercise appraisal rights to pay them the amount, if any, to which they are entitled under chapter 13. Where the surviving entity is a domestic unincorporated entity, it will be similarly liable to the shareholders of the converting corporation pursuant to section 9.55(a)(2).

Section 9.55(d) preserves liability only for owner liabilities to the extent they arise before the conversion. Owner liability is not preserved for subsequent changes in an underlying liability, regardless of whether a change is voluntary or involuntary.

This section does not address the issue that could arise in an entity conversion where a person who had authority to bind the converting entity loses that authority because of the conversion and yet purports to act to bind the surviving entity. For example, in a conversion of a general partnership into a corporation, a person who is a general partner but does not become an officer of the corporation will lose the authority of a general partner to bind the business to obligations incurred in the ordinary course, but might purport to commit the corporation to such an obligation in dealing with a person who does not have knowledge of the conversion. Instances in which this occurs will be rare and, in the limited instances in which it does occur, general principles of agency law are sufficient to resolve the problems created.

§ 9.56   Abandonment of an Entity Conversion

(a) Unless otherwise provided in a plan of entity conversion of a domestic business corporation, after the plan has been adopted and approved as required by this subchapter, and at any time before the entity conversion has become effective, it may be abandoned by the board of directors without action by the shareholders.

(b) If an entity conversion is abandoned after articles of entity conversion or articles of charter surrender have been filed with the secretary of state but before the entity conversion has become effective, a statement that the entity conversion has been abandoned in accordance with this section, executed by an officer or other duly authorized representative, shall be delivered to the secretary of state for filing prior to the effective date of the entity conversion. Upon filing, the statement shall take effect and the entity conversion shall be deemed abandoned and shall not become effective.

Official Comment

Unless otherwise provided in a plan of entity conversion, a domestic business corporation proposing to convert to an unincorporated entity may abandon the transaction without shareholder approval, even though it has been previously approved by the shareholders. Whether or not the conversion of an unincorporated entity to a domestic business corporation may be abandoned is determined by the law under which the unincorporated entity is organized, except that the rule of this section will apply to the extent provided in section 9.50(c).

Chapter 10

AMENDMENT OF ARTICLES OF INCORPORATION AND BYLAWS

Subchapter A.

AMENDMENT OF ARTICLES OF INCORPORATION

§ 10.01 Authority to Amend

(a) A corporation may amend its articles of incorporation at any time to add or change a provision that is required or permitted in the articles of incorporation as of the effective date of the amendment or to delete a provision that is not required to be contained in the articles of incorporation.

(b) A shareholder of the corporation does not have a vested property right resulting from any provision in the articles of incorporation, including provisions relating to management, control, capital structure, dividend entitlement, or purpose or duration of the corporation.

Official Comment

Section 10.01(a) authorizes a corporation to amend its articles of incorporation by adding a new provision to its articles of incorporation, modifying an existing provision, or deleting a provision in its entirety. The sole test for the validity of an amendment is whether the provision could lawfully have been included in (or in the case of a deletion, omitted from) the articles of incorporation as of the effective date of the amendment.

The power of amendment must be exercised pursuant to the procedures set forth in chapter 10. Section 10.03 requires most amendments to be approved by a majority of the votes cast on the proposed amendment at a meeting at which a quorum consisting of at least a majority of the votes entitled to be cast is present. This requirement is supplemented by section 10.04, which governs voting by voting groups on amendments that directly affect a single class or series of shares, and by section 7.27, which governs amendments that change the voting requirements for future amendments.

Section 10.01(b) restates the policy embodied in earlier versions of the Act and in all modern state corporation statutes, that a shareholder "does not have a vested property right" in any provision of the articles of incorporation. Under section 1.02, corporations and their shareholders are also subject to amendments of the governing statute.

Section 10.01 should be construed liberally to achieve the fundamental purpose of this chapter of permitting corporate adjustment and change by majority vote. Section 10.01(b) rejects decisions by a few courts that have applied a vested right or property right doctrine to restrict or invalidate amendments to articles of incorporation because they modified particular rights conferred on shareholders by the original articles of incorporation.

Under general corporation law and under the Act, a provision in the articles of incorporation is subject to amendment under section 10.01 even though the provision is described, referred to, or stated in a share certificate, information statement, or other document issued by the corporation that reflects provisions of the articles of incorporation. The only exception to this unlimited power of amendment is section 6.27, which provides that without the consent of the holder, amendments cannot impose share transfer restrictions on previously issued shares.

However, section 10.01 does not concern obligations of a corporation to its shareholders based upon contracts independent of the articles of incorporation. An amendment permitted by this section may constitute a breach of such a contract or of a contract between the shareholders themselves. A shareholder with contractual rights (or who otherwise is concerned about possible onerous amendments) may obtain complete protection against these amendments by establishing procedures in the articles of incorporation or bylaws that limit the power of amendment without the shareholder's consent. In appropriate cases, a shareholder may be able to enjoin an amendment that constitutes a breach of a contract.

Minority shareholders are protected from the power of the majority to impose onerous or objectionable amendments in several ways. First, such shareholders may have the right to vote on amendments by separate voting groups (section 10.04). Second, a decision by a majority shareholder or a control group to exercise the powers granted by this section in a way that may breach a duty to minority or noncontrolling interests may be reviewable by a court under its inherent equity power to review transactions for good faith and fair dealing to the minority shareholders. McNulty v. W. & J. Sloane, 184 Misc. 835, 54 N.Y.S.2d 253 (Sup. Ct. 1945); Kamena v. Janssen Dairy Corp., 133 N.J.Eq. 214, 31 A.2d 200, 202 (Ch. 1943), aff'd, 134 N.J.Eq. 359, 35 A.2d 894 (1944) (where the court stated that it "is more a question of fair dealing between the strong and the weak than it is a question of percentages or proportions of the votes favoring the plan"). See also Teschner v. Chicago Title & Trust Co., 59 Ill. 2d 452, 322 N.E.2d 54, 57 (1974), where the court, in upholding a transaction that had a reasonable business purpose, relied partially on the fact that there was "no claim of fraud or deceptive conduct ... [or] that the exchange offer was unfair or that the price later offered for the shares was inadequate."

Because of the broad power of amendment contained in this section, it is unnecessary to make any reference to, or reserve, an express power to amend in the articles of incorporation.

§ 10.02   Amendment Before Issuance of Shares

If a corporation has not yet issued shares, its board of directors, or its incorporators if it has no board of directors, may adopt one or more amendments to the corporation's articles of incorporation.

Official Comment

Section 10.02 provides that, before any shares are issued, amendments may be made by the persons empowered to complete the organization of the corporation. Under section 2.04 the organizers may be either the incorporators or the initial directors named in the articles of incorporation.

§ 10.03   Amendment By Board of Directors and Shareholders

If a corporation has issued shares, an amendment to the articles of incorporation shall be adopted in the following manner:

(a) The proposed amendment must be adopted by the board of directors.

(b) Except as provided in sections 10.05, 10.07, and 10.08, after adopting the proposed amendment the board of directors must submit the amendment to the shareholders for their approval. The board of directors must also transmit to the shareholders a recommendation that the shareholders approve the amendment, unless the board of directors makes a determination that because of conflicts of interest or other special circumstances it should not make such a recommendation, in which case the board of directors must transmit to the shareholders the basis for that determination.

(c) The board of directors may condition its submission of the amendment to the shareholders on any basis.

(d) If the amendment is required to be approved by the shareholders, and the approval is to be given at a meeting, the corporation must notify each shareholder, whether or not entitled to vote, of the meeting of shareholders at which the amendment is to be submitted for approval. The notice must state that the purpose, or one of the purposes, of the meeting is to consider the amendment and must contain or be accompanied by a copy of the amendment.

(e) Unless the articles of incorporation, or the board of directors acting pursuant to subsection (c), requires a greater vote or a greater number of shares to be present, approval of the amendment requires the approval of the shareholders at a meeting at which a quorum consisting of at least a majority of the votes entitled to be cast on the amendment exists, and, if any class or series of shares is entitled to vote as a separate group on the amendment, except as provided in section 10.04(c), the approval of each such separate voting group at a meeting at which a quorum of the voting group consisting of at least a majority of the votes entitled to be cast on the amendment by that voting group exists.

Official Comment

1. In General

Under section 10.03, if a corporation has issued shares, a proposed amendment to the articles of incorporation must be adopted by the board. Thereafter, the board must submit the amendment to the shareholders for their approval, except as provided in sections 10.05, 10.07, and 10.08.

2. Submission to the Shareholders

Section 10.03 requires the board of directors, after having adopted an amendment, to submit the amendment to the shareholders for approval except as otherwise provided by sections 10.05, 10.07, and 10.08. When submitting the amendment, the board of directors must make a recommendation to the shareholders that the amendment be approved, unless the board of directors makes a determination that because of conflicts of interest or other special circumstances it should make no recommendation. For example, the board of directors may make such a determination where there is not a sufficient number of directors free of a conflicting interest to approve the amendment or because the board of directors is evenly divided as to the merits of an amendment but is able to agree that shareholders should be permitted to consider the amendment. If the board of directors makes such a determination, it must describe the conflict of interest or special circumstances, and communicate the basis for the determination, when submitting the amendment to the shareholders. The exception for conflicts of interest or other special circumstances is intended to be sparingly available. Generally, shareholders should not be asked to act on an amendment in the absence of a recommendation by the board of directors. The exception is not intended to relieve the board of directors of its duty to consider carefully the amendment and the interests of shareholders.

Section 10.03(c) permits the board of directors to condition its submission of an amendment on any basis. Among the conditions that a board might impose are that the amendment will not be deemed approved (i) unless it is approved by a specified vote of the shareholders, or by one or more specified classes or series of shares, voting as a separate voting group, or by a specified percentage of disinterested shareholders, or (ii) if shareholders holding more than a specified fraction of outstanding shares assert appraisal rights. The board of directors is not limited to conditions of these types.

3. Quorum and Voting

Section 10.03(e) provides that approval of an amendment requires approval of the shareholders at a meeting at which a quorum consisting of at least a majority of the votes entitled to be cast on the amendment exists, including, if any class or series of shares is entitled to vote as a separate group on the amendment, the approval of each such separate group, at a meeting at which a similar quorum of the voting group exists. If a quorum exists, then under sections 7.25 and 7.26 the amendment will be approved if more votes are cast in favor of the amendment than against it by the voting group or separate voting groups entitled to vote on the plan. This represents a change from the Act's previous voting rule for amendments, which required approval by a majority of votes cast, with no minimum quorum, for some amendments, and approval by a majority of the votes entitled to be cast by a voting group, for others.

If an amendment would affect the voting requirements on future amendments, it must also be approved by the vote required by section 7.27.

§ 10.04 Voting on Amendments By Voting Groups

(a) If a corporation has more than one class of shares outstanding, the holders of the outstanding shares of a class are entitled to vote as a separate voting group (if shareholder voting is otherwise required by this Act) on a proposed amendment to the articles of incorporation if the amendment would:

    (1) effect an exchange or reclassification of all or part of the shares of the class into shares of another class;

    (2) effect an exchange or reclassification, or create the right of exchange, of all or part of the shares of another class into shares of the class;

    (3) change the rights, preferences, or limitations of all or part of the shares of the class;

    (4) change the shares of all or part of the class into a different number of shares of the same class;

    (5) create a new class of shares having rights or preferences with respect to distributions or to dissolution that are prior or superior to the shares of the class;

    (6) increase the rights, preferences, or number of authorized shares of any class that, after giving effect to the amendment, have rights or preferences with respect to distributions or to dissolution that are prior or superior to the shares of the class;

    (7) limit or deny an existing preemptive right of all or part of the shares of the class; or

> (8) cancel or otherwise affect rights to distributions that have accumulated but not yet been authorized on all or part of the shares of the class.

(b) If a proposed amendment would affect a series of a class of shares in one or more of the ways described in subsection (a), the holders of shares of that series are entitled to vote as a separate voting group on the proposed amendment.

(c) If a proposed amendment that entitles the holders of two or more classes or series of shares to vote as separate voting groups under this section would affect those two or more classes or series in the same or a substantially similar way, the holders of shares of all the classes or series so affected must vote together as a single voting group on the proposed amendment, unless otherwise provided in the articles of incorporation or required by the board of directors.

(d) A class or series of shares is entitled to the voting rights granted by this section although the articles of incorporation provide that the shares are nonvoting shares.

Official Comment

Section 10.04(a) requires separate approval by voting groups for certain types of amendments to the articles of incorporation where the corporation has more than one class of shares outstanding. In general, section 10.04 carries forward provisions of the prior Act, but certain changes have been made. Under the prior Act, approval by a class, voting as a separate voting group, was required for an amendment that would increase or decrease the aggregate number of shares of the class. That provision does not appear in the present Act. Also, in the prior Act approval by a class, voting as a separate voting group, was required for an amendment that would create a new class of shares having rights or preferences with respect to dissolution that would be prior, superior, or substantially equal to the class, and for an amendment that would increase the rights, preferences, or number of authorized shares of any class that, after giving effect to the amendment, would have rights or preferences with respect to distributions or dissolution that would be prior, superior, or substantially equal to the shares of the class. Under the present Act, approval by a class, voting as a separate voting group, is required in these cases only when the new or other class would have rights with respect to distributions or dissolution that would be prior or superior to the class, not when the rights would be substantially equal.

Shares are entitled to vote as separate voting groups under this section even though they are designated as nonvoting shares in the articles of incorporation, or the articles of incorporation purport to deny them entirely the right to vote on the proposal in question, or purport to allow other classes or series of shares to vote as part of the same voting group. However, an amendment that does not require shareholder approval does not trigger the right to vote by voting groups under this section. This would include a determination by the board of directors, pursuant to authority granted in the articles of incorporation, of the preferences, limitations and relative rights of any class prior to the issuance of any shares of that class, or of one or more series within a class before the issuance of any shares of that series (see section 6.02(a)).

The right to vote as a separate voting group provides a major protection for classes or series of shares with preferential rights, or classes or series of limited or nonvoting shares, against amendments that are especially burdensome to that class or series. This section, however, does not make the right to vote by separate voting group dependent on an evaluation of whether the amendment is detrimental to the class or series; if the amendment is one of those described in section 10.04(a), the class or series is automatically entitled to vote as a separate voting group on the amendment. The question whether an amendment is detrimental is often a question of judgment, and approval by the affected class or series is required irrespective of whether the board or other shareholders believe it is beneficial or detrimental to the affected class or series.

Under subsection (a)(4), a class is entitled to vote as a separate voting group on an amendment that would change the shares of all or part of the class into a different number of shares of the same class. An amendment that changes the number of shares owned by one of more shareholders of a class into a fraction of a share, through a "reverse split," falls within subsection (a)(4) and therefore requires approval by the class, voting as a separate voting group, whether or not the fractional share is to be acquired for cash under section 6.04.

Sections 7.25 and 7.26 set forth the mechanics of voting by multiple voting groups.

Subsection (b) extends the privilege of voting by separate voting group to a series of a class of shares if the series has financial or voting provisions unique to the series that are affected in one or more of the ways described in subsection (a). Any significant distinguishing feature of a series, which an amendment affects or alters, should trigger the right of voting by separate voting group for that series. However, under subsection (c) if a proposed amendment that entitles two or more classes or series of shares to vote as separate voting groups would affect those classes or series in the same or a substantially similar way, the shares of all the class or series so affected must vote together, as a single voting group, unless otherwise provided in the articles of incorporation or required by the board of directors.

The application of subsections (b) and (c) may best be illustrated by examples.

First, assume there is a class of shares, with preferential rights, comprised of three series, each with different preferential dividend rights. A proposed amendment would reduce the rate of dividend applicable to the "Series A" shares and would change the dividend right of the "Series B" shares from a cumulative to a noncumulative right. The amendment would not affect the preferential dividend right of the "Series C" shares. Both Series A and B would be entitled to vote as separate voting groups on the proposed amendment; the holders of the Series C shares, not directly affected by the amendment, would not be entitled to vote at all, unless otherwise provided, or unless the shares are voting shares under the articles of incorporation, in which case they would not vote as a separate voting group but in the voting group consisting of all shares with general voting rights under the articles of incorporation.

Second, if the proposed amendment would reduce the dividend right of Series A and change the dividend right of both Series B and C from a cumulative to a noncumulative right, the holders of Series A would be entitled to vote as a single voting group, and the holders of Series B and C would be required to vote together as a single, separate voting group.

Third, assume that a corporation has common stock and two classes of preferred stock. A proposed amendment would create a new class of senior preferred that would have priority in distribution rights over both the common stock and the existing classes of preferred stock. Because the creation of the new senior preferred would affect all three classes of stock in the same or a substantially similar way, all three classes would vote together as a single voting group on the proposed amendment.

Under the prior version of section 10.04(c), series that were affected by an amendment in the same or a substantially similar manner were required to vote together, but classes that were affected by an amendment in the same or a substantially similar manner voted separately. Thus under the prior version of section 10.04(c) if, in the second example, the A, B, and C stock had been denominated as classes rather than series, then the A, B, and C holders would have been required to vote separately rather than together. Similarly, in the third example, under the prior version of section 10.04(c) the Common and existing Preferred would have been required to vote separately rather than together, because each was a separate class. The distinction between classes and series for this purpose seems artificial, and therefore has been eliminated in the current version of section 10.04(c).

Section 10.04(d) makes clear that the right to vote by separate voting groups provided by section 10.04 may not be narrowed or eliminated by the articles of incorporation. Even if a class or series of shares is described as "nonvoting" and the articles purport to make that class or series nonvoting "for all purposes," that class or series nevertheless has the voting right provided by this section. No inference should be drawn from section 10.04(d) as to whether other, unrelated sections of the Act may be modified by provisions in the articles of incorporation.

§ 10.05   Amendment By Board of Directors

Unless the articles of incorporation provide otherwise, a corporation's board of directors may adopt amendments to the corporation's articles of incorporation without shareholder approval:

(1) to extend the duration of the corporation if it was incorporated at a time when limited duration was required by law;

(2) to delete the names and addresses of the initial directors;

(3) to delete the name and address of the initial registered agent or registered office, if a statement of change is on file with the secretary of state;

(4) if the corporation has only one class of shares outstanding:

    (a) to change each issued and unissued authorized share of the class into a greater number of whole shares of that class; or

    (b) to increase the number of authorized shares of the class to the extent necessary to permit the issuance of shares as a share dividend;

(5) to change the corporate name by substituting the word "corporation," "incorporated," "company," "limited," or the abbreviation "corp.," "inc.," "co.," or "ltd.," for a similar word or abbreviation in the name, or by adding, deleting, or changing a geographical attribution for the name;

(6) to reflect a reduction in authorized shares, as a result of the operation of section 6.31(b), when the corporation has acquired its own shares and the articles of incorporation prohibit the reissue of the acquired shares;

(7) to delete a class of shares from the articles of incorporation, as a result of the operation of section 6.31(b), when there are no remaining shares of the class because the corporation has acquired all shares of the class and the articles of incorporation prohibit the reissue of the acquired shares; or

(8) to make any change expressly permitted by section 6.02(a) or (b) to be made without shareholder approval.

Official Comment

The amendments described in clauses (1) through (8) are so routine and "housekeeping" in nature as not to require approval by shareholders. None affects substantive rights in any meaningful way.

Section 10.05(4)(a) authorizes the board of directors to change each issued and unissued share of an outstanding class of shares into a greater number of whole shares if the corporation has only that class of shares outstanding. All shares of the class being changed must be treated identically under this clause. Section 10.05(4)(b) authorizes the board of directors to increase the number of shares of the class to the extent necessary to permit the issuance of shares as a share dividend, if the corporation has only that one class of stock outstanding.

Amendments provided for in this section may be included in restated articles of incorporation under section 10.07 or in articles of merger under chapter 11.

§ 10.06 Articles of Amendment

After an amendment to the articles of incorporation has been adopted and approved in the manner required by this Act and by the articles of incorporation, the corporation shall deliver to the secretary of state, for filing, articles of amendment, which shall set forth:

(1) the name of the corporation;

(2) the text of each amendment adopted, or the information required by section 1.20(k)(5);

(3) if an amendment provides for an exchange, reclassification, or cancellation of issued shares, provisions for implementing the amendment (if not contained in the amendment itself), which may be made dependent upon facts objectively ascertainable outside the articles of amendment in accordance with section 1.20(k);

(4) the date of each amendment's adoption; and

(5) if an amendment:

    (a) was adopted by the incorporators or board of directors without shareholder approval, a statement that the amendment was duly approved by the incorporators or by the board of directors, as the case may be, and that shareholder approval was not required;

    (b) required approval by the shareholders, a statement that the amendment was duly approved by the shareholders in the manner required by this Act and by the articles of incorporation; or

    (c) is being filed pursuant to section 1.20(k)(5), a statement to that effect.

Official Comment

Section 10.06(3) requires the articles of amendment to contain a statement of the manner in which an exchange, reclassification, or cancellation of issued shares is to be put into effect if not set forth in the amendment itself. This requirement avoids any possible confusion that may arise as to how the amendment is to be put into effect and also permits the amendment itself to be limited to provisions of permanent applicability, with transitional provisions having no long-range effect appearing only in the articles of amendment.

§ 10.07   Restated Articles of Incorporation

(a) A corporation's board of directors may restate its articles of incorporation at any time, with or without shareholder approval, to consolidate all amendments into a single document.

(b) If the restated articles include one or more new amendments that require shareholder approval, the amendments must be adopted and approved as provided in section 10.03.

(c) A corporation that restates its articles of incorporation shall deliver to the secretary of state for filing articles of restatement setting forth the name of the corporation and the text of the restated articles of incorporation together with a certificate which states that the restated articles consolidate all amendments into a single document and, if a new amendment is included in the restated articles, which also includes the statements required under section 10.06.

(d) Duly adopted restated articles of incorporation supersede the original articles of incorporation and all amendments thereto.

(e) The secretary of state may certify restated articles of incorporation as the articles of incorporation currently in effect, without including the certificate information required by subsection (c).

Official Comment

Restated articles of incorporation serve the useful purpose of permitting articles of incorporation that have been amended from time to time, or are being concurrently amended, to be consolidated into a single document.

A restatement of a corporation's articles of incorporation is not an amendment of the articles of incorporation, but only a consolidation of amendments into a single document. A corporation that is restating its articles may concurrently amend the articles, and include the new amendments in the restated articles. In such a case, the provisions of this chapter that govern amendments of the articles of incorporation would apply to the new amendments. In case of doubt whether a provision of a restatement of the articles of incorporation might be deemed to be an amendment, rather than a consolidation, the prudent course for the corporation is to treat that provision as an amendment, and follow the procedures that apply to amendments under this chapter.

Where the articles of incorporation are amended at the same time they are restated, a combined articles of amendment and restatement may be filed.

§ 10.08   Amendment Pursuant to Reorganization

(a) A corporation's articles of incorporation may be amended without action by the board of directors or shareholders to carry out a plan of reorganization ordered or decreed by a court of competent jurisdiction under the authority of a law of the United States.

(b) The individual or individuals designated by the court shall deliver to the secretary of state for filing articles of amendment setting forth:

   (1) the name of the corporation;

   (2) the text of each amendment approved by the court;

   (3) the date of the court's order or decree approving the articles of amendment;

   (4) the title of the reorganization proceeding in which the order or decree was entered; and

   (5) a statement that the court had jurisdiction of the proceeding under federal statute.

(c) This section does not apply after entry of a final decree in the reorganization proceeding even though the court retains jurisdiction of the proceeding for limited purposes unrelated to consummation of the reorganization plan.

Official Comment

Section 10.08 provides a simplified method of conforming corporate documents filed under state law with the federal statutes relating to corporate reorganization. If a federal court confirms a plan of reorganization that requires articles of amendment to be filed, those amendments may be prepared and filed by the persons designated by the court and the approval of neither the shareholders nor the board of directors is required.

This section applies only to amendments in articles of incorporation approved before the entry of a final decree in the reorganization.

§ 10.09   Effect of Amendment

An amendment to the articles of incorporation does not affect a cause of action existing against or in favor of the corporation, a proceeding to which the corporation is a party, or the existing rights of persons other than shareholders of the corporation. An amendment changing a corporation's name does not abate a proceeding brought by or against the corporation in its former name.

Official Comment

Under section 10.09, amendments to articles of incorporation do not interrupt the corporate existence and do not abate a proceeding by or against the corporation even though the amendment changes the name of the corporation.

Amendments are effective when filed unless a delayed effective date is elected. See section 1.23.

Subchapter B.

AMENDMENT OF BYLAWS

§ 10.20 Amendment By Board of Directors or Shareholders

(a) A corporation's shareholders may amend or repeal the corporation's bylaws.

(b) A corporation's board of directors may amend or repeal the corporation's bylaws, unless:

(1) the articles of incorporation or section 10.21 reserve that power exclusively to the shareholders in whole or part; or

(2) the shareholders in amending, repealing, or adopting a bylaw expressly provide that the board of directors may not amend, repeal, or reinstate that bylaw.

Official Comment

The power to amend or repeal bylaws is shared by the board of directors and the shareholders, unless that power is reserved exclusively to the shareholders by an appropriate provision in the articles of incorporation. Section 10.20(b)(1) provides that the power to amend or repeal the bylaws may be reserved to the shareholders "in whole or part." This language permits the reservation of power to be limited to specific articles or sections of the bylaws or to specific subjects or topics addressed in the bylaws.

Section 10.20(b)(2) permits the shareholders to amend, repeal, or adopt a bylaw and reserve exclusively to themselves the power to amend, repeal, or reinstate that bylaw if the reservation is express.

Section 10.21 limits the power of directors to adopt or amend supermajority provisions in bylaws. See section 10.21 and the Official Comment thereto.

§ 10.21 Bylaw Increasing Quorum or Voting Requirement for Directors

(a) A bylaw that increases a quorum or voting requirement for the board of directors may be amended or repealed:

(1) if adopted by the shareholders, only by the shareholders, unless the bylaw otherwise provides;

(2) if adopted by the board of directors, either by the shareholders or by the board of directors.

(b) A bylaw adopted or amended by the shareholders that increases a quorum or voting requirement for the board of directors may provide that it can be amended or repealed only by a specified vote of either the shareholders or the board of directors.

(c) Action by the board of directors under subsection (a) to amend or repeal a bylaw that changes the quorum or voting requirement for the board of directors must meet the same quorum requirement and be adopted by the same vote required to take action under the quorum and voting requirement then in effect or proposed to be adopted, whichever is greater.

Official Comment

Provisions that increase a quorum or voting requirement for the board over the requirement that would otherwise apply under this Act or that was previously set forth in the bylaws ("supermajority requirements") may be placed in the bylaws of the corporation without specific authorization in the articles of incorporation. See section 8.24(a) and (c). Like other bylaw provisions, they may be adopted either by the shareholders or by the board of directors. See section 10.20. Such provisions may be amended or repealed by the board of directors or shareholders as provided in this section.

Section 10.21(a)(1) provides that if a supermajority requirement is imposed by a bylaw adopted by the shareholders, only the shareholders may amend or repeal it. Under section 10.21(b), such a bylaw may impose restrictions on the manner in which it may be thereafter amended or repealed by the shareholders. If a supermajority requirement is imposed in a bylaw adopted by the board of directors, the bylaw may be amended either by the shareholders or the board of directors (see section 10.21(a)(2)). However, if such an amendment is amended by the board of directors, section 10.21(c) requires approval by the supermajority requirement then in effect or proposed to be adopted, whichever is greater. Compare section 7.27.

Chapter 11

MERGERS AND SHARE EXCHANGES

§ 11.01 Definitions

As used in this chapter:

(a) "Merger" means a business combination pursuant to section 11.02.

(b) "Party to a merger" or "party to a share exchange" means any domestic or foreign corporation or eligible entity that will either:

   (1) merge under a plan of merger;

   (2) acquire shares or eligible interests of another corporation or an eligible entity in a share exchange; or

(3) have all of its shares or interests or all of one or more classes or series of its shares or eligible interests acquired in a share exchange.

(c) "Share exchange" means a business combination pursuant to section 11.03.

(d) "Survivor" in a merger means the corporation or eligible entity into which one or more other corporations or eligible entities are merged. A survivor of a merger may preexist the merger or be created by the merger.

Official Comment

1. In General

The definition of what constitutes an "eligible entity" in section 1.40(7B) determines the kinds of entities, other than corporations, with which a corporation may merge. The definition of "voting power" in section 1.40 also has important substantive implications, because whether shareholder approval is required for a transaction under chapter 11 depends in part on the proportion of voting power that is carried by shares that would be issued and issuable as a result of the transaction.

2. Interests

The term "interests" as defined in section 1.40(13B) includes such interests as general and limited partnership interests in limited partnerships, equity interests in limited liability companies, and any other form of equity or ownership interests in an unincorporated entity, as defined in section 1.40(24A), however denominated. For purposes of this chapter, the definition of "eligible interests" in section 1.40(7C) adds to those types of interests any form of membership in a domestic or foreign nonprofit corporation.

3. Organic Documents

The definition of the term "organic documents" which was previously found in section 11.01(c) is now set forth in section 1.40(15A).

4. Survivor

The term "survivor" is used in chapter 11 as a defined technical term and therefore is not always used in a manner that is equivalent to the ordinary meaning of the term. For example, a corporation may be the "survivor" of a merger within the meaning of section 11.01(g) even if it is created by the merger, and therefore had no existence before the merger.

§ 11.02 Merger

(a) One or more domestic business corporations may merge with one or more domestic or foreign business corporations or eligible entities pursuant to a plan of merger, or two or more foreign business corporations or domestic or foreign eligible entities may merge into a new domestic business corporation to be created in the merger in the manner provided in this chapter.

(b) A foreign business corporation, or a foreign eligible entity, may be a party to a merger with a domestic business corporation, or may be created by the terms of the plan of merger, only if the merger is permitted by the laws under which the foreign business corporation or eligible entity is organized or by which it is governed.

(b.1) If the organic law of a domestic eligible entity does not provide procedures for the approval of a merger, a plan of merger may be adopted and approved, the merger effectuated, and appraisal rights exercised in accordance with the procedures in this chapter and chapter 13. For the purposes of applying this chapter and chapter 13:

(1) the eligible entity, its members or interest holders, eligible interests and organic documents taken together shall be deemed to be a domestic business corporation, shareholders, shares and articles of incorporation, respectively and vice versa as the context may require; and

(2) if the business and affairs of the eligible entity are managed by a group of persons that is not identical to the members or interest holders, that group shall be deemed to be the board of directors.

(c) The plan of merger must include:

(1) the name of each domestic or foreign business corporation or eligible entity that will merge and the name of the domestic or foreign business corporation or eligible entity that will be the survivor of the merger;

(2) the terms and conditions of the merger;

(3) the manner and basis of converting the shares of each merging domestic or foreign business corporation and eligible interests of each merging domestic or foreign eligible entity into shares or other securities, eligible interests, obligations, rights to acquire shares, other securities or eligible interests, cash, other property, or any combination of the foregoing;

(4) the articles of incorporation of any domestic or foreign business or nonprofit corporation, or the organic documents of any domestic or foreign unincorporated entity, to be created by the merger, or if a new domestic or foreign business or nonprofit corporation or unincorporated entity is not to be created by the

merger, any amendments to the survivor's articles of incorporation or organic documents.

(d) Terms of a plan of merger may be made dependant on facts objectively ascertainable outside the plan in accordance with section 1.20(k).

(e) The plan of merger may also include a provision that the plan may be amended prior to filing articles of merger, but if the shareholders of a domestic corporation that is a party to the merger are required or permitted to vote on the plan, the plan must provide that subsequent to approval of the plan by such shareholders the plan may not be amended to change:

(1) the amount or kind of shares or other securities, eligible interests, obligations, rights to acquire shares, other securities or eligible interests, cash, or other property to be received under the plan by the shareholders of or owners of eligible interests in any party to the merger;

(2) the articles of incorporation of any corporation, or the organic documents of any unincorporated entity, that will survive or be created as a result of the merger, except for changes permitted by section 10.05 or by comparable provisions of the organic laws of any such foreign business or nonprofit corporation or domestic or foreign unincorporated entity; or

(3) any of the other terms or conditions of the plan if the change would adversely affect such shareholders in any material respect.

[*(f) Property held in trust or for charitable purposes under the laws of this state by a domestic or foreign eligible entity shall not be diverted by a merger from the objects for which it was donated, granted or devised, unless and until the eligible entity obtains an order of [court] [the attorney general] specifying the disposition of the property to the extent required by and pursuant to [cite state statutory cy pres or other nondiversion statute].*]

Official Comment

1. In General

Section 11.02 authorizes mergers between one or more domestic business corporations, or between one or more domestic business corporations and one or more foreign business corporations or domestic or foreign eligible entities. The section also authorizes a merger in which none of the merging parties is a domestic business corporation but the surviving party created in the merger is a domestic business corporation. Upon the effective date of the merger the survivor becomes vested with all the assets of the corporations or eligible entities that merge into the survivor and becomes subject to their liabilities, as provided in section 11.07.

2. Applicability

A merger of a domestic business corporation with a foreign business corporation or a foreign eligible entity is authorized by chapter 11 only if the merger is permitted by the laws under which the foreign business corporation or eligible entity is organized, and in effecting the merger the foreign business corporation or eligible entity complies with such laws. Whether and on what terms a foreign business corporation or a foreign eligible entity is authorized to merge with a domestic business corporation is a matter that is governed by the laws under which that corporation or eligible entity is organized or by which it is governed, not by chapter 11.

Nevertheless, certain provisions of chapter 11 have an indirect effect on a foreign business corporation or foreign eligible entity that proposes to or does merge with a domestic business corporation, because they set conditions concerning the effectiveness and effect of the merger. For example, section 11.02(c) sets forth certain requirements for the contents of a plan of merger. This section is directly applicable only to domestic business corporations, but has an indirect effect on a foreign corporation or eligible entity that is a party to a proposed merger with a domestic business corporation.

In some cases, the impact of chapter 11 on a foreign corporation or eligible entity is more direct. For example, section 11.07(d) provides that upon a merger becoming effective, a foreign corporation or eligible entity that is the survivor of the merger is deemed to appoint the secretary of state as its agent for service of process in a proceeding to enforce the rights of shareholders of each domestic corporation that is a party to the merger to exercise appraisal rights and to agree that it will promptly pay to such shareholders the amount, if any, to which they are entitled under chapter 13.

If the law under which a domestic eligible entity is organized does not expressly authorize it to merge with a domestic business corporation, it is intended that section 11.02(a) will provide the necessary authority. Until such time as the various laws governing the organization of each form of eligible entity have been amended to provide procedures for adopting and approving a plan of merger, section 11.02(b.1) provides those procedures by reference to the provisions of this subchapter applicable to domestic business corporations.

3. Terms and Conditions of Merger

Chapter 11 imposes virtually no restrictions or limitations on the terms or conditions of a merger, except for those set forth in section 11.02(e) concerning provisions in a plan of merger for amendment of the plan after it has been approved by shareholders. Owners of shares or eligible interests in a party to the merger that merges into the survivor may receive shares or other securities of the survivor, shares or other securities of a party other than the survivor, eligible interests, obligations, rights to acquire shares, other securities or eligible interests, cash, or other property. The capitalization of the survivor may be restructured in the merger, and its articles or organic documents may be amended by the articles of merger, in any way deemed appropriate.

Although chapter 11 imposes virtually no restrictions or limitations on the terms or conditions of a merger, section 11.02(c) requires that the terms and conditions be set forth in the plan of merger. The present Act clarifies that the plan of merger need not be set forth in the articles of merger that are to be delivered to the secretary of state for filing after the merger has been adopted and approved. See section 11.06.

Section 11.02(c)(4) provides that a plan of merger must set forth the articles of incorporation of any business or nonprofit corporation, and the organic documents of any unincorporated entity, to be created by the merger, or if a new corporation or unincorporated entity is not to be created by the merger, any amendments to the survivor's articles of incorporation or organic documents. If a domestic corporation is merged into an existing domestic or foreign corporation or eligible entity, section 11.02(c) does not require that the survivor's articles of incorporation or organic documents be included in the plan of merger. However, if approval of the plan of merger by the shareholders of a domestic corporation to be merged into another party to the merger is required under section 11.04, section 11.04(d) requires that the shareholders be furnished with a copy or summary of those articles of incorporation or organic documents in connection with voting on approval of the merger.

The list in section 11.02(c) of required provisions in a plan of merger is not exhaustive and the plan may include any other provisions that may be desired.

4. Amendments of Articles of Incorporation

Under Section 11.02, a corporation's articles of incorporation may be amended by a merger. Under section 11.02(c)(4), a plan of merger must include any amendments to the survivor's articles of incorporation or organic documents. If the plan of merger is approved, the amendments will be effective.

5. Adoption and Approval; Abandonment

A merger must be adopted and approved as set forth in sections 11.04 and 11.05. Under section 11.08, the board of directors may abandon a merger before its effective date even if the plan of merger has already been approved by the corporation's shareholders.

6. Effective Date of Merger

A merger takes effect on the date the articles of merger are filed, unless a later date, not more than 90 days after filing, is specified in the articles. See section 11.06 and the Official Comment thereto.

7. Appraisal Rights

Shareholders of a domestic corporation that is a party to a merger may have appraisal rights. See chapter 13.

8. Protection of Restricted Property

This section permits a nonprofit corporation or unincorporated nonprofit association to merge into a for-profit corporation or unincorporated entity. The laws of some states governing the nondiversion of charitable and trust property to other uses may not be worded in a fashion that will cover a merger under section 11.02. To prevent a merger from being used to avoid restrictions on the use of property held by nonprofit entities, optional section 11.02(f) may be used to require approval of mergers by the appropriate arm of government having supervision of nonprofit entities.

§ 11.03   Share Exchange

(a) Through a share exchange:

    (1) a domestic business corporation may acquire all of the shares of one or more classes or series of shares of another domestic or foreign business corporation, or all of the eligible interests of one or more classes or series of eligible interests of a domestic or foreign eligible entity, in exchange for shares, other securities, eligible interests, obligations, rights to acquire shares, other securities or eligible interests, cash, other property, or any combination of the foregoing, pursuant to a plan of share exchange, or

    (2) all of the shares of one or more classes or series of shares of a domestic business corporation may be acquired by another domestic or foreign business corporation or eligible entity, in exchange for shares, other securities, eligible interests, obligations, rights to acquire shares, other securities or eligible interests, cash, other property, or any combination of the foregoing, pursuant to a plan of share exchange.

(b) A foreign corporation or eligible entity may be a party to a share exchange only if the share exchange is permitted by the laws under which the corporation or eligible entity is organized or by which it is governed.

(b.1) If the organic law of a domestic eligible entity does not provide procedures for the approval of a share exchange, a plan of share exchange may be adopted and approved, and the share exchange effectuated, in accordance with the procedures, if any, for a merger. If the organic law of a domestic eligible entity does not provide procedures for the approval of either a share exchange or a merger, a plan of share exchange may be adopted and approved, the share exchange effectuated, and appraisal rights exercised, in accordance with the procedures in this chapter and chapter 13. For the purposes of applying this chapter and chapter 13:

(1) the eligible entity, its members or interest holders, eligible interests and organic documents taken together shall be deemed to be a domestic business corporation, shareholders, shares and articles of incorporation, respectively and vice versa as the context may require; and

(2) if the business and affairs of the eligible entity are managed by a group of persons that is not identical to the members or interest holders, that group shall be deemed to be the board of directors.

(c) The plan of share exchange must include:

(1) the name of each corporation or eligible entity whose shares or eligible interests will be acquired and the name of the corporation or eligible entity that will acquire those shares or eligible interests;

(2) the terms and conditions of the share exchange;

(3) the manner and basis of exchanging shares of a corporation or eligible interests in an eligible entity whose shares or eligible interests will be acquired under the share exchange into shares, other securities, eligible interests, obligations, rights to acquire shares, other securities, or eligible interests, cash, other property, or any combination of the foregoing.

(d) Terms of a plan of share exchange may be made dependent on facts objectively ascertainable outside the plan in accordance with section 1.20(k).

(e) The plan of share exchange may also include a provision that the plan may be amended prior to filing articles of share exchange, but if the shareholders of a domestic corporation that is a party to the share exchange are required or permitted to vote on the plan, the plan must provide that subsequent to approval of the plan by such shareholders the plan may not be amended to change:

(1) the amount or kind of shares, other securities, eligible interests, obligations, rights to acquire shares, other securities or eligible interests, cash, or other property to be issued by the corporation or to be received under the plan by the shareholders of or holders of eligible interests in any party to the share exchange; or

    (2) any of the other terms or conditions of the plan if the change would adversely affect such shareholders in any material respect.

(f) Section 11.03 does not limit the power of a domestic corporation to acquire shares of another corporation or eligible interests in an eligible entity in a transaction other than a share exchange.

Official Comment

1. In General

It is often desirable to structure a corporate combination so that the separate existence of one or more parties to the combination does not cease although another corporation or eligible entity obtains ownership of the shares or eligible interests of those parties. This objective is often particularly important in the formation of insurance and bank holding companies, but is not limited to those contexts. In the absence of the procedure authorized in section 11.03, this kind of result often can be accomplished only by a triangular merger, which involves the formation by a corporation, A, of a new subsidiary, followed by a merger of that subsidiary with another party to the merger, B, effected through the exchange of A's securities for securities of B. Section 11.03 authorizes a more straightforward procedure to accomplish the same result.

Under section 11.03, the acquiring corporation in a share exchange must acquire all of the shares or eligible interests of the class or series of shares or eligible interests that is being acquired. The shares or eligible interests of one or more other classes or series of the acquired corporation or eligible entity may be excluded from the share exchange or may be included on different bases. After the plan of share exchange is adopted and approved as required by section 11.04, it is binding on all holders of the class or series to be acquired. Accordingly, a share exchange may operate in a mandatory fashion on some holders of the class or series of shares or eligible interests acquired.

Section 11.03(f) makes clear that the authorization of share exchange combinations under section 11.03 does not limit the power of corporations to acquire shares or eligible interests without using the share-exchange procedure, either as part of a corporate combination or otherwise.

In contrast to mergers, the articles of incorporation of a party to a share exchange may not be amended by a plan of share exchange. Such an amendment may, however, be effected under chapter 10 as a separate element of a corporate combination that involves a share exchange.

2. Applicability

Whether and on what terms a foreign business corporation or a foreign eligible entity is authorized to enter into a share exchange with a domestic business corporation is a matter that is governed by the laws under which that corporation or eligible entity is organized or by which it is governed, not by chapter 11. Therefore, for example, section 11.04, which governs the manner in which a plan of share exchange must be adopted, applies only to adoption of a plan of share exchange by a domestic business corporation.

Nevertheless, certain provisions of chapter 11 have an indirect effect on a foreign business corporation or foreign eligible entity that proposes to or does engage in a share exchange with a domestic business corporation, because they set conditions concerning the effectiveness and effect of the share exchange. For example, section 11.03(c) sets forth certain requirements for the contents of a plan of share exchange. This section is directly applicable only to domestic corporations, but has an indirect effect on a foreign corporation or eligible entity that is a party to a proposed share exchange with a domestic corporation.

If the law under which a domestic eligible entity is organized does not expressly authorize it to participate in a share (or eligible interest) exchange with a domestic business corporation, it is intended that section 11.03(a) will provide the necessary authority. Until such time as the various laws governing the organization of each form of eligible entity have been amended to provide procedures for adopting and approving a plan of share (or eligible interest) exchange, section 11.03(b.1) provides those procedures by reference to the provisions of this subchapter applicable to domestic business corporations.

3. Terms and Conditions of Share Exchange

Chapter 11 imposes virtually no restrictions or limitations on the terms and conditions of a share exchange, except for those contained in section 11.03(e) concerning provisions in a plan of share exchange for amendment of the plan after it has been approved by shareholders, and the requirement in section 11.03(a) that the acquiring party must acquire all the shares of the acquired class or series of stock or eligible interests. Owners of shares or eligible interests in a party whose shares are acquired under Section 11.03(a)(2) may receive securities or eligible interests of the acquiring party, securities or eligible interests of a party other than the acquiring party, or cash or other property.

Although chapter 11 imposes virtually no restrictions or limitations on the terms or conditions of a share exchange, section 11.03(c) requires that the terms and conditions be set forth in the plan of share exchange. The present Act clarifies that the plan of share exchange need not be set forth in the articles of share exchange that are to be delivered to the secretary of state for filing after the share exchange has been adopted and approved. See section 11.06.

The list in section 11.03(c) of required provisions in a plan of share exchange is not exhaustive and the plan may include any other provisions that may be desired.

4. Adoption And Approval; Abandonment

A share exchange must be adopted and approved as set forth in section 11.04. Under section 11.08, the board of directors may abandon a share exchange before its effective date even if the plan of share exchange has already been approved by the corporation's shareholders.

5. Effective Date Of Share Exchange

A share exchange takes effect on the date the articles of share exchange are filed, unless a later date, not more than 90 days after filing, is specified in the articles. See section 11.06 and the Official Comment thereto.

6. Appraisal Rights

Holders of a class or series of shares of a domestic corporation that is acquired in a share exchange may have appraisal rights. See chapter 13.

§ 11.04 Action on a Plan of Merger or Share Exchange

In the case of a domestic corporation that is a party to a merger or share exchange:

(a) The plan of merger or share exchange must be adopted by the board of directors.

(b) Except as provided in subsection (g) and in section 11.05, after adopting the plan of merger or share exchange the board of directors must submit the plan to the shareholders for their approval. The board of directors must also transmit to the shareholders a recommendation that the shareholders approve the plan, unless the board of directors makes a determination that because of conflicts of interest or other special circumstances it should not make such a recommendation, in which case the board of directors must transmit to the shareholders the basis for that determination.

(c) The board of directors may condition its submission of the plan of merger or share exchange to the shareholders on any basis.

(d) If the plan of merger or share exchange is required to be approved by the shareholders, and if the approval is to be given at a meeting, the corporation must notify each shareholder, whether or not entitled to vote, of the meeting of shareholders at which the plan is to be submitted for approval. The notice must state that the purpose, or one of the purposes, of the meeting is to consider the plan and must contain or be accompanied by a copy or summary of the plan. If the corporation is to be merged into an existing corporation or eligible entity, the notice shall also include or be accompanied by a copy or summary of the articles of incorporation or organic documents of that corporation or eligible entity. If the corporation is to be merged into a corporation or eligible entity that is to be created pursuant to the merger, the notice shall include or be accompanied by a copy or a summary of the articles of incorporation or organic documents of the new corporation or eligible entity.

(e) Unless the articles of incorporation, or the board of directors acting pursuant to subsection (c), requires a greater vote or a greater number of votes to be present, approval of the plan of merger or share exchange requires the approval of the shareholders at a meeting at which a quorum consisting of at least a majority of the votes entitled to be cast on the plan exists, and, if any class or series of shares is entitled to vote as a separate group on the plan of merger or share exchange, the approval of each such separate voting group at a meeting at which a quorum of the voting group consisting of at least a majority of the votes entitled to be cast on the merger or share exchange by that voting group is present.

(f) Separate voting by voting groups is required:

    (1) on a plan of merger, by each class or series of shares that:

        (i) are to be converted under the plan of merger into other securities, eligible interests, obligations, rights to acquire shares, other securities or eligible interests, cash, other property, or any combination of the foregoing; or

        (ii) would be entitled to vote as a separate group on a provision in the plan that, if contained in a proposed amendment to articles of incorporation, would require action by separate voting groups under section 10.04;

    (2) on a plan of share exchange, by each class or series of shares included in the exchange, with each class or series constituting a separate voting group; and

    (3) on a plan of merger or share exchange, if the voting group is entitled under the articles of incorporation to vote as a voting group to approve a plan of merger or share exchange.

(g) Unless the articles of incorporation otherwise provide, approval by the corporation's shareholders of a plan of merger or share exchange is not required if:

    (1) the corporation will survive the merger or is the acquiring corporation in a share exchange;

    (2) except for amendments permitted by section 10.05, its articles of incorporation will not be changed;

    (3) each shareholder of the corporation whose shares were outstanding immediately before the effective date of the merger or share

exchange will hold the same number of shares, with identical preferences, limitations, and relative rights, immediately after the effective date of change; and

(4) the issuance in the merger or share exchange of shares or other securities convertible into or rights exercisable for shares does not require a vote under section 6.21(f).

(h) If as a result of a merger or share exchange one or more shareholders of a domestic business corporation would become subject to owner liability for the debts, obligations or liabilities of any other person or entity, approval of the plan of merger or share exchange shall require the execution, by each such shareholder, of a separate written consent to become subject to such owner liability.

Official Comment

1. In General

Under section 11.04, a plan of merger or share exchange must be adopted by the board. Thereafter, the board must submit the plan to the shareholders for their approval, unless the conditions stated in section 11.04(g) or section 11.05 are satisfied. A plan of share exchange must always be approved by the shareholders of the class or series that is being acquired in a share exchange. Similarly, a plan of merger must always be approved by the shareholders of a corporation that is merged into another party in a merger, unless the corporation is a subsidiary and the merger falls within section 11.05. However, under section 11.04(g) approval of a plan of merger or share exchange by the shareholders of a surviving corporation in a merger or of an acquiring corporation in a share exchange is not required if the conditions stated in that section, including the fundamental rule of section 6.21(f), are satisfied.

Section 11.04(f) provides that a class or series has a right to vote on a plan of merger as a separate voting group if, pursuant to the merger, the class or series would be converted into other securities, eligible interests, obligations, rights to acquire shares, other securities or eligible interests, cash, or other property. A class or series also is entitled to vote as a separate voting group if the class or series would be entitled to vote as a separate group on a provision in the plan that, if contained in an amendment to the articles of incorporation, would require approval by that class or series, voting as a separate voting group, under section 10.04. Under this latter requirement, a class or series will be entitled to vote as a separate voting group if the terms of that class or series are being changed or the shares of that class or series are being converted into shares of any other class or series. Where the surviving entity is a foreign business corporation, it is not intended that immaterial changes in the terms of a class or series that conform to the usage of the laws of the foreign jurisdiction will alone create an entitlement to vote as a separate group.

If a merger would amend the articles of incorporation in such a way as to affect the voting requirements on future amendments, the transaction must also be approved by the vote required by section 7.27.

2. Submission to the Shareholders

Section 11.04(b) requires the board of directors, after having adopted the plan of merger or share exchange, to submit the plan of merger or share exchange to the shareholders for approval, except as provided in subsection (g) and section 11.05. When submitting the plan of merger or share exchange the board of directors must make a recommendation to the shareholders that the plan be approved, unless the board of directors makes a determination that because of conflicts of interest or other special circumstances it should make no recommendation. For example, the board or directors may make such a determination where there is not a sufficient number of directors free of a conflicting interest to approve the transaction or because the board of directors is evenly divided as to the merits of a transaction but is able to agree that shareholders should be permitted to consider the transaction. If the board of directors makes such a determination, it must describe the conflict of interest or special circumstances, and communicate the basis for the determination, when submitting the plan of merger or share exchange to the shareholders. The exception for conflicts of interest or other special circumstances is intended to be sparingly available. Generally, shareholders should not be asked to act on a merger or share exchange in the absence of a recommendation by the board of directors. The exception is not intended to relieve the board of directors of its duty to consider carefully the proposed transaction and the interests of shareholders.

Section 11.04(c) permits the board of directors to condition its submission of a plan of merger or share exchange on any basis. Among the conditions that a board might impose are that the plan will not be deemed approved (i) unless it is approved by a specified vote of the shareholders, or by one or more specified classes or series of shares, voting as a separate voting group, or by a specified percentage of disinterested shareholders or (ii) if shareholders holding more than a specified fraction of the outstanding shares assert appraisal rights. The board of directors is not limited to conditions of these types.

Section 11.04(d) provides that if the plan of merger or share exchange is required to be approved by the shareholders, and if the approval is to be given at a meeting, the corporation must notify each shareholder, whether or not entitled to vote, of the meeting of shareholders at which the plan is to be submitted. Requirements concerning the timing and content of a notice of meeting are set out in section 7.05. Section 11.04(d) does not itself require that notice be given to nonvoting shareholders where the merger is approved, without a meeting, by unanimous consent. However, that requirement is imposed by section 7.04(d).

3. Quorum and Voting

Section 11.04(e) provides that approval of a plan of merger or share exchange requires approval of the shareholders at a meeting at which a quorum consisting of a majority of the votes entitled to be cast on the plan exists and, if any class or series of shares are entitled to vote as a separate group on the plan, the approval of each such separate group at a meeting at which a quorum consisting of at least a majority of the votes entitled to be cast on the plan by that class or series exists. If a quorum is present, then under sections 7.25 and 7.26 the plan will be approved if more votes are cast in favor of the plan than against it by the voting group or separate voting groups entitled to vote on the plan. This represents a change from the Act's previous voting rule for mergers and share exchanges, which required approval by a majority of outstanding shares.

In lieu of approval at a shareholders' meeting, approval can be given by the consent of all the shareholders entitled to vote on the merger or share exchange, under the procedures set forth in section 7.04.

4. Abandonment of Merger or Share Exchange

Under section 11.08, the board of directors may abandon a merger or share exchange before its effective date even if the plan of merger or share exchange has already been approved by the corporation's shareholders.

5. Personal Liability of Shareholders

Section 11.04(h) applies only in situations where a shareholder is becoming subject to "owner liability" as defined in section 1.40(15C), for example, where a corporation is merging into a general partnership. Where an unincorporated entity whose interest holders have owner liability, such as a general partnership, is merging into a corporation, the effect of the transaction on the owner liability of the interest holders in the unincorporated entity will be determined by section 11.07(e).

§ 11.05 Merger Between Parent and Subsidiary or Between Subsidiaries

(a) A domestic parent corporation that owns shares of a domestic or foreign subsidiary corporation that carry at least 90 percent of the voting power of each class and series of the outstanding shares of the subsidiary that have voting power may merge the subsidiary into itself or into another such subsidiary, or merge itself into the subsidiary, without the approval of the board of directors or shareholders of the subsidiary, unless the articles of incorporation of any of the corporations otherwise provide, and unless, in the case of a foreign subsidiary, approval by the subsidiary's board of directors or shareholders is required by the laws under which the subsidiary is organized.

(b) If under subsection (a) approval of a merger by the subsidiary's shareholders is not required, the parent corporation shall, within ten days after the effective date of the merger, notify each of the subsidiary's shareholders that the merger has become effective.

(c) Except as provided in subsections (a) and (b), a merger between a parent and a subsidiary shall be governed by the provisions of chapter 11 applicable to mergers generally.

Official Comment

Under section 11.05, if a parent owns 90 percent of the voting power of each class and series of the outstanding shares of a subsidiary that have voting power, the subsidiary may be merged into the parent or another such subsidiary, or the parent may be merged into the subsidiary, without the approval of the subsidiary's shareholders or board of directors, subject to certain informational and notice requirements. Approval by the subsidiary's shareholders is not required partly because if a parent already owns 90 percent or more of the voting power of each class and series of a subsidiary's shares, approval of a merger by the subsidiary's shareholders would be a foregone conclusion, and partly to facilitate the simplification of corporate structure where only a very small fraction of stock is held by outside shareholders. Approval by the subsidiary's board of directors is not required because if the parent owns 90 percent or more of the voting power of each class and series of the subsidiary's outstanding shares, the subsidiary's directors cannot be expected to be independent of the parent, so that the approval by the subsidiary's board of directors would also be a foregone conclusion. In other respects, mergers between parents and 90 percent-owned subsidiaries are governed by the provisions of chapter 11.

Section 11.05 dispenses with approval by the board of directors or the shareholders of a subsidiary that is merged into the parent or another subsidiary if the conditions of the section are met. Section 11.05 does not in itself dispense with approval by the shareholders of the parent. Under section 11.04(g), a merger of the kind described in section 11.05 in which the subsidiary is merged upstream into the parent would usually not require approval of the parent's shareholders, because in such cases the parent's articles of incorporation are usually not affected by the merger and the parent usually does not issue stock carrying more than 20 percent of its voting power. If, however, a parent is merged downstream into the subsidiary, approval by the parent's shareholders would be required under section 11.04.

§ 11.06   Articles of Merger or Share Exchange

(a) After a plan of merger or share exchange has been adopted and approved as required by this Act, articles of merger or share exchange shall be executed on behalf of each party to the merger or share exchange by any officer or other duly authorized representative. The articles shall set forth:

(1) the names of the parties to the merger or share exchange;

(2) if the articles of incorporation of the survivor of a merger are amended, or if a new corporation is created as a result of a merger, the amendments to the survivor's articles of incorporation or the articles of incorporation of the new corporation;

(3) if the plan of merger or share exchange required approval by the shareholders of a domestic corporation that was a party to the merger or share exchange, a statement that the plan was duly approved by the shareholders and, if voting by any separate voting group was required, by each such separate voting group, in the manner required by this Act and the articles of incorporation;

(4) if the plan of merger or share exchange did not require approval by the shareholders of a domestic corporation that was a party to the merger or share exchange, a statement to that effect; and

(5) as to each foreign corporation or eligible entity that was a party to the merger or share exchange, a statement that the participation of the foreign corporation or eligible entity was duly authorized as required by the organic law of the corporation or eligible entity.

(b) Articles of merger or share exchange shall be delivered to the secretary of state for filing by the survivor of the merger or the acquiring corporation or eligible entity in a share exchange, and shall take effect at the effective time provided in section 1.23. Articles of merger or share exchange filed under this section may be combined with any filing required under the organic law of any domestic eligible entity involved in the transaction if the combined filing satisfies the requirements of both this section and the other organic law.

Official Comment

The filing of articles of merger or share exchange makes the transaction a matter of public record. The requirements of filing are set forth in section 1.20. The effective date of the articles is the effective date of their filing, unless otherwise specified. Under section 1.23, a document may specify a delayed effective time and date, and if it does so the document becomes effective at the time and date specified, except that a delayed effective date may not be later than the 90th day after the date the document is filed.

If a merger or share exchange involves a domestic eligible entity whose organic law also requires a filing to effectuate the transaction, section 11.06(b) permits the filings under that organic law and this section to be combined so that only one document need be filed with the secretary of state.

§ 11.07 Effect of Merger or Share Exchange

(a) When a merger becomes effective:

(1) the corporation or eligible entity that is designated in the plan of merger as the survivor continues or comes into existence, as the case may be;

(2) the separate existence of every corporation or eligible entity that is merged into the survivor ceases;

(3) all property owned by, and every contract right possessed by, each corporation or eligible entity that merges into the survivor is vested in the survivor without reversion or impairment;

(4) all liabilities of each corporation or eligible entity that is merged into the survivor are vested in the survivor;

(5) the name of the survivor may, but need not be, substituted in any pending proceeding for the name of any party to the merger whose separate existence ceased in the merger;

(6) the articles of incorporation or organic documents of the survivor are amended to the extent provided in the plan of merger;

(7) the articles of incorporation or organic documents of a survivor that is created by the merger become effective; and

(8) the shares of each corporation that is a party to the merger, and the eligible interests in an eligible entity that is a party to a merger, that are to be converted under the plan of merger into shares, eligible interests, obligations, rights to acquire shares, other securities, or eligible interests, cash, other property, or any combination of the foregoing, are converted, and the former holders of such shares or eligible interests are entitled only to the rights provided to them in the plan of merger or to any appraisal rights they may have under chapter 13 or the organic law of the eligible entity.

(b) When a share exchange becomes effective, the shares of each domestic corporation that are to be exchanged for shares, other securities, eligible interests, obligations, rights to acquire shares, other securities, or eligible interests, cash, other property, or any combination of the foregoing, are entitled only to the rights provided to them in the plan of share exchange or to any rights they may have under chapter 13.

(c) A person who becomes subject to owner liability for some or all of the debts, obligations or liabilities of any entity as a result of a merger or share exchange shall have owner liability only to the extent provided in the organic law of the entity and only for those debts, obligations and liabilities that arise after the effective time of the articles of merger or share exchange.

(d) Upon a merger becoming effective, a foreign corporation, or a foreign eligible entity, that is the survivor of the merger is deemed to:

   (1) appoint the secretary of state as its agent for service of process in a proceeding to enforce the rights of shareholders of each domestic corporation that is a party to the merger who exercise appraisal rights, and

   (2) agree that it will promptly pay the amount, if any, to which such shareholders are entitled under chapter 13.

(e) The effect of a merger or share exchange on the owner liability of a person who had owner liability for some or all of the debts, obligations or liabilities of a party to the merger or share exchange shall be as follows:

   (1) The merger or share exchange does not discharge any owner liability under the organic law of the entity in which the person was a shareholder, member or interest holder to the extent any such owner liability arose before the effective time of the articles of merger or share exchange.

   (2) The person shall not have owner liability under the organic law of the entity in which the person was a shareholder, member or interest holder prior to the merger or share exchange for any debt, obligation or liability that arises after the effective time of the articles of merger or share exchange.

   (3) The provisions of the organic law of any entity for which the person had owner liability before the merger or share exchange shall continue to apply to the collection or discharge of any owner liability preserved by paragraph (1), as if the merger or share exchange had not occurred.

   (4) The person shall have whatever rights of contribution from other persons are provided by the organic law of the entity for which the person had owner liability with respect to any owner liability preserved by paragraph (1), as if the merger or share exchange had not occurred.

Official Comment

Under section 11.07(a), in the case of a merger the survivor and the parties that merge into the survivor become one. The survivor automatically becomes the owner of all real and personal property and becomes subject to all the liabilities, actual or contingent, of each party that is merged into it. A merger is not a conveyance, transfer, or assignment. It does not give rise to claims of reverter or impairment of title based on a prohibited conveyance, transfer or assignment. It does not give rise to a claim that a contract with a party to the merger is no longer in effect on the ground of nonassignability, unless the contract specifically provides that it does not survive a merger. All pending proceedings involving either the survivor or a party whose separate existence ceased as a result of the merger are continued. Under section 11.07(a)(5), the name of the survivor may be, but need not be, substituted in any pending proceeding for the name of a party to the merger whose separate existence ceased as a result of the merger. The substitution may be made whether the survivor is a complainant or a respondent, and may be made at the instance of either the survivor or an opposing party. Such a substitution has no substantive effect, because whether or not the survivor's name is substituted it succeeds to the claims of, and is subject to the liabilities of, any party to the merger whose separate existence ceased as a result of the merger.

In contrast to a merger, a share exchange does not in and of itself affect the separate existence of the parties, vest in the acquiring party the assets of the party whose stock or eligible interests are to be acquired, or render the acquiring party liable for the liabilities of the party whose stock or eligible interests the acquiring party acquires.

Under section 11.07(a)(8), on the effective date of a merger the former shareholders of a corporation that is merged into the survivor are entitled only to the rights provided in the plan of merger (which would include any rights they have as holders of the consideration they acquire) or to any rights they may have under chapter 13. Similarly, under section 11.07(b), on the effective date of a share exchange the former shareholders of a corporation whose shares are acquired are entitled only to the rights provided in the plan of share exchange (which would include any rights they have as holders of the consideration they acquire) or to any rights they may have under chapter 13. These provisions are not intended to preclude an otherwise proper question concerning the merger's validity, or to override or otherwise affect any provisions of chapter 13 concerning the exclusiveness of rights under that chapter.

Under section 11.07(d), when a merger becomes effective a foreign corporation or eligible entity that is the survivor of the merger is deemed to appoint the secretary of state as its agent for service of process in a proceeding to enforce the rights of any shareholders of each domestic corporation that is a party to the merger who exercise appraisal rights, and to agree that is will promptly pay the amount, if any, to which such shareholders are entitled under chapter 13. This result is based on the implied consent of such a foreign corporation or eligible entity to the terms of chapter 11 by virtue of entering into an agreement that is governed by this chapter.

Section 11.07(e) preserves liability only for owner liabilities to the extent they arise before the merger or share exchange. Owner liability is not preserved for subsequent changes in an underlying liability, regardless of whether a change is voluntary or involuntary.

Under section 11.04(h), a merger cannot have the effect of making any shareholder of a domestic corporation subject to owner liability for the debts, obligations or liabilities of any other person or entity unless each such shareholder has executed a separate written consent to become subject to such owner liability.

This section does not address the issue that could arise in a merger where a person who had authority to bind a party to the merger loses that authority because of the merger and yet purports to act to bind the survivor of the merger. For example, in a merger of a general partnership into a corporation, a person who is a general partner but does not become an officer of the corporation will lose the authority of a general partner to bind the business to obligations incurred in the ordinary course, but might purport to commit the corporation to such an obligation in dealing with a person who does not have knowledge of the merger. Instances in which this occurs are rare and, in the limited instances in which it does occur, general principles of agency law are sufficient to resolve the problems created.

§ 11.08   Abandonment of a Merger or Share Exchange

(a) Unless otherwise provided in a plan of merger or share exchange or in the laws under which a foreign business corporation or a domestic or foreign eligible entity that is a party to a merger or a share exchange is organized or by which it is governed, after the plan has been adopted and approved as required by this chapter, and at any time before the merger or share exchange has become effective, it may be abandoned by a domestic business corporation that is a party thereto without action by its shareholders, in accordance with any procedures set forth in the plan of merger or share exchange or, if no such procedures are set forth in the plan, in the manner determined by the board of directors, subject to any contractual rights of other parties to the merger or share exchange.

(b) If a merger or share exchange is abandoned under subsection (a) after articles of merger or share exchange have been filed with the secretary of state but before the merger or share exchange has become effective, a statement that the merger or share exchange has been abandoned in accordance with this section, executed on behalf of a party to the merger or share exchange by an officer or other duly authorized representative, shall be delivered to the secretary of state for filing prior to the effective date of the merger or share exchange.

Upon filing, the statement shall take effect and the merger or share exchange shall be deemed abandoned and shall not become effective.

Official Comment

Under section 11.08, unless otherwise provided in the plan of merger or share exchange, a domestic business corporation that is a party to a merger or share exchange may abandon the transaction without shareholder approval, even though the transaction has been previously approved by the shareholders. The power under section 11.08 to abandon a transaction without shareholder approval does not affect any contract rights that other parties may have. The power of a foreign business corporation or a domestic or foreign eligible entity to abandon a transaction will be determined by the organic law of the corporation or eligible entity, except as provided in sections 11.02(b.1) and 11.03(b.1).

Chapter 12

DISPOSITION OF ASSETS

§ 12.01 Disposition of Assets Not Requiring Shareholder Approval

No approval of the shareholders of a corporation is required, unless the articles of incorporation otherwise provide:

(1) to sell, lease, exchange, or otherwise dispose of any or all of the corporation's assets in the usual and regular course of business;

(2) to mortgage, pledge, dedicate to the repayment of indebtedness (whether with or without recourse), or otherwise encumber any or all of the corporation's assets, whether or not in the usual and regular course of business;

(3) to transfer any or all of the corporation's assets to one or more corporations or other entities all of the shares or interests of which are owned by the corporation; or

(4) to distribute assets pro rata to the holders of one or more classes or series of the corporation's shares.

Official Comment

Section 12.01 provides that no approval of the shareholders is required for dispositions of assets of the types described therein, unless the articles of incorporation otherwise provide. Dispositions other than those described in section 12.01 require shareholder approval if they fall within section 12.02.

Under subsection (1), shareholder approval is not required for a disposition of the corporation's assets in the usual and regular course of business, regardless of the size of the transaction. Examples of such dispositions would include the sale of a building that was the corporation's only major asset where the corporation was formed for the purpose of constructing and selling that building, or the sale by a corporation of its only major business where the corporation was formed to buy and sell businesses and the proceeds of the sale are to be reinvested in the purchase of a new business, or an open- or closed-end investment company whose portfolio turns over many times in short periods.

Subsection (3) provides that no approval of shareholders is required to transfer any or all of the corporation's assets to a wholly owned subsidiary or other entity. This provision may not be used as a device to avoid a vote of shareholders by a multi-step transaction.

Subsection (4) provides that no approval of the shareholders is required to distribute assets pro rata to the holders of one or more classes of the corporation's shares. A traditional spin-off—that is, a pro rata distribution of the shares of a subsidiary to the holders of one or more classes of shares—falls within this subsection. A split-off—that is, a non pro rata distribution of shares of a subsidiary to some or all shareholders in exchange for some of their shares—would require shareholder approval if the disposition left the parent without a significant continuing business activity under subsection 12.02(a). A split-up—that is, a distribution of the shares of two or more subsidiaries in complete liquidation to shareholders—would be governed by section 14.02 (dissolution), not by chapter 12. In each of the foregoing situations, the subsidiary or subsidiaries could be historical or newly created.

§ 12.02   Shareholder Approval of Certain Dispositions

(a) A sale, lease, exchange, or other disposition of assets, other than a disposition described in section 12.01, requires approval of the corporation's shareholders if the disposition would leave the corporation without a significant continuing business activity. If a corporation retains a business activity that represented at least 25 percent of total assets at the end of the most recently completed fiscal year, and 25 percent of either income from continuing operations before taxes or revenues from continuing operations for that fiscal year, in each case of the corporation and its subsidiaries on a consolidated basis, the corporation will conclusively be deemed to have retained a significant continuing business activity.

(b) A disposition that requires approval of the shareholders under subsection (a) shall be initiated by a resolution by the board of directors authorizing the disposition. After adoption of such a resolution, the board of directors shall submit the proposed disposition to the shareholders for their approval. The board of directors shall also transmit to the shareholders a recommendation that the shareholders approve the proposed disposition, unless the board of directors makes a determination that because of conflicts of interest or other special circumstances it should not make such a recommendation, in which case the board of directors shall transmit to the shareholders the basis for that determination.

(c) The board of directors may condition its submission of a disposition to the shareholders under subsection (b) on any basis.

(d) If a disposition is required to be approved by the shareholders under subsection (a), and if the approval is to be given at a meeting, the corporation shall notify each shareholder, whether or not entitled to vote, of the meeting of shareholders at which the disposition is to be submitted for approval. The notice shall state that the purpose, or one of the purposes, of the meeting is to consider the disposition and shall contain a description of the disposition, including the terms and conditions thereof and the consideration to be received by the corporation.

(e) Unless the articles of incorporation or the board of directors acting pursuant to subsection (c) requires a greater vote, or a greater number of votes to be present, the approval of a disposition by the shareholders shall require the approval of the shareholders at a meeting at which a quorum consisting of at least a majority of the votes entitled to be cast on the disposition exists.

(f) After a disposition has been approved by the shareholders under subsection (b), and at any time before the disposition has been consummated, it may be abandoned by the corporation without action by the shareholders, subject to any contractual rights of other parties to the disposition.

(g) A disposition of assets in the course of dissolution under chapter 14 is not governed by this section.

(h) The assets of a direct or indirect consolidated subsidiary shall be deemed the assets of the parent corporation for the purposes of this section.

Official Comment

1. In General

Section 12.02(a) requires shareholder approval for a sale, lease, exchange or other disposition by a corporation that would leave the corporation without a significant continuing business activity. The test employed in section 12.02(a) for whether a disposition of assets requires shareholder approval differs verbally from the test employed in past versions of the Model Act, which centered on whether a sale involves "all or substantially all" of a corporation's assets. The "all or substantially all" test has also been used in most corporate statutes. In practice, however, courts interpreting these statutes have commonly employed a test comparable to that embodied in 12.02(a). For example, in Gimbel v. Signal Cos., 316 A.2d 599 (Del.Ch.), aff'd, 316 A.2d 619 (Del.1974), the court stated that "While it is true that [the all or substantially all] test does not lend itself to a strict mathematical standard to be applied in every case, the qualitative factor can be defined to some degree.... If the sale is of assets quantitatively vital to the operation of the corporation and is out of the ordinary [course] and substantially affects the existence and purpose of the corporation then it is beyond the power of the Board of Directors." In Thorpe v. Cerbco, Inc., 676 A.2d 436 (Del.1996), a major issue was whether the sale by a corporation, CERB-CO, of one of its subsidiaries, East, would have been a sale of all or substantially all of the corporation's assets, and therefore would have required shareholder approval under the Delaware statute. The court, quoting Oberly v. Kirby, 592 A.2d 445 (Del.1991), stated:

> "[T]he rule announced in Gimbel v. Signal Cos., Del.Ch., 316 A.2d 599, aff'd, Del. Supr., 316 A.2d 619 (1974), makes it clear that the need for shareholder ... approval is to be measured not by the size of a sale alone, but also by its qualitative effect upon the corporation. Thus, it is relevant to ask whether a transaction 'is out of the ordinary and substantially affects the existence and purpose of the corporation.' [Gimbel, 316 A.2d] at 606."

In the opinion below, the Chancellor determined that the sale of East would constitute a radical transformation of CERBCO. In addition, CERBCO's East stock accounted for 68 [percent] of CERBCO's assets in 1990 and this stock was its primary income generating asset. We therefore affirm the decision that East stock constituted "substantially all" of CERBCO's assets as consistent with Delaware law.

See also Katz v. Bregman, 431 A.2d 1274 (Del.Ch.), appeal refused sub nom. Plant Industries, Inc. v. Katz, 435 A.2d 1044 (Del.1981); Stiles v. Aluminum Products Co., 338 Ill.App. 48, 86 N.E.2d 887 (1949); Campbell v. Vose, 515 F.2d 256 (10th Cir.1975); South End Improvement Group, Inc. v. Mulliken, 602 So.2d 1327 (Fla.App.1992); Schwadel v. Uchitel, 455 So.2d 401 (Fla.App.1984).

Whether a disposition leaves a corporation with a significant continuing business activity, within the meaning of section 12.02(a), depends primarily on whether the corporation will have a remaining business activity that is significant when compared to the corporation's business prior to the disposition. The addition of a safe harbor, embodied in the second sentence of section 12.02(a), under which a significant business activity exists if the continuing business activity represented at least 25 percent of the total assets and 25 percent of either income from continuing operations before income taxes or revenues from continuing operations, in each case of the company and its subsidiaries on a consolidated basis for the most recent full fiscal year, the corporation will conclusively be deemed to have retained a significant continuing business activity, represents a policy judgment that a greater measure of certainty than is provided by interpretations of the current case law is highly desirable. The application of this bright-line safe-harbor test should, in most cases, produce a reasonably clear result substantially in conformity with the approaches taken in the better case law developing the "quantitative" and "qualitative" analyses. The test is to be applied to assets, revenue, and income as of the time immediately before the decision to make the disposition in question.

If a corporation disposes of assets for the purpose of reinvesting the proceeds of the disposition in substantially the same business in a somewhat different form (for example, by selling the corporation's only plant for the purpose of buying or building a replacement plant), the disposition and reinvestment should be treated together, so that the transaction should not be deemed to leave the corporation without a significant continuing business activity.

In determining whether a disposition would leave a corporation without a significant continuing business activity, the term "the corporation" includes subsidiaries that are or should be consolidated with the parent under generally accepted accounting principles. Accordingly, if, for example, a corporation's only significant business is owned by a wholly or almost wholly owned subsidiary, a sale of that business requires approval of the parent's shareholders under section 12.02. See Schwadel v. Uchitel, 455 So.2d 401 (Fla.App.1984). Correspondingly, if a corporation owns one significant business directly, and several other significant businesses through one or more wholly or almost wholly owned subsidiaries, a sale by the corporation of the single business it owns directly does not require shareholder approval under section 12.02.

If all or a large part of a corporation's assets are held for investment, the corporation actively manages those assets, and it has no other significant business, for purposes of the statute the corporation should be considered to be in the business of investing in such assets, so that a sale of most of those assets without a reinvestment should be considered a sale that would leave the corporation without a significant continuing business activity. In applying the 25 percent tests of section 12.02(a), an issue could arise if a corporation had more than one business activity, one or more of which might be traditional operating activities such as manufacturing or distribution, and another of which might be considered managing investments in other securities or enterprises. If the activity constituting the management of investments is to be a continuing business activity as a result of the active engagement of the management of the corporation in that process, and the 25 percent tests were met upon the disposition of the other businesses, shareholder approval would not be required.

As under section 6.40(d) (determination of whether a dividend is permissible), and for the same reasons, the board of directors may base a determination that a retained continuing business falls within the 25 percent bright-line tests of the safe harbor embodied in the second sentence of section 12.02(a) either on accounting principles and practices that are reasonable in the circumstances or (in applying the asset test) on a fair valuation or other method that is reasonable in the circumstances. See section 6.40(d) and Comment 4 thereto.

The utilization of the term "significant," and the specific 25 percent safe harbor test for purposes of this section, should not be read as implying a standard for the test of significance or materiality for any other purposes under the Act or otherwise.

2. Submission to Shareholders

Section 12.02(b) requires the board of directors, after having adopted a resolution authorizing a disposition that requires shareholder approval, to submit the disposition to the shareholders for approval. When submitting the disposition to the shareholders, the board of directors must make a recommendation to the shareholders that the disposition be approved, unless the board makes a determination that because of conflicts of interests or other special circumstances it should make no recommendation. For example, the board of directors may make such a determination where there is not a sufficient number of directors free of a conflicting interest to approve the transaction or because the board of directors is evenly divided as to the merits of a transaction but is able to agree that shareholders should be permitted to consider the transaction. If the board of directors makes such a determination, it must describe the conflicts of interests or special circumstances, and communicate the basis for the determination, when submitting the disposition to the shareholders. The exception for conflicts of interest or other special circumstances is intended to be sparingly available. Generally, shareholders should not be asked to act on a disposition in the absence of a recommendation by the board of directors. The exception is not intended to relieve the board of directors of its duty to consider carefully the proposed transaction and the interests of shareholders.

Section 12.02(c) permits the board of directors to condition its submission of a proposed disposition to the shareholders. Among the conditions that board might impose are that the disposition will not be deemed approved: (i) unless it is approved by a specified percentage of the shareholders, or by one or more specified classes or series of shares, voting as a separate voting group, or by a specified percentage of disinterested shareholders, or (ii) if shareholders holding more than a specified fraction of the outstanding shares assert appraisal rights. The board of directors is not limited to conditions of these types.

3. Quorum and Voting

Section 12.02(e) provides that approval of a [disposition by the shareholders] requires approval of the shareholders at a meeting at which at least a majority of the votes entitled to be cast on the plan is present, including, if any class or series of shares are entitled to vote as a separate group on the plan, the approval of each such separate group at a meeting at which a similar quorum of the voting group exists. If a quorum is present, then under sections 7.25 and 7.26 the [disposition] will be approved if more votes are cast in favor of the [disposition] than against it by the voting group or separate voting groups entitled to vote on the [disposition]. This represents a change from the Act's previous voting rule, which required approval by a majority of outstanding shares.

In lieu of approval at a shareholders' meeting, approval can be given by the consent of all the shareholders entitled to vote on the merger or share exchange, under the procedures set forth in section 7.04.

4. Appraisal Rights

Shareholders of a domestic corporation that engages in a disposition that requires shareholder approval under section 12.02 may have appraisal rights. See chapter 13.

Chapter 13

DISSENTERS' RIGHTS

Subchapter A

§ 13.01 Definitions

In this chapter:

(1) "Affiliate" means a person that directly or indirectly through one or more intermediaries controls, is controlled by, or is under common control with another person or is a senior executive thereof. For purposes of section 13.02(b)(4), a person is deemed to be an affiliate of its senior executives.

(2) "Beneficial shareholder" means a person who is the beneficial owner of shares held in a voting trust or by a nominee on the beneficial owner's behalf.

(3) "Corporation" means the issuer of the shares held by a shareholder demanding appraisal and, for matters covered in sections 13.22–13.31, includes the surviving entity in a merger.

(4) "Fair value" means the value of the corporation's shares determined:

   (i) immediately before the effectuation of the corporate action to which the shareholder objects;

   (ii) using customary and current valuation concepts and techniques generally employed for similar businesses in the context of the transaction requiring appraisal; and

   (iii) without discounting for lack of marketability or minority status except, if appropriate, for amendments to the articles pursuant to section 13.02(a)(5).

(5) "Interest" means interest from the effective date of the corporate action until the date of payment, at the rate of interest on judgments in this state on the effective date of the corporate action.

(6) "Preferred shares" means a class or series of shares whose holders have preferences over any other class or series with respect to distributions.

(7) "Record shareholder" means the person in whose name shares are registered in the records of the corporation or the beneficial owner of shares to the extent of the rights granted by a nominee certificate on file with the corporation.

(8) "Senior executive" means the chief executive officer, chief operating officer, chief financial officer, and anyone in charge of a principal business unit or function.

(9) "Shareholder" means both a record shareholder and a beneficial shareholder.

Official Comment

1. Overview

Chapter 13 deals with the tension between the desire of the corporate leadership to be able to enter new fields, acquire new enterprises, and rearrange investor rights, and the desire of investors to adhere to the rights and the risks on the basis of which they invested. Contemporary corporation statutes in the United States attempt to resolve this tension through a combination of two devices. On the one hand, through their approval of an amendment to the articles of incorporation, a merger, share exchange or disposition of assets, the majority may change the nature and shape of the enterprise and the rights of all its shareholders. On the other hand, shareholders who object to these changes may withdraw the fair value of their investment in cash through their exercise of appraisal rights.

The traditional accommodation has been sharply criticized from two directions. From the viewpoint of investors who object to the transaction, the appraisal process is criticized for providing little help to the ordinary investor because its technicalities make its use difficult, expensive, and risky. From the viewpoint of the corporate leadership, the appraisal process is criticized because it fails to protect the corporation from demands that are motivated by the hope of a nuisance settlement or by fanciful conceptions of value. See generally Bayless Manning, "The Shareholders' Appraisal Remedy: An Essay for Frank Coker," 72 Yale L.J. 223 (1962).

Chapter 13 is a compromise between these opposing points of view. It is designed to increase the frequency with which assertion of appraisal rights leads to economical and satisfying solutions, and to decrease the frequency with which such assertion leads to delay, expense, and dissatisfaction. It seeks to achieve these goals primarily by simplifying and clarifying the appraisal process, as well as by motivating the parties to settle their differences in private negotiations without resort to judicial appraisal proceedings.

Chapter 13 proceeds from the premise that judicial appraisal should be provided by statute only when two conditions co-exist. First, the proposed corporate action as approved by the majority will result in a fundamental change in the shares to be affected by the action. Second, uncertainty concerning the fair value of the affected shares may cause reasonable persons to differ about the fairness of the terms of the corporate action. Uncertainty is greatly reduced, however, in the case of publicly-traded shares. This explains both the market exception described below and the limits provided to the exception.

Appraisal rights in connection with mergers and share exchanges under chapter 11 and dispositions of assets requiring shareholder approval under chapter 12 are provided when these two conditions co-exist. Each of these actions will result in a fundamental change in the shares that a disapproving shareholder may feel was not adequately compensated by the terms approved by the majority. Except for shareholders of a subsidiary corporation that is merged under section 11.05 (the "short-form" merger), only those shareholders who are entitled to vote on a transaction are entitled to appraisal rights. The linkage between voting and appraisal rights is justified because the right to a shareholder vote is a good proxy for assessing the seriousness of the change contemplated by the corporate action. This is especially true where the action triggers group-voting provisions.

Notwithstanding this linkage, amended chapter 13 eliminates appraisal for voting shareholders in several instances where it would have been available under the 1984 Act. Shareholders who are entitled to vote on a corporate action, whether because such shareholders have general voting rights or because group voting provisions are triggered, are not entitled to appraisal if the change will not alter the terms of the class or series of securities that they hold. Thus, statutory appraisal rights are not available for shares of any class of the surviving corporation in a merger or any class of shares that is not included in a share exchange. Appraisal is also not triggered by a voluntary dissolution under chapter 14 because that action does not affect liquidation rights—the only rights that are relevant following a shareholder vote to dissolve.

With the exception of reverse stock splits that result in cashing out some of the shares of a class or series, amended chapter 13 also eliminates appraisal in connection with all amendments to the articles of incorporation. This change in amended chapter 13 does not reflect a judgment that an amendment changing the terms of a particular class or series may not have significant economic effects. Rather, it reflects a judgment that distinguishing among different types of amendments for the purposes of statutory appraisal is necessarily arbitrary and thus may not accurately reflect the actual demand of shareholders for appraisal in specific instances. Instead, amended chapter 13 permits a high degree of private-ordering by delineating a list of transactions for which the corporation may voluntarily choose to provide appraisal and by permitting a provision in the articles of incorporation that eliminates, in whole or in part, statutory appraisal rights for preferred shares.

Chapter 13 also is unique in its approach to appraisal rights for publicly-traded shares. Approximately half of the general corporation statutes in the United States provide exceptions to appraisal for publicly-traded shares, on the theory that it is not productive to expose the corporation to the time, expense and cash drain imposed by appraisal demands when shareholders who are dissatisfied with the consideration offered in an appraisal-triggering transaction could sell their shares and obtain cash from the market. This exception to appraisal is generally known as the "market-out" and is referred to here as the "market exception." Opponents of the market exception argue that it results in unfairness where neither the consideration offered in connection with the transaction nor the market price reflects the fair value of the shares, particularly if the corporate decision-makers have a conflict of interest.

Chapter 13 seeks to accommodate both views by providing a market exception that is limited to those situations where shareholders are likely to receive fair value when they sell their shares in the market after the announcement of an appraisal-triggering transaction. For the market exception to apply under chapter 13, there must first be a liquid market. Second, unique to chapter 13, the market exception does not apply in specified circumstances where the appraisal-triggering action is deemed to be a conflict-of-interest transaction.

2. Definitions

Section 13.01 contains specialized definitions applicable only to chapter 13. . . .

Fair value

Subsection (i) of the definition of "fair value" in section 13.01(4) makes clear that fair value is to be determined immediately before the effectuation of the corporate action, rather than, as is the case under most state statutes that address the issue, the date of the shareholders' vote. . . .

The new formulation in paragraph (ii), which is patterned on section 7.22 of the Principles of Corporate Governance promulgated by the American Law Institute, directs courts to keep the methodology chosen in appraisal proceedings consistent with evolving economic concepts and adopts that part of section 7.22 which provides that fair value should be determined using "customary valuation concepts and techniques generally employed . . . for similar businesses in the context of the transaction requiring appraisal." Subsection (ii) adopts the accepted view that different transactions and different contexts may warrant different valuation methodologies. Customary valuation concepts and techniques will typically take into account numerous relevant factors, including assigning a higher valuation to corporate assets that would be more productive if acquired in a comparable transaction but excluding any element of value attributable to the unique synergies of the actual purchaser of the corporation or its assets. For example, if the corporation's assets include undeveloped real estate that is located in a prime commercial area, the court should consider the value that would be attributed to the real estate as commercial development property in a comparable transaction. The court should not, however, assign any additional value based upon the specific plans or special use of the actual purchaser.

Modern valuation methods will normally result in a range of values, not a particular single value. When a transaction falls within that range, "fair value" has been established. Absent unusual circumstances, it is expected that the consideration in an arm's-length transaction will fall within the range of "fair value" for purposes of section 13.01(4). Section 7.22 of the ALI Principles of Corporate Governance also provides that in situations that do not involve certain types of specified conflicts of interest, "the aggregate price accepted by the board of directors of the subject corporation should be presumed to represent the fair value of the corporation, or of the assets sold in the case of an asset sale, unless the plaintiff can prove otherwise by clear and convincing evidence." That presumption has not been included in the definition of "fair value" in section 13.01(4) because the framework of defined types of conflict transactions which is a predicate for the ALI's presumption is not contained in the Model Act. Nonetheless, under section 13.01(4), a court determining fair value should give great deference to the aggregate consideration accepted or approved by a disinterested board of directors for an appraisal-triggering transaction.

Subsection (iii) of the definition of "fair value" establishes that valuation discounts for lack of marketability or minority status are inappropriate in most appraisal actions, both because most transactions that trigger appraisal rights affect the corporation as a whole and because such discounts give the majority the opportunity to take advantage of minority shareholders who have been forced against their will to accept the appraisal-triggering transaction. Subsection (iii), in conjunction with the lead-in language to the definition, is also designed to adopt the more modern view that appraisal should generally award a shareholder his or her proportional interest in the corporation after valuing the corporation as a whole, rather than the value of the shareholder's shares when valued alone. If, however, the corporation voluntarily grants appraisal fights for transactions that do not affect the entire corporation—such as certain amendments to the articles of incorporation—the court should use its discretion in applying discounts if appropriate. As the introductory clause of section 13.01 notes, the definition of "fair value" applies only to chapter 13. See the Official Comment to section 14.34 which recognizes that a minority discount may be appropriate under that section....

§ 13.02   Right to Appraisal

(a) A shareholder is entitled to appraisal rights, and to obtain payment of the fair value of that shareholder's shares, in the event of any of the following corporate actions:

   (1) consummation of a merger to which the corporation is a party (i) if shareholder approval is required for the merger by section 11.04 and the shareholder is entitled to vote on the merger, except that appraisal rights shall not be available to any shareholder of the corporation with respect to shares of any class or series that remain outstanding after consummation of the merger, or (ii) if the corporation is a subsidiary and the merger is governed by section 11.05;

   (2) consummation of a share exchange to which the corporation is a party as the corporation whose shares will be acquired if the shareholder is entitled to vote on the exchange, except that appraisal rights shall not be available to any shareholder of the corporation with respect to any class or series of shares of the corporation that is not exchanged;

   (3) consummation of a disposition of assets pursuant to section 12.02 if the shareholder is entitled to vote on the disposition;

   (4) an amendment of the articles of incorporation with respect to a class or series of shares that reduces the number of shares of a class or series owned by the shareholder to a fraction of a share if the corporation has the obligation or right to repurchase the fractional share so created;

   (5) any other amendment to the articles of incorporation, merger, share exchange or disposition of assets to the extent provided by the articles of incorporation, bylaws or a resolution of the board of directors;

   (6) consummation of a domestication if the shareholder does not receive shares in the foreign corporation resulting from the domestication that have terms as favorable to the shareholder in all material respects, and represent at least the same percentage interest of the total voting rights of the outstanding shares of the corporation, as the shares held by the shareholder before the domestication;

   (7) consummation of a conversion of the corporation to nonprofit status pursuant to subchapter 9C; or

   (8) consummation of a conversion of the corporation to an unincorporated entity pursuant to subchapter 9E.

(b) Notwithstanding subsection (a), the availability of appraisal rights under subsection (a)(1), (2), (3), (4), (6) and (8) shall be limited in accordance with the following provisions:

(1) Appraisal rights shall not be available for the holders of shares of any class or series of shares which is:

    (i) listed on the New York Stock Exchange or the American Stock Exchange or designated as a national market system security on an interdealer quotation system by the National Association of Securities Dealers, Inc.; or

    (ii) not so listed or designated, but has at least 2,000 shareholders and the outstanding shares of such class or series has a market value of at least $20 million (exclusive of the value of such shares held by its subsidiaries, senior executives, directors and beneficial shareholders owning more than 10 percent of such shares).

(2) The applicability of subsection (b)(1) shall be determined as of:

    (i) the record date fixed to determine the shareholders entitled to receive notice of, and to vote at, the meeting of shareholders to act upon the corporate action requiring appraisal rights; or

    (ii) the day before the effective date of such corporate action if there is no meeting of shareholders.

(3) Subsection (b)(1) shall not be applicable and appraisal rights shall be available pursuant to subsection (a) for the holders of any class or series of shares who are required by the terms of the corporate action requiring appraisal rights to accept for such shares anything other than cash or shares of any class or any series of shares of any corporation, or any other proprietary interest of any other entity, that satisfies the standards set forth in subsection (b)(1) at the time the corporate action becomes effective.

(4) Subsection (b)(1) shall not be applicable and appraisal rights shall be available pursuant to subsection (a) for the holders of any class or series of shares where:

    (i) any of the shares or assets of the corporation are being acquired or converted, whether by merger, share exchange or otherwise, pursuant to the corporate action by a person, or by an affiliate of a person, who:

        (A) is, or at any time in the one-year period immediately preceding approval by the board of directors of the corporate action requiring appraisal rights was, the beneficial owner of 20 percent or more of the voting power of the corporation, excluding any shares acquired pursuant to an offer for all shares having voting power if such offer was made within one year prior to the corporate action requiring appraisal rights for consideration of the same kind and of a value equal to or less than that paid in connection with the corporate action; or

        (B) directly or indirectly has, or at any time in the one-year period immediately preceding approval by the board of directors of the corporation of the corporate action requiring appraisal rights had, the power, contractually or otherwise, to cause the appointment or election of 25 percent or more of the directors to the board of directors of the corporation; or

(ii) any of the shares or assets of the corporation are being acquired or converted, whether by merger, share exchange or otherwise, pursuant to such corporate action by a person, or by an affiliate of a person, who is, or at any time in the one-year period immediately preceding approval by the board of directors of the corporate action requiring appraisal rights was, a senior executive or director of the corporation or a senior executive of any affiliate thereof, and that senior executive or director will receive, as a result of the corporate action, a financial benefit not generally available to other shareholders as such, other than:

(A) employment, consulting, retirement or similar benefits established separately and not as part of or in contemplation of the corporate action; or

(B) employment, consulting, retirement or similar benefits established in contemplation of, or as part of, the corporate action that are not more favorable than those existing before the corporate action or, if more favorable, that have been approved on behalf of the corporation in the same manner as is provided in section 8.62; or

(C) in the case of a director of the corporation who will, in the corporate action, become a director of the acquiring entity in the corporate action or one of its affiliates, rights and benefits as a director that are provided on the same basis as those afforded by the acquiring entity generally to other directors of such entity or such affiliate.

(5) For the purposes of paragraph (4) only, the term "beneficial owner" means any person who, directly or indirectly, through any contract, arrangement, or understanding, other than a revocable proxy, has or shares the power to vote, or to direct the voting of, shares, provided that a member of a national securities exchange shall not be deemed to be a beneficial owner of securities held directly or indirectly by it on behalf of another person solely because such member is the record holder of such securities if the member is precluded by the rules of such exchange from voting without instruction on contested matters or matters that may affect substantially the rights or privileges of the holders of the securities to be voted. When two or more persons agree to act together for the purpose of voting their shares of the corporation, each member of the group formed thereby shall be deemed to have acquired beneficial ownership, as of the date of such agreement, of all voting shares of the corporation beneficially owned by any member of the group.

(c) Notwithstanding any other provision of section 13.02, the articles of incorporation as originally filed or any amendment thereto may limit or eliminate appraisal rights for any class or series of preferred shares, but, any such limitation or elimination contained in an amendment to the articles of incorporation that limits or eliminates appraisal rights for any of such shares that are outstanding immediately prior to the effective date of such amendment or that the corporation is or may be required to issue or sell thereafter pursuant to any conversion, exchange or other right existing immediately before the effective date of such amendment shall not apply to any corporate action that becomes effective within one year of that date if such action would otherwise afford appraisal rights.

(d) A shareholder entitled to appraisal rights under this section may not challenge a completed corporate action for which appraisal rights are available unless such corporate action:

   (1) was not effectuated in accordance with the applicable provisions of chapters 10, 11 or 12 or the corporation's articles of incorporation, bylaws or board of directors' resolution authorizing the corporate action; or

   (2) was procured as a result of fraud or material misrepresentation.

Official Comment ...

2. Market Exception to Appraisal Rights

Chapter 13 provides a limited exception to appraisal rights for those situations where shareholders can either accept the consideration offered in the appraisal-triggering transaction or can obtain the fair value of their shares by selling them in the market. This provision is predicated on the theory that where an efficient market exists, the market price will be an adequate proxy for the fair value of the corporation's shares, thus making appraisal unnecessary. Furthermore, after the corporation announces an appraisal-triggering action, the market operates at maximum efficiency with respect to that corporation's shares because interested parties and market professionals evaluate the offer and competing offers may be generated if the original offer is deemed inadequate. Moreover, the market exception reflects an evaluation that the uncertainty, costs and time commitment involved in any appraisal proceeding are not warranted where shareholders can sell their shares in an efficient, fair and liquid market. For these reasons, approximately half of the states have enacted market exceptions to their appraisal statutes.

For purposes of this chapter, the market exception is provided for a class or series if two criteria are met: the market in which the class or series is traded must be "liquid" and the value of the shares established by the appraisal-triggering event must be "reliable." Liquidity is defined in section 13.02(b)(1) and requires the class or series of stock to satisfy either of two requirements: the class or series is either listed on the New York Stock Exchange or the American Stock Exchange or is designated as a national market system security on an interdealer quotation system by the National Association of Securities Dealers, Inc.; or, although not so listed or designated, the class or series has at least 2,000 record or beneficial shareholders, provided that using both concepts does not result in duplication. In this instance, the outstanding class or series must also have a market value of at least $20 million, excluding the value of shares held by the corporation's subsidiaries, senior executives, directors and beneficial shareholders owning more than 10 percent of the class or series.

Because section 13.02(b)(3) excludes from the market exception those transactions that require shareholders to accept anything other than cash or securities that also meet the liquidity tests of section 13.02(b)(1), shareholders are assured of receiving either appraisal rights, cash from the transaction, or shares or other proprietary interests in the survivor entity that are liquid. Section 13.02(b)(2) provides that the corporation generally must satisfy the requirements of section 13.02(b)(1) on the record date for a shareholder vote on the appraisal-triggering transaction. For purposes of subsection 13.02(a)(1)(ii), the requirements of section 13.02(b)(1) must be met as of the day before the corporate action becomes effective.

3.   Appraisal Rights in Conflict Transactions

The premise of the market exception is that the market must be liquid and the valuation assigned to the relevant shares must be "reliable." Section 13.02(b)(1) is designed to assure liquidity. For purposes of these provisions, section 13.02(b)(4) is designed to assure reliability by recognizing that the market price of, or consideration for, shares of a corporation that proposes to engage in a section 13.02(a) transaction may be subject to influences where a corporation's management, controlling shareholders or directors have conflicting interests that could, if not dealt with appropriately adversely affect the consideration that otherwise could have been expected. Section 13.02(b)(4) addresses two groups of conflict transactions: those in clause (i), which involve controlling shareholders; and those in clause (ii), which involve senior executives and directors.

Section 13.02(b)(4)(i) covers two possible conflict situations: subsection (A) covers the acquisition or exchange of shares or assets of the corporation by a shareholder or an affiliate of the shareholder that could be considered controlling by virtue of ownership of a substantial amount of voting stock (20 percent); and subsection (B) covers the acquisition or exchange of shares or assets of the corporation by an individual or group, or by an affiliate of such individual or group, that has the ability to exercise control, through contract, stock ownership, or some other means, over at least one fourth of the board's membership. The definition of "beneficial owner" in section 13.02(b)(5) serves to identify possible conflict situations by deeming each member of a group that agrees to vote in tandem to be a beneficial owner of all the voting shares owned by the group. In contrast, the term "beneficial shareholder," as defined in section 13.01(2), is used to identify those persons entitled to appraisal rights. The last portion of subsection (A) recognizes that an acquisition effected in two steps (a tender offer followed by a merger) within one year, where the two steps are either on the same terms or the second step is on terms that are more favorable to target shareholders, is properly considered a single transaction for purposes of identifying conflict transactions, regardless of whether the second-step merger is governed by sections 11.04 or 11.05.

Section 13.02(b)(4)(ii) covers the acquisition or exchange of shares or assets of the corporation by a person, or an affiliate of a person, who is, or in the year leading up to the transaction was, a senior executive or director of the corporation. The section eliminates the market exception for management buyouts because participation in the buyout group is itself "a financial benefit not available to other shareholders as such." The market exception is also not available for transactions involving other types of economic benefits (in addition to benefits afforded to shareholders generally, as such) afforded to senior executives (as defined in section 13.01(8)) and directors in specified conflict situations, unless specific objective or procedural standards are met. Section 13.01(1) specially defines the term "affiliate" for purposes of section 13.02(b)(4) to include an entity of which a person is a senior executive. Due to this specialized definition, if a senior executive of the corporation is to continue and is to receive enumerated employment and other financial benefits after the transaction, the availability of the market exception will depend on meeting one of the three conditions specified in clauses (A), (B) and (C) of section 13.02(b)(4)(ii). . . .

5. Exclusivity of Appraisal Rights

With three exceptions, section 13.02(d) provides that appraisal is the exclusive remedy for a corporate action that has been completed.

The theory underlying this section is that when a majority of shareholders has approved a corporate change, the corporation should be permitted to proceed even if a minority considers the change unwise or disadvantageous. The very existence of the appraisal remedy recognizes that shareholders may disagree about the financial consequences that a corporate action may have and some may hold such strong views that they will want to vindicate them in a judicial proceeding. Since a judicial proceeding is insulated from the dynamics of an actual negotiation, it is not surprising that the two processes could produce different valuations. Accordingly, if such a proceeding results in an award of additional consideration to the shareholders who pursued appraisal, no inference should be drawn that the judgment of the majority was wrong or that compensation is now owed to shareholders who did not seek appraisal. Thus, an exclusivity principle is generally justified.

Nevertheless, there may be exceptional circumstances where judicial review of a completed transaction is warranted. The same reasoning that supports the provision of appraisal rights for conflict of interest transactions described in section 13.02(b)(3) and (4) supports the decision in the first clause of section 13.02(d) not to preclude judicial review of such transactions for fairness. Similarly, there may be instances where the process by which the corporate action was approved was so flawed that it is appropriate to provide more general relief on behalf of all affected shareholders. Thus section 13.02(d)(1) does not preclude challenges to serious procedural defects in approving the action, such as a failure to obtain the votes required by statute or by the corporation's own articles, bylaws, or board resolution authorizing the transaction. Similarly, subsection (2) creates an exception for cases where fraud or material misrepresentation have affected the shareholder vote to such an extent as to have caused the corporate action to be approved mistakenly. The concept of misrepresentation includes the omission of a material fact necessary to make statements made not misleading.

Although section 13.02(d) does not address the question of remedies, such as injunctive relief, that may be available before the corporate action is effected, it should be noted that a complaint based solely on adequacy of consideration is not actionable unless accompanied by credible allegations of wrongdoing. Since section 13.02(d) is concerned with challenges only to the corporate action, it does not address remedies, if any, that shareholders may have against directors or other persons as a result of the corporate action. See section 8.31 and Official Comment.

§ 13.03   Assertion of Rights by Nominees and Beneficial Owners

(a) A record shareholder may assert appraisal rights as to fewer than all the shares registered in the record shareholder's name but owned by a beneficial shareholder only if the record shareholder objects with respect to all shares of the class or series owned by the beneficial shareholder and notifies the corporation in writing of the name and address of each beneficial shareholder on whose behalf appraisal rights are being asserted. The rights of a record shareholder who asserts appraisal rights for only part of the shares held of record in the record shareholder's name under this subsection shall be determined as if the shares as to which the record shareholder objects and the record shareholder's other shares were registered in the names of different record shareholders.

(b) A beneficial shareholder may assert appraisal rights as to shares of any class or series held on behalf of the shareholder only if such shareholder:

(1) submits to the corporation the record shareholder's written consent to the assertion of such rights no later than the date referred to in section 13.22(b)(2)(ii); and

(2) does so with respect to all shares of the class or series that are beneficially owned by the beneficial shareholder.

Subchapter B

Procedure for Exercise of Appraisal Rights

§ 13.20 Notice of Appraisal Rights

(a) Where any corporate action specified in section 13.02(a) is to be submitted to a vote at a shareholders' meeting, the meeting notice must state that the corporation has concluded that the shareholders are, are not or may be entitled to assert appraisal rights under this chapter. If the corporation concludes that appraisal rights are or may be available, a copy of this chapter must accompany the meeting notice sent to those record shareholders entitled to exercise appraisal rights.

(b) In a merger pursuant to section 11.05, the parent corporation must notify in writing all record shareholders of the subsidiary who are entitled to assert appraisal rights that the corporate action became effective. Such notice must be sent within 10 days after the corporate action became effective and include the materials described in section 13.22.

(c) Where any corporate action specified in section 13.02(a) is to be approved by written consent of the shareholders pursuant to section 7.04:

    (1) written notice that appraisal rights are, are not or may be available must be given to each record shareholder from whom a consent is solicited at the time consent of such shareholder is first solicited and, if the corporation has concluded that appraisal rights are or may be available, must be accompanied by a copy of this chapter; and

    (2) written notice that appraisal rights are, are not or may be available must be delivered together with the notice to nonconsenting and nonvoting shareholders required by sections 7.04(e) and (f), may include the materials described in section 13.22 and, if the corporation has concluded that appraisal rights are or may be available, must be accompanied by a copy of this chapter.

§ 13.21 Notice of Intent to Demand Payment

(a) If a corporate action specified in section 13.02(a) is submitted to a vote at a shareholders' meeting, a shareholder who wishes to assert appraisal rights with respect to any class or series of shares:

    (1) must deliver to the corporation, before the vote is taken, written notice of the shareholder's intent to demand payment if the proposed action is effectuated; and

(2) must not vote, or cause or permit to be voted, any shares of such class or series in favor of the proposed action.

(b) If a corporate action specified in section 13.02(a) is to be approved by less than unanimous written consent, a shareholder who wishes to assert appraisal rights with respect to any class or series of shares must not execute a consent in favor of the proposed action with respect to that class or series of shares.

(c) A shareholder who fails to satisfy the requirements of subsection (a) or (b) is not entitled to payment under this chapter.

§ 13.22   Appraisal Notice and Form

(a) If proposed corporate action requiring appraisal rights under section 13.02(a) becomes effective, the corporation must deliver a written appraisal notice and form required by subsection (b)(1) to all shareholders who satisfied the requirements of section 13.21. In the case of a merger under section 11.05, the parent must deliver a written appraisal notice and form to all record shareholders who may be entitled to assert appraisal rights.

(b) The appraisal notice must be sent no earlier than the date the corporate action became effective and no later than ten days after such date and must:

(1) supply a form that specifies the date of the first announcement to shareholders of the principal terms of the proposed corporate action and requires the shareholder asserting appraisal rights to certify (i) whether or not beneficial ownership of those shares for which appraisal rights are asserted was acquired before that date and (ii) that the shareholder did not vote for the transaction;

(2) state:

(i) where the form must be sent and where certificates for certificated shares must be deposited and the date by which those certificates must be deposited, which date may not be earlier than the date for receiving the required form under subsection (2)(ii);

(ii) a date by which the corporation must receive the form which date may not be fewer than 40 nor more than 60 days after the date the subsection (a) appraisal notice and form are sent, and state that the shareholder shall have waived the right to demand appraisal with respect to the shares unless the form is received by the corporation by such specified date;

(iii) the corporation's estimate of the fair value of the shares;

(iv) that, if requested in writing, the corporation will provide, to the shareholder so requesting, within ten days after the date specified in subsection (2)(ii) the number of shareholders who return the forms by the specified date and the total number of shares owned by them; and

(v) the date by which the notice to withdraw under section
13.23 must be received, which date must be within 20 days
after the date specified in subsection (2)(ii); and

(3) be accompanied by a copy of this chapter.

Official Comment ...

Sections 13.22(b)(1) and (2)(i) require the corporation to specify in
the form supplied for demanding payment where the form must be sent
as well as the date of the first announcement of the terms of the
proposed corporate action. This is the critical date for determining the
rights of shareholder-transferees: persons who became shareholders
prior to that date are entitled to full appraisal rights, while persons who
became shareholders on or after that date are entitled only to the more
limited rights provided by section 13.25. See the Official Comments to
sections 13.23 and 13.25. The date set forth in the form should be the
date the principal terms of the transaction were announced by the
corporation to shareholders. This may be the day the terms were
communicated directly to the shareholders, included in a public filing
with the Securities and Exchange Commission, published in a newspaper
of general circulation that can be expected to reach the financial community, or any earlier date on which such terms were first announced by
any other person or entity to such persons or sources. Any announcement to news media or to shareholders that relates to the proposed
transaction but does not contain the principal terms of the transaction to
be authorized at the shareholders' meeting is not considered to be an
announcement for the purposes of section 13.22. . . .

§ 13.23 Perfection of Rights; Right to Withdraw

(a) A shareholder who receives notice pursuant to section 13.22 and who
wishes to exercise appraisal rights must sign and return the form
sent by the corporation and, in the case of certificated shares, deposit
the shareholder's certificates in accordance with the terms of the
notice by the date referred to in the notice pursuant to section
13.22(b)(2)(ii). In addition, if applicable, the shareholder must certify
on the form whether the beneficial owner of such shares acquired
beneficial ownership of the shares before the date required to be set
forth in the notice pursuant to section 13.22(b)(1). If a shareholder
fails to make this certification, the corporation may elect to treat the
shareholder's shares as after-acquired shares under section 13.25.
Once a shareholder deposits that shareholder's certificates or, in the
case of uncertificated shares, returns the signed forms, that shareholder loses all rights as a shareholder, unless the shareholder
withdraws pursuant to subsection (b).

(b) A shareholder who has complied with subsection (a) may nevanthe-
less decline to exercise appraisal rights and withdraw from the
appraisal process by so notifying the corporation in writing by the
date set forth in the appraisal notice pursuant to section

13.22(b)(2)(v). A shareholder who fails to so withdraw from the appraisal process may not thereafter withdraw without the corporation's written consent.

(c) A shareholder who does not execute and return the form and, in the case of certificated shares, deposit that shareholder's share certificates where required, each by the date set forth in the notice described in section 13.22(b), shall not be entitled to payment under this chapter.

Official Comment . . .

If required, the shareholder should include on the appraisal form a certification as to whether the date on which the beneficial shareholder acquired beneficial ownership of the shares was before (or on or after) the date the transaction was announced. See section 13.22(b)(1). This information permits the corporation to exercise its right under section 13.25 to defer payment of compensation for certain shares. The corporation may elect to proceed under section 13.25 with respect to those shareholders who were required to make the certification but did not do so.

Section 13.23(a) also requires persons with certificated shares who file the required form to deposit their share certificates as directed by the corporation in its appraisal notice. Once a shareholder deposits that shareholder's shares, that shareholder loses all rights as a shareholder unless the shareholder withdraws from the appraisal process pursuant to section 13.23(b). . . .

§ 13.24 Payment

(a) Except as provided in section 13.25, within 30 days after the form required by section 13.22(b)(2)(ii) is due, the corporation shall pay in cash to those shareholders who complied with section 13.23(a) the amount the corporation estimates to be the fair value of the shares, plus interest.

(b) The payment to each shareholder pursuant to subsection (a) must be accompanied by:

    (1) financial statements of the corporation that issued the shares to be appraised, consisting of a balance sheet as of the end of a fiscal year ending not more than 16 months before the date of payment, an income statement for that year, a statement of changes in shareholders' equity for that year, and the latest available interim financial statements, if any;

    (2) a statement of the corporation's estimate of the fair value of the shares, which estimate must equal or exceed the corporation's estimate given pursuant to section 13.22(b)(2)(iii);

    (3) a statement that shareholders described in subsection (a) have the right to demand further payment under section 13.26 and that if any such shareholder does not do so within the time

period specified therein, such shareholder shall be deemed to have accepted such payment in full satisfaction of the corporation's obligations under this chapter.

Official Comment

Section 13.24 is applicable both to shareholders who have complied with section 13.23(a), as well as to shareholders who are described in section 13.25(a) if the corporation so chooses. The corporation must, however, elect to treat all shareholders described in section 13.25(a) either under section 13.24 or under section 13.25; it may not elect to treat some shareholders from this group under section 13.24 but treat others under section 13.25. Considerations of simplicity and harmony may prompt the corporation to elect to treat all shareholders under section 13.24.

Section 13.24 changes the relative balance between the corporation and shareholders demanding appraisal by requiring the corporation to pay in cash within 30 days after the required form is due the corporation's estimate of the fair value of the stock plus interest. Section 13.24(b)(2) requires that estimate to at least equal the corporation's estimate of fair value given pursuant to section 13.22(b)(2)(iii). Since under section 13.23(a) all rights as a shareholder are terminated with the deposit of that shareholder's shares, the former shareholder should have immediate use of such money. A difference of opinion over the total amount to be paid should not delay payment of the amount that is undisputed. Thus, the corporation must pay its estimate of fair value, plus interest from the effective date of the corporate action, without waiting for the conclusion of the appraisal proceeding. . . .

§ 13.25 After–Acquired Shares

(a) A corporation may elect to withhold payment required by section 13.24 from any shareholder who was required to, but did not certify that beneficial ownership of all of the shareholder's shares for which appraisal rights are asserted was acquired before the date set forth in the appraisal notice sent pursuant to section13.22(b)(1).

(b) If the corporation elected to withhold payment under subsection (a), it must, within 30 days after the form required by section 13.22(b)(2)(ii) is due, notify all shareholders who are described in subsection (a):

  (1) of the information required by section 13.24(b)(1);

  (2) of the corporation's estimate of fair value pursuant to section 13.24(b)(2);

  (3) that they may accept the corporation's estimate of fair value, plus interest, in full satisfaction of their demands or demand appraisal under section 13.26;

  (4) that those shareholders who wish to accept such offer must so notify the corporation of their acceptance of the corporation's offer within 30 days after receiving the offer; and

(5) that those shareholders who do not satisfy the requirements for demanding appraisal under section 13.26 shall be deemed to have accepted the corporation's offer.

(c) Within ten days after receiving the shareholder's acceptance pursuant to subsection (b), the corporation must pay in cash the amount it offered under subsection (b)(2) to each shareholder who agreed to accept the corporation's offer in full satisfaction of the shareholder's demand.

(d) Within 40 days after sending the notice described in subsection (b), the corporation must pay in cash the amount it offered to pay under subsection (b)(2) to each shareholder described in subsection(b)(5).

Official Comment

If a public announcement of the proposed corporate action is made, section 13.25(a) gives the corporation the option to treat differently shares acquired on or after the date of that announcement. The date of any public announcement is required to be specified by the corporation in its appraisal notice under section 13.22(b)(1). At the corporation's option, holders of shares acquired on or after this date, or shareholders who are required to but do not certify otherwise under section 13.23(a), are not entitled to immediate payment under section 13.24. Instead, shareholders described in subsection (a) may receive only an offer of payment which is conditioned on their agreement to accept it in full satisfaction of their claim. If the right of unconditional immediate payment were granted as to all after-acquired shares, speculators and others might be tempted to buy shares merely for the purpose of demanding appraisal. Since the function of appraisal rights is to protect investors against unforeseen changes, there is no need to give equally favorable treatment to purchasers who knew or should have known about the proposed changes.

The date used as a cut-off for determining the application of this section is when "the principal terms" of the transaction are first announced to shareholders or to a newspaper of general circulation that can be expected to reach the financial community or included in a public filing with the Securities and Exchange Commission. The cut-off should not be set at an earlier date, such as when the first public statement that the corporate action was under consideration was made, because the goal of this section is to prevent use of appraisal rights as a speculative device after the terms of the transaction are announced. . . .

§ 13.26 Procedure if Shareholder Dissatisfied With Payment or Offer

(a) A shareholder paid pursuant to section 13.24 who is dissatisfied with the amount of the payment must notify the corporation in writing of that shareholder's estimate of the fair value of the shares and demand payment of that estimate plus interest (less any payment under section 13.24). A shareholder offered payment under section 13.25 who is dissatisfied with that offer must reject the offer and demand payment of the shareholder's stated estimate of the fair value of the shares plus interest.

(b) A shareholder who fails to notify the corporation in writing of that shareholder's demand to be paid the shareholder's stated estimate of the fair value plus interest under subsection (a) within 30 days after receiving the corporation's payment or offer of payment under section 13.24 or section 13.25, respectively, waives the right to demand payment under this section and shall be entitled only to the payment made or offered pursuant to those respective sections.

Official Comment

A shareholder who is not content with the corporation's remittance under section 13.24, or offer of remittance under section 13.25, and wishes to pursue appraisal rights further must state in writing the amount the shareholder is willing to accept. A shareholder whose demand is deemed arbitrary, unreasonable or not in good faith, however, runs the risk of being assessed litigation expenses under section 13.31. These provisions are designed to encourage settlement without a judicial proceeding.

A shareholder to whom the corporation has made payment (or who has been offered payment under section 13.25) must make a supplemental demand within 30 days after receipt of the payment or offer of payment in order to permit the corporation to make an early decision on initiating appraisal proceedings. A failure to make such demand causes the shareholder to relinquish under section 13.26(b) anything beyond the amount the corporation paid or offered to pay.

Subchapter C

Judicial Appraisal of Shares

§ 13.30 Court Action

(a) If a shareholder makes demand for payment under section 13.26 which remains unsettled, the corporation shall commence a proceeding within 60 days after receiving the payment demand and petition the court to determine the fair value of the shares and accrued interest. If the corporation does not commence the proceeding within the 60–day period, it shall pay in cash to each shareholder the amount the shareholder demanded pursuant to section 13.26 plus interest.

(b) The corporation shall commence the proceeding in the appropriate court of the county where the corporation's principal office (or, if none, its registered office) in this state is located. If the corporation is a foreign corporation without a registered office in this state, it shall commence the proceeding in the county in this state where the principal office or registered office of the domestic corporation merged with the foreign corporation was located at the time of the transaction.

(c) The corporation shall make all shareholders (whether or not residents of this state) whose demands remain unsettled parties to the proceeding as in an action against their shares, and all parties must be served with a copy of the petition. Nonresidents may be served by registered or certified mail or by publication as provided by law.

(d) The jurisdiction of the court in which the proceeding is commenced under subsection (b) is plenary and exclusive. The court may appoint one or more persons as appraisers to receive evidence and recommend a decision on the question of fair value. The appraisers shall have the powers described in the order appointing them, or in any amendment to it. The shareholders demanding appraisal rights are entitled to the same discovery rights as parties in other civil proceedings. There shall be no right to a jury trial.

(e) Each shareholder made a party to the proceeding is entitled to judgment (i) for the amount, if any, by which the court finds the fair value of the shareholder's shares, plus interest, exceeds the amount paid by the corporation to the shareholder for such shares or (ii) for the fair value, plus interest, of the shareholder's shares for which the corporation elected to withhold payment under section 13.25.

§ 13.31   Court Costs and Expenses

(a) The court in an appraisal proceeding commenced under section 13.30 shall determine all court costs of the proceeding, including the reasonable compensation and expenses of appraisers appointed by the court. The court shall assess the court costs against the corporation, except that the court may assess court costs against all or some of the shareholders demanding appraisal, in amounts the court finds equitable, to the extent the court finds such shareholders acted arbitrarily vexatiously, or not in good faith with respect to the rights provided by this chapter.

(b) The court in an appraisal proceeding may also assess the expenses of the respective parties, in amounts the court finds equitable:

   (1) against the corporation and in favor of any or all shareholders demanding appraisal if the court finds the corporation did not substantially comply with the requirements of sections 13.20, 13.22, 13.24 or 13.25; or

   (2) against either the corporation or a shareholder demanding appraisal, in favor of any other party, if the court finds that the party against whom the expenses are assessed acted arbitrarily vexatiously, or not in good faith with respect to the rights provided by this chapter.

(c) If the court in an appraisal proceeding finds that the expenses incurred by any shareholder were of substantial benefit to other shareholders similarly situated, and that such expenses should not be assessed against the corporation, the court may direct that such expenses be paid out of the amounts awarded the shareholders who were benefitted.

(d) To the extent the corporation fails to make a required payment pursuant to sections 13.24, 13.25, or 13.26, the shareholder may sue directly for the amount owed and, to the extent successful, shall be entitled to recover from the corporation all expenses of the suit.

Chapter 14

DISSOLUTION

Subchapter A

Voluntary Dissolution

§ 14.01 Dissolution by Incorporators or Initial Directors

A majority of the incorporators or initial directors of a corporation that has not issued shares or has not commenced business may dissolve the corporation by delivering to the secretary of state for filing articles of dissolution that set forth:

(1) the name of the corporation;

(2) the date of its incorporation;

(3) either (i) that none of the corporation's shares has been issued or (ii) that the corporation has not commenced business;

(4) that no debt of the corporation remains unpaid;

(5) that the net assets of the corporation remaining after winding up have been distributed to the shareholders, if shares were issued; and

(6) that a majority of the incorporators or initial directors authorized the dissolution.

§ 14.02 Dissolution by Board of Directors and Shareholders

(a) A corporation's board of directors may propose dissolution for submission to the shareholders.

(b) For a proposal to dissolve to be adopted:

(1) the board of directors must recommend dissolution to the shareholders unless the board of directors determines that because of conflict of interest or other special circumstances it should make no recommendation and communicates the basis for its determination to the shareholders; and

(2) the shareholders entitled to vote must approve the proposal to dissolve as provided in subsection (e).

(c) The board of directors may condition its submission of the proposal for dissolution on any basis.

(d) The corporation shall notify each shareholder, whether or not entitled to vote, of the proposed shareholders' meeting. The notice must
also state that the purpose, or one of the purposes, of the meeting is
to consider dissolving the corporation.

(e) Unless the articles of incorporation or the board of directors acting
pursuant to subsection (c) require a greater vote, a greater number
of shares to be present, or a vote by voting groups, adoption of the
proposal to dissolve shall require the approval of the shareholders at
a meeting at which a quorum consisting of at least a majority of the
votes entitled to be cast exists.

Official Comment

Section 14.02(b) requires the board of directors, after approving a
proposal to dissolve, to submit the proposal to the shareholders for their
approval. When submitting the proposal the board of directors must
make a recommendation to the shareholders that the plan be approved,
unless the board of directors makes a determination that because of
conflicts of interest or other special circumstances it should make no
recommendation. For example, the board or directors may make such a
determination where there is not a sufficient number of directors free of
a conflicting interest to approve the proposal or because the board of
directors is evenly divided as to the merits of the proposal but is able to
agree that shareholders should be permitted to consider dissolution. If
the board of directors makes such a determination, it must describe the
conflict of interest or special circumstances, and communicate the basis
for the determination, when submitting the proposal to dissolve to the
shareholders. The exception for conflicts of interest or other special
circumstances is intended to be sparingly available. Generally, shareholders should not be asked to act on a proposal for dissolution in the
absence of a recommendation by the board of directors. The exception is
not intended to relieve the board of directors of its duty to consider
carefully the proposed dissolution and the interests of shareholders.

Section 14.02(c) permits the board of directors to condition its
submission of a proposal for dissolution on any basis. Among the
conditions that a board might impose are that the proposal will not be
deemed approved unless it is approved by a specified vote of the
shareholders, or by one or more specified classes or series of shares,
voting as a separate voting group, or by a specified percentage of
disinterested shareholders. The board of directors is not limited to
conditions of these types.

Section 14.02(d) provides that if the proposal is required to be
approved by the shareholders, and if the approval is to be given at a
meeting, the corporation must notify each shareholder, whether or not
entitled to vote, of the meeting of shareholders at which the proposal is
to be submitted. Requirements concerning the timing and content of a
notice of meeting are set out in section 7.05. Section 14.02(d) does not

itself require that notice be given to nonvoting shareholders where the proposal is approved, without a meeting, by unanimous consent. However, that requirement is imposed by section 7.04(d).

Section 14.02(e) provides that approval of a proposal for dissolution requires approval of the shareholders at a meeting at which a quorum consisting of a majority of the votes entitled to be cast on the proposal exists. If a quorum is present, then under sections 7.25 and 7.26 the proposal will be approved if more votes are cast in favor of the proposal than against it by the voting group or separate voting groups entitled to vote on the proposal. This represents a change from the Act's previous voting rule for dissolution, which required approval by a majority of outstanding shares.

The Act does not mandate separate voting by voting groups or appraisal rights in relation to dissolution proposals on the theory that, upon dissolution, the rights or all classes or series of shares are fixed by the articles of incorporation. Of course, group voting rights may be conferred by the articles of incorporation or by the board of directors, acting pursuant to subsection (c).

§ 14.03   Articles of Dissolution

(a) At any time after dissolution is authorized, the corporation may dissolve by delivering to the secretary of state for filing articles of dissolution setting forth:

   (1) the name of the corporation;

   (2) the date dissolution was authorized; and

   (3) if dissolution was approved by the shareholders, a statement that the proposal to dissolve was duly approved by the shareholders in the manner required by this Act and by the articles of incorporation.

(b) A corporation is dissolved upon the effective date of its articles of dissolution.

(c) For purposes of this subchapter, ''dissolved corporation'' means a corporation whose articles of dissolution have become effective and includes a successor entity to which the remaining assets of the corporation are transferred subject to its liabilities for purposes of liquidation.

§ 14.04   Revocation of Dissolution

(a) A corporation may revoke its dissolution within 120 days of its effective date.

(b) Revocation of dissolution must be authorized in the same manner as the dissolution was authorized unless that authorization permitted revocation by action of the board of directors alone, in which event the board of directors may revoke the dissolution without shareholder action.

(c) After the revocation of dissolution is authorized, the corporation may revoke the dissolution by delivering to the secretary of state for filing articles of revocation of dissolution, together with a copy of its articles of dissolution, that set forth:

(1) the name of the corporation;

(2) the effective date of the dissolution that was revoked;

(3) the date that the revocation of dissolution was authorized;

(4) if the corporation's board of directors (or incorporators) revoked the dissolution, a statement to that effect;

(5) if the corporation's board of directors revoked a dissolution authorized by the shareholders, a statement that revocation was permitted by action by the board of directors alone pursuant to that authorization; and

(6) if shareholder action was required to revoke the dissolution, the information required by section 14.03(a)(3).

(d) Revocation of dissolution is effective upon the effective date of the articles of revocation of dissolution.

(e) When the revocation of dissolution is effective, it relates back to and takes effect as of the effective date of the dissolution and the corporation resumes carrying on its business as if dissolution had never occurred.

§ 14.05 Effect of Dissolution

(a) A dissolved corporation continues its corporate existence but may not carry on any business except that appropriate to wind up and liquidate its business and affairs, including:

(1) collecting its assets;

(2) disposing of its properties that will not be distributed in kind to its shareholders;

(3) discharging or making provision for discharging its liabilities;

(4) distributing its remaining property among its shareholders according to their interests; and

(5) doing every other act necessary to wind up and liquidate its business and affairs.

(b) Dissolution of a corporation does not:

(1) transfer title to the corporation's property;

(2) prevent transfer of its shares or securities, although the authorization to dissolve may provide for closing the corporation's share transfer records;

(3) subject its directors or officers to standards of conduct different from those prescribed in chapter 8;

(4) change quorum or voting requirements for its board of directors or shareholders; change provisions for selection, resignation, or removal of its directors or officers or both; or change provisions for amending its bylaws;

(5) prevent commencement of a proceeding by or against the corporation in its corporate name;

(6) abate or suspend a proceeding pending by or against the corporation on the effective date of dissolution; or

(7) terminate the authority of the registered agent of the corporation.

Official Comment

Section 14.05(a) provides that dissolution does not terminate the corporate existence but simply requires the corporation thereafter to devote itself to winding up its affairs and liquidating its assets; after dissolution, the corporation may not carry on its business except as may be appropriate for winding-up.

The Model Act uses the term "dissolution" in the specialized sense described above and not to describe the final step in the liquidation of the corporate business. This is made clear by section 14.05(b), which provides that chapter 14 dissolution does not have any of the characteristics of common law dissolution, which treated corporate dissolution as analogous to the death of a natural person and abated lawsuits, vested equitable title to corporate property in the shareholders, imposed the fiduciary duty of trustees on directors who had custody of corporate assets, and revoked the authority of the registered agent. Section 14.05(b) expressly reverses all of these common law attributes of dissolution and makes clear that the rights, powers, and duties of shareholders, the directors, and the registered agent are not affected by dissolution and that suits by or against the corporation are not affected in any way.

§ 14.06 Known Claims Against Dissolved Corporation

(a) A dissolved corporation may dispose of the known claims against it by notifying its known claimants in writing of the dissolution at any time after its effective date.

(b) The written notice must:

(1) describe information that must be included in a claim;

(2) provide a mailing address where a claim may be sent;

(3) state the deadline, which may not be fewer than 120 days from the effective date of the written notice, by which the dissolved corporation must receive the claim; and

(4) state that the claim will be barred if not received by the deadline.

(c) A claim against the dissolved corporation is barred:

   (1) if a claimant who was given written notice under subsection (b) does not deliver the claim to the dissolved corporation by the deadline; or

   (2) if a claimant whose claim was rejected by the dissolved corporation does not commence a proceeding to enforce the claim within 90 days from the effective date of the rejection notice.

(d) For purposes of this section, "claim" does not include a contingent liability or a claim based on an event occurring after the effective date of dissolution.

§ 14.07 Other Claims Against Dissolved Corporation

(a) A dissolved corporation may also publish notice of its dissolution and request that persons with claims against the dissolved corporation present them in accordance with the notice.

(b) The notice must:

   (1) be published one time in a newspaper of general circulation in the county where the dissolved corporation's principal office (or, if none in this state, its registered office) is or was last located;

   (2) describe the information that must be included in a claim and provide a mailing address where the claim may be sent; and

   (3) state that a claim against the dissolved corporation will be barred unless a proceeding to enforce the claim is commenced within three years after the publication of the notice.

(c) If the dissolved corporation publishes a newspaper notice in accordance with subsection (b), the claim of each of the following claimants is barred unless the claimant commences a proceeding to enforce the claim against the dissolved corporation within three years after the publication date of the newspaper notice:

   (1) a claimant who was not given written notice under section 14.06;

   (2) a claimant whose claim was timely sent to the dissolved corporation but not acted on;

   (3) a claimant whose claim is contingent or based on an event occurring after the effective date of dissolution.

(d) A claim that is not barred by section 14.06(c) or section 14.07(c) may be enforced:

   (1) against the dissolved corporation, to the extent of its undistributed assets; or

   (2) except as provided in section 14.08(d), if the assets have been distributed in liquidation, against a shareholder of the dissolved corporation to the extent of the shareholder's pro rata share of

the claim or the corporate assets distributed to the shareholder in liquidation, whichever is less, but a shareholder's total liability for all claims under this section may not exceed the total amount of assets distributed to the shareholder.

Official Comment

Earlier versions of the Model Act did not recognize the serious problem created by possible claims that might arise long after the dissolution process was completed and the corporate assets distributed to shareholders. Most of these claims were based on personal injuries occurring after dissolution, but caused by allegedly defective products sold before dissolution. The application of the Model Act provision (and of the state dissolution statutes phrased in different terms) to this problem led to confusing and inconsistent results. The problems raised by these claims are intractable: on the one hand, the application of a mechanical limitation period to a claim for injury that occurs after the period has expired involves obvious injustice to the plaintiff. On the other hand, to permit these suits generally makes it impossible ever to complete the winding up of the corporation, make suitable provision for creditors, and distribute the balance of the corporate assets to the shareholders. Evolving legal rules make estimating future liability for personal injury claims difficult.

In some circumstances successor liability theories have been applied to allow plaintiffs incurring post-dissolution injuries to bring suit against the person that acquired the corporate assets. Some courts have refused to broaden these doctrines, particularly when the purchaser of the corporate assets has not continued the business of the dissolved corporation. In these cases, the remedy of the plaintiff is limited to claims against the dissolved corporation and its shareholders receiving assets pursuant to the dissolution.

The solution adopted in section 14.07 is to continue the liability of a dissolved corporation for subsequent claims for a period of three years after it publishes notice of dissolution. It is recognized that a three year cut-off is itself arbitrary, but it is believed that the bulk of post-dissolution claims that can be estimated will arise during this period. This provision is therefore believed to be a reasonable compromise between the competing considerations of providing a remedy to injured plaintiffs and providing a basis for directors to estimate liabilities so that dissolved corporations may distribute remaining assets free of all claims and shareholders may receive them secure in the knowledge that they may not be reclaimed. The period of three years for asserting claims is within the range of time periods adopted by state statutes.

Directors must generally discharge or make provision for discharging the corporation's liabilities before distributing the remaining assets to the shareholders. See section 14.09(a). Many claims covered by this section are of a type for which provision may be made by the purchase of insurance or by the setting aside of a portion of the assets, thereby permitting prompt distributions in liquidation. Claimants, of course, may always have recourse to the remaining assets of the dissolved corporation. See section 14.07(d)(1). Further, where unbarred claims arise after distributions have been made to shareholders in liquidation, section 14.07(d)(2) authorizes recovery against the shareholders receiving the earlier distributions. The recovery, however, is limited to the smaller of the recipient shareholders' pro rata share of the claim or the total amount of assets received as liquidating distributions by the shareholder from the corporation. The provision ensures that claimants seeking to recover distributions from shareholders will try to recover from the entire class of shareholders rather than concentrating only on the larger shareholders and protects the limited liability of shareholders. Shareholders also may be liable to directors for recoupment under section 8.33(b)(2).

§ 14.08   Court Proceedings

(a) A dissolved corporation that has published a notice under section 14.07 may file an application with the [name or describe] court of the county where the dissolved corporation's principal office (or, if none in this state, its registered office) is located for a determination of the amount and form of security to be provided for payment of claims that are contingent or have not been made known to the dissolved corporation or that are based on an event occurring after the effective date of dissolution but that, based on the facts known to the dissolved corporation, are reasonably estimated to arise after the effective date of dissolution. Provision need not be made for any claim that is or is reasonably anticipated to be barred under section 14.07(c).

(b) Within 10 days after the filing of the application, notice of the proceeding shall be given by the dissolved corporation to each claimant holding a contingent claim whose contingent claim is shown on the records of the dissolved corporation.

(c) The court may appoint a guardian ad litem to represent all claimants whose identities are unknown in any proceeding brought under this section. The reasonable fees and expenses of such guardian, including all reasonable expert witness fees, shall be paid by the dissolved corporation.

(d) Provision by the dissolved corporation for security in the amount and the form ordered by the court under section 14.08(a) shall satisfy the dissolved corporation's obligations with respect to claims that are contingent, have not been made known to the dissolved corporation or are based on an event occurring after the effective date of dissolution, and such claims may not be enforced against a shareholder who received assets in liquidation.

Official Comment

Section 14.08 adds a provision to the Model Act allowing a dissolved corporation to initiate a proceeding to establish the provision that should be made for unknown or contingent claims before a distribution in liquidation is made to shareholders. Similar proceedings are authorized in several states to remove the risk of director and shareholder liability for inadequate provision for claims.

Section 14.08(a) authorizes the proceeding and specifies that provision for unknown and contingent claims can only be for those claims that are estimated to arise after dissolution that are not expected to be barred by section 14.07(d). The same analysis may be made by the board of directors under section 14.09 if court proceedings are not used. As a result, estimates for unknown or contingent claims, such as product liability injury claims that might arise after dissolution, need only be made for those claims that the court determines are reasonably anticipated to be asserted within three years after dissolution. Such estimates might reasonably be based on the claims experience of the corporation prior to its dissolution.

If the dissolved corporation elects to initiate a proceeding, it must give notice of the proceeding within 10 days after filing the court application to each holder of a contingent claim whose claim is shown on the records of the corporation. Notice to holders of guarantees made by the corporation typically would be required under this subsection.

Subsection (c) allows the court to appoint a guardian ad litem for unknown claimants, but does not make the appointment mandatory. Reasonable fees and expenses of the guardian ad litem are to be paid by the dissolved corporation. Section 14.08 is designed to permit the court to adopt procedures appropriate to the circumstances.

If the proceeding is completed, section 14.08(d) establishes that the dissolved corporation is deemed to have satisfied its obligation to discharge or make provision for discharging its liabilities (see section 14.05(a)(3)). With respect to claims that have not matured, directors are protected from liability by section 14.09(b), and shareholders are protected from claims under section 14.08(d).

If a court determines that the corporation is dissolving for the primary purpose of avoiding anticipated claims of future tort claimants, it is expected that the court will use its general discretionary powers and deny the protections of section 14.08 to the dissolved corporation.

§ 14.09 Director Duties

(a) Directors shall cause the dissolved corporation to discharge or make reasonable provision for the payment of claims and make distributions of assets to shareholders after payment or provision for claims.

(b) Directors of a dissolved corporation which has disposed of claims under sections 14.06, 14.07, or 14.08 shall not be liable for breach of section 14.09(a) with respect to claims against the dissolved corporation that are barred or satisfied under sections 14.06, 14.07, or 14.08.

Official Comment

New section 14.09(a) establishes the duty of directors to discharge or make provision for claims and to make distributions of the remaining assets to shareholders. The earlier version of chapter 14 inferred the obligation from sections 14.05(3) and (4) concerning the powers of the corporation to pay claims and make distributions upon dissolution. Liability of directors formerly was based on violations of section 6.40 concerning distributions. New section 6.40(h) removed distributions in liquidation from the coverage of section 6.40.

Section 14.09(b) provides that directors of a dissolved corporation that complies with sections 14.06, 14.07, or 14.08 are not liable for breach of section 14.09(a) with respect to claims that are disposed of under those sections. For example, directors need not make provision for claims of known creditors who are barred under section 14.06 for failure to file a claim or commence a proceeding within the specified times, for contingent claimants whose estimated claims are barred by the three-year period after publication, pursuant to section 14.07(c), or for claimants such as guarantors if provision for the claims have been approved by a court under section 14.08(d).

Section 14.09(b) leaves unchanged the section 8.33 provision that director liability is to the corporation. There are, however, cases that under various theories recognize liability directly to creditors for wrongful payments in liquidation. While there might be circumstances under which direct creditor claims are appropriate, the basic approach of chapter 14 is that claims for breach of duty of directors for breach of section 14.09(a) and claims against shareholders for recoupment of amounts improperly distributed in liquidation should be mediated through the corporation.

Subchapter B

Administrative Dissolution

§ 14.20   Grounds for Administrative Dissolution

The secretary of state may commence a proceeding under section 14.21 to administratively dissolve a corporation if:

(1) the corporation does not pay within 60 days after they are due any franchise taxes or penalties imposed by this Act or other law;

(2) the corporation does not deliver its annual report to the secretary of state within 60 days after it is due;

(3) the corporation is without a registered agent or registered office in this state for 60 days or more;

(4) the corporation does not notify the secretary of state within 60 days that its registered agent or registered office has been changed, that its registered agent has resigned, or that its registered office has been discontinued; or

(5) the corporation's period of duration stated in its articles of incorporation expires.

Subchapter C

Judicial Dissolution

§ 14.30   Grounds for Judicial Dissolution

The [name or describe court or courts] may dissolve a corporation:

(a) (1) in a proceeding by the attorney general if it is established that:

    (i) the corporation obtained its articles of incorporation through fraud; or

    (ii) the corporation has continued to exceed or abuse the authority conferred upon it by law;

(2) in a proceeding by a shareholder if it is established that:

    (i) the directors are deadlocked in the management of the corporate affairs, the shareholders are unable to break the deadlock, and irreparable injury to the corporation is threatened or being suffered, or the business and affairs of the corporation can no longer be conducted to the advantage of the shareholders generally, because of the deadlock;

    (ii) the directors or those in control of the corporation have acted, are acting, or will act in a manner that is illegal, oppressive, or fraudulent;

    (iii) the shareholders are deadlocked in voting power and have failed, for a period that includes at least two consecutive annual meeting dates, to elect successors to directors whose terms have expired; or

    (iv) the corporate assets are being misapplied or wasted;

(3) in a proceeding by a creditor if it is established that:

    (i) the creditor's claim has been reduced to judgment, the execution on the judgment returned unsatisfied, and the corporation is insolvent; or

    (ii) the corporation has admitted in writing that the creditor's claim is due and owing and the corporation is insolvent; or

(4) in a proceeding by the corporation to have its voluntary dissolution continued under court supervision.

(5) in a proceeding by a shareholder if the corporation has abandoned its business and has failed within a reasonable time to liquidate and distribute its assets and dissolve.

(b) Section 14.30(a)(2) shall not apply in the case of a corporation that, on the date of the filing of the proceeding, has shares that are

(i) listed on the New York Stock Exchange, the American Stock Exchange or on any exchange owned or operated by the NASDAQ Stock Market LLC, or listed or quoted on a system owned or operated by the National Association of Securities Dealers, Inc.; or

(ii) not so listed or quoted, but are held by at least 300 shareholders and the shares outstanding have a market value of at least $20 million (exclusive of the value of such shares held by the corporation's subsidiaries, senior executives, directors and beneficial shareholders owning more than 10 percent of such shares).

(c) In this section, "beneficial shareholder" has the meaning specified in section 13.01(2).

Official Comment

Section 14.30(a) provides grounds for judicial dissolution of corporations at the request of the state, a shareholder, a creditor, or a corporation which has commenced voluntary dissolution. The section states that a court "may" order dissolution if a ground for dissolution exists. Thus, there is discretion on the part of the court as to whether dissolution is appropriate even though grounds exist under the specific circumstances. The grounds listed in section 14.30(a)(2) are available only if the corporation does not meet the tests for being publicly traded set forth in section 14.30(b)....

2. Involuntary Dissolution by Shareholders

Section 14.30(a)(2) provides for involuntary dissolution at the suit of a shareholder under circumstances involving deadlock or significant abuse of power by controlling shareholders or directors. The remedy of judicial dissolution under section 14.30(a)(2) is appropriate only for shareholders of corporations that are not widely-held. Even in those situations, however, the court can take into account the number of shareholders and the nature of the trading market for the shares in deciding whether to exercise its discretion to order dissolution. Shareholders of corporations that meet the tests of section 14.30(b) will normally have the ability to sell their shares if they are dissatisfied with current management. In addition, (i) they may seek traditional remedies for breach of fiduciary duty; (ii) they may seek judicial removal of directors in case of fraud, gross abuse of power, or the intentional infliction of harm on the corporation, under section 8.09, or (iii) in the narrow circumstances covered in section 7.48(a), if irreparable injury is occurring or threatened, they may seek the appointment of a custodian or receiver outside the context of a dissolution proceeding. In contrast, a resort to litigation may result in an irreparable breach of personal relationships among the shareholders of a non-public corporation, making it impossible for them to continue in business to their mutual advantage, and making liquidation and dissolution (subject to the buy-out provisions of section 14.34) the appropriate solution. The grounds for dissolution under section 14.30(a)(2) are broader than those required to be shown for the appointment of a custodian or receiver under section 7.48(a). The difference is attributable to the different focus of the two proceedings. While some of the grounds listed in 14.30(a)(2), such as deadlock, may implicate the welfare of the corporation as a whole, the primary focus is on the effect of actions by those in control on the value of the complaining shareholder's individual investment: for example, the "oppression" ground in section 14.30(a)(2)(ii) is often cited in complaints for dissolution and generally describes action directed against a particular shareholder. In contrast, the primary focus of an action to appoint a custodian or receiver under section 7.48(a) is the corporate entity, and the action is intended to protect the interests of all shareholders, creditors and others who may have an interest therein. In other instances, action that is "illegal" or "fraudulent" under 14.30(a)(2) may be severely prejudicial to the interests of the individual complaining shareholder, whereas conduct that is illegal with respect to the corporation may be remedied by other causes of action available to shareholders, and "fraudulent" conduct or a board deadlock under section 7.48(a) must be accompanied by or threaten irreparable harm to warrant the appointment of a custodian or receiver. An action under section 7.48(a) may be brought by a shareholder of any corporation. . . .

§ 14.31 Procedure for Judicial Dissolution

(a) Venue for a proceeding by the attorney general to dissolve a corporation lies in [name the county or counties]. Venue for a proceeding brought by any other party named in section 14.30 lies in the county where a corporation's principal office (or, if none in this state, its registered office) is or was last located.

(b) It is not necessary to make shareholders parties to a proceeding to dissolve a corporation unless relief is sought against them individually.

(c) A court in a proceeding brought to dissolve a corporation may issue injunctions, appoint a receiver or custodian pendente lite with all powers and duties the court directs, take other action required to preserve the corporate assets wherever located, and carry on the business of the corporation until a full hearing can be held.

(d) Within 10 days of the commencement of a proceeding under section 14.30(2) to dissolve a corporation that is not a public corporation, the corporation must send to all shareholders, other than the petitioner, a notice stating that the shareholders are entitled to avoid the dissolution of the corporation by electing to purchase the petitioner's shares under section 14.34 and accompanied by a copy of section 14.34.

§ 14.32   Receivership or Custodianship

(a) Unless an election to purchase has been filed under section 14.34, a court in a judicial proceeding brought to dissolve a corporation may appoint one or more receivers to wind up and liquidate, or one or more custodians to manage, the business and affairs of the corporation. The court shall hold a hearing, after notifying all parties to the proceeding and any interested persons designated by the court, before appointing a receiver or custodian. The court appointing a receiver or custodian has jurisdiction over the corporation and all of its property wherever located.

(b) The court may appoint an individual or a domestic or foreign corporation (authorized to transact business in this state) as a receiver or custodian. The court may require the receiver or custodian to post bond, with or without sureties, in an amount the court directs.

(c) The court shall describe the powers and duties of the receiver or custodian in its appointing order, which may be amended from time to time. Among other powers:

   (1) the receiver (i) may dispose of all or any part of the assets of the corporation wherever located, at a public or private sale, if authorized by the court; and (ii) may sue and defend in his own name as receiver of the corporation in all courts of this state;

   (2) the custodian may exercise all of the powers of the corporation, through or in place of its board of directors or officers, to the extent necessary to manage the affairs of the corporation in the best interests of its shareholders and creditors.

(d) The court during a receivership may redesignate the receiver a custodian, and during a custodianship may redesignate the custodian a receiver, if doing so is in the best interests of the corporation, its shareholders, and creditors.

(e) The court from time to time during the receivership or custodianship may order compensation paid and expenses paid or reimbursed to the receiver or custodian from the assets of the corporation or proceeds from the sale of the assets.

§ 14.33 Decree of Dissolution

(a) If after a hearing the court determines that one or more grounds for judicial dissolution described in section 14.30 exist, it may enter a decree dissolving the corporation and specifying the effective date of the dissolution, and the clerk of the court shall deliver a certified copy of the decree to the secretary of state, who shall file it.

(b) After entering the decree of dissolution, the court shall direct the winding up and liquidation of the corporation's business and affairs in accordance with section 14.05 and the notification of claimants in accordance with sections 14.06 and 14.07.

§ 14.34 Election to Purchase in Lieu of Dissolution

(a) In a proceeding under section 14.30(2) to dissolve a corporation, the corporation may elect or, if it fails to elect, one or more shareholders may elect to purchase all shares owned by the petitioning shareholder at the fair value of the shares. An election pursuant to this section shall be irrevocable unless the court determines that it is equitable to set aside or modify the election.

(b) An election to purchase pursuant to this section may be filed with the court at any time within 90 days after the filing of the petition under section 14.30(2) or at such later time as the court in its discretion may allow. If the election to purchase is filed by one or more shareholders, the corporation shall, within 10 days thereafter, give written notice to all shareholders, other than the petitioner. The notice must state the name and number of shares owned by the petitioner and the name and number of shares owned by each electing shareholder and must advise the recipients of their right to join in the election to purchase shares in accordance with this section. Shareholders who wish to participate must file notice of their intention to join in the purchase no later than 30 days after the effective date of the notice to them. All shareholders who have filed an election or notice of their intention to participate in the election to purchase thereby become parties to the proceeding and shall participate in the purchase in proportion to their ownership of shares as of the date the first election was filed, unless they otherwise agree or the court otherwise directs. After an election has been filed by the corporation or one or more shareholders, the proceeding under section 14.30(2) may not be discontinued or settled, nor may the petitioning shareholder sell or otherwise dispose of his shares, unless the court determines that it would be equitable to the corporation and the shareholders, other than the petitioner, to permit such discontinuance, settlement, sale, or other disposition.

(c) If, within 60 days of the filing of the first election, the parties reach agreement as to the fair value and terms of purchase of the petitioner's shares, the court shall enter an order directing the purchase of petitioner's shares upon the terms and conditions agreed to by the parties.

(d) If the parties are unable to reach an agreement as provided for in subsection (c), the court, upon application of any party, shall stay the section 14.30(2) proceedings and determine the fair value of the petitioner's shares as of the day before the date on which the petition under section 14.30(2) was filed or as of such other date as the court deems appropriate under the circumstances.

(e) Upon determining the fair value of the shares, the court shall enter an order directing the purchase upon such terms and conditions as the court deems appropriate, which may include payment of the purchase price in installments, where necessary in the interests of equity, provision for security to assure payment of the purchase price and any additional costs, fees, and expenses as may have been awarded, and, if the shares are to be purchased by shareholders, the allocation of shares among them. In allocating petitioner's shares among holders of different classes of shares, the court should attempt to preserve the existing distribution of voting rights among holders of different classes insofar as practicable and may direct that holders of a specific class or classes shall not participate in the purchase. Interest may be allowed at the rate and from the date determined by the court to be equitable, but if the court finds that the refusal of the petitioning shareholder to accept an offer of payment was arbitrary or otherwise not in good faith, no interest shall be allowed. If the court finds that the petitioning shareholder had probable grounds for relief under paragraphs (ii) or (iv) of section 14.30(2), it may award to the petitioning shareholder reasonable fees and expenses of counsel and of any experts employed by him.

(f) Upon entry of an order under subsections (c) or (e), the court shall dismiss the petition to dissolve the corporation under section 14.30, and the petitioning shareholder shall no longer have any rights or status as a shareholder of the corporation, except the right to receive the amounts awarded to him by the order of the court which shall be enforceable in the same manner as any other judgment.

(g) The purchase ordered pursuant to subsection (e), shall be made within 10 days after the date the order becomes final unless before that time the corporation files with the court a notice of its intention to adopt articles of dissolution pursuant to sections 14.02 and 14.03, which articles must then be adopted and filed within 50 days thereafter. Upon filing of such articles of dissolution, the corporation shall be dissolved in accordance with the provisions of sections 14.05 through 07, and the order entered pursuant to subsection (e) shall no longer be of any force or effect, except that the court may award the petitioning shareholder reasonable fees and expenses in accordance with the provisions of the last sentence of subsection (e) and the petitioner may continue to pursue any claims previously asserted on behalf of the corporation.

(h) Any payment by the corporation pursuant to an order under subsections (c) or (e), other than an award of fees and expenses pursuant to subsection (e), is subject to the provisions of section 6.40.

Official Comment

The proceeding for judicial dissolution has become an increasingly important remedy for minority shareholders of closely-held corporations who believe that the value of their investment is threatened by reason of circumstances or conduct described in section 14.30(2). If the petitioning shareholder proves one or more grounds under section 14.30(2), he is entitled to some form of relief but many courts have hesitated to award dissolution, the only form of relief explicitly provided, because of its adverse effects on shareholders, employees, and others who may have an interest in the continuation of the business.

Commentators have observed that it is rarely necessary to dissolve the corporation and liquidate its assets in order to provide relief: the rights of the petitioning shareholder are fully protected by liquidating only his interest and paying the fair value of his shares while permitting the remaining shareholders to continue the business. In fact, it appears that most dissolution proceedings result in a buyout of one or another of the disputants' shares either pursuant to a statutory buyout provision or a negotiated settlement. See generally Hetherington & Dooley, Illiquidity and Exploitation: A Proposed Statutory Solution to the Remaining Close Corporation Problem, 63 Va.L.Rev. 1 (1977); Haynsworth, The Effectiveness of Involuntary Dissolution Suits As a Remedy for Close Corporation Dissension, 35 Clev.St.L.Rev. 25 (1987). Accordingly, section 14.34 affords an orderly procedure by which a dissolution proceeding under section 14.30(2) can be terminated upon payment of the fair value of the petitioner's shares.

1. Availability

There are two prerequisites to filing an election to purchase under section 14.34. First, a proceeding to dissolve the corporation under section 14.30(2) must have been commenced. Second, the election may be made only by the corporation or by shareholders other than the shareholder who is seeking to dissolve the corporation under section 14.30(2).

2. Effect of Filing

The election to purchase is wholly voluntary, but it can be made as a matter of right within 90 days after the filing of the petition under section 14.30(2). After 90 days, leave of court is required. Once an election is filed:

(i) The election is irrevocable and may not be set aside or modified (as to one or more parties) unless the court determines it is equitable to do so; and

(ii) The dissolution proceeding under section 14.30(2) may not be discontinued or settled and the petitioning shareholder may not dispose of his shares without court approval.

These provisions are intended to reduce the risk that either the dissolution proceeding or the buyout election will be used for strategic purposes. For example, the Official Comment to section 14.30 cautions courts to distinguish between dissolution petitions predicated on "genuine abuse" and those brought for other reasons. Section 14.34 makes strategic use of section 14.30(2) a high-risk proposition for the petitioning shareholder because his shares are, in effect, subject to a "call" for 90 days after commencement of the section 14.30(2) proceeding. The petitioner becomes irrevocably committed to sell his shares pursuant to section 14.34 once an election is filed and may not thereafter discontinue the dissolution proceeding or dispose of his shares outside of section 14.34 without permission of the court, which is specifically directed to consider whether such action would be equitable from the standpoint of the corporation and the other shareholders.

By the same token, if the corporation or the other shareholders fail to elect to purchase the petitioner's shares within the first 90 days, they run the risk that the court will decline to accept a subsequent election and will, instead, allow the dissolution proceeding to go forward. Note also that the dissolution proceeding is not affected by the mere filing of an election; it will be stayed only upon application to the court to determine the fair value of the petitioner's shares after the expiration of the 60 day negotiating period provided for in section 14.34(c).

Once an election is filed, it may be set aside or modified only for reasons that the court finds equitable. If the court sets aside the election, the corporation or the electing shareholders are released from their obligation to purchase the petitioner's shares. Under section 14.34(a), the court also has discretion to "modify" the election by releasing one or more electing shareholders without releasing the others.

3.   Election by Corporation or Shareholders

Any change in the allocation of shareholdings in a closely-held corporation may upset control or other arrangements that have been previously negotiated by the parties. It is therefore desirable that the purchase of petitioner's shares under section 14.34 be made in ways that are least disruptive of existing arrangements. Accordingly, an election by the corporation is given preference during the 90 day period provided for in section 14.34(b). This preference does not affect the order of filing, and any shareholder may file an election (thus triggering the provisions of subsection (b)) as soon as the dissolution proceeding is commenced. If the corporation thereafter files an election within the 90 day period, its election takes precedence over any previously filed election by shareholders. An election by the corporation after 90 days may be filed only with the court's approval and would not be entitled to the same preemptive weight. Section 14.34 does not affect an agreement between the corporation and the other shareholders to participate jointly in the purchase of the petitioner's shares.

Concern over preserving existing control arrangements makes it inadvisable to extend purchase rights to holders of shares that have only preferential rights to distributions or assets but do not have any right to vote (other than as provided bylaw). On the other hand, control arrangements are not disturbed if shareholders having voting rights elect to purchase nonvoting shares of a petitioning shareholder, and such elections are permitted. If the election to purchase is made by one or more shareholders, section 14.34(b) requires the corporation to notify all other shareholders of their right to join in the purchase "in proportion to their ownership of shares as of the date the first election was filed." This raises the question of whether shareholders of a class different from the class of shares owned by the petitioner may participate in the purchase. Given the wide variety of capital structures adopted by closely-held corporations, it is not possible to state a general rule that would be appropriate in all cases. Any allocation that is agreed to by the electing shareholders controls regardless of whether the other terms and conditions of the purchase are set by the parties' agreement pursuant to subsection (c) or are determined by the court pursuant to subsection (e). If electing shareholders cannot agree, the court, under subsection (e), must determine an allocation.

In making this determination, the court should be guided by the desirability of preserving existing arrangements, so far as that is practicable. . . .

4. Court Order

If the parties are unable to reach agreement, any or all terms of the purchase may be set by the court under subsection (d). Section 14.34 does not specify the components of "fair value," and the court may find it useful to consider valuation methods that would be relevant to a judicial appraisal of shares under section 13.30. The two proceedings are not wholly analogous, however, and the court should consider all relevant facts and circumstances of the particular case in determining fair value. For example, liquidating value may be relevant in cases of deadlock but an inappropriate measure in other cases. If the court finds that the value of the corporation has been diminished by the wrongful conduct of controlling shareholders, it would be appropriate to include as an element of fair value the petitioner's proportional claim for any compensable corporate injury. In cases where there is dissension but no evidence of wrongful conduct, "fair value" should be determined with reference to what the petitioner would likely receive in a voluntary sale of shares to a third party, taking into account his minority status. If the parties have previously entered into a shareholders' agreement that defines or provides a method for determining the fair value of shares to be sold, the court should look to such definition or method unless the court decides it would be unjust or inequitable to do so in light of the facts and circumstances of the particular case. The valuation date is set as the day before the filing of the petition under section 14.30, although the court may choose an earlier or later date if appropriate under the circumstances of the particular case....

Chapter 15

FOREIGN CORPORATIONS

Subchapter A

Certificate of Authority

§ 15.01   Authority to Transact Business Required

(a) A foreign corporation may not transact business in this state until it obtains a certificate of authority from the secretary of state.

(b) The following activities, among others, do not constitute transacting business within the meaning of subsection (a):

   (1)   maintaining, defending, or settling any proceeding;

   (2)   holding meetings of the board of directors or shareholders or carrying on other activities concerning internal corporate affairs;

   (3)   maintaining bank accounts;

   (4)   maintaining offices or agencies for the transfer, exchange, and registration of the corporation's own securities or maintaining trustees or depositaries with respect to those securities;

   (5)   selling through independent contractors;

   (6)   soliciting or obtaining orders, whether by mail or through employees or agents or otherwise, if the orders require acceptance outside this state before they become contracts;

   (7)   creating or acquiring indebtedness, mortgages, and security interests in real or personal property;

(8) securing or collecting debts or enforcing mortgages and security interests in property securing the debts;

(9) owning, without more, real or personal property;

(10) conducting an isolated transaction that is completed within 30 days and that is not one in the course of repeated transactions of a like nature;

§ 15.02 Consequences of Transacting Business Without Authority

(a) A foreign corporation transacting business in this state without a certificate of authority may not maintain a proceeding in any court in this state until it obtains a certificate of authority.

(b) The successor to a foreign corporation that transacted business in this state without a certificate of authority and the assignee of a cause of action arising out of that business may not maintain a proceeding based on that cause of action in any court in this state until the foreign corporation or its successor obtains a certificate of authority.

(c) A court may stay a proceeding commenced by a foreign corporation, its successor, or assignee until it determines whether the foreign corporation or its successor requires a certificate of authority. If it so determines, the court may further stay the proceeding until the foreign corporation or its successor obtains the certificate.

(d) A foreign corporation is liable for a civil penalty of $_____ for each day, but not to exceed a total of $_____ for each year, it transacts business in this state without a certificate of authority. The attorney general may collect all penalties due under this subsection.

(e) Notwithstanding subsections (a) and (b), the failure of a foreign corporation to obtain a certificate of authority does not impair the validity of its corporate acts or prevent it from defending any proceeding in this state.

§ 15.03 Application for Certificate of Authority

(a) A foreign corporation may apply for a certificate of authority to transact business in this state by delivering an application to the secretary of state for filing. The application must set forth:

(1) The name of the foreign corporation or, if its name is unavailable for use in this state, a corporate name that satisfies the requirements of section 15.06;

(2) The name of the state or country under whose law it is incorporated;

(3) Its date of incorporation and period of duration;

(4) The street address of its principal office;

(5) The address of its registered office in this state and the name of its registered agent at that office; and

(6) The names and usual business addresses of its current directors and officers.

(b) The foreign corporation shall deliver with the completed application a certificate of existence (or a document of similar import) duly authenticated by the secretary of state or other official having custody of corporate records in the state or country under whose law it is incorporated.

§ 15.05   Effect of Certificate of Authority

(a) A certificate of authority authorizes the foreign corporation to which it is issued to transact business in this state subject, however, to the right of the state to revoke the certificate as provided in this Act.

(b) A foreign corporation with a valid certificate of authority has the same but no greater rights and has the same but no greater privileges as, and except as otherwise provided by this Act is subject to the same duties, restrictions, penalties, and liabilities now or later imposed on, a domestic corporation of like character.

(c) This Act does not authorize this state to regulate the organization or internal affairs of a foreign corporation authorized to transact business in this state.

Chapter 16

RECORDS AND REPORTS

Subchapter A

Records

§ 16.01   Corporate Records

(a) A corporation shall keep as permanent records minutes of all meetings of its shareholders and board of directors, a record of all actions taken by the shareholders or board of directors without a meeting, and a record of all actions taken by a committee of the board of directors in place of the board of directors on behalf of the corporation.

(b) A corporation shall maintain appropriate accounting records.

(c) A corporation or its agent shall maintain a record of its shareholders, in a form that permits preparation of a list of the names and addresses of all shareholders, in alphabetical order by class of shares showing the number and class of shares held by each.

(d) A corporation shall maintain its records in written form or in another form capable of conversion into written form within a reasonable time.

(e) A corporation shall keep a copy of the following records at its principal office:

(1) its articles or restated articles of incorporation, all amendments to them currently in effect and any notices to shareholders referred to in section 1.20(k)(5) regarding facts on which a filed document is dependent;

(2) its bylaws or restated bylaws and all amendments to them currently in effect;

(3) resolutions adopted by its board of directors creating one or more classes or series of shares, and fixing their relative rights, preferences, and limitations, if shares issued pursuant to those resolutions are outstanding;

(4) the minutes of all shareholders' meetings, and records of all action taken by shareholders without a meeting, for the past three years;

(5) all written communications to shareholders generally within the past three years, including the financial statements furnished for the past three years under section 16.20;

(6) a list of the names and business addresses of its current directors and officers; and

(7) its most recent annual report delivered to the secretary of state under section 16.22.

§ 16.02 Inspection of Records by Shareholders

(a) A shareholder of a corporation is entitled to inspect and copy, during regular business hours at the corporation's principal office, any of the records of the corporation described in section 16.01(e) if he gives the corporation written notice of his demand at least five business days before the date on which he wishes to inspect and copy.

(b) A shareholder of a corporation is entitled to inspect and copy, during regular business hours at a reasonable location specified by the corporation, any of the following records of the corporation if the shareholder meets the requirements of subsection (c) and gives the corporation written notice of his demand at least five business days before the date on which he wishes to inspect and copy:

(1) excerpts from minutes of any meeting of the board of directors, records of any action of a committee of the board of directors while acting in place of the board of directors on behalf of the corporation, minutes of any meeting of the shareholders, and records of action taken by the shareholders or board of directors

without a meeting, to the extent not subject to inspection under section 16.02(a);

(2) accounting records of the corporation; and

(3) the record of shareholders.

(c) A shareholder may inspect and copy the records described in subsection (b) only if:

(1) his demand is made in good faith and for a proper purpose;

(2) he describes with reasonable particularity his purpose and the records he desires to inspect; and

(3) the records are directly connected with his purpose.

(d) The right of inspection granted by this section may not be abolished or limited by a corporation's articles of incorporation or bylaws.

(e) This section does not affect:

(1) the right of a shareholder to inspect records under section 7.20 or, if the shareholder is in litigation with the corporation, to the same extent as any other litigant;

(2) the power of a court, independently of this Act, to compel the production of corporate records for examination.

(f) For purposes of this section, "shareholder" includes a beneficial owner whose shares are held in a voting trust or by a nominee on his behalf.

§ 16.03   Scope of Inspection Right

(a) A shareholder's agent or attorney has the same inspection and copying rights as the shareholder represented.

(b) The right to copy records under section 16.02 includes, if reasonable, the right to receive copies by xerographic or other means, including copies through an electronic transmission if available and so requested by the shareholder.

(c) The corporation may comply at its expense with a shareholder's demand to inspect the record of shareholders under section 16.02(b)(3) by providing the shareholder with a list of shareholders that was compiled no earlier than the date of the shareholder's demand.

(d) The corporation may impose a reasonable charge, covering the costs of labor and material, for copies of any documents provided to the shareholder. The charge may not exceed the estimated cost of production, reproduction or transmission of the records.

Official Comment ...

Under applicable law, a list of shareholders generally will include underlying information in the corporation's possession relating to stock ownership, including, where applicable, breakdowns of stock holdings by nominees and non-objecting beneficial ownership (NOBO) lists. However, a corporation generally is not required to generate this information for the requesting shareholder and is only required to provide NOBO and other similar lists to the extent such information is in the corporation's possession.

Section 7.20 creates a right of shareholders to inspect a list of shareholders in advance of and at a meeting that is independent of the rights of shareholders to inspect corporate records under chapter 16.

§ 16.04 Court–Ordered Inspection

(a) If a corporation does not allow a shareholder who complies with section 16.02(a) to inspect and copy any records required by that subsection to be available for inspection, the [name or describe court] of the county where the corporation's principal office (or, if none in this state, its registered office) is located may summarily order inspection and copying of the records demanded at the corporation's expense upon application of the shareholder.

(b) If a corporation does not within a reasonable time allow a shareholder to inspect and copy any other record, the shareholder who complies with sections 16.02(b) and (c) may apply to the [name or describe court] in the county where the corporation's principal office (or, if none in this state, its registered office) is located for an order to permit inspection and copying of the records demanded. The court shall dispose of an application under this subsection on an expedited basis.

(c) If the court orders inspection and copying of the records demanded, it shall also order the corporation to pay the shareholder's expenses incurred to obtain the order unless the corporation proves that it refused inspection in good faith because it had a reasonable basis for doubt about the right of the shareholder to inspect the records demanded.

(d) If the court orders inspection and copying of the records demanded, it may impose reasonable restrictions on the use or distribution of the records by the demanding shareholder.

Official Comment ...

Earlier versions of the Model Act and the statutes of many states imposed a penalty upon the corporation or its officers for refusal to permit inspection of books and records by shareholders who (1) had been shareholders for at least six months or (2) owned five percent or more of the outstanding shares. This provision has been omitted. A penalty unrelated to the expenses of securing inspection was arbitrary and, as a result, was seldom actually enforced; further, a qualification based on the size or duration of the shareholder's holding unrelated to his actual purpose was subject to the criticism that it constituted unreasonable discrimination against small shareholders.

§ 16.05   Inspection of Records by Directors

(a) A director of a corporation is entitled to inspect and copy the books, records and documents of the corporation at any reasonable time to the extent reasonably related to the performance of the director's duties as a director, including duties as a member of a committee, but not for any other purpose or in any manner that would violate any duty to the corporation.

(b) The [*name or describe the court*] of the county where the corporation's principal office (or if none in this state, its registered office) is located may order inspection and copying of the books, records and documents at the corporation's expense, upon application of a director who has been refused such inspection rights, unless the corporation establishes that the director is not entitled to such inspection rights. The court shall dispose of an application under this subsection on an expedited basis.

(c) If an order is issued, the court may include provisions protecting the corporation from undue burden or expense, and prohibiting the director from using information obtained upon exercise of the inspection rights in a manner that would violate a duty to the corporation, and may also order the corporation to reimburse the director for the director's expenses incurred in connection with the application.

Official Comment . . .

Under subsection (a), a director typically would be entitled to review books, records and documents relating to matters such as (i) compliance by a corporation with applicable law, (ii) adequacy of the corporation's system of internal controls to provide accurate and timely financial statements and disclosure documents, or (iii) the proper operation, maintenance and protection of the corporation's assets. In addition, a director would be entitled to review records and documents to the extent required to consider and make decisions with respect to matters placed before the Board.

Subsection (b) provides a director with the right to seek on an expedited basis a court order permitting inspection and copying of the books, records and documents of the corporation, at the corporation's expense. There is a presumption that significant latitude and discretion should be granted to the director, and the corporation has the burden of establishing that a director is not entitled to inspection of the documents requested. Circumstances where the director's inspection rights might be denied include requests which (i) are not reasonably related to performance of a director's duties (*e.g.*, seeking a specified confidential document not necessary for the performance of a director's duties), (ii) impose an unreasonable burden and expense on the corporation *(e.g.,* compliance with the request would be duplicative of information already provided or would be unreasonably expensive and time-consuming), (iii) violate the director's duty to the corporation *(e.g.,* the director could reasonably be expected to use or exploit confidential information in personal or third-party transactions), or (iv) violate any applicable law *(e.g.,* the director does not have the necessary governmental security clearance to see the requested classified information). . . .

§ 16.06 Exception to Notice Requirement

(a) Whenever notice is required to be given under any provision of this Act to any shareholder, such notice shall not be required to be given if;

    (i) Notice of two consecutive annual meetings, and all notices of meetings during the period between such two consecutive annual meetings, have been sent to such shareholder at such shareholder's address as shown on the records of the corporation and have been returned undeliverable; or

    (ii) All, but not less than two, payments of dividends on securities during a twelve-month period, or two consecutive payments of dividends on securities during a period of more than twelve months, have been sent to such shareholder at such shareholder's address as shown on the records of the corporation and have been returned undeliverable.

(b) If any such shareholder shall deliver to the corporation a written notice setting forth such shareholder's then-current address, the requirement that notice be given to such shareholder shall be reinstated.

Subchapter B

Reports

§ 16.20 Financial Statements for Shareholders

(a) A corporation shall furnish its shareholders annual financial statements, which may be consolidated or combined statements of the corporation and one or more of its subsidiaries, as appropriate, that include a balance sheet as of the end of the fiscal year, an income statement for that year, and a statement of changes in shareholders' equity for the year unless that information appears elsewhere in the financial statements. If financial statements are prepared for the corporation on the basis of generally accepted accounting principles, the annual financial statements must also be prepared on that basis.

(b) If the annual financial statements are reported upon by a public accountant, his report must accompany them. If not, the statements must be accompanied by a statement of the president or the person responsible for the corporation's accounting records:

(1) stating his reasonable belief whether the statements were prepared on the basis of generally accepted accounting principles and, if not, describing the basis of preparation; and

(2) describing any respects in which the statements were not prepared on a basis of accounting consistent with the statements prepared for the preceding year.

(c) A corporation shall mail the annual financial statements to each shareholder within 120 days after the close of each fiscal year. Thereafter, on written request from a shareholder who was not mailed the statements, the corporation shall mail him the latest financial statements.

§ 16.22   Annual Report for Secretary of State

(a) Each domestic corporation, and each foreign corporation authorized to transact business in this state, shall deliver to the secretary of state for filing an annual report that sets forth:

(1) the name of the corporation and the state or country under whose law it is incorporated;

(2) the address of its registered office and the name of its registered agent at that office in this state;

(3) the address of its principal office;

(4) the names and business addresses of its directors and principal officers;

(5) a brief description of the nature of its business;

(6) the total number of authorized shares, itemized by class and series, if any, within each class; and

(7) the total number of issued and outstanding shares, itemized by class and series, if any, within each class.

(b) Information in the annual report must be current as of the date the annual report is executed on behalf of the corporation.

(c) The first annual report must be delivered to the secretary of state between January 1 and April 1 of the year following the calendar year in which a domestic corporation was incorporated or a foreign corporation was authorized to transact business. Subsequent annual reports must be delivered to the secretary of state between January 1 and April 1 of the following calendar years.

(d) If an annual report does not contain the information required by this section, the secretary of state shall promptly notify the reporting domestic or foreign corporation in writing and return the report to it for correction. If the report is corrected to contain the information required by this section and delivered to the secretary of state within

30 days after the effective date of notice, it is deemed to be timely filed.

APPENDIX: PRIOR VERSIONS OF SELECTED PROVISIONS OF THE MODEL ACT

Note: This Appendix contains versions of selected provisions of the Model Act that have been superseded in the Model Act itself, but may not be immediately adopted by all Model Act states.

---

§ 8.30　General Standards for Director Conduct*

(a) A director shall discharge his duties as a director, including his duties as a member of a committee:

　(1) In good faith;

　(2) with the care an ordinarily prudent person in a like position would exercise under similar circumstances; and

　(3) in a manner he reasonably believes to be in the best interests of the corporation.

(b) In discharging his duties a director is entitled to rely on information, opinions, reports, or statements, including financial statements and other financial data, if prepared or presented by:

　(1) one or more officers or employees of the corporation whom the director reasonably believes to be reliable and competent in the matters presented;

　(2) legal counsel, public accountants, or other persons as to matters the director reasonably believes are within the person's professional or expert competence; or

　(3) a committee of the board of directors of which he is not a member if the director reasonably believes the committee merits confidence.

(c) A director is not acting in good faith if he has knowledge concerning the matter in question that makes reliance otherwise permitted by subsection (b) unwarranted.

(d) A director is not liable for any action taken as a director, or any failure to take any action, if he performed the duties of his office in compliance with this section.

---

* Prior Section 8.30 has been replaced by new Sections 8.30–8.31, supra.

§ 8.31 Director Conflict of Interest [†]

(a) A conflict of interest transaction is a transaction with the corporation in which a director of the corporation has a direct or indirect interest. A conflict of interest transaction is not voidable by the corporation solely because of the director's interest in the transaction if any one of the following is true:

    (1) the material facts of the transaction and the director's interest were disclosed or known to the board of directors or a committee of the board of directors and the board of directors or committee authorized, approved, or ratified the transaction;

    (2) the material facts of the transaction and the director's interest were disclosed or known to the shareholders entitled to vote and they authorized, approved, or ratified the transaction; or

    (3) the transaction was fair to the corporation.

(b) For purposes of this section, a director of the corporation has an indirect interest in a transaction if (1) another entity in which he has a material financial interest or in which he is a general partner is a party to the transaction or (2) another entity of which he is a director, officer, or trustee is a party to the transaction and the transaction is or should be considered by the board of directors of the corporation.

(c) For purposes of subsection (a)(1), a conflict of interest transaction is authorized, approved, or ratified if it receives the affirmative vote of a majority of the directors on the board of directors (or on the committee) who have no direct or indirect interest in the transaction, but a transaction may not be authorized, approved, or ratified under this section by a single director. If a majority of the directors who have no direct or indirect interest in the transaction vote to authorize, approve, or ratify the transaction, a quorum is present for the purpose of taking action under this section. The presence of, or a vote cast by, a director with a direct or indirect interest in the transaction does not affect the validity of any action taken under subsection (a)(1) if the transaction is otherwise authorized, approved, or ratified as provided in that subsection.

(d) For purposes of subsection (a)(2), a conflict of interest transaction is authorized, approved, or ratified if it receives the vote of a majority of the shares entitled to be counted under this subsection. Shares owned by or voted under the control of a director who has a direct or indirect interest in the transaction, and shares owned by or voted under the control of an entity described in subsection (b)(1), may not be counted in a vote of shareholders to determine whether to authorize, approve, or ratify a conflict of interest transaction under subsection (a)(2). The vote of those shares, however, is counted in

[†] Prior Section 8.31 has been replaced by new Sections 8.60–8.63, supra.

determining whether the transaction is approved under other sections of this Act. A majority of the shares, whether or not present, that are entitled to be counted in a vote on the transaction under this subsection constitutes a quorum for the purpose of taking action under this section.

Official Comment

1. Conflict of Interest Transactions in General

Section 8.31 deals only with "conflict of interest" transactions by a director with the corporation, that is, transactions in which the director has an interest either (1) directly or (2) indirectly through an entity in which the director has a financial or managerial interest covered by section 8.31(b). A conflict of interest transaction does not include transactions in which the director participates in the transaction only as a shareholder and receives only a proportionate share of the advantage or benefit of the transaction. Section 8.31 deals only with conflict of interest transactions involving directors; it does not address analogous transactions entered into by officers, employees, or substantial or dominating shareholders unless they are also directors.

Section 8.31 rejects the common law view that all conflict of interest transactions entered into by directors are automatically voidable at the option of the corporation without regard to the fairness of the transaction or the manner in which the transaction was approved by the corporation. Section 8.31(a) makes any automatic rule of voidability inapplicable to transactions that are fair or that have been approved by directors or shareholders in the manner provided by the balance of section 8.31. The approval mechanisms set forth in section 8.31(c) and (d) relate only to the elimination of this automatic rule of voidability and do not address the manner in which the transactions must be approved under other sections of this Act. This is made clear by the express limitations in sections 8.31(c) and (d) that they are applicable only "for the purposes of this section" as well as the language of the second and third sentences of section 8.31(d).

The elimination of the automatic rule of voidability does not mean that all transactions that meet one or more of the tests set forth in section 8.31(a) are automatically valid. These transactions may be subject to attack on a variety of grounds independent of section 8.31—for example, that the transaction constituted waste, that it was not authorized by the appropriate corporate body, that it violated other sections of the Model Business Corporation Act, or that it was unenforceable under other common law principles. The sole purpose of section 8.31 is to sharply limit the common law principle of automatic voidability and in this respect section 8.31 follows earlier versions of the Model Act and the statutes of many states dealing with conflict of interest transactions.

2. Requirements for Approval of Conflict of Interest Transactions

Sections 8.31(c) and (d) provide special rules for determining whether the board of directors (or a committee thereof) or the shareholders have authorized, approved, or ratified a conflict of interest transaction so as to bring subsections (a)(1) or (a)(2) into play. Basically, these subsections require the transaction in question to be approved by an absolute majority of the directors (on the board of directors, or on the committee, as the case may be) or shares whose votes may be counted in determining whether the transaction should be authorized, approved, or ratified. If these votes are not obtained the transaction is tested under the fairness test of subsection (a)(3). The vote required for authorization, approval, or ratification of a conflict of interest transaction is more onerous than the standard applicable to normal voting requirements for approval of corporate actions—i.e., that a quorum be present and only the votes of directors or shares present or represented at that meeting be considered—because of the importance of assuring that conflict of interest transactions receive as broad consideration within the corporation as possible if independent review on the basis of fairness is to be avoided....

b. *Consideration by the shareholders* ....

In some situations, the prohibition of section 8.31(d) will result in the conflict of interest issue being resolved by a majority of a minority of the shares. This will occur, for example, whenever a director who is the majority shareholder of the corporation is interested in a transaction. The vote on the conflict of interest issue under section 8.31, however, must be distinguished from the vote on the approval of the transaction itself under other sections of the Model Act, in which there is no prohibition against the voting of shares owned or controlled by an interested director. For example, if a parent corporation wishes to merge its 60–percent–owned subsidiary into itself, and the majority shareholder of the parent is a director of the subsidiary, the votes of the shares owned by the parent corporation may not be counted under section 8.31(d) (since the shares are owned by an entity which is a party to the transaction and which the director controls). The shares nevertheless may be voted on the merger proposal itself under chapter 11 of the Model Act, and the merger will, of course, normally be approved solely by the vote of the shares owned by the parent corporation. On the other hand, the test of section 8.31(a)(2) is not met unless the transaction is approved by at least a majority of the votes cast by the holders of the 40 percent of the shares not owned by the parent corporation. If this requirement is not met, the transaction may be evaluated under the fairness test of section 8.31(a)(3).

3. Indirect Conflicts of Interest

Section 8.31 is applicable to "indirect" as well as direct conflicts; "indirect" is defined in section 8.31(b) to cover transactions between the corporation and an entity in which the director has a material financial interest or is a general partner. Further, section 8.31(b) covers indirect conflicts where the director is an officer or director of another entity (but does not have a material financial interest in the transaction) if the transaction is of sufficient importance that it is or should be considered by the board of directors of the corporation. The purpose of this last clause is to permit normal business transactions between large business entities that may have a common director to go forward without concern about the technical rules relating to conflict of interest unless the transaction is of such importance that it is or should be considered by the board of directors or the director may be deemed to have a material financial interest in the transaction. Thus, section 8.31 covers transactions between corporations with interlocking or common directors as well as the direct "interested director" transaction.

4. "Fairness" of a Transaction

The fairness of a transaction for purposes of section 8.31 should be evaluated on the basis of the facts and circumstances as they were known or should have been known at the time the transaction was entered into. For example, the terms of a transaction subject to section 8.31 should normally be deemed "fair" if they are within the range that might have been entered into at arm's-length by disinterested persons.

5. An "Interested" Director

The Model Act does not attempt to define precisely when a director should be viewed as "interested" for purposes of participating in the decision to adopt, approve, or ratify a conflict of interest transaction. Section 8.31(b) does, however, define one aspect of this concept—the "indirect" interest. For purposes of section 8.31 a director should normally be viewed as interested in a transaction if he or the immediate members of his family have a financial interest in the transaction or a relationship with the other parties to the transaction such that the relationship might reasonably be expected to affect his judgment in the particular matter in a manner adverse to the corporation.

Prior Model Act Chapter 10*

AMENDMENT OF ARTICLES OF INCORPORATION AND BYLAWS

Subchapter A

Amendment of Articles of Incorporation

§ 10.01 Authority to Amend

(a) A corporation may amend its articles of incorporation at any time to add or change a provision that is required or permitted in the articles of incorporation or to delete a provision not required in the articles of incorporation. Whether a provision is required or permitted in the articles of incorporation is determined as of the effective date of the amendment.

(b) A shareholder of the corporation does not have a vested property right resulting from any provision in the articles of incorporation, including provisions relating to management, control, capital structure, dividend entitlement, or purpose or duration of the corporation.

§ 10.02 Amendment by Board of Directors

Unless the articles of incorporation provide otherwise, a corporation's board of directors may adopt one or more amendments to the corporation's articles of incorporation without shareholder action:

(1) to extend the duration of the corporation if it was incorporated at a time when limited duration was required by law;

(2) to delete the names and addresses of the initial directors;

(3) to delete the name and address of the initial registered agent or registered office, if a statement of change is on file with the secretary of state;

(4) to change each issued and unissued authorized share of an outstanding class into a greater number of whole shares if the corporation has only shares of that class outstanding;

(5) to change the corporate name by substituting the word "corporation," "incorporated," "company," "limited," or the abbreviation "corp.," "inc.," "co.," or "ltd.," for a similar word or abbreviation in the name, or by adding, deleting, or changing a geographical attribution for the name; or

(6) to make any other change expressly permitted by this Act to be made without shareholder action.

* Prior Chapter 10 of the Model Act has been replaced by new Chapter 10, supra.

§ 10.03 Amendment by Board of Directors and Shareholders

(a) A corporation's board of directors may propose one or more amendments to the articles of incorporation for submission to the shareholders.

(b) For the amendment to be adopted:

    (1) the board of directors must recommend the amendment to the shareholders unless the board of directors determines that because of conflict of interest or other special circumstances it should make no recommendation and communicates the basis for its determination to the shareholders with the amendment; and

    (2) the shareholders entitled to vote on the amendment must approve the amendment as provided in subsection (e).

(c) The board of directors may condition its submission of the proposed amendment on any basis.

(d) The corporation shall notify each shareholder, whether or not entitled to vote, of the proposed shareholders' meeting in accordance with section 7.05. The notice of meeting must also state that the purpose, or one of the purposes, of the meeting is to consider the proposed amendment and contain or be accompanied by a copy or summary of the amendment.

(e) Unless this Act, the articles of incorporation, or the board of directors (acting pursuant to subsection (c)) require a greater vote or a vote by voting groups, the amendment to be adopted must be approved by:

    (1) a majority of the votes entitled to be cast on the amendment by any voting group with respect to which the amendment would create dissenters' rights; and

    (2) the votes required by sections 7.25 and 7.26 by every other voting group entitled to vote on the amendment.

§ 10.04 Voting on Amendments by Voting Groups

(a) The holders of the outstanding shares of a class are entitled to vote as a separate voting group (if shareholder voting is otherwise required by this Act) on a proposed amendment if the amendment would:

    (1) increase or decrease the aggregate number of authorized shares of the class;

    (2) effect an exchange or reclassification of all or part of the shares of the class into shares of another class;

    (3) effect an exchange or reclassification, or create the right of exchange, of all or part of the shares of another class into shares of the class;

(4) change the designation, rights, preferences, or limitations of all or part of the shares of the class;

(5) change the shares of all or part of the class into a different number of shares of the same class;

(6) create a new class of shares having rights or preferences with respect to distributions or to dissolution that are prior, superior, or substantially equal to the shares of the class;

(7) increase the rights, preferences, or number of authorized shares of any class that, after giving effect to the amendment, have rights or preferences with respect to distributions or to dissolution that are prior, superior, or substantially equal to the shares of the class;

(8) limit or deny an existing preemptive right of all or part of the shares of the class; or

(9) cancel or otherwise affect rights to distributions or dividends that have accumulated but not yet been declared on all or part of the shares of the class.

(b) If a proposed amendment would affect a series of a class of shares in one or more of the ways described in subsection (a), the shares of that series are entitled to vote as a separate voting group on the proposed amendment.

(c) If a proposed amendment that entitles two or more series of shares to vote as separate voting groups under this section would affect those two or more series in the same or a substantially similar way, the shares of all the series so affected must vote together as a single voting group on the proposed amendment.

(d) A class or series of shares is entitled to the voting rights granted by this section although the articles of incorporation provide that the shares are nonvoting shares.

§ 10.05   Amendment Before Issuance of Shares

If a corporation has not yet issued shares, its incorporators or board of directors may adopt one or more amendments to the corporation's articles of incorporation.

§ 10.06   Articles of Amendment

A corporation amending its articles of incorporation shall deliver to the secretary of state for filing articles of amendment setting forth:

(1) the name of the corporation;

(2) the text of each amendment adopted;

(3) if an amendment provides for an exchange, reclassification, or cancellation of issued shares, provisions for implementing the amendment if not contained in the amendment itself;

(4) the date of each amendment's adoption;

(5) if an amendment was adopted by the incorporators or board of directors without shareholder action, a statement to that effect and that shareholder action was not required;

(6) if an amendment was approved by the shareholders:

   (i) the designation, number of outstanding shares, number of votes entitled to be cast by each voting group entitled to vote separately on the amendment, and number of votes of each voting group indisputably represented at the meeting;

   (ii) either the total number of votes cast for and against the amendment by each voting group entitled to vote separately on the amendment or the total number of undisputed votes cast for the amendment by each voting group and a statement that the number cast for the amendment by each voting group was sufficient for approval by that voting group.

§ 10.09   Effect of Amendment

An amendment to articles of incorporation does not affect a cause of action existing against or in favor of the corporation, a proceeding to which the corporation is a party, or the existing rights of persons other than shareholders of the corporation. An amendment changing a corporation's name does not abate a proceeding brought by or against the corporation in its former name.

Subchapter B

Amendment of Bylaws

§ 10.20   Amendment by Board of Directors or Shareholders

(a) A corporation's board of directors may amend or repeal the corporation's bylaws unless:

   (1) the articles of incorporation or this Act reserve this power exclusively to the shareholders in whole or part; or

   (2) the shareholders in amending or repealing a particular bylaw provide expressly that the board of directors may not amend or repeal that bylaw.

(b) A corporation's shareholders may amend or repeal the corporation's bylaws even though the bylaws may also be amended or repealed by its board of directors.

§ 10.21   Bylaw Increasing Quorum or Voting Requirement for Shareholders

(a) If authorized by the articles of incorporation, the shareholders may adopt or amend a bylaw that fixes a greater quorum or voting requirement for shareholders (or voting groups of shareholders) than is required by this Act. The adoption or amendment of a bylaw that adds, changes, or deletes a greater quorum or voting requirement for shareholders must meet the same quorum requirement and be adopted by the same vote and voting groups required to take action under the quorum and voting requirement then in effect or proposed to be adopted, whichever is greater.

(b) A bylaw that fixes a greater quorum or voting requirement for shareholders under subsection (a) may not be adopted, amended, or repealed by the board of directors.

§ 10.22 Bylaw Increasing Quorum or Voting Requirement for Directors

(a) A bylaw that fixes a greater quorum or voting requirement for the board of directors may be amended or repealed:

(1) if originally adopted by the shareholders, only by the shareholders;

(2) if originally adopted by the board of directors, either by the shareholders or by the board of directors.

(b) A bylaw adopted or amended by the shareholders that fixes a greater quorum or voting requirement for the board of directors may provide that it may be amended or repealed only by a specified vote of either the shareholders or the board of directors.

(c) Action by the board of directors under subsection (a)(2) to adopt or amend a bylaw that changes the quorum or voting requirement for the board of directors must meet the same quorum requirement and be adopted by the same vote required to take action under the quorum and voting requirement then in effect or proposed to be adopted, whichever is greater.

––––––––

Prior Model Act Chapter 11*

MERGER AND SHARE EXCHANGE

§ 11.01 Merger

(a) One or more corporations may merge into another corporation if the board of directors of each corporation adopts and its shareholders (if required by section 11.03) approve a plan of merger.

(b) The plan of merger must set forth:

*Prior Chapter 11 of the Model Act has been replaced by new Chapter 11, supra.

(1) the name of each corporation planning to merge and the name of the surviving corporation into which each other corporation plans to merge;

(2) the terms and conditions of the merger; and

(3) the manner and basis of converting the shares of each corporation into shares, obligations, or other securities of the surviving or any other corporation or into cash or other property in whole or part.

(c) The plan of merger may set forth:

(1) amendments to the articles of incorporation of the surviving corporation; and

(2) other provisions relating to the merger.

Official Comment ...

2. Equivalent Nonstatutory Transactions

A transaction may have the same economic effect as a statutory merger even though it is cast in the form of a nonstatutory transaction. For example, assets of the disappearing corporations may be sold for consideration in the form of shares of the surviving corporation, followed by the distribution of those shares by the disappearing corporations to their shareholders and their subsequent dissolution. Transactions have sometimes been structured in nonstatutory form for tax reasons or in an effort to avoid some of the consequences of a statutory merger, particularly appraisal rights to dissenting shareholders. Faced with these transactions, a few courts have developed or accepted the "de facto merger" concept which, to some uncertain extent, grants to dissenting shareholders the rights they would have had if the transaction had been structured as a statutory merger. See Folk, "De Facto Mergers in Delaware: Hariton v. Arco Electronics, Inc.," 49 Va.L.Rev. 1261 (1963). These problems should not occur under the Model Act since the procedural requirements for authorization and consequences of various types of transactions are largely standardized. For example, dissenters' rights are granted not only in mergers but also in share exchanges, in sales of all or substantially all the corporate assets, and in amendments to articles of incorporation that significantly affect rights of shareholders.

§ 11.02 Share Exchange

(a) A corporation may acquire all of the outstanding shares of one or more classes or series of another corporation if the board of directors of each corporation adopts and its shareholders (if required by section 11.03) approve the exchange.

(b) The plan of exchange must set forth:

(1) the name of the corporation whose shares will be acquired and the name of the acquiring corporation;

(2) the terms and conditions of the exchange;

(3) the manner and basis of exchanging the shares to be acquired for shares, obligations, or other securities of the acquiring or any other corporation or for cash or other property in whole or part.

(c) The plan of exchange may set forth other provisions relating to the exchange.

(d) This section does not limit the power of a corporation to acquire all or part of the shares of one or more classes or series of another corporation through a voluntary exchange or otherwise.

§ 11.03   Action on Plan

(a) After adopting a plan of merger or share exchange, the board of directors of each corporation party to the merger, and the board of directors of the corporation whose shares will be acquired in the share exchange, shall submit the plan of merger (except as provided in subsection (g)) or share exchange for approval by its shareholders.

(b) For a plan of merger or share exchange to be approved:

(1) the board of directors must recommend the plan of merger or share exchange to the shareholders, unless the board of directors determines that because of conflict of interest or other special circumstances it should make no recommendation and communicates the basis for its determination to the shareholders with the plan; and

(2) the shareholders entitled to vote must approve the plan.

(c) The board of directors may condition its submission of the proposed merger or share exchange on any basis.

(d) The corporation shall notify each shareholder, whether or not entitled to vote, of the proposed shareholders' meeting in accordance with section 7.05. The notice must also state that the purpose, or one of the purposes, of the meeting is to consider the plan of merger or share exchange and contain or be accompanied by a copy or summary of the plan.

(e) Unless this Act, the articles of incorporation, or the board of directors (acting pursuant to subsection (c)) require a greater vote or a vote by voting groups, the plan of merger or share exchange to be authorized must be approved by each voting group entitled to vote separately on the plan by a majority of all the votes entitled to be cast on the plan by that voting group.

(f) Separate voting by voting groups is required:

(1) on a plan of merger if the plan contains a provision that, if contained in a proposed amendment to articles of incorporation, would require action by one or more separate voting groups on the proposed amendment under section 10.04;

(2) on a plan of share exchange by each class or series of shares included in the exchange, with each class or series constituting a separate voting group.

(g) Action by the shareholders of the surviving corporation on a plan of merger is not required if:

    (1) the articles of incorporation of the surviving corporation will not differ (except for amendments enumerated in section 10.02) from its articles before the merger;

    (2) each shareholder of the surviving corporation whose shares were outstanding immediately before the effective date of the merger will hold the same number of shares, with identical designations, preferences, limitations, and relative rights, immediately after;

    (3) the number of voting shares outstanding immediately after the merger, plus the number of voting shares issuable as a result of the merger (either by the conversion of securities issued pursuant to the merger or the exercise of rights and warrants issued pursuant to the merger), will not exceed by more than 20 percent the total number of voting shares of the surviving corporation outstanding immediately before the merger; and

    (4) the number of participating shares outstanding immediately after the merger, plus the number of participating shares issuable as a result of the merger (either by the conversion of securities issued pursuant to the merger or the exercise of rights and warrants issued pursuant to the merger), will not exceed by more than 20 percent the total number of participating shares outstanding immediately before the merger.

(h) As used in subsection (g):

    (1) "Participating shares" means shares that entitle their holders to participate without limitation in distributions.

    (2) "Voting shares" means shares that entitle their holders to vote unconditionally in elections of directors.

(i) After a merger or share exchange is authorized, and at any time before articles of merger or share exchange are filed, the planned merger or share exchange may be abandoned (subject to any contractual rights), without further shareholder action, in accordance with the procedure set forth in the plan of merger or share exchange or, if none is set forth, in the manner determined by the board of directors.

Official Comment ...

2. When Surviving Corporation Shareholder Approval is Not Required

Section 11.03(g) describes when approval by the shareholders of the surviving corporation is not required. The theory behind this subsection is that shareholders' votes should be required only if the transaction fundamentally alters the character of the enterprise or substantially reduces the shareholders' participation in voting or profit distribution. It is believed that the transactions for which shareholder approval is not required by subsection (g) do not alter the investors' prospects any more than many other management decisions, and thus should not require a shareholder vote. In particular, the 20 percent requirement of subsections (g)(3) and (4) is broadly consistent with the statutes of several states, including Delaware (20 percent), Michigan (20 percent), and Pennsylvania (15 percent), and also with the New York Stock Exchange requirement that shareholders must be consulted if the number of outstanding shares is to be increased by more than 18.5 percent.

The requirement that shareholders of the surviving corporation in a statutory merger have a right to vote if the increase in the number of shares exceeds 20 percent may be avoided by arranging the transaction in the form of a merger involving a subsidiary of the acquiring corporation or as a share exchange under section 11.02. This anomaly reflects a compromise among basically conflicting points of view.

The 20 percent requirement is applicable only if the corporation has available enough authorized shares to permit it to issue the shares without amending its articles of incorporation to increase authorized capital. If it must amend its articles of incorporation to authorize the shares necessary to complete the transaction, a shareholder vote on the amendment will be necessary in all cases. See section 10.03....

§ 11.04   Merger of Subsidiary

(a) A parent corporation owning at least 90 percent of the outstanding shares of each class of a subsidiary corporation may merge the subsidiary into itself without approval of the shareholders of the parent or subsidiary.

(b) The board of directors of the parent shall adopt a plan of merger that sets forth:

    (1) the names of the parent and subsidiary; and

    (2) the manner and basis of converting the shares of the subsidiary into shares, obligations, or other securities of the parent or any other corporation or into cash or other property in whole or part.

(c) The parent shall mail a copy or summary of the plan of merger to each shareholder of the subsidiary who does not waive the mailing requirement in writing.

(d) The parent may not deliver articles of merger to the secretary of state for filing until at least 30 days after the date it mailed a copy of the plan of merger to each shareholder of the subsidiary who did not waive the mailing requirement.

(e) Articles of merger under this section may not contain amendments to the articles of incorporation of the parent corporation (except for amendments enumerated in section 10.02).

Official Comment

Section 11.04(a) defines a "parent" corporation as one that owns at least 90 percent of the outstanding shares of each class of another corporation, and a "subsidiary" corporation as one whose shares are so owned. Section 11.04 permits merger of a subsidiary into its parent corporation upon adoption of a plan of merger by the board of directors of the parent alone. Separate action by the board of directors of the subsidiary is unnecessary because the share ownership of the parent corporation is normally sufficient to permit it to elect or remove the subsidiary's board of directors.

Further, the merger transaction need not be approved by the shareholders of either corporation. Approval by the shareholders of the subsidiary is meaningless because the parent's share ownership is sufficient to ensure the plan will be approved. Approval by the parent's shareholders is also unnecessary because the transaction does not materially change their rights: the ownership of the parent corporation is being changed only from 90 percent indirect ownership to 100 percent direct ownership of the same assets, and no significant amendment of the parent's articles of incorporation is being made. For the same reason, shareholders of the parent corporation do not have the right to dissent from the transaction under chapter 13.

Minority shareholders of the subsidiary corporation may receive shares, obligations, or other securities of the parent or any other corporation, or cash or other property in whole or in part in exchange for their shares. These shareholders are entitled to 30 days' notice of the plan of merger before it is effectuated.

Shareholders of the subsidiary corporation have a right to dissent from the merger transaction under chapter 13. . . .

§ 11.05 Articles of Merger or Share Exchange

(a) After a plan of merger or share exchange is approved by the shareholders, or adopted by the board of directors if shareholder approval is not required, the surviving or acquiring corporation shall deliver to the secretary of state for filing articles of merger or share exchange setting forth:

  (1) the plan of merger or share exchange;

  (2) if shareholder approval was not required, a statement to that effect;

  (3) if approval of the shareholders of one or more corporations party to the merger or share exchange was required:

(i) the designation, number of outstanding shares, and number of votes entitled to be cast by each voting group entitled to vote separately on the plan as to each corporation; and

(ii) either the total number of votes cast for and against the plan by each voting group entitled to vote separately on the plan or the total number of undisputed votes cast for the plan separately by each voting group and a statement that the number cast for the plan by each voting group was sufficient for approval by that voting group.

(b) A merger or share exchange takes effect upon the effective date of the articles of merger or share exchange.

§ 11.06   Effect of Merger or Share Exchange

(a) When a merger takes effect:

(1) every other corporation party to the merger merges into the surviving corporation and the separate existence of every corporation except the surviving corporation ceases;

(2) the title to all real estate and other property owned by each corporation party to the merger is vested in the surviving corporation without reversion or impairment;

(3) the surviving corporation has all liabilities of each corporation party to the merger;

(4) a proceeding pending against any corporation party to the merger may be continued as if the merger did not occur or the surviving corporation may be substituted in the proceeding for the corporation whose existence ceased;

(5) the articles of incorporation of the surviving corporation are amended to the extent provided in the plan of merger; and

(6) the shares of each corporation party to the merger that are to be converted into shares, obligations, or other securities of the surviving or any other corporation or into cash or other property are converted, and the former holders of the shares are entitled only to the rights provided in the articles of merger or to their rights under chapter 13.

(b) When a share exchange takes effect, the shares of each acquired corporation are exchanged as provided in the plan, and the former holders of the shares are entitled only to the exchange rights provided in the articles of share exchange or to their rights under chapter 13.

Prior Model Act Chapter 12*

SALE OF ASSETS

§ 12.01 Sale of Assets in Regular Course of Business and Mortgage of Assets

(a) A corporation may, on the terms and conditions and for the consideration determined by the board of directors:

(1) sell, lease, exchange, or otherwise dispose of all, or substantially all, of its property in the usual and regular course of business;

(2) mortgage, pledge, dedicate to the repayment of indebtedness (whether with or without recourse), or otherwise encumber any or all of its property whether or not in the usual and regular course of business; or

(3) transfer any or all of its property to a corporation all the shares of which are owned by the corporation.

(b) Unless the articles of incorporation require it, approval by the shareholders of a transaction described in subsection (a) is not required.

Official Comment

A sale of "all or substantially all" the corporate assets in the regular course of business is governed by section 12.01. Mortgages of all of the corporation's assets or redeployment of those assets through a wholly owned subsidiary are also covered by section 12.01. All other sales of "all or substantially all" the corporate assets are governed by section 12.02. Dispositions or transfers of property that do not involve "all or substantially all" the property of the corporation are not controlled by statute and may be approved by the board of directors (or authorized corporate officer) in the same manner as any other corporate transaction.

1. The Meaning of "All or Substantially All"

The phrase "all or substantially all," chosen by the draftsmen of the Model Act, is intended to mean what it literally says, "all or substantially all." The phrase "substantially all" is synonymous with "nearly all" and was added merely to make it clear that the statutory requirements could not be avoided by retention of some minimal or nominal residue of the original assets. A sale of all the corporate assets other than cash or cash equivalents is normally the sale of "all or substantially all" of the corporation's property. A sale of several distinct manufacturing lines while retaining one or more lines is normally not a sale of "all or

---

* Prior Chapter 12 of the Model Act has been replaced by new Chapter 12, supra.

substantially all" even though the lines being sold are substantial and include a significant fraction of the corporation's former business. If the lines retained are viewed only as a temporary operation or as a pretext to avoid the "all or substantially all" requirements, however, the statutory requirements of chapter 12 must be complied with. Similarly, a sale of a plant but retention of operating assets (e.g., machinery and equipment), accounts receivable, good will, and the like with a view toward continuing the operation at another location is not a sale of "all or substantially all" the corporation's property.

Some court decisions have adopted a narrower construction of somewhat similar statutory language. These decisions should be viewed as resting on the diverse statutory language involved in those cases and should not be viewed as illustrating the meaning of "all or substantially all" intended by the draftsmen of the Model Act.

2. Transfers of "All or Substantially All" of a Corporation's Assets That Do Not Require Shareholder Approval....

b. Sales in the Usual and Regular Course of Business

Most transfers of "all or substantially all" the corporate property (as defined above) are, almost by definition, not in the usual and regular course of business; sales by real estate corporations and by corporations organized to liquidate a business are examples of sales that may be included in this part of section 12.01(a). Typically, sales falling within the usual and regular course of business do not involve the sale of the corporate name or good will....

§ 12.02 Sale of Assets Other Than in Regular Course of Business

(a) A corporation may sell, lease, exchange, or otherwise dispose of all, or substantially all, of its property (with or without the good will), otherwise than in the usual and regular course of business, on the terms and conditions and for the consideration determined by the corporation's board of directors, if the board of directors proposes and its shareholders approve the proposed transaction.

(b) For a transaction to be authorized:

    (1) the board of directors must recommend the proposed transaction to the shareholders unless the board of directors determines that because of conflict of interest or other special circumstances it should make no recommendation and communicates the basis for its determination to the shareholders with the submission of the proposed transaction; and

    (2) the shareholders entitled to vote must approve the transaction.

(c) The board of directors may condition its submission of the proposed transaction on any basis.

(d) The corporation shall notify each shareholder, whether or not entitled to vote, of the proposed shareholders' meeting in accordance with section 7.05. The notice must also state that the purpose, or one of the purposes, of the meeting is to consider the sale, lease, exchange, or other disposition of all, or substantially all, the property of the corporation and contain or be accompanied by a description of the transaction.

(e) Unless the articles of incorporation or the board of directors (acting pursuant to subsection (c)) require a greater vote or a vote by voting groups, the transaction to be authorized must be approved by a majority of all the votes entitled to be cast on the transaction.

(f) After a sale, lease, exchange, or other disposition of property is authorized, the transaction may be abandoned (subject to any contractual rights) without further shareholder action.

(g) A transaction that constitutes a distribution is governed by section 6.40 and not by this section.

Official Comment

Certain corporate divisions, often called "spin offs," "split offs," or "split ups," sometimes involve transactions that may be formally characterized as sales of "all or substantially all" the corporate assets when in fact they are only a step in a corporate division that does not give rise to the problem of a major change in corporate direction and therefore does not need shareholder approval. Section 12.02(g) is designed to make clear that transactions like this, which actually constitute a distribution, are not subject to section 12.02. See Siegal, "When Corporations Divide: A Statutory and Financial Analysis," 79 Harv.L.Rev. 534 (1966).

Prior Model Act Chapter 13*

DISSENTER'S RIGHTS

Subchapter A

Right to Dissent and Obtain Payment for Shares

§ 13.01 Definitions

In this chapter:

(1) "Corporation" means the issuer of the shares held by a dissenter before the corporate action, or the surviving or acquiring corporation by merger or share exchange of that issuer.

* Prior Chapter 13 of the Model Act has been replaced by new Chapter 13, supra.

(2) "Dissenter" means a shareholder who is entitled to dissent from corporate action under section 13.02 and who exercises that right when and in the manner required by sections 13.20 through 13.28.

(3) "Fair value," with respect to a dissenter's shares, means the value of the shares immediately before the effectuation of the corporate action to which the dissenter objects, excluding any appreciation or depreciation in anticipation of the corporate action unless exclusion would be inequitable.

(4) "Interest" means interest from the effective date of the corporate action until the date of payment, at the average rate currently paid by the corporation on its principal bank loans or, if none, at a rate that is fair and equitable under all the circumstances.

(5) "Record shareholder" means the person in whose name shares are registered in the records of a corporation or the beneficial owner of shares to the extent of the rights granted by a nominee certificate on file with a corporation.

(6) "Beneficial shareholder" means the person who is a beneficial owner of shares held in a voting trust or by a nominee as the record shareholder.

(7) "Shareholder" means the record shareholder or the beneficial shareholder.

Official Comment

Section 13.01 contains specialized definitions applicable only to chapter 13. . . .

(2) The definition of "dissenter" in section 13.01(2) is phrased in terms of a "shareholder," a term that is itself specially defined in section 13.01(7). . . .

. . . Under this definition, a shareholder who initially objects but fails to perform any of these conditions within the times specified by this chapter loses his status as "dissenter" under this section.

(3) The definition of "fair value" in section 13.01(3) leaves to the parties (and ultimately to the courts) the details by which "fair value" is to be determined within the broad outlines of the definition. This definition thus leaves untouched the accumulated case law about market value, value based on prior sales, capitalized earnings value, and asset value. It specifically preserves the former language excluding appreciation and depreciation in anticipation of the proposed corporate action, but permits an exception for equitable considerations. The purpose of this exception ("unless exclusion would be inequitable") is to permit consideration of factors similar to those approved by the Supreme Court of Delaware in Weinberger v. UOP, Inc., 457 A.2d 701 (Del.1983), a case in which the court found that the transaction did not involve fair dealing or fair price: "In our

view this includes the elements of [rescissory] damages if the Chancellor considers them susceptible of proof and a remedy appropriate to all the issues of fairness before him." Consideration of appreciation or depreciation which might result from other corporate actions is permitted; these effects in the past have often been reflected either in market value or capitalized earnings value.

"Fair value" is to be determined immediately before the effectuation of the corporate action, instead of the date of the shareholder's vote, as is the case under most state statutes that address the issue. This comports with the plan of this chapter to preserve the dissenter's prior rights as a shareholder until the effective date of the corporate action, rather than leaving him in a twilight zone where he has lost his former rights, but has not yet gained his new ones.

(4) The definition of "interest" in section 13.01(4) is included to make interest computations under this chapter more realistic. The right to receive interest is based on the elementary consideration that the corporation has the use of the dissenter's money, and the dissenter has no use of it, from the effective date of the corporate action until the date of payment. . . .

§ 13.02 Right to Dissent

(a) A shareholder is entitled to dissent from, and obtain payment of the fair value of his shares in the event of, any of the following corporate actions:

(1) consummation of a plan of merger to which the corporation is a party (i) if shareholder approval is required for the merger by section 11.03 or the articles of incorporation and the shareholder is entitled to vote on the merger or (ii) if the corporation is a subsidiary that is merged with its parent under section 11.04;

(2) consummation of a plan of share exchange to which the corporation is a party as the corporation whose shares will be acquired, if the shareholder is entitled to vote on the plan;

(3) consummation of a sale or exchange of all, or substantially all, of the property of the corporation other than in the usual and regular course of business, if the shareholder is entitled to vote on the sale or exchange, including a sale in dissolution, but not including a sale pursuant to court order or a sale for cash pursuant to a plan by which all or substantially all of the net proceeds of the sale will be distributed to the shareholders within one year after the date of sale;

(4) an amendment of the articles of incorporation that materially and adversely affects rights in respect of a dissenter's shares because it:

(i) alters or abolishes a preferential right of the shares;

    (ii) creates, alters, or abolishes a right in respect of redemption, including a provision respecting a sinking fund for the redemption or repurchase, of the shares;

    (iii) alters or abolishes a preemptive right of the holder of the shares to acquire shares or other securities;

    (iv) excludes or limits the right of the shares to vote on any matter, or to cumulate votes, other than a limitation by dilution through issuance of shares or other securities with similar voting rights; or

    (v) reduces the number of shares owned by the shareholder to a fraction of a share if the fractional share so created is to be acquired for cash under section 6.04; or

(5) any corporate action taken pursuant to a shareholder vote to the extent the articles of incorporation, bylaws, or a resolution of the board of directors provides that voting or nonvoting shareholders are entitled to dissent and obtain payment for their shares.

(b) A shareholder entitled to dissent and obtain payment for his shares under this chapter may not challenge the corporate action creating his entitlement unless the action is unlawful or fraudulent with respect to the shareholder or the corporation.

Official Comment

1. Transactions Giving Rise to Dissenters' Rights

Section 13.02(a) establishes the scope of a shareholder's right to dissent (and his resulting right to obtain payment for his shares) by defining the transactions with respect to which a right to dissent exists. These transactions are:

(1) A plan of merger if the shareholder (i) is entitled to vote on the merger under section 11.03 or pursuant to provisions in the articles of incorporation, or (ii) is a shareholder of a subsidiary that is merged with a parent under section 11.04. The right to vote on a merger under section 11.03 extends to corporations whose separate existence disappears in the merger and to the surviving corporations if the number of its outstanding shares is increased by more than 20 percent as a result of the merger.

(2) A share exchange under section 11.02 if the corporation is a party whose shares are being acquired by the plan and the shareholder is entitled to vote on the exchange.

(3) A sale or exchange of all or substantially all of the property of the corporation not in the usual course of business under section 12.02 if the shareholder is entitled to vote on the sale or exchange. Section 13.02(a)(3) generally grants dissenters' rights in connection with sales in the process of dissolution but excludes them in connection

with sales by court order and sales for cash that require substantially all the proceeds to be distributed to the shareholders within one year. The inclusion of sales in dissolution is designed to ensure that the right to dissent cannot be avoided by characterizing sales as made in the process of dissolution long before distribution is made. An exception is provided for sales for cash pursuant to a plan that provides for distribution within one year. These transactions are unlikely to be unfair to minority shareholders since majority and minority are being treated in precisely the same way and all shareholders will ultimately receive cash for their shares. A sale other than for cash gives rise to a right of dissent since property sometimes cannot be converted into cash until long after receipt and a minority shareholder should not be compelled to assume the risk of delays or market declines. Similarly, a plan that provides for a prompt distribution of the property received gives rise to the right of dissent since the minority shareholder should not be compelled to accept for his shares different securities or other property that may not be readily marketable.

The exclusion of court-ordered sales from the dissenter's right is based on the view that court review and approval ensures that an independent appraisal of the fairness of the transaction has been made.

(4) Amendments to articles of incorporation that impair the shareholders' rights as shareholders in any of the enumerated ways. The reasons for granting a right of dissent in these situations are similar to those granting such rights in cases of merger and transfer of assets. The grant of these rights increases the security of investors by allowing them to escape when the nature of their investment rights is fundamentally altered or they are compelled to accept cash for their investment in an amount established by the corporation. The grant also enhances the freedom of the majority to make changes, because the existence of an escape hatch makes fair and reasonable a change that might be unfair if it forced a fundamental change of rights upon unwilling investors without giving them a reasonable alternative. . . .

Generally, only shareholders who are entitled to vote on the transaction are entitled to assert dissenters' rights with respect to the transaction. The right to vote may be based on the articles of incorporation or other provisions of the Model Act. For example, a class of nonvoting shares may nevertheless be entitled to vote (either as a separate voting group or as part of the general voting group) on an amendment to the articles of incorporation that affects them as provided in one of the ways set forth in section 10.04; such a class is entitled to assert dissenters' rights if the transaction also falls within section 13.02. On the other hand, such a class does not have the right to vote on a sale of substantially all the corporation's assets not in the ordinary course of business, and therefore that class is not entitled to assert dissenters' rights with respect to that sale. One exception to this principle is the merger of a subsidiary into its parent under section 11.04 in which minority shareholders of the subsidiary have the right to assert dissenters' rights even though they have no right to vote.

2. Exclusivity of Dissenters' Rights

Section 13.02(b) basically adopts the New York formula as to exclusivity of the dissenters' remedy of this chapter. The remedy is the exclusive remedy unless the transaction is "unlawful" or "fraudulent." The theory underlying this section is as follows: when a majority of shareholders has approved a corporate change, the corporation should be permitted to proceed even if a minority considers the change unwise or disadvantageous, and persuades a court that this is correct. Since dissenting shareholders can obtain the fair value of their shares, they are protected from pecuniary loss. Thus in general terms an exclusivity principle is justified. But the prospect that shareholders may be "paid off" does not justify the corporation in proceeding unlawfully or fraudulently. If the corporation attempts an action in violation of the corporation law on voting, in violation of clauses in articles of incorporation prohibiting it, by deception of shareholders, or in violation of a fiduciary duty—to take some examples—the court's freedom to intervene should be unaffected by the presence or absence of dissenters' rights under this chapter. Because of the variety of situations in which unlawfulness and fraud may appear, this section makes no attempt to specify particular illustrations. Rather, it is designed to recognize and preserve the principles that have developed in the case law of Delaware, New York and other states with regard to the effect of dissenters' rights on other remedies of dissident shareholders. See Weinberger v. UOP, Inc., 457 A.2d 701 (Del.1983) (appraisal remedy may not be adequate "where fraud, misrepresentation, self-dealing, deliberate waste of corporate assets, or gross or palpable overreaching are involved"). See also Vorenberg, "Exclusiveness of the Dissenting Stockholders' Appraisal Right," 77 Harv.L.Rev. 1189 (1964).

§ 13.03 Dissent by Nominees and Beneficial Owners

(a) A record shareholder may assert dissenters' rights as to fewer than all the shares registered in his name only if he dissents with respect to all shares beneficially owned by any one person and notifies the corporation in writing of the name and address of each person on whose behalf he asserts dissenters' rights. The rights of a partial dissenter under this subsection are determined as if the shares as to which he dissents and his other shares were registered in the names of different shareholders.

(b) A beneficial shareholder may assert dissenters' rights as to shares held on his behalf only if:

(1) he submits to the corporation the record shareholder's written consent to the dissent not later than the time the beneficial shareholder asserts dissenters' rights; and

(2) he does so with respect to all shares of which he is the beneficial shareholder or over which he has power to direct the vote.

Subchapter B

Procedure for Exercise of Dissenters' Rights

§ 13.20 Notice of Dissenters' Rights

(a) If proposed corporate action creating dissenters' rights under section 13.02 is submitted to a vote at a shareholders' meeting, the meeting notice must state that shareholders are or may be entitled to assert dissenters' rights under this chapter and be accompanied by a copy of this chapter.

(b) If corporate action creating dissenters' rights under section 13.02 is taken without a vote of shareholders, the corporation shall notify in writing all shareholders entitled to assert dissenters' rights that the action was taken and send them the dissenters' notice described in section 13.22.

§ 13.21 Notice of Intent to Demand Payment

(a) If proposed corporate action creating dissenters' rights under section 13.02 is submitted to a vote at a shareholders' meeting, a shareholder who wishes to assert dissenters' rights (1) must deliver to the corporation before the vote is taken written notice of his intent to demand payment for his shares if the proposed action is effectuated and (2) must not vote his shares in favor of the proposed action.

(b) A shareholder who does not satisfy the requirements of subsection (a) is not entitled to payment for his shares under this chapter.

§ 13.22 Dissenters' Notice

(a) If proposed corporate action creating dissenters' rights under section 13.02 is authorized at a shareholders' meeting, the corporation shall deliver a written dissenters' notice to all shareholders who satisfied the requirements of section 13.21.

(b) The dissenters' notice must be sent no later than 10 days after the corporate action was taken, and must:

(1) state where the payment demand must be sent and where and when certificates for certificated shares must be deposited;

(2) inform holders of uncertificated shares to what extent transfer of the shares will be restricted after the payment demand is received;

1053

(3) supply a form for demanding payment that includes the date of the first announcement to news media or to shareholders of the terms of the proposed corporate action and requires that the person asserting dissenters' rights certify whether or not he acquired beneficial ownership of the shares before that date;

(4) set a date by which the corporation must receive the payment demand, which date may not be fewer than 30 nor more than 60 days after the date the subsection (a) notice is delivered; and

(5) be accompanied by a copy of this chapter.

§ 13.23   Duty to Demand Payment

(a) A shareholder sent a dissenters' notice described in section 13.22 must demand payment, certify whether he acquired beneficial ownership of the shares before the date required to be set forth in the dissenters' notice pursuant to section 13.22(b)(3), and deposit his certificates in accordance with the terms of the notice.

(b) The shareholder who demands payment and deposits his share certificates under section (a) retains all other rights of a shareholder until these rights are cancelled or modified by the taking of the proposed corporate action.

(c) A shareholder who does not demand payment or deposit his share certificates where required, each by the date set in the dissenters' notice, is not entitled to payment for his shares under this chapter.

§ 13.24   Share Restrictions

(a) The corporation may restrict the transfer of uncertificated shares from the date the demand for their payment is received until the proposed corporate action is taken or the restrictions released under section 13.26.

(b) The person for whom dissenters' rights are asserted as to uncertificated shares retains all other rights of a shareholder until these rights are cancelled or modified by the taking of the proposed corporate action.

§ 13.25   Payment

(a) Except as provided in section 13.27, as soon as the proposed corporate action is taken, or upon receipt of a payment demand, the corporation shall pay each dissenter who complied with section 13.23 the amount the corporation estimates to be the fair value of his shares, plus accrued interest.

(b) The payment must be accompanied by:

(1) the corporation's balance sheet as of the end of a fiscal year ending not more than 16 months before the date of payment, an

income statement for that year, a statement of changes in share-holders' equity for that year, and the latest available interim financial statements, if any;

(2) a statement of the corporation's estimate of the fair value of the shares;

(3) an explanation of how the interest was calculated;

(4) a statement of the dissenter's right to demand payment under section 13.28; and

(5) a copy of this chapter.

Official Comment

Section 13.25 changes the relative balance between corporation and dissenting shareholders by requiring immediate payment by the corporation upon the completion of the transaction or (if the transaction did not need shareholder approval and has been completed) upon receipt of the demand for payment. The corporation may not wait for a final agreement on value before making payment, and the shareholder has the immediate use of the amount determined by the corporation to represent fair value without waiting for the conclusion of appraisal proceedings.

This obligation to make immediate payment is based on the view that since the person's rights as a shareholder are terminated with the completion of the transaction, he should have immediate use of the money to which the corporation agrees it has no further claim. A difference of opinion over the total amount to be paid should not delay payment of the amount that is undisputed....

§ 13.26 Failure to Take Action

(a) If the corporation does not take the proposed action within 60 days after the date set for demanding payment and depositing share certificates, the corporation shall return the deposited certificates and release the transfer restrictions imposed on uncertificated shares.

(b) If after returning deposited certificates and releasing transfer restrictions, the corporation takes the proposed action, it must send a new dissenters' notice under section 13.22 and repeat the payment demand procedure.

§ 13.27 After–Acquired Shares

(a) A corporation may elect to withhold payment required by section 13.25 from a dissenter unless he was the beneficial owner of the shares before the date set forth in the dissenters' notice as the date of the first announcement to news media or to shareholders of the terms of the proposed corporate action.

(b) To the extent the corporation elects to withhold payment under subsection (a), after taking the proposed corporate action, it shall estimate the fair value of the shares, plus accrued interest, and shall pay this amount to each dissenter who agrees to accept it in full satisfaction of his demand. The corporation shall send with its offer a statement of its estimate of the fair value of the shares, an explanation of how the interest was calculated, and a statement of the dissenter's right to demand payment under section 13.28.

§ 13.28 Procedure if Shareholder Dissatisfied With Payment or Offer

(a) A dissenter may notify the corporation in writing of his own estimate of the fair value of his shares and amount of interest due, and demand payment of his estimate (less any payment under section 13.25), or reject the corporation's offer under section 13.27 and demand payment of the fair value of his shares and interest due, if:

    (1) the dissenter believes that the amount paid under section 13.25 or offered under section 13.27 is less than the fair value of his shares or that the interest due is incorrectly calculated;

    (2) the corporation fails to make payment under section 13.25 within 60 days after the date set for demanding payment; or

    (3) the corporation, having failed to take the proposed action, does not return the deposited certificates or release the transfer restrictions imposed on uncertificated shares within 60 days after the date set for demanding payment.

(b) A dissenter waives his right to demand payment under this section unless he notifies the corporation of his demand in writing under subsection (a) within 30 days after the corporation made or offered payment for his shares.

Subchapter C

Judicial Appraisal of Shares

§ 13.30 Court Action

(a) If a demand for payment under section 13.28 remains unsettled, the corporation shall commence a proceeding within 60 days after receiving the payment demand and petition the court to determine the fair value of the shares and accrued interest. If the corporation does not commence the proceeding within the 60–day period, it shall pay each dissenter whose demand remains unsettled the amount demanded.

(b) The corporation shall commence the proceeding in the [name or describe] court of the county where a corporation's principal office (or, if none in this state, its registered office) is located. If the corporation is a foreign corporation without a registered office in this state, it shall commence the proceeding in the county in this state where the registered office of the domestic corporation merged with or whose shares were acquired by the foreign corporation was located.

(c) The corporation shall make all dissenters (whether or not residents of this state) whose demands remain unsettled parties to the proceeding as in an action against their shares and all parties must be served with a copy of the petition. Nonresidents may be served by registered or certified mail or by publication as provided by law.

(d) The jurisdiction of the court in which the proceeding is commenced under subsection (b) is plenary and exclusive. The court may appoint one or more persons as appraisers to receive evidence and recommend decision on the question of fair value. The appraisers have the powers described in the order appointing them, or in any amendment to it. The dissenters are entitled to the same discovery rights as parties in other civil proceedings.

(e) Each dissenter made a party to the proceeding is entitled to judgment (1) for the amount, if any, by which the court finds the fair value of his shares, plus interest, exceeds the amount paid by the corporation or (2) for the fair value, plus accrued interest, of his after-acquired shares for which the corporation elected to withhold payment under section 13.27.

Official Comment

All demands for payment made under section 13.28 are to be resolved in a single proceeding brought in the county where the corporation's principal office is located or, if none, in other specified counties. All shareholders making section 13.28 demands must be made parties, with service by publication authorized if necessary. . . .

§ 13.31 Court Costs and Counsel Fees

(a) The court in an appraisal proceeding commenced under section 13.30 shall determine all costs of the proceeding, including the reasonable compensation and expenses of appraisers appointed by the court. The court shall assess the costs against the corporation, except that the court may assess costs against all or some of the dissenters, in amounts the court finds equitable, to the extent the court finds the dissenters acted arbitrarily, vexatiously, or not in good faith in demanding payment under section 13.28.

(b) The court may also assess the fees and expenses of counsel and experts for the respective parties, in amounts the court finds equitable:

(1) against the corporation and in favor of any or all dissenters if the court finds the corporation did not substantially comply with the requirements of sections 13.20 through 13.28; or

    (2) against either the corporation or a dissenter, in favor of any other party, if the court finds that the party against whom the fees and expenses are assessed acted arbitrarily, vexatiously, or not in good faith with respect to the rights provided by this chapter.

(c) If the court finds that the services of counsel for any dissenter were of substantial benefit to other dissenters similarly situated, and that the fees for those services should not be assessed against the corporation, the court may award to these counsel reasonable fees to be paid out of the amounts awarded the dissenters who were benefited.

CALIFORNIA CORPORATIONS CODE
(SELECTED PROVISIONS)

TITLE 1

CORPORATIONS

GENERAL PROVISIONS

Chapter 1

GENERAL PROVISIONS AND DEFINITIONS

Chapter 2

ORGANIZATION AND BYLAWS

Chapter 3

DIRECTORS AND MANAGEMENT

Chapter 4

SHARES AND SHARE CERTIFICATES

Chapter 5

DIVIDENDS AND REACQUISITIONS OF SHARES

Chapter 6

SHAREHOLDERS' MEETINGS AND CONSENTS

Chapter 7

VOTING OF SHARES

Chapter 8

SHAREHOLDER DERIVATIVE ACTIONS

Chapter 9

AMENDMENT OF ARTICLES

Chapter 22

CRIMES AND PENALTIES

TITLE 4

SECURITIES

TITLE 1

CORPORATIONS

CORPORATIONS CODE
GENERAL PROVISIONS

§ 20. Electronic transmission by the corporation defined

"Electronic transmission by the corporation" means a communication (a) delivered by (1) facsimile telecommunication or electronic mail when directed to the facsimile number or electronic mail address, respectively, for that recipient on record with the corporation, (2) posting on an electronic message board or network which the corporation has designated for those communications, together with a separate notice to the recipient of the posting, which transmission shall be validly delivered upon the later of the posting or delivery of the separate notice thereof, or (3) other means of electronic communication, (b) to a recipient who has provided an unrevoked consent to the use of those means of transmission for communications under or pursuant to this code, and (c) that creates a record that is capable of retention, retrieval, and review, and that may thereafter be rendered into clearly legible tangible form. However, an electronic transmission by a corporation to an individual shareholder or member under this code is not authorized unless, in addition to satisfying the requirements of this section, the transmission satisfies the requirements applicable to consumer consent to electronic records as set forth in the Electronic Signatures in Global and National Commerce Act (15 U.S.C. Sec. 7001(c)(1)).

§ 21. Electronic transmission to the corporation defined

"Electronic transmission to the corporation" means a communication (a) delivered by (1) facsimile telecommunication or electronic mail when directed to the facsimile number or electronic mail address, respectively, which the corporation has provided from time to time to shareholders or members and directors for sending communications to the corporation, (2) posting on an electronic message board or network which the corporation has designated for those communications, and which transmission shall be validly delivered upon the posting, or (3) other means of electronic communication, (b) as to which the corporation has placed in effect reasonable measures to verify that the sender is the shareholder or member (in person or by proxy) or director purporting to send the transmission, and (c) that creates a record that is capable of retention, retrieval, and review, and that may thereafter be rendered into clearly legible tangible form.

Chapter 1

GENERAL PROVISIONS AND DEFINITIONS

§ 114. Financial Statements and Accounting Items

All references in this division to financial statements, balance sheets, income statements and statements of changes in financial position of a corporation and all references to assets, liabilities, earnings, retained earnings and similar accounting items of a corporation mean such financial statements or such items prepared or determined in conformity with generally accepted accounting principles then applicable, fairly presenting in conformity with generally accepted accounting principles the matters which they purport to present, subject to any specific accounting treatment required by a particular section of this division. Unless otherwise expressly stated, all references in this division to such financial statements mean, in the case of a corporation which has subsidiaries, consolidated statements of the corporation and such of its subsidiaries as are required ... to be included in such consolidated statements under generally accepted accounting principles then applicable and all references to such accounting items mean such items determined on a consolidated basis in accordance with such consolidated financial statements. Financial statements other than annual statements may be condensed or otherwise presented as permitted by authoritative accounting pronouncements.

§ 150. Affiliate; Affiliated

A corporation is an "affiliate" of, or a corporation is "affiliated" with, another specified corporation if it directly, or indirectly through one or more intermediaries, controls, is controlled by or is under common control with the other specified corporation.

§ 151. Approved by (or Approval of) the Board

"Approved by (or approval of) the board" means approved or ratified by the vote of the board or by the vote of a committee authorized to exercise the powers of the board....

§ 152. Approved by (or Approval of) the Outstanding Shares

"Approved by (or approval of) the outstanding shares" means approved by the affirmative vote of a majority of the outstanding shares entitled to vote. Such approval shall include the affirmative vote of a majority of the outstanding shares of each class or series entitled, by any provision of the articles or of this division, to vote as a class or series on the subject matter being voted upon and shall also include the affirmative vote of such greater proportion (including all) of the outstanding shares of any class or series if such greater proportion is required by the articles or this division.

§ 153. Approved by (or Approval of) the Shareholders

"Approved by (or approval of) the shareholders" means approved or ratified by the affirmative vote of a majority of the shares ... represented and voting at a duly held meeting at which a quorum is present (which shares voting affirmatively also constitute at least a majority of the required quorum) or by the written consent of shareholders ... or by the affirmative vote or written consent of such greater proportion (including all) of the shares of any class or series as may be provided in the articles or in this division for all or any specified shareholder action.

§ 158. Close Corporation

(a) "Close corporation" means a corporation whose articles contain, in addition to the provisions required by Section 202 [Articles of Incorporation; Required Provisions], a provision that all of the corporation's issued shares of all classes shall be held of record by not more than a specified number of persons, not exceeding 35, and a statement "This corporation is a close corporation."

(b) The special provisions referred to in subdivision (a) may be included in the articles by amendment, but if such amendment is adopted after the issuance of shares only by the affirmative vote of all of the issued and outstanding shares of all classes.

(c) The special provisions referred to in subdivision (a) may be deleted from the articles by amendment, or the number of shareholders specified may be changed by amendment, but if such amendment is adopted after the issuance of shares only by the affirmative vote of at least two-thirds of each class of the outstanding shares; provided, however, that the articles may provide for a lesser vote, but not less than a majority of the outstanding shares, or may deny a vote to any class, or both.

(d) In determining the number of shareholders for the purposes of the provision in the articles authorized by this section, a husband and wife and the personal representative of either shall be counted as one regardless of how shares may be held by either or both of them, a trust or personal representative of a decedent holding shares shall be counted as one regardless of the number of trustees or beneficiaries and a partnership or corporation or business association holding shares shall be counted as one (except that any such trust or entity the primary purpose of which was the acquisition or voting of the shares shall be counted according to the number of beneficial interests therein).

(e) A corporation shall cease to be a close corporation upon the filing of an amendment to its articles pursuant to subdivision (c) or if it shall have more than the maximum number of holders of record of its shares specified in its articles as a result of an inter vivos transfer of shares which is not void under subdivision (d) of Section 418, the transfer of shares on distribution by will or pursuant to the laws of descent and distribution, the dissolution of a partnership or corporation or business association or the termination of a trust which holds shares, by court decree upon dissolution of a marriage or otherwise by operation of law. Promptly upon acquiring more than the specified number of holders of record of its shares, a close corporation shall execute and file an amendment to its articles deleting the special provisions referred to in subdivision (a) and deleting any other provisions not permissible for a corporation which is not a close corporation, which amendment shall be promptly approved and filed by the board and need not be approved by the outstanding shares.

(f) Nothing contained in this section shall invalidate any agreement among the shareholders to vote for the deletion from the articles of the special provisions referred to in subdivision (a) upon the lapse of a specified period of time or upon the occurrence of a certain event or condition or otherwise....

(g) The following sections contain specific references to close corporations: 186, ... 204, 300, 418 ... 1201, 1800....

§ 160. Control

(a) Except as provided in subdivision (b), "control" means the possession, direct or indirect, of the power to direct or cause the direction of the management and policies of a corporation.

(b) "Control" in Sections 181, 1001 and 1200 means the ownership directly or indirectly of shares or equity securities possessing more than 50 percent of the voting power of a domestic corporation, a foreign corporation, or an other business entity.

§ 161. Constituent Corporation

"Constituent corporation" means a corporation which is merged with or into one or more other corporations or one or more other business entities and includes a surviving corporation.

§ 161.7 Constituent Other Business Entity

"Constituent other business entity" means an other business entity that is merged with or into one or more corporations and includes the surviving other business entity.

§ 161.9 Conversion

"Conversion" means a conversion pursuant to Chapter 11.5. . . .

§ 163.1 Cumulative Dividends in Arrears

For purposes of Section 503, "cumulative dividends in arrears" means only cumulative dividends that have not been paid as required on a scheduled payment date set forth in, or determined pursuant to, the articles of incorporation, regardless of whether those dividends had been declared prior to that scheduled payment date.

§ 165. Disappearing Corporation

"Disappearing corporation" means a constituent corporation which is not the surviving corporation.

§ 166. Distribution to Its Shareholders

"Distribution to its shareholders" means the transfer of cash or property by a corporation to its shareholders without consideration, whether by way of dividend or otherwise, except a dividend in shares of the corporation, or the purchase or redemption of its shares for cash or property, including the transfer, purchase, or redemption by a subsidiary of the corporation. The time of any distribution by way of dividend shall be the date of declaration thereof and the time of any distribution by purchase or redemption of shares shall be the date cash or property is transferred by the corporation, whether or not pursuant to a contract of an earlier date; provided, that where a debt obligation that is a security (as defined in Section 8102 of the Commercial Code) is issued in exchange for shares the time of the distribution is the date when the corporation acquires the shares in the exchange. In the case of a sinking fund payment, cash or property is transferred within the meaning of this section at the time that it is delivered to a trustee for the holders of preferred shares to be used for the redemption of the shares or physically segregated by the corporation in trust for that purpose. "Distribution to its shareholders" shall not include (a) satisfaction of a final judgment of a court or tribunal of appropriate jurisdiction ordering the rescission of the issuance of shares, (b) the rescission by a corporation of the issuance of its shares, if the board determines (with any director who is, or would be, a party to the transaction not being entitled to vote) that (1) it is reasonably likely that the holder or holders of the shares in question could legally enforce a claim for the rescission, (2) that the rescission is in the best interests of the corporation, and (3) the corporation is likely to be able to meet its liabilities (except those for which payment is otherwise adequately provided) as they mature, or (c) the repurchase by a corporation of its shares issued by it pursuant to Section 408 [Employee Stock Purchase or Stock Option Plans], if the board determines (with any director who is, or would be, a party to the transaction not being entitled to vote) that (1) the repurchase is in the best interests of the corporation and that (2) the corporation is likely to be able to meet its liabilities (except those for which payment is otherwise adequately provided) as they mature.

§ 167.8 Disappearing Other Business Entity

"Disappearing other business entity" means a constituent other business entity that is not the surviving other business entity.

§ 168. Equity Security

"Equity security" in Sections 181, 1001, 1113, 1200, and 1201 means any share or membership of a domestic or foreign corporation; any partnership interest, membership interest, or equivalent equity interest in an other business entity; and any security convertible with or without consideration into, shares or any warrant or right to subscribe to or purchase, any of the foregoing.

§ 171.1 Initial Transaction Statement

"Initial transaction statement" means a statement signed by or on behalf of the issuer sent to the new registered owner or registered pledgee, and "written statements," when used in connection with uncertificated securities, means the written statements that are periodically, or at the request of the registered owner or registered pledgee, sent by the issuer to the registered owner or registered pledgee describing the issue of which the uncertificated security is a part.

§ 172. Liquidation Price; Liquidation Preference

"Liquidation price" or "liquidation preference" means amounts payable on shares of any class upon voluntary or involuntary dissolution, winding up or distribution of the entire assets of the corporation, including any cumulative dividends accrued and unpaid, in priority to shares of another class or classes.

§ 174.5 Other Business Entity

"Other business entity" means a domestic or foreign limited liability company, limited partnership, [or] general partnership. . . .

§ 175. Parent

Except as used in Sections 1001, 1101, and 1113, a "parent" of a specified corporation is an affiliate in control (Section 160(a)) of that corporation directly or indirectly through one or more intermediaries. In Sections 1001, 1101, and 1113, "parent" means a person in control (Section 160(b)) of a domestic corporation, a foreign corporation, or an other business entity.

§ 180. Redemption Price

"Redemption price" means the amount or amounts (in cash, property or securities, or any combination thereof) payable on shares of any class or series upon the redemption of the shares. Unless otherwise expressly provided, the redemption price is payable in cash.

§ 181. Reorganization

"Reorganization" means either:

(a) A merger pursuant to Chapter 11 (commencing with Section 1100) other than a short-form merger (a "merger reorganization").

(b) The acquisition by one domestic corporation, foreign corporation, or other business entity in exchange, in whole or in part, for its equity securities (or the equity securities of a domestic corporation, a foreign corporation, or an other business entity which is in control of the acquiring entity) of equity securities of another domestic corporation, foreign corporation, or other business entity if, immediately after the acquisition, the acquiring entity has control of the other entity (an "exchange reorganization").

(c) The acquisition by one domestic corporation, foreign corporation, or other business entity in exchange in whole or in part for its equity securities (or the equity securities of a domestic corporation, a foreign corporation, or an other business entity which is in control of the acquiring entity) or for its debt securities (or debt securities of a domestic corporation, foreign corporation, or other business entity which is in control of the acquiring entity) which are not adequately secured and which have a maturity date in excess of five years after the consummation of the reorganization, or both, of all or substantially all of the assets of another domestic corporation, foreign corporation, or other business entity (a "sale-of-assets reorganization").

§ 183.5 Share Exchange Tender Offer

"Share exchange tender offer" means any acquisition by one corporation in exchange in whole or in part for its equity securities (or the equity securities of a corporation which is in control of the acquiring corporation) of shares of another corporation, other than an exchange reorganization (subdivision (b) of Section 181).

§ 186. Shareholders' Agreement

"Shareholders' agreement" means a written agreement among all of the shareholders of a close corporation, or if a close corporation has only one shareholder between such shareholder and the corporation, as authorized by subdivision (b) of Section 300.

§ 187. Short Form Merger

"Short-form merger" means a merger pursuant to Section 1110.

§ 189. Subsidiary

(a) Except as provided in subdivision (b), "subsidiary" of a specified corporation means a corporation shares of which possessing more than 50 percent of the voting power are owned directly or indirectly through one or more subsidiaries by the specified corporation.

(b) For the purpose of Section 703, "subsidiary" of a specified corporation means a corporation shares of which possessing more than 25 percent of the voting power are owned directly or indirectly through one or more subsidiaries as defined in subdivision (a) by the specified corporation.

§ 190. Surviving Corporation

"Surviving corporation" means a corporation into which one or more other corporations or one or more other business entities are merged.

§ 190.5 Surviving Limited Partnership

"Surviving limited partnership" means a limited partnership into which one or more other limited partnerships or one or more corporations are merged.

§ 190.7   Surviving Other Business Entity

"Surviving other business entity" means an other business entity into which one or more other business entities or one or more corporations are merged.

§ 194.   Vote

"Vote" includes authorization by written consent, subject to the provisions of subdivision (b) of Section 307 and subdivision (d) of Section 603.*

§ 194.5   Voting Power

"Voting power" means the power to vote for the election of directors at the time any determination of voting power is made and does not include the right to vote upon the happening of some condition or event which has not yet occurred. In any case where different classes of shares are entitled to vote as separate classes for different members of the board, the determination of percentage of voting power shall be made on the basis of the percentage of the total number of authorized directors which the shares in question (whether of one or more classes) have the power to elect in an election at which all shares then entitled to vote for the election of any directors are voted.

§ 194.7   Voting Shift

"Voting shift" means a change, pursuant to or by operation of a provision of the articles, in the relative rights of the holders of one or more classes or series of shares, voting as one or more separate classes or series, to elect one or more directors.

§ 195.   Written; In Writing

"Written" or "in writing" includes facsimile, telegraphic, and other electronic communication when authorized by this code, including an electronic transmission by a corporation that satisfies the requirements of Section 20.

Chapter 2

ORGANIZATION AND BYLAWS

§ 204.   Articles of Incorporation; Optional Provisions

The articles of incorporation may set forth:

(a) Any or all of the following provisions, which shall not be effective unless expressly provided in the articles:

---

* Section 603(d) provides that directors may not be elected by written consent ex-cept by unanimous written consent. (Footnote by ed.)

(1) Granting, with or without limitations, the power to levy assessments upon the shares or any class of shares.

(2) Granting to shareholders preemptive rights to subscribe to any or all issues of shares or securities.

(3) Special qualifications of persons who may be shareholders.

(4) A provision limiting the duration of the corporation's existence to a specified date.

(5) A provision requiring, for any or all corporate actions (except as provided in Section 303, subdivision (b) of Section 402.5, subdivision (c) of Section 708 and Section 1900) the vote of a larger proportion or of all of the shares of any class or series, or the vote or quorum for taking action of a larger proportion or of all of the directors, than is otherwise required by this division.

(6) A provision limiting or restricting the business in which the corporation may engage or the powers which the corporation may exercise or both.

(7) A provision conferring upon the holders of any evidences of indebtedness, issued or to be issued by the corporation, the right to vote in the election of directors and on any other matters on which shareholders may vote.

(8) A provision conferring upon shareholders the right to determine the consideration for which shares shall be issued.

(9) A provision requiring the approval of the shareholders (Section 153) or the approval of the outstanding shares (Section 152) for any corporate action, even though not otherwise required by this division.

(10) Provisions eliminating or limiting the personal liability of a director for monetary damages in an action brought by or in the right of the corporation for breach of a director's duties to the corporation and its shareholders, as set forth in Section 309, provided, however, that (A) such a provision may not eliminate or limit the liability of directors (i) for acts or omissions that involve intentional misconduct or a knowing and culpable violation of law, (ii) for acts or omissions that a director believes to be contrary to the best interests of the corporation or its shareholders or that involve the absence of good faith on the part of the director, (iii) for any transaction from which a director derived an improper personal benefit, (iv) for acts or omissions that show a reckless disregard for the director's duty to the corporation or its shareholders in circumstances in which the director was aware, or should have been aware, in the ordinary course of performing a director's duties, of a risk of serious injury to the corporation or its shareholders, (v) for acts or omissions that constitute an unexcused pattern of inattention that amounts to an abdication of the director's duty to the corporation or its shareholders, (vi) under Section 310, or (vii) under Section 316, (B) no such provision shall eliminate or limit the liability of a director for any

act or omission occurring prior to the date when the provision becomes effective, and (C) no such provision shall eliminate or limit the liability of an officer for any act or omission as an officer, notwithstanding that the officer is also a director or that his or her actions, if negligent or improper, have been ratified by the directors.

(11) A provision authorizing, whether by bylaw, agreement, or otherwise, the indemnification of agents (as defined in Section 317) in excess of that expressly permitted by Section 317 for those agents of the corporation for breach of duty to the corporation and its stockholders, provided, however, that the provision may not provide for indemnification of any agent for any acts or omissions or transactions from which a director may not be relieved of liability as set forth in the exception to paragraph (10) or as to circumstances in which indemnity is expressly prohibited by Section 317.

Notwithstanding this subdivision, in the case of a close corporation any of the provisions referred to above may be validly included in a shareholders' agreement. Notwithstanding this subdivision, bylaws may require for all or any actions by the board the affirmative vote of a majority of the authorized number of directors. Nothing contained in this subdivision shall affect the enforceability, as between the parties thereto, of any lawful agreement not otherwise contrary to public policy.

(b) Reasonable restrictions upon the right to transfer or hypothecate shares of any class or classes or series, but no restriction shall be binding with respect to shares issued prior to the adoption of the restriction unless the holders of such shares voted in favor of the restriction.

(c) The names and addresses of the persons appointed to act as initial directors.

(d) Any other provision, not in conflict with law, for the management of the business and for the conduct of the affairs of the corporation, including any provision which is required or permitted by this division to be stated in the bylaws.

§ 212. Bylaws; Contents

(a) The bylaws shall set forth (unless such provision is contained in the articles, in which case it may only be changed by an amendment of the articles) the number of directors of the corporation; or that the number of directors shall be not less than a stated minimum nor more than a stated maximum (which in no case shall be greater than two times the stated minimum minus one), with the exact number of directors to be fixed, within the limits specified, by approval of the board or the shareholders (Section 153) in the manner provided in the bylaws, subject to paragraph (5) of subdivision (a) of Section 204. The number or minimum number of directors shall not be less than three; provided, however, that (1) before shares are issued, the number may be one, (2) before shares are issued, the number may be two, (3) so long as the corporation has only one shareholder, the number may be one, (4) so long as the corporation has only one shareholder, the number may be two, and (5) so long as the corporation has only two shareholders, the number may be two. After the issuance of shares, a bylaw specifying or changing a fixed number of directors or the maximum or minimum number or changing from a fixed to a variable board or vice versa may only be adopted by approval of the outstanding shares (Section 152); provided, however that a bylaw or amendment of the articles reducing the fixed number or the minimum number of directors to a number less than five cannot be adopted if the votes cast against its adoption at a meeting or the shares not consenting in the case of action by written consent are equal to more than 16⅔ percent of the outstanding shares entitled to vote.

(b) The bylaws may contain any provision, not in conflict with law or the articles for the management of the business and for the conduct of the affairs of the corporation, including but not limited to:

(1) Any provision referred to in subdivision (b), (c) or (d) of Section 204.

(2) The time, place and manner of calling, conducting and giving notice of shareholders', directors' and committee meetings.

(3) The manner of execution, revocation and use of proxies.

(4) The qualifications, duties and compensation of directors; the time of their annual election; and the requirements of a quorum for directors' and committee meetings.

(5) The appointment and authority of committees of the board.

(6) The appointment, duties, compensation and tenure of officers.

(7) The mode of determination of holders of record of its shares.

(8) The making of annual reports and financial statements to the shareholders.

Chapter 3

DIRECTORS AND MANAGEMENT

§ 300. Powers of Board; Delegation; Close Corporations; Shareholders' Agreements; Validity; Liability; Failure to Observe Formalities

(a) Subject to the provisions of this division and any limitations in the articles relating to action required to be approved by the shareholders (Section 153) or by the outstanding shares (Section 152), or by a less than majority vote of a class or series of preferred shares (Section 402.5), the business and affairs of the corporation shall be managed and all corporate powers shall be exercised by or under the direction of the board. The board may delegate the management of the day-to-day operation of the business of the corporation to a management company or other person provided that the business and affairs of the corporation shall be managed and all corporate powers shall be exercised under the ultimate direction of the board.

(b) Notwithstanding subdivision (a) or any other provision of this division, but subject to subdivision (c), no shareholders' agreement, which relates to any phase of the affairs of a close corporation, including but not limited to management of its business, division of its profits or distribution of its assets on liquidation, shall be invalid as between the parties thereto on the ground that it so relates to the conduct of the affairs of the corporation as to interfere with the discretion of the board or that it is an attempt to treat the corporation as if it were a partnership or to arrange their relationships in a manner that would be appropriate only between partners. A transferee of shares covered by such an agreement which is filed with the secretary of the corporation for inspection by any prospective purchaser of shares, who has actual knowledge thereof or notice thereof by a notation on the certificate pursuant to Section 418, is bound by its provisions and is a party thereto for the purposes of subdivision (d). Original issuance of shares by the corporation to a new shareholder who does not become a party to the agreement terminates the agreement, except that if the agreement so provides it shall continue to the extent it is enforceable apart from this subdivision. The agreement may not be modified, extended or revoked without the consent of such a transferee, subject to any provision of the agreement permitting modification, extension or revocation by less than unanimous agreement of the parties. A transferor of shares covered by such an agreement ceases to be a party thereto upon ceasing to be a shareholder of the corporation unless the transferor is a party thereto other than as a shareholder. An agreement made pursuant to this subdivision shall terminate when the corporation ceases to be a close corporation, except that if the agreement so provides it shall continue to the extent it is enforceable apart from this subdivision. This subdivision does not apply to an agreement authorized by subdivision (a) of Section 706.

(c) No agreement entered into pursuant to subdivision (b) may alter or waive any of the provisions of Sections 158, 417, 418, 500, 501, and 1111, subdivision (e) of Section 1201, Sections 2009, 2010, and 2011, or of Chapters 15 (commencing with Section 1500), 16 (commencing with Section 1600), 18 (commencing with Section 1800), and 22 (commencing with Section 2200). All other provisions of this division may be altered or waived as between the parties thereto in a shareholders' agreement, except the required filing of any document with the Secretary of State.

(d) An agreement of the type referred to in subdivision (b) shall, to the extent and so long as the discretion or powers of the board in its management of corporate affairs is controlled by such agreement, impose upon each shareholder who is a party thereto liability for managerial acts performed or omitted by such person pursuant thereto that is otherwise imposed by this division upon directors, and the directors shall be relieved to that extent from such liability.

(e) The failure of a close corporation to observe corporate formalities relating to meetings of directors or shareholders in connection with the management of its affairs, pursuant to an agreement authorized by subdivision (b), shall not be considered a factor tending to establish that the shareholders have personal liability for corporate obligations.

§ 301. Directors; Election; Term

(a) Except as provided in Section 301.5, at each annual meeting of shareholders, directors shall be elected to hold office until the next annual meeting. However, to effectuate a voting shift (Section 194.7) the articles may provide that directors hold office for a shorter term. The articles may provide for the election of one or more directors by the holders of the shares of any class or series voting as a class or series.

(b) Each director, including a director elected to fill a vacancy, shall hold office until the expiration of the term for which elected and until a successor has been elected and qualified.

§ 301.5 Listed Corporations; Classes of Directors; Cumulative Voting; Election of Directors; Amendment of Articles and Bylaws

(a) A listed corporation may, by amendment of its articles or bylaws, adopt provisions to divide the board of directors into two or three classes to serve for terms of two or three years respectively, or to eliminate cumulative voting, or both. After the issuance of shares, a corporation which is not a listed corporation may, by amendment of its articles or bylaws, adopt provisions to be effective when the corporation becomes a listed corporation to divide the board of directors into two or three classes to serve for terms of two or three years respectively, or to eliminate cumulative voting, or both. An article or bylaw amendment providing for division of the board of directors into classes, or any change in the number of classes, or the elimination of cumulative voting may only be adopted by the approval of the board and the outstanding shares (Section 152) voting as a single class . . . .

(b) If the board of directors is divided into two classes pursuant to subdivision (a), the authorized number of directors shall be no less than six and one-half of the directors or as close an approximation as possible shall be elected at each annual meeting of shareholders. If the board of directors is divided into three classes, the authorized number of directors shall be no less than nine and one-third of the directors or as close an approximation as possible shall be elected at each annual meeting of shareholders. Directors of a listed corporation may be elected by classes at a meeting of shareholders at which an amendment to the articles or bylaws described in subdivision (a) is approved, but the extended terms for directors are contingent on that approval, and in the case of an amendment to the articles, the filing of any necessary amendment to the articles. . . .

(c) If directors for more than one class are to be elected by the shareholders at any one meeting of shareholders and the election is by cumulative voting pursuant to Section 708, votes may be cumulated only for directors to be elected within each class.

(d) For purposes of this section, a "listed corporation" means any of the following:

(1) A corporation with outstanding shares listed on the New York Stock Exchange or the American Stock Exchange.

(2) A corporation with outstanding securities listed on the National Market System or the Nasdaq Stock Market (or any successor to that entity).

(e) Subject to subdivision (h), if a listed corporation having a board of directors divided into classes pursuant to subdivision (a) ceases to be a listed corporation for any reason, unless the articles of incorporation or bylaws of the corporation provide for the elimination of classes of directors at an earlier date or dates, the board of directors of the corporation shall cease to be divided into classes as to each class of directors on the date of the expiration of the term of the directors in that class and the term of each director serving at the time the corporation ceases to be a listed corporation (and the term of each director elected to fill a vacancy resulting from the death, resignation, or removal of any of those directors) shall continue until its expiration as if the corporation had not ceased to be a listed corporation.

(f) Subject to subdivision (h), if a listed corporation having a provision in its articles or bylaws eliminating cumulative voting pursuant to subdivision (a) or permitting noncumulative voting in the election of directors pursuant to that subdivision, or both, ceases to be a listed corporation for any reason, the shareholders shall be entitled to cumulate their votes pursuant to Section 708 at any election of directors occurring while the corporation is not a listed corporation notwithstanding that provision in its articles of incorporation or bylaws.

(g) Subject to subdivision (i), if a corporation that is not a listed corporation adopts amendments to its articles of incorporation or bylaws to divide its board of directors into classes or to eliminate cumulative voting, or both, pursuant to subdivision (a) and then becomes a listed corporation, unless the articles of incorporation or bylaws provide for those provisions to become effective at some other time and, in cases where classes of directors are provided for, identify the directors who, or the directorships that, are to be in each class or the method by which those directors or directorships are to be identified, the provisions shall become effective for the next election of directors after the corporation becomes a listed corporation at which all directors are to be elected.

(h) If a corporation ceases to be a listed corporation on or after the record date for a meeting of shareholders and prior to the conclusion of the meeting, including the conclusion of the meeting after an adjournment or postponement that does not require or result in the setting of a new record date, then, solely for purposes of subdivisions (e) and (f), the corporation shall not be deemed to have ceased to be a listed corporation until the conclusion of the meeting of shareholders.

(i) If a corporation becomes a listed corporation on or after the record date for a meeting of shareholders and prior to the conclusion of the meeting, including the conclusion of the meeting after an adjournment or postponement that does not require or result in the setting of a new record date, then, solely for purposes of subdivision (g), the corporation shall not be deemed to have become a listed corporation until the conclusion of the meeting of shareholders.

(j) If an article amendment referred to in subdivision (a) is adopted by a listed corporation, the certificate of amendment shall include a statement of the facts showing that the corporation is a listed corporation within the meaning of subdivision (d). If an article or bylaw amendment referred to in subdivision (a) is adopted by a corporation which is not a listed corporation, the provision as adopted, shall include the following statement or the substantial equivalent: "This provision shall become effective only when the corporation becomes a listed corporation within the meaning of Section 301.5 of the Corporations Code."

§ 302. Directors; Vacancy; Grounds for Declaration

The board may declare vacant the office of a director who has been declared of unsound mind by an order of court or convicted of a felony.

§ 303. Directors; Removal Without Cause

(a) Any or all of the directors may be removed without cause if such removal is approved by the outstanding shares (Section 152), subject to the following:

(1) Except for a corporation to which paragraph (3) is applicable, no director may be removed (unless the entire board is removed) when the votes cast against removal, or not consenting in writing to the removal, would be sufficient to elect the director if voted cumulatively at an election at which the same total number of votes were cast (or, if the action is taken by written consent, all shares entitled to vote were voted) and the entire number of directors authorized at the time of the director's most recent election were then being elected.

(2) When by the provisions of the articles the holders of the shares of any class or series, voting as a class or series, are entitled to elect one or more directors, any director so elected may be removed only by the applicable vote of the holders of the shares of that class or series.

(3) A director of a corporation whose board of directors is classified pursuant to Section 301.5 may not be removed if the votes cast against removal of the director, or not consenting in writing to the removal, would be sufficient to elect the director if voted cumulatively (without regard to whether shares may otherwise be voted cumulatively) at an election at which the same total number of votes were cast (or, if the action is taken by written consent, all shares entitled to vote were voted) and either the number of directors elected at the most recent annual meeting of shareholders, or if greater, the number of directors for whom removal is being sought, were then being elected.

(b) Any reduction of the authorized number of directors or amendment reducing the number of classes of directors does not remove any director prior to the expiration of such director's term of office.

(c) Except as provided in this section and Sections 302 and 304, a director may not be removed prior to the expiration of the director's term of office.

§ 304. Removal for Cause; Shareholders Suit

The superior court of the proper county may, at the suit of shareholders holding at least 10 percent of the number of outstanding shares of any class, remove from office any director in case of fraudulent or dishonest acts or gross abuse of authority or discretion with reference to the corporation and may bar from reelection any director so removed for a period prescribed by the court. The corporation shall be made a party to such action.

§ 307. Meetings

(a) Unless otherwise provided in the articles or, subject to paragraph (5) of subdivision (a) of Section 204, in the bylaws. . . .

(6) Members of the board may participate in a meeting through use of conference telephone, electronic video screen communication, or electronic transmission by and to the corporation (Sections 20 and 21). Participation in a meeting through use of conference telephone or electronic video screen transmission pursuant to this subdivision constitutes presence in person at that meeting as long as all members participating in the meeting are able to hear one another. Participation in a meeting through electronic transmission by and to the corporation (other than conference telephone and electronic video screen transmission) pursuant to this subdivision constitutes presence in person at that meeting if both of the following apply:

(A) Each member participating in the meeting can communicate with all of the other members concurrently.

(B) Each member is provided the means of participating in all matters before the board, including, without limitation, the capacity to propose, or to interpose an objection to, a specific action to be taken by the corporation.

(7) A majority of the authorized number of directors constitutes a quorum of the board for the transaction of business. The articles or bylaws may not provide that a quorum shall be less than one-third the authorized number of directors or less than two, whichever is larger, unless the authorized number of directors is one, in which case one director constitutes a quorum.

(8) An act or decision done or made by a majority of the directors present at a meeting duly held at which a quorum is present is the act of the board, subject to the provisions of Section 310 and subdivision (e) of Section 317 [authorization of indemnification]. The articles or bylaws may not provide that a lesser vote than a majority of the directors present at a meeting is the act of the board. A meeting at which a quorum is initially present may continue to transact business notwithstanding the withdrawal of directors, if any action taken is approved by at least a majority of the required quorum for that meeting. . . .

(b) An action required or permitted to be taken by the board may be taken without a meeting, if all members of the board shall individually or collectively consent in writing to that action and if the number of members of the board serving at the time constitutes a quorum. The written consent or consents shall be filed with the minutes of the proceedings of the board. For purposes of this subdivision only, "all members of the board" shall include an "interested director" as described in subdivision (a) of Section 310 or a "common director" as described in subdivision (b) of Section 310 who abstains in writing from providing consent, where the disclosures required by Section 310 have been made to the noninterested or noncommon directors, as applicable, prior to their execution of the written consent or consents, the specified disclosures are conspicuously included in the written consent or consents executed by the noninterested or noncommon directors, and the noninterested or noncommon directors, as applicable, approve the action by a vote that is sufficient without counting the votes of the interested or common directors. If written consent is provided by the directors in accordance with the immediately preceding sentence and the disclosures made regarding the action that is the subject of the consent do not comply with the requirements of Section 310, the action that is the subject of the consent shall be deemed approved, but in any suit brought to challenge the action, the party asserting the validity of the action shall have the burden of proof in establishing that the action was just and reasonable to the corporation at the time it was approved.

§ 308. Deadlock on Board With Even Number of Directors; Provisional Director; Appointment; Powers

(a) If a corporation has an even number of directors who are equally divided and cannot agree as to the management of its affairs, so that its business can no longer be conducted to advantage or so that there is danger that its property and business will be impaired or lost, the superior court of the proper county may, notwithstanding any provisions of the articles or bylaws and whether or not an action is pending for an involuntary winding up or dissolution of the corporation, appoint a provisional director pursuant to this section. Action for such appointment may be brought by any director or by the holders of not less than 33⅓ percent of the voting power.

(b) If the shareholders of a corporation are deadlocked so that they cannot elect the directors to be elected at an annual meeting of shareholders, the superior court of the proper county may, notwithstanding any provisions of the articles or bylaws, upon petition of a shareholder or shareholders holding 50 percent of the voting power, appoint a provisional director or directors pursuant to this section or order such other equitable relief as the court deems appropriate.

(c) A provisional director shall be an impartial person, who is neither a shareholder nor a creditor of the corporation, nor related by consanguinity or affinity within the third degree according to the common law to any of the other directors of the corporation or to any judge of the court by which such provisional director is appointed. A provisional director shall have all the rights and powers of a director until the deadlock in the board or among shareholders is broken or until such provisional director is removed by order of the court or by approval of the outstanding shares (Section 152). Such person shall be entitled to such compensation as shall be fixed by the court unless otherwise agreed with the corporation. . . .

§ 309. Performance of Duties by Director; Liability

(a) A director shall perform the duties of a director, including duties as a member of any committee of the board upon which the director may serve, in good faith, in a manner such director believes to be in the best interests of the corporation and its shareholders and with such care, including reasonable inquiry, as an ordinarily prudent person in a like position would use under similar circumstances.

(b) In performing the duties of a director, a director shall be entitled to rely on information, opinions, reports or statements, including financial statements and other financial data, in each case prepared or presented by any of the following:

(1) One or more officers or employees of the corporation whom the director believes to be reliable and competent in the matters presented.

(2) Counsel, independent accountants or other persons as to matters which the director believes to be within such person's professional or expert competence.

(3) A committee of the board upon which the director does not serve, as to matters within its designated authority, which committee the director believes to merit confidence, so long as, in any such case, the director acts in good faith, after reasonable inquiry when the need therefor is indicated by the circumstances and without knowledge that would cause such reliance to be unwarranted.

(c) A person who performs the duties of a director in accordance with subdivisions (a) and (b) shall have no liability based upon any alleged failure to discharge the person's obligations as a director. In addition, the liability of a director for monetary damages may be eliminated or limited in a corporation's articles to the extent provided in paragraph (10) of subdivision (a) of Section 204.

§ 310. Contracts in Which Director Has Material Financial Interest; Validity

(a) No contract or other transaction between a corporation and one or more of its directors, or between a corporation and any corporation, firm or association in which one or more of its directors has a material financial interest, is either void or voidable because such director or directors or such other corporation, firm or association are parties or because such director or directors are present at the meeting of the board or a committee thereof which authorizes, approves or ratifies the contract or transaction, if

(1) The material facts as to the transaction and as to such director's interest are fully disclosed or known to the shareholders and such contract or transaction is approved by the shareholders (Section 153) in good faith, with the shares owned by the interested director or directors not being entitled to vote thereon, or

(2) The material facts as to the transaction and as to such director's interest are fully disclosed or known to the board or committee, and the board or committee authorizes, approves or ratifies the contract or transaction in good faith by a vote sufficient without counting the vote of the interested director or directors and the contract or transaction is just and reasonable as to the corporation at the time it is authorized, approved or ratified, or

(3) As to contracts or transactions not approved as provided in paragraph (1) or (2) of this subdivision, the person asserting the validity of the contract or transaction sustains the burden of proving that the contract or transaction was just and reasonable as to the corporation at the time it was authorized, approved or ratified.

A mere common directorship does not constitute a material financial interest within the meaning of this subdivision. A director is not interested within the meaning of this subdivision in a resolution fixing the compensation of another director as a director, officer or employee of the corporation, notwithstanding the fact that the first director is also receiving compensation from the corporation.

(b) No contract or other transaction between a corporation and any corporation or association of which one or more of its directors are directors is either void or voidable because such director or directors are present at the meeting of the board or a committee thereof which authorizes, approves or ratifies the contract or transaction, if

(1) The material facts as to the transaction and as to such director's other directorship are fully disclosed or known to the board or committee, and the board or committee authorizes, approves or ratifies the contract or transaction in good faith by a vote sufficient without counting the vote of the common director or directors or the contract or transaction is approved by the shareholders (Section 153) in good faith, or

(2) As to contracts or transactions not approved as provided in paragraph (1) of this subdivision, the contract or transaction is just and reasonable as to the corporation at the time it is authorized, approved or ratified.

This subdivision does not apply to contracts or transactions covered by subdivision (a).

(c) Interested or common directors may be counted in determining the presence of a quorum at a meeting of the board or a committee thereof which authorizes, approves or ratifies a contract or transaction.

§ 312. Officers; Election; Term; Resignation

(a) A corporation shall have a chairman of the board or a president or both, a secretary, a chief financial officer and such other officers with such titles and duties as shall be stated in the bylaws or determined by the board and as may be necessary to enable it to sign instruments and share certificates. The president, or if there is no president the chairman of the board, is the general manager and chief executive officer of the corporation, unless otherwise provided in the articles or bylaws. Any number of offices may be held by the same person unless the articles or bylaws provide otherwise.

(b) Except as otherwise provided by the articles or bylaws, officers shall be chosen by the board and serve at the pleasure of the board, subject to the rights, if any, of an officer under any contract of employment. Any officer may resign at any time upon written notice to the corporation without prejudice to the rights, if any, of the corporation under any contract to which the officer is a party.

§ 313. Instrument in Writing and Assignment or Endorsement Thereof; Signatures; Validity

Subject to the provisions of subdivision (a) of Section 208, any note, mortgage, evidence of indebtedness, contract, share certificate, initial transaction statement or written statement, conveyance, or other instrument in writing, and any assignment or endorsement thereof, executed or entered into between any corporation and any other person, when signed by the chairman of the board, the president or any vice president and the secretary, any assistant secretary, the chief financial officer or any assistant treasurer of such corporation, is not invalidated as to the corporation by any lack of authority of the signing officers in the absence of actual knowledge on the part of the other person that the signing officers had no authority to execute the same.

§ 316. Corporate Actions Subjecting Directors to Joint and Several Liability; Actions; Damages

(a) Subject to the provisions of Section 309, directors of a corporation who approve any of the following corporate actions shall be jointly and severally liable to the corporation for the benefit of all of the creditors or shareholders entitled to institute an action under subdivision (c):

(1) The making of any distribution to its shareholders to the extent that it is contrary to the provisions of Sections 500 to 503, inclusive.

(2) The distribution of assets to shareholders after institution of dissolution proceedings of the corporation, without paying or adequately providing for all known liabilities of the corporation, excluding any claims not filed by creditors within the time limit set by the court in a notice given to creditors under Chapters 18 (commencing with Section 1800), 19 (commencing with Section 1900) and 20 (commencing with Section 2000).

(3) The making of any loan or guaranty contrary to Section 315 [Loans or guarantees of obligations of directors, officers, or other persons].

(b) A director who is present at a meeting of the board, or any committee thereof, at which action specified in subdivision (a) is taken and who abstains from voting shall be considered to have approved the action.

(c) Suit may be brought in the name of the corporation to enforce the liability (1) under paragraph (1) of subdivision (a) against any or all directors liable by the persons entitled to sue under subdivision (b) of Section 506, (2) under paragraph (2) or (3) of subdivision (a) against any or all directors liable by any one or more creditors of the corporation whose debts or claims arose prior to the time of any of the corporate actions specified in paragraph (2) or (3) of subdivision (a) and who have not consented to the corporate action, whether or not they have reduced their claims to judgment, or (3) under paragraph (3) of subdivision (a) against any or all directors liable by any one or more holders of shares outstanding at the time of any corporate action specified in paragraph (3) of subdivision (a) who have not consented to the corporate action, without regard to the provisions of Section 800.

(d) The damages recoverable from a director under this section shall be the amount of the illegal distribution (or if the illegal distribution consists of property, the fair market value of that property at the time of the illegal distribution) plus interest thereon from the date of the distribution at the legal rate on judgments until paid, together with all reasonably incurred costs of appraisal or other valuation, if any, of that property or loss suffered by the corporation as a result of the illegal loan or guaranty, as the case may be, but not exceeding the liabilities of the corporation owed to nonconsenting creditors at the time of the violation and the injury suffered by nonconsenting shareholders, as the case may be.

(e) Any director sued under this section may implead all other directors liable and may compel contribution, either in that action or in an independent action against directors not joined in that action.

(f) Directors liable under this section shall also be entitled to be subrogated to the rights of the corporation:

(1) With respect to paragraph (1) of subdivision (a), against shareholders who received the distribution.

(2) With respect to paragraph (2) of subdivision (a), against shareholders who received the distribution of assets.

(3) With respect to paragraph (3) of subdivision (a), against the person who received the loan or guaranty. Any director sued under this section may file a cross-complaint against the person or persons who are liable to the director as a result of the subrogation provided for in this subdivision or may proceed against them in an independent action.

§ 317. Indemnification of Agent of Corporation in Proceedings or Actions

(a) For the purposes of this section, "agent" means any person who is or was a director, officer, employee or other agent of the corporation, or is or was serving at the request of the corporation as a director, officer, employee or agent of another foreign or domestic corporation, partnership, joint venture, trust or other enterprise, or was a director, officer, employee or agent of a foreign or domestic corporation which was a predecessor corporation of the corporation or of another enterprise at the request of the predecessor corporation; "proceeding" means any threatened, pending or completed action or proceeding, whether civil, criminal, administrative or investigative; and "expenses" includes without limitation attorneys' fees and any expenses of establishing a right to indemnification under subdivision (d) or paragraph (4) of subdivision (e).

(b) A corporation shall have power to indemnify any person who was or is a party or is threatened to be made a party to any proceeding (other than an action by or in the right of the corporation to procure a judgment in its favor) by reason of the fact that the person is or was an agent of the corporation, against expenses, judgments, fines, settlements, and other amounts actually and reasonably incurred in connection with the proceeding if that person acted in good faith and in a manner the person reasonably believed to be in the best interests of the corporation and, in the case of a criminal proceeding, had no reasonable cause to believe the conduct of the person was unlawful. The termination of any proceeding by judgment, order, settlement, conviction, or upon a plea of nolo contendere or its equivalent shall not, of itself, create a presumption that the person did not act in good faith and in a manner which the person reasonably believed to be in the best interests of the corporation or that the person had reasonable cause to believe that the person's conduct was unlawful.

(c) A corporation shall have power to indemnify any person who was or is a party or is threatened to be made a party to any threatened, pending, or completed action by or in the right of the corporation to procure a judgment in its favor by reason of the fact that the person is or was an agent of the corporation, against expenses actually and reasonably incurred by that person in connection with the defense or settlement of the action if the person acted in good faith, in a manner the person believed to be in the best interests of the corporation and its shareholders.

No indemnification shall be made under this subdivision for any of the following:

(1) In respect of any claim, issue or matter as to which the person shall have been adjudged to be liable to the corporation in the performance of that person's duty to the corporation and its shareholders, unless and only to the extent that the court in which the proceeding is or was pending shall determine upon application that, in view of all the circumstances of the case, the person is fairly and reasonably entitled to indemnity for expenses and then only to the extent that the court shall determine.

(2) Of amounts paid in settling or otherwise disposing of a pending action without court approval.

(3) Of expenses incurred in defending a pending action which is settled or otherwise disposed of without court approval.

(d) To the extent that an agent of a corporation has been successful on the merits in defense of any proceeding referred to in subdivision (b) or (c) or in defense of any claim, issue, or matter therein, the agent shall be indemnified against expenses actually and reasonably incurred by the agent in connection therewith.

(e) Except as provided in subdivision (d), any indemnification under this section shall be made by the corporation only if authorized in the specific case, upon a determination that indemnification of the agent is proper in the circumstances because the agent has met the applicable standard of conduct set forth in subdivision (b) or (c), by any of the following:

(1) A majority vote of a quorum consisting of directors who are not parties to such proceeding.

(2) If such a quorum of directors is not obtainable, by independent legal counsel in a written opinion.

(3) Approval of the shareholders (Section 153), with the shares owned by the person to be indemnified not being entitled to vote thereon.

(4) The court in which the proceeding is or was pending upon application made by the corporation or the agent or the attorney or other person rendering services in connection with the defense, whether or not the application by the agent, attorney or other person is opposed by the corporation.

(f) Expenses incurred in defending any proceeding may be advanced by the corporation prior to the final disposition of the proceeding upon receipt of an undertaking by or on behalf of the agent to repay that amount if it shall be determined ultimately that the agent is not entitled to be indemnified as authorized in this section. The provisions of subdivision (a) of Section 315 do not apply to advances made pursuant to this subdivision.

(g) The indemnification authorized by this section shall not be deemed exclusive of any additional rights to indemnification for breach of duty to the corporation and its shareholders while acting in the capacity of a director or officer of the corporation to the extent the additional rights to indemnification are authorized in an article provision adopted pursuant to paragraph (11) of subdivision (a) of Section 204. The indemnification provided by this section for acts, omissions, or transactions while acting in the capacity of, or while serving as, a director or officer of the corporation but not involving breach of duty to the corporation and its shareholders shall not be deemed exclusive of any other rights to which those seeking indemnification may be entitled under any bylaw, agreement, vote of shareholders or disinterested directors, or otherwise, to the extent the additional rights to indemnification are authorized in the articles of the corporation. An article provision authorizing indemnification "in excess of that otherwise permitted by Section 317" or "to the fullest extent permissible under California law" or the substantial equivalent thereof shall be construed to be both a provision for additional indemnification for breach of duty to the corporation and its shareholders as referred to in, and with the limitations required by, paragraph (11) of subdivision (a) of Section 204 and a provision for additional indemnification as referred to in the second sentence of this subdivision. The rights to indemnity hereunder shall continue as to a person who has ceased to be a director, officer, employee, or agent and shall inure to the benefit of the heirs, executors, and administrators of the person. Nothing contained in this section shall affect any right to indemnification to which persons other than the directors and officers may be entitled by contract or otherwise.

(h) No indemnification or advance shall be made under this section, except as provided in subdivision (d) or paragraph (4) of subdivision (e), in any circumstance where it appears:

(1) That it would be inconsistent with a provision of the articles, bylaws, a resolution of the shareholders, or an agreement in effect at the time of the accrual of the alleged cause of action asserted in the proceeding in which the expenses were incurred or other amounts were paid, which prohibits or otherwise limits indemnification.

(2) That it would be inconsistent with any condition expressly imposed by a court in approving a settlement.

(i) A corporation shall have power to purchase and maintain insurance on behalf of any agent of the corporation against any liability asserted against or incurred by the agent in that capacity or arising out of the agent's status as such whether or not the corporation would have the power to indemnify the agent against that liability under this section. The fact that a corporation owns all or a portion of the shares of the company issuing a policy of insurance shall not render this subdivision inapplicable if either of the following conditions are satisfied: (1) if the articles authorize indemnification in excess of that authorized in this section and the insurance provided by this subdivision is limited as indemnification is required to be limited by paragraph (11) of subdivision (a) of Section 204; or (2)(A) the company issuing the insurance policy is organized, licensed, and operated in a manner that complies with the insurance laws and regulations applicable to its jurisdiction of organization, (B) the company issuing the policy provides procedures for processing claims that do not permit that company to be subject to the direct control of the corporation that purchased that policy, and (C) the policy issued provides for some manner of risk sharing between the issuer and purchaser of the policy, on one hand, and some unaffiliated person or persons, on the other, such as by providing for more than one unaffiliated owner of the company issuing the policy or by providing that a portion of the coverage furnished will be obtained from some unaffiliated insurer or reinsurer.

(j) This section does not apply to any proceeding against any trustee, investment manager, or other fiduciary of an employee benefit plan in that person's capacity as such, even though the person may also be an agent as defined in subdivision (a) of the employer corporation. A corporation shall have power to indemnify such a trustee, investment manager or other fiduciary to the extent permitted by subdivision (f) of Section 207 [corporate powers].

Chapter 4

SHARES AND SHARE CERTIFICATES

§ 407. Fractional Shares

A corporation may, but is not required to, issue fractions of a share originally or upon transfer. If it does not issue fractions of a share, it shall in connection with any original issuance of shares (a) arrange for the disposition of fractional interests by those entitled thereto, (b) pay in cash the fair value of fractions of a share as of the time when those entitled to receive those fractions are determined or (c) issue scrip or warrants in registered form, as certificated securities or uncertificated securities, or [in] bearer form as certificated securities, which shall entitle the holder to receive a certificate for a full share upon the surrender of such script or warrants aggregating a full share; provided, however, that if the fraction of a share that any person would otherwise be entitled to receive in a merger, conversion, or reorganization is less than one-half of 1 percent of the total shares that person is entitled to receive, a merger, conversion, or reorganization agreement may provide that fractions of a share will be disregarded or that shares issuable in the merger will be rounded off to the nearest whole share; and provided, further, that a corporation may not pay cash for fractional shares if that action would result in the cancellation of more than 10 percent of the outstanding shares of any class. A determination by the board of the fair value of fractions of a share shall be conclusive in the absence of fraud. A certificate for a fractional share shall, but scrip or warrants shall not unless otherwise provided therein, entitle the holder to exercise voting rights, to receive dividends thereon and to participate in any of the assets of the corporation in the event of liquidation. The board may cause scrip or warrants to be issued subject to the condition that they shall become void if not exchanged for full shares before a specified date or that the shares for which scrip or warrants are exchangeable may be sold by the corporation and the proceeds thereof distributed to the holder of the scrip or warrants or any other condition that the board may impose.

§ 418.   Certificates or Initial Transaction Statements; Required Contents of Statements on Face of Documents; Failure to State; Enforceability; Close Corporations; Validity of Transfers

(a) There shall also appear on the certificate, the initial transaction statement, and written statements (unless stated or summarized under subdivision (a) or (b) of Section 417) the statements required by all of the following clauses to the extent applicable:

(1) The fact that the shares are subject to restrictions upon transfer.

(2) If the shares are assessable or are not fully paid, a statement that they are assessable or the statements required by subdivision (d) of Section 409 if they are not fully paid.

(3) The fact that the shares are subject to a voting agreement under subdivision (a) of Section 706 or an irrevocable proxy under subdivision (e) of Section 705 or restrictions upon voting rights contractually imposed by the corporation.

(4) The fact that the shares are redeemable.

(5) The fact that the shares are convertible and the period for conversion.

Any such statement or reference thereto (Section 174) on the face of the certificate, the initial transaction statement, and written statements required by paragraph (1) or (2) shall be conspicuous.

(b) Unless stated on the certificate, the initial transaction statement, and written statements as required by subdivision (a), no restriction upon transfer, no right of redemption and no voting agreement under subdivision (a) of Section 706, no irrevocable proxy under subdivision (e) of Section 705, and no voting restriction imposed by the corporation shall be enforceable against a transferee of the shares without actual knowledge of such restriction, right, agreement of proxy. With regard only to liability to assessment or for the unpaid portion of the subscription price, unless stated on the certificate as required by subdivision (a), that liability shall not be enforceable against a transferee of the shares. For the purpose of this subdivision, "transferee" includes a purchaser from the corporation.

(c) All certificates representing shares of a close corporation shall contain in addition to any other statements required by this section, the following conspicuous legend on the face thereof: "This corporation is a close corporation. The number of holders of record of its shares of all classes cannot exceed _____ [a number not in excess of 35]. Any attempted voluntary inter vivos transfer which would violate this requirement is void. Refer to the articles, bylaws and any agreements on file with the secretary of the corporation for further restrictions."

(d) Any attempted voluntary inter vivos transfer of the shares of a close corporation which would result in the number of holders of record of its shares exceeding the maximum number specified in its articles is void if the certificate contains the legend required by subdivision (c).

Chapter 5

DIVIDENDS AND REACQUISITIONS OF SHARES

§ 500. Distributions; Retained Earnings or Assets Remaining After Completion

Neither a corporation nor any of its subsidiaries shall make any distribution to the corporation's shareholders (Section 166) except as follows:

(a) The distribution may be made if the amount of the retained earnings of the corporation immediately prior thereto equals or exceeds the amount of the proposed distribution; or

(b) The distribution may be made if immediately after giving effect thereto:

(1) The sum of the assets of the corporation (exclusive of goodwill, capitalized research and development expenses and deferred charges) would be at least equal to 1¼ times its liabilities (not including deferred taxes, deferred income and other deferred credits); and

(2) The current assets of the corporation would be at least equal to its current liabilities or, if the average of the earnings of the corporation before taxes on income and before interest expense for the two preceding fiscal years was less than the average of the interest expense of the corporation for those fiscal years, at least equal to 1¼ times its current liabilities; provided, however, that in determining the amount of the assets of the corporation profits derived from an exchange of assets shall not be included unless the assets received are currently realizable in cash; and provided, further, that for the purpose of this subdivision "current assets" may include net amounts which the board has determined in good faith may reasonably be expected to be received from customers during the 12–month period used in calculating current liabilities pursuant to existing contractual relationships obligating those customers to make fixed or periodic payments during the term of the contract or, in the case of public utilities, pursuant to service connections with customers, after in each case giving effect to future costs not then included in current liabilities but reasonably expected to be incurred by the corporation in performing those contracts or providing service to utility customers. Paragraph (2) of subdivision (b) is not applicable to a corporation which does not classify its assets into current and fixed under generally accepted accounting principles.

(c) The amount of any distribution payable in property shall, for the purposes of this chapter, be determined on the basis of the value at which such property is carried on the corporation's financial statements in accordance with generally accepted accounting principles.

(d) For the purpose of applying this section to a distribution by a corporation of cash or property in payment by the corporation in connection with the purchase of its shares, there shall be added to retained earnings all amounts that had been previously deducted there-from with respect to obligations incurred in connection with the corporation's repurchase of its shares and reflected on the corporation's balance sheet, but not in excess of the principal of the obligations that remain unpaid immediately prior to the distribution. In addition, there shall be deducted from liabilities all amounts that had been previously added thereto with respect to the obligations incurred in connection with the corporation's repurchase of its shares and reflected on the corporation's balance sheet, but not in excess of the principal of the obligations that will remain unpaid after the distribution, provided that no addition to retained earnings or deduction from liabilities under this subdivision shall occur on account of any obligation that is a distribution to the corporation's shareholders (Section 166) at the time the obligation is incurred....

Legislative Committee Comment ...

... Under prior law dividends may generally be declared only out of earned surplus.... There are several exceptions to this general rule. Dividends may be paid in some circumstances out of net profits for a six to twelve month period ("nimble" dividends), paid-in surplus or surplus resulting from the reduction of stated capital.... However, a dividend may not be declared in any event where the corporation would thereby be rendered insolvent....

As a practical matter, these general restrictions do not provide adequate protection to creditors, particularly trade creditors. This results from the fact that all but an insignificant amount of the money originally received from the shareholders can be designated as paid-in surplus rather than stated capital.

Similarly, the general rule under prior law is that a corporation may acquire shares issued by it only from earned surplus.... Exceptions to this rule permit purchases of such shares from reduction surplus, and redemption of shares subject to redemption from any surplus....

This distinction between the sources from which shares may be purchased and those from which dividends may be paid is anomalous, as a purchase of shares on a pro rata basis has exactly the same effect as a dividend with regard to the protection of creditors and senior shareholders.

For the purpose of establishing meaningful protection for creditors and shareholders and to rationalize restrictions upon the payment of dividends and repurchase of shares, this section provides restrictions upon a corporation in the making of any "distribution to its shareholders" based upon the current financial condition of the corporation ["Distribution to its shareholder" is a defined term. See § 166]. This approach eliminates the concepts of "stated capital" and "surplus" in favor of balance sheet tests.

The corporation may make a distribution to its shareholders if either of two tests is met. First, a corporation may make a distribution out of its retained earnings.

Second, if there are not retained earnings, a corporation may make a distribution provided that after giving effect to the distribution the assets of the corporation (exclusive of certain intangibles) are at least equal to one and a quarter times its liabilities (excluding certain deferred items) and its current assets are at least equal to its current liabilities.

With regard to the liquidity portion of this test, if the average of the earnings of the corporation before taxes on income and before interest expense for the two proceeding fiscal years is not at least equal to the average of the interest expense of the corporation for such years, the current assets must be at least one and a quarter times the current liabilities. However, this liquidity test is inapplicable to any corporation not classifying its assets into current and fixed under generally accepted accounting principles.

This section prohibits, in determining the amount of the assets of a corporation, the inclusion of any appreciation in value not yet realized (except with respect to readily marketable securities) and profits derived from exchange of assets unless the assets received are currently realizable in cash. . . . The amount of any distribution payable in property is the value at which such property is carried on the corporation's financial statements [All references to financial statements, as well as other specified terms, mean consolidated financial statements or other items prepared or determined in accordance with generally accepted accounting principles then applicable. See § 114.].

In appropriate cases where income within a "current" period is definitely assured and determinable, such income although not yet received may be included in the calculation of current assets subject to certain adjustments.

Any distribution to the corporation's shareholders permitted by this section is subject to the solvency limitation of § 501.

§ 501. Inability to Meet Liabilities as They Mature; Prohibition of Distribution

Neither a corporation nor any of its subsidiaries shall make any distribution to the corporation's shareholders (Section 166) if the corporation or the subsidiary making the distribution is, or as a result thereof would be, likely to be unable to meet its liabilities (except those whose payment is otherwise adequately provided for) as they mature.

§ 502. Distribution to Junior Shares if Excess of Assets Over Liabilities Less Than Liquidation Preference of Senior Shares; Prohibition

Neither a corporation nor any of its subsidiaries shall make any distribution to the corporation's shareholders (Section 166) on any shares of its stock of any class or series that are junior to outstanding shares of any class or series with respect to distribution of assets on liquidation if, after giving effect thereto, the excess of its assets (exclusive of goodwill, capitalized research and development expenses and deferred charges) over its liabilities (not including deferred taxes, deferred income and other deferred credits) would be less than the liquidation preference of all shares having a preference on liquidation over the class or series to which the distribution is made; provided, however, that for the purpose of applying this section to a distribution by a corporation of cash or property in payment by the corporation in connection with the purchase of its shares, there shall be deducted from liabilities all amounts that had been previously added thereto with respect to obligations incurred in connection with the corporation's repurchase of its shares and reflected on the corporation's balance sheet, but not in excess of the principal of the obligations that will remain unpaid after the distribution; provided, further, that no deduction from liabilities shall occur on account of any obligation that is a distribution to the corporation's shareholders (Section 166) at the time the obligation is incurred.

§ 503. Retained Earnings Necessary to Allow Distribution to Junior Shares

Neither a corporation nor any of its subsidiaries shall make any distribution to the corporation's shareholders (Section 166) on any shares of its stock of any class or series that are junior to outstanding shares of any other class or series with respect to payment of dividends, and as to which senior class or series the corporation has cumulative dividends in arrears, unless the amount of the retained earnings of the corporation immediately prior thereto equals or exceeds the amount of the proposed distribution plus the aggregate amount of the cumulative dividends in arrears on all shares having a preference with respect to payment of dividends over the class or series to which the distribution is made; provided, however, that for the purpose of applying this section to a distribution by a corporation of cash or property in payment by the corporation in connection with the purchase of its shares, there shall be added to retained earnings all amounts that had been previously deducted therefrom with respect to obligations incurred in connection with the corporation's repurchase of its shares and reflected on the corporation's balance sheet, but not in excess of the principal of the obligations that remain unpaid immediately prior to the distribution; provided, further, that no addition to retained earnings shall occur on account of any obligation that is a distribution to the corporation's shareholders (Section 166) at the time the obligation is incurred.

§ 506. Receipt of Prohibited Dividend; Liability of Shareholder; Suit by Creditors or Other Shareholders; Fraudulent Transfers

(a) Any shareholder who receives any distribution prohibited by this chapter with knowledge of facts indicating the impropriety thereof is liable to the corporation for the benefit of all of the creditors or shareholders entitled to institute an action under subdivision (b) for the amount so received by such shareholder with interest thereon at the legal rate on judgments until paid, but not exceeding the liabilities of the corporation owed to nonconsenting creditors at the time of the violation and the injury suffered by nonconsenting shareholders, as the case may be. For purposes of this chapter, in the event that any shareholder receives any distribution of the corporation's property that is prohibited by this chapter, the shareholder receiving that illegal distribution shall be liable to the corporation for an amount equal to the fair market value of the property at the time of the illegal distribution plus interest thereon from the date of the distribution at the legal rate on judgments until paid, together with all reasonably incurred costs of appraisal or other valuation, if any, of that property, but not exceeding the liabilities of the corporation owed to nonconsenting creditors at the time of the violation and the injury suffered by nonconsenting shareholders, as the case may be.

(b) Suit may be brought in the name of the corporation to enforce the liability (1) to creditors arising under subdivision (a) for a violation of Section 500 or 501 against any or all shareholders liable by any one or more creditors of the corporation whose debts or claims arose prior to the time of the distribution to shareholders and who have not consented thereto, whether or not they have reduced their claims to judgment, or (2) to shareholders arising under subdivision (a) for a violation of Section 502 or 503 against any or all shareholders liable by any one or more holders of preferred shares outstanding at the time of the distribution who have not consented thereto, without regard to the provisions of Section 800.

(c) Any shareholder sued under this section may implead all other shareholders liable under this section and may compel contribution, either in that action or in an independent action against shareholders not joined in that action.

(d) Nothing contained in this section affects any liability which any shareholder may have under Chapter 1 (commencing with Section 3439) of Title 2 of Part 2 of Division 4 of the Civil Code [Uniform Fraudulent Transfer Act].

§ 507. Dividend Not Chargeable to Retained Earnings; Notice to Shareholders

Each dividend other than one chargeable to retained earnings shall be identified in a notice to shareholders as being made from a source other than retained earnings, stating the accounting treatment thereof. The notice shall accompany the dividend or shall be given within three months after the end of the fiscal year in which the dividend is paid.

§ 510. Acquisition of Own Shares; Status; Prohibition of Reissue by Articles; Reduction in Authorized Shares; Amendment of Articles; Filing

(a) When a corporation reacquires its own shares, those shares are restored to the status of authorized but unissued shares, unless the articles prohibit the reissuance thereof.

(b) When a corporation reacquires authorized shares of a class or series and the articles prohibit the reissuance of those shares:

(1) If all of the authorized shares of that class or series, as the case may be, are reacquired, then (A) that class or series is automatically eliminated, (B) in the case of reacquisition of all of the authorized shares of a series, the authorized number of shares of the class to which the shares belonged is reduced by the number of shares so reacquired, and (C) the articles shall be amended to eliminate any statement of rights, preferences, privileges, and restrictions relating solely to that class or series.

(2) If less than all of the authorized shares but all of the issued and outstanding shares of that class or series, as the case may be, are reacquired, the authorized number of shares of the class or series is automatically reduced by the number of shares so reacquired, and the board shall determine either (A) to eliminate that class or series, whereupon the articles shall be amended to eliminate any statement of rights, preferences, privileges, and restrictions relating solely to that class or series, or (B) not to eliminate that class or series, whereupon the articles shall be amended to reflect that reduction of the number of authorized shares of that class or series by the shares so reacquired.

(3) If less than all of the authorized shares and less than all of the issued and outstanding shares of a class or series, as the case may be, are reacquired, the authorized number of shares of that class or series shall be automatically reduced by the number of shares reacquired, and the articles shall be amended to reflect that reduction.

(c) When a corporation reacquires authorized shares of a series of shares and the articles only prohibit the reissuance of those shares as shares of the same series:

(1) If all of the authorized shares of that series are reacquired, then that series is automatically eliminated, the articles shall be amended to eliminate any statement of rights, preferences, privileges, and restrictions relating solely to that series, and the board shall determine either (A) to return those shares to the status of authorized but undesignated shares of the class to which they belong or (B) to eliminate those shares entirely, whereupon the articles in either case shall be amended to reflect the reduction in the authorized shares of that series and the effect, if any, on the class to which that series belongs.

(2) If all of the issued and outstanding shares of that series (but less than all of the authorized shares of that series) are reacquired, the board shall determine either (A) to eliminate that series, whereupon the articles shall be amended to eliminate any statement of rights, preferences, privileges, and restrictions relating solely to that series, or (B) not to eliminate that series, whereupon the articles shall be amended to reflect the return of the reacquired shares to the status of authorized but undesignated shares of the class to which they belong.

(3) If less than all of the issued and outstanding shares of that series are reacquired, the authorized number of shares of that series shall be automatically reduced by the number of shares reacquired, and the board shall determine either (A) to return those shares to the status of authorized but undesignated shares of the class to which they belong, or (B) to eliminate those shares entirely, whereupon the articles in either case shall be amended to reflect the reduction in the authorized shares of that series and the effect, if any, on the class to which that series belongs.

(d) "Reacquires" as used in this section means that a corporation purchases, redeems, acquires by way of conversion to another class or series, or otherwise acquires its own shares or that issued and outstanding shares cease to be outstanding.

(e) The provisions of this section are subject to any contrary or inconsistent provision in the articles.

(f) A certificate of amendment shall be filed in accordance with the requirements of Chapter 9 (commencing with Section 900) reflecting any elimination or reduction of authorized shares set forth in subdivisions (b) and (c), and any related elimination from the articles of the designation and the rights, preferences, privileges, and restrictions of any series or class of stock that is eliminated, except that approval by the outstanding shares (Section 152) shall not be required to adopt any such amendment. . . .

Chapter 6

SHAREHOLDERS' MEETINGS AND CONSENTS

§ 602. Quorum; Votes; Withdrawal During Meeting Leaving Less Than Quorum

(a) Unless otherwise provided in the articles, a majority of the shares entitled to vote, represented in person or by proxy, shall constitute a quorum at a meeting of the shareholders, but in no event shall a quorum consist of less than one-third . . . of the shares entitled to vote at the meeting or, except in the case of a close corporation, of more than a majority of the shares entitled to vote at the meeting. Except as provided in subdivision (b), the affirmative vote of a majority of the shares represented and voting at a duly held meeting at which a quorum is present (which shares voting affirmatively also constitute at least a majority of the required quorum) shall be the act of the shareholders, unless the vote of a greater number or voting by classes is required by this division or the articles.

(b) The shareholders present at a duly called or held meeting at which a quorum is present may continue to transact business until adjournment notwithstanding the withdrawal of enough shareholders to leave less than a quorum, if any action taken (other than adjournment) is approved by at least a majority of the shares required to constitute a quorum or, if required by this division or the articles, the vote of a greater number or voting by class.

(c) In the absence of a quorum, any meeting of shareholders may be adjourned from time to time by the vote of a majority of the shares represented either in person or by proxy, but no other business may be transacted, except as provided in subdivision (b).

§ 604. Proxies or Written Consents; Contents; Form

(a) Any form of proxy or written consent distributed to 10 or more shareholders of a corporation with outstanding shares held of record by 100 or more persons shall afford an opportunity on the proxy or form of written consent to specify a choice between approval and disapproval of each matter or group of related matters intended to be acted upon at the meeting for which the proxy is solicited or by such written consent, other than elections to office, and shall provide, subject to reasonable specified conditions, that where the person solicited specifies a choice with respect to any such matter the shares will be voted in accordance therewith.

(b) In any election of directors, any form of proxy in which the directors to be voted upon are named therein as candidates and which is marked by a shareholder "withhold" or otherwise marked in a manner indicating that the authority to vote for the election of directors is withheld shall not be voted for the election of a director.

(c) Failure to comply with this section shall not invalidate any corporate action taken, but may be the basis for challenging any proxy at a meeting and the superior court may compel compliance therewith at the suit of any shareholder.

(d) This section does not apply to any corporation with an outstanding class of securities registered under Section 12 of the Securities Exchange Act of 1934 or whose securities are exempted from such registration by Section 12(g)(2) of that act.

Chapter 7

VOTING OF SHARES

§ 703. Shares in Name of Other Corporations, [Shares Owned by] Subsidiary or Held in Fiduciary Capacity by Issuing Corporation

(a) Shares standing in the name of another corporation, domestic or foreign, may be voted by an officer, agent, or proxyholder as the bylaws of the other corporation may prescribe or, in the absence of such provision, as the board of the other corporation may determine or, in the absence of that determination, by the chairman of the board, president or any vice president of the other corporation, or by any other person authorized to do so by the chairman of the board, president, or any vice president of the other corporation. Shares which are purported to be voted or any proxy purported to be executed in the name of a corporation (whether or not any title of the person signing is indicated) shall be presumed to be voted or the proxy executed in accordance with the provisions of this subdivision, unless the contrary is shown.

(b) Shares of a corporation owned by its subsidiary shall not be entitled to vote on any matter.

(c) Shares held by the issuing corporation in a fiduciary capacity, and shares of an issuing corporation held in a fiduciary capacity by its subsidiary, shall not be entitled to vote on any matter, except as follows:

(1) To the extent that the settlor or beneficial owner possesses and exercises a right to vote or to give the corporation binding instructions as to how to vote such shares.

(2) Where there are one or more cotrustees who are not affected by the prohibition of this subdivision, in which case the shares may be voted by the cotrustees as if it or they are the sole trustee.

§ 705. Proxies; Validity; Expiration; Revocation; Irrevocable Proxies

(a) Every person entitled to vote shares may authorize another person or persons to act by proxy with respect to such shares. Any proxy purporting to be executed in accordance with the provisions of this division shall be presumptively valid.

(b) No proxy shall be valid after the expiration of 11 months from the date thereof unless otherwise provided in the proxy. Every proxy continues in full force and effect until revoked by the person executing it prior to the vote pursuant thereto, except as otherwise provided in this section. Such revocation may be effected by a writing delivered to the corporation stating that the proxy is revoked or by a subsequent proxy executed by the person executing the prior proxy and presented to the meeting, or as to any meeting by attendance at such meeting and voting in person by the person executing the proxy. The dates contained on the forms of proxy presumptively determine the order of execution, regardless of the postmark dates on the envelopes in which they are mailed.

(c) A proxy is not revoked by the death or incapacity of the maker unless, before the vote is counted, written notice of such death or incapacity is received by the corporation.

(d) Except when other provision shall have been made by written agreement between the parties, the recordholder of shares which such person holds as pledgee or otherwise as security or which belong to another shall issue to the pledgor or to the owner of such shares, upon demand therefor and payment of necessary expenses thereof, a proxy to vote or take other action thereon.

(e) A proxy which states that it is irrevocable is irrevocable for the period specified therein (notwithstanding subdivision (c)) when it is held by any of the following or a nominee of any of the following:

(1) A pledgee.

(2) A person who has purchased or agreed to purchase or holds an option to purchase the shares or a person who has sold a portion of such person's shares in the corporation to the maker of the proxy.

(3) A creditor or creditors of the corporation or the shareholder who extended or continued credit to the corporation or the shareholder in consideration of the proxy if the proxy states that it was given in consideration of such extension or continuation of credit and the name of the person extending or continuing credit.

(4) A person who has contracted to perform services as an employee of the corporation, if a proxy is required by the contract of employment and if the proxy states that it was given in consideration of such contract of employment, the name of the employee and the period of employment contracted for.

(5) A person designated by or under an agreement under Section 706.

(6) A beneficiary of a trust with respect to shares held by the trust.

Notwithstanding the period of irrevocability specified, the proxy becomes revocable when the pledge is redeemed, the option or agreement to purchase is terminated or the seller no longer owns any shares of the corporation or dies, the debt of the corporation or the shareholder is paid, the period of employment provided for in the contract of employment has terminated, the agreement under Section 706 has terminated, or the person ceases to be a beneficiary of the trust. In addition to the foregoing clauses (1) through (5), a proxy may be made irrevocable (notwithstanding subdivision (c)) if it is given to secure the performance of a duty or to protect a title, either legal or equitable, until the happening of events which, by its terms, discharge the obligations secured by it.

(f) A proxy may be revoked, notwithstanding a provision making it irrevocable, by a transferee of shares without knowledge of the existence of the provision unless the existence of the proxy and its irrevocability appears, in the case of certificated securities, on the certificate representing such shares, or in the case of uncertificated securities, on the initial transaction statement and written statements.

§ 706. Agreement Between Two or More Shareholders of a Corporation; Voting Trust Agreements

(a) Notwithstanding any other provision of this division, an agreement between two or more shareholders of a corporation, if in writing and signed by the parties thereto, may provide that in exercising any voting rights the shares held by them shall be voted as provided by the agreement, or as the parties may agree or as determined in accordance with a procedure agreed upon by them, and the parties may but need not transfer the shares covered by such an agreement to a third party or parties with authority to vote them in accordance with the terms of the agreement. Such an agreement shall not be denied specific performance by a court on the ground that the remedy at law is adequate or on other grounds relating to the jurisdiction of a court of equity.

(b) Shares in any corporation may be transferred by written agreement to trustees in order to confer upon them the right to vote and otherwise represent the shares for such period of time, not exceeding 10 years, as may be specified in the agreement. The validity of a voting trust agreement, otherwise lawful, shall not be affected during a period of 10 years from the date when it was created or last extended as hereinafter provided by the fact that under its terms it will or may last beyond such 10-year period. At any time within two years prior to the time of expiration of any voting trust agreement as originally fixed or as last extended as provided in this subdivision, one or more beneficiaries under the voting trust agreement may, by written agreement and with the written consent of the voting trustee or trustees, extend the duration of the voting trust agreement with respect to their shares for an additional period not exceeding 10 years from the expiration date of the trust as originally fixed or as last extended as provided in this subdivision. A duplicate of the voting trust agreement and any extension thereof shall be filed with the secretary of the corporation and shall be open to inspection by a shareholder, a holder of a voting trust certificate or the agent of either, upon the same terms as the record of shareholders of the corporation is open to inspection.

(c) No agreement made pursuant to subdivision (a) shall be held to be invalid or unenforceable on the ground that it is a voting trust that does not comply with subdivision (b) or that it is a proxy that does not comply with Section 705.

(d) This section shall not invalidate any voting or other agreement among shareholders or any irrevocable proxy complying with subdivision (e) of Section 705, which agreement or proxy is not otherwise illegal.

§ 708. Directors; Cumulative Voting; Election by Ballot

(a) Except as provided in Section 301.5, every shareholder complying with subdivision (b) and entitled to vote at any election of directors may cumulate such shareholder's votes and give one candidate a number of votes equal to the number of directors to be elected multiplied by the number of votes to which the shareholder's shares are normally entitled, or distribute the shareholder's votes on the same principle among as many candidates as the shareholder thinks fit.

(b) No shareholder shall be entitled to cumulate votes (i.e., cast for any candidate a number of votes greater than the number of votes which such shareholder normally is entitled to cast) unless such candidate or candidates' names have been placed in nomination prior to the voting and the shareholder has given notice at the meeting prior to the voting of the shareholder's intention to cumulate the shareholder's votes. If any one shareholder has given such notice, all shareholders may cumulate their votes for candidates in nomination.

(c) In any election of directors, the candidates receiving the highest number of affirmative votes of the shares entitled to be voted for them up to the number of directors to be elected by such shares are elected; votes against the director and votes withheld shall have no legal effect. . . .

(e) Elections for directors need not be by ballot unless a shareholder demands election by ballot at the meeting and before the voting begins or unless the bylaws so require.

§ 710. Supermajority Vote Requirement; Approval; Duration; Readoption

(a) This section applies to a corporation with outstanding shares held of record by 100 or more persons (determined as provided in Section 605) [shares deemed "held of record"] which files an amendment of articles or certificate of determination containing a "supermajority vote" provision on or after January 1, 1989; provided that this section shall not apply to a corporation which files an amendment of articles or certificate of determination on or after January 1, 1994, if, at the time of filing, the corporation has (1) outstanding shares of more than one class or series of stock; (2) no class of equity securities registered under Section 12(b) or 12(g) of the Securities Exchange Act of 1934; and (3) outstanding securities held of record by fewer than 300 persons determined as provided by Section 605.

(b) A "supermajority vote" is a requirement set forth in the articles or in a certificate of determination authorized under any provision of this division that specified corporate action or actions be approved by a larger proportion of the outstanding shares than a majority, or by a larger proportion of the outstanding shares of a class or series than a majority, but no supermajority vote which is subject to this section shall require a vote in excess of 66⅔ percent of the outstanding shares or 66⅔ percent of the outstanding shares of any class or series of those shares.

(c) An amendment of the articles or a certificate of determination that includes a supermajority vote requirement shall be approved by at least as large a proportion of the outstanding shares (Section 152) as is required pursuant to that amendment or certificate of determination for the approval of the specified corporate action or actions. The supermajority vote requirement shall cease to be effective two years after the filing of the most recent filing of the amendment or certificate of determination to adopt or readopt the supermajority vote requirement. At any time within one year before the applicable expiration date, a supermajority vote requirement may be renewed, and at any time after the expiration date, a supermajority vote requirement may again be made effective for another two-year period, by readopting the provision and filing a certificate of amendment pursuant to, and subject to the limitations of, this subdivision. If the provision is not readopted in this manner, then the particular corporate action or actions previously subject to the supermajority vote shall thereafter require a vote of only a majority of either the outstanding shares or the shares of the specified class or series which had previously been subject to the supermajority vote provision, whichever the case may be. . . .

§ 711. **Maintenance by Holding Legal Owners and Disclosure to Persons on Whose Behalf Shares Are Voted; Charges; Actions to Enforce Section; Payment of Costs and Attorney's Fees** . . .

(a) The Legislature finds and declares that:

Many of the residents of this state are the legal and beneficial owners or otherwise the ultimate beneficiaries of shares of stock of domestic and foreign corporations, title to which may be held by a variety of intermediate owners as defined in subdivision (b). The informed and active involvement of such beneficial owners and beneficiaries in holding legal owners and, through them, management, accountable in their exercise of corporate power is essential to the interest of those beneficiaries and beneficial owners and to the economy and well-being of this state.

The purpose of this section is to serve the public interest by ensuring that voting records are maintained and disclosed as provided in this section. In the event that by statute or regulation pursuant to the federal Employee Retirement Income Security Act of 1974 (29 U.S.C. Sec. 1001 et seq.), there are imposed upon investment managers as defined in Sec. 2(38) thereof, duties substantially the same as those set forth in this section, compliance with those statutory or regulatory requirements by persons subject to this section shall be deemed to fulfill the obligations contained in this section.

This section shall be construed liberally to achieve that purpose.

(b) For purposes of this section, a person on whose behalf shares are voted includes, but is not limited to:

(1) A participant or beneficiary of an employee benefit plan with regard to shares held for the benefit of the participant or beneficiary.

(2) A shareholder, beneficiary, or contract owner of any entity (or of any portfolio of any entity) as defined in Section 3(a) of the federal Investment Company Act of 1940 (15 U.S.C. Sec. 80a–1 et seq.), as amended, to the extent the entity (or portfolio) holds the shares for which the record is requested.

(c) For the purposes of this section, a person on whose behalf shares are voted does not include:

(1) A person who possesses the right to terminate or withdraw from the shareholder, contract owner, participant, or beneficiary relationship with any entity (or any portfolio of any entity) defined in subdivision (b). This exclusion does not apply in the event the right of termination or withdrawal cannot be exercised without automatic imposition of a tax penalty. The right to substitute a relationship with an entity or portfolio, the shares of which are voted by or subject to the direction of the investment adviser (as defined in Section 2 of the federal Investment Company Act of 1940 (15 U.S.C. Sec. 80a–1 et seq.), as amended), of the prior entity or portfolio, or an affiliate of the investment adviser, shall not be deemed to be a right of termination or withdrawal within the meaning of this subdivision.

(2) A person entitled to receive information about a trust pursuant to Section 16061 of the Probate Code.

(3) A beneficiary, participant, contract owner, or shareholder whose interest is funded through the general assets of a life insurance company authorized to conduct business in this state.

(d) Every person possessing the power to vote shares of stock on behalf of another shall maintain a record of the manner in which the shares were voted. The record shall be maintained for a period of 12 consecutive months from the effective date of the vote.

(e) Upon a reasonable written request, the person possessing the power to vote shares of stock on behalf of another, or a designated agent, shall disclose the voting record with respect to any matter involving a specific security or securities in accordance with the following procedures:

(1) Except as set forth in paragraph (2), disclosure shall be made to the person making the request. The person making the disclosure may require identification sufficient to identify the person making the request as a person on whose behalf the shares were voted. A request for identification, if made, shall be reasonable, shall be made promptly, and may include a request for the person's social security number.

(2) If the person possessing the power to vote shares on behalf of another holds that power pursuant to an agreement entered into with a party other than the person making the request for disclosure, the person maintaining and disclosing the record pursuant to this section may, instead, make the requested disclosure to that party. Disclosure to that party shall be deemed compliance with the disclosure requirement of this section. If disclosure is made to that party and not to the person making the request, subdivision (i) shall not apply. However, nothing herein shall prohibit that party and the person possessing the power to vote on shares from entering into an agreement between themselves for the payment or assessment of a reasonable charge to defray expenses of disclosing the record.

(f) Where the entity subject to the requirements of this section is organized as a unit investment trust as defined in Section 4(2) of the federal Investment Company Act of 1940 (15 U.S.C. Sec. 80a–1 et seq.), the open-ended investment companies underlying the unit investment trust shall promptly make available their proxy voting records to the unit investment trust upon evidence of a bona fide request for voting record information pursuant to subdivision (e).

(g) Signing a proxy on another's behalf and forwarding it for disposition or receiving voting instructions does not constitute the power to vote. A person forwarding proxies or receiving voting instructions shall disclose the identity of the person having the power to vote shares upon reasonable written request by a person entitled to request a voting record under subdivision (c).

(h) For purposes of this section, if one or more persons has the power to vote shares on behalf of another, unless a governing instrument provides otherwise, the person or persons may designate an agent who shall maintain and disclose the record in accordance with subdivisions (b) and (c).

(i) Except as provided in paragraph (2) of subdivision (e), or as otherwise provided by law or a governing instrument, a person maintaining and disclosing a record pursuant to this section may assess a reasonable charge to the requesting person in order to defray expenses of disclosing the record in accordance with subdivision (e). Disclosure shall be made within a reasonable period after payment is received.

(j) Upon the petition of any person who successfully brings an action pursuant to or to enforce this section, the court may award costs and reasonable attorney's fees if the court finds that the defendant willfully violated this section....

Chapter 8

SHAREHOLDER DERIVATIVE ACTIONS

§ 800. Conditions; Security; Motion for Order; Determination....

(b) No action may be instituted or maintained in right of any domestic or foreign corporation by any holder of shares or of voting trust certificates of ... the corporation unless both of the following conditions exist:

(1) The plaintiff alleges in the complaint that plaintiff was a shareholder, of record or beneficially, or the holder of voting trust certificates at the time of the transaction or any part thereof of which plaintiff complains or that plaintiff's shares or voting trust certificates thereafter devolved upon plaintiff by operation of law from a holder who was a holder at the time of the transaction or any part thereof complained of; provided, that any shareholder who does not meet ... these requirements may nevertheless be allowed in the discretion of the court to maintain ... the action on a preliminary showing to and determination by the court, by motion and after a hearing, at which the court shall consider such evidence, by affidavit or testimony, as it deems material, that (i) there is a strong prima facie case in favor of the claim asserted on behalf of the corporation, (ii) no other similar action has been or is likely to be instituted, (iii) the plaintiff acquired the shares before there was disclosure to the public or to the plaintiff of the wrongdoing of which plaintiff complains, (iv) unless the action can be maintained the defendant may retain a gain derived from defendant's willful breach of a fiduciary duty, and (v) the requested relief will not result in unjust enrichment of the corporation or any shareholder of the corporation; and

(2) The plaintiff alleges in the complaint with particularity plaintiff's efforts to secure from the board such action as plaintiff desires, or the reasons for not making such effort, and alleges further that plaintiff has either informed the corporation or the board in writing of the

ultimate facts of each cause of action against each defendant or delivered to the corporation or the board a true copy of the complaint which plaintiff proposes to file.

(c) In any action referred to in subdivision (b), at any time within 30 days after service of summons upon the corporation or upon any defendant who is an officer or director of the corporation, or held such office at the time of the acts complained of, the corporation or ... the defendant may move the court for an order, upon notice and hearing, requiring the plaintiff to furnish ... a bond as hereinafter provided. The motion shall be based upon one or both of the following grounds:

(1) That there is no reasonable possibility that the prosecution of the cause of action alleged in the complaint against the moving party will benefit the corporation or its shareholders.

(2) That the moving party, if other than the corporation, did not participate in the transaction complained of in any capacity.

The court on application of the corporation or any defendant may, for good cause shown, extend the 30–day period for an additional period or periods not exceeding 60 days.

(d) At the hearing upon any motion pursuant to subdivision (c), the court shall consider such evidence, written or oral, by witnesses or affidavit, as may be material (1) to the ground or grounds upon which the motion is based, or (2) to a determination of the probable reasonable expenses, including attorneys' fees, of the corporation and the moving party which will be incurred in the defense of the action. If the court determines, after hearing the evidence adduced by the parties, that the moving party has established a probability in support of any of the grounds upon which the motion is based, the court shall fix the ... amount of the bond, not to exceed fifty thousand dollars ($50,000), to be furnished by the plaintiff for reasonable expenses, including attorneys' fees, which may be incurred by the moving party and the corporation in connection with the action, including expenses for which the corporation may become liable pursuant to Section 317 [Indemnification]. A ruling by the court on the motion shall not be a determination of any issue in the action or of the merits thereof.... If the court, upon the motion, makes a determination that ... a bond shall be furnished by the plaintiff as to any one or more defendants, the action shall be dismissed as to ... the defendant or defendants, unless the bond required by the court ... has been furnished within such reasonable time as may be fixed by the court....

(e) If the plaintiff shall, either before or after a motion is made pursuant to subdivision (c), or any order or determination pursuant to ... the motion, ... furnish a bond in the aggregate amount of fifty thousand dollars ($50,000) to secure the reasonable expenses of the parties entitled to make the motion, the plaintiff has complied with the requirements of this section and with any order for ... a bond theretofore made ..., and any such motion then pending shall be dismissed and no further or additional bond ... shall be required.

(f) If a motion is filed pursuant to subdivision (c), no pleadings need be filed by the corporation or any other defendant and the prosecution of the action shall be stayed until 10 days after the motion has been disposed of.

Chapter 9

AMENDMENT OF ARTICLES

§ 900. Authorization; Prohibited Amendments

(a) By complying with the provisions of this chapter, a corporation may amend its articles from time to time, in any and as many respects as may be desired, so long as its articles as amended contain only such provisions as it would be lawful to insert in original articles filed at the time of the filing of the amendment and, if a change in shares or the rights of shareholders or an exchange, reclassification or cancellation of shares or rights of shareholders is to be made, such provisions as may be necessary to effect such change, exchange, reclassification or cancellation. It is the intent of the Legislature in adopting this section to exercise to the fullest extent the reserve power of the state over corporations and to authorize any amendment of the articles covered by the preceding sentence regardless of whether any provision contained in the amendment was permissible at the time of the original incorporation of the corporation.

(b) A corporation shall not amend its articles to alter any statement which may appear in the original articles of the names and addresses of the first directors, nor the name and address of the initial agent, except to correct an error in the statement or to delete either after the corporation has filed a statement under Section 1502 [Annual statement of general information and agents for service of process].

Chapter 10

SALES OF ASSETS

§ 1001. Sale, Lease, Exchange, etc.....; of Property or Assets; Approval; Abandonment; Terms, Conditions and Consideration

(a) A corporation may sell, lease, convey, exchange, transfer or otherwise dispose of all or substantially all of its assets when the principal terms are approved by the board, and, unless the transaction is in the usual and regular course of its business, approved by the outstanding shares (Section 152), either before or after approval by the board and before or after the transaction. A transaction constituting a reorganization (Section 181) is subject to the provisions of Chapter 12 (commencing with Section 1200) and not this section (other than subdivision (d)). A transaction constituting a conversion (Section 161.9) is subject to the provisions of Chapter 11.5 (commencing with Section 1150) and not this section.

(b) Notwithstanding approval of the outstanding shares (Section 152), the board may abandon the proposed transaction without further action by the shareholders, subject to the contractual rights, if any, of third parties.

(c) The sale, lease, conveyance, exchange, transfer or other disposition may be made upon those terms and conditions and for that consideration as the board may deem in the best interests of the corporation. The consideration may be money, securities, or other property.

(d) If the acquiring party in a transaction pursuant to subdivision (a) of this section or subdivision (g) of Section 2001 [sale of assets in dissolution] is in control of or under common control with the dissolving corporation, the principal terms of the sale must be approved by at least 90 percent of the voting power of the disposing corporation unless the disposition is to a domestic or foreign corporation or other business entity in consideration of the nonredeemable common shares or nonredeemable equity securities of the acquiring party or its parent.

(e) Subdivision (d) does not apply to any transaction if the Commissioner of Corporations, the Commissioner of Financial Institutions, the Insurance Commissioner or the Public Utilities Commission has approved the terms and conditions. . . .

Chapter 11

MERGER

§ 1101. Agreement of Merger; Approval of Boards; Contents

The board of each corporation which desires to merge shall approve an agreement of merger. The constituent corporations shall be parties to the agreement of merger and other persons, including a parent party (Section 1200), may be parties to the agreement of merger. The agreement shall state all of the following:

(a) The terms and conditions of the merger.

(b) The amendments . . . to the articles of the surviving corporation to be effected by the merger, if any. If any amendment changes the name of the surviving corporation the new name may be the same as or similar to the name of a disappearing domestic or foreign corporation . . . .

(c) The name and place of incorporation of each constituent corporation and which of the constituent corporations is the surviving corporation.

(d) The manner of converting the shares of each of the constituent corporations into shares or other securities of the surviving corporation and, if any shares of any of the constituent corporations are not to be converted solely into shares or other securities of the surviving corporation, the cash, rights, securities, or other property which the holders of those shares are to receive in exchange for the shares, which cash, rights, securities, or other property may be in addition to or in lieu of shares or other securities of the surviving corporation, or that the shares are cancelled without consideration.

(e) Other details or provisions as are desired, if any, including, without limitation, a provision for the payment of cash in lieu of fractional shares or for any other arrangement with respect thereto consistent with the provisions of Section 407.

Each share of the same class or series of any constituent corporation (other than the cancellation of shares held by a constituent corporation or its parent or a wholly owned subsidiary of either in another constituent corporation) shall, unless all shareholders of the class or series consent and except as provided in Section 407, be treated equally with respect to any distribution of cash, rights, securities, or other property. Notwithstanding subdivision (d), except in a short-form merger, and in the merger of a corporation into its subsidiary in which it owns at least 90 percent of the outstanding shares of each class, the nonredeemable common shares or nonredeemable equity securities of a constituent corporation may be converted only into nonredeemable common shares of the surviving party or a parent party if a constituent corporation or its parent owns, directly or indirectly, prior to the merger, shares of another constituent corporation representing more than 50 percent of the voting power of the other constituent corporation prior to the merger, unless all of the shareholders of the class consent and except as provided in Section 407.

§ 1101.1 Agreement of Merger; Approval by Governmental Officer or Commission

... [T]he last two sentences of Section 1101 do not apply to any transaction if the Commissioner of Corporations, the Commissioner of Financial Institutions, the Insurance Commissioner ... or the Public Utilities Commission has approved the terms and conditions of the transaction and the fairness of those terms and conditions. ...

Chapter 12

REORGANIZATIONS

§ 1200. Approval by Board

A reorganization (Section 181) or a share exchange tender offer (Section 183.5) shall be approved by the board of:

(a) Each constituent corporation in a merger reorganization;

(b) The acquiring corporation in an exchange reorganization;

(c) The acquiring corporation and the corporation whose property and assets are acquired in a sale-of-assets reorganization;

(d) The acquiring corporation in a share exchange tender offer (Section 183.5); and

(e) The corporation in control of any constituent or acquiring domestic or foreign corporation or other business entity under subdivision (a), (b) or (c) and whose equity securities are issued, transferred, or exchanged in the reorganization (a "parent party").

Legislative Committee Comment . . .

Under the new law, various methods of corporate fusion are treated as different means to the same end for the purpose of codifying the "de facto merger" doctrine.

As a basis for this approach, "reorganization" is defined to encompass the three basic methods of combination. . . . This section generally requires a reorganization to be approved by the board of each party, as well as the board of any "parent party" to the transaction. Taken together, these provisions specify the transactions (including the so-called "upside-down" and "triangular" transactions) in which § 1201 may require shareholder approval and, in turn, § 1300 may require dissenters' rights.

§ 1201. Approval of Shareholders; Abandonment by Board; Actions to Attack Validity if Party Directly or Indirectly Controlled by Other Party

(a) The principal terms of a reorganization shall be approved by the outstanding shares (Section 152) of each class of each corporation the approval of whose board is required under Section 1200, except as provided in subdivision (b) and except that (unless otherwise provided in the articles) no approval of any class of outstanding preferred shares of the surviving or acquiring corporation or parent party shall be required if the rights, preferences, privileges and restrictions granted to or imposed upon that class of shares remain unchanged (subject to the provisions of subdivision (c)). For the purpose of this subdivision, two classes of common shares differing only as to voting rights shall be considered as a single class of shares.

(b) No approval of the outstanding shares (Section 152) is required by subdivision (a) in the case of any corporation if that corporation, or its shareholders immediately before the reorganization, or both, shall own (immediately after the reorganization) equity securities, other than any warrant or right to subscribe to or purchase those equity securities, of the surviving or acquiring corporation or a parent party (subdivision (d)of Section 1200) possessing more than five-sixths of the voting power of the surviving or acquiring corporation or parent party. In making the determination of ownership by the shareholders of a corporation, immediately after the reorganization, of equity securities pursuant to the preceding sentence, equity securities which they owned immediately before the reorganization as shareholders of another party to the transaction shall be disregarded. For the purpose of this section only, the voting power of a corporation shall be calculated by assuming the conversion of all equity securities convertible (immediately or at some future time) into shares entitled to vote but not assuming the exercise of any warrant or right to subscribe to or purchase those shares.

(c) Notwithstanding subdivision (b), the principal terms of a reorganization shall be approved by the outstanding shares (Section 152) of the surviving corporation in a merger reorganization if any amendment is made to its articles which would otherwise require that approval.

(d) Notwithstanding subdivision (b), the principal terms of a reorganization shall be approved by the outstanding shares (Section 152) of any class of a corporation which is a party to a merger or sale-of-assets reorganization if holders of shares of that class receive shares of the surviving or acquiring corporation or parent party having different rights, preferences, privileges or restrictions than those surrendered. Shares in a foreign corporation received in exchange for shares in a domestic corporation have different rights, preferences, privileges and restrictions within the meaning of the preceding sentence.

(e) Notwithstanding subdivisions (a) and (b), the principal terms of a reorganization shall be approved by the affirmative vote of at least two-thirds of each class of the outstanding shares of any close corporation if the reorganization would result in their receiving shares of a corporation which is not a close corporation. However, the articles may provide for a lesser vote, but not less than a majority of the outstanding shares of each class.

(f) Notwithstanding subdivisions (a) and (b), the principal terms of a reorganization shall be approved by the outstanding shares (Section 152) of any class of a corporation which is a party to a merger reorganization if holders or shares of that class receive interests of a surviving other business entity [§ 174.5] in the merger.

(g) Notwithstanding subdivisions (a) and (b), the principal terms of a reorganization shall be approved by all shareholders of any class or series if, as a result of the reorganization, the holders of that class or series become personally liable for any obligations of a party to the reorganization, unless all holders of that class or series have the dissenters' rights provided in Chapter 13 (commencing with Section 1300).

(h) Any approval required by this section may be given before or after the approval by the board. Notwithstanding approval required by this section, the board may abandon the proposed reorganization without further action by the shareholders, subject to the contractual rights, if any, of third parties.

§ 1201.5 Share Exchange Tender Offer; Approval of Principal Terms

(a) The principal terms of a share exchange tender offer (Section 183.5) shall be approved by the outstanding shares (Section 152) of each class of the corporation making the tender offer or whose shares are to be used in the tender offer, except as provided in subdivision (b) and except that (unless otherwise provided in the articles) no approval of any class of outstanding preferred shares of either corporation shall be required, if the rights, preferences, privileges, and restrictions granted to or imposed upon that class of shares remain unchanged. For the purpose of this subdivision, two classes of common shares differing only as to voting rights shall be considered as a single class of shares.

(b) No approval of the outstanding shares (Section 152) is required by subdivision (a) in the case of any corporation if the corporation, or its shareholders immediately before the tender offer, or both, shall own (immediately after the completion of the share exchange proposed in the tender offer) equity securities, (other than any warrant or right to subscribe to or purchase the equity securities), of the corporation making the tender offer or of the corporation whose shares were used in the tender offer, possessing more than five-sixths of the voting power of either corporation. In making the determination of ownership by the shareholders of a corporation, immediately after the tender offer, of equity securities pursuant to the preceding sentence, equity securities which they owned immediately before the tender offer as shareholders of another party to the transaction shall be disregarded. For the purpose of this section only, the voting power of a corporation shall be calculated by assuming the conversion of all equity securities convertible (immediately or at some future time) into shares entitled to vote but not assuming the exercise of any warrant or right to subscribe to, or purchase, shares.

§ 1202. Terms of Merger Reorganization or Sale-of-Assets Reorganization; Approval by Shareholders; Foreign Corporations

(a) In addition to the requirements of Section 1201, the principal terms of a merger reorganization shall be approved by all the outstanding shares of a corporation if the agreement of merger provides that all the outstanding shares of that corporation are canceled without consideration in the merger.

(b) In addition to the requirements of Section 1201, if the terms of a merger reorganization or sale-of-assets reorganization provide that a class or series of preferred shares is to have distributed to it a lesser amount than would be required by applicable article provisions, the principal terms of the reorganization shall be approved by the same percentage of outstanding shares of that class or series which would be required to approve an amendment of the article provisions to provide for the distribution of that lesser amount.

(c) If a parent party within the meaning of Section 1200 is a foreign corporation (other than a foreign corporation to which subdivision (a) of Section 2115 is applicable), any requirement or lack of a requirement for approval by the outstanding shares of the foreign corporation shall be based, not on the application of Sections 1200 and 1201, but on the application of the laws of the state or place of incorporation of the foreign corporation.

§ 1203. Interested Party Proposal or Tender Offer to Shareholders; Affirmative Opinion; Delivery; Approval; Later Proposal or Tender Offer; Withdrawal of Vote, Consent, or Proxy; Procedures

(a) If a tender offer, including a share exchange tender offer (Section 183.5), or a written proposal for approval of a reorganization subject to Section 1200 or for a sale of assets subject to subdivision (a) of Section 1001 is made to some or all of a corporation's shareholders by an interested party (herein referred to as an "Interested Party Proposal"), an affirmative opinion in writing as to the fairness of the consideration to the shareholders of that corporation shall be delivered as follows:

(1) If no shareholder approval or acceptance is required for the consummation of the transaction, the opinion shall be delivered to the corporation's board of directors not later than the time that consummation of the transaction is authorized and approved by the board of directors.

(2) If a tender offer is made to the corporation's shareholders, the opinion shall be delivered to the shareholders at the time that the tender offer is first made in writing to the shareholders. However, if the tender offer is commenced by publication and tender offer materials are subsequently mailed or otherwise distributed to the shareholders, the opinion may be omitted in that publication if the opinion is included in the materials distributed to the shareholders.

(3) If a shareholders' meeting is to be held to vote on approval of the transaction, the opinion shall be delivered to the shareholders with the notice of the meeting (Section 601).

(4) If consents of all shareholders entitled to vote are solicited in writing (Section 603), the opinion shall be delivered at the same time as that solicitation.

(5) If the consents of all shareholders are not solicited in writing, the opinion shall be delivered to each shareholder whose consent is

solicited prior to that shareholder's consent being given, and to all other shareholders at the time they are given the notice required by subdivision (b) of Section 603.

For purposes of this section, the term "interested party" means a person who is a party to the transaction and (A) directly or indirectly controls the corporation that is the subject of the tender offer or proposal, (B) is, or is directly or indirectly controlled by, an officer or director of the subject corporation, or (C) is an entity in which a material financial interest (subdivision (a) of Section 310) is held by any director or executive officer of the subject corporation. For purposes of the preceding sentence, "any executive officer" means the president, any vice president in charge of a principal business unit, division, or function such as sales, administration, research or development, or finance, and any other officer or other person who performs a policymaking function or has the same duties as those of a president or vice president. The opinion required by this subdivision shall be provided by a person who is not affiliated with the offeror and who, for compensation, engages in the business of advising others as to the value of properties, businesses, or securities. The fact that the opining person previously has provided services to the offeror or a related entity or is simultaneously engaged in providing advice or assistance with respect to the proposed transaction in a manner which makes its compensation contingent on the success of the proposed transaction shall not, for those reasons, be deemed to affiliate the opining person with the offeror. Nothing in this subdivision shall limit the applicability of the standards of review of the transaction in the event of a challenge thereto under Section 310 or subdivision (c) of Section 1312.

This subdivision shall not apply to an Interested Party Proposal if the corporation that is the subject thereof does not have shares held of record by 100 or more persons . . . , or if the transaction has been qualified under Section 25113 [Qualification by permit; application; contents; effective date] or 25120 [Necessity of qualification of security or exemption of security or transaction] and no order under Section 25140 [Issuance of stop orders affecting qualification of securities; refusal to issue or suspension or revocation of permits; grounds] or subdivision (a) of Section 25143 [Postponement or suspension of effectiveness of qualification; notice; hearing] is in effect with respect to that qualification.

(b) If a tender of shares or a vote or written consent is being sought pursuant to an Interested Party Proposal and a later tender offer or written proposal for a reorganization subject to Section 1200 or sale of assets subject to subdivision (a) of Section 1001 that would require a vote or written consent of shareholders is made to the corporation or its shareholders (herein referred to as a "Later Proposal") by any other person at least 10 days prior to the date for acceptance of the tendered shares or the vote or notice of shareholder approval on the Interested Party Proposal, then each of the following shall apply:

(1) The shareholders shall be informed of the Later Proposal and any written material provided for this purpose by the later offeror shall be forwarded to the shareholders at that offeror's expense.

(2) The shareholders shall be afforded a reasonable opportunity to withdraw any vote, consent, or proxy previously given before the vote or written consent on the Interested Party Proposal becomes effective, or a reasonable time to withdraw any tendered shares before the purchase of the shares pursuant to the Interested Party Proposal. For purposes of this subdivision, a delay of 10 days from the notice or publication of the Later Proposal shall be deemed to provide a reasonable opportunity or time to effect that withdrawal.

Chapter 13

DISSENTERS' RIGHTS

§ 1300. Reorganization or Short–Form Merger; Dissenting Shares; Corporate Purchase at Fair Market Value; Definitions

(a) If the approval of the outstanding shares (Section 152) of a corporation is required for a reorganization under subdivisions (a) and (b) or subdivision (e) or (f) of Section 1201, each shareholder of the corporation entitled to vote on the transaction and each shareholder of a subsidiary corporation in a short-form merger may, by complying with this chapter, require the corporation in which the shareholder holds shares to purchase for cash at their fair market value the shares owned by the shareholder which are dissenting shares as defined in subdivision (b). The fair market value shall be determined as of the day before the first announcement of the terms of the proposed reorganization or short-form merger, excluding any appreciation or depreciation in consequence of the proposed action, but adjusted for any stock split, reverse stock split or share dividend which becomes effective thereafter.

(b) As used in this chapter, "dissenting shares" means shares which come within all of the following descriptions:

(1) Which were not immediately prior to the reorganization or short-form merger either (A) listed on any national securities exchange certified by the Commissioner of Corporations under subdivision (*o*) of Section 25100 or (B) listed on the National Market System of the NASDAQ Stock Market, and the notice of meeting of shareholders to act upon the reorganization summarizes this section and Sections 1301, 1302, 1303 and 1304; provided, however, that this provision does not apply to any shares with respect to which there exists any restriction on transfer imposed by the corporation or by any law or regulation; and

provided, further, that this provision does not apply to any class of shares described in subparagraph (A) or (B) if demands for payment are filed with respect to 5 percent or more of the outstanding shares of that class.

(2) Which were outstanding on the date for the determination of shareholders entitled to vote on the reorganization and (A) were not voted in favor of the reorganization or, (B) if described in subparagraph (A) or (B) of paragraph (1) (without regard to the provisos in that paragraph), were voted against the reorganization, or which were held of record on the effective date of a short-form merger; provided, however, that subparagraph (A) rather than subparagraph (B) of this paragraph applies in any case where the approval required by Section 1201 is sought by written consent rather than at a meeting.

(3) Which the dissenting shareholder has demanded that the corporation purchase at their fair market value, in accordance with Section 1301.

(4) Which the dissenting shareholder has submitted for endorsement, in accordance with Section 1302.

(c) As used in this chapter, "dissenting shareholder" means the recordholder of dissenting shares and includes a transferee of record.

§ 1311. Exempt Shares

This chapter, except Section 1312, does not apply to classes of shares whose terms and provisions specifically set forth the amount to be paid in respect to such shares in the event of a reorganization or merger.

§ 1312. Right of Dissenting Shareholder to Attack, Set Aside or Rescind Merger or Reorganization; Restraining Order or Injunction; Conditions

(a) No shareholder of a corporation who has a right under this chapter to demand payment of cash for the shares held by the shareholder shall have any right at law or in equity to attack the validity of the reorganization or short-form merger, or to have the reorganization or short-form merger set aside or rescinded, except in an action to test whether the number of shares required to authorize or approve the reorganization have been legally voted in favor thereof; but any holder of shares of a class whose terms and provisions specifically set forth the amount to be paid in respect to them in the event of a reorganization or short-form merger is entitled to payment in accordance with those terms and provisions, or, if the principal terms of the reorganization are approved pursuant to subdivision (b) or Section 1202, is entitled to payment in accordance with the terms and provisions of the approved reorganization.

(b) If one of the parties to a reorganization or short-form merger is directly or indirectly controlled by, or under common control with, another party to the reorganization or short-form merger, subdivision (a) shall not apply to any shareholder of such party who has not demanded payment of cash for such shareholder's shares pursuant to this chapter; but if the shareholder institutes any action to attack the validity of the reorganization or short-form merger or to have the reorganization or short-form merger set aside or rescinded, the shareholder shall not thereafter have any right to demand payment of cash for the shareholder's shares pursuant to this chapter. The court in any action attacking the validity of the reorganization or short-form merger or to have the reorganization or short-form merger set aside or rescinded shall not restrain or enjoin the consummation of the transaction except upon 10 days' prior notice to the corporation and upon a determination by the court that clearly no other remedy will adequately protect the complaining shareholder or the class of shareholders of which such shareholder is a member.

(c) If one of the parties to a reorganization or short-form merger is directly or indirectly controlled by, or under common control with, another party to the reorganization or short-form merger, in any action to attack the validity of the reorganization or short-form merger or to have the reorganization or short-form merger set aside or rescinded, (1) a party to a reorganization or short-form merger which controls another party to the reorganization or short-form merger shall have the burden of proving that the transaction is just and reasonable as to the shareholders of the controlled party, and (2) a person who controls two or more parties to a reorganization shall have the burden of proving that the transaction is just and reasonable as to the shareholders of any party so controlled.

Chapter 15

RECORDS AND REPORTS

§ 1501. Annual Report; Time of Sending to Shareholders; Contents; Quarterly Financial Statements; Written Request; Inspection; Expenses in Actions

(a) The board shall cause an annual report to be sent to the shareholders not later than 120 days after the close of the fiscal year, unless in the case of a corporation with less than 100 holders of record of its shares ... this requirement is expressly waived in the bylaws. Unless otherwise provided by the articles or bylaws and if approved by the board of directors, that report and any accompanying material sent pursuant to this section may be sent by electronic transmission by the corporation (Section 20). This report shall contain a balance sheet as of the end of that fiscal year and an income statement and statement of changes in financial position for that fiscal year, accompanied by any report thereon of independent accountants or, if there is no such report, the certificate of an authorized officer of the corporation that the statements were prepared without audit from the books and records of the corporation.

Unless so waived, the report shall be sent to the shareholders at least 15 (or, if sent by third-class mail, 35) days prior to the annual meeting of shareholders to be held during the next fiscal year, but this requirement shall not limit the requirement for holding an annual meeting as required by Section 600.

Notwithstanding Section 114, the financial statements of any corporation with fewer than 100 holders of record of its shares ... required to be furnished by this subdivision and subdivision (c) ... are not required to be prepared in conformity with generally accepted accounting principles if they reasonably set forth the assets and liabilities and the income and expense of the corporation and disclose the accounting basis used in their preparation.

(b) In addition to the financial statements required by subdivision (a), the annual report of any corporation having 100 or more holders of record of its shares ... either not subject to the reporting requirements of Section 13 of the Securities Exchange Act of 1934, or exempted from those reporting requirements by Section 12(g)(2) of that act, shall also describe briefly both of the following:

(1) Any transaction (excluding compensation of officers and directors) during the previous fiscal year involving an amount in excess of forty thousand dollars ($40,000) (other than contracts let at competitive bid or services rendered at prices regulated by law) to which the corporation or its parent or subsidiary was a party and in which any director or officer of the corporation or of a subsidiary or (if known to the corporation or its parent or subsidiary) any holder of more than 10 percent of the outstanding voting shares of the corporation had a direct or indirect material interest, naming the person and stating the person's relationship to the corporation, the nature of the person's interest in the transaction and, where practicable, the amount of the interest; provided ... that in the case of a transaction with a partnership of which the person is a partner, only the interest of the partnership need be stated; and provided ... further that no such report need be made in the case of any transaction approved by the shareholders (Section 153).

(2) The amount and circumstances of any indemnification or advances aggregating more than ten thousand dollars ($10,000) paid during the fiscal year to any officer or director of the corporation ... ; provided ... that no such report need be made in the case of indemnification approved by the shareholders. ...

(c) If no annual report for the last fiscal year has been sent to shareholders, the corporation shall, upon the written request of any shareholder made more than 120 days after the close of that fiscal year, deliver or mail to the person making the request within 30 days thereafter the financial statements required by subdivision (a) for that year. A shareholder or shareholders holding at least 5 percent of the outstanding shares of any class of a corporation may make a written request to the corporation for an income statement of the corporation for the three-month, six-month or nine-month period of the current fiscal year ended more than 30 days prior to the date of the request and a balance sheet of the corporation as of the end of the period and, in addition, if no annual report for the last fiscal year has been sent to shareholders, the statements referred to in subdivision (a) for the last fiscal year. The statements shall be delivered or mailed to the person making the request within 30 days thereafter. A copy of the statements shall be kept on file in the principal office of the corporation for 12 months and it shall be exhibited at all reasonable times to any share-holder demanding an examination of the statements or a copy shall be mailed to the shareholder.

(d) The quarterly income statements and balance sheets referred to in this section shall be accompanied by the report thereon, if any, of any independent accountants engaged by the corporation or the certificate of an authorized officer of the corporation that the financial statements were prepared without audit from the books and records of the corporation.

(e) In addition to the [financial] penalties provided for in Section 2200, the superior court of the proper county shall enforce the duty of making and mailing or delivering the information and financial statements required by this section and, for good cause shown, may extend the time therefor.

(f) In any action or proceeding under this section, if the court finds the failure of the corporation to comply with the requirements of this section to have been without justification, the court may award an amount sufficient to reimburse the shareholder for the reasonable expenses incurred by the shareholder, including attorneys' fees, in connection with the action or proceeding.

(g) This section applies to any domestic corporation and also to a foreign corporation having its principal executive office in this state or customarily holding meetings of its board in this state.

§ 1502. Statement of Information; Timing and Contents of Filing; Additional Contents for Publicly Traded Companies; Agent for Service of Process; Updated Information; Public Inspection; Certification

(a) Every corporation shall file, within 90 days after the filing of its original articles and annually thereafter during the applicable filing period, on a form prescribed by the Secretary of State, a statement containing all of the following:

(1) The names and complete business or residence addresses of its incumbent directors.

(2) The number of vacancies on the board, if any.

(3) The names and complete business or residence addresses of its chief executive officer, secretary, and chief financial officer.

(4) The street address of its principal executive office.

(5) If the address of its principal executive office is not in this state, the street address of its principal business office in this state, if any.

(6) A statement of the general type of business that constitutes the principal business activity of the corporation (for example, manufacturer of aircraft; wholesale liquor distributor; or retail department store)....

(h) The statement required by subdivision (a) shall be available and open to the public for inspection. The Secretary of State ... shall provide access to all information contained in this statement by means of an online database....

(j) A corporation shall certify that the information it provides pursuant to subdivisions (a) and (b) is true and correct. No claim may be made against the state for inaccurate information contained in the statements.

§ 1502.1 Statement of Information Pertaining to Independent Auditors, Members of the Board of Directors, and Executive Officers; Definitions; Public Inspection; Certification

(a) In addition to the statement required pursuant to Section 1502, every publicly traded corporation shall file annually, within 150 days after the end of its fiscal year, a statement, on a form prescribed by the Secretary of State, that includes all of the following information:

(1) The name of the independent auditor that prepared the most recent auditor's report on the corporation's annual financial statements.

(2) A description of other services, if any, performed for the corporation during its two most recent fiscal years and the period between the end of its most recent fiscal year and the date of the statement by the foregoing independent auditor, by its parent corporation, or by a subsidiary or corporate affiliate of the independent auditor or its parent corporation.

(3) The name of the independent auditor employed by the corporation on the date of the statement, if different from the independent auditor listed pursuant to paragraph (1).

(4) The compensation for the most recent fiscal year of the corporation paid to each member of the board of directors and paid to each of the five most highly compensated executive officers of the corporation who are not members of the board of directors, including the number of any shares issued, options for shares granted, and similar equity-based compensation granted to each of those persons. If the chief executive officer is not among the five most highly compensated executive officers of the corporation, the compensation paid to the chief executive officer shall also be included.

(5) A description of any loan, including the amount and terms of the loan, made to any member of the board of directors by the corporation during the corporation's two most recent fiscal years at an interest rate lower than the interest rate available from unaffiliated commercial lenders generally to a similarly-situated borrower.

(6) A statement indicating whether an order for relief has been entered in a bankruptcy case with respect to the corporation, its executive officers, or members of the board of directors of the corporation during the 10 years preceding the date of the statement.

(7) A statement indicating whether any member of the board of directors or executive officer of the corporation was convicted of fraud during the 10 years preceding the date of the statement, if the conviction has not been overturned or expunged.

(8) A description of any material pending legal proceedings, other than ordinary routine litigation incidental to the business, to which the corporation or any of its subsidiaries is a party or of which any of their property is the subject, as specified by Item 103 of Regulation S–K of the Securities Exchange Commission (Section 229.103 of Title 12 of the Code of Federal Regulations). A description of any material legal proceeding during which the corporation was found legally liable by entry of a final judgment or final order that was not overturned on appeal during the five years preceding the date of the statement.

(b) For purposes of this section, the following definitions apply:

(1) "Publicly traded corporation" means a corporation, as defined in Section 162, that is an issuer as defined in Section 3 of the Securities Exchange Act of 1934, as amended (15 U.S.C. Sec. 78c), and has at least one class of securities listed or admitted for trading on a national securities exchange, on the National or Small-Cap Markets of the NASDAQ Stock Market, on the OTC–Bulletin Board, or on the electronic service operated by Pink Sheets, LLC.

(2) "Executive officer" means the chief executive officer, president, any vice president in charge of a principal business unit, division, or function, any other officer of the corporation who

performs a policymaking function, or any other person who performs similar policymaking functions for the corporation.

(3) "Compensation" as used in paragraph (4) of subdivision (a) means all plan and nonplan compensation awarded to, earned by, or paid to the person for all services rendered in all capacities to the corporation and to its subsidiaries, as the compensation is specified by Item 402 of Regulation S–K of the Securities and Exchange Commission (Section 229.402 of Title 17 of the Code of Federal Regulations).

(4) "Loan" as used in paragraph (5) of subdivision (a) excludes an advance for expenses permitted under subdivision (d) of Section 315, the corporation's payment of life insurance premiums permitted under subdivision (e) of Section 315, and an advance of expenses permitted under Section 317.

(c) This statement shall be available and open to the public for inspection. The Secretary of State . . . shall provide access to all information contained in this statement by means of an online database.

(d) A corporation shall certify that the information it provides pursuant to this section is true and correct. No claim may be made against the state for inaccurate information contained in statements filed under this section with the Secretary of State.

Chapter 16

RIGHTS OF INSPECTION

§ 1600. List of Shareholders' Names, Addresses and Shareholdings; Time for Compliance After Demand; Delay; Postponement of Shareholders' Meeting; Inspection and Copying

(a) A shareholder or shareholders holding at least 5 percent in the aggregate of the outstanding voting shares of a corporation or who hold at least 1 percent of those voting shares and have filed a Schedule 14A with the United States Securities and Exchange Commission . . . shall have an absolute right to do either or both of the following: (1) inspect and copy the record of shareholders' names and addresses and shareholdings during usual business hours upon five business days' prior written demand upon the corporation, or (2) obtain from the transfer agent for the corporation, upon written demand and upon the tender of its usual charges for such a list (the amount of which charges shall be stated to the shareholder by the transfer agent upon request), a list of the shareholders' names and addresses, who are entitled to vote for the election of directors, and their shareholdings, as of the most recent record date for which it has been compiled or as of a date specified by the shareholder subsequent to the date of demand. The list shall be made available on or before the later of five business days after the demand is received or the date specified therein as the date as of which the list is to be compiled. A corporation shall have the responsibility to cause its transfer agent to comply with this subdivision.

(b) Any delay by the corporation or the transfer agent in complying with a demand under subdivision (a) beyond the time limits specified therein shall give the shareholder or shareholders properly making the demand a right to obtain from the superior court, upon the filing of a verified complaint in the proper county and after a hearing, notice of which shall be given to such persons and in such manner as the court may direct, an order postponing any shareholders' meeting previously noticed for a period equal to the period of such delay. Such right shall be in addition to any other legal or equitable remedies to which the shareholder may be entitled.

(c) The record of shareholders shall also be open to inspection and copying by any shareholder or holder of a voting trust certificate at any time during usual business hours upon written demand on the corporation, for a purpose reasonably related to such holder's interests as a shareholder or holder of a voting trust certificate.

(d) Any inspection and copying under this section may be made in person or by agent or attorney. The rights provided in this section may not be limited by the articles or bylaws. This section applies to any domestic corporation and to any foreign corporation having its principal executive office in this state or customarily holding meetings of its board in this state.

§ 1601. Accounting Books and Records and Minutes of Meetings; Inspection Upon Demand by Shareholder or Holder of Voting Trust Certificate; Nature of Right

(a) The accounting books and records and minutes of proceedings of the shareholders and the board and committees of the board of any domestic corporation, and of any foreign corporation keeping any such records in this state or having its principal executive office in this state, shall be open to inspection upon the written demand on the corporation of any shareholder or holder of a voting trust certificate at any reasonable time during usual business hours, for a purpose reasonably related to such holder's interests as a shareholder or as the holder of such voting trust certificate. The right of inspection created by this subdivision shall extend to the records of each subsidiary of a corporation subject to this subdivision.

(b) Such inspection by a shareholder or holder of a voting trust certificate may be made in person or by agent or attorney, and the right of inspection includes the right to copy and make extracts. The right of the shareholders to inspect the corporate records may not be limited by the articles or bylaws.

§ 1602. Directors

Every director shall have the absolute right at any reasonable time to inspect and copy all books, records and documents of every kind and to inspect the physical properties of the corporation of which such person is a director and also of its subsidiary corporations, domestic or foreign. Such inspection by a director may be made in person or by agent or attorney and the right of inspection includes the right to copy and make extracts. This section applies to a director of any foreign corporation having its principal executive office in this state or customarily holding meetings of its board in this state.

§ 1603. Action to Enforce Right; Appointment of Inspector or Accountant; Report; Penalty for Failure to Produce Records; Expenses of Suit

(a) Upon refusal of a lawful demand for inspection, the superior court of the proper county, may enforce the right of inspection with just and proper conditions or may, for good cause shown, appoint one or more competent inspectors or accountants to audit the books and records kept in this state and investigate the property, funds and affairs of any domestic corporation or any foreign corporation keeping records in this state and of any subsidiary corporation thereof, domestic or foreign, keeping records in this state and to report thereon in such manner as the court may direct.

(b) All officers and agents of the corporation shall produce to the inspectors or accountants so appointed all books and documents in their custody or power, under penalty of punishment for contempt of court.

(c) All expenses of the investigation or audit shall be defrayed by the applicant unless the court orders them to be paid or shared by the corporation.

Chapter 18

INVOLUNTARY DISSOLUTION

§ 1800. Verified Complaint; Plaintiffs; Grounds; Intervention by Shareholder or Creditor; Exempt Corporations

(a) A verified complaint for involuntary dissolution of a corporation on any one or more of the grounds specified in subdivision (b) may be filed in the superior court of the proper county by any of the following persons:

(1) One-half or more of the directors in office.

(2) A shareholder or shareholders who hold shares representing not less than 33⅓ percent of (i) the total number of outstanding shares (assuming conversion of any preferred shares convertible into common

shares) or (ii) the outstanding common shares or (iii) the equity of the corporation, exclusive in each case of shares owned by persons who have personally participated in any of the transactions enumerated in paragraph (4) of subdivision (b), or any shareholder or shareholders of a close corporation.

(3) Any shareholder if the ground for dissolution is that the period for which the corporation was formed has terminated without extension thereof.

(4) Any other person expressly authorized to do so in the articles.

(b) The grounds for involuntary dissolution are that:

(1) The corporation has abandoned its business for more than one year.

(2) The corporation has an even number of directors who are equally divided and cannot agree as to the management of its affairs, so that its business can no longer be conducted to advantage or so that there is danger that its property and business will be impaired or lost, and the holders of the voting shares of the corporation are so divided into factions that they cannot elect a board consisting of an uneven number.

(3) There is internal dissension and two or more factions of shareholders in the corporation are so deadlocked that its business can no longer be conducted with advantage to its shareholders or the shareholders have failed at two consecutive annual meetings at which all voting power was exercised, to elect successors to directors whose terms have expired or would have expired upon election of their successors.

(4) Those in control of the corporation have been guilty of or have knowingly countenanced persistent and pervasive fraud, mismanagement or abuse of authority or persistent unfairness toward any shareholders or its property is being misapplied or wasted by its directors or officers.

(5) In the case of any corporation with 35 or fewer shareholders (determined as provided in Section 605), liquidation is reasonably necessary for the protection of the rights or interests of the complaining shareholder or shareholders.

(6) The period for which the corporation was formed has terminated without extension of such period.

(c) At any time prior to the trial of the action any shareholder or creditor may intervene therein.

(d) This section does not apply to any corporation subject to the Banking Law ... , the Public Utilities Act ..., [or] the Savings and Loan Association Law....

(e) For the purposes of this section, "shareholder" includes a beneficial owner of shares who has entered into an agreement under Section 300 or 706.

§ 1802. Provisional Director; Appointment; Deadlocked Board

If the ground for the complaint for involuntary dissolution of the corporation is a deadlock in the board as set forth in subdivision (b)(2) of Section 1800, the court may appoint a provisional director. The provisions of subdivision (c) of Section 308 apply to any such provisional director so appointed.

§ 1804. Decree for Winding Up and Dissolution; Other Judicial Relief

After hearing the court may decree a winding up and dissolution of the corporation if cause therefor is shown or, with or without winding up and dissolution, may make such orders and decrees and issue such injunctions in the case as justice and equity require.

Chapter 19

VOLUNTARY DISSOLUTION

§ 1900. Election by Shareholders; Required Vote; Election by Board; Grounds

(a) Any corporation may elect voluntarily to wind up and dissolve by the vote of shareholders holding shares representing 50 percent or more of the voting power.

(b) Any corporation which comes within one of the following descriptions may elect by approval by the board to wind up and dissolve:

(1) A corporation ... as to which an order for relief has been entered under Chapter 7 of the federal bankruptcy law.

(2) A corporation which has disposed of all its assets and has not conducted any business for a period of five years immediately preceding the adoption of the resolution electing to dissolve the corporation.

(3) A corporation which has issued no shares.

Chapter 20

GENERAL PROVISIONS RELATING TO DISSOLUTION

§ 2000. Avoidance of Dissolution by Purchase of Plaintiffs' Shares; Valuation; Vote Required; Stay of Dissolution Proceedings; Appraisal Under Court Order; Confirmation by Court; Appeal

(a) Subject to any contrary provision in the articles, in any suit for involuntary dissolution, or in any proceeding for voluntary dissolution initiated by the vote of shareholders representing only 50 percent of the voting power, the corporation or, if it does not elect to purchase, the holders of 50 percent or more of the voting power of the corporation (the "purchasing parties") may avoid the dissolution of the corporation and the appointment of any receiver by purchasing for cash the shares owned by the plaintiffs or by the shareholders so initiating the proceeding (the "moving parties") at their fair value. The fair value shall be determined on the basis of the liquidation value as of the valuation date but taking into account the possibility, if any, of sale of the entire business as a going concern in a liquidation. In fixing the value, the amount of any damages resulting if the initiation of the dissolution is a breach by any moving party or parties of an agreement with the purchasing party or parties may be deducted from the amount payable to such moving party or parties, unless the ground for dissolution is that specified in paragraph (4) of subdivision (b) of Section 1800. The election of the corporation to purchase may be made by the approval of the outstanding shares (Section 152) excluding shares held by the moving parties.

(b) If the purchasing parties (1) elect to purchase the shares owned by the moving parties, and (2) are unable to agree with the moving parties upon the fair value of such shares, and (3) give bond with sufficient security to pay the estimated reasonable expenses (including attorneys' fees) of the moving parties if such expenses are recoverable under subdivision (c), the court upon application of the purchasing parties, either in the pending action or in a proceeding initiated in the superior court of the proper county by the purchasing parties in the case of a voluntary election to wind up and dissolve, shall stay the winding up and dissolution proceeding and shall proceed to ascertain and fix the fair value of the shares owned by the moving parties.

(c) The court shall appoint three disinterested appraisers to appraise the fair value of the shares owned by the moving parties, and shall make an order referring the matter to the appraisers so appointed for the purpose of ascertaining such value. The order shall prescribe the time and manner of producing evidence, if evidence is required. The award of the appraisers or of a majority of them, when confirmed by the court, shall be final and conclusive upon all parties. The court shall enter a decree which shall provide in the alternative for winding up and dissolution of the corporation unless payment is made for the shares within the time specified by the decree. If the purchasing parties do not make payment for the shares within the time specified, judgment shall be entered against them and the surety or sureties on the bond for the amount of the expenses (including attorneys' fees) of the moving parties. Any shareholder aggrieved by the action of the court may appeal therefrom.

(d) If the purchasing parties desire to prevent the winding up and dissolution, they shall pay to the moving parties the value of their shares ascertained and decreed within the time specified pursuant to this section, or, in case of an appeal, as fixed on appeal. On receiving such payment or the tender thereof, the moving parties shall transfer their shares to the purchasing parties.

(e) For the purposes of this section, "shareholder" includes a beneficial owner of shares who has entered into an agreement under Section 300 or 706.

(f) For the purposes of this section, the valuation date shall be (1) in the case of a suit for involuntary dissolution under Section 1800, the date upon which that action was commenced, or (2) in the case of a proceeding for voluntary dissolution initiated by the vote of shareholders representing only 50 percent of the voting power, the date upon which that proceeding was initiated. However, in either case the court may, upon the hearing of a motion by any party, and for good cause shown, designate some other date as the valuation date.

Chapter 21

FOREIGN CORPORATIONS

§ 2115. Foreign Corporations Subject to Corporate Laws of State; Tests to Determine Subject Corporations; Laws Applicable; Time of Application

(a) A foreign corporation (other than a foreign association or foreign nonprofit corporation but including a foreign parent corporation even though it does not itself transact intrastate business) is subject to the requirements of subdivision (b) commencing on the date specified in subdivision (d) and continuing until the date specified in subdivision (e) if:

(1) the average of the property factor, the payroll factor and the sales factor (as defined in Sections 25129, 25132 and 25134 of the Revenue and Taxation Code) with respect to it is more than 50 percent during its latest full income year and

(2) more than one-half of its outstanding voting securities are held of record by persons having addresses in this state appearing on the books of the corporation on the record date for the latest meeting of shareholders held during its latest full income year or, if no meeting was held during that year, on the last day of the latest full income year. The property factor, payroll factor and sales factor shall be those used in computing the portion of its income allocable to this state in its franchise tax return or, with respect to corporations the allocation of whose income is governed by special formulas or that are not required to file separate or any tax returns, which would have been so used if they were governed by this three-factor formula. The determination of these factors with respect to any parent corporation shall be made on a consolidated basis, including in a unitary computation (after elimination of intercompany transactions) the property, payroll and sales of the parent and all of its subsidiaries in which it owns directly or indirectly more than 50 percent of the outstanding shares entitled to vote for the election of directors, but deducting a percentage of the property, payroll and sales of any subsidiary equal to the percentage minority ownership, if any, in the subsidiary. For the purpose of this subdivision, any securities held to the knowledge of the issuer in the names of broker-dealers, nominees for broker-dealers (including clearing corporations), or banks, associations, or other entities holding securities in a nominee name or otherwise on behalf of a beneficial owner (collectively "nominee holders"), shall not be considered outstanding. However, if the foreign corporation requests all nominee holders to certify, with respect to all beneficial owners for whom securities are held, the number of shares held for those beneficial owners having addresses (as shown on the records of the nominee holder) in this state and outside of this state, then all shares so certified shall be considered outstanding and held of record by persons having addresses either in this state or outside of this state as so certified, provided that the certification so provided shall be retained with the record of shareholders and made available for inspection and copying in the same manner as provided in Section 1600 with respect to that record. A current list of beneficial owners of a foreign corporation's securities provided to the corporation by one or more Nominee Holders or their agent pursuant to the requirements of Rule 14b–1(b)(3) or 14b–2(b)(3) as adopted on January 6, 1992, promulgated under the Securities Exchange Act of 1934 shall constitute an acceptable certification with respect to beneficial owners for the purposes of this subdivision.

(b) Except as provided in subdivision (c), the following chapters and sections of this division shall apply to a foreign corporation as defined in subdivision (a) (to the exclusion of the law of the jurisdiction in which it is incorporated):

Chapter 1 (general provisions and definitions), to the extent applicable to the following provisions;

Section 301 (annual election of directors);

Section 303 (removal of directors without cause);

Section 304 (removal of directors by court proceedings);

Section 305, subdivision (c) (filing of director vacancies where less than a majority in office elected by shareholders);

Section 309 (directors' standard of care);

Section 310 (super-majority requirement);

Section 316 (excluding paragraph (3) of subdivision (a) and paragraph (3) of subdivision (f)) (liability of directors for unlawful distributions);

Section 317 (indemnification of directors, officers and others);

Sections 500 to 505, inclusive (limitations on corporate distributions in cash or property);

Section 506 (liability of shareholder who receives unlawful distribution);

Section 600, subdivisions (b) and (c) (requirement for annual shareholders' meeting and remedy if same not timely held);

Section 708, subdivisions (a), (b) and (c) (shareholder's right to cumulate votes at any election of directors);

Section 710 (supermajority vote requirement);

Section 1001, subdivision (d) (limitations on sale of assets);

Section 1101 (provisions following subdivision (e)) (limitations on mergers); . . .

Chapter 12 (commencing with Section 1200) (reorganizations);

Chapter 13 (commencing with Section 1300) (dissenters' rights);

Sections 1500 and 1501 (records and reports);

Section 1508 (action by Attorney General);

Chapter 16 (commencing with Section 1600) (rights of inspection).

(c) This section does not apply to any corporation (1) with outstanding securities listed on the New York Stock Exchange or the American Stock Exchange, or (2) with outstanding securities designated as qualified for trading on the Nasdaq National market (or any successor thereto) of the Nasdaq Stock Market operated by the Nasdaq Stock Market Inc., or (3) if all of its voting shares (other than directors' qualifying shares) are owned directly or indirectly by a corporation or corporations not subject to this section.

(d) For purposes of subdivision (a), the requirements of subdivision (b) shall become applicable to a foreign corporation only upon the first day of the first income year of the corporation (1) commencing on or after the 135th day of the income year immediately following the latest income year with respect to which the tests referred to in subdivision (a) have been met or (2) commencing on or after the entry of a final order by a court of competent jurisdiction declaring that those tests have been met.

(e) For purposes of subdivision (a), the requirements of subdivision (b) shall cease to be applicable to a foreign corporation (1) at the end of the first income year of the corporation immediately following the latest income year with respect to which at least one of the tests referred to in subdivision (a) is not met or (2) at the end of the income year of the corporation during which a final order has been entered by a court of competent jurisdiction declaring that one of those tests is not met, provided that a contrary order has not been entered before the end of the income year.

(f) Any foreign corporation that is subject to the requirements of subdivision (b) shall advise any shareholder of record, any officer, director, employee, or other agent ... and any creditor of the corporation in writing, within 30 days of receipt of written request for that information, whether or not it is subject to subdivision (b) at the time the request is received. [If any party] obtains a final determination by a court of competent jurisdiction that the corporation failed to provide to the party information required to be provided by this subdivision or provided the party information of the kind required to be provided by this subdivision that was incorrect, then the court, in its discretion, shall have the power to include in its judgment recovery by the party from the corporation of all courts costs and reasonable attorneys' fees incurred in that legal proceeding to the extent they relate to obtaining that final determination.

§ 2117. Statement of Information; Timing and Contents of Filing; Additional Contents for Publicly Traded Companies; Agent for Service of Process; Public Inspection; Notice of Change of Information

(a) Every foreign corporation (other than a foreign association) qualified to transact intrastate business shall file, annually during the applicable filing period, on a form prescribed by the Secretary of State, a statement containing:

(1) The names and complete business or residence addresses of its chief executive officer, secretary, and chief financial officer.

(2) The street address of its principal executive office.

(3) The street address of its principal business office in this state, if any.

(4) A statement of the general type of business that constitutes the principal business activity of the corporation (for example, manufacturer of aircraft; wholesale liquor distributor; or retail department store).

(b) The statement required by subdivision (a) shall also designate, as the agent of the corporation for the purpose of service of process, a natural person residing in this state or a corporation that has complied with Section 1505 and whose capacity to act as the agent has not terminated. If a natural person is designated, the statement shall set forth the person's complete business or residence address. If a corporate agent is designated, no address for it shall be set forth.

(c) The statement ... required by subdivision (a) shall be available and open to the public for inspection. The Secretary of State shall provide access to all information contained in the statement by means of an online database. . . .

§ 2117.1 Statement of Information Pertaining to Independent Auditors, Members of the Board of Directors, and Executive Officers; Definitions; Public Inspection; Certification

(a) In addition to the statement required pursuant to Section 2117, every publicly traded foreign corporation shall file annually, within 150 days after the end of its fiscal year, on a form prescribed by the Secretary of State, a statement that includes all of the following information:

(1) The name of the independent auditor that prepared the most recent auditor's report on the publicly traded foreign corporation's annual financial statements.

(2) A description of other services, if any, performed for the publicly traded foreign corporation during its two most recent fiscal years and the period between the end of its most recent fiscal year and the date of the statement by the foregoing independent auditor, by its parent corporation, or by a subsidiary or corporate affiliate of the independent auditor or its parent corporation.

(3) The name of the independent auditor employed by the foreign corporation on the date of the statement, if different from the independent auditor listed pursuant to paragraph (1).

(4) The compensation for the most recent fiscal year of the publicly traded foreign corporation paid to each member of the board of directors and paid to each of the five most highly compensated executive officers of the foreign corporation who are not members of the board of directors, including the number of any shares issued, options for shares granted, and similar equity-based compensation granted to each of those persons. If the chief executive officer is not among the five most highly compensated executive officers of the corporation, the compensation paid to the chief executive officer shall also be included.

(5) A description of any loan, including the amount and terms of the loans, made to any member of the board of directors by the publicly traded foreign corporation during the foreign corporation's two most recent fiscal years at an interest rate lower than the interest rate available from unaffiliated commercial lenders generally to a similarly situated borrower.

(6) A statement indicating whether an order for relief has been entered in a bankruptcy case with respect to the foreign corporation, its executive officers, or members of the board of directors of the foreign corporation during the 10 years preceding the date of the statement.

(7) A statement indicating whether any member of the board of directors or executive officer of the publicly traded foreign corporation was convicted of fraud during the 10 years preceding the date of the statement, which conviction has not been overturned or expunged.

(8) A description of any material pending legal proceedings, other than ordinary routine litigation incidental to the business, to which the corporation or any of its subsidiaries is a party or of which any of their property is the subject, as specified by Item 103 of Regulation S–K of the Securities Exchange Commission (Section 229.103 of Title 12 of the Code of Federal Regulations). A description of any material legal proceeding during which the corporation was found legally liable by entry of a final judgment or final order that was not overturned on appeal during the five years preceding the date of the statement.

(b) For purposes of this section, the following definitions apply:

(1) "Publicly traded foreign corporation" means a foreign corporation, as defined in Section 171, that is an issuer as defined in Section 3 of the Securities Exchange Act of 1934, as amended (15 U.S.C. Sec. 78c), and has at least one class of securities listed or admitted for trading on a national securities exchange, on the National or Small-Cap Markets of the NASDAQ Stock Market, on the OTC–Bulletin Board, or on the electronic service operated by Pink Sheets, LLC.

(2) "Executive officer" means the chief executive officer, president, any vice president in charge of a principal business unit, division, or function, any other officer of the corporation who performs a policymaking function, or any other person who performs similar policymaking functions for the corporation.

(3) "Compensation" as used in paragraph (4) of subdivision (a) means all plan and nonplan compensation awarded to, earned by, or paid to the person for all services rendered in all capacities to the corporation and to its subsidiaries, as the compensation is specified

by Item 402 of Regulation S–K of the Securities and Exchange Commission (Section 229.402 of Title 17 of the Code of Federal Regulations).

(4) "Loan" as used in paragraph (5) of subdivision (a) excludes an advance for expenses, the foreign corporation's payment of life insurance premiums, and an advance of litigation expenses, in each instance as permitted according to the applicable law of the state or place of incorporation or organization of the foreign corporation.

(c) This statement shall be available and open to the public for inspection. The Secretary of State . . . shall provide access to all information contained in this statement by means of an online database.

(d) A foreign corporation shall certify that the information it provides pursuant to this section is true and correct. No claim may be made against the state for inaccurate information contained in statements filed under this section with the Secretary of State.

Chapter 22

CRIMES AND PENALTIES

§ 2200. Neglect, Failure or Refusal to Keep Record of Shareholders or Books of Account or Prepare or Submit Financial Statements; Penalty; Payment to Shareholder

Every corporation that neglects, fails, or refuses: (a) to keep or cause to be kept or maintained the record of shareholders or books of account required by this division to be kept or maintained, (b) to prepare or cause to be prepared or submitted the financial statements required by this division to be prepared or submitted, or (c) to give any shareholder of record the advice required by subdivision (f) of Section 2215, is subject to penalty as provided in this section.

The penalty shall be twenty-five dollars ($25) for each day that the failure or refusal continues, up to a maximum of one thousand five hundred dollars ($1,500), beginning 30 days after the receipt of the written request that the duty be performed from one entitled to make the request, except that, in the case of a failure to give advice required by subdivision (f) of Section 2115, the 30–day period shall run from the date of receipt of the request made pursuant to subdivision (f) of Section 2115, and no additional request is required by this section.

The penalty shall be paid to the shareholder or shareholders jointly making the request for performance of the duty, and damaged by the neglect, failure, or refusal, if suit therefor is commenced within 90 days after the written request is made, including any request made pursuant to subdivision (f) of Section 2115; but the maximum daily penalty because of failure to comply with any number of separate requests made on any one day or for the same act shall be two hundred fifty dollars ($250).

§ 2207. Liability of Corporation for Civil Penalty for Failure to Notify Attorney General or Appropriate Government Agency and Shareholders or Investors With Respect to Knowledge of Certain Enumerated Acts

(a) A corporation is liable for a civil penalty in an amount not exceeding one million dollars ($1,000,000) if the corporation does both of the following:

(1) Has actual knowledge that an officer, director, manager, or agent of the corporation does any of the following:

(A) Makes, publishes, or posts, or has made, published, or posted either generally or privately to the shareholders or other persons either of the following:

(i) An oral, written, or electronically transmitted report, exhibit, notice, or statement of its affairs or pecuniary condition that contains a material statement or omission that is false and intended to give the shares of stock in the corporation a materially greater or a materially less apparent market value than they really possess.

(ii) An oral, written, or electronically transmitted report, prospectus, account, or statement of operations, values, business, profits, or expenditures, that includes a material false statement or omission intended to give the shares of stock in the corporation a materially greater or a materially less apparent market value than they really possess.

(B) Refuses or has refused to make any book entry or post any notice required by law in the manner required by law.

(C) Misstates or conceals or has misstated or concealed from a regulatory body a material fact in order to deceive a regulatory body to avoid a statutory or regulatory duty, or to avoid a statutory or regulatory limit or prohibition.

(2) Within 30 days after actual knowledge is acquired of the actions described in paragraph (1), the corporation knowingly fails to do both of the following:

(A) Notify the Attorney General or appropriate government agency in writing, unless the corporation has actual knowledge that the Attorney General or appropriate government agency has been notified.

(B) Notify its shareholders in writing, unless the corporation has actual knowledge that the shareholders have been notified.

(b) The requirement for notification under this section is not applicable if the action taken or about to be taken by the corporation, or by an officer, director, manager, or agent of the corporation under paragraph (1) of subdivision (a) is abated within the time prescribed for reporting, unless the appropriate government agency requires disclosure by regulation.

(c) If the action reported to the Attorney General pursuant to this section implicates the government authority of an agency other than the Attorney General, the Attorney General shall promptly forward the written notice to that agency.

(d) If the Attorney General was not notified pursuant to subparagraph (A) of paragraph (2) of subdivision (a), but the corporation reasonably and in good faith believed that it had complied with the notification requirements of this section by notifying a government agency listed in paragraph (4) of subdivision (e), no penalties shall apply.

(e) For purposes of this section:

(1) "Manager" means a person having both of the following:

(A) Management authority over a business entity.

(B) Significant responsibility for an aspect of a business that includes actual authority for the financial operations or financial transactions of the business.

(2) "Agent" means a person or entity authorized by the corporation to make representations to the public about the corporation's financial condition and who is acting within the scope of the agency when the representations are made.

(3) "Shareholder" means a person or entity that is a shareholder of the corporation at the time the disclosure is required pursuant to subparagraph (B) of paragraph (2) of subdivision (a).

(4) "Notify its shareholders" means to give sufficient description of an action taken or about to be taken that would constitute acts or omissions as described in paragraph (1) of subdivision (a). A notice or report filed by a corporation with the United States Securities and Exchange Commission that relates to the facts and circumstances giving rise to an obligation under paragraph (1) of subdivision (a) shall satisfy all notice requirements arising under paragraph (2) of subdivision (a), but shall not be the exclusive means of satisfying the notice requirements, provided that the Attorney General or appropriate agency is informed in writing that the filing has been made together with a copy of the filing or an electronic link where it is available online without charge.

(5) "Appropriate government agency" means an agency on the following list that has regulatory authority with respect to the financial operations of a corporation:

(A) Department of Corporations.

(B) Department of Insurance.

(C) Department of Financial Institutions.

(D) Department of Managed Health Care.

(E) United States Securities and Exchange Commission.

(6) "Actual knowledge of the corporation" means the knowledge an officer or director of a corporation actually possesses or does not consciously avoid possessing, based on an evaluation of information provided pursuant to the corporation's disclosure controls and procedures.

(7) "Refuse to make a book entry" means the intentional decision not to record an accounting transaction when all of the following conditions are satisfied:

(A) The independent auditors required recordation of an accounting transaction during the course of an audit.

(B) The audit committee of the corporation has not approved the independent auditor's recommendation.

(C) The decision is made for the primary purpose of rendering the financial statements materially false or misleading.

(8) "Refuse to post any notice required by law" means an intentional decision not to post a notice required by law when all of the following conditions exist:

(A) The decision not to post the notice has not been approved by the corporation's audit committee.

(B) The decision is intended to give the shares of stock in the corporation a materially greater or a materially less apparent market value than they really possess.

(9) "Misstate or conceal material facts from a regulatory body" means an intentional decision not to disclose material facts when all of the following conditions exist:

(A) The decision not to disclose material facts has not been approved by the corporation's audit committee.

(B) The decision is intended to give the shares of stock in the corporation a materially greater or a materially less apparent market value than they really possess.

(10) "Material false statement or omission" means an untrue statement of material fact or an omission to state a material fact necessary in order to make the statements made under the circumstances under which they were made not misleading.

(11) "Officer" means any person as set forth in Rule 16A-1 promulgated under the Securities Exchange Act of 1934 or any

successor regulation thereto, except an officer of a subsidiary corporation who is not also an officer of the parent corporation.

(f) This section only applies to corporations that are issuers, as defined in Section 2 of the Sarbanes–Oxley Act of 2002 (15 U.S.C. Sec. 7201 and following).

(g) An action to enforce this section may only be brought by the Attorney General or a district attorney or city attorney in the name of the people of the State of California.

TITLE 4

SECURITIES

§ 25402. Purchase or Sale of Securities by Person Having Access to Material Information Not Available to Public Through Special Relationship With Issuer

It is unlawful for an issuer or any person who is an officer, director or controlling person of an issuer or any other person whose relationship to the issuer gives him access, directly or indirectly, to material information about the issuer not generally available to the public, to purchase or sell any security of the issuer in this state at a time when he knows material information about the issuer gained from such relationship which would significantly affect the market price of that security and which is not generally available to the public, and which he knows is not intended to be so available, unless he has reason to believe that the person selling to or buying from him is also in possession of the information.

§ 25502. Violation of Section 25402; Damages

Any person who violates Section 25402 shall be liable to the person who purchases a security from him or sells a security to him, for damages equal to the difference between the price at which such security was purchased or sold and the market value which such security would have had at the time of the purchase or sale if the information known to the defendant had been publicly disseminated prior to that time and a reasonable time had elapsed for the market to absorb the information, plus interest at the legal rate, unless the defendant proves that the plaintiff knew the information or that the plaintiff would have purchased or sold at the same price even if the information had been revealed to him.

§ 25502.5 Liability to Issuer of Violator of Insider Trading Prohibitions; Allegation by Shareholder; Consideration by Board

(a) Any person other than the issuer who violates Section 25402 shall be liable to the issuer of the security purchased or sold in violation of Section 25402 for damages in an amount up to three times the difference between the price at which the security was purchased or sold and the market value which the security would have had at the time of the purchase or sale if the information known to the defendant had been publicly disseminated prior to that time and a reasonable time had elapsed for the market to absorb the information and shall be liable to the issuer of the security or to a person who institutes an action under this section in the right of the issuer of the security for reasonable costs and attorney's fees.

(b) The amounts recoverable under this section by the issuer shall be reduced by any amount paid by the defendant in a proceeding brought by the Securities and Exchange Commission with respect to the same transaction or transactions under the federal Insider Trading Sanctions Act of 1984 (15 U.S.C. Secs. 78a, 78c, 78o, 78t, 78u, and 78ff) or any other act regardless of whether the amount was paid pursuant to a judgment or settlement or paid before or after the filing of an action by the plaintiff against the defendant. If a proceeding has been commenced by the Securities and Exchange Commission but has not been finally resolved, the court shall delay entering a judgment for the plaintiff under this section until that proceeding is resolved.

(c) If any shareholder of an issuer alleges to the board that there has been a violation of this section, the board shall be required to consider the allegation in good faith, and if the allegation involves misconduct by any director, that director shall not be entitled to vote on any matter involving the allegation. However, that director may be counted in determining the presence of a quorum at a meeting of the board or a committee of the board.

(d) This section shall only apply to issuers who have total assets in excess of one million dollars ($1,000,000) and have a class of equity security held of record by 500 or more persons.

CONNECTICUT GENERAL STATUTES
ANN. § 33–756

§ 33–756. General standards for directors

(a) A director shall discharge his duties as a director, including his duties as a member of a committee: (1) In good faith; (2) with the care an ordinarily prudent person in a like position would exercise under similar circumstances; and (3) in a manner he reasonably believes to be in the best interests of the corporation.

(b) In discharging his duties a director is entitled to rely on information, opinions, reports or statements, including financial statements and other financial data, if prepared or presented by: (1) One or more officers or employees of the corporation whom the director reasonably believes to be reliable and competent in the matters presented; (2) legal counsel, public accountants or other persons as to matters the director reasonably believes are within the person's professional or expert competence; or (3) a committee of the board of directors of which he is not a member if the director reasonably believes the committee merits confidence.

(c) A director is not acting in good faith if he has knowledge concerning the matter in question that makes reliance otherwise permitted by subsection (b) of this section unwarranted.

(d) For purposes of sections 33–817 [merger], 33–830 [sale of substantially all assets in the usual course of business], 33–831 [sale of substantially all assets otherwise than in the regular course of business], 33–841 [certain business combinations] and 33–844 [certain business combinations] of this act, a director of a corporation which has a class of voting stock registered pursuant to Section 12 of the Securities Exchange Act of 1934, as the same has been or hereafter may be amended from time to time, in addition to complying with the provisions of subsections (a) to (c), inclusive, of this section, shall consider, in determining what he reasonably believes to be in the best interests of the corporation, (1) the long-term as well as the short-term interests of the corporation, (2) the interests of the shareholders, long-term as well as short-term, including the possibility that those interests may be best served by the continued independence of the corporation, (3) the interests of the corporation's employees, customers, creditors and suppliers, and (4) community and societal considerations including those of any community in which any office or other facility of the corporation is located. A director may also in his discretion consider any other factors he reasonably considers appropriate in determining what he reasonably believes to be in the best interests of the corporation.

(e) A director is not liable for any action taken as a director, or any failure to take any action, if he performed the duties of his office in compliance with this section.

IND. CODE ANN.
TITLE 23

**[Standards of Conduct for Directors;
Control Share Acquisitions]**

Chapter 35

STANDARDS OF CONDUCT FOR DIRECTORS

§ 23–1–35–1 Standards of conduct; liability; reaffirmation of corporate governance rules; presumption

(a) A director shall, based on facts then known to the director, discharge the duties as a director, including the director's duties as a member of a committee:

(1) in good faith;

(2) with the care an ordinarily prudent person in a like position would exercise under similar circumstances; and

(3) in a manner the director reasonably believes to be in the best interests of the corporation.

(b) In discharging the director's duties a director is entitled to rely on information, opinions, reports, or statements, including financial statements and other financial data, if prepared or presented by:

(1) one (1) or more officers or employees of the corporation whom the director reasonably believes to be reliable and competent in the matters presented;

(2) legal counsel, public accountants, or other persons as to matters the director reasonably believes are within the person's professional or expert competence; or

(3) a committee of the board of directors of which the director is not a member if the director reasonably believes the committee merits confidence.

(c) A director is not acting in good faith if the director has knowledge concerning the matter in question that makes reliance otherwise permitted by subsection (b) unwarranted.

(d) A director may, in considering the best interests of a corporation, consider the effects of any action on shareholders, employees, suppliers, and customers of the corporation, and communities in which offices or other facilities of the corporation are located, and any other factors the director considers pertinent.

1144

(e) A director is not liable for any action taken as a director, or any failure to take any action, unless:

  (1) the director has breached or failed to perform the duties of the director's office in compliance with this section; and

  (2) the breach or failure to perform constitutes willful misconduct or recklessness.

(f) In enacting this article, the general assembly established corporate governance rules for Indiana corporations, including in this chapter, the standards of conduct applicable to directors of Indiana corporations, and the corporate constituent groups and interests that a director may take into account in exercising the director's business judgment. The general assembly intends to reaffirm certain of these corporate governance rules to ensure that the directors of Indiana corporations, in exercising their business judgment, are not required to approve a proposed corporate action if the directors in good faith determine, after considering and weighing as they deem appropriate the effects of such action on the corporation's constituents, that such action is not in the best interests of the corporation. In making such determination, directors are not required to consider the effects of a proposed corporate action on any particular corporate constituent group or interest as a dominant or controlling factor. Without limiting the generality of the foregoing, directors are not required to render inapplicable any of the provisions of [§] 23–1–43 [business combinations], to redeem any rights under or to render inapplicable a shareholder rights plan adopted pursuant to [§] 23–1–26–5 [rights, options or warrants], or to take or decline to take any other action under this article, solely because of the effect such action might have on a proposed acquisition of control of the corporation or the amounts that might be paid to shareholders under such an acquisition. Certain judicial decisions in Delaware and other jurisdictions, which might otherwise be looked to for guidance in interpreting Indiana corporate law, including decisions relating to potential change of control transactions that impose a different or higher degree of scrutiny on actions taken by directors in response to a proposed acquisition of control of the corporation, are inconsistent with the proper application of the business judgment rule under this article. Therefore, the general assembly intends:

  (1) to reaffirm that this section allows directors the full discretion to weigh the factors enumerated in subsection (d) as they deem appropriate; and

  (2) to protect both directors and the validity of corporate action taken by them in the good faith exercise of their business judgment after reasonable investigation.

(g) In taking or declining to take any action, or in making or declining to make any recommendation to the shareholders of the corporation with respect to any matter, a board of directors may, in its discretion, consider both the short term and long term best interests of the corporation, taking into account, and weighing as the directors deem appropriate, the effects thereof on the corporation's shareholders and the other corporate constituent groups and interests listed or described in subsection (d), as well as any other factors deemed pertinent by the directors under subsection (d). If a determination is made with respect to the foregoing with the approval of a majority of the disinterested directors of the board of directors, that determination shall conclusively be presumed to be valid unless it can be demonstrated that the determination was not made in good faith after reasonable investigation.

(h) For the purposes of subsection (g), a director is disinterested if:

(1) the director does not have a conflict of interest, within the meaning of section 2 of this chapter [conflict-of-interest transactions], in connection with the action or recommendation in question;

(2) in connection with matters described in [§] 23–1–32 [derivative actions] the director is disinterested (as defined in [§] 23–1–32–4(d));

(3) in connection with any matter involving or otherwise affecting:

(A) a control share acquisition (as defined in [§] 23–1–42–2) or any matter related to a control share acquisition ...;

(B) a business combination (as defined in [§] 23–1–43–5) or any matter related to a business combination ...;

(C) any transaction that may result in a change of control (as defined in [§] 23–1–22–4) of the corporation;

the director is not an employee of the corporation; and

(4) in connection with any matter involving or otherwise affecting:

(A) a control share acquisition (as defined in [§] 23–1–42–2) or any matter related to a control share acquisition ...;

(B) a business combination (as defined in [§] 23–1–43–5) or any matter related to a business combination ...;

(C) any transaction that may result in a change of control (as defined in [§] 23–1–22–4) of the corporation;

the director is not an affiliate or associate of, or was not nominated or designated as a director by, a person proposing any of the transactions described in clause (A), (B), or (C).

(i) A person may be disinterested under this section even though the person is a director or shareholder of the corporation....

Chapter 42

CONTROL SHARE ACQUISITIONS

§ 23–1–42–1 "Control shares" defined

As used in this chapter, "control shares" means shares that, except for this chapter, would have voting power with respect to shares of an issuing public corporation that, when added to all other shares of the issuing public corporation owned by a person or in respect to which that person may exercise or direct the exercise of voting power, would entitle that person, immediately after acquisition of the shares (directly or indirectly, alone or as a part of a group), to exercise or direct the exercise of the voting power of the issuing public corporation in the election of directors within any of the following ranges of voting power:

(1) One-fifth (⅕) or more but less than one-third (⅓) of all voting power.

(2) One-third (⅓) or more but less than a majority of all voting power.

(3) A majority or more of all voting power.

§ 23–1–42–2 "Control share acquisition" defined

(a) As used in this chapter, "control share acquisition" means the acquisition (directly or indirectly) by any person of ownership of, or the power to direct the exercise of voting power with respect to, issued and outstanding control shares.

(b) For purposes of this section, shares acquired within ninety (90) days or shares acquired pursuant to a plan to make a control share acquisition are considered to have been acquired in the same acquisition.

(c) For purposes of this section, a person who acquires shares in the ordinary course of business for the benefit of others in good faith and not for the purpose of circumventing this chapter has voting power only of shares in respect of which that person would be able to exercise or direct the exercise of votes without further instruction from others.

(d) The acquisition of any shares of an issuing public corporation does not constitute a control share acquisition if the acquisition is consummated in any of the following circumstances: ...

(3) Pursuant to the laws of descent and distribution.

(4) Pursuant to the satisfaction of a pledge or other security interest created in good faith and not for the purpose of circumventing this chapter.

(5) Pursuant to a merger or plan of share exchange effected in compliance with [Indiana Code] 23-1-40 [merger and share exchange] if the issuing public corporation is a party to the agreement of merger or plan of share exchange.

(e) The acquisition of shares of an issuing public corporation in good faith and not for the purpose of circumventing this chapter by or from:

(1) any person whose voting rights had previously been authorized by shareholders in compliance with this chapter; or

(2) any person whose previous acquisition of shares of an issuing public corporation would have constituted a control share acquisition but for subsection (d);

does not constitute a control share acquisition, unless the acquisition entitles any person (directly or indirectly, alone or as a part of a group) to exercise or direct the exercise of voting power of the corporation in the election of directors in excess of the range of the voting power otherwise authorized.

§ 23-1-42-3 "Interested shares" defined

As used in this chapter, "interested shares" means the shares of an issuing public corporation in respect of which any of the following persons may exercise or direct the exercise of the voting power of the corporation in the election of directors:

(1) An acquiring person or member of a group with respect to a control share acquisition.

(2) Any officer of the issuing public corporation.

(3) Any employee of the issuing public corporation who is also a director of the corporation.

§ 23-1-42-4 "Issuing public corporation" defined

(a) As used in this chapter, "issuing public corporation" means a corporation that has:

(1) one hundred (100) or more shareholders;

(2) its principal place of business, its principal office, or substantial assets within Indiana; and

(3) either:

    (A) more than ten percent (10%) of its shareholders resident in Indiana;

    (B) more than ten percent (10%) of its shares owned by Indiana residents; or

    (C) ten thousand (10,000) shareholders resident in Indiana.

(b) The residence of a shareholder is presumed to be the address appearing in the records of the corporation.

(c) Shares held by banks (except as trustee or guardian), brokers or nominees shall be disregarded for purposes of calculating the percentages or numbers described in this section.*

§ 23–1–42–5 Voting rights under [§] 23–1–42–9

Unless the corporation's articles of incorporation or bylaws provide that this chapter does not apply to control share acquisitions of shares of the corporation before the control share acquisition, control shares of an issuing public corporation acquired in a control share acquisition have only such voting rights as are conferred by section 9 of this chapter.

§ 23–1–42–6 Acquiring person statement

Any person who proposes to make or has made a control share acquisition may at the person's election deliver an acquiring person statement to the issuing public corporation at the issuing public corporation's principal office. The acquiring person statement must set forth all of the following:

(1) The identity of the acquiring person and each other member of any group of which the person is a part for purposes of determining control shares.

(2) A statement that the acquiring person statement is given pursuant to this chapter.

(3) The number of shares of the issuing public corporation owned (directly or indirectly) by the acquiring person and each other member of the group.

(4) The range of voting power under which the control share acquisition falls or would, if consummated, fall.

(5) If the control share acquisition has not taken place:

    (A) a description in reasonable detail of the terms of the proposed control share acquisition; and

---

* Under § 23–1–20–5, "corporation" means a corporation incorporated in Indiana. [Footnote by ed.]

(B) representations of the acquiring person, together with a statement in reasonable detail of the facts upon which they are based, that the proposed control share acquisition, if consummated, will not be contrary to law, and that the acquiring person has the financial capacity to make the proposed control share acquisition.

§ 23-1-42-7 Special meeting of shareholders

(a) If the acquiring person so requests at the time of delivery of an acquiring person statement and gives an undertaking to pay the corporation's expenses of a special meeting, within ten (10) days thereafter, the directors of the issuing public corporation shall call a special meeting of shareholders of the issuing public corporation for the purpose of considering the voting rights to be accorded the shares acquired or to be acquired in the control share acquisition.

(b) Unless the acquiring person agrees in writing to another date, the special meeting of shareholders shall be held within fifty (50) days after receipt by the issuing public corporation of the request.

(c) If no request is made, the voting rights to be accorded the shares acquired in the control share acquisition shall be presented to the next special or annual meeting of shareholders.

(d) If the acquiring person so requests in writing at the time of delivery of the acquiring person statement, the special meeting must not be held sooner than thirty (30) days after receipt by the issuing public corporation of the acquiring person statement.

§ 23-1-42-8 Notice

(a) If a special meeting is requested, notice of the special meeting of shareholders shall be given as promptly as reasonably practicable by the issuing public corporation to all shareholders of record as of the record date set for the meeting, whether or not entitled to vote at the meeting.

(b) Notice of the special or annual shareholder meeting at which the voting rights are to be considered must include or be accompanied by both of the following:

(1) A copy of the acquiring person statement delivered to the issuing public corporation pursuant to this chapter.

(2) A statement by the board of directors of the corporation, authorized by its directors, of its position or recommendation, or that it is taking no position or making no recommendation, with respect to the proposed control share acquisition.

§ 23-1-42-9 Voting rights of acquired control shares; resolution

(a) Control shares acquired in a control share acquisition have the same voting rights as were accorded the shares before the control share acquisition only to the extent granted by resolution approved by the shareholders of the issuing public corporation.

(b) To be approved under this section, the resolution must be approved by:

(1) each voting group entitled to vote separately on the proposal by a majority of all the votes entitled to be cast by that voting group, with the holders of the outstanding shares of a class being entitled to vote as a separate voting group if the proposed control share acquisition would, if fully carried out, result in any of the changes described in [Indiana Code] 23–1–38–4(a) [class voting on amendments]; and

(2) each voting group entitled to vote separately on the proposal by a majority of all the votes entitled to be cast by that group, excluding all interested shares.

§ 23–1–42–10 Redemption of acquired control shares

(a) If authorized in a corporation's articles of incorporation or bylaws before a control share acquisition has occurred, control shares acquired in a control share acquisition with respect to which no acquiring person statement has been filed with the issuing public corporation may, at any time during the period ending sixty (60) days after the last acquisition of control shares by the acquiring person, be subject to redemption by the corporation at the fair value thereof pursuant to the procedures adopted by the corporation.

(b) Control shares acquired in a control share acquisition are not subject to redemption after an acquiring person statement has been filed unless the shares are not accorded full voting rights by the shareholders as provided in section 9 of this chapter.

§ 23–1–42–11 Dissenters' rights; "fair value" defined

(a) Unless otherwise provided in a corporation's articles of incorporation or bylaws before a control share acquisition has occurred, in the event control shares acquired in a control share acquisition are accorded full voting rights and the acquiring person has acquired control shares with a majority or more of all voting power, all shareholders of the issuing public corporation have dissenters' rights as provided in this chapter.

(b) As soon as practicable after such events have occurred, the board of directors shall cause a notice to be sent to all shareholders of the corporation advising them of the facts and that they have dissenters' rights to receive the fair value of their shares pursuant to [Indiana Code] 23–1–44 [dissenters' rights].

(c) As used in this section, "fair value" means a value not less than the highest price paid per share by the acquiring person in the control share acquisition.

MARYLAND ANN. CODE
CORPORATIONS AND ASSOCIATIONS, TITLE 4

[Close Corporations]

TITLE 4.

CLOSE CORPORATIONS.

Subtitle 1.　Definitions; General Provisions.

§ 4–101.　Definitions

(a) *In general.*—In this title the following words have the meanings indicated.

(b) *Close corporation.*—"Close corporation" means a corporation which elects to be a close corporation in accordance with § 4–201 of this title.

(c) *Unanimous stockholders' agreement.*—"Unanimous stockholders' agreement" means an agreement to which every stockholder of a close corporation actually has assented and which is contained in its charter or bylaws or in a written instrument signed by all the stockholders.

§ 4–102.　Execution of documents

Notwithstanding any contrary provision of law, an individual who holds more than one office in a close corporation may act in more than one capacity to execute, acknowledge, or verify any instrument required to be executed, acknowledged, or verified by more than one officer.

Subtitle 2.　Election to Be a Close Corporation.

§ 4–201.　Statement of election

(a) *Statement to be contained in charter.*—A corporation may elect to be a close corporation under this title by including in its charter a statement that it is a close corporation.

(b) *Procedure.*—The statement that a corporation is a close corporation shall be:

(1) Contained in the articles of incorporation originally filed with the Department; or

(2) Added to the charter by an amendment which is approved:

(i) Under the provisions of § 2–603 [Charter amendment— No stock outstanding or subscribed for] of this article, if at the time of the adoption of the amendment no stock of the corporation is either outstanding or subscribed for; or

(ii) By the affirmative vote of every stockholder and every subscriber for stock of the corporation.

§ 4–202.　Required references to close corporation status

(a) *Clear reference required.*—Clear reference to the fact that the corporation is a close corporation shall appear prominently:

(1) At the head of the charter document in which the election to be a close corporation is made;

(2) In each subsequent charter document of the corporation; and

(3) On each certificate representing outstanding stock of the corporation.

(b) *Absence of reference.*—The status of a corporation as a close corporation is not affected by the failure of any charter document or stock certificate to contain the reference required by this section.

§ 4–203.　Removal of statement from charter

The charter of a close corporation may be amended to remove the statement of election to be a close corporation, but only by the affirmative vote of every stockholder and every subscriber for stock of the corporation.

Subtitle 3.　Board of Directors.

§ 4–301.　At least one director required initially

A close corporation shall have at least one director until an election by the corporation in its charter to have no board of directors becomes effective.

§ 4–302.　Election to have no board of directors

(a) *Effective time of election.*—An election to have no board of directors becomes effective at the later of:

(1) The time that the organization meeting of directors and the issuance of at least one share of stock of the corporation are completed;

(2) The time the charter document in which the election is made becomes effective; or

(3) The time specified in the charter document in which the election is made.

(b) *Cessation of director's status.*—A director automatically ceases to be a director when an election to have no board of directors becomes effective.

§ 4–303.　Effect of election to have no board of directors

If there is an election to have no board of directors:

(1) The stockholders may exercise all powers of directors, and the business and affairs of the corporation shall be managed under their direction;

(2) The stockholders of the corporation are responsible for taking any action required by law to be taken by the board of directors;

(3) Action by stockholders shall be taken by the voting of shares of stock as provided in this article;

(4) The stockholders may take any action for which this article otherwise would require both a resolution of directors and a vote of stockholders;

(5) By the affirmative vote of a majority of all the votes entitled to be cast, the stockholders may take any action for which this article otherwise would require a vote of a majority of the entire board of directors;

(6) A statement that the corporation is a close corporation which has no board of directors satisfies any requirement that an instrument filed with the Department contain a statement that a specified action was taken by the board of directors;

(7) The special liabilities imposed on directors by § 2–312(a) of this article and the provisions of §§ 2–312(b) and 2–410 of this article apply to the stockholders of the corporation and, for this purpose, "present" in § 2–410 of this article means present in person or by proxy *; and

(8) A stockholder is not liable for any action taken as a result of a vote of the stockholders, unless he was entitled to vote on the action.

Subtitle 4. Stockholders.

§ 4–401. Unanimous stockholders' agreement

(a) *Governing the corporation.*—Under a unanimous stockholders' agreement, the stockholders of a close corporation may regulate any aspect of the affairs of the corporation or the relations of the stockholders, including:

(1) The management of the business and affairs of the corporation;

(2) Restrictions on the transfer of stock;

(3) The right of one or more stockholders to dissolve the corporation at will or on the occurrence of a specified event or contingency;

(4) The exercise or division of voting power;

---

* Section 2–312 concerns the liability of directors. Section 2–410 concerns the dis- sent of a director to an action of the board. (Footnote by ed.)

(5) The terms and conditions of employment of an officer or employee of the corporation, without regard to the period of his employment;

(6) The individuals who are to be directors and officers of the corporation; and

(7) The payment of dividends or the division of profits.

(b) *Amending unanimous stockholders' agreement.*—A unanimous stockholders' agreement may be amended, but only by the unanimous written consent of the stockholders then parties to the agreement.

(c) *Acquisition of stock subject to unanimous stockholders' agreement.*—A stockholder who acquires his stock after a unanimous stockholders' agreement becomes effective is considered to have actually assented to the agreement and is a party to it:

(1) Whether or not he has actual knowledge of the existence of the agreement at the time he acquires the stock, if acquired by gift or bequest from a person who was a party to the agreement; and

(2) If he has actual knowledge of the existence of the agreement at the time he acquires the stock, if acquired in any other manner.

(d) *Enforcement of unanimous stockholders' agreement.*—(1) A court of equity may enforce a unanimous stockholders' agreement by injunction or by any other relief which the court in its discretion determines to be fair and appropriate in the circumstances.

(2) As an alternative to the granting of an injunction or other equitable relief, on motion of a party to the proceeding, the court may order dissolution of the corporation under the provisions of Subtitle 6 of this title.

(e) *Inapplicability of section to other agreements.*—This section does not affect any otherwise valid agreement among stockholders of a close corporation or of any other corporation.

§ 4–402. Stockholders' annual meeting

(a) *General rule.*—The bylaws of a close corporation shall provide for an annual meeting of stockholders in accordance with Title 2 of this article, but the meeting need not be held unless requested by a stockholder.

(b) *Written request for annual meeting.*—A request for an annual meeting shall be in writing and delivered to the president or secretary of the corporation:

(1) At least 30 days before the date specified in the bylaws for the meeting; or

(2) If the bylaws specify a period during which the date for the meeting may be set, at least 30 days before the beginning of that period.

§ 4–403. Stockholders' right of inspection

A stockholder of a close corporation or his agent may inspect and copy during usual business hours any records or documents of the corporation relevant to its business and affairs, including any:

(1) Bylaws;

(2) Minutes of the proceedings of the stockholders and directors;

(3) Annual statement of affairs;

(4) Stock ledger; and

(5) Books of account.

§ 4–404. Statement of affairs

(a) *Stockholders' right to request.*—Once during each calendar year, each stockholder of a close corporation may present to any officer of the corporation a written request for a statement of its affairs.

(b) *Duty to prepare and file; verification.*—Within 20 days after a request is made for a statement of a close corporation's affairs, the corporation shall prepare and have available on file at its principal office a statement verified under oath by its president or treasurer or one of its vice-presidents or assistant treasurers which sets forth in reasonable detail the corporation's assets and liabilities as of a reasonably current date.

Subtitle 5. Stock Restrictions.

§ 4–501. Restriction on issuance or sale of stock

If there is any stock of a close corporation outstanding, the corporation may not issue or sell any of its stock, including treasury stock, unless the issuance or sale is:

(1) Approved by the affirmative vote of the holders of all outstanding stock; or

(2) Permitted by a unanimous stockholders' agreement.

§ 4–502. Certain securities and stock options prohibited

A close corporation may not have outstanding any:

(1) Securities which are convertible into its stock;

(2) Voting securities other than stock; or

(3) Options, warrants, or other rights to subscribe for or purchase any of its stock, unless they are nontransferable.

§ 4–503. Restrictions on transfer of stock

(a) *"Transfer" defined.*—(1) In this section, "transfer" means the transfer of any interest in the stock of a close corporation, except:

    (i) A transfer by operation of law to a personal representative, trustee in bankruptcy, receiver, guardian, or similar legal representative;

    (ii) The acquisition of a lien or power of sale by an attachment, levy, or similar procedure; or

    (iii) The creation or assignment of a security interest.

(2) A foreclosure sale or other transfer by a person who acquired his interest or power in a transaction described in paragraph (1) of this subsection is a transfer subject to all the provisions of this section. For purposes of the transfer, the person effecting the foreclosure sale or other transfer shall be treated as and have the rights of a holder of the stock under this section and § 4–602(b) of this title.

(b) *Enumeration of restrictions.*—A transfer of the stock of a close corporation is invalid unless:

(1) Every stockholder of the corporation consents to the transfer in writing within the 90 days before the date of the transfer; or

(2) The transfer is made under a provision of a unanimous stockholders' agreement permitting the transfer to the corporation or to or in trust for the principal benefit of:

    (i) One or more of the stockholders or security holders of the corporation or their wives, children, or grandchildren; or

    (ii) One or more persons named in the agreement.

§ 4–504. Denial or restriction of voting rights; unanimous stockholder vote

(a) *Denial or restriction of voting rights.*—A close corporation may deny or restrict the voting rights of any of its stock as provided in this article. Notwithstanding any denial or restriction, all stock has voting rights on any matter required by this title to be authorized by the affirmative vote of every stockholder or every subscriber for stock of a close corporation.

(b) *Unanimous stockholder vote.*—Notwithstanding the provisions of § 2–104(b)(5) * of this article, the charter of a close corporation may not lower the proportion of votes required to approve any action for which this title requires the affirmative vote or assent of every stockholder or every subscriber for stock of the corporation.

---

* Section 2–104(b)(5) provides that the articles of incorporation may include certain provisions that reduce the shareholder note that would otherwise be required. (Footnote by ed.)

Subtitle 6. Termination of Existence.

§ 4–601. Consolidation, merger, share exchange, or transfer of assets

A consolidation, merger, share exchange, or transfer of assets of a close corporation shall be made in accordance with the provisions of Title 3 of this article [Extraordinary Actions]. However, approval of a proposed consolidation or merger, a transfer of its assets, or an acquisition of its stock in a share exchange requires the affirmative vote of every stockholder of the corporation.

§ 4–602. Involuntary dissolution

(a) *Dissolution by stockholder generally.*—Any stockholder of a close corporation may petition a court of equity for dissolution of the corporation on the grounds set forth in § 3–413 of this article [Grounds for petition for involuntary dissolution] or on the ground that there is such internal dissension among the stockholders of the corporation that the business and affairs of the corporation can no longer be conducted to the advantage of the stockholders generally.

(b) *Dissolution by stockholder desiring to transfer stock.*—(1) Unless a unanimous stockholders' agreement provides otherwise, a stockholder of a close corporation has the right to require dissolution of the corporation if:

(i) The stockholder made a written request for consent to a proposed bona fide transfer of his stock in accordance with the provisions of § 4–503(b)(1) of this title, specifying the proposed transferee and consideration, and the consent was not received by him within 30 days after the date of the request; or

(ii) Another party to a unanimous stockholders' agreement defaulted in an obligation, set forth in or arising under the agreement, to purchase or cause to be purchased stock of the stockholder, and the default was not remedied within 30 days after the date for performance of the obligation.

(2) A petition for dissolution under this subsection shall be filed within 60 days after the date of the request or the default, as the case may be.

(c) *Proceeding to be in accordance with § 3–414.*—A proceeding for dissolution authorized by this section shall be in accordance with the provisions of § 3–414 of this article [Appointment of receiver in involuntary dissolution].

§ 4–603. Avoidance of dissolution by purchase of petitioner's stock

(a) *Stockholder's right to avoid dissolution.*—Any one or more stockholders who desire to continue the business of a close corporation may avoid the dissolution of the corporation or the appointment of a receiver by electing to purchase the stock owned by the petitioner at a price equal to its fair value.

(b) *Court to determine fair value of stock.*—

(1) If a stockholder who makes the election is unable to reach an agreement with the petitioner as to the fair value of the stock, then, if the electing stockholder gives bond or other security sufficient to assure payment to the petitioner of the fair value of the stock, the court shall stay the proceeding and determine the fair value of the stock.

(2) Fair value shall be determined in accordance with the procedure set forth in Title 3, Subtitle 2 of this article [Rights of Objecting Shareholders], as of the close of business on the day on which the petition for dissolution was filed.

(c) *Court order.*—After the fair value of the stock is determined, the order of the court directing the purchase shall set the purchase price and the time within which payment shall be made. The court may order other appropriate terms and conditions of sale, including:

(1) Payment of the purchase price in installments; and

(2) The allocation of shares of stock among electing stockholders.

(d) *Interest on purchase price; cessation of other rights.*—The petitioner:

(1) Is entitled to interest on the purchase price of his stock from the date the petition is filed; and

(2) Ceases to have any other rights with respect to the stock, except the right to receive payment of its fair value.

(e) *Costs of proceeding.*—The costs of the proceeding, as determined by the court, shall be divided between the petitioner and the purchasing stockholder. The costs shall include the reasonable compensation and expenses of appraisers, but may not include fees and expenses of counsel or of other experts retained by a party.

(f) *Transfer of stock.*—The petitioner shall transfer his shares of stock to the purchasing stockholder:

(1) At a time set by the court; or

(2) If the court sets no time, at the time the purchase price is paid in full.

MICH. COMP. LAWS § 450.1489

450.1489. Shareholders' actions; relief; exclusions

Sec. 489. (1) A shareholder may bring an action in the circuit court of the county in which the principal place of business or registered office of the corporation is located to establish that the acts of the directors or those in control of the corporation are illegal, fraudulent, or willfully unfair and oppressive to the corporation or to the shareholder. If the shareholder establishes grounds for relief, the circuit court may make an order or grant relief as it considers appropriate, including, without limitation, an order providing for any of the following:

(a) The dissolution and liquidation of the assets and business of the corporation.

(b) The cancellation or alteration of a provision contained in the articles of incorporation, an amendment of the articles of incorporation, or the bylaws of the corporation.

(c) The cancellation, alteration, or injunction against a resolution or other act of the corporation.

(d) The direction or prohibition of an act of the corporation or of shareholders, directors, officers, or other persons party to the action.

(e) The purchase at fair value of the shares of a shareholder, either by the corporation or by the officers, directors, or other shareholders responsible for the wrongful acts.

(f) *An award of damages to the corporation or a shareholder.* An action seeking an award of damages must be commenced within 3 years after the cause of action under this section has accrued, or within 2 years after the shareholder discovers or reasonably should have discovered the cause of action under this section, whichever occurs first.

(2) No action under this section shall be brought by a shareholder whose shares are listed on a national securities exchange or regularly traded in a market maintained by 1 or more members of a national or affiliated securities association.

(3) As used in this section, "willfully unfair and oppressive conduct" means a continuing course of conduct or a significant action or series of actions that substantially interferes with the interests of the shareholder as a shareholder. Willfully unfair an oppressive conduct may include the termination of employment or limitations on employment benefits to the extent that the actions interfere with distributions or other shareholder interests disproportionately as to the affected shareholder. The term does not include conduct or actions that are permitted by an agreement, the articles of incorporation, the bylaws, or a consistently applied written corporate policy or procedure.

302A.751. Judicial intervention; equitable remedies or dissolution

Subdivision 1. When permitted. A court may grant any equitable relief it deems just and reasonable in the circumstances or may dissolve a corporation and liquidate its assets and business:

(a) In a supervised voluntary dissolution pursuant to section 302A.741;

(b) In an action by a shareholder when it is established that:

(1) the directors or the persons having the authority otherwise vested in the board are deadlocked in the management of the corporate affairs and the shareholders are unable to break the deadlock;

(2) the directors or those in control of the corporation have acted fraudulently or illegally toward one or more shareholders in their capacities as shareholders or directors, or as officers or employees of a closely held corporation;

(3) the directors or those in control of the corporation have acted in a manner unfairly prejudicial toward one or more shareholders in their capacities as shareholders or directors of a corporation that is not a publicly held corporation, or as officers or employees of a closely held corporation;

(4) the shareholders of the corporation are so divided in voting power that, for a period the includes the time when two consecutive regular meetings were held, they have failed to elect successors to directors whose terms have expired or would have expired upon the election and qualification of their successors;

(5) the corporate assets are being misapplied or wasted; or

(6) the period of duration as provided in the articles has expired and has not been extended as provided in section 302A.801;

(c) In an action by a creditor when:

(1) the claim of the creditor has been reduced to judgment and an execution thereon has been returned unsatisfied; or

(2) the corporation has admitted in writing that the claim of the creditor is due and owing and it is established that the corporation is unable to pay its debts in the ordinary course of business; or

(d) In an action by the attorney general to dissolve the corporation in accordance with section 302A.757 when it is established that a decree of dissolution is appropriate.

Subd. 2. Buy-out on motion. In an action under subdivision 1, clause (b), involving a corporation that is not a publicly held corporation at the time the action is commenced and in which one or more of the circumstances described in that clause is established, the court may, upon motion of a corporation or a shareholder or beneficial owner of shares of the corporation, order the sale by plaintiff or a defendant of all shares of the corporation held by the plaintiff or defendant to either the corporation or the moving shareholders, whichever is specified in the motion, if the court determines in its discretion that an order would be fair and equitable to all parties under all of the circumstances of the case.

The purchase price of any shares so sold shall be the fair value of the shares as of the date of the commencement of the action or as of another date found equitable by the court, provided that, if the shares in question are then subject to sale and purchase pursuant to the bylaws of the corporation, a shareholder control agreement, the terms of the shares, or otherwise, the court shall order the sale for the price and on the terms set forth in them, unless the court determines that the price or terms are unreasonable under all the circumstances of the case.

Within five days after the entry of the order, the corporation shall provide each selling shareholder or beneficial owner with the information it is required to provide under section 302A.473, subdivision 5, paragraph (a).

If the parties are unable to agree on fair value within 40 days of entry of the order, the court shall determine the fair value of the shares under the provisions of section 302A.473, subdivision 7, and may allow interest or costs as provided in section 302A.473, subdivisions 1 and 8.

The purchase price shall be paid in one or more installments as agreed on by the parties, or, if no agreement can be reached within 40 days of entry of the order, as ordered by the court. Upon entry of an order for the sale of shares under this subdivision and provided that the corporation or the moving shareholders post a bond in adequate amount with sufficient sureties or otherwise satisfy the court that the full purchase price of the shares, plus such additional costs, expenses, and fees as may be awarded, will be paid when due and payable, the selling shareholders shall no longer have any rights or status as shareholders, officers, or directors, except the right to receive the fair value of their shares plus such other amounts as might be awarded.

Subd. 3. Condition of corporation. In determining whether to order equitable relief, dissolution, or a buy-out, the court shall take into consideration the financial condition of the corporation but shall not refuse to order equitable relief, dissolution, or a buy-out solely on the ground that the corporation has accumulated or current operating profits.

Subd. 3a. Considerations in granting relief involving closely held corporations. In determining whether to order equitable relief, dissolution, or a buy-out, the court shall take into consideration the duty which all shareholders in a closely held corporation owe one another to act in an honest, fair, and reasonable manner in the operation of the corporation and the reasonable expectations of all shareholders as they exist at the inception and develop during the course of the shareholders' relationship with the corporation and with each other. For purposes of this section, any written agreements, including employment agreements and buy-sell agreements, between or among shareholders or between or among one or more shareholders and the corporation are presumed to reflect the parties' reasonable expectations concerning matters dealt with in the agreements.

Subd. 3b. Dissolution as remedy. In deciding whether to order dissolution, the court shall consider whether lesser relief suggested by one or more parties, such as any form of equitable relief, a buy-out, or a partial liquidation, would be adequate to permanently relieve the circumstances established under subdivision 1, clause (b) or (c). Lesser relief may be ordered in any case where it would be appropriate under all the facts and circumstances of the case.

Subd. 4. Expenses. If the court finds that a party to a proceeding brought under this section has acted arbitrarily, vexatiously, or otherwise not in good faith, it may in its discretion award reasonable expenses, including attorneys' fees and disbursements, to any of the other parties.

Subd. 5. Venue; parties. Proceedings under this section shall be brought in a court within the county in which the registered office of the corporation is located. It is not necessary to make shareholders parties to the action or proceeding unless relief is sought against them personally.

NEW YORK BUSINESS CORPORATION LAW

(Selected Provisions)

ARTICLE 1. SHORT TITLE; DEFINITIONS; APPLICATION; CERTIFICATES; MISCELLANEOUS

ARTICLE 2. CORPORATE PURPOSES AND POWERS

ARTICLE 4. FORMATION OF CORPORATIONS

ARTICLE 5. CORPORATE FINANCE

ARTICLE 6. SHAREHOLDERS

ARTICLE 7. DIRECTORS AND OFFICERS

ARTICLE 1

SHORT TITLE; DEFINITIONS; APPLICATION; CERTIFICATES; MISCELLANEOUS

§ 102. Definitions

(a) As used in this chapter, unless the context otherwise requires, the term....

(8) "Insolvent" means being unable to pay debts as they become due in the usual course of the debtor's business.

1167

(9) "Net assets" means the amount by which the total assets exceed the total liabilities. Stated capital and surplus are not liabilities....

(12) "Stated capital" means the sum of (A) the par value of all shares with par value that have been issued, (B) the amount of the consideration received for all shares without par value that have been issued, except such part of the consideration therefor as may have been allocated to surplus in a manner permitted by law, and (C) such amounts not included in clauses (A) and (B) as have been transferred to stated capital, whether upon the distribution of shares or otherwise, minus all reductions from such sums as have been effected in a manner permitted by law.

(13) "Surplus" means the excess of net assets over stated capital.

(14) "Treasury shares" means shares which have been issued, have been subsequently acquired, and are retained uncancelled by the corporation. Treasury shares are issued shares, but not outstanding shares, and are not assets....

ARTICLE 2
CORPORATE PURPOSES AND POWERS

§ 201. Purposes

(a) A corporation may be formed under this chapter for any lawful business purpose or purposes except to do in this state any business for which formation is permitted under any other statute of this state unless such statute permits formation under this chapter. If, immediately prior to the effective date of this chapter, a statute of this state permitted the formation of a corporation under the stock corporation law for a purpose or purposes specified in such other statute, such statute shall be deemed and construed to permit formation of such corporation under this chapter, and any conditions, limitations or restrictions in such other statute upon the formation of such corporation under the stock corporation law shall apply to the formation thereof under this chapter.

(b) The approval of the industrial board of appeals is required for the filing with the department of state of any certificate of incorporation, certificate of merger or consolidation or application of a foreign corporation for authority to do business in this state which states as the purpose or one of the purposes of the corporation the formation of an organization of groups of working men or women or wage earners, or the performance, rendition or sale of services as labor consultant or as advisor on labor-management relations or as arbitrator or negotiator in labor-management disputes.

(c) In time of war or other national emergency, a corporation may do any lawful business in aid thereof, notwithstanding the purpose or purposes set forth in its certificate of incorporation, at the request or direction of any competent governmental authority.

(d) A corporation may not include as its purpose or among its purposes the establishment or operation of a day care center for children, unless its certificate of incorporation shall so state and such certificate shall have annexed thereto the approval of the commissioner of social services.

(e) A corporation may not include as its purpose or among its purposes the establishment or maintenance of a hospital or facility providing health related services, as those terms are defined in article twenty-eight of the public health law unless its certificate of incorporation shall so state and such certificate shall have annexed thereto the approval of the public health council.

§ 202. General Powers

(a) Each corporation, subject to any limitations provided in this chapter or any other statute of this state or its certificate of incorporation, shall have power in furtherance of its corporate purposes:

(1) To have perpetual duration.

(2) To sue and be sued in all courts and to participate in actions and proceedings, whether judicial, administrative, arbitrative or otherwise, in like cases as natural persons.

(3) To have a corporate seal, and to alter such seal at pleasure, and to use it by causing it or a facsimile to be affixed or impressed or reproduced in any other manner.

(4) To purchase, receive, take by grant, gift, devise, bequest or otherwise, lease, or otherwise acquire, own, hold, improve, employ, use and otherwise deal in and with, real or personal property, or any interest therein, wherever situated.

(5) To sell, convey, lease, exchange, transfer or otherwise dispose of, or mortgage or pledge, or create a security interest in, all or any of its property, or any interest therein, wherever situated.

(6) To purchase, take, receive, subscribe for, or otherwise acquire, own, hold, vote, employ, sell, lend, lease, exchange, transfer, or otherwise dispose of, mortgage, pledge, use and otherwise deal in and with, bonds and other obligations, shares, or other securities or interests issued by others, whether engaged in similar or different business, governmental, or other activities.

(7) To make contracts, give guarantees and incur liabilities, borrow money at such rates of interest as the corporation may determine, issue its notes, bonds and other obligations, and secure any of its obligations by mortgage or pledge of all or any of its property or any interest therein, wherever situated.

(8) To lend money, invest and reinvest its funds, and take and hold real and personal property as security for the payment of funds so loaned or invested.

(9) To do business, carry on its operations, and have offices and exercise the powers granted by this chapter in any jurisdiction within or without the United States.

(10) To elect or appoint officers, employees and other agents of the corporation, define their duties, fix their compensation and the compensation of directors, and to indemnify corporate personnel.

(11) To adopt, amend or repeal by-laws, including emergency by-laws made pursuant to subdivision seventeen of section twelve of the state defense emergency act, relating to the business of the corporation, the conduct of its affairs, its rights or powers or the rights or powers of its shareholders, directors or officers.

(12) To make donations, irrespective of corporate benefit, for the public welfare or for community fund, hospital, charitable, educational, scientific, civic or similar purposes, and in time of war or other national emergency in aid thereof.

(13) To pay pensions, establish and carry out pension, profit-sharing, share bonus, share purchase, share option, savings, thrift and other retirement, incentive and benefit plans, trusts and provisions for any or all of its directors, officers and employees.

(14) To purchase, receive, take, or otherwise acquire, own, hold, sell, lend, exchange, transfer or otherwise dispose of, pledge, use and otherwise deal in and with its own shares.

(15) To be a promoter, partner, member, associate or manager of other business enterprises or ventures, or to the extent permitted in any other jurisdiction to be an incorporator of other corporations of any type or kind.

(16) To have and exercise all powers necessary or convenient to effect any or all of the purposes for which the corporation is formed.

(b) No corporation shall do business in New York state under any name, other than that appearing in its certificate of incorporation, without compliance with the filing provisions of section one hundred thirty of the general business law governing the conduct of business under an assumed name.

§ 203. Defense of Ultra Vires

(a) No act of a corporation and no transfer of real or personal property to or by a corporation, otherwise lawful, shall be invalid by reason of the fact that the corporation was without capacity or power to do such act or to make or receive such transfer, but such lack of capacity or power may be asserted:

(1) In an action by a shareholder against the corporation to enjoin the doing of any act or the transfer of real or personal property by or to the corporation. If the unauthorized act or transfer sought to be enjoined is being, or is to be, performed or made under any contract to which the corporation is a party, the court may, if all of the parties to the contract are parties to the action and if it deems the same to be equitable, set aside and enjoin the performance of such contract, and in so doing may allow to the corporation or to the other parties to the contract, as the case may be, such compensation as may be equitable for the loss or damage sustained by any of them from the action of the court in setting aside and enjoining the performance of such contract; provided that anticipated profits to be derived from the performance of the contract shall not be awarded by the court as a loss or damage sustained.

(2) In an action by or in the right of the corporation to procure a judgment in its favor against an incumbent or former officer or director of the corporation for loss or damage due to his unauthorized act.

(3) In an action or special proceeding by the attorney-general to annul or dissolve the corporation or to enjoin it from the doing of unauthorized business.

ARTICLE 4

FORMATION OF CORPORATIONS

§ 401. Incorporators

One or more natural persons of the age of eighteen years or over may act as incorporators of a corporation to be formed under this chapter.

§ 402. Certificate of Incorporation; Contents

(a) A certificate, entitled "Certificate of incorporation of _____ (name of corporation) under section 402 of the Business Corporation Law", shall be signed by each incorporator, with his name and address included in such certificate[,] and delivered to the department of state. It shall set forth:

(1) The name of the corporation.

(2) The purpose or purposes for which it is formed, it being sufficient to state, either alone or with other purposes, that the purpose of the corporation is to engage in any lawful act or activity for which corporations may be organized under this chapter, provided that it also state that it is not formed to engage in any act or activity requiring the consent or approval of any state official, department, board, agency or other body without such consent or approval first being obtained. By such statement all lawful acts and activities shall be within the purposes

of the corporation, except for express limitations therein or in this chapter, if any.

(3) The county within this state in which the office of the corporation is to be located.

(4) The aggregate number of shares which the corporation shall have the authority to issue; if such shares are to consist of one class only, the par value of the shares or a statement that the shares are without par value; or, if the shares are to be divided into classes, the number of shares of each class and the par value of the shares having par value and a statement as to which shares, if any, are without par value.

(5) If the shares are to be divided into classes, the designation of each class and a statement of the relative rights, preferences and limitations of the shares of each class.

(6) If the shares of any preferred class are to be issued in series, the designation of each series and a statement of the variations in the relative rights, preferences and limitations as between series insofar as the same are to be fixed in the certificate of incorporation, a statement of any authority to be vested in the board to establish and designate series and to fix the variations in the relative rights, preferences and limitations as between series and a statement of any limit on the authority of the board of directors to change the number of shares of any series of preferred shares as provided in paragraph (e) of section 502 (Issue of any class of preferred shares in series).

(7) A designation of the secretary of state as agent of the corporation upon whom process against it may be served and the post office address within or without this state to which the secretary of state shall mail a copy of any process against it served upon him.

(8) If the corporation is to have a registered agent, his name and address within this state and a statement that the registered agent is to be the agent of the corporation upon whom process against it may be served.

(9) The duration of the corporation if other than perpetual.

(b) The certificate of incorporation may set forth a provision eliminating or limiting the personal liability of directors to the corporation or its shareholders for damages for any breach of duty in such capacity, provided that no such provision shall eliminate or limit:

(1) the liability of any director if a judgment or other final adjudication adverse to him establishes that his acts or omissions were in bad faith or involved intentional misconduct or a knowing violation of law or that he personally gained in fact a financial profit or other advantage to which he was not legally entitled or that his acts violated section 719, or

(2) the liability of any director for any act or omission prior to the adoption of a provision authorized by this paragraph.

(c) The certificate of incorporation may set forth any provision, not inconsistent with this chapter or any other statute of this state, relating to the business of the corporation, its affairs, its rights or powers, or the rights or powers of its shareholders, directors or officers including any provision relating to matters which under this chapter are required or permitted to be set forth in the by-laws. It is not necessary to set forth in the certificate of incorporation any of the powers enumerated in this chapter.

§ 403. Certificate of Incorporation; Effect

Upon the filing of the certificate of incorporation by the department of state, the corporate existence shall begin, and such certificate shall be conclusive evidence that all conditions precedent have been fulfilled and that the corporation has been formed under this chapter, except in an action or special proceeding brought by the attorney-general. Notwithstanding the above, a certificate of incorporation may set forth a date subsequent to filing, not to exceed ninety days after filing, upon which date corporate existence shall begin.

ARTICLE 5

CORPORATE FINANCE

§ 501. Authorized Shares

(a) Every corporation shall have power to create and issue the number of shares stated in its certificate of incorporation. Such shares may be all of one class or may be divided into two or more classes. Each class shall consist of either shares with par value or shares without par value, having such designation and such relative voting, dividend, liquidation and other rights, preferences and limitations, consistent with this chapter, as shall be stated in the certificate of incorporation. The certificate of incorporation may deny, limit or otherwise define the voting rights and may limit or otherwise define the dividend or liquidation rights of shares of any class, but no such denial, limitation or definition of voting rights shall be effective unless at the time one or more classes of outstanding shares or bonds, singly or in the aggregate, are entitled to full voting rights, and no such limitation or definition of dividend or liquidation rights shall be effective unless at the time one or more classes of outstanding shares, singly or in the aggregate, are entitled to unlimited dividend and liquidation rights.

(b) If the shares are divided into two or more classes, the shares of each class shall be designated to distinguish them from the shares of all other classes. Shares which are entitled to preference in the distribution of dividends or assets shall not be designated as common shares. Shares which are not entitled to preference in the distribution of dividends or assets shall be common shares, even if identified by a class or other designation, and shall not be designated as preferred shares.

(c) Subject to the designations, relative rights, preferences and limitations applicable to separate series and except as otherwise permitted by subparagraph two of paragraph (a) of section five hundred five of this article, each share shall be equal to every other share of the same class....

§ 502. Issue of Any Class of Preferred Shares in Series

(a) If the certificate of incorporation so provides, a corporation may issue any class of preferred shares in series. Shares of each such series when issued, shall be designated to distinguish them from shares of all other series.

(b) The number of shares included in any or all series of any classes of preferred shares and any or all of the designations, relative rights, preferences and limitations of any or all such series may be fixed in the certificate of incorporation, subject to the limitation that, unless the certificate of incorporation provides otherwise, if the stated dividends and amounts payable on liquidation are not paid in full, the shares of all series of the same class shall share ratably in the payment of dividends including accumulations, if any, in accordance with the sums which would be payable on such shares if all dividends were declared and paid in full, and in any distribution of assets other than by way of dividends in accordance with the sums which would be payable on such distribution if all sums payable were discharged in full.

(c) If any such number of shares or any such designation, relative right, preference or limitation of the shares of any series is not fixed in the certificate of incorporation, it may be fixed by the board, to the extent authorized by the certificate of incorporation. Unless otherwise provided in the certificate of incorporation, the number of preferred shares of any series so fixed by the board may be increased (but not above the total number of authorized shares of the class) or decreased (but not below the number of shares thereof then outstanding) by the board. In case the number of such shares shall be decreased, the number of shares by which the series is decreased shall, unless eliminated pursuant to paragraph (e) of this section, resume the status which they had prior to being designated as part of a series of preferred shares.

(d) Before the issue of any shares of a series established by the board, a certificate of amendment under section 805 (Certificate of amendment; contents) shall be delivered to the department of state. Such certificate shall set forth:

(1) The name of the corporation, and, if it has been changed, the name under which it was formed.

(2) The date the certificate of incorporation was filed by the department of state.

(3) That the certificate of incorporation is thereby amended by the addition of a provision stating the number, designation, relative rights, preferences, and limitations of the shares of the series as fixed by the board, setting forth in full the text of such provision.

(e) Action by the board to increase or decrease the number of preferred shares of any series pursuant to paragraph (c) of this section shall become effective by delivering to the department of state a certificate of amendment under section 805 (Certificate of amendment; contents) which shall set forth:

(1) The name of the corporation, and, if it has been changed, the name under which it was formed.

(2) The date its certificate of incorporation was filed with the department of state.

(3) That the certificate of incorporation is thereby amended to increase or decrease, as the case may be, the number of preferred shares of any series so fixed by the board, setting forth the specific terms of the amendment and the number of shares so authorized following the effectiveness of the amendment.

When no shares of any such series are outstanding, either because none were issued or because no issued shares of any such series remain outstanding, the certificate of amendment under section 805 may also set forth a statement that none of the authorized shares of such series are outstanding and that none will be issued subject to the certificate of incorporation, and, when such certificate becomes accepted for filing, it shall have the effect of eliminating from the certificate of incorporation all matter set forth therein with respect to such series of preferred shares.

§ 503. Subscription for Shares; Time of Payment, Forfeiture for Default

(a) Unless otherwise provided by the terms of the subscription, a subscription for shares of a corporation to be formed shall be irrevocable, except with the consent of all other subscribers or the corporation, for a period of three months from its date.

(b) A subscription, whether made before or after the formation of a corporation, shall not be enforceable unless in writing and signed by the subscriber.

(c) Unless otherwise provided by the terms of the subscription, subscriptions for shares, whether made before or after the formation of a corporation, shall be paid in full at such time, or in such installments and at such times, as shall be determined by the board. Any call made by the board for payment on subscriptions shall be uniform as to all shares of the same class or of the same series. If a receiver of the corporation has been appointed, all unpaid subscriptions shall be paid at such times and in such installments as such receiver or the court may direct.

(d) In the event of default in the payment of any installment or call when due, the corporation may proceed to collect the amount due in the same manner as any debt due the corporation or the board may declare a forfeiture of the subscriptions. The subscription agreement may prescribe other penalties, not amounting to forfeiture, for failure to pay installments or calls that may become due. No forfeiture of the subscription shall be declared as against any subscriber unless the amount due thereon shall remain unpaid for a period of thirty days after written demand has been made therefor. If mailed, such written demand shall be deemed to be made when deposited in the United States mail in a sealed envelope addressed to the subscriber at his last post office address known to the corporation, with postage thereon prepaid. Upon forfeiture of the subscription, if at least fifty percent of the subscription price has been paid, the shares subscribed for shall be offered for sale for cash or a binding obligation to pay cash at a price at least sufficient to pay the full balance owed by the delinquent subscriber plus the expenses incidental to such sale, and any excess of net proceeds realized over the amount owed on such shares shall be paid to the delinquent subscriber or to his legal representative. If no prospective purchaser offers a cash price or binding obligation to pay cash sufficient to pay the full balance owed by the delinquent subscriber plus the expenses incidental to such sale, or if less than fifty percent of the subscription price has been paid, the shares subscribed for shall be cancelled and restored to the status of authorized but unissued shares and all previous payments thereon shall be forfeited to the corporation and transferred to capital surplus.

(e) Notwithstanding the provisions of paragraph (d) of this section, in the event of default in payment or other performance under the instrument evidencing a subscriber's binding obligation to pay a portion of the subscription price or perform services, the corporation may pursue such remedies as are provided in such instrument or a related agreement or under law.

§ 504. Consideration and Payment for Shares

(a) Consideration for the issue of shares shall consist of money or other property, tangible or intangible; labor or services actually received by or performed for the corporation or for its benefit or in its formation or reorganization; a binding obligation to pay the purchase price or the subscription price in cash or other property; a binding obligation to perform services having an agreed value; or a combination thereof. In the absence of fraud in the transaction, the judgment of the board or shareholders, as the case may be, as to the value of the consideration received for shares shall be conclusive.

(c) Shares with par value may be issued for such consideration, not less than the par value thereof, as is fixed from time to time by the board.

(d) Shares without par value may be issued for such consideration as is fixed from time to time by the board unless the certificate of incorporation reserves to the shareholders the right to fix the consideration. If such right is reserved as to any shares, a vote of the shareholders shall either fix the consideration to be received for the shares or authorize the board to fix such consideration.

(e) Treasury shares may be disposed of by a corporation on such terms and conditions as are fixed from time to time by the board.

(f) Upon distribution of authorized but unissued shares to shareholders, that part of the surplus of a corporation which is concurrently transferred to stated capital shall be the consideration for the issue of such shares.

(g) In the event of a conversion of bonds or shares into shares, or in the event of an exchange of bonds or shares for shares, with or without par value, the consideration for the shares so issued in exchange or conversion shall be the sum of (1) either the principal sum of, and accrued interest on, the bonds so exchanged or converted, or the stated capital then represented by the shares so exchanged or converted, plus (2) any additional consideration paid to the corporation for the new shares, plus (3) any stated capital not theretofore allocated to any designated class or series which is thereupon allocated to the new shares, plus (4) any surplus thereupon transferred to stated capital and allocated to the new shares.

(h) Certificates for shares may not be issued until the amount of the consideration therefor determined to be stated capital pursuant to section 506 (Determination of stated capital) has been paid in the form of cash, services rendered, personal or real property or a combination thereof and consideration for the balance (if any) complying with paragraph (a) of this section has been provided, except as provided in paragraphs (e) and (f) of section 505 (Rights and options to purchase shares; issue of rights and options to directors, officers and employees).

(i) When the consideration for shares has been provided in compliance with paragraph (h) of this section, the subscriber shall be entitled to all the rights and privileges of a holder of such shares and to a certificate representing his shares, and such shares shall be fully paid and nonassessable.

(j) Notwithstanding that such shares may be fully paid and nonassessable, the corporation may place in escrow shares issued for a binding obligation to pay cash or other property or to perform future services, or make other arrangements to restrict the transfer of the shares, and may credit distributions in respect of the shares against the obligation, until the obligation is performed. If the obligation is not performed in whole or in part, the corporation may pursue such remedies as are provided in the instrument evidencing the obligation or a related agreement or under law.

§ 505. Rights and Options to Purchase Shares; Issue of Rights and Options to Directors, Officers and Employees

(a)(1) Except as otherwise provided in this section or in the certificate of incorporation, a corporation may create and issue, whether or not in connection with the issue and sale of any of its shares or bonds, rights or options entitling the holders thereof to purchase from the corporation, upon such consideration, terms and conditions as may be fixed by the board, shares of any class or series, whether authorized but unissued shares, treasury shares or shares to be purchased or acquired or assets of the corporation.

(2)(i) In the case of a domestic corporation that has a class of voting stock registered with the Securities and Exchange Commission pursuant to section twelve of the Exchange Act, the terms and conditions of such rights or options may include, without limitation, restrictions or conditions that preclude or limit the exercise, transfer or receipt of such rights or options by an interested shareholder or any transferee of any such interested shareholder or that invalidate or void such rights or options held by any such interested shareholder or any such transferee. For the purposes of this subparagraph, the terms "voting stock", "Exchange Act" and "interested shareholder" shall have the same meanings as set forth in section nine hundred twelve of this chapter.

(ii) Determinations of the board of directors whether to impose, enforce or waive or otherwise render ineffective such limitations or conditions as are permitted by clause (i) of this subparagraph shall be subject to judicial review in an appropriate proceeding in which the courts formulate or apply appropriate standards in order to insure that such limitations or conditions are imposed, enforced or waived in the best long-term interests and short-term interests of the corporation and its shareholders considering, without limitation, the prospects for potential growth, development, productivity and profitability of the corporation.

(b) The consideration for shares to be purchased under any such right or option shall comply with the requirements of section 504 (Consideration and payment for shares).

(c) The terms and conditions of such rights or options, including the time or times at or within which and the price or prices at which they may be exercised and any limitations upon transferability, shall be set forth or incorporated by reference in the instrument or instruments evidencing such rights or options.

(d) The issue of such rights or options to one or more directors, officers or employees of the corporation or a subsidiary or affiliate thereof, as an incentive to service or continued service with the corporation, a subsidiary or affiliate thereof, or to a trustee on behalf of such directors, officers or employees, shall be authorized as required by the policies of all stock exchanges or automated quotation systems on which the corporation's shares are listed or authorized for trading, or if the corporation's shares are not so listed or authorized, by a majority of the votes cast at a meeting of shareholders by the holders of shares entitled to vote thereon, or authorized by and consistent with a plan adopted by such vote of shareholders. If, under the certificate of incorporation, there are preemptive rights to any of the shares to be thus subject to rights or options to purchase, either such issue or such plan, if any shall also be approved by the vote or written consent of the holders of a majority of the shares entitled to exercise preemptive rights with respect to such shares and such vote or written consent shall operate to release the preemptive rights with respect thereto of the holders of all the shares that were entitled to exercise such preemptive rights.

In the absence of preemptive rights, nothing in this paragraph shall require shareholder approval for the issuance of rights or options to purchase shares of the corporation in substitution for, or upon the assumption of, rights or options issued by another corporation, if such substitution or assumption is in connection with such other corporation's merger or consolidation with, or the acquisition of its shares or all or part of its assets by, the corporation or its subsidiary.

(e) A plan adopted by the shareholders for the issue of rights or options to directors, officers or employees shall include the material terms and conditions upon which such rights or options are to be issued, such as, but without limitation thereof, any restrictions on the number of shares that eligible individuals may have the right or option to purchase, the method of administering the plan, the terms and conditions of payment for shares in full or in installments, the issue of certificates for shares to be paid for in installments, any limitations upon the transferability of such shares and the voting and dividend rights to which the holders of such shares may be entitled, though the full amount of the consideration therefor has not been paid; provided that under this section no certificate for shares shall be delivered to a shareholder, prior to full payment therefor, unless the fact that the shares are partly paid is noted conspicuously on the face or back of such certificate.

(f) If there is shareholder approval for the issue of rights or options to individual directors, officers or employees, but not under an approved plan under paragraph (e), the terms and conditions of issue set forth in paragraph (e) shall be permissible except that the grantees of such rights or options shall not be granted voting or dividend rights until the consideration for the shares to which they are entitled under such rights or options has been fully paid.

(g) If there is shareholder approval for the issue of rights and options, such approval may provide that the board is authorized by certificate of amendment under section 805 (Certificate of amendment; contents) to increase the authorized shares of any class or series to such number as will be sufficient, when added to the previously authorized but unissued shares of such class or series, to satisfy any such rights or options entitling the holders thereof to purchase from the corporation authorized but unissued shares of such class or series.

(h) In the absence of fraud in the transaction, the judgment of the board shall be conclusive as to the adequacy of the consideration, tangible or intangible, received or to be received by the corporation for the issue of rights or options for the purchase from the corporation of its shares.

(i) The provisions of this section are inapplicable to the rights of the holders of convertible shares or bonds to acquire shares upon the exercise of conversion privileges under section 519 (Convertible shares and bonds).

§ 506. Determination of Stated Capital

(a) Upon issue by a corporation of shares with a par value, the consideration received therefor shall constitute stated capital to the extent of the par value of such shares.

(b) Upon issue by a corporation of shares without par value, the entire consideration received therefor shall constitute stated capital unless the board within a period of sixty days after issue allocates to surplus a portion, but not all, of the consideration received for such shares. No such allocation shall be made of any portion of the consideration received for shares without par value having a preference in the assets of the corporation upon involuntary liquidation except all or part of the amount, if any, of such consideration in excess of such preference, nor shall such allocation be made of any portion of the consideration for the issue of shares without par value which is fixed by the shareholders pursuant to a right reserved in the certificate of incorporation, unless such allocation is authorized by vote of the shareholders.

(c) The stated capital of a corporation may be increased from time to time by resolution of the board transferring all or part of the surplus of the corporation to stated capital. The board may direct that the amount so transferred shall be stated capital in respect of any designated class or series of shares.

§ 510. Dividends or Other Distributions in Cash or Property

(a) A corporation may declare and pay dividends or make other distributions in cash or its bonds or its property, including the shares or bonds of other corporations, on its outstanding shares, except when currently the corporation is insolvent or would thereby be made insolvent, or when the declaration, payment or distribution would be contrary to any restrictions contained in the certificate of incorporation.

(b) Dividends may be declared or paid and other distributions may be made out of surplus only, so that the net assets of the corporation remaining after such declaration, payment or distribution shall at least equal the amount of its stated capital; except that a corporation engaged in the exploitation of natural resources or other wasting assets, including patents, or formed primarily for the liquidation of specific assets, may declare and pay dividends or make other distributions in excess of its surplus, computed after taking due account of depletion and amortization, to the extent that the cost of the wasting or specific assets has been recovered by depletion reserves, amortization or sale, if the net assets remaining after such dividends or distributions are sufficient to cover the liquidation preferences of shares having such preferences in involuntary liquidation.

§ 511. Share Distributions and Changes

(a) A corporation may make pro rata distributions of its authorized but unissued shares to holders of any class or series of its outstanding shares, subject to the following conditions:

(1) If a distribution of shares having a par value is made, such shares shall be issued at not less than the par value thereof and there shall be transferred to stated capital at the time of such distribution an amount of surplus equal to the aggregate par value of such shares.

(2) If a distribution of shares without par value is made, the amount of stated capital to be represented by each such share shall be fixed by the board, unless the certificate of incorporation reserves to the shareholders the right to fix the consideration for the issue of such shares, and there shall be transferred to stated capital at the time of such distribution an amount of surplus equal to the aggregate stated capital represented by such shares.

(3) A distribution of shares of any class or series may be made to holders of the same or any other class or series of shares unless the certificate of incorporation provides otherwise, provided, however, that in the case of a corporation incorporated prior to [February 22, 1998] then so long as any shares of such class remain outstanding a distribution of shares of any class or series of shares of such corporation may be made only to holders of the same class or series of shares unless the certificate of incorporation permits distribution to holders of another class or series, or unless such distribution is approved by the affirmative vote or the written consent of the holders of a majority of the outstanding shares of the class or series to be distributed.

(4) A distribution of any class or series of shares shall be subject to the preemptive rights, if any, applicable to such shares pursuant to this chapter.

(b) A corporation making a pro rata distribution of authorized but unissued shares to the holders of any class or series of outstanding shares may at its option make an equivalent distribution upon treasury shares of the same class or series, and any shares so distributed shall be treasury shares.

(c) A change of issued shares of any class which increases the stated capital represented by those shares may be made if the surplus of the corporation is sufficient to permit the transfer, and a transfer is concurrently made, from surplus to stated capital, of an amount equal to such increase.

(d) No transfer from surplus to stated capital need be made by a corporation making a distribution of its treasury shares to holders of any class of outstanding shares; nor upon a split up or division of issued shares of any class into a greater number of shares of the same class, or a combination of issued shares of any class into a lesser number of shares of the same class, if there is no increase in the aggregate stated capital represented by them.

(e) Nothing in this section shall prevent a corporation from making other transfers from surplus to stated capital in connection with share distributions or otherwise.

(f) Every distribution to shareholders of certificates representing a share distribution or a change of shares which affects stated capital or surplus shall be accompanied by a written notice (1) disclosing the amounts by which such distribution or change affects stated capital and surplus, or (2) if such amounts are not determinable at the time of such notice, disclosing the approximate effect of such distribution or change upon stated capital and surplus and stating that such amounts are not yet determinable.

(g) When issued shares are changed in any manner which affects stated capital or surplus, and no distribution to shareholders of certificates representing any shares resulting from such change is made, disclosure of the effect of such change upon the stated capital and surplus shall be made in the next financial statement covering the period in which such change is made that is furnished by the corporation to holders of shares of the class or series so changed or, if practicable, in the first notice of dividend or share distribution or change that is furnished to such shareholders between the date of the change of shares and the next such financial statement, and in any event within six months of the date of such change.

§ 512. Redeemable Shares

(a) Subject to the restrictions contained in section 513 (Purchase, redemption and certain other transactions by a corporation with respect to its own shares) and paragraph (b) of this section, a corporation may provide in its certificate of incorporation for one or more classes or series of shares which are redeemable, in whole or in part, at the option of the corporation the holder or another person or upon the happening of a specified event.

(b) No redeemable common shares, other than shares of an open-end investment company, as defined in an act of congress entitled "Investment Company Act of 1940", as amended, or of a member corporation of a national securities exchange registered under a statute of the United States such as the Securities Exchange Act of 1934, as amended, or of a corporation described in this paragraph, shall be issued or redeemed unless the corporation at the time has outstanding a class of common shares that is not subject to redemption. Any common shares of a corporation which directly or through a subsidiary has a license or franchise to conduct its business, which license or franchise is conditioned upon some or all of the holders of such corporation's common shares possessing prescribed qualifications, may be made subject to redemption by the corporation to the extent necessary to prevent the loss of, or to reinstate, such license or franchise.

(c) Shares of any class or series which may be made redeemable under this section may be redeemed for cash, other property, indebtedness or other securities of the same or another corporation, at such time or times, price or prices, or rate or rates, and with such adjustments, as shall be stated in the certificate of incorporation.

(d) Nothing in this section shall prevent a corporation from creating sinking funds for the redemption or purchase of its shares to the extent permitted by section 513 (Purchase, redemption and certain other transactions by a corporation with respect to its own shares).

§ 513. Purchase, Redemption and Certain Other Transactions by a Corporation With Respect to Its Own Shares

(a) Notwithstanding any authority contained in the certificate of incorporation, the shares of a corporation may not be purchased by the corporation, or, if redeemable, convertible or exchangeable shares, may not be redeemed, converted or exchanged, in each case for or into cash, other property, indebtedness or other securities of the corporation (other than shares of the corporation and rights to acquire such shares) if the corporation is then insolvent or would thereby be made insolvent. Shares may be purchased or redeemed only out of surplus.

(b) When its redeemable, convertible or exchangeable shares are purchased by the corporation within the period during which such shares may be redeemed, converted or exchanged at the option of the corporation, the purchase price thereof shall not exceed the applicable redemption, conversion or exchange price stated in the certificate of incorporation. Upon a redemption, conversion or exchange, the amount payable by the corporation for shares having a cumulative preference on dividends may include the stated redemption, conversion or exchange price plus accrued dividends to the next dividend date following the date of redemption, conversion or exchange of such shares.

(c) No domestic corporation which is subject to the provisions of section nine hundred twelve of this chapter shall purchase or agree to purchase more than ten percent of the stock of the corporation from a shareholder for more than the market value thereof unless such purchase or agreement to purchase is approved by the affirmative vote of the board of directors and a majority of the votes of all outstanding shares entitled to vote thereon at a meeting of shareholders unless the certificate of incorporation requires a greater percentage of the votes of the outstanding shares to approve.

The provisions of this paragraph shall not apply when the corporation offers to purchase shares from all holders of stock or for stock which the holder has been the beneficial owner of for more than two years.

The terms "stock", "beneficial owner", and "market value" shall be as defined in section nine hundred twelve of this chapter.

§ 514. Agreements for Purchase by a Corporation of Its Own Shares

(a) An agreement for the purchase by a corporation of its own shares shall be enforceable by the shareholder and the corporation to the extent such purchase is permitted at the time of purchase by section 513 (Purchase or redemption by a corporation of its own shares).

(b) The possibility that a corporation may not be able to purchase its shares under section 513 shall not be a ground for denying to either party specific performance of an agreement for the purchase by a corporation of its own shares, if at the time for performance the corporation can purchase all or part of such shares under section 513.

§ 515. Reacquired Shares

(a) Shares that have been issued and have been purchased, redeemed or otherwise reacquired by a corporation shall be cancelled if they are reacquired out of stated capital, or if they are converted shares, or if the certificate of incorporation requires that such shares be cancelled upon reacquisition.

(b) Any shares reacquired by the corporation and not required to be cancelled may be either retained as treasury shares or cancelled by the board at the time of reacquisition or at any time thereafter.

(c) Neither the retention of reacquired shares as treasury shares, nor their subsequent distribution to shareholders or disposition for a consideration shall change the stated capital. When treasury shares are disposed of for a consideration, the surplus shall be increased by the full amount of the consideration received.

(d) Shares cancelled under this section are restored to the status of authorized but unissued shares. However, if the certificate of incorporation prohibits the reissue of any shares required or permitted to be cancelled under this section, the board by certificate of amendment under section 805 (Certificate of amendment; contents) shall reduce the number of authorized shares accordingly.

§ 516. Reduction of Stated Capital in Certain Cases

(a) Except as otherwise provided in the certificate of incorporation, the board may at any time reduce the stated capital of a corporation in any of the following ways:

(1) by eliminating from stated capital any portion of amounts previously transferred by the board from surplus to stated capital and not allocated to any designated class or series of shares;

(2) by reducing or eliminating any amount of stated capital represented by issued shares having a par value which exceeds the aggregate par value of such shares;

(3) by reducing the amount of stated capital represented by issued shares without par value; or

(4) by applying to an otherwise authorized purchase, redemption, conversion or exchange of outstanding shares some or all of the stated capital represented by the shares being purchased, redeemed, converted or exchanged, or some or all of any stated capital that has been allocated to any particular shares, or both. Notwithstanding the foregoing, if the consideration for the issue of shares without par value was fixed by the shareholders under section 504 (Consideration and payment for shares), the board shall not reduce the stated capital represented by such shares except to the extent, if any, that the board was authorized by the shareholders to allocate any portion of such consideration to surplus.

(b) No reduction of stated capital shall be made under this section unless after such reduction the stated capital exceeds the aggregate preferential amounts payable upon involuntary liquidation upon all issued shares having preferential rights in the assets plus the par value of all other issued shares with par value.

(c) When a reduction of stated capital has been effected under this section, the amount of such reduction shall be disclosed in the next financial statement covering the period in which such reduction is made that is furnished by the corporation to all its shareholders or, if practicable, in the first notice of dividend or share distribution that is furnished to the holders of each class or series of its shares between the date of such reduction and the next such financial statement, and in any event to all its shareholders within six months of the date of such reduction.

§ 518. Corporate Bonds

(a) No corporation shall issue bonds except for money or other property, tangible or intangible, or labor or services actually received by or performed for the corporation or for its benefit or in its formation or reorganization; a binding obligation to pay the purchase price thereof in cash or other property; a binding obligation to perform services having an agreed value; or a combination thereof. In the absence of fraud in the transaction, the judgment of the board as to the value of the consideration received shall be conclusive.

(b) If a distribution of its own bonds is made by a corporation to holders of any class or series of its outstanding shares, there shall be concurrently transferred to the liabilities of the corporation in respect of such bonds an amount of surplus equal to the principal amount of, and any accrued interest on, such bonds. The amount of the surplus so transferred shall be the consideration for the issue of such bonds.

(c) A corporation may, in its certificate of incorporation, confer upon the holders of any bonds issued or to be issued by the corporation, rights to inspect the corporate books and records and to vote in the election of directors and on any other matters on which shareholders of the corporation may vote.

§ 520. Liability for Failure to Disclose Required Information

Failure of the corporation to comply in good faith with the notice or disclosure provisions of paragraphs (f) and (g) of section 511 (Share distributions and changes), or paragraph (c) of section 516 (Reduction of stated capital in certain cases), shall make the corporation liable for any damage sustained by any shareholder in consequence thereof.

ARTICLE 6

SHAREHOLDERS

§ 601. By-Laws

(a) The initial by-laws of a corporation shall be adopted by its incorporator or incorporators at the organization meeting. Thereafter, subject to section 613 (Limitations on right to vote), by-laws may be adopted, amended or repealed by a majority of the votes cast by the shares at the time entitled to vote in the election of any directors. When so provided in the certificate of incorporation or a by-law adopted by the shareholders, by-laws may also be adopted, amended or repealed by the board by such vote as may be therein specified, which may be greater than the vote otherwise prescribed by this chapter, but any by-law adopted by the board may be amended or repealed by the shareholders entitled to vote thereon as herein provided. Any reference in this chapter to a "by-law adopted by the shareholders" shall include a by-law adopted by the incorporator or incorporators.

(b) The by-laws may contain any provision relating to the business of the corporation, the conduct of its affairs, its rights or powers or the rights or powers of its shareholders, directors or officers, not inconsistent with this chapter or any other statute of this state or the certificate of incorporation.

§ 602. Meetings of Shareholders

(a) Meetings of shareholders may be held at such place, within or without this state, as may be fixed by or under the by-laws, or if not so fixed, at the office of the corporation in this state.

(b) A meeting of shareholders shall be held annually for the election of directors and the transaction of other business on a date fixed by or under the by-laws. A failure to hold the annual meeting on the date so fixed or to elect a sufficient number of directors to conduct the business of the corporation shall not work a forfeiture or give cause for dissolution of the corporation, except as provided in paragraph (c) of section 1104 (Petition in case of deadlock among directors or shareholders).

(c) Special meetings of the shareholders may be called by the board and by such person or persons as may be so authorized by the certificate of incorporation or the by-laws. At any such special meeting only such business may be transacted which is related to the purpose or purposes set forth in the notice required by section 605 (Notice of meetings of shareholders).

(d) Except as otherwise required by this chapter, the by-laws may designate reasonable procedures for the calling and conduct of a meeting of shareholders, including but not limited to specifying: (i) who may call and who may conduct the meeting, (ii) the means by which the order of business to be conducted shall be established, (iii) the procedures and requirements for the nomination of directors, (iv) the procedures with respect to the making of shareholder proposals, and (v) the procedures to be established for the adjournment of any meeting of shareholders. No amendment of the by-laws pertaining to the election of directors or the procedures for the calling and conduct of a meeting of shareholders shall affect the election of directors or the procedures for the calling or conduct in respect of any meeting of shareholders unless adequate notice thereof is given to the shareholders in a manner reasonably calculated to provide shareholders with sufficient time to respond thereto prior to such meeting.

§ 603. Special Meeting for Election of Directors

(a) If, for a period of one month after the date fixed by or under the by-laws for the annual meeting of shareholders, or if no date has been so fixed, for a period of thirteen months after the formation of the corporation or the last annual meeting, there is a failure to elect a sufficient number of directors to conduct the business of the corporation, the board shall call a special meeting for the election of directors. If such special meeting is not called by the board within two weeks after the expiration of such period or if it is so called but there is a failure to elect such directors for a period of two months after the expiration of such period, holders of ten percent of the votes of the shares entitled to vote in an election of directors may, in writing, demand the call of a special meeting for the election of directors specifying the date and month thereof, which shall not be less than sixty nor more than ninety days from the date of such written demand. The secretary of the corporation upon receiving the written demand shall promptly give notice of such meeting, or if he fails to do so within five business days thereafter, any shareholder signing such demand may give such notice. The meeting shall be held at the place fixed in the by-laws or, if not so fixed, at the office of the corporation.

(b) At any such special meeting called on demand of shareholders, notwithstanding section 608 (Quorum of shareholders), the shareholders attending, in person or by proxy, and entitled to vote in an election of directors shall constitute a quorum for the purpose of electing directors, but not for the transaction of any other business.

§ 604. Fixing Record Date

(a) For the purpose of determining the shareholders entitled to notice of or to vote at any meeting of shareholders or any adjournment thereof, or to express consent to or dissent from any proposal without a meeting, or for the purpose of determining shareholders entitled to receive payment of any dividend or the allotment of any rights, or for the purpose of any other action, the by-laws may provide for fixing or, in the absence of such provision, the board may fix, in advance, a date as the record date for any such determination of shareholders. Such date shall not be more than sixty nor less than ten days before the date of such meeting, nor more than sixty days prior to any other action.

(b) If no record date is fixed:

(1) The record date for the determination of shareholders entitled to notice of or to vote at a meeting of shareholders shall be at the close of business on the day next preceding the day on which notice is given, or, if no notice is given, the day on which the meeting is held.

(2) The record date for determining shareholders for any purpose other than that specified in subparagraph (1) shall be at the close of

business on the day on which the resolution of the board relating thereto is adopted.

(c) When a determination of shareholders of record entitled to notice of or to vote at any meeting of shareholders has been made as provided in this section, such determination shall apply to any adjournment thereof, unless the board fixes a new record date under this section for the adjourned meeting.

§ 605. Notice of Meetings of Shareholders

(a) Whenever under the provisions of this chapter shareholders are required or permitted to take any action at a meeting, notice shall be given stating the place, date and hour of the meeting and, unless it is the annual meeting, indicating that it is being issued by or at the direction of the person or persons calling the meeting. Notice of a special meeting shall also state the purpose or purposes for which the meeting is called. Notice of any meeting of shareholders may be written or electronic. If, at any meeting, action is proposed to be taken which would, if taken, entitle shareholders fulfilling the requirements of section 623 (Procedure to enforce shareholder's right to receive payment for shares) to receive payment for their shares, the notice of such meeting shall include a statement of that purpose and to that effect and shall be accompanied by a copy of section 623 or an outline of its material terms. Notice of any meeting shall be given not fewer than ten nor more than sixty days before the date of the meeting, provided, however, that such notice may be given by third class mail not fewer than twenty-four nor more than sixty days before the date of the meeting, to each shareholder entitled to vote at such meeting. If mailed, such notice is given when deposited in the United States mail, with postage thereon prepaid, directed to the shareholder at the shareholder's address as it appears on the record of shareholders, or, if the shareholder shall have filed with the secretary of the corporation a request that notices to the shareholder be mailed to some other address, then directed to him at such other address. If transmitted electronically, such notice is given when directed to the shareholder's electronic mail address as supplied by the shareholder to the secretary of the corporation or as otherwise directed pursuant to the shareholder's authorization or instructions. An affidavit of the secretary or other person giving the notice or of a transfer agent of the corporation that the notice required by this section has been given shall, in the absence of fraud, be prima facie evidence of the facts therein stated.

(b) When a meeting is adjourned to another time or place, it shall not be necessary, unless the by-laws require otherwise, to give any notice of the adjourned meeting if the time and place to which the meeting is adjourned are announced at the meeting at which the adjournment is taken, and at the adjourned meeting any business may be transacted that might have been transacted on the original date of the meeting. However, if after the adjournment the board fixes a new record date for the adjourned meeting, a notice of the adjourned meeting shall be given to each shareholder of record on the new record date entitled to notice under paragraph (a).

§ 606. Waivers of Notice

Notice of meeting need not be given to any shareholder who submits a waiver of notice whether before or after the meeting. Waiver of notice may be written or electronic. If written, the waiver must be executed by the shareholder or the shareholder's authorized officer, director, employee or agent by signing such waiver or causing his or her signature to be affixed to such waiver by any reasonable means, including, but not limited to, facsimile signature. If electronic, the transmission of the waiver must either set forth or be submitted with information from which it can reasonably be determined that the transmission was authorized by the shareholder. The attendance of any shareholder at a meeting, in person or by proxy, without protesting prior to the conclusion of the meeting the lack of notice of such meeting, shall constitute a waiver of notice by such shareholder.

§ 607. List of Shareholders at Meetings

A list of shareholders as of the record date, certified by the corporate officer responsible for its preparation or by a transfer agent, shall be produced at any meeting of shareholders upon the request thereat or prior thereto of any shareholder. If the right to vote at any meeting is challenged, the inspectors of election, or person presiding thereat, shall require such list of shareholders to be produced as evidence of the right of the persons challenged to vote at such meeting, and all persons who appear from such list to be shareholders entitled to vote thereat may vote at such meeting.

§ 608. Quorum of Shareholders

(a) The holders of a majority of the votes of shares entitled to vote thereat shall constitute a quorum at a meeting of shareholders for the transaction of any business, provided that when a specified item of business is required to be voted on by a particular class or series of shares, voting as a class, the holders of a majority of the votes of shares of such class or series shall constitute a quorum for the transaction of such specified item of business.

(b) The certificate of incorporation or by-laws may provide for any lesser quorum not less than one-third of the votes of shares entitled to vote, and the certificate of incorporation may, under section 616 (Greater requirement as to quorum and vote of shareholders), provide for a greater quorum.

(c) When a quorum is once present to organize a meeting, it is not broken by the subsequent withdrawal of any shareholders.

(d) The shareholders present may adjourn the meeting despite the absence of a quorum.

§ 609. Proxies

(a) Every shareholder entitled to vote at a meeting of shareholders or to express consent or dissent without a meeting may authorize another person or persons to act for him by proxy.

(b) No proxy shall be valid after the expiration of eleven months from the date thereof unless otherwise provided in the proxy. Every proxy shall be revocable at the pleasure of the shareholder executing it, except as otherwise provided in this section.

(c) The authority of the holder of a proxy to act shall not be revoked by the incompetence or death of the shareholder who executed the proxy unless, before the authority is exercised, written notice of an adjudication of such incompetence or of such death is received by the corporate officer responsible for maintaining the list of shareholders.

(d) Except when other provision shall have been made by written agreement between the parties, the record holder of shares which he holds as pledgee or otherwise as security or which belong to another, shall issue to the pledgor or to such owner of such shares, upon demand therefor and payment of necessary expenses thereof, a proxy to vote or take other action thereon.

(e) A shareholder shall not sell his vote or issue a proxy to vote to any person for any sum of money or anything of value, except as authorized in this section and section 620 (Agreements as to voting; provision in certificate of incorporation as to control of directors), provided, however, that this paragraph shall not apply to votes, proxies or consents given by holders of preferred shares in connection with a proxy or consent solicitation made available on identical terms to all holders of shares of the same class or series and remaining open for acceptance for at least twenty business days.

(f) A proxy which is entitled "irrevocable proxy" and which states that it is irrevocable, is irrevocable when it is held by any of the following or a nominee of any of the following:

(1) A pledgee;

(2) A person who has purchased or agreed to purchase the shares;

(3) A creditor or creditors of the corporation who extend or continue credit to the corporation in consideration of the proxy if the proxy states that it was given in consideration of such extension or continuation of credit, the amount thereof, and the name of the person extending or continuing credit;

(4) A person who has contracted to perform services as an officer of the corporation, if a proxy is required by the contract of employment, if

the proxy states that it was given in consideration of such contract of employment, the name of the employee and the period of employment contracted for;

(5) A person designated by or under an agreement under paragraph (a) of section 620.

(g) Notwithstanding a provision in a proxy, stating that it is irrevocable, the proxy becomes revocable after the pledge is redeemed, or the debt of the corporation is paid, or the period of employment provided for in the contract of employment has terminated, or the agreement under paragraph (a) of section 620 has terminated; and, in a case provided for in subparagraphs (f)(3) or (4), becomes revocable three years after the date of the proxy or at the end of the period, if any, specified therein, whichever period is less, unless the period of irrevocability is renewed from time to time by the execution of a new irrevocable proxy as provided in this section. This paragraph does not affect the duration of a proxy under paragraph (b).

(h) A proxy may be revoked, notwithstanding a provision making it irrevocable, by a purchaser of shares without knowledge of the existence of the provision unless the existence of the proxy and its irrevocability is noted conspicuously on the face or back of the certificate representing such shares.

(i) Without limiting the manner in which a shareholder may authorize another person or persons to act for him as proxy pursuant to paragraph (a) of this section, the following shall constitute a valid means by which a shareholder may grant such authority.

(1) A shareholder may execute a writing authorizing another person or persons to act from him as proxy. Execution may be accomplished by the shareholder or the shareholder's authorized officer, director, employee or agent signing such writing or causing his or her signature to be affixed to such writing by any reasonable means including, but not limited to, by facsimile signature.

(2) A shareholder may authorize another person or persons to act for the shareholder as proxy by transmitting or authorizing the transmission of a telegram, cablegram or other means of electronic transmission to the person who will be the holder of the proxy or to a proxy solicitation firm, proxy support service organization or like agent duly authorized by the person who will be the holder of the proxy to receive such transmission, provided that any such telegram, cablegram or other means of electronic transmission must either set forth or be submitted with information from which it can be reasonably determined that the telegram, cablegram or other electronic transmission was authorized by the shareholder. If it is determined that such telegrams, cablegrams or other electronic transmissions are valid, the inspectors or, if there are no inspectors, such other persons making that determination shall specify the nature of the information upon which they relied.

(j) Any copy, facsimile telecommunication or other reliable reproduction of the writing or transmission created pursuant to paragraph (i) of this section may be substituted or used in lieu of the original writing or transmission for any and all purposes for which the original writing or transmission could be used, provided that such copy, facsimile telecommunication or other reproduction shall be a complete reproduction of the entire original writing or transmission.

§ 614. Vote of Shareholders

(a) Directors shall, except as otherwise required by this chapter or by the certificate of incorporation as permitted by this chapter, be elected by a plurality of the votes cast at a meeting of shareholders by the holders of shares entitled to vote in the election.

(b) Whenever any corporate action, other than the election of directors, is to be taken under this chapter by vote of the shareholders, it shall, except as otherwise required by this chapter or by the certificate of incorporation as permitted by this chapter or by the specific provisions of a by-law adopted by the shareholders, be authorized by a majority of the votes cast in favor of or against such action at a meeting of shareholders by the holders of shares entitled to vote thereon. Except as otherwise provided in the certificate of incorporation or the specific provision of a by-law adopted by the shareholders, an abstention shall not constitute a vote cast.

§ 615. Written Consent of Shareholders, Subscribers or Incorporators Without a Meeting

(a) Whenever under this chapter shareholders are required or permitted to take any action by vote, such action may be taken without a meeting on written consent, setting forth the action so taken, signed by the holders of all outstanding shares entitled to vote thereon or, if the certificate of incorporation so permits, signed by the holders of outstanding shares having not less than the minimum number of votes that would be necessary to authorize or take such action at a meeting at which all shares entitled to vote thereon were present and voted. In addition, this paragraph shall not be construed to alter or modify the provisions of any section or any provision in a certificate of incorporation not inconsistent with this chapter under which the written consent of the holders of less than all outstanding shares is sufficient for corporate action.

(b) No written consent shall be effective to take the corporate action referred to therein unless, within sixty days of the earliest dated consent delivered in the manner required by this paragraph to the corporation, written consents signed by a sufficient number of holders to take action are delivered to the corporation by delivery to its registered office in this state, its principal place of business, or an officer or agent of the corporation having custody of the book in which proceedings of meetings of shareholders are recorded. Delivery made to a corporation's registered office shall be by hand or by certified or registered mail, return receipt requested.

(c) Prompt notice of the taking of the corporate action without a meeting by less than unanimous written consent shall be given to those shareholders who have not consented in writing.

(d) Written consent thus given by the holders of such number of shares as is required under paragraph (a) of this section shall have the same effect as a valid vote of holders of such number of shares, and any certificate with respect to the authorization or taking of any such action which is to be delivered to the department of state shall recite that written consent has been given in accordance with this section and that written notice has been given as and to the extent required by this section.

(e) When there are no shareholders of record, such action may be taken on the written consent signed by a majority in interest of the subscribers for shares whose subscriptions have been accepted or their successors in interest or, if no subscription has been accepted, on the written consent signed by the incorporator or a majority of the incorporators. When there are two or more incorporators, if any dies or is for any reason unable to act, the other or others may act. If there is no incorporator able to act, any person for whom an incorporator was acting as agent may act in his stead, or if such other person also dies or is for any reason unable to act, his legal representative may act.

§ 616. Greater Requirement as to Quorum and Vote of Shareholders

(a) The certificate of incorporation may contain provisions specifying either or both of the following:

(1) That the proportion of votes of shares, or the proportion of votes of shares of any class or series thereof, the holders of which shall be present in person or by proxy at any meeting of shareholders ... in order to constitute a quorum for the transaction of any business or of any specified item of business, including amendments to the certificate of incorporation, shall be greater than the proportion prescribed by this chapter in the absence of such provision.

(2) That the proportion of votes of shares, or votes of shares of a particular class or series of shares, that shall be necessary at any meeting of shareholders for the transaction of any business or of any specified item of business, including amendments to the certificate of incorporation, shall be greater than the proportion prescribed by this chapter in the absence of such provision.

(b) An amendment of the certificate of incorporation which changes or strikes out a provision permitted by this section, shall be authorized at a meeting of shareholders by two-thirds of the votes of the shares entitled to vote thereon, or of such greater proportion of votes of shares, or votes of shares of a particular class or series of shares, as may be provided specifically in the certificate of incorporation for changing or striking out a provision permitted by this section.

(c) If the certificate of incorporation of any corporation contains a provision authorized by this section, the existence of such provision shall be noted conspicuously on the face or back of every certificate for shares issued by such corporation, except that this requirement shall not apply to any corporation having any class of any equity security registered pursuant to Section twelve of the Securities Exchange Act of 1934, as amended.

§ 617. Voting by Class or Classes of Shares

(a) The certificate of incorporation may contain provisions specifying that any class or classes of shares or of any series thereof shall vote as a class in connection with the transaction of any business or of any specified item of business at a meeting of shareholders, including amendments to the certificate of incorporation.

(b) Where voting as a class is provided in the certificate of incorporation, it shall be by the proportionate vote so provided or, if no proportionate vote is provided, in the election of directors, by a plurality of the votes cast at such meeting by the holders of shares of such class entitled to vote in the election, or for any other corporate action, by a majority of the votes cast at such meeting by the holders of shares of such class entitled to vote thereon.

(c) Such voting by class shall be in addition to any other vote, including vote by class, required by this chapter and by the certificate of incorporation as permitted by this chapter.

§ 619. Powers of Supreme Court Respecting Elections

Upon the petition of any shareholder aggrieved by an election, and upon notice to the persons declared elected thereat, the corporation and such other persons as the court may direct, the supreme court at a special term held within the judicial district where the office of the corporation is located shall forthwith hear the proofs and allegations of the parties, and confirm the election, order a new election, or take such other action as justice may require.

§ 620. Agreements as to Voting; Provision in Certificate of Incorporation as to Control of Directors

(a) An agreement between two or more shareholders, if in writing and signed by the parties thereto, may provide that in exercising any voting rights, the shares held by them shall be voted as therein provided, or as they may agree, or as determined in accordance with a procedure agreed upon by them.

(b) A provision in the certificate of incorporation otherwise prohibited by law because it improperly restricts the board in its management of the business of the corporation, or improperly transfers to one or more shareholders or to one or more persons or corporations to be selected by him or them, all or any part of such management otherwise within the authority of the board under this chapter, shall nevertheless be valid:

(1) If all the incorporators or holders of record of all outstanding shares, whether or not having voting power, have authorized such provision in the certificate of incorporation or an amendment thereof; and

(2) If, subsequent to the adoption of such provision, shares are transferred or issued only to persons who had knowledge or notice thereof or consented in writing to such provision.

(c) A provision authorized by paragraph (b) shall be valid only so long as no shares of the corporation are listed on a national securities exchange or regularly quoted in an over-the-counter market by one or more members of a national or affiliated securities association.

(d)(1) Except as provided in paragraph (e), an amendment to strike out a provision authorized by paragraph (b) shall be authorized at a meeting of shareholders by (A)(i) for any corporation in existence on [February 22, 1998], two-thirds of the votes of the shares entitled to vote thereon and (ii) for any corporation in existence on the effective date of this clause the certificate of incorporation of which expressly provides such and for any corporation incorporated after the effective date of subparagraph (2) of this paragraph, a majority of the votes of the shares entitled to vote thereon or (B) in either case, by such greater proportion of votes of shares as may be required by the certificate of incorporation for that purpose.

(2) Any corporation may adopt an amendment of the certificate of incorporation in accordance with the applicable clause or subclause of paragraph (1) of this paragraph to provide that any further amendment of the certificate of incorporation that strikes out a provision authorized by paragraph (b) of this section shall be authorized at a meeting of the shareholders by a specified proportion of votes of the shares, or votes of a particular class or series of shares, entitled to vote thereon, provided that such proportion may not be less than a majority.

(e) Alternatively, if a provision authorized by paragraph (b) shall have ceased to be valid under this section, the board may authorize a certificate of amendment under section 805 (Certificate of amendment; contents) striking out such provision. Such certificate shall set forth the event by reason of which the provision ceased to be valid.

(f) The effect of any such provision authorized by paragraph (b) shall be to relieve the directors and impose upon the shareholders authorizing the same or consenting thereto the liability for managerial acts or omissions that is imposed on directors by this chapter to the extent that and so long as the discretion or powers of the board in its management of corporate affairs is controlled by any such provision.

(g) If the certificate of incorporation of any corporation contains a provision authorized by paragraph (b), the existence of such provision shall be noted conspicuously on the face or back of every certificate for shares issued by such corporation.

§ 621. Voting Trust Agreements

(a) Any shareholder or shareholders, under an agreement in writing, may transfer his or their shares to a voting trustee or trustees for the purpose of conferring the right to vote thereon for a period not exceeding ten years upon the terms and conditions therein stated. The certificates for shares so transferred shall be surrendered and cancelled and new certificates therefor issued to such trustee or trustees stating that they are issued under such agreement, and in the entry of such ownership in the record of the corporation that fact shall also be noted, and such trustee or trustees may vote the shares so transferred during the term of such agreement.

(b) The trustee or trustees shall keep available for inspection by holders of voting trust certificates at his or their office or at a place designated in such agreement or of which the holders of voting trust certificates have been notified in writing, correct and complete books and records of account relating to the trust, and a record containing the names and addresses of all persons who are holders of voting trust certificates and the number and class of shares represented by the certificates held by them and the dates when they became the owners thereof. The record may be in written form or any other form capable of being converted into written form within a reasonable time.

(c) A duplicate of every such agreement shall be filed in the office of the corporation and it and the record of voting trust certificate holders shall be subject to the same right of inspection by a shareholder of record or a holder of a voting trust certificate, in person or by agent or attorney, as are the records of the corporation under section 624 (Books and records; right of inspection, prima facie evidence). The shareholder or holder of a voting trust certificate shall be entitled to the remedies provided in that section.

(d) At any time within six months before the expiration of such voting trust agreement as originally fixed or as extended one or more times under this paragraph, one or more holders of voting trust certificates may, by agreement in writing, extend the duration of such voting trust agreement, nominating the same or substitute trustee or trustees, for an additional period not exceeding ten years. Such extension agreement shall not affect the rights or obligations of persons not parties thereto and shall in every respect comply with and be subject to all the provisions of this section applicable to the original voting trust agreement.

§ 622. Preemptive Rights

(a) As used in this section, the term:

(1) "Unlimited dividend rights" means the right without limitation as to amount either to all or to a share of the balance of current or liquidating dividends after the payment of dividends on any shares entitled to a preference.

(2) "Equity shares" means shares of any class, whether or not preferred as to dividends or assets, which have unlimited dividend rights.

(3) "Voting rights" means the right to vote for the election of one or more directors, excluding a right so to vote which is dependent on the happening of an event specified in the certificate of incorporation which would change the voting rights of any class of shares.

(4) "Voting shares" means shares of any class which have voting rights, but does not include bonds on which voting rights are conferred under section 518 (Corporate bonds).

(5) "Preemptive right" means the right to purchase shares or other securities to be issued or subject to rights or options to purchase, as such right is defined in this section.

(b)(1) With respect to any corporation incorporated prior to [February 22, 1998], except as otherwise provided in the certificate of incorporation, and except as provided in this section, the holders of equity shares of any class, in case of the proposed issuance by the corporation of, or the proposed granting by the corporation of rights or options to purchase, its equity shares of any class or any shares or other securities convertible into or carrying rights or options to purchase its equity shares of any class, shall, if the issuance of the equity shares proposed to be issued or issuable upon exercise of such rights or options or upon conversion of such other securities would adversely affect the unlimited dividend rights of such holders, have the right during a reasonable time and on reasonable conditions, both to be fixed by the board, to purchase such shares or other securities in such proportions as shall be determined as provided in this section.

(2) With respect to any corporation incorporated on or after [February 22, 1998], the holders of such shares shall not have any preemptive right, except as otherwise expressly provided in the certificate of incorporation.

(c) Except as otherwise provided in the certificate of incorporation, and except as provided in this section, the holders of voting shares of any class having any preemptive right under this paragraph on the date immediately prior to [February 22, 1998], in case of the proposed issuance by the corporation of, or the proposed granting by the corporation of rights or options to purchase, its voting shares of any class or any shares or other securities convertible into or carrying rights or options to purchase its voting shares of any class, shall, if the issuance of the voting shares proposed to be issued or issuable upon exercise of such rights or options or upon conversion of such other securities would adversely affect the voting rights of such holders, have the right during a reasonable time and on reasonable conditions, both to be fixed by the board, to purchase such shares or other securities in such proportions as shall be determined as provided in this section.

(d) The preemptive right provided for in paragraphs (b) and (c) shall entitle shareholders having such rights to purchase the shares or other securities to be offered or optioned for sale as nearly as practicable in such proportions as would, if such preemptive right were exercised, preserve the relative unlimited dividend rights and voting rights of such holders and at a price or prices not less favorable than the price or prices at which such shares or other securities are proposed to be offered for sale to others, without deduction of such reasonable expenses of and compensation for the sale, underwriting or purchase of such shares or other securities by underwriters or dealers as may lawfully be paid by the corporation. In case each of the shares entitling the holders thereof to preemptive rights does not confer the same unlimited dividend right or voting right, the board shall apportion the shares or other securities to be offered or optioned for sale among the shareholders having preemptive rights to purchase them in such proportions as in the opinion of the board shall preserve as far as practicable the relative unlimited dividend rights and voting rights of the holders at the time of such offering. The apportionment made by the board shall, in the absence of fraud or bad faith, be binding upon all shareholders.

(e) Unless otherwise provided in the certificate of incorporation, shares or other securities offered for sale or subjected to rights or options to purchase shall not be subject to preemptive rights under paragraph (b) or (c) of this section if they:

(1) Are to be issued by the board to effect a merger or consolidation or offered or subjected to rights or options for consideration other than cash;

(2) Are to be issued or subjected to rights or options under paragraph (d) of section 505 (Rights and options to purchase shares; issue of rights and options to directors, officers and employees);

(3) Are to be issued to satisfy conversion or option rights theretofore granted by the corporation;

(4) Are treasury shares;

(5) Are part of the shares or other securities of the corporation authorized in its original certificate of incorporation and are issued, sold or optioned within two years from the date of filing such certificate; or

(6) Are to be issued under a plan of reorganization approved in a proceeding under any applicable act of congress relating to reorganization of corporations.

(f) Shareholders of record entitled to preemptive rights on the record date fixed by the board under section 604 (Fixing record date), or, if no record date is fixed, then on the record date determined under section 604, and no others shall be entitled to the right defined in this section.

(g) The board shall cause to be given to each shareholder entitled to purchase shares or other securities in accordance with this section, a notice directed to him in the manner provided in section 605 (Notice of meetings of shareholders) setting forth the time within which and the terms and conditions upon which the shareholder may purchase such shares or other securities and also the apportionment made of the right to purchase among the shareholders entitled to preemptive rights. Such notice shall be given personally or by mail at least fifteen days prior to the expiration of the period during which the shareholder shall have the right to purchase. All shareholders entitled to preemptive rights to whom notice shall have been given as aforesaid shall be deemed conclusively to have had a reasonable time in which to exercise their preemptive rights.

(h) Shares or other securities which have been offered to shareholders having preemptive rights to purchase and which have not been purchased by them within the time fixed by the board may thereafter, for a period of not exceeding one year following the expiration of the time during which shareholders might have exercised such preemptive rights, be issued, sold or subjected to rights or options to any other person or persons at a price, without deduction of such reasonable expenses of and compensation for the sale, underwriting or purchase of such shares by underwriters or dealers as may lawfully be paid by the corporation, not less than that at which they were offered to such shareholders. Any such shares or other securities not so issued, sold or subjected to rights or options to others during such one year period shall thereafter again be subject to the preemptive rights of shareholders.

(i) Except as otherwise provided in the certificate of incorporation and except as provided in this section, no holder of any shares of any class shall as such holder have any preemptive right to purchase any other shares or securities of any class which at any time may be sold or offered for sale by the corporation. Unless otherwise provided in the certificate of incorporation, holders of bonds on which voting rights are conferred under section 518 shall have no preemptive rights.

§ 623. Procedure to Enforce Shareholder's Right to Receive Payment for Shares

(a) A shareholder intending to enforce his right under a section of this chapter to receive payment for his shares if the proposed corporate action referred to therein is taken shall file with the corporation, before the meeting of shareholders at which the action is submitted to a vote, or at such meeting but before the vote, written objection to the action. ...

(c) Within twenty days after the giving of notice to him, any shareholder from whom written objection was not required and who elects to dissent shall file with the corporation a written notice of such election, stating his name and residence address, the number and classes of shares as to which he dissents and a demand for payment of the fair value of his shares. ...

(g) Within fifteen days after the expiration of the period within which shareholders may file their notices of election to dissent, or within fifteen days after the proposed corporate action is consummated, whichever is later (but in no case later than ninety days from the shareholders' authorization date), the corporation or, in the case of a merger or consolidation, the surviving or new corporation, shall make a written offer by registered mail to each shareholder who has filed such notice of election to pay for his shares at a specified price which the corporation considers to be their fair value. Such offer shall be accompanied by a statement setting forth the aggregate number of shares with respect to which notices of election to dissent have been received and the aggregate number of holders of such shares. If the corporate action has been consummated, such offer shall also be accompanied by (1) advance payment to each such shareholder who has submitted the certificates representing his shares to the corporation, as provided in paragraph (f), of an amount equal to eighty percent of the amount of such offer, or (2) as to each shareholder who has not yet submitted his certificates a statement that advance payment to him of an amount equal to eighty percent of the amount of such offer will be made by the corporation promptly upon submission of his certificates. If the corporate action has not been consummated at the time of the making of the offer, such advance payment or statement as to advance payment shall be sent to each shareholder entitled thereto forthwith upon consummation of the corporate action. Every advance payment or statement as to advance payment shall include advice to the shareholder to the effect that acceptance of such payment does not constitute a waiver of any dissenters' rights. ...;

(h) The following procedure shall apply if the corporation fails to make such offer within such period of fifteen days, or if it makes the offer and any dissenting shareholder or shareholders fail to agree with it within the period of thirty days thereafter upon the price to be paid for their shares:

(1) The corporation shall, within twenty days after the expiration of whichever is applicable of the two periods last mentioned, institute a special proceeding in the supreme court in the judicial district in which the office of the corporation is located to determine the rights of dissenting shareholders and to fix the fair value of their shares. If, in the case of merger or consolidation, the surviving or new corporation is a foreign corporation without an office in this state, such proceeding shall be brought in the county where the office of the domestic corporation, whose shares are to be valued, was located.

(2) If the corporation fails to institute such proceeding within such period of twenty days, any dissenting shareholder may institute such proceeding for the same purpose not later than thirty days after the expiration of such twenty day period. If such proceeding is not instituted within such thirty day period, all dissenter's rights shall be lost unless the supreme court, for good cause shown, shall otherwise direct.

(3) All dissenting shareholders, excepting those who, as provided in paragraph (g), have agreed with the corporation upon the price to be paid for their shares, shall be made parties to such proceeding, which shall have the effect of an action quasi in rem against their shares. The corporation shall serve a copy of the petition in such proceeding upon each dissenting shareholder who is a resident of this state in the manner provided by law for the service of a summons, and upon each nonresident dissenting shareholder either by registered mail and publication, or in such other manner as is permitted by law. The jurisdiction of the court shall be plenary and exclusive.

(4) The court shall determine whether each dissenting shareholder, as to whom the corporation requests the court to make such determination, is entitled to receive payment for his shares. If the corporation does not request any such determination or if the court finds that any dissenting shareholder is so entitled, it shall proceed to fix the value of the shares, which, for the purposes of this section, shall be the fair value as of the close of business on the day prior to the shareholders' authorization date. In fixing the fair value of the shares, the court shall consider the nature of the transaction giving rise to the shareholder's right to receive payment for shares and its effects on the corporation and its shareholders, the concepts and methods then customary in the relevant securities and financial markets for determining fair value of shares of a corporation engaging in a similar transaction under comparable circumstances and all other relevant factors. The court shall determine the fair value of the shares without a jury and without referral to an appraiser or referee. Upon application by the corporation or by any shareholder who is a party to the proceeding, the court may, in its discretion, permit pretrial disclosure, including, but not limited to, disclosure of any expert's reports relating to the fair value of the shares whether or not intended for use at the trial in the proceeding....

§ 624. Books and Records; Right of Inspection, Prima Facie Evidence

(a) Each corporation shall keep correct and complete books and records of account and shall keep minutes of the proceedings of its shareholders, board and executive committee, if any, and shall keep at the office of the corporation in this state or at the office of its transfer agent or registrar in this state, a record containing the names and addresses of all shareholders, the number and class of shares held by each and the dates when they respectively became the owners of record thereof. Any of the foregoing books, minutes or records may be in written form or in any other form capable of being converted into written form within a reasonable time.

(b) Any person who shall have been a shareholder of record of a corporation upon at least five days' written demand shall have the right to examine in person or by agent or attorney, during usual business hours, its minutes of the proceedings of its shareholders and record of shareholders and to make extracts therefrom for any purpose reasonably related to such person's interest as a shareholder. Holders of voting trust certificates representing shares of the corporation shall be regarded as shareholders for the purpose of this section. Any such agent or attorney shall be authorized in a writing that satisfies the requirements of a writing under paragraph (b) of section 609 (Proxies). A corporation requested to provide information pursuant to this paragraph shall make available such information in written form and in any format in which such information is maintained by the corporation and shall not be required to provide such information in any other format. If a request made pursuant to this paragraph includes a request to furnish information regarding beneficial owners, the corporation shall make available such information in its possession regarding beneficial owners as is provided to the corporation by a registered broker or dealer or a bank, association or other entity that exercises fiduciary powers in connection with the forwarding of information to such owners. The corporation shall not be required to obtain information about beneficial owners not in its possession.

(c) An inspection authorized by paragraph (b) may be denied to such shareholder or other person upon his refusal to furnish to the corporation, its transfer agent or registrar an affidavit that such inspection is not desired for a purpose which is in the interest of a business or object other than the business of the corporation and that he has not within five years sold or offered for sale any list of shareholders of any corporation of any type or kind, whether or not formed under the laws of this state, or aided or abetted any person in procuring any such record of shareholders for any such purpose.

(d) Upon refusal by the corporation or by an officer or agent of the corporation to permit an inspection of the minutes of the proceedings of its shareholders or of the record of shareholders as herein provided, the person making the demand for inspection may apply to the supreme court in the judicial district where the office of the corporation is located, upon such notice as the court may direct, for an order directing the corporation, its officer or agent to show cause why an order should not be granted permitting such inspection by the applicant. Upon the return day of the order to show cause, the court shall hear the parties summarily, by affidavit or otherwise, and if it appears that the applicant is qualified and entitled to such inspection, the court shall grant an order compelling such inspection and awarding such further relief as to the court may seem just and proper.

(e) Upon the written request of any shareholder the corporation shall give or mail to such shareholder an annual balance sheet and profit and loss statement for the preceding fiscal year, and, if any interim balance sheet or profit and loss statement has been distributed to its shareholders or otherwise made available to the public, the most recent such interim balance sheet or profit and loss statement. The corporation shall be allowed a reasonable time to prepare such annual balance sheet and profit and loss statement.

(f) Nothing herein contained shall impair the power of courts to compel the production for examination of the books and records of a corporation.

(g) The books and records specified in paragraph (a) shall be prima facie evidence of the facts therein stated in favor of the plaintiff in any action or special proceeding against such corporation or any of its officers, directors or shareholders.

§ 626. Shareholders' Derivative Action Brought in the Right of the Corporation to Procure a Judgment in Its Favor

(a) An action may be brought in the right of a domestic or foreign corporation to procure a judgment in its favor, by a holder of shares or of voting trust certificates of the corporation or of a beneficial interest in such shares or certificates.

(b) In any such action, it shall be made to appear that the plaintiff is such a holder at the time of bringing the action and that he was such a holder at the time of the transaction of which he complains, or that his shares or his interest therein devolved upon him by operation of law.

(c) In any such action, the complaint shall set forth with particularity the efforts of the plaintiff to secure the initiation of such action by the board or the reasons for not making such effort.

(d) Such action shall not be discontinued, compromised or settled, without the approval of the court having jurisdiction of the action. If the court shall determine that the interests of the shareholders or any class or classes thereof will be substantially affected by such discontinuance, compromise, or settlement, the court, in its discretion, may direct that notice, by publication or otherwise, shall be given to the shareholders or class or classes thereof whose interest it determines will be so affected; if notice is so directed to be given, the court may determine which one or more of the parties to the action shall bear the expense of giving the same, in such amount as the court shall determine and find to be reasonable in the circumstances, and the amount of such expense shall be awarded as special costs of the action and recoverable in the same manner as statutory taxable costs.

(e) If the action on behalf of the corporation was successful, in whole or in part, or if anything was received by the plaintiff or plaintiffs or a claimant or claimants as the result of a judgment, compromise or settlement of an action or claim, the court may award the plaintiff or plaintiffs, claimant or claimants, reasonable expenses, including reasonable attorney's fees, and shall direct him or them to account to the corporation for the remainder of the proceeds so received by him or them. This paragraph shall not apply to any judgment rendered for the benefit of injured shareholders only and limited to a recovery of the loss or damage sustained by them.

§ 627. Security for Expenses in Shareholders' Derivative Action Brought in the Right of the Corporation to Procure a Judgment in Its Favor

In any action specified in section 626 (Shareholders' derivative action brought in the right of the corporation to procure a judgment in its favor), unless the plaintiff or plaintiffs hold five percent or more of any class of the outstanding shares or hold voting trust certificates or a beneficial interest in shares representing five percent or more of any class of such shares, or the shares, voting trust certificates and beneficial interest of such plaintiff or plaintiffs have a fair value in excess of fifty thousand dollars, the corporation in whose right such action is brought shall be entitled at any stage of the proceedings before final judgment to require the plaintiff or plaintiffs to give security for the reasonable expenses, including attorney's fees, which may be incurred by it in connection with such action and by the other parties defendant in connection therewith for which the corporation may become liable under this chapter, under any contract or otherwise under law, to which the corporation shall have recourse in such amount as the court having jurisdiction of such action shall determine upon the termination of such action. The amount of such security may thereafter from time to time be increased or decreased in the discretion of the court having jurisdiction of such action upon showing that the security provided has or may become inadequate or excessive.

§ 628. Liability of Subscribers and Shareholders

(a) A holder of or subscriber for shares of a corporation shall be under no obligation to the corporation for payment for such shares other than the obligation to pay the unpaid portion of his subscription which in no event shall be less than the amount of the consideration for which such shares could be issued lawfully.

(b) Any person becoming an assignee or transferee of shares or of a subscription for shares in good faith and without knowledge or notice that the full consideration therefor has not been paid shall not be personally liable for any unpaid portion of such consideration, but the transferor shall remain liable therefor.

(c) No person holding shares in any corporation as collateral security shall be personally liable as a shareholder but the person pledging such shares shall be considered the holder thereof and shall be so liable. No executor, administrator, guardian, trustee or other fiduciary shall be personally liable as a shareholder, but the estate and funds in the hands of such executor, administrator, guardian, trustee or other fiduciary shall be liable.

§ 629. Certain Transfers or Assignments by Shareholders or Subscribers; Effect

Any transfer or assignment by a shareholder of his shares, or by a subscriber for shares of his interest in the corporation, shall not relieve him of any liability as a shareholder or subscriber if at the time of such transfer or assignment the aggregate of the corporation's property, exclusive of any property which it may have conveyed, transferred, concealed, removed, or permitted to be concealed or removed, with intent to defraud, hinder or delay its creditors, is not at a fair valuation sufficient in amount to pay its debts, or if such condition is imminent.

§ 630. Liability of Shareholders for Wages Due to Laborers, Servants or Employees

(a) The ten largest shareholders, as determined by the fair value of their beneficial interest as of the beginning of the period during which the unpaid services referred to in this section are performed, of every corporation (other than an investment company registered as such under an act of congress entitled "Investment Company Act of 1940"), no shares of which are listed on a national securities exchange or regularly quoted in an over-the-counter market by one or more members of a national or an affiliated securities association, shall jointly and severally be personally liable for all debts, wages or salaries due and owing to any of its laborers, servants or employees other than contractors, for services performed by them for such corporation. Before such laborer, servant or employee shall charge such shareholder for such services, he shall give notice in writing to such shareholder that he intends to hold him liable under this section. Such notice shall be given within one hundred and eighty days after termination of such services, except that if, within such period, the laborer, servant or employee demands an examination of the record of shareholders under paragraph (b) of section 624 (Books and records; right of inspection, prima facie evidence), such notice may be given within sixty days after he has been given the opportunity to examine the record of shareholders. An action to enforce such liability shall be commenced within ninety days after the return of an execution unsatisfied against the corporation upon a judgment recovered against it for such services.

(b) For the purposes of this section, wages or salaries shall mean all compensation and benefits payable by an employer to or for the account of the employee for personal services rendered by such employee. These shall specifically include but not be limited to salaries, overtime, vacation, holiday and severance pay; employer contributions to or payments of insurance or welfare benefits; employer contributions to pension or annuity funds; and any other moneys properly due or payable for services rendered by such employee.

(c) A shareholder who has paid more than his pro rata share under this section shall be entitled to contribution pro rata from the other shareholders liable under this section with respect to the excess so paid, over and above his pro rata share, and may sue them jointly or severally or any number of them to recover the amount due from them. Such recovery may be had in a separate action. As used in this paragraph, "pro rata" means in proportion to beneficial share interest. Before a shareholder may claim contribution from other shareholders under this paragraph, he shall, unless they have been given notice by a laborer, servant or employee under paragraph (a), give them notice in writing that he intends to hold them so liable to him. Such notice shall be given by him within twenty days after the date that notice was given to him by a laborer, servant or employee under paragraph (a).

ARTICLE 7

DIRECTORS AND OFFICERS

§ 701. Board of Directors

Subject to any provision in the certificate of incorporation authorized by paragraph (b) of section 620 (Agreements as to voting; provision in certificate of incorporation as to control of directors) or by paragraph (b) of section 715 (Officers), the business of a corporation shall be managed under the direction of its board of directors, each of whom shall be at least eighteen years of age. The certificate of incorporation or the by-laws may prescribe other qualifications for directors.

§ 702. Number of Directors

(a) The board of directors shall consist of one or more members. The number of directors constituting the board may be fixed by the bylaws, or by action of the shareholders or of the board under the specific provisions of a by-law adopted by the shareholders. If not otherwise fixed under this paragraph, the number shall be one. As used in this article, "entire board" means the total number of directors which the corporation would have if there were no vacancies.

(b) The number of directors may be increased or decreased by amendment of the by-laws, or by action of the shareholders or of the board under the specific provisions of a by-law adopted by the shareholders, subject to the following limitations.

(1) If the board is authorized by the by-laws to change the number of directors, whether by amending the by-laws or by taking action under the specific provisions of a by-law adopted by the shareholders, such amendment or action shall require the vote of a majority of the entire board.

(2) No decrease shall shorten the term of any incumbent director.

§ 703. Election and Term of Directors

(a) At each annual meeting of shareholders, directors shall be elected to hold office until the next annual meeting except as authorized by section 704 (Classification of directors). The certificate of incorporation may provide for the election of one or more directors by the holders of the shares of any class or series, or by the holders of bonds entitled to vote in the election of directors pursuant to section 518 (Corporate bonds), voting as a class.

(b) Each director shall hold office until the expiration of the term for which he is elected, and until his successor has been elected and qualified.

§ 704. Classification of Directors

(a) The certificate of incorporation or the specific provisions of a by-law adopted by the shareholders may provide that the directors be divided into either two, three or four classes. All classes shall be as nearly equal in number as possible. The terms of office of the directors initially classified shall be as follows: that of the first class shall expire at the next annual meeting of shareholders, the second class at the second succeeding annual meeting, the third class, if any, at the third succeeding annual meeting, and the fourth class, if any, at the fourth succeeding annual meeting.

(b) At each annual meeting after such initial classification, directors to replace those whose terms expire at such annual meting shall be elected to hold office until the second succeeding annual meeting if there are two classes, the third succeeding annual meeting if there are three classes, or the fourth succeeding annual meeting if there are four classes.

(c) If directors are classified and the number of directors is thereafter changed:

(1) Any newly created directorships or any decrease in directorships shall be so apportioned among the classes as to make all classes as nearly equal in number as possible.

(2) When the number of directors is increased by the board and any newly created directorships are filled by the board, there shall be no classification of the additional directors until the next annual meeting of shareholders.

§ 705. Newly Created Directorships and Vacancies

(a) Newly created directorships resulting from an increase in the number of directors and vacancies occurring in the board for any reason except the removal of directors without cause may be filled by vote of the board. If the number of the directors then in office is less than a quorum, such newly created directorships and vacancies may be filled by vote of a majority of the directors then in office. Nothing in this paragraph shall affect any provision of the certificate of incorporation or the by-laws which provides that such newly created directorships or vacancies shall be filled by vote of the shareholders, or any provision of the certificate of incorporation specifying greater requirements as permitted under section 709 (Greater requirements as to quorum and vote of directors).

(b) Unless the certificate of incorporation or the specific provisions of a by-law adopted by the shareholders provide that the board may fill vacancies occurring in the board by reason of the removal of directors without cause, such vacancies may be filled only by vote of the shareholders.

(c) A director elected to fill a vacancy, unless elected by the shareholders, shall hold office until the next meeting of shareholders at which the election of directors is in the regular order of business, and until his successor has been elected and qualified.

(d) Unless otherwise provided in the certificate of incorporation or by-laws, notwithstanding the provisions of paragraphs (a) and (b) of this section, whenever the holders of any class or classes of shares or series thereof are entitled to elect one or more directors by the certificate of incorporation, any vacancy that may be filled by the board or a majority of the directors then in office, as the case may be, shall be filled by a majority of the directors elected by such class or classes or series thereof then in office, or, if no such director is in office, then as provided in paragraph (a) or (b) of this section, as the case may be.

§ 706. Removal of Directors

(a) Any or all of the directors may be removed for cause by vote of the shareholders. The certificate of incorporation or the specific provisions of a by-law adopted by the shareholders may provide for such removal by action of the board, except in the case of any director elected by cumulative voting, or by the holders of the shares of any class or series, or holders of bonds, voting as a class, when so entitled by the provisions of the certificate of incorporation.

(b) If the certificate of incorporation or the by-laws so provide, any or all of the directors may be removed without cause by vote of the shareholders.

(c) The removal of directors, with or without cause, as provided in paragraphs (a) and (b) is subject to the following:

(1) In the case of a corporation having cumulative voting, no director may be removed when the votes cast against his removal would be sufficient to elect him if voted cumulatively at an election at which the same total number of votes were cast and the entire board, or the entire class of directors of which he is a member, were then being elected; and

(2) When by the provisions of the certificate of incorporation the holders of the shares of any class or series, or holders of bonds, voting as a class, are entitled to elect one or more directors, any director so elected may be removed only by the applicable vote of the holders of the shares of that class or series, or the holders of such bonds, voting as a class.

(d) An action to procure a judgment removing a director for cause may be brought by the attorney-general or by the holders of ten percent of the outstanding shares, whether or not entitled to vote. The court may bar from re-election any director so removed for a period fixed by the court.

§ 707. Quorum of Directors

Unless a greater proportion is required by the certificate of incorporation, a majority of the entire board shall constitute a quorum for the transaction of business or of any specified item of business, except that the certificate of incorporation or the by-laws may fix the quorum at less than a majority of the entire board but not less than one-third thereof.

§ 708. Action by the Board

(a) Except as otherwise provided in this chapter, any reference in this chapter to corporate action to be taken by the board shall mean such action at a meeting of the board.

(b) Unless otherwise restricted by the certificate of incorporation or the by-laws, any action required or permitted to be taken by the board or any committee thereof may be taken without a meeting if all members of the board or the committee consent in writing to the adoption of a resolution authorizing the action. The resolution and the written consents thereto by the members of the board or committee shall be filed with the minutes of the proceedings of the board or committee.

(c) Unless otherwise restricted by the certificate of incorporation or the by-laws, any one or more members of the board or any committee thereof may participate in a meeting of such board or committee by means of a conference telephone or similar communications equipment allowing all persons participating in the meeting to hear each other at the same time. Participation by such means shall constitute presence in person at a meeting.

(d) Except as otherwise provided in this chapter, the vote of a majority of the directors present at the time of the vote, if a quorum is present at such time, shall be the act of the board.

§ 709. Greater Requirement as to Quorum and Vote of Directors

(a) The certificate of incorporation may contain provisions specifying either or both of the following:

(1) That the proportion of directors that shall constitute a quorum for the transaction of business or of any specified item of business shall be greater than the proportion prescribed by this chapter in the absence of such provision.

(2) That the proportion of votes of directors that shall be necessary for the transaction of business or of any specified item of business shall be greater than the proportion prescribed by this chapter in the absence of such provision.

(b)(1) An amendment of the certificate of incorporation which changes or strikes out a provision permitted by this section shall be authorized at a meeting of shareholders by (A)(i) for any corporation in existence on [February 22, 1998], two-thirds of the votes of all outstanding shares entitled to vote thereon, and (ii) for any corporation in existence on [February 22, 1998], the certificate of incorporation of which expressly provides such and for any corporation incorporated after the effective date of subparagraph (2) of this paragraph, a majority of the votes of all outstanding shares entitled to vote thereon or (B) in either case, such greater proportion of votes of shares, or votes of a class or series of shares, as may be provided specifically in the certificate of incorporation for changing or striking out a provision permitted by the section.

(2) Any corporation may adopt an amendment of the certificate of incorporation in accordance with any applicable clause or subclause of subparagraph (1) of this paragraph to provide that any further amendment of the certificate of incorporation that changes or strikes out a provision permitted by this section shall be authorized at a meeting of the shareholders by a specified proportion of the votes of shares, or particular class or series of shares, entitled to vote thereon, provided that such proportion may not be less than a majority.

§ 712. Executive Committee and Other Committees

(a) If the certificate of incorporation or the by-laws so provide, the board, by resolution adopted by a majority of the entire board, may designate from among its members an executive committee and other committees, each consisting of one or more directors, and each of which, to the extent provided in the resolution or in the certificate of incorporation or by-laws, shall have all the authority of the board, except that no such committee shall have authority as to the following matters:

(1) The submission to shareholders of any action that needs shareholders' approval under this chapter.

(2) The filling of vacancies in the board of directors or in any committee.

(3) The fixing of compensation of the directors for serving on the board or on any committee.

(4) The amendment or repeal of the by-laws, or the adoption of new by-laws.

(5) The amendment or repeal of any resolution of the board which by its terms shall not be so amendable or repealable.

(b) The board may designate one or more directors as alternate members of any such committee, who may replace any absent or disqualified member or members at any meeting of such committee.

(c) Each such committee shall serve at the pleasure of the board. The designation of any such committee, the delegation thereto of authority, or action by any such committee pursuant to such authority shall not alone constitute performance by any member of the board who is not a member of the committee in question, of his duty to the corporation under section 717 (Duty of directors).

§ 713. Interested Directors

(a) No contract or other transaction between a corporation and one or more of its directors, or between a corporation and any other corporation, firm, association or other entity in which one or more of its directors are directors or officers, or have a substantial financial interest, shall be either void or voidable for this reason alone or by reason alone that such director or directors are present at the meeting of the board, or of a committee thereof, which approves such contract or transaction, or that his or their votes are counted for such purpose:

(1) If the material facts as to such director's interest in such contract or transaction and as to any such common directorship, officership or financial interest are disclosed in good faith or known to the board or committee, and the board or committee approves such contract or transaction by a vote sufficient for such purpose without counting the vote of such interested director or, if the votes of the disinterested

directors are insufficient to constitute an act of the board as defined in section 708 (Action by the board), by unanimous vote of the disinterested directors; or

(2) If the material facts as to such director's interest in such contract or transaction and as to any such common directorship, officership or financial interest are disclosed in good faith or known to the shareholders entitled to vote thereon, and such contract or transaction is approved by vote of such shareholders.

(b) If a contract or other transaction between a corporation and one or more of its directors, or between a corporation and any other corporation, firm, association or other entity in which one or more of its directors are directors or officers, or have a substantial financial interest, is not approved in accordance with paragraph (a), the corporation may avoid the contract or transaction unless the party or parties thereto shall establish affirmatively that the contract or transaction was fair and reasonable as to the corporation at the time it was approved by the board, a committee or the shareholders.

(c) Common or interested directors may be counted in determining the presence of a quorum at a meeting of the board or of a committee which approves such contract or transaction.

(d) The certificate of incorporation may contain additional restrictions on contracts or transactions between a corporation and its directors and may provide that contracts or transactions in violation of such restrictions shall be void or voidable by the corporation.

(e) Unless otherwise provided in the certificate of incorporation or the by-laws, the board shall have authority to fix the compensation of directors for services in any capacity.

§ 714. Loans to Directors

(a) A corporation may not lend money to or guarantee the obligation of a director of the corporation unless:

(1) the particular loan or guarantee is approved by the shareholders, with the holders of a majority of the votes of the shares entitled to vote thereon constituting a quorum, but shares held of record or beneficially by directors who are benefitted by such loan or guarantee shall not be entitled to vote or to be included in the determination of a quorum; or

(2) with respect to any corporation in existence on the effective date of this subparagraph (2) the certificate of incorporation of which expressly provides such and with respect to any corporation incorporated after the effective date of this subparagraph (2), the board determines that the loan or guarantee benefits the corporation and either approves the specific loan or guarantee or a general plan authorizing loans and guarantees.

(b) The fact that a loan or guarantee is made in violation of this section does not affect the borrower's liability on the loan.

§ 715. Officers

(a) The board may elect or appoint a president, one or more vice-presidents, a secretary and a treasurer, and such other officers as it may determine, or as may be provided in the by-laws.

(b) The certificate of incorporation may provide that all officers or that specified officers shall be elected by the shareholders instead of by the board.

(c) Unless otherwise provided in the certificate of incorporation or the by-laws, all officers shall be elected or appointed to hold office until the meeting of the board following the next annual meeting of shareholders or, in the case of officers elected by the shareholders, until the next annual meeting of shareholders.

(d) Each officer shall hold office for the term for which he is elected or appointed, and until his successor has been elected or appointed and qualified.

(e) Any two or more offices may be held by the same person. When all of the issued and outstanding stock of the corporation is owned by one person, such person may hold all or any combination of offices.

(f) The board may require any officer to give security for the faithful performance of his duties.

(g) All officers as between themselves and the corporation shall have such authority and perform such duties in the management of the corporation as may be provided in the by-laws or, to the extent not so provided, by the board.

(h) An officer shall perform his duties as an officer in good faith and with that degree of care which an ordinarily prudent person in a like position would use under similar circumstances. In performing his duties, an officer shall be entitled to rely on information, opinions, reports or statements including financial statements and other financial data, in each case prepared or presented by:

(1) one or more other officers or employees of the corporation or of any other corporation of which at least fifty percentum of the outstanding shares of stock entitling the holders thereof to vote for the election of directors is owned directly or indirectly by the corporation, whom the officer believes to be reliable and competent in the matters presented, or

(2) counsel, public accountants or other persons as to matters which the officer believes to be within such person's professional or expert competence, so long as in so relying he shall be acting in good faith and with such degree of care, but he shall not be considered to be acting in good faith if he has knowledge concerning the matter in question that

would cause such reliance to be unwarranted. A person who so performs his duties shall have no liability by reason of being or having been an officer of the corporation.

§ 716. Removal of Officers

(a) Any officer elected or appointed by the board may be removed by the board with or without cause. An officer elected by the shareholders may be removed, with or without cause, only by vote of the shareholders, but his authority to act as an officer may be suspended by the board for cause.

(b) The removal of an officer without cause shall be without prejudice to his contract rights, if any. The election or appointment of an officer shall not of itself create contract rights.

(c) An action to procure a judgment removing an officer for cause may be brought by the attorney-general or by ten percent of the votes of the outstanding shares, whether or not entitled to vote. The court may bar from re-election or reappointment any officer so removed for a period fixed by the court.

§ 717. Duty of Directors

(a) A director shall perform his duties as a director, including his duties as a member of any committee of the board upon which he may serve, in good faith and with that degree of care which an ordinarily prudent person in a like position would use under similar circumstances. In performing his duties, a director shall be entitled to rely on information, opinions, reports or statements including financial statements and other financial data, in each case prepared or presented by:

(1) one or more officers or employees of the corporation or of any other corporation of which at least fifty percentum of the outstanding shares of stock entitling the holders thereof to vote for the election of directors is owned directly or indirectly by the corporation, whom the director believes to be reliable and competent in the matters presented,

(2) counsel, public accountants or other persons as to matters which the director believes to be within such person's professional or expert competence, or

(3) a committee of the board upon which he does not serve, duly designated in accordance with a provision of the certificate of incorporation or the by-laws, as to matters within its designated authority, which committee the director believes to merit confidence, so long as in so relying he shall be acting in good faith and with such degree of care, but he shall not be considered to be acting in good faith if he has knowledge concerning the matter in question that would cause such reliance to be unwarranted. A person who so performs his duties shall

have no liability by reason of being or having been a director of the corporation.

(b) In taking action, including, without limitation, action which may involve or relate to a change or potential change in the control of the corporation, a director shall be entitled to consider, without limitation, (1) both the long-term and the short-term interests of the corporation and its shareholders and (2) the effects that the corporation's actions may have in the short-term or in the long-term upon any of the following:

(i) the prospects for potential growth, development, productivity and profitability of the corporation;

(ii) the corporation's current employees;

(iii) the corporation's retired employees and other beneficiaries receiving or entitled to receive retirement, welfare or similar benefits from or pursuant to any plan sponsored, or agreement entered into, by the corporation;

(iv) the corporation's customers and creditors; and

(v) the ability of the corporation to provide, as a going concern, goods, services, employment opportunities and employment benefits and otherwise to contribute to the communities in which it does business.

Nothing in this paragraph shall create any duties owed by any director to any person or entity to consider or afford any particular weight to any of the foregoing or abrogate any duty of the directors, either statutory or recognized by common law or court decisions.

For purposes of this paragraph, "control" shall mean the possession, directly or indirectly, of the power to direct or cause the direction of the management and policies of the corporation, whether through the ownership of voting stock, by contract, or otherwise.

§ 719. Liability of Directors in Certain Cases

(a) Directors of a corporation who vote for or concur in any of the following corporate actions shall be jointly and severally liable to the corporation for the benefit of its creditors or shareholders, to the extent of any injury suffered by such persons, respectively, as a result of such action:

(1) The declaration of any dividend or other distribution to the extent that it is contrary to the provisions of paragraphs (a) and (b) of section 510 (Dividends or other distributions in cash or property).

(2) The purchase of the shares of the corporation to the extent that it is contrary to the provisions of section 513 (Purchase or redemption by a corporation of its own shares).

(3) The distribution of assets to shareholders after dissolution of the corporation without paying or adequately providing for all known liabili-

ties of the corporation, excluding any claims not filed by creditors within the time limit set in a notice given to creditors under articles 10 (Nonjudicial dissolution) or 11 (Judicial dissolution).

(4) The making of any loan contrary to section 714 (Loans to directors).

(b) A director who is present at a meeting of the board, or any committee thereof, when action specified in paragraph (a) is taken shall be presumed to have concurred in the action unless his dissent thereto shall be entered in the minutes of the meeting, or unless he shall submit his written dissent to the person acting as the secretary of the meeting before the adjournment thereof, or shall deliver or send by registered mail such dissent to the secretary of the corporation promptly after the adjournment of the meeting. Such right to dissent shall not apply to a director who voted in favor of such action. A director who is absent from a meeting of the board, or any committee thereof, when such action is taken shall be presumed to have concurred in the action unless he shall deliver or send by registered mail his dissent thereto to the secretary of the corporation or shall cause such dissent to be filed with the minutes of the proceedings of the board or committee within a reasonable time after learning of such action.

(c) Any director against whom a claim is successfully asserted under this section shall be entitled to contribution from the other directors who voted for or concurred in the action upon which the claim is asserted.

(d) Directors against whom a claim is successfully asserted under this section shall be entitled, to the extent of the amounts paid by them to the corporation as a result of such claims:

(1) Upon payment to the corporation of any amount of an improper dividend or distribution, to be subrogated to the rights of the corporation against shareholders who received such dividend or distribution with knowledge of facts indicating that it was not authorized by section 510, in proportion to the amounts received by them respectively.

(2) Upon payment to the corporation of any amount of the purchase price of an improper purchase of shares, to have the corporation rescind such purchase of shares and recover for their benefit, but at their expense, the amount of such purchase price from any seller who sold such shares with knowledge of facts indicating that such purchase of shares by the corporation was not authorized by section 513.

(3) Upon payment to the corporation of the claim of any creditor by reason of a violation of subparagraph (a)(3), to be subrogated to the rights of the corporation against shareholders who received an improper distribution of assets.

(4) Upon payment to the corporation of the amount of any loan made contrary to section 714, to be subrogated to the rights of the corporation against a director who received the improper loan.

(e) A director shall not be liable under this section if, in the circumstances, he performed his duty to the corporation under paragraph (a) of section 717.

(f) This section shall not affect any liability otherwise imposed by law upon any director.

§ 720. Action Against Directors and Officers for Misconduct

(a) An action may be brought against one or more directors or officers of a corporation to procure a judgment for the following relief:

(1) Subject to any provision of the certificate of incorporation authorized pursuant to paragraph (b) of section 402, to compel the defendant to account for his official conduct in the following cases:

(A) The neglect of, or failure to perform, or other violation of his duties in the management and disposition of corporate assets committed to his charge.

(B) The acquisition by himself, transfer to others, loss or waste of corporate assets due to any neglect of, or failure to perform, or other violation of his duties.

(2) To set aside an unlawful conveyance, assignment or transfer of corporate assets, where the transferee knew of its unlawfulness.

(3) To enjoin a proposed unlawful conveyance, assignment or transfer of corporate assets, where there is sufficient evidence that it will be made.

(b) An action may be brought for the relief provided in this section, and in paragraph (a) of section 719 (Liability of directors in certain cases) by a corporation, or a receiver, trustee in bankruptcy, officer, director or judgment creditor thereof, or, under section 626 (Shareholders' derivative action brought in the right of the corporation to procure a judgment in its favor), by a shareholder, voting trust certificate holder, or the owner of a beneficial interest in shares thereof.

(c) This section shall not affect any liability otherwise imposed by law upon any director or officer.

§ 721. Nonexclusivity of Statutory Provisions for Indemnification of Directors and Officers

The indemnification and advancement of expenses granted pursuant to, or provided by, this article shall not be deemed exclusive of any other rights to which a director or officer seeking indemnification or advancement of expenses may be entitled, whether contained in the certificate of incorporation or the by-laws or, when authorized by such certificate of incorporation or by-laws, (i) a resolution of shareholders, (ii) a resolution of directors, or (iii) an agreement providing for such indemnification, provided that no indemnification may be made to or on behalf of any director or officer if a judgment or other final adjudication adverse to the director or officer establishes that his acts were committed in bad faith or were the result of active and deliberate dishonesty and were material to the cause of action so adjudicated, or that he personally gained in fact a financial profit or other advantage to which he was not legally entitled. Nothing contained in this article shall affect any rights to indemnification to which corporate personnel other than directors and officers may be entitled by contract or otherwise under law.

§ 722. Authorization for Indemnification of Directors and Officers

(a) A corporation may indemnify any person made, or threatened to be made, a party to an action or proceeding (other than one by or in the right of the corporation to procure a judgment in its favor), whether civil or criminal, including an action by or in the right of any other corporation of any type or kind, domestic or foreign, or any partnership, joint venture, trust, employee benefit plan or other enterprise, which any director or officer of the corporation served in any capacity at the request of the corporation, by reason of the fact that he, his testator or intestate, was a director or officer of the corporation, or served such other corporation, partnership, joint venture, trust, employee benefit plan or other enterprise in any capacity, against judgments, fines, amounts paid in settlement and reasonable expenses, including attorneys' fees actually and necessarily incurred as a result of such action or proceeding, or any appeal therein, if such director or officer acted, in good faith, for a purpose which he reasonably believed to be in, or, in the case of service for any other corporation or any partnership, joint venture, trust, employee benefit plan or other enterprise, not opposed to, the best interests of the corporation and, in criminal actions or proceedings, in addition, had no reasonable cause to believe that his conduct was unlawful.

(b) The termination of any such civil or criminal action or proceeding by judgment, settlement, conviction or upon a plea of nolo contendere, or its equivalent, shall not in itself create a presumption that any such director or officer did not act, in good faith, for a purpose which he reasonably believed to be in, or, in the case of service for any other corporation or any partnership, joint venture, trust, employee benefit plan or other enterprise, not opposed to, the best interests of the corporation or that he had reasonable cause to believe that his conduct was unlawful.

(c) A corporation may indemnify any person made, or threatened to be made, a party to an action by or in the right of the corporation to procure a judgment in its favor by reason of the fact that he, his testator or intestate, is or was a director or officer of the corporation, or is or was serving at the request of the corporation as a director or officer of any other corporation of any type or kind, domestic or foreign, [or] of any partnership, joint venture, trust, employee benefit plan or other enterprise, against amounts paid in settlement and reasonable expenses, including attorneys' fees, actually and necessarily incurred by him in connection with the defense or settlement of such action, or in connection with an appeal therein, if such director or officer acted, in good faith, for a purpose which he reasonably believed to be in, or, in the case of service for any other corporation or any partnership, joint venture, trust, employee benefit plan or other enterprise, not opposed to, the best interests of the corporation, except that no indemnification under this paragraph shall be made in respect of (1) a threatened action, or a pending action which is settled or otherwise disposed of, or (2) any claim, issue or matter as to which such person shall have been adjudged to be liable to the corporation, unless and only to the extent that the court in which the action was brought, or, if no action was brought, any court of competent jurisdiction, determines upon application that, in view of all the circumstances of the case, the person is fairly and reasonably entitled to indemnity for such portion of the settlement amount and expenses as the court deems proper.

(d) For the purpose of this section, a corporation shall be deemed to have requested a person to serve an employee benefit plan where the performance by such person of his duties to the corporation also imposes duties on, or otherwise involves services by, such person to the plan or participants or beneficiaries of the plan; excise taxes assessed on a person with respect to an employee benefit plan pursuant to applicable law shall be considered fines; and action taken or omitted by a person with respect to an employee benefit plan in the performance of such person's duties for a purpose reasonably believed by such person to be in the interest of the participants and beneficiaries of the plan shall be deemed to be for a purpose which is not opposed to the best interests of the corporation.

§ 723. Payment of Indemnification Other Than by Court Award

(a) A person who has been successful, on the merits or otherwise, in the defense of a civil or criminal action or proceeding of the character described in section 722 shall be entitled to indemnification as authorized in such section.

(b) Except as provided in paragraph (a), any indemnification under section 722 or otherwise permitted by section 721, unless ordered by a court under section 724 (Indemnification of directors and officers by a court), shall be made by the corporation, only if authorized in the specific case:

(1) By the board acting by a quorum consisting of directors who are not parties to such action or proceeding upon a finding that the director or officer has met the standard of conduct set forth in section 722 or established pursuant to section 721, as the case may be, or,

(2) If a quorum under subparagraph (1) is not obtainable or, even if obtainable, a quorum of disinterested directors so directs;

(A) By the board upon the opinion in writing of independent legal counsel that indemnification is proper in the circumstances because the applicable standard of conduct set forth in such sections has been met by such director or officer, or

(B) By the shareholders upon a finding that the director or officer has met the applicable standard of conduct set forth in such sections.

(C) Expenses incurred in defending a civil or criminal action or proceeding may be paid by the corporation in advance of the final disposition of such action or proceeding upon receipt of an undertaking by or on behalf of such director or officer to repay such amount as, and to the extent, required by paragraph (a) of section 725.

§ 724. Indemnification of Directors and Officers by a Court

(a) Notwithstanding the failure of a corporation to provide indemnification, and despite any contrary resolution of the board or of the shareholders in the specific case under section 723 (Payment of indemnification other than by court award), indemnification shall be awarded by a court to the extent authorized under section 722 (Authorization for indemnification of directors and officers), and paragraph (a) of section 723. Application therefor may be made, in every case, either:

(1) In the civil action or proceeding in which the expenses were incurred or other amounts were paid, or

(2) To the supreme court in a separate proceeding, in which case the application shall set forth the disposition of any previous application made to any court for the same or similar relief and also reasonable cause for the failure to make application for such relief in the action or proceeding in which the expenses were incurred or other amounts were paid.

(b) The application shall be made in such manner and form as may be required by the applicable rules of court or, in the absence thereof, by direction of a court to which it is made. Such application shall be upon notice to the corporation. The court may also direct that notice be given at the expense of the corporation to the shareholders and such other persons as it may designate in such manner as it may require.

(c) Where indemnification is sought by judicial action, the court may allow a person such reasonable expenses, including attorneys' fees, during the pendency of the litigation as are necessary in connection with his defense therein, if the court shall find that the defendant has by his pleadings or during the course of the litigation raised genuine issues of fact or law.

§ 725. Other Provisions Affecting Indemnification of Directors and Officers

(a) All expenses incurred in defending a civil or criminal action or proceeding which are advanced by the corporation under paragraph (c) of section 723 (Payment of indemnification other than by court award) or allowed by a court under paragraph (c) of section 724 (Indemnification of directors and officers by a court) shall be repaid in case the person receiving such advancement or allowance is ultimately found, under the procedure set forth in this article, not to be entitled to indemnification or, where indemnification is granted, to the extent the expenses so advanced by the corporation or allowed by the court exceed the indemnification to which he is entitled.

(b) No indemnification, advancement or allowance shall be made under this article in any circumstance where it appears:

(1) That the indemnification would be inconsistent with the law of the jurisdiction of incorporation of a foreign corporation which prohibits or otherwise limits such indemnification;

(2) That the indemnification would be inconsistent with a provision of the certificate of incorporation, a by-law, a resolution of the board or of the shareholders, an agreement or other proper corporate action, in effect at the time of the accrual of the alleged cause of action asserted in the threatened or pending action or proceeding in which the expenses were incurred or other amounts were paid, which prohibits or otherwise limits indemnification; or

(3) If there has been a settlement approved by the court, that the indemnification would be inconsistent with any condition with respect to indemnification expressly imposed by the court in approving the settlement.

(c) If any expenses or other amounts are paid by way of indemnification, otherwise than by court order or action by the shareholders, the corporation shall, not later than the next annual meeting of shareholders unless such meeting is held within three months from the date of such payment, and, in any event, within fifteen months from the date of such payment, mail to its shareholders of record at the time entitled to vote for the election of directors a statement specifying the persons paid, the amounts paid, and the nature and status at the time of such payment of the litigation or threatened litigation.

(d) If any action with respect to indemnification of directors and officers is taken by way of amendment of the by-laws, resolution of directors, or by agreement, then the corporation shall, not later than the next annual meeting of shareholders, unless such meeting is held within three months from the date of such action, and, in any event, within fifteen months from the date of such action, mail to its shareholders of record at the time entitled to vote for the election of directors a statement specifying the action taken. . . .

(f) The provisions of this article relating to indemnification of directors and officers and insurance therefor shall apply to domestic corporations and foreign corporations doing business in this state, except as provided in section 1320 (Exemption from certain provisions).

§ 726. Insurance for Indemnification of Directors and Officers

(a) Subject to paragraph (b), a corporation shall have power to purchase and maintain insurance:

(1) To indemnify the corporation for any obligation which it incurs as a result of the indemnification of directors and officers under the provisions of this article, and

(2) To indemnify directors and officers in instances in which they may be indemnified by the corporation under the provisions of this article, and

(3) To indemnify directors and officers in instances in which they may not otherwise be indemnified by the corporation under the provisions of this article provided the contract of insurance covering such directors and officers provides, in a manner acceptable to the superintendent of insurance, for a retention amount and for co-insurance.

(b) No insurance under paragraph (a) may provide for any payment, other than cost of defense, to or on behalf of any director or officer:

(1) if a judgment or other final adjudication adverse to the insured director or officer establishes that his acts of active and deliberate dishonesty were material to the cause of action so adjudicated, or that he personally gained in fact a financial profit or other advantage to which he was not legally entitled, or

(2) in relation to any risk the insurance of which is prohibited under the insurance law of this state.

(c) Insurance under any or all subparagraphs of paragraph (a) may be included in a single contract or supplement thereto. Retrospective rated contracts are prohibited.

(d) The corporation shall, within the time and to the persons provided in paragraph (c) of section 725 (Other provisions affecting indemnification of directors or officers), mail a statement in respect of any insurance it has purchased or renewed under this section, specifying the insurance carrier, date of the contract, cost of the insurance, corporate positions insured, and a statement explaining all sums, not previously reported in a statement to shareholders, paid under any indemnification insurance contract.

(e) This section is the public policy of this state to spread the risk of corporate management, notwithstanding any other general or special law of this state or of any other jurisdiction including the federal government.

ARTICLE 8

AMENDMENTS AND CHANGES

§ 801. Right to Amend Certificate of Incorporation

(a) A corporation may amend its certificate of incorporation, from time to time, in any and as many respects as may be desired, if such amendment contains only such provisions as might be lawfully contained in an original certificate of incorporation filed at the time of making such amendment.

(b) In particular, and without limitation upon such general power of amendment, a corporation may amend its certificate of incorporation, from time to time, so as:

(1) To change its corporate name.

(2) To enlarge, limit or otherwise change its corporate purposes.

(3) To specify or change the location of the office of the corporation.

(4) To specify or change the post office address to which the secretary of state shall mail a copy of any process against the corporation served upon him.

(5) To make, revoke or change the designation of a registered agent, or to specify or change the address of its registered agent.

(6) To extend the duration of the corporation or, if the corporation ceased to exist because of the expiration of the duration in its certificate of incorporation, to revive its existence.

(7) To increase or decrease the aggregate number of shares, or shares of any class or series, with or without par value, which the corporation shall have to issue.

(8) To remove from authorized shares any class of shares, or any shares of any class, whether issued or unissued.

(9) To increase the par value of any authorized shares of any class with par value, whether issued or unissued.

(10) To reduce the par value of any authorized shares of any class with par value, whether issued or unissued.

(11) To change any authorized shares, with or without par value, whether issued or unissued, into a different number of shares of the same class or into the same or a different number of shares of any one or more classes or any series thereof, either with or without par value.

(12) To fix, change or abolish the designation of any authorized class or any series thereof or any of the relative rights, preferences and

limitations of any shares of any authorized class or any series thereof, whether issued or unissued, including any provisions in respect of any undeclared dividends, whether or not cumulative or accrued, or the redemption of any shares, or any sinking fund for the redemption or purchase of any shares, or any preemptive right to acquire shares or other securities.

(13) As to the shares of any preferred class, then or theretofore authorized, which may be issued in series, to grant authority to the board or to change or revoke the authority of the board to establish and designate series and to fix the number of shares and the relative rights, preferences and limitation as between series.

(14) To strike out, change or add any provision, not inconsistent with this chapter or any other statute, relating to the business of the corporation, its affairs, its rights or powers, or the rights or powers of its shareholders, directors or officers, including any provision which under this chapter is required or permitted to be set forth in the by-laws, except that a certificate of amendment may not be filed wherein the duration of the corporation shall be reduced.

(c) A corporation created by special act may accomplish any or all amendments permitted in this article, in the manner and subject to the conditions in this article.

§ 802. Reduction of Stated Capital by Amendment

(a) A corporation may reduce its stated capital by an amendment of its certificate of incorporation under section 801 (Right to amend certificate of incorporation) which:

(1) Reduces the par value of any issued shares with par value.

(2) Changes issued shares under subparagraph (b)(11) of section 801 that results in a reduction of stated capital.

(3) Removes from authorized shares, shares that have been issued, reacquired and cancelled by the corporation.

(b) This section shall not prevent a corporation from reducing its stated capital in any other manner permitted by this chapter.

§ 804. Class Voting on Amendment

(a) Notwithstanding any provision in the certificate of incorporation, the holders of shares of a class shall be entitled to vote and to vote as a class upon the authorization of amendment and, in addition to the authorization of the amendment by a majority of the votes of all outstanding shares entitled to vote thereon, the amendment shall be authorized by a majority of the votes of all outstanding shares of the class when a proposed amendment would:

(1) Exclude or limit their right to vote on any matter, except as such right may be limited by voting rights given to new shares then being authorized of any existing or new class or series.

(2) Change their shares under subparagraphs (b) (10), (11) or (12) of section 801 (Right to amend certificate of incorporation) or provide that their shares may be converted into shares of any other class or into shares of any other series of the same class, or alter the terms or conditions upon which their shares are convertible or change the shares issuable upon conversion of their shares, if such action would adversely affect such holders, or

(3) Subordinate their rights, by authorizing shares having preferences which would be in any respect superior to their rights.

(b) If any proposed amendment referred to in paragraph (a) would adversely affect the rights of the holders of shares of only one or more series of any class, but not the entire class, then only the holders of those series whose rights would be affected shall be considered a separate class for the purposes of this section.

ARTICLE 9

MERGER OR CONSOLIDATION; GUARANTEE; DISPOSITION OF ASSETS

§ 912. Requirements Relating to Certain Business Combinations

(a) For the purposes of this section:

(1) "Affiliate" means a person that directly, or indirectly through one or more intermediaries, controls, or is controlled by, or is under common control with, a specified person.

(2) "Announcement date", when used in reference to any business combination, means the date of the first public announcement of the final, definitive proposal for such business combination.

(3) "Associate", when used to indicate a relationship with any person, means (A) any corporation or organization of which such person is an officer or partner or is, directly or indirectly, the beneficial owner of ten percent or more of any class of voting stock, (B) any trust or other estate in which such person has a substantial beneficial interest or as to which such person serves as trustee or in a similar fiduciary capacity, and (C) any relative or spouse of such person, or any relative of such spouse, who has the same home as such person.

(4) "Beneficial owner", when used with respect to any stock, means a person:

(A) that, individually or with or through any of its affiliates or associates, beneficially owns such stock, directly or indirectly; or

(B) that, individually or with or through any of its affiliates or associates, has (i) the right to acquire such stock (whether such right is exercisable immediately or only after the passage of time), pursuant to any agreement, arrangement or understanding (whether or not in writing), or upon the exercise of conversion rights, exchange rights, warrants or options, or otherwise; provided, however, that a person shall not be deemed the beneficial owner of stock tendered pursuant to a tender or exchange offer made by such person or any of such person's affiliates or associates until such tendered stock is accepted for purchase or exchange; or (ii) the right to vote such stock pursuant to any agreement, arrangement or understanding (whether or not in writing); provided, however, that a person shall not be deemed the beneficial owner of any stock under this item if the agreement, arrangement or understanding to vote such stock (X) arises solely from a revocable proxy or consent given in response to a proxy or consent solicitation made in accordance with the applicable rules and regulations under the Exchange Act and (Y) is not then reportable on a Schedule 13D under the Exchange Act (or any comparable or successor report); or

(C) that has any agreement, arrangement or understanding (whether or not in writing), for the purpose of acquiring, holding, voting (except voting pursuant to a revocable proxy or consent as described in item (ii) of clause (B) of this subparagraph), or disposing of such stock with any other person that beneficially owns, or whose affiliates or associates beneficially own, directly or indirectly, such stock.

(5) "Business combination", when used in reference to any domestic corporation and any interested shareholder of such corporation, means:

(A) any merger or consolidation of such corporation or any subsidiary of such corporation with (i) such interested shareholder or (ii) any other corporation (whether or not itself an interested shareholder of such corporation) which is, or after such merger or consolidation would be, an affiliate or associate of such interested shareholder;

(B) any sale, lease, exchange, mortgage, pledge, transfer or other disposition (in one transaction or a series of transactions) to or with such interested shareholder or any affiliate or associate of such interested shareholder of assets of such corporation or any subsidiary of such corporation (i) having an aggregate market value equal to ten percent or more of the aggregate market value of all the assets, determined on a consolidated basis, of such corporation, (ii) having an aggregate market value equal to ten percent or more of the aggregate market value of all the outstanding stock of such corporation, or (iii) representing ten percent or more of the earning power or net income, determined on a consolidated basis, of such corporation;

(C) the issuance or transfer by such corporation or any subsidiary of such corporation (in one transaction or a series of transactions) of any stock of such corporation or any subsidiary of such corporation which has an aggregate market value equal to five percent or more of the aggregate market value of all the outstanding stock of such corporation to such interested shareholder or any affiliate or associate of such interested shareholder except pursuant to the exercise of warrants or rights to purchase stock offered, or a dividend or distribution paid or made, pro rata to all shareholders of such corporation;

(D) the adoption of any plan or proposal for the liquidation or dissolution of such corporation proposed by, or pursuant to any agreement, arrangement or understanding (whether or not in writing) with, such interested shareholder or any affiliate or associate of such interested shareholder;

(E) any reclassification of securities (including, without limitation, any stock split, stock dividend, or other distribution of stock in respect of stock, or any reverse stock split), or recapitalization of such corporation, or any merger or consolidation of such corporation with any subsidiary of such corporation, or any other transaction (whether or not with or into or otherwise involving such interested shareholder), proposed by, or pursuant to any agreement, arrangement or understanding (whether or not in writing) with, such interested shareholder or any affiliate or associate of such interested shareholder, which has the effect, directly or indirectly, of increasing the proportionate share of the outstanding shares of any class or series of voting stock or securities convertible into voting stock of such corporation or any subsidiary of such corporation which is directly or indirectly owned by such interested shareholder or any affiliate or associate of such interested shareholder, except as a result of immaterial changes due to fractional share adjustments; or

(F) any receipt by such interested shareholder or any affiliate or associate of such interested shareholder of the benefit, directly or indirectly (except proportionately as a shareholder of such corporation) of any loans, advances, guarantees, pledges or other financial assistance or any tax credits or other tax advantages provided by or through such corporation.

(6) "Common stock" means any stock other than preferred stock.

(7) "Consummation date", with respect to any business combination, means the date of consummation of such business combination, or, in the case of a business combination as to which a shareholder vote is taken, the later of the business day prior to the vote or twenty days prior to the date of consummation of such business combination.

(8) "Control", including the terms "controlling", "controlled by" and "under common control with", means the possession, directly or indirectly, of the power to direct or cause the direction of the management and policies of a person, whether through the ownership of voting stock, by contract, or otherwise. A person's beneficial ownership of ten percent or more of a corporation's outstanding voting stock shall create a presumption that such person has control of such corporation. Notwith-

standing the foregoing, a person shall not be deemed to have control of a corporation if such person holds voting stock, in good faith and not for the purpose of circumventing this section, as an agent, bank, broker, nominee, custodian or trustee for one or more beneficial owners who do not individually or as a group have control of such corporation.

(9) "Exchange Act" means the Act of Congress known as the Securities Exchange Act of 1934, as the same has been or hereafter may be amended from time to time.

(10) "Interested shareholder", when used in reference to any domestic corporation, means any person (other than such corporation or any subsidiary of such corporation) that

(A)(i) is the beneficial owner, directly or indirectly, of twenty percent or more of the outstanding voting stock of such corporation; or

(ii) is an affiliate or associate of such corporation and at any time within the five-year period immediately prior to the date in question was the beneficial owner, directly or indirectly, of twenty percent or more of the then outstanding voting stock of such corporation; provided that

(B) for the purpose of determining whether a person is an interested shareholder, the number of shares of voting stock of such corporation deemed to be outstanding shall include shares deemed to be beneficially owned by the person through application of subparagraph four of this paragraph but shall not include any other unissued shares of voting stock of such corporation which may be issuable pursuant to any agreement, arrangement or understanding, or upon exercise of conversion rights, warrants or options, or otherwise.

(11) "Market value", when used in reference to stock or property of any domestic corporation, means:

(A) in the case of stock, the highest closing sale price during the thirty-day period immediately preceding the date in question of a share of such stock on the composite tape for New York stock exchange-listed stocks, or, if such stock is not quoted on such composite tape or if such stock is not listed on such exchange, on the principal United States securities exchange registered under the Exchange Act on which such stock is listed, or, if such stock is not listed on any such exchange, the highest closing bid quotation with respect to a share of such stock during the thirty-day period preceding the date in question on the National Association of Securities Dealers, Inc. Automated Quotations System or any system then in use, or if no such quotations are available, the fair market value on the date in question of a share of such stock as determined by the board of directors of such corporation in good faith; and

(B) in the case of property other than cash or stock, the fair market value of such property on the date in question as determined by the board of directors of such corporation in good faith.

(12) "Preferred stock" means any class or series of stock of a domestic corporation which under the by-laws or certificate of incorporation of such corporation is entitled to receive payment of dividends prior to any payment of dividends on some other class or series of stock, or is entitled in the event of any voluntary liquidation, dissolution or winding up of the corporation to receive payment or distribution of a preferential amount before any payments or distributions are received by some other class or series of stock.

(14) "Stock" means:

(A) any stock or similar security, any certificate of interest, any participation in any profit sharing agreement, any voting trust certificate, or any certificate of deposit for stock; and

(B) any security convertible, with or without consideration, into stock, or any warrant, call or other option or privilege of buying stock without being bound to do so, or any other security carrying any right to acquire, subscribe to or purchase stock.

(15) "Stock acquisition date", with respect to any person and any domestic corporation, means the date that such person first becomes an interested shareholder of such corporation.

(16) "Subsidiary" of any person means any other corporation of which a majority of the voting stock is owned, directly or indirectly, by such person.

(17) "Voting stock" means shares of capital stock of a corporation entitled to vote generally in the election of directors.

(b) Notwithstanding anything to the contrary contained in this chapter (except the provisions of paragraph (d) of this section), no domestic corporation shall engage in any business combination with any interested shareholder of such corporation for a period of five years following such interested shareholder's stock acquisition date unless such business combination or the purchase of stock made by such interested shareholder on such interested shareholder's stock acquisition date is approved by the board of directors of such corporation prior to such interested shareholder's stock acquisition date. If a good faith proposal is made in writing to the board of directors of such corporation regarding a business combination, the board of directors shall respond, in writing, within thirty days or such shorter period, if any, as may be required by the Exchange Act, setting forth its reasons for its decision regarding such proposal. If a good faith proposal to purchase stock is made in writing to the board of directors of such corporation, the board of directors, unless it responds affirmatively in writing within thirty days or such shorter period, if any, as may be required by the Exchange Act, shall be deemed to have disapproved such stock purchase.

(c) Notwithstanding anything to the contrary contained in this chapter (except the provisions of paragraphs (b) and (d) of this section), no domestic corporation shall engage at any time in any business combination with any interested shareholder of such corporation other than a business combination specified in any one of subparagraph (1), (2) or (3):

(1) A business combination approved by the board of directors of such corporation prior to such interested shareholder's stock acquisition date, or where the purchase of stock made by such interested shareholder on such interested shareholder's stock acquisition date had been approved by the board of directors of such corporation prior to such interested shareholder's stock acquisition date.

(2) A business combination approved by the affirmative vote of the holders of a majority of the outstanding voting stock not beneficially owned by such interested shareholder or any affiliate or associate of such interested shareholder at a meeting called for such purpose no earlier than five years after such interested shareholder's stock acquisition date.

(3) A business combination that meets all of the following conditions:

(A) The aggregate amount of the cash and the market value as of the consummation date of consideration other than cash to be received per share by holders of outstanding shares of common stock of such corporation in such business combination is [at] least equal to the higher of the following:

(i) the highest per share price paid by such interested shareholder at a time when he was the beneficial owner, directly or indirectly, of five percent or more of the outstanding voting stock of such corporation, for any shares of common stock of the same class or series acquired by it (X) within the five-year period immediately prior to the announcement date with respect to such business combination, or (Y) within the five-year period immediately prior to, or in, the transaction in which such interested shareholder became an interested shareholder, whichever is higher; plus, in either case, interest compounded annually from the earliest date on which such highest per share acquisition price was paid through the consummation date at the rate for one-year United States treasury obligations from time to time in effect; less the aggregate amount of any cash dividends paid, and the market value of any dividends paid other than in cash, per share of common stock since such earliest date, up to the amount of such interest; and

(ii) the market value per share of common stock on the announcement date with respect to such business combination or on such interested shareholder's stock acquisition date, whichever is higher; plus interest compounded annually from such date through the consummation date at the rate for one-year United States treasury obligations from time to time in effect; less the aggregate amount of any cash dividends paid, and the market value of any dividends paid other than in cash, per share of common stock since such date, up to the amount of such interest.

(B) The aggregate amount of the cash and the market value as of the consummation date of consideration other than cash to be received per share by holders of outstanding shares of any class or series of stock, other than common stock, of such corporation is at least equal to the highest of the following (whether or not such interested shareholder has previously acquired any shares of such class or series of stock):

(i) the highest per share price paid by such interested share-holder at a time when he was the beneficial owner, directly or indirectly, of five percent or more of the outstanding voting stock of such corporation, for any shares of such class or series of stock acquired by it (X) within the five-year period immediately prior to the announcement date with respect to such business combination, or (Y) within the five-year period immediately prior to, or in, the transaction in which such interested shareholder became an interested shareholder, whichever is higher; plus, in either case, interest compounded annually from the earliest date on which such highest per share acquisition price was paid through the consummation date at the rate for one-year United States treasury obligations from time to time in effect; less the aggregate amount of any cash dividends paid, and the market value of any dividends paid other than in cash, per share of such class or series of stock since such earliest date, up to the amount of such interest;

(ii) the highest preferential amount per share to which the holders of shares of such class or series of stock are entitled in the event of any voluntary liquidation, dissolution or winding up of such corporation, plus the aggregate amount of any dividends declared or due as to which such holders are entitled prior to payment of dividends on some other class or series of stock (unless the aggregate amount of such dividends is included in such preferential amount); and

(iii) the market value per share of such class or series of stock on the announcement date with respect to such business combination or on such interested shareholder's stock acquisition date, whichever is higher; plus interest compounded annually from such date through the consummation date at the rate for one-year United States treasury obligations from time to time in effect; less the aggregate amount of any cash dividends paid, and the market value of any dividends paid other than in cash, per share of such class or series of stock since such date, up to the amount of such interest.

(C) The consideration to be received by holders of a particular class or series of outstanding stock (including common stock) of such corporation in such business combination is in cash or in the same form as the interested shareholder has used to acquire the largest number of shares of such class or series of stock previously acquired by it, and such consideration shall be distributed promptly.

(D) The holders of all outstanding shares of stock of such corporation not beneficially owned by such interested shareholder immediately prior to the consummation of such business combination are entitled to receive in such business combination cash or other consideration for such shares in compliance with clauses (A), (B) and (C) of this subparagraph.

(E) After such interested shareholder's stock acquisition date and prior to the consummation date with respect to such business combination, such interested shareholder has not become the beneficial owner of any additional shares of voting stock of such corporation except:

(i) as part of the transaction which resulted in such interested shareholder becoming an interested shareholder;

(ii) by virtue of proportionate stock splits, stock dividends or other distributions of stock in respect of stock not constituting a business combination under clause (E) of subparagraph five of paragraph (a) of this section;

(iii) through a business combination meeting all of the conditions of paragraph (b) of this section and this paragraph; or

(iv) through purchase by such interested shareholder at any price which, if such price had been paid in an otherwise permissible business combination the announcement date and consummation date of which were the date of such purchase, would have satisfied the requirements of clauses (A), (B) and (C) of this subparagraph.

(d) The provisions of this section shall not apply:

(1) to any business combination of a domestic corporation that does not have a class of voting stock registered with the Securities and Exchange Commission pursuant to section twelve of the Exchange Act, unless the certificate of incorporation provides otherwise; or

(2) to any business combination of a domestic corporation whose certificate of incorporation has been amended to provide that such corporation shall be subject to the provisions of this section, which did not have a class of voting stock registered with the Securities and Exchange Commission pursuant to section twelve of the Exchange Act on the effective date of such amendment, and which is a business combination with an interested shareholder whose stock acquisition date is prior to the effective date of such amendment; or

(3) to any business combination of a domestic corporation (i) the original certificate of incorporation of which contains a provision expressly electing not to be governed by this section, or (ii) which adopts an amendment to such corporation's by-laws prior to March thirty-first, nineteen hundred eighty-six, expressly electing not to be governed by

this section, or (iii) which adopts an amendment to such corporation's by-laws, approved by the affirmative vote of a majority of votes of the outstanding voting stock of such corporation, excluding the voting stock of interested shareholders and their affiliates and associates, expressly electing not to be governed by this section, provided that such amendment to the by-laws shall not be effective until eighteen months after such vote of such corporation's shareholders and shall not apply to any business combination of such corporation with an interested shareholder whose stock acquisition date is on or prior to the effective date of such amendment; or

(4) to any business combination of a domestic corporation with an interested shareholder of such corporation which became an interested shareholder inadvertently, if such interested shareholder (i) as soon as practicable, divests itself of a sufficient amount of the voting stock of such corporation so that it no longer is the beneficial owner, directly or indirectly, of twenty percent or more of the outstanding voting stock of such corporation, and (ii) would not at any time within the five-year period preceding the announcement date with respect to such business combination have been an interested shareholder but for such inadvertent acquisition; or

(5) to any business combination with an interested shareholder who was the beneficial owner, directly or indirectly, of five per cent or more of the outstanding voting stock of such corporation on October thirtieth, nineteen hundred eighty-five, and remained so to such interested shareholder's stock acquisition date.

ARTICLE 10

NON–JUDICIAL DISSOLUTION

§ 1001. Authorization of Dissolution

(a) A corporation may be dissolved under this article. Such dissolution shall be authorized at a meeting of shareholders by (i) for corporations the certificate of incorporation of which expressly provides such or corporations incorporated after [February 22, 1998], a majority of the votes of all outstanding shares entitled to vote thereon or (ii) for other corporations, two-thirds of the votes of all outstanding shares entitled to vote thereon, except, in either case, as otherwise provided under section 1002 (Dissolution under provision in certificate of incorporation).

(b) Any corporation may adopt an amendment of the certificate of incorporation providing that such dissolution shall be authorized at a meeting of shareholders by a specified proportion of votes of all outstanding shares entitled to vote thereon, provided that such proportion may not be less than a majority.

§ 1002. Dissolution Under Provision in Certificate of Incorporation

(a) The certificate of incorporation may contain a provision that any shareholder, or the holders of any specified number or proportion of shares or votes of shares, or of any specified number or proportion of shares or votes of shares of any class or series thereof, may require the dissolution of the corporation at will or upon the occurrence of a specified event. If the certificate of incorporation contains such a provision, a certificate of dissolution under section 1003 (Certificate of dissolution; contents) may be signed, verified and delivered to the department of state as provided in section 104 (Certificate; requirements, signing, filing, effectiveness) when authorized by a holder or holders of the number or proportion of shares or votes of shares specified in such provision, given in such manner as may be specified therein, or if no manner is specified therein, when authorized on written consent signed by such holder or holders; or such certificate may be signed, verified and delivered to the department by such holder or holders or by such of them as are designated by them.

(b) An amendment of the certificate of incorporation which adds a provision permitted by this section, or which changes or strikes out such a provision, shall be authorized at a meeting of shareholders by vote of all outstanding shares, whether or not otherwise entitled to vote on any amendment, or of such lesser proportion of shares and of such class or series of shares, but not less than a majority of all outstanding shares entitled to vote on any amendment, as may be provided specifically in the certificate of incorporation for adding, changing or striking out a provision permitted by this section.

(c) If the certificate of incorporation of any corporation contains a provision authorized by this section, the existence of such provision shall be noted conspicuously on the face or back of every certificate for shares issued by such corporation.

ARTICLE 11

JUDICIAL DISSOLUTION

§ 1101. Attorney–General's Action for Judicial Dissolution

(a) The attorney-general may bring an action for the dissolution of a corporation upon one or more of the following grounds:

(1) That the corporation procured its formation through fraudulent misrepresentation or concealment of a material fact.

(2) That the corporation has exceeded the authority conferred upon it by law, or has violated any provision of law whereby it has forfeited its charter, or carried on, conducted or transacted its business in a persis-

tently fraudulent or illegal manner, or by the abuse of its powers contrary to the public policy of the state has become liable to be dissolved. ...

§ 1102. Directors' Petition for Judicial Dissolution

If a majority of the board adopts a resolution that finds that the assets of a corporation are not sufficient to discharge its liabilities or that a dissolution will be beneficial to the shareholders, it may present a petition for its dissolution.

§ 1103. Shareholders' Petition for Judicial Dissolution

(a) If the shareholders of a corporation adopt a resolution stating that they find that its assets are not sufficient to discharge its liabilities, or that they deem a dissolution to be beneficial to the shareholders, the shareholders or such of them as are designated for that purpose in such resolution may present a petition for its dissolution.

(b) A shareholders' meeting to consider such a resolution may be called, notwithstanding any provision in the certificate of incorporation, by the holders of shares representing ten percent of the votes of all outstanding shares entitled to vote thereon, or if the certificate of incorporation authorizes a lesser proportion of votes of shares to call the meeting, by such lesser proportion. A meeting under this paragraph may not be called more often than once in any period of twelve consecutive months.

(c) Such a resolution may be adopted at a meeting of shareholders by vote of a majority of the votes of all outstanding shares entitled to vote thereon or if the certificate of incorporation requires a greater proportion of votes to adopt such a resolution, by such greater proportion.

§ 1104. Petition in Case of Deadlock Among Directors or Shareholders

(a) Except as otherwise provided in the certificate of incorporation under section 613 (Limitations on right to vote), the holders of shares representing one-half of the votes of all outstanding shares of a corporation entitled to vote in an election of directors may present a petition for dissolution on one or more of the following grounds:

(1) That the directors are so divided respecting the management of the corporation's affairs that the votes required for action by the board cannot be obtained.

(2) That the shareholders are so divided that the votes required for the election of directors cannot be obtained.

(3) That there is internal dissension and two or more factions of shareholders are so divided that dissolution would be beneficial to the shareholders.

(b) If the certificate of incorporation provides that the proportion of votes required for action by the board, or the proportion of votes of shareholders required for election of directors, shall be greater than that otherwise required by this chapter, such a petition may be presented by the holders of shares representing more than one-third of the votes of all outstanding shares entitled to vote on non-judicial dissolution under section 1001 (Authorization of dissolution).

(c) Notwithstanding any provision in the certificate of incorporation, any holder of shares entitled to vote at an election of directors of a corporation, may present a petition for its dissolution on the ground that the shareholders are so divided that they have failed, for a period which includes at least two consecutive annual meeting dates, to elect successors to directors whose terms have expired or would have expired upon the election and qualification of their successors.

§ 1104–a.   Petition for Judicial Dissolution Under Special Circumstances

(a) The holders of shares representing twenty percent or more of the votes of all outstanding shares of a corporation, other than a corporation registered as an investment company under an act of congress entitled "Investment Company Act of 1940", no shares of which are listed on a national securities exchange or regularly quoted in an over-the-counter market by one or more members of a national or an affiliated securities association, entitled to vote in an election of directors may present a petition of dissolution on one or more of the following grounds:

(1) The directors or those in control of the corporation have been guilty of illegal, fraudulent or oppressive actions toward the complaining shareholders;

(2) The property or assets of the corporation are being looted, wasted, or diverted for non-corporate purposes by its directors, officers or those in control of the corporation.

(b) The court, in determining whether to proceed with involuntary dissolution pursuant to this section, shall take into account:

(1) Whether liquidation of the corporation is the only feasible means whereby the petitioners may reasonably expect to obtain a fair return on their investment; and

(2) Whether liquidation of the corporation is reasonably necessary for the protection of the rights and interests of any substantial number of shareholders or of the petitioners.

(c) In addition to all other disclosure requirements, the directors or those in control of the corporation, no later than thirty days after the filing of a petition hereunder, shall make available for inspection and copying to the petitioners under reasonable working conditions the corporate financial books and records for the three preceding years.

(d) The court may order stock valuations be adjusted and may provide for a surcharge upon the directors or those in control of the corporation upon a finding of wilful or reckless dissipation or transfer of assets or corporate property without just or adequate compensation therefor.

§ 1111. Judgment or Final Order of Dissolution

(a) In an action or special proceeding under this article if, in the court's discretion, it shall appear that the corporation should be dissolved, it shall make a judgment or final order dissolving the corporation.

(b) In making its decision, the court shall take into consideration the following criteria:

(1) In an action brought by the attorney-general, the interest of the public is of paramount importance.

(2) In a special proceeding brought by directors or shareholders, the benefit to the shareholders of a dissolution is of paramount importance.

(3) In a special proceeding brought under section 1104 (Petition in case of deadlock among directors or shareholders) or section 1104–a (Petition for judicial dissolution under special circumstances) dissolution is not to be denied merely because it is found that the corporate business has been or could be conducted at a profit.

(c) If the judgment or final order shall provide for a dissolution of the corporation, the court may, in its discretion, provide therein for the distribution of the property of the corporation to those entitled thereto according to their respective rights.

(d) The clerk of the court or such other person as the court may direct shall transmit certified copies of the judgment or final order of dissolution to the department of state and to the clerk of the county in which the office of the corporation was located at the date of the judgment or order. Upon filing by the department of state, the corporation shall be dissolved.

(e) The corporation shall promptly thereafter transmit a certified copy of the judgment or final order to the clerk of each other county in which its certificate of incorporation was filed.

§ 1118. Purchase of Petitioner's Shares; Valuation

(a) In any proceeding brought pursuant to section eleven hundred four-a of this chapter, any other shareholder or shareholders or the corporation may, at any time within ninety days after the filing of such petition or at such later time as the court in its discretion may allow, elect to purchase the shares owned by the petitioners at their fair value and upon such terms and conditions as may be approved by the court, including the conditions of paragraph (c) herein. An election pursuant to this section shall be irrevocable unless the court, in its discretion, for just and equitable considerations, determines that such election be revocable.

(b) If one or more shareholders or the corporation elect to purchase the shares owned by the petitioner but are unable to agree with the petitioner upon the fair value of such shares, the court, upon the application of such prospective purchaser or purchasers or the petitioner, may stay the proceedings brought pursuant to section 1104–a of this chapter and determine the fair value of the petitioner's shares as of the day prior to the date on which such petition was filed, exclusive of any element of value arising from such filing but giving effect to any adjustment or surcharge found to be appropriate in the proceeding under section 1104–a of this chapter. In determining the fair value of the petitioner's shares, the court, in its discretion, may award interest from the date the petition is filed to the date of payment for the petitioner's share at an equitable rate upon judicially determined fair value of his shares.

(c) In connection with any election to purchase pursuant to this section:

(1) If such election is made beyond ninety days after the filing of the petition, and the court allows such petition, the court, in its discretion, may award the petitioner his reasonable expenses incurred in the proceeding prior to such election, including reasonable attorneys' fees;

(2) The court, in its discretion, may require, at any time prior to the actual purchase of petitioner's shares, the posting of a bond or other acceptable security in an amount sufficient to secure petitioner for the fair value of his shares.

ARTICLE 13

FOREIGN CORPORATIONS

§ 1315. Record of Shareholders

(a) Any resident of this state who shall have been a shareholder of record of a foreign corporation doing business in this state upon at least five days' written demand may require such foreign corporation to produce a record of its shareholders setting forth the names and addresses of all shareholders, the number and class of shares held by each and the dates when they respectively became the owners of record thereof and shall have the right to examine in person or by agent or attorney at the office of the foreign corporation in this state or at the office of its transfer agent or registrar in this state or at such other place in the county in this state in which the foreign corporation is doing business as may be designated by the foreign corporation, during the usual business hours, the record of shareholders or an exact copy thereof certified as correct by the corporate officer or agent responsible for keeping or producing such record and to make extracts therefrom. Resident holders of voting trust certificates representing shares of the foreign corporation shall for the purpose of this section be regarded as shareholders. Any such agent or authority shall be authorized in a writing that satisfies the requirements of a writing under paragraph (b) of section 609 (proxies). A corporation requested to provide information pursuant to this paragraph shall make available such information in the format in which such information is maintained by the corporation and shall not be required to provide such information in any other format. If a request made pursuant to this paragraph includes a request to furnish information regarding beneficial owners, the corporation shall make available such information in its possession regarding beneficial owners as is provided to the corporation by a registered broker or dealer or a bank, association or other entity that exercises fiduciary powers in connection with the forwarding of information to such owners. The corporation shall not be required to obtain information about beneficial owners not in its possession.

(b) An examination authorized by paragraph (a) may be denied to such shareholder or other person upon his refusal to furnish to the foreign corporation or its transfer agent or registrar an affidavit that such inspection is not desired for a purpose which is in the interest of a business or object other than the business of the foreign corporation and that such shareholder or other person has not within five years sold or offered for sale any list of shareholders of any corporation of any type or kind, whether or not formed under the laws of this state, or aided or abetted any person in procuring any such record of shareholders for any such purpose.

(c) Upon refusal by the foreign corporation or by an officer or agent of the foreign corporation to produce for examination or to permit an examination of the record of shareholders as herein provided, the person making the demand for production and examination may apply to the supreme court in the judicial district where the office of the foreign corporation within this state is located, upon such notice as the court may direct, for an order directing the foreign corporation, its officer or agent, to show cause why an order should not be granted directing such production and permitting such examination by the applicant. Upon the return day of the order to show cause, the court shall hear the parties summarily, by affidavit or otherwise, and if its appears that the applicant is qualified and entitled to such examination, the court shall grant an order compelling such production for examination and awarding such further relief as to the court may seem just and proper.

(d) Nothing herein contained shall impair the power of courts to compel the production for examination of the books of a foreign corporation. The record of shareholders specified in paragraph (a) shall be prima facie evidence of the facts therein stated in favor of the plaintiff in any action or special proceeding against such foreign corporation or any of its officers, directors or shareholders.

§ 1317. Liabilities of Directors and Officers of Foreign Corporations

(a) Except as otherwise provided in this chapter, the directors and officers of a foreign corporation doing business in this state are subject, to the same extent as directors and officers of a domestic corporation, to the provisions of:

(1) Section 719 (Liability of directors in certain cases) except subparagraph (a)(3) thereof, and

(2) Section 720 (Action against directors and officers for misconduct.)

(b) Any liability imposed by paragraph (a) may be enforced in, and such relief granted by, the courts in this state, in the same manner as in the case of a domestic corporation.

§ 1318. Liability of Foreign Corporations for Failure to Disclose Required Information

A foreign corporation doing business in this state shall, in the same manner as a domestic corporation, disclose to its shareholders of record who are residents of this state the information required under paragraph (c) of section 510 (Dividends or other distributions in cash or property), paragraphs (f) and (g) of section 511 (Share distributions and changes), paragraph (d) of section 515 (Reacquired shares), paragraph (c) of section 516 (Reduction of stated capital in certain cases), and shall be liable as provided in section 520 (Liability for failure to disclose required information) for failure to comply in good faith with these requirements.

§ 1319. Applicability of Other Provisions

(a) In addition to articles 1 (Short title; definitions; application; certificates; miscellaneous) and 3 (Corporate name and service of process) and the other sections of article 13, the following provisions, to the extent provided therein, shall apply to a foreign corporation doing business in this state, its directors, officers and shareholders:

(1) Section 623 (Procedure to enforce shareholder's right to receive payment for shares).

(2) Section 626 (Shareholders' derivative action brought in the right of the corporation to procure a judgment in its favor).

(3) Section 627 (Security for expenses in shareholders' derivative action brought in the right of the corporation to procure a judgment in its favor).

(4) Sections 721 (Exclusivity of statutory provisions for indemnification of directors and officers) through 727 (Insurance for indemnification of directors and officers), inclusive.

(5) Section 808 (Reorganization under act of congress).

(6) Section 907 (Merger or consolidation of domestic and foreign corporations).

§ 1320.　Exemption From Certain Provisions

(a) Notwithstanding any other provision of this chapter, a foreign corporation doing business in this state which is authorized under this article, its directors, officers and shareholders, shall be exempt from the provisions of paragraph (e) of section 1316 (Voting trust records), subparagraph (a)(1) of section 1317 (Liabilities of directors and officers of foreign corporations), section 1318 (Liability of foreign corporations for failure to disclose required information) and subparagraph (a)(4) of section 1319 (Applicability of other provisions) if when such provision would otherwise apply:

(1) Shares of such corporation were listed on a national securities exchange, or

(2) Less than one-half of the total of its business income for the preceding three fiscal years, or such portion thereof as the foreign corporation was in existence, was allocable to this state for franchise tax purposes under the tax law.

PENNSYLVANIA CONSOL. STATS. ANN. TITLE 15

(Excerpts)

TITLE 15

CORPORATIONS AND UNINCORPORATED ASSOCIATIONS

PART II

CORPORATIONS

SUBPART B

BUSINESS CORPORATIONS

ARTICLE A

PRELIMINARY PROVISIONS

Chapter 11

GENERAL PROVISIONS

ARTICLE B

DOMESTIC CORPORATIONS GENERALLY

Chapter 17

OFFICERS, DIRECTORS, AND SHAREHOLDERS

Subchapter B

Fiduciary Duty

ARTICLE C

DOMESTIC CORPORATION ANCILLARIES

Chapter 25

REGISTERED CORPORATIONS

Subchapter A

Preliminary Provisions

Subchapter F

Business Combinations

Subchapter G

Control–Share Acquisitions

Subchapter H

Disgorgement by Certain Controlling Shareholders Following Attempts to Acquire Control

Subchapter I

Severance Compensation for Employees Terminated Following Certain Control–Share Acquisitions

Subchapter J

Business Combination Transactions—Labor Contracts

SUBPART B

BUSINESS CORPORATIONS

ARTICLE A

PRELIMINARY PROVISIONS

Chapter 11

GENERAL PROVISIONS

§ 1103. Definitions

"Exchange Act." The Securities Exchange Act of 1934 (48 Stat. 881, 15 U.S.C. § 78a et seq.)....

"Registered corporation." A corporation defined in section 2502 (relating to registered corporation status)....

ARTICLE B

DOMESTIC CORPORATIONS GENERALLY

Chapter 17

OFFICERS, DIRECTORS, AND SHAREHOLDERS

Subchapter B

Fiduciary Duty

§ 1711. Alternative provisions

(a) **General rule.**—Section 1716 (relating to alternative standard) shall not be applicable to any business corporation to which section 1715 (relating to exercise of powers generally) is applicable.

(b) **Exceptions.**—Section 1715 shall be applicable to:

(1) Any registered corporation described in section 2502(1)(i) (relating to registered corporation status), except a corporation:

(i) the bylaws of which explicitly provide that section 1715 ... shall not be applicable to the corporation by amendment adopted by the board of directors on or before July 26, 1990, in the case of a corporation that was a registered corporation described in section 2502(1)(i) on April 27, 1990; or

(ii) in any other case, the articles of which explicitly provide that section 1715 ... shall not be applicable to the corporation by a provision included in the original articles, or by an articles amendment adopted on or before 90 days after the corporation first becomes a registered corporation described in section 2502(1)(i).

(2) Any registered corporation described solely in section 2502(1)(ii), except a corporation:

(i) the bylaws of which explicitly provide that section 1715 ... shall not be applicable to the corporation by amendment adopted by the board of directors on or before April 27, 1991, in the case of a corporation that was a registered corporation described solely in section 2502(1)(ii) on April 27, 1990; or

(ii) in any other case, the articles of which explicitly provide that section 1715 ... shall not be applicable to the corporation by a provision included in the original articles, or by an articles amendment adopted on or before one year after the corporation first becomes a registered corporation described in section 2502(1)(ii).

(3) Any business corporation that is not a registered corporation described in section 2502(1), except a corporation:

(i) the bylaws of which explicitly provide that section 1715 ... shall not be applicable to the corporation by amendment adopted by the board of directors on or before April 27, 1991, in the case of a corporation that was a business corporation on April 27, 1990; or

(ii) in any other case, the articles of which explicitly provide that section 1715 or corresponding provisions of prior law shall not be applicable to the corporation by a provision included in the original articles, or by an articles amendment adopted on or before one year after the corporation first becomes a business corporation. . . .

§ 1712. Standard of care and justifiable reliance

(a) Directors.—A director of a business corporation shall stand in a fiduciary relation to the corporation and shall perform his duties as a director, including his duties as a member of any committee of the board upon which he may serve, in good faith, in a manner he reasonably believes to be in the best interests of the corporation and with such care, including reasonable inquiry, skill and diligence, as a person of ordinary prudence would use under similar circumstances. In performing his duties, a director shall be entitled to rely in good faith on information, opinions, reports or statements, including financial statements and other financial data, in each case prepared or presented by any of the following:

(1) One or more officers or employees of the corporation whom the director reasonably believes to be reliable and competent in the matters presented.

(2) Counsel, public accountants or other persons as to matters which the director reasonably believes to be within the professional or expert competence of such person.

(3) A committee of the board upon which he does not serve, duly designated in accordance with law, as to matters within its designated authority, which committee the director reasonably believes to merit confidence.

(b) Effect of actual knowledge.—A director shall not be considered to be acting in good faith if he has knowledge concerning the matter in question that would cause his reliance to be unwarranted.

(c) Officers.—Except as otherwise provided in the bylaws, an officer shall perform his duties as an officer in good faith, in a manner he reasonably believes to be in the best interests of the corporation and with such care, including reasonable inquiry, skill and diligence, as a person of ordinary prudence would use under similar circumstances. A person who so performs his duties shall not be liable by reason of having been an officer of the corporation.

§ 1713. Personal liability of directors

(a) General rule.—If a bylaw adopted by the shareholders of a business corporation so provides, a director shall not be personally liable, as such, for monetary damages for any action taken unless:

(1) the director has breached or failed to perform the duties of his office under this subchapter; and

(2) the breach or failure to perform constitutes self-dealing, willful misconduct or recklessness.

(b) Exceptions.—

Subsection (a) shall not apply to:

(1) the responsibility or liability of a director pursuant to any criminal statute; or

(2) the liability of a director for the payment of taxes pursuant to Federal, State or local law.

§ 1715. Exercise of powers generally

(a) General rule.—In discharging the duties of their respective positions, the board of directors, committees of the board and individual directors of a business corporation may, in considering the best interests of the corporation, consider to the extent they deem appropriate:

(1) The effects of any action upon any or all groups affected by such action, including shareholders, employees, suppliers, customers and creditors of the corporation, and upon communities in which offices or other establishments of the corporation are located.

(2) The short-term and long-term interests of the corporation, including benefits that may accrue to the corporation from its long-term plans and the possibility that these interests may be best served by the continued independence of the corporation.

(3) The resources, intent and conduct (past, stated and potential) of any person seeking to acquire control of the corporation.

(4) All other pertinent factors.

(b) Consideration of interests and factors.—The board of directors, committees of the board and individual directors shall not be required, in considering the best interests of the corporation or the effects of any action, to regard any corporate interest or the interests of any particular group affected by such action as a dominant or controlling interest or factor. The consideration of interests and factors in the manner described in this subsection and in subsection (a) shall not constitute a violation of section 1712 (relating to standard of care and justifiable reliance).

(c) Specific applications.—In exercising the powers vested in the corporation, including, without limitation, those powers pursuant to section 1502 (relating to general powers), and in no way limiting the discretion of the board of directors, committees of the board and individual directors pursuant to subsections (a) and (b), the fiduciary duty of directors shall not be deemed to require them:

(1) to redeem any rights under, or to modify or render inapplicable, any shareholder rights plan, including, but not limited to, a plan adopted pursuant or made subject to section 2513 (relating to disparate treatment of certain persons);

(2) to render inapplicable, or make determinations under, the provisions of Subchapter E (relating to control transactions), F (relating to business combinations), G (relating to control-share acquisitions) or H (relating to disgorgement by certain controlling shareholders following attempts to acquire control) of Chapter 25 or under any other provision of this title relating to or affecting acquisitions or potential or proposed acquisitions of control; or

(3) to act as the board of directors, a committee of the board or an individual director solely because of the effect such action might have on an acquisition or potential or proposed acquisition of control of the corporation or the consideration that might be offered or paid to shareholders in such an acquisition.

(d) Presumption.—Absent breach of fiduciary duty, lack of good faith or self-dealing, any act as the board of directors, a committee of the board or an individual director shall be presumed to be in the best interests of the corporation. In assessing whether the standard set forth in section 1712 has been satisfied, there shall not be any greater obligation to justify, or higher burden of proof with respect to, any act as the board of directors, any committee of the board or any individual director relating to or affecting an acquisition or potential or proposed acquisition of control of the corporation than is applied to any other act as a board of directors, any committee of the board or any individual director. Notwithstanding the preceding provisions of this subsection, any act as the board of directors, a committee of the board or an individual director relating to or affecting an acquisition or potential or proposed acquisition of control to which a majority of the disinterested directors shall have assented shall be presumed to satisfy the standard set forth in section 1712, unless it is proven by clear and convincing evidence that the disinterested directors did not assent to such act in good faith after reasonable investigation.

(e) Definition.—The term "disinterested director" as used in subsection (d) and for no other purpose means:

(1) A director of the corporation other than:

(i) A director who has a direct or indirect financial or other interest in the person acquiring or seeking to acquire control of the corporation or who is an affiliate or associate, as defined in section 2552 (relating to definitions), of, or was nominated or designated as a director by, a person acquiring or seeking to acquire control of the corporation.

(ii) Depending on the specific facts surrounding the director and the act under consideration, an officer or employee or former officer or employee of the corporation.

(2) A person shall not be deemed to be other than a disinterested director solely by reason of any or all of the following:

(i) The ownership by the director of shares of the corporation.

(ii) The receipt as a holder of any class or series of any distribution made to all owners of shares of that class or series.

(iii) The receipt by the director of director's fees or other consideration as a director.

(iv) Any interest the director may have in retaining the status or position of director.

(v) The former business or employment relationship of the director with the corporation.

(vi) Receiving or having the right to receive retirement or deferred compensation from the corporation due to service as a director, officer or employee.

(f) Cross reference.—See section 1711 (relating to alternative provisions).

§ 1716. Alternative standard

(a) General rule.—In discharging the duties of their respective positions, the board of directors, committees of the board and individual directors of a business corporation may, in considering the best interests of the corporation, consider the effects of any action upon employees, upon suppliers and customers of the corporation and upon communities in which offices or other establishments of the corporation are located, and all other pertinent factors. The consideration of those factors shall not constitute a violation of section 1712 (relating to standard of care and justifiable reliance).

(b) Presumption.—Absent breach of fiduciary duty, lack of good faith or self-dealing, actions taken as a director shall be presumed to be in the best interests of the corporation.

(c) Cross reference.—See section 1711 (relating to alternative provisions).

§ 1717. Limitation on standing

The duty of the board of directors, committees of the board and individual directors under section 1712 (relating to standard of care and justifiable reliance) is solely to the business corporation and may be enforced directly by the corporation or may be enforced by a shareholder, as such, by an action in the right of the corporation, and may not be enforced directly by a shareholder or by any other person or group. Notwithstanding the preceding sentence, sections 1715(a) and (b) (relating to exercise of powers generally) and 1716(a) (relating to alternative standard) do not impose upon the board of directors, committees of the board and individual directors any legal or equitable duties, obligations or liabilities or create any right or cause of action against, or basis for standing to sue, the board of directors, committees of the board and individual directors.

ARTICLE C

DOMESTIC CORPORATION ANCILLARIES

Chapter 25

REGISTERED CORPORATIONS

Subchapter A

Preliminary Provisions

§ 2502. Registered corporation status

Subject to additional definitions contained in subsequent provisions of this chapter which are applicable to specific subchapters of this chapter, as used in this chapter, the term "registered corporation" shall mean:

(1) A domestic business corporation:

(i) that:

(A) has a class or series of shares entitled to vote generally in the election of directors of the corporation registered under the [Exchange Act]; or . . .

(ii) that is:

(A) subject to the reporting obligations imposed by section 15(d) of the Exchange Act by reason of having filed a registration statement which has become effective under the Securities Act of 1933 relating to shares of a class or series of its equity securities entitled to vote generally in the election of directors. . . .

A corporation which satisfies both subparagraphs (i) and (ii) shall be deemed to be described solely in subparagraph (i) for the purposes of this chapter.

(2) A domestic business corporation all of the shares of which are owned, directly or indirectly, by one or more registered corporations. . . .

Subchapter F

Business Combinations

§ 2552. Definitions

The following words and phrases when used in this subchapter shall have the meanings given to them in this section unless the context clearly indicates otherwise: . . .

"Beneficial owner." When used with respect to any shares, a person:

(1) that, individually or with or through any of its affiliates or associates, beneficially owns such shares, directly or indirectly;

(2) that, individually or with or through any of its affiliates or associates, has:

    (i) the right to acquire such shares (whether the right is exercisable immediately or only after the passage of time), pursuant to any agreement, arrangement or understanding (whether or not in writing), or upon the exercise of conversion rights, exchange rights, warrants or options, or otherwise, except that a person shall not be deemed the beneficial owner of shares tendered pursuant to a tender or exchange offer made by such person or the affiliates or associates of any such person until the tendered shares are accepted for purchase or exchange; or

    (ii) the right to vote such shares pursuant to any agreement, arrangement or understanding (whether or not in writing), except that a person shall not be deemed the beneficial owner of any shares under this subparagraph if the agreement, arrangement or understanding to vote such shares:

        (A) arises solely from a revocable proxy or consent given in response to a proxy or consent solicitation made in accordance with the applicable rules and regulations under the Exchange Act; and

        (B) is not then reportable on a Schedule 13D under the Exchange Act, (or any comparable or successor report); or

(3) that has any agreement, arrangement or understanding (whether or not in writing), for the purpose of acquiring, holding, voting (except voting pursuant to a revocable proxy or consent as described in paragraph (2)(ii)), or disposing of such shares with any other person that beneficially owns, or whose affiliates or associates beneficially own, directly or indirectly, such shares. . . .

"Voting shares." Shares of a corporation entitled to vote generally in the election of directors.

Subchapter G

Control–Share Acquisitions

§ 2562. Definitions

The following words and phrases when used in this subchapter shall have the meanings given to them in this section unless the context clearly indicates otherwise. . . .

"Publicly disclosed or caused to be disclosed." Includes, but is not limited to, any disclosure (whether or not required by law) that becomes public made by a person:

(1) with the intent or expectation that such disclosure become public; or

(2) to another where the disclosing person knows, or reasonably should have known, that the receiving person was not under an obligation to refrain from making such disclosure, directly or indirectly, to the public and such receiving person does make such disclosure, directly or indirectly, to the public. . . .

Subchapter H

Disgorgement by Certain Controlling Shareholders Following Attempts to Acquire Control

§ 2571. Application and effect of subchapter

(a) General rule.—Except as otherwise provided in this section, this subchapter shall apply to every registered corporation.

(b) Exceptions.—This subchapter shall not apply to any transfer of an equity security:

(1) Of a registered corporation described in section 2502(1)(ii) or (2) (relating to registered corporation status).

(2) Of a corporation:

(i) the bylaws of which explicitly provide that this subchapter shall not be applicable to the corporation by amendment adopted by the board of directors on or before July 26, 1990, in the case of a corporation:

(A) which on April 27, 1990, was a registered corporation described in section 2502(1)(i); and

(B) did not on that date have outstanding one or more classes or series of preference shares entitled, upon the occurrence of a default in the payment of dividends or another similar contingency, to elect a majority of the members of the board of directors (a bylaw adopted on or before July 26, 1990, by a corporation excluded from the scope of this subparagraph by this clause shall be ineffective unless ratified under subparagraph (ii));

(ii) the bylaws of which explicitly provide that this subchapter shall not be applicable to the corporation by amendment ratified by the board of directors on or after December 19, 1990, and on or before March 19, 1991, in the case of a corporation:

(A) which on April 27, 1990, was a registered corporation described in section 2502(1)(i);

(B) which on that date had outstanding one or more classes or series of preference shares entitled, upon the occurrence of a default in the payment of dividends or another similar contingency, to elect a majority of the members of the board of directors; and

(C) the bylaws of which on that date contained a provision described in subparagraph (i); or

(iii) in any other case, the articles of which explicitly provide that this subchapter shall not be applicable to the corporation by a provision included in the original articles, or by an articles amendment adopted at any time while it is a corporation other than a registered corporation described in section 2502(1)(i) or on or before 90 days after the corporation first becomes a registered corporation described in section 2502(1)(i). . . .

(6) Consummated by:

(i) The corporation or any of its subsidiaries.

(ii) Any savings, stock ownership, stock option or other benefit plan of the corporation or any of its subsidiaries, or any fiduciary with respect to any such plan when acting in such capacity, or by any participant in any such plan with respect to any equity security acquired pursuant to any such plan or any equity security acquired as a result of the exercise or conversion of any equity security (specifically including any options, warrants or rights) issued to such participant by the corporation pursuant to any such plan. . . .

(7)(i) where the acquisition of the equity security has been approved by a resolution adopted prior to the acquisition of the equity security; or

(ii) where the disposition of the equity security has been approved by a resolution adopted prior to the disposition of the equity security if the equity security at the time of the adoption of the resolution is beneficially owned by a person or group that is or was a controlling person or group with respect to the corporation and is in control of the corporation if:

the resolution in either subparagraph (i) or (ii) is approved by the board of directors and ratified by the affirmative vote of the shareholders entitled to cast at least a majority of the votes which all shareholders are entitled to cast thereon and identifies the specific person or group that proposes such acquisition or disposition, the specific purpose of such acquisition or disposition and the specific number of equity securities that are proposed to be acquired or disposed of by such person or group.

(d) Formation of group.—For the purposes of this subchapter, if there is no change in the beneficial ownership of an equity security held by a person, then the formation of or participation in a group involving the person shall not be deemed to constitute an acquisition of the beneficial ownership of such equity security by the group.

§ 2572. Policy and purpose

(a) General rule.—The purpose of this subchapter is to protect certain registered corporations and legitimate interests of various groups related to such corporations from certain manipulative and coercive actions. Specifically, this subchapter seeks to:

(1) Protect registered corporations from being exposed to and paying "greenmail."

(2) Promote a stable relationship among the various parties involved in registered corporations, including the public whose confidence in the future of a corporation tends to be undermined when a corporation is put "in play."

(3) Ensure that speculators who put registered corporations "in play" do not misappropriate corporate values for themselves at the expense of the corporation and groups affected by corporate actions.

(4) Discourage such speculators from putting registered corporations "in play" through any means, including, but not limited to, offering to purchase at least 20% of the voting shares of the corporation or threatening to wage or waging a proxy contest in connection with or as a means toward or part of a plan to acquire control of the corporation, with the effect of reaping short-term speculative profits.

Moreover, this subchapter recognizes the right and obligation of the Commonwealth to regulate and protect the corporations it creates from abuses resulting from the application of its own laws affecting generally corporate governance and particularly director obligations, mergers and related matters. Such laws, and the obligations imposed on directors or others thereunder, should not be the vehicles by which registered corporations are manipulated in certain instances for the purpose of obtaining short-term profits.

(b) Limitations.—The purpose of this subchapter is not to affect legitimate shareholder activity that does not involve putting a corporation "in play" or involve seeking to acquire control of the corporation. Specifically, the purpose of this subchapter is not to:

(1) curtail proxy contests on matters properly submitted for shareholder action under applicable State or other law, including, but not limited to, certain elections of directors, corporate governance matters such as cumulative voting or staggered boards, or other corporate matters such as environmental issues or conducting business in a particular country if, in any such instance, such proxy contest is not utilized in connection with or as a means toward or part of a plan to put the corporation "in play" or to seek to acquire control of the corporation; or

(2) affect the solicitation of proxies or consents by or on behalf of the corporation in connection with shareholder meetings or actions of the corporation.

§ 2573. Definitions

The following words and phrases when used in this subchapter shall have the meanings given to them in this section unless the context clearly indicates otherwise:

"Beneficial owner." The term shall have the meaning specified in section 2552 (relating to definitions).

"Control." The power, whether or not exercised, to direct or cause the direction of the management and policies of a person, whether through the ownership of voting shares, by contract or otherwise.

"Controlling person or group."

(1)(i) A person or group who has acquired, offered to acquire or, directly or indirectly, publicly disclosed or caused to be disclosed (other than for the purpose of circumventing the intent of this subchapter) the intention of acquiring voting power over voting shares of a registered corporation that would entitle the holder thereof to cast at least 20% of the votes that all shareholders would be entitled to cast in an election of directors of the corporation; or

(ii) a person or group who has otherwise, directly or indirectly, publicly disclosed or caused to be disclosed (other than for the purpose of circumventing the intent of this subchapter) that it may seek to acquire control of a corporation through any means.

(2) Two or more persons acting in concert, whether or not pursuant to an express agreement, arrangement, relationship or understanding, including as a partnership, limited partnership, syndicate, or through any means of affiliation whether or not formally organized, for the purpose of acquiring, holding, voting or disposing of equity securities of a corporation shall be deemed a group for

purposes of this subchapter. Notwithstanding any other provision of this subchapter to the contrary, and regardless of whether a group has been deemed to acquire beneficial ownership of an equity security under this subchapter, each person who participates in a group, where such group is a controlling person or group as defined in this subchapter, shall also be deemed to be a controlling person or group for the purposes of this subchapter. ...

"Equity security." Any security, including all shares, stock or similar security, and any security convertible into (with or without additional consideration) or exercisable for any such shares, stock or similar security, or carrying any warrant, right or option to subscribe to or purchase such shares, stock or similar security or any such warrant, right, option or similar instrument.…

"Profit." The positive value, if any, of the difference between:

(1) the consideration received from the disposition of equity securities less only the usual and customary broker's commissions actually paid in connection with such disposition; and

(2) the consideration actually paid for the acquisition of such equity securities plus only the usual and customary broker's commissions actually paid in connection with such acquisition.

"Proxy." Includes any proxy, consent or authorization.

"Proxy solicitation" or **"solicitation of proxies."** Includes any solicitation of a proxy, including a solicitation of a revocable proxy of the nature and under the circumstances described in section 2574(b)(3) (relating to controlling person or group safe harbor).

"Publicly disclosed or caused to be disclosed." The term shall have the meaning specified in section 2562 (relating to definitions).

"Transfer." Acquisition or disposition.

"Voting shares." The term shall have the meaning specified in section 2552 (relating to definitions).

§ 2574. Controlling person or group safe harbor

(a) Nonparticipant.—For the purpose of this subchapter, a person or group shall not be deemed a controlling person or group, absent significant other activities indicating that a person or group should be deemed a controlling person or group, by reason of voting or giving a proxy or consent as a shareholder of the corporation if the person or group is one who or which:

(1) did not acquire any voting shares of the corporation with the purpose of changing or influencing control of the corporation or seeking to acquire control of the corporation or in connection with or as a participant in any agreement, arrangement, relationship, understanding or otherwise having any such purpose;

(2) if control were acquired, would not be a person or group or a participant in a group that has control over the corporation and will not receive, directly or indirectly, any consideration from a person or group that has control over the corporation other than consideration offered proportionately to all holders of voting shares of the corporation; and

(3) if a proxy or consent is given, executes a revocable proxy or consent given without consideration in response to a proxy or consent solicitation made in accordance with the applicable rules and regulations under the Exchange Act under circumstances not then reportable on Schedule 13D under the Exchange Act (or any comparable or successor report) by the person or group who gave the proxy or consent.

(b) Certain holders.—For the purpose of this subchapter, a person or group shall not be deemed a controlling person or group under subparagraph (1)(i) of the definition of "controlling person or group" in section 2573 (relating to definitions) if such person or group holds voting power:

(1) in good faith and not for the purpose of circumventing this subchapter, as an agent, bank, broker, nominee or trustee for one or more beneficial owners who do not individually or, if they are a group acting in concert, as a group have the voting power specified in subparagraph (1)(i) of the definition of "controlling person or group" in section 2573;

(2) in connection with the solicitation of proxies or consents by or on behalf of the corporation in connection with shareholder meetings or actions of the corporation; or

(3) in the amount specified in subparagraph (1)(i) of the definition of "controlling person or group" in section 2573 as a result of the solicitation of revocable proxies or consents with respect to voting shares if such proxies or consents both:

(i) are given without consideration in response to a proxy or consent solicitation made in accordance with the applicable rules and regulations under the exchange act; and

(ii) do not empower the holder thereof, whether or not this power is shared with any other person, to vote such shares except on the specific matters described in such proxy or consent and in accordance with the instructions of the giver of such proxy or consent. . . .

§ 2575. Ownership by corporation of profits resulting from certain transactions

Any profit realized by any person or group who is or was a controlling person or group with respect to a registered corporation from the disposition of any equity security of the corporation to any person ... including, without limitation, to the corporation ... or to another member of the controlling person or group, shall belong to and be recoverable by the corporation where the profit is realized by such person or group:

> (1) from the disposition of the equity security within 18 months after the person or group obtained the status of a controlling person or group; and

> (2) the equity security had been acquired by the controlling person or group within 24 months prior to or 18 months subsequent to the obtaining by the person or group of the status of a controlling person or group.

Any transfer by a controlling person or group of the ownership of any equity security may be suspended on the books of the corporation, and certificates representing such securities may be duly legended, to enforce the rights of the corporation under this subchapter.

§ 2576. Enforcement actions

(a) **Venue.**—Actions to recover any profit due under this subchapter may be commenced in any court of competent jurisdiction by the registered corporation issuing the equity security or by any holder of any equity security of the corporation in the name and on behalf of the corporation if the corporation fails or refuses to bring the action within 60 days after written request by a holder or shall fail to prosecute the action diligently. If a judgment requiring the payment of any such profits is entered, the party bringing such action shall recover all costs, including reasonable attorney fees, incurred in connection with enforcement of this subchapter.

(b) **Jurisdiction.**—By engaging in the activities necessary to become a controlling person or group and thereby becoming a controlling person or group, the person or group and all persons participating in the group consent to personal jurisdiction in the courts of this Commonwealth for enforcement of this subchapter. Courts of this Commonwealth may exercise personal jurisdiction over any controlling person or group in actions to enforce this subchapter.... Service of process may be made upon such persons outside this Commonwealth in accordance with the procedures specified by 42 Pa.C.S. § 5323 (relating to service of process on persons outside this Commonwealth).

(c) **Limitation.**—Any action to enforce this subchapter shall be brought within two years from the date any profit recoverable by the corporation was realized.

Subchapter I

Severance Compensation for Employees Terminated Following Certain Control–Share Acquisitions

Sec.
2581. Definitions.
2582. Severance compensation.
2583. Enforcement and remedies.

§ 2581. Definitions

The following words and phrases when used in this subchapter shall have the meanings given to them in this section unless the context clearly indicates otherwise:

"Acquiring person." The term shall have the meaning specified in section 2562 (relating to definitions).

"Control-share acquisition." The term shall have the meaning specified in section 2562.

"Control-share approval."

(1) The occurrence of both:

(i) a control-share acquisition to which Subchapter G (relating to control-share acquisitions) applies with respect to a registered corporation described in section 2502(1)(i) (relating to registered corporation status) by an acquiring person; and

(ii) the according by such registered corporation of voting rights pursuant to section 2564(a) (relating to voting rights of shares acquired in a control-share acquisition) in connection with such control-share acquisition to control shares of the acquiring person.

(2) The term shall also include a control-share acquisition effected by an acquiring person, other than a control-share acquisition described in section 2561(b)(3), (4) or (5) (other than subparagraph 2561(b)(5)(vii)) (relating to application and effect of subchapter) if the control-share acquisition:

(i)(A) occurs primarily in response to the actions of another acquiring person where Subchapter G (relating to control-share acquisitions) applies to a control-share acquisition or proposed control-share acquisition by such other acquiring person; and

(B) either:

(I) pursuant to an agreement or plan [of merger, consolidation, or share exchange] described in section 2561(b)(5)(vii);

1260

(II) after adoption of an amendment to the articles of the registered corporation [which provide that Subchapter G shall not be applicable to the corporation] pursuant to section 2561(b)(2)(iii); or

(III) after reincorporation of the registered corporation in another jurisdiction;

if the agreement or plan is approved or the amendment or reincorporation is adopted by the board of directors of the corporation during the period commencing after the satisfaction by such other acquiring person of the requirements of section 2565(a) or (b) (relating to procedure for establishing voting rights of control shares) and ending 90 days after the date such issue is voted on by the shareholders, is withdrawn from consideration or becomes moot; or

(ii) is consummated in any manner by a person who satisfied, within two years prior to such acquisition, the requirements of section 2565(a) or (b).

"Control shares." The term shall have the meaning specified in section 2562.

"Eligible employee." Any employee of a registered corporation (or any subsidiary thereof) if:

(1) the registered corporation was the subject of a control-share approval;

(2) the employee was an employee of such corporation (or any subsidiary thereof) within 90 days before or on the day of the control-share approval and had been so employed for at least two years prior thereto; and

(3) the employment of the employee is in this Commonwealth.

"Employee." Any person lawfully employed by an employer.

"Employment in this Commonwealth."

(1) The entire service of an employee, performed inside and outside of this Commonwealth, if the service is localized in this Commonwealth.

(2) Service shall be deemed to be localized in this Commonwealth if:

(i) the service is performed entirely inside this Commonwealth; or

(ii) the service is performed both inside and outside of this Commonwealth but the service performed outside of this Commonwealth is incidental to the service of the employee inside this Commonwealth, as where such service is temporary or transitory in nature or consists of isolated transactions.

(3) Employment in this Commonwealth shall also include service of the employee, performed inside and outside of this Commonwealth, if the service is not localized in any state, but some of the service is performed in this Commonwealth, and:

> (i) the base of operations of the employee is in this Commonwealth;

> (ii) there is no base of operations, and the place from which such service is directed or controlled is in this Commonwealth; or

> (iii) the base of operations of the employee or place from which such service is directed or controlled is not in any state in which some part of the service is performed, but the residence of the employee is in this Commonwealth.

"**Minimum severance amount.**" With respect to an eligible employee, the weekly compensation of the employee multiplied by the number of the completed years of service of the employee, up to a maximum of 26 times the weekly compensation of the employee.

"**Subsidiary.**" The term shall have the meaning specified in section 2552 (relating to definitions).

"**Termination of employment.**" The layoff of at least six months, or the involuntary termination of an employee, except that any employee employed in a business operation who is continued or employed or offered employment (within 60 days) by the purchaser of such business operation, on substantially the same terms (including geographic location) as those pursuant to which the employee was employed in such business operation, shall not be deemed to have been laid off or involuntarily terminated for the purposes of this subchapter by such transfer of employment to the purchaser, but the purchaser shall make the lump-sum payment under this subchapter in the event of a layoff of at least six months or the involuntary termination of the employee within the period specified in section 2582 (relating to severance compensation).

"**Weekly compensation.**" The average regular weekly compensation of an employee based on normal schedule of hours in effect for such employee over the last three months preceding the control-share approval.

"**Year of service.**" Each full year during which the employee has been employed by the employer.

§ 2582. Severance compensation

(a) **General rule.**—Any eligible employee whose employment is terminated, other than for willful misconduct connected with the work of the employee, within 90 days before the control-share approval with respect to the registered corporation if such termination was pursuant to an agreement, arrangement or understanding, whether formal or informal, with the acquiring person whose control shares were accorded voting rights in connection with such control-share approval or within 24 calendar months after the control-share approval with respect to the registered corporation shall receive a one-time, lump-sum payment from the employer equal to:

(1) the minimum severance amount with respect to the employee; less

(2) any payments made to the employee by the employer due to termination of employment, whether pursuant to any contract, policy, plan or otherwise, but not including any final wage payments to the employee or payments to the employee under pension, savings, retirement or similar plans.

(b) Limitation.—If the amount specified in subsection (a)(2) is at least equal to the amount specified in subsection (a)(1), no payment shall be required to be made under this subchapter.

(c) Due date of payment.—Severance compensation under this subchapter to eligible employees shall be made within one regular pay period after the last day of work of the employee, in the case of a layoff known at such time to be at least six months or an involuntary termination and in all other cases within 30 days after the eligible employee first becomes entitled to compensation under this subchapter.

§ 2583. Enforcement and remedies

(a) Notice.—Within 30 days of the control-share approval, the employer shall provide written notice to each eligible employee and to the collective bargaining representative, if any, of the rights of eligible employees under this subchapter.

(b) Remedies.—In the event any eligible employee is denied a lump-sum payment in violation of this subchapter or the employer fails to provide the notice required by subsection (a), the employee on his or her own behalf or on behalf of other employees similarly situated, or the collective bargaining representative, if any, on the behalf of the employee, may, in addition to all other remedies available at law or in equity, bring an action to remedy such violation. In any such action, the court may order such equitable or legal relief as it deems just and proper.

(c) Civil penalty.—In the case of violations of subsection (a), the court may order the employer to pay to each employee who was subject to a termination of employment and entitled to severance compensation under this subchapter a civil penalty not to exceed $75 per day for each business day that notice was not provided to such employee.

(d) Successor liability.—The rights under this subchapter of any individual who was an eligible employee at the time of the control-share approval shall vest at that time, and, in any action based on a violation of this subchapter, recovery may be secured against:

 (1) a merged, consolidated or resulting domestic or foreign corporation or other successor employer; or

 (2) the corporation after its status as a registered corporation has terminated;

notwithstanding any provision of law to the contrary.

Subchapter J

Business Combination Transactions—Labor Contracts

Sec.

§ 2585. Application and effect of subchapter

 (a) General rule.—Except as otherwise provided in this section, this subchapter shall apply to every business combination transaction relating to a business operation if such business operation was owned by a registered corporation (or any subsidiary thereof) at the time of a control-share approval with respect to the corporation (regardless of the fact, if such be the case, that such operation after the control-share approval is owned by the registered corporation or any other person).

 (b) Exceptions.—This subchapter shall not apply to:

 (1) Any business combination transaction occurring more than five years after the control-share approval of the registered corporation.

 (2) Any business operation located other than in this Commonwealth.

§ 2586. Definitions

 The following words and phrases when used in this subchapter shall have the meanings given to them in this section unless the context clearly indicates otherwise:

 "Business combination transaction." Any merger or consolidation, sale, lease, exchange or other disposition, in one transaction or a series of transactions, whether affecting all or substantially all the property and assets, including its good will, of the business operation that is the subject of the labor contract referred to in section 2587 (relating to labor contracts preserved in business combination transactions) or any transfer of a controlling interest in such business operation.

"Control-share approval." The term shall have the meaning specified in section 2581 (relating to definitions).

"Covered labor contract." Any labor contract if such contract:

(1) covers persons engaged in employment in this Commonwealth;

(2) was negotiated by a labor organization or by a collective bargaining agent or other representative;

(3) relates to a business operation that was owned by the registered corporation (or any subsidiary thereof) at the time of the control-share approval with respect to such corporation; and

(4) was in effect and covered such business operation and such employees at the time of such control-share approval.

"Employee" and **"employment in this Commonwealth."** The terms shall have the meanings specified in section 2581.

"Subsidiary." The term shall have the meaning specified in section 2552 (relating to definitions).

§ 2587. Labor contracts preserved in business combination transactions

No business combination transaction shall result in the termination or impairment of the provisions of any covered labor contract, and the contract shall continue in effect pursuant to its terms until it is terminated pursuant to any termination provision contained therein or until otherwise agreed upon by the parties to such contract or their successors.

§ 2588. Civil remedies

(a) General rule.—In the event that an employee is denied or fails to receive wages, benefits or wage supplements or suffers any contractual loss as a result of a violation of this subchapter, the employee on his or her own behalf or on behalf of other employees similarly situated, or the labor organization or collective bargaining agent party to the labor contract, may, in addition to all other remedies available at law or in equity, bring an action in any court of competent jurisdiction to recover such wages, benefits, wage supplements or contractual losses and to enjoin the violation of this subchapter.

(b) Successor liability.—The rights under this subchapter of any employee at the time of the control-share approval shall vest at that time, and, in any action based on a violation of this subchapter, recovery may be secured against:

(1) a merged, consolidated or resulting domestic or foreign corporation or other successor employer; or

(2) the corporation after its status as a registered corporation has terminated;

notwithstanding any provision of law to the contrary.

VIRGINIA CORPORATIONS
CODE § 13.1–690

§ 13.1–690 General standards of conduct for director

A. A director shall discharge his duties as a director, including his duties as a member of a committee, in accordance with his good faith business judgment of the best interests of the corporation.

B. Unless he has knowledge or information concerning the matter in question that makes reliance unwarranted, a director is entitled to rely on information, opinions, reports or statements, including financial statements and other financial data, if prepared or presented by:

1. One or more officers or employees of the corporation whom the director believes, in good faith, to be reliable and competent in the matters presented;

2. Legal counsel, public accountants, or other persons as to matters the director believes, in good faith, are within the person's professional or expert competence; or

3. A committee of the board of directors of which he is not a member if the director believes, in good faith, that the committee merits confidence.

C. A director is not liable for any action taken as a director, or any failure to take any action, if he performed the duties of his office in compliance with this section.

D. A person alleging a violation of this section has the burden of proving the violation.

§ 8–204. Effect of Issuer's Restriction on Transfer

A restriction on transfer of a security imposed by the issuer, even if otherwise lawful, is ineffective against a person without knowledge of the restriction unless:

(1) the security is certificated and the restriction is noted conspicuously on the security certificate; or

(2) the security is uncertificated and the registered owner has been notified of the restriction.

Official Comment

1. Restrictions on transfer of securities are imposed by issuers in a variety of circumstances and for a variety of purposes, such as to retain control of a close corporation or to ensure compliance with federal securities laws. Other law determines whether such restrictions are permissible. This section deals only with the consequences of failure to note the restriction on a security certificate.

This section imposes no bar to enforcement of a restriction on transfer against a person who has actual knowledge of it.

2. A restriction on transfer of a certificated security is ineffective against a person without knowledge of the restriction unless the restriction is noted conspicuously on the certificate. The word "noted" is used to make clear that the restriction need not be set forth in full text. Refusal by an issuer to register a transfer on the basis of an unnoted restriction would be a violation of the issuer's duty to register under Section 8–401 [Duty of Issuer to Register Transfer].

3. ... A purchaser who takes delivery of a certificated security is entitled to rely on the terms stated on the certificate. That policy obviously does not apply to uncertificated securities. For uncertificated securities, this section requires only that the registered owner has been notified of the restriction. Suppose, for example, that A is the registered owner of an uncertificated security, and that the issuer has notified A of a restriction on transfer. A agrees to sell the security to B, in violation of the restriction. A completes a written instruction directing the issuer to register transfer to B, and B pays A for the security at the time A delivers the instruction to B. A does not inform B of the restriction, and B does not otherwise have notice or knowledge of it at the time B pays and receives the instruction. B presents the instruction to the issuer, but the issuer refuses to register the transfer on the grounds that it

would violate the restriction. The issuer has complied with this section, because it did notify the registered owner A of the restriction. The issuer's refusal to register transfer is not wrongful. B has an action against A for breach of transfer warranty.... B's mistake was treating an uncertificated security transaction in the fashion appropriate only for a certificated security. The mechanism for transfer of uncertificated securities is registration of transfer on the books of the issuer; handing over an instruction only initiates the process. The purchaser should make arrangements to ensure that the price is not paid until it knows that the issuer has or will register transfer.

4. In the indirect holding system, investors neither take physical delivery of security certificates nor have uncertificated securities registered in their names. So long as the requirements of this section have been satisfied at the level of the relationship between the issuer and the securities intermediary that is a direct holder, this section does not preclude the issuer from enforcing a restriction on transfer....

5. This section deals only with restrictions imposed by the issuer. Restrictions imposed by statute are not affected. See Quiner v. Marblehead Social Co., 10 Mass. 476 (1813); Madison Bank v. Price, 79 Kan. 289, 100 P. 280 (1909); Healey v. Steele Center Creamery Ass'n, 115 Minn. 451, 133 N.W. 69 (1911). Nor does it deal with private agreements between stockholders containing restrictive covenants as to the sale of the security.

FEDERAL RULES OF CIVIL PROCEDURE

RULES 11, 23, 23.1

Rule 11. Signing of Pleadings, Motions, and Other Papers; Representations to Court; Sanctions

(a) Signature. Every pleading, written motion, and other paper shall be signed by at least one attorney of record in the attorney's individual name, or, if the party is not represented by an attorney, shall be signed by the party. Each paper shall state the signer's address and telephone number, if any. Except when otherwise specifically provided by rule or statute, pleadings need not be verified or accompanied by affidavit. An unsigned paper omission of the signature is corrected promptly after being called to the attention of the attorney or party.

(b) Representations to Court. By presenting to the court (whether by signing, filing, submitting, or later advocating) a pleading, written motion, or other paper, an attorney or unrepresented party is certifying that to the best of the person's knowledge, information, and belief, formed after an inquiry reasonable under the circumstances,—

(1) it is not being presented for any improper purpose, such as to harass or to cause unnecessary delay or needless increase in the cost of litigation;

(2) the claims, defenses, and other legal contentions therein are warranted by existing law or by a nonfrivolous argument for the extension, modification, or reversal of existing law or the establishment of new law;

(3) the allegations and other factual contentions have evidentiary support or, if specifically so identified, are likely to have evidentiary support after a reasonable opportunity for further investigation or discovery; and

(4) the denials of factual contentions are warranted on the evidence or, if specifically so identified, are reasonably based on a lack of information or belief.

(c) Sanctions. If, after notice and a reasonable opportunity to respond, the court determines that subdivision (b) has been violated, the court may, subject to the conditions stated below, impose an appropriate sanction upon the attorneys, law firms, or parties that have violated subdivision (b) or are responsible for the violation.

(1) How Initiated.

(A) *By Motion.* A motion for sanctions under this rule shall be made separately from other motions or requests and shall describe the specific conduct alleged to violate subdivision (b). It shall be served as provided in Rule 5, but shall not be filed with or presented to the court unless, within 21 days after service of the motion (or such other period as the court may prescribe), the challenged paper, claim, defense, contention, allegation, or denial is not withdrawn or appropriately corrected. If warranted, the court may award to the party prevailing on the motion the reasonable expenses and attorney's fees incurred in presenting or opposing the motion. Absent exceptional circumstances, a law firm shall be held jointly responsible for violations committed by its partners, associates, and employees.

(B) *On Court's Initiative.* On its own initiative, the court may enter an order describing the specific conduct that appears to violate subdivision (b) and directing an attorney, law firm, or party to show cause why it has not violated subdivision (b) with respect thereto.

(2) Nature of Sanction; Limitations. A sanction imposed for violation of this rule shall be limited to what is sufficient to deter repetition of such conduct or comparable conduct by others similarly situated. Subject to the limitations in subparagraphs (A) and (B), the sanction may consist of, or include, directives of a nonmonetary nature, an order to pay a penalty into court, or, if imposed on motion and warranted for effective deterrence, an order directing payment to the movant of some or all of the reasonable attorneys' fees and other expenses incurred as a direct result of the violation.

(A) Monetary sanctions may not be awarded against a represented party for a violation of subdivision (b)(2).

(B) Monetary sanctions may not be awarded on the court's initiative unless the court issues its order to show cause before a voluntary dismissal or settlement of the claims made by or against the party which is, or whose attorneys are, to be sanctioned.

(3) Order. When imposing sanctions, the court shall describe the conduct determined to constitute a violation of this rule and explain the basis for the sanction imposed.

(d) Inapplicability to Discovery. Subdivisions (a) through (c) of this rule do not apply to disclosures and discovery requests, responses, objections, and motions that are subject to the provisions of Rules 26 through 37.

Rule 23.   Class Actions

(a) **Prerequisites to a Class Action.** One or more members of a class may sue or be sued as representative parties on behalf of all only if (1) the class is so numerous that joinder of all members is impracticable, (2) there are questions of law or fact common to the class, (3) the claims or defenses of the representative parties are typical of the claims or defenses of the class, and (4) the representative parties will fairly and adequately protect the interests of the class.

(b) **Class Actions Maintainable.** An action may be maintained as a class action if the prerequisites of subdivision (a) are satisfied, and in addition:

(1) the prosecution of separate actions by or against individual members of the class would create a risk of

(A) inconsistent or varying adjudications with respect to individual members of the class which would establish incompatible standards of conduct for the party opposing the class, or

(B) adjudications with respect to individual members of the class which would as a practical matter be dispositive of the interests of the other members not parties to the adjudications or substantially impair or impede their ability to protect their interests; or

(2) the party opposing the class has acted or refused to act on grounds generally applicable to the class, thereby making appropriate final injunctive relief or corresponding declaratory relief with respect to the class as a whole; or

(3) the court finds that the questions of law or fact common to the members of the class predominate over any questions affecting only individual members, and that a class action is superior to other available methods for the fair and efficient adjudication of the controversy. The matters pertinent to the findings include: (A) the interest of members of the class in individually controlling the prosecution or defense of separate actions; (B) the extent and nature of any litigation concerning the controversy already commenced by or against members of the class; (C) the desirability or undesirability of concentrating the litigation of the claims in the particular forum; (D) the difficulties likely to be encountered in the management of a class action.

(c) **Determining by Order Whether to Certify a Class Action; Appointing Class Counsel; Notice and Membership in Class; Judgment; Multiple Classes and Subclasses.**

(1)(A) When a person sues or is sued as a representative of a class, the court must—at an early practicable time—determine by order whether to certify the action as a class action.

(B) An order certifying a class action must define the class and the class claims, issues, or defenses, and must appoint class counsel under Rule 23(g).

(C) An order under Rule 23(c)(1) may be altered or amended before final judgment.

(2)(A) For any class certified under Rule 23(b)(1) or (2), the court may direct appropriate notice to the class.

(B) For any class certified under Rule 23(b)(3), the court must direct to class members the best notice practicable under the circumstances, including individual notice to all members who can be identified through reasonable effort. The notice must concisely and clearly state in plain, easily understood language:

- the nature of the action,

- the definition of the class certified,

- the class claims, issues, or defenses,

- that a class member may enter an appearance through counsel if the member so desires,

- that the court will exclude from the class any member who requests exclusion, stating when and how members may elect to be excluded, and

- the binding effect of a class judgment on class members under Rule 23(c)(3).

(3) The judgment in an action maintained as a class action under subdivision (b)(1) or (b)(2), whether or not favorable to the class, shall include and describe those whom the court finds to be members of the class. The judgment in an action maintained as a class action under subdivision (b)(3), whether or not favorable to the class, shall include and specify or describe those to whom the notice provided in subdivision (c)(2) was directed, and who have not requested exclusion, and whom the court finds to be members of the class.

(4) When appropriate (A) an action may be brought or maintained as a class action with respect to particular issues, or (B) a class may be divided into subclasses and each subclass treated as a class, and the provisions of this rule shall then be construed and applied accordingly.

(d) Orders in Conduct of Actions. In the conduct of actions to which this rule applies, the court may make appropriate orders: (1) determining the course of proceedings or prescribing measures to prevent undue repetition or complication in the presentation of evidence or argument; (2) requiring, for the protection of the members of the class or otherwise for the fair conduct of the action, that notice be given in such manner as the court may direct to some or all of the members of any step in the action, or of the proposed extent of the judgment, or of the opportunity of members to signify whether they consider the representation fair and adequate, to intervene and present claims or defenses, or otherwise to come into the action; (3) imposing conditions on the representative parties or on intervenors; (4) requiring that the pleadings be amended to eliminate therefrom allegations as to representation of absent persons, and that the action proceed accordingly; (5) dealing with similar procedural matters. The orders may be combined with an order under Rule 16 [Pre-Trial Procedure; Formulating Issues], and may be altered or amended as may be desirable from time to time.

(e) Settlement, Voluntary Dismissal, or Compromise.

(1)(A) The court must approve any settlement, voluntary dismissal, or compromise of the claims, issues, or defenses of a certified class.

(B) The court must direct notice in a reasonable manner to all class members who would be bound by a proposed settlement, voluntary dismissal, or compromise.

(C) The court may approve a settlement, voluntary dismissal, or compromise that would bind class members only after a hearing and on finding that the settlement, voluntary dismissal, or compromise is fair, reasonable, and adequate.

(2) The parties seeking approval of a settlement, voluntary dismissal, or compromise under Rule 23(e)(1) must file a statement identifying any agreement made in connection with the proposed settlement, voluntary dismissal, or compromise.

(3) In an action previously certified as a class action under Rule 23(b)(3), the court may refuse to approve a settlement unless it affords a new opportunity to request exclusion to individual class members who had an earlier opportunity to request exclusion but did not do so.

(4)(A) Any class member may object to a proposed settlement, voluntary dismissal, or compromise that requires court approval under Rule 23(e)(1)(A).

(B) An objection made under Rule 23(e)(4)(A) may be withdrawn only with the court's approval.

(f) Appeals.
A court of appeals may in its discretion permit an appeal from an order of a district court granting or denying class action certification under this rule if application is made to it within ten days after entry of the order. An appeal does not stay proceedings in the district court unless the district judge or the court of appeals so orders.

(g) Class Counsel.

(1) Appointing Class Counsel.

(A) Unless a statute provides otherwise, a court that certifies a class must appoint class counsel.

(B) An attorney appointed to serve as class counsel must fairly and adequately represent the interests of the class.

(C) In appointing class counsel, the court

(i) must consider:

- the work counsel has done in identifying or investigating potential claims in the action,
- counsel's experience in handling class actions, other complex litigation, and claims of the type asserted in the action,
- counsel's knowledge of the applicable law, and
- the resources counsel will commit to representing the class;

(ii) may consider any other matter pertinent to counsel's ability to fairly and adequately represent the interests of the class;

(iii) may direct potential class counsel to provide information on any subject pertinent to the appointment and to propose terms for attorney fees and nontaxable costs; and

(iv) may make further orders in connection with the appointment.

(2) Appointment Procedure.

(A) The court may designate interim counsel to act on behalf of the putative class before determining whether to certify the action as a class action.

(B) When there is one applicant for appointment as class counsel, the court may appoint that applicant only if the applicant is adequate under Rule 23(g)(1)(B) and (C). If more than one adequate applicant seeks appointment as class counsel, the court must appoint the applicant best able to represent the interests of the class.

(C) The order appointing class counsel may include provisions about the award of attorney fees or nontaxable costs under Rule 23(h).

(h) Attorney Fees Award. In an action certified as a class action, the court may award reasonable attorney fees and nontaxable costs authorized by law or by agreement of the parties as follows:

(1) Motion for Award of Attorney Fees. A claim for an award of attorney fees and nontaxable costs must be made by motion under Rule 54(d)(2), subject to the provisions of this subdivision, at a time set by the court. Notice of the motion must be served on all parties and, for motions by class counsel, directed to class members in a reasonable manner.

(2) Objections to Motion. A class member, or a party from whom payment is sought, may object to the motion.

(3) Hearing and Findings. The court may hold a hearing and must find the facts and state its conclusions of law on the motion under Rule 52(a).

(4) Reference to Special Master or Magistrate Judge. The court may refer issues related to the amount of the award to a special master or to a magistrate judge as provided in Rule 54(d)(2)(D).

Rule 23.1   Derivative Actions by Shareholders

In a derivative action brought by one or more shareholders or members to enforce a right of a corporation or of an unincorporated association, the corporation or association having failed to enforce a right which may properly be asserted by it, the complaint shall be verified and shall allege (1) that the plaintiff was a shareholder or member at the time of the transaction of which the plaintiff complains or that the plaintiff's share or membership thereafter devolved on the plaintiff by operation of law, and (2) that the action is not a collusive one to confer jurisdiction on a court of the United States which it would not otherwise have. The complaint shall also allege with particularity the efforts, if any, made by the plaintiff to obtain the action the plaintiff desires from the directors or comparable authority and, if necessary, from the shareholders or members, and the reasons for the plaintiff's failure to obtain the action or for not making the effort. The derivative action may not be maintained if it appears that the plaintiff does not fairly and adequately represent the interests of the shareholders or members similarly situated in enforcing the right of the corporation or association. The action shall not be dismissed or compromised without the approval of the court, and notice of the proposed dismissal or compromise shall be given to shareholders or members in such manner as the court directs.

UNIFORM FRAUDULENT TRANSFER ACT

(Selected Provisions)

§ 1. Definitions ....

As used in this [Act]:

(1) "Affiliate" means:

(i) a person who directly or indirectly owns, controls, or holds with power to vote, 20 percent or more of the outstanding voting securities of the debtor, other than a person who holds the securities,

(A) as a fiduciary or agent without sole discretionary power to vote the securities; or

(B) solely to secure a debt, if the person has not exercised the power to vote;

(ii) a corporation 20 percent or more of whose outstanding voting securities are directly or indirectly owned, controlled, or held with power to vote, by the debtor or a person who directly or indirectly owns, controls, or holds, with power to vote, 20 percent or more of the outstanding voting securities of the debtor, other than a person who holds the securities,

(A) as a fiduciary or agent without sole power to vote the securities; or

(B) solely to secure a debt, if the person has not in fact exercised the power to vote;

(iii) a person whose business is operated by the debtor under a lease or other agreement, or a person substantially all of whose assets are controlled by the debtor; or

(iv) a person who operates the debtor's business under a lease or other agreement or controls substantially all of the debtor's assets....

(7) "Insider" includes ...

(ii) if the debtor is a corporation,

(A) a director of the debtor;

(B) an officer of the debtor;

(C) a person in control of the debtor;

(D) a partnership in which the debtor is a general partner;

(E) a general partner in a partnership described in clause (D); or

(F) a relative of a general partner, director, officer, or person in control of the debtor;

(iii) if the debtor is a partnership,

(A) a general partner in the debtor;

(B) a relative of a general partner in, a general partner of, or a person in control of the debtor;

(C) another partnership in which the debtor is a general partner;

(D) a general partner in a partnership described in clause (C); or

(E) a person in control of the debtor;

(iv) an affiliate, or an insider of an affiliate as if the affiliate were the debtor; and

(v) a managing agent of the debtor....

(12) "Transfer" means every mode, direct or indirect, absolute or conditional, voluntary or involuntary, of disposing of or parting with an asset or an interest in an asset, and includes payment of money, release, lease, and creation of a lien or other encumbrance.

§ 2. Insolvency

(a) A debtor is insolvent if the sum of the debtor's debts is greater than all of the debtor's assets at a fair valuation....

(b) A debtor who is generally not paying his [or her] debts as they become due is presumed to be insolvent.

(c) A partnership is insolvent under subsection (a) if the sum of the partnership's debts is greater than the aggregate, at a fair valuation, of all of the partnership's assets and the sum of the excess of the value of each general partner's nonpartnership assets over the partner's nonpartnership debts....

§ 4. Transfers Fraudulent as to Present and Future Creditors

(a) A transfer made or obligation incurred by a debtor is fraudulent as to a creditor, whether the creditor's claim arose before or after the transfer was made or the obligation was incurred, if the debtor made the transfer or incurred the obligation:

      (1) with actual intent to hinder, delay, or defraud any creditor of the debtor; or

      (2) without receiving a reasonably equivalent value in exchange for the transfer or obligation, and the debtor:

            (i) was engaged or was about to engage in a business or a transaction for which the remaining assets of the debtor were unreasonably small in relation to the business or transaction; or

            (ii) intended to incur, or believed or reasonably should have believed that he [or she] would incur, debts beyond his [or her] ability to pay as they became due.

  (b) In determining actual intent under subsection (a)(1), consideration may be given, among other factors, to whether:

      (1) the transfer or obligation was to an insider;

      (2) the debtor retained possession or control of the property transferred after the transfer; . . .

      (8) the value of the consideration received by the debtor was reasonably equivalent to the value of the asset transferred or the amount of the obligation incurred;

      (9) the debtor was insolvent or became insolvent shortly after the transfer was made or the obligation was incurred;

      (10) the transfer occurred shortly before or shortly after a substantial debt was incurred; and

      (11) the debtor transferred the essential assets of the business to a lienor who transferred the assets to an insider of the debtor.

§ 5.   Transfers Fraudulent as to Present Creditors

  (a) A transfer made or obligation incurred by a debtor is fraudulent as to a creditor whose claim arose before the transfer was made or the obligation was incurred if the debtor made the transfer or incurred the obligation without receiving a reasonably equivalent value in exchange for the transfer or obligation and the debtor was insolvent at that time or the debtor became insolvent as a result of the transfer or obligation.

  (b) A transfer made by a debtor is fraudulent as to a creditor whose claim arose before the transfer was made if the transfer was made to an insider for an antecedent debt, the debtor was insolvent at that time, and the insider had reasonable cause to believe that the debtor was insolvent.

§ 7. Remedies of Creditors

(a) In an action for relief against a transfer or obligation under this [Act], a creditor . . . may obtain:

(1) avoidance of the transfer or obligation to the extent necessary to satisfy the creditor's claim . . .

. . . .

(3) subject to applicable principles of equity and in accordance with applicable rules of civil procedure,

(i) an injunction against further disposition by the debtor or a transferee, or both, of the asset transferred or of other property;

(ii) appointment of a receiver to take charge of the asset transferred or of other property of the transferee; or

(iii) any other relief the circumstances may require.

(b) If a creditor has obtained a judgment on a claim against the debtor, the creditor, if the court so orders, may levy execution on the asset transferred or its proceeds.

§ 8. Defenses, Liability, and Protection of Transferee

(a) A transfer or obligation is not voidable under Section 4(a)(1) against a person who took in good faith and for a reasonably equivalent value or against any subsequent transferee or obligee.

(b) Except as otherwise provided in this section, to the extent a transfer is voidable in an action by a creditor under Section 7(a)(1), the creditor may recover judgment for the value of the asset transferred [at the time of the transfer, subject to adjustment as the equities may require], or the amount necessary to satisfy the creditor's claim, whichever is less. The judgment may be entered against:

(1) the first transferee of the asset or the person for whose benefit the transfer was made; or

(2) any subsequent transferee other than a good faith transferee who took for value or from any subsequent transferee. . . .

(d) Notwithstanding voidability of a transfer or an obligation under this [Act], a good-faith transferee or obligee is entitled, to the extent of the value given the debtor for the transfer or obligation, to

(1) a lien on or a right to retain any interest in the asset transferred;

(2) enforcement of any obligation incurred; or

(3) a reduction in the amount of the liability on the judgment. . . .

§ 9.   Extinguishment of [Claim for Relief] [Cause of Action]

A [claim for relief] [cause of action] with respect to a fraudulent transfer or obligation under this [Act] is extinguished unless action is brought....

(b) under Section 4(a)(2) or 5(a), within 4 years after the transfer was made or the obligation was incurred....

BANKRUPTCY CODE
11 U.S.C.A. §§ 101(31), 548(a)

§ 101. Definitions...

(32) "insolvent" means—

(A) with reference to an entity other than a partnership ... financial condition such that the sum of such entity's debts is greater than all of such entity's property, at a fair valuation....

Historical and Revision Notes

The definition of "insolvent" is ... the traditional bankruptcy balance sheet test of insolvency.

§ 548. Fraudulent Transfers and Obligations

(a)(1) The trustee [in bankruptcy] may avoid any transfer (including any transfer to or for the benefit of an insider under an employment contract) of an interest of the debtor in property, or any obligation (including any obligation to or for the benefit of an insider under an employment contract) incurred by the debtor, that was made or incurred on or within two years before the date of the filing of the petition, if the debtor voluntarily or involuntarily—

(A) made such transfer or incurred such obligation with actual intent to hinder, delay, or defraud any entity to which the debtor was or became, on or after the date that such transfer was made or such obligation was incurred, indebted; or

(B)(i) received less than a reasonably equivalent value in exchange for such transfer or obligation; and

(ii)(I) was insolvent on the date that such transfer was made or such obligation was incurred, or became insolvent as a result of such transfer or obligation;

(II) was engaged in business or a transaction, or was about to engage in business or a transaction, for which any property remaining with the debtor was an unreasonably small capital;

(III) intended to incur, or believed that the debtor would incur, debts that would be beyond the debtor's ability to pay as such debts matured; or

(IV) made such transfer to or for the benefit of an insider, or incurred such obligation to or for the benefit of an insider, under an employment contract and not in the ordinary course of business.

INTERNAL REVENUE CODE § 162(m)

§ 162. Trade or Business Expenses ...

(m) Certain Excessive Employee Remuneration.—

(1) In General.—In the case of any publicly held corporation, no deduction shall be allowed under this chapter for applicable employee remuneration with respect to any covered employee to the extent that the amount of such remuneration for the taxable year with respect to such employee exceeds $1,000,000.

(2) Publicly Held Corporation.—For purposes of this subsection, the term "publicly held corporation" means any corporation issuing any class of common equity securities required to be registered under section 12 of the Securities Exchange Act of 1934.

(3) Covered Employee.—For purposes of this subsection, the term "covered employee" means any employee of the taxpayer if—

(A) as of the close of the taxable year, such employee is the chief executive officer of the taxpayer or is an individual acting in such a capacity, or

(B) the total compensation of such employee for the taxable year is required to be reported to shareholders under the Securities Exchange Act of 1934 by reason of such employee being among the 4 highest compensated officers for the taxable year (other than the chief executive officer).

(4) Applicable Employee Remuneration.—For purposes of this subsection—

(A) In general.—Except as otherwise provided in this paragraph, the term "applicable employee remuneration" means, with respect to any covered employee for any taxable year, the aggregate amount allowable as a deduction under this chapter for such taxable year (determined without regard to this subsection) for remuneration for services performed by such employee (whether or not during the taxable year).

(B) Exception for remuneration payable on commission basis.—The term "applicable employee remuneration" shall not include any remuneration payable on a commission basis solely on account of income generated directly by the individual performance of the individual to whom such remuneration is payable.

(C) Other performance-based compensation.—The term "applicable employee remuneration" shall not include any remuneration payable solely on account of the attainment of one or more performance goals, but only if—

(i) the performance goals are determined by a compensation committee of the board of directors of the taxpayer which is comprised solely of 2 or more outside directors,

(ii) the material terms under which the remuneration is to be paid, including the performance goals, are disclosed to shareholders and approved by a majority of the vote in a separate shareholder vote before the payment of such remuneration, and

(iii) before any payment of such remuneration, the compensation committee referred to in clause (i) certifies that the performance goals and any other material terms were in fact satisfied.

(D) Exception for existing binding contracts.—The term "applicable employee remuneration" shall not include any remuneration payable under a written binding contract which was in effect on February 17, 1993, and which was not modified thereafter in any material respect before such remuneration is paid.

(E) Remuneration.—For purposes of this paragraph, the term "remuneration" includes any remuneration (including benefits) in any medium other than cash....

REGULATIONS UNDER INTERNAL REVENUE CODE § 162(m) (26 C.F.R. § 1.162–27)

§ 1.162–27 Certain employee remuneration in excess of $1,000,000

(b) *Limitation on deduction.* Section 162(m) precludes a deduction under chapter 1 of the Internal Revenue Code by any publicly held corporation for compensation paid to any covered employee to the extent that the compensation for the taxable year exceeds $1,000,000....

(e) *Exception for qualified performance-based compensation—*

(1) *In general.* The deduction limit in paragraph (b) of this section does not apply to qualified performance-based compensation. Qualified performance-based compensation is compensation that meets all of the requirements of paragraphs (e)(2) through (e)(5) of this section.

(2) *Performance goal requirement—*

(i) *Preestablished goal.* Qualified performance-based compensation must be paid solely on account of the attainment of one or more preestablished, objective performance goals. A performance goal is considered preestablished if it is established in writing by the compensation committee not later than 90 days after the commencement of the period of service to which the performance goal relates, provided that the outcome is substantially uncertain at the time the compensation committee actually establishes the goal. However, in no event will a performance goal be considered to be preestablished if it is established after 25 percent of the period of service (as scheduled in good faith at the time the goal is established) has elapsed. A performance goal is objective if a third party having knowledge of the relevant facts could determine whether the goal is met. Performance goals can be based on one or more business criteria that apply to the individual, a business unit, or the corporation as a whole. Such business criteria could include, for example, stock price, market share, sales, earnings per share, return on equity, or costs. A performance goal need not, however, be based upon an increase or positive result under a business criterion and could include, for example, maintaining the status quo or limiting economic losses (measured, in each case, by reference to a specific business criterion). A performance goal does not include the mere continued employment of the covered employee. Thus, a vesting provision based solely on continued employment would not constitute a performance goal. See paragraph (e)(2)(vi) of this section for rules on compensation that is based on an increase in the price of stock.

(ii) *Objective compensation formula.* A preestablished performance goal must state, in terms of an objective formula or standard, the method for computing the amount of compensation payable to the employee if the goal is attained. A formula or standard is objective if a third party having knowledge of the relevant performance results could calculate the amount to be paid to the employee. In addition, a formula or standard must specify the individual employees or class of employees to which it applies.

(iii) *Discretion.*

(A) The terms of an objective formula or standard must preclude discretion to increase the amount of compensation payable that would otherwise be due upon attainment of the goal. A performance goal is not discretionary for purposes of this paragraph (e)(2)(iii) merely because the compensation committee reduces or eliminates the compensation or other economic benefit that was due upon attainment of the goal. However, the exercise of negative discretion with respect to one employee is not permitted to result in an increase in the amount payable to another employee. Thus, for example, in the case of a bonus pool, if the amount payable to each employee is stated in terms of a percentage of the pool, the sum of these individual percentages of the pool is not permitted to exceed 100 percent. If the terms of an objective formula or standard fail to preclude discretion to increase the amount of compensation merely because the amount of compensation to be paid upon attainment of the performance goal is based, in whole or in part, on a percentage of salary or base pay and the dollar amount of the salary or base pay is not fixed at the time the performance goal is established, then the objective formula or standard will not be considered discretionary for purposes of this paragraph (e)(2)(iii) if the maximum dollar amount to be paid is fixed at that time. . . .

(v) *Compensation contingent upon attainment of performance goal.* Compensation does not satisfy the requirements of this paragraph (e)(2) if the facts and circumstances indicate that the employee would receive all or part of the compensation regardless of whether the performance goal is attained. Thus, if the payment of compensation under a grant or award is only nominally or partially contingent on attaining a performance goal, none of the compensation payable under the grant or award will be considered performance-based. For example, if an employee is entitled to a bonus under either of two arrangements, where payment under a nonperformance-based arrangement is contingent upon the failure to attain the performance goals under an otherwise performance-based arrangement, then neither arrangement provides for compensation that satisfies the requirements of this paragraph (e)(2). Compensation does not fail to be qualified performance-based compensation merely because the plan allows the compensation to be payable upon death, disability, or change of ownership or control, although compensation actually paid on account of those events prior to the attainment of the performance goal would not satisfy the requirements of this paragraph (e)(2)....

(vi) *Application of requirements to stock options and stock appreciation rights—*

(A) *In general.* Compensation attributable to a stock option or a stock appreciation right is deemed to satisfy the requirements of this paragraph (e)(2) if the grant or award is made by the compensation committee; the plan under which the option or right is granted states the maximum number of shares with respect to which options or rights may be granted during a specified period to any employee; and, under the terms of the option or right, the amount of compensation the employee could receive is based solely on an increase in the value of the stock after the date of the grant or award. Conversely, if the amount of compensation the employee will receive under the grant or award is not based solely on an increase in the value of the stock after the date of grant or award (e.g., in the case of restricted stock, or an option that is granted with an exercise price that is less than the fair market value of the stock as of the date of grant), none of the compensation attributable to the grant or award is qualified performance-based compensation because it does not satisfy the requirement of this paragraph (e)(2)(vi)(A). Whether a stock option grant is based solely on an increase in the value of the stock after the date of grant is determined without regard to any dividend equivalent that may be payable, provided that payment of the dividend equivalent is not made contingent on the exercise of the option. The rule that the compensation attributable to a stock option or stock appreciation right must be based solely on an increase in the value of the stock after the date of grant or award does not apply if the grant or award is made on account of, or if the vesting or exercisability of the grant or award is contingent on, the attainment of a performance goal that satisfies the requirements of this paragraph (e)(2).

(B) *Cancellation and repricing.* Compensation attributable to a stock option or stock appreciation right does not satisfy the requirements of this paragraph (e)(2) to the extent that the number of options granted exceeds the maximum number of shares for which options may be granted to the employee as specified in the plan. If an option is canceled, the canceled option continues to be counted against the maximum number of shares for which options may be granted to the employee under the plan. If, after grant, the exercise price of an option is reduced, the transaction is treated as a cancellation of the option and a grant of a new option. In such case, both the option that is deemed to be canceled and the option that is deemed to be granted reduce the maximum number of shares for which options may be granted to the employee under the plan. This paragraph (e)(2)(vi)(B) also applies in the case of a stock appreciation right where, after the award is made, the base amount on which stock appreciation is calculated is reduced to reflect a reduction in the fair market value of stock. . . .

(3) *Outside directors*—

(i) *General rule.* The performance goal under which compensation is paid must be established by a compensation committee comprised solely of two or more outside directors. A director is an outside director if the director—. . .

(B) Is not a former employee of the publicly held corporation who receives compensation for prior services (other than benefits under a tax-qualified retirement plan) during the taxable year;

(C) Has not been an officer of the publicly held corporation; and

(D) Does not receive remuneration from the publicly held corporation, either directly or indirectly, in any capacity other than as a director. For this purpose, remuneration includes any payment in exchange for goods or services.

(ii) *Remuneration received.* For purposes of this paragraph (e)(3), remuneration is received, directly or indirectly, by a director in each of the following circumstances:

(A) If remuneration is paid, directly or indirectly, to the director personally or to an entity in which the director has a beneficial ownership interest of greater than 50 percent. For this purpose, remuneration is considered paid when actually paid (and throughout the remainder of that taxable year of the corporation) and, if earlier, throughout the period when a contract or agreement to pay remuneration is outstanding.

(B) If remuneration, other than de minimis remuneration, was paid by the publicly held corporation in its preceding taxable year to an entity in which the director has a beneficial ownership interest of at least 5 percent but not more than 50 percent. For this purpose, remuneration is considered paid when actually paid or, if earlier, when the publicly held corporation becomes liable to pay it.

(C) If remuneration, other than de minimis remuneration, was paid by the publicly held corporation in its preceding taxable year to an entity by which the director is employed or self-employed other than as a director. For this purpose, remuneration is considered paid when actually paid or, if earlier, when the publicly held corporation becomes liable to pay it.

(iii) *De minimis remuneration*—

(A) *In general.* For purposes of paragraphs (e)(3)(ii)(B) and (C) of this section, remuneration that was paid by the publicly held corporation in its preceding taxable year to an entity is de minimis if payments to the entity did not exceed 5 percent of the gross revenue of the entity for its taxable year ending with or within that preceding taxable year of the publicly held corporation.

(B) *Remuneration for personal services and substantial owners.* Notwithstanding paragraph (e)(3)(iii)(A) of this section, remuneration in excess of $60,000 is not de minimis if the remuneration is paid to an entity described in paragraph (e)(3)(ii)(B) of this section, or is paid for personal services to an entity described in paragraph (e)(3)(ii)(C) of this section.

(iv) *Remuneration for personal services.* For purposes of paragraph (e)(3)(iii)(B) of this section, remuneration from a publicly held corporation is for personal services if—

(A) The remuneration is paid to an entity for personal or professional services, consisting of legal, accounting, investment banking, and management consulting services (and other similar services that may be specified by the Commissioner in revenue rulings, notices, or other guidance published in the Internal Revenue Bulletin), performed for the publicly held corporation, and the remuneration is not for services that are incidental to the purchase of goods or to the purchase of services that are not personal services; and

(B) The director performs significant services (whether or not as an employee) for the corporation, division, or similar organization (within the entity) that actually provides the services described in paragraph (e)(3)(iv)(A) of this section to the publicly held corporation, or more than 50 percent of the entity's gross revenues (for the entity's preceding taxable year) are derived from that corporation, subsidiary, or similar organization....

(4) *Shareholder approval requirement*—

(i) *General rule.* The material terms of the performance goal under which the compensation is to be paid must be disclosed to and subsequently approved by the shareholders of the publicly held corporation before the compensation is paid. The requirements of this paragraph (e)(4) are not satisfied if the compensation would be paid regardless of whether the material terms are approved by shareholders. The material terms include the employees eligible to receive compensation; a description of the business criteria on which the performance goal is based; and either the maximum amount of compensation that could be paid to any employee or the formula used to calculate the amount of compensation to be paid to the employee if the performance goal is attained (except that, in the case of a formula that fails to preclude discretion to increase the amount of compensation (as described in paragraph (e)(2)(iii)(A) of this section) merely because the amount of compensation to be paid is based, in whole or in part, on a percentage of salary or base pay and the dollar amount of the salary or base pay is not fixed at the time the performance goal is established, the maximum dollar amount of compensation that could be paid to the employee must be disclosed). . . .

(iii) *Description of business criteria—*

(A) *In general.* Disclosure of the business criteria on which the performance goal is based need not include the specific targets that must be satisfied under the performance goal. For example, if a bonus plan provides that a bonus will be paid if earnings per share increase by 10 percent, the 10–percent figure is a target that need not be disclosed to shareholders. However, in that case, disclosure must be made that the bonus plan is based on an earnings-per-share business criterion. In the case of a plan under which employees may be granted stock options or stock appreciation rights, no specific description of the business criteria is required if the grants or awards are based on a stock price that is no less than current fair market value.

(B) *Disclosure of confidential information.* The requirements of this paragraph (e)(4) may be satisfied even though information that otherwise would be a material term of a performance goal is not disclosed to shareholders, provided that the compensation committee determines that the information is confidential commercial or business information, the disclosure of which would have an adverse effect on the publicly held corporation. Whether disclosure would adversely affect the corporation is determined on the basis of the facts and circumstances. If the compensation committee makes such a determination, the disclosure to shareholders must state the compensation committee's belief that the information is confidential commercial or business information, the disclosure of which would adversely affect the company. In addition, the ability not to disclose confidential information does not eliminate the requirement that disclosure be made of the maximum amount of compensation that is payable to an individual under a performance goal. Confidential information does not include the identity of an executive or the class of executives to which a performance goal applies or the amount of compensation that is payable if the goal is satisfied.

(iv) *Description of compensation.* Disclosure as to the compensation payable under a performance goal must be specific enough so that shareholders can determine the maximum amount of compensation that could be paid to any employee during a specified period. If the terms of the performance goal do not provide for a maximum dollar amount, the disclosure must include the formula under which the compensation would be calculated. Thus, for example, if compensation attributable to the exercise of stock options is equal to the difference in the exercise price and the current value of the stock, disclosure would be required of the maximum number of shares for which grants may be made to any employee and the exercise price of those options (*e.g.,* fair market value on date of grant). In that case, shareholders could calculate the maximum amount of compensation that would be attributable to the exercise of options on the basis of their assumptions as to the future stock price.

(v) *Disclosure requirements of the Securities and Exchange Commission.* To the extent not otherwise specifically provided in this paragraph (e)(4), whether the material terms of a performance goal are adequately disclosed to shareholders is determined under the same standards as apply under the Exchange Act.

(vi) *Frequency of disclosure.* Once the material terms of a performance goal are disclosed to and approved by shareholders, no additional disclosure or approval is required unless the compensation committee changes the material terms of the performance goal. If, however, the compensation committee has authority to change the targets under a performance goal after shareholder approval of the goal, material terms of the performance goal must be disclosed to and reapproved by shareholders no later than the first shareholder meeting that occurs in the fifth year following the year in which shareholders previously approved the performance goal.

(vii) *Shareholder vote.* For purposes of this paragraph (e)(4), the material terms of a performance goal are approved by shareholders if, in a separate vote, a majority of the votes cast on the issue (including abstentions to the extent abstentions are counted as voting under applicable state law) are cast in favor of approval. . . .

(5) *Compensation committee certification.* The compensation committee must certify in writing prior to payment of the compensation that the performance goals and any other material terms were in fact satisfied. For this purpose, approved minutes of the compensation committee meeting in which the certification is made are treated as a written certification. Certification by the compensation committee is not required for compensation that is attributable solely to the increase in the value of the stock of the publicly held corporation. . . .

NEW YORK STOCK EXCHANGE LISTED COMPANY MANUAL

(Excerpts)

202.01   Internal Handling of Confidential Corporate Matters

Unusual market activity or a substantial price change has on occasion occurred in a company's securities shortly before the announcement of an important corporate action or development. Such incidents are extremely embarrassing and damaging to both the company and the Exchange since the public may quickly conclude that someone acted on the basis of inside information.

Negotiations leading to mergers and acquisitions, stock splits, the making of arrangements preparatory to an exchange or tender offer, changes in dividend rates or earnings, calls for redemption, and new contracts, products, or discoveries are the type of developments where the risk of untimely and inadvertent disclosure of corporate plans are most likely to occur. Frequently, these matters require extensive discussion and study by corporate officials before final decisions can be made. Accordingly, extreme care must be used in order to keep the information on a confidential basis.

Where it is possible to confine formal or informal discussions to a small group of the top management of the company or companies involved, and their individual confidential advisors where adequate security can be maintained, premature public announcement may properly be avoided. In this regard, the market action of a company's securities should be closely watched at a time when consideration is being given to important corporate matters. If unusual market activity should arise, the company should be prepared to make an immediate public announcement of the matter.

At some point it usually becomes necessary to involve other persons to conduct preliminary studies or assist in other preparations for contemplated transactions, e.g., business appraisals, tentative financing arrangements, attitude of large outside holders, availability of major blocks of stock, engineering studies and market analyses and surveys. Experience has shown that maintaining security at this point is virtually impossible. Accordingly, fairness requires that the company make an immediate public announcement as soon as disclosures relating to such important matters are made to outsiders.

The extent of the disclosures will depend upon the stage of discussions, studies, or negotiations. So far as possible, public statements should be definite as to price, ratio, timing and/or any other pertinent information necessary to permit a reasonable evaluation of the matter. As a minimum, they should include those disclosures made to outsiders. Where an initial announcement cannot be specific or complete, it will need to be supplemented from time to time as more definitive or different terms are discussed or determined.

Corporate employees, as well as directors and officers, should be regularly reminded as a matter of policy that they must not disclose confidential information they may receive in the course of their duties and must not attempt to take advantage of such information themselves.

In view of the importance of this matter and the potential difficulties involved, the Exchange suggests that a periodic review be made by each company of the manner in which confidential information is being handled within its own organization. A reminder notice of the company's policy to those in sensitive areas might also be helpful.

A sound corporate disclosure policy is essential to the maintenance of a fair and orderly securities market. It should minimize the occasions where the Exchange finds it necessary to temporarily halt trading in a security due to information leaks or rumors in connection with significant corporate transactions.

While the procedures are directed primarily at situations involving two or more companies, they are equally applicable to major corporate developments involving a single company.

202.02 Relationship Between Company Officials and Others

(A) Security Analysts, Institutional Investors, Etc.

Security analysts play an increasingly important role in the evaluation and interpretation of the financial affairs of listed companies. Annual reports, quarterly reports, and interim releases cannot by their nature provide all of the financial and statistical data that should be available to the investing public. The Exchange recommends that companies observe an "open door" policy in their relations with security analysts, financial writers, shareholders, and others who have legitimate investment interest in the company's affairs.

A company should not give information to one inquirer which it would not give to another, nor should it reveal information it would not willingly give or has not given to the press for publication. Thus, for companies to give advance earnings, dividend, stock split, merger, or tender information to analysts, whether representing an institution, brokerage house, investment advisor, large shareholder, or anyone else, would clearly violate Exchange policy. On the other hand, it should not withhold information in which analysts or other members of the investment public have a warrantable interest.

If during the course of a discussion with analysts substantive material not previously published is disclosed, that material should be simultaneously released to the public. The various security analysts societies usually have a regular procedure to be followed where formal presentations are made. The company should follow these same precautions when dealing with groups of industry analysts in small or closed meetings....

202.03   Dealing With Rumors or Unusual Market Activity

The market activity of a company's securities should be closely watched at a time when consideration is being given to significant corporate matters. If rumors or unusual market activity indicate that information on impending developments has leaked out, a frank and explicit announcement is clearly required. If rumors are in fact false or inaccurate, they should be promptly denied or clarified. A statement to the effect that the company knows of no corporate developments to account for the unusual market activity can have a salutary effect. It is obvious that if such a public statement is contemplated, management should be checked prior to any public comment so as to avoid any embarrassment or potential criticism. If rumors are correct or there are developments, an immediate candid statement to the public as to the state of negotiations or of development of corporate plans in the rumored area must be made directly and openly. Such statements are essential despite the business inconvenience which may be caused and even though the matter may not as yet have been presented to the company's Board of Directors for consideration.

The Exchange recommends that its listed companies contact their Exchange representative if they become aware of rumors circulating about their company. Exchange Rule 435 provides that no member, member organization or allied member shall circulate in any manner rumors of a sensational character which might reasonably be expected to affect market conditions on the Exchange. Information provided concerning rumors will be promptly investigated.

202.04   Exchange Market Surveillance

The Exchange maintains a continuous market surveillance program through its Market Surveillance and Evaluation Division. An "on-line" computer system has been developed which monitors the price movement of every listed stock—on a trade-to-trade basis—throughout the trading session. The program is designed to closely review the markets in those securities in which unusual price and volume changes occur or where there is a large unexplained influx of buy or sell orders. If the price movement of a stock exceeds a predetermined guideline, it is immediately "flagged" and review of the situation is immediately undertaken to seek the causes of the exceptional activity. Under these circumstances, the company may be called by its Exchange representative to inquire about any company developments which have not been publicly announced but which could be responsible for unusual market activity. Where the market appears to reflect undisclosed information, the company will normally be requested to make the information public immediately. Occasionally it may be necessary to carry out a review of the trading after the fact, and the Exchange may request such information from the company as may be necessary to complete the inquiry.

The Listing Agreement provides that a company must furnish the Exchange with such information concerning the company as the Exchange may reasonably require. . . .

202.05 Timely Disclosure of Material News Developments

A listed company is expected to release quickly to the public any news or information which might reasonably be expected to materially affect the market for its securities. This is one of the most important and fundamental purposes of the listing agreement which the company enters into with the Exchange.

A listed company should also act promptly to dispel unfounded rumors which result in unusual market activity or price variations. . . .

202.06 Procedure for Public Release of Information

(A) Immediate Release Policy

The normal method of publication of important corporate data is by means of a press release. This may be either by telephone or in written form. Any release of information that could reasonably be expected to have an impact on the market for a company's securities should be given to the wire services and the press *"For Immediate Release."*

The spirit of the immediate release policy is not considered to be violated on weekends where a "Hold for Sunday or Monday A.M.'s" is used to obtain a broad public release of the news. This procedure facilitates the combination of a press release with a mailing to shareholders.

Annual and quarterly earnings, dividend announcements, mergers, acquisitions, tender offers, stock splits, major management changes, and any substantive items of unusual or non-recurrent nature are examples of news items that should be handled on an immediate release basis.

News of major new products, contract awards, expansion plans, and discoveries very often fall into the same category. Unfavorable news should be reported as promptly and candidly as favorable news. Reluctance or unwillingness to release a negative story or an attempt to disguise unfavorable news endangers management's reputation for integrity. Changes in accounting methods to mask such occurrences can have a similar impact. . . .

302.00   Annual Meetings

Listed companies are required to hold an annual shareholders' meeting during each fiscal year.

303A.   Corporate Governance Standards

303A.00   Introduction

General Application

Companies listed on the Exchange must comply with certain standards regarding corporate governance as codified in this Section 303A. Consistent with the NYSE's traditional approach, as well as the requirements of the Sarbanes–Oxley Act of 2002, certain provisions of Section 303A are applicable to some listed companies but not to others.

Equity Listings

Section 303A applies in full to all companies listing common equity securities, with the following exceptions:

Controlled Companies. A listed company of which more than 50% of the voting power is held by an individual, a group or another company need not comply with the requirements of Sections 303A.01, 303A.04 or 303A.05. A controlled company that chooses to take advantage of any or all of these exemptions must disclose that choice, that it is a controlled company and the basis for the determination in its annual proxy statement or, if the company does not file an annual proxy statement, in the company's annual report on Form 10–K filed with the SEC. Controlled companies must comply with the remaining provisions of Section 303A. . . .

303A.01   Independent Directors

Listed companies must have a majority of independent directors.

> *Commentary:* Effective boards of directors exercise independent judgment in carrying out their responsibilities. Requiring a majority of independent directors will increase the quality of board oversight and lessen the possibility of damaging conflicts of interest.

303A.02 Independence Tests

In order to tighten the definition of "independent director" for purposes of these standards:

(a) No director qualifies as "independent" unless the board of directors affirmatively determines that the director has no material relationship with the listed company (either directly or as a partner, shareholder or officer of an organization that has a relationship with the company). Companies must identify which directors are independent and disclose the basis for that determination.

Commentary: It is not possible to anticipate, or explicitly to provide for, all circumstances that might signal potential conflicts of interest, or that might bear on the materiality of a director's relationship to a listed company (references to "company" would include any parent or subsidiary in a consolidated group with the company). Accordingly, it is best that boards making "independence" determinations broadly consider all relevant facts and circumstances. In particular, when assessing the materiality of a director's relationship with the listed company, the board should consider the issue not merely from the standpoint of the director, but also from that of persons or organizations with which the director has an affiliation. Material relationships can include commercial, industrial, banking, consulting, legal, accounting, charitable and familial relationships, among others. However, as the concern is independence from management, the Exchange does not view ownership of even a significant amount of stock, by itself, as a bar to an independence finding.

The identity of the independent directors and the basis for a board determination that a relationship is not material must be disclosed in the listed company's annual proxy statement or, if the company does not file an annual proxy statement, in the company's annual report on Form 10–K filed with the SEC. In this regard, a board may adopt and disclose categorical standards to assist it in making determinations of independence and may make a general disclosure if a director meets these standards. Any determination of independence for a director who does not meet these standards must be specifically explained. A company must disclose any standard it adopts. It may then make the general statement that the independent directors meet the standards set by the board without detailing particular aspects of the immaterial relationships between individual directors and the company. In the event that a director with a business or other relationship that does not fit within the disclosed standards is determined to be independent, a board must disclose the basis for its determination in the manner described above. This approach provides investors with an adequate means of assessing the quality of a board's independence and its independence determinations while avoiding excessive disclosure of immaterial relationships.

(b) In addition, a director is not independent if:

(i) The director is, or has been within the last three years, an employee of the listed company, or an immediate family member is, or has been within the last three years, an executive officer,[1] of the listed company.

> *Commentary:* Employment as an interim Chairman or CEO or other executive officer shall not disqualify a director from being considered independent following that employment.

(ii) The director has received, or has an immediate family member who has received, during any twelve-month period within the last three years, more than $100,000 in direct compensation from the listed company, other than director and committee fees and pension or other forms of deferred compensation for prior service (provided such compensation is not contingent in any way on continued service).

> *Commentary:* Compensation received by a director for former service as an interim Chairman or CEO or other executive officer need not be considered in determining independence under this test. Compensation received by an immediate family member for service as an employee of the listed company (other than an executive officer) need not be considered in determining independence under this test.

(iii)(A) The director or an immediate family member is a current partner of a firm that is the company's internal or external auditor; (B) the director is a current employee of such a firm; (C) the director has an immediate family member who is a current employee of such a firm and who participates in the firm's audit, assurance or tax compliance (but not tax planning) practice; or (D) the director or an immediate family member was within the last three years (but is no longer) a partner or employee of such a firm and personally worked on the listed company's audit within that time.

(iv) The director or an immediate family member is, or has been within the last three years, employed as an executive officer of another company where any of the listed company's present executive officers at the same time serves or served on that company's compensation committee.

---

1. For purposes of Section 303A, the term "executive officer" has the same meaning specified for the term "officer" in Rule 16a–1(f) under the Securities Exchange Act of 1934.

(v) The director is a current employee, or an immediate family member is a current executive officer, of a company that has made payments to, or received payments from, the listed company for property or services in an amount which, in any of the last three fiscal years, exceeds the greater of $1 million, or 2% of such other company's consolidated gross revenues.

Commentary: In applying the test in Section 303A.02(b)(v), both the payments and the consolidated gross revenues to be measured shall be those reported in the last completed fiscal year. The look-back provision for this test applies solely to the financial relationship between the listed company and the director or immediate family member's current employer; a listed company need not consider former employment of the director or immediate family member.

Contributions to tax exempt organizations shall not be considered "payments" for purposes of Section 303A.02(b)(v), provided however that a listed company shall disclose in its annual proxy statement, or if the listed company does not file an annual proxy statement, in the company's annual report on Form 10–K filed with the SEC, any such contributions made by the listed company to any tax exempt organization in which any independent director serves as an executive officer if, within the preceding three years, contributions in any single fiscal year from the listed company to the organization exceeded the greater of $1 million, or 2% of such tax exempt organization's consolidated gross revenues. Listed company boards are reminded of their obligations to consider the materiality of any such relationship in accordance with Section 303A.02(a) above.

General Commentary to Section 303A.02(b): An "immediate family member" includes a person's spouse, parents, children, siblings, mothers and fathers-in-law, sons and daughters-in-law, brothers and sisters-in-law, and anyone (other than domestic employees) who shares such person's home. When applying the look-back provisions in Section 303A.02(b), listed companies need not consider individuals who are no longer immediate family members as a result of legal separation or divorce, or those who have died or become incapacitated.

In addition, references to the "company" would include any parent or subsidiary in a consolidated group with the company....

303A.03 Executive Sessions

To empower non-management directors to serve as a more effective check on management, the non-management directors of each listed company must meet at regularly scheduled executive sessions without management.

Commentary: To promote open discussion among the non-management directors, companies must schedule regular executive sessions in which those directors meet without management participation. "Non-management" directors are all those who are not executive officers, and includes such directors who are not independent by virtue of a material relationship, former status or family membership, or for any other reason.

Regular scheduling of such meetings is important not only to foster better communication among non-management directors, but also to prevent any negative inference from attaching to the calling of executive sessions. A non-management director must preside over each executive session of the non-management directors, although the same director is not required to preside at all executive sessions of the non-management directors. If one director is chosen to preside at all of these meetings, his or her name must be disclosed in the listed company's annual proxy statement or, if the company does not file an annual proxy statement, in the company's annual report on Form 10–K filed with the SEC. Alternatively, if the same individual is not the presiding director at every meeting, a listed company must disclose the procedure by which a presiding director is selected for each executive session. For example, a listed company may wish to rotate the presiding position among the chairs of board committees.

In order that interested parties may be able to make their concerns known to the non-management directors, a listed company must disclose a method for such parties to communicate directly with the presiding director or with the non-management directors as a group. Such disclosure must be made in the listed company's annual proxy statement or, if the company does not file an annual proxy statement, in the company's annual report on Form 10–K filed with the SEC. Companies may, if they wish, utilize for this purpose the same procedures they have established to comply with the requirement of Rule 10A–3(b)(3) under the Exchange Act, as applied to listed companies through Section 303A.06.

While this Section 303A.03 refers to meetings of non-management directors, if that group includes directors who are not independent under this Section 303A, listed companies should at least once a year schedule an executive session including only independent directors.

303A.04   Nominating/Corporate Governance Committee

(a) Listed companies must have a nominating/corporate governance committee composed entirely of independent directors.

(b) The nominating/corporate governance committee must have a written charter that addresses:

(i) the committee's purpose and responsibilities—which, at minimum, must be to: identify individuals qualified to become board members, consistent with criteria approved by the board, and to select, or to recommend that the board select, the director nominees for the next annual meeting of shareholders; develop and recommend to the board a set of corporate governance guidelines applicable to the corporation; and oversee the evaluation of the board and management; and

(ii) an annual performance evaluation of the committee.

Commentary: A nominating/corporate governance committee is central to the effective functioning of the board. New director and board committee nominations are among a board's most important functions. Placing this responsibility in the hands of an independent nominating/corporate governance committee can enhance the independence and quality of nominees. The committee is also responsible for taking a leadership role in shaping the corporate governance of a corporation.

If a listed company is legally required by contract or otherwise to provide third parties with the ability to nominate directors (for example, preferred stock rights to elect directors upon a dividend default, shareholder agreements, and management agreements), the selection and nomination of such directors need not be subject to the nominating committee process.

The nominating/corporate governance committee charter should also address the following items: committee member qualifications; committee member appointment and removal; committee structure and operations (including authority to delegate to subcommittees); and committee reporting to the board. In addition, the charter should give the nominating/corporate governance committee sole authority to retain and terminate any search firm to be used to identify director candidates, including sole authority to approve the search firm's fees and other retention terms.

Boards may allocate the responsibilities of the nominating/corporate governance committee to committees of their own denomination, provided that the committees are composed entirely of independent directors. Any such committee must have a published committee charter.

303A.05 Compensation Committee

(a) Listed companies must have a compensation committee composed entirely of independent directors.

(b) The compensation committee must have a written charter that addresses:

(i) the committee's purpose and responsibilities—which, at minimum, must be to have direct responsibility to:

(A) review and approve corporate goals and objectives relevant to CEO compensation, evaluate the CEO's performance in light of those goals and objectives, and, either as a committee or together with the other independent directors (as directed by the board), determine and approve the CEO's compensation level based on this evaluation; and

(B) make recommendations to the board with respect to non-CEO executive officer compensation, and incentive-compensation and equity-based plans that are subject to board approval; and

(C) produce a compensation committee report on executive officer compensation as required by the SEC to be included in the listed company's annual proxy statement or annual report on Form 10–K filed with the SEC;

(ii) an annual performance evaluation of the compensation committee.

Commentary: In determining the long-term incentive component of CEO compensation, the committee should consider the listed company's performance and relative shareholder return, the value of similar incentive awards to CEOs at comparable companies, and the awards given to the listed company's CEO in past years. To avoid confusion, note that the compensation committee is not precluded from approving awards (with or without ratification of the board) as may be required to comply with applicable tax laws (i.e., Rule 162(m)). Note also that nothing in Section 303A.05(b)(i)(B) is intended to preclude the board from delegating its authority over such matters to the compensation committee.

The compensation committee charter should also address the following items: committee member qualifications; committee member appointment and removal; committee structure and operations (including authority to delegate to subcommittees); and committee reporting to the board.

Additionally, if a compensation consultant is to assist in the evaluation of director, CEO or executive officer compensation, the compensation committee charter should give that committee sole authority to retain and terminate the consulting firm, including sole authority to approve the firm's fees and other retention terms.

Boards may allocate the responsibilities of the compensation committee to committees of their own denomination, provided that the committees are composed entirely of independent directors. Any such committee must have a published committee charter.

Nothing in this provision should be construed as precluding discussion of CEO compensation with the board generally, as it is not the intent of this standard to impair communication among members of the board.

303A.06 Audit Committee

Listed companies must have an audit committee that satisfies the requirements of Rule 10A–3 under the Exchange Act.

303A.07 Audit Committee Additional Requirements

(a) The audit committee must have a minimum of three members.

Commentary: Each member of the audit committee must be financially literate, as such qualification is interpreted by the listed company's board in its business judgment, or must become financially literate within a reasonable period of time after his or her appointment to the audit committee. In addition, at least one member of the audit committee must have accounting or related financial management expertise, as the listed company's board interprets such qualification in its business judgment. While the Exchange does not require that a listed company's audit committee include a person who satisfies the definition of audit committee financial expert set out in Item 401(h) of Regulation S–K, a board may presume that such a person has accounting or related financial management expertise.

Because of the audit committee's demanding role and responsibilities, and the time commitment attendant to committee membership, each prospective audit committee member should evaluate carefully the existing demands on his or her time before accepting this important assignment. Additionally, if an audit committee member simultaneously serves on the audit committees of more than three public companies, and the listed company does not limit the number of audit committees on which its audit committee members serve to three or less, then in each case, the board must determine that such simultaneous service would not impair the ability of such member to effectively serve on the listed company's audit committee and disclose such determination in the listed company's annual proxy statement or, if the company does not file an annual proxy statement, in the company's annual report on Form 10–K filed with the SEC.

(b) In addition to any requirement of Rule 10A–3(b)(1), all audit committee members must satisfy the requirements for independence set out in Section 303A.02.

(c) The audit committee must have a written charter that addresses:

(i) the committee's purpose—which, at minimum, must be to:

(A) assist board oversight of (1) the integrity of the listed company's financial statements, (2) the listed company's compliance with legal and regulatory requirements, (3) the independent auditor's qualifications and independence, and (4) the performance of the listed company's internal audit function and independent auditors; and

(B) prepare an audit committee report as required by the SEC to be included in the listed company's annual proxy statement;

(ii) an annual performance evaluation of the audit committee; and

(iii) the duties and responsibilities of the audit committee—which, at a minimum, must include those set out in Rule 10A–3(b)(2), (3), (4) and (5) of the Exchange Act, as well as to:

(A) at least annually, obtain and review a report by the independent auditor describing: the firm's internal quality-control procedures; any material issues raised by the most recent internal quality-control review, or peer review, of the firm, or by any inquiry or investigation by governmental or professional authorities, within the preceding five years, respecting one or more independent audits carried out by the firm, and any steps taken to deal with any such issues; and (to assess the auditor's independence) all relationships between the independent auditor and the listed company;

Commentary: After reviewing the foregoing report and the independent auditor's work throughout the year, the audit committee will be in a position to evaluate the auditor's qualifications, performance and independence. This evaluation should include the review and evaluation of the lead partner of the independent auditor. In making its evaluation, the audit committee should take into account the opinions of management and the listed company's internal auditors (or other personnel responsible for the internal audit function). In addition to assuring the regular rotation of the lead audit partner as required by law, the audit committee should further consider whether, in order to assure continuing auditor independence, there should be regular rotation of the audit firm itself. The audit committee should present its conclusions with respect to the independent auditor to the full board.

(B) meet to review and discuss the listed company's annual audited financial statements and quarterly financial statements with management and the independent auditor, including reviewing the company's specific disclosures under "Management's Discussion and Analysis of Financial Condition and Results of Operations";

(C) discuss the listed company's earnings press releases, as well as financial information and earnings guidance provided to analysts and rating agencies;

Commentary: The audit committee's responsibility to discuss earnings releases, as well as financial information and earnings guidance, may be done generally (i.e., discussion of the types of information to be disclosed and the type of presentation to be made). The audit committee need not discuss in advance each earnings release or each instance in which a listed company may provide earnings guidance.

(D) discuss policies with respect to risk assessment and risk management;

Commentary: While it is the job of the CEO and senior management to assess and manage the listed company's exposure to risk, the audit committee must discuss guidelines and policies to govern the process by which this is handled. The audit committee should discuss the listed company's major financial risk exposures and the steps management has taken to monitor and control such exposures. The audit committee is not required to be the sole body responsible for risk assessment and management, but, as stated above, the committee must discuss guidelines and policies to govern the process by which risk assessment and management is undertaken. Many companies, particularly financial companies, manage and assess their risk through mechanisms other than the audit committee. The processes these companies have in place should be reviewed in a general manner by the audit committee, but they need not be replaced by the audit committee.

(E) meet separately, periodically, with management, with internal auditors (or other personnel responsible for the internal audit function) and with independent auditors;

Commentary: To perform its oversight functions most effectively, the audit committee must have the benefit of separate sessions with management, the independent auditors and those responsible for the internal audit function. As noted herein, all listed companies must have an internal audit function. These separate sessions may be more productive than joint sessions in surfacing issues warranting committee attention.

(F) review with the independent auditor any audit problems or difficulties and management's response;

Commentary: The audit committee must regularly review with the independent auditor any difficulties the auditor encountered in the course of the audit work, including any restrictions on the scope of the independent auditor's activities or on access to requested information, and any significant disagreements with management. Among the items the audit committee may want to review with the auditor are: any accounting adjustments that were noted or proposed by the auditor but were "passed" (as immaterial or otherwise); any communications between the audit team and the audit firm's national office respecting auditing or accounting issues presented by the engagement; and any "management" or "internal control" letter issued, or proposed to be issued, by the audit firm to the listed company. The review should also include discussion of the responsibilities, budget and staffing of the listed company's internal audit function.

(G) set clear hiring policies for employees or former employees of the independent auditors; and

Commentary: Employees or former employees of the independent auditor are often valuable additions to corporate management. Such individuals' familiarity with the business, and personal rapport with the employees, may be attractive qualities when filling a key opening. However, the audit committee should set hiring policies taking into account the pressures that may exist for auditors consciously or subconsciously seeking a job with the company they audit.

(H) report regularly to the board of directors.

Commentary: The audit committee should review with the full board any issues that arise with respect to the quality or integrity of the listed company's financial statements, the company's compliance with legal or regulatory requirements, the performance and independence of the company's independent auditors, or the performance of the internal audit function.

General Commentary to Section 303A.07(c): While the fundamental responsibility for the listed company's financial statements and disclosures rests with management and the independent auditor, the audit committee must review: (A) major issues regarding accounting principles and financial statement presentations, including any significant changes in the company's selection or application of accounting principles, and major issues as to the adequacy of the company's internal controls and any special audit steps adopted in light of material control deficiencies; (B) analyses prepared by management and/or the independent auditor setting forth significant financial reporting issues and judgments made in connection with the preparation of the financial statements, including analyses of the effects of alternative GAAP methods on the financial statements; (C) the effect of regulatory and accounting initiatives, as well as off-balance sheet structures, on the financial statements of the listed company; and (D) the type and presentation of information to be included in earnings press releases (paying particular attention to any use of "pro forma," or "adjusted" non-GAAP, information), as well as review any financial information and earnings guidance provided to analysts and rating agencies.

(d) Each listed company must have an internal audit function.

Commentary: Listed companies must maintain an internal audit function to provide management and the audit committee with ongoing assessments of the company's risk management processes and system of internal control. A listed company may choose to outsource this function to a third party service provider other than its independent auditor.

General Commentary to Section 303A.07: To avoid any confusion, note that the audit committee functions specified in Section 303A.07 are the sole responsibility of the audit committee and may not be allocated to a different committee.

303A.08 Shareholder Approval of Equity Compensation Plans

Shareholders must be given the opportunity to vote on all equity-compensation plans and material revisions thereto, with limited exemptions explained below.

Equity-compensation plans can help align shareholder and management interests, and equity-based awards are often very important components of employee compensation. To provide checks and balances on the potential dilution resulting from the process of earmarking shares to be used for equity-based awards, the Exchange requires that all equity-compensation plans, and any material revisions to the terms of such plans, be subject to shareholder approval, with the limited exemptions explained below.

Definition of Equity–Compensation Plan

An "equity-compensation plan" is a plan or other arrangement that provides for the delivery of equity securities (either newly issued or treasury shares) of the listed company to any employee, director or other service provider as compensation for services. Even a compensatory grant of options or other equity securities that is not made under a plan is, nonetheless, an "equity-compensation plan" for these purposes.

However, the following are not "equity-compensation plans" even if the brokerage and other costs of the plan are paid for by the listed company:

- Plans that are made available to shareholders generally, such as a typical dividend reinvestment plan.

- Plans that merely allow employees, directors or other service providers to elect to buy shares on the open market or from the listed company for their current fair market value, regardless of whether:

—the shares are delivered immediately or on a deferred basis; or

—the payments for the shares are made directly or by giving up compensation that is otherwise due (for example, through payroll deductions).

Material Revisions

A "material revision" of an equity-compensation plan includes (but is not limited to), the following:

- A material increase in the number of shares available under the plan (other than an increase solely to reflect a reorganization, stock split, merger, spinoff or similar transaction).

—If a plan contains a formula for automatic increases in the shares available (sometimes called an "evergreen formula") or for automatic grants pursuant to a formula, each such increase or grant will be considered a revision requiring shareholder approval *unless* the plan has a term of not more than ten years.

This type of plan (regardless of its term) is referred to below as a "formula plan." Examples of automatic grants pursuant to a formula are (1) annual grants to directors of restricted stock having a certain dollar value, and (2) "matching contributions," whereby stock is credited to a participant's account based upon the amount of compensation the participant elects to defer.

—If a plan contains no limit on the number of shares available and is not a formula plan, then each grant under the plan will require separate shareholder approval *regardless* of whether the plan has a term of not more than ten years.

This type of plan is referred to below as a "discretionary plan." A requirement that grants be made out of treasury shares or repurchased shares will not, in itself, be considered a limit or pre-established formula so as to prevent a plan from being considered a discretionary plan.

- An expansion of the types of awards available under the plan.

- A material expansion of the class of employees, directors or other service providers eligible to participate in the plan.

- A material extension of the term of the plan.

- A material change to the method of determining the strike price of options under the plan.

—A change in the method of determining "fair market value" from the closing price on the date of grant to the average of the high and low price on the date of grant is an example of a change that the Exchange would not view as material.

- The deletion or limitation of any provision prohibiting repricing of options. See the next section for details.

Note that an amendment will not be considered a "material revision" if it curtails rather than expands the scope of the plan in question.

Repricings

A plan that does not contain a provision that specifically *permits* repricing of options will be considered for purposes of this listing standard as *prohibiting* repricing. Accordingly any actual repricing of options will be considered a material revision of a plan even if the plan itself is not revised. This consideration will not apply to a repricing through an exchange offer that commenced before the date this listing standard became effective.

"Repricing" means any of the following or any other action that has the same effect:

- Lowering the strike price of an option after it is granted.

- Any other action that is treated as a repricing under generally accepted accounting principles.

- Canceling an option at a time when its strike price exceeds the fair market value of the underlying stock, in exchange for another option, restricted stock, or other equity, unless the cancellation and exchange occurs in connection with a merger, acquisition, spin-off or other similar corporate transaction.

Exemptions

This listing standard does not require shareholder approval of employment inducement awards, certain grants, plans and amendments in the context of mergers and acquisitions, and certain specific types of plans, all as described below. However, these exempt grants, plans and amendments may be made only with the approval of the company's independent compensation committee or the approval of a majority of the company's independent directors. Companies must also notify the Exchange in writing when they use one of these exemptions.

Employment Inducement Awards

An employment inducement award is a grant of options or other equity-based compensation as a material inducement to a person or persons being hired by the listed company or any of its subsidiaries, or being rehired following a bona fide period of interruption of employment. Inducement awards include grants to new employees in connection with a merger or acquisition. Promptly following a grant of any inducement award in reliance on this exemption, the listed company must disclose in a press release the material terms of the award, including the recipient(s) of the award and the number of shares involved.

Mergers and Acquisitions

Two exemptions apply in the context of corporate acquisitions and mergers.

First, shareholder approval will not be required to convert, replace or adjust outstanding options or other equity-compensation awards to reflect the transaction.

Second, shares available under certain plans acquired in corporate acquisitions and mergers may be used for certain post-transaction grants without further shareholder approval.

This exemption applies to situations where a party that is not a listed company following the transaction has shares available for grant under pre-existing plans that were previously approved by shareholders. A plan adopted in contemplation of the merger or acquisition transaction would not be considered "pre-existing" for purposes of this exemption.

Shares available under such a pre-existing plan may be used for post-transaction grants of options and other awards with respect to equity of the entity that is the listed company after the transaction, either under the pre-existing plan or another plan, without further shareholder approval, so long as:

- the number of shares available for grants is appropriately adjusted to reflect the transaction;

- the time during which those shares are available is not extended beyond the period when they would have been available under the pre-existing plan, absent the transaction; and

- the options and other awards are not granted to individuals who were employed, immediately before the transaction, by the post-transaction listed company or entities that were its subsidiaries immediately before the transaction.

Any shares reserved for listing in connection with a transaction pursuant to either of these exemptions would be counted by the Exchange in determining whether the transaction involved the issuance of 20% or more of the company's outstanding common stock and thus required shareholder approval under Listed Company Manual Section 312.03(c).

These merger-related exemptions will not result in any increase in the aggregate potential dilution of the combined enterprise. Further, mergers or acquisitions are not routine occurrences, and are not likely to be abused. Therefore, the Exchange considers both of these exemptions to be consistent with the fundamental policy involved in this standard.

Qualified Plans, Parallel Excess Plans and Section 423 Plans

The following types of plans (and material revisions thereto) are exempt from the shareholder approval requirement:

- plans intended to meet the requirements of Section 401(a) of the Internal Revenue Code (e.g., ESOPs);

- plans intended to meet the requirements of Section 423 of the Internal Revenue Code; and

- "parallel excess plans" as defined below.

Section 401(a) plans and Section 423 plans are already regulated under the Internal Revenue Code and Treasury regulations. Section 423 plans, which are stock purchase plans under which an employee can purchase no more than $25,000 worth of stock per year at a plan-specified discount capped at 15%, are also required by the Internal Revenue Code to receive shareholder approval. While Section 401(a) plans and parallel excess plans are not required to be approved by shareholders, U.S. GAAP requires that the shares issued under these plans be "expensed" (i.e., treated as a compensation expense on the income statement) by the company issuing the shares.

An equity-compensation plan that provides non-U.S. employees with substantially the same benefits as a comparable Section 401(a) plan, Section 423 plan or parallel excess plan that the listed company provides to its U.S. employees, but for features necessary to comply with applicable foreign tax law, are also exempt from shareholder approval under this section.

The term "parallel excess plan" means a plan that is a "pension plan" within the meaning of the Employee Retirement Income Security Act ("ERISA") that is designed to work in parallel with a plan intended to be qualified under Internal Revenue Code Section 401(a) to provide benefits that exceed the limits set forth in Internal Revenue Code Section 402(g) (the section that limits an employee's annual pre-tax contributions to a 401(k) plan), Internal Revenue Code Section 401(a)(17) (the section that limits the amount of an employee's compensation that can be taken into account for plan purposes) and/or Internal Revenue Code Section 415 (the section that limits the contributions and benefits under qualified plans) and/or any successor or similar limitations that may hereafter be enacted. A plan will not be considered a parallel excess plan unless (1) it covers all or substantially all employees of an employer who are participants in the related qualified plan whose annual compensation is in excess of the limit of Code Section 401(a)(17) (or any successor or similar limits that may hereafter be enacted); (2) its terms are substantially the same as the qualified plan that it parallels except for the elimination of the limits described in the preceding sentence and the limitation described in clause (3); and (3) no participant receives employer equity contributions under the plan in excess of 25% of the participant's cash compensation. . . .

303A.09 Corporate Governance Guidelines

Listed companies must adopt and disclose corporate governance guidelines.

Commentary: No single set of guidelines would be appropriate for every listed company, but certain key areas of universal importance include director qualifications and responsibilities, responsibilities of key board committees, and director compensation. Given the importance of corporate governance, each listed company's website must include its corporate governance guidelines and the charters of its most important committees (including at least the audit, and if applicable, compensation and nominating committees). The listed company must state in its annual proxy statement or, if the company does not file an annual proxy statement, in the company's annual report on Form 10–K filed with the SEC that the foregoing information is available on its website, and that the information is available in print to any shareholder who requests it. Making this information publicly available should promote better investor understanding of the listed company's policies and procedures, as well as more conscientious adherence to them by directors and management.

The following subjects must be addressed in the corporate governance guidelines:

- **Director qualification standards.** These standards should, at minimum, reflect the independence requirements set forth in Sections 303A.01 and 303A.02. Companies may also address other substantive qualification requirements, including policies limiting the number of boards on which a director may sit, and director tenure, retirement and succession.

- **Director responsibilities.** These responsibilities should clearly articulate what is expected from a director, including basic duties and responsibilities with respect to attendance at board meetings and advance review of meeting materials.

- **Director access to management and, as necessary and appropriate, independent advisors.**

- **Director compensation.** Director compensation guidelines should include general principles for determining the form and amount of director compensation (and for reviewing those principles, as appropriate). The board should be aware that questions as to directors' independence may be raised when directors' fees and emoluments exceed what is customary. Similar concerns may be raised when the listed company makes substantial charitable contributions to organizations in which a director is affiliated, or enters into consulting contracts with (or provides other indirect forms of compensation to) a director. The board should critically evaluate each of these matters when determining the form and amount of director compensation, and the independence of a director.

- **Director orientation and continuing education.**

- **Management succession.** Succession planning should include policies and principles for CEO selection and performance review, as well as policies regarding succession in the event of an emergency or the retirement of the CEO.

- **Annual performance evaluation of the board.** The board should conduct a self-evaluation at least annually to determine whether it and its committees are functioning effectively.

303A.10 Code of Business Conduct and Ethics

Listed companies must adopt and disclose a code of business conduct and ethics for directors, officers and employees, and promptly disclose any waivers of the code for directors or executive officers.

Commentary: No code of business conduct and ethics can replace the thoughtful behavior of an ethical director, officer or employee. However, such a code can focus the board and management on areas of ethical risk, provide guidance to personnel to help them recognize and deal with ethical issues, provide mechanisms to report unethical conduct, and help to foster a culture of honesty and accountability.

Each code of business conduct and ethics must require that any waiver of the code for executive officers or directors may be made only by the board or a board committee and must be promptly disclosed to shareholders. This disclosure requirement should inhibit casual and perhaps questionable waivers, and should help assure that, when warranted, a waiver is accompanied by appropriate controls designed to protect the listed company. It will also give shareholders the opportunity to evaluate the board's performance in granting waivers.

Each code of business conduct and ethics must also contain compliance standards and procedures that will facilitate the effective operation of the code. These standards should ensure the prompt and consistent action against violations of the code. Each listed company's website must include its code of business conduct and ethics. The listed company must state in its annual proxy statement or, if the company does not file an annual proxy statement, in the company's annual report on Form 10–K filed with the SEC, that the foregoing information is available on its website and that the information is available in print to any shareholder who requests it.

Each listed company may determine its own policies, but all listed companies should address the most important topics, including the following:

- **Conflicts of interest.** A "conflict of interest" occurs when an individual's private interest interferes in any way—or even appears to interfere—with the interests of the corporation as a whole. A conflict situation can arise when an employee, officer or director takes actions or has interests that may make it difficult to perform his or her company work objectively and effectively. Conflicts of interest also arise when an employee, officer or director, or a member of his or her family, receives improper personal benefits as a result of his or her position in the company. Loans to, or guarantees of obligations of, such persons are of special concern. The listed company should have a policy prohibiting such conflicts of interest, and providing a means for employees, officers and directors to communicate potential conflicts to the listed company.

- **Corporate opportunities.** Employees, officers and directors should be prohibited from (a) taking for themselves personally opportunities that are discovered through the use of corporate property, information or position; (b) using corporate property, information, or position for personal gain; and (c) competing with the company. Employees, officers and directors owe a duty to the company to advance its legitimate interests when the opportunity to do so arises.

- **Confidentiality.** Employees, officers and directors should maintain the confidentiality of information entrusted to them by the listed company or its customers, except when disclosure is authorized or legally mandated. Confidential information includes all non-public information that might be of use to competitors, or harmful to the company or its customers, if disclosed.

- **Fair dealing.** Each employee, officer and director should endeavor to deal fairly with the company's customers, suppliers, competitors and employees. None should take unfair advantage of anyone through manipulation, concealment, abuse of privileged information, misrepresentation of material facts, or any other unfair-dealing practice. Listed companies may write their codes in a manner that does not alter existing legal rights and obligations of companies and their employees, such as "at will" employment arrangements.

- **Protection and proper use of company assets.** All employees, officers and directors should protect the company's assets and ensure their efficient use. Theft, carelessness and waste have a direct impact on the listed company's profitability. All company assets should be used for legitimate business purposes.

- **Compliance with laws, rules and regulations (including insider trading laws).** The listed company should proactively promote compliance with laws, rules and regulations, including insider trading laws. Insider trading is both unethical and illegal, and should be dealt with decisively.

- **Encouraging the reporting of any illegal or unethical behavior.** The listed company should proactively promote ethical behavior. The company should encourage employees to talk to supervisors, managers or other appropriate personnel when in doubt about the best course of action in a particular situation. Additionally, employees should report violations of laws, rules, regulations or the code of business conduct to appropriate personnel. To encourage employees to report such violations, the listed company must ensure that employees know that the company will not allow retaliation for reports made in good faith.

303A.11 Foreign Private Issuer Disclosure

Listed foreign private issuers must disclose any significant ways in which their corporate governance practices differ from those followed by domestic companies under NYSE listing standards.

Commentary: Foreign private issuers must make their U.S. investors aware of the significant ways in which their corporate governance practices differ from those required of domestic companies under NYSE listing standards. However, foreign private issuers are not required to present a detailed, item-by-item analysis of these differences. Such a disclosure would be long and unnecessarily complicated. Moreover, this requirement is not intended to suggest that one country's corporate governance practices are better or more effective than another. The Exchange believes that U.S. shareholders should be aware of the significant ways that the governance of a listed foreign private issuer differs from that of a U.S. listed company. The Exchange underscores that what is required is a brief, general summary of the significant differences, not a cumbersome analysis.

Listed foreign private issuers may provide this disclosure either on their web site (provided it is in the English language and accessible from the United States) and/or in their annual report as distributed to shareholders in the United States ... (again, in the English language). If the disclosure is only made available on the web site, the annual report shall so state and provide the web address at which the information may be obtained.

303A.12   Certification Requirements

(a) Each listed company CEO must certify to the NYSE each year that he or she is not aware of any violation by the company of NYSE corporate governance listing standards, qualifying the certification to the extent necessary.

Commentary: The CEO's annual certification regarding the NYSE's corporate governance listing standards will focus the CEO and senior management on the listed company's compliance with the listing standards. Both this certification to the NYSE, including any qualifications to that certification, and any CEO/CFO certifications required to be filed with the SEC regarding the quality of the listed company's public disclosure, must be disclosed in the company's annual report to shareholders or, if the company does not prepare an annual report to shareholders, in the company's annual report on Form 10–K filed with the SEC.

(b) Each listed company CEO must promptly notify the NYSE in writing after any executive officer of the listed company becomes aware of any material non-compliance with any applicable provisions of this Section 303A.

(c) Each listed company must submit an executed Written Affirmation annually to the NYSE. In addition, each listed company must submit an interim Written Affirmation each time a change occurs to the board or any of the committees subject to

Section 303A. The annual and interim Written Affirmations must be in the form specified by the NYSE.

303A.13   Public Reprimand Letter

The NYSE may issue a public reprimand letter to any listed company that violates a NYSE listing standard.

> *Commentary:* Suspending trading in or delisting a listed company can be harmful to the very shareholders that the NYSE listing standards seek to protect; the NYSE must therefore use these measures sparingly and judiciously. For this reason it is appropriate for the NYSE to have the ability to apply a lesser sanction to deter companies from violating its corporate governance (or other) listing standards. Accordingly, the NYSE may issue a public reprimand letter to any listed company, regardless of type of security listed or country of incorporation, that it determines has violated a NYSE listing standard. For companies that repeatedly or flagrantly violate NYSE listing standards, suspension and delisting remain the ultimate penalties. For clarification, this lesser sanction is not intended for use in the case of companies that fall below the financial and other continued listing standards provided in Chapter 8 of the Listed Company Manual or that fail to comply with the audit committee standards set out in Section 303A.06. The processes and procedures provided for in Chapter 8 govern the treatment of companies falling below those standards.

304.00   Classified Boards of Directors.

The Exchange expects that Boards of Directors will be elected by all of the shareholders entitled to vote as a class except where special representation is required by the default provisions of a class or classes of preferred stock.

The Exchange will refuse to authorize listing where the Board of Directors is divided into more than three classes. Where classes are provided, they should be of approximately equal size and tenure and directors' terms of office should not exceed three years.

308.00   Defensive Tactics.

For many years, the Exchange has encouraged the broadening of share ownership in a climate of corporate democracy and has endeavored to preserve the basic right of shareholders to participate in the corporate affairs of the companies which they own by requiring an informed and convenient method of voting in proportion to their investment in the company. Since 1926 the Exchange has refused to list non-voting common stock and currently will delist the voting common stock of a company which creates a class of nonvoting common stock or fails to solicit proxies for meetings of its shareholders. All common stocks listed on the Exchange have the right to vote.

The Exchange has an ongoing concern as to the possible implications of certain so-called "defensive tactics" which would in effect discriminate among shareholders.

Generally speaking, an arrangement which could be applied uniformly to all transactions of similar nature and without regard to the parties involved, normally, would not be viewed as objectionable. On the other hand, any proposal which results in either discrimination against an existing substantial shareholder or discouragement of anyone seeking to make a substantial investment would appear to raise substantial questions as to whether or not it constitutes an infringement upon the voting philosophy of the Exchange. In this connection, the Exchange would find objectionable such things as the imposition of a "right of first refusal" on acquired securities, or similar kinds of "call" provisions, or the use of irrevocable proxies.

As a matter of policy, the Exchange will refuse to list additional common stock of a company when restrictions exist such as voting trusts, irrevocable proxies, disproportionate voting power or classification of Boards of Directors into more than three classes of approximately equal size and tenure, or when unusual voting provisions are created which tend to nullify or restrict the voting of a class of stock or the right to veto the action of another class are created.

The Exchange would also be concerned about the issuance of preferred stock which by its terms would vote separately as a class from the common stock on the approval of mergers and acquisitions, unless required by federal or state statute.

It is suggested that companies consult with their Exchange representatives while corporate planning is in an early stage to be certain that Exchange voting rights policies are not violated. In any event, copies of preliminary proxy materials should be furnished to the Exchange for review, preferably before formal filing. This will avoid problems that otherwise might arise as to a company's continued listing status.

312.00   Shareholder Approval Policy

312.03   Shareholder Approval

Shareholder approval is a prerequisite to listing in the following situations:

(a) Shareholder approval is required for equity compensation plans. See Section 303A.08.

(b) Shareholder approval is required prior to the issuance of common stock, or of securities convertible into or exercisable for common stock, to:

> (1) a director, officer or substantial security holder of the company (a "Related Party");

(2) a subsidiary, affiliate or other closely-related person of a Related Party; or

(3) any company or entity in which a Related Party has a substantial direct or indirect interest; if the number of shares of common stock to be issued, or if the number of shares of common stock into which the securities may be convertible or exercisable, exceeds either one percent of the number of shares of common stock or one percent of the voting power outstanding before the issuance.

However, if the Related Party involved in the transaction is classified as such solely because such person is a substantial security holder, and if the issuance relates to a sale of stock for cash at a price at least as great as each of the book and market value of the issuer's common stock, then shareholder approval will not be required unless the number of shares of common stock to be issued, or unless the number of shares of common stock into which the securities may be convertible or exercisable, exceeds either five percent of the number of shares of common stock or five percent of the voting power outstanding before the issuance.

(c) Shareholder approval is required prior to the issuance of common stock, or of securities convertible into or exercisable for common stock, in any transaction or series of related transactions if:

(1) the common stock has, or will have upon issuance, voting power equal to or in excess of 20 percent of the voting power outstanding before the issuance of such stock or of securities convertible into or exercisable for common stock; or

(2) the number of shares of common stock to be issued is, or will be upon issuance, equal to or in excess of 20 percent of the number of shares of common stock outstanding before the issuance of the common stock or of securities convertible into or exercisable for common stock.

However, shareholder approval will not be required for any such issuance involving:

- any public offering for cash;

- any bona fide private financing, if such financing involves a sale of:

- common stock, for cash, at a price at least as great as each of the book and market value of the issuer's common stock; or

- securities convertible into or exercisable for common stock, for cash, if the conversion or exercise price is at least as great as each of the book and market value of the issuer's common stock.

(d) Shareholder approval is required prior to an issuance that will result in a change of control of the issuer.

312.04   For the Purpose of Para. 312.03

For the purpose of Para. 312.03:

(a) Shareholder approval is required if any of the subparagraphs of Para. 312.03 require such approval, notwithstanding the fact that the transaction does not require approval under one or more of the other subparagraphs.

(b) Pursuant to subparagraphs (b) and (c) of Para. 312.03, shareholder approval is required for the issuance of securities convertible into or exercisable for common stock if the stock that can be issued upon conversion or exercise exceeds the applicable percentages. This is the case even if such convertible or exchangeable securities are not to be listed on the Exchange. . . .

(c) Only shares actually issued and outstanding (excluding treasury shares or shares held by a subsidiary) are to be used in making any calculation provided for in that paragraph. Unissued shares reserved for issuance upon conversion of securities or upon exercise of options or warrants will not be regarded as outstanding.

(d) An interest consisting of less than either five percent of the number of shares of common stock or five percent of the voting power outstanding of a company or entity shall not be considered a substantial interest or cause the holder of such an interest to be regarded as a substantial security holder.

(e) "Voting power outstanding" refers to the aggregate number of votes that may be cast by holders of those securities outstanding that entitle the holders thereof to vote generally on all matters submitted to the company's security holders for a vote.

(f) "Bona fide private financing" refers to a sale in which either:

- a registered broker-dealer purchases the securities from the issuer with a view to the private sale of such securities to one or more purchasers; or

- the issuer sells the securities to multiple purchasers, and no one such purchaser, or group of related purchasers, acquires, or has the right to acquire upon exercise or conversion of the securities, more than five percent of the shares of the issuer's common stock or more than five percent of the issuer's voting power before the sale.

(g) "Officer" has the same meaning as defined by the Securities and Exchange Commission in Rule 16a–1(f) under the Securities Exchange Act of 1934, or any successor rule.

312.05   Exceptions

Exceptions may be made to the shareholder approval policy in Para. 312.03 upon application to the Exchange when (1) the delay in securing stockholder approval would seriously jeopardize the financial viability of the enterprise and (2) reliance by the company on this exception is expressly approved by the Audit Committee of the Board.

A company relying on this exception must mail to all shareholders not later than 10 days before issuance of the securities a letter alerting them to its omission to seek the shareholder approval that would otherwise be required under the policy of the Exchange and indicating that the Audit Committee of the Board has expressly approved the exception.

312.07 Where shareholder approval is a prerequisite to the listing of any additional or new securities of a listed company, the minimum vote which will constitute shareholder approval for listing purposes is defined as approval by a majority of votes cast on a proposal in a proxy bearing on the particular matter, provided that the total vote cast on the proposal represents over 50% in interest of all securities entitled to vote on the proposal.

313.00 Voting Rights

(A) Voting Rights Policy....

Voting rights of existing shareholders of publicly traded common stock under Section 12 of the Exchange Act cannot be disparately reduced or restricted through any corporate action or issuance. Examples of such corporate action or issuance include, but are not limited to, the adoption of time phased voting plans, the adoption of capped voting rights plans, the issuance of super voting stock, or the issuance of stock with voting rights less than the per share voting rights of the existing common stock through an exchange offer.

Supplementary Material:

.10 Companies with Dual Class Structures—The restriction against the issuance of super voting stock is primarily intended to apply to the issuance of a new class of stock, and companies with existing dual class capital structures would generally be permitted to issue additional shares of the existing super voting stock without conflict with this Policy.

.20 Consultation with the Exchange—Violation of the Exchange's Voting Rights Policy could result in the loss of an Issuers's Exchange market or public trading market. The Policy can apply to a variety of corporate actions and securities issuances, not just super voting or so-called "time phase" voting common stock....

(B) Non–Voting Common Stock

The Exchange's voting rights policy permits the listing of the voting common stock of a company which also has outstanding a non-voting common stock as well as the listing of non-voting common stock.

However, certain safeguards must be provided to holders of a listed non-voting common stock:

(1) Any class of non-voting common stock that is listed on the Exchange must meet all original listing standards. The rights of the holders of the non-voting common stock should, except for voting rights, be substantially the same as those of the holders of the company's voting common stock.

(2) The requirement that listed companies publish at least once a year and submit to shareholders an annual report ... applies equally to holders of voting common stock and to holders of listed non-voting common stock.

(3) In addition, although the holders of shares of listed non-voting common stock are not entitled to vote generally on matters submitted for shareholder action, holders of any listed non-voting common stock must receive all communications, including proxy material, sent generally to the holders of the voting securities of the listed company.

(C) Preferred Stock, Minimum Voting Rights Required

Preferred stock, voting as a class, should have the right to elect a minimum of two directors upon default of the equivalent of six quarterly dividends. The right to elect directors should accrue regardless of whether defaulted dividends occurred in consecutive periods.

The right to elect directors should remain in effect until cumulative dividends have been paid in full or until non-cumulative dividends have been paid regularly for at least a year. The preferred stock quorum should be low enough to ensure that the right to elect directors can be exercised as soon as it accrues. In no event should the quorum exceed the percentage required for a quorum of the common stock required for the election of directors. The Exchange prefers that no quorum requirement be fixed in respect of the right of a preferred stock, voting as a class, to elect directors when dividends are in default....

ABA MODEL RULES OF PROFESSIONAL CONDUCT, RULES 1.6, 1.7, 1.13

Rule 1.6. Confidentiality of Information

(a) A lawyer shall not reveal information relating to the representation of a client unless the client gives informed consent, the disclosure is impliedly authorized in order to carry out the representation or the disclosure is permitted by paragraph (b).

(b) A lawyer may reveal information relating to the representation of a client to the extent the lawyer reasonably believes necessary:

(1) to prevent reasonably certain death or substantial bodily harm;

(2) to prevent the client from committing a crime or fraud that is reasonably certain to result in substantial injury to the financial interests or property of another and in furtherance of which the client has used or is using the lawyer's services;

(3) to prevent, mitigate or rectify substantial injury to the financial interests or property of another that is reasonably certain to result or has resulted from the client's commission of a crime or fraud in furtherance of which the client has used the lawyer's services;

(4) to secure legal advice about the lawyer's compliance with these Rules;

(5) to establish a claim or defense on behalf of the lawyer in a controversy between the lawyer and the client, to establish a defense to a criminal charge or civil claim against the lawyer based upon conduct in which the client was involved, or to respond to allegations in any proceeding concerning the lawyer's representation of the client; or

(6) to comply with other law or a court order.

Comment ...

Disclosure Adverse to Client

[6] Although the public interest is usually best served by a strict rule requiring lawyers to preserve the confidentiality of information relating to the representation of their clients, the confidentiality rule is subject to limited exceptions. Paragraph (b)(1) recognizes the overriding value of life and physical integrity and permits disclosure reasonably necessary to prevent reasonably certain death or substantial bodily harm. Such harm is reasonably certain to occur if it will be suffered imminently or if there is a present and substantial threat that a person

will suffer such harm at a later date if the lawyer fails to take action necessary to eliminate the threat. Thus, a lawyer who knows that a client has accidentally discharged toxic waste into a town's water supply may reveal this information to the authorities if there is a present and substantial risk that a person who drinks the water will contract a life-threatening or debilitating disease and the lawyer's disclosure is necessary to eliminate the threat or reduce the number of victims. . . .

[7] Paragraph (b)(2) is a limited exception to the rule of confidentiality that permits the lawyer to reveal information to the extent necessary to enable affected persons or appropriate authorities to prevent the client from committing a crime or fraud . . . that is reasonably certain to result in substantial injury to the financial or property interests of another and in furtherance of which the client has used or is using the lawyer's services. Such a serious abuse of the client-lawyer relationship by the client forfeits the protection of this Rule. The client can, of course, prevent such disclosure by refraining from the wrongful conduct. Although paragraph (b)(2) does not require the lawyer to reveal the client's misconduct, the lawyer may not counsel or assist the client in conduct the lawyer knows is criminal or fraudulent. See Rule 1.2(d). See also Rule 1.16 with respect to the lawyer's obligation or right to withdraw from the representation of the client in such circumstances, and Rule 1.13(c), which permits the lawyer, where the client is an organization, to reveal information relating to the representation in limited circumstances.

[8] Paragraph (b)(3) addresses the situation in which the lawyer does not learn of the client's crime or fraud until after it has been consummated. Although the client no longer has the option of preventing disclosure by refraining from the wrongful conduct, there will be situations in which the loss suffered by the affected person can be prevented, rectified or mitigated. In such situations, the lawyer may disclose information relating to the representation to the extent necessary to enable the affected persons to prevent or mitigate reasonably certain losses or to attempt to recoup their losses. Paragraph (b)(3) does not apply when a person who has committed a crime or fraud thereafter employs a lawyer for representation concerning that offense. . . .

Rule 1.7. Conflict of Interest: Current Clients

(a) Except as provided in paragraph (b), a lawyer shall not represent a client if the representation involves a concurrent conflict of interest. A concurrent conflict of interest exists if:

(1) the representation of one client will be directly adverse to another client; or

(2) there is a significant risk that the representation of one or more clients will be materially limited by the lawyer's responsibili-

ties to another client, a former client or a third person or by a personal interest of the lawyer.

(b) Notwithstanding the existence of a concurrent conflict of interest under paragraph (a), a lawyer may represent a client if:

(1) the lawyer reasonably believes that the lawyer will be able to provide competent and diligent representation to each affected client;

(2) the representation is not prohibited by law;

(3) the representation does not involve the assertion of a claim by one client against another client represented by the lawyer in the same litigation or other proceeding before a tribunal; and

(4) each affected client gives informed consent, confirmed in writing.

Comment ...

Organizational Clients

[34] A lawyer who represents a corporation or other organization does not, by virtue of that representation, necessarily represent any constituent or affiliated organization, such as a parent or subsidiary. See Rule 1.13(a). Thus, the lawyer for an organization is not barred from accepting representation adverse to an affiliate in an unrelated matter, unless the circumstances are such that the affiliate should also be considered a client of the lawyer, there is an understanding between the lawyer and the organizational client that the lawyer will avoid representation adverse to the client's affiliates, or the lawyer's obligations to either the organizational client or the new client are likely to limit materially the lawyer's representation of the other client.

[35] A lawyer for a corporation or other organization who is also a member of its board of directors should determine whether the responsibilities of the two roles may conflict. The lawyer may be called on to advise the corporation in matters involving actions of the directors. Consideration should be given to the frequency with which such situations may arise, the potential intensity of the conflict, the effect of the lawyer's resignation from the board and the possibility of the corporation's obtaining legal advice from another lawyer in such situations. If there is material risk that the dual role will compromise the lawyer's independence of professional judgment, the lawyer should not serve as a director or should cease to act as the corporation's lawyer when conflicts of interest arise. The lawyer should advise the other members of the board that in some circumstances matters discussed at board meetings while the lawyer is present in the capacity of director might not be protected by the attorney-client privilege and that conflict of interest considerations might require the lawyer's recusal as a director or might

require the lawyer and the lawyer's firm to decline representation of the corporation in a matter.

Rule 1.13. Organization as Client

(a) A lawyer employed or retained by an organization represents the organization acting through its duly authorized constituents.

(b) If a lawyer for an organization knows that an officer, employee or other person associated with the organization is engaged in action, intends to act or refuses to act in a matter related to the representation that is a violation of a legal obligation to the organization, or a violation of law that reasonably might be imputed to the organization, and that is likely to result in substantial injury to the organization, then the lawyer shall proceed as is reasonably necessary in the best interest of the organization. Unless the lawyer reasonably believes that it is not necessary in the best interest of the organization to do so, the lawyer shall refer the matter to higher authority in the organization, including, if warranted by the circumstances, to the highest authority that can act on behalf of the organization as determined by applicable law.

(c) Except as provided in paragraph (d), if

(1) despite the lawyer's efforts in accordance with paragraph (b) the highest authority that can act on behalf of the organization insists upon or fails to address in a timely and appropriate manner an action or a refusal to act, that is clearly a violation of law, and

(2) the lawyer reasonably believes that the violation is reasonably certain to result in substantial injury to the organization,

then the lawyer may reveal information relating to the representation whether or not Rule 1.6 permits such disclosure, but only if and to the extent the lawyer reasonably believes necessary to prevent substantial injury to the organization.

(d) Paragraph (c) shall not apply with respect to information relating to a lawyer's representation of an organization to investigate an alleged violation of law, or to defend the organization or an officer, employee or other constituent associated with the organization against a claim arising out of an alleged violation of law.

(e) A lawyer who reasonably believes that he or she has been discharged because of the lawyer's actions taken pursuant to paragraphs (b) or (c), or who withdraws under circumstances that require or permit the lawyer to take action under either of those paragraphs, shall proceed as the lawyer reasonably believes necessary to assure that the organization's highest authority is informed of the lawyer's discharge or withdrawal.

(f) In dealing with an organization's directors, officers, employees, members, shareholders or other constituents, a lawyer shall explain the identity of the client when the lawyer knows or reasonably should know that the organization's interests are adverse to those of the constituents with whom the lawyer is dealing.

(g) A lawyer representing an organization may also represent any of its directors, officers, employees, members, shareholders or other constituents, subject to the provisions of Rule 1.7. If the organization's consent to the dual representation is required by Rule 1.7, the consent shall be given by an appropriate official of the organization other than the individual who is to be represented, or by the shareholders.

Comment

The Entity as the Client

[1] An organizational client is a legal entity, but it cannot act except through its officers, directors, employees, shareholders and other constituents. Officers, directors, employees and shareholders are the constituents of the corporate organizational client. The duties defined in this Comment apply equally to unincorporated associations. "Other constituents" as used in this Comment means the positions equivalent to officers, directors, employees and shareholders held by persons acting for organizational clients that are not corporations.

[2] When one of the constituents of an organizational client communicates with the organization's lawyer in that person's organizational capacity, the communication is protected by Rule 1.6. Thus, by way of example, if an organizational client requests its lawyer to investigate allegations of wrongdoing, interviews made in the course of that investigation between the lawyer and the client's employees or other constituents are covered by Rule 1.6. This does not mean, however, that constituents of an organizational client are the clients of the lawyer. The lawyer may not disclose to such constituents information relating to the representation except for disclosures explicitly or impliedly authorized by the organizational client in order to carry out the representation or as otherwise permitted by Rule 1.6.

[3] When constituents of the organization make decisions for it, the decisions ordinarily must be accepted by the lawyer even if their utility or prudence is doubtful. Decisions concerning policy and operations, including ones entailing serious risk, are not as such in the lawyer's province. Paragraph (b) makes clear, however, that when the lawyer knows that the organization is likely to be substantially injured by action of an officer or other constituent that violates a legal obligation to the organization or is in violation of law [and] that might be imputed to the organization, the lawyer must proceed as is reasonably necessary in the best interest of the organization. . . . [K]nowledge can be inferred from circumstances, and a lawyer cannot ignore the obvious.

[4] In determining how to proceed under paragraph (b), the lawyer should give due consideration to the seriousness of the violation and its consequences, the responsibility in the organization and the apparent

motivation of the person involved, the policies of the organization concerning such matters, and any other relevant considerations. Ordinarily, referral to a higher authority would be necessary. In some circumstances, however, it may be appropriate for the lawyer to ask the constituent to reconsider the matter; for example, if the circumstances involve a constituent's innocent misunderstanding of law and subsequent acceptance of the lawyer's advice, the lawyer may reasonably conclude that the best interest of the organization does not require that the matter be referred to higher authority. If a constituent persists in conduct contrary to the lawyer's advice, it will be necessary for the lawyer to take steps to have the matter reviewed by a higher authority in the organization. If the matter is of sufficient seriousness and importance or urgency to the organization, referral to higher authority in the organization may be necessary even if the lawyer has not communicated with the constituent. Any measures taken should, to the extent practicable, minimize the risk of revealing information relating to the representation to persons outside the organization. Even in circumstances where a lawyer is not obligated by Rule 1.13 to proceed, a lawyer may bring to the attention of an organizational client, including its highest authority, matters that the lawyer reasonably believes to be of sufficient importance to warrant doing so in the best interest of the organization.

[5] Paragraph (b) also makes clear that when it is reasonably necessary to enable the organization to address the matter in a timely and appropriate manner, the lawyer must refer the matter to higher authority, including, if warranted by the circumstances, the highest authority that can act on behalf of the organization under applicable law. The organization's highest authority to whom a matter may be referred ordinarily will be the board of directors or similar governing body. However, applicable law may prescribe that under certain conditions the highest authority reposes elsewhere, for example, in the independent directors of a corporation.

Relation to Other Rules

[6] The authority and responsibility provided in this Rule are concurrent with the authority and responsibility provided in other Rules.... Paragraph (c) of this Rule supplements Rule 1.6(b) by providing an additional basis upon which the lawyer may reveal information relating to the representation, but does not modify, restrict, or limit the provisions of Rule 1.6(b)(1)–(6). Under Paragraph (c) the lawyer may reveal such information only when the organization's highest authority insists upon or fails to address threatened or ongoing action that is clearly a violation of law, and then only to the extent the lawyer reasonably believes necessary to prevent reasonably certain substantial injury to the organization. It is not necessary that the lawyer's services be used in furtherance of the violation, but it is required that the matter be related to the lawyer's representation of the organization. If the

lawyer's services are being used by an organization to further a crime or fraud by the organization, Rules 1.6(b)(2) and 1.6(b)(3) may permit the lawyer to disclose confidential information....

[7] Paragraph (d) makes clear that the authority of a lawyer to disclose information relating to a representation in circumstances described in paragraph (c) does not apply with respect to information relating to a lawyer's engagement by an organization to investigate an alleged violation of law or to defend the organization or an officer, employee or other person associated with the organization against a claim arising out of an alleged violation of law. This is necessary in order to enable organizational clients to enjoy the full benefits of legal counsel in conducting an investigation or defending against a claim.

[8] A lawyer who reasonably believes that he or she has been discharged because of the lawyer's actions taken pursuant to Paragraph (b) or (c), or who withdraws in circumstances that require or permit the lawyer to take action under either of these Paragraphs, must proceed as the lawyer reasonably believes necessary to assure that the organization's highest authority is informed of the lawyer's discharge or withdrawal, and what the lawyer reasonably believes is the basis for his or her discharge or withdrawal.

Government Agency

[9] The duty defined in this Rule applies to governmental organizations. Defining precisely the identity of the client and prescribing the resulting obligations of such lawyers may be more difficult in the government context and is a matter beyond the scope of these Rules.... Although in some circumstances the client may be a specific agency, it may also be a branch of government, such as the executive branch, or the government as a whole. For example, if the action or failure to act involves the head of a bureau, either the department of which the bureau is a part or the relevant branch of government may be the client for purposes of this Rule. Moreover, in a matter involving the conduct of government officials, a government lawyer may have authority under applicable law to question such conduct more extensively than that of a lawyer for a private organization in similar circumstances. Thus, when the client is a governmental organization, a different balance may be appropriate between maintaining confidentiality and assuring that the wrongful act is prevented or rectified, for public business is involved. In addition, duties of lawyers employed by the government or lawyers in military service may be defined by statutes and regulation. This Rule does not limit that authority....

Clarifying the Lawyer's Role

[10] There are times when the organization's interest may be or become adverse to those of one or more of its constituents. In such circumstances the lawyer should advise any constituent, whose interest

the lawyer finds adverse to that of the organization of the conflict or potential conflict of interest, that the lawyer cannot represent such constituent, and that such person may wish to obtain independent representation. Care must be taken to assure that the individual understands that, when there is such adversity of interest, the lawyer for the organization cannot provide legal representation for that constituent individual, and that discussions between the lawyer for the organization and the individual may not be privileged.

[11] Whether such a warning should be given by the lawyer for the organization to any constituent individual may turn on the facts of each case.

Dual Representation

[12] Paragraph (g) recognizes that a lawyer for an organization may also represent a principal officer or major shareholder.

Derivative Actions

[13] Under generally prevailing law, the shareholders or members of a corporation may bring suit to compel the directors to perform their legal obligations in the supervision of the organization. Members of unincorporated associations have essentially the same right. Such an action may be brought nominally by the organization, but usually is, in fact, a legal controversy over management of the organization.

[14] The question can arise whether counsel for the organization may defend such an action. The proposition that the organization is the lawyer's client does not alone resolve the issue. Most derivative actions are a normal incident of an organization's affairs, to be defended by the organization's lawyer like any other suit. However, if the claim involves serious charges of wrongdoing by those in control of the organization, a conflict may arise between the lawyer's duty to the organization and the lawyer's relationship with the board. In those circumstances, Rule 1.7 governs who should represent the directors and the organization.

AMERICAN LAW INSTITUTE
PRINCIPLES OF CORPORATE GOVERNANCE: ANALYSIS AND RECOMMENDATIONS (1994) *

PART I

DEFINITIONS

* Most or all Sections of the Principles of Corporate Governance employ terms that are defined in Part I (Definitions). Normally, the first time a defined term is used in the text or Comment of each Section it is followed by a cross-reference, set in brackets, to the Section of Part I in which the term is defined. Usually, however, if the same term is used again in that Section, the term is not accompanied by further cross-references to Part I.

Italics. Italics are used in the text where a number recommended for a bright-line test is deemed preferable, but not clearly superior, to somewhat higher or lower numbers.

** Omitted.

PART II

THE OBJECTIVE AND CONDUCT OF THE CORPORATION

PART III

CORPORATE STRUCTURE: FUNCTIONS AND POWERS OF DIRECTORS AND OFFICERS; AUDIT COMMITTEE IN LARGE PUBLICLY HELD CORPORATIONS

PART III–A

RECOMMENDATIONS OF CORPORATE PRACTICE CONCERNING THE BOARD AND THE PRINCIPAL OVERSIGHT COMMITTEES

PART I

DEFINITIONS

§ 1.01 Effect of Definitions

The definitions in Part I apply for the purposes of Parts I–VII unless the context requires otherwise.

§ 1.02 Approved by the Shareholders

(a) "Approved by the shareholders" means approval by a majority of the voting shares, unless a greater percentage is required by the corporation's charter documents [§ 1.05] pursuant to Subsection (b).

(b) Any provision in a charter document (other than a fair-price provision) that increases the percentage of shares whose approval is required to more than a majority shall be approved by the same vote as is set forth in the provision.

(c) A change in the corporation's charter documents that affects shareholders' rights or control [§ 1.08] of the corporation that is made by the board of directors is to be considered as having been approved by the shareholders if the shareholders have clearly empowered the board of directors to adopt the change or provision.

§ 1.03 Associate

(a) "Associate" means:

(1)(A) The spouse (or a parent or sibling thereof) of a director [§ 1.13], senior executive [§ 1.33], or shareholder, or a child, grandchild, sibling, or parent (or the spouse of any thereof) of a director, senior executive, or shareholder, or an individual having the same home as a director, senior executive, or shareholder, or a trust or estate of which an individual specified in this Subsection (A) is a substantial beneficiary; or (B) a trust, estate, incompetent, conservatee, or minor of which a director, senior executive, or shareholder is a fiduciary; or

(2) A person [§ 1.28] with respect to whom a director, senior executive, or shareholder has a business, financial, or similar relationship that would reasonably be expected to affect the person's judgment with respect to the transaction or conduct in question in a manner adverse to the corporation.

(b) Notwithstanding § 1.03(a)(2), a business organization [§ 1.04] is not an associate of a director, senior executive, or shareholder solely because the director, senior executive, or shareholder is a director or principal manager [§ 1.29] of the business organization. A business organization in which a director, senior executive, or shareholder is the beneficial or record holder of not more than 10 percent of any class of equity interest [§ 1.19] is not presumed to be associate of the holder by reason of the holding, unless the value of the interest to the holder would reasonably be expected to affect the holder's judgment with respect to the transaction in question in a manner adverse to the corporation. A business organization in which a director, senior executive, or shareholder is the beneficial or record holder (other than in a custodial capacity) of more than 10 percent of any class of equity interest is presumed to be an associate of the holder by reason of the holding, unless the value of the interest to the holder would not reasonably be expected to affect the holder's judgment with respect to the transaction or conduct in question in a manner adverse to the corporation.

§ 1.04 Business Organization

"Business organization" means an organization of any form (other than an agency or instrumentality of government) that is primarily engaged in business, including a corporation, a partnership or any other form of association, a sole proprietorship, or any form of trust or estate.

§ 1.05 Charter Documents

"Charter documents" means the articles or certificate of incorporation; documents supplementary thereto that set forth the rights, preferences, and privileges of equity securities [§ 1.20] and any limitations thereon; and the bylaws of the corporation.

§ 1.06 Closely Held Corporation

"Closely held corporation" means a corporation the equity securities [§ 1.20] of which are owned by a small number of persons, and for which securities no active trading market exists.

§ 1.07 Commercial Payment

"Commercial payment" means any payment except the following: a payment of interest on securities, a pro rata distribution to a class of shareholders, a payment to a corporation for its stock, a loan, a repayment of principal, a payment by an insurer on account of an insured loss, a payment to a public utility at a regulated rate, a director's fee, or a payment on behalf of a third party.

§ 1.08 Control

(a) "Control" means the power, directly or indirectly, either alone or pursuant to an arrangement or understanding with one or more other persons [§ 1.28], to exercise a controlling influence over the management or policies of a business organization [§ 1.04], through the ownership of or power to vote equity interests [§ 1.19], through one or more intermediary persons, by contract, or otherwise.

(b) A person who, either alone or pursuant to an arrangement or understanding with one or more other persons, owns or has the power to vote more than 25 percent of the equity interests in a business organization is presumed to be in control of the organization, unless some other person, either alone or pursuant to an arrangement or understanding with one or more other persons, owns or has the power to vote a greater percentage of equity interests. A person who does not, either alone or pursuant to an arrangement or understanding with one or more other persons, own or have the power to vote more than 25 percent of the equity interests in a business organization is not presumed to be in control of the business organization by virtue solely of ownership of or power to vote equity interests in that organization.

(c) A person is not in control of a business organization solely because the person is a director [§ 1.13] or principal manager [§ 1.29] of the organization.

§ 1.09 Control Group

"Control group" means a group of persons [§ 1.28] who act in concert to exercise a controlling influence over the management or policies of a business organization [§ 1.04] pursuant to an arrangement or understanding with each other.

§ 1.10 Controlling Shareholder

(a) A "controlling shareholder" means a person [§ 1.28] who, either alone or pursuant to an arrangement or understanding with one or more other persons:

> (1) Owns and has the power to vote more than 50 percent of the outstanding voting equity securities [§ 1.40] of a corporation; or

> (2) Otherwise exercises a controlling influence over the management or policies of the corporation or the transaction or conduct in question by virtue of the person's position as a shareholder.

(b) A person who, either alone or pursuant to an arrangement or understanding with one or more other persons, owns or has the power to vote more than 25 percent of the outstanding voting equity securities of a corporation is presumed to exercise a controlling influence over the management or policies of the corporation, unless some other person, either alone or pursuant to an arrangement or understanding with one or more other persons, owns or has the power to vote a greater percentage of the voting equity securities. A person who does not, either alone or pursuant to an arrangement with one or more other persons, own or have the power to vote more than 25 percent of the outstanding voting equity securities of a corporation is not presumed to be in control of the corporation by virtue solely of ownership of or power to vote voting equity securities.

§ 1.11 Corporate Decisionmaker

"Corporate decisionmaker" means that corporate official or body with the authority to make a particular decision for the corporation.

§ 1.12 Corporation

(a) A "corporation" means a corporation incorporated under a business corporation law or an analogue thereof.

(b) For purposes of the obligations imposed upon a corporation under § 7.23(c)–(e) (procedural standards for appraisal), including the obligation to pay fair value on the occurrence of the events specified in § 7.21 (Corporate Transactions Giving Rise to Appraisal Rights), "corporation" includes the surviving, successor, or acquiring entity in the case of a business combination that gives rise to appraisal rights under that section.

§ 1.13 Director

"Director" means an individual designated as a director by the corporation or an individual who acts in place of a director under applicable law or a standard of the corporation [§ 1.36].

§ 1.14 Disclosure

(a) *Disclosure Concerning a Conflict of Interest.* A director [§ 1.13], senior executive [§ 1.33], or controlling shareholder [§ 1.10] makes "disclosure concerning a conflict of interest" if the director, senior executive, or controlling shareholder discloses to the corporate decisionmaker [§ 1.11] who authorizes in advance or ratifies the transaction in question the material facts [§ 1.25] known to the director, senior executive, or controlling shareholder concerning the conflict of interest, or if the corporate decisionmaker knows of those facts at the time the transaction is authorized or ratified.

(b) *Disclosure Concerning a Transaction.* A director, senior executive, or controlling shareholder makes "disclosure concerning a transaction" if the director, senior executive, or controlling shareholder discloses to the corporate decisionmaker who authorizes in advance or ratifies the transaction in question the material facts known to the director, senior executive, or controlling shareholder concerning the transaction, or if the corporate decisionmaker knows of those facts at the time the transaction is authorized or ratified.

§ 1.15 Disinterested Directors

A provision that gives a specified effect to action by "disinterested directors" requires the affirmative vote of a majority, but not less than two, of the directors on the board or on an appropriate committee who are not interested [§ 1.23] in the transaction or conduct in question.

§ 1.16 Disinterested Shareholders

A provision that gives a specified effect to action by "disinterested shareholders" requires approval by a majority of the votes cast by shareholders who are not interested [§ 1.23] in the transaction or conduct in question. In the case of § 5.15 (Transfer of Control in Which a Director or Principal Senior Executive Is Interested), such approval shall be deemed to have been given when there has been a tender offer and it has been accepted by a majority of the shares for which the tender offer has been made.

§ 1.17 Eligible Holder

(a) "Eligible holder" means the holder [§ 1.22] of one or more shares, whether common or preferred, that (1) carry voting rights with respect to the election of directors, (2) are entitled to share in all or any portion of current or liquidating dividends after the payment of dividends on any shares entitled to a preference, or (3) are adversely affected by an amendment of the certificate of incorporation as described in § 7.21(d), in each case as of the date of the shareholder vote or other corporate action under § 7.21 (Corporate Transactions Giving Rise to Appraisal Rights).

(b) No person shall be deemed an eligible holder if (1) the shares owned by such person were voted in favor of the proposed transaction or provision, (2) the person fails to elect appraisal with respect to all shares of the class owned by the person, or (3) in the case of a beneficial owner who is not the record holder [§ 1.32] of the shares, the beneficial owner fails to submit to the corporation the record holder's written consent to the beneficial owner's dissent not later than 20 days after the date of the corporate action giving rise to appraisal rights (or such later date on which notice thereof is first given to shareholders).

§ 1.19   Equity Interest

"Equity interest" means an equity security [§ 1.20] in a corporation, or a beneficial interest in any other form of business organization [§ 1.04].

§ 1.20   Equity Security

"Equity security" means (a) a share in a corporation or similar security, or (b) a security convertible, with or without consideration, into such a security, or carrying a warrant or right to subscribe for or buy such a security, if the warrant or right or convertible security is issued by the issuer of that security.

§ 1.21   Family Group

"Family group" means a group of persons [§ 1.28], all of whom act in concert concerning the corporation's affairs and who are either individuals related by blood, marriage, or adoption, or trusts or other organizations created or acting primarily for the benefit of such individuals.

§ 1.22   Holder

A "holder" is a person [§ 1.28] having a legal or substantial beneficial interest in an equity security [§ 1.20].

§ 1.23   Interested

(a) A director [§ 1.13] or officer [§ 1.27] is "interested" in a transaction or conduct if either:

(1) The director or officer, or an associate [§ 1.03] of the director or officer, is a party to the transaction or conduct;

(2) The director or officer has a business, financial, or familial relationship with a party to the transaction or conduct, and that relationship would reasonably be expected to affect the director's or officer's judgment with respect to the transaction or conduct in a manner adverse to the corporation;

(3) The director or officer, an associate of the director or officer, or a person with whom the director or officer has a business, financial, or familial relationship, has a material pecuniary interest in the transaction or conduct (other than usual and customary directors' fees and benefits) and that interest and (if present) that relationship would reasonably be expected to affect the director's or officer's judgment in a manner adverse to the corporation; or

(4) The director or officer is subject to a controlling influence by a party to the transaction or conduct or a person who has a material pecuniary interest in the transaction or conduct, and that controlling influence could reasonably be expected to affect the director's or officer's judgment with respect to the transaction or conduct in a manner adverse to the corporation.

(b) A shareholder is interested in a transaction or conduct if either the shareholder or, to the shareholder's knowledge, an associate of the shareholder is a party to the transaction or conduct, or the shareholder is also an interested director or officer with respect to the same transaction or conduct.

(c) A director is interested in an action within the meaning of Part VII, Chapter 1 (The Derivative Action), but not elsewhere in these Principles, if:

(1) The director is interested, within the meaning of Subsection (a), in the transaction or conduct that is the subject of the action, or

(2) The director is a defendant in the action, except that the fact a director is named as a defendant does not make the director interested under this section if the complaint against the director:

(A) is based only on the fact that the director approved of or acquiesced in the transaction or conduct that is the subject of the action, and

(B) does not otherwise allege with particularity facts that, if true, raise a significant prospect that the director would be adjudged liable to the corporation or its shareholders.

§ 1.24 Large Publicly Held Corporation

"Large publicly held corporation" means a corporation that as of the record date for its most recent annual shareholders' meeting had both 2,000 or more record holders [§ 1.32] of its equity securities [§ 1.20] and $100 million or more of total assets [§ 1.37]; but a corporation shall not cease to be a large publicly held corporation because its total assets fall below $100 million unless total assets remain below $100 million for *two* consecutive fiscal years.

§ 1.25 Material Fact

A fact is "material" if there is a substantial likelihood that a reasonable person would consider it important under the circumstances in determining the person's course of action.

§ 1.26 Member of the Immediate Family

"Member of the immediate family" of an individual means a spouse (or a parent or sibling thereof) of the individual, or a child, grandchild, sibling, parent (or spouse of any thereof) of the individual, or a natural person having the same home as the individual.

§ 1.27 Officer

"Officer" means (a) the chief executive, operating, financial, legal, and accounting officers of a corporation; (b) to the extent not encompassed by the foregoing, the chairman of the board of directors (unless the chairman neither performs a policymaking function other than as a director nor receives a material amount of compensation in excess of director's fees), president, treasurer, and secretary, and a vice-president or vice-chairman who is in charge of a principal business unit, division, or function (such as sales, administration, or finance) or performs a major policymaking function for the corporation; and (c) any other individual designated by the corporation as an officer.

§ 1.28 Person

"Person" means (a) an individual, (b) any form of organization, including a corporation, a partnership or any other form of association, any form of trust or estate, a government or any political subdivision, or an agency or instrumentality of government, or (c) any other legal or commercial entity.

§ 1.29 Principal Manager

"Principal manager" means a senior executive [§ 1.33] of a corporation, a general partner of a partnership, a person holding a comparable position in any other business organization [§ 1.04], or a trustee of a trust.

§ 1.30 Principal Senior Executive

"Principal senior executive" means an officer described in Subsection (a) of § 1.27 (Officer).

§ 1.31 Publicly Held Corporation

"Publicly held corporation" means a corporation that as of the record date for its most recent annual shareholders' meeting had both 500 or more record holders [§ 1.32] of its equity securities [§ 1.20] and

$5 million or more of total assets [§ 1.37]; but a corporation shall not cease to be a publicly held corporation because its total assets fall below $5 million, unless total assets remain below $5 million for *two* consecutive fiscal years.

§ 1.32   Record Holder

A "record holder" of equity securities [§ 1.20] means a person [§ 1.28] identified as the owner of such securities on the record of security holders maintained by or on behalf of the corporation, except that: (a) a group of persons holding as co-owners or co-fiduciaries shall be treated as a single person; and (b) for purposes of §§ ..., 1.24 (Large Publicly Held Corporation), 1.31 (Publicly Held Corporation), and 1.35 (Small Publicly Held Corporation), there shall be included as record holders the number of beneficial owners of equity securities held in the name of a voting trustee, trustee of an employee stock ownership trust, stock depository, stockbroker, or nominee, and the number of owners of equity securities held in bearer form, that the corporation has a reasonable basis for estimating.

§ 1.33   Senior Executive

"Senior executive" means an officer described in Subsection (a) or (b) of § 1.27 (Officer).

§ 1.34   Significant Relationship

(a) Except as provided in § 1.34(b), a director has a "significant relationship" with the senior executives [§ 1.33] of a corporation if, as of the end of the corporation's last fiscal year, either:

(1) The director is employed by the corporation, or was so employed within the *two* preceding years;

(2) The director is a member of the immediate family [§ 1.26] of an individual who (A) is employed by the corporation as an officer [§ 1.27], or (B) was employed by the corporation as a senior executive within the *two* preceding years;

(3) The director has made to or received from the corporation during either of its *two* preceding years, commercial payments [§ 1.07] which exceeded *$200,000,* or the director owns or has power to vote an equity interest [§ 1.19] in a business organization [§ 1.04] to which the corporation made, or from which the corporation received, during either of its *two* preceding years, commercial payments that, when multiplied by the director's percentage equity interest in the organization, exceeded *$200,000;*

(4) The director is a principal manager [§ 1.29] of a business organization to which the corporation made, or from which the corporation received, during either of the organization's *two* preced-

ing years, commercial payments that exceeded *five percent* of the organization's consolidated gross revenues for that year, or *$200,000,* whichever is more; or

(5) The director is affiliated in a professional capacity with a law firm that was the primary legal adviser to the corporation with respect to general corporate or securities law matters, or with an investment banking firm that was retained by the corporation in an advisory capacity or acted as a managing underwriter in an issue of the corporation's securities, within the *two* preceding years, or was so affiliated with such a law or investment banking firm when it was so retained or so acted.

(b) A director shall not be deemed to have a significant relationship with the senior executives under § 1.34(a)(3)–(5) if, on the basis of countervailing or other special circumstances, it could not reasonably be believed that the judgment of a person in the director's position would be affected by the relationship under § 1.34(a)(3)–(5) in a manner adverse to the corporation.

(c) For purposes of § 1.34 (and § 1.27, to the extent it is incorporated in § 1.34 by reference) the term "the corporation" includes any corporation that controls [§ 1.08] the corporation, and any subsidiary or other business organization that is controlled by the corporation.

§ 1.35   Small Publicly Held Corporation

A "small publicly held corporation" is a publicly held corporation [§ 1.31] other than a large publicly held corporation [§ 1.24].

§ 1.36   Standard of the Corporation

"Standard of the corporation" means a valid certificate or bylaw provision or board of directors or shareholder resolution.

§ 1.37   Total Assets

A corporation's "total assets" means the total assets shown on the balance sheet for its most recent fiscal year-end.

§ 1.38   Transaction in Control

(a) Subject to Subsection (b), a "transaction in control" with respect to a corporation means:

(1) A business combination effected through (i) a merger, (ii) a consolidation, (iii) an issuance of voting equity securities [§ 1.40] to effect an acquisition of the assets of another corporation that would constitute a transaction in control under Subsection (a)(2) with respect to the other corporation, or (iv) an issuance of voting equity securities in exchange for at least a majority of the voting equity

securities of another corporation, in each case whether effected directly or by means of a subsidiary;

(2) A sale of assets that would leave the corporation without a significant continuing business; or

(3) An issuance of securities or any other transaction by the corporation (other than pursuant to a transaction described in Subsection (a)(1)) that, alone or in conjunction with other transactions or circumstances, would cause a change in control [§ 1.08] of the corporation;

(b) A transaction is not a transaction in control within § 1.38(a) if the transaction consists of:

(1) The issuance of voting equity securities (other than pursuant to a transaction described in Subsection (a)(1)) in a widely distributed offering;

(2) The issuance of debt or equity securities that would constitute a transaction in control only because the securities carry the right to approve transactions in control, and such right serves to protect dividend, interest, sinking fund, conversion, exchange, or other rights of the securities, or to protect against the issuance of additional securities that would be on a parity with or superior to the securities; or

(3) A transaction described in Subsection (a)(1) if those persons [§ 1.28] who were the holders of voting equity securities in the corporation immediately before the transaction would own immediately after the transaction at least 75 percent of the surviving corporation's voting equity securities, in substantially the same proportions in relation to other preexisting shareholders of the corporation.

§ 1.39 Unsolicited Tender Offer

"Unsolicited tender offer" means an offer to purchase or invitation to tender made to holders of voting equity securities [§ 1.40] of a corporation, without the approval of the corporation's board of directors, to effect a change in control [§ 1.08] of the corporation by purchasing the holders' securities for cash, securities, other consideration, or any combination thereof.

§ 1.40 Voting Equity Security

"Voting equity security" means an equity security [§ 1.20] that is a voting security [§ 1.41].

§ 1.41 Voting Security

(a) "Voting security" means a security that currently entitles its record holder [§ 1.32] to vote for the election of directors.

(b) A specified percentage of the voting securities of a corporation means whatever amount of its outstanding voting securities entitles the record holders to cast that specified percentage of the aggregate votes that the record holders of all the outstanding voting securities are entitled to cast in the election of directors.

§ 1.42   Waste of Corporate Assets

A transaction constitutes a "waste of corporate assets" if it involves an expenditure of corporate funds or a disposition of corporate assets for which no consideration is received in exchange and for which there is no rational business purpose, or, if consideration is received in exchange, the consideration the corporation receives is so inadequate in value that no person of ordinary sound business judgment would deem it worth that which the corporation has paid.

PART II

THE OBJECTIVE AND CONDUCT OF THE CORPORATION

§ 2.01   The Objective and Conduct of the Corporation

(a) Subject to the provisions of Subsection (b) and § 6.02 (Action of Directors That Has the Foreseeable Effect of Blocking Unsolicited Tender Offers), a corporation [§ 1.12] should have as its objective the conduct of business activities with a view to enhancing corporate profit and shareholder gain.

(b) Even if corporate profit and shareholder gain are not thereby enhanced, the corporation, in the conduct of its business:

(1) Is obliged, to the same extent as a natural person, to act within the boundaries set by law;

(2) May take into account ethical considerations that are reasonably regarded as appropriate to the responsible conduct of business; and

(3) May devote a reasonable amount of resources to public welfare, humanitarian, educational, and philanthropic purposes.

Comment . . .

f. The economic objective. In very general terms, Subsection (a) may be thought of as a broad injunction to enhance economic returns, while Subsection (b) makes clear that certain kinds of conduct must or may be pursued whether or not they enhance such returns (that is, even if the conduct either yields no economic return or entails a net economic loss). In most cases, however, the kinds of conduct described in Subsection (b) could be pursued even under the principle embodied in Subsection (a). Such conduct will usually be consistent with economic self-interest, because the principle embodied in Subsection (a)—that the objective of the corporation is to conduct business activities with a view to enhancing corporate profit and shareholder gain—does not mean that the objective of the corporation must be to realize corporate profit and shareholder gain in the short run. . . .

Illustrations:

1. Corporation A is a publicly held corporation with annual earnings in the range of $2–3 million. A has entered into a contract that is unenforceable against it under the Statute of Frauds. Performance of the contract will involve a loss of $70,000. A performs the contract, because the relevant corporate decisionmaker makes a judgment, in a manner that meets the standards of § 4.01 (Duty of Care of Directors and Officers; the Business Judgment Rule), that the loss is likely to be exceeded by long-run profits from preserving confidence in A's willingness to honor its commitments. A's action does not involve a departure from the economic objective stated in § 2.01(a).

2. B Corporation is a publicly held corporation with annual earnings in the range of $6–8 million. White, a long-time middle-manager of B, is forced to retire because of serious injuries sustained in an automobile accident. B has a pension plan covering White, but the plan was installed only recently, and White's benefits are only 30 percent vested. B purchases an annuity for White at a cost of $50,000 to bring White's retirement income up to a reasonable amount, because the relevant corporate decisionmaker makes a judgment, in a manner that meets the standards of § 4.01, that the cost of the annuity will be exceeded by long-run economic benefits from improving the morale of B's remaining employees. B's action does not involve a departure from the economic objective stated in § 2.01(a). . . .

g. Compliance with legal rules. Under § 2.01(b)(1), the corporation is obliged, to the same extent as a natural person, to act within the boundaries set by law. It is sometimes maintained that whether a corporation should adhere to a given legal rule may properly depend on a kind of cost-benefit analysis, in which probable corporate gains are weighed against either probable social costs, measured by the dollar liability imposed for engaging in such conduct, or probable corporate losses, measured by potential dollar liability discounted for likelihood of detection. Section 2.01 does not adopt this position. With few exceptions, dollar liability is not a "price" that can properly be paid for the privilege of engaging in legally wrongful conduct. Cost-benefit analysis may have a place in the state's determination whether a given type of conduct should be deemed legally wrongful. Once that determination has been made, however, the resulting legal rule normally represents a community decision that the conduct is wrongful as such, so that cost-benefit analysis whether to obey the rule is out of place. . . .

Illustrations:

    7.   F Corporation is a publicly held corporation with annual earnings in the range of $3–5 million. F hopes to be awarded a supply contract by P, a large publicly held corporation. The anticipated profits on the contract are $5 million over a two-year period. A vice-president of P has approached Brown, the relevant corporate decisionmaker of F, with the suggestion that if F pays the vice-president $20,000, F will be awarded the contract. Brown knows such a payment would be illegal, but correctly regards the risk of detection as extremely small. After carefully weighing that risk and the consequences of detection, Brown causes F to pay the $20,000. F's action involves a departure from the principle stated in § 2.01(b)(1).

    8.   G Corporation owns and operates 15 plants that were traditionally non-union. For the last several years, Union U has been attempting to organize G's workers, and has won elections at three of G's plants. Although G does not have a good faith belief that the elections were invalid, it adopts a strategy of refusing to bargain at these three plants and harassing members, adherents, and supporters of U at G's other 12 plants. The relevant corporate decisionmaker knows that the conduct violates the National Labor Relations Act, but believes that a long time will elapse before sanctions are imposed, and that the profit from this conduct will far exceed the cost of possible sanctions. G's action involves a departure from the principle stated in § 2.01(b)(1). . . .

    h. Ethical considerations. Section 2.01(b)(2) provides that a corporation may take into account ethical considerations that are reasonably regarded as appropriate to the responsible conduct of business. . . . [O]bservation suggests that corporate decisions are not infrequently made on the basis of ethical considerations even when doing so would not enhance corporate profit or shareholder gain. Such behavior is not only appropriate, but desirable. Corporate officials are not less morally obliged than any other citizens to take ethical considerations into account, and it would be unwise social policy to preclude them from doing so.

    This does not mean that corporate officials can properly take into account any ethical consideration, no matter how idiosyncratic. Because such officials are dealing with other people's money, they will act properly in taking ethical principles into account only where those considerations are reasonably regarded as appropriate to the responsible conduct of business. In this connection, however, it should be recognized that new principles may emerge over time. A corporate official therefore should be permitted to take into account emerging ethical principles, reasonably regarded as appropriate to the responsible conduct of business, that have significant support although less-than-universal acceptance....

Illustrations:

11. The facts being otherwise as stated in Illustration 1, A is about to be dissolved. A nevertheless honors the contract, because ethical considerations that it reasonably regards as appropriate to the responsible conduct of business suggest that seriously made business promises should be kept even if there is a technical excuse for nonperformance. A's action can be justified under § 2.01(b)(2), and therefore does not involve a departure from the principles stated in § 2.01....

i. Public welfare, humanitarian, educational, and philanthropic purposes. Section 2.01(b)(3) permits the corporation to devote a reasonable amount of resources to public welfare, humanitarian, educational, and philanthropic purposes, even if corporate profit and shareholder gain are not thereby enhanced. As in the case of ethical considerations, conduct that appears to be based on public welfare, humanitarian, educational, or philanthropic considerations may be intended to enhance corporate profit and shareholder gain. For example, a donation to public television may be made for reasons comparable to those for sponsoring a commercial, and a contribution to local Red Cross or Community Chest activities may be made for reasons of employee well-being and morale....

Section 2.01(b)(3) goes beyond these justifications and allows corporate resources to be devoted to public welfare, humanitarian, educational, and philanthropic purposes even without a showing of expected profits or ethical norms.... Social policy ... favors humane behavior by major social institutions. [Social policy also] favors the maintenance of diversity in educational and philanthropic activity, and this objective would be more difficult to achieve if corporations, which control a great share of national resources, were not allowed to devote a portion of those resources to those ends. However, corporate activity that is justified solely by social considerations should be subject to a limit of reasonableness....

Illustrations:

13. The facts being otherwise as stated in Illustration 2, B is about to liquidate. Accordingly, it will have no remaining employees and therefore cannot justify the purchase of an annuity for White on the basis of long-term profitability. B's assets net of liabilities are $30 million. White is the only employee whom the liquidation will leave without retirement security. The relevant decisionmaker causes B to purchase an annuity, at a cost of $50,000, to bring White's retirement income up to a reasonable amount,

partly for humanitarian reasons, and partly because ethical considerations that B reasonably regards as appropriate to the responsible
conduct of business suggest that a business should make reasonable
provision for a faithful long-term employee who has made a contribution to the business, and is forced by ill health to retire while in
the corporation's employ. B's action can be justified under both
§ 2.01(b)(2) and § 2.01(b)(3), and therefore does not involve a
departure from the principles stated in § 2.01....

19.   O, a publicly held corporation, has assets of $100 million
and annual earnings in the range of $13–15 million. O owns three
aluminum plants, which are profitable, and one plastics plant, which
is losing $4 million a year. The plastics plant shows no sign of ever
becoming profitable, because of its very high operating costs, and
there is no evidence that the plant and the underlying real estate
will increase in value. O decides to sell the plastics plant. The only
bidder for the plant is Gold, who intends to use the plant for a new
purpose, introduce automation, and replace all existing employees.
O turns down Gold's bid and keeps the plastics plant operating
indefinitely for the purpose of preserving the employees' jobs. O's
action involves a departure from the principles stated in § 2.01.
The action is for a humanitarian purpose, but cannot be justified
under § 2.01(b)(3), because the expenditures involved are unreasonable in amount in relation to earnings. It cannot be justified under
§ 2.01(b)(2), because a corporation is not ethically obliged to continue indefinitely the operation of a business that is losing large
amounts of money, equal to more than one fourth of the corporation's earnings, for the purpose of keeping workers employed. The
action cannot be justified under § 2.01(a), because the action is not
motivated by profit considerations, and on the facts it would not be
within the realm of business judgment to conclude that the action
will result in short- or long-term profits exceeding the costs involved.

20.   The facts being otherwise as stated in Illustration 19, the
only person who bids on the plant is a real-estate developer who
plans to close the plant and hold the land for investment. The
developer is agreeable to leasing the plant back to O at a moderate
rent for up to 12 months. O enters into a three-month lease, and
continues to operate the plant during that period, at a loss of
$500,000, so as to provide the employees at the plant a period of
adjustment prior to its closing. This action is taken partly out of
humanitarian considerations, and partly because ethical considerations that are reasonably regarded as appropriate to the responsible
conduct of business suggest that an enterprise should make reasonable provision to cushion the transition of long-term employees who
are about to be discharged. O's action can be justified under

§ 2.01(b)(2) and § 2.01(b)(3), and therefore does not involve a departure from the principles stated in § 2.01....

PART III

CORPORATE STRUCTURE: FUNCTIONS AND POWERS OF DIRECTORS AND OFFICERS; AUDIT COMMITTEE IN LARGE PUBLICLY HELD CORPORATIONS

§ 3.01 Management of the Corporation's Business: Functions and Powers of Principal Senior Executives and Other Officers

The management of the business of a publicly held corporation [§ 1.31] should be conducted by or under the supervision of such principal senior executives [§ 1.30] as are designated by the board of directors, and by those other officers [§ 1.27] and employees to whom the management function is delegated by the board or those executives, subject to the functions and powers of the board under § 3.02.

§ 3.02 Functions and Powers of the Board of Directors

Except as otherwise provided by statute:

(a) The board of directors of a publicly held corporation [§ 1.31] should perform the following functions:

(1) Select, regularly evaluate, fix the compensation of, and, where appropriate, replace the principal senior executives [§ 1.30];

(2) Oversee the conduct of the corporation's business to evaluate whether the business is being properly managed;

(3) Review and, where appropriate, approve the corporation's financial objectives and major corporate plans and actions;

(4) Review and, where appropriate, approve major changes in, and determinations of other major questions of choice respecting, the appropriate auditing and accounting principles and practices to be used in the preparation of the corporation's financial statements;

(5) Perform such other functions as are prescribed by law, or assigned to the board under a standard of the corporation [§ 1.36].

(b) A board of directors also has power to:

(1) Initiate and adopt corporate plans, commitments, and actions;

(2) Initiate and adopt changes in accounting principles and practices;

(3) Provide advice and counsel to the principal senior executives;

(4) Instruct any committee, principal senior executive, or other officer [§ 1.27], and review the actions of any committee, principal senior executive, or other officer;

(5) Make recommendations to shareholders;

(6) Manage the business of the corporation;

(7) Act as to all other corporate matters not requiring shareholder approval.

(c) Subject to the board's ultimate responsibility for oversight under Subsection (a)(2), the board may delegate to its committees authority to perform any of its functions and exercise any of its powers.

Comment . . .

d. The oversight function. In the publicly held corporation, the management function is normally vested in the principal senior executives. A basic function of the board is to select these executives and to oversee their performance (using the term "oversee" to refer to general observation and oversight, not active supervision or day-to-day scrutiny) to determine whether the business is being properly managed, having in mind the objective and conduct of the corporation under § 2.01. This oversight function is usually performed, not directly by actively supervising the principal senior executives, but indirectly by evaluating the performance of those executives and replacing any who are not meeting reasonable expectations concerning job performance. . . .

§ 3.03 Directors' Informational Rights

(a) Every director has the right, within the limits of § 3.03(b) (and subject to other applicable law), to inspect and copy all books, records, and documents of every kind, and to inspect the physical properties, of the corporation and of its subsidiaries, domestic or foreign, at any reasonable time, in person or by an attorney or other agent.

(b)(1) A judicial order to enforce such right should be granted unless the corporation establishes that the information to be obtained by the exercise of the right is not reasonably related to the performance of directorial functions and duties, or that the director or the director's agent is likely to use the information in a manner that would violate the director's fiduciary obligation to the corporation.

(2) An application for such an order should be decided expeditiously and may be decided on the basis of affidavits.

(3) Such an order may contain provisions protecting the corporation from undue burden or expense, and prohibiting the director from using the information in a manner that would violate the director's fiduciary obligation to the corporation.

(4) A director who makes an application for such an order after the corporation has denied a request should, if successful, be reimbursed by the corporation for expenses (including attorney's fees) reasonably incurred in connection with the application.

§ 3.04 Right of Directors Who Have No Significant Relationship With the Corporation's Senior Executives to Retain Outside Experts

The directors of a publicly held corporation [§ 1.31] who have no significant relationship [§ 1.34] with the corporation's senior executives [§ 1.33] should be entitled, acting as a body by the vote of a majority of such directors, to retain legal counsel, accountants, or other experts, at the corporation's expense, to advise them on problems arising in the exercise of their functions and powers (§ 3.02), if:

(a) Payment of such expense is authorized by the board; or

(b) A court approves an application for the payment of such expense upon a finding that the board had been requested to authorize the payment of such expense and had declined to do so, and the directors who have no relationship with the corporation's senior executives reasonably believed that (i) retention of an outside expert was required for the proper performance of the directors' functions and powers, (ii) the amount involved was reasonable in relation to both the importance of the problem and the corporation's assets and income, and (iii) assistance by corporate staff or corporate counsel was inappropriate or inadequate.

§ 3.05 Audit Committee in Large Publicly Held Corporations

Every large publicly held corporation [§ 1.24] should have an audit committee to implement and support the oversight function of the board (§ 3.02) by reviewing on a periodic basis the corporation's processes for producing financial data, its internal controls, and the independence of the corporation's external auditor. The audit committee should consist of at least three members, and should be composed exclusively of directors who are neither employed by the corporation nor were so employed within the two preceding years, including at least a majority of members who have no significant relationship [§ 1.34] with the corporation's senior executives.

Comment:

a. Comparison with present law and practice. An audit committee is not required as a matter of state law, except in Connecticut. However, the New York Stock Exchange requires listed companies to establish and maintain an audit committee "comprised solely of directors independent of management and free from any relationship that, in the opinion of its Board of Directors, would interfere with the exercise of indepen-

dent judgment as a committee member." ... The American Stock
Exchange and NASDAQ also recommend or require audit committees,
and the employment of such committees in publicly held corporations is
now prevalent practice....

PART III–A

RECOMMENDATIONS OF CORPORATE PRACTICE CONCERNING THE BOARD AND THE PRINCIPAL OVERSIGHT COMMITTEES

§ 3A.01 Composition of the Board in Publicly Held Corporations

It is recommended as a matter of corporate practice that:

(a) The board of every large publicly held corporation [§ 1.24]
should have a majority of directors who are free of any significant
relationship [§ 1.34] with the corporation's senior executives
[§ 1.33], unless a majority of the corporation's voting securities
[§ 1.41] are owned by a single person [§ 1.28], a family group
[§ 1.21], or a control group [§ 1.09].

(b) The board of a publicly held corporation [§ 1.31] that does
not fall within Subsection (a) should have at least three directors
who are free of any significant relationship with the corporation's
senior executives.

REPORTER'S NOTE ....

3. Data from various sources show that the concepts embodied in
§ 3A.01 have taken firm hold in practice. A 1991 study by Korn/Ferry
reported that the boards of responding corporations had an average
number of three inside and nine outside directors. Korn/Ferry, *Board of
Directors* 5, 15 (1991). In 1985, Korn/Ferry had found that the comparable average was 10 outside directors and four inside directors; in 1975,
the average had been eight outside directors and five inside directors.
Id. at 3, 5. The 1990 Korn/Ferry study predicts that in the next decade,
the number of insiders on the board will drop even further, from three to
two, and that increasingly the only insiders on the board will be the chief
executive officer and the chief operating officer. Id. at 3. Two studies
by Heidrick & Struggles in the 1980s, using different samples, found
that "independent" directors (defined as those who were neither management nor affiliated nonmanagement directors) made up 61 percent of
the boards of responding companies in one sample, and 59 percent in the
other. Heidrick & Struggles, *The Changing Board* 3 (1983); Heidrick &
Struggles, *Director Data* 1.

§ 3A.02 Audit Committee in Small Publicly Held Corporations

It is recommended as a matter of corporate practice that every small publicly held corporation [§ 1.35] should have an audit committee to implement and support the oversight function of the board (§ 3.02) by reviewing on a periodic basis the corporation's processes for producing financial data, its internal controls, and the independence of the corporation's external auditor. The audit committee should consist of at least three members, and should be composed exclusively of directors who are neither employed by the corporation nor were so employed within the previous two years, including a majority of members who have no significant relationship [§ 1.34] with the corporation's senior executives.

§ 3A.03 Functions and Powers of Audit Committees

It is recommended as a matter of corporate practice that:

The audit committee of a publicly held corporation established under §§ 3.05 (Audit Committee in Large Publicly Held Corporations) or 3A.02 (Audit Committee in Small Publicly Held Corporations) should:

(a) Recommend the firm to be employed as the corporation's external auditor and review the proposed discharge of any such firm;

(b) Review the external auditor's compensation, the proposed terms of its engagement, and its independence;

(c) Review the appointment and replacement of the senior internal auditing executive, if any;

(d) Serve as a channel of communication between the external auditor and the board and between the senior internal auditing executive, if any, and the board;

(e) Review the results of each external audit of the corporation, the report of the audit, any related management letter, management's responses to recommendations made by the external auditor in connection with the audit, reports of the internal auditing department that are material to the corporation as a whole, and management's responses to those reports;

(f) Review the corporation's annual financial statements, any certification, report, opinion, or review rendered by the external auditor in connection with those financial statements, and any significant disputes between management and the external auditor that arose in connection with the preparation of those financial statements;

(g) Consider, in consultation with the external auditor and the senior internal auditing executive, if any, the adequacy of the corporation's internal controls;

(h) Consider major changes and other major questions of choice respecting the appropriate auditing and accounting principles and practices to be used in the preparation of the corporation's financial statements, when presented by the external auditor, a principal senior executive [§ 1.30], or otherwise.

§ 3A.04   Nominating Committee in Publicly Held Corporations: Composition, Powers, and Functions

It is recommended as a matter of corporate practice that:

(a) Every publicly held corporation [§ 1.31], except corporations a majority of whose voting securities are owned by a single person [§ 1.28], a family group [§ 1.21], or a control group [§ 1.09], should establish a nominating committee composed exclusively of directors who are not officers [§ 1.27] or employees of the corporation, including at least a majority of members who have no significant relationship [§ 1.34] with the corporation's senior executives [§ 1.33].

(b) The nominating committee should:

(1) Recommend to the board candidates for all directorships to be filled by the shareholders or the board.

(2) Consider, in making its recommendations, candidates for directorships proposed by the chief executive officer and, within the bounds of practicability, by any other senior executive or any director or shareholder.

(3) Recommend to the board directors to fill the seats on board committees.

Reporter's Note

... A 1990 study by Heidrick & Struggles, based on 1989 data, reported that 60 percent of the respondents had nominating committees.... A 1990 study by Korn/Ferry, based on 1989 data, reported that 57 percent of the respondents had nominating committees....

§ 3A.05   Compensation Committee in Large Publicly Held Corporations: Composition, Powers, and Functions

It is recommended as a matter of corporate practice that:

(a) Every large publicly held corporation [§ 1.24] should establish a compensation committee to implement and support the oversight function of the board in the area of compensation. The committee should be composed exclusively of directors who are not officers [§ 1.27] or employees of the corporation, including at least a majority of members who have no significant relationship [§ 1.34] with the corporation's senior executives [§ 1.33].

(b) The compensation committee should:

(1) Review and recommend to the board, or determine, the annual salary, bonus, stock options, and other benefits, direct and indirect, of the senior executives.

(2) Review new executive compensation programs; review on a periodic basis the operation of the corporation's executive compensation programs to determine whether they are properly coordinated; establish and periodically review policies for the administration of executive compensation programs; and take steps to modify any executive compensation programs that yield payments and benefits that are not reasonably related to executive performance.

(3) Establish and periodically review policies in the area of management perquisites.

Reporter's Note

... A 1990 study by Heidrick & Struggles, based on 1989 data, reported that 93 percent of the respondents had compensation committees.... A 1990 study by Korn/Ferry, based on 1989 data, reported that 91 percent of the respondents had compensation committees....

PART IV

DUTY OF CARE AND THE BUSINESS JUDGMENT RULE

§ 4.01 Duty of Care of Directors and Officers; the Business Judgment Rule

(a) A director or officer has a duty to the corporation to perform the director's or officer's functions in good faith, in a manner that he or she reasonably believes to be in the best interests of the corporation, and with the care that an ordinarily prudent person would reasonably be expected to exercise in a like position and under similar circumstances. This Subsection (a) is subject to the provisions of Subsection (c) (the business judgment rule) where applicable.

(1) The duty in Subsection (a) includes the obligation to make, or cause to be made, an inquiry when, but only when, the circumstances would alert a reasonable director or officer to the need therefor. The extent of such inquiry shall be such as the director or officer reasonably believes to be necessary.

(2) In performing any of his or her functions (including oversight functions), a director or officer is entitled to rely on materials and persons in accordance with §§ 4.02 and 4.03 (reliance on directors, officers, employees, experts, other persons, and committees of the board).

(b) Except as otherwise provided by statute or by a standard of the corporation [§ 1.36] and subject to the board's ultimate responsibility for oversight, in performing its functions (including oversight functions), the board may delegate, formally or informally by course of conduct, any function (including the function of identifying matters requiring the attention of the board) to committees of the board or to directors, officers, employees, experts, or other persons; a director may rely on such committees and persons in fulfilling the duty under this Section with respect to any delegated function if the reliance is in accordance with §§ 4.02 and 4.03.

(c) A director or officer who makes a business judgment in good faith fulfills the duty under this Section if the director or officer:

(1) is not interested [§ 1.23] in the subject of the business judgment;

(2) is informed with respect to the subject of the business judgment to the extent the director or officer reasonably believes to be appropriate under the circumstances; and

(3) rationally believes that the business judgment is in the best interests of the corporation.

(d) A person challenging the conduct of a director or officer under this Section has the burden of proving a breach of the duty of care, including the inapplicability of the provisions as to the fulfillment of duty under Subsection (b) or (c), and, in a damage action, the burden of proving that the breach was the legal cause of damage suffered by the corporation.

Comment to § 4.01(a), first paragraph: ...

Illustrations:

> 6. C, who is rich and charming, has been a director of Y Corporation for several years. C's only significant contribution to Y has been a willingness to entertain important customers. C has said: "I do not have the capacity to oversee Y's business," and has made no attempt to oversee it. Y Corporation has gone into bankruptcy because of mismanagement. C, as a result of the failure to oversee the conduct of Y's business, has committed a breach of the duty of care. The fact that C may not have the capacity of an "ordinarily prudent person" is no defense. C will be held to an objective standard. . . .

Comment to § 4.01(a)(1)–(a)(2):

Illustrations ...

> 1. Last year X Corporation, which had annual sales of $900,000,000 and a wide distribution system for its consumer products, was fined $1 million for horizontal price fixing, a

criminal violation of the Sherman Act. It also had to settle a number of civil antitrust actions by paying an aggregate of $16.8 million. The directors of X Corporation have never been concerned with the existence of an antitrust compliance program, and X Corporation still has no company statement on antitrust policy and no compliance program. A new horizontal price-fixing violation has just occurred. It is clear, however, that the directors of X Corporation had no knowledge of the new antitrust violation. The directors of X Corporation may well have violated their duty of care. The recent antitrust violations, the size of X Corporation, and its wide distribution system should have made compliance with the antitrust laws a particularly prominent concern. Unless other facts were present, such as the delegation of antitrust law compliance functions to the general counsel and proper reliance on the general counsel in accordance with § 4.01(b), the failure of the directors of X Corporation to be reasonably concerned with the existence of an antitrust compliance program would constitute a breach of the directors' duty of care.

2. The facts being otherwise as stated in Illustration 1, after the $1 million fine was paid, X Corporation did in fact install an antitrust compliance program which required X's local staff attorneys to refer all antitrust questions—and report all suspicious circumstances—to a designated staff attorney at company headquarters. An attorney in one regional office has, however, failed to report questionable conduct that may constitute a *per se* antitrust violation. X's directors have not failed to meet their duty of care due to an isolated breakdown in the compliance program. No violation of § 4.01(a) has occurred....

Comment to § 4.01(c) ...

c. Prerequisite of a conscious exercise of judgment. Section 4.01(c) affords protection only to a "business judgment." This means that to be afforded protection a decision must have been consciously made and judgment must, in fact, have been exercised. For efficiency reasons, corporate decisionmakers should be permitted to act decisively and with relative freedom from a judge's or jury's subsequent second-guessing. It is desirable to encourage directors and officers to enter new markets, develop new products, innovate, and take other business risks.

There is, however, no reason to provide special protection where no business decisionmaking is to be found. If, for example, directors have failed to oversee the conduct of the corporation's business (§ 3.02(a)(2)) by not even considering the need for an effective audit process, and this permits an executive to abscond with corporate funds, business judgment rule protection would be manifestly undesirable. The same would be true where a director received but did not read basic financial information, over a period of time, and thus allowed his corporation to be looted. Cf. Hoye v. Meek, 795 F.2d 893 (10th Cir.1986); DePinto v. Provident Security Life Insur. Co., 374 F.2d 37 (9th Cir.1967), cert. denied 389 U.S. 822, 88 S.Ct. 48, 19 L.Ed.2d 74 (1967); Francis v. United Jersey Bank, 87 N.J. 15, 432 A.2d 814 (1981). In these and other "omission" situations, the director or officer would be judged under the reasonable care standards of § 4.01(a) and not protected by § 4.01(c). See, e.g., Aronson v. Lewis, 473 A.2d 805, 813 (Del.1984) ("the business judgment rule operates only in the context of director action.... [I]t has no role where directors have either abdicated their functions, or absent a conscious decision, failed to act."); Arsht, The Business Judgment Rule Revisited, 8 Hofstra L.Rev. 93, 112 (1979); Block & Prussin, The Business Judgment Rule and Shareholder Derivative Actions: Viva Zapata?, 37 Bus.Law. 27, 33 (1981) ("The [business judgment] rule does not apply where the director has in fact made no decision")....

e. *Prerequisite of an informed decision.* The great weight of case law and commentator authority supports the proposition that an informed decision (made, for example, on the basis of explanatory information presented to the board) is a prerequisite to the legal insulation afforded by the business judgment rule. In a much quoted statement, the court in Casey v. Woodruff, 49 N.Y.S.2d 625, 643 (1944), observed: "When courts say that they will not interfere in matters of business judgment, it is presupposed that judgment— reasonable diligence—has in fact been exercised." See ... Arsht, The Business Judgment Rule Revisited, 8 Hofstra L.Rev. 93, 111 (1979) (the business judgment rule should not be available to directors who do "not exercise due care to ascertain the relevant and available facts before voting")....

f. *The "rationally believes" requirement.* If the requirements of "good faith" and § 4.01(c)(1)–(c)(2) are met, § 4.01(c)(3) will protect a director or officer from liability for a business judgment if the director or officer "rationally believes that the business judgment is in the best interests of the corporation." The term "rationally believes" has both an objective and a subjective content. A director or officer must actually believe that the business judgment is in the best interests of the corporation and that belief must be rational....

There have been varying approaches taken in the cases and by commentators to the proper standard for judicial review of business judgments. Some courts have stated that a director's or officer's business judgment must be "reasonable" to be upheld.... On the other hand, a few cases have simply said that a director's or officer's judgment would be upheld if made with disinterest, in an informed manner, and in good faith. . . .

Sound public policy dictates that directors and officers be given greater protection than courts and commentators using a "reasonableness" test would afford. . . .

On the other hand, courts that have articulated only a "good faith" test may, depending on the court's meaning, provide too much legal insulation for directors and officers. A "good faith" test could be interpreted broadly to achieve the same result as the "rationally believes" standard. For example, in Sam Wong & Son v. New York Mercantile Exchange, 735 F.2d 653, 671, 678 n. 32 (2d Cir.1984), Judge Friendly held that the rationality of a decision by the Board of Governors of the Mercantile Exchange was relevant in determining whether the Board had acted in good faith, and concluded that "[a]bsent some basis in reason, action could hardly be in good faith even apart from ulterior motive." . . . . Serious problems arise, however, if the phrase "good faith" is interpreted narrowly to mean only the absence of subjective "bad motives." There is no reason to insulate an objectively irrational business decision—one so removed from the realm of reason that it should not be sustained—solely on the basis that it was made in subjective good faith. . . .

§ 4.02 Reliance on Directors, Officers, Employees, Experts, and Other Persons

In performing his or her duties and functions, a director or officer who acts in good faith, and reasonably believes that reliance is warranted, is entitled to rely on information, opinions, reports, statements (including financial statements and other financial data), decisions, judgments, and performance (including decisions, judgments, and performance within the scope of § 4.01(b)) prepared, presented, made, or performed by:

(a) One or more directors, officers, or employees of the corporation, or of a business organization [§ 1.04] under joint control or common control [§ 1.08] with the corporation, who the director or officer reasonably believes merit confidence; or

(b) Legal counsel, public accountants, engineers, or other persons who the director or officer reasonably believes merit confidence.

§ 4.03 Reliance on a Committee of the Board

In performing his or her duties and functions, a director who acts in good faith, and reasonably believes that reliance is warranted, is entitled to rely on:

(a) The decisions, judgments, and performance (including decisions, judgments, and performance within the scope of § 4.01(b)), of a duly authorized committee of the board upon which the director does not serve, with respect to matters delegated to that committee, provided that the director reasonably believes the committee merits confidence.

(b) Information, opinions, reports, and statements (including financial statements and other financial data), prepared or presented by a duly authorized committee of the board upon which the director does not serve, provided that the director reasonably believes the committee merits confidence.

PART V

DUTY OF FAIR DEALING

Chapter 1

GENERAL PRINCIPLE

§ 5.01 Duty of Fair Dealing of Directors, Senior Executives, and Controlling Shareholders

Directors [§ 1.13], senior executives [§ 1.33], and controlling shareholders [§ 1.10], when interested [§ 1.23] in a matter affecting the corporation, are under a duty of fair dealing, which may be fulfilled as set forth in Chapters 2 and 3 of Part V. This duty includes the obligation to make appropriate disclosure as provided in such Chapters.

Chapter 2

DUTY OF FAIR DEALING OF DIRECTORS AND SENIOR EXECUTIVES

§ 5.02 Transactions With the Corporation

(a) *General Rule.* A director [§ 1.13] or senior executive [§ 1.33] who enters into a transaction with the corporation (other than a transaction involving the payment of compensation) fulfills the duty of fair dealing with respect to the transaction if:

(1) Disclosure concerning the conflict of interest [§ 1.14(a)] and the transaction [§ 1.14(b)] is made to the corporate decisionmaker [§ 1.11] who authorizes in advance or ratifies the transaction; and

(2) either:

(A) The transaction is fair to the corporation when entered into;

(B) The transaction is authorized in advance, following disclosure concerning the conflict of interest and the transaction, by disinterested directors [§ 1.15], or in the case of a senior executive who is not a director by a disinterested superior, who could reasonably have concluded that the transaction was fair to the corporation at the time of such authorization;

(C) The transaction is ratified, following such disclosure, by disinterested directors who could reasonably have concluded that the transaction was fair to the corporation at the time it was entered into, provided (i) a corporate decisionmaker who is not interested [§ 1.23] in the transaction acted for the corporation in the transaction and could reasonably have concluded that the transaction was fair to the corporation; (ii) the interested director or senior executive made disclosure to such decisionmaker pursuant to Subsection (a)(1) to the extent he or she then knew of the material facts; (iii) the interested director or senior executive did not act unreasonably in failing to seek advance authorization of the transaction by disinterested directors or a disinterested superior; and (iv) the failure to obtain advance authorization of the transaction by disinterested directors or a disinterested superior did not adversely affect the interests of the corporation in a significant way; or

(D) the transaction is authorized in advance or ratified, following such disclosure, by disinterested shareholders [§ 1.16], and does not constitute a waste of corporate assets [§ 1.42] at the time of the shareholder action.

(b) *Burden of Proof.* A party who challenges a transaction between a director or senior executive and the corporation has the burden of proof, except that if such party establishes that none of Subsections (a)(2)(B), (a)(2)(C), or (a)(2)(D) is satisfied, the director or senior executive has the burden of proving that the transaction was fair to the corporation.

(c) *Ratification of Disclosure or Nondisclosure.* The disclosure requirements of § 5.02(a)(1) will be deemed to be satisfied if at any time (but no later than a reasonable time after suit is filed challenging the transaction) the transaction is ratified, following such disclosure, by the directors, the shareholders, or the corporate decisionmaker who initially approved the transaction or the decisionmaker's successor.

Comment to § 5.02(a)(1) ...

A director or senior executive may not deal with the corporation as a stranger at arm's length. Even where the conflict of interest is made known, there is a relationship of "trust and confidence" with the corporation, so as to require disclosure of "material matters," rather than the relationship of a stranger to the corporation with a much more limited duty of disclosure. Compare Restatement, Second, Torts § 551(2)(a) with Restatement, Second, Torts § 551(2)(e). See also Restatement, Second, Torts § 551, Comments *e, f* and *k*. The duty of one who occupies a relationship of trust and confidence to disclose material facts is widely recognized. See, e.g., Restatement, Second, Contracts § 161, Comment *f;* Restatement, Second, Agency § 390; Restatement of Restitution § 191, Comment on Clause (b). A director or senior executive owes a duty to the corporation not only to avoid misleading it by misstatements or omissions, but affirmatively to disclose the material facts known to the director or senior executive. The interested director or senior executive also has an obligation to explain the implications of a transaction, when he or she is in a position to realize those implications and the disinterested superior or director reviewing the transaction is not in a position to do so. See Globe Woolen Co. v. Utica Gas & Elec. Co., 224 N.Y. 483, 121 N.E. 378 (1918).

Section 1.14 sets forth the required elements of disclosure and § 1.25 sets forth the definition of material facts which are required to be disclosed. Under § 5.02, a director or senior executive who fails to make required disclosure has failed to fulfill the duty of fair dealing, even if the terms of the transaction are fair. A contract price might be fair in the sense that it corresponds to market price, and yet the corporation might have refused to make the contract if a given material fact had been disclosed. See, e.g., Illustrations 4 and 6. Furthermore, as pointed out in paragraph d of the Introductory Note, fairness is often a range, rather than a point, and disclosure of a material fact might have induced the corporation to bargain the price down lower in the range....

Illustrations ...

4. X Corporation is seeking a new headquarters building. D, a vice president of X Corporation, owns all the stock of R Corporation, which owns an office building. D causes a real estate agent to offer R Corporation's building to X Corporation, but does not disclose his ownership of R Corporation. X Corporation's board of directors agrees to purchase the building for a fair price. Two weeks later, X Corporation learns of D's interest in R Corporation. D has not fulfilled his duty to the corporation under [§] 5.02(a)(1)....

6. The facts being otherwise as stated in Illustration 4, D discloses to X Corporation, prior to the acquisition, his interest in R Corporation. D fails to disclose, however, that he has information, not publicly available, that the State Highway Department has formally decided to run a highway through the property on which R Corporation's building stands, and to condemn the building under its power of eminent domain. The price paid by X Corporation is fair, even taking the proposed condemnation into account, since the condemnation award is likely to equal or exceed the price. Two weeks after the acquisition, X Corporation learns of the Highway Department's decision. D has not fulfilled his duty to the corporation under § 5.02(a)(1)....

Illustrations [to Section 5.02(a)(2)(B)];

9. Corporation C is engaged in commercial agriculture. C's Board consists of L, its president, and N, O, and P, who own other types of agricultural businesses. C is potentially in the market for a new headquarters building. L recently inherited a commercial building that is somewhat rundown and only partially rented. Although L has no experience in real estate, she is convinced that with a $1 million renovation the building will be worth $9 million. L offered the building to a number of sophisticated buyers, whose bids ranged between $3 and 5 million. Subsequently, L listed the building with a commercial real estate broker for six months at a price of $7.5 million, but received no offers. L then offered the building to C's board for $7.5 million, making full disclosure, but arguing that this was a bargain price. N, O, and P, who are disinterested within the meaning of § 1.15, consulted a real estate expert, who advised that the building might conceivably be worth $7.5 million, but this was an extremely high price, and the expert would not pay it. The board nevertheless accepted L's offer. N, O, and P did not act irrationally, since real estate cannot be precisely valued, and the value that will be added to a building by renovation is always somewhat problematic. However, the $7.5 million price could not reasonably be regarded as fair, considering that the building had been extensively marketed to sophisticated real estate investors who were aware of the possibility of renovation; that none of these investors was willing to pay more than $5 million; and that N, O, and P were not themselves experts in real estate. The transaction fails to meet the standard of § 5.02(a)(2)(B), and an action may be brought against L to rescind the transaction. However, N, O, and P are protected from liability as individuals since they meet the standard of the business judgment rule [§ 4.01(c)]....

§ 5.03 Compensation of Directors and Senior Executives

(a) *General Rule.* A director [§ 1.13] or senior executive [§ 1.33] who receives compensation from the corporation for services in that capacity fulfills the duty of fair dealing with respect to the compensation if either:

(1) The compensation is fair to the corporation when approved;

(2) The compensation is authorized in advance by disinterested directors [§ 1.15] or, in the case of a senior executive who is not a director, authorized in advance by a disinterested superior, in a manner that satisfies the standards of the business judgment rule [§ 4.01(c)];

(3) The compensation is ratified by disinterested directors [§ 1.15] who satisfy the requirements of the business judgment rule [§ 4.01(c)], provided (i) a corporate decisionmaker who was not

interested [§ 1.23] in receipt of the compensation acted for the corporation in determining the compensation and satisfied the requirements of the business judgment rule; (ii) the interested director or senior executive did not act unreasonably in failing to seek advance authorization of the compensation by disinterested directors or a disinterested superior; and (iii) the failure to obtain advance authorization of the compensation by disinterested directors or a disinterested superior did not adversely affect the interests of the corporation in a significant way; or

(4) The compensation is authorized in advance or ratified by disinterested shareholders [§ 1.16], and does not constitute a waste of corporate assets [§ 1.42] at the time of the shareholder action.

(b) *Burden of Proof.* A party who challenges a transaction involving the payment of compensation to a director or senior executive has the burden of proof, except that if such party establishes that the requirements of neither Subsections (a)(2), (a)(3), nor (a)(4) are met, the director or the senior executive has the burden of proving that the transaction was fair to the corporation.

§ 5.04 Use by a Director or Senior Executive of Corporate Property, Material Non-public Corporate Information, or Corporate Position

(a) *General Rule.* A director [§ 1.13] or senior executive [§ 1.33] may not use corporate property, material non-public corporate information, or corporate position to secure a pecuniary benefit, unless either:

(1) Value is given for the use and the transaction meets the standards of § 5.02 (Transactions with the Corporation);

(2) The use constitutes compensation and meets the standards of § 5.03 (Compensation of Directors and Senior Executives);

(3) The use is solely of corporate information, and is not in connection with trading of the corporation's securities, is not a use of proprietary information of the corporation, and does not harm the corporation;

(4) The use is subject neither to § 5.02 nor § 5.03 but is authorized in advance or ratified by disinterested directors [§ 1.15] or disinterested shareholders [§ 1.16], and meets the requirements and standards of disclosure and review set forth in § 5.02 as if that Section were applicable to the use; or

(5) The benefit is received as a shareholder and is made proportionately available to all other similarly situated shareholders,

and the use is not otherwise unlawful.

(b) *Burden of Proof.* A party who challenges the conduct of a director or senior executive under Subsection (a) has the burden of proof, except that if value was given for the benefit, the burden of proving whether the value was fair should be allocated as provided in § 5.02 in the case of a transaction with the corporation.

(c) *Special Rule on Remedies.* A director or senior executive is subject to liability under this Section only to the extent of any improper benefit received and retained, except to the extent that any foreseeable harm caused by the conduct of the director or senior executive exceeds the value of the benefit received, and multiple liability based on receipt of the same benefit is not to be imposed.

§ 5.05 Taking of Corporate Opportunities by Directors or Senior Executives

(a) *General Rule.* A director [§ 1.13] or senior executive [§ 1.33] may not take advantage of a corporate opportunity unless:

(1) The director or senior executive first offers the corporate opportunity to the corporation and makes disclosure concerning the conflict of interest [§ 1.14(a)] and the corporate opportunity [§ 1.14(b)];

(2) The corporate opportunity is rejected by the corporation; and

(3) either:

(A) The rejection of the opportunity is fair to the corporation;

(B) The opportunity is rejected in advance, following such disclosure, by disinterested directors [§ 1.15], or, in the case of a senior executive who is not a director, by a disinterested superior, in a manner that satisfies the standards of the business judgment rule [§ 4.01(c)]; or

(C) The rejection is authorized in advance or ratified, following such disclosure, by disinterested shareholders [§ 1.16], and the rejection is not equivalent to a waste of corporate assets [§ 1.42].

(b) *Definition of a Corporate Opportunity.* For purposes of this Section, a corporate opportunity means:

(1) Any opportunity to engage in a business activity of which a director or senior executive becomes aware, either:

(A) In connection with the performance of functions as a director or senior executive, or under circumstances that should reasonably lead the director or senior executive to believe that the person offering the opportunity expects it to be offered to the corporation; or

(B) Through the use of corporate information or property, if the resulting opportunity is one that the director or senior

1367

executive should reasonably be expected to believe would be of interest to the corporation; or

(2) Any opportunity to engage in a business activity of which a senior executive becomes aware and knows is closely related to a business in which the corporation is engaged or expects to engage.

(c) *Burden of Proof.* A party who challenges the taking of a corporate opportunity has the burden of proof, except that if such party establishes that the requirements of Subsection (a)(3)(B) or (C) are not met, the director or the senior executive has the burden of proving that the rejection and the taking of the opportunity were fair to the corporation.

(d) *Ratification of Defective Disclosure.* A good faith but defective disclosure of the facts concerning the corporate opportunity may be cured if at any time (but no later than a reasonable time after suit is filed challenging the taking of the corporate opportunity) the original rejection of the corporate opportunity is ratified, following the required disclosure, by the board, the shareholders, or the corporate decisionmaker who initially approved the rejection of the corporate opportunity, or such decisionmaker's successor.

(e) *Special Rule Concerning Delayed Offering of Corporate Opportunities.* Relief based solely on failure to first offer an opportunity to the corporation under Subsection (a)(1) is not available if: (1) such failure resulted from a good faith belief that the business activity did not constitute a corporate opportunity, and (2) not later than a reasonable time after suit is filed challenging the taking of the corporate opportunity, the corporate opportunity is to the extent possible offered to the corporation and rejected in a manner that satisfies the standards of Subsection (a).

§ 5.06 Competition With the Corporation

(a) *General Rule.* Directors [§ 1.13] and senior executives [§ 1.33] may not advance their pecuniary interests by engaging in competition with the corporation unless either:

(1) Any reasonably foreseeable harm to the corporation from such competition is outweighed by the benefit that the corporation may reasonably be expected to derive from allowing the competition to take place, or there is no reasonably foreseeable harm to the corporation from such competition;

(2) The competition is authorized in advance or ratified, following disclosure concerning the conflict of interest [§ 1.14(a)] and the competition [§ 1.14(b)], by disinterested directors [§ 1.15], or in the case of a senior executive who is not a director, is authorized in advance by a disinterested superior, in a manner that satisfies the standards of the business judgment rule [§ 4.01(c)]; or

(3) The competition is authorized in advance or ratified, following such disclosure, by disinterested shareholders [§ 1.16], and the shareholders' action is not equivalent to a waste of corporate assets [§ 1.42].

(b) *Burden of Proof.* A party who challenges a director or senior executive for advancing the director's or senior executive's pecuniary interest by competing with the corporation has the burden of proof, except that if such party establishes that neither Subsection (a)(2) nor (3) is satisfied, the director or the senior executive has the burden of proving that any reasonably foreseeable harm to the corporation from such competition is outweighed by the benefit that the corporation may reasonably be expected to derive from allowing the competition to take place, or that there is no reasonably foreseeable harm to the corporation.

§ 5.07 Transactions Between Corporations With Common Directors or Senior Executives

(a) A transaction between two corporations is not to be treated as a transaction subject to the provisions of § 5.02 (Transactions With the Corporation) solely on the ground that the same person is a director [§ 1.13] or senior executive [§ 1.33] of both corporations unless:

(1) The director or senior executive participates personally and substantially in negotiating the transaction for either of the corporations; or

(2) The transaction is approved by the board of either corporation, and a director on that board who is also a director or senior executive of the other corporation casts a vote that is necessary to approve the transaction.

(b) If a transaction falls within Subsection (a)(1) or (a)(2), it will be reviewed under § 5.02.

§ 5.08 Conduct on Behalf of Associates of Directors or Senior Executives

A director [§ 1.13] or senior executive [§ 1.33] fails to fulfill the duty of fair dealing to the corporation if the director or senior executive knowingly advances the pecuniary interest of an associate [§ 1.03] in a manner that would fail to comply with the provisions of this Chapter 2 had the director or senior executive acted for himself or herself.

§ 5.09 Effect of a Standard of the Corporation

If a director [§ 1.13] or senior executive [§ 1.33] acts in reliance upon a standard of the corporation [§ 1.36] that authorizes a director or senior executive to either:

(a) Enter into a transaction with the corporation that is of a specified type and that could be expected to recur in the ordinary course of business of the corporation;

(b) Use corporate position or corporate property in a specified manner that is not unlawful and that could be expected to recur in the ordinary course of business of the corporation;

(c) Take advantage of a specified type of corporate opportunity of which the director or senior executive becomes aware other than (i) in connection with the performance of directorial or executive functions, or (ii) under circumstances that should reasonably lead the director or senior executive to believe that the person [§ 1.28] offering the opportunity expected it to be offered to the corporation, or (iii) through the use of corporate information or property; or

(d) Engage in competition of a specified type;

and the standard was authorized in advance by disinterested directors [§ 1.15] or disinterested shareholders [§ 1.16], following disclosure concerning the effect of the standard and of the type of transaction or conduct intended to be covered by the standard, then the standard is to be deemed equivalent to an authorization of the action in advance by disinterested directors or shareholders under §§ 5.02 (Transactions with the Corporation), 5.03 (Compensation of Directors and Senior Executives), 5.04 (Use by a Director or Senior Executive of Corporate Property, Material Non–Public Corporate Information, or Corporate Position), 5.05 (Taking of Corporate Opportunities by Directors or Senior Executives), or 5.06 (Competition with the Corporation), as the case may be.

Chapter 3

DUTY OF FAIR DEALING OF CONTROLLING SHAREHOLDERS

§ 5.10 Transactions by a Controlling Shareholder With the Corporation

(a) *General Rule.* A controlling shareholder [§ 1.10] who enters into a transaction with the corporation fulfills the duty of fair dealing to the corporation with respect to the transaction if:

(1) The transaction is fair to the corporation when entered into; or

(2) The transaction is authorized in advance or ratified by disinterested shareholders [§ 1.16], following disclosure concerning the conflict of interest [§ 1.14(a)] and the transaction [§ 1.14(b)], and does not constitute a waste of corporate assets [§ 1.42] at the time of the shareholder action.

(b) *Burden of Proof.* If the transaction was authorized in advance by disinterested directors [§ 1.15], or authorized in advance or ratified by disinterested shareholders, following such disclosure, the party challenging the transaction has the burden of proof. The party challenging the transaction also has the burden of proof if the transaction was ratified by disinterested directors and the failure to obtain advance authorization did not adversely affect the interests of the corporation in a significant way. If the transaction was not so authorized or ratified, the controlling shareholder has the burden of proof, except to the extent otherwise provided in Subsection (c).

(c) *Transactions in the Ordinary Course of Business.* In the case of a transaction between a controlling shareholder and the corporation that was in the ordinary course of the corporation's business, a party who challenges the transaction has the burden of coming forward with evidence that the transaction was unfair, whether or not the transaction was authorized in advance or ratified by disinterested directors or disinterested shareholders.

§ 5.11 Use by a Controlling Shareholder of Corporate Property, Material Non-public Corporate Information, or Corporate Position

(a) *General Rule.* A controlling shareholder may not use corporate property, its controlling position, or (when trading in the corporation's securities) material non-public corporate information to secure a pecuniary benefit, unless:

(1) Value is given for the use and the transaction meets the standards of § 5.10 (Transactions by a Controlling Shareholder with the Corporation), or

(2) Any resulting benefit to the controlling shareholder either is made proportionally available to the other similarly situated shareholders or is derived only from the use of controlling position and is not unfair to other shareholders,

and the use is not otherwise unlawful.

(b) *Burden of Proof.* A party who challenges the conduct of a controlling shareholder under Subsection (a) has the burden of proof, except that if value was given for the benefit, the burden of proving whether the value was fair should be determined as provided in § 5.10 in the case of a transaction with the corporation.

(c) *Special Rule on Remedies.* A controlling shareholder is subject to liability under this section only to the extent of any improper benefit received and retained, except to the extent that any foreseeable harm caused by the shareholder's conduct exceeds the value of the benefit received, and multiple liability based on receipt of the same benefit is not to be imposed.

§ 5.12 Taking of Corporate Opportunities by a Controlling Shareholder

(a) *General Rule.* A controlling shareholder [§ 1.10] may not take advantage of a corporate opportunity unless:

(1) The taking of the opportunity is fair to the corporation; or

(2) The taking of the opportunity is authorized in advance or ratified by disinterested shareholders [§ 1.16], following disclosure concerning the conflict of interest [§ 1.14(a)] and the corporate opportunity [§ 1.14(b)], and the taking of the opportunity is not equivalent to a waste of corporate assets [§ 1.42].

(b) *Definition of a Corporate Opportunity.* For purposes of this Section, a corporate opportunity means any opportunity to engage in a business activity that:

(1) Is developed or received by the corporation, or comes to the controlling shareholder primarily by virtue of its relationship to the corporation; or

(2) Is held out to shareholders of the corporation by the controlling shareholder, or by the corporation with the consent of the controlling shareholder, as being a type of business activity that will be within the scope of the business in which the corporation is engaged or expects to engage and will not be within the scope of the controlling shareholder's business.

(c) *Burden of Proof.* A party who challenges the taking of a corporate opportunity has the burden of proof, except that the controlling shareholder has the burden of proving that the taking of the opportunity is fair to the corporation if the taking of the opportunity was not authorized in advance or ratified by disinterested directors or disinterested shareholders, following the disclosure required by Subsection (a)(2).

§ 5.13 Conduct on Behalf of Associates of a Controlling Shareholder

A controlling shareholder [§ 1.10] fails to fulfill the duty of fair dealing to the corporation if it knowingly advances the pecuniary interest of an associate [§ 1.03] of the controlling shareholder in a manner that would fail to comply with the provisions of this Chapter 3 had the controlling shareholder acted for itself.

Chapter 4

TRANSFER OF CONTROL

§ 5.15 Transfer of Control in Which a Director or Principal Senior Executive Is Interested

(a) If directors or principal senior executives [§ 1.30] of a corporation are interested [§ 1.23] in a transaction in control [§ 1.38] or a tender offer that results in a transfer of control [§ 1.08] of the corporation to another person [§ 1.28], then those directors or principal senior executives have the burden of proving that the transaction was fair to the shareholders of the corporation unless (1) the transaction involves a transfer by a controlling shareholder [§ 1.10] or (2) the conditions of Subsection (b) are satisfied.

(b) If in connection with a transaction described in Subsection (a) involving a publicly held corporation [§ 1.31]:

(1) Public disclosure of the proposed transaction is made;

(2) Responsible persons who express an interest are provided relevant information concerning the corporation and given a reasonable opportunity to submit a competing proposal;

(3) The transaction is authorized in advance by disinterested directors [§ 1.15] after the procedures set forth in Subsections (1) and (2) have been complied with; and

(4) The transaction is authorized or ratified by disinterested shareholders [§ 1.16] (or, if the transaction is effected by a tender offer, the offer is accepted by disinterested shareholders), after disclosure concerning the conflict of interest [§ 1.14(a)] and the transaction [§ 1.14(b)] has been made;

then a party challenging the transaction has the burden of proving that the terms of the transaction are equivalent to a waste of corporate assets [§ 1.42].

(c) The fact that holders of equity securities are entitled to an appraisal remedy reflecting the general principles embodied in §§ 7.21–7.23 with respect to a transaction specified in Subsection (a) does not make an appraisal proceeding the exclusive remedy of a shareholder who proposes to challenge the transaction, unless the transaction falls within § 7.25 (Transactions in Control Involving Corporate Combinations to Which a Majority Shareholder Is a Party).

§ 5.16 Disposition of Voting Equity Securities by a Controlling Shareholder to Third Parties

A controlling shareholder [§ 1.10] has the same right to dispose of voting equity securities [§ 1.40] as any other shareholder, including the right to dispose of those securities for a price that is not made proportionally available to other shareholders, but the controlling shareholder does not satisfy the duty of fair dealing to the other shareholders if:

(a) The controlling shareholder does not make disclosure concerning the transaction [§ 1.14(b)] to other shareholders with whom the controlling shareholder deals in connection with the transaction; or

(b) It is apparent from the circumstances that the purchaser is likely to violate the duty of fair dealing under Part V in such a way as to obtain a significant financial benefit for the purchaser or an associate [§ 1.03].

PART VI

ROLE OF DIRECTORS AND SHAREHOLDERS IN TRANSACTIONS IN CONTROL AND TENDER OFFERS

§ 6.01 Role of Directors and Holders of Voting Equity Securities With Respect to Transactions in Control Proposed to the Corporation

(a) The board of directors, in the exercise of its business judgment [§ 4.01(c)], may approve, reject, or decline to consider a proposal to the corporation to engage in a transaction in control [§ 1.38].

(b) A transaction in control of the corporation to which the corporation is a party should require approval by the shareholders [§ 1.02].

§ 6.02 Action of Directors That Has the Foreseeable Effect of Blocking Unsolicited Tender Offers

(a) The board of directors may take an action that has the foreseeable effect of blocking an unsolicited tender offer [§ 1.39], if the action is a reasonable response to the offer.

(b) In considering whether its action is a reasonable response to the offer:

(1) The board may take into account all factors relevant to the best interests of the corporation and shareholders, including, among other things, questions of legality and whether the offer, if successful, would threaten the corporation's essential economic prospects; and

(2) The board may, in addition to the analysis under § 6.02(b)(1), have regard for interests or groups (other than shareholders) with respect to which the corporation has a legitimate concern if to do so would not significantly disfavor the long-term interests of shareholders.

(c) A person who challenges an action of the board on the ground that it fails to satisfy the standards of Subsection (a) has the burden of proof that the board's action is an unreasonable response to the offer.

(d) An action that does not meet the standards of Subsection (a) may be enjoined or set aside, but directors who authorize such an action are not subject to liability for damages if their conduct meets the standard of the business judgment rule [§ 4.01(c)].

PART VII

REMEDIES

INTRODUCTION ...

REPORTER'S NOTE

1. *The empirical evidence.* Critiques of the derivative action are not new. In the 1904s, the Chamber of Commerce of the State of New York sponsored a study by Franklin Wood that examined 1400 derivative actions filed between 1936 and 1942 in New York City. Wood reported a consistent pattern in which (1) the plaintiff's stockholdings were generally nominal, (2) the plaintiff seldom secured a litigated victory, and (3) private settlements (in which the corporation often received nothing) were common. F. Wood, Survey and Report Regarding Stockholders' Derivative Suits, 32 (1944) (the "Wood Report"). He concluded that the benefits of the action were outweighed by its costs. Partly as a result of the Wood Report and similar commentary, and partly because of the bar's uneasiness with an action in which the attorney was frequently the real party in interest, the derivative action was frequently derided as a "strike suit" that served no interests other than those of the plaintiff's attorney.

In response, legislative treatment of the action was generally skeptical and constraining: statutes requiring security for expenses' bonds were enacted, common law defenses were tightened, and an extraordinary procedural complexity developed around such questions as jurisdiction, alignment of the parties, demand on the board and shareholders, and settlement and dismissal. Later, other commentators re-analyzed Wood's data and, after excluding those cases that were still pending or in which the disposition was unknown, concluded that the overall rate of plaintiff's "success" (i.e., cases in which some recovery was secured) was about 44 percent, and thus compared favorably with the rate of plaintiff's success in similar forms of civil litigation. See Conard, A Behavioral Analysis of Directors' Liability for Negligence, 1972 Duke L.J. 895, 901 n.21; Hornstein, The Death Knell of Stockholders' Derivative Suits in New York, 32 Calif.L.Rev. 123, 127–28 (1944).

Important empirical work has been done in this area since the time of the original Wood study, but an overall evaluation of the derivative action remains difficult to reach. One such effort casts some partial light on the disputed benefits of the derivative action. An eight-year study followed 531 derivative and class action suits brought against the officers or directors of 205 publicly held corporations between 1971 and 1978. See Jones, An Empirical Examination of the Resolution of Shareholder Derivative and Class Action Lawsuits, 60 B.U.L.Rev. 542 (1980). The following results of that study seem salient:

(1) In roughly 75 percent of the cases, plaintiffs obtained some form of relief, typically by way of settlement (70%), but in less than one percent did plaintiffs win a litigated judgment. Although this study concluded that "the notion that shareholder plaintiffs rarely obtain relief is clearly a myth" (Id. at 545), it is uncertain at what price this relief came. Because data were not collected with respect to the size or adequacy of the settlement funds in these actions, and because direct and derivative actions were not carefully distinguished, it remains an open question whether these actions yielded a net compensatory benefit to their corporations.

(2) The incidence of "primary" shareholder litigation (i.e., litigation directed at corporate officials personally) did not significantly rise over the period from 1971 to 1978, and, if adjustment is made for a sudden spurt of "illegal payments" cases in the mid–1970s, probably fell slightly over this period.

(3) Derivative ligation tended to focus on self-dealing transactions and duty of loyalty issues and only infrequently involved challenges to arm's-length business decisions.

(4) Only a minority of publicly held corporations experienced such litigation. About 30 percent of the large publicly held corporations surveyed were involved in any form of shareholder litigation, direct or derivative, during the eight-year period. Once the impact of multiple suits arising out of the same event or transaction was adjusted for, the study concluded that the typical publicly held firm would be involved in such a suit only once every 17.6 years on average. See Jones, An Empirical Evaluation of the Incidence of Shareholder Derivative and Class Action Lawsuits, 1971–1978, 60 B.U.L.Rev. 306, 312–13 (1980).

Recently, social scientists have reanalyzed the data collected in the foregoing study. Although they found important information to be lacking from much of the sample, they still noted that, when the amount of the recovery was indicated, "one-third of the total reported settlements involved no monetary relief, and six of the fifteen cases in which attorney fees were reported involved only 'procedural changes,' but significant attorney fees." This pattern suggests the existence of a substantial conflict of interest may exist between the plaintiff's attorney and his nominal clients, the shareholders. See Garth, Nagel and Plager, The Role of Empirical Research in Assessing the Efficacy of the Shareholders' Derivative Suit: Promise and Potential, 48 Law and Contemp.Probs. 137, 146–47 (1985). See also Rosenfeld, An Empirical Test of Class Action Settlements, 5 J.Legal Stud. 113, 119 (1976); Coffee, The Unfaithful Champion: The Plaintiff as Monitor in Shareholder Litigation, 48 Law and Contemp.Probs. 5, 26–33 (1985).

The most recent study of shareholder litigation examined a random sample of 535 public corporations over a period extending from the late 1960s to 1987. See Romano, The Shareholder Suit: Litigation Without Foundation?, 7 J.Law, Econ., & Org. 55 (1991). Its findings underline the relative infrequency of derivative actions and the centrality of the settlement stage. Only 19 percent of the corporations in the sample experienced a derivative suit, but some corporations attracted recurrent litigation, and there was an increase in litigation frequency during the 1980s. Although very few judgments for plaintiffs were obtained, the most striking fact about derivative litigation in this study was the high rate of settlement. Eighty-three out of 128 actions resolved during this period (or roughly 65%) were settled. Id. at 60. Yet, only half of the settlements (46 out of 83) involved any monetary recovery; however, the vast majority (75 out of 83) involved fee awards to the plaintiffs' attorneys. In another 25 cases, the settlement afforded non-pecuniary structural relief (there was also a monetary recovery in four of the suits). In those cases where the settlement fund could be valued (39 out of 83), the average recovery was $9 million, but there was substantial variation within this class (as the median recovery was only $2 million). Interestingly, the average recovery in derivative actions was found to be about half that in class actions. Id. at 61. These results can be interpreted in various ways. Some would explain them on the hypothesis that a significant percentage of shareholder litigation is without merit; another hypothesis is that plaintiffs' attorneys in such actions have serious conflicts of interest that lead them not to maximize the possible recovery to their class. Yet, a paradox arises here: another recent study has found that securities class actions tend to settle at 25 percent of the asserted potential damages. See Alexander, Do the Merits Matter? A Study of Settlements in Securities Class Actions, 43 Stan.L.Rev. 497, 500 (1991). Although such findings can similarly be interpreted to show an excessive incentive to litigate and to settle, the puzzle is that the two contexts are closely related. Indeed, typically, the same plaintiffs' attorneys are suing similarly situated defendants in both types of actions. In this light, the difference in outcomes between class and derivative actions (and the greater recoveries in the former) may reflect the greater legal barriers surrounding the derivative action. Overbroad rules that deny standing to plaintiffs in derivative actions in which the underlying allegations have legal merit could explain the lesser apparent settlement value of legal claims in the derivative action context.

Some preliminary efforts have been made to use econometric techniques to study the impact of the termination of derivative actions on the stock prices of companies in whose name the action was brought. Early results have reported a marginally negative market reaction to the suit's termination, but one that was statistically insignificant. See Fischel and Bradley, The Role of Liability Rules and the Derivative Suit in Corporate Law: A Theoretical and Empirical Analysis, 71 Cornell L.Rev. 261, 277–83 (1986). However, both because the methodology underlying these studies makes questionable assumptions about the stock market's sensitivity to the prospect of relatively small recoveries and because there is no evidence that the market's expectation was frustrated by the suit's termination (i.e., the market may assume that most suits will be terminated, whatever their merit), little reliance is here placed on such data. Even if reliable data that showed an insignificant or negative trend in the wake of an action's filing were available, the interpretation that should be placed on such data would remain open to debate. Stock market indifference to derivative litigation could be explained as based on the expectation that such actions were likely to result in collusive or cosmetic settlements in which any recovery would be consumed by costly attorneys' fees and other expenses. In addition, if the principal benefit of such actions lies in their general deterrent effect on all corporate managements, the stock price reaction of any single corporation would not reveal this benefit.

The existing state of the empirical data does not answer many important questions. First, it does not tell us whether derivative actions yield on average a net compensatory benefit for the corporation (after appropriate deduction is made for the cost of attorneys' fees and indemnification). Second, although the data shows little evidence of any recent explosion in the rate of shareholder litigation and suggests that such litigation only infrequently concerns business decisions not complicated by an alleged conflict of interest, it is possible that directors' perception of such litigation may be very different, and it is the perceived threat that may shape their willingness to serve on boards. Finally, recent institutional changes—such as the decreased availability of liability insurance and the change in incidence of takeover contests—may not be reflected in historical data. Still, the empirical evidence does clearly highlight the centrality of the settlement stage and the possibility that the conflicts of interest attending this stage may weaken the ability of derivative litigation to serve shareholders' interests.

Chapter 1

THE DERIVATIVE ACTION

§ 7.01 Direct and Derivative Actions Distinguished

(a) A derivative action may be brought in the name or right of a corporation by a holder [§ 1.22], as provided in § 7.02 (Standing to Commence and Maintain a Derivative Action), to redress an injury sustained by, or enforce a duty owed to, a corporation. An action in which the holder can prevail only by showing an injury or breach of duty to the corporation should be treated as a derivative action.

(b) A direct action may be brought in the name and right of a holder to redress an injury sustained by, or enforce a duty owed to, the holder. An action in which the holder can prevail without showing an injury or breach of duty to the corporation should be treated as a direct action that may be maintained by the holder in an individual capacity.

(c) If a transaction gives rise to both direct and derivative claims, a holder may commence and maintain direct and derivative actions simultaneously, and any special restrictions or defenses pertaining to the maintenance, settlement, or dismissal of either action should not apply to the other.

(d) In the case of a closely held corporation [§ 1.06], the court in its discretion may treat an action raising derivative claims as a direct action, exempt it from those restrictions and defenses applicable only to derivative actions, and order an individual recovery, if it finds that to do so will not (i) unfairly expose the corporation or the defendants to a multiplicity of actions, (ii) materially prejudice the interests of creditors of the corporation, or (iii) interfere with a fair distribution of the recovery among all interested persons.

§ 7.02 Standing to Commence and Maintain a Derivative Action

(a) A holder [§ 1.22] of an equity security [§ 1.20] has standing to commence and maintain a derivative action if the holder:

(1) Acquired the equity security either (A) before the material facts relating to the alleged wrong were publicly disclosed or were known by, or specifically communicated to, the holder, or (B) by devolution of law, directly or indirectly, from a prior holder who acquired the security as described in the preceding Clause (A);

(2) Continues to hold the equity security until the time of judgment, unless the failure to do so is the result of corporate action in which the holder did not acquiesce, and either (A) the derivative action was commenced prior to the corporate action terminating the holder's status, or (B) the court finds that the holder is better able to represent the interests of the shareholders than any other holder who has brought suit;

(3) Has complied with the demand requirement of § 7.03 (Exhaustion of Intracorporate Remedies: The Demand Rule) or was excused by its terms; and

(4) Is able to represent fairly and adequately the interests of the shareholders.

(b) On a timely motion, a holder of an equity security should be permitted to intervene in a derivative action, unless the court finds that the interests to be represented by the intervenor are already fairly and adequately represented or that the intervenor is unable to represent fairly and adequately the interests of the shareholders.

(c) A director [§ 1.13] of a corporation has standing to commence and maintain a derivative action unless the court finds that the director is unable to represent fairly and adequately the interests of the shareholders.

§ 7.03 Exhaustion of Intracorporate Remedies: The Demand Rule

(a) Before commencing a derivative action, a holder [§ 1.22] or a director [§ 1.13] should be required to make a written demand upon the board of directors of the corporation, requesting it to prosecute the action or take suitable corrective measures, unless demand is excused under § 7.03(b). The demand should give notice to the board, with reasonable specificity, of the essential facts relied upon to support each of the claims made therein.

(b) Demand on the board should be excused only if the plaintiff makes a specific showing that irreparable injury to the corporation would otherwise result, and in such instances demand should be made promptly after commencement of the action.

(c) Demand on shareholders should not be required.

(d) Except as provided in § 7.03(b), the court should dismiss a derivative action that is commenced prior to the response of the board or a committee thereof to the demand required by § 7.03(a), unless the board or committee fails to respond within a reasonable time.

§ 7.04 Pleading, Demand Rejection, Procedure, and Costs in a Derivative Action

The legal standards applicable to a derivative action should provide that:

(a) *Particularity; Demand Rejection.*

(1) *In General.* The complaint shall plead with particularity facts that, if true, raise a significant prospect that the transaction or conduct complained of did not meet the applicable requirements of Parts IV (Duty of Care and the Business Judgment Rule), V (Duty of Fair Dealing), or VI (Role of Directors and Shareholders in Transactions in Control and Tender Offers), in light of any approvals of the transaction or conduct communicated to the plaintiff by the corporation.

(2) *Demand Rejection.* If a corporation rejects the demand made on the board pursuant to § 7.03, and if, at or following the

1380

rejection, the corporation delivers to the plaintiff a written reply to the demand which states that the demand was rejected by directors who were not interested [§ 1.23] in the transaction or conduct described in and forming the basis for the demand and that such directors constituted a majority of the entire board and were capable as a group of objective judgment in the circumstances, and provides specific reasons for those statements, then the complaint shall also plead with particularity facts that, if true, raise a significant prospect that either:

(A) The statements in the reply are not correct;

(B) If Part IV, V, or VI provides that the underlying transaction or conduct would be reviewed under the standard of the business judgment rule, that the rejection did not satisfy the requirements of the business judgment rule as specified in § 4.01(c); or

(C) If Part IV, V, or VI provides that the underlying transaction or conduct would be reviewed under a standard other than the business judgment rule, either (i) that the disinterested directors who rejected the demand did not satisfy the good faith and informational requirements (§ 4.01(c)(2)) of the business judgment rule or (ii) that disinterested directors could not reasonably have determined that rejection of the demand was in the best interests of the corporation.

If the complaint fails to set forth sufficiently such particularized facts, defendants shall be entitled to dismissal of the complaint prior to discovery.

(b) *Attorney's Certification.* Each party's attorney of record shall sign every pleading, motion, and other paper filed on behalf of the party, and such signature shall constitute the attorney's certification that (i) to the best of the attorney's knowledge, information, and belief, formed after reasonable inquiry, the pleading, motion, or other paper is well grounded in fact and is warranted by existing law or by a good faith argument for the extension, modification, or reversal of existing law, and (ii) the pleading, motion, or other paper is not interposed for any improper purpose, such as to harass or to cause unnecessary delay or needless increase in the cost of litigation.

(c) *Security for Expenses.* Except as authorized by statute or judicial rule applicable to civil actions generally, no bond, undertaking, or other security for expenses shall be required.

(d) *Award of Costs.* The court may award applicable costs, including reasonable attorney's fees and expenses, against a party, or a party's counsel:

(1) At any time, if the court finds that any specific claim for relief or defense was asserted or any pleading, motion, request for

discovery, or other action was made or taken in bad faith or without reasonable cause; or

(2) Upon final judgment, if the court finds, in light of all the evidence, and considering both the state and trend of the substantive law, that the action taken as a whole was brought, prosecuted, or defended in bad faith or in an unreasonable manner.

Comment . . .

d. Section 7.04(a)(2) . . .

Section 7.04(a)(1) and § 7.04(a)(2) state separate tests, so both are required to be met. There is nevertheless an interrelationship between the two tests. In applying § 7.04(a), a court should balance the strength and seriousness of the case set out by the particularized pleading of the plaintiff, as tested under § 7.04(a)(1), with that required under § 7.04(a)(2). The stronger and more serious the case set out by the plaintiff's particularized pleading, as tested under § 7.04(a)(1), the less the complaint must allege with particularity to establish under § 7.04(a)(2) that there is a significant prospect the directors could not have satisfied the business judgment rule under § 7.04(a)(2)(B), or could not reasonably have determined that rejection of the demand was in the best interests of the corporation under § 7.04(a)(2)(C).

§ 7.05 Board or Committee Authority in Regard to a Derivative Action

(a) The board of a corporation in whose name or right a derivative action is brought has standing on behalf of the corporation to:

(1) Move to dismiss the action on account of the plaintiff's lack of standing under § 7.02 (Standing to Commence and Maintain a Derivative Action) or the plaintiff's failure to comply with § 7.03 (Exhaustion of Intracorporate Remedies: The Demand Rule) or § 7.04(a) or (b) (Pleading, Demand Rejection, Procedure, and Costs in a Derivative Action) or move for dismissal of the complaint or for summary judgment;

(2) Move for a stay of the action, including discovery, as provided by § 7.06 (Authority of Court to Stay a Derivative Action);

(3) Move to dismiss the action as contrary to the best interests of the corporation, as provided in §§ 7.07–7.12 (dismissal of a derivative action based on a motion requesting dismissal by the board, a board committee, the shareholders, or a special panel);

(4) Oppose injunctive or other relief materially affecting the corporation's interests;

(5) Adopt or pursue the action in the corporation's right;

(6) Comment on, object to, or recommend any proposed settlement, discontinuance, compromise, or voluntary dismissal by agree-

ment between the plaintiff and any defendant under § 7.14 (Settlement of a Derivative Action by Agreement Between the Plaintiff and a Defendant), or any award of attorney's fees and other expenses under § 7.17 (Plaintiff's Attorney's Fees and Expenses); and

(7) Seek to settle the action without agreement of the plaintiff under § 7.15 (Settlement of a Derivative Action Without the Agreement of the Plaintiff).

Except as provided above, the corporation may not otherwise defend the action in the place of, or raise defenses on behalf of, other defendants.

(b) The board of a corporation in whose name or right a derivative action is brought may:

(1) Delegate its authority to take any action specified in § 7.05(a) to a committee of directors; or

(2) Request the court to appoint a special panel in lieu of a committee of directors, or a special member of a committee, under § 7.12 (Special Panel or Special Committee Members).

§ 7.06 Authority of Court to Stay a Derivative Action

In the absence of special circumstances, the court should stay discovery and all further proceedings by the plaintiff in a derivative action on the motion of the corporation and upon such conditions as the court deems appropriate pending the court's determination of any motion made by the corporation under § 7.04(a)(2) and the completion within a reasonable period of any review and evaluation undertaken and diligently pursued pursuant to § 7.09 (Procedures for Requesting Dismissal of a Derivative Action). On the same basis, the court may stay discovery and further proceedings pending (a) the resolution of a related action or (b) such other event or development as the interests of justice may require.

§ 7.07 Dismissal of a Derivative Action Based on a Motion Requesting Dismissal by the Board or a Committee: General Statement

(a) The court having jurisdiction over a derivative action should dismiss the action as against one or more of the defendants based on a motion by the board or a properly delegated committee requesting dismissal of the action as in the best interests of the corporation, if:

(1) In the case of an action against a person [§ 1.28] other than a director [§ 1.13], senior executive [§ 1.33], or person in control [§ 1.08] of the corporation, or an associate [§ 1.03] of any such person, the determinations of the board or committee underlying the motion satisfy the requirements of the business judgment rule as specified in § 4.01;

(2) In the case of an action against a director, senior executive, or person in control of the corporation, or an associate of any such person, the conditions specified in § 7.08 (Dismissal of a Derivative Action Against Directors, Senior Executives, Controlling Persons, or Associates Based on a Motion Requesting Dismissal by the Board or a Committee) are satisfied; or

(3) In any case, the shareholders approve a resolution requesting dismissal of the action in the manner provided in § 7.11 (Dismissal of a Derivative Action Based Upon Action by the Shareholders).

(b) Regardless of whether a corporation chooses to proceed under § 7.08 or § 7.11, it is free to make any other motion available to it under the law, including a motion to dismiss the complaint or for summary judgment.

§ 7.08 Dismissal of a Derivative Action Against Directors, Senior Executives, Controlling Persons, or Associates Based on a Motion Requesting Dismissal by the Board or a Committee

The court should, subject to the provisions of § 7.10(b) (retention of significant improper benefit), dismiss a derivative action against a defendant who is a director [§ 1.13], a senior executive [§ 1.33], or a person [§ 1.28] in control [§ 1.08] of the corporation, or an associate [§ 1.03] of any such person, if:

(a) The board of directors or a properly delegated committee thereof (either in response to a demand or following commencement of the action) has determined that the action is contrary to the best interests of the corporation and has requested dismissal of the action;

(b) The procedures specified in § 7.09 (Procedures for Requesting Dismissal of a Derivative Action) for the conduct of a review and evaluation of the action were substantially complied with (either in response to a demand or following commencement of the action), or any material departures therefrom were justified under the circumstances; and

(c) The determinations of the board or committee satisfy the applicable standard of review set forth in § 7.10(a) (Standard of Judicial Review with Regard to a Board or Committee Motion Requesting Dismissal of a Derivative Action Under § 7.08).

§ 7.09 Procedures for Requesting Dismissal of a Derivative Action

(a) The following procedural standards should apply to the review and evaluation of a derivative action by the board or committee under

§ 7.08 (Dismissal of a Derivative Action Against Directors, Senior Executives, Controlling Persons, or Associates Based on a Motion Requesting Dismissal by the Board or a Committee) or § 7.11 (Dismissal of a Derivative Action Based Upon Action by the Shareholders):

(1) The board or committee should be composed of two or more persons, no participating member of which was interested [§ 1.23] in the action, and should as a group be capable of objective judgment in the circumstances;

(2) The board or committee should be assisted by counsel of its choice and such other agents as it reasonably considers necessary;

(3) The determinations of the board or committee should be based upon a review and evaluation that was sufficiently informed to satisfy the standards applicable under § 7.10(a); and

(4) If the board or committee determines to request dismissal of the derivative action, it shall prepare and file with the court a report or other written submission setting forth its determinations in a manner sufficient to enable the court to conduct the review required under § 7.10 (Standard of Judicial Review with Regard to a Board or Committee Motion Requesting Dismissal of a Derivative Action Under § 7.08).

(b) If the court is unwilling to grant a motion to dismiss under § 7.08 or § 7.11 because the procedures followed by the board or committee departed materially from the standards specified in § 7.09(a), the court should permit the board or committee to supplement its procedures, and make such further reports or other written submissions, as will satisfy the standards specified in § 7.09(a), unless the court decides that (i) the board or committee did not act on the basis of a good faith belief that its procedures and report were justified in the circumstances; (ii) unreasonable delay or prejudice would result; or (iii) there is no reasonable prospect that such further steps would support dismissal of the action.

§ 7.10 Standard of Judicial Review With Regard to a Board or Committee Motion Requesting Dismissal of a Derivative Action Under § 7.08

(a) *Standard of Review.* In deciding whether an action should be dismissed under § 7.08 (Dismissal of a Derivative Action Against Directors, Senior Executives, Controlling Persons, or Associates Based on a Motion Requesting Dismissal by the Board or a Committee), the court should apply the following standards of review:

(1) If the gravamen of the claim is that the defendant violated a duty set forth in Part IV (Duty of Care and the Business Judgment Rule), other than by committing a knowing and culpable violation of law that is alleged with particularity, or if the underlying transac-

tion or conduct would be reviewed under the business judgment rule under § 5.03, § 5.04, § 5.05, § 5.06, § 5.08, or § 6.02, the court should dismiss the claim unless it finds that the board's or committee's determinations fail to satisfy the requirements of the business judgment rule as specified in § 4.01(c).

(2) In other cases governed by Part V (Duty of Fair Dealing) or Part VI (Role of Directors and Shareholders in Transactions in Control and Tender Offers), or to which the business judgment rule is not applicable, including cases in which the gravamen of the claim is that defendant committed a knowing and culpable violation of law in breach of Part IV, the court should dismiss the action if the court finds, in light of the applicable standards under Part IV, V, or VI that the board or committee was adequately informed under the circumstances and reasonably determined that dismissal was in the best interests of the corporation, based on grounds that the court deems to warrant reliance.

(3) In cases arising under either Subsection (a)(1) or (a)(2), the court may substantively review and determine any issue of law.

(b) *Retention of Significant Improper Benefit.* The court shall not dismiss an action if the plaintiff establishes that dismissal would permit a defendant, or an associate [§ 1.03], to retain a significant improper benefit where:

(1) The defendant, either alone or collectively with others who are also found to have received a significant improper benefit arising out of the same transaction, possesses control [§ 1.08] of the corporation; or

(2) Such benefit was obtained:

(A) As the result of a knowing and material misrepresentation or omission or other fraudulent act; or

(B) Without advance authorization or the requisite ratification of such benefit by disinterested directors [§ 1.15] (or, in the case of a non-director senior executive, advance authorization by a disinterested superior), or authorization or ratification by disinterested shareholders [§ 1.16], and in breach of § 5.02 (Transactions with the Corporation) or § 5.04 (Use by a Director or Senior Executive of Corporate Property, Material Non–Public Corporate Information, or Corporate Position);

unless the court determines, in light of specific reasons advanced by the board or committee, that the likely injury to the corporation from continuation of the action convincingly outweighs any adverse impact on the public interest from dismissal of the action.

(c) *Subsequent Developments.* In determining whether the standards of § 7.10(a) are satisfied or whether § 7.10(b) or any of the exceptions set forth therein are applicable, the court may take into account considerations set forth by the board or committee (or otherwise brought to the court's attention) that reflect material developments subsequent to the time of the underlying transaction or conduct or to the time of the motion by the board or committee requesting dismissal.

§ 7.11 Dismissal of a Derivative Action Based Upon Action by the Shareholders

The court should dismiss a derivative action against any defendant upon approval by the shareholders of a resolution requesting dismissal of the action as in the best interests of the corporation if the court finds that:

(a) A resolution recommending such dismissal to the shareholders was adopted by the board of directors, or a properly delegated committee thereof, after a review and evaluation that substantially complied with the procedures specified in § 7.09(a)(1)–(3) (Procedures for Requesting Dismissal of a Derivative Action) or in which any material departures from those procedures were justified under the circumstances;

(b) Disclosure was made to the shareholders of all material facts [§ 1.25] concerning the derivative action and the board's resolution recommending its dismissal to the shareholders and, if requested by plaintiff, the disclosure statement included a brief statement by the plaintiff summarizing the plaintiff's views of the action and of the board's or committee's resolutions;

(c) The resolution was approved by a vote of disinterested shareholders [§ 1.16]; and

(d) Dismissal would not constitute a waste of corporate assets [§ 1.42].

§ 7.12 Special Panel or Special Committee Members

(a) On motion made by a corporation in whose name or right a derivative action is brought or upon which a demand has been made, the court may appoint one or more individuals to serve as a panel in lieu of a committee of directors for purposes of § 7.08 (Dismissal of a Derivative Action Against Directors, Senior Executives, Controlling Persons, or Associates Based on a Motion Requesting Dismissal by the Board or a Committee) or § 7.11 (Dismissal of a Derivative Action Based Upon Action by the Shareholders), none of whom should be interested [§ 1.23] in the action or have a significant relationship [§ 1.34] with a senior executive [§ 1.33] of the corporation or a similar relationship with any defendant or plaintiff. The panel so appointed should conduct a review and evaluation and prepare a report or other written submission as to the advisability of terminating the action, in compliance with the procedures specified in § 7.09 (Procedures for Requesting Dismissal of a Derivative Action). Any report or other written submission so prepared should have the same status under § 7.08, § 7.10, § 7.11, or § 7.13

(Judicial Procedures on Motions to Dismiss a Derivative Action Under § 7.08 or § 7.11) as a report or other written submission of the board or a properly delegated committee thereof. The costs of the inquiry and report or other written submission should be borne by the corporation, unless the court directs otherwise.

(b) In lieu of the appointment of a panel under § 7.12(a), the court on motion of a corporation may appoint one or more individuals who are not directors of the corporation and who meet the qualifications specified in § 7.12(a) to serve on a committee established by the corporation under § 7.05(b)(1).

§ 7.13   Judicial Procedures on Motions to Dismiss a Derivative Action Under § 7.08 or § 7.11

(a) *Filing of Report or Other Written Submission.* Upon a motion to dismiss an action under § 7.08 (Dismissal of a Derivative Action Against Directors, Senior Executives, Controlling Persons, or Associates Based on a Motion Requesting Dismissal by the Board or a Committee) or § 7.11 (Dismissal of a Derivative Action Based Upon Action by the Shareholders), the corporation shall file with the court a report or other written submission setting forth the procedures and determinations of the board or committee, or the resolution of the shareholders. A copy of the report or other written submission, including any supporting documentation filed by the corporation, shall be given to the plaintiff's counsel.

(b) *Protective Order.* The court may issue a protective order concerning such materials, where appropriate.

(c) *Discovery.* Subject to § 7.06 (Authority of Court to Stay a Derivative Action), if the plaintiff has demonstrated that a substantial issue exists whether the applicable standards of § 7.08, § 7.09, § 7.10, § 7.11, or § 7.12 have been satisfied and if the plaintiff is unable without undue hardship to obtain the information by other means, the court may order such limited discovery or limited evidentiary hearing, as to issues specified by the court, as the court finds to be (i) necessary to enable it to render a decision on the motion under the applicable standards of § 7.08, § 7.09, § 7.10, § 7.11, or § 7.12, and (ii) consistent with an expedited resolution of the motion. In the absence of special circumstances, the court should limit on a similar basis any discovery that is sought by the plaintiff in response to a motion for summary judgment by the corporation or any defendant to those facts likely to be in dispute. The results of any such discovery may be made subject to a protective order on the same basis as under § 7.13(b).

(d) *Burdens of Proof.* The plaintiff has the burden of proof in the case of a motion (1) under § 7.08 where the standard of judicial review is determined under § 7.10(a)(1) because the basis of the claim involves a breach of a duty set forth in Part IV (Duty of Care and the Business

Judgment Rule) or because the underlying transaction would be reviewed under the business judgment rule, or (2) under § 7.07(a)(1) (suits against third parties and lesser corporate officials). The corporation has the burden of proof in the case of a motion under § 7.08 where the standard of judicial review is determined under § 7.10(a)(2) because the underlying transaction would be reviewed under a standard other than the business judgment rule, except that the plaintiff retains the burden of proof in all cases to show (i) that a defendant's conduct involved a knowing and culpable violation of law, (ii) that the board or committee as a group was not capable of objective judgment in the circumstances as required by § 7.09(a)(1), and (iii) that dismissal of the action would permit a defendant or an associate [§ 1.03] thereof to retain a significant improper benefit under § 7.10(b). The corporation shall also have the burden of proving under § 7.10(b) that the likely injury to the corporation from continuation of the action convincingly outweighs any adverse impact on the public interest from dismissal of the action. In the case of a motion under § 7.11 (Dismissal of a Derivative Action Based Upon Action by the Shareholders), the plaintiff has the burden of proof with respect to § 7.11(b), (c), and (d), and the corporation has the burden of proof with respect to § 7.11(a).

(e) *Privilege.* The plaintiff's counsel should be furnished a copy of related legal opinions received by the board or committee if any opinion is tendered to the court under § 7.13(a). Subject to that requirement, communications, both oral and written, between the board or committee and its counsel with respect to the subject matter of the action do not forfeit their privileged character, and documents, memoranda, or other material qualifying as attorney's work product do not become subject to discovery, on the grounds that the action is derivative or that the privilege was waived by the production to the plaintiff or the filing with the court of a report, other written submission, or supporting documents pursuant to § 7.13.

§ 7.14 Settlement of a Derivative Action by Agreement Between the Plaintiff and a Defendant

(a) A derivative action should not be settled, discontinued, compromised, or voluntarily dismissed by agreement between the plaintiff and a defendant, except with the approval of the court.

(b) The court should approve a proposed settlement or other disposition if the balance of corporate interests warrants approval and the settlement or other disposition is consistent with public policy. In evaluating a proposed settlement, the court should place special weight on the net benefit, including pecuniary and non-pecuniary elements, to the corporation.

(c) In the absence of circumstances leading the court to find that the interests of the shareholders will not be substantially affected by the settlement or other disposition, the court's approval should be preceded by notice (which should be on an individual basis to the extent practicable) to, and an opportunity of a hearing for, affected shareholders. At such a hearing, objecting shareholders should have a reasonable opportunity to contest a proposed settlement or other disposition, including an opportunity with the court's approval to present and to cross-examine witnesses, and the court may allow, upon good cause shown, reasonable discovery consistent with avoiding undue delay.

§ 7.15   Settlement of a Derivative Action Without the Agreement of the Plaintiff

(a) Once a derivative action is commenced, the board or a properly delegated committee, without the agreement of a plaintiff, may with the approval of the court enter into a settlement with, or grant a release to, a director [§ 1.13], a senior executive [§ 1.33], or a person [§ 1.28] in control [§ 1.08] of the corporation, or an associate [§ 1.03] of any such person, with respect to any claim raised on behalf of the corporation in the action. The court should approve the settlement or release if it finds, in response to a motion made on behalf of the corporation by its board of directors or a properly delegated committee, that the following conditions are satisfied:

(1) The board or a properly delegated committee, whose participating members in either case were not interested [§ 1.23] in the action, entered into the proposed settlement after conducting an adequately informed review and evaluation, and filed with the court a report or other written submission that was substantially in conformity with the requirements applicable to a motion requesting dismissal by the board or a committee under § 7.09 (Procedures for Requesting Dismissal of a Derivative Action), or any material departures from those procedures were justified in the circumstances.

(2) The provisions of § 7.14 (Settlement of a Derivative Action by Agreement Between the Plaintiff and a Defendant) applicable to notice and an opportunity for a hearing to affected shareholders in the case of a settlement between the plaintiff and a defendant were substantially complied with.

(3) On the basis of the entire record, the balance of corporate interests warrants approval and the settlement or release is consistent with public policy. In evaluating a proposed settlement, the court should place special weight on the net benefit, including pecuniary and nonpecuniary elements, to the corporation.

(b) Any settlement or release entered into in accordance with § 7.15(a) constitutes a valid affirmative defense with respect to the claims and liabilities covered to the same extent as a settlement entered into with the plaintiff and approved pursuant to § 7.14.

(c) In lieu of a report or other written submission from the board or a committee, the court may consider and rely upon the determinations and conclusions of a special panel appointed under procedures that were substantially in conformity with the procedures of § 7.12 (Special Panel or Special Committee Members) applicable to a panel appointed to consider whether a derivative action should be dismissed.

§ 7.16 Disposition of Recovery in a Derivative Action

Except in the special circumstances specified in § 7.18(e) (pro-rata recovery), the recovery in a derivative action should accrue exclusively to the corporation. Any plaintiff or attorney who brings (or threatens to bring) an action in the name or right of the corporation and who receives property or money (including reimbursement for expenses) from the corporation or any defendant, as a result of the settlement, compromise, discontinuance, or dismissal of an actual or threatened derivative action, should be required to account to the corporation therefor, unless such money or property was received pursuant to a judicial order or a judicially approved settlement.

§ 7.17 Plaintiff's Attorney's Fees and Expenses

A successful plaintiff in a derivative action should be entitled to recover reasonable attorney's fees and other reasonable litigation expenses from the corporation, as determined by the court having jurisdiction over the action, but in no event should the attorney's fee award exceed a reasonable proportion of the value of the relief (including nonpecuniary relief) obtained by the plaintiff for the corporation.

Comment ...

... Because individual shareholders would find it infeasible to organize and tax themselves the costs necessary for a successful action, the well-established rule that a successful plaintiff in a derivative action may look to the corporation for reimbursement of attorney's fees and expenses is a precondition to an effective litigation remedy. In effect, this rule represents the common law's efficient solution to the well-recognized "free rider" problem that arises whenever an individual must incur costs to benefit a group of which the individual is a member. Unless some mechanism exists by which to allocate these costs among the group in proportion to the respective benefits to be received, the individual (here, the plaintiff shareholder) has an inadequate incentive to proceed.

Although the foregoing logic is widely accepted, there is less agreement as to the appropriate formula by which to determine the amount of the fee. Two basic approaches exist. Under the traditional "salvage value" approach, courts have calculated counsel fees by awarding a percentage of the total recovery.... The alternative approach, recommended by the Manual for Complex Litigation, Second § 24.12 (1986), and prevalent among federal courts, focuses principally on the value of the attorney's time at the attorney's customary hourly rate, and then adjusts this "lodestar figure" upward (or downward) to reflect the risk assumed by the attorney and the quality of the work done. . . . Recently, there appears to have been a trend toward greater use of the percentage method, and in some Circuits a 30 percent fee award has now become presumptive. . . . Other courts have expressly used high multipliers under the lodestar formula in order to achieve the same desired percentage of the recovery. . . .

Both the lodestar and the percentage-of-the-recovery approaches have well-recognized deficiencies if they are applied literally and without a sense of their impact upon the incentives held out to the plaintiff's attorney. Because a time-based formula, such as the "lodestar" method, compensates attorneys for the hours they expend, a number of commentators have suggested that such a formula gives rise to an incentive to expend unnecessary time and engage in dilatory tactics in order to maximize the attorney's recovery. Such an incentive is unfortunate not only because it delays the progress of the litigation, but also because it aggravates a latent conflict of interest between the attorney and the class he or she represents; the greater the fee, the smaller the net recovery will typically be for the shareholders. In addition, if the defendant strategically delays any settlement offer until just before the moment of trial or judgment, the defendant can further exacerbate this conflict, because at this point an inadequate settlement offer should produce nearly the same attorney's fee under a time-based formula as would a highly successful litigated victory. Thus, the plaintiff's attorney may have an incentive to accept an offer that is not in the best interests of the client in order to avoid the risk of trial and an adverse decision.

In contrast, a percentage-of-the-recovery formula avoids these problems (because the attorney's fee grows only in proportion to the recovery), but encounters others. First, a percentage formula may sometimes encourage premature settlements that are not in the best interests of the class. . . . Second, a percentage formula clearly does not work with respect to nonpecuniary recoveries, such as injunctive or equitable relief, where the value of the benefit conferred cannot be easily quantified. Finally, such a formula may produce windfall profits (such as where a case is settled immediately), which may evoke public criticism and erode respect for the law. Accordingly, § 7.17 proposes a compromise that attempts to retain the best of both formulas while avoiding their deficiencies. Section 7.17 permits the use of the percentage-of-the-recovery formula, but does not require it. Where it is not employed as the measure of the fee award, however, it should set a ceiling on the maximum fee allowable under any formula. The effect is to reduce the incentive to expend time needlessly, to minimize the danger of collusive settlements, and to align better the attorney's self-interest with that of the client; in addition, the danger of unjustified "windfall" profits is better avoided.

Chapter 2

RECOVERY FOR BREACH OF DUTY

§ 7.18 Recovery Resulting From a Breach of Duty: General Rules

(a) Except as otherwise provided in § 7.19 (Limitation on Damages for Certain Violations of the Duty of Care), a defendant who violates the standards of conduct set forth in Part IV (Duty of Care and the Business Judgment Rule), Part V (Duty of Fair Dealing), or Part VI (Role of Directors and Shareholders in Transactions in Control and Tender Offers) is subject to liability for the losses to the corporation (or, to the extent that a direct action lies under § 7.01 (Direct and Derivative Actions Distinguished), to its shareholders) of which the violation is a legal cause, and, in the case of a violation of the standards set forth in Part V, for any additional gains derived by the defendant or an associate [§ 1.03] to the extent necessary to make equitable restitution.

(b) A violation of the standards of conduct set forth in Part IV, Part V, or Part VI is the legal cause of loss if the plaintiff proves that (i) satisfaction of the applicable standard would have been a substantial factor in averting the loss, and (ii) the likelihood of injury would have been foreseeable to an ordinarily prudent person in like position to that of the defendant and in similar circumstances. It is not a defense to liability in such cases that damage to the corporation would not have resulted but for the acts or omissions of other individuals.

(c) A plaintiff bears the burden of proving causation and the amount of damages suffered by, or other recovery due to, the corporation or the shareholders as the result of a defendant's violation of a standard of conduct set forth in Part IV, Part V, or Part VI. The court may permit a defendant to offset against such liability any gains to the corporation that the defendant can establish arose out of the same transaction and whose recognition in this manner is not contrary to public policy.

(d) The losses deemed to be legally caused by a knowing violation of a standard of conduct set forth in Part V include the costs and expenses to which the corporation was subjected as a result of the violation, including the counsel fees and expenses of a successful plaintiff in a derivative action, except to the extent the court determines that inclusion of some or all of such costs and expenses would be inequitable in the circumstances.

(e) The court having jurisdiction over a derivative action may direct that all or a portion of the award be paid directly to individual shareholders, on a pro-rata basis, when such a payment is equitable in the circumstances and adequate provision has been made for the creditors of the corporation.

§ 7.19 Limitation on Damages for Certain Violations of the Duty of Care

Except as otherwise provided by statute, if a failure by a director [§ 1.13] or an officer [§ 1.27] to meet the standard of conduct specified in Part IV (Duty of Care and the Business Judgment Rule) did not either:

> (1) Involve a knowing and culpable violation of law by the director or officer;

> (2) Show a conscious disregard for the duty of the director or officer to the corporation under circumstances in which the director or officer was aware that the conduct or omission created an unjustified risk of serious injury to the corporation; or

> (3) Constitute a sustained and unexcused pattern of inattention that amounted to an abdication of the defendant's duty to the corporation;

and the director or officer, or an associate [§ 1.03], did not receive a benefit that was improper under Part V (Duty of Fair Dealing), then a provision in a certificate of incorporation that limits damages against an officer or a director for such failure to an amount not less than such person's annual compensation from the corporation should be given effect, if the provision is adopted by a vote of disinterested shareholders [§ 1.16] after disclosure [§ 1.14(b)] concerning the provision, may be repealed by the shareholders at any annual meeting without prior action by the board, and does not reduce liability with respect to pending actions or losses incurred prior to its adoption.

Chapter 3

INDEMNIFICATION AND INSURANCE

§ 7.20 Indemnification and Insurance

(a) *General Rule.* Subject to the limitations set forth in Subsection (b):

> (1) A corporation should have the power to indemnify a person who is or was a director [§ 1.13] or officer [§ 1.27] for liabilities and reasonable expenses incurred in connection with any threatened, pending, or completed action, suit, or other proceeding, formal or informal, whether civil, criminal, administrative, or investigative, to which the director or officer is or may be made a party or in connection with which the director or officer is or may be otherwise required to appear:

(A) Because such person was acting in his or her capacity as a director or officer of the corporation, or acting in some capacity on behalf of a third party at the request of the corporation, if such person was acting in good faith or otherwise engaged in good faith conduct in such capacity, or

(B) Solely because of the fact that such person is or was a director or officer.

(2) A corporation should have the power to pay expenses incurred by a person who is or was a director or officer in connection with a proceeding described in Subsection (a)(1) in advance of the final disposition of such proceeding, upon receipt of an undertaking by or on behalf of the director or officer to repay such expenses, if it is ultimately determined that the person is not entitled to be indemnified by the corporation.

(3) A corporation should be obligated to indemnify a person who is or was a director or officer for liabilities and reasonable expenses incurred in connection with a proceeding described in Subsection (a)(1) if:

(A) the director or officer was wholly successful, on the merits or otherwise, in the defense of such proceeding, or

(B) the corporation properly obligates itself to so indemnify the director or officer, to the extent permitted by this Section, by a provision in its charter documents or by contract.

(4) A corporation should have the power to purchase insurance on behalf of a person who is or was a director or officer against liability asserted against or expenses incurred by the person in connection with a proceeding described in Subsection (a)(1), whether or not the corporation would have the power to indemnify the person against the same liability or expenses.

(b) *Limitations on Indemnification and Insurance*

(1) A corporation should not have the power or be obligated to indemnify a director or officer for liabilities and reasonable expenses incurred in connection with a proceeding described in Subsection (a)(1):

(A) If the conduct for which indemnification is sought directly involved a knowing and culpable violation of law or a significant pecuniary benefit was obtained to which the director or officer was not legally entitled;

(B) To the extent that the indemnification would involve any amount paid in satisfaction of a fine, civil penalty, or similar judgment as a result of violation of statutory law, the policy of which clearly precludes indemnification;

(C) If the indemnification would involve any amount paid in settlement of the proceeding and the conduct directly involved a violation of statutory law, the policy of which clearly precludes indemnification; or

(D) To the extent that the indemnification would involve amounts paid (i) in satisfaction of a judgment or in settlement of an action that was brought by or in the right of the corporation, or (ii) for expenses incurred in any such proceeding in which the director or officer was adjudged liable to the corporation, except as provided in Subsection (c).

In the absence of a judicial determination, the applicability of Subsection (b)(1) may be determined by disinterested directors, disinterested shareholders, or independent counsel, but if a determination so made is adverse to the director or officer, the director or officer should have standing to seek a de novo court determination thereof.

(2) A corporation should not be entitled to purchase insurance pursuant to Subsection (a)(4), to the extent that the insurance would furnish protection against liability for conduct directly involving a knowing and culpable violation of law or involving a significant pecuniary benefit obtained by an insured person to which the person is not legally entitled.

(c) *Court–Ordered Indemnification*

(1) A court should order the payment of indemnification in the circumstances described in Subsection (a)(3) and should also order the corporation to pay the reasonable expenses incurred by the director or officer in successfully obtaining court-ordered indemnification.

(2) A court may order the indemnification of amounts paid in settlement of an action brought by or in the right of the corporation (other than amounts paid in settlement of an action in which the court determines that there was a substantial likelihood that the director or officer received a significant pecuniary benefit to which the director or officer was not legally entitled), or for expenses in any proceeding referred to in Subsection (b)(1)(A) or (D), if it determines that indemnification is fair and reasonable, in whole or in part, in view of all the circumstances.

(d) *Report to Shareholders Concerning Indemnification in Derivative Actions.* If a corporation indemnifies or advances expenses to a director or officer in connection with a proceeding by or in the right of the corporation, the corporation should report the indemnification or advance to the shareholders at or before the time notice of the next shareholders' meeting is sent.

(e) *Nonexclusivity of Indemnification Provisions.* Subject to the limitations set forth in Subsection (b): (1) a corporation should have the power to provide indemnification and the payment of expenses under a standard of the corporation [§ 1.36], agreement, or otherwise, and (2) this Section should not be deemed exclusive of any other rights to which a director or officer seeking indemnification or the payment of expenses may be entitled.

(f) *Legal Successors.* The power or obligation to indemnify or pay expenses under this section shall extend to executors, administrators, trustees, and other successors in interest of directors and officers against whom liabilities are threatened or asserted.

Chapter 4

THE APPRAISAL REMEDY

§ 7.21 Corporate Transactions Giving Rise to Appraisal Rights

An eligible holder [§ 1.17] of the corporation [§ 1.12(b)] should be entitled on demand to be paid in cash the fair value of the shares owned by the eligible holder as provided in §§ 7.22 (Standards for Determining Fair Value) and 7.23 (Procedural Standards) in the event of:

(a) A merger, a consolidation, a mandatory share exchange, or an exchange by the corporation of its stock for substantial assets or equity securities [§ 1.20] of another corporation (hereinafter collectively referred to as a "business combination"), whether effected directly or by means of a subsidiary, unless those persons who were shareholders of the corporation immediately before the combination own 60 percent or more of the total voting power of the surviving or issuing corporation immediately thereafter, in approximately the same proportions (in relation to the other preexisting shareholders) as before the combination;

(b) Any business combination, amendment of the corporation's charter documents [§ 1.05], or other corporate act or transaction that has the effect of involuntarily eliminating the eligible holder's equity interest [§ 1.19] (other than the elimination of less than a round lot in a publicly traded corporation or a similar elimination of a comparably insignificant interest in a non-publicly traded corporation);

(c) A sale, lease, exchange, or other disposition of substantial assets by the corporation that

(1) Falls within § 5.15(a) (Transfer of Control in Which a Director or Principal Senior Executive Is Interested) and the assets so disposed of would account for a majority of the corporation's earnings or total assets [§ 1.37] as of the end of its most recent fiscal year, unless (A) the procedures specified in § 5.15(b)(1)–(3) are complied with, and (B) at least one class of equity securities [§ 1.20]

of the corporation is listed on a national securities exchange or is included within NASDAQ's National Market System; or

(2) Leaves the corporation without a significant continuing business, unless the sale (A) is in the ordinary course of business, or (B) is for cash or for cash equivalents that are to be liquidated for cash or used to satisfy corporate obligations, and is pursuant to a plan of complete dissolution by which all or substantially all of the net assets will be distributed to the shareholders within one year after the date of such transaction;

(d) An amendment of the charter documents [§ 1.05], whether accomplished directly or through a merger or consolidation, whose effect is to (1) materially and adversely alter or abolish a preferential, preemptive, redemption, or conversion right applicable to the eligible holder's shares, (2) reduce the number of shares owned by the eligible holder (other than a holder of less than a round lot in a publicly traded corporation or a similar holder of a comparably insignificant interest in a non-publicly traded corporation) to a fraction of a share or less, (3) create a right to redeem the eligible holder's shares, or (4) exclude or limit the voting rights of shares with respect to any matter, other than simply through the authorization of new shares of an existing or new class or the elimination of cumulative voting rights; or

(e) Any corporate action as to which the charter documents, other than the bylaws, provide that eligible holders have applicable appraisal rights.

§ 7.22   Standards for Determining Fair Value

(a) The fair value of shares under § 7.21 (Corporate Transactions Giving Rise to Appraisal Rights) should be the value of the eligible holder's [§ 1.17] proportionate interest in the corporation, without any discount for minority status or, absent extraordinary circumstances, lack of marketability. Subject to Subsections (b) and (c), fair value should be determined using the customary valuation concepts and techniques generally employed in the relevant securities and financial markets for similar businesses in the context of the transaction giving rise to appraisal.

(b) In the case of a business combination that gives rise to appraisal rights, but does not fall within § 5.10 (Transactions by a Controlling Shareholder with the Corporation), § 5.15 (Transfer of Control in Which a Director or Principal Senior Executive Is Interested), or § 7.25 (Transactions in Control Involving Corporate Combinations to Which a Majority Shareholder Is a Party), the aggregate price accepted by the board of directors of the subject corporation should be presumed to represent the fair value of the corporation, or of the assets sold in the case of an asset sale, unless the plaintiff can prove otherwise by clear and convincing evidence.

(c) If the transaction giving rise to appraisal falls within § 5.10, § 5.15, or § 7.25, the court generally should give substantial weight to the highest realistic price that a willing, able, and fully informed buyer would pay for the corporation as an entirety. In determining what such a buyer would pay, the court may include a proportionate share of any gain reasonably to be expected to result from the combination, unless special circumstances would make such an allocation unreasonable.

§ 7.23 Procedural Standards

(a) *Notice.* A corporation that proposes to engage in a transaction giving rise to appraisal rights under § 7.21 (Corporate Transactions Giving Rise to Appraisal Rights) should:

(i) Notify each record holder [§ 1.32] as of the record date set for the shareholder vote, and attempt in good faith to notify each other beneficial holder [§ 1.22] of shares as of such date who is known to it, of the right to exercise appraisal reasonably in advance of the date on which the transaction is to be voted upon by the shareholders, or, if no shareholder vote is required, the date on which the corporate action giving rise to appraisal is to be taken;

(ii) Describe the method for exercising the right, including the procedures in § 7.23(f);

(iii) Disclose the material facts [§ 1.25] concerning the transaction or other action and furnish copies of the corporation's financial statements; and

(iv) Provide a reasonable means by which eligible holders [§ 1.17] can easily and effectively indicate their election to dissent.

(b) *Shareholder Response.* To perfect a right to dissent, an eligible holder should be required only to utilize the means provided for under § 7.23(a)(iv), or otherwise deliver a written instrument expressing an election to dissent, at or before the shareholders' meeting, or, if no shareholder vote is to be taken, on or before the day preceding the date on which the corporate action giving rise to the right to appraisal is to be taken; provided, however, that eligible holders should have a reasonable period in which to elect to dissent from the time notice is first sent by the corporation pursuant to § 7.23(a)(i). Any eligible holder who so responds should be deemed a "dissenting holder" for purposes of § 7.23. If notice is not given as required under § 7.23(a), any eligible holder may initiate an appraisal proceeding without taking any other action.

(c) *Mandatory Prepayment.* Promptly after the transaction that gives rise to appraisal under § 7.21 is consummated and upon the tender of the dissenting holder's shares to the corporation's transfer agent for the notation of an appropriate legend to reflect the payment required under this § 7.23(c), the corporation should pay to such dissenting holder the amount in cash that it reasonably estimates to be the fair value of the shares plus any interest due. Acceptance of such prepayment shall not constitute a waiver of the dissenting holder's rights under § 7.21.

(d) *Costs and Expenses.* If payment of the amount required under § 7.23(c) is not made within *30* days after the later of the date on which the transaction is consummated or the date on which shares are tendered under § 7.23(c), or if the amount so paid is materially less than the amount ultimately determined by the court to constitute fair value, the corporation should be required to pay all costs and expenses of the appraisal proceeding, including such dissenting holder's reasonable attorney's and experts' fees. In all other circumstances, the costs and expenses of the action shall be assessed or apportioned as the court deems equitable, except that the corporation's attorney's fees may be assessed or apportioned against a shareholder only where the court finds the shareholder's action to have been arbitrary, vexatious, or not in good faith.

(e) *Interest.* Interest on the amount awarded by the court (less the amount of prepayment) should be paid at the time of the payment of the award and should be computed from the time the relevant transaction is consummated at an appropriate market rate for the corporation.

(f) *Consolidation.* If there are any dissenting holders, the corporation should commence a consolidated proceeding in the state of incorporation under § 7.21 to fix fair value and determine eligibility to dissent. All dissenting holders should be made parties to the action. If such a consolidated action is not commenced by the corporation within a reasonable time after consummation of the transaction that gives rise to the appraisal right, it may be commenced by any dissenting holder. The court may appoint a lead counsel or steering committee to coordinate discovery and the trial of the proceeding and to represent any dissenting holders who have not secured other counsel. The court should also require the corporation to provide it with the names and addresses of all dissenting holders known to the corporation, and, subject to appropriate restrictions, such list should be available for inspection by dissenting holders or their agents.

§ 7.24 Transactions in Control Involving Corporate Combinations in Which Directors, Principal Senior Executives, and Controlling Shareholders Are Not Interested

(a) An appraisal proceeding is the exclusive remedy of an eligible holder [§ 1.17] to challenge a transaction in control [§ 1.38] involving a corporate combination that requires shareholder approval and is not subject to § 5.10 (Transactions by a Controlling Shareholder with the Corporation), § 5.15 (Transfer of Control in Which a Director or Principal Senior Executive Is Interested), or § 7.25 (Transactions in Control

Involving Corporate Combinations to Which a Majority Shareholder Is a Party), if:

(1) Disclosure concerning the transaction [§ 1.14(b)] is made to the shareholders who are entitled to authorize the transaction;

(2) The transaction is approved pursuant to, and is otherwise in accordance with, applicable provisions of law and the corporation's charter documents [§ 1.05]; and

(3) Eligible holders who are entitled to but do not vote to approve the transaction are entitled to an appraisal remedy reflecting the general principles embodied in §§ 7.22 (Standards for Determining Fair Value) and 7.23 (Procedural Standards).

(b) A party who challenges a transaction subject to this Section has the burden of proving failure to comply with Subsections (a)(1)–(3).

(c) If Subsections (a)(1) and (a)(2) are satisfied, but Subsection (a)(3) is not, the transaction may be challenged on the ground that it constituted a waste of corporate assets [§ 1.42].

(d) The availability of an appraisal remedy does not preclude a proceeding against a director, officer, controlling shareholder, or an associate of any of the foregoing, for a violation of Part V (Duty of Fair Dealing).

§ 7.25 Transactions in Control Involving Corporate Combinations to Which a Majority Shareholder Is a Party

(a) An appraisal proceeding is the exclusive remedy of an eligible holder [§ 1.17] to challenge a transaction in control [§ 1.38] involving a corporate combination to which a shareholder who holds sufficient voting shares of a corporation to approve the corporate combination under the law of the relevant jurisdiction, or its associate [§ 1.03], is a party if:

(1) The directors who approve the transaction on behalf of the corporation (or the directors of the shareholder if the directors of the corporation are not required by law to approve the transaction) have an adequate basis, grounded on substantial objective evidence, for believing that the consideration offered to the minority shareholders in the transaction constitutes fair value for their shares, as determined in accordance with the standards provided in § 7.22 (Standards for Determining Fair Value);

(2) Disclosure concerning the transaction [§ 1.14(b)] (including representations of the directors' belief with respect to the fair value of minority shares and the basis for such belief) and the conflict of interest [§ 1.14(a)] is made to the minority shareholders, as contemplated by § 7.23(a);

(3) The transaction is approved pursuant to, and is otherwise in accordance with, applicable provisions of law and the corporation's charter documents [§ 1.05]; and

(4) Holders of equity securities who do not vote to approve the transaction are entitled to an appraisal remedy reflecting the general principles embodied in §§ 7.22 (Standards for Determining Fair Value) and 7.23 (Procedural Standards).

(b) A party who challenges a transaction that is subject to this Section has the burden of proving a failure to comply with Subsections (a)(1)–(4) if the transaction was authorized in advance by disinterested directors [§ 1.15] and authorized in advance or ratified by disinterested shareholders [§ 1.16], following the disclosure set forth in Subsection (a)(2); otherwise, the burden is on the majority shareholder to prove compliance with Subsections (a)(1)–(4).

(c) If Subsections (a)(1)–(3) are satisfied but Subsection (a)(4) is not, then:

(1) If the transaction was approved by disinterested shareholders following the disclosure required by Subsection (a)(2), it may be challenged on the ground that it was not fair, with the burden on the challenging party to prove that the transaction was unfair to the minority shareholders; and

(2) If the transaction was not so approved, it may be challenged on the ground that it was not fair, with the burden on the majority shareholder to prove that the transaction was fair to the minority shareholders.

(d) The exclusivity provisions of this Section are not applicable to closely held corporations [§ 1.06].

OECD PRINCIPLES OF CORPORATE GOVERNANCE*

2004

ORGANIZATION FOR ECONOMIC CO–OPERATION AND DEVELOPMENT

Pursuant to Article 1 of the Convention signed in Paris on 14th December 1960, and which came into force on 30th September 1961, the Organization for Economic Co-operation and Development (OECD) shall promote policies designed:

—to achieve the highest sustainable economic growth and employment and a rising standard of living in member countries, while maintaining financial stability, and thus to contribute to the development of the world economy;

—to contribute to sound economic expansion in member as well as non-member countries in the process of economic development; and

—to contribute to the expansion of world trade on a multilateral, non-discriminatory basis in accordance with international obligations.

The original member countries of the OECD are Austria, Belgium, Canada, Denmark, France, Germany, Greece, Iceland, Ireland, Italy, Luxembourg, the Netherlands, Norway, Portugal, Spain, Sweden, Switzerland, Turkey, the United Kingdom and the United States. The following countries became members subsequently through accession at the dates indicated hereafter: Japan (28th April 1964), Finland (28th January 1969), Australia (7th June 1971), New Zealand (29th May 1973), Mexico (18th May 1994), the Czech Republic (21st December 1995), Hungary (7th May 1996), Poland (22nd November 1996), Korea (12th December 1996) and the Slovak Republic (14th December 2000). The Commission of the European Communities takes part in the work of the OECD (Article 13 of the OECD Convention).

Foreword

The *OECD Principles of Corporate Governance* were endorsed by OECD Ministers in 1999 and have since become an international benchmark for policy makers, investors, corporations and other stakeholders worldwide. They have advanced the corporate governance agenda and

* OECD Principles of Corporate Governance—2004 Edition, © OECD 2004. For ease of reading, where the English and American spelling of words used in the OECD Principles differ, American spellings have been submitted for the English spellings. For example, "recognize" has been substituted for "recognise" and "safe harbor" has been substituted for "safe harbour." (Footnote by ed.)

provided specific guidance for legislative and regulatory initiatives in both OECD and non OECD countries. The Financial Stability Forum has designated the *Principles* as one of the 12 key standards for sound financial systems. The *Principles* also provide the basis for an extensive programme of cooperation between OECD and non-OECD countries and underpin the corporate governance component of World Bank/IMF Reports on the Observance of Standards and Codes (ROSC).

The *Principles* have now been thoroughly reviewed to take account of recent developments and experiences in OECD member and non-member countries. Policy makers are now more aware of the contribution good corporate governance makes to financial market stability, investment and economic growth. Companies better understand how good corporate governance contributes to their competitiveness. Investors—especially collective investment institutions and pension funds acting in a fiduciary capacity—realize they have a role to play in ensuring good corporate governance practices, thereby underpinning the value of their investments. In today's economies, interest in corporate governance goes beyond that of shareholders in the performance of individual companies. As companies play a pivotal role in our economies and we rely increasingly on private sector institutions to manage personal savings and secure retirement incomes, good corporate governance is important to broad and growing segments of the population.

The review of the *Principles* was undertaken by the OECD Steering Group on Corporate Governance under a mandate from OECD Ministers in 2002. The review was supported by a comprehensive survey of how member countries addressed the different corporate governance challenges they faced. It also drew on experiences in economies outside the OECD area where the OECD, in co-operation with the World Bank and other sponsors, organizes Regional Corporate Governance Roundtables to support regional reform efforts.

The review process benefited from contributions from many parties. Key international institutions participated and extensive consultations were held with the private sector, labour, civil society and representatives from non-OECD countries. The process also benefited greatly from the insights of internationally recognized experts who participated in two high level informal gatherings I convened. Finally, many constructive suggestions were received when a draft of the *Principles* was made available for public comment on the internet.

The *Principles* are a living instrument offering non-binding standards and good practices as well as guidance on implementation, which can be adapted to the specific circumstances of individual countries and regions. The OECD offers a forum for ongoing dialogue and exchange of experiences among member and non-member countries. To stay abreast of constantly changing circumstances, the OECD will closely follow developments in corporate governance, identifying trends and seeking remedies to new challenges.

These *Revised Principles* will further reinforce OECD's contribution and commitment to collective efforts to strengthen the fabric of corporate governance around the world in the years ahead. This work will not eradicate criminal activity, but such activity will be made more difficult as rules and regulations are adopted in accordance with the *Principles*.

Importantly, our efforts will also help develop a culture of values for professional and ethical behavior on which well functioning markets depend. Trust and integrity play an essential role in economic life and for the sake of business and future prosperity we have to make sure that they are properly rewarded.

Donald J. Johnston OECD Secretary–General

Table of Contents

Part One

The OECD Principles of Corporate Governance

Part Two

Annotations to the OECD Principles of Corporate Governance

PART ONE

THE OECD PRINCIPLES OF CORPORATE GOVERNANCE

I. Ensuring the Basis for an Effective Corporate Governance Framework

The corporate governance framework should promote transparent and efficient markets, be consistent with the rule of law and clearly articulate the division of responsibilities among different supervisory, regulatory and enforcement authorities.

A. The corporate governance framework should be developed with a view to its impact on overall economic performance, market integrity and the incentives it creates for market participants and the promotion of transparent and efficient markets.

B. The legal and regulatory requirements that affect corporate governance practices in a jurisdiction should be consistent with the rule of law, transparent and enforceable.

C. The division of responsibilities among different authorities in a jurisdiction should be clearly articulated and ensure that the public interest is served.

D. Supervisory, regulatory and enforcement authorities should have the authority, integrity and resources to fulfil their duties in a professional and objective manner. Moreover, their rulings should be timely, transparent and fully explained.

II. *The Rights of Shareholders and Key Ownership Functions*

The corporate governance framework should protect and facilitate the exercise of shareholders' rights.

A. Basic shareholder rights should include the right to: 1) secure methods of ownership registration; 2) convey or transfer shares; 3) obtain relevant and material information on the corporation on a timely and regular basis; 4) participate and vote in general shareholder meetings; 5) elect and remove members of the board; and 6) share in the profits of the corporation.

B. Shareholders should have the right to participate in, and to be sufficiently informed on, decisions concerning fundamental corporate changes such as: 1) amendments to the statutes, or articles of incorporation or similar governing documents of the company; 2) the authorization of additional shares; and 3) extraordinary transactions, including the transfer of all or substantially all assets, that in effect result in the sale of the company.

C. Shareholders should have the opportunity to participate effectively and vote in general shareholder meetings and should be informed of the rules, including voting procedures, that govern general shareholder meetings:

1. Shareholders should be furnished with sufficient and timely information concerning the date, location and agenda of general meetings, as well as full and timely information regarding the issues to be decided at the meeting.

2. Shareholders should have the opportunity to ask questions to the board, including questions relating to the annual external audit, to place items on the agenda of general meetings, and to propose resolutions, subject to reasonable limitations.

3. Effective shareholder participation in key corporate governance decisions, such as the nomination and election of board members, should be facilitated. Shareholders should be able to make their views known on the remuneration policy for board members and key executives. The equity component of compensation schemes for board members and employees should be subject to shareholder approval.

4. Shareholders should be able to vote in person or in absentia, and equal effect should be given to votes whether cast in person or in absentia.

D. Capital structures and arrangements that enable certain shareholders to obtain a degree of control disproportionate to their equity ownership should be disclosed.

E. Markets for corporate control should be allowed to function in an efficient and transparent manner.

1. The rules and procedures governing the acquisition of corporate control in the capital markets, and extraordinary transactions such as mergers, and sales of substantial portions of corporate assets, should be clearly articulated and disclosed so that investors understand their rights and recourse. Transactions should occur at transparent prices and under fair conditions that protect the rights of all shareholders according to their class.

2. Anti-take-over devices should not be used to shield management and the board from accountability.

F. The exercise of ownership rights by all shareholders, including institutional investors, should be facilitated.

1. Institutional investors acting in a fiduciary capacity should disclose their overall corporate governance and voting policies with respect to their investments, including the procedures that they have in place for deciding on the use of their voting rights.

2. Institutional investors acting in a fiduciary capacity should disclose how they manage material conflicts of interest that may affect the exercise of key ownership rights regarding their investments.

G. Shareholders, including institutional shareholders, should be allowed to consult with each other on issues concerning their basic shareholder rights as defined in the Principles, subject to exceptions to prevent abuse.

III. The Equitable Treatment of Shareholders

The corporate governance framework should ensure the equitable treatment of all shareholders, including minority and foreign shareholders. All shareholders should have the opportunity to obtain effective redress for violation of their rights.

A. All shareholders of the same series of a class should be treated equally.

   1. Within any series of a class, all shares should carry the same rights. All investors should be able to obtain information about the rights attached to all series and classes of shares before they purchase. Any changes in voting rights should be subject to approval by those classes of shares which are negatively affected.

   2. Minority shareholders should be protected from abusive actions by, or in the interest of, controlling shareholders acting either directly or indirectly, and should have effective means of redress.

   3. Votes should be cast by custodians or nominees in a manner agreed upon with the beneficial owner of the shares.

   4. Impediments to cross border voting should be eliminated.

   5. Processes and procedures for general shareholder meetings should allow for equitable treatment of all shareholders. Company procedures should not make it unduly difficult or expensive to cast votes.

B. Insider trading and abusive self-dealing should be prohibited.

C. Members of the board and key executives should be required to disclose to the board whether they, directly, indirectly or on behalf of third parties, have a material interest in any transaction or matter directly affecting the corporation.

IV. *The Role of Stakeholders in Corporate Governance*

The corporate governance framework should recognize the rights of stakeholders established by law or through mutual agreements and encourage active co-operation between corporations and stakeholders in creating wealth, jobs, and the sustainability of financially sound enterprises.

A. The rights of stakeholders that are established by law or through mutual agreements are to be respected.

B. Where stakeholder interests are protected by law, stakeholders should have the opportunity to obtain effective redress for violation of their rights.

C. Performance-enhancing mechanisms for employee participation should be permitted to develop.

D. Where stakeholders participate in the corporate governance process, they should have access to relevant, sufficient and reliable information on a timely and regular basis.

E. Stakeholders, including individual employees and their representative bodies, should be able to freely communicate their concerns about illegal or unethical practices to the board and their rights should not be compromised for doing this.

F. The corporate governance framework should be complemented by an effective, efficient insolvency framework and by effective enforcement of creditor rights.

V. *Disclosure and Transparency*

The corporate governance framework should ensure that timely and accurate disclosure is made on all material matters regarding the corporation, including the financial situation, performance, ownership, and governance of the company.

A. Disclosure should include, but not be limited to, material information on:

1. The financial and operating results of the company.

2. Company objectives.

3. Major share ownership and voting rights.

4. Remuneration policy for members of the board and key executives, and information about board members, including their qualifications, the selection process, other company directorships and whether they are regarded as independent by the board.

5. Related party transactions.

6. Foreseeable risk factors.

7. Issues regarding employees and other stakeholders.

8. Governance structures and policies, in particular, the content of any corporate governance code or policy and the process by which it is implemented.

B. Information should be prepared and disclosed in accordance with high quality standards of accounting and financial and non-financial disclosure.

C. An annual audit should be conducted by an independent, competent and qualified, auditor in order to provide an external and objective assurance to the board and shareholders that the financial statements fairly represent the financial position and performance of the company in all material respects.

D. External auditors should be accountable to the shareholders and owe a duty to the company to exercise due professional care in the conduct of the audit.

E. Channels for disseminating information should provide for equal, timely and cost efficient access to relevant information by users.

F. The corporate governance framework should be complemented by an effective approach that addresses and promotes the provision of analysis or advice by analysts, brokers, rating agencies and others, that is relevant to decisions by investors, free from material conflicts of interest that might compromise the integrity of their analysis or advice.

VI. *The Responsibilities of the Board*

The corporate governance framework should ensure the strategic guidance of the company, the effective monitoring of management by the board, and the board's accountability to the company and the shareholders.

A.   Board members should act on a fully informed basis, in good faith, with due diligence and care, and in the best interest of the company and the shareholders.

B.   Where board decisions may affect different shareholder groups differently, the board should treat all shareholders fairly.

C.   The board should apply high ethical standards. It should take into account the interests of stakeholders.

D.   The board should fulfil certain key functions, including:

1.   Reviewing and guiding corporate strategy, major plans of action, risk policy, annual budgets and business plans; setting performance objectives; monitoring implementation and corporate performance; and overseeing major capital expenditures, acquisitions and divestitures.

2.   Monitoring the effectiveness of the company's governance practices and making changes as needed.

3.   Selecting, compensating, monitoring and, when necessary, replacing key executives and overseeing succession planning.

4.   Aligning key executive and board remuneration with the longer term interests of the company and its shareholders.

5.   Ensuring a formal and transparent board nomination and election process.

6.   Monitoring and managing potential conflicts of interest of management, board members and shareholders, including misuse of corporate assets and abuse in related party transactions.

7.   Ensuring the integrity of the corporation's accounting and financial reporting systems, including the independent audit, and that appropriate systems of control are in place, in particular, systems for risk management, financial and operational control, and compliance with the law and relevant standards.

8.   Overseeing the process of disclosure and communications.

E.   The board should be able to exercise objective independent judgement on corporate affairs.

1. Boards should consider assigning a sufficient number of non-executive board members capable of exercising independent judgement to tasks where there is a potential for conflict of interest. Examples of such key responsibilities are ensuring the integrity of financial and non-financial reporting, the review of related party transactions, nomination of board members and key executives, and board remuneration.

2. When committees of the board are established, their mandate, composition and working procedures should be well defined and disclosed by the board.

3. Board members should be able to commit themselves effectively to their responsibilities.

F. In order to fulfil their responsibilities, board members should have access to accurate, relevant and timely information.

PART TWO

ANNOTATIONS TO THE OECD PRINCIPLES OF CORPORATE GOVERNANCE

I. *Ensuring the Basis for an Effective Corporate Governance Framework*

The corporate governance framework should promote transparent and efficient markets, be consistent with the rule of law and clearly articulate the division of responsibilities among different supervisory, regulatory and enforcement authorities.

To ensure an effective corporate governance framework, it is necessary that an appropriate and effective legal, regulatory and institutional foundation is established upon which all market participants can rely in establishing their private contractual relations. This corporate governance framework typically comprises elements of legislation, regulation, self regulatory arrangements, voluntary commitments and business practices that are the result of a country's specific circumstances, history and tradition. The desirable mix between legislation, regulation, self-regulation, voluntary standards, etc. in this area will therefore vary from country to country. As new experiences accrue and business circumstances change, the content and structure of this framework might need to be adjusted.

Countries seeking to implement the Principles should monitor their corporate governance framework, including regulatory and listing requirements and business practices, with the objective of maintaining and strengthening its contribution to market integrity and economic performance. As part of this, it is important to take into account the interactions and complementarity between different elements of the corporate governance framework and its overall ability to promote ethical, responsible and transparent corporate governance practices. Such analysis should be viewed as an important tool in the process of developing an effective corporate governance framework. To this end, effective and continuous consultation with the public is an essential element that is widely regarded as good practice. Moreover, in developing a corporate governance framework in each jurisdiction, national legislators and regulators should duly consider the need for, and the results from, effective international dialogue and cooperation. If these conditions are met, the governance system is more likely to avoid over-regulation, support the exercise of entrepreneurship and limit the risks of damaging conflicts of interest in both the private sector and in public institutions.

A. The corporate governance framework should be developed with a view to its impact on overall economic performance, market integrity and the incentives it creates for market participants and the promotion of transparent and efficient markets.

The corporate form of organization of economic activity is a powerful force for growth. The regulatory and legal environment within which corporations operate is therefore of key importance to overall economic outcomes. Policy makers have a responsibility to put in place a framework that is flexible enough to meet the needs of corporations operating in widely different circumstances, facilitating their development of new opportunities to create value and to determine the most efficient deployment of resources. To achieve this goal, policy makers should remain focused on ultimate economic outcomes and when considering policy options, they will need to undertake an analysis of the impact on key variables that affect the functioning of markets, such as incentive structures, the efficiency of self-regulatory systems and dealing with systemic conflicts of interest. Transparent and efficient markets serve to discipline market participants and to promote accountability.

B. The legal and regulatory requirements that affect corporate governance practices in a jurisdiction should be consistent with the rule of law, transparent and enforceable.

If new laws and regulations are needed, such as to deal with clear cases of market imperfections, they should be designed in a way that makes them possible to implement and enforce in an efficient and even handed manner covering all parties. Consultation by government and other regulatory authorities with corporations, their representative organizations and other stakeholders, is an effective way of doing this. Mechanisms should also be established for parties to protect their rights. In order to avoid over-regulation, unenforceable laws, and unintended consequences that may impede or distort business dynamics, policy measures should be designed with a view to their overall costs and benefits. Such assessments should take into account the need for effective enforcement, including the ability of authorities to deter dishonest behavior and to impose effective sanctions for violations.

Corporate governance objectives are also formulated in voluntary codes and standards that do not have the status of law or regulation. While such codes play an important role in improving corporate governance arrangements, they might leave shareholders and other stakeholders with uncertainty concerning their status and implementation. When codes and principles are used as a national standard or as an explicit substitute for legal or regulatory provisions, market credibility requires that their status in terms of coverage, implementation, compliance and sanctions is clearly specified.

C. **The division of responsibilities among different authorities in a jurisdiction should be clearly articulated and ensure that the public interest is served.**

Corporate governance requirements and practices are typically influenced by an array of legal domains, such as company law, securities regulation, accounting and auditing standards, insolvency law, contract law, labor law and tax law. Under these circumstances, there is a risk that the variety of legal influences may cause unintentional overlaps and even conflicts, which may frustrate the ability to pursue key corporate governance objectives. It is important that policy-makers are aware of this risk and take measures to limit it. Effective enforcement also requires that the allocation of responsibilities for supervision, implementation and enforcement among different authorities is clearly defined so that the competencies of complementary bodies and agencies are respected and used most effectively. Overlapping and perhaps contradictory regulations between national jurisdictions is also an issue that should be monitored so that no regulatory vacuum is allowed to develop (i.e. issues slipping through in which no authority has explicit responsibility) and to minimize the cost of compliance with multiple systems by corporations.

When regulatory responsibilities or oversight are delegated to non-public bodies, it is desirable to explicitly assess why, and under what circumstances, such delegation is desirable. It is also essential that the governance structure of any such delegated institution be transparent and encompass the public interest.

D. **Supervisory, regulatory and enforcement authorities should have the authority, integrity and resources to fulfil their duties in a professional and objective manner. Moreover, their rulings should be timely, transparent and fully explained.**

Regulatory responsibilities should be vested with bodies that can pursue their functions without conflicts of interest and that are subject to judicial review. As the number of public companies, corporate events and the volume of disclosures increase, the resources of supervisory, regulatory and enforcement authorities may come under strain. As a result, in order to follow developments, they will have a significant demand for fully qualified staff to provide effective oversight and investigative capacity which will need to be appropriately funded. The ability to attract staff on competitive terms will enhance the quality and independence of supervision and enforcement.

II. *The Rights of Shareholders and Key Ownership Functions*

The corporate governance framework should protect and facilitate the exercise of shareholders' rights.

Equity investors have certain property rights. For example, an equity share in a publicly traded company can be bought, sold, or transferred. An equity share also entitles the investor to participate in the profits of the corporation, with liability limited to the amount of the investment. In addition, ownership of an equity share provides a right to information about the corporation and a right to influence the corporation, primarily by participation in general shareholder meetings and by voting.

As a practical matter, however, the corporation cannot be managed by shareholder referendum. The shareholding body is made up of individuals and institutions whose interests, goals, investment horizons and capabilities vary. Moreover, the corporation's management must be able to take business decisions rapidly. In light of these realities and the complexity of managing the corporation's affairs in fast moving and ever changing markets, shareholders are not expected to assume responsibility for managing corporate activities. The responsibility for corporate strategy and operations is typically placed in the hands of the board and a management team that is selected, motivated and, when necessary, replaced by the board.

Shareholders' rights to influence the corporation center on certain fundamental issues, such as the election of board members, or other means of influencing the composition of the board, amendments to the company's organic documents, approval of extraordinary transactions, and other basic issues as specified in company law and internal company statutes. This Section can be seen as a statement of the most basic rights of shareholders, which are recognized by law in virtually all OECD countries. Additional rights such as the approval or election of auditors, direct nomination of board members, the ability to pledge shares, the approval of distributions of profits, etc., can be found in various jurisdictions.

A. Basic shareholder rights should include the right to: 1) secure methods of ownership registration; 2) convey or

transfer shares; 3) obtain relevant and material information on the corporation on a timely and regular basis; 4) participate and vote in general shareholder meetings; 5) elect and remove members of the board; and 6) share in the profits of the corporation.

B. Shareholders should have the right to participate in, and to be sufficiently informed on, decisions concerning fundamental corporate changes such as: 1) amendments to the statutes, or articles of incorporation or similar governing documents of the company; 2) the authorization of additional shares; and 3) extraordinary transactions, including the transfer of all or substantially all assets, that in effect result in the sale of the company.

The ability of companies to form partnerships and related companies and to transfer operational assets, cash flow rights and other rights and obligations to them is important for business flexibility and for delegating accountability in complex organizations. It also allows a company to divest itself of operational assets and to become only a holding company. However, without appropriate checks and balances such possibilities may also be abused.

C. Shareholders should have the opportunity to participate effectively and vote in general shareholder meetings and should be informed of the rules, including voting procedures, that govern general shareholder meetings:

1. Shareholders should be furnished with sufficient and timely information concerning the date, location and agenda of general meetings, as well as full and timely information regarding the issues to be decided at the meeting.

2. Shareholders should have the opportunity to ask questions to the board, including questions relating to the annual external audit, to place items on the agenda of general meetings, and to propose resolutions, subject to reasonable limitations.

In order to encourage shareholder participation in general meetings, some companies have improved the ability of shareholders to place items on the agenda by simplifying the process of filing amendments and resolutions. Improvements have also been made in order to make it easier for shareholders to submit questions in advance of the general meeting and to obtain replies from management and board members. Shareholders should also be able to ask questions relating to the external audit report. Companies are justified in assuring that abuses of such opportunities do not occur. It is reasonable, for example, to require that in order for shareholder resolutions to be placed on the agenda, they need to be supported by shareholders holding a specified market value or percentage of shares or voting rights.

This threshold should be determined taking into account the degree of ownership concentration, in order to ensure that minority shareholders are not effectively prevented from putting any items on the agenda. Shareholder resolutions that are approved and fall within the competence of the shareholders' meeting should be addressed by the board.

3. **Effective shareholder participation in key corporate governance decisions, such as the nomination and election of board members, should be facilitated. Shareholders should be able to make their views known on the remuneration policy for board members and key executives. The equity component of compensation schemes for board members and employees should be subject to shareholder approval.**

To elect the members of the board is a basic shareholder right. For the election process to be effective, shareholders should be able to participate in the nomination of board members and vote on individual nominees or on different lists of them. To this end, shareholders have access in a number of countries to the company's proxy materials which are sent to shareholders, although sometimes subject to conditions to prevent abuse. With respect to nomination of candidates, boards in many companies have established nomination committees to ensure proper compliance with established nomination procedures and to facilitate and coordinate the search for a balanced and qualified board. It is increasingly regarded as good practice in many countries for independent board members to have a key role on this committee. To further improve the selection process, the Principles also call for full disclosure of the experience and background of candidates for the board and the nomination process, which will allow an informed assessment of the abilities and suitability of each candidate.

The Principles call for the disclosure of remuneration policy by the board. In particular, it is important for shareholders to know the specific link between remuneration and company performance when they assess the capability of the board and the qualities they should seek in nominees for the board. Although board and executive contracts are not an appropriate subject for approval by the general meeting of shareholders, there should be a means by which they can express their views. Several countries have introduced an advisory vote which conveys the strength and tone of shareholder sentiment to the board without endangering employment contracts. In the case of equity-based schemes, their potential to dilute shareholders' capital and to powerfully determine managerial incentives means that they should be approved by shareholders, either for individuals or for the policy of the scheme as a whole. In an increasing number of jurisdictions, any material changes to existing schemes must also be approved.

4. **Shareholders should be able to vote in person or in absentia, and equal effect should be given to votes whether cast in person or in absentia.**

The Principles recommend that voting by proxy be generally accepted. Indeed, it is important to the promotion and protection of shareholder rights that investors can place reliance upon directed proxy voting. The corporate governance framework should ensure that proxies are voted in accordance with the direction of the proxy holder and that disclosure is provided in relation to how undirected proxies will be voted. In those jurisdictions where companies are allowed to obtain proxies, it is important to disclose how the Chairperson of the meeting (as the usual recipient of shareholder proxies obtained by the company) will exercise the voting rights attaching to undirected proxies. Where proxies are held by the board or management for company pension funds and for employee stock ownership plans, the directions for voting should be disclosed.

The objective of facilitating shareholder participation suggests that companies consider favorably the enlarged use of information technology in voting, including secure electronic voting in absentia.

D. **Capital structures and arrangements that enable certain shareholders to obtain a degree of control disproportionate to their equity ownership should be disclosed.**

Some capital structures allow a shareholder to exercise a degree of control over the corporation disproportionate to the shareholders' equity ownership in the company. Pyramid structures, cross shareholdings and shares with limited or multiple voting rights can be used to diminish the capability of noncontrolling shareholders to influence corporate policy.

In addition to ownership relations, other devices can affect control over the corporation. Shareholder agreements are a common means for groups of shareholders, who individually may hold relatively small shares of total equity, to act in concert so as to constitute an effective majority, or at least the largest single block of shareholders. Shareholder agreements usually give those participating in the agreements preferential rights to purchase shares if other parties to the agreement wish to sell. These agreements can also contain provisions that require those accepting the agreement not to sell their shares for a specified time. Shareholder agreements can cover issues such as how the board or the Chairman will be selected. The agreements can also oblige those in the agreement to vote as a block. Some countries have found it necessary to closely monitor such agreements and to limit their duration.

Voting caps limit the number of votes that a shareholder may cast, regardless of the number of shares the shareholder may actually possess. Voting caps therefore redistribute control and may affect the incentives for shareholder participation in shareholder meetings.

Given the capacity of these mechanisms to redistribute the influence of shareholders on company policy, shareholders can reasonably expect that all such capital structures and arrangements be disclosed.

E. Markets for corporate control should be allowed to function in an efficient and transparent manner.

1. **The rules and procedures governing the acquisition of corporate control in the capital markets, and extraordinary transactions such as mergers, and sales of substantial portions of corporate assets, should be clearly articulated and disclosed so that investors understand their rights and recourse. Transactions should occur at transparent prices and under fair conditions that protect the rights of all shareholders according to their class.**

2. **Anti-take-over devices should not be used to shield management and the board from accountability.**

    In some countries, companies employ anti-take-over devices. However, both investors and stock exchanges have expressed concern over the possibility that widespread use of anti-take-over devices may be a serious impediment to the functioning of the market for corporate control. In some instances, take-over defences can simply be devices to shield the management or the board from shareholder monitoring. In implementing any anti-takeover devices and in dealing with take-over proposals, the fiduciary duty of the board to shareholders and the company must remain paramount.

F. The exercise of ownership rights by all shareholders, including institutional investors, should be facilitated.

As investors may pursue different investment objectives, the Principles do not advocate any particular investment strategy and do not seek to prescribe the optimal degree of investor activism. Nevertheless, in considering the costs and benefits of exercising their ownership rights, many investors are likely to conclude that positive financial returns and growth can be obtained by undertaking a reasonable amount of analysis and by using their rights.

1. **Institutional investors acting in a fiduciary capacity should disclose their overall corporate governance and voting policies with respect to their investments, including the procedures that they have in place for deciding on the use of their voting rights.**

    It is increasingly common for shares to be held by institutional investors. The effectiveness and credibility of the entire corporate governance system and company oversight will, therefore, to a large extent depend on institutional investors that can make informed use of their shareholder rights and effectively exercise their ownership functions in companies in which they invest. While this principle does not require institutional investors to vote their shares, it calls for disclosure of how they exercise their ownership rights with due consideration to cost effectiveness. For institutions acting in a fiduciary capacity, such as pension funds, collective investment schemes and some activities of insurance companies, the right to vote can be considered part of the value of the investment being undertaken on behalf of their clients. Failure to exercise the ownership rights could result in a loss to the investor who should therefore be made aware of the policy to be followed by the institutional investors.

    In some countries, the demand for disclosure of corporate governance policies to the market is quite detailed and includes requirements for explicit strategies regarding the circumstances in which the institution will intervene in a company; the approach they will use for such intervention; and how they will assess the effectiveness of the strategy. In several countries institutional investors are either required to disclose their actual voting records or it is regarded as good practice and implemented on an "apply or explain" basis. Disclosure is either to their clients (only with respect to the securities of each client) or, in the case of investment advisors to registered investment companies, to the market, which is a less costly procedure. A complementary approach to participation in shareholders' meetings is to establish a continuing dialogue with portfolio companies. Such a dialogue between institutional investors and companies should be encouraged, especially by lifting unnecessary regulatory barriers, although it is incumbent on the company to treat all investors equally and not to divulge information to the institutional investors which is not at the same time made available to the market. The additional information provided by a company would normally therefore include general background information about the markets in which the company is operating and further elaboration of information already available to the market.

When fiduciary institutional investors have developed and disclosed a corporate governance policy, effective implementation requires that they also set aside the appropriate human and financial resources to pursue this policy in a way that their beneficiaries and portfolio companies can expect.

2. **Institutional investors acting in a fiduciary capacity should disclose how they manage material conflicts of interest that may affect the exercise of key ownership rights regarding their investments.**

The incentives for intermediary owners to vote their shares and exercise key ownership functions may, under certain circumstances, differ from those of direct owners. Such differences may sometimes be commercially sound but may also arise from conflicts of interest which are particularly acute when the fiduciary institution is a subsidiary or an affiliate of another financial institution, and especially an integrated financial group.

When such conflicts arise from material business relationships, for example, through an agreement to manage the portfolio company's funds, such conflicts should be identified and disclosed.

At the same time, institutions should disclose what actions they are taking to minimize the potentially negative impact on their ability to exercise key ownership rights. Such actions may include the separation of bonuses for fund management from those related to the acquisition of new business elsewhere in the organization.

G. **Shareholders, including institutional shareholders, should be allowed to consult with each other on issues concerning their basic shareholder rights as defined in the Principles, subject to exceptions to prevent abuse.**

It has long been recognized that in companies with dispersed ownership, individual shareholders might have too small a stake in the company to warrant the cost of taking action or for making an investment in monitoring performance. Moreover, if small shareholders did invest resources in such activities, others would also gain without having contributed (i.e. they are "free riders"). This effect, which serves to lower incentives for monitoring, is probably less of a problem for institutions, particularly financial institutions acting in a fiduciary capacity, in deciding whether to increase their ownership to a significant stake in individual companies, or to rather simply diversify. However, other costs with regard to holding a significant stake might still be high. In many instances institutional investors are prevented from doing this because it is beyond their capacity or would require investing more of their assets in one company than may be prudent. To overcome this asymmetry which favors diversification, they should be allowed, and even encouraged, to co-operate and co-ordinate their actions in nominating and electing board members, placing proposals on the agenda and holding discussions directly with a company in order to improve its corporate governance. More generally, shareholders should be allowed to communicate with each other without having to comply with the formalities of proxy solicitation.

It must be recognized, however, that co-operation among investors could also be used to manipulate markets and to obtain control over a company without being subject to any takeover regulations. Moreover, co-operation might also be for the purposes of circumventing competition law. For this reason, in some countries, the ability of institutional investors to co-operate on their voting strategy is either limited or prohibited. Shareholder agreements may also be closely monitored. However, if co-operation does not involve issues of corporate control, or conflict with concerns about market efficiency and fairness, the benefits of more effective ownership may still be obtained.

Necessary disclosure of co-operation among investors, institutional or otherwise, may have to be accompanied by provisions which prevent trading for a period so as to avoid the possibility of market manipulation.

III. The Equitable Treatment of Shareholders

The corporate governance framework should ensure the equitable treatment of all shareholders, including minority and foreign shareholders. All shareholders should have the opportunity to obtain effective redress for violation of their rights.

Investors' confidence that the capital they provide will be protected from misuse or misappropriation by corporate managers, board members or controlling shareholders is an important factor in the capital markets.

Corporate boards, managers and controlling shareholders may have the opportunity to engage in activities that may advance their own interests at the expense of non-controlling shareholders. In providing protection to investors, a distinction can usefully be made between ex-ante and ex-post shareholder rights. Ex-ante rights are, for example, pre-emptive rights and qualified majorities for certain decisions. Ex-post rights allow the seeking of redress once rights have been violated. In jurisdictions where the enforcement of the legal and regulatory framework is weak, some countries have found it desirable to strengthen the ex-ante rights of shareholders such as by low share ownership thresholds for placing items on the agenda of the shareholders meeting or by requiring a supermajority of shareholders for certain important decisions. The Principles support equal treatment for foreign and domestic shareholders in corporate governance. They do not address government policies to regulate foreign direct investment.

One of the ways in which shareholders can enforce their rights is to be able to initiate legal and administrative proceedings against management and board members. Experience has shown that an important determinant of the degree to which shareholder rights are protected is whether effective methods exist to obtain redress for grievances at a reasonable cost and without excessive delay. The confidence of minority investors is enhanced when the legal system provides mechanisms for minority shareholders to bring lawsuits when they have reasonable grounds to believe that their rights have been violated. The provision of such enforcement mechanisms is a key responsibility of legislators and regulators.

There is some risk that a legal system, which enables any investor to challenge corporate activity in the courts, can become prone to excessive litigation. Thus, many legal systems have introduced provisions to protect management and board members against litigation abuse in the form of tests for the sufficiency of shareholder complaints, so-called safe harbors for management and board member actions (such as the business judgement rule) as well as safe harbors for the disclosure of information. In the end, a balance must be struck between allowing investors to seek remedies for infringement of ownership rights and avoiding excessive litigation. Many countries have found that alternative adjudication procedures, such as administrative hearings or arbitration procedures organized by the securities regulators or other regulatory bodies, are an efficient method for dispute settlement, at least at the first instance level.

A. All shareholders of the same series of a class should be treated equally.

1. Within any series of a class, all shares should carry the same rights. All investors should be able to obtain information about the rights attached to all series and classes of shares before they purchase. Any changes in voting rights should be subject to approval by those classes of shares which are negatively affected.

The optimal capital structure of the firm is best decided by the management and the board, subject to the approval of the shareholders. Some companies issue preferred (or preference) shares which have a preference in respect of receipt of the profits of the firm but which normally have no voting rights. Companies may also issue participation certificates or shares without voting rights, which would presumably trade at different prices than shares with voting rights. All of these structures may be effective in distributing risk and reward in ways that are thought to be in the best interests of the company and to cost-efficient financing. The Principles do not take a position on the concept of "one share one vote". However, many institutional investors and shareholder associations support this concept.

Investors can expect to be informed regarding their voting rights before they invest. Once they have invested, their rights should not be changed unless those holding voting shares have had the opportunity to participate in the decision. Proposals to change the voting rights of different series and classes of shares should be submitted for approval at general shareholders meetings by a specified majority of voting shares in the affected categories.

2. **Minority shareholders should be protected from abusive actions by, or in the interest of, controlling shareholders acting either directly or indirectly, and should have effective means of redress.**

Many publicly traded companies have a large controlling shareholder. While the presence of a controlling shareholder can reduce the agency problem by closer monitoring of management, weaknesses in the legal and regulatory framework may lead to the abuse of other shareholders in the company. The potential for abuse is marked where the legal system allows, and the market accepts, controlling shareholders to exercise a level of control which does not correspond to the level of risk that they assume as owners through exploiting legal devices to separate ownership from control, such as pyramid structures or multiple voting rights. Such abuse may be carried out in various ways, including the extraction of direct private benefits via high pay and bonuses for employed family members and associates, inappropriate related party transactions, systematic bias in business decisions and changes in the capital structure through special issuance of shares favoring the controlling shareholder.

In addition to disclosure, a key to protecting minority shareholders is a clearly articulated duty of loyalty by board members to the company and to all shareholders. Indeed, abuse of minority shareholders is most pronounced in those countries where the legal and regulatory framework is weak in this regard. A particular issue arises in some jurisdictions where groups of companies are prevalent and where the duty of loyalty of a board member might be ambiguous and even interpreted as to the group.

In these cases, some countries are now moving to control negative effects by specifying that a transaction in favor of another group company must be offset by receiving a corresponding benefit from other companies of the group.

Other common provisions to protect minority shareholders, which have proven effective, include pre-emptive rights in relation to share issues, qualified majorities for certain shareholder decisions and the possibility to use cumulative voting in electing members of the board. Under certain circumstances, some jurisdictions require or permit controlling shareholders to buy-out the remaining shareholders at a share-price that is established through an independent appraisal. This is particularly important when controlling shareholders decide to de-list an enterprise. Other means of improving minority shareholder rights include derivative and class action law suits. With the common aim of improving market credibility, the choice and ultimate design of different provisions to protect minority shareholders necessarily depends on the overall regulatory framework and the national legal system.

3. **Votes should be cast by custodians or nominees in a manner agreed upon with the beneficial owner of the shares.**

In some OECD countries it was customary for financial institutions which held shares in custody for investors to cast the votes of those shares.

Custodians such as banks and brokerage firms holding securities as nominees for customers were sometimes required to vote in support of management unless specifically instructed by the shareholder to do otherwise.

The trend in OECD countries is to remove provisions that automatically enable custodian institutions to cast the votes of shareholders. Rules in some countries have recently been revised to require custodian institutions to provide shareholders with information concerning their options in the use of their voting rights. Shareholders may elect to delegate all voting rights to custodians. Alternatively, shareholders may choose to be informed of all upcoming shareholder votes and may decide to cast some votes while delegating some voting rights to the custodian. It is necessary to draw a reasonable balance between assuring that shareholder votes are not cast by custodians without regard for the wishes of shareholders and not imposing excessive burdens on custodians to secure shareholder approval before casting votes. It is sufficient to disclose to the shareholders that, if no instruction to the contrary is received, the custodian will vote the shares in the way it deems consistent with shareholder interest.

It should be noted that this principle does not apply to the exercise of voting rights by trustees or other persons acting under a special legal mandate (such as, for example, bankruptcy receivers and estate executors).

Holders of depository receipts should be provided with the same ultimate rights and practical opportunities to participate in corporate governance as are accorded to holders of the underlying shares. Where the direct holders of shares may use proxies, the depositary, trust office or equivalent body should therefore issue proxies on a timely basis to depository receipt holders. The depository receipt holders should be able to issue binding voting instructions with respect to the shares, which the depositary or trust office holds on their behalf.

4. **Impediments to cross border voting should be eliminated.**

Foreign investors often hold their shares through chains of intermediaries. Shares are typically held in accounts with securities intermediaries, that in turn hold accounts with other intermediaries and central securities depositories in other jurisdictions, while the listed company resides in a third country. Such cross-border chains cause special challenges with respect to determining the entitlement of foreign investors to use their voting rights, and the process of communicating with such investors. In combination with business practices which provide only a very short notice period, shareholders are often left with only very limited time to react to a convening notice by the company and to make informed decisions concerning items for decision. This makes cross border voting difficult. The legal and regulatory framework should clarify who is entitled to control the voting rights in cross border situations and where necessary to simplify the depository chain. Moreover, notice periods should ensure that foreign investors in effect have similar opportunities to exercise their ownership functions as domestic investors. To further facilitate voting by foreign investors, laws, regulations and corporate practices should allow participation through means which make use of modern technology.

5. **Processes and procedures for general shareholder meetings should allow for equitable treatment of all shareholders. Company procedures should not make it unduly difficult or expensive to cast votes.**

The right to participate in general shareholder meetings is a fundamental shareholder right. Management and controlling investors have at times sought to discourage non-controlling or foreign investors from trying to influence the direction of the company. Some companies have charged fees for voting. Other impediments included prohibitions on proxy voting and the requirement of personal attendance at general shareholder meetings to vote. Still other procedures may make it practically impossible to exercise ownership rights. Proxy materials may be sent too close to the time of general shareholder meetings to allow investors adequate time for reflection and consultation. Many companies in OECD countries are seeking to develop better channels of communication and decision-making with shareholders. Efforts by companies to remove artificial barriers to participation in general meetings are encouraged and the corporate governance framework should facilitate the use of electronic voting in absentia.

B. Insider trading and abusive self-dealing should be prohibited.

Abusive self-dealing occurs when persons having close relationships to the company, including controlling shareholders, exploit those relationships to the detriment of the company and investors. As insider trading entails manipulation of the capital markets, it is prohibited by securities regulations, company law and/or criminal law in most OECD countries. However, not all jurisdictions prohibit such practices, and in some cases enforcement is not vigorous. These practices can be seen as constituting a breach of good corporate governance inasmuch as they violate the principle of equitable treatment of shareholders.

The Principles reaffirm that it is reasonable for investors to expect that the abuse of insider power be prohibited. In cases where such abuses are not specifically forbidden by legislation or where enforcement is not effective, it will be important for governments to take measures to remove any such gaps.

C. Members of the board and key executives should be required to disclose to the board whether they, directly, indirectly or on behalf of third parties, have a material interest in any transaction or matter directly affecting the corporation.

Members of the board and key executives have an obligation to inform the board where they have a business, family or other special relationship outside of the company that could affect their judgement with respect to a particular transaction or matter affecting the company. Such special relationships include situations where executives and board members have a relationship with the company via their association with a shareholder who is in a position to exercise control. Where a material interest has been declared, it is good practice for that person not to be involved in any decision involving the transaction or matter.

IV. *The Role of Stakeholders in Corporate Governance*

The corporate governance framework should recognize the rights of stakeholders established by law or through mutual

agreements and encourage active co-operation between corporations and stakeholders in creating wealth, jobs, and the sustainability of financially sound enterprises.

A key aspect of corporate governance is concerned with ensuring the flow of external capital to companies both in the form of equity and credit. Corporate governance is also concerned with finding ways to encourage the various stakeholders in the firm to undertake economically optimal levels of investment in firm-specific human and physical capital. The competitiveness and ultimate success of a corporation is the result of teamwork that embodies contributions from a range of different resource providers including investors, employees, creditors, and suppliers. Corporations should recognize that the contributions of stakeholders constitute a valuable resource for building competitive and profitable companies. It is, therefore, in the long-term interest of corporations to foster wealth-creating cooperation among stakeholders. The governance framework should recognize that the interests of the corporation are served by recognizing the interests of stakeholders and their contribution to the long-term success of the corporation.

A. The rights of stakeholders that are established by law or through mutual agreements are to be respected.

In all OECD countries, the rights of stakeholders are established by law (e.g. labour, business, commercial and insolvency laws) or by contractual relations. Even in areas where stakeholder interests are not legislated, many firms make additional commitments to stakeholders, and concern over corporate reputation and corporate performance often requires the recognition of broader interests.

B. Where stakeholder interests are protected by law, stakeholders should have the opportunity to obtain effective redress for violation of their rights.

The legal framework and process should be transparent and not impede the ability of stakeholders to communicate and to obtain redress for the violation of rights.

C. Performance-enhancing mechanisms for employee participation should be permitted to develop.

The degree to which employees participate in corporate governance depends on national laws and practices, and may vary from company to company as well. In the context of corporate governance, performance enhancing mechanisms for participation may benefit companies directly as well as indirectly through the readiness by employees to invest in firm specific skills. Examples of mechanisms for employee participation include: employee representation on boards; and governance processes such as works councils that consider employee viewpoints in certain key decisions. With respect to performance enhancing mechanisms, employee stock ownership plans or other profit sharing mechanisms are to be found in many countries. Pension commitments are also often an element of the relationship between the company and its past and present employees. Where such commitments involve establishing an independent fund, its trustees should be independent of the company's management and manage the fund for all beneficiaries.

D. Where stakeholders participate in the corporate governance process, they should have access to relevant, sufficient and reliable information on a timely and regular basis.

Where laws and practice of corporate governance systems provide for participation by stakeholders, it is important that stakeholders have access to information necessary to fulfil their responsibilities.

E. Stakeholders, including individual employees and their representative bodies, should be able to freely communicate their concerns about illegal or unethical practices to the board and their rights should not be compromised for doing this.

Unethical and illegal practices by corporate officers may not only violate the rights of stakeholders but also be to the detriment of the company and its shareholders in terms of reputation effects and an increasing risk of future financial liabilities. It is therefore to the advantage of the company and its shareholders to establish procedures and safe-harbors for complaints by employees, either personally or through their representative bodies, and others outside the company, concerning illegal and unethical behavior. In many countries the board is being encouraged by laws and or principles to protect these individuals and representative bodies and to give them confidential direct access to someone independent on the board, often a member of an audit or an ethics committee. Some companies have established an ombudsman to deal with complaints. Several regulators have also established confidential phone and e-mail facilities to receive allegations. While in certain countries representative employee bodies undertake the tasks of conveying concerns to the company, individual employees should not be precluded from, or be less protected, when acting alone. When there is an inadequate response to a complaint regarding contravention of the law, the OECD Guidelines for Multinational Enterprises encourage them to report their bona fide complaint to the competent public authorities. The company should refrain from discriminatory or disciplinary actions against such employees or bodies.

F. The corporate governance framework should be complemented by an effective, efficient insolvency framework and by effective enforcement of creditor rights.

Especially in emerging markets, creditors are a key stakeholder and the terms, volume and type of credit extended to firms will depend importantly on their rights and on their enforceability. Companies with a good corporate governance record are often able to borrow larger sums and on more favorable terms than those with poor records or which operate in nontransparent markets. The framework for corporate insolvency varies widely across countries. In some countries, when companies are nearing insolvency, the legislative framework imposes a duty on directors to act in the interests of creditors, who might therefore play a prominent role in the governance of the company. Other countries have mechanisms which encourage the debtor to reveal timely information about the company's difficulties so that a consensual solution can be found between the debtor and its creditors.

Creditor rights vary, ranging from secured bond holders to unsecured creditors. Insolvency procedures usually require efficient mechanisms for reconciling the interests of different classes of creditors. In many jurisdictions provision is made for special rights such as through "debtor in possession" financing which provides incentives/protection for new funds made available to the enterprise in bankruptcy.

V. Disclosure and Transparency

The corporate governance framework should ensure that timely and accurate disclosure is made on all material matters regarding the corporation, including the financial situation, performance, ownership, and governance of the company.

In most OECD countries a large amount of information, both mandatory and voluntary, is compiled on publicly traded and large unlisted enterprises, and subsequently disseminated to a broad range of users. Public disclosure is typically required, at a minimum, on an annual basis though some countries require periodic disclosure on a semi-annual or quarterly basis, or even more frequently in the case of material developments affecting the company. Companies often make voluntary disclosure that goes beyond minimum disclosure requirements in response to market demand.

A strong disclosure regime that promotes real transparency is a pivotal feature of market-based monitoring of companies and is central to shareholders' ability to exercise their ownership rights on an informed basis. Experience in countries with large and active equity markets shows that disclosure can also be a powerful tool for influencing the behavior of companies and for protecting investors. A strong disclosure regime can help to attract capital and maintain confidence in the capital markets. By contrast, weak disclosure and non-transparent practices can contribute to unethical behavior and to a loss of market integrity at great cost, not just to the company and its shareholders but also to the economy as a whole. Shareholders and potential investors require access to regular, reliable and comparable information in sufficient detail for them to assess the stewardship of management, and make informed decisions about the valuation, ownership and voting of shares. Insufficient or unclear information may hamper the ability of the markets to function, increase the cost of capital and result in a poor allocation of resources.

Disclosure also helps improve public understanding of the structure and activities of enterprises, corporate policies and performance with respect to environmental and ethical standards, and companies' relationships with the communities in which they operate. The OECD Guidelines for Multinational Enterprises are relevant in this context.

Disclosure requirements are not expected to place unreasonable administrative or cost burdens on enterprises. Nor are companies expected to disclose information that may endanger their competitive position unless disclosure is necessary to fully inform the investment decision and to avoid misleading the investor. In order to determine what information should be disclosed at a minimum, many countries apply the concept of materiality.

Material information can be defined as information whose omission or misstatement could influence the economic decisions taken by users of information.

The Principles support timely disclosure of all material developments that arise between regular reports. They also support simultaneous reporting of information to all shareholders in order to ensure their equitable treatment. In maintaining close relations with investors and market participants, companies must be careful not to violate this fundamental principle of equitable treatment.

A. Disclosure should include, but not be limited to, material information on:

1. The financial and operating results of the company.

> Audited financial statements showing the financial performance and the financial situation of the company (most typically including the balance sheet, the profit and loss statement, the cash flow statement and notes to the financial statements) are the most widely used source of information on companies. In their current form, the two principal goals of financial statements are to enable appropriate monitoring to take place and to provide the basis to value securities. Management's discussion and analysis of operations is typically included in annual reports. This discussion is most useful when read in conjunction with the accompanying financial statements. Investors are particularly interested in information that may shed light on the future performance of the enterprise.

Arguably, failures of governance can often be linked to the failure to disclose the "whole picture", particularly where off-balance sheet items are used to provide guarantees or similar commitments between related companies. It is therefore important that transactions relating to an entire group of companies be disclosed in line with high quality internationally recognized standards and include information about contingent liabilities and off-balance sheet transactions, as well as special purpose entities.

2. **Company objectives.**

In addition to their commercial objectives, companies are encouraged to disclose policies relating to business ethics, the environment and other public policy commitments. Such information may be important for investors and other users of information to better evaluate the relationship between companies and the communities in which they operate and the steps that companies have taken to implement their objectives.

3. **Major share ownership and voting rights.**

One of the basic rights of investors is to be informed about the ownership structure of the enterprise and their rights vis-à-vis the rights of other owners. The right to such information should also extend to information about the structure of a group of companies and intra-group relations. Such disclosures should make transparent the objectives, nature and structure of the group. Countries often require disclosure of ownership data once certain thresholds of ownership are passed. Such disclosure might include data on major shareholders and others that, directly or indirectly, control or may control the company through special voting rights, shareholder agreements, the ownership of controlling or large blocks of shares, significant cross shareholding relationships and cross guarantees.

Particularly for enforcement purposes, and to identify potential conflicts of interest, related party transactions and insider trading, information about record ownership may have to be complemented with information about beneficial ownership. In cases where major shareholdings are held through intermediary structures or arrangements, information about the beneficial owners should therefore be obtainable at least by regulatory and enforcement agencies and/or through the judicial process. The OECD template Options for Obtaining Beneficial Ownership and Control Information can serve as a useful self-assessment tool for countries that wish to ensure necessary access to information about beneficial ownership.

4. **Remuneration policy for members of the board and key executives, and information about board members, in-**

cluding their qualifications, the selection process, other company directorships and whether they are regarded as independent by the board.

Investors require information on individual board members and key executives in order to evaluate their experience and qualifications and assess any potential conflicts of interest that might affect their judgement. For board members, the information should include their qualifications, share ownership in the company, membership of other boards and whether they are considered by the board to be an independent member. It is important to disclose membership of other boards not only because it is an indication of experience and possible time pressures facing a member of the board, but also because it may reveal potential conflicts of interest and makes transparent the degree to which there are inter-locking boards.

A number of national principles, and in some cases laws, lay down specific duties for board members who can be regarded as independent and in some instances recommend that a majority of the board should be independent. In many countries, it is incumbent on the board to set out the reasons why a member of the board can be considered independent. It is then up to the shareholders, and ultimately the market, to determine if those reasons are justified. Several countries have concluded that companies should disclose the selection process and especially whether it was open to a broad field of candidates. Such information should be provided in advance of any decision by the general shareholder's meeting or on a continuing basis if the situation has changed materially.

Information about board and executive remuneration is also of concern to shareholders. Of particular interest is the link between remuneration and company performance. Companies are generally expected to disclose information on the remuneration of board members and key executives so that investors can assess the costs and benefits of remuneration plans and the contribution of incentive schemes, such as stock option schemes, to company performance. Disclosure on an individual basis (including termination and retirement provisions) is increasingly regarded as good practice and is now mandated in several countries. In these cases, some jurisdictions call for remuneration of a certain number of the highest paid executives to be disclosed, while in others it is confined to specified positions.

5. **Related party transactions.**

It is important for the market to know whether the company is being run with due regard to the interests of all its investors. To this end, it is essential for the company to fully disclose material related party transactions to the market, either individually, or on a grouped basis, including whether they have been executed at arms-length and on normal market terms. In a number of jurisdictions this is indeed already a legal requirement. Related parties can include entities that control or are under common control with the company, significant shareholders including members of their families and key management personnel. Transactions involving the major shareholders (or their close family, relations etc.), either directly or indirectly, are potentially the most difficult type of transactions. In some jurisdictions, shareholders above a limit as low as 5 per cent shareholding are obliged to report transactions.

Disclosure requirements include the nature of the relationship where control exists and the nature and amount of transactions with related parties, grouped as appropriate. Given the inherent opaqueness of many transactions, the obligation may need to be placed on the beneficiary to inform the board about the transaction, which in turn should make a disclosure to the market. This should not absolve the firm from maintaining its own monitoring, which is an important task for the board.

6. **Foreseeable risk factors.**

Users of financial information and market participants need information on reasonably foreseeable material risks that may include: risks that are specific to the industry or the geographical areas in which the company operates; dependence on commodities; financial market risks including interest rate or currency risk; risk related to derivatives and off-balance sheet transactions; and risks related to environmental liabilities. The Principles do not envision the disclosure of information in greater detail than is necessary to fully inform investors of the material and foreseeable risks of the enterprise. Disclosure of risk is most effective when it is tailored to the particular industry in question. Disclosure about the system for monitoring and managing risk is increasingly regarded as good practice.

7. **Issues regarding employees and other stakeholders.**

Companies are encouraged, and in some countries even obliged, to provide information on key issues relevant to employees and other stakeholders that may materially affect the performance of the company. Disclosure may include management/employee relations, and relations with other stakeholders such as creditors, suppliers, and local communities.

Some countries require extensive disclosure of information on human resources. Human resource policies, such as programs for human resource development and training, retention rates of employees and employee share ownership plans, can communicate important information on the competitive strengths of companies to market participants.

8. Governance structures and policies, in particular, the content of any corporate governance code or policy and the process by which it is implemented.

Companies should report their corporate governance practices, and in a number of countries such disclosure is now mandated as part of the regular reporting. In several countries, companies must implement corporate governance principles set, or endorsed, by the listing authority with mandatory reporting on a "comply or explain" basis. Disclosure of the governance structures and policies of the company, in particular the division of authority between shareholders, management and board members is important for the assessment of a company's governance. As a matter of transparency, procedures for shareholders meetings should ensure that votes are properly counted and recorded, and that a timely announcement of the outcome is made.

B. Information should be prepared and disclosed in accordance with high quality standards of accounting and financial and non-financial disclosure.

The application of high quality standards is expected to significantly improve the ability of investors to monitor the company by providing increased reliability and comparability of reporting, and improved insight into company performance. The quality of information substantially depends on the standards under which it is compiled and disclosed. The Principles support the development of high quality internationally recognized standards, which can serve to improve transparency and the comparability of financial statements and other financial reporting between countries. Such standards should be developed through open, independent, and public processes involving the private sector and other interested parties such as professional associations and independent experts. High quality domestic standards can be achieved by making them consistent with one of the internationally recognized accounting standards. In many countries, listed companies are required to use these standards.

C. An annual audit should be conducted by an independent, competent and qualified .... auditor in order to provide an external and objective assurance to the board and shareholders that the financial statements fairly represent the financial position and performance of the company in all material respects.

In addition to certifying that the financial statements represent fairly the financial position of a company, the audit statement should also include an opinion on the way in which financial statements have been prepared and presented. This should contribute to an improved control environment in the company.

Many countries have introduced measures to improve the independence of auditors and to tighten their accountability to shareholders. A number of countries are tightening audit oversight through an independent entity. Indeed, the Principles of Auditor Oversight issued by IOSCO in 2002 states that effective auditor oversight generally includes, inter alia, mechanisms: "... to provide that a body, acting in the public interest, provides oversight over the quality and implementation, and ethical standards used in the jurisdiction, as well as audit quality control environments"; and " ... to require auditors to be subject to the discipline of an auditor oversight body that is independent of the audit profession, or, if a professional body acts as the oversight body, is overseen by an independent body". It is desirable for such an auditor oversight body to operate in the public interest, and have an appropriate membership, an adequate charter of responsibilities and powers, and adequate funding that is not under the control of the auditing profession, to carry out those responsibilities.

It is increasingly common for external auditors to be recommended by an independent audit committee of the board or an equivalent body and to be appointed either by that committee/body or by shareholders directly. Moreover, the IOSCO Principles of Auditor Independence and the Role of Corporate Governance in Monitoring an Auditor's Independence states that, "standards of auditor independence should establish a framework of principles, supported by a combination of prohibitions, restrictions, other policies and procedures and disclosures, that addresses at least the following threats to independence: self-interest, self-review, advocacy, familiarity and intimidation".

The audit committee or an equivalent body is often specified as providing oversight of the internal audit activities and should also be charged with overseeing the overall relationship with the external auditor including the nature of non-audit services provided by the auditor to the company. Provision of non-audit services by the external auditor to a company can significantly impair their independence and might involve them auditing their own work.

To deal with the skewed incentives which may arise, a number of countries now call for disclosure of payments to external auditors for non-audit services. Examples of other provisions to underpin auditor independence include, a total ban or severe limitation on the nature of non-audit work which can be undertaken by an auditor for their audit client, mandatory rotation of auditors (either partners or in some cases the audit partnership), a temporary ban on the employment of an ex-auditor by the audited company and prohibiting auditors or their dependents from having a financial stake or management role in the companies they audit. Some countries take a more direct regulatory approach and limit the percentage of non-audit income that the auditor can receive from a particular client or limit the total percentage of auditor income that can come from one client.

An issue which has arisen in some jurisdictions concerns the pressing need to ensure the competence of the audit profession. In many cases there is a registration process for individuals to confirm their qualifications. This needs, however, to be supported by ongoing training and monitoring of work experience to ensure an appropriate level of professional competence.

D. External auditors should be accountable to the shareholders and owe a duty to the company to exercise due professional care in the conduct of the audit.

The practice that external auditors are recommended by an independent audit committee of the board or an equivalent body and that external auditors are appointed either by that committee/body or by the shareholders' meeting directly can be regarded as good practice since it clarifies that the external auditor should be accountable to the shareholders. It also underlines that the external auditor owes a duty of due professional care to the company rather than any individual or group of corporate managers that they may interact with for the purpose of their work.

E. Channels for disseminating information should provide for equal, timely and cost-efficient access to relevant information by users.

Channels for the dissemination of information can be as important as the content of the information itself. While the disclosure of information is often provided for by legislation, filing and access to information can be cumbersome and costly. Filing of statutory reports has been greatly enhanced in some countries by electronic filing and data retrieval systems. Some countries are now moving to the next stage by integrating different sources of company information, including shareholder filings. The Internet and other information technologies also provide the opportunity for improving information dissemination.

A number of countries have introduced provisions for ongoing disclosure (often prescribed by law or by listing rules) which includes periodic disclosure and continuous or current disclosure which must be provided on an ad hoc basis. With respect to continuous/current disclosure, good practice is to call for "immediate" disclosure of material developments, whether this means "as soon as possible" or is defined as a prescribed maximum number of specified days. The IOSCO Principles for Ongoing Disclosure and Material Development Reporting by Listed Entities set forth common principles of ongoing disclosure and material development reporting for listed companies.

F. The corporate governance framework should be complemented by an effective approach that addresses and promotes the provision of analysis or advice by analysts, brokers, rating agencies and others, that is relevant to decisions by investors, free from material conflicts of interest that might compromise the integrity of their analysis or advice.

In addition to demanding independent and competent auditors, and to facilitate timely dissemination of information, a number of countries have taken steps to ensure the integrity of those professions and activities that serve as conduits of analysis and advice to the market. These intermediaries, if they are operating free from conflicts and with integrity, can play an important role in providing incentives for company boards to follow good corporate governance practices.

Concerns have arisen, however, in response to evidence that conflicts of interest often arise and may affect judgement. This could be the case when the provider of advice is also seeking to provide other services to the company in question, or where the provider has a direct material interest in the company or its competitors. The concern identifies a highly relevant dimension of the disclosure and transparency process that targets the professional standards of stock market research analysts, rating agencies, investment banks, etc.

Experience in other areas indicates that the preferred solution is to demand full disclosure of conflicts of interest and how the entity is choosing to manage them. Particularly important will be disclosure about how the [intermediary] is structuring the incentives of its employees in order to eliminate the potential conflict of interest. Such disclosure allows investors to judge the risks involved and the likely bias in the advice and information. IOSCO has developed statements of principles relating to analysts and rating agencies (IOSCO Statement of Principles for Addressing Sell-side Securities Analyst Conflicts of Interest; IOSCO Statement of Principles Regarding the Activities of Credit Rating Agencies).

VI. *The Responsibilities of the Board*

The corporate governance framework should ensure the strategic guidance of the company, the effective monitoring of management by the board, and the board's accountability to the company and the shareholders.

Board structures and procedures vary both within and among OECD countries. Some countries have two-tier boards that separate the supervisory function and the management function into different bodies. Such systems typically have a "supervisory board" composed of non-executive board members and a "management board" composed entirely of executives. Other countries have "unitary" boards, which bring together executive and nonexecutive board members. In some countries there is also an additional statutory body for audit purposes. The Principles are intended to be sufficiently general to apply to whatever board structure is charged with the functions of governing the enterprise and monitoring management. Together with guiding corporate strategy, the board is chiefly responsible for monitoring managerial performance and achieving an adequate return for shareholders, while preventing conflicts of interest and balancing competing demands on the corporation. In order for boards to effectively fulfil their responsibilities they must be able to exercise objective and independent judgement. Another important board responsibility is to oversee systems designed to ensure that the corporation obeys applicable laws, including tax, competition, labour, environmental, equal opportunity, health and safety laws. In some countries, companies have found it useful to explicitly articulate the responsibilities that the board assumes and those for which management is accountable.

The board is not only accountable to the company and its shareholders but also has a duty to act in their best interests. In addition, boards are expected to take due regard of, and deal fairly with, other stakeholder interests including those of employees, creditors, customers, suppliers and local communities. Observance of environmental and social standards is relevant in this context.

A. Board members should act on a fully informed basis, in good faith, with due diligence and care, and in the best interest of the company and the shareholders.

In some countries, the board is legally required to act in the interest of the company, taking into account the interests of shareholders, employees, and the public good. Acting in the best interest of the company should not permit management to become entrenched.

This principle states the two key elements of the fiduciary duty of board members: the duty of care and the duty of loyalty. The duty of care requires board members to act on a fully informed basis, in good faith, with due diligence and care. In some jurisdictions there is a standard of reference which is the behavior that a reasonably prudent person would exercise in similar circumstances. In nearly all jurisdictions, the duty of care does not extend to errors of business judgement so long as board members are not grossly negligent and a decision is made with due diligence etc. The principle calls for board members to act on a fully informed basis. Good practice takes this to mean that they should be satisfied that key corporate information and compliance systems are fundamentally sound and underpin the key monitoring role of the board advocated by the Principles. In many jurisdictions this meaning is already considered an element of the duty of care, while in others it is required by securities regulation, accounting standards etc.

The duty of loyalty is of central importance, since it underpins effective implementation of other principles in this document relating to, for example, the equitable treatment of shareholders, monitoring of related party transactions and the establishment of remuneration policy for key executives and board members. It is also a key principle for board members who are working within the structure of a group of companies: even though a company might be controlled by another enterprise, the duty of loyalty for a board member relates to the company and all its shareholders and not to the controlling company of the group.

B. Where board decisions may affect different shareholder groups differently, the board should treat all shareholders fairly.

In carrying out its duties, the board should not be viewed, or act, as an assembly of individual representatives for various constituencies. While specific board members may indeed be nominated or elected by certain shareholders (and sometimes contested by others) it is an important feature of the board's work that board members when they assume their responsibilities carry out their duties in an even-handed manner with respect to all shareholders. This principle is particularly important to establish in the presence of controlling shareholders that de facto may be able to select all board members.

C. The board should apply high ethical standards. It should take into account the interests of stakeholders.

The board has a key role in setting the ethical tone of a company, not only by its own actions, but also in appointing and overseeing key executives and consequently the management in general. High ethical standards are in the long term interests of the company as a means to make it credible and trustworthy, not only in day-to-day operations but also with respect to longer term commitments. To make the objectives of the board clear and operational, many companies have found it useful to develop company codes of conduct based on, inter alia, professional standards and sometimes broader codes of behavior. The latter might include a voluntary commitment by the company (including its subsidiaries) to comply with the OECD Guidelines for Multinational Enterprises which reflect all four principles contained in the ILO Declaration on Fundamental Labour Rights.

Company-wide codes serve as a standard for conduct by both the board and key executives, setting the framework for the exercise of judgement in dealing with varying and often conflicting constituencies. At a minimum, the ethical code should set clear limits on the pursuit of private interests, including dealings in the shares of the company. An overall framework for ethical conduct goes beyond compliance with the law, which should always be a fundamental requirement.

D. The board should fulfil certain key functions, including:

1. Reviewing and guiding corporate strategy, major plans of action, risk policy, annual budgets and business plans; setting performance objectives; monitoring implementation and corporate performance; and overseeing major capital expenditures, acquisitions and divestitures.

An area of increasing importance for boards and which is closely related to corporate strategy is risk policy. Such policy will involve specifying the types and degree of risk that a company is willing to accept in pursuit of its goals. It is thus a crucial guideline for management that must manage risks to meet the company's desired risk profile.

2. Monitoring the effectiveness of the company's governance practices and making changes as needed.

Monitoring of governance by the board also includes continuous review of the internal structure of the company to ensure that there are clear lines of accountability for management throughout the organization. In addition to requiring the monitoring and disclosure of corporate governance practices on a regular basis, a number of countries have moved to recommend or indeed mandate self-assessment by boards of their performance as well as performance reviews of individual board members and the CEO/Chairman.

3. Selecting, compensating, monitoring and, when necessary, replacing key executives and overseeing succession planning.

In two tier board systems the supervisory board is also responsible for appointing the management board which will normally comprise most of the key executives.

4. Aligning key executive and board remuneration with the longer term interests of the company and its shareholders.

In an increasing number of countries it is regarded as good practice for boards to develop and disclose a remuneration policy statement covering board members and key executives. Such policy statements specify the relationship between remuneration and performance, and include measurable standards that emphasize the longer run interests of the company over short term considerations. Policy statements generally tend to set conditions for payments to board members for extra-board activities, such as consulting. They also often specify terms to be observed by board members and key executives about holding and trading the stock of the company, and the procedures to be followed in granting and re-pricing of options. In some countries, policy also covers the payments to be made when terminating the contract of an executive.

It is considered good practice in an increasing number of countries that remuneration policy and employment contracts for board members and key executives be handled by a special committee of the board comprising either wholly or a majority of independent directors. There are also calls for a remuneration committee that excludes executives that serve on each others' remuneration committees, which could lead to conflicts of interest.

5. **Ensuring a formal and transparent board nomination and election process.**

These Principles promote an active role for shareholders in the nomination and election of board members. The board has an essential role to play in ensuring that this and other aspects of the nominations and election process are respected. First, while actual procedures for nomination may differ among countries, the board or a nomination committee has a special responsibility to make sure that established procedures are transparent and respected. Second, the board has a key role in identifying potential members for the board with the appropriate knowledge, competencies and expertise to complement the existing skills of the board and thereby improve its value-adding potential for the company. In several countries there are calls for an open search process extending to a broad range of people.

6. **Monitoring and managing potential conflicts of interest of management, board members and shareholders, including misuse of corporate assets and abuse in related party transactions.**

It is an important function of the board to oversee the internal control systems covering financial reporting and the use of corporate assets and to guard against abusive related party transactions. These functions are sometimes assigned to the internal auditor which should maintain direct access to the board. Where other corporate officers are responsible such as the general counsel, it is important that they maintain similar reporting responsibilities as the internal auditor.

In fulfilling its control oversight responsibilities it is important for the board to encourage the reporting of unethical/unlawful behavior without fear of retribution. The existence of a company code of ethics should aid this process which should be underpinned by legal protection for the individuals concerned. In a number of companies either the audit committee or an ethics committee is specified as the contact point for employees who wish to report concerns about unethical or illegal behavior that might also compromise the integrity of financial statements.

7. **Ensuring the integrity of the corporation's accounting and financial reporting systems, including the independent audit, and that appropriate systems of control are in place, in particular, systems for risk management, financial and operational control, and compliance with the law and relevant standards.**

Ensuring the integrity of the essential reporting and monitoring systems will require the board to set and enforce clear lines of responsibility and accountability throughout the organization. The board will also need to ensure that there is appropriate oversight by senior management. One way of doing this is through an internal audit system directly reporting to the board. In some jurisdictions it is considered good practice for the internal auditors to report to an independent audit committee of the board or an equivalent body which is also responsible for managing the relationship with the external auditor, thereby allowing a coordinated response by the board. It should also be regarded as good practice for this committee, or equivalent body, to review and report to the board the most critical accounting policies which are the basis for financial reports. However, the board should retain final responsibility for ensuring the integrity of the reporting systems. Some countries have provided for the chair of the board to report on the internal control process.

Companies are also well advised to set up internal programs and procedures to promote compliance with applicable laws, regulations and standards, including statutes to criminalize bribery of foreign officials that are required to be enacted by the OECD Anti-bribery Convention and measures designed to control other forms of bribery and corruption. Moreover, compliance must also relate to other laws and regulations such as those covering securities, competition and work and safety conditions. Such compliance programs will also underpin the company's ethical code. To be effective, the incentive structure of the business needs to be aligned with its ethical and professional standards so that adherence to these values is rewarded and breaches of law are met with dissuasive consequences or penalties. Compliance programs should also extend where possible to subsidiaries.

8. Overseeing the process of disclosure and communications.

The functions and responsibilities of the board and management with respect to disclosure and communication need to be clearly established by the board. In some companies there is now an investment relations officer who reports directly to the board.

E. The board should be able to exercise objective independent judgement on corporate affairs.

In order to exercise its duties of monitoring managerial performance, preventing conflicts of interest and balancing competing demands on the corporation, it is essential that the board is able to exercise objective judgement. In the first instance this will mean independence and objectivity with respect to management with important implications for the composition and structure of the board. Board independence in these circumstances usually requires that a sufficient number of board members will need to be independent of management. In a number of countries with single tier board systems, the objectivity of the board and its independence from management may be strengthened by the separation of the role of chief executive and chairman, or, if these roles are combined, by designating a lead non-executive director to convene or chair sessions of the outside directors. Separation of the two posts may be regarded as good practice, as it can help to achieve an appropriate balance of power, increase accountability and improve the board's capacity for decision making independent of management. The designation of a lead director is also regarded as a good practice alternative in some jurisdictions. Such mechanisms can also help to ensure high quality governance of the enterprise and the effective functioning of the board. The Chairman or lead director may, in some countries, be supported by a company secretary. In the case of two tier board systems, consideration should be given to whether corporate governance concerns might arise if there is a tradition for the head of the lower board becoming the Chairman of the Supervisory Board on retirement.

The manner in which board objectivity might be underpinned also depends on the ownership structure of the company. A dominant shareholder has considerable powers to appoint the board and the management. However, in this case, the board still has a fiduciary responsibility to the company and to all shareholders including minority shareholders.

The variety of board structures, ownership patterns and practices in different countries will thus require different approaches to the issue of board objectivity. In many instances objectivity requires that a sufficient number of board members not be employed by the company or its affiliates and not be closely related to the company or its management through significant economic, family or other ties. This does not prevent shareholders from being board members. In others, independence from controlling shareholders or another controlling body will need to be emphasized, in particular if the ex ante rights of minority shareholders are weak and opportunities to obtain redress are limited. This has led to both codes and the law in some jurisdictions to call for some board members to be independent of dominant shareholders, independence extending to not being their representative or having close business ties with them. In other cases, parties such as particular creditors can also exercise significant influence. Where there is a party in a special position to influence the company, there should be stringent tests to ensure the objective judgement of the board.

In defining independent members of the board, some national principles of corporate governance have specified quite detailed presumptions for nonindependence which are frequently reflected in listing requirements. While establishing necessary conditions, such "negative" criteria defining when an individual is not regarded as independent can usefully be complemented by "positive" examples of qualities that will increase the probability of effective independence.

Independent board members can contribute significantly to the decision-making of the board. They can bring an objective view to the evaluation of the performance of the board and management. In addition, they can play an important role in areas where the interests of management, the company and its shareholders may diverge such as executive remuneration, succession planning, changes of corporate control, take-over defences, large acquisitions and the audit function. In order for them to play this key role, it is desirable that boards declare who they consider to be independent and the criterion for this judgement.

1. **Boards should consider assigning a sufficient number of non-executive board members capable of exercising independent judgement to tasks where there is a potential for conflict of interest. Examples of such key responsibilities are ensuring the integrity of financial and non-financial reporting, the review of related party transactions, nomination of board members and key executives, and board remuneration.**

   While the responsibility for financial reporting, remuneration and nomination are frequently those of the board as a whole, independent nonexecutive board members can provide additional assurance to market participants that their interests are defended. The board may also consider establishing specific committees to consider questions where there is a potential for conflict of interest. These committees may require a minimum number or be composed entirely of non-executive members. In some countries, shareholders have direct responsibility for nominating and electing non-executive directors to specialized functions.

2. **When committees of the board are established, their mandate, composition and working procedures should be well defined and disclosed by the board.**

While the use of committees may improve the work of the board they may also raise questions about the collective responsibility of the board and of individual board members. In order to evaluate the merits of board committees it is therefore important that the market receives a full and clear picture of their purpose, duties and composition. Such information is particularly important in the increasing number of jurisdictions where boards are establishing independent audit committees with powers to oversee the relationship with the external auditor and to act in many cases independently. Other such committees include those dealing with nomination and compensation. The accountability of the rest of the board and the board as a whole should be clear. Disclosure should not extend to committees set up to deal with, for example, confidential commercial transactions

3. **Board members should be able to commit themselves effectively to their responsibilities.**

Service on too many boards can interfere with the performance of board members. Companies may wish to consider whether multiple board memberships by the same person are compatible with effective board performance and disclose the information to shareholders. Some countries have limited the number of board positions that can be held. Specific limitations may be less important than ensuring that members of the board enjoy legitimacy and confidence in the eyes of shareholders. Achieving legitimacy would also be facilitated by the publication of attendance records for individual board members (e.g. whether they have missed a significant number of meetings) and any other work undertaken on behalf of the board and the associated remuneration.

In order to improve board practices and the performance of its members, an increasing number of jurisdictions are now encouraging companies to engage in board training and voluntary self-evaluation that meets the needs of the individual company. This might include that board members acquire appropriate skills upon appointment, and thereafter remain abreast of relevant new laws, regulations, and changing commercial risks through in-house training and external courses.

F. In order to fulfil their responsibilities, board members should have access to accurate, relevant and timely information.

Board members require relevant information on a timely basis in order to support their decision-making. Non-executive board members do not typically have the same access to information as key managers within the company. The contributions of non-executive board members to the company can be enhanced by providing access to certain key managers within the company such as, for example, the company secretary and the internal auditor, and recourse to independent external advice at the expense of the company. In order to fulfil their responsibilities, board members should ensure that they obtain accurate, relevant and timely information.

CORPORATE FORMS

SIMPLE FORM OF CERTIFICATE OF INCORPORATION

[From 3 R. Balotti & J. Finkelstein, The Delaware Law of
Corporations and Business Organizations,
Form 1.5 (3d ed. 1998).]

CERTIFICATE OF INCORPORATION
OF
_____ CORPORATION

I, the undersigned, for the purpose of incorporating and organizing a corporation under the General Corporation Law of the State of Delaware, do execute this Certificate of Incorporation and do hereby certify as follows:

FIRST. The name of the corporation is _____.

SECOND. The address of the corporation's registered office in the State of Delaware is One Rodney Square, 10th Floor, Tenth and King Streets, in the City of Wilmington, County of New Castle, 19801. The name of its registered agent at such address is RL&F Service Corp.

THIRD. The purpose of the corporation is to engage in any lawful act or activity for which corporations may be organized under the General Corporation Law of the State of Delaware.

FOURTH. The total number of shares of stock which the corporation shall have authority to issue is _____. All such shares are to be Common Stock, par value of $_____ per share and are to be of one class.

FIFTH. The incorporator of the corporation is _____, whose mailing address is One Rodney Square, P.O. Box 551, Wilmington, Delaware 19899.

SIXTH. Unless and except to the extent that the by-laws of the corporation shall so require, the election of directors of the corporation need not be by written ballot.

SEVENTH. In furtherance and not in limitation of the powers conferred by the laws of the State of Delaware, the Board of Directors of the corporation is expressly authorized to make, alter and repeal the by-laws of the corporation, subject to the power of the stockholders of the corporation to alter or repeal any by-law whether adopted by them or otherwise.

EIGHTH. A director of the corporation shall not be liable to the corporation or its stockholders for monetary damages for breach of fiduciary duty as a director, except to the extent such exemption from liability or limitation thereof is not permitted under the General Corporation Law of the State of Delaware as the same exists or may hereafter be amended. Any amendment, modification or repeal of the foregoing sentence shall not adversely affect any right or protection of a director of the corporation hereunder in respect of any act or omission occurring prior to the time of such amendment, modification or repeal.

NINTH. The corporation reserves the right at any time, and from time to time, to amend, alter, change or repeal any provision contained in this Certificate of Incorporation, and other provisions authorized by the laws of the State of Delaware at the time in force may be added or inserted, in the manner now or hereafter prescribed by law; and all rights, preferences and privileges of whatsoever nature conferred upon stockholders, directors or any other persons whomsoever by and pursuant to this Certificate of Incorporation in its present form or as hereafter amended are granted subject to the rights reserved in this article.

TENTH. The powers of the incorporator are to terminate upon the filing of this Certificate of Incorporation. The name and mailing address of the person who is to serve as the initial director of the corporation until the first annual meeting of stockholders of the corporation, or until his successor is elected and qualifies, is: _____.

The undersigned incorporator hereby acknowledges that the foregoing certificate of incorporation is his act and deed on this _____ day of _____ 199__.

_____
Incorporator

FORM OF BY–LAWS

[From 3 R. Balotti & J. Finkelstein, The Delaware Law of
Corporations and Business Organizations,
Form 1.17 (3d ed. 1998).]

BY–LAWS
OF
_____ CORPORATION

ARTICLE I
Stockholders

Section 1.1. *Annual Meetings.* An annual meeting of stockholders shall be held for the election of directors at such date, time and place, either within or without the State of Delaware, as may be designated by resolution of the Board of Directors from time to time. Any other proper business may be transacted at the annual meeting.

Section 1.2. *Special Meetings.* Special meetings of stockholders for any purpose or purposes may be called at any time by the Board of Directors, or by a committee of the Board of Directors that has been duly designated by the Board of Directors and whose powers and authority, as expressly provided in a resolution of the Board of Directors, include the power to call such meetings, but such special meetings may not be called by any other person or persons.

Section 1.3. *Notice of Meetings.* Whenever stockholders are required or permitted to take any action at a meeting, a written notice of the meeting shall be given that shall state the place, date and hour of the meeting and, in the case of a special meeting, the purpose or purposes for which the meeting is called. Unless otherwise provided by law, the certificate of incorporation or these by-laws, the written notice of any meeting shall be given not less than ten nor more than sixty days before the date of the meeting to each stockholder entitled to vote at such meeting. If mailed, such notice shall be deemed to be given when deposited in the United States mail, postage prepaid, directed to the stockholder at his address as it appears on the records of the corporation.

Section 1.4. *Adjournments.* Any meeting of stockholders, annual or special, may adjourn from time to time to reconvene at the same or some other place, and notice need not be given of any such adjourned meeting if the time and place thereof are announced at the meeting at which the adjournment is taken. At the adjourned meeting the corporation may transact any business which might have been transacted at the original meeting. If the adjournment is for more than thirty days, or if after the adjournment a new record date is fixed for the adjourned meeting, notice of the adjourned meeting shall be given to each stock-holder of record entitled to vote at the meeting.

Section 1.5. *Quorum.* Except as otherwise provided by law, the certificate of incorporation or these by-laws, at each meeting of stock-holders the presence in person or by proxy of the holders of shares of stock having a majority of the votes which could be cast by the holders of all outstanding shares entitled to vote at the meeting shall be necessary and sufficient to constitute a quorum. In the absence of a quorum, the stockholders so present may, by majority vote, adjourn the meeting from time to time in the manner provided in Section 1.4 of these by-laws until a quorum shall attend. Shares of its own stock belonging to the corporation or to another corporation, if a majority of the shares entitled to vote in the election of directors of such other corporation is held, directly or indirectly, by the corporation, shall neither be entitled to vote nor be counted for quorum purposes; provided, however, that the foregoing shall not limit the right of the corporation to vote stock, including but not limited to its own stock, held by it in a fiduciary capacity.

Section 1.6. *Organization.* Meetings of stockholders shall be pre-sided over by the Chairman of the Board, if any, or in his absence by the Vice Chairman of the Board, if any, or in his absence by the President, or in his absence by a Vice President, or in the absence of the foregoing persons by a chairman designated by the Board of Directors, or in the absence of such designation by a chairman chosen at the meeting. The Secretary shall act as secretary of the meeting, but in his absence the chairman of the meeting may appoint any person to act as secretary of the meeting. The chairman of the meeting shall announce at the meeting of stockholders the date and time of the opening and the closing of the polls for each matter upon which the stockholders will vote.

Section 1.7. *Voting; Proxies.* Except as otherwise provided by the certificate of incorporation, each stockholder entitled to vote at any meeting of stockholders shall be entitled to one vote for each share of stock held by him which has voting power upon the matter in question. Each stockholder entitled to vote at a meeting of stockholders or to express consent or dissent to corporate action in writing without a meeting may authorize another person or persons to act for him by proxy, but no such proxy shall be voted or acted upon after three years from its date, unless the proxy provides for a longer period. A proxy shall be irrevocable if it states that it is irrevocable and if, and only as long as, it is coupled with an interest sufficient in law to support an irrevocable power. A stockholder may revoke any proxy which is not irrevocable by attending the meeting and voting in person or by filing an instrument in writing revoking the proxy or by delivering a proxy in accordance with applicable law bearing a later date to the Secretary of the corporation. Voting at meetings of stockholders need not be by written ballot and, unless otherwise required by law, need not be conducted by inspectors of election unless so determined by the holders of shares of stock having a majority of the votes which could be cast by the holders of all outstanding shares of stock entitled to vote thereon which are present in person or by proxy at such meeting. At all meetings of stockholders for the election of directors a plurality of the votes cast shall be sufficient to elect. All other elections and questions shall, unless otherwise provided by law, the certificate of incorporation or these by-laws, be decided by the vote of the holders of shares of stock having a majority of the votes which could be cast by the holders of all shares of stock outstanding and entitled to vote thereon.

Section 1.8. *Fixing Date for Determination of Stockholders of Record.* In order that the corporation may determine the stockholders entitled to notice of or to vote at any meeting of stockholders or any adjournment thereof, or to express consent to corporate action in writing without a meeting, or entitled to receive payment of any dividend or other distribution or allotment of any rights, or entitled to exercise any rights in respect of any change, conversion or exchange of stock or for the purpose of any other lawful action, the Board of Directors may fix a record date, which record date shall not precede the date upon which the resolution fixing the record date is adopted by the Board of Directors and which record date: (1) in the case of determination of stockholders entitled to vote at any meeting of stockholders or adjournment thereof, shall, unless otherwise required by law, not be more than sixty nor less than ten days before the date of such meeting; (2) in the case of determination of stockholders entitled to express consent to corporate action in writing without a meeting, shall not be more than ten days from the date upon which the resolution fixing the record date is adopted by the Board of Directors; and (3) in the case of any other action, shall not be more than sixty days prior to such other action. If no record date is fixed: (1) the record date for determining stockholders entitled to notice of or to vote at a meeting of stockholders shall be at the close of business on the day next preceding the day on which notice is given, or, if notice is waived, at the close of business on the day next preceding the day on which the meeting is held; (2) the record date for determining stockholders entitled to express consent to corporate action in writing without a meeting when no prior action of the Board of Directors is required by law, shall be the first date on which a signed written consent setting forth the action taken or proposed to be taken is delivered to the corporation in accordance with applicable law, or, if prior action by the Board of Directors is required by law, shall be at the close of business on the day on which the Board of Directors adopts the resolution taking such prior action; and (3) the record date for determining stockholders for any other purpose shall be at the close of business on the day on which the Board of Directors adopts the resolution relating thereto. A determination of stockholders of record entitled to notice of or to vote at a meeting of stockholders shall apply to any adjournment of the meeting;

provided, however, that the Board of Directors may fix a new record date for the adjourned meeting.

Section 1.9. *List of Stockholders Entitled to Vote.* The Secretary shall prepare and make, at least ten days before every meeting of stockholders, a complete list of the stockholders entitled to vote at the meeting, arranged in alphabetical order, and showing the address of each stockholder and the number of shares registered in the name of each stockholder. Such list shall be open to the examination of any stockholder, for any purpose germane to the meeting, during ordinary business hours, for a period of at least ten days prior to the meeting, either at a place within the city where the meeting is to be held, which place shall be specified in the notice of the meeting, or if not so specified, at the place where the meeting is to be held. The list shall also be produced and kept at the time and place of the meeting during the whole time thereof and may be inspected by any stockholder who is present. Upon the willful neglect or refusal of the directors to produce such a list at any meeting for the election of directors, they shall be ineligible for election to any office at such meeting. The stock ledger shall be the only evidence as to who are the stockholders entitled to examine the stock ledger, the list of stockholders or the books of the corporation, or to vote in person or by proxy at any meeting of stockholders.

Section 1.10. *Action By Consent of Stockholders.* Unless otherwise restricted by the certificate of incorporation, any action required or permitted to be taken at any annual or special meeting of the stockholders may be taken without a meeting, without prior notice and without a vote, if a consent or consents in writing, setting forth the action so taken, shall be signed by the holders of outstanding stock having not less than the minimum number of votes that would be necessary to authorize or take such action at a meeting at which all shares entitled to vote thereon were present and voted and shall be delivered (by hand or by certified or registered mail, return receipt requested) to the corporation by delivery to its registered office in the State of Delaware, its principal place of business, or an officer or agent of the corporation having custody of the book in which proceedings of minutes of stockholders are recorded. Prompt notice of the taking of the corporate action without a meeting by less than unanimous written consent shall be given to those stockholders who have not consented in writing.

Section 1.11. *Conduct of Meetings.* The Board of Directors of the corporation may adopt by resolution such rules and regulations for the conduct of the meeting of stockholders as it shall deem appropriate. Except to the extent inconsistent with such rules and regulations as adopted by the Board of Directors, the chairman of any meeting of stockholders shall have the right and authority to prescribe such rules, regulations and procedures and to do all such acts as, in the judgment of such chairman, are appropriate for the proper conduct of the meeting. Such rules, regulations or procedures, whether adopted by the Board of

Directors or prescribed by the chairman of the meeting, may include, without limitation, the following: (i) the establishment of an agenda or order of business for the meeting; (ii) rules and procedures for maintaining order at the meeting and the safety of those present; (iii) limitations on attendance at or participation in the meeting to stockholders of record of the corporation, their duly authorized and constituted proxies or such other persons as the chairman of the meeting shall determine; (iv) restrictions on entry to the meeting after the time fixed for the commencement thereof; and (v) limitations on the time allotted to questions or comments by participants. Unless and to the extent determined by the Board of Directors or the chairman of the meeting, meetings of stockholders shall not be required to be held in accordance with the rules of parliamentary procedure.

ARTICLE II

Board of Directors

Section 2.1. *Number; Qualifications.* The Board of Directors shall consist of one or more members, the number thereof to be determined from time to time by resolution of the Board of Directors. Directors need not be stockholders.

Section 2.2. *Election: Resignation: Removal: Vacancies.* The Board of Directors shall initially consist of the persons named as directors by the incorporator, and each director so elected shall hold office until the first annual meeting of stockholders or until his successor is elected and qualified. At the first annual meeting of stockholders and at each annual meeting thereafter, the stockholders shall elect directors each of whom shall hold office for a term of one year or until his successor is elected and qualified. Any director may resign at any time upon written notice to the corporation. Any newly created directorship or any vacancy occurring in the Board of Directors for any cause may be filled by a majority of the remaining members of the Board of Directors, although such majority is less than a quorum, or by a plurality of the votes cast at a meeting of stockholders, and each director so elected shall hold office until the expiration of the term of office of the director whom he has replaced or until his successor is elected and qualified.

Section 2.3. *Regular Meetings.* Regular meetings of the Board of Directors may be held at such places within or without the State of Delaware and at such times as the Board of Directors may from time to time determine, and if so determined notices thereof need not be given.

Section 2.4. *Special Meetings.* Special meetings of the Board of Directors may be held at any time or place within or without the State of Delaware whenever called by the President, any Vice President, the Secretary, or by any member of the Board of Directors. Notice of a special meeting of the Board of Directors shall be given by the person or persons calling the meeting at least twenty-four hours before the special meeting.

Section 2.5. *Telephonic Meetings Permitted.* Members of the Board of Directors, or any committee designated by the Board of Directors, may participate in a meeting thereof by means of conference telephone or similar communications equipment by means of which all persons participating in the meeting can hear each other, and participation in a meeting pursuant to this by-law shall constitute presence in person at such meeting.

Section 2.6. *Quorum: Vote Required for Action.* At all meetings of the Board of Directors a majority of the whole Board of Directors shall constitute a quorum for the transaction of business. Except in cases in which the certificate of incorporation or these by-laws otherwise provide, the vote of a majority of the directors present at a meeting at which a quorum is present shall be the act of the Board of Directors.

Section 2.7. *Organization.* Meetings of the Board of Directors shall be presided over by the Chairman of the Board, if any, or in his absence by the Vice Chairman of the Board, if any, or in his absence by the President, or in their absence by a chairman chosen at the meeting. The Secretary shall act as secretary of the meeting, but in his absence the chairman of the meeting may appoint any person to act as secretary of the meeting.

Section 2.8. *Informal Action by Directors.* Unless otherwise restricted by the certificate of incorporation or these by-laws, any action required or permitted to be taken at any meeting of the Board of Directors, or of any committee thereof, may be taken without a meeting if all members of the Board of Directors or such committee, as the case may be, consent thereto in writing, and the writing or writings are filed with the minutes of proceedings of the Board of Directors or such committee.

ARTICLE III

Committees

Section 3.1. *Committees.* The Board of Directors may, by resolution passed by a majority of the whole Board of Directors, designate one or more committees, each committee to consist of one or more of the directors of the corporation. The Board of Directors may designate one or more directors as alternate members of any committee, who may replace any absent or disqualified member at any meeting of the committee. In the absence or disqualification of a member of the committee, the member or members thereof present at any meeting and not disqualified from voting, whether or not he or they constitute a quorum, may unanimously appoint another member of the Board of Directors to act at the meeting in place of any such absent or disqualified member. Any such committee, to the extent permitted by law and to the extent provided in the resolution of the Board of Directors, shall have and may exercise all the powers and authority of the Board of Directors in the management of the business and affairs of the corporation, and may authorize the seal of the corporation to be affixed to all papers which may require it.

Section 3.2. *Committee Rules.* Unless the Board of Directors otherwise provides, each committee designated by the Board of Directors may make, alter and repeal rules for the conduct of its business. In the absence of such rules each committee shall conduct its business in the same manner as the Board of Directors conducts its business pursuant to Article II of these by-laws.

ARTICLE IV
Officers

Section 4.1. *Executive Officers; Election; Qualifications; Term of Office; Resignation; Removal; Vacancies.* The Board of Directors shall elect a President and Secretary, and it may, if it so determines, choose a Chairman of the Board and a Vice Chairman of the Board from among its members. The Board of Directors may also choose one or more Vice Presidents, one or more Assistant Secretaries, a Treasurer and one or more Assistant Treasurers. Each such officer shall hold office until the first meeting of the Board of Directors after the annual meeting of stockholders next succeeding his election, and until his successor is elected and qualified or until his earlier resignation or removal. Any officer may resign at any time upon written notice to the corporation. The Board of Directors may remove any officer with or without cause at any time, but such removal shall be without prejudice to the contractual rights of such officer, if any, with the corporation. Any number of offices may be held by the same person. Any vacancy occurring in any office of the corporation by death, resignation, removal or otherwise may be filled for the unexpired portion of the term by the Board of Directors at any regular or special meeting.

Section 4.2. *Powers and Duties of Executive Officers.* The officers of the corporation shall have such powers and duties in the management of the corporation as may be prescribed in a resolution by the Board of Directors and, to the extent not so provided, as generally pertain to their respective offices, subject to the control of the Board of Directors. The Board of Directors may require any officer, agent or employee to give security for the faithful performance of his duties.

ARTICLE V
Stock

Section 5.1. *Certificates.* Every holder of stock shall be entitled to have a certificate signed by or in the name of the corporation by the Chairman or Vice Chairman of the Board of Directors, if any, or the

President or a Vice President, and by the Treasurer or an Assistant Treasurer, or the Secretary or an Assistant Secretary, of the corporation certifying the number of shares owned by him in the corporation. Any of or all the signatures on the certificate may be a facsimile. In case any officer, transfer agent or registrar who has signed or whose facsimile signature has been placed upon a certificate shall have ceased to be such officer, transfer agent, or registrar before such certificate is issued, it may be issued by the corporation with the same effect as if he were such officer, transfer agent, or registrar at the date of issue.

Section 5.2. *Lost, Stolen or Destroyed Stock Certificates; Issuance of New Certificates.* The corporation may issue a new certificate of stock in the place of any certificate theretofore issued by it, alleged to have been lost, stolen or destroyed, and the corporation may require the owner of the lost, stolen or destroyed certificate, or his legal representative, to give the corporation a bond sufficient to indemnify it against any claim that may be made against it on account of the alleged loss, theft or destruction of any such certificate or the issuance of such new certificate.

ARTICLE VI

Indemnification

Section 6.1. *Right to Indemnification.* The corporation shall indemnify and hold harmless, to the fullest extent permitted by applicable law as it presently exists or may hereafter be amended, any person who was or is made or is threatened to be made a party or is otherwise involved in any action, suit or proceeding, whether civil, criminal, administrative or investigative (a "proceeding") by reason of the fact that he, or a person for whom he is the legal representative, is or was a director or officer of the corporation or is or was serving at the request of the corporation as a director, officer, employee or agent of another corporation or of a partnership, joint venture, trust, enterprise or nonprofit entity, including service with respect to employee benefit plans, against all liability and loss suffered and expenses (including attorneys' fees) reasonably incurred by such person. The corporation shall be required to indemnify a person in connection with a proceeding (or part thereof) initiated by such person only if the proceeding (or part thereof) was authorized by the Board of Directors of the corporation.

Section 6.2. *Prepayment of Expenses.* The corporation may, in its discretion, pay the expenses (including attorneys' fees) incurred in defending any proceeding in advance of its final disposition, provided, however, that the payment of expenses incurred by a director or officer in advance of the final disposition of the proceeding shall be made only upon receipt of an undertaking by the director or officer to repay all amounts advanced if it should be ultimately determined that the director or officer is not entitled to be indemnified under this Article or otherwise.

Section 6.3. *Claims.* If a claim for indemnification or payment of expenses under this Article is not paid in full within sixty days after a written claim therefor has been received by the corporation, the claimant may file suit to recover the unpaid amount of such claim and, if successful in whole or in part, shall be entitled to be paid the expense of prosecuting such claim. In any such action the corporation shall have the burden of proving that the claimant was not entitled to the requested indemnification or payment of expenses under applicable law.

Section 6.4. *Non–Exclusivity of Rights.* The rights conferred on any person by this Article VI shall not be exclusive of any other rights which such person may have or hereafter acquire under any statute, provision of the certificate of incorporation, these by-laws, agreement, vote of stockholders or disinterested directors or otherwise.

Section 6.5. *Other Indemnification.* The corporation's obligation, if any, to indemnify any person who was or is serving at its request as a director, officer, employee or agent of another corporation, partnership, joint venture, trust, enterprise or nonprofit entity shall be reduced by any amount such person may collect as indemnification from such other corporation, partnership, joint venture, trust, enterprise or nonprofit enterprise.

Section 6.6. *Amendment or Repeal.* Any repeal or modification of the foregoing provisions of this Article VI shall not adversely affect any right or protection hereunder of any person in respect of any act or omission occurring prior to the time of such repeal or modification.

ARTICLE VII

Miscellaneous

Section 7.1. *Fiscal Year.* The fiscal year of the corporation shall be determined by resolution of the Board of Directors.

Section 7.2. *Seal.* The corporate seal shall have the name of the corporation inscribed thereon and shall be in such form as may be approved from time to time by the Board of Directors.

Section 7.3. *Waiver of Notice of Meetings of Stockholders, Directors and Committees.* Any written waiver of notice, signed by the person entitled to notice, whether before or after the time stated therein, shall be deemed equivalent to notice. Attendance of a person at a meeting shall constitute a waiver of notice of such meeting, except when the person attends a meeting for the express purpose of objecting, at the beginning of the meeting, to the transaction of any business because the meeting is not lawfully called or convened. Neither the business to be transacted at nor the purpose of any regular or special meeting of the stockholders, directors, or members of a committee of directors need be specified in any written waiver of notice.

Section 7.4. *Interested Directors; Quorum.* No contract or transaction between the corporation and one or more of its directors or officers, or between the corporation and any other corporation, partnership, association, or other organization in which one or more of its directors or officers are directors or officers, or have a financial interest, shall be void or voidable solely for this reason, or solely because the director or officer is present at or participates in the meeting of the Board of Directors or committee thereof which authorizes the contract or transaction, or solely because his or their votes are counted for such purpose, if: (1) the material facts as to his relationship or interest and as to the contract or transaction are disclosed or are known to the Board of Directors or the committee, and the Board of Directors or committee in good faith authorizes the contract or transaction by the affirmative votes of a majority of the disinterested directors, even though the disinterested directors be less than a quorum; or (2) the material facts as to his relationship or interest and as to the contract or transaction are disclosed or are known to the stockholders entitled to vote thereon, and the contract or transaction is specifically approved in good faith by vote of the stockholders; or (3) the contract or transaction is fair as to the corporation as of the time it is authorized, approved or ratified, by the Board of Directors, a committee thereof, or the stockholders. Common or interested directors may be counted in determining the presence of a quorum at a meeting of the Board of Directors or of a committee which authorizes the contract or transaction.

Section 7.5. *Form of Records.* Any records maintained by the corporation in the regular course of its business, including its stock ledger, books of account, and minute books, may be kept on, or be in the form of, punch cards, magnetic tape, photographs, microphotographs, or any other information storage device, provided that the records so kept can be converted into clearly legible form within a reasonable time.

Section 7.6. *Amendment of By-Laws.* These by-laws may be altered or repealed, and new by-laws made, by the Board of Directors, but the stockholders may make additional by-laws and may alter and repeal any by-laws whether adopted by them or otherwise.

FORM OF MINUTES OF ORGANIZATION MEETING

[From 3 R. Balotti & J. Finkelstein, The Delaware Law of
Corporations and Business Organizations,
Form 1.24 (3d ed. 1998).]

MINUTES OF THE FIRST MEETING OF THE
BOARD OF DIRECTORS OF _____

The first meeting of the Board of Directors of _____, a Delaware
corporation (the "Corporation"), was held on _____, 199_ at _____
_.m., at _____. Present were _____, _____ and _____, being a
majority of the Directors and a quorum. Present by invitation were
_____.

By unanimous vote, _____ was chosen Chairman of the meeting,
and _____ was chosen Secretary of the meeting. The Secretary
presented a Waiver of Notice of the meeting signed by all of the
Directors of the Corporation. The Chairman directed that the original
of such Waiver be prefixed to the Minutes of this meeting.

The Secretary presented a certified copy of the Certificate of Incorporation, and upon motion made and duly carried, it was:

RESOLVED, that the original Certificate of Incorporation of this Corporation, filed in the office of the Secretary of State of the State of
Delaware on _____, 199_, is hereby approved.

RESOLVED, FURTHER, that all of the actions taken by the incorporator
of this Corporation to effect the incorporation of this Corporation
are hereby approved, ratified, confirmed and adopted by and on
behalf of this Corporation.

The Secretary presented a form of By-laws for the regulation of the
affairs of the Corporation. Upon motion made and duly carried, it was:

RESOLVED, FURTHER, that the By-laws for the regulation of the affairs
of this Corporation, attached hereto as Exhibit A and incorporated
herein by reference, are hereby ratified, adopted and approved as
the By-laws of this Corporation and shall be filed with the minutes
of the Corporation.

RESOLVED, FURTHER, that pursuant to Section 2.1 of the By-laws of
this Corporation, the Board of Directors shall consist of _____
members.

The Secretary submitted to the meeting a seal proposed to be used
as the corporate seal of the Corporation. Upon motion made and duly
carried, it was:

RESOLVED, FURTHER, that the form of corporate seal, an impression of which is imprinted at the margin of this Consent, is adopted as the official corporate seal of the Corporation.

The Secretary presented to the meeting a proposed form of certificate for the Corporation's Common stock. The Chairman directed that a specimen of such form of certificate be annexed to the Minutes of this meeting. Upon motion made and duly carried, it was:

RESOLVED, FURTHER, that the form of stock certificate representing shares of Common Stock, par value _____ ($__) per share, a specimen of which is attached hereto as Exhibit B, is adopted as the form of stock certificate for the Common Stock of the Corporation.

The following persons were nominated to hold the offices of the Corporation set forth opposite their respective names. Upon motion made and duly adopted, it was:

RESOLVED, FURTHER, that the following persons be and each of them hereby is elected to serve in the offices of the Corporation set opposite their respective names, each to hold such offices until his respective successor is duly elected and qualified or until his earlier resignation or removal:

Name	Office
1	Chief Executive Officer
2	President
3	Executive Vice President
4	Vice President
5	Secretary
6	Assistant Secretary
7	Treasurer
8	Assistant Treasurer

The Chairman stated that the Corporation had received an offer from _____ to purchase _____ shares of the Corporation's common stock for a purchase price of _____. Upon motion made and duly carried, it was:

RESOLVED, FURTHER, that in consideration of $_____ in cash paid to the Corporation by _____, such consideration being at least equal to the par value of such shares, the Corporation shall immediately issue _____ shares of its Common Stock to _____, which shares shall be fully paid, nonassessable Common Stock of the Corporation.

RESOLVED, FURTHER, that the President and the Secretary of the Corporation be and each of them hereby is authorized to issue to _____ a stock certificate or certificates evidencing the ownership of _____ shares of Common Stock of the Corporation.

RESOLVED, FURTHER, that of the $_____ in cash to be received in exchange for the issuance of shares of Common Stock of the Corporation to _____ pursuant to the foregoing resolution, $_____ ($___ per share) is hereby designated and specified as the stated capital of such shares, and said amount shall constitute the capital of the Corporation in respect of such shares.

RESOLVED, FURTHER, that of the $_____ in cash to be received in exchange for the issuance of shares of Common Stock of the Corporation to _____ pursuant to the foregoing resolution, $_____ ($___ per share) is hereby accepted as a capital surplus contribution from _____, and the Treasurer of this Corporation is hereby authorized and directed to cause this capital surplus contribution to be reflected in the accounting books and records of this Corporation.

The Chairman stated that the Corporation may wish to qualify to do business in other jurisdictions in order to carry on the business of the Corporation. Upon motion made and duly carried, it was:

RESOLVED, FURTHER, that for the purpose of authorizing the Corporation to do business in any jurisdiction in which it is necessary or expedient for the Corporation to transact business, the officers of the Corporation be and each of them hereby is authorized to appoint and substitute all necessary agents or attorneys for service of process, to designate and change the location of all necessary statutory offices and under the corporate seal if required, to make and file all necessary certificates, reports, powers of attorney and other instruments as may be required by the laws of such jurisdiction to authorize the Corporation to transact business therein, and whenever it is expedient for the Corporation to cease doing business therein and withdraw therefrom, to revoke any appointment of agent or attorney for service of process and to file such certificates, reports, revocations of appointment, or surrenders of authority as may be necessary to terminate the authority of the Corporation to do business in any such jurisdiction.

The Chairman next stated that it would be desirable to designate a depository of the funds of the Corporation. The Secretary presented to the meeting a form of resolutions supplied by the bank with respect to establishing one or more accounts with the bank. Upon motion made and duly carried, it was:

RESOLVED, FURTHER, that the Chairman of the Board of Directors, the President and the Treasurer of the Corporation (the "Designated Officers") be and each of them hereby is authorized for and on behalf of the Corporation to designate from time to time one or more banks, trust companies or other banking institutions (any thereof being hereinafter referred to as a "bank") to act as depository or depositories for the funds of the Corporation for and during such period as he may from time to time deem necessary or desirable in the interests of the Corporation and to open or close out from time to time accounts in any such depository so selected or reselected.

RESOLVED, FURTHER, that the proper officers of the Corporation be and each of them hereby is authorized and directed, in the name and on behalf of the Corporation, to take any and all action that they may deem necessary or advisable in order to establish bank accounts at _____ from time to time for the efficient conduct of the Corporation's business.

RESOLVED, FURTHER, that the form of resolutions supplied by _____ for the establishment of the Corporation's checking account, attached hereto as Exhibit C and incorporated herein by reference, are hereby adopted as the resolutions of this Board of Directors.

RESOLVED, FURTHER, that the President of the Corporation be and he hereby is authorized to designate those officers or agents of the Corporation who may be authorized from time to time to sign checks on any of such bank accounts.

The Chairman suggested that the Treasurer of the Corporation be authorized to pay all expenses and reimburse all persons for expenditures made in connection with the organization of the Corporation, and that the Secretary and the Treasurer be authorized to procure proper books for the maintenance of the records of the Corporation. Upon motion made and duly carried, it was:

RESOLVED, FURTHER, that the President, any Vice President, Secretary and Treasurer be, and each of them hereby is, authorized and directed, for and on behalf of the Corporation, to pay all charges and expenses incident to or arising out of the incorporation of the Corporation and to reimburse the persons who have made any disbursements therefor.

RESOLVED, FURTHER, that the officers of the Corporation be and each of them hereby is authorized and empowered on behalf of the Corporation to pay any other such fees and expenses and to do such other acts and things as they may deem necessary or advisable in connection with the carrying out of any of the matters or purposes set forth in the foregoing resolutions.

RESOLVED, FURTHER, that the Secretary and the Treasurer of this Corporation be and hereby are authorized and directed to procure all appropriate corporate books, books of account and stock books that may be deemed necessary or appropriate in connection with the business of this Corporation.

The Chairman suggested that the Corporation adopt a fiscal year end and set a date for the annual meeting of the Stockholders and Directors of the Corporation. Upon motion made and duly carried, it was:

RESOLVED, FURTHER, that the date for the annual meeting of the Corporation be and the same hereby is fixed as the day of _____ of _____ each year, with the first such meeting to be held _____, 19__, at _____.

RESOLVED, FURTHER, that the fiscal year of the Corporation shall commence on the _____ day of _____ and shall end on the day of _____ of each year.

The Chairman indicated that the Stockholder of the Corporation desired the Corporation to be qualified with the Internal Revenue Service as an S Corporation. Upon motion made and duly carried, it was:

RESOLVED, FURTHER, that the appropriate officers of this Corporation be and each of them hereby is authorized and directed to take any action deemed necessary or advisable to qualify this Corporation as an S Corporation under Section 1361 of the Internal Revenue Code.

There being no further business to come before the meeting, upon motion made and duly carried, the meeting was adjourned.

_____
Secretary of the Meeting

FORM OF STOCK CERTIFICATE

[From 3 R. Balotti & J. Finkelstein, The Delaware Law of
Corporations and Business Organizations,
Form 5.1 (2d ed. 1990).]

COMMON STOCK CERTIFICATE

FORM OF STOCK CERTIFICATE

The corporation will furnish without charge to each stockholder who so requests the powers, designations, preferences and relative, participating, optional or other special rights of each class of stock or series thereof of the corporation, and the qualifications, limitations or restrictions of such preferences and/or rights. Such request may be made to the corporation or the transfer agent.

The following abbreviations, when used in the inscription on the face of this certificate, shall be construed as though they were written out in full according to applicable laws or regulations:

TEN COM — as tenants in common
TEN ENT — as tenants by the entireties
JT TEN — as joint tenants with right of survivorship and
                 not as tenants in common
UNIF GIFT MIN ACT — _____ Custodian _____
                        (Cust)   (Minor)

       under Uniform Gifts to Minors Act

                            (State)

Additional abbreviations may also be used though not in the above list.

For value received, _____ hereby sell, assign and transfer unto

Please insert social security or other
identifying number of assignee

(Please print or typewrite name and address, including zip code, of assignee)

_____ Shares
of the capital stock represented by the within Certificate, and do hereby irrevocably constitute and appoint

_____ Attorney
to transfer the said stock on the books of the within named Corporation with full power of substitution in the premises.

Dated: _____

Notice: The signature to this assignment must correspond with the name as written upon the face of the certificate in every particular, without alteration or enlargement or any change whatever.

FORM OF PROXY STATEMENT
AND FORM OF PROXY

The Coca-Cola Company

NOTICE OF ANNUAL MEETING OF SHAREOWNERS

TO THE OWNERS OF COMMON STOCK
OF THE COCA-COLA COMPANY

The Annual Meeting of Shareowners of The Coca-Cola Company (the "Company") will be held at the Hotel du Pont, 11th and Market Streets, Wilmington, Delaware 19801, on Tuesday, April 19, 2005, at 10:30 a.m., local time. The purposes of the meeting are:

1. To elect fourteen Directors to serve until the 2006 Annual Meeting of Shareowners,

2. To ratify the appointment of Ernst & Young LLP as independent auditors of the Company to serve for the 2005 fiscal year,

3. To vote on three proposals submitted by shareowners if properly presented at the meeting, and

4. To transact such other business as may properly come before the meeting and at any adjournments or postponements of the meeting.

The Board of Directors set February 22, 2005 as the record date for the meeting. This means that owners of record of Common Stock at the close of business on that date are entitled to:

- receive this notice of the meeting, and

- vote at the meeting and any adjournments or postponements of the meeting.

We will make available a list of shareowners as of the close of business on February 22, 2005 for inspection by shareowners during normal business hours from April 8 through April 18, 2005 at the Company's principal place of business, One Coca-Cola Plaza, Atlanta, Georgia 30313. This list also will be available to shareowners at the meeting.

By Order of the Board of Directors
CAROL CROFOOT HAYES
Assistant Secretary

FORM OF PROXY STATEMENT AND FORM OF PROXY

Atlanta, Georgia
March 8, 2005

We urge each shareowner to promptly sign and return the enclosed proxy card or to use telephone or Internet voting. See our question and answer section for information about voting by telephone or Internet, how to revoke a proxy, and how to vote shares in person.

TABLE OF CONTENTS

FORM OF PROXY STATEMENT AND FORM OF PROXY

THE COCA-COLA COMPANY
One Coca-Cola Plaza
Atlanta, Georgia 30313

March 8, 2005

PROXY STATEMENT
FOR ANNUAL MEETING OF SHAREOWNERS
TO BE HELD APRIL 19, 2005*

Our Board of Directors (the "Board") is furnishing you this proxy statement to solicit proxies on its behalf to be voted at the 2005 Annual Meeting of Shareowners of The Coca-Cola Company (the "Company"). The meeting will be held at the Hotel du Pont, Wilmington, Delaware, on April 19, 2005, at 10:30 a.m., local time. The proxies also may be voted at any adjournments or postponements of the meeting.

The mailing address of our principal executive offices is The Coca-Cola Company, P.O. Box 1734, Atlanta, Georgia 30301. We are first sending the proxy materials to shareowners on March 8, 2005.

All properly executed written proxies, and all properly completed proxies submitted by telephone or by the Internet, that are delivered pursuant to this solicitation will be voted at the meeting in accordance with the directions given in the proxy, unless the proxy is revoked prior to voting at the meeting.

Only owners of record of shares of Common Stock of the Company (the "Common Stock") at the close of business on February 22, 2005, the record date, are entitled to notice of and to vote at the meeting, or at adjournments or postponements of the meeting. Each owner of record on the record date is entitled to one vote for each share of Common Stock held. On February 22, 2005, there were 2,410,078,480 shares of Common Stock issued and outstanding.

QUESTIONS AND ANSWERS ABOUT
THE MEETING AND VOTING

1. **What is a proxy?**

It is your legal designation of another person to vote the stock you own. That other person is called a proxy. If you designate someone as your proxy in a written document, that document also is called a proxy or a proxy card. We have designated three of our officers as proxies for the 2005 Annual Meeting of Shareowners. These three officers are Gary P. Fayard, Geoffrey J. Kelly and Cynthia McCague.

2. **What is a proxy statement?**

---

* Certain footnotes omitted.

It is a document that the Securities and Exchange Commission ("SEC") regulations require us to give you when we ask you to sign a proxy card designating Gary P. Fayard, Geoffrey J. Kelly and Cynthia McCague, as proxies to vote on your behalf.

3. **What is the difference between a shareowner of record and a shareowner who holds stock in street name?**

If your shares are registered in your name, you are a shareowner of record.

If your shares are held in the name of your broker or bank, your shares are held in street name.

4. **How do I get an admission card to attend the meeting?**

If you are a shareowner of record, your admission card is attached to your proxy card. You will need to bring it with you to the meeting.

If you own shares in street name, bring your most recent brokerage statement with you to the meeting. We can use that to verify your ownership of Common Stock and admit you to the meeting; *however, you will not be able to vote your shares at the meeting without a legal proxy (described in question 5)*. Please note that if you own shares in street name and you request a legal proxy, any previously executed proxy will be revoked, and your vote will not be counted unless you appear at the meeting and vote in person or legally appoint another proxy to vote on your behalf.

You will also need to bring a photo ID to gain admission.

5. **How can I vote at the meeting if I own shares in street name?**

You will need to ask your broker or bank for a legal proxy. You will need to bring the legal proxy with you to the meeting. You will not be able to vote your shares at the meeting without a legal proxy. Please note that if you request a legal proxy, any previously executed proxy will be revoked, and your vote will not be counted unless you appear at the meeting and vote in person or legally appoint another proxy to vote on your behalf. If you do not receive the legal proxy in time, you can follow the procedures as described in Question 4 to gain admission to the meeting.

6. **How can I view the live webcast of the meeting?**

You can view the live webcast of the meeting by logging on to our website at www.coca-cola.com and clicking on "Investors" and then on the link to the webcast. An archived copy of the webcast also will be available until May 19, 2005.

We have included the website address for reference only. The information contained on our website is not incorporated by reference into this proxy statement.

7.   **What different methods can I use to vote?**

By Written Proxy. All shareowners can vote by written proxy card.

By Telephone and Internet Proxy. All shareowners of record also can vote by touchtone telephone from the U.S. and Canada, using the toll-free telephone number on the proxy card, or through the Internet, using the procedures and instructions described on the proxy card and other enclosures. Street name holders may vote by telephone or through the Internet if their bank or broker makes those methods available, in which case the bank or broker will enclose the instructions with the proxy statement. The telephone and Internet voting procedures are designed to authenticate shareowners' identities, to allow shareowners to vote their shares, and to confirm that their instructions have been properly recorded.

In Person. All shareowners may vote in person at the meeting (unless they are street name holders without a legal proxy, as described in question 5).

8.   **What is the record date and what does it mean?**

The record date for the 2005 Annual Meeting of Shareowners is February 22, 2005. The record date is established by the Board as required by Delaware law. Owners of record of Common Stock at the close of business on the record date are entitled to:

(a)   receive notice of the meeting, and

(b)   vote at the meeting and any adjournments or postponements of the meeting.

9.   **How can I revoke a proxy?**

Shareowners can revoke a proxy prior to the completion of voting at the meeting by:

(a)   giving written notice to the Office of the Secretary of the Company,

(b)   delivering a later-dated proxy, or

(c)   voting in person at the meeting (unless they are street name holders without a legal proxy, as described in question5).

10.   **Are votes confidential? Who counts the votes?**

We will continue our long-standing practice of holding the votes of all shareowners in confidence from Directors, officers and employees except:

(a)   as necessary to meet applicable legal requirements and to assert or defend claims for or against the Company,

1471

(b)   in case of a contested proxy solicitation,

(c)   if a shareowner makes a written comment on the proxy card or otherwise communicates his or her vote to management, or

(d)   to allow the independent inspectors of election to certify the results of the vote.

We will also continue, as we have for many years, to retain an independent tabulator to receive and tabulate the proxies and independent inspectors of election to certify the results.

11.   **What are my voting choices when voting for Director nominees, and what vote is needed to elect Directors?**

In the vote on the election of fourteen Director nominees to serve until the 2006 Annual Meeting of Shareowners, shareowners may:

(a)   vote in favor of all nominees,

(b)   withhold votes as to all nominees, or

(c)   withhold votes as to specific nominees.

Directors will be elected by a plurality vote.

The Board recommends a vote FOR each of the nominees.

12.   **What are my voting choices when voting on the ratification of the appointment of Ernst & Young LLP as independent auditors, and what vote is needed to ratify their appointment?**

In the vote on the ratification of the appointment of Ernst & Young LLP as independent auditors, shareowners may:

(a)   vote in favor of the ratification,

(b)   vote against the ratification, or

(c)   abstain from voting on the ratification.

The proposal to ratify the appointment of Ernst & Young LLP as independent auditors will require approval by a majority of the votes cast by the holders of the shares of Common Stock voting in person or by proxy at the meeting.

The Board recommends a vote FOR this proposal.

13.   What are my voting choices when voting on each shareowner proposal properly presented at the meeting, and what vote is needed to approve any of the shareowner proposals?

A separate vote will be held on each of the three shareowner proposals that is properly presented at the meeting. In voting on each of the proposals, shareowners may:

(a)   vote in favor of the proposal,

(b)   vote against the proposal, or

(c)   abstain from voting on the proposal.

In order to be approved, each shareowner proposal will require approval by a majority of the votes cast by the holders of the shares of Common Stock voting in person or by proxy at the meeting.

The Board recommends a vote AGAINST each of the three shareowner proposals.

14.   What if I do not specify a choice for a matter when returning a proxy?

Shareowners should specify their choice for each matter on the enclosed proxy. If no specific instructions are given, proxies which are signed and returned will be voted FOR the election of all Director nominees, FOR the proposal to ratify the appointment of Ernst & Young LLP as independent auditors, and AGAINST each of the three shareowner proposals that is properly presented at the meeting.

15.   How are abstentions and broker non-votes counted?

Abstentions and broker non-votes will not be included in vote totals and will not affect the outcome of the vote.

16.   Does the Company have a policy about Directors' attendance at the Annual Meeting of Shareowners?

The Company does not have a policy about Directors' attendance at the Annual Meeting of Shareowners. All of the Directors, except one, attended the 2004 Annual Meeting of Shareowners.

17.   How are proxies solicited and what is the cost?

We bear all expenses incurred in connection with the solicitation of proxies. We have engaged Georgeson Shareholder Communications Inc. to assist with the solicitation of proxies for an estimated fee of $25,000 plus expenses. We will reimburse brokers, fiduciaries and custodians for their costs in forwarding proxy materials to beneficial owners of Common Stock held in their names.

FORM OF PROXY STATEMENT AND FORM OF PROXY

Our Directors, officers and employees may also solicit proxies by mail, telephone and personal contact. They will not receive any additional compensation for these activities.

ELECTION OF DIRECTORS

(Item 1)

Board of Directors

The Company's By-Laws provide for the annual election of Directors.

The terms of Herbert A. Allen, Ronald W. Allen, Cathleen P. Black, Warren E. Buffett, Barry Diller, Donald R. Keough, Maria Elena Lagomasino, Donald F. McHenry, Robert L. Nardelli, Sam Nunn, J. Pedro Reinhard, James D. Robinson III, Peter V. Ueberroth and James B. Williams will expire at the 2005 Annual Meeting of Shareowners. The term of E. Neville Isdell, who was appointed by the Board, also expires at the 2005 Annual Meeting of Shareowners. The Board has nominated each of (i) Herbert A. Allen, Ronald W. Allen, Cathleen P. Black, Warren E. Buffett, Barry Diller, Donald R. Keough, Maria Elena Lagomasino, Donald F. McHenry, Sam Nunn, J. Pedro Reinhard, James D. Robinson III, Peter V. Ueberroth and James B. Williams to stand for reelection and (ii) E. Neville Isdell to stand for election at the meeting to hold office until our 2006 Annual Meeting of Shareowners and until his or her successor is elected and qualified.

Mr. Nardelli has announced his decision not to stand for reelection citing increasing demands on his time as Chairman, President and Chief Executive Officer of The Home Depot, Inc., a position he has held since December 2000. From 1995 to December 2000, he served as President and Chief Executive Officer of GE Power Systems.

At its February 2005 meeting, the Board reduced the number of Directors constituting the Board to fourteen, effective immediately prior to the 2005 Annual Meeting of Shareowners.

We have no reason to believe that any of the nominees will be unable or unwilling for good cause to serve if elected. However, if any nominee should become unable for any reason or unwilling for good cause to serve, proxies may be voted for another person nominated as a substitute by the Board, or the Board may reduce the number of Directors.

The Board of Directors recommends a vote FOR the election of Herbert A. Allen, Ronald W. Allen, Cathleen P. Black, Warren E. Buffett, Barry Diller, E. Neville Isdell, Donald R. Keough, Maria Elena Lagomasino, Donald F. McHenry, Sam Nunn, J. Pedro Reinhard, James D. Robinson III, Peter V. Ueberroth and James B. Williams.

HERBERT A. ALLEN   Director since 1982

Age 65

Mr. Allen is President and Chief Executive Officer and a Director of Allen & Company Incorporated, a privately held investment firm, and has held these positions for more than the past five years. Mr. Allen was a Managing Director of Allen & Company LLC, a privately held investment banking firm, from September 2002 to February 2003. He is a Director of Convera Corporation.

RONALD W. ALLEN   Director since 1991
Age 63

Mr. Allen is a consultant to and Advisory Director of Delta Air Lines, Inc., a major U.S. air transportation company, and has held these positions since July 1997. He retired as Delta's Chairman of the Board, President and Chief Executive Officer in July 1997, and had been its Chairman of the Board and Chief Executive Officer since 1987. He is a Director of Aaron Rents, Inc.

CATHLEEN P. BLACK   Director since 1993
Age 60

Ms. Black is President, Hearst Magazines, a unit of The Hearst Corporation, a major media and communications company, and has held this position since November 1995. Ms. Black has been a Director of The Hearst Corporation since January 1996. From May 1991 to November 1995, she served as President and Chief Executive Officer of Newspaper Association of America, a newspaper industry organization. She served as a Director of the Company from April 1990 to May 1991, and was again elected as a Director in October 1993. Ms. Black is a Director of International Business Machines Corporation and iVillage Inc.

WARREN E. BUFFETT Director since 1989
Age 74

Mr. Buffett is Chairman of the Board and Chief Executive Officer of Berkshire Hathaway Inc., a diversified holding company, and has held these

positions for more than the past five years. He is a Director of The Washington Post Company.

BARRY DILLER   Director since 2002
  Age 63

Mr. Diller is Chairman of the Board and Chief Executive Officer of IAC/InterActiveCorp, an interactive commerce company. He has held this position with IAC/InterActiveCorp or its predecessors since August 1995. He was Chairman of the Board and Chief Executive Officer of QVC, Inc. from December 1992 through December 1994. From 1984 to 1992, Mr. Diller served as the Chairman of the Board and Chief Executive Officer of Fox, Inc. Prior to joining Fox, Inc., Mr. Diller served for ten years as Chairman of the Board and Chief Executive Officer of Paramount Pictures Corporation. He is a Director of The Washington Post Company.

E. NEVILLE ISDELL   Director since 2004
  Age 61

Mr. Isdell is Chairman of the Board and Chief Executive Officer of the Company, and has held these positions since June 1, 2004. From January 2002 to May 2004, Mr. Isdell was an international consultant to the Company. He was Chief Executive Officer of Coca-Cola Hellenic Bottling Company S.A. from September 2000 to May 2001 and Vice Chairman from May 2001 to December 2001. He was Chairman and Chief Executive Officer of Coca-Cola Beverages Plc from July 1998 to September 2000. Mr. Isdell joined the Coca-Cola system in 1966 with a local bottling company in Zambia. He held a variety of positions prior to serving as Senior Vice President of the Company from January 1989 until February 1998. He also served as President of the Greater Europe Group from January 1995 to February 1998. He is a Director of SunTrust Banks, Inc.

DONALD R. KEOUGH Director since 2004
  Age 78

1476

Mr. Keough is Chairman of the Board of Allen & Company Incorporated, a privately held investment firm, and has held this position for more than the past five years. Mr. Keough retired as President, Chief Operating Officer and a Director of the Company in April 1993. He is a Director of IAC/InterActiveCorp, Convera Corporation and Berkshire Hathaway Inc.

MARIA ELENA LAGOMASINO Director since 2003
Age 55

Ms. Lagomasino is Chairman and Chief Executive Officer of J.P. Morgan Private Bank, a unit of J.P. Morgan Chase & Co. Prior to assuming this position in September 2001, Ms. Lagomasino was Managing Director at The Chase Manhattan Bank in charge of its Global Private Banking Group. Ms. Lagomasino had been with Chase Manhattan since 1983 in various positions in private banking. Prior to 1983, she was a Vice President at Citibank. Ms. Lagomasino is a Director of Avon Products, Inc.

DONALD F. McHENRY   Director since 1981
Age 68

Mr. McHenry is Distinguished Professor in the Practice of Diplomacy and International Affairs at the School of Foreign Service, Georgetown University, and a principal owner and President of The IRC Group, LLC, a Washington, D.C. consulting firm. He has held these positions for more than the past five years. He is a Director of AT&T Corporation and International Paper Company.

SAM NUNN   Director since 1997
Age 66

Mr. Nunn is Co-Chairman and Chief Executive Officer of the Nuclear Threat Initiative, a position he has held since 2001. The Nuclear Threat Initiative is a charitable organization working to reduce the global threats from nuclear, biological and chemical weapons. Mr. Nunn was a partner in

the law firm of King & Spalding from 1997 to December 2003. He served as a member of the United States Senate from 1972 through 1996. He is a Director of ChevronTexaco Corporation, Dell Inc., General Electric Company, Internet Security Systems, Inc. and Scientific-Atlanta, Inc.

J. PEDRO REINHARD   Director since 2003
  Age 59

Mr. Reinhard is Executive Vice President and Chief Financial Officer of The Dow Chemical Company, a company engaged in the manufacture and sale of chemicals, plastic materials, agricultural and other specialized products and services, a position he has held for more than the past five years. He is a Director of The Dow Chemical Company, Dow Corning Corporation, Royal Bank of Canada and Sigma-Aldrich Corporation.

JAMES D. ROBINSON III   Director since 1975
Age 69

Mr. Robinson is co-founder and General Partner of RRE Ventures and Chairman of RRE Investors, LLC, private information technology focused venture capital firms, and has held these positions since 1994. He is also President of JD Robinson, Inc., a strategic advisory firm. Mr. Robinson previously served as non-executive Chairman of Violy, Byorum & Partners Holdings, LLC from 1996 to 2003. He previously served as Chairman and Chief Executive Officer of American Express Company from 1977 to 1993. Mr. Robinson is a Director of Bristol-Myers Squibb Company, First Data Corporation and Novell, Inc.

PETER V. UEBERROTH   Director since 1986
Age 67

Mr. Ueberroth is an investor and Chairman of the Contrarian Group, Inc., a business management company, and has held this position since 1989. He is

also Co-Chairman of Pebble Beach Company. He is Chairman of Ambassadors International, Inc. and is a Director of Adecco S.A. and Hilton Hotels Corporation.

JAMES B. WILLIAMS Director since 1979
Age 71

Mr. Williams retired in March 1998 as Chairman of the Board and Chief Executive Officer of SunTrust Banks, Inc., a bank holding company, which positions he had held for more than five years. He is a Director of Genuine Parts Company, Georgia-Pacific Corporation, Marine Products Corporation, Rollins, Inc. and RPC, Inc.

Ownership of Equity Securities in the Company

The following table sets forth information regarding beneficial ownership of Common Stock by each Director, each individual named in the Summary Compensation Table on page 28, and our Directors and executive officers as a group, all as of February 22, 2005, except as noted.

Name	Aggregate Number of Shares Beneficially Owned	Percent of Outstanding Shares
Herbert A. Allen	8,642,710[1]	*
Ronald W. Allen	22,602[2]	*
Cathleen P. Black	32,112[3]	*
Warren E. Buffett	200,020,871[4]	8.30%
Barry Diller	8,631[5]	*
Donald R. Keough	5,138,673[6]	*
Maria Elena Lagomasino	6,620[7]	*
Donald F. McHenry	38,883[8]	*
Robert L. Nardelli	8,631[9]	*
Sam Nunn	18,172[10]	*
J. Pedro Reinhard	4,259[11]	*

James D. Robinson III	299,984[12]	*
Peter V. Ueberroth	94,219[13]	*
James B. Williams	104,554,320[14]	4.34%
E. Neville Isdell	505,619[15]	*
Gary P. Fayard	679,977[16]	*
Mary E. Minnick	513,843[17]	*
José Octavio Reyes	373,373[18]	*
Alexander B. Cummings, Jr.	238,321[19]	*
Douglas N. Daft	2,631,964[20]	*
Steven J. Heyer	1,454,678[21]	*
All Directors and Executive Officers as a Group (29 Persons)	327,276,841[22]	13.53%

* Less than 1% of issued and outstanding shares of Common Stock. . . .

Principal Shareowners

Set forth in the table below is information as of December 31, 2004 about persons we know to be the beneficial owners of more than five percent of the issued and outstanding Common Stock:

Name and Address	Number of Shares Beneficially Owned	Percent of Class as of December 31, 2004
Berkshire Hathaway Inc. 440 Kiewit Plaza Omaha, Nebraska 68131 . . .	200,000,000	8.30%

Information About the Board of Directors and Corporate Governance

The Board is elected by the shareowners to oversee their interest in the long-term health and the overall success of the business and its financial strength. The Board serves as the ultimate decision-making body of the Company, except for those matters reserved to or shared with the shareowners. The Board selects and oversees the members of senior management, who are charged by the Board with conducting the business of the Company.

The Committee on Directors and Corporate Governance periodically reviews and assesses the Company's corporate governance policies.

The Chairman of the Committee on Directors and Corporate Governance presides at all meetings of non-management Directors. These meetings include the evaluation of the Chief Executive Officer. The Committee on Directors and Corporate Governance leads the Board of Director's process of Board and Committee evaluation and carefully examines the performance

1480

and qualifications of each incumbent Director before deciding whether to recommend him or her to the Board for renomination.

Independence Determination

No Director will be deemed to be independent unless the Board of Directors affirmatively determines that the Director has no material relationship with the Company, directly, or as an officer, shareowner or partner of an organization that has a relationship with the Company. The Board observes all criteria for independence established by the SEC, the Exchange and other governing laws and regulations.

The Company has adopted categorical standards which provide that the following relationships will not be considered material relationships that would impact a director's independence:

- the director is an executive officer or employee or any member of his or her immediate family is an executive officer of any other organization that does business with the Company and the annual sales to, or purchases from, the Company are less than $1 million or 1% of the consolidated gross revenues of such organization, whichever is more;

- the director or any member of his or her immediate family is an executive officer of any other organization which is indebted to the Company, or to which the Company is indebted, and the total amount of either company's indebtedness to the other is less than $1 million or 1% of the total consolidated assets of the organization on which the director or any member of his or her immediate family serves as an executive officer, whichever is more;

- the director is a director or trustee, but not an executive officer, of any other organization that does business with, or receives donations from, the Company;

- the director or any member of his or her immediate family holds a less than 5% interest in any other organization that has a relationship with the Company; or

- the director or any member of his or her immediate family serves as an executive officer of a charitable or educational organization which receives contributions from the Company in a single fiscal year of less than $1 million or 2% of that organization's consolidated gross revenues, whichever is more.

In its annual review of Director independence, the Board considers all commercial, banking, consulting, legal, accounting, charitable or other business relationships any Director may have with the Company. As a result of its annual review, the Board has determined that none of the following Directors has a material relationship with the Company and, as a result, such directors are determined to be independent: Ronald W. Allen, Cathleen P. Black, Warren E. Buffett, Barry Diller, Maria Elena Lagomasino, Robert L. Nardelli, Sam Nunn, J. Pedro Reinhard, James D. Robinson III, Peter V. Ueberroth or James B. Williams. None of the

Directors who were determined to be independent had any relationships that were outside the categorical standards identified above. The independent Directors, who constitute a majority of the Board of Directors, are also identified by an asterisk on the next table. Even though they are not currently determined to be independent, Messrs. Allen, Keough and McHenry have contributed greatly to the Board of Directors and the Company through their wealth of experience, expertise and judgment.

The Board and Board Committees

In 2004, the Board of Directors held eight meetings and Committees of the Board of Directors held a total of 35 meetings. Overall attendance at such meetings was 95%. Each Director attended more than 75% of the aggregate of all meetings of the Board of Directors and the Committees on which he or she served during 2004.

The Board of Directors has an Audit Committee, a Committee on Directors and Corporate Governance, a Compensation Committee, an Executive Committee, a Finance Committee, a Management Development Committee and a Public Issues and Diversity Review Committee. The Board of Directors has adopted a written charter for each of these Committees. The full text of each charter and the Company's Corporate Governance Guidelines are available on the Company's website located at www.coca-cola.com. Additionally, a copy of the Audit Committee Charter is attached as Appendix I hereto.

The following table describes the current members of each of the Committees and the number of meetings held during 2004.

	AUDIT	COMPENSATION	DIRECTORS AND CORPORATE GOVERNANCE	EXECUTIVE	FINANCE	MANAGEMENT DEVELOPMENT	PUBLIC ISSUES AND DIVERSITY REVIEW
Herbert A. Allen				X	X	X	
Ronald W. Allen*	X						X
Cathleen P. Black*	X	Chair					
Warren E. Buffett*	X			X	X		
Barry Diller*			X	X	X	X	
E. Neville Isdell				Chair			
Donald R. Keough						Chair	
Maria Elena Lagomasino*		X	X				
Donald F. McHenry							Chair
Robert L. Nardelli*	X	X					
Sam Nunn*				X	X		X
J. Pedro Reinhard*	X						
James D. Robinson III*			Chair			X	X
Peter V. Ueberroth*	Chair	X					

James B. Williams*				X	Chair	X	
Number of Meetings	7	10	4	0	5	5	4

* Independent Directors.

The Audit Committee

Under the terms of its charter, the Audit Committee represents and assists the Board in fulfilling its oversight responsibility relating to the integrity of the Company's financial statements and the financial reporting process, the systems of internal accounting and financial controls, the internal audit function, the annual independent audit of the Company's financial statements, the Company's compliance with legal and regulatory requirements and its ethics program, the independent auditors' qualifications and independence, the performance of the Company's internal audit function and the performance of its independent auditors. In fulfilling its duties, the Audit Committee, among other things, shall:

- have the sole authority and responsibility to hire, evaluate and, where appropriate, replace the independent auditors;

- meet and review with management and the independent auditors the interim financial statements and the Company's disclosures under Management's Discussion and Analysis of Financial Condition and Results of Operations prior to the filing of the Company's Quarterly Reports on Form 10-Q;

- meet and review with management and the independent auditors the financial statements to be included in the Company's Annual Report on Form 10-K (or the annual report to shareowners) including (a) their judgment about the quality, not just acceptability, of the Company's accounting principles, including significant financial reporting issues and judgments made in connection with the preparation of the financial statements; (b) the clarity of the disclosures in the financial statements; and (c) the Company's disclosures under Management's Discussion and Analysis of Financial Condition and Results of Operations, including critical accounting policies;

- review and discuss with management, the internal auditors and the independent auditors the Company's policies with respect to risk assessment and risk management;

- review and discuss with management, the internal auditors and the independent auditors the Company's internal controls, the results of the internal audit program, and the Company's disclosure controls and procedures and quarterly assessment of such controls and procedures;

- establish procedures for handling complaints regarding accounting, internal accounting controls, and auditing matters, including procedures for confidential, anonymous submission of concerns by employees regarding accounting and auditing matters; and

- review and discuss with management, the internal auditors and the independent auditors the overall adequacy and effectiveness of the Company's legal, regulatory and ethical compliance programs.

Each member of the Audit Committee meets the independence requirements of the Exchange, the 1934 Act and the Company's Corporate Governance Guidelines. Each member of the Audit Committee is financially literate, knowledgeable and qualified to review financial statements. The "audit committee financial expert" designated by the Board is J. Pedro Reinhard, Executive Vice President and Chief Financial Officer of The Dow Chemical Company.

The Compensation Committee

Under the terms of its charter, the Compensation Committee has overall responsibility for evaluating and approving the officer compensation plans, policies and programs of the Company. In fulfilling its duties, the Compensation Committee, among other things, shall:

- review and approve all corporate goals and objectives relevant to the compensation of the Chief Executive Officer;

- evaluate the performance of the Chief Executive Officer in light of approved corporate goals, performance goals and objectives;

- review and approve compensation of the Chief Executive Officer, other elected officers and all key senior executives based on their evaluation;

- review and approve any employment agreements, severance agreements or arrangements, retirement arrangements, change in control agreements/provisions, and any special or supplemental benefits for each officer of the Company;

- approve, disapprove, modify or amend all non-equity plans designed and intended to provide compensation primarily for officers;

- make recommendations to the Board of Directors regarding adoption of equity plans; and

- administer, modify or amend the stock option plans and restricted stock plans.

Each member of the Compensation Committee meets the independence requirements of the Exchange, the Internal Revenue Code of 1986, as amended (the "Code"), and the Company's Corporate Governance Guidelines.

1484

The Committee on Directors and Corporate Governance

Under the terms of its charter, the Committee on Directors and Corporate Governance is responsible for considering and making recommendations concerning the function and needs of the Board, and the review and development of corporate governance guidelines. In fulfilling its duties, the Committee on Directors and Corporate Governance, among other things, shall:

- seek individuals qualified to be Board members consistent with criteria established by the Board including evaluating persons suggested by shareowners or others;

- recommend to the Board nominees for the next annual meeting of shareowners;

- oversee the evaluation of the Board and management;

- consider issues involving related party transactions with Directors and similar issues; and

- review and recommend all matters pertaining to fees and retainers paid to Directors.

The Chairman of the Committee on Directors and Corporate Governance presides at all meetings of non-management Directors, including the meeting in which the Chief Executive Officer's performance is evaluated.

Each member of the Committee on Directors and Corporate Governance meets the independence requirements of the Exchange and the Company's Corporate Governance Guidelines.

The Finance Committee

Under the terms of its charter, the Finance Committee is appointed to assist the Board in discharging its responsibilities relating to oversight of the Company's financial affairs. In fulfilling its duties, the Finance Committee, among other things, shall:

- formulate and recommend for approval to the Board the financial policies of the Company;

- maintain oversight of the budget and financial operations of the Company;

- review and recommend capital expenditures;

- evaluate the performance of and returns on approved capital expenditures; and

- recommend dividend policy to the Board.

The Public Issues and Diversity Review Committee

Under the terms of its charter, the Public Issues and Diversity Review Committee aids the Board in discharging its responsibilities relating to public issues and diversity. In fulfilling its duties, the Public Issues and Diversity Review Committee, among other things, shall:

- review the Company's policy and practice relating to significant public issues of concern to shareowners, the Company, the business community and the general public;

- monitor the Company's progress towards its diversity goals, compliance with its responsibilities as an equal opportunity employer and compliance with any legal obligation arising out of employment discrimination class action litigation; and

- review and recommend the Board's position on shareowner proposals in the annual proxy statement.

The Executive Committee

Under the terms of its charter, the Executive Committee has the authority to exercise the power and authority of the Board between meetings, except the powers reserved for the Board or the shareowners by the Delaware General Corporation Law.

The Management Development Committee

Under the terms of its charter, the Management Development Committee aids the Board in discharging its responsibilities relating to succession planning and oversight of talent development for senior positions.

Director Compensation

Officers who are also Directors do not receive any fee or remuneration for services as members of the Board or of any Committee of the Board. During 2004, non-management Directors received an annual retainer fee of $125,000, of which $50,000 was paid in cash and $75,000 accrued in share units to the account of each Director under the Director Deferred Compensation Plan. During 2004, non-management Directors also received a $1,000 fee for each Board or Committee meeting attended, the chairman of the Audit Committee received a committee chairman fee of $25,000 and the chairpersons of the other committees each received a $3,000 committee chairman fee. The Company also provides its products to Directors.

In addition to the required deferral of a portion of Director compensation into share units (as noted above), the Director Deferred Compensation Plan provides that non-management Directors may elect to defer receipt of all or part of the $50,000 cash portion of the retainer fee until date(s) no earlier than the year following the year in which they leave the Board. Under this plan, cash retainer fees may be deferred in share units or cash. Cash deferrals are credited with interest at the prime lending rate of SunTrust Bank. Share units accrue phantom dividends and appreciate (or depreciate) as would an actual share of Common Stock purchased on the deferral date. After service as a Director terminates, both cash deferrals and share unit deferrals will be paid in cash.

In addition, the Company provides insurance benefits to non-management Directors, including $30,000 term life insurance for each Director, $100,000 group accidental death and dismemberment insurance and $200,000 group travel accident insurance coverage while traveling on Company business. The Company also offers medical and dental coverage. Costs for all these benefits for 2004 totaled $33,916.

Director Nominations

The Committee on Directors and Corporate Governance will consider recommendations for directorships submitted by shareowners. Shareowners who wish the Committee on Directors and Corporate Governance to consider their recommendations for nominees for the position of Director should submit their recommendations in writing to the Committee on Directors and Corporate Governance in care of the Office of the Secretary, The Coca-Cola Company, P.O. Box 1734, Atlanta, Georgia 30301. Recommendations by shareowners that are made in accordance with these procedures will receive the same consideration given to nominees of the Committee on Directors and Corporate Governance.

In its assessment of each potential candidate, the Committee on Directors and Corporate Governance will review the nominee's judgment, experience, independence, understanding of the Company's or other related industries and such other factors the Committee on Directors and Corporate Governance determines are pertinent in light of the current needs of the Board. Diversity of race, ethnicity, gender and age are factors in evaluating candidates for Board membership. The Committee on Directors and Corporate Governance will also take into account the ability of a Director to devote the time and effort necessary to fulfill his or her responsibilities to the Company.

Nominees may be suggested by Directors, members of management, shareowners or, in some cases, by a third party firm. In identifying and considering candidates for nomination to the Board, the Committee on Directors and Corporate Governance considers, in addition to the requirements set out in the Company's Corporate Governance Guidelines and its charter, quality of experience, the needs of the Company and the range of talent and experience represented on the Board.

The Committee on Directors and Corporate Governance sometimes uses the services of a third party executive search firm to assist it in identifying and evaluating possible nominees for Director.

Certain Transactions and Relationships

SunTrust

FORM OF PROXY STATEMENT AND FORM OF PROXY

SunTrust Banks, Inc. ("SunTrust"), which during a portion of 2004 was a 5% owner of Common Stock, engages in ordinary course of business banking transactions with the Company and its subsidiaries, including the making of loans on customary terms, for which we paid fees totaling approximately $504,000 in 2004. SunTrust Bank, an indirect subsidiary of SunTrust, has extended a $100 million 364-day line of credit and an approximate $12 million letter of credit, subsequently reduced to approximately $9 million in July 2004, to the Company and an approximate $16.3 million letter of credit, subsequently reduced to approximately $14.5 million in February 2004, to a Company subsidiary for which we paid fees totaling approximately $109,000 in 2004. In 2004, the Company also paid SunTrust Bank $2.75 million with respect to certain contracts sold to SunTrust Bank by certain vendors of the Company. The Company expects to pay approximately $3 million pursuant to these contracts in 2005. The Company has also guaranteed an obligation in the original principal amount of $45 million to SunTrust Bank on behalf of a third party. SunTrust leases office space in a building owned by one of our subsidiaries and located at 711 Fifth Avenue, New York, New York. In 2004, our subsidiary was paid approximately $465,000 under both the current lease and a new lease for additional office space entered into with SunTrust and its subsidiary, SunTrust Capital Markets. We expect that the Company will be paid a greater amount in 2005 for this additional office space under the terms of the new lease. In the opinion of management, the terms of such banking and credit arrangements and leases are fair and reasonable and as favorable to the Company and its subsidiaries as those which could have been obtained from unrelated third parties at the time of their execution.

SunTrust filed an amendment to its Schedule 13G on February 16, 2005 indicating that, as of December 31, 2004, it owned less than 5% of the issued and outstanding Common Stock.

Warren E. Buffett

Warren E. Buffett, one of our Directors, is Chairman of the Board, Chief Executive Officer and the major shareowner of Berkshire Hathaway. Berkshire Hathaway is a significant shareowner of the Company. McLane Company, Inc. ("McLane") is a wholly owned subsidiary of Berkshire Hathaway. In 2004, McLane made payments totaling approximately $170.2 million to the Company to purchase fountain syrup and other products in the ordinary course of business. Also in 2004, McLane received from the Company approximately $9.8 million in agency commissions relating to the sale of the Company's products to customers, and approximately $298,000 in freight cost associated with the transport of syrup, each in the ordinary course of business. McLane also received from the Company approximately $140,000 for advertising and marketing payments and other fees in the ordinary course of business. This business relationship was in place prior to Berkshire Hathaway's acquisition of McLane in 2003 and is on terms similar to the Company's relationships with other customers.

International Dairy Queen, Inc. ("IDQ") is a wholly owned subsidiary of Berkshire Hathaway. In 2004, IDQ and its subsidiaries made payments totaling approximately $2.1 million to the Company directly and through bottlers and other agents to purchase fountain syrup and other products in the ordinary course of business. Also in 2004, IDQ and its subsidiaries received promotional and marketing incentives for corporate and franchised stores totaling approximately $1.1 million from the Company and its subsidiaries in the ordinary course of business. This business relationship was in place for many years prior to Berkshire Hathaway's acquisition of IDQ and is on terms substantially similar to the Company's relationships with other customers.

FlightSafety International, Inc. ("FlightSafety") is also a wholly owned subsidiary of Berkshire Hathaway. In 2002, the Company entered into a four-year agreement with FlightSafety to provide pilot, flight attendant and mechanic training services to the Company. In 2004, the Company paid FlightSafety approximately $592,000 for providing these services to the Company in the ordinary course of business. Berkshire Hathaway holds a significant equity interest in Moody's Corporation, to which the Company paid fees of $99,000 in 2004 for rating our commercial paper programs. Berkshire Hathaway holds a significant equity interest in The FINOVA Group, Inc. ("FINOVA"). In 2004, one of our subsidiaries paid approximately $79,000 to a subsidiary of FINOVA for the lease of coolers in the ordinary course of business and approximately $123,000 to purchase leased coolers. The original lease was entered into prior to Berkshire Hathaway's acquisition of its interest in FINOVA. In the opinion of management, the terms of the Flight Safety contract and the lease are fair and reasonable and as favorable to the Company as those which could have been obtained from unrelated third parties at the time of their execution.

Berkshire Hathaway also holds a significant equity interest in American Express Company ("American Express"). In 2004, the Company paid fees for credit card memberships, business travel and other services in the ordinary course of business to American Express or its subsidiaries. Additionally in 2004, American Express and its subsidiaries made payments totaling approximately $99,000 to the Company to purchase fountain syrup in the ordinary course of business. XTRA Corporation is a wholly owned subsidiary of Berkshire Hathaway. In 2004, the Company paid approximately $235,000 to XTRA Corporation for equipment leases of trailers used to transport and store product in the ordinary course of business. In the opinion of management, the terms of the lease are fair and reasonable and as favorable to the Company as those which could have been obtained from unrelated third parties at the time of its execution.

Herbert A. Allen

Herbert A. Allen, one of our Directors, is President and Chief Executive Officer and a Director of Allen & Company Incorporated ("ACI") and a principal shareowner of ACI's parent. ACI has leased and subleased office space since 1977 in a building owned by one of our subsidiaries and located at 711 Fifth Avenue, New York, New York. In 2004, ACI paid approximately $3.8 million and it is expected that it will pay a similar amount in 2005 under the terms of the current lease. In the opinion of management, the terms of the lease, as modified in 2002, are fair and reasonable and as favorable to the Company as those which could have been obtained from unrelated third parties at the time of its execution.

Donald R. Keough

Donald R. Keough, one of our Directors, is Chairman of the Board of ACI. The Company's transactions with ACI are described above.

REPORT OF THE COMPENSATION COMMITTEE
OF THE BOARD OF DIRECTORS OF THE COCA-COLA COMPANY
ON EXECUTIVE COMPENSATION

This is the Report of the Compensation Committee of the Board of Directors of The Coca-Cola Company (the "Committee") on compensation policies for executive officers and the Chief Executive Officer of The Coca-Cola Company (the "Company").

We believe that executive compensation policies and practices at the Company should be consistent with and linked to the Company's strategic business objectives and the creation of shareowner value.

Within that framework, we undertake to compensate executives based on performance, at a level competitive with the market, in a manner that would attract and retain strong talent and with an emphasis on the equity component of compensation. Our goal is to be consistent with our philosophy, competitive with the market, and transparent in our thinking and our actions with respect to compensation for Company executives.

The Committee enlists the help of an independent consultant, Towers Perrin. The following discussion reflects the executive compensation philosophy and programs of the Company.

Background

The Company's executive compensation programs are designed to serve the Company's broader strategic goals of profitable growth and the creation of long-term shareowner value. The programs are designed to meet the following objectives:

Performance and Accountability. Our programs are fundamentally pay-for-performance programs. The rewards earned and delivered through the Company's executive compensation plans are directly linked to the desired performance for the Company and its operating units. Individual performance and contributions are considered at the time awards are delivered. Measures selected align rewards with both top and bottom line growth goals and shareowner interests.

Competitiveness. We assess competitiveness using a peer group of global companies. These companies include large companies in the consumer goods/services sector, companies with broad global scale and scope, companies with significant brand equity and companies that are recognized for best practices or with whom the Company competes for talent. The companies selected for comparison of total compensation differ from those included in the Performance Graph because the Company seeks talent from a broader group of companies than the Food, Beverage and Tobacco Groups against which performance is compared. We emphasize and assess total compensation opportunities, both short and long term, while at the same time focusing attention on the competitiveness of each component of compensation.

Management Development. To support the Board in fulfilling its responsibility to identify future leaders of the Company, we structure compensation opportunities to attract and retain those individuals who can maximize the creation of shareowner value.

Equity Orientation. Equity-based plans comprise the major part of the total compensation package to instill ownership thinking and to link compensation to corporate performance and shareowner interests. Consistent with this philosophy, the Company has established stock ownership guidelines which require executives to own appropriate levels of Common Stock. Compliance with these guidelines is monitored.

These principles are not mechanical, but rather inform the Committee's judgment. We have the flexibility to target individual components of pay at higher or lower levels on an individual basis, depending on the executive's experience, the criticality of the position, individual performance, potential for advancement, years of service in level/position and other considerations.

Actual bonus payouts, actual value received from long-term incentive awards and actual overall compensation levels may vary from the targeted levels based on corporate, business unit and individual performance, and overall Company stock price.

The overall mix of pay components is monitored and compared to peer company practices to ensure appropriate pay leverage is maintained in the overall compensation package, and in equity-based incentives which emphasize long-term shareowner value creation.

Components of Executive Compensation

The basic components of executive compensation are:

- *Annual Cash Compensation,* including base salary and annual incentives; and

- *Long-Term Incentive Compensation,* including stock options and performance share units resulting in future awards of restricted stock if certain performance targets are met.

Annual Cash Compensation

Base Salary. The purpose of base salary is to create a secure base of cash compensation for executives that is competitive with the market for global talent.

Executives' salary increases do not follow a preset schedule or formula; however, the following will be considered when determining appropriate salary levels and increases:

- The individual's current and sustained performance results and the methods utilized to achieve such results; and

- Non-financial performance indicators to include strategic developments for which an executive has responsibility (such as quality, acquisitions, environmental efforts or product development) and managerial performance (such as diversity management, succession planning and social responsibility).

We exercise discretion in making salary decisions taking into account, among other things, each individual's performance and the Company's overall performance. With regard to individual performance, we rely to a large extent on the Chief Executive Officer's evaluations of each individual executive officer's performance.

Annual Incentives. The purpose of annual incentive plans is to provide cash compensation on an annual basis that is at-risk and contingent on the achievement of annual business and operating objectives. Annual incentive funding will reflect overall Company performance and operating group and division performance, where appropriate. Actual incentive awards reflect achievement of individual performance goals and contributions to business unit and Company results. Annual incentive awards vary within a range of 0% to approximately 200% of targeted award amounts.

Long-Term Incentive Compensation

Long-term incentives comprise the largest portion of the total compensation package for executives. There are two forms of long-term incentives normally used for executives: stock options and performance share units. In any given year, executives will generally receive awards from one or both of these two programs to effectively align awards with long-term Company performance and stock price growth.

Grant levels will be determined for each executive based on individual performance and potential, history of past grants, time in current job and level of, or significant changes in, responsibility.

- *Stock Options.* The purpose of stock options is to provide equity compensation whose value is at-risk directly related to the creation of shareowner value and the increase in Company stock price. Stock options provide executives a vehicle to increase equity ownership and share in the appreciation of the value of Company stock.

- *Performance Share Units.* Performance Share Unit awards are agreements to grant restricted stock at a future date based upon the Company achieving pre-determined long-term performance goals. Awards of Performance Share Units provide equity compensation whose value is at-risk and based on the achievement of sustained performance of Company goals and the enhancement of shareowner value over time. They also serve to help retain key executive talent over the long term.

Grant size under both these plans varies based on individual performance, contribution and potential. Adjustments are made within the framework of the Company's long-term incentive grant guidelines.

The ultimate value delivered from long-term incentive awards will vary directly with changes in shareowner returns and stock price appreciation.

Approximately 5,900 employees received option awards in 2004. The named executive officers received option awards for 1,420,000 shares in 2004, or 4% of options awarded.

Approximately 55 executives received Performance Share Units in 2004. The named executive officers received Performance Share Unit awards for 271,102 shares in 2004, or 28.4% of Performance Share Units awarded.

Additional Information

Benefits. Benefits offered to executive officers serve a different purpose than do the other elements of total compensation. In general, they are designed to provide a safety net of protection against the financial catastrophes that can result from illness, disability or death, and to provide a reasonable level of retirement income based on years of service with the Company. Benefits offered to executive officers are those that are offered to the general employee population, with some variation, primarily to promote tax efficiency and replacement of benefit opportunities lost due to regulatory limits.

Tax Compliance Policy. A feature of the Omnibus Budget Reconciliation Act of 1993 limits deductibility of certain compensation for the Chief Executive Officer and the four other executive officers who are highest paid and employed at year end to $1 million per year, effective for tax years beginning on or after January 1, 1994. If certain conditions are met, compensation may be excluded from the $1 million limit. However, we have not designed compensation programs solely for tax purposes.

The Company's shareowner approved incentive plans, Stock Option Plans and certain awards under the 1989 Restricted Stock Plan meet the conditions necessary for deductibility. However, we will continue to exercise discretion in those instances where the mechanistic approaches necessary under tax law considerations would compromise the interests of shareowners in rewarding performance which increases the value of the Company.

Compensation for the Chairman and Chief Executive Officer

E. Neville Isdell

The Committee awarded Mr. Isdell a competitive compensation package (salary and short and long-term target opportunities) upon his employment that, in our opinion, is reasonable and competitive compared to peer company CEOs. Importantly, the package is more heavily weighted in performance-based equity awards.

In addition, the Committee awarded a special restricted stock award that is intended to keep Mr. Isdell whole for his overall net income, not related to his current employment, that was adversely affected by accepting U.S. employment. The award is not meant to be a performance-based award, but its eventual value to Mr. Isdell will be contingent upon Company stock price performance. The award is not released to Mr. Isdell until six months following his retirement (with approval by the Board and no earlier than June 1, 2008). The award contains a provision that, in the event the shares are forfeited for any reason other than for termination for cause, Mr. Isdell will receive a cash payment to compensate him for additional taxes he would have paid on his non-Company related income during the period of his U.S. residency while Chairman and CEO.

In February, after full Company results were reviewed, the Committee reviewed and awarded Mr. Isdell awards for his performance. Those awards include:

- An annual incentive award of $2,864,862

- A stock option award of 620,690 shares

- A Performance Share Unit target award of 139,740 shares.

In our opinion, the awards for Mr. Isdell are reasonable and competitive, and reflect both his contributions thus far and our expectations of his performance. Both Mr. Isdell and the Board are clear that the results of Mr. Isdell's work will be a focused organization with clear growth goals and the ability to successfully execute against them and, as a result, drive shareowner value. Both Mr. Isdell and the Board are clear that this effort will take time. In the months Mr. Isdell has been Chairman, he has completed a comprehensive assessment of the Company's situation and has established new goals for the Company going forward aimed at restoring growth to the Company. He is focusing on developing management talent and refining succession plans as well as ensuring effective management routines and overall employee engagement.

Douglas N. Daft

Mr. Daft announced his decision to retire at the end of 2004. Related to that decision, the Committee reviewed provisions of his retirement and allowed the release of 200,000 restricted shares granted to him during the period from April 1992 to October 1998. The terms of these grants provided that the restricted shares would be released upon retirement after age 62 but not earlier than five years from the date of grant. The Committee determined to release the shares in recognition of Mr. Daft's 27 years of service to the Company and the fact that he turns 62 in March of 2005. Mr. Daft forfeited 500,000 shares of restricted stock granted to him in November 2000 since as of the date of his retirement he had not held these shares for five years from the date of grant. In addition, Mr. Daft forfeited 1,000,000 shares of performance-based restricted stock since he will have retired prior to the completion of the performance period. The Committee also approved payment of $1,002,430 under the Long-Term Incentive Program. Achievement of performance against three-year compound growth in economic profit and average operating profit resulted in the award, which was determined against the range originally set by the Committee for performance. No annual incentive was paid for 2004.

Summary

We believe the executive compensation policies and programs described in this report serve the interests of the shareowners and the Company. Pay delivered to executives is aligned with Company, business unit where applicable, and individual performance. We will continue to evaluate and, as necessary, update our compensation programs to assure that they remain performance-driven, reward competitively, serve to attract, motivate and retain the best talent and reinforce equity ownership. Through these principles, we believe executives will be motivated to achieve the long-term sustainable growth of the Company. We invite shareowners to review the following tables for details of specific awards.

Cathleen P. Black,
Chairman
Maria Elena Lagomasino
Robert L. Nardelli
Peter V. Ueberroth

EXECUTIVE COMPENSATION

The following tables and footnotes discuss the compensation paid in 2004, 2003 and 2002 to (i) our Chief Executive Officer, (ii) our four other most highly compensated executive officers, (iii) Douglas N. Daft who served as Chief Executive Officer through May 31, 2004, and (iv) Steven J. Heyer who was an executive officer during a portion of the fiscal year ended December 31, 2004 and would have been one of the four most highly compensated executive officers for 2004 but for the fact that he was not an executive officer as of December 31, 2004.

Summary Compensation Table

		Annual Compensation			Long-Term Compensation			
Name and Principal Position	Year	Salary (a)	Bonus (b)	Other Annual Compensation (c)	Restricted Stock Awards (d)	Securities Underlying Options/SAR Awards (e)	LTIP Payout (f)	All Other Compensation (g)
E. Neville Isdell[1] Chairman of the Board and Chief Executive Officer	2004 2003 2002	$ 875,000 — —	$2,864,862 — —	$ 296,281 — —	$6,855,800 — —	450,000 — —	$ — — —	$ 26,250 — —
Gary P. Fayard[2] Executive Vice President and	2004 2003 2002	540,750 533,333 475,000	838,500 650,000 750,000	— — —	0 0 0	125,000 112,000 175,000	374,634 0 0	35,723 36,250 32,063

Name and Title	Year							
Chief Financial Officer								
Mary E. Minnick[3] Executive Vice President and President and Chief Operating Officer, Asia	2004	570,625	744,500	—	0	130,000	345,735	37,382
	2003	558,333	589,875	—	0	112,000	0	44,993
	2002	500,000	800,000	—	2,344,000	175,000	240,100	36,620
José Octavio Reyes[4] Executive Vice President and President and Chief Operating Officer, Latin America	2004	518,716	698,700	83,011	0	160,000	172,088	5,042
	2003	456,278	614,250	58,572	0	112,000	0	1,932
	2002	407,258	350,000	79,922	0	57,813	333,156	2,110
Alexander B. Cummings, Jr.[5] Executive Vice President and President and Chief Operating Officer, Africa	2004	492,812	638,300	75,000	0	125,000	233,155	34,133
	2003	483,500	629,375	66,000	0	112,000	0	36,210
	2002	425,000	675,000	45,000	0	85,313	97,020	23,717
Douglas N. Daft[6] Former Chairman of the Board and Chief Executive Officer	2004	1,494,792	0	130,027	0	0	1,002,430	164,844
	2003	1,500,000	4,000,000	199,593	0	0	0	165,000
	2002	1,500,000	4,000,000	180,785	0	0	0	150,000
Steven J. Heyer[7] Former President and Chief Operating Officer	2004	996,154	1,036,547	96,628	0	430,000	682,500	7,136,885
	2003	1,000,000	1,500,000	57,763	0	0	0	75,000
	2002	885,000	2,000,000	—	0	450,000	—	107,053

1. The amounts reflected for Mr. Isdell include the following:
   (a) Salary for period of June 1, 2004 to December 31, 2004.
   (b) Payments based on Company and individual performance from one or more incentive plans of the Company.
   (c) For 2004, other annual compensation includes $112,402 paid under an international consulting arrangement between Mr. Isdell and the Company which was terminated prior to his becoming Chairman and Chief Executive Officer of the Company. Also includes $183,878 for personal use of Company aircraft including a gross-up for taxes due. The figure represents the incremental direct operating cost to the Company for personal aircraft use. Mr. Isdell is required by the Company to use Company aircraft for all travel. In prior years, the standard industry fare level ("SIFL") rates set by the Internal Revenue Service were used to value personal aircraft use. In order to provide a comparison with prior years, the SIFL value for Mr. Isdell for 2004 would have been $55,582, including a gross-up for taxes due.

(d) An award of 140,000 shares of restricted stock was made to Mr. Isdell on July 22, 2004. The value at year-end of this award was $5,829,600. Dividends on these restricted shares are paid at the same rate and at the same time as paid to all shareowners.

(g) For 2004, includes $6,150 contributed by the Company to the Thrift Plan and $20,100 accrued under the thrift portion of the Supplemental Plan.

2. The amounts reflected for Mr. Fayard include the following:

(b) Payments based on Company and individual performance from one or more incentive plans of the Company.

(d) The value at year-end of 89,000 shares of restricted stock granted previously, including 75,000 performance-based restricted shares, was $3,705,960. Dividends on all restricted shares, including performance-based restricted shares that have not vested, are paid at the same rate and at the same time as paid to all shareowners.

(f) Payment of the Long-Term Performance Incentive Program award for the 2002-2004 performance period. One half of this amount is payable in March 2005; the other half is payable in March 2007.

(g) For 2004, includes $6,150 contributed by the Company to the Thrift Plan and $29,573 accrued under the thrift portion of the Supplemental Plan.

3. The amounts reflected for Ms. Minnick include the following:

(b) Payments based on Company and individual performance from one or more incentive plans of the Company.

(d) The value at year-end of 100,000 shares of performance-based restricted stock granted previously was $4,164,000. Dividends on all restricted shares, including performance-based restricted shares that have not vested, are paid at the same rate and at the same time as paid to all shareowners.

(f) • For 2004, represents the Long-Term Performance Incentive Program award for the 2002-2004 performance period. One half of this amount is payable in March 2005; the other half is payable in March 2007.

• For 2002, represents payment under an overseas long-term performance plan which operated on similar terms to the Long-Term Performance Incentive Program . . . . The performance targets for this plan were based on the results of the applicable operating segment. This plan is no longer in use and the last three-year performance period ended December 31, 2002.

(g) For 2004, includes $6,150 contributed by the Company to the Thrift Plan and $31,232 accrued under the thrift portion of the Supplemental Plan.

4. The amounts reflected for Mr. Reyes include the following:

(a) Includes $37,550, $43,269 and $38,627 for statutorily required payments in 2004, 2003 and 2002, respectively.

(b) Payments based on Company and individual performance from one or more incentive plans of the Company.

(c) • For 2004, other annual compensation includes $35,687 for costs relating to the personal use of a Company driver and $45,467 reimbursement for certain tax expenses. Although Mr. Reyes is not an International Service Associate, the

Company applies certain tax equalization provisions of that policy to Mr. Reyes because he incurs U.S. tax obligations due to his work responsibilities in the United States. This reimbursement is intended to ensure that Mr. Reyes is not advantaged or disadvantaged from a tax standpoint.

- For 2003, other annual compensation includes $45,012 for costs relating to the personal use of a Company driver and $12,073 for personal use of Company aircraft based on the SIFL rates.
- For 2002, other annual compensation includes $48,015 for the costs of a second Company car assigned to Mr. Reyes and $30,284 for costs relating to the personal use of a Company driver.

(d) Mr. Reyes does not hold any restricted stock.

(f)
- For 2004, payment of the Long-Term Performance Incentive Program award for the 2002-2004 performance period. One half of this amount is payable in March 2005; the other half is payable in March 2007.
- For 2002, represents payment under an overseas long-term performance plan which operated on similar terms to the Long-Term Performance Incentive Program . . . . The performance targets for this plan were based on the results of the applicable operating segment. This plan is no longer in use and the last three-year performance period ended December 31, 2002.

(g) For 2004, includes $1,894 contributed by the Company to the savings fund portion of the Plan Futura (the "Mexico Plan") and $3,148 contributed to the equity portion of the Mexico Plan.

5. The amounts reflected for Mr. Cummings include the following:

(b) Payments based on Company and individual performance from one or more incentive plans of the Company.

(c) Other annual compensation includes $75,000, $66,000 and $45,000 in dividend equivalents paid in each of 2004, 2003 and 2002, respectively, in connection with a performance-based promise to award 75,000 shares of restricted stock.

(d) Mr. Cummings does not hold any restricted stock.

(f)
- For 2004, payment of the Long-Term Performance Incentive Program award for the 2002-2004 performance period. One half of this amount is payable in March 2005; the other half is payable in March 2007.
- For 2002, represents payment under an overseas long-term performance plan which operated on similar terms to the Long-Term Performance Incentive Program . . . . The performance targets for this plan were based on the results of the applicable operating segment. This plan is no longer in use and the last three-year performance period ended December 31, 2002.

(g) For 2004, includes $6,150 contributed by the Company to the Thrift Plan and $27,983 accrued under the thrift portion of the Supplemental Plan.

6. Mr. Daft resigned as Chairman and Chief Executive Officer on May 31, 2004 and retired from the Company effective as of December 31, 2004. The amounts reflected for Mr. Daft include the following:

(a) Salary for period of January 1, 2004 to December 30, 2004.

(b) Payments based on Company and individual performance from one or more incentive plans of the Company.

(c) • For 2004, other annual compensation includes $114,950 for personal use of Company aircraft. This figure represents the incremental direct operating cost to the Company for personal aircraft use. In prior years, SIFL rates were used to value personal aircraft use. In order to provide a comparison with prior years, the SIFL value for Mr. Daft for 2004 would have been $55,760 including a gross-up for taxes due.

　　• For 2003, other annual compensation includes $181,993 for personal use of Company aircraft based on the SIFL rates.

　　• For 2002, other annual compensation includes $152,738 for personal use of Company aircraft based on the SIFL rates.

While Chairman, Mr. Daft was required by the Company to use Company aircraft for all travel. The amounts include a gross-up for taxes due.

(d) Effective upon his retirement, all restrictions on 200,000 shares of restricted stock with a value on December 30, 2004 of $8,323,000 were released. Mr. Daft also forfeited 1,500,000 shares of restricted stock on that date.

(f) Payment of the Long-Term Performance Incentive Program award for the 2002-2004 performance period. According to the plan, the full award will be paid in March 2005 due to Mr. Daft's retirement.

(g) For 2004, includes $6,150 contributed by the Company to the Thrift Plan and $158,694 accrued under the thrift portion of the Supplemental Plan.

7. Mr. Heyer separated from the Company effective as of December 31, 2004. The amounts reflected for Mr. Heyer include the following:

(a) Salary for period of January 1, 2004 to December 30, 2004.

(b) • Payments based on Company and individual performance from one or more incentive plans of the Company.

　　• For 2002, the amount in the Bonus column includes $500,000 payable pursuant to his employment contract.

(c) • For 2004, other annual compensation includes $76,711 for personal use of Company aircraft. This figure represents the incremental direct operating cost to the Company for personal aircraft use. In prior years, the SIFL rates were used to value personal aircraft use. In order to provide a comparison with prior years, the SIFL value for Mr. Heyer for 2004 would have been $44,496.

　　• For 2003, other annual compensation includes $57,588 for personal use of Company aircraft based on the SIFL rates.

(d) • The value at year-end of Mr. Heyer's 125,000 performance-based restricted shares was $5,205,000. Release of the restrictions on these performance-based restricted shares is dependent upon Company performance for the 2001-2005 performance period. Dividends on all restricted shares, including performance-based restricted shares that have not vested, are paid at the same rate and at the same time as paid to all shareowners. Additionally all restrictions on 50,000 shares of restricted stock with a value on December 30, 2004 of $2,080,750 were released pursuant to the terms of his employment contract.

(f) Payment of the Long-Term Performance Incentive Program award for the 2002-

2004 performance period. This amount will be paid in March 2005 pursuant to the terms of his employment contract.

(g) For 2004, includes $7,062,000 payable to Mr. Heyer upon his separation from the Company pursuant to his employment contract. Also includes $6,150 contributed by the Company to the Thrift Plan and $68,735 accrued under the thrift portion of the Supplemental Plan.

Option/SAR Grants in Last Fiscal Year

	Individual Grants				
Name	Number of Securities Underlying Options/SARs Granted (#)[1]	% of Total Options/ SARs Granted to Employees in Fiscal Year	Exercise or Base Price (S/Share)	Expiration Date	Grant Date Value*
E. Neville Isdell[2]	450,000	1.43%	$ 48.89	07/21/2014	$ 6,583,500
Gary P. Fayard	125,000	.40%	41.27	12/15/2014	1,442,500
Mary E. Minnick	130,000	.41%	41.27	12/15/2014	1,500,200
José Octavio Reyes	160,000	.51%	41.27	12/15/2014	1,846,400
Alexander B. Cummings, Jr.	125,000	.40%	41.27	12/15/2014	1,442,500
Douglas N. Daft	0	—	—	—	—
Steven J. Heyer[3]	430,000	1.36%	51.115	02/18/2014	7,073,500

[1] These awards were made pursuant to The Coca-Cola Company 2002 Stock Option Plan (the "2002 Stock Option Plan"). Options awarded vest one-fourth on the first, second, third and fourth anniversaries of the grant date. The 2004 grants have a term of 10 years from the date of grant.

[2] An option grant for Mr. Isdell was made at the February 2005 Compensation Committee meeting, following an appraisal of his 2004 performance by the Compensation Committee taking into account input from the Board. This award does not appear in the table because the award was not made in fiscal 2004. The Compensation Committee awarded Mr. Isdell 620,690 options with an exercise price of $43.08 with term provisions as noted above. The award to Mr. Isdell provides for specific vesting and exercise provisions in the event of his retirement.

[3] These options were forfeited effective as of December 31, 2004 upon Mr. Heyer's separation from the Company.

* The grant date values are based on different Black-Scholes valuations per option utilizing the following assumptions:

	Grant made on 02/19/2004 to Mr. Heyer	Grant made on 07/22/2004 to Mr. Isdell	Grants made on 12/16/2004

Black-Scholes Value		$16.45	$14.63	$11.54
(a)	Exercise price	$51.115	$48.89	$41.27
(b)	Time horizon	10 years	10 years	10 years
(c)	Volatility	22.64%	21.27%	20.63%
(d)	Risk-free interest rate (10 years)	4.59%	4.41%	4.41%
(e)	Dividend yield	1.77%	1.90%	2.08%

Accounting rules require the Company to use a Black-Scholes calculation to determine the stock option expense for purposes of the Company's financial statements that is different than the values shown above. These rules require that the expected life of an option be used in the calculation, instead of its full term which the Company uses to determine value delivered (as shown above). The difference in valuation is primarily due to the assumed time horizon. Annually, at the time of our grant to employees, we obtain two independent market quotes to ensure the best market-based assumptions were used. Our Black-Scholes value was not materially different from the independent quotes.

Aggregated Option/SAR Exercises in Last Fiscal Year and FY-End Options/SAR Values

Name	Shares Acquired on Exercise	Value Realized	Number of Securities Underlying Unexercised Options/SARs at FY-End (#) Exercisable/ Unexercisable	Value of Unexercised In-the-Money Options/SARs at FY-End ($) (Based on $41.64 Per Share) Exercisable/ Unexercisable
E. Neville Isdell	80,000[1]	$ 1,137,907	165,000[2]/ 450,000	$ 0/ 0
Gary P. Fayard	4,000	59,999	570,750/ 371,500	180,450/ 46,250
Mary E. Minnick	11,000	194,825	367,070/ 324,000	96,240/ 48,100
José Octavio Reyes	12,450	234,247	330,157/ 295,406	102,255/ 59,200
Alexander B. Cummings, Jr.	0	N/A	231,897/ 282,906	0/ 46,250
Douglas N. Daft	40,000	711,843	2,007,000/ 0	300,750/ 0
Steven J. Heyer	0	N/A	1,285,000/ 0[3]	0/ 0

[1] Mr. Isdell exercised these options prior to his reemployment.

[2] Represents exercisable options held by Mr. Isdell prior to his reemployment.

[3] Mr. Heyer forfeited 740,000 unvested options upon his separation from the Company.

Long-Term Performance Plans

Long-term awards in the form of Performance Share Unit awards were made by the Compensation Committee under the 1989 Restricted Stock Award Plan and are for the three-year performance period beginning January 1, 2005 and ending December 31, 2007.

Long-Term Incentive Plans—Awards in Last Fiscal Year[1]

| Name | Number of Shares, Units or Other Rights (#) | Performance or Other Period Until Maturation or Payout | Estimated Future Payouts Under Non-Stock Price-Based Plan[2] | | |
			Threshold ($ or #)	Target ($ or #)	Maximum ($ or #)
E. Neville Isdell[3]	0	—	—	—	—
Gary P. Fayard	42,246	3 years	27,882	42,246	63,369
Mary E. Minnick	45,999	3 years	30,359	45,999	68,999
José Octavio Reyes	35,000	3 years	23,100	35,000	52,500
Alexander B. Cummings, Jr.	38,623	3 years	25,491	38,623	57,935
Douglas N. Daft[4]	0	—	—	—	—
Steven J. Heyer[5]	109,234	3 years	54,617	109,234	163,851

[1] The Company has established a program to provide Performance Share Unit Awards under The Coca-Cola Company 1989 Restricted Stock Award Plan (the "Restricted Stock Award Plan") to executives (the "Program"). The Compensation Committee made awards for the 2005-2007 Performance Period in December 2004 to executives participating in the Program with the exception of Mr. Isdell whose award was made in February 2005. The Compensation Committee, which administers the plan, sets award targets for participating executives. The target is expressed as a number of share units and cannot be increased. The Committee also sets a matrix which describes the percentage, which ranges from 0 - 150% of the target award, to be granted after performance has been certified. The Performance Measure for the plan is compound annual growth in earnings per share. At the end of the three-year Performance Period, subject to the participant's continued employment and international tax considerations, the Compensation Committee will grant a restricted stock award under the Restricted Stock Award Plan, which will contain restrictions for an additional two years. The awards have specific rules related to the treatment of the award, either during or after the Performance Period, in such events as death, disability, retirement, transfer to a Related Company and Involuntary Separation (other than for cause).

[2] If actual Company performance falls below certain thresholds, no payouts are made. The applicable percentage of the target award is granted if performance targets are achieved.

[3] A Performance Share Unit Award was made to Mr. Isdell at the February 2005 Compensation Committee meeting, following an appraisal of his 2004 performance by the Compensation Committee taking into account input from the Board. No award appears in the table because the award was not made in fiscal 2004. The Compensation Committee awarded Mr. Isdell 139,740 Performance Share Units, with a threshold award of 92,228 and a maximum award of 209,610. The Performance Period and other terms for the award are generally the same as for the other named executive officers. The award contains specific provisions in the event of his retirement.

[4] Due to his announced retirement, Mr. Daft was not considered for participation for the 2005-2007 Performance Period.

[5] The Performance Share Unit Award shown for Mr. Heyer was made in February 2004 and was for the 2004-2006 Performance Period. The Award was forfeited upon Mr. Heyer's separation from the Company effective December 31, 2004. Due to his announced departure, Mr. Heyer was not considered for participation for the 2005-2007 Performance Period.

Pension Plan Tables

Domestic

The table below sets forth the *annual* retirement benefits payable under the Employee Retirement Plan of The Coca-Cola Company (the "Retirement Plan"), the retirement portion of the Supplemental Plan and The Coca-Cola Company Key Executive Retirement Plan (the "Key Executive Plan") upon retirement at age 65 or later. These plans are described beginning on page 37. The calculations assume actual retirement on January 1, 2005. The benefits listed in the table do not take into account any reduction for Social Security or other offset amounts. However, when paid, some of these benefits may be subject to offset by benefits paid by other Company-sponsored retirement plans or statutory payments under plans to which the Company has contributed on the participant's behalf.

Assumed Average Annual Compensation for Five-Year Period Preceding Retirement	Years of Credited Service with the Company				
	15 Years	20 Years	25 Years	30 Years	35 Years
$ 500,000	$ 175,000	$ 200,000	$ 225,000	$ 250,000	$ 275,000
1,000,000	350,000	400,000	450,000	500,000	550,000
1,500,000	525,000	600,000	675,000	750,000	825,000
2,000,000	700,000	800,000	900,000	1,000,000	1,100,000
2,500,000	875,000	1,000,000	1,125,000	1,250,000	1,375,000

3,000,000	1,050,000	1,200,000	1,350,000	1,500,000	1,650,000
3,500,000	1,225,000	1,400,000	1,575,000	1,750,000	1,925,000
4,000,000	1,400,000	1,600,000	1,800,000	2,000,000	2,200,000
4,500,000	1,575,000	1,800,000	2,025,000	2,250,000	2,475,000
5,000,000	1,750,000	2,000,000	2,250,000	2,500,000	2,750,000
5,500,000	1,925,000	2,200,000	2,475,000	2,750,000	3,025,000

Generally, compensation utilized for pension formula purposes includes salary and annual bonus reported in the Summary Compensation Table. Cash awards under the Long-Term Performance Incentive Plan are generally also included in the computation of pension benefits under the Retirement Plan, the Key Executive Plan and the Supplemental Plan. Company contributions received under the Thrift Plan and the thrift portion of the Supplemental Plan and amounts related to stock options, performance share units or restricted stock are not included in the calculation of compensation for purposes of the pension benefit.

The years of credited service under the retirement plans described above as of December 31, 2004 are as follows: Mr. Isdell 29.9 years; Mr. Fayard 10.8 years; Ms. Minnick 21.6 years; Mr. Cummings 7.5 years; Mr. Daft 28.3 years; and Mr. Heyer 3.8 years. Pursuant to a contractual arrangement, Mr. Heyer is credited with an additional ten years of service for purposes of determining benefits under the retirement plans with such amounts to be paid outside of the retirement plans.*

International

The table below sets forth the *annual* retirement benefits under The Coca-Cola Export Corporation Overseas Retirement Plan (the "Overseas Plan") upon retirement at age 65 or later. The calculations assume actual retirement on January 1, 2005. The benefits listed in the table do not take into account any reduction for any statutory plans or other offset amounts. However, these benefits are subject to offset by any benefits paid by other Company-sponsored retirement plans or statutory payments under plans to which the Company has contributed on the participant's behalf.

Assumed Average Annual Compensation for Five-Year Period Preceding Retirement	Years of Credited Service with the Company				
	15 Years	20 Years	25 Years	30 Years	35 Years
$ 1,000,000	$ 240,000	$ 320,000	$ 400,000	$ 480,000	$ 560,000
1,500,000	360,000	480,000	600,000	720,000	840,000
2,000,000	480,000	640,000	800,000	960,000	1,120,000
2,500,000	600,000	800,000	1,000,000	1,200,000	1,400,000

3,000,000					
	720,000	960,000	1,200,000	1,440,000	1,680,000
3,500,000					
	840,000	1,120,000	1,400,000	1,680,000	1,960,000
4,000,000					
	960,000	1,280,000	1,600,000	1,920,000	2,240,000
4,500,000					
	1,080,000	1,440,000	1,800,000	2,160,000	2,520,000
5,000,000					
	1,200,000	1,600,000	2,000,000	2,400,000	2,800,000
5,500,000					
	1,320,000	1,760,000	2,200,000	2,640,000	3,080,000

Compensation utilized for pension formula purposes under the Overseas Plan is similar to that used for the Retirement Plan, the Key Executive Plan and the Supplemental Plan.

The years of credited service under the Overseas Plan as of December 31, 2004 are as follows: Mr. Isdell 20.4 years and Mr. Daft 15.0 years.*

Mexico

The table below sets forth the *lump sum* retirement benefit under the pension equity portion of the Mexico Plan upon retirement at age 60 or later. The calculations assume actual retirement on January 1, 2005. The benefits listed in the table do not take into account any reduction for any statutory plans or other offset amounts and are paid in a lump sum.

Assumed Average Annual Compensation Salary (U.S. Dollars)	Years of Credited Service with the Company				
	15 Years	20 Years	25 Years	30 Years	35 Years
$ 600,000	$ 1,050,000	$ 1,250,000	$ 1,250,000	$ 1,250,000	$ 1,250,000
720,000	1,260,000	1,500,000	1,500,000	1,500,000	1,500,000
840,000	1,470,000	1,750,000	1,750,000	1,750,000	1,750,000
960,000	1,680,000	2,000,000	2,000,000	2,000,000	2,000,000
1,080,000	1,890,000	2,250,000	2,250,000	2,250,000	2,250,000
1,200,000	2,100,000	2,500,000	2,500,000	2,500,000	2,500,000

Compensation utilized for pension formula purposes generally includes salary, annual incentive, savings fund and other payments made in accordance with Mexican laws and customary business practice.

The years of credited service for Mr. Reyes under the Mexico Plan as of December 31, 2004 were 18 years.*

*   *Where employees participate in multiple pension plans, the plans include provisions that prohibit duplication of benefits.*

Summary of Plans

The following section provides information on Company-sponsored plans noted in the Compensation Committee Report or in the tables.

Retirement Plans

The Retirement Plan.   The Retirement Plan is a tax-qualified defined benefit plan and generally bases pension benefits on a percentage of (a) the employee's final average compensation (the five highest consecutive calendar years of compensation out of the employee's last eleven years of vesting service) or (b) $205,000 for 2004 (the limit set by the Code), whichever is lower, multiplied by the employee's years of credited service. Age requirements and benefit reductions for early retirement are reduced for participants who terminate for any reason within two years after a change in control. The term "compensation" includes salary, overtime, commissions and cash incentive awards of the participants, but excludes any amounts related to stock options, performance share units or restricted stock.

The Supplemental Plan.   The Supplemental Plan also provides a benefit to eligible persons whenever 100% of their pension benefits under the Retirement Plan are not permitted to be funded or paid through that plan because of limits imposed by the Code and/or because of deferrals under any deferred compensation plan. In 2004, the maximum annual benefit at age 65 under the Retirement Plan is $165,000. If a participant terminates employment before early retirement age (for any reason other than death), the participant forfeits the supplemental benefit, except any amounts attributable to deferred compensation under any deferred compensation plan. In that case, the supplemental benefit will generally vest according to the same provisions as the Retirement Plan. In addition, a participant will forfeit all rights to future pension benefits under the Supplemental Plan if the participant competes against the Company following termination of employment.

If a participant is entitled to a pension benefit from the Retirement Plan because of termination of employment for any reason within two years after a change in control, then the change in control provisions in the Retirement Plan will apply to the calculation of the participant's pension benefit under the Supplemental Plan.

Additionally, the Supplemental Plan makes up in share units any shortfall on the Company's matching contributions under the Thrift Plan caused by the limits in the Code and/or because of deferrals under any deferred compensation plan. Payouts from the thrift portion of the Supplemental Plan are made in cash upon termination of employment.

- Mr. Isdell, Mr. Fayard, Ms. Minnick, Mr. Cummings, Mr. Daft and Mr. Heyer participated in the Retirement Plan and the Supplemental Plan in 2004.

- Prior to his reemployment, Mr. Isdell was paid $10,775 in 2004 under the Retirement Plan. Further payments under the Retirement Plan are suspended during his employment with the Company.

The Key Executive Plan. This plan is being phased out and no current employees accrue benefits under this plan.

The Key Executive Plan pays annually, upon retirement, 20% of the participant's average pay, including cash awards pursuant to the Long-Term Performance Incentive Program, for the five highest consecutive years of vesting service increased 1% for each year of credited service with the Company up to a maximum of 35 years (i.e., up to 55%). The plan excludes any amounts related to stock options, performance share units or restricted stock. The amount any participant will receive under the Key Executive Plan is offset by amounts payable under the Retirement Plan, the Supplemental Plan and the Overseas Plan. There is also a benefit to a participant's surviving spouse. A participant will forfeit all rights to future benefits under the Key Executive Plan if the participant competes against the Company following termination of employment. In the event of a change in control, all benefits accrued to a participant would immediately vest and, if a participant's employment terminates within two years after a change in control, his or her benefits would be paid in cash in a lump sum. The Company would pay the employee an additional amount equal to the liability, if any, under Section 4999 of the Code attributable to lump sum payments under the Key Executive Plan.

- Of the individuals named in the Summary Compensation Table, only Mr. Daft receives a benefit from the Key Executive Plan.

- Prior to his return to the Company on June 1, 2004, Mr. Isdell was receiving benefits under the Key Executive Plan. However, his benefits under the Key Executive Plan are suspended and he will not accrue further service or compensation credit under this plan due to his reemployment. Prior to the suspension of benefits, Mr. Isdell was paid $53,270 in 2004 under the Key Executive Plan.

The Overseas Plan. The Overseas Plan provides a retirement benefit to International Service Associates ("ISAs") of the Company who are not U.S. citizens, who cannot participate in the Retirement Plan during their international assignments and who do not participate in a local pension plan. Participants in the Overseas Plan become vested after five years of service and can choose to retire as early as age 55 with ten years of service. Benefits under the Overseas Plan are offset by any benefits paid by other Company-sponsored plans or statutory payments under plans to which the Company has contributed on the participants' behalf. Participants have the option of electing a lump sum payment under the Overseas Plan.

- Mr. Isdell participated in the Overseas Plan while he was an ISA earlier in his career, and received a benefit from the Overseas Plan upon his retirement in 1998. Mr. Isdell will not accrue any additional years of benefit service under the Overseas Plan as a result of his reemployment. However, Mr. Isdell will receive an additional benefit upon his retirement as a result of his increased salary due to his reemployment.

- Mr. Daft participated in the Overseas Plan while he was an ISA earlier in his career and a portion of his total retirement benefit was paid from the Overseas Plan upon his retirement.

The Thrift Plan.   The Thrift Plan is a tax-qualified defined contribution plan. The Company contributes to each participant's account an amount equal to 100% of the participant's contributions but not more than (a) 3% of the participant's earnings or (b) the amount allowable under the limits imposed under Sections 401(a) and 415(c) of the Code, whichever is lower. The Company's matching contribution is invested in Common Stock.

- Mr. Isdell, Mr. Fayard, Ms. Minnick, Mr. Cummings, Mr. Daft and Mr. Heyer participated in the Thrift Plan in 2004.

The International Thrift Plan.   The International Thrift Plan operates similarly to the thrift portion of the Supplemental Plan. The participants are ISAs who are not U.S. citizens. The International Thrift Plan provides a contribution in hypothetical Company share units equivalent to 3% of the ISA's eligible compensation. The value of the accumulated share units, including dividend equivalents, is paid in cash to the individual at termination of employment.

- Mr. Reyes and Mr. Daft participated in the International Thrift Plan during previous assignments.

The Mexico Plan.   The Mexico Plan consists of a pension equity plan and a defined contribution plan. The plan operates under Mexico's Labor Department rules and regulations.

The pension equity plan is a defined benefit plan that pays a lump sum amount at retirement, based on the employee's final average salary and points accumulated during employment. An employee earns from 8 to 15 points for each year of service based on age. A maximum of 250 points can be accumulated. The lump sum benefit is the employee's final monthly average salary multiplied by the total accumulated points, then divided by 10. Generally compensation for purposes of the final average salary includes salary, annual incentive, savings fund and other payments made in accordance with Mexican laws and customary business practice.

The defined contribution plan is a savings plan in which employees can contribute up to 5% of their compensation on a pre-tax basis. The Company makes a matching contribution equal to 50% of the employee's contribution.

- Mr. Reyes participates in the Mexico Plan.

The DCP. The Coca-Cola Company Deferred Compensation Plan (the "DCP") is a non-qualified and unfunded deferred compensation program offered to a select group of U.S.-based management or highly compensated employees. Eligible participants may defer up to 80% of base salary and up to 100% of their incentive, with gains and losses credited based on a variety of deemed investment choices as elected by the participant. A participant's account may or may not appreciate depending on the performance of their deemed investment choices. None of the deemed investment choices provide interest at above-market rates. All deferrals are paid out in cash upon distribution.

- Mr. Isdell, Mr. Fayard, Ms. Minnick, Mr. Daft and Mr. Heyer have elected to participate in the DCP.

Incentive Plans

Annual Incentive Plans

The Company maintains two annual incentive programs for employees. Executive officers may be selected for participation in either of these programs, but not both. Each program is described below.

Executive Plans

The first program consists of the Executive Performance Incentive Program ("EPIP") and the Executive Incentive Plan ("EIP") which work in conjunction to provide an annual award to those executives whose compensation may be subject to the provisions of Section 162(m) of the Code. The EPIP provides the part of the award that is defined by objective measures (and therefore meets tax deductibility rules). The EIP is used to allow the Compensation Committee to award achievement of subjective goals such as those related to diversity, quality and the environment.

- *Executive Performance Incentive Program.* The EPIP is a part of the Company's Executive and Long-Term Performance Incentive Plan. The Committee may approve some or all of the executive officers for participation in this program each year. Target annual incentives are established for each approved executive officer. Below a threshold level of performance, no awards may be granted. Payments from this program are intended to qualify as tax-deductible performance-based compensation under the terms of Section 162(m) of the Code. Under the terms of the program, the Committee may designate one or more performance factors from the list of performance factors set forth in the program.

- *Executive Incentive Plan.* Used only in conjunction with the EPIP, this plan allows executive officers covered under the EPIP to be rewarded for individual performance and for achievement of goals such as those related to diversity, quality and the environment, which are not currently part of the shareowner-approved EPIP. Payments from this plan are not intended to qualify as tax-deductible performance-based compensation under the terms of Section 162(m) of the Code.

Performance Incentive Plan

The second program is the Performance Incentive Plan. Any executive officers not selected for the first program, all other officers and certain employees are eligible to participate in this plan. Generally, performance measures under this plan are similar to or the same as those under the EPIP.

- *Performance Incentive Plan.* Target annual incentives are established for certain key executives. Below a threshold level of performance, no awards may be granted. Executive officers who participate in the EPIP are not eligible for participation in the Performance Incentive Plan.

Under all of these annual incentive plans, in the event of a change in control, participants earn the right to receive awards equal to the target percentage of their annual salaries as if their performance goals had been met, prorated to reflect the number of months a participant was employed in the plan year.

Long-Term Incentive Plans

Stock Option Plans. Stock option plans provide equity compensation whose value is at-risk based upon the increase in Company stock price and the creation of shareowner value. Stock options comprise the long-term equity component of compensation for eligible employees below the senior executive level and a part of the long-term equity component for senior executives.

The Company currently grants options from the 2002 Stock Option Plan. The 2002 Stock Option Plan generally provides that the option price must be not less than 100% of the fair market value of Common Stock on the date the option is granted. The fair market value of a share of Common Stock is the average of the high and low sales prices on the date of grant. The grants provide that stock options generally may not be exercised during the first twelve months after the date of grant. Generally, options vest 25% each year beginning on the first anniversary of the grant date.

The 2002 Stock Option Plan allows shares of Common Stock to be used to satisfy any resulting Federal, state and local tax liabilities. Change of control, death, disability and retirement, with certain exceptions, cause the acceleration of vesting.

Restricted Stock Award Plan. The Restricted Stock Award Plan is designed to focus executives on the long-term performance of the Company. The Restricted Stock Award Plan allows the Compensation Committee flexibility related to grant terms and conditions.

There are currently three types of awards which have been made under the Restricted Stock Award Plan and are outstanding:

- *Time-Based Restricted Stock.* Restrictions lapse on a certain date or on retirement;

- *Performance-Based Restricted Stock.* Restrictions lapse when certain performance targets are met; and

- *Performance Share Units.* Restricted stock is awarded only after performance targets based on pre-determined performance criteria are met. The performance period is generally three years and after determination of performance, the grants contain an additional restriction period. In certain circumstances, for participating executives overseas for international tax considerations, the restricted stock award will not occur at the end of the Performance Period but will be made after the additional restriction period. Dividends or, when applicable, hypothetical dividends are paid during the additional restriction period.

The majority of outstanding grants are Performance Share Units tied to Company long-term performance measures, such as Earnings Per Share growth. The Compensation Committee generally uses time-based restricted stock sparingly for purposes of attraction and retention or other special awards.

Upon a change in control of the Company, the restrictions on restricted shares lapse.

Long-Term Performance Incentive Program. As a result of the comprehensive review of the Company's executive compensation programs in 2003, the Compensation Committee determined to make no further grants from the Long-Term Performance Incentive Program (a part of the Company's Executive and Long-Term Performance Incentive Plan) and the program will no longer be used after the 2003-2005 performance period ends. Performance periods currently in progress will continue in accordance with the terms of the program.

The Long-Term Performance Incentive Program provides cash awards for three-year performance periods. The program is not based on the price of Common Stock. Subject to continued employment of the participant, unless death, disability or retirement occurs, one-third of each award earned is paid at the close of each three-year performance period. Payment of the balance of each award, the "Contingent Award," is deferred and paid one-half after one year and the balance after two years. The Contingent Award is subject to forfeiture if the participant's employment with the Company terminates for any reason other than death, disability, retirement or a change in control of the Company. The participant is entitled to accrued interest on the Contingent Award during the two-year period, calculated at prevailing market interest rates. Prior to the 2003-2005 performance period, 50% of each award was paid at the end of the performance period and the balance was deferred for a two-year period. Upon a change in control of the Company, all awards or portions of awards earned up until such date become fully vested and payable, and additional payments will be made in an amount equal to the participant's liability for any taxes attributable to such payments.

Other Compensation Matters

FORM OF PROXY STATEMENT AND FORM OF PROXY

The Company has arrangements with each individual as described below:

Steven J. Heyer.   The Company entered into an agreement with Mr. Heyer on March 2, 2001 for a five-year period beginning April 1, 2001. The arrangement includes an annual salary of $850,000, subject to increase, as well as cash incentive and participation in long-term incentive plans. Mr. Heyer's contract also calls for the grant of annual equity awards in the range of $9 to $12 million based upon Black-Scholes valuations, with the final award within the stated range to be subject to the discretion of the Compensation Committee. The agreement with Mr. Heyer includes an additional ten years of service credit to be calculated under the Retirement Plan and the Supplemental Plan. These payments are to be paid outside of such plans. The Company took specific actions not to renew Mr. Heyer's contract in June 2004, which triggered the agreement's "Good Reason" provisions. The contract has specific provisions for treatment of all compensation in the event of Mr. Heyer's termination.

Pursuant to the "Good Reason" provisions of his contract, Mr. Heyer received an annual incentive award of $1,036,547, which was determined, prorated and paid according to the terms of the annual incentive program and a lump sum payment of $7,062,000, equivalent to three times base salary plus the average of the three preceding bonus payments. Additionally, the 805,000 option grant received by Mr. Heyer to compensate for options forfeited at his former employer became fully vested and the 50,000 share restricted stock award was released. Other stock option and restricted stock awards shall be paid according to their terms, and he will be entitled to elect Company-paid COBRA coverage. Upon reaching retirement age, he will be entitled to the pension credit.

E. Neville Isdell.   Mr. Isdell's compensation arrangements include an annual base salary of $1,500,000, subject to increase, and participation in the Company's annual incentive program and long-term incentive plans. For 2004, Mr. Isdell's annual incentive opportunity was 200% of his base salary for that year. In recognition of his new role, on July 22, 2004, Mr. Isdell was granted a stock option award of 450,000 shares and a restricted stock award of 140,000 shares. The transfer restrictions on the restricted stock award lapse six months following retirement (with the consent of the Board), provided retirement occurs no earlier than June 1, 2008. In the event that the shares of restricted stock are forfeited for any reason other than termination for cause, Mr. Isdell will receive a special cash payment that will compensate him for the additional taxes that he will have paid on his non-Company related income during the period of time that he was a U.S. resident. Mr. Isdell participates in the Retirement Plan and the Supplemental Plan; upon his retirement, Mr. Isdell's benefits under the Retirement Plan, the Supplemental Plan and the Overseas Plan will be adjusted to reflect his reemployment. Since Mr. Isdell had the requisite service to be retirement eligible prior to his reemployment, he will be considered retirement eligible at whatever time he leaves the Company in the future. Payments to Mr. Isdell under the Retirement Plan and the Key Executive Plan were suspended as of his reemployment.

The Company has made previous filings under the Securities Act of 1933, as amended, or the Securities Exchange Act of 1934, as amended, that incorporate future filings, including this proxy statement, in whole or in part. However, the Report of the Compensation Committee, the Report of the Audit Committee and the following Performance Graph shall not be incorporated by reference into any such filings.

Performance Graph

Comparison of Five-Year Cumulative Total Return Among
The Coca-Cola Company, the Food, Beverage and Tobacco Groups and the S&P 500 Index

Total Return
Stock Price Plus Reinvested Dividends

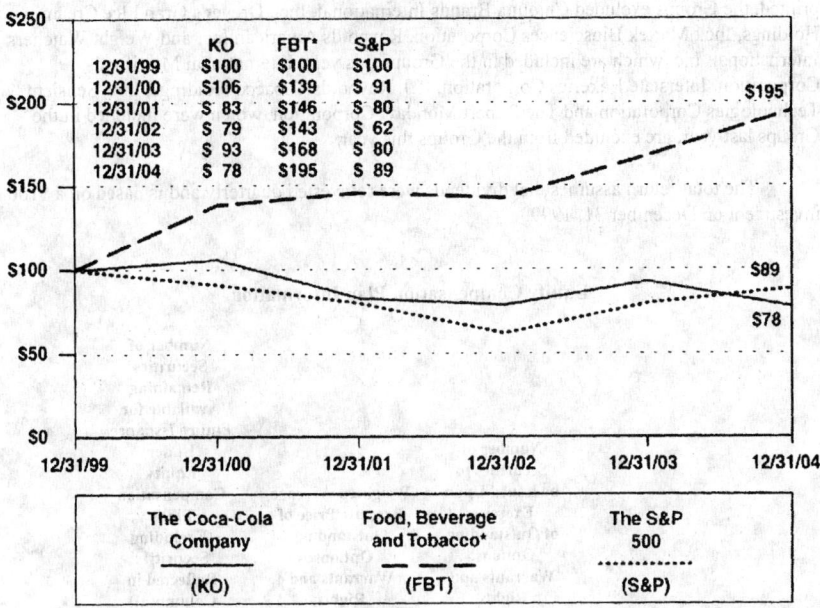

	KO	FBT*	S&P
12/31/99	$100	$100	$100
12/31/00	$106	$139	$ 91
12/31/01	$ 83	$146	$ 80
12/31/02	$ 79	$143	$ 62
12/31/03	$ 93	$168	$ 80
12/31/04	$ 78	$195	$ 89

The Coca-Cola Company	Food, Beverage and Tobacco*	The S&P 500
(KO)	(FBT)	(S&P)

* Based on information for a self-constructed peer group of the Food, Beverage and Tobacco Groups of companies as published in *The Wall Street Journal*, which includes the following companies, but from which the Company has been excluded:

Adolph Coors Company, Altria Group, Inc., American Italian Pasta Company, Anheuser-Busch Companies, Inc., Archer-Daniels-Midland Company, Brown-Forman Corporation, Bunge Limited, Campbell Soup Company, Chiquita Brands International, Inc., Coca-Cola Enterprises

Inc., ConAgra Foods, Inc., Constellation Brands, Inc., Corn Products International, Inc., Dean Foods Company, Del Monte Foods Company, Dreyer's Grand Ice Cream Holdings, Inc., Flowers Foods, Inc., General Mills, Inc., H.J. Heinz Company, Hershey Foods Corporation, Hormel Foods Corporation, Kellogg Company, Kraft Foods Inc., Lancaster Colony Corporation, Loews Corporation (Carolina Group tracking stock), Martek Biosciences Corporation, McCormick & Company, Incorporated, NBTY, Inc., PepsiAmericas, Inc., PepsiCo, Inc., Ralcorp Holdings, Inc., Reynolds American Inc., Sara Lee Corporation, Smithfield Foods, Inc., The Hain Celestial Group, Inc., The J.M. Smucker Company,

The Pepsi Bottling Group, Inc., Tootsie Roll Industries, Inc., Tyson Foods, Inc., Universal Corporation, UST Inc., Weight Watchers International, Inc. and Wm. Wrigley Jr. Company.

The Wall Street Journal periodically changes the companies reported as a part of the Food, Beverage and Tobacco Groups of companies. At the time last year's proxy statement was printed, the Groups excluded Chiquita Brands International, Inc., Dreyer's Grand Ice Cream Holdings, Inc., Martek Biosciences Corporation, Reynolds American Inc. and Weight Watchers International, Inc. which are included in the Groups this year. International Multifoods Corporation, Interstate Bakeries Corporation, R.J. Reynolds Tobacco Holdings, Inc., Sensient Technologies Corporation and The Robert Mondavi Corporation, which were included in the Groups last year, are excluded from the Groups this year.

The total return assumes that dividends were reinvested quarterly and is based on a $100 investment on December 31, 1999.

Equity Compensation Plan Information

Plan Category	Number of Securities to be Issued Upon Exercise of Outstanding Options, Warrants and Rights (a)	Weighted-Average Exercise Price of Outstanding Options, Warrants and Rights (b)	Number of Securities Remaining Available for Future Issuance Under Equity Compensation Plans (Excluding Securities Reflected in Column(a)) (c)
Equity Compensation Plans Approved by Security Holders	183,369,896[1]	$ 49.41	116,283,180[2]
Equity Compensation Plans Not Approved by Security Holders	0	N/A	—[3]

Total	183,369,896	116,283,180[3]

[1] Shares issuable pursuant to outstanding options under The Coca-Cola Company 1991 Stock Option Plan, The Coca-Cola Company 1999 Stock Option Plan and The Coca-Cola Company 2002 Stock Option Plan (collectively, the "Stock Option Plans").

[2] Represents shares of Common Stock which may be issued pursuant to future awards under the Stock Option Plans, the 1983 Restricted Stock Plan of The Coca-Cola Company and the 1989 Restricted Stock Plan of The Coca-Cola Company (including shares which may be issued pursuant to outstanding Performance Share Units).

[3] The number of shares issuable pursuant to the plans described below are not presently determinable.

The Company facilitates employee share ownership through matching contributions pursuant to The Coca-Cola Export Corporation Employee Share Plan (the "Export Plan"), the Employees' Savings and Share Ownership Plan of Coca-Cola Ltd. (the "Canadian Plan"), the Employee Stockholding Program (the "Japanese Plan") and the Share Savings Plan (the "Danish Plan"). Pursuant to the Export Plan, the Company matches contributions made by participating employees to a maximum of £1,500 per year; however, shares cannot be withdrawn before a five-year holding period without adverse tax consequences. The participant is immediately vested in the matching contribution. Pursuant to the Canadian Plan, the Company matches 50% of the contributions made by participating employees to a maximum of 4% of such participant's salary per year. The participant is immediately vested in the matching contribution; however an employee cannot withdraw any matching contributions until termination of employment. Pursuant to the Japanese Plan, the Company matches contributions made by participating employees up to 3% of such employee's pay. The participant is immediately vested in the matching contribution. Employees may withdraw shares at termination of employment or at specified limited periods by withdrawing from the stockholding association. Pursuant to the Danish Plan, the Company matches contributions made by participating employees up to a maximum of 3% of such participant's salary per year. The participant is immediately vested in the matching contribution; however, the shares are held in trust and a participant is not entitled to withdraw the shares purchased for a period of five years without tax liability. Under each of the plans, the Company contributes the matching amounts in cash to the trustee of the plan who acquires the shares of Common Stock on the open market. There is no limit on the number of shares that may be purchased pursuant to the Export Plan, the Canadian Plan, the Japanese Plan or the Danish Plan. The shares, which are already issued, are acquired on the open market. These plans are exempt from the shareowner approval requirement of the Exchange.

The Company also sponsors employee share purchase plans in numerous jurisdictions. The Company does not grant or issue any shares of Common Stock pursuant to such plans, but rather facilitates the acquisition of shares of Common·Stock by employees in a cost efficient manner. These plans are not equity compensation plans.

Shares that may be issued under the Thrift Plan or share units credited under the thrift portion of the Supplemental Plan, the International Thrift Plan, the Director Deferred Compensation Plan and the DCP are not included. . . . The Director Deferred Compensation Plan is described on page 19. Share units accrued under the thrift portion of the Supplemental Plan, the International Thrift Plan and the Director Deferred Compensation Plan are paid in cash.

Compensation Committee Interlocks and Insider Participation

The Compensation Committee of the Company is composed of the following four independent Directors: Cathleen P. Black, Chairman, Maria Elena Lagomasino, Robert L. Nardelli and Peter V. Ueberroth.

CERTAIN INVESTEE COMPANIES

The Company and its subsidiaries together currently hold approximately 36% of the issued and outstanding shares of Coca-Cola Enterprises Inc. ("Enterprises") and approximately 40% of the issued and outstanding shares of Coca-Cola FEMSA, S.A. de C.V. ("Coca-Cola FEMSA"). We call Enterprises and Coca-Cola FEMSA the "Investee Companies" in the proxy statement.

Certain Transactions and Relationships with Enterprises

SunTrust

SunTrust, which during a portion of 2004 was a 5% owner of Common Stock, engaged in ordinary course of business banking transactions in 2004, and is expected to engage in similar transactions in 2005, with Enterprises and its subsidiaries, including the making of loans on customary terms. Fees for these transactions of approximately $1.9 million were paid in 2004. Also in 2004, Enterprises paid SunTrust approximately $323,000 for letter of credit fees, approximately $490,000 for investment management fees relating to Enterprises' benefit plans and approximately $68,000 in credit facility fees. A subsidiary of SunTrust also holds equipment leases for freight line tractors and blow mold equipment under which Enterprises paid approximately $2.3 million in 2004. SunTrust filed an amendment to its Schedule 13G on February 16, 2005 indicating that, as of December 31, 2004, it owned less than 5% of the Company's issued and outstanding Common Stock.

Warren E. Buffett

Warren E. Buffett, one of our Directors, is Chairman of the Board, Chief Executive Officer and a major shareowner of Berkshire Hathaway. McLane Company, Inc. ("McLane") is a wholly owned subsidiary of Berkshire Hathaway. In 2004, a subsidiary of McLane made payments totaling approximately $3.5 million to Enterprises to purchase products in the ordinary course of business. Berkshire Hathaway is a major shareowner of the Company. Berkshire

Hathaway holds a significant equity interest in Moody's Corporation to which Enterprises paid approximately $308,000 in 2004 for providing long-term and short-term credit ratings services. In 2004, Enterprises paid XTRA Corporation, a wholly owned subsidiary of Berkshire Hathaway, approximately $696,000 for equipment leases of trailers used to store and transport finished product in the ordinary course of business.

Ownership of Securities in Investee Companies

The following table sets forth information regarding ownership of the stock of the Investee Companies, if any, by each Director, each individual named in the Summary Compensation Table on page 28, and our Directors and executive officers as a group, all as of February 22, 2005, except as noted.

Name	Company	Aggregate Number of Shares Beneficially Owned	Percent of Outstanding Shares[6]
Herbert A. Allen	Coca-Cola	500[2]	*
	FEMSA		
Donald R. Keough	Enterprises	25,508	*
Donald F. McHenry	Enterprises	1,035	*
	Coca-Cola	3,000	*
	FEMSA		
Steven J. Heyer	Enterprises	19,747[3]	*
Gary P. Fayard	Enterprises	20,715[4]	*
All Directors and Executive Officers as a Group (29 Persons)[1]	Enterprises	69,081[5]	*
	Coca-Cola	3,500	*
	FEMSA		

* Less than 1% of issued and outstanding shares of common stock of the indicated entity.

[1] Includes holdings of Douglas N. Daft and Steven J. Heyer.

[2] Shares held by Allen & Company Incorporated.

[3] Information is as of December 31, 2004, the effective date of Mr. Heyer's separation from the Company. Includes 7,498 shares which may be acquired upon the exercise of options which are presently exercisable or which will become exercisable on or before April 29, 2005.

[4] Includes 5,715 phantom units issued under the Coca-Cola Enterprises Inc. Deferred Compensation Plan for Non-Employee Director Compensation (the "Enterprises Plan") and 15,000 shares which may be acquired upon the exercise of options which are presently exercisable or which will become exercisable on or before April 29, 2005.

[5] Includes 7,791 phantom units issued under the Enterprises Plan and 22,498 shares which may be acquired upon the exercise of options which are presently exercisable or which will become exercisable on or before April 29, 2005.

[6] Phantom units issued under the Enterprises Plan are not counted as outstanding in calculating these percentages.

REPORT OF THE AUDIT COMMITTEE

For many years, the Company's Audit Committee has been composed entirely of non-management directors. The members of the Audit Committee meet the independence and experience requirements of the New York Stock Exchange and the SEC. In 2004, the Audit Committee held five regularly scheduled meetings and two special meetings. The Audit Committee has a charter outlining the practices it follows, which it annually reviews. In December 2004, the Board of Directors amended the charter; a copy of the charter is attached as Appendix I to this proxy statement. The charter complies with all current regulatory requirements. Additionally, the Committee has continued its long-standing practice of having independent legal counsel.

During 2004, at each of its regularly scheduled meetings, the Audit Committee met with the senior members of the Company's financial management team, the director of internal audit, the general counsel or his designee, the ethics and compliance officer and our independent auditors. The Audit Committee's agenda is established by the Audit Committee's chairman and the director of internal audit. The Audit Committee had separate private sessions, at each of its regularly scheduled meetings, with the Company's general counsel or his designee, independent auditors, and the director of internal audit, at which candid discussions regarding financial management, legal, accounting, auditing, and internal control issues took place.

The Audit Committee has been updated quarterly on management's process to assess the adequacy of the Company's system of internal control over financial reporting, the framework used to make the assessment, and management's conclusions on the effectiveness of the Company's internal control over financial reporting. The Audit Committee has also discussed with the independent auditor the Company's internal control assessment process, management's assessment with respect thereto and the independent auditor's evaluation of the Company's system of internal control over financial reporting.

The Audit Committee reviewed with senior members of management, including the director of internal audit and the general counsel, and the independent auditors, the Company's policies and procedures with respect to risk assessment and risk management. The overall adequacy and effectiveness of the Company's legal, regulatory and ethical compliance programs, including the Company's Code of Business Conduct, were also reviewed.

The Audit Committee recommended to the Board of Directors the engagement of Ernst & Young LLP as the Company's independent auditors for the year ended December 31, 2004 and reviewed with senior members of the Company's financial management team, the independent auditors, and the director of internal audit, the overall audit scope and plans, the results of internal and external audit examinations, evaluations by management and the independent auditors of the Company's internal controls over financial reporting and the quality of the Company's financial reporting. Although the Audit Committee has the sole authority to appoint the independent auditors, the Audit Committee will continue its long-standing practice of recommending that the Board ask the shareowners, at their annual meeting, to ratify their appointment of the independent auditors.

Management has reviewed the audited financial statements in the Annual Report on Form 10-K with the Audit Committee including a discussion of the quality, not just the acceptability, of the accounting principles, the reasonableness of significant accounting judgments and estimates, and the clarity of disclosures in the financial statements. In addressing the quality of management's accounting judgments, members of the Audit Committee asked for management's representations and reviewed certifications prepared by the Chief Executive Officer and Chief Financial Officer that the unaudited quarterly and audited consolidated financial statements of the Company fairly present, in all material respects, the financial condition, results of operations and cash flows of the Company, and have expressed to both management and the auditors their general preference for conservative policies when a range of accounting options is available.

In its meetings with representatives of the independent auditors, the Audit Committee asks them to address, and discuss their responses to several questions that the Audit Committee believes are particularly relevant to its oversight. These questions include:

- Are there any significant accounting judgments or estimates made by management in preparing the financial statements that would have been made differently had the auditors themselves prepared and been responsible for the financial statements?

- Based on the auditors' experience, and their knowledge of the Company, do the Company's financial statements fairly present to investors, with clarity and completeness, the Company's financial position and performance for the reporting period in accordance with generally accepted accounting principles, and SEC disclosure requirements?

- Based on the auditors' experience, and their knowledge of the Company, has the Company implemented internal controls and internal audit procedures that are appropriate for the Company?

The Audit Committee believes that, by thus focusing its discussions with the independent auditors, it can promote a meaningful dialogue that provides a basis for its oversight judgments.

The Audit Committee also discussed with the independent auditors other matters required to be discussed by the auditors with the Audit Committee under Statement on Auditing Standards No. 61, as amended by Statement on Auditing Standards No. 90 (communications with audit committees). The Audit Committee received and discussed with the auditors their annual written report on their independence from the Company and its management, which is made under

FORM OF PROXY STATEMENT AND FORM OF PROXY

Independence Standards Board Standard No. 1 (independence discussions with audit committees), and considered with the auditors whether the provision of non-audit services provided by them to the Company during 2004 was compatible with the auditors' independence.

In performing all of these functions, the Audit Committee acts in an oversight capacity. The Audit Committee reviews the Company's quarterly and annual reports on Form 10-Q and Form 10-K prior to filing with the SEC. In its oversight role the Audit Committee relies on the work and assurances of the Company's management, which has the primary responsibility for establishing and maintaining adequate internal controls over financial reporting and for preparing the financial statements, and other reports, and of the independent auditors, who are engaged to audit and report on the consolidated financial statements of the Company and subsidiaries, management's assessment of the effectiveness of the Company's internal control over financial reporting, and the effectiveness of the Company's internal control over financial reporting.

In reliance on these reviews and discussions, and the reports of the independent auditors, the Audit Committee has recommended to the Board of Directors, and the Board has approved, that the audited financial statements be included in the Company's Annual Report on Form 10-K for the year ended December 31, 2004, for filing with the SEC.

Peter V. Ueberroth
Chairman
Ronald W. Allen
Cathleen P. Black
Warren E. Buffett
Robert L. Nardelli
J. Pedro Reinhard

RATIFICATION OF THE APPOINTMENT OF INDEPENDENT AUDITORS

(Item 2)

The Audit Committee has appointed Ernst & Young LLP to serve as independent auditors for the fiscal year ending December 31, 2005, subject to ratification of the appointment by the shareowners. Ernst & Young LLP has served as the Company's independent auditors for many years and is considered by management to be well qualified.

Audit Fees and All Other Fees

Audit Fees

Fees for audit services totaled approximately $23.7 million in 2004 and $16.9 million in 2003, including fees associated with the annual audit and the audit of internal control over financial reporting in 2004, the reviews of the Company's quarterly reports on Form 10-Q, and statutory audits required internationally.

Audit Related Fees

Fees for audit related services totaled approximately $2.8 million in 2004 and $2.6 million in 2003. Audit related services principally include due diligence in connection with acquisitions, consultation on accounting and internal control matters, audits in connection with proposed or consummated acquisitions, information systems audits and other attest services.

Tax Fees

Fees for tax services, including tax compliance, tax advice and tax planning, totaled approximately $8.0 million in 2004 and $8.6 million in 2003.

All Other Fees

Fees for all other services not described above totaled approximately $1.7 million in 2004 and $2.4 million in 2003, principally including services related to the Company's expatriate program, and advisory services in connection with the Company's process improvement initiatives.

The Company has been advised by Ernst & Young LLP that neither the firm, nor any member of the firm, has any financial interest, direct or indirect, in any capacity in the Company or its subsidiaries.

One or more representatives of Ernst & Young LLP will be present at this year's Annual Meeting of Shareowners. The representatives will have an opportunity to make a statement if they desire to do so and will be available to respond to appropriate questions.

Audit Committee Pre-Approval of Audit and Permissible Non-Audit Services of Independent Auditors

The Audit Committee pre-approves all audit and permissible non-audit services provided by the independent auditors. These services may include audit services, audit-related services, tax services and other services. The Audit Committee has adopted a policy for the pre-approval of services provided by the independent auditors.

Under the policy, pre-approval is generally provided for work associated with registration statements under the Securities Act of 1933 (for example, comfort letters or consents); statutory or other financial audit work for non-U.S. subsidiaries that is not required for the 1934 Act audits; due diligence work for potential acquisitions or disposals; attest services not required by statute or regulation; adoption of new accounting pronouncements or auditing and disclosure requirements and accounting or regulatory consultations; internal control reviews and assistance with internal control reporting requirements; review of information systems security and controls; tax compliance, tax planning and related tax services, excluding any tax service prohibited by regulatory or other oversight authorities; expatriate and other individual tax services; and assistance and consultation on questions raised by regulatory agencies. For each proposed service, the independent auditors are required to provide detailed back-up documentation at the time of approval to permit the Audit Committee to make a determination whether the provision of such services would impair the independent auditors' independence.

The Audit Committee has approved in advance certain permitted services whose scope is routine across business units. These services are (i) statutory or other financial audit work for non-U.S. subsidiaries that is not required for the 1934 Act audit and (ii) individual tax preparation and related administration under the International Service Associate programs, including the related local expatriate tax programs (not including any individual tax services for executive officers).

Ratification of the appointment of the independent auditors requires the affirmative vote of a majority of the votes cast by the holders of the shares of Common Stock voting in person or by proxy at the Annual Meeting of Shareowners. If the shareowners should not ratify the appointment of Ernst & Young LLP, the Audit Committee will reconsider the appointment.

The Board of Directors recommends a vote
FOR
the ratification of the appointment of Ernst & Young LLP as independent auditors.

PROPOSALS OF SHAREOWNERS

Items 3 through 5

The following three proposals were submitted by shareowners. If the shareowner proponent, or a representative who is qualified under state law, is present and submits such proposal for a vote, then the proposal will be voted upon at the Annual Meeting of Shareowners. In accordance with Federal securities regulations, we include the shareowner proposals plus any supporting statement exactly as submitted by the proponents. To make sure readers can easily distinguish between material provided by the proponents and material provided by the Company, we have put a box around material provided by the proponents. If proposals are submitted by more than one shareowner, we will only list the primary filer's name, address and number of shares held. We will provide the information regarding co-filers to shareowners promptly if we receive an oral or written request for the information.

Shareowner Proposal Regarding an Independent Delegation of Inquiry to Colombia (Item 3)

New York City Employees' Retirement System and the New York City Teachers' Retirement System, 1 Centre Street, New York, NY 10007-2341, owners of 5,340,332 shares of Common Stock, submitted, along with co-filers, the following proposal:

WHEREAS, Coca-Cola's Latin American affiliate, Coca-Cola/FEMSA, operates bottling plants in Colombia, and

WHEREAS, since 1995, union officials and unionized employees of Coca-Cola's Colombian affiliate have been subjected to numerous attacks and physical threats from paramilitary forces, and

WHEREAS, Sindicato Nacional de Trabajadores de Industrias Alimenticias (SINALTRAINAL), a union representing employees at Coca-Cola's Colombian plants, have made allegations of collusion between paramilitary forces and officials of Coca-Cola's Colombian bottling affiliate, and

WHEREAS, these allegations of collusion have led to negative publicity, lawsuits, public protests, and calls for consumer boycotts of Coca-Cola products, and

WHEREAS, the Washington Post (April 22, 2004) reported that Coca-Cola's General Counsel promised in October, 2003, that he would mount an independent investigation of the charges of collusion against managers and officials of Coca-Cola's bottling affiliate, and

WHEREAS, the Washington Post reported that the Company's then chief executive Douglas N. Daft, after giving early encouragement about mounting an independent investigation, changed his mind and turned down the General Counsel's idea, and

THEREFORE, BE IT RESOLVED, that the shareholders request that the Company sponsor the sending of an independent delegation of inquiry to Colombia to examine the charges of collusion in anti-union violence that have been made against officials of Coca-Cola's bottling plants in that country, and that that delegation includes representatives from U.S. and Colombian human rights organizations.

SUPPORTING STATEMENT

The Board of Trustees of the New York City Employees' Retirement System, the New York City Teachers' Retirement, the New York City Fire Department Fund, and the New York City Police Pension Fund believe that it is time for management to seriously review its policies in this area. Significant commercial advantages can accrue to our company by the rigorous implementation of human rights policies guaranteeing freedom of association based on the Universal Declaration of Human Rights. These include an enhanced corporate reputation, improved employee recruitment and retention, improved community and stakeholder relations, and a reduced risk of adverse publicity, divestment and boycott campaigns, and lawsuits.

We therefore urge you to vote FOR this proposal.

Statement Against Shareowner Proposal Regarding an Independent Delegation of Inquiry to Colombia

The Board is recommending a vote against this proposal because we believe that an alternate approach, now being implemented by our Company, is the best and most appropriate way for our business to address the concerns of the proponents.

Our Company and our bottling partners do business in many challenging places—perhaps none more difficult than Colombia. A 40-year civil war has claimed thousands of lives and made violence a tragic part of daily life. Our business is not exempt from this brutality. Our workers and those of our bottlers have been threatened, kidnapped and some have even been murdered.

In the midst of this complex situation, a small number of activists have accused The Coca-Cola Company of perpetrating or condoning this violence against our employees and our bottlers' employees. The allegations made against us in Colombia are not merely false; they are repugnant to all of us at The Coca-Cola Company.

We agree with the proponents that our Company must clearly demonstrate that we and our bottling partners support human and labor rights and oppose all forms of violence. Our desire is for Coca-Cola to be seen as part of the solution to some of the business issues in Colombia today. We are convinced our current approach will allow for that outcome.

We are undertaking a comprehensive, long term and integrated approach that includes the initiatives outlined below. To develop these initiatives, we incorporated input from a number of our stakeholders, including investors, labor unions and non-governmental organizations.

The first initiative is an assessment process being piloted in different Company and bottler locations around the world, including Colombia. These assessments are being conducted by an independent third party and will evaluate current workplace practices including wages and hours, facility security, freedom of association, collective bargaining, and health and safety measures.

The process is much broader than Colombia. Working with our key bottling partners, we will assess, and where necessary, enhance the model for providing industry-leading work environments for our respective employees.

Findings from the assessments will be shared with the public.

In another important initiative, our Company will undertake a review of its current policies related to human rights. This is an exercise that has been recommended by a number of stakeholders, including the proponents. We will work through this review process with a group of our investors who have experience in this area, with a goal towards ensuring that our policies and practices around human rights are robust.

This proposal recommends an inquiry to examine charges of collusion in anti-union violence. While we believe that the initiatives outlined above constitute a more appropriate and comprehensive approach for our business, it is important for our shareowners to know that these charges have, in fact, been investigated. Two different independent inquiries in Colombia—a judicial inquiry by a Colombian Court, and an inquiry by the Colombian Attorney General's office—examined the specific issue of whether managers at a bottling plant were complicit in the murder of a trade unionist. They found no evidence to support the allegation. Further, based on internal investigations conducted by our Company and by our bottling partners, we are confident that allegations the bottlers engaged paramilitaries to intimidate trade unionists are false.

**The Board of Directors recommends a vote
AGAINST
the proposal regarding an independent delegation of inquiry to Colombia.**

—

Shareowner Proposal Regarding Restricted Stock (Item 4)

Elton W. Shepard, 720 Buff Drive, N.E., Atlanta, Georgia 30342, owner of 26,542 shares of Common Stock, submitted the following proposal:

In June, 2004, The Wall Street Journal Attributed This Quote To Warren Buffett...

"there has been more misdirected compensation in corporate America in the last 5 years than in the previous 100."

From 1999-2003, Coca-Cola Paid Former CEO Daft $34,000,000 More Than Director Buffett.

CEO	Base	Bonus	Stock Value	Dividends	Total	Weekly Pay
			Free Restricted Stock			
Daft	$ 6,229,000	$ 14,500,000	$ 9,000,000*	$ 5,364,000	$ 35,093,000	$ 135,000
Buffett	$ 500,000	$ 0	$ 0	$ 0	$ 500,000	$ 2,000

Mr. Daft also received 1,775,000 stock options.

*Released in 2004.

While Mr. Daft Received $135,000 Weekly, PepsiCo Outperformed Coca-Cola by +40%.

	12-31-98	12-31-03	Return
	\$100 Investment — Stock Price Appreciation Plus Dividends		
Coca-Cola	$ 100	$ 82	-18%
PepsiCo	$ 100	$ 122	+22%

Coca-Cola peaked at $89 in 1998.

Restricted Stock is Free.

It includes dividends;

Voting rights;

Dilutes the ownership interest of common shareowners;

And, guarantees recipients a profit, *even if our stock price decreases.*

Coca-Cola's Restricted Stock Plan Permits Our Board To Prematurely Release Free Restricted Shares Without A Shareowners Vote.

I believe this is undemocratic.

Restrictions On Free Restricted Stock Lapse 1) On A Date At Least Five Years After The Award, And 2) Upon Retirement At Age 62. However, Our Board Has Repeatedly Released Free Restricted Shares To Departing Executives Who Did Not Meet These Two Requirements.

Former Executive	Value Of Free Restricted Shares Upon Release
Ivester	$ 98,000,000
Stahl	$ 19,100,000
Daft	$ 9,000,000
Frenette	$ 3,600,000
Dunn	$ 2,500,000
Heyer	$ 2,000,000
Ware	$ 1,600,000
Total	**$ 135,800,000**

36,000,000 Free Restricted Shares Have Been Granted Since 1983.

If these shares were still in our Treasury, they would have a market value of $1,440,000,000.

Coca-Cola Grants Another Form Of Free Restricted Stock Called Performance Share Units. But, . . .

PSU grants vest in just 3 years, not at age 62.

And, our Board can prematurely release PSU grants *without a shareowner vote.*

PSU Grants Are Tied To Earnings Per Share. But, Coca-Cola Reserves The Right To Adjust EPS For. . .

Significant structural changes;

Accounting changes;

And, other operating and non-operating charges and gains disclosed separately.

Former PepsiCo CEO Roger Enrico, Who For Years Donated His Base Salary To An Employee Scholarship Endowment, Said In A New York Times Interview. . .

"you are likely as CEO to have more money that you can spend."

In Congressional Testimony, Fed Chairman Greenspan Described Some Corporate Conduct As "Infectious Greed."

I believe "infectious greed" describes Coca-Cola's compensation program.

In A Speech Entitled "What Went Wrong With America", John Bogle, Founder Of The Vanguard Mutual Fund Group, Said. . .

"as Directors often turned over to managers the virtually unfettered power to place their own interests first, the concept of stewardship became conspicuously absent from corporate America."

Last Year My Proposal Received 476,000,000 Votes Or 28% Of The Total.

Thanks.

Resolved That Shareowners Urge Coca-Cola's Board That A Significant Percentage Of Future Awards Of Free Restricted Stock And Performance Share Units...

Are performance based;

Are tied to company specific performance metrics, performance targets and timeframes clearly communicated to shareowners;

And, can not be prematurely released or substantially altered *without shareowner approval.*

Statement Against Shareowner Proposal Regarding Restricted Stock

The Board respectfully submits that the provisions of this proposal are already met.

1.   A significant percentage of currently outstanding awards of restricted stock and performance share units are performance-based.

2.   Those awards are tied to specific performance metrics, targets and timeframes and are clearly communicated to shareowners. In fact, shareowners have approved the performance criteria that may be used for performance awards.

3. The awards can only be altered as outlined in the plan shareowners have previously approved.

The Board considers this proposal unnecessary because it proposes to further modify what shareowners have already approved. This proposal and a similar proposal were previously submitted by this shareowner. In neither case did shareowners elect to adopt the change being suggested.

The Board's Compensation Committee is made up of independent directors and makes decisions about executive compensation. That Committee uses an independent advisor who counsels it on decisions related to executive compensation.

The Committee recognizes that not every shareowner agrees with every decision related to executive pay. Over the past few years the Committee has also reviewed shareowner opinions on executive compensation that ranged from providing only cash-based compensation to providing only restricted stock. The role of the Committee is to set compensation strategy that links to shareowners' interests while balancing and synthesizing the varied feedback from shareowners. The Board believes our compensation philosophy serves shareowner interests.

The Board understands and agrees that executive compensation is an important and appropriate focus for shareowners; it is also the focus of the Board's Compensation Committee. To that end, the Committee primarily uses plans and programs that have been approved by shareowners.

The Board of Directors recommends a vote
AGAINST
the proposal regarding restricted stock.

Shareowner Proposal Regarding Severance Agreements (Item 5)

International Brotherhood of Teamsters General Fund, 25 Louisiana Avenue, N.W., Washington, D.C. 20001, owner of 100 shares of Common Stock, submitted the following proposal:

RESOLVED: That the shareholders of the Coca-Cola Company ("Coke" or the "Company") urge the Board of Directors to seek shareholder approval for future severance agreements with senior executives that provide benefits in an amount exceeding 2.99 times the sum of the executive's base salary plus bonus. "Severance pay" means "payment by an employer to an employee beyond his or her base pay and bonus upon termination of his/her employment." "Future severance agreements" include employment agreements containing severance provisions; retirement agreements; and, agreements renewing, modifying or extending existing such agreements. "Benefits" include lump-sum cash payments (including payments in lieu of medical and other benefits) and the estimated present value of periodic retirement payments, fringe benefits and consulting fees (including reimbursable expenses) to be paid to the executive.

SUPPORTING STATEMENT: As part of his severance agreement, Coke's former Chairman of the Board and CEO, Mr. Douglas Ivester, received a six-year consulting agreement worth $675,000, office space, furniture, supplies, a company car, home security service, and club dues. In total Mr. Ivester's retirement package was reportedly worth $119 million. Steven Heyer, Coke's former COO, received a severance package reportedly worth at least $24 million after only three years on the job. Jack Stahl, the Company's former president and COO, received a severance package reportedly worth over $25 million. Douglas Daft, former Chairman of the board and CEO, was paid over $36 million when he left the Company's Board in 2004.

Despite disappointing profits and a federal investigation into Coke's accounting practices, Coke's board continues to reward leaders that have failed to meet shareholders' performance expectations. Our Company's history of paying exorbitant pay packages to departing executives subverts the idea of pay for performance.

In light of gross corporate abuses at companies like Enron, Tyco, and WorldCom, shareholders are taking a closer look at executive compensation practices and seemingly limitless severance packages for senior executives. Requiring shareholder approval for severance agreements—whether entered into prior to or at the time of termination—will insulate the Board from manipulation and will avoid rewarding bad management or poor performance.

Severance agreements may be appropriate in some circumstances. Nonetheless, we believe that the potential cost of such agreements entitles shareholders to be heard when a company contemplates paying out more than twice the amount of an executive's last salary and bonus. Because it is not always practical to obtain prior shareholder approval, the Company would have the option, if it implemented this proposal, of seeking approval after the material terms of the agreement were agreed upon.

Several other companies, including Sprint, Norfolk-Southern, and Bank of America have adopted similar resolutions. In the spirit of improving financial transparency and accountability to shareholders, Coca-Cola should reform its excessive compensation practices and policies.

For these reasons, we urge shareholders to vote **FOR** this proposal.

Statement Against Shareowner Proposal Regarding Severance Agreements

We do not believe this proposal is in the best interests of our shareowners because it would substitute an arbitrary numeric standard for the judgment of an independent Compensation Committee. It would also put the Company at a competitive disadvantage by substantially undermining the ability to attract and retain the talent required to deliver business results for shareowners. Finally, we believe the costs to shareowners of this proposal should be considered.

This proposal would dictate an absolute numeric standard for all severance arrangements, without regard to the circumstances of the particular individual involved. These types of individual circumstances include, but are not limited to, the executive's term of employment, past accomplishments and reasons for separation from the Company. The proposal would not differentiate executives who have left the Company after long and distinguished tenures having added to shareowner value over the course of their careers from those who have parted ways with the company after a shorter tenure. Currently, our Compensation Committee does consider these factors.

Also, flexibility to prepare an appropriate severance package would be substantially undermined by a requirement for shareowner approval. Although the proposal states that the shareowner approval can be obtained after the material terms of an arrangement are agreed upon, this solution is not practical. Separation from the company can be a trying experience for any employee—executive or non-executive. Prolonging the process to gain shareowner approval would be unproductive to an effective process, unfair to the individual and disruptive to the business. It is also unlikely that many executives would agree to such a provision of employment, leaving the Company at a disadvantage to its peers.

Shareowners should also be aware that shareowner approval for these agreements would involve a significant cost. Seeking shareowner approval for one of these agreements outside of the regular annual meeting cycle, which would almost certainly be necessary, would cost the Company and its shareowners nearly $2.5 million.

Finally, the Board believes it is important for shareowners to know that, except in rare circumstances, the Company has not entered into severance arrangements as a condition of employment. At the point of an executive's separation from our Company, the Compensation Committee determines whether the Company should enter into separation arrangements and separation payments generally are calculated pursuant to formulas contained in the Company's severance plan.

The Board believes our Compensation Committee has the expertise and familiarity with the market necessary to make prudent decisions about compensation.

The Board of Directors recommends a vote
AGAINST
the proposal regarding severance agreements.

QUESTIONS AND ANSWERS ABOUT
COMMUNICATIONS, SHAREOWNER PROPOSALS AND COMPANY DOCUMENTS

1. How do I submit a shareowner proposal?

We must receive proposals of shareowners intended to be presented at the 2006 Annual Meeting of Shareowners on or before November 8, 2005, in order for the proposals to be eligible for inclusion in our proxy statement and proxy relating to that meeting. These proposals should be sent to the Office of the Secretary by fax to (404) 515-0358 or by mail to the Office of the Secretary, The Coca-Cola Company, P.O. Box 1734, Atlanta, Georgia 30301 or by e-mail to shareowneraffairs@na.ko.com.

According to our By-Laws, a proposal for action to be presented by any shareowner at the 2006 Annual Meeting of Shareowners shall be out of order and shall not be acted upon unless:

- specifically described in our notice to all shareowners of the meeting and the matters to be acted upon thereat; or

- the proposal shall have been submitted in writing to the Office of the Secretary at the above fax number or mailing address or e-mail address and received at our principal executive offices prior to December 20, 2005, and such proposal is, under law, an appropriate subject for shareowner action.

2. How can I communicate with the Company's outside Directors?

Mail can be addressed to Directors in care of the Office of the Secretary, The Coca-Cola Company, P.O. Box 1734, Atlanta, Georgia 30301. At the direction of the Board, all mail received will be opened and screened for security purposes. The mail will then be logged in. All mail, other than trivial or obscene items, will be forwarded. Trivial items will be delivered to the Directors at the next scheduled Board meeting. Mail addressed to a particular Director will be forwarded or delivered to that Director. Mail addressed to "Outside Directors" or "Non-Management Directors" will be forwarded or delivered to the Chairman of the Committee on Directors and Corporate Governance. Mail addressed to the "Board of Directors" will be forwarded or delivered to the Chairman of the Board.

3. What is householding?

As permitted by the 1934 Act, only one copy of this proxy statement is being delivered to shareowners residing at the same address, unless such shareowners have notified the Company of their desire to receive multiple copies of the proxy statement. This is known as householding.

The Company will promptly deliver, upon oral or written request, a separate copy of the proxy statement to any shareowner residing at an address to which only one copy was mailed. Requests for additional copies should be directed to Shareowner Affairs.

Shareowners of record residing at the same address and currently receiving only one copy of the proxy statement may contact Shareowner Affairs to request multiple copies of the proxy statement in the future.

Shareowners of record residing at the same address and currently receiving multiple copies of the proxy statement may contact Shareowner Affairs to request that only a single copy of the proxy statement be mailed in the future. Contact Shareowner Affairs by fax at (404) 515-0358 or by mail to Shareowner Affairs, The Coca-Cola Company, P.O. Box 1734, Atlanta, Georgia 30301 or by e-mail to shareowneraffairs@na.ko.com.

4. Where can I see the Company's corporate documents and SEC filings?

1531

The Company's website contains the Company's Certificate of Incorporation, By-Laws, Corporate Governance Guidelines, the Committee Charters, the Code of Business Conduct and the Company's SEC filings. To view the Certificate of Incorporation, By-Laws, Corporate Governance Guidelines, Committee Charters or Code of Business Conduct, go to www.coca-cola.com, click on "The Coca-Cola Company", then click on "Investors" and then click on "Corporate Governance". To view the Company's SEC filings and Forms 3, 4 and 5 filed by the Company's Directors and Executive Officers, go to www.coca-cola.com, click on "The Coca-Cola Company," then click on "Investors" and then click on "SEC Filings."

5. How can I obtain copies of the Corporate Governance Guidelines, Committee Charters or the Code of Business Conduct?

The Company will promptly deliver free of charge, upon request, a copy of the Corporate Governance Guidelines, the Committee Charters or the Code of Business Conduct to any shareowner requesting a copy. Requests should be directed to Shareowner Affairs, The Coca-Cola Company, P.O. Box 1734, Atlanta, Georgia 30301.

6. How can I obtain copies of the Company's Annual Report on Form 10-K?

The Company will promptly deliver free of charge, upon request, a copy of the Company's Annual Report on Form 10-K to any shareowner requesting a copy. Requests should be directed to the Company's Consumer and Industry Affairs Department, The Coca-Cola Company, P.O. Box 1734, Atlanta, Georgia 30301.

OTHER INFORMATION

Management does not know of any items, other than those referred to in the accompanying Notice of Annual Meeting of Shareowners, which may properly come before the meeting or other matters incident to the conduct of the meeting.

As to any other item or proposal that may properly come before the meeting, including voting on a proposal omitted from this proxy statement pursuant to the rules of the SEC, it is intended that proxies will be voted in accordance with the discretion of the proxy holders.

The form of proxy and this proxy statement have been approved by the Board of Directors and are being mailed and delivered to shareowners by its authority.

CAROL CROFOOT HAYES
Assistant Secretary

Atlanta, Georgia
March 8, 2005

———————

FORM OF PROXY STATEMENT AND FORM OF PROXY

The 2004 Annual Report on Form 10-K includes our financial statements for the fiscal year ended December 31, 2004. We have mailed the 2004 Annual Report on Form 10-K to all shareowners. The 2004 Annual Report on Form 10-K does not form any part of the material for the solicitation of proxies.

APPENDIX I

AUDIT COMMITTEE CHARTER

Purpose

The Committee will represent and assist the Board in fulfilling its oversight responsibility to the shareowners and others relating to the integrity of the Company's financial statements and the financial reporting process, the systems of internal accounting and financial controls, the internal audit function, the annual independent audit of the Company's financial statements, the Company's compliance with legal and regulatory requirements, and its ethics programs as established by management and the Board, including the Company's Code of Business Conduct. The Committee shall also oversee the independent auditors' qualifications and independence. The Committee will evaluate the performance of the Company's internal audit function (responsibilities, budget and staffing) and the Company's independent auditors, including a review and evaluation of the engagement partner and coordinating partner. In so doing, it is the responsibility of the Committee to maintain free and open communication between the Committee, independent auditors, the internal auditors and management of the Company. The Committee is also responsible for producing an annual report for inclusion in the Company's proxy statement.

Committee Membership

The Committee shall be appointed by the Board and shall comprise at least three directors. Each Committee member shall meet the requirements of the New York Stock Exchange listing standards, and federal laws and regulations, with respect to audit committees, as they may become applicable from time to time, as well as the requirements of the Company's Corporate Governance Guidelines. No member may serve on the audit committees of more than three public companies. Committee members may receive no compensation from the Company other than director's fees. All Committee members will be financially literate, and at least one member of the Committee will meet the definition of "audit committee financial expert" set forth in rules and regulations of the Securities and Exchange Commission. The Board will designate a Chairman for the Committee. The Committee may form and delegate authority to subcommittees when appropriate.

Committee Authority and Responsibilities

The primary responsibility of the Committee is to oversee the Company's financial controls and reporting processes on behalf of the Board and report the results of its activities to the Board. Management is responsible for preparing the Company's financial statements, and the independent auditors are responsible for auditing those financial statements. The Committee in carrying out its responsibilities believes its policies and procedures should remain flexible, in order to best react to changing conditions and circumstances. The Committee should take the appropriate actions to set the overall corporate "tone" for quality financial reporting, sound business risk practices, and ethical behavior.

The following shall be the principal recurring processes of the Committee in carrying out its oversight responsibilities. The Committee may perform such other duties and responsibilities as are consistent with its purpose and as the Board or the Committee deems appropriate.

1. *Independent Auditors.* The Committee shall have a clear understanding with management and the independent auditors that the independent auditors are ultimately accountable to the Committee and the Board, as representatives of the Company's shareowners. The Committee shall have the sole authority and responsibility to hire, evaluate and, where appropriate, replace the independent auditors and, in its capacity as a committee of the Board, shall be directly responsible for the appointment, compensation and general oversight of the work of the independent auditors. The Committee shall discuss the auditors' qualifications and independence from management and the Company, including whether the auditors' performance of permissible non-audit services is compatible with their independence. This process will include, at least annually, the Committee's review of the independent auditors' internal control procedures, any material issues raised by the most recent internal quality-control review, or peer review, of the independent auditors, or by any inquiry or investigation by governmental or professional authorities, within the preceding five years, respecting one or more independent audits carried out by the independent auditors, and any steps taken to deal with any such issues; and (to assess the auditors' independence) all relationships between the independent auditors and the Company. Annually, the Committee will review the qualifications and performance of the Company's current independent auditors, and select the Company's independent auditors for the next year, subject to shareowner ratification.

2. *Audit Services.* The Committee shall discuss with the internal auditors and the independent auditors the overall scope and plans for their respective audits including their respective responsibilities and the adequacy of staffing and compensation. The Committee shall approve in advance all audit engagement fees and the terms of all audit services to be provided by the independent auditors.

3. *Permissible Non-audit Services.* The Committee shall establish policies and procedures for the engagement of the independent auditors to provide permissible non-audit services, which shall include pre-approval of any permissible non-audit services to be provided by the independent auditors. No non-audit services shall be provided by the independent auditors, except as approved in advance by the Committee.

4. *Review of Interim Financial Statements and Earnings Releases.* The Committee shall meet and review the interim financial statements, and the Company's disclosures under

Management's Discussion and Analysis of Financial Condition and Results of Operations, with management and the independent auditors prior to the filing of each of the Company's Quarterly Reports on Form 1O-Q. The Committee will discuss the Company's policies and procedures with respect to earnings releases and review financial information included in releases and earnings guidance provided to analysts and rating agencies. The Committee will discuss the results of the quarterly review and any other matters required to be communicated to the Committee by the independent auditors under generally accepted auditing standards.

5. *Review of Annual Audited Financial Statements.*   The Committee shall meet and review with management and the independent auditors the financial statements to be included in the Company's Annual Report on Form 10-K (or the annual report to shareowners if distributed prior to the filing of the Form 10-K), including (a) their judgment about the quality, not just acceptability, of the Company's accounting principles, including significant financial reporting issues and judgments made in connection with the preparation of the financial statements; (b) the clarity of the disclosures in the financial statements; and (c) the Company's disclosures under Management's Discussion and Analysis of Financial Condition and Results of Operations, including critical accounting policies.

The Committee will also review with management and the independent auditors (a) major issues regarding accounting principles and financial statement presentations, including significant changes in the selection or application of accounting principles; (b) major issues regarding the adequacy of internal controls and steps taken in light of material deficiencies; and, (c) the effects of regulatory and accounting initiatives on the financial statements.

The Committee will discuss the results of the annual audit and any difficulties the independent auditors encountered in the course of their audit work, including any restrictions on the scope of the auditors' activities or on access to requested information, and any significant disagreements with management. The Committee will also discuss any other matters required to be communicated to the Committee by the independent auditors under generally accepted auditing standards, and the annual report on internal controls by the Chief Executive Officer and Chief Financial Officer, as reviewed by the independent auditors.

Based on these reviews, the Committee will make a recommendation to the Board as to whether the audited financial statements should be included in the Company's Annual Report on Form 10-K.

6. *Risk Assessment and Risk Management.*   The Committee will review and discuss with management, the internal auditors, and the independent auditors the Company's policies and procedures with respect to risk assessment and risk management.

7. *Internal Controls, Disclosure Controls and Procedures.*   The Committee will discuss with management, the internal auditors, and the independent auditors the Company's internal controls (with particular emphasis on the scope and performance of the internal audit function), and review and discuss with the internal auditors the results of the internal audit program. The Committee will review and discuss the Company's disclosure controls and

procedures, and the quarterly assessments of such controls and procedures by the Chief Executive Officer and Chief Financial Officer.

8. *Complaint Procedures.* The Committee shall establish procedures for handling complaints regarding accounting, internal accounting controls, and auditing matters, including procedures for confidential, anonymous submission of concerns by employees regarding accounting and auditing matters.

9. *Compliance Programs.* The Committee shall periodically review and discuss with management, the internal auditors, and the independent auditors the overall adequacy and effectiveness of the Company's legal, regulatory and ethical compliance programs, including the Company's Code of Business Conduct.

10. *Report for Inclusion in Proxy Statement.* The Committee shall prepare the report that SEC rules require to be included in the Company's annual proxy statement.

11. *Hiring of Auditor Personnel.* The Committee shall set hiring policies with regard to employees and former employees of the independent auditors.

12. *Charter.* The Committee shall periodically review and reassess the adequacy of this Charter and recommend any proposed changes to the Board for approval.

13. *Annual Performance Evaluation.* The Committee shall annually review its own performance.

14. *Investigative Authority.* In discharging its oversight role, the Committee is empowered to investigate any matter brought to its attention with full access to all books, records, facilities and personnel of the Company.

Outside Advisors

The Committee shall have the authority to retain such outside counsel, accountants, experts and other advisors as it deems appropriate to assist the Committee in the performance of its functions.

The Committee shall be provided with appropriate funding, as determined by the Committee, for payment of compensation to such outside counsel, accountants, experts and other advisors.

Meetings

The Committee will meet as often as may be deemed necessary or appropriate in its judgment, at least quarterly each year, and at such times and places as the Committee shall determine. The majority of the members of the Committee shall constitute a quorum. The Committee will meet separately, at least quarterly, with the internal auditors, the independent auditors, the general counsel and other senior management to discuss any matters that they wish to bring to the Committee's attention or that the Committee wishes to bring to their attention.

The Committee shall report to the Board with respect to its meetings, including any significant issues that arise with respect to the quality or integrity of the Company's financial statements, the Company's compliance with legal or regulatory requirements, the performance and independence of the Company's independent auditors, or the performance of the internal audit function.

FORM OF PROXY STATEMENT AND FORM OF PROXY

NOTICE OF ANNUAL MEETING OF SHAREOWNERS

The Annual Meeting of Shareowners of The Coca-Cola Company (the "Company") will be held at the Hotel du Pont, 11th and Market Streets, Wilmington, Delaware 19801, on Tuesday, April 19, 2005, at 10:30 a.m., local time. The purposes of the meeting are:

1. To elect fourteen Directors to serve until the 2006 Annual Meeting of Shareowners,

2. To ratify the appointment of Ernst & Young LLP as independent auditors of the Company to serve for the 2005 fiscal year,

3. To vote on three proposals submitted by shareowners if properly presented at the meeting, and

4. To transact such other business as may properly come before the meeting and at any adjournments or postponements of the meeting.

The Board of Directors set February 22, 2005, as the record date for the meeting. This means that owners of Common Stock at the close of business on that date are entitled to:

- receive this notice of the meeting, and

- vote at the meeting and any adjournments or postponements of the meeting.

We will make available a list of shareowners as of the close of business on February 22, 2005, for inspection by shareowners during normal business hours from April 8 through April 18, 2005, at the Company's principal place of business, One Coca-Cola Plaza, Atlanta, Georgia 30313. This list also will be available to shareowners at the meeting.

By Order of the
Board of Directors
Carol Crofoot Hayes
Assistant Secretary

/ **FOLD AND DETACH HERE** /

The Coca-Cola Company

FORM OF PROXY STATEMENT AND FORM OF PROXY

**This Proxy is Solicited on Behalf of the Board of Directors
of The Coca-Cola Company**

The undersigned, having received the Notice of Annual Meeting and Proxy Statement, hereby (i) appoints Gary P. Fayard, Geoffrey J. Kelly and Cynthia P. McCague, each of them, proxies with full power of substitution, for and in the name of the undersigned, to vote all shares of Common Stock of The Coca-Cola Company owned of record by the undersigned, and (ii) directs (a) Merrill Lynch Trust Company, FSB, Trustee under The Coca-Cola Company Thrift & Investment Plan, and/or (b) Banco Santander De Puerto Rico, Inc., Trustee under the Caribbean Refrescos, Inc. Thrift Plan, and/or (c) Putnam Fiduciary Trust Company, Trustee under the Coca-Cola Enterprises Inc. Matched Employee Savings and Investment Plan, Coca-Cola Enterprises Inc. Bargaining 401(k) Plan, The Lansing Matched Employee Savings and Investment Plan, The Coca-Cola Bottling Company of New York, Inc. Savings Plan for Southern New England, Central States Coca-Cola Bottling Company 401(k) Plan for St. Louis Bargaining Employees, to vote in person or by proxy all shares of Common Stock of The Coca-Cola Company allocated to any accounts of the undersigned under such Plans, and which the undersigned is entitled to vote, in each case, on all matters which may come before the 2005 Annual Meeting of Shareowners to be held at the Hotel du Pont, 11th and Market Streets, Wilmington, Delaware 19801, on April 19, 2005, at 10:30 a.m. local time, and any adjournments or postponements thereof, unless otherwise specified herein. **The proxies, in their discretion, are further authorized to vote (x) for the election of a person to the Board of Directors if any nominee named herein becomes unable to serve or for good cause will not serve, (y) on any matter which the Board of Directors did not know would be presented at the 2005 Annual Meeting of Shareowners by a reasonable time before the proxy solicitation was made, and (z) on other matters which may properly come before the 2005 Annual Meeting of Shareowners and any adjournments or postponements thereof.**

Election of Directors:
  Nominees for reelection (terms expiring in 2006)
   01. Herbert A. Allen   02. Ronald W. Allen   03. Cathleen P. Black   04. Warren E. Buffett   05. Barry Diller
   06. E. Neville Isdell   07. Donald R. Keough   08. Maria Elena Lagomasino   09. Donald F. McHenry
   10. Sam Nunn   11. J. Pedro Reinhard   12. James D. Robinson III   13. Peter V. Ueberroth   14. James B. Williams

You are encouraged to specify your choices by marking the appropriate boxes (SEE REVERSE SIDE), but you need not mark any boxes if you wish to vote in accordance with the Board of Directors' recommendations. The proxies cannot vote your shares unless you sign and return this card.

**SEE
REVERSE
SIDE**

The Coca-Cola Company

**C/O EQUISERVE TRUST COMPANY N.A.
P.O. BOX 8080
EDISON, NJ 08818-8080**

To vote your shares electronically, use one of the methods below and follow the instructions provided once you access the system.

1538

FORM OF PROXY STATEMENT AND FORM OF PROXY

Your electronic vote authorizes the named proxies in the same manner as if you marked, signed, dated and returned the proxy card. If you choose to vote your shares electronically, there is no need for you to mail back your proxy card.

_____

_____

Your vote is important. Please vote immediately.

Vote-by-Internet

OR

Vote-by-Telephone

- Log on to the Internet and go to the web site **http://www.eproxyvote.com/ko**

- On a touch-tone telephone, call **1-877-PRX-VOTE (1-877-779-8683)** 24 hours a day, 7 days a week

Sign up to receive next year's annual report and proxy materials via the Internet. Next year when the materials are available, we will send you an e-mail with instructions which will enable you to review these materials on-line. To sign up for this optional service, visit www.econsent.com/ko

/ FOLD AND DETACH HERE /

Please mark your votes as in this example.

COC

This proxy when properly signed will be voted in the manner directed herein. If no direction is made, this proxy will be voted "FOR" all of the Board of Directors' nominees, "FOR" proposal 2, and "AGAINST" proposals 3, 4 and 5.

The Board of Directors recommends a vote FOR:

		FOR	WITHHELD
1.	Election of Directors (see reverse)	☐	☐

☐ For, except vote withheld from the following nominee(s):

_____

		FOR	AGAINST	ABSTAIN
2.	Ratification of the appointment of Ernst & Young LLP as independent auditors	☐	☐	☐

The Board of Directors recommends a vote AGAINST:

		FOR	AGAINST	ABSTAIN
3.	Shareowner Proposal regarding an Independent Delegation of Inquiry to Colombia	☐	☐	☐

1539

FORM OF PROXY STATEMENT AND FORM OF PROXY

4.	Shareowner Proposal regarding Restricted Stock	☐	☐	☐
5.	Shareowner Proposal regarding Severance Agreements	☐	☐	☐

SPECIAL ACTION   Mark here if you plan to
                                                             attend the Annual
                                                             Meeting.   ☐

SIGNATURE(S):   DATE:

Note: Please sign exactly as name appears hereon. Joint owners should each sign. When signing as attorney, executor, administrator, Trustee or guardian, please give full title as such.

AMERICAN BAR FOUNDATION, COMMENTARIES ON DEBENTURES 410–411 (1971)

II. Discussion

Debenture indentures frequently contain a covenant of the Company to the effect that it will not make any distributions to its shareholders after a certain date (the "peg date") if, after giving effect thereto, the total of all such distributions would exceed the aggregate (or a stated percentage) of the net earnings accumulated since the peg date plus, in many cases, a specific amount representing a portion of earned surplus at the peg date and all or a portion of the proceeds received from the issuance of shares after the peg date. The peg date is usually the beginning of the fiscal year in which the debt is issued....

1. Net Income and the Proceeds of Stock Issues.

... [T]he covenant restricting distributions to shareholders is generally expressed in terms of limiting such distributions to an amount comprised of three items which are discussed below: *first,* all or part of the accumulated net earnings of the borrower after the peg date until the time of the declaration or payment, taken as one accounting period; *second,* the proceeds from the issuance or sale of stock after the peg date; and *third,* an additional dollar amount which in effect allows the borrower the flexibility of making distributions to shareholders out of a portion of the net earnings previously accumulated and existing as earned surplus at the peg date.[5]

(a) *Net Income.* One portion of the maximum amount of permitted distribution to shareholders under such a formula is all or some fraction of the net income of the Company after the peg date. Sometimes the peg date may be much earlier, even several years earlier, than the beginning of the current fiscal year in order to permit the Company to use a greater portion of the earnings accumulated before the negotiations for the new issue or to make the new restriction no more onerous than that under an outstanding debt issue.

For the purpose of considering allowable distributions to shareholders, the net income of the Company includes all net income from the peg date until a specified date at or close to the dividend, other distribution or purchase of shares. Many indentures provide that the specified date shall be the date of the declaration of the dividend or the date of the disbursement of any other distribution on or purchase of shares. Un-

---

5. The third item, permitting the use of a specified amount of existing earned sur- plus, is sometimes referred to as the "dip".

doubtedly exact figures for such entire period would not be available at the date of declaration or distribution, but could only be approximated. This will be sufficient unless the question of whether or not there is a violation of the covenant is a close one. To avoid such a problem, some indentures fix the end of the period as the end of a specified month or quarter prior to the dividend, distribution or acquisition.

Net income will be stated as either that of the Company or that of the Company and some or all of its subsidiaries on a consolidated basis. Net income may be defined for other covenants of the indenture, but, if not, some definition is frequently used in connection with the dividend covenant itself. Frequently the definition is that net income shall be that determined in accordance with generally accepted accounting principles. The parties may, however, desire to vary from generally accepted accounting principles in some respects, or may feel that the reference to such principles may leave questions as to certain items, and therefore will agree upon a more detailed definition of net income. . . .

4. Maintenance of Working Capital.

Dividends payable in cash necessarily reduce working capital as well as net worth and therefore indentures frequently include, as a condition to the declaration or payment of a dividend, that working capital be at least a specified amount.

As has been indicated, some indentures contain a separate covenant requiring the maintenance of working capital at a prescribed minimum level, and a decline below that level, whether because of a dividend payment, decline in sales, or for any other reason, is a default.

In other situations the parties may agree that declines in working capital should not create a default under the indenture unless they result from a voluntary distribution made while working capital is already at a low level. This is accomplished by including in the dividend covenant a condition that the working capital remaining after the distribution on stock will be in excess of a prescribed minimum.

Some indentures include both tests on the theory that the absolute maintenance test establishes a rock-bottom level and voluntary distributions ought to be restricted at a somewhat higher level.

Following are sample dividend covenants which illustrate some of the numerous variations which are common.

III. Sample Covenants . . .

SAMPLE COVENANT 4

(Expanded Form Covering Practically All Types of Payments and Distributions to Shareholders)

To avoid a multiplicity of examples, which in any event could not cover the many combinations of elements which the parties might negotiate, the following Sample Covenant sets forth an expanded form covering practically all types of payments and distributions to shareholders.

§ 10–12. Limitations on Dividends and Other Stock Payments.

The Company will not declare any dividends on any class of its stock or make any payment on account of, or set apart money for a sinking or other analogous fund for, the purchase, redemption or other retirement of any shares of such stock, or make any distribution in respect thereof, either directly or indirectly, and whether in cash or property or in obligations of the Company (such dividends, payments and distributions being herein called *"Stock Payments"*), unless such dividends are declared to be payable not more than 60 days after the date of declaration, and unless, after giving effect to such proposed Stock Payment, all of the conditions set forth in the following *Subsections A to D,* inclusive, shall exist at the date of such declaration (in the case of a dividend) or at the date of such setting apart in the case of any such fund, or the date of such other payment or distribution in the case of any other Stock Payment (each such date being herein called a *"Computation Date"*):

A. no Event of Default [under the Indenture] has occurred which has not been cured.

B. the sum of

(1) $ [the dip];

(2) plus (or minus in the case of a deficit) [10] the Consolidated Net Income of the Company and its Consolidated Subsidiaries computed for the period beginning [the peg date] [11] to and including the Computation Date;

(3) plus the aggregate amount of all contributions to capital (including the fair value of property other than cash) received by the Company during such period;

(4) plus the aggregate net proceeds (including the fair value of property other than cash) received by the Company from the issue or sale of any class of its stock during such period;

shall be greater than all Stock Payments declared (in the case of dividends) or set apart (in the case of any such fund) or made (in the case of any other Stock Payment) during such period.

C. the Consolidated Working Capital [Consolidated Net Tangible Assets] [Consolidated Tangible Net Worth] of the Company and its Consolidated Subsidiaries shall be at least $_____.

---

10. If only a portion of such net income is to be included in the formula, there will be inserted at this point such words as "an amount equal to ...% of".

11. Usually the peg date will be the same throughout the Section although special circumstances may dictate that different dates be used for different purposes.

D.   After deducting from both Consolidated Current Assets and Consolidated Current Liabilities of the Company and its Consolidated Subsidiaries an amount equal to the aggregate amount included in Consolidated Current Liabilities

(1) as provision for taxes (to the extent not then due, or if due, payable without penalty) measured by income or profits or by salaries or wages, and

(2) as liabilities to the federal or any state government, or to any subdivision or agency of any thereof, on account of amounts withheld or collected from salaries or wages of persons in its employ under any income tax law or any social security law applicable to such persons, or on account of amounts withheld or collected from employees for the purpose of purchasing obligations of the federal government, the remaining Consolidated Current Assets of the Company and its Consolidated Subsidiaries shall be at least ___% of the remaining Consolidated Current Liabilities of the Company and its Consolidated Subsidiaries.

Provided, however, that this Section shall not apply to, and the term "Stock Payment" shall not include, dividends payable solely in any class of stock of the Company, or the purchase, redemption or other retirement of any stock of any class of the Company by exchange for, or out of the proceeds of the substantially concurrent sale of, shares of any other class of stock of the Company, or the application to the redemption, purchase or other retirement of any such stock of any moneys previously and properly set apart for and then held in a sinking or other analogous fund established for such stock.

For the purposes of this Section, the amount of any Stock Payment declared or paid or distributed in property of the Company shall be deemed to be the book value of such property (after deducting related reserves for depreciation, depletion and amortization) at the Computation Date, and the amount of any Stock Payment declared or paid or distributed in obligations of the Company shall be deemed to be the value of such obligations as of the date of the adoption of the Board Resolution authorizing such Stock Payment, as determined by such Board Resolution.   The fair value of any obligations of the Company received by the Company as a contribution to capital or as the consideration for the issuance of stock of the Company (whether upon conversion of such obligations or otherwise) shall be the principal amount of such obligations.

Without regard to the foregoing restrictions of this Section, the Company may pay regular dividends upon shares of the _____ Preferred Stock of the Company outstanding on _____, and may set apart money and apply the same to the purchase or redemption of shares of said Preferred Stock through the operation of the sinking fund provided for by the Company's Certificate of Incorporation as in effect on _____, but all amounts so paid, set apart and/or applied shall be included in all subsequent computations of Stock Payments for the purposes of this Section.

The Company will not permit any Subsidiary to purchase any stock of any class of the Company.

WACHTELL, LIPTON, ROSEN & KATZ
SHARE PURCHASE
RIGHTS PLAN

INTRODUCTION ...
The Share Purchase Rights Plan
Background of the Rights Plan

The basic objectives of the rights plan are to deter abusive takeover tactics by making them unacceptably expensive to the raider and to encourage prospective acquirors to negotiate with the board of directors of the target rather than to attempt a hostile takeover.

The plan includes a "flip-in" feature designed to deter creeping accumulations of a company's stock. The "flip-in" feature is structured to be available from a 10% to a 15% ownership threshold. If triggered, the flip-in feature would give shareholders, other than the holder triggering the flip-in, the right to purchase shares of the company at a discount to market price (thereby diluting the triggering shareholder). The plan also has a "flip-over" feature which provides shareholders protection against being forced to dispose of their equity interest in the company. The flip-over feature would give shareholders the right to purchase shares of the acquiring company at a discount in the event of a freeze-out merger or similar transaction (thereby diluting the acquiring company).

The rights issued pursuant to the plan are redeemable for a nominal amount prior to the acquisition of 15% of the target's shares. The plan also allows the board of directors to lower the threshold to not less than 10% if the Board determines it is appropriate in light of specific circumstances. Thus, the effect of the plan is to force potential acquirors to deal with the company's board of directors (or conduct a proxy contest to replace directors) before acquiring shares in excess of the threshold level. This increases the negotiating power of the Board. Part II of this memorandum contains a summary of the terms of our recommended plan....

Terms of Recommended Rights Plan*

Issuance: One right to buy one one-hundredth of a share of a new series of preferred stock as a dividend on each outstanding share of

---

* These terms are as they would be set by a company that uses authorized blank check preferred stock, with terms that make 1/100th of a share of the preferred stock the economic equivalent of one share of common stock, as the security for which the rights are exercisable.

common stock of the company. Until the rights become exercisable, all further issuances of common stock, including common stock issuable upon exercise of outstanding options, would include issuances of rights.

Term: 10 years.

Exercise price: An amount per one one-hundredth of a share of the preferred stock which approximates the board's view of the long-term value of the company's common stock. Factors to be considered in setting the exercise price include the company's business and prospects, its long-term plans and market conditions. The exercise price is subject to certain anti-dilution adjustments. For illustration only, assume an exercise price of $120 per one one-hundredth of a share.

Rights detach and become exercisable: The rights are not exercisable and are not transferable apart from the company's common stock until the tenth day after such time as a person or group acquires beneficial ownership of 15% or more of the company's common stock or the tenth business day (or such later time as the board of directors may determine) after a person or group commences a tender or exchange offer the consummation of which would result in beneficial ownership by a person or group of 15% or more of the company's common stock. As soon as practicable after the rights become exercisable, separate right certificates would be issued and the rights would become transferable apart from the company's common stock.

Protection against creeping acquisition/open market purchases: In the event a person or group were to acquire a 15% or greater position in the company, each right then outstanding would "flip in" and become a right to buy that number of shares of common stock of the company which at the time of the 15% acquisition had a market value of two times the exercise price of the rights. The acquiror who triggered the rights would be excluded from the "flip-in" because his rights would have become null and void upon his triggering acquisition. Thus, if the company's common stock at the time of the "flip-in" were trading at $30 per share and the exercise price of the rights at such time were $120, each right would thereafter be exercisable at $120 for eight shares of the company's common stock. The amendment provision of the Rights Agreement provides that the 15% threshold can be lowered to not less than 10%. The board can utilize this provision to provide additional protection against creeping accumulations.

Protection against squeezeout: If, after the rights have been triggered, an acquiring company were to merge or otherwise combine with the company, or the company were to sell 50% or more of its assets or earning power to an acquiring company, each right then outstanding (other than rights held by the acquiring company) would "flip over" and thereby would become a right to buy that number of shares of common stock of the acquiring company which at the time of such transaction would have a market value of two times the exercise price of the rights. Thus, if the acquiring company's common stock at the time of such transaction were trading at $30 per share and the exercise price of the rights at such time were $120, each right would thereafter be exercisable at $120 for eight shares (*i.e.*, the number of shares that could be purchased for $240, or two times the exercise price of the rights) of the acquiring company's common stock.

Exchange: At any time after the acquisition by a person or group of affiliated or associated persons of beneficial ownership of 15% or more of the outstanding common stock of the company and before the acquisition by a person or group of 50% or more of the outstanding common stock of the company, the board of directors may exchange the rights (other than rights owned by such person or group, which have become void), in whole or in part, at an exchange ratio of one share of the company's common stock (or one one-hundredth of a share of junior participating preferred stock) per right, subject to adjustment.

Redemption: The rights are redeemable by the company's board of directors at a price of $.01 per right at any time prior to the acquisition by a person or group of beneficial ownership of 15% or more of the company's common stock. The redemption of the rights may be made effective at such time, on such basis, and with such conditions as the board of directors in its sole discretion may establish. Thus, the rights would not interfere with a negotiated merger or a white knight transaction, even after a hostile tender offer has been commenced. The rights may prevent a white knight transaction after a 15% acquisition (unless the exchange feature described above is used to eliminate the rights and the white knight's price is adjusted for the issuance of the additional shares).

Voting: The rights would not have any voting rights.

Terms of preferred stock: The preferred stock issuable upon exercise of the rights would be non-redeemable and rank junior to all other series of the company's preferred stock. The dividend, liquidation and voting rights, and non-redemption features of the preferred stock are designed so that the value of the one one-hundredth interest in a share of new preferred stock purchasable with each right will approximate the value of one share of common stock. Each whole share of preferred stock would be entitled to receive a quarterly preferential dividend of $1 per share but would be entitled to receive, in the aggregate, a dividend of 100 times the dividend declared on the common stock. In the event of liquidation, the holders of the new preferred stock would be entitled to receive a preferential liquidation payment of $100 per share but would be entitled to receive, in the aggregate, a liquidation payment equal to 100 times the payment made per share of common stock. Each share of preferred stock would have 100 votes, voting together with the common stock. Finally, in the event of any merger, consolidation or other transaction in which shares of common stock are exchanged for or changed into other stock or securities, cash and/or other property, each share of preferred stock would be entitled to receive 100 times the amount received per share of common stock. The foregoing rights are protected against dilution in the event additional shares of common stock are issued. Since the "out of the money" rights would not be exercisable immediately, registration of the preferred stock issuable upon exercise of the rights with the Securities and Exchange Commission need not be effective until the rights become exercisable and are "in the money" or are so close to being "in the money" so as to make exercise economically possible.

Federal income tax consequences: The Internal Revenue Service has published a revenue ruling holding that the adoption of a rights plan is not a taxable event for the company or its shareholders under the federal income tax laws. The physical distribution of rights certificates upon the rights becoming exercisable should not result in any tax. After such physical distribution, the rights would be treated for tax purposes as capital assets in the hands of most shareholders, the tax basis of each right would be zero in most cases (or, in certain cases, an allocable part of the tax basis of the stock with respect to which the right was issued) and the holding period of each right would include the holding period of the stock with respect to which such right was issued. Upon the rights becoming rights to purchase an acquiror's common stock, holders of rights probably would be taxed even if the rights were not exercised. Upon the rights becoming rights to purchase additional common stock of the company, holders of rights probably would not have a taxable event. The redemption of the rights for cash and, most likely, the acquisition of the rights by the company for its stock would each be taxable events. The use of company stock (with the rights attached) will not interfere with the company's ability to engage in tax-free acquisitions nor will it affect any net operating losses of the company.

Accounting consequences: The initial issuance of the rights has no accounting or financial reporting impact. Since the rights would be "out of the money" when issued, they would not dilute earnings per share. Because the redemption date of the rights is neither fixed nor determinable, the accounting guidelines do not require the redemption amount to be accounted for as a long-term obligation of the company.

Miscellaneous: The Rights Agreement provides that the company may not enter into any transaction of the sort which would give rise to the "flip-over" right if, in connection therewith, there are outstanding securities or there are agreements or arrangements intended to counteract the protective provisions of the rights. The Rights Agreement may be amended from time to time in any manner prior to the acquisition of a 15% position (or a 10% position if the board lowers the triggering threshold).

FORM OF PLAN

_____, INC.

and

_____

Rights Agreement

Dated as of _____, 200__

TABLE OF CONTENTS

Agreement, dated as of _____, 200_, between _____, Inc., a _____ corporation (the "Company"), and _____, as rights agent (the "Rights Agent").

The Board of Directors of the Company has authorized and declared a dividend of one preferred share purchase right (a "Right") for each Common Share (as hereinafter defined) of the Company outstanding on _____ , 200_ (the "Record Date"), each Right representing the right to purchase one one-hundredth of a Preferred Share (as hereinafter defined), upon the terms and subject to the conditions herein set forth, and has further authorized and directed the issuance of one Right with respect to each Common Share that shall become outstanding between the Record Date and the earliest of the Distribution Date, the Redemption Date and the Final Expiration Date (as such terms are hereinafter defined).

Accordingly, in consideration of the premises and the mutual agreements herein set forth, the parties hereby agree as follows:

Section 1. Definitions. For purposes of this Agreement, the following terms have the meanings indicated:

(a) "Acquiring Person" shall mean any Person who or which, together with all Affiliates and Associates of such Person, shall be the Beneficial Owner of 15% or more of the Common Shares of the Company then outstanding, but shall not include the Company, any Subsidiary of the Company, any employee benefit plan of the Company or any Subsidiary of the Company, or any entity holding Common Shares for or pursuant to the terms of any such plan. Notwithstanding the foregoing, no Person shall become an "Acquiring Person" as the result of an acquisition of Common Shares by the Company which, by reducing the number of Common Shares of the Company outstanding, increases the proportionate number of Common Shares of the Company beneficially owned by such Person to 15% or more of the Common Shares of the Company then outstanding; provided, however, that, if a Person shall

1551

become the Beneficial Owner of 15% or more of the Common Shares of the Company then outstanding by reason of share purchases by the Company and shall, after such share purchases by the Company, become the Beneficial Owner of any additional Common Shares of the Company, then such Person shall be deemed to be an "Acquiring Person." Notwithstanding the foregoing, if the Board of Directors of the Company determines in good faith that a Person who would otherwise be an "Acquiring Person," as defined pursuant to the foregoing provisions of this paragraph (a), has become such inadvertently, and such Person divests as promptly as practicable a sufficient number of Common Shares so that such Person would no longer be an "Acquiring Person," as defined pursuant to the foregoing provisions of this paragraph (a), then such Person shall not be deemed to be an "Acquiring Person" for any purposes of this Agreement.

(b) "Affiliate" shall have the meaning ascribed to such term in Rule 12b–2 of the General Rules and Regulations under the Exchange Act as in effect on the date of this Agreement.

(c) "Associate" shall have the meaning ascribed to such term in Rule 12b–2 of the General Rules and Regulations under the Exchange Act as in effect on the date of this Agreement.

(d) A Person shall be deemed the "Beneficial Owner" of and shall be deemed to "beneficially own" any securities:

(i) which such Person or any of such Person's Affiliates or Associates beneficially owns, directly or indirectly;

(ii) which such Person or any of such Person's Affiliates or Associates has (A) the right to acquire (whether such right is exercisable immediately or only after the passage of time) pursuant to any agreement, arrangement or understanding (other than customary agreements with and between underwriters and selling group members with respect to a bona fide public offering of securities), or upon the exercise of conversion rights, exchange rights, rights (other than these Rights), warrants or options, or otherwise; provided, however, that a Person shall not be deemed the Beneficial Owner of, or to beneficially own, securities tendered pursuant to a tender or exchange offer made by or on behalf of such Person or any of such Person's Affiliates or Associates until such tendered securities are accepted for purchase or exchange; or (B) the right to vote pursuant to any agreement, arrangement or understanding; provided, however, that a Person shall not be deemed the Beneficial Owner of, or to beneficially own, any security if the agreement, arrangement or understanding to vote such security (1) arises solely from a revocable proxy or consent given to such Person in response to a public proxy or consent solicitation made pursuant to, and in accordance with, the applicable rules and regulations promulgated under the Exchange Act and (2) is not also then reportable on Schedule 13D under the Exchange Act (or any comparable or successor report); or

(iii) which are beneficially owned, directly or indirectly, by any other Person with which such Person or any of such Person's Affiliates or Associates has any agreement, arrangement or understanding (other than customary agreements with and between underwriters and selling group members with respect to a bona fide public offering of securities) for the purpose of acquiring, holding, voting (except to the extent contemplated by the proviso to Section 1(d)(ii)(B) hereof) or disposing of any securities of the Company.

Notwithstanding anything in this definition of Beneficial Ownership to the contrary, the phrase "then outstanding," when used with reference to a Person's Beneficial Ownership of securities of the Company, shall mean the number of such securities then issued and outstanding together with the number of such securities not then actually issued and outstanding which such Person would be deemed to own beneficially hereunder.

(e) "Business Day" shall mean any day other than a Saturday, a Sunday, or a day on which banking institutions in [State of Rights Agent] are authorized or obligated by law or executive order to close.

(f) "Close of Business" on any given date shall mean 5:00 P.M., [City of Rights Agent] time, on such date; provided, however, that, if such date is not a Business Day, it shall mean 5:00 P.M., [City of Rights Agent] time, on the next succeeding Business Day.

(g) "Common Shares" when used with reference to the Company shall mean the shares of common stock, par value $____ per share, of the Company. "Common Shares" when used with reference to any Person other than the Company shall mean the capital stock (or equity interest) with the greatest voting power of such other Person or, if such other Person is a Subsidiary of another Person, the Person or Persons which ultimately control such first-mentioned Person.

(h) "Distribution Date" shall have the meaning set forth in Section 3(a) hereof.

(i) "Exchange Act" shall mean the Securities Exchange Act of 1934, as amended.

(j) "Exchange Ratio" shall have the meaning set forth in Section 24(a) hereof.

(k) "Final Expiration Date" shall have the meaning set forth in Section 7(a) hereof.

(l) "NASDAQ" shall mean the National Association of Securities Dealers, Inc. Automated Quotation System.

(m) "Person" shall mean any individual, firm, corporation or other entity, and shall include any successor (by merger or otherwise) of such entity.

(n) "Preferred Shares" shall mean shares of Series A Junior Participating Preferred Stock, par value $____ per share, of the Company having the rights and preferences set forth in the Form of Certificate of Designations attached to this Agreement as Exhibit A.

(o) "Purchase Price" shall have the meaning set forth in Section 4 hereof.

(p) "Record Date" shall have the meaning set forth in the second paragraph hereof.

(q) "Redemption Date" shall have the meaning set forth in Section 7(a) hereof.

(r) "Redemption Price" shall have the meaning set forth in Section 23(a) hereof.

(s) "Right" shall have the meaning set forth in the second paragraph hereof.

(t) "Right Certificate" shall have the meaning set forth in Section 3(a) hereof.

(u) "Shares Acquisition Date" shall mean the first date of public announcement by the Company or an Acquiring Person that an Acquiring Person has become such.

(v) "Subsidiary" of any Person shall mean any corporation or other entity of which a majority of the voting power of the voting equity securities or equity interest is owned, directly or indirectly, by such Person.

(w) "Summary of Rights" shall have the meaning set forth in Section 3(b) hereof.

(x) "Trading Day" shall have the meaning set forth in Section 11(d) hereof.

Section 2. Appointment of Rights Agent. The Company hereby appoints the Rights Agent to act as agent for the Company and the holders of the Rights (who, in accordance with Section 3 hereof, shall, prior to the Distribution Date, also be the holders of the Common Shares of the Company) in accordance with the terms and conditions hereof, and the Rights Agent hereby accepts such appointment. The Company may from time to time appoint such co-Rights Agents as it may deem necessary or desirable.

Section 3. Issue of Right Certificates. (a) Until the earlier of (i) the tenth day after the Shares Acquisition Date or (ii) the tenth Business Day (or such later date as may be determined by action of the Board of Directors of the Company prior to such time as any Person becomes an

Acquiring Person) after the date of the commencement by any Person (other than the Company, any Subsidiary of the Company, any employee benefit plan of the Company or of any Subsidiary of the Company or any entity holding Common Shares of the Company for or pursuant to the terms of any such plan) of a tender or exchange offer the consummation of which would result in any Person becoming the Beneficial Owner of Common Shares of the Company aggregating 15% or more of the then outstanding Common Shares of the Company (including any such date which is after the date of this Agreement and prior to the issuance of the Rights; the earlier of such dates being herein referred to as the "Distribution Date"), (x) the Rights will be evidenced (subject to the provisions of Section 3(b) hereof) by the certificates for Common Shares of the Company registered in the names of the holders thereof (which certificates shall also be deemed to be Right Certificates) and not by separate Right Certificates, and (y) the right to receive Right Certificates will be transferable only in connection with the transfer of Common Shares of the Company. As soon as practicable after the Distribution Date, the Company will prepare and execute, the Rights Agent will countersign, and the Company will send or cause to be sent (and the Rights Agent will, if requested, send) by first-class, insured, postage-prepaid mail, to each record holder of Common Shares of the Company as of the Close of Business on the Distribution Date, at the address of such holder shown on the records of the Company, a Right Certificate, in substantially the form of Exhibit B hereto (a "Right Certificate"), evidencing one Right for each Common Share so held. As of the Distribution Date, the Rights will be evidenced solely by such Right Certificates.

(b) On the Record Date, or as soon as practicable thereafter, the Company will send a copy of a Summary of Rights to Purchase Preferred Shares, in substantially the form of Exhibit C hereto (the "Summary of Rights"), by first-class, postage-prepaid mail, to each record holder of Common Shares as of the Close of Business on the Record Date, at the address of such holder shown on the records of the Company. With respect to certificates for Common Shares of the Company outstanding as of the Record Date, until the Distribution Date, the Rights will be evidenced by such certificates registered in the names of the holders thereof together with a copy of the Summary of Rights attached thereto. Until the Distribution Date (or the earlier of the Redemption Date or the Final Expiration Date), the surrender for transfer of any certificate for Common Shares of the Company outstanding on the Record Date, with or without a copy of the Summary of Rights attached thereto, shall also constitute the transfer of the Rights associated with the Common Shares of the Company represented thereby.

(c) Certificates for Common Shares which become outstanding (including, without limitation, reacquired Common Shares referred to in the last sentence of this paragraph (c)) after the Record Date but prior to the earliest of the Distribution Date, the Redemption Date or the Final

Expiration Date shall have impressed on, printed on, written on or otherwise affixed to them the following legend:

> This certificate also evidences and entitles the holder hereof to certain rights as set forth in an Agreement between _____ , Inc. and _____ , dated as of _____ , 200_, as it may be amended from time to time (the "Agreement"), the terms of which are hereby incorporated herein by reference and a copy of which is on file at the principal executive offices of _____ , Inc. Under certain circumstances, as set forth in the Agreement, such Rights (as defined in the Agreement) will be evidenced by separate certificates and will no longer be evidenced by this certificate. _____ , Inc. will mail to the holder of this certificate a copy of the Agreement without charge after receipt of a written request therefor. As set forth in the Agreement, Rights beneficially owned by any Person (as defined in the Agreement) who becomes an Acquiring Person (as defined in the Agreement) become null and void.

With respect to such certificates containing the foregoing legend, until the Distribution Date, the Rights associated with the Common Shares of the Company represented by such certificates shall be evidenced by such certificates alone, and the surrender for transfer of any such certificate shall also constitute the transfer of the Rights associated with the Common Shares of the Company represented thereby. In the event that the Company purchases or acquires any Common Shares of the Company after the Record Date but prior to the Distribution Date, any Rights associated with such Common Shares of the Company shall be deemed cancelled and retired so that the Company shall not be entitled to exercise any Rights associated with the Common Shares of the Company which are no longer outstanding.

Section 4. <u>Form of Right Certificates</u>. The Right Certificates (and the forms of election to purchase Preferred Shares and of assignment to be printed on the reverse thereof) shall be substantially the same as Exhibit B hereto, and may have such marks of identification or designation and such legends, summaries or endorsements printed thereon as the Company may deem appropriate and as are not inconsistent with the provisions of this Agreement, or as may be required to comply with any applicable law or with any applicable rule or regulation made pursuant thereto or with any applicable rule or regulation of any stock exchange or the National Association of Securities Dealers, Inc., or to conform to usage. Subject to the provisions of Section 22 hereof, the Right Certificates shall entitle the holders thereof to purchase such number of one one-hundredths of a Preferred Share as shall be set forth therein at the price per one one-hundredth of a Preferred Share set forth therein (the "Purchase Price"), but the number of such one one-hundredths of a Preferred Share and the Purchase Price shall be subject to adjustment as provided herein.

Section 5. <u>Countersignature and Registration.</u> The Right Certificates shall be executed on behalf of the Company by its Chairman of the Board, its Chief Executive Officer, its President, any of its Vice Presidents or its Treasurer, either manually or by facsimile signature, shall have affixed thereto the Company's seal or a facsimile thereof, and shall be attested by the Secretary or an Assistant Secretary of the Company, either manually or by facsimile signature. The Right Certificates shall be manually countersigned by the Rights Agent and shall not be valid for any purpose unless countersigned. In case any officer of the Company who shall have signed any of the Right Certificates shall cease to be such officer of the Company before countersignature by the Rights Agent and issuance and delivery by the Company, such Right Certificates, nevertheless, may be countersigned by the Rights Agent and issued and delivered by the Company with the same force and effect as though the individual who signed such Right Certificates had not ceased to be such officer of the Company; and any Right Certificate may be signed on behalf of the Company by any individual who, at the actual date of the execution of such Right Certificate, shall be a proper officer of the Company to sign such Right Certificate, although at the date of the execution of this Agreement any such individual was not such an officer.

Following the Distribution Date, the Rights Agent will keep or cause to be kept, at its principal office, books for registration and transfer of the Right Certificates issued hereunder. Such books shall show the names and addresses of the respective holders of the Right Certificates, the number of Rights evidenced on its face by each of the Right Certificates and the date of each of the Right Certificates.

Section 6. <u>Transfer, Split Up, Combination and Exchange of Right Certificates; Mutilated, Destroyed, Lost or Stolen Right Certificates.</u> Subject to the provisions of Section 14 hereof, at any time after the Close of Business on the Distribution Date, and at or prior to the Close of Business on the earlier of the Redemption Date or the Final Expiration Date, any Right Certificate or Right Certificates (other than Right Certificates representing Rights that have become void pursuant to Section 11(a)(ii) hereof or that have been exchanged pursuant to Section 24 hereof) may be transferred, split up, combined or exchanged for another Right Certificate or Right Certificates entitling the registered holder to purchase a like number of one one-hundredths of a Preferred Share as the Right Certificate or Right Certificates surrendered then entitled such holder to purchase. Any registered holder desiring to transfer, split up, combine or exchange any Right Certificate or Right Certificates shall make such request in writing delivered to the Rights Agent, and shall surrender the Right Certificate or Right Certificates to be transferred, split up, combined or exchanged at the principal office of the Rights Agent. Thereupon the Rights Agent shall countersign and deliver to the Person entitled thereto a Right Certificate or Right Certificates, as the case may be, as so requested. The Company may require payment of a sum sufficient to cover any tax or governmental charge that may be imposed in connection with any transfer, split up, combination or exchange of Right Certificates.

Upon receipt by the Company and the Rights Agent of evidence reasonably satisfactory to them of the loss, theft, destruction or mutilation of a Right Certificate, and, in case of loss, theft or destruction, of indemnity or security reasonably satisfactory to them, and, at the Company's request, reimbursement to the Company and the Rights Agent of all reasonable expenses incidental thereto, and upon surrender to the Rights Agent and cancellation of the Right Certificate if mutilated, the Company will make and deliver a new Right Certificate of like tenor to the Rights Agent for delivery to the registered holder in lieu of the Right Certificate so lost, stolen, destroyed or mutilated.

Section 7. <u>Exercise of Rights; Purchase Price; Expiration Date of Rights</u>. (a) The registered holder of any Right Certificate may exercise the Rights evidenced thereby (except as otherwise provided herein), in whole or in part, at any time after the Distribution Date, upon surrender of the Right Certificate, with the form of election to purchase on the reverse side thereof duly executed, to the Rights Agent at the principal office of the Rights Agent, together with payment of the Purchase Price for each one one-hundredth of a Preferred Share as to which the Rights are exercised, at or prior to the earliest of (i) the Close of Business on _____, 201_ (the "Final Expiration Date"), (ii) the time at which the Rights are redeemed as provided in Section 23 hereof (the "<u>Redemption Date</u>"), or (iii) the time at which such Rights are exchanged as provided in Section 24 hereof.

(b) The Purchase Price for each one one-hundredth of a Preferred Share purchasable pursuant to the exercise of a Right shall initially be $_____ , and shall be subject to adjustment from time to time as provided in Section 11 or 13 hereof, and shall be payable in lawful money of the United States of America in accordance with paragraph (c) below.

(c) Upon receipt of a Right Certificate representing exercisable Rights, with the form of election to purchase duly executed, accompanied by payment of the Purchase Price for the shares to be purchased and an amount equal to any applicable transfer tax required to be paid by the holder of such Right Certificate in accordance with Section 9 hereof by certified check, cashier's check or money order payable to the order of the Company, the Rights Agent shall thereupon promptly (i) (A) requisition from any transfer agent of the Preferred Shares certificates for the number of Preferred Shares to be purchased and the Company hereby irrevocably authorizes any such transfer agent to comply with all such requests, or (B) requisition from the depositary agent depositary receipts representing such number of one one-hundredths of a Preferred Share as are to be purchased (in which case certificates for the Preferred Shares represented by such receipts shall be deposited by the transfer agent of the Preferred Shares with such depositary agent) and the Company hereby directs such depositary agent to comply with such request; (ii) when appropriate, requisition from the Company the amount of cash to be paid in lieu of issuance of fractional shares in accordance with Section 14 hereof; (iii) promptly after receipt of such certificates or depositary receipts, cause the same to be delivered to or upon the order of the registered holder of such Right Certificate, registered in such name or names as may be designated by such holder; and (iv) when appropriate, after receipt, promptly deliver such cash to or upon the order of the registered holder of such Right Certificate.

(d) In case the registered holder of any Right Certificate shall exercise less than all the Rights evidenced thereby, a new Right Certificate evidencing Rights equivalent to the Rights remaining unexercised shall be issued by the Rights Agent to registered holder of such Right Certificate or to such holder's duly authorized assigns, subject to the provisions of Section 14 hereof.

Section 8. <u>Cancellation and Destruction of Right Certificates</u>. All Right Certificates surrendered for the purpose of exercise, transfer, split up, combination or exchange shall, if surrendered to the Company or to any of its agents, be delivered to the Rights Agent for cancellation or in cancelled form, or, if surrendered to the Rights Agent, shall be cancelled by it, and no Right Certificates shall be issued in lieu thereof except as expressly permitted by any of the provisions of this Agreement. The Company shall deliver to the Rights Agent for cancellation and retirement, and the Rights Agent shall so cancel and retire, any other Right Certificate purchased or acquired by the Company otherwise than upon the exercise thereof. The Rights Agent shall deliver all cancelled Right Certificates to the Company, or shall, at the written request of the Company, destroy such cancelled Right Certificates, and, in such case, shall deliver a certificate of destruction thereof to the Company.

Section 9. <u>Availability of Preferred Shares</u>. The Company covenants and agrees that it will cause to be reserved and kept available out of its authorized and unissued Preferred Shares or any Preferred Shares held in its treasury the number of Preferred Shares that will be sufficient to permit the exercise in full of all outstanding Rights in accordance with Section 7 hereof. The Company covenants and agrees that it will take all such action as may be necessary to ensure that all Preferred Shares delivered upon exercise of Rights shall, at the time of delivery of the certificates for such Preferred Shares (subject to payment of the Purchase Price), be duly and validly authorized and issued and fully paid and nonassessable shares.

The Company further covenants and agrees that it will pay when due and payable any and all federal and state transfer taxes and charges which may be payable in respect of the issuance or delivery of the Right Certificates or of any Preferred Shares upon the exercise of Rights. The

Company shall not, however, be required to pay any transfer tax which may be payable in respect of any transfer or delivery of Right Certificates to a Person other than, or the issuance or delivery of certificates or depositary receipts for the Preferred Shares in a name other than that of, the registered holder of the Right Certificate evidencing Rights surrendered for exercise or to issue or to deliver any certificates or depositary receipts for Preferred Shares upon the exercise of any Rights until any such tax shall have been paid (any such tax being payable by the holder of such Right Certificate at the time of surrender) or until it has been established to the Company's reasonable satisfaction that no such tax is due.

Section 10. Preferred Shares Record Date. Each Person in whose name any certificate for Preferred Shares is issued upon the exercise of Rights shall for all purposes be deemed to have become the holder of record of the Preferred Shares represented thereby on, and such certificate shall be dated, the date upon which the Right Certificate evidencing such Rights was duly surrendered and payment of the Purchase Price (and any applicable transfer taxes) was made; provided, however, that, if the date of such surrender and payment is a date upon which the Preferred Shares transfer books of the Company are closed, such Person shall be deemed to have become the record holder of such shares on, and such certificate shall be dated, the next succeeding Business Day on which the Preferred Shares transfer books of the Company are open. Prior to the exercise of the Rights evidenced thereby, the holder of a Right Certificate shall not be entitled to any rights of a holder of Preferred Shares for which the Rights shall be exercisable, including, without limitation, the right to vote, to receive dividends or other distributions or to exercise any preemptive rights, and shall not be entitled to receive any notice of any proceedings of the Company, except as provided herein.

Section 11. Adjustment of Purchase Price, Number of Shares or Number of Rights. The Purchase Price, the number of Preferred Shares covered by each Right and the number of Rights outstanding are subject to adjustment from time to time as provided in this Section 11.

(a) (i) In the event the Company shall at any time after the date of this Agreement (A) declare a dividend on the Preferred Shares payable in Preferred Shares, (B) subdivide the outstanding Preferred Shares, (C) combine the outstanding Preferred Shares into a smaller number of Preferred Shares or (D) issue any shares of its capital stock in a reclassification of the Preferred Shares (including any such reclassification in connection with a consolidation or merger in which the Company is the continuing or surviving corporation), except as otherwise provided in this Section 11(a), the Purchase Price in effect at the time of the record date for such dividend or of the effective date of such subdivision, combination or reclassification, and the number and kind of shares of capital stock issuable on such date, shall be proportionately adjusted so that the holder of any Right exercised after such time shall be entitled to receive the aggregate number and kind of shares of capital stock which, if such Right had been exercised immediately prior to such date and at a time when the Preferred Shares transfer books of the Company were open, such holder would have owned upon such exercise and been entitled to receive by virtue of such dividend, subdivision, combination or reclassification; provided, however, that in no event shall the consideration to be paid upon the exercise of one Right be less than the aggregate par value of the shares of capital stock of the Company issuable upon exercise of one Right.

(ii) Subject to Section 24 hereof, in the event any Person becomes an Acquiring Person, each holder of a Right shall thereafter have a right to receive, upon exercise thereof at a price equal to the then current Purchase Price multiplied by the number of one one-hundredths of a Preferred Share for which a Right is then exercisable, in accordance with the terms of this Agreement and in lieu of Preferred Shares, such number of Common Shares of the Company as shall equal the result obtained by (A) multiplying the then current Purchase Price by the number of one one-hundredths of a Preferred Share for which a Right is then exercisable and dividing that product by (B) 50% of the then current per share market price of the Common Shares of the Company (determined pursuant to Section 11(d) hereof) on the date of the occurrence of such event. In the event that any Person shall become an Acquiring Person and the Rights shall then be outstanding, the Company shall not take any action which would eliminate or diminish the benefits intended to be afforded by the Rights.

From and after the occurrence of such event, any Rights that are or were acquired or beneficially owned by any Acquiring Person (or any Associate or Affiliate of such Acquiring Person) shall be void, and any holder of such Rights shall thereafter have no right to exercise such Rights under any provision of this Agreement. No Right Certificate shall be issued pursuant to Section 3 hereof that represents Rights beneficially owned by an Acquiring Person whose Rights would be void pursuant to the preceding sentence or any Associate or Affiliate thereof; no Right Certificate shall be issued at any time upon the transfer of any Rights to an Acquiring Person whose Rights would be void pursuant to the preceding sentence or any Associate or Affiliate thereof or to any nominee of such Acquiring Person, Associate or Affiliate; and any Right Certificate delivered to the Rights Agent for transfer to an Acquiring Person whose Rights would be void pursuant to the preceding sentence shall be cancelled.

(iii) In the event that there shall not be sufficient Common Shares issued but not outstanding or authorized but unissued to permit the exercise in full of the Rights in accordance with subparagraph (ii) above, the Company shall take all such action as may be necessary to authorize additional Common Shares for issuance upon exercise of the Rights. In the event the Company shall, after good faith effort, be unable to take all such action as may be necessary to authorize such additional Common Shares, the Company shall substitute, for each Common Share that would otherwise be issuable upon exercise of a Right, a number of Preferred Shares or fraction thereof such that the current per share market price of one Preferred Share multiplied by such number or fraction is equal to the current per share market price of one Common Share as of the date of issuance of such Preferred Shares or fraction thereof.

(b) In case the Company shall fix a record date for the issuance of rights, options or warrants to all holders of Preferred Shares entitling them (for a period expiring within 45 calendar days after such record date) to subscribe for or purchase Preferred Shares (or shares having the same rights, privileges and preferences as the Preferred Shares ("equivalent preferred shares")) or securities convertible into Preferred Shares or equivalent preferred shares at a price per Preferred Share or equivalent preferred share (or having a conversion price per share, if a security convertible into Preferred Shares or equivalent preferred shares) less than the then current per share market price of the Preferred Shares (as defined in Section 11(d)) on such record date, the Purchase Price to be in effect after such record date shall be determined by multiplying the Purchase Price in effect immediately prior to such record date by a fraction, the numerator of which shall be the number of Preferred Shares outstanding on such record date plus the number of Preferred Shares which the aggregate offering price of the total number of Preferred Shares and/or equivalent preferred shares so to be offered (and/or the aggregate initial conversion price of the convertible securities so to be offered) would purchase at such current market price and the denominator of which shall be the number of Preferred Shares outstanding on such record date plus the number of additional Preferred Shares and/or equivalent preferred shares to be offered for subscription or purchase (or into which the convertible securities so to be offered are initially convertible); provided, however, that in no event shall the consideration to be paid upon the exercise of one Right be less than the aggregate par value of the shares of capital stock of the Company issuable upon exercise of one Right. In case such subscription price may be paid in a consideration part or all of which shall be in a form other than cash, the value of such consideration shall be as determined in good faith by the Board of Directors of the Company, whose determination shall be described in a statement filed with the Rights Agent and shall be binding on the Rights Agent and holders of the Rights. Preferred Shares owned by or held for the account of the Company shall not be deemed outstanding for the purpose of any such computation. Such adjustment shall be made successively whenever such a record date is fixed; and, in the event that such rights, options or warrants are not so issued, the Purchase Price shall be adjusted to be the Purchase Price which would then be in effect if such record date had not been fixed.

(c) In case the Company shall fix a record date for the making of a distribution to all holders of the Preferred Shares (including any such distribution made in connection with a consolidation or merger in which the Company is the continuing or surviving corporation) of evidences of indebtedness or assets (other than a regular quarterly cash dividend or a dividend payable in Preferred Shares) or subscription rights or warrants (excluding those referred to in Section 11(b) hereof), the Purchase Price to be in effect after such record date shall be determined by multiplying the Purchase Price in effect immediately prior to such record date by a fraction, the numerator of which shall be the then-current per share market price of the Preferred Shares on such record date, less the fair market value (as determined in good faith by the Board of Directors of the Company, whose determination shall be described in a statement filed with the Rights Agent and shall be binding on the Rights Agent and holders of the Rights) of the portion of the assets or evidences of indebtedness so to be distributed or of such subscription rights or warrants applicable to one Preferred Share and the denominator of which shall be such then-current per share market price of the Preferred Shares on such record date; provided, however, that in no event shall the consideration to be paid upon the exercise of one Right be less than the aggregate par value of the shares of capital stock of the Company to be issued upon exercise of one Right. Such adjustments shall be made successively whenever such a record date is fixed; and, in the event that such distribution is not so made, the Purchase Price shall again be adjusted to be the Purchase Price which would then be in effect if such record date had not been fixed.

(d) (i) For the purpose of any computation hereunder, the "current per share market price" of any security (a "Security" for the purpose of this Section 11(d)(i)) on any date shall be deemed to be the average of the daily closing prices per share of such Security for the 30 consecutive Trading Days immediately prior to such date; provided, however, that, in the event that the current per share market price of the Security is determined during a period following the announcement by the issuer of such Security of (A) a dividend or distribution on such Security payable in shares of such Security or Securities convertible into such shares, or (B) any subdivision, combination or reclassification of such Security and prior to the expiration of 30 Trading Days after the ex-dividend date for such dividend or distribution, or the record date for such subdivision, combination or reclassification, then, and in each such case, the current per share market price shall be appropriately adjusted to reflect the current market price per share equivalent of such Security. The closing price for each day shall be the last sale price, regular way, reported at or prior to 4:00 P.M. Eastern time or, in case no such sale takes place on such day, the average of the bid and asked prices, regular way, reported as of 4:00 P.M. Eastern time, in either case, as reported in the principal consolidated transaction reporting system with respect to securities listed or admitted to trading on the New York Stock Exchange or, if the Security is not listed or admitted to trading on the New York Stock Exchange, as reported in the principal consolidated transaction reporting system with respect to securities listed on the principal national securities exchange on which the Security is listed or admitted to trading or, if the Security is not listed or admitted to trading on any national securities exchange, the last quoted price reported at or prior to 4:00 P.M. Eastern time or, if not so quoted, the average of the high bid and low asked prices in the over-the-counter market, as reported as of 4:00 P.M. Eastern time by NASDAQ or such other system then in use, or, if on any such date the Security is not quoted by any such organization, the average of the closing bid and asked prices as furnished by a professional market maker making a market in the Security selected by the Board of Directors of the Company. The term "Trading Day" shall mean a day on which the principal national securities exchange on which the Security is listed or admitted to trading is open for the transaction of business, or, if the Security is not listed or admitted to trading on any national securities exchange, a Business Day.

(ii) For the purpose of any computation hereunder, the "current per share market price" of the Preferred Shares shall be determined in accordance with the method set forth in Section 11(d)(i). If the Preferred Shares are not publicly traded, the "current per share market price" of the Preferred Shares shall be conclusively deemed to be the current per share market price of the Common Shares as determined pursuant to Section 11(d)(i) hereof (appropriately adjusted to reflect any stock split, stock dividend or similar transaction occurring after the date hereof), multiplied by one hundred. If neither the Common Shares nor the Preferred Shares are publicly held or so listed or traded, "current per share market price" shall mean the fair value per share as determined in good faith by the Board of Directors of the Company, whose determination shall be described in a statement filed with the Rights Agent.

(e) No adjustment in the Purchase Price shall be required unless such adjustment would require an increase or decrease of at least 1% in the Purchase Price; provided, however, that any adjustments which by reason of this Section 11(e) are not required to be made shall be carried forward and taken into account in any subsequent adjustment. All calculations under this Section 11 shall be made to the nearest cent or to the nearest one one-millionth of a Preferred Share or one ten-thousandth of any other share or security as the case may be. Notwithstanding the first sentence of this Section 11(e), any adjustment required by this Section 11 shall be made no later than the earlier of (i) three years from the date of the transaction which requires such adjustment or (ii) the date of the expiration of the right to exercise any Rights.

(f) If, as a result of an adjustment made pursuant to Section 11(a) hereof, the holder of any Right thereafter exercised shall become entitled to receive any shares of capital stock of the Company other than Preferred Shares, thereafter the number of such other shares so receivable upon exercise of any Right shall be subject to adjustment from time to time in a manner and on terms as nearly equivalent as practicable to the provisions with respect to the Preferred Shares contained in Section 11(a) through (c) hereof, inclusive, and the provisions of Sections 7, 9, 10 and 13 hereof with respect to the Preferred Shares shall apply on like terms to any such other shares.

(g) All Rights originally issued by the Company subsequent to any adjustment made to the Purchase Price hereunder shall evidence the right to purchase, at the adjusted Purchase Price, the number of one one-hundredths of a Preferred Share purchasable from time to time hereunder upon exercise of the Rights, all subject to further adjustment as provided herein.

(h) Unless the Company shall have exercised its election as provided in Section 11(i) hereof, upon each adjustment of the Purchase Price as a result of the calculations made in Sections 11(b) and (c) hereof, each Right outstanding immediately prior to the making of such adjustment shall thereafter evidence the right to purchase, at the adjusted Purchase Price, that number of one one-hundredths of a Preferred Share (calculated to the nearest one one-millionth of a Preferred Share) obtained by (A) multiplying (x) the number of one one-hundredths of a share covered by a Right immediately prior to this adjustment by (y) the Purchase Price in effect immediately prior to such adjustment of the Purchase Price and (B) dividing the product so obtained by the Purchase Price in effect immediately after such adjustment of the Purchase Price.

(i) The Company may elect, on or after the date of any adjustment of the Purchase Price, to adjust the number of Rights in substitution for any adjustment in the number of one one-hundredths of a Preferred Share purchasable upon the exercise of a Right. Each of the Rights outstanding after such adjustment of the number of Rights shall be exercisable for the number of one one-hundredths of a Preferred Share for which a Right was exercisable immediately prior to such adjustment. Each Right held of record prior to such adjustment of the number of Rights shall become that number of Rights (calculated to the nearest one ten-thousandth) obtained by dividing the Purchase Price in effect immediately prior to adjustment of the Purchase Price by the Purchase Price in effect immediately after adjustment of the Purchase Price. The Company shall make a public announcement of its election to adjust the number of Rights, indicating the record date for the adjustment, and, if known at the time, the amount of the adjustment to be made. This record date may be the date on which the Purchase Price is adjusted or any day thereafter, but, if the Right Certificates have been issued, shall be at least 10 days later than the date of the public announcement. If

Right Certificates have been issued, upon each adjustment of the number of Rights pursuant to this Section 11(i), the Company shall, as promptly as practicable, cause to be distributed to holders of record of Right Certificates on such record date Right Certificates evidencing, subject to Section 14 hereof, the additional Rights to which such holders shall be entitled as a result of such adjustment, or, at the option of the Company, shall cause to be distributed to such holders of record in substitution and replacement for the Right Certificates held by such holders prior to the date of adjustment, and upon surrender thereof, if required by the Company, new Right Certificates evidencing all the Rights to which such holders shall be entitled after such adjustment. Right Certificates so to be distributed shall be issued, executed and countersigned in the manner provided for herein, and shall be registered in the names of the holders of record of Right Certificates on the record date specified in the public announcement.

(j) Irrespective of any adjustment or change in the Purchase Price or in the number of one one-hundredths of a Preferred Share issuable upon the exercise of the Rights, the Right Certificates theretofore and thereafter issued may continue to express the Purchase Price and the number of one one-hundredths of a Preferred Share which were expressed in the initial Right Certificates issued hereunder.

(k) Before taking any action that would cause an adjustment reducing the Purchase Price below one one-hundredth of the then par value, if any, of the Preferred Shares issuable upon exercise of the Rights, the Company shall take any corporate action which may, in the opinion of its counsel, be necessary in order that the Company may validly and legally issue fully paid and nonassessable Preferred Shares at such adjusted Purchase Price.

(*l*) In any case in which this Section 11 shall require that an adjustment in the Purchase Price be made effective as of a record date for a specified event, the Company may elect to defer until the occurrence of such event the issuing to the holder of any Right exercised after such record date of the Preferred Shares and other capital stock or securities of the Company, if any, issuable upon such exercise over and above the Preferred Shares and other capital stock or securities of the Company, if any, issuable upon such exercise on the basis of the Purchase Price in effect prior to such adjustment; provided, however, that the Company shall deliver to such holder a due bill or other appropriate instrument evidencing such holder's right to receive such additional shares upon the occurrence of the event requiring such adjustment.

(m) Anything in this Section 11 to the contrary notwithstanding, the Company shall be entitled to make such reductions in the Purchase Price, in addition to those adjustments expressly required by this Section 11, as and to the extent that it, in its sole discretion, shall determine to be advisable in order that any consolidation or subdivision of the Preferred Shares, issuance wholly for cash of any Preferred Shares at less than the current market price, issuance wholly for cash of Preferred Shares or securities which by their terms are convertible into or exchangeable for Preferred Shares, dividends on Preferred Shares payable in Preferred Shares or issuance of rights, options or warrants referred to in Section 11(b) hereof, hereafter made by the Company to holders of the Preferred Shares shall not be taxable to such stockholders.

(n) In the event that, at any time after the date of this Agreement and prior to the Distribution Date, the Company shall (i) declare or pay any dividend on the Common Shares payable in Common Shares, or (ii) effect a subdivision, combination or consolidation of the Common Shares (by reclassification or otherwise than by payment of dividends in Common Shares) into a greater or lesser number of Common Shares, then, in any such case, (A) the number of one one-hundredths of a Preferred Share purchasable after such event upon proper exercise of each Right shall be determined by multiplying the number of one one-hundredths of a Preferred Share so purchasable immediately prior to such event by a fraction, the numerator of which is the number of Common Shares outstanding immediately before such event and the denominator of which is the number of Common Shares outstanding immediately after such event, and (B) each Common Share outstanding immediately after such event shall have issued with respect to it that number of Rights which each Common Share outstanding immediately prior to such event had issued with respect to it. The adjustments provided for in this Section 11(n) shall be made successively whenever such a dividend is declared or paid or such a subdivision, combination or consolidation is effected.

Section 12. <u>Certificate of Adjusted Purchase Price or Number of Shares</u>. Whenever an adjustment is made as provided in Section 11 or 13 hereof, the Company shall promptly (a) prepare a certificate setting forth such adjustment and a brief statement of the facts accounting for such adjustment, (b) file with the Rights Agent and with each transfer agent for the Common Shares or the Preferred Shares and the Securities and Exchange Commission a copy of such certificate and (c) if such adjustment occurs at any time after the Distribution Date, mail a brief summary thereof to each holder of a Right Certificate in accordance with Section 25 hereof.

Section 13. <u>Consolidation, Merger or Sale or Transfer of Assets or Earning Power</u>. In the event, directly or indirectly, at any time after a Person has become an Acquiring Person, (a) the Company shall consolidate with, or merge with and into, any other Person, (b) any Person shall consolidate with the Company, or merge with and into the Company and the Company shall be the continuing or surviving corporation of such merger and, in connection with such merger, all or part of the Common Shares shall be changed into or exchanged for stock or other securities of any other Person (or the Company) or cash or any other property, or (c) the Company shall sell or otherwise transfer (or one or more of its Subsidiaries shall sell or otherwise transfer), in one or more transactions, assets or earning power aggregating 50% or more of the assets or earning power of the Company and its Subsidiaries (taken as a whole) to any other Person other than the Company or one or more of its wholly-owned Subsidiaries, then, and in each such case, proper provision shall be made so that (i) each holder of a Right (except as otherwise provided herein) shall thereafter have the right to receive, upon the exercise thereof at a price equal to the then current Purchase Price multiplied by the number of one one-hundredths of a Preferred Share for which a Right is then exercisable, in accordance with the terms of this Agreement and in lieu of Preferred Shares, such number of Common Shares of such other Person (including the Company as successor thereto or as the surviving corporation) as shall equal the result obtained by (A) multiplying the then current Purchase Price by the number of one one-hundredths of a Preferred Share for which a Right is then exercisable and dividing that product by (B) 50% of the then current per share market price of the Common Shares of such other Person (determined pursuant to Section 11(d) hereof) on the date of consummation of such consolidation, merger, sale or transfer; (ii) the issuer of such Common Shares shall thereafter be liable for, and shall assume, by virtue of such consolidation, merger, sale or transfer, all the obligations and duties of the Company pursuant to this Agreement; (iii) the term "Company" shall thereafter be deemed to refer to such issuer; and (iv) such issuer shall take such steps (including, but not limited to, the reservation of a sufficient number of its Common Shares in accordance with Section 9 hereof) in connection with such consummation as may be necessary to assure that the provisions hereof shall thereafter be applicable, as nearly as reasonably may be, in relation to the Common Shares of the Company thereafter deliverable upon the exercise of the Rights. The Company shall not consummate any such consolidation, merger, sale or transfer unless, prior thereto, the Company and such issuer shall have executed and delivered to the Rights Agent a supplemental agreement so providing. The Company shall not enter into any transaction of the kind referred to in this Section 13 if at the time of such transaction there are any rights, warrants, instruments or securities outstanding or any agreements or arrangements which, as a result of the consummation of such transaction, would eliminate or substantially diminish the benefits intended to be afforded by the Rights. The provisions of this Section 13 shall similarly apply to successive mergers or consolidations or sales or other transfers.

Section 14. <u>Fractional Rights and Fractional Shares</u>. (a) The Company shall not be required to issue fractions of Rights or to distribute Right Certificates which evidence fractional Rights. In lieu of such fractional Rights, there shall be paid to the registered holders of the Right

Certificates with regard to which such fractional Rights would otherwise be issuable, an amount in cash equal to the same fraction of the current market value of a whole Right. For the purposes of this Section 14(a), the current market value of a whole Right shall be the closing price of the Rights for the Trading Day immediately prior to the date on which such fractional Rights would have been otherwise issuable. The closing price for any day shall be the last sale price, regular way, or, in case no such sale takes place on such day, the average of the closing bid and asked prices, regular way, in either case, as reported in the principal consolidated transaction reporting system with respect to securities listed or admitted to trading on the New York Stock Exchange or, if the Rights are not listed or admitted to trading on the New York Stock Exchange, as reported in the principal consolidated transaction reporting system with respect to securities listed on the principal national securities exchange on which the Rights are listed or admitted to trading or, if the Rights are not listed or admitted to trading on any national securities exchange, the last quoted price or, if not so quoted, the average of the high bid and low asked prices in the over-the-counter market, as reported by NASDAQ or such other system then in use or, if on any such date the Rights are not quoted by any such organization, the average of the closing bid and asked prices as furnished by a professional market maker making a market in the Rights selected by the Board of Directors of the Company. If on any such date no such market maker is making a market in the Rights, the fair value of the Rights on such date as determined in good faith by the Board of Directors of the Company shall be used.

(b) The Company shall not be required to issue fractions of Preferred Shares (other than fractions which are integral multiples of one one-hundredth of a Preferred Share) upon exercise of the Rights or to distribute certificates which evidence fractional Preferred Shares (other than fractions which are integral multiples of one one-hundredth of a Preferred Share). Fractions of Preferred Shares in integral multiples of one one-hundredth of a Preferred Share may, at the election of the Company, be evidenced by depositary receipts, pursuant to an appropriate agreement between the Company and a depositary selected by it; provided that such agreement shall provide that the holders of such depositary receipts shall have all the rights, privileges and preferences to which they are entitled as beneficial owners of the Preferred Shares represented by such depositary receipts. In lieu of fractional Preferred Shares that are not integral multiples of one one-hundredth of a Preferred Share, the Company shall pay to the registered holders of Right Certificates at the time such Rights are exercised as herein provided an amount in cash equal to the same fraction of the current market value of one Preferred Share. For the purposes of this Section 14(b), the current market value of a Preferred Share shall be the closing price of a Preferred Share (as determined pursuant to the second sentence of

Section 11(d)(i) hereof) for the Trading Day immediately prior to the date of such exercise.

(c) The holder of a Right, by the acceptance of the Right, expressly waives such holder's right to receive any fractional Rights or any fractional shares upon exercise of a Right (except as provided above).

Section 15. <u>Rights of Action</u>. All rights of action in respect of this Agreement, excepting the rights of action given to the Rights Agent under Section 18 hereof, are vested in the respective registered holders of the Right Certificates (and, prior to the Distribution Date, the registered holders of the Common Shares); and any registered holder of any Right Certificate (or, prior to the Distribution Date, of the Common Shares), without the consent of the Rights Agent or of the holder of any other Right Certificate (or, prior to the Distribution Date, of the Common Shares), may, in such holder's own behalf and for such holder's own benefit, enforce, and may institute and maintain any suit, action or proceeding against the Company to enforce, or otherwise act in respect of, such holder's right to exercise the Rights evidenced by such Right Certificate in the manner provided in such Right Certificate and in this Agreement. Without limiting the foregoing or any remedies available to the holders of Rights, it is specifically acknowledged that the holders of Rights would not have an adequate remedy at law for any breach of this Agreement, and will be entitled to specific performance of the obligations under, and injunctive relief against actual or threatened violations of the obligations of any Person subject to, this Agreement.

Section 16. <u>Agreement of Right Holders</u>. Every holder of a Right, by accepting the same, consents and agrees with the Company and the Rights Agent and with every other holder of a Right that:

(a) prior to the Distribution Date, the Rights will be transferable only in connection with the transfer of the Common Shares;

(b) after the Distribution Date, the Right Certificates are transferable only on the registry books of the Rights Agent if surrendered at the principal office of the Rights Agent, duly endorsed or accompanied by a proper instrument of transfer; and

(c) the Company and the Rights Agent may deem and treat the person in whose name the Right Certificate (or, prior to the Distribution Date, the associated Common Shares certificate) is registered as the absolute owner thereof and of the Rights evidenced thereby (notwithstanding any notations of ownership or writing on the Right Certificate or the associated Common Shares certificate made by anyone other than the Company or the Rights Agent) for all purposes whatsoever, and neither the Company nor the Rights Agent shall be affected by any notice to the contrary.

Section 17. <u>Right Certificate Holder Not Deemed a Stockholder</u>. No holder, as such, of any Right Certificate shall be entitled to vote, receive dividends or be deemed for any purpose the holder of the Preferred Shares or any other securities of the Company which may at any time be issuable on the exercise of the Rights represented thereby, nor shall anything contained herein or in any Right Certificate be construed to confer upon the holder of any Right Certificate, as such, any of the rights of a stockholder of the Company or any right to vote for the election of directors or upon any matter submitted to stockholders at any meeting thereof, or to give or withhold consent to any corporate action, or to receive notice of meetings or other actions affecting stockholders (except as provided in Section 25 hereof), or to receive dividends or subscription rights, or otherwise, until the Right or Rights evidenced by such Right Certificate shall have been exercised in accordance with the provisions hereof.

Section 18. <u>Concerning the Rights Agent</u>. The Company agrees to pay to the Rights Agent reasonable compensation for all services rendered by it hereunder, and, from time to time, on demand of the Rights Agent, its reasonable expenses and counsel fees and other disbursements incurred in the administration and execution of this Agreement and the exercise and performance of its duties hereunder. The Company also agrees to indemnify the Rights Agent for, and to hold it harmless against, any loss, liability, or expense incurred without negligence, bad faith or willful misconduct on the part of the Rights Agent, for anything done or omitted by the Rights Agent in connection with the acceptance and administration of this Agreement, including the costs and expenses of defending against any claim of liability in the premises.

The Rights Agent shall be protected and shall incur no liability for, or in respect of any action taken, suffered or omitted by it in connection with, its administration of this Agreement in reliance upon any Right Certificate or certificate for the Preferred Shares or Common Shares or for other securities of the Company, instrument of assignment or transfer, power of attorney, endorsement, affidavit, letter, notice, direction, consent, certificate, statement, or other paper or document believed by it to be genuine and to be signed, executed and, where necessary, verified or acknowledged, by the proper person or persons, or otherwise upon the advice of counsel as set forth in Section 20 hereof.

Section 19. <u>Merger or Consolidation or Change of Name of Rights Agent</u>. Any corporation into which the Rights Agent or any successor Rights Agent may be merged or with which it may be consolidated, or any corporation resulting from any merger or consolidation to which the Rights Agent or any successor Rights Agent shall be a party, or any corporation succeeding to the stock transfer or corporate trust powers of the Rights Agent or any successor Rights Agent, shall be the successor to the Rights Agent under this Agreement without the execution or filing of any paper or any further act on the part of any of the parties hereto; <u>provided</u> that such corporation would be eligible for appointment as a successor Rights Agent under the provisions of Section 21 hereof. In case at the time such successor Rights Agent shall succeed to the agency created by this Agreement, any of the Right Certificates shall have been countersigned but not delivered, any such successor Rights Agent may adopt the countersignature of the predecessor Rights Agent and deliver such Right Certificates so countersigned; and, in case at that time any of the Right Certificates shall not have been countersigned, any successor Rights Agent may countersign such Right Certificates either in the name of the predecessor Rights Agent or in the name of the successor Rights Agent; and, in all such cases, such Right Certificates shall have the full force provided in the Right Certificates and in this Agreement.

In case at any time the name of the Rights Agent shall be changed and at such time any of the Right Certificates shall have been countersigned but not delivered, the Rights Agent may adopt the countersignature under its prior name and deliver Right Certificates so countersigned; and, in case at that time any of the Right Certificates shall not have been countersigned, the Rights Agent may countersign such Right Certificates either in its prior name or in its changed name; and, in all such cases, such Right Certificates shall have the full force provided in the Right Certificates and in this Agreement.

Section 20. Duties of Rights Agent. The Rights Agent undertakes the duties and obligations imposed by this Agreement upon the following terms and conditions, by all of which the Company and the holders of Right Certificates, by their acceptance thereof, shall be bound:

(a) The Rights Agent may consult with legal counsel (who may be legal counsel for the Company), and the opinion of such counsel shall be full and complete authorization and protection to the Rights Agent as to any action taken or omitted by it in good faith and in accordance with such opinion.

(b) Whenever in the performance of its duties under this Agreement the Rights Agent shall deem it necessary or desirable that any fact or matter be proved or established by the Company prior to taking or suffering any action hereunder, such fact or matter (unless other evidence in respect thereof be herein specifically prescribed) may be deemed to be conclusively proved and established by a certificate signed by any one of the Chairman of the Board, the Chief Executive Officer, the President, any Vice President, the Treasurer or the Secretary of the Company and delivered to the Rights Agent; and such certificate shall be full authorization to the Rights Agent for any action taken or suffered in good faith by it under the provisions of this Agreement in reliance upon such certificate.

(c) The Rights Agent shall be liable hereunder to the Company and any other Person only for its own negligence, bad faith or willful misconduct.

(d) The Rights Agent shall not be liable for or by reason of any of the statements of fact or recitals contained in this Agreement or in the

Right Certificates (except its countersignature thereof) or be required to verify the same, but all such statements and recitals are and shall be deemed to have been made by the Company only.

(e) The Rights Agent shall not be under any responsibility in respect of the validity of this Agreement or the execution and delivery hereof (except the due execution hereof by the Rights Agent) or in respect of the validity or execution of any Right Certificate (except its countersignature thereof); nor shall it be responsible for any breach by the Company of any covenant or condition contained in this Agreement or in any Right Certificate; nor shall it be responsible for any change in the exercisability of the Rights (including the Rights becoming void pursuant to Section 11(a)(ii) hereof) or any adjustment in the terms of the Rights (including the manner, method or amount thereof) provided for in Section 3, 11, 13, 23 or 24 hereof, or the ascertaining of the existence of facts that would require any such change or adjustment (except with respect to the exercise of Rights evidenced by Right Certificates after actual notice that such change or adjustment is required); nor shall it by any act hereunder be deemed to make any representation or warranty as to the authorization or reservation of any Preferred Shares to be issued pursuant to this Agreement or any Right Certificate or as to whether any Preferred Shares will, when issued, be validly authorized and issued, fully paid and nonassessable.

(f) The Company agrees that it will perform, execute, acknowledge and deliver or cause to be performed, executed, acknowledged and delivered all such further and other acts, instruments and assurances as may reasonably be required by the Rights Agent for the carrying out or performing by the Rights Agent of the provisions of this Agreement.

(g) The Rights Agent is hereby authorized and directed to accept instructions with respect to the performance of its duties hereunder from any one of the Chairman of the Board, the Chief Executive Officer, the President, any Vice President, the Secretary or the Treasurer of the Company, and to apply to such officers for advice or instructions in connection with its duties, and it shall not be liable for any action taken or suffered by it in good faith in accordance with instructions of any such officer or for any delay in acting while waiting for those instructions.

(h) The Rights Agent and any stockholder, director, officer or employee of the Rights Agent may buy, sell or deal in any of the Rights or other securities of the Company or become pecuniarily interested in any transaction in which the Company may be interested, or contract with or lend money to the Company or otherwise act as fully and freely as though it were not Rights Agent under this Agreement. Nothing herein shall preclude the Rights Agent from acting in any other capacity for the Company or for any other legal entity.

(i) The Rights Agent may execute and exercise any of the rights or powers hereby vested in it or perform any duty hereunder either itself or by or through its attorneys or agents, and the Rights Agent shall not be answerable or accountable for any act, default, neglect or misconduct of any such attorneys or agents or for any loss to the Company resulting from any such act, default, neglect or misconduct, provided that reasonable care was exercised in the selection and continued employment thereof.

Section 21. <u>Change of Rights Agent</u>. The Rights Agent or any successor Rights Agent may resign and be discharged from its duties under this Agreement upon 30 days' notice in writing mailed to the Company and to each transfer agent of the Common Shares or Preferred Shares by registered or certified mail, and to the holders of the Right Certificates by first-class mail. The Company may remove the Rights Agent or any successor Rights Agent upon 30 days' notice in writing, mailed to the Rights Agent or successor Rights Agent, as the case may be, and to each transfer agent of the Common Shares or Preferred Shares by registered or certified mail, and to the holders of the Right Certificates by first-class mail. If the Rights Agent shall resign or be removed or shall otherwise become incapable of acting, the Company shall appoint a successor to the Rights Agent. If the Company shall fail to make such appointment within a period of 30 days after giving notice of such removal or after it has been notified in writing of such resignation or incapacity by the resigning or incapacitated Rights Agent or by the holder of a Right Certificate (which holder shall, with such notice, submit such holder's Right Certificate for inspection by the Company), then the registered holder of any Right Certificate may apply to any court of competent jurisdiction for the appointment of a new Rights Agent. Any successor Rights Agent, whether appointed by the Company or by such a court, shall be a corporation organized and doing business under the laws of the United States or of the State of [State of Rights Agent] (or of any other state of the United States so long as such corporation is authorized to do business as a banking institution in the State of [State of Rights Agent]), in good standing, having an office in the State of [State of Rights Agent], which is authorized under such laws to exercise corporate trust or stock transfer powers and is subject to supervision or examination by federal or state authority and which has at the time of its appointment as Rights Agent a combined capital and surplus of at least $50 million. After appointment, the successor Rights Agent shall be vested with the same powers, rights, duties and responsibilities as if it had been originally named as Rights Agent without further act or deed; but the predecessor Rights Agent shall deliver and transfer to the successor Rights Agent any property at the time held by it hereunder, and execute and deliver any further assurance, conveyance, act or deed necessary for the purpose. Not later than the effective date of any such appointment, the Company shall file notice thereof in writing with the predecessor Rights Agent and each transfer agent of the Common Shares or Preferred Shares, and mail a notice thereof in writing to the registered holders of the Right Certificates. Failure to give any notice provided for in this Section 21, however, or any defect therein, shall not affect the legality or validity of the resignation or removal of the Rights Agent or the appointment of the successor Rights Agent, as the case may be.

Section 22. Issuance of New Right Certificates. Notwithstanding any of the provisions of this Agreement or of the Rights to the contrary, the Company may, at its option, issue new Right Certificates evidencing Rights in such form as may be approved by the Board of Directors of the Company to reflect any adjustment or change in the Purchase Price and the number or kind or class of shares or other securities or property purchasable under the Right Certificates made in accordance with the provisions of this Agreement.

Section 23. Redemption. (a) The Board of Directors of the Company may, at its option, at any time prior to such time as any Person becomes an Acquiring Person, redeem all but not less than all the then outstanding Rights at a redemption price of $.01 per Right, appropriately adjusted to reflect any stock split, stock dividend or similar transaction occurring after the date hereof (such redemption price being hereinafter referred to as the "Redemption Price"). The redemption of the Rights by the Board of Directors of the Company may be made effective at such time, on such basis and with such conditions as the Board of Directors of the Company, in its sole discretion, may establish.

(b) Immediately upon the action of the Board of Directors of the Company ordering the redemption of the Rights pursuant to paragraph (a) of this Section 23, and without any further action and without any notice, the right to exercise the Rights will terminate and the only right thereafter of the holders of Rights shall be to receive the Redemption Price. The Company shall promptly give public notice of any such redemption; provided, however, that the failure to give, or any defect in, any such notice shall not affect the validity of such redemption. Within 10 days after such action of the Board of Directors of the Company ordering the redemption of the Rights, the Company shall mail a notice of redemption to all the holders of the then outstanding Rights at their last addresses as they appear upon the registry books of the Rights Agent or, prior to the Distribution Date, on the registry books of the transfer agent for the Common Shares. Any notice which is mailed in the manner herein provided shall be deemed given, whether or not the holder receives the notice. Each such notice of redemption will state the method by which the payment of the Redemption Price will be made. Neither the Company nor any of its Affiliates or Associates may redeem, acquire or purchase for value any Rights at any time in any manner other than that specifically set forth in this Section 23 or in Section 24 hereof, and other than in connection with the purchase of Common Shares prior to the Distribution Date.

Section 24. <u>Exchange</u>. (a) The Board of Directors of the Company may, at its option, at any time after any Person becomes an Acquiring Person, exchange all or part of the then outstanding and exercisable Rights (which shall not include Rights that have become void pursuant to the provisions of Section 11(a)(ii) hereof) for Common Shares at an exchange ratio of one Common Share per Right, appropriately adjusted to reflect any adjustment in the number of Rights pursuant to Section 11(i) (such exchange ratio being hereinafter referred to as the "<u>Exchange Ratio</u>"). Notwithstanding the foregoing, the Board of Directors of the Company shall not be empowered to effect such exchange at any time after any Person (other than the Company, any Subsidiary of the Company, any employee benefit plan of the Company or any such Subsidiary, or any entity holding Common Shares for or pursuant to the terms of any such plan), together with all Affiliates and Associates of such Person, becomes the Beneficial Owner of 50% or more of the Common Shares then outstanding.

(b) Immediately upon the action of the Board of Directors of the Company ordering the exchange of any Rights pursuant to paragraph (a) of this Section 24 and without any further action and without any notice, the right to exercise such Rights shall terminate and the only right thereafter of a holder of such Rights shall be to receive that number of Common Shares equal to the number of such Rights held by such holder multiplied by the Exchange Ratio. The Company shall promptly give public notice of any such exchange; <u>provided</u>, <u>however</u>, that the failure to give, or any defect in, such notice shall not affect the validity of such exchange. The Company promptly shall mail a notice of any such exchange to all of the holders of such Rights at their last addresses as they appear upon the registry books of the Rights Agent. Any notice which is mailed in the manner herein provided shall be deemed given, whether or not the holder receives the notice. Each such notice of exchange will state the method by which the exchange of the Common Shares for Rights will be effected, and, in the event of any partial exchange, the number of Rights which will be exchanged. Any partial exchange shall be effected <u>pro rata</u> based on the number of Rights (other than Rights which have become void pursuant to the provisions of Section 11(a)(ii) hereof) held by each holder of Rights.

(c) In the event that there shall not be sufficient Common Shares issued but not outstanding or authorized but unissued to permit any exchange of Rights as contemplated in accordance with this Section 24, the Company shall take all such action as may be necessary to authorize additional Common Shares for issuance upon exchange of the Rights. In the event the Company shall, after good faith effort, be unable to take all such action as may be necessary to authorize such additional Common Shares, the Company shall substitute, for each Common Share that would otherwise be issuable upon exchange of a Right, a number of Preferred Shares or fraction thereof such that the current per share market price of one Preferred Share multiplied by such number or fraction is equal to the current per share market price of one Common Share as of the date of issuance of such Preferred Shares or fraction thereof.

(d) The Company shall not be required to issue fractions of Common Shares or to distribute certificates which evidence fractional Common Shares. In lieu of such fractional Common Shares, the Company shall pay to the registered holders of the Right Certificates with regard to which such fractional Common Shares would otherwise be issuable an amount in cash equal to the same fraction of the current market value of a whole Common Share. For the purposes of this paragraph (d), the current market value of a whole Common Share shall be the closing price of a Common Share (as determined pursuant to the second sentence of Section 11(d)(i) hereof) for the Trading Day immediately prior to the date of exchange pursuant to this Section 24.

Section 25. Notice of Certain Events. (a) In case the Company shall, at any time after the Distribution Date, propose (i) to pay any dividend payable in stock of any class to the holders of the Preferred Shares or to make any other distribution to the holders of the Preferred Shares (other than a regular quarterly cash dividend), (ii) to offer to the holders of the Preferred Shares rights or warrants to subscribe for or to purchase any additional Preferred Shares or shares of stock of any class or any other securities, rights or options, (iii) to effect any reclassification of the Preferred Shares (other than a reclassification involving only the subdivision of outstanding Preferred Shares), (iv) to effect any consolidation or merger into or with, or to effect any sale or other transfer (or to permit one or more of its Subsidiaries to effect any sale or other transfer), in one or more transactions, of 50% or more of the assets or earning power of the Company and its Subsidiaries (taken as a whole) to, any other Person, (v) to effect the liquidation, dissolution or winding up of the Company, or (vi) to declare or pay any dividend on the Common Shares payable in Common Shares or to effect a subdivision, combination or consolidation of the Common Shares (by reclassification or otherwise than by payment of dividends in Common Shares), then, in each such case, the Company shall give to each holder of a Right Certificate, in accordance with Section 26 hereof, a notice of such proposed action, which shall specify the record date for the purposes of such stock dividend, or distribution of rights or warrants, or the date on which such reclassification, consolidation, merger, sale, transfer, liquidation, dissolution, or winding up is to take place and the date of participation therein by the holders of the Common Shares and/or Preferred Shares, if any such date is to be fixed, and such notice shall be so given in the case of any action covered by clause (i) or (ii) above at least 10 days prior to the record date for determining holders of the Preferred Shares for purposes of such action, and, in the case of any such other action, at least 10 days prior to the date of the taking of such proposed action or the date of participation therein by the holders of the Common Shares and/or Preferred Shares, whichever shall be the earlier.

(b) In case the event set forth in Section 11(a)(ii) hereof shall occur, then the Company shall, as soon as practicable thereafter, give to each holder of a Right Certificate, in accordance with Section 26 hereof, a notice of the occurrence of such event, which notice shall describe such event and the consequences of such event to holders of Rights under Section 11(a)(ii) hereof.

Section 26. <u>Notices</u>. Notices or demands authorized by this Agreement to be given or made by the Rights Agent or by the holder of any Right Certificate to or on the Company shall be sufficiently given or made if sent by first-class mail, postage prepaid, addressed (until another address is filed in writing with the Rights Agent) as follows:

    _____, Inc.

    Attention: Corporate Secretary

Subject to the provisions of Section 21 hereof, any notice or demand authorized by this Agreement to be given or made by the Company or by the holder of any Right Certificate to or on the Rights Agent shall be sufficiently given or made if sent by first-class mail, postage prepaid, addressed (until another address is filed in writing with the Company) as follows:

    [Name of Rights Agent]

    Attention:

Notices or demands authorized by this Agreement to be given or made by the Company or the Rights Agent to the holder of any Right Certificate shall be sufficiently given or made if sent by first-class mail, postage prepaid, addressed to such holder at the address of such holder as shown on the registry books of the Company.

Section 27. <u>Supplements and Amendments</u>. The Company may from time to time supplement or amend this Agreement without the approval of any holders of Right Certificates in order to cure any ambiguity, to correct or supplement any provision contained herein which may be defective or inconsistent with any other provisions herein, or to make any other provisions with respect to the Rights which the Company may deem necessary or desirable, any such supplement or amendment to be evidenced by a writing signed by the Company and the Rights Agent; <u>provided</u>, <u>however</u>, that, from and after such time as any Person becomes an Acquiring Person, this Agreement shall not be amended in any manner which would adversely affect the interests of the holders of Rights. Without limiting the foregoing, the Company may at any time prior to such time as any Person becomes an Acquiring Person amend this Agreement to lower the thresholds set forth in Section 1(a) and 3(a) hereof to not less than 10% (the "Reduced Threshold"); provided, however, that no Person who beneficially owns a number of Common Shares equal to or greater than the Reduced Threshold shall become an Acquiring Person unless such Person shall, after the public announcement of the Reduced Threshold, increase its beneficial ownership of the then outstanding Common Shares (other than as a result of an acquisition of Common Shares by the Company) to an amount equal to or greater than the greater of (x) the Reduced Threshold or (y) the sum of (i) the lowest beneficial ownership of such Person as a percentage of the outstanding Common Shares as of any date on or after the date of the public announcement of such Reduced Threshold plus (ii) .001%.

Section 28. Successors. All the covenants and provisions of this Agreement by or for the benefit of the Company or the Rights Agent shall bind and inure to the benefit of their respective successors and assigns hereunder.

Section 29. Benefits of this Agreement. Nothing in this Agreement shall be construed to give to any Person other than the Company, the Rights Agent and the registered holders of the Right Certificates (and, prior to the Distribution Date, the Common Shares) any legal or equitable right, remedy or claim under this Agreement; but this Agreement shall be for the sole and exclusive benefit of the Company, the Rights Agent and the registered holders of the Right Certificates (and, prior to the Distribution Date, the Common Shares).

Section 30. Severability. If any term, provision, covenant or restriction of this Agreement is held by a court of competent jurisdiction or other authority to be invalid, void or unenforceable, the remainder of the terms, provisions, covenants and restrictions of this Agreement shall remain in full force and effect and shall in no way be affected, impaired or invalidated.

Section 31. Governing Law. This Agreement and each Right Certificate issued hereunder shall be deemed to be a contract made under the laws of the State of _____ and for all purposes shall be governed by and construed in accordance with the laws of such state applicable to contracts to be made and performed entirely within such state.

Section 32. Counterparts. This Agreement may be executed in any number of counterparts and each of such counterparts shall for all purposes be deemed to be an original, and all such counterparts shall together constitute but one and the same instrument.

Section 33. Descriptive Headings. Descriptive headings of the several Sections of this Agreement are inserted for convenience only and shall not control or affect the meaning or construction of any of the provisions hereof.

IN WITNESS WHEREOF, the parties hereto have caused this Agreement to be duly executed and attested, all as of the day and year first above written.

Attest: _____, INC.

By: _____   By: _____
    Name: Name:
    Title: Title:

Attest: [Rights Agent]

By: _____   By: _____
    Name: Name:
    Title: Title

SUMMARY OF RIGHTS TO PURCHASE PREFERRED SHARES ...

The Rights. Our Board authorized the issuance of a Right with respect to each outstanding share of common stock on _____ __, 200_. The Rights will initially trade with, and will be inseparable from, the common stock. The Rights are evidenced only by certificates that represent shares of common stock. New Rights will accompany any new shares of common stock we issue after _____ __, 200_ until the Distribution Date described below.

Exercise Price. Each Right will allow its holder to purchase from our Company one one-hundredth of a share of Series A Junior Participating Preferred Stock ("Preferred Share") for $___, once the Rights become exercisable. This portion of a Preferred Share will give the stockholder approximately the same dividend, voting, and liquidation rights as would one share of common stock. Prior to exercise, the Right does not give its holder any dividend, voting, or liquidation rights.

Exercisability. The Rights will not be exercisable until

- 10 days after the public announcement that a person or group has become an "Acquiring Person" by obtaining beneficial ownership of 15% or more of our outstanding common stock, or, if earlier,

- 10 business days (or a later date determined by our Board before any person or group becomes an Acquiring Person) after a person or group begins a tender or exchange offer which, if completed, would result in that person or group becoming an Acquiring Person.

We refer to the date when the Rights become exercisable as the "Distribution Date." Until that date, the common stock certificates will also evidence the Rights, and any transfer of shares of common stock will constitute a transfer of Rights. After that date, the Rights will separate from the common stock and be evidenced by book-entry credits or by Rights certificates that we will mail to all eligible holders of common stock. Any Rights held by an Acquiring Person are void and may not be exercised.

Our Board may reduce the threshold at which a person or group becomes an Acquiring Person from 15% to not less than 10% of the outstanding common stock.

Consequences of a Person or Group Becoming an Acquiring Person.

- *Flip In.* If a person or group becomes an Acquiring Person, all holders of Rights except the Acquiring Person may, for $___, purchase shares of our common stock with a market value of $___, based on the market price of the common stock prior to such acquisition.

- *Flip Over.* If our Company is later acquired in a merger or similar transaction after the Rights Distribution Date, all holders of Rights except the Acquiring Person may, for $___, purchase shares of the acquiring corporation with a market value of $___ based on the market price of the acquiring corporation's stock, prior to such merger.

Preferred Share Provisions.

Each one one-hundredth of a Preferred Share, if issued:

- will not be redeemable.

- will entitle holders to quarterly dividend payments of $.01 per share, or an amount equal to the dividend paid on one share of common stock, whichever is greater.

- will entitle holders upon liquidation either to receive $1 per share or an amount equal to the payment made on one share of common stock, whichever is greater.

- will have the same voting power as one share of common stock.

- if shares of our common stock are exchanged via merger, consolidation, or a similar transaction, will entitle holders to a per share payment equal to the payment made on one share of common stock.

The value of one one-hundredth interest in a Preferred Share should approximate the value of one share of common stock.

Expiration. The Rights will expire on _____ __, 201_.

Redemption. Our Board may redeem the Rights for $.01 per Right at any time before any person or group becomes an Acquiring Person. If our Board redeems any Rights, it must redeem all of the Rights. Once the Rights are redeemed, the only right of the holders of Rights will be to receive the redemption price of $.01 per Right. The redemption price will be adjusted if we have a stock split or stock dividends of our common stock.

Exchange. After a person or group becomes an Acquiring Person, but before an Acquiring Person owns 50% or more of our outstanding common stock, our Board may extinguish the Rights by exchanging one share of common stock or an equivalent security for each Right, other than Rights held by the Acquiring Person.

Anti-Dilution Provisions. Our Board may adjust the purchase price of the Preferred Shares, the number of Preferred Shares issuable and the number of outstanding Rights to prevent dilution that may occur from a stock dividend, a stock split, a reclassification of the Preferred Shares or common stock. No adjustments to the Exercise Price of less than 1% will be made.

Amendments. The terms of the Rights Agreement may be amended by our Board without the consent of the holders of the Rights. However, our Board may not amend the Rights Agreement to lower the threshold at which a person or group becomes an Acquiring Person to below 10% of our outstanding common stock. In addition, the Board may not cause a person or group to become an Acquiring Person by lowering this threshold below the percentage interest that such person or group already owns. After a person or group becomes an Acquiring Person, our Board may not amend the agreement in a way that adversely affects holders of the Rights.

FORM OF CHUBB'S DIRECTORS AND OFFICERS LIABILITY POLICY

Executive Protection Portfolio [SM]
*Executive Liability and Entity Securities
Liability Coverage Section*

In consideration of payment of the premium and subject to the Declarations, the General Terms and Conditions, and the limitations, conditions, provisions and other terms of this coverage section, the Company and the Insureds agree as follows:

Insuring Clauses

Executive Liability Coverage Insuring Clause 1

1. The Company shall pay, on behalf of each of the **Insured Persons**, **Loss** for which the **Insured Person** is not indemnified by the **Organization** and which the **Insured Person** becomes legally obligated to pay on account of any **Claim** first made against the **Insured Person**, individually or otherwise, during the **Policy Period** or, if exercised, during the Extended Reporting Period, for a **Wrongful Act** committed, attempted, or allegedly committed or attempted by such **Insured Person** before or during the **Policy Period**, but only if such **Claim** is reported to the Company in writing in the manner and within the time provided in Subsection 15 of this coverage section.

Executive Indemnification Coverage Insuring Clause 2

2. The Company shall pay, on behalf of the **Organization**, **Loss** for which the **Organization** grants indemnification to an **Insured Person**, as permitted or required by law, and which the **Insured Person** becomes legally obligated to pay on account of any **Claim** first made against the **Insured Person**, individually or otherwise, during the **Policy Period** or, if exercised, during the Extended Reporting Period, for a **Wrongful Act** committed, attempted, or allegedly committed or attempted by such **Insured Person** before or during the **Policy Period**, but only if such **Claim** is reported to the Company in writing in the manner and within the time provided in Subsection 15 of this coverage section.

Entity Securities Coverage Insuring Clause 3

3. The Company shall pay, on behalf of the **Organization**, **Loss** which the **Organization** becomes legally obligated to pay on account of any **Securities Claim** first made against the **Organization** during the **Policy Period** or, if exercised, during the Extended Reporting Period, for a **Wrongful Act** committed, attempted, or allegedly committed or attempted by the **Organization** or the **Insured Persons** before or during the **Policy Period**, but only if such **Securities Claim** is reported to the Company in writing in the manner and within the time provided in Subsection 15 of this coverage section.

Securityholder Derivative Demand Coverage Insuring Clause 4

4. The Company shall pay, on behalf of the **Organization**, **Investigative Costs** resulting from a **Securityholder Derivative Demand** first received by the **Organization** during the **Policy Period** or, if exercised, during the Extended Reporting Period, for a **Wrongful Act** committed, attempted, or allegedly committed or attempted before or during the **Policy Period**, but only if such **Securityholder Derivative Demand** is reported to the Company in writing in the manner and within the time provided in Subsection 15 of this coverage section.

Executive Protection Portfolio [SM]
Executive Liability and Entity Securities
Liability Coverage Section

Definitions

5.   When used in this coverage section:

Application means all signed applications, including attachments and other materials submitted therewith or incorporated therein, submitted by the **Insureds** to the Company for this coverage section or for any coverage section or policy of which this coverage section is a direct or indirect renewal or replacement.

Application shall also include, for each **Organization**, all of the following documents whether or not submitted with or attached to any such signed application: (i) the Annual Report (including financial statements) last issued to shareholders before this policy's inception date; (ii) the report last filed with the Securities and Exchange Commission on Form 10-K before this policy's inception date; (iii) the report last filed with the Securities and Exchange Commission on Form 10-Q before this policy's inception date; (iv) the proxy statement and (if different) definitive proxy statement last filed with the Securities and Exchange Commission before this policy's inception date; (v) all reports filed with the Securities and Exchange Commission on Form 8-K during the twelve months preceding this policy's inception date; and (vi) all reports filed with the Securities and Exchange Commission on Schedule 13D, with respect to any equity securities of such **Organization**, during the twelve months preceding this policy's inception date. All such applications, attachments, materials and other documents are deemed attached to, incorporated into and made a part of this coverage section.

Claim means:

(1)   when used in reference to the coverage provided by Insuring Clause 1 or 2:

  (a)   a written demand for monetary damages or non-monetary relief;

  (b)   a civil proceeding commenced by the service of a complaint or similar pleading; or

  (c)   a formal civil administrative or civil regulatory proceeding commenced by the filing of a notice of charges or similar document or by the entry of a formal order of investigation or similar document,

  against an **Insured Person** for a **Wrongful Act**, including any appeal therefrom;

(2)   when used in reference to the coverage provided by Insuring Clause 3:

  (a)   a written demand for monetary damages or non-monetary relief;

  (b)   a civil proceeding commenced by the service of a complaint or similar pleading; or

  (c)   a formal civil administrative or civil regulatory proceeding commenced by the filing of a notice of charges or similar document or by the entry of a formal order of investigation or similar document, but only while such proceeding is also pending against an **Insured Person**,

  against an **Organization** for a **Wrongful Act**, including any appeal therefrom; or

(3)   when used in reference to the coverage provided by Insuring Clause 4, a **Securityholder Derivative Demand**.

Except as may otherwise be provided in Subsection 12, Subsection 13(g),or Subsection 15(b) of this coverage section, a **Claim** will be deemed to have first been made when such **Claim** is commenced as set forth in this definition (or, in the case of a written demand, including but not limited to any **Securityholder Derivative Demand**, when such demand is first received by an **Insured**).

Defense Costs means that part of **Loss** consisting of reasonable costs, charges, fees (including but not limited to attorneys' fees and experts' fees) and expenses (other than regular or overtime wages, salaries, fees or benefits of the directors, officers or employees of the **Organization**) incurred in defending any **Claim** and the premium for appeal, attachment or similar bonds.

Domestic Partner means any natural person qualifying as a domestic partner under the provisions of any applicable federal, state or local law or under the provisions of any formal program established by the **Organization**.

Financial Impairment means the status of an **Organization** resulting from:

(a)   the appointment by any state or federal official, agency or court of any receiver, conservator, liquidator, trustee, rehabilitator or similar official to take control of, supervise, manage or liquidate such **Organization**; or

(b)   such **Organization** becoming a debtor in possession under the United States bankruptcy law or the equivalent of a debtor in possession under the law of any other country.

Insured means the **Organization** and any **Insured Person**.

Insured Capacity means the position or capacity of an **Insured Person** that causes him or her to meet the definition of **Insured Person** set forth in this coverage section. **Insured Capacity** does not include any position or capacity held by an **Insured Person** in any organization other than the **Organization**, even if the **Organization** directed or requested the **Insured Person** to serve in such position or capacity in such other organization.

Insured Person means any natural person who was, now is or shall become:

(a)   a duly elected or appointed director, officer, **Manager**, or the in-house general counsel of any **Organization** chartered in the United States of America;

(b)   a holder of a position equivalent to any position described in (a) above in an **Organization** that is chartered in any jurisdiction other than the United States of America; or

(c)   solely with respect to **Securities Claims**, any other employee of an **Organization**, provided that such other employees shall not, solely by reason of their status as employees, be **Insured Persons** for purposes of Exclusion 6(c).

Investigative Costs means reasonable costs, charges, fees (including but not limited to attorneys' fees and experts' fees) and expenses (other than regular or overtime wages, salaries, fees, or benefits of the directors, officers or employees of the **Organization**)

1585

Executive Protection Portfolio [SM]
Executive Liability and Entity Securities
Liability Coverage Section

incurred by the **Organization** (including its Board of Directors or any committee of its Board of Directors) in investigating or evaluating on behalf of the **Organization** whether it is in the best interest of the **Organization** to prosecute the claims alleged in a **Securityholder Derivative Demand**.

Loss means:

(a) the amount that any **Insured Person** (for purposes of Insuring Clauses 1 and 2) or the **Organization** (for purposes of Insuring Clause 3) becomes legally obligated to pay on account of any covered **Claim**, including but not limited to damages (including punitive or exemplary damages, if and to the extent that such punitive or exemplary damages are insurable under the law of the jurisdiction most favorable to the insurability of such damages provided such jurisdiction has a substantial relationship to the relevant **Insureds**, to the Company, or to the **Claim** giving rise to the damages), judgments, settlements, pre-judgment and post-judgment interest and **Defense Costs**; or

(b) for purposes of Insuring Clause 4, covered **Investigative Costs**.

Loss does not include:

(a) any amount not indemnified by the **Organization** for which an **Insured Person** is absolved from payment by reason of any covenant, agreement or court order;

(b) any costs incurred by the **Organization** to comply with any order for injunctive or other non-monetary relief, or to comply with an agreement to provide such relief;

(c) any amount incurred by an **Insured** in the defense or investigation of any action, proceeding or demand that is not then a **Claim** even if (i) such amount also benefits the defense of a covered **Claim**, or (ii) such action, proceeding or demand subsequently gives rise to a **Claim**;

(d) taxes, fines or penalties, or the multiple portion of any multiplied damage award, except as provided above with respect to punitive or exemplary damages;

(e) any amount not insurable under the law pursuant to which this coverage section is construed, except as provided above with respect to punitive or exemplary damages;

(f) any amount allocated to non-covered loss pursuant to Subsection 17 of this coverage section; or

(g) any amount that represents or is substantially equivalent to an increase in the consideration paid (or proposed to be paid) by an **Organization** in connection with its purchase of any securities or assets.

Manager means any natural person who was, now is or shall become a manager, member of the Board of Managers or equivalent executive of an **Organization** that is a limited liability company.

Executive Protection Portfolio [SM]
Executive Liability and Entity Securities
Liability Coverage Section

Organization means, collectively, those organizations designated in Item 5 of the Declarations for this coverage section, including any such organization in its capacity as a debtor in possession under the United States bankruptcy law or in an equivalent status under the law of any other country.

Pollutants means (a) any substance located anywhere in the world exhibiting any hazardous characteristics as defined by, or identified on a list of hazardous substances issued by, the United States Environmental Protection Agency or any state, county, municipality or locality counterpart thereof, including, without limitation, solids, liquids, gaseous or thermal irritants, contaminants or smoke, vapor, soot, fumes, acids, alkalis, chemicals or waste materials, or (b) any other air emission, odor, waste water, oil or oil products, infectious or medical waste, asbestos or asbestos products or any noise.

Related Claims means all **Claims** for **Wrongful Acts** based upon, arising from, or in consequence of the same or related facts, circumstances, situations, transactions or events or the same or related series of facts, circumstances, situations, transactions or events.

Securities Claim means that portion of a **Claim** which:

(a) is brought by a securityholder of an **Organization**

   (i) in his or her capacity as a securityholder of such **Organization**, with respect to his or her interest in securities of such **Organization**, and against such **Organization** or any of its **Insured Persons**; or

   (ii) derivatively, on behalf of such **Organization**, against an **Insured Person** of such **Organization**; or

(b) alleges that an **Organization** or any of its **Insured Persons**

   (i) violated a federal, state, local or foreign securities law or a rule or regulation promulgated under any such securities law; or

   (ii) committed a **Wrongful Act** that constitutes or arises from a purchase, sale, or offer to purchase or sell securities of such **Organization**,

provided that **Securities Claim** does not include any **Claim** by or on behalf of a former, current, future or prospective employee of the **Organization** that is based upon, arising from, or in consequence of any offer, grant or issuance, or any plan or agreement relating to the offer, grant or issuance, by the **Organization** to such employee in his or her capacity as such of stock, stock warrants, stock options or other securities of the **Organization**, or any payment or instrument the amount or value of which is derived from the value of securities of the **Organization**; and provided, further, that **Securities Claim** does not include any **Securityholder Derivative Demand**.

Securityholder Derivative Demand means:

(a) any written demand, by a securityholder of an **Organization**, upon the Board of Directors or Board of **Managers** of such **Organization** to bring a civil proceeding in a court of law against an **Insured Person** for a **Wrongful Act**; or

(b) any lawsuit by a securityholder of an **Organization**, brought derivatively on behalf of such **Organization** against an **Insured Person** for a **Wrongful Act** without first making a demand as described in (a) above, provided such demand or lawsuit is brought and maintained without any active assistance or participation of, or solicitation by, any **Insured Person**.

Subsidiary, either in the singular or plural, means any organization while more than fifty percent (50%) of the outstanding securities or voting rights representing the present right to vote for election of or to appoint directors or **Managers** of such organization are owned or controlled, directly or indirectly, in any combination, by one or more **Organizations**.

Wrongful Act means:

(a) any error, misstatement, misleading statement, act, omission, neglect, or breach of duty committed, attempted, or allegedly committed or attempted by an **Insured Person** in his or her **Insured Capacity**, or for purposes of coverage under Insuring Clause 3, by the **Organization**, or

(b) any other matter claimed against an **Insured Person** solely by reason of his or her serving in an **Insured Capacity**.

Exclusions

Applicable To All Insuring Clauses

6. The Company shall not be liable for **Loss** on account of any **Claim**:

(a) based upon, arising from, or in consequence of any fact, circumstance, situation, transaction, event or **Wrongful Act** that, before the inception date set forth in Item 2 of the Declarations of the General Terms and Conditions, was the subject of any notice given under any policy or coverage section of which this coverage section is a direct or indirect renewal or replacement;

(b) based upon, arising from, or in consequence of any demand, suit or other proceeding pending against, or order, decree or judgment entered for or against any **Insured**, on or prior to the Pending or Prior Date set forth in Item 7 of the Declarations for this coverage section, or the same or substantially the same fact, circumstance or situation underlying or alleged therein;

(c) brought or maintained by or on behalf of any **Insured** in any capacity; provided that this Exclusion 6(c) shall not apply to:

(i) a **Claim** brought or maintained derivatively on behalf of the **Organization** by one or more securityholders of the **Organization**, provided such **Claim** is brought and maintained without any active assistance or participation of, or solicitation by, any **Insured Person**;

(ii) an employment **Claim** brought or maintained by or on behalf of an **Insured Person**;

(iii) a **Claim** brought or maintained by an **Insured Person** for contribution or indemnity, if such **Claim** directly results from another **Claim** covered under this coverage section; or

Executive Protection Portfolio ^{SM}
*Executive Liability and Entity Securities
Liability Coverage Section*

(iv)   a **Claim** brought by an **Insured Person** who has not served in an **Insured Capacity** for at least four (4) years prior to the date such **Claim** is first made and who brings and maintains such **Claim** without any active assistance or participation of, or solicitation by, the **Organization** or any other **Insured Person** who is serving or has served in an **Insured Capacity** within such four (4) year period;

(d)   based upon, arising from, or in consequence of:

(i)   any actual, alleged, or threatened exposure to, or generation, storage, transportation, discharge, emission, release, dispersal, escape, treatment, removal or disposal of any **Pollutants**; or

(ii)   any regulation, order, direction or request to test for, monitor, clean up, remove, contain, treat, detoxify or neutralize any **Pollutants**, or any action taken in contemplation or anticipation of any such regulation, order, direction or request,

including but not limited to any **Claim** for financial loss to the **Organization**, its securityholders or its creditors based upon, arising from, or in consequence of any matter described in clause (i) or clause (ii) of this Exclusion 6(d);

(e)   for bodily injury, mental anguish, emotional distress, sickness, disease or death of any person or damage to or destruction of any tangible property including loss of use thereof whether or not it is damaged or destroyed; provided that this Exclusion 6(e) shall not apply to mental anguish or emotional distress for which a claimant seeks compensation in an employment **Claim**;

(f)   for an actual or alleged violation of the responsibilities, obligations or duties imposed on fiduciaries by the Employee Retirement Income Security Act of 1974, or any amendments thereto, or any rules or regulations promulgated thereunder, or any similar provisions of any federal, state, or local statutory law or common law anywhere in the world;

(g)   for **Wrongful Acts** of an **Insured Person** in his or her capacity as a director, officer, manager, trustee, regent, governor or employee of any entity other than the **Organization**, even if the **Insured Person's** service in such capacity is with the knowledge or consent or at the request of the **Organization**; or

(h)   made against a **Subsidiary** or an **Insured Person** of such **Subsidiary** for any **Wrongful Act** committed, attempted, or allegedly committed or attempted during any time when such entity was not a **Subsidiary**.

Applicable To Insuring Clauses 1 and 2 Only

7.   The **Company** shall not be liable under Insuring Clause 1 or 2 for **Loss** on account of any **Claim** made against any **Insured Person**:

(a)   for an accounting of profits made from the purchase or sale by such **Insured Person** of securities of the **Organization** within the meaning of Section 16(b) of the Securities Exchange Act of 1934, any amendments thereto, or any similar provision of any federal, state, or local statutory law or common law anywhere in the world; or

Executive Protection Portfolio ^{SM}
Executive Liability and Entity Securities
Liability Coverage Section

(b)   based upon, arising from, or in consequence of:

   (i)   the committing in fact of any deliberately fraudulent act or omission or any willful violation of any statute or regulation by such **Insured Person**; or

   (ii)   such **Insured Person** having gained in fact any profit, remuneration or advantage to which such **Insured Person** was not legally entitled,

   as evidenced by (A) any written statement or written document by any **Insured** or (B) any judgment or ruling in any judicial, administrative or alternative dispute resolution proceeding.

Applicable To Insuring Clause 3 Only

8.   The Company shall not be liable under Insuring Clause 3 for **Loss** on account of any **Securities Claim** made against any **Organization**:

   (a)   based upon, arising from, or in consequence of:

      (i)   the committing in fact of any deliberately fraudulent act or omission or any willful violation of any statute or regulation by an **Organization** or by any past, present or future chief financial officer, in-house general counsel, president, chief executive officer or chairperson of an **Organization**; or

      (ii)   such **Organization** having gained in fact any profit, remuneration or advantage to which such **Organization** was not legally entitled,

      as evidenced by (A) any written statement or written document by any **Insured** or (B) any judgment or ruling in any judicial, administrative or alternative dispute resolution proceeding; or

   (b)   for any actual or alleged liability of an **Organization** under any contract or agreement that relates to the purchase, sale, or offer to purchase or sell any securities; provided that this Exclusion 8(b) shall not apply to liability that would have attached to such **Organization** in the absence of such contract or agreement.

Severability of Exclusions

9.   (a)   No fact pertaining to or knowledge possessed by any **Insured Person** shall be imputed to any other **Insured Person** for the purpose of applying the exclusions in Subsection 7 of this coverage section.

      (b)   Only facts pertaining to and knowledge possessed by any past, present, or future chief financial officer, in-house general counsel, president, chief executive officer or chairperson of an **Organization** shall be imputed to such **Organization** for the purpose of applying the exclusions in Subsection 8 of this coverage section.

Spouses, Estates and Legal Representatives

10. Subject otherwise to the General Terms and Conditions and the limitations, conditions, provisions and other terms of this coverage section, coverage shall extend to **Claims** for the **Wrongful Acts** of an **Insured Person** made against:

    (a) the estate, heirs, legal representatives or assigns of such **Insured Person** if such **Insured Person** is deceased or the legal representatives or assigns of such **Insured Person** if such **Insured Person** is incompetent, insolvent or bankrupt; or

    (b) the lawful spouse or **Domestic Partner** of such **Insured Person** solely by reason of such spouse or **Domestic Partner's** status as a spouse or **Domestic Partner**, or such spouse or **Domestic Partner's** ownership interest in property which the claimant seeks as recovery for an alleged **Wrongful Act** of such **Insured Person**.

    All terms and conditions of this coverage section, including without limitation the Retention, applicable to **Loss** incurred by the **Insured Persons**, shall also apply to loss incurred by the estates, heirs, legal representatives, assigns, spouses and **Domestic Partners** of such **Insured Persons**. The coverage provided by this Subsection 10 shall not apply with respect to any loss arising from an act or omission by an **Insured Person's** estate, heirs, legal representatives, assigns, spouse or **Domestic Partner**.

Coordination With Employment Practices Liability Coverage Section

11. Any **Loss** otherwise covered by both (i) this coverage section and (ii) any employment practices liability coverage section or policy issued by the Company or by any affiliate of the Company (an "Employment Practices Liability Coverage") first shall be covered as provided in, and shall be subject to the limit of liability, retention and coinsurance percentage applicable to such Employment Practices Liability Coverage. Any remaining **Loss** otherwise covered by this coverage section which is not paid under such Employment Practices Liability Coverage shall be covered as provided in, and shall be subject to the Limit of Liability, Retention and Coinsurance Percentage applicable to this coverage section; provided the Retention applicable to such **Loss** under this coverage section shall be reduced by the amount of **Loss** otherwise covered by this coverage section which is paid by the **Insureds** as the retention under such Employment Practices Liability Coverage.

Extended Reporting Period

12. If the Company or the **Parent Organization** terminates or does not renew this coverage section, other than termination by the Company for nonpayment of premium, the **Parent Organization** and the **Insured Persons** shall have the right, upon payment of the additional premium set forth in Item 6(B) of the Declarations for this coverage section, to an extension of the coverage granted by this coverage section for **Claims** that are (i) first made during the period set forth in Item 6(A) of the Declarations for this coverage section (the "Extended Reporting Period") following the effective date of termination or nonrenewal, and (ii) reported to the Company in writing within the time provided in Subsection 15(a) of this coverage section, but only to the extent such **Claims** are for **Wrongful Acts** committed, attempted, or allegedly committed or attempted before the earlier of the effective date of termination or nonrenewal or the date of the first merger, consolidation or acquisition event described in Subsection 21 below. The offer of renewal terms and conditions or premiums different from those in effect prior to renewal shall not constitute

Executive Protection Portfolio ^{SM}
Executive Liability and Entity Securities
Liability Coverage Section

refusal to renew. The right to purchase an extension of coverage as described in this Subsection shall lapse unless written notice of election to purchase the extension, together with payment of the additional premium due, is received by the Company within thirty (30) days after the effective date of termination or nonrenewal. Any **Claim** made during the Extended Reporting Period shall be deemed to have been made during the immediately preceding **Policy Period**. The entire additional premium for the Extended Reporting Period shall be deemed fully earned at the inception of such Extended Reporting Period.

Limit of Liability, Retention and Coinsurance

13. (a) The Company's maximum liability for all **Loss** on account of each **Claim**, whether covered under one or more Insuring Clauses, shall be the Limit of Liability set forth in Item 2(A) of the Declarations for this coverage section. The Company's maximum aggregate liability for all **Loss** on account of all **Claims** first made during the **Policy Period**, whether covered under one or more Insuring Clauses, shall be the Limit of Liability for each **Policy Period** set forth in Item 2(B) of the Declarations for this coverage section.

(b) The Company's maximum aggregate liability under Insuring Clause 4 for all **Investigative Costs** on account of all **Securityholder Derivative Demands** shall be the Sublimit set forth in Item 2(C) of the Declarations for this coverage section. Such Sublimit is part of, and not in addition to, the Limits of Liability set forth in Items 2(A) and 2(B) of the Declarations.

(c) **Defense Costs** are part of, and not in addition to, the Limits of Liability set forth in Item 2 of the Declarations for this coverage section, and the payment by the Company of **Defense Costs** shall reduce and may exhaust such applicable Limits of Liability.

(d) The Company's liability under Insuring Clause 2 or 3 shall apply only to that part of covered **Loss** (as determined by any applicable provision in Subsection 17 of this coverage section) on account of each **Claim** which is excess of the applicable Retention set forth in Item 4 of the Declarations for this coverage section. Such Retention shall be depleted only by **Loss** otherwise covered under this coverage section and shall be borne by the **Insureds** uninsured and at their own risk. Except as otherwise provided in Subsection 14, no Retention shall apply to any **Loss** under Insuring Clause 1 or 4.

(e) If different parts of a single **Claim** are subject to different Retentions, the applicable Retentions will be applied separately to each part of such **Claim**, but the sum of such Retentions shall not exceed the largest applicable Retention.

(f) To the extent that **Loss** resulting from a **Securities Claim** is covered under Insuring Clause 2 or 3 (as determined by Subsection 17(a) of this coverage section) and is in excess of the applicable Retention, the **Insureds** shall bear uninsured and at their own risk that percentage of such **Loss** specified as the Coinsurance Percentage in Item 3(A) of the Declarations for this coverage section, and the Company's liability shall apply only to the remaining percentage of such **Loss**. To the extent that **Loss** resulting from a **Claim** other than a **Securities Claim** is covered under Insuring Clause 2 or 3 (as determined by Subsection 17(b) of this coverage section) and is in excess of the applicable Retention, the **Insureds** shall bear uninsured and at their own risk that percentage of such **Loss** specified as the Coinsurance Percentage in

Executive Protection Portfolio^{SM}
Executive Liability and Entity Securities
Liability Coverage Section

Item 3(B) of the Declarations for this coverage section, and the Company's liability shall apply only to the remaining percentage of such **Loss**.

(g) All **Related Claims** shall be treated as a single **Claim** first made on the date the earliest of such **Related Claims** was first made, or on the date the earliest of such **Related Claims** is treated as having been made in accordance with Subsection 15(b) below, regardless of whether such date is before or during the **Policy Period**.

(h) The limit of liability available during the Extended Reporting Period (if exercised) shall be part of, and not in addition to, the Company's maximum aggregate limit of liability for all **Loss** on account of all **Claims** first made during the immediately preceding **Policy Period**.

Presumptive Indemnification

14. If the **Organization** fails or refuses, other than for reason of **Financial Impairment**, to indemnify an **Insured Person** for **Loss**, or to advance **Defense Costs** on behalf of an **Insured Person**, to the fullest extent permitted by statutory or common law, then, notwithstanding any other conditions, provisions or terms of this coverage section to the contrary, any payment by the Company of such **Defense Costs** or other **Loss** shall be subject to:

(i) the applicable Insuring Clause 2 Retention set forth in Item 4 of the Declarations for this coverage section; and

(ii) the applicable Coinsurance Percentage set forth in Item 3 of the Declarations for this coverage section.

Reporting and Notice

15. (a) The **Insureds** shall, as a condition precedent to exercising any right to coverage under this coverage section, give to the Company written notice of any **Claim** as soon as practicable, but in no event later than the earliest of the following dates:

(i) sixty (60) days after the date on which any **Organization's** chief financial officer, in-house general counsel, risk manager, president, chief executive officer or chairperson first becomes aware that the **Claim** has been made;

(ii) if this coverage section expires (or is otherwise terminated) without being renewed and if no Extended Reporting Period is purchased, sixty (60) days after the effective date of such expiration or termination; or

(iii) the expiration date of the Extended Reporting Period, if purchased;

provided that if the Company sends written notice to the **Parent Organization**, at any time before the date set forth in (i) above with respect to any **Claim**, stating that this coverage section is being terminated for nonpayment of premium, the **Insureds** shall give to the Company written notice of such **Claim** prior to the effective date of such termination.

Executive Protection Portfolio ^{SM}

Executive Liability and Entity Securities
Liability Coverage Section

(b)   If during the **Policy Period** an **Insured**:

    (i)   becomes aware of circumstances which could give rise to a **Claim** and gives written notice of such circumstances to the Company;

    (ii)   receives a written request to toll or waive a statute of limitations applicable to **Wrongful Acts** committed, attempted, or allegedly committed or attempted before or during the **Policy Period** and gives written notice of such request and of such alleged **Wrongful Acts** to the Company; or

    (iii)   gives written notice to the Company of a **Securityholder Derivative Demand**,

    then any **Claim** subsequently arising from the circumstances referred to in (i) above, from the **Wrongful Acts** referred to in (ii) above, or from the **Securityholder Derivative Demand** referred to in (iii) above, shall be deemed to have been first made during the **Policy Period** in which the written notice described in (i), (ii) or (iii) above was first given by an **Insured** to the Company, provided any such subsequent **Claim** is reported to the Company as set forth in Subsection 15(a) above. With respect to any such subsequent **Claim**, no coverage under this coverage section shall apply to loss incurred prior to the date such subsequent **Claim** is actually made.

(c)   The **Insureds** shall, as a condition precedent to exercising any right to coverage under this coverage section, give to the Company such information, assistance, and cooperation as the Company may reasonably require; and shall include in any notice under Subsection 15(a) or (b) a description of the **Claim**, circumstances, or **Securityholder Derivative Demand**, the nature of any alleged **Wrongful Acts**, the nature of the alleged or potential damage, the names of all actual or potential claimants, the names of all actual or potential defendants, and the manner in which such **Insured** first became aware of the **Claim**, circumstances, or **Securityholder Derivative Demand**.

Defense and Settlement

16.   (a)   It shall be the duty of the **Insureds** and not the duty of the Company to defend **Claims** made against the **Insureds**.

    (b)   The **Insureds** agree not to settle or offer to settle any **Claim**, incur any **Defense Costs** or otherwise assume any contractual obligation or admit any liability with respect to any **Claim** without the Company's prior written consent. The Company shall not be liable for any element of **Loss** incurred, for any obligation assumed, or for any admission made, by any **Insured** without the Company's prior written consent. Provided the **Insureds** comply with Subsections 16(c) and (d) below, the Company shall not unreasonably withhold any such consent.

    (c)   With respect to any **Claim** that appears reasonably likely to be covered in whole or in part under this coverage section, the Company shall have the right and shall be given the opportunity to effectively associate with the **Insureds**, and shall be consulted in advance by the **Insureds**, regarding the investigation, defense and settlement of such **Claim**, including but not limited to selecting appropriate defense counsel and negotiating any settlement.

Executive Protection Portfolio ^{SM}
*Executive Liability and Entity Securities
Liability Coverage Section*

(d) The **Insureds** agree to provide the Company with all information, assistance and cooperation which the Company may reasonably require and agree that in the event of a **Claim** the **Insureds** will do nothing that could prejudice the Company's position or its potential or actual rights of recovery.

(e) Any advancement of **Defense Costs** shall be repaid to the Company by the **Insureds**, severally according to their respective interests, if and to the extent it is determined that such **Defense Costs** are not insured under this coverage section.

Allocation

17. (a) If in any **Securities Claim** the **Insureds** incur both **Loss** that is covered under this coverage section and loss that is not covered under this coverage section, the **Insureds** and the Company shall allocate such amount between covered **Loss** and non-covered loss as follows:

    (i) The portion, if any, of such amount that is in part covered and in part not covered under Insuring Clause 2 shall be allocated in its entirety to covered **Loss**, subject, however, to the applicable Retention and Coinsurance Percentage set forth in Items 4(C) and 3(A) of the Declarations for this coverage section, respectively; and

    (ii) The portion, if any, of such amount that is in part covered and in part not covered under Insuring Clause 1 or 3 shall be allocated between covered **Loss** and non-covered loss based on the relative legal and financial exposures of the **Insureds** to covered and non-covered matters and, in the event of a settlement in such **Securities Claim**, based also on the relative benefits to the **Insureds** from settlement of the covered matters and from settlement of the non-covered matters; provided that the amount so allocated to covered **Loss** under Insuring Clause 3 shall be subject to the Retention and Coinsurance Percentage set forth in Items 4(C) and 3(A) of the Declarations for this coverage section, respectively.

    The Company shall not be liable under this coverage section for the portion of such amount allocated to non-covered loss. The allocation described in (i) above shall be final and binding on the Company and the **Insureds** under Insuring Clause 2, but shall not apply to any allocation under Insuring Clauses 1 and 3.

    (b) If in any **Claim** other than a **Securities Claim** the **Insured Persons** incur both **Loss** that is covered under this coverage section and loss that is not covered under this coverage section, either because such **Claim** includes both covered and non-covered matters or because such **Claim** is made against both **Insured Persons** and others (including the **Organization**), the **Insureds** and the Company shall allocate such amount between covered **Loss** and non-covered loss based on the relative legal and financial exposures of the parties to covered and non-covered matters and, in the event of a settlement in such **Claim**, based also on the relative benefits to the parties from such settlement. The Company shall not be liable under this coverage section for the portion of such amount allocated to non-covered loss.

    (c) If the **Insureds** and the Company agree on an allocation of **Defense Costs**, the Company shall advance on a current basis **Defense Costs** allocated to the covered **Loss**. If the **Insureds** and the Company cannot agree on an allocation:

    (i)   no presumption as to allocation shall exist in any arbitration, suit or other proceeding;

    (ii)   the Company shall advance on a current basis **Defense Costs** which the Company believes to be covered under this coverage section until a different allocation is negotiated, arbitrated or judicially determined; and

    (iii)   the Company, if requested by the **Insureds**, shall submit the dispute to binding arbitration. The rules of the American Arbitration Association shall apply except with respect to the selection of the arbitration panel, which shall consist of one arbitrator selected by the **Insureds**, one arbitrator selected by the Company, and a third independent arbitrator selected by the first two arbitrators.

(d)   Any negotiated, arbitrated or judicially determined allocation of **Defense Costs** on account of a **Claim** shall be applied retroactively to all **Defense Costs** on account of such **Claim**, notwithstanding any prior advancement to the contrary. Any allocation or advancement of **Defense Costs** on account of a **Claim** shall not apply to or create any presumption with respect to the allocation of other **Loss** on account of such **Claim**.

Other Insurance

18.   If any **Loss** under this coverage section is insured under any other valid insurance policy(ies), then this coverage section shall cover such **Loss**, subject to its limitations, conditions, provisions and other terms, only to the extent that the amount of such **Loss** is in excess of the applicable retention (or deductible) and limit of liability under such other insurance, whether such other insurance is stated to be primary, contributory, excess, contingent or otherwise, unless such other insurance is written only as specific excess insurance over the Limits of Liability provided in this coverage section. Any payment by **Insureds** of a retention or deductible under such other insurance shall reduce, by the amount of such payment which would otherwise have been covered under this coverage section, the applicable Retention under this coverage section.

Payment of Loss

19.   In the event payment of **Loss** is due under this coverage section but the amount of such **Loss** in the aggregate exceeds the remaining available Limit of Liability for this coverage section, the Company shall:

(a)   first pay such **Loss** for which coverage is provided under Insuring Clause 1 of this coverage section; then

(b)   to the extent of any remaining amount of the Limit of Liability available after payment under (a) above, pay such **Loss** for which coverage is provided under any other Insuring Clause of this coverage section.

Except as otherwise provided in this Subsection 19, the Company may pay covered **Loss** as it becomes due under this coverage section without regard to the potential for other future payment obligations under this coverage section.

Changes in Exposure

Acquisition /Creation of Another Organization

20. If before or during the **Policy Period** any **Organization**:

(a) acquires securities or voting rights in another organization or creates another organization, which as a result of such acquisition or creation becomes a **Subsidiary**; or

(b) acquires another organization by merger into or consolidation with an **Organization** such that the **Organization** is the surviving entity,

such other organization and its **Insured Persons** shall be **Insureds** under this coverage section, but only with respect to **Wrongful Acts** committed, attempted, or allegedly committed or attempted after such acquisition or creation unless the Company agrees, after presentation of a complete application and all other appropriate information, to provide coverage by endorsement for **Wrongful Acts** committed, attempted, or allegedly committed or attempted by such **Insureds** before such acquisition or creation.

If the total assets of any such acquired organization or new **Subsidiary** exceed ten percent (10%) of the total assets of the **Parent Organization** (as reflected in the most recent audited consolidated financial statements of such organization and the **Parent Organization**, respectively, as of the date of such acquisition or creation), the **Parent Organization** shall give written notice of such acquisition or creation to the Company as soon as practicable, but in no event later than sixty (60) days after the date of such acquisition or creation, together with such other information as the Company may require and shall pay any reasonable additional premium required by the Company. If the **Parent Organization** fails to give such notice within the time specified in the preceding sentence, or fails to pay the additional premium required by the Company, coverage for such acquired or created organization and its **Insured Persons** shall terminate with respect to **Claims** first made more than sixty (60) days after such acquisition or creation. Coverage for any acquired or created organization described in this paragraph, and for the **Insured Persons** of such organization, shall be subject to such additional or different terms, conditions and limitations of coverage as the Company in its sole discretion may require.

Acquisition by Another Organization

21. If:

(a) the **Parent Organization** merges into or consolidates with another organization and the **Parent Organization** is not the surviving entity; or

(b) another organization or person or group of organizations and/or persons acting in concert acquires securities or voting rights which result in ownership or voting control by the other organization(s) or person(s) of more than fifty percent (50%) of the outstanding securities or voting rights representing the present right to vote for the election of or to appoint directors or **Managers** of the **Parent Organization**,

coverage under this coverage section shall continue until termination of this coverage section, but only with respect to **Claims** for **Wrongful Acts** committed, attempted, or allegedly committed or attempted by **Insureds** before such merger, consolidation or

Executive Protection Portfolio ^{SM}

Executive Liability and Entity Securities
Liability Coverage Section

acquisition. Upon the occurrence of any event described in (a) or (b) of this Subsection 21, the entire premium for this coverage section shall be deemed fully earned.

The **Parent Organization** shall give written notice of such merger, consolidation or acquisition to the Company as soon as practicable, but in no event later than sixty (60) days after the date of such merger, consolidation or acquisition, together with such other information as the Company may require. Upon receipt of such notice and information and at the request of the **Parent Organization**, the Company shall provide to the **Parent Organization** a quotation for an extension of coverage (for such period as may be negotiated between the Company and the **Parent Organization**) with respect to **Claims** for **Wrongful Acts** committed, attempted, or allegedly committed or attempted by **Insureds** before such merger, consolidation or acquisition. Any coverage extension pursuant to such quotation shall be subject to such additional or different terms, conditions and limitations of coverage, and payment of such additional premium, as the Company in its sole discretion may require.

Cessation of Subsidiary

22. In the event an organization ceases to be a **Subsidiary** before or during the **Policy Period**, coverage with respect to such **Subsidiary** and its **Insured Persons** shall continue until termination of this coverage section, but only with respect to **Claims** for **Wrongful Acts** committed, attempted, or allegedly committed or attempted while such organization was a **Subsidiary**.

Related Entity Public Offering

23. If any **Organization** files or causes to be filed, with the United States Securities and Exchange Commission or an equivalent agency or government department in any country other than the United States of America, any registration statement in contemplation of a public offering of equity securities by any entity other than the **Parent Organization** (irrespective of whether such public offering is an initial public offering or a secondary or other offering subsequent to an initial public offering), then the Company shall not be liable for **Loss** on account of any **Claim** based upon, arising from, or in consequence of such registration statement or the sale, offer to sell, distribution or issuance of any securities pursuant to such registration statement, unless (i) the Company receives written notice at least thirty (30) days prior to the effective date of such registration statement providing full details of the contemplated offering, and (ii) the Company, in its sole discretion, agrees by written endorsement to this coverage section to provide coverage for such **Claims** upon such terms and conditions, subject to such limitations and other provisions, and for such additional premium as the Company may require. If the Company in its sole discretion agrees to provide coverage for such **Claims**, the additional premium specified by the Company shall be payable to the Company in full not later than the date on which such registration statement becomes effective.

Representations and Severability

24. In issuing this coverage section the Company has relied upon the statements, representations and information in the **Application**. All of the **Insureds** acknowledge and agree that all such statements, representations and information (i) are true and accurate, (ii) were made or provided in order to induce the Company to issue this coverage section,

and (iii) are material to the Company's acceptance of the risk to which this coverage section applies.

In the event that any of the statements, representations or information in the **Application** are not true and accurate, this coverage section shall be void with respect to (i) any **Insured** who knew as of the effective date of the **Application** the facts that were not truthfully and accurately disclosed (whether or not the **Insured** knew of such untruthful disclosure in the **Application**) or to whom knowledge of such facts is imputed, and (ii) the **Organization** under Insuring Clause 2 to the extent it indemnifies an **Insured Person** who had such actual or imputed knowledge. For purposes of the preceding sentence:

(a) the knowledge of any **Insured Person** who is a past, present or future chief financial officer, in-house general counsel, chief executive officer, president or chairperson of an **Organization** shall be imputed to such **Organization** and its **Subsidiaries**;

(b) the knowledge of the person(s) who signed the **Application** for this coverage section shall be imputed to all of the **Insureds**; and

(c) except as provided in (a) above, the knowledge of an **Insured Person** who did not sign the **Application** shall not be imputed to any other **Insured**.

SPECIMEN

SECURITIES ACT OF 1933

15 U.S.C. §§ 77a et seq.

Schedules of Information Required in Registration Statement

* Omitted.

§ 1. Short Title

This subchapter may be cited as the "Securities Act of 1933."

§ 2. Definitions; Promotion of Efficiency, Competition, and Capital Formation

(a) Definitions

When used in this subchapter, unless the context otherwise requires—

(1) The term "security" means any note, stock, treasury stock, security future, bond, debenture, evidence of indebtedness, certificate of interest or participation in any profit-sharing agreement, collateral-trust certificate, preorganization certificate or subscription, transferable share, investment contract, voting-trust certificate, certificate of deposit for a security, fractional undivided interest in oil, gas, or other mineral rights, any put, call, straddle, option, or privilege on any security, certificate of deposit, or group or index of securities (including any interest therein or based on the value thereof), or any put, call, straddle, option, or privilege entered into on a national securities exchange relating to foreign currency, or, in general, any interest or instrument commonly known as a "security", or any certificate of interest or participation in, temporary or interim certificate for, receipt for, guarantee of, or warrant or right to subscribe to or purchase, any of the foregoing.

(2) The term "person" means an individual, a corporation, a partnership, an association, a joint-stock company, a trust, any unincorporated organization, or a government or political subdivision thereof. As used in this paragraph the term "trust" shall include only a trust where the interest or interests of the beneficiary or beneficiaries are evidenced by a security.

(3) The term "sale" or "sell" shall include every contract of sale or disposition of a security or interest in a security, for value. The term "offer to sell", "offer for sale", or "offer" shall include every attempt or offer to dispose of, or solicitation of an offer to buy, a security or interest in a security, for value. The terms defined in this paragraph and the term "offer to buy" as used in subsection (c) of section 5 of this title shall not include preliminary negotiations or agreements between an issuer (or any person directly or indirectly controlling or controlled by an issuer, or under direct or indirect common control with an issuer) and any underwriter or among underwriters who are or are to be in privity of contract with an issuer (or any person directly or indirectly controlling or controlled by an issuer, or under direct or indirect common control with an issuer). Any security given or delivered with, or as a bonus on account of, any purchase of securities or any other thing, shall be

conclusively presumed to constitute a part of the subject of such purchase and to have been offered and sold for value. The issue or transfer of a right or privilege, when originally issued or transferred with a security, giving the holder of such security the right to convert such security into another security of the same issuer or of another person, or giving a right to subscribe to another security of the same issuer or of another person, which right cannot be exercised until some future date, shall not be deemed to be an offer or sale of such other security; but the issue or transfer of such other security upon the exercise of such right of conversion or subscription shall be deemed a sale of such other security. Any offer or sale of a security futures product by or on behalf of the issuer of the securities underlying the security futures product, an affiliate of the issuer, or an underwriter, shall constitute a contract for sale of, sale of, offer for sale, or offer to sell the underlying securities.

(4) The term "issuer" means every person who issues or proposes to issue any security; except that with respect to certificates of deposit, voting-trust certificates, or collateral-trust certificates, or with respect to certificates of interest or shares in an unincorporated investment trust not having a board of directors (or persons performing similar functions) or of the fixed, restricted management, or unit type, the term "issuer" means the person or persons performing the acts and assuming the duties of depositor or manager pursuant to the provisions of the trust or other agreement or instrument under which such securities are issued; except that in the case of an unincorporated association which provides by its articles for limited liability of any or all of its members, or in the case of a trust, committee, or other legal entity, the trustees or members thereof shall not be individually liable as issuers of any security issued by the association, trust, committee, or other legal entity; except that with respect to equipment-trust certificates or like securities, the term "issuer" means the person by whom the equipment or property is or is to be used; and except that with respect to fractional undivided interests in oil, gas, or other mineral rights, the term "issuer" means the owner of any such right or of any interest in such right (whether whole or fractional) who creates fractional interests therein for the purpose of public offering.

(5) The term "Commission" means the Securities and Exchange Commission.

(6) The term "Territory" means Puerto Rico, Canal Zone, the Virgin Islands, and the insular possessions of the United States.

(7) The term "interstate commerce" means trade or commerce in securities or any transportation or communication relating thereto among the several States or between the District of Columbia or any Territory of the United States and any State or other Territory,

or between any foreign country and any State, Territory, or the District of Columbia, or within the District of Columbia.

(8) The term "registration statement" means the statement provided for in section 6 of this title, and includes any amendment thereto and any report, document, or memorandum filed as part of such statement or incorporated therein by reference.

(9) The term "write" or "written" shall include printed, lithographed, or any means of graphic communication.

(10) The term "prospectus" means any prospectus, notice, circular, advertisement, letter, or communication, written or by radio or television, which offers any security for sale or confirms the sale of any security; except that (a) a communication sent or given after the effective date of the registration statement (other than a prospectus permitted under subsection (b) of section 10 of this title) shall not be deemed a prospectus if it is proved that prior to or at the same time with such communication a written prospectus meeting the requirements of subsection (a) of section 10 of this title at the time of such communication was sent or given to the person to whom the communication was made, and (b) a notice, circular, advertisement, letter, or communication in respect of a security shall not be deemed to be a prospectus if it states from whom a written prospectus meeting the requirements of section 10 of this title may be obtained and, in addition, does no more than identify the security, state the price thereof, state by whom orders will be executed, and contain such other information as the Commission, by rules or regulations deemed necessary or appropriate in the public interest and for the protection of investors, and subject to such terms and conditions as may be prescribed therein, may permit.

(11) The term "underwriter" means any person who has purchased from an issuer with a view to, or offers or sells for an issuer in connection with, the distribution of any security, or participates or has a direct or indirect participation in any such undertaking, or participates or has a participation in the direct or indirect underwriting of any such undertaking; but such term shall not include a person whose interest is limited to a commission from an underwriter or dealer not in excess of the usual and customary distributors' or sellers' commission. As used in this paragraph the term "issuer" shall include, in addition to an issuer, any person directly or indirectly controlling or controlled by the issuer, or any person under direct or indirect common control with the issuer.

(12) The term "dealer" means any person who engages either for all or part of his time, directly or indirectly, as agent, broker, or principal, in the business of offering, buying, selling, or otherwise dealing or trading in securities issued by another person.

(13) The term "insurance company" means a company which is organized as an insurance company, whose primary and predominant business activity is the writing of insurance or the reinsuring of risks underwritten by insurance companies, and which is subject to supervision by the insurance commissioner, or a similar official or agency, of a State or territory or the District of Columbia; or any receiver or similar official or any liquidating agent for such company, in his capacity as such.

(14) The term "separate account" means an account established and maintained by an insurance company pursuant to the laws of any State or territory of the United States, the District of Columbia, or of Canada or any province thereof, under which income, gains and losses, whether or not realized, from assets allocated to such account, are, in accordance with the applicable contract, credited to or charged against such account without regard to other income, gains, or losses of the insurance company.

(15) The term "accredited investor" shall mean—

(i) a bank as defined in section 3(a)(2) whether acting in its individual or fiduciary capacity; an insurance company as defined in paragraph (13) of this subsection; an investment company registered under the Investment Company Act of 1940 or a business development company as defined in section 2(a)(48) of that Act; a Small Business Investment Company licensed by the Small Business Administration; or an employee benefit plan, including an individual retirement account, which is subject to the provisions of the Employee Retirement Income Security Act of 1974, if the investment decision is made by a plan fiduciary, as defined in section 3(21) of such Act, which is either a bank, insurance company, or registered investment adviser; or

(ii) any person who, on the basis of such factors as financial sophistication, net worth, knowledge, and experience in financial matters, or amount of assets under management qualifies as an accredited investor under rules and regulations which the Commission shall prescribe.

(16) The terms "security future" ... and "security futures product" have the same meanings as provided in section 3(a)(55) of the Securities Exchange Act of 1934.

(b) Consideration of promotion of efficiency, competition, and capital formation

Whenever pursuant to this subchapter the Commission is engaged in rulemaking and is required to consider or determine whether an action is necessary or appropriate in the public interest, the Commission shall also consider, in addition to the protection of investors, whether the action will promote efficiency, competition, and capital formation.

§ 3. Classes of Securities Under This Subchapter

(a) Exempted securities

Except as hereinafter expressly provided, the provisions of this subchapter shall not apply to any of the following classes of securities:

(1) Any security which, prior to or within sixty days after May 27, 1933, has been sold or disposed of by the issuer or bona fide offered to the public, but this exemption shall not apply to any new offering of any such security by an issuer or underwriter subsequent to such sixty days;

(2) Any security issued or guaranteed by the United States or any territory thereof, or by the District of Columbia, or by any State of the United States, or by any political subdivision of a State or territory, or by any public instrumentality of one or more States or territories, or by any person controlled or supervised by and acting as an instrumentality of the Government of the United States pursuant to authority granted by the Congress of the United States; or any certificate of deposit for any of the foregoing; or any security issued or guaranteed by any bank; or any security issued by or representing an interest in or a direct obligation of a Federal Reserve bank....

(3) Any note, draft, bill of exchange, or banker's acceptance which arises out of a current transaction or the proceeds of which have been or are to be used for current transactions, and which has a maturity at the time of issuance of not exceeding nine months, exclusive of days of grace, or any renewal thereof the maturity of which is likewise limited;

(4) Any security issued by a person organized and operated exclusively for religious, educational, benevolent, fraternal, charitable, or reformatory purposes and not for pecuniary profit, and no part of the net earnings of which inures to the benefit of any person, private stockholder, or individual ...;

(5) Any security issued ... by a savings and loan association, building and loan association, cooperative bank, homestead association, or similar institution, which is supervised and examined by State or Federal authority having supervision over any such institution ...;

(6) Any interest in a railroad equipment trust. For purposes of this paragraph "interest in a railroad equipment trust" means any interest in an equipment trust, lease, conditional sales contract, or other similar arrangement entered into, issued, assumed, guaranteed by, or for the benefit of, a common carrier to finance the acquisition of rolling stock, including motive power;

(7) Certificates issued by a receiver or by a trustee or debtor in possession in a case under title 11, with the approval of the court;

(8) Any insurance or endowment policy or annuity contract or optional annuity contract, issued by a corporation subject to the supervision of the insurance commissioner, bank commissioner, or any agency or officer performing like functions, of any State or Territory of the United States or the District of Columbia;

(9) Except with respect to a security exchanged in a case under title 11, any security exchanged by the issuer with its existing security holders exclusively where no commission or other remuneration is paid or given directly or indirectly for soliciting such exchange;

(10) Except with respect to a security exchanged in a case under title 11, any security which is issued in exchange for one or more bona fide outstanding securities, claims or property interests, or partly in such exchange and partly for cash, where the terms and conditions of such issuance and exchange are approved, after a hearing upon the fairness of such terms and conditions at which all persons to whom it is proposed to issue securities in such exchange shall have the right to appear, by any court, or by any official or agency of the United States, or by any State or Territorial banking or insurance commission or other governmental authority expressly authorized by law to grant such approval;

(11) Any security which is a part of an issue offered and sold only to persons resident within a single State or Territory, where the issuer of such security is a person resident and doing business within or, if a corporation, incorporated by and doing business within, such State or Territory. . . .

(b) Additional exemptions

The Commission may from time to time by its rules and regulations, and subject to such terms and conditions as may be prescribed therein, add any class of securities to the securities exempted as provided in this section, if it finds that the enforcement of this subchapter with respect to such securities is not necessary in the public interest and for the protection of investors by reason of the small amount involved or the limited character of the public offering; but no issue of securities shall be exempted under this subsection where the aggregate amount at which such issue is offered to the public exceeds $5,000,000.

(c) Securities issued by small investment company

The Commission may from time to time by its rules and regulations and subject to such terms and conditions as may be prescribed therein, add to the securities exempted as provided in this section any class of securities issued by a small business investment company under the Small Business Investment Act of 1958 [15 U.S.C. 661 et seq.] if it finds, having regard to the purposes of that Act, that the enforcement of this subchapter with respect to such securities is not necessary in the public interest and for the protection of investors.

§ 4. Exempted Transactions

The provisions of section 5 of this title shall not apply to—

(1) transactions by any person other than an issuer, underwriter, or dealer.

(2) transactions by an issuer not involving any public offering.

(3) transactions by a dealer (including an underwriter no longer acting as an underwriter in respect of the security involved in such transaction), except—

    (A) transactions taking place prior to the expiration of forty days after the first date upon which the security was bona fide offered to the public by the issuer or by or through an underwriter,

    (B) transactions in a security as to which a registration statement has been filed taking place prior to the expiration of forty days after the effective date of such registration statement or prior to the expiration of forty days after the first date upon which the security was bona fide offered to the public by the issuer or by or through an underwriter after such effective date, whichever is later (excluding in the computation of such forty days any time during which a stop order issued under section 8 of this title is in effect as to the security), or such shorter period as the Commission may specify by rules and regulations or order, and

    (C) transactions as to securities constituting the whole or a part of an unsold allotment to or subscription by such dealer as a participant in the distribution of such securities by the issuer or by or through an underwriter.

With respect to transactions referred to in clause (B), if securities of the issuer have not previously been sold pursuant to an earlier effective registration statement the applicable period, instead of forty days, shall be ninety days, or such shorter period as the Commission may specify by rules and regulations or order.

(4) brokers' transactions executed upon customers' orders on any exchange or in the over-the-counter market but not the solicitation of such orders. . . .

(6) transactions involving offers or sales by an issuer solely to one or more accredited investors, if the aggregate offering price of an issue of securities offered in reliance on this paragraph does not exceed the amount allowed under section 3(b) of this title, if there is no advertising or public solicitation in connection with the transac-

tion by the issuer or anyone acting on the issuer's behalf, and if the issuer files such notice with the Commission as the Commission shall prescribe.

§ 5. Prohibitions Relating to Interstate Commerce and the Mails

(a) Sale or delivery after sale of unregistered securities

Unless a registration statement is in effect as to a security, it shall be unlawful for any person, directly or indirectly—

(1) to make use of any means or instruments of transportation or communication in interstate commerce or of the mails to sell such security through the use or medium of any prospectus or otherwise; or

(2) to carry or cause to be carried through the mails or in interstate commerce, by any means or instruments of transportation, any such security for the purpose of sale or for delivery after sale.

(b) Necessity of prospectus meeting requirements of section 10 of this title

It shall be unlawful for any person, directly or indirectly—

(1) to make use of any means or instruments of transportation or communication in interstate commerce or of the mails to carry or transmit any prospectus relating to any security with respect to which a registration statement has been filed under this subchapter, unless such prospectus meets the requirements of section 10 of this title; or

(2) to carry or cause to be carried through the mails or in interstate commerce any such security for the purpose of sale or for delivery after sale, unless accompanied or preceded by a prospectus that meets the requirements of subsection (a) of section 10 of this title.

(c) Necessity of filing registration statement

It shall be unlawful for any person, directly or indirectly, to make use of any means or instruments of transportation or communication in interstate commerce or of the mails to offer to sell or offer to buy through the use or medium of any prospectus or otherwise any security, unless a registration statement has been filed as to such security, or while the registration statement is the subject of a refusal order or stop order or (prior to the effective date of the registration statement) any public proceeding or examination under section 8 of this title.

§ 6. Registration of Securities

(a) Method of registration

Any security may be registered with the Commission under the terms and conditions hereinafter provided, by filing a registration statement in triplicate, at least one of which shall be signed by each issuer, its principal executive officer or officers, its principal financial officer, its comptroller or principal accounting officer, and the majority of its board of directors or persons performing similar functions (or, if there is no board of directors or persons performing similar functions, by the majority of the persons or board having the power of management of the issuer), and in case the issuer is a foreign or Territorial person by its duly authorized representative in the United States; except that when such registration statement relates to a security issued by a foreign government, or political subdivision thereof, it need be signed only by the underwriter of such security. Signatures of all such persons when written on the said registration statements shall be presumed to have been so written by authority of the person whose signature is so affixed and the burden of proof, in the event such authority shall be denied, shall be upon the party denying the same. The affixing of any signature without the authority of the purported signer shall constitute a violation of this subchapter. A registration statement shall be deemed effective only as to the securities specified therein as proposed to be offered....

§ 7. Information Required in Registration Statement

(a) The registration statement, when relating to a security other than a security issued by a foreign government, or political subdivision thereof, shall contain the information, and be accompanied by the documents, specified in Schedule A of section 27 of this title, and when relating to a security issued by a foreign government, or political subdivision thereof, shall contain the information, and be accompanied by the documents, specified in Schedule B of section 27 of this title; except that the Commission may by rules or regulations provide that any such information or document need not be included in respect of any class of issuers or securities if it finds that the requirement of such information or document is inapplicable to such class and that disclosure fully adequate for the protection of investors is otherwise required to be included within the registration statement. If any accountant, engineer, or appraiser, or any person whose profession gives authority to a statement made by him, is named as having prepared or certified any part of the registration statement, or is named as having prepared or certified a report or valuation for use in connection with the registration statement, the written consent of such person shall be filed with the registration statement. If any such person is named as having prepared or certified a report or valuation (other than a public official document or statement) which is used in connection with the registration statement, but is not named as having prepared or certified such report or

1609

valuation for use in connection with the registration statement, the written consent of such person shall be filed with the registration statement unless the Commission dispenses with such filing as impracticable or as involving undue hardship on the person filing the registration statement. Any such registration statement shall contain such other information, and be accompanied by such other documents, as the Commission may by rules or regulations require as being necessary or appropriate in the public interest or for the protection of investors.

(b)(1) The Commission shall prescribe special rules with respect to registration statements filed by any issuer that is a blank check company. Such rules may, as the Commission determines necessary or appropriate in the public interest or for the protection of investors—

(A) require such issuers to provide timely disclosure, prior to or after such statement becomes effective under section 8, of (i) information regarding the company to be acquired and the specific application of the proceeds of the offering, or (ii) additional information necessary to prevent such statement from being misleading;

(B) place limitations on the use of such proceeds and the distribution of securities by such issuer until the disclosures required under subparagraph (A) have been made; and

(C) provide a right of rescission to shareholders of such securities.

(2) The Commission may, as it determines consistent with the public interest and the protection of investors, by rule or order exempt any issuer or class of issuers from the rules prescribed under paragraph (1).

(3) For purposes of paragraph (1) of this subsection, the term "blank check company" means any development stage company that is issuing a penny stock (within the meaning of section 3(a)(51) of the Securities Exchange Act of 1934) and that—

(A) has no specific business plan or purpose; or

(B) has indicated that its business plan is to merge with an unidentified company or companies.

§ 8. Taking Effect of Registration Statements and Amendments Thereto

(a) Effective date of registration statement

Except as hereinafter provided, the effective date of a registration statement shall be the twentieth day after the filing thereof or such earlier date as the Commission may determine, having due regard to the adequacy of the information respecting the issuer theretofore available to the public, to the facility with which the nature of the securities to be registered, their relationship to the capital structure of the issuer and the rights of holders thereof can be understood, and to the public interest and the protection of investors. If any amendment to any such statement is filed prior to the effective date of such statement, the registration statement shall be deemed to have been filed when such amendment was filed; except that an amendment filed with the consent of the Commission, prior to the effective date of the registration statement, or filed pursuant to an order of the Commission, shall be treated as a part of the registration statement.

(b) Incomplete or inaccurate registration statement

If it appears to the Commission that a registration statement is on its face incomplete or inaccurate in any material respect, the Commission may, after notice by personal service or the sending of confirmed telegraphic notice not later than ten days after the filing of the registration statement, and opportunity for hearing (at a time fixed by the Commission) within ten days after such notice by personal service or the sending of such telegraphic notice, issue an order prior to the effective date of registration refusing to permit such statement to become effective until it has been amended in accordance with such order. When such statement has been amended in accordance with such order the Commission shall so declare and the registration shall become effective at the time provided in subsection (a) of this section or upon the date of such declaration, whichever date is the later.

(c) Effective Date of Amendment to Registration Statement

An amendment filed after the effective date of the registration statement, if such amendment, upon its face, appears to the Commission not to be incomplete or inaccurate in any material respect, shall become effective on such date as the Commission may determine, having due regard to the public interest and the protection of investors.

(d) Untrue statements or omissions in registration statement

If it appears to the Commission at any time that the registration statement includes any untrue statement of a material fact or omits to state any material fact required to be stated therein or necessary to make the statements therein not misleading, the Commission may, after notice by personal service or the sending of confirmed telegraphic notice, and after opportunity for hearing (at a time fixed by the Commission) within fifteen days after such notice by personal service or the sending of such telegraphic notice, issue a stop order suspending the effectiveness of the registration statement. When such statement has been amended in accordance with such stop order, the Commission shall so declare and thereupon the stop order shall cease to be effective.

(e) Examination for issuance of stop order

The Commission is empowered to make an examination in any case in order to determine whether a stop order should issue under subsection (d) of this section. In making such examination the Commission or any officer or officers designated by it shall have access to and may demand the production of any books and papers of, and may administer oaths and affirmations to and examine, the issuer, underwriter, or any other person, in respect of any matter relevant to the examination, and may, in its discretion, require the production of a balance sheet exhibiting the assets and liabilities of the issuer, or its income statement, or both, to be certified to by a public or certified accountant approved by the Commission. If the issuer or underwriter shall fail to cooperate, or shall obstruct or refuse to permit the making of an examination, such conduct shall be proper ground for the issuance of a stop order.

(f)   Notice requirements

Any notice required under this section shall be sent to or served on the issuer, or, in case of a foreign government or political subdivision thereof, to or on the underwriter, or, in the case of a foreign or Territorial person, to or on its duly authorized representative in the United States named in the registration statement, properly directed in each case of telegraphic notice to the address given in such statement.

§ 8A.   Cease-and-Desist Proceedings

(a)   Authority of the Commission

If the Commission finds, after notice and opportunity for hearing, that any person is violating, has violated, or is about to violate any provision of this title, or any rule or regulation thereunder, the Commission may publish its findings and enter an order requiring such person, and any other person that is, was, or would be a cause of the violation, due to an act or omission the person knew or should have known would contribute to such violation, to cease and desist from committing or causing such violation and any future violation of the same provision, rule, or regulation. Such order may, in addition to requiring a person to cease and desist from committing or causing a violation, require such person to comply, or to take steps to effect compliance, with such provision, rule, or regulation, upon such terms and conditions and within such time as the Commission may specify in such order. Any such order may, as the Commission deems appropriate, require future compliance or steps to effect future compliance, either permanently or for such period of time as the Commission may specify, with such provision, rule, or regulation with respect to any security, any issuer, or any other person....

(e)   Authority to enter an order requiring an accounting and disgorgement

In any cease-and-desist proceeding under subsection (a), the Commission may enter an order requiring accounting and disgorgement, including reasonable interest. The Commission is authorized to adopt rules, regulations, and orders concerning payments to investors, rates of interest, periods of accrual, and such other matters as it deems appropriate to implement this subsection.

(f) Authority of the Commission to Prohibit Persons From Serving as Officers or Directors.

In any cease-and-desist proceeding under subsection (a), the Commission may issue an order to prohibit, conditionally or unconditionally, and permanently or for such period of time as it shall determine, any person who has violated section 17(a)(l) or the rules or regulations thereunder, from acting as an officer or director of any issuer that has a class of securities registered pursuant to section 12 of the Securities Exchange Act of 1934, or that is required to file reports pursuant to section 15(d) of that Act, if the conduct of that person demonstrates unfitness to serve as an officer or director of any such issuer.

§ 9. Court Review of Orders

(a) Any person aggrieved by an order of the Commission may obtain a review of such order in the Court of Appeals of the United States, within any circuit wherein such person resides or has his principal place of business, or in the United States Court of Appeals for the District of Columbia, by filing in such court, within sixty days after the entry of such order, a written petition praying that the order of the Commission be modified or be set aside in whole or in part. A copy of such petition shall be forthwith transmitted by the clerk of the court to the Commission, and thereupon the Commission shall file in the court the record upon which the order complained of was entered, as provided in section 2112 of title 28. No objection to the order of the Commission shall be considered by the court unless such objection shall have been urged before the Commission. The finding of the Commission as to the facts, if supported by evidence, shall be conclusive. If either party shall apply to the court for leave to adduce additional evidence, and shall show to the satisfaction of the court that such additional evidence is material and that there were reasonable grounds for failure to adduce such evidence in the hearing before the Commission, the court may order such additional evidence to be taken before the Commission and to be adduced upon the hearing in such manner and upon such terms and conditions as to the court may seem proper. The Commission may modify its findings as to the facts, by reason of the additional evidence so taken, and it shall file such modified or new findings, which, if supported by evidence, shall be conclusive, and its recommendation, if any, for the modification or setting aside of the original order. The jurisdiction of the court shall be exclusive and its judgment and decree, affirming, modifying, or setting aside, in whole or in part, any order of the Commission, shall be final, subject to review by the Supreme Court of the United States upon certiorari or certification as provided in section 1254 of title 28.

(b) The commencement of proceedings under subsection (a) of this section shall not, unless specifically ordered by the court, operate as a stay of the Commission's order.

§ 10.   Information Required in Prospectus

(a)   Information in registration statement; documents not required

Except to the extent otherwise permitted or required pursuant to this subsection or subsections (c), (d), or (e) of this section—

(1) a prospectus relating to a security other than a security issued by a foreign government or political subdivision thereof, shall contain the information contained in the registration statement....

(3) notwithstanding the provisions of paragraphs (1) and (2) of this subsection when a prospectus is used more than nine months after the effective date of the registration statement, the information contained therein shall be as of a date not more than sixteen months prior to such use, so far as such information is known to the user of such prospectus or can be furnished by such user without unreasonable effort or expense;

(4) there may be omitted from any prospectus any of the information required under this subsection which the Commission may by rules or regulations designate as not being necessary or appropriate in the public interest or for the protection of investors.

(b)   Summarizations and omissions allowed by rules and regulations

In addition to the prospectus permitted or required in subsection (a) of this section, the Commission shall by rules or regulations deemed necessary or appropriate in the public interest or for the protection of investors permit the use of a prospectus for the purposes of subsection (b)(1) of section 5 of this title which omits in part or summarizes information in the prospectus specified in subsection (a) of this section. A prospectus permitted under this subsection shall, except to the extent the Commission by rules or regulations deemed necessary or appropriate in the public interest or for the protection of investors otherwise provides, be filed as part of the registration statement but shall not be deemed a part of such registration statement for the purposes of section 11 of this title. The Commission may at any time issue an order preventing or suspending the use of a prospectus permitted under this subsection, if it has reason to believe that such prospectus has not been filed (if required to be filed as part of the registration statement) or includes any untrue statement of a material fact or omits to state any material fact required to be stated therein or necessary to make the statements therein, in the light of the circumstances under which such prospectus is or is to be used, not misleading. Upon issuance of an order under this subsection, the Commission shall give notice of the issuance of such order and opportunity for hearing by personal service or the sending of confirmed telegraphic notice. The Commission shall vacate or modify the order at any time for good cause or if such prospectus has been filed or amended in accordance with such order.

(c) Additional information required by rules and regulations

Any prospectus shall contain such other information as the Commission may by rules or regulations require as being necessary or appropriate in the public interest or for the protection of investors.

(d) Classification of prospectuses

In the exercise of its powers under subsections (a), (b), or (c) of this section, the Commission shall have authority to classify prospectuses according to the nature and circumstances of their use or the nature of the security, issue, issuer, or otherwise, and, by rules and regulations and subject to such terms and conditions as it shall specify therein, to prescribe as to each class the form and contents which it may find appropriate and consistent with the public interest and the protection of investors.

(e) Information in conspicuous part of prospectus

The statements or information required to be included in a prospectus by or under authority of subsections (a), (b), (c), or (d) of this section, when written, shall be placed in a conspicuous part of the prospectus and, except as otherwise permitted by rules or regulations, in type as large as that used generally in the body of the prospectus.

(f) Prospectus consisting of radio or television broadcast

In any case where a prospectus consists of a radio or television broadcast, copies thereof shall be filed with the Commission under such rules and regulations as it shall prescribe. The Commission may by rules and regulations require the filing with it of forms and prospectuses used in connection with the offer or sale of securities registered under this subchapter.

§ 11. Civil Liabilities on Account of False Registration Statement

(a) Persons possessing cause of action; persons liable

In case any part of the registration statement, when such part became effective, contained an untrue statement of a material fact or omitted to state a material fact required to be stated therein or necessary to make the statements therein not misleading, any person acquiring such security (unless it is proved that at the time of such acquisition he knew of such untruth or omission) may, either at law or in equity, in any court of competent jurisdiction, sue—

(1) every person who signed the registration statement;

(2) every person who was a director of (or person performing similar functions) or partner in the issuer at the time of the filing of the part of the registration statement with respect to which his liability is asserted;

(3) every person who, with his consent, is named in the registration statement as being or about to become a director, person performing similar functions, or partner;

(4) every accountant, engineer, or appraiser, or any person whose profession gives authority to a statement made by him, who has with his consent been named as having prepared or certified any part of the registration statement, or as having prepared or certified any report or valuation which is used in connection with the registration statement, with respect to the statement in such registration statement, report, or valuation, which purports to have been prepared or certified by him;

(5) every underwriter with respect to such security.

If such person acquired the security after the issuer has made generally available to its security holders an earning statement covering a period of at least twelve months beginning after the effective date of the registration statement, then the right of recovery under this subsection shall be conditioned on proof that such person acquired the security relying upon such untrue statement in the registration statement or relying upon the registration statement and not knowing of such omission, but such reliance may be established without proof of the reading of the registration statement by such person.

(b) Persons exempt from liability upon proof of issues

Notwithstanding the provisions of subsection (a) of this section no person, other than the issuer, shall be liable as provided therein who shall sustain the burden of proof—

(1) that before the effective date of the part of the registration statement with respect to which his liability is asserted (A) he had resigned from or had taken such steps as are permitted by law to resign from, or ceased or refused to act in, every office, capacity, or relationship in which he was described in the registration statement as acting or agreeing to act, and (B) he had advised the Commission and the issuer in writing that he had taken such action and that he would not be responsible for such part of the registration statement; or

(2) that if such part of the registration statement became effective without his knowledge, upon becoming aware of such fact

he forthwith acted and advised the Commission, in accordance with paragraph (1) of this subsection, and, in addition, gave reasonable public notice that such part of the registration statement had become effective without his knowledge; or

(3) that (A) as regards any part of the registration statement not purporting to be made on the authority of an expert, and not purporting to be a copy of or extract from a report or valuation of an expert, and not purporting to be made on the authority of a public official document or statement, he had, after reasonable investigation, reasonable ground to believe and did believe, at the time such part of the registration statement became effective, that the statements therein were true and that there was no omission to state a material fact required to be stated therein or necessary to make the statements therein not misleading; and (B) as regards any part of the registration statement purporting to be made upon his authority as an expert or purporting to be a copy of or extract from a report or valuation of himself as an expert, (i) he had, after reasonable investigation, reasonable ground to believe and did believe, at the time such part of the registration statement became effective, that the statements therein were true and that there was no omission to state a material fact required to be stated therein or necessary to make the statements therein not misleading, or (ii) such part of the registration statement did not fairly represent his statement as an expert or was not a fair copy of or extract from his report or valuation as an expert; and (C) as regards any part of the registration statement purporting to be made on the authority of an expert (other than himself) or purporting to be a copy of or extract from a report or valuation of an expert (other than himself), he had no reasonable ground to believe and did not believe, at the time such part of the registration statement became effective, that the statements therein were untrue or that there was an omission to state a material fact required to be stated therein or necessary to make the statements therein not misleading, or that such part of the registration statement did not fairly represent the statement of the expert or was not a fair copy of or extract from the report or valuation of the expert; and (D) as regards any part of the registration statement purporting to be a statement made by an official person or purporting to be a copy of or extract from a public official document, he had no reasonable ground to believe and did not believe, at the time such part of the registration statement became effective, that the statements therein were untrue, or that there was an omission to state a material fact required to be stated therein or necessary to make the statements therein not misleading, or that such part of the registration statement did not fairly represent the statement made by the official person or was not a fair copy of or extract from the public official document.

(c)   Standard of reasonableness

In determining, for the purpose of paragraph (3) of subsection (b) of this section, what constitutes reasonable investigation and reasonable ground for belief, the standard of reasonableness shall be that required of a prudent man in the management of his own property.

(d)   Effective date of registration statement with regard to underwriters

If any person becomes an underwriter with respect to the security after the part of the registration statement with respect to which his liability is asserted has become effective, then for the purposes of paragraph (3) of subsection (b) of this section such part of the registration statement shall be considered as having become effective with respect to such person as of the time when he became an underwriter.

(e)   Measure of damages; undertaking for payment of costs

The suit authorized under subsection (a) of this section may be to recover such damages as shall represent the difference between the amount paid for the security (not exceeding the price at which the security was offered to the public) and (1) the value thereof as of the time such suit was brought, or (2) the price at which such security shall have been disposed of in the market before suit, or (3) the price at which such security shall have been disposed of after suit but before judgment if such damages shall be less than the damages representing the difference between the amount paid for the security (not exceeding the price at which the security was offered to the public) and the value thereof as of the time such suit was brought: *Provided,* That if the defendant proves that any portion or all of such damages represents other than the depreciation in value of such security resulting from such part of the registration statement, with respect to which his liability is asserted, not being true or omitting to state a material fact required to be stated therein or necessary to make the statements therein not misleading, such portion of or all such damages shall not be recoverable. In no event shall any underwriter (unless such underwriter shall have knowingly received from the issuer for acting as an underwriter some benefit, directly or indirectly, in which all other underwriters similarly situated did not share in proportion to their respective interests in the underwriting) be liable in any suit or as a consequence of suits authorized under subsection (a) of this section for damages in excess of the total price at which the securities underwritten by him and distributed to the public were offered to the public. In any suit under this or any other section of this subchapter the court may, in its discretion, require an undertaking for the payment of the costs of such suit, including reasonable attorney's fees, and if judgment shall be rendered against a party litigant, upon the motion of the other party litigant, such costs may be assessed in favor of such party litigant (whether or not such undertaking has been required) if the court believes the suit or the defense to have been without merit, in an amount sufficient to reimburse him for the reasonable expenses incurred by him, in connection with such suit, such costs to be taxed in the manner usually provided for taxing of costs in the court in which the suit was heard.

(f) Joint and several liability

(1) Except as provided in paragraph (2), all or any one or more of the persons specified in subsection (a) of this section shall be jointly and severally liable, and every person who becomes liable to make any payment under this section may recover contribution as in cases of contract from any person who, if sued separately, would have been liable to make the same payment, unless the person who has become liable was, and the other was not, guilty of fraudulent misrepresentation.

(2)(A) The liability of an outside director under subsection (e) of this section shall be determined in accordance with section 21D(f) of the Securities Exchange Act of 1934.

(B) For purposes of this paragraph, the term "outside director" shall have the meaning given such term by rule or regulation of the Commission.

(g) Offering price to public as maximum amount recoverable

In no case shall the amount recoverable under this section exceed the price at which the security was offered to the public.

§ 12. Civil Liabilities Arising in Connection With Prospectuses and Communications

(a) In General

Any person who—

(1) offers or sells a security in violation of section 5 of this title, or

(2) offers or sells a security (whether or not exempted by the provisions of section 3 of this title, other than paragraphs (2) and (14) of subsection (a) of said section), by the use of any means or instruments of transportation or communication in interstate commerce or of the mails, by means of a prospectus or oral communication, which includes an untrue statement of a material fact or omits to state a material fact necessary in order to make the statements, in the light of the circumstances under which they were made, not misleading (the purchaser not knowing of such untruth or omission), and who shall not sustain the burden of proof that he did not know, and in the exercise of reasonable care could not have known, of such untruth or omission,

shall be liable, subject to subsection (b), to the person purchasing such security from him, who may sue either at law or in equity in any court of competent jurisdiction, to recover the consideration paid for such security with interest thereon, less the amount of any income received thereon, upon the tender of such security, or for damages if he no longer owns the security.

(b) Loss Causation

In an action described in subsection (a)(2), if the person who offered or sold such security proves that any portion or all of the amount recoverable under subsection (a)(2) represents other than the depreciation in value of the subject security resulting from such part of the prospectus or oral communication, with respect to which the liability of that person is asserted, not being true or omitting to state a material fact required to be stated therein or necessary to make the statement not misleading, then such portion or amount, as the case may be, shall not be recoverable.

§ 13. Limitation of Actions

No action shall be maintained to enforce any liability created under section 11 or 12(a)(2) of this title unless brought within one year after the discovery of the untrue statement or the omission, or after such discovery should have been made by the exercise of reasonable diligence, or, if the action is to enforce a liability created under section 12(a)(1) of this title, unless brought within one year after the violation upon which it is based. In no event shall any such action be brought to enforce a liability created under section 11 or 12(a)(1) of this title more than three years after the security was bona fide offered to the public, or under section 12(a)(2) of this title more than three years after the sale.

§ 14. Contrary Stipulations Void

Any condition, stipulation, or provision binding any person acquiring any security to waive compliance with any provision of this subchapter or of the rules and regulations of the Commission shall be void.

§ 15. Liability of Controlling Persons

Every person who, by or through stock ownership, agency, or otherwise, or who, pursuant to or in connection with an agreement or understanding with one or more other persons by or through stock ownership, agency, or otherwise, controls any person liable under sections 11 or 12 of this title, shall also be liable jointly and severally with and to the same extent as such controlled person to any person to whom such controlled person is liable, unless the controlling person had no knowledge of or reasonable ground to believe in the existence of the facts by reason of which the liability of the controlled person is alleged to exist.

§ 16. Additional Remedies; Limitations on Remedies

(a) *Remedies Additional.*—Except as provided in subsection (b), the rights and remedies provided by this title shall be in addition to any and all other rights and remedies that may exist at law or in equity.

(b) *Class Action Limitations.*—No covered class action based upon the statutory or common law of any State or subdivision thereof may be maintained in any State or Federal court by any private party alleging—

(1) an untrue statement or omission of a material fact in connection with the purchase or sale of a covered security; or

(2) that the defendant used or employed any manipulative or deceptive device or contrivance in connection with the purchase or sale of a covered security.

(c) *Removal of Covered Class Actions.*—Any covered class action brought in any State court involving a covered security, as set forth in subsection (b), shall be removable to the Federal district court for the district in which the action is pending, and shall be subject to subsection (b).

(d) *Preservation of Certain Actions.*—

(1) *Actions under state law of state of incorporation.*—

(A) *Actions preserved.*—Notwithstanding subsection (b) or (c), a covered class action described in subparagraph (B) of this paragraph that is based upon the statutory or common law of the State in which the issuer is incorporated (in the case of a corporation) or organized (in the case of any other entity) may be maintained in a State or Federal court by a private party.

(B) *Permissible actions.*—A covered class action is described in this subparagraph if it involves—

(i) the purchase or sale of securities by the issuer or an affiliate of the issuer exclusively from or to holders of equity securities of the issuer; or

(ii) any recommendation, position, or other communication with respect to the sale of securities of the issuer that—

(I) is made by or on behalf of the issuer or an affiliate of the issuer to holders of equity securities of the issuer; and

(II) concerns decisions of those equity holders with respect to voting their securities, acting in response to a tender or exchange offer, or exercising dissenters' or appraisal rights.

(2) *State actions.—*

(A) *In general.*—Notwithstanding any other provision of this section, nothing in this section may be construed to preclude a State or political subdivision thereof or a State pension plan from bringing an action involving a covered security on its own behalf, or as a member of a class comprised solely of other States, political subdivisions, or State pension plans that are named plaintiffs, and that have authorized participation, in such action.

(B) *State pension plan defined.*—For purposes of this paragraph, the term "State pension plan" means a pension plan established and maintained for its employees by the government of the State or political subdivision thereof, or by any agency or instrumentality thereof.

(3) *Actions under contractual agreements between issuers and indenture trustees.*—Notwithstanding subsection (b) or (c), a covered class action that seeks to enforce a contractual agreement between an issuer and an indenture trustee may be maintained in a State or Federal court by a party to the agreement or a successor to such party.

(4) *Remand of removed actions.*—In an action that has been removed from a State court pursuant to subsection (c), if the Federal court determines that the action may be maintained in State court pursuant to this subsection, the Federal court shall remand such action to such State court.

(e) *Preservation of State Jurisdiction.*—The securities commission (or any agency or office performing like functions) of any State shall retain jurisdiction under the laws of such State to investigate and bring enforcement actions.

(f) *Definitions.*—For purposes of this section, the following definitions shall apply:

(1) *Affiliate of the issuer.*—The term "affiliate of the issuer" means a person that directly or indirectly, through one or more intermediaries, controls or is controlled by or is under common control with, the issuer.

(2) *Covered class action.*—

(A) *In general.*—The term "covered class action" means—

(i) any single lawsuit in which—

(I) damages are sought on behalf of more than 50 persons or prospective class members, and questions of law or fact common to those persons or members of the prospective class, without reference to issues of individualized reliance on an alleged misstatement or omission, predominate over any questions affecting only individual persons or members; or

> (II) one or more named parties seek to recover damages on a representative basis on behalf of themselves and other unnamed parties similarly situated, and questions of law or fact common to those persons or members of the prospective class predominate over any questions affecting only individual persons or members; or

(ii) any group of lawsuits filed in or pending in the same court and involving common questions of law or fact, in which—

> (I) damages are sought on behalf of more than 50 persons; and

> (II) the lawsuits are joined, consolidated, or otherwise proceed as a single action for any purpose.

(B) *Exception for derivative actions.*—Notwithstanding subparagraph (A), the term "covered class action" does not include an exclusively derivative action brought by one or more shareholders on behalf of a corporation.

(C) *Counting of certain class members.*—For purposes of this paragraph, a corporation, investment company, pension plan, partnership, or other entity, shall be treated as one person or prospective class member, but only if the entity is not established for the purpose of participating in the action.

(D) *Rule of construction.*—Nothing in this paragraph shall be construed to affect the discretion of a State court in determining whether actions filed in such court should be joined, consolidated, or otherwise allowed to proceed as a single action.

(3) *Covered security.*—The term "covered security" means a security that satisfies the standards for a covered security specified in paragraph (1) or (2) of section 18(b) at the time during which it is alleged that the misrepresentation, omission, or manipulative or deceptive conduct occurred, except that such term shall not include any debt security that is exempt from registration under this title pursuant to rules issued by the Commission under section 4(2).

§ 17. Fraudulent Interstate Transactions

(a) Use of interstate commerce for purpose of fraud or deceit

It shall be unlawful for any person in the offer or sale of any securities ... by the use of any means or instruments of transportation or communication in interstate commerce or by the use of the mails, directly or indirectly—

(1) to employ any device, scheme, or artifice to defraud, or

(2) to obtain money or property by means of any untrue statement of a material fact or any omission to state a material fact necessary in order to make the statements made, in the light of the circumstances under which they were made, not misleading, or

(3) to engage in any transaction, practice, or course of business which operates or would operate as a fraud or deceit upon the purchaser.

(b) Use of interstate commerce for purpose of offering for sale

It shall be unlawful for any person, by the use of any means or instruments of transportation or communication in interstate commerce or by the use of the mails, to publish, give publicity to, or circulate any notice, circular, advertisement, newspaper, article, letter, investment service, or communication which, though not purporting to offer a security for sale, describes such security for a consideration received or to be received, directly or indirectly, from an issuer, underwriter, or dealer, without fully disclosing the receipt, whether past or prospective, of such consideration and the amount thereof.

(c) Exemptions of section 3 not applicable to this section

The exemptions provided in section 3 of this title shall not apply to the provisions of this section. . . .

§ 18. Exemption From State Regulation of Securities Offerings

(a) Scope of exemption

Except as otherwise provided in this section, no law, rule, regulation, or order, or other administrative action of any State or any political subdivision thereof—

(1) requiring, or with respect to, registration or qualification of securities, or registration or qualification of securities transactions, shall directly or indirectly apply to a security that—

(A) is a covered security; or

(B) will be a covered security upon completion of the transaction;

(2) shall directly or indirectly prohibit, limit, or impose any conditions upon the use of—

(A) with respect to a covered security described in subsection (b) of this section, any offering document that is prepared by or on behalf of the issuer; or

(B) any proxy statement, report to shareholders, or other disclosure document relating to a covered security or the issuer thereof that is required to be and is filed with the Commission or any national securities organization registered under section 15A of the Securities Exchange Act, except that this subparagraph does not apply to the laws, rules, regulations, or orders, or other administrative actions of the State of incorporation of the issuer; or

(3) shall directly or indirectly prohibit, limit, or impose conditions, based on the merits of such offering or issuer, upon the offer or sale of any security described in paragraph (1).

(b) Covered securities

For purposes of this section, the following are covered securities:

(1) *Exclusive Federal registration of nationally traded securities*

A security is a covered security if such security is—

(A) listed, or authorized for listing, on the New York Stock Exchange or the American Stock Exchange, or listed, or authorized for listing, on the National Market System of the Nasdaq Stock Market (or any successor to such entities);

(B) listed, or authorized for listing, on a national securities exchange (or tier or segment thereof) that has listing standards that the Commission determines by rule (on its own initiative or on the basis of a petition) are substantially similar to the listing standards applicable to securities described in subparagraph (A); or

(C) is a security of the same issuer that is equal in seniority or that is a senior security to a security described in subparagraph (A) or (B).

(2) *Exclusive Federal registration of investment companies*

A security is a covered security if such security is a security issued by an investment company that is registered, or that has filed a registration statement, under the Investment Company Act of 1940.

(3) *Sales to qualified purchasers*

A security is a covered security with respect to the offer or sale of the security to qualified purchasers, as defined by the Commission by rule. In prescribing such rule, the Commission may define the term "qualified purchaser" differently with respect to different categories of securities, consistent with the public interest and the protection of investors.

(4) *Exemption in connection with certain exempt offerings*

A security is a covered security with respect to a transaction that is exempt from registration under this subchapter pursuant to—

(A) paragraph (1) or (3) of section 4, and the issuer of such security files reports with the Commission pursuant to section 13 or 15(d) of the Securities Exchange Act;

(B) section 4(4);

(C) section 3(a), other than the offer or sale of a security that is exempt from such registration pursuant to paragraph (4), (10), or (11) of such section, except that a municipal security that is exempt from such registration pursuant to paragraph (2) of such section is not a covered security with respect to the offer or sale of such security in the State in which the issuer of such security is located; or

(D) Commission rules or regulations issued under section 4(2), except that this subparagraph does not prohibit a State from imposing notice filing requirements that are substantially similar to those required by rule or regulation under section 4(2) that are in effect on September 1, 1996.

(c) Preservation of authority

(1) *Fraud authority*

Consistent with this section, the securities commission (or any agency or officer performing like functions) of any State shall retain jurisdiction under the laws of such State to investigate and bring enforcement actions with respect to fraud or deceit, or unlawful conduct by a broker or dealer, in connection with securities or securities transactions.

(2) *Preservation of filing requirements*

(A) *Notice filings permitted*

Nothing in this section prohibits the securities commission (or any agency or office performing like functions) of any State from requiring the filing of any document filed with the Commission pursuant to this subchapter, together with annual or periodic reports of the value of securities sold or offered to be sold to persons located in the State (if such sales data is not included in documents filed with the Commission), solely for notice purposes and the assessment of any fee, together with a consent to service of process and any required fee.

(B) *Preservation of fees*

(i) *In general*

Until otherwise provided by law, rule, regulation, or order, or other administrative action of any State, or any political subdivision thereof, adopted after October 11, 1996, filing or registration fees with respect to securities or securities transactions shall continue to be collected in amounts determined pursuant to State law as in effect on the day before such date.

(ii) *Schedule*

The fees required by this subparagraph shall be paid, and all necessary supporting data on sales or offers for sales required under subparagraph (A), shall be reported on the same schedule as would have been applicable had the issuer not relied on the exemption provided in subsection (a) of this section.

(C) *Availability of preemption contingent on payment of fees*

(i) *In general*

During the period beginning on October 11, 1996, and ending 3 years after October 11, 1996, the securities commission (or any agency or office performing like functions) of any State may require the registration of securities issued by any issuer who refuses to pay the fees required by subparagraph (B).

(ii) *Delays*

For purposes of this subparagraph, delays in payment of fees or underpayments of fees that are promptly remedied shall not constitute a refusal to pay fees.

(D) *Fees not permitted on listed securities*

Notwithstanding subparagraphs (A), (B), and (C), no filing or fee may be required with respect to any security that is a covered security pursuant to subsection (b)(1) of this section, or will be such a covered security upon completion of the transaction, or is a security of the same issuer that is equal in seniority or that is a senior security to a security that is a covered security pursuant to subsection (b)(1) of this section.

(3) *Enforcement of requirements*

Nothing in this section shall prohibit the securities commission (or any agency or office performing like functions) of any State from suspending the offer or sale of securities within such State as a result of the failure to submit any filing or fee required under law and permitted under this section.

(d) Definitions

For purposes of this section, the following definitions shall apply:

(1) *Offering document*

The term "offering document"—

(A) has the meaning given the term "prospectus" in section 2(a)(10) of this title, but without regard to the provisions of subparagraphs (a) and (b) of that section; and

(B) includes a communication that is not deemed to offer a security pursuant to a rule of the Commission.

(2) *Prepared by or on behalf of the issuer*

Not later than 6 months after the date of enactment of the National Securities Market Improvement Act of 1996, the Commission shall, by rule, define the term "prepared by or on behalf of the issuer" for purposes of this section.

(3) *State*

The term "State" has the same meaning as in section 3.

(4) *Senior security*

The term "senior security" means any bond, debenture, note, or similar obligation or instrument constituting a security and evidencing indebtedness, and any stock of a class having priority over any other class as to distribution of assets or payment of dividends.

§ 19. Special Powers of Commission

(a) The Commission shall have authority from time to time to make, amend, and rescind such rules and regulations as may be necessary to carry out the provisions of this subchapter, including rules and regulations governing registration statements and prospectuses for various classes of securities and issuers, and defining accounting, technical, and trade terms used in this subchapter. Among other things, the Commission shall have authority, for the purposes of this subchapter, to prescribe the form or forms in which required information shall be set forth, the items or details to be shown in the balance sheet and earning statement, and the methods to be followed in the preparation of accounts, in the appraisal or valuation of assets and liabilities, in the determination of depreciation and depletion, in the differentiation of recurring and nonrecurring income, in the differentiation of investment and operating income, and in the preparation, where the Commission deems it necessary or desirable, of consolidated balance sheets or income accounts of any person directly or indirectly controlling or controlled by the issuer, or any person under direct or indirect common control with the issuer. The rules and regulations of the Commission shall be effective upon publication in the manner which the Commission shall prescribe. No provision of this subchapter imposing any liability shall apply to any act done or omitted in good faith in conformity with any rule or regulation of the Commission, notwithstanding that such rule or regulation may, after such act or omission, be amended or rescinded or be determined by judicial or other authority to be invalid for any reason.

(b) Recognition of accounting standards

(1) *In general.*—In carrying out its authority under subsection (a) and under section 13(b) of the Securities Exchange Act of 1934, the Commission may recognize, as "generally accepted" for purposes of the securities laws, any accounting principles established by a standard setting body—

(A) that—

(i) is organized as a private entity;

(ii) has, for administrative and operational purposes, a board of trustees (or equivalent body) serving in the public interest, the majority of whom are not, concurrent with their service on such board, and have not been during the 2–year period preceding such service, associated persons of any registered public accounting firm; ...

(iv) has adopted procedures to ensure prompt consideration, by majority vote of its members, of changes to accounting principles necessary to reflect emerging accounting issues and changing business practices; and

(v) considers, in adopting accounting principles, the need to keep standards current in order to reflect changes in the business environment, the extent to which international convergence on high quality accounting standards is necessary or appropriate in the public interest and for the protection of investors; and

(B) that the Commission determines has the capacity to assist the Commission in fulfilling the requirements of subsection (a) and section 13(b) of the Securities Exchange Act of 1934, because, at a minimum, the standard setting body is capable of improving the accuracy and effectiveness of financial reporting and the protection of investors under the securities laws.

(2) *Annual report.*—A standard setting body described in paragraph (1) shall submit an annual report to the Commission and the public, containing audited financial statements of that standard setting body.

(c) For the purpose of all investigations which, in the opinion of the Commission, are necessary and proper for the enforcement of this subchapter, any member of the Commission or any officer or officers designated by it are empowered to administer oaths and affirmations, subpoena witnesses, take evidence, and require the production of any books, papers, or other documents which the Commission deems relevant or material to the inquiry. Such attendance of witnesses and the production of such documentary evidence may be required from any place in the United States or any Territory at any designated place of hearing. . . .

§ 20.　Injunctions and Prosecution of Offenses. . . .

(b)　Action for injunction or criminal prosecution in district court

Whenever it shall appear to the Commission that any person is engaged or about to engage in any acts or practices which constitute or will constitute a violation of the provisions of this subchapter, or of any rule or regulation prescribed under authority thereof, it may in its discretion, bring an action in any district court of the United States or United States court of any Territory, to enjoin such acts or practices, and upon a proper showing a permanent or temporary injunction or restraining order shall be granted without bond.　The Commission may transmit such evidence as may be available concerning such acts or practices to the Attorney General who may, in his discretion, institute the necessary criminal proceedings under this subchapter.　Any such criminal proceeding may be brought either in the district wherein the transmittal of the prospectus or security complained of begins, or in the district wherein such prospectus or security is received. . . .

(d)　Money penalties in civil actions

(1) *Authority of commission.*　Whenever it shall appear to the Commission that any person has violated any provision of this title, the rules or regulations thereunder, or a cease-and-desist order entered by the Commission pursuant to section 8A of this title, other than by committing a violation subject to a penalty pursuant to section 21A of the Securities Exchange Act of 1934, the Commission may bring an action in a United States district court to seek, and the court shall have jurisdiction to impose, upon a proper showing, a civil penalty to be paid by the person who committed such violation.

(2) *Amount of penalty.*

(A) *First tier.*　The amount of the penalty shall be determined by the court in light of the facts and circumstances.　For each violation, the amount of the penalty shall not exceed the greater of (i) [$6,500]* for a natural person or [$65,000] for any other person, or (ii) the gross amount of pecuniary gain to such defendant as a result of the violation.

(B) *Second tier.*　Notwithstanding subparagraph (A), the amount of penalty for each such violation shall not exceed the

---

* The bracketed figures in this section have been adjusted for inflation by the SEC under the Debt Collection Act of 1996, which requires the Commission to make inflationary adjustments to civil penalties in the Securities Act, the Exchange Act, and other Acts that the Commission administers. (Footnote by ed.)

greater of (i) [$65,000] for a natural person or [$325,000] for any other person, or (ii) the gross amount of pecuniary gain to such defendant as a result of the violation, if the violation described in paragraph (1) involved fraud, deceit, manipulation, or deliberate or reckless disregard of a regulatory requirement.

(C) *Third tier.* Notwithstanding subparagraphs (A) and (B), the amount of penalty for each such violation shall not exceed the greater of (i) [$130,000] for a natural person or [$650,000] for any other person, or (ii) the gross amount of pecuniary gain to such defendant as a result of the violation, if—

(I) the violation described in paragraph (1) involved fraud, deceit, manipulation, or deliberate or reckless disregard of a regulatory requirement; and

(II) such violation directly or indirectly resulted in substantial losses or created a significant risk of substantial losses to other persons.

(3) *Procedures for collection.*

(A) *Payment of penalty to treasury.* A penalty imposed under this section shall be payable into the Treasury of the United States, except as otherwise provided in section 308 of the Sarbanes–Oxley Act of 2002.

(B) *Collection of penalties.* If a person upon whom such a penalty is imposed shall fail to pay such penalty within the time prescribed in the court's order, the Commission may refer the matter to the Attorney General who shall recover such penalty by action in the appropriate United States district court.

(C) *Remedy not exclusive.* The actions authorized by this subsection may be brought in addition to any other action that the Commission or the Attorney General is entitled to bring.

(D) *Jurisdiction and venue.* For purposes of section 22 of this title, actions under this section shall be actions to enforce a liability or a duty created by this title.

(4) *Special provisions relating to a violation of a cease-and-desist order.* In an action to enforce a cease-and-desist order entered by the Commission pursuant to section 8A, each separate violation of such order shall be a separate offense, except that in the case of a violation through a continuing failure to comply with such an order, each day of the failure to comply with the order shall be deemed a separate offense.

(e) Authority of a court to prohibit persons from serving as Officers and Directors

In any proceeding under subsection (b), the court may prohibit, conditionally or unconditionally, and permanently or for such period of time as it shall determine, any person who violated section 17(a)(1) of this title from acting as an officer or director of any issuer that has a class of securities registered pursuant to section 12 of the Securities Exchange Act of 1934 or that is required to file reports pursuant to section 15(d) of such Act if the person's conduct demonstrates unfitness to serve as an officer or director of any such issuer.

(f) Prohibition of Attorneys' Fees Paid From Commission Disgorgement Funds

Except as otherwise ordered by the court upon motion by the Commission, or, in the case of an administrative action, as otherwise ordered by the Commission, funds disgorged as the result of an action brought by the Commission in Federal court, or as a result of any Commission administrative action, shall not be distributed as payment for attorneys' fees or expenses incurred by private parties seeking distribution of the disgorged funds.

(g) Authority of a court to prohibit persons from participating in an offering of penny stock

(1) *In general.*—In any proceeding under subsection (a) against any person participating in, or, at the time of the alleged misconduct, who was participating in, an offering of penny stock, the court may prohibit that person from participating in an offering of penny stock, conditionally or unconditionally, and permanently or for such period of time as the court shall determine.

(2) *Definition.*—For purposes of this subsection, the term "person participating in an offering of penny stock" includes any person engaging in activities with a broker, dealer, or issuer for purposes of issuing, trading, or inducing or attempting to induce the purchase or sale of, any penny stock. The Commission may, by rule or regulation, define such term to include other activities, and may, by rule, regulation, or order, exempt any person or class of persons, in whole or in part, conditionally or unconditionally, from inclusion in such term.

§ 22. Jurisdiction of Offenses and Suits

(a) Federal and State courts; venue; service of process; review; removal; costs

The district courts of the United States, and the United States courts of any Territory, shall have jurisdiction of offenses and violations under this subchapter and under the rules and regulations promulgated by the Commission in respect thereto, and, concurrent with State and Territorial courts, except as provided in section 16 with respect to covered class actions, of all suits in equity and actions at law brought to enforce any liability or duty created by this subchapter. Any such suit or action may be brought in the district wherein the defendant is found or is an inhabitant or transacts business, or in the district where the offer or sale took place, if the defendant participated therein, and process in such cases may be served in any other district of which the defendant is an inhabitant or wherever the defendant may be found. Judgments and decrees so rendered shall be subject to review as provided in sections 1254, 1291, and 1292 of title 28. Except as provided in section 16(c), no case arising under this subchapter and brought in any State court of competent jurisdiction shall be removed to any court of the United States. No costs shall be assessed for or against the Commission in any proceeding under this subchapter brought by or against it in the Supreme Court or such other courts.

(b) Contumacy or refusal to obey subpoena: contempt

In case of contumacy or refusal to obey a subpoena issued to any person, any of the said United States courts, within the jurisdiction of which said person guilty of contumacy or refusal to obey is found or resides, upon application by the Commission may issue to such person an order requiring such person to appear before the Commission, or one of its examiners designated by it, there to produce documentary evidence if so ordered, or there to give evidence touching the matter in question; and any failure to obey such order of the court may be punished by said court as a contempt thereof.

§ 23. Unlawful Representations

Neither the fact that the registration statement for a security has been filed or is in effect nor the fact that a stop order is not in effect with respect thereto shall be deemed a finding by the Commission that the registration statement is true and accurate on its face or that it does not contain an untrue statement of fact or omit to state a material fact, or be held to mean that the Commission has in any way passed upon the merits of, or given approval to, such security. It shall be unlawful to make, or cause to be made to any prospective purchaser any representation contrary to the foregoing provisions of this section.

§ 24. Penalties

Any person who willfully violates any of the provisions of this subchapter, or the rules and regulations promulgated by the Commission under authority thereof, or any person who willfully, in a registration statement filed under this subchapter, makes any untrue statement of a material fact or omits to state any material fact required to be stated therein or necessary to make the statements therein not misleading, shall upon conviction be fined not more than $10,000 or imprisoned not more than five years, or both....

§ 27. Private Securities Litigation

(a) Private Class Actions

(1) *In general.*—The provisions of this subsection shall apply to each private action arising under this title that is brought as a plaintiff class action pursuant to the Federal Rules of Civil Procedure.

(2) *Certification filed with complaint.*—

(A) In general.—Each plaintiff seeking to serve as a representative party on behalf of a class shall provide a sworn certification, which shall be personally signed by such plaintiff and filed with the complaint, that—

(i) states that the plaintiff has reviewed the complaint and authorized its filing;

(ii) states that the plaintiff did not purchase the security that is the subject of the complaint at the direction of plaintiff's counsel or in order to participate in any private action arising under this title;

(iii) states that the plaintiff is willing to serve as a representative party on behalf of a class, including providing testimony at deposition and trial, if necessary;

(iv) sets forth all of the transactions of the plaintiff in the security that is the subject of the complaint during the class period specified in the complaint;

(v) identifies any other action under this title, filed during the 3–year period preceding the date on which the certification is signed by the plaintiff, in which the plaintiff has sought to serve, or served, as a representative party on behalf of a class; and

(vi) states that the plaintiff will not accept any payment for serving as a representative party on behalf of a class beyond the plaintiff's pro rata share of any recovery, except as ordered or approved by the court in accordance with paragraph (4).

(B) Nonwaiver of attorney-client privilege.—The certification filed pursuant to subparagraph (A) shall not be construed to be a waiver of the attorney-client privilege.

(3) *Appointment of lead plaintiff.*—

(A) Early notice to class members.—

(i) In general.—Not later than 20 days after the date on which the complaint is filed, the plaintiff or plaintiffs shall cause to be published, in a widely circulated national business-oriented publication or wire service, a notice advising members of the purported plaintiff class—

(I) of the pendency of the action, the claims asserted therein, and the purported class period; and

(II) that, not later than 60 days after the date on which the notice is published, any member of the purported class may move the court to serve as lead plaintiff of the purported class.

(ii) Multiple actions.—If more than one action on behalf of a class asserting substantially the same claim or claims arising under this title is filed, only the plaintiff or plaintiffs in the first filed action shall be required to cause notice to be published in accordance with clause (i).

(iii) Additional notices may be required under federal rules.—Notice required under clause (i) shall be in addition to any notice required pursuant to the Federal Rules of Civil Procedure.

(B) Appointment of lead plaintiff.—

(i) In general.—Not later than 90 days after the date on which a notice is published under subparagraph (A)(i), the court shall consider any motion made by a purported class member in response to the notice, including any motion by a class member who is not individually named as a plaintiff in the complaint or complaints, and shall appoint as lead plaintiff the member or members of the purported plaintiff class that the court determines to be most capable of adequately representing the interests of class members (hereafter in this paragraph referred to as the "most adequate plaintiff") in accordance with this subparagraph.

(ii) Consolidated actions.—If more than one action on behalf of a class asserting substantially the same claim or claims arising under this title has been filed, and any party has sought to consolidate those actions for pretrial purposes or for trial, the court shall not make the determination required by clause (i) until after the decision on the motion to consolidate is rendered. As soon as practicable after such decision is rendered, the court shall appoint the most adequate plaintiff as lead plaintiff for the consolidated actions in accordance with this subparagraph.

(iii) Rebuttable presumption.—

(I) In general.—Subject to subclause (II), for purposes of clause (i), the court shall adopt a presumption that the most adequate plaintiff in any private action arising under this title is the person or group of persons that—

(aa) has either filed the complaint or made a motion in response to a notice under subparagraph (A)(i);

(bb) in the determination of the court, has the largest financial interest in the relief sought by the class; and

(cc) otherwise satisfies the requirements of Rule 23 of the Federal Rules of Civil Procedure.

(II) Rebuttal evidence.—The presumption described in subclause (I) may be rebutted only upon proof by a member of the purported plaintiff class that the presumptively most adequate plaintiff—

(aa) will not fairly and adequately protect the interests of the class; or

(bb) is subject to unique defenses that render such plaintiff incapable of adequately representing the class.

(iv) Discovery.—For purposes of this subparagraph, discovery relating to whether a member or members of the purported plaintiff class is the most adequate plaintiff may be conducted by a plaintiff only if the plaintiff first demonstrates a reasonable basis for a finding that the presumptively most adequate plaintiff is incapable of adequately representing the class.

(v) Selection of lead counsel.—The most adequate plaintiff shall, subject to the approval of the court, select and retain counsel to represent the class.

(vi) Restrictions on professional plaintiffs.—Except as the court may otherwise permit, consistent with the purposes of this section, a person may be a lead plaintiff, or an officer, director, or fiduciary of a lead plaintiff, in no more than 5 securities class actions brought as plaintiff class actions pursuant to the Federal Rules of Civil Procedure during any 3–year period.

(4) *Recovery by plaintiffs.*—The share of any final judgment or of any settlement that is awarded to a representative party serving on behalf of a class shall be equal, on a per share basis, to the portion of the final judgment or settlement awarded to all other members of the class. Nothing in this paragraph shall be construed to limit the award of reasonable costs and expenses (including lost wages) directly relating to the representation of the class to any representative party serving on behalf of the class.

(5) *Restrictions on settlements under seal.*—The terms and provisions of any settlement agreement of a class action shall not be filed under seal, except that on motion of any party to the settlement, the court may order filing under seal for those portions of a settlement agreement as to which good cause is shown for such filing under seal. For purposes of this paragraph, good cause shall exist only if publication of a term or provision of a settlement agreement would cause direct and substantial harm to any party.

(6) *Restrictions on payment of attorneys' fees and expenses.*—Total attorneys' fees and expenses awarded by the court to counsel for the plaintiff class shall not exceed a reasonable percentage of the amount of any damages and prejudgment interest actually paid to the class.

(7) *Disclosure of settlement terms to class members.*—Any proposed or final settlement agreement that is published or otherwise disseminated to the class shall include each of the following statements, along with a cover page summarizing the information contained in such statements:

(A) Statement of plaintiff recovery.—The amount of the settlement proposed to be distributed to the parties to the action, determined in the aggregate and on an average per share basis.

(B) Statement of potential outcome of case.—

(i) Agreement on amount of damages.—If the settling parties agree on the average amount of damages per share that would be recoverable if the plaintiff prevailed on each claim alleged under this title, a statement concerning the average amount of such potential damages per share.

(ii) Disagreement on amount of damages.—If the parties do not agree on the average amount of damages per share that would be recoverable if the plaintiff prevailed on each claim alleged under this title, a statement from each settling party concerning the issue or issues on which the parties disagree.

(iii) Inadmissibility for certain purposes.—A statement made in accordance with clause (i) or (ii) concerning the amount of damages shall not be admissible in any Federal or State judicial action or administrative proceeding, other than an action or proceeding arising out of such statement.

(C) Statement of attorneys' fees or costs sought.—If any of the settling parties or their counsel intend to apply to the court for an award of attorneys' fees or costs from any fund established as part of the settlement, a statement indicating which parties or counsel intend to make such an application, the amount of fees and costs that will be sought (including the amount of such fees and costs determined on an average per share basis), and a brief explanation supporting the fees and costs sought.

(D) *Identification of lawyers' representatives.*—The name, telephone number, and address of one or more representatives of counsel for the plaintiff class who will be reasonably available to answer questions from class members concerning any matter contained in any notice of settlement published or otherwise disseminated to the class.

(E) *Reasons for settlement.*—A brief statement explaining the reasons why the parties are proposing the settlement.

(F) *Other information.*—Such other information as may be required by the court.

(8) *Attorney conflict of interest.*—If a plaintiff class is represented by an attorney who directly owns or otherwise has a beneficial interest in the securities that are the subject of the litigation, the court shall make a determination of whether such ownership or other interest constitutes a conflict of interest sufficient to disqualify the attorney from representing the plaintiff class.

(b) Stay of Discovery; Preservation of Evidence

(1) *In general.*—In any private action arising under this title, all discovery and other proceedings shall be stayed during the pendency of any motion to dismiss, unless the court finds, upon the motion of any party, that particularized discovery is necessary to preserve evidence or to prevent undue prejudice to that party.

(2) *Preservation of evidence.*—During the pendency of any stay of discovery pursuant to this subsection, unless otherwise ordered by the court, any party to the action with actual notice of the allegations contained in the complaint shall treat all documents, data compilations (including electronically recorded or stored data), and tangible objects that are in the custody or control of such person and that are relevant to the allegations, as if they were the subject of a continuing request for production of documents from an opposing party under the Federal Rules of Civil Procedure.

(3) *Sanction for willful violation.*—A party aggrieved by the willful failure of an opposing party to comply with paragraph (2) may apply to the court for an order awarding appropriate sanctions.

(4) *Circumvention of stay of discovery.*—Upon a proper showing, a court may stay discovery proceedings in any private action in a State court as necessary in aid of its jurisdiction, or to protect or effectuate its judgments, in an action subject to a stay of discovery pursuant to this subsection.

(c) Sanctions for Abusive Litigation

(1) *Mandatory review by court.*—In any private action arising under this title, upon final adjudication of the action, the court shall include in the record specific findings regarding compliance by each party and each attorney representing any party with each requirement of Rule 11(b) of the Federal Rules of Civil Procedure as to any complaint, responsive pleading, or dispositive motion.

(2) *Mandatory sanctions.*—If the court makes a finding under paragraph (1) that a party or attorney violated any requirement of Rule 11(b) of the Federal Rules of Civil Procedure as to any complaint, responsive pleading, or dispositive motion, the court shall impose sanctions on such party or attorney in accordance with Rule 11 of the Federal Rules of Civil Procedure. Prior to making a finding that any party or attorney has violated Rule 11 of the Federal Rules of Civil Procedure, the court shall give such party or attorney notice and an opportunity to respond.

(3) *Presumption in favor of attorneys' fees and costs.*—

(A) In general.—Subject to subparagraphs (B) and (C), for purposes of paragraph (2), the court shall adopt a presumption that the appropriate sanction—

(i) for failure of any responsive pleading or dispositive motion to comply with any requirement of Rule 11(b) of the Federal Rules of Civil Procedure is an award to the opposing party of the reasonable attorneys' fees and other expenses incurred as a direct result of the violation; and

(ii) for substantial failure of any complaint to comply with any requirement of Rule 11(b) of the Federal Rules of Civil Procedure is an award to the opposing party of the reasonable attorneys' fees and other expenses incurred in the action.

(B) Rebuttal evidence.—The presumption described in subparagraph (A) may be rebutted only upon proof by the party or attorney against whom sanctions are to be imposed that—

(i) the award of attorneys' fees and other expenses will impose an unreasonable burden on that party or attorney and would be unjust, and the failure to make such an award would not impose a greater burden on the party in whose favor sanctions are to be imposed; or

(ii) the violation of Rule 11(b) of the Federal Rules of Civil Procedure was de minimis.

(C) Sanctions.—If the party or attorney against whom sanctions are to be imposed meets its burden under subparagraph (B), the court shall award the sanctions that the court deems appropriate pursuant to Rule 11 of the Federal Rules of Civil Procedure.

(d) Defendant's Right to Written Interrogatories

In any private action arising under this title in which the plaintiff may recover money damages only on proof that a defendant acted with a particular state of mind, the court shall, when requested by a defendant, submit to the jury a written interrogatory on the issue of each such defendant's state of mind at the time the alleged violation occurred.

§ 27A. Application of Safe Harbor for Forward–Looking Statements

(a) Applicability

This section shall apply only to a forward-looking statement made by—

(1) an issuer that, at the time that the statement is made, is subject to the reporting requirements of section 13(a) or section 15(d) of the Securities Exchange Act of 1934;

(2) a person acting on behalf of such issuer;

(3) an outside reviewer retained by such issuer making a statement on behalf of such issuer; or

(4) an underwriter, with respect to information provided by such issuer or information derived from information provided by the issuer.

(b) Exclusions

Except to the extent otherwise specifically provided by rule, regulation, or order of the Commission, this section shall not apply to a forward-looking statement—

(1) that is made with respect to the business or operations of the issuer, if the issuer—

(A) during the 3–year period preceding the date on which the statement was first made—

(i) was convicted of any felony or misdemeanor described in clauses (i) through (iv) of section 15(b)(4)(B) of the Securities Exchange Act of 1934; or

(ii) has been made the subject of a judicial or administrative decree or order arising out of a governmental action that—

(I) prohibits future violations of the antifraud provisions of the securities laws;

(II) requires that the issuer cease and desist from violating the antifraud provisions of the securities laws; or

(III) determines that the issuer violated the antifraud provisions of the securities laws;

(B) makes the forward-looking statement in connection with an offering of securities by a blank check company;

(C) issues penny stock;

(D) makes the forward-looking statement in connection with a rollup transaction; or

(E) makes the forward-looking statement in connection with a going private transaction; or

(2) that is—

(A) included in a financial statement prepared in accordance with generally accepted accounting principles;

(B) contained in a registration statement of, or otherwise issued by, an investment company;

(C) made in connection with a tender offer;

(D) made in connection with an initial public offering;

(E) made in connection with an offering by, or relating to the operations of, a partnership, limited liability company, or a direct participation investment program; or

(F) made in a disclosure of beneficial ownership in a report required to be filed with the Commission pursuant to section 13(d) of the Securities Exchange Act of 1934.

(c) Safe Harbor

(1) *In general.*—Except as provided in subsection (b), in any private action arising under this title that is based on an untrue statement of a material fact or omission of a material fact necessary to make the statement not misleading, a person referred to in subsection (a) shall not be liable with respect to any forward-looking statement, whether written or oral, if and to the extent that—

(A) the forward-looking statement is—

(i) identified as a forward-looking statement, and is accompanied by meaningful cautionary statements identifying important factors that could cause actual results to differ materially from those in the forward-looking statement; or

(ii) immaterial; or

(B) the plaintiff fails to prove that the forward-looking statement—

(i) if made by a natural person, was made with actual knowledge by that person that the statement was false or misleading; or

(ii) if made by a business entity; was—

(I) made by or with the approval of an executive officer of that entity, and

(II) made or approved by such officer with actual knowledge by that officer that the statement was false or misleading.

(2) *Oral forward-looking statements.*—In the case of an oral forward-looking statement made by an issuer that is subject to the reporting requirements of section 13(a) or section 15(d) of the Securities Exchange Act of 1934, or by a person acting on behalf of such issuer, the requirement set forth in paragraph (1)(A) shall be deemed to be satisfied—

(A) if the oral forward-looking statement is accompanied by a cautionary statement—

(i) that the particular oral statement is a forward-looking statement; and

(ii) that the actual results could differ materially from those projected in the forward-looking statement; and

(B) if—

(i) the oral forward-looking statement is accompanied by an oral statement that additional information concerning factors that could cause actual results to differ materially from those in the forward-looking statement is contained in a readily available written document, or portion thereof;

(ii) the accompanying oral statement referred to in clause (i) identifies the document, or portion thereof, that contains the additional information about those factors relating to the forward-looking statement; and

(iii) the information contained in that written document is a cautionary statement that satisfies the standard established in paragraph (1)(A).

(3) *Availability.*—Any document filed with the Commission or generally disseminated shall be deemed to be readily available for purposes of paragraph (2).

(4) *Effect on other safe harbors.*—The exemption provided for in paragraph (1) shall be in addition to any exemption that the Commission may establish by rule or regulation under subsection (g).

(d) Duty to Update

Nothing in this section shall impose upon any person a duty to update a forward-looking statement.

(e) Dispositive Motion

On any motion to dismiss based upon subsection (c)(1), the court shall consider any statement cited in the complaint and cautionary statement accompanying the forward-looking statement, which are not subject to material dispute, cited by the defendant.

(f) Stay Pending Decision on Motion

In any private action arising under this title, the court shall stay discovery (other than discovery that is specifically directed to the applicability of the exemption provided for in this section) during the pendency of any motion by a defendant for summary judgment that is based on the grounds that—

>   (1) the statement or omission upon which the complaint is based is a forward-looking statement within the meaning of this section; and

>   (2) the exemption provided for in this section precludes a claim for relief.

(g) Exemption Authority

In addition to the exemptions provided for in this section, the Commission may, by rule or regulation, provide exemptions from or under any provision of this title, including with respect to liability that is based on a statement or that is based on projections or other forward-looking information, if and to the extent that any such exemption is consistent with the public interest and the protection of investors, as determined by the Commission.

(h) Effect on Other Authority of Commission

Nothing in this section limits, either expressly or by implication, the authority of the Commission to exercise similar authority or to adopt similar rules and regulations with respect to forward-looking statements under any other statute under which the Commission exercises rulemaking authority.

(i) Definitions

For purposes of this section, the following definitions shall apply:

>   (1) *Forward-looking statement.*—The term "forward-looking statement" means—

>>   (A) a statement containing a projection of revenues, income (including income loss), earnings (including earnings loss) per share, capital expenditures, dividends, capital structure, or other financial items;

(B) a statement of the plans and objectives of management for future operations, including plans or objectives relating to the products or services of the issuer;

(C) a statement of future economic performance, including any such statement contained in a discussion and analysis of financial condition by the management or in the results of operations included pursuant to the rules and regulations of the Commission;

(D) any statement of the assumptions underlying or relating to any statement described in subparagraph (A), (B), or (C);

(E) any report issued by an outside reviewer retained by an issuer, to the extent that the report assesses a forward-looking statement made by the issuer; or

(F) a statement containing a projection or estimate of such other items as may be specified by rule or regulation of the Commission.

(2) *Investment company.*—The term "investment company" has the same meaning as in section 3(a) of the Investment Company Act of 1940.

(3) *Penny stock.*—The term "penny stock" has the same meaning as in section 3(a)(51) of the Securities Exchange Act of 1934, and the rules and regulations, or orders issued pursuant to that section.

(4) *Going private transaction.*—The term "going private transaction" has the meaning given that term under the rules or regulations of the Commission issued pursuant to section 13(e) of the Securities Exchange Act of 1934.

(5) *Securities laws.*—The term "securities laws" has the same meaning as in section 3 of the Securities Exchange Act of 1934.

(6) *Person acting on behalf of an issuer.*—The term "person acting on behalf of an issuer" means an officer, director, or employee of the issuer.

(7) *Other terms.*—The terms "blank check company", "roll-up transaction", "partnership", "limited liability company", "executive officer of an entity" and "direct participation investment program", have the meanings given those terms by rule or regulation of the Commission.

§ 28. General Exemptive Authority

The Commission, by rule or regulation, may conditionally or unconditionally exempt any person, security, or transaction, or any class or classes of persons, securities, or transactions, from any provision or provisions of this subchapter or of any rule or regulation issued under subchapter, to the extent that such exemption is necessary or appropriate in the public interest, and is consistent with the protection of investors.

RULES AND FORMS UNDER THE
SECURITIES ACT OF 1933
(Selected Provisions)

17 C.F.R. §§ 230.00 et seq.

GENERAL

* Omitted.

REGULATION D—RULES GOVERNING THE LIMITED OFFER AND SALE OF SECURITIES WITHOUT REGISTRATION UNDER THE SECURITIES ACT OF 1933

GENERAL

Rule 134. Communications Not Deemed a Prospectus

Except as provided in paragraphs (e) and (g) of this section, the terms "prospectus" as defined in section 2(a)(10) of the Act or "free writing prospectus" as defined in Rule 405 shall not include a communication limited to the statements required or permitted by this section, provided that the communication is published or transmitted to any person only after a registration statement relating to the offering that includes a prospectus satisfying the requirements of section 10 of the Act (except as otherwise permitted in paragraph (a) of this section) has been filed.

(a) Such communication may include any one or more of the following items of information, which need not follow the numerical sequence of this paragraph, provided that, except as to paragraphs (a)(4), (a)(5), (a)(6), and (a)(17), the prospectus included in the filed registration statement does not have to include a price range otherwise required by rule:

(1) Factual information about the legal identity and business location of the issuer limited to the following: the name of the issuer of the security, the address, phone number, and e-mail address of the issuer's

principal offices and contact for investors, the issuer's country of organization, and the geographic areas in which it conducts business;

(2) The title of the security or securities and the amount or amounts being offered, which title may include a designation as to whether the securities are convertible, exercisable, or exchangeable, and as to the ranking of the securities;

(3) A brief indication of the general type of business of the issuer, limited to the following:

(i) In the case of a manufacturing company, the general type of manufacturing, the principal products or classes of products manufactured, and the segments in which the company conducts business;

(ii) In the case of a public utility company, the general type of services rendered, a brief indication of the area served, and the segments in which the company conducts business;

(iii) In the case of an asset-backed issuer, the identity of key parties, such as sponsor, depositor, issuing entity, servicer or servicers, and trustee, the asset class of the transaction, and the identity of any credit enhancement or other support; and

(iv) In the case of any other type of company, a corresponding statement;

(4) The price of the security, or if the price is not known, the method of its determination or the *bona fide* estimate of the price range as specified by the issuer or the managing underwriter or underwriters;

(5) In the case of a fixed income security, the final maturity and interest rate provisions or, if the final maturity or interest rate provisions are not known, the probable final maturity or interest rate provisions, as specified by the issuer or the managing underwriter or underwriters;

(6) In the case of a fixed income security with a fixed (non-contingent) interest rate provision, the yield or, if the yield is not known, the probable yield range, as specified by the issuer or the managing underwriter or underwriters and the yield of fixed income securities with comparable maturity and security rating as referred to in paragraph (a)(17) of this section;

(7) A brief description of the intended use of proceeds of the offering, if then disclosed in the prospectus that is part of the filed registration statement;

(8) The name, address, phone number, and e-mail address of the sender of the communication and the fact that it is participating, or expects to participate, in the distribution of the security;

(9) The type of underwriting, if then included in the disclosure in the prospectus that is part of the filed registration statement;

(10) The names of underwriters participating in the offering of the securities, and their additional roles, if any, within the underwriting syndicate;

(11) The anticipated schedule for the offering (including the approximate date upon which the proposed sale to the public will begin) and a description of marketing events (including the dates, times, locations, and procedures for attending or otherwise accessing them);

(12) A description of the procedures by which the underwriters will conduct the offering and the procedures for transactions in connection with the offering with the issuer or an underwriter or participating dealer (including procedures regarding account opening and submitting indications of interest and conditional offers to buy), and procedures regarding directed share plans and other participation in offerings by officers, directors, and employees of the issuer;

(13) Whether, in the opinion of counsel, the security is a legal investment for savings banks, fiduciaries, insurance companies, or similar investors under the laws of any State or Territory or the District of Columbia, and the permissibility or status of the investment under the Employee Retirement Income Security Act of 1974;

(14) Whether, in the opinion of counsel, the security is exempt from specified taxes, or the extent to which the issuer has agreed to pay any tax with respect to the security or measured by the income therefrom;

(15) Whether the security is being offered through rights issued to security holders, and, if so, the class of securities the holders of which will be entitled to subscribe, the subscription ratio, the actual or proposed record date, the date upon which the rights were issued or are expected to be issued, the actual or anticipated date upon which they will expire, and the approximate subscription price, or any of the foregoing;

(16) Any statement or legend required by any state law or administrative authority;

(17) With respect to the securities being offered:

(i) Any security rating assigned, or reasonably expected to be assigned, by a *nationally recognized statistical rating organization* as defined in Rule 15c3–1(c)(2)(vi)(F) of the Securities Exchange Act of 1934 and the name or names of the nationally recognized statistical rating organization(s) that assigned or is or are reasonably expected to assign the rating(s); and

(ii) If registered on Form F–9, any security rating assigned, or reasonably expected to be assigned, by any other rating organization specified in the Instruction to paragraph A.(2) of General Instruction I of Form F–9;

(18) The names of selling security holders, if then disclosed in the prospectus that is part of the filed registration statement;

(19) The names of securities exchanges or other securities markets where any class of the issuer's securities are, or will be, listed;

(20) The ticker symbols, or proposed ticker symbols, of the issuer's securities;

(21) The CUSIP number as defined in Rule 17Ad–19(a)(5) of the Securities Exchange Act of 1934 assigned to the securities being offered; and

(22) Information disclosed in order to correct inaccuracies previously contained in a communication permissibly made pursuant to this section.

(b) Except as provided in paragraph (c) of this section, every communication used pursuant to this section shall contain the following:

(1) If the registration statement has not yet become effective, the following statement: A registration statement relating to these securities has been filed with the Securities and Exchange Commission but has not yet become effective. These securities may not be sold nor may offers to buy be accepted prior to the time the registration statement becomes effective; and

(2) The name and address of a person or persons from whom a written prospectus for the offering meeting the requirements of section 10 of the Act (other than a free writing prospectus as defined in Rule 405) including as to the identified paragraphs above a price range where required by rule, may be obtained.

(c) Any of the statements or information specified in paragraph (b) of this section may, but need not, be contained in a communication which:

(1) Does no more than state from whom and include the uniform resource locator (URL) where a written prospectus meeting the requirements of section 10 of the Act (other than a free writing prospectus as defined in Rule 405) may be obtained, identify the security, state the price thereof and state by whom orders will be executed; or

(2) Is accompanied or preceded by a prospectus or a summary prospectus, other than a free writing prospectus as defined in Rule 405, which meets the requirements of section 10 of the Act, including a price range where required by rule, at the date of such preliminary communication.

(d) A communication sent or delivered to any person pursuant to this section which is accompanied or preceded by a prospectus which meets the requirements of section 10 of the Act (other than a free writing prospectus as defined in Rule 405), including a price range where required by rule, at the date of such communication, may solicit from the recipient of the communication an offer to buy the security or request the recipient to indicate whether he or she might be interested in the security, if the communication contains substantially the following statement:

> No offer to buy the securities can be accepted and no part of the purchase price can be received until the registration statement has become effective, and any such offer may be withdrawn or revoked, without obligation or commitment of any kind, at any time prior to notice of its acceptance given after the effective date.

Provided, that such statement need not be included in such a communication to a dealer.

(e) A section 10 prospectus included in any communication pursuant to this section shall remain a prospectus for all purposes under the Act.

(f) The provision in paragraphs (c)(2) and (d) of this section that a prospectus that meets the requirements of section 10 of the Act precede or accompany a communication will be satisfied if such communication is an electronic communication containing an active hyperlink to such prospectus.

(g) This section does not apply to a communication relating to an investment company registered under the Investment Company Act of 1940 or a business development company as defined in section 2(a)(48) of the Investment Company Act of 1940.

Rule 135.   Notice of Proposed Registered Offerings

(a) *When notice is not an offer*. For purposes of section 5 of the Act only, an issuer or a selling security holder (and any person acting on behalf of either of them) that publishes through any medium a notice of a proposed offering to be registered under the Act will not be deemed to offer its securities for sale through that notice if:

(1) *Legend*. The notice includes a statement to the effect that it does not constitute an offer of any securities for sale; and

(2) *Limited notice content*. The notice otherwise includes no more than the following information:

(i) The name of the issuer;

(ii) The title, amount and basic terms of the securities offered;

(iii) The amount of the offering, if any, to be made by selling security holders;

(iv) The anticipated timing of the offering;

(v) A brief statement of the manner and the purpose of the offering, without naming the underwriters;

(vi) Whether the issuer is directing its offering to only a particular class of purchasers;

(vii) Any statements or legends required by the laws of any state or foreign country or administrative authority; and

(viii) In the following offerings, the notice may contain additional information, as follows:

(A) *Rights offering.* In a rights offering to existing security holders:

(1) The class of security holders eligible to subscribe;

(2) The subscription ratio and expected subscription price;

(3) The proposed record date;

(4) The anticipated issuance date of the rights; and

(5) The subscription period or expiration date of the rights offering.

(B) *Offering to employees.* In an offering to employees of the issuer or an affiliated company:

(1) The name of the employer;

(2) The class of employees being offered the securities;

(3) The offering price; and

(4) The duration of the offering period.

(C) *Exchange offer.* In an exchange offer:

(1) The basic terms of the exchange offer;

(2) The name of the subject company;

(3) The subject class of securities sought in the exchange offer.

(D) *Rule 145(a) offering.* In a Rule 145(a) offering:

(1) The name of the person whose assets are to be sold in exchange for the securities to be offered;

(2) The names of any other parties to the transaction;

(3) A brief description of the business of the parties to the transaction;

(4) The date, time and place of the meeting of security holders to vote on or consent to the transaction; and

(5) A brief description of the transaction and the basic terms of the transaction.

(b) *Corrections of misstatements about the offering.* A person that publishes a notice in reliance on this section may issue a notice that contains no more information than is necessary to correct inaccuracies published about the proposed offering.

Rule 135c.   Notice of Certain Proposed Unregistered Offerings

(a) For the purposes only of Section 5 of the Act, a notice given by an issuer required to file reports pursuant to Section 13 or 15(d) of the Securities Exchange Act of 1934 or a foreign issuer that is exempt from registration under the Securities Exchange Act of 1934 pursuant to Rule 12g3–2(b) that it proposes to make, is making or has made an offering of securities not registered or required to be registered under the Act shall not be deemed to offer any securities for sale if:

(1) Such notice is not used for the purpose of conditioning the market in the United States for any of the securities offered;

(2) Such notice states that the securities offered will not be or have not been registered under the Act and may not be offered or sold in the United States absent registration or an applicable exemption from registration requirements; and

(3) Such notice contains no more than the following additional information:

(i) The name of the issuer;

(ii) The title, amount and basic terms of the securities offered, the amount of the offering, if any, made by selling security holders, the time of the offering and a brief statement of the manner and purpose of the offering without naming the underwriters;

(iii) In the case of a rights offering to security holders of the issuer, the class of securities the holders of which will be or were entitled to subscribe to the securities offered, the subscription ratio, the record date, the date upon which the rights are proposed to be or were issued, the term or expiration date of the rights and the subscription price, or any of the foregoing;

(iv) In the case of an offering of securities in exchange for other securities of the issuer or of another issuer, the name of the issuer and the title of the securities to be surrendered in exchange for the securities offered, the basis upon which the exchange may be made, or any of the foregoing;

(v) In the case of an offering to employees of the issuer or to employees of any affiliate of the issuer, the name of the employer and class or classes of employees to whom the securities are offered, the offering price or basis of the offering and the period during which the offering is to be or was made or any of the foregoing; and

(vi) Any statement or legend required by State or foreign law or administrative authority.

(b) Any notice contemplated by this section may take the form of a news release or a written communication directed to security holders or employees, as the case may be, or other published statements.

(c) Notwithstanding the provisions of paragraphs (a) and (b) of this section, in the case of a rights offering of a security listed or subject to unlisted trading privileges on a national securities exchange or quoted on the NASDAQ inter-dealer quotation system information with respect to the interest rate, conversion ratio and subscription price may be disseminated through the facilities of the exchange, the consolidated transaction reporting system, the NASDAQ system or the Dow Jones broad tape, provided such information is already disclosed in a Form 8–K on file with the Commission, in a Form 6–K furnished to the Commission or, in the case of an issuer relying on Rule 12g3–2(b), in a submission made pursuant to that Rule to the Commission.

(d) The issuer shall file any notice contemplated by this section with the Commission under cover of Form 8–K or furnish such notice under Form 6–K, as applicable, and, if relying on Rule 12g3–2(b), shall furnish such notice to the Commission in accordance with the provisions of that exemptive Section.

Rule 137. Publications or Distributions of Research Reports by Brokers or Dealers that are not Participating in an Issuer's Registered Distribution of Securities

Under the following conditions, the terms "offers," "participates," or "participation" in section 2(a)(11) of the Act shall not be deemed to apply to the publication or distribution of research reports with respect to the securities of an issuer which is the subject of an offering pursuant to a registration statement that the issuer proposes to file, or has filed, or that is effective:

(a) The broker or dealer (and any affiliate) that has distributed the report and, if different, the person (and any affiliate) that has published the report have not participated, are not participating, and do not propose to participate in the distribution of the securities that are or will be the subject of the registered offering.

(b) In connection with the publication or distribution of the research report, the broker or dealer (and any affiliate) that has distributed the report and, if different, the person (and any affiliate) that has published the report are not receiving and have not received consideration directly or indirectly from, and are not acting under any direct or indirect arrangement or understanding with:

(1) The issuer of the securities;

(2) A selling security holder;

(3) Any participant in the distribution of the securities that are or will be the subject of the registration statement; or

(4) Any other person interested in the securities that are or will be the subject of the registration statement.

Instruction to Rule 137(b).

This paragraph (b) does not preclude payment of:

1. The regular price being paid by the broker or dealer for independent research, so long as the conditions of this paragraph (b) are satisfied; or

2. The regular subscription or purchase price for the research report.

(c) The broker or dealer publishes or distributes the research report in the regular course of its business....

(e) *Definition of research report.* For purposes of this section, *research report* means a written communication, as defined in Rule 405, that includes information, opinions, or recommendations with respect to securities of an issuer or an analysis of a security or an issuer, whether or not it provides information reasonably sufficient upon which to base an investment decision.

Rule 138. Publications or Distributions of Research Reports by Brokers or Dealers About Securities Other Than Those They Are Distributing

(a) *Registered offerings.* Under the following conditions, a broker's or dealer's publication or distribution of research reports about securities of an issuer shall be deemed for purposes of sections 2(a)(10) and 5(c) of the Act not to constitute an offer for sale or offer to sell a security which is the subject of an offering pursuant to a registration statement that the issuer proposes to file, or has filed, or that is effective, even if the broker or dealer is participating or will participate in the registered offering of the issuer's securities:

(1)(i) The research report relates solely to the issuer's common stock, or debt securities, or preferred stock convertible into its common stock, and the offering involves solely the issuer's non-convertible debt securities or non-convertible, non-participating preferred stock; or

(ii) The research report relates solely to the issuer's non-convertible debt securities or non-convertible, non-participating preferred stock, and the offering involves solely the issuer's common stock, or debt securities, or preferred stock convertible into its common stock.

(2) The issuer as of the date of reliance on this section:

... Is required to file reports, and has filed all periodic reports required during the preceding 12 months (or such shorter time that the issuer was required to file such reports) on Forms 10–K, 10–KSB, 10–Q, 10–QSB, and 20–F pursuant to section 13 or section 15(d) of the Securities Exchange Act of 1934....

(3) The broker or dealer publishes or distributes research reports on the types of securities in question in the regular course of its business....

(b) *Rule 144A offerings.* If the conditions in paragraph (a) of this section are satisfied, a broker's or dealer's publication or distribution of a research report shall not be considered an offer for sale or an offer to sell a security or general solicitation or general advertising, in connection with an offering relying on Rule 144A.

(c) *Regulation S offerings.* If the conditions in paragraph (a) of this section are satisfied, a broker's or dealer's publication or distribution of a research report shall not:

(1) Constitute directed selling efforts as defined in Rule 902(c) for offerings under Regulation S. . . .

(d) *Definition of research report.* For purposes of this section, *research report* means a written communication, as defined in Rule 405, that includes information, opinions, or recommendations with respect to securities of an issuer or an analysis of a security or an issuer, whether or not it provides information reasonably sufficient upon which to base an investment decision.

Rule 139. Publications or Distributions of Research Reports by Brokers or Dealers Distributing Securities

(a) *Registered offerings.* Under the conditions of paragraph (a)(1) or (a)(2) of this section, a broker's or dealer's publication or distribution of a research report about an issuer or any of its securities shall be deemed for purposes of sections 2(a)(10) and 5(c) of the Act not to constitute an offer for sale or offer to sell a security that is the subject of an offering pursuant to a registration statement that the issuer proposes to file, or has filed, or that is effective, even if the broker or dealer is participating or will participate in the registered offering of the issuer's securities:

(1) *Issuer-specific research reports.*

(i) The issuer either:

(A)(*1*) At the later of the time of filing its most recent Form S–3 . . . or the time of its most recent amendment to such registration statement for purposes of complying with section 10(a)(3) of the Act or, if no Form S–3 . . . has been filed, at the date of reliance on this section, meets the registrant requirements of such Form S–3 . . . and:

(*i*) At such date, meets the minimum float provisions of General Instruction I.B.1 of such Forms; or

(*ii*) At the date of reliance on this section, is, or if a registration statement has not been filed, will be, offering securities meeting the requirements for the offering of investment grade securities pursuant to General Instruction I.B.2 of Form S–3 . . .; or

(*iii*) At the date of reliance on this section is a well-known seasoned issuer as defined in Rule 405, other than a majority-owned subsidiary that is a well-known seasoned issuer by virtue of paragraph (1)(ii) of the definition of well-known seasoned issuer in Rule 405; and

(*2*) As of the date of reliance on this section, has filed all periodic reports required during the preceding 12 months on Forms 10–K, . . ., 10–Q, . . . pursuant to section 13 or section 15(d) of the Securities Exchange Act of 1934; or

(iii) The broker or dealer publishes or distributes research reports in the regular course of its business and such publication or distribution does not represent the initiation of publication of research reports about such issuer or its securities or reinitiation of such publication following discontinuation of publication of such research reports.

(2) *Industry reports.*

(i) The issuer is required to file reports pursuant to section 13 or section 15(d) of the Securities Exchange Act of 1934 or satisfies the conditions in paragraph (a)(1)(i)(B) of this section;

(ii) The condition in paragraph (a)(1)(ii) of this section is satisfied;

(iii) The research report includes similar information with respect to a substantial number of issuers in the issuer's industry or sub-industry, or contains a comprehensive list of securities currently recommended by the broker or dealer; (iv) The analysis regarding the issuer or its securities is given no materially greater space or prominence in the publication than that given to other securities or issuers; and

(v) The broker or dealer publishes or distributes research reports in the regular course of its business and, at the time of the publication or distribution of the research report, is including similar information about the issuer or its securities in similar reports.

(b) *Rule 144A offerings.* If the conditions in paragraph (a)(1) or (a)(2) of this section are satisfied, a broker's or dealer's publication or distribution of a research report shall not be considered an offer for sale or an offer to sell a security or general solicitation or general advertising, in connection with an offering relying on Rule 144A.

(c) *Regulation S offerings.* If the conditions in paragraph (a)(1) or (a)(2) of this section are satisfied, a broker's or dealer's publication or distribution of a research report shall not:

(1) Constitute directed selling efforts as defined in Rule 902(c) for offerings under Regulation S. . . .

(d) *Definition of research report.* For purposes of this section, *research report* means a written communication, as defined in Rule 405, that includes information, opinions, or recommendations with respect to securities of an issuer or an analysis of a security or an issuer, whether or not it provides information reasonably sufficient upon which to base an investment decision.

Rule 144. Persons Deemed Not to Be Engaged in a Distribution and Therefore Not Underwriters

Preliminary Note

Rule 144 is designed to implement the fundamental purposes of the Act, as expressed in its preamble, "To provide full and fair disclosure of the character of the securities sold in interstate commerce and through the mails, and to prevent fraud in the sale thereof ...'' The rule is designed to prohibit the creation of public markets in securities of issuers concerning which adequate current information is not available to the public. At the same time, where adequate current information concerning the issuer is available to the public, the rule permits the public sale in ordinary trading transactions of limited amounts of securities owned by persons controlling, controlled by or under common control with the issuer and by persons who have acquired restricted securities of the issuer.

Certain basic principles are essential to an understanding of the requirement of registration in the Act:

1. If any person utilizes the jurisdictional means to sell any nonexempt security to any other person, the security must be registered unless a statutory exemption can be found for the transaction.

2. In addition to the exemptions found in section 3, four exemptions applicable to transactions in securities are contained in section 4. Three of these section 4 exemptions are clearly not available to anyone acting as an ''underwriter'' of securities. (The fourth, found in section 4(4), is available only to those who act as brokers under certain limited circumstances.) An understanding of the term ''underwriter'' is therefore important to anyone who wishes to determine whether or not an exemption from registration is available for his sale of securities.

The term underwriter is broadly defined in section 2(11) of the Act to mean any person who has purchased from an issuer with a view to, or offers or sells for an issuer in connection with, the distribution of any security, or participates, or has a direct or indirect participation in any such undertaking, or participates or has a participation in the direct or indirect underwriting of any such undertaking. The interpretation of this definition has traditionally focused on the words ''with a view to'' in the phrase ''purchased from an issuer with a view to ... distribution.'' Thus, an investment banking firm which arranges with an issuer for the public sale of its securities is clearly an ''underwriter'' under that section. Individual investors who are not professionals in the securities business may also be ''underwriters'' within the meaning of that term as used in the Act if they act as links in a chain of transactions through which securities move from an issuer to the public. Since it is difficult to ascertain the mental state of the purchaser at the time of his acquisition, subsequent acts and circumstances have been considered to determine whether such person took with a view to distribution at the time of his acquisition. Emphasis has been placed on factors such as the length of time the person has held the securities and whether there has been an unforeseeable change in circumstances of the holder. Experience has shown, however, that reliance upon such factors as the above has not assured adequate protection of investors through the maintenance of informed trading markets and has led to uncertainty in the application of the registration provisions of the Act.

It should be noted that the statutory language of section 2(11) is in the disjunctive. Thus, it is insufficient to conclude that a person is not an underwriter solely because he did not purchase securities from an issuer with a view to their distribution. It must also be established that the person is not offering or selling for an issuer in connection with the distribution of the securities, does not participate or have a direct or indirect participation in any such undertaking, and does not participate or have a participation in the direct or indirect underwriting of such an undertaking.

In determining when a person is deemed not to be engaged in a distribution several factors must be considered.

First, the purpose and underlying policy of the Act to protect investors requires that there be adequate current information concerning the issuer, whether the resales of securities by persons result in a distribution or are effected in trading transactions. Accordingly, the availability of the rule is conditioned on the existence of adequate current public information.

Secondly, a holding period prior to resale is essential, among other reasons, to assure that those persons who buy under a claim of a section 4(2) exemption have assumed the economic risks of investment, and therefore are not acting as conduits for sale to the public of unregistered securities, directly or indirectly, on behalf of an issuer. It should be noted that there is nothing in section 2(11) which places a time limit on a person's status as an underwriter. The public has the same need for protection afforded by registration whether the securities are distributed shortly after their purchase or after a considerable length of time.

A third factor, which must be considered in determining what is deemed not to constitute a "distribution", is the impact of the particular transaction or transactions on the trading markets. Section 4(1) was intended to exempt only routine trading transactions between individual investors with respect to securities already issued and not to exempt distributions by issuers or acts of other individuals who engage in steps necessary to such distributions. Therefore, a person reselling securities under section 4(1) of the Act must sell the securities in such limited quantities and in such a manner as not to disrupt the trading markets. The larger the amount of securities involved, the more likely it is that such resales may involve methods of offering and amounts of compensation usually associated with a distribution rather than routine trading transactions. Thus, solicitation of buy orders or the payment of extra compensation are not permitted by the rule.

In summary, if the sale in question is made in accordance with all of the provisions of the section as set forth below, any person who sells restricted securities shall be deemed not to be engaged in a distribution of such securities and therefore not an underwriter thereof. The rule also provides that any person who sells restricted or other securities on behalf of a person in a control relationship with the issuer shall be deemed not to be engaged in a distribution of such securities and therefore not to be an underwriter thereof, if the sale is made in accordance with all the conditions of the section.

(a) *Definitions*. The following definitions shall apply for the purposes of this section.

(1) An "affiliate" of an issuer is a person that directly, or indirectly through one or more intermediaries, controls, or is controlled by, or is under common control with, such issuer. ...

(3) The term "restricted securities" means:

(i) securities that are acquired directly or indirectly from the issuer, or from an affiliate of the issuer, in a transaction or chain of transactions not involving any public offering;

(ii) securities acquired from the issuer that are subject to the resale limitations of Rule 502(d) under Regulation D ...;

(iii) securities acquired in a transaction or chain of transactions meeting the requirements of Rule 144A....

(b) *Conditions to be met*. Any affiliate or other person who sells restricted securities of an issuer for his own account, or any person who sells restricted or any other securities for the account of an affiliate of the issuer of such securities, shall be deemed not to be engaged in a distribution of such securities and therefore not to be an underwriter thereof within the meaning of section 2(11) of the Act if all of the conditions of this section are met.

(c) *Current public information*. There shall be available adequate current public information with respect to the issuer of the securities. Such information shall be deemed to be available only if either of the following conditions is met:

(1) *Filing of reports*. The issuer has securities registered pursuant to section 12 of the Securities Exchange Act of 1934, has been subject to the reporting requirements of section 13 of that Act for a period of at least 90 days immediately preceding the sale of the securities and has filed all the reports required to be filed thereunder during the 12 months preceding such sale (or for such shorter period that the issuer was required to file such reports), other than form 8–K reports; or has securities registered pursuant to the Securities Act of 1933, has been subject to the reporting requirements of section 15(d) of the Securities Exchange Act of 1934 for a period of at least 90 days immediately preceding the sale of the securities and has filed all the reports required to be filed thereunder during the 12 months preceding such sale (or for such shorter period that the issuer was required to file such reports) other than Form 8–K reports. The person for whose account the

securities are to be sold shall be entitled to rely upon a statement in whichever is the most recent report, quarterly or annual, required to be filed and filed by the issuer that such issuer has filed all reports required to be filed by section 13 or 15(d) of the Securities Exchange Act of 1934 during the preceding 12 months (or for such shorter period that the issuer was required to file such reports), other than Form 8–K reports, and has been subject to such filing requirements for the past 90 days, unless he knows or has reason to believe that the issuer has not complied with such requirements. Such person shall also be entitled to rely upon a written statement from the issuer that it has complied with such reporting requirements unless he knows or has reasons to believe that the issuer has not complied with such requirements.

(2) *Other public information.* If the issuer is not subject to section 13 or 15(d) of the Securities Exchange Act of 1934, there is publicly available the information concerning the issuer specified in paragraph (a)(5)(i) to (xiv), inclusive, and paragraph (a)(5)(xvi) of Rule 15c2–11 [under the 1934 Act]. . . .

(d) *Holding period for restricted securities.* If the securities sold are restricted securities, the following provisions apply:

(1) *General rule.* A minimum of one year must elapse between the later of the date of the acquisition of the securities from the issuer or from an affiliate of the issuer, and any resale of such securities in reliance on this section for the account of either the acquiror or any subsequent holder of those securities. If the acquiror takes the securities by purchase, the one-year period shall not begin until the full purchase price or other consideration is paid or given by the person acquiring the securities from the issuer or from an affiliate of the issuer. . . .

(e) *Limitation on amount of securities sold.* Except as hereinafter provided, the amount of securities which may be sold in reliance upon this rule shall be determined as follows:

(1) *Sales by affiliates.* If restricted or other securities are sold for the account of an affiliate of the issuer, the amount of securities sold, together with all sales of restricted and other securities of the same class for the account of such person within the preceding three months, shall not exceed the greater of

(i) One percent of the shares or other units of the class outstanding as shown by the most recent report or statement published by the issuer, or

(ii) The average weekly reported volume of trading in such securities on all national securities exchanges and/or reported through the automated quotation system of a registered securities association during the four calendar weeks preceding the filing of notice required by paragraph (h), or if no such notice is required the date of receipt of the order to execute the transaction by the broker or the date of execution of the transaction directly with a market maker, or

(iii) The average weekly volume of trading in such securities reported through the consolidated transaction reporting system contemplated by Rule 11Aa3–1 under the Securities Exchange Act of 1934 ... during the four-week period specified in paragraph (e)(1)(ii) of this section.

(2) *Sales by persons other than affiliates.* The amount of restricted securities sold for the account of any person other than an affiliate of the issuer, together with all other sales of restricted securities of the same class for the account of such person within the preceding three months, shall not exceed the amount specified in paragraphs (e)(1)(i), (ii) or (iii) of this section, whichever is applicable, unless the conditions of paragraph (k) of this rule are satisfied. ...

(f) *Manner of sale.* The securities shall be sold in "brokers' transactions" within the meaning of section 4(4) of the Act or in transactions directly with a "market maker," as that term is defined in section 3(a)(38) of the Securities Exchange Act of 1934, and the person selling the securities shall not (1) solicit or arrange for the solicitation of orders to buy the securities in anticipation of or in connection with such transaction, or (2) make any payment in connection with the offer or sale of the securities to any person other than the broker who executes an order to sell the securities. ...

(g) *Brokers' transactions.* The term "brokers' transactions" in section 4(4) of the Act shall for the purposes of this rule be deemed to include transactions by a broker in which such broker:

(1) Does no more than execute the order or orders to sell the securities as agent for the person for whose account the securities are sold; and receives no more than the usual and customary broker's commission;

(2) Neither solicits nor arranges for the solicitation of customers' orders to buy the securities in anticipation of or in connection with the transaction ....

(h) *Notice of proposed sale.* If the amount of securities to be sold in reliance upon the rule during any period of three months exceeds 500 shares or other units or has an aggregate sale price in excess of $10,000, three copies of a notice on Form 144 shall be filed with the Commission at its principal office in Washington, D.C.; and if such securities are admitted to trading on any national securities exchange, one copy of such notice shall also be transmitted to the principal exchange on which such securities are so admitted. The Form 144 shall be signed by the person for whose account the securities are to be sold and shall be transmitted for filing concurrently with either the placing with a broker of an order to execute a sale of securities in reliance upon this rule or the execution directly with a market maker of such a sale. Neither the filing of such notice nor the failure of the Commission to comment thereon shall be deemed to preclude the Commission from taking any action it deems necessary or appropriate with respect to the sale of the securities referred to in such notice. The requirements of this paragraph, however, shall not apply to securities sold for the account of any person other than an affiliate of the issuer, provided the conditions of paragraph (k) of this rule are satisfied.

(i) *Bona fide intention to sell.* The person filing the notice required by paragraph (h) of this section shall have a bona fide intention to sell the securities referred to therein within a reasonable time after the filing of such notice.

(j) *Non-exclusive rule.* Although this rule provides a means for reselling restricted securities and securities held by affiliates without registration, it is not the exclusive means for reselling such securities in that manner. Therefore, it does not eliminate or otherwise affect the availability of any exemption for resales under the Securities Act that a person or entity may be able to rely upon.

(k) *Termination of certain restrictions on sales of restricted securities by persons other than affiliates.* The requirements of paragraphs (c), (e), (f) and (h) of this rule shall not apply to restricted securities sold for the account of a person who is not an affiliate of the issuer at the time of the sale and has not been an affiliate during the preceding three months, provided a period of at least two years has elapsed since the later of the date the securities were acquired from the issuer or from an affiliate of the issuer. The two-year period shall be calculated as described in paragraph (d) of this rule. . . .

Rule 144A. Private Resales of Securities to Institutions

Preliminary Notes

1. This section relates solely to the application of Section 5 of the Act and not to antifraud or other provisions of the federal securities laws.

2. Attempted compliance with this section does not act as an exclusive election; any seller hereunder may also claim the availability of any other applicable exemption from the registration requirements of the Act.

3. In view of the objective of this section and the policies underlying the Act, this section is not available with respect to any transaction or series of transactions that, although in technical compliance with this section, is part of a plan or scheme to evade the registration provisions of the Act. In such cases, registration under the Act is required.

4. Nothing in this section obviates the need for any issuer or any other person to comply with the securities registration or broker-dealer

registration requirements of the Securities Exchange Act of 1934 (the "Exchange Act"), whenever such requirements are applicable.

5. Nothing in this section obviates the need for any person to comply with any applicable state law relating to the offer or sale of securities.

6. Securities acquired in a transaction made pursuant to the provisions of this section are deemed to be "restricted securities" within the meaning of Rule 144(a)(3).

7. The fact that purchasers of securities from the issuer thereof may purchase such securities with a view to reselling such securities pursuant to this section will not affect the availability to such issuer of an exemption under Section 4(2) of the Act, or Regulation D under the Act, from the registration requirements of the Act.

(a) *Definitions*

(1) For purposes of this section, "qualified institutional buyer" shall mean:

(i) Any of the following entities, acting for its own account or the accounts of other qualified institutional buyers, that in the aggregate owns and invests on a discretionary basis at least $100 million in securities of issuers that are not affiliated with the entity:

(A) Any *insurance company* as defined in Section 2(13) of the Act;

> NOTE: A purchase by an insurance company for one or more of its separate accounts, as defined by section 2(a)(37) of the Investment Company Act of 1940 (the "Investment Company Act"), which are neither registered under section 8 of the Investment Company Act nor required to be so registered, shall be deemed to be a purchase for the account of such insurance company.

(B) Any *investment company* registered under the Investment Company Act or any *business development company* as defined in Section 2(a)(48) of that Act;

(C) Any *Small Business Investment Company* licensed by the U.S. Small Business Administration under Section 301(c) or (d) of the Small Business Investment Act of 1958;

(D) Any *plan* established and maintained by a state, its political subdivisions, or any agency or instrumentality of a state or its political subdivisions, for the benefit of its employees;

(E) Any *employee benefit plan* within the meaning of Title I of the Employee Retirement Income Security Act of 1974;

(F) Any *trust fund* whose trustee is a bank or trust company and whose participants are exclusively plans of the types identified in paragraph (a)(1)(i)(D) or (E) of this section, except trust funds that include as participants individual retirement accounts or H.R. 10 plans.

(G) Any *business development company* as defined in Section 202(a)(22) of the Investment Advisers Act of 1940;

(H) Any *organization described in Section 501(c)(3)* of the Internal Revenue Code, corporation (other than a bank as defined in Section 3(a)(2) of the Act or a savings and loan association or other institution referenced in Section 3(a)(5)(A) of the Act or a foreign bank or savings and loan association or equivalent institution), partnership, or Massachusetts or similar business trust; and

(I) Any *investment adviser* registered under the Investment Advisers Act.

(ii) Any *dealer* registered pursuant to Section 15 of the Exchange Act, acting for its own account or the accounts of other qualified institutional buyers, that in the aggregate owns and invests on a discretionary basis at least $10 million of securities of issuers that are not affiliated with the dealer, *provided that* securities constituting the whole or a part of an unsold allotment to or subscription by a dealer as a participant in a public offering shall not be deemed to be owned by such dealer;

(iii) Any *dealer* registered pursuant to Section 15 of the Exchange Act acting in a riskless principal transaction on behalf of a qualified institutional buyer . . .;

(iv) Any investment company registered under the Investment Company Act, acting for its own account or for the accounts of other qualified institutional buyers, that is part of a *family of investment companies* which own in the aggregate at least $100 million in securities of issuers, other than issuers that are affiliated with the investment company or are part of such family of investment companies. "Family of investment companies" means any two or more investment companies registered under the Investment Company Act, except for a unit investment trust whose assets consist solely of shares of one or more registered investment companies, that have the same investment adviser (or, in the case of unit investment trusts, the same depositor) . . .;

(v) Any entity, all of the equity owners of which are qualified institutional buyers, acting for its own account or the accounts of other qualified institutional buyers; and

(vi) Any *bank* as defined in Section 3(a)(2) of the Act, any *savings and loan association* or other institution as referenced in Section 3(a)(5)(A) of the Act, *or any foreign bank or savings and loan association or equivalent institution*, acting for its own account or the accounts of other qualified institutional buyers, that in the aggregate owns and invests on a discretionary basis at least $100 million in securities of issuers that are not affiliated with it and that has an audited net worth of at least $25 million as demonstrated in its latest annual financial statements, as of a date not more than 16 months preceding the date of sale ... in the case of a U.S. bank or savings and loan association, and not more than 18 months preceding such date of sale for a foreign bank or savings and loan association or equivalent institution.

(2) In determining the aggregate amount of securities owned and invested on a discretionary basis by an entity, the following instruments and interests shall be excluded: bank deposit notes and certificates of deposit; loan participations; repurchase agreements; securities owned but subject to a repurchase agreement; and currency, interest rate and commodity swaps.

(3) The aggregate value of securities owned and invested on a discretionary basis by an entity shall be the cost of such securities, except where the entity reports its securities holdings in its financial statements on the basis of their market value, and no current information with respect to the cost of those securities has been published. In the latter event, the securities may be valued at market for purposes of this section....

(5) For purposes of this section, "riskless principal transaction" means a transaction in which a dealer buys a security from any person and makes a simultaneous offsetting sale of such security to a qualified institutional buyer, including another dealer acting as riskless principal for a qualified institutional buyer....

(b) *Sales by Persons Other Than Issuers or Dealers.* Any person, other than the issuer or a dealer, who offers or sells securities in compliance with the conditions set forth in paragraph (d) of this section shall be deemed not to be engaged in a distribution of such securities and therefore not to be an underwriter of such securities within the meaning of Sections 2(11) and 4(1) of the Act.

(c) *Sales by Dealers.* Any dealer who offers or sells securities in compliance with the conditions set forth in paragraph (d) of this section shall be deemed not to be a participant in a distribution of such securities within the meaning of Section 4(3)(C) of the Act and not to be an underwriter of such securities within the meaning of Section 2(11) of the Act, and such securities shall be deemed not to have been offered to the public within the meaning of Section 4(3)(A) of the Act.

(d) *Conditions to Be Met.* To qualify for exemption under this section, an offer or sale must meet the following conditions:

(1) The securities are offered or sold only to a qualified institutional buyer or to an offeree or purchaser that the seller and any person acting on behalf of the seller reasonably believe is a qualified institutional buyer....;

(2) The seller and any person acting on its behalf takes reasonable steps to ensure that the purchaser is aware that the seller may rely on the exemption from the provisions of Section 5 of the Act provided by this section;

(3) The securities offered or sold:

(i) Were not, when issued, of the same class as securities listed on a national securities exchange registered under Section 6 of the Exchange Act or quoted in a U.S. automated inter-dealer quotation system . . . ; and

(ii) Are not securities of an open-end investment company, unit investment trust or face-amount certificate company that is or is required to be registered under Section 8 of the Investment Company Act; and

(4)(i) In the case of securities of an issuer that is neither subject to Section 13 or 15(d) of the Exchange Act, nor exempt from reporting pursuant to Rule 12g3–2(b) under the Exchange Act, nor a foreign government as defined in Rule 405 eligible to register securities under Schedule B of the Act, the holder and a prospective purchaser designated by the holder have the right to obtain from the issuer, upon request of the holder, and the prospective purchaser has received from the issuer, the seller, or a person acting on either of their behalf, at or prior to the time of sale, upon such prospective purchaser's request to the holder or the issuer, the following information (which shall be reasonably current in relation to the date of resale under this section): a very brief statement of the nature of the business of the issuer and the products and services it offers; and the issuer's most recent balance sheet and profit and loss and retained earnings statements, and similar financial statements for such part of the two preceding fiscal years as the issuer has been in operation (the financial statements should be audited to the extent reasonably available).

(ii) The requirement that the information be "reasonably current" will be presumed to be satisfied if:

(A) the balance sheet is as of a date less than 16 months before the date of resale, the statements of profit and loss and retained earnings are for the 12 months preceding the date of such balance sheet, and if such balance sheet is not as of a date less than 6 months before the date of resale, it shall be accompanied by additional statements of profit and loss and retained earnings for the period from the date of such balance sheet to a date less than 6 months before the date of resale; and

(B) the statement of the nature of the issuer's business and its products and services offered is as of a date within 12 months prior to the date of resale; or

(C) with regard to foreign private issuers, the required information meets the timing requirements of the issuer's home country or principal trading markets.

(e) Offers and sales of securities pursuant to this section shall be deemed not to affect the availability of any exemption or safe harbor relating to any previous or subsequent offer or sale of such securities by the issuer or any prior or subsequent holder thereof.

Rule 145. Reclassification of Securities, Mergers, Consolidations and Acquisitions of Assets

Preliminary Note

Rule 145 ... is designed to make available the protection provided by registration under the Securities Act of 1933, as amended (Act), to persons who are offered securities in a business combination of the type described in paragraphs (a)(1), (2) and (3) of the rule. The thrust of the rule is that an "offer," "offer to sell," "offer for sale," or "sale" occurs when there is submitted to security holders a plan or agreement pursuant to which such holders are required to elect, on the basis of what is in substance a new investment decision, whether to accept a new or different security in exchange for their existing security. Rule 145 embodies the Commission's determination that such transactions are subject to the registration requirements of the Act . . . .

Transactions for which statutory exemptions under the Act, including those contained in sections 3(a)(9), (10), (11) and 4(2), are otherwise available are not affected by Rule 145. . . .

Note 2: A reclassification of securities covered by Rule 145 would be exempt from registration pursuant to section 3(a)(9) or (11) of the Act if the conditions of either of these sections are satisfied.

(a) *Transactions within this section.* An "offer," "offer to sell," "offer for sale," or "sale" shall be deemed to be involved, within the meaning of section 2(3) of the Act, so far as the security holders of a corporation or other person are concerned where, pursuant to statutory provisions of the jurisdiction under which such corporation or other person is organized, or pursuant to provisions contained in its certificate of incorporation or similar controlling instruments, or otherwise, there is submitted for the vote or consent of such security holders a plan or agreement for:

(1) *Reclassifications.* A reclassification of securities of such corporation or other person, other than a stock split, reverse stock split, or change in par value, which involves the substitution of a security for another security;

(2) *Mergers of Consolidations.* A statutory merger or consolidation or similar plan or acquisition in which securities of such corporation or other person held by such security holders will become or be exchanged

for securities of any person, unless the sole purpose of the transaction is to change an issuer's domicile solely within the United States; or

(3) *Transfers of assets.* A transfer of assets of such corporation or other person, to another person in consideration of the issuance of securities of such other person or any of its affiliates, if:

(i) Such plan or agreement provides for dissolution of the corporation or other person whose security holders are voting or consenting; or

(ii) Such plan or agreement provides for a pro rata or similar distribution of such securities to the security holders voting or consenting; or

(iii) The board of directors or similar representatives of such corporation or other person, adopts resolutions relative to paragraph (a)(3)(i) or (ii) of this section within 1 year after the taking of such vote or consent; or

(iv) The transfer of assets is a part of a preexisting plan for distribution of such securities, notwithstanding paragraph (a)(3)(i), (ii), or (iii) of this section.

(b) *Communications before a Registration Statement is filed.* Communications made in connection with or relating to a transaction described in paragraph (a) of this section that will be registered under the Act may be made under Rule 135, 165 or 166.

(c) *Persons and parties deemed to be underwriters.* For purposes of this section, any party to any transaction specified in paragraph (a) of this section, other than the issuer, or any person who is an affiliate of such party at the time any such transaction is submitted for vote or consent, who publicly offers or sells securities of the issuer acquired in connection with any such transaction, shall be deemed to be engaged in a distribution and therefore to be an underwriter thereof within the meaning of section 2(11) of the Act. The term "party" as used in this paragraph (c) shall mean the corporations, business entities, or other persons, other than the issuer, whose assets or capital structure are affected by the transactions specified in paragraph (a) of this section.

(d) *Resale provisions for persons and parties deemed underwriters.* Notwithstanding the provisions of paragraph (c), a person or party specified therein shall not be deemed to be engaged in a distribution and therefore not to be an underwriter of registered securities acquired in a transaction specified in paragraph (a) of this section if:

(1) Such securities are sold by such person or party in accordance with the provisions of paragraphs (c), (e), (f) and (g) of Rule 144;

(2) Such person or party is not an affiliate of the issuer and a period of at least one year, as determined in accordance with paragraph (d) of Rule 144, has elapsed since the date the securities were acquired from

the issuer in such transaction, and the issuer meets the requirements of paragraph (c) of Rule 144; or

(3) Such person or party is not, and has not been for at least three months, an affiliate of the issuer, and a period of at least two years, as determined in accordance with paragraph (d) of Rule 144, has elapsed since the date the securities were acquired from the issuer in such transaction. . . .

Rule 147. "Part of an Issue," "Person Resident," and "Doing Business Within" for Purposes of Section 3(a)(11)

Preliminary Notes

1.   This rule shall not raise any presumption that the exemption provided by section 3(a)(11) of the Act is not available for transactions by an issuer which do not satisfy all of the provisions of the rule.

2.   Nothing in this rule obviates the need for compliance with any state law relating to the offer and sale of the securities.

3.   Section 5 of the Act requires that all securities offered by the use of the mails or by any means or instruments of transportation or communication in interstate commerce be registered with the Commission.   Congress, however, provided certain exemptions in the Act from such registration provisions where there was no practical need for registration or where the benefits of registration were too remote. Among those exemptions is that provided by section 3(a)(11) of the Act for transactions in "any security which is a part of an issue offered and sold only to persons resident within a single State or Territory, where the issuer of such security is a person resident and doing business within . . . such State or Territory."   The legislative history of that Section suggests that the exemption was intended to apply only to issues genuinely local in character, which in reality represent local financing by local industries, carried out through local investment.   Rule 147 is intended to provide more objective standards upon which responsible local businessmen intending to raise capital from local sources may rely in claiming the section 3(a)(11) exemption.

All of the terms and conditions of the rule must be satisfied in order for the rule to be available.   These are: (i) That the issuer be a resident of and doing business within the state or territory in which all offers and sales are made;   and (ii) that no part of the issue be offered or sold to non-residents within the period of time specified in the rule.   For purposes of the rule the definition of "issuer" in section 2(4) of the Act shall apply.

All offers, offers to sell, offers for sale, and sales which are part of the same issue must meet all of the conditions of Rule 147 for the rule to be available.   The determination whether offers, offers to sell, offers for sale and sales of securities are part of the same issue (i.e., are deemed to be "integrated") will continue to be a question of fact and will depend on the particular circumstances. See Securities Act of 1933 Release No. 4434 (December 6, 1961) (26 FR 9158). Securities Act Release No. 4434 indicated that in determining whether offers and sales should be regarded as part of the same issue and thus should be integrated any one or more of the following factors may be determinative:

(i) Are the offerings part of a single plan of financing;

(ii) Do the offerings involve issuance of the same class of securities;

(iii) Are the offerings made at or about the same time;

(iv) Is the same type of consideration to be received; and

(v) Are the offerings made for the same general purpose.

Subparagraph (b)(2) of the rule, however, is designed to provide certainty to the extent feasible by identifying certain types of offers and sales of securities which will be deemed not part of an issue, for purposes of the rule only.

Persons claiming the availability of the rule have the burden of proving that they have satisfied all of its provisions. However, the rule does not establish exclusive standards for complying with the section 3(a)(11) exemption. The exemption would also be available if the issuer satisfied the standards set forth in relevant administrative and judicial interpretations at the time of the offering but the issuer would have the burden of proving the availability of the exemption. Rule 147 relates to transactions exempted from the registration requirements of section 5 of the Act by section 3(a)(11). Neither the rule nor section 3(a)(11) provides an exemption from the registration requirements of section 12(g) of the Securities Exchange Act of 1934, the anti-fraud provisions of the federal securities laws, the civil liability provisions of section 12(2) of the Act or other provisions of the federal securities laws.

Finally, in view of the objectives of the rule and the purposes and policies underlying the Act, the rule shall not be available to any person with respect to any offering which, although in technical compliance with the rule, is part of a plan or scheme by such person to make interstate offers or sales of securities. In such cases registration pursuant to the Act is required.

4. The rule provides an exemption for offers and sales by the issuer only. It is not available for offers or sales of securities by other persons. Section 3(a)(11) of the Act has been interpreted to permit offers and sales by persons controlling the issuer, if the exemption provided by that section would have been available to the issuer at the time of the offering. See Securities Act Release No. 4434. Controlling persons who want to offer or sell securities pursuant to section 3(a)(11) may continue to do so in accordance with applicable judicial and administrative interpretations.

(a) *Transactions covered.* Offers, offers to sell, offers for sale and sales by an issuer of its securities made in accordance with all of the terms and conditions of this rule shall be deemed to be part of an issue offered and sold only to persons resident within a single state or territory where the issuer is a person resident and doing business within such state or territory, within the meaning of section 3(a)(11) of the Act.

(b) *Part of an issue.* (1) For purposes of this rule, all securities of the issuer which are part of an issue shall be offered, offered for sale or sold in accordance with all of the terms and conditions of this rule.

(2) For purposes of this rule only, an issue shall be deemed not to include offers, offers to sell, offers for sale or sales of securities of the issuer pursuant to the exemption provided by section 3 or section 4(2) of the Act or pursuant to a registration statement filed under the Act, that take place prior to the six month period immediately preceding or after the six month period immediately following any offers, offers for sale or sales pursuant to this rule, *Provided,* That, there are during either of said six month periods no offers, offers for sale or sales of securities by or for the issuer of the same or similar class as those offered, offered for sale or sold pursuant to the rule.

(c) *Nature of the issuer.* The issuer of the securities shall at the time of any offers and the sales be a person resident and doing business within the state or territory in which all of the offers, offers to sell, offers for sale and sales are made.

(1) The issuer shall be deemed to be a resident of the state or territory in which:

(i) It is incorporated or organized, if a corporation, limited partnership, trust or other form of business organization that is organized under state or territorial law;

(ii) Its principal office is located, if a general partnership or other form of business organization that is not organized under any state or territorial law;

(iii) His principal residence is located if an individual.

(2) The issuer shall be deemed to be doing business within a state or territory if:

(i) The issuer derived at least 80 percent of its gross revenues and those of its subsidiaries on a consolidated basis

(A) For its most recent fiscal year, if the first offer of any part of the issue is made during the first six months of the issuer's current fiscal year; or

(B) For the first six months of its current fiscal year or during the twelve-month fiscal period ending with such six-month period, if the first offer of any part of the issue is made during the last six months of the issuer's current fiscal year

from the operation of a business or of real property located in or from the rendering of services within such state or territory; provided, however, that this provision does not apply to any issuer which has not had gross revenues in excess of $5,000 from the sale of products or services or other conduct of its business for its most recent twelve-month fiscal period;

(ii) The issuer had at the end of its most recent semi-annual fiscal period prior to the first offer of any part of the issue, at least 80 percent of its assets and those of its subsidiaries on a consolidated basis located within such state or territory;

(iii) The issuer intends to use and uses at least 80 percent of the net proceeds to the issuer from sales made pursuant to this rule in connection with the operation of a business or of real property, the purchase of real property located in, or the rendering of services within such state or territory; and

(iv) The principal office of the issuer is located within such state or territory.

(d) *Offerees and purchasers: Person Resident.* Offers, offers to sell, offers for sale and sales of securities that are part of an issue shall be made only to persons resident within the state or territory of which the issuer is a resident. For purposes of determining the residence of offerees and purchasers:

(1) A corporation, partnership, trust or other form of business organization shall be deemed to be a resident of a state or territory if, at the time of the offer and sale to it, it has its principal office within such state or territory.

(2) An individual shall be deemed to be a resident of a state or territory if such individual has, at the time of the offer and sale to him, his principal residence in the state or territory.

(3) A corporation, partnership, trust or other form of business organization which is organized for the specific purpose of acquiring part of an issue offered pursuant to this rule shall be deemed not to be a resident of a state or territory unless all of the beneficial owners of such organization are residents of such state or territory.

(e) *Limitation of resales.* During the period in which securities that are part of an issue are being offered and sold by the issuer, and for a period of nine months from the date of the last sale by the issuer of such securities, all resales of any part of the issue, by any person, shall be made only to persons resident within such state or territory.

(f) *Precautions against interstate offers and sales.* (1) The issuer shall, in connection with any securities sold by it pursuant to this rule:

(i) Place a legend on the certificate or other document evidencing the security stating that the securities have not been registered under the Act and setting forth the limitations on resale contained in paragraph (e) of this section;

(ii) Issue stop transfer instructions to the issuer's transfer agent, if any, with respect to the securities, or, if the issuer transfers its own securities make a notation in the appropriate records of the issuer; and

(iii) Obtain a written representation from each purchaser as to his residence.

(2) The issuer shall, in connection with the issuance of new certificates for any of the securities that are part of the same issue that are presented for transfer during the time period specified in paragraph (e), take the steps required by paragraphs (f)(1)(i) and (ii) of this section.

(3) The issuer shall, in connection with any offers, offers to sell, offers for sale or sales by it pursuant to this rule, disclose, in writing, the limitations on resale contained in paragraph (e) and the provisions of paragraphs (f)(1)(i) and (ii) and paragraph (f)(2) of this section.

Rule 153.   Definition of "Preceded By A Prospectus" As Used in Section 5(b)(2) of the Act, In Relation to Certain Transactions

(a) *Definition of preceded by a prospectus.* The term preceded by a prospectus as used in section 5(b)(2) of the Act, regarding any requirement of a broker or dealer to deliver a prospectus to a broker or dealer as a result of a transaction effected between such parties on or through a national securities exchange or facility thereof, trading facility of a national securities association, or an alternative trading system, shall mean the satisfaction of the conditions in paragraph (b) of this section.

(b) *Conditions.* Any requirement of a broker or dealer to deliver a prospectus for transactions covered by paragraph (a) of this section will be satisfied if:

(1) Securities of the same class as the securities that are the subject of the transaction are trading on that national securities exchange or facility thereof, trading facility of a national securities association, or alternative trading system;

(2) The registration statement relating to the offering is effective and is not the subject of any pending proceeding or examination under section 8(d) or 8(e) of the Act;

(3) Neither the issuer, nor any underwriter or participating dealer is the subject of a pending proceeding under section 8A of the Act in connection with the offering; and

(4) The issuer has filed or will file with the Commission a prospectus that satisfies the requirements of section 10(a) of the Act.

(c) *Definitions.*

(1) The term *national securities exchange,* as used in this section, shall mean a securities exchange registered as a national securities exchange under section 6 of the Securities Exchange Act of 1934.

(2) The term *trading facility*, as used in this section, shall mean a trading facility sponsored and governed by the rules of a registered securities association or a national securities exchange.

(3) The term *alternative trading system*, as used in this section, shall mean an alternative trading system as defined in Rule 300(a) of Regulation ATS under the Securities Exchange Act of 1934 registered with the Commission pursuant to Rule 301 of Regulation ATS under the Securities Exchange Act of 1934.

Rule 155. Integration of Abandoned Offerings

Preliminary Note: Compliance with paragraph (b) or (c) of this section provides a non-exclusive safe harbor from integration of private and registered offerings. Because of the objectives of Rule 155 and the policies underlying the Act, Rule 155 is not available to any issuer for any transaction or series of transactions that, although in technical compliance with the rule, is part of a plan or scheme to evade the registration requirements of the Act.

(a) *Definition of terms.* For the purposes of this section only, a private offering means an unregistered offering of securities that is exempt from registration under Section 4(2) or 4(6) of the Act or Rule 506 of Regulation D.

(b) *Abandoned private offering followed by a registered offering.* A private offering of securities will not be considered part of an offering for which the issuer later files a registration statement if:

(1) No securities were sold in the private offering;

(2) The issuer and any person(s) acting on its behalf terminate all offering activity in the private offering before the issuer files the registration statement;

(3) The Section 10(a) final prospectus and any Section 10 preliminary prospectus used in the registered offering disclose information about the abandoned private offering, including:

(i) The size and nature of the private offering;

(ii) The date on which the issuer abandoned the private offering;

(iii) That any offers to buy or indications of interest given in the private offering were rejected or otherwise not accepted; and

(iv) That the prospectus delivered in the registered offering supersedes any offering materials used in the private offering; and

(4) The issuer does not file the registration statement until at least 30 calendar days after termination of all offering activity in the private offering, unless the issuer and any person acting on its behalf offered

securities in the private offering only to persons who were (or who the issuer reasonably believes were):

(i) Accredited investors (as that term is defined in Rule 501(a)); or

(ii) Persons who satisfy the knowledge and experience standard of Rule 506(b)(2)(ii).

(c) *Abandoned registered offering followed by a private offering.* An offering for which the issuer filed a registration statement will not be considered part of a later commenced private offering if:

(1) No securities were sold in the registered offering;

(2) The issuer withdraws the registration statement under Rule 477;

(3) Neither the issuer nor any person acting on the issuer's behalf commences the private offering earlier than 30 calendar days after the effective date of withdrawal of the registration statement under Rule 477;

(4) The issuer notifies each offeree in the private offering that:

(i) The offering is not registered under the Act;

(ii) The securities will be "restricted securities" (as that term is defined in Rule 144(a)(3)) and may not be resold unless they are registered under the Act or an exemption from registration is available;

(iii) Purchasers in the private offering do not have the protection of Section 11 of the Act; and

(iv) A registration statement for the abandoned offering was filed and withdrawn, specifying the effective date of the withdrawal; and

(5) Any disclosure document used in the private offering discloses any changes in the issuer's business or financial condition that occurred after the issuer filed the registration statement that are material to the investment decision in the private offering.

Rule 159. Information Available to Purchaser at Time of Contract of Sale

(a) For purposes of section 12(a)(2) of the Act only, and without affecting any other rights a purchaser may have, for purposes of determining whether a prospectus or oral statement included an untrue statement of a material fact or omitted to state a material fact necessary in order to make the statements, in the light of the circumstances under which they were made, not misleading at the time of sale (including, without limitation, a contract of sale), any information conveyed to the purchaser only after such time of sale (including such contract of sale) will not be taken into account.

(b) For purposes of section 17(a)(2) of the Act only, and without affecting any other rights the Commission may have to enforce that section, for purposes of determining whether a statement includes or represents any untrue statement of a material fact or any omission to state a material fact necessary in order to make the statements made, in light of the circumstances under which they were made, not misleading at the time of sale (including, without limitation, a contract of sale), any information conveyed to the purchaser only after such time of sale (including such contract of sale) will not be taken into account.

(c) For purposes of section 12(a)(2) of the Act only, knowing of such untruth or omission in respect of a sale (including, without limitation, a contract of sale), means knowing at the time of such sale (including such contract of sale).

Rule 159A. Certain Definitions for Purposes of Section 12(a)(2) of the Act

(a) *Definition of seller for purposes of section 12(a)(2) of the Act.* For purposes of section 12(a)(2) of the Act only, in a primary offering of securities of the issuer, regardless of the underwriting method used to sell the issuer's securities, *seller* shall include the issuer of the securities sold to a person as part of the initial distribution of such securities, and the issuer shall be considered to offer or sell the securities to such person, if the securities are offered or sold to such person by means of any of the following communications:

(1) Any preliminary prospectus or prospectus of the issuer relating to the offering required to be filed pursuant to Rule 424 or Rule 497;

(2) Any free writing prospectus as defined in Rule 405 relating to the offering prepared by or on behalf of the issuer or used or referred to by the issuer and, in the case of an issuer that is an open-end management company registered under the Investment Company Act of 1940, any profile relating to the offering provided pursuant to Rule 498;

(3) The portion of any other free writing prospectus (or, in the case of an issuer that is an investment company registered under the Investment Company Act of 1940 or a business development company as defined in section 2(a)(48) of the Investment Company Act of 1940, any advertisement pursuant to Rule 482) relating to the offering containing material information about the issuer or its securities provided by or on behalf of the issuer; and

(4) Any other communication that is an offer in the offering made by the issuer to such person.

(b) *Definition of by means of for purposes of section 12(a)(2) of the Act.*

(1) For purposes of section 12(a)(2) of the Act only, an offering participant other than the issuer shall not be considered to offer or sell securities that are the subject of a registration statement by means of a

free writing prospectus as to a purchaser unless one or more of the following circumstances shall exist:

(i) The offering participant used or referred to the free writing prospectus in offering or selling the securities to the purchaser;

(ii) The offering participant offered or sold securities to the purchaser and participated in planning for the use of the free writing prospectus by one or more other offering participants and such free writing prospectus was used or referred to in offering or selling securities to the purchaser by one or more of such other offering participants; or

(iii) The offering participant was required to file the free writing prospectus pursuant to the conditions to use in Rule 433.

(2) For purposes of section 12(a)(2) of the Act only, a person will not be considered to offer or sell securities by means of a free writing prospectus solely because another person has used or referred to the free writing prospectus or filed the free writing prospectus with the Commission pursuant to Rule 433.

Rule 162. Submission of Tenders in Registered Exchange Offers

(a) Notwithstanding section 5(a) of the Act, offerors may solicit tenders of securities in an exchange offer subject to Rule 13e–4(e) or Rule 14d–4(b) [under the Securities Exchange Act] before a registration statement is effective as to the security offered, so long as no securities are purchased until the registration statement is effective and the tender offer has expired in accordance with the tender offer rules.

(b) Notwithstanding section 5(b)(2) of the Act, a prospectus that meets the requirements of section 10(a) of the Act need not be delivered to security holders in an exchange offer subject to Rule 12e–4(e) or 14d–4(b), so long as a preliminary prospectus, prospectus supplements and revised prospectuses are delivered to security holders in accordance with Rule 13e–4(e)(2) or Rule 14d–4(b) of this chapter, as applicable.

Rule 163. Exemption from Section 5(c) of the Act for Certain Communications by or on Behalf of Well-known Seasoned Issuers

Preliminary Note to Rule 163

Attempted compliance with this section does not act as an exclusive election and the issuer also may claim the availability of any other applicable exemption or exclusion. Reliance on this section does not affect the availability of any other exemption or exclusion from the requirements of section 5 of the Act.

(a) In an offering by or on behalf of a well-known seasoned issuer, as defined in Rule 405, that will be or is at the time intended to be registered under the Act, an offer by or on behalf of such issuer is exempt from the prohibitions in section 5(c) of the Act on offers to sell, offers for sale, or offers to buy its securities before a registration statement has been filed, provided that:

(1) Any written communication that is an offer made in reliance on this exemption will be a free writing prospectus as defined in Rule 405 and a prospectus under section 2(a)(10) of the Act relating to a public offering of securities to be covered by the registration statement to be filed; and

(2) The exemption from section 5(c) of the Act provided in this section for such written communication that is an offer shall be conditioned on satisfying the conditions in paragraph (b) of this section.

(b) *Conditions*.

(1) *Legend*.

(i) Every written communication that is an offer made in reliance on this exemption shall contain substantially the following legend:

The issuer may file a registration statement (including a prospectus) with the SEC for the offering to which this communication relates. Before you invest, you should read the prospectus in that registration statement and other documents the issuer has filed with the SEC for more complete information about the issuer and this offering. You may get these documents for free by visiting EDGAR on the SEC Web site at www.sec.gov. Alternatively, the company will arrange to send you the prospectus after filing if you request it by calling toll-free 1–8[xx-xxxxxxx].

(ii) The legend also may provide an e-mail address at which the documents can be requested and may indicate that the documents also are available by accessing the issuer's Web site, and provide the Internet address and the particular location of the documents on the Web site.

(iii) An immaterial or unintentional failure to include the specified legend in a free writing prospectus required by this section will not result in a violation of section 5(c) of the Act or the loss of the ability to rely on this section so long as:

(A) A good faith and reasonable effort was made to comply with the specified legend condition;

(B) The free writing prospectus is amended to include the specified legend as soon as practicable after discovery of the omitted or incorrect legend; and

(C) If the free writing prospectus has been transmitted without the specified legend, the free writing prospectus is retransmitted with the legend by substantially the same means as, and directed to substantially the same prospective purchasers to whom, the free writing prospectus was originally transmitted.

(2) *Filing condition.*

(i) Subject to paragraph (b)(2)(ii) of this section, every written communication that is an offer made in reliance on this exemption shall be filed by the issuer with the Commission promptly upon the filing of the registration statement, if one is filed, or an amendment, if one is filed, covering the securities that have been offered in reliance on this exemption.

(ii) The condition that an issuer shall file a free writing prospectus with the Commission under this section shall not apply in respect of any communication that has previously been filed with, or furnished to, the Commission or that the issuer would not be required to file with the Commission pursuant to the conditions of Rule 433 if the communication was a free writing prospectus used after the filing of the registration statement. The condition that the issuer shall file a free writing prospectus with the Commission under this section shall be satisfied if the issuer satisfies the filing conditions (other than timing of filing which is provided in this section) that would apply under Rule 433 if the communication was a free writing prospectus used after the filing of the registration statement.

(iii) An immaterial or unintentional failure to file or delay in filing a free writing prospectus to the extent provided in this section will not result in a violation of section 5(c) of the Act or the loss of the ability to rely on this section so long as:

(A) A good faith and reasonable effort was made to comply with the filing condition; and

(B) The free writing prospectus is filed as soon as practicable after discovery of the failure to file.

(3) *Ineligible offerings.* The exemption in paragraph (a) of this section shall not be available to:

(i) Communications relating to business combination transactions that are subject to Rule 165 or Rule 166; . . .

(c) For purposes of this section, a communication is made by or on behalf of an issuer if the issuer or an agent or representative of the issuer, other than an offering participant who is an underwriter or dealer, authorizes or approves the communication before it is made.

(d) For purposes of this section, a communication for which disclosure would be required under section 17(b) of the Act as a result of consideration given or to be given, directly or indirectly, by or on behalf of an issuer is deemed to be an offer by the issuer and, if a written communication, is deemed to be a free writing prospectus of the issuer.

(e) A communication exempt from section 5(c) of the Act pursuant to this section will not be considered to be in connection with a securities offering registered under the Securities Act for purposes of Rule 100(b)(2)(iv) of Regulation FD under the Securities Exchange Act of 1934.

Rule 163A. Exemption from Section 5(c) of the Act for Certain Communications Made by or on Behalf of Issuers More Than 30 days Before a Registration Statement is Filed

Preliminary Note to Rule 163A

Attempted compliance with this section does not act as an exclusive election and the issuer also may claim the availability of any other applicable exemption or exclusion. Reliance on this section does not affect the availability of any other exemption or exclusion from the requirements of section 5 of the Act.

(a) Except as excluded pursuant to paragraph (b) of this section, in all registered offerings by issuers, any communication made by or on behalf of an issuer more than 30 days before the date of the filing of the registration statement that does not reference a securities offering that is or will be the subject of a registration statement shall not constitute an offer to sell, offer for sale, or offer to buy the securities being offered under the registration statement for purposes of section 5(c) of the Act, provided that the issuer takes reasonable steps within its control to prevent further distribution or publication of such communication during the 30 days immediately preceding the date of filing the registration statement.

(b) The exemption in paragraph (a) of this section shall not be available with respect to the following communications:

. . . Communications relating to business combination transactions that are subject to Rule 165 or Rule 166; . . .

(c) For purposes of this section, a communication is made by or on behalf of an issuer if the issuer or an agent or representative of the issuer, other than an offering participant who is an underwriter or dealer, authorizes or approves the communication before it is made.

(d) A communication exempt from section 5(c) of the Act pursuant to this section will not be considered to be in connection with a securities offering registered under the Securities Act for purposes of Rule 100(b)(2)(iv) of Regulation FD under the Securities Exchange Act of 1934.

Rule 164. Post-filing Free Writing Prospectuses in Connection with Certain Registered Offerings

Preliminary Notes to Rule 164

1. This section is not available for any communication that, although in technical compliance with this section, is part of a plan or scheme to evade the requirements of section 5 of the Act.

2. Attempted compliance with this section does not act as an exclusive election and the person relying on this section also may

claim the availability of any other applicable exemption or exclusion. Reliance on this section does not affect the availability of any other exemption or exclusion from the requirements of section 5 of the Act.

(a) In connection with a registered offering of an issuer meeting the requirements of this section, a free writing prospectus, as defined in Rule 405, of the issuer or any other offering participant, including any underwriter or dealer, after the filing of the registration statement will be a section 10(b) prospectus for purposes of section 5(b)(1) of the Act provided that the conditions set forth in Rule 433 are satisfied.

(b) An immaterial or unintentional failure to file or delay in filing a free writing prospectus as necessary to satisfy the filing conditions contained in Rule 433 will not result in a violation of section 5(b)(1) of the Act or the loss of the ability to rely on this section so long as:

(1) A good faith and reasonable effort was made to comply with the filing condition; and

(2) The free writing prospectus is filed as soon as practicable after discovery of the failure to file.

(c) An immaterial or unintentional failure to include the specified legend in a free writing prospectus as necessary to satisfy the legend condition contained in Rule 433 will not result in a violation of section 5(b)(1) of the Act or the loss of the ability to rely on this section so long as:

(1) A good faith and reasonable effort was made to comply with the legend condition;

(2) The free writing prospectus is amended to include the specified legend as soon as practicable after discovery of the omitted or incorrect legend; and

(3) If the free writing prospectus has been transmitted without the specified legend, the free writing prospectus must be retransmitted with the legend by substantially the same means as, and directed to substantially the same prospective purchasers to whom, the free writing prospectus was originally transmitted.

(d) Solely for purposes of this section, an immaterial or unintentional failure to retain a free writing prospectus as necessary to satisfy the record retention condition contained in Rule 433 will not result in a violation of section 5(b)(1) of the Act or the loss of the ability to rely on this section so long as a good faith and reasonable effort was made to comply with the record retention condition. Nothing in this paragraph will affect, however, any other record retention provisions applicable to the issuer or any offering participant.

(e) *Ineligible issuers* (1) This section and Rule 433 are available only if at the eligibility determination date for the offering in question, determined pursuant to paragraph (h) of this section, the issuer is not an ineligible issuer as defined in Rule 405 (or in the case of any offering participant, other than the issuer, the participant has a reasonable belief that the issuer is not an ineligible issuer);

(2) Notwithstanding paragraph (e)(1) of this section, this section and Rule 433 are available to an ineligible issuer with respect to a free writing prospectus that contains only descriptions of the terms of the securities in the offering or the offering. . . .

(g) *Excluded offerings.* This section and Rule 433 are not available if the issuer is registering a business combination transaction as defined in Rule 165(f)(1) or the issuer, other than a well-known seasoned issuer, is registering an offering on Form S–8.

(h) For purposes of this section and Rule 433, the determination date as to whether an issuer is an ineligible issuer in respect of an offering shall be:

(1) Except as provided in paragraph (h)(2) of this section, the time of filing of the registration statement covering the offering; or

(2) If the offering is being registered pursuant to Rule 415, the earliest time after the filing of the registration statement covering the offering at which the issuer, or in the case of an underwritten offering the issuer or another offering participant, makes a *bona fide* offer, including without limitation through the use of a free writing prospectus, in the offering.

Rule 165.   Offers Made in Connection with a Business Combination Transaction

Preliminary Note: This section is available only to communications relating to business combinations. The exemption does not apply to communications that may be in technical compliance with this section, but have the primary purpose or effect of conditioning the market for another transaction, such as a capital-raising or resale transaction.

(a) *Communications before a registration statement is filed.* Notwithstanding section 5(c) of the Act, the offeror of securities in a business combination transaction to be registered under the Act may make an offer to sell or solicit an offer to buy those securities from and including the first public announcement until the filing of a registration statement related to the transaction, so long as any written communication (other than non-public communications among participants) made in connection with or relating to the transaction (i.e., prospectus) is filed in accordance with Rule 425 and the conditions in paragraph (c) of this section are satisfied.

(b) *Communications after a registration statement is filed.* Notwithstanding section 5(b)(1) of the Act, any written communication (other than non-public communications among participants) made in connection with or relating to a business combination transaction (i.e., prospectus) after the filing of a registration statement related to the transaction need not satisfy the requirements of section 10 of the Act, so long as the prospectus is filed in accordance with Rule 424 or Rule 425 and the conditions in paragraph (c) of this section are satisfied.

(c) *Conditions.* To rely on paragraphs (a) and (b) of this section:

(1) Each prospectus must contain a prominent legend that urges investors to read the relevant documents filed or to be filed with the Commission because they contain important information. The legend also must explain to investors that they can get the documents for free at the Commission's web site and describe which documents are available free from the offeror; and

(2) In an exchange offer, the offer must be made in accordance with the applicable tender offer rules (Rules 14d–1 through 14e–8); and, in a transaction involving the vote of security holders, the offer must be made in accordance with the applicable proxy or information statement rules (Rules 14a–1 through 14a–101 and 14c–1 through 14c–101 [under the Securities Exchange Act]).

(d) *Applicability.* This section is applicable not only to the offeror of securities in a business combination transaction, but also to any other participant that may need to rely on and complies with this section in communicating about the transaction.

(e) *Failure to file or delay in filing.* An immaterial or unintentional failure to file or delay in filing a prospectus described in this section will not result in a violation of section 5(b)(1) or (c) of the Act, so long as:

(1) A good faith and reasonable effort was made to comply with the filing requirement; and

(2) The prospectus is filed as soon as practicable after discovery of the failure to file.

(f) *Definitions.*

(1) *A business combination transaction* means any transaction specified in Rule 145(a) or exchange offer;

(2) A *participant* is any person or entity that is a party to the business combination transaction and any persons authorized to act on their behalf; and

(3) *Public announcement* is any oral or written communication by a participant that is reasonably designed to, or has the effect of, informing the public or security holders in general about the business combination transaction.

Rule 166. Exemption from Section 5(c) for Certain Communications in Connection with Business Combination Transactions

Preliminary Note: This section is available only to communications relating to business combinations. The exemption does not apply to communications that may be in technical compliance with this section, but have the primary purpose or effect of conditioning the market for another transaction, such as a capital-raising or resale transaction.

(a) *Communications.* In a registered offering involving a business combination transaction, any communication made in connection with or relating to the transaction before the first public announcement of the offering will not constitute an offer to sell or a solicitation of an offer to buy the securities offered for purposes of section 5(c) of the Act, so long as the participants take all reasonable steps within their control to prevent further distribution or publication of the communication until either the first public announcement is made or the registration statement related to the transaction is filed.

(b) *Definitions.* The terms business combination transaction, participant and public announcement have the same meaning as set forth in Rule 165(f).

Rule 168. Exemption from Sections 2(a)(10) and 5(c) of the Act for Certain Communications of Regularly Released Factual Business Information and Forward-looking Information

Preliminary Notes to Rule 168.

1. This section is not available for any communication that, although in technical compliance with this section, is part of a plan or scheme to evade the requirements of section 5 of the Act.

2. This section provides a non-exclusive safe harbor for factual business information and forward-looking information released or disseminated as provided in this section. Attempted compliance with this section does not act as an exclusive election and the issuer also may claim the availability of any other applicable exemption or exclusion. Reliance on this section does not affect the availability of any other exemption or exclusion from the definition of prospectus in section 2(a)(10) or the requirements of section 5 of the Act.

3. The availability of this section for a release or dissemination of a communication that contains or incorporates factual business information or forward-looking information will not be affected by another release or dissemination of a communication that contains all or a portion of the same factual business information or forward-looking information that does not satisfy the conditions of this section.

(a) For purposes of sections 2(a)(10) and 5(c) of the Act, the regular release or dissemination by or on behalf of an issuer (and, in the case of an asset-backed issuer, the other persons specified in paragraph (a)(3) of this section) of communications containing factual business information or forward-looking information shall be deemed not to constitute an offer to sell or offer for sale of a security which is the subject of an offering pursuant to a registration statement that the issuer proposes to file, or has filed, or that is effective, if the conditions of this section are satisfied by any of the following:

(1) An issuer that is required to file reports pursuant to section 13 or section 15(d) of the Securities Exchange Act of 1934. . . .

(b) *Definitions.*

(1) *Factual business information* means some or all of the following information that is released or disseminated under the conditions in paragraph (d) of this section, including, without limitation, such factual business information contained in reports or other materials filed with, furnished to, or submitted to the Commission pursuant to the Securities Exchange Act of 1934:

(i) Factual information about the issuer, its business or financial developments, or other aspects of its business;

(ii) Advertisements of, or other information about, the issuer's products or services; and

(iii) Dividend notices.

(2) *Forward-looking information* means some or all of the following information that is released or disseminated under the conditions in paragraph (d) of this section, including, without limitation, such forward-looking information contained in reports or other materials filed with, furnished to, or submitted to the Commission pursuant to the Securities Exchange Act of 1934:

(i) Projections of the issuer's revenues, income (loss), earnings (loss) per share, capital expenditures, dividends, capital structure, or other financial items;

(ii) Statements about the issuer management's plans and objectives for future operations, including plans or objectives relating to the products or services of the issuer;

(iii) Statements about the issuer's future economic performance, including statements of the type contemplated by the management's discussion and analysis of financial condition and results of operation described in Item 303 of Regulations S–B and S–K. . . .

(iv) Assumptions underlying or relating to any of the information described in paragraphs (b)(2)(i), (b)(2)(ii) and (b)(2)(iii) of this section.

(3) For purposes of this section, the release or dissemination of a communication is by or on behalf of the issuer if the issuer or an agent or representative of the issuer, other than an offering participant who is an underwriter or dealer, authorizes or approves such release or dissemination before it is made.

(4) For purposes of this section, in the case of communications of a person specified in paragraph (a)(3) of this section other than the asset-backed issuer, the release or dissemination of a communication is by or on behalf of such other person if such other person or its agent or representative, other than an underwriter or dealer, authorizes or approves such release or dissemination before it is made.

(c) *Exclusion.* A communication containing information about the registered offering or released or disseminated as part of the offering activities in the registered offering is excluded from the exemption of this section.

(d) *Conditions to exemption.* The following conditions must be satisfied:

(1) The issuer ... has previously released or disseminated information of the type described in this section in the ordinary course of its business;

(2) The timing, manner, and form in which the information is released or disseminated is consistent in material respects with similar past releases or disseminations....

Rule 169. Exemption from Sections 2(a)(10) and 5(c) of the Act for Certain Communications of Regularly Released Factual Business Information

Preliminary Notes to Rule 169

1. This section is not available for any communication that, although in technical compliance with this section, is part of a plan or scheme to evade the requirements of section 5 of the Act.

2. This section provides a non-exclusive safe harbor for factual business information released or disseminated as provided in this section. Attempted compliance with this section does not act as an exclusive election and the issuer also may claim the availability of any other applicable exemption or exclusion. Reliance on this section does not affect the availability of any other exemption or exclusion from the definition of prospectus in section 2(a)(10) or the requirements of section 5 of the Act.

3. The availability of this section for a release or dissemination of a communication that contains or incorporates factual business information will not be affected by another release or dissemination of a communication that contains all or a portion of the same factual business information that does not satisfy the conditions of this section.

(a) For purposes of sections 2(a)(10) and 5(c) of the Act, the regular release or dissemination by or on behalf of an issuer of communications containing factual business information shall be deemed not to constitute an offer to sell or offer for sale of a security by an issuer which is the subject of an offering pursuant to a registration statement that the issuer proposes to file, or has filed, or that is effective, if the conditions of this section are satisfied.

(b) *Definitions*.

(1) *Factual business information* means some or all of the following information that is released or disseminated under the conditions in paragraph (d) of this section:

(i) Factual information about the issuer, its business or financial developments, or other aspects of its business; and

(ii) Advertisement of, or other information about, the issuer's products or services.

(2) For purposes of this section, the release or dissemination of a communication is by or on behalf of the issuer if the issuer or an agent or representative of the issuer, other than an offering participant who is an underwriter or dealer, authorizes or approves such release or dissemination before it is made.

(c) *Exclusions*. A communication containing information about the registered offering or released or disseminated as part of the offering activities in the registered offering is excluded from the exemption of this section.

(d) *Conditions to exemption*. The following conditions must be satisfied:

(1) The issuer has previously released or disseminated information of the type described in this section in the ordinary course of its business;

(2) The timing, manner, and form in which the information is released or disseminated is consistent in material respects with similar past releases or disseminations;

(3) The information is released or disseminated for intended use by persons, such as customers and suppliers, other than in their capacities as investors or potential investors in the issuer's securities, by the issuer's employees or agents who historically have provided such information. . . .

Rule 172. Delivery of Prospectuses

(a) *Sending confirmations and notices of allocations*. After the effective date of a registration statement, the following are exempt from the provisions of section 5(b)(1) of the Act if the conditions set forth in paragraph (c) of this section are satisfied:

(1) Written confirmations of sales of securities in an offering pursuant to a registration statement that contain information limited to that called for in Rule 10b–10 under the Securities Exchange Act of 1934 and other information customarily included in written confirmations of sales

of securities, which may include notices provided pursuant to Rule 173; and

(2) Notices of allocation of securities sold or to be sold in an offering pursuant to the registration statement that may include information identifying the securities (including the CUSIP number) and otherwise may include only information regarding pricing, allocation and settlement, and information incidental thereto.

(b) *Transfer of the security.* Any obligation under section 5(b)(2) of the Act to have a prospectus that satisfies the requirements of section 10(a) of the Act precede or accompany the carrying or delivery of a security in a registered offering is satisfied if the conditions in paragraph (c) of this section are met.

(c) *Conditions.*

(1) The registration statement relating to the offering is effective and is not the subject of any pending proceeding or examination under section 8(d) or 8(e) of the Act;

(2) Neither the issuer, nor an underwriter or participating dealer is the subject of a pending proceeding under section 8A of the Act in connection with the offering; and

(3) The issuer has filed with the Commission a prospectus with respect to the offering that satisfies the requirements of section 10(a) of the Act or the issuer will make a good faith and reasonable effort to file such a prospectus within the time required under Rule 424 and, in the event that the issuer fails to file timely such a prospectus, the issuer files the prospectus as soon as practicable thereafter.

(4) The condition in paragraph (c)(3) of this section shall not apply to transactions by dealers requiring delivery of a final prospectus pursuant to section 4(3) of the Act.

(d) *Exclusions.* This section shall not apply to. . . .

. . . A business combination transaction as defined in Rule 165(f)(1). . . .

Rule 173. Notice of Registration

(a) In a transaction that represents a sale by the issuer or an underwriter, or a sale where there is not an exclusion or exemption from the requirement to deliver a final prospectus meeting the requirements of section 10(a) of the Act pursuant to section 4(3) of the Act or Rule 174, each underwriter or dealer selling in such transaction shall provide to each purchaser from it, not later than two business days following the completion of such sale, a copy of the final prospectus or, in lieu of such prospectus, a notice to the effect that the sale was made pursuant to a registration statement or in a transaction in which a final prospectus would have been required to have been delivered in the absence of Rule 172.

(b) If the sale was by the issuer and was not effected by or through an underwriter or dealer, the responsibility to send a prospectus, or in lieu of such prospectus, such notice as set forth in paragraph (a) of this section, shall be the issuer's.

(c) Compliance with the requirements of this section is not a condition to reliance on Rule 172.

(d) A purchaser may request from the person responsible for sending a notice a copy of the final prospectus if one has not been sent.

(e) After the effective date of the registration statement with respect to an offering, notices as set forth in paragraph (a) of this section, are exempt from the provisions of section 5(b)(1) of the Act.

(f) *Exclusions.* This section shall not apply to any ... 1940;

... business combination transaction as defined in Rule 165(f)(1) ...

Rule 174. Delivery of Prospectus by Dealers: Exemptions Under Section 4(3) of the Act

The obligations of a dealer (including an underwriter no longer acting as an underwriter in respect of the security involved in such transactions) to deliver a prospectus in transactions in a security as to which a registration statement has been filed taking place prior to the expiration of the 40– or 90–day period specified in section 4(3) of the Act after the effective date of such registration statement or prior to the expiration of such period after the first date upon which the security was bona fide offered to the public by the issuer or by or through an underwriter after such effective date, whichever is later, shall be subject to the following provisions ...

(b) No prospectus need be delivered if the issuer is subject, immediately prior to the time of filing the registration statement, to the reporting requirements of section 13 or 15(d) of the Securities Exchange Act of 1934.

(c) Where a registration statement relates to offerings to be made from time to time no prospectus need be delivered after the expiration of the initial prospectus delivery period specified in section 4(3) of the Act following the first bona fide offering of securities under such registration statement.

(d) If (1) the registration statement relates to the security of an issuer that is not subject, immediately prior to the time of filing the registration statement, to the reporting requirements of Section 13 or 15(d) of the Securities Exchange Act of 1934, and (2) as of the offering date, the security is listed on a registered national securities exchange or authorized for inclusion in an electronic interdealer quotation system sponsored and governed by the rules of a registered securities association, no prospectus need be delivered after the expiration of twenty-five calendar days after the offering date. For purposes of this provision, the term "offering date" refers to the later of the effective date of the registration statement or the first date on which the security was bona fide offered to the public.

(e) Notwithstanding the foregoing, the period during which a prospectus must be delivered by a dealer shall be:

(1) As specified in section 4(3) of the Act if the registration statement was the subject of a stop order issued under section 8 of the Act; or

(2) As the Commission may provide upon application or on its own motion in a particular case.

(f) Nothing in this section shall affect the obligation to deliver a prospectus pursuant to the provisions of section 5 of the Act by a dealer who is acting as an underwriter with respect to the securities involved or who is engaged in a transaction as to securities constituting the whole or a part of an unsold allotment to or subscription by such dealer as a participant in the distribution of such securities by the issuer or by or through an underwriter. . . .

(h) Any obligation pursuant to Section 4(3) of the Act and this section to deliver a prospectus, other than pursuant to paragraph (g) of this section, may be satisfied by compliance with the provisions of Rule 172.

Rule 175. Liability for Certain Statements by Issuers

(a) A statement within the coverage of paragraph (b) of this section which is made by or on behalf of an issuer or by an outside reviewer retained by the issuer shall be deemed not to be a fraudulent statement (as defined in paragraph (d) of this section), unless it is shown that such statement was made or reaffirmed without a reasonable basis or was disclosed other than in good faith.

(b) This rule applies to the following statements:

(1) A forward-looking statement (as defined in paragraph (c) of this section) made in a document filed with the Commission, in Part I of a quarterly report on Form 10–Q . . ., or in an annual report to shareholders meeting the requirements of Rules 14a–3(b) and (c) or 14c–3(a) and (b) under the Securities Exchange Act of 1934, a statement reaffirming such forward-looking statement subsequent to the date the document was filed or the annual report was made publicly available, or a forward-looking statement made prior to the date the document was filed or the date the annual report was publicly available if such statement is reaffirmed in a filed document, in Part I of a quarterly report on Form 10–Q, or in an annual report made publicly available within a reasonable time after the making of such forward-looking statement; *Provided,* That

(i) At the time such statements are made or reaffirmed, either the issuer is subject to the reporting requirements of section 13(a) or 15(d) of the Securities Exchange Act of 1934 and has complied with the requirements of Rule 13a–1 or 15d–1 thereunder, if applicable, to file its most recent annual report on Form 10–K ...; or if the issuer is not subject to the reporting requirements of section 13(a) or 15(d) of the Securities Exchange Act of 1934, the statements are made in a registration statement filed under [the Securities Act of 1933], offering statement or solicitation of interest written document or broadcast script under Regulation A or pursuant to section 12(b) or (g) of the Securities Exchange Act of 1934, and

(ii) The statements are not made by or on behalf of an issuer that is an investment company registered under the Investment Company Act of 1940; and

(2) Information which is disclosed in a document filed with the Commission, in Part I of a quarterly report on Form 10–Q ... or in an annual report to shareholders meeting the requirements of Rules 14a–3(b) and (c) or 14c–3(a) and (b) under the Securities Exchange Act of 1934 ... and which relates to (i) the effects of changing prices on the business enterprise, ... or (ii) the value of proved oil and gas reserves. ...

(c) For the purpose of this rule, the term "forward-looking statement" shall mean and shall be limited to:

(1) A statement containing a projection of revenues, income (loss), earnings (loss) per share, capital expenditures, dividends, capital structure or other financial items;

(2) A statement of management's plans and objectives for future operations;

(3) A statement of future economic performance contained in management's discussion and analysis of financial condition and results of operations included pursuant to Item 303 of Regulation S–K ... or

(4) Disclosed statements of the assumptions underlying or relating to any of the statements described in paragraphs (c)(1), (2), or (3) of this section.

(d) For the purpose of this rule the term "fraudulent statement" shall mean a statement which is an untrue statement of a material fact, a statement false or misleading with respect to any material fact, an omission to state a material fact necessary to make a statement not misleading, or which constitutes the employment of a manipulative, deceptive, or fraudulent device, contrivance, scheme, transaction, act, practice, course of business, or an artifice to defraud, as those terms are used in the Securities Act of 1933 or the rules or regulations promulgated thereunder.

Rule 176. Circumstances Affecting the Determination of What Constitutes Reasonable Investigation and Reasonable Grounds for Belief Under Section 11 of the Securities Act

In determining whether or not the conduct of a person constitutes a reasonable investigation or a reasonable ground for belief meeting the standard set forth in section 11(c), relevant circumstances include, with respect to a person other than the issuer.

(a) The type of issuer;

(b) The type of security;

(c) The type of person;

(d) The office held when the person is an officer;

(e) The presence or absence of another relationship to the issuer when the person is a director or proposed director;

(f) Reasonable reliance on officers, employees, and others whose duties should have given them knowledge of the particular facts (in the light of the functions and responsibilities of the particular person with respect to the issuer and the filing);

(g) When the person is an underwriter, the type of underwriting arrangement, the role of the particular person as an underwriter and the availability of information with respect to the registrant; and

(h) Whether, with respect to a fact or document incorporated by reference, the particular person had any responsibility for the fact or document at the time of the filing from which it was incorporated. . . .

Rule 215. Accredited Investor

The term "accredited investor" as used in section 2(15)(ii) of the Securities Act of 1933 . . . shall include the following persons:

(a) Any savings and loan association or other institution specified in section 3(a)(5)(A) of the Act whether acting in its individual or fiduciary capacity; any broker or dealer registered pursuant to section 15 of the Securities Exchange Act of 1934; any plan established and maintained by a state, its political subdivisions, or any agency or instrumentality of a state or its political subdivisions, for the benefit of its employees, if such plan has total assets in excess of $5,000,000; any employee benefit plan within the meaning of Title I of the Employee Retirement Income Security Act of 1974, if the investment decision is made by a plan fiduciary, as defined in section 3(21) of such Act, which is a savings and loan association, or if the employee benefit plan has total assets in excess of $5,000,000 or, if a self-directed plan, with investment decisions made solely by persons that are accredited investors;

(b) Any private business development company as defined in section 202(a)(22) of the Investment Advisers Act of 1940;

1693

(c) Any organization described in section 501(c)(3) of the Internal Revenue Code, corporation, Massachusetts or similar business trust, or partnership, not formed for the specific purpose of acquiring the securities offered, with total assets in excess of $5,000,000;

(d) Any director, executive officer, or general partner of the issuer of the securities being offered or sold, or any director, executive officer, or general partner of a general partner of that issuer;

(e) Any natural person whose individual net worth, or joint net worth with that person's spouse, at the time of his purchase exceeds $1,000,000;

(f) Any natural person who had an individual income in excess of $200,000 in each of the two most recent years or joint income with that person's spouse in excess of $300,000 in each of those years and has a reasonable expectation of reaching the same income level in the current year;

(g) Any trust, with total assets in excess of $5,000,000, not formed for the specific purpose of acquiring the securities offered, whose purchase is directed by a sophisticated person as described in Rule 506(b)(2)(ii); and

(h) Any entity in which all of the equity owners are accredited investors.

REGULATION A—CONDITIONAL SMALL ISSUES EXEMPTION

Rule 251. Scope of Exemption

A public offer or sale of securities that meets the following terms and conditions shall be exempt under section 3(b) from the registration requirements of the Securities Act of 1933 (the "Securities Act"):

(a) *Issuer.* The issuer of the securities:

(1) is an entity organized under the laws of the United States or Canada, or any State, Province, Territory or possession thereof, or the District of Columbia, with its principal place of business in the United States or Canada;

(2) is not subject to section 13 or 15(d) of the Securities Exchange Act of 1934 (the "Exchange Act") immediately before the offering;

(3) is not a development stage company that either has no specific business plan or purpose, or has indicated that its business plan is to merge with an unidentified company or companies;

(4) is not an investment company registered or required to be registered under the Investment Company Act of 1940;

(5) is not issuing fractional undivided interests in oil or gas rights ..., or a similar interest in other mineral rights; and

(6) is not disqualified because of Rule 262.

(b) *Aggregate Offering Price.* The sum of all cash and other consideration to be received for the securities ("aggregate offering price") shall not exceed $5,000,000, including no more than $1,500,000 offered by all selling security holders, less the aggregate offering price for all securities sold within the twelve months before the start of and during the offering of securities in reliance upon Regulation A. No affiliate resales are permitted if the issuer has not had net income from continuing operations in at least one of its last two fiscal years. . . .

(c) *Integration With Other Offerings.* Offers and sales made in reliance on this Regulation A will not be integrated with:

(1) prior offers or sales of securities; or

(2) subsequent offers or sales of securities that are:

(i) registered under the Securities Act, except as provided in Rule 254(d);

(ii) made in reliance on Rule 701;

(iii) made pursuant to an employee benefit plan;

(iv) made in reliance on Regulation S; or

(v) made more than six months after the completion of the Regulation A offering.

NOTE: If the issuer offers or sells securities for which the safe harbor rules are unavailable, such offers and sales still may not be integrated with the Regulation A offering, depending on the particular facts and circumstances. . . .

(d) *Offering Conditions.*

(1) *Offers.*

(i) Except as allowed by Rule 254, no offer of securities shall be made unless a Form 1–A offering statement has been filed with the Commission.

(ii) After the Form 1–A offering statement has been filed:

(A) oral offers may be made;

(B) written offers under Rule 255 may be made;

(C) printed advertisements may be published or radio or television broadcasts made, if they state from whom a Preliminary Offering Circular or Final Offering Circular may be obtained, and contain no more than the following information:

(*1*) The name of the issuer of the security;

(*2*) the title of the security, the amount being offered and the per unit offering price to the public;

(*3*) the general type of the issuer's business; and

(*4*) a brief statement as to the general character and location of its property.

(iii) after the Form 1–A offering statement has been qualified, other written offers may be made, but only if accompanied with or preceded by a Final Offering Circular.

(2) *Sales.*

(i) No sale of securities shall be made until:

(A) the Form 1–A offering statement has been qualified;

(B) a Preliminary Offering Circular or Final Offering Circular is furnished to the prospective purchaser at least 48 hours prior to the mailing of the confirmation of sale to that person; and

(C) a Final Offering Circular is delivered to the purchaser with the confirmation of sale, unless it has been delivered to that person at an earlier time.

(ii) Sales by a dealer (including an underwriter no longer acting in that capacity for the security involved in such transaction) that take place within 90 days after the qualification of the Regulation A offering statement may be made only if the dealer delivers a copy of the current offering circular to the purchaser before or with the confirmation of sale. The issuer or underwriter of the offering shall provide requesting dealers with reasonable quantities of the offering circular for this purpose.

(3) *Continuous or delayed offerings.* Continuous or delayed offerings may be made under this Regulation A if permitted by Rule 415.

Rule 252.   Offering Statement

(a) *Documents to Be Included.* The offering statement consists of the facing sheet of Form 1–A, the contents required by the form and any other material information necessary to make the required statements, in the light of the circumstances under which they are made, not misleading. . . .

(e) *Number of Copies and Where to File.* Seven copies of the offering statement, at least one of which is manually signed, shall be filed with the Commission's main office in Washington, D.C. . . .

(g) *Qualification.* (1) If there is no delaying notation as permitted by paragraph (g)(2) of this section or suspension proceeding under Rule 258, an offering statement is qualified without Commission action on the 20th calendar day after its filing.

(2) An offering statement containing the following notation can be qualified only by order of the Commission, unless such notation is

removed prior to Commission action as described in paragraph (g)(3) of this section:

This offering statement shall only be qualified upon order of the Commission, unless a subsequent amendment is filed indicating the intention to become qualified by operation of the terms of Regulation A.

(3) The delaying notation specified in paragraph (g)(2) of this section can be removed only by an amendment to the offering statement that contains the following language:

This offering statement shall become qualified on the 20th calendar day following the filing of this amendment.

(h) *Amendments.*

(1) If any information in the offering statement is amended, an amendment, signed in the same manner as the initial filing, shall be filed. Seven copies of every amendment shall be filed with the Commission's main office in Washington, D.C.

(2) An amendment to include a delaying notation pursuant to paragraph (g)(2) or to remove one pursuant to paragraph (g)(3) of this section after the initial filing of an offering statement may be made by telegram, letter or facsimile transmission. Each such telegraphic amendment shall be confirmed in writing within a reasonable time by filing a signed copy. Such confirmation shall not be deemed an amendment.

Rule 253. Offering Circular

(a) *Contents.* An offering circular shall include the narrative and financial information required by Form 1–A.

(b) *Presentation of Information.* Information in the offering circular shall be presented in a clear, concise and understandable manner and in a type size that is easily readable. Repetition of information should be avoided; cross-referencing of information within the document is permitted.

(c) *Date.* An offering circular shall be dated approximately as of the date of the qualification of the offering statement of which it is a part.

(d) *Cover Page Legend.* The cover page of every offering circular shall display the following statement in capital letters printed in bold-faced type at least as large as that used generally in the body of such offering circular:

THE UNITED STATES SECURITIES AND EXCHANGE COMMISSION DOES NOT PASS UPON THE MERITS OF OR GIVE ITS APPROVAL TO ANY SECURITIES OFFERED OR THE TERMS OF THE OFFERING, NOR DOES IT PASS UPON THE ACCURACY OR COMPLETENESS OF ANY OF-

FERING CIRCULAR OR OTHER SELLING LITERATURE. THESE SECURITIES ARE OFFERED PURSUANT TO AN EXEMPTION FROM REGISTRATION WITH THE COMMISSION; HOWEVER, THE COMMISSION HAS NOT MADE AN INDEPENDENT DETERMINATION THAT THE SECURITIES OFFERED HEREUNDER ARE EXEMPT FROM REGISTRATION.

(e) *Revisions.* (1) An offering circular shall be revised during the course of an offering whenever the information it contains has become false or misleading in light of existing circumstances, material developments have occurred, or there has been a fundamental change in the information initially presented.

(2) An offering circular for a continuous offering shall be updated to include, among other things, updated financial statements, 12 months after the date the offering statement was qualified.

(3) Every revised or updated offering circular shall be filed as an amendment to the offering statement and requalified in accordance with Rule 252.

Rule 254.   Solicitation of Interest Document for Use Prior to an Offering Statement

(a) An issuer may publish or deliver to prospective purchasers a written document or make scripted radio or television broadcasts to determine whether there is any interest in a contemplated securities offering. Following submission of the written document or script of the broadcast to the Commission, as required by paragraph (b) of this section, oral communications with prospective investors and other broadcasts are permitted. The written documents, broadcasts and oral communications are each subject to the antifraud provisions of the federal securities laws. No solicitation or acceptance of money or other consideration, nor of any commitment, binding or otherwise, from any prospective investor is permitted. No sale may be made until qualification of the offering statement.

(b) While not a condition to any exemption pursuant to this section:

(1) On or before the date of its first use, the issuer shall submit a copy of any written document or the script of any broadcast with the Commission's main office in Washington, D.C. (*Attention:* Office of Small Business Review). The document or broadcast script shall either contain or be accompanied by the name and telephone number of a person able to answer questions about the document or the broadcast.

    NOTE: Only solicitation of interest material that contains substantive changes from or additions to previously submitted material needs to be submitted.

(2) The written document or script of the broadcast shall:

(i) state that no money or other consideration is being solicited, and if sent in response, will not be accepted;

(ii) state that no sales of the securities will be made or commitment to purchase accepted until delivery of an offering circular that includes complete information about the issuer and the offering;

(iii) state that an indication of interest made by a prospective investor involves no obligation or commitment of any kind; and

(iv) identify the chief executive officer of the issuer and briefly and in general its business and products.

(3) Solicitations of interest pursuant to this provision may not be made after the filing of an offering statement.

(4) Sales may not be made until 20 calendar days after the last publication or delivery of the document or radio or television broadcast.

(c) Any written document under this section may include a coupon, returnable to the issuer indicating interest in a potential offering, revealing the name, address and telephone number of the prospective investor.

(d) Where an issuer has a bona fide change of intention and decides to register an offering after using the process permitted by this section without having filed the offering statement prescribed by Rule 252, the Regulation A exemption for offers made in reliance upon this section will not be subject to integration with the registered offering, if at least 30 calendar days have elapsed between the last solicitation of interest and the filing of the registration statement with the Commission, and all solicitation of interest documents have been submitted to the Commission. With respect to integration with other offerings, see Rule 251(c).

(e) Written solicitation of interest materials submitted to the Commission and otherwise in compliance with this section shall not be deemed to be a prospectus as defined in Section 2(10) of the Securities Act.

Rule 255. Preliminary Offering Circulars

(a) Prior to qualification of the required offering statement, but after its filing, a written offer of securities may be made if it meets the following requirements:

(1) The outside front cover page of the material bears the caption "Preliminary Offering Circular," the date of issuance, and the following statement, which shall run along the left hand margin of the page and be printed perpendicular to the text, in boldfaced type at least as large as that used generally in the body of such offering circular:

An offering statement pursuant to Regulation A relating to these securities has been filed with the Securities and Exchange Commission.

Information contained in this Preliminary Offering Circular is subject to completion or amendment. These securities may not be sold nor may offers to buy be accepted prior to the time an offering circular which is not designated as a Preliminary Offering Circular is delivered and the offering statement filed with the Commission becomes qualified. This Preliminary Offering Circular shall not constitute an offer to sell or the solicitation of an offer to buy nor shall there be any sales of these securities in any state in which such offer, solicitation or sale would be unlawful prior to registration or qualification under the laws of any such state.

(2) The Preliminary Offering Circular contains substantially the information required in an offering circular by Form 1–A, except that information with respect to offering price, underwriting discounts or commissions, discounts or commissions to dealers, amount of proceeds, conversions rates, call prices, or other matters dependent upon the offering price may be omitted. The outside front cover page of the Preliminary Offering Circular shall include a bona fide estimate of the range of the maximum offering price and maximum number of shares or other units of securities to be offered or a bona fide estimate of the principal amount of debt securities to be offered.

(3) The material is filed as a part of the offering statement.

(b) If a Preliminary Offering Circular is inaccurate or inadequate in any material respect, a revised Preliminary Offering Circular or a complete Offering Circular shall be furnished to all persons to whom securities are to be sold at least 48 hours prior to the mailing of any confirmation of sale to such persons, or shall be sent to such persons under such circumstances that it would normally be received by them 48 hours prior to receipt of confirmation of the sale.

Rule 256. Filing of Sales Material

While not a condition to an exemption pursuant to this provision, seven copies of any advertisement or written communication, or the script of any radio or television broadcast, shall be filed with the main office of the Commission in Washington, D.C.

> *NOTE:* Only sales material that contains substantive changes from or additions from previously filed material needs to be filed.

Rule 257. Reports of Sales and Use of Proceeds

While not a condition to an exemption pursuant to this provision, the issuer and/or each selling security holder shall file seven copies of a report concerning sales and use of proceeds on Form 2–A, or other prescribed form with the main office of the Commission in Washington, D.C. This report shall be filed at the following times:

(a) every six months after the qualification of the offering statement or any amendment until substantially all the proceeds have been applied; and

(b) within 30 calendar days after the termination, completion or final sale of securities in the offering, or the application of the proceeds from the offering, whichever is the latest event. This report should be labelled the final report. For purposes of this section, the temporary investment of proceeds pending final application shall not constitute application of the proceeds.

Rule 258. Suspension of the Exemption

(a) The Commission may at any time enter an order temporarily suspending a Regulation A exemption if it has reason to believe that:

(1) no exemption is available or any of the terms, conditions or requirements of the Regulation have not been complied with, including failures to provide the Commission a copy of the document or broadcast script under Rule 254, to file any sales material as required by Rule 256 or report as required by Rule 257;

(2) the offering statement [or] any sales or solicitation of interest material contains any untrue statement of a material fact or omits to state a material fact necessary in order to make the statements made, in light of the circumstances under which they are made, not misleading;

(3) the offering is being made or would be made in violation of section 17 of the Securities Act;

(4) an event has occurred after the filing of the offering statement which would have rendered the exemption hereunder unavailable if it had occurred prior to such filing;

(5) any person specified in paragraph (a) of Rule 262 has been indicted for any crime or offense of the character specified in paragraph (a)(3) of Rule 262, or any proceeding has been initiated for the purpose of enjoining any such person from engaging in or continuing any conduct or practice of the character specified in paragraph (a)(4) of Rule 262;

(6) any person specified in paragraph (b) of Rule 262 has been indicted for any crime or offense of the character specified in paragraph (b)(1) of Rule 262, or any proceeding has been initiated for the purpose of enjoining any such person from engaging in or continuing any conduct or practice of the character specified in paragraph (b)(2) of Rule 262; or

(7) the issuer or any promoter, officer, director or underwriter has failed to cooperate, or has obstructed or refused to permit the making of an investigation by the Commission in connection with any offering made or proposed to be made in reliance on Regulation A.

(b) Upon the entry of an order under paragraph (a) of this section, the Commission will promptly give notice to the issuer, any underwriter and any selling security holder:

(1) that such order has been entered, together with a brief statement of the reasons for the entry of the order; and

(2) that the Commission upon receipt of a written request within 30 calendar days after the entry of the order, will within 20 calendar days after receiving the request, order a hearing at a place to be designated by the Commission.

(c) If no hearing is requested and none is ordered by the Commission, an order entered under paragraph (a) of this section shall become permanent on the 30th calendar day after its entry and shall remain in effect unless or until it is modified or vacated by the Commission. Where a hearing is requested or is ordered by the Commission, the Commission will, after notice of and opportunity for such hearing, either vacate the order or enter an order permanently suspending the exemption.

(d) The Commission may, at any time after notice of and opportunity for hearing, enter an order permanently suspending the exemption for any reason upon which it could have entered a temporary suspension order under paragraph (a) of this section. Any such order shall remain in effect until vacated by the Commission.

(e) All notices required by this section shall be given by personal service, registered or certified mail to the addresses given by the issuer, any underwriter and any selling security holder in the offering statement.

Rule 259. Withdrawal or Abandonment of Offering Statements

(a) If none of the securities which are the subject of an offering statement have been sold and such offering statement is not the subject of a proceeding under Rule 258, the offering statement may be withdrawn with the Commission's consent. The application for withdrawal shall state the reason the offering statement is to be withdrawn, shall be signed by an authorized representative of the issuer and shall be provided to the main office of the Commission in Washington, D.C.

(b) When an offering statement has been on file with the Commission for nine months without amendment and has not become qualified, the Commission may, in its discretion, proceed in the following manner to determine whether such offering statement has been abandoned by the issuer. If the offering statement has been amended, the 9–month period shall be computed from the date of the latest amendment.

(1) Notice will be sent to the issuer, and to any counsel for the issuer named in the offering statement, by registered or certified mail, return receipt requested, addressed to the most recent addresses for the issuer and issuer's counsel as reflected in the offering statement. Such notice will inform the issuer and issuer's counsel that the offering statement or amendments thereto is out of date and must be either

amended to comply with applicable requirements of Regulation A or be withdrawn within 30 calendar days after the notice.

(2) If the issuer or issuer's counsel fail to respond to such notice by filing a substantive amendment or withdrawing the offering statement or does not furnish a satisfactory explanation as to why the issuer has not done so within 30 calendar days, the Commission may declare the offering statement abandoned.

Rule 260. Insignificant Deviations From a Term, Condition or Requirement of Regulation A

(a) A failure to comply with a term, condition or requirement of Regulation A will not result in the loss of the exemption from the requirements of section 5 of the Securities Act for any offer or sale to a particular individual or entity, if the person relying on the exemption establishes:

(1) the failure to comply did not pertain to a term, condition or requirement directly intended to protect that particular individual or entity;

(2) the failure to comply was insignificant with respect to the offering as a whole, provided that any failure to comply with paragraphs (a), (b), (d)(1) and (3) of Rule 251 shall be deemed to be significant to the offering as a whole; and

(3) a good faith and reasonable attempt was made to comply with all applicable terms, conditions and requirements of Regulation A.

(b) A transaction made in reliance upon Regulation A shall comply with all applicable terms, conditions and requirements of the regulation. Where an exemption is established only through reliance upon paragraph (a) of this section, the failure to comply shall nonetheless be actionable by the Commission under section 20 of the Act.

(c) This provision provides no relief or protection from a proceeding under Rule 258.

Rule 261. Definitions

As used in this Regulation A, all terms have the same meanings as in Rule 405, except that all references to "registrant" in those definitions shall refer to the issuer of the securities to be offered and sold under Regulation A. In addition, these terms have the following meanings:

(a) Final Offering Circular—The current offering circular contained in a qualified offering statement;

(b) Preliminary Offering Circular—The offering circular described in Rule 255(a).

Rule 262. Disqualification Provisions

Unless, upon a showing of good cause and without prejudice to any other action by the Commission, the Commission determines that it is not necessary under the circumstances that the exemption provided by this Regulation A be denied, the exemption shall not be available for the offer or sale of securities, if:

(a) the issuer, any of its predecessors or any affiliated issuer:

(1) has filed a registration statement which is the subject of any pending proceeding or examination under section 8 of the Act, or has been the subject of any refusal order or stop order thereunder within 5 years prior to the filing of the offering statement required by Rule 252;

(2) is subject to any pending proceeding under Rule 258 or any similar section adopted under section 3(b) of the Securities Act, or to an order entered thereunder within 5 years prior to the filing of such offering statement;

(3) has been convicted within 5 years prior to the filing of such offering statement of any felony or misdemeanor in connection with the purchase or sale of any security or involving the making of any false filing with the Commission;

(4) is subject to any order, judgment, or decree of any court of competent jurisdiction temporarily or preliminarily restraining or enjoining, or is subject to any order, judgment or decree of any court of competent jurisdiction, entered within 5 years prior to the filing of such offering statement, permanently restraining or enjoining, such person from engaging in or continuing any conduct or practice in connection with the purchase or sale of any security or involving the making of any false filing with the Commission; or

(5) is subject to a United States Postal Service false representation order entered under 39 U.S.C. § 3005 within 5 years prior to the filing of the offering statement, or is subject to a temporary restraining order or preliminary injunction entered under 39 U.S.C. § 3007 with respect to conduct alleged to have violated 39 U.S.C. § 3005. The entry of an order, judgment or decree against any affiliated entity before the affiliation with the issuer arose, if the affiliated entity is not in control of the issuer and if the affiliated entity and the issuer are not under the common control of a third party who was in control of the affiliated entity at the time of such entry does not come within the purview of this paragraph (a) of this section.

(b) any director, officer or general partner of the issuer, beneficial owner of 10 percent or more of any class of its equity securities, any promoter of the issuer presently connected with it in any capacity, any underwriter of the securities to be offered, or any partner, director or officer of any such underwriter:

(1) has been convicted within 10 years prior to the filing of the offering statement required by Rule 252 of any felony or misdemeanor in connection with the purchase or sale of any security, involving the making of a false filing with the Commission, or arising out of the conduct of the business of an underwriter, broker, dealer, municipal securities dealer, or investment adviser;

(2) is subject to any order, judgment, or decree of any court of competent jurisdiction temporarily or preliminarily enjoining or restraining, or is subject to any order, judgment, or decree of any court of competent jurisdiction, entered within 5 years prior to the filing of such offering statement, permanently enjoining or restraining such person from engaging in or continuing any conduct or practice in connection with the purchase or sale of any security, involving the making of a false filing with the Commission, or arising out of the conduct of the business of an underwriter, broker, dealer, municipal securities dealer, or investment adviser;

(3) is subject to an order of the Commission entered pursuant to section 15(b), 15B(a), or 15B(c) of the Exchange Act, or section 203(e) or (f) of the Investment Advisers Act of 1940;

(4) is suspended or expelled from membership in, or suspended or barred from association with a member of, a national securities exchange registered under section 6 of the Exchange Act or a national securities association registered under section 15A of the Exchange Act for any act or omission to act constituting conduct inconsistent with just and equitable principles of trade; or

(5) is subject to a United States Postal Service false representation order entered under 39 U.S.C. § 3005 within 5 years prior to the filing of the offering statement required by Rule 252, or is subject to a restraining order or preliminary injunction entered under 39 U.S.C. § 3007 with respect to conduct alleged to have violated 39 U.S.C. § 3005.

(c) any underwriter of such securities was an underwriter or was named as an underwriter of any securities:

(1) covered by any registration statement which is the subject of any pending proceeding or examination under section 8 of the Act, or is the subject of any refusal order or stop order entered thereunder within 5 years prior to the filing of the offering statement required by Rule 252; or

(2) covered by any filing which is subject to any pending proceeding under Rule 258 or any similar rule adopted under section 3(b) of the Securities Act, or to an order entered thereunder within 5 years prior to the filing of such offering statement.

FORM 1–A—REGULATION A OFFERING STATEMENT

SECURITIES AND EXCHANGE COMMISSION

FORM 1–A

REGULATION A OFFERING STATEMENT UNDER THE SECURITIES ACT OF 1933

_____

(Exact name of issuer as specified in its charter)

_____

(State or other jurisdiction of incorporation or organization)

_____

(Address, including zip code, and telephone number, including area code of issuer's principal executive offices)

_____

(Name, address, including zip code, and telephone number, including area code, of agent for service)

_____

(Primary Standard Industrial Classification Code Number)   (I.R.S. Employer Identification Number)

. . .

GENERAL INSTRUCTIONS

1. Eligibility Requirements for Use of Form 1–A.

This form is to be used for securities offerings made pursuant to Regulation A. . . . Careful attention should be directed to the terms, conditions and requirements of the regulation, especially Rule 251, inasmuch as the exemption is not available to all issuers or to every type of securities transaction. Further, the aggregate offering amount of securities which may be sold in any 12 month period is strictly limited to $5 million.

II. Preparation and Filing of the Offering Statement.

An offering statement shall be prepared by all persons seeking exemption pursuant to the provisions of Regulation A. Parts I, II and III shall be addressed by all issuers. Part II of the form which relates to the content of the required offering circular provides several alternate formats depending upon the nature and/or business of the issuer; only one format needs to be followed and provided in the offering statement. General information regarding the preparation, format, content of, and where to file the offering statement is contained in Rule 252. Requirements relating to the offering circular are contained in Rules 253 and 255. The offering statement may be printed, mimeographed, lithographed, or typewritten or prepared by any similar process which will result in clearly legible copies.

III. Supplemental Information.

The following information shall be furnished to the Commission as supplemental information:

(1) A statement as to whether or not the amount of compensation to be allowed or paid to the underwriter has been cleared with the NASD.

(2) Any engineering, management or similar report referenced in the offering circular.

(3) Such other information as requested by the staff in support of statements, representations and other assertions contained in the offering statement.

[The balance of Form 1–A is omitted.]

REGULATION C—REGISTRATION....

GENERAL REQUIREMENTS....

Rule 405. Definitions of Terms

Unless the context otherwise requires, all terms used in 400 to 494, inclusive, or in the forms for registration have the same meanings as in the Act and in the general rules and regulations. In addition, the following definitions apply, unless the context otherwise requires:

Affiliate. An "affiliate" of, or person "affiliated" with, a specified person, is a person that directly, or indirectly through one or more intermediaries, controls or is controlled by, or is under common control with, the person specified....

Associate. The term "associate," when used to indicate a relationship with any person, means (1) a corporation or organization (other than the registrant or a majority-owned subsidiary of the registrant) of which such person is an officer or partner or is, directly or indirectly, the beneficial owner of 10 percent or more of any class of equity securities, (2) any trust or other estate in which such person has a substantial beneficial interest or as to which such person serves as trustee or in a similar capacity, and (3) any relative or spouse of such person, or any relative of such spouse, who has the same home as such person or who is a director or officer of the registrant or any of its parents or subsidiaries....

Automatic shelf registration statement. The term *automatic shelf registration statement* means a registration statement filed on Form S–3 or Form F–3 by a well-known seasoned issuer pursuant to General Instruction I.D. or I.C. of such forms, respectively....

1707

Control. The term "control" (including the terms "controlling," "controlled by" and "under common control with") means the possession, direct or indirect, of the power to direct or cause the direction of the management and policies of a person, whether through the ownership of voting securities, by contract, or otherwise. . . .

Equity security. The term "equity security" means any stock or similar security, certificate of interest or participation in any profit sharing agreement, preorganization certificate or subscription, transferable share, voting trust certificate or certificate of deposit for an equity security, limited partnership interest, interest in a joint venture, or certificate of interest in a business trust; any security future on any such security; or any security convertible, with or without consideration into such a security, or carrying any warrant or right to subscribe to or purchase such a security; or any such warrant or right; or any put, call, straddle, or other option or privilege of buying such a security from or selling such a security to another without being bound to do so.

Executive officer. The term "executive officer," when used with reference to a registrant, means its president, any vice president of the registrant in charge of a principal business unit, division or function (such as sales, administration or finance), any other officer who performs a policy making function or any other person who performs similar policy making functions for the registrant. Executive officers of subsidiaries may be deemed executive officers of the registrant if they perform such policy making functions for the registrant. . . .

Free writing prospectus. Except as otherwise specifically provided or the context otherwise requires, a *free writing prospectus* is any written communication as defined in this section that constitutes an offer to sell or a solicitation of an offer to buy the securities relating to a registered offering that is used after the registration statement in respect of the offering is filed (or, in the case of a well-known seasoned issuer, whether or not such registration statement is filed) and is made by means other than:

(1) A prospectus satisfying the requirements of section 10(a) of the Act, Rule 430, Rule 430A, Rule 430B, Rule 430C, or Rule 431;

(2) A written communication used in reliance on Rule 167 and Rule 426; or

(3) A written communication that constitutes an offer to sell or solicitation of an offer to buy such securities that falls within the exception from the definition of prospectus in clause (a) of section 2(a)(10) of the Act. . . .

Graphic communication. The term *graphic communication*, which appears in the definition of "write, written" in section 2(a)(9) of the Act and in the definition of written communication in this section, shall include all forms of electronic media, including, but not limited to, audiotapes, videotapes, facsimiles, CD–ROM, electronic mail, Internet Web sites, substantially similar messages widely distributed (rather than individually distributed) on telephone answering or voice mail systems, computers, computer networks and other forms of computer data compilation. Graphic communication shall not include a communication that, at the time of the communication, originates live, in real-time to a live audience and does not originate in recorded form or otherwise as a graphic communication, although it is transmitted through graphic means. . . .

Ineligible issuer. (1) An *ineligible issuer* is an issuer with respect to which any of the following is true as of the relevant date of determination:

(i) Any issuer that is required to file reports pursuant to section 13 or 15(d) of the Securities Exchange Act of 1934 that has not filed all reports and other materials required to be filed during the preceding 12 months (or for such shorter period that the issuer was required to file such reports pursuant to sections 13 or 15(d) of the Securities Exchange Act of 1934), other than reports on Form 8–K required solely pursuant to an item specified in General Instruction I.A.3(b) of Form S–3. . . .;

(iv) Within the past three years, a petition under the federal bankruptcy laws or any state insolvency law was filed by or against the issuer, or a court appointed a receiver, fiscal agent or similar officer with respect to the business or property of the issuer. . . .

(v) Within the past three years, the issuer or any entity that at the time was a subsidiary of the issuer was convicted of any felony or misdemeanor described in paragraphs (i) through (iv) of section 15(b)(4)(B) of the Securities Exchange Act of 1934;

(vi) Within the past three years (but in the case of a decree or order agreed to in a settlement, not before December 1, 2005), the issuer or any entity that at the time was a subsidiary of the issuer was made the subject of any judicial or administrative decree or order arising out of a governmental action that:

(A) Prohibits certain conduct or activities regarding, including future violations of, the anti-fraud provisions of the federal securities laws;

(B) Requires that the person cease and desist from violating the anti-fraud provisions of the federal securities laws; or

(C) Determines that the person violated the anti-fraud provisions of the federal securities laws;

(vii) The issuer has filed a registration statement that is the subject of any pending proceeding or examination under section 8 of the Act or has been the subject of any refusal order or stop order under section 8 of the Act within the past three years; or

(viii) The issuer is the subject of any pending proceeding under section 8A of the Act in connection with an offering.

(2) An issuer shall not be an ineligible issuer if the Commission determines, upon a showing of good cause, that it is not necessary under the circumstances that the issuer be considered an ineligible issuer. Any such determination shall be without prejudice to any other action by the Commission in any other proceeding or matter with respect to the issuer or any other person.

(3) The date of determination of whether an issuer is an ineligible issuer is as follows:

(i) For purposes of determining whether an issuer is a well-known seasoned issuer, at the date specified for purposes of such determination in paragraph (2) of the definition of well-known seasoned issuer in this section; and

(ii) For purposes of determining whether an issuer or offering participant may use free writing prospectuses in respect of an offering in accordance with the provisions of Rules 164 and 433, at the date in respect of the offering specified in paragraph (h) of Rule 164. . . .

Material. The term "material," when used to qualify a requirement for the furnishing of information as to any subject, limits the information required to those matters to which there is a substantial likelihood that a reasonable investor would attach importance in determining whether to purchase the security registered.

Officer. The term "officer" means a president, vice president, secretary, treasurer or principal financial officer, comptroller or principal accounting officer, and any person routinely performing corresponding functions with respect to any organization whether incorporated or unincorporated.

Parent. A "parent" of a specified person is an affiliate controlling such person directly, or indirectly through one or more intermediaries. . . .

Principal underwriter. The term "principal underwriter" means an underwriter in privity of contract with the issuer of the securities as to which he is underwriter, the term "issuer" having the meaning given in sections 2(4) and 2(11) of the Act.

Promoter. (1) The term "promoter" includes:

(i) Any person who, acting alone or in conjunction with one or more other persons, directly or indirectly takes initiative in founding and organizing the business or enterprise of an issuer; or

(ii) Any person who, in connection with the founding and organizing of the business or enterprise of an issuer, directly or indirectly receives in consideration of services or property, or both services and property, 10 percent or more of any class of securities of the issuer or 10 percent or more of the proceeds from the sale of any class of such securities. However, a person who receives such securities or proceeds either solely as underwriting commissions or solely in consideration of property shall not be deemed a promoter within the meaning of this paragraph if such person does not otherwise take part in founding and organizing the enterprise.

(2) All persons coming within the definition of "promoter" in paragraph (1) of this definition may be referred to as "founders" or "organizers" or by another term provided that such term is reasonably descriptive of those persons' activities with respect to the issuer. . . .

Small Business Issuer. The term "small business issuer" means an entity that meets the following criteria:

(1) has revenues of less than $25,000,000;

(2) is a U.S. or Canadian issuer;

(3) is not an investment company; and

(4) if a majority owned subsidiary, the parent corporation is also a small business issuer.

Provided however, that an entity is not a small business issuer if it has a public float (the aggregate market value of the outstanding voting and non-voting common equity held by nonaffiliates) of $25,000,000 or more. . . .

Subsidiary. A "subsidiary" of a specified person is an affiliate controlled by such person directly, or indirectly through one or more intermediaries. . . .

Voting securities. The term "voting securities" means securities the holders of which are presently entitled to vote for the election of directors. . . .

Well-known seasoned issuer. A *well-known seasoned issuer* is an issuer that, as of the most recent determination date determined pursuant to paragraph (2) of this definition:

(1)(i) Meets all the registrant requirements of General Instruction I.A. of Form S–3 . . . F–3 and either:

(A) As of a date within 60 days of the determination date, has a worldwide market value of its outstanding voting and non-voting common equity held by non-affiliates of $700 million or more; or

(B)(*1*) As of a date within 60 days of the determination date, has issued in the last three years at least $1 billion aggregate principal amount of non-convertible securities, other than common equity, in primary offerings for cash, not exchange, registered under the Act; and

(*2*) Will register only non-convertible securities, other than common equity, and full and unconditional guarantees permitted pursuant to paragraph (1)(ii) of this definition unless, at the determination date, the issuer also is eligible to register a primary offering of its securities relying on General Instruction I.B.1. of Form S–3....

(*3*) Provided that as to a parent issuer only, for purposes of calculating the aggregate principal amount of outstanding non-convertible securities under paragraph (1)(i)(B)(*1*) of this definition, the parent issuer may include the aggregate principal amount of non-convertible securities, other than common equity, of its majority-owned subsidiaries issued in registered primary offerings for cash, not exchange, that it has fully and unconditionally guaranteed, within the meaning of Rule 3–10 of Regulation S–X in the last three years; or

(ii) Is a majority-owned subsidiary of a parent that is a well-known seasoned issuer pursuant to paragraph (1)(i) of this definition and, as to the subsidiaries' securities that are being or may be offered on that parent's registration statement:

(A) The parent has provided a full and unconditional guarantee, as defined in Rule 3–10 of Regulation S–X, of the payment obligations on the subsidiary's securities and the securities are non-convertible securities, other than common equity;

(B) The securities are guarantees of:

(*1*) Non-convertible securities, other than common equity, of its parent being registered; or

(*2*) Non-convertible securities, other than common equity, of another majority-owned subsidiary being registered where there is a full and unconditional guarantee, as defined in Rule 3–10 of Regulation S–X, of such non-convertible securities by the parent; or

(C) The securities of the majority-owned subsidiary meet the conditions of General Instruction I.B.2 of Form S–3....

(iii) Is not an ineligible issuer as defined in this section....

(2) For purposes of this definition, the determination date as to whether an issuer is a well-known seasoned issuer shall be the latest of:

(i) The time of filing of its most recent shelf registration statement; or

(ii) The time of its most recent amendment (by post-effective amendment, incorporated report filed pursuant to section 13 or 15(d) of the Securities Exchange Act of 1934, or form of prospectus) to a shelf registration statement for purposes of complying with section 10(a)(3) of the Act (or if such amendment has not been made within the time period required by section 10(a)(3) of the Act, the date on which such amendment is required); or

(iii) In the event that the issuer has not filed a shelf registration statement or amended a shelf registration statement for purposes of complying with section 10(a)(3) of the Act for sixteen months, the time of filing of the issuer's most recent annual report on Form 10–K ... (or if such report has not been filed by its due date, such due date).

Written communication. Except as otherwise specifically provided or the context otherwise requires, a *written communication* is any communication that is written, printed, a radio or television broadcast, or a graphic communication as defined in this section.

Note to definition of "written communication." A communication that is a radio or television broadcast is a written communication regardless of the means of transmission of the broadcast.

Rule 408. Additional Information.

(a) In addition to the information expressly required to be included in a registration statement, there shall be added such further material information, if any, as may be necessary to make the required statements, in the light of the circumstances under which they are made, not misleading.

(b) Notwithstanding paragraph (a) of this section, unless otherwise required to be included in the registration statement, the failure to include in a registration statement information included in a free writing prospectus will not, solely by virtue of inclusion of the information in a free writing prospectus (as defined in Rule 405), be considered an omission of material information required to be included in the registration statement.

Rule 415. Delayed or Continuous Offering and Sale of Securities

(a) Securities may be registered for an offering to be made on a continuous or delayed basis in the future, *Provided,* That:

(1) The registration statement pertains only to:

(i) Securities which are to be offered or sold solely by or on behalf of a person or persons other than the registrant, a subsidiary of the registrant or a person of which the registrant is a subsidiary;

(ii) Securities which are to be offered and sold pursuant to a dividend or interest reinvestment plan or an employee benefit plan of the registrant;

(iii) Securities which are to be issued upon the exercise of outstanding options, warrants or rights;

(iv) Securities which are to be issued upon conversion of other outstanding securities;

(v) Securities which are pledged as collateral ...;

(vii) Mortgage related securities, including such securities as mortgage backed debt and mortgage participation or pass through certificates;

(viii) Securities which are to be issued in connection with business combination transactions;

(ix) Securities the offering of which will be commenced promptly, will be made on a continuous basis and may continue for a period in excess of 30 days from the date of initial effectiveness;

(x) Securities registered (or qualified to be registered) on Form S–3 ... which are to be offered and sold on an immediate, continuous or delayed basis by or on behalf of the registrant, a majority-owned subsidiary of the registrant or a person of which the registrant is a majority-owned subsidiary. . . .

(2) Securities in paragraph (a)(1)(viii) of this section and securities in paragraph (a)(1)(ix) of this section that are not registered on Form S–3 ... may only be registered in an amount which, at the time the registration statement becomes effective, is reasonably expected to be offered and sold within two years from the initial effective date of the registration.

(3) The registrant furnishes the undertakings required by Item 512(a) of Regulation S–K. . . .

(4) In the case of a registration statement pertaining to an at the market offering of equity securities by or on behalf of the registrant, the offering must come within paragraph (a)(1)(x) of this section. As used in this paragraph, the term "at the market offering" means an offering of equity securities into an existing trading market for outstanding shares of the same class at other than a fixed price.

(5) Securities registered on an automatic shelf registration statement and securities described in paragraphs (a)(1)(vii), (ix), and (x) of this section may be offered and sold only if not more than three years have elapsed since the initial effective date of the registration statement under which they are being offered and sold, *provided, however*, that if a new registration statement has been filed pursuant to paragraph (a)(6) of this section:

(i) If the new registration statement is an automatic shelf registration statement, it shall be immediately effective . . . ; or

(ii) If the new registration statement is not an automatic shelf registration statement:

(A) Securities covered by the prior registration statement may continue to be offered and sold until the earlier of the effective date of the new registration statement or 180 days after the third anniversary of the initial effective date of the prior registration statement; and

(B) A continuous offering of securities covered by the prior registration statement that commenced within three years of the initial effective date may continue until the effective date of the new registration statement if such offering is permitted under the new registration statement.

(6) Prior to the end of the three-year period described in paragraph (a)(5) of this section, an issuer may file a new registration statement covering securities described in such paragraph (a)(5) of this section, which may, if permitted, be an automatic shelf registration statement. The new registration statement and prospectus included therein must include all the information that would be required at that time in a prospectus relating to all offering(s) that it covers. Prior to the effective date of the new registration statement (including at the time of filing in the case of an automatic shelf registration statement), the issuer may include on such new registration statement any unsold securities covered by the earlier registration statement by identifying on the bottom of the facing page of the new registration statement or latest amendment thereto the amount of such unsold securities being included and any filing fee paid in connection with such unsold securities, which will continue to be applied to such unsold securities. The offering of securities on the earlier registration statement will be deemed terminated as of the date of effectiveness of the new registration statement.

Rule 421. Presentation of information in prospectuses....

(b) You must present the information in a prospectus in a clear, concise and understandable manner. You must prepare the prospectus using the following standards:

(1) Present information in clear, concise sections, paragraphs, and sentences. Whenever possible, use short, explanatory sentences and bullet lists;

(2) Use descriptive headings and subheadings;

(3) Avoid frequent reliance on glossaries or defined terms as the primary means of explaining information in the prospectus. Define terms in a glossary or other section of the document only if the meaning is unclear from the context. Use a glossary only if it facilitates understanding of the disclosure; and

(4) Avoid legal and highly technical business terminology.

Note to Rule 421(b):

In drafting the disclosure to comply with this section, you should avoid the following:

1. Legalistic or overly complex presentations that make the substance of the disclosure difficult to understand;

2. Vague "boilerplate" explanations that are imprecise and readily subject to different interpretations;

3. Complex information copied directly from legal documents without any clear and concise explanation of the provision(s); and

4. Disclosure repeated in different sections of the document that increases the size of the document but does not enhance the quality of the information. . . .

(d)(1) To enhance the readability of the prospectus, you must use plain English principles in the organization, language, and design of the front and back cover pages, the summary, and the risk factors section.

(2) You must draft the language in these sections so that at a minimum it substantially complies with each of the following plain English writing principles:

(i) Short sentences;

(ii) Definite, concrete, everyday words;

(iii) Active voice;

(iv) Tabular presentation or bullet lists for complex material, whenever possible;

(v) No legal jargon or highly technical business terms; and

(vi) No multiple negatives.

(3) In designing these sections or other sections of the prospectus, you may include pictures, logos, charts, graphs, or other design elements so long as the design is not misleading and the required information is clear. You are encouraged to use tables, schedules, charts and graphic illustrations of the results of operations, balance sheet, or other financial data that present the data in an understandable manner. Any presentation must be consistent with the financial statements and non-financial information in the prospectus. You must draw the graphs and charts to scale. Any information you provide must not be misleading.

Rule 425. Filing of Certain Prospectuses and Communications under Rule 135 in Connection with Business Combination Transactions

(a) All written communications made in reliance on Rule 165 are prospectuses that must be filed with the Commission under this section on the date of first use.

(b) All written communications that contain no more information than that specified in Rule 135 must be filed with the Commission on or before the date of first use except as provided in paragraph (d)(1) of this section. A communication limited to the information specified in Rule 135 will not be deemed an offer in accordance with Rule 135 even though it is filed under this section.

(c) Each prospectus or Rule 135 communication filed under this section must identify the filer, the company that is the subject of the offering and the Commission file number for the related registration statement or, if that file number is unknown, the subject company's

Exchange Act or Investment Company Act file number, in the upper right corner of the cover page.

(d) Notwithstanding paragraph (a) of this section, the following need not be filed under this section:

(1) Any written communication that is limited to the information specified in Rule 135 and does not contain new or different information from that which was previously publicly disclosed and filed under this section.

(2) Any research report used in reliance on Rule 137, Rule 138 and Rule 139;

(3) Any confirmation described in Rule 10b–10 [under the Securities Exchange Act]; and

(4) Any prospectus filed under Rule 424.

Rule 427.   Contents of Prospectus Used After Nine Months

There may be omitted from any prospectus used more than 9 months after the effective date of the registration statement any information previously required to be contained in the prospectus insofar as later information covering the same subjects, including the latest available certified financial statement, as of a date not more than 16 months prior to the use of the prospectus is contained therein.

Rule 430.   Prospectus for Use Prior to Effective Date

A form of prospectus filed as a part of the registration statement shall be deemed to meet the requirements of section 10 of the Act for the purpose of section 5(b)(1) thereof prior to the effective date of the registration statement, provided such form of prospectus contains substantially the information required by the Act and the rules and regulations thereunder to be included in a prospectus meeting the requirements of section 10(a) of the Act for the securities being registered, or contains substantially that information except for the omission of information with respect to the offering price, underwriting discounts or commissions, discounts or commissions to dealers, amount of proceeds, conversion rates, call prices, or other matters dependent upon the offering price. Every such form of prospectus shall be deemed to have been filed as a part of the registration statement for the purpose of section 7 of the Act.

Rule 431.   Summary Prospectuses

(a) A summary prospectus prepared and filed as a part of a registration statement in accordance with this rule shall be deemed to be a prospectus permitted under section 10(b) of the Act for the purpose of section 5(b)(1) of the Act if the form used for registration of the securities to be offered provides for the use of a summary prospectus and, if the issuer is not a registered open-end investment company, the following conditions are met:

(1)(i) The registrant is organized under the laws of the United States or any State or Territory or the District of Columbia and has its principal business operations in the United States or its territories; or

(ii) The registrant is a foreign private issuer eligible to use Form F–2 . . .;

(2) The registrant has a class of securities registered pursuant to section 12(b) of the Securities Exchange Act of 1934 or has a class of equity securities registered pursuant to section 12(g) of that Act or is required to file reports pursuant to section 15(d) of that Act;

(3) The registrant: (i) Has been subject to the requirements of section 12 or 15(d) of the Securities Exchange Act of 1934 and has filed all the material required to be filed pursuant to sections 13, 14 or 15(d) of that Act for a period of at least thirty-six calendar months immediately preceding the filing of the registration statement; and (ii) has filed in a timely manner all reports required to be filed during the twelve calendar months and any portion of a month immediately preceding the filing of the registration statement and . . .

(4) Neither the registrant nor any of its consolidated or unconsolidated subsidiaries has, since the end of its last fiscal year for which certified financial statements of the registrant and its consolidated subsidiaries were included in a report filed pursuant to section 13(a) or 15(d) of the Securities Exchange Act of 1934: (i) failed to pay any dividend or sinking fund installment on preferred stock; or (ii) defaulted on any installment or installments on indebtedness for borrowed money, or on any rental on one or more long term leases, which defaults in the aggregate are material to the financial position of the registrant and its consolidated and unconsolidated subsidiaries, taken as a whole.

(b) A summary prospectus shall contain the information specified in the instructions as to summary prospectuses in the form used for registration of the securities to be offered. Such prospectus may include any other information the substance of which is contained in the registration statement except as otherwise specifically provided in the instructions as to summary prospectuses in the form used for registration. It shall not include any information the substance of which is not contained in the registration statement except that a summary prospectus may contain any information specified in Rule 134(a). . . .

(c) All information included in a summary prospectus, other than the statement required by paragraph (e) of this section, may be expressed in such condensed or summarized form as may be appropriate in the light of the circumstances under which the prospectus is to be used. The information need not follow the numerical sequence of the items of the form used for registration. Every summary prospectus shall be dated approximately as of the date of its first use.

(d) When used prior to the effective date of the registration statement, a summary prospectus shall be captioned a "Preliminary Summary Prospectus" and shall comply with the applicable requirements relating to a preliminary prospectus.

(e) A statement to the following effect shall be prominently set forth in conspicuous print at the beginning or at the end of every summary prospectus:

"Copies of a more complete prospectus may be obtained from" (Insert name(s), address(es) and telephone number(s)).

Copies of a summary prospectus filed with the Commission pursuant to paragraph (g) of this section may omit the names of persons from whom the complete prospectus may be obtained.

(f) Any summary prospectus published in a newspaper, magazine or other periodical need only be set in type at least as large as 7 point modern type. Nothing in this rule shall prevent the use of reprints of a summary prospectus published in a newspaper, magazine, or other periodical, if such reprints are clearly legible.

(g) Eight copies of every proposed summary prospectus shall be filed as a part of the registration statement, or as an amendment thereto, at least 5 days (exclusive of Saturdays, Sundays and holidays) prior to the use thereof, or prior to the release for publication by any newspaper, magazine or other person, whichever is earlier. The Commission may, however, in its discretion, authorize such use or publication prior to the expiration of the 5-day period upon a written request for such authorization. Within 7 days after the first use or publication thereof, 5 additional copies shall be filed in the exact form in which it was used or published. . . .

Rule 432. Additional Information Required to be Included in Prospectuses Relating to Tender Offers

Notwithstanding the provisions of any form for the registration of securities under the Act, any prospectus relating to securities to be offered in connection with a tender offer for, or a request or invitation for tenders of, securities subject to either Rule 13e–4 or section 14(d) of the Securities Exchange Act of 1934 must include the information required by Rule 13e–4(d)(1) or Rule 14d–6(d)(1), as applicable, in all tender offers, requests or invitations that are published, sent or given to security holders.

Rule 433. Conditions to Permissible Post-filing Free Writing Prospectuses

(a) *Scope of section.* This section applies to any free writing prospectus with respect to securities of any issuer (except as set forth in Rule

164) that are the subject of a registration statement that has been filed under the Act. Such a free writing prospectus that satisfies the conditions of this section may include information the substance of which is not included in the registration statement. Such a free writing prospectus that satisfies the conditions of this section will be a prospectus permitted under section 10(b) of the Act for purposes of sections 2(a)(10), 5(b)(1), and 5(b)(2) of the Act and will, for purposes of considering it a prospectus, be deemed to be public, without regard to its method of use or distribution, because it is related to the public offering of securities that are the subject of a filed registration statement.

(b) *Permitted use of free writing prospectus.* Subject to the conditions of this paragraph (b) and satisfaction of the conditions set forth in paragraphs (c) through (g) of this section, a free writing prospectus may be used under this section and Rule 164 in connection with a registered offering of securities:

(1) *Eligibility and prospectus conditions for seasoned issuers and well-known seasoned issuers.* Subject to the provisions of Rule 164(e), (f), and (g), the issuer or any other offering participant may use a free writing prospectus in the following offerings after a registration statement relating to the offering has been filed that includes a prospectus that, other than by reason of this section or Rule 431, satisfies the requirements of section 10 of the Act:

(i) Offerings of securities registered on Form S–3 pursuant to General Instruction I.B.1, I.B.2, I.B.5, I.C., or I.D. thereof; . . .

(iii) Any other offering not excluded from reliance on this section and Rule 164 of securities of a well-known seasoned issuer; and . . .

(2) *Eligibility and prospectus conditions for non-reporting and unseasoned issuers.* If the issuer does not fall within the provisions of paragraph (b)(1) of this section, then, subject to the provisions of Rule 164(e), (f), and (g), any person participating in the offer or sale of the securities may use a free writing prospectus as follows:

(i) If the free writing prospectus is or was prepared by or on behalf of or used or referred to by an issuer or any other offering participant, if consideration has been or will be given by the issuer or other offering participant for the dissemination (in any format) of any free writing prospectus (including any published article, publication, or advertisement), or if section 17(b) of the Act requires disclosure that consideration has been or will be given by the issuer or other offering participant for any activity described therein in connection with the free writing prospectus, then a registration statement relating to the offering must have been filed that includes a prospectus that, other than by reason of this section or Rule 431, satisfies the requirements of section 10 of the Act, including a price range where required by rule, and the free writing prospectus shall be accompanied or preceded by the most recent such prospectus; *provided, however,* that use of the free writing prospectus is not conditioned on providing the most recent such prospectus if a prior such prospectus has been provided and there is no material change from the prior prospectus reflected in the most recent prospectus; *provided, further* that after effectiveness and availability of a final prospectus meeting the requirements of section 10(a) of the Act, no such earlier prospectus may be provided in satisfaction of this condition, and such final prospectus must precede or accompany any free writing prospectus provided after such availability, whether or not an earlier prospectus had been previously provided. For purposes of paragraph (f) of this section, the prospectus included in the registration statement relating to the offering that has been filed does not have to include a price range otherwise required by rule.

(c) *Information in a free writing prospectus.*

(1) A free writing prospectus used in reliance on this section may include information the substance of which is not included in the registration statement but such information shall not conflict with:

(i) Information contained in the filed registration statement, including any prospectus or prospectus supplement that is part of the registration statement ... and not superseded or modified; or

(ii) Information contained in the issuer's periodic and current reports filed or furnished to the Commission pursuant to section 13 or 15(d) of the Securities Exchange Act of 1934 that are incorporated by reference into the registration statement and not superseded or modified.

(2)(i) A free writing prospectus used in reliance on this section shall contain substantially the following legend:

> The issuer has filed a registration statement (including a prospectus) with the SEC for the offering to which this communication relates. Before you invest, you should read the prospectus in that registration statement and other documents the issuer has filed with the SEC for more complete information about the issuer and this offering. You may get these documents for free by visiting EDGAR on the SEC Web site at www.sec.gov. Alternatively, the issuer, any underwriter or any dealer participating in the offering will arrange to send you the prospectus if you request it by calling toll-free 1–8[xx-xxx-xxxx].

(ii) The legend also may provide an e-mail address at which the documents can be requested and may indicate that the documents also are available by accessing the issuer's Web site and provide the Internet address and the particular location of the documents on the Web site....

(h) *Definitions. For purposes of this section*:

(1) An *issuer free writing prospectus* means a free writing prospectus prepared by or on behalf of the issuer or used or referred to by the issuer....

(2) *Issuer information* means material information about the issuer or its securities that has been provided by or on behalf of the issuer.

(3) A written communication or information is prepared or provided by or on behalf of a person if the person or an agent or representative of the person authorizes the communication or information or approves the communication or information before it is used. An offering participant other than the issuer shall not be an agent or representative of the issuer solely by virtue of its acting as an offering participant. . . .

Rule 460. Distribution of Preliminary Prospectus

(a) Pursuant to the statutory requirement that the Commission in ruling upon requests for acceleration of the effective date of a registration statement shall have due regard to the adequacy of the information respecting the issuer theretofore available to the public, the Commission may consider whether the persons making the offering have taken reasonable steps to make the information contained in the registration statement conveniently available to underwriters and dealers who it is reasonably anticipated will be invited to participate in the distribution of the security to be offered or sold.

(b) As a minimum, reasonable steps to make the information conveniently available would involve the distribution, to each underwriter and dealer who it is reasonably anticipated will be invited to participate in the distribution of the security, a reasonable time in advance of the anticipated effective date of the registration statement, of as many copies of the proposed form of preliminary prospectus permitted by Rule 430 . . . as appears to be reasonable to secure adequate distribution of the preliminary prospectus. . . .

Rule 461. Acceleration of Effective Date

(a) Requests for acceleration of the effective date of a registration statement shall be made by the registrant and the managing underwriters of the proposed issue, or, if there are no managing underwriters, by the principal underwriters of the proposed issue, and shall state the date upon which it is desired that the registration statement shall become effective. Such requests may be made in writing or orally, provided that, if an oral request is to be made, a letter indicating that fact and stating that the registrant and the managing or principal underwriters are aware of their obligations under the Act must accompany the registration statement (or a pre-effective amendment thereto) at the time of filing with the Commission. Written requests may be sent to the Commission by facsimile transmission. If by reason of the expected arrangement in connection with the offering, it is to be requested that the registration statement shall become effective at a particular hour of the day, the Commission must be advised to that effect not later than the second business day before the day which it is desired that the registration statement shall become effective. A person's request for acceleration will be considered confirmation of such person's awareness of the person's obligations under the Act. Not later than the time of filing the last amendment prior to the effective date of the registration statement, the registrant shall inform the Commission as to whether or not the amount of compensation to be allowed or paid to the underwriters and any other arrangements among the registrant, the underwriters and other broker dealers participating in the distribution, as described in the registration statement, have been reviewed to the extent required by the National Association of Securities Dealers, Inc. and such Association has issued a statement expressing no objections to the compensation and other arrangements.

(b) Having due regard to the adequacy of information respecting the registrant theretofore available to the public, to the facility with which the nature of the securities to be registered, their relationship to the capital structure of the registrant issuer and the rights of holders thereof can be understood, and to the public interest and the protection of investors, as provided in section 8(a) of the Act, it is the general policy of the Commission, upon request, as provided in paragraph (a) of this section, to permit acceleration of the effective date of the registration statement as soon as possible after the filing of appropriate amendments, if any. In determining the date on which a registration statement shall become effective, the following are included in the situations in which the Commission considers that the statutory standards of section 8(a) may not be met and may refuse to accelerate the effective date:

(1) Where there has not been a bona fide effort to make the prospectus reasonably concise, readable, and in compliance with the plain English requirements of Rule 421(d) of Regulation C in order to facilitate an understanding of the information in the prospectus.

(2) Where the form of preliminary prospectus, which has been distributed by the issuer or underwriter, is found to be inaccurate or inadequate in any material respect, until the Commission has received satisfactory assurance that appropriate correcting material has been sent to all underwriters and dealers who received such preliminary prospectus or prospectuses in quantity sufficient for their information and the information of others to whom the inaccurate or inadequate material was sent.

(3) Where the Commission is currently making an investigation of the issuer, a person controlling the issuer, or one of the underwriters, if any, of the securities to be offered, pursuant to any of the Acts administered by the Commission. . . .

(5) Where there have been transactions in securities of the registrant by persons connected with or proposed to be connected with the offering which may have artificially affected or may artificially affect the market price of the security being offered.

(6) Where the amount of compensation to be allowed or paid to the underwriters and any other arrangements among the registrant, the underwriters and other broker dealers participating in the distribution, as described in the registration statement, if required to be reviewed by the National Association of Securities Dealers, Inc. (NASD), have been reviewed by the NASD and the NASD has not issued a statement expressing no objections to the compensation and other arrangements.

(c) Insurance against liabilities arising under the Act, whether the cost of insurance is borne by the registrant, the insured or some other person, will not be considered a bar to acceleration, unless the registrant is a registered investment company or a business development company and the cost of such insurance is borne by other than an insured officer or director of the registrant. In the case of such a registrant, the Commission may refuse to accelerate the effective date of the registration statement when the registrant is organized or administered pursuant to any instrument (including a contract for insurance against liabilities arising under the Act) that protects or purports to protect any director or officer of the company against any liability to the company or its security holders to which he or she would otherwise be subject by reason of willful misfeasance, bad faith, gross negligence or reckless disregard of the duties involved in the conduct of his or her office.

REGULATION D—RULES GOVERNING THE LIMITED OFFER AND SALE OF SECURITIES WITHOUT REGISTRATION UNDER THE SECURITIES ACT OF 1933

Preliminary Notes

1. The following rules relate to transactions exempted from the registration requirements of section 5 of the Securities Act of 1933 (the "Act").... Such transactions are not exempt from the antifraud, civil liability, or other provisions of the federal securities laws. Issuers are reminded of their obligation to provide such further material information, if any, as may be necessary to make the information required under this regulation, in light of the circumstances under which it is furnished, not misleading....

3. Attempted compliance with any rule in Regulation D does not act as an exclusive election; the issuer can also claim the availability of any other applicable exemption. For instance, an issuer's failure to satisfy all the terms and conditions of Rule 506 shall not raise any presumption that the exemption provided by section 4(2) of the Act is not available....

5. These rules may be used for business combinations that involve sales by virtue of Rule 145(a) ... or otherwise.

6. In view of the objectives of these rules and the policies underlying the Act, Regulation D is not available to any issuer for any transaction or chain of transactions that, although in technical compliance with these rules, is part of a plan or scheme to evade the registration provisions of the Act. In such cases, registration under the Act is required. . . .

Rule 501. Definitions and Terms Used in Regulation D

As used in Regulation D (Rules 501–506), the following terms shall have the meaning indicated:

(a) *Accredited investor*. "Accredited investor" shall mean any person who comes within any of the following categories, or who the issuer reasonably believes comes within any of the following categories, at the time of the sale of the securities to that person:

(1) Any bank as defined in section 3(a)(2) of the Act, or any savings and loan association or other institution as defined in section 3(a)(5)(A) of the Act whether acting in its individual or fiduciary capacity; any broker or dealer registered pursuant to section 15 of the Securities Exchange Act of 1934; any insurance company as defined in section 2(13) of the Act; any investment company registered under the Investment Company Act of 1940 or a business development company as defined in section 2(a)(48) of that Act; any Small Business Investment Company licensed by the U.S. Small Business Administration under section 301(c) or (d) of the Small Business Investment Act of 1958; any plan established and maintained by a state, its political subdivisions, or any agency or instrumentality of a state or its political subdivisions, for the benefit of its employees, if such plan has total assets in excess of $5,000,000; any employee benefit plan within the meaning of the Employee Retirement Income Security Act of 1974 if the investment decision is made by a plan fiduciary, as defined in section 3(21) of such Act, which is either a bank, savings and loan association, insurance company, or registered investment adviser, or if the employee benefit plan has total assets in excess of $5,000,000 or, if a self-directed plan, with investment decisions made solely by persons that are accredited investors;

(2) Any private business development company as defined in section 202(a)(22) of the Investment Advisers Act of 1940;

(3) Any organization described in section 501(c)(3) of the Internal Revenue Code, corporation, Massachusetts or similar business trust, or partnership, not formed for the specific purpose of acquiring the securities offered, with total assets in excess of $5,000,000;

(4) Any director, executive officer, or general partner of the issuer of the securities being offered or sold, or any director, executive officer, or general partner of a general partner of that issuer;

(5) Any natural person whose individual net worth, or joint net worth with that person's spouse, at the time of his purchase exceeds $1,000,000;

(6) Any natural person who had an individual income in excess of $200,000 in each of the two most recent years or joint income with that person's spouse in excess of $300,000 in each of those years and has a reasonable expectation of reaching the same income level in the current year;

(7) Any trust, with total assets in excess of $5,000,000, not formed for the specific purpose of acquiring the securities offered, whose purchase is directed by a sophisticated person as described in Rule 506(b)(2)(ii); and

(8) Any entity in which all of the equity owners are accredited investors.

(b) *Affiliate.* An "affiliate" of, or person "affiliated" with, a specified person shall mean a person that directly, or indirectly through one or more intermediaries, controls or is controlled by, or is under common control with, the person specified.

(c) *Aggregate offering price.* "Aggregate offering price" shall mean the sum of all cash, services, property, notes, cancellation of debt, or other consideration to be received by an issuer for issuance of its securities. . . .

(d) *Business combination.* "Business combination" shall mean any transaction of the type specified in paragraph (a) of Rule 145 under the Act . . . and any transaction involving the acquisition by one issuer, in exchange for all or a part of its own or its parent's stock, of stock of another issuer if, immediately after the acquisition, the acquiring issuer has control of the other issuer (whether or not it had control before the acquisition).

(e) *Calculation of number of purchasers.* For purposes of calculating the number of purchasers under Rules 505(b) and 506(b) only, the following shall apply:

(1) The following purchasers shall be excluded:

(i) Any relative, spouse or relative of the spouse of a purchaser who has the same principal residence as the purchaser;

(ii) Any trust or estate in which a purchaser and any of the persons related to him as specified in paragraph (e)(1)(i) or (e)(1)(iii) of this Rule 501 collectively have more than 50 percent of the beneficial interest (excluding contingent interests);

(iii) Any corporation or other organization of which a purchaser and any of the persons related to him as specified in paragraph (e)(1)(i) or (e)(1)(ii) of this section collectively are beneficial owners of more than 50 percent of the equity securities (excluding directors' qualifying shares) or equity interests; and

(iv) Any accredited investor....

(f) *Executive officer.* "Executive officer" shall mean the president, any vice president in charge of a principal business unit, division or function (such as sales, administration or finance), any other officer who performs a policy making function, or any other person who performs similar policy making functions for the issuer. Executive officers of subsidiaries may be deemed executive officers of the issuer if they perform such policy making functions for the issuer. ...

(h) *Purchaser representative.* "Purchaser representative" shall mean any person who satisfies all of the following conditions or who the issuer reasonably believes satisfies all of the following conditions:

(1) Is not an affiliate, director, officer or other employee of the issuer, or beneficial owner of 10 percent or more of any class of the equity securities or 10 percent or more of the equity interest in the issuer ...;

(2) Has such knowledge and experience in financial and business matters that he is capable of evaluating, alone, or together with other purchaser representatives of the purchaser, or together with the purchaser, the merits and risks of the prospective investment;

(3) Is acknowledged by the purchaser in writing, during the course of the transaction, to be his purchaser representative in connection with evaluating the merits and risks of the prospective investment; and

(4) Discloses to the purchaser in writing a reasonable time prior to the sale of securities to that purchaser any material relationship between himself or his affiliates and the issuer or its affiliates that then exists, that is mutually understood to be contemplated, or that has existed at any time during the previous two years, and any compensation received or to be received as a result of such relationship.

Rule 502. General Conditions to Be Met

The following conditions shall be applicable to offers and sales made under Regulation D (Rules 501–506):

(a) *Integration.* All sales that are part of the same Regulation D offering must meet all of the terms and conditions of Regulation D. Offers and sales that are made more than six months before the start of a Regulation D offering or are made more than six months after completion of a Regulation D offering will not be considered part of that Regulation D offering, so long as during those six month periods there are no offers or sales of securities by or for the issuer that are of the same or a similar class as those offered or sold under Regulation D, other than those offers or sales of securities under an employee benefit plan....

NOTE: The term "offering" is not defined in the Act or in Regulation D. If the issuer offers or sells securities for which the safe harbor rule in paragraph (a) of this Rule 502 is unavailable, the determination as to whether separate sales of securities are part of the same offering (i.e. are considered "integrated") depends on the particular facts and circumstances. . . .

The following factors should be considered in determining whether offers and sales should be integrated for purposes of the exemptions under Regulation D:

(a) whether the sales are part of a single plan of financing;

(b) whether the sales involve issuance of the same class of securities;

(c) whether the sales have been made at or about the same time;

(d) whether the same type of consideration is received; and

(e) whether the sales are made for the same general purpose. . . .

(b) *Information requirements* —(1) *When information must be furnished.* If the issuer sells securities under Rule 505 or Rule 506 to any purchaser that is not an accredited investor, the issuer shall furnish the information specified in paragraph (b)(2) of this section to such purchaser a reasonable time prior to sale. The issuer is not required to furnish the specified information to purchasers when it sells securities under Rule 504, or to any accredited investor.

NOTE: When an issuer provides information to investors pursuant to paragraph (b)(1), it should consider providing such information to accredited investors as well, in view of the anti-fraud provisions of the federal securities laws.

(2) *Type of information to be furnished.*

(i) If the issuer is not subject to the reporting requirements of section 13 or 15(d) of the Exchange Act, at a reasonable time prior to the sale of securities the issuer shall furnish to the purchaser, to the extent material to an understanding of the issuer, its business and the securities being offered:

(A) *Non-financial statement information.* If the issuer is eligible to use Regulation A, the same kind of information as would be required in Part II of Form 1–A. If the issuer is not eligible to use Regulation A, the same kind of information as required in Part I of a registration statement filed under the Securities Act on the form that the issuer would be entitled to use.

(B) *Financial statement information.* *(1) Offering up to $2,000,000.* The information required in Item 310 of Regulation S–B, except that only the issuer's balance sheet, which shall be dated within 120 days of the start of the offering, must be audited.

(2) Offerings up to $7,500,000. The financial statement information required in Form SB–2. If an issuer, other than a limited partnership, cannot obtain audited financial statements without unreasonable effort or expense, then only the issuer's balance sheet, which shall be dated within 120 days of the start of the offering, must be audited. If the issuer is a limited partnership and cannot obtain the required financial statements without unreasonable effort or expense, it may furnish financial statements that have been prepared on the basis of Federal income tax requirements and examined and reported on in accordance with generally accepted auditing standards by an independent public or certified accountant.

(3) Offerings over $7,500,000. The financial statement as would be required in a registration statement filed under the Act on the form that the issuer would be entitled to use. If an issuer, other than a limited partnership, cannot obtain audited financial statements without unreasonable effort or expense, then only the issuer's balance sheet, which shall be dated within 120 days of the start of the offering, must be audited. If the issuer is a limited partnership and cannot obtain the required financial statements without unreasonable effort or expense, it may furnish financial statements that have been prepared on the basis of Federal income tax requirements and examined and reported on in accordance with generally accepted auditing standards by an independent public or certified accountant....

(ii) If the issuer is subject to the reporting requirements of section 13 or 15(d) of the Exchange Act, at a reasonable time prior to the sale of securities the issuer shall furnish to the purchaser the information specified in paragraph (b)(2)(ii)(A) or (B) of this section, and in either event the information specified in paragraph (b)(2)(ii)(C) of this section:

(A) The issuer's annual report to shareholders for the most recent fiscal year, if such annual report meets the requirements of Rule 14a–3 or 14c–3 under the Exchange Act, the definitive proxy statement filed in connection with that annual report, and, if requested by the purchaser in writing, a copy of the issuer's most recent Form 10–K ... under the Exchange Act.

(B) The information contained in an annual report on Form 10–K ... under the Exchange Act or in a registration statement on Form S–1, Form S–11, or Form S–18 ..., under the Act or on Form 10 under the Exchange Act, whichever filing is the most recent required to be filed.

(C) The information contained in any reports or documents required to be filed by the issuer under sections 13(a), 14(a), 14(c), and 15(d) of the Exchange Act since the distribution or filing of the report or registration statement specified in paragraphs (b)(2)(ii)(A) or (B), and a brief description of the securities being offered, the use of the proceeds from the offering, and any material changes in the issuer's affairs that are not disclosed in the documents furnished. . . .

(iii) Exhibits required to be filed with the Commission as part of a registration statement or report, other than an annual report to shareholders or parts of that report incorporated by reference in a Form 10–K . . . report, need not be furnished to each purchaser that is not an accredited investor if the contents of material exhibits are identified and such exhibits are made available to the purchaser, upon his written request, a reasonable time prior to his purchase.

(iv) At a reasonable time prior to the sale of securities to any purchaser that is not an accredited investor in a transaction under Rule 505 or Rule 506, the issuer shall furnish to the purchaser a brief description in writing of any material written information concerning the offering that has been provided by the issuer to any accredited investor but not previously delivered to such unaccredited purchaser. The issuer shall furnish any portion or all of this information to the purchaser, upon his written request a reasonable time prior to his purchase.

(v) The issuer shall also make available to each purchaser at a reasonable time prior to his purchase of securities in a transaction under Rule 505 or 506 the opportunity to ask questions and receive answers concerning the terms and conditions of the offering and to obtain any additional information which the issuer possesses or can acquire without unreasonable effort or expense that is necessary to verify the accuracy of information furnished under paragraph (b)(2)(i) or (ii) of this Rule 502.

(vi) For business combinations or exchange offers, in addition to information required by Form S–4, the issuer shall provide to each purchaser at the time the plan is submitted to security holders, or, with an exchange, during the course of the transaction and prior to sale, written information about any terms or arrangements of the proposed transactions that are materially different from those for all other security holders. . . .

(vii) At a reasonable time prior to the sale of securities to any purchaser that is not an accredited investor in a transaction under Rules 505 or 506, the issuer shall advise the purchaser of the limitations on resale in the manner contained in paragraph (d)(2) of this Rule. Such disclosure may be contained in other materials required to be provided by this paragraph.

(c) *Limitation on manner of offering.* Except as provided in Rule 504(b)(1), neither the issuer nor any person acting on its behalf shall offer or sell the securities by any form of general solicitation or general advertising, including, but not limited to, the following:

(1) Any advertisement, article, notice or other communication published in any newspaper, magazine, or similar media or broadcast over television or radio; and

(2) Any seminar or meeting whose attendees have been invited by any general solicitation or general advertising;

Provided, however, that publication by an issuer of a notice in accordance with Rule 135c shall not be deemed to constitute general solicitation or general advertising for purposes of this section. . . .

(d) *Limitations on resale.* Except as provided in Rule 504(b)(1), securities acquired in a transaction under Regulation D shall have the status of securities acquired in a transaction under section 4(2) of the Act and cannot be resold without registration under the Act or an exemption therefrom. The issuer shall exercise reasonable care to assure that the purchasers of the securities are not underwriters within the meaning of section 2(11) of the Act, which reasonable care may be demonstrated by the following:

(1) Reasonable inquiry to determine if the purchaser is acquiring the securities for himself or for other persons;

(2) Written disclosure to each purchaser prior to sale that the securities have not been registered under the Act and, therefore, cannot be resold unless they are registered under the Act or unless an exemption from registration is available; and

(3) Placement of a legend on the certificate or other document that evidences the securities stating that the securities have not been registered under the Act and setting forth or referring to the restrictions on transferability and sale of the securities.

While taking these actions will establish the requisite reasonable care, it is not the exclusive method to demonstrate such care. Other actions by the issuer may satisfy this provision. In addition, Rule 502(b)(2)(vii) requires the delivery of written disclosure of the limitations on resale to investors in certain instances.

Rule 503. Filing of Notice of Sales

(a) An issuer offering or selling securities in reliance on Rule 504, Rule 505 or Rule 506 shall file with the Commission five copies of a notice on Form D no later than 15 days after the first sale of securities.

(b) One copy of every notice on Form D shall be manually signed by a person duly authorized by the issuer.

(c) If sales are made under Rule 505, the notice shall contain an undertaking by the issuer to furnish to the Commission, upon the written request of its staff, the information furnished by the issuer under Rule 502(b)(2) to any purchaser that is not an accredited investor.
. . .

Rule 504. Exemption for Limited Offerings and Sales of Securities Not Exceeding $1,000,000

(a) *Exemption.* Offers and sales of securities that satisfy the conditions in paragraph (b) of this Rule 504 by an issuer that is not:

(1) subject to the reporting requirements of section 13 or 15(d) of the Exchange Act;

(2) an investment company; or

(3) a development stage company that either has no specific business plan or purpose or has indicated that its business plan is to engage in a merger or acquisition with an unidentified company or companies, or other entity or person, shall be exempt from the provision of section 5 of the Act under section 3(b) of the Act.

(b) *Conditions to be met.*

(1) *General conditions.* To qualify for exemption under this Rule 504, offers and sales must satisfy the terms and conditions of Rules 501 and Rule 502(a), (c) and (d), except that the provisions of Rule 502(c) and (d) will not apply to offers and sales of securities under this Rule 504 that are made:

(i) Exclusively in one or more states that provide for the registration of the securities, and require the public filing and delivery to investors of a substantive disclosure document before sale, and are made in accordance with those state provisions;

(ii) In one or more states that have no provision for the registration of the securities or the public filing or delivery of a disclosure document before sale, if the securities have been registered in at least one state that provides for such registration, public filing and delivery before sale, offers and sales are made in that state in accordance with such provisions, and the disclosure document is delivered before sale to all purchasers (including those in the states that have no such procedure); or

(iii) Exclusively according to state law exemptions from registration that permit general solicitation and general advertising so long as sales are made only to "accredited investors" as defined in Rule 501(a).

(2) The aggregate offering price for an offering of securities under this Rule 504, as defined in Rule 501(c), shall not exceed $1,000,000, less the aggregate offering price for all securities sold within the twelve months before the start of and during the offering of securities under this Rule 504, in reliance on any exemption under section 3(b), or in violation of section 5(a) of the Securities Act.

NOTE 1: The calculation of the aggregate offering price is illustrated as follows:

If an issuer sold $900,000 on June 1, 1987 under this Rule 504 and an additional $4,100,000 on December 1, 1987 under Rule 505, the issuer could not sell any of its securities under this Rule 504 until December 1, 1988. Until then the issuer must count the December 1, 1987 sale towards the $1,000,000 limit within the preceding twelve months.

NOTE 2: If a transaction under Rule 504 fails to meet the limitation on the aggregate offering price, it does not affect the availability of this Rule 504 for the other transactions considered in applying such limitation. For example, if an issuer sold $1,000,000 worth of its securities on January 1, 1988 under this Rule 504 and an additional $500,000 worth on July 1, 1988, this Rule 504 would not be available for the later sale, but would still be applicable to the January 1, 1988 sale.

Rule 505. Exemption for Limited Offers and Sales of Securities Not Exceeding $5,000,000

(a) *Exemption.* Offers and sales of securities that satisfy the conditions in paragraph (b) of this Rule 505 by an issuer that is not an investment company shall be exempt from the provisions of section 5 of the Act under section 3(b) of the Act.

(b) *Conditions to be met* —(1) *General conditions.* To qualify for exemption under this section, offers and sales must satisfy the terms and conditions of Rules 501 and 502.

(2) *Specific conditions* —(i) *Limitation on aggregate offering price.* The aggregate offering price for an offering of securities under this Rule 505, as defined in Rule 501(c), shall not exceed $5,000,000, less the aggregate offering price for all securities sold within the twelve months before the start of and during the offering of securities under this section in reliance on any exemption under section 3(b) of the Act or in violation of section 5(a) of the Act.

(ii) *Limitation on number of purchasers.* There are no more than or the issuer reasonably believes that there are no more than 35 purchasers of securities from the issuer in any offering under this section.

(iii) *Disqualifications.* No exemption under this section shall be available for the securities of any issuer described in Rule 262 of Regulation A, except that for purposes of this section only:

(A) The term "filing of the offering statement required by Rule 252" as used in Rule 262(a), (b) and (c) shall mean the first sale of securities under this Rule 505;

(B) The term "underwriter" as used in Rule 262(b) and (c) shall mean a person that has been or will be paid directly or indirectly remuneration for solicitation of purchasers in connection with sales of securities under this Rule 505; and

(C) Paragraph (b)(2)(iii) of this Rule 505 shall not apply to any issuer if the Commission determines, upon a showing of good cause, that it is not necessary under the circumstances that the exemption be denied. Any such determination shall be without prejudice to any other action by the Commission in any other proceeding or matter with respect to the issuer or any other person.

Rule 506. Exemption for Limited Offers and Sales Without Regard to Dollar Amount of Offering

(a) *Exemption.* Offers and sales of securities by an issuer that satisfy the conditions in paragraph (b) of this section shall be deemed to be transactions not involving any public offering within the meaning of section 4(2) of the Act.

(b) *Conditions to be met*—(1) *General conditions.* To qualify for an exemption under this Rule 506, offers and sales must satisfy all the terms and conditions of Rules 501 and 502.

(2) *Specific conditions*—(i) *Limitation on number of purchasers.* There are no more than or the issuer reasonably believes that there are no more than 35 purchasers of securities from the issuer in any offering under this section.

(ii) *Nature of purchasers.* Each purchaser who is not an accredited investor either alone or with his purchaser representative(s) has such knowledge and experience in financial and business matters that he is capable of evaluating the merits and risks of the prospective investment, or the issuer reasonably believes immediately prior to making any sale that such purchaser comes within this description.

Rule 507. Disqualifying Provision Relating to Exemptions Under Rule 504, Rule 505 and Rule 506

(a) No exemption under Rule 504, Rule 505 or Rule 506 shall be available for an issuer if such issuer, any of its predecessors or affiliates have been subject to any order, judgment, or decree of any court of competent jurisdiction temporarily, preliminarily or permanently enjoining such person for failure to comply with Rule 503.

(b) Paragraph (a) of this section shall not apply if the Commission determines, upon a showing of good cause, that it is not necessary under the circumstances that the exemption be denied.

Rule 508. Insignificant Deviations From a Term, Condition or Requirement of Regulation D

(a) A failure to comply with a term, condition or requirement of Rule 504, Rule 505 or Rule 506 will not result in the loss of the exemption from the requirements of section 5 of the Act for any offer or sale to a particular individual or entity, if the person relying on the exemption shows:

(1) the failure to comply did not pertain to a term, condition or requirement directly intended to protect that particular individual or entity; and

(2) The failure to comply was insignificant with respect to the offering as a whole, provided that any failure to comply with paragraph (c) of Rule 502, paragraph (b)(2) of Rule 504, paragraphs (b)(2)(i) and (ii) of Rule 505 and paragraph (b)(2)(i) of Rule 506 shall be deemed to be significant to the offering as a whole; and

(3) a good faith and reasonable attempt was made to comply with all applicable terms, conditions and requirements of Rule 504, Rule 505 or Rule 506.

(b) A transaction made in reliance on Rule 504, Rule 505 or Rule 506 shall comply with all applicable terms, conditions and requirements of Regulation D. Where an exemption is established only through reliance upon paragraph (a) of this section, the failure to comply shall nonetheless be actionable by the Commission under section 20 of the Act.

FORM S-1

REGISTRATION STATEMENT UNDER
THE SECURITIES ACT OF 1933

(Exact name of registrant as specified in its charter)

(State or other jurisdiction of incorporation or organization)

(Primary Standard Industrial Classification Code Number)

(I.R.S. Employer Identification No.)

(Address, including zip code, and telephone number, including area code, of registrant's principal executive offices)

(Name, address, including zip code, and telephone number, including area code, of agent for service)

Approximate date of commencement of proposed sale to the public

_____ . . . .

GENERAL INSTRUCTIONS
I. Eligibility Requirements for Use of Form S-1

This Form shall be used for the registration under the Securities Act of 1933 ("Securities Act") of securities of all registrants for which no other form is authorized or prescribed, except that this Form shall not be used for securities of foreign governments or political subdivisions thereof....

PART I—INFORMATION REQUIRED IN PROSPECTUS....

Item 3. Summary Information, Risk Factors and Ratio of Earnings to Fixed Charges....

Item 4. Use of Proceeds....

Item 5. Determination of Offering Price....

Item 6. Dilution....

Item 7. Selling Security Holders....

Item 8. Plan of Distribution....

Item 9. Description of Securities to Be Registered....

Item 10. Interests of Named Experts and Counsel....

Item 11. Information With Respect to the Registrant. Furnish the following information with respect to the registrant:

(a) Information required by Item 101 of Regulation S–K ... [concerning] description of business;

(b) Information required by Item 102 of Regulation S–K ... [concerning] description of property;

(c) Information required by Item 103 of Regulation S–K ... [concerning] legal proceedings;

(d) Where common equity securities are being offered, information required by Item 201 of Regulation S–K ... [concerning] market price of and dividends on the registrant's common equity and related stockholder matters;

(e) Financial statements meeting the requirements of Regulation S–X ...

(f) Information required by Item 301 of Regulation S–K ... [concerning] selected financial data;

(g) Information required by Item 302 of Regulation S–K ... [concerning] supplementary financial information;

(h) Information required by Item 303 of Regulation S–K ... [concerning] management's discussion and analysis of financial condition and results of operations;

(i) Information required by Item 304 of Regulation S–K ... [concerning] changes in and disagreements with accountants on accounting and financial disclosure;

(j) Information required by Item 401 of Regulation S–K ... [concerning] directors and executive officers;

(k) Information required by Item 402 of Regulation S–K ... [concerning] executive compensation;

(*l*) Information required by Item 403 of Regulation S–K ... [concerning] security ownership of certain beneficial owners and management;

(m) Information required by Item 404 of Regulation S–K ... [concerning] certain relationships and related transactions. ...

Item 11A. Material Changes.

If the registrant elects to incorporate information by reference pursuant to General Instruction VII., describe any and all material changes in the registrant's affairs which have occurred since the end of the latest fiscal year for which audited financial statements were included in the latest Form 10–K ... and which have not been described in a Form 10–Q ... or Form 8–K filed under the Exchange Act.

Item 12. Incorporation of Certain Information by Reference.

If the registrant elects to incorporate information by reference pursuant to General Instruction VII.:

(a) It must specifically incorporate by reference into the prospectus contained in the registration statement the following documents by means of a statement to that effect in the prospectus listing all such documents:

(1) The registrant's latest annual report on Form 10–K ... filed pursuant to Section 13(a) or Section 15(d) of the Exchange Act which contains financial statements for the registrant's latest fiscal year for which a Form 10–K ... was required to have been filed; and

(2) All other reports filed pursuant to Section 13(a) or 15(d) of the Exchange Act or proxy or information statements filed pursuant to Section 14 of the Exchange Act since the end of the fiscal year covered by the annual report referred to in paragraph (a)(1) above.

(b)(1) The registrant must state:

(i) That it will provide to each person, including any beneficial owner, to whom a prospectus is delivered, a copy of any or all of the reports or documents that have been incorporated by reference in the prospectus contained in the registration statement but not delivered with the prospectus;

(ii) That it will provide these reports or documents upon written or oral request;

(iii) That it will provide these reports or documents at no cost to the requester;

(iv) The name, address, telephone number, and e-mail address, if any, to which the request for these reports or documents must be made; and

(v) The registrant's Web site address, including the uniform resource locator (URL) where the incorporated reports and other documents may be accessed.

(2) The registrant must:

(i) Identify the reports and other information that it files with the SEC; and

(ii) State that the public may read and copy any materials it files with the SEC at the SEC's Public Reference Room at 100 F Street, N.E., Washington, DC 20549. State that the public may obtain information on the operation of the Public Reference Room by calling the SEC at 1–800–SEC–0330. If the registrant is an electronic filer, state that the SEC maintains an Internet site that contains reports, proxy and information statements, and other information regarding issuers that file electronically with the SEC and state the address of that site (http://www.sec.gov).

PART II—INFORMATION NOT REQUIRED IN PROSPECTUS

Item 13.   Other Expenses of Issuance and Distribution....

Item 14.   Indemnification of Directors and Officers....

Item 15.   Recent Sales of Unregistered Securities....

Item 16.   Exhibits and Financial Statement Schedules....

Item 17.   Undertakings....

FORM S–3

SECURITIES AND EXCHANGE COMMISSION

REGISTRATION STATEMENT UNDER
THE SECURITIES ACT OF 1933

(Exact name of registrant as specified in its charter)

(State or other jurisdiction of incorporation or organization)

(I.R.S. Employer Identification No.)

(Address, including zip code, and telephone number,
including area code, of registrant's principal
executive offices)

(Name, address, including zip code, and telephone
number, including area code, of agent for service)

Approximate date of commencement of proposed sale to the public
————. ...

GENERAL INSTRUCTIONS

I. Eligibility Requirements for Use of Form S–3

This instruction sets forth registrant requirements and transaction requirements for the use of Form S–3. Any registrant which meets the requirements of I.A. below ("Registrant Requirements") may use this Form for the registration of securities under the Securities Act of 1933 ("Securities Act") which are offered in any transaction specified in I.B. below ("Transaction Requirement") provided that the requirement applicable to the specified transaction are met.... With respect to well-known seasoned issuers and majority-owned subsidiaries of well-known seasoned issuers, see Instruction I.D. below.

A. *Registrant Requirements.* Registrants must meet the following conditions in order to use this Form for registration under the Securities Act of securities offered in the transactions specified in I.B. below:

1. The registrant is organized under the laws of the United States or any State or Territory or the District of Columbia and has its principal business operations in the United States or its territories.

2. The registrant has a class of securities registered pursuant to Section 12(b) of the Securities Exchange Act of 1934 ("Exchange Act") or a class of equity securities registered pursuant to Section 12(g) of the Exchange Act or is required to file reports pursuant to Section 15(d) of the Exchange Act.

3. The registrant: (a) has been subject to the requirements of Section 12 or 15(d) of the Exchange Act and has filed all the material required to be filed pursuant to Sections 13, 14 or 15(d) for a period of at least twelve calendar months immediately preceding the filing of the registration statement on this Form; and (b) has filed in a timely manner all reports required to be filed during the twelve calendar months and any portion of a month immediately preceding the filing of the registration statement, other than a report that is required solely pursuant to Item 1.01, 1.02, 2.03, 2.04, 2.05, 2.06, 4.02(a), 6.01, 6.03 or 6.05 of Form 8–K....

5. Neither the registrant nor any of its consolidated or unconsolidated subsidiaries have, since the end of the last fiscal year for which certified financial statements of the registrant and its consolidated subsidiaries were included in a report filed pursuant to Section 13(a) or 15(d) of the Exchange Act: (a) failed to pay any dividend or sinking fund installment on preferred stock; or (b) defaulted (i) on any installment or installments on indebtedness for borrowed money, or (ii) on any rental on one or more long term leases, which defaults in the aggregate are

material to the financial position of the registrant and its consolidated and unconsolidated subsidiaries, taken as a whole. . . .

B. *Transaction Requirements.* Security offerings meeting any of the following conditions and made by a registrant meeting the Registrant Requirements specified in I.A. above may be registered on this Form:

1. *Primary Offerings by Certain Registrants.* Securities to be offered for cash by or on behalf of a registrant, or outstanding securities to be offered for cash for the account of any person other than the registrant, including securities acquired by standby underwriters in connection with the call or redemption by the registrant of warrants or a class of convertible securities; *provided* that the aggregate market value of the voting stock held by non-affiliates of the registrant is $75 million or more. . . .

2. *Primary Offerings of Non-convertible Investment Grade Securities.* Non-convertible securities to be offered for cash by or on behalf of a registrant, provided such securities at the time of sale are "investment grade securities," as defined below. A non-convertible security is an "investment grade security" if, at the time of sale, at least one nationally recognized statistical rating organization . . . has rated the security in one of its generic rating categories which signifies investment grade; typically, the four highest rating categories (within which there may be sub-categories or gradations indicating relative standing) signify investment grade.

3. *Transactions Involving Secondary Offerings.* Outstanding securities to be offered for the account of any person other than the issuer . . . if securities of the same class are listed and registered on a national securities exchange or are quoted on the automated quotation system of a national securities association. . . .

D. Automatic Shelf Offerings by Well–Known Seasoned Issuers.

Any registrant that is a well-known seasoned issuer, as defined in Rule 405, at the most recent eligibility determination date specified in paragraph (2) of that definition may use this Form for registration under the Securities Act of securities offerings, other than pursuant to Rule 415(a)(1)(vii) or (viii), as follows:

1. The securities to be offered are:

(a) Any securities to be offered pursuant to Rule 415, Rule 430A [Prospectus in a Registration Statement at the Time of Effectiveness], or Rule 430B [Prospectus in a Registration Statement After the Effective Date] by:

(i) A registrant that is a well-known seasoned issuer by reason of paragraph (1)(i)(A) of the definition in Rule 405; or

(ii) A registrant that is a well-known seasoned issuer only by reason of paragraph (1)(i)(B) of the definition in Rule 405 if the registrant also is eligible to register a primary offering of its securities pursuant to Transaction Requirement I.B.1 of this Form. . . .

II. Application of General Rules and Regulations

. . .

C. A "small business issuer," defined in Rule 405, that is eligible to use Form S–3 shall refer to the disclosure items in Regulation S–B and not Regulation S–K. For example, while Item 1 of Form S–3 requires the information required by Item 501 of Regulation S–K, small business issuers shall provide the information in Item 501 of Regulation S–B. Where Regulation S–B does not contain a comparable Item, for example there is no Item "301" in Regulation S–B, then small business issuers may omit the Item. Small business issuers shall provide the financial information called for by Item 310 of Regulation S–B in lieu of the financial information called for by Item 11. . . .

IV. Registration of Additional Securities and Additional Classes of Securities . . .

B. Registration of Additional Securities or Classes of Securities or Additional Registrants After Effectiveness. A well-known seasoned issuer relying on General Instruction I.D. of this Form may register additional securities or classes of securities, pursuant to Rule 413(b) [Registration of Additional Securities] by filing a post-effective amendment to the effective registration statement. The well-known seasoned issuer may add majority-owned subsidiaries as additional registrants whose securities are eligible to be sold as part of the automatic shelf registration statement by filing a post-effective amendment identifying the additional registrants, and the registrant and the additional registrants and other persons required to sign the registration statement must sign the post-effective amendment. The post-effective amendment must consist of the facing page; any disclosure required by this Form that is necessary to update the registration statement to reflect the additional securities, additional classes of securities, or additional registrants; any required opinions and consents; and the signature page. Required information, consents, or opinions may be included in the prospectus and the registration statement through a post-effective amendment or may be provided through a document incorporated or deemed incorporated by reference into the registration statement and the prospectus that is part of the registration statement, or, as to the required information only, contained in a prospectus filed pursuant to Rule 424(b) [Filing of Prospectuses] that is deemed part of and included in the registration statement and prospectus that is part of the registration statement.

PART I—INFORMATION REQUIRED IN PROSPECTUS

Item 3. Summary Information, Risk Factors and Ratio of Earnings to Fixed Charges....

Item 4. Use of Proceeds....

Item 5. Determination of Offering Price....

Item 6. Dilution....

Item 7. Selling Security Holders....

Item 8. Plan of Distribution....

Item 9. Description of Securities to be Registered....

Item 10. Interests of Named Experts and Counsel....

Item 11. Material Changes. (a) Describe any and all material changes in the registrant's affairs which have occurred since the end of the latest fiscal year for which certified financial statements were included in the latest annual report to security holders and which have not been described in a report on Form 10–Q ... or Form 8–K ... filed under the Exchange Act....

PART II—INFORMATION NOT REQUIRED IN PROSPECTUS

Item 14. Other Expenses of Issuance and Distribution....

Item 15. Indemnification of Directors and Officers....

Item 16. Exhibits....

Item 17. Undertakings....

––––––––

FORM SB–2

REGISTRATION STATEMENT UNDER THE SECURITIES ACT OF 1933 ...

_____

(Name of small business issuer in its charter)

(State or jurisdiction of incorporation or organization)	(Primary Standard Industrial Classification Code Number)	(I.R.S. Employer Identification No.)

_____

(Address and telephone number of principal executive offices)

_____

(Address of principal place of business or intended principal place of business)

_____

(Name, address and telephone number of agent for service)

Approximate date of commencement of proposed sale to the public
_____ ...

GENERAL INSTRUCTIONS

A. *Use of Form and Place of Filing.*

1. A "small business issuer," defined in Rule 405 of the Securities Act of 1933 (the "Securities Act") may use this form to register securities to be sold for cash. See also Item 10(a) of Regulation S–B ...

PART I—INFORMATION REQUIRED IN PROSPECTUS

Item 1. Front of Registration Statement and Outside Front Cover of Prospectus.

Furnish the information required by Item 501 of Regulation S–B.

Item 2. Inside Front and Outside Back Cover Pages of Prospectus.

Furnish the information required by Item 502 of Regulation S–B.

Item 3. Summary Information and Risk Factors.

Furnish the information required by Item 503 of Regulation S–B.

Item 4. Use of Proceeds.

Furnish the information required by Item 504 of Regulation S–B.

Item 5. Determination of Offering Price.

Furnish the information required by Item 505 of Regulation S–B.

Item 6. Dilution.

Furnish the information required by Item 506 of Regulation S–B.

Item 7. Selling Security Holders.

Furnish the information required by Item 507 of Regulation S–B.

Item 8. Plan of Distribution.

Furnish the information required by Item 508 of Regulation S–B.

Item 9. Legal Proceedings.

Furnish the information required by Item 103 of Regulation S–B.

Item 10. Directors, Executive Officers, Promoters and Control Persons.

Furnish the information required by Item 401 of Regulation S–B.

Item 11. Security Ownership of Certain Beneficial Owners and Management.

Furnish the information required by Item 403 of Regulation S–B.

Item 12. Description of Securities.

Furnish the information required by Item 202 of Regulation S–B.

Item 13. Interest of Named Experts and Counsel.

Furnish the information required by Item 509 of Regulation S–B.

Item 14.   Disclosure of Commission Position on Indemnification for Securities Act Liabilities.

Furnish the information required by Item 510 of Regulation S–B.

Item 15.   Organization Within Last Five Years.

Furnish the information required by Item 404 of Regulation S–B.

Item 16.   Description of Business.

Furnish the information required by Item 101 of Regulation S–B.

Item 17.   Management's Discussion and Analysis or Plan of Operation.

Furnish the information required by Item 303 of Regulation S–B.

Item 18.   Description of Property.

Furnish the information required by Item 102 of Regulation S–B.

Item 19.   Certain Relationships and Related Transactions.

Furnish the information required by Item 404 of Regulation S–B.

Item 20.   Market for Common Equity and Related Stockholder Matters.

Furnish the information required by Item 201 of Regulation S–B.

Item 21.   Executive Compensation.

Furnish the information required by Item 402 of Regulation S–B.

Item 22.   Financial Statements.

Furnish the information required by Item 310 of Regulation S–B.

Item 23.   Changes In and Disagreements With Accountants on Accounting and Financial Disclosure.

Furnish the information required by Item 304 of Regulation S–B.

PART II—INFORMATION NOT REQUIRED IN PROSPECTUS

Item 24.   Indemnification of Directors and Officers.

Furnish the information required by Item 702 of Regulation S–B.

Item 25.   Other Expenses of Issuance and Distribution.

Furnish the information required by Item 511 of Regulation S–B.

Item 26.   Recent Sales of Unregistered Securities.

Furnish the information required by Item 701 of Regulation S–B.

Item 27.   Exhibits.

Furnish the exhibits required by Item 601 of Regulation S–B.

Item 28.   Undertakings.

Furnish the undertakings required by Item 512 of Regulation S–B....

[The balance of Form SB–2 is omitted.]

––––––––

REGULATION S–B—INTEGRATED DISCLOSURE SYSTEM FOR SMALL BUSINESS ISSUERS (EXCERPTS)

17 C.F.R. §§ 228.10 et seq.

* Omitted.

Item 10. General

(a) *Application of Regulation S–B.* Regulation S–B is the source of disclosure requirements for "small business issuer" filings under the Securities Act of 1933 (the "Securities Act") and the Securities Exchange Act of 1934 (the "Exchange Act").

(1) *Definition of small business issuer.* A small business issuer is defined as a company that meets all of the following criteria:

(i) has revenues of less than $25,000,000;

(ii) is a U.S. or Canadian issuer;

(iii) is not an investment company; and

(iv) if a majority owned subsidiary, the parent corporation is also a small business issuer.

Provided however, that an entity is not a small business issuer if it has a public float (the aggregate market value of the issuer's outstanding securities held by non-affiliates) of $25,000,000 or more. . . .

(2) *Entering and Exiting the Small Business Disclosure System.* (i) A company that meets the definition of small business issuer may use Form SB–2 for registration of its securities under the Securities Act; Form 10–SB for registration of its securities under the Exchange Act; and Forms 10–KSB and 10–QSB for its annual and quarterly reports.

(ii) For a non-reporting company entering the disclosure system for the first time either by filing a registration statement under the Securities Act on Form SB–2 or a registration statement under the Exchange Act on Form 10–SB, the determination as to whether a company is a small business issuer is made with reference to its revenues during its last fiscal year and public float as of a date within 60 days of the date the registration statement is filed. . . .

(iii) Once a small business issuer becomes a reporting company it will remain a small business issuer until it exceeds the revenue limit or the public float limit at the end of two consecutive years. For example, if a company exceeds the revenue limit for two consecutive years, it will no longer be considered a small business. However, if it exceeds the revenue limit in one year and the next year exceeds the public float limit, but not the revenue limit, it will still be considered a small business. . . .

(iv) A reporting company that is not a small business company must meet the definition of a small business issuer at the end of two consecutive fiscal years before it will be considered a small business issuer for purposes of using Form SB–2, Form 10–SB, Form 10–KSB and Form 10–QSB.

(v) The determination as to the reporting category (small business issuer or other issuer) made for a non-reporting company at the time it enters the disclosure system governs all reports relating to the remainder of the fiscal year. The determination made for a reporting company at the end of its fiscal year governs all reports relating to the next fiscal year. An issuer may not change from one category to another with respect to its reports under the Exchange Act for a single fiscal year. A company may, however, choose not to use a Form SB–2 for a registration under the Securities Act.

(b) *Definitions of terms.*

(1) *Common equity*—means the small business issuer's common stock. If the small business issuer is a limited partnership, the term refers to the equity interests in the partnership.

(2) *Public market*—no public market shall be deemed to exist unless, within the past 60 business days, both bid and asked quotations at fixed prices (excluding "bid wanted" or "offer wanted" quotations) have appeared regularly in any established quotation system on at least half of such business days. Transactions arranged without the participation of a broker or dealer functioning as such are not indicative of a "public market."

(3) *Reporting company*—means a company that is obligated to file periodic reports with the Securities and Exchange Commission under section 15(d) or 13(a) of the Exchange Act.

(4) *Small business issuer*—refers to the issuer and all of its consolidated subsidiaries.

(c) *Preparing the disclosure document.* (1) The purpose of a disclosure document is to inform investors. Hence, information should be presented in a clear, concise and understandable fashion. Avoid unnecessary details, repetition or the use of technical language. The responses to the items of this Regulation should be brief and to the point.

(2) Small business issuers should consult the General Rules and Regulations under the Securities Act and Exchange Act for requirements concerning the preparation and filing of documents. Small business issuers should be aware that there are special rules concerning such matters as the kind and size of paper that is allowed and how filings should be bound. These special rules are located in Regulation C of the Securities Act and in Regulation 12B of the Exchange Act.

(d) *Commission policy on projections.* The Commission encourages the use of management's projections of future economic performance that have a reasonable basis and are presented in an appropriate format. The guidelines below set forth the Commission's views on important factors to be considered in preparing and disclosing such projections. (*See also* Rule 175 . . .).

(1) *Basis for projections.* Management has the option to present in Commission filings its good faith assessment of a small business issuer's future performance. Management, however, must have a reasonable basis for such an assessment. An outside review of management's

projections may furnish additional support in this regard. If management decides to include a report of such a review in a Commission filing, it should also disclose the qualifications of the reviewer, the extent of the review, the relationship between the reviewer and the registrant, and other material factors concerning the process by which any outside review was sought or obtained. Moreover, in the case of a registration statement under the Securities Act, the reviewer would be deemed an expert and an appropriate consent must be filed with the registration statement.

(2) *Format for projections.* Traditionally, projections have been given for three financial items generally considered to be of primary importance to investors (revenues, net income (loss) and earnings (loss) per share) . . . [P]rojection information need not necessarily be limited to these three items. However, management should take care to assure that the choice of items projected is not susceptible to misleading inferences through selective projection of only favorable items. It generally would be misleading to present sales or revenue projections without one of the foregoing measures of income. The period that appropriately may be covered by a projection depends to a large extent on the particular circumstances of the company involved. For certain companies in certain industries, a projection covering a two or three year period may be entirely reasonable. Other companies may not have a reasonable basis for projections beyond the current year.

(3) *Investor understanding.* Disclosures accompanying the projections should facilitate investor understanding of the basis for and limitations of projections. The Commission believes that investor understanding would be enhanced by disclosure of the assumptions which in management's opinion are most significant to the projections or are the key factors upon which the financial results of the enterprise depend and encourages disclosure of assumptions in a manner that will provide a frame-work for analysis of the projection. Management also should consider whether disclosure of the accuracy or inaccuracy of previous projections would provide investors with important insights into the limitations of projections.

(e) *Commission policy on security ratings.* In view of the importance of security ratings ("ratings") to investors and the marketplace, the Commission permits small business issuers to disclose ratings assigned by rating organizations to classes of debt securities, convertible debt securities and preferred stock in registration statements and periodic reports. In addition, the Commission permits, disclosure of ratings assigned by any nationally recognized statistical rating organizations ("NRSROs") in certain communications deemed not to be a prospectus ("tombstone advertisements"). Below are the Commission's views on important matters to be considered in disclosing security ratings.

(1)(i) If a small business issuer includes in a filing any rating(s) assigned to a class of securities, it should consider including any other rating assigned by a different NRSRO that is materially different. A statement that a security rating is not a recommendation to buy, sell or hold securities and that it may be subject to revision or withdrawal at any time by the assigning rating organization should also be included.

(ii)(A) If the rating is included in a filing under the Securities Act, the written consent of any rating organization that is not a NRSRO whose rating is included should be filed. The consent of any NRSRO is not required. ...

(B) If a change in a rating already included is available before effectiveness of the registration statement, the small business issuer should consider including such rating change in the prospectus. If the rating change is material, consideration should be given to recirculating the preliminary prospectus.

(C) If a materially different additional NRSRO rating or a material change in a rating already included becomes available during any period in which offers or sales are being made, the small business issuer should consider disclosing this information in a sticker to the prospectus.

(iii) If there is a material change in the rating(s) assigned by any NRSRO(s) to any outstanding class(es) of securities of a reporting company, the registrant should consider filing a report on Form 8–K ... or other appropriate report under the Exchange Act disclosing such rating change....

QUALIFICATIONS AND REPORTS
OF ACCOUNTANTS

17 C.F.R. Part 210

Rule 2–01. Qualifications of accountants ...

(a) The Commission will not recognize any person as a certified public accountant who is not duly registered and in good standing as such under the laws of the place of his residence or principal office. The Commission will not recognize any person as a public accountant who is not in good standing and entitled to practice as such under the laws of the place of his residence or principal office.

(b) The Commission will not recognize an accountant as independent, with respect to an audit client, if the accountant is not, or a reasonable investor with knowledge of all relevant facts and circumstances would conclude that the accountant is not, capable of exercising objective and impartial judgment on all issues encompassed within the accountant's engagement. In determining whether an accountant is independent, the Commission will consider all relevant circumstances, including all relationships between the accountant and the audit client, and not just those relating to reports filed with the Commission.

(c) This paragraph sets forth a non-exclusive specification of circumstances inconsistent with paragraph (b) of this section.

(1) *Financial relationships.* An accountant is not independent if, at any point during the audit and professional engagement period, the accountant has a direct financial interest or a material indirect financial interest in the accountant's audit client, such as:

(i) *Investments in audit clients.* An accountant is not independent when:

(A) The accounting firm, any covered person in the firm, or any of his or her immediate family members, has any direct investment in an audit client, such as stocks, bonds, notes, options, or other securities. The term direct investment includes an investment in an audit client through an intermediary if:

(1) The accounting firm, covered person, or immediate family member, alone or together with other persons, supervises or participates in the intermediary's investment decisions or has control over the intermediary; or

(2) The intermediary is not a diversified management investment company, as defined by section 5(b)(1) of the Investment Company Act of 1940, and has an investment in the audit client that amounts to 20% or more of the value of the intermediary's total investments.

1750

(B) Any partner, principal, shareholder, or professional employee of the accounting firm, any of his or her immediate family members, any close family member of a covered person in the firm, or any group of the above persons has filed a Schedule 13D or 13G with the Commission indicating beneficial ownership of more than five percent of an audit client's equity securities or controls an audit client, or a close family member of a partner, principal, or shareholder of the accounting firm controls an audit client.

(C) The accounting firm, any covered person in the firm, or any of his or her immediate family members, serves as voting trustee of a trust, or executor of an estate, containing the securities of an audit client, unless the accounting firm, covered person in the firm, or immediate family member has no authority to make investment decisions for the trust or estate.

(D) The accounting firm, any covered person in the firm, any of his or her immediate family members, or any group of the above persons has any material indirect investment in an audit client. For purposes of this paragraph, the term material indirect investment does not include ownership by any covered person in the firm, any of his or her immediate family members, or any group of the above persons of 5% or less of the outstanding shares of a diversified management investment company, as defined by section 5(b)(1) of the Investment Company Act of 1940, that invests in an audit client.

(E) The accounting firm, any covered person in the firm, or any of his or her immediate family members:

(1) Has any direct or material indirect investment in an entity where:

(i) An audit client has an investment in that entity that is material to the audit client and has the ability to exercise significant influence over that entity; or

(ii) The entity has an investment in an audit client that is material to that entity and has the ability to exercise significant influence over that audit client;

(2) Has any material investment in an entity over which an audit client has the ability to exercise significant influence; or

(3) Has the ability to exercise significant influence over an entity that has the ability to exercise significant influence over an audit client.

(ii) *Other financial interests in audit client.* An accountant is not independent when the accounting firm, any covered person in the firm, or any of his or her immediate family members has:

(A) *Loans/debtor-creditor relationship.* Any loan (including any margin loan) to or from an audit client, or an audit client's officers, directors, or record or beneficial owners of more than ten percent of the audit client's equity securities, except for the following loans obtained from a financial institution under its normal lending procedures, terms, and requirements:

(1) Automobile loans and leases collateralized by the automobile;

(2) Loans fully collateralized by the cash surrender value of an insurance policy;

(3) Loans fully collateralized by cash deposits at the same financial institution; and

(4) A mortgage loan collateralized by the borrower's primary residence provided the loan was not obtained while the covered person in the firm was a covered person.

(B) *Savings and checking accounts.* Any savings, checking, or similar account at a bank, savings and loan, or similar institution that is an audit client, if the account has a balance that exceeds the amount insured by the Federal Deposit Insurance Corporation or any similar insurer, except that an accounting firm account may have an uninsured balance provided that the likelihood of the bank, savings and loan, or similar institution experiencing financial difficulties is remote.

(C) *Broker-dealer accounts.* Brokerage or similar accounts maintained with a broker-dealer that is an audit client, if:

(1) Any such account includes any asset other than cash or securities (within the meaning of "security" provided in the Securities Investor Protection Act of 1970 ("SIPA"));

(2) The value of assets in the accounts exceeds the amount that is subject to a Securities Investor Protection Corporation advance, for those accounts, under Section 9 of SIPA; or

(3) With respect to non-U.S. accounts not subject to SIPA protection, the value of assets in the accounts exceeds the amount insured or protected by a program similar to SIPA.

(D) *Futures commission merchant accounts.* Any futures, commodity, or similar account maintained with a futures commission merchant that is an audit client.

(E) *Credit cards.* Any aggregate outstanding credit card balance owed to a lender that is an audit client that is not reduced to $10,000 or less on a current basis taking into consideration the payment due date and any available grace period.

(F) *Insurance* products. Any individual policy issued by an insurer that is an audit client unless:

(1) The policy was obtained at a time when the covered person in the firm was not a covered person in the firm; and

(2) The likelihood of the insurer becoming insolvent is remote.

(G) *Investment companies*. Any financial interest in an entity that is part of an investment company complex that includes an audit client.

(iii) *Exceptions*. Notwithstanding paragraphs (c)(1)(i) and (c)(1)(ii) of this section, an accountant will not be deemed not independent if:

(A) *Inheritance and gift*. Any person acquires an unsolicited financial interest, such as through an unsolicited gift or inheritance, that would cause an accountant to be not independent under paragraph (c)(1)(i) or (c)(1)(ii) of this section, and the financial interest is disposed of as soon as practicable, but no later than 30 days after the person has knowledge of and the right to dispose of the financial interest.

(B) *New audit engagement*. Any person has a financial interest that would cause an accountant to be not independent under paragraph (c)(1)(i) or (c)(1)(ii) of this section, and:

(1) The accountant did not audit the client's financial statements for the immediately preceding fiscal year; and

(2) The accountant is independent under paragraph (c)(1)(i) and (c)(1)(ii) of this section before the earlier of:

(i) Signing an initial engagement letter or other agreement to provide audit, review, or attest services to the audit client; or

(ii) Commencing any audit, review, or attest procedures (including planning the audit of the client's financial statements).

(C) *Employee compensation and benefit plans*. An immediate family member of a person who is a covered person in the firm only by virtue of paragraphs (f)(11)(iii) or (f)(11)(iv) of this section has a financial interest that would cause an accountant to be not independent under paragraph (c)(1)(i) or (c)(1)(ii) of this section, and the acquisition of the financial interest was an unavoidable consequence of participation in his or her employer's employee compensation or benefits program, provided that the financial interest, other than unexercised employee stock options, is disposed of as soon as practicable, but no later than 30 days after the person has the right to dispose of the financial interest.

(iv) *Audit clients' financial relationships*. An accountant is not independent when:

(A) *Investments by the audit client in the accounting firm*. An audit client has, or has agreed to acquire, any direct investment in the accounting firm, such as stocks, bonds, notes, options, or other securities, or the audit client's officers or directors are record or beneficial owners of more than 5% of the equity securities of the accounting firm.

(B) *Underwriting*. An accounting firm engages an audit client to act as an underwriter, broker-dealer, market-maker, promoter, or analyst with respect to securities issued by the accounting firm.

(2) *Employment relationships*. An accountant is not independent if, at any point during the audit and professional engagement period, the

accountant has an employment relationship with an audit client, such as:

(i) *Employment at audit client of accountant.* A current partner, principal, shareholder, or professional employee of the accounting firm is employed by the audit client or serves as a member of the board of directors or similar management or governing body of the audit client.

(ii) *Employment at audit client of certain relatives of accountant.* A close family member of a covered person in the firm is in an accounting role or financial reporting oversight role at an audit client, or was in such a role during any period covered by an audit for which the covered person in the firm is a covered person.

(iii) *Employment at audit client of former employee of accounting firm.*

(A) A former partner, principal, shareholder, or professional employee of an accounting firm is in an accounting role or financial reporting oversight role at an audit client, unless the individual:

(1) Does not influence the accounting firm's operations or financial policies;

(2) Has no capital balances in the accounting firm; and

(3) Has no financial arrangement with the accounting firm other than one providing for regular payment of a fixed dollar amount (which is not dependent on the revenues, profits, or earnings of the accounting firm):

(i) Pursuant to a fully funded retirement plan, rabbi trust, or, in jurisdictions in which a rabbi trust does not exist, a similar vehicle; or

(ii) In the case of a former professional employee who was not a partner, principal, or shareholder of the accounting firm and who has been disassociated from the accounting firm for more than five years, that is immaterial to the former professional employee; and

(B) A former partner, principal, shareholder, or professional employee of an accounting firm is in a financial reporting oversight role at an issuer (as defined in section 10A(f) of the Securities Exchange Act of 1934), except an issuer that is an investment company registered under section 8 of the Investment Company Act of 1940, unless the individual:

(1) Employed by the issuer was not a member of the audit engagement team of the issuer during the one year period preceding the date that audit procedures commenced for the fiscal period that included the date of initial employment of the audit engagement team member by the issuer;

(2) For purposes of paragraph (c)(2)(iii)(B)(1) of this section, the following individuals are not considered to be members of the audit engagement team:

(i) Persons, other than the lead partner and the concurring partner, who provided ten or fewer hours of audit, review, or attest services during the period covered by paragraph (c)(2)(iii)(B)(1) of this section;

(ii) Individuals employed by the issuer as a result of a business combination between an issuer that is an audit client and the employing entity, provided employment was not in contemplation of the business combination and the audit committee of the successor issuer is aware of the prior employment relationship; and

(iii) Individuals that are employed by the issuer due to an emergency or other unusual situation provided that the audit committee determines that the relationship is in the interest of investors;

(3) For purposes of paragraph (c)(2)(iii)(B)(1) of this section, audit procedures are deemed to have commenced for a fiscal period the day following the filing of the issuer's periodic annual report with the Commission covering the previous fiscal period; or

(C) A former partner, principal, shareholder, or professional employee of an accounting firm is in a financial reporting oversight role with respect to an investment company registered under section 8 of the Investment Company Act of 1940, if:

(1) The former partner, principal, shareholder, or professional employee of an accounting firm is employed in a financial reporting oversight role related to the operations and financial reporting of the registered investment company at an entity in the investment company complex, as defined in (f)(14) of this section, that includes the registered investment company; and

(2) The former partner, principal, shareholder, or professional employee of an accounting firm employed by the registered investment company or any entity in the investment company complex was a member of the audit engagement team of the registered investment company or any other registered investment company in the investment company complex during the one year period preceding the date that audit procedures commenced that included the date of initial employment of the audit engagement team member by the registered investment company or any entity in the investment company complex.

(3) For purposes of paragraph (c)(2)(iii)(C)(2) of this section, the following individuals are not considered to be members of the audit engagement team:

(i) Persons, other than the lead partner and concurring partner, who provided ten or fewer hours of audit, review or attest services during the period covered by paragraph (c)(2)(iii)(C)(2) of this section;

(ii) Individuals employed by the registered investment company or any entity in the investment company complex as a result of a business combination between a registered investment company or any entity in the investment company complex that is an audit client and the employing entity, provided employment was not in contemplation of the business combination and the audit committee of the registered investment company is aware of the prior employment relationship; and

(iii) Individuals that are employed by the registered investment company or any entity in the investment company complex due to an emergency or other unusual situation provided that the audit committee determines that the relationship is in the interest of investors.

(4) For purposes of paragraph (c)(2)(iii)(C)(2) of this section, audit procedures are deemed to have commenced the day following the filing of the registered investment company's periodic annual report with the Commission.

(3) *Business relationships.* An accountant is not independent if, at any point during the audit and professional engagement period, the accounting firm or any covered person in the firm has any direct or material indirect business relationship with an audit client, or with persons associated with the audit client in a decision-making capacity, such as an audit client's officers, directors, or substantial stockholders. The relationships described in this paragraph do not include a relationship in which the accounting firm or covered person in the firm provides professional services to an audit client or is a consumer in the ordinary course of business.

(4) *Non-audit services.* An accountant is not independent if, at any point during the audit and professional engagement period, the accountant provides the following non-audit services to an audit client:

(i) *Bookkeeping or other services related to the accounting records or financial statements of the audit client.* Any service, unless it is reasonable to conclude that the results of these services will not be subject to audit procedures during an audit of the audit client's financial statements, including:

(A) Maintaining or preparing the audit client's accounting records;

(B) Preparing the audit client's financial statements that are filed with the Commission or that form the basis of financial statements filed with the Commission; or

(C) Preparing or originating source data underlying the audit client's financial statements.

(ii) *Financial information systems design and implementation.* Any service, unless it is reasonable to conclude that the results of these services will not be subject to audit procedures during an audit of the audit client's financial statements, including:

(A) Directly or indirectly operating, or supervising the operation of, the audit client's information system or managing the audit client's local area network; or

1756

(B) Designing or implementing a hardware or software system that aggregates source data underlying the financial statements or generates information that is significant to the audit client's financial statements or other financial information systems taken as a whole.

(iii) Appraisal or valuation services, fairness opinions, or contribution-in-kind reports. Any appraisal service, valuation service, or any service involving a fairness opinion or contribution-in-kind report for an audit client, unless it is reasonable to conclude that the results of these services will not be subject to audit procedures during an audit of the audit client's financial statements.

(iv) *Actuarial services.* Any actuarially-oriented advisory service involving the determination of amounts recorded in the financial statements and related accounts for the audit client other than assisting a client in understanding the methods, models, assumptions, and inputs used in computing an amount, unless it is reasonable to conclude that the results of these services will not be subject to audit procedures during an audit of the audit client's financial statements.

(v) *Internal audit outsourcing services.* Any internal audit service that has been outsourced by the audit client that relates to the audit client's internal accounting controls, financial systems, or financial statements, for an audit client unless it is reasonable to conclude that the results of these services will not be subject to audit procedures during an audit of the audit client's financial statements.

(vi) *Management functions.* Acting, temporarily or permanently, as a director, officer, or employee of an audit client, or performing any decision-making, supervisory, or ongoing monitoring function for the audit client.

(vii) *Human resources.*

(A) Searching for or seeking out prospective candidates for managerial, executive, or director positions;

(B) Engaging in psychological testing, or other formal testing or evaluation programs;

(C) Undertaking reference checks of prospective candidates for an executive or director position;

(D) Acting as a negotiator on the audit client's behalf, such as determining position, status or title, compensation, fringe benefits, or other conditions of employment; or

(E) Recommending, or advising the audit client to hire, a specific candidate for a specific job (except that an accounting firm may, upon request by the audit client, interview candidates and advise the audit client on the candidate's competence for financial accounting, administrative, or control positions).

(viii) *Broker-dealer, investment adviser, or investment banking services.* Acting as a broker-dealer (registered or unregistered), promoter, or underwriter, on behalf of an audit client, making investment decisions on behalf of the audit client or otherwise having discretionary authority over an audit client's investments, executing a transaction to buy or sell an audit client's investment, or having custody of assets of the audit client, such as taking temporary possession of securities purchased by the audit client.

(ix) *Legal services.* Providing any service to an audit client that, under circumstances in which the service is provided, could be provided only by someone licensed, admitted, or otherwise qualified to practice law in the jurisdiction in which the service is provided.

(x) *Expert services unrelated to the audit.* Providing an expert opinion or other expert service for an audit client, or an audit client's legal representative, for the purpose of advocating an audit client's interests in litigation or in a regulatory or administrative proceeding or investigation. In any litigation or regulatory or administrative proceeding or investigation, an accountant's independence shall not be deemed to be impaired if the accountant provides factual accounts, including in testimony, of work performed or explains the positions taken or conclusions reached during the performance of any service provided by the accountant for the audit client.

(5) *Contingent fees.* An accountant is not independent if, at any point during the audit and professional engagement period, the accountant provides any service or product to an audit client for a contingent fee or a commission, or receives a contingent fee or commission from an audit client.

(6) *Partner rotation.*

(i) Except as provided in paragraph (c)(6)(ii) of this section, an accountant is not independent of an audit client when:

(A) Any audit partner as defined in paragraph (f)(7)(ii) of this section performs:

(1) The services of a lead partner, as defined in paragraph (f)(7)(ii)(A) of this section, or concurring partner, as defined in paragraph (f)(7)(ii)(B) of this section, for more than five consecutive years; or

(2) One or more of the services defined in paragraphs (f)(7)(ii)(C) and (D) of this section for more than seven consecutive years;

(B) Any audit partner:

(1) Within the five consecutive year period following the performance of services for the maximum period permitted under paragraph (c)(6)(i)(A)(1) of this section, performs for that audit client the services of a lead partner, as defined in paragraph (f)(7)(ii)(A) of this section, or

concurring partner, as defined in paragraph (f)(7)(ii)(B) of this section, or a combination of those services, or

(2) Within the two consecutive year period following the performance of services for the maximum period permitted under paragraph (c)(6)(i)(A)(2) of this section, performs one or more of the services defined in paragraph (f)(7)(ii) of this section.

(ii) Any accounting firm with less than five audit clients that are issuers (as defined in section 10A(f) of the Securities Exchange Act of 1934 (15 U.S.C. 78j–1(f))) and less than ten partners shall be exempt from paragraph (c)(6)(i) of this section provided the Public Company Accounting Oversight Board conducts a review at least once every three years of each of the audit client engagements that would result in a lack of auditor independence under this paragraph.

(iii) For purposes of paragraph (c)(6)(i) of this section, an audit client that is an investment company registered under section 8 of the Investment Company Act of 1940 (15 U.S.C. 80a–8), does not include an affiliate of the audit client that is an entity in the same investment company complex, as defined in paragraph (f)(14) of this section, except for another registered investment company in the same investment company complex. For purposes of calculating consecutive years of service under paragraph (c)(6)(i) of this section with respect to investment companies in an investment company complex, audits of registered investment companies with different fiscal year-ends that are performed in a continuous 12–month period count as a single consecutive year.

(7) *Audit committee administration of the engagement.* An accountant is not independent of an issuer (as defined in section 10A(f) of the Securities Exchange Act of 1934), . . . unless:

(i) In accordance with Section 10A(i) of the Securities Exchange Act of 1934 either:

(A) Before the accountant is engaged by the issuer or its subsidiaries, or the registered investment company or its subsidiaries, to render audit or non-audit services, the engagement is approved by the issuer's or registered investment company's audit committee; or

(B) The engagement to render the service is entered into pursuant to pre-approval policies and procedures established by the audit committee of the issuer or registered investment company, provided the policies and procedures are detailed as to the particular service and the audit committee is informed of each service and such policies and procedures do not include delegation of the audit committees responsibilities under the Securities Exchange Act of 1934 to management; or

(C) With respect to the provision of services other than audit, review or attest services the pre-approval requirement is waived if:

(1) The aggregate amount of all such services provided constitutes no more than five percent of the total amount of revenues paid by the

audit client to its accountant during the fiscal year in which the services are provided;

(2) Such services were not recognized by the issuer or registered investment company at the time of the engagement to be non-audit services; and

(3) Such services are promptly brought to the attention of the audit committee of the issuer or registered investment company and approved prior to the completion of the audit by the audit committee or by one or more members of the audit committee who are members of the board of directors to whom authority to grant such approvals has been delegated by the audit committee.

(ii) A registered investment company's audit committee also must pre-approve its accountant's engagements for non-audit services with the registered investment company's investment adviser (not including a sub-adviser whose role is primarily portfolio management and is sub-contracted or overseen by another investment adviser) and any entity controlling, controlled by, or under common control with the investment adviser that provides ongoing services to the registered investment company in accordance with paragraph (c)(7)(i) of this section, if the engagement relates directly to the operations and financial reporting of the registered investment company, except that with respect to the waiver of the pre-approval requirement under paragraph (c)(7)(i)(C) of this section, the aggregate amount of all services provided constitutes no more than five percent of the total amount of revenues paid to the registered investment company's accountant by the registered investment company, its investment adviser and any entity controlling, controlled by, or under common control with the investment adviser that provides ongoing services to the registered investment company during the fiscal year in which the services are provided that would have to be pre-approved by the registered investment company's audit committee pursuant to this section.

(8) *Compensation.* An accountant is not independent of an audit client if, at any point during the audit and professional engagement period, any audit partner earns or receives compensation based on the audit partner procuring engagements with that audit client to provide any products or services other than audit, review or attest services. Any accounting firm with fewer than ten partners and fewer than five audit clients that are issuers (as defined in section 10A(f) of the Securities Exchange Act of 1934) shall be exempt from the requirement stated in the previous sentence.

(d) *Quality controls.* An accounting firm's independence will not be impaired solely because a covered person in the firm is not independent of an audit client provided:

(1) The covered person did not know of the circumstances giving rise to the lack of independence;

(2) The covered person's lack of independence was corrected as promptly as possible under the relevant circumstances after the covered person or accounting firm became aware of it; and

(3) The accounting firm has a quality control system in place that provides reasonable assurance, taking into account the size and nature of the accounting firm's practice, that the accounting firm and its employees do not lack independence, and that covers at least all employees and associated entities of the accounting firm participating in the engagement, including employees and associated entities located outside of the United States.

(4) For an accounting firm that annually provides audit, review, or attest services to more than 500 companies with a class of securities registered with the Commission under section 12 of the Securities Exchange Act of 1934, a quality control system will not provide such reasonable assurance unless it has at least the following features:

(i) Written independence policies and procedures;

(ii) With respect to partners and managerial employees, an automated system to identify their investments in securities that might impair the accountant's independence;

(iii) With respect to all professionals, a system that provides timely information about entities from which the accountant is required to maintain independence;

(iv) An annual or on-going firm-wide training program about auditor independence;

(v) An annual internal inspection and testing program to monitor adherence to independence requirements;

(vi) Notification to all accounting firm members, officers, directors, and employees of the name and title of the member of senior management responsible for compliance with auditor independence requirements;

(vii) Written policies and procedures requiring all partners and covered persons to report promptly to the accounting firm when they are engaged in employment negotiations with an audit client, and requiring the firm to remove immediately any such professional from that audit client's engagement and to review promptly all work the professional performed related to that audit client's engagement; and

(viii) A disciplinary mechanism to ensure compliance with this section. . . .

(f) *Definition of terms.* For purposes of this section:

(1) *Accountant*, as used in paragraphs (b) through (e) of this section, means a registered public accounting firm, certified public accountant or public accountant performing services in connection with an engagement for which independence is required. References to the accountant include

any accounting firm with which the certified public accountant or public accountant is affiliated.

(2) *Accounting firm* means an organization (whether it is a sole proprietorship, incorporated association, partnership, corporation, limited liability company, limited liability partnership, or other legal entity) that is engaged in the practice of public accounting and furnishes reports or other documents filed with the Commission or otherwise prepared under the securities laws, and all of the organization's departments, divisions, parents, subsidiaries, and associated entities, including those located outside of the United States. Accounting firm also includes the organization's pension, retirement, investment, or similar plans.

(3)(i) *Accounting role* means a role in which a person is in a position to or does exercise more than minimal influence over the contents of the accounting records or anyone who prepares them.

(ii) *Financial reporting oversight role* means a role in which a person is in a position to or does exercise influence over the contents of the financial statements or anyone who prepares them, such as when the person is a member of the board of directors or similar management or governing body, chief executive officer, president, chief financial officer, chief operating officer, general counsel, chief accounting officer, controller, director of internal audit, director of financial reporting, treasurer, or any equivalent position.

(4) *Affiliate of the audit client* means:

(i) An entity that has control over the audit client, or over which the audit client has control, or which is under common control with the audit client, including the audit client's parents and subsidiaries;

(ii) An entity over which the audit client has significant influence, unless the entity is not material to the audit client;

(iii) An entity that has significant influence over the audit client, unless the audit client is not material to the entity; and

(iv) Each entity in the investment company complex when the audit client is an entity that is part of an investment company complex.

(5) *Audit and professional engagement period* includes both:

(i) The period covered by any financial statements being audited or reviewed (the "audit period"); and

(ii) The period of the engagement to audit or review the audit client's financial statements or to prepare a report filed with the Commission (the "professional engagement period"):

(A) The professional engagement period begins when the accountant either signs an initial engagement letter (or other agreement to review or audit a client's financial statements) or begins audit, review, or attest procedures, whichever is earlier; and

(B) The professional engagement period ends when the audit client or the accountant notifies the Commission that the client is no longer that accountant's audit client.

(iii) For audits of the financial statements of foreign private issuers, the "audit and professional engagement period" does not include periods ended prior to the first day of the last fiscal year before the foreign private issuer first filed, or was required to file, a registration statement or report with the Commission, provided there has been full compliance with home country independence standards in all prior periods covered by any registration statement or report filed with the Commission.

(6) *Audit client* means the entity whose financial statements or other information is being audited, reviewed, or attested and any affiliates of the audit client, other than, for purposes of paragraph (c)(1)(i) of this section, entities that are affiliates of the audit client only by virtue of paragraph (f)(4)(ii) or (f)(4)(iii) of this section.

(7)(i) *Audit engagement team* means all partners, principals, shareholders and professional employees participating in an audit, review, or attestation engagement of an audit client, including audit partners and all persons who consult with others on the audit engagement team during the audit, review, or attestation engagement regarding technical or industry-specific issues, transactions, or events.

(ii) *Audit partner* means a partner or persons in an equivalent position, other than a partner who consults with others on the audit engagement team during the audit, review, or attestation engagement regarding technical or industry-specific issues, transactions, or events, who is a member of the audit engagement team who has responsibility for decision-making on significant auditing, accounting, and reporting matters that affect the financial statements, or who maintains regular contact with management and the audit committee and includes the following:

(A) The lead or coordinating audit partner having primary responsibility for the audit or review (the "lead partner");

(B) The partner performing a second level of review to provide additional assurance that the financial statements subject to the audit or review are in conformity with generally accepted accounting principles and the audit or review and any associated report are in accordance with generally accepted auditing standards and rules promulgated by the Commission or the Public Company Accounting Oversight Board (the "concurring or reviewing partner");

(C) Other audit engagement team partners who provide more than ten hours of audit, review, or attest services in connection with the annual or interim consolidated financial statements of the issuer or an investment company registered under section 8 of the Investment Company Act of 1940; and

(D) Other audit engagement team partners who serve as the "lead partner" in connection with any audit or review related to the annual or interim financial statements of a subsidiary of the issuer whose assets or revenues constitute 20% or more of the assets or revenues of the issuer's respective consolidated assets or revenues.

(8) *Chain of command* means all persons who:

(i) Supervise or have direct management responsibility for the audit, including at all successively senior levels through the accounting firm's chief executive;

(ii) Evaluate the performance or recommend the compensation of the audit engagement partner; or

(iii) Provide quality control or other oversight of the audit.

(9) *Close family members* means a person's spouse, spousal equivalent, parent, dependent, nondependent child, and sibling.

(10) *Contingent fee* means, except as stated in the next sentence, any fee established for the sale of a product or the performance of any service pursuant to an arrangement in which no fee will be charged unless a specified finding or result is attained, or in which the amount of the fee is otherwise dependent upon the finding or result of such product or service. Solely for the purposes of this section, a fee is not a "contingent fee" if it is fixed by courts or other public authorities, or, in tax matters, if determined based on the results of judicial proceedings or the findings of governmental agencies. Fees may vary depending, for example, on the complexity of services rendered.

(11) *Covered persons in the firm* means the following partners, principals, shareholders, and employees of an accounting firm:

(i) The "audit engagement team";

(ii) The "chain of command";

(iii) Any other partner, principal, shareholder, or managerial employee of the accounting firm who has provided ten or more hours of non-audit services to the audit client for the period beginning on the date such services are provided and ending on the date the accounting firm signs the report on the financial statements for the fiscal year during which those services are provided, or who expects to provide ten or more hours of non-audit services to the audit client on a recurring basis; and

(iv) Any other partner, principal, or shareholder from an "office" of the accounting firm in which the lead audit engagement partner primarily practices in connection with the audit.

(12) *Group* means two or more persons who act together for the purposes of acquiring, holding, voting, or disposing of securities of a registrant.

1764

(13) *Immediate family members* means a person's spouse, spousal equivalent, and dependents. . . .

(15) *Office* means a distinct sub-group within an accounting firm, whether distinguished along geographic or practice lines.

(16) *Rabbi trust* means an irrevocable trust whose assets are not accessible to the accounting firm until all benefit obligations have been met, but are subject to the claims of creditors in bankruptcy or insolvency.

(17) *Audit committee* means a committee (or equivalent body) as defined in section 3(a)(58) of the Securities Exchange Act of 1934. . . .

Rule 2–07. Communication with audit committees.

(a) Each registered public accounting firm that performs for an audit client that is an issuer (as defined in section 10A(f) of the Securities Exchange Act of 1934) . . . any audit required under the securities laws shall report, prior to the filing of such audit report with the Commission (or in the case of a registered investment company, annually, and if the annual communication is not within 90 days prior to the filing, provide an update, in the 90 day period prior to the filing, of any changes to the previously reported information), to the audit committee of the issuer or registered investment company:

(1) All critical accounting policies and practices to be used;

(2) All alternative treatments within Generally Accepted Accounting Principles for policies and practices related to material items that have been discussed with management of the issuer or registered investment company, including:

(i) Ramifications of the use of such alternative disclosures and treatments; and

(ii) The treatment preferred by the registered public accounting firm;

(3) Other material written communications between the registered public accounting firm and the management of the issuer or registered investment company, such as any management letter or schedule of unadjusted differences. . . .

REGULATION S–T—GENERAL RULES AND REGULATIONS FOR ELECTRONIC FILINGS

17 C.F.R. Part 232

§ 232.101. Mandated Electronic Submissions and Exceptions.

(a) *Mandated electronic submissions.*

(1) The following filings, including any related correspondence and supplemental information, except as otherwise provided, shall be submitted in electronic format:

(i) Registration statements and prospectuses filed pursuant to the Securities Act or registration statements filed pursuant to Sections 12(b) or 12(g) of the Exchange Act....

(iii) Statements, reports and schedules filed with the Commission pursuant to sections 13, 14, 15(d) or 16(a) of the Exchange Act, and proxy materials required to be furnished for the information of the Commission in connection with annual reports on Form 10–K....

REGULATION S–K—STANDARD INSTRUCTIONS FOR FILING FORMS UNDER SECURITIES ACT OF 1933 [AND] SECURITIES EXCHANGE ACT OF 1934 (SELECTED PROVISIONS)

17 C.F.R. §§ 229.10 et seq.

Subpart 200—Securities of the Registrant

Item 201. Market Price of and Dividends on the Registrant's Common Equity and Related Stockholder Matters....

(d) *Securities authorized for issuance under equity compensation plans.*

(1) In the following tabular format, provide the information specified in paragraph (d)(2) of this Item as of the end of the most recently completed fiscal year with respect to compensation plans (including individual compensation arrangements) under which equity securities of the registrant are authorized for issuance, aggregated as follows:

(i) All compensation plans previously approved by security holders; and

(ii) All compensation plans not previously approved by security holders.

Plan Category	Number of securities to be issued upon exercise of outstanding options, warrents and rights (a)	Weighted-average exercise price of outstanding options, warrants and rights (b)	Number of securities remaining available for future issuance under equity compensation plans (excluding securities reflected in column (a)) (c)
Equity compensation plans approved by security holders			
Equity compensation plans not approved by security holders			
Total			

(2) The table shall include the following information as of the end of the most recently completed fiscal year for each category of equity compensation plan described in paragraph (d)(1) of this Item:

(i) The number of securities to be issued upon the exercise of outstanding options, warrants and rights (column (a));

(ii) The weighted-average exercise price of the outstanding options, warrants and rights disclosed pursuant to paragraph (d)(2)(i) of this Item (column (b)); and

(iii) Other than securities to be issued upon the exercise of the outstanding options, warrants and rights disclosed in paragraph (d)(2)(i) of this Item, the number of securities remaining available for future issuance under the plan (column (c)).

(3) For each compensation plan under which equity securities of the registrant are authorized for issuance that was adopted without the approval of security holders, describe briefly, in narrative form, the material features of the plan.

Instructions to Paragraph (d).

1. Disclosure shall be provided with respect to any compensation plan and individual compensation arrangement of the registrant (or parent, subsidiary or affiliate of the registrant) under which equity securities of the registrant are authorized for issuance to employees or non-employees (such as directors, consultants, advisors, vendors, customers, suppliers or lenders) in exchange for consideration in the form of goods or services. . . .

Subpart 300—

Item 301. Selected Financial Data

Furnish in comparative columnar form the selected financial data for the registrant referred to below, for

(a) Each of the last five fiscal years of the registrant (or for the life of the registrant and its predecessors, if less), and

(b) Any additional fiscal years necessary to keep the information from being misleading.

Instructions to Item 301.

1. The purpose of the selected financial data shall be to supply in a convenient and readable format selected financial data which highlight certain significant trends in the registrant's financial condition and results of operations.

2. Subject to appropriate variation to conform to the nature of the registrant's business, the following items shall be included in the

table of financial data: net sales or operating revenues; income (loss) from continuing operations; income (loss) from continuing operations per common share; total assets; long-term obligations and redeemable preferred stock . . . .

Briefly describe, or cross-reference to a discussion thereof, factors such as accounting changes, business combinations or dispositions of business operations, that materially affect the comparability of the information reflected in selected financial data. Discussion of, or reference to, any material uncertainties should also be included where such matters might cause the data reflected herein not to be indicative of the registrant's future financial condition or results of operations. . . .

Item 303. Management's Discussion and Analysis of Financial Condition and Results of Operations

(a) *Full fiscal years.* Discuss registrant's financial condition, changes in financial condition and results of operations. The discussion shall provide information as specified in paragraphs (a)(1) through (a)(5) of this Item and also shall provide such other information that the registrant believes to be necessary to an understanding of its financial condition, changes in financial condition and results of operations. Discussions of liquidity and capital resources may be combined whenever the two topics are interrelated. Where in the registrant's judgment a discussion of segment information or of other subdivisions of the registrant's business would be appropriate to an understanding of such business, the discussion shall focus on each relevant, reportable segment or other subdivision of the business and on the registrant as a whole.

(1) *Liquidity.* Identify any known trends or any known demands, commitments, events or uncertainties that will result in or that are reasonably likely to result in the registrant's liquidity increasing or decreasing in any material way. If a material deficiency is identified, indicate the course of action that the registrant has taken or proposes to take to remedy the deficiency. Also identify and separately describe internal and external sources of liquidity, and briefly discuss any material unused sources of liquid assets.

(2) *Capital resources.* (i) Describe the registrant's material commitments for capital expenditures as of the end of the latest fiscal period, and indicate the general purpose of such commitments and the anticipated source of funds needed to fulfill such commitments.

(ii) Describe any known material trends, favorable or unfavorable, in the registrant's capital resources. Indicate any expected material changes in the mix and relative cost of such resources. The discussion shall consider changes between equity, debt and any off-balance sheet financing arrangements.

(3) *Results of operations.* (i) Describe any unusual or infrequent events or transactions or any significant economic changes that materially affected the amount of reported income from continuing operations and, in each case, indicate the extent to which income was so affected. In addition, describe any other significant components of revenues or expenses that, in the registrant's judgment, should be described in order to understand the registrant's results of operations.

(ii) Describe any known trends or uncertainties that have had or that the registrant reasonably expects will have a material favorable or unfavorable impact on net sales or revenues or income from continuing operations. If the registrant knows of events that will cause a material change in the relationship between costs and revenues (such as known future increases in costs of labor or materials or price increases or inventory adjustments), the change in the relationship shall be disclosed.

(iii) To the extent that the financial statements disclose material increases in net sales or revenues, provide a narrative discussion of the extent to which such increases are attributable to increases in prices or to increases in the volume or amount of goods or services being sold or to the introduction of new products or services.

(iv) For the three most recent fiscal years of the registrant ... or for those fiscal years in which the registrant has been engaged in business, whichever period is shortest, discuss the impact of inflation and changing prices on the registrant's net sales and revenues and on income from continuing operations.

(4) *Off-balance sheet arrangements.* (i) In a separately-captioned section, discuss the registrant's off-balance sheet arrangements that have or are reasonably likely to have a current or future effect on the registrant's financial condition, changes in financial condition, revenues or expenses, results of operations, liquidity, capital expenditures or capital resources that is material to investors. The disclosure shall include the items specified in paragraphs (a)(4)(i)(A), (B), (C) and (D) of this Item to the extent necessary to an understanding of such arrangements and effect and shall also include such other information that the registrant believes is necessary for such an understanding.

(A) The nature and business purpose to the registrant of such off-balance sheet arrangements;

(B) The importance to the registrant of such off-balance sheet arrangements in respect of its liquidity, capital resources, market risk support, credit risk support or other benefits;

(C) The amounts of revenues, expenses and cash flows of the registrant arising from such arrangements; the nature and amounts of any interests retained, securities issued and other indebtedness incurred by the registrant in connection with such arrangements; and the nature and amounts of any other obligations or liabilities (including contingent obligations or liabilities) of the registrant arising from such arrangements that are or are reasonably likely to become material and the triggering events or circumstances that could cause them to arise; and

(D) Any known event, demand, commitment, trend or uncertainty that will result in or is reasonably likely to result in the termination, or material reduction in availability to the registrant, of its off-balance sheet arrangements that provide material benefits to it, and the course of action that the registrant has taken or proposes to take in response to any such circumstances.

(ii) As used in this paragraph (a)(4), the term off-balance sheet arrangement means any transaction, agreement or other contractual arrangement to which an entity unconsolidated with the registrant is a party, under which the registrant has:

(A) Any obligation under a guarantee contract that has any of the characteristics identified in paragraph 3 of FASB Interpretation No. 45, Guarantor's Accounting and Disclosure Requirements for Guarantees, Including Indirect Guarantees of Indebtedness of Others (November 2002) ("FIN 45"), as may be modified or supplemented, and that is not excluded from the initial recognition and measurement provisions of FIN 45 pursuant to paragraphs 6 or 7 of that Interpretation;

(B) A retained or contingent interest in assets transferred to an unconsolidated entity or similar arrangement that serves as credit, liquidity or market risk support to such entity for such assets;

(C) Any obligation, including a contingent obligation, under a contract that would be accounted for as a derivative instrument, except that it is both indexed to the registrant's own stock and classified in stockholders' equity in the registrant's statement of financial position, and therefore excluded from the scope of FASB Statement of Financial Accounting Standards No. 133, Accounting for Derivative Instruments and Hedging Activities (June 1998), pursuant to paragraph 11(a) of that Statement, as may be modified or supplemented; or

(D) Any obligation, including a contingent obligation, arising out of a variable interest (as referenced in FASB Interpretation No. 46, Consolidation of Variable Interest Entities (January 2003), as may be modified or supplemented) in an unconsolidated entity that is held by, and material to, the registrant, where such entity provides financing, liquidity, market risk or credit risk support to, or engages in leasing, hedging or research and development services with, the registrant.

(5) *Tabular disclosure of contractual obligations.* (i) In a tabular format, provide the information specified in this paragraph (a)(5) as of the latest fiscal year end balance sheet date with respect to the registrant's known contractual obligations specified in the table that follows this paragraph (a)(5)(i). The registrant shall provide amounts, aggregated by type of contractual obligation. The registrant may disaggregate the

specified categories of contractual obligations using other categories suitable to its business, but the presentation must include all of the obligations of the registrant that fall within the specified categories. A presentation covering at least the periods specified shall be included. The tabular presentation may be accompanied by footnotes to describe provisions that create, increase or accelerate obligations, or other pertinent data to the extent necessary for an understanding of the timing and amount of the registrant's specified contractual obligations.

Contractual obligations	Payments due by period				
	Total	Less than 1 year	1–3 years	3–5 years	More than 5 years
[Long–Term Debt Obligations]	. . . .	. . . .	. . . .	. . . .	. . . .
[Capital (Finance) Lease Obligations]	. . . .	. . . .	. . . .	. . . .	. . . .
[Operating Lease Obligations]	. . . .	. . . .	. . . .	. . . .	. . . .
[Purchase Obligations]	. . . .	. . . .	. . . .	. . . .	. . . .
[Other Long–Term Liabilities] Reflected on the Company's Balance Sheet under the GAAP of the primary financial statements	. . . .	. . . .	. . . .	. . . .	. . . .
Total	. . . .	. . . .	. . . .	. . . .	. . . .

(ii) Definitions: The following definitions apply to this paragraph (a)(5):

(A) Long–Term Debt Obligation means a payment obligation under long-term borrowings referenced in FASB Statement of Financial Accounting Standards No. 47 Disclosure of Long–Term Obligations (March 1981), as may be modified or supplemented.

(B) Capital Lease Obligation means a payment obligation under a lease classified as a capital lease pursuant to FASB Statement of Financial Accounting Standards No. 13 Accounting for Leases (November 1976), as may be modified or supplemented.

(C) Operating Lease Obligation means a payment obligation under a lease classified as an operating lease and disclosed pursuant to FASB Statement of Financial Accounting Standards No. 13 Accounting for Leases (November 1976), as may be modified or supplemented.

(D) Purchase Obligation means an agreement to purchase goods or services that is enforceable and legally binding on the registrant that specifies all significant terms, including: fixed or minimum quantities to be purchased; fixed, minimum or variable price provisions; and the approximate timing of the transaction.

Instructions to Paragraph 303(a). . . . .

3. The discussion and analysis shall focus specifically on material events and uncertainties known to management that would cause reported financial information not to be necessarily indicative

of future operating results or of future financial condition. This would include descriptions and amounts of (A) matters that would have an impact on future operations and have not had an impact in the past, and (B) matters that have had an impact on reported operations and are not expected to have an impact upon future operations.

4. Where the consolidated financial statements reveal material changes from year to year in one or more line items, the causes for the changes shall be described to the extent necessary to an understanding of the registrant's businesses as a whole....

7. Any forward-looking information supplied is expressly covered by the safe harbor rule for projections. See Rule 175 under the Securities Act....

(b) *Interim periods.* If interim period financial statements are included or are required to be included [under] Regulation S–X ..., a management's discussion and analysis of the financial condition and results of operations shall be provided so as to enable the reader to assess material changes in financial condition and results of operations....

(c) *Safe harbor.* (1) The safe harbor provided in section 27A of the Securities Act of 1933 and section 21E of the Securities Exchange Act of 1934 ("statutory safe harbors") shall apply to forward-looking information provided pursuant to paragraphs (a)(4) and (5) of this Item, provided that the disclosure is made by: an issuer; a person acting on behalf of the issuer; an outside reviewer retained by the issuer making a statement on behalf of the issuer; or an underwriter, with respect to information provided by the issuer or information derived from information provided by the issuer.

Item 304. Changes in and Disagreements With Accountants on Accounting and Financial Disclosure

(a)(1) If during the registrant's two most recent fiscal years or any subsequent interim period, an independent accountant who was previously engaged as the principal accountant to audit the registrant's financial statements, or an independent accountant who was previously engaged to audit a significant subsidiary and on whom the principal accountant expressed reliance in its reports, has resigned (or indicated it has declined to stand for re-election after the completion of the current audit) or was dismissed, then the registrant shall:

(i) State whether the former accountant resigned, declined to stand for re-election or was dismissed and the date thereof.

(ii) State whether the principal accountant's report on the financial statements for either of the past two years contained an adverse opinion or a disclaimer of opinion, or was qualified or modified as to uncertainty, audit scope, or accounting principles; and also describe the nature of each such adverse opinion, disclaimer of opinion, modification, or qualification.

(iii) State whether the decision to change accountants was recommended or approved by:

(A) any audit or similar committee of the board of directors, if the issuer has such a committee; or

(B) the board of directors, if the issuer has no such committee.

(iv) State whether during the registrant's two most recent fiscal years and any subsequent interim period preceding such resignation, declination or dismissal there were any disagreements with the former accountant on any matter of accounting principles or practices, financial statement disclosure, or auditing scope or procedure, which disagreement(s), if not resolved to the satisfaction of the former accountant, would have caused it to make reference to the subject matter of the disagreement(s) in connection with its report. Also, (A) describe each such disagreement; (B) state whether any audit or similar committee of the board of directors, or the board of directors, discussed the subject matter of each of such disagreements with the former accountant; and (C) state whether the registrant has authorized the former accountant to respond fully to the inquiries of the successor accountant concerning the subject matter of each of such disagreements and, if not, describe the nature of any limitation thereon and the reason therefore. The disagreements required to be reported in response to this Item include both those resolved to the former accountant's satisfaction and those not resolved to the former accountant's satisfaction. Disagreements contemplated by this Item are those that occur at the decision-making level, i.e., between personnel of the registrant responsible for presentation of its financial statements and personnel of the accounting firm responsible for rendering its report.

(v) Provide the information required by paragraph (a)(1)(iv) of this Item for each of the kinds of events (even though the registrant and the former accountant did not express a difference of opinion regarding the event) listed in paragraphs (A) through (D) below, that occurred within the registrant's two most recent fiscal years and any subsequent interim period preceding the former accountant's resignation, declination to stand for re-election, or dismissal ("reportable events"). If the event led to a disagreement or difference of opinion, then the event should be reported as a disagreement under paragraph (a)(1)(iv) and need not be repeated under this paragraph.

(A) [t]he accountant's having advised the registrant that the internal controls necessary for the registrant to develop reliable financial statements do not exist;

(B) the accountant's having advised the registrant that information has come to the accountant's attention that has led it to no longer be able to rely on management's representations, or that has made it unwilling to be associated with the financial statements prepared by management;

(C)*(1)* the accountant's having advised the registrant of the need to expand significantly the scope of its audit, or that information has come to the accountant's attention during the time period covered by Item 304(a)(1)(iv), that if further investigated may *(i)* materially impact the fairness or reliability of either: a previously issued audit report or the underlying financial statements; or the financial statements issued or to be issued covering the fiscal period(s) subsequent to the date of the most recent financial statements covered by an audit report (including information that may prevent it from rendering an unqualified audit report on those financial statements), or *(ii)* cause it to be unwilling to rely on management's representations or be associated with the registrant's financial statements, and *(2)* due to the accountant's resignation (due to audit scope limitations or otherwise) or dismissal, or for any other reason, the accountant did not so expand the scope of its audit or conduct such further investigation; or

(D)*(1)* the accountant's having advised the registrant that information has come to the accountant's attention that it has concluded materially impacts the fairness or reliability of either *(i)* a previously issued audit report or the underlying financial statements, or *(ii)* the financial statements issued or to be issued covering the fiscal period(s) subsequent to the date of the most recent financial statements covered by an audit report (including information that, unless resolved to the accountant's satisfaction, would prevent it from rendering an unqualified audit report on those financial statements), and *(2)* due to the accountant's resignation, dismissal or declination to stand for re-election, or for any other reason, the issue has not been resolved to the accountant's satisfaction prior to its resignation, dismissal or declination to stand for re-election.

(2) If during the registrant's two most recent fiscal years or any subsequent interim period, a new independent accountant has been engaged as either the principal accountant to audit the registrant's financial statements, or as an independent accountant to audit a significant subsidiary and on whom the principal accountant is expected to express reliance in its report, then the registrant shall identify the newly engaged accountant and indicate the date of such accountant's engagement. In addition, if during the registrant's two most recent fiscal years, and any subsequent interim period prior to engaging that accountant, the registrant (or someone on its behalf) consulted the newly engaged accountant regarding (i) either: the application of accounting principles to a specified transaction, either completed or proposed; or the type of audit opinion that might be rendered on the registrant's financial statements, and either a written report was provided to the registrant or oral advice was provided that the new accountant conclud-

ed was an important factor considered by the registrant in reaching a decision as to the accounting, auditing or financial reporting issue; or (ii) any matter that was either the subject of a disagreement (as defined in paragraph 304(a)(1)(iv) and the related instructions to this item) or a reportable event (as described in paragraph 304(a)(1)(v)), then the registrant shall:

(A) so state and identify the issues that were the subjects of those consultations;

(B) briefly describe the views of the newly engaged accountant as expressed orally or in writing to the registrant on each such issue and, if written views were received by the registrant, file them as an exhibit to the report or registration statement requiring compliance with this Item 304(a);

(C) state whether the former accountant was consulted by the registrant regarding any such issues, and if so, provide a summary of the former accountant's views; and

(D) request the newly engaged accountant to review the disclosure required by this Item 304(a) before it is filed with the Commission and provide the new accountant the opportunity to furnish the registrant with a letter addressed to the Commission containing any new information, clarification of the registrant's expression of its views, or the respects in which it does not agree with the statements made by the registrant in response to Item 304(a). The registrant shall file any such letter as an exhibit to the report or registration statement containing the disclosure required by this Item.

(3) The registrant shall provide the former accountant with a copy of the disclosures it is making in response to this Item 304(a) that the former accountant shall receive no later than the day that the disclosures are filed with the Commission. The registrant shall request the former accountant to furnish the registrant with a letter addressed to the Commission stating whether it agrees with the statements made by the registrant in response to this Item 304(a) and, if not, stating the respects in which it does not agree. The registrant shall file the former accountant's letter as an exhibit to the report or registration statement containing this disclosure. If the former accountant's letter is unavailable at the time of filing such report or registration statement, then the registrant shall request the former accountant to provide the letter as promptly as possible so that the registrant can file the letter with the Commission within ten business days after the filing of the report or registration statement. Notwithstanding the ten business day period, the registrant shall file the letter by amendment within two business days of receipt; if the letter is received on a Saturday, Sunday or holiday on which the Commission is not open for business, then the two business day period shall begin to run on and shall include the first business day thereafter. The former accountant may provide the registrant with an

interim letter highlighting specific areas of concern and indicating that a more detailed letter will be forthcoming within the ten business day period noted above. If not filed with the report or registration statement containing the registrant's disclosure under this Item 304(a), then the interim letter, if any, shall be filed by the registrant by amendment within two business days of receipt.

(b) If, (1) in connection with a change in accountants subject to paragraph (a) of this Item 304, there was any disagreement of the type described in paragraph (a)(1)(iv) or any reportable event as described in paragraph (a)(1)(v) of this Item; (2) during the fiscal year in which the change in accountants took place or during the subsequent fiscal year, there have been any transactions or events similar to those which involved such disagreement or reportable event and (3) such transactions or events were material and were accounted for or disclosed in a manner different from that which the former accountants apparently would have concluded was required, the registrant shall state the existence and nature of the disagreement or reportable event and also state the effect on the financial statements if the method had been followed which the former accountants apparently would have concluded was required. These disclosures need not be made if the method asserted by the former accountants ceases to be generally accepted because of authoritative standards or interpretations subsequently issued.

Instructions to Item 304....

4. The term "disagreements" as used in this Item shall be interpreted broadly, to include any difference of opinion concerning any matter of accounting principles or practices, financial statement disclosure, or auditing scope or procedure which (if not resolved to the satisfaction of the former accountant) would have caused it to make reference to the subject matter of the disagreement in connection with its report. It is not necessary for there to have been an argument to have had a disagreement, merely a difference of opinion. For purposes of this Item, however, the term disagreements does not include initial differences of opinion based on incomplete facts or preliminary information that were later resolved to the former accountant's satisfaction by, and providing the registrant and the accountant do not continue to have a difference of opinion upon, obtaining additional relevant facts or information.

5. In determining whether any disagreement or reportable event has occurred, an oral communication from the engagement partner or another person responsible for rendering the accounting firm's opinion (or their designee) will generally suffice as the accountant advising the registrant of a reportable event or as a statement of a disagreement at the "decision-making level" within the accounting firm and require disclosure under this Item.

Item 306. Audit Committee Report

(a) The audit committee must state whether:

(1) The audit committee has reviewed and discussed the audited financial statements with management;

(2) The audit committee has discussed with the independent auditors the matters required to be discussed by SAS 61, as may be modified or supplemented;

(3) The audit committee has received the written disclosures and the letter from the independent accountants required by Independence Standards Board Standard No. 1 (Independence Standards Board, *Standard No. 1, Independence Discussions with Audit Committees*), as may be modified or supplemented, and has discussed with the independent accountant the independent accountant's independence; and

(4) Based on the review and discussions referred to in paragraphs (a)(1) through (a)(3) of this Item, the audit committee recommended to the Board of Directors that the audited financial statements be included in the company's Annual Report on Form 10–K . . . for the last fiscal year for filing with the Commission.

(b) The name of each member of the company's audit committee (or, in the absence of an audit committee, the board committee performing equivalent functions or the entire board of directors) must appear below the disclosure required by this Item.

(c) The information required by paragraphs (a) and (b) of this Item shall not be deemed to be "soliciting material," or to be "filed" with the Commission or subject to Regulation 14A or 14C, other than as provided in this Item, or to the liabilities of section 18 of the Exchange Act, except to the extent that the company specifically requests that the information be treated as soliciting material or specifically incorporates it by reference into a document filed under the Securities Act or the Exchange Act.

(d) The information required by paragraphs (a) and (b) of this Item need not be provided in any filings other than a registrant proxy or information statement relating to an annual meeting of security holders at which directors are to be elected (or special meeting or written consents in lieu of such meeting). Such information will not be deemed to be incorporated by reference into any filing under the Securities Act or the Exchange Act, except to the extent that the registrant specifically incorporates it by reference.

Item 307. Disclosure Controls and Procedures

Disclose the conclusions of the registrant's principal executive and principal financial officers, or persons performing similar functions, regarding the effectiveness of the registrant's disclosure controls and procedures (as defined in Rule 13a–15(e) or Rule 15d–15(e)) as of the end of the period covered by the report, based on the evaluation of these controls and procedures required by paragraph (b) of Rule 13a–15 or Rule 15d–15.

Item 308.   Internal Control Over Financial Reporting

(a) *Management's annual report on internal control over financial reporting.* Provide a report of management on the registrant's internal control over financial reporting (as defined in Rule 13a–15(f) or Rule 15d–15(f)) that contains:

(1) A statement of management's responsibility for establishing and maintaining adequate internal control over financial reporting for the registrant;

(2) A statement identifying the framework used by management to evaluate the effectiveness of the registrant's internal control over financial reporting as required by paragraph (c) Rule 13a–15 or Rule 15d–15;

(3) Management's assessment of the effectiveness of the registrant's internal control over financial reporting as of the end of the registrant's most recent fiscal year, including a statement as to whether or not internal control over financial reporting is effective. This discussion must include disclosure of any material weakness in the registrant's internal control over financial reporting identified by management. Management is not permitted to conclude that the registrant's internal control over financial reporting is effective if there are one or more material weaknesses in the registrant's internal control over financial reporting; and

(4) A statement that the registered public accounting firm that audited the financial statements included in the annual report containing the disclosure required by this Item has issued an attestation report on management's assessment of the registrant's internal control over financial reporting.

(b) *Attestation report of the registered public accounting firm.* Provide the registered public accounting firm's attestation report on management's assessment of the registrant's internal control over financial reporting in the registrant's annual report containing the disclosure required by this Item.

(c) *Changes in internal control over financial reporting.* Disclose any change in the registrant's internal control over financial reporting identified in connection with the evaluation required by paragraph (d) of Rule 13a–15 or Rule 15d–15 that occurred during the registrant's last fiscal quarter (the registrant's fourth fiscal quarter in the case of an annual report) that has materially affected, or is reasonably likely to materially affect, the registrant's internal control over financial reporting.

Instructions to Item 308

1. The registrant must maintain evidential matter, including documentation, to provide reasonable support for management's assessment of the effectiveness of the registrant's internal control over financial reporting. . . .

Subpart 400—Management and Certain Security Holders

Item 401. Directors, Executive Officers, Promoters and Control Persons

(a) *Identification of directors.* List the names and ages of all directors of the registrant and all persons nominated or chosen to become directors; indicate all positions and offices with the registrant held by each such person; state his term of office as director and any period(s) during which he has served as such; describe briefly any arrangement or understanding between him and any other person(s) (naming such person(s)) pursuant to which he was or is to be selected as a director or nominee. . . .

(b) *Identification of executive officers.* List the names and ages of all executive officers of the registrant and all persons chosen to become executive officers; indicate all positions and offices with the registrant held by each such person; state his term of office as officer and the period during which he has served as such and describe briefly any arrangement or understanding between him and any other person(s) (naming such person) pursuant to which he was or is to be selected as an officer.

(c) *Identification of certain significant employees.* Where the registrant employs persons such as production managers, sales managers, or research scientists who are not executive officers but who make or are expected to make significant contributions to the business of the registrant, such persons shall be identified and their background disclosed to the same extent as in the case of executive officers. Such disclosure need not be made if the registrant was subject to section 13(a) or 15(d) of the Exchange Act or was exempt from section 13(a) by section 12(g)(2)(G) of such Act immediately prior to the filing of the registration statement, report, or statement to which this Item is applicable.

(d) *Family relationships.* State the nature of any family relationship between any director, executive officer, or person nominated or chosen by the registrant to become a director or executive officer.

Instruction to Paragraph 401(d).

The term "family relationship" means any relationship by blood, marriage, or adoption, not more remote than first cousin.

(e) *Business experience* —(1) *Background.* Briefly describe the business experience during the past five years of each director, executive officer, person nominated or chosen to become a director or executive officer, and each person named in answer to paragraph (c) of Item 401, including: Each person's principal occupations and employment during the past five years; the name and principal business of any corporation or other organization in which such occupations and employment were carried on; and whether such corporation or organization is a parent, subsidiary or other affiliate of the registrant. When an executive officer or person named in response to paragraph (c) of Item 401 has been employed by the registrant or a subsidiary of the registrant for less than five years, a brief explanation shall be included as to the nature of the responsibility undertaken by the individual in prior positions to provide adequate disclosure of his prior business experience. What is required is information relating to the level of his professional competence, which may include, depending upon the circumstances, such specific information as the size of the operation supervised.

(2) *Directorships.* Indicate any other directorships held by each director or person nominated or chosen to become a director in any company with a class of securities registered pursuant to section 12 of the Exchange Act or subject to the requirements of section 15(d) of such Act....

(f) *Involvement in certain legal proceedings.* Describe any of the following events that occurred during the past five years and that are material to an evaluation of the ability or integrity of any director, person nominated to become a director or executive officer of the registrant:

(1) A petition under the Federal bankruptcy laws or any state insolvency law was filed by or against, or a receiver, fiscal agent or similar officer was appointed by a court for the business or property of such person, or any partnership in which he was a general partner at or within two years before the time of such filing, or any corporation or business association of which he was an executive officer at or within two years before the time of such filing;

(2) Such person was convicted in a criminal proceeding or is a named subject of a pending criminal proceeding (excluding traffic violations and other minor offenses);

(3) Such person was the subject of any order, judgment, or decree, not subsequently reversed, suspended or vacated, of any court of competent jurisdiction, permanently or temporarily enjoining him from, or otherwise limiting, the following activities:

(i) Acting as a futures commission merchant, introducing broker, commodity trading advisor, commodity pool operator, floor broker, leverage transaction merchant, any other person regulated by the Commodity Futures Trading Commission, or an associated person of any of the foregoing, or as an investment adviser, underwriter, broker or dealer in securities, or as an affiliated person, director or employee of any investment company, bank, savings and loan association or insurance company, or engaging in or continuing any conduct or practice in connection with such activity;

(ii) Engaging in any type of business practice; or

(iii) Engaging in any activity in connection with the purchase or sale of any security or commodity or in connection with any violation of Federal or State securities laws or Federal commodities laws....

(g) *Promoters and control persons.* (1) Registrants, which have not been subject to the reporting requirements of section 13(a) or 15(d) of the Exchange Act for the twelve months immediately prior to the filing of the registration statement, report, or statement to which this Item is applicable, and which were organized within the last five years, shall describe with respect to any promoter, any of the events enumerated in [paragraph (f)] that occurred during the past five years and that are material to a voting or investment decision.

(2) Registrants, which have not been subject to the reporting requirements of section 13(a) or 15(d) of the Exchange Act for the twelve months immediately prior to the filing of the registration statement, report, or statement to which this Item is applicable, shall describe with respect to any control person, any of the events enumerated in [paragraph (f)] that occurred during the past five years and that are material to a voting or investment decision....

(h) *Audit committee financial expert.* (1)(i) Disclose that the registrant's board of directors has determined that the registrant either:

(A) Has at least one audit committee financial expert serving on its audit committee; or

(B) Does not have an audit committee financial expert serving on its audit committee.

(ii) If the registrant provides the disclosure required by paragraph (h)(1)(i)(A) of this Item, it must disclose the name of the audit committee financial expert and whether that person is independent, as that term is used in Item 7(d)(3)(iv) of Schedule 14A under the Exchange Act.

(iii) If the registrant provides the disclosure required by paragraph (h)(1)(i)(B) of this Item, it must explain why it does not have an audit committee financial expert.

Instruction to paragraph (h)(1) *of Item 401.*

If the registrant's board of directors has determined that the registrant has more than one audit committee financial expert serving on its audit committee, the registrant may, but is not required to, disclose the names of those additional persons. A registrant choosing to identify such persons must indicate whether they are independent pursuant to Item 401(h)(1)(ii).

(2) For purposes of this Item, an audit committee financial expert means a person who has the following attributes:

(i) An understanding of generally accepted accounting principles and financial statements;

(ii) The ability to assess the general application of such principles in connection with the accounting for estimates, accruals and reserves;

(iii) Experience preparing, auditing, analyzing or evaluating financial statements that present a breadth and level of complexity of accounting issues that are generally comparable to the breadth and complexity of issues that can reasonably be expected to be raised by the registrant's financial statements, or experience actively supervising one or more persons engaged in such activities;

(iv) An understanding of internal control over financial reporting; and

(v) An understanding of audit committee functions.

(3) A person shall have acquired such attributes through:

(i) Education and experience as a principal financial officer, principal accounting officer, controller, public accountant or auditor or experience in one or more positions that involve the performance of similar functions;

(ii) Experience actively supervising a principal financial officer, principal accounting officer, controller, public accountant, auditor or person performing similar functions;

(iii) Experience overseeing or assessing the performance of companies or public accountants with respect to the preparation, auditing or evaluation of financial statements; or

(iv) Other relevant experience.

(4) *Safe Harbor.* (i) A person who is determined to be an audit committee financial expert will not be deemed an expert for any purpose, including without limitation for purposes of section 11 of the Securities Act of 1933, as a result of being designated or identified as an audit committee financial expert pursuant to this Item 401.

(ii) The designation or identification of a person as an audit committee financial expert pursuant to this Item 401 does not impose on such person any duties, obligations or liability that are greater than the duties, obligations and liability imposed on such person as a member of the audit committee and board of directors in the absence of such designation or identification.

(iii) The designation or identification of a person as an audit committee financial expert pursuant to this Item 401 does not affect the duties, obligations or liability of any other member of the audit committee or board of directors.

Instructions to Item 401(h).

1. The registrant need not provide the disclosure required by this Item 401(h) in a proxy or information statement unless that registrant is electing to incorporate this information by reference from the proxy or information statement into its annual report pursuant to general instruction G(3) to Form 10–K.

2. If a person qualifies as an audit committee financial expert by means of having held a position described in paragraph (h)(3)(iv) of this Item, the registrant shall provide a brief listing of that person's relevant experience. Such disclosure may be made by reference to disclosures required under paragraph (e) of this Item 401....

(i) *Identification of the audit committee.* (1) If you meet the following requirements, provide the disclosure in paragraph (i)(2) of this section:

(i) You are a listed issuer, as defined in Rule 10A–3 of this chapter;

(ii) You are filing either an annual report on Form 10–K or 10–KSB, or a proxy statement or information statement pursuant to the Exchange Act if action is to be taken with respect to the election of directors ...

(2)(i) State whether or not the registrant has a separately-designated standing audit committee established in accordance with section 3(a)(58)(A) of the Exchange Act, or a committee performing similar functions. If the registrant has such a committee, however designated, identify each committee member. If the entire board of directors is acting as the registrant's audit committee as specified in section 3(a)(58)(B) of the Exchange Act, so state....

(j) Describe any material changes to the procedures by which security holders may recommend nominees to the registrant's board of directors, where those changes were implemented after the registrant last provided disclosure in response to the requirements of Item 7(d)(2)(ii)(G) of Schedule 14A, or this Item.

Item 402. Executive Compensation

(a) *General....*

(3) *Persons Covered.* Disclosure shall be provided pursuant to this item for each of the following (the "named executive officers"):

(i) all individuals serving as the registrant's chief executive officer or acting in a similar capacity during the last completed fiscal year ("CEO"), regardless of compensation level;

(ii) the registrant's four most highly compensated executive officers other than the CEO who were serving as executive officers at the end of the last completed fiscal year; and

(iii) up to two additional individuals for whom disclosure would have been provided pursuant to paragraph (a)(3)(ii) of this item but for the fact that the individual was not serving as an executive officer of the registrant at the end of the last completed fiscal year.

Instructions to Item 402(a)(3).

1. *Determination of Most Highly Compensated Executive Officers.* The determination as to which executive officers are most highly compensated shall be made by reference to total annual salary and bonus for the last completed fiscal year (as required to be disclosed pursuant to paragraph (b) ... of this item), ... *provided, however,* that no disclosure need be provided for any executive officer, other than the CEO, whose total annual salary and bonus ... does not exceed $100,000.

2. *Inclusion of Executive Officer of Subsidiary.* It may be appropriate in certain circumstances for a registrant to include an executive officer of a subsidiary in the disclosure required by this item. *See* Rule 3b–7 under the Exchange Act....

(7) *Definitions.* For purposes of this item:

(i) The term "stock appreciation rights" ("SARs") refers to SARs payable in cash or stock, including SARs payable in cash or stock at the election of the registrant or a named executive officer.

(ii) The term "plan" includes, but is not limited to, the following: any plan, contract, authorization or arrangement, whether or not set forth in any formal documents, pursuant to which the following may be received: cash, stock, restricted stock or restricted stock units, phantom stock, stock options, SARs, stock options in tandem with SARs, warrants, convertible securities, performance units and performance shares, and similar instruments. A plan may be applicable to one person. Registrants may omit information regarding group life, health, hospitalization, medical reimbursement or relocation plans that do not discriminate in scope, terms or operation, in favor of executive officers or directors of the registrant and that are available generally to all salaried employees.

(iii) The term "long-term incentive plan" means any plan providing compensation intended to serve as incentive for performance to occur over a period longer than one fiscal year, whether such performance is measured by reference to financial performance of the registrant or an affiliate, the registrant's stock price, or any other measure, but excluding restricted stock, stock option and SAR plans.

(8) *Location of Specified Information.* The information required by paragraphs (i), (k) and (*l*) of this item need not be provided in any filings other than a registrant proxy or information statement relating to an annual meeting of security holders at which directors are to be elected (or special meeting or written consents in lieu of such meeting). Such information will not be deemed to be incorporated by reference into any filing under the Securities Act or the Exchange Act, except to the extent that the registrant specifically incorporates it by reference.

(9) *Liability for Specified Information.* The information required by paragraphs (k) and (*l*) of this item shall not be deemed to be "soliciting material" or to be "filed" with the Commission or subject to Regulations 14A or 14C, other than as provided in this item, or to the liabilities of Section 18 of the Exchange Act, except to the extent that the registrant specifically requests that such information be treated as soliciting material or specifically incorporates it by reference into a filing under the Securities Act or the Exchange Act.

(b) *Summary Compensation Table. (1) General.* The information specified in paragraph (b)(2) of this item, concerning the compensation of the named executive officers for each of the registrant's last three completed fiscal years shall be provided in a Summary Compensation Table, in the tabular format specified below.

				SUMMARY COMPENSATION TABLE				
		Annual Compensation			Long Term Compensation			
						Awards	Payouts	
(a)	(b)	(c)	(d)	(e)	(f)	(g)	(h)	(i)
Name and Principal Position and Principal Position	Year	Salary ($)	Bonus ($)	Other Annual Compensation ($) Annual Compensation ($)	Restricted Stock Award(s) ($) Restricted Stock Award(s) ($)	Securities Underlying Options/ SARs (#) Securities Underlying Options/ SARs (#)	LTIP Payouts ($) LTIP Pay-Outs ($)	All Other Compensation ($) Other Compensation ($)
	Year	Salary ($)	Bonus ($)					
CEO	___							
	___							
	___							
A	___							
	___							
B	___							
	___							
C	___							
	___							
D	___							
	___							

(2) The Table shall include . . .

(iii) Annual compensation . . . including. . . .

(C) The dollar value of other annual compensation not properly categorized as salary or bonus, as follows (column (e)):

(1) Perquisites and other personal benefits, securities or property, unless the aggregate amount of such compensation is the lesser of either $50,000 or 10% of the total of annual salary and bonus reported for the named executive officer in columns (c) and (d) . . .; and

(5) The dollar value of the difference between the price paid by a named executive officer for any security of the registrant or its subsidiaries purchased from the registrant or its subsidiaries (through deferral of salary or bonus, or otherwise), and the fair market value of such security at the date of purchase, unless that discount is available generally, either to all security holders or to all salaried employees of the registrant.

Instructions to Item 402(b)(2)(iii)(C).

1. Each perquisite or other personal benefit exceeding 25% of the total perquisites and other personal benefits reported for a named executive officer must be identified by type and amount in a footnote or accompanying narrative discussion to column (e).

2. Perquisites and other personal benefits shall be valued on the basis of the aggregate incremental cost to the registrant and its subsidiaries. . . .

(iv) Long-term compensation (columns (f), (g) and (h)), including:

(A) The dollar value (net of any consideration paid by the named executive officer) of any award of restricted stock, including share units (calculated by multiplying the closing market price of the registrant's unrestricted stock on the date of grant by the number of shares awarded) (column (f));

(B) The sum of the number of securities underlying stock options granted, with or without tandem SARs, and the number of freestanding SARs (column (g)): and

(C) The dollar value of all payouts pursuant to long-term incentive plans ("LTIPs") as defined in paragraph (a)(7)(iii) of this item (column (h)).

(c) *Option/SAR Grants Table.*

(1) The [following] information . . . concerning individual grants of stock options (whether or not in tandem with SARs), and freestanding SARs made during the last completed fiscal year to each of the named executive officers shall be provided in the tabular format specified below:

(2) The Table shall include, with respect to each grant . . .

(ii) The number of securities underlying option SARs granted (column (b)). . . .

(vi) Either (A) the potential realizable value of each grant of options or freestanding SARs or (B) the present value of each grant, as follows:

					Potential Realizable Value at Assumed Annual Rates of Stock Price Appreciation for Option Term		Alternative to (f) and (g): Grant Date Value
		Individual Grants					
(a)	(b)	(c)	(d)	(e)	(f)	(g)	(f)
Name	Number of Securities Underlying Options/ SARs Granted (#)	% of Total Options/ SARs Granted to Employees in Fiscal Year	Exercise or Base Price ($/Sh)	Expiration Date	5% ($)	10% ($)	Grant Date Present Value $
CEO							
A							
B							
C							
D							

Option/SAR Grants in Last Fiscal Year

(A) The potential realizable value of each grant of options or free-standing SARs, assuming that the market price of the underlying security appreciates in value from the date of grant to the end of the option or SAR term, at the following annualized rates:

(1) 5% (column (f));

(2) 10% (column (g)); and

(3) If the exercise or base price was below the market price of the underlying security at the date of grant, provide an additional column labeled 0%, to show the value at grant-date market price; or

(B) The present value of the grant at the date of grant, under any option pricing model (alternative column (f)).

Instructions to Item 402(c). . . .

7. The potential realizable dollar value of a grant (columns (f) and (g)) shall be the product of: (a) the difference between: (i) the product of the per-share market price at the time of the grant and the sum of 1 plus the adjusted stock price appreciation rate (the assumed rate of appreciation compounded annually over the term of the option or SAR); and (ii) the per-share exercise price of the option or SAR; and (b) the number of securities underlying the grant at fiscal year end. . . .

9. Where the registrant chooses to use the grant-date valuation alternative specified in paragraph (c)(2)(vi)(B) of this item, the valuation shall be footnoted to describe the valuation method used. Where the registrant has used a variation of the Black–Scholes or binomial option pricing model, the description shall identify the use of such pricing model and describe the assumptions used relating to the expected volatility, risk-free rate of return, dividend yield and time of exercise. Any adjustments for non-transferability or risk of

forfeiture also shall be disclosed. In the event another valuation method is used, the registrant is required to describe the methodology as well as any material assumption.

(d) *Aggregated Option/SAR Exercises and Fiscal Year–End Option/SAR Value Table.*

(1) The [following] information ... concerning each exercise of stock options (or tandem SARs) and freestanding SARs during the last completed fiscal year by each of the named executive officers and the fiscal year-end value of unexercised options and SARs, shall be provided on an aggregated basis in the tabular format specified below:

Aggregated Option/SAR Exercises in Last Fiscal Year and FY–End Option/SAR Values				
(a)	(b)	(c)	(d) Number of Securities Underlying Unexercised Options/SARs at FY–End (#)	(e) Value of Unexercised In-the-Money Options/SARs at FY–End ($)
Name	Shares Acquired on Exercise (#)	Value Realized ($)	Exercisable/ Unexercisable	Exercisable/ Unexercisable
CEO				
A				
B				
C				
D				

(e) *Long–Term Incentive Plan ("LTIP") Awards Table.*

(1) The [following] information ... regarding each award made to a named executive officer in the last completed fiscal year under any LTIP, shall be provided in the tabular format specified below:

Long–Term Incentive Plans—Awards in Last Fiscal Year			Estimated Future Payouts under Non–Stock Price–Based Plans		
(a)	(b) Number of Shares, Units or Other Rights (#)	(c) Performances or Other Period Until Maturation or Payout	(d) Threshold ($ or #)	(e) Target ($ or #)	(f) Maximum ($ or #)
Name					
CEO					
A					
B					
C					
D					

Instructions to Item 402(e).

1. For purposes of this paragraph, the term "long-term incentive plan" or "LTIP" shall be defined in accordance with paragraph (a)(7)(iii) of this item.

2. Describe in a footnote or in narrative text accompanying this table the material terms of any award, including a general description of the formula or criteria to be applied in determining the amounts payable. Registrants are not required to disclose any factor, criterion or performance-related or other condition to payout or maturation of a particular award that involves confidential commercial or business information, disclosure of which would adversely affect the registrant's competitive position. . . .

4. For column (d), "threshold" refers to the minimum amount payable for a certain level of performance under the plan. For column (e), "target" refers to the amount payable if the specified performance target(s) are reached. For column (f), "maximum" refers to the maximum payout possible under the plan. . . .

(f) *Defined Benefit or Actuarial Plan Disclosure.*

(1) *Pension Plan Table.*

(i) For any defined benefit or actuarial plan under which benefits are determined primarily by final compensation (or average final compensation) and years of service, provide a separate Pension Plan Table showing estimated annual benefits payable upon retirement (including amounts attributable to any defined benefit supplementary or excess pension award plans) in specified compensation and years of service classifications in the format specified below.

			PENSION PLAN TABLE		
			Years of Service		
Remuneration	15	20	25	30	35
125,000					
150,000					
175,000					
200,000					
225,000					
250,000					
300,000					
400,000					
450,000					
500,000					

(ii) Immediately following the Table, the registrant shall disclose:
. . .

(B) The estimated credited years of service for each of the named executive officers; and

(C) A statement as to the basis upon which benefits are computed (e.g., straight-life annuity amounts), and whether or not the benefits listed in the Pension Plan Table are subject to any deduction for Social Security or other offset amounts.

(2) *Alternative Pension Plan Disclosure.* For any defined benefit or actuarial plan under which benefits are not determined primarily by

final compensation (or average final compensation) and years of service, the registrant shall state in narrative form:

(i) The formula by which benefits are determined; and

(ii) The estimated annual benefits payable upon retirement at normal retirement age for each of the named executive officers.

Instructions to Item 402(f).

1. *Pension Levels.* Compensation set forth in the Pension Plan Table pursuant to paragraph (f)(1)(i) of this item shall allow for reasonable increases in existing compensation levels; alternatively, registrants may present as the highest compensation level in the Pension Plan Table an amount equal to 120% of the amount of covered compensation of the most highly compensated individual named in the Summary Compensation Table required by paragraph (b)(2) of this item . . . .

(g) *Compensation of Directors.*

(1) *Standard Arrangements.* Describe any standard arrangements, stating amounts, pursuant to which directors of the registrant are compensated for any services provided as a director, including any additional amounts payable for committee participation or special assignments.

(2) *Other Arrangements.* Describe any other arrangements pursuant to which any director of the registrant was compensated during the registrant's last completed fiscal year for any service provided as a director, stating the amount paid and the name of the director.

Instruction to Item 402(g)(2).

The information required by paragraph (g)(2) of this item shall include any arrangement, including consulting contracts, entered into in consideration of the director's service on the board. The material terms of any such arrangement shall be included.

(h) *Employment Contracts and Termination of Employment and Change-in-Control Arrangements.* Describe the terms and conditions of each of the following contracts or arrangements:

(1) Any employment contract between the registrant and a named executive officer; and

(2) Any compensatory plan or arrangement, including payments to be received from the registrant, with respect to a named executive officer, if such plan or arrangement results or will result from the resignation, retirement or any other termination of such executive officer's employment with the registrant and its subsidiaries or from a change-in-control of the registrant or a change in the named executive officer's responsibilities following a change-in-control and the amount

involved, including all periodic payments or installments, exceeds $100,000.

(i) *Report on Repricing of Options/SARs.* (1) If at any time during the last completed fiscal year, the registrant, while a reporting company pursuant to Section 13(a) or 15(d) of the Exchange Act, has adjusted or amended the exercise price of stock options or SARs previously awarded to any of the named executive officers, whether through amendment, cancellation or replacement grants, or any other means ("repriced"), the registrant shall provide the information specified in paragraphs (i)(2) and (i)(3) of this item.

(2) The compensation committee (or other board committee performing equivalent functions or, in the absence of any such committee, the entire board of directors) shall explain in reasonable detail any such repricing of options and/or SARs held by a named executive officer in the last completed fiscal year, as well as the basis for each such repricing.

(3)(i) The [following] information ... concerning all such repricings of options and SARs held by *any* executive officer during the last ten completed fiscal years, shall be provided in the tabular format specified below:

			Ten–Year Option/SAR Repricings			
(a)	(b)	(c)	(d)	(e)	(f)	(g)
		Number of Securities Underlying Options/ SARs Repriced or	Market Price of Stock at Time of Repricing or	Exercise Price At Time of Repricing or	New Exercise	Length of Original Option Term Remaining at Date of Repricing or
Name	Date	Amended (#)	Amendment ($)	Amendment ($)	Price ($)	Amendment

Instructions to Item 402(i).

1. The required report shall be made over the name of each member of the registrant's compensation committee, or other board committee performing equivalent functions or, in the absence of any such committee, the entire board of directors....

(j) *Additional Information with Respect to Compensation Committee Interlocks and Insider Participation in Compensation Decisions.* Under the caption "Compensation Committee Interlocks and Insider Participation,"

(1) The registrant shall identify each person who served as a member of the compensation committee of the registrant's board of directors (or board committee performing equivalent functions) during the last completed fiscal year, indicating each committee member who:

(i) was, during the fiscal year, an officer or employee of the registrant or any of its subsidiaries;

(ii) was formerly an officer of the registrant or any of its subsidiaries; or

(iii) had any relationship requiring disclosure by the registrant under any paragraph of Item 404 of Regulation S–K. In this event, the disclosure required by Item 404 shall accompany such identification.

(2) If the registrant has no compensation committee (or other board committee performing equivalent functions), the registrant shall identify each officer and employee of the registrant or any of its subsidiaries, and any former officer of the registrant or any of its subsidiaries, who, during the last completed fiscal year, participated in deliberations of the registrant's board of directors concerning executive officer compensation.

(3) The registrant shall describe any of the following relationships that existed during the last completed fiscal year:

(i) an executive officer of the registrant served as a member of the compensation committee (or other board committee performing equivalent functions or, in the absence of any such committee, the entire board of directors) of another entity, one of whose executive officers served on the compensation committee (or other board committee performing equivalent functions or, in the absence of any such committee, the entire board of directors) of the registrant;

(ii) an executive officer of the registrant served as a director of another entity, one of whose executive officers served on the compensation committee (or other board committee performing equivalent functions or, in the absence of any such committee, the entire board of directors) of the registrant; and

(iii) an executive officer of the registrant served as a member of the compensation committee (or other board committee performing equivalent functions or, in the absence of any such committee, the entire board of directors) of another entity, one of whose executive officers served as a director of the registrant.

(4) Disclosure required under paragraph (j)(3) of this item regarding any compensation committee member or other director of the registrant who also served as an executive officer of another entity shall be accompanied by the disclosure called for by Item 404 with respect to that person....

(k) *Board Compensation Committee Report on Executive Compensation.*

(1) Disclosure of the compensation committee's compensation policies applicable to the registrant's executive officers (including the named executive officers), including the specific relationship of corporate performance to executive compensation, is required with respect to compensation reported for the last completed fiscal year.

(2) Discussion is required of the compensation committee's bases for the CEO's compensation reported for the last completed fiscal year, including the factors and criteria upon which the CEO's compensation was based. The committee shall include a specific discussion of the relationship of the registrant's performance to the CEO's compensation for the last completed fiscal year, describing each measure of the registrant's performance, whether qualitative or quantitative, on which the CEO's compensation was based.

(3) The required disclosure shall be made over the name of each member of the registrant's compensation committee (or other board committee performing equivalent functions or, in the absence of any such committee, the entire board of directors). If the board of directors modified or rejected in any material way any action or recommendation by such committee with respect to such decisions in the last completed fiscal year, the disclosure must so indicate and explain the reasons for the board's actions, and be made over the names of all members of the board....

(l) Performance Graph.

(1) Provide a line graph comparing the yearly percentage change in the registrant's cumulative total shareholder return on a class of common stock registered under Section 12 of the Exchange Act (as measured by dividing (i) the sum of (A) the cumulative amount of dividends for the measurement period, assuming dividend reinvestment, and (B) the difference between the registrant's share price at the end and the beginning of the measurement period; by (ii) the share price at the beginning of the measurement period) with

(i) the cumulative total return of a broad equity market index assuming reinvestment of dividends, that includes companies whose equity securities are traded on the same exchange or NASDAQ market or are of comparable market capitalization; *provided, however,* that if the registrant is a company within the Standard & Poor's 500 Stock Index, the registrant must use that index; and

(ii) the cumulative total return, assuming reinvestment of dividends, of:

(A) a published industry or line-of-business index;

(B) peer issuer(s) selected in good faith. If the registrant does not select its peer issuer(s) on an industry or line-of-business basis, the registrant shall disclose the basis for its selection; or

(C) [i]ssuer(s) with similar market capitalization(s), but only if the registrant does not use a published industry or line-of-business index and does not believe it can reasonably identify a peer group. If the registrant uses this alternative, the graph shall be accompanied by a statement of the reasons for this selection.

(2) For purposes of paragraph (*l*)(1) of this item, the term "meas-urement period" shall be the period beginning at the "measurement point" established by the market close on the last trading day before the beginning of the registrant's fifth preceding fiscal year, through and including the end of the registrant's last completed fiscal year. If the class of securities has been registered under section 12 of the Exchange Act for a shorter period of time, the period covered by the comparison may correspond to that time period.

(3) For purposes of paragraph (*l*)(1)(ii)(A) of this item, the term "published industry or line-of-business index" means any index that is prepared by a party other than the registrant or an affiliate and is accessible to the registrant's security holders; provided, however, that registrants may use an index prepared by the registrant or affiliate if such index is widely recognized and used.

(4) If the registrant selects a different index from an index used for the immediately preceding fiscal year, explain the reason(s) for this change and also compare the registrant's total return with that of both the newly selected index and the index used in the immediately preced-ing fiscal year.

Instructions to Item 402(l)....

4. Registrants may include comparisons using performance measures in addition to total return, such as return on average common shareholders' equity, so long as the registrant's compensa-tion committee (or other board committee performing equivalent functions or, in the absence of any such committee, the entire board of directors) describes the link between that measure and the level of executive compensation in the statement required by paragraph (k) of this Item.

Item 403. Security Ownership of Certain Beneficial Owners and Management

(a) *Security ownership of certain beneficial owners.* Furnish the following information, as of the most recent practicable date, substan-tially in the tabular form indicated, with respect to any person (including any "group" as that term is used in section 13(d)(3) of the Exchange Act) who is known to the registrant to be the beneficial owner of more than five percent of any class of the registrant's voting securities. The address given in column (2) may be a business, mailing or residence address. Show in column (3) the total number of shares beneficially owned and in column (4) the percentage of class so owned. Of the number of shares shown in column (3), indicate by footnote or otherwise the amount known to be shares with respect to which such listed beneficial owner has the right to acquire beneficial ownership, as speci-fied in Rule 13d–3(d)(1) under the Exchange Act....

(1) Title of class	(2) Name and address of beneficial owner	(3) Amount and nature of beneficial ownership	(4) Percent of class

(b) *Security ownership of management.* Furnish the following information, as of the most recent practicable date, in substantially the tabular form indicated, as to each class of equity securities of the registrant or any of its parents or subsidiaries other than directors' qualifying shares, beneficially owned by all directors and nominees, naming them, each of the named executive officers as defined in Item 402(a)(3), and directors and executive officers of the registrant as a group, without naming them. Show in column (3) the total number of shares beneficially owned and in column (4) the percent of class so owned. Of the number of shares shown in column (3), indicate, by footnote or otherwise, the amount of shares with respect to which such persons have the right to acquire beneficial ownership as specified in Rule 13d–3(d)(1) [under the Exchange Act].

(1) Title of class	(2) Name of beneficial owner	(3) Amount and Nature of beneficial ownership	(4) Percent of class

(c) *Changes in control.* Describe any arrangements, known to the registrant, including any pledge by any person of securities of the registrant or any of its parents, the operation of which may at a subsequent date result in a change in control of the registrant.

Item 404. Certain Relationships and Related Transactions

(a) *Transactions with management and others.* Describe briefly any transaction, or series of similar transactions, since the beginning of the registrant's last fiscal year, or any currently proposed transaction, or series of similar transactions, to which the registrant or any of its subsidiaries was or is to be a party, in which the amount involved exceeds $60,000 and in which any of the following persons had, or will have, a direct or indirect material interest, naming such person and indicating the person's relationship to the registrant, the nature of such person's interest in the transaction(s), the amount of such transaction(s) and, where practicable, the amount of such person's interest in the transaction(s):

(1) Any director or executive officer of the registrant;

(2) Any nominee for election as a director;

(3) Any security holder who is known to the registrant to own of record or beneficially more than five percent of any class of the registrant's voting securities; and

(4) Any member of the immediate family of any of the foregoing persons.

Instructions to Paragraph (a) of Item 404.

1. The materiality of any interest is to be determined on the basis of the significance of the information to investors in light of all the circumstances of the particular case. The importance of the interest to the person having the interest, the relationship of the parties to the transaction with each other and the amount involved in the transactions are among the factors to be considered in determining the significance of the information to investors.

2. For purposes of paragraph (a), a person's immediate family shall include such person's spouse; parents; children; siblings; mothers and fathers-in-law; sons and daughters-in-law; and brothers and sisters-in-law.

3. In computing the amount involved in the transaction or series of similar transactions, include all periodic installments in the case of any lease or other agreement providing for periodic payments or installments.

4. The amount of the interest of any person specified in paragraphs (a)(1) through (4) shall be computed without regard to the amount of the profit or loss involved in the transaction(s).

5. In describing any transaction involving the purchase or sale of assets by or to the registrant or any of its subsidiaries, otherwise than in the ordinary course of business, state the cost of the assets to the purchaser and, if acquired by the seller within two years prior to the transaction, the cost thereof to the seller. Indicate the principle followed in determining the registrant's purchase or sale price and the name of the person making such determination.

6. Information shall be furnished in answer to paragraph (a) with respect to transactions that involve remuneration from the registrant or its subsidiaries, directly or indirectly, to any of the persons specified in paragraphs (a)(1) through (4) for services in any capacity unless the interest of such person arises solely from the ownership individually and in the aggregate of less than ten percent of any class of equity securities of another corporation furnishing the services to the registrant or its subsidiaries.

7. No information need be given in answer to paragraph (a) as to any transactions where:

A. The rates or charges involved in the transaction are determined by competitive bids, or the transaction involves the rendering of services as a common or contract carrier, or public utility, at rates or charges fixed in conformity with law or governmental authority;

B.   The transaction involves services as a bank depositary of funds, transfer agent, registrar, trustee under a trust indenture, or similar services; or

C.   The interest of the person specified in paragraphs (a)(1) through (4) arises solely from the ownership of securities of the registrant and such person receives no extra or special benefit not shared on a pro rata basis.

8.   Paragraph (a) requires disclosure of indirect, as well as direct, material interests in transactions. A person who has a position or relationship with a firm, corporation, or other entity that engages in a transaction with the registrant or its subsidiaries may have an indirect interest in such transaction by reason of such position or relationship. Such an interest, however, shall not be deemed "material" within the meaning of paragraph (a) where:

A.   The interest arises only: (i) From such person's position as a director of another corporation or organization which is a party to the transaction; or (ii) from the direct or indirect ownership by such person and all other persons specified in paragraphs (a)(1) through (4), in the aggregate, of less than a ten percent equity interest in another person (other than a partnership) which is a party to the transaction; or (iii) from both such position and ownership;

B.   The interest arises only from such person's position as a limited partner in a partnership in which the person and all other persons specified in paragraphs (a)(1) through (4) have an interest of less than ten percent; or

C.   The interest of such person arises solely from the holding of an equity interest (including a limited partnership interest, but excluding a general partnership interest) or a creditor interest in another person that is a party to the transaction with the registrant or any of its subsidiaries, and the transaction is not material to such other person.

9.   There may be situations where, although these instructions do not expressly authorize nondisclosure, the interest of a person specified in paragraphs (a)(1) through (4) in a particular transaction or series of transactions is not a direct or indirect material interest. In that case, information regarding such interest and transaction is not required to be disclosed in response to this paragraph.

(b) *Certain business relationships.* Describe any of the following relationships regarding directors or nominees for director that exist, or have existed during the registrant's last fiscal year, indicating the identity of the entity with which the registrant has such a relationship, the name of the nominee or director affiliated with such entity and the nature of such nominee's or director's affiliation, the relationship between such entity and the registrant and the amount of the business done between the registrant and the entity during the registrant's last full fiscal year or proposed to be done during the registrant's current fiscal year:

(1) If the nominee or director is, or during the last fiscal year has been, an executive officer of, or owns, or during the last fiscal year has owned, of record or beneficially in excess of ten percent equity interest in, any business or professional entity that has made during the registrant's last full fiscal year, or proposes to make during the registrant's current fiscal year, payments to the registrant or its subsidiaries for property or services in excess of five percent of (i) the registrant's consolidated gross revenues for its last full fiscal year, or (ii) the other entity's consolidated gross revenues for its last full fiscal year;

(2) If the nominee or director is, or during the last fiscal year has been, an executive officer of, or owns, or during the last fiscal year has owned, of record or beneficially in excess of ten percent equity interest in, any business or professional entity to which the registrant or its subsidiaries has made during the registrant's last full fiscal year, or proposes to make during the registrant's current fiscal year, payments for property or services in excess of five percent of (i) the registrant's consolidated gross revenues for its last full fiscal year, or (ii) the other entity's consolidated gross revenues for its last full fiscal year;

(3) If the nominee or director is, or during the last fiscal year has been, an executive officer of, or owns, or during the last fiscal year has owned, of record or beneficially in excess of ten percent equity interest in, any business or professional entity to which the registrant or its subsidiaries was indebted at the end of the registrant's last full fiscal year in an aggregate amount in excess of five percent of the registrant's total consolidated assets at the end of such fiscal year;

(4) If the nominee or director is, or during the last fiscal year has been, a member of, or of counsel to, a law firm that the issuer has retained during the last fiscal year or proposes to retain during the current fiscal year; *Provided, however,* that the dollar amount of fees paid to a law firm by the registrant need not be disclosed if such amount does not exceed five percent of the law firm's gross revenues for that firm's last full fiscal year;

(5) If the nominee or director is, or during the last fiscal year has been, a partner or executive officer of any investment banking firm that has performed services for the registrant, other than as a participating underwriter in a syndicate, during the last fiscal year or that the registrant proposes to have perform services during the current year; *Provided, however,* That the dollar amount of compensation received by an investment banking firm need not be disclosed if such amount does not exceed five percent of the investment banking firm's consolidated gross revenues for that firm's last full fiscal year; or

(6) Any other relationships that the registrant is aware of between the nominee or director and the registrant that are substantially similar in nature and scope to those relationships listed in paragraphs (b)(1) through (5).

Instructions to Paragraph (b) of Item 404. ...

2. In calculating payments for property and services the following may be excluded:

A. Payments where the rates or charges involved in the transaction are determined by competitive bids, or the transaction involves the rendering of services as a common contract carrier, or public utility, at rates or charges fixed in conformity with law or governmental authority;

B. Payments that arise solely from the ownership of securities of the registrant and no extra or special benefit not shared on a pro rata basis by all holders of the class of securities is received. . . .

3. In calculating indebtedness the following may be excluded:

A. Debt securities that have been publicly offered, admitted to trading on a national securities exchange, or quoted on the automated quotation system of a registered securities association;

B. Amounts due for purchases subject to the usual trade terms. . . .

(c) *Indebtedness of management.* If any of the following persons has been indebted to the registrant or its subsidiaries at any time since the beginning of the registrant's last fiscal year in an amount in excess of $60,000, indicate the name of such person, the nature of the person's relationship by reason of which such person's indebtedness is required to be described, the largest aggregate amount of indebtedness outstanding at any time during such period, the nature of the indebtedness and of the transaction in which it was incurred, the amount thereof outstanding as of the latest practicable date and the rate of interest paid or charged thereon:

(1) Any director or executive officer of the registrant;

(2) Any nominee for election as a director;

(3) Any member of the immediate family of any of the persons specified in paragraph (c)(1) or (2);

(4) Any corporation or organization (other than the registrant or a majority-owned subsidiary of the registrant) of which any of the persons specified in paragraph (c)(1) or (2) is an executive officer or partner or is, directly or indirectly, the beneficial owner of ten percent or more of any class of equity securities; and

(5) Any trust or other estate in which any of the persons specified in paragraph (c)(1) or (2) has a substantial beneficial interest or as to which such person serves as a trustee or in a similar capacity.

Instructions to Paragraph (c) of Item 404.

1. For purposes of paragraph (c), the members of a person's immediate family are those persons specified in Instruction 2 to Item 404(a).

2. Exclude from the determination of the amount of indebtedness all amounts due from the particular person for purchases subject to usual trade terms, for ordinary travel and expense payments and for other transactions in the ordinary course of business.

3. If the lender is a bank, savings and loan association, or broker-dealer extending credit under Federal Reserve Regulation T ... and the loans are not disclosed as nonaccrual, past due, restructured or potential problems ... disclosure may consist of a statement, if such is the case, that the loans to such persons (A) were made in the ordinary course of business, (B) were made on substantially the same terms, including interest rates and collateral, as those prevailing at the time for comparable transactions with other persons, and (C) did not involve more than the normal risk of collectibility or present other unfavorable features.

4. If any indebtedness required to be described arose under section 16(b) of the Exchange Act and has not been discharged by payment, state the amount of any profit realized, that such profit will inure to the benefit of the registrant or its subsidiaries and whether suit will be brought or other steps taken to recover such profit. If, in the opinion of counsel, a question reasonably exists as to the recoverability of such profit, it will suffice to state all facts necessary to describe the transactions, including the prices and number of shares involved.

(d) *Transactions with promoters.* Registrants that have been organized within the past five years and that are filing a registration statement on Form S–1 under the Securities Act ... or on Form 10 under the Exchange Act ... shall:

(1) State the names of the promoters, the nature and amount of anything of value (including money, property, contracts, options or rights of any kind) received or to be received by each promoter, directly or indirectly, from the registrant and the nature and amount of any assets, services or other consideration therefore received or to be received by the registrant; and

(2) As to any assets acquired or to be acquired by the registrant from a promoter, state the amount at which the assets were acquired or are to be acquired and the principle followed or to be followed in determining such amount and identify the persons making the determi-

nation and their relationship, if any, with the registrant or any promoter. If the assets were acquired by the promoter within two years prior to their transfer to the registrant, also state the cost thereof to the promoter.

Item 405. Compliance With Section 16(a) of the Exchange Act

Every registrant having a class of equity securities registered pursuant to Section 12 of the Exchange Act . . . shall:

(a) Based solely upon a review of Forms 3 and 4 and amendments thereto furnished to the registrant under Rule 16a–3(e) during its most recent fiscal year and Forms 5 and amendments thereto furnished to the registrant with respect to its most recent fiscal year, and any written representation referred to in paragraph (b)(1) of this section:

(1) Under the caption "Section 16(a) Beneficial Ownership Reporting Compliance," identify each person who, at any time during the fiscal year, was a director, officer, [or] beneficial owner of more than ten percent of any class of equity securities of the registrant registered pursuant to Section 12 of the Exchange Act . . . ("reporting person") that failed to file on a timely basis, as disclosed in the above Forms, reports required by Section 16(a) of the Exchange Act during the most recent fiscal year or prior fiscal years.

(2) For each such person, set forth the number of late reports, the number of transactions that were not reported on a timely basis, and any known failure to file a required Form. A known failure to file would include, but not be limited to, a failure to file a Form 3, which is required of all reporting persons, and a failure to file a Form 5 in the absence of the written representation referred to in paragraph (b)(1) of this section, unless the registrant otherwise knows that no Form 5 is required.

(b) With respect to the disclosure required by paragraph (a) of this section, if the registrant:

(1) Receives a written representation from the reporting person that no Form 5 is required; and

(2) Maintains the representation for two years, making a copy available to the Commission or its staff upon request,

the registrant need not identify such reporting person pursuant to paragraph (a) of this section as having failed to file a Form 5 with respect to that fiscal year.

Item 406. Code of Ethics

(a) Disclose whether the registrant has adopted a code of ethics that applies to the registrant's principal executive officer, principal financial officer, principal accounting officer or controller, or persons performing similar functions. If the registrant has not adopted such a code of ethics, explain why it has not done so.

(b) For purposes of this Item 406, the term code of ethics means written standards that are reasonably designed to deter wrongdoing and to promote:

    (1) Honest and ethical conduct, including the ethical handling of actual or apparent conflicts of interest between personal and professional relationships;

    (2) Full, fair, accurate, timely, and understandable disclosure in reports and documents that a registrant files with, or submits to, the Commission and in other public communications made by the registrant;

    (3) Compliance with applicable governmental laws, rules and regulations;

    (4) The prompt internal reporting of violations of the code to an appropriate person or persons identified in the code; and

    (5) Accountability for adherence to the code.

(c) The registrant must:

    (1) File with the Commission a copy of its code of ethics that applies to the registrant's principal executive officer, principal financial officer, principal accounting officer or controller, or persons performing similar functions, as an exhibit to its annual report;

    (2) Post the text of such code of ethics on its Internet website and disclose, in its annual report, its Internet address and the fact that it has posted such code of ethics on its Internet Web site; or

    (3) Undertake in its annual report filed with the Commission to provide to any person without charge, upon request, a copy of such code of ethics and explain the manner in which such request may be made.

(d) If the registrant intends to satisfy the disclosure requirement under Item 10 of Form 8–K regarding an amendment to, or a waiver from, a provision of its code of ethics that applies to the registrant's principal executive officer, principal financial officer, principal accounting officer or controller, or persons performing similar functions and that relates to any element of the code of ethics definition enumerated in paragraph (b) of this Item by posting such information on its Internet website, disclose the registrant's Internet address and such intention.

Instructions to Item 406.

    1. A registrant may have separate codes of ethics for different types of officers. Furthermore, a code of ethics within the meaning of paragraph (b) of this Item may be a portion of a broader document that addresses additional topics or that applies to more

persons than those specified in paragraph (a). In satisfying the requirements of paragraph (c), a registrant need only file, post or provide the portions of a broader document that constitutes a code of ethics as defined in paragraph (b) and that apply to the persons specified in paragraph (a).

2.   If a registrant elects to satisfy paragraph (c) of this Item by posting its code of ethics on its website pursuant to paragraph (c)(2), the code of ethics must remain accessible on its Web site for as long as the registrant remains subject to the requirements of this Item and chooses to comply with this Item by posting its code on its Web site pursuant to paragraph (c)(2)....

Subpart 500—Registration Statement and Prospectus Provisions....

Item 512.   Undertakings

Include each of the following undertakings that is applicable to the offering being registered.

(a) *Rule 415 Offering.*   Include the following if the securities are registered pursuant to Rule 415 under the Securities Act . . . :

The undersigned registrant hereby undertakes:

(1) To file, during any period in which offers or sales are being made, a post-effective amendment to this registration statement:

(i) To include any prospectus required by section 10(a)(3) of the Securities Act of 1933;

(ii) To reflect in the prospectus any facts or events arising after the effective date of the registration statement (or the most recent post-effective amendment thereof) which, individually or in the aggregate, represent a fundamental change in the information set forth in the registration statement. Notwithstanding the foregoing, any increase or decrease in volume of securities offered (if the total dollar value of securities offered would not exceed that which was registered) and any deviation from the low or high end of the estimated maximum offering range may be reflected in the form of prospectus filed with the Commission pursuant to Rule 424(b) . . . if, in the aggregate, the changes in volume and price represent no more than a 20% change in the maximum aggregate offering price set forth in the "Calculation of Registration Fee" table in the effective registration statement.

(iii) To include any material information with respect to the plan of distribution not previously disclosed in the registration statement or any material change to such information in the registration statement;

Provided, however, That . . .

(B) Paragraphs (a)(1)(i), (a)(1)(ii) and (a)(1)(iii) of this section do not apply if the registration statement is on Form S–3 ... and the information required to be included in a post-effective amendment by those paragraphs is contained in reports filed with or furnished to the Commission by the registrant pursuant to section 13 or section 15(d) of the Securities Exchange Act of 1934 that are incorporated by reference in the registration statement, or is contained in a form of prospectus filed pursuant to Rule 424(b) [Filing of Prospectuses; Number of Copies] that is part of the registration statement.

(C) Paragraphs (a)(1)(i) and (a)(1)(ii) of this section do not apply if the registration statement is on Form S–3, Form S–8 or Form F–3, and the information required to be included in a post-effective amendment by those paragraphs is contained in periodic reports filed with or furnished to the Commission by the registrant pursuant to section 13 or section 15(d) of the Securities Exchange Act of 1934 that are incorporated by reference in the registration statement....

(2) That, for the purpose of determining any liability under the Securities Act of 1933, each such post-effective amendment shall be deemed to be a new registration statement relating to the securities offered therein, and the offering of such securities at that time shall be deemed to be the initial bona fide offering thereof.

(3) To remove from registration by means of a post-effective amendment any of the securities being registered which remain unsold at the termination of the offering. ...

(6) That, for the purpose of determining liability of the registrant under the Securities Act of 1933 to any purchaser in the initial distribution of the securities:

The undersigned registrant undertakes that in a primary offering of securities of the undersigned registrant pursuant to this registrant statement, regardless of the underwriting method used to sell the securities to the purchaser, if the securities are offered or sold to such purchaser by means of any of the following communications, the undersigned registrant will be a seller to the purchaser and will be considered to offer or sell such securities to such purchaser:

(i) Any preliminary prospectus or prospectus of the undersigned registrant relating to the offering required to be filed pursuant to Rule 424;

(ii) Any free writing prospectus relating to the offering prepared by or on behalf of the undersigned registrant or used or referred to by the undersigned registrant;

(iii) The portion of any other free writing prospectus relating to the offering containing material information about the undersigned registrant or its securities provided by or on behalf of the undersigned registrant; and

(iv) Any other communication that is an offer in the offering made by the undersigned registrant to the purchaser.

(b) *Filings incorporating subsequent Exchange Act documents by reference.* Include the following if the registration statement incorporates by reference any Exchange Act document filed subsequent to the effective date of the registration statement:

> The undersigned registrant hereby undertakes that, for purposes of determining any liability under the Securities Act of 1933, each filing of the registrant's annual report pursuant to section 13(a) or section 15(d) of the Securities Exchange Act of 1934 (and, where applicable, each filing of an employee benefit plan's annual report pursuant to section 15(d) of the Securities Exchange Act of 1934) that is incorporated by reference in the registration statement shall be deemed to be a new registration statement relating to the securities offered therein, and the offering of such securities at that time shall be deemed to be the initial bona fide offering thereof. . . .

(h) *Request for acceleration of effective date or filing of registration statement becoming effective upon filing.* Include the following if acceleration is requested of the effective date of the registration statement pursuant to Rule 461 under the Securities Act, [or] if a Form S–3 or . . . will become effective upon filing with the Commission pursuant to Rule 462 (e) or (f) [Immediate Effectiveness of Certain Registration Statements and Post–Effective Amendments] under the Securities Act, and: (1) any provision or arrangement exists whereby the registrant may indemnify a director, officer or controlling person of the registrant against liabilities arising under the Securities Act, or (2) the underwriting agreement contains a provision whereby the registrant indemnifies the underwriter or controlling persons of the underwriter against such liabilities and a director, officer or controlling person of the registrant is such an underwriter or controlling person thereof or a member of any firm which is such an underwriter, and (3) the benefits of such indemnification are not waived by such persons:

> Insofar as indemnification for liabilities arising under the Securities Act of 1933 may be permitted to directors, officers and controlling persons of the registrant pursuant to the foregoing provisions, or otherwise, the registrant has been advised that in the opinion of the Securities and Exchange Commission such indemnification is against public policy as expressed in the Act and is, therefore, unenforceable. In the event that a claim for indemnification against such liabilities (other than the payment by the registrant of expenses incurred or paid by a director, officer or controlling person of the registrant in the successful defense of any action, suit or proceeding) is asserted by such director, officer or controlling person in connection with the securities being registered, the regis-

trant will, unless in the opinion of its counsel the matter has been settled by controlling precedent, submit to a court of appropriate jurisdiction the question whether such indemnification by it is against public policy as expressed in the Act and will be governed by the final adjudication of such issue. . . .

Subpart 600—Exhibits

Item 601. Exhibits. . . .

(b) Description of Exhibits . . .

(10) Material Contracts . . .

(ii) . . .

(B) Any compensatory plan, contract or arrangement adopted without the approval of security holders pursuant to which equity may be awarded, including, but not limited to, options, warrants or rights (or if not set forth in any formal document, a written description thereof), in which any employee (whether or not an executive officer of the registrant) participates shall be filed unless immaterial in amount or significance. . . .

(14) *Code of ethics*. Any code of ethics, or amendment thereto, that is the subject of the disclosure required by Item 406 of Regulation S–K or Item 10 of Form 8–K, to the extent that the registrant intends to satisfy the Item 406 or Item 10 requirements through filing of an exhibit. . . .

(17) *Correspondence on departure of director*. Any written correspondence from a former director concerning the circumstances surrounding the former director's retirement, resignation, refusal to stand for re-election or removal, including any letter from the former director to the registrant stating whether the former director agrees with statements made by the registrant describing the former director's departure. . . .

(31)(i) The certifications required by Rule 13a–14(a) or Rule 15d–14(a) exactly as set forth below. . . .

CERTIFICATIONS*

I, [identify the certifying individual], certify that:

1. I have reviewed this [specify report] of [identify registrant];

2. Based on my knowledge, this report does not contain any untrue statement of a material fact or omit to state a material fact necessary to make the statements made, in light of the circumstances under which

---

* Provide a separate certification for each principal executive officer and principal financial officer of the registrant. See Rules 13a–14(a) and 15d–14(a).

such statements were made, not misleading with respect to the period covered by this report;

3. Based on my knowledge, the financial statements, and other financial information included in this report, fairly present in all material respects the financial condition, results of operations and cash flows of the registrant as of, and for, the periods presented in this report;

4. The registrant's other certifying officer(s) and I are responsible for establishing and maintaining disclosure controls and procedures (as defined in Exchange Act Rules 13a–15(e) and 15d–15(e)) and internal control over financial reporting (as defined in Exchange Act Rules 13a–15(f) and 15d–15(f)) for the registrant and have:

(a) Designed such disclosure controls and procedures, or caused such disclosure controls and procedures to be designed under our supervision, to ensure that material information relating to the registrant, including its consolidated subsidiaries, is made known to us by others within those entities, particularly during the period in which this report is being prepared;

(b) Designed such internal control over financial reporting, or caused such internal control over financial reporting to be designed under our supervision, to provide reasonable assurance regarding the reliability of financial reporting and the preparation of financial statements for external purposes in accordance with generally accepted accounting principles;

(c) Evaluated the effectiveness of the registrant's disclosure controls and procedures and presented in this report our conclusions about the effectiveness of the disclosure controls and procedures, as of the end of the period covered by this report based on such evaluation; and

(d) Disclosed in this report any change in the registrant's internal control over financial reporting that occurred during the registrant's most recent fiscal quarter (the registrant's fourth fiscal quarter in the case of an annual report) that has materially affected, or is reasonably likely to materially affect, the registrant's internal control over financial reporting; and

5. The registrant's other certifying officer(s) and I have disclosed, based on our most recent evaluation of internal control over financial reporting, to the registrant's auditors and the audit committee of the registrant's board of directors (or persons performing the equivalent functions):

(a) All significant deficiencies and material weaknesses in the design or operation of internal control over financial reporting which are reasonably likely to adversely affect the registrant's ability to record, process, summarize and report financial information; and

(b) Any fraud, whether or not material, that involves management or other employees who have a significant role in the registrant's internal control over financial reporting.

Date: ....

                                      _____

                                       [Signature]
                                       [Title]

(32) *Section 1350 Certifications.*

(i) The certifications required by Rule 13a–14(b) or Rule 15d–14(b) and Section 1350 of Chapter 63 of Title 18 of the United States.

(ii) A certification furnished pursuant to this item will not be deemed "filed" for purposes of Section 18 of the Exchange Act, or otherwise subject to the liability of that section. Such certification will not be deemed to be incorporated by reference into any filing under the Securities Act or the Exchange Act, except to the extent that the registrant specifically incorporates it by reference....

Subpart 900—Roll–Up Transactions

Item 901.   **[Definitions]** ...

(b)(1) *Partnership* means any:

(i) Finite-life limited partnership; or

(ii) Other finite-life entity.

(2)(i) Except as provided in paragraph (b)(2)(ii) of this Item ..., a limited partnership or other entity is "finite-life" if:

(A) It operates as a conduit vehicle for investors to participate in the ownership of assets for a limited period of time; and

(B) It has as a policy or purpose distributing to investors proceeds from the sale, financing or refinancing of assets or cash from operations, rather than reinvesting such proceeds or cash in the business (whether for the term of the entity or after an initial period of time following commencement of operations).

(ii) A real estate investment trust as defined in I.R.C. section 856 is not *finite-life* solely because of the distribution to investors of net income as provided by the I.R.C. if its policies or purposes do not include the distribution to investors of proceeds from the sale, financing or refinancing of assets, rather than the reinvestment of such proceeds in the business....

(c)(1) Except as provided in paragraph (c)(2) or (c)(3) of this Item, *roll-up transaction* means a transaction involving the combination or reorganization of one or more partnerships, directly or indirectly, in which some or all of the investors in any of such partnerships will receive new securities, or securities in another entity.

(2) Notwithstanding paragraph (c)(1) of this Item, *roll-up transaction* shall not include:

(i) A transaction wherein the interests of all of the investors in each of the partnerships are repurchased, recalled, or exchanged in accordance with the terms of the preexisting partnership agreement for securities in an operating company specifically identified at the time of the formation of the original partnership;

(ii) A transaction in which the securities to be issued or exchanged are not required to be and are not registered under the Securities Act of 1933 . . .;

(iii) A transaction that involves only issuers that are not required to register or report under Section 12 of the Securities Exchange Act of 1934, . . . both before and after the transaction;

(iv) A transaction that involves the combination or reorganization of one or more partnerships in which a non-affiliated party succeeds to the interests of a general partner or sponsor, if:

(A) Such action is approved by not less than 66⅔% of the outstanding units of each of the participating partnerships; and

(B) As a result of the transaction, the existing general partners will receive only compensation to which they are entitled as expressly provided for in the preexisting partnership agreements; . . .

. . .

(C) For purposes of paragraph (c)(2)(v) of this item . . ., a *regularly traded* security means any security with a minimum closing price of $2.00 or more for a majority of the business days during the preceding three-month period and a six-month minimum average daily trading volume of 1,000 shares . . .;

(vii) A transaction in which the investors in any of the partnerships involved in the transaction are not subject to a significant adverse change with respect to voting rights, the terms of existence of the entity, management compensation or investment objectives; or

(viii) A transaction in which all investors are provided an option to receive or retain a security under substantially the same terms and conditions as the original issue. . . .

Item 908. Reasons for and Alternatives to the Roll–Up Transaction

(a) Describe the reason(s) for the roll-up transaction.

(b)(1) If the general partner or sponsor considered alternatives to the roll-up transaction being proposed, describe such alternative(s) and state the reason(s) for their rejection.

(2) Whether or not described in response to paragraph (b)(1) of this Item, describe in reasonable detail the potential alternative of continuation of the partnerships in accordance with their existing business plans, including the effects of such continuation and the material risks and benefits that likely would arise in connection therewith, and, if applicable, the general partner's reasons for not considering such alternative.

(3) Whether or not described in response to paragraph (b)(1) of this Item, describe in reasonable detail the potential alternative of liquidation of the partnerships, the procedures required to accomplish liquidation, the effects of liquidation, the material risks and benefits that likely would arise in connection with liquidation, and, if applicable, the general partner's reasons for not considering such alternative.

(c) State the reasons for the structure of the roll-up transaction and for undertaking such transaction at this time.

(d) State whether the general partner initiated the roll-up transaction and, if not, whether the general partner participated in the structuring of the transaction.

(e) State whether the general partner recommends the roll-up transaction and briefly describe the reasons for such recommendation.

Item 909. Conflicts of Interest

(a) Briefly describe the general partner's fiduciary duties to each partnership subject to the roll-up transaction and each actual or potential material conflict of interest between the general partner and the investors relating to the roll-up transaction.

(b)(1) State whether or not the general partner has retained an unaffiliated representative to act on behalf of investors for purposes of negotiating the terms of the roll-up transaction. If no such representative has been retained, describe the reasons therefor and the risks arising from the absence of separate representation. . . .

Item 910. Fairness of the Transaction

(a) State whether the general partner reasonably believes that the roll-up transaction is fair or unfair to investors and the reasons for such belief. Such discussion must address the fairness of the roll-up transaction to investors in each of the partnerships and as a whole. If the roll-up transaction may be completed with a combination of partnerships consisting of less than all partnerships, or with portions of partnerships, the belief stated must address each possible combination.

(b) Discuss in reasonable detail the material factors upon which the belief stated in paragraph (a) of this Item is based and, to the extent practicable, the weight assigned to each such factor. Such discussion should include an analysis of the extent, if any, to which such belief is based on the factors set forth in Instructions (2) and (3) to this Item, paragraph (b)(1) of Item 909 ... and Item 911.... This discussion also must:

(1) Compare the value of the consideration to be received in the roll-up transaction to the value of the consideration that would be received pursuant to each of the alternatives discussed in response to Item 908(b) ...; and

(2) Describe any material differences among the partnerships (e.g., different types of assets or different investment objectives) relating to the fairness of the transaction.

(c) If any offer of the type described in Instruction (2)(viii) to this Item has been received, describe such offer and state the reason(s) for its rejection.

(d) Describe any factors known to the general partner that may affect materially the value of the consideration to be received by investors in the roll-up transaction, the values assigned to the partnerships for purposes of the comparisons to alternatives required by paragraph (b) of this Item and the fairness of the transaction to investors.

(e) State whether the general partner's statements in response to paragraphs (a) and (b) of this Item are based, in whole or in part, on any report, opinion or appraisal described in response to Item 911 of this subpart. If so, describe any material uncertainties known to the general partner that relate to the conclusions in any such report, opinion or appraisal including, but not limited to, developments or trends that have affected or are reasonably likely to affect materially such conclusions.

Instructions to Item 910.

(1) A statement that the general partner has no reasonable belief as to the fairness of the roll-up transaction to investors will not be considered sufficient disclosure in response to paragraph (a) of this Item.

(2) The factors which are important in determining the fairness of a roll-up transaction to investors and the weight, if any, which should be given to them in a particular context will vary. Normally such factors will include, among others, those referred to in paragraph (b)(1) of Item 909 and whether the consideration offered to investors constitutes fair value in relation to:

(i) Current market prices, if any;

(ii) Historic market prices, if any;

(iii) Net book value;

(iv) Going concern value;

(v) Liquidation value;

(vi) Purchases of limited partnership interests by the general partner or sponsor or their affiliates since the commencement of the partnership's second full fiscal year preceding the date of filing of the disclosure document for the roll-up transaction;

(vii) Any report, opinion, or appraisal described in Item 911; and

(viii) Offers of which the general partner or sponsor is aware made during the preceding eighteen months for a merger, consolidation, or combination of any of the partnerships; an acquisition of any of the partnerships or a material amount of their assets; a tender offer for or other acquisition of securities of any class issued by any of the partnerships; or a change in control of any of the partnerships.

(3) The discussion concerning fairness should specifically address material terms of the transaction including whether the consideration offered to investors constitutes fair value in relation to:

(i) The form and amount of consideration to be received by investors and the sponsor in the roll-up transaction;

(ii) The methods used to determine such consideration; and

(iii) The compensation to be paid to the sponsor in the future.

(4) Conclusory statements, such as "The roll-up transaction is fair to investors in relation to net book value, going concern value, liquidation value and future prospects of the partnership," will not be considered sufficient disclosure in response to paragraph (b) of this Item....

Item 911. Reports, Opinions and Appraisals

(a)(1) *All material reports, opinions or appraisals.* State whether or not the general partner or sponsor has received any report, opinion (other than an opinion of counsel) or appraisal from an outside party which is materially related to the roll-up transaction including, but not limited to, any such report, opinion or appraisal relating to the consideration or the fairness of the consideration to be offered to investors in connection with the roll-up transaction or the fairness of such transaction to the general partner or investors....

(b) *Fairness Opinions:* (1) If any report, opinion or appraisal relates to the fairness of the roll-up transaction to investors in the partnerships, state whether or not the report, opinion or appraisal addresses the fairness of:

(i) The roll-up transaction as a whole and to investors in each partnership; and

(ii) All possible combinations of partnerships in the roll-up transaction (including portions of partnerships if the transaction is structured to permit portions of partnerships to participate). If all possible combinations are not addressed:

(A) Identify the combinations that are addressed;

(B) Identify the person(s) that determined which combinations would be addressed and state the reasons for the selection of the combinations; and

(C) State that if the roll-up transaction is completed with a combination of partnerships not addressed, no report, opinion or appraisal concerning the fairness of the roll-up transaction will have been obtained.

(2) If the sponsor or the general partner has not obtained any opinion on the fairness of the proposed roll-up transaction to investors in each of the affected partnerships, state the sponsor's or general partner's reasons for concluding that such an opinion is not necessary in order to permit the limited partners or shareholders to make an informed decision on the proposed transaction. . . .

REGULATION M–A

Item 1000. Definitions

The following definitions apply to the terms used in Regulation M–A, unless specified otherwise:

(a) *Associate* has the same meaning as in Rule 12b–2;

(b) *Instruction C* means General Instruction C to Schedule 13E–3 and General Instruction C to Schedule TO.

(c) *Issuer tender offer* has the same meaning as in Rule 13e–4(a)(2);

(d) *Offeror* means any person who makes a tender offer or on whose behalf a tender offer is made;

(e) *Rule 13e–3 transaction* has the same meaning as in Rule 13e–3(a)(3);

(f) *Subject company* means the company or entity whose securities are sought to be acquired in the transaction (e.g., the target), or that is otherwise the subject of the transaction;

(g) *Subject securities* means the securities or class of securities that are sought to be acquired in the transaction or that are otherwise the subject of the transaction; and

(h) *Third-party tender offer* means a tender offer that is not an issuer tender offer.

Item 1001. Summary Term Sheet

Summary term sheet. Provide security holders with a summary term sheet that is written in plain English. The summary term sheet must briefly describe in bullet point format the most material terms of the proposed transaction. The summary term sheet must provide security holders with sufficient information to understand the essential features and significance of the proposed transaction. The bullet points must cross-reference a more detailed discussion contained in the disclosure document that is disseminated to security holders.

Item 1002. Subject Company Information

(a) *Name and address.* State the name of the subject company (or the issuer in the case of an issuer tender offer), and the address and telephone number of its principal executive offices.

(b) *Securities.* State the exact title and number of shares outstanding of the subject class of equity securities as of the most recent practicable date. This may be based upon information in the most recently available filing with the Commission by the subject company unless the filing person has more current information.

(c) *Trading market and price.* Identify the principal market in which the subject securities are traded and state the high and low sales prices for the subject securities in the principal market (or, if there is no principal market, the range of high and low bid quotations and the source of the quotations) for each quarter during the past two years. If there is no established trading market for the securities (except for limited or sporadic quotations), so state.

(d) *Dividends.* State the frequency and amount of any dividends paid during the past two years with respect to the subject securities. Briefly describe any restriction on the subject company's current or future ability to pay dividends. If the filing person is not the subject company, furnish this information to the extent known after making reasonable inquiry.

(e) *Prior public offerings.* If the filing person has made an underwritten public offering of the subject securities for cash during the past three years that was registered under the Securities Act of 1933 or exempt from registration under Regulation A [under that Act], state the date of the offering, the amount of securities offered, the offering price per share (adjusted for stock splits, stock dividends, etc. as appropriate) and the aggregate proceeds received by the filing person.

(f) *Prior stock purchases.* If the filing person purchased any subject securities during the past two years, state the amount of the securities purchased, the range of prices paid and the average purchase price for each quarter during that period. Affiliates need not give information for purchases made before becoming an affiliate.

Item 1003.   Identity and Background of Filing Person

(a) *Name and address.* State the name, business address and business telephone number of each filing person. Also state the name and address of each person specified in Instruction C to the schedule (except for Schedule 14D–9). If the filing person is an affiliate of the subject company, state the nature of the affiliation. If the filing person is the subject company, so state.

(b) *Business and background of entities.* If any filing person (other than the subject company) or any person specified in Instruction C to the schedule is not a natural person, state the person's principal business, state or other place of organization, and the information required by paragraphs (c)(3) and (c)(4) of this section for each person.

(c) Business and background of natural persons. If any filing person or any person specified in Instruction C to the schedule is a natural person, provide the following information for each person:

(1) Current principal occupation or employment and the name, principal business and address of any corporation or other organization in which the employment or occupation is conducted;

(2) Material occupations, positions, offices or employment during the past five years, giving the starting and ending dates of each and the name, principal business and address of any corporation or other organization in which the occupation, position, office or employment was carried on;

(3) A statement whether or not the person was convicted in a criminal proceeding during the past five years (excluding traffic violations or similar misdemeanors). If the person was convicted, describe the criminal proceeding, including the dates, nature of conviction, name and location of court, and penalty imposed or other disposition of the case;

(4) A statement whether or not the person was a party to any judicial or administrative proceeding during the past five years (except for matters that were dismissed without sanction or settlement) that resulted in a judgment, decree or final order enjoining the person from future violations of, or prohibiting activities subject to, federal or state securities laws, or a finding of any violation of federal or state securities laws. Describe the proceeding, including a summary of the terms of the judgment, decree or final order; and

(5) Country of citizenship.

(d) *Tender offer.* Identify the tender offer and the class of securities to which the offer relates, the name of the offeror and its address (which may be based on the offeror's Schedule TO filed with the Commission).

Item 1004.   Terms of the Transaction

(a) *Material terms.* State the material terms of the transaction.

(1) *Tender offers*. In the case of a tender offer, the information must include:

(i) The total number and class of securities sought in the offer;

(ii) The type and amount of consideration offered to security holders;

(iii) The scheduled expiration date;

(iv) Whether a subsequent offering period will be available, if the transaction is a third-party tender offer;

(v) Whether the offer may be extended, and if so, how it could be extended;

(vi) The dates before and after which security holders may withdraw securities tendered in the offer;

(vii) The procedures for tendering and withdrawing securities;

(viii) The manner in which securities will be accepted for payment;

(ix) If the offer is for less than all securities of a class, the periods for accepting securities on a pro rata basis and the offeror's present intentions in the event that the offer is oversubscribed;

(x) An explanation of any material differences in the rights of security holders as a result of the transaction, if material;

(xi) A brief statement as to the accounting treatment of the transaction, if material; and

(xii) The federal income tax consequences of the transaction, if material.

(2) *Mergers or similar transactions*. In the case of a merger or similar transaction, the information must include:

(i) A brief description of the transaction;

(ii) The consideration offered to security holders;

(iii) The reasons for engaging in the transaction;

(iv) The vote required for approval of the transaction;

(v) An explanation of any material differences in the rights of security holders as a result of the transaction, if material;

(vi) A brief statement as to the accounting treatment of the transaction, if material; and

(vii) The federal income tax consequences of the transaction, if material.

(b) *Purchases*. State whether any securities are to be purchased from any officer, director or affiliate of the subject company and provide the details of each transaction.

(c) *Different terms*. Describe any term or arrangement in the Rule 13e–3 transaction that treats any subject security holders differently from other subject security holders.

(d) *Appraisal rights*. State whether or not dissenting security holders are entitled to any appraisal rights. If so, summarize the appraisal rights. If there are no appraisal rights available under state law for security holders who object to the transaction, briefly outline any other rights that may be available to security holders under the law.

(e) *Provisions for unaffiliated security holders*. Describe any provision made by the filing person in connection with the transaction to grant unaffiliated security holders access to the corporate files of the filing person or to obtain counsel or appraisal services at the expense of the filing person. If none, so state.

(f) *Eligibility for listing or trading*. If the transaction involves the offer of securities of the filing person in exchange for equity securities held by unaffiliated security holders of the subject company, describe whether or not the filing person will take steps to assure that the securities offered are or will be eligible for trading on an automated quotations system operated by a national securities association.

Item 1005. Past Contacts, Transactions, Negotiations and Agreements

(a) *Transactions*. Briefly state the nature and approximate dollar amount of any transaction, other than those described in paragraphs (b) or (c) of this section, that occurred during the past two years, between the filing person (including any person specified in Instruction C of the schedule) and;

(1) The subject company or any of its affiliates that are not natural persons if the aggregate value of the transactions is more than one percent of the subject company's consolidated revenues for:

(i) The fiscal year when the transaction occurred; or

(ii) The past portion of the current fiscal year, if the transaction occurred in the current year; and

(2) Any executive officer, director or affiliate of the subject company that is a natural person if the aggregate value of the transaction or series of similar transactions with that person exceeds $60,000.

(b) *Significant corporate events*. Describe any negotiations, transactions or material contacts during the past two years between the filing person (including subsidiaries of the filing person and any person specified in Instruction C of the schedule) and the subject company or its affiliates concerning any:

(1) Merger;

(2) Consolidation;

(3) Acquisition;

(4) Tender offer for or other acquisition of any class of the subject company's securities;

(5) Election of the subject company's directors; or

(6) Sale or other transfer of a material amount of assets of the subject company.

(c) *Negotiations or contacts*. Describe any negotiations or material contacts concerning the matters referred to in paragraph (b) of this section during the past two years between:

(1) Any affiliates of the subject company; or

(2) The subject company or any of its affiliates and any person not affiliated with the subject company who would have a direct interest in such matters.

(d) *Conflicts of interest*. If material, describe any agreement, arrangement or understanding and any actual or potential conflict of interest between the filing person or its affiliates and:

(1) The subject company, its executive officers, directors or affiliates; or

(2) The offeror, its executive officers, directors or affiliates.

(e) *Agreements involving the subject company's securities*. Describe any agreement, arrangement, or understanding, whether or not legally enforceable, between the filing person (including any person specified in Instruction C of the schedule) and any other person with respect to any securities of the subject company. Name all persons that are a party to the agreements, arrangements, or understandings and describe all material provisions.

Item 1006. Purposes of the Transaction and Plans or Proposals

(a) *Purposes*. State the purposes of the transaction.

(b) *Use of securities acquired*. Indicate whether the securities acquired in the transaction will be retained, retired, held in treasury, or otherwise disposed of.

(c) *Plans*. Describe any plans, proposals or negotiations that relate to or would result in:

(1) Any extraordinary transaction, such as a merger, reorganization or liquidation, involving the subject company or any of its subsidiaries;

(2) Any purchase, sale or transfer of a material amount of assets of the subject company or any of its subsidiaries;

(3) Any material change in the present dividend rate or policy, or indebtedness or capitalization of the subject company;

(4) Any change in the present board of directors or management of the subject company, including, but not limited to, any plans or proposals to change the number or the term of directors or to fill any existing vacancies on the board or to change any material term of the employment contract of any executive officer;

(5) Any other material change in the subject company's corporate structure or business;

(6) Any class of equity securities of the subject company to be delisted from a national securities exchange or cease to be authorized to be quoted in an automated quotations system operated by a national securities association;

(7) Any class of equity securities of the subject company becoming eligible for termination of registration under section 12(g)(4) of the Securities Exchange Act;

(8) The suspension of the subject company's obligation to file reports under Section 15(d) of the Securities Exchange Act;

(9) The acquisition by any person of additional securities of the subject company, or the disposition of securities of the subject company; or

(10) Any changes in the subject company's charter, bylaws or other governing instruments or other actions that could impede the acquisition of control of the subject company.

(d) *Subject company negotiations*. If the filing person is the subject company:

(1) State whether or not that person is undertaking or engaged in any negotiations in response to the tender offer that relate to:

(i) A tender offer or other acquisition of the subject company's securities by the filing person, any of its subsidiaries, or any other person; or

(ii) Any of the matters referred to in paragraphs (c)(1) through (c)(3) of this section; and

(2) Describe any transaction, board resolution, agreement in principle, or signed contract that is entered into in response to the tender offer that relates to one or more of the matters referred to in paragraph (d)(1) of this section.

Item 1007. Source and Amount of Funds or other Consideration

(a) *Source of funds*. State the specific sources and total amount of funds or other consideration to be used in the transaction. If the transaction involves a tender offer, disclose the amount of funds or other consideration required to purchase the maximum amount of securities sought in the offer.

(b) *Conditions*. State any material conditions to the financing discussed in response to paragraph (a) of this section. Disclose any alternative financing arrangements or alternative financing plans in the event the primary financing plans fall through. If none, so state.

(c) *Expenses*. Furnish a reasonably itemized statement of all expenses incurred or estimated to be incurred in connection with the transaction including, but not limited to, filing, legal, accounting and appraisal fees, solicitation expenses and printing costs and state whether or not the subject company has paid or will be responsible for paying any or all expenses.

(d) *Borrowed funds*. If all or any part of the funds or other consideration required is, or is expected, to be borrowed, directly or indirectly, for the purpose of the transaction:

(1) Provide a summary of each loan agreement or arrangement containing the identity of the parties, the term, the collateral, the stated and effective interest rates, and any other material terms or conditions of the loan; and

(2) Briefly describe any plans or arrangements to finance or repay the loan, or, if no plans or arrangements have been made, so state.

Item 1008. Interest In Securities of the Subject Company

(a) *Securities ownership*. State the aggregate number and percentage of subject securities that are beneficially owned by each person named in response to Item 1003 of Regulation M–A and by each associate and majority-owned subsidiary of those persons. Give the name and address of any associate or subsidiary.

(b) *Securities transactions*. Describe any transaction in the subject securities during the past 60 days. The description of transactions required must include, but not necessarily be limited to:

(1) The identity of the persons specified in the Instruction to this section who effected the transaction;

(2) The date of the transaction;

(3) The amount of securities involved;

(4) The price per share; and

(5) Where and how the transaction was effected.

Instructions to Item 1008(b):

1. Provide the required transaction information for the following persons:

(a) The filing person (for all schedules);

(b) Any person named in Instruction C of the schedule and any associate or majority-owned subsidiary of the issuer of filing person (for all schedules except Schedule 14D–9)....

Item 1009. Persons/Assets, Retained, Employed, Compensated or Used

(a) *Solicitations or recommendations*. Identify all persons and classes of persons that are directly or indirectly employed, retained, or to be compensated to make solicitations or recommendations in connection with the transaction. Provide a summary of all material terms of employment, retainer or other arrangement for compensation.

(b) *Employees and corporate assets*. Identify any officer, class of employees or corporate assets of the subject company that has been or will be employed or used by the filing person in connection with the transaction. Describe the purpose for their employment or use.

Item 1010. Financial Statements

(a) *Financial information*. Furnish the following financial information:

(1) Audited financial statements for the two fiscal years required to be filed with the company's most recent annual report under sections 13 and 15(d) of the Exchange Act;

(2) Unaudited balance sheets, comparative year-to-date income statements and related earnings per share data, statements of cash flows, and comprehensive income required to be included in the company's most recent quarterly report filed under the Exchange Act;

(3) Ratio of earnings to fixed charges ... for the two most recent fiscal years and the interim periods provided under paragraph (a)(2) of this section; and

(4) Book value per share as of the date of the most recent balance sheet presented.

(b) *Pro forma information*. If material, furnish pro forma information disclosing the effect of the transaction on:

(1) The company's balance sheet as of the date of the most recent balance sheet presented under paragraph (a) of this section;

(2) The company's statement of income, earnings per share, and ratio of earnings to fixed charges for the most recent fiscal year and the latest interim period provided under paragraph (a)(2) of this section; and

(3) The company's book value per share as of the date of the most recent balance sheet presented under paragraph (a) of this section.

(c) *Summary information.* Furnish a fair and adequate summary of the information specified in paragraphs (a) and (b) of this section for the same periods specified. A fair and adequate summary includes:

(1) The summarized financial information specified in § 210.1–02(bb)(1) of this chapter;

(2) Income per common share from continuing operations (basic and diluted, if applicable);

(3) Net income per common share (basic and diluted, if applicable);

(4) Ratio of earnings to fixed charges . . .;

(5) Book value per share as of the date of the most recent balance sheet; and

(6) If material, pro forma data for the summarized financial information specified in paragraphs (c)(1) through (c)(5) of this section disclosing the effect of the transaction.

Item 1011. Additional Information

(a) *Agreements, regulatory requirements and legal proceedings.* If material to a security holder's decision whether to sell, tender or hold the securities sought in the tender offer, furnish the following information:

(1) Any present or proposed material agreement, arrangement, understanding or relationship between the offeror or any of its executive officers, directors, controlling persons or subsidiaries and the subject company or any of its executive officers, directors, controlling persons or subsidiaries (other than any agreement, arrangement or understanding disclosed under any other sections of Regulation M–A);

(2) To the extent known by the offeror after reasonable investigation, the applicable regulatory requirements which must be complied with or approvals which must be obtained in connection with the tender offer;

(3) The applicability of any anti-trust laws;

(4) The applicability of margin requirements under section 7 of the [Securities Exchange] Act and the applicable regulations; and

(5) Any material pending legal proceedings relating to the tender offer, including the name and location of the court or agency in which the proceedings are pending, the date instituted, the principal parties, and a brief summary of the proceedings and the relief sought.

(b) *Other material information.* Furnish such additional material information, if any, as may be necessary to make the required statements, in light of the circumstances under which they are made, not materially misleading.

Item 1012.   The Solicitation or Recommendation

(a) *Solicitation or recommendation.* State the nature of the solicitation or the recommendation. If this statement relates to a recommendation, state whether the filing person is advising holders of the subject securities to accept or reject the tender offer or to take other action with respect to the tender offer and, if so, describe the other action recommended. If the filing person is the subject company and is not making a recommendation, state whether the subject company is expressing no opinion and is remaining neutral toward the tender offer or is unable to take a position with respect to the tender offer.

(b) *Reasons.* State the reasons for the position (including the inability to take a position) stated in paragraph (a) of this section.   Conclusory statements such as "The tender offer is in the best interests of shareholders" are not considered sufficient disclosure.

(c) *Intent to tender.* To the extent known by the filing person after making reasonable inquiry, state whether the filing person or any executive officer, director, affiliate or subsidiary of the filing person currently intends to tender, sell or hold the subject securities that are held of record or beneficially owned by that person.

(d) *Intent to tender or vote in a going-private transaction.* To the extent known by the filing person after making reasonable inquiry, state whether or not any executive officer, director or affiliate of the issuer (or any person specified in Instruction C to the schedule) currently intends to tender or sell subject securities owned or held by that person and/or how each person currently intends to vote subject securities, including any securities the person has proxy authority for. State the reasons for the intended action.

(e) *Recommendations of others.* To the extent known by the filing person after making reasonable inquiry, state whether or not any person specified in paragraph (d) of this section has made a recommendation either in support of or opposed to the transaction and the reasons for the recommendation.

Item 1013.   Purposes, Alternatives, Reasons and Effects in a Going–Private Transaction

(a) *Purposes.* State the purposes for the Rule 13e–3 transaction.

(b) *Alternatives.* If the subject company or affiliate considered alternative means to accomplish the stated purposes, briefly describe the alternatives and state the reasons for their rejection.

(c) *Reasons.* State the reasons for the structure of the Rule 13e–3 transaction and for undertaking the transaction at this time.

(d) *Effects.* Describe the effects of the Rule 13e–3 transaction on the subject company, its affiliates and unaffiliated security holders, including the federal tax consequences of the transaction.

Instructions to Item 1013:

1. Conclusory statements will not be considered sufficient disclosure in response to this section.

2. The description required by paragraph (d) of this section must include a reasonably detailed discussion of both the benefits and detriments of the Rule 13e–3 transaction to the subject company, its affiliates and unaffiliated security holders. The benefits and detriments of the Rule 13e–3 transaction must be quantified to the extent practicable.

3. If this statement is filed by an affiliate of the subject company, the description required by paragraph (d) of this section must include, but not be limited to, the effect of the Rule 13e–3 transaction on the affiliate's interest in the net book value and net earnings of the subject company in terms of both dollar amounts and percentages.

Item 1014. Fairness of the Going–Private Transaction

(a) *Fairness.* State whether the subject company or affiliate filing the statement reasonably believes that the Rule 13e–3 transaction is fair or unfair to unaffiliated security holders. If any director dissented to or abstained from voting on the Rule 13e–3 transaction, identify the director, and indicate, if known, after making reasonable inquiry, the reasons for the dissent or abstention.

(b) *Factors considered in determining fairness.* Discuss in reasonable detail the material factors upon which the belief stated in paragraph (a) of this section is based and, to the extent practicable, the weight assigned to each factor. The discussion must include an analysis of the extent, if any, to which the filing person's beliefs are based on the factors described in Instruction 2 of this section, paragraphs (c), (d) and (e) of this section and Item 1015 of Regulation M–A.

(c) *Approval of security holders.* State whether or not the transaction is structured so that approval of at least a majority of unaffiliated security holders is required.

(d) *Unaffiliated representative.* State whether or not a majority of directors who are not employees of the subject company has retained an unaffiliated representative to act solely on behalf of unaffiliated security holders for purposes of negotiating the terms of the Rule 13e–3 transaction and/or preparing a report concerning the fairness of the transaction.

(e) *Approval of directors.* State whether or not the Rule 13e–3 transaction was approved by a majority of the directors of the subject company who are not employees of the subject company.

(f) *Other offers.* If any offer of the type described in paragraph (viii) of Instruction 2 to this section has been received, describe the offer and state the reasons for its rejection.

Instructions to Item 1014:

1. A statement that the issuer or affiliate has no reasonable belief as to the fairness of the Rule 13e–3 transaction to unaffiliated security holders will not be considered sufficient disclosure in response to paragraph (a) of this section.

2. The factors that are important in determining the fairness of a transaction to unaffiliated security holders and the weight, if any, that should be given to them in a particular context will vary. Normally such factors will include, among others, those referred to in paragraphs (c), (d) and (e) of this section and whether the consideration offered to unaffiliated security holders constitutes fair value in relation to:

(i) Current market prices;

(ii) Historical market prices;

(iii) Net book value;

(iv) Going concern value;

(v) Liquidation value;

(vi) Purchase prices paid in previous purchases disclosed in response to Item 1002(f) of Regulation M–A;

(vii) Any report, opinion, or appraisal described in Item 1015 of Regulation M–A; and

(viii) Firm offers of which the subject company or affiliate is aware made by any unaffiliated person, other than the filing persons, during the past two years for:

(A) The merger or consolidation of the subject company with or into another company, or vice versa;

(B) The sale or other transfer of all or any substantial part of the assets of the subject company; or

(C) A purchase of the subject company's securities that would enable the holder to exercise control of the subject company.

3. Conclusory statements, such as "The Rule 13e–3 transaction is fair to unaffiliated security holders in relation to net book value, going concern value and future prospects of the issuer" will not be considered sufficient disclosure in response to paragraph (b) of this section.

Item 1015. Reports, Opinions, Appraisals and Negotiations

(a) *Report, opinion or appraisal.* State whether or not the subject company or affiliate has received any report, opinion (other than an opinion of counsel) or appraisal from an outside party that is materially related to the Rule 13e–3 transaction, including, but not limited to: Any report, opinion or appraisal relating to the consideration or the fairness of the consideration to be offered to security holders or the fairness of the transaction to the issuer or affiliate or to security holders who are not affiliates.

(b) *Preparer and summary of the report, opinion or appraisal.* For each report, opinion or appraisal described in response to paragraph (a) of this section or any negotiation or report described in response to Item 1014(d) of Regulation M–A or Item 14(b)(6) of Schedule 14A concerning the terms of the transaction:

(1) Identify the outside party and/or unaffiliated representative;

(2) Briefly describe the qualifications of the outside party and/or unaffiliated representative;

(3) Describe the method of selection of the outside party and/or unaffiliated representative;

(4) Describe any material relationship that existed during the past two years or is mutually understood to be contemplated and any compensation received or to be received as a result of the relationship between:

(i) The outside party, its affiliates, and/or unaffiliated representative; and

(ii) The subject company or its affiliates;

(5) If the report, opinion or appraisal relates to the fairness of the consideration, state whether the subject company or affiliate determined the amount of consideration to be paid or whether the outside party recommended the amount of consideration to be paid; and

(6) Furnish a summary concerning the negotiation, report, opinion or appraisal. The summary must include, but need not be limited to, the procedures followed; the findings and recommendations; the bases for and methods of arriving at such findings and recommendations; instructions received from the subject company or affiliate; and any limitation imposed by the subject company or affiliate on the scope of the investigation.

(c) *Availability of documents.* Furnish a statement to the effect that the report, opinion or appraisal will be made available for inspection and copying at the principal executive offices of the subject company or affiliate during its regular business hours by any interested equity security holder of the subject company or representative who has been so designated in writing. This statement also may provide that a copy of the report, opinion or appraisal will be transmitted by the subject company or affiliate to any interested equity security holder of the subject company or representative who has been so designated in writing upon written request and at the expense of the requesting security holder.

Item 1016. Exhibits

File as an exhibit to the schedule:

(a) Any disclosure materials furnished to security holders by or on behalf of the filing person, including:

(1) Tender offer materials (including transmittal letter);

(2) Solicitation or recommendation (including those referred to in Item 1012 of Regulation M–A);

(3) Going-private disclosure document;

(4) Prospectus used in connection with an exchange offer where securities are registered under the Securities Act of 1933; and

(5) Any other disclosure materials;

(b) Any loan agreement referred to in response to Item 1007(d) of Regulation M–A;

(c) Any report, opinion or appraisal referred to in response to Item 1014(d) or Item 1015 of Regulation M–A;

(d) Any document setting forth the terms of any agreement, arrangement, understanding or relationship referred to in response to Item 1005(e) or Item 1011(a)(1) of Regulation M–A;

(e) Any agreement, arrangement or understanding referred to in response to Item 1005(d), or the pertinent portions of any proxy statement, report or other communication containing the disclosure required by Item 1005(d) of Regulation M–A;

(f) A detailed statement describing security holders' appraisal rights and the procedures for exercising those appraisal rights referred to in response to Item 1004(d) of Regulation M–A;

(g) Any written instruction, form or other material that is furnished to persons making an oral solicitation or recommendation by or on behalf of the filing person for their use directly or indirectly in connection with the transaction; and

(h) Any written opinion prepared by legal counsel at the filing person's request and communicated to the filing person pertaining to the tax consequences of the transaction. . . .

SECURITIES EXCHANGE ACT OF 1934

15 U.S.C. §§ 78a et seq.

* Omitted.

§ 1. Short Title

This chapter may be cited as the "Securities Exchange Act of 1934."

. . .

§ 3. Definitions and Application

(a) Definitions

When used in this chapter, unless the context otherwise requires. . . .

(4) The term "broker" means any person engaged in the business of effecting transactions in securities for the account of others, but does not include a bank.

(5) The term "dealer" means any person engaged in the business of buying and selling securities for his own account, through a broker or otherwise, but does not include a bank, or any person insofar as he buys or sells securities for his own account, either individually or in some fiduciary capacity, but not as a part of a regular business. . . .

(8) The term "issuer" means any person who issues or proposes to issue any security. . . .

(10) The term "security" means any note, stock, treasury stock, security future, bond, debenture, certificate of interest or participation in

* Omitted.

any profit-sharing agreement or in any oil, gas, or other mineral royalty or lease, any collateral-trust certificate, preorganization certificate or subscription, transferable share, investment contract, voting-trust certificate, certificate of deposit for a security, any put, call, straddle, option, or privilege on any security, certificate of deposit, or group or index of securities (including any interest therein or based on the value thereof), or any put, call, straddle, option, or privilege entered into on a national securities exchange relating to foreign currency, or in general, any instrument commonly known as a "security"; or any certificate of interest or participation in, temporary or interim certificate for, receipt for, or warrant or right to subscribe to or purchase, any of the foregoing; but shall not include currency or any note, draft, bill of exchange, or banker's acceptance which has a maturity at the time of issuance of not exceeding nine months, exclusive of days of grace, or any renewal thereof the maturity of which is likewise limited.

(11) The term "equity security" means any stock or similar security; or any security future on any such security; or any security convertible, with or without consideration, into such a security, or carrying any warrant or right to subscribe to or purchase such a security; or any such warrant or right; or any other security which the Commission shall deem to be of similar nature and consider necessary or appropriate, by such rules and regulations as it may prescribe in the public interest or for the protection of investors, to treat as an equity security.

(12)(A) The term "exempted security" or "exempted securities" includes—

(i) government securities, as defined in paragraph (42) of this subsection;

(ii) municipal securities, as defined in paragraph (29) of this subsection;

(iii) any interest or participation in any common trust fund or similar fund maintained by a bank exclusively for the collective investment and reinvestment of assets contributed thereto by such bank in its capacity as trustee, executor, administrator, or guardian;

(iv) any interest or participation in a single trust fund, or a collective trust fund maintained by a bank, or any security arising out of a contract issued by an insurance company, which interest, participation, or security is issued in connection with a qualified plan as defined in subparagraph (C) of this paragraph;

(v) any security issued by or any interest or participation in any pooled income fund, collective trust fund, collective investment fund, or similar fund that is excluded from the definition of an investment company under section 3(c)(10)(B) of the Investment Company Act of 1940; . . .

(vii) such other securities (which may include, among others, unregistered securities, the market in which is predominantly intrastate) as the Commission may, by such rules and regulations as it deems consistent with the public interest and the protection of investors, either unconditionally or upon specified terms and conditions or for stated periods, exempt from the operation of any one or more provisions of this chapter which by their terms do not apply to an "exempted security" or to "exempted securities" . . . .

(13) The terms "buy" and "purchase" each include any contract to buy, purchase, or otherwise acquire . . . .

(14) The terms "sale" and "sell" each include any contract to sell or otherwise dispose of . . . .

(26) The term "self-regulatory organization" means any national securities exchange, registered securities association, or registered clearing agency . . . .

(27) The term "rules of an exchange", "rules of an association", or "rules of a clearing agency" means the constitution, articles of incorporation, bylaws, and rules, or instruments corresponding to the foregoing, of an exchange, association of brokers and dealers, or clearing agency, respectively, and such of the stated policies, practices, and interpretations of such exchange, association, or clearing agency as the Commission, by rule, may determine to be necessary or appropriate in the public interest or for the protection of investors to be deemed to be rules of such exchange, association, or clearing agency.

(28) The term "rules of a self-regulatory organization" means the rules of an exchange which is a national securities exchange, the rules of an association of brokers and dealers which is a registered securities association, the rules of a clearing agency which is a registered clearing agency or the rules of the Municipal Securities Rulemaking Board . . . .

(29) The term "municipal securities" means securities which are direct obligations of, or obligations guaranteed as to principal or interest by, a State or any political subdivision thereof, or any agency or instrumentality of a State or any political subdivision thereof, or any municipal corporate instrumentality of one or more States . . . .

(42) The term "government securities" means—

(A) securities which are direct obligations of, or obligations guaranteed as to principal or interest by, the United States;

(B) securities which are issued or guaranteed by corporations in which the United States has a direct or indirect interest and which are designated by the Secretary of the Treasury for exemption as necessary or appropriate in the public interest or for the protection of investors;

(C) securities issued or guaranteed as to principal or interest by any corporation the securities of which are designated, by statute specifically naming such corporation, to constitute exempt securities within the meaning of the laws administered by the Commission....

(51)(A) The term "penny stock" means any equity security other than a security that is—

(i) registered or approved for registration and traded on a national securities exchange that meets such criteria as the Commission shall prescribe by rule or regulation for purposes of this paragraph;

(ii) authorized for quotation on an automated quotation system sponsored by a registered securities association, if such system (I) was established and in operation before January 1, 1990, and (II) meets such criteria as the Commission shall prescribe by rule or regulation for purposes of this paragraph;

(iii) issued by an investment company registered under the Investment Company Act of 1940;

(iv) excluded, on the basis of exceeding a minimum price, net tangible assets of the issuer, or other relevant criteria, from the definition of such term by rule or regulation which the Commission shall prescribe for purposes of this paragraph; or

(v) exempted, in whole or in part, conditionally or unconditionally, from the definition of such term by rule, regulation, or order prescribed by the Commission.

(B) The Commission may, by rule, regulation, or order, designate any equity security or class of equity securities described in clause (i) or (ii) of subparagraph (A) as within the meaning of the term "penny stock" if such security or class of securities is traded other than on a national securities exchange or through an automated quotation system described in clause (ii) of subparagraph (A).

(C) In exercising its authority under this paragraph to prescribe rules, regulations, and orders, the Commission shall determine that such rule, regulation, or order is consistent with the public interest and the protection of investors....

(55)(A) The term "security future" means a contract of sale for future delivery of a single security....

(56) The term "security futures product" means a security future or any put, call, straddle, option, or privilege on any security future....

(58) Audit Committee.—The term "audit committee" means—

(A) a committee (or equivalent body) established by and amongst the board of directors of an issuer for the purpose of overseeing the accounting and financial reporting processes of the issuer and audits of the financial statements of the issuer; and

(B) if no such committee exists with respect to an issuer, the entire board of directors of the issuer.

(59) Registered Public Accounting Firm.—The term "registered public accounting firm" has the same meaning as in section 2 of the Sarbanes–Oxley Act of 2002.

(f) Consideration of promotion of efficiency, competition, and capital formation

Whenever pursuant to this chapter the Commission is engaged in rulemaking, or in the review of a rule of a self-regulatory organization, and is required to consider or determine whether an action is necessary or appropriate in the public interest, the Commission shall also consider, in addition to the protection of investors, whether the action will promote efficiency, competition, and capital formation. . . .

§ 4. Securities and Exchange Commission

(a) Establishment; composition; limitations on commissioners; terms of office

There is hereby established a Securities and Exchange Commission (hereinafter referred to as the "Commission") to be composed of five commissioners to be appointed by the President by and with the advice and consent of the Senate. Not more than three of such commissioners shall be members of the same political party, and in making appointments members of different political parties shall be appointed alternately as nearly as may be practicable. . . .

§ 4C. Appearance and Practice Before the Commission.

(a) Authority to censure

The Commission may censure any person, or deny, temporarily or permanently, to any person the privilege of appearing or practicing before the Commission in any way, if that person is found by the Commission, after notice and opportunity for hearing in the matter—

(1) not to possess the requisite qualifications to represent others;

(2) to be lacking in character or integrity, or to have engaged in unethical or improper professional conduct; or

(3) to have willfully violated, or willfully aided and abetted the violation of, any provision of the securities laws or the rules and regulations issued thereunder.

(b) Definition

With respect to any registered public accounting firm or associated person, for purposes of this section, the term "improper professional conduct" means—

(1) intentional or knowing conduct, including reckless conduct, that results in a violation of applicable professional standards; and

(2) negligent conduct in the form of—

(A) a single instance of highly unreasonable conduct that results in a violation of applicable professional standards in circumstances in which the registered public accounting firm or associated person knows, or should know, that heightened scrutiny is warranted; or

(B) repeated instances of unreasonable conduct, each resulting in a violation of applicable professional standards, that indicate a lack of competence to practice before the Commission.

§ 5. Transactions on Unregistered Exchanges

It shall be unlawful for any broker, dealer, or exchange, directly or indirectly, to make use of the mails or any means or instrumentality of interstate commerce for the purpose of using any facility of an exchange within or subject to the jurisdiction of the United States to effect any transaction in a security, or to report any such transaction, unless such exchange (1) is registered as a national securities exchange under section 6 of this title, or (2) is exempted from such registration upon application by the exchange because, in the opinion of the Commission, by reason of the limited volume of transactions effected on such exchange, it is not practicable and not necessary or appropriate in the public interest or for the protection of investors to require such registration.

§ 6. National Securities Exchanges

(a) Registration; Application

An exchange may be registered as a national securities exchange under the terms and conditions hereinafter provided in this section and in accordance with the provisions of section 19(a) of this title, by filing with the Commission an application for registration in such form as the Commission, by rule, may prescribe containing the rules of the exchange and such other information and documents as the Commission, by rule, may prescribe as necessary or appropriate in the public interest or for the protection of investors....

(b) Determination by Commission requisite to registration of applicant as national securities exchange....*

An exchange shall not be registered as a national securities exchange unless the Commission determines that ...

(9) The rules of the exchange prohibit the listing of any security issued in a limited partnership rollup transaction (as such term is defined in paragraphs (4) and (5) of section 14(h)), unless such transac-

_____
* Section 6(b)(9) is effective December 17, 1994. (Footnote by ed.)

tion was conducted in accordance with procedures designed to protect the rights of limited partners, including—

    (A) the right of dissenting limited partners to one of the following:

        (i) an appraisal and compensation;

        (ii) retention of a security under substantially the same terms and conditions as the original issue;

        (iii) approval of the limited partnership rollup transaction by not less than 75 percent of the outstanding securities of each of the participating limited partnerships;

        (iv) the use of a committee of limited partners that is independent, as determined in accordance with rules prescribed by the exchange, of the general partner or sponsor, that has been approved by a majority of the outstanding units of each of the participating limited partnerships, and that has such authority as is necessary to protect the interest of limited partners, including the authority to hire independent advisors, to negotiate with the general partner or sponsor on behalf of the limited partners, and to make a recommendation to the limited partners with respect to the proposed transaction; or

        (v) other comparable rights that are prescribed by rule by the exchange and that are designed to protect dissenting limited partners;

    (B) the right not to have their voting power unfairly reduced or abridged;

    (C) the right not to bear an unfair portion of the costs of a proposed limited partnership rollup transaction that is rejected; and

    (D) restrictions on the conversion of contingent interests or fees into non-contingent interests or fees and restrictions on the receipt of a non-contingent equity interest in exchange for fees for services which have not yet been provided.

As used in this paragraph, the term "dissenting limited partner" means a person who, on the date on which soliciting material is mailed to investors, is a holder of a beneficial interest in a limited partnership that is the subject of a limited partnership rollup transaction, and who casts a vote against the transaction and complies with procedures established by the exchange, except that for purposes of an exchange or tender offer, such person shall file an objection in writing under the rules of the exchange during the period during which the offer is outstanding. . . .

§ 9.   Manipulation of Security Prices

(a)   Transactions relating to purchase or sale of security

    It shall be unlawful for any person, directly or indirectly, by the use of the mails or any means or instrumentality of interstate commerce, or of any facility of any national securities exchange, or for any member of a national securities exchange—

(1) For the purpose of creating a false or misleading appearance of active trading in any security registered on a national securities exchange, or a false or misleading appearance with respect to the market for any such security, (A) to effect any transaction in such security which involves no change in the beneficial ownership thereof, or (B) to enter an order or orders for the purchase of such security with the knowledge that an order or orders of substantially the same size, at substantially the same time, and at substantially the same price, for the sale of any such security, has been or will be entered by or for the same or different parties, or (C) to enter any order or orders for the sale of any such security with the knowledge that an order or orders of substantially the same size, at substantially the same time, and at substantially the same price, for the purchase of such security, has been or will be entered by or for the same or different parties.

(2) To effect, alone or with one or more other persons, a series of transactions in any security registered on a national securities exchange ... creating actual or apparent active trading in such security or raising or depressing the price of such security, for the purpose of inducing the purchase or sale of such security by others.

(3) If a dealer or broker, or other person selling or offering for sale or purchasing or offering to purchase the security ..., to induce the purchase or sale of any security registered on a national securities exchange ... by the circulation or dissemination in the ordinary course of business of information to the effect that the price of any such security will or is likely to rise or fall because of market operations of any one or more persons conducted for the purpose of raising or depressing the prices of such security.

(4) If a dealer or broker, or the person selling or offering for sale or purchasing or offering to purchase the security ... with respect to such security, to make, regarding any security registered on a national securities exchange ..., for the purpose of inducing the purchase or sale of such security, any statement which was at the time and in the light of the circumstances under which it was made, false or misleading with respect to any material fact, and which he knew or had reasonable ground to believe was so false or misleading.

(5) For a consideration, received directly or indirectly from a dealer or broker, or other person selling or offering for sale or purchasing or offering to purchase the security ... with respect to such security, to induce the purchase of any security registered on a national securities exchange or any security-based swap agreement ... with respect to such security by the circulation or dissemination

of information to the effect that the price of any such security will or is likely to rise or fall because of the market operations of any one or more persons conducted for the purpose of raising or depressing the price of such security.

(6) To effect either alone or with one or more other persons any series of transactions for the purchase and/or sale of any security registered on a national securities exchange for the purpose of pegging, fixing, or stabilizing the price of such security in contravention of such rules and regulations as the Commission may prescribe as necessary or appropriate in the public interest or for the protection of investors.

(b)   Transactions relating to puts, calls, straddles, or options

It shall be unlawful for any person to effect, by use of any facility of a national securities exchange, in contravention of such rules and regulations as the Commission may prescribe as necessary or appropriate in the public interest or for the protection of investors—

(1) any transaction in connection with any security whereby any party to such transaction acquires (A) any put, call, straddle, or other option or privilege of buying the security from or selling the security to another without being bound to do so; or (B) any security futures product on the security; or

(2) any transaction in connection with any security with relation to which he has, directly or indirectly, any interest in any (A) such put, call, straddle, option, or privilege; or (B) such security futures product; or

(3) any transaction in any security for the account of any person who he has reason to believe has, and who actually has, directly or indirectly, any interest in any (A) such put, call, straddle, option, or privilege or (B) such security futures product with relation to such security. . . .

(e)   Persons liable; suits at law or in equity

Any person who willfully participates in any act or transaction in violation of subsections (a), (b), or (c) of this section, shall be liable to any person who shall purchase or sell any security at a price which was affected by such act or transaction, and the person so injured may sue in law or in equity in any court of competent jurisdiction to recover the damages sustained as a result of any such act or transaction. In any such suit the court may, in its discretion, require an undertaking for the payment of the costs of such suit, and assess reasonable costs, including reasonable attorneys' fees, against either party litigant. Every person who becomes liable to make any payment under this subsection may recover contribution as in cases of contract from any person who, if joined in the original suit, would have been liable to make the same payment. No action shall be maintained to enforce any liability created under this section, unless brought within one year after the discovery of the facts constituting the violation and within three years after such violation.

(f) Subsection (a) not applicable to exempted securities

The provisions of subsection (a) of this section shall not apply to an exempted security....

(h) Limitations on practices that affect market volatility

It shall be unlawful for any person, by the use of the mails or any means or instrumentality of interstate commerce or of any facility of any national securities exchange, to use or employ any act or practice in connection with the purchase or sale of any equity security in contravention of such rules or regulations as the Commission may adopt, consistent with the public interest, the protection of investors, and the maintenance of fair and orderly markets—

(1) to prescribe means reasonably designed to prevent manipulation of price levels of the equity securities market or a substantial segment thereof; and

(2) to prohibit or constrain, during periods of extraordinary market volatility, any trading practice in connection with the purchase or sale of equity securities that the Commission determines (A) has previously contributed significantly to extraordinary levels of volatility that have threatened the maintenance of fair and orderly markets; and (B) is reasonably certain to engender such levels of volatility if not prohibited or constrained.

In adopting rules under paragraph (2), the Commission shall, consistent with the purposes of this subsection, minimize the impact on the normal operations of the market and a natural person's freedom to buy or sell any equity security....

§ 10. Manipulative and Deceptive Devices

It shall be unlawful for any person, directly or indirectly, by the use of any means or instrumentality of interstate commerce or of the mails, or of any facility of any national securities exchange—

(a)(1) To effect a short sale, or to use or employ any stop-loss order in connection with the purchase or sale, of any security registered on a national securities exchange, in contravention of such rules and regulations as the Commission may prescribe as necessary or appropriate in the public interest or for the protection of investors....

(b) To use or employ, in connection with the purchase or sale of any security registered on a national securities exchange or any security not so registered, ... any manipulative or deceptive device or contrivance in contravention of such rules and regulations as the Commission may prescribe as necessary or appropriate in the public interest or for the protection of investors.....

§ 10A. Audit Requirements

(a) In general.

Each audit required pursuant to this title of the financial statements of an issuer by a registered public accounting firm shall include, in accordance with generally accepted auditing standards, as may be modified or supplemented from time to time by the Commission—

(1) procedures designed to provide reasonable assurance of detecting illegal acts that would have a direct and material effect on the determination of financial statement amounts;

(2) procedures designed to identify related party transactions that are material to the financial statements or otherwise require disclosure therein; and

(3) an evaluation of whether there is substantial doubt about the ability of the issuer to continue as a going concern during the ensuing fiscal year.

(b) Required response to audit discoveries

(1) *Investigation and report to management.*—If, in the course of conducting an audit pursuant to this title to which subsection (a) applies, the registered public accounting firm detects or otherwise becomes aware of information indicating that an illegal act (whether or not perceived to have a material effect on the financial statements of the issuer) has or may have occurred, the firm shall, in accordance with generally accepted auditing standards, as may be modified or supplemented from time to time by the Commission—

(A)

(i) determine whether it is likely that an illegal act has occurred; and

(ii) if so, determine and consider the possible effect of the illegal act on the financial statements of the issuer, including any contingent monetary effects, such as fines, penalties, and damages; and

(B) as soon as practicable, inform the appropriate level of the management of the issuer and assure that the audit committee of the issuer, or the board of directors of the issuer in the absence of such a committee, is adequately informed with respect to illegal acts that have been detected or have otherwise come to the attention of such accountant in the course of the audit, unless the illegal act is clearly inconsequential.

(2) *Response to failure to take remedial action.*—If, after determining that the audit committee of the board of directors of the issuer, or the board of directors of the issuer in the absence of an audit committee, is adequately informed with respect to illegal acts that have been detected or have otherwise come to the attention of the firm in the course of the audit of such firm, the registered public accounting firm concludes that—

(A) the illegal act has a material effect on the financial statements of the issuer;

(B) the senior management has not taken, and the board of directors has not caused senior management to take, timely and appropriate remedial actions with respect to the illegal act; and

(C) the failure to take remedial action is reasonably expected to warrant departure from a standard report of the auditor, when made, or warrant resignation from the audit engagement;

the registered public accounting firm shall, as soon as practicable, directly report its conclusions to the board of directors.

(3) *Notice to commission; response to failure to notify.*—An issuer whose board of directors receives a report under paragraph (2) shall inform the Commission by notice not later than 1 business day after the receipt of such report and shall furnish the registered public accounting firm making such report with a copy of the notice furnished to the Commission. If the registered public accounting firm fails to receive a copy of the notice before the expiration of the required 1–business–day period, the registered public accounting firm shall—

(A) resign from the engagement; or

(B) furnish to the Commission a copy of its report (or the documentation of any oral report given) not later than 1 business day following such failure to receive notice.

(4) *Report after resignation.*—If a registered public accounting firm resigns from an engagement under paragraph (3)(A), the firm shall, not later than 1 business day following the failure by the issuer to notify the Commission under paragraph (3), furnish to the Commission a copy of the report of the firm (or the documentation of any oral report given).

(c) Auditor liability limitation

No registered public accounting firm shall be liable in a private action for any finding, conclusion, or statement expressed in a report made pursuant to paragraph (3) or (4) of subsection (b), including any rule promulgated pursuant thereto.

(d) Civil penalties in cease-and-desist proceedings

If the Commission finds, after notice and opportunity for hearing in a proceeding instituted pursuant to section 21C, that an independent public accountant has willfully violated paragraph (3) or (4) of subsection (b), the Commission may, in addition to entering an order under section 21C, impose a civil penalty against the registered public accounting firm and any other person that the Commission finds was a cause of such violation. The determination to impose a civil penalty and the amount of the penalty shall be governed by the standards set forth in section 21B.

(e) Preservation of existing authority

Except as provided in subsection (d), nothing in this section shall be held to limit or otherwise affect the authority of the Commission under this title.

(f) Definitions

As used in this section, the term "illegal act" means an act or omission that violates any law, or any rule or regulation having the force of law.

As used in this section, the term "issuer" means an issuer (as defined in section 3), the securities of which are registered under section 12, or that is required to file reports pursuant to section 15(d), or that files or has filed a registration statement that has not yet become effective under the Securities Act of 1933 (15 U.S.C. 77a et seq.), and that it has not withdrawn.

(g) Prohibited activities

Except as provided in subsection (h), it shall be unlawful for a registered public accounting firm (and any associated person of that firm, to the extent determined appropriate by the Commission) that performs for any issuer any audit required by this title or the rules of the Commission under this title or, beginning 180 days after the date of commencement of the operations of the Public Company Accounting Oversight Board established under section 101 of the Sarbanes–Oxley Act of 2002 (in this section referred to as the "Board"), the rules of the Board, to provide to that issuer, contemporaneously with the audit, any non-audit service, including—

(1) bookkeeping or other services related to the accounting records or financial statements of the audit client;

(2) financial information systems design and implementation;

(3) appraisal or valuation services, fairness opinions, or contribution-in-kind reports;

(4) actuarial services;

(5) internal audit outsourcing services;

(6) management functions or human resources;

(7) broker or dealer, investment adviser, or investment banking services;

(8) legal services and expert services unrelated to the audit; and

(9) any other service that the Board determines, by regulation, is impermissible.

(h) Preapproval required for non–audit services

A registered public accounting firm may engage in any non-audit service, including tax services, that is not described in any of paragraphs (1) through (9) of subsection (g) for an audit client, only if the activity is approved in advance by the audit committee of the issuer, in accordance with subsection (i).

(i) Preapproval requirements

(1) *In General.—*

(A) *Audit Committee Action.—*All auditing services (which may entail providing comfort letters in connection with securities underwritings or statutory audits required for insurance companies for purposes of State law) and non-audit services, other than as provided in subparagraph (B), provided to an issuer by the auditor of the issuer shall be preapproved by the audit committee of the issuer.

(B) *De Minimus Exception.—*The preapproval requirement under subparagraph (A) is waived with respect to the provision of non-audit services for an issuer, if-

(i) the aggregate amount of all such non-audit services provided to the issuer constitutes not more than 5 percent of the total amount of revenues paid by the issuer to its auditor during the fiscal year in which the nonaudit services are provided;

(ii) such services were not recognized by the issuer at the time of the engagement to be non-audit services; and

(iii) such services are promptly brought to the attention of the audit committee of the issuer and approved prior to the completion of the audit by the audit committee or by 1 or more members of the audit committee who are members of the board of directors to whom authority to grant such approvals has been delegated by the audit committee.

(2) *Disclosure to Investors.—*Approval by an audit committee of an issuer under this subsection of a non-audit service to be per-

formed by the auditor of the issuer shall be disclosed to investors in periodic reports required by section 13(a).

(3) *Delegation Authority.*—The audit committee of an issuer may delegate to 1 or more designated members of the audit committee who are independent directors of the board of directors, the authority to grant preapprovals required by this subsection. The decisions of any member to whom authority is delegated under this paragraph to preapprove an activity under this subsection shall be presented to the full audit committee at each of its scheduled meetings.

(4) *Approval of Audit Services for Other Purposes.*—In carrying out its duties under subsection (m)(2), if the audit committee of an issuer approves an audit service within the scope of the engagement of the auditor, such audit service shall be deemed to have been preapproved for purposes of this subsection.

(j) Audit partner rotation

It shall be unlawful for a registered public accounting firm to provide audit services to an issuer if the lead (or coordinating) audit partner (having primary responsibility for the audit), or the audit partner responsible for reviewing the audit, has performed audit services for that issuer in each of the 5 previous fiscal years of that issuer.

(k) Reports to audit committees

Each registered public accounting firm that performs for any issuer any audit required by this title shall timely report to the audit committee of the issuer—

(1) all critical accounting policies and practices to be used;

(2) all alternative treatments of financial information within generally accepted accounting principles that have been discussed with management officials of the issuer, ramifications of the use of such alternative disclosures and treatments, and the treatment preferred by the registered public accounting firm; and

(3) other material written communications between the registered public accounting firm and the management of the issuer, such as any management letter or schedule of unadjusted differences.

(*l*) Conflicts of interest

It shall be unlawful for a registered public accounting firm to perform for an issuer any audit service required by this title, if a chief executive officer, controller, chief financial officer, chief accounting officer, or any person serving in an equivalent position for the issuer, was employed by that registered independent public accounting firm and participated in any capacity in the audit of that issuer during the 1–year period preceding the date of the initiation of the audit.

(m) Standards relating to audit committees

(1) *Commission Rules.*—

(A) *In General.*—Effective not later than 270 days after the date of enactment of this subsection, the Commission shall, by rule, direct the national securities exchanges and national securities associations to prohibit the listing of any security of an issuer that is not in compliance with the requirements of any portion of paragraphs (2) through (6).

(B) *Opportunity to Cure Defects.*—The rules of the Commission under subparagraph (A) shall provide for appropriate procedures for an issuer to have an opportunity to cure any defects that would be the basis for a prohibition under subparagraph (A), before the imposition of such prohibition.

(2) *Responsibilities Relating to Registered Public Accounting Firms.*—The audit committee of each issuer, in its capacity as a committee of the board of directors, shall be directly responsible for the appointment, compensation, and oversight of the work of any registered public accounting firm employed by that issuer (including resolution of disagreements between management and the auditor regarding financial reporting) for the purpose of preparing or issuing an audit report or related work, and each such registered public accounting firm shall report directly to the audit committee.

(3) *Independence*

(A) *In General.*—Each member of the audit committee of the issuer shall be a member of the board of directors of the issuer, and shall otherwise be independent.

(B) *Criteria.*—In order to be considered to be independent for purposes of this paragraph, a member of an audit committee of an issuer may not, other than in his or her capacity as a member of the audit committee, the board of directors, or any other board committee—

(i) accept any consulting, advisory, or other compensatory fee from the issuer; or

(ii) be an affiliated person of the issuer or any subsidiary thereof.

(C) *Exemption Authority.*—The Commission may exempt from the requirements of subparagraph (B) a particular relationship with respect to audit committee members, as the Commission determines appropriate in light of the circumstances.

(4) *Complaints.*—Each audit committee shall establish procedures for—

(A) the receipt, retention, and treatment of complaints received by the issuer regarding accounting, internal accounting controls, or auditing matters; and

(B) the confidential, anonymous submission by employees of the issuer of concerns regarding questionable accounting or auditing matters.

(5) *Authority to Engage Advisers.*—Each audit committee shall have the authority to engage independent counsel and other advisers, as it determines necessary to carry out its duties.

(6) *Funding.*—Each issuer shall provide for appropriate funding, as determined by the audit committee, in its capacity as a committee of the board of directors, for payment of compensation—

(A) to the registered public accounting firm employed by the issuer for the purpose of rendering or issuing an audit report; and

(B) to any advisers employed by the audit committee under paragraph (5).

§ 12. Registration Requirements for Securities

(a) General requirement of registration

It shall be unlawful for any member, broker, or dealer to effect any transaction in any security (other than an exempted security) on a national securities exchange unless a registration is effective as to such security for such exchange in accordance with the provisions of this chapter and the rules and regulations thereunder. The provisions of this subsection shall not apply in respect of a security futures product traded on a national securities exchange.

(b) Procedure for registration; information

A security may be registered on a national securities exchange by the issuer filing an application with the exchange (and filing with the Commission such duplicate originals thereof as the Commission may require), which application shall contain—

(1) Such information, in such detail, as to the issuer and any person directly or indirectly controlling or controlled by, or under direct or indirect common control with, the issuer, and any guarantor of the security as to principal or interest or both, as the Commission may by rules and regulations require, as necessary or appropriate in the public interest or for the protection of investors, in respect of the following:

(A) the organization, financial structure, and nature of the business;

(B) the terms, position, rights, and privileges of the different classes of securities outstanding;

(C) the terms on which their securities are to be, and during the preceding three years have been, offered to the public or otherwise;

(D) the directors, officers, and underwriters, and each security holder of record holding more than 10 per centum of any class of any equity security of the issuer (other than an exempted security), their remuneration and their interests in the securities of, and their material contracts with, the issuer and any person directly or indirectly controlling or controlled by, or under direct or indirect common control with, the issuer;

(E) remuneration to others than directors and officers exceeding $20,000 per annum;

(F) bonus and profit-sharing arrangements;

(G) management and service contracts;

(H) options existing or to be created in respect of their securities;

(I) material contracts, not made in the ordinary course of business, which are to be executed in whole or in part at or after the filing of the application or which were made not more than two years before such filing, and every material patent or contract for a material patent right shall be deemed a material contract;

(J) balance sheets for not more than the three preceding fiscal years, certified if required by the rules and regulations of the Commission by a registered public accounting firm;

(K) profit and loss statements for not more than the three preceding fiscal years, certified if required by the rules and regulations of the Commission by a registered public accounting firm; and

(L) any further financial statements which the Commission may deem necessary or appropriate for the protection of investors.

(2) Such copies of articles of incorporation, bylaws, trust indentures, or corresponding documents by whatever name known, underwriting arrangements, and other similar documents of, and voting trust agreements with respect to, the issuer and any person directly or indirectly controlling or controlled by, or under direct or indirect common control with, the issuer as the Commission may require as necessary or appropriate for the proper protection of investors and to insure fair dealing in the security.

(3) Such copies of material contracts, referred to in paragraph (1)(I) above, as the Commission may require as necessary or appropriate for the proper protection of investors and to insure fair dealing in the security. . . .

(g) Registration of securities by issuer; exemptions

(1) Every issuer which is engaged in interstate commerce, or in a business affecting interstate commerce, or whose securities are traded by use of the mails or any means or instrumentality of interstate commerce shall— . . .

(B) within one hundred and twenty days after the last day of its first fiscal year . . . on which the issuer has total assets exceeding $1,000,000 and a class of equity security (other than an exempted security) held of record by five hundred or more . . . persons,

register such security by filing with the Commission a registration statement (and such copies thereof as the Commission may require) with respect to such security containing such information and documents as the Commission may specify comparable to that which is required in an application to register a security pursuant to subsection (b) of this section. Each such registration statement shall become effective sixty days after filing with the Commission or within such shorter period as the Commission may direct. Until such registration statement becomes effective it shall not be deemed filed for the purposes of section 18 of this title. Any issuer may register any class of equity security not required to be registered by filing a registration statement pursuant to the provisions of this paragraph. The Commission is authorized to extend the date upon which any issuer or class of issuers is required to register a security pursuant to the provisions of this paragraph.

(2) The provisions of this subsection shall not apply in respect of—

(A) any security listed and registered on a national securities exchange.

(B) any security issued by an investment company registered pursuant to section 80a–8 of this title. . . .

(G) any security issued by an insurance company if all of the following conditions are met:

(i) Such insurance company is required to and does file an annual statement with the Commissioner of Insurance (or other officer or agency performing a similar function) of its domiciliary State, and such annual statement conforms to that prescribed by the National Association of Insurance Commissioners or in the determination of such State commissioner, officer or agency substantially conforms to that so prescribed.

(ii) Such insurance company is subject to regulation by its domiciliary State of proxies, consents, or authorizations in respect of securities issued by such company and such regulation conforms to that prescribed by the National Association of Insurance Commissioners.

(iii) ... [T]he purchase and sales of securities issued by such insurance company by beneficial owners, directors, or officers of such company are subject to regulation (including reporting) by its domiciliary State substantially in the manner provided in section 16 of this title. . . .

(3) The Commission may by rules or regulations or, on its own motion, after notice and opportunity for hearing, by order, exempt from this subsection any security of a foreign issuer, including any certificate of deposit for such a security, if the Commission finds that such exemption is in the public interest and is consistent with the protection of investors.

(4) Registration of any class of security pursuant to this subsection shall be terminated ninety days, or such shorter period as the Commission may determine, after the issuer files a certification with the Commission that the number of holders of record of such class of security is reduced to less than three hundred persons. The Commission shall after notice and opportunity for hearing deny termination of registration if it finds that the certification is untrue. Termination of registration shall be deferred pending final determination on the question of denial.

(5) For the purposes of this subsection the term "class" shall include all securities of an issuer which are of substantially similar character and the holders of which enjoy substantially similar rights and privileges. The Commission may for the purpose of this subsection define by rules and regulations the terms "total assets" and "held of record" as it deems necessary or appropriate in the public interest or for the protection of investors in order to prevent circumvention of the provisions of this subsection. For purposes of this subsection, a security futures product shall not be considered a class of equity security of the issuer of the securities underlying the security futures product.

(h) Exemption by rules and regulations from certain provisions of section

The Commission may by rules and regulations, or upon application of an interested person, by order, after notice and opportunity for hearing, exempt in whole or in part any issuer or class of issuers from the provisions of subsection (g) of this section or from section 13, 14, or 15(d) of this title or may exempt from section 16 of this title any officer, director, or beneficial owner of securities of any issuer, any security of which is required to be registered pursuant to subsection (g) hereof, upon such terms and conditions and for such period as it deems necessary or appropriate, if the Commission finds, by reason of the number of public investors, amount of trading interest in the securities, the nature and extent of the activities of the issuer, income or assets of the issuer, or otherwise, that such action is not inconsistent with the public interest or the protection of investors. The Commission may, for the purposes of any of the above-mentioned sections or subsections of this chapter, classify issuers and prescribe requirements appropriate for each such class. . . .

(j) Denial, suspension, or revocation of registration; notice and hearing

The Commission is authorized, by order, as it deems necessary or appropriate for the protection of investors to deny, to suspend the effective date of, to suspend for a period not exceeding twelve months, or to revoke the registration of a security, if the Commission finds, on the record after notice and opportunity for hearing, that the issuer of such security has failed to comply with any provision of this chapter or the rules and regulations thereunder. No member of a national securities exchange, broker, or dealer shall make use of the mails or any means or instrumentality of interstate commerce to effect any transaction in, or to induce the purchase or sale of, any security the registration of which has been and is suspended or revoked pursuant to the preceding sentence.

(k) Trading suspensions; emergency authority

(1) *Trading Suspensions.* If in its opinion the public interest and the protection of investors so require, the Commission is authorized by order—

> (A) summarily to suspend trading in any security (other than an exempted security) for a period not exceeding 10 business days, and

> (B) summarily to suspend all trading on any national securities exchange or otherwise, in securities other than exempted securities, for a period not exceeding 90 calendar days.

The action described in subparagraph (B) shall not take effect unless the Commission notifies the President of its decision and the President notifies the Commission that the President does not disapprove of such decision. . . .

(2) *Emergency orders.* (A) The Commission, in an emergency, may by order summarily take such action to alter, supplement, suspend, or impose requirements or restrictions with respect to any matter or action subject to regulation by the Commission or a self-regulatory organization under this title, as the Commission determines is necessary in the public interest and for the protection of investors—

> (i) to maintain or restore fair and orderly securities markets (other than markets in exempted securities); or

(ii) to ensure prompt, accurate, and safe clearance and settlement of transactions in securities (other than exempted securities).

(B) An order of the Commission under this paragraph (2) shall continue in effect for the period specified by the Commission, and may be extended, except that in no event shall the Commission's action continue in effect for more than 10 business days, including extensions. . . .

(3) *Termination of Emergency Actions by president.* The President may direct that action taken by the Commission under paragraph (1)(B) or paragraph (2) of this subsection shall not continue in effect. . . .

. . . .

(6) *Definition of emergency.* For purposes of this subsection, the term "emergency" means a major market disturbance characterized by or constituting—

(A) sudden and excessive fluctuations of securities prices generally, or a substantial threat thereof, that threaten fair and orderly markets, or

(B) a substantial disruption of the safe or efficient operation of the national system for clearance and settlement of securities, or a substantial threat thereof.

(*l*) Issuance of any security in contravention of rules and regulations; application to annuity contracts and variable life policies

It shall be unlawful for an issuer, any class of whose securities is registered pursuant to this section or would be required to be so registered except for the exemption from registration provided by subsection (g)(2)(B) or (g)(2)(G) of this section, by the use of any means or instrumentality of interstate commerce, or of the mails, to issue, either originally or upon transfer, any of such securities in a form or with a format which contravenes such rules and regulations as the Commission may prescribe as necessary or appropriate for the prompt and accurate clearance and settlement of transactions in securities. The provisions of this subsection shall not apply to variable annuity contracts or variable life policies issued by an insurance company or its separate accounts. . . .

§ 13. Periodical and Other Reports

(a) Reports by issuer of security; contents

Every issuer of a security registered pursuant to section 12 of this title shall file with the Commission, in accordance with such rules and regulations as the Commission may prescribe as necessary or appropriate for the proper protection of investors and to insure fair dealing in the security—

(1) such information and documents (and such copies thereof) as the Commission shall require to keep reasonably current the information and documents required to be included in or filed with an application or registration statement filed pursuant to section 12 of this title....

(2) such annual reports (and such copies thereof), certified if required by the rules and regulations of the Commission by independent public accountants, and such quarterly reports (and such copies thereof), as the Commission may prescribe.

Every issuer of a security registered on a national securities exchange shall also file a duplicate original of such information, documents, and reports with the exchange.

(b)   Form of report; books, records, and internal accounting; directives

(1) The Commission may prescribe, in regard to reports made pursuant to this chapter, the form or forms in which the required information shall be set forth, the items or details to be shown in the balance sheet and the earning statement, and the methods to be followed in the preparation of reports, in the appraisal or valuation of assets and liabilities, in the determination of depreciation and depletion, in the differentiation of recurring and nonrecurring income, in the differentiation of investment and operating income, and in the preparation, where the Commission deems it necessary or desirable, of separate and/or consolidated balance sheets or income accounts of any person directly or indirectly controlling or controlled by the issuer, or any person under direct or indirect common control with the issuer....

(2) Every issuer which has a class of securities registered pursuant to section 12 of this title and every issuer which is required to file reports pursuant to section 15(d) of this title shall—

(A) make and keep books, records, and accounts, which, in reasonable detail, accurately and fairly reflect the transactions and dispositions of the assets of the issuer;

(B) devise and maintain a system of internal accounting controls sufficient to provide reasonable assurances that—

(i) transactions are executed in accordance with management's general or specific authorization;

(ii) transactions are recorded as necessary (I) to permit preparation of financial statements in conformity with generally accepted accounting principles or any other criteria applicable to such statements, and (II) to maintain accountability for assets;

(iii) access to assets is permitted only in accordance with management's general or specific authorization; and

(iv) the recorded accountability for assets is compared with the existing assets at reasonable intervals and appropriate action is taken with respect to any differences. . . .

(d) Reports by persons acquiring more than five per centum of certain classes of securities

(1) Any person who, after acquiring directly or indirectly the beneficial ownership of any equity security of a class which is registered pursuant to section 12 of this title, or any equity security of an insurance company which would have been required to be so registered except for the exemption contained in section 12(g)(2)(G) of this title, or any equity security issued by a closed-end investment company registered under the Investment Company Act of 1940, is directly or indirectly the beneficial owner of more than 5 per centum of such class shall, within ten days after such acquisition, send to the issuer of the security at its principal executive office, by registered or certified mail, send to each exchange where the security is traded, and file with the Commission, a statement containing such of the following information, and such additional information, as the Commission may by rules and regulations, prescribe as necessary or appropriate in the public interest or for the protection of investors—

(A) the background, and identity, residence, and citizenship of, and the nature of such beneficial ownership by, such person and all other persons by whom or on whose behalf the purchases have been or are to be effected;

(B) the source and amount of the funds or other consideration used or to be used in making the purchases, and if any part of the purchase price is represented or is to be represented by funds or other consideration borrowed or otherwise obtained for the purpose of acquiring, holding, or trading such security, a description of the transaction and the names of the parties thereto, except that where a source of funds is a loan made in the ordinary course of business by a bank, . . . if the person filing such statement so requests, the name of the bank shall not be made available to the public;

(C) if the purpose of the purchases or prospective purchases is to acquire control of the business of the issuer of the securities, any plans or proposals which such persons may have to liquidate such issuer, to sell its assets to or merge it with any other persons, or to make any other major change in its business or corporate structure;

(D) the number of shares of such security which are beneficially owned, and the number of shares concerning which there is a right to acquire, directly or indirectly, by (i) such person, and (ii) by each associate of such person, giving the background, identity, residence, and citizenship of each such associate; and

(E) information as to any contracts, arrangements, or understandings with any person with respect to any securities of the issuer, including but not limited to transfer of any of the securities, joint ventures, loan or option arrangements, puts or calls, guaranties of loans, guaranties against loss or guaranties of profits, division of losses or profits, or the giving or withholding of proxies, naming the persons with whom such contracts, arrangements, or understandings have been entered into, and giving the details thereof.

(2) If any material change occurs in the facts set forth in the statements to the issuer and the exchange, and in the statement filed with the Commission, an amendment shall be transmitted to the issuer and the exchange and shall be filed with the Commission, in accordance with such rules and regulations as the Commission may prescribe as necessary or appropriate in the public interest or for the protection of investors.

(3) When two or more persons act as a partnership, limited partnership, syndicate, or other group for the purpose of acquiring, holding, or disposing of securities of an issuer, such syndicate or group shall be deemed a "person" for the purposes of this subsection.

(4) In determining, for purposes of this subsection, any percentage of a class of any security, such class shall be deemed to consist of the amount of the outstanding securities of such class, exclusive of any securities of such class held by or for the account of the issuer or a subsidiary of the issuer.

(5) The Commission, by rule or regulation or by order, may permit any person to file in lieu of the statement required by paragraph (1) of this subsection or the rules and regulations thereunder, a notice stating the name of such person, the number of shares of any equity securities subject to paragraph (1) which are owned by him, the date of their acquisition and such other information as the Commission may specify, if it appears to the Commission that such securities were acquired by such person in the ordinary course of his business and were not acquired for the purpose of and do not have the effect of changing or influencing the control of the issuer nor in connection with or as a participant in any transaction having such purpose or effect.

(6) The provisions of this subsection shall not apply to—

(A) any acquisition or offer to acquire securities made or proposed to be made by means of a registration statement under the Securities Act of 1933;

(B) any acquisition of the beneficial ownership of a security which, together with all other acquisitions by the same person of securities of the same class during the preceding twelve months, does not exceed 2 per centum of that class;

(C) any acquisition of an equity security by the issuer of such security;

(D) any acquisition or proposed acquisition of a security which the Commission, by rules or regulations or by order, shall exempt from the provisions of this subsection as not entered into for the purpose of, and not having the effect of, changing or influencing the control of the issuer or otherwise as not comprehended within the purposes of this subsection.

(e)   Purchase of securities by issuer

(1) It shall be unlawful for an issuer which has a class of equity securities registered pursuant to section 12 of this title, or which is a closed-end investment company registered under the Investment Company Act of 1940, to purchase any equity security issued by it if such purchase is in contravention of such rules and regulations as the Commission, in the public interest or for the protection of investors, may adopt (A) to define acts and practices which are fraudulent, deceptive, or manipulative, and (B) to prescribe means reasonably designed to prevent such acts and practices. Such rules and regulations may require such issuer to provide holders of equity securities of such class with such information relating to the reasons for such purchase, the source of funds, the number of shares to be purchased, the price to be paid for such securities, the method of purchase, and such additional information, as the Commission deems necessary or appropriate in the public interest or for the protection of investors, or which the Commission deems to be material to a determination whether such security should be sold.

(2) For the purpose of this subsection, a purchase by or for the issuer or any person controlling, controlled by, or under common control with the issuer, or a purchase subject to control of the issuer or any such person, shall be deemed to be a purchase by the issuer. The Commission shall have power to make rules and regulations implementing this paragraph in the public interest and for the protection of investors, including exemptive rules and regulations covering situations in which the Commission deems it unnecessary or inappropriate that a purchase of the type described in this paragraph shall be deemed to be a purchase by the issuer for purposes of some or all of the provisions of paragraph (1) of this subsection. . . .

(g)   Statement of equity security ownership

(1) Any person who is directly or indirectly the beneficial owner of more than 5 per centum of any security of a class described in subsection (d)(1) of this section shall send to the issuer of the security and shall file with the Commission a statement setting forth, in such form and at such time as the Commission may, by rule, prescribe—

(A) such person's identity, residence, and citizenship; and

(B) the number and description of the shares in which such person has an interest and the nature of such interest.

(2) If any material change occurs in the facts set forth in the statement sent to the issuer and filed with the Commission, an amendment shall be transmitted to the issuer and shall be filed with the Commission, in accordance with such rules and regulations as the Commission may prescribe as necessary or appropriate in the public interest or for the protection of investors.

(3) When two or more persons act as a partnership, limited partnership, syndicate, or other group for the purpose of acquiring, holding, or disposing of securities of an issuer, such syndicate or group shall be deemed a "person" for the purposes of this subsection.

(4) In determining, for purposes of this subsection, any percentage of a class of any security, such class shall be deemed to consist of the amount of the outstanding securities of such class, exclusive of any securities of such class held by or for the account of the issuer or a subsidiary of the issuer.

(5) In exercising its authority under this subsection, the Commission shall take such steps as it deems necessary or appropriate in the public interest or for the protection of investors (A) to achieve centralized reporting of information regarding ownership, (B) to avoid unnecessarily duplicative reporting by and minimize the compliance burden on persons required to report, and (C) to tabulate and promptly make available the information contained in any report filed pursuant to this subsection in a manner which will, in the view of the Commission, maximize the usefulness of the information to other Federal and State agencies and the public.

(6) The Commission may, by rule or order, exempt, in whole or in part, any person or class of persons from any or all of the reporting requirements of this subsection as it deems necessary or appropriate in the public interest or for the protection of investors....

(h) Large trader reporting

(1) Identification requirements for large traders.

For the purpose of monitoring the impact on the securities markets of securities transactions involving a substantial volume or a large fair market value or exercise value and for the purpose of otherwise assisting the Commission in the enforcement of this title, each large trader shall—

(A) provide such information to the Commission as the Commission may by rule or regulation prescribe as necessary or appropriate, identifying such large trader and all accounts in or through which such large trader effects such transactions; and

(B) identify, in accordance with such rules or regulations as the Commission may prescribe as necessary or appropriate, to any registered broker or dealer by or through whom such large trader directly or indirectly effects securities transactions, such large trader and all accounts directly or indirectly maintained with such broker or dealer by such large trader in or through which such transactions are effected.

(2) Recordkeeping and reporting requirements for brokers and dealers. Every registered broker or dealer shall make and keep for prescribed periods such records as the Commission by rule or regulation prescribes as necessary or appropriate in the public interest, for the protection of investors, or otherwise in furtherance of the purposes of this title, with respect to securities transactions that equal or exceed the reporting activity level effected directly or indirectly by or through such registered broker or dealer of or for any person that such broker or dealer knows is a large trader, or any person that such broker or dealer has reason to know is a large trader on the basis of transactions in securities effected by or through such broker or dealer. Such records shall be available for reporting to the Commission, or any self-regulatory organization that the Commission shall designate to receive such reports, on the morning of the day following the day the transactions were effected, and shall be reported to the Commission or a self-regulatory organization designated by the Commission immediately upon request by the Commission or such a self-regulatory organization. Such records and reports shall be in a format and transmitted in a manner prescribed by the Commission (including, but not limited to, machine readable form)....

(8) Definitions. For purposes of this subsection—

(A) the term "large trader" means every person who, for his own account or an account for which he exercises investment discretion, effects transactions for the purchase or sale of any publicly traded security or securities by use of any means or instrumentality of interstate commerce or of the mails, or of any facility of a national securities exchange, directly or indirectly by or through a registered broker or dealer in an aggregate amount equal to or in excess of the identifying activity level;

(B) the term "publicly traded security" means any equity security (including an option on individual equity securities, and an option on a group or index of such securities) listed, or admitted to unlisted trading privileges, on a national securities exchange, or quoted in an automated interdealer quotation system;

(C) the term "identifying activity level" means transactions in publicly traded securities at or above a level of volume, fair market value, or exercise value as shall be fixed from time to time by the Commission by rule or regulation, specifying the time interval during which such transactions shall be aggregated;

(D) the term "reporting activity level" means transactions in publicly traded securities at or above a level of volume, fair market value, or exercise value as shall be fixed from time to time by the Commission by rule, regulation, or order, specifying the time interval during which such transactions shall be aggregated; and

(E) the term "person" has the meaning given in section 3(a)(9) of this title and also includes two or more persons acting as a partnership, limited partnership, syndicate, or other group, but does not include a foreign central bank.

(i) Accuracy of financial reports

Each financial report that contains financial statements, and that is required to be prepared in accordance with (or reconciled to) generally accepted accounting principles under this title and filed with the Commission shall reflect all material correcting adjustments that have been identified by a registered public accounting firm in accordance with generally accepted accounting principles and the rules and regulations of the Commission.

(j) Off-balance sheet transactions

Not later than 180 days after the date of enactment of the Sarbanes–Oxley Act of 2002, the Commission shall issue final rules providing that each annual and quarterly financial report required to be filed with the Commission shall disclose all material off-balance sheet transactions, arrangements, obligations (including contingent obligations), and other relationships of the issuer with unconsolidated entities or other persons, that may have a material current or future effect on financial condition, changes in financial condition, results of operations, liquidity, capital expenditures, capital resources, or significant components of revenues or expenses.

(k) Prohibition on personal loans to executives

(1) *In general.*—It shall be unlawful for any issuer (as defined in section 2 of the Sarbanes–Oxley Act of 2002), directly or indirectly, including through any subsidiary, to extend or maintain credit, to arrange for the extension of credit, or to renew an extension of credit, in the form of a personal loan to or for any director or executive officer (or equivalent thereof) of that issuer. An extension of credit maintained by the issuer on the date of enactment of this subsection shall not be subject to the provisions of this subsection, provided that there is no material modification to any term of any

such extension of credit or any renewal of any such extension of credit on or after that date of enactment.

(2) *Limitation.*—Paragraph (1) does not preclude any home improvement and manufactured home loans (as that term is defined in section 5 of the Home Owners' Loan Act (12 U.S.C. 1464)), consumer credit (as defined in section 103 of the Truth in Lending Act (15 U.S.C. 1602)), or any extension of credit under an open end credit plan (as defined in section 103 of the Truth in Lending Act (15 U.S.C. 1602)), or a charge card (as defined in section 127(c)(4)(e) of the Truth in Lending Act (15 U.S.C. 1637(c)(4)(e)), or any extension of credit by a broker or dealer registered under section 15 of this title to an employee of that broker or dealer to buy, trade, or carry securities, that is permitted under rules or regulations of the Board of Governors of the Federal Reserve System pursuant to section 7 of this title (other than an extension of credit that would be used to purchase the stock of that issuer), that is—

    (A) made or provided in the ordinary course of the consumer credit business of such issuer;

    (B) of a type that is generally made available by such issuer to the public; and

    (C) made by such issuer on market terms, or terms that are no more favorable than those offered by the issuer to the general public for such extensions of credit. . . .

(*l*) Real time issuer disclosures

Each issuer reporting under section 13(a) or 15(d) shall disclose to the public on a rapid and current basis such additional information concerning material changes in the financial condition or operations of the issuer, in plain English, which may include trend and qualitative information and graphic presentations, as the Commission determines, by rule, is necessary or useful for the protection of investors and in the public interest.

§ 14. Proxies

(a) Solicitation of proxies in violation of rules and regulations

It shall be unlawful for any person, by the use of the mails or by any means or instrumentality of interstate commerce or of any facility of a national securities exchange or otherwise, in contravention of such rules and regulations as the Commission may prescribe as necessary or appropriate in the public interest or for the protection of investors, to solicit or to permit the use of his name to solicit any proxy or consent or authorization in respect of any security (other than an exempted security) registered pursuant to section 12 of this title. . . .

(b) Giving or refraining from giving proxy in respect of any security carried for account of customer; disclosure of beneficial owners

(1) It shall be unlawful for any member of a national securities exchange, or any broker or dealer registered under this chapter, or any bank, association, or other entity that exercises fiduciary powers, in contravention of such rules and regulations as the Commission may prescribe as necessary or appropriate in the public interest or for the protection of investors, to give, or to refrain from giving a proxy, consent, authorization, or information statement in respect of any security registered pursuant to section 12 of this title, or any security issued by an investment company registered under the Investment Company Act of 1940, and carried for the account of a customer....

(c) Information to holders of record prior to annual or other meeting

Unless proxies, consents, or authorizations in respect of a security registered pursuant to section 12 of this title, or a security issued by an investment company registered under the Investment Company Act of 1940, are solicited by or on behalf of the management of the issuer from the holders of record of such security in accordance with the rules and regulations prescribed under subsection (a) of this section, prior to any annual or other meeting of the holders of such security, such issuer shall, in accordance with rules and regulations prescribed by the Commission, file with the Commission and transmit to all holders of record of such security information substantially equivalent to the information which would be required to be transmitted if a solicitation were made....

(d) Tender offer by owner of more than five per centum of class of securities; exceptions

(1) It shall be unlawful for any person, directly or indirectly, by use of the mails or by any means or instrumentality of interstate commerce or of any facility of a national securities exchange or otherwise, to make a tender offer for, or a request or invitation for tenders of, any class of any equity security which is registered pursuant to section 12 of this title, or any equity security of an insurance company which would have been required to be so registered except for the exemption contained in section 12(g)(2)(G) of this title, or any equity security issued by a closed-end investment company registered under the Investment Company Act of 1940, if, after consummation thereof, such person would, directly or indirectly, be the beneficial owner of more than 5 per centum of such class, unless at the time copies of the offer or request or invitation are first published or sent or given to security holders such person has filed with the Commission a statement containing such of the information specified in section 13(d) of this title, and such additional information as

the Commission may by rules and regulations prescribe as necessary or appropriate in the public interest or for the protection of investors. All requests or invitations for tenders or advertisements making a tender offer or requesting or inviting tenders of such a security shall be filed as a part of such statement and shall contain such of the information contained in such statement as the Commission may by rules and regulations prescribe. Copies of any additional material soliciting or requesting such tender offers subsequent to the initial solicitation or request shall contain such information as the Commission may by rules and regulations prescribe as necessary or appropriate in the public interest or for the protection of investors, and shall be filed with the Commission not later than the time copies of such material are first published or sent or given to security holders. Copies of all statements, in the form in which such material is furnished to security holders and the Commission, shall be sent to the issuer not later than the date such material is first published or sent or given to any security holders.

(2) When two or more persons act as a partnership, limited partnership, syndicate, or other group for the purpose of acquiring, holding, or disposing of securities of an issuer, such syndicate or group shall be deemed a "person" for purposes of this subsection.

(3) In determining, for purposes of this subsection, any percentage of a class of any security, such class shall be deemed to consist of the amount of the outstanding securities of such class, exclusive of any securities of such class held by or for the account of the issuer or a subsidiary of the issuer.

(4) Any solicitation or recommendation to the holders of such a security to accept or reject a tender offer or request or invitation for tenders shall be made in accordance with such rules and regulations as the Commission may prescribe as necessary or appropriate in the public interest or for the protection of investors.

(5) Securities deposited pursuant to a tender offer or request or invitation for tenders may be withdrawn by or on behalf of the depositor at any time until the expiration of seven days after the time definitive copies of the offer or request or invitation are first published or sent or given to security holders, and at any time after sixty days from the date of the original tender offer or request or invitation, except as the Commission may otherwise prescribe by rules, regulations, or order as necessary or appropriate in the public interest or for the protection of investors.

(6) Where any person makes a tender offer, or request or invitation for tenders, for less than all the outstanding equity securities of a class, and where a greater number of securities is deposited pursuant thereto within ten days after copies of the offer or request or invitation are first published or sent or given to security holders than such person is bound or willing to take up and pay for, the securities taken up shall be taken

up as nearly as may be pro rata, disregarding fractions, according to the number of securities deposited by each depositor. The provisions of this subsection shall also apply to securities deposited within ten days after notice of an increase in the consideration offered to security holders, as described in paragraph (7), is first published or sent or given to security holders.

(7) Where any person varies the terms of a tender offer or request or invitation for tenders before the expiration thereof by increasing the consideration offered to holders of such securities, such person shall pay the increased consideration to each security holder whose securities are taken up and paid for pursuant to the tender offer or request or invitation for tenders whether or not such securities have been taken up by such person before the variation of the tender offer or request or invitation.

(8) The provisions of this subsection shall not apply to any offer for, or request or invitation for tenders of, any security—

    (A) if the acquisition of such security, together with all other acquisitions by the same person of securities of the same class during the preceding twelve months, would not exceed 2 per centum of that class;

    (B) by the issuer of such security; or

    (C) which the Commission, by rules or regulations or by order, shall exempt from the provisions of this subsection as not entered into for the purpose of, and not having the effect of, changing or influencing the control of the issuer or otherwise as not comprehended within the purposes of this subsection.

(e) Untrue statement of material fact or omission of fact with respect to tender offer

It shall be unlawful for any person to make any untrue statement of a material fact or omit to state any material fact necessary in order to make the statements made, in the light of the circumstances under which they are made, not misleading, or to engage in any fraudulent, deceptive, or manipulative acts or practices, in connection with any tender offer or request or invitation for tenders, or any solicitation of security holders in opposition to or in favor of any such offer, request, or invitation. The Commission shall, for the purposes of this subsection, by rules and regulations define, and prescribe means reasonably designed to prevent, such acts and practices as are fraudulent, deceptive, or manipulative.

(f) Election or designation of majority of directors of issuer by owner of more than five per centum of class of securities at other than meeting of security holders

If, pursuant to any arrangement or understanding with the person or persons acquiring securities in a transaction subject to subsection (d) of this section or subsection (d) of section 13 of this title, any persons are to be elected or designated as directors of the issuer, otherwise than at a meeting of security holders, and the persons so elected or designated will constitute a majority of the directors of the issuer, then, prior to the time any such person takes office as a director, and in accordance with rules and regulations prescribed by the Commission, the issuer shall file with the Commission, and transmit to all holders of record of securities of the issuer who would be entitled to vote at a meeting for election of directors, information substantially equivalent to the information which would be required by subsection (a) or (c) of this section to be transmitted if such person or persons were nominees for election as directors at a meeting of such security holders. . . .

(h) Proxy solicitations and tender offers in connection with limited partnership rollup transactions

(1) Proxy rules to contain special provisions

It shall be unlawful for any person to solicit any proxy, consent, or authorization concerning a limited partnership rollup transaction, or to make any tender offer in furtherance of a limited partnership rollup transaction, unless such transaction is conducted in accordance with rules prescribed by the Commission under subsections (a) and (d) of this section as required by this subsection. Such rules shall—

> **(A)** permit any holder of a security that is the subject of the proposed limited partnership rollup transaction to engage in preliminary communications for the purpose of determining whether to solicit proxies, consents, or authorizations in opposition to the proposed limited partnership rollup transaction, without regard to whether any such communication would otherwise be considered a solicitation of proxies, and without being required to file soliciting material with the Commission prior to making that determination, except that—
>
>> **(i)** nothing in this subparagraph shall be construed to limit the application of any provision of this chapter prohibiting, or reasonably designed to prevent, fraudulent, deceptive, or manipulative acts or practices under this chapter; and
>>
>> **(ii)** any holder of not less than 5 percent of the outstanding securities that are the subject of the proposed limited partnership rollup transaction who engages in the business of buying and selling limited partnership interests in the secondary market shall be required to disclose such ownership interests and any potential conflicts of interests in such preliminary communications;
>
> **(B)** require the issuer to provide to holders of the securities that are the subject of the limited partnership rollup transaction such list of the holders of the issuer's securities as the Commission

may determine in such form and subject to such terms and conditions as the Commission may specify;

(C) prohibit compensating any person soliciting proxies, consents, or authorizations directly from security holders concerning such a limited partnership rollup transaction—

(i) on the basis of whether the solicited proxy, consent, or authorization either approves or disapproves the proposed limited partnership rollup transaction; or

(ii) contingent on the approval, disapproval, or completion of the limited partnership rollup transaction;

(D) set forth disclosure requirements for soliciting material distributed in connection with a limited partnership rollup transaction, including requirements for clear, concise, and comprehensible disclosure with respect to—

(i) any changes in the business plan, voting rights, form of ownership interest, or the compensation of the general partner in the proposed limited partnership rollup transaction from each of the original limited partnerships;

(ii) the conflicts of interest, if any, of the general partner;

(iii) whether it is expected that there will be a significant difference between the exchange values of the limited partnerships and the trading price of the securities to be issued in the limited partnership rollup transaction;

(iv) the valuation of the limited partnerships and the method used to determine the value of the interests of the limited partners to be exchanged for the securities in the limited partnership rollup transaction;

(v) the differing risks and effects of the limited partnership rollup transaction for investors in different limited partnerships proposed to be included, and the risks and effects of completing the limited partnership rollup transaction with less than all limited partnerships;

(vi) the statement by the general partner required under subparagraph (E);

(vii) such other matters deemed necessary or appropriate by the Commission;

(E) require a statement by the general partner as to whether the proposed limited partnership rollup transaction is fair or unfair to investors in each limited partnership, a discussion of the basis for that conclusion, and an evaluation and a description by the general partner of alternatives to the limited partnership rollup transaction, such as liquidation;

(F) provide that, if the general partner or sponsor has obtained any opinion (other than an opinion of counsel), appraisal, or report that is prepared by an outside party and that is materially related to the limited partnership rollup transaction, such soliciting materials shall contain or be accompanied by clear, concise, and comprehensible disclosure with respect to—

 (i) the analysis of the transaction, scope of review, preparation of the opinion, and basis for and methods of arriving at conclusions, and any representations and undertakings with respect thereto;

 (ii) the identity and qualifications of the person who prepared the opinion, the method of selection of such person, and any material past, existing, or contemplated relationships between the person or any of its affiliates and the general partner, sponsor, successor, or any other affiliate;

 (iii) any compensation of the preparer of such opinion, appraisal, or report that is contingent on the transaction's approval or completion; and

 (iv) any limitations imposed by the issuer on the access afforded to such preparer to the issuer's personnel, premises, and relevant books and records;

(G) provide that, if the general partner or sponsor has obtained any opinion, appraisal, or report as described in subparagraph (F) from any person whose compensation is contingent on the transaction's approval or completion or who has not been given access by the issuer to its personnel and premises and relevant books and records, the general partner or sponsor shall state the reasons therefor;

(H) provide that, if the general partner or sponsor has not obtained any opinion on the fairness of the proposed limited partnership rollup transaction to investors in each of the affected partnerships, such soliciting materials shall contain or be accompanied by a statement of such partner's or sponsor's reasons for concluding that such an opinion is not necessary in order to permit the limited partners to make an informed decision on the proposed transaction;

(I) require that the soliciting material include a clear, concise, and comprehensible summary of the limited partnership rollup transaction (including a summary of the matters referred to in clauses (i) through (vii) of subparagraph (D) and a summary of the matter referred to in subparagraphs (F), (G), and (H)), with the risks of the limited partnership rollup transaction set forth prominently in the fore part thereof;

(J) provide that any solicitation or offering period with respect to any proxy solicitation, tender offer, or information statement in a limited partnership rollup transaction shall be for not less than the lesser of 60 calendar days or the maximum number of days permitted under applicable State law; and

(K) contain such other provisions as the Commission determines to be necessary or appropriate for the protection of investors in limited partnership rollup transactions.

(2) Exemptions

The Commission may, consistent with the public interest, the protection of investors, and the purposes of this chapter, exempt by rule or order any security or class of securities, any transaction or class of transactions, or any person or class of persons, in whole or in part, conditionally or unconditionally, from the requirements imposed pursuant to paragraph (1) or from the definition contained in paragraph (4).

(3) Effect on Commission authority

Nothing in this subsection limits the authority of the Commission under subsection (a) or (d) of this section or any other provision of this chapter or precludes the Commission from imposing, under subsection (a) or (d) of this section or any other provision of this chapter, a remedy or procedure required to be imposed under this subsection.

(4) Definition of limited partnership rollup transaction

Except as provided in paragraph (5), as used in this subsection, the term "limited partnership rollup transaction" means a transaction involving the combination or reorganization of one or more limited partnerships, directly or indirectly, in which—

(A) some or all of the investors in any of such limited partnerships will receive new securities, or securities in another entity, that will be reported under a transaction reporting plan declared effective before December 17, 1993, by the Commission under section 11A of this title;

(B) any of the investors' limited partnership securities are not, as of the date of filing, reported under a transaction reporting plan declared effective before December 17, 1993, by the Commission under section 11A of this title;

(C) investors in any of the limited partnerships involved in the transaction are subject to a significant adverse change with respect to voting rights, the term of existence of the entity, management compensation, or investment objectives; and

(D) any of such investors are not provided an option to receive or retain a security under substantially the same terms and conditions as the original issue.

(5) Exclusions from definition

Notwithstanding paragraph (4), the term "limited partnership roll-up transaction" does not include—

(A) a transaction that involves only a limited partnership or partnerships having an operating policy or practice of retaining cash available for distribution and reinvesting proceeds from the sale, financing, or refinancing of assets in accordance with such criteria as the Commission determines appropriate;

(B) a transaction involving only limited partnerships wherein the interests of the limited partners are repurchased, recalled, or exchanged in accordance with the terms of the preexisting limited partnership agreements for securities in an operating company specifically identified at the time of the formation of the original limited partnership;

(C) a transaction in which the securities to be issued or exchanged are not required to be and are not registered under the Securities Act of 1933;

(D) a transaction that involves only issuers that are not required to register or report under section 12 of this title, both before and after the transaction;

(E) a transaction, except as the Commission may otherwise provide by rule for the protection of investors, involving the combination or reorganization of one or more limited partnerships in which a non-affiliated party succeeds to the interests of a general partner or sponsor, if—

  (i) such action is approved by not less than 66⅔ percent of the outstanding units of each of the participating limited partnerships; and

  (ii) as a result of the transaction, the existing general partners will receive only compensation to which they are entitled as expressly provided for in the preexisting limited partnership agreements; or

(F) a transaction, except as the Commission may otherwise provide by rule for the protection of investors, in which the securities offered to investors are securities of another entity that are reported under a transaction reporting plan declared effective before December 17, 1993, by the Commission under section 11A of this title, if—

  (i) such other entity was formed, and such class of securities was reported and regularly traded, not less than 12 months before the date on which soliciting material is mailed to investors; and

(ii) the securities of that entity issued to investors in the transaction do not exceed 20 percent of the total outstanding securities of the entity, exclusive of any securities of such class held by or for the account of the entity or a subsidiary of the entity.

§ 15. Registration and Regulation of Brokers and Dealers

(a) Registration of all persons utilizing exchange facilities to effect transactions; exemptions

(1) It shall be unlawful for any broker or dealer which is either a person other than a natural person or a natural person not associated with a broker or dealer which is a person other than a natural person (other than such a broker or dealer whose business is exclusively intrastate and who does not make use of any facility of a national securities exchange) to make use of the mails or any means or instrumentality of interstate commerce to effect any transactions in, or to induce or attempt to induce the purchase or sale of, any security (other than an exempted security or commercial paper, bankers' acceptances, or commercial bills) unless such broker or dealer is registered in accordance with subsection (b) of this section. . . .

(d) Filing of supplementary and periodic information

Each issuer which has filed a registration statement containing an undertaking which is or becomes operative under this subsection as in effect prior to August 20, 1964, and each issuer which shall after such date file a registration statement which has become effective pursuant to the Securities Act of 1933 ... shall file with the Commission, in accordance with such rules and regulations as the Commission may prescribe as necessary or appropriate in the public interest or for the protection of investors, such supplementary and periodic information, documents, and reports as may be required pursuant to section 13 of this title in respect of a security registered pursuant to section 12 of this title. The duty to file under this subsection shall be automatically suspended if and so long as any issue of securities of such issuer is registered pursuant to section 12 of this title. The duty to file under this subsection shall also be automatically suspended as to any fiscal year, other than the fiscal year within which such registration statement became effective, if, at the beginning of such fiscal year, the securities of each class to which the registration statement relates are held of record by less than three hundred persons. For the purposes of this subsection, the term "class" shall be construed to include all securities of an issuer which are of substantially similar character and the holders of which enjoy substantially similar rights and privileges. The Commission may, for the purpose of this subsection, define by rules and regulations the term "held of record" as it deems necessary or appropriate in the public interest or for the protection of investors in order to prevent circumvention of the provisions of this subsection. . . .

(f) Prevention of misuse of nonpublic information

Every registered broker or dealer shall establish, maintain, and enforce written policies and procedures reasonably designed, taking into consideration the nature of such broker's or dealer's business, to prevent the misuse in violation of this title, or the rules or regulations thereunder, of material, nonpublic information by such broker or dealer or any person associated with such broker or dealer. The Commission, as it deems necessary or appropriate in the public interest or for the protection of investors, shall adopt rules or regulations to require specific policies or procedures reasonably designed to prevent misuse in violation of this title (or the rules or regulations thereunder) of material, nonpublic information.

(g) Requirements for transactions in penny stocks

(1) *In general.* No broker or dealer shall make use of the mails or any means or instrumentality of interstate commerce to effect any transaction in, or to induce or attempt to induce the purchase or sale of, any penny stock by any customer except in accordance with the requirements of this subsection and the rules and regulations prescribed under this subsection.

(2) *Risk disclosure with respect to penny stocks.* Prior to effecting any transaction in any penny stock, a broker or dealer shall give the customer a risk disclosure document that—

 (A) contains a description of the nature and level of risk in the market for penny stocks in both public offerings and secondary trading;

 (B) contains a description of the broker's or dealer's duties to the customer and of the rights and remedies available to the customer with respect to violations of such duties or other requirements of Federal securities laws;

 (C) contains a brief, clear, narrative description of a dealer market, including "bid" and "ask" prices for penny stocks and the significance of the spread between the bid and ask prices. . . .

(3) *Commission rules relating to disclosure.* The Commission shall adopt rules setting forth additional standards for the disclosure by brokers and dealers to customers of information concerning transactions in penny stocks. Such rules—

 (A) shall require brokers and dealers to disclose to each customer, prior to effecting any transaction in, and at the time of confirming any transaction with respect to any penny stock, in accordance with such procedures and methods as the Commission may require consistent with the public interest and the protection of investors—

> (i) the bid and ask prices for penny stock, or such other information as the Commission may, by rule, require to provide customers with more useful and reliable information relating to the price of such stock;

> (ii) the number of shares to which such bid and ask prices apply, or other comparable information relating to the depth and liquidity of the market for such stock; and

> (iii) the amount and a description of any compensation that the broker or dealer and the associated person thereof will receive or has received in connection with such transaction. . . .

(5) *Regulations.* It shall be unlawful for any person to violate such rules and regulations as the Commission shall prescribe in the public interest or for the protection of investors or to maintain fair and orderly markets—

> (A) as necessary or appropriate to carry out this subsection; or

> (B) as reasonably designed to prevent fraudulent, deceptive, or manipulative acts and practices with respect to penny stocks. . . .

§ 15D. Securities Analysts and Research Reports

(a) Analyst protections

The Commission, or upon the authorization and direction of the Commission, a registered securities association or national securities exchange, shall have adopted, not later than 1 year after the date of enactment of this section, rules reasonably designed to address conflicts of interest that can arise when securities analysts recommend equity securities in research reports and public appearances, in order to improve the objectivity of research and provide investors with more useful and reliable information, including rules designed—

> (1) to foster greater public confidence in securities research, and to protect the objectivity and independence of securities analysts, by—

> > (A) restricting the prepublication clearance or approval of research reports by persons employed by the broker or dealer who are engaged in investment banking activities, or persons not directly responsible for investment research, other than legal or compliance staff;

(B) limiting the supervision and compensatory evaluation of securities analysts to officials employed by the broker or dealer who are not engaged in investment banking activities; and

(C) requiring that a broker or dealer and persons employed by a broker or dealer who are involved with investment banking activities may not, directly or indirectly, retaliate against or threaten to retaliate against any securities analyst employed by that broker or dealer or its affiliates as a result of an adverse, negative, or otherwise unfavorable research report that may adversely affect the present or prospective investment banking relationship of the broker or dealer with the issuer that is the subject of the research report, except that such rules may not limit the authority of a broker or dealer to discipline a securities analyst for causes other than such research report in accordance with the policies and procedures of the firm;

(2) to define periods during which brokers or dealers who have participated, or are to participate, in a public offering of securities as underwriters or dealers should not publish or otherwise distribute research reports relating to such securities or to the issuer of such securities;

(3) to establish structural and institutional safeguards within registered brokers or dealers to assure that securities analysts are separated by appropriate informational partitions within the firm from the review, pressure, or oversight of those whose involvement in investment banking activities might potentially bias their judgment or supervision; and

(4) to address such other issues as the Commission, or such association or exchange, determines appropriate.

(b) Disclosure

The Commission, or upon the authorization and direction of the Commission, a registered securities association or national securities exchange, shall have adopted, not later than 1 year after the date of enactment of this section, rules reasonably designed to require each securities analyst to disclose in public appearances, and each registered broker or dealer to disclose in each research report, as applicable, conflicts of interest that are known or should have been known by the securities analyst or the broker or dealer, to exist at the time of the appearance or the date of distribution of the report, including—

(1) the extent to which the securities analyst has debt or equity investments in the issuer that is the subject of the appearance or research report;

(2) whether any compensation has been received by the registered broker or dealer, or any affiliate thereof, including the securi-

ties analyst, from the issuer that is the subject of the appearance or research report, subject to such exemptions as the Commission may determine appropriate and necessary to prevent disclosure by virtue of this paragraph of material non-public information regarding specific potential future investment banking transactions of such issuer, as is appropriate in the public interest and consistent with the protection of investors;

(3) whether an issuer, the securities of which are recommended in the appearance or research report, currently is, or during the 1–year period preceding the date of the appearance or date of distribution of the report has been, a client of the registered broker or dealer, and if so, stating the types of services provided to the issuer;

(4) whether the securities analyst received compensation with respect to a research report, based upon (among any other factors) the investment banking revenues (either generally or specifically earned from the issuer being analyzed) of the registered broker or dealer; and

(5) such other disclosures of conflicts of interest that are material to investors, research analysts, or the broker or dealer as the Commission, or such association or exchange, determines appropriate.

(c) Definitions.—In this section—

(1) the term "securities analyst" means any associated person of a registered broker or dealer that is principally responsible for, and any associated person who reports directly or indirectly to a securities analyst in connection with, the preparation of the substance of a research report, whether or not any such person has the job title of "securities analyst"; and

(2) the term "research report" means a written or electronic communication that includes an analysis of equity securities of individual companies or industries, and that provides information reasonably sufficient upon which to base an investment decision.

§ 16.   Directors, Officers, and Principal Stockholders

(a) Disclosures required

(1) *Directors, officers, and principal stockholders required to file.*—Every person who is directly or indirectly the beneficial owner of more than 10 percent of any class of any equity security (other than an exempted security) which is registered pursuant to section 12, or who is a director or an officer of the issuer of such security, shall file the statements required by this subsection with the Commission (and, if such security is registered on a national securities exchange, also with the exchange).

(2) *Time of filing.*—The statements required by this subsection shall be filed—

(A) at the time of the registration of such security on a national securities exchange or by the effective date of a registration statement filed pursuant to section 12(g);

(B) within 10 days after he or she becomes such beneficial owner, director, or officer;

(C) if there has been a change in such ownership, or if such person shall have purchased or sold a security-based swap agreement (as defined in section 20 6(b) of the Gramm–Leach–Bliley Act (15 U.S.C. 78c note)) involving such equity security, before the end of the second business day following the day on which the subject transaction has been executed, or at such other time as the Commission shall establish, by rule, in any case in which the Commission determines that such 2–day period is not feasible.

(3) *Contents of statements.*—A statement filed—

(A) under subparagraph (A) or (B) of paragraph (2) shall contain a statement of the amount of all equity securities of such issuer of which the filing person is the beneficial owner; and

(B) under subparagraph (C) of such paragraph shall indicate ownership by the filing person at the date of filing, any such changes in such ownership, and such purchases and sales of the security-based swap agreements as have occurred since the most recent such filing under such subparagraph.

(4) *Electronic filing and availability.*—Beginning not later than 1 year after July 30, 2002—

(A) a statement filed under subparagraph (C) of paragraph (2) shall be filed electronically;

(B) the Commission shall provide each such statement on a publicly accessible Internet site not later than the end of the business day following that filing; and

(C) the issuer (if the issuer maintains a corporate website) shall provide that statement on that corporate website, not later than the end of the business day following that filing.

(b) Profits from purchase and sale of security within six months

For the purpose of preventing the unfair use of information which may have been obtained by such beneficial owner, director, or officer by reason of his relationship to the issuer, any profit realized by him from any purchase and sale, or any sale and purchase, of any equity security of such issuer (other than an exempted security) ... involving any such equity security within any period of less than six months, unless such security ... was acquired in good faith in connection with a debt previously contracted, shall inure to and be recoverable by the issuer, irrespective of any intention on the part of such beneficial owner, director, or officer in entering into such transaction of holding the security ... purchased or of not repurchasing the security ... sold for a period exceeding six months. Suit to recover such profit may be instituted at law or in equity in any court of competent jurisdiction by the issuer, or by the owner of any security of the issuer in the name and in behalf of the issuer if the issuer shall fail or refuse to bring such suit within sixty days after request or shall fail diligently to prosecute the same thereafter; but no such suit shall be brought more than two years after the date such profit was realized. This subsection shall not be construed to cover any transaction where such beneficial owner was not such both at the time of the purchase and sale, or the sale and purchase, of the security ... involved, or any transaction or transactions which the Commission by rules and regulations may exempt as not comprehended within the purpose of this subsection.

(c) Conditions for sale of security by beneficial owner, director, or officer

It shall be unlawful for any such beneficial owner, director, or officer, directly or indirectly, to sell any equity security of such issuer (other than an exempted security), if the person selling the security or his principal (1) does not own the security sold, or (2) if owning the security, does not deliver it against such sale within twenty days thereafter, or does not within five days after such sale deposit it in the mails or other usual channels of transportation; but no person shall be deemed to have violated this subsection if he proves that notwithstanding the exercise of good faith he was unable to make such delivery or deposit within such time, or that to do so would cause undue inconvenience or expense....

§ 18. Liability for Misleading Statements

(a) Persons liable; persons entitled to recover; defense of good faith; suit at law or in equity; costs, etc.

Any person who shall make or cause to be made any statement in any application, report, or document filed pursuant to this chapter or any rule or regulation thereunder or any undertaking contained in a registration statement as provided in subsection (d) of section 15 of this title, which statement was at the time and in the light of the circumstances under which it was made false or misleading with respect to any material fact, shall be liable to any person (not knowing that such statement was false or misleading) who, in reliance upon such statement, shall have purchased or sold a security at a price which was affected by such statement, for damages caused by such reliance, unless the person sued shall prove that he acted in good faith and had no knowledge that such statement was false or misleading. A person seeking to enforce such liability may sue at law or in equity in any court of competent jurisdiction. In any such suit the court may, in its discretion, require an undertaking for the payment of the costs of such suit, and assess reasonable costs, including reasonable attorneys' fees, against either party litigant.

(b) Contribution

Every person who becomes liable to make payment under this section may recover contribution as in cases of contract from any person who, if joined in the original suit, would have been liable to make the same payment.

(c) Period of limitations

No action shall be maintained to enforce any liability created under this section unless brought within one year after the discovery of the facts constituting the cause of action and within three years after such cause of action accrued.

§ 19. Registration, Responsibilities, and Oversight of Self–Regulatory Organizations. . . .

(b) Proposed rule changes; notice; proceedings

(1) Each self-regulatory organization shall file with the Commission, in accordance with such rules as the Commission may prescribe, copies of any proposed rule or any proposed change in, addition to, or deletion from the rules of such self-regulatory organization (hereinafter in this subsection collectively referred to as a "proposed rule change") accompanied by a concise general statement of the basis and purpose of such proposed rule change. The Commission shall, upon the filing of any proposed rule change, publish notice thereof together with the terms of substance of the proposed rule change or a description of the subjects and issues involved. The Commission shall give interested persons an opportunity to submit written data, views, and arguments concerning such proposed rule change. No proposed rule change shall take effect unless approved by the Commission or otherwise permitted in accordance with the provisions of this subsection.

(2) Within thirty-five days of the date of publication of notice of the filing of a proposed rule change in accordance with paragraph (1) of this subsection, or within such longer period as the Commission may designate up to ninety days of such date if it finds such longer period to be appropriate and publishes its reasons for so finding or as to which the self-regulatory organization consents, the Commission shall—

(A) by order approve such proposed rule change, or

(B) institute proceedings to determine whether the proposed rule change should be disapproved. Such proceedings shall include notice of the grounds for disapproval under consideration and opportunity for hearing and be concluded within one hundred eighty days of the date of publication of notice of the filing of the proposed rule change. At the conclusion of such proceedings the Commission, by order, shall approve or disapprove such proposed rule change. The Commission may extend the time for conclusion of such proceedings for up to sixty days if it finds good cause for such extension and publishes its reasons for so finding or for such longer period as to which the self-regulatory organization consents.

The Commission shall approve a proposed rule change of a self-regulatory organization if it finds that such proposed rule change is consistent with the requirements of this chapter and the rules and regulations thereunder applicable to such organization. The Commission shall disapprove a proposed rule change of a self-regulatory organization if it does not make such finding. The Commission shall not approve any proposed rule change prior to the thirtieth day after the date of publication of notice of the filing thereof, unless the Commission finds good cause for so doing and publishes its reasons for so finding....

(c) Amendment by Commission of rules of self-regulatory organizations

The Commission, by rule, may abrogate, add to, and delete from (hereinafter in this subsection collectively referred to as "amend") the rules of a self-regulatory organization (other than a registered clearing agency) as the Commission deems necessary or appropriate to insure the fair administration of the self-regulatory organization, to conform its rules to requirements of this chapter and the rules and regulations thereunder applicable to such organization, or otherwise in furtherance of the purposes of this chapter, in the following manner:

(1) The Commission shall notify the self-regulatory organization and publish notice of the proposed rulemaking in the Federal Register. The notice shall include the text of the proposed amendment to the rules of the self-regulatory organization and a statement of the Commission's reasons, including any pertinent facts, for commencing such proposed rulemaking.

(2) The Commission shall give interested persons an opportunity for the oral presentation of data, views, and arguments, in addition to an opportunity to make written submissions. A transcript shall be kept of any oral presentation.

(3) A rule adopted pursuant to this subsection shall incorporate the text of the amendment to the rules of the self-regulatory organization and a statement of the Commission's basis for and purpose in so amending such rules. This statement shall include an

identification of any facts on which the Commission considers its determination so to amend the rules of the self-regulatory agency to be based, including the reasons for the Commission's conclusions as to any of such facts which were disputed in the rulemaking.

(4)(A) Except as provided in paragraphs (1) through (3) of this subsection, rulemaking under this subsection shall be in accordance with the procedures specified in section 553 of title 5 for rulemaking not on the record.

(B) Nothing in this subsection shall be construed to impair or limit the Commission's power to make, or to modify or alter the procedures the Commission may follow in making, rules and regulations pursuant to any other authority under this chapter.

(C) Any amendment to the rules of a self-regulatory organization made by the Commission pursuant to this subsection shall be considered for all purposes of this chapter to be part of the rules of such self-regulatory organization and shall not be considered to be a rule of the Commission. . . .

§ 20. Liability of Controlling Persons and Persons Who Aid and Abet Violations

(a) Joint and several liability; good faith defense

Every person who, directly or indirectly, controls any person liable under any provision of this chapter or of any rule or regulation thereunder shall also be liable jointly and severally with and to the same extent as such controlled person to any person to whom such controlled person is liable, unless the controlling person acted in good faith and did not directly or indirectly induce the act or acts constituting the violation or cause of action.

(b) Unlawful activity through or by means of any other person

It shall be unlawful for any person, directly or indirectly, to do any act or thing which it would be unlawful for such person to do under the provisions of this chapter or any rule or regulation thereunder through or by means of any other person.

(c) Hindering, delaying, or obstructing the making or filing of any document, report, or information

It shall be unlawful for any director or officer of, or any owner of any securities issued by, any issuer required to file any document, report, or information under this chapter or any rule or regulation thereunder without just cause to hinder, delay, or obstruct the making or filing of any such document, report, or information. . . .

(d) Liability for trading in securities while in possession of material nonpublic information

Wherever communicating, or purchasing or selling a security while in possession of, material nonpublic information would violate, or results in liability to any purchaser or seller of the security under any provision of this title, or any rule or regulation thereunder, such conduct in connection with a purchase or sale of a put, call, straddle, option, privilege, or security-based swap agreement ... with respect to such security or with respect to a group or index of securities including such security, shall also violate and result in comparable liability to any purchaser or seller of that security under such provision, rule, or regulation.

(e) Prosecution of persons who aid and abet violations

For purposes of any action brought by the Commission under paragraph (1) or (3) of section 21(d), any person that knowingly provides substantial assistance to another person in violation of a provision of this title, or of any rule or regulation issued under this title, shall be deemed to be in violation of such provision to the same extent as the person to whom such assistance is provided....

§ 20A. Liability to Contemporaneous Traders for Insider Trading

(a) Private rights of action based on contemporaneous trading

Any person who violates any provision of this title or the rules or regulations thereunder by purchasing or selling a security while in possession of material, nonpublic information shall be liable in an action in any court of competent jurisdiction to any person who, contemporaneously with the purchase or sale of securities that is the subject of such violation, has purchased (where such violation is based on a sale of securities) or sold (where such violation is based on a purchase of securities) securities of the same class.

(b) Limitations on liability

(1) *Contemporaneous trading actions limited to profit gained or loss avoided.* The total amount of damages imposed under subsection (a) shall not exceed the profit gained or loss avoided in the transaction or transactions that are the subject of the violation.

(2) *Offsetting disgorgements against liability.* The total amount of damages imposed against any person under subsection (a) shall be diminished by the amounts, if any, that such person may be required to disgorge, pursuant to a court order obtained at the instance of the Commission, in a proceeding brought under section 21(d) of this title [Investigations; Injunctions and Prosecution of Offenses] relating to the same transaction or transactions.

(3) *Controlling person liability.* No person shall be liable under this section solely by reason of employing another person who is liable under this section, but the liability of a controlling person under this section shall be subject to section 20(a) of this title.

(4) *Statute of limitations.* No action may be brought under this section more than 5 years after the date of the last transaction that is the subject of the violation.

(c) Joint and several liability for communicating

Any person who violates any provision of this title or the rules or regulations thereunder by communicating material, nonpublic information shall be jointly and severally liable under subsection (a) with, and to the same extent as, any person or persons liable under subsection (a) to whom the communication was directed.

(d) Authority not to restrict other express or implied rights of action

Nothing in this section shall be construed to limit or condition the right of any person to bring an action to enforce a requirement of this title or the availability of any cause of action implied from a provision of this title.

(e) Provisions not to affect public prosecutions

This section shall not be construed to bar or limit in any manner any action by the Commission or the Attorney General under any other provision of this title, nor shall it bar or limit in any manner any action to recover penalties, or to seek any other order regarding penalties.

§ 21. Investigations and Actions . . .

(d)(1) Wherever it shall appear to the Commission that any person is engaged or is about to engage in acts or practices constituting a violation of any provision of this chapter, the rules or regulations thereunder, the rules of a national securities exchange or registered securities association of which such person is a member or a person associated with a member, the rules of a registered clearing agency in which such person is a participant, the rules of the Public Company Accounting Oversight Board, of which such person is a registered public accounting firm or a person associated with such a firm, or the rules of the Municipal Securities Rulemaking Board, it may in its discretion bring an action in the proper district court of the United States, the United States District Court for the District of Columbia, or the United States courts of any territory or other place subject to the jurisdiction of the United States, to enjoin such acts or practices, and upon a proper showing a permanent or temporary injunction or restraining order shall be granted without bond. The Commission may transmit such evidence as may be available concerning such acts or practices as may constitute a violation of any provision of this chapter or the rules or regulations thereunder to the Attorney General, who may, in his discretion, institute the necessary criminal proceedings under this chapter.

(2) *Authority of a court to prohibit persons from serving as officers and directors.* In any proceeding under paragraph (1) of this subsection, the court may prohibit, conditionally or unconditionally, and permanently or for such period of time as it shall determine, any person who violated section 10(b) of this title or the rules or regulations thereunder from acting as an officer or director of any issuer that has a class of securities registered pursuant to section 12 of this title or that is required to file reports pursuant to section 15(d) of this title if the person's conduct demonstrates unfitness to serve as an officer or director of any such issuer.

(3) *Money penalties in civil actions.*

(A) *Authority of commission.* Whenever it shall appear to the Commission that any person has violated any provision of this title, the rules or regulations thereunder, or a cease-and-desist order entered by the Commission pursuant to section 21C of this title, other than by committing a violation subject to a penalty pursuant to section 21A, the Commission may bring an action in a United States district court to seek, and the court shall have jurisdiction to impose, upon a proper showing, a civil penalty to be paid by the person who committed such violation.

(B) *Amount of penalty.*

(i) *First tier.* The amount of the penalty shall be determined by the court in light of the facts and circumstances. For each violation, the amount of the penalty shall not exceed the greater of (I) [$6,500]* for a natural person or [$65,000] for any other person, or (II) the gross amount of pecuniary gain to such defendant as a result of the violation.

(ii) *Second tier.* Notwithstanding clause (i), the amount of penalty for each such violation shall not exceed the greater of (I) [$65,000] for a natural person or [$325,-000] for any other person, or (II) the gross amount of pecuniary gain to such defendant as a result of the violation, if the violation described in subparagraph (A) involved fraud, deceit, manipulation, or deliberate or reckless disregard of a regulatory requirement.

---

* The bracketed figures in this section have been adjusted for inflation by the SEC under the Debt Collection Act of 1996, which requires the Commission to make inflationary adjustments to civil penalties in the Securities Act, the Exchange Act, and other Acts that the Commission administers. (Footnote by ed.)

(iii) *Third tier.* Notwithstanding clauses (i) and (ii), the amount of penalty for each such violation shall not exceed the greater of (I) [$130,000] for a natural person or [$650,000] for any other person, or (II) the gross amount of pecuniary gain to such defendant as a result of the violation, if—

(aa) the violation described in subparagraph (A) involved fraud, deceit, manipulation, or deliberate or reckless disregard of a regulatory requirement; and

(bb) such violation directly or indirectly resulted in substantial losses or created a significant risk of substantial losses to other persons....

(4) *Prohibition of attorneys' fees paid from commission disgorgement funds*—Except as otherwise ordered by the court upon motion by the Commission, or, in the case of an administrative action, as otherwise ordered by the Commission, funds disgorged as the result of an action brought by the Commission in Federal court, or as a result of any Commission administrative action, shall not be distributed as payment for attorneys' fees or expenses incurred by private parties seeking distribution of the disgorged funds....

(5) *Equitable relief.*—In any action or proceeding brought or instituted by the Commission under any provision of the securities laws, the Commission may seek, and any Federal court may grant, any equitable relief that may be appropriate or necessary for the benefit of investors.

(6) *Authority of a court to prohibit persons from participating in an offering of penny stock*—

(A) *In general.*—In any proceeding under paragraph (1) against any person participating in, or, at the time of the alleged misconduct who was participating in, an offering of penny stock, the court may prohibit that person from participating in an offering of penny stock, conditionally or unconditionally, and permanently or for such period of time as the court shall determine.

(B) *Definition.*—For purposes of this paragraph, the term "person participating in an offering of penny stock" includes any person engaging in activities with a broker, dealer, or issuer for purposes of issuing, trading, or inducing or attempting to induce the purchase or sale of, any penny stock. The Commission may, by rule or regulation, define such term to include other activities, and may, by rule, regulation, or order, exempt any person or class of persons, in whole or in part, conditionally or unconditionally, from inclusion in such term.

§ 21A. Civil Penalties for Insider Trading

(a) Authority to impose civil penalties

(1) *Judicial actions by commission authorized.* Whenever it shall appear to the Commission that any person has violated any provision of this title or the rules or regulations thereunder by purchasing or selling a security ... while in possession of material, nonpublic information in, or has violated any such provision by communicating such information in connection with, a transaction on or through the facilities of a national securities exchange or from or through a broker or dealer, and which is not part of a public offering by an issuer of securities other than standardized options or security futures products, the Commission—

(A) may bring an action in a United States district court to seek, and the court shall have jurisdiction to impose, a civil penalty to be paid by the person who committed such violation; and

(B) may, subject to subsection (b)(1), bring an action in a United States district court to seek, and the court shall have jurisdiction to impose, a civil penalty to be paid by a person who, at the time of the violation, directly or indirectly controlled the person who committed such violation.

(2) *Amount of penalty for person who committed violation.* The amount of the penalty which may be imposed on the person who committed such violation shall be determined by the court in light of the facts and circumstances, but shall not exceed three times the profit gained or loss avoided as a result of such unlawful purchase, sale, or communication.

(3) *Amount of penalty for controlling person.* The amount of the penalty which may be imposed on any person who, at the time of the violation, directly or indirectly controlled the person who committed such violation, shall be determined by the court in light of the facts and circumstances, but shall not exceed the greater of [$1,275,000],* or three times the amount of the profit gained or loss avoided as a result of such controlled person's violation. If such controlled person's violation was a violation by communication, the profit gained or loss avoided as a result of the violation shall, for purposes of this paragraph only, be deemed to be limited to the profit gained or loss avoided by the person or persons to whom the controlled person directed such communication.

---

* The bracketed figure in this section has been adjusted for inflation by the SEC under the Debt Collection Act of 1996, which requires the Commission to make inflation- ary adjustments to civil penalties in the Securities Act, the Exchange Act, and other Acts that the Commission administers. (Footnote by ed.)

(b) Limitations on liability

(1) *Liability of controlling persons.* No controlling person shall be subject to a penalty under subsection (a)(1)(B) unless the Commission establishes that—

(A) such controlling person knew or recklessly disregarded the fact that such controlled person was likely to engage in the act or acts constituting the violation and failed to take appropriate steps to prevent such act or acts before they occurred; or

(B) such controlling person knowingly or recklessly failed to establish, maintain, or enforce any policy or procedure required under section 15(f) of this title or section 204A of the Investment Advisers Act of 1940 and such failure substantially contributed to or permitted the occurrence of the act or acts constituting the violation.

(2) *Additional restrictions on liability.* No person shall be subject to a penalty under subsection (a) solely by reason of employing another person who is subject to a penalty under such subsection, unless such employing person is liable as a controlling person under paragraph (1) of this subsection. Section 20(a) of this title shall not apply to actions under subsection (a) of this section....

(e) Authority to award bounties to informants

Notwithstanding the provisions of subsection (d)(1), there shall be paid from amounts imposed as a penalty under this section and recovered by the Commission or the Attorney General, such sums, not to exceed 10 percent of such amounts, as the Commission deems appropriate, to the person or persons who provide information leading to the imposition of such penalty. Any determinations under this subsection, including whether, to whom, or in what amount to make payments, shall be in the sole discretion of the Commission, except that no such payment shall be made to any member, officer, or employee of any appropriate regulatory agency, the Department of Justice, or a self-regulatory organization. Any such determination shall be final and not subject to judicial review.

(f) Definition

For purposes of this section, "profit gained" or "loss avoided" is the difference between the purchase or sale price of the security and the value of that security as measured by the trading price of the security a reasonable period after public dissemination of the nonpublic information....

§ 21B. Civil Remedies in Administrative Proceedings

(a) Commission authority to assess money penalties

In any proceeding instituted pursuant to sections 15(b)(4), 15(b)(6), 15B, 15C, 15D, or 17A of this title against any person, the Commission or the appropriate regulatory agency may impose a civil penalty if it finds, on the record after notice and opportunity for hearing, that such person—

(1) has willfully violated any provision of the Securities Act of 1933, the Investment Company Act of 1940, the Investment Advisers Act of 1940, or this title, or the rules or regulations thereunder, or the rules of the Municipal Securities Rulemaking Board;

(2) has willfully aided, abetted, counseled, commanded, induced, or procured such a violation by any other person;

(3) has willfully made or caused to be made in any application for registration or report required to be filed with the Commission or with any other appropriate regulatory agency under this title, or in any proceeding before the Commission with respect to registration, any statement which was, at the time and in the light of the circumstances under which it was made, false or misleading with respect to any material fact, or has omitted to state in any such application or report any material fact which is required to be stated therein; or

(4) has failed reasonably to supervise, within the meaning of section 15(b)(4)(E) of this title, with a view to preventing violations of the provisions of such statutes, rules and regulations, another person who commits such a violation, if such other person is subject to his supervision;

and that such penalty is in the public interest.

(b) Maximum amount of penalty

(1) *First tier.*—The maximum amount of penalty for each act or omission described in subsection (a) shall be [$6,500]* for a natural person or [$65,000] for any other person.

(2) *Second tier.*—Notwithstanding paragraph (1), the maximum amount of penalty for each such act or omission shall be [$65,000] for a natural person or [$325,000] for any other person if the act or omission described in subsection (a) involved fraud, deceit, manipulation, or deliberate or reckless disregard of a regulatory requirement.

(3) *Third tier.*—Notwithstanding paragraphs (1) and (2), the maximum amount of penalty for each such act or omission shall be [$130,000] for a natural person or [$650,000] for any other person if—

* The bracketed figures in this section have been adjusted for inflation by the SEC under the Debt Collection Act of 1996, which requires the Commission to make inflationary adjustments to civil penalties in the Securities Act, the Exchange Act, and other Acts that the Commission administers. (Footnote by ed.)

(A) The act or omission described in subsection (a) involved fraud, deceit, manipulation, or deliberate or reckless disregard of a regulatory requirement; and

(B) such act or omission directly or indirectly resulted in substantial losses or created a significant risk of substantial losses to other persons or resulted in substantial pecuniary gain to the person who committed the act or omission.

(c) Determination of public interest

In considering under this section whether a penalty is in the public interest, the Commission or the appropriate regulatory agency may consider—

(1) whether the act or omission for which such penalty is assessed involved fraud, deceit, manipulation, or deliberate or reckless disregard of a regulatory requirement;

(2) the harm to other persons resulting either directly or indirectly from such act or omission;

(3) the extent to which any person was unjustly enriched, taking into account any restitution made to persons injured by such behavior;

(4) whether such person previously has been found by the Commission, another appropriate regulatory agency, or a self-regulatory organization to have violated the Federal securities laws, State securities laws, or the rules of a self-regulatory organization, has been enjoined by a court of competent jurisdiction from violations of such laws or rules, or has been convicted by a court of competent jurisdiction of violations of such laws or of any felony or misdemeanor described in section 15(b)(4)(B) of this title;

(5) the need to deter such person and other persons from committing such acts or omissions; and

(6) such other matters as justice may require.

(d) Evidence concerning ability to pay

In any proceeding in which the Commission or the appropriate regulatory agency may impose a penalty under this section, a respondent may present evidence of the respondent's ability to pay such penalty. The Commission or the appropriate regulatory agency may, in its discretion, consider such evidence in determining whether such penalty is in the public interest. Such evidence may relate to the extent of such person's ability to continue in business and the collectability of a penalty, taking into account any other claims of the United States or third parties upon such person's assets and the amount of such person's assets.

(e) Authority to enter an order requiring an accounting and disgorgement

In any proceeding in which the Commission or the appropriate regulatory agency may impose a penalty under this section, the Commission or the appropriate regulatory agency may enter an order requiring accounting and disgorgement, including reasonable interest. The Commission is authorized to adopt rules, regulations, and orders concerning payments to investors, rates of interest, periods of accrual, and such other matters as it deems appropriate to implement this subsection.

§ 21C. Cease–and–Desist Proceedings

(a) Authority of the Commission

If the Commission finds, after notice and opportunity for hearing, that any person is violating, has violated, or is about to violate any provision of this title, or any rule or regulation thereunder, the Commission may publish its findings and enter an order requiring such person, and any other person that is, was, or would be a cause of the violation, due to an act or omission the person knew or should have known would contribute to such violation, to cease and desist from committing or causing such violation and any future violation of the same provision, rule, or regulation. Such order may, in addition to requiring a person to cease and desist from committing or causing a violation, require such person to comply, or to take steps to effect compliance, with such provision, rule, or regulation, upon such terms and conditions and within such time as the Commission may specify in such order. Any such order may, as the Commission deems appropriate, require future compliance or steps to effect future compliance, either permanently or for such period of time as the Commission may specify, with such provision, rule, or regulation with respect to any security, any issuer, or any other person. . . .

(e) Authority to enter an order requiring an accounting and disgorgement

In any cease-and-desist proceeding under subsection (a), the Commission may enter an order requiring accounting and disgorgement, including reasonable interest. The Commission is authorized to adopt rules, regulations, and orders concerning payments to investors, rates of interest, periods of accrual, and such other matters as it deems appropriate to implement this subsection.

(f) Authority of the Commission to prohibit persons from serving as officers or directors

In any cease-and-desist proceeding under subsection (a), the Commission may issue an order to prohibit, conditionally or unconditionally, and permanently or for such period of time as it shall determine, any person who has violated section 10(b) or the rules or regulations there-under, from acting as an officer or director of any issuer that has a class of securities registered pursuant to section 12, or that is required to file reports pursuant to section 15(d), if the conduct of that person demonstrates unfitness to serve as an officer or director of any such issuer.

§ 21D. Private Securities Litigation

(a) Private class actions

(1) *In general.*—The provisions of this subsection shall apply in each private action arising under this title that is brought as a plaintiff class action pursuant to the Federal Rules of Civil Procedure.

(2) *Certification filed with complaint.*—

(A) In General.—Each plaintiff seeking to serve as a representative party on behalf of a class shall provide a sworn certification, which shall be personally signed by such plaintiff and filed with the complaint, that—

(i) states that the plaintiff has reviewed the complaint and authorized its filing;

(ii) states that the plaintiff did not purchase the security that is the subject of the complaint at the direction of plaintiff's counsel or in order to participate in any private action arising under this title;

(iii) states that the plaintiff is willing to serve as a representative party on behalf of a class, including providing testimony at deposition and trial, if necessary;

(iv) sets forth all of the transactions of the plaintiff in the security that is the subject of the complaint during the class period specified in the complaint;

(v) identifies any other action under this title, filed during the 3–year period preceding the date on which the certification is signed by the plaintiff, in which the plaintiff has sought to serve as a representative party on behalf of a class; and

(vi) states that the plaintiff will not accept any payment for serving as a representative party on behalf of a class beyond the plaintiff's pro rata share of any recovery, except as ordered or approved by the court in accordance with paragraph (4).

(B) *Nonwaiver of attorney-client privilege.*—The certification filed pursuant to subparagraph (A) shall not be construed to be a waiver of the attorney-client privilege.

(3) *Appointment of lead plaintiff.*

(A) *Early notice to class members.—*

(i) *In General.*—Not later than 20 days after the date on which the complaint is filed, the plaintiff or plaintiffs shall cause to be published, in a widely circulated national business-oriented publication or wire service, a notice advising members of the purported plaintiff class—

(I) of the pendency of the action, the claims asserted therein, and the purported class period; and

(II) that, not later than 60 days after the date on which the notice is published, any member of the purported class may move the court to serve as lead plaintiff of the purported class.

(ii) *Multiple actions.*—If more than one action on behalf of a class asserting substantially the same claim or claims arising under this title is filed, only the plaintiff or plaintiffs in the first filed action shall be required to cause notice to be published in accordance with clause (i).

(iii) *Additional notices may be required under federal rules.*—Notice required under clause (i) shall be in addition to any notice required pursuant to the Federal Rules of Civil Procedure.

(B) *Appointment of lead plaintiff.—*

(i) *In general.*—Not later than 90 days after the date on which a notice is published under subparagraph (A)(i), the court shall consider any motion made by a purported class member in response to the notice, including any motion by a class member who is not individually named as a plaintiff in the complaint or complaints, and shall appoint as lead plaintiff the member or members of the purported plaintiff class that the court determines to be most capable of adequately representing the interests of class members (hereafter in this paragraph referred to as the "most adequate plaintiff") in accordance with this subparagraph.

(ii) *Consolidated actions.*—If more than one action on behalf of a class asserting substantially the same claim or claims arising under this title has been filed, and any party has sought to consolidate those actions for pretrial purposes or for trial, the court shall not make the determination required by clause (i) until after the decision on the motion to consolidate is rendered. As soon as practicable after such decision is rendered, the court shall appoint the most adequate plaintiff as lead plaintiff for the consolidated actions in accordance with this paragraph.

(iii) *Rebuttable presumption.—*

(I) *In general.—*Subject to subclause (II), for purposes of clause (i), the court shall adopt a presumption that the most adequate plaintiff in any private action arising under this title is the person or group of persons that—

(aa) has either filed the complaint or made a motion in response to a notice under subparagraph (A)(i);

(bb) in the determination of the court, has the largest financial interest in the relief sought by the class; and

(cc) otherwise satisfies the requirements of Rule 23 of the Federal Rules of Civil Procedure.

(II) Rebuttal evidence.—The presumption described in subclause (I) may be rebutted only upon proof by a member of the purported plaintiff class that the presumptively most adequate plaintiff—

(aa) will not fairly and adequately protect the interests of the class; or

(bb) is subject to unique defenses that render such plaintiff incapable of adequately representing the class.

(iv) *Discovery.—*For purposes of this subparagraph, discovery relating to whether a member or members of the purported plaintiff class is the most adequate plaintiff may be conducted by a plaintiff only if the plaintiff first demonstrates a reasonable basis for a finding that the presumptively most adequate plaintiff is incapable of adequately representing the class.

(v) *Selection of lead counsel.—*The most adequate plaintiff shall, subject to the approval of the court, select and retain counsel to represent the class.

(vi) *Restrictions on professional plaintiffs.—*Except as the court may otherwise permit, consistent with the purposes of this section, a person may be a lead plaintiff, or an officer, director, or fiduciary of a lead plaintiff, in no more than 5 securities class actions brought as plaintiff class actions pursuant to the Federal Rules of Civil Procedure during any 3–year period.

(4) *Recovery by plaintiffs.—*The share of any final judgment or of any settlement that is awarded to a representative party serving on behalf of a class shall be equal, on a per share basis, to the portion of the final judgment or settlement awarded to all other members of the class. Nothing in this paragraph shall be construed to limit the award of reasonable costs and expenses (including lost

wages) directly relating to the representation of the class to any representative party serving on behalf of a class.

(5) *Restrictions on settlements under seal.*—The terms and provisions of any settlement agreement of a class action shall not be filed under seal, except that on motion of any party to the settlement, the court may order filing under seal for those portions of a settlement agreement as to which good cause is shown for such filing under seal. For purposes of this paragraph, good cause shall exist only if publication of a term or provision of a settlement agreement would cause direct and substantial harm to any party.

(6) *Restrictions on payment of attorneys' fees and expenses.*— Total attorneys' fees and expenses awarded by the court to counsel for the plaintiff class shall not exceed a reasonable percentage of the amount of any damages and prejudgment interest actually paid to the class.

(7) *Disclosure of settlement terms to class members.*—Any proposed or final settlement agreement that is published or otherwise disseminated to the class shall include each of the following statements, along with a cover page summarizing the information contained in such statements:

(A) *Statement of plaintiff recovery.*—The amount of the settlement proposed to be distributed to the parties to the action, determined in the aggregate and on an average per share basis.

(B) *Statement of potential outcome of case.*—

(i) *Agreement on amount of damages.*—If the settling parties agree on the average amount of damages per share that would be recoverable if the plaintiff prevailed on each claim alleged under this title, a statement concerning the average amount of such potential damages per share.

(ii) *Disagreement on amount of damages.*—If the parties do not agree on the average amount of damages per share that would be recoverable if the plaintiff prevailed on each claim alleged under this title, a statement from each settling party concerning the issue or issues on which the parties disagree.

(iii) *Inadmissibility for certain purposes.*—A statement made in accordance with clause (i) or (ii) concerning the amount of damages shall not be admissible in any Federal or State judicial action or administrative proceeding, other than an action or proceeding arising out of such statement.

(C) *Statement of attorneys' fees or costs sought.*—If any of the settling parties or their counsel intend to apply to the court for an award of attorneys' fees or costs from any fund estab-

1892

lished as part of the settlement, a statement indicating which parties or counsel intend to make such an application, the amount of fees and costs that will be sought (including the amount of such fees and costs determined on an average per share basis), and a brief explanation supporting the fees and costs sought. Such information shall be clearly summarized on the cover page of any notice to a party of any proposed or final settlement agreement.

(D) *Identification of lawyers' representatives.*—The name, telephone number, and address of one or more representatives of counsel for the plaintiff class who will be reasonably available to answer questions from class members concerning any matter contained in any notice of settlement published or otherwise disseminated to the class.

(E) *Reasons for settlement.*—A brief statement explaining the reasons why the parties are proposing the settlement.

(F) *Other information.*—Such other information as may be required by the court.

(8) *Security for payment of costs in class actions.*—In any private action arising under this title that is certified as a class action pursuant to the Federal Rules of Civil Procedure, the court may require an undertaking from the attorneys for the plaintiff class, the plaintiff class, or both, or from the attorneys for the defendant, the defendant, or both, in such proportions and at such times as the court determines are just and equitable, for the payment of fees and expenses that may be awarded under this subsection.

(9) *Attorney conflict of interest.*—If a plaintiff class is represented by an attorney who directly owns or otherwise has a beneficial interest in the securities that are the subject of the litigation, the court shall make a determination of whether such ownership or other interest constitutes a conflict of interest sufficient to disqualify the attorney from representing the plaintiff class.

(b) Requirements for securities fraud actions

(1) *Misleading statements and omissions.*—In any private action arising under this title in which the plaintiff alleges that the defendant—

(A) made an untrue statement of a material fact; or

(B) omitted to state a material fact necessary in order to make the statements made, in the light of the circumstances in which they were made, not misleading;

the complaint shall specify each statement alleged to have been misleading, the reason or reasons why the statement is misleading, and, if an allegation regarding the statement or omission is made on information and belief, the complaint shall state with particularity all facts on which that belief is formed.

(2) *Required state of mind.*—In any private action arising under this title in which the plaintiff may recover money damages only on proof that the defendant acted with a particular state of mind, the complaint shall, with respect to each act or omission alleged to violate this title, state with particularity facts giving rise to a strong inference that the defendant acted with the required state of mind.

(3) *Motion to dismiss; stay of discovery.*—

(A) *Dismissal for failure to meet pleading requirements.*—In any private action arising under this title, the court shall, on the motion of any defendant, dismiss the complaint if the requirements of paragraphs (1) and (2) are not met.

(B) *Stay of discovery.*—In any private action arising under this title, all discovery and other proceedings shall be stayed during the pendency of any motion to dismiss, unless the court finds upon the motion of any party that particularized discovery is necessary to preserve evidence or to prevent undue prejudice to that party.

(C) *Preservation of evidence.*—

(i) In general.—During the pendency of any stay of discovery pursuant to this paragraph, unless otherwise ordered by the court, any party to the action with actual notice of the allegations contained in the complaint shall treat all documents, data compilations (including electronically recorded or stored data), and tangible objects that are in the custody or control of such person and that are relevant to the allegations, as if they were the subject of a continuing request for production of documents from an opposing party under the Federal Rules of Civil Procedure.

(ii) Sanction for willful violation.—A party aggrieved by the willful failure of an opposing party to comply with clause (i) may apply to the court for an order awarding appropriate sanctions.

(D) *Circumvention of stay of discovery.*—Upon a proper showing, a court may stay discovery proceedings in any private action in a State court, as necessary in aid of its jurisdiction, or to protect or effectuate its judgments, in an action subject to a stay of discovery pursuant to this paragraph.

(4) *Loss causation.*—In any private action arising under this title, the plaintiff shall have the burden of proving that the act or omission of the defendant alleged to violate this title caused the loss for which the plaintiff seeks to recover damages.

(c) Sanctions for abusive litigation

(1) *Mandatory review by court.*—In any private action arising under this title, upon final adjudication of the action, the court shall include in the record specific findings regarding compliance by each party and each attorney representing any party with each requirement of Rule 11(b) of the Federal Rules of Civil Procedure as to any complaint, responsive pleading, or dispositive motion.

(2) *Mandatory sanctions.*—If the court makes a finding under paragraph (1) that a party or attorney violated any requirement of Rule 11(b) of the Federal Rules of Civil Procedure as to any complaint, responsive pleading, or dispositive motion, the court shall impose sanctions on such party or attorney in accordance with Rule 11 of the Federal Rules of Civil Procedure. Prior to making a finding that any party or attorney has violated Rule 11 of the Federal Rules of Civil Procedure, the court shall give such party or attorney notice and an opportunity to respond.

(3) *Presumption in favor of attorneys' fees and costs.*—

(A) *In general.*—Subject to subparagraphs (B) and (C), for purposes of paragraph (2), the court shall adopt a presumption that the appropriate sanction—

(i) for failure of any responsive pleading or dispositive motion to comply with any requirement of Rule 11(b) of the Federal Rules of Civil Procedure is an award to the opposing party of the reasonable attorneys' fees and other expenses incurred as a direct result of the violation; and

(ii) for substantial failure of any complaint to comply with any requirement of Rule 11(b) of the Federal Rules of Civil Procedure is an award to the opposing party of the reasonable attorneys' fees and other expenses incurred in the action.

(B) *Rebuttal evidence.*—The presumption described in subparagraph (A) may be rebutted only upon proof by the party or attorney against whom sanctions are to be imposed that—

(i) the award of attorneys' fees and other expenses will impose an unreasonable burden on that party or attorney and would be unjust, and the failure to make such an award would not impose a greater burden on the party in whose favor sanctions are to be imposed; or

(ii) the violation of Rule 11(b) of the Federal Rules of Civil Procedure was de minimis.

(C) *Sanctions.*—If the party or attorney against whom sanctions are to be imposed meets its burden under subparagraph (B), the court shall award the sanctions that the court

1895

deems appropriate pursuant to Rule 11 of the Federal Rules of Civil Procedure.

(d) Defendant's right to written interrogatories

In any private action arising under this title in which the plaintiff may recover money damages, the court shall, when requested by a defendant, submit to the jury a written interrogatory on the issue of each such defendant's state of mind at the time the alleged violation occurred.

(e) Limitation on damages

(1) *In general.*—Except as provided in paragraph (2), in any private action arising under this title in which the plaintiff seeks to establish damages by reference to the market price of a security, the award of damages to the plaintiff shall not exceed the difference between the purchase or sale price paid or received, as appropriate, by the plaintiff for the subject security and the mean trading price of that security during the 90–day period beginning on the date on which the information correcting the misstatement or omission that is the basis for the action is disseminated to the market.

(2) *Exception.*—In any private action arising under this title in which the plaintiff seeks to establish damages by reference to the market price of a security, if the plaintiff sells or repurchases the subject security prior to the expiration of the 90–day period described in paragraph (1), the plaintiff's damages shall not exceed the difference between the purchase or sale price paid or received, as appropriate, by the plaintiff for the security and the mean trading price of the security during the period beginning immediately after dissemination of information correcting the misstatement or omission and ending on the date on which the plaintiff sells or repurchases the security.

(3) *Definition.*—For purposes of this subsection, the "mean trading price" of a security shall be an average of the daily trading price of that security, determined as of the close of the market each day during the 90–day period referred to in paragraph (1).

(f) Proportionate liability

(1) *Applicability.*—Nothing in this subsection shall be construed to create, affect, or in any manner modify, the standard for liability associated with any action arising under the securities laws.

(2) *Liability for damages.*—

(A) Joint and several liability.—Any covered person against whom a final judgment is entered in a private action shall be liable for damages jointly and severally only if the trier of fact specifically determines that such covered person knowingly committed a violation of the securities laws.

(B) Proportionate liability.—

(i) In general.—Except as provided in subparagraph (A), a covered person against whom a final judgment is entered in a private action shall be liable solely for the portion of the judgment that corresponds to the percentage of responsibility of that covered person, as determined under paragraph (3).

(ii) Recovery by and costs of covered person.—In any case in which a contractual relationship permits, a covered person that prevails in any private action may recover the attorney's fees and costs of that covered person in connection with the action.

(3) *Determination of responsibility.*—

(A) *In general.*—In any private action, the court shall instruct the jury to answer special interrogatories, or if there is no jury, shall make findings, with respect to each covered person and each of the other persons claimed by any of the parties to have caused or contributed to the loss incurred by the plaintiff, including persons who have entered into settlements with the plaintiff or plaintiffs, concerning—

(i) whether such person violated the securities laws;

(ii) the percentage of responsibility of such person, measured as a percentage of the total fault of all persons who caused or contributed to the loss incurred by the plaintiff; and

(iii) whether such person knowingly committed a violation of the securities laws.

(B) *Contents of special interrogatories or findings.*—The responses to interrogatories, or findings, as appropriate, under subparagraph (A) shall specify the total amount of damages that the plaintiff is entitled to recover and the percentage of responsibility of each covered person found to have caused or contributed to the loss incurred by the plaintiff or plaintiffs.

(C) *Factors for consideration.*—In determining the percentage of responsibility under this paragraph, the trier of fact shall consider—

(i) the nature of the conduct of each covered person found to have caused or contributed to the loss incurred by the plaintiff or plaintiffs; and

(ii) the nature and extent of the causal relationship between the conduct of each such person and the damages incurred by the plaintiff or plaintiffs.

(4) *Uncollectible share.*—

(A) *In general.*—Notwithstanding paragraph (2)(B), [if] upon motion made not later than 6 months after a final judgment is entered in any private action, the court determines that all or part of the share of the judgment of the covered person is not collectible against that covered person, and is also not collectible against a covered person described in paragraph (2)(A), each covered person described in paragraph (2)(B) shall be liable for the uncollectible share as follows:

(i) Percentage of net worth.—Each covered person shall be jointly and severally liable for the uncollectible share if the plaintiff establishes that—

(I) the plaintiff is an individual whose recoverable damages under the final judgment are equal to more than 10 percent of the net worth of the plaintiff; and

(II) the net worth of the plaintiff is equal to less than $200,000.

(ii) Other plaintiffs.—With respect to any plaintiff not described in subclauses (I) and (II) of clause (i), each covered person shall be liable for the uncollectible share in proportion to the percentage of responsibility of that covered person, except that the total liability of a covered person under this clause may not exceed 50 percent of the proportionate share of that covered person, as determined under paragraph (3)(B).

(iii) Net worth.—For purposes of this subparagraph, net worth shall be determined as of the date immediately preceding the date of the purchase or sale (as applicable) by the plaintiff of the security that is the subject of the action, and shall be equal to the fair market value of assets, minus liabilities, including the net value of the investments of the plaintiff in real and personal property (including personal residences).

(B) *Overall limit.*—In no case shall the total payments required pursuant to subparagraph (A) exceed the amount of the uncollectible share.

(C) *Covered persons subject to contribution.*—A covered person against whom judgment is not collectible shall be subject to contribution and to any continuing liability to the plaintiff on the judgment.

(5) *Right of contribution.*—To the extent that a covered person is required to make an additional payment pursuant to paragraph (4), that covered person may recover contribution—

(A) from the covered person originally liable to make the payment;

(B) from any covered person liable jointly and severally pursuant to paragraph (2)(A);

(C) from any covered person held proportionately liable pursuant to this paragraph who is liable to make the same payment and has paid less than his or her proportionate share of that payment; or

(D) from any other person responsible for the conduct giving rise to the payment that would have been liable to make the same payment.

(6) *Nondisclosure to jury.*—The standard for allocation of damages under paragraphs (2) and (3) and the procedure for reallocation of uncollectible shares under paragraph (4) shall not be disclosed to members of the jury.

(7) *Settlement discharge.*—

(A) *In general.*—A covered person who settles any private action at any time before final verdict or judgment shall be discharged from all claims for contribution brought by other persons. Upon entry of the settlement by the court, the court shall enter a bar order constituting the final discharge of all obligations to the plaintiff of the settling covered person arising out of the action. The order shall bar all future claims for contribution arising out of the action—

(i) by any person against the settling covered person; and

(ii) by the settling covered person against any person, other than a person whose liability has been extinguished by the settlement of the settling covered person.

(B) *Reduction.*—If a covered person enters into a settlement with the plaintiff prior to final verdict or judgment, the verdict or judgment shall be reduced by the greater of—

(i) an amount that corresponds to the percentage of responsibility of that covered person; or

(ii) the amount paid to the plaintiff by that covered person.

(8) *Contribution.*—A covered person who becomes jointly and severally liable for damages in any private action may recover contribution from any other person who, if joined in the original

action, would have been liable for the same damages. A claim for contribution shall be determined based on the percentage of responsibility of the claimant and of each person against whom a claim for contribution is made.

(9) *Statute of limitations for contribution.*—In any private action determining liability, an action for contribution shall be brought not later than 6 months after the entry of a final, nonappealable judgment in the action, except that an action for contribution brought by a covered person who was required to make an additional payment pursuant to paragraph (4) may be brought not later than 6 months after the date on which such payment was made.

(10) *Definitions.*—For purposes of this subsection—

(A) a covered person "knowingly commits a violation of the securities laws"—

(i) with respect to an action that is based on an untrue statement of material fact or omission of a material fact necessary to make the statement not misleading, if—

(I) that covered person makes an untrue statement of a material fact, with actual knowledge that the representation is false, or omits to state a fact necessary in order to make the statement made not misleading, with actual knowledge that, as a result of the omission, one of the material representations of the covered person is false; and

(II) persons are likely to reasonably rely on that misrepresentation or omission; and

(ii) with respect to an action that is based on any conduct that is not described in clause (i), if that covered person engages in that conduct with actual knowledge of the facts and circumstances that make the conduct of that covered person a violation of the securities laws;

(B) reckless conduct by a covered person shall not be construed to constitute a knowing commission of a violation of the securities laws by that covered person;

(C) the term "covered person" means—

(i) a defendant in any private action arising under this title; or

(ii) a defendant in any private action arising under section 11 of the Securities Act of 1933, who is an outside director of the issuer of the securities that are the subject of the action; and

(D) the term "outside director" shall have the meaning given such term by rule or regulation of the Commission.

§ 21E. Application of Safe Harbor for Forward–Looking Statements

(a) Applicability

This section shall apply only to a forward-looking statement made by—

(1) an issuer that, at the time that the statement is made, is subject to the reporting requirements of section 13(a) or section 15(d);

(2) a person acting on behalf of such issuer;

(3) an outside reviewer retained by such issuer making a statement on behalf of such issuer; or

(4) an underwriter, with respect to information provided by such issuer or information derived from information provided by such issuer.

(b) Exclusions

Except to the extent otherwise specifically provided by rule, regulation, or order of the Commission, this section shall not apply to a forward-looking statement—

(1) that is made with respect to the business or operations of the issuer, if the issuer—

(A) during the 3–year period preceding the date on which the statement was first made—

(i) was convicted of any felony or misdemeanor described in clauses (i) through (iv) of section 15(b)(4)(B); or

(ii) has been made the subject of a judicial or administrative decree or order arising out of a governmental action that—

(I) prohibits future violations of the antifraud provisions of the securities laws;

(II) requires that the issuer cease and desist from violating the antifraud provisions of the securities laws; or

(III) determines that the issuer violated the antifraud provisions of the securities laws;

(B) makes the forward-looking statement in connection with an offering of securities by a blank check company;

(C) issues penny stock;

(D) makes the forward-looking statement in connection with a rollup transaction; or

(E) makes the forward-looking statement in connection with a going private transaction; or

(2) that is—

(A) included in a financial statement prepared in accordance with generally accepted accounting principles;

(B) contained in a registration statement of, or otherwise issued by, an investment company;

(C) made in connection with a tender offer;

(D) made in connection with an initial public offering;

(E) made in connection with an offering by, or relating to the operations of, a partnership, limited liability company, or a direct participation investment program; or

(F) made in a disclosure of beneficial ownership in a report required to be filed with the Commission pursuant to section 13(d).

(c) Safe harbor

(1) *In general.*—Except as provided in subsection (b), in any private action arising under this title that is based on an untrue statement of a material fact or omission of a material fact necessary to make the statement not misleading, a person referred to in subsection (a) shall not be liable with respect to any forward-looking statement, whether written or oral, if and to the extent that—

(A) the forward-looking statement is—

(i) identified as a forward-looking statement, and is accompanied by meaningful cautionary statements identifying important factors that could cause actual results to differ materially from those in the forward-looking statement; or

(ii) immaterial; or

(B) the plaintiff fails to prove that the forward-looking statement—

(i) if made by a natural person, was made with actual knowledge by that person that the statement was false or misleading; or

(ii) if made by a business entity; was—

(I) made by or with the approval of an executive officer of that entity; and

(II) made or approved by such officer with actual knowledge by that officer that the statement was false or misleading.

(2) *Oral forward-looking statements.*—In the case of an oral forward-looking statement made by an issuer that is subject to the reporting requirements of section 13(a) or section 15(d), or by a person acting on behalf of such issuer, the requirement set forth in paragraph (1)(A) shall be deemed to be satisfied—

(A) if the oral forward-looking statement is accompanied by a cautionary statement—

(i) that the particular oral statement is a forward-looking statement; and

(ii) that the actual results might differ materially from those projected in the forward-looking statement; and

(B) if—

(i) the oral forward-looking statement is accompanied by an oral statement that additional information concerning factors that could cause actual results to materially differ from those in the forward-looking statement is contained in a readily available written document, or portion thereof;

(ii) the accompanying oral statement referred to in clause (i) identifies the document, or portion thereof, that contains the additional information about those factors relating to the forward-looking statement; and

(iii) the information contained in that written document is a cautionary statement that satisfies the standard established in paragraph (1)(A).

(3) *Availability.*—Any document filed with the Commission or generally disseminated shall be deemed to be readily available for purposes of paragraph (2).

(4) *Effect on other safe harbors.*—The exemption provided for in paragraph (1) shall be in addition to any exemption that the Commission may establish by rule or regulation under subsection (g).

(d) Duty to update

Nothing in this section shall impose upon any person a duty to update a forward-looking statement.

(e) Dispositive motion

On any motion to dismiss based upon subsection (c)(1), the court shall consider any statement cited in the complaint and any cautionary statement accompanying the forward-looking statement, which are not subject to material dispute, cited by the defendant.

(f) Stay pending decision on motion

In any private action arising under this title, the court shall stay discovery (other than discovery that is specifically directed to the applicability of the exemption provided for in this section) during the pendency of any motion by a defendant for summary judgment that is based on the grounds that—

> (1) the statement or omission upon which the complaint is based is a forward-looking statement within the meaning of this section; and

> (2) the exemption provided for in this section precludes a claim for relief.

(g) Exemption authority

In addition to the exemptions provided for in this section, the Commission may, by rule or regulation, provide exemptions from or under any provision of this title, including with respect to liability that is based on a statement or that is based on projections or other forward-looking information, if and to the extent that any such exemption is consistent with the public interest and the protection of investors, as determined by the Commission.

(h) Effect on other authority of commission

Nothing in this section limits, either expressly or by implication, the authority of the Commission to exercise similar authority or to adopt similar rules and regulations with respect to forward-looking statements under any other statute under which the Commission exercises rulemaking authority.

(i) Definitions

For purposes of this section, the following definitions shall apply:

> (1) *Forward-looking statement.*—The term "forward-looking statement" means—

>> (A) a statement containing a projection of revenues, income (including income loss), earnings (including earnings loss) per share, capital expenditures, dividends, capital structure, or other financial items;

>> (B) a statement of the plans and objectives of management for future operations, including plans or objectives relating to the products or services of the issuer;

>> (C) a statement of future economic performance, including any such statement contained in a discussion and analysis of

financial condition by the management or in the results of operations included pursuant to the rules and regulations of the Commission;

(D) any statement of the assumptions underlying or relating to any statement described in subparagraph (A), (B), or (C);

(E) any report issued by an outside reviewer retained by an issuer, to the extent that the report assesses a forward-looking statement made by the issuer; or

(F) a statement containing a projection or estimate of such other items as may be specified by rule or regulation of the Commission.

(2) *Investment Company.*—The term "investment company" has the same meaning as in section 3(a) of the Investment Company Act of 1940.

(3) *Going Private Transaction.*—The term "going private transaction" has the meaning given that term under the rules or regulations of the Commission issued pursuant to section 13(e).

(4) *Person acting on behalf of an issuer.*—The term "person acting on behalf of an issuer" means any officer, director, or employee of such issuer.

(5) *Other terms.*—The terms "blank check company", "rollup transaction", "partnership", "limited liability company", "executive officer of an entity" and "direct participation investment program", have the meanings given those terms by rule or regulation of the Commission.

§ 27. Jurisdiction of Offenses and Suits

The district courts of the United States, and the United States courts of any Territory or other place subject to the jurisdiction of the United States shall have exclusive jurisdiction of violations of this chapter or the rules and regulations thereunder, and of all suits in equity and actions at law brought to enforce any liability or duty created by this chapter or the rules and regulations thereunder. Any criminal proceeding may be brought in the district wherein any act or transaction constituting the violation occurred. Any suit or action to enforce any liability or duty created by this chapter or rules and regulations thereunder, or to enjoin any violation of such chapter or rules and regulations, may be brought in any such district or in the district wherein the defendant is found or is an inhabitant or transacts business, and process in such cases may be served in any other district of which the defendant is an inhabitant or wherever the defendant may be found. . . .

§ 27A. Special Provision Relating to Statute of Limitations on Private Causes of Action

(a) Effect on pending causes of action

The limitation period for any private civil action implied under section 10(b) of this Act that was commenced on or before June 19, 1991, shall be the limitation period provided by the laws applicable in the jurisdiction, including principles of retroactivity, as such laws existed on June 19, 1991.

(b) Effect on dismissed causes of action

Any private civil action implied under section 10(b) of this Act that was commenced on or before June 19, 1991—

(1) which was dismissed as time barred subsequent to June 19, 1991, and

(2) which would have been timely filed under the limitation period provided by the laws applicable in the jurisdiction, including principles of retroactivity, as such laws existed on June 19, 1991,

shall be reinstated on motion by the plaintiff not later than 60 days after the date of enactment of this section.

§ 28. Effect on Existing Law

(a) Addition of rights and remedies; recovery of actual damages; State Securities Commissions

Except as provided in subsection (f), the rights and remedies provided by this chapter shall be in addition to any and all other rights and remedies that may exist at law or in equity; but no person permitted to maintain a suit for damages under the provisions of this chapter shall recover, through satisfaction of judgment in one or more actions, a total amount in excess of his actual damages on account of the act complained of. Except as otherwise specifically provided in this chapter, nothing in this chapter shall affect the jurisdiction of the securities commission (or any agency or officer performing like functions) of any State over any security or any person insofar as it does not conflict with the provisions of this chapter or the rules and regulations thereunder. No State law which prohibits or regulates the making or promoting of wagering or gaming contracts, or the operation of "bucket shops" or other similar or related activities, shall invalidate any put, call, straddle, option, privilege, or other security subject to this chapter, or apply to any activity which is incidental or related to the offer, purchase, sale, exercise, settlement, or closeout of any such security. . . .

(f) Limitations on remedies—

(1) *Class action limitations.*—No covered class action based upon the statutory or common law of any State or subdivision thereof may be maintained in any State or Federal court by any private party alleging—

(A) a misrepresentation or omission of a material fact in connection with the purchase or sale of a covered security; or

(B) that the defendant used or employed any manipulative or deceptive device or contrivance in connection with the purchase or sale of a covered security.

(2) *Removal of covered class actions.*—Any covered class action brought in any State court involving a covered security, as set forth in paragraph (1), shall be removable to the Federal district court for the district in which the action is pending, and shall be subject to paragraph (1).

(3) *Preservation of certain actions.*—

(A) *Actions under the state law of state of incorporation.*—

(i) *Actions preserved.*—Notwithstanding paragraph (1) or (2), a covered class action described in clause (ii) of this subparagraph that is based upon the statutory or common law of the State in which the issuer is incorporated (in the case of a corporation) or organized (in the case of any other entity) may be maintained in a State or Federal court by a private party.

(ii) *Permissible actions.*—A covered class action is described in this clause if it involves—

(I) the purchase or sale of securities by the issuer or an affiliate of the issuer exclusively from or to holders of equity securities of the issuer; or

(II) any recommendation, position, or other communication with respect to the sale of securities of an issuer that—

(aa) is made by or on behalf of the issuer or an affiliate of the issuer to holders of equity securities of the issuer; and

(bb) concerns decisions of such equity holders with respect to voting their securities, acting in response to a tender or exchange offer, or exercising dissenters' or appraisal rights.

(B) *State actions.*—

(i) *In general.*—Notwithstanding any other provision of this subsection, nothing in this subsection may be construed to preclude a State or political subdivision thereof or a State pension plan from bringing an action involving a covered security on its own behalf, or as a member of a class comprised solely of other States, political subdivisions, or State pension plans that are named plaintiffs, and that have authorized participation, in such action.

(ii) *State pension plan defined.*—For purposes of this subparagraph, the term "State pension plan" means a pension plan established and maintained for its employees by the government of a State or political subdivision thereof, or by any agency or instrumentality thereof.

(C) *Actions under contractual agreements between issuers and indenture trustees.*—Notwithstanding paragraph (1) or (2), a covered class action that seeks to enforce a contractual agreement between an issuer and an indenture trustee may be maintained in a State or Federal court by a party to the agreement or a successor to such party.

(D) *Remand of removed actions.*—In an action that has been removed from a State court pursuant to paragraph (2), if the Federal court determines that the action may be maintained in State court pursuant to this subsection, the Federal court shall remand such action to such State court.

(4) *Preservation of state jurisdiction.*—The securities commission (or any agency or office performing like functions) of any State shall retain jurisdiction under the laws of such State to investigate and bring enforcement actions.

(5) *Definitions.*—For purposes of this subsection, the following definitions shall apply:

(A) *Affiliate of the issuer.*—The term "affiliate of the issuer" means a person that directly or indirectly, through one or more intermediaries, controls or is controlled by or is under common control with, the issuer.

(B) *Covered class action.*—The term "covered class action" means—

(i) any single lawsuit in which—

(I) damages are sought on behalf of more than 50 persons or prospective class members, and questions of law or fact common to those persons or members of the prospective class, without reference to issues of individualized reliance on an alleged misstatement or omission, predominate over any questions affecting only individual persons or members; or

(II) one or more named parties seek to recover damages on a representative basis on behalf of themselves and other unnamed parties similarly situated, and questions of law or fact common to those persons or members of the prospective class predominate over any questions affecting only individual persons or members; or

(ii) any group of lawsuits filed in or pending in the same court and involving common questions of law or fact, in which—

(I) damages are sought on behalf of more than 50 persons; and

(II) the lawsuits are joined, consolidated, or otherwise proceed as a single action for any purpose.

(C) *Exception for derivative actions.*—Notwithstanding subparagraph (B), the term "covered class action" does not include an exclusively derivative action brought by one or more shareholders on behalf of a corporation.

(D) *Counting of certain class members.*—For purposes of this paragraph, a corporation, investment company, pension plan, partnership, or other entity, shall be treated as one person or prospective class member, but only if the entity is not established for the purpose of participating in the action.

(E) *Covered security.*—The term "covered security" means a security that satisfies the standards for a covered security specified in paragraph (1) or (2) of section 18(b) of the Securities Act of 1933, at the time during which it is alleged that the misrepresentation omission, or manipulative or deceptive conduct occurred, except that such term shall not include any debt security that is exempt from registration under the Securities Act of 1933 pursuant to rules issued by the Commission under section 4(2) of that Act.

(F) *Rule of construction.*—Nothing in this paragraph shall be construed to affect the discretion of a State court in determining whether actions filed in such court should be joined, consolidated, or otherwise allowed to proceed as a single action.

§ 29. Validity of Contracts

(a) Waiver provisions

Any condition, stipulation, or provision binding any person to waive compliance with any provision of this chapter or of any rule or regulation thereunder, or of any rule of an exchange required thereby shall be void.

(b) Contract provisions in violation of chapter

Every contract made in violation of any provision of this chapter or of any rule or regulation thereunder, and every contract (including any contract for listing a security on an exchange) heretofore or hereafter made, the performance of which involves the violation of, or the continuance of any relationship or practice in violation of, any provision of this chapter or any rule or regulation thereunder, shall be void (1) as regards the rights of any person who, in violation of any such provision, rule, or regulation, shall have made or engaged in the performance of any such contract, and (2) as regards the rights of any person who, not being a party to such contract, shall have acquired any right thereunder with actual knowledge of the facts by reason of which the making or performance of such contract was in violation of any such provision, rule, or regulation. . . .

§ 30A. Prohibited Foreign Trade Practices by Issuers

(a) Prohibition

It shall be unlawful for any issuer which has a class of securities registered pursuant to section 12 of this title or which is required to file reports under section 15(d) of this title, or for any officer, director, employee, or agent of such issuer or any stockholder thereof acting on behalf of such issuer, to make use of the mails or any means or instrumentality of interstate commerce corruptly in furtherance of an offer, payment, promise to pay, or authorization of the payment of any money, or offer, gift, promise to give, or authorization of the giving of anything of value to—

   (1) any foreign official for purposes of—

      (A)(i) influencing any act or decision of such foreign official in his official capacity, (ii) inducing such foreign official to do or omit to do any act in violation of the lawful duty of such official, or (iii) securing any improper advantage; or

      (B) inducing such foreign official to use his influence with a foreign government or instrumentality thereof to affect or influence any act or decision of such government or instrumentality,

in order to assist such issuer in obtaining or retaining business for or with, or directing business to, any person;

   (2) any foreign political party or official thereof or any candidate for foreign political office for purposes of—

      (A)(i) influencing any act or decision of such party, official, or candidate in its or his official capacity, (ii) inducing such party, official, or candidate to do or omit to do an act in violation of the lawful duty of such party, official, or candidate, or (iii) securing any improper advantage; or

      (B) inducing such party, official, or candidate to use its or his influence with a foreign government or instrumentality thereof to affect or influence any act or decision of such government or instrumentality

in order to assist such issuer in obtaining or retaining business for or with, or directing business to, any person; or

   (3) any person, while knowing that all or a portion of such money or thing of value will be offered, given, or promised, directly

or indirectly, to any foreign official, to any foreign political party or official thereof, or to any candidate for foreign political office, for purposes of—

(A)(i) influencing any act or decision of such foreign official, political party, party official, or candidate in his or its official capacity, (ii) inducing such foreign official, political party, party official, or candidate to do or omit to do any act in violation of the lawful duty of such foreign official, political party, party official, or candidate, or (iii) securing any improper advantage; or

(B) inducing such foreign official, political party, party official, or candidate to use his or its influence with a foreign government or instrumentality thereof to affect or influence any act or decision of such government or instrumentality

in order to assist such issuer in obtaining or retaining business for or with, or directing business to, any person.

(b) Exception for routine governmental action

Subsections (a) and (g) of this section shall not apply to any facilitating or expediting payment to a foreign official, political party, or party official the purpose of which is to expedite or to secure the performance of a routine governmental action by a foreign official, political party, or party official.

(c) Affirmative defenses

It shall be an affirmative defense to actions under subsections (a) and (g) of this section that—

(1) the payment, gift, offer, or promise of anything of value that was made, was lawful under the written laws and regulations of the foreign official's, political party's, party official's, or candidate's country; or

(2) the payment, gift, offer, or promise of anything of value that was made, was a reasonable and bona fide expenditure, such as travel and lodging expenses, incurred by or on behalf of a foreign official, party, party official, or candidate and was directly related to—

(A) the promotion, demonstration, or explanation of products or services; or

(B) the execution or performance of a contract with a foreign government or agency thereof. . . .

(f) Definitions

For purposes of this section:

(1)(A) The term "foreign official" means any officer or employee of a foreign government or any department, agency, or instrumentality thereof, or of a public international organization, or any person acting in an official capacity for or on behalf of any such government or department, agency, or instrumentality, or for or on behalf of any such public international organization.

(B) For purposes of subparagraph (A), the term "public international organization" means—

(i) an organization that is designated by Executive order pursuant to section 1 of the International Organizations Immunities Act; or

(ii) any other international organization that is designated by the President by Executive order for the purposes of this section, effective as of the date of publication of such order in the Federal Register.

(2)(A) A person's state of mind is "knowing" with respect to conduct, a circumstance, or a result if—

(i) such person is aware that such person is engaging in such conduct, that such circumstance exists, or that such result is substantially certain to occur; or

(ii) such person has a firm belief that such circumstance exists or that such result is substantially certain to occur.

(B) When knowledge of the existence of a particular circumstance is required for an offense, such knowledge is established if a person is aware of a high probability of the existence of such circumstance, unless the person actually believes that such circumstance does not exist.

(3)(A) The term "routine governmental action" means only an action which is ordinarily and commonly performed by a foreign official in—

(i) obtaining permits, licenses, or other official documents to qualify a person to do business in a foreign country;

(ii) processing governmental papers, such as visas and work orders;

(iii) providing police protection, mail pick-up and delivery, or scheduling inspections associated with contract performance or inspections related to transit of goods across country;

(iv) providing phone service, power and water supply, loading and unloading cargo, or protecting perishable products or commodities from deterioration; or

(v) actions of a similar nature.

(B) The term "routine governmental action" does not include any decision by a foreign official whether, or on what terms, to award new business to or to continue business with a particular party, or any action taken by a foreign official involved in the decision-making process to encourage a decision to award new business to or continue business with a particular party.

(g) Alternative jurisdiction—

(1) It shall also be unlawful for any issuer organized under the laws of the United States, or a State, territory, possession, or commonwealth of the United States or a political subdivision thereof and which has a class of securities registered pursuant to section 12 of this title or which is required to file reports under section 15(d) of this title, or for any United States person that is an officer, director, employee, or agent of such issuer or a stockholder thereof acting on behalf of such issuer, to corruptly do any act outside the United States in furtherance of an offer, payment, promise to pay, or authorization of the payment of any money, or offer, gift, promise to give, or authorization of the giving of anything of value to any of the persons or entities set forth in paragraphs (1), (2), and (3) of subsection (a) of this section for the purposes set forth therein, irrespective of whether such issuer or such officer, director, employee, agent, or stockholder makes use of the mails or any means or instrumentality of interstate commerce in furtherance of such offer, gift, payment, promise, or authorization.

(2) As used in this subsection, the term "United States person" means a national of the United States (as defined in section 101 of the Immigration and Nationality Act), or any corporation, partnership, association, joint-stock company, business trust, unincorporated organization, or sole proprietorship organized under the laws of the United States or any State, territory, possession, or commonwealth of the United States, or any political subdivision thereof.

§ 32. Penalties

(a) Willful violations; false and misleading statements

Any person who willfully violates any provision of this chapter (other than section 30A of this title), or any rule or regulation thereunder the violation of which is made unlawful or the observance of which is required under the terms of this chapter, or any person who willfully and knowingly makes, or causes to be made, any statement in any application, report, or document required to be filed under this chapter or any rule or regulation thereunder or any undertaking contained in a registration statement as provided in subsection (d) of section 15 of this title, or by any self-regulatory organization in connection with an application for membership or participation therein or to become associated with a member thereof, which statement was false or misleading with respect to any material fact, shall upon conviction be fined not more than $5,000,000, or imprisoned not more than 20 years, or both, except that when such person is a person other than a natural person, a fine not exceeding $25,000,000 may be imposed; but no person shall be subject to imprisonment under this section for the violation of any rule or regulation if he proves that he had no knowledge of such rule or regulation.

(b)   Failure to file information, documents, or reports

Any issuer which fails to file information, documents, or reports required to be filed under subsection (d) of section 15 of this title or any rule or regulation thereunder shall forfeit to the United States the sum of [$110]* for each and every day such failure to file shall continue. Such forfeiture, which shall be in lieu of any criminal penalty for such failure to file which might be deemed to arise under subsection (a) of this section, shall be payable into the Treasury of the United States and shall be recoverable in a civil suit in the name of the United States.

(c)   Violations by issuers, officers, directors, stockholders, employees, or agents of issuers

(1)(A) Any issuer that violates subsection (a) or (g) of section 30A of this title shall be fined no more than $2,000,000.

(B) Any issuer that violates subsection (a) or (g) of section 30A of this title shall be subject to a civil penalty of not more than [$11,000] imposed in an action brought by the Commission.

(2)(A) Any officer, director, employee, or agent of an issuer, or stockholder acting on behalf of such issuer, who willfully violates subsection (a) or (g) of section 30A of this title shall be fined not more than $100,000, or imprisoned not more than 5 years, or both.

(B) Any officer, director, employee, or agent of an issuer, or stockholder acting on behalf of such issuer, who violates subsection (a) or (g) of section 30A of this title shall be subject to a civil penalty of not more than $10,000 imposed in an action brought by the Commission.

(3) Whenever a fine is imposed under paragraph (2) upon any officer, director, employee, agent, or stockholder of an issuer, such fine may not be paid, directly or indirectly, by such issuer.

§ 36.   General Exemptive Authority

(a) Authority

(1) *In general*

Except as provided in subsection (b) of this section, but notwithstanding any other provision of this chapter, the Commission, by

---

* The bracketed figures in this section have been adjusted for inflation by the SEC under the Debt Collection Act of 1996, which requires the Commission to make inflationary adjustments to civil penalties in the Securities Act, the Exchange Act, and other Acts that the Commission administers. (Footnote by ed.)

rule, regulation, or order, may conditionally or unconditionally exempt any person, security, or transaction, or any class or classes of persons, securities, or transactions, from any provision or provisions of this chapter or of any rule or regulation thereunder, to the extent that such exemption is necessary or appropriate in the public interest, and is consistent with the protection of investors.

(2) *Procedures*

The Commission shall, by rule or regulation, determine the procedures under which an exemptive order under this section shall be granted and may, in its sole discretion, decline to entertain any application for an order of exemption under this section.

(b) Limitation

The Commission may not, under this section, exempt any person, security, or transaction, or any class or classes of persons, securities, or transactions from section 15C [Government Securities Brokers and Dealers] or the rules or regulations issued thereunder....

RULES AND FORMS UNDER THE SECURITIES EXCHANGE ACT OF 1934 (SELECTED PROVISIONS)

17 C.F.R. §§ 240.0–1 et seq.

DEFINITIONS

MANIPULATIVE AND DECEPTIVE DEVICES AND CONTRIVANCES

REPORTS UNDER SECTION 10A

REGULATION 12B: REGISTRATION AND REPORTING

EXTENSIONS AND TEMPORARY EXEMPTIONS; DEFINITIONS

REGULATION 13A: REPORTS OF ISSUERS OF SECURITIES REGISTERED PURSUANT TO SECTION 12

REGULATION 15D: REPORTS OF REGISTRANTS UNDER THE SECURITIES ACT OF 1933

REPORTS OF DIRECTORS, OFFICERS, AND PRINCIPAL SHAREHOLDERS

EXEMPTION OF CERTAIN TRANSACTIONS FROM SECTION 16(b)

DEFINITIONS ...

Rule 3a11–1. Definition of the Term "Equity Security"

The term "equity security" is hereby defined to include any stock or similar security, certificate of interest or participation in any profit sharing agreement, preorganization certificate or subscription, transferable share, voting trust certificate or certificate of deposit for an equity security, limited partnership interest, interest in a joint venture, or certificate of interest in a business trust; any security future on any such security; or any security convertible, with or without consideration into such a security, or carrying any warrant or right to subscribe to or purchase such a security; or any such warrant or right; or any put, call, straddle, or other option or privilege of buying such a security from or selling such a security to another without being bound to do so.

Rule 3b–2. Definition of "Officer"

The term "officer" means a president, vice president, secretary, treasurer or principal financial officer, comptroller or principal accounting officer, and any person routinely performing corresponding functions with respect to any organization whether incorporated or unincorporated.

Rule 3b–6. Liability for Certain Statements by Issuers

(a) A statement within the coverage of paragraph (b) of this section which is made by or on behalf of an issuer or by an outside reviewer retained by the issuer shall be deemed not to be a fraudulent statement . (as defined in paragraph (d) of this section), unless it is shown that such statement was made or reaffirmed without a reasonable basis or was disclosed other than in good faith.

(b) This rule applies to the following statements:

(1) A forward-looking statement (as defined in paragraph (c) of this section) made in a document filed with the Commission, in Part I of a quarterly report on Form 10–Q ... or in an annual report to shareholders meeting the requirements of Rules 14a–3(b) and (c) or 14c–3(a) and (b) under the Securities Exchange Act of 1934, a statement reaffirming such forward-looking statement subsequent to the date the document was filed or the annual report was made publicly available, or a forward-looking statement made prior to the date the document was filed or the date the annual report was made publicly available if such statement is reaffirmed in a filed document, in Part I of a quarterly report on Form 10–Q ... or in an annual report made publicly available within a reasonable time after the making of such forward-looking statement; *Provided,* That:

(i) At the time such statements are made or reaffirmed, either the issuer is subject to the reporting requirements of section 13(a) or 15(d) of the Securities Exchange Act of 1934 and has complied with the requirements of Rule 13a–1 or 15d–1 thereunder, if applicable, to file its most recent annual report on Form 10–K ..., or if the issuer is not subject to the reporting requirements of section 13(a) or 15(d) of the Securities Exchange Act of 1934, the statements are made in a registration statement filed under the Securities Act of 1933 offering statement or solicitation of interest[,] written document or broadcast script under Regulation A or pursuant to section 12(b) or (g) of the Securities Exchange Act of 1934, and . . .

(2) Information which is disclosed in a document filed with the Commission in Part I of a quarterly report on Form 10–Q. . . .

(c) For the purpose of this rule, the term *forward-looking statement* shall mean and shall be limited to:

(1) A statement containing a projection of revenues, income (loss), earnings (loss) per share, capital expenditures, dividends, capital structure or other financial items;

(2) A statement of management's plans and objectives for future operations;

(3) A statement of future economic performance contained in management's discussion and analysis of financial condition and results of operations included pursuant to Item 303 of Regulation S–K . . .

(4) Disclosed statements of the assumptions underlying or relating to any of the statements described in paragraphs (c)(1), (2), or (3) of this section.

(d) For the purpose of this rule the term *fraudulent statement* shall mean a statement which is an untrue statement of a material fact, a statement false or misleading with respect to any material fact, an omission to state a material fact necessary to make a statement not misleading, or which constitutes the employment of a manipulative, deceptive, or fraudulent device, contrivance, scheme, transaction, act, practice, course of business, or an artifice to defraud, as those terms are used in the Securities Exchange Act of 1934 or the rules or regulations promulgated thereunder.

Rule 3b–7.   Definition of "Executive Officer"

The term "executive officer," when used with reference to a registrant, means its president, any vice president of the registrant in charge of a principal business unit, division or function (such as sales, administration, or finance), any other officer who performs a policy making function or any other person who performs similar policy making functions for the registrant.   Executive officers of subsidiaries may be deemed executive officers of the registrant if they perform such policy making functions for the registrant.

Rule 3b–11.   Definitions Relating to Limited Partnership Roll-Up Transactions for Purposes of Sections 6(b)(9), 14(h) and 15A(b)(12)–(13)

For purposes of Sections 6(b)(9), 14(h) and 15A(b)(12)–(13) of the Act . . .;

(a) The term *limited partnership roll-up transaction* does not include a transaction involving only entities that are not "finite-life" as defined in Item 901(b)(2) of Regulation S–K. . . .

(c) The term "regularly traded" shall be defined as in Item 901(c)(2)(v)(C) of Regulation S–K.

MANIPULATIVE AND DECEPTIVE DEVICES AND CONTRIVANCES. . . .

Rule 10b–5.   Employment of Manipulative and Deceptive Devices

It shall be unlawful for any person, directly or indirectly, by the use of any means or instrumentality of interstate commerce, or of the mails or of any facility of any national securities exchange,

(a) To employ any device, scheme, or artifice to defraud,

(b) To make any untrue statement of a material fact or to omit to state a material fact necessary in order to make the statements made, in the light of the circumstances under which they were made, not misleading, or

(c) To engage in any act, practice, or course of business which operates or would operate as a fraud or deceit upon any person,

in connection with the purchase or sale of any security.

Rule 10b5–1.   Trading on the Basis of Material Nonpublic Information in Insider Trading Cases

Preliminary Note to Rule 10b5–1: This provision defines when a purchase or sale constitutes trading "on the basis of" material nonpublic information in insider trading cases brought under Section 10(b) of the Act and Rule 10b–5 thereunder. The law of insider trading is otherwise defined by judicial opinions construing Rule 10b–5, and Rule 10b5–1 does not modify the scope of insider trading law in any other respect.

(a) *General*. The "manipulative and deceptive devices" prohibited by Section 10(b) of the Act and Rule 10b–5 thereunder include, among other things, the purchase or sale of a security of any issuer, on the basis of material nonpublic information about that security or issuer, in breach of a duty of trust or confidence that is owed directly, indirectly, or derivatively, to the issuer of that security or the shareholders of that issuer, or to any other person who is the source of the material nonpublic information.

(b) *Definition of "on the basis of."* Subject to the affirmative defenses in paragraph (c) of this section, a purchase or sale of a security of an issuer is "on the basis of" material nonpublic information about that security or issuer if the person making the purchase or sale was aware of the material nonpublic information when the person made the purchase or sale.

(c) *Affirmative defenses.*

(1)(i) Subject to paragraph (c)(1)(ii) of this section, a person's purchase or sale is not "on the basis of" material nonpublic information if the person making the purchase or sale demonstrates that:

(A) Before becoming aware of the information, the person had:

(1) Entered into a binding contract to purchase or sell the security,

(2) Instructed another person to purchase or sell the security for the instructing person's account, or

(3) Adopted a written plan for trading securities;

(B) The contract, instruction, or plan described in paragraph (c)(1)(i)(A) of this Section:

(1) Specified the amount of securities to be purchased or sold and the price at which and the date on which the securities were to be purchased or sold;

(2) Included a written formula or algorithm, or computer program, for determining the amount of securities to be purchased or sold and the price at which and the date on which the securities were to be purchased or sold; or

(3) Did not permit the person to exercise any subsequent influence over how, when, or whether to effect purchases or sales; provided, in addition, that any other person who, pursuant to the contract, instruction, or plan, did exercise such influence must not have been aware of the material nonpublic information when doing so; and

(C) The purchase or sale that occurred was pursuant to the contract, instruction, or plan. A purchase or sale is not "pursuant to a contract, instruction, or plan" if, among other things, the person who entered into the contract, instruction, or plan altered or deviated from the contract, instruction, or plan to purchase or sell securities (whether by changing the amount, price, or timing of the purchase or sale), or entered into or altered a corresponding or hedging transaction or position with respect to those securities.

(ii) Paragraph (c)(1)(i) of this section is applicable only when the contract, instruction, or plan to purchase or sell securities was given or entered into in good faith and not as part of a plan or scheme to evade the prohibitions of this section.

(iii) This paragraph (c)(1)(iii) defines certain terms as used in paragraph (c) of this Section.

(A) *Amount.* "Amount" means either a specified number of shares or other securities or a specified dollar value of securities.

(B) *Price.* "Price" means the market price on a particular date or a limit price, or a particular dollar price.

(C) *Date.* "Date" means, in the case of a market order, the specific day of the year on which the order is to be executed (or as soon thereafter as is practicable under ordinary principles of best execution). "Date" means, in the case of a limit order, a day of the year on which the limit order is in force.

(2) A person other than a natural person also may demonstrate that a purchase or sale of securities is not "on the basis of" material nonpublic information if the person demonstrates that:

(i) The individual making the investment decision on behalf of the person to purchase or sell the securities was not aware of the information; and

(ii) The person had implemented reasonable policies and procedures, taking into consideration the nature of the person's business, to ensure that individuals making investment decisions would not violate the laws prohibiting trading on the basis of material nonpublic information. These policies and procedures may include those that restrict any purchase, sale, and causing any purchase or sale of any security as to which the person has material nonpublic information, or those that prevent such individuals from becoming aware of such information.

Rule 10b5–2. Duties of Trust or Confidence in Misappropriation Insider Trading Cases

Preliminary Note to Rule 10b5–2: This section provides a nonexclusive definition of circumstances in which a person has a duty of trust or confidence for purposes of the "misappropriation" theory of insider trading under Section 10(b) of the Act and Rule 10b–5. The law of insider trading is otherwise defined by judicial opinions construing Rule 10b–5, and Rule 10b5–2 does not modify the scope of insider trading law in any other respect.

(a) *Scope of Rule.* This section shall apply to any violation of Section 10(b) of the Act and Rule 10b–5 thereunder that is based on the purchase or sale of securities on the basis of, or the communication of, material nonpublic information misappropriated in breach of a duty of trust or confidence.

(b) *Enumerated "duties of trust or confidence."* For purposes of this section, a "duty of trust or confidence" exists in the following circumstances, among others:

(1) Whenever a person agrees to maintain information in confidence;

(2) Whenever the person communicating the material nonpublic information and the person to whom it is communicated have a history, pattern, or practice of sharing confidences, such that the recipient of the information knows or reasonably should know that the person communicating the material nonpublic information expects that the recipient will maintain its confidentiality; or

(3) Whenever a person receives or obtains material nonpublic information from his or her spouse, parent, child, or sibling; provided, however, that the person receiving or obtaining the information may demonstrate that no duty of trust or confidence existed with respect to the information, by establishing that he or she neither knew nor reasonably should have known that the person who was the source of the information expected that the person would keep the information confidential, because of the parties' history, pattern, or practice of sharing and maintaining confidences, and because there was no agreement or understanding to maintain the confidentiality of the information.

Rule 10b–18. Purchases of Certain Equity Securities by the Issuer and Others
Preliminary Notes to Rule 10b–18

1. Rule 10b–18 provides an issuer (and its affiliated purchasers) with a "safe harbor" from liability for manipulation under sections 9(a)(2) of the Act and Rule 10b–5 under the Act *solely* by reason of the manner, timing, price, and volume of their repurchases when they repurchase the issuer's common stock in the market in accordance with the section's manner, timing, price, and volume conditions. As a safe harbor, compliance with Rule 10b–18 is voluntary. To come within the safe harbor, however, an issuer's repurchases must satisfy (on a daily basis) each of the section's four conditions. Failure to meet any one of the four conditions will remove all of the issuer's repurchases from the safe harbor for that day. The safe harbor, moreover, is not available for repurchases that, although made in technical compliance with the section, are part of a plan or scheme to evade the federal securities laws....

(a) *Definitions.* Unless otherwise provided, all terms used in this section shall have the same meaning as in the Act. In addition, the following definitions shall apply:

(1) *ADTV* means the average daily trading volume reported for the security during the four calendar weeks preceding the week in which the Rule 10b–18 purchase is to be effected.

(2) *Affiliate* means any person that directly or indirectly controls, is controlled by, or is under common control with, the issuer.

(3) *Affiliated purchaser* means:

(i) A person acting, directly or indirectly, in concert with the issuer for the purpose of acquiring the issuer's securities; or

(ii) An affiliate who, directly or indirectly, controls the issuer's purchases of such securities, whose purchases are controlled by the issuer, or whose purchases are under common control with those of the issuer; *Provided, however*, that "affiliated purchaser" shall not include a broker, dealer, or other person solely by reason of such broker, dealer, or other person effecting Rule 10b–18 purchases on behalf of the issuer or for its account, and shall not include an officer or director of the issuer solely by reason of that officer or director's participation in the decision to authorize Rule 10b–18 purchases by or on behalf of the issuer....

(5) *Block* means a quantity of stock that either:

(i) Has a purchase price of $200,000 or more; or

(ii) Is at least 5,000 shares and has a purchase price of at least $50,000; or

(iii) Is at least 20 round lots of the security and totals 150 percent or more of the trading volume for that security or, in the event that trading volume data are unavailable, is at least 20 round lots of the security and totals at least one-tenth of one percent (.001) of the outstanding shares of the security, exclusive of any shares owned by any affiliate;

Provided, however, That a block under paragraph (a)(5)(i), (ii), and (iii) shall not include any amount a broker or dealer, acting as principal, has accumulated for the purpose of sale or resale to the issuer or to any affiliated purchaser of the issuer if the issuer or such affiliated purchaser knows or has reason to know that such amount was accumulated for such purpose, nor shall it include any amount that a broker or dealer has sold short to the issuer or to any affiliated purchaser of the issuer if the issuer or such affiliated purchaser knows or has reason to know that the sale was a short sale.

(6) *Consolidated system* means a consolidated transaction or quotation reporting system that collects and publicly disseminates on a current and continuous basis transaction or quotation information in common equity securities pursuant to an effective transaction reporting plan....

(7) *Market-wide trading suspension* means a market-wide trading halt of 30 minutes or more that is:

(i) Imposed pursuant to the rules of a national securities exchange or a national securities association in response to a market-wide decline during a single trading session; or

(ii) Declared by the Commission pursuant to its authority under section 12(k) of the Act....

(9) *Principal market* for a security means the single securities market with the largest reported trading volume for the security during

the six full calendar months preceding the week in which the Rule 10b–18 purchase is to be effected. . . .

(11) *Purchase price* means the price paid per share as reported, exclusive of any commission paid to a broker acting as agent, or commission equivalent, mark-up, or differential paid to a dealer.

(12) *Riskless principal transaction* means a transaction in which a broker or dealer after having received an order from an issuer to buy its security, buys the security as principal in the market at the same price to satisfy the issuer's buy order. The issuer's buy order must be effected at the same price per-share at which the broker or dealer bought the shares to satisfy the issuer's buy order, exclusive of any explicitly disclosed markup or markdown, commission equivalent, or other fee. In addition, only the first leg of the transaction, when the broker or dealer buys the security in the market as principal, is reported under the rules of a self-regulatory organization or under the Act. For purposes of this section, the broker or dealer must have written policies and procedures in place to assure that, at a minimum, the issuer's buy order was received prior to the offsetting transaction; the offsetting transaction is allocated to a riskless principal account or the issuer's account within 60 seconds of the execution; and the broker or dealer has supervisory systems in place to produce records that enable the broker or dealer to accurately and readily reconstruct, in a time-sequenced manner, all orders effected on a riskless principal basis.

(13) *Rule 10b–18 purchase* means a purchase (or any bid or limit order that would effect such purchase) of an issuer's common stock (or an equivalent interest, including a unit of beneficial interest in a trust or limited partnership or a depository share) by or for the issuer or any affiliated purchaser (including riskless principal transactions). However, it does *not* include any purchase of such security:

(i) Effected during the applicable restricted period of a distribution that is subject to § 242.102 of this chapter;

(ii) Effected by or for an issuer plan by an agent independent of the issuer;

(iii) Effected as a fractional share purchase (a fractional interest in a security) evidenced by a script certificate, order form, or similar document;

(iv) Effected during the period from the time of public announcement (as defined in Rule 165(f)) of a merger, acquisition, or similar transaction involving a recapitalization, until the earlier of the completion of such transaction or the completion of the vote by target shareholders. This exclusion does *not* apply to Rule 10b–18 purchases:

(A) Effected during such transaction in which the consideration is solely cash and there is no valuation period; or

(B) Where:

(1) The total volume of Rule 10b–18 purchases effected on any single day does not exceed the lesser of 25% of the security's four-week ADTV or the issuer's average daily Rule 10b–18 purchases during the three full calendar months preceding the date of the announcement of such transaction;

(2) The issuer's block purchases effected pursuant to paragraph (b)(4) of this section do not exceed the average size and frequency of the issuer's block purchases effected pursuant to paragraph (b)(4) of this section during the three full calendar months preceding the date of the announcement of such transaction; and

(3) Such purchases are not otherwise restricted or prohibited;

(v) Effected pursuant to Rule 13e–1;

(vi) Effected pursuant to a tender offer that is subject to Rule 13e–4 or specifically excepted from Rule 13e–4; or

(vii) Effected pursuant to a tender offer that is subject to section 14(d) of the Act and the rules and regulations thereunder.

(b) *Conditions to be met.* Rule 10b–18 purchases shall not be deemed to have violated the anti-manipulation provisions of sections 9(a)(2) or 10(b) of the Act or Rule 10b–5 under the Act, solely by reason of the time, price, or amount of the Rule 10b–18 purchases, or the number of brokers or dealers used in connection with such purchases, if the issuer or affiliated purchaser of the issuer effects the Rule 10b–18 purchases according to each of the following conditions:

(1) *One broker or dealer.* Rule 10b–18 purchases must be effected from or through only one broker or dealer on any single day; *Provided, however,* that:

(i) The "one broker or dealer" condition shall not apply to Rule 10b–18 purchases that are not solicited by or on behalf of the issuer or its affiliated purchaser(s);

(ii) Where Rule 10b–18 purchases are effected by or on behalf of more than one affiliated purchaser of the issuer (or the issuer and one or more of its affiliated purchasers) on a single day, the issuer and all affiliated purchasers must use the same broker or dealer; and

(iii) Where Rule 10b–18 purchases are effected on behalf of the issuer by a broker-dealer that is not an electronic communication network (ECN) or other alternative trading system (ATS), that broker-dealer can access ECN or other ATS liquidity in order to execute repurchases on behalf of the issuer (or any affiliated purchaser of the issuer) on that day.

(2) *Time of purchases.* Rule 10b–18 purchases must not be:

(i) The opening (regular way) purchase reported in the consolidated system;

(ii) Effected during the 10 minutes before the scheduled close of the primary trading session in the principal market for the security, and the 10 minutes before the scheduled close of the primary trading session in the market where the purchase is effected, for a security that has an ADTV value of $1 million or more and a public float value of $150 million or more; and

(iii) Effected during the 30 minutes before the scheduled close of the primary trading session in the principal market for the security, and the 30 minutes before the scheduled close of the primary trading session in the market where the purchase is effected, for all other securities;

(iv) However, for purposes of this section, Rule 10b–18 purchases may be effected following the close of the primary trading session until the termination of the period in which last sale prices are reported in the consolidated system so long as such purchases are effected at prices that do not exceed the lower of the closing price of the primary trading session in the principal market for the security and any lower bids or sale prices subsequently reported in the consolidated system, and all of this section's conditions are met. However, for purposes of this section, the issuer may use one broker or dealer to effect Rule 10b–18 purchases during this period that may be different from the broker or dealer that it used during the primary trading session. However, the issuer's Rule 10b–18 purchase may not be the opening transaction of the session following the close of the primary trading session.

(3) *Price of purchases.* Rule 10b–18 purchases must be effected at a purchase price that:

(i) Does not exceed the highest independent bid or the last independent transaction price, whichever is higher, quoted or reported in the consolidated system at the time the Rule 10b–18 purchase is effected;

(ii) For securities for which bids and transaction prices are not quoted or reported in the consolidated system, Rule 10b–18 purchases must be effected at a purchase price that does not exceed the highest independent bid or the last independent transaction price, whichever is higher, displayed and disseminated on any national securities exchange or on any inter-dealer quotation system ... that displays at least two priced quotations for the security, at the time the Rule 10b–18 purchase is effected; and

(iii) For all other securities, Rule 10b–18 purchases must be effected at a price no higher than the highest independent bid obtained from three independent dealers.

(4) *Volume of purchases.* The total volume of Rule 10b–18 purchases effected by or for the issuer and any affiliated purchasers effected on any single day must not exceed 25 percent of the ADTV for that security; *However,* once each week, in lieu of purchasing under the 25 percent of

ADTV limit for that day, the issuer or an affiliated purchaser of the issuer may effect one block purchase if:

(i) No other Rule 10b–18 purchases are effected that day, and

(ii) The block purchase is *not* included when calculating a security's four week ADTV under this section.

(c) *Alternative conditions*. The conditions of paragraph (b) of this section shall apply in connection with Rule 10b–18 purchases effected during a trading session following the imposition of a market-wide trading suspension, except:

(1) That the time of purchases condition in paragraph (b)(2) of this section shall not apply, either:

(i) From the reopening of trading until the scheduled close of trading on the day that the market-wide trading suspension is imposed; or

(ii) At the opening of trading on the next trading day until the scheduled close of trading that day, if a market-wide trading suspension was in effect at the close of trading on the preceding day; and

(2) The volume of purchases condition in paragraph (b)(4) of this section is modified so that the amount of Rule 10b–18 purchases must not exceed 100 percent of the ADTV for that security.

(d) *Other purchases*. No presumption shall arise that an issuer or an affiliated purchaser has violated the anti-manipulation provisions of sections 9(a)(2) or 10(b) of the Act, or Rule 10b–5 under the Act, if the Rule 10b–18 purchases of such issuer or affiliated purchaser do not meet the conditions specified in paragraph (b) or (c) of this section.

REPORTS UNDER SECTION 10A

Rule 10A–1.   Notice to the Commission Pursuant to Section 10A of the Act

(a)(1) If any issuer with a reporting obligation under the Act receives a report requiring a notice to the Commission in accordance with section 10A(b)(3) of the Act, the issuer shall submit such notice to the Commission's Office of the Chief Accountant within the time period prescribed in that section. The notice may be provided by facsimile, telegraph, personal delivery, or any other means, *provided* it is received by the Office of the Chief Accountant within the required time period.

(2) The notice specified in paragraph (a)(1) of this section shall be in writing and:

(i) Shall identify the issuer (including the issuer's name, address, phone number, and file number assigned to the issuer's filings by the Commission) and the independent accountant (including the independent accountant's name and phone number, and the address of the independent accountant's principal office);

(ii) Shall state the date that the issuer received from the independent accountant the report specified in section 10A(b)(2) of the Act;

(iii) Shall provide, at the election of the issuer, either:

(A) A summary of the independent accountant's report, including a description of the act that the independent accountant has identified as a likely illegal act and the possible effect of that act on all affected financial statements of the issuer or those related to the most current three-year period, whichever is shorter; or

(B) A copy of the independent accountant's report; and

(iv) May provide additional information regarding the issuer's views of and response to the independent accountant's report.

(3) Reports of the independent accountant submitted by the issuer to the Commission's Office of the Chief Accountant in accordance with paragraph (a)(2)(iii)(B) of this section shall be deemed to have been made pursuant to section 10A(b)(3) or section 10A(b)(4) of the Act, for purposes of the safe harbor provided by section 10A(c) of the Act.

(4) Submission of the notice in paragraphs (a)(1) and (a)(2) of this section shall not relieve the issuer from its obligations to comply fully with all other reporting requirements, including, without limitation:

(i) The filing requirements of Form 8–K ... regarding a change in the issuer's certifying accountant and

(ii) The disclosure requirements of ... or item 304 of Regulation S–K.

(b)(1) Any independent accountant furnishing to the Commission a copy of a report (or the documentation of any oral report) in accordance with section 10A(b)(3) or section 10A(b)(4) of the Act, shall submit that report (or documentation) to the Commission's Office of the Chief Accountant within the time period prescribed by the appropriate section of the Act. The report (or documentation) may be submitted to the Commission's Office of the Chief Accountant by facsimile, telegraph, personal delivery, or any other means, provided it is received by the Office of the Chief Accountant within the time period set forth in section 10A(b)(3) or 10A(b)(4) of the Act, whichever is applicable in the circumstances.

(2) If the report (or documentation) submitted to the Office of the Chief Accountant in accordance with paragraph (b)(1) of this section does not clearly identify both the issuer (including the issuer's name, address, phone number, and file number assigned to the issuer's filings with the Commission) and the independent accountant (including the independent accountant's name and phone number, and the address of the independent accountant's principal office), then the independent

accountant shall place that information in a prominent attachment to the report (or documentation) and shall submit that attachment to the Office of the Chief Accountant at the same time and in the same manner as the report (or documentation) is submitted to that Office.

(3) Submission of the report (or documentation) by the independent accountant as described in paragraphs (b)(1) and (b)(2) of this section shall not replace, or otherwise satisfy the need for, the newly engaged and former accountants' letters under items 304(a)(2)(D) and 304(a)(3) of Regulation S–K, and shall not limit, reduce, or affect in any way the independent accountant's obligations to comply fully with all other legal and professional responsibilities, including, without limitation, those under generally accepted auditing standards and the rules or interpretations of the Commission that modify or supplement those auditing standards.

(c) A notice or report submitted to the Office of the Chief Accountant in accordance with paragraphs (a) and (b) of this section shall be deemed to be an investigative record and shall be non-public and exempt from disclosure pursuant to the Freedom of Information Act to the same extent and for the same periods of time that the Commission's investigative records are non-public and exempt from disclosure.... Nothing in this paragraph, however, shall relieve, limit, delay, or affect in any way, the obligation of any issuer or any independent accountant to make all public disclosures required by law, by any Commission disclosure item, rule, report, or form, or by any applicable accounting, auditing, or professional standard....

Rule 10A–2. Auditor Independence

It shall be unlawful for an auditor not to be independent under Rule 2–01(c)(2)(iii)(B), (c)(4), (c)(6), (c)(7), and Rule 2–07.

Rule 10A–3. Listing Standards Relating to Audit Committees....

(a) Pursuant to section 10A(m) of the [Securities Exchange] Act and section 3 of the Sarbanes–Oxley Act of 2002:

(1) *National securities exchanges.* The rules of each national securities exchange registered pursuant to section 6 of the Act must, in accordance with the provisions of this section, prohibit the initial or continued listing of any security of an issuer that is not in compliance with the requirements of any portion of paragraph (b) or (c) of this section.

(2) *National securities associations.* The rules of each national securities association registered pursuant to section 15A of the Act must, in accordance with the provisions of this section, prohibit the initial or continued listing in an automated inter-dealer quotation system of any

security of an issuer that is not in compliance with the requirements of any portion of paragraph (b) or (c) of this section....

(4) *Notification of noncompliance.* The rules required by paragraphs (a)(1) and (a)(2) of this section must include a requirement that a listed issuer must notify the applicable national securities exchange or national securities association promptly after an executive officer of the listed issuer becomes aware of any material noncompliance by the listed issuer with the requirements of this section....

(b) *Required standards.*

(1) *Independence.*

(i) Each member of the audit committee must be a member of the board of directors of the listed issuer, and must otherwise be independent;....

(ii) *Independence requirements for non-investment company issuers.* In order to be considered to be independent for purposes of this paragraph (b)(1), a member of an audit committee of a listed issuer that is not an investment company may not, other than in his or her capacity as a member of the audit committee, the board of directors, or any other board committee:

(A) Accept directly or indirectly any consulting, advisory, or other compensatory fee from the issuer or any subsidiary thereof, provided that, unless the rules of the national securities exchange or national securities association provide otherwise, compensatory fees do not include the receipt of fixed amounts of compensation under a retirement plan (including deferred compensation) for prior service with the listed issuer (provided that such compensation is not contingent in any way on continued service); or

(B) Be an affiliated person of the issuer or any subsidiary thereof....

(2) *Responsibilities relating to registered public accounting firms.* The audit committee of each listed issuer, in its capacity as a committee of the board of directors, must be directly responsible for the appointment, compensation, retention and oversight of the work of any registered public accounting firm engaged (including resolution of disagreements between management and the auditor regarding financial reporting) for the purpose of preparing or issuing an audit report or performing other audit, review or attest services for the listed issuer, and each such registered public accounting firm must report directly to the audit committee.

(3) *Complaints.* Each audit committee must establish procedures for:

(i) The receipt, retention, and treatment of complaints received by the listed issuer regarding accounting, internal accounting controls, or auditing matters; and

(ii) The confidential, anonymous submission by employees of the listed issuer of concerns regarding questionable accounting or auditing matters.

(4) *Authority to engage advisers*. Each audit committee must have the authority to engage independent counsel and other advisers, as it determines necessary to carry out its duties.

(5) *Funding*. Each listed issuer must provide for appropriate funding, as determined by the audit committee, in its capacity as a committee of the board of directors, for payment of:

(i) Compensation to any registered public accounting firm engaged for the purpose of preparing or issuing an audit report or performing other audit, review or attest services for the listed issuer;

(ii) Compensation to any advisers employed by the audit committee under paragraph (b)(4) of this section; and

(iii) Ordinary administrative expenses of the audit committee that are necessary or appropriate in carrying out its duties. . . .

(e) *Definitions*. Unless the context otherwise requires, all terms used in this section have the same meaning as in the Act. In addition, unless the context otherwise requires, the following definitions apply for purposes of this section:

(1)(i) The term *affiliate* of, or a person *affiliated* with, a specified person, means a person that directly, or indirectly through one or more intermediaries, controls, or is controlled by, or is under common control with, the person specified.

(ii)(A) A person will be deemed not to be in control of a specified person for purposes of this section if the person:

(1) Is not the beneficial owner, directly or indirectly, of more than 10% of any class of voting equity securities of the specified person; and

(2) Is not an executive officer of the specified person.

(B) Paragraph (e)(1)(ii)(A) of this section only creates a safe harbor position that a person does not control a specified person. The existence of the safe harbor does not create a presumption in any way that a person exceeding the ownership requirement in paragraph (e)(1)(ii)(A)(1) of this section controls or is otherwise an affiliate of a specified person.

(iii) The following will be deemed to be affiliates:

(A) An executive officer of an affiliate;

(B) A director who also is an employee of an affiliate;

(C) A general partner of an affiliate; and

(D) A managing member of an affiliate....

(3) In the case of a listed issuer that is a limited partnership or limited liability company where such entity does not have a board of directors or equivalent body, the term *board of directors* means the board of directors of the managing general partner, managing member or equivalent body.

(4) The term *control* (including the terms *controlling, controlled by* and under *common control with*) means the possession, direct or indirect, of the power to direct or cause the direction of the management and policies of a person, whether through the ownership of voting securities, by contract, or otherwise.

(6) The term *executive officer* has the meaning set forth in Rule 3b–7....

(8) The term *indirect* acceptance by a member of an audit committee of any consulting, advisory or other compensatory fee includes acceptance of such a fee by a spouse, a minor child or stepchild or a child or stepchild sharing a home with the member or by an entity in which such member is a partner, member, an officer such as a managing director occupying a comparable position or executive officer, or occupies a similar position (except limited partners, non-managing members and those occupying similar positions who, in each case, have no active role in providing services to the entity) and which provides accounting, consulting, legal, investment banking or financial advisory services to the issuer or any subsidiary of the issuer.

(9) The terms *listed* and *listing* refer to securities listed on a national securities exchange or listed in an automated inter-dealer quotation system of a national securities association or to issuers of such securities.

REGULATION 12B: REGISTRATION AND REPORTING

GENERAL

Rule 12b–2.   Definitions

Unless the context otherwise requires, the following terms, when used in the rules contained in this regulation or in Regulation 13A or 15D or in the forms for statements and reports filed pursuant to sections 12, 13 or 15(d) of the act, shall have the respective meanings indicated in this rule:

Accelerated filer and large accelerated filer.

(1) *Accelerated filer.* The term *accelerated filer* means an issuer after it first meets the following conditions as of the end of its fiscal year:

(i) The issuer had an aggregate worldwide market value of the voting and non-voting common equity held by its non-affiliates of $75 million or more, but less than $700 million, as of the last business day of the issuer's most recently completed second fiscal quarter;

(ii) The issuer has been subject to the requirements of section 13(a) or 15(d) of the Act for a period of at least twelve calendar months;

(iii) The issuer has filed at least one annual report pursuant to section 13(a) or 15(d) of the Act . . . .

(2) *Large accelerated filer.* The term *large accelerated filer* means an issuer after it first meets the following conditions as of the end of its fiscal year:

(i) The issuer had an aggregate worldwide market value of the voting and non-voting common equity held by its non-affiliates of $700 million or more, as of the last business day of the issuer's most recently completed second fiscal quarter;

(ii) The issuer has been subject to the requirements of section 13(a) or 15(d) of the Act for a period of at least twelve calendar months;

(iii) The issuer has filed at least one annual report pursuant to section 13(a) or 15(d) of the Act . . . .

(3) *Entering and exiting accelerated filer and large accelerated filer status.*

(i) The determination at the end of the issuer's fiscal year for whether a non-accelerated filer becomes an accelerated filer, or whether a non-accelerated filer or accelerated filer becomes a large accelerated filer, governs the deadlines for the annual report to be filed for that fiscal year, the quarterly and annual reports to be filed for the subsequent fiscal year and all annual and quarterly reports to be filed thereafter while the issuer remains an accelerated filer or large accelerated filer.

(ii) Once an issuer becomes an accelerated filer, it will remain an accelerated filer unless the issuer determines at the end of a fiscal year that the aggregate worldwide market value of the voting and non-voting common equity held by non-affiliates of the issuer was less than $50 million, as of the last business day of the issuer's most recently completed second fiscal quarter. An issuer making this determination becomes a non-accelerated filer. The issuer will not become an accelerated filer again unless it subsequently meets the conditions in paragraph (1) of this definition.

(iii) Once an issuer becomes a large accelerated filer, it will remain a large accelerated filer unless the issuer determines at the end of a fiscal year that the aggregate worldwide market value of the voting and non-voting common equity held by non-affiliates of the issuer was less than $500 million, as of the last business day of the issuer's most recently completed second fiscal quarter. If the issuer's aggregate worldwide market value was $50 million or more, but less than $500 million, as of the last business day of the issuer's most recently completed second fiscal quarter, the issuer becomes an accelerated filer. If the issuer's aggregate worldwide market value was less than $50 million, as of the last business day of the issuer's most recently completed second fiscal quarter, the issuer becomes a non-accelerated filer. An issuer will not become a large accelerated filer again unless it subsequently meets the conditions in paragraph (2) of this definition.

(iv) The determination at the end of the issuer's fiscal year for whether an accelerated filer becomes a non-accelerated filer, or a large accelerated filer becomes an accelerated filer or a non-accelerated filer, governs the deadlines for the annual report to be filed for that fiscal year, the quarterly and annual reports to be filed for the subsequent fiscal year and all annual and quarterly reports to be filed thereafter while the issuer remains an accelerated filer or non-accelerated filer.

Affiliate. An "affiliate" of, or a person "affiliated" with, a specified person, is a person that directly, or indirectly through one or more intermediaries, controls, or is controlled by, or is under common control with, the person specified....

Associate. The term "associate" used to indicate a relationship with any person, means (1) any corporation or organization (other than the registrant or a majority-owned subsidiary of the registrant) of which such person is an officer or partner or is, directly or indirectly, the beneficial owner of 10 percent or more of any class of equity securities, (2) any trust or other estate in which such person has a substantial beneficial interest or as to which such person serves as trustee or in a similar fiduciary capacity, and (3) any relative or spouse of such person, or any relative of such spouse, who has the same home as such person or who is a director or officer of the registrant or any of its parents or subsidiaries....

Control. The term "control" (including the terms "controlling," "controlled by" and "under common control with") means the possession, direct or indirect, of the power to direct or cause the direction of the management and policies of a person, whether through the ownership of voting securities, by contract, or otherwise....

Small Business Issuer. The term "small business issuer" means an entity that meets the following criteria:

(1) has revenues of less than $25,000,000;

(2) is a U.S. or Canadian issuer;

(3) is not an investment company and is not an asset-backed issuer; and

(4) if a majority owned subsidiary, the parent corporation is also a small business issuer.

Provided however, that an entity is not a small business issuer if it has a public float (the aggregate market value of the issuer's outstanding voting and non-voting common equity held by non-affiliates) of $25,000,000 or more.

NOTE: The public float of a reporting company shall be computed by use of the price at which the stock was last sold, or the average of the bid and asked prices of such stock, on a date within 60 days prior to the end of its most recent fiscal year. The public float of a company filing an initial registration statement under the Exchange Act shall be determined as of a date within 60 days of the date the registration statement is filed. In the case of an initial public offering of securities, public float shall be computed on the basis of the number of shares outstanding prior to the offering and the estimated public offering price of the securities.

Subsidiary. A "subsidiary" of a specified person is an affiliate controlled by such person directly, or indirectly through one or more intermediaries....

EXTENSIONS AND TEMPORARY EXEMPTIONS: DEFINITIONS

Rule 12g–1. Exemption From Section 12(g)

An issuer shall be exempt from the requirement to register any class of equity securities pursuant to section 12(g)(1) if on the last day of its most recent fiscal year the issuer had total assets not exceeding $10 million and, with respect to a foreign private issuer, such securities were not quoted in an automated inter-dealer quotation system.

Rule 12g3–2. Exemptions for ... Certain Foreign Securities....

(b)(1) Securities of any foreign private issuer shall be exempt from section 12(g) of the Act if the issuer, or a government official or agency of the country of the issuer's domicile or in which it is incorporated or organized:

(i) Shall furnish to the Commission whatever information in each of the following categories the issuer since the beginning of its last fiscal year (A) has made or is required to make public pursuant to the law of the country of its domicile or in which it is incorporated or organized, (B) has filed or is required to file with a stock exchange on which its securities are traded and which was made public by such exchange, or (C) has distributed or is required to distribute to its security holders....

(3) The information required to be furnished under this paragraph (b) is information material to an investment decision such as: the financial condition or results of operations; changes in business; acquisitions or dispositions of assets; issuance, redemption or acquisitions of their securities; changes in management or control; the granting of

options or the payment of other remuneration to directors or officers; and transactions with directors, officers or principal security holders....

REGULATION 13A: REPORTS OF ISSUERS OF SECURITIES REGISTERED PURSUANT TO SECTION 12

Rule 13a–1. Requirements of Annual Reports

Every issuer having securities registered pursuant to section 12 of the Act shall file an annual report on the appropriate form authorized or prescribed therefor for each fiscal year after the last full fiscal year for which financial statements were filed in its registration statement....

Rule 13a–11. Current Reports on Form 8–K

(a) Except as provided in paragraph (b) of this section, every registrant subject to Rule 13a–1 shall file a current report on Form 8–K within the period specified in that form....

Rule 13a–13. Quarterly Reports on Form 10–Q ...

(a) Except as provided in paragraphs (b) and (c) of this section, every issuer that has securities registered pursuant to section 12 of the Act and which is required to file annual reports pursuant to section 13 of the Act on Form 10–K ... shall file a quarterly report on Form 10–Q ... for each of the first three fiscal quarters of each fiscal year of the issuer....

Rule 13a–14. Certification of Disclosure in Annual and Quarterly Reports

(a) Each report ... filed on Form 10–Q ... [or] Form 10–K ... must include certifications in the form specified in the applicable exhibit filing requirements of such report and such certifications must be filed as an exhibit to such report. Each principal executive and principal financial officer of the issuer, or persons performing similar functions, at the time of filing of the report must sign a certification.

(b) Each periodic report containing financial statements filed by an issuer pursuant to section 13(a) of the [Securities Exchange] Act must be accompanied by the certifications required by Section 1350 of Chapter 63 of Title 18 of the United States Code (18 U.S.C. 1350) and such certifications must be furnished as an exhibit to such report as specified in the applicable exhibit requirements for such report. Each principal executive and principal financial officer of the issuer (or equivalent thereof) must sign a certification. This requirement may be satisfied by a single certification signed by an issuer's principal executive and principal financial officers.

(c) A person required to provide a certification specified in paragraph (a) or (b) of this section may not have the certification signed on his or her behalf pursuant to a power of attorney or other form of confirming authority. . . .

Rule 13a–15. Controls and Procedures

(a) Every issuer that has a class of securities registered pursuant to section 12 of the Act . . . must maintain disclosure controls and procedures (as defined in paragraph (e) of this section) and internal control over financial reporting (as defined in paragraph (f) of this section).

(b) Each such issuer's management must evaluate, with the participation of the issuer's principal executive and principal financial officers, or persons performing similar functions, the effectiveness of the issuer's disclosure controls and procedures, as of the end of each fiscal quarter. . . .

(c) The management of each such issuer . . . must evaluate, with the participation of the issuer's principal executive and principal financial officers, or persons performing similar functions, the effectiveness, as of the end of each fiscal year, of the issuer's internal control over financial reporting. The framework on which management's evaluation of the issuer's internal control over financial reporting is based must be a suitable, recognized control framework that is established by a body or group that has followed due-process procedures, including the broad distribution of the framework for public comment.

(d) The management of each such issuer . . . must evaluate, with the participation of the issuer's principal executive and principal financial officers, or persons performing similar functions, any change in the issuer's internal control over financial reporting, that occurred during each of the issuer's fiscal quarters, or fiscal year in the case of a foreign private issuer, that has materially affected, or is reasonably likely to materially affect, the issuer's internal control over financial reporting.

(e) For purposes of this section, the term *disclosure controls and procedures* means controls and other procedures of an issuer that are designed to ensure that information required to be disclosed by the issuer in the reports that it files or submits under the [Securities Exchange] Act is recorded, processed, summarized and reported, within the time periods specified in the Commission's rules and forms. Disclosure controls and procedures include, without limitation, controls and procedures designed to ensure that information required to be disclosed by an issuer in the reports that it files or submits under the Act is accumulated and communicated to the issuer's management, including its principal executive and principal financial officers, or persons performing similar functions, as appropriate to allow timely decisions regarding required disclosure.

(f) The term *internal control over financial reporting* is defined as a process designed by, or under the supervision of, the issuer's principal executive and principal financial officers, or persons performing similar functions, and effected by the issuer's board of directors, management and other personnel, to provide reasonable assurance regarding the reliability of financial reporting and the preparation of financial statements for external purposes in accordance with generally accepted accounting principles and includes those policies and procedures that:

(1) Pertain to the maintenance of records that in reasonable detail accurately and fairly reflect the transactions and dispositions of the assets of the issuer;

(2) Provide reasonable assurance that transactions are recorded as necessary to permit preparation of financial statements in accordance with generally accepted accounting principles, and that receipts and expenditures of the issuer are being made only in accordance with authorizations of management and directors of the issuer; and

(3) Provide reasonable assurance regarding prevention or timely detection of unauthorized acquisition, use or disposition of the issuer's assets that could have a material effect on the financial statements.

FORM 8–K

Current Report

Pursuant to Section 13 or 15(d) of the
Securities Exchange Act of 1934

* * * * *

GENERAL INSTRUCTIONS ...

B. Events to be Reported and Time for Filing of Reports.

1. A report on this form is required to be filed or furnished, as applicable, upon the occurrence of any one or more of the events specified in the items in Sections 1–6 and 9 of this form. Unless otherwise specified, a report is to be filed or furnished within four business days after occurrence of the event. If the event occurs on a Saturday, Sunday or holiday on which the Commission is not open for business, then the four business day period shall begin to run on, and include, the first business day thereafter. A registrant either furnishing a report on this form under Item 7.01 (Regulation FD Disclosure) or electing to file a report on this form under Item 8.01 (Other Events) solely to satisfy its obligations under Regulation FD must furnish such report or make such filing, as applicable, in accordance with the require-

ments of Rule 100(a) of Regulation FD, including the deadline for furnishing or filing such report.

2. The information in a report furnished pursuant to Item 2.02 (Results of Operations and Financial Condition) or Item 7.01 (Regulation FD Disclosure) shall not be deemed to be "filed" for purposes of Section 18 of the Exchange Act or otherwise subject to the liabilities of that section, unless the registrant specifically states that the information is to be considered "filed" under the Exchange Act or incorporates it by reference into a filing under the Securities Act or the Exchange Act. If a report on Form 8–K contains disclosures under Item 2.02 or Item 7.01, whether or not the report contains disclosures regarding other items, all exhibits to such report relating to Item 2.02 or Item 7.01 will be deemed furnished, and not filed, unless the registrant specifies, under Item 9.01 (Financial Statements and Exhibits), which exhibits, or portions of exhibits, are intended to be deemed filed rather than furnished pursuant to this instruction. . . .

6. A registrant's report under Item 7.01 (Regulation FD Disclosure) or Item 8.01 (Other Events) will not be deemed an admission as to the materiality of any information in the report that is required to be disclosed solely by Regulation FD.

* * * * *

Information to Be Included in the Report

Section 1—Registrant's Business and Operations

Item 1.01.   Entry into a Material Definitive Agreement

(a) If the registrant has entered into a material definitive agreement not made in the ordinary course of business of the registrant, or into any amendment of such agreement that is material to the registrant, disclose the following information:

(1) the date on which the agreement was entered into or amended, the identity of the parties to the agreement or amendment and a brief description of any material relationship between the registrant or its affiliates and any of the parties, other than in respect of the material definitive agreement or amendment; and

(2) a brief description of the terms and conditions of the agreement or amendment that are material to the registrant.

(b) For purposes of this Item 1.01, a *material definitive agreement* means an agreement that provides for obligations that are material to and enforceable against the registrant, or rights that are material to the registrant and enforceable by the registrant against one or more other parties to the agreement, in each case whether or not subject to conditions.

Instructions

1. Any material definitive agreement of the registrant not made in the ordinary course of the registrant's business must be disclosed under this Item 1.01. An agreement is deemed to be not made in the ordinary course of a registrant's business even if the agreement is such as ordinarily accompanies the kind of business conducted by the registrant if it involves the subject matter identified in Item 601(b)(10)(ii)(A)—(D) of Regulation S–K....

2. A registrant must provide disclosure under this Item 1.01 if the registrant succeeds as a party to the agreement or amendment to the agreement by assumption or assignment (other than in connection with a merger or acquisition or similar transaction)....

Item 1.02. Termination of a Material Definitive Agreement

(a) If a material definitive agreement which was not made in the ordinary course of business of the registrant and to which the registrant is a party is terminated otherwise than by expiration of the agreement on its stated termination date, or as a result of all parties completing their obligations under such agreement, and such termination of the agreement is material to the registrant, disclose the following information:

(1) the date of the termination of the material definitive agreement, the identity of the parties to the agreement and a brief description of any material relationship between the registrant or its affiliates and any of the parties other than in respect of the material definitive agreement;

(2) a brief description of the terms and conditions of the agreement that are material to the registrant;

(3) a brief description of the material circumstances surrounding the termination; and

(4) any material early termination penalties incurred by the registrant.

(b) For purposes of this Item 1.02, the term *material definitive agreement* shall have the same meaning as set forth in Item 1.01(b).

Instructions

1. No disclosure is required solely by reason of this Item 1.02 during negotiations or discussions regarding termination of a material definitive agreement unless and until the agreement has been terminated.

2. No disclosure is required solely by reason of this Item 1.02 if the registrant believes in good faith that the material definitive agreement has not been terminated, unless the registrant has received a notice of termination pursuant to the terms of agreement....

Item 1.03. Bankruptcy or Receivership

(a) If a receiver, fiscal agent or similar officer has been appointed for a registrant or its parent, in a proceeding under the U.S. Bankruptcy Code or in any other proceeding under state or federal law in which a court or governmental authority has assumed jurisdiction over substantially all of the assets or business of the registrant or its parent, or if such jurisdiction has been assumed by leaving the existing directors and officers in possession but subject to the supervision and orders of a court or governmental authority, disclose the following information:

(1) the name or other identification of the proceeding;

(2) the identity of the court or governmental authority;

(3) the date that jurisdiction was assumed; and

(4) the identity of the receiver, fiscal agent or similar officer and the date of his or her appointment.

(b) If an order confirming a plan of reorganization, arrangement or liquidation has been entered by a court or governmental authority having supervision or jurisdiction over substantially all of the assets or business of the registrant or its parent, disclose the following;

(1) the identity of the court or governmental authority;

(2) the date that the order confirming the plan was entered by the court or governmental authority;

(3) a summary of the material features of the plan and, pursuant to Item 9.01 (Financial Statements and Exhibits), a copy of the plan as confirmed;

(4) the number of shares or other units of the registrant or its parent issued and outstanding, the number reserved for future issuance in respect of claims and interests filed and allowed under the plan, and the aggregate total of such numbers; and

(5) information as to the assets and liabilities of the registrant or its parent as of the date that the order confirming the plan was entered, or a date as close thereto as practicable.

Instructions

> 1. The information called for in paragraph (b)(5) of this Item 1.03 may be presented in the form in which it was furnished to the court or governmental authority....

Section 2—Financial Information

Item 2.01. Completion of Acquisition or Disposition of Assets

If the registrant or any of its majority-owned subsidiaries has completed the acquisition or disposition of a significant amount of assets, otherwise than in the ordinary course of business, disclose the following information:

(a) the date of completion of the transaction;

(b) a brief description of the assets involved;

(c) the identity of the person(s) from whom the assets were acquired or to whom they were sold and the nature of any material relationship, other than in respect of the transaction, between such person(s) and the registrant or any of its affiliates, or any director or officer of the registrant, or any associate of any such director or officer;

(d) the nature and amount of consideration given or received for the assets and, if any material relationship is disclosed pursuant to paragraph (c) of this Item 2.01, the formula or principle followed in determining the amount of such consideration;

(e) if the transaction being reported is an acquisition and if a material relationship exists between the registrant or any of its affiliates and the source(s) of the funds used in the acquisition, the identity of the source(s) of the funds unless all or any part of the consideration used is a loan made in the ordinary course of business by a bank as defined by Section 3(a)(6) of the Act, in which case the identity of such bank may be omitted provided the registrant:

(1) has made a request for confidentiality pursuant to Section 13(d)(1)(B) of the Act; and

(2) states in the report that the identity of the bank has been so omitted and filed separately with the Commission ...

Instructions

1. No information need be given as to:

(i) any transaction between any person and any wholly-owned subsidiary of such person;

(ii) any transaction between two or more wholly-owned subsidiaries of any person; or

(iii) the redemption or other acquisition of securities from the public, or the sale or other disposition of securities to the public, by the issuer of such securities or by a wholly-owned subsidiary of that issuer.

2. The term *acquisition* includes every purchase, acquisition by lease, exchange, merger, consolidation, succession or other acquisition, except that the term does not include the construction or development of property by or for the registrant or its subsidiaries or the acquisition of materials for such purpose. The term *disposition* includes every sale, disposition by lease, exchange, merger, consolidation, mortgage, assignment or hypothecation of assets,

whether for the benefit of creditors or otherwise, abandonment, destruction, or other disposition.

3.   The information called for by this Item 2.01 is to be given as to each transaction or series of related transactions of the size indicated. The acquisition or disposition of securities is deemed the indirect acquisition or disposition of the assets represented by such securities if it results in the acquisition or disposition of control of such assets.

4.   An acquisition or disposition shall be deemed to involve a significant amount of assets:

> (i) if the registrant's and its other subsidiaries' equity in the net book value of such assets or the amount paid or received for the assets upon such acquisition or disposition exceeded 10% of the total assets of the registrant and its consolidated subsidiaries; or

> (ii) if it involved a business ... that is significant (see 17 CFR 210.11–01(b)).*

Acquisitions of individually insignificant businesses are not required to be reported pursuant to this Item 2.01 unless they are related businesses ... and are significant in the aggregate.

5.   Attention is directed to the requirements in Item 9.01 (Financial Statements and Exhibits) with respect to the filing of:

* 17 C.F.R./210.11–01(b) provides that:

A business combination or disposition of a business shall be considered significant if:

(1) A comparison of the most recent annual financial statements of the business acquired or to be acquired and the registrant's most recent annual consolidated financial statements filed at or prior to the date of acquisition indicates that the business would be a significant subsidiary pursuant to the conditions specified in § 210.1–02(w), substituting 20 percent for 10 percent for each place it appears therein; or

(2) The business to be disposed of meets the conditions of a significant subsidiary in § 210.1–02(w)....

17 C.F.R. § 210.1–02(w) provides that:

The term "significant subsidiary" means a subsidiary, including its subsidiaries, which meets any of the following conditions:

(1) The registrant's and its other subsidiaries' investments in and advances to the subsidiary exceed 10 percent of the total assets of the registrant and its subsidiaries consolidated as of the end of the most recently completed fiscal year (for a proposed business combination to be accounted for as a pooling of interests, this condition is also met when the number of common shares exchanged or to be exchanged by the registrant exceeds 10 percent of its total common shares outstanding at the date the combination is initiated); or

(2) The registrant's and its other subsidiaries' proportionate share of the total assets (after intercompany eliminations) of the subsidiary exceeds 10 percent of the total assets of the registrants and its subsidiaries consolidated as of the end of the most recently completed fiscal year; or

(3) The registrant's and its other subsidiaries' equity in the income from continuing operations before income taxes, extraordinary items and cumulative effect of a change in accounting principle of the subsidiary exceeds 10 percent of such income of the registrant and its subsidiaries consolidated for the most recently completed fiscal year.... (Footnote by ed.)

    (i) financial statements of businesses acquired;

    (ii) *pro forma* financial information; and

    (iii) copies of the plans of acquisition or disposition as exhibits to the report.

Item 2.02. Results of Operations and Financial Condition

(a) If a registrant, or any person acting on its behalf, makes any public announcement or release (including any update of an earlier announcement or release) disclosing material non-public information regarding the registrant's results of operations or financial condition for a completed quarterly or annual fiscal period, the registrant shall disclose the date of the announcement or release, briefly identify the announcement or release and include the text of that announcement or release as an exhibit.

(b) A Form 8–K is not required to be furnished to the Commission under this Item 2.02 in the case of disclosure of material non-public information that is disclosed orally, telephonically, by webcast, by broadcast, or by similar means if:

(1) the information is provided as part of a presentation that is complementary to, and initially occurs within 48 hours after, a related, written announcement or release that has been furnished on Form 8–K pursuant to this Item 2.02 prior to the presentation;

(2) the presentation is broadly accessible to the public by dial-in conference call, by webcast, by broadcast or by similar means;

(3) the financial and other statistical information contained in the presentation is provided on the registrant's website . . .; and

(4) the presentation was announced by a widely disseminated press release, that included instructions as to when and how to access the presentation and the location on the registrant's website where the information would be available.

Instructions

    1. The requirements of this Item 2.02 are triggered by the disclosure of material non-public information regarding a completed fiscal year or quarter. Release of additional or updated material non-public information regarding a completed fiscal year or quarter would trigger an additional Item 2.02 requirement. . . .

    3. Issuers that make earnings announcements or other disclosures of material non-public information regarding a completed fiscal year or quarter in an interim or annual report to shareholders are permitted to specify which portion of the report contains the information required to be furnished under this Item 2.02.

4. This Item 2.02 does not apply in the case of a disclosure that is made in a quarterly report filed with the Commission on Form 10–Q ... or an annual report filed with the Commission on Form 10–K. . . .

Item 2.03. Creation of a Direct Financial Obligation or an Obligation under an Off–Balance Sheet Arrangement of a Registrant

(a) If the registrant becomes obligated on a direct financial obligation that is material to the registrant, disclose the following information:

(1) the date on which the registrant becomes obligated on the direct financial obligation and a brief description of the transaction or agreement creating the obligation;

(2) the amount of the obligation, including the terms of its payment and, if applicable, a brief description of the material terms under which it may be accelerated or increased and the nature of any recourse provisions that would enable the registrant to recover from third parties; and

(3) a brief description of the other terms and conditions of the transaction or agreement that are material to the registrant.

(b) If the registrant becomes directly or contingently liable for an obligation that is material to the registrant arising out of an off-balance sheet arrangement, disclose the following information:

(1) the date on which the registrant becomes directly or contingently liable on the obligation and a brief description of the transaction or agreement creating the arrangement and obligation;

(2) a brief description of the nature and amount of the obligation of the registrant under the arrangement, including the material terms whereby it may become a direct obligation, if applicable, or may be accelerated or increased and the nature of any recourse provisions that would enable the registrant to recover from third parties;

(3) the maximum potential amount of future payments (undiscounted) that the registrant may be required to make, if different; and

(4) a brief description of the other terms and conditions of the obligation or arrangement that are material to the registrant.

(c) For purposes of this Item 2.03, *direct financial obligation* means any of the following:

(1) a long-term debt obligation, as defined in Item 303(a)(5)(ii)(A) of Regulation S–K;

(2) a capital lease obligation, as defined in Item 303(a)(5)(ii)(B) of Regulation S–K . . .;

(3) an operating lease obligation, as defined in Item 303(a)(5)(ii)(C) of Regulation S–K ...; or

(4) a short-term debt obligation that arises other than in the ordinary course of business.

(d) For purposes of this Item 2.03, *off-balance sheet arrangement* has the meaning set forth in Item 303(a)(4)(ii) of Regulation S–K....

(e) For purposes of this Item 2.03, *short-term debt obligation* means a payment obligation under a borrowing arrangement that is scheduled to mature within one year, or, for those registrants that use the operating cycle concept of working capital, within a registrant's operating cycle that is longer than one year, as discussed in Accounting Research Bulletin No. 43, Chapter 3A, *Working Capital.*

Instructions

1. A registrant has no obligation to disclose information under this Item 2.03 until the registrant enters into an agreement enforceable against the registrant, whether or not subject to conditions, under which the direct financial obligation will arise or be created or issued. If there is no such agreement, the registrant must provide the disclosure within four business days after the occurrence of the closing or settlement of the transaction or arrangement under which the direct financial obligation arises or is created.

2. A registrant must provide the disclosure required by paragraph (b) of this Item 2.03 whether or not the registrant is also a party to the transaction or agreement creating the contingent obligation arising under the off-balance sheet arrangement. In the event that neither the registrant nor any affiliate of the registrant is also a party to the transaction or agreement creating the contingent obligation arising under the off-balance sheet arrangement in question, the four business day period for reporting the event under this Item 2.03 shall begin on the earlier of (i) the fourth business day after the contingent obligation is created or arises, and (ii) the day on which an executive officer, as defined in Rule 3b–7, of the registrant becomes aware of the contingent obligation.

3. In the event that an agreement, transaction or arrangement requiring disclosure under this Item 2.03 comprises a facility, program or similar arrangement that creates or may give rise to direct financial obligations of the registrant in connection with multiple transactions, the registrant shall:

(i) disclose the entering into of the facility, program or similar arrangement if the entering into of the facility is material to the registrant; and

(ii) as direct financial obligations arise or are created under the facility or program, disclose the required information under this Item 2.03 to the extent that the obligations are material to the registrant (including when a series of previously undisclosed individually immaterial obligations become material in the aggregate).

4. For purposes of Item 2.03(b)(3), the maximum amount of future payments shall not be reduced by the effect of any amounts that may possibly be recovered by the registrant under recourse or collateralization provisions in any guarantee agreement, transaction or arrangement.

5. If the obligation required to be disclosed under this Item 2.03 is a security, or a term of a security, that has been or will be sold pursuant to an effective registration statement of the registrant, the registrant is not required to file a Form 8–K pursuant to this Item 2.03, *provided* that the prospectus relating to that sale contains the information required by this Item 2.03. . . .

Item 2.04. Triggering Events That Accelerate or Increase a Direct Financial Obligation or an Obligation under an Off-Balance Sheet Arrangement

(a) If a triggering event causing the increase or acceleration of a direct financial obligation of the registrant occurs and the consequences of the event, taking into account those described in paragraph (a)(4) of this Item 2.04, are material to the registrant, disclose the following information:

(1) the date of the triggering event and a brief description of the agreement or transaction under which the direct financial obligation was created and is increased or accelerated;

(2) a brief description of the triggering event;

(3) the amount of the direct financial obligation, as increased if applicable, and the terms of payment or acceleration that apply; and

(4) any other material obligations of the registrant that may arise, increase, be accelerated or become direct financial obligations as a result of the triggering event or the increase or acceleration of the direct financial obligation.

(b) If a triggering event occurs causing an obligation of the registrant under an off-balance sheet arrangement to increase or be accelerated, or causing a contingent obligation of the registrant under an off-balance sheet arrangement to become a direct financial obligation of the registrant, and the consequences of the event, taking into account those described in paragraph (b)(4) of this Item 2.04, are material to the registrant, disclose the following information:

(1) the date of the triggering event and a brief description of the off-balance sheet arrangement;

(2) a brief description of the triggering event;

(3) the nature and amount of the obligation, as increased if applicable, and the terms of payment or acceleration that apply; and

(4) any other material obligations of the registrant that may arise, increase, be accelerated or become direct financial obligations as a result of the triggering event or the increase or acceleration of the obligation under the off-balance sheet arrangement or its becoming a direct financial obligation of the registrant.

(c) For purposes of this Item 2.04, the term *direct financial obligation* has the meaning provided in Item 2.03 of this form, but shall also include an obligation arising out of an off-balance sheet arrangement that is accrued under FASB Statement of Financial Accounting Standards No. 5, *Accounting for Contingencies* (SFAS No. 5) as a probable loss contingency.

(d) For purposes of this Item 2.04, the term *off-balance sheet arrangement* has the meaning provided in Item 2.03 of this form.

(e) For purposes of this Item 2.04, a *triggering event* is an event, including an event of default, event of acceleration or similar event, as a result of which a direct financial obligation of the registrant or an obligation of the registrant arising under an off-balance sheet arrangement is increased or becomes accelerated or as a result of which a contingent obligation of the registrant arising out of an off-balance sheet arrangement becomes a direct financial obligation of the registrant.

Instructions

1. Disclosure is required if a triggering event occurs in respect of an obligation of the registrant under an off-balance sheet arrangement and the consequences are material to the registrant, whether or not the registrant is also a party to the transaction or agreement under which the triggering event occurs.

2. No disclosure is required under this Item 2.04 unless and until a triggering event has occurred in accordance with the terms of the relevant agreement, transaction or arrangement, including, if required, the sending to the registrant of notice of the occurrence of a triggering event pursuant to the terms of the agreement, transaction or arrangement and the satisfaction of all conditions to such occurrence, except the passage of time.

3. No disclosure is required solely by reason of this Item 2.04 if the registrant believes in good faith that no triggering event has occurred, unless the registrant has received a notice described in Instruction 2 to this Item 2.04.

4. Where a registrant is subject to an obligation arising out of an off-balance sheet arrangement, whether or not disclosed pursuant to Item 2.03 of this form, if a triggering event occurs as a result of which under that obligation an accrual for a probable loss is

required under SFAS No. 5, the obligation arising out of the off-balance sheet arrangement becomes a direct financial obligation as defined in this Item 2.04. In that situation, if the consequences as determined under Item 2.04(b) are material to the registrant, disclosure is required under this Item 2.04. . . .

Item 2.05.   Costs Associated with Exit or Disposal Activities

If the registrant's board of directors, a committee of the board of directors or the officer or officers of the registrant authorized to take such action if board action is not required, commits the registrant to an exit or disposal plan, or otherwise disposes of a long-lived asset or terminates employees under a plan of termination described in paragraph 8 of FASB Statement of Financial Accounting Standards No. 146, *Accounting for Costs Associated with Exit or Disposal Activities* (SFAS No. 146), under which material charges will be incurred under generally accepted accounting principles applicable to the registrant, disclose the following information:

(a) the date of the commitment to the course of action and a description of the course of action, including the facts and circumstances leading to the expected action and the expected completion date;

(b) for each major type of cost associated with the course of action (for example, one-time termination benefits, contract termination costs and other associated costs), an estimate of the total amount or range of amounts expected to be incurred in connection with the action;

(c) an estimate of the total amount or range of amounts expected to be incurred in connection with the action; and

(d) the registrant's estimate of the amount or range of amounts of the charge that will result in future cash expenditures, *provided, however*, that if the registrant determines that at the time of filing it is unable in good faith to make a determination of an estimate required by paragraphs (b), (c) or (d) of this Item 2.05, no disclosure of such estimate shall be required; *provided further, however*, that in any such event, the registrant shall file an amended report on Form 8–K under this Item 2.05 within four business days after it makes a determination of such an estimate or range of estimates.

Item 2.06.   Material Impairments

If the registrant's board of directors, a committee of the board of directors or the officer or officers of the registrant authorized to take such action if board action is not required, concludes that a material charge for impairment to one or more of its assets, including, without limitation, impairments of securities or goodwill, is required under generally accepted accounting principles applicable to the registrant, disclose the following information:

(a) the date of the conclusion that a material charge is required and a description of the impaired asset or assets and the facts and circumstances leading to the conclusion that the charge for impairment is required;

(b) the registrant's estimate of the amount or range of amounts of the impairment charge; and

(c) the registrant's estimate of the amount or range of amounts of the impairment charge that will result in future cash expenditures,

provided, however, that if the registrant determines that at the time of filing it is unable in good faith to make a determination of an estimate required by paragraphs (b) or (c) of this Item 2.06, no disclosure of such estimate shall be required; *provided further, however*, that in any such event, the registrant shall file an amended report on Form 8–K under this Item 2.06 within four business days after it makes a determination of such an estimate or range of estimates.

Instruction

No filing is required under this Item 2.06 if the conclusion is made in connection with the preparation, review or audit of financial statements required to be included in the next periodic report due to be filed under the Exchange Act, the periodic report is filed on a timely basis and such conclusion is disclosed in the report.

Section 3—Securities and Trading Markets

Item 3.01. Notice of Delisting or Failure to Satisfy a Continued Listing Rule or Standard; Transfer of Listing

(a) If the registrant has received notice from the national securities exchange or national securities association (or a facility thereof) that maintains the principal listing for any class of the registrant's common equity (as defined in Exchange Act Rule 12b–2) that:

- the registrant or such class of the registrant's securities does not satisfy a rule or standard for continued listing on the exchange or association;

- the exchange has submitted an application under Exchange Act Rule 12d2–2 to the Commission to delist such class of the registrant's securities; or

- the association has taken all necessary steps under its rules to delist the security from its automated inter-dealer quotation system,

the registrant must disclose:

(i) the date that the registrant received the notice;

(ii) the rule or standard for continued listing on the national securities exchange or national securities association that the registrant fails, or has failed to, satisfy; and

(iii) any action or response that, at the time of filing, the registrant has determined to take in response to the notice.

(b) If the registrant has notified the national securities exchange or national securities association (or a facility thereof) that maintains the principal listing for any class of the registrant's common equity (as defined in Exchange Act Rule 12b–2) that the registrant is aware of any material noncompliance with a rule or standard for continued listing on the exchange or association, the registrant must disclose:

(i) the date that the registrant provided such notice to the exchange or association;

(ii) the rule or standard for continued listing on the exchange or association that the registrant fails, or has failed, to satisfy; and

(iii) any action or response that, at the time of filing, the registrant has determined to take regarding its noncompliance.

(c) If the national securities exchange or national securities association (or a facility thereof) that maintains the principal listing for any class of the registrant's common equity (as defined in Exchange Act Rule 12b–2), in lieu of suspending trading in or delisting such class of the registrant's securities, issues a public reprimand letter or similar communication indicating that the registrant has violated a rule or standard for continued listing on the exchange or association, the registrant must state the date, and summarize the contents of the letter or communication.

(d) If the registrant's board of directors, a committee of the board of directors or the officer or officers of the registrant authorized to take such action if board action is not required, has taken definitive action to cause the listing of a class of its common equity to be withdrawn from the national securities exchange, or terminated from the automated inter-dealer quotation system of a registered national securities association, where such exchange or association maintains the principal listing for such class of securities, including by reason of a transfer of the listing or quotation to another securities exchange or quotation system, describe the action taken and state the date of the action.

Item 3.02. Unregistered Sales of Equity Securities

(a) If the registrant sells equity securities in a transaction that is not registered under the Securities Act, furnish the information set forth in paragraphs (a) and (c) through (e) of Item 701 of Regulation S–K. For purposes of determining the required filing date for the Form 8–K under this Item 3.02(a), the registrant has no obligation to disclose information under this Item 3.02 until the registrant enters into an agreement enforceable against the registrant, whether or not subject to conditions, under which the equity securities are to be sold. If there is no such agreement, the registrant must provide the disclosure within four business days after the occurrence of the closing or settlement of the transaction or arrangement under which the equity securities are to be sold.

(b) No report need be filed under this Item 3.02 if the equity securities sold, in the aggregate since its last report filed under this Item 3.02 or its last periodic report, whichever is more recent, constitute less than 1% of the number of shares outstanding of the class of equity securities sold. In the case of a small business issuer, no report need be filed if the equity securities sold, in the aggregate since its last report filed under this Item 3.02 or its last periodic report, whichever is more recent, constitute less than 5% of the number of shares outstanding of the class of equity securities sold.

Instructions

1. For purposes of this Item 3.02, "the number of shares outstanding" refers to the actual number of shares of equity securities of the class outstanding and does not include outstanding securities convertible into or exchangeable for such equity securities....

Item 3.03. Material Modification to Rights of Security Holders

(a) If the constituent instruments defining the rights of the holders of any class of registered securities of the registrant have been materially modified, disclose the date of the modification, the title of the class of securities involved and briefly describe the general effect of such modification upon the rights of holders of such securities.

(b) If the rights evidenced by any class of registered securities have been materially limited or qualified by the issuance or modification of any other class of securities by the registrant, briefly disclose the date of the issuance or modification, [and] the general effect of the issuance or modification of such other class of securities upon the rights of the holders of the registered securities.

Instruction

Working capital restrictions and other limitations upon the payment of dividends must be reported pursuant to this Item 3.03.

Section 4—Matters Related to Accountants and Financial Statements

Item 4.01. Changes in Registrant's Certifying Accountant

(a) If an independent accountant who was previously engaged as the principal accountant to audit the registrant's financial statements, or an independent accountant upon whom the principal accountant expressed reliance in its report regarding a significant subsidiary, resigns (or indicates that it declines to stand for re-appointment after completion of the current audit) or is dismissed, disclose the information required by Item 304(a)(1) of Regulation S–K ..., including compliance with Item 304(a)(3) of Regulation S–K.

(b) If a new independent accountant has been engaged as either the principal accountant to audit the registrant's financial statements or as an independent accountant on whom the principal accountant is expected to express reliance in its report regarding a significant subsidiary, the registrant must disclose the information required by Item 304(a)(2).

Instruction

The resignation or dismissal of an independent accountant, or its refusal to stand for re-appointment, is a reportable event separate from the engagement of a new independent accountant. On some occasions, two reports on Form 8–K are required for a single change in accountants, the first on the resignation (or refusal to stand for re-appointment) or dismissal of the former accountant and the second when the new accountant is engaged. Information required in the second Form 8–K in such situations need not be provided to the extent that it has been reported previously in the first Form 8–K.

Item 4.02. Non–Reliance on Previously Issued Financial Statements or a Related Audit Report or Completed Interim Review

(a) If the registrant's board of directors, a committee of the board of directors or the officer or officers of the registrant authorized to take such action if board action is not required, concludes that any previously issued financial statements, covering one or more years or interim periods for which the registrant is required to provide financial statements under Regulation S–X ..., should no longer be relied upon because of an error in such financial statements as addressed in Accounting Principles Board Opinion No. 20, as may be modified, supplemented or succeeded, disclose the following information:

(1) the date of the conclusion regarding the non-reliance and an identification of the financial statements and years or periods covered that should no longer be relied upon;

(2) a brief description of the facts underlying the conclusion to the extent known to the registrant at the time of filing; and

(3) a statement of whether the audit committee, or the board of directors in the absence of an audit committee, or authorized officer or officers, discussed with the registrant's independent accountant the matters disclosed in the filing pursuant to this Item 4.02(a).

(b) If the registrant is advised by, or receives notice from, its independent accountant that disclosure should be made or action should be taken to prevent future reliance on a previously issued audit report or completed interim review related to previously issued financial statements, disclose the following information:

(1) the date on which the registrant was so advised or notified;

(2) identification of the financial statements that should no longer be relied upon;

(3) a brief description of the information provided by the accountant; and

(4) a statement of whether the audit committee, or the board of directors in the absence of an audit committee, or authorized officer or officers, discussed with the independent accountant the matters disclosed in the filing pursuant to this Item 4.02(b).

(c) If the registrant receives advisement or notice from its independent accountant requiring disclosure under paragraph (b) of this Item 4.02, the registrant must:

(1) provide the independent accountant with a copy of the disclosures it is making in response to this Item 4.02 that the independent accountant shall receive no later than the day that the disclosures are filed with the Commission;

(2) request the independent accountant to furnish to the registrant as promptly as possible a letter addressed to the Commission stating whether the independent accountant agrees with the statements made by the registrant in response to this Item 4.02 and, if not, stating the respects in which it does not agree; and

(3) amend the registrant's previously filed Form 8–K by filing the independent accountant's letter as an exhibit to the filed Form 8–K no later than two business days after the registrant's receipt of the letter.

Section 5—Corporate Governance and Management

Item 5.01.   Changes in Control of Registrant

(a) If, to the knowledge of the registrant's board of directors, a committee of the board of directors or authorized officer or officers of the registrant, a change in control of the registrant has occurred, furnish the following information:

(1) the identity of the person(s) who acquired such control;

(2) the date and a description of the transaction(s) which resulted in the change in control;

(3) the basis of the control, including the percentage of voting securities of the registrant now beneficially owned directly or indirectly by the person(s) who acquired control;

(4) the amount of the consideration used by such person(s);

(5) the source(s) of funds used by the person(s), *unless* all or any part of the consideration used is a loan made in the ordinary course of business by a bank as defined by Section 3(a)(6) of the Act, in which case the identity of such bank may be omitted provided the person who acquired control:

(i) has made a request for confidentiality pursuant to Section 13(d)(1)(B) of the Act; and

(ii) states in the report that the identity of the bank has been so omitted and filed separately with the Commission.

(6) the identity of the person(s) from whom control was assumed;

(7) any arrangements or understandings among members of both the former and new control groups and their associates with respect to election of directors or other matters.

(b) Furnish the information required by Item 403(c) of Regulation S–K. . . .

Item 5.02. Departure of Directors or Principal Officers; Election of Directors; Appointment of Principal Officers

(a)(1) If a director has resigned or refuses to stand for re-election to the board of directors since the date of the last annual meeting of shareholders because of a disagreement with the registrant, known to an executive officer of the registrant, as defined in Rule 3b–7, on any matter relating to the registrant's operations, policies or practices, or if a director has been removed for cause from the board of directors, disclose the following information:

(i) the date of such resignation, refusal to stand for re-election or removal;

(ii) any positions held by the director on any committee of the board of directors at the time of the director's resignation, refusal to stand for re-election or removal; and

(iii) a brief description of the circumstances representing the disagreement that the registrant believes caused, in whole or in part, the director's resignation, refusal to stand for re-election or removal.

(2) If the director has furnished the registrant with any written correspondence concerning the circumstances surrounding his or her resignation, refusal or removal, the registrant shall file a copy of the document as an exhibit to the report on Form 8–K.

(3) The registrant also must:

(i) provide the director with a copy of the disclosures it is making in response to this Item 5.02 no later than the day the registrant file the disclosures with the Commission;

(ii) provide the director with the opportunity to furnish the registrant as promptly as possible with a letter addressed to the registrant stating whether he or she agrees with the statements made by the registrant in response to this Item 5.02 and, if not, stating the respects in which he or she does not agree; and

(iii) file any letter received by the registrant from the director with the Commission as an exhibit by an amendment to the previously filed Form 8–K within two business days after receipt by the registrant.

(b) If the registrant's principal executive officer, president, principal financial officer, principal accounting officer, principal operating officer or any person performing similar functions retires, resigns or is terminated from that position, or if a director retires, resigns, is removed, or refuses to stand for re-election (except in circumstances described in paragraph (a) of this Item 5.02), disclose the fact that the event has occurred and the date of the event.

(c) If the registrant appoints a new principal executive officer, president, principal financial officer, principal accounting officer, principal operating officer or person performing similar functions, disclose the following information with respect to the newly appointed officer:

(1) the name and position of the newly appointed officer and the date of the appointment;

(2) the information required by Items 401(b), (d), (e) and Item 404(a) of Regulation S–K . . .; and

(3) a brief description of the material terms of any employment agreement between the registrant and that officer.

Item 5.03. Amendments to Articles of Incorporation or Bylaws; Change in Fiscal Year

(a) If a registrant with a class of equity securities registered under Section 12 of the Exchange Act amends its articles of incorporation or bylaws and a proposal for the amendment was not disclosed in a proxy statement or information statement filed by the registrant, disclose the following information:

(1) the effective date of the amendment; and

(2) a description of the provision adopted or changed by amendment and, if applicable, the previous provision.

(b) If the registrant determines to change the fiscal year from that used in its most recent filing with the Commission other than by means of:

(1) a submission to a vote of security holders through the solicitation of proxies or otherwise; or

(2) an amendment to its articles of incorporation or bylaws,

disclose the date of such determination, the date of the new fiscal year end and the form (for example, Form 10–K . . .) on which the report covering the transition period will be filed. . . .

Item 5.05. Amendments to the Registrant's Code of Ethics, or Waiver of a Provision of the Code of Ethics

(a) Briefly describe the date and nature of any amendment to a provision of the registrant's code of ethics that applies to the registrant's principal executive officer, principal financial officer, principal accounting officer or controller or persons performing similar functions and that relates to any element of the code of ethics definition enumerated in Item 406(b) of [Regulation] S–K. . . .

(b) If the registrant has granted a waiver, including an implicit waiver, from a provision of the code of ethics to an officer or person described in paragraph (a) of this Item 5.05, and the waiver relates to one or more of the elements of the code of ethics definition referred to in paragraph (a) of this Item 5.05, briefly describe the nature of the waiver, the name of the person to whom the waiver was granted, and the date of the waiver.

(c) The registrant does not need to provide any information pursuant to this Item 5.05 if it discloses the required information on its Internet website within four business days following the date of the amendment or waiver and the registrant has disclosed in its most recently filed annual report its Internet address and intention to provide disclosure in this manner. If the registrant elects to disclose the information required by this Item 5.05 through its website, such information must remain available on the website for at least a 12–month period. Following the 12–month period, the registrant must retain the information for a period of not less than five years. Upon request, the registrant must furnish to the Commission or its staff a copy of any or all information retained pursuant to this requirement. . . .

Section 7—Regulation FD

Item 7.01. Regulation FD Disclosure

Unless filed under Item 8.01, disclose under this item only information that the registrant elects to disclose through Form 8–K pursuant to Regulation FD.

Section 8—Other Events

Item 8.01. Other Events

The registrant may, at its option, disclose under this Item 8.01 any events, with respect to which information is not otherwise called for by this form, that the registrant deems of importance to security holders. The registrant may, at its option, file a report under this Item 8.01 disclosing the nonpublic information required to be disclosed by Regulation FD. . . .

FORM 10–Q

GENERAL INSTRUCTIONS

A. Rule as to Use of Form 10–Q.

1. Form 10–Q shall be used for quarterly reports under Section 13 or 15(d) of the Securities Exchange Act of 1934, filed pursuant to Rule 13a–13 or Rule 15d–13. A quarterly report on this form pursuant to Rule 13a–13 or Rule 15d–13 shall be filed within the following period after the end of each of the first three fiscal quarters of each fiscal year, but no report need be filed for the fourth quarter of any fiscal year:

a. 40 days after the end of the fiscal quarter for large accelerated filers and accelerated filers (as defined in Rule 12b–2); and

b. 45 days after the end of the fiscal quarter for all other registrants.

Quarterly Report Under Section 13 or 15(d) of the Securities Exchange Act of 1934

For the Quarterly Period Ended _____

* * *

Commission file number _____

_____
(Exact name of registrant as specified in its charter)

_____
(State or other jurisdiction of incorporation   (I.R.S. Employer
or organization)   Identification No.)

_____
(Address of principal executive offices) (Zip Code)

_____
(Registrant's telephone number, including area code)

_____
(Former name, former address and former fiscal year, if changed since last report.)

PART 1—FINANCIAL INFORMATION

Item 1.   Financial Statements.

Provide the information required by Rule 10–01 of Regulation S–X [Interim Financial Statements]....

Item 2.   Management's Discussion and Analysis of Financial Condition and Results of Operations.

Furnish the information required by Item 303 of Regulation S–K ...

Item 4. Controls and Procedures.

Furnish the information required by Item 307 of Regulation S–K and 308(c) of Regulation S–K.

PART II—OTHER INFORMATION....

Item 1. Legal Proceedings.

Furnish the information required by Item 103 of Regulation S–K [Legal Proceedings]. As to such proceedings which have been terminated during the period covered by the report, provide similar information, including the date of termination and a description of the disposition thereof with respect to the registrant and its subsidiaries.

Item 1A. Risk Factors.

Set forth any material changes from risk factors as previously disclosed in the registrant's Form 10–K in response to Item 1A. to Part I of Form 10–K.

Item 2. Changes in Securities.

(a) If the constituent instruments defining the rights of the holders of any class of registered securities have been materially modified, give the title of the class of securities involved and state briefly the general effect of such modification upon the rights of holders of such securities.

(b) If the rights evidenced by any class of registered securities have been materially limited or qualified by the issuance or modification of any other class of securities, state briefly the general effect of the issuance or modification of such other class of securities upon the rights of the holders of the registered securities....

Item 3. Defaults Upon Senior Securities.

(a) If there has been any material default in the payment of principal, interest, a sinking or purchase fund installment, or any other material default not cured within 30 days, with respect to any indebtedness of the registrant or any of its significant subsidiaries exceeding 5 percent of the total assets of the registrant and its consolidated subsidiaries, identify the indebtedness and state the nature of the default. In the case of such a default in the payment of principal, interest, or a sinking or purchase fund installment, state the amount of the default and the total arrearage on the date of filing this report.

(b) If any material arrearage in the payment of dividends has occurred or if there has been any other material delinquency not cured within 30 days, with respect to any class of preferred stock of the registrant which is registered or which ranks prior to any class of registered securities, or with respect to any class of preferred stock of any significant subsidiary of the registrant, give the title of the class and state the nature of the arrearage or delinquency. In the case of an arrearage in the payment of dividends, state the amount and the total arrearage on the date of filing this report....

Item 4. Submission of Matters to a Vote of Security Holders.

If any matter has been submitted to a vote of security holders during the period covered by this report, through the solicitation of proxies or otherwise, furnish the following information:

(a) The date of the meeting and whether it was an annual or special meeting.

(b) If the meeting involved the election of directors, the name of each director elected at the meeting and the name of each other director whose term of office as a director continued after the meeting.

(c) A brief description of each matter voted upon at the meeting and state the number of votes cast for, against or withheld, as well as the number of abstentions and broker non-votes, as to each such matter, including a separate tabulation with respect to each nominee for office.

(d) A description of the terms of any settlement between the registrant and any other participant (as defined in Rule 14a–11 ... of Regulation 14A under the Act) terminating any solicitation subject to Rule 14a–11, including the cost or anticipated cost to the registrant....

SIGNATURES

Pursuant to the requirements of the Securities Exchange Act of 1934, the registrant has duly caused this report to be signed on its behalf by the undersigned thereunto duly authorized.

	_____
	(Registrant)

_____	_____
(Date)	(Signature)**
_____	_____
(Date)	(Signature)**

FORM 10–K

Annual Report Pursuant to Section 13 or 15(d)
of The Securities Exchange Act of 1934
GENERAL INSTRUCTIONS....

A. Rule as to Use of Form 10–K.

(1) This Form shall be used for annual reports pursuant to Section 13 or 15(d) of the Securities Exchange Act of 1934 for which no other

form is prescribed. This Form also shall be used for transition reports filed pursuant to Section 13 or 15(d) of the Act.

(2) Annual reports on this Form shall be filed within the following period:

(a) 60 days after the end of the fiscal year covered by the report ... for large accelerated filers (as defined in Rule 12b–2):

(b) 75 days after the end of the fiscal year covered by the report for accelerated filers (as defined in Rule 12b–2); and

(c) 90 days after the end of the fiscal year covered by the report for all other registrants. . . .

For the fiscal year ended _____ Commission file number _____

_____

(Exact name of registrant as specified in its charter)

_____ _____

(State or other jurisdiction of incorporation or organization)   (I.R.S. Employer Identification No.)

_____ _____

(Address of principal executive offices)   (Zip Code)

Registrant's telephone number, including area code _____

Securities registered pursuant to Section 12(b) of the Act:

Title of each class	Name of each exchange on which registered
_____	_____
_____	_____

Securities registered pursuant to section 12(g) of the Act:

_____

(Title of class)

. . .

PART I ...

Item 1. Business. . . .

Item 1A. Risk Factors.

Set forth, under the caption "Risk Factors," where appropriate, the risk factors described in Item 503(c) of Regulation S–K applicable to the registrant. Provide any discussion of risk factors in plain English in accordance with Rule 421(d) of the Securities Act of 1933.

Item 1B. Unresolved Staff Comments.

If the registrant is an accelerated filer as defined in Rule 12b–2 of the Exchange Act or is a well-known seasoned issuer as defined in Rule 405 of the Securities Act and has received written comments from the Commission staff regarding its periodic or current reports under the Act not less than 180 days before the end of its fiscal year to which the annual report relates, and such comments remain unresolved, disclose the substance of any such unresolved comments that the registrant believes are material. Such disclosure may provide other information including the position of the registrant with respect to any such comment.

Item 2.   Properties. . . .

Item 3.   Legal Proceedings. . . .

Item 4.   Submission of Matters to a Vote of Security Holders.

If any matter was submitted during the fourth quarter of the fiscal year covered by this report to a vote of security holders, through the solicitation of proxies or otherwise, furnish the following information:

(a) The date of the meeting and whether it was an annual or special meeting.

(b) If the meeting involved the election of directors, the name of each director elected at the meeting and the name of each other director whose term of office as a director continued after the meeting.

(c) A brief description of each matter voted upon at the meeting and state the number of votes cast for, against or withheld, as well as the number of abstentions and broker non-votes as to each such matter, including a separate tabulation with respect to each nominee for office.

(d) A description of the terms of any settlement between the registrant and any other participant (as defined in Rule 14a–11 of Regulation 14A under the Act) terminating any solicitation subject to Rule 14a–11, including the cost or anticipated cost to the registrant.

PART II . . .

Item 5.   Market for Registrant's Common Equity and Related Stockholder Matters. . . .

Item 6.   Selected Financial Data.

Furnish the information required by Item 301 of Regulation S–K. . . .

Item 7.   Management's Discussion and Analysis of Financial Condition and Results of Operation.

Furnish the information required by Item 303 of Regulation S–K. . . .

Item 8.   Financial Statements and Supplementary Data. . . .

Furnish financial statements meeting the requirements of Regulation S–X. . . .

Item 9.   Changes in and Disagreements With Accountants on Accounting and Financial Disclosure.

Furnish the information required by Item 304 of Regulation S–K. . . .

Item 9A.   Controls and Procedures.

Furnish the information required by Items 307 and 308 of Regulation S–K. . . .

PART III . . .

Item 10.   Directors and Executive Officers of the Registrant.

Furnish the information required by Items 401, 403, and 405 of Regulation S–K. . . .

Item 11.   Executive Compensation.

Furnish the information required by Item 402 Regulation S–K. . . .

Item 12.   Security Ownership of Certain Beneficial Owners and Management.

Furnish the information required by Item 201(d) of Regulation S–K and by Item 403 of Regulation S–K. . . .

Item 13.   Certain Relationships and Related Transactions.

Furnish the information required by Item 404 of Regulation S–K. . . .

Item 14.   Principal Accountant Fees and Services.

Furnish the information required by Item 9(e) of Schedule 14A.

(1) Disclose, under the caption Audit Fees, the aggregate fees billed for each of the last two fiscal years for professional services rendered by the principal accountant for the audit of the registrant's annual financial statements and review of financial statements included in the registrant's Form 10–Q or 10–QSB or services that are normally provided by the accountant in connection with statutory and regulatory filings or engagements for those fiscal years.

(2) Disclose, under the caption Audit–Related Fees, the aggregate fees billed in each of the last two fiscal years for assurance and related services by the principal accountant that are reasonably related to the performance of the audit or review of the registrant's financial statements and are not reported under Item 9(e)(1) of Schedule 14A. Registrants shall describe the nature of the services comprising the fees disclosed under this category.

(3) Disclose, under the caption Tax Fees, the aggregate fees billed in each of the last two fiscal years for professional services rendered by the principal accountant for tax compliance, tax advice, and tax planning. Registrants shall describe the nature of the services comprising the fees disclosed under this category.

(4) Disclose, under the caption All Other Fees, the aggregate fees billed in each of the last two fiscal years for products and services

provided by the principal accountant, other than the services reported in Items 9(e)(1) through 9(e)(3) of Schedule 14A. Registrants shall describe the nature of the services comprising the fees disclosed under this category.

(5)(i) Disclose the audit committee's pre-approval policies and procedures. . . .

(ii) Disclose the percentage of services described in each of Items 9(e)(2) through 9(e)(4) of Schedule 14A that were approved by the audit committee. . . .

(6) If greater than 50 percent, disclose the percentage of hours expended on the principal accountant's engagement to audit the registrant's financial statements for the most recent fiscal year that were attributed to work performed by persons other than the principal accountant's full-time, permanent employees.

*****

SIGNATURES . . .

Pursuant to the requirements of Section 13 or 15(d) of the Securities Exchange Act of 1934, the registrant has duly caused this report to be signed on its behalf by the undersigned, thereunto duly authorized.

(Registrant) _____

By (Signature and Title) _____

Date _____

Pursuant to the requirements of the Securities Exchange Act of 1934, this report has been signed below by the following persons on behalf of the registrant and in the capacities and on the dates indicated.

By (Signature and Title) _____

Date _____

By (Signature and Title) _____

Date _____

Rule 13b2–2. Representations and conduct in connection with the preparation of required reports and documents.

(a) No director or officer of an issuer shall, directly or indirectly:

(1) Make or cause to be made a materially false or misleading statement to an accountant in connection with; or

(2) Omit to state, or cause another person to omit to state, any material fact necessary in order to make statements made, in light of the

circumstances under which such statements were made, not misleading, to an accountant in connection with:

(i) Any audit, review or examination of the financial statements of the issuer required to be made pursuant to this subpart; or

(ii) The preparation or filing of any document or report required to be filed with the Commission pursuant to this subpart or otherwise.

(b)(1) No officer or director of an issuer, or any other person acting under the direction thereof, shall directly or indirectly take any action to coerce, manipulate, mislead, or fraudulently influence any independent public or certified public accountant engaged in the performance of an audit or review of the financial statements of that issuer that are required to be filed with the Commission pursuant to this subpart or otherwise if that person knew or should have known that such action, if successful, could result in rendering the issuer's financial statements materially misleading.

(2) For purposes of paragraphs (b)(1) and (c)(2) of this section, actions that, "if successful, could result in rendering the issuer's financial statements materially misleading" include, but are not limited to, actions taken at any time with respect to the professional engagement period to coerce, manipulate, mislead, or fraudulently influence an auditor:

(i) To issue or reissue a report on an issuer's financial statements that is not warranted in the circumstances (due to material violations of generally accepted accounting principles, generally accepted auditing standards, or other professional or regulatory standards);

(ii) Not to perform audit, review or other procedures required by generally accepted auditing standards or other professional standards;

(iii) Not to withdraw an issued report; or

(iv) Not to communicate matters to an issuer's audit committee. . . .

REGULATION 13D

Rule 13d–1. Filing of Schedules 13D and 13G

(a) Any person who, after acquiring directly or indirectly the beneficial ownership of any equity security of a class which is specified in paragraph (i) of this section, is directly or indirectly the beneficial owner of more than five percent of the class shall, within 10 days after such acquisition, file with the Commission, a statement containing the information required by Schedule 13D. . . .

(b)(1) A person who would otherwise be obligated under paragraph (a) of this section to file a statement on Schedule 13D may, in lieu thereof, file with the Commission, a short-form statement on Schedule 13G, provided, that:

(i) Such person has acquired such securities in the ordinary course of his business and not with the purpose nor with the effect of changing or influencing the control of the issuer, nor in connection with or as a participant in any transaction having such purpose or effect, including any transaction subject to Rule 13d–3(b); and

(ii) Such person is:

(A) A broker or dealer registered under section 15 of the Act;

(B) A bank as defined in section 3(a)(6) of the Act;

(C) An insurance company as defined in section 3(a)(19) of the Act;

(D) An investment company registered under section 8 of the Investment Company Act of 1940;

(E) Any person registered as an investment adviser under Section 203 of the Investment Advisers Act of 1940 or under the laws of any state;

(F) An employee benefit plan as defined in Section 3(3) of the Employee Retirement Income Security Act of 1974, as amended, 29 U.S.C. 1001 et seq. ("ERISA") that is subject to the provisions of ERISA, or any such plan that is not subject to ERISA that is maintained primarily for the benefit of the employees of a state or local government or instrumentality, or an endowment fund;

(G) A parent holding company or control person, provided the aggregate amount held directly by the parent or control person, and directly and indirectly by their subsidiaries or affiliates that are not persons specified in Rule 13d–1(b)(1)(ii)(A) through (I), does not exceed one percent of the securities of the subject class;

(H) A savings association as defined in Section 3(b) of the Federal Deposit Insurance Act (12 U.S.C. 1813);

(I) A church plan that is excluded from the definition of an investment company under section 3(c)(14) of the Investment Company Act of 1940; and

(J) A group, provided that all the members are persons specified in Rule 13d–1(b)(1)(ii)(A) through (I); and

(iii) Such person has promptly notified any other person (or group within the meaning of section 13(d)(3) of the Act) on whose behalf it holds, on a discretionary basis, securities exceeding five percent of the class, of any acquisition or transaction on behalf of such other person which might be reportable by that person under section 13(d) of the Act. This paragraph only requires notice to the account owner of information which the filing person reasonably should be expected to know and which would advise the account owner of an obligation he may have to file a statement pursuant to section 13(d) of the Act or an amendment thereto.

(2) The Schedule 13G filed pursuant to paragraph (b)(1) of this section shall be filed within 45 days after the end of the calendar year in which the person became obligated under paragraph (b)(1) of this section to report the person's beneficial ownership as of the last day of the calendar year, Provided, That it shall not be necessary to file a Schedule 13G unless the percentage of the class of equity security specified in paragraph (i) of this section beneficially owned as of the end of the calendar year is more than five percent; However, if the person's direct or indirect beneficial ownership exceeds 10 percent of the class of equity securities prior to the end of the calendar year, the initial Schedule 13G shall be filed within 10 days after the end of the first month in which the person's direct or indirect beneficial ownership exceeds 10 percent of the class of equity securities, computed as of the last day of the month....

(c) A person who would otherwise be obligated under paragraph (a) of this section to file a statement on Schedule 13D may, in lieu thereof, file with the Commission, within 10 days after an acquisition described in paragraph (a) of this section, a short-form statement on Schedule 13G. *Provided*, That the person:

(1) Has not acquired the securities with any purpose, or with the effect of, changing or influencing the control of the issuer, or in connection with or as a participant in any transaction having that purpose or effect, including any transaction subject to Rule 13d–3(b); ...

(3) Is not directly or indirectly the beneficial owner of 20 percent or more of the class....

(d) Any person who, as of the end of any calendar year, is or becomes directly or indirectly the beneficial owner of more than five percent of any equity security of a class specified in paragraph (i) of this section and who is not required to file a statement under paragraph (a) of this section by virtue of the exemption provided by Section 13(d)(6)(A) or (B) of the Act, or because the beneficial ownership was acquired prior to December 22, 1970, or because the person otherwise (except for the exemption provided by Section 13(d)(6)(C) of the Act) is not required to file a statement, shall file with the Commission, within 45 days after the end of the calendar year in which the person became obligated to report under this paragraph (d), a statement containing the information required by Schedule 13G....

(e)(1) Notwithstanding [paragraph (c)] of this section and Rule 13d–2(b), a person that has reported that it is the beneficial owner of more than five percent of a class of equity securities in a statement on Schedule 13G pursuant to paragraph ... (c) of this section, or is required to report the acquisition but has not yet filed the schedule, shall immediately become subject to Rules 13d–1(a) and 13d–2(a) and shall file a statement on Schedule 13D within 10 days if, and shall remain subject to those requirements for so long as, the person:

(i) Has acquired or holds the securities with a purpose or effect of changing or influencing control of the issuer, or in connection with or as a participant in any transaction having that purpose or effect, including any transaction subject to Rule 13d–3(b); and

(ii) Is at that time the beneficial owner of more than five percent of a class of equity securities described in Rule 13d–1(i).

(2) From the time the person has acquired or holds the securities with a purpose or effect of changing or influencing control of the issuer, or in connection with or as a participant in any transaction having that purpose or effect until the expiration of the tenth day from the date of the filing of the Schedule 13D pursuant to this section, that person shall not:

(i) Vote or direct the voting of the securities described therein; or

(ii) Acquire an additional beneficial ownership interest in any equity securities of the issuer of the securities, nor of any person controlling the issuer.

(f)(1) Notwithstanding paragraph (c) of this section and Rule 13d–2(b), persons reporting on Schedule 13G pursuant to paragraph (c) of this section shall immediately become subject to Rule 13d–1(a) and Rule 13d–2(a) and shall remain subject to those requirements for so long as, and shall file a statement on Schedule 13D within 10 days of the date on which, the person's beneficial ownership equals or exceeds 20 percent of the class of equity securities.

(2) From the time of the acquisition of 20 percent or more of the class of equity securities until the expiration of the tenth day from the date of the filing of the Schedule 13D pursuant to this section, the person shall not:

(i) Vote or direct the voting of the securities described therein, or

(ii) Acquire an additional beneficial ownership interest in any equity securities of the issuer of the securities, nor of any person controlling the issuer. . . .

(g) Any person who has reported an acquisition of securities in a statement on Schedule 13G pursuant to paragraph (b) of this section, or has become obligated to report on the Schedule 13G (Rule 13d–102) but has not yet filed the Schedule, and thereafter ceases to be a person specified in paragraph (b)(1)(ii) of this section or determines that it no longer has acquired or holds the securities in the ordinary course of business shall immediately become subject to Rule 13d–1(a) or Rule 13d–1(c) (if the person satisfies the requirements specified in Rule 13d–1(c)), and Rule 13d–2 (a), (b) or (d), and shall file, within 10 days thereafter, a statement on Schedule 13D or amendment to Schedule 13G, as applicable, if the person is a beneficial owner at that time of more than five percent of the class of equity securities. . . .

(h) Any person who has filed a Schedule 13D pursuant to paragraph [(e) or (f)] of this section may again report its beneficial ownership on Schedule 13G pursuant to [paragraph] (c) of this section provided the person qualifies thereunder, as applicable, by filing a Schedule 13G once the person determines that the provisions of paragraph [(e) or (f)] of this section no longer apply.

(i) For the purpose of this regulation, the term "equity security" means any equity security of a class which is registered pursuant to section 12 of that Act, or any equity security of any insurance company which would have been required to be so registered except for the exemption contained in section 12(g)(2)(G) of the Act, or any equity security issued by a closed-end investment company registered under the Investment Company Act of 1940; *Provided,* Such term shall not include securities of a class of non-voting securities....

(k)(1) Whenever two or more persons are required to file a statement containing the information required by Schedule 13D or Schedule 13G with respect to the same securities, only one statement need be filed: provided, that:

(i) Each person on whose behalf the statement is filed is individually eligible to use the Schedule on which the information is filed;

(ii) Each person on whose behalf the statement is filed is responsible for the timely filing of such statement and any amendments thereto, and for the completeness and accuracy of the information concerning such person contained therein; such person is not responsible for the completeness or accuracy of the information concerning the other persons making the filing, unless such person knows or has reason to believe that such information is inaccurate; and

(iii) Such statement identifies all such persons, contains the required information with regard to each such person, indicates that such statement is filed on behalf of all such persons, and includes, as an exhibit, their agreement in writing that such a statement is filed on behalf of each of them.

(2) A group's filing obligation may be satisfied either by a single joint filing or by each of the group's members making an individual filing. If the group's members elect to make their own filings, each such filing should identify all members of the group but the information provided concerning the other persons making the filing need only reflect information which the filing person knows or has reason to know.

Rule 13d–2.   Filing of Amendments to Schedules 13D or 13G

(a) If any material change occurs in the facts set forth in the Schedule 13D required by Rule 13d–1(a), including, but not limited to, any material increase or decrease in the percentage of the class beneficially owned, the person or persons who were required to file the statement shall promptly file or cause to be filed with the Commission an amendment disclosing that change. An acquisition or disposition of beneficial ownership of securities in an amount equal to one percent or more of the class of securities shall be deemed "material" for purposes of this section; acquisitions or dispositions of less than those amounts may be material, depending upon the facts and circumstances. . . .

Rule 13d–3. Determination of Beneficial Owner

(a) For the purposes of sections 13(d) and 13(g) of the Act a beneficial owner of a security includes any person who, directly or indirectly, through any contract, arrangement, understanding, relationship, or otherwise has or shares:

(1) Voting power which includes the power to vote, or to direct the voting of, such security; and/or,

(2) Investment power which includes the power to dispose, or to direct the disposition of, such security.

(b) Any person who, directly or indirectly, creates or uses a trust, proxy, power of attorney, pooling arrangement or any other contract, arrangement, or device with the purpose or effect of divesting such person of beneficial ownership of a security or preventing the vesting of such beneficial ownership as part of a plan or scheme to evade the reporting requirements of section 13(d) or (g) of the Act shall be deemed for purposes of such sections to be the beneficial owner of such security.

(c) All securities of the same class beneficially owned by a person, regardless of the form which such beneficial ownership takes, shall be aggregated in calculating the number of shares beneficially owned by such person.

(d) Notwithstanding the provisions of paragraphs (a) and (c) of this rule:

(1)(i) A person shall be deemed to be the beneficial owner of a security, subject to the provisions of paragraph (b) of this rule, if that person has the right to acquire beneficial ownership of such security, as defined in Rule 13d–3(a) . . . within sixty days, including but not limited to any right to acquire: (A) Through the exercise of any option, warrant or right; (B) through the conversion of a security; (C) pursuant to the power to revoke a trust, discretionary account, or similar arrangement; or (D) pursuant to the automatic termination of a trust, discretionary account or similar arrangement; provided, however, any person who acquires a security or power specified in paragraphs (d)(1)(i)(A), (B) or (C), of this section, with the purpose or effect of changing or influencing the control of the issuer, or in connection with or as a participant in any transaction having such purpose or effect, immediately upon such acquisition shall be deemed to be the beneficial owner of the securities which may be acquired through the exercise or conversion of such security or power. Any securities not outstanding which are subject to such options, warrants, rights or conversion privileges shall be deemed to be outstanding for the purpose of computing the percentage of outstanding securities of the class owned by such person but shall not be deemed to be outstanding for the purpose of computing the percentage of the class [owned] by any other person.

(ii) Paragraph (d)(1)(i) of this section remains applicable for the purpose of determining the obligation to file with respect to the underlying security even though the option, warrant, right or convertible security is of a class of equity security, as defined in Rule 13d–1(i), and may therefore give rise to a separate obligation to file....

(2) A member of a national securities exchange shall not be deemed to be a beneficial owner of securities held directly or indirectly by it on behalf of another person solely because such member is the record holder of such securities and, pursuant to the rules of such exchange, may direct the vote of such securities, without instruction, on other than contested matters or matters that may affect substantially the rights or privileges of the holders of the securities to be voted, but is otherwise precluded by the rules of such exchange from voting without instruction.

(3) A person who in the ordinary course of his business is a pledgee of securities under a written pledge agreement shall not be deemed to be the beneficial owner of such pledged securities until the pledgee has taken all formal steps necessary which are required to declare a default and determines that the power to vote or to direct the vote or to dispose or to direct the disposition of such pledged securities will be exercised, provided, that:

(i) The [pledge] agreement is bona fide and was not entered into with the purpose nor with the effect of changing or influencing the control of the issuer, nor in connection with any transaction having such purpose or effect, including any transaction subject to Rule 13d–3(b);

(ii) The pledgee is a person specified in Rule 13d–1(b)(ii), including persons meeting the conditions set forth in paragraph (G) thereof; and

(iii) The [pledge] agreement, prior to default, does not grant to the pledgee;

(A) The power to vote or to direct the vote of the pledged securities; or

(B) The power to dispose or direct the disposition of the pledged securities, other than the grant of such power(s) pursuant to a pledge agreement under which credit is extended subject to regulation T (12 CFR 220.1 to 220.8) and in which the pledgee is a broker or dealer registered under section 15 of the act.

(4) A person engaged in business as an underwriter of securities who acquires securities through his participation in good faith in a firm commitment underwriting registered under the Securities Act of 1933 shall not be deemed to be the beneficial owner of such securities until the expiration of forty days after the date of such acquisition.

Rule 13d–4. Disclaimer of Beneficial Ownership

Any person may expressly declare in any statement filed that the filing of such statement shall not be construed as an admission that such person is, for the purposes of sections 13(d) or 13(g) of the Act, the beneficial owner of any securities covered by the statement.

Rule 13d–5. Acquisition of Securities

(a) A person who becomes a beneficial owner of securities shall be deemed to have acquired such securities for purposes of section 13(d)(1) of the Act, whether such acquisition was through purchase or otherwise. . . .

(b)(1) When two or more persons agree to act together for the purpose of acquiring, holding, voting or disposing of equity securities of an issuer, the group formed thereby shall be deemed to have acquired beneficial ownership, for purposes of sections 13(d) and (g) of the Act, as of the date of such agreement, of all equity securities of that issuer beneficially owned by any such persons. . . .

Rule 13d–7. Dissemination

One copy of the Schedule filed pursuant to Rules 13d–1 and 13d–2 shall be sent to the issuer of the security at its principal executive office, by registered or certified mail. A copy of Schedules filed pursuant to Rules 13d–1(a) and 13d–2(a) shall also be sent to each national securities exchange where the security is traded.

SCHEDULE 13D. INFORMATION TO BE INCLUDED IN STATEMENTS FILED PURSUANT TO RULE 13d–1(a) and ... RULE 13d–2(a)

(Name of Issuer)

(Title of Class of Securities)

(CUSIP Number)

(Name, Address and Telephone Number of Person Authorized
to Receive Notices and Communications)

(Date of Event Which Requires Filing of This Statement). . . .

GENERAL INSTRUCTIONS ...

Item 1.   Security and Issuer.   State the title of the class of equity securities to which this statement relates and the name and address of the principal executive offices of the issuer of such securities.

Item 2.   Identity and Background. If the person filing this statement ... is a corporation, general partnership, limited partnership, syndicate or other group of persons, state its name, the state or other place of its organization, its principal business, the address of its principal office and the information required by (d) and (e) of this Item. If the person filing this statement or any person enumerated in Instruction C is a natural person, provide the information specified in (a) through (f) of this Item with respect to such person(s).

(a) Name;

(b) Residence or business address;

(c) Present principal occupation or employment and the name, principal business and address of any corporation or other organization in which such employment is conducted;

(d) Whether or not, during the last five years, such person has been convicted in a criminal proceeding (excluding traffic violations or similar misdemeanors) and, if so, give the dates, nature of conviction, name and location of court, any penalty imposed, or other disposition of the case;

(e) Whether or not, during the last five years, such person was a party to a civil proceeding of a judicial or administrative body of competent jurisdiction and as a result of such proceeding was or is subject to a judgment, decree or final order enjoining future violations of, or prohibiting or mandating activities subject to, federal or state securities laws or finding any violation with respect to such laws; and, if so, identify and describe such proceedings and summarize the terms of such judgment, decree or final order; and

(f) Citizenship.

Item 3. Source and Amount of Funds or Other Consideration. State the source and the amount of funds or other consideration used or to be used in making the purchases, and if any part of the purchase price is or will be represented by funds or other consideration borrowed or otherwise obtained for the purpose of acquiring, holding, trading or voting the securities, a description of the transaction and the names of the parties thereto. Where material, such information should also be provided with respect to prior acquisitions not previously reported pursuant to this regulation. If the source of all or any part of the funds is a loan made in the ordinary course of business by a bank ..., the name of the bank shall not be made available to the public if the person at the time of filing the statement so requests in writing and files such request, naming such bank, with the Secretary of the Commission. If the securities were acquired other than by purchase, describe the method of acquisition.

Item 4. Purpose of Transaction. State the purpose or purposes of the acquisition of securities of the issuer. Describe any plans or proposals which the reporting persons may have which relate to or would result in:

(a) The acquisition by any person of additional securities of the issuer, or the disposition of securities of the issuer;

(b) An extraordinary corporate transaction, such as a merger, reorganization or liquidation, involving the issuer or any of its subsidiaries;

(c) A sale or transfer of a material amount of assets of the issuer or any of its subsidiaries;

(d) Any change in the present board of directors or management of the issuer, including any plans or proposals to change the number or term of directors or to fill any existing vacancies on the board;

(e) Any material change in the present capitalization or dividend policy of the issuer;

(f) Any other material change in the issuer's business or corporate structure . . . ;

(g) Changes in the issuer's charter, bylaws or instruments corresponding thereto or other actions which may impede the acquisition of control of the issuer by any person;

(h) Causing a class of securities of the issuer to be delisted from a national securities exchange or to cease to be authorized to be quoted in an inter-dealer quotation system of a registered national securities association;

(i) A class of equity securities of the issuer becoming eligible for termination of registration pursuant to section 12(g)(4) of the Act; or

(j) Any action similar to any of those enumerated above.

Item 5. Interest in Securities of the Issuer. (a) State the aggregate number and percentage of the class of securities identified pursuant to Item 1 . . . beneficially owned (identifying those shares which there is a right to acquire) by each person named in Item 2. The above mentioned information should also be furnished with respect to persons who, together with any of the persons named in Item 2, comprise a group within the meaning of section 13(d)(3) of the Act;

(b) For each person named in response to paragraph (a), indicate the number of shares as to which there is sole power to vote or to direct the vote, sole power to dispose or to direct the disposition, or shared power to dispose or to direct the disposition. Provide the applicable information required by Item 2 with respect to each person with whom the power to vote or to direct the vote or to dispose or direct the disposition is shared;

(c) Describe any transactions in the class of securities reported on that were effected during the past sixty days or since the most recent filing of Schedule 13D ... whichever is less, by the persons named in response to paragraph (a). ...

Item 6. Contracts, Arrangements, Understandings or Relationships With Respect to Securities of the Issuer. Describe any contracts, arrangements, understandings or relationships (legal or otherwise) among the persons named in Item 2 and between such persons and any person with respect to any securities of the issuer, including but not limited to transfer or voting of any of the securities, finder's fees, joint ventures, loan or option arrangements, puts or calls, guarantees of profits, division of profits or loss, or the giving or withholding of proxies, naming the persons with whom such contracts, arrangements, understandings or relationships have been entered into. Include such information for any of the securities that are pledged or otherwise subject to a contingency the occurrence of which would give another person voting power or investment power over such securities except that disclosure of standard default and similar provisions contained in loan agreements need not be included. . . .

SCHEDULE 13G. INFORMATION TO BE INCLUDED IN STATEMENTS FILED PURSUANT TO RULE 13(d)(1)[c] . . .

SECURITIES AND EXCHANGE COMMISSION
Washington, D. C. 20549
SCHEDULE 13G
Under the Securities Exchange Act of 1934
(Amendment No. ___)

_____
(Name of Issuer)

_____
(Title of Class of Securities)

_____
(CUSIP Number)

_____
(Date of Event Which Requires Filing of This Statement)

Instructions . . .

Item 3 . . .

If this statement is filed pursuant to Rule 13d–1(c), check this box [   ].

Item 4

Ownership

Provide the following information regarding the aggregate number and percentage of the class of securities of the issuer. . . .

1978

(a) Amount beneficially owned: _____

(b) Percent of class: _____

(c) Number of shares as to which the person has: _____

    (i) Sole power to vote or to direct the vote _____

    (ii) Shared power to vote or to direct the vote _____

    (iii) Sole power to dispose or to direct the disposition of _____

    (iv) Shared power to dispose or to direct the disposition of ___

Item 10

Certifications. . . .

(b) The following certification shall be included if the statement is filed pursuant to Rule 13d–1(c):

By signing below I certify that, to the best of my knowledge and belief, the securities referred to above were not acquired and are not held for the purpose of or with the effect of changing or influencing the control of the issuer of the securities and were not acquired and are not held in connection with or as a participant in any transaction having that purpose or effect.

Rule 13e–1. Purchase of Securities by the Issuer During a Third–Party Tender Offer

An issuer that has received notice that it is the subject of a tender offer made under Section 14(d)(1) of the Act, that has commenced under Rule 14d–2 must not purchase any of its equity securities during the tender offer unless the issuer first:

(a) Files a statement with the Commission containing the following information:

(1) The title and number of securities to be purchased;

(2) The names of the persons or classes of persons from whom the issuer will purchase the securities;

(3) The name of any exchange, inter-dealer quotation system or any other market on or through which the securities will be purchased;

(4) The purpose of the purchase;

(5) Whether the issuer will retire the securities, hold the securities in its treasury, or dispose of the securities. If the issuer intends to dispose of the securities, describe how it intends to do so; and

(6) The source and amount of funds or other consideration to be used to make the purchase. If the issuer borrows any funds or other consideration to make the purchase or enters any agreement for the purpose of acquiring, holding, or trading the securities, describe the transaction and agreement and identify the parties; and

(b) Pays the fee required . . . when it files the initial statement.

(c) This section does not apply to periodic repurchases in connection with an employee benefit plan or other similar plan of the issuer so long as the purchases are made in the ordinary course and not in response to the tender offer.

Rule 13e–3.   Going Private Transactions by Certain Issuers or Their Affiliates

(a) *Definitions*.   Unless indicated otherwise or the context otherwise requires, all terms used in this section and in Schedule 13E–3 . . . shall have the same meaning as in the Act or elsewhere in the General Rules and Regulations thereunder.   In addition, the following definitions apply:

(1) An "affiliate" of an issuer is a person that directly or indirectly through one or more intermediaries controls, is controlled by, or is under common control with such issuer.   For the purposes of this section only, a person who is not an affiliate of an issuer at the commencement of such person's tender offer for a class of equity securities of such issuer will not be deemed an affiliate of such issuer prior to the stated termination of such tender offer and any extensions thereof;

(2) The term "purchase" means any acquisition for value including, but not limited to, (i) any acquisition pursuant to the dissolution of an issuer subsequent to the sale or other disposition of substantially all the assets of such issuer to its affiliate, (ii) any acquisition pursuant to a merger, (iii) any acquisition of fractional interests in connection with a reverse stock split, and (iv) any acquisition subject to the control of an issuer or an affiliate of such issuer;

(3) A "Rule 13e–3 transaction" is any transaction or series of transactions involving one or more of the transactions described in paragraph (a)(3)(i) of this section which has either a reasonable likelihood or a purpose of producing, either directly or indirectly, any of the effects described in paragraph (a)(3)(ii) of this section;

(i) The transactions referred to in paragraph (a)(3) of this section are:

(A) A purchase of any equity security by the issuer of such security or by an affiliate of such issuer;

(B) A tender offer for or request or invitation for tenders of any equity security made by the issuer of such class of securities or by an affiliate of such issuer; or

(C) A solicitation subject to Regulation 14A . . . of any proxy, consent or authorization of, or a distribution subject to Regulation 14C . . . of information statements to, any equity security holder by the issuer of the class of securities or by an affiliate of such issuer, in connection with: a merger, consolidation, reclassification, recapitalization, reorganization or similar corporate transaction of an issuer or between an issuer (or its subsidiaries) and its affiliate; a sale of substantially all the assets of an issuer to its affiliate or group of affiliates; or a reverse stock split of any class of equity securities of the issuer involving the purchase of fractional interests.

(ii) The effects referred to in paragraph (a)(3) of this section are:

(A) Causing any class of equity securities of the issuer which is subject to section 12(g) or section 15(d) of the Act to be held of record by less than 300 persons; or

(B) Causing any class of equity securities of the issuer which is either listed on a national securities exchange or authorized to be quoted in an inter-dealer quotation system of a registered national securities association to be neither listed on any national securities exchange nor authorized to be quoted on an inter-dealer quotation system of any registered national securities association. . . .

(b) *Application of section to an issuer (or an affiliate of such issuer) subject to section 12 of the Act.* (1) It shall be a fraudulent, deceptive or manipulative act or practice, in connection with a Rule 13e–3 transaction, for an issuer which has a class of equity securities registered pursuant to section 12 of the Act or which is a closed-end investment company registered under the Investment Company Act of 1940, or an affiliate of such issuer, directly or indirectly

(i) To employ any device, scheme or artifice to defraud any person;

(ii) To make any untrue statement of a material fact or to omit to state a material fact necessary in order to make the statements made, in light of the circumstances under which they were made, not misleading; or

(iii) To engage in any act, practice or course of business which operates or would operate as a fraud or deceit upon any person.

(2) As a means reasonably designed to prevent fraudulent, deceptive or manipulative acts or practices in connection with any Rule 13e–3 transaction, it shall be unlawful for an issuer which has a class of equity securities registered pursuant to section 12 of the Act, or an affiliate of such issuer, to engage, directly or indirectly, in a Rule 13e–3 transaction unless:

(i) Such issuer or affiliate complies with the requirements of paragraphs (d), (e) and (f) of this section; and

(ii) The Rule 13e–3 transaction is not in violation of paragraph (b)(1) of this section. . . .

(d) *Material required to be filed.* The issuer or affiliate engaging in a Rule 13e–3 transaction must file with the Commission:

(1) A Schedule 13E–3, including all exhibits;

(2) An amendment to Schedule 13E–3 reporting promptly any material changes in the information set forth in the schedule previously filed; and

(3) A final amendment to Schedule 13E–3 reporting promptly the results of the Rule 13e–3 transaction.

(e) *Disclosure of information to security holders.*

(1) In addition to disclosing the information required by any other applicable rule or regulation under the federal securities laws, the issuer or affiliate engaging in a Rule 13e–3 transaction must disclose to security holders of the class that is the subject of the transaction, as specified in paragraph (f) of this section, the following:

(i) The information required by Item 1 of Schedule 13E–3 (Summary Term Sheet);

(ii) The information required by Items 7, 8 and 9 of Schedule 13E–3, which must be prominently disclosed in a "Special Factors" section in the front of the disclosure document;

(iii) A prominent legend on the outside front cover page that indicates that neither the Securities and Exchange Commission nor any state securities commission has: approved or disapproved of the transaction; passed upon the merits or fairness of the transaction; or passed upon the adequacy or accuracy of the disclosure in the document. The legend also must make it clear that any representation to the contrary is a criminal offense;

(iv) The information concerning appraisal rights required by Item 1016(f) of [Regulation S–K]; and

(v) The information required by the remaining items of Schedule 13E–3, except for Item 1016 of [Regulation S–K] (exhibits), or a fair and adequate summary of the information. . . .

Rule 13e–4.   Tender Offers by Issuers

(a) *Definitions.*   Unless the context otherwise requires, all terms used in this section and in Schedule TO . . . shall have the same meaning as in the Act or elsewhere in the General Rules and Regulations thereunder.   In addition, the following definitions shall apply:

(1) The term "issuer" means any issuer which has a class of equity security registered pursuant to section 12 of the Act, or which is required to file periodic reports pursuant to section 15(d) of the Act, or which is a closed-end investment company registered under the Investment Company Act of 1940.

(2) The term "issuer tender offer" refers to a tender offer for, or a request or invitation for tenders of, any class of equity security, made by the issuer of such class of equity security or by an affiliate of such issuer. . . .

(b) *Filing, disclosure and dissemination.* As soon as practicable on the date of commencement of the issuer tender offer, the issuer or affiliate making the issuer tender offer must comply with:

(1) The filing requirements of paragraph (c)(2) of this section;

(2) The disclosure requirements of paragraph (d)(1) of this section; and

(3) The dissemination requirements of paragraph (e) of this section.

(c) *Material required to be filed.* The issuer or affiliate making the issuer tender offer must file with the Commission:

(1) All written communications made by the issuer or affiliate relating to the issuer tender offer, from and including the first public announcement, as soon as practicable on the date of the communication;

(2) A Schedule TO, including all exhibits;

(3) An amendment to Schedule TO reporting promptly any material changes in the information set forth in the schedule previously filed; and

(4) A final amendment to Schedule TO reporting promptly the results of the issuer tender offer.

Instructions to Rule 13e–4(c): . . .

5. "Public announcement" is any oral or written communication by the issuer, affiliate or any person authorized to act on their behalf that is reasonably designed to, or has the effect of, informing the public or security holders in general about the issuer tender offer.

(d) *Disclosure of tender offer information to security holders.*

(1) The issuer or affiliate making the issuer tender offer must disclose, in a manner prescribed by paragraph (e)(1) of this section, the following:

(i) The information required by Item 1 of Schedule TO (summary term sheet); and

(ii) The information required by the remaining items of Schedule TO for issuer tender offers, except for Item 12 (exhibits), or a fair and adequate summary of the information.

(2) If there are any material changes in the information previously disclosed to security holders, the issuer or affiliate must disclose the changes promptly to security holders in a manner specified in paragraph (e)(3) of this section.

(3) If the issuer or affiliate disseminates the issuer tender offer by means of summary publication as described in paragraph (e)(1)(iii) of this section, the summary advertisement must not include a transmittal

letter that would permit security holders to tender securities sought in the offer and must disclose at least the following information:

(i) The identity of the issuer or affiliate making the issuer tender offer;

(ii) The information required by 1004(a)(1) and 1006(a) of [Regulation S–K];

(iii) Instructions on how security holders can obtain promptly a copy of the statement required by paragraph (d)(1) of this section, at the issuer or affiliate's expense; and

(iv) A statement that the information contained in the statement required by paragraph (d)(1) of this section is incorporated by reference.

(e) *Dissemination of tender offers to security holders.* An issuer tender offer will be deemed to be published, sent or given to security holders if the issuer or affiliate making the issuer tender offer complies fully with one or more of the methods described in this section.

(1) For issuer tender offers in which the consideration offered consists solely of cash and/or securities exempt from registration under section 3 of the Securities Act of 1933:

(i) *Dissemination of cash issuer tender offers by long-form publication*: By making adequate publication of the information required by paragraph (d)(1) of this section in a newspaper or newspapers, on the date of commencement of the issuer tender offer.

(ii) *Dissemination of any issuer tender offer by use of stockholder and other lists*:

(A) By mailing or otherwise furnishing promptly a statement containing the information required by paragraph (d)(1) of this section to each security holder whose name appears on the most recent stockholder list of the issuer;

(B) By contacting each participant on the most recent security position listing of any clearing agency within the possession or access of the issuer or affiliate making the issuer tender offer, and making inquiry of each participant as to the approximate number of beneficial owners of the securities sought in the offer that are held by the participant;

(C) By furnishing to each participant a sufficient number of copies of the statement required by paragraph (d)(1) of this section for transmittal to the beneficial owners; and

(D) By agreeing to reimburse each participant promptly for its reasonable expenses incurred in forwarding the statement to beneficial owners.

(iii) *Dissemination of certain cash issuer tender offers by summary publication*:

(A) If the issuer tender offer is not subject to Rule 13e–3, by making adequate publication of a summary advertisement containing the information required by paragraph (d)(3) of this section in a newspaper or newspapers, on the date of commencement of the issuer tender offer; and

(B) By mailing or otherwise furnishing promptly the statement required by paragraph (d)(1) of this section and a transmittal letter to any security holder who requests a copy of the statement or transmittal letter.

Instruction to paragraph (e)(1): . . .

(2) For tender offers in which the consideration consists solely or partially of securities registered under the Securities Act of 1933, a registration statement containing all of the required information, including pricing information, has been filed and a preliminary prospectus or a prospectus that meets the requirements of Section 10(a) of the Securities Act, including a letter of transmittal, is delivered to security holders. However, for going-private transactions (as defined by Rule 13e–3) and roll-up transactions (as described by Item 901 of Regulation S–K), a registration statement registering the securities to be offered must have become effective and only a prospectus that meets the requirements of Section 10(a) of the Securities Act may be delivered to security holders on the date of commencement.

(f) *Manner of making tender offer.* (1) The issuer tender offer, unless withdrawn, shall remain open until the expiration of:

(i) At least twenty business days from its commencement; and

(ii) At least ten business days from the date that notice of an increase or decrease in the percentage of the class of securities being sought or the consideration offered or the dealer's soliciting fee to be given is first published, sent or given to security holders.

Provided, however, That, for purposes of this paragraph, the acceptance for payment by the issuer or affiliate of an additional amount of securities not to exceed two percent of the class of securities that is the subject of the tender offer shall not be deemed to be an increase. For purposes of this paragraph, the percentage of a class of securities shall be calculated in accordance with section 14(d)(3) of the Act.

(2) The issuer or affiliate making the issuer tender offer shall permit securities tendered pursuant to the issuer tender offer to be withdrawn:

(i) At any time during the period such issuer tender offer remains open; and

(ii) If not yet accepted for payment, after the expiration of forty business days from the commencement of the issuer tender offer.

(3) If the issuer or affiliate makes a tender offer for less than all of the outstanding equity securities of a class, and if a greater number of securities is tendered pursuant thereto than the issuer or affiliate is bound or willing to take up and pay for, the securities taken up and paid for shall be taken up and paid for as nearly as may be pro rata, disregarding fractions, according to the number of securities tendered by each security holder during the period such offer remains open; *Provided, however,* That this provision shall not prohibit the issuer or affiliate making the issuer tender offer from:

(i) Accepting all securities tendered by persons who own, beneficially or of record, an aggregate of not more than a specified number which is less than one hundred shares of such security and who tender all their securities, before prorating securities tendered by others; or

(ii) Accepting by lot securities tendered by security holders who tender all securities held by them and who, when tendering their securities, elect to have either all or none or at least a minimum amount or none accepted, if the issuer or affiliate first accepts all securities tendered by security holders who do not so elect;

(4) In the event the issuer or affiliate making the issuer tender increases the consideration offered after the issuer tender offer has commenced, such issuer or affiliate shall pay such increased consideration to all security holders whose tendered securities are accepted for payment by such issuer or affiliate.

(5) The issuer or affiliate making the tender offer shall either pay the consideration offered, or return the tendered securities, promptly after the termination or withdrawal of the tender offer.

(6) Until the expiration of at least ten business days after the date of termination of the issuer tender offer, neither the issuer nor any affiliate shall make any purchases, otherwise than pursuant to the tender offer, of:

(i) Any security which is the subject of the issuer tender offer, or any security of the same class and series, or any right to purchase any such securities; and

(ii) In the case of an issuer tender offer which is an exchange offer, any security being offered pursuant to such exchange offer, or any security of the same class and series, or any right to purchase any such security.

(7) The time periods for the minimum offering periods pursuant to this section shall be computed on a concurrent as opposed to a consecutive basis.

(8) No issuer or affiliate shall make a tender offer unless:

(i) The tender offer is open to all security holders of the class of securities subject to the tender offer; and

(ii) The consideration paid to any security holder pursuant to the tender offer is the highest consideration paid to any other security holder during such tender offer....

(j)(1) It shall be a fraudulent, deceptive or manipulative act or practice, in connection with an issuer tender offer, for an issuer or an affiliate of such issuer, in connection with an issuer tender offer:

(i) To employ any device, scheme or artifice to defraud any person;

(ii) To make any untrue statement of a material fact or to omit to state a material fact necessary in order to make the statements made, in the light of the circumstances under which they were made, not misleading; or

(iii) To engage in any act, practice or course of business which operates or would operate as a fraud or deceit upon any person.

(2) As a means reasonably designed to prevent fraudulent, deceptive or manipulative acts or practices in connection with any issuer tender offer, it shall be unlawful for an issuer or an affiliate of such issuer to make an issuer tender offer unless:

(i) Such issuer or affiliate complies with the requirements of paragraphs (b), (c), (d), (e) and (f) of this section; and

(ii) The issuer tender offer is not in violation of paragraph (j)(1) of this section.

SCHEDULE 13E-3. TRANSACTION STATEMENT UNDER SECTION 13(e)....

(Name of the Issuer)

(Name of Person(s) Filing Statement)

(Title of Class of Securities)

(CUSIP Number of Class of Securities)

(Name, address and telephone number of person authorized to receive notices and communications on behalf of persons filing statement) ...

General Instructions....

C. If the statement is filed by a general or limited partnership, syndicate or other group, the information called for by Items 3, 5, 6, 10 and 11 must be given with respect to: (i) each partner of the general partnership; (ii) each partner who is, or functions as, a general partner of the limited partnership; (iii) each member of the syndicate or group; and (iv) each person controlling the partner or member. If the statement is filed by a corporation ... the information called for by the items specified above must be given with respect to: (a) each executive officer and director of the corporation; (b) each person controlling the corporation; and (c) each executive officer and director of any corporation or other person ultimately in control of the corporation....

Item 1. Summary Term Sheet

Furnish the information required by Item 1001 of Regulation M–A unless information is disclosed to security holders in a prospectus that meets the requirements of Rule 421(d) [under the Securities Act].

Item 2. Subject Company Information

Furnish the information required by Item 1002(a) through (c) of Regulation M-A.

Item 3. Identity and Background of Filing Person

Furnish the information required by Item 1003(a) through (c) of Regulation M-A.

Item 4. Terms of the Transaction

Furnish the information required by Item 1004(a) of Regulation M-A.

Item 5. Past Contacts, Transactions, Negotiations and Agreements

Furnish the information required by Item 1005(a) and (b) of Regulation M-A.

Item 6. Purposes of the Transaction and Plans or Proposals

Furnish the information required by Item 1006(a) and (c)(1) through (7) of Regulation M-A.

Item 7. Purposes, Alternatives, Reasons and Effects

Furnish the information required by Item 1013 of Regulation M-A.

Item 8. Fairness of the Transaction

Furnish the information required by Item 1014 of Regulation M-A.

Item 9. Reports, Opinions, Appraisals and Negotiations

Furnish the information required by Item 1015 of Regulation M-A.

Item 10. Source and Amounts of Funds or Other Consideration

Furnish the information required by Item 1007 of Regulation M-A.

Item 11. Interest in Securities of the Subject Company

Furnish the information required by Item 1008 of Regulation M-A.

Item 12. The Solicitation or Recommendation

Furnish the information required by Item 1012(d) and (e) of Regulation M-A.

Item 13. Financial Statements

Furnish the information required by Item 1010(a) through (b) of Regulation M-A for the issuer of the subject class of securities.

Item 14. Persons/Assets, Retained, Employed, Compensated or Used

Furnish the information required by Item 1009 of Regulation M–A.

Item 15. Additional Information

Furnish the information required by Item 1011(b) of Regulation M–A.

Item 16. Exhibits

File as an exhibit to the Schedule all documents specified in Item 1016(a) through (d), (f) and (g) of Regulation M–A....

REGULATION 14A: SOLICITATION OF PROXIES

Rule 14a–1. Definitions

Unless the context otherwise requires, all terms used in this regulation have the same meanings as in the Act or elsewhere in the general rules and regulations thereunder. In addition, the following definitions apply unless the context otherwise requires:

(a) *Associate.* The term "associate," used to indicate a relationship with any person, means:

(1) Any corporation or organization (other than the registrant or a majority owned subsidiary of the registrant) of which such person is an officer or partner or is, directly or indirectly, the beneficial owner of 10 percent or more of any class of equity securities;

(2) Any trust or other estate in which such person has a substantial beneficial interest or as to which such person serves as trustee or in a similar fiduciary capacity; and

(3) Any relative or spouse of such person, or any relative of such spouse, who has the same home as such person or who is a director or officer of the registrant or any of its parents or subsidiaries....

(f) *Proxy.* The term "proxy" includes every proxy, consent or authorization within the meaning of section 14(a) of the Act. The consent or authorization may take the form of failure to object or to dissent.

(g) *Proxy statement.* The term "proxy statement" means the statement required by Rule 14a–3(a) whether or not contained in a single document....

(j) *Registrant.* The term "registrant" means the issuer of the securities in respect of which proxies are to be solicited....

(k) *Respondent bank.* For purposes of Rules 14a–13, 14b–1 and 14b–2, the term "respondent bank" means any bank, association or other entity that exercises fiduciary powers which holds securities on behalf of beneficial owners and deposits such securities for safekeeping with another bank, association or other entity that exercises fiduciary powers.

(*l*) *Solicitation.* (1) The terms "solicit" and "solicitation" include:

(i) Any request for a proxy whether or not accompanied by or included in a form of proxy;

(ii) Any request to execute or not to execute, or to revoke, a proxy; or

(iii) The furnishing of a form of proxy or other communication to security holders under circumstances reasonably calculated to result in the procurement, withholding or revocation of a proxy.

(2) The terms do not apply, however, to:

(i) The furnishing of a form of proxy to a security holder upon the unsolicited request of such security holder;

(ii) The performance by the registrant of acts required by Rule 14a–7;

(iii) The performance by any person of ministerial acts on behalf of a person soliciting a proxy; or

(iv) A communication by a security holder who does not otherwise engage in a proxy solicitation (other than a solicitation exempt under Rule 14a–2) stating how the security holder intends to vote and the reasons therefor, provided that the communication:

(A) is made by means of speeches in public forums, press releases, published or broadcast opinions, statements, or advertisements appearing in a broadcast media, or newspaper, magazine or other bona fide publication disseminated on a regular basis,

(B) is directed to persons to whom the security holder owes a fiduciary duty in connection with the voting of securities of a registrant held by the security holder, or

(C) is made in response to unsolicited requests for additional information with respect to a prior communication by the security holder made pursuant to this paragraph (*l*)(2)(iv).

Rule 14a–2. Solicitations to Which Rule 14a–3 to Rule 14a–15 Apply

Rules 14a–3 to 14a–15, except as specified below, apply to every solicitation of a proxy with respect to securities registered pursuant to

Section 12 of the Act whether or not trading in such securities has been suspended. To the extent specified below, certain of these sections also apply to roll-up transactions that do not involve an entity with securities registered pursuant to Section 12 of the Act.

(a) Rules 14a–3 to 14a–15 do not apply to the following:

(1) Any solicitation by a person in respect to securities carried in his name or in the name of his nominee (otherwise than as voting trustee) or held in his custody, if such person—

(i) Receives no commission or remuneration for such solicitation, directly or indirectly, other than reimbursement of reasonable expenses,

(ii) Furnishes promptly to the person solicited (or such person's household in accordance with Rule 14a–3(e)(i)) a copy of all soliciting material with respect to the same subject matter or meeting received from all persons who shall furnish copies thereof for such purpose and who shall, if requested, defray the reasonable expenses to be incurred in forwarding such material, and

(iii) In addition, does no more than impartially instruct the person solicited to forward a proxy to the person, if any, to whom the person solicited desires to give a proxy, or impartially request from the person solicited instructions as to the authority to be conferred by the proxy and state that a proxy will be given if no instructions are received by a certain date.

(2) Any solicitation by a person in respect of securities of which he is the beneficial owner....

(6) Any solicitation through the medium of a newspaper advertisement which informs security holders of a source from which they may obtain copies of a proxy statement, form of proxy and any other soliciting material and does no more than:

(i) Name the registrant,

(ii) State the reason for the advertisement, and

(iii) Identify the proposal or proposals to be acted upon by security holders.

(b) Rules 14a–3 to 14a–6 (other than Rules 14a–6(g)), 14a–8, and 14a–10 to 14a–15 do not apply to the following:

(1) Any solicitation by or on behalf of any person who does not, at any time during such solicitation, seek directly or indirectly, either on its own or another's behalf, the power to act as proxy for a security holder and does not furnish or otherwise request, or act on behalf of a person who furnishes or requests, a form of revocation, abstention, consent or authorization. *Provided, however,* that the exemption set forth in this paragraph shall not apply to:

(i) the registrant or an affiliate or associate of the registrant (other than an officer or director or any person serving in a similar capacity);

(ii) an officer or director of the registrant or any person serving in a similar capacity engaging in a solicitation financed directly or indirectly by the registrant;

(iii) an officer, director, affiliate or associate of a person that is ineligible to rely on the exemption set forth in this paragraph (other than persons specified in paragraph (b)(1)(i) of this section), or any person serving in a similar capacity;

(iv) any nominee for whose election as a director proxies are solicited;

(v) any person soliciting in opposition to a merger, recapitalization, reorganization, sale of assets or other extraordinary transaction recommended or approved by the board of directors of the registrant who is proposing or intends to propose an alternative transaction to which such person or one of its affiliates is a party;

(vi) any person who is required to report beneficial ownership of the registrant's equity securities on a Schedule 13D, unless such person has filed a Schedule 13D and has not disclosed pursuant to Item 4 thereto an intent, or reserved the right, to engage in a control transaction, or any contested solicitation for the election of directors;

(vii) Any person who received compensation from an ineligible person directly related to the solicitation of proxies, other than pursuant to Rule 14a–13; . . .

(ix) any person who, because of a substantial interest in the subject matter of the solicitation, is likely to receive a benefit from a successful solicitation that would not be shared pro rata by all other holders of the same class of securities, other than a benefit arising from the person's employment with the registrant; and

(x) any person acting on behalf of any of the foregoing.

(2) Any solicitation made otherwise than on behalf of the registrant where the total number of persons solicited is not more than ten; and

(3) The furnishing of proxy voting advice by any person (the "advisor") to any other person with whom the advisor has a business relationship, if:

(i) The advisor renders financial advice in the ordinary course of his business;

(ii) The advisor discloses to the recipient of the advice any significant relationship with the registrant or any of its affiliates, or a security holder proponent of the matter on which advice is given, as well as any material interests of the advisor in such matter;

(iii) The advisor receives no special commission or remuneration for furnishing the proxy voting advice from any person other than a recipient of the advice and other persons who receive similar advice under this subsection; and

(iv) The proxy voting advice is not furnished on behalf of any person soliciting proxies or on behalf of a participant in an election subject to the provisions of Rule 14a–11.

(4) Any solicitation in connection with a roll-up transaction as defined in Item 901(c) of Regulation S–K ... in which the holder of a security that is the subject of a proposed roll-up transaction engages in preliminary communications with other holders of securities that are the subject of the same limited partnership roll-up transaction for the purpose of determining whether to solicit proxies, consents, or authorizations in opposition to the proposed limited partnership roll-up transaction; *provided, however,* that:

(i) This exemption shall not apply to a security holder who is an affiliate of the registrant or general partner or sponsor; and

(ii) This exemption shall not apply to a holder of five percent (5%) or more of the outstanding securities of a class that is the subject of the proposed roll-up transaction who engages in the business of buying and selling limited partnership interests in the secondary market unless that holder discloses to the persons to whom the communications are made such ownership interest and any relations of the holder to the parties [to] the transaction or to the transaction itself, as required by Rule 14a–6(n)(1) and specified in the Notice of Exempt Preliminary Roll-up Communication (Rule 14a–104). If the communication is oral, this disclosure may be provided to the security holder orally. Whether the communication is written or oral, the notice required by Rule 14a–6(n) and Rule 14a–104 shall be furnished to the Commission.

(5) Publication or distribution by a broker or a dealer of a research report in accordance with Rule 138 or Rule 139 during a transaction in which the broker or dealer or its affiliate participates or acts in an advisory role.

Rule 14a–3. Information to Be Furnished to Security Holders

(a) No solicitation subject to this regulation shall be made unless each person solicited is concurrently furnished or has previously been furnished with a publicly filed preliminary or definitive written proxy statement containing the information specified in Schedule 14A....

(b) If the solicitation is made on behalf of the registrant and relates to an annual (or special meeting in lieu of the annual) meeting of security holders, or written consent in lieu of such meeting, at which directors are to be elected, each proxy statement furnished pursuant to paragraph (a) of this section shall be accompanied or preceded by an annual report to security holders as follows:

Note to Small Business Issuers. A "small business issuer," defined under Rule 12b–2 of the Exchange Act, shall refer to the disclosure items in Regulation S–B rather than Regulation S–K. If there is no comparable disclosure item in Regulation S–B, a small business issuer need not provide the information requested. A small business issuers shall provide the information in Item 310(a) of Regulation S–B in lieu of the financial information required by Rule 14a–3(b)(1)....

(1) The report shall include, for the registrant and its subsidiaries[,] consolidated, audited balance sheets as of the end of each of the two most recent fiscal years and audited statements of income and cash flows for each of the three most recent fiscal years prepared in accordance with Regulation S–X....

(3) The report shall contain the supplementary financial information required by Item 302 of Regulation S–K....

(4) The report shall contain information concerning changes in and disagreements with accountants on accounting and financial disclosure required by Item 304 of Regulation S–K....

(5)(i) The report shall contain the selected financial data required by Item 301 of Regulation S–K....

(ii) The report shall contain management's discussion and analysis of financial condition and results of operations required by Item 303 of Regulation S–K....

(6) The report shall contain a brief description of the business done by the registrant and its subsidiaries during the most recent fiscal year which will, in the opinion of management, indicate the general nature and scope of the business of the registrant and its subsidiaries.

(7) The report shall contain information relating to the registrant's industry segments, classes of similar products or services, foreign and domestic operations and exports sales required by paragraphs (b), (c)(1)(i) and (d) of Item 101 of Regulation S–K [Description of Business]....

(8) The report shall identify each of the registrant's directors and executive officers, and shall indicate the principal occupation or employment of each such person and the name and principal business of any organization by which such person is employed.

(9) The report shall contain the market price of and dividends on the registrant's common equity and related security holder matters required by Item 201 ... of Regulation S–K [Market Price of and Dividends on the Registrant's Common Equity and Related Stockholder Matters]....

(10) The registrant's proxy statement, or the report, shall contain an undertaking in bold face or otherwise reasonably prominent type to

provide without charge to each person solicited upon the written request of any such person, a copy of the registrant's annual report on Form 10–K, ... including the financial statements and the financial statement schedules, required to be filed with the Commission pursuant to Rule 13a–1 under the Act for the registrant's most recent fiscal year, and shall indicate the name and address (including title or department) of the person to whom such a written request is to be directed.... If the registrant's annual report to security holders complies with all of the disclosure requirements of Form 10–K ... and is filed with the Commission in satisfaction of its Form 10–K ... filing requirements, such registrant need not furnish a separate Form 10–K ... to security holders who receive a copy of such annual report....

(c) Seven copies of the report sent to security holders pursuant to this rule shall be mailed to the Commission, solely for its information, not later than the date on which such report is first sent or given to security holders or the date on which preliminary copies, or definitive copies, if preliminary filing was not required, of solicitation material are filed with the Commission pursuant to Rule 14a–6, whichever date is later. The report is not deemed to be "soliciting material" or to be "filed" with the Commission or subject to this regulation otherwise than as provided in this Rule, or to the liabilities of section 18 of the Act, except to the extent that the registrant specifically requests that it be treated as a part of the proxy soliciting material or incorporates it in the proxy statement or other filed report by reference....

(e)(1)(i) A registrant will be considered to have delivered an annual report or proxy statement to all security holders of record who share an address if:

(A) The registrant delivers one annual report or proxy statement, as applicable, to the shared address;

(B) The registrant addresses the annual report or proxy statement, as applicable, to the security holders as a group (for example, "ABC Fund [or Corporation] Security Holders," "Jane Doe and Household," "The Smith Family"), to each of the security holders individually (for example, "John Doe and Richard Jones") or to the security holders in a form to which each of the security holders has consented in writing....

(C) The security holders consent ... to delivery of one annual report or proxy statement, as applicable;

(D) With respect to delivery of the proxy statement, the registrant delivers, together with or subsequent to delivery of the proxy statement, a separate proxy card for each security holder at the shared address; and

(E) The registrant includes an undertaking in the proxy statement to deliver promptly upon written or oral request a separate copy of the annual report or proxy statement, as applicable, to a security holder at a shared address to which a single copy of the document was delivered. . . .

(f) The provisions of paragraph (a) of this section shall not apply to a communication made by means of speeches in public forums, press releases, published or broadcast opinions, statements, or advertisements appearing in a broadcastmedia, newspaper, magazine or other bona fide publication disseminated on a regular basis, provided that:

(1) no form of proxy, consent or authorization or means to execute the same is provided to a security holder in connection with the communication; and

(2) at the time the communication is made, a definitive proxy statement is on file with the Commission pursuant to Rule 14a–6(b).

Rule 14a–4. Requirements as to Proxy

(a) The form of proxy (1) shall indicate in bold-face type whether or not the proxy is solicited on behalf of the registrant's board of directors or, if provided other than by a majority of the board of directors, shall indicate in bold-face type on whose behalf the solicitation is made;

(2) Shall provide a specifically designated blank space for dating the proxy card; and

(3) Shall identify clearly and impartially each separate matter intended to be acted upon, whether or not related to or conditioned on the approval of other matters, and whether proposed by the registrant or by security holders. No reference need be made, however, to proposals as to which discretionary authority is conferred pursuant to paragraph (c) of this section.

(b)(1) Means shall be provided in the form of proxy whereby the person solicited is afforded an opportunity to specify by boxes a choice between approval or disapproval of, or abstention with respect to each separate matter referred to therein as intended to be acted upon, other than elections to office. A proxy may confer discretionary authority with respect to matters as to which a choice is not specified by the security holder provided that the form of proxy states in bold-face type how it is intended to vote the shares represented by the proxy in each such case.

(2) A form of proxy which provides for the election of directors shall set forth the names of persons nominated for election as directors. Such form of proxy shall clearly provide any of the following means for security holders to withhold authority to vote for each nominee:

(i) A box opposite the name of each nominee which may be marked to indicate that authority to vote for such nominee is withheld; or

(ii) An instruction in bold-face type which indicates that the security holder may withhold authority to vote for any nominee by lining through or otherwise striking out the name of any nominee; or

(iii) Designated blank spaces in which the security holder may enter the names of nominees with respect to whom the security holder chooses to withhold authority to vote; or

(iv) Any other similar means, provided that clear instructions are furnished indicating how the security holder may withhold authority to vote for any nominee.

Such form of proxy also may provide a means for the security holder to grant authority to vote for the nominees set forth, as a group, provided that there is a similar means for the security holder to withhold authority to vote for such group of nominees. Any such form of proxy which is executed by the security holder in such manner as not to withhold authority to vote for the election of any nominee shall be deemed to grant such authority, provided that the form of proxy so states in bold-face type.

> *Instructions.* 1. Paragraph (2) does not apply in the case of a merger, consolidation or other plan if the election of directors is an integral part of the plan.
>
> 2. If applicable state law gives legal effect to votes cast against a nominee, then in lieu of, or in addition to, providing a means for security holders to withhold authority to vote, the registrant should provide a similar means for security holders to vote against each nominee.

(c) A proxy may confer discretionary authority to vote on any of the following matters:

(1) For an annual meeting of shareholders, if the registrant did not have notice of the matter at least 45 days before the date on which the registrant first mailed its proxy materials for the prior year's annual meeting of shareholders (or date specified by an advance notice provision), and a specific statement to that effect is made in the proxy statement or form of proxy. If during the prior year the registrant did not hold an annual meeting, or if the date of the meeting has changed more than 30 days from the prior year, then notice must not have been received a reasonable time before the registrant mails its proxy materials for the current years.

(2) In the case in which the registrant has received timely notice in connection with an annual meeting of shareholders (as determined under paragraph (c)(1) of this section), if the registrant includes, in the proxy statement, advice on the nature of the matter and how the registrant intends to exercise its discretion to vote on each matter. However, even if the registrant includes this information in its proxy statement, it may not exercise discretionary voting authority on a particular proposal if the proponent:

(i) Provides the registrant with a written statement, within the time-frame determined under paragraph (c)(1) of this section, that the proponent intends to deliver a proxy statement and form of proxy to holders of at least the percentage of the company's voting shares required under applicable law to carry the proposal;

(ii) Includes the same statement in its proxy materials filed under Rule 14a–6; and

(iii) Immediately after soliciting the percentage of shareholders required to carry the proposal, provides the registrant with a statement from any solicitor or other person with knowledge that the necessary steps have been taken to deliver a proxy statement and form of proxy to holders of at least the percentage of the company's voting shares required under applicable law to carry the proposal.

(3) For solicitations other than for annual meetings or for solicitations by persons other than the registrant, matters which the persons making the solicitation do not know, a reasonable time before the solicitation, are to be presented at the meeting, if a specific statement to that effect is made in the proxy statement or form of proxy.

(4) Approval of the minutes of the prior meeting if such approval does not amount to ratification of the action taken at that meeting;

(5) The election of any person to any office for which a bona fide nominee is named in the proxy statement and such nominee is unable to serve or for good cause will not serve.

(6) Any proposal omitted from the proxy statement and form of proxy pursuant to Rule 14a–8 or 14a–9 of this chapter.

(7) Matters incident to the conduct of the meeting.

(d) No proxy shall confer authority:

(1) To vote for the election of any person to any office for which a bona fide nominee is not named in the proxy statement,

(2) To vote at any annual meeting other than the next annual meeting (or any adjournment thereof) to be held after the date on which the proxy statement and form of proxy are first sent or given to security holders,

(3) To vote with respect to more than one meeting (and any adjournment thereof) or more than one consent solicitation or

(4) To consent to or authorize any action other than the action proposed to be taken in the proxy statement, or matters referred to in paragraph (c) of this rule. A person shall not be deemed to be a bona fide nominee and he shall not be named as such unless he has consented to being named in the proxy statement and to serve if elected.

Provided, however, that nothing in this Rule 4a–4 shall prevent any person soliciting in support of nominees who, if elected, would constitute a minority of the board of directors, from seeking authority to vote for nominees named in the registrant's proxy statement, so long as the soliciting party:

(i) seeks authority to vote in the aggregate for the number of director positions then subject to election;

(ii) represents that it will vote for all the registrant nominees, other than those registrant nominees specified by the soliciting party;

(iii) provides the security holder an opportunity to withhold authority with respect to any other registrant nominee by writing the name of that nominee on the form of proxy; and

(iv) states on the form of proxy and in the proxy statement that there is no assurance that the registrant's nominees will serve if elected with any of the soliciting party's nominees.

(e) The proxy statement or form of proxy shall provide, subject to reasonable specified conditions, that the shares represented by the proxy will be voted and that where the person solicited specifies by means of a ballot provided pursuant to paragraph (b) of this section a choice with respect to any matter to be acted upon, the shares will be voted in accordance with the specifications so made.

(f) No person conducting a solicitation subject to this regulation shall deliver a form of proxy, consent or authorization to any security holder unless the security holder concurrently receives, or has previously received, a definitive proxy statement that has been filed with the Commission pursuant to Rule 14a–6(b).

Rule 14a–5. Presentation of Information in Proxy Statement

(a) The information included in the proxy statement shall be clearly presented and the statements made shall be divided into groups according to subject matter and the various groups of statements shall be preceded by appropriate headings. The order of items and sub-items in the schedule need not be followed. Where practicable and appropriate, the information shall be presented in tabular form. All amounts shall be stated in figures. Information required by more than one applicable item need not be repeated. No statement need be made in response to any item or sub-item which is inapplicable.

(b) Any information required to be included in the proxy statement as to terms of securities or other subject matter which from a standpoint of practical necessity must be determined in the future may be stated in terms of present knowledge and intention. To the extent practicable, the authority to be conferred concerning each such matter shall be confined within limits reasonably related to the need for discretionary authority. Subject to the foregoing, information which is not known to the persons on whose behalf the solicitation is to be made and which it is not reasonably within the power of such persons to ascertain or procure may be omitted, if a brief statement of the circumstances rendering such information unavailable is made.

(c) Any information contained in any other proxy soliciting material which has been furnished to each person solicited in connection with the same meeting or subject matter may be omitted from the proxy statement, if a clear reference is made to the particular document containing such information.

(d) All printed proxy statements shall be in roman type at least as large and as legible as 10–point modern type, except that to the extent necessary for convenient presentation financial statements and other tabular data, but not the notes thereto, may be in roman type at least as large and as legible as 8–point modern type. All such type shall be leaded at least 2 points.

(e) All proxy statements shall disclose, under an appropriate caption, the following dates:

(1) The deadline for submitting shareholder proposals for inclusion in the registrant's proxy statement and form of proxy for the registrant's next annual meeting, calculated in the manner provided in Rule 14a–8(d) (Question 4); and

(2) The date after which notice of a shareholder proposal submitted outside the processes of Rule 14a–8 is considered untimely, either calculated in the manner provided by Rule 14a–4(c)(1) or as established by the registrant's advance notice provision, if any, authorized by applicable state law.

(f) If the date of the next annual meeting is subsequently advanced or delayed by more than 30 calendar days from the date of the annual meeting to which the proxy statement relates, the registrant shall, in a timely manner, inform shareholders of such change, and the new dates referred to in paragraphs (e)(1) and (e)(2) of this section, by including a notice, under Item 5, in its earliest possible quarterly report on Form 10–Q . . ., or, if impracticable, any means reasonably calculated to inform shareholders.

Rule 14a–6. Filing Requirements

(a) *Preliminary proxy statement.* Five preliminary copies of the proxy statement and form of proxy shall be filed with the Commission at least 10 calendar days prior to the date definitive copies of such material are first sent or given to security holders, or such shorter period prior to that date as the Commission may authorize upon a showing of good cause thereunder. A registrant, however, shall not file with the Commission a preliminary proxy statement, form of proxy or other soliciting material to be furnished to security holders concurrently therewith if the solicitation relates to an annual (or special meeting in lieu of the annual) meeting, . . . if the solicitation relates to any meeting of security holders at which the only matters to be acted upon are: (1) the election of directors; (2) the election, approval or ratification of accountant(s); [or] (3) a security holder proposal included pursuant to Rule 14a-8.... This exclusion from filing preliminary proxy material does not apply if the registrant comments upon or refers to a solicitation in opposition in connection with the meeting in its proxy material.

(b) *Definitive proxy statement and other soliciting material.* Eight definitive copies of the proxy statement, form of proxy and all other soliciting materials, in the same form as the materials sent to security holders, must be filed with the Commission no later than the date they are first sent or given to security holders. Three copies of these materials also must be filed with, or mailed for filing to, each national securities exchange on which the registrant has a class of securities listed and registered.

(c) *Personal solicitation materials.* If part or all of the solicitation involves personal solicitation, then eight copies of all written instructions or other materials that discuss, review or comment on the merits of any matter to be acted on, that are furnished to persons making the actual solicitation for their use directly or indirectly in connection with the solicitation, must be filed with the Commission no later than the date the materials are first sent or given to these persons.

(d) *Release dates.* All preliminary proxy statements and forms of proxy filed pursuant to paragraph (a) of this section shall be accompanied by a statement of the date on which definitive copies thereof filed pursuant to paragraph (b) of this section are intended to be released to security holders. All definitive material filed pursuant to paragraph (b) of this section shall be accompanied by a statement of the date on which copies of such material were released to security holders, or, if not released, the date on which copies thereof are intended to be released. All material filed pursuant to paragraph (c) of this section shall be accompanied by a statement of the date on which copies thereof were released to the individual who will make the actual solicitation or if not released, the date on which copies thereof are intended to be released.

(e)(1) *Public Availability of Information.* All copies of preliminary proxy statements and forms of proxy filed pursuant to paragraph (a) of this section shall be clearly marked "Preliminary Copies," and shall be deemed immediately available for public inspection unless confidential treatment is obtained pursuant to paragraph (e)(2) of this section.

(2) *Confidential treatment.* If action will be taken on any matter specified in Item 14 of Schedule 14A, all copies of the preliminary proxy statement and form of proxy filed under paragraph (a) of this section will be for the information of the Commission only and will not be deemed available for public inspection until filed with the Commission in definitive form so long as:

(i) The proxy statement does not relate to a matter or proposal subject to Rule 13e–3 or a roll-up transaction as defined in Item 901(c) of Regulation S–K;

(ii) Neither the parties to the transaction nor any persons authorized to act on their behalf have made any public communications relating to the transaction except for statements where the content is limited to the information specified in Rule 135 [under the Securities Act]; and

(iii) The materials are filed in paper and marked "Confidential, For Use of the Commission Only." In all cases, the materials may be disclosed to any department or agency of the United States Government and to the Congress, and the Commission may make any inquiries or investigation into the materials as may be necessary to conduct an adequate review by the Commission.

(g) *Solicitations subject to Rule 14a–2(b)(1).*

(1) Any person who:

(i) engages in a solicitation pursuant to Rule 14a–2(b)(1), and

(ii) at the commencement of that solicitation owns beneficially securities of the class which is the subject of the solicitation with a market value of over $5 million, shall furnish or mail to the Commission, not later than three days after the date the written solicitation is first sent or given to any security holder, five copies of a statement containing the information specified in the [Form of] Notice of Exempt Solicitation which statement shall attach as an exhibit all written soliciting materials. Five copies of an amendment to such statement shall be furnished or mailed to the Commission, in connection with dissemination of any additional communications, not later than three days after the date the additional material is first sent or given to any security holder. Three copies of the Notice of Exempt Solicitation and amendments thereto shall, at the same time the materials are furnished or mailed to the Commission, be furnished or mailed to each national securities exchange upon which any class of securities of the registrant is listed and registered.

(2) Notwithstanding paragraph (g)(1) of this section, no such submission need be made with respect to oral solicitations (other than with respect to scripts used in connection with such oral solicitations), speeches delivered in a public forum, press releases, published or broadcast opinions, statements, and advertisements appearing in a broadcast media, or a newspaper, magazine or other bona fide publication disseminated on a regular basis. . . .

(n) *Solicitations subject to Rule 14a–2(b)(4).* Any person who:

(1) Engages in a solicitation pursuant to Rule 14a–2(b)(4), and

(2) At the commencement of that solicitation both owns five percent (5%) or more of the outstanding securities of a class that is the subject of the proposed roll-up transaction, and engages in the business of buying and selling limited partnership interests in the secondary market, shall furnish or mail to the Commission, not later than three days after the date an oral or written solicitation by that person is first made, sent or provided to any security holder, five copies of a statement containing the information specified in the Notice of Exempt Preliminary Roll-up Communication (Rule 14a–104). Five copies of any amendment to such statement shall be furnished or mailed to the Commission not later than three days after a communication containing revised material is first made, sent or provided to any security holder.

(*o*) *Solicitations before furnishing a definitive proxy statement.* Solicitations that are published, sent or given to security holders before they have been furnished a definitive proxy statement must be made in accordance with Rule 14a–12 unless there is an exemption available under Rule 14a–2.

Rule 14a–7. Obligations of Registrants to Provide a List of, or Mail Soliciting Material to, Security Holders

(a) If the registrant has made or intends to make a proxy solicitation in connection with a security holder meeting or action by consent or authorization, upon the written request by any record or beneficial holder of securities of the class entitled to vote at the meeting, or to execute a consent or authorization to provide a list of security holders or to mail the requesting security holder's materials, regardless of whether the request references this section, the registrant shall:

(1) deliver to the requesting security holder within five business days after receipt of the request:

(i) notification as to whether the registrant has elected to mail the security holder's soliciting materials or provide a security holder list if the election under paragraph (b) of this section is to be made by the registrant;

(ii) a statement of the approximate number of record holders and beneficial holders, separated by type of holder and class, owning securities in the same class or classes as holders which have been or are to be solicited on management's behalf, or any more limited group of such holders designated by the security holder if available or retrievable under the registrant's or its transfer agent's security holder data systems; and

(iii) the estimated cost of mailing a proxy statement, form of proxy or other communication to such holders, including to the extent known or reasonably available, the estimated costs of any bank, broker, and similar person through whom the registrant has solicited or intends to solicit beneficial owners in connection with the security holder meeting or action;

(2) perform the acts set forth in either paragraphs (a)(2)(i) or (a)(2)(ii) of this section, at the registrant's or requesting security holder's option, as specified in paragraph (b) of this section:

(i) Mail copies of any proxy statement, form of proxy or other soliciting material furnished by the security holder to the record holders, including banks, brokers, and similar entities, designated by the security holder. A sufficient number of copies must be mailed to the banks, brokers and similar entities for distribution to all beneficial owners designated by the security holder. If the registrant has received affirmative written or implied consent to deliver a single proxy statement to security holders at a shared address in accordance with the procedures in Rule 14a–3(e)(1), a single copy of the proxy statement furnished by the security holder shall be mailed to that address. The registrant shall mail the security holder material with reasonable promptness after tender of the material to be mailed, envelopes or other containers therefor, postage or payment for postage and other reasonable expenses of effecting such mailing. The registrant shall not be responsible for the content of the material; or

(ii) Deliver the following information to the requesting security holder within five business days of receipt of the request: a reasonably current list of the names, addresses and security positions of the record holders, including banks, brokers and similar entities, holding securities in the same class or classes as holders which have been or are to be solicited on management's behalf, or any more limited group of such holders designated by the security holder if available or retrievable under the registrant's or its transfer agent's security holder data systems; the most recent list of names, addresses and security positions of beneficial owners as specified in Rule 14a–13(b), in the possession, or which subsequently comes into the possession, of the registrant. If the registrant has received affirmative written or implied consent to deliver a single proxy statement to security holders at a shared address in accordance with the procedures in Rule 14a–3(e)(1), a single copy of the proxy statement furnished by the security holder shall be mailed to that address. All security holder list information shall be in the form requested by the security holder to the extent that such form is available to the registrant without undue burden or expense. The registrant shall furnish the security holder with updated record holder information on a daily basis or, if not available on a daily basis, at the shortest reasonable intervals, *provided, however,* the registrant need not provide beneficial or record holder information more current than the record date for the meeting or action.

(b)(1) The requesting security holder shall have the options set forth in paragraph (a)(2) of this section, and the registrant shall have corresponding obligations, if the registrant or general partner or sponsor is soliciting or intends to solicit with respect to:

(i) A proposal that is subject to Rule 13e–3;

(ii) A roll-up transaction as defined in Item 901(c) of Regulation S–K that involves an entity with securities registered pursuant to Section 12 of the Act;

(iii) A roll-up transaction as defined in Item 901(c) of Regulation S–K that involves a limited partnership. . . .

(2) With respect to all other requests pursuant to this section, the registrant shall have the option to either mail the security holder's material or furnish the security holder list as set forth in this section.

(c) At the time of a list request, the security holder making the request shall:

(1) if holding the registrant's securities through a nominee, provide the registrant with a statement by the nominee or other independent third party, or a copy of a current filing made with the Commission and furnished to the registrant, confirming such holder's beneficial ownership; and

(2) provide the registrant with an affidavit, declaration, affirmation or other similar document provided for under applicable state law identifying the proposal or other corporate action that will be the subject of the security holder's solicitation or communication and attesting that:

(i) the security holder will not use the list information for any purpose other than to solicit security holders with respect to the same meeting or action by consent or authorization for which the registrant is soliciting or intends to solicit or to communicate with security holders with respect to a solicitation commenced by the registrant; and

(ii) the security holder will not disclose such information to any person other than a beneficial owner for whom the request was made and an employee or agent to the extent necessary to effectuate the communication or solicitation.

(d) The security holder shall not use the information furnished by the registrant pursuant to paragraph (a)(2)(ii) of this section for any purpose other than to solicit security holders with respect to the same meeting or action by consent or authorization for which the registrant is soliciting or intends to solicit or to communicate with security holders with respect to a solicitation commenced by the registrant; or disclose such information to any person other than an employee, agent, or beneficial owner for whom a request was made to the extent necessary to effectuate the communication or solicitation. The security holder shall return the information provided pursuant to paragraph (a)(2)(ii) of this section and shall not retain any copies thereof or of any information derived from such information after the termination of the solicitation.

(e) The security holder shall reimburse the reasonable expenses incurred by the registrant in performing the acts requested pursuant to paragraph (a) of this section.

Rule 14a–8.   Shareholder Proposals

This section addresses when a company must include a shareholder's proposal in its proxy statement and identify the proposal in its form of proxy when the company holds an annual or special meeting of shareholders. In summary, in order to have your shareholder proposal included on a company's proxy card, and included along with any supporting statement in its proxy statement, you must be eligible and follow certain procedures. Under a few specific circumstances, the company is permitted to exclude your proposal, but only after submitting its reasons to the Commission. We structured this section in a question-and-answer format so that it is easier to understand. The references to "you" are to a shareholder seeking to submit the proposal.

(a) **Question 1: What is a proposal?**

A shareholder proposal is your recommendation or requirement that the company and/or its board of directors take action, which you intend to present at a meeting of the company's shareholders. Your proposal should state as clearly as possible the course of action that you believe the company should follow. If your proposal is placed on the company's proxy card, the company must also provide in the form of proxy means for shareholders to specify by boxes a choice between approval or disapproval, or abstention. Unless otherwise indicated, the word "proposal" as used in this section refers both to your proposal, and to your corresponding statement in support of your proposal (if any).

(b) **Question 2: Who is eligible to submit a proposal, and how do I demonstrate to the company that I am eligible?**

(1) In order to be eligible to submit a proposal, you must have continuously held at least $2,000 in market value, or 1%, of the company's securities entitled to be voted on the proposal at the meeting for at least one year by the date you submit the proposal. You must continue to hold those securities through the date of the meeting.

(2) If you are the registered holder of your securities, which means that your name appears in the company's records as a shareholder, the company can verify your eligibility on its own, although you will still have to provide the company with a written statement that you intend to continue to hold the securities through the date of the meeting of shareholders. However, if like many shareholders you are not a registered holder, the company likely does not know that you are a shareholder, or how many shares you own. In this case, at the time you submit your proposal, you must prove your eligibility to the company in one of two ways:

(i) The first way is to submit to the company a written statement from the "record" holder of your securities (usually a broker or bank) verifying that, at the time you submitted your proposal, you continuously held the securities for at least one year. You must also include your own written statement that you intend to continue to hold the securities through the date of the meeting of shareholders; or

(ii) The second way to prove ownership applies only if you have filed a Schedule 13D, Schedule 13G, Form 3, Form 4 and/or Form 5, or amendments to those documents or updated forms, reflecting your ownership of the shares as of or before the date on which the one-year eligibility period begins. If you have filed one of these documents with the SEC, you may demonstrate your eligibility by submitting to the company:

(A) A copy of the schedule and/or form, and any subsequent amendments reporting a change in your ownership level;

(B) Your written statement that you continuously held the required number of shares for the one-year period as of the date of the statement;

(C) Your written statement that you intend to continue ownership of the shares through the date of the company's annual or special meeting.

(c) **Question 3: How many proposals may I submit?**

Each shareholder may submit no more than one proposal to a company for a particular shareholders' meeting.

(d) **Question 4: How long can my proposal be?**

The proposal, including any accompanying supporting statement, may not exceed 500 words.

(e) **Question 5: What is the deadline for submitting a proposal?**

(1) If you are submitting your proposal for the company's annual meeting, you can in most cases find the deadline in last year's proxy statement. However, if the company did not hold an annual meeting last year, or has changed the date of its meeting for this year more than 30 days from the last year's meeting, you can usually find the deadline in one of the company's quarterly reports on Form 10–Q.... In order to avoid controversy, shareholders should submit their proposals by means, including electronic means, that permit them to prove the date of delivery.

(2) The deadline is calculated in the following manner if the proposal is submitted for a regularly scheduled annual meeting. The proposal must be received at the company's principal executive offices not less than 120 calendar days before the date of the company's proxy statement

released to shareholders in connection with the previous year's annual meeting. However, if the company did not hold an annual meeting the previous year, or if the date of this year's annual meeting has been changed by more than 30 days from the date of the previous year's meeting, then the deadline is a reasonable time before the company begins to print or mail its proxy materials.

(3) If you are submitting your proposal for a meeting of shareholders other than a regularly scheduled annual meeting, the deadline is a reasonable time before the company begins to print and mail its proxy materials.

(f) **Question 6: What if I fail to follow one of the eligibility or procedural requirements explained in answers to Questions 1 through 4 of this section?**

(1) The company may exclude your proposal, but only after it has notified you of the problem, and you have failed adequately to correct it. Within 14 calendar days of receiving your proposal, the company must notify you in writing of any procedural or eligibility deficiencies, as well as of the time frame for your response. Your response must be post-marked, or transmitted electronically, no later than 14 days from the date you received the company's notification. A company need not provide you such notice of a deficiency if the deficiency cannot be remedied, such as if you fail to submit a proposal by the company's properly determined deadline. If the company intends to exclude the proposal, it will later have to make a submission under Rule 14a–8 and provide you with a copy under Question 10 below, Rule 14a–8(j).

(2) If you fail in your promise to hold the required number of securities through the date of the meeting of shareholders, then the company will be permitted to exclude all of your proposals from its proxy materials for any meeting held in the following two calendar years.

(g) **Question 7: Who has the burden of persuading the Commission or its staff that my proposal can be excluded?**

Except as otherwise noted, the burden is on the company to demonstrate that it is entitled to exclude a proposal.

(h) **Question 8: Must I appear personally at the shareholders' meeting to present the proposal?**

(1) Either you, or your representative who is qualified under state law to present the proposal on your behalf, must attend the meeting to present the proposal. Whether you attend the meeting yourself or send a qualified representative to the meeting in your place, you should make sure that you, or your representative, follow the proper state law procedures for attending the meeting and/or presenting your proposal.

(2) If the company holds its shareholder meeting in whole or in part via electronic media, and the company permits you or your representative to present your proposal via such media, then you may appear

through electronic media rather than traveling to the meeting to appear in person.

(3) If you or your qualified representative fail to appear and present the proposed, without good cause, the company will be permitted to exclude all of your proposals from its proxy materials for any meetings held in the following two calendar years.

(i) **Question 9: If I have complied with the procedural requirements, on what other bases may a company rely to exclude my proposal?**

(1) **Improper under state law:** If the proposal is not a proper subject for action by shareholders under the laws of the jurisdiction of the company's organization;

Note to paragraph (i)(1): Depending on the subject matter, some proposals are not considered proper under state law if they would be binding on the company if approved by shareholders. In our experience, most proposals that are cast as recommendations or requests that the board of directors take specified action are proper under state law. Accordingly, we will assume that a proposal drafted as a recommendation or suggestion is proper unless the company demonstrates otherwise.

(2) **Violation of law:** If the proposal would, if implemented, cause the company to violate any state, federal, or foreign law to which it is subject;

Note to paragraph (i)(2): We will not apply this basis for exclusion to permit exclusion of a proposal on grounds that it would violate foreign law if compliance with the foreign law would result in a violation of any state or federal law.

(3) **Violation of proxy rules:** If the proposal or supporting statement is contrary to any of the Commission's proxy rules, including Rule 14a–9, which prohibits materially false or misleading statements in proxy soliciting materials;

(4) **Personal grievance; special interest:** If the proposal relates to the redress of a personal claim or grievance against the company or any other person, or if it is designed to result in a benefit to you, or to further a personal interest, which is not shared by the other shareholders at large;

(5) **Relevance:** If the proposal relates to operations which account for less than 5 percent of the company's total assets at the end of its most recent fiscal year, and for less than 5 percent of its net earnings and gross sales for its most recent fiscal year, and is not otherwise significantly related to the company's business;

(6) **Absence of power/authority:** If the company would lack the power or authority to implement the proposal;

(7) **Management functions:** If the proposal deals with a matter relating to the company's ordinary business operations;

(8) **Relates to election:** If the proposal relates to an election for membership on the company's board of directors or analogous governing body;

(9) **Conflicts with company's proposal:** If the proposal conflicts in substance with one of the company's own proposals to be submitted to shareholders at the same meeting;

Note to paragraph (i)(9): A company's submission to the Commission under this section shall specify the points of conflict with the company's proposal.

(10) **Substantially implemented:** If the company has already substantially implemented the proposal;

(11) **Duplication:** If the proposal substantially duplicates another proposal previously submitted to the company by another proponent that will be included in the company's proxy materials for the same meeting;

(12) **Resubmissions:** If the proposal deals with substantially the same subject matter as another proposal or proposals that has or have been previously included in the company's proxy materials within the preceding 5 calendar years, a company may exclude it from its proxy materials for any meeting held within 3 calendar years of the last time it was included if the proposal received:

(i) Less than 3% of the vote if proposed once within the preceding 5 calendar years;

(ii) Less than 6% of the vote on its last submission to shareholders if proposed twice previously within the preceding 5 calendar years; or

(iii) Less than 10% of the vote on its last submission to shareholders if proposed three times or more previously within the preceding 5 calendar years; and

(13) **Specific amount of dividends:** If the proposal relates to specific amounts of cash or stock dividends.

(j) **Question 10: What procedures must the company follow if it intends to exclude my proposal?**

(1) If the company intends to exclude a proposal from its proxy materials, it must file its reasons with the Commission no later than 80 calendar days before it files its definitive proxy statement and form of proxy with the Commission. The company must simultaneously provide you with a copy of its submission. The Commission staff may permit the company to make its submission later than 80 days before the company files its definitive proxy statement and form of proxy, if the company demonstrates good cause for missing the deadline.

2010

(2) The company must file six paper copies of the following:

(i) The proposal;

(ii) An explanation of why the company believes that it may exclude the proposal, which should, if possible, refer to the most recent applicable authority, such as prior Division letters issued under the rule; and

(iii) A supporting opinion of counsel when such reasons are based on matters of state or foreign law.

(k) **Question 11: May I submit my own statement to the Commission responding to the company's arguments?**

Yes, you may submit a response, but it is not required. You should try to submit any response to us, with a copy to the company, as soon as possible after the company makes its submission. This way, the Commission staff will have time to consider fully your submission before it issues its response. You should submit six paper copies of your response.

(*l*) **Question 12: If the company includes my shareholder proposal in its proxy materials, what information about me must it include along with the proposal itself?**

(1) The company's proxy statement must include your name and address, as well as the number of the company's voting securities that you hold. However, instead of providing that information, the company may instead include a statement that it will provide the information to shareholders promptly upon receiving an oral or written request.

(2) The company is not responsible for the contents of your proposal or supporting statement.

(m) **Question 13: What can I do if the company includes in its proxy statement reasons why it believes shareholders should not vote in favor of my proposal, and I disagree with some of its statements?**

(1) The company may elect to include in its proxy statement reasons why it believes shareholders should vote against your proposal. The company is allowed to make arguments reflecting its own point of view, just as you may express your own point of view in your proposal's supporting statement.

(2) However, if you believe that the company's opposition to your proposal contains materially false or misleading statements that may violate our anti-fraud rule, Rule 14a–9, you should promptly send to the Commission staff and the company a letter explaining the reasons for your view, along with a copy of the company's statements opposing your proposal. To the extent possible, your letter should include specific factual information demonstrating the inaccuracy of the company's claims. Time permitting, you may wish to try to work out your differ-

ences with the company by yourself before contacting the Commission staff.

(3) We require the company to send a copy of its statements opposing your proposal before it mails its proxy materials, so that you may bring to our attention any materially false or misleading statements, under the following timeframes.

(i) If our no-action response requires that you make revisions to your proposal or supporting statement as a condition to requiring the company to include it in its proxy materials, then the company must provide you with a copy of its opposition statements no later than 5 calendar days after the company receives a copy of your proposal; or

(ii) In all other cases, the company must provide you with a copy of its opposition statements no later than 30 calendar days before its files definitive copies of its proxy statement and form of proxy under Rule 14a–6.

Rule 14a–9. False or Misleading Statements

(a) No solicitation subject to this regulation shall be made by means of any proxy statement, form of proxy, notice of meeting or other communication, written or oral, containing any statement which, at the time and in the light of the circumstances under which it is made, is false or misleading with respect to any material fact, or which omits to state any material fact necessary in order to make the statements therein not false or misleading or necessary to correct any statement in any earlier communication with respect to the solicitation of a proxy for the same meeting or subject matter which has become false or misleading.

(b) The fact that a proxy statement, form of proxy or other soliciting material has been filed with or examined by the Commission shall not be deemed a finding by the Commission that such material is accurate or complete or not false or misleading, or that the Commission has passed upon the merits of or approved any statement contained therein or any matter to be acted upon by security holders. No representation contrary to the foregoing shall be made. . . .

Rule 14a–10. Prohibition of Certain Solicitations

No person making a solicitation which is subject to Rules 14a–1 to 14a–10 shall solicit:

(a) Any undated or postdated proxy; or

(b) Any proxy which provides that it shall be deemed to be dated as of any date subsequent to the date on which it is signed by the security holder.

Rule 14a–12.   Solicitation Before Furnishing a Proxy Statement

(a) Notwithstanding the provisions of Rule 14a–3(a), a solicitation may be made before furnishing security holders with a proxy statement meeting the requirements of Rule 14a–3(a) if:

(1) Each written communication includes:

(i) The identity of the participants in the solicitation (as defined in Instruction 3 to Item 4 of Schedule 14A) and a description of their direct or indirect interests, by security holdings or otherwise, or a prominent legend in clear, plain language advising security holders where they can obtain that information; and

(ii) A prominent legend in clear, plain language advising security holders to read the proxy statement when it is available because it contains important information.   The legend also must explain to investors that they can get the proxy statement, and any other relevant documents, for free at the Commission's web site and describe which documents are available free from the participants; and

(2) A definitive proxy statement meeting the requirements of Rule 14a–3(a) is sent or given to security holders solicited in reliance on this section before or at the same time as the forms of proxy, consent or authorization are furnished to or requested from security holders.

(b) Any soliciting material published, sent or given to security holders in accordance with paragraph (a) of this section must be filed with the Commission no later than the date the material is first published, sent or given to security holders.   Three copies of the material must at the same time be filed with, or mailed for filing to, each national securities exchange upon which any class of securities of the registrant is listed and registered.   The soliciting material must include a cover page in the form set forth in Schedule 14A and the appropriate box on the cover page must be marked. Soliciting material in connection with a registered offering is required to be filed only under Rule 424 or Rule 425 [under the Securities Exchange Act], and will be deemed filed under this section.

(c) Solicitations by any person or group of persons for the purpose of opposing a solicitation subject to this regulation by any other person or group of persons with respect to the election or removal of directors at any annual or special meeting of security holders also are subject to the following provisions:

(1) *Application of this rule to annual report.*   Notwithstanding the provisions of Rule 14a–3 (b) and (c), any portion of the annual report referred to in Rule 14a–3(b) that comments upon or refers to any solicitation subject to this rule, or to any participant in the solicitation, other than the solicitation by the management, must be filed with the Commission as proxy material subject to this regulation.   This must be filed in electronic format . . .

(2) *Use of reprints or reproductions.*   In any solicitation subject to this Rule 14a–12(c), soliciting material that includes, in whole or part, any reprints or reproductions of any previously published material must:

(i) State the name of the author and publication, the date of prior publication, and identify any person who is quoted without being named in the previously published material.

(ii) Except in the case of a public or official document or statement, state whether or not the consent of the author and publication has been obtained to the use of the previously published material as proxy soliciting material.

(iii) If any participant using the previously published material, or anyone on his or her behalf, paid, directly or indirectly, for the preparation or prior publication of the previously published material, or has made or proposes to make any payments or give any other consideration in connection with the publication or republication of the material, state the circumstances.

Rule 14a–15. Differential and Contingent Compensation in Connection With Roll–Up Transactions

(a) It shall be unlawful for any person to receive compensation for soliciting proxies, consents, or authorizations directly from security holders in connection with a roll-up transaction as provided in paragraph (b) of this section, if the compensation is:

(1) Based on whether the solicited proxy, consent, or authorization either approves or disapproves the proposed roll-up transaction; or

(2) Contingent on the approval, disapproval, or completion of the roll-up transaction.

(b) This section is applicable to a roll-up transaction as defined in Item 901(c) of Regulation S–K, except for a transaction involving only:

(1) Finite-life entities that are not limited partnerships....

SCHEDULE 14A. INFORMATION REQUIRED IN PROXY STATEMENT....

Item 1.   Date, time and place information.   (a) State the date, time and place of the meeting of security holders, and the complete mailing address, including ZIP Code, of the principal executive offices of the registrant, unless such information is otherwise disclosed in material furnished to security holders with or preceding the proxy statement. If action is to be taken by written consent, state the date by which consents are to be submitted if state law requires that such a date be specified or if the person soliciting intends to set a date.

(b) On the first page of the proxy statement, as delivered to security holders, state the approximate date on which the proxy statement and form of proxy are first sent or given to security holders.

(c) Furnish the information required to be in the proxy statement by Rule 14a–5(e)....

Item 2. Revocability of proxy. State whether or not the person giving the proxy has the power to revoke it. If the right of revocation before the proxy is exercised is limited or is subject to compliance with any formal procedure, briefly describe such limitation or procedure.

Item 3. Dissenters' right of appraisal. Outline briefly the rights of appraisal or similar rights of dissenters with respect to any matter to be acted upon and indicate any statutory procedure required to be followed by dissenting security holders in order to perfect such rights. Where such rights may be exercised only within a limited time after the date of adoption of a proposal, the filing of a charter amendment or other similar act, state whether the persons solicited will be notified of such date.

> *Instruction.* Indicate whether a security holder's failure to vote against a proposal will constitute a waiver of his appraisal or similar rights and whether a vote against a proposal will be deemed to satisfy any notice requirements under State law with respect to appraisal rights. If the State law is unclear, state what position will be taken in regard to these matters.

Item 4. Persons Making the Solicitation —(a) *Solicitations not subject to Rule 14a–12(c)....* (1) If the solicitation is made by the registrant, so state. Give the name of any director of the registrant who has informed the registrant in writing that he intends to oppose any action intended to be taken by the registrant and indicate the action which he intends to oppose.

(2) If the solicitation is made otherwise than by the registrant, so state and give the names of the participants in the solicitation, as defined in paragraphs (a)(iii), (iv), (v) and (vi) of Instruction 3 to this Item.

(3) If the solicitation is to be made otherwise than by the use of the mails, describe the methods to be employed. If the solicitation is to be made by specially engaged employees or paid solicitors, state (i) the material features of any contract or arrangement for such solicitation and identify the parties, and (ii) the cost or anticipated cost thereof.

(4) State the names of the persons by whom the cost of solicitation has been or will be borne, directly or indirectly.

(b) *Solicitations subject to Rule 14a–12(c)....* (1) State by whom the solicitation is made and describe the methods employed and to be employed to solicit security holders.

(2) If regular employees of the registrant or any other participant in a solicitation have been or are to be employed to solicit security holders, describe the class or classes of employees to be so employed, and the manner and nature of their employment for such purpose.

(3) If specially engaged employees, representatives or other persons have been or are to be employed to solicit security holders, state (i) the material features of any contract or arrangement for such solicitation and the identity of the parties, (ii) the cost or anticipated cost thereof and (iii) the approximate number of such employees or employees of any other person (naming such other person) who will solicit security holders.

(4) State the total amount estimated to be spent and the total expenditures to date for, in furtherance of, or in connection with the solicitation of security holders.

(5) State by whom the cost of the solicitation will be borne. If such cost is to be borne initially by any person other than the registrant, state whether reimbursement will be sought from the registrant, and, if so, whether the question of such reimbursement will be submitted to a vote of security holders.

(6) If any such solicitation is terminated pursuant to a settlement between the registrant and any other participant in such solicitation, describe the terms of such settlement, including the cost or anticipated cost thereof to the registrant....

Instructions....

3. For purposes of this Item 4 and Item 5 of this Schedule 14A:

(a) The terms "participant" and "participant in a solicitation" include the following:

(i) the registrant;

(ii) any director of the registrant, and any nominee for whose election as a director proxies are solicited;

(iii) any committee or group which solicits proxies, any member of such committee or group, and any person whether or not named as a member who, acting alone or with one or more other persons, directly or indirectly takes the initiative, or engages, in organizing, directing, or arranging for the financing of any such committee or group;

(iv) any person who finances or joins with another to finance the solicitation of proxies, except persons who contribute not more than $500 and who are not otherwise participants;

(v) any person who lends money or furnishes credit or enters into any other arrangements, pursuant to any contract or understanding with a participant, for the purpose of financing or otherwise inducing the purchase, sale, holding or voting of securities of the registrant by any participant or other persons, in support of or in opposition to a participant; except that such terms do not include a bank, broker or dealer who, in the ordinary course of business, lends money or executes orders for the purchase or sale of securities and who is not otherwise a participant; and

(vi) any person who solicits proxies.

(b) The terms "participant" and "participant in a solicitation" do not include:

(i) any person or organization retained or employed by a participant to solicit security holders and whose activities are limited to the duties required to be performed in the course of such employment;

(ii) any person who merely transmits proxy soliciting material or performs other ministerial or clerical duties;

(iii) any person employed by a participant in the capacity of attorney, accountant, or advertising, public relations or financial adviser, and whose activities are limited to the duties required to be performed in the course of such employment;

(iv) any person regularly employed as an officer or employee of the registrant or any of its subsidiaries who is not otherwise a participant; or

(v) any officer or director of, or any person regularly employed by, any other participant, if such officer, director or employee is not otherwise a participant.

Item 5.   Interest of certain persons in matters to be acted upon—(a) *Solicitations not subject to Rule 14a–12(c)*.... Describe briefly any substantial interest, direct or indirect, by security holdings or otherwise, of each of the following persons in any matter to be acted upon, other than elections to office:

(1) If the solicitation is made on behalf of the registrant, each person who has been a director or executive officer of the registrant at any time since the beginning of the last fiscal year.

(2) If the solicitation is made otherwise than on behalf of the registrant, each participant in the solicitation, as defined in paragraphs (a)(iii), (iv), (v), and (vi) of Instruction 3 to Item 4 of this Schedule 14A.

(3) Each nominee for election as a director of the registrant.

(4) Each associate of any of the foregoing persons....

(b) *Solicitation subject to Rule 14a–12(c)*.   With respect to any solicitation subject to Rule 14a–12(c):

(1) Describe briefly any substantial interest, direct or indirect, by security holdings or otherwise, of each participant as defined in paragraphs (a)(ii), (iii), (iv), (v) and (vi) of Instruction 3 to Item 4 of this

Schedule 14A, in any matter to be acted upon at the meeting, and include with respect to each participant the following information, or a fair and accurate summary thereof:

(i) Name and business address of the participant.

(ii) The participant's present principal occupation or employment and the name, principal business and address of any corporation or other organization in which such employment is carried on.

(iii) State whether or not, during the past ten years, the participant has been convicted in a criminal proceeding (excluding traffic violations or similar misdemeanors) and, if so, give dates, nature of conviction, name and location of court, and penalty imposed or other disposition of the case. A negative answer need not be included in the proxy statement or other soliciting material.

(iv) State the amount of each class of securities of the registrant which the participant owns beneficially, directly or indirectly.

(v) State the amount of each class of securities of the registrant which the participant owns of record but not beneficially.

(vi) State with respect to all securities of the registrant purchased or sold within the past two years, the dates on which they were purchased or sold and the amount purchased or sold on each such date.

(vii) If any part of the purchase price or market value of any of the shares specified in paragraph (b)(1)(vi) of this Item is represented by funds borrowed or otherwise obtained for the purpose of acquiring or holding such securities, so state and indicate the amount of the indebtedness as of the latest practicable date. If such funds were borrowed or obtained otherwise than pursuant to a margin account or bank loan in the regular course of business of a bank, broker or dealer, briefly describe the transaction, and state the names of the parties.

(viii) State whether or not the participant is, or was within the past year, a party to any contract, arrangements or understandings with any person with respect to any securities of the registrant, including, but not limited to joint ventures, loan or option arrangements, puts or calls, guarantees against loss or guarantees of profit, division of losses or profits, or the giving or withholding of proxies. If so, name the parties to such contracts, arrangements or understandings and give the details thereof.

(ix) State the amount of securities of the registrant owned beneficially, directly or indirectly, by each of the participant's associates and the name and address of each such associate.

(x) State the amount of each class of securities of any parent or subsidiary of the registrant which the participant owns beneficially, directly or indirectly.

(xi) Furnish for the participant and associates of the participant the information required by Item 404(a) of Regulation S–K.

(xii) State whether or not the participant or any associates of the participant have any arrangement or understanding with any person—

(A) with respect to any future employment by the registrant or its affiliates; or

(B) with respect to any future transactions to which the registrant or any of its affiliates will or may be a party.

If so, describe such arrangement or understanding and state the names of the parties thereto.

(2) With respect to any person, other than a director or executive officer of the registrant acting solely in that capacity, who is a party to an arrangement or understanding pursuant to which a nominee for election as director is proposed to be elected, describe any substantial interest, direct or indirect, by security holdings or otherwise, that such person has in any matter to be acted upon at the meeting, and furnish the information called for by paragraphs (b)(1)(xi) and (xii) of this Item. . . .

Item 6. Voting securities and principal holders thereof. (a) As to each class of voting securities of the registrant entitled to be voted at the meeting (or by written consents or authorizations if no meeting is held), state the number of shares outstanding and the number of votes to which each class is entitled.

(b) State the record date, if any, with respect to this solicitation. If the right to vote or give consent is not to be determined, in whole or in part, by reference to a record date, indicate the criteria for the determination of security holders entitled to vote or give consent.

(c) If action is to be taken with respect to the election of directors and if the persons solicited have cumulative voting rights: (1) Make a statement that they have such rights, (2) briefly describe such rights, (3) state briefly the conditions precedent to the exercise thereof, and (4) if discretionary authority to cumulate votes is solicited, so indicate.

(d) Furnish the information required by Item 403 of Regulation S–K . . . to the extent known by the persons on whose behalf the solicitation is made.

(e) If, to the knowledge of the persons on whose behalf the solicitation is made, a change in control of the registrant has occurred since the beginning of its last fiscal year, state the name of the person(s) who acquired such control, the amount and the source of the consideration used by such person or persons; the basis of the control, the date and a description of the transaction(s) which resulted in the change of control and the percentage of voting securities of the registrant now beneficially owned directly or indirectly by the person(s) who acquired control; and the identity of the person(s) from whom control was assumed. If the source of all or any part of the consideration used is a loan made in the ordinary course of business by a bank ..., the identity of such bank shall be omitted provided a request for confidentiality has been made ... by the person(s) who acquired control. In lieu thereof, the material shall indicate that the identity of the bank has been so omitted and filed separately with the Commission.

> *Instruction.* 1. State the terms of any loans or pledges obtained by the new control group for the purpose of acquiring control, and the names of the lenders or pledgees.

> 2. Any arrangements or understandings among members of both the former and new control groups and their associates with respect to election of directors or other matters should be described.

Item 7. Directors and executive officers. If action is to be taken with respect to the election of directors, furnish the following information in tabular form to the extent practicable. If, however, the solicitation is made on behalf of persons other than the registrant, the information required need be furnished only as to nominees of the persons making the solicitation.

(a) The information required by instruction 4 to Item 103 of Regulation S–K [Legal Proceedings] ... with respect to directors and executive officers.

(b) The information required by Items 401, 404(a) and (c), and 405 of Regulation S–K. . . .

(c) With respect to registrants other than investment companies registered under the Investment Company Act of 1940, furnish the information required by Item 404(b) of Regulation S–K. . . .

(d)(1) State whether or not the registrant has standing audit, nominating and compensation committees of the Board of Directors, or committees performing similar functions. If the registrant has such committees, however designated, identify each committee member, state the number of committee meetings held by each such committee during the last fiscal year and describe briefly the functions performed by such committees. . . .

(2)(i) If the registrant does not have a standing nominating committee or committee performing similar functions, state the basis for the view of the board of directors that it is appropriate for the registrant not to have such a committee and identify each director who participates in the consideration of director nominees;

(ii) Provide the following information regarding the registrant's director nomination process:

(A) If the nominating committee has a charter, disclose whether a current copy of the charter is available to security holders on the registrant's website. If the nominating committee has a charter and a current copy of the charter is available to security holders on the registrant's website, provide the registrant's website address. If the nominating committee has a charter and a current copy of the charter is not available to security holders on the registrant's website, include a copy of the charter as an appendix to the registrant's proxy statement at least once every three fiscal years. If a current copy of the charter is not available to security holders on the registrant's website, and is not included as an appendix to the registrant's proxy statement, identify in which of the prior fiscal years the charter was so included in satisfaction of this requirement;

(B) If the nominating committee does not have a charter, state that fact;

(C) If the registrant is a listed issuer (as defined in Rule 10A–3) whose securities are listed on a national securities exchange registered pursuant to section 6(a) of the Act or in an automated inter-dealer quotation system of a national securities association registered pursuant to section 15A(a) of the Act that has independence requirements for nominating committee members, disclose whether the members of the nominating committee are independent, as independence for nominating committee members is defined in the listing standards applicable to the listed issuer;

(D) If the registrant is not a listed issuer (as defined in Rule 10A–3), disclose whether each of the members of the nominating committee is independent. In determining whether a member is independent, the registrant must use a definition of independence of a national securities exchange registered pursuant to section 6(a) of the Act or a national securities association registered pursuant to section 15A(a) of the Act that has been approved by the Commission (as that definition may be modified or supplemented), and state which definition it used. Whatever definition the registrant chooses, it must apply that definition consistently to all members of the nominating committee and use the independence standards of the same national securities exchange or national securities association for purposes of nominating committee disclosure under this requirement and audit committee disclosure required under paragraph (d)(3)(iv) of Item 7 of Schedule 14A;

(E) If the nominating committee has a policy with regard to the consideration of any director candidates recommended by security holders, provide a description of the material elements of that policy, which shall include, but need not be limited to, a statement as to whether the committee will consider director candidates recommended by security holders;

(F) If the nominating committee does not have a policy with regard to the consideration of any director candidates recommended by security holders, state that fact and state the basis for the view of the board of directors that it is appropriate for the registrant not to have such a policy;

(G) If the nominating committee will consider candidates recommended by security holders, describe the procedures to be followed by security holders in submitting such recommendations;

(H) Describe any specific, minimum qualifications that the nominating committee believes must be met by a nominating committee-recommended nominee for a position on the registrant's board of directors, and describe any specific qualities or skills that the nominating committee believes are necessary for one or more of the registrant's directors to possess;

(I) Describe the nominating committee's process for identifying and evaluating nominees for director, including nominees recommended by security holders, and any differences in the manner in which the nominating committee evaluates nominees for director based on whether the nominee is recommended by a security holder;

(J) With regard to each nominee approved by the nominating committee for inclusion on the registrant's proxy card (other than nominees who are executive officers or who are directors standing for re-election), state which one or more of the following categories of persons or entities recommended that nominee: security holder, non-management director, chief executive officer, other executive officer, third-party search firm, or other, specified source. With regard to each such nominee approved by a nominating committee of an investment company, state which one or more of the following additional categories of persons or entities recommended that nominee: security holder, director, chief executive officer, other executive officer, or employee of the investment company's investment adviser, principal underwriter, or any affiliated person of the investment adviser or principal underwriter;

(K) If the registrant pays a fee to any third party or parties to identify or evaluate or assist in identifying or evaluating potential nominees, disclose the function performed by each such third party; and

(L) If the registrant's nominating committee received, by a date not later than the 120th calendar day before the date of the registrant's proxy statement released to security holders in connection with the previous year's annual meeting, a recommended nominee from a security holder that beneficially owned more than 5% of the registrant's voting common stock for at least one year as of the date the recommendation was made, or from a group of security holders that beneficially owned, in the aggregate, more than 5% of the registrant's voting common stock, with each of the securities used to calculate that ownership held for at least one year as of the date the recommendation was made, identify the candidate and the security holder or security holder group that recommended the candidate and disclose whether the nominating committee chose to nominate the candidate, provided, however, that no such identification or disclosure is required without the written consent of both the security holder or security holder group and the candidate to be so identified.

(3) If the registrant has an audit committee:

(i) Provide the information required by Item 306 of Regulation S–K.

(ii) State whether the registrant's Board of Directors has adopted a written charter for the audit committee.

(iii) Include a copy of the written charter, if any, as an appendix to the registrant's proxy statement, unless a copy has been included as an appendix to the registrant's proxy statement within the registrant's past three fiscal years.

(iv)(A) If the registrant is a listed issuer, as defined in Rule 10A–3:

(1) Disclose whether the members of the audit committee are independent, as independence for audit committee members is defined in the listing standards applicable to the listed issuer. If the registrant does not have a separately designated audit committee, or committee performing similar functions, the registrant must provide the disclosure with respect to all members of its board of directors.

(2) If the listed issuer's board of directors determines, in accordance with the listing standards applicable to the listed issuer, to appoint a director to the audit committee who is not independent (apart from the requirements in Rule 10A–3) because of exceptional or limited or similar circumstances, disclose the nature of the relationship that makes that individual not independent and the reasons for the board of directors' determination.

(B) If the registrant, including a small business issuer, is not a listed issuer, disclose whether the registrant has an audit committee established in accordance with section 3(a)(58)(A) of the [Securities Exchange] Act and, if so, whether the members of the committee are independent. In determining whether a member is independent, the registrant must use a definition for audit committee member independence of a national securities exchange registered pursuant to section 6(a) of the Act or a national securities association registered pursuant to section 15A(a) of the Act that has been approved by the Commission (as such definition may be modified or supplemented), and state which definition was used. Whichever definition is chosen must be applied consistently to all members of the audit committee.

(v) The information required by paragraph (d)(3) of this Item shall not be deemed to be "soliciting material," or to be "filed" with the Commission or subject to Regulation 14A or 14C, other than as provided in this Item, or to the liabilities of section 18 of the Exchange Act, except to the extent that the registrant specifically requests that the information be treated as soliciting material or specifically incorporates it by reference into a document filed under the Securities Act or the Exchange

Act. Such information will not be deemed to be incorporated by reference into any filing under the Securities Act or the Exchange Act, except to the extent that the registrant specifically incorporates it by reference.

(vi) The disclosure required by this paragraph (d)(3) need only be provided one time during any fiscal year. . . .

(f) State the total number of meetings of the board of directors (including regularly scheduled and special meetings) which were held during the last full fiscal year. Name each incumbent director who during the last full fiscal year attended fewer than 75 percent of the aggregate of (1) the total number of meetings of the board of directors (held during the period for which he has been a director) and (2) the total number of meetings held by all committees of the board on which he served (during the periods that he served).

(g) If a director has resigned or declined to stand for re-election to the board of directors since the date of the last annual meeting of security holders because of a disagreement with the registrant on any matter relating to the registrant's operations, policies or practices, and if the director has furnished the registrant with a letter describing such disagreement and requesting that the matter be disclosed, the registrant shall state the date of resignation or declination to stand for re-election and summarize the director's description of the disagreement.

If the registrant believes that the description provided by the director is incorrect or incomplete, it may include a brief statement presenting its view of the disagreement.

(h)(1) State whether or not the registrant's board of directors provides a process for security holders to send communications to the board of directors and, if the registrant does not have such a process for security holders to send communications to the board of directors, state the basis for the view of the board of directors that it is appropriate for the registrant not to have such a process;

(2) If the registrant has a process for security holders to send communications to the board of directors:

(i) Describe the manner in which security holders can send communications to the board and, if applicable, to specified individual directors; and

(ii) If all security holder communications are not sent directly to board members, describe the registrant's process for determining which communications will be relayed to board members; and

(3) Describe the registrant's policy, if any, with regard to board members' attendance at annual meetings and state the number of board members who attended the prior year's annual meeting.

Item 8. Compensation of directors and executive officers. Furnish the information required by Item 402 of Regulation S–K if action is to be taken with regard to:

(a) the election of directors;

(b) any bonus, profit sharing or other compensation plan, contract or arrangement in which any director, nominee for election as a director, or executive officer of the registrant will participate;

(c) any pension or retirement plan in which any such person will participate; or

(d) the granting or extension to any such person of any options, warrants or rights to purchase any securities, other than warrants or rights issued to security holders as such, on a pro rata basis. However, if the solicitation is made on behalf of persons other than the registrant, the information required need be furnished only as to nominees of the persons making the solicitation and associates of such nominees....

Item 9. Independent public accountants. If the solicitation is made on behalf of the registrant and relates to: (1) The annual (or special meeting in lieu of annual) meeting of security holders at which directors are to be elected, or a solicitation of consents or authorizations in lieu of such meeting or (2) the election, approval or ratification of the registrant's accountant, furnish the following information describing the registrant's relationship with its independent public accountant:

(a) The name of the principal accountant selected or being recommended to security holders for election, approval or ratification for the current year. If no accountant has been selected or recommended, so state and briefly describe the reasons therefor.

(b) The name of the principal accountant for the fiscal year most recently completed if different from the accountant selected or recommended for the current year or if no accountant has yet been selected or recommended for the current year.

(c) The proxy statement shall indicate: (1) Whether or not representatives of the principal accountant for the current year and for the most recently completed fiscal year are expected to be present at the security holders' meeting, (2) whether or not they will have the opportunity to make a statement if they desire to do so, and (3) whether or not such representatives are expected to be available to respond to appropriate questions.

(d) If during the registrant's two most recent fiscal years or any subsequent interim period, (1) an independent accountant who was previously engaged as the principal accountant to audit the registrant's financial statements, or an independent accountant on whom the principal accountant expressed reliance in its report regarding a significant subsidiary, has resigned (or indicated it has declined to stand for re-election after the completion of the current audit) or was dismissed, or

(2) a new independent accountant has been engaged as either the principal accountant to audit the registrant's financial statements or as an independent accountant on whom the principal accountant has expressed or is expected to express reliance in its report regarding a significant subsidiary, then, notwithstanding any previous disclosure, provide the information required by Item 304(a) of Regulation S–K.

(e)(1) Disclose, under the caption Audit Fees, the aggregate fees billed for each of the last two fiscal years for professional services rendered by the principal accountant for the audit of the registrant's annual financial statements and review of financial statements included in the registrant's Form 10–Q or 10–QSB for services that are normally provided by the accountant in connection with statutory and regulatory filings or engagements for those fiscal years.

(2) Disclose, under the caption Audit–Related Fees, the aggregate fees billed in each of the last two fiscal years for assurance and related services by the principal accountant that are reasonably related to the performance of the audit or review of the registrant's financial statements and are not reported under paragraph (e)(1) of this section. Registrants shall describe the nature of the services comprising the fees disclosed under this category.

(3) Disclose, under the caption Tax Fees, the aggregate fees billed in each of the last two fiscal years for professional services rendered by the principal accountant for tax compliance, tax advice, and tax planning. Registrants shall describe the nature of the services comprising the fees disclosed under this category.

(4) Disclose, under the caption All Other Fees, the aggregate fees billed in each of the last two fiscal years for products and services provided by the principal accountant, other than the services reported in paragraphs (e)(1) through (e)(3) of this section. Registrants shall describe the nature of the services comprising the fees disclosed under this category.

(5)(i) Disclose the audit committee's pre-approval policies and procedures described in 17 CFR 210.2–01(c)(7)(i).

(ii) Disclose the percentage of services described in each of paragraphs (e)(2) through (e)(4) of this section that were approved by the audit committee pursuant to 17 CFR 210.2–01(c)(7)(i)(C).

(6) If greater than 50 percent, disclose the percentage of hours expended on the principal accountant's engagement to audit the registrant's financial statements for the most recent fiscal year that were attributed to work performed by persons other than the principal accountant's full-time, permanent employees. . . .

Item 10.   Compensation Plans. If action is to be taken with respect to any plan pursuant to which cash or noncash compensation may be paid or distributed, furnish the following information:

(a) *Plans Subject to Security Holder Action.*

(1) Describe briefly the material features of the plan being acted upon, identify each class of persons who will be eligible to participate therein, indicate the approximate number of persons in each such class, and state the basis of such participation.

(2)(i) In the tabular format specified below, disclose the benefits or amounts that will be received by or allocated to each of the following under the plan being acted upon, if such benefits or amounts are determinable:

NEW PLAN BENEFITS		
	Plan Name	
Name and Position	Dollar Value ($)	Number of Units
CEO		
A		
B		
C		
D		
Executive Group		
Non–Executive Director Group		
Non–Executive Officer Employee Group		

(ii) The table required by paragraph (a)(2)(i) of this Item shall provide information as to the following persons:

(A) Each person (stating name and position) specified in paragraph (a)(3) of Item 402 of Regulation S–K;

(B) All current executive officers as a group;

(C) All current directors who are not executive officers as a group; and

(D) All employees, including all current officers who are not executive officers, as a group. . . .

(b)(1) *Additional Information Regarding Specified Plans Subject to Security Holder Action.* With respect to any pension or retirement plan submitted for security holder action, state:

(i) The approximate total amount necessary to fund the plan with respect to past services, the period over which such amount is to be paid and the estimated annual payments necessary to pay the total amount over such period; and

(ii) The estimated annual payment to be made with respect to current services. In the case of a pension or retirement plan, information called for by paragraph (a)(2) of this Item may be furnished in the format specified by paragraph (f)(1) of Item 402 of Regulation S–K.

(2)(i) With respect to any specific grant of or any plan containing options, warrants or rights submitted for security holder action, state:

(A) The title and amount of securities underlying such options, warrants or rights;

(B) The prices, expiration dates and other material conditions upon which the options, warrants or rights may be exercised;

(C) The consideration received or to be received by the registrant or subsidiary for the granting or extension of the options, warrants or rights;

(D) The market value of the securities underlying the option, warrants, or rights as of the latest practicable date; and

(E) In the case of options, the federal income tax consequences of the issuance and exercise of such options to the recipient and the registrant; and

(ii) State separately the amount of such options received or to be received by the following persons if such benefits or amounts are determinable:

(A) Each person (stating name and position) specified in paragraph (a)(3) of Item 402 of Regulation S–K;

(B) All current executive officers as a group;

(C) All current directors who are not executive officers as a group;

(D) Each nominee for election as a director;

(E) Each associate of any of such directors, executive officers or nominees;

(F) Each other person who received or is to receive 5 percent of such options, warrants or rights; and

(G) All employees, including all current officers who are not executive officers, as a group. . . .

(c) *Information regarding plans and other arrangements not subject to security holder action.* Furnish the information required by Item 201(d) of Regulation S–K. . . .

Item 18. Matters not required to be submitted. If action is to be taken with respect to any matter which is not required to be submitted to a vote of security holders, state the nature of such matter, the reasons for submitting it to a vote of security holders and what action is intended to be taken by the registrant in the event of a negative vote on the matter by the security holders. . . .

Item 21. Voting Procedures. As to each matter which is to be submitted to a vote of security holders, furnish the following information:

(a) State the vote required for approval or election, other than for the approval of auditors.

(b) Disclose the method by which votes will be counted, including the treatment and effect of abstentions and broker non-votes under applicable state law as well as registrant charter and by-law provisions....

[FORM OF] NOTICE OF EXEMPT SOLICITATION— INFORMATION TO BE INCLUDED IN STATEMENTS SUBMITTED BY OR ON BEHALF OF A PERSON PURSUANT TO RULE 6(g)

Notice of Exempt Solicitation

1. Name of the Registrant:

---

2. Name of person relying on exemption:

---

3. Address of person relying on exemption:

---

4. Written materials. Attach written material required to be submitted pursuant to Rule 14a–6(g)(1).

Rule 14b–1. Obligation of Registered Brokers and Dealers in Connection With the Prompt Forwarding of Certain Communications to Beneficial Owners

(a) *Definitions.* Unless the context otherwise requires, all terms used in this section shall have the same meanings as in the Act and, with respect to proxy soliciting material, as in Rule 14a–1 thereunder and, with respect to information statements, as in Rule 14c–1 thereunder. In addition, as used in this section, the term "registrant" means:

(1) The issuer of a class of securities registered pursuant to Section 12 of the Act....

(2) An investment company registered under the Investment Company Act of 1940.

(b) *Dissemination and beneficial owner information requirements.* A broker or dealer registered under Section 15 of the Act shall comply with the following requirements for disseminating certain communications to beneficial owners and providing beneficial owner information to registrants.

(1) The broker or dealer shall respond, by first class mail or other equally prompt means, directly to the registrant no later than seven

business days after the date it receives an inquiry ... by indicating, by means of a search card or otherwise:

(i) The approximate number of customers of the broker or dealer who are beneficial owners of the registrant's securities that are held of record by the broker, dealer, or its nominee;

(ii) The number of customers of the broker or dealer who are beneficial owners of the registrant's securities who have objected to disclosure of their names, addresses, and securities positions if the registrant has indicated ... that it will distribute the annual report to security holders to beneficial owners of its securities whose names, addresses and securities positions are disclosed pursuant to paragraph (b)(3) of this section; ...

(2) The broker or dealer shall, upon receipt of the proxy, other proxy soliciting material, information statement, and/or annual reports to security holders, forward such materials to its customers who are beneficial owners of the registrant's securities no later than five business days after receipt of the proxy material, information statement or annual reports.

(3) The broker or dealer shall, through its agent or directly:

(i) Provide the registrant, upon the registrant's request, with the names, addresses, and securities positions, compiled as of a date specified in the registrant's request which is no earlier than five business days after the date the registrant's request is received, of its customers who are beneficial owners of the registrant's securities and who have not objected to disclosure of such information ...; and

(ii) Transmit the data specified in paragraph (b)(3)(i) of this section to the registrant no later than five business days after the record date or other date specified by the registrant....

(c) *Exceptions to dissemination and beneficial owner information requirements* ....

(2) A broker or dealer need not satisfy:

(i) Its obligations under paragraphs (b)(2) and (b)(3) of this section if a registrant does not provide assurance of reimbursement of the broker's or dealer's reasonable expenses, both direct and indirect, incurred in connection with performing the obligations imposed by paragraphs (b)(2) and (b)(3) of this section....

Rule 14b–2.   Obligation of Banks, Associations and Other Entities That Exercise Fiduciary Powers in Connection With the Prompt Forwarding of Certain Communications to Beneficial Owners

(a) *Definitions.* Unless the context otherwise requires, all terms used in this section shall have the same meanings as in the Act and, with respect to proxy soliciting material, as in Rule 14a–1 thereunder and, with respect to information statements, as in Rule 14c–1 thereunder. In addition, as used in this section, the following terms shall apply:

(1) The term "bank" means a bank, association, or other entity that exercises fiduciary powers.

(2) The term "beneficial owner" includes any person who has or shares, pursuant to an instrument, agreement, or otherwise, the power to vote, or to direct the voting of a security. . . .

(3) The term "registrant" means:

(i) The issuer of a class of securities registered pursuant to Section 12 of the Act.

(ii) . . . .

(b) *Dissemination and beneficial owner information requirements.* A bank shall comply with the following requirements for disseminating certain communications to beneficial owners and providing beneficial owner information to registrants.

(1) The bank shall:

(i) Respond, by first class mail or other equally prompt means, directly to the registrant, no later than one business day after the date it receives an inquiry . . . by indicating the name and address of each of its respondent banks that holds the registrant's securities on behalf of beneficial owners, if any; and

(ii) Respond, by first class mail or other equally prompt means, directly to the registrant no later than seven business days after the date it receives an inquiry . . . by indicating, by means of a search card or otherwise:

(A) The approximate number of customers of the bank who are beneficial owners of the registrant's securities that are held of record by the bank or its nominee;

(B) If the registrant has indicated . . . that it will distribute the annual report to security holders to beneficial owners of its securities, whose names, addresses, and securities positions are disclosed pursuant to paragraphs (b)(4)(ii) and (iii) of this section:

(1) With respect to customer accounts opened on or before December 28, 1986, the number of beneficial owners of the registrant's securities who have affirmatively consented to disclosure of their names, addresses, and securities positions; and

(2) With respect to customer accounts opened after December 28, 1986, the number of beneficial owners of the registrant's securities who have not objected to disclosure of their names, addresses, and securities positions; and

(C) The identity of its designated agent, if any, acting on its behalf in fulfilling its obligations under paragraphs (b)(4)(ii) and (iii) of this section; . . .

(2) Where proxies are solicited, the bank shall, within five business days after the record date:

(i) Execute an omnibus proxy, including a power of substitution, in favor of its respondent banks and forward such proxy to the registrant; and

(ii) Furnish a notice to each respondent bank in whose favor an omnibus proxy has been executed that it has executed such a proxy, including a power of substitution, in its favor pursuant to paragraph (b)(2)(i) of this section.

(3) Upon receipt of the proxy, other proxy soliciting material, information statement, and/or annual reports to security holders, the bank shall forward such materials to each beneficial owner on whose behalf it holds securities, no later than five business days after the date it receives such material and, where a proxy is solicited, the bank shall forward, with the other proxy soliciting material and/or the annual report, either:

(i) A properly executed proxy:

(A) indicating the number of securities held for such beneficial owner;

(B) bearing the beneficial owner's account number or other form of identification, together with instructions as to the procedures to vote the securities;

(C) briefly stating which other proxies, if any, are required to permit securities to be voted under the terms of the instrument creating that voting power or applicable state law; and

(D) being accompanied by an envelope addressed to the registrant or its agent, if not provided by the registrant; or

(ii) A request for voting instructions (for which registrant's form of proxy may be used and which shall be voted by the record holder bank or respondent bank in accordance with the instructions received), together with an envelope addressed to the record holder bank or respondent bank.

(4) The bank shall:

(i) Respond, by first class mail or other equally prompt means, directly to the registrant no later than one business day after the date it receives an inquiry made in accordance with Rule 14a–13(b)(1) or Rule 14c–7(b)(1) by indicating the name and address of each of its respondent banks that holds the registrant's securities on behalf of beneficial owners, if any;

(ii) Through its agent or directly, provide the registrant, upon the registrant's request, and within the time specified in paragraph (b)(4)(iii) of this section, with the names, addresses, and securities position, compiled as of a date specified in the registrant's request which is no earlier than five business days after the date the registrant's request is received, of:

(A) With respect to customer accounts opened on or before December 28, 1986, beneficial owners of the registrant's securities on whose behalf it holds securities who have consented affirmatively to disclosure of such information, subject to paragraph (b)(5) of this section; and

(B) With respect to customer accounts opened after December 28, 1986, beneficial owners of the registrant's securities on whose behalf it holds securities who have not objected to disclosure of such information;
. . .

(iii) Through its agent or directly, transmit the data specified in paragraph (b)(4)(ii) of this section to the registrant no later than five business days after the date specified by the registrant. . . .

(5) For customer accounts opened on or before December 28, 1986, unless the bank has made a good faith effort to obtain affirmative consent to disclosure of beneficial owner information pursuant to paragraph (b)(4)(ii) of this section, the bank shall provide such information as to beneficial owners who do not object to disclosure of such information. A good faith effort to obtain affirmative consent to disclosure of beneficial owner information shall include, but shall not be limited to, making an inquiry:

(i) Phrased in neutral language, explaining the purpose of the disclosure and the limitations on the registrant's use thereof:

(ii) Either in at least one mailing separate from other account mailings or in repeated mailings; and

(iii) In a mailing that includes a return card, postage paid enclosure.

(c) *Exceptions to dissemination and beneficial owner information requirements. . . .*

(2) The bank need not satisfy:

(i) Its obligations under paragraphs (b)(2), (b)(3), and (b)(4) of this section if a registrant does not provide assurance of reimbursement of its reasonable expenses, both direct and indirect, incurred in connection with performing the obligations imposed by paragraphs (b)(2), (b)(3), and (b)(4) of this section. . . .

REGULATION 14C: DISTRIBUTION OF INFORMATION PURSUANT TO SECTION 14(c) ...

Rule 14c-2. Distribution of Information Statement

(a) In connection with every annual or other meeting of the holders of the class of securities registered pursuant to section 12 of the Act ..., including the taking of corporate action by the written authorization or consent of security holders, the registrant shall transmit a written information statement containing the information specified in Schedule 14C ..., and containing the information specified in such form, to every security holder of the class that is entitled to vote or give an authorization or consent in regard to any matter to be acted upon and from whom proxy authorization or consent is not solicited on behalf of the registrant pursuant to Section 14(a) of the Act....

Rule 14c-3. Annual Report to Be Furnished Security Holders

(a) If the information statement relates to an annual (or special meeting in lieu of the annual) meeting, or written consent in lieu of such meeting, of security holders at which directors are to be elected, it shall be accompanied or preceded by an annual report to such security holders....

(1) The annual report shall contain the information specified in paragraphs (b)(1) through (b)(11) of Rule 14a-3....

SCHEDULE 14C. INFORMATION REQUIRED IN INFORMATION STATEMENT ...

Note: Where any item, other than Item 4, calls for information with respect to any matter to be acted upon at the meeting or, if no meeting is being held, by written authorization or consent, such item need be answered only with respect to proposals to be made by the registrant....

Item 1. Information required by Items of Schedule 14A.... Furnish the information called for by all of the items of Schedule 14A of Regulation 14A (other than Items 1(c), 2, 4 and 5 thereof) which would be applicable to any matter to be acted upon at the meeting if proxies were to be solicited in connection with the meeting....

Item 2. Statement that proxies are not solicited. The following statement shall be set forth on the first page of the information statement in bold-face type:

WE ARE NOT ASKING YOU FOR A PROXY AND YOU ARE REQUESTED NOT TO SEND US A PROXY

Item 3. Interest of certain persons in or opposition to matters to be acted upon. (a) Describe briefly any substantial interest, direct or indirect, by security holdings or otherwise, of each of the following persons in any matter to be acted upon, other than elections to office:

(1) Each person who has been a director or officer of the registrant at any time since the beginning of the last fiscal year;

(2) Each nominee for election as a director of the registrant;

(3) Each associate of any of the foregoing persons.

(b) Give the name of any director of the registrant who has informed the registrant in writing that he intends to oppose any action to be taken by the registrant at the meeting and indicate the action which he intends to oppose.

Item 4. Proposals by security holders. If any security holder entitled to vote at the meeting or by written authorization or consent has submitted to the registrant a reasonable time before the information statement is to be transmitted to security holders a proposal, other than elections to office, which is accompanied by notice of his intention to present the proposal for action at the meeting the registrant shall, if a meeting is held, make a statement to that effect, identify the proposal and indicate the disposition proposed to be made of the proposal by the registrant at the meeting. . . .

REGULATION 14D

Rule 14d–1. Scope of and Definitions Applicable to Regulations 14D and 14E

(a) *Scope.* Regulation 14D . . . shall apply to any tender offer which is subject to section 14(d)(1) of the Act, including, but not limited to, any tender offer for securities of a class described in that section which is made by an affiliate of the issuer of such class. Regulation 14E (Rules 14e–1 and 14e–2) shall apply to any tender offer for securities (other than exempted securities) unless otherwise noted therein. . . .

(2) *Definitions.* Unless the context otherwise requires, all terms used in Regulation 14D and Regulation 14E have the same meaning as in the Act and in Rule 12b–2 . . . promulgated thereunder. In addition, for purposes of sections 14(d) and 14(e) of the Act and Regulations 14D and 14E, the following definitions apply:

(1) The term *bidder* means any person who makes a tender offer or on whose behalf a tender offer is made: *Provided, however,* That the

term does not include an issuer which makes a tender offer for securities of any class of which it is the issuer;

(2) The term *subject company* means any issuer of securities which are sought by a bidder pursuant to a tender offer;

(3) The term *security holders* means holders of record and beneficial owners of securities which are the subject of a tender offer; . . .

(5) The term *tender offer material* means:

(i) The bidder's formal offer, including all the material terms and conditions of the tender offer and all amendments thereto;

(ii) The related transmittal letter (whereby securities of the subject company which are sought in the tender offer may be transmitted to the bidder or its depositary) and all amendments thereto; and

(iii) Press releases, advertisements, letters and other documents published by the bidder or sent or given by the bidder to security holders which, directly or indirectly, solicit, invite or request tenders of the securities being sought in the tender offer;

(6) The term *business day* means any day, other than Saturday, Sunday or a federal holiday. . . .

Rule 14d–2.   Commencement of a Tender Offer

(a) *Date of commencement.*   A bidder will have commenced its tender offer for purposes of section 14(d) of the Act and the rules under that section at 12:01 a.m. on the date when the bidder has first published, sent or given the means to tender to security holders.   For purposes of this section, the means to tender includes the transmittal form or a statement regarding how the transmittal form may be obtained.

(b) *Pre-commencement communications.*   A communication by the bidder will not be deemed to constitute commencement of a tender offer if:

(1) It does not include the means for security holders to tender their shares into the offer; and

(2) All written communications relating to the tender offer, from and including the first public announcement, are filed under cover of Schedule TO with the Commission no later than the date of the communication.   The bidder also must deliver to the subject company and any other bidder for the same class of securities the first communication relating to the transaction that is filed, or required to be filed, with the Commission.

Instructions to paragraph (b)(2) . . .

5.   "Public announcement" is any oral or written communication by the bidder, or any person authorized to act on the bidder's

behalf, that is reasonably designed to, or has the effect of, informing the public or security holders in general about the tender offer.

(c) *Filing and other obligations triggered by commencement.* As soon as practicable on the date of commencement, a bidder must comply with the filing requirements of Rule 14d–3(a), the dissemination requirements of Rule 14d–4(a) or (b), and the disclosure requirements of Rule 14d–6(a).

Rule 14d–3. Filing and Transmission of Tender Offer Statement

(a) *Filing and transmittal.* No bidder shall make a tender offer if, after consummation thereof, such bidder would be the beneficial owner of more than 5 percent of the class of the subject company's securities for which the tender offer is made, unless as soon as practicable on the date of the commencement of the tender offer such bidder:

(1) Files with the Commission a Tender Offer Statement on Schedule TO ..., including all exhibits thereto;

(2) Delivers a copy of such Schedule TO, including all exhibits thereto:

(i) To the subject company at its principal executive office; and

(ii) To any other bidder, which has filed a Schedule TO with the Commission relating to a tender offer which has not yet terminated for the same class of securities of the subject company, at such bidder's principal executive office or at the address of the person authorized to receive notices and communications (which is disclosed on the cover sheet of such other bidder's Schedule TO);

(3) Gives telephonic notice of the information required by Rule 14d–6(e)(2)(i) and (ii) and mails by means of first class mail a copy of such Schedule TO, including all exhibits thereto:

(i) To each national securities exchange where such class of the subject company's securities is registered and listed for trading ... which telephonic notice shall be made when practicable prior to the opening of each such exchange; and

(ii) To the National Association of Securities Dealers, Inc. ("NASD") if such class of the subject company's securities is authorized for quotation in the NASDAQ interdealer quotation system....

Rule 14d–4. Dissemination of Tender Offers to Security Holders

As soon as practicable on the date of commencement of a tender offer, the bidder must publish, send or give the disclosure required by Rule 14d–6 to security holders of the class of securities that is the subject of the offer, by complying with all of the requirements of any of the following:

(a) *Cash tender offers and exempt securities offers.* For tender offers in which the consideration consists solely of cash and/or securities exempt from registration under section 3 of the Securities Act of 1933:

(1) *Long-form publication.* The bidder makes adequate publication in a newspaper or newspapers of long-form publication of the tender offer.

(2) *Summary publication.* (i) If the tender offer is not subject to Rule 13e–3 ..., the bidder makes adequate publication in a newspaper or newspapers of a summary advertisement of the tender offer; and

(ii) Mails by first class mail or otherwise furnishes with reasonable promptness the bidder's tender offer materials to any security holder who requests such tender offer materials pursuant to the summary advertisement or otherwise....

(b) *Registered securities offers.* For tender offers in which the consideration consists solely or partially of securities registered under the Securities Act of 1933, a registration statement containing all of the required information, including pricing information, has been filed and a preliminary prospectus or a prospectus that meets the requirements of section 10(a) of the Securities Act, including a letter of transmittal, is delivered to security holders. However, for going-private transactions (as defined by Rule 13e–3) and roll-up transactions (as described by Item 901 of Regulation S–K), a registration statement registering the securities to be offered must have become effective and only a prospectus that meets the requirements of section 10(a) of the Securities Act may be delivered to security holders on the date of commencement.

(c) *Adequate publication.* Depending on the facts and circumstances involved, adequate publication of a tender offer pursuant to this section may require publication in a newspaper with a national circulation or may only require publication in a newspaper with metropolitan or regional circulation or may require publication in a combination thereof: *Provided, however,* That publication in all editions of a daily newspaper with a national circulation shall be deemed to constitute adequate publication....

Rule 14d–6.   Disclosure of Tender Offer Information to Security Holders

(a) *Information required on date of commencement.*—(1) Long-form publication. If a tender offer is published, sent or given to security holders on the date of commencement by means of long-form publication under Rule 14d–4(a)(1), the long-form publication must include the information required by paragraph (d)(1) of this section.

(2) *Summary publication.* If a tender offer is published, sent or given to security holders on the date of commencement by means of summary publication under Rule 14d–4(a)(2):

(i) The summary advertisement must contain at least the information required by paragraph (d)(2) of this section; and

(ii) The tender offer materials furnished by the bidder upon request of any security holder must include the information required by paragraph (d)(1) of this section.

(3) *Use of stockholder lists and security position listings.* If a tender offer is published, sent or given to security holders on the date of commencement by the use of stockholder lists and security position listings under Rule 14d–4(a)(3):

(i) The summary advertisement must contain at least the information required by paragraph (d)(2) of this section; and

(ii) The tender offer materials transmitted to security holders pursuant to such lists and security position listings and furnished by the bidder upon the request of any security holder must include the information required by paragraph (d)(1) of this section.

(4) *Other tender offers.* If a tender offer is published or sent or given to security holders other than pursuant to Rule 14d–4(a), the tender offer materials that are published or sent or given to security holders on the date of commencement of such offer must include the information required by paragraph (d)(1) of this section.

(b) *Information required in other tender offer materials published after commencement.* Except for tender offer materials described in paragraphs (a)(2)(ii) and (a)(3)(ii) of this section, additional tender offer materials published, sent or given to security holders after commencement must include:

(1) The identities of the bidder and subject company;

(2) The amount and class of securities being sought;

(3) The type and amount of consideration being offered; and

(4) The scheduled expiration date of the tender offer, whether the tender offer may be extended and, if so, the procedures for extension of the tender offer.

(c) *Material changes.* A material change in the information published or sent or given to security holders must be promptly disclosed to security holders in additional tender offer materials.

(d) *Information to be included.*—(1) *Tender offer materials other than summary publication.* The following information is required by paragraphs (a)(1), (a)(2)(ii), (a)(3)(ii) and (a)(4) of this section:

(i) The information required by Item 1of Schedule TO (Summary Term Sheet); and

(ii) The information required by the remaining items of Schedule TO for third-party tender offers, except for Item 12 (exhibits) of Schedule TO, or a fair and adequate summary of the information.

(2) *Summary Publication.* The following information is required in a summary advertisement under paragraphs (a)(2)(i) and (a)(3)(i) of this section:

(i) The identity of the bidder and the subject company;

(ii) The information required by Item 1004(a)(1) of Regulation M–A;

(iii) If the tender offer is for less than all of the outstanding securities of a class of equity securities, a statement as to whether the purpose or one of the purposes of the tender offer is to acquire or influence control of the business of the subject company;

(iv) A statement that the information required by paragraph (d)(1) of this section is incorporated by reference into the summary advertisement;

(v) Appropriate instructions as to how security holders may obtain promptly, at the bidder's expense, the bidder's tender offer materials; and

(vi) In a tender offer published or sent or given to security holders by use of stockholder lists and security position listings under Rule 14d–4(a)(3), a statement that a request is being made for such lists and listings. The summary publication also must state that tender offer materials will be mailed to record holders and will be furnished to brokers, banks and similar persons whose name appears or whose nominee appears on the list of security holders or, if applicable, who are listed as participants in a clearing agency's security position listing for subsequent transmittal to beneficial owners of such securities. If the list furnished to the bidder also included beneficial owners pursuant to Rule 14d–5(c)(1) and tender offer materials will be mailed directly to beneficial holders, include a statement to that effect.

(3) *No transmittal letter.* Neither the initial summary advertisement nor any subsequent summary advertisement may include a transmittal letter (the letter furnished to security holders for transmission of securities sought in the tender offer) or any amendment to the transmittal letter.

Rule 14d–7. Additional Withdrawal Rights

(a)(1) *Rights.* In addition to the provisions of section 14(d)(5) of the Act, any person who has deposited securities pursuant to a tender offer has the right to withdraw any such securities during the period such offer, request or invitation remains open.

(2) *Exemption during subsequent offering period.* Notwithstanding the provisions of section 14(d)(5) of the Act and paragraph (a) of this section, the bidder need not offer withdrawal rights during a subsequent offering period.

(b) *Notice of withdrawal.* Notice of withdrawal pursuant to this section shall be deemed to be timely upon the receipt by the bidder's depositary of a written notice of withdrawal specifying the name(s) of the tendering stockholder(s), the number or amount of the securities to be withdrawn and the name(s) in which the certificate(s) is (are) registered, if different from that of the tendering security holder(s). A bidder may impose other reasonable requirements, including certificate numbers and a signed request for withdrawal accompanied by a signature guarantee, as conditions precedent to the physical release of withdrawn securities.

Rule 14d–8. Exemption From Statutory Pro Rata Requirements

Notwithstanding the pro rata provisions of section 14(d)(6) of the Act, if any person makes a tender offer or request or invitation for tenders, for less than all of the outstanding equity securities of a class, and if a greater number of securities are deposited pursuant thereto than such person is bound or willing to take up and pay for, the securities taken up and paid for shall be taken up and paid for as nearly as may be pro rata, disregarding fractions, according to the number of securities deposited by each depositor during the period such offer, request or invitation remains open.

Rule 14d–9. Recommendation or Solicitation by the Subject Company and Others

(a) *Pre-commencement communications.* A communication by a person described in paragraph (e) of this section with respect to a tender offer will not be deemed to constitute a recommendation or solicitation under this section if:

(1) The tender offer has not commenced under Rule 14d–2; and

(2) The communication is filed under cover of Schedule 14D–9 with the Commission no later than the date of the communication.

(b) *Post-commencement communications.* After commencement by a bidder under Rule 14d–2, no solicitation or recommendation to security holders may be made by any person described in paragraph (e) of this section with respect to a tender offer for such securities unless as soon as practicable on the date such solicitation or recommendation is first published or sent or given to security holders such person complies with the following:

(1) Such person shall file with the Commission a Tender Offer Solicitation/Recommendation Statement on Schedule 14D–9 ... and

(2) If such person is either the subject company or an affiliate of the subject company,

(i) Such person shall hand deliver a copy of the Schedule 14D–9 to the bidder at its principal office ...; and

(ii) Such person shall give telephonic notice (which notice to the extent possible shall be given prior to the opening of the market) of the information required by Items 1003(d) and 1012(a) of Regulation M–A and shall mail a copy of the Schedule to each national securities exchange where the class of securities is registered and listed for trading and, if the class is authorized for quotation in the NASDAQ interdealer quotation system, to the National Association of Securities Dealers, Inc. ("NASD").

(3) If such person is neither the subject company nor an affiliate of the subject company,

(i) Such person shall mail a copy of the schedule to the bidder at its principal office . . .; and

(ii) Such person shall mail a copy of the Schedule to the subject company at its principal office. . . .

(d) *Information required in solicitation or recommendation.* Any solicitation or recommendation to holders of a class of securities referred to in section 14(d)(1) of the Act with respect to a tender offer for such securities shall include the name of the person making such solicitation or recommendation and the information required by Items 1 through 8 of Schedule 14D–9 . . . or a fair and adequate summary thereof: *Provided, however,* That such solicitation or recommendation may omit any of such information previously furnished to security holders of such class of securities by such person with respect to such tender offer.

(e) *Applicability.* (1) Except as is provided in paragraphs (e)(2) and (f) of this section, this section shall only apply to the following persons:

(i) The subject company, any director, officer, employee, affiliate or subsidiary of the subject company;

(ii) Any record holder or beneficial owner of any security issued by the subject company, by the bidder, or by any affiliate of either the subject company or the bidder; and

(iii) Any person who makes a solicitation or recommendation to security holders on behalf of any of the foregoing or on behalf of the bidder other than by means of a solicitation or recommendation to security holders which has been filed with the Commission pursuant to this section or Rule 14d–3. . . .

(2) Notwithstanding paragraph (e)(1) of this section, this section shall not apply to the following persons:

(i) A bidder who has filed a Schedule TO . . . pursuant to Rule 14d–3 . . .;

(ii) Attorneys, banks, brokers, fiduciaries or investment advisers who are not participating in a tender offer in more than a ministerial capacity and who furnish information and/or advice regarding such tender offer to their customers or clients on the unsolicited request of such customers or clients or solely pursuant to a contract or a relationship providing for advice to the customer or client to whom the information and/or advice is given. . . .

(f) *Stop-look-and-listen communication.* This section shall not apply to the subject company with respect to a communication by the subject company to its security holders which only:

(1) Identifies the tender offer by the bidder;

(2) States that such tender offer is under consideration by the subject company's board of directors and/or management;

(3) States that on or before a specified date (which shall be no later than 10 business days from the date of commencement of such tender offer) the subject company will advise such security holders of (i) whether the subject company recommends acceptance or rejection of such tender offer; expresses no opinion and remains neutral toward such tender offer; or is unable to take a position with respect to such tender offer and (ii) the reason(s) for the position taken by the subject company with respect to the tender offer (including the inability to take a position); and

(4) Requests such security holders to defer making a determination whether to accept or reject such tender offer until they have been advised of the subject company's position with respect thereto pursuant to paragraph (f)(3) of this section.

(g) *Statement of management's position.* A statement by the subject company of its position with respect to a tender offer which is required to be published or sent or given to security holders pursuant to Rule 14e–2 shall be deemed to constitute a solicitation or recommendation within the meaning of this section and section 14(d)(4) of the Act.

Rule 14d–10. Equal Treatment of Security Holders

(a) No bidder shall make a tender offer unless:

(1) The tender offer is open to all security holders of the class of securities subject to the tender offer; and

(2) The consideration paid to any security holder pursuant to the tender offer is the highest consideration paid to any other security holder during such tender offer....

Rule 14d–11. Subsequent Offering Period

A bidder may elect to provide a subsequent offering period of three business days to 20 business days during which tenders will be accepted if:

(a) The initial offering period of at least 20 business days has expired;

(b) The offer is for all outstanding securities of the class that is the subject of the tender offer, and if the bidder is offering security holders a choice of different forms of consideration, there is no ceiling on any form of consideration offered;

(c) The bidder immediately accepts and promptly pays for all securities tendered during the initial offering period;

(d) The bidder announces the results of the tender offer, including the approximate number and percentage of securities deposited to date, no later than 9:00 a.m. Eastern time on the next business day after the expiration date of the initial offering period and immediately begins the subsequent offering period;

(e) The bidder immediately accepts and promptly pays for all securities as they are tendered during the subsequent offering period; and

(f) The bidder offers the same form and amount of consideration to security holders in both the initial and the subsequent offering period.

SCHEDULE TO.   TENDER OFFER STATEMENT UNDER SECTION 14(d)(1) OR 13(e)(1)

Schedule TO

Tender Offer Statement under Section 14(d)(1) or 13(e)(1) of the Securities Exchange Act of 1934 ...

(Name of Subject Company (user))

(Names of Filing Persons (identifying status as offeror, issuer or other person))

(Title of Class of Securities)

(CUSIP Number of Class of Securities)

(Name, address, and telephone numbers of person authorized to receive notices and communications on behalf of filing persons) ...

General Instructions . . . .

C. If the statement is filed by a general or limited partnership, syndicate or other group, the information called for by Items 3, 5, 6, 10 and 11 must be given with respect to: (i) each partner of the general partnership; (ii) each partner who is, or functions as, a general partner of the limited partnership; (iii) each member of the syndicate or group; and (iv) each person controlling the partner or member. If the statement is filed by a corporation ... the information called for by the items specified above must be given with respect to: (a) each executive officer and director of the corporation; (b) each person controlling the corporation; and (c) each executive officer and director of any corporation or other person ultimately in control of the corporation. . . .

Item 1. *Summary Term Sheet*

Furnish the information required by Item 1001 of Regulation M–A unless information is disclosed to security holders in a prospectus that meets the requirements of Rule 421(d) [under the Securities Act].

Item 2. *Subject Company Information*

Furnish the information required by Item 1002 of Regulation M–A.

Item 3. *Identity and Background of Filing Person*

Furnish the information required by Item 1003(a) through (c) of Regulation M–A for a third-party tender offer and the information required by Item 1003(a) of Regulation M–A.

Item 4. *Terms of the Transaction*

Furnish the information required by Item 1004(a) of Regulation M–A for a third-party tender offer and the information required by Item 1004(a) through (b) of Regulation M–A for an issuer tender offer.

Item 5. *Past Contacts, Transactions, Negotiations and Agreements*

Furnish the information required by Item 1005(a) and (b) of Regulation M–A for a third-party tender offer and the information required by Item 1005(e) of Regulation M–A for an issuer tender offer.

Item 6. *Purposes of the Transaction and Plans or Proposals*

Furnish the information required by Item 1006(a) and (c)(1) through (7) of Regulation M–A for a third-party tender offer and the information required by Item 1006(a) through (c) of Regulation M–A for an issuer tender offer.

Item 7. *Source and Amount of Funds or Other Consideration*

Furnish the information required by Item 1007(a), (b) and (d) of Regulation M-A.

Item 8. *Interest in Securities of the Subject Company*

Furnish the information required by Item 1008 of Regulation M–A.

Item 9. *Persons/Assets, Retained, Employed, Compensated or Used*

Furnish the information required by Item 1009(a) of Regulation M-A.

Item 10. *Financial Statements*

If material, furnish the information required by Item 1010(a) and (b) of Regulation M–A for the issuer in an issuer tender offer and for the offeror in a third-party tender offer.

Instructions to Item 10:

1. Financial statements must be provided when the offeror's financial condition is material to security holder's decision whether to sell, tender or hold the securities sought. The facts and circumstances of a tender offer, particularly the terms of the tender offer, may influence a determination as to whether financial statements are material, and thus required to be disclosed.

2. Financial statements are not considered material when: (a) The consideration offered consists solely of cash; (b) the offer is not subject to any financing condition; and either: (c) the offeror is a public reporting company under Section 13(a) or 15(d) of the Act that files reports electronically.... , or (d) the offer is for all outstanding securities of the subject class. Financial information may be required, however, in a two-tier transaction....

Item 11. *Additional Information*

Furnish the information required by Item 1011 of Regulation M–A.

Item 12. *Exhibits*

File as an exhibit to the Schedule all documents specified by Item 1016 (a), (b), (d), (g) and (h) of Regulation M–A.

Item 13. *Information Required by Schedule 13E–3*

If the Schedule TO is combined with Schedule 13E–3, set forth the information required by Schedule 13E–3 that is not included or covered by the items in Schedule TO....

_____

SCHEDULE 14D–9. SOLICITATION/RECOMMENDATION STATEMENT UNDER SECTION 14(d)(4) OF THE SECURITIES EXCHANGE ACT OF 1934

_____

(Name of Subject Company)

_____

(Names of Persons Filing Statement)

_____

(Title of Class of Securities)

_____

(CUSIP Number of Class of Securities)

(Name, address, and telephone numbers of person authorized to receive notices and communications on behalf of the persons filing statement)

Item 1. Subject Company Information

Furnish the information required by Item1002(a) and (b) of Regulation
M-A.

Item 2. Identity and Background of Filing Person

Furnish the information required by Item 1003(a) and (d) of Regulation
M-A.

Item 3. Past Contacts, Transactions, Negotiations and Agreements

Furnish the information required by Item 1005(d) of Regulation
M-A.

Item 4. The Solicitation or Recommendation

Furnish the information required by Item 1012(a) through (c) of Regulation
M-A.

Item 5. Person/Assets, Retained, Employed, Compensated or Used

Furnish the information required by Item 1009(a) of Regulation
M-A.

Item 6. Interest in Securities of the Subject Company

Furnish the information required by Item 1008(b) of Regulation
M-A.

Item 7. Purposes of the Transaction and Plans or Proposals

Furnish the information required by Item 1006(d) of Regulation
M-A.

Item 8. Additional Information

Furnish the information required by Item 1011(b) of Regulation
M-A.

Item 9. Exhibits

File as an exhibit to the Schedule all documents specified by Item
1016(a), (e) and (g) of Regulation M-A. . . .

REGULATION 14E

Note: For the scope of and definitions applicable to Regulation 14E,
refer to Rule 14d-1.

Rule 14e-1. Unlawful Tender Offer Practices

As a means reasonably designed to prevent fraudulent, deceptive or
manipulative acts or practices within the meaning of section 14(e) of the
Act, no person who makes a tender offer shall:

(a) Hold such tender offer open for less than twenty business days from the date such tender offer is first published or sent or given to security holders ...;

(b) Increase or decrease the percentage of the class of securities being sought or the consideration offered or the dealer's soliciting fee to be given in a tender offer unless such tender offer remains open for at least ten business days from the date that notice of such increase or decrease is first published or sent or given to security holders....

(c) Fail to pay the consideration offered or return the securities deposited by or on behalf of security holders promptly after the termination or withdrawal of a tender offer....

Rule 14e–2.   Position of Subject Company With Respect to a Tender Offer

(a) *Position of subject company.*   As a means reasonably designed to prevent fraudulent, deceptive or manipulative acts or practices within the meaning of section 14(e) of the Act, the subject company, no later than 10 business days from the date the tender offer is first published or sent or given, shall publish, send or give to security holders a statement disclosing that the subject company:

(1) Recommends acceptance or rejection of the bidder's tender offer;

(2) Expresses no opinion and is remaining neutral toward the bidder's tender offer; or

(3) Is unable to take a position with respect to the bidder's tender offer.   Such statement shall also include the reason(s) for the position (including the inability to take a position) disclosed therein.

(b) *Material change.*   If any material change occurs in the disclosure required by paragraph (a) of this section, the subject company shall promptly publish or send or give a statement disclosing such material change to security holders....

Rule 14e–3.   Transactions in Securities on the Basis of Material, Nonpublic Information in the Context of Tender Offers

(a) If any person has taken a substantial step or steps to commence, or has commenced, a tender offer (the "offering person"), it shall constitute a fraudulent, deceptive or manipulative act or practice within the meaning of section 14(e) of the Act for any other person who is in possession of material information relating to such tender offer which information he knows or has reason to know is nonpublic and which he knows or has reason to know has been acquired directly or indirectly from:

(1) The offering person,

(2) The issuer of the securities sought or to be sought by such tender offer, or

(3) Any officer, director, partner or employee or any other person acting on behalf of the offering person or such issuer,

to purchase or sell or cause to be purchased or sold any of such securities or any securities convertible into or exchangeable for any such securities or any option or right to obtain or to dispose of any of the foregoing securities, unless within a reasonable time prior to any purchase or sale such information and its source are publicly disclosed by press release or otherwise.

(b) A person other than a natural person shall not violate paragraph (a) of this section if such person shows that:

(1) The individual(s) making the investment decision on behalf of such person to purchase or sell any security described in paragraph (a) of this section or to cause any such security to be purchased or sold by or on behalf of others did not know the material, nonpublic information; and

(2) Such person had implemented one or a combination of policies and procedures, reasonable under the circumstances, taking into consideration the nature of the person's business, to ensure that individual(s) making investment decision(s) would not violate paragraph (a) of this section, which policies and procedures may include, but are not limited to, (i) those which restrict any purchase, sale and causing any purchase and sale of any such security or (ii) those which prevent such individual(s) from knowing such information.

(c) Notwithstanding anything in paragraph (a) of this section to the contrary, the following transactions shall not be violations of paragraph (a) of this section:

(1) Purchase(s) of any security described in paragraph (a) of this section by a broker or by another agent on behalf of an offering person; or

(2) Sale(s) by any person of any security described in paragraph (a) of this section to the offering person.

(d)(1) As a means reasonably designed to prevent fraudulent, deceptive or manipulative acts or practices within the meaning of section 14(e) of the Act, it shall be unlawful for any person described in paragraph (d)(2) of this section to communicate material, nonpublic information relating to a tender offer to any other person under circumstances in which it is reasonably foreseeable that such communication is likely to result in a violation of this section *except* that this paragraph shall not apply to a communication made in good faith.

(i) To the officers, directors, partners or employees of the offering person, to its advisors or to other persons, involved in the planning, financing, preparation or execution of such tender offer;

(ii) To the issuer whose securities are sought or to be sought by such tender offer, to its officers, directors, partners, employees or advisors or to other persons, involved in the planning, financing, preparation or execution of the activities of the issuer with respect to such tender offer; or

(iii) To any person pursuant to a requirement of any statute or rule or regulation promulgated thereunder.

(2) The persons referred to in paragraph (d)(1) of this section are:

(i) The offering person or its officers, directors, partners, employees or advisors;

(ii) The issuer of the securities sought or to be sought by such tender offer or its officers, directors, partners, employees or advisors;

(iii) Anyone acting on behalf of the persons in paragraph (d)(2)(i) of this section or the issuer or persons in paragraph (d)(2)(ii) of this section; and

(iv) Any person in possession of material information relating to a tender offer which information he knows or has reason to know is nonpublic and which he knows or has reason to know has been acquired directly or indirectly from any of the above.

Rule 14e–4. Prohibited Transactions in Connection With Partial Tender Offers

(a) *Definitions.* For purposes of this section:

(1) The amount of a person's "net long position" in a subject security shall equal the excess, if any, of such person's "long position" over such person's "short position." For the purposes of determining the net long position as of the end of the proration period and for tendering concurrently to two or more partial tender offers, securities that have been tendered in accordance with the Rule and not withdrawn are deemed to be part of the person's long position.

(i) Such person's "long position," is the amount of subject securities that such person:

(A) or his agent has title to or would have title to but for having lent such securities; or

(B) has purchased, or has entered into an unconditional contract, binding on both parties thereto, to purchase but has not yet received; or

(C) has exercised a standardized call option for; or

(D) has converted, exchanged, or exercised an equivalent security for; or

(E) is entitled to receive upon conversion, exchange, or exercise of an equivalent security.

(ii) Such person's "short position," is the amount of subject securities or subject securities underlying equivalent securities that such person:

(A) has sold, or has entered into an unconditional contract, binding on both parties thereto, to sell; or

(B) has borrowed; or

(C) has written a non-standardized call option, or granted any other right pursuant to which his shares may be tendered by another person; or

(D) is obligated to deliver upon exercise of a standardized call option sold on or after the date that a tender offer is first publicly announced or otherwise made known by the bidder to holders of the security to be acquired, if the exercise price of such option is lower than the highest tender offer price or stated amount of the consideration offered for the subject security. For the purpose of this paragraph, if one or more tender offers for the same security are ongoing on such date, the announcement date shall be that of the first announced offer.

(2) The term "equivalent security" means:

(i) Any security (including any option, warrant, or other right to purchase the subject security), issued by the person whose securities are the subject of the offer, that is immediately convertible into, or exchangeable or exercisable for, a subject security, or

(ii) Any other right or option (other than a standardized call option) that entitles the holder thereof to acquire a subject security, but only if the holder thereof reasonably believes that the maker or writer of the right or option has title to and possession of the subject security and upon exercise will promptly deliver the subject security.

(3) The term "subject security" means a security that is the subject of any tender offer or request or invitation for tenders.

(4) For purposes of this rule, a person shall be deemed to "tender" a security if he:

(i) Delivers a subject security pursuant to an offer,

(ii) Causes such delivery to be made,

(iii) Guarantees delivery of a subject security pursuant to a tender offer,

(iv) Causes a guarantee of such delivery to be given by another person, or

(v) Uses any other method by which acceptance of a tender offer may be made.

(5) The term "partial tender offer" means a tender offer or request or invitation for tenders for less than all of the outstanding securities subject to the offer in which tenders are accepted either by lot or on a *pro rata* basis for a specified period, or a tender offer for all of the outstanding shares that offers a choice of consideration in which tenders for different forms of consideration may be accepted either by lot or on a *pro rata* basis for a specified period.

(6) The term "standardized call option" means any call option that is traded on an exchange, or for which quotation information is disseminated in an electronic interdealer quotation system of a registered national securities association.

(b) It shall be unlawful for any person acting alone or in concert with others, directly or indirectly, to tender any subject security in a partial tender offer:

(1) For his own account unless at the time of tender, and at the end of the proration period or period during which securities are accepted by lot (including any extensions thereof), he has a net long position equal to or greater than the amount tendered in:

(i) the subject security and will deliver or cause to be delivered such security for the purpose of tender to the person making the offer within the period specified in the offer; or

(ii) an equivalent security and, upon the acceptance of his tender will acquire the subject security by conversion, exchange, or exercise of such equivalent security to the extent required by the terms of the offer, and will deliver or cause to be delivered the subject security acquired for the purpose of tender to the person making the offer within the period specified in the offer; or

(2) For the account of another person unless the person making the tender:

(i) Possesses the subject security or an equivalent security, or

(ii) Has a reasonable belief that, upon information furnished by the person on whose behalf the tender is made, such person owns the subject security or an equivalent security and will promptly deliver the subject security or such equivalent security for the purpose of tender to the person making the tender.

(c) This rule shall not prohibit any transaction or transactions which the Commission, upon written request or upon its own motion, exempts, either unconditionally or on specified terms and conditions.

Rule 14e–5. Prohibiting Purchases Outside of a Tender Offer

(a) *Unlawful activity.* As a means reasonably designed to prevent fraudulent, deceptive or manipulative acts or practices in connection with a tender offer for equity securities, no covered person may directly or indirectly purchase or arrange to purchase any subject securities or any related securities except as part of the tender offer. This prohibition applies from the time of public announcement of the tender offer until the tender offer expires. . . .

(b) *Excepted activity.* The following transactions in subject securities or related securities are not prohibited by paragraph (a) of this section:

(1) *Exercises of securities.* Transactions by covered persons to convert, exchange, or exercise related securities into subject securities, if the covered person owned the related securities before public announcement;

(2) *Purchases for plans.* Purchases or arrangements to purchase by or for a plan that are made by an agent independent of the issuer;

(3) *Purchases during odd-lot offers.* . . .

(4) *Purchases as intermediary.* Purchases by or through a dealer-manager or its affiliates that are made in the ordinary course of business and made either:

(i) On an agency basis not for a covered person; or

(ii) As principal for its own account if the dealer-manager or its affiliate is not a market maker, and the purchase is made to offset a contemporaneous sale after having received an unsolicited order to buy from a customer who is not a covered person;

(5) *Basket transactions.* Purchases or arrangements to purchase a basket of securities containing a subject security or a related security if the following conditions are satisfied:

(i) The purchase or arrangement to purchase is made in the ordinary course of business and not to facilitate the tender offer;

(ii) The basket contains 20 or more securities; and

(iii) Covered securities and related securities do not comprise more than 5% the value of the basket;

(6) *Covering transactions.* Purchases or arrangements to purchase that are made to satisfy an obligation to deliver a subject security or a

related security arising from a short sale or from the exercise of an option by a non-covered person if:

(i) The short sale or option transaction was made in the ordinary course of business and not to facilitate the offer;

(ii) In the case of a short sale, the short sale was entered into before public announcement of the tender offer; and

(iii) In the case of an exercise of an option, the covered person wrote the option before public announcement of the tender offer;

(7) *Purchases pursuant to contractual obligations.* Purchases or arrangements to purchase pursuant to a contract if the following conditions are satisfied:

(i) The contract was entered into before public announcement of the tender offer;

(ii) The contract is unconditional and binding on both parties; and

(iii) The existence of the contract and all material terms including quantity, price and parties are disclosed in the offering materials;

(8) *Purchases or arrangements to purchase by an affiliate of the dealer-manager.* Purchases or arrangements to purchase by an affiliate of a dealer-manager if the following conditions are satisfied:

(i) The dealer-manager maintains and enforces written policies and procedures reasonably designed to prevent the flow of information to or from the affiliate that might result in a violation of the federal securities laws and regulations;

(ii) The dealer-manager is registered as a broker or dealer under Section 15(a) of the Act;

(iii) The affiliate has no officers (or persons performing similar functions) or employees (other than clerical, ministerial, or support personnel) in common with the dealer-manager that direct, effect, or recommend transactions in securities; and

(iv) The purchases or arrangements to purchase are not made to facilitate the tender offer. . . .

(c) *Definitions.* For purposes of this section, the term:

(1) *Affiliate* has the same meaning as in Rule 12b–2; . . .

(3) *Covered person* means:

(i) The offeror and its affiliates;

(ii) The offeror's dealer-manager and its affiliates;

(iii) Any advisor to any of the persons specified in paragraph (c)(3)(i) and (ii) of this section, whose compensation is dependent on the completion of the offer; and

(iv) Any person acting, directly or indirectly, in concert with any of the persons specified in this paragraph (c)(3) in connection with any purchase or arrangement to purchase any subject securities or any related securities; ...

(5) *Public announcement* is any oral or written communication by the offeror or any person authorized to act on the offeror's behalf that is reasonably designed to, or has the effect of, informing the public or security holders in general about the tender offer;

(6) *Related securities* means securities that are immediately convertible into, exchangeable for, or exercisable for subject securities; and

(7) *Subject securities* has the same meaning as in [Regulation M–A, Item 1000].

(d) *Exemptive authority.* Upon written application or upon its own motion, the Commission may grant an exemption from the provisions of this section, either unconditionally or on specified terms or conditions, to any transaction or class of transactions or any security or class of security, or any person or class of persons.

Rule 14e–7. Unlawful Tender Offer Practices in Connection With Roll–Ups

In order to implement Section 14(h) of the Act:

(a)(1) It shall be unlawful for any person to receive compensation for soliciting tenders directly from security holders in connection with a roll-up transaction as provided in paragraph (a)(2) of this section, if the compensation is:

    (i) Based on whether the solicited person participates in the tender offer; or

    (ii) Contingent on the success of the tender offer.

(2) Paragraph (a)(1) of this section is applicable to a roll-up transaction as defined in Item 901(c) of Regulation S–K, structured as a tender offer, except for a transaction involving only:

    (i) Finite-life entities that are not limited partnerships....

(b)(1) It shall be unlawful for any finite-life entity that is the subject of a roll-up transaction as provided in paragraph (b)(2) of this section to fail to provide a security holder list or mail communications related to a tender offer that is in furtherance of the roll-up transaction, at the option of a requesting security holder, pursuant to the procedures set forth in Rule 14a–7.

(2) Paragraph (b)(1) of this section is applicable to a roll-up transaction as defined in Item 901(c) of Regulation S–K, structured as a tender offer, that involves:

    (i) An entity with securities registered pursuant to Section 12 of the Act; or

(ii) A limited partnership....

Rule 14e–8.   Prohibited Conduct in Connection with Pre-commencement Communications

It is a fraudulent, deceptive or manipulative act or practice within the meaning of section 14(e) of the Act for any person to publicly announce that the person (or a party on whose behalf the person is acting) plans to make a tender offer that has not yet been commenced, if the person:

(a) Is making the announcement of a potential tender offer without the intention to commence the offer within a reasonable time and complete the offer;

(b) Intends, directly or indirectly, for the announcement to manipulate the market price of the stock of the bidder or subject company; or

(c) Does not have the reasonable belief that the person will have the means to purchase securities to complete the offer.

Rule 14f–1.   Change in Majority of Directors

If, pursuant to any arrangement or understanding with the person or persons acquiring securities in a transaction subject to section 13(d) or 14(d) of the Act, any persons are to be elected or designated as directors of the issuer, otherwise than at a meeting of security holders, and the persons so elected or designated will constitute a majority of the directors of the issuer, then, not less than 10 days prior to the date any such person take office as a director, or such shorter period prior to that date as the Commission may authorize upon a showing of good cause therefor, the issuer shall file with the Commission and transmit to all holders of record of securities of the issuer who would be entitled to vote at a meeting for election of directors, information substantially equivalent to the information which would be required by Items 6(a), (d) and (e), 7 and 8 of Schedule 14A of Regulation 14A ... to be transmitted if such person or persons were nominees for election as directors at a meeting of such security holders. Eight copies of such information shall be filed with the Commission.

REGULATION 15D.   REPORTS OF REGISTRANTS UNDER THE SECURITIES ACT OF 1933

Rule 15d–1.   Requirement of Annual Reports

Every registrant under the Securities Act of 1933 shall file an annual report, on the appropriate form authorized or prescribed therefor, for the fiscal year in which the registration statement under the

Securities Act of 1933 became effective and for each fiscal year thereafter, unless the registrant is exempt from such filing by section 15(d) of the Act or rules thereunder. . . .

Rule 15d–11. Current Reports on Form 8–K . . .

(a) Except as provided in paragraph (b) of this section, every registrant subject to Rule 15d–1 shall file a current report on Form 8–K within the period specified in that form unless substantially the same information as that required by Form 8–K has been previously reported by the registrant. . . .

Rule 15d–13. Quarterly Reports on Form 10–Q . . .

(a) Except as provided in paragraphs (b) and (c) of this section, every issuer that has securities registered pursuant to the Securities Act of 1933 and which is required to file annual reports pursuant to section 15(d) of the Securities Exchange Act of 1934 on Form 10–K . . . shall file a quarterly report on Form 10–Q . . . for each of the first three fiscal quarters of each fiscal year of the issuer. . . .

Rule 15d–14. Certification of Disclosure in Annual and Quarterly Reports

(a) Each report, including transition reports, filed on Form 10–Q [or] . . . Form 10–K, under section 15(d) of the [Securities Exchange] Act . . . must include certifications in the form specified in the applicable exhibit filing requirements of such report and such certifications must be filed as an exhibit to such report. Each principal executive and principal financial officer of the issuer, or persons performing similar functions, at the time of filing of the report must sign a certification.

(b) Each periodic report containing financial statements filed by an issuer pursuant to section 15(d) of the Act must be accompanied by the certifications required by Section 1350 of Chapter 63 of Title 18 of the United States Code and such certifications must be furnished as an exhibit to such report as specified in the applicable exhibit requirements for such report. Each principal executive and principal financial officer of the issuer (or equivalent thereof) must sign a certification. This requirement may be satisfied by a single certification signed by an issuer's principal executive and principal financial officers.

(c) A person required to provide a certification specified in paragraph [(a) or (b)] of this section may not have the certification signed on his or her behalf pursuant to a power of attorney or other form of confirming authority. . . .

Rule 15d–15. Controls and Procedures

(a) Every issuer that files reports under section 15(d) of the Act . . . must maintain disclosure controls and procedures (as defined in paragraph (e) of this section) and internal control over financial reporting (as defined in paragraph (f) of this section).

(b) Each such issuer's management must evaluate, with the participation of the issuer's principal executive and principal financial officers, or persons performing similar functions, the effectiveness of the issuer's disclosure controls and procedures, as of the end of each fiscal quarter. . . .

(c) The management of each such issuer . . . must evaluate, with the participation of the issuer's principal executive and principal financial officers, or persons performing similar functions, the effectiveness, as of the end of each fiscal year, of the issuer's internal control over financial reporting. The framework on which management's evaluation of the issuer's internal control over financial reporting is based must be a suitable, recognized control framework that is established by a body or group that has followed due-process procedures, including the broad distribution of the framework for public comment.

(d) The management of each such issuer, other than an investment company registered under section 8 of the Investment Company Act of 1940, must evaluate, with the participation of the issuer's principal executive and principal financial officers, or persons performing similar functions, any change in the issuer's internal control over financial reporting, that occurred during each of the issuer's fiscal quarters, or fiscal year in the case of a foreign private issuer, that has materially affected, or is reasonably likely to materially affect, the issuer's internal control over financial reporting.

(e) For purposes of this section, the term *disclosure controls and procedures* means controls and other procedures of an issuer that are designed to ensure that information required to be disclosed by the issuer in the reports that it files or submits under the Act (15 U.S.C. 78a et seq.) is recorded, processed, summarized and reported, within the time periods specified in the Commission's rules and forms. Disclosure controls and procedures include, without limitation, controls and procedures designed to ensure that information required to be disclosed by an issuer in the reports that it files or submits under the Act is accumulated and communicated to the issuer's management, including its principal executive and principal financial officers, or persons performing similar functions, as appropriate to allow timely decisions regarding required disclosure.

(f) The term *internal control over financial reporting* is defined as a process designed by, or under the supervision of, the issuer's principal executive and principal financial officers, or persons performing similar functions, and effected by the issuer's board of directors, management and other personnel, to provide reasonable assurance regarding the reliability of financial reporting and the preparation of financial statements for external purposes in accordance with generally accepted accounting principles and includes those policies and procedures that:

(1) Pertain to the maintenance of records that in reasonable detail accurately and fairly reflect the transactions and dispositions of the assets of the issuer;

(2) Provide reasonable assurance that transactions are recorded as necessary to permit preparation of financial statements in accordance with generally accepted accounting principles, and that receipts and expenditures of the issuer are being made only in accordance with authorizations of management and directors of the issuer; and

(3) Provide reasonable assurance regarding prevention or timely detection of unauthorized acquisition, use or disposition of the issuer's assets that could have a material effect on the financial statements.

REPORTS OF DIRECTORS, OFFICERS, AND PRINCIPAL SHAREHOLDERS

Rule 16a–1. Definition of Terms

Terms defined in this Rule shall apply solely to Section 16 of the Act and the rules thereunder. These terms shall not be limited to Section 16(a) of the Act but also shall apply to all other subsections under Section 16 of the Act.

(a) The term "beneficial owner" shall have the following applications:

(1) Solely for purposes of determining whether a person is a beneficial owner of more than ten percent of any class of equity securities registered pursuant to Section 12 of the Act, the term "beneficial owner" shall mean any person who is deemed a beneficial owner pursuant to Section 13(d) of the Act and the rules thereunder; *provided, however,* that the following institutions or persons shall not be deemed the beneficial owner of securities of such class held for the benefit of third parties or in customer or fiduciary accounts in the ordinary course of business ... as long as such shares are acquired by such institutions or persons without the purpose or effect of changing or influencing control of the issuer or engaging in any arrangement subject to Rule 13d–3(b):

(i) A broker or dealer ...;

(ii) A bank ...;

(iii) An insurance company ...;

(iv) An investment company ...;

(v) ... an investment adviser ...;

(vi) An employee benefit plan....

Note to paragraph (a). Pursuant to this section, a person deemed a beneficial owner of more than ten percent of any class of equity securities registered under Section 12 of the Act would file a Form 3, but the securities holdings disclosed on Form 3, and changes in beneficial ownership reported on subsequent Forms 4 or 5, would be determined by the definition of "beneficial owner" in paragraph (a)(2) of this section.

(2) Other than for purposes of determining whether a person is a beneficial owner of more than ten percent of any class of equity securities registered under Section 12 of the Act, the term "beneficial owner" shall mean any person who, directly or indirectly, through any contract, arrangement, understanding, relationship or otherwise, has or shares a direct or indirect pecuniary interest in the equity securities, subject to the following:

(i) The term "pecuniary interest" in any class of equity securities shall mean the opportunity, directly or indirectly, to profit or share in any profit derived from a transaction in the subject securities.

(ii) The term "indirect pecuniary interest" in any class of equity securities shall include, but not be limited to:

(A) securities held by members of a person's immediate family sharing the same household; *provided, however,* that the presumption of such beneficial ownership may be rebutted . . . ,

(B) a general partner's proportionate interest in the portfolio securities held by a general or limited partnership. . . .

(E) A person's interest in securities held by a trust . . . ; and

(F) A person's right to acquire equity securities through the exercise or conversion of any derivative security, whether or not presently exercisable.

(iii) A shareholder shall not be deemed to have a pecuniary interest in the portfolio securities held by a corporation or similar entity in which the person owns securities if the shareholder is not a controlling shareholder of the entity and does not have or share investment control over the entity's portfolio. . . .

(b) The term "call equivalent position" shall mean a derivative security position that increases in value as the value of the underlying equity increases, including, but not limited to, a long convertible security, a long call option, and a short put option position.

(c) The term "derivative securities" shall mean any option, warrant, convertible security, stock appreciation right, or similar right with an exercise or conversion privilege at a price related to an equity security, or similar securities with a value derived from the value of an equity security . . . .

(d) The term "equity security of such issuer" shall mean any equity security or derivative security relating to an issuer, whether or not issued by that issuer.

(e) The term "immediate family" shall mean any child, stepchild, grandchild, parent, stepparent, grandparent, spouse, sibling, mother-in-law, father-in-law, son-in-law, daughter-in-law, brother-in-law, or sister-in-law, and shall include adoptive relationships.

(f) The term "officer" shall mean an issuer's president, principal financial officer, principal accounting officer (or, if there is no such accounting officer, the controller), any vice-president of the issuer in charge of a principal business unit, division or function (such as sales, administration or finance), any other officer who performs a policy-making function, or any other person who performs similar policy-making functions for the issuer. Officers of the issuer's parent(s) or subsidiaries shall be deemed officers of the issuer if they perform such policy-making functions for the issuer. . . .

(g) The term "portfolio securities" shall mean all securities owned by an entity, other than securities issued by the entity.

(h) The term "put equivalent position" shall mean a derivative security position that increases in value as the value of the underlying equity decreases, including, but not limited to, a long put option and a short call option position.

Rule 16a–2.   Persons and Transactions Subject to Section 16

Any person who is the beneficial owner, directly or indirectly, of more than ten percent of any class of equity securities ("ten percent beneficial owner") registered pursuant to Section 12 of the Act, any director or officer of the issuer of such securities, and any person specified in Section 17(a) of the Public Utility Holding Company Act of 1935 or Section 30(h) of the Investment Company Act of 1940, . . . shall be subject to the provisions of Section 16 of the Act. The rules under Section 16 of the Act apply to any class of equity securities of an issuer whether or not registered under Section 12 of the Act. . . . With respect to transactions by persons subject to Section 16 of the Act:

(a) A transaction(s) carried out by a director or officer in the six months prior to the director or officer becoming subject to Section 16 of the Act shall be subject to Section 16 of the Act and reported on the first required Form 4 only if the transaction(s) occurred within six months of the transaction giving rise to the Form 4 filing obligation and the director or officer became subject to Section 16 of the Act solely as a result of the issuer registering a class of equity securities pursuant to Section 12 of the Act.

(b) A transaction(s) following the cessation of director or officer status shall be subject to section 16 of the Act only if:

(1) Executed within a period of less than six months of an opposite transaction subject to section 16(b) of the Act that occurred while that person was a director or officer; and

(2) Not otherwise exempted from section 16(b) of the Act pursuant to the provisions of this chapter.

Note to Paragraph (b): For purposes of this paragraph, an acquisition and a disposition each shall be an opposite transaction with respect to the other.

(c) The transaction that results in a person becoming a ten percent beneficial owner is not subject to Section 16 of the Act unless the person otherwise is subject to Section 16 of the Act. A ten percent beneficial owner not otherwise subject to Section 16 of the Act must report only those transactions conducted while the beneficial owner of more than ten percent of a class of equity securities of the issuer registered pursuant to Section 12 of the Act....

Rule 16a–3. Reporting Transactions and Holdings

(a) Initial statements of beneficial ownership of equity securities required by Section 16(a) of the Act shall be filed on Form 3. Statements of changes in beneficial ownership required by that Section shall be filed on Form 4. Annual statements shall be filed on Form 5. At the election of the reporting person, any transaction required to be reported on Form 5 may be reported on an earlier filed Form 4. All such statements shall be prepared and filed in accordance with the requirements of the applicable form....

(e) Any person required to file a statement under Section 16(a) of the Act shall, not later than the time the statement is transmitted for filing with the Commission, send or deliver a duplicate to the person designated by the issuer to receive such statements, or, in the absence of such a designation, to the issuer's corporate secretary or person performing equivalent functions.

(f)(1) A Form 5 shall be filed by every person who at any time during the issuer's fiscal year was subject to Section 16 of the Act with respect to such issuer, except as provided in paragraph (2) below. The Form shall be filed within 45 days after the issuer's fiscal year end, and shall disclose the following holdings and transactions not reported previously on Forms 3, 4 or 5:

(i) All transactions during the most recent fiscal year that were exempt from section 16(b) of the Act, except:

(A) Exercises and conversions of derivative securities exempt under either Rule 16b–3 or Rule 16b–6(b), and any transaction exempt under Rule 16b–3(d), Rule 16b–3(e), or Rule 16b–3(f) (these are required to be reported on Form 4);

(B) Transactions exempt from section 16(b) of the Act pursuant to Rule 16b–3(c), which shall be exempt from section 16(a) of the Act; and

(C) Transactions exempt from section 16(a) of the Act pursuant to another rule;

(ii) Transactions that constituted small acquisitions pursuant to Rule 16a–6(a);

(iii) all holdings and transactions that should have been reported during the most recent fiscal year, but were not; and

(iv) with respect to the first Form 5 requirement for a reporting person, all holdings and transactions that should have been reported in each of the issuer's last two fiscal years but were not, based on the reporting person's reasonable belief in good faith in the completeness and accuracy of the information.

(2) Notwithstanding the above, no Form 5 shall be required where all transactions otherwise required to be reported on the Form 5 have been reported before the due date of the Form 5.

Note: Persons no longer subject to Section 16 of the Act, but who were subject to the Section at any time during the issuer's fiscal year, must file a Form 5 unless paragraph (f)(2) is satisfied. See also Rule 16a–2(b) regarding the reporting obligations of persons ceasing to be officers or directors.

(g)(1) A Form 4 must be filed to report: all transactions not exempt from section 16(b) of the Act; all transactions exempt from section 16(b) of the Act pursuant to 16b–3(d), 16b–3(e), or 16b–3(f); and all exercises and conversions of derivative securities, regardless of whether exempt from section 16(b) of the Act. Form 4 must be filed before the end of the second business day following the day on which the subject transaction has been executed.

(2) Solely for purposes of section 16(a)(2)(C) of the Act and paragraph (g)(1) of this section, the date on which the executing broker, dealer or plan administrator notifies the reporting person of the execution of the transaction is deemed the date of execution for a transaction where the following conditions are satisfied:

(i) the transaction is pursuant to a contract, instruction or written plan for the purchase or sale of equity securities of the issuer (as defined in Rule 16a–1(d)) that satisfies the affirmative defense conditions of Rule 10b5–1(c) of this chapter; and

(ii) the reporting person does not select the date of execution.

(3) Transactions that are exempted by operation of any rule pursuant to Section 16(b) of the Act, other than exercises and conversions of derivative securities exempted pursuant to Rule 16b–6(b), shall be reported on either Form 5, or, at the option of the reporting person, Form 4, but in no event later than the due date of the Form 5 with respect to the fiscal year in which the transaction occurred. . . .

(k) Any issuer that maintains a corporate website shall post on that website by the end of the business day after filing any Form 3, 4 or 5 filed under section 16(a) of the Act as to the equity securities of that issuer. Each such form shall remain accessible on such issuer's website for at least a 12–month period. In the case of an issuer that is an investment company and that does not maintain its own website, if any of the issuer's investment adviser, sponsor, depositor, trustee, administrator, principal underwriter, or any affiliated person of the investment company maintains a website that includes the name of the issuer, the issuer shall comply with the posting requirements by posting the forms on one such website.

Rule 16a–4.   Derivative Securities

(a) For purposes of Section 16 of the Act, both derivative securities and the underlying securities to which they relate shall be deemed to be the same class of equity securities, *except that* the acquisition or disposition of any derivative security shall be separately reported. . . .

Rule 16a–6.   Small Acquisitions

(a) Any acquisition of an equity security or the right to acquire such securities, other than an acquisition from the issuer (including an employee benefit plan sponsored by the issuer), not exceeding $10,000 in market value shall be reported on Form 5, subject to the following conditions:

(1) Such acquisition, when aggregated with other acquisitions of securities of the same class (including securities underlying derivative securities, but excluding acquisitions exempted by rule from section 16(b) or previously reported on Form 4 or Form 5) within the prior six months, does not exceed a total of $10,000 in market value; and

(2) The person making the acquisition does not within six months thereafter make any disposition, other than by a transaction exempt from section 16(b) of the Act.

(b) If an acquisition no longer qualifies for the reporting deferral in paragraph (a) of this section, all such acquisitions that have not yet been reported must be reported on Form 4 before the end of the second business day following the day on which the conditions of paragraph (a) of this section are no longer met.

Rule 16a–8. Trusts

(a) *Persons Subject to Section 16.*

(1) *Trusts.* A trust shall be subject to section 16 of the Act with respect to securities of the issuer if the trust is a beneficial owner, pursuant to Rule 16a–1(a)(1), of more than ten percent of any class of equity securities of the issuer registered pursuant to section 12 of the Act ("ten percent beneficial owner").

(2) *Trustees, Beneficiaries, and Settlors.* In determining whether a trustee, beneficiary, or settlor is a ten percent beneficial owner with respect to the issuer:

(i) such persons shall be deemed the beneficial owner of the issuer's securities held by the trust, to the extent specified by Rule 16a–1(a)(1); and

(ii) settlors shall be deemed the beneficial owner of the issuer's securities held by the trust where they have the power to revoke the trust without the consent of another person. . . .

Rule 16a–9. Stock Splits, Stock Dividends, and Pro Rata Rights

The following shall be exempt from Section 16 of the Act:

(a) The increase or decrease in the number of securities held as a result of a stock split or stock dividend applying equally to all securities of a class, including a stock dividend in which equity securities of a different issuer are distributed; and

(b) the acquisition of rights, such as shareholder or preemptive rights, pursuant to a pro rata grant to all holders of the same class of equity securities registered under Section 12 of the Act. . . .

Rule 16a–10. Exemptions Under Section 16(a)

Except as provided in Rule 16a–6, any transaction exempted from the requirements of Section 16(a) of the Act, insofar as it is otherwise subject to the provisions of Section 16(b), shall be likewise exempt from Section 16(b) of the Act.

Rule 16a–12. Domestic Relations Orders

The acquisition or disposition of equity securities pursuant to a domestic relations order, as defined in the Internal Revenue Code or Title I of the Employee Retirement Income Security Act, or the rules thereunder, shall be exempt from section 16 of the Act.

Rule 16a–13.   Change in Form of Beneficial Ownership

A transaction, other than the exercise or conversion of a derivative security or deposit into or withdrawal from a voting trust, that effects only a change in the form of beneficial ownership without changing a person's pecuniary interest in the subject equity securities shall be exempt from section 16 of the Act.

EXEMPTION OF CERTAIN TRANSACTIONS
FROM SECTION 16(b) ...

Rule 16b–3.   Transactions Between an Issuer and Its Officers or Directors

(a) *General.*   A transaction between the issuer (including an employee benefit plan sponsored by the issuer) and an officer or director of the issuer that involves issuer equity securities shall be exempt from section 16(b) of the Act if the transaction satisfies the applicable conditions set forth in this section.

(b) *Definitions.*

(1) A *Discretionary Transaction* shall mean a transaction pursuant to an employee benefit plan that:

(i) Is at the volition of a plan participant;

(ii) Is not made in connection with the participant's death, disability, retirement or termination of employment;

(iii) Is not required to be made available to a plan participant pursuant to a provision of the Internal Revenue Code; and

(iv) Results in either an intra-plan transfer involving an issuer equity securities fund, or a cash distribution funded by a volitional disposition of an issuer equity security.

(2) An *Excess Benefit Plan* shall mean an employee benefit plan that is operated in conjunction with a Qualified Plan, and provides only the benefits or contributions that would be provided under a Qualified Plan but for any benefit or contribution limitations set forth in the Internal Revenue Code of 1986, or any successor provisions thereof.

(3)(i) A *Non–Employee Director* shall mean a director who:

(A) Is not currently an officer (as defined in Rule 16a–1(f)) of the issuer or a parent or subsidiary of the issuer, or otherwise currently employed by the issuer or a parent or subsidiary of the issuer;

(B) Does not receive compensation, either directly or indirectly, from the issuer or a parent or subsidiary of the issuer, for services rendered as a consultant or in any capacity other than as a director, except for an amount that does not exceed the dollar amount for which disclosure would be required pursuant to Item 404(a) [under Regulation S–U];

(C) Does not possess an interest in any other transaction for which disclosure would be required pursuant to Item 404(a) [under Regulation S–K]; and

(D) Is not engaged in a business relationship for which disclosure would be required pursuant to Item 404(b). . . .

(4) A *Qualified Plan* shall mean an employee benefit plan that satisfies the coverage and participation requirements of sections 410 and 401(a)(26) of the Internal Revenue Code of 1986, or any successor provisions thereof.

(5) A *Stock Purchase Plan* shall mean an employee benefit plan that satisfies the coverage and participation requirements of sections 423(b)(3) and 423(b)(5), or section 410, of the Internal Revenue Code of 1986, or any successor provisions thereof.

(c) *Tax-conditioned plans.* Any transaction (other than a Discretionary Transaction) pursuant to a Qualified Plan, an Excess Benefit Plan, or a Stock Purchase Plan shall be exempt without condition.

(d) *Acquisitions from the issuer.* Any transaction, other than a Discretionary Transaction, involving an acquisition from the issuer (including without limitation a grant or award), whether or not intended for a compensatory or other particular purpose, shall be exempt if:

(1) The transaction is approved by the board of directors of the issuer, or a committee of the board of directors that is composed solely of two or more Non–Employee Directors;

(2) The transaction is approved or ratified, in compliance with section 14 of the Act, by either: the affirmative votes of the holders of a majority of the securities of the issuer present, or represented, and entitled to vote at a meeting duly held in accordance with the applicable laws of the state or other jurisdiction in which the issuer is incorporated; or the written consent of the holders of a majority of the securities of the issuer entitled to vote; *provided that* such ratification occurs no later than the date of the next annual meeting of shareholders; or

(3) The issuer equity securities so acquired are held by the officer or director for a period of six months following the date of such acquisition, *provided that* this condition shall be satisfied with respect to a derivative security if at least six months elapse from the

date of acquisition of the derivative security to the date of disposition of the derivative security (other than upon exercise or conversion) or its underlying equity security.

(e) *Dispositions to the issuer.* Any transaction, other than a Discretionary Transaction, involving the disposition to the issuer of issuer equity securities, whether or not intended for a compensatory or other particular purpose, shall be exempt, provided that the terms of such disposition are approved in advance in the manner prescribed by either paragraph (d)(1) or paragraph (d)(2) of this section.

(f) *Discretionary Transactions.* A Discretionary Transaction shall be exempt only if effected pursuant to an election made at least six months following the date of the most recent election, with respect to any plan of the issuer, that effected a Discretionary Transaction that was:

(1) An acquisition, if the transaction to be exempted would be a disposition; or

(2) A disposition, if the transaction to be exempted would be an acquisition.

Notes to Rule 16b–3:

Note (1): The exercise or conversion of a derivative security that does not satisfy the conditions of this section is eligible for exemption from section 16(b) of the Act to the extent that the conditions of Rule 16b–6(b) are satisfied.

Note (2): Section 16(a) reporting requirements applicable to transactions exempt pursuant to this section are set forth in Rule 16a–3(f) and (g) and Rule 16a–4.

Note (3): The approval conditions of paragraphs (d)(1), (d)(2) and (e) of this section require the approval of each specific transaction, and are not satisfied by approval of a plan in its entirety except for the approval of a plan pursuant to which the terms and conditions of each transaction are fixed in advance, such as a formula plan. Where the terms of a subsequent transaction (such as the exercise price of an option, or the provision of an exercise or tax withholding right) are provided for in a transaction as initially approved pursuant to paragraphs (d)(1), (d)(2) or (e), such subsequent transaction shall not require further specific approval.

Rule 16b–5.   Bona Fide Gifts and Inheritance

Both the acquisition and the disposition of equity securities shall be exempt from the operation of Section 16(b) of the Act if they are: (a) bona fide gifts; or (b) transfers of securities by will or the laws of descent and distribution.

Rule 16b–6. Derivative Securities

(a) The establishment of or increase in a call equivalent position or liquidation of or decrease in a put equivalent position shall be deemed a purchase of the underlying security for purposes of Section 16(b) of the Act, and the establishment of or increase in a put equivalent position or liquidation of or decrease in a call equivalent position shall be deemed a sale of the underlying securities for purposes of Section 16(b) of the Act . . . .

(b) The closing of a derivative security position as a result of its exercise or conversion shall be exempt from the operation of Section 16(b) of the Act, and the acquisition of underlying securities at a fixed exercise price due to the exercise or conversion of a call equivalent position or the disposition of underlying securities at a fixed exercise price due to the exercise of a put equivalent position shall be exempt from the operation of Section 16(b) of the Act . . . .

(c) In determining the short-swing profit recoverable pursuant to Section 16(b) of the Act from transactions involving the purchase and sale or sale and purchase of derivative and other securities, the following rules apply:

(1) Short-swing profits in transactions involving the purchase and sale or sale and purchase of derivative securities that have identical characteristics (*e.g.,* purchases and sales of call options of the same strike price and expiration date, or purchases and sales of the same series of convertible debentures) shall be measured by the actual prices paid or received in the short-swing transactions.

(2) Short-swing profits in transactions involving the purchase and sale or sale and purchase of derivative securities having different characteristics but related to the same underlying security (*e.g.,* the purchase of a call option and the sale of a convertible debenture) or derivative securities and underlying securities shall not exceed the difference in price of the underlying security on the date of purchase or sale and the date of sale or purchase . . . .

Rule 16b–7. Mergers, Reclassifications, and Consolidations

(a) The following transactions shall be exempt from the provisions of section 16(b) of the Act:

(1) The acquisition of a security of a company, pursuant to a merger, reclassification or consolidation, in exchange for a security of a company that before the merger, reclassification or consolidation, owned 85 percent or more of either:

(i) The equity securities of all other companies involved in the merger, reclassification or consolidation, or in the case of a consolidation, the resulting company; or

(ii) The combined assets of all the companies involved in the merger, reclassification or consolidation, computed according to their book values before the merger, reclassification or consolidation as determined by reference to their most recent available financial statements for a 12 month period before the merger, reclassification or consolidation, or such shorter time as the company has been in existence.

(2) The disposition of a security, pursuant to a merger, reclassification or consolidation, of a company that before the merger, reclassification or consolidation, owned 85 percent or more of either:

(i) The equity securities of all other companies involved in the merger, reclassification or consolidation or, in the case of a consolidation, the resulting company; or

(ii) The combined assets of all the companies undergoing merger, reclassification or consolidation, computed according to their book values before the merger, reclassification or consolidation as determined by reference to their most recent available financial statements for a 12 month period before the merger, reclassification or consolidation.

(b) A merger within the meaning of this section shall include the sale or purchase of substantially all the assets of one company by another in exchange for equity securities which are then distributed to the security holders of the company that sold its assets.

(c) The exemption provided by this section applies to any securities transaction that satisfies the conditions specified in this section and is not conditioned on the transaction satisfying any other conditions.

(d) Notwithstanding the foregoing, if a person subject to section 16 of the Act makes any non-exempt purchase of a security in any company involved in the merger, reclassification or consolidation and any non-exempt sale of a security in any company involved in the merger, reclassification or consolidation within any period of less than six months during which the merger, reclassification or consolidation took place, the exemption provided by this section shall be unavailable to the extent of such purchase and sale.

FORM 3

UNITED STATES SECURITIES AND EXCHANGE COMMISSION

Washington, D.C. 20549

FORM 3

INITIAL STATEMENT OF BENEFICIAL OWNERSHIP OF SECURITIES ...

GENERAL INSTRUCTIONS

1. Who Must File

(a) This Form must be filed by the following persons ("reporting person"):

(i) any director or officer of an issuer with a class of equity securities registered pursuant to Section 12 of the Securities Exchange Act of 1934 ("Exchange Act"); (*Note:* Title is not determinative for purposes of determining "officer" status. See Rule 16a–1(f) for the definition of "officer");

(ii) any beneficial owner of greater than 10% of a class of equity securities registered under Section 12 of the Exchange Act, as determined by voting or investment control over the securities pursuant to Rule 16a–1(a)(1) ("ten percent holder"); ...

(v) any trust, trustee, beneficiary or settlor required to report pursuant to Rule 16a–8....

(c) If a person described above does not beneficially own any securities required to be reported (*see* Rule 16a–1 and Instruction 5), the person is required to file this Form and state that no securities are beneficially owned.

2. When Form Must Be Filed

... This Form must be filed within 10 days after the event by which the person becomes a reporting person (*i.e.*, officer, director, ten percent holder or other person)....

3. Where Form Must Be Filed

(a) A reporting person must file this Form in electronic format via the Commission's Electronic Data Gathering Analysis and Retrieval System (EDGAR)....

(b) At the time this Form or any amendment is filed with the Commission, file one copy with each Exchange on which any class of securities of the issuer is registered....

4. Class of Securities Reported

... Persons reporting pursuant to Section 16(a) of the Exchange Act shall include information as to their beneficial ownership of any class of equity securities of the issuer, even though one or more of such classes may not be registered pursuant to Section 12 of the Exchange Act....

5. Holdings Required to Be Reported

(a) *General Requirements*

Report holdings of each class of securities of the issuer beneficially owned as of the date of the event requiring the filing of this Form. See Instruction 4 as to securities required to be reported.

(b) *Beneficial Ownership Reported (Pecuniary Interest)*

(i) Although, for purposes of determining status as a ten percent holder, a person is deemed to beneficially own securities over which that person has voting or investment control (*see* Rule 16a–1(a)(1)), for reporting purposes, a person is deemed to be the beneficial owner of securities if that person has or shares the opportunity, directly or indirectly, to profit or share in any profit derived from a transaction in the securities ("pecuniary interest"). *See* Rule 16a–1(a)(2)....

(ii) Both direct and indirect beneficial ownership of securities shall be reported. Securities beneficially owned directly are those held in the reporting person's name or in the name of a bank, broker or nominee for the account of the reporting person. In addition, securities held as joint tenants, tenants in common, tenants by the entirety, or as community property are to be reported as held directly. If a person has a pecuniary interest, by reason of any contract, understanding or relationship (including a family relationship or arrangement), in securities held in the name of another person, that person is an indirect beneficial owner of those securities. *See* Rule 16a–1(a)(2)(ii) for certain indirect beneficial ownerships.

(iii) Report securities beneficially owned directly on a separate line from those beneficially owned indirectly. Report different forms of indirect ownership on separate lines. The nature of indirect ownership shall be stated as specifically as possible; for example, "By Self as Trustee for X," "By Spouse," "By X Trust," "By Y Corporation," etc.

(iv) In stating the amount of securities owned indirectly through a partnership, corporation, trust, or other entity, report the number of securities representing the reporting person's proportionate interest in securities beneficially owned by that entity....

FORM 3

UNITED STATES SECURITIES AND EXCHANGE COMMISSION
Washington, D.C. 20549
Form 3
INITIAL STATEMENT OF BENEFICIAL OWNERSHIP OF SECURITIES

Filed pursuant to Section 16(a) of the Securities Exchange Act of 1934, Section 17(a) of the Public Utility
Holding Company Act of 1935 or Section 30(h) of the Investment Company Act of 1940

OMB APPROVAL	
OMB Number:	3235-0104
Expires:	January 31, 2005
Estimated average burden hours per response. 0.5	

(Print or Type Responses)

1. Name and Address of Reporting Person*	2. Date of Event Requiring Statement (Month/Day/Year)	3. Issuer Name and Ticker or Trading Symbol
(Last) (First) (Middle)		
(Street)		4. Relationship of Reporting Person(s) to Issuer (Check all applicable)
		____ Director ____ 10% Owner
		____ Officer (give ____ Other (specify
		title below) below)
(City) (State) (Zip)		

5. If Amendment, Date Original Filed (Month/Day/Year)
6. Individual or Joint/Group Filing (Check Applicable Line)
____ Form filed by One Reporting Person
____ Form filed by More than One Reporting Person

Table I — Non-Derivative Securities Beneficially Owned

1. Title of Security (Instr. 4)	2. Amount of Securities Beneficially Owned (Instr. 4)	3. Ownership Form: Direct (D) or Indirect (I) (Instr. 5)	4. Nature of Indirect Beneficial Ownership (Instr. 5)

Reminder: Report on a separate line for each class of securities beneficially owned directly or indirectly.
* If the form is filed by more than one reporting person, *see* Instruction 5(b)(v).

**Potential persons who are to respond to the collection of information contained in this form are not
required to respond unless the form displays a currently valid OMB control number.**

SEC 1473 (6-03) (Over)

Form 3

SECURITIES EXCHANGE ACT OF 1934

FORM 3 (continued)   Table II — Derivative Securities Beneficially Owned (*e.g.*, puts, calls, warrants, options, convertible securities)

1. Title of Derivative Security (Instr. 4)	2. Date Exercisable and Expiration Date (Month/Day/Year)		3. Title and Amount of Securities Underlying Derivative Security (Instr. 4)		4. Conversion or Exercise Price of Derivative Security	5. Ownership Form of Derivative Security: Direct (D) or Indirect (I) (Instr. 5)	6. Nature of Indirect Beneficial Ownership (Instr. 5)
	Date Exercisable	Expiration Date	Title	Amount or Number of Shares			

Explanation of Responses:

** Intentional misstatements or omissions of facts constitute Federal Criminal Violations.
See 18 U.S.C. 1001 and 15 U.S.C. 78ff(a).

Note: File three copies of this Form, one of which must be manually signed. If space is insufficient, *See* Instruction 6 for procedure.

Potential persons who are to respond to the collection of information contained in this form are not required to respond unless the form displays a currently valid OMB Number.

**Signature of Reporting Person   Date

Page 2

FORM 4

UNITED STATES SECURITIES AND EXCHANGE COMMISSION

Washington, D.C. 20549

FORM 4

STATEMENT OF CHANGES OF BENEFICIAL OWNERSHIP OF SECURITIES ...

GENERAL INSTRUCTIONS

1. When Form Must Be Filed

(a) This Form must be filed before the end of the second business day following the day on which a transaction resulting in a change in beneficial ownership has been executed (see Rule 16a–1(a)(2) and Instruction 4 regarding the meaning of "beneficial owner," and Rule 16a–3(g) regarding determination of the date of execution for specified transactions). This Form and any amendment is deemed filed with the Commissions or the Exchange on the date it is received by the Commission or the Exchange, respectively. *See*, however, Rule 16a–3(h) regarding delivery to a third party business that guarantees delivery of the filing no later than the specified due date.

(b) A reporting person no longer subject to Section 16 of the Securities Exchange Act of 1934 ("Exchange Act") must check the exit box appearing on this Form. However, Form 4 and 5 obligations may continue to be applicable. *See* Rule 16a–3(f); *see also* Rule 16a–2(b) (transactions after termination of insider status). Form 5 transactions to date may be included on this Form and subsequent Form 5 transactions may be reported on a later Form 4 or Form 5, provided all transactions are reported by the required date.

(c) A separate Form shall be filed to reflect beneficial ownership of securities of each issuer, except that a single statement shall be filed with respect to the securities of a registered public utility holding company and all of its subsidiary companies.

(d) If a reporting person is not an officer, director, or ten percent holder, the person should check "other" in Item 6 (Relationship of Reporting Person to Issuer) and describe the reason for reporting status in the space provided.

Form 4 *SECURITIES EXCHANGE ACT OF 1934*

2. Where Form Must Be Filed . . .*

3. Class of Securities Reported . . .

4. Transactions and Holdings Required to be Reported

   (a) *General Requirements*

      (i) Report, in accordance with Rules 16a–3(g):

         (1) all transactions not exempt from § 16(b);

         (2) all transactions exempt from Section 16(b) pursuant to Rule 16b–3(d), Rule 16b–3(e), or Rule 16b–3(f); and

         (3) all exercises and conversions of derivative securities, regardless of whether exempt from Section 16(b) of the Act.

         Every transaction must be reported even though acquisitions and dispositions are equal. Report total beneficial ownership following the reported transaction(s) for each class of securities in which a transaction was reported. . . .

   (b) *Beneficial Ownership Reported (Pecuniary Interest)*

      (i) Although for purposes of determining status as a ten percent holder, a person is deemed to beneficially own securities over which that person exercises voting or investment control (*see* Rule 16a–1(a)(1)), for reporting transactions and holdings, a person is deemed to be the beneficial owner of securities if that person has the opportunity, directly or indirectly, to profit or share in any profit derived from a transaction in the securities ("pecuniary interest"). *See* Rule 16a–1(a)(2). *See also* Rule 16a–8 for the application of the beneficial ownership definition to trust holdings and transactions.

      (ii) Both direct and indirect beneficial ownership of securities shall be reported. Securities beneficially owned directly are those held in the reporting person's name or in the name of a bank, broker or nominee for the account of the reporting person. In addition, securities held as joint tenants, tenants in common, tenants by the entirety, or as community property are to be reported as held directly. If a person has a pecuniary interest, by reason of any contract, understanding or relationship (including a family relationship or arrangement), in securities held in the name of another person, that person is an indirect beneficial owner of the securities. *See* Rule 16a–1(a)(2)(ii) for certain indirect beneficial ownerships. . . .

---

* Instructions 2, 3, and 4(b) parallel instructions 3, 4, and 5(b) for Form 3, supra.   (Footnote by ed.)

FORM 4

☐ Check this box if no longer subject to Section 16. Form 4 or Form 5 obligations may continue. *See Instruction 1(b).*

OMB APPROVAL
OMB Number: 3235-0287
Expires: January 31, 2005
Estimated average burden
hours per response 0.5

UNITED STATES SECURITIES AND EXCHANGE COMMISSION
Washington, D.C. 20549

STATEMENT OF CHANGES IN BENEFICIAL OWNERSHIP

Filed pursuant to Section 16(a) of the Securities Exchange Act of 1934, Section 17(a) of the Public Utility Holding Company Act of 1935 or Section 30(h) of the Investment Company Act of 1940

(Print or Type Responses)

1. Name and Address of Reporting Person*	2. Issuer Name and Ticker or Trading Symbol	5. Relationship of Reporting Person(s) to Issuer (Check all applicable)

(Last) (First) (Middle)

(Street)

(City) (State) (Zip)

3. Date of Earliest Transaction Required to be Reported (Month/Day/Year)

4. If Amendment, Date Original Filed (Month/Day/Year)

5. Relationship of Reporting Person(s) to Issuer (Check all applicable)
_____ Director _____ 10% Owner
_____ Officer (give _____ Other (specify title below) below)

6. Individual or Joint/Group Filing (Check Applicable Line)
_____ Form filed by One Reporting Person
_____ Form filed by More than One Reporting Person

Table I — Non-Derivative Securities Acquired, Disposed of, or Beneficially Owned

1. Title of Security (Instr. 3)	2. Transaction Date (Month/Day/Year)	2A. Deemed Execution Date, if any (Month/Day/Year)	3. Transaction Code (Instr. 8)		4. Securities Acquired (A) or Disposed of (D) (Instr. 3, 4 and 5)			5. Amount of Securities Beneficially Owned Following Reported Transaction (s) (Instr. 3 and 4)	6. Ownership Form: Direct (D) or Indirect (I) (Instr. 4)	7. Nature of Indirect Beneficial Ownership (Instr. 4)
			Code	V	Amount	(A) or (D)	Price			

Reminder: Report on a separate line for each class of securities beneficially owned directly or indirectly.

* If the form is filed by more than one reporting person, *see* Instruction 4(b)(v).

(Over)
SEC 1474 (06-03)

FORM 4 (continued)

Table II — Derivative Securities Acquired, Disposed of, or Beneficially Owned
(e.g. puts, calls, warrants, options, convertible securities)

1. Title of Derivative Security (Instr. 3)	2. Conversion or Exercise Price of Derivative Security	3. Transaction Date (Month/ Day/ Year)	3A. Deemed Execution Date, if any (Month/ Day/ Year)	4. Transaction Code (Instr. 8)		5. Number of Derivative Securities Acquired (A) or Disposed of (D) (Instr. 3, 4, and 5)		6. Date Exercisable and Expiration Date (Month/Day/Year)		7. Title and Amount of Underlying Securities (Instr. 3 and 4)		8. Price of Derivative Security (Instr. 5)	9. Number of derivative Securities Beneficially Owned following Reported Transaction(s)(Instr. 4)	10. Ownership Form of Derivative Security: Direct (D) or Indirect (I) (Instr. 4)	11. Nature of Indirect Beneficial Ownership (Instr. 4)
				Code	V	(A)	(D)	Date Exercisable	Expiration Date	Title	Amount or Number of Shares				

Explanation of Responses:

_____   _____
**Signature of Reporting Person   Date

** Intentional misstatements or omissions of facts constitute Federal Criminal Violations.
See 18 U.S.C. 1001 and 15 U.S.C. 78ff(a).

Note: File three copies of this Form, one of which must be manually signed. If space is insufficient,
see Instruction 6 for procedure.

Potential persons who are to respond to the collection of information contained in this form are not
required to respond unless the form displays a currently valid OMB Number.

FORM 5

UNITED STATES SECURITIES AND EXCHANGE COMMISSION

Washington, D.C. 20549

FORM 5

ANNUAL STATEMENT OF BENEFICIAL OWNERSHIP OF SECURITIES ...

GENERAL INSTRUCTIONS

1. When Form Must Be Filed

(a) This Form must be filed on or before the 45th day after the end of the issuer's fiscal year in accordance with Rule 16a–3(f)....

(b) A reporting person no longer subject to Section 16 of the Securities Exchange Act of 1934 ("Exchange Act") must check the exit box appearing on this Form. Transactions and holdings previously reported are not required to be included on this Form. Form 4 or Form 5 obligations may continue to be applicable. *See* Rules 16a–3(f) and 16a–2(b)....

2. Where Form Must Be Filed ...*

3. Class of Securities Reported ...

4. Transactions and Holdings Required to Be Reported

(a) *General Requirements*

(i) Pursuant to Rule 16a–3(f), if not previously reported, the following transactions, and total beneficial ownership as of the end of the issuer's fiscal year (or the earlier date applicable to a person ceasing to be an insider during the fiscal year) for any class of securities for which a transaction is reported, shall be reported:

(A) any transaction during the issuer's most recent fiscal year that was exempt from Section 16(b) of the Act, except: (1) any transaction exempt from Section 16(b) pursuant to Rule 16b–3(d), Rule 16b–3(e) or Rule 16b–3(f) (these are required to be reported on Form 4); (2) any exercise or conversion of derivative securities exempt under either Rule 16b–3 or Rule 16b–6(b) (these are required to be reported on Form 4); (3) any transaction exempt from Section 16(b) of the Act pursuant to Rule 16b–3(c), which is exempt from Section 16(a) of the Act;

---

* Instructions 2, 3, and 4(b) generally parallel the corresponding instructions 3, 4, and 5(b) for Form 3, supra. (Footnote by ed.)

and (4) any transaction exempt from Section 16 of the Act pursuant to another Section 16(a) rule;

(B) any small acquisition or series of acquisitions in a six month period during the issuer's fiscal year not exceeding $10,000 in market value (*see* Rule 16a–6);

(C) any transactions or holdings that should have been reported during the issuer's fiscal year on a Form 3 or Form 4, but were not reported. The first Form 5 filing obligation shall include all holdings and transactions that should have been reported in each of the issuer's last two fiscal years but were not.....

FORM 5

☐ **Check box if no longer subject to
Section 16. Form 4 or Form 5 obligations may continue. See Instruction 1(b).**
☐ **Form 3 Holdings Reported**
☐ **Form 4 Transactions Reported**

UNITED STATES SECURITIES AND EXCHANGE COMMISSION
Washington, D.C. 20549

ANNUAL STATEMENT OF CHANGES IN BENEFICIAL OWNERSHIP OF SECURITIES

Filed pursuant to Section 16(a) of the Securities Exchange Act of 1934, Section 17(a) of the Public Utility
Holding Company Act of 1935 or Section 30(h) of the Investment Company Act of 1940

OMB APPROVAL
OMB Number: 3235-0362
Expires: January 31, 2005
Estimated average burden
hours per response. 1.0

1. Name and Address of Reporting Person*	2. Issuer Name and Ticker or Trading Symbol	5. Relationship of Reporting Person(s) to Issuer (Check all applicable)

1. Name and Address of Reporting Person*

(Last)   (First)   (Middle)

(Street)

(City)   (State)   (Zip)

2. Issuer Name and Ticker or Trading Symbol

3. Statement for Issuer's Fiscal Year Ended (Month/Day/Year)

4. If Amendment, Date Original Filed (Month/Day/Year)

5. Relationship of Reporting Person(s) to Issuer (Check all applicable)
____ Director   ____ 10% Owner
____ Officer (give   ____ Other (specify
title   below)
below)

6. Individual or Joint/Group Reporting (check applicable line)
____ Form Filed by One Reporting Person
____ Form Filed by More than One Reporting Person

Table I — Non-Derivative Securities Acquired, Disposed of, or Beneficially Owned

1. Title of Security (Instr. 3)	2. Transaction Date (Month/Day/Year)	2A. Deemed Execution Date, if any (Month/Day/Year)	3. Transaction Code (Instr. 8)		4. Securities Acquired (A) or Disposed of (D) (Instr. 3, 4 and 5)			5. Amount of Securities Beneficially Owned at end of Issuer's Fiscal Year (Instr. 3 and 4)	6. Ownership Form: Direct (D) or Indirect (I) (Instr. 4)	7. Nature of Indirect Beneficial Ownership (Instr. 4)
					Amount	(A) or (D)	Price			

Reminder: Report on a separate line for each class of securities beneficially owned directly or indirectly.
* If the form is filed by more than one reporting person, see Instruction 4(b)(v).

Potential persons who are to respond to the collection of information contained in this form are not required to respond unless the form displays a currently valid OMB control number.

(Over)   SEC 2270 (7-03)

2081

Form 5   SECURITIES EXCHANGE ACT OF 1934

FORM 5 (continued)   Table II — Derivative Securities Acquired, Disposed of, or Beneficially Owned
                                  (e.g., puts, calls, warrants, options, convertible securities)

1. Title of Derivative Security (Instr. 3)	2. Conversion or Exercise Price of Derivative Security	3. Transaction Date (Month/Day/Year)	3A. Deemed Execution Date, if any (Month/Day/Year)	4. Transaction Code (Instr. 8)	5. Number of Derivative Securities Acquired (A) or Disposed of (D) (Instr. 3, 4, and 5)		6. Date Exercisable and Expiration Date (Month/Day/Year)		7. Title and Amount of Underlying Securities (Instr. 3 and 4)		8. Price of Derivative Security (Instr. 5)	9. Number of Derivative Securities Beneficially Owned at End of Issuer's Fiscal Year (Instr. 4)	10. Ownership Form of Derivative Securities: Direct (D) or Indirect (I) (Instr. 4)	11. Nature of Indirect Beneficial Ownership (Instr. 4)
					(A)	(D)	Date Exercisable	Expiration Date	Title	Amount or Number of Shares				

Explanation of Responses:

_____   _____
** Signature of Reporting Person   Date

** Intentional misstatements or omissions of facts constitute Federal Criminal Violations.
   See 18 U.S.C. 1001 and 15 U.S.C. 78ff(a).

Note: File three copies of this Form, one of which must be manually signed.
       If space provided is insufficient, see Instruction 6 for procedure.

Potential persons who are to respond to the collection of information contained in this form are not required to respond unless the form displays a currently valid OMB number.

Page 2

REGULATION FD

Rule 100. General Rule Regarding Selective Disclosure.

(a) Whenever an issuer, or any person acting on its behalf, discloses any material nonpublic information regarding that issuer or its securities to any person described in paragraph (b)(1) of this section, the issuer shall make public disclosure of that information as provided in Rule 101(e):

(1) Simultaneously, in the case of an intentional disclosure; and

(2) Promptly, in the case of a non-intentional disclosure.

(b)(1) Except as provided in paragraph (b)(2) of this section, paragraph (a) of this section shall apply to a disclosure made to any person outside the issuer:

(i) Who is a broker or dealer, or a person associated with a broker or dealer, as those terms are defined in Section 3(a) of the Securities Exchange Act of 1934;

(ii) Who is an investment adviser, as that term is defined in Section 202(a)(11) of the Investment Advisers Act of 1940; an institutional investment manager, as that term is defined in Section 13(f)(5) of the Securities Exchange Act of 1934 . . . or a person associated with either of the foregoing. . . .

(iv) In connection with a securities offering registered under the Securities Act, other than an offering of the type described in any of Rule 415(a)(1)(i) through (vi) under the Securities Act (except an offering of the type described in Rule 415(a)(1)(i) under the Securities Act also involving a registered offering, whether or not underwritten, for capital formation purposes for the account of the issuer (unless the issuer's offering is being registered for the purpose of evading the requirements of this section)), if the disclosure is by any of the following means:

(A) A registration statement filed under the Securities Act, including a prospectus contained therein;

(B) A free writing prospectus used after filing of the registration statement for the offering or a communication falling within the exception to the definition of prospectus contained in clause (a) of section 2(a)(10) of the Securities Act;

(C) Any other Section 10(b) prospectus;

(D) A notice permitted by Rule 135 under the Securities Act;

(E) A communication permitted by Rule 134 under the Securities Act; or

(F) An oral communication made in connection with the registered securities offering after filing of the registration statement for the offering under the Securities Act.

Rule 101. Definitions.

This section defines certain terms as used in Regulation FD (Rules 100–103).

(a) *Intentional*. A selective disclosure of material nonpublic information is "intentional" when the person making the disclosure either knows, or is reckless in not knowing, that the information he or she is communicating is both material and nonpublic.

(b) *Issuer*. An "issuer" subject to this regulation is one that has a class of securities registered under Section 12 of the Securities Exchange Act of 1934, or is required to file reports under Section 15(d) of the Securities Exchange Act of 1934....

(c) *Person acting on behalf of an issuer*. "Person acting on behalf of an issuer" means any senior official of the issuer (or, in the case of a closed-end investment company, a senior official of the issuer's investment adviser), or any other officer, employee, or agent of an issuer who regularly communicates with any person described in Rule 100(b)(1)(i), (ii), or (iii), or with holders of the issuer's securities. An officer, director, employee, or agent of an issuer who discloses material nonpublic information in breach of a duty of trust or confidence to the issuer shall not be considered to be acting on behalf of the issuer.

(d) *Promptly*. "Promptly" means as soon as reasonably practicable (but in no event after the later of 24 hours or the commencement of the next day's trading on the New York Stock Exchange) after a senior official of the issuer (or, in the case of a closed-end investment company, a senior official of the issuer's investment adviser) learns that there has been a non-intentional disclosure by the issuer or person acting on behalf of the issuer of information that the senior official knows, or is reckless in not knowing, is both material and nonpublic.

(e) *Public disclosure*. (1) Except as provided in paragraph (e)(2) of this section, an issuer shall make the "public disclosure" of information required by Rule 100(a) by furnishing to or filing with the Commission a Form 8–K disclosing that information.

(2) An issuer shall be exempt from the requirement to furnish or file a Form 8–K if it instead disseminates the information through another method (or combination of methods) of disclosure that is reasonably designed to provide broad, non-exclusionary distribution of the information to the public.

(f) *Senior official*. "Senior official" means any director, executive officer [as defined in Rule 3b–7 under the Securities Act], investor relations or public relations officer, or other person with similar functions.

(g) *Securities offering.* For purposes of Rule 100(b)(2)(iv):

(1) *Underwritten offerings.* A securities offering that is underwritten commences when the issuer reaches an understanding with the broker-dealer that is to act as managing underwriter and continues until the later of the end of the period during which a dealer must deliver a prospectus or the sale of the securities (unless the offering is sooner terminated);

(2) *Non-underwritten offerings.* A securities offering that is not underwritten:

(i) If covered by Rule 415(a)(1)(x) [under the Securities Act], commences when the issuer makes its first bona fide offer in a takedown of securities and continues until the later of the end of the period during which each dealer must deliver a prospectus or the sale of the securities in that takedown (unless the takedown is sooner terminated);

(ii) If a business combination as defined in Rule 165(f)(1) [under the Securities Act], commences when the first public announcement of the transaction is made and continues until the completion of the vote or the expiration of the tender offer, as applicable (unless the transaction is sooner terminated);

(iii) If an offering other than those specified in paragraphs (a) and (b) of this section, commences when the issuer files a registration statement and continues until the later of the end of the period during which each dealer must deliver a prospectus or the sale of the securities (unless the offering is sooner terminated).

Rule 102.   No Effect on Antifraud Liability.

No failure to make a public disclosure required solely by Rule 100 shall be deemed to be a violation of Rule 10b–5 under the Securities Exchange Act.

Rule 103.   No effect on Exchange Act Reporting Status.

A failure to make a public disclosure required solely by Rule 100 shall not affect whether:

(a) For purposes of Forms S–2, S–3 and S–8 under the Securities Act, an issuer is deemed to have filed all the material required to be filed pursuant to Section 13 or 15(d) of the Securities Exchange Act of 1934 or, where applicable, has made those filings in a timely manner; or

(b) There is adequate current public information about the issuer for purposes of Rule 144(c) [under the Securities Act].

SECURITIES AND EXCHANGE COMMISSION RELEASE NO. 33-7881 (2000)

SELECTIVE DISCLOSURE AND INSIDER TRADING ...

II. Selective Disclosure: Regulation FD

A. *Background*

... [W]e we have become increasingly concerned about the selective disclosure of material information by issuers. As reflected in recent publicized reports, many issuers are disclosing important nonpublic information, such as advance warnings of earnings results, to securities analysts or selected institutional investors or both, before making full disclosure of the same information to the general public. Where this has happened, those who were privy to the information beforehand were able to make a profit or avoid a loss at the expense of those kept in the dark.

We believe that the practice of selective disclosure leads to a loss of investor confidence in the integrity of our capital markets. Investors who see a security's price change dramatically and only later are given access to the information responsible for that move rightly question whether they are on a level playing field with market insiders.

Issuer selective disclosure bears a close resemblance in this regard to ordinary "tipping" and insider trading. In both cases, a privileged few gain an informational edge—and the ability to use that edge to profit— from their superior access to corporate insiders, rather than from their skill, acumen, or diligence. Likewise, selective disclosure has an adverse impact on market integrity that is similar to the adverse impact from illegal insider trading: Investors lose confidence in the fairness of the markets when they know that other participants may exploit "unerodable informational advantages" derived not from hard work or insights, but from their access to corporate insiders. The economic effects of the two practices are essentially the same. Yet, as a result of judicial interpretations, tipping and insider trading can be severely punished under the antifraud provisions of the federal securities laws, whereas the status of issuer selective disclosure has been considerably less clear.

Regulation FD is also designed to address another threat to the integrity of our markets: the potential for corporate management to treat material information as a commodity to be used to gain or maintain favor with particular analysts or investors.... [I]n the absence of a prohibition on selective disclosure, analysts may feel pressured to report favorably about a company or otherwise slant their analysis in order to have continued access to selectively disclosed information. We are concerned, in this regard, with reports that analysts who publish negative views of an issuer are sometimes excluded by that issuer from calls and meetings to which other analysts are invited.

Finally, ... technological developments have made it much easier for issuers to disseminate information broadly. Whereas issuers once may have had to rely on analysts to serve as information intermediaries, issuers now can use a variety of methods to communicate directly with the market. In addition to press releases, these methods include, among others, Internet webcasting and teleconferencing. Accordingly, technological limitations no longer provide an excuse for abiding the threats to market integrity that selective disclosure represents.

To address the problem of selective disclosure, we proposed Regulation FD. It targets the practice by establishing new requirements for full and fair disclosure by public companies....

B. *Discussion of Regulation FD*

Rule 100 of Regulation FD sets forth the basic rule regarding selective disclosure. Under this rule, whenever:

(1) an issuer, or person acting on its behalf,

(2) discloses material nonpublic information,

(3) to certain enumerated persons (in general, securities market professionals or holders of the issuer's securities who may well trade on the basis of the information),

(4) the issuer must make public disclosure of that same information:

(a) simultaneously (for intentional disclosures), or

(b) promptly (for non-intentional disclosures).

As a whole, the regulation requires that when an issuer makes an intentional disclosure of material nonpublic information to a person covered by the regulation, it must do so in a manner that provides general public disclosure, rather than through a selective disclosure. For a selective disclosure that is non-intentional, the issuer must publicly disclose the information promptly after it knows (or is reckless in not knowing) that the information selectively disclosed was both material and nonpublic....

1. *Scope of Communications and Issuer Personnel Covered by the Regulation* ...

[Regulation FD] is designed to address the core problem of selective disclosure made to those who would reasonably be expected to trade securities on the basis of the information or provide others with advice about securities trading. Accordingly, Rule 100(a) of Regulation FD ... makes clear that the general rule against selective disclosure applies only to disclosures made to the categories of persons enumerated in Rule 100(b)(1).

Rule 100(b)(1) enumerates four categories of persons to whom selective disclosure may not be made absent a specified exclusion. The first three are securities market professionals—(1) broker-dealers and their associated persons, (2) investment advisers, certain institutional investment managers and their associated persons, and (3) investment companies, hedge funds, and affiliated persons. These categories will include sell-side analysts, many buy-side analysts, large institutional investment managers, and other market professionals who may be likely to trade on the basis of selectively disclosed information. The fourth category of person included in Rule 100(b)(1) is any holder of the issuer's securities, under circumstances in which it is reasonably foreseeable that such person would purchase or sell securities on the basis of the information. Thus, as a whole, Rule 100(b)(1) will cover the types of persons most likely to be the recipients of improper selective disclosure, but should not cover persons who are engaged in ordinary-course business communications with the issuer, or interfere with disclosures to the media or communications to government agencies.

Rule 100(b)(2) sets out four exclusions from coverage. The first, as proposed, is for communications made to a person who owes the issuer a duty of trust or confidence—*i.e.*, a "temporary insider"—such as an attorney, investment banker, or accountant. The second exclusion is for communications made to any person who expressly agrees to maintain the information in confidence. Any misuse of the information for trading by the persons in these two exclusions would thus be covered under either the "temporary insider" or the misappropriation theory of insider trading. This approach recognizes that issuers and their officials may properly share material nonpublic information with outsiders, for legitimate business purposes, when the outsiders are subject to duties of confidentiality.

The third exclusion from coverage in Rule 100(b)(2) is for disclosures to an entity whose primary business is the issuance of credit ratings, provided the information is disclosed solely for the purpose of developing a credit rating and the entity's ratings are publicly available.... [R]atings organizations often obtain nonpublic information in the course of their ratings work. We are not aware, however, of any incidents of selective disclosure involving ratings organizations. Ratings organizations, like the media, have a mission of public disclosure; the objective and result of the ratings process is a widely available publication of the rating when it is completed. And under this provision, for the exclusion to apply, the ratings organization must make its credit ratings publicly available. For these reasons, we believe it is appropriate to provide this exclusion from the coverage of Regulation FD.

The fourth exclusion from coverage is for communications made in connection with most offerings of securities registered under the Securities Act....

b. *Disclosures by a Person Acting on an Issuer's Behalf.* ...

... We define the term ["person acting on behalf of an issuer"] to mean: (1) Any senior official of the issuer[1] or (2) any other officer, employee, or agent of an issuer who regularly communicates with any of the persons described in Rule 100(b)(1)(i), (ii), or (iii), or with the issuer's security holders. [Under this definition, Regulation FD covers senior management, investor relations professionals, and others who regularly interact with securities market professionals or security holders]. Of course, neither an issuer nor such a covered person could avoid the reach of the regulation merely by having a non-covered person make a selective disclosure. Thus, to the extent that another employee had been *directed* to make a selective disclosure by a member of senior management, that member of senior management would be responsible for having made the selective disclosure. *See* Section 20(b) of the Exchange Act. In addition ... the definition expressly states that a person who communicates material nonpublic information in breach of a duty to the issuer would not be considered to be acting on behalf of the issuer. Thus, an issuer is not responsible under Regulation FD when one of its employees improperly trades or tips.

2. *Disclosures of Material Nonpublic Information*

[Regulation FD] applies to disclosures of "material nonpublic" information about the issuer or its securities. The regulation does not define the terms "material" and "nonpublic," but relies on existing definitions of these terms established in the case law. Information is material if "there is a substantial likelihood that a reasonable shareholder would consider it important" in making an investment decision. To fulfill the materiality requirement, there must be a substantial likelihood that a fact "would have been viewed by the reasonable investor as having significantly altered the total mix of information made available." Information is nonpublic if it has not been disseminated in a manner making it available to investors generally....

... While it is not possible to create an exhaustive list, the following items are some types of information or events that should be reviewed carefully to determine whether they are material: (1) Earnings information; (2) mergers, acquisitions, tender offers, joint ventures, or changes in assets; (3) new products or discoveries, or developments regarding customers or suppliers (*e.g.*, the acquisition or loss of a contract); (4) changes in control or in management; (5) change in auditors or auditor notification that the issuer may no longer rely on an auditor's audit

---

1. "Senior official" is defined in Rule 101(f) as any director, executive officer, in- vestor relations or public relations officer, or other person with similar functions....

report; (6) events regarding the issuer's securities—*e.g.,* defaults on senior securities, calls of securities for redemption, repurchase plans, stock splits or changes in dividends, changes to the rights of security holders, public or private sales of additional securities; and (7) bankruptcies or receiverships.

By including this list, we do not mean to imply that each of these items is *per se* material. The information and events on this list still require determinations as to their materiality (although some determinations will be reached more easily than others). For example, some new products or contracts may clearly be material to an issuer; yet that does not mean that *all* product developments or contracts will be material. This demonstrates, in our view, why no "bright-line" standard or list of items can adequately address the range of situations that may arise. Furthermore, we do not and cannot create an exclusive list of events and information that have a higher probability of being considered material.

One common situation that raises special concerns about selective disclosure has been the practice of securities analysts seeking "guidance" from issuers regarding earnings forecasts. When an issuer official engages in a private discussion with an analyst who is seeking guidance about earnings estimates, he or she takes on a high degree of risk under Regulation FD. If the issuer official communicates selectively to the analyst nonpublic information that the company's anticipated earnings will be higher than, lower than, or even the same as what analysts have been forecasting, the issuer likely will have violated Regulation FD. This is true whether the information about earnings is communicated expressly or through indirect "guidance," the meaning of which is apparent though implied. Similarly, an issuer cannot render material information immaterial simply by breaking it into ostensibly non-material pieces.

At the same time, an issuer is not prohibited from disclosing a non-material piece of information to an analyst, even if, unbeknownst to the issuer, that piece helps the analyst complete a "mosaic" of information that, taken together, is material. Similarly, since materiality is an objective test keyed to the reasonable investor, Regulation FD will not be implicated where an issuer discloses immaterial information whose significance is discerned by the analyst. Analysts can provide a valuable service in sifting through and extracting information that would not be significant to the ordinary investor to reach material conclusions. We do not intend, by Regulation FD, to discourage this sort of activity. The focus of Regulation FD is on whether the issuer discloses material nonpublic information, not on whether an analyst, through some combination of persistence, knowledge, and insight, regards as material information whose significance is not apparent to the reasonable investor.

... Rule 101(a) states that a person acts "intentionally" only if the person knows, or is reckless in not knowing, that the information he or she is communicating is both material and nonpublic.... [T]his aspect of the regulation provides additional protection that issuers need not fear being second-guessed by the Commission in enforcement actions for mistaken judgments about materiality in close cases.

3. *Intentional and Non-intentional Selective Disclosures: Timing of Required Public Disclosures*

A key provision of Regulation FD is that the timing of required public disclosure differs depending on whether the issuer has made an "intentional" selective disclosure or a selective disclosure that was not intentional. For an "intentional" selective disclosure, the issuer is required to publicly disclose the same information simultaneously.

a. *Standard of "Intentional" Selective Disclosure.* Under the regulation, a selective disclosure is "intentional" when the issuer or person acting on behalf of the issuer making the disclosure either knows, or is reckless in not knowing, prior to making the disclosure, that the information he or she is communicating is both material and nonpublic....

b. *"Prompt" Public Disclosure After Non-intentional Selective Disclosures.*

Under Rule 100(a)(2), when an issuer makes a covered non-intentional disclosure of material nonpublic information, it is required to make public disclosure promptly....

Commenters expressed varying views on the definition of "promptly" provided in the rule. Some said that the time period provided for disclosure was appropriate; others said it was too short; and still others said that it was too specific, and should require disclosure only as soon as reasonably possible or practicable. We believe that it is preferable for issuers and the investing public that there be a clear delineation of when "prompt" disclosure is required. We also believe that the 24–hour requirement strikes the appropriate balance between achieving broad, non-exclusionary disclosure and permitting issuers time to determine how to respond after learning of the non-intentional selective disclosure. However, recognizing that sometimes non-intentional selective disclosures will arise close to or over a weekend or holiday, we have slightly modified the final rule to state that the outer boundary for prompt disclosure is the later of 24 hours or the commencement of the next day's trading on the New York Stock Exchange, after a senior official learns of the disclosure and knows (or is reckless in not knowing) that the information disclosed was material and nonpublic....

4. *"Public Disclosure" Required by Regulation FD*

Rule 101(e) defines the type of "public disclosure" that will satisfy the requirements of Regulation FD. As proposed, Rule 101(e) gave issuers considerable flexibility in determining how to make required public disclosure. The proposal stated that issuers could meet Regulation

FD's "public disclosure" requirement by filing a Form 8–K, by distributing a press release through a widely disseminated news or wire service, or by any other non-exclusionary method of disclosure that is reasonably designed to provide broad public access—such as announcement at a conference of which the public had notice and to which the public was granted access, either by personal attendance, or telephonic or electronic access. This definition was designed to permit issuers to make use of current technologies, such as webcasting of conference calls, that provide broad public access to issuer disclosure events. . . .

We believe that issuers could use the following model, which employs a combination of methods of disclosure, for making a planned disclosure of material information, such as a scheduled earnings release:

 • First, issue a press release, distributed through regular channels, containing the information;

 • Second, provide adequate notice, by a press release and/or website posting, of a scheduled conference call to discuss the announced results, giving investors both the time and date of the conference call, and instructions on how to access the call; and

 • Third, hold the conference call in an open manner, permitting investors to listen in either by telephonic means or through Internet webcasting.[2]

By following these steps, an issuer can use the press release to provide the initial broad distribution of the information, and then discuss its release with analysts in the subsequent conference call, without fear that if it should disclose additional material details related to the original disclosure it will be engaging in a selective disclosure of material information. . . .

5. *Issuers Subject to Regulation FD*

Regulation FD will apply to all issuers with securities registered under Section 12 of the Exchange Act, and all issuers required to file reports under Section 15(d) of the Exchange Act, including closed-end investment companies, but not including other investment companies, foreign governments, or foreign private issuers. . . .

7. *Liability Issues*

We recognize that the prospect of private liability for violations of Regulation FD could contribute to a "chilling effect" on issuer communications. Issuers might refrain from some informal communications with outsiders if they feared that engaging in such communications, even when appropriate, would lead to their being charged in private lawsuits with violations of Regulation FD. . . .

. . . Rule 102 . . . expressly provides that no failure to make a public disclosure required solely by Regulation FD shall be deemed to be a

---

2. Giving the public the opportunity to listen to the call does not also require that the issuer give all members of the public the opportunity to ask questions.

violation of Rule 10b–5. This provision makes clear that Regulation FD does not create a new duty for purposes of Rule 10b–5 liability. Accordingly, private plaintiffs cannot rely on an issuer's violation of Regulation FD as a basis for a private action alleging Rule 10b–5 violations.

Rule 102 is designed to exclude Rule 10b–5 liability for cases that would be based "solely" on a failure to make a public disclosure required by Regulation FD. As such, it does not affect any existing grounds for liability under Rule 10b–5. Thus, for example, liability for "tipping" and insider trading under Rule 10b–5 may still exist if a selective disclosure is made in circumstances that meet the *Dirks* "personal benefit" test. In addition, an issuer's failure to make a public disclosure still may give rise to liability under a "duty to correct" or "duty to update" theory in certain circumstances. And an issuer's contacts with analysts may lead to liability under the "entanglement" or "adoption" theories. In addition, if an issuer's report or public disclosure made under Regulation FD contained false or misleading information, or omitted material information, Rule 102 would not provide protection from Rule 10b–5 liability.

Finally, if an issuer failed to comply with Regulation FD, it would be subject to an SEC enforcement action alleging violations of Section 13(a) or 15(d) of the Exchange Act . . . and Regulation FD. We could bring an administrative action seeking a cease-and-desist order, or a civil action seeking an injunction and/or civil money penalties.[3] In appropriate cases, we could also bring an enforcement action against an individual at the issuer responsible for the violation, either as "a cause of" the violation in a cease-and-desist proceeding,[4] or as an aider and abetter of the violation in an injunctive action.[5]

III. Insider Trading Rules . . .

A. Rule 10b5–1: Trading "On the Basis of" Material Nonpublic Information

1. Background

. . . [O]ne unsettled issue in insider trading law has been what, if any, causal connection must be shown between the trader's possession of

---

3. Regulation FD does not expressly require issuers to adopt policies and procedures to avoid violations, but we expect that most issuers will use appropriate disclosure policies as a safeguard against selective disclosure. We are aware that many, if not most, issuers already have policies and regarding disclosure practices, the dissemination of material information, and the question of which issuer personnel are authorized to speak to analysts, the media, or investors. The existence of an appropriate policy, and the issuer's general adherence to it, may often be relevant to determining the issuer's intent with regard to a selective disclosure.

4. Section 21C of the Exchange Act, *15 U.S.C. 78u–3.* A failure to file or otherwise make required public disclosure under Regulation FD will be considered a violation for as long as the failure continues; in our enforcement actions, we likely will seek more severe sanctions for violations that continue for a longer period of time.

5. Section 20(e) of the Exchange Act, *15 U.S.C. 78t*(e).

inside information and his or her trading. In enforcement cases, we have argued that a trader may be liable for trading while in "knowing possession" of the information. The contrary view is that a trader is not liable unless it is shown that he or she "used" the information for trading. Until recent years, there has been little case law discussing this issue. Although the Supreme Court has variously described an insider's violations as trading "on"[6] or "on the basis of"[7] material nonpublic information, it has not addressed the use/possession issue. Three recent courts of appeals cases addressed the issue but reached different results.[8]

. . . [I]n our view, the goals of insider trading prohibitions—protecting investors and the integrity of securities markets—are best accomplished by a standard closer to the "knowing possession" standard than to the "use" standard. At the same time, we recognize that an absolute standard based on knowing possession, or awareness, could be overbroad in some respects. The new rule attempts to balance these considerations by means of a general rule based on "awareness" of the material nonpublic information, with several carefully enumerated affirmative defenses. This approach will better enable insiders and issuers to conduct themselves in accordance with the law. . . .

. . . Scienter remains a necessary element for liability under Section 10(b) of the Exchange Act and Rule 10b–5 thereunder, and Rule 10b5–1 does not change this.

2. Provisions of Rule 10b5–1

We are adopting . . . the general rule set forth in Rule 10b5–1(a), and the definition of "on the basis of" material nonpublic information in Rule 10b5–1(b). A trade is on the basis of material nonpublic information if the trader was aware of the material, nonpublic information when the person made the purchase or sale.

. . . The awareness standard reflects the common sense notion that a trader who is aware of inside information when making a trading decision inevitably makes use of the information. Additionally, a clear awareness standard will provide greater clarity and certainty than a presumption or "strong inference" approach.[9] Accordingly, we have determined to adopt the awareness standard. . . .

---

6. *See Dirks v. SEC*, 463 U.S. 646, 654 (1983).

7. *See O'Hagan*, 521 U.S. at 651–52.

8. *Compare United States v. Teicher*, 987 F.2d 112, 120–21 (2d Cir.), cert. denied, 510 U.S. 976 (1993) (suggesting that "knowing possession" is sufficient) with *SEC v. Adler*, 137 F.3d 1325, 1337 (11th Cir.1998) ("use" required, but proof of possession provides strong inference of use) and *United States v. Smith*, 155 F.3d 1051, 1069 & n. 27 (9th Cir.1998), cert. denied, 525 U.S. 1071 (1999) (requiring that "use" be proven in a criminal case).

9. Some commenters stated that "aware" was an unclear term that may be interpreted to mean something less than "knowing possession." We disagree. "Aware" is a commonly used and well-defined English word, meaning "having knowledge; conscious; cognizant." We believe that "awareness" has a much clearer meaning that "knowing possession," which has not been defined by case law.

.... [T]he affirmative defense [in Rule 10b5–1] allows purchases and sales pursuant to contracts, instructions, and plans. [The defense provides] appropriate flexibility to persons who wish to structure securities trading plans and strategies when they are not aware of material nonpublic information, and do not exercise any influence over the transaction once they do become aware of such information.

As adopted, paragraph (c)(1)(i) sets forth an affirmative defense from the general rule, which applies both to individuals and entities that trade. To satisfy this provision, a person must establish several factors.

- First, the person must demonstrate that before becoming aware of the information, he or she had entered into a binding contract to purchase or sell the security, provided instructions to another person to execute the trade for the instructing person's account, or adopted a written plan for trading securities.

- Second, the person must demonstrate that, with respect to the purchase or sale, the contract, instructions, or plan either: (1) expressly specified the amount, price, and date; (2) provided a written formula or algorithm, or computer program, for determining amounts, prices, and dates; or (3) did not permit the person to exercise any subsequent influence over how, when, or whether to effect purchases or sales; provided, in addition, that any other person who did exercise such influence was not aware of the material nonpublic information when doing so.

- Third, the person must demonstrate that the purchase or sale that occurred was pursuant to the prior contract, instruction, or plan. A purchase or sale is not pursuant to a contract, instruction, or plan if, among other things, the person who entered into the contract, instruction, or plan altered or deviated from the contract, instruction, or plan or entered into or altered a corresponding or hedging transaction or position with respect to those securities.[10]

Under paragraph (c)(1)(ii), ... the exclusion provided in paragraph (c)(1)(i) will be available only if the contract, instruction, or plan was entered into in good faith and not as part of a scheme to evade the prohibitions of this section.

Paragraph (c)(1)(iii) defines several key terms in the exclusion.... ["Amount"] means either a specified number of shares or a specified dollar value of securities.... [Price] means market price on a particular date or a limit price or a particular dollar price. "Date" means either the specific day of the year on which a market order is to be executed, or a day or days of the year on which a limit order is in force.

---

10. Rule 10b5–1(c)(1)(i)(C). However, a person acting in good faith may modify a prior contract, instruction, or plan before becoming aware of material nonpublic information. In that case, a purchase or sale that complies with the modified contract, instruction, or plan will be considered pursuant to a new contract, instruction, or plan.

Taken as a whole, the ... defense is designed to cover situations in which a person can demonstrate that the material nonpublic information was not a factor in the trading decision. We believe this provision will provide appropriate flexibility to those who would like to plan securities transactions in advance at a time when they are not aware of material nonpublic information, and then carry out those pre-planned transactions at a later time, even if they later become aware of material nonpublic information.

For example, an issuer operating a repurchase program will not need to specify with precision the amounts, prices, and dates on which it will repurchase its securities. Rather, an issuer could adopt a written plan, when it is not aware of material nonpublic information, that uses a written formula to derive amounts, prices, and dates. Or the plan could simply delegate all the discretion to determine amounts, prices, and dates to another person who is not aware of the information—provided that the plan did not permit the issuer to (and in fact the issuer did not) exercise any subsequent influence over the purchases or sales.

Similarly, an employee wishing to adopt a plan for exercising stock options and selling the underlying shares could, while not aware of material nonpublic information, adopt a written plan that contained a formula for determining the specified percentage of the employee's vested options to be exercised and/or sold at or above a specific price. The formula could provide, for example, that the employee will exercise options and sell the shares one month before each date on which her son's college tuition is due, and link the amount of the trade to the cost of the tuition.

An employee also could acquire company stock through payroll deductions under an employee stock purchase plan or a Section 401(k) plan. The employee could provide oral instructions as to his or her plan participation, or proceed by means of a written plan. The transaction price could be computed as a percentage of market price, and the transaction amount could be based on a percentage of salary to be deducted under the plan. The date of a plan transaction could be determined pursuant to a formula set forth in the plan. Alternatively, the date of a plan transaction could be controlled by the plan's administrator or investment manager, assuming that he or she is not aware of the material, nonpublic information at the time of executing the transaction, and the employee does not exercise influence over the timing of the transaction....

The [rule includes] an additional affirmative defense available only to trading parties that are entities.... [T]his defense is available to entities as an alternative to the other enumerated defenses described above.

Under this provision, an entity will not be liable if it demonstrates that the individual making the investment decision on behalf of the entity was not aware of the information, and that the entity had implemented reasonable policies and procedures to prevent insider trading. . . .

B. *Rule 10b–2: Duties of Trust or Confidence in Misappropriation Insider Trading Cases*

1. *Background*

. . . [A]n unsettled issue in insider trading law has been under what circumstances certain non-business relationships, such as family and personal relationships, may provide the duty of trust or confidence required under the misappropriation theory. Case law has produced the following anomalous result. A family member who receives a "tip" (within the meaning of *Dirks*) and then trades violates Rule 10b–5. A family member who trades in breach of an express promise of confidentiality also violates Rule 10b–5. A family member who trades in breach of a reasonable expectation of confidentiality, however, does not necessarily violate Rule 10b–5.

. . . [W]e think that this anomalous result harms investor confidence in the integrity and fairness of the nation's securities markets. The family member's trading has the same impact on the market and investor confidence in the third example as it does in the first two examples. In all three examples, the trader's informational advantage stems from "contrivance, not luck," and the informational disadvantage to other investors "cannot be overcome with research or skill." Additionally, the need to distinguish among the three types of cases may require an unduly intrusive examination of the details of particular family relationships. Accordingly, we believe there is good reason for the broader approach we adopt today for determining when family or personal relationships create "duties of trust or confidence" under the misappropriation theory.

. . . [Rule 10b5–2] is not designed to interfere with particular family or personal relationships; rather, its goal is to protect investors and the fairness and integrity of the nation's securities markets against improper trading on the basis of inside information. Moreover, we do not believe that the rule will require a more intrusive examination of family relationships than would be required under existing case law without the rule. Current case law . . . already establishes a regime under which questions of liability turn on the nature of the details of the relationships between family members, such as their prior history and patterns of sharing confidences. By providing more of a bright-line test for certain enumerated close family relationships, we believe the rule will mitigate, to some degree, the need to examine the details of particular relationships in the course of investigating suspected insider trading.

2. *Provisions of Rule 10b5–2*

[Rule 10b5–2] sets forth a non-exclusive list of three situations in which a person has a duty of trust or confidence for purposes of the "misappropriation" theory of the Exchange Act and Rule 10b–5 thereunder.

First ... we provide that a duty of trust or confidence exists whenever a person agrees to maintain information in confidence.

Second, we provide that a duty of trust or confidence exists when two people have a history, pattern, or practice of sharing confidences such that the recipient of the information knows or reasonably should know that the person communicating the material nonpublic information expects that the recipient will maintain its confidentiality. This is a "facts and circumstances" test based on the expectation of the parties in light of the overall relationship. Some commenters were concerned that, as proposed, this provision examined the reasonable expectation of confidentiality of the person communicating the material nonpublic information rather than examining the expectations of the recipient of the information and/or both parties to the communication. We believe that mutuality was implicit in the proposed rule because an inquiry into the reasonableness of the recipient's expectation necessarily involves considering the relationship as a whole, including the other party's expectations. Nevertheless, we have revised the provision to make this mutuality explicit. . . .

Third, we are adopting as proposed a bright-line rule that states that a duty of trust or confidence exists when a person receives or obtains material nonpublic information from certain enumerated close family members: spouses, parents, children, and siblings. An affirmative defense permits the person receiving or obtaining the information to demonstrate that under the facts and circumstances of that family relationship, no duty of trust or confidence existed. Some commenters noted that the enumerated relationships do not include domestic partners, step-parents, or step-children. We have determined not to include these relationships in this paragraph, although paragraphs (b)(1) and (b)(2) could reach them. Our experience in this area indicates that most instances of insider trading between or among family members involve spouses, parents and children, or siblings; therefore, we have enumerated these relationships and not others. . . .

DIVISION OF CORPORATION FINANCE: STAFF LEGAL BULLETIN NO. 14A

SHAREHOLDER PROPOSALS

Date: July 12, 2002

Rule 14a–8 provides an opportunity for a shareholder owning a relatively small amount of a company's securities to have his or her proposal placed alongside management's proposals in that company's proxy materials for presentation to a vote at an annual or special meeting of shareholders. The rule generally requires the company to include the proposal unless the shareholder has not complied with the rule's procedural requirements or the proposal falls within one of the rule's 13 substantive bases for exclusion.

Rule 14a–8(i)(7) is one of the substantive bases for exclusion in rule 14a–8. It provides a basis for excluding a proposal that deals with a matter relating to the company's ordinary business operations. The fact that a proposal relates to ordinary business matters does not conclusively establish that a company may exclude the proposal from its proxy materials. As the Commission stated in Exchange Act Release No. 40018, proposals that relate to ordinary business matters but that focus on "sufficiently significant social policy issues ... would not be considered to be excludable because the proposals would transcend the day-to-day business matters."

In the 2001–2002 proxy season, shareholders submitted proposals to several companies relating to equity compensation plans. Some of these proposals requested that the companies submit for shareholder approval all equity compensation plans that potentially would result in material dilution to existing shareholders. We received four no-action requests from companies seeking to exclude these proposals from their proxy materials in reliance on rule 14a–8(i)(7). In each instance, we took the view that the proposal could be excluded in reliance on rule 14a–8(i)(7) because the proposal related to general employee compensation, an ordinary business matter.

The Commission has stated that proposals involving "the management of the workforce, such as the hiring, promotion, and termination of employees," relate to ordinary business matters. Our position to date with respect to equity compensation proposals is consistent with this guidance and the Division's historical approach to compensation proposals. Since 1992, we have applied a bright-line analysis to proposals concerning equity or cash compensation:

- We agree with the view of companies that they may exclude proposals that relate to general employee compensation matters in reliance on rule 14a–8(i)(7); and

● We do not agree with the view of companies that they may exclude proposals that concern only senior executive and director compensation in reliance on rule 14a–8(i)(7).

The Commission has previously taken the position that proposals relating to ordinary business matters "but focusing on sufficiently significant social policy issues … generally would not be considered to be excludable, because the proposals would transcend the day-to-day business matters and raise policy issues so significant that it would be appropriate for a shareholder vote." The Division has noted many times that the presence of widespread public debate regarding an issue is among the factors to be considered in determining whether proposals concerning that issue "transcend the day-to-day business matters."

We believe that the public debate regarding shareholder approval of equity compensation plans has become significant in recent months. Consequently, in view of the widespread public debate regarding shareholder approval of equity compensation plans and consistent with our historical analysis of the "ordinary business" exclusion, we are modifying our treatment of proposals relating to this topic. Going forward, we will take the following approach to rule 14a–8(i)(7) submissions concerning proposals that relate to shareholder approval of equity compensation plans:

● *Proposals that focus on equity compensation plans that may be used to compensate only senior executive officers and directors.* As has been our position since 1992, companies may not rely on rule 14a–8(i)(7) to omit these proposals from their proxy materials.

● *Proposals that focus on equity compensation plans that may be used to compensate senior executive officers, directors and the general workforce.* If the proposal seeks to obtain shareholder approval of all such equity compensation plans, without regard to their potential dilutive effect, a company may rely on rule 14a–8(i)(7) to omit the proposal from its proxy materials. If the proposal seeks to obtain shareholder approval of all such equity compensation plans that potentially would result in material dilution to existing shareholders, a company may not rely on rule 14a–8(i)(7) to omit the proposal from its proxy materials.

● *Proposals that focus on equity compensation plans that may be used to compensate the general workforce only, with no senior executive officer or director participation.* If the proposal seeks to obtain shareholder approval of all such equity compensation plans, without regard to their potential dilutive effect, a company may rely on rule 14a–8(i)(7) to omit the proposal from its proxy materials. If the proposal seeks to obtain shareholder approval of all such equity compensation plans that potentially would result in material dilution to existing shareholders, a company may not rely on rule 14a–8(i)(7) to omit the proposal from its proxy materials. . . .

17 C.F.R. PART 205—STANDARDS OF PROFESSIONAL CONDUCT FOR ATTORNEYS APPEARING AND PRACTICING BEFORE THE COMMISSION IN THE REPRESENTATION OF AN ISSUER

§ 205.1.   Purpose and Scope

This part sets forth minimum standards of professional conduct for attorneys appearing and practicing before the Commission in the representation of an issuer. These standards supplement applicable standards of any jurisdiction where an attorney is admitted or practices and are not intended to limit the ability of any jurisdiction to impose additional obligations on an attorney not inconsistent with the application of this part. Where the standards of a state or other United States jurisdiction where an attorney is admitted or practices conflict with this part, this part shall govern.

§ 205.2.   Definitions

For purposes of this part, the following definitions apply:

(a) *Appearing and practicing before the Commission:*

(1) Means:

(i) Transacting any business with the Commission, including communications in any form;

(ii) Representing an issuer in a Commission administrative proceeding or in connection with any Commission investigation, inquiry, information request, or subpoena;

(iii) Providing advice in respect of the United States securities laws or the Commission's rules or regulations thereunder regarding any document that the attorney has notice will be filed with or submitted to, or incorporated into any document that will be filed with or submitted to, the Commission, including the provision of such advice in the context of preparing, or participating in the preparation of, any such document; or

(iv) Advising an issuer as to whether information or a statement, opinion, or other writing is required under the United States securities laws or the Commission's rules or regulations thereunder to be filed with or submitted to, or incorporated into any document that will be filed with or submitted to, the Commission; but

(2) Does not include an attorney who:

(i) Conducts the activities in paragraphs (a)(1)(i) through (a)(1)(iv) of this section other than in the context of providing legal services to an issuer with whom the attorney has an attorney-client relationship; or

(ii) Is a non-appearing foreign attorney.

(b) *Appropriate response* means a response to an attorney regarding reported evidence of a material violation as a result of which the attorney reasonably believes:

(1) That no material violation, as defined in paragraph (i) of this section, has occurred, is ongoing, or is about to occur;

(2) That the issuer has, as necessary, adopted appropriate remedial measures, including appropriate steps or sanctions to stop any material violations that are ongoing, to prevent any material violation that has yet to occur, and to remedy or otherwise appropriately address any material violation that has already occurred and to minimize the likelihood of its recurrence; or

(3) That the issuer, with the consent of the issuer's board of directors, a committee thereof to whom a report could be made pursuant to Rule 205.3(b)(3), or a qualified legal compliance committee, has retained or directed an attorney to review the reported evidence of a material violation and either:

(i) Has substantially implemented any remedial recommendations made by such attorney after a reasonable investigation and evaluation of the reported evidence; or

(ii) Has been advised that such attorney may, consistent with his or her professional obligations, assert a colorable defense on behalf of the issuer (or the issuer's officer, director, employee, or agent, as the case may be) in any investigation or judicial or administrative proceeding relating to the reported evidence of a material violation.

(c) *Attorney* means any person who is admitted, licensed, or otherwise qualified to practice law in any jurisdiction, domestic or foreign, or who holds himself or herself out as admitted, licensed, or otherwise qualified to practice law.

(d) *Breach of fiduciary duty* refers to any breach of fiduciary or similar duty to the issuer recognized under an applicable Federal or State statute or at common law, including but not limited to misfeasance, nonfeasance, abdication of duty, abuse of trust, and approval of unlawful transactions.

(e) *Evidence of a material violation* means credible evidence, based upon which it would be unreasonable, under the circumstances, for a prudent and competent attorney not to conclude that it is reasonably likely that a material violation has occurred, is ongoing, or is about to occur. . . .

(g) *In the representation of an issuer* means providing legal services as an attorney for an issuer, regardless of whether the attorney is employed or retained by the issuer.

(h) *Issuer* means an issuer (as defined in section 3 of the Securities Exchange Act of 1934), the securities of which are registered under section 12 of that Act, or that is required to file reports under section 15(d) of that Act, or that files or has filed a registration statement that has not yet become effective under the Securities Act of 1933, and that it has not withdrawn. . . . For purposes of paragraphs (a) and (g) of this section, the term "issuer" includes any person controlled by an issuer, where an attorney provides legal services to such person on behalf of, or at the behest, or for the benefit of the issuer, regardless of whether the attorney is employed or retained by the issuer.

(i) *Material violation* means a material violation of an applicable United States federal or state securities law, a material breach of fiduciary duty arising under United States federal or state law, or a similar material violation of any United States federal or state law. . . .

(k) *Qualified legal compliance committee* means a committee of an issuer (which also may be an audit or other committee of the issuer) that:

(1) Consists of at least one member of the issuer's audit committee (or, if the issuer has no audit committee, one member from an equivalent committee of independent directors) and two or more members of the issuer's board of directors who are not employed, directly or indirectly, by the issuer and who are not, in the case of a registered investment company, "interested persons" as defined in section 2(a)(19) of the Investment Company Act of 1940;

(2) Has adopted written procedures for the confidential receipt, retention, and consideration of any report of evidence of a material violation under Rule 205.3;

(3) Has been duly established by the issuer's board of directors, with the authority and responsibility:

(i) To inform the issuer's chief legal officer and chief executive officer (or the equivalents thereof) of any report of evidence of a material violation (except in the circumstances described in Rule 205.3(b)(4));

(ii) To determine whether an investigation is necessary regarding any report of evidence of a material violation by the issuer, its officers, directors, employees or agents and, if it determines an investigation is necessary or appropriate, to:

(A) Notify the audit committee or the full board of directors;

(B) Initiate an investigation, which may be conducted either by the chief legal officer (or the equivalent thereof) or by outside attorneys; and

(C) Retain such additional expert personnel as the committee deems necessary; and

(iii) At the conclusion of any such investigation, to:

(A) Recommend, by majority vote, that the issuer implement an appropriate response to evidence of a material violation; and

(B) Inform the chief legal officer and the chief executive officer (or the equivalents thereof) and the board of directors of the results of any such investigation under this section and the appropriate remedial measures to be adopted; and

(4) Has the authority and responsibility, acting by majority vote, to take all other appropriate action, including the authority to notify the Commission in the event that the issuer fails in any material respect to implement an appropriate response that the qualified legal compliance committee has recommended the issuer to take.

(*l*) *Reasonable* or *reasonably denotes*, with respect to the actions of an attorney, conduct that would not be unreasonable for a prudent and competent attorney.

(m) *Reasonably believes* means that an attorney believes the matter in question and that the circumstances are such that the belief is not unreasonable.

(n) *Report* means to make known to directly, either in person, by telephone, by e-mail, electronically, or in writing.

§ 205.3. Issuer as Client

(a) *Representing an issuer*. An attorney appearing and practicing before the Commission in the representation of an issuer owes his or her professional and ethical duties to the issuer as an organization. That the attorney may work with and advise the issuer's officers, directors, or employees in the course of representing the issuer does not make such individuals the attorney's clients.

(b) *Duty to report evidence of a material violation.*

(1) If an attorney, appearing and practicing before the Commission in the representation of an issuer, becomes aware of evidence of a material violation by the issuer or by any officer, director, employee, or agent of the issuer, the attorney shall report such evidence to the issuer's chief legal officer (or the equivalent thereof) or to both the issuer's chief legal officer and its chief executive officer (or the equivalents thereof) forthwith. By communicating such information to the issuer's officers or directors, an attorney does not reveal client confidences or secrets or privileged or otherwise protected information related to the attorney's representation of an issuer.

(2) The chief legal officer (or the equivalent thereof) shall cause such inquiry into the evidence of a material violation as he or she reasonably believes is appropriate to determine whether the material violation described in the report has occurred, is ongoing, or is about to occur. If the chief legal officer (or the equivalent thereof) determines no material violation has occurred, is ongoing, or is about to occur, he or she shall notify the reporting attorney and advise the reporting attorney of the basis for such determination. Unless the chief legal officer (or the equivalent thereof) reasonably believes that no material violation has occurred, is ongoing, or is about to occur, he or she shall take all reasonable steps to cause the issuer to adopt an appropriate response, and shall advise the reporting attorney thereof. In lieu of causing an inquiry under this paragraph (b), a chief legal officer (or the equivalent thereof) may refer a report of evidence of a material violation to a qualified legal compliance committee under paragraph (c)(2) of this section if the issuer has duly established a qualified legal compliance committee prior to the report of evidence of a material violation.

(3) Unless an attorney who has made a report under paragraph (b)(1) of this section reasonably believes that the chief legal officer or the chief executive officer of the issuer (or the equivalent thereof) has provided an appropriate response within a reasonable time, the attorney shall report the evidence of a material violation to:

(i) The audit committee of the issuer's board of directors;

(ii) Another committee of the issuer's board of directors consisting solely of directors who are not employed, directly or indirectly, by the issuer . . .; or

(iii) The issuer's board of directors (if the issuer's board of directors has no committee consisting solely of directors who are not employed, directly or indirectly, by the issuer). . . .

(4) If an attorney reasonably believes that it would be futile to report evidence of a material violation to the issuer's chief legal officer and chief executive officer (or the equivalents thereof) under

paragraph (b)(1) of this section, the attorney may report such evidence as provided under paragraph (b)(3) of this section.

(5) An attorney retained or directed by an issuer to investigate evidence of a material violation reported under paragraph (b)(1), (b)(3), or (b)(4) of this section shall be deemed to be appearing and practicing before the Commission. Directing or retaining an attorney to investigate reported evidence of a material violation does not relieve an officer or director of the issuer to whom such evidence has been reported under paragraph (b)(1), (b)(3), or (b)(4) of this section from a duty to respond to the reporting attorney.

(6) An attorney shall not have any obligation to report evidence of a material violation under this paragraph (b) if:

(i) The attorney was retained or directed by the issuer's chief legal officer (or the equivalent thereof) to investigate such evidence of a material violation and:

(A) The attorney reports the results of such investigation to the chief legal officer (or the equivalent thereof); and

(B) Except where the attorney and the chief legal officer (or the equivalent thereof) each reasonably believes that no material violation has occurred, is ongoing, or is about to occur, the chief legal officer (or the equivalent thereof) reports the results of the investigation to the issuer's board of directors, a committee thereof to whom a report could be made pursuant to paragraph (b)(3) of this section, or a qualified legal compliance committee; or

(ii) The attorney was retained or directed by the chief legal officer (or the equivalent thereof) to assert, consistent with his or her professional obligations, a colorable defense on behalf of the issuer (or the issuer's officer, director, employee, or agent, as the case may be) in any investigation or judicial or administrative proceeding relating to such evidence of a material violation, and the chief legal officer (or the equivalent thereof) provides reasonable and timely reports on the progress and outcome of such proceeding to the issuer's board of directors, a committee thereof to whom a report could be made pursuant to paragraph (b)(3) of this section, or a qualified legal compliance committee.

(7) An attorney shall not have any obligation to report evidence of a material violation under this paragraph (b) if such attorney was retained or directed by a qualified legal compliance committee:

(i) To investigate such evidence of a material violation; or

(ii) To assert, consistent with his or her professional obligations, a colorable defense on behalf of the issuer (or the issuer's officer, director, employee, or agent, as the case may be) in any investigation or judicial or administrative proceeding relating to such evidence of a material violation.

(8) An attorney who receives what he or she reasonably believes is an appropriate and timely response to a report he or she has made pursuant to paragraph (b)(1), (b)(3), or (b)(4) of this section need do nothing more under this section with respect to his or her report.

(9) An attorney who does not reasonably believe that the issuer has made an appropriate response within a reasonable time to the report or reports made pursuant to paragraph (b)(1), (b)(3), or (b)(4) of this section shall explain his or her reasons therefor to the chief legal officer (or the equivalent thereof), the chief executive officer (or the equivalent thereof), and directors to whom the attorney reported the evidence of a material violation pursuant to paragraph (b)(1), (b)(3), or (b)(4) of this section.

(10) An attorney formerly employed or retained by an issuer who has reported evidence of a material violation under this part and reasonably believes that he or she has been discharged for so doing may notify the issuer's board of directors or any committee thereof that he or she believes that he or she has been discharged for reporting evidence of a material violation under this section.

(c) *Alternative reporting procedures for attorneys retained or employed by an issuer that has established a qualified legal compliance committee.*

(1) If an attorney, appearing and practicing before the Commission in the representation of an issuer, becomes aware of evidence of a material violation by the issuer or by any officer, director, employee, or agent of the issuer, the attorney may, as an alternative to the reporting requirements of paragraph (b) of this section, report such evidence to a qualified legal compliance committee, if the issuer has previously formed such a committee. An attorney who reports evidence of a material violation to such a qualified legal compliance committee has satisfied his or her obligation to report such evidence and is not required to assess the issuer's response to the reported evidence of a material violation.

(2) A chief legal officer (or the equivalent thereof) may refer a report of evidence of a material violation to a previously established qualified legal compliance committee in lieu of causing an inquiry to be conducted under paragraph (b)(2) of this section. The chief legal officer (or the equivalent thereof) shall inform the reporting attorney that the report has been referred to a qualified legal compliance committee. Thereafter, pursuant to the requirements under § 205.2(k), the qualified legal compliance committee shall be responsible for responding to the evidence of a material violation reported to it under this paragraph (c).

(d) *Issuer confidences.*

(1) Any report under this section (or the contemporaneous record thereof) or any response thereto (or the contemporaneous record thereof) may be used by an attorney in connection with any investigation, proceeding, or litigation in which the attorney's compliance with this part is in issue.

(2) An attorney appearing and practicing before the Commission in the representation of an issuer may reveal to the Commission, without the issuer's consent, confidential information related to the representation to the extent the attorney reasonably believes necessary:

(i) To prevent the issuer from committing a material violation that is likely to cause substantial injury to the financial interest or property of the issuer or investors;

(ii) To prevent the issuer, in a Commission investigation or administrative proceeding from committing perjury, proscribed in 18 U.S.C. 1621; suborning perjury, proscribed in 18 U.S.C. 1622; or committing any act proscribed in 18 U.S.C. 1001 that is likely to perpetrate a fraud upon the Commission; or

(iii) To rectify the consequences of a material violation by the issuer that caused, or may cause, substantial injury to the financial interest or property of the issuer or investors in the furtherance of which the attorney's services were used.

§ 205.4. Responsibilities of Supervisory Attorneys

(a) An attorney supervising or directing another attorney who is appearing and practicing before the Commission in the representation of an issuer is a supervisory attorney. An issuer's chief legal officer (or the equivalent thereof) is a supervisory attorney under this section.

(b) A supervisory attorney shall make reasonable efforts to ensure that a subordinate attorney, as defined in Rule 205.5(a), that he or she supervises or directs conforms to this part. To the extent a subordinate attorney appears and practices before the Commission in the representation of an issuer, that subordinate attorney's supervisory attorneys also appear and practice before the Commission.

(c) A supervisory attorney is responsible for complying with the reporting requirements in Rule 205.3 when a subordinate attorney has reported to the supervisory attorney evidence of a material violation.

(d) A supervisory attorney who has received a report of evidence of a material violation from a subordinate attorney under Rule 205.3 may report such evidence to the issuer's qualified legal compliance committee if the issuer has duly formed such a committee.

§ 205.5. Responsibilities of a Subordinate Attorney

(a) An attorney who appears and practices before the Commission in the representation of an issuer on a matter under the supervision or direction of another attorney (other than under the direct supervision or direction of the issuer's chief legal officer (or the equivalent thereof)) is a subordinate attorney.

(b) A subordinate attorney shall comply with this part notwithstanding that the subordinate attorney acted at the direction of or under the supervision of another person.

(c) A subordinate attorney complies with Rule 205.3 if the subordinate attorney reports to his or her supervising attorney under Rule 205.3(b) evidence of a material violation of which the subordinate attorney has become aware in appearing and practicing before the Commission.

(d) A subordinate attorney may take the steps permitted or required by Rule 205.3(b) or (c) if the subordinate attorney reasonably believes that a supervisory attorney to whom he or she has reported evidence of a material violation under Rule 205.3(b) has failed to comply with Rule 205.3.

§ 205.6. Sanctions and Discipline

(a) A violation of this part by any attorney appearing and practicing before the Commission in the representation of an issuer shall subject such attorney to the civil penalties and remedies for a violation of the federal securities laws available to the Commission in an action brought by the Commission thereunder.

(b) An attorney appearing and practicing before the Commission who violates any provision of this part is subject to the disciplinary authority of the Commission, regardless of whether the attorney may also be subject to discipline for the same conduct in a jurisdiction where the attorney is admitted or practices. An administrative disciplinary proceeding initiated by the Commission for violation of this part may result in an attorney being censured, or being temporarily or permanently denied the privilege of appearing or practicing before the Commission.

(c) An attorney who complies in good faith with the provisions of this part shall not be subject to discipline or otherwise liable under inconsistent standards imposed by any state or other United States jurisdiction where the attorney is admitted or practices.

(d) An attorney practicing outside the United States shall not be required to comply with the requirements of this part to the extent that such compliance is prohibited by applicable foreign law.

§ 205.7. **No Private Right of Action**

(a) Nothing in this part is intended to, or does, create a private right of action against any attorney, law firm, or issuer based upon compliance or noncompliance with its provisions.

(b) Authority to enforce compliance with this part is vested exclusively in the Commission.

PROXY VOTING

DISCLOSURE OF PROXY VOTING POLICIES AND PROXY VOTING RECORDS BY MUTUAL FUNDS AND OTHER REGISTERED MANAGEMENT INVESTMENT COMPANIES [FORMS N1–A AND N–PX]

Form N–1A (Registration Statement of Open–End Management Investment Companies)

Item 13. Management of the Fund ...

(f) *Proxy Voting Policies.* Unless the Fund invests exclusively in non-voting securities, describe the policies and procedures that the Fund uses to determine how to vote proxies relating to portfolio securities, including the procedures that the Fund uses when a vote presents a conflict between the interests of Fund shareholders, on the one hand, and those of the Fund's investment adviser; principal underwriter; or any affiliated person of the Fund, its investment adviser, or its principal underwriter, on the other. Include any policies and procedures of the Fund's investment adviser, or any other third party, that the Fund uses, or that are used on the Fund's behalf, to determine how to vote proxies relating to portfolio securities. Also, state that information regarding how the Fund voted proxies relating to portfolio securities during the most recent 12–month period ended June 30 is available (1) without charge, upon request, by calling a specified toll-free (or collect) telephone number; or on or through the Fund's Web site at a specified Internet address; or both; and (2) on the Commission's Web site at http://www.sec.gov.

Instructions.

1. A Fund may satisfy the requirement to provide a description of the policies and procedures that it uses to determine how to vote proxies relating to portfolio securities by including a copy of the policies and procedures themselves.

2. If a Fund discloses that the Fund's proxy voting record is available by calling a toll-free (or collect) telephone number, and the Fund (or financial intermediary through which shares of the Fund may be purchased or sold) receives a request for this information, the Fund (or financial intermediary) must send the information disclosed in the Fund's most recently filed report on Form N–PX, within three business days of receipt of the request, by first-class mail or other means designed to ensure equally prompt delivery.

3. If a Fund discloses that the Fund's proxy voting record is available on or through its Web site, the Fund must make available free of charge the information disclosed in the Fund's most recently filed report on Form N–PX on or through its Web site as soon as reasonably practicable after filing the report with the Commission....

Item 22. Financial Statements

(b) *Annual Report* ...

(7) A statement that a description of the policies and procedures that the Fund uses to determine how to vote proxies relating to portfolio securities is available (i) without charge, upon request, by calling a specified toll-free (or collect) telephone number; (ii) on the Fund's Web site, if applicable; and (iii) on the Commission's Web site at http://www.sec.gov.

(8) A statement that information regarding how the Fund voted proxies relating to portfolio securities during the most recent 12–month period ended June 30 is available (i) without charge, upon request, by calling a specified toll-free (or collect) telephone number; or on or through the Fund's Web site at a specified Internet address; or both; and (ii) on the Commission's Web site at http://www.sec.gov.

Form N–PX (Annual Report of Proxy Voting Record of Registered Management Investment Company) ...

Form N–PX is to be used by a registered management investment company ... to file reports with the Commission, not later than August 31 of each year, containing the registrant's proxy voting record for the most recent twelve-month period ended June 30....

Item 1. Proxy Voting Record

Disclose the following information for each matter relating to a portfolio security considered at any shareholder meeting held during the period covered by the report and with respect to which the registrant was entitled to vote:

(a) The name of the issuer of the portfolio security;

(b) The exchange ticker symbol of the portfolio security;

(c) The Council on Uniform Securities Identification Procedures ("CUSIP") number for the portfolio security;

(d) The shareholder meeting date;

(e) A brief identification of the matter voted on;

(f) Whether the matter was proposed by the issuer or by a security holder;

(g) Whether the registrant cast its vote on the matter;

(h) How the registrant cast its vote (e.g., for or against proposal, or abstain; for or withhold regarding election of directors); and

(i) Whether the registrant cast its vote for or against management.

VOTING ACTIVITIES BY INVESTMENT ADVISERS

[17 C.F.R. Part 275—Rules 204–2, 275–6 Under the Investment Advisers Act]

Rule 204–2. Books and Records to be Maintained by Investment Advisers....

(c) ...

(2) Every investment adviser [registered or required to be registered under section 203 of the Investment Advisers Act] that exercises voting authority with respect to client securities shall, with respect to those clients, make and retain the following:

(i) Copies of all policies and procedures required by Rule 275.

(ii) A copy of each proxy statement that the investment adviser receives regarding client securities. An investment adviser may satisfy this requirement by relying on a third party to make and retain, on the investment adviser's behalf, a copy of a proxy statement (provided that the adviser has obtained an undertaking from the third party to provide a copy of the proxy statement promptly upon request) or may rely on obtaining a copy of a proxy statement from the Commission's Electronic Data Gathering, Analysis, and Retrieval (EDGAR) system.

(iii) A record of each vote cast by the investment adviser on behalf of a client. An investment adviser may satisfy this requirement by relying on a third party to make and retain, on the investment adviser's behalf, a record of the vote cast (provided that the adviser has obtained an undertaking from the third party to provide a copy of the record promptly upon request).

(iv) A copy of any document created by the adviser that was material to making a decision how to vote proxies on behalf of a client or that memorializes the basis for that decision.

(v) A copy of each written client request for information on how the adviser voted proxies on behalf of the client, and a copy of any written response by the investment adviser to any (written or oral) client request for information on how the adviser voted proxies on behalf of the requesting client....

(e)(1) All books and records required to be made under the provisions of [paragraph (c)(2)] shall be maintained and preserved in an easily accessible place for a period of not less than five years from the end of the fiscal year during which the last entry was made on such record, the first two years in an appropriate office of the investment adviser.

Rule 275-6. Proxy Voting.

If you are an investment adviser registered or required to be registered under section 203 of the [Investment Advisors] Act, it is a fraudulent, deceptive, or manipulative act, practice or course of business within the meaning of section 206(4) of the Act, for you to exercise voting authority with respect to client securities, unless you:

(a) Adopt and implement written policies and procedures that are reasonably designed to ensure that you vote client securities in the best interest of clients, which procedures must include how you address material conflicts that may arise between your interests and those of your clients;

(b) Disclose to clients how they may obtain information from you about how you voted with respect to their securities; and

(c) Describe to clients your proxy voting policies and procedures and, upon request, furnish a copy of the policies and procedures to the requesting client.

REGULATION AC (ANALYST CERTIFICATION)

17 C.F.R. §§ 242.500–505

Rule 500. Definitions.
Rule 501. Certifications in Connection with Research Reports.
Rule 502. Certifications in Connection with Public Appearances.
Rule 503. Certain Foreign Research Reports.
Rule 504. Notification to Associated Persons.
Rule 505. Exclusion for News Media.

Rule 500. Definitions.

For purposes of Regulation AC the term:

Covered person of a broker or dealer means an associated person of that broker or dealer but does not include:

(1) An associated person:*

    (i) If the associated person has no officers (or persons performing similar functions) or employees in common with the broker or dealer who can influence the activities of research analysts or the content of research reports; and

    (ii) If the broker or dealer maintains and enforces written policies and procedures reasonably designed to prevent the broker or dealer, any controlling persons, officers (or persons performing similar functions), and employees of the broker or dealer from influencing the activities of research analysts and the content of research reports prepared by the associated person....

Foreign person means any person who is not a U.S. person.

Foreign security means a security issued by a foreign issuer for which a U.S. market is not the principal trading market.

Public appearance means any participation by a research analyst in a seminar, forum (including an interactive electronic forum), or radio or television or other interview, in which the research analyst makes a specific recommendation or provides information reasonably sufficient upon which to base an investment decision about a security or an issuer.

---

  * The term "person associated with a broker or dealer" is defined in section 3(a)(18) of the Securities Exchange Act to mean "... any partner, officer, director, or branch manager of such broker or dealer (or any person occupying a similar status or performing similar functions), any person directly or indirectly controlling, controlled by, or under common control with such broker or dealer, or any employee of such broker or dealer...." (Footnote by ed.)

Registered broker or dealer means a broker or dealer registered or required to register pursuant to section 15 or section 15B of the Securities Exchange Act of 1934 or a government securities broker or government securities dealer registered or required to register pursuant to section 15C(a)(1)(A) of the Securities Exchange Act of 1934.

Research analyst means any natural person who is primarily responsible for the preparation of the content of a research report.

Research report means a written communication (including an electronic communication) that includes an analysis of a security or an issuer and provides information reasonably sufficient upon which to base an investment decision.

Third party research analyst means:

(1) With respect to a broker or dealer, any research analyst not employed by that broker or dealer or any associated person of that broker or dealer; and

(2) With respect to a covered person of a broker or dealer, any research analyst not employed by that covered person, by the broker or dealer with whom that covered person is associated, or by any other associated person of the broker or dealer with whom that covered person is associated. . . .

Rule 501. Certifications in Connection with Research Reports.

(a) A broker or dealer or covered person that publishes, circulates, or provides a research report prepared by a research analyst to a U.S. person in the United States shall include in that research report a clear and prominent certification by the research analyst containing the following:

(1) A statement attesting that all of the views expressed in the research report accurately reflect the research analyst's personal views about any and all of the subject securities or issuers; and

(2)(i) A statement attesting that no part of the research analyst's compensation was, is, or will be, directly or indirectly, related to the specific recommendations or views expressed by the research analyst in the research report; or

(ii) A statement:

(A) Attesting that part or all of the research analyst's compensation was, is, or will be, directly or indirectly, related to the specific recommendations or views expressed by the research analyst in the research report;

(B) Identifying the source, amount, and purpose of such compensation; and

(C) Further disclosing that the compensation could influence the recommendations or views expressed in the research report.

(b) A broker or dealer or covered person that publishes, circulates, or provides a research report prepared by a third party research analyst to a U.S. person in the United States shall be exempt from the requirements of this section with respect to such research report if the following conditions are satisfied:

(1) The employer of the third party research analyst has no officers (or persons performing similar functions) or employees in common with the broker or dealer or covered person; and

(2) The broker or dealer (or, with respect to a covered person, the broker or dealer with whom the covered person is associated) maintains and enforces written policies and procedures reasonably designed to prevent the broker or dealer, any controlling persons, officers (or persons performing similar functions), and employees of the broker or dealer from influencing the activities of the third party research analyst and the content of research reports prepared by the third party research analyst.

Rule 502. Certifications in Connection with Public Appearances.

(a) If a broker or dealer publishes, circulates, or provides a research report prepared by a research analyst employed by the broker or dealer or covered person to a U.S. person in the United States, the broker or dealer must make a record within 30 days after any calendar quarter in which the research analyst made a public appearance that contains the following:

(1) A statement by the research analyst attesting that the views expressed by the research analyst in all public appearances during the calendar quarter accurately reflected the research analyst's personal views at that time about any and all of the subject securities or issuers; and

(2) A statement by the research analyst attesting that no part of the research analyst's compensation was, is, or will be, directly or indirectly, related to the specific recommendations or views expressed by the research analyst in such public appearances.

(b) If the broker or dealer does not obtain a statement by the research analyst in accordance with paragraph (a) of this section:

(1) The broker or dealer shall promptly notify in writing its examining authority, designated pursuant to section 17(d) of the Securities Exchange Act of 1934 and Rule 17d–2 of this chapter, that the research analyst did not provide the certifications specified in paragraph (a) of this section; and

(2) For 120 days following notification pursuant to paragraph (b)(1) of this section, the broker or dealer shall disclose in any research report prepared by the research analyst and published, circulated, or provided to a U.S. person in the United States that the research analyst did not provide the certifications specified in paragraph (a) of this section.

(c) In the case of a research analyst who is employed outside the United States by a foreign person located outside the United States, this section shall only apply to a public appearance while the research analyst is physically present in the United States.

(d) A broker or dealer shall preserve the records specified in paragraphs (a) and (b) of this section in accordance with Rule 17a–4 of this chapter and for a period of not less than 3 years, the first 2 years in an accessible place.

Rule 503. Certain Foreign Research Reports.

A foreign person, located outside the United States and not associated with a registered broker or dealer, who prepares a research report concerning a foreign security and provides it to a U.S. person in the United States in accordance with the provisions of § 240.15a–6(a)(2) of this chapter shall be exempt from the requirements of this regulation.

Rule 504. Notification to Associated Persons.

A broker or dealer shall notify any person with whom that broker or dealer is associated who publishes, circulates, or provides research reports:

(a) Whether the broker or dealer maintains and enforces written policies and procedures reasonably designed to prevent the broker or dealer, any controlling persons, officers (or persons performing similar functions), or employees of the broker or dealer from influencing the activities of research analysts and the content of research reports prepared by the associated person; and

(b) Whether the associated person has any officers (or persons performing similar functions) or employees in common with the broker or dealer who can influence the activities of research analysts or the content of research reports and, if so, the identity of those persons.

Rule 505. Exclusion for News Media.

No provision of this Regulation AC shall apply to any person who:

(a) Is the publisher of any bona fide newspaper, news magazine or business or financial publication of general and regular circulation; and

(b) Is not registered or required to be registered with the Commission as a broker or dealer or investment adviser.

SARBANES–OXLEY ACT OF 2002

15 U.S.C.A. §§ 7201 et seq.

TABLE OF CONTENTS

* Omitted

* Omitted

SECTION 1. SHORT TITLE

(a) SHORT TITLE.—This Act may be cited as the "Sarbanes–Oxley Act of 2002" . . .

SEC. 2. DEFINITIONS.

(a) IN GENERAL.—In this Act, the following definitions shall apply:

(1) APPROPRIATE STATE REGULATORY AUTHORITY.—The term "appropriate State regulatory authority" means the State agency or other authority responsible for the licensure or other regulation of the practice of accounting in the State or States having jurisdiction over a registered public accounting firm or associated person thereof, with respect to the matter in question.

* Omitted

2122

(2) AUDIT.—The term "audit" means an examination of the financial statements of any issuer by an independent public accounting firm in accordance with the rules of the Board or the Commission (or, for the period preceding the adoption of applicable rules of the Board under section 103, in accordance with then-applicable generally accepted auditing and related standards for such purposes), for the purpose of expressing an opinion on such statements.

(3) AUDIT COMMITTEE.—The term "audit committee" means—

(A) a committee (or equivalent body) established by and amongst the board of directors of an issuer for the purpose of overseeing the accounting and financial reporting processes of the issuer and audits of the financial statements of the issuer; and

(B) if no such committee exists with respect to an issuer, the entire board of directors of the issuer.

(4) AUDIT REPORT.—The term "audit report" means a document or other record—

(A) prepared following an audit performed for purposes of compliance by an issuer with the requirements of the securities laws; and

(B) in which a public accounting firm either—

(i) sets forth the opinion of that firm regarding a financial statement, report, or other document; or

(ii) asserts that no such opinion can be expressed.

(5) BOARD.—The term "Board" means the Public Company Accounting Oversight Board established under section 101.

(6) COMMISSION.—The term "Commission" means the Securities and Exchange Commission.

(7) ISSUER.—The term "issuer" means an issuer (as defined in section 3 of the Securities Exchange Act of 1934 (15 U.S.C. 78c)), the securities of which are registered under section 12 of that Act (15 U.S.C. 78l), or that is required to file reports under section 15(d) (15 U.S.C. 78o(d)), or that files or has filed a registration statement that has not yet become effective under the Securities Act of 1933 (15 U.S.C. 77a et seq.), and that it has not withdrawn.

(8) NON–AUDIT SERVICES.—The term "non-audit services" means any professional services provided to an issuer by a registered public accounting firm, other than those provided to an issuer in connection with an audit or a review of the financial statements of an issuer.

(9) PERSON ASSOCIATED WITH A PUBLIC ACCOUNTING FIRM.—

(A) IN GENERAL.—The terms "person associated with a public accounting firm" (or with a "registered public accounting firm") and "associated person of a public accounting firm" (or of a "registered public accounting firm") mean any individual proprietor, partner, shareholder, principal, accountant, or other professional employee of a public accounting firm, or any other independent contractor or entity that, in connection with the preparation or issuance of any audit report—

(i) shares in the profits of, or receives compensation in any other form from, that firm; or

(ii) participates as agent or otherwise on behalf of such accounting firm in any activity of that firm.

(B) EXEMPTION AUTHORITY.—The Board may, by rule, exempt persons engaged only in ministerial tasks from the definition in subparagraph (A), to the extent that the Board determines that any such exemption is consistent with the purposes of this Act, the public interest, or the protection of investors.

(10) PROFESSIONAL STANDARDS.—The term "professional standards" means—(A) accounting principles that are—

(i) established by the standard setting body described in section 19(b) of the Securities Act of 1933, as amended by this Act, or prescribed by the Commission under section 19(a) of that Act (15 U.S.C. 17a(s)) or section 13(b) of the Securities Exchange Act of 1934 (15 U.S.C. 78a(m)); and

(ii) relevant to audit reports for particular issuers, or dealt with in the quality control system of a particular registered public accounting firm; and

(B) auditing standards, standards for attestation engagements, quality control policies and procedures, ethical and competency standards, and independence standards (including rules implementing title II) that the Board or the Commission determines—

(i) relate to the preparation or issuance of audit reports for issuers; and

(ii) are established or adopted by the Board under section 103(a), or are promulgated as rules of the Commission.

(11) PUBLIC ACCOUNTING FIRM.—The term "public accounting firm" means—

(A) a proprietorship, partnership, incorporated association, corporation, limited liability company, limited liability partnership, or other legal entity that is engaged in the practice of public accounting or preparing or issuing audit reports; and

(B) to the extent so designated by the rules of the Board, any associated person of any entity described in subparagraph (A).

(12) REGISTERED PUBLIC ACCOUNTING FIRM.—The term "registered public accounting firm" means a public accounting firm registered with the Board in accordance with this Act.

(13) RULES OF THE BOARD.—The term "rules of the Board" means the bylaws and rules of the Board (as submitted to, and approved, modified, or amended by the Commission, in accordance with section 107), and those stated policies, practices, and interpretations of the Board that the Commission, by rule, may deem to be rules of the Board, as necessary or appropriate in the public interest or for the protection of investors.

(14) SECURITY.—The term "security" has the same meaning as in section 3(a) of the Securities Exchange Act of 1934 (15 U.S.C.A. § 78c(a)).

(15) SECURITIES LAWS.—The term "securities laws" means the provisions of law referred to in section 3(a)(47) of the Securities Exchange Act of 1934 (15 U.S.C.A. § 78c(a)(47)), as amended by this Act, and includes the rules, regulations, and orders issued by the Commission thereunder.

(16) STATE.—The term "State" means any State of the United States, the District of Columbia, Puerto Rico, the Virgin Islands, or any other territory or possession of the United States. . . .

SEC. 3. COMMISSION RULES AND ENFORCEMENT

(a) REGULATORY ACTION.—The Commission shall promulgate such rules and regulations, as may be necessary or appropriate in the public interest or for the protection of investors, and in furtherance of this Act.

(b) ENFORCEMENT.—

(1) IN GENERAL.—A violation by any person of this Act, any rule or regulation of the Commission issued under this Act, or any rule of the Board shall be treated for all purposes in the same manner as a violation of the Securities Exchange Act of 1934 (15 U.S.C.A. §§ 78a et seq.) or the rules and regulations issued thereunder, consistent with the provisions of this Act, and any such person shall be subject to the same penalties, and to the same extent, as for a violation of that Act or such rules or regulations. . . .

(c) EFFECT ON COMMISSION AUTHORITY.—Nothing in this Act or the rules of the Board shall be construed to impair or limit—

(1) the authority of the Commission to regulate the accounting profession, accounting firms, or persons associated with such firms for purposes of enforcement of the securities laws;

(2) the authority of the Commission to set standards for accounting or auditing practices or auditor independence, derived from other provisions of the securities laws or the rules or regulations thereunder, for purposes of the preparation and issuance of any audit report, or otherwise under applicable law; or

(3) the ability of the Commission to take, on the initiative of the Commission, legal, administrative, or disciplinary action against any registered public accounting firm or any associated person thereof.

TITLE I—PUBLIC COMPANY ACCOUNTING OVERSIGHT BOARD

SEC. 101. ESTABLISHMENT; ADMINISTRATIVE PROVISIONS.

(a) ESTABLISHMENT OF BOARD.—There is established the Public Company Accounting Oversight Board, to oversee the audit of public companies that are subject to the securities laws, and related matters, in order to protect the interests of investors and further the public interest in the preparation of informative, accurate, and independent audit reports for companies the securities of which are sold to, and held by and for, public investors. The Board shall be a body corporate, operate as a nonprofit corporation, and have succession until dissolved by an Act of Congress.

(b) STATUS.—The Board shall not be an agency or establishment of the United States Government, and, except as otherwise provided in this Act, shall be subject to, and have all the powers conferred upon a nonprofit corporation by, the District of Columbia Nonprofit Corporation Act. No member or person employed by, or agent for, the Board shall be deemed to be an officer or employee of or agent for the Federal Government by reason of such service.

(c) DUTIES OF THE BOARD.—The Board shall, subject to action by the Commission under section 107, and once a determination is made by the Commission under subsection (d) of this section—

(1) register public accounting firms that prepare audit reports for issuers, in accordance with section 102;

(2) establish or adopt, or both, by rule, auditing, quality control, ethics, independence, and other standards relating to the preparation of audit reports for issuers, in accordance with section 103;

(3) conduct inspections of registered public accounting firms, in accordance with section 104 and the rules of the Board;

(4) conduct investigations and disciplinary proceedings concerning, and impose appropriate sanctions where justified upon, registered public accounting firms and associated persons of such firms, in accordance with section 105;

(5) perform such other duties or functions as the Board (or the Commission, by rule or order) determines are necessary or appropriate to promote high professional standards among, and improve the quality of audit services offered by, registered public accounting firms and associated persons thereof, or otherwise to carry out this Act, in order to protect investors, or to further the public interest;

(6) enforce compliance with this Act, the rules of the Board, professional standards, and the securities laws relating to the preparation and issuance of audit reports and the obligations and liabilities of accountants with respect thereto, by registered public accounting firms and associated persons thereof; and

(7) set the budget and manage the operations of the Board and the staff of the Board.

(d) COMMISSION DETERMINATION.—The members of the Board shall take such action (including hiring of staff, proposal of rules, and adoption of initial and transitional auditing and other professional standards) as may be necessary or appropriate to enable the Commission to determine, not later than 270 days after the date of enactment of this Act, that the Board is so organized and has the capacity to carry out the requirements of this title, and to enforce compliance with this title by registered public accounting firms and associated persons thereof. The Commission shall be responsible, prior to the appointment of the Board, for the planning for the establishment and administrative transition to the Board's operation.

(e) BOARD MEMBERSHIP.—

(1) COMPOSITION.—The Board shall have 5 members, appointed from among prominent individuals of integrity and reputation who have a demonstrated commitment to the interests of investors and the public, and an understanding of the responsibilities for and nature of the financial disclosures required of issuers under the securities laws and the obligations of accountants with respect to the preparation and issuance of audit reports with respect to such disclosures.

(2) LIMITATION.—Two members, and only 2 members, of the Board shall be or have been certified public accountants pursuant to the laws of 1 or more States, provided that, if 1 of those 2 members is the chairperson, he or she may not have been a practicing certified public accountant for at least 5 years prior to his or her appointment to the Board.

(3) FULL–TIME INDEPENDENT SERVICE.—Each member of the Board shall serve on a full-time basis, and may not, concurrent with service on the Board, be employed by any other person or engage in any other professional or business activity. No member of the Board may share in any of the profits of, or receive payments from, a public accounting firm (or any other person, as determined by rule of the Commission), other than fixed continuing payments, subject to such conditions as the Commission may impose, under standard arrangements for the retirement of members of public accounting firms.

(4) APPOINTMENT OF BOARD MEMBERS.—

(A) INITIAL BOARD.—Not later than 90 days after the date of enactment of this Act, the Commission, after consultation with the Chairman of the Board of Governors of the Federal Reserve System and the Secretary of the Treasury, shall appoint the chairperson and other initial members of the Board, and shall designate a term of service for each.

(B) VACANCIES.—A vacancy on the Board shall not affect the powers of the Board, but shall be filled in the same manner as provided for appointments under this section.

(5) TERM OF SERVICE.—

(A) IN GENERAL.—The term of service of each Board member shall be 5 years, and until a successor is appointed, except that—

(i) the terms of office of the initial Board members (other than the chairperson) shall expire in annual increments, 1 on each of the first 4 anniversaries of the initial date of appointment; and

(ii) any Board member appointed to fill a vacancy occurring before the expiration of the term for which the predecessor was appointed shall be appointed only for the remainder of that term.

(B) TERM LIMITATION.—No person may serve as a member of the Board, or as chairperson of the Board, for more than 2 terms, whether or not such terms of service are consecutive.

(6) REMOVAL FROM OFFICE.—A member of the Board may be removed by the Commission from office, in accordance with section 107(d)(3), for good cause shown before the expiration of the term of that member.

(f) POWERS OF THE BOARD.—In addition to any authority granted to the Board otherwise in this Act, the Board shall have the power, subject to section 107—

(1) to sue and be sued, complain and defend, in its corporate name and through its own counsel, with the approval of the Commission, in any Federal, State, or other court;

(2) to conduct its operations and maintain offices, and to exercise all other rights and powers authorized by this Act, in any State, without regard to any qualification, licensing, or other provision of law in effect in such State (or a political subdivision thereof);

(3) to lease, purchase, accept gifts or donations of or otherwise acquire, improve, use, sell, exchange, or convey, all of or an interest in any property, wherever situated;

(4) to appoint such employees, accountants, attorneys, and other agents as may be necessary or appropriate, and to determine their qualifications, define their duties, and fix their salaries or other compensation (at a level that is comparable to private sector self-regulatory, accounting, technical, supervisory, or other staff or management positions);

(5) to allocate, assess, and collect accounting support fees established pursuant to section 109, for the Board, and other fees and charges imposed under this title; and

(6) to enter into contracts, execute instruments, incur liabilities, and do any and all other acts and things necessary, appropriate, or incidental to the conduct of its operations and the exercise of its obligations, rights, and powers imposed or granted by this title.

(g) RULES OF THE BOARD.—The rules of the Board shall, subject to the approval of the Commission—

(1) provide for the operation and administration of the Board, the exercise of its authority, and the performance of its responsibilities under this Act;

(2) permit, as the Board determines necessary or appropriate, delegation by the Board of any of its functions to an individual member or employee of the Board, or to a division of the Board, including functions with respect to hearing, determining, ordering, certifying, reporting, or otherwise acting as to any matter, except that—

(A) the Board shall retain a discretionary right to review any action pursuant to any such delegated function, upon its own motion;

(B) a person shall be entitled to a review by the Board with respect to any matter so delegated, and the decision of the Board upon such review shall be deemed to be the action of the Board for all purposes (including appeal or review thereof); and

(C) if the right to exercise a review described in subparagraph (A) is declined, or if no such review is sought within the time stated in the rules of the Board, then the action taken by the holder of such delegation shall for all purposes, including appeal or review thereof, be deemed to be the action of the Board;

(3) establish ethics rules and standards of conduct for Board members and staff, including a bar on practice before the Board (and the Commission, with respect to Board-related matters) of 1 year for former members of the Board, and appropriate periods (not to exceed 1 year) for former staff of the Board; and

(4) provide as otherwise required by this Act.

(h) ANNUAL REPORT TO THE COMMISSION.—The Board shall submit an annual report (including its audited financial statements) to the Commission, and the Commission shall transmit a copy of that report to the Committee on Banking, Housing, and Urban Affairs of the Senate, and the Committee on Financial Services of the House of Representatives, not later than 30 days after the date of receipt of that report by the Commission.

SEC. 102. REGISTRATION WITH THE BOARD

(a) MANDATORY REGISTRATION.—Beginning 180 days after the date of the determination of the Commission under section 101(d), it shall be unlawful for any person that is not a registered public accounting firm to prepare or issue, or to participate in the preparation or issuance of, any audit report with respect to any issuer.

(b) APPLICATIONS FOR REGISTRATION.—

(1) FORM OF APPLICATION.—A public accounting firm shall use such form as the Board may prescribe, by rule, to apply for registration under this section.

(2) CONTENTS OF APPLICATIONS.—Each public accounting firm shall submit, as part of its application for registration, in such detail as the Board shall specify—

(A) the names of all issuers for which the firm prepared or issued audit reports during the immediately preceding calendar year, and for which the firm expects to prepare or issue audit reports during the current calendar year;

(B) the annual fees received by the firm from each such issuer for audit services, other accounting services, and non-audit services, respectively;

(C) such other current financial information for the most recently completed fiscal year of the firm as the Board may reasonably request;

(D) a statement of the quality control policies of the firm for its accounting and auditing practices;

(E) a list of all accountants associated with the firm who participate in or contribute to the preparation of audit reports, stating the license or certification number of each such person, as well as the State license numbers of the firm itself;

(F) information relating to criminal, civil, or administrative actions or disciplinary proceedings pending against the firm or any associated person of the firm in connection with any audit report;

(G) copies of any periodic or annual disclosure filed by an issuer with the Commission during the immediately preceding calendar year which discloses accounting disagreements between such issuer and the firm in connection with an audit report furnished or prepared by the firm for such issuer; and

(H) such other information as the rules of the Board or the Commission shall specify as necessary or appropriate in the public interest or for the protection of investors.

(3) CONSENTS.—Each application for registration under this subsection shall include—

(A) a consent executed by the public accounting firm to cooperation in and compliance with any request for testimony or the production of documents made by the Board in the furtherance of its authority and responsibilities under this title (and an agreement to secure and enforce similar consents from each of the associated persons of the public accounting firm as a condition of their continued employment by or other association with such firm); and

(B) a statement that such firm understands and agrees that cooperation and compliance, as described in the consent required by subparagraph (A), and the securing and enforcement of such consents from its associated persons, in accordance with the rules of the Board, shall be a condition to the continuing effectiveness of the registration of the firm with the Board.

(c) ACTION ON APPLICATIONS.—

(1) TIMING.—The Board shall approve a completed application for registration not later than 45 days after the date of receipt of the application, in accordance with the rules of the Board, unless the Board, prior to such date, issues a written notice of disapproval to, or requests more information from, the prospective registrant.

(2) TREATMENT.—A written notice of disapproval of a completed application under paragraph (1) for registration shall be treated as a disciplinary sanction for purposes of sections 105(d) and 107(c).

(d) PERIODIC REPORTS.—Each registered public accounting firm shall submit an annual report to the Board, and may be required to report more frequently, as necessary to update the information contained in its application for registration under this section, and to provide to the Board such additional information as the Board or the Commission may specify, in accordance with subsection (b)(2).

(e) PUBLIC AVAILABILITY.—Registration applications and annual reports required by this subsection, or such portions of such applications or reports as may be designated under rules of the Board, shall be made available for public inspection, subject to rules of the Board or the Commission, and to applicable laws relating to the confidentiality of proprietary, personal, or other information contained in such applications or reports, provided that, in all events, the Board shall protect from public disclosure information reasonably identified by the subject accounting firm as proprietary information.

(f) REGISTRATION AND ANNUAL FEES.—The Board shall assess and collect a registration fee and an annual fee from each registered public accounting firm, in amounts that are sufficient to recover the costs of processing and reviewing applications and annual reports.

SEC. 103. AUDITING, QUALITY CONTROL, AND INDEPENDENCE STANDARDS AND RULES.

(a) AUDITING, QUALITY CONTROL, AND ETHICS STANDARDS.—

(1) IN GENERAL.—The Board shall, by rule, establish, including, to the extent it determines appropriate, through adoption of standards proposed by 1 or more professional groups of accountants designated pursuant to paragraph (3)(A) or advisory groups convened pursuant to paragraph (4), and amend or otherwise modify or alter, such auditing and related attestation standards, such quality control standards, and such ethics standards to be used by registered public accounting firms in the preparation and issuance of audit reports, as required by this Act or the rules of the Commission, or as may be necessary or appropriate in the public interest or for the protection of investors.

(2) RULE REQUIREMENTS.—In carrying out paragraph (1), the Board—

(A) shall include in the auditing standards that it adopts, requirements that each registered public accounting firm shall—

(i) prepare, and maintain for a period of not less than 7 years, audit work papers, and other information related to any audit report, in sufficient detail to support the conclusions reached in such report;

(ii) provide a concurring or second partner review and approval of such audit report (and other related information), and concurring approval in its issuance, by a qualified person (as prescribed by the Board) associated with the public accounting firm, other than the person in charge of the audit, or by an independent reviewer (as prescribed by the Board); and

(iii) describe in each audit report the scope of the auditor's testing of the internal control structure and procedures of the issuer, required by section 404(b), and present (in such report or in a separate report)—

(I) the findings of the auditor from such testing;

(II) an evaluation of whether such internal control structure and procedures—

(aa) include maintenance of records that in reasonable detail accurately and fairly reflect the transactions and dispositions of the assets of the issuer;

(bb) provide reasonable assurance that transactions are recorded as necessary to permit preparation of financial statements in accordance with generally accepted accounting principles, and that receipts and expenditures of the issuer are being made only in accordance with authorizations of management and directors of the issuer; and

(III) a description, at a minimum, of material weaknesses in such internal controls, and of any material noncompliance found on the basis of such testing.

(B) shall include, in the quality control standards that it adopts with respect to the issuance of audit reports, requirements for every registered public accounting firm relating to—

(i) monitoring of professional ethics and independence from issuers on behalf of which the firm issues audit reports;

(ii) consultation within such firm on accounting and auditing questions;

(iii) supervision of audit work;

(iv) hiring, professional development, and advancement of personnel;

(v) the acceptance and continuation of engagements;

(vi) internal inspection; and

(vii) such other requirements as the Board may prescribe, subject to subsection (a)(1).

(3) AUTHORITY TO ADOPT OTHER STANDARDS.—

(A) IN GENERAL.—In carrying out this subsection, the Board—

(i) may adopt as its rules, subject to the terms of section 107, any portion of any statement of auditing standards or other professional standards that the Board determines satisfy the requirements of paragraph (1), and that were proposed by 1 or more professional groups of accountants that shall be designated or recognized by the Board, by rule, for such purpose, pursuant to this paragraph or 1 or more advisory groups convened pursuant to paragraph (4); and

(ii) notwithstanding clause (i), shall retain full authority to modify, supplement, revise, or subsequently amend, modify, or repeal, in whole or in part, any portion of any statement described in clause (i).

(B) INITIAL AND TRANSITIONAL STANDARDS.—The Board shall adopt standards described in subparagraph (A)(i) as initial or transitional standards, to the extent the Board determines necessary, prior to a determination of the Commission under section 101(d), and such standards shall be separately approved by the Commission at the time of that determination, without regard to the procedures required by section 107 that otherwise would apply to the approval of rules of the Board.

(4) ADVISORY GROUPS.—The Board shall convene, or authorize its staff to convene, such expert advisory groups as may be appropriate, which may include practicing accountants and other experts, as well as representatives of other interested groups, subject to such rules as the Board may prescribe to prevent conflicts of interest, to make recommendations concerning the content (including proposed drafts) of auditing, quality control, ethics, independence, or other standards required to be established under this section.

(b) INDEPENDENCE STANDARDS AND RULES.—The Board shall establish such rules as may be necessary or appropriate in the public interest or for the protection of investors, to implement, or as authorized under, title II of this Act.

(c) COOPERATION WITH DESIGNATED PROFESSIONAL GROUPS OF ACCOUNTANTS AND ADVISORY GROUPS.—

(1) IN GENERAL.—The Board shall cooperate on an ongoing basis with professional groups of accountants designated under subsection (a)(3)(A) and advisory groups convened under subsection (a)(4) in the examination of the need for changes in any standards subject to its authority under subsection (a), recommend issues for inclusion on the agendas of such designated professional groups of

accountants or advisory groups, and take such other steps as it deems appropriate to increase the effectiveness of the standard setting process.

(2) BOARD RESPONSES.—The Board shall respond in a timely fashion to requests from designated professional groups of accountants and advisory groups referred to in paragraph (1) for any changes in standards over which the Board has authority.

(d) EVALUATION OF STANDARD SETTING PROCESS.—The Board shall include in the annual report required by section 101(h) the results of its standard setting responsibilities during the period to which the report relates, including a discussion of the work of the Board with any designated professional groups of accountants and advisory groups described in paragraphs (3)(A) and (4) of subsection (a), and its pending issues agenda for future standard setting projects.

SEC. 104. INSPECTIONS OF REGISTERED PUBLIC ACCOUNTING FIRMS.

(a) IN GENERAL.—The Board shall conduct a continuing program of inspections to assess the degree of compliance of each registered public accounting firm and associated persons of that firm with this Act, the rules of the Board, the rules of the Commission, or professional standards, in connection with its performance of audits, issuance of audit reports, and related matters involving issuers.

(b) INSPECTION FREQUENCY.—

(1) IN GENERAL.—Subject to paragraph (2), inspections required by this section shall be conducted—

(A) annually with respect to each registered public accounting firm that regularly provides audit reports for more than 100 issuers; and

(B) not less frequently than once every 3 years with respect to each registered public accounting firm that regularly provides audit reports for 100 or fewer issuers.

(2) ADJUSTMENTS TO SCHEDULES.—The Board may, by rule, adjust the inspection schedules set under paragraph (1) if the Board finds that different inspection schedules are consistent with the purposes of this Act, the public interest, and the protection of investors. The Board may conduct special inspections at the request of the Commission or upon its own motion.

(c) PROCEDURES.—The Board shall, in each inspection under this section, and in accordance with its rules for such inspections—

(1) identify any act or practice or omission to act by the registered public accounting firm, or by any associated person thereof, revealed by such inspection that may be in violation of this Act,

the rules of the Board, the rules of the Commission, the firm's own quality control policies, or professional standards;

(2) report any such act, practice, or omission, if appropriate, to the Commission and each appropriate State regulatory authority; and

(3) begin a formal investigation or take disciplinary action, if appropriate, with respect to any such violation, in accordance with this Act and the rules of the Board.

(d) CONDUCT OF INSPECTIONS.—In conducting an inspection of a registered public accounting firm under this section, the Board shall—

(1) inspect and review selected audit and review engagements of the firm (which may include audit engagements that are the subject of ongoing litigation or other controversy between the firm and 1 or more third parties), performed at various offices and by various associated persons of the firm, as selected by the Board;

(2) evaluate the sufficiency of the quality control system of the firm, and the manner of the documentation and communication of that system by the firm; and

(3) perform such other testing of the audit, supervisory, and quality control procedures of the firm as are necessary or appropriate in light of the purpose of the inspection and the responsibilities of the Board.

(e) RECORD RETENTION.—The rules of the Board may require the retention by registered public accounting firms for inspection purposes of records whose retention is not otherwise required by section 103 or the rules issued thereunder.

(f) PROCEDURES FOR REVIEW.—The rules of the Board shall provide a procedure for the review of and response to a draft inspection report by the registered public accounting firm under inspection. The Board shall take such action with respect to such response as it considers appropriate (including revising the draft report or continuing or supplementing its inspection activities before issuing a final report), but the text of any such response, appropriately redacted to protect information reasonably identified by the accounting firm as confidential, shall be attached to and made part of the inspection report.

(g) REPORT.—A written report of the findings of the Board for each inspection under this section, subject to subsection (h), shall be—

(1) transmitted, in appropriate detail, to the Commission and each appropriate State regulatory authority, accompanied by any letter or comments by the Board or the inspector, and any letter of response from the registered public accounting firm; and

(2) made available in appropriate detail to the public (subject to section 105(b)(5)(A), and to the protection of such confidential and

proprietary information as the Board may determine to be appropriate, or as may be required by law), except that no portions of the inspection report that deal with criticisms of or potential defects in the quality control systems of the firm under inspection shall be made public if those criticisms or defects are addressed by the firm, to the satisfaction of the Board, not later than 12 months after the date of the inspection report.

(h) INTERIM COMMISSION REVIEW.—

(1) REVIEWABLE MATTERS.—A registered public accounting firm may seek review by the Commission, pursuant to such rules as the Commission shall promulgate, if the firm—

(A) has provided the Board with a response, pursuant to rules issued by the Board under subsection (f), to the substance of particular items in a draft inspection report, and disagrees with the assessments contained in any final report prepared by the Board following such response; or

(B) disagrees with the determination of the Board that criticisms or defects identified in an inspection report have not been addressed to the satisfaction of the Board within 12 months of the date of the inspection report, for purposes of subsection (g)(2).

(2) TREATMENT OF REVIEW.—Any decision of the Commission with respect to a review under paragraph (1) shall not be reviewable under section 25 of the Securities Exchange Act of 1934 (15 U.S.C. 78y), or deemed to be "final agency action" for purposes of section 704 of title 5, United States Code.

(3) TIMING.—Review under paragraph (1) may be sought during the 30–day period following the date of the event giving rise to the review under subparagraph (A) or (B) of paragraph (1).

SEC. 105. INVESTIGATIONS AND DISCIPLINARY PROCEEDINGS.

(a) IN GENERAL.—The Board shall establish, by rule, subject to the requirements of this section, fair procedures for the investigation and disciplining of registered public accounting firms and associated persons of such firms.

(b) INVESTIGATIONS.—

(1) AUTHORITY.—In accordance with the rules of the Board, the Board may conduct an investigation of any act or practice, or omission to act, by a registered public accounting firm, any associated person of such firm, or both, that may violate any provision of this Act, the rules of the Board, the provisions of the securities laws relating to the preparation and issuance of audit reports and the obligations and liabilities of accountants with respect thereto, in-

cluding the rules of the Commission issued under this Act, or professional standards, regardless of how the act, practice, or omission is brought to the attention of the Board.

(2) TESTIMONY AND DOCUMENT PRODUCTION.—In addition to such other actions as the Board determines to be necessary or appropriate, the rules of the Board may—

(A) require the testimony of the firm or of any person associated with a registered public accounting firm, with respect to any matter that the Board considers relevant or material to an investigation;

(B) require the production of audit work papers and any other document or information in the possession of a registered public accounting firm or any associated person thereof, wherever domiciled, that the Board considers relevant or material to the investigation, and may inspect the books and records of such firm or associated person to verify the accuracy of any documents or information supplied;

(C) request the testimony of, and production of any document in the possession of, any other person, including any client of a registered public accounting firm that the Board considers relevant or material to an investigation under this section, with appropriate notice, subject to the needs of the investigation, as permitted under the rules of the Board; and

(D) provide for procedures to seek issuance by the Commission, in a manner established by the Commission, of a subpoena to require the testimony of, and production of any document in the possession of, any person, including any client of a registered public accounting firm, that the Board considers relevant or material to an investigation under this section.

(3) NONCOOPERATION WITH INVESTIGATIONS.—

(A) IN GENERAL.—If a registered public accounting firm or any associated person thereof refuses to testify, produce documents, or otherwise cooperate with the Board in connection with an investigation under this section, the Board may—

(i) suspend or bar such person from being associated with a registered public accounting firm, or require the registered public accounting firm to end such association;

(ii) suspend or revoke the registration of the public accounting firm; and

(iii) invoke such other lesser sanctions as the Board considers appropriate, and as specified by rule of the Board.

(B) PROCEDURE.—Any action taken by the Board under this paragraph shall be subject to the terms of section 107(c).

(4) COORDINATION AND REFERRAL OF INVESTIGA-TIONS.—

(A) COORDINATION.—The Board shall notify the Commission of any pending Board investigation involving a potential violation of the securities laws, and thereafter coordinate its work with the work of the Commission's Division of Enforcement, as necessary to protect an ongoing Commission investigation.

(B) REFERRAL.—The Board may refer an investigation under this section—

(i) to the Commission;

(ii) to any other Federal functional regulator (as defined in section 509 of the Gramm–Leach–Bliley Act (15 U.S.C. 6809)), in the case of an investigation that concerns an audit report for an institution that is subject to the jurisdiction of such regulator; and

(iii) at the direction of the Commission, to—

(I) the Attorney General of the United States;

(II) the attorney general of 1 or more States; and

(III) the appropriate State regulatory authority.

(5) USE OF DOCUMENTS.—

(A) CONFIDENTIALITY.—Except as provided in subparagraph (B), all documents and information prepared or received by or specifically for the Board, and deliberations of the Board and its employees and agents, in connection with an inspection under section 104 or with an investigation under this section, shall be confidential and privileged as an evidentiary matter (and shall not be subject to civil discovery or other legal process) in any proceeding in any Federal or State court or administrative agency, and shall be exempt from disclosure, in the hands of an agency or establishment of the Federal Government, under the Freedom of Information Act (5 U.S.C. 552a), or otherwise, unless and until presented in connection with a public proceeding or released in accordance with subsection (c).

(B) AVAILABILITY TO GOVERNMENT AGENCIES.—Without the loss of its status as confidential and privileged in the hands of the Board, all information referred to in subparagraph (A) may—

(i) be made available to the Commission; and

(ii) in the discretion of the Board, when determined by the Board to be necessary to accomplish the purposes of this Act or to protect investors, be made available to—

(I) the Attorney General of the United States;

(II) the appropriate Federal functional regulator (as defined in section 509 of the Gramm–Leach–Bliley Act (15 U.S.C. 6809)), other than the Commission, with respect to an audit report for an institution subject to the jurisdiction of such regulator;

(III) State attorneys general in connection with any criminal investigation; and

(IV) any appropriate State regulatory authority, each of which shall maintain such information as confidential and privileged.

(6) IMMUNITY.—Any employee of the Board engaged in carrying out an investigation under this Act shall be immune from any civil liability arising out of such investigation in the same manner and to the same extent as an employee of the Federal Government in similar circumstances.

(c) DISCIPLINARY PROCEDURES.—

(1) NOTIFICATION; RECORDKEEPING.—The rules of the Board shall provide that in any proceeding by the Board to determine whether a registered public accounting firm, or an associated person thereof, should be disciplined, the Board shall—

(A) bring specific charges with respect to the firm or associated person;

(B) notify such firm or associated person of, and provide to the firm or associated person an opportunity to defend against, such charges; and

(C) keep a record of the proceedings.

(2) PUBLIC HEARINGS.—Hearings under this section shall not be public, unless otherwise ordered by the Board for good cause shown, with the consent of the parties to such hearing.

(3) SUPPORTING STATEMENT.—A determination by the Board to impose a sanction under this subsection shall be supported by a statement setting forth—

(A) each act or practice in which the registered public accounting firm, or associated person, has engaged (or omitted to engage), or that forms a basis for all or a part of such sanction;

(B) the specific provision of this Act, the securities laws, the rules of the Board, or professional standards which the Board determines has been violated; and

(C) the sanction imposed, including a justification for that sanction.

(4) SANCTIONS.—If the Board finds, based on all of the facts and circumstances, that a registered public accounting firm or associated person thereof has engaged in any act or practice, or omitted to act, in violation of this Act, the rules of the Board, the provisions of the securities laws relating to the preparation and issuance of audit reports and the obligations and liabilities of accountants with respect thereto, including the rules of the Commission issued under this Act, or professional standards, the Board may impose such disciplinary or remedial sanctions as it determines appropriate, subject to applicable limitations under paragraph (5), including—

(A) temporary suspension or permanent revocation of registration under this title;

(B) temporary or permanent suspension or bar of a person from further association with any registered public accounting firm;

(C) temporary or permanent limitation on the activities, functions, or operations of such firm or person (other than in connection with required additional professional education or training);

(D) a civil money penalty for each such violation, in an amount equal to—

(i) not more than $100,000 for a natural person or $2,000,000 for any other person; and

(ii) in any case to which paragraph (5) applies, not more than $750,000 for a natural person or $15,000,000 for any other person;

(E) censure;

(F) required additional professional education or training; or

(G) any other appropriate sanction provided for in the rules of the Board.

(5) INTENTIONAL OR OTHER KNOWING CONDUCT.—The sanctions and penalties described in subparagraphs (A) through (C) and (D)(ii) of paragraph (4) shall only apply to—

(A) intentional or knowing conduct, including reckless conduct, that results in violation of the applicable statutory, regulatory, or professional standard; or

(B) repeated instances of negligent conduct, each resulting in a violation of the applicable statutory, regulatory, or professional standard.

(6) FAILURE TO SUPERVISE.—

(A) IN GENERAL.—The Board may impose sanctions under this section on a registered accounting firm or upon the supervisory personnel of such firm, if the Board finds that—

(i) the firm has failed reasonably to supervise an associated person, either as required by the rules of the Board relating to auditing or quality control standards, or otherwise, with a view to preventing violations of this Act, the rules of the Board, the provisions of the securities laws relating to the preparation and issuance of audit reports and the obligations and liabilities of accountants with respect thereto, including the rules of the Commission under this Act, or professional standards; and

(ii) such associated person commits a violation of this Act, or any of such rules, laws, or standards.

(B) RULE OF CONSTRUCTION.—No associated person of a registered public accounting firm shall be deemed to have failed reasonably to supervise any other person for purposes of subparagraph (A), if—

(i) there have been established in and for that firm procedures, and a system for applying such procedures, that comply with applicable rules of the Board and that would reasonably be expected to prevent and detect any such violation by such associated person; and

(ii) such person has reasonably discharged the duties and obligations incumbent upon that person by reason of such procedures and system, and had no reasonable cause to believe that such procedures and system were not being complied with.

(7) EFFECT OF SUSPENSION.—

(A) ASSOCIATION WITH A PUBLIC ACCOUNTING FIRM.—It shall be unlawful for any person that is suspended or barred from being associated with a registered public accounting firm under this subsection willfully to become or remain associated with any registered public accounting firm, or for any registered public accounting firm that knew, or, in the exercise of reasonable care should have known, of the suspension or bar, to permit such an association, without the consent of the Board or the Commission.

(B) ASSOCIATION WITH AN ISSUER.—It shall be unlawful for any person that is suspended or barred from being associated with an issuer under this subsection willfully to become or remain associated with any issuer in an accountancy or a financial management capacity, and for any issuer that knew, or in the exercise of reasonable care should have known, of such suspension or bar, to permit such an association, without the consent of the Board or the Commission.

(d) REPORTING OF SANCTIONS.—

(1) RECIPIENTS.—If the Board imposes a disciplinary sanction, in accordance with this section, the Board shall report the sanction to—

(A) the Commission;

(B) any appropriate State regulatory authority or any foreign accountancy licensing board with which such firm or person is licensed or certified; and

(C) the public (once any stay on the imposition of such sanction has been lifted).

(2) CONTENTS.—The information reported under paragraph (1) shall include—

(A) the name of the sanctioned person;

(B) a description of the sanction and the basis for its imposition; and

(C) such other information as the Board deems appropriate.

(e) STAY OF SANCTIONS.—

(1) IN GENERAL.—Application to the Commission for review, or the institution by the Commission of review, of any disciplinary action of the Board shall operate as a stay of any such disciplinary action, unless and until the Commission orders (summarily or after notice and opportunity for hearing on the question of a stay, which hearing may consist solely of the submission of affidavits or presentation of oral arguments) that no such stay shall continue to operate.

(2) EXPEDITED PROCEDURES.—The Commission shall establish for appropriate cases an expedited procedure for consideration and determination of the question of the duration of a stay pending review of any disciplinary action of the Board under this subsection.

SEC. 107. COMMISSION OVERSIGHT OF THE BOARD.

(a) GENERAL OVERSIGHT RESPONSIBILITY.—The Commission shall have oversight and enforcement authority over the Board, as provided in this Act. The provisions of section 17(a)(1) of the Securities Exchange Act of 1934 (15 U.S.C. 78q(a)(1)), and of section 17(b)(1) of the Securities Exchange Act of 1934 (15 U.S.C. 78q(b)(1)) shall apply to the Board as fully as if the Board were a "registered securities association" for purposes of those sections 17(a)(1) and 17(b)(1).

(b) RULES OF THE BOARD.—

(1) DEFINITION.—In this section, the term "proposed rule" means any proposed rule of the Board, and any modification of any such rule.

(2) PRIOR APPROVAL REQUIRED.—No rule of the Board shall become effective without prior approval of the Commission in accordance with this section, other than as provided in section 103(a)(3)(B) with respect to initial or transitional standards.

(3) APPROVAL CRITERIA.—The Commission shall approve a proposed rule, if it finds that the rule is consistent with the requirements of this Act and the securities laws, or is necessary or appropriate in the public interest or for the protection of investors.

(4) PROPOSED RULE PROCEDURES.—The provisions of paragraphs (1) through (3) of section 19(b) of the Securities Exchange Act of 1934 (15 U.S.C.A. § 78s(b)) shall govern the proposed rules of the Board, as fully as if the Board were a "registered securities association" for purposes of that section 19(b), except that, for purposes of this paragraph—

(A) the phrase "consistent with the requirements of this title and the rules and regulations thereunder applicable to such organization" in section 19(b)(2) of that Act shall be deemed to read "consistent with the requirements of title I of the Sarbanes–Oxley Act of 2002, and the rules and regulations issued thereunder applicable to such organization, or as necessary or appropriate in the public interest or for the protection of investors"; and

(B) the phrase "otherwise in furtherance of the purposes of this title" in section 19(b)(3)(C) of that Act shall be deemed to read "otherwise in furtherance of the purposes of title I of the Sarbanes–Oxley Act of 2002".

(5) COMMISSION AUTHORITY TO AMEND RULES OF THE BOARD.—The provisions of section 19(c) of the Securities Exchange Act of 1934 (15 U.S.C. 78s(c)) shall govern the abrogation, deletion, or addition to portions of the rules of the Board by the Commission as fully as if the Board were a "registered securities association" for purposes of that section 19(c), except that the phrase "to conform its rules to the requirements of this title and the rules and regulations thereunder applicable to such organization, or otherwise in furtherance of the purposes of this title" in section 19(c) of that Act shall, for purposes of this paragraph, be deemed to read "to assure the fair administration of the Public Company Accounting Oversight Board, conform the rules promulgated by that Board to the requirements of title I of the Sarbanes–Oxley Act of 2002, or otherwise further the purposes of that Act, the securities laws, and the rules and regulations thereunder applicable to that Board".

(c) COMMISSION REVIEW OF DISCIPLINARY ACTION TAKEN BY THE BOARD.—

(1) NOTICE OF SANCTION.—The Board shall promptly file notice with the Commission of any final sanction on any registered public accounting firm or on any associated person thereof, in such form and containing such information as the Commission, by rule, may prescribe.

(2) REVIEW OF SANCTIONS.—The provisions of sections 19(d)(2) and 19(e)(1) of the Securities Exchange Act of 1934 (15 U.S.C. 78s (d)(2) and (e)(1)) shall govern the review by the Commission of final disciplinary sanctions imposed by the Board (including sanctions imposed under section 105(b)(3) of this Act for noncooperation in an investigation of the Board), as fully as if the Board were a self-regulatory organization and the Commission were the appropriate regulatory agency for such organization for purposes of those sections 19(d)(2) and 19(e)(1), except that,for purposes of this paragraph—

(A) section 105(e) of this Act (rather than that section 19(d)(2)) shall govern the extent to which application for, or institution by the Commission on its own motion of, review of any disciplinary action of the Board operates as a stay of such action;

(B) references in that section 19(e)(1) to "members" of such an organization shall be deemed to be references to registered public accounting firms;

(C) the phrase "consistent with the purposes of this title" in that section 19(e)(1) shall be deemed to read "consistent with the purposes of this title and title I of the Sarbanes–Oxley Act of 2002";

(D) references to rules of the Municipal Securities Rulemaking Board in that section 19(e)(1) shall not apply; and

(E) the reference to section 19(e)(2) of the Securities Exchange Act of 1934 shall refer instead to section 107(c)(3) of this Act.

(3) COMMISSION MODIFICATION AUTHORITY.—The Commission may enhance, modify, cancel, reduce, or require the remission of a sanction imposed by the Board upon a registered public accounting firm or associated person thereof, if the Commission, having due regard for the public interest and the protection of investors, finds, after a proceeding in accordance with this subsection, that the sanction—

(A) is not necessary or appropriate in furtherance of this Act or the securities laws; or

(B) is excessive, oppressive, inadequate, or otherwise not appropriate to the finding or the basis on which the sanction was imposed.

(d) CENSURE OF THE BOARD; OTHER SANCTIONS.—

(1) RESCISSION OF BOARD AUTHORITY.—The Commission, by rule, consistent with the public interest, the protection of investors, and the other purposes of this Act and the securities laws, may relieve the Board of any responsibility to enforce compliance with any provision of this Act, the securities laws, the rules of the Board, or professional standards.

(2) CENSURE OF THE BOARD; LIMITATIONS.—The Commission may, by order, as it determines necessary or appropriate in the public interest, for the protection of investors, or otherwise in furtherance of the purposes of this Act or the securities laws, censure or impose limitations upon the activities, functions, and operations of the Board, if the Commission finds, on the record, after notice and opportunity for a hearing, that the Board—

(A) has violated or is unable to comply with any provision of this Act, the rules of the Board, or the securities laws; or

(B) without reasonable justification or excuse, has failed to enforce compliance with any such provision or rule, or any professional standard by a registered public accounting firm or an associated person thereof.

(3) CENSURE OF BOARD MEMBERS; REMOVAL FROM OFFICE.—The Commission may, as necessary or appropriate in the public interest, for the protection of investors, or otherwise in furtherance of the purposes of this Act or the securities laws, remove from office or censure any member of the Board, if the Commission finds, on the record, after notice and opportunity for a hearing, that such member—

(A) has willfully violated any provision of this Act, the rules of the Board, or the securities laws;

(B) has willfully abused the authority of that member; or

(C) without reasonable justification or excuse, has failed to enforce compliance with any such provision or rule, or any professional standard by any registered public accounting firm or any associated person thereof.

SEC. 108. ACCOUNTING STANDARDS.

(a) AMENDMENT TO SECURITIES ACT OF 1933. [This section amends Securities Act § 19. See this Supplement, supra.]

(b) COMMISSION AUTHORITY.—The Commission shall promulgate such rules and regulations to carry out section 19(b) of the Securities Act of 1933, as added by this section, as it deems necessary or appropriate in the public interest or for the protection of investors.

(c) NO EFFECT ON COMMISSION POWERS.—Nothing in this Act, including this section and the amendment made by this section, shall be construed to impair or limit the authority of the Commission to establish accounting principles or standards for purposes of enforcement of the securities laws. . . .

TITLE II—AUDITOR INDEPENDENCE

SEC. 201. SERVICES OUTSIDE THE SCOPE OF PRACTICE OF AUDITORS.

[This section adds Securities Exchange Act § 10A(g). See this Supplement, supra.]

(b) EXEMPTION AUTHORITY.—The Board may, on a case by case basis, exempt any person, issuer, public accounting firm, or transaction from the prohibition on the provision of services under section 10A(g) of the Securities Exchange Act of 1934 (as added by this section), to the extent that such exemption is necessary or appropriate in the public interest and is consistent with the protection of investors, and subject to review by the Commission in the same manner as for rules of the Board under section 107.

SEC. 202. PREAPPROVAL REQUIREMENTS.

[This section adds Securities Exchange Act § 10A(i). See this Supplement, supra.]

SEC. 203. AUDIT PARTNER ROTATION.

[This section adds Securities Exchange Act § 10A(j). See this Supplement, supra.]

SEC. 204. AUDITOR REPORTS TO AUDIT COMMITTEES.

[This section adds Securities Exchange Act § 10A(k). See this Supplement, supra.]

SEC. 206. CONFLICTS OF INTEREST

[This section adds Securities Exchange Act § 10A(l). See this Supplement, supra.]

SEC. 207. STUDY OF MANDATORY ROTATION OF REGISTERED PUBLIC ACCOUNTING FIRMS.

(a) STUDY AND REVIEW REQUIRED.—The Comptroller General of the United States shall conduct a study and review of the potential effects of requiring the mandatory rotation of registered public accounting firms.

(b) REPORT REQUIRED.—Not later than 1 year after the date of enactment of this Act, the Comptroller General shall submit a report to the Committee on Banking, Housing, and Urban Affairs of the Senate and the Committee on Financial Services of the House of Representatives on the results of the study and review required by this section.

(c) DEFINITION.—For purposes of this section, the term "mandatory rotation" refers to the imposition of a limit on the period of years in which a particular registered public accounting firm may be the auditor of record for a particular issuer.

SEC. 208. COMMISSION AUTHORITY.

(a) COMMISSION REGULATIONS.—Not later than 180 days after the date of enactment of this Act, the Commission shall issue final regulations to carry out each of subsections (g) through (l) of section 10A of the Securities Exchange Act of 1934, as added by this title.

(b) AUDITOR INDEPENDENCE.—It shall be unlawful for any registered public accounting firm (or an associated person thereof, as applicable) to prepare or issue any audit report with respect to any issuer, if the firm or associated person engages in any activity with respect to that issuer prohibited by any of subsections (g) through (l) of section 10A of the Securities Exchange Act of 1934, as added by this title, or any rule or regulation of the Commission or of the Board issued thereunder.

SEC. 209. CONSIDERATIONS BY APPROPRIATE STATE REGULATORY AUTHORITIES.

In supervising nonregistered public accounting firms and their associated persons, appropriate State regulatory authorities should make an independent determination of the proper standards applicable, particularly taking into consideration the size and nature of the business of the accounting firms they supervise and the size and nature of the business of the clients of those firms. The standards applied by the Board under this Act should not be presumed to be applicable for purposes of this section for small and medium sized nonregistered public accounting firms.

TITLE III—CORPORATE RESPONSIBILITY

SEC. 301. PUBLIC COMPANY AUDIT COMMITTEES.

[This section adds Securities Exchange Act § 10A(m). See this Supplement, supra.]

SEC. 302. CORPORATE RESPONSIBILITY FOR FINANCIAL REPORTS.

(a) REGULATIONS REQUIRED.—The Commission shall, by rule, require, for each company filing periodic reports under section 13(a) or

15(d) of the Securities Exchange Act of 1934 (15 U.S.C. 78m, 78o(d)), that the principal executive officer or officers and the principal financial officer or officers, or persons performing similar functions, certify in each annual or quarterly report filed or submitted under either such section of such Act that—

(1) the signing officer has reviewed the report;

(2) based on the officer's knowledge, the report does not contain any untrue statement of a material fact or omit to state a material fact necessary in order to make the statements made, in light of the circumstances under which such statements were made, not misleading;

(3) based on such officer's knowledge, the financial statements, and other financial information included in the report, fairly present in all material respects the financial condition and results of operations of the issuer as of, and for, the periods presented in the report;

(4) the signing officers—

(A) are responsible for establishing and maintaining internal controls;

(B) have designed such internal controls to ensure that material information relating to the issuer and its consolidated subsidiaries is made known to such officers by others within those entities, particularly during the period in which the periodic reports are being prepared;

(C) have evaluated the effectiveness of the issuer's internal controls as of a date within 90 days prior to the report; and

(D) have presented in the report their conclusions about the effectiveness of their internal controls based on their evaluation as of that date;

(5) the signing officers have disclosed to the issuer's auditors and the audit committee of the board of directors (or persons fulfilling the equivalent function)—

(A) all significant deficiencies in the design or operation of internal controls which could adversely affect the issuer's ability to record, process, summarize, and report financial data and have identified for the issuer's auditors any material weaknesses in internal controls; and

(B) any fraud, whether or not material, that involves management or other employees who have a significant role in the issuer's internal controls; and

(6) the signing officers have indicated in the report whether or not there were significant changes in internal controls or in other factors that could significantly affect internal controls subsequent to

the date of their evaluation, including any corrective actions with regard to significant deficiencies and material weaknesses.

(b) FOREIGN REINCORPORATIONS HAVE NO EFFECT.—Nothing in this section 302 shall be interpreted or applied in any way to allow any issuer to lessen the legal force of the statement required under this section 302, by an issuer having reincorporated or having engaged in any other transaction that resulted in the transfer of the corporate domicile or offices of the issuer from inside the United States to outside of the United States.

(c) DEADLINE.—The rules required by subsection (a) shall be effective not later than 30 days after the date of enactment of this Act.

SEC. 303. IMPROPER INFLUENCE ON CONDUCT OF AUDITS.

(a) RULES TO PROHIBIT.—It shall be unlawful, in contravention of such rules or regulations as the Commission shall prescribe as necessary and appropriate in the public interest or for the protection of investors, for any officer or director of an issuer, or any other person acting under the direction thereof, to take any action to fraudulently influence, coerce, manipulate, or mislead any independent public or certified accountant engaged in the performance of an audit of the financial statements of that issuer for the purpose of rendering such financial statements materially misleading.

(b) ENFORCEMENT.—In any civil proceeding, the Commission shall have exclusive authority to enforce this section and any rule or regulation issued under this section.

(c) NO PREEMPTION OF OTHER LAW.—The provisions of subsection (a) shall be in addition to, and shall not supersede or preempt, any other provision of law or any rule or regulation issued thereunder.

(d) DEADLINE FOR RULEMAKING.—The Commission shall—

(1) propose the rules or regulations required by this section, not later than 90 days after the date of enactment of this Act; and

(2) issue final rules or regulations required by this section, not later than 270 days after that date of enactment.

SEC. 304. FORFEITURE OF CERTAIN BONUSES AND PROFITS.

(a) ADDITIONAL COMPENSATION PRIOR TO NONCOMPLIANCE WITH COMMISSION FINANCIAL REPORTING REQUIREMENTS.—If an issuer is required to prepare an accounting restatement due to the material noncompliance of the issuer, as a result of misconduct, with any financial reporting requirement under the securities laws, the chief executive officer and chief financial officer of the issuer shall reimburse the issuer for—

(1) any bonus or other incentive-based or equity-based compensation received by that person from the issuer during the 12–month period following the first public issuance or filing with the Commission (whichever first occurs) of the financial document embodying such financial reporting requirement; and

(2) any profits realized from the sale of securities of the issuer during that 12–month period.

(b) COMMISSION EXEMPTION AUTHORITY.—The Commission may exempt any person from the application of subsection (a), as it deems necessary and appropriate.

SEC. 305. OFFICER AND DIRECTOR BARS AND PENALTIES.

[This section amends Securities Exchange Act §§ 20(3), 21(d). See this Supplement, *supra*.]

SEC. 306. INSIDER TRADES DURING PENSION FUND BLACK-OUT PERIODS. (a) PROHIBITION OF INSIDER TRADING DURING PENSION FUND BLACKOUT PERIODS.—

(1) IN GENERAL.—Except to the extent otherwise provided by rule of the Commission pursuant to paragraph (3), it shall be unlawful for any director or executive officer of an issuer of any equity security (other than an exempted security), directly or indirectly, to purchase, sell, or otherwise acquire or transfer any equity security of the issuer (other than an exempted security) during any blackout period with respect to such equity security if such director or officer acquires such equity security in connection with his or her service or employment as a director or executive officer.

(2) REMEDY.—

(A) IN GENERAL.—Any profit realized by a director or executive officer referred to in paragraph (1) from any purchase, sale, or other acquisition or transfer in violation of this subsection shall inure to and be recoverable by the issuer, irrespective of any intention on the part of such director or executive officer in entering into the transaction.

(B) ACTIONS TO RECOVER PROFITS.—An action to recover profits in accordance with this subsection may be instituted at law or in equity in any court of competent jurisdiction by the issuer, or by the owner of any security of the issuer in the name and in behalf of the issuer if the issuer fails or refuses to bring such action within 60 days after the date of request, or fails diligently to prosecute the action thereafter, except that no such suit shall be brought more than 2 years after the date on which such profit was realized.

(3) RULEMAKING AUTHORIZED.—The Commission shall, in consultation with the Secretary of Labor, issue rules to clarify the application of this subsection and to prevent evasion thereof. Such rules shall provide for the application of the requirements of paragraph (1) with respect to entities treated as a single employer with respect to an issuer under section 414(b), (c), (m), or (o) of the Internal Revenue Code of 1986 to the extent necessary to clarify the application of such requirements and to prevent evasion thereof. Such rules may also provide for appropriate exceptions from the requirements of this subsection, including exceptions for purchases pursuant to an automatic dividend reinvestment program or purchases or sales made pursuant to an advance election.

(4) BLACKOUT PERIOD.—For purposes of this subsection, the term "blackout period", with respect to the equity securities of any issuer—

(A) means any period of more than 3 consecutive business days during which the ability of not fewer than 50 percent of the participants or beneficiaries under all individual account plans maintained by the issuer to purchase, sell, or otherwise acquire or transfer an interest in any equity of such issuer held in such an individual account plan is temporarily suspended by the issuer or by a fiduciary of the plan; and

(B) does not include, under regulations which shall be prescribed by the Commission—

(i) a regularly scheduled period in which the participants and beneficiaries may not purchase, sell, or otherwise acquire or transfer an interest in any equity of such issuer, if such period is—

(I) incorporated into the individual account plan; and

(II) timely disclosed to employees before becoming participants under the individual account plan or as a subsequent amendment to the plan; or

(ii) any suspension described in subparagraph (A) that is imposed solely in connection with persons becoming participants or beneficiaries, or ceasing to be participants or beneficiaries, in an individual account plan by reason of a corporate merger, acquisition, divestiture, or similar transaction involving the plan or plan sponsor.

(5) INDIVIDUAL ACCOUNT PLAN.—For purposes of this subsection, the term "individual account plan" has the meaning provided in section 3(34) of the Employee Retirement Income Security Act of 1974 (29 U.S.C. 1002(34)), except that such term shall not include a one-participant retirement plan (within the meaning of section 101(i)(8)(B) of such Act).

(6) NOTICE TO DIRECTORS, EXECUTIVE OFFICERS, AND THE COMMISSION.—In any case in which a director or executive officer is subject to the requirements of this subsection in connection with a blackout period (as defined in paragraph (4)) with respect to any equity securities, the issuer of such equity securities shall timely notify such director or officer and the Securities and Exchange Commission of such blackout period. . . .

SEC. 307. RULES OF PROFESSIONAL RESPONSIBILITY FOR ATTORNEYS.

Not later than 180 days after the date of enactment of this Act, the Commission shall issue rules, in the public interest and for the protection of investors, setting forth minimum standards of professional conduct for attorneys appearing and practicing before the Commission in any way in the representation of issuers, including a rule—

(1) requiring an attorney to report evidence of a material violation of securities law or breach of fiduciary duty or similar violation by the company or any agent thereof, to the chief legal counsel or the chief executive officer of the company (or the equivalent thereof); and

(2) if the counsel or officer does not appropriately respond to the evidence (adopting, as necessary, appropriate remedial measures or sanctions with respect to the violation), requiring the attorney to report the evidence to the audit committee of the board of directors of the issuer or to another committee of the board of directors comprised solely of directors not employed directly or indirectly by the issuer, or to the board of directors.

SEC. 308. FAIR FUNDS FOR INVESTORS.

(a) CIVIL PENALTIES ADDED TO DISGORGEMENT FUNDS FOR THE RELIEF OF VICTIMS.—If in any judicial or administrative action brought by the Commission under the securities laws (as such term is defined in section 3(a)(47) of the Securities Exchange Act of 1934) the Commission obtains an order requiring disgorgement against any person for a violation of such laws or the rules or regulations thereunder, or such person agrees in settlement of any such action to such disgorgement, and the Commission also obtains pursuant to such laws a civil penalty against such person, the amount of such civil penalty shall, on the motion or at the direction of the Commission, be added to and become part of the disgorgement fund for the benefit of the victims of such violation.

(b) ACCEPTANCE OF ADDITIONAL DONATIONS.—The Commission is authorized to accept, hold, administer, and utilize gifts, bequests and devises of property, both real and personal, to the United States for a disgorgement fund described in subsection (a). Such gifts, bequests, and devises of money and proceeds from sales of other property received as gifts, bequests, or devises shall be deposited in the disgorgement fund and shall be available for allocation in accordance with subsection (a)....

TITLE IV—ENHANCED FINANCIAL DISCLOSURES

SEC. 401. DISCLOSURES IN PERIODIC REPORTS.

(a) DISCLOSURES REQUIRED.—[This section adds Securities Exchange Act § 13(i), (j). See this Supplement, supra.]

(b) COMMISSION RULES ON PRO FORMA FIGURES.—Not later than 180 days after the date of enactment of the Sarbanes–Oxley Act of 2002, the Commission shall issue final rules providing that pro forma financial information included in any periodic or other report filed with the Commission pursuant to the securities laws, or in any public disclosure or press or other release, shall be presented in a manner that—

(1) does not contain an untrue statement of a material fact or omit to state a material fact necessary in order to make the pro forma financial information, in light of the circumstances under which it is presented, not misleading; and

(2) reconciles it with the financial condition and results of operations of the issuer under generally accepted accounting principles....

SEC. 402. ENHANCED CONFLICT OF INTEREST PROVISIONS.

[This section adds Securities Exchange Act § 13(k). See this Supplement, supra.]

SEC. 403. DISCLOSURES OF TRANSACTIONS INVOLVING MANAGEMENT AND PRINCIPAL STOCKHOLDERS.

[This section adds Securities Exchange Act § 16(a). See this Supplement, supra.]

SEC. 404. MANAGEMENT ASSESSMENT OF INTERNAL CONTROLS.

(a) RULES REQUIRED.—The Commission shall prescribe rules requiring each annual report required by section 13(a) or 15(d) of the Securities Exchange Act of 1934 to contain an internal control report, which shall—

(1) state the responsibility of management for establishing and maintaining an adequate internal control structure and procedures for financial reporting; and

(2) contain an assessment, as of the end of the most recent fiscal year of the issuer, of the effectiveness of the internal control structure and procedures of the issuer for financial reporting.

(b) INTERNAL CONTROL EVALUATION AND REPORTING.—
With respect to the internal control assessment required by subsection
(a), each registered public accounting firm that prepares or issues the
audit report for the issuer shall attest to, and report on, the assessment
made by the management of the issuer. An attestation made under this
subsection shall be made in accordance with standards for attestation
engagements issued or adopted by the Board. Any such attestation shall
not be the subject of a separate engagement.

SEC. 406. CODE OF ETHICS FOR SENIOR FINANCIAL OFFI- CERS.

(a) CODE OF ETHICS DISCLOSURE.—The Commission shall is-
sue rules to require each issuer, together with periodic reports required
pursuant to section 13(a) or 15(d) of the Securities Exchange Act of
1934, to disclose whether or not, and if not, the reason therefor, such
issuer has adopted a code of ethics for senior financial officers, applicable
to its principal financial officer and comptroller or principal accounting
officer, or persons performing similar functions.

(b) CHANGES IN CODES OF ETHICS.—The Commission shall
revise its regulations concerning matters requiring prompt disclosure on
Form 8–K (or any successor thereto) to require the immediate disclosure,
by means of the filing of such form, dissemination by the Internet or by
other electronic means, by any issuer of any change in or waiver of the
code of ethics for senior financial officers.

(c) DEFINITION.—In this section, the term "code of ethics" means
such standards as are reasonably necessary to promote—

(1) honest and ethical conduct, including the ethical handling of
actual or apparent conflicts of interest between personal and professional relationships;

(2) full, fair, accurate, timely, and understandable disclosure in
the periodic reports required to be filed by the issuer; and

(3) compliance with applicable governmental rules and regulations. . . .

SEC. 407. DISCLOSURE OF AUDIT COMMITTEE FINANCIAL EXPERT.

(a) RULES DEFINING "FINANCIAL EXPERT".—The Commis-
sion shall issue rules, as necessary or appropriate in the public interest
and consistent with the protection of investors, to require each issuer,
together with periodic reports required pursuant to sections 13(a) and
15(d) of the Securities Exchange Act of 1934, to disclose whether or not,
and if not, the reasons therefor, the audit committee of that issuer is
comprised of at least 1 member who is a financial expert, as such term is
defined by the Commission.

(b) CONSIDERATIONS.—In defining the term "financial expert" for purposes of subsection (a), the Commission shall consider whether a person has, through education and experience as a public accountant or auditor or a principal financial officer, comptroller, or principal accounting officer of an issuer, or from a position involving the performance of similar functions—

(1) an understanding of generally accepted accounting principles and financial statements;

(2) experience in—

(A) the preparation or auditing of financial statements of generally comparable issuers; and

(B) the application of such principles in connection with the accounting for estimates, accruals, and reserves;

(3) experience with internal accounting controls; and

(4) an understanding of audit committee functions. . . .

SEC. 408. ENHANCED REVIEW OF PERIODIC DISCLOSURES BY ISSUERS.

(a) REGULAR AND SYSTEMATIC REVIEW.—The Commission shall review disclosures made by issuers reporting under section 13(a) of the Securities Exchange Act of 1934 (including reports filed on Form 10-K), and which have a class of securities listed on a national securities exchange or traded on an automated quotation facility of a national securities association, on a regular and systematic basis for the protection of investors. Such review shall include a review of an issuer's financial statement.

(b) REVIEW CRITERIA.—For purposes of scheduling the reviews required by subsection (a), the Commission shall consider, among other factors—

(1) issuers that have issued material restatements of financial results;

(2) issuers that experience significant volatility in their stock price as compared to other issuers;

(3) issuers with the largest market capitalization;

(4) emerging companies with disparities in price to earning ratios;

(5) issuers whose operations significantly affect any material sector of the economy; and

(6) any other factors that the Commission may consider relevant.

(c) MINIMUM REVIEW PERIOD.—In no event shall an issuer required to file reports under section 13(a) or 15(d) of the Securities

Exchange Act of 1934 be reviewed under this section less frequently than once every 3 years.

SEC. 409. REAL TIME ISSUER DISCLOSURES.

[This section adds Securities Exchange Act § 13(l). See this Supplement, supra.]

TITLE V—ANALYST CONFLICTS OF INTEREST

SEC. 501. TREATMENT OF SECURITIES ANALYSTS BY REGISTERED SECURITIES ASSOCIATIONS AND NATIONAL SECURITIES EXCHANGES.

[This section adds Securities Exchange Act § 15D. See this Supplement, supra.]

TITLE VI—COMMISSION RESOURCES AND AUTHORITY

SEC. 602. APPEARANCE AND PRACTICE BEFORE THE COMMISSION.

[This section adds Securities Exchange Act § 4C. See this Supplement, supra.]

SEC. 603. FEDERAL COURT AUTHORITY TO IMPOSE PENNY STOCK BARS.

[This section adds Securities Exchange Act §§ 20, 21(d). See this Supplement, supra.]

TITLE VIII—CORPORATE AND CRIMINAL FRAUD ACCOUNTABILITY

SEC. 806. PROTECTION FOR EMPLOYEES OF PUBLICLY TRADED COMPANIES WHO PROVIDE EVIDENCE OF FRAUD.

(a) IN GENERAL.—Chapter 73 of title 18, United States Code, is amended by inserting after section 1514 the following:

"§ 1514A. Civil action to protect against retaliation in fraud cases

"(a) WHISTLEBLOWER PROTECTION FOR EMPLOYEES OF PUBLICLY TRADED COMPANIES.—No company with a class of securities registered under section 12 of the Securities Exchange Act of 1934 or that is required to file reports under section 15(d) of the Securities Exchange Act of 1934, or any officer, employee, contractor, subcontractor, or agent of such company, may discharge, demote, suspend, threaten, harass, or in any other manner discriminate against an employee in the terms and conditions of employment because of any lawful act done by the employee—

"(1) to provide information, cause information to be provided, or otherwise assist in an investigation regarding any conduct which the employee reasonably believes constitutes a violation of section 1341, 1343, 1344, or 1348, any rule or regulation of the Securities and Exchange Commission, or any provision of Federal law relating to fraud against shareholders, when the information or assistance is provided to or the investigation is conducted by—

"(A) a Federal regulatory or law enforcement agency;

"(B) any Member of Congress or any committee of Congress; or

"(C) a person with supervisory authority over the employee (or such other person working for the employer who has the authority to investigate, discover, or terminate misconduct); or

"(2) to file, cause to be filed, testify, participate in, or otherwise assist in a proceeding filed or about to be filed (with any knowledge of the employer) relating to an alleged violation of section 1341, 1343, 1344, or 1348, any rule or regulation of the Securities and Exchange Commission, or any provision of Federal law relating to fraud against shareholders.

"(b) ENFORCEMENT ACTION.—

"(1) IN GENERAL.—A person who alleges discharge or other discrimination by any person in violation of subsection (a) may seek relief under subsection (c), by—

"(A) filing a complaint with the Secretary of Labor; or

"(B) if the Secretary has not issued a final decision within 180 days of the filing of the complaint and there is no showing that such delay is due to the bad faith of the claimant, bringing an action at law or equity for de novo review in the appropriate district court of the United States, which shall have jurisdiction over such an action without regard to the amount in controversy.

"(2) PROCEDURE.—

"(A) IN GENERAL.—An action under paragraph (1)(A) shall be governed under the rules and procedures set forth in section 42121(b) of title 49, United States Code.

"(B) EXCEPTION.—Notification made under section 42121(b)(1) of title 49, United States Code, shall be made to the person named in the complaint and to the employer.

"(C) BURDENS OF PROOF.—An action brought under paragraph (1)(B) shall be governed by the legal burdens of proof set forth in section 42121(b) of title 49, United States Code.

"(D) STATUTE OF LIMITATIONS.—An action under paragraph (1) shall be commenced not later than 90 days after the date on which the violation occurs.

"(c) REMEDIES.—

"(1) IN GENERAL.—An employee prevailing in any action under subsection (b)(1) shall be entitled to all relief necessary to make the employee whole.

"(2) COMPENSATORY DAMAGES.—Relief for any action under paragraph (1) shall include—

"(A) reinstatement with the same seniority status that the employee would have had, but for the discrimination;

"(B) the amount of back pay, with interest; and

"(C) compensation for any special damages sustained as a result of the discrimination, including litigation costs, expert witness fees, and reasonable attorney fees.

"(d) RIGHTS RETAINED BY EMPLOYEE.—Nothing in this section shall be deemed to diminish the rights, privileges, or remedies of any employee under any Federal or State law, or under any collective bargaining agreement. . . ."

SEC. 807. CRIMINAL PENALTIES FOR DEFRAUDING SHARE-HOLDERS OF PUBLICLY TRADED COMPANIES.

[This section adds 18 U.S.C. § 1348. See this Supplement, infra.]

TITLE IX—WHITE–COLLAR CRIME PENALTY ENHANCEMENTS

SEC. 906. CORPORATE RESPONSIBILITY FOR FINANCIAL REPORTS.

(a) IN GENERAL.—Chapter 63 of title 18, United States Code, is amended by inserting after section 1349, as created by this Act, the following:

"§ 1350. Failure of corporate officers to certify financial reports

(a) CERTIFICATION OF PERIODIC FINANCIAL RE-PORTS.—Each periodic report containing financial statements filed by an issuer with the Securities Exchange Commission pursuant to section 13(a) or 15(d) of the Securities Exchange Act of 1934 shall be accompanied by a written statement by the chief executive officer and chief financial officer (or equivalent thereof) of the issuer.

"(b) CONTENT.—The statement required under subsection (a) shall certify that the periodic report containing the financial statements fully complies with the requirements of section 13(a) or 15(d) of the Securities Exchange Act pf 1934 and that information contained in the periodic report fairly presents, in all material respects, the financial condition and results of operations of the issuer.

"(c) CRIMINAL PENALTIES.—Whoever—

"(1) certifies any statement as set forth in subsections (a) and (b) of this section knowing that the periodic report accompanying the statement does not comport with all the requirements set forth in this section shall be fined not more than $1,000,000 or imprisoned not more than 10 years, or both; or

"(2) willfully certifies any statement as set forth in subsections (a) and (b) of this section knowing that the periodic report accompanying the statement does not comport with all the requirements set forth in this section shall be fined not more than $5,000,000, or imprisoned not more than 20 years, or both.".

TITLE XI—CORPORATE FRAUD ACCOUNTABILITY

SEC. 1101. SHORT TITLE.

This title may be cited as the "Corporate Fraud Accountability Act of 2002".

SEC. 1102. TAMPERING WITH A RECORD OR OTHERWISE IMPEDING AN OFFICIAL PROCEEDING.

Section 1512 of title 18, United States Code, is amended . . .

(2) by inserting after subsection (b) the following new subsection:

"(c) Whoever corruptly—

"(1) alters, destroys, mutilates, or conceals a record, document, or other object, or attempts to do so, with the intent to impair the object's integrity or availability for use in an official proceeding; or

"(2) otherwise obstructs, influences, or impedes any official proceeding, or attempts to do so, shall be fined under this title or imprisoned not more than 20 years, or both.

SEC. 1105. AUTHORITY OF THE COMMISSION TO PROHIBIT PERSONS FROM SERVING AS OFFICERS OR DIRECTORS.

[This section adds Securities Exchange Act §§ 21C(f), 8A(f). See this Supplement, supra.]

SEC. 1106. INCREASED CRIMINAL PENALTIES UNDER SECURITIES EXCHANGE ACT OF 1934.

[This section amends Securities Exchange Act § 32(a). See this Supplement, supra.]

SEC. 1107. RETALIATION AGAINST INFORMANTS.

(a) IN GENERAL.—Section 1513 of title 18, United States Code, is amended by adding at the end the following:

"(e) Whoever knowingly, with the intent to retaliate, takes any action harmful to any person, including interference with the lawful employment or livelihood of any person, for providing to a law enforcement officer any truthful information relating to the commission or possible commission of any Federal offense, shall be fined under this title or imprisoned not more than 10 years, or both.".

FEDERAL MAIL FRAUD ACT

18 U.S.C. §§ 1341 et seq.

§ 1341. Frauds and swindles

Whoever, having devised or intending to devise any scheme or artifice to defraud, or for obtaining money or property by means of false or fraudulent pretenses, representations, or promises, or to sell, dispose of, loan, exchange, alter, give away, distribute, supply, or furnish or procure for unlawful use any counterfeit or spurious coin, obligation, security, or other article, or anything represented to be or intimated or held out to be such counterfeit or spurious article, for the purpose of executing such scheme or artifice or attempting so to do, places in any post office or authorized depository for mail matter, any matter or thing whatever to be sent or delivered by the Postal Service, or deposits or causes to be deposited any matter or thing whatever to be sent or delivered by any private or commercial interstate carrier, or takes or receives therefrom, any such matter or thing, or knowingly causes to be delivered by mail according to the direction thereon, or at the place at which it is directed to be delivered by the person to whom it is addressed, any such matter or thing, shall be fined under this title or imprisoned not more than 20 years, or both. If the violation affects a financial institution, such person shall be fined not more than $1,000,000 or imprisoned not more than 30 years, or both.

§ 1343. Fraud by wire, radio, or television

Whoever, having devised or intending to devise any scheme or artifice to defraud, or for obtaining money or property by means of false or fraudulent pretenses, representations, or promises, transmits or causes to be transmitted by means of wire, radio, or television communication in interstate or foreign commerce, any writings, signs, signals, pictures, or sounds for the purpose of executing such scheme or artifice, shall be fined under this title or imprisoned not more than 20 years, or both. If the violation affects a financial institution, such person shall be fined not more than $1,000,000 or imprisoned not more than 30 years, or both.

§ 1348. Securities fraud

Whoever knowingly executes, or attempts to execute, a scheme or artifice—

(1) to defraud any person in connection with any security of an issuer with a class of securities registered under section 12 of the Securities Exchange Act of 1934 or that is required to file reports under section 15(d) of the Securities Exchange Act of 1934; or

(2) to obtain, by means of false or fraudulent pretenses, representations, or promises, any money or property in connection with the purchase or sale of any security of an issuer with a class of securities registered under section 12 of the Securities Exchange Act of 1934;

shall be fined under this title, or imprisoned not more than 25 years, or both.

28 U.S.C. § 1658

[Statute of Limitations]

(a) Except as otherwise provided by law, a civil action arising under an Act of Congress enacted after the date of the enactment of this section may not be commenced later than 4 years after the cause of action accrues.

(b) Notwithstanding subsection (a), a private right of action that involves a claim of fraud, deceit, manipulation, or contrivance in contravention of a regulatory requirement concerning the securities laws, as defined in section 3(a)(47) of the Securities Exchange Act of 1934, may be brought not later than the earlier of—

    (1) 2 years after the discovery of the facts constituting the violation; or

    (2) 5 years after such violation.

RACKETEER INFLUENCED AND CORRUPT ORGANIZATIONS (RICO)

18 U.S.C. § 1961 et seq.

§ 1961. Definitions

As used in this chapter—

(1) "racketeering activity" means (A) any act or threat involving murder, kidnaping, gambling, arson, robbery, bribery, [or] extortion, . . . which is chargeable under State law and punishable by imprisonment for more than one year; . . . (D) any offense involving fraud connected with a case under title 11 . . . [or] fraud in the sale of securities, . . . [or] (E) any act which is indictable under the Currency and Foreign Transactions Reporting Act. . . .

(4) "enterprise" includes any individual, partnership, corporation, association, or other legal entity, and any union or group of individuals associated in fact although not a legal entity;

(5) "pattern of racketeering activity" requires at least two acts of racketeering activity, one of which occurred after the effective date of this chapter and the last of which occurred within ten years (excluding any period of imprisonment) after the commission of a prior act of racketeering activity . . . .

§ 1962. Prohibited Activities

(a) It shall be unlawful for any person who has received any income derived, directly or indirectly, from a pattern of racketeering activity . . . to use or invest, directly or indirectly, any part of such income, or the proceeds of such income, in [the] acquisition of any interest in, or the establishment or operation of, any enterprise which is engaged in, or the activities of which affect, interstate or foreign commerce. A purchase of securities on the open market for purposes of investment, and without the intention of controlling or participating in the control of the issuer, or of assisting another to do so, shall not be unlawful under this

* Omitted.

2165

subsection if the securities of the issuer held by the purchaser, the members of his immediate family, and his or their accomplices in any pattern or racketeering activity ... do not amount in the aggregate to one percent of the outstanding securities of any one class, and do not confer, either in law or in fact, the power to elect one or more directors of the issuer.

(b) It shall be unlawful for any person through a pattern of racketeering activity ... to acquire or maintain, directly or indirectly, any interest in or control of any enterprise which is engaged in, or the activities of which affect, interstate or foreign commerce.

(c) It shall be unlawful for any person employed by or associated with any enterprise engaged in, or the activities of which affect, interstate or foreign commerce, to conduct or participate, directly or indirectly, in the conduct of such enterprise's affairs through a pattern of racketeering activity....

(d) It shall be unlawful for any person to conspire to violate any of the provisions of subsection (a), (b), or (c) of this section.

§ 1963. Criminal Penalties

(a) Whoever violates any provision of section 1962 of this chapter shall be fined under this title or imprisoned not more than 20 years (or for life if the violation is based on a racketeering activity for which the maximum penalty includes life imprisonment), or both, and shall forfeit to the United States, irrespective of any provision of State law—

(1) any interest the person has acquired or maintained in violation of section 1962;

(2) any—

(A) interest in;

(B) security of;

(C) claim against; or

(D) property or contractual right of any kind affording a source of influence over;

any enterprise which the person has established, operated, controlled, conducted, or participated in the conduct of in violation of section 1962; and

(3) any property constituting, or derived from, any proceeds which the person obtained, directly or indirectly, from racketeering activity ... in violation of section 1962....

§ 1964. Civil Remedies

(a) The district courts of the United States shall have jurisdiction to prevent and restrain violations of section 1962 of this chapter by issuing appropriate orders, including, but not limited to: ordering any person to divest himself of any interest, direct or indirect, in any enterprise; imposing reasonable restrictions on the future activities or investments of any person, including, but not limited to, prohibiting any person from engaging in the same type of endeavor as the enterprise engaged in, the activities of which affect interstate or foreign commerce; or ordering dissolution or reorganization of any enterprise, making due provision for the rights of innocent persons.

(b) The Attorney General may institute proceedings under this section. Pending final determination thereof, the court may at any time enter such restraining orders or prohibitions, or take such other actions, including the acceptance of satisfactory performance bonds, as it shall deem proper.

(c) Any person injured in his business or property by reason of a violation of section 1962 of this chapter may sue therefor in any appropriate United States district court and shall recover threefold the damages he sustains and the cost of the suit, including a reasonable attorney's fee, except that no person may rely upon any conduct that would have been actionable as fraud in the purchase or sale of securities to establish a violation of section 1962. The exception contained in the preceding sentence does not apply to an action against any person that is criminally convicted in connection with the fraud, in which case the statute of limitations shall start to run on the date on which the conviction becomes final.

(d) A final judgment or decree rendered in favor of the United States in any criminal proceeding brought by the United States under this chapter shall estop the defendant from denying the essential allegations of the criminal offense in any subsequent civil proceeding brought by the United States. . . .

HART–SCOTT–RODINO ANTITRUST IMPROVEMENTS ACT

15 U.S.C. § 18a, Clayton Act § 7A

§ 18a. Premerger Notification and Waiting Period

(a) Filing

Except as exempted pursuant to subsection (c), no person shall acquire, directly or indirectly, any voting securities or assets of any other person, unless both persons (or in the case of a tender offer, the acquiring person) file notification pursuant to rules under subsection (d)(1) and the waiting period described in subsection (b)(1) has expired, if—

(1) the acquiring person, or the person whose voting securities or assets are being acquired, is engaged in commerce or in any activity affecting commerce;

(2) as a result of such acquisition, the acquiring person would hold an aggregate total amount of the voting securities and assets of the acquired person—

(A) in excess of $200,000,000 [adjusted periodically based on percentage changes in the gross national product];

(B) (i) in excess of $50,000,000 (as so adjusted . . .) but not in excess of $200,000,000 (as so adjusted . . .); and

(ii) (I) any voting securities or assets of a person engaged in manufacturing which has annual net sales or total assets of $10,000,000 (as so adjusted . . .) or more are being acquired by any person which has total assets or annual net sales of $100,000,000 (as so adjusted . . .) or more;

(II) any voting securities or assets of a person not engaged in manufacturing which has total assets of $10,000,000 (as so adjusted . . .) or more are being acquired by any person which has total assets or annual net sales of $100,000,000 (as so adjusted . . .) or more; or

(III) any voting securities or assets of a person with annual net sales or total assets of $100,000,000 (as so adjusted . . .) or more are being acquired by any person with total assets or annual net sales of $10,000,000 (as so adjusted . . .) or more.

In the case of a tender offer, the person whose voting securities are sought to be acquired by a person required to file notification under this subsection shall file notification pursuant to rules under subsection (d).

(b) Waiting period; publication; voting securities

(1) The waiting period required under subsection (a) of this section shall—

(A) begin on the date of the receipt by the Federal Trade Commission and the Assistant Attorney General in charge of the Antitrust Division of the Department of Justice (hereinafter referred to in this section as the "Assistant Attorney General") of—

(i) the completed notification required under subsection (a), or

(ii) if such notification is not completed, the notification to the extent completed and a statement of the reasons for such noncompliance,

from both persons, or, in the case of a tender offer, the acquiring person; and

(B) end on the thirtieth day after the date of such receipt (or in the case of a cash tender offer, the fifteenth day), or on such later date as may be set under subsection (e)(2) or (g)(2).

(2) The Federal Trade Commission and the Assistant Attorney General may, in individual cases, terminate the waiting period specified in paragraph (1) and allow any person to proceed with any acquisition subject to this section, and promptly shall cause to be published in the Federal Register a notice that neither intends to take any action within such period with respect to such acquisition.

(3) As used in this section—

(A) The term "voting securities" means any securities which at present or upon conversion entitle the owner or holder thereof to vote for the election of directors of the issuer or, with respect to unincorporated issuers, persons exercising similar functions.

(B) The amount or percentage of voting securities or assets of a person which are acquired or held by another person shall be determined by aggregating the amount or percentage of such voting securities or assets held or acquired by such other person and each affiliate thereof.

(c) Exempt transactions

The following classes of transactions are exempt from the requirements of this section—

(1) acquisitions of goods or realty transferred in the ordinary course of business;

(2) acquisitions of bonds, mortgages, deeds of trust, or other obligations which are not voting securities;

(3) acquisitions of voting securities of an issuer at least 50 per centum of the voting securities of which are owned by the acquiring person prior to such acquisition;

(4) transfers to or from a Federal agency or a State or political subdivision thereof;

(5) transactions specifically exempted from the antitrust laws by Federal statute;

(6) transactions specifically exempted from the antitrust laws by Federal statute if approved by a Federal agency, if copies of all information and documentary material filed with such agency are contemporaneously filed with the Federal Trade Commission and the Assistant Attorney General; . . .

(9) acquisitions, solely for the purpose of investment, of voting securities, if, as a result of such acquisition, the securities acquired or held do not exceed 10 per centum of the outstanding voting securities of the issuer;

(10) acquisitions of voting securities, if, as a result of such acquisition, the voting securities acquired do not increase, directly or indirectly, the acquiring person's per centum share of outstanding voting securities of the issuer; . . .

(12) such other acquisitions, transfers, or transactions, as may be exempted under subsection (d)(2)(B).

(d) Commission rules

The Federal Trade Commission, with the concurrence of the Assistant Attorney General . . . consistent with the purposes of this section—

(1) shall require that the notification required under subsection (a) be in such form and contain such documentary material and information relevant to a proposed acquisition as is necessary and appropriate to enable the Federal Trade Commission and the Assistant Attorney General to determine whether such acquisition may, if consummated, violate the antitrust laws; and

(2) may—

(A) define the terms used in this section;

(B) exempt, from the requirements of this section, classes of persons, acquisitions, transfers, or transactions which are not likely to violate the antitrust laws; and

(C) prescribe such other rules as may be necessary and appropriate to carry out the purposes of this section.

(e) Additional information; waiting period extensions

(1)(A) The Federal Trade Commission or the Assistant Attorney General may, prior to the expiration of the 30-day waiting period (or in the case of a cash tender offer, the 15-day waiting period) specified in subsection (b)(1) of this section, require the submission of additional information or documentary material relevant to the proposed acquisition, from a person required to file notification with respect to such acquisition under subsection (a) of this section prior to the expiration of the waiting period specified in subsection (b)(1) of this section, or from any officer, director, partner, agent, or employee of such person. . . .

(2) The Federal Trade Commission or the Assistant Attorney General, in its or his discretion, may extend the 30-day waiting period (or in the case of a cash tender offer, the 15-day waiting period) specified in subsection (b)(1) of this section for an additional period of not more than 30 days (or in the case of a cash tender offer, 10 days) after the date on which the Federal Trade Commission or the Assistant Attorney General, as the case may be, receives from any person to whom a request is made under paragraph (1), or in the case of tender offers, the acquiring person, (A) all the information and documentary material required to be submitted pursuant to such a request, or (B) if such request is not fully complied with, the information and documentary material submitted and a statement of the reasons for such noncompliance. . . .

(g) Civil penalty; compliance; power of court

(1) Any person, or any officer, director, or partner thereof, who fails to comply with any provision of this section shall be liable to the United States for a civil penalty of not more than $10,000 for each day during which such person is in violation of this section. Such penalty may be recovered in a civil action brought by the United States.

(2) If any person, or any officer, director, partner, agent, or employee thereof, fails substantially to comply with the notification requirement under subsection (a) or any request for the submission of additional information or documentary material under subsection (e)(1) of this section within the waiting period specified in subsection (b)(1) and as may be extended under subsection (e)(2), the United States district court—

(A) may order compliance;

(B) shall extend the waiting period specified in subsection (b)(1) and as may have been extended under subsection (e)(2) until there has been substantial compliance, except that, in the case of a tender offer, the court may not extend such waiting period on the basis of a failure, by the person whose stock is sought to be acquired, to comply substantially with such notification requirement or any such request; and

(C) may grant such other equitable relief as the court in its discretion determines necessary or appropriate,

upon application of the Federal Trade Commission or the Assistant Attorney General. . . .

REGULATIONS UNDER THE HART–SCOTT–RODINO ANTITRUST IMPROVEMENTS ACT

16 C.F.R. § 800.1 et seq.

§ 801.1 Definitions

When used in the act and these rules ...

(h) *Notification threshold.* The term "notification threshold" means:

(1) An aggregate total amount of voting securities of the acquired person valued at greater than $50 million (as adjusted) but less than $100 million (as adjusted);

(2) An aggregate total amount of voting securities of the acquired person valued at $100 million (as adjusted) or greater but less than $500 million (as adjusted);

(3) An aggregate total amount of voting securities of the acquired person valued at $500 million (as adjusted) or greater;

(4) Twenty-five percent of the outstanding voting securities of an issuer if valued at greater than $1 billion (as adjusted); or

(5) Fifty percent of the outstanding voting securities of an issuer if valued at greater than $50 million (as adjusted).

(i)(1) *Solely for the purpose of investment.* Voting securities are held or acquired "solely for the purpose of investment" if the person holding or acquiring such voting securities has no intention of participating in the formulation, determination, or direction of the basic business decisions of the issuer....

(n)(*as adjusted*). The parenthetical "(as adjusted)" refers to the adjusted values published in the Federal Register notice titled "Revised Jurisdictional Threshold for Section 7A of the Clayton Act." This Federal Register notice will be published in January of each year and the values contained therein will be effective as of the effective date published in the Federal Register notice and will remain effective until superseded in the next calendar year. The notice will also be available at http://www.ftc.gov. Such adjusted values will be calculated in accordance with Section 7A(a)(2)(A) and will be rounded up to the next highest $100,000.

§ 801.13 Voting Securities or Assets to Be Held as a Result of Acquisition

(a) *Voting securities.* (1) Subject to the provisions of § 801.15, and paragraph (a)(3) of this section, all voting securities of the issuer which will be held by the acquiring person after the consummation of an acquisition shall be deemed voting securities held as a result of the acquisition. The value of such voting securities shall be the sum of the value of the voting securities to be acquired . . . and the value of the voting securities held by the acquiring person prior to the acquisition, determined in accordance with paragraph (a)(2) of this section. . . .

(3) Voting securities held by the acquiring person prior to an acquisition shall not be deemed voting securities held as a result of that subsequent acquisition if:

(i) The acquiring person is, in the subsequent acquisition, acquiring only assets; and

(ii) The acquisition of the previously acquired voting securities was subject to the filing and waiting requirements of the act (and such requirements were observed) or was exempt pursuant to § 802.21. . . .

§ 802.21 Acquisitions of Voting Securities Not Meeting or Exceeding Greater Notification Threshold

(a) An acquisition of voting securities shall be exempt from the requirements of the act if:

(1) The acquiring person and all other persons required by the act and these rules to file notification filed notification with respect to an earlier acquisition of voting securities of the same issuer;

(2) The waiting period with respect to the earlier acquisition has expired . . . and the acquisition will be consummated within 5 years of such expiration or termination; and

(3) The acquisition will not increase the holdings of the acquiring person to meet or exceed a notification threshold (as adjusted) greater than the greatest notification threshold met or exceeded in the earlier acquisition.

†

Partnership, → S.O is RUPA (1997)

UPA = partnership is an aggregate of the parties } fall-back provisions
RUPA = partnership is an actual entity

RUPA §103(b) → what must be done, can not waive provisions

RUPA §101 ⁽ᵈ⁾→ leads to §202(a)

RUPA § 201, 203, 204 = partnership can own property (UPA §§)

R §501, 502 - UPA §26

R §404 with 103 = waiver of some fiduciary duties

R §304 UPA §13, 14 = liability of partnership
   307, 405(b)

R §306, 307 = partners jointly and severally liable for obligations of partner

UPA §15 = partners jointly not severally liable in K, both in tort

How do they grow? ① existing owners ② outside lenders ③ new investors ④ earnings from business

RUPA §401 (i) = consent of ALL existing partners for new partner allowed in

R   §306(b) = not held responsible for liability incurred before

R §401 = account credited w/ equal money + property
         initial contribution + allocation of profit/loss - distributions

R §401(b) = partner entitled to equal share of profits = UPA §18(a)

R §502 = transferable interest = UPA §26

R §503 = unanimous consent to sell to 3P

Vanishing Partner = sells rights to distributions, any vote, can not get unanimous
         is cashed out

R §504 = creditor can get distribution until individual debt paid

☆ Withdrawal of a partner   RUPA terminology
     (a) dissociation
     (b) dissolution
     (c) winding up
     (d) termination
     (e) RUPA § 601, 603 (a) switching mechanism, where to go from here ie §801

R 602 = all partners have power to dissociate at any time

R §701 = wrongful dissociate

R §603 = dissociation

R §801 = dissolution

R article 8 - dissolution, winding up termination
R article 7 - lead to buy out or continuation

R§ 801, 802 (b) = what causes dissolution

R§ 807 = who is responsible for partnership losses

Exit your Review
- ownership interest in partnership may end by
    - freeze out
    - expulsion
    - withdrawal
    - sale to existing partner
    - sale to 3P of transferable interest

- Typical method for end
    - dissolution
    - wind up
    - termination

Limited Partnership
- has limited partner and at least one general partner
- limited partner not personally responsible for debt
- subject to Limited Partnership Law - fall back to UPA
- an entity
- subject to fed. sec. laws

RULPA §201

Draw - monthly checks

Corporations

MBCA § 2.02 and 2.03 = what is a corporation and how to become one

Corporation is ① separate and legal entity ② has limited liability

Corporate Law is ① state statute ② Articles of Incorporation, By laws and other agreements
     ③ case law ④ federal statutes

AOI = article of incorporation → must set forth
     ① corporate name ② number of shares authorized to issue ③ street address of corp
     initial registered office and registered agent ④ name and address of each incorporator

§ 203, 2.03(a)(b), 2.06(b) → corp begins at filing of AOI

Min Capitalization Statute - in S.D. need $1000

§ 707(a) - by laws may fix record date
§ 7.21(a) - outstanding share gets 1 vote, unless AOI change

MBCA § 6.03(a) = issuing stock

     § 2.04 = promoter jointly and severally liable if they state "knowingly" an corporation

     § 6.02 = terms of class or series determined by BOD

MBCA § 6.21 Issuance of Shares - BOD can authorize shares issued for consideration of tangible or intangible

     § 8.30 and 8.31 = protection for shareholder if BOD issuing stock for intangible property or benefit

     § 6.22(b) = protects shareholders from liability
          ↳ directly address limited liability see § 6.21(c)

     § 8.01 = BOD control of corp, make decisions → requirement for Duties of BOD - limited by § 7.32

     § 7.32 = shareholder Agreements - used often for closely held corp.

     § 8.40 and § 8.41 - allow by-laws to designate what officers the corp will have and their duties
     § 8.40 - officers
     § 8.41 - duties of officers

Changes needing shareholder votes
     ① amendment to AOI
     ② dissolution
     ③ merger
     ④ sale of all or substantially all assets of corp

§ 7.22 - Proxies   Rule 14a-9 and 14a-8 → shareholder proposals
                    ↳ no false or misleading statements

Promoter - someone who acts on behalf of corporation not yet formed - duty of care and loyalty

Issuance - sale of stock by corporation

Novation - substitute of a new party for a party to the K

Acquiescence - corp may be bound by promoter K given corp knowledge and passage of time

Par value - S.D. Has

Internal Affairs Doctrine - law of state of inc. should govern most intra-corp relationships

Subsidiary - corp whose stock is owned by another corp

Parent - corp stock owned by in majority or wholly by another corp.

Cumulative voting formula to determine how many shares needed to elect 1 director

$$\left(\frac{S}{D+1}\right)+1$$
  S = total shares voting
  D = # of directors to be elected

Annual Meeting - meeting held annually §7.01

Special Meeting - any meeting that is not annual meeting §7.02

Record Owner - person who has legal right to vote at annual or special meeting §7.05 and §7.20

Record Date - whoever is on record date gets notice and may vote §7.07

Derivative Suit - claim to be asserted is the corp. } §7.40 - 7.47

Class Action - asserting personal claims

Market Value - price per share × shares outstanding

§6.40 - when distributions are not allowed
§14.30 - grounds for judicial dissolution
§6.30 - adopt "opt in" for preemptive rights
§16.01 - what corp must keep records of
§16.02 - inspection of records by shareholders
§16.20 - financial statements for shareholders
§16.22 - Annual reports for Sec. of State
§7.30 - voting Trusts - valid not more than 10 years, extendable, need to let corp know
§7.31 - voting agreements - enforceable, must be in writing and signed by all participants, no statute of limitations, do not have to let corp know
§8.57 - authorizes corporation to buy liability for directors and officers → D and O ins.
§8.51 - corp can indemnify directors
§8.55 - corp are required to indemnify

Piercing Corporate Veil §6.22

Entity Theory → whenever recognition of corp. form would extend principle of incorporation beyond its legitimate purposes and produce injustice or inequitable consequences. Corp and shareholders will be regarded as identical

Alter Ego Theory — corp is a facade for dominant shareholder

Factors ① grossly undercapitalized for endeavor

② failure to observe corporate formalities (issuing stock certificates, holding meetings, electing officers, documenting loans and other transactions)

③ nonpaying dividends

④ insolvency of debtor corp at the time of debt

⑤ siphoning funds of the corp by dominant shareholder

⑥ nonfunctioning of other officers or directors

⑦ absence of corp records

⑧ intermixing affairs (blurring concerns of corp and owner)

‡ Fact intensive so rarely done on summary judgment, totality of circumstances

Alter Ego Theory of corp as parent

Totality of circumstances
1 - parent and sub have common BOD or officers
2 - p and s have common business dept.
3 - file consolidated financial statement and tax returns
4 - p finances s
5 - p cause inc of s
6 - s operates w/ grossly inadequate capital
7 - p pays salary and other expenses for s
8 - s receives no business except from p
9 - p uses s property as own
10 - daily operations of both are not separate
11 - s does not observe basic business formalities

Piercing the Corp Veil — structural settings

① Personal Shareholder Liability - shareholder liable not BOD or officers

Plaintiff → Corp → shareholder

② Parent Subsidiary

‡ → subsidiary → Parent Corp → Ind. shareholder (possible) double pierce

③ Brother - Sister Corp → Reverse Pierce

Corp legal responsibilities

① duty of care → business judgment rule = rational basis for BOD decisions

§ 8.30 standard of conduct for directors   see Schlensky v. Wrigley

    ① good faith

    ② manner directors reasonably believes is in best interest of corp

② Duty of loyalty - arises when ⓐ director competes w/ corp. ⓑ takes for themselves a corp. opportunity ⓒ has personal pecuniary interest in corp. decision   Cookies case

Corporate 0

How do corp grow
- borrow money
- issue more stocks

☆ Rule 10 b-5 = Constraints on Any Stock Issuance

It shall be unlawful for any person, directly or indirectly, by the use of any means of or instrumentalities of interstate commerce, or the mails or any facility of any national securities exchange,

(a) to employ any device scheme or artifice to defraud

(b) to make any untrue statements of material fact or to omit to state a material fact necessary to make the statements made, in the light of the circumstances under which they were made, not misleading, or

(c) to engage in any act, practice or course of business which operates or would operate as a fraud or deceit upon any person, in connection w/ the purchase or sale of any security

Fraud on Market Theory - price of co. stock based on available material info regarding the co. and its business so can not put out misleading info

Rule 16 (a) - disclosure requires directors, officers, and principal stockholders to file

Rule 16 (b) - profits from purchase and sale of security w/in 6 months

Buy-Sell Agreement
① what triggers obligation to sell or buy
② what is purchase price
③ where is money coming from

Corporate Opportunity rule - may take advantage of it

① first offer the corp opportunity and makes disclosure of conflict of interest and corp opportunity

② corp opportunity rejected by corp

③ either ⓐ rejection is fair to corp

ⓑ opportunity reject in advance by disinterested directors

ⓒ rejection authorized in advance or ratified by disinterested shareholders

Courts Test ① corp financially able to exploit opportunity

② opportunity w/in corp line of business

③ corp has interest or expectancy in opportunity _and_

④ by taking opportunity for himself, corp fiduciary placed in position inimitable to

duties to corp

Where BOD can self deal RMBCA   Lewis's case

① disclosure to board

② disclosure to voting shareholders

③ & or transaction is fair

Limited Liability Company

Members have

① protection from liability for the business's debt

② same pass through income tax of partnership

ULLCA = Uniform Limited Liability Company Act (1996)

- § 202(b) = company begins when articles of org filed

- Operating Agreement = most important document

- member liable to 3P

- members ~~liable~~ and managers liable to the co.

End Zone

A. Dissolution - majority of directors and 2/3 of voting shares
  ↳ corp continues after dissolution for purposes of winding - up

B. Merger - 2 or more businesses combine into one

  MBCA §11.06 effect of Merger or Share Exchange

4. 6 million tax returns in 1996
  50% less than $100 K assets
  75% less than $250 K assets

Directors
  ① inside = officer of co, works for co.
  ② outside = independent director, no job working for co.

S.D. has cumulative voting by ~~state~~ Constitution

Directors/managers business responsibility
  ① duty of care both action and inaction of BOD
  ② duty of loyalty
  ③ covenant/duty of Good Faith

Hayes v. National Service Industries Inc.

knew business agent / lawyer settled
- lawyer can do express authority

Derivative Suit Jury Trial
  - state = default says no
  - federal = right to jury trial

Caremark Int'l Inc Derivative Litigation

Facts: Derivative suit alleging BOD violated duty of care by failing to supervise conduct of employees

Issue:

Holding: BOD obligation includes duty to attempt in good faith to assure a corp info and reporting system which is adequate exists and failure may make BOD liable for losses caused by noncompliance

→ If director makes good faith effort to know all relevant info, not held liable for not knowing specifics which led to indictment

Cookies BBQ Sauce Inc

Facts: π alleges Herrig breached fiduciary duty of loyalty by executing self dealing Ks and fraudulently misappropriated and converted corp funds

Issue: Does self dealing violate duty of loyalty?

Holding: needs to show fees were reasonable and fair. They were

Donahue v. Rodd Electrotype Company of New England Inc.

Facts: controlling shareholder of closely held sold most of his shares at a price and π wanted corp to buy his shares in same manner and price. Co. refused. π said sale was breach of fiduciary duty owed to minor shareholder by not offering equal opportunity

Issue: Does minor shareholder have right to sell stock when given to major shareholder?

Holding: Yes, no real market to sell closely held corp, like a partnership
Equal opportunity to sell a ratable number of shares of corp at identical price

Landstrom v. Shaver

Facts: Owner of Rmc died and left shares in trust for children and gave Shaver ownership interest. Had a buy-sell agreement for no sale to 3P during Shaver's lifetime. By 1987 amendment said Shaver could rate sale of stock by any S/H. Daughter wanted out of co and demanded price for stock not in buy sell agreement formula. Trial court Shaver breached fiduciary to Landstrom by not informing of amendment

Issue: Was Landstrom oppressed by agreement?

Holding: Yes by ① reasonable expectations of minority S/H or ② burdensome, harsh, wrong by major S/H

Kansas Gas Electric Co. v. Ross
Jeff

Facts: bid signed by Jeff Ross owner of Ross Service Co. Ross Service did not pay all of K. Jeff Ross minority S/H in Ross Service, listed as director, signed note as "Treasurer".

Trial Court: Ross had some control .3½ 25% as manager but Ross Service not alter ego

Issue: Whether Ross was alter ego of Ross Service

Holding: set any 2 prong test ① was there unity of interest and ownership that separate personalities are indistinct or non-existent ② would adherence to the fiction of separate corp existence sanction fraud, promote injustice or inequitable consequences or lead to an evasion of legal obligations

→ its not ① not ②